# THE WORLD BOOK ENCYCLOPEDIA

## S

### Volume 17

FIELD ENTERPRISES EDUCATIONAL CORPORATION

CHICAGO   LONDON   ROME   SYDNEY   TORONTO

# THE WORLD BOOK ENCYCLOPEDIA

COPYRIGHT © 1970, U.S.A.

*by* FIELD ENTERPRISES EDUCATIONAL CORPORATION

*All rights reserved. This volume may not be reproduced in whole or in part in any form without written permission from the publishers.*

"WORLD BOOK" Reg. U.S. Pat. Off.    Marca Registrada

Copyright © 1969, 1968, 1967, 1966, 1965, 1964, 1963, 1962, 1961, 1960, 1959, 1958, 1957 by Field Enterprises Educational Corporation. Copyright © 1957, 1956, 1955, 1954, 1953, 1952, 1951, 1950, 1949, 1948 by Field Enterprises, Inc. Copyright 1948, 1947, 1946, 1945, 1944, 1943, 1942, 1941, 1940, 1939, 1938 by The Quarrie Corporation. Copyright 1937, 1936, 1935, 1934, 1933, 1931, 1930, 1929 by W. F. Quarrie & Company. THE WORLD BOOK, Copyright 1928, 1927, 1926, 1925, 1923, 1922, 1921, 1919, 1918, 1917 by W. F. Quarrie & Company. Copyrights renewed 1969, 1968, 1967, 1966, 1965, 1964, 1963, 1962, 1961, 1960, 1958 by Field Enterprises Educational Corporation. Copyrights renewed 1957, 1956, 1955, 1954, 1953, 1952, 1950 by Field Enterprises, Inc.

*International Copyright © 1970, 1969, 1968, 1967, 1966, 1965, 1964, 1963, 1962, 1961, 1960, 1959, 1958, 1957 by Field Enterprises Educational Corporation. International Copyright © 1957, 1956, 1955, 1954, 1953, 1952, 1951, 1950, 1949, 1948 by Field Enterprises, Inc. International Copyright 1948, 1947 by The Quarrie Corporation.*

Printed in the United States of America

LIBRARY OF CONGRESS CATALOG CARD NUMBER 70-79247

# THE WORLD BOOK

**S s** is the 19th letter in our alphabet. It was also a letter in the alphabet of the ancient Semites, who once lived in Syria and Palestine. They called the letter *shin*, meaning tooth. The Phoenicians took over the Semitic letter and gave it a more regular shape, and the Greeks turned it on its side. See ALPHABET.

**Uses.** *S* or *s* is about the eighth most frequently used letter in books, newspapers, and other printed material in English. When used on a report card, *S* may mean *superior* or *satisfactory*. As a geographic abbreviation, it stands for *south* or *southern*. As an abbreviation in titles, *S* often means *society*, *state*, or *school*. In music, *s* is used as an abbreviation for *soprano* or *solo*. It stands for *shilling* in English money, for the element *sulfur* in chemistry, and for *singular* number in grammars and dictionaries. It is also used as an abbreviation for *size* in advertisements and catalogues.

**Pronunciation.** *S* has two common sounds in English. It can have a hissing sound, as in *sat*. A person produces this sound by forcing his breath through his open lips with his tongue below the lower teethridge and his vocal cords relaxed. *S* can also be pronounced as *z* in the middle or at the end of a word *(season, has)*. This sound is produced in much the same way, but with the vocal cords vibrating. In such words as *aisle* or *debris*, the *s* is silent. *S* has the same sounds in French, German, and most other European languages that it has in English. See PRONUNCIATION.    I. J. GELB and J. M. WELLS

The 19th letter took its shape from a letter used by the ancient Semites. Its sound came from their name for the letter, *shin*, their word for *tooth*.

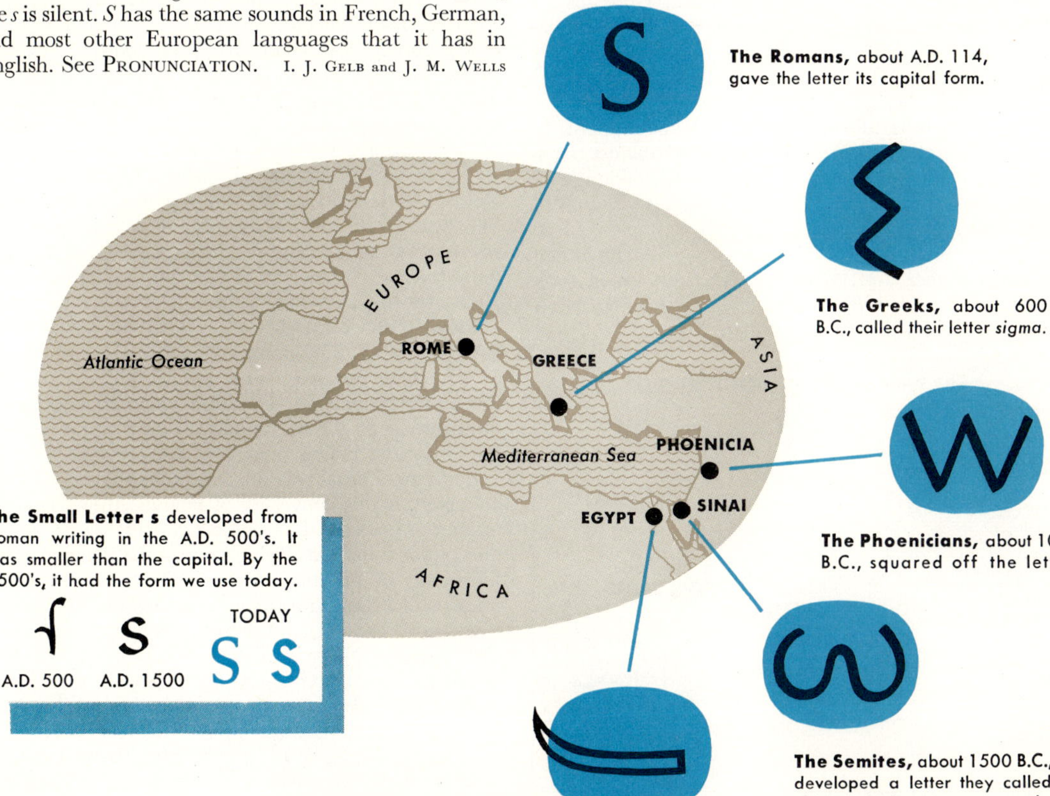

**The Romans,** about A.D. 114, gave the letter its capital form.

**The Greeks,** about 600 B.C., called their letter *sigma*.

**The Phoenicians,** about 1000 B.C., squared off the letter.

**The Semites,** about 1500 B.C., developed a letter they called *shin*, which means *tooth*.

**The Egyptians,** about 3000 B.C., drew this symbol of a tusk.

**The Small Letter s** developed from Roman writing in the A.D. 500's. It was smaller than the capital. By the 1500's, it had the form we use today.

A.D. 500 — A.D. 1500 — TODAY S s

# SAADI

**SAADI,** *sah DE* (1184?-1291), was a famous Persian writer and poet. Under the protection of his patron, the ruler of Fārs, he studied in Baghdad, and won fame by his writings. The Mongols deposed his patron in 1226, and Saadi became a wanderer. He finally went to Jerusalem, where he lived as a hermit until he was captured by some Frankish crusaders. He was rescued and returned home. Most important of his 22 works are *Bostān* (Orchard) and the *Gulistān* (Rose Garden), in prose and verse. Saadi's works were the first Persian literature to be introduced into Europe. Moslems honor Saadi as a saint. He was born in Shiraz. WALTER J. FISCHEL

**SAAR,** *zahr*, is a state in West Germany on the Franco-German border. Its population is 1,123,500. It is named after the Saar River, which flows through the area. The region is also called the Saar Territory, or the Saar Basin. It covers 991 square miles in the western Rhineland near Lorraine and Luxembourg. The Saar is valuable for its many coal mines and steel plants. Its capital is Saarbrücken.

Before World War I, the Saar belonged to Germany. After the war, France wanted to annex the Saar in payment for war damages. The Treaty of Versailles gave France the use of the Saar coal mines for 15 years in payment for French losses.

The League of Nations governed the Saar during the French occupation. The governing body included one Frenchman, one German, and three persons of other nationalities. Germany protested against this, and in 1930 the League ordered an end to the allied control. Most of the persons living in the Saar were Germans and they voted in 1935 to become part of Germany.

After World War II, France occupied the Saar, directing its defense and foreign relations and controlling its heavy industries. The Saar also joined in a customs and currency union with France.

The Saar was allowed partial self-government in 1947. In October, 1955, the people voted against transferring the responsibilities of defense and foreign relations from France to the Western European Union. On Dec. 18, 1955, they elected a parliament pledged to unite the Saar with West Germany. By agreement between France and West Germany, this union took place on Jan. 1, 1957. FRANK O. AHNERT

See also GERMANY (political map).

**The Saar Is Part of West Germany.**

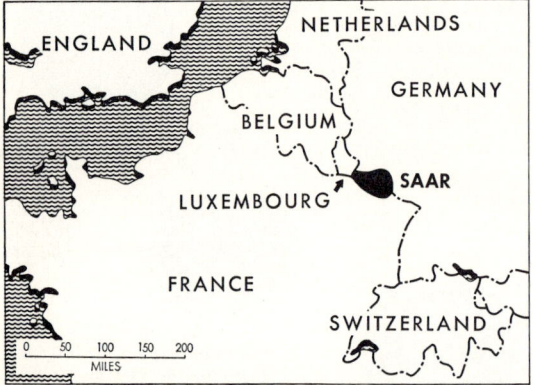

Knoll Associates, Inc.
**Eero Saarinen**

**SAARINEN,** *SAH rih nen*, is the family name of two noted architects, father and son.

**Eliel Saarinen** (1873-1950) began his career in Finland. Examples of his work include the Helsinki railroad station, designs for the Finnish parliament house, a city plan for Reval, and a plan for the decentralization of Helsinki.

Saarinen won second prize in 1922 for a design of the Chicago Tribune Tower. This entry had a profound influence on later skyscraper design.

In 1923, Saarinen and his family moved to the U.S. His work in the U.S. includes the educational groups for the Cranbrook Foundation at Bloomfield Hills, Mich., the Kleinhans Music Hall in Buffalo, N.Y., the Tabernacle Church of Christ in Columbus, Ind., the Crow Island School in Winnetka, Ill., and many planning projects. In 1947, he received the gold medal of the American Institute of Architects, the highest architectural award in the United States. Saarinen wrote *The City: Its Growth, Its Decay, Its Future* (1943) and *Search for Form* (1948). He was born in Helsinki.

**Eero Saarinen** (1910-1961), son of Eliel Saarinen, believed that each building employing the forms and technology of our day must have a look of its own. But at the same time it must fit in with its surroundings.

Saarinen's works include the Dulles International Airport outside Washington, D.C.; the women's dormitory group at Drake University; the 25-building group at the General Motors technical center near Detroit; and the U.S. embassy in London. He also designed the auditorium and chapel at the Massachusetts Institute of Technology. In 1948, he won a competition for the Jefferson National Expansion Memorial in St. Louis. His design was a 630-foot arch of stainless steel. He was born at Kyrkslatt, Finland. See also ARCHITECTURE (picture: Architecture Today); CHICAGO (picture: University of Chicago); MASSACHUSETTS INSTITUTE OF TECHNOLOGY (picture). WILLIAM T. ARNETT

**SAAVEDRA LAMAS,** *SAH ah VAY thrah LAH mahs*, **CARLOS** (1878-1959), received the Nobel peace prize in 1936. He served Argentina at the Montevideo and Buenos Aires conferences in 1933 and 1936, and figured prominently in the settlement of the dispute between Paraguay and Bolivia over the Chaco region.

Saavedra Lamas was born in Buenos Aires, and was educated at the University of Buenos Aires. He wrote numerous books and pamphlets on educational, social, and political matters. He was one of the founders of the University of La Plata. From 1932 to 1938, he was minister of foreign affairs. He sponsored the 1933 Argentine Anti-War Pact, and presided over the Assembly of the League of Nations in 1936. DONALD E. WORCESTER

**SABA** (pop. 1,000) is a volcanic islet in the Netherlands Antilles. It covers an area of 5 square miles. Most of the people are fishermen. Saba was first occupied by the Dutch in the 1600's. See NETHERLANDS ANTILLES.

**SABAH.** See BORNEO.

**SABATIER, PAUL.** See HYDROGENATION.

**SABATINI,** *SAH bah TE nee*, **RAFAEL** (1875-1950), was an English novelist, short-story writer, and playwright. He became known for historical romances. His works had become popular by 1921 when his best-selling novel, *Scaramouche*, was published. He also wrote *The Sea Hawk* (1915) and *Columbus* (1942). He was born in Jesi, Italy. Sabatini attended the École Cantonale at Zoug (Zug), Switzerland. R. W. STALLMAN

**SABBATH,** *SAB uth*, is the rest day of the Jews. It comes on Saturday, the seventh day of the week. Today, Christians also use the word *Sabbath* for their Sunday.

In ancient Hebrew history, the Sabbath was a joyous, holy day. On the Sabbath people stopped working, visited the temple, and offered a double number of sacrifices. One of the Ten Commandments (Exod. 20:8-11) is about observing the Sabbath.

After the Babylonian exile, Sabbath observance became very strict. The Jews suffered many losses and insults rather than break the Sabbath laws. In the oral law, 39 major and minor kinds of labor were forbidden. These included bearing burdens, gathering sticks, lighting fires, and traveling more than a Sabbath day's journey (less than a mile). Many Jews today still keep strict Sabbath regulations. The Jewish Sabbath begins at sunset Friday evening and lasts until sunset Saturday. Christians have generally adopted Sunday as the Sabbath because they believe Jesus Christ rose from the dead on the first day of the week. But the Seventh-day Adventist group, a Christian sect, observes Saturday as the sabbath. LOUIS L. MANN

See also SUNDAY.

**SABENA.** See AIRLINE.

**SABER.** See FENCING.

**SABER-TOOTHED CAT,** or SABER-TOOTHED TIGER, was a catlike prehistoric animal. It was one of many catlike species that had enlarged *canine teeth* (the long, pointed teeth near the front of the mouth). The teeth were shaped like *sabers* (curved swords), and were about 8 inches long. The first saber-toothed cats lived about 40 million years ago. The species became extinct about 12,000 years ago. Fossils of saber-toothed cats have been found in Africa, Europe, and North and South America. The cats were probably as heavy as today's tigers. They probably ate thick-skinned animals, including elephants, mastodons, and ground sloths.

**Scientific Classification.** Saber-toothed cats belonged to the cat family, *Felidae*. There were many genera. The most common American species was *Smilodon californicus*. SAMUEL PAUL WELLES

**The Saber-Toothed Cat Had Two Long, Fanglike Teeth.**
Painting by Charles R. Knight, from the American Museum of Natural History

The Metropolitan Museum of Art, New York, Dick Fund, 1946
**Early Romans Kidnaped the Sabine Women** because they needed wives, according to a legend. Nicolas Poussin portrayed the incident in his oil painting, *The Rape of the Sabine Women*.

**SABIN, ALBERT B.** (1906-    ), an American virologist, developed a polio vaccine that can be taken by mouth (see POLIOMYELITIS). It was approved for use in the United States in 1961. Born in Bialystok, Russia, Sabin was graduated from the New York University College of Medicine in 1931. He joined the staff of University of Cincinnati College of Medicine in 1939. In 1963, Sabin began a study of viruses and human cells to find out how normal cells become cancerous.

**SABIN, FLORENCE RENA** (1871-1953), was an American scientist. Born in Central City, Colo., she studied and taught at Johns Hopkins Medical School. From 1925 until 1938 she worked at the Rockefeller Institute for Medical Research where she studied cells, the blood stream, and tuberculosis. After her retirement she became famous for her public health work. A statue of Florence Sabin represents Colorado in Statuary Hall in the United States Capitol.

**SABINE,** *SAY bine*, was a member of an ancient Italian tribe. The Sabines lived northeast of Rome, and were among the ancestors of the Romans. The Sabines are famous for a legend told about them. According to the legend, few women lived in Rome when Romulus founded the city. Romulus asked neighboring cities to allow Romans to choose wives from among their women. When the cities refused, Romulus invited all the surrounding people to attend a great festival. During the festival games, the Romans carried off young Sabine women by force. The Sabines went to war with the Romans, but the women persuaded the two tribes to stop fighting and unite as one nation. HERBERT M. HOWE

See also ROMULUS AND REMUS; TARPEIAN ROCK.

**SABINE PASS.** See SABINE RIVER.

**SABINE RIVER** is an important waterway of Texas and Louisiana. It forms two-thirds of the boundary between these states. It rises in Hunt County in northeast Texas, and flows southeast for about half of its 360-mile course before turning south between Texas and Louisiana. The river empties into Sabine Lake, which flows through Sabine Pass into the Gulf of Mexico. For location, see LOUISIANA (physical map). H. BAILEY CARROLL

**SABLE,** *SAY b'l*, is a small animal in the weasel family. It has the most valuable pelt of all weasels.

3

*Sovfoto*
**Sable Farms** were started in central Siberia when hunters killed most of the wild animals to meet the great demand for the fur.

It lives in Siberia, and is closely related to the North American *pine marten*, or *American sable* (see MARTEN). The sable measures about 20 inches long, including its 5-inch tail. Its lustrous fur ranges in color from dark brown to almost black, with a grayish-yellow patch on the throat. The sable's coat does not change to white in winter, as do those of some animals. In Europe, sable is used in the robes of rulers and officials. Furriers make it into women's expensive fur clothing (see FUR).

Sables range from eastern Russia across Siberia to Hokkaido, in northern Japan. Because of the demand for the fur, trappers have killed off the animals in the western and southwestern portions of the Russian range. Sables are rare almost everywhere. Russia has closed the trapping season several times, and has experimented successfully with raising sables.

**Scientific Classification.** The Siberian sable belongs to the family *Mustelidae*. It is classified as genus *Martes*, species *M. zibellina*. E. LENDELL COCKRUM

**SABLE, JEAN BAPTISTE POINT DU.** See DU SABLE, JEAN BAPTISTE POINT.

**SABLE ISLAND,** known to sailors as the *graveyard of the Atlantic*, lies in the North Atlantic shipping lane between North America and Europe. It is about 90 miles from Nova Scotia. Shaped like a half moon, the island is 20 miles long and one mile wide. It is made up of white sand dunes. Cranberries flourish on the island, but no trees or shrubs grow there. The Canadian government maintains a life-saving station, wireless station, meteorological station, and two lighthouses on Sable Island. Only the people who man these stations live on the island. A small herd of wild ponies roams the dunes. Supposedly they are the descendants of horses that survived a shipwreck in the 1500's.

Long, dangerous, submerged sand bars lie near the island. So many ships were wrecked off the island in the 1700's that numerous adventurers came there to pillage the cargoes. Finally, in 1804, Nova Scotia established a lifeboat crew and armed guard there. Radar and other aids to navigators now prevent most accidents. Tremendous seas break on Sable Island in the autumn and winter, and the west end is gradually washing away. Since the mid-1800's, the west lighthouse has had to be moved several times. THOMAS H. RADDALL

**SABOTAGE,** *SAB uh tahzh*, is any means of deliberately wasting or damaging the tools, machinery, or production of an employer or government. The word originated in the 1800's when French workers would throw their *sabots* (wooden shoes) into machines to halt production. In Spain, France, and Italy, sabotage was used by the *syndicalists*, members of anarchist trade unions. In England, forms of sabotage were called "ca'canny" or "soldiering" on the job.

For about 10 years before World War I, the Industrial Workers of the World (IWW) advocated sabotage as part of the workers' strategy in disputes in the United States. Unions today favor strikes instead of sabotage.

In wartime, sabotage by trained agents called *saboteurs* (pronounced *SAB uh TURS*) is a means of damaging war production and communications in enemy countries. Enemy attempts at sabotage against the United States have never caused important damage to U.S. war efforts. ROBERT D. PATTON

See also FIFTH COLUMN.

**SAC.** See STRATEGIC AIR COMMAND.

**SAC INDIANS.** See SAUK INDIANS.

**SACAGAWEA,** *SAK uh juh WEE uh*, SACAJAWEA, or SAKAKAWEA (1787?-1812?), was the interpreter for the Lewis and Clark Expedition to the Pacific Ocean in 1804 and 1805. Sacagawea's name means *Bird Woman*. She was born among the Shoshoni, or Snake, Indians of Idaho. Enemy Indians captured her, and sold her as a slave to a French-Canadian trader, Toussaint Charbonneau. Charbonneau and Sacagawea joined the Lewis and Clark Expedition as it passed up the Missouri River. Sacagawea was the principal guide of the expedition. While crossing the Continental Divide, the explorers met relatives of Sacagawea among the Shoshoni. She was able to get food and horses that the travelers needed to continue their journey to the Pacific Ocean and back (see LEWIS AND CLARK EXPEDITION).

Almost nothing was known of Sacagawea for a hundred years after the journey. According to one account, she died on the Missouri River in 1812. Others have contended that she died and was buried on the Wind River Reservation in Wyoming in 1884. An entry in Captain Clark's journal of 1825-1828 lists her as dead.

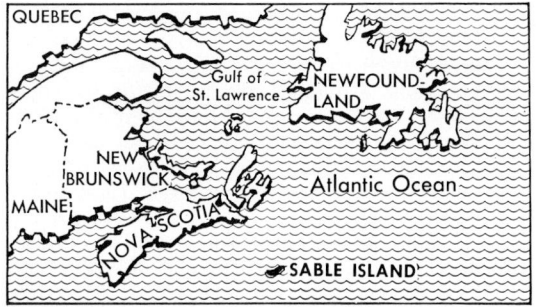

**Sable Island Is Part of Canada.**

Historical Society of Montana, Jorud Photo

**Sacagawea Points Out the Country of Her Childhood** to Lewis and Clark at her right. The daring explorers are standing at Three Forks in western Montana. Sacagawea's husband, a French-Canadian trader, stands at her left.

Sacagawea has been honored by having a river, a peak, and a mountain pass named after her. Monuments and memorials to her stand at Portland, Ore., Armstead, Mont., Three Forks, Mont., Bismarck, N. Dak., and Lewiston, Ida.   WILLIAM H. GILBERT

**SACCHARIDES,** *SACK uh rides*, are carbohydrates that differ in chemical structure. Carbohydrates can be classified according to the number of *monosaccharides* (simple saccharide units). Monosaccharides, such as the sugar *glucose*, are made up of a chain of five or six carbon atoms, which cannot be broken down by enzymes or dilute acids. Carbohydrates called *disaccharides*, such as the sugar *sucrose*, contain two monosaccharide units linked by an oxygen atom. *Oligosaccharides* are made up of from two to ten monosaccharide units with oxygen links. *Polysaccharides*, such as starch and cellulose, may contain thousands of units. Most oxygen links can be split easily by acids or specific enzymes. See also CARBOHYDRATE; STARCH.   DEXTER FRENCH

**SACCHARIMETER,** *SACK uh RIM ee ter*, is an instrument that measures the amount of sugar in a liquid. See POLARIZED LIGHT (Uses of Polarized Light).

**SACCHARIN,** *SACK uh rin* (chemical formula, $C_6H_4SO_2NHCO$), a white crystal powder, is used for sweetening. Saccharin is a compound made from toluene, which is made from coal tar and from petroleum. It is 400 to 500 times as sweet as table sugar, but contains no carbohydrates and has no food value. It is used primarily in diseases such as diabetes, where it is harmful for the patient to use sugar. Persons dieting to lose weight often use saccharin in place of sugar. Since saccharin has no food value, United States Pure Food and Drug laws bar its use in most commercial foods.

Saccharin is made into tiny tablets. It is also manufactured in liquid form. It was discovered in 1879 by a German chemist, Constantin Fahlberg, and an American chemist, Ira Remsen.

**SACCO-VANZETTI CASE** was a famous trial in the United States in the 1920's. It attracted world-wide attention because of the political beliefs of the defendants. Two Italian aliens, Nicola Sacco and Bartolomeo Vanzetti, were accused of killing a paymaster and his guard in South Braintree, Mass., and stealing about $16,000. After many legal delays, the two were executed in August, 1927. Many persons believed they were convicted because they were philosophical anarchists, not because of the evidence presented (see ANARCHISM).

**SACHS,** *zahks*, **HANS** (1494-1576), a German shoemaker and poet, was the most famous of the mastersingers. Though Richard Wagner glorified him in his opera *Die Meistersinger von Nürnberg*, his songs are forgotten. But he is remembered for his poems and plays, including *The Travelling Scholar in Paradise, Saint Peter with the Goat*, and other homespun and instructive tales. Sachs was born in Nuremberg.   WERNER P. FRIEDERICH

**SACHS, JULIUS VON** (1832-1897), a German botanist, was a distinguished teacher and the founder of the science of plant physiology. His epoch-making *Textbook of Botany* (1868) had great influence in the United States by emphasizing the use of living plants in teaching botany. His *History of Botany* (1875) is one of the best sources of information about all aspects of botany up to 1860. Sachs was noted for his wide interests, and his insistence upon critical thought. He was born in Breslau, Germany (now Wrocław, Poland).   ROGERS MCVAUGH

**SACHS, NELLY** (1891-   ), is a German-born poet and dramatist. She shared the 1966 Nobel prize for literature with Shmuel Yosef Agnon "for her outstanding lyrical and dramatic writing, which interprets Israel's destiny with touching strength." Her lyric poetry and verse plays are filled with compassion for the suffering and persecution the Jewish people have endured throughout their history. She writes in German. Her poetry has been collected in *And No One Knows Where to*

# SACKVILLE

*Go* (1957) and *Flight and Metamorphosis* (1959). Her best-known play is *Eli: A Miracle Play of the Sufferings of Israel* (1950).

Nelly Sachs was born in Berlin. She fled to Sweden in 1940 when threatened with arrest by the Nazis. She later became a Swedish subject and has translated the works of many Swedish poets into German.

**SACKVILLE,** New Brunswick (pop. 3,186; alt. 25 ft.), a town near Nova Scotia, lies about 127 miles east of Saint John. For location, see NEW BRUNSWICK (political map). It lies at the edge of the Tantramar Marshes, around which the early settlers built dikes. The name *Tantramar* comes from a French word meaning a *racket* or *hubbub*. The noise comes from ducks and geese who live there during the spring and the fall.

Sackville is the center of a farming district noted for the growing of small fruits, especially strawberries. Rich hay is grown on the marshes. The town has a number of industries, including stove foundries, and woodworking and box factories. Canada's International Short Wave Service, the *Voice of Canada*, is in Sackville. Mount Allison University is also there. W. S. MACNUTT

**SACKVILLE-WEST, VICTORIA MARY** (1892-1962), was an English writer whose books reflect her aristocratic, country family background. Her best-known novel, *The Edwardians* (1930), examines English upper-class life during the reign of Edward VII in the early 1900's. Set against a background of country houses and estates, the book attempts to capture the social and emotional flavor of that time.

Miss Sackville-West also wrote of country living in the novels *All Passion Spent* (1931) and *The Dark Island* (1934); in the nonfiction books *Country Notes* (1939), *English Country Houses* (1941), and *In Your Garden* (1951); and in many of her poems. Her best-known book of poetry is *The Land* (1929).

Victoria Sackville-West was born in Knole Castle, a country house given to her ancestors by Queen Elizabeth I. She traveled widely with her husband, diplomat-author Sir Harold Nicolson. They bought an estate in Kent in the 1930's, and she died there. JOHN ESPEY

**SACO RIVER.** See MAINE (Rivers and Lakes); NEW HAMPSHIRE (Rivers and Lakes).

**SACRAMENT,** *SACK ruh munt*, is a solemn observance in the Christian Church. It is an outward sign that a faithful worshiper is receiving the grace of God. The Eastern and Roman Catholic churches have seven sacraments—Baptism, Confirmation, Holy Eucharist, Penance, Extreme Unction (now called Anointing of the Sick in the Roman Catholic Church), Holy Orders, and Matrimony. Most Protestant churches recognize two sacraments—Baptism and Communion, or Lord's Supper. Quakers do not observe outward forms, but consider all life a sacrament. Roman Catholics believe sacraments aid salvation. Most Protestants see them as visible signs of agreement between God and individuals. See also ROMAN CATHOLIC CHURCH (The Sacraments); EASTERN ORTHODOX CHURCHES (Sacraments); ANOINTING OF THE SICK; BAPTISM; CONFIRMATION; COMMUNION; MARRIAGE. FULTON J. SHEEN

**SACRAMENTO,** *SACK ruh MEN toh*, Calif. (pop. 237,712; met. area 625,503; alt. 30 ft.), is the state capital and a historic city of the American West.

**Sacramento** lies along the Sacramento River. The domed state Capitol towers above other government buildings that surround Capitol Park, at the edge of the business district.
Division of Highways, Sacramento

Captain John A. Sutter founded it in 1839 as New Helvetia on a land grant from Mexico. The settlement became the first outpost of white civilization in inland California. Today, Sacramento is the industrial, financial, shipping, and trading center of California's Central Valley. The city lies on the Sacramento River, about 75 miles northeast of San Francisco, and covers 13.7 square miles (see CALIFORNIA [political map]).

The city's population includes such nationality groups as Mexicans, Italians, Chinese, Japanese, and Filipinos, as well as many descendants of pioneer German and Swiss settlers. Many families are descendants of people who came to California with the general westward movement of the 1850's.

The chief industries of Sacramento are connected with processing, packing, and shipping the products of the farming region surrounding the city. There are large fruit and vegetable canneries, slaughtering and meat-packing plants, flour and feed mills, dairy-products plants, and other food-processing industries. At least one crop is harvested and processed each month. The production of rocket engines is another industry.

Large boats can sail up the Sacramento River to load freight shipments at the Sacramento wharves. The city is served by four railroad lines and by motor-freight and bus routes. There are several civilian airports in addition to Mather Air Force Base and McClellan Air Force Base. The U.S. Army maintains the nearby Sacramento Signal Depot.

Captain Sutter's New Helvetia was formally laid out as a town in 1848 and the name was then changed to Sacramento. Nearby Sutter's Fort was the western terminal of the wagon trains of the early pioneers of the West. Sacramento became the center of mining activities in the great gold rush following the discovery of the precious metal at Sutter's Mill in 1848.

In 1850 the first California legislature incorporated Sacramento as a city and selected it as the site of its first assembly. The city became the permanent capital in 1854. The Central Pacific (now Southern Pacific), a link in the first transcontinental railway, was begun there in 1863. The city has a council-manager government. GEORGE SHAFTEL

See also CALIFORNIA (color picture: State Capitol); PIONEER LIFE IN AMERICA (picture: Sutter's Fort).

**SACRAMENTO RIVER** is the largest waterway in California. It drains the fertile Sacramento Valley in the northern part of the Central Valley of California. The river rises near the slope of Mount Shasta and flows south into Suisun Bay. For location, see CALIFORNIA (physical map). The Sacramento River is 382 miles long. Small boats can sail to Red Bluff, 256 miles above the river's mouth. Larger boats can sail 67 miles to the city of Sacramento.

The main branches of the Sacramento flow into it from the Sierra Nevada. Many smaller streams join the river from the Sierra Nevada and from the Coast Ranges. The Feather River is the chief eastern tributary of the Sacramento.

In 1945, the U.S. Bureau of Reclamation completed the Shasta Dam and Reservoir. This is part of the Central Valley Project. See CENTRAL VALLEY PROJECT; SHASTA DAM. C. LANGDON WHITE

**SACRAMENTO STATE COLLEGE** is a state-controlled coeducational school at Sacramento, Calif. It offers courses in applied science, business administration, chemistry, civil engineering, liberal arts, nursing, recreational therapy, and teacher education. The Sacramento State College was chartered in 1947. For enrollment, see UNIVERSITIES AND COLLEGES (table).

**SACRED BAND.** See PELOPIDAS.

**SACRED COLLEGE** is the entire body of cardinals, who are appointed by the pope and share with him the government of the Roman Catholic Church. In influence and position they are second only to the pope himself.

For the number of cardinals in the Sacred College, see CARDINAL.

Traditionally, there are three orders of cardinals in the Sacred College: cardinal bishops, cardinal priests, and cardinal deacons. In general, their duties consist of administering the affairs of the church under the direction of the pope. But their greatest responsibility comes after the pope dies. Then they must meet to elect someone, customarily one of their own members, as his successor. During this election they have no contacts with the outer world. FULTON J. SHEEN

See also CONCLAVE; POPE; ROMAN CATHOLIC CHURCH.

**SACRED HEART, COLLEGE OF THE.** See UNIVERSITIES AND COLLEGES (table).

**SACRED HEART COLLEGE.** See UNIVERSITIES AND COLLEGES (table).

# SACRISTY

**SACRED HEART OF JESUS, SOCIETY OF THE,** is a Roman Catholic society of women, established for the education of youth and to provide centers for retreats. It was founded in Paris in 1800 by St. Madeleine Sophie Barat. The society has 188 houses, which include colleges, academies, and elementary and high schools. The schools are located in 32 different countries, including the United States, Canada, and Mexico. The mother house is in Rome. FULTON J. SHEEN

**SACRED HEART SEMINARY.** See UNIVERSITIES AND COLLEGES (table).

**SACRED MUSIC** is music written with a religious subject or theme. It is used chiefly in church services, and also by many types of musical organizations.

The music of the Middle Ages about which we know most was mainly a religious art. It was sung by choral groups in the Roman Catholic Church. The earliest form of sacred music was the *plain song*. This was a melody without regular rhythm or accompaniment sung by a group of voices chanting together in unison.

The first organized example of the plain song was the Ambrosian chant, which dates from about the middle of the A.D. 300's. Another early example is the Gregorian chant, which became a part of the church liturgy about A.D. 600.

Church congregations had little part in singing services until the time of the Protestant Reformation. Martin Luther was one of the first persons to make congregational singing possible. He composed several hymns and chorales. Other types of vocal sacred music include anthems, cantatas, and oratorios. Bach, Handel, and Mendelssohn are among the composers who wrote church music. RAYMOND KENDALL

Related Articles in WORLD BOOK include:

| | |
|---|---|
| A Cappella | Hymn |
| Ave Maria | Magnificat |
| Cantata | Music (History) |
| Carol | Oratorio |
| Chorale | Passion Music |
| Christmas (Music) | Spiritual |

**SACRED WAY.** See ROME (Forums).

**SACRIFICE** is a religious ceremony in which something is given to a god or the gods, thus becoming "holy." The word comes from two Latin terms meaning *to make holy*. Persons making the sacrifice expect to receive some physical or spiritual good. Sacrifices have included food, animals, and even people.

There are many theories about the origin of sacrifice. Some persons claim that it was divinely instituted. Others believe that it developed from men's inner conflicts, uncertainties, or feelings of guilt and remorse. Fear of the gods and the unknown, and desire for favors, probably helped it emerge. Psychiatrists point out that persons troubled by feelings of guilt are often prone to accidents as a kind of disguised sacrifice.

Many religions include a ritual of sacrifice, often symbolically. Orthodox Christianity teaches that the sacrifice of Jesus makes other sacrifices unnecessary. The Jews have not used sacrifice since A.D. 70, when the Temple in Jerusalem was destroyed. Some religions, such as Buddhism, oppose sacrifice. FLOYD H. ROSS

See also ALTAR; ATONEMENT; GEHENNA; HECATOMB; MOLOCH.

**SACRISTY.** See CLOISTER.

# SACROILIAC JOINT

**SACROILIAC JOINT,** SAY *kroh IL ee ack*, connects the backbone with the pelvis. The V-shaped sacrum bone near the bottom of the backbone fits like a wedge between the wide wings of the hipbone (ilium). Ligaments and plates made up of cartilage connect the bones. Inflammation or strain on this joint often causes aching in the lower back. W. B. YOUMANS

**SACRUM.** See PELVIS.

**SADDLE** is a seat used by a rider on a horse. There are many different kinds of saddles. They range from a mere blanket, such as the Indians used, to the saddles of the feudal knights, which supported them firmly on their horses when they were struck with a lance or spear.

The main parts of most saddles are a *seat*, usually made of leather; a *girth* (strap) underneath the horse, which may be tightened to secure the saddle; and *stirrups* for the rider's feet. There is usually a *pad* under the seat to protect the horse's back from irritation, and a leather *skirt*, which hangs down on both sides of the horse to protect its sides.

The two most common saddles in America are the *English* and the *Western*. The English saddle is almost flat, with only a slight curve in the seat. The front of the seat comes to a slight point called the *pommel*, while the back is wider and slightly raised to form the *cantle*. The Western saddle has wide stirrups, a high cantle, and a pommel raised to make a *horn* to which a lariat may be fastened. GEORG MANN

See also HORSE (Riding Equipment).

**SADDUCEE,** *SAD yoo see*, was a member of a religious group that was active in Judea until Jerusalem fell in A.D. 70. The Sadducees gained influence in Judea when Rome ruled the land. They opposed the Pharisees in religious beliefs and practices. They accepted only the written law of the Hebrew Bible, and refused to recognize the Oral Law as binding upon them (see ORAL LAW). The Sadducees did not believe in immortality, as the Pharisees did. They said that the soul died with the body. They believed that each person had free will and was responsible for whatever good or evil befell him. See also PHARISEE; TALMUD. LOUIS L. MANN

**SADI,** an alternate spelling of Saadi. See SAADI.
**SADOWA, BATTLE OF.** See SEVEN WEEKS' WAR.
**S.A.E. RATING.** See HORSEPOWER.
**SAFARI,** *suh FAR ee*, is an organized hunt in Africa. Hunters join safaris for a chance to kill cape buffaloes, elephants, leopards, lions, rhinoceroses, or other big game. An organized trip to photograph wild animals is also called a safari.

Most safaris last from three to six weeks. Most of them are organized by a safari company that provides a guide or professional hunter to lead the safari, cooks, game skinners, game trackers, gunbearers, clothing, and camping and cooking equipment.

Many African countries limit the number and kind of wild animals that may be killed by hunters. Some also specify the type of weapons that may be used to kill certain animals.

See also ROOSEVELT, THEODORE (Later Years).

Shostal

**Hunters and Photographers Live at Safari Camps** while they search for wild game in Kenya and other parts of Africa.

**SAFE HARBOR DAM** is a privately owned concrete dam at Safe Harbor, Pa., near the Pennsylvania-Maryland state line. It was built in 1931 to generate electric power for industry. It measures 4,869 feet long and 62 feet high, and its power plant has a capacity of 230,000 kilowatts.

See also DAM.

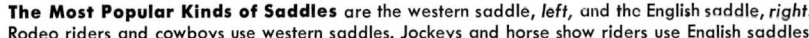

**The Most Popular Kinds of Saddles** are the western saddle, *left*, and the English saddle, *right*. Rodeo riders and cowboys use western saddles. Jockeys and horse show riders use English saddles.

WORLD BOOK illustration by James Teason

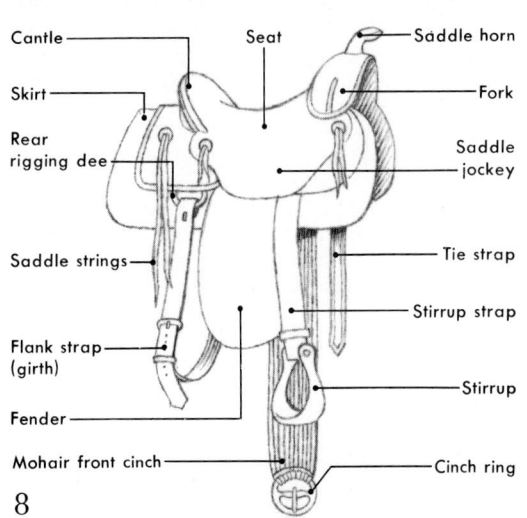
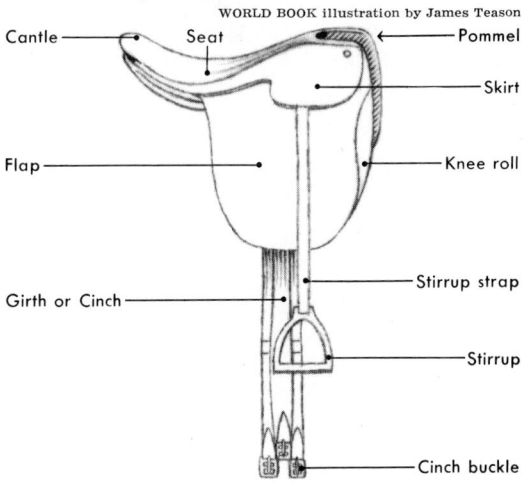

WORLD BOOK photo by Rie Gaddis

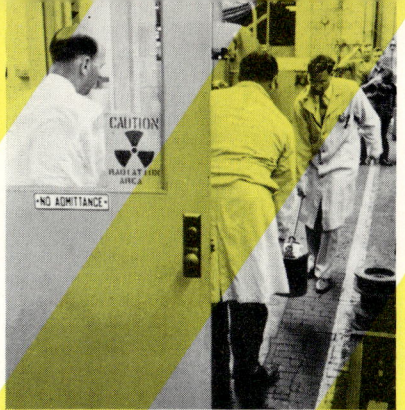

International Harvester WORLD

United Press Int.

# SAFETY

**SAFETY** has always been one of man's greatest concerns. Primitive man lived in caves or treetops to protect himself from dangerous wild beasts and enemy tribes. He soon learned to cover the entrance to his cave with a huge rock or to pull his ladder of vines up out of reach.

As time went on, man invented tools and weapons. He learned to build stronger and safer places in which to live. His cave or tree house became a stone-walled castle. The rock blocking the entrance became a door, his ladder of vines a moat.

Man gradually overcame many of the dangers and discomforts that surrounded him. Many of the dangerous animals died out.

But as natural dangers disappeared, new perils took their place. The machines man built to serve him often betrayed and destroyed him. Man invented machines quickly but did not know how to use them safely. He built better roads and bridges, but invented dangerous vehicles to drive over them. He sailed bigger and safer ships, but to more distant and dangerous places. Fire became his enemy as well as his friend.

Today's crowded living conditions have also brought new dangers. People rely on one another more today than ever before. The careless act of one person, driving an automobile or a bicycle, flying an airplane, or operating a machine can affect the safety of many.

Despite these new and greater dangers, people live more safely today than at any time in history. Since the early 1900's, accidents in the United States have declined by more than one-third, in proportion to the population.

Most accidents can be prevented by combining proper engineering, enforcement, and education. Safety *engineering* produces such safety devices as seat belts for automobiles and airplanes, and guards and shields that protect persons operating machines. Safety *enforcement* includes rules in sports, in schools, on transportation, and in industry that require individuals to take the proper safety precautions and wear the proper equipment. Safety *education* makes people aware of hazardous conditions and teaches them how to perform the most dangerous tasks safely.

Living safely does not mean living a dull life. The greatest safety precautions of all are required for those tasks that are the most dangerous and exciting. Astronauts, explorers, deep-sea divers, and others who live under the most dangerous conditions, take every possible precaution. Otherwise they could not hope to accomplish their missions. Without safety precautions, most of history's great adventures would have been halted by accidents.

# SAFETY/HOME

Most people think of their homes as the safest place. But the home may be the most dangerous place of all, according to the National Safety Council. About 40 per cent of all accidental injuries and 25 per cent of all accidental deaths occur in the home. Nearly every home accident occurs because someone carelessly breaks a simple rule of safety or does not realize the dangers involved.

**Falls** cause nearly half of all the accidental deaths that occur in homes. Slippery floors, unmended worn spots in rugs, loose treads on stairs, and objects carelessly littered about the home are major causes of falls.

If you and the people in your home follow these simple rules, your home will be a safer place in which to live:

All stairways should have handrails that are in good condition. Stair treads should be firm and uniform.

Place lights and light switches at both ends of stairways and halls.

Walk up and down stairs carefully.

Never leave objects on stairs or floors.

Buff waxed floors to make them less slippery.

Do not place small rugs on slippery floors.

Use rubber underpads to anchor rugs.

Keep rugs and carpets mended.

Wipe up spilled liquids immediately.

Cover icy sidewalks with salt, sand, or ashes.

Place rubber mats in showers and bathtubs.

Put gates at the head and foot of stairs, and strong hooks on window screens to protect small children.

Fasten children securely into carriages and high chairs.

Never overburden yourself with large packages or heavy objects.

Turn on lights before entering dark rooms.

Do not sit on window sills, lean out windows, or tilt back on chairs.

**Burns and Scalds** rank second only to falls as a cause of accidental deaths in the home. Nearly every burn results from carelessness or ignorance of safety rules. Hot or burning objects such as cigarettes, matches, stoves, fireplaces, furnaces, and outdoor barbecues cause most burns and scalds. A little bit of extra care around such objects can help keep your home and the people in it safe from fires, burns, and scalds. See BURNS AND SCALDS; FIRE PREVENTION.

Here are some rules to follow:

Keep matches in a safe, fireproof container, out of the reach of small children and away from heat sources.

Always strike matches away from your body so the head of the match will not burn you if it should fly off.

Never use lighted matches in closets, or near any flammable materials.

Be sure that smokers put cigarettes, cigars, and pipe ashes in ash trays.

Place candles or fuel burning lanterns on a firm base so they won't fall or tip over. Be sure that the last person to go to bed or to leave the house puts them out.

**Keep Stairways Clear** of toys and other objects that might cause you or someone in your family to trip and fall.

**Never Climb On Chairs**, tables, or boxes to reach high places, *left*. Use a stepladder to avoid injury from a fall.

**Avoid Burns and Scalds** by turning pot and pan handles toward the back of the stove, *below*. Keep matches away from youngsters and heat sources.

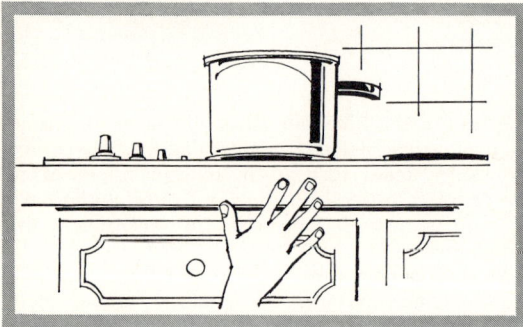

WORLD BOOK illustrations by Jim Joseph

**Keep Medicine Locked Up** and out of reach, *below*. Be sure containers are clearly marked.

**Overloaded Wall Sockets**, *below*, and poorly placed cords cause many damaging fires.
WORLD BOOK photos by Rie Gaddis

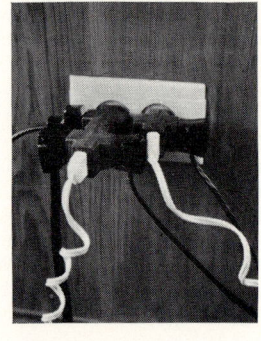

Never clean with flammable dry-cleaning fluids.
Never start fires with gasoline or similar products.
Use charcoal lighter fluids or kerosene to start fires. But never use these devices to restart fires from embers.

Cover fireplaces with spark screens.

Keep fireplaces, flues, and chimneys free of obstructions.

Turn pots and pans so their handles point to the rear of the cooking surface out of reach.

Open both the broiler and oven doors when lighting gas ovens. Turn the gas on after striking the match, never before.

Smother burning fat with a metal cover or bicarbonate of soda. Never use flour. It may explode.

Be sure that all furnaces and heat sources, and all cooking appliances, are in good working condition.

**Poisoning** causes many accidental deaths in homes each year. Potential danger areas are medicine cabinets, and places such as garages or basements where such poisonous substances as cleansers, paints, and insecticides are stored.

Extra care should be taken in these areas when children and pets are present. If anyone should swallow a substance you think may be poisonous, read the instructions on the label to find a quick remedy, then call a physician immediately. If possible, tell the physician the brand name and contents of the product so he can determine the best remedy as quickly as possible. See ANTIDOTE; FIRST AID.

These simple rules will help avoid accidents from poisoning: before they happen:

Lock all medicine cabinets and all places where poisonous substances are stored. Keep poisons out of reach of children.

Label all bottles clearly.

Never take medicine without reading the label.

Never take medicine in the dark.

Inspect medicine cabinets regularly and throw away medicines that are no longer being used.

Put away all poisonous substances immediately after using them.

Keep children and pets away from areas recently painted or covered with insecticides, plant sprays, or other poisonous substances.

Throw away food that is no longer fresh.

**Asphyxiation.** Many persons die needlessly from gas poisoning or from choking on food or other objects. Faulty gas stoves, furnaces, or other gas-fueled appliances and poor ventilation cause most gas poisoning. Automobiles with motors running in closed or poorly ventilated garages also cause many deaths. See FIRST AID (Stoppage of Breathing).

Here are some ways to prevent asphyxiation:

Have heating equipment inspected regularly.

Never operate automobile engines or gasoline-powered motors in closed areas such as a closed garage. They produce poisonous carbon monoxide gas.

Be sure that all heating and cooking appliances are properly vented to dispose of gas.

Make all gas connections with metal piping, never with rubber hose. Be sure that all fittings are tight.

Report all gas leaks to the utility company the instant you notice them.

Do not let young children play with coins, marbles, or other small objects they might choke on.

Never give popcorn or food with nuts to children under four years of age.

**Cuts and Scratches** usually cause only minor injuries. But if they are not treated properly, they may be serious.

Most cuts and scratches can be avoided by handling tacks, nails, broken glass, knives and other cutting tools, and metal objects with sharp edges carefully. Such a seemingly harmless object as paper can also cause painful cuts.

Here are some ways to avoid cuts and scratches:

Keep sharp or pointed objects out of the reach of children.

Pick up tacks, pins, needles, and other sharp objects immediately.

Remove all nails and splinters from boards before the boards are stored.

Sweep up broken glass immediately. Always pick up glass slivers with a paper towel, never with your bare hands.

Learn the right way to use cutting tools before starting to work with them. The right way is always the safe way.

Treat all cuts or scratches that break the skin.

Serious cuts, or bleeding that will not stop, should be treated by a physician as soon as possible.

**Safety With Electricity.** Faulty electrical wiring can cause fires, dangerous electric shocks, and even death. All electrical appliances and areas where electrical wiring is used are potential danger spots. See ELECTRICITY (How to Use Electricity Safely).

Here are some rules to follow:

Have all wiring done by a competent electrician.

Electrical wiring and appliances should bear the Underwriter's Laboratories label on all parts.

Replace any cords and plugs showing frayed or cracked insulation or other signs of wear.

Never run cords over radiators, under rugs, or through doorways.

Have extra outlets installed by an electrician instead of using long extension cords.

Never touch electric cords, wires, or fixtures if your hands, feet, or shoes are damp.

Never jerk cords out of outlets. Grip the plug only.

**Other Home Hazards.** Most new home appliances require some safety measures. Power mowers and snow shovels, electric hedge clippers, and power tools are examples of these.

For safety follow these rules:

Never repair, service, or fuel machines or tools when they are operating.

Always learn to use a new tool safely before you attempt to use it.

Follow manufacturers' instructions to the letter when assembling, repairing, servicing, and using all products.

I 11

# SAFETY/SCHOOL

Except for their homes, young people spend more time in schools than they do anywhere else. Special safety rules apply to school buildings. For example, doors should open easily, even for the smallest children. Exits, fire escapes, and emergency equipment should be clearly marked.

Accidents that occur in schools are especially tragic when they result from carelessness, faulty equipment, rowdyness, or foolish horseplay.

Each student must recognize his responsibility not only for his own safety, but also for the safety of other students. This responsibility is especially true for older students.

**Corridors, Stairs, and Classrooms.** Accidents can occur easily in corridors and on stairways. Everyone is in a hurry to get to the next class or to go home. Crowded corridors and stairways are like streets and highways during rush-hour traffic. Just as automobiles move faster and safer with traffic regulations, students will get where they are going faster and safer by following a few simple traffic rules in corridors and on stairways.

Classrooms are usually less dangerous than corridors and stairways. But serious and painful injuries can also occur there unless normal safety regulations are observed.

These rules will help avoid accidents:

Keep to the right in corridors and on stairways. Do not crowd or shove.

Walk, do not run.

Use each step going up and down stairs. Be ready to grab the handrail if you slip.

Keep classroom aisles and cloakrooms clear of obstacles.

Hang up coats and keep overshoes and umbrellas out of the way.

Report broken seats, desks, and other damaged equipment.

Put away materials you are not using.

Keep feet out of aisles.

Do not tip chairs back.

Carry pens, pencils, scissors, and other sharp objects with points down and protected. Be careful when using them.

**Gymnasiums and Athletic Fields** are where more than half of all school accidents occur. Some injuries can be expected during vigorous physical activity, but many of them could be avoided. Proper equipment and good physical condition are essential. Sportsmanship also promotes safety.

The best players in any sports are those who follow the rules. They are less likely to be injured, so they are more valuable to themselves and to their teams. Precautions must be taken by students and by school authorities as well.

Here are some ways to avoid injuries in gymnasiums and on athletic fields:

Cover pillars and walls and other obstacles close to playing areas with padding.

Keep fields clear of broken glass, bits of metal, sticks, and trash of all kinds.

Keep gymnasium floors and playing fields smooth and in good repair.

Inspect equipment, grounds, and facilities regularly and keep them in good condition.

Always have first aid equipment handy and know how to use it.

Be sure you are in proper physical condition and well trained in the fundamentals before you participate in any sport.

Understand the rules of the game and apply them strictly.

# SAFETY/INSTRUCTION

**Safety Instruction** has assumed an important place in schools today. With safety engineering and safety enforcement, safety education is one of the three essential factors in maintaining and improving safety conditions.

Safety education neither begins nor ends in the classroom. But schools play an important role in making safety a recognized part of everyday life. Safety education begins in the home during infancy. By the time a child reaches school age, safety has become so much a part of his knowledge and experience that he has no need to think about it.

Many states require safety instruction in school. But required or not, it is part of everyday classroom activities, from the earliest grades through high school and college. It continues on the job and in the home, all through life.

Specific safety courses are not taught in school. Each school subject relates to safety in its own way.

Safety receives greater emphasis in such courses as physical education, driver education, vocational courses, fine and practical arts, and social studies, where it relates specifically to the subject matter. But safety is so much a part of life itself that safety education is often taught and learned without the instructor or student realizing it.

**School Safety Organizations.** Most classroom safety instruction deals with safety as it applies to specific classroom situations or to life in general. But safety also applies to activities and conditions in and around school. For example, perhaps a stairway is poorly lighted. Students may tend to congregate in a particular place in the corridors, creating a bad traffic problem. Perhaps a leaky radiator has made a certain stretch of corridor dangerously slippery. Or there may be a dangerous corner near the school building where a number of traffic accidents have occurred. Either these conditions must be corrected, or students must

Never participate in any sport without using the proper equipment. Be sure the equipment is in good condition. Playing without equipment, or with poor equipment can be dangerous.

Report all dangerous conditions.

Report any injuries to yourself or others at once, whether or not they seem serious.

Do not lose your temper during rough play or physical contact.

Keep spectators clear of the playing area.

Be careful in locker rooms and showers. Accidents there can be even more serious than those that occur on the playing field.

**Shops and Laboratories,** the training grounds for future scientists, engineers, and industrial workers, have conditions similar to those found in industry. Students learn how to work with the equipment and how to solve the problems they will have to face later on the job.

Schools should also teach students about the hazards found in shops and laboratories and how to protect themselves against them. Shop and laboratory safety precautions should teach students the attitudes toward industrial safety that future employers will expect them to have.

The following common sense rules are important to shop and laboratory safety:

Organize shop and laboratory safety procedures along the same lines as those in industry.

Use the proper safety equipment and wear the proper clothing.

Students should learn how to handle machinery and equipment before they use them.

Inspect tools and equipment regularly. Worn or damaged equipment should be repaired or replaced immediately.

**Proper Equipment,** *above,* helps to prevent gymnasium injuries and to ensure safety.

**Blocked Classroom Aisles,** *below, can cause accidents.*

WORLD BOOK photos by Ric Gaddis

**Courtesy On Stairways,** *above,* helps school safety.

**Wear Safety Equipment** while working in the school shop or laboratory, *below.*

WORLD BOOK illustrations by Jim Joseph

be warned of the dangers so they can take precautions against them.

Many schools have created safety organizations made up of students elected by their classmates to help improve safety conditions. The job of the safety organization is to discover hazards in and around the school, and either eliminate them or take precautions against them. Students must cooperate in order that the organization may do its job effectively. Students should follow its recommendations and help by reporting hazardous conditions.

A valuable way to eliminate accidents is by "reporting the accident that almost happened." For example, suppose a bar of steel falls from a storage rack in a machine shop, narrowly missing a student. This incident could easily go unnoticed, because no one was injured and no damage occurred. By someone reporting the mishap to the proper authority the condition can be corrected. Perhaps by sending out a daily or weekly report of "accidents that almost happened," the safety organization can alert students to unsafe conditions around them.

**Safety Patrols and School Bus Patrols.** Safety patrol boys and girls help students cross streets at the proper places. If a traffic officer is present, the patrol boy or girl works under his supervision. Accepted rules and policies for school safety patrols have been devised by the American Automobile Association, International Association of Chiefs of Police, National Commission on Safety Education of the National Education Association, National Congress of Parents and Teachers, National Safety Council, and the United States Office of Education.

In areas where school buses carry students to and from school, student bus patrols are often formed from older pupils on board. The patrols help drivers take roll, maintain order, and help children on and off the bus and across roads safely.

# SAFETY/COLOR /////

**Hunters Wear Red,** as a safety measure, *above.* They never shoot at anything red.

**A Policeman's Safety Vest** has bright red and white stripes. The colors help you to see him when he directs traffic, *left.*

**Fire Protection Red,** *right,* tells you instantly where you will find fire fighting equipment and emergency fire exits.

WORLD BOOK photos by Rie Gaddis

WORLD BOOK illustrations by Jim Joseph

**Precautionary Blue** warns you. It marks equipment that is out of order and not to be used.

**Emergency Green** leads you quickly to first aid equipment, *above,* when you need it.

**Warning Yellow,** *right,* alerts you to take special care in avoiding hazards.

# SAFETY/INDUSTRY /////////////////////////

WORLD BOOK photo by Rie Gaddis, courtesy General Motors E.M.D.

**Color Is Important in Industrial Safety.** Colors play a major part in helping to maintain the safety of workers in industrial plants. How many safety colors do you see here?

Industrial safety improvements since 1900 prove that accident prevention works. Organized accident prevention began in 1913 with the founding of the National Council of Industrial Safety. It soon changed its name to the National Safety Council, extending its program to include prevention of all accidents.

In 1912, the year before the safety council was founded, work accidents killed about 21 out of every 100,000 persons in the United States. By the mid-1960's, the yearly rate was about 7 out of every 100,000.

The first steps toward industrial safety came in engineering. Safer machines and equipment reduced accidents. Next came better working procedures, and rules to enforce them. Lectures, motion pictures, and posters are now used to teach safety methods to workers.

Employers demand safe work methods. They know that safety not only reduces accidents and deaths, but that it reduces costs as well.

14

# SAFETY/RECREATION

Injuries are never pleasant. But perhaps the worst injuries are those that keep you from doing things you want to do, or that make you stop in the midst of having a good time. Yet, skiers break legs, boaters drown, hunters are shot accidentally, campers lose their way in the woods. In almost every case, these mishaps result from carelessness.

It is easy to relax your guard against accidents during a boat ride or while participating in or watching a baseball game. But accidents are more likely to occur when you do things that are not a part of your everyday routine.

Some activities appear more dangerous than others because the hazards are easier to see. But hidden hazards often cause the worst accidents. As a result, the most "dangerous" activities often have better accident records than the so-called "safe" ones.

Safety precautions that apply to gymnasiums and athletic fields apply also to most forms of outdoor recreation. Proper clothing, equipment, physical conditioning, and training are essential to safety.

**Water Safety.** Drowning ranks fourth among the causes of accidental death. Most drowning victims could have saved themselves if they had known how to swim.

Nearly everyone spends some time either in or near water. Anyone who goes near water without knowing how to swim, takes unnecessary chances. Swimming is easy to learn and lessons are available to most people. Children can learn to swim at very early ages. School age children should learn to take care of themselves in depths over their heads. Adults can learn to swim at public and private pools and at recreation centers. See ARTIFICIAL RESPIRATION; BOATS AND BOATING; CANOEING (picture, How to Handle a Canoe); DROWNING.

Instruction in all water sports emphasizes safety. Here are a few basic water safety rules:

Always swim with a companion.

If you do not know how to swim well stay in shallow water.

Never go in the water until at least an hour after eating.

At least one member of a swimming party should have training in lifesaving, resuscitation, and first aid if no lifeguard is on duty.

Before diving, make sure the water is deep enough and free of obstructions.

When swimming for distance, swim parallel to the shore or have someone accompany you in a boat.

Watch small children closely when they are in or near water.

Do not swim near diving boards or in areas where people are diving.

Never engage in horseplay in the water.

Never swim during storms.

Be sure you know water traffic regulations before sailing a boat.

Never pilot any boat without mastering the skills required to operate it safely.

Only skilled and experienced sailors should venture out alone.

Always wear a life jacket when in a boat if you cannot swim.

Only expert swimmers should water ski or skin dive, and only after receiving adequate instructions.

**Hiking and Camping** can be enjoyed by almost everyone. What could be more delightful than strolling in the woods, pitching a tent, and surrounding yourself with nature for a few days? Hiking and camping are easy ways "to get away from it all." The nearest woods may contain a world completely different from the world in which you live.

Although they may seem safer than some more vigorous recreational activities, hiking and camping trips are filled with hidden hazards. Some of the dangers that hikers and campers may face are wild animals, hidden streams, tree stumps, and holes in the ground. They also may lose their way in strange country. Sudden changes in weather may bring unexpected and sometimes serious hardships.

Before starting on a trip you should learn about the difficulties that may lie ahead of you. You can learn much about hiking and camping by reading books and magazines, and through such groups as the Boy Scouts and Girl Scouts, and American Youth Hostels. But once you take basic precautions, the best way to find out about hiking and camping is through experience.

If you follow these suggestions, your hiking or camping trip will be safer and more enjoyable:

Start with short trips. Work toward long, rugged trips by easy stages.

Keep as warm, dry, and comfortable as possible. Always prepare yourself for sudden changes in weather.

Choose clothing to fit the country and climate in which you will hike or camp.

Always carry sufficient changes of underclothes and socks. Have a sweater or jacket to wear when it turns cool at night.

Wear sturdy shoes, and heavy socks of wool or similar material that does not hold moisture as does cotton.

**Follow Playground Rules.** You are responsible for the safety of yourself and others. Carelessness causes injuries.

**Swim in Safe Places** and never be careless in the water. Always swim near a lifeguard and remain close to shore.

WORLD BOOK illustrations by Jim Joseph

# SAFETY/RECREATION (continued)

Never try to catch, handle, or pet wild animals. They are not pets.

Take a guide with you when you enter strange, wild country.

Know where you are going. Always carry a compass, maps, and other guides to help you find your way.

Carry a flashlight and extra batteries.

Take enough food and water for the entire trip.

Carry a first aid handbook and kit.

**Winter Sports** require safety precautions similar to those of most other sports. But winter sports enthusiasts must also protect against severe weather. The major dangers include thin ice, dangerous ski or toboggan slopes, inadequate training or equipment, and poor physical conditioning.

Here are some suggestions to follow:

Wear clothing that is warm, comfortable, and suited to the activity.

Be sure you have adequate equipment.

Do not attempt difficult slopes until you have developed skiing skills.

Never go beyond the skiing area unless a guide accompanies you.

Skate on supervised ice skating rinks when possible. Have ropes or planks available to help anyone who falls through the ice on natural bodies of water.

Check ice thickness on ponds or streams to make sure it is safe for skating.

Avoid skating above moving water. Varying ice thickness and strong currents make this dangerous.

Never go sledding or tobogganing on public streets, unless they have been closed off for that purpose.

Never pack snowballs with stones or ice, or to ice-like hardness.

**Firearms.** Serious accidents involving guns rarely occur on target ranges. People die each year in hunting accidents, but more than half of the deaths involving firearms occur at home.

A hunter safety course is recommended for all new hunters. Some states require this. Instructions in hunter safety, marksmanship, and gun safety are available from the National Rifle Association, 1600 Rhode Island Ave., NW, Washington, D.C. 20018. State rifle associations, some state departments of conservation, and a number of local shooting and hunting clubs also give instructions.

Anyone who uses firearms should follow these rules:

Learn to handle a gun safely before you use it.

Keep guns unloaded, in locked cabinets. Keep ammunition locked in a separate place.

Keep all guns away from children.

Never handle a gun without first looking into the chamber and feeling inside to make absolutely sure it is unloaded.

Always point the muzzle of a gun in a safe direction. Keep the safety catch on until you are about to shoot.

# SAFETY/TRANSPORTATION

Motor vehicle accidents present the greatest safety problem in the United States. They cause almost half of all accidental deaths, despite constant efforts to make automobiles, highways, and drivers safer. Each year, more drivers and greater numbers of automobiles travel over the roads and highways.

**Driver Education** is one of the most valuable tools in traffic safety. More than 60 per cent of the high schools in the United States offer some form of driver education. In many schools the course lasts a full semester. Some schools offer less than the recommended minimum of 30 hours of classroom instruction and six hours of behind-the-wheel laboratory work. Drivers who have completed driver education courses have fewer accidents than do other drivers. See AUTOMOBILE (Driving Safely).

**Pedestrian Safety.** A great many motor vehicle accidents involve pedestrians. Although the driver is often at fault, many pedestrians could avoid serious injury or death by taking precautions.

Pedestrians should observe these safety rules:

Never walk on streets or highways unless there are no sidewalks to walk on.

When you must walk in streets or roads, always walk toward oncoming traffic. Step off the road whenever cars approach.

Cross streets only at intersections or in designated crosswalks. Obey traffic signals regardless of whether or not traffic is approaching.

Avoid stepping into the street away from intersections or from between parked cars. If you must do this, be extra careful.

Children should never play in streets.

Playgrounds and playing fields near streets or parking lots should be fenced in so children cannot dart out in front of cars.

**Bicycles and Wheel Toys** present hazards to motorists. Children riding tricycles, or using roller skates, wagons, scooters, or other wheel toys should stay on sidewalks, or in yards or playgrounds. Any cyclist not old enough to know, understand, or accept traffic regulations must not ride a bicycle in the street. See BICYCLE (diagram).

Here are some safety rules to follow:

Learn and follow the same traffic rules that automobile drivers follow.

Ride in the same direction as automobile traffic.

Stay close to the right edge of the road so cars can pass easily.

See that front and rear lights, horn or bell, and brakes are in good working order.

Always signal when turning a corner or stopping.

Slow up at intersections. Walk your bicycle across busy intersections.

16

# SAFETY

Make no sudden stops or motions that might confuse a driver.

Always ride in single file when riding with a group of cyclists.

Never try stunts or ride more than one person on a bicycle.

Avoid heavy traffic. Use bicycle paths when they are available.

Children should never take wheel toys in the street. They should learn to watch for cars backing out of driveways. They should be courteous to persons using the sidewalks.

**Commercial Transportation** has a much better safety record than private automobiles. This is true for streetcars, buses, trains, ships, and airplanes. Operators and crews of commercial forms of transportation are trained to watch out for the safety of their passengers. In the late 1960's passenger automobiles averaged more than 2 deaths per 100 million passenger-miles. Rates for all forms of commercial transportation combined averaged less than 0.6 per 100 million miles.

Passengers should take the following precautions:

Follow all posted rules for safety and comfort.

Never get on or off moving vehicles.

Wait in safety zones or on curbs for streetcars or buses.

In safety zones, face oncoming traffic to remain alert to any approaching danger.

When getting off buses or streetcars, remain in the safety zone until you are sure you can cross the street safely.

Take special care when crossing in front of or behind any vehicle.

Always get into or out of taxicabs or automobiles on the curb side.

Keep your arms inside the vehicle.

Never talk to the driver of the vehicle.

*Critically reviewed by* NATIONAL SAFETY COUNCIL

**Related Articles** in WORLD BOOK include:

### PUBLIC SAFETY

Civil Defense
Fallout Shelter
Fire Fighting
National Safety Council
Police
Public Health
Pure Food and
  Drug Laws
Sanitation
Smoke Prevention
Sprinkler System

### SAFETY AT HOME

Asphyxiation
Bandage
Bleeding
Botulism
Burns and Scalds
Emetic
Fire Extinguisher
Fire Prevention
First Aid
Insulator,
  Electric
Lightning Rod
Match (Matches Can Be
  Dangerous)
Mushroom (Poisonous
  Mushrooms)
Ptomaine Poisoning
Resuscitator
Tourniquet
Wound

### SAFETY IN INDUSTRY

Coal (Mine Safety
  Measures)
Disease (Occupational
  Diseases)
Dust Explosion
Lead Poisoning
Radiation
Radiation Sickness
Radium
  (Dangers of Radium)
Safety Lamp
Safety Valve
Ventilation

### SAFETY IN RECREATION

Artificial Respiration
Bicycle (Bicycle Safety)
Boats and Boating
  (diagram: Boating
  Safety)
Camping (Camping
  Precautions)
Drowning
Life Jacket
Poisonous Plant
Snake Bite
Sunburn
Sunstroke
Swimming (Water Safety
  Rules; Lifesaving)

### SAFETY IN TRANSPORTATION

Airplane (Instruments and
  Safety Devices)
Airport (Safety Devices)
Automobile (Driving Safely)
Aviation (To Ensure Safety)
Coast Guard, United
  States
Ice Patrol, International
Radar (Law Enforcement; pictures)
Railroad (Signals and
  Safety Devices)

### OTHER RELATED ARTICLES

Health
Insurance
Lightning (pictures:
  Lightning Safety Rules)
Protection
Weather Bureau,
  United States

### Outline

I. **Safety/Home**
  A. Falls
  B. Burns and Scalds
  C. Poisoning
  D. Asphyxiation
  E. Cuts and Scratches
  F. Safety With Electricity
  G. Other Home Hazards
II. **Safety/School**
  A. Corridors, Stairs, and Classrooms
  B. Gymnasiums and Athletic Fields
  C. Shops and Laboratories
III. **Safety/Instruction**
  A. Safety Instruction
  B. School Safety Organizations
  C. Safety Patrols and School Bus Patrols
IV. **Safety/Color**
V. **Safety/Industry**
VI. **Safety/Recreation**
  A. Water Safety
  B. Hiking and Camping
  C. Winter Sports
  D. Firearms
VII. **Safety/Transportation**
  A. Driver Education
  B. Pedestrian Safety
  C. Bicycles and Wheel Toys
  D. Commercial Transportation

### Questions

Is mankind safer since natural dangers have decreased?

What proportion of injuries and deaths occur in the home? What is the most common cause of home accidents?

How are most good electrical wiring and appliances marked?

Where do the greatest number of school accidents occur? How can they be prevented?

What does an employer expect a recent graduate to have learned in school about safety?

How can reporting "the accident that almost happened" help in a school safety program?

What rules should swimmers observe?

What should be done with firearms and ammunition kept in the home?

What safety precautions should hunters observe?

What is the safe way to get on or off a bus?

# SAFETY CAR

**SAFETY CAR.** See AUTOMOBILE (The Automobile Tomorrow [picture]).

**SAFETY COUNCIL, NATIONAL.** See NATIONAL SAFETY COUNCIL.

**SAFETY DEPOSIT BOX.** See BANKS AND BANKING (How Banks Serve Us).

**SAFETY GLASS.** See GLASS (Specialty Glasses).

**SAFETY LAMP** is a lamp designed to warn coal miners of the presence of firedamp, a gas that can cause destructive explosions. Firedamp, composed chiefly of methane and air, is formed by the decay of coal.

The safety lamp burns oil. Inside the lamp a wire gauze cylinder of fine mesh forms a cage around the flame. Firedamp can be detected by lowering the wick on the lamp. If firedamp is present, a pale blue flame appears around the central flame. This warns a miner to leave the spot immediately.

Mine Safety Appliance Co., Pittsburgh
**A Miner's Safety Lamp** detects the presence of firedamp but will not ignite the gas that may surround it.

The heat of the flame will not pass beyond the gauze covering and light the gas on the outside until the wire becomes as hot as the flame. The wire around the miner's safety lamp has good conducting power and will not heat up before the miner has time to escape. Most safety lamps are locked to prevent miners from opening them. Some lamps go out when opened. Firedamp detectors based on electricity and light have been invented, but the safety lamp is still widely used.

The safety lamp is based on a principle discovered by the English chemist Sir Humphry Davy. Davy produced the first really successful safety lamp in 1815. GEORGE B. CLARK

See also COAL (picture: Mining in Safety); DAMP; DAVY, SIR HUMPHRY.

**SAFETY MATCH.** See MATCH.

**SAFETY PATROL, SCHOOL.** See SAFETY (Patrols).

**SAFETY PIN.** See PIN.

**SAFETY VALVE** is attached to a steam boiler to release some of the steam if the pressure becomes higher than the boiler can safely stand. It consists of a cone-shaped vent into which a plug is fitted. This plug is held in place by a lever bearing a weight. The maximum steam pressure in the boiler can be increased or decreased by shifting the weight on the lever. Many safety valves use a spring instead of a weight. This is because a spring is less subject to accident. Spring safety valves are called *pop* safety valves. The tension of the spring can be regulated so that the valve will "pop" at any desired pressure. Hot water heaters also have safety valves. OTTO A. UYEHARA

USDA
**The Safflower Has a Blossom at the End of Each Branch.**

**SAFFLOWER** is a thistlelike plant with large heads of flowers. The blooms vary in color from white to a brilliant red. The plant grows about 3 feet high, and has coarse, branching stems. The broad leaves are usually spiny. The seeds must be planted each year.

The safflower has been grown in the dry areas of Asia, Africa, and Europe for many hundreds of years. At one time, people used its flowers to make red dye. Today, gardeners cultivate the plant in the western United States, and in the Canadian provinces of Saskatchewan and Manitoba. The chief interest is in the oil and meal made from safflower seeds. The oil is used in diets for persons suffering from heart diseases and hypertension. It is also used as a drying agent in varnishes and paints. The meal is fed to livestock.

**Scientific Classification.** Safflowers belong to the composite family, *Compositae*. They are classified as genus *Carthamus*, species *C. tinctorius*. HAROLD NORMAN MOLDENKE

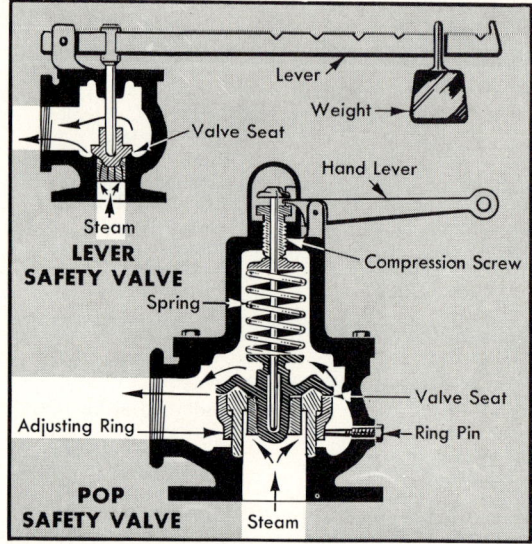

**SAFFRON,** *SAF run,* is a brilliant yellow dye and a food flavoring. It is produced by drying the stigmas and part of the styles of the purple autumn crocus. About 4,000 flowers yield about one ounce of commercial saffron. Saffron has a sweet odor, but tastes bitter. It is used in cooking, and in flavoring and coloring candy. People in Europe and India use saffron to season various foods. See also CROCUS. LEONE RUTLEDGE CARROLL

**SAGA** is the name given to a large body of literature written in Iceland between the 1100's and the 1300's. The word *saga* is related to the Icelandic verb meaning "to say" or "to tell." Any story—especially an adventure story—may be called a saga.

The earliest sagas were biographies of Icelandic bishops and Norwegian kings. The greatest achievement in this early historical writing was a complete history of the Norwegian kings composed by Snorri Sturluson in the 1200's. About 40 of the estimated 400 Icelandic sagas have been preserved.

The classic sagas were composed in the 1200's. They are usually known in English as *Icelandic Family Sagas* and in Icelandic as *Sagas of Icelanders.* They are anonymous and vary in length from short stories to full-length novels, and were composed in a concise but highly expressive style. Scholars once believed these sagas were transmitted orally from generation to generation until finally scribes wrote them down in the 1200's. However, most scholars now believe the Icelandic sagas were conscious artistic creations, based on both oral and written tradition.

The sagas were composed during a period of civil war and social decline. They glorified the moral and social codes of a "golden age" that occurred between 850 and 1050 during the early settlement of Iceland. They are tales of legal disputes and blood vengeance, and provide a detailed picture of social and cultural conditions at that time. The longest and finest is *Njal's Saga,* an impressive tale of honor and loyalty, death and vengeance.

During the 1200's, the European literature of chivalry began to influence Icelandic writers. Sagas became more romantic and fantastic. By the early 1300's, the nature of sagas had completely changed. These later sagas described the adventures of many traditional Germanic heroes such as Sigurd the Dragon Slayer and Rollo. Generally, critics consider these sagas inferior to the earlier ones. KENNETH G. CHAPMAN

See also SNORRI STURLUSON; SIGURD.

**SAGE.** See AIR FORCE, UNITED STATES (Defense).

**SAGE** is a somewhat shrubby garden plant known for its sweet odor and the flavor of its leaves and stems. The sage belongs to the mint family. It came from the southern part of Europe, and gardeners grow it throughout North America. Sage stands from 6 to 15 inches high. It has rough, woolly, grayish-green leaves, and a white, woolly stem. The flowers may be blue, white, or purple. They grow in groups. The sage is reproduced by seeds or by planting slips or cuttings. It needs much sun and a rich soil to grow properly. Cooks use the leaves and stems of the sage in making seasonings for sausages and cheeses, dressings for meat, and sauces. There are also several other species of wild and cultivated sage.

**Scientific Classification.** Sage belongs to the mint family, *Labiatae.* Garden sage is classified as genus *Salvia,* species *S. officinalis.* HAROLD NORMAN MOLDENKE

# SAGE OF MONTICELLO

**SAGE, RUSSELL** (1816-1906), was an American banker and philanthropist. He served two terms as a Whig member of the House of Representatives in the 1850's. Later, he joined Jay Gould, the railway promoter, and made a fortune in railway promotions and in stocks (see GOULD [Jay]). Sage was born in Oneida County, New York.

Margaret Sage (1828-1918), his second wife, used his fortune in many projects (see SAGE FOUNDATION, RUSSELL). She left money to 18 colleges, including Russell Sage College. Mrs. Sage also bought 70,000 acres on Marsh Island, in the Gulf of Mexico off the coast of Louisiana, for a bird refuge. She also made large bequests to the American Museum of Natural History and the Metropolitan Museum of Art, both of which are in New York City. V. E. CANGELOSI and R. E. WESTMEYER

**SAGE FOUNDATION, RUSSELL,** is an institution whose chief aim is to remove the causes for poverty and allow people to earn enough to have sanitary homes, wholesome food, and healthy children. The foundation was incorporated in 1907 by the widow of Russell Sage, who gave an endowment of $10 million for the improvement of social and living conditions in the United States. Soon afterward the endowment was increased by $5 million. For assets, see FOUNDATIONS (table).

The foundation includes a research program, a welfare organization, a department that promotes new ways of helping needy and retarded children, a child-hygiene department, and a housing project for persons with low incomes. It conducts its activities directly under its own auspices or jointly with selected organizations. It does not relieve directly either individual or family needs. Headquarters are at 230 Park Avenue, New York, N.Y. 10017. CARTER ALEXANDER

**SAGE OF MONTICELLO.** See JEFFERSON, THOMAS (The Sage of Monticello).

**The Tangy-Smelling Sage Plant** has been used for hundreds of years to improve the taste of food. Chopped or powdered sage is often used in sausage and in dressings for meat, fowl, and fish.
J. Horace McFarland

19

# SAGEBRUSH

**SAGEBRUSH** is a bushy plant known for its sweet odor and bitter taste. The sagebrush grows in the dry plains of the western part of the United States, particularly in northeastern California, eastern Oregon, Nevada, Utah, Wyoming, and Colorado. It may grow to any height from 2 to 12 feet, and has a straight stiff stem. The leaves are small and grow close together. The flowers of the sagebrush grow at the top of the stem, and may be yellow or white. Each flower is made up of many tiny flowers called *florets*.

The sagebrush is a perennial. It flourishes in the dry soil of the western plains, where many other plants cannot grow. But it also grows on mountain slopes. Sometimes the heat and dryness in the summer dry up the plant so much that it shows no sign of being alive. Then, the wind often uproots the sagebrush and blows it all over the plains, much as the wind blows tumbleweed. The seeds of the sagebrush are scattered in this way. Often the sagebrush is the only plant life for hundreds and hundreds of miles.

Sagebrush is not true sage, a plant used widely for seasoning (see SAGE). Sagebrush received its common name from the sweet, sagelike odor of its crushed foliage. There are several types of sagebrush. Some are used as food for sheep in the winter. Some people use sagebrush for fuel, because the dry wood burns with a hot flame and gives off a sweet-smelling smoke. Sagebrush can also be cultivated for domestic gardens.

**Scientific Classification.** Sagebrush belongs to the composite family, *Compositae*. The common sagebrush is genus *Artemisia*, species *A. tridentata*. J. J. LEVISON

See also NEVADA (color picture, State Flower).

**SAGEBRUSH STATE.** See NEVADA.

**SAGINAW,** SAG *uh naw*, Mich. (pop. 98,265; met. area 190,752; alt. 595 ft.), is a manufacturing city with about 220 industrial plants. The city stands beside the Saginaw River, about 85 miles northwest of Detroit and about 20 miles south of Saginaw Bay. See MICHIGAN (political map).

Farms near Saginaw produce large crops of sugar beets. Sugar processing and shipping is a major industry in the Saginaw area. The city also has one of the world's largest bean elevators. Products include automobile parts, boilers, furniture, graphite products, machinery, measuring instruments, railway equipment, and venetian blinds. Saginaw, with nearby Midland, is an important producer of chemicals. The city has about 160 wholesale firms.

Large ships can sail down the Saginaw River from the city to the mouth of Saginaw Bay. The city has an airport, and rail and bus service.

A settlement called Saginaw was founded on the west bank of the river, following the building of Fort Saginaw about 1820. A second settlement, called East Saginaw, began on the opposite bank in 1849. The two united as Saginaw in 1889. Fur trading flourished until the first sawmill was erected in 1834. Saginaw became a lumber center until most commercially valuable Michigan forests were cut down in the late 1800's.

Saginaw was never incorporated as a village. It received a city charter in 1857. The city is the seat of Saginaw County, and has a council-manager form of government. WILLIS F. DUNBAR

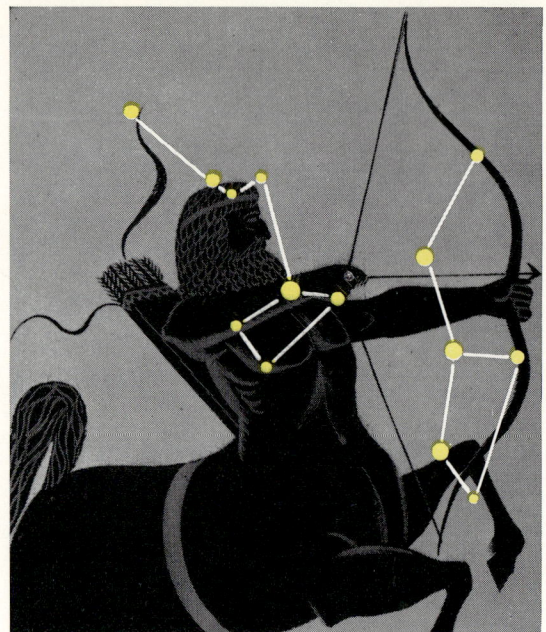

**The Constellation Sagittarius, the Archer**

**SAGITTARIUS,** SAJ *ih* TA *rih us*, THE ARCHER, is a *constellation* (group of stars) located in the Milky Way. It is the ninth sign of the zodiac (see ZODIAC). Sagittarius has no bright stars, but it can be seen in the southern part of the sky in late summer. The sun, the earth, and Sagittarius are in a straight line in the sky on December 22, the beginning of winter.

In Greek mythology, the constellations Sagittarius and Centaurus were placed in the sky to honor Chiron, the wise *centaur* (mythical half-man, half-horse). See also ASTRONOMY (Skies of the Seasons); CENTAURUS. I. M. LEVITT

**SAGO,** SAY *goh*, is a starch found in the spongy center, or pith, of various tropical palm trees. A type of flour, called *sago flour*, is made from sago. The largest supply of sago comes from the East Indies. Large quantities of sago are sent to Europe and North America for cooking purposes. Sago flour is used mostly in making puddings and as a thickening for soups. The flour is nourishing and easy to digest. Sago is one of the principal foods of East Indian people.

The fruit of the palm trees from which sago is produced is not allowed to ripen fully. The full ripening completes the life cycle of the tree and exhausts the starch center. It leaves the trunk a hollow shell and causes the tree to die. Workers cut down the palms when they are about 15 years old, at which time they are just ready to flower. The stems, which grow to a height of 30 feet, are split up. The starch pith is taken from the stems and ground to a powder. A single palm yields about 800 pounds of starch. The powder is kneaded in water over a cloth or sieve. It passes into a trough where it settles. After a few washings, the sago flour is ready to be used in making puddings and soups. Sago is further refined and prepared for export purposes. LEONE RUTLEDGE CARROLL

See also ARROWROOT; CORNSTARCH; TAPIOCA.

**A Camel Caravan** slowly plods across the shifting sand dunes of the Sahara. Such "ships of the desert" have provided transportation across the world's largest desert for hundreds of years.

**SAGUARO.** See Cactus (Kinds of Cacti); Flower (color picture: Flowers of the Desert); Saguaro National Monument.

**SAGUARO NATIONAL MONUMENT** is in southern Arizona near Tucson. The cacti after which the monument has been named may grow as high as 50 feet, and may weigh 10 tons. Wildlife in the 78,644-acre monument includes the coyote, black bear, and elf owl. The monument was established in 1933.

See also Arizona (color picture).

**SAGUENAY RIVER,** SAG uh NAY, is an important waterway in the Canadian province of Quebec. This river begins at the eastern end of Lac Saint-Jean in Quebec. It flows eastward for about 100 miles, and empties into the St. Lawrence River about 120 miles northeast of the city of Quebec. For location, see Quebec (physical map).

The river is not navigable for its first 35 miles. It drops more than 300 feet in this stretch, which extends from Lac Saint-Jean to Chicoutimi. However, this upper branch of the Saguenay has been harnessed for a power output of over 2 million horsepower.

The Lower Saguenay begins just below Chicoutimi, where the river forms a small inlet called Ha Ha Bay. The chief harbors on Ha Ha Bay are Port Alfred for industrial traffic, and Bagotville for passenger ships. The Lower Saguenay is navigable for the 65 miles from Chicoutimi to the St. Lawrence River. It becomes a fiord in this stretch, averaging 800 feet deep. Capes Trinity and Eternity, the most famous of the river's cliffs, tower over the Lower Saguenay. Both cliffs are more than 1,600 feet high.

Tourist cruises have been conducted on the Saguenay River since 1849. The Saguenay is a major lumber-transportation route. Tadoussac, at the mouth of the river, is a well-known resort area. M. G. BALLANTYNE

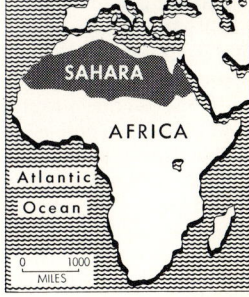

**SAHARA** is the largest desert in the world. It stretches across North Africa from the Atlantic Ocean to the Red Sea, and from the Mediterranean Sea to the Sudan. It combines with the Sudan in a zone of steppe vegetation. Only a narrow strip of fertile land along the Nile River and scattered *oases* (places where palms and grasses grow) break up this vast desert land. *Sahara* means *desert region.*

The Sahara is almost as large as the United States. It covers about 3 million square miles. Its greatest length, from east to west, is about 3,200 miles, or greater than the distance between New York City and San Francisco, Calif. The Sahara is from 800 to 1,400 miles wide from north to south.

The Sahara covers most of Algeria, Libya, and Egypt, and parts of Morocco, Tunisia, and the Sudan. This vast desert also includes large parts of Chad, Niger, Mauritania, and Mali, and Spanish Sahara, a Spanish province in Africa.

Part of the Sahara consists of mile upon mile of hot, shifting sand dunes. Great stretches of the desert, however, have a hard and rocky surface. A central plateau extends about three-fourths of the distance across the desert from northeast to southwest. This plateau is from 1,900 to 2,500 feet above sea level. Three mountain ranges, the Ahaggar, the Tibesti, and the Aïr, rise above this plateau. The highest peaks are from 6,000 to nearly 10,000 feet above sea level. Many fertile river valleys lie in this mountain region. The western Sahara is a vast sand waste. The Libyan Desert, north and east of the central plateau, is a gravelly waste.

21

# SAHARA

**Climate.** The northeast trade wind that blows constantly across Africa from the Red Sea to the Atlantic dries up the moisture of the Sahara. In summer, the equatorial sun often pushes the temperature to between 120° F. and 130° F. during the day. In winter, the sand cools so quickly that there may be frost during the night. Sometimes the temperature falls quickly when the wind becomes cutting and cold. It seldom snows in the lower areas of the desert but higher mountains are sometimes snow-covered. Blinding sandstorms often occur.

There is no part of the Sahara that does not get some rain, but in many places there are only a few scanty showers. Sometimes rain falls, but evaporates before it strikes the ground.

**Oases** are watered spots in the desert. There are many of these areas in the Sahara. They range in size from less than a square mile to those so large that several million date palms may be grown by the use of irrigation. Most of the oases are watered by springs that are fed from underground water. This water collects on a layer of clay beneath the sand. Some oases have been enlarged by digging new wells, and the soil has been improved enough to grow tropical fruits and grain.

**Animal Life** is scarce on the Sahara, because of the small natural food supply. The camel and the ostrich find a natural environment in the sandy wastes. On the borders of the desert, where there is some water, there are lions, panthers, hyenas, jackals, foxes, and several kinds of apes. There are many snakes.

**The People of the Sahara** include Arabs, Berbers, Tuareg, Tibbu, and Negroes. They have fitted their way of life to the desert conditions. The Arabs and Berbers live along the northern border of the desert near the Mediterranean Sea. The wandering Arabs of the desert are often called Bedouins. Tuareg robber bands wander over many sections of the middle Sahara. The Tibbu are a Negro people of mixed ancestry who live in the southeastern part of the desert. Negroes inhabit the southern section of the Sahara. Most of these people follow the Islamic faith. See ARAB; BEDOUIN; BERBER.

**Industry and Trade.** Camel caravans have crossed the Sahara desert since very early times. There is some evidence that the caravan routes are about 4,000 years old. But thirst and starvation, sandstorms, or attack by bandit tribes often threatened those who attempted to cross the desert before the motor truck was developed. In 1923, the French government sent track-type tractors across the width of the Sahara for the first time. Today, motorbuses and trucks make regular trips across the Sahara. Filling stations are situated at many of the oases, near the springs where camels still stop to drink and rest. The telegraph provides communication.

Many persons believe the Sahara has a great industrial future. Natural resources which have already been discovered in commercial quantities in the rocky regions of the Sahara include oil, uranium, iron ore, coal, copper, and phosphate. France used the Sahara for nuclear bomb tests in the 1960's. ELDRED D. WILSON

**Related Articles** in WORLD BOOK include:

| | | |
|---|---|---|
| Africa (color picture) | Harmattan | Oasis |
| Camel | Khamsin | Simoom |
| Desert (picture) | Libyan Desert | Sirocco |

**SAID PASHA.** See DE LESSEPS, FERDINAND M.

**SAIGON,** *sye GAHN* (pop. 1,400,000; alt. 30 ft.), the capital of South Vietnam, is the country's main seaport and center of commerce and industry (see VIETNAM [color map]). Saigon produces textiles, bottles, rice wine, tobacco, matches, and soap. This beautiful city is called the *Paris of the Orient.* About 170,000 Chinese people live in Cholon, a section of Saigon.

**SAIGON RIVER.** See MEKONG RIVER.

**SAIL.** See SAILING; SHIP AND SHIPPING; SHIP MODEL.

**SAILFISH** is a large fish that has a large dorsal fin that spreads out like a sail. Sport fishermen catch these game fighting fishes on light rod-and-reel tackle in the warm ocean waters off both coasts of the United States, and Central and South America. Sailfish around Florida are sometimes 6 feet long and weigh 120 pounds. The largest caught in Pacific waters weighed 221 pounds. The flesh is good to eat. The upper jaw of the sailfish is sharp and long, like that of the swordfish, to which it is related. Sailfish are sometimes called *billfish.*

See also FISH (color picture, Salt-Water Fishes); FISHING (table, Game-Fishing World Records).

**Scientific Classification.** Sailfish belong to the marlin family, *Istiophoridae.* The Atlantic sailfish is classified as genus *Istiophorus,* species *I. americanus.* The Pacific sailfish is classified as *I. greyi.* LEONARD P. SCHULTZ

Boubat, Photo Researchers

**A Sahara Nomad** carries dry wood for a campfire. An oil derrick, *background,* rises from the sand and stones. The French discovered oil in the Sahara in 1956.

# SAILING

Morris Rosenfeld

**SAILING** is an exciting water sport. The thrill of sailing a boat in a fresh breeze attracts thousands of sailors to seashores, lakes, and rivers in all parts of the world. They take to the water in sailboats that range in size from tiny dinghies to large yachts that can cross an ocean. Many persons enjoy racing their boats against other craft. For some, sailing brings the pleasure of leisurely hours on the water. All sailors love the challenge sailing offers to their skill as seamen.

For hundreds of years, all great navies and merchant fleets consisted of sailing vessels. Tall-masted ships with huge, billowing canvas sails traveled to all parts of the world. During the 1800's, steamships replaced sailing vessels for military and commercial purposes (see SHIP AND SHIPPING [History]). The development of sailing as a sport began when sailing ships declined in commercial importance.

Professional boatbuilders make most pleasure sailboats. Many boats have hulls made of wooden planking fastened over frames. But newer materials, such as fiber glass and molded plywood, have become increasingly popular. Many amateurs build small sailboats at home. Sometimes the manufacturer supplies the parts in a kit and the buyer simply fits them together. This is an especially popular way of building small boats called *prams*. These boats are 8 feet long and have blunt ends similar to the baby carriages known as prams. They are the smallest practical sailboats, and are excellent for beginning sailors to use in learning sailing fundamentals.

## The Parts of a Sailboat

Each part of a sailboat has a special name. Sailors everywhere take great pride in using the proper terms. The main parts of a sailboat include (1) the hull, (2) the spars, (3) the sails, and (4) the rigging.

**Hull** is the body of a sailboat. The front of the hull is called the *bow*, and the rear is called the *stern*. *Forward*, or *fore*, means *front*, and *aft* means *rear*. Almost all sailboats have either a *keel* or a *centerboard*. These flat pieces of metal or wood extend into the water from the bottom of the hull to prevent movement to either side. A keel is fixed in place. But a centerboard can be raised or

23

## PARTS OF A SAILBOAT

*MARCONI-RIGGED SLOOP*

bottom by a boom. They received this name because the tall masts necessary to hold these sails looked like the antennas for the radio developed by the Italian electrical engineer Guglielmo Marconi.

Nearly all pleasure and racing boats are also *fore-and-aft-rigged*. One end of the boom or gaff is joined to the mast and holds the sail out backward from the mast and parallel to the length of the boat.

**Sails.** The *mainsail* (largest sail on a sailboat) is fastened to the back of the mainmast. A smaller, triangular sail in front of the mainmast is called a *jib*. A large jib that overlaps the mast and stretches far back next to the mainsail is called a *Genoa jib*, after the Italian port where it was first used. The *spinnaker* is a large, balloon-shaped sail used for added speed when a boat sails with the wind. Spinnakers are often made in red, blue, and other bright colors. Dacron has largely replaced cotton as a material for sails. This material is strong and tightly woven, and holds its shape well no matter how strong the wind blows. But spinnakers are usually made of nylon, which is strong, light, and elastic. Nylon is too elastic for regular sails.

**Rigging** includes the *lines* (ropes) used on a sailboat. *Standing rigging* is permanent and supports the masts. It includes *shrouds* that run from the sides of the boat to the mast, and *stays* that run from the bow to the mast. *Running rigging* consists of the lines used to adjust the sails and booms. The lines that raise and lower the sails are called *halyards*. Those used to *trim* (adjust) the sails are called *sheets*.

### Kinds of Sailboats

Sailboats are classified according to their size and the way their sails and masts are *rigged* (arranged). There are many combinations of sails and masts. The most common rigs include catboats, sloops, yawls, ketches,

**Skipper's View of a Sailing Sloop.** The boom, top, extends back overhead from the mast. The doorway leads to the cabin.
Robert E. Mann

lowered through a slot in the bottom of a hull. Some boats, such as inland scows, may have two centerboards known as *bilge boards*. Other craft, such as sailing canoes, have *leeboards*, one on each side of the hull. Bilge boards and leeboards serve the same purpose as keels and centerboards. A crewman steers the boat with the *rudder*, a flat piece of metal or wood that extends vertically into the water near the stern of the boat. On small sailboats, he turns the rudder with a long handle called a *tiller*, and on larger boats with a *wheel*.

**Spars** are the poles that support the sails. They include masts, booms, and gaffs. *Masts* are the upright poles that hold the sails. The *mainmast* holds the largest sail. Some large sailboats also have a shorter mast, called a *mizzenmast*, toward the stern, or a shorter *foremast* toward the bow.

*Booms* and *gaffs* are the poles that extend at right angles to the masts and hold the sails straight out. Booms are fastened to the bottom of the sail, and gaffs are fastened to the top. Few pleasure or racing sailboats used in the United States today are *gaff-rigged* (have sails hung from a gaff). Nearly all American sailboats are *Marconi-rigged*, with triangular sails held out at the

24

## TYPES OF SAILBOATS

and schooners. Most small sailboats are catboats and sloops. Larger sailboats, especially those capable of ocean trips, are usually yawls, ketches, or schooners.

**Catboats and Sloops,** the most popular sailboats, are easy to sail and comparatively cheap. A *catboat* has one mast far forward in the bow, and only one sail. One type of small catboat especially popular with children is called a *sailing dinghy*. A *sloop* has one mast toward the middle of the boat, and two sails, a mainsail and jib. A large sloop with two jibs is sometimes called a *cutter*. *Inland scows* are popular on lakes. These light, fast boats are usually sloop-rigged. They have a rounded bow and a square stern, and are flat-bottomed. Scows usually have two bilge boards and two rudders.

There are several hundred classes of catboats and sloops. Each is built slightly differently as to the design and size of its hull, sails, and rigging. These sailboats are known as *one-design* classes. That is, all the boats in a particular class are built to exactly the same measurements. Each class has its own name, such as *Snipe*, *Penguin*, *Lightning*, and *Star*. The *Snipe* ranks as the world's most popular sailboat, with more than 10,000 boats registered in about 25 countries.

**Yawls, Ketches, and Schooners** are large, expensive boats. All have two masts and may be more than 70 feet in length. A *yawl* has at least three sails—a jib, a mainsail, and a mizzensail. The mizzenmast stands in the stern behind the rudder post. A *ketch* also carries three or more sails, but the mizzenmast stands in front of the rudder post. A *schooner* has a mainmast in about the middle of the boat, and a foremast. A schooner carries the most sails, including one or more jibs, a foresail, and a mainsail. These larger boats may have comfortable living quarters that make them popular for long trips. When they have engines to help them sail into and out of harbors, they are called *sailing auxiliaries*.

### Sailing a Boat

Even a log raft with a goatskin tied to a pole will sail before the wind. To sail in other directions, a boat must

**The Wheel** is used to turn the rudder and steer the sailboat. Lines near the wheel *trim* (adjust) the mainsail.

Robert E. Mann

**The Galley (Kitchen)** makes up part of the boat's cabin area. Sleeping quarters are beyond the door in the front of the cabin.

Morgan Yacht Corp.

25

## SAILING

be designed and rigged so that the force of the wind moves it across the wind or into the wind, as well as moving it with the wind.

**Controlling Direction.** A boat with no means of control will travel straight *downwind* (in the direction toward which the wind is blowing). It will do this no matter which direction its bow or stern is pointing. It may even go sideways. Using a rudder is the first step in controlling a boat. With a rudder, the bow of the boat can be pointed in the desired direction.

But a rudder is not enough to control a boat. A boat must also have something to keep it from sliding sideways when moving across the wind. This is done with a keel, centerboard, bilge boards, or leeboards. Boats with keels can sail only in water deeper than the keel. Boats with centerboards and bilge boards can sail in shallower water, because the centerboard or bilge boards can be raised or lowered as needed. Leeboards are a simple way of changing a canoe or rowboat into a sailboat. They can be swung out of the water when not needed.

With a rudder for steering and a keel or centerboard to prevent sideward movement, a sailboat can travel in many directions. The bow of a sailboat is usually sharply pointed, so it can cut through the water easily.

**Why a Boat Sails.** A sail has curved edges so it will be shaped like the wing of an airplane when the wind fills it out. The side of the sail to *leeward* (away from the wind), corresponds to the top of an airplane wing. The action of the wind blowing across this curved surface creates a lift similar to the force that enables an airplane to stay in the air (see AERODYNAMICS). In a sailboat, this lifting force becomes a pull away from the sail and toward the bow of the boat. At the same time, the wind also exerts a push against the other side of the sail. In this way, the action of the wind on the sail combines in two ways to force the boat forward. These forces make it possible to sail a boat in almost any direction, no matter which way the wind is blowing.

**Basic Sailing Maneuvers.** There are three basic sailing maneuvers: (1) sailing into the wind, (2) sailing across the wind, and (3) sailing before the wind.

*Sailing into the Wind* is called *tacking to windward, sailing on the wind,* or *beating to windward.* No boat can sail directly into the wind. If it does so, the sail flaps like a flag and becomes useless. But a boat can sail upwind by *tacking,* or following a zig-zag course. In general, a sailboat can head to within 45 degrees of the direction from which the wind is blowing before its sail starts to *luff* (flap) and lose its driving force.

Sailing to windward requires great skill. The wind almost never blows constantly with the same force from the same direction. The speed with which a sailor's tacks bring him to a certain point upwind depends on his ability to feel the little shifts and changes in the wind, and to adjust his sails accordingly.

*Sailing Across the Wind*, with the wind *abeam*, is called *reaching.* Sailboats can usually move faster when sailing across the wind than in any other direction. Some light sailboats with flat bottoms can move fast enough in a good breeze to lift out of the water and *plane* on the surface like a motorboat. This gives a great sensation of speed even though the boats seldom travel more than 20 miles an hour.

*Sailing Before the Wind* is called *running.* Contrary to what might be expected, running is not so fast as reaching or sailing to windward. In running, the sail is simply pushed along by the wind and makes its own resistance at the same time. When sailing downwind, many racing boats use spinnakers for added speed. These huge sails lift the boat along.

**Trimming and Tacking** are two basic skills all sailors must learn in order to handle their boats effectively.

*Trimming* means adjusting the sails to obtain the full

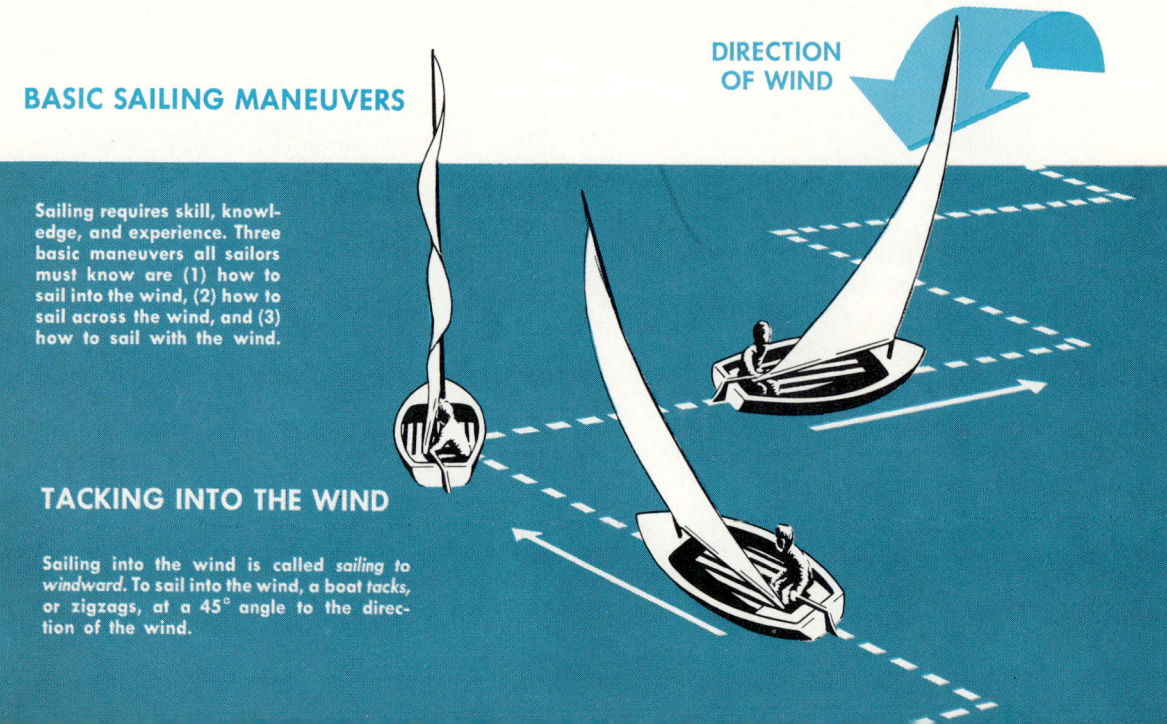

**BASIC SAILING MANEUVERS**

Sailing requires skill, knowledge, and experience. Three basic maneuvers all sailors must know are (1) how to sail into the wind, (2) how to sail across the wind, and (3) how to sail with the wind.

**DIRECTION OF WIND**

**TACKING INTO THE WIND**

Sailing into the wind is called *sailing to windward.* To sail into the wind, a boat *tacks,* or zigzags, at a 45° angle to the direction of the wind.

# SAILING

**With Jib Sail Flapping,** the *Intrepid* tacks into the wind and heads toward victory in the 1967 America's Cup race. *Wide World*

advantage of the available wind. A sailor must always know the wind direction in order to trim his sails correctly. When the boat is running before the wind, the mainsail is at right angles to the boat's direction. If a spinnaker is used, it is rigged out on one side of the mast on its own boom, called a *spinnaker pole*. The mainsail is on the other side of the mast. When the boat is sailing across wind, the mainsail extends about halfway out from the boat, or at about a 45-degree angle to its direction of travel. When the boat is sailing into the wind, the sails should be trimmed as parallel as possible to the boat's direction.

Small sailboats can easily *capsize* (overturn) if mishandled. Experienced sailors know where to place their weight and how to relieve dangerous pressure on the sails if a boat tips too far. This is done by *slacking off* (letting the sails out) so some of the wind spills from them. If a boat does capsize, the crew should hang on to it until rescued. All sailors, especially those who are weak swimmers, should always wear life jackets. See SWIMMING (Water Safety).

*Tacking* involves turning the boat so that the wind comes at it from the opposite side. When sailing into the wind, this is called *coming about*. In coming about, the bow is turned so that the wind crosses it. This is a comparatively safe maneuver. When the stern is to the wind, a turn that brings the wind to the other side of the boat is called *jibing*. Then, the wind crosses the stern quickly, and the sail slams across the boat. This quick shift of forces can capsize a boat if the maneuver is not handled carefully and with skill.

## Sailboat Racing

**One-Design Races.** The largest number of races are held for the catboats and sloops that make up the many one-design classes of boats. The boats usually sail over triangular courses in protected waters near a local yacht or boating club. These are evenly matched races, because all the boats in a particular class are designed and built alike. This makes the skill of the skipper and his crew the most important factor in winning a sailboat race.

But the care with which a crew maintains its boat and prepares it for a race is also important. The way the crew members *tune* (adjust the rigging) and mount the sails has much to do with a boat's speed. A bad paint job on a sailboat's hull will slow it down, because the hull will not slip through the water easily.

**Handicap Races** involve boats of different sizes and designs. All the boats cross the starting line together, but the smaller boats have a *handicap* (time allowance). A smaller boat can win even though it finishes far behind a larger boat. Most long ocean races for larger

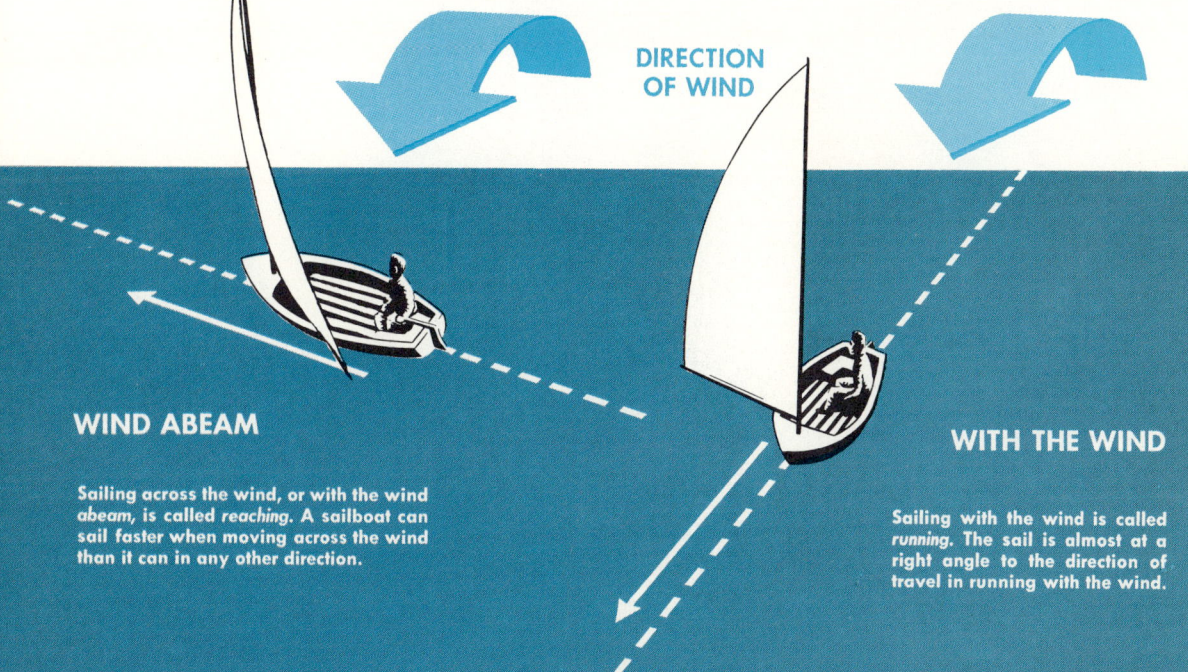

**WIND ABEAM**

Sailing across the wind, or with the wind *abeam*, is called *reaching*. A sailboat can sail faster when moving across the wind than it can in any other direction.

**DIRECTION OF WIND**

**WITH THE WIND**

Sailing with the wind is called *running*. The sail is almost at a right angle to the direction of travel in running with the wind.

# SAILING

sailboats are handicap races. Some of the best-known races are from Miami, Fla., to Nassau in the Bahama Islands; from Los Angeles, Calif., to Honolulu, Hawaii; and the Mackinac Races on Lake Michigan from Chicago and Detroit to Mackinac Island in the Straits of Mackinac.

**America's Cup Race** is the world's most famous sailboat race. In this race, a boat from another nation challenges the New York Yacht Club for a cup first won by the schooner *America* in 1851. Since then, the race has been held an average of once every six years, with most of the challenges by British yachts. Sir Thomas Lipton, a British tea merchant, made five efforts to win the race between 1899 and 1930. However, no country has yet won the cup from the United States.

In 1962, the American sloop *Weatherly* successfully defended the cup for the 18th time by beating the Australian yacht *Gretel*. In 1967, the American yacht *Intrepid* was the successful defender, beating Australia's *Dame Pattie*. WILLIAM W. ROBINSON

**Related Articles** in WORLD BOOK include:

| | | |
|---|---|---|
| Boats and Boating | Frigate | United States Coast |
| Brig | Galleon | Guard Academy |
| Caravel | Galley | (picture: Aboard |
| Chichester, | Junk | the *Eagle*) |
|   Sir Francis | Lipton, Sir T. J. | Yawl |
| Clipper Ship | Ship and Shipping | |

### Outline

**I. The Parts of a Sailboat**
  A. Hull
  B. Spars
  C. Sails
  D. Rigging

**II. Kinds of Sailboats**
  A. Catboats and Sloops
  B. Yawls, Ketches, and Schooners

**III. Sailing a Boat**
  A. Controlling Direction
  B. Why a Boat Sails
  C. Basic Sailing Maneuvers
  D. Trimming and Tacking

**IV. Sailboat Racing**
  A. One-Design Races
  B. Handicap Races
  C. America's Cup Race

### Questions

How does a sloop differ from a yawl?
What sail was named after an Italian port?
In what direction would a boat be sailing if it is *reaching*? *Running*?
When would a *spinnaker* be used?
What is the world's most famous sailboat race?
Why is Dacron an excellent material for sails?
On what basis are the various sailboats classified?
How does a *sailing auxiliary* differ from the standard large sailboat?
Why is a *jibing* turn difficult for a sailboat?
How does a centerboard enable a sailboat to enter shallow water?

**SAILOR'S-CHOICE.** See GRUNT.

**SAILPLANE.** See GLIDER (Sailplanes).

**Under Full Sail,** the *Columbia* sails across the wind through a calm sea. This schooner won the 1871 America's Cup race. The race dates from 1851, when the schooner *America* defeated 14 British ships.

Wide World

28

**SAINT** is a holy person who becomes a religious hero by exemplifying a virtue or virtues of his or her religion. The word comes from the Latin word *sanctus*, meaning *a holy one*.

The followers of a religion regard its saints as unusually blessed. They believe these saints are able to give special blessings and to exercise certain superhuman powers. All the world's major religions *revere* (deeply respect) saints, but in different ways. Some religions have formal procedures for officially granting sainthood to certain men and women. Other religions do not formally recognize saints, but they have religious practices that honor holy persons.

Many persons achieve sainthood because they played a major role in the history of their religion or symbolize a traditional feature of it. For example, Saint Paul converted to Christianity from another religion and became a great missionary who sought other converts. Some saints are martyrs who died for a holy cause. Many Christians who died rather than give up their faith during early Christianity are now considered saints.

A number of saints are considered especially close to God. Roman Catholics believe that the Virgin Mary is so loved by God that she rose bodily to heaven.

Some saints, such as Buddha, are believed to have gained superhuman or special knowledge about, or insight into, holy mysteries. Eastern Orthodox Christians revere Saint John Chrysostom for his wisdom.

Some persons are revered as saints because before or after death they performed miracles and pleaded with God for blessings or curses on particular persons. Others achieved sainthood because their *relics* (remains or possessions) or some place associated with them came to be regarded as holy.

Still others are considered saints because before or after death they became *demigods* (partly a god and partly human) and had divine powers. Before World War II, believers in one form of Shintoism regarded the emperor of Japan as divine.

### Non-Christian Saints

Judaism forbids praying to any being other than God. But Jews honor saintly persons as heroes. In Jewish worship, the heroic deeds of holy persons may be recited as examples of faithfulness to God. Such early heroes as Jacob and David sometimes broke Jewish laws. But later Jewish saints were learned in the *Torah* (religious law) and firm in following its rules of behavior. Jewish saints have been called "toilers in the Torah." The most famous Jewish saints include Hillel the Elder and Akiba ben Joseph.

Islam credits supernatural powers only to *Allah* (God). All Moslems acknowledge as saints such heroes as Mohammed and Ali. The Islamic holy book, the Koran, does not provide for the worship of saints, but each locality cherishes a saint called *wali* (benefactor, companion, or friend). Moslem saints are considered to be close to God but not divine. The spiritual powers they exercised as living persons increase when they die. Then, their influence centers on their tombs and relics, especially their robes. Moslems believe each saint can perform a special miracle. A visit to a saint's tomb, with its holy objects and often its pool or fountain, is believed to provide advice, to cure a disease, or to grant children to a childless woman.

The Oriental religions have a greater variety of practices and beliefs regarding saints than do the Western religions. Buddhism honors the buddhas and their close disciples, along with relics and sacred places associated with them. Buddhist monks and nuns recognize patron saints as special guardians, and Buddhist martyrs are honored as religious heroes. Hinduism has no official saints for all Hindus. There are many ranks of semidivine local or regional saints. A Hindu village, tribe, or religious order may raise its own heroes or protectors to sainthood. Confucianism has holy men who are *sages* (wise men) of intellectual and moral superiority. The most famous sage is Confucius. Shintoism has no human saints or martyrs because its holy persons are considered divine.

### Christian Saints

The more traditional Christian denominations emphasize the honoring of saints. The Eastern Orthodox Churches, the Roman Catholic Church, some Lutheran churches, and the churches of the Anglican Communion regard many of the same persons as saints.

A *canonized* saint is a person whose name is included in a *canon* (official list). Christian saints were first considered saints by common agreement among people in a certain area, and later by regional bishops. Gradually, the authority to canonize saints for Latin Christians centered on the pope.

The earliest Christian writings call all believers *saints*. This practice has been renewed by several modern denominations, including the Mormons (Latter-day Saints). During the 200's, the term *saint* referred specifically to martyrs, and in the 300's to bishops. By the 500's, the term referred to all departed heroes of Christianity who were honored in worship services. In the early forms of honoring a martyr, believers living in his locality gathered at his tomb on the anniversary of his death. The fame of certain saints gradually spread to other congregations, and by the 500's some famous saints were revered throughout the Christian world.

After many martyrs, bishops, monks, scholars, miracle-workers, and other heroes had entered the list of saints, their relics were considered able to give special blessings. Believers asked the saints to plead with God for special favors. The Christian saints were popularly regarded as holy before they became officially recognized as saints. During the Middle Ages, popular religious sentiment sometimes disregarded the difference between worshiping or adoring God and *venerating* (showing religious devotion to) saints. By the early 1500's, many people prayed to the saints and their relics for special assurances of salvation. Certain practices developed around the veneration of some Christian saints, but were later considered superstitious. For example, many people thought St. Lazarus could cure measles if a person who had the disease prayed to him.

During the Reformation, both Protestants and Catholics attacked abuses in the worship of saints. Most Protestants refused to revere any persons as saints except certain heroes mentioned in the New Testament. After the Reformation, the Roman Catholic Church re-

## SAINT

stated the manner in which followers could call on saints for help or protection. Catholic saints were clearly ranked lower than God, and superstitious or other *impious* (disrespectful) practices regarding them were outlawed. Roman Catholics, members of Eastern Orthodox churches, and some Protestants still ask saints to plead with God in their behalf.

### Roman Catholic Saints

Present Roman Catholic procedures of canonization were officially established in the 1600's. A commission appointed by the church strictly examines the subject's life and works and any miracles associated with the person. If the investigation produces enough evidence, the person is eligible for *beatification*. That is, he or she may officially be declared "blessed." If further investigation produces proof of two miracles associated with the person, he may be canonized as a saint.

Canonization consists of declaring that a person believed to be holy was indeed a saint during his lifetime and is in heaven with God. This official status does not approve all that the individual said, did, or wrote. Among Roman Catholics, only the pope can grant official recognition to a person nominated for beatification or canonization.

In 1969, the Vatican announced a revision of the church's liturgical calendar, which lists the feast days of saints celebrated by the church. The new calendar listed 58 saints. But many more saints could continue to be venerated locally. The church also made optional the celebration of the feast days of other saints.

Children of Catholic parents and many others are named after a saint, often the saint on whose day the child was born or baptized. That saint becomes the child's special guardian or patron. A number of cities, especially in the Western Hemisphere, are named after saints. They include Saint Louis, Mo., and Sao Paulo (Saint Paul), Brazil. In many denominations, parish churches or congregations take the names of saints. Many Christians, recognizing that many holy men and women have never been canonized, celebrate them on All Saints' Day, November 1. WILLIAM A. CLEBSCH

*Related Articles.* See CANONIZATION; ALL SAINTS' DAY; and the table of popes with the POPE article. Other related articles in WORLD BOOK include:

Agnes, Saint
Albertus Magnus, Saint
Alphonsus Liguori, Saint
Ambrose, Saint
Andrew, Saint
Anne, Saint
Anselm, Saint
Anthony of Padua, Saint
Anthony of Thebes, Saint
Aquinas, Saint Thomas
Athanasius, Saint
Augustine, Saint
Augustine of Canterbury, Saint
Bartholomew, Saint
Basil, Saint
Becket, Saint Thomas à
Bellarmine, Saint Robert
Bernadette, Saint
Bonaventure, Saint
Boniface, Saint
Borromeo, Saint Charles
Bosco, Saint John
Brébeuf, Saint Jean de
Bridget, Saint
Cabrini, Saint Frances Xavier
Canisius, Saint Peter
Catherine of Siena, Saint
Cecilia, Saint
Christopher, Saint
Chrysostom, Saint John
Cyril of Alexandria, Saint
Cyril of Jerusalem, Saint
David, Saint
Denis, Saint
Dismas, Saint
Dominic, Saint
Dunstan, Saint
Edward the Confessor
Elizabeth, Saint
Fisher, Saint John
Francis de Sales, Saint
Francis of Assisi, Saint
George, Saint
Gonzaga, Saint Aloysius
Ignatius, Saint
Irenaeus, Saint
James (saints)
James, Saint
Jean Baptiste de la Salle, Saint
Jerome, Saint
Joan of Arc, Saint
Jogues, Saint Isaac
John the Baptist
John the Evangelist, Saint
Joseph
Jude, Saint
Justin the Martyr, Saint
Louis (IX)
Loyola, Saint Ignatius
Luke, Saint
Mark, Saint
Matthew, Saint
Matthias, Saint
Michael, Saint
More, Saint Thomas
Neri, Saint Philip
Nicholas, Saint
Patrick, Saint
Paul, Saint
Paul of the Cross, Saint
Peter, Saint
Philip of Bethsaida, Saint
Polycarp, Saint
Rose of Lima, Saint
Sebastian, Saint
Simeon Stylites
Simon the Canaanite, Saint
Stanislas, Saint
Stephen, Saint
Swithin, Saint
Theresa, Saint
Thérèse of Lisieux, Saint
Thomas, Saint
Ursula, Saint
Valentine, Saint
Veronica, Saint
Virgin Mary
Vladimir I
Xavier, Saint Francis

**SAINT, THOMAS.** See SEWING MACHINE (History).

**SAINT ALBANS,** Vt. (pop. 8,806; alt. 385 ft.), is called the *Maple Syrup Capital of the U.S.* It lies in Franklin County, which is a leading producer of maple syrup. St. Albans serves as the headquarters of the Central Vermont Railway, a branch of the Canadian National Railways. The city lies in the northwestern corner of Vermont, 19 miles south of the Canadian border. For location, see VERMONT (political map). Dairy products, flashlight cases, paper food containers, and sugar-making equipment are made there.

On Oct. 19, 1864, Confederate soldiers who fled to Canada attacked the North in the *Saint Albans Raid.* The Fenians, Irish patriots, used the city as a base in trying to attack Canada in 1866. St. Albans has a council-manager government. WALTER R. HARD, JR.

**SAINT ALBERT'S COLLEGE.** See UNIVERSITIES AND COLLEGES (table).

**SAINT ALPHONSUS COLLEGE.** See UNIVERSITIES AND COLLEGES (table).

**SAINT AMBROSE COLLEGE.** See UNIVERSITIES AND COLLEGES (table).

**SAINT ANDREWS** (pop. 10,396; alt. 20 ft.) lies on the east coast of Scotland between Edinburgh and Dundee. This farm town is sometimes called the *Capital of Golf.* The Royal and Ancient Golf Club, founded here in 1758, establishes many of the rules for the game. Scotland's oldest university, the University of St. Andrews, was founded in 1411. WILLIAM A. HANCE

**SAINT ANDREWS,** New Brunswick (pop. 1,719; alt. 23 ft.), is often called *Saint Andrews-by-the-Sea.* St. Andrews lies on Passamaquoddy Bay, about 60 miles west of St. John, and about five miles east of the United States border. For location, see NEW BRUNSWICK (political map). The many small islands in Passamaquoddy Bay and the ocean shoreline make the town a popular tourist center. St. Andrews was founded in 1784 by United Empire Loyalists (see UNITED EMPIRE LOYALIST). W. S. MACNUTT

**SAINT ANDREW'S CROSS.** See CROSS (picture).

**SAINT ANDREW'S DAY** commemorates the martyrdom of Saint Andrew in about A.D. 70. It is also known as *Andry's Day* or *Andermass.* Many branches of the

Christian Church celebrate November 30 as his feast day. Saint Andrew was the brother of Saint Peter, and one of the 12 Apostles of Jesus Christ. He became the patron saint of Scotland. Scottish people have organized Saint Andrew's societies to help the poor. See also ANDREW, SAINT.   RAYMOND HOYT JAHN

**SAINT ANDREWS PRESBYTERIAN COLLEGE.** See UNIVERSITIES AND COLLEGES (table).

**SAINT ANSELM'S COLLEGE.** See UNIVERSITIES AND COLLEGES (table).

**SAINT ANTHONY, FALLS OF.** See MINNEAPOLIS (History).

**SAINT ANTHONY'S CHAPEL.** See IOWA (Places to Visit).

**SAINT ANTHONY'S CROSS.** See CROSS (picture).

**SAINT ANTHONY'S FIRE.** See ERGOT; ERYSIPELAS.

**SAINT AUGUSTINE,** Fla. (pop. 14,734; alt. 10 ft.), is the oldest city in the United States. It was founded in 1565 by the Spaniard Pedro Menéndez de Avilés. The Spanish explorer Juan Ponce de León had visited the present-day St. Augustine area as early as 1513. The city lies on the Atlantic Coast in northeastern Florida (see FLORIDA [political map]). St. Augustine's historic sites and fine beaches attract many tourists. The city has a council-manager form of government. See also FOUNTAIN OF YOUTH.   KATHRYN ABBEY HANNA

**SAINT AUGUSTINE'S COLLEGE.** See UNIVERSITIES AND COLLEGES (table).

**SAINT BARTHOLOMEW'S DAY, MASSACRE OF,** was a slaughter of French *Huguenots* (Protestants). The massacre began on Aug. 24, 1572, in Paris. The massacre spread throughout France, and thousands of Huguenots were killed before the violence ended.

During the mid-1500's, the French Roman Catholics and Huguenots fought bitterly. The Huguenots had become so numerous that the Roman Catholics feared they would take control of the French government. A civil war began in 1562 and lasted eight years. In 1570, the Peace of Saint-Germain granted the Huguenots liberty. But fear of the growing Huguenot political power led Catherine de Médicis, the mother of King Charles IX, and other Roman Catholic leaders to plot the assassination of leading Huguenots. The attempted murder of Gaspard de Coligny, one of the most respected Huguenot leaders, caused great tension in Paris.

Catherine convinced King Charles that the Huguenots would attack the palace and might kill him. Charles then ordered the death of leading Huguenots. He reportedly said, "Kill them all so that not a single one be left to reproach me." Henry de Guise, Coligny's enemy, led a group who murdered Coligny on St. Bartholomew's Day. Other well-known Huguenots were killed in Paris. Mobs then killed thousands of Huguenots throughout France.   EDWIN J. WESTERMANN

See also HUGUENOTS; CATHERINE DE MÉDICIS; COLIGNY, GASPARD DE; CHARLES (IX) of France.

**SAINT BENEDICT, COLLEGE OF.** See UNIVERSITIES AND COLLEGES (table).

**SAINT BENEDICT'S COLLEGE.** See UNIVERSITIES AND COLLEGES (table).

# SAINT BERNARD

Ylla

**The Saint Bernard Has a Huge, Sad-looking Face.**

**SAINT BERNARD** is a large intelligent dog that has become famous for rescuing lost travelers. The dog gets its name from the fact that it was developed by a group of monks in the monastery of St. Bernard, in the Alps of Switzerland. There were formerly foot travelers in the Alps. They often lost their way, or became buried in sudden snowdrifts or snowstorms. The St. Bernard was trained to rescue such persons. With its wonderful sense of smell, the St. Bernard could find persons who were buried several feet under the snow. After it had found the lost traveler, it called out for help by barking loudly. They were also trained to guide travelers over treacherous trails, giving warning of dangerous footing. An English artist, Sir Edwin Landseer, painted a popular picture of the dog with a small cask hanging from a collar around its neck. But authorities say the St. Bernard never carried casks on rescue missions.

The St. Bernard is valued throughout the world as a watchdog. It is also an excellent guide dog and pet. It is strong and very tall, measuring about $2\frac{1}{2}$ feet from the shoulder to the ground. It weighs from 140 to 220 pounds, and is one of the heaviest of all dogs. The dog has a red and white body with some black on its head. Its hair may be either long or short, though in America

**The Gates of St. Augustine, Fla.,** formed part of the city's defenses. These stone gates were built in 1804.

Louis C. Williams

29

**Hospice of Saint Bernard** stands in Great Saint Bernard Pass in the Alps, on the Swiss border with Italy. For nearly 1,000 years, the hospice has been a refuge for travelers during severe Alpine winters.

Swiss National Tourist Office

the most common type has long hair. The St. Bernard has a large, square head, a short muzzle, and a short neck.   OLGA DAKAN

See also DOG (color picture: Working Dogs).

**SAINT BERNARD, GREAT,** and **SAINT BERNARD, LITTLE,** are high passes across the Swiss Alps. The Romans used them as military roads. Today, motor roads cross the passes. Each pass has a *hospice* (refuge for travelers). The 3½-mile Great St. Bernard Tunnel for automobiles, linking Italy and Switzerland, was opened to traffic in 1964. For location, see SWITZERLAND (color map).

**Great Saint Bernard.** The road leading across Great St. Bernard begins at Martigny, in the Rhône Valley. It follows the Val d'Entremont to an elevation of 8,110 feet. The road then descends into northwestern Italy by way of Val d'Aosta. The gray stone St. Bernard Hospice stands at the highest point in the pass. It was founded in the 1000's by Saint Bernard of Menthon. Augustine monks offer refuge for travelers at the hospice. During the severe winter months, the monks and their famous St. Bernard dogs save the lives of many wayfarers. In normal winters, the road leading to the pass is only partially open, leaving the hospice completely isolated from the outside world. Food supplies and mail must then be carried to the top of the pass by lay brothers and monks. The life of the monks is so severe that only young men are chosen to serve. Most of the monks are excellent mountain guides, climbers, and skiers. Many summer travelers visit the hospice, which has room for over 300 persons. But no one may stay there longer than one day except in an emergency.

**Little Saint Bernard** lies about 25 miles southwest of Great St. Bernard. Its hospice dates from 962, and is nestled in the pass at an elevation of 7,170 feet. It is 10 miles south of Mont Blanc, one of the highest peaks in Europe.   FRANKLIN C. ERICKSON

See also ALPS; SAINT BERNARD.

**SAINT BERNARD COLLEGE.** See UNIVERSITIES AND COLLEGES (table).

**SAINT BONAVENTURE UNIVERSITY.** See UNIVERSITIES AND COLLEGES (table).

**SAINT BONIFACE,** Manitoba (pop. 43,214; alt. 763 ft.), on the east bank of the Red River, forms part of the Winnipeg metropolitan and industrial area. For location, see MANITOBA (political map).

One of Canada's largest stockyards operates in St. Boniface. The city also has canning and packing plants, flour mills, paint and soap works, and a large concrete and masonry industry. The French explorer Pierre Gaultier, Sieur de la Vérendrye, visited the site in 1738. He established Fort Rouge nearby in 1738. French colonists settled there in 1818.

Manitoba's Roman Catholic culture is centered in St. Boniface where western Canada's largest cathedral, the Basilica of St. Boniface, is located.   W. L. MORTON

**SAINT CATHARINES,** Ontario (pop. 97,101; alt. 347 ft.), is the center of a rich fruit-growing area on the Niagara peninsula. It stands beside the Welland Canal. For location, see ONTARIO (political map).

In addition to packing and canning fruits and vegetables, industries there manufacture farm tools, automotive parts, paper and wood products, and textiles. Ridley College, a boys' school, is located there. The Henley Rowing Regatta and the St. Catharines Horse Show are held there each year. St. Catharines was settled about 1796.   D. M. L. FARR

**SAINT CATHERINE, COLLEGE OF.** See UNIVERSITIES AND COLLEGES (table).

**SAINT CHRISTOPHER-NEVIS-ANGUILLA.** See WEST INDIES ASSOCIATED STATES.

**SAINT CLAIR, ARTHUR** (1736-1818), was a Scottish-American soldier and statesman. He served as a British army officer in America during the French and Indian War. When the Revolutionary War broke out, he joined the colonial army, and organized the New Jersey troops. St. Clair fought at Trenton and Princeton, and became a major general. He commanded Fort Ticonderoga, but did not try to defend it against General John Burgoyne. His failure to defend the fort caused much criticism, and he was recalled from service.

After the war, St. Clair won a seat in the Continental Congress as a representative for Pennsylvania. In 1787, he became president of Congress, and, in 1789, governor of the Northwest Territory. After a defeat in battle by the Miami Indians in 1791, he resigned his army command. In 1802, St. Clair objected to the law which made Ohio a state, and had to resign as governor of the Northwest Territory. He was born in Thurso, County Caithness, Scotland. JOHN R. ALDEN

**SAINT CLAIR, LAKE.** See LAKE SAINT CLAIR.

**SAINT CLAIR SHORES,** Mich. (pop. 76,657; alt. 580 ft.), lies northeast of Detroit on the western shore of Lake Saint Clair. Fine harbors for boating have given it the nickname, *Boating Capital of Michigan*. Saint Clair Shores was incorporated as a village in 1925 and as a city in 1950. It has a council-manager form of government. For location, see MICHIGAN (political map). WILLIS F. DUNBAR

**SAINT CLOUD,** Minn. (pop. 33,815; alt. 1,045 ft.), is a center of the granite industry. The city ranks high in the production and processing of colored granite. It lies on the Mississippi River, about 70 miles northwest of Minneapolis (see MINNESOTA [political map]).

Leading products include optical lenses and railway freight cars. The city serves as a central Minnesota wholesale and retail shipping center.

Ole Bergeson, a Norwegian, staked the original claim to the site of Saint Cloud in the early 1850's. In 1853, John L. Wilson, a pioneer from Maine, paid Bergeson $250 for the 325 acres where the Saint Cloud business district now stands. Wilson named the settlement Saint Cloud after a suburb of Paris, France. In the 1850's and 1860's, Saint Cloud was a terminal of a stage line that extended from the Mississippi River to the Red River Colony (now Winnipeg, Canada). Saint Cloud received its city charter in 1868. It is the seat of Stearns County, and has a mayor-council government. HAROLD T. HAGG

**SAINT CLOUD STATE COLLEGE.** See UNIVERSITIES AND COLLEGES (table).

**SAINT CROIX.** See VIRGIN ISLANDS.

**SAINT CROIX ISLAND NATIONAL MONUMENT,** on the Canadian border in eastern Maine, is the site of one of the first French settlements in North America. Explorers Sieur de Monts and Samuel de Champlain established a colony there in 1604, but it was abandoned in 1605. The 56½-acre site is on St. Croix Island in the St. Croix River, and on the southern bank of the river. Congress authorized the monument in 1949, but the government did not acquire all the land until 1967.

**SAINT CROIX RIVER.** See MAINE (Rivers and Lakes).

**SAINT DAVID'S DAY** is celebrated on March 1 in honor of the patron saint of Wales. He was born in the British Isles, probably in the A.D. 400's, and became bishop of a Roman port, now St. David's. Legend says he was a relative of King Arthur, a pilgrim to Jerusalem, and a leader against the Saxons. The day has been celebrated in America since 1729. RAYMOND HOYT JAHN

**SAINT DENIS, RUTH** (1877?-1968), was an American dancer, dance teacher, and *choreographer* (dance composer). For more than 70 years, she devoted herself to proving that dance could express "the noblest thoughts of man."

Ruth St. Denis was born in Newark, N.J. She considered the dances she saw as a girl to be superficial, and turned to the East for ideas about dance as a spiritual art. She choreographed and performed in *Radha* (1906), a dance about a Hindu goddess. She also composed and danced in the Japanese ballet *O-Mika* (1913) and in other adaptations of Oriental material. In 1915, she and her husband, Ted Shawn, opened the Denishawn school in Los Angeles and formed the Denishawn dance company. Their students included Martha Graham, Doris Humphrey, and Charles Weidman. The company toured the U.S. from 1915 to 1931. Miss St. Denis devoted much of her later life to composing religious dances that were staged in churches. SELMA JEANNE COHEN

See also SHAWN, TED.

**SAINT DUNSTAN'S UNIVERSITY** is a private liberal arts university in Charlottetown, Prince Edward Island. Bachelor's degrees are awarded in arts, business administration, education, and general science. Saint Dunstan's also offers the first three years of a five-year engineering course. It was founded in 1855. For enrollment, see CANADA (table: Universities and Colleges). G. A. MACDONALD

**SAINT EDWARD'S UNIVERSITY.** See UNIVERSITIES AND COLLEGES (table).

**SAINT ELIAS MOUNTAINS** are a rugged series of the world's highest coastal mountains. They stand along the southeastern boundary of Alaska and the Yukon Territory. The range is nearly 300 miles long. It has a maximum width of 100 miles, excluding the coastal plain and foothill belt. The international boundary is 30 miles from the coast between Mount Saint Elias and Mount Fairweather (see ALASKA [physical map]).

The second and fourth highest peaks in North America stand in the Saint Elias Mountains. They are Mount Logan (19,850 feet) in the Yukon Territory, and Mount

**Ruth Saint Denis** was fascinated by Eastern and Oriental dances. She danced *Siamese Ballet* with her partner, Ted Shawn.

Photo by Lou Goodale Bigelow
(The Dance Collection, New York Public Library)

## SAINT ELIZABETH, COLLEGE OF

Saint Elias (18,008 feet) in Alaska. Twelve other peaks in the range are higher than any peaks in the United States, excluding Alaska. These peaks include Mounts Vancouver, Fairweather, and Hubbard.

The ruggedness of the range prevents extensive exploration. Many peaks are unnamed. The mountains are composed chiefly of sedimentary and volcanic rocks of the Paleozoic and Mesozoic ages (see EARTH [table: Outline of Earth History]). The range has frequent rains. Glaciers can be found throughout the mountain area. The largest glacier, called Malaspina, is larger than the state of Rhode Island. LYMAN E. ALLEN

See also ALASKA (Land Regions); GLACIER; MOUNT LUCANIA.

**SAINT ELIZABETH, COLLEGE OF.** See UNIVERSITIES AND COLLEGES (table).

**SAINT ELMO'S FIRE** is the name given to a round flash of light that is seen around ships in a thunderstorm. This flash of light gets its name from the fact that it looks like fire. It is actually a charge of electricity caused by the storm. In stormy weather it can be seen around airplanes, the masts of ships, at steeple tops, and at tree tops. It also may be seen around horses' manes and people's heads. The name *Saint Elmo* is a shorter form of the name of *Saint Erasmus*, who was considered the patron saint of Mediterranean sailors.

See also JACK-O'-LANTERN.

**SAINT-ÉTIENNE,** *SAN tay TYEN* (pop. 201,242; met. area 289,958; alt. 1,675 ft.), is a leading industrial city 31 miles southwest of Lyon, in south-central France. It stands on the slopes of the Furens River valley. With Lyon and Roanne, Saint-Étienne forms the major industrial triangle of central France. Its industries include blast furnaces, iron foundries, steel mills, armament plants, and ribbon factories. Its ribbon industry dates from the 1400's. For location, see FRANCE (political map).

**SAINT-EXUPÉRY,** *SAN TEG ZYOO PAY REE*, **ANTOINE DE** (1900-1944), was the chief influence in the creation of the literature of aviation. He was a flier himself, and died an aviator's death, disappearing while on an Allied reconnaissance mission during World War II. Saint-Exupéry was an air pioneer, opening routes over Africa, the South Atlantic, and the Andes Mountains.

During the campaign of France from May to June, 1940, he led a squadron in an unequal fight against superior German air forces. He wrote *Night Flight* (1932), *Wind, Sand and Stars* (1939), and *The Little Prince* (1943). He often used his books about aviation to discuss his personal philosophy of life. Saint-Exupéry was born in Lyon, France. HENRI PEYRE

**SAINT FRANCIS, COLLEGE OF.** See UNIVERSITIES AND COLLEGES (table).

**SAINT FRANCIS COLLEGE.** See UNIVERSITIES AND COLLEGES (table).

**SAINT FRANCIS RIVER.** See QUEBEC (Rivers).

**SAINT FRANCIS SEMINARY.** See UNIVERSITIES AND COLLEGES (table).

**SAINT FRANCIS XAVIER UNIVERSITY** is a coeducational Roman Catholic university in Antigonish, N.S. It was founded in 1853. The main campus has faculties of arts and science. It also includes the Coady International Institute, an extension department, and the two-

Brown Bros.

*The Standing Lincoln* **by Augustus Saint-Gaudens** is in Lincoln Park in Chicago. Saint-Gaudens carved many other public monuments in the United States.

year Xavier College at Sydney, N.S. Mount St. Bernard College and St. Martha's School of Nursing are affiliated with it. For enrollment, see CANADA (table: Universities and Colleges). MALCOLM MACLELLAN

**SAINT-GAUDENS,** *GAW d'nz*, **AUGUSTUS** (1848-1907), was an American sculptor whose work is noted for its lifelike qualities. He became famous overnight in 1880 with his statue of Admiral David Farragut, which now stands in Madison Square in New York City. His works include *The Puritan* or *Deacon Chapin* in Springfield, Mass., *The Standing Lincoln* in Chicago, and *Captain Randall* on Staten Island. Saint-Gaudens' first statue was *Hiawatha*, completed in 1871. He designed the statue of *Diana* on the tower of the old Madison Square Garden that stood at Madison Avenue and East 26th Street in New York City. Saint-Gaudens is also noted for his *Shaw Memorial* in Boston, and *Adoration of the Cross*, a bas-relief statue in St. Thomas Church in New York City.

Saint-Gaudens was born in Dublin, Ireland. He attended school in New York, but left at 13 to work for a cameo cutter. He studied drawing at Cooper Union, the National Academy of Design, and the École des Beaux-Arts. Saint-Gaudens' earliest work was a bronze bust of his father. JEAN LIPMAN

See also UNITED STATES (The Arts in the U.S.).

**SAINT GEORGE,** Utah (pop. 5,130; alt. 2,880 ft.), is the site of a $1 million Mormon Temple, the first completed in Utah. The city is in the southwest corner of the state, about seven miles north of the Arizona border (see UTAH [political map]). In 1892, St. George experienced the hottest temperature recorded in Utah, 116° F. Early settlers called the area "Utah's Dixie," because the climate encouraged them to grow and mill cotton. The region is famous for fruit, and is a tourist center. A. R. MORTENSEN

**SAINT GEORGE ISLAND.** See PRIBILOF ISLANDS.

**SAINT GEORGE'S CHANNEL** is an arm of the Atlantic Ocean which separates Wales from southern Ireland. It is about 100 miles long, and from 60 to 100 miles wide. The channel runs from Holyhead and Dublin to Saint David's Head, joining the Irish Sea with the Atlantic Ocean. For the channel's location, see GREAT BRITAIN (color map).

**SAINT GEORGE'S CROSS.** See CROSS (Other Crosses; picture).

**SAINT GERMAIN,** *saynt jer MAIN,* or *SAN ZHER MAN,* **TREATY OF.** The Allied powers of World War I and the republic of Austria signed the Treaty of Saint Germain on September 10, 1919. Twenty-seven Allied and associated countries signed the agreement which broke Austria's power. Romania and Yugoslavia were the only two Allied countries which delayed signing. These countries objected to treaty guarantees given to minority groups. Several months passed before they were persuaded to sign the document. The Austrian National Assembly ratified the Treaty of Saint Germain on October 17, 1919, and the agreement went into force on July 16, 1920.

The Treaty of Saint Germain was much like the Treaty of Versailles. Part I of the treaty provided that Austria could be admitted to the League of Nations after a period of good behavior. Part II reduced Austria's territory from about 115,000 square miles to only 32,369 square miles. The population was thereby reduced from 30 million to about 6 million. Eight clauses guaranteed the independence and safety of minority groups living in Austria.

The Treaty of Saint Germain gave complete independence to Poland, Yugoslavia, Czechoslovakia, and Hungary. These nations, together with Italy, also gained much territory that Austria had controlled before the war. Military clauses reduced the Austrian army to 30,000 soldiers. Only one factory could manufacture military armaments. Much of the Austro-Hungarian navy passed into the hands of the Allies, and Austria was left with only four patrol boats. Even these were only for inland-water protection, for Austria had lost all its seaports.

One of the important clauses of the Treaty of Saint Germain forbade union between the countries of Austria and Germany. But in 1938 Hitler forced a union with Austria. World War II set aside the Treaty of Saint Germain. DWIGHT E. LEE

**SAINT GOTTHARD PASS,** *GOT urd,* is a famous mountain pass in the Lepontine Alps of southern Switzerland. It is a level depression, surrounded by a number of small lakes. The Rhine and Rhône rivers begin near the pass. A road with many hairpin turns crosses the pass at 6,935 feet above sea level. The southern end of the pass leads to the rich farming and industrial valley of the Po River in northern Italy.

Travelers first used the pass in the 1200's. The League of Three Cantons, the first three "states" of early Switzerland, guarded approaches to the pass during these early years. A hospice was founded in Saint Gotthard Pass in the 1300's to give aid to travelers. JACK R. VILLMOW

**SAINT GOTTHARD TUNNEL** is a railroad tunnel that runs through the Alps in southern Switzerland. The tunnel is 9.3 miles long and lies 4,000 feet above sea level. It provides an easy and scenic crossing of the Lepontine Alps by way of Zurich, Switzerland, and Milan in northern Italy. For location, see SWITZERLAND (color map).

Construction of the tunnel began in 1872, and it was completed in 1888. Workmen were hampered by extensive illness, high temperatures in the tunnel, water rushing into the tunnel, and collapsing walls. JACK R. VILLMOW

**SAINT HELENA,** *saynt huh LEE nuh,* is a British island in the Atlantic Ocean. It lies about 1,200 miles off the southwest coast of Africa, and about 700 miles southeast of Ascension Island, which is the nearest land. For location, see AFRICA (political map). Saint Helena is famous in history because Napoleon Bonaparte was forced to live there from 1815 until his death on May 5, 1821 (see NAPOLEON I). The Portuguese discovered Saint Helena in 1502, but the island has belonged to Britain since 1673. It serves as the administrative center for certain other British islands in the southern part of the Atlantic Ocean. These include Ascension Island and the Tristan da Cunha group, which consists of Tristan da Cunha, Gough, Inaccessible, and Nightingale islands.

Saint Helena is rough and mountainous. It covers an area of 47 square miles of lonely, volcanic wasteland. Barren cliffs rise 1,000 feet above sea level at some points. The only village and port on the island is Jamestown, the island capital. It lies at the mouth of a small mountain stream near James Bay. Saint Helena has a population of about 5,000. The people are Europeans, East Indians, and Africans.

Less than a third of Saint Helena can be used for raising crops. The chief crop is New Zealand flax. Grasslands where cattle and sheep graze cover part of the island. The government has helped set up factories to make fiber mats. Other industries include fish curing and lacemaking. H. F. RAUP

See also ASCENSION; JAMESTOWN.

**Longwood, Napoleon's Home in Exile,** stands near Jamestown on St. Helena Island. Napoleon lived there from 1815 to 1821.

Camera Press, Pix

# SAINT HELENS, MOUNT

**SAINT HELENS, MOUNT.** See WASHINGTON (Land Regions).

**SAINT JAMES'S PALACE** is a royal mansion in London, England. It stands in Westminster, north of the Mall (see LONDON [Map of Inner London]). The palace served as the official London residence of the British sovereign until 1837. At that time, Queen Victoria moved the royal residence to Buckingham Palace. The British court is still officially known as "The Court of St. James's." Henry VIII built the palace in 1532.

**SAINT JOHN.** See VIRGIN ISLANDS.

**SAINT JOHN,** New Brunswick (pop. 51,567; met. area 101,192; alt. 42 ft.), became the first incorporated city in Canada in 1785. New Brunswick's largest city, it lies on the Bay of Fundy at the mouth of the Saint John River (see NEW BRUNSWICK [political map]). It is one of two winter ports on Canada's east coast. The waters in its harbors never freeze. Saint John has one of the largest dry docks in the world. Steamers from all parts of the world dock at this port, especially ships from the West Indies. The famous Reversing Falls lie nearby on the Saint John River.

Saint John has many industries, including lumber manufacturing, oil refining, pulp and paper processing, shipbuilding, steel fabricating, and sugar processing. It also has a brush factory. The Canadian National Railways and Canadian Pacific Railway serve the city.

The river was discovered by Samuel de Champlain on the feast day of Saint John the Baptist in 1604. The first settlement in this region was a fur-trading post. Rival French traders and the English fought over the settlement. American colonists, known as United Empire Loyalists, founded the city in 1783. It has a mayor-council form of government. W. S. MACNUTT

For information on the monthly weather in Saint John, see NEW BRUNSWICK (Climate).

**Saint John, New Brunswick,** is a leading industrial city. It is also one of Canada's two Atlantic Coast winter ports.
Saint John Port and Industrial Development Commission

**SAINT JOHN, KNIGHTS OF.** See KNIGHTS OF SAINT JOHN.

**SAINT JOHN COLLEGE OF CLEVELAND.** See UNIVERSITIES AND COLLEGES (table).

**SAINT JOHN FISHER COLLEGE.** See UNIVERSITIES AND COLLEGES (table).

**SAINT JOHN LATERAN.** See LATERAN.

**SAINT JOHN RIVER** is the main waterway of New Brunswick, Canada. It is 390 miles long, and drains an area of more than 21,500 square miles. The Saint John is formed by the joining of several small streams, which rise on or near the boundary between Quebec and northwestern Maine. The river flows northeast to cross the northwest corner of Maine, then forms the boundary between Maine and New Brunswick. After the Saint John river enters New Brunswick, it continues south for over 200 miles, and finally empties into the Bay of Fundy.

The Saint John, often called the *Rhine of America*, is one of the most beautiful rivers in the Atlantic Provinces. Three miles after the stream leaves Maine and enters New Brunswick, it plunges over the Grand Falls, a drop of 75 feet. The rapids continue for nearly a mile below the falls, and the river drops another 75 feet as it surges through this section. Small boats can travel up the Saint John about 260 miles. Near the river's mouth are the famous Reversing Falls of Saint John (see REVERSING FALLS OF SAINT JOHN). W. S. MACNUTT

**SAINT JOHN THE DIVINE, CATHEDRAL OF,** between 110th and 113th streets in New York City, is the world's largest Gothic cathedral. The cornerstone was laid on Dec. 17, 1892. Builders partly finished this Episcopal church in a combination of Byzantine, Romanesque, and Gothic styles. In 1911, plans were changed to copy late Gothic styles. Construction methods, such as using stone rather than reinforced concrete, follow medieval customs. Work continues on the unfinished cathedral. G. HOLMES PERKINS

See also NEW YORK CITY (picture: Famous Churches); RELIGION (color picture: Christianity).

**SAINT JOHN'S,** Newfoundland (pop. 79,884; met. area 101,161; alt. 110 ft.), is the capital and industrial center of the province (see NEWFOUNDLAND [political map]). According to tradition, John Cabot found the harbor of Saint John's on the feast day of Saint John the Baptist (June 24) in 1497, and named it for the saint. Both the city's Anglican and Roman Catholic cathedrals are named for this saint, and June 24 is a public holiday in Saint John's. Saint John's, settled in the 1500's, is one of the oldest cities in North America to be continuously occupied.

Saint John's is on the eastern shore of Newfoundland, about 5 miles from Cape Spear, the easternmost point in North America. Two hills, Signal Hill and Southside Hill, guard the harbor's entrance, which is 1,400 feet wide at this point. On the peak of a slope on the northern side of the harbor is the Roman Catholic Basilica, one of the largest churches of its kind in North America.

Saint John's is the home of the Memorial University of Newfoundland. The Saint John's Gosling Memorial Library is the center of Newfoundland's public library service. The Anglican Cathedral in Saint John's is one of the finest examples of Gothic architecture in North America.

**Saint John's Stands on This Deep, Well-Sheltered Harbor Which Can Accommodate Ocean-Going Ships.**

Saint John's produces fishing equipment, rope, paints, varnishes, soaps, butterine, biscuits, and jams. Materials shipped to the city are made into tobacco products, furniture, clothing, tinware, and ironware.

The French and the English prized Saint John's as a cod-fishing port in the 1600's and 1700's. The Treaty of Utrecht gave Newfoundland to England in 1713, and Saint John's remained the capital. During the Revolutionary War and the War of 1812, the British fleet made the city a major base. It also served as a naval base during World War II. In 1949, the city became the capital of the newly created province of Newfoundland. FRED W. ROWE

**SAINT JOHN'S-BREAD.** See CAROB.

**SAINT JOHN'S COLLEGE,** Calif. See UNIVERSITIES AND COLLEGES (table).

**SAINT JOHN'S COLLEGE** is a private, coeducational, liberal arts school. Its main campus is in Annapolis, Md. A branch campus located in Santa Fe, N.Mex., opened in 1964.

The college's course of study is unusual. Instead of textbooks, students read more than 125 books by the world's greatest thinkers. For example, they read Plato and Aristotle, the Bible and St. Thomas Aquinas, Locke and Rousseau, and Darwin and Freud. They discuss the books in evening classes called *seminars*. There are no faculty departments and no majors. Students study English, foreign languages, mathematics, and music in classes called *tutorials*. Tutorials emphasize discussion. Students also study science in laboratories for four years. St. John's grants a B.A. degree.

Saint John's College was founded as King William's School, an academy, in 1696. It was chartered as a college in 1784. For enrollment, see UNIVERSITIES AND COLLEGES (table). RICHARD D. WEIGLE

**SAINT JOHNS RIVER.** See FLORIDA (Rivers, Lakes, and Springs).

**SAINT JOHN'S UNIVERSITY,** Minn. See UNIVERSITIES AND COLLEGES (table).

**SAINT JOHN'S UNIVERSITY** is a Roman Catholic coeducational school in New York City. It is governed by a board of trustees consisting of eight laymen and seven priests of the Vincentian Fathers. It includes St. John's College for Men. Saint John's offers courses in the liberal arts, business administration, science, law, education, pharmacy, and nursing. The school was founded in 1870. For enrollment, see UNIVERSITIES AND COLLEGES (table). EDWARD J. BURKE

**SAINT JOHN'S-WORT,** or HYPERICUM, is a handsome shrub with large yellow flowers. Gardeners often use it for borders. Most Saint John's-worts grow in the temperate and warmer regions of the Northern Hemisphere. They are usually low shrubs. Some are evergreen. The flowers bloom in clusters during the summer. Pink and purplish flowers are rare. These bushes grow well in loam or moist, sandy soil. Most

**Saint John's-Wort**
J. Horace McFarland

35

## SAINT JOHNSBURY

of them should have some shade. The larger Saint John's-worts form rounded bushes when they grow alone. The smaller Saint John's-worts make good low borders or ground cover. The goldflower is a hybrid. There are over 300 known *species* (kinds) of Saint John's-worts.

**Scientific Classification.** The Saint John's-wort belongs to the Saint John's-wort family, *Hypericaceae*. The goldflower is classified as genus *Hypericum*, species *H. moserianum*.
ALFRED C. HOTTES

**SAINT JOHNSBURY,** Vt. (pop. 6,809; alt. 555 ft.), is the largest community in northeastern Vermont. It is about 30 miles northeast of Montpelier, on the Passumpsic and Moose rivers (see VERMONT [political map]). Saint Johnsbury is the home of a million-dollar maple sugar processing industry. Other manufactures include wood products and machinery. The manufacture of weighing scales began in 1831, when Thaddeus Fairbanks invented the platform scale there. The village is the seat of Caledonia County, and has a council-manager form of government. Saint Johnsbury was settled in 1786.
WALTER R. HARD, JR.

**SAINT JOSEPH,** Mo. (pop. 79,673; met. area 90,581; alt. 850 ft.), is the trading center for a large fruit, livestock, and grain-producing region. The city lies on the east bank of the Missouri River in the northwest part of Missouri, 55 miles northwest of Kansas City. For location, see MISSOURI (political map).

St. Joseph has the largest plant in the United States for producing cholera serum for hogs. One of America's largest paper-tablet and stationery factories is located in St. Joseph.

Saint Joseph has one of the largest livestock and meat-packing industries in the state. It is an important flour and cereal milling center. Many dry-goods concerns operate in the city.

Manufacturing plants in Saint Joseph make textiles, clothing, candy, beverages, dairy goods, harnesses and saddles, chemicals, drugs, paper boxes, and iron goods. The city is the transportation center for northwest Missouri.

The city was founded in 1826 by Joseph Robidoux, a French fur trader. It received a city charter in 1851. The city has a mayor-council form of government. In 1860, the Pony Express began operating between Saint Joseph and Sacramento, Calif. (see PONY EXPRESS). Jesse James, a famous western outlaw, was killed in Saint Joseph in 1882.
NOEL P. GIST

**SAINT JOSEPH COLLEGE.** See UNIVERSITIES AND COLLEGES (table).

**SAINT JOSEPH'S COLLEGE.** See UNIVERSITIES AND COLLEGES (table).

**SAINT JOSEPH'S COLLEGE FOR WOMEN.** See UNIVERSITIES AND COLLEGES (table).

**SAINT JOSEPH'S SEMINARY.** See UNIVERSITIES AND COLLEGES (table).

**SAINT JOSEPH'S SEMINARY AND COLLEGE.** See UNIVERSITIES AND COLLEGES (table).

**SAINT KITTS-NEVIS-ANGUILLA.** See WEST INDIES ASSOCIATED STATES.

**SAINT LAURENT,** *SAN LAW RAHN*, Quebec (pop. 59,479; alt. 140 ft.), is a suburb of Montreal, about 3 miles northwest of the city. St. Laurent produces iron and steel products, transportation equipment, and chemicals. Basile Moreau College, St. Laurent College, and St. Croix Seminary are located there. St. Laurent was founded in 1845.

St. Laurent became a city in 1954. It has a mayor-council form of government. For location, see QUEBEC (political map).
HUBERT CHARBONNEAU

**Saint Joseph, Mo., An Important Industrial Center, Lies Beside the Missouri River.**
St. Joseph, Missouri, Chamber of Commerce

Newfoundland became the 10th Canadian province in 1949 during the administration of Louis S. St. Laurent.

## LOUIS S. ST. LAURENT
### Prime Minister of Canada
### 1948-1957

**SAINT LAURENT,** SAN law RAHN, **LOUIS STEPHEN** (1882-    ), served as Prime Minister of Canada from 1948 to 1957. He was the second French-Canadian to hold the office. Like Sir Wilfrid Laurier, the first French-Canadian Prime Minister, he was a Liberal.

Under St. Laurent's leadership, Canada took an increasingly important part in world affairs. St. Laurent was one of the chief architects of the North Atlantic Treaty Organization (NATO), a military alliance of 15 Western nations. In 1949, Canada dropped the word "Dominion" from its name, but maintained its relationship with Britain in the British Commonwealth of Nations. Also in 1949, Newfoundland became the 10th Canadian province. St. Laurent, who was half Irish and half French, considered his outstanding contribution to be the promotion of greater understanding and cooperation between English-speaking Canadians and French-speaking Canadians.

Louis St. Laurent entered public service unusually late in life. He was 59 years old when he became Canada's minister of justice and 66 when he took office as Prime Minister. He had already earned a reputation as an outstanding lawyer. Many Canadians thought St. Laurent was too modest and reserved to be an effective politician. But he led the Liberals to victory with overwhelming majorities in the 1949 and 1953 elections.

A lean, quick-moving man, St. Laurent had a shy manner and a friendly smile. He had piercing black eyes, white hair, and a neat white mustache. St. Laurent spoke French and English equally well. When he used English, listeners could hear a trace of Irish brogue. St. Laurent's gestures, particularly an expressive hunch of the shoulders, were French.

### Early Life

**Boyhood and Education.** Louis S. St. Laurent was born on Feb. 1, 1882, in the town of Compton, Que., a few miles north of the Canadian border with Vermont. He was one of the six children of Jean Baptiste Moïse St. Laurent, a storekeeper, and Ann Mary Broderick St. Laurent, a former schoolteacher. His father was descended from French settlers. His mother's parents were Irish immigrants. Louis grew up learning to speak French with his father and English with his mother.

As a boy, Louis became keenly interested in politics. His political hero was Wilfrid Laurier. During the 1896 election, the wall telephone in his father's store was the town's only source of election news. Louis enthusiastically relayed bulletins as they brought the news that Laurier and the Liberals had won.

During the 1900 election, Louis was in college. He could not leave his dormitory after a certain hour, so he lowered a pail from his window and hauled up election bulletins. In 1903, while studying law, St. Laurent reported Quebec politics for the *Sherbrooke Record*. He took the job so he could watch the Quebec parliament in action from the press gallery.

St. Laurent attended St. Charles Seminary in Sherbrooke, Que., and received a bachelor's degree in 1902. He then studied law at Laval University in Quebec and earned his law degree in 1905. St. Laurent refused the offer of a Rhodes Scholarship to Oxford University because he wanted to begin practicing law immediately. He went to work in a Quebec law office for $50 a month.

**Marriage.** In 1906, St. Laurent met Jeanne Renault (1886-1966), the daughter of a Beauceville East, Que., businessman. She later recalled: "As soon as I saw Louis, I said to myself, 'That's the man I'm going to marry.'" She and St. Laurent were married in May, 1908. They had two sons and three daughters. Both sons became lawyers. One of them, Jean Paul, served in parliament from 1955 to 1958.

**Lawyer.** St. Laurent quickly earned a reputation as a brilliant lawyer. In 1914, he became a professor of law at Laval University. He served as president of the Canadian Bar Association from 1930 to 1932. St. Laurent ranked as one of the top Canadian authorities on constitutional law. From 1937 to 1939, he served as senior counsel of the Royal Commission on federalism.

### Entry Into Public Life

In November, 1941, minister of justice Ernest Lapointe died. He had been the principal voice of French-Canadians in the Liberal party. Prime Minister Mac-

36a

## IMPORTANT EVENTS DURING ST. LAURENT'S ADMINISTRATION

**NATO** was set up in 1949 with Canada as a member. St. Laurent helped form the alliance.

**Supreme Court of Canada** became the final court of appeals for Canadians in 1949.

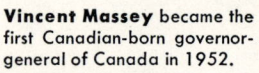

**Vincent Massey** became the first Canadian-born governor-general of Canada in 1952.

**Heading Canada's Delegation** to the United Nations in 1947, St. Laurent, *left*, conferred with alternate delegate Lester B. Pearson.

by Hans Zander for WORLD BOOK

National Film Board

kenzie King asked the 59-year-old St. Laurent to take Lapointe's place. St. Laurent agreed "as a matter of patriotic duty" to serve for the duration of World War II. He took office as minister of justice on Dec. 10, 1941.

As wartime minister of justice, St. Laurent encouraged unity between English- and French-Canadians by supporting *conscription* (drafting men for military service). During World War I, English-Canadians had favored conscription but French-Canadians had hotly opposed it (see BORDEN, SIR ROBERT LAIRD [Conscription Crisis]).

In February, 1942, St. Laurent won election to Lapointe's old parliament seat from Quebec East. He was re-elected in 1945. After World War II ended in 1945, St. Laurent wanted to return to private life. But King persuaded him to stay in office.

On Sept. 4, 1946, King named St. Laurent secretary of state for external affairs. In 1946 and 1947, St. Laurent led the Canadian delegations to the UN General Assembly in London and New York City.

In 1948, Prime Minister King announced his plans to retire. He urged the Liberal party to name St. Laurent as his successor as party leader. On Aug. 7, 1948, St. Laurent was elected leader of the Liberal party.

### Prime Minister (1948-1957)

At the age of 66, Louis St. Laurent took office as Prime Minister of Canada on Nov. 15, 1948. During his term, Canada's international reputation soared. St. Laurent realized that Canada would have to adopt a more international outlook than ever before. He and his minister of external affairs, Lester B. Pearson, led in forming the North Atlantic Treaty Organization.

In 1949, Great Britain granted the Canadian parliament the power to amend Canada's constitution in matters pertaining to the federal government. Previously, only the British parliament had made amendments to the Canadian constitution. Also in 1949, the Supreme Court of Canada became the final court of appeals for Canadians. Until this time, Canadian legal appeals had gone to the Privy Council in England.

In 1952, upon St. Laurent's recommendation, Vincent Massey became the first Canadian-born governor-general of Canada (see MASSEY, VINCENT). St. Laurent explained his choice: "I would not like to think that a Canadian, alone of the Queen's subjects, would not be considered to represent the Queen in Canada."

---- IMPORTANT DATES IN ST. LAURENT'S LIFE ----

1882 (Feb. 1) Born in Compton, Que.
1908 (May 19) Married Jeanne Renault.
1930 Elected president of Canadian Bar Association.
1941 (Dec. 10) Became minister of justice.
1942 Elected to parliament.
1946 (Sept. 4) Appointed secretary of state for external affairs.
1948 (Aug. 7) Elected leader of Liberal party.
1948 (Nov. 15) Became Prime Minister of Canada.
1949 Great Britain gave Canada the power to amend its own constitution.
   Newfoundland became Canada's 10th province.
1957 (June 21) Resigned as Prime Minister.
1958 (January) Resigned as Liberal party leader.

After being in power for 22 years, the Liberals lost the election of June, 1957. They won only 105 seats in parliament, compared to 112 for the Progressive Conservatives and 44 for other parties. The Progressive Conservatives took over the government and John G. Diefenbaker became Prime Minister. The defeat of the Liberals resulted partly from a public feeling that they had ruled too long and no longer understood the people's wishes. It was also due to a rising new national spirit in Canada which the energetic Diefenbaker seemed to represent.

St. Laurent himself was re-elected to parliament. But he did not seek re-election after parliament was dissolved on Feb. 1, 1958. St. Laurent retired as party leader in January, 1958, and the Liberals elected Lester B. Pearson to succeed him.

### Later Years

In 1958, St. Laurent returned to the practice of law in Quebec. He also lectured on law at Laval University and served on the boards of several large Canadian corporations. St. Laurent did not withdraw completely from political life. He continued to speak publicly on behalf of the Liberal party.    WILFRID EGGLESTON

**Related Articles** in WORLD BOOK include:

Canada, Government of
Canada, History of
Diefenbaker, John George
King, William Lyon Mackenzie
Laurier, Sir Wilfrid
Pearson, Lester Bowles
Political Party (Political Parties in Canada)

**SAINT LAWRENCE, GULF OF.** See GULF OF SAINT LAWRENCE.

**SAINT LAWRENCE ISLANDS NATIONAL PARK.** See CANADA (National Parks).

36b

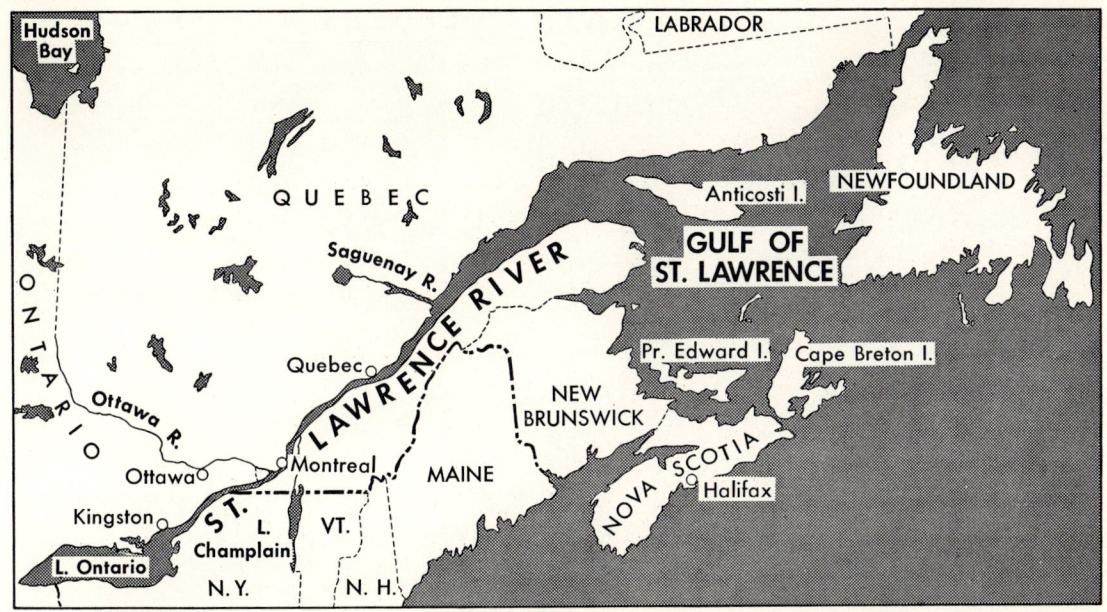

**The Saint Lawrence River Drains the Great Lakes and Flows Into the Gulf of Saint Lawrence.**

**SAINT LAWRENCE RIVER** is the largest river in Canada and one of the largest rivers in the world. It is often called the *Mother of Canada*. Its wide, deep course was the first highway of the explorers, fur traders, and colonists who came to Canada in early days.

Some authorities estimate that the Saint Lawrence is second only to the Amazon in the total amount of water that it pours into the ocean every day. The river drains more than 500,000 square miles, including the Great Lakes and southeastern Canada.

**Sources.** The Saint Lawrence begins at the northeast end of Lake Ontario, and flows in a northeasterly direction until it enters the Gulf of Saint Lawrence. But the source of this vast river system is the Saint Louis River, which rises in northeastern Minnesota and enters into Lake Superior at Duluth. The Saint Marys River connects Lake Superior to Lake Huron. The Saint Clair and Detroit rivers connect lakes Huron and Erie. And the waters of the Niagara River "shake the earth" at the great falls and rapids between lakes Erie and Ontario. The Saint Lawrence River proper from Lake Ontario to its mouth in the Gulf of Saint Lawrence is 710 miles long. The Greater Saint Lawrence River—from the head of its most distant source, the Saint Louis River in Minnesota, to the Gulf of Saint Lawrence—is about 1,900 miles long.

Many smaller streams empty tons of water each day into the broad Saint Lawrence. Some of these smaller bodies of water include the Ottawa River which pours its flood of water from the north into the clear waters of the main stream at the island of Montreal (see OTTAWA RIVER). Other branches that enter the Saint Lawrence from the north include the Saint Maurice River, which is noted for its high falls, the Montmorency River, famed for its cascade, and the Saguenay. From the south, the Saint Lawrence receives the waters of the Saint Regis, which rises in the foothills of the Adirondacks. The Richelieu, which is the outlet for Lake Champlain, the Chaudière, and a number of less important streams also enter the Saint Lawrence from the south.

**General Description.** The Saint Lawrence has an average width of a mile and a quarter as it flows from Lake Ontario to Quebec. In some places, the great river narrows to less than a mile, but in others it expands to form "lakes." The most famous of these lakes are Lake Saint Francis, a 30-mile long stretch of water above Montreal, and Lake Saint Peter, 28 miles long, which is located halfway between Montreal and Quebec. The channel of the Saint Lawrence slowly broadens below Quebec to form the great *estuary* (sunken river mouth) that blends with the Gulf of Saint Lawrence at Anticosti Island. Below the Isle of Orleans, the channel of the river is never less than 10 miles wide. The river is 25 miles wide where the Saguenay empties into it, and opposite Gaspé, it is 90 miles wide.

The river drops 245 feet between Lake Ontario and the city of Quebec. Most of this fall is above the city of Montreal. Between Lake Ontario and Montreal, there are about 30 miles of rapids. The tide goes up the Saint Lawrence River as far as the Saint Maurice River, at Three Rivers. There, the water may rise as high as 19 feet. The rise at Quebec is nearly as great.

Bad floods on the Saint Lawrence are unknown, because the waters of the Great Lakes do not rise and fall suddenly. Mud and silt that flow into the Great Lakes settle to the bottom, leaving the Saint Lawrence clean. However, the lakes and river have recently been *polluted* (made dirty) by sewage, industry, and ship wastes.

During the 1960's, light rainfall and low water levels caused many problems along the Saint Lawrence. In 1964, the International Joint Commission, a U.S.-Canadian agency, began studies on the Saint Lawrence pollution and low-water level problems.   W. R. WILLOUGHBY

**Related Articles** in WORLD BOOK include:

| | |
|---|---|
| Great Lakes | River (chart) |
| Gulf of Saint Lawrence | Saint Lawrence |
| Lake Saint Lawrence | Seaway |
| Ontario (picture: Thousand Islands) | Thousand Islands |

37

# SAINT LAWRENCE SEAWAY

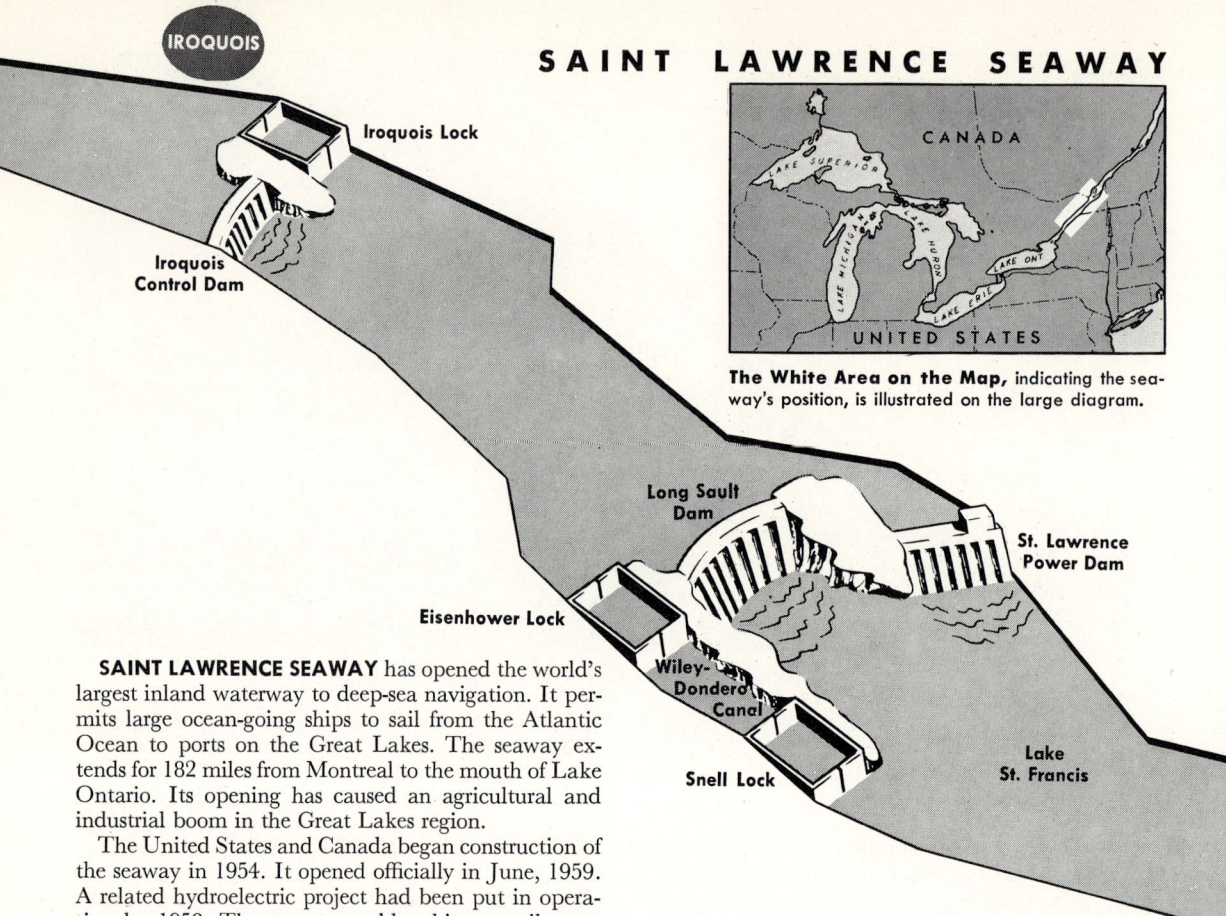

**The White Area on the Map,** indicating the seaway's position, is illustrated on the large diagram.

**SAINT LAWRENCE SEAWAY** has opened the world's largest inland waterway to deep-sea navigation. It permits large ocean-going ships to sail from the Atlantic Ocean to ports on the Great Lakes. The seaway extends for 182 miles from Montreal to the mouth of Lake Ontario. Its opening has caused an agricultural and industrial boom in the Great Lakes region.

The United States and Canada began construction of the seaway in 1954. It opened officially in June, 1959. A related hydroelectric project had been put in operation by 1958. The seaway enables ships to sail more than 2,300 miles inland from the Atlantic Ocean. By using it, about 80 per cent of the world's cargo ships can now sail as far west as Lake Superior.

### Saint Lawrence System

The vast Saint Lawrence River system has its source in the Saint Louis River in northeastern Minnesota. The system follows the Great Lakes to the northeastern end of Lake Ontario. Here the Saint Lawrence River itself begins. It flows northeast until it enters the Gulf of Saint Lawrence and flows into the Atlantic Ocean.

*W. R. Willoughby, the contributor of this article, is Professor of Political Science at the University of New Brunswick and author of* The St. Lawrence Waterway.

Before the seaway was completed, most of the huge waterway was deep enough for large-scale navigation. All but the largest ocean ships could sail for more than 1,000 miles from the Atlantic to Montreal. The river is 35 feet deep for this distance. Lake ships, carrying up to 25,000 tons, could sail from Ogdensburg, N.Y., to Lake Superior. The waterway's minimum depth in this 1,000-mile stretch is 27 feet.

However, navigation was hampered by five changes in elevation. These changes raise the waters from sea level at the ocean to about 600 feet above sea level at Lake Superior. The first step is a minor 20-foot increase in the 1,000 miles below Montreal. Then the upper Saint Lawrence River from Montreal to Lake Ontario jumps 225 feet in 182 miles. The last 68 miles of this area form the Thousand Islands section. The Niagara River accounts for an increase of about 326 feet between lakes Ontario and Erie. The fourth step is an 8-foot rise on the Detroit and Saint Clair rivers. The fifth is a 21.5-foot step on the Saint Marys River, between Lakes Huron and Superior.

**Canals.** Canada completed the Welland Ship Canal in 1932. The 27-mile canal has eight locks between Lakes Erie and Ontario. The United States and Canadian Soo Canals permit ships to pass between Lakes Superior and Huron. During the late 1800's, Canada built a series of 14-foot canals in what is now the Saint Lawrence Seaway area. These canals overcame the 225-foot drop caused by rapids and falls between Montreal and Ogdensburg, N.Y. The canals extended for 46 miles and had 22 locks, each 252 feet long, 44 feet wide, and 14 feet deep. Until the 1950's, all ships had to squeeze through these narrow locks. The channel was restricted to ships with a capacity under 3,000 tons. The United States and Canada began the Saint Lawrence Seaway in 1954 to remove this bottleneck.

**Navigation Project.** The United States' share of the seaway has included digging the Wiley-Dondero Canal in the International Rapids section near Massena, N.Y. The canal is 8 miles long and 27 feet deep. It has two locks, the Dwight D. Eisenhower and the Bertrand H. Snell. Each is 800 feet long, 80 feet wide, and 30 feet deep. The United States has also dredged the Thousand Islands section to a 27-foot depth. Between 1957 and 1964, the United States deepened the connecting channels of the Great Lakes to 27 feet. Shippers have urged that the channels be deepened to 35 feet.

Canada has built a short canal and lock to bypass the Iroquois Control Dam. Canada has also constructed canals with five locks. The Côte Ste. Catherine and St. Lambert locks are on the South Shore Canal, and two Beauharnois locks were built near Montreal. The Iroquois Lock is near Iroquois, Ontario. The Canadian locks are identical to those of the United States in size and depth. The Canadians also deepened the Welland Canal to 27 feet and dredged the 68-mile section between Cornwall, Ontario, and Montreal.

The United States spent $130 million for its share of the navigation project. The U.S. Army Corps of Engineers directed the construction, under the supervision of the Saint Lawrence Seaway Development Corporation. Canada spent $366$\frac{1}{2}$ million. The Saint Lawrence Seaway Authority of Canada directed the Canadian construction. Tolls were fixed by Canadian-United States agreement to pay off bonds.

**Power Project.** New York state and the province of Ontario began the power project in August, 1954. The state and province paid equal shares of the $600 million cost. About 38,000 acres of farmland were flooded to create a 28-mile-long lake in the Massena, N.Y.-Cornwall, Ont., region. Seven Canadian towns and

**Huge Circuit Breakers** are used as part of the Saint Lawrence Seaway power system. Electric power from the plants along the seaway flows to New York, Vermont, and Ontario.

**Diagram of the Saint Lawrence Seaway** illustrates the major installations of the waterway, and traces the Saint Lawrence River between Montreal, Que., and Iroquois, Ont.

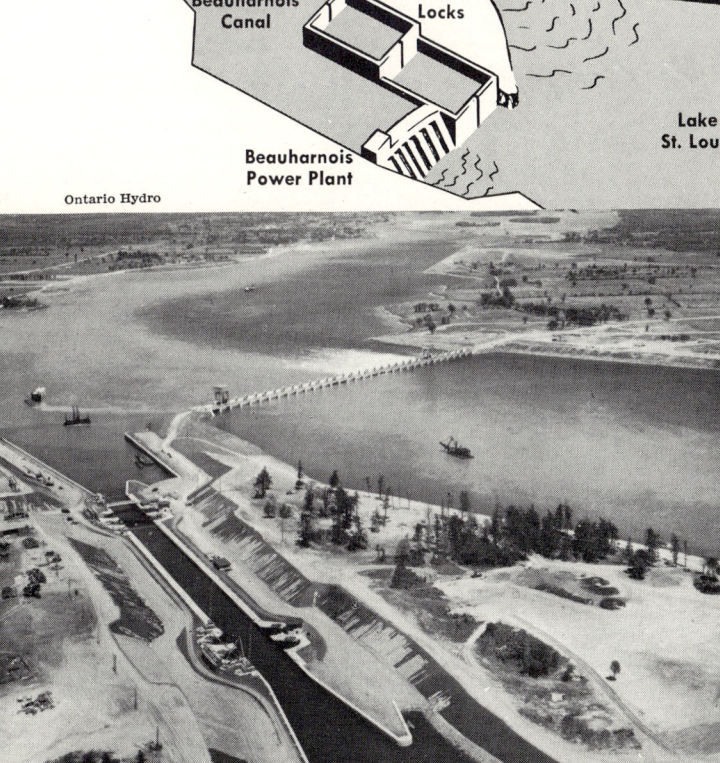

**The Iroquois Control Dam,** center, crosses the Saint Lawrence between Canada and the United States, near the Iroquois Lock, left foreground.

39

Power Authority of the State of New York

**Lake Saint Lawrence** was created by waters confined by the Saint Lawrence Power and Long Sault dams. The dams flooded an area between Massena, N.Y., and Cornwall, Ont. Ships go through the Snell and Eisenhower locks, and the Wiley-Dondero Canal.

part of an eighth were also flooded. Most of the residents moved to four newly-created communities nearby. The power project includes a powerhouse dam, a spillway dam, and a control dam. The powerhouse dam, called Robert Moses-Robert H. Saunders St. Lawrence Power Dam, stretches between the eastern end of Barnhart Island and the Canadian mainland. The spillway dam (Long Sault Dam) is across the south channel. It connects the western end of Barnhart Island with the United States mainland. The Iroquois Control Dam is 25 miles upstream from the Long Sault Dam.

The Power Authority of New York directed the state's share of the construction. The Hydro-Electric Power Commission of Ontario supervised the province's share. The project produces about 12,600,000,000 kilowatt-hours of electricity annually.

### History

French explorer Jacques Cartier discovered the Saint Lawrence River in 1535. He hoped the river would open into the Northwest Passage to the Orient. However, he was stopped by the Lachine Rapids near the site of Montreal. French fur traders and missionaries built a shallow canal with a wooden lock around these rapids in 1700. The Canadians continued to build canals during the next 200 years. By 1903, they had completed a navigable channel, 14 feet deep, from the Atlantic Ocean to Lake Erie. In 1823, the United States began to improve the channels between the Great Lakes. By 1914, the United States had provided channels 25 feet deep from Lake Superior to Lake Erie.

The improved channels were soon outmoded by the growth of shipping and the increased number of large ships. By the 1890's, many citizens of Canada and the United States were urging the cooperative development of the Saint Lawrence resources. The International Joint Commission was created in 1911, with authority over the boundary waters of the United States and Canada. In 1920, the two countries asked the commission to investigate the resources of the upper Saint Lawrence region. The commission, made up of three members from each country, issued a report in 1921. The members recommended that a joint power-and-navigation project be undertaken.

**Treaty of 1932.** A treaty was signed by representatives of the United States and Canada in 1932. It provided for the cooperative construction of a waterway, 27 feet deep, from the Atlantic Ocean to the head of Lake Superior. It also provided for development of hydroelectric power in the International Rapids section of the Saint Lawrence River. Power and costs were to be shared equally by the two governments.

President Franklin D. Roosevelt urged the United States Senate to approve the measure. However, rail-

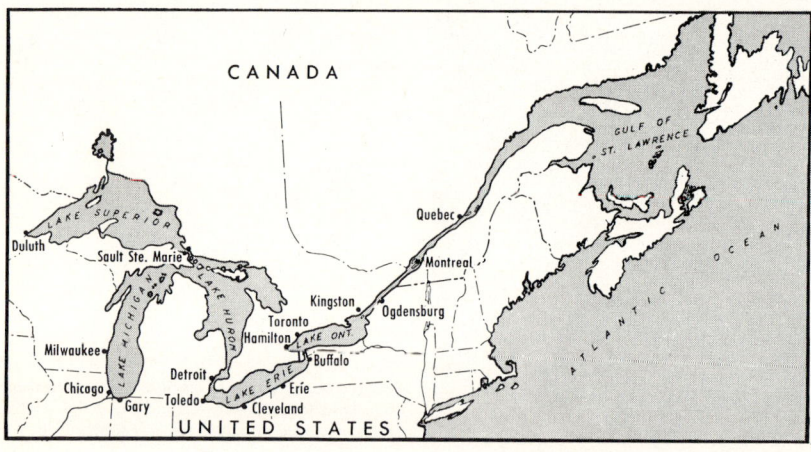

**Inland Cities** on the Saint Lawrence River system have become international ports since the development of the waterway. The seaway has opened the interior of the North American continent to ocean ships.

40

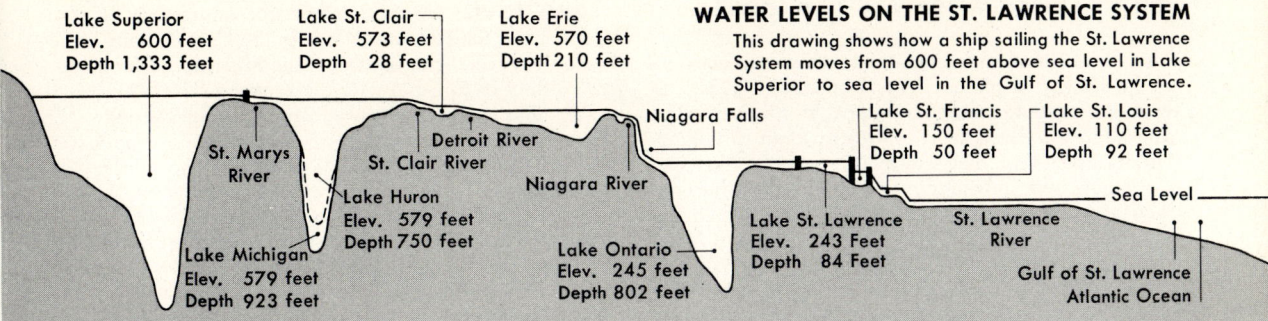

roads, shipping interests, and Eastern and Gulf ports opposed the proposal. Private utility companies and the coal-mining industry also feared the competition of Saint Lawrence power. In 1934, the United States Senate refused to ratify the treaty with Canada.

**Agreement of 1941.** World War II renewed interest in the seaway by creating a demand for electricity and shipbuilding resources. A new Canadian-United States understanding was signed in March, 1941. It included plans for the redevelopment of Niagara Falls, as well as the previous proposals for navigation and power development. It was subject to approval by a simple majority in both houses of the United States Congress. The House Committee on Rivers and Harbors supported the agreement. But the attack on Pearl Harbor in December, 1941, pushed the bill aside in favor of more urgent matters. An acute power shortage developed on both sides of the Canadian-United States boundary. In 1942, President Roosevelt considered using executive authority to start the power development. He decided not to when he learned that three years would be required to obtain electricity from the development.

Early in 1948, officials of Ontario and of New York state tried to end the deadlock. They proposed a separation of the power and navigation projects. The separation would have enabled the province and state to proceed at once with the power project. The navigation project would have remained a joint federal undertaking.

The new procedure called for the approval of both federal governments. New York state had to secure a license from the Federal Power Commission. The approval of the International Joint Commission was necessary in order to change the level of the Saint Lawrence River. At first, President Harry S. Truman and key members of the Canadian cabinet opposed the measure. They feared that the separation of the two projects would seriously delay the navigation improvements. For months, they refused to transmit the applications to the International Joint Commission. New York state also encountered difficulties in obtaining a license from the Federal Power Commission. Hearings extended over more than a two-year period. Finally, in 1950, the commissioners rejected the state's application. They recommended that the federal governments proceed at once with the combined navigation-and-power project.

Months passed and Congress did not approve the 1941 agreement. In 1951, Canadian officials offered to build the seaway as a Canadian project. The Canadians created the Saint Lawrence Seaway Authority to direct the undertaking. In return, they asked the United States to permit the Ontario Hydro-Electric Power Commission and some American company or agency to develop the power resources. The President agreed to support the Canadian action if an early start on the joint project could not be made.

In June, 1952, the two federal governments submitted applications to the International Joint Commission. They asked for the construction of power works in the International Rapids section by the Ontario Hydro-Electric Power Commission and a United States "entity." Three months later, the Federal Power Commission agreed to reconsider New York state's application for a license. The International Joint Commission speedily granted permission for the construction of the power development. However, 21 months passed before the United States government selected the cooperating "entity." The government finally chose the Power Authority of New York to direct the state's phase of the power project.

The long delay placed a serious strain on United States-Canadian relations. It also gave the United States a final opportunity to obtain a share in the seaway. The Wiley-Dondero bill passed both houses of Congress in May, 1954. President Dwight D. Eisenhower signed the measure several days later. The Wiley-Dondero Act created the Saint Lawrence Seaway Development Corporation. The Act provided for a channel, 27 feet deep, from the Atlantic Ocean to Lake Erie. The navigation phase of the project was to be a joint federal undertaking. The power phase was to be undertaken by the province of Ontario and the state of New York. The Canadian government agreed to readmit the United States to the project.

**Construction Begins.** Workmen began blasting operations for the hydroelectric project in August, 1954. A month later, construction started on the navigation phase. Congress passed the Blatnik Act in March, 1956, giving the U.S. Army Corps of Engineers authority to deepen the Great Lakes connecting channels to 27 feet. The hydroelectric project generated its first power during the summer of 1958. The seaway was officially opened to ocean shipping the following spring.

Improvements to the seaway are made in winter when ice floes force the seaway to close. Some major ports, such as Chicago, Detroit, and Montreal, have added dock facilities to handle the heavier traffic.

**Results.** The Saint Lawrence Seaway opened up the interior of North America to international shipping. On April 30, 1959, the *Prins Johan Willem Friso*, a Dutch ship, docked in the Chicago harbor. It was the first ocean-going ship to travel through the seaway to this great port of the St. Lawrence-Great Lakes

## SAINT LAWRENCE SEAWAY DEV. CORP.

water route. Ships carried about 20 million tons of cargo on the seaway in its first year of operation. This was twice the amount carried on the old St. Lawrence canals. Ships on the seaway now carry about 50 million tons of cargo a year. The seaway is expected to increase population and industry in such cities as Chicago, Cleveland, Detroit, Milwaukee, and Montreal. Such cargo as grains from the Midwest and ores from Minnesota and Labrador can be shipped at low rates on the seaway. The huge power plant in the International Rapids section has stimulated industry. Two aluminum plants and an automobile factory have been built near Massena, N.Y., to make use of the increased power. The three installations of the power plant have increased the power supply about 20 per cent.     W. R. WILLOUGHBY

**Related Articles** in WORLD BOOK include:

| | | |
|---|---|---|
| Great Lakes | Saint Lawrence | Soo Canals |
| Inland Waterway | Seaway Development | Welland |
| Saint Lawrence | Corporation | Ship |
| River | | Canal |

**SAINT LAWRENCE SEAWAY DEVELOPMENT CORPORATION** is an agency of the United States government. It was created in 1954 to construct the United States share of the Saint Lawrence Seaway. It also was given the job of deepening the Thousand Islands section of the Saint Lawrence River, so that larger ships could use it. The corporation operates and maintains the navigation works, in cooperation with the Saint Lawrence Seaway Authority of Canada.

The corporation is managed by an Administrator and a five-man Advisory Board. These officials are appointed by the President of the United States, with the consent of the Senate. The corporation is a part of the Department of Transportation.     W. R. WILLOUGHBY

**SAINT LAWRENCE UNIVERSITY** is a private coeducational arts and sciences school at Canton, N.Y. The nondenominational university includes a theological school, which grants the Bachelor of Divinity degree. The university also offers an engineering program in cooperation with Columbia University School of Engineering, Massachusetts Institute of Technology, and Rensselaer Polytechnic Institute. The Frederick A. Moran Memorial Institute on Delinquency and Crime is held on campus each summer. The university was founded in 1856. For enrollment, see UNIVERSITIES AND COLLEGES (table).

**SAINT LAZARUS, ORDER OF,** was a religious order of the Roman Catholic Church founded in Jerusalem about 1150. Its purpose was to care for sick pilgrims, especially lepers. Branches were started in various parts of Europe, with the most important one at Boigny, France. The order was later merged into that of Our Lady of Mount Carmel.     FULTON J. SHEEN

**SAINT LEGER,** *LEJ ur,* **BARRY** (1737-1789), a British soldier, fought against the Americans in the Revolutionary War. St. Leger's retreat to Canada after the Battle of Oriskany in 1777 was instrumental in upsetting the British campaign plan, and contributed to Burgoyne's surrender at Saratoga (see BURGOYNE, JOHN). St. Leger also fought in the French and Indian Wars.     W. B. WILLCOX

**SAINT LEO COLLEGE.** See UNIVERSITIES AND COLLEGES (table).

42

**SAINT LOUIS,** *saynt LOO is,* is the largest city in Missouri and the 10th largest city in the United States. St. Louis lies on the west bank of the Mississippi River, just south of its junction with the Missouri River. This location has made the city an important midwestern center of industry, trade, and transportation.

French fur traders built a post on the site of the present city in 1764. It was a convenient point for Indians to reach by canoe, bringing furs to trade. Even today, St. Louis is still the largest raw-fur market in the world. In the 1850's, St. Louis became a main port for Mississippi steamboats. The river is still important to the business of the city. But of greater importance is a large railroad network spreading out from St. Louis. The city ranks second to Chicago as a rail center.

**Location and Description.** St. Louis lies about halfway between the Appalachian Mountains to the east and the Rocky Mountains to the west. It is on the main course of the Mississippi River, about midway between Minneapolis, Minn., and New Orleans, La. For location, see MISSOURI (political map).

For rainfall and monthly temperature in St. Louis, see MISSOURI (Climate).

St. Louis is shaped somewhat like a fan. The Mississippi sweeps past the city, forming the 19-mile eastern border of the city. However, the metropolitan area of St. Louis spills across the Mississippi into Illinois. Nearly half the metropolitan area lies in Illinois.

The historic riverfront section between Third Street and the Mississippi has been cleared for the Jefferson National Expansion Memorial. This memorial honors Thomas Jefferson, the Louisiana Purchase, and the pioneers who settled the West. The memorial includes a stadium, parks, and the Gateway Arch. The 630-foot-high arch symbolizes the *Gateway to the West.* Capsule-cars within the arch carry visitors to the top.

The downtown district lies between Third Street and Twelfth Boulevard. A number of industrial districts spread out to the north, south, and west.

Eight bridges across the Mississippi link St. Louis with the Illinois part of its metropolitan area. The famous Eads Bridge extends from the foot of Washington Avenue to East St. Louis (see EADS BRIDGE).

---
**FACTS IN BRIEF**
---

**Population:** 750,026; metropolitan area, 2,104,669 (1,617,471 in Missouri; 487,198 in Illinois).

**Area:** 61 square miles; metropolitan area, 2,987 square miles (1,586 in Missouri; 1,401 in Illinois).

**Altitude:** 455 feet above sea level.

**Government:** Mayor-council (4-year terms).

**Founded:** 1764; incorporated as a town, 1808; as a city, 1822.

**Flag:** A golden disk containing a blue fleur-de-lis, lies left of center on a red background. Blue and white wavy lines extend from the left corners and the right center edge, to meet at the disk. See CITY (color picture).

**Seal:** It shows a steamboat on the Mississippi.

**Winged Horse and Warrior** guard the Soldiers Memorial Building. On top of the Civil Courts Building, *right*, are a Greek temple and Egyptian pyramid.

**Old Cathedral,** a Roman Catholic church on the St. Louis river front, was completed in 1834. A bell in its sanctuary was cast in 1772.

**Meeting of the Waters Fountain** creates graceful water patterns in front of Union Station. The fountain, with its 14 bronze figures, was designed by sculptor Carl Milles.

**Metropolitan St. Louis** is shown in light gray on the small map, *right*. The city is in black. The dotted line encloses the area covered by the large map, *above*.

**Gateway Arch** and Busch Memorial Stadium, *left*, were completed in 1966. The arch, 630 feet high, towers over the Mississippi.

**Saint Louis the Crusader,** *far right*, a statue by Charles H. Niehaus, stands in Forest Park. It was completed in 1907.

# SAINT LOUIS

**The People.** Many persons of German descent live on the north and south sides of the city. St. Louis also has citizens of English, French, Italian, Scottish, and Spanish ancestry. Negroes make up more than a fourth of the population.

**Industry and Trade.** The St. Louis raw-fur market is the largest in the world. Valuable skins from all parts of the world are sent to the city for processing. Furriers throughout the United States buy the skins and make them into coats and other garments. The city also ranks as a leading American grain market. The St. Louis Livestock Exchange, at East St. Louis, Ill., is the country's chief hog-shipping center. St. Louis manufactures more shoes than any other city in the world. Other manufactured products include automobiles, beer, bricks, chemicals, dresses, drugs, enamelware, macaroni, stoves, railroad cars, and terra-cotta tile.

**Transportation.** Eighteen major railroads serve St. Louis, the nation's second largest rail center. Union Station is one of the world's largest railroad terminals. St. Louis is a main port for barges that travel the Mississippi. The Lambert-St. Louis Municipal Airport lies 11 miles northwest of the downtown area.

**Communication.** The city's leading daily newspapers are the morning *Globe-Democrat* and the afternoon *Post-Dispatch*. Joseph Pulitzer founded the *Post-Dispatch* in 1878. The Pulitzer prizes were created with money left in his will (see PULITZER, JOSEPH). Sixteen radio and five television stations broadcast from St. Louis.

**Education.** The St. Louis public school system has made several notable contributions to education. In 1873, William Torrey Harris, the city's superintendent of schools, established the first public kindergarten in the United States at the Des Peres School. The St. Louis Manual Training School, established in 1880, became a model for schools of this type. Today, the city has over 130 public schools, and Lutheran and Roman Catholic parochial school systems.

St. Louis University and Washington University are the city's largest institutions of higher education. St. Louis University was founded in 1818 and is the oldest university west of the Mississippi River. Other schools include Cardinal Glennon College, Fontbonne College, Harris Teachers College, Marillac College, Maryville College of the Sacred Heart, St. Louis College of Pharmacy, a campus of the University of Missouri, and Webster College. The Central Public Library of St. Louis owns more than a million books, and operates 19 branch libraries. The Mercantile Library specializes in frontier art and literature. The Missouri Historical Society is a research center that deals with the history of the West.

**What to See and Do in St. Louis.** Forest Park is one of the largest city parks in the United States. Its 1,380 acres of natural beauty include streams, pools, lagoons, waterfalls, bridges, golf links, bridle paths, an ice skating rink, and picnic areas. The City Art Museum, on Art Hill in Forest Park, displays more than 7,000 works of art. The museum is famous for its collection of Chinese art. The St. Louis Zoo and the Municipal Open-Air Theater are located in the park. The theater is the home of the St. Louis Municipal Opera, which offers light opera and musical comedy in the summer. The Jewel Box has flower exhibits.

The Missouri Botanical Garden, near Tower Grove Park, displays over 12,000 kinds of plants from all parts of the world. It features the Climatron, a modern greenhouse that displays various plants in their native climates. The garden was established by Henry Shaw (1800-1889), a St. Louis merchant. It is often called *Shaw's Garden*. St. Louis has two other large parks, Carondelet and Fairgrounds.

The St. Louis Symphony Orchestra is the second oldest in the United States. It was founded as a choral group in 1880, 38 years after the New York Philharmonic Orchestra.

St. Louis has two professional athletic teams called the Cardinals. The baseball team competes in the National League, and the football team is a member of the National Football League. The St. Louis Blues play in the National Hockey League.

Other interesting places to visit include:

**Aloe Plaza,** on Market Street, features the *Meeting of the Waters* fountain designed by the sculptor Carl Milles. The fountain portrays the meeting of the Mississippi and Missouri rivers.

**Eugene Field Birthplace.** The St. Louis Board of Education maintains this three-story red brick building as a museum and a shrine to the *poet of childhood*.

**Memorial Plaza,** facing Aloe Plaza, honors St. Louis servicemen of World Wars I and II. Many of the city's outstanding civic buildings stand around the plaza. They include the Civil Courts Building, the United States Courthouse, City Hall, the Municipal Courts Building, and the Henry W. Kiel Municipal Auditorium.

**National Museum of Transport** is devoted to the history of transportation.

**Riverfront.** This area includes the Old Courthouse, completed in 1862; the Old Cathedral, built in 1834; and the Lisa Warehouse, used by the army in the early 1800's. Old-time melodramas are presented nightly on the *Goldenrod*, a historic showboat. The top of Gateway Arch offers a magnificent view of St. Louis.

**Government.** St. Louis is one of the nation's few cities that is not in a county. In 1877, St. Louis withdrew from St. Louis County and became an independent city. The city did this so it could elect its own officials who would take a special interest in the city's affairs. The city is not officially a county. But it has the status of a county so it can be represented in the state legislature. St. Louis County now rims the city in Missouri. The city has often tried to extend its borders, but the county has opposed such changes.

Unlike most cities, St. Louis does not control its own police department or its department of elections. They are managed by boards of commissioners appointed by the governor of Missouri. The city has a mayor and a 28-member council and council president. All these officials are elected to four-year terms.

**History.** Two French fur traders, Pierre Laclède Liguest (1724?-1778) and René Auguste Chouteau, established a trading post on the site of St. Louis in 1764. Laclède named the settlement after Louis IX, a French king who had been made a saint. At the end of the French and Indian War in 1763, France gave all its territory west of the Mississippi River to Spain. The French gave their land east of the river to Great Britain. St. Louis grew rapidly as French settlers crossed the river and settled around the post. These settlers preferred Spanish to British rule. See CHOUTEAU.

On March 10, 1804, the transfer of the northern

part of the Louisiana Purchase region to the United States took place in St. Louis. The town soon became a key point in the westward expansion of the United States. The expeditions of Meriwether Lewis and William Clark and of Zebulon M. Pike started from St. Louis. Keelboats, and later steamboats, traveled up the Missouri River and its tributaries, and returned with fortunes in furs.

After the Civil War, railroad construction and the expanding trade of the Southwest brought steady growth to St. Louis. Eads Bridge was completed in 1874. The Illinois coal fields then became easier to reach from St. Louis, and the city's Illinois suburbs began to grow.

The Louisiana Purchase Exposition, held in Forest Park in 1904, stimulated trade and culture in St. Louis. See LOUISIANA PURCHASE EXPOSITION.

Bond issues totaling more than $100 million were passed in 1926 and 1934. They helped finance street widening, new public buildings, and various other projects.

In 1954, the city charter was amended to permit a tax on individual and business earnings. This tax made possible a program to build new expressways and docks and to improve public buildings. In 1955, aroused by growing slums and city-wide deterioration, St. Louis voters approved three bond issues totaling more than $165 million. The funds were marked for schools, expressways, and other public works. In the 1960's, a 10-year program moved ahead to improve Mill Creek Valley, a 465-acre slum area that was located in the heart of St. Louis. IRVING DILLIARD

**SAINT LOUIS COLLEGE OF PHARMACY.** See UNIVERSITIES AND COLLEGES (table).

**SAINT LOUIS UNIVERSITY** is a private, coeducational school in St. Louis, Mo. It is sponsored by the Society of Jesus, and governed by a board of trustees composed of Jesuits and laymen. Divisions of St. Louis University include the schools of arts and sciences, commerce and finance, dentistry, engineering, aeronautical engineering, philosophy and letters, nursing and health services, law, medicine, social service, divinity, and the graduate school. Its medical, dental, and nursing schools, and hospitals and clinics make up the world's largest Catholic medical center. The school's Pius XII Memorial Library contains on microfilm the general collection, and 12 million pages of manuscript from the Vatican Library. Founded in 1818, the school is the oldest university west of the Mississippi River. For enrollment, see UNIVERSITIES AND COLLEGES (table). PAUL C. REINERT

**SAINT LUCIA.** See WEST INDIES ASSOCIATED STATES.

**SAINT LUCIA'S DAY.** See CHRISTMAS (In Sweden).

**SAINT MARK, CATHEDRAL OF,** is a famous Roman Catholic church in Venice, Italy. It is named for St. Mark the Evangelist, the patron saint of Venice. The cathedral used to be the private chapel of the Doge, the ruler of Venice. It is now the cathedral of the city. The Cathedral of Saint Mark is one of the finest examples of Byzantine architecture in western Europe (see VENICE [picture]).

The building is in the form of a Greek cross, 250 feet long and 220 feet wide at the widest point. A dome, 42 feet in diameter, rises over the center of the church, and smaller domes rise over each arm. The inside of

Gendreau

**The Cathedral of Saint Mark in Venice, Italy,** is an outstanding example of Byzantine architecture. The church is decorated with beautiful carvings, mosaics, and religious statues. Four huge bronze horses stand above the center door.

the cathedral is entirely covered with mosaics. Marbles, carvings, and the famous *Pala d'Oro*, or Altar of Gold, also add to the interior beauty of the cathedral. Four bronze horses, brought from Constantinople (now Istanbul) in 1204, stand over the center door. A *campanile* (bell tower) stands in the Square of Saint Mark (see CAMPANILE).

When St. Mark's was built, beginning about A.D. 1050, Venice maintained close trade relations with the East. By law, every merchant who traveled to the Orient had to bring back some object for the church. This built an art collection. OTTO G. VON SIMSON

See also MOSAIC (picture: Byzantine Mosaics).

**SAINT MARTIN'S COLLEGE** is a coeducational Roman Catholic school at Olympia, Wash. Courses lead to B.A. and B.S. degrees in liberal arts, business administration, and civil engineering. Saint Martin's College was founded in 1895. For enrollment, see UNIVERSITIES AND COLLEGES (table).

**SAINT MARTIN'S SUMMER.** See INDIAN SUMMER.

**SAINT MARY, COLLEGE OF.** See UNIVERSITIES AND COLLEGES (table).

**SAINT MARY COLLEGE.** See UNIVERSITIES AND COLLEGES (table).

**SAINT MARY OF THE PLAINS COLLEGE.** See UNIVERSITIES AND COLLEGES (table).

**SAINT MARY-OF-THE-WOODS COLLEGE** is a women's school at St. Mary-of-the-Woods, Ind. It is conducted by the Sisters of Providence of the Roman Catholic Church. Courses are offered in the liberal arts, fine arts, and sciences. The school was founded in 1840. For enrollment, see UNIVERSITIES AND COLLEGES (table).

**SAINT MARY'S CITY.** See MARYLAND (Places to Visit).

**SAINT MARY'S COLLEGE** is a liberal arts school for men at Winona, Minn. It is controlled by the Brothers of the Christian Schools, a Roman Catholic lay organization. Courses are offered leading to A.B. and B.S.

45

## SAINT MARY'S COLLEGE

degrees. St. Mary's was founded in 1912. For enrollment, see UNIVERSITIES AND COLLEGES (table).

**SAINT MARY'S COLLEGE** is a Roman Catholic liberal arts school for women at Notre Dame, Ind. Courses lead to B.A., B.S., and B.M. degrees. Saint Mary's College was founded in 1844. For enrollment, see UNIVERSITIES AND COLLEGES (table).

**SAINT MARY'S COLLEGE OF CALIFORNIA** in the town of St. Mary's College is a Roman Catholic men's school. Courses are offered in liberal arts, economics, prelaw, business administration, premedicine, and predentistry. It was founded in 1863. For enrollment, see UNIVERSITIES AND COLLEGES (table).

**SAINT MARY'S DOMINICAN COLLEGE** is a Roman Catholic liberal arts school for women at New Orleans, La. It is under the direction of the Dominican Sisters. Upon graduation, students receive either an A.B. or B.S. degree. St. Mary's was founded in 1910. For enrollment, see UNIVERSITIES AND COLLEGES (table).

**SAINT MARYS RIVER** is the stream that carries the waters of Lake Superior into Lake Huron. It is about 40 miles long, and forms part of the boundary between Ontario and Upper Michigan. Islands divide the river into two main channels, and each channel spreads out into several lakelike bays. The Saint Marys Rapids are near the northern end of the river. Here there is a fall of nearly 20 feet within a mile. The Soo (Sault Sainte Marie) canals and locks have been built on the Canadian and American sides so ships can by-pass the dangerous rapids.

The rapids furnish power for industry. A railroad bridge crosses the rapids. The two-mile International Bridge carries traffic across the Saint Marys River at Sault Ste. Marie. WILLIS F. DUNBAR

**SAINT MARY'S SEMINARY.** See UNIVERSITIES AND COLLEGES (table).

**SAINT MARY'S SEMINARY AND UNIVERSITY** is a Roman Catholic school for men in Baltimore, Md. Its courses are aimed at educating men for the priesthood. Founded in 1791, St. Mary's is the oldest Catholic seminary in the United States. For enrollment, see UNIVERSITIES AND COLLEGES (table).

**SAINT MARY'S UNIVERSITY** is located at Halifax, N.S. It is conducted by the Roman Catholic Jesuit Fathers of Upper Canada. It grants bachelor's degrees in commerce, education, engineering, liberal arts, and science, and grants master's degrees in education and philosophy. It was founded in 1841. For enrollment, see CANADA (table: Universities and Colleges). C. J. FISCHER

**SAINT MARY'S UNIVERSITY OF SAN ANTONIO** has a school of arts and sciences, a business school, and a law school. The university is in San Antonio, Tex. It is affiliated with the Roman Catholic Church, and is coeducational. It grants bachelor's and master's degrees. St. Mary's was founded in 1852. For enrollment, see UNIVERSITIES AND COLLEGES (table).

**SAINT MAURICE RIVER.** See SAINT LAWRENCE RIVER (Sources); QUEBEC (color pictures).

**SAINT MEINRAD SEMINARY.** See UNIVERSITIES AND COLLEGES (table).

**SAINT MICHAEL, FEAST OF.** See MICHAEL, SAINT.

**SAINT MICHAEL'S COLLEGE.** See UNIVERSITIES AND COLLEGES (table).

**SAINT MIHIEL.** See WORLD WAR I (The Last Campaigns).

**SAINT MORITZ,** SAYNT moh RITZ (pop. 3,751), is a famous resort town in Switzerland. It lies at 6,037 feet above sea level, in the Engadine, the upper part of the great Inn River Valley. For location, see SWITZERLAND (color map). St. Moritz is one of the highest villages in the valley, and has a magnificent view. Visitors come to St. Moritz from all parts of the world. Its baths have been famous since the 1500's. St. Moritz is one of the most popular ski resorts in Europe. FRANKLIN C. ERICKSON

**SAINT NICHOLAS, FEAST OF,** falls on December 6. People in many European countries celebrate it as a special holiday. In some places, children believe that Saint Nicholas appears on the eve of his feast day with gifts for good boys and girls. Dutch settlers brought the customs of celebrating his feast day to America. The Feast of Saint Nicholas gradually became part of the American tradition of Christmas. See also CHRISTMAS; NICHOLAS, SAINT; SANTA CLAUS.

**SAINT NORBERT COLLEGE.** See UNIVERSITIES AND COLLEGES (table).

**SAINT OLAF COLLEGE.** See UNIVERSITIES AND COLLEGES (table).

**SAINT PATRICK'S CATHEDRAL** is a famous Roman Catholic church on Fifth Avenue in New York City. It is the seat of the Archdiocese of New York. St. Patrick's was the first major cathedral built in the neo-Gothic style in the United States. The cornerstone was laid in 1858 and the building opened in 1879. The cathedral resembles several French and English Gothic churches, including the church at St. Ouen in Rouen, France. Much of the decoration in the cathedral is of European workmanship. G. HOLMES PERKINS

See also NEW YORK CITY (picture: Famous Churches).

**SAINT PATRICK'S COLLEGE** is a coeducational Roman Catholic college in Ottawa, Ont. St. Patrick's offers courses in business administration, the liberal arts, and the social sciences which lead to bachelor's and master's degrees. The school is operated by the Congregation of the Oblates of Mary Immaculate. It was founded in 1929.

**SAINT PATRICK'S COLLEGE.** See UNIVERSITIES AND COLLEGES (table).

**SAINT PATRICK'S DAY** is celebrated on March 17 in honor of the patron saint of Ireland. Many legends have grown up about St. Patrick. One of them is that he used the shamrock to illustrate the idea of the Trinity.

His death on March 17, in about 461, has been observed in America since colonial days. The Friendly Sons of St. Patrick was organized in Philadelphia. In New York, Irishmen of the Roman Catholic and Presbyterian faiths organized another chapter of the society. Observance of the day since 1845 has become nationwide. It is celebrated in homes, churches, schools, and places of entertainment. Merchants sell special wearing apparel, flowers, shamrocks, and greeting cards. Some cities hold parades. Each year, arrangements for New York's St. Patrick's Day parade begin shortly after New Year's. The organization committee enlists the help of businessmen, churches, and government officials and employees throughout the city to make the parade "a great day for the Irish." RAYMOND HOYT JAHN

See also PATRICK, SAINT; SHAMROCK.

# SAINT PAUL

Saint Paul Area Chamber of Commerce

**The Wabasha Street Bridge Leads to Downtown Saint Paul, Minn.**

**SAINT PAUL** (pop. 313,411; alt. 780 ft.) is the capital of Minnesota. Saint Paul and its sister city, Minneapolis, form Minnesota's "Twin Cities." Their metropolitan area population is 1,482,030. Saint Paul serves as a manufacturing, retail, and wholesale center for one of the country's richest farming areas.

**Location and Description.** Saint Paul lies in eastern Minnesota, about 400 miles northwest of Chicago. Most of the city stands on the north side of the Mississippi River. For location, see MINNESOTA (political map).

Saint Paul stretches along three terraces, hundreds of feet above the river. The first terrace has railroad yards and factories. The second terrace contains the business district. Homes occupy the third and highest terrace. The state Capitol, constructed of white marble and native granite, stands on a hill overlooking the city. Paintings on the inside walls of the building portray incidents in the history of Minnesota. The City Hall and Ramsey County Courthouse occupy a single modern building. The main hall is a memorial to servicemen killed in World War I. A statue of an Indian god by sculptor Carl Milles stands in the hall.

Other important buildings in the city include the Federal Building, the Minnesota Historical Building, the Municipal Auditorium, the Roman Catholic Cathedral of Saint Paul, and the Saint Paul Public Library. The Minnesota State Fair Grounds are in Saint Paul.

**Industry and Trade.** Factories in the city produce abrasives, adhesives, electrical equipment, fur goods, machinery, malt beverages, meat and food products, paper products, and refrigerators. The West Publishing Company is the largest law-book publishing firm in the United States. The Ford Company's plant on the riverbank is one of the city's largest factories. Mississippi River barges annually carry over 2 million tons of freight to and from the city. Several airlines, railroads, and truck lines serve the city.

**Cultural Life.** Saint Paul is the home of Bethel College and Seminary, the College of St. Catherine, the College of St. Thomas, Concordia College, Hamline University, Macalester College, and the Saint Paul Seminary. The University of Minnesota's College of Agriculture, Forestry, and Home Economics is located in Saint Paul. The Roman Catholic Archdiocese of Saint Paul has headquarters there. The city also has a civic opera and a concert orchestra.

**Recreation.** Most of the city's boulevards follow the riverbank. Kellogg Boulevard stretches for a mile along the downtown river front. Parks, drives, and playgrounds cover about 2,000 acres in the city. Como Park has a famous zoo. Lakes in and near the city provide water sports. The annual Saint Paul Winter Carnival attracts many visitors each winter. The Minnesota Twins of the American Baseball League and the Minnesota Vikings of the National Football League play in Bloomington, a nearby suburb.

**History and Government.** Father Louis Hennepin, a missionary explorer, visited the site of Saint Paul in

## SAINT PAUL

1680. In 1805, the federal government sent Lieutenant Zebulon M. Pike to explore the area. The United States had acquired the territory from Great Britain by the Treaty of Paris after the Revolutionary War. Pike made a treaty with the Sioux Indians and obtained a land grant. Around 1820, Fort Snelling was built about five miles from the site of Saint Paul. The first settler was a French-Canadian trader nicknamed "Pig's Eye." The community adopted the name *Pig's Eye*. In 1841, Father Lucien Galtier built Saint Paul's Chapel on what is now Kellogg Boulevard and Minnesota Street. At that time, the community's name was changed to *Saint Paul's Landing*. The earliest settlers were Swiss and French Canadians. Pioneers from Germany, France, Ireland, New England, and Scandinavia came later. Saint Paul became a busy river port and trading center. Railroad builder James Hill stimulated civic, cultural, and industrial development in the late 1800's. He gave the city a library, and donated funds to build the Saint Paul Cathedral. Archbishop John Ireland was a civic and religious leader in this largely Roman Catholic community in the late 1800's and early 1900's. He established settlers on thousands of acres in the archdiocese. The land was acquired by purchase and federal grant.

Saint Paul was incorporated and became the capital when Minnesota was made a territory in 1849. The city received its charter in 1854. It remained the capital when Minnesota was admitted to the Union in 1858. Saint Paul is the seat of Ramsey County. It has a commission form of government.

HAROLD T. HAGG

See also MINNESOTA (color picture, The State Capitol).

**SAINT PAUL ISLAND.** See PRIBILOF ISLANDS.

**SAINT PAUL SEMINARY.** See UNIVERSITIES AND COLLEGES (table).

**SAINT PAUL'S CATHEDRAL.** See LONDON (Churches; picture).

**SAINT PAUL'S COLLEGE.** See UNIVERSITIES AND COLLEGES (table).

**SAINT PETER'S CHURCH,** in Vatican City, is the largest Christian church in the world. Also called SAINT PETER'S BASILICA, it is the second church to stand above the *crypt* (tomb) which is believed to contain the body of Saint Peter, the first pope.

Saint Peter's is built in the shape of a cross. The church is almost 700 feet long and about 450 feet across at its widest point. It covers an area of about 15,500 square yards. The *nave* (center aisle) is 150 feet high. The building's most outstanding architectural feature is its magnificent dome, designed by Michelangelo. The dome rises more than 400 feet from the floor of the church, and measures 138 feet in diameter.

**The Exterior.** The church was given an impressive setting by Giovanni Lorenzo Bernini, one of its archi-

**Saint Peter's Church in Vatican City** stands over the tomb believed to contain Saint Peter's body. Only the pope, or a cardinal representing him, is permitted to celebrate Mass at the high altar in Saint Peter's. The altar is in the center of the church, underneath a great bronze canopy. The church can hold over 50,000 persons.

Forum, Black Star

tects. From a great distance, the whole church appears to be set on a stage. A mile-long avenue leads from the Tiber River to the *Piazza di San Pietro* (Square of Saint Peter), a large open space in front of the church. Double colonnades arranged in semicircles on two sides of the piazza seem to draw the visitor into the church.

In the center of the piazza stands a red granite *obelisk* (shaft) that is 85 feet high. It was brought to Rome from Egypt about A.D. 37, and was moved to the piazza in 1586.

**The Interior** of the church is decorated in baroque style. Its most famous features are the work of Bernini, who was also a sculptor. He built the elaborate bronze *baldacchino* (canopy) over the main altar, which stands beneath the dome. Marble, gilding, and mosaics decorate the walls and ceiling of the church. Chapels, altars, and tombs line the walls. Michelangelo's famous sculpture, the *Pietà*, stands in one of the chapels.

**History.** The first Saint Peter's, called the Basilica of Constantine, was begun by Constantine the Great about 325. He built the church to symbolize his acceptance of Christianity as the official religion of the Roman Empire.

The church was modeled on the *basilica*, a rectangular building used as a meeting hall by the Romans (see BASILICA). Four rows of columns, extending almost the length of the church, divided it into a nave with two aisles on either side. Throughout the Middle Ages, many persons made pilgrimages to the church, and many great medieval churches were copied from its design. In 1506, Pope Julius II decided to rebuild the church completely. He demolished it so thoroughly that only the tomb and a few small details from it remain.

Rebuilding Saint Peter's took almost 150 years. During this time, 10 different architects worked on the church and changed its design. The first architect was Donato Bramante. He designed a domed, perfectly symmetrical church in the form of a *Greek cross* (a cross with four arms of equal length). But the nave was lengthened in the 1600's, so that the church took the form of a Latin cross. Only the gigantic scale and dimensions of Bramante's work remain.

The most important architects were Michelangelo and Bernini. Michelangelo became the church's architect in the 1540's, when he was over 70 years old. He changed Bramante's plan for a balanced and restful dome into a dynamic construction. He put a *drum* (ring) at the base of the dome that appears to be squeezing the dome and forcing its sides to spring upwards.

Bernini began his work on Saint Peter's in 1623. The building was dedicated in 1626 by Pope Urban VIII, but other parts were added later. JOACHIM SMET

**Related Articles** in WORLD BOOK include:

| Architecture | Dome | Rome (Churches, |
| (Renaissance | (picture) | Palaces, and |
| [picture]) | Michelangelo | Fountains) |
| Bramante, Donato | Pope (picture) | Vatican City |

**SAINT PETER'S COLLEGE.** See UNIVERSITIES AND COLLEGES (table).

**SAINT PETERSBURG.** See LENINGRAD.

**SAINT PETERSBURG,** Fla. (pop. 181,298; alt. 20 ft.), is a popular resort city in Florida. Saint Petersburg is often called the *Sunshine City*. It was named for Saint Petersburg (now Leningrad), Russia. Saint Petersburg lies on the west coast of Florida, covering the southern tip of the peninsula that separates Tampa Bay from the Gulf of Mexico (see FLORIDA [political map]). Gandy Bridge, seven miles long, shortens the land journey from Tampa to the southwest. The 15-mile-long Sunshine Skyway bridge spans Tampa Bay and links Saint Petersburg with the city of Bradenton. Saint Petersburg and Tampa form a metropolitan area with a population of over 770,000.

The tourist trade gives the city more than $50 million worth of business every year. Saint Petersburg has a large fishing industry. It is a market for truck-garden products and citrus fruits grown nearby. Its excellent harbor can accommodate large steamships. Railways and airlines serve the city. The Saint Petersburg Coast Guard Air Station covers 84 acres on Tampa Bay. Florida Presbyterian College is located in the city.

Antonio Maximo settled the peninsula in 1843, and started a fishing camp. But hurricanes destroyed his holdings. The present city was established by John C. Williams, son of an early founder of Detroit, and Peter Demens, a Russian engineer who built the first railroad into town in 1888. It was incorporated in 1903 and has a council-manager government. KATHRYN ABBEY HANNA

**SAINT PIERRE AND MIQUELON,** *MICK uh lahn,* are two small French islands about 10 miles south of Newfoundland. The islands cover a total area of 93 square miles, and have a population of about 5,000. They are ruled by an administrator who is assisted by a *privy council,* made up of chiefs of departments. The *general council,* made up of 14 elected members, manages financial and other local affairs. The islands constitute an overseas territory of France.

The islands are barren and rocky, and are important only as a French fishing center. During the fishing season, they export many tons of codfish. The chief town is Saint Pierre. It has a good harbor.

France first occupied the islands in 1635. England and France controlled them in turn until 1814, when France took final possession. In 1956, the French government gave them self-government. ROBERT E. DICKINSON

**SAINT PROCOPIUS COLLEGE.** See UNIVERSITIES AND COLLEGES (table).

**SAINT ROCH,** a ship. See VANCOUVER (What to See and Do in Vancouver); NORTHWEST PASSAGE.

**SAINT ROSE, COLLEGE OF.** See UNIVERSITIES AND COLLEGES (table).

**SAINT-SAËNS,** *san SAHNS,* **CAMILLE** (1835-1921), was a French composer. He composed large quantities of music for a great variety of instrumental and vocal combinations. He wrote easily, "as an apple tree produces fruit," he said once. But many of his works are no longer played. Probably his best-known composition is the opera *Samson and Delilah* (1877).

Saint-Saëns composed a "zoological fantasy," *Carnival of Animals,* for two

Camille Saint-Saëns
Brown Bros.

## SAINT SCHOLASTICA, COLLEGE OF

pianos and orchestra in 1886. In this humorous piece, he used the instruments to describe the elephant, kangaroo, cuckoo, lion, swan, and other animals. Saint-Saëns was born in Paris. At the age of 13, he entered the Paris Conservatory. He became a famous pianist and organist. HOMER ULRICH

**SAINT SCHOLASTICA, COLLEGE OF.** See UNIVERSITIES AND COLLEGES (table).

**SAINT-SIMON,** SAN SEE MAWN, **COMTE DE** (1760-1825), CLAUDE HENRI DE ROUVROY, was a founder of French socialism. His ambition was to work for the betterment of mankind. He wanted to bring about a new society in which everyone would have to work, and in which each would receive rewards equal to his labor. No person would be allowed to inherit wealth, and all men would start life on an equal basis. Saint-Simon wanted to base his social theories on scientific evidence, but actually his conclusions were unsystematic.

Saint-Simon was born in Paris. He went to America in his youth and fought bravely in the Revolutionary War. Saint-Simon took no active part in the French Revolution, although he welcomed it. W. T. JONES

Ewing Galloway

**Saint Sophia in Istanbul** was originally built as a Christian cathedral. It became a Moslem mosque in 1453 and a museum in 1933. Its marble-lined walls have beautiful designs.

**SAINT SOPHIA,** so FIE uh, is the finest and most famous example of Byzantine architecture in the world. It was built as a Christian cathedral by Justinian the Great between A.D. 532 and 537 in Constantinople (now Istanbul). After an earthquake damaged the original dome, a higher one was built between 558 and 563. The building was used as a *mosque* (Moslem temple) after 1453 when the Turks conquered the city. Since 1933, Saint Sophia has served as a museum. It is more accurately called *Hagia Sophia*, which means Holy Wisdom.

The inside appearance is one of great space, height, and richness. The rare and costly building materials were brought from many parts of the Roman Empire. The marble-lined walls have many colors and designs. Mosaics decorate the vaults. These were covered over by the Turks. After the building became a museum, the mosaics were uncovered. Many beautiful pictures were found. Among these are figures of Christ, the Virgin Mary, the Archangel Gabriel, and a number of portraits of rulers and officials.

The floor plan is oblong. The building is 250 feet from east to west and 235 feet from north to south. Over the center is the great dome, 185 feet high and 107 feet across. WILLIAM G. SINNIGEN

See also BYZANTINE ART (pictures: Saint Sophia); ARCHITECTURE (color pictures); DOME (picture: Saint Sophia's Church).

**SAINT STEPHEN'S COLLEGE.** See UNIVERSITIES AND COLLEGES (table).

**SAINT SWITHIN'S DAY,** the feast day of that saint, is July 15. He was bishop of Winchester and the trusted councilor of Ethelwulf, King of the West Saxons, who had him made bishop about 852 (see SWITHIN, SAINT). St. Swithin's name is connected with this rhyme:

> St. Swithin's day if thou dost rain,
> For forty days it will remain;
> St. Swithin's day if thou be fair,
> For forty days 'twill rain nae mair. FULTON J. SHEEN

**SAINT TERESA, COLLEGE OF,** is a liberal arts college for women in Winona, Minn. It was founded in 1907, and is conducted by the Roman Catholic Sisters of St. Francis. For enrollment, see UNIVERSITIES AND COLLEGES (table).

**SAINT THOMAS.** See VIRGIN ISLANDS.

**SAINT THOMAS, COLLEGE OF,** is a men's school in St. Paul, Minn. It is controlled by the Roman Catholic Church, but admits students of all faiths. Courses are offered in all the major departments of the liberal arts. The college has a graduate program in education, and a cooperative liberal arts-engineering program with the University of Notre Dame. The school was founded in 1885. For enrollment, see UNIVERSITIES AND COLLEGES (table). JAMES P. SHANNON

**SAINT THOMAS, UNIVERSITY OF.** See UNIVERSITIES AND COLLEGES (table).

**SAINT THOMAS SEMINARY.** See UNIVERSITIES AND COLLEGES (table).

**SAINT VALENTINE'S DAY.** See VALENTINE'S DAY.

**SAINT VINCENT.** See WEST INDIES ASSOCIATED STATES.

**SAINT VINCENT, CAPE.** See CAPE SAINT VINCENT.

**SAINT VINCENT COLLEGE** is a liberal arts school for men in Latrobe, Pa. The college is controlled by the Roman Catholic Church, but students of all faiths may enroll. Saint Vincent offers work leading to degrees in the prelegal, pre-engineering, predental, premedical, business, natural and social sciences, humanities, and music fields. Saint Vincent was founded in 1846. For enrollment, see UNIVERSITIES AND COLLEGES (table).

**SAINT VITUS'S DANCE.** See CHOREA.

**SAINT XAVIER COLLEGE.** See UNIVERSITIES AND COLLEGES (table).

**SAINTE ANNE DE BEAUPRÉ,** BOH PRAY, is a Roman Catholic shrine in Montmorency County, Quebec. It is a place where many miracles are said to have been

**The Basilica of Sainte Anne de Beaupré** is one of the most frequently visited religious shrines in North America.

Ministère Du Tourisme, Quebec

performed. Hundreds of thousands of ill and crippled men and women have made pilgrimages to the shrine. Hundreds have left their crutches in the church as tokens of their healing. Sainte Anne de Beaupré is known as "the American Lourdes." Lourdes is a French shrine where many are said to have been healed.

An old legend tells how the first chapel was built there during the early days of French settlement in Canada. A boatload of Breton sailors was being tossed about wildly by the waves on the Saint Lawrence River. The frightened sailors prayed to Saint Anne, the patron saint of sailors. They promised to build a chapel in her honor if they were saved. When the storm passed, they landed where the Saint Lawrence joins the Sainte Anne River near Quebec. There they built a church in 1658.

In 1876, a new church was built nearby. Eleven years later, it was created a basilica by papal decree. The splendid church was destroyed in 1922 by a fire which began in the pile of crutches. But a monk saved the relic of Saint Anne and a statue of the saint. The church has since been rebuilt.   FULTON J. SHEEN

**SAINTE-BEUVE,** *sant BUHV,* **CHARLES AUGUSTIN** (1804-1869), a French critic, was the greatest exponent of the biographical method of literary criticism. His works reveal that his primary interest was in human psychology and the origin of a literary work in the creator's mind, his family, his friends, and his time.

Sainte-Beuve possessed excellent taste and tireless curiosity. Writing in a delicate and subtle style, he ranged over the entire field of arts and letters, and probably did more than any other man to determine attitudes on French literature in his time. His brilliant essays were published in *Literary Portraits* (1829-1846), *Contemporary Portraits* (1846), 15 volumes of *Monday Chats* (1853-1862), and 10 volumes of *More Monday Chats* (1863-1872).

## SAKE

Sainte-Beuve was also an outstanding historian of French aesthetic and intellectual movements. *Tableau of French Poetry* (1828) is a sympathetic study of the French origins of romanticism. *History of Port-Royal* (1840-1860) examines Port-Royal, a French convent that became the center of a religious and literary movement in the 1600's. *Chateaubriand and His Literary Circle* (1860) is a critical assessment of the French statesman and author and his literary circle during the First Empire in the early 1800's. Sainte-Beuve also wrote poetry and a fine, partly autobiographical novel, *Volupté* (*Pleasures of the Senses*, 1834).

Sainte-Beuve was born in Boulogne-sur-Mer. He studied medicine from 1823 to 1827 before he decided to make his career in literature. Sainte-Beuve spent much of his career writing for newspapers and for literary magazines.   ROBERT J. NIESS

**SAINTE-CLAIRE DEVILLE, HENRI ÉTIENNE.** See ALUMINUM (History).

**SAINTPAULIA.** See AFRICAN VIOLET.

**SAINTS PETER AND PAUL, CATHEDRAL OF.** See WASHINGTON CATHEDRAL.

**SAIPAN,** *sy PAN,* is the second largest island in the Mariana Islands, in the western Pacific Ocean. It lies about 1,600 miles east of Luzon Island in the Philippines, and about the same distance southeast of Tokyo. For location, see PACIFIC ISLANDS (color map). Saipan has an area of 48 square miles and a population of about 8,500. Its former chief town, Garapan, was destroyed during World War II, but its harbor remains one of the best in the Marianas. The island belonged to Spain until 1899, when Germany bought it. A mandate of the League of Nations gave Japan control after World War I. The Japanese planted sugar cane, and built large sugar refineries and heavy fortifications.

Saipan was the scene of heavy fighting during World War II. United States forces landed there in June, 1944, and captured the island after several weeks of fierce fighting. Saipan then became an important American air base for further attacks on Japan. After the war, Saipan became a United Nations trust territory under the direct control of the United States. The headquarters of the Trust Territory of the Pacific Islands was moved from Guam to Saipan in 1962.   EDWIN H. BRYAN, JR.

**The *Enola Gay*** returns to Saipan after dropping an atomic bomb on Hiroshima, Japan, near the end of World War II.

U.S. Air Force

**SAJAMA.** See ANDES MOUNTAINS (Physical Features).
**SAKAKAWEA.** See SACAGAWEA.
**SAKE.** See ALCOHOLIC DRINK (Other Fermented Drinks).

51

# SAKHALIN

**SAKHALIN,** *SACK uh leen,* is a long and narrow island which lies off the eastern coast of Siberia. It is about 600 miles long, and from 16 to 100 miles wide. It has a population of 631,000 and an area of 29,100 square miles. For location, see RUSSIA (physical map).

Pine and spruce forests cover almost all of Sakhalin. It has a changeable climate and the land is not suited to farming. Most of the people make a living by fishing, and fish is their most important food. Many fur-bearing animals live on the island, and some of the men are fur traders. Coal mining and lumbering are carried on and wood pulp is manufactured.

Dutch navigators were the first to discover Sakhalin. For many years Russia and Japan quarreled over the island. In 1875, Japan recognized Russia's ownership. But disputes continued until 1905, when Russia and Japan divided Sakhalin between them after the Russo-Japanese War of 1904-1905. Russia took the northern half of the island, and Japan took over the southern half. The Ainu, a race of white men believed to have been the first people in Japan, still live in southern Sakhalin (see AINU).

The discovery of oil on Sakhalin led the Russians to colonize the island in 1931. The defeat of Japan in World War II gave Russia complete control of the island. THEODORE SHABAD

**SAKI.** See MUNRO, HECTOR HUGH.

**SAKIEH.** See EGYPT (Agriculture).

**SAL AMMONIAC** (chemical formula, $NH_4Cl$) is a white crystal compound made up of nitrogen, hydrogen, and chlorine. Sal ammoniac is known chemically as *ammonium chloride*. It dissolves easily in water, and gives it a sharp, salty taste. Manufacturers make sal ammoniac by combining liquid ammonia with hydrochloric acid. This compound is then evaporated and purified. Sal ammoniac is sometimes found as a mineral in the lava which is poured forth by volcanoes.

Sal ammoniac has many uses in industry and medicine. Its main use is in the manufacture of electric dry cells. It is also used in making the flux for soldering, in gold refining, and in the textile industry. As a medicine, sal ammoniac is often used to induce spitting up or vomiting in bronchitis, pneumonia, and stomach disorders. GEORGE L. BUSH

**SAL SODA.** See SODA.

**SALADIN,** *SAL uh din* (1138-1193), was the greatest Moslem warrior of the 1100's. He brought about the Third Crusade by capturing Jerusalem in 1187 (see CRUSADES [The Third Crusade]). The Moslems regarded Saladin as a saintly hero, and even the Christians honored him for his honesty and bravery.

Saladin served as a soldier in the army of Nur-ed-din, Sultan of Syria. The sultan sent Saladin with an army to aid the Egyptian ruler, who was caliph of the Shiite branch of Islam and a rival of the Sunnite caliph of Baghdad (see CALIPH; ISLAM [Sects]).

Saladin entered the service of the Egyptian caliph, and through his ability as a soldier, became *vizier,* or real head of the government. He worked to change Egypt to the Sunnite branch of Islam. Saladin achieved this aim shortly before the Egyptian caliph died in 1171. Then the caliph of Baghdad recognized Saladin as sultan of Egypt.

Historical Pictures Service
**Saladin** led Moslem troops against the Christians who tried to recapture Jerusalem during the Third Crusade (1189-1192).

Saladin extended his rule northward over Damascus, Aleppo, Mosul, and Edessa, and fought the Christian states along the coast. Some of his troops were besieged at Acre in 1189. They surrendered after two years to Richard the Lion-Hearted (see RICHARD [I]). Saladin and Richard made a truce in 1192 which gave the coast to the Christians, the interior to the Moslems, and allowed Christian pilgrims to enter Jerusalem.

Saladin is remembered also for his support of theologians and other scholars. He built schools, dikes, and canals to help his subjects, and mosques for their worship. When Saladin died, his lands were divided among his less able heirs.

Saladin was born in the castle of Tekrit on the Tigris River in Mesopotamia. His father, a Kurd general, later became governor of Damascus, the center of Moslem learning. FRANKLIN D. SCOTT

**SALAMANDER** is a timid, harmless animal that looks like a lizard but is related to the frogs and toads. Most salamanders are small, but the giant salamander of Japan grows 5 feet long.

Salamanders are cold-blooded animals with moist, slimy skins. They usually have four legs and a long tail. Their bodies can replace lost parts, such as the tail and legs. Salamanders live in streams and ponds, on the land beneath stones, and in caves or rotting logs where it is cool, dark, and moist. They eat grubs, slugs, worms, and insects.

The female salamander usually lays her eggs in early spring. The eggs are deposited one by one, in groups or in long strings. The *larvae* (young) hatch from the eggs at different times. In some *species* (kinds), the larva does not leave the egg. The larva breathes through external gills until it changes into an adult. But some kinds of salamanders keep their larval characteristics throughout their lives.

The *spotted salamander* of North America is one of the best-known species. It is approximately 6 inches long and it has yellow spots on its smooth, dark colored skin. The spotted salamander secretes a milky fluid

# SALEM

American Museum of Natural History
**Red Salamanders Grow About Six Inches Long.**

through its skin when it is roughly handled. This fluid is poisonous to some animals, and protects the salamander from some of its enemies.

**Scientific Classification.** Salamanders belong to the class *Amphibia* and the order *Caudata*. The spotted salamander is a member of the mole salamander family, *Ambystomidae*. It belongs to the genus *Ambystoma*, and is species *A. maculatum*. W. FRANK BLAIR

See also HELLBENDER; MUD PUPPY; NEWT.

**SALAMIS,** *SAL uh mis,* is a horseshoe-shaped Greek island in the Saronic Gulf, about 10 miles west of the city of Athens. Salamis covers an area of 36 square miles. For location, see GREECE (color map). Much of the land on Salamis is rocky and mountainous. Most of the inhabitants are Albanians. They raise grapes, olives, and grain in the valleys and coastal regions. Salamis is also known by a modern name, *Kuluri*, which means *baker's crescent*. The island has a population of about 20,650.

The Greeks and Persians fought a great sea battle near Salamis in 480 B.C. When the Persians advanced after the Battle of Thermopylae, the Athenians sought safety on Salamis. In the Battle of Salamis, Persian ships tried to block the retreat of Greek vessels. The Greeks destroyed half the Persian fleet. C. BRADFORD WELLES

See also NAVY (Famous Sea Battles of History); ARISTIDES; THEMISTOCLES; XERXES.

**SALARIUM.** See SALT (History).

**SALAZAR,** *suh luh ZAHR,* **ANTONIO DE OLIVEIRA** (1889-    ), served as dictator of Portugal from 1933 to 1968. He became prime minister in 1932. The next year he proclaimed a new constitution that made him a virtual dictator. He suffered a stroke in 1968 and was unable to carry out his duties. He was replaced as prime minister by Marcello Caetano.

Salazar was a financial expert, and a professor of economics at Coimbra University before he entered government service. He refused the position of minister of finance in 1926, because he felt he would

**Antonio de Salazar**
Consulate General of Portugal

not have enough power to solve Portugal's financial problems. By 1928, Portugal's finances were in such poor condition that the government gave Salazar the power he wanted. He gradually took control of the government.

Salazar set up a police state. He put trade unions under government control, and abolished freedom of the press and political expression. He put Portugal's finances on a firm basis, but he did so at the expense of wages, education, and the well-being of many of the Portuguese people.

During World War II, Salazar kept Portugal neutral. The capital, Lisbon, became the main link between Allied and Axis nations, and their agents operated freely in the country. Yet Salazar maintained Portugal's traditional ties to Great Britain, and granted the Allies naval and air bases in Portugal's Azores Islands.

Political opposition to Salazar began growing in Portugal in the late 1950's. His policies toward Angola, Mozambique, and the other Portuguese colonies in Africa attracted international attention in the late 1960's. Salazar maintained Portuguese domination over the colonies despite disapproval by the United Nations and rebellion by some Africans. STANLEY G. PAYNE

**SALE, BILL OF.** See BILL OF SALE.

**SALEM,** Mass. (pop. 39,211; alt. 9 ft.), is one of New England's most historic cities. It was the site of the famous witchcraft trials of the 1690's. Around 1850, Salem became a center of the cotton industry. Today, the city's products include cables, flashbulbs, games, lamps, plastics, radio tubes, tannery and leather products, and valves.

**Location and Description.** Salem lies on a fine harbor, 16 miles northeast of Boston. For location, see MASSACHUSETTS (political map). The Air-Sea Rescue Service of the U.S. Coast Guard operates from an air base on Winter Island in the harbor.

Salem State College is located in Salem. The city's many historic houses include the birthplace of Nathaniel Hawthorne and the House of Seven Gables, about which he wrote his famous novel. Other beautiful homes, built by wealthy sea merchants, line Chestnut Street. The Essex Institute and the Peabody Museum have preserved many relics from the voyages of Salem ships. The Salem Maritime National Historic Site, which covers 10.73 acres, contains buildings that were significant in New England's maritime, architectural, and literary history. The first settlement in Salem has been reconstructed as Pioneer Village. Another historic site is the Witch House, where the preliminary hearings for the witch trials were held.

**History.** Roger Conant and colonists from Cape Ann established the first settlement on the site of Salem in 1626. In 1628, John Endecott led a group of settlers into the area for the Massachusetts Bay Company.

Salem's witchcraft scare began in 1692. One of the servants of a local minister was a West Indian slave girl named Tituba. She told voodoo tales to a group of young girls. The girls became so excited by her stories that they shivered and screamed at night. A physician who examined them said they were bewitched. Tituba and two other women were accused of being witches and were sentenced to death. The witchcraft scare continued

53

**The Harbor at Salem, Mass., Became the Home Base for Many Privateers Who Operated in the Revolutionary War.**

for about a year. Nineteen persons were hanged as witches on Gallows Hill and one was pressed to death. See SEWALL, SAMUEL; WITCHCRAFT.

During the Revolutionary War, Salem became a great privateering port. When peace came, Salem merchant ships sailed to all parts of the world. Salem captains traveled around the Cape of Good Hope to reach the Far East. Salem again became a privateering port in the War of 1812. However, war losses, the increasing shallowness of the harbor, and the opening of the Erie Canal ruined Salem's trade.

Salem received its city charter in 1836. The seat of Essex County, Salem has a mayor-council type of government. WILLIAM J. REID

See also COLONIAL LIFE IN AMERICA (picture: Witch House).

**SALEM,** Ore. (pop. 58,808; met. area 147,411; alt. 160 ft.), the state capital, lies on the Willamette River about 50 miles south of Portland. It has food-processing and metal, paper, and wood products industries. Salem began as the village, Chemeketa. It was named Salem in 1846, and received a city charter in 1857. Salem was chosen as the state capital in 1864. It is the home of Willamette University, and Marion County seat. Salem has a council-manager form of government. For location, see OREGON (political map). RICHARD M. HIGHSMITH, JR.

See also OREGON (picture: The State Capitol).

**SALEM COLLEGE.** See UNIVERSITIES AND COLLEGES (table).

**SALEM STATE COLLEGE.** See UNIVERSITIES AND COLLEGES (table).

**SALEM WITCHCRAFT.** See SALEM (Mass.); WITCHCRAFT.

**SALERATUS.** See SODA.

**SALERNO,** *sah LAIR noh* (pop. 123,589; alt. 80 ft.), is the seaport capital of the province of Salerno in Italy. An Italian Mediterranean shipping center, it lies on the Gulf of Salerno, about 30 miles from Naples (see ITALY [political map]).

Salerno was the seat of an early medical school from the 1000's to the end of the 1200's. Some of the churches in the city, including the Cathedral of San Matteo, were built during the same period, when the Normans controlled Salerno. During World War II, Allied troops landed at Salerno in September, 1943, and captured the city from the Germans. SHEPARD B. CLOUGH

**SALES, SAINT FRANCIS DE.** See FRANCIS DE SALES, SAINT.

**SALES ENGINEER.** See ENGINEERING (Engineers at Work).

**SALES TAX** is levied on the sale of goods and services. The tax is a certain percentage of the sale. The sales tax may be used by a city, state or province, or national government. It can be collected by the producer, manufacturer, wholesaler, or retailer. It may be levied on selected items or on every sale. The rate is usually low, although a high rate may be levied on luxury goods such as furs, or on such items as gasoline, tobacco, and food.

The main objection to most sales taxes is that they fall heavily on low-income groups. Persons with low incomes must spend much of their wages on consumers' goods. So they pay more sales tax in relation to their incomes than wealthy people do. The main advantages of the sales tax are that it produces a great deal of money, it reduces government reliance on income taxes, and it is relatively easy to administer. CHARLES J. GAA

**SALESIAN.** See BOSCO, SAINT JOHN.

Rie Gaddis

**Good Salesmanship** uses the same techniques, whether the salesman is selling shirts or houses. A good real estate salesman tries to find the house that fills the needs and wishes of his customer.

**SALESMANSHIP** is the capacity to get people to act. It is the ability to persuade other persons to support an idea willingly and happily, to buy a product, or to take a service.

Some persons used to say that salesmen are born, not made. But most persons now know that many specific methods of salesmanship not only *can* be learned, but also *must* be learned, if a person is to lead the most happy and most successful life of which he is capable.

### Everybody Is a Salesman

Salesmanship is an art, and it also approaches being a science. It is perhaps the most human of arts and sciences, because it has the most human basis of all the arts and sciences. In its broad meaning, salesmanship enters into almost every human activity. The boy who persuades his playmates that they would rather play one game than another is using salesmanship. The job-seeker must use salesmanship to convince the employer that he is worth hiring. An employer, too, often has to use salesmanship to hire an employee whom he wants, and then to get him to do his work in certain ways.

Salesmanship is used in almost every occupation and profession. A man who repairs automobiles in a garage seldom thinks of himself as a salesman. But the courtesy with which he does his work, and the way in which he explains what needs to be done and how he proposes to do it, may determine whether or not the owner of the car will return to the garage for more service.

It is almost as important for a doctor to inspire the confidence of his patients as it is for him to have a broad knowledge of medicine. His "bedside manner" is salesmanship of a high order. A trial lawyer's job is much like that of a salesman. He must convince a judge or jury of the truth and justice of his case. That, too, is salesmanship.

The genius of a great scientist or inventor would never be of maximum benefit to mankind without being accompanied by good salesmanship. The electric light, the washing machine, and the refrigerator might still be laboratory toys if there had not been men with the power to convince people that such new-fangled gadgets would benefit them. In a very real sense, salesmanship is education of the people to higher and better standards of living.

### Salesmanship as an Occupation

In its narrower and more common meaning, salesmanship refers to the processes by which most goods and services are sold for use, or for resale. There are many different kinds of salesmen. There are those who sell such products as vacuum cleaners, insurance, or common household products, by approaching their customers directly in their homes or offices. Other salesmen sell products which are to be used in certain kinds of businesses or factories. These salesmen visit only those companies which are likely to use their product. Still other salesmen represent wholesale houses which sell their products for resale to stores. The stores themselves have retail clerks who make up another class of sales personnel. Still another class of persons sell their services.

# SALESMANSHIP

They include laundry operators, automobile repairmen, television and home-appliance servicemen, and dry cleaners.

## History of Salesmanship

Salesmanship has existed in a crude form since very early times. Primitive tribes traded food they raised or articles they made for the goods of other tribes. Early people bargained with each other to get as much as possible in return for their products. And in their bargaining they used many of the basic principles of salesmanship for personal persuasion.

Salesmanship took another step forward when money came into use. We know that the early Phoenician traders used money in their trade. Through the use of money they made it possible to sell goods without having to receive anything of practical value in exchange. The use of money expanded trade and in turn expanded salesmanship. But salesmanship as we know it today is a fairly recent development. Until about two hundred years ago the vast majority of all peoples bought very little goods. They made at home nearly everything they needed. They grew their own food, and they made their own clothing. They made the implements they needed for doing their work.

However, some peoples made more articles or grew more food than they actually needed, and they traded these goods for things which they were not able to make for themselves. In the towns, people began to make special kinds of goods. Cobblers made shoes, tailors made clothing, and metalsmiths made tableware and jewelry. Some of these made fairly large quantities of goods and during the Middle Ages some persons traveled from one place to another to sell or trade their surplus goods for raw materials.

But communication and transportation were so limited that selling goods at a distance was difficult. Carrying products over great distances made them too expensive for the average person to buy. So selling was only on a small scale. Yet in England during the time of Queen Elizabeth I, some merchant trading organizations developed in the manufacturing towns. They collected goods and took them to coastal towns where they were exchanged for foreign goods. In turn their goods were shipped to foreign markets.

Modern salesmanship began to develop during the Industrial Revolution of the 1700's and 1800's. The Industrial Revolution introduced into selling three major elements. These were mass production, the invention of radically different products, and competition in business.

**Mass Production.** The most important thing the Industrial Revolution did was to replace hand labor with machinery. Machines produced articles more quickly and more cheaply than people could make them by hand. Soon there began to be more articles than people actually needed, and they were produced so cheaply that the common people could afford to buy them. Luxury goods came into the reach of the average person.

But people did not start buying merely because goods were available. It was necessary to educate and to persuade people to buy. Goods had to be sold rapidly if the manufacturer was to stay in business. Many manufacturers did not have time to find their own markets and sell their own goods. So there developed the sales agent for the manufacturer. These agents, or wholesalers, bought the manufactured goods and took the risk of distributing them. They sent salesmen to the various cities to sell the goods. At first the salesmen took the goods with them. But in those days, roads were often unsafe because there were many robbers. Also it proved to be expensive to haul goods great distances, when it was not certain that they would be sold. So these "chapmen," or "bagmen," as the salesmen were called, began to take only samples of their wares with them. They showed them to prospective customers and took orders for the goods. The goods were delivered only after orders were taken. These salesmen became the first traveling salesmen as we know them today.

**Invention of New Products.** Another development of the Industrial Revolution was the invention of many new products. However, people often had to be persuaded that the new articles would be useful to them. At first many new inventions were laughed at. For example, Elias Howe patented the first practical sewing machine. But it took Isaac M. Singer to sell the public on the value of the sewing machine in the home.

Most people are naturally slow to try the new. They must be convinced that a new product is good and useful. The salesman acts as a teacher to explain to people how they can make their lives more comfortable by using new products. In this way salesmen have improved the world's standards of living.

**Competition.** As the Industrial Revolution progressed, there was greater and greater competition among manufacturers. Soon many different plants were making similar products. It took salesmen to convince the public that one product was better than another.

Nowadays, selling is a vital part of the economic system. Even when goods are scarce and it is comparatively easy to find customers, salesmen are needed to distribute goods, to act as the servicing and informational link between seller and buyer, and to maintain good-will relationships.

Salesmen also play a large part in creating the wealth that makes production of goods possible. This is brought about in the following manner. The salesmen get people to buy goods. The money that the salesmen bring to their companies makes it possible for those companies to improve their products and to make them in greater quantities. Greater production creates more jobs, and the workers use their wages to buy other products.

## Basic Selling Techniques

Selling is essentially a human relationship, so it is not possible or practical to confine its procedures to any rigid rules. But there are certain fairly well defined paths which successful salesmen follow and some basic techniques of salesmanship on which most salesmen are generally agreed.

**Finding the Prospect.** The income of the average salesman is based on how much he sells. His income will be low if he spends his time in trying to sell his goods to persons who are not likely to buy. He can save time in the long run by carefully selecting and qualifying possible customers, or prospects.

The problems of finding prospects depend largely

on what the salesman has to sell. For salesmen who sell essentially needed products, this problem is not great. For example, the salesman of shoemaking machinery knows that only shoe factories will buy his goods. Similarly, the salesman of a brand of expensive food would not try to sell his goods to a store whose customers had little money.

The salesman may find customers by writing letters to possible prospects before he calls, with a view to developing inquiries or requests for more information from such prospects. The salesman then calls only on the people who have made inquiries. This way of getting "leads" is called "direct mail." See LETTER WRITING.

Salesmen of products which are in general use may rely on door-to-door canvassing. Tactful questioning of buyers may give the salesmen the names of neighbors or friends who would be good prospects.

**Preparing for the Interview.** A sales interview should be carefully planned. The salesman who goes to see a prospect with little idea of what he is going to say or do will not last long. Many sales manuals prepared by companies for their salesmen provide outlines of presentations. Other manuals give sales talks with directions as complete as the stage directions of a play. These companies require that a salesman should rehearse his interview as carefully as an actor rehearses a play. And he is asked to learn his part so well that he gives a sincere and convincing performance. Other companies prefer that their salesmen rely on no memorized presentation, but that they follow certain general patterns of persuasion which other salesmen have proved to be effective.

In any event, a salesman should enter his sales interview with a specific idea about how his product can be useful to the prospect. Therefore, it is necessary that he have as full an understanding as possible of the nature of his prospect's business.

Knowledge of the prospect's business involves also knowledge of whom the salesman should see to make his sale. Some companies have buyers or purchasing agents who make the decisions on what should be bought. Generally these decisions are influenced by certain specifications or requirements which the engineering or production departments of their companies have developed. Other companies rely on their department heads or their presidents to decide on purchases.

A salesman must be prepared to make a quick estimate of his prospect's characteristics and to adapt himself to them. Some persons like to work rapidly and come to a quick decision. Other persons' minds move more slowly. They prefer to come to a decision only after considerable discussion. The salesman should try to judge the mental inclinations of his prospect and shape his sales talk to fit such habits of thinking. Some prospects tend to be distrustful. Others tend to be emotional in their make-up. Still others are coldly logical. A few are very professional in insisting that certain "pet" ideas of their own be complied with. By engaging the prospect in preliminary discussion of other matters, the salesman often can gauge the prospect's probable manner of thinking.

**The Sales Presentation.** What is said in a sales talk depends largely on what is to be sold. A clerk in a grocery store usually does not need to do much more than arrange the merchandise attractively and con-

### THE ELEMENTS OF SALESMANSHIP
The salesman has much in common with other callings.

**Like a Lawyer,** he must be able to express his ideas clearly and convincingly.

**Like a Minister,** he must be sincere, and honest, and firm in his beliefs.

**Like a Teacher,** he must be able to explain the points of his product clearly.

**Like a Parent,** he should be a master of psychology in dealing with people.

**Like a Librarian,** he understands and fits his product to public taste.

**Like the Statesman,** he must both shape and follow the will of the people.

# SALESMANSHIP

veniently and help the shopper meet her immediate needs. But a grocery clerk can increase sales by emphasizing the reliability of certain brands of goods. He can also make helpful suggestions about the use of new products that have come on the market.

But the salesman who is trying, for instance, to get a large manufacturing corporation to use the packing cartons which his own company makes has an entirely different problem. He knows his prospect is a possible customer. He knows also that the prospect has to be convinced of the superior value of the salesman's product.

The most successful salesman is the one who can put himself in the position of the prospect, and understand his problems, his needs, and his desires.

**Motives and Emotions.** There are a number of basic human motives and deep-running emotions that are mainsprings to action. Every one, for example, seeks to acquire and to own different forms of wealth. These may be lands, goods, or money. Some people like to own farms or homes. Others like to possess automobiles, clothes, and jewelry. Still others like to make profits, accumulate money as such, or to own stocks and bonds.

The alert salesman may show that his lands or goods will produce more money, or more additional goods and lands than the prospect can get by keeping his money. He shows that what he sells will produce more for the prospect than the price asked for it. Profit is the motive for buying.

Every person likes to be well thought of by others. He strives for a good name. If the salesman can show that the "best people" are joining his association, or supporting his program, many prospects will be persuaded to follow their example.

When the salesman can show that what he proposes will make a man's heart stouter, his head quicker, or his mind faster or better informed, he employs still another motive for buying. That is why people buy books and magazines, why they join reading clubs, and why they seek education.

If a salesman can show that his article will ensure health and prolong life, he has a strong selling motive. Medicines, tonics, vitamins, sanitariums, rest retreats, and travel tours are sold on this basis.

Almost every one will act for the benefit of some one whom they love, for their family, or for their friends. Men buy homes to please their wives and children. They take out insurance to protect them. They send their children to school to educate them.

We all like things of beauty, objects of art, and of personal adornment, beautiful sunsets, good music, moving drama, and delicious foods. They all create pleasurable sensations. Good salesmen show that their product has pleasing proportions, harmonious colorings, and that it is good to the eyes or to the taste.

Wealth, profits, good name and fame, personal power, fine health, worthwhile service, and pleasurable sensations are some of many motives that inspire action.

Emotions also are highly important when it comes to getting action. Confidence and fear, pride and shame, love and hate, envy and admiration, respect and contempt, courage and caution—all these emotions play their part in moving people to act.

Effective salesmen combine appeals to motives and emotions to good advantage; at the beginning or in the middle of their presentation they show how their product, service, or idea will add wealth, health, reputation, power, or pleasure. Then toward the end of their presentation, they inspire their prospects with confidence and pride in taking the action which they propose. They show the position of honor and respect that accompanies such action. They point out how the purchaser may be the envy of others, or what joy they will afford their families. The motives and emotions, thus taken together, make for action.

Selling is not entirely a matter of talking about the product. Many a buyer has bought one product instead of another equally good product simply because the salesman of the first product showed more sincerity and eagerness to serve than did the salesman of the other product. Once the salesman is fully informed about his product and its uses, and the reputation, achievements, and capacity of his company, he will do well to add his own qualities of personal agreeableness. He should like the prospect, and seek to get the prospect to like him. Liking often grows out of common interests. The successful salesman will try to find out if his prospect likes golf, fishing, or stamp collecting. He will then try to build up a personal relationship through such interests. But he should not rely on this personal relationship alone to sell his goods.

**The Introduction and Description of the Product** itself is an important element in a sales presentation. First of all, the salesman must believe wholeheartedly in his product. He must understand how it works, how it is made, and how it can be used. He must be able to answer all questions about it without any hesitation and with complete directness.

It is not enough for the salesman to present his product and let it sell itself. He must in a sense act as the eyes of his prospect. Some buyers know exactly what they are looking for in a product, and are expert enough to judge the product without the salesman's help. But most persons must have a product explained to them, and have its good qualities pointed out. The successful salesman does this.

The salesman should develop the ability to dramatize his product. The successful actor makes himself felt by his audience as a distinct personality. The successful salesman makes his product recognized as something special. He may do this by pointing out how it is better than other similar products. Or he may describe the special research that was conducted to make the product as good as it is. He may make a demonstration of his product. Or he may use special literature to describe its qualities. The salesman must plan how to present his product in the best possible way.

**Overcoming Sales Resistance.** One thing which the salesman must learn to handle is "sales resistance." Most people are naturally cautious about spending their money, and they may make many objections to a product before they buy it. A salesman may train himself to meet many of these objections beforehand. The salesman can develop certain fairly standard answers for certain typical objections that he frequently receives. Much of this understanding comes only through experience.

A salesman should anticipate his customer's objections. He always should treat such objections with respect, even though he knows that they are not valid ones. Quite often such objections are based on fears instead of on facts. In such cases, the salesman can say, "I know how you feel. Some of our customers felt the same way at first, but here is what they have found out."

He must be trained to answer quickly any questions his customers may ask, and be ready to admit faults that are obvious, but be quick to show that the merits outweigh the faults. Failure to do so will make the prospect doubt the salesman's honesty and sincerity.

Often, objections can be turned to the salesman's advantage. Suppose the prospect says the price is too high. The salesman can then point out the valid reasons why the price of his product is higher than that of other comparable products. He can show that his product is made of better materials, has better workmanship, and will last longer. He may be able to show that his product is cheaper in the long run than other, less well-made products.

**Repeat Sales.** One of the main problems of a salesman is the assurance of repeat sales. The bases of successful repeat salesmanship are satisfactory quality, pricing, and service by the company, and complete honesty by the salesman. A buyer will continue to buy from a firm's salesman only if he has complete confidence in him, in the firm, and in its product. A salesman's honesty appears in several stages of the selling process. First, he must never make claims about his product which are not true. The buyer will soon find out that they are not true and will not buy again.

Second, a salesman should not try to sell a product to a person who does not really need it. He may succeed in making the first sale, because of his salesmanship ability. But in the long run the customer will feel that he has been led into making a bad purchase, and the salesman will lose his good will.

Third, the salesman should never make promises unless he is sure they can be fulfilled. If a customer asks for a certain service, the salesman should not promise to perform the service if he or his firm cannot perform it. Yet the salesman can do many things to build good will and to help his customers. For example, a salesman whose product is sold in retail stores can give the proprietor ideas on displays which will help sales. This, in turn, will allow the salesman to sell more of his product to the store owner.

Repeat sales depend a great deal on the personality of the salesman. "High-pressure" salesmen who exaggerate values, make strong statements without proof, and rush their prospects into action without giving them time for investigation or reflection, may be successful in first sales. But they often lose out in repeat sales because their tactics anger their customers. The most successful salesmen in the long run are those who are straightforward in their dealings.

**Other Aids to Selling.** There are many modern aids to salesmanship. The wise salesman makes the fullest use of these aids. One of the greatest selling aids is advertising. Often a customer first becomes acquainted with a product through a radio or newspaper advertisement. The salesman should closely follow the advertising of his product and make full use of the selling points which it offers him. See ADVERTISING.

The salesman is also often equipped with literature and with picture displays which he can use effectively in his work. Sometimes he has samples of his product to show, or models by which he can demonstrate the product. Such visual aids to selling are very helpful. It has been proved that most persons can understand something they see much more easily than something they hear about.

Magazines and books on products or on the art of salesmanship are also helpful to salesmen. Nearly all businesses have trade publications which describe the latest developments in their fields. The salesman should keep up to date not only on his own company's improvements, but also on those of his competitors. He should look constantly for new ideas in salesmanship.

## Qualifications of a Good Salesman

There are a few basic qualities which are helpful to almost all persons who want to sell.

**Industry.** A salesman does not punch a time clock. Moreover, even though he works long hours, as he should, his actual talking time to prospects is seldom more than two hours a day. This requires that the salesman be alert to find the "free time" of his prospect, and fit his calls and hours accordingly. It means also that he should so organize his day's work and his calls that he uses the least possible time in going from place to place. Where possible, appointments should be made in advance to cut down the time of waiting to see prospects.

**Loyalty.** The salesman must be loyal to his employer and to his company's products and policies. But he need not be a rubber stamp, blindly doing as he is ordered. He is expected to offer new ideas and critical suggestions. But once the company has made a decision as to how its business is to be conducted, the salesman should follow that decision. The success of a company as a whole depends a great deal upon the uniform way in which a sales program is carried out.

**Initiative and Originality.** The salesman should always be alert to the need for changes in his personal selling methods. He should be sensitive to his prospect's attitude and be ready to adapt himself to it.

**Sincerity and Enthusiasm.** No one should ever try to sell a product about which he is not enthusiastic. Prospects are quick to sense that the salesman does not believe what he is saying. A successful salesman must have complete confidence in himself and his product. This confidence will then be carried over to the prospect.

**Courage and Foresight.** Business conditions constantly change. The salesman should have the imagination and the knowledge of his field necessary to foresee these changes. And he should have the courage to change his methods to fit new conditions. He also must have the determination to keep on presenting his product, no matter how discouraging immediate results may be. In the long run, he is certain to enjoy reasonable success if he has the heart to continue to make as many presentations each day as he can crowd in.

**Leadership.** The qualities that make up a good salesman are much the same as those that make people good leaders. The boy who leads the games at a party, the girl who organizes the school clubs, the woman who does the real work in organizing public-welfare cam-

# SALESMANSHIP

paigns—these people are likely to make good salespersons. They have the extra drive and the willingness to work which make for success.

**Understanding.** A salesman should have a thorough understanding of human nature. His job is basically a job of personal relationship. He must make people like him and respect him through his sympathetic understanding of others.

**Personality.** Psychologists sometimes divide people into two classes, which they call *introverts* and *extroverts*. Introverts are "turned in" on themselves. Their primary concern is their own problems. The extroverts are "turned out." They are more interested in other persons than in their own inner thoughts and worries. Most successful salesmen are extroverts. Their cheerfulness, enthusiasm, diplomacy, and open-mindedness make it easy for them to get along with people.

**Ability to Talk.** A salesman is, in a sense, a showman. Like a showman, he must be able to talk well and intelligently. If he talks hesitantly and without confidence, he annoys his prospects. They doubt the truth of what he is saying. At the same time, a salesman should be a good listener, and, at the start of his interview, a good questioner, so that he can know his prospect's situation, and so determine how his company and his product can best be of use.

**Personal Appearance.** A salesman should always be careful of his personal appearance. Some people make up their minds about a person from their first impression of him. Personal mannerisms are also important. Peculiar habits of speech often make a prospect feel uncomfortable, or even dislike the salesman. A salesman must try to see himself as others see him. He should try to analyze his own behavior and see whether he has any bad mannerisms which will tend to annoy people.

**Good Manners.** Courtesy and tact play a large part in successful salesmanship. The successful salesman is one who makes his prospect happy to buy, not just happy to get rid of him. He must be convinced that he is doing his prospect a service by trying to sell him his product. But he must never give the appearance of trying to force his prospect to buy.

## Careers in Selling

More persons in the United States are employed in selling jobs than in any other occupation. Salesmanship offers almost unlimited opportunities for personal advancement to energetic young men or women.

The best training for salesmanship is a broad, general education. But certain specific courses are valuable for the would-be salesman. Courses in English, psychology, logic, letter writing, bookkeeping, and other commercial subjects will help him acquire helpful skills in business and knowledge of business practices. Many high schools and colleges also give courses in merchandising and salesmanship. A training in public speaking and in dramatics may develop the salesman's ability to talk and give him more confidence. There are also special books on salesmanship which will help him.

**Selecting the Job.** A sales job should be selected as carefully as any other occupation. Working conditions vary considerably from one selling position to another. Many salesmen must travel a great deal. For persons who do not like to be away from home for long periods, such jobs would not prove satisfactory. Selling demands hard work and long hours. People who do not have much physical strength can not perform such a job satisfactorily. Possibilities for advancement also influence the selection of a selling job.

Perhaps the most important point in selecting a selling job is the salesman's major interest in any product. Is it in how it works? Or is it in what it does? If the salesman's special interest is in how a product works, he probably will be more successful in selling to manufacturers and wholesalers. If his special interest is in what a product does, he very likely will be more successful in selling to consumers, or users.

**Income Possibilities.** There is perhaps a greater range in the income of salesmen than in any other occupation. In the mid-1960's, the *median* annual income for salesmen was about $12,000. As many salesmen had incomes above $12,000 as had incomes below that figure. About a fourth of all salesmen had earnings of $15,000 or higher. Some salesmen work on a salary basis, usually with bonuses for good sales records. Sometimes bonuses earned in a year amount to more than the annual salary. Other salesmen work entirely on commission.

**Advancement Possibilities.** A salesman has an excellent chance to gain a broad knowledge of his company and the industry in which it operates. Often, salesmen with special ability rise to important positions in their firms. Salesmen may become district or general managers of the sales organizations, and from there they may be promoted to executive positions in the home office.

BENJAMIN F. BILLS

**Related Articles.** See the sections on Careers in various articles in WORLD BOOK. For example, see: AIR CONDITIONING; AUTOMOBILE; BUSINESS; INSURANCE; IRON AND STEEL; PETROLEUM; PLASTICS; PUBLISHING; RADIO; REAL ESTATE; TELEVISION.

### Outline
I. Everybody Is a Salesman
II. Salesmanship as an Occupation
III. History of Salesmanship
IV. Basic Selling Techniques
    A. Finding the Prospect
    B. Preparing for the Interview
    C. The Sales Presentation
    D. Motives and Emotions
    E. The Introduction and Description of the Product
    F. Overcoming Sales Resistance
    G. Repeat Sales
    H. Other Aids to Selling
V. Qualifications of a Good Salesman
    A. Industry
    B. Loyalty
    C. Initiative and Originality
    D. Sincerity and Enthusiasm
    E. Courage and Foresight
    F. Leadership
    G. Understanding
    H. Personality
    I. Ability to Talk
    J. Personal Appearance
    K. Good Manners
VI. Careers in Selling

### Questions
What is salesmanship? Explain.
How may an employer, a doctor, or a lawyer have to use salesmanship?
How did the first use of money affect salesmanship?
Who were perhaps the first modern traveling salesmen?
What is "sales resistance"? How does the salesman try to overcome it?
What training is especially desirable for a salesman?
What is perhaps the most important point in selecting a selling job?

**SALFORD,** *SAWL furd* (pop. 143,430; alt. 255 ft.), is an English manufacturing city a few miles west of Manchester. It has large cotton, iron, and chemical factories. It is on the Manchester Ship Canal. For location, see GREAT BRITAIN (political map).

**SALIAN.** See FRANK; SALIC LAW.

**SALIC LAW** was a set of laws written in Latin and founded on Germanic customs and procedure. Historians believe Clovis (466?-511), king of the Salian Franks, had the Salic laws drawn up during his reign. Parts of the Salic Law listed fines payable to relatives of free persons who were killed, injured, or insulted.

In the 1300's, the Salic Law played an important part in the history of France. The last son of Philip IV died without leaving any direct male heirs. French lawyers used the Salic Law to keep Edward III of England from gaining the throne of France. Edward was the son of a daughter of Philip IV, and the French argued that a kingdom could not be inherited through a woman. Actually, the Salic Law had said nothing about the inheritance of kingdoms. It simply stated that Salic land could not be inherited by women.

The French recognized Philip VI, the son of a brother of Philip IV, as king of France. As a result, Salic Law came to mean that a woman or descendants of a woman could not inherit royal authority. WILLIAM F. MCDONALD

**SALICIN.** See WILLOW.

**SALICYLIC ACID,** *SAL uh SILL ik* (chemical formula, $C_6H_4(OH)COOH$), is the foundation of one of the most popular home remedies, *aspirin* (acetylsalicylic acid). The pain-relieving qualities of this compound, together with its comparative harmlessness, make it a popular drug throughout the world. Another salicylic acid derivative is *oil of wintergreen* (methyl salicylate). This oil is a flavoring for candies, chewing gum, and soft drinks.

Salicylic acid occurs as colorless needle-shaped crystals of a sweetish acid taste. It dissolves a little in cold water and readily in hot water, ether, or alcohol. It may be extracted from oil of wintergreen, but more often it is made from sodium phenate and carbon dioxide.

Salicylic acid is a powerful poison for the bacteria that cause food to spoil, and formerly was used as a food preservative. Salicylic acid is used in treating ringworm and eczema, and in making dyes. GEORGE L. BUSH

See also ASPIRIN; SALOL.

**SALINA,** Kans. (pop. 43,202; alt. 1,225 ft.), is the chief business center of north-central Kansas. It stands on the banks of the Smoky Hill River, about 180 miles west of Kansas City (see KANSAS [political map]). Salina lies in the hard winter-wheat belt of the Middle West, and ranks high in the production of flour. Other important products of Salina include farm implements, flour mill machinery, playground equipment, and foodstuffs. It is the home of Kansas Wesleyan University, St. John's Military School, and Marymount College. Salina is the seat of Saline County, and it has a council-manager government. WILLIAM F. ZORNOW

**SALINGER, J. D.** (1919-    ), is an American author whose novel *The Catcher in the Rye* (1951) ranks as a minor classic. The book became especially popular among American high school and college students. The hero and narrator of the story is Holden Caulfield, a prep school dropout in search of self-understanding and a meaning for his life. His misadventures in New York City—with his sister, a girl friend, a prostitute, and others—are comic on the surface but agonizing for Holden. In the end, Holden learns to face the ugliness in life and the weakness in himself.

Salinger also wrote *Nine Stories* (1953) which, like *The Catcher in the Rye*, deals with the loveless. His later fiction has centered on the Glass family in such books as *Franny and Zooey* (1961); and *Raise High the Roof Beam, Carpenters* and *Seymour, an Introduction*, published together in 1963. Of the seven Glass children, Seymour, who commits suicide, best represents the desperate search for lost innocence and the mystic bliss that is glimpsed by Salinger's major characters. Salinger was born JEROME DAVID SALINGER in New York City. EUGENE K. GARBER

**SALISBURY,** *SAWLZ bur ee*, or NEW SARUM (pop. 35,990; alt. 305 ft.), lies about 80 miles southwest of London, in southern England (see GREAT BRITAIN [political map]). Salisbury is famous for its cathedral, the top of whose spire is 404 feet from the ground. The cathedral was built as part of a new town to replace the town of Old Sarum in the 1200's. All that remains of Old Sarum is a large mound with *ramparts* (defensive banks) made of earth. Stonehenge, the largest prehistoric structure in western Europe, stands near Salisbury (see STONEHENGE). JOHN W. WEBB

**SALISBURY,** Md. (pop. 16,302; alt. 25 ft.), is the largest town on the Eastern Shore of Maryland. It ranks second only to Baltimore among the ports of the state. Salisbury lies near the center of the Delmarva Peninsula (see DELMARVA PENINSULA). Its plants produce canned goods, building materials, paper boxes, creosoted products, brass, iron, shirts, gasoline pumps, and ships. Salisbury was founded in 1732. It is the seat of Wicomico County and has a mayor-council government. FRANCIS C. HABER

**SALISBURY** (pop. 324,800; alt. 4,700 ft.) is the capital of Rhodesia (formerly Southern Rhodesia). Until 1963, it was the capital of the Federation of Rhodesia and Nyasaland. The city lies on a plain near the Hunyani River, in a healthful area that produces tobacco and corn. About a fourth of the people of Salisbury are Europeans. Salisbury is a modern city. Cecil Square, in the center of the city, was named for Cecil Rhodes, the founder of Rhodesia. HIBBERD V. B. KLINE, JR.

**SALISBURY, MARQUIS OF** (1830-1903), ROBERT ARTHUR TALBOT GASCOYNE-CECIL, was a distinguished British statesman who served as prime minister three times. He entered the Cabinet in 1867 and again in 1874 as secretary of state for India under Prime Minister Benjamin Disraeli. In 1878, he became secretary of state for foreign affairs. When Disraeli died in 1881, Salisbury became leader of the Conservative Party and then prime minister. He served from June 24, 1885, to Feb. 6, 1886; from Aug. 3, 1886, to Aug. 8, 1892; and from July 2, 1895 to July 12, 1902. During most of this period of Conservative domination, Salisbury also served as secretary of state for foreign affairs.

Salisbury was born at Hatfield in Hertfordshire, and was educated at Oxford University. He was elected to the House of Commons in 1853, and remained a member until the death of his father in 1868 gave him a seat in the House of Lords. JAMES L. GODFREY

**SALISBURY CATHEDRAL.** See ENGLAND (The Arts).

# SALISBURY STATE COLLEGE

**SALISBURY STATE COLLEGE.** See UNIVERSITIES AND COLLEGES (table).

**SALIVA**, *suh LY vuh*, a sticky fluid produced in the mouth, is important to the digestion of food. It has a colorless and watery appearance. It contains some mucus and produces an *alkaline* (acid-neutralizing) chemical action. Saliva contains an enzyme called *ptyalin*. Ptyalin changes starches into simpler substances called *maltose*.

Saliva moistens and softens all food that is taken into the mouth. It helps in the chewing and swallowing of food. It also keeps the mouth moist, which is important to comfort. Its most important action is on starchy foods. Saliva breaks down all starches into maltose, the first step in digestion.

Three pairs of glands in the mouth and cheeks, known as *salivary glands*, produce saliva. One pair of glands, the *parotid*, is located in front of the ears. Another pair, the *submandibular*, is located under the lower jaw. The third pair of glands is located under the tongue and is known as the *sublingual*. There are several other small glands in the mucous membrane of the mouth that aid in producing saliva.     EWALD E. SELKURT

See also MASTICATION.

**Saliva** is produced by three pairs of glands, the *sublingual*, the *parotid*, and the *submandibular*. Saliva helps digest food.

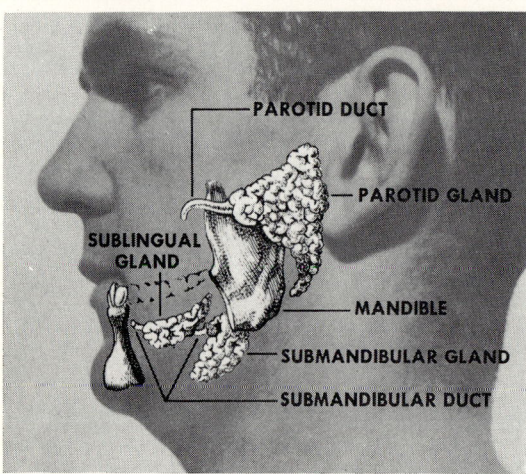

**SALIVARY GLANDS.** See SALIVA.

**SALK, JONAS EDWARD** (1914-    ), an American research scientist, works in the field of preventive medicine. He gained his greatest recognition for developing a vaccine that became the first effective weapon in preventing poliomyelitis (see POLIOMYELITIS). Albert B. Sabin later developed an effective oral polio vaccine (see SABIN, ALBERT B.). Salk also made significant contributions to our understanding of influenza, a severe infectious disease. Both poliomyelitis and influenza are caused by viruses, the microorganisms which are the smallest germs (see VIRUS).

Vast amounts of material relative to immunity had accumulated since "the golden age of bacteriology" during the last half of the 1800's. Salk's task was to dis-

The Salk Institute
**Jonas E. Salk**

till this information and apply the findings to his preparation of a polio vaccine. He found it necessary to weaken the virus with formalin without knocking out its ability to stimulate the body to produce protective antibodies. Since each type of microorganism has its own antibodies, Salk's vaccine contained all three polio virus types recognized at the time (see ANTIBODY).

**The Salk Vaccine.** In 1953, Salk announced the development of a trial vaccine. The viruses it contained had been killed with a formaldehyde solution. Among the first to receive the vaccine were Salk, his wife, and their three sons. The vaccine was found safe, and there was considerable evidence that it was effective.

It was further tested during a mass trial in 1954, when 1,830,000 schoolchildren took part in a testing program. This trial was sponsored by the National Foundation for Infantile Paralysis, which had given $1,700,000 to Salk and his research workers for their polio project. The vaccine was pronounced safe and effective in April, 1955. Salk received many honors, including a citation from President Eisenhower and a Congressional gold medal for "great achievement in the field of medicine." He refused to accept any cash awards, and returned to the university to improve the vaccine.

**His Early Life.** Salk was born in New York City, the oldest of a garment industry worker's three sons. He helped pay for his education by working after school and by earning scholarships. He was graduated from the New York University School of Medicine in 1939. There he did research with viruses in the laboratory of Thomas Francis, Jr.

In 1942, Salk went to the University of Michigan on a research fellowship, and advanced to assistant professor of epidemiology (the science of treating epidemics). Francis had become head of the department of epidemiology at Michigan's school of public health. Salk worked with Francis to develop influenza vaccines. Later, Francis directed the evaluation of the mass tests of the Salk antipolio vaccine.

Salk went to the University of Pittsburgh School of Medicine in 1947, and became research professor of bacteriology and director of the Virus Research Laboratory. In 1955, a $25,000-a-year Chair of Preventive Medicine was created at the university, and Salk was given the new post.     STANLEY E. WEDBERG

**SALLUST**, *SAL ust* (86-34 B.C.), was a noted Roman historian and politician. He was the first Roman to treat history as more than just a chronicle of events. Sallust's writings contain the reasons for each event, and character studies of the people involved. His works include *The Conspiracy of Catiline* and *The Jugurthine War*.

Sallust was born of a poor family, in Amiternum in central Italy. He became a friend of Julius Caesar, who named him proconsul, or governor, of Numidia, a territory in northern Africa. He made a fortune there by dishonest practices. He then returned to Rome and devoted himself to writing.     THOMAS A. BRADY

**SALMON,** *SAM un,* is one fish that nearly everybody knows at least by taste. Millions of cans of its firm, pink or red flesh are sold every year. Salmon, ready-cooked so that it can be eaten directly out of the can, has had tremendous importance in enlarging the diets of soldiers, prospectors, explorers, and peoples in the far-flung corners of the earth. The salmon is one of the chief food fishes of the world.

The salmon has a fascinating life story. It spends its adult life in the sea. Then, when the time comes for the salmon to *spawn* (lay its eggs), it is driven by some mysterious urge. It battles rushing currents and leaps headlong up swift waterfalls to reach the quiet inland streams where it shapes its underwater nest. Pacific salmon die soon after spawning, but Atlantic salmon return to spawn a number of times.

In spite of the vast amount of study that has been made of the salmon's habits, there is still more to learn about the lives of the various kinds of salmon.

In the United States, when we speak of salmon, we usually mean any one of the five different members of the Pacific salmons that live in the rivers and coastal waters of the North Pacific Ocean. These are found from California up the coast to Alaska and across to Siberia. The Atlantic salmon, another kind, lives in the North Atlantic Ocean. The Pacific salmons and the Atlantic salmon belong to the same family, the *Salmonidae*. But the *Salmonidae* also includes a large number of fishes that we know by other names. Some of these other fishes are the trout, the grayling, and various whitefishes. All are found in the North Temperate Zone around the world. The fishes we know as "salmon" were originally found only on the American and Asiatic sides of the North Pacific, and in North Atlantic coastal waters. Small numbers are now also found in Australia and New Zealand.

The five kinds of Pacific salmon belong to the genus *Oncorhynchus*, a term that comes from two Greek words that mean *hooked snout.* The hooked snout is a characteristic that develops in males of all five species of Pacific salmon during spawning time.

The kind of salmon generally known as the "Atlantic salmon" is found along the North Atlantic Coast of America and Europe, and is known scientifically as *Salmo salar.* It differs somewhat from the Pacific salmon in both appearance and habit.

One extraordinary thing about the Atlantic salmon is that it is often found to be landlocked in the lakes of Maine, New Hampshire, Vermont, and northward into Canada. This means that these salmon are compelled to spend their lives in fresh water without making the migrations to salt water. Landlocked salmon are also found among some of the species of Pacific salmon, notably the *Kokanee*. This fish is a landlocked form of the sockeye salmon.

The Atlantic salmon are not as common today in the waters of the United States as they were in colonial

Annan Photo Features

**Salmon Swimming Upstream** to spawn do remarkable acrobatics. They may leap more than 10 feet over rugged, swirling rapids.

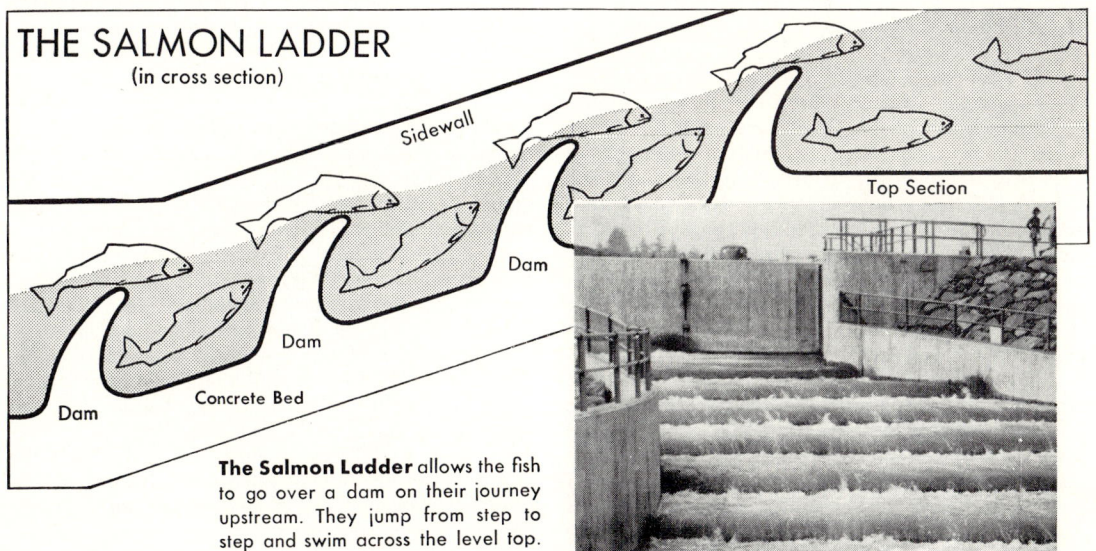

**The Salmon Ladder** allows the fish to go over a dam on their journey upstream. They jump from step to step and swim across the level top.

# THE LIFE STORY OF A SALMON

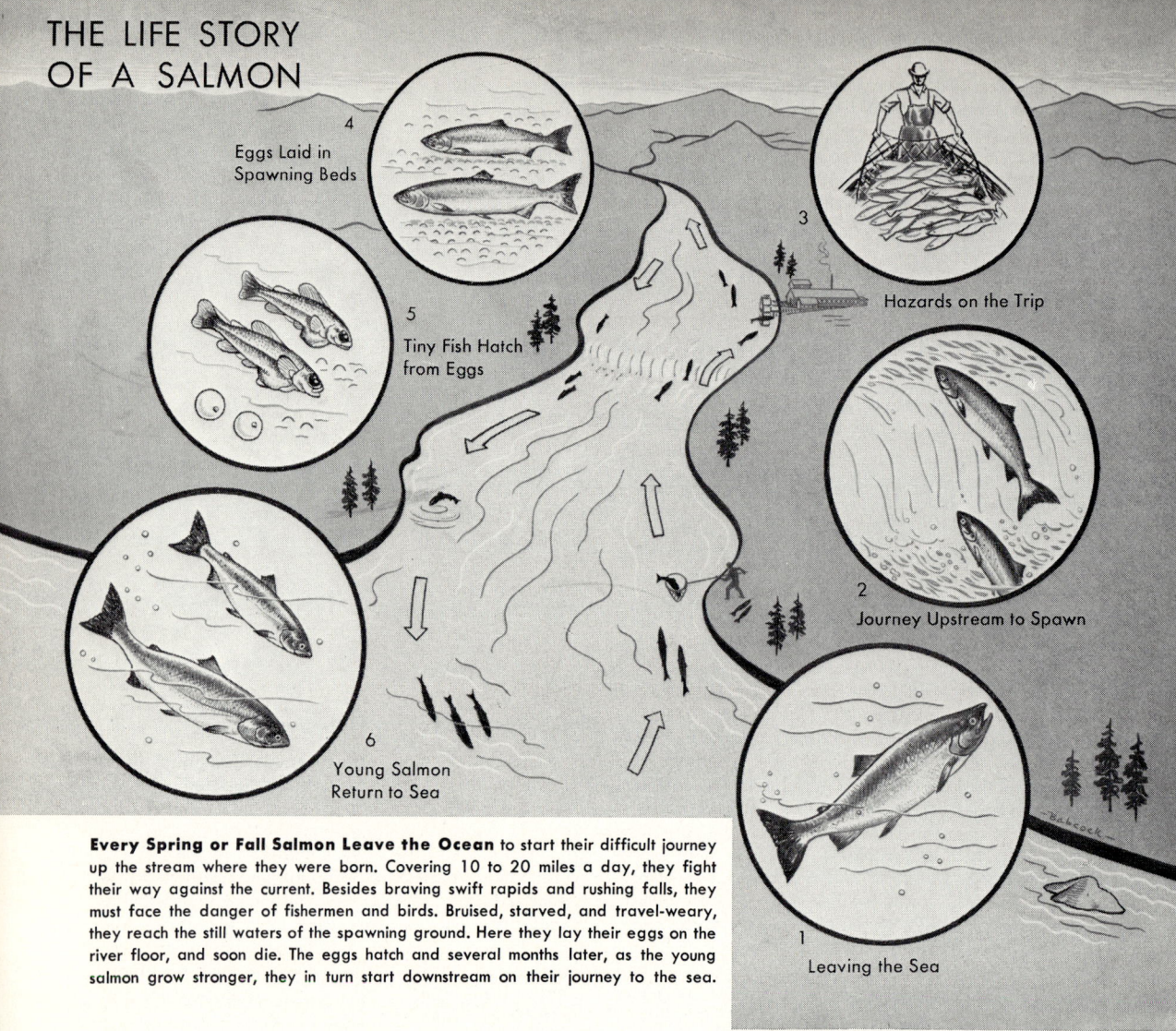

**Every Spring or Fall Salmon Leave the Ocean** to start their difficult journey up the stream where they were born. Covering 10 to 20 miles a day, they fight their way against the current. Besides braving swift rapids and rushing falls, they must face the danger of fishermen and birds. Bruised, starved, and travel-weary, they reach the still waters of the spawning ground. Here they lay their eggs on the river floor, and soon die. The eggs hatch and several months later, as the young salmon grow stronger, they in turn start downstream on their journey to the sea.

times. But the ones that remain rank among the finest of game fishes.

### Life History

All species of salmon differ in certain respects. But the Chinook salmon is a good example of the whole group. Its looks come close to what an artist might call "the way a fish ought to look." It has grace and strength. Its silvery body glistens and shimmers. It is dotted with black spots on the back and fins.

Let us follow a typical salmon from its hatching until the time comes for it to produce the next generation and die. The story begins on an autumn day far up the fresh-water streams that wind down the slopes to the sea in the Pacific Northwest. Salmon prefer to lay eggs in water just a few feet deep. Usually they lay the eggs at the head of a riffle where fast running water seeps into the gravelly bed of the streams and brings supplies of oxygen to the eggs. There the female clears a *redd* (nest) in the loose stones. Vigorous swishes of her tail and body scatter the mud and tiny plants that cling to the stones. When the redd—which may be 5 to 6 feet across—is clean and "dustless," the female is ready to lay her eggs. Great numbers of eggs are dropped among the stones. A female may deposit 10,000 of the pinkish, pea-sized globules. Simultaneously, the male gives off a milky substance called *milt*, which fertilizes the eggs. Such factors as water level and temperature help determine the number that hatch.

Once their eggs are deposited and fertilized, the salmon begin to float downstream. Soon they die and are washed ashore or fished out by hungry bears.

Meantime, life has been stirring among the eggs. In about two and a half months the young, called *alevins*, burst forth. Carrying a huge yolk sac which nourishes them in the early weeks, they lie hidden from larger fish and many other enemies that they will meet in later life. They rest for another two and a half months until they begin to take on the familiar shape of little fishes and are ready to emerge as free-swimming *fry*.

In a few months to about a year, a fish gets the urge to leave the familiar waters where it was hatched. It may be about 5 inches long by this time. It is a vigorous, lively creature already old enough and big

*Friends Magazine*

**Packaged Salt** comes in many different weights, sizes, and forms. Coming down a conveyor belt, *above*, are 50- and 100-pound bags of salt. Salt is also pressed into blocks, *right*, for livestock feeding.

good health. Among many peoples, salt is still used as a sign of honor, friendship, and hospitality. The Arabs say "there is salt between us," meaning "we have eaten together, and are friends."

Salt was a chief economic product of the ancient world. It was important in the development of the earliest highways of trade. Roman soldiers built the *Via Salaria* (Salt Road), one of the great military roads in history, from the saltworks at Ostia to Rome.

Salt was once so scarce and precious that it was used as money. Caesar's soldiers received part of their pay in common salt. This part of their pay was known as their *salarium*, and it is from this that the word *salary* comes. Also dating back to the days when workers were paid either all or part of their wages in salt, is the modern expression "not worth his salt." It literally meant that a man did not earn his wages. — DANIEL PETERKIN, JR.

See also COLOMBIA (picture: Guajira Indian Women); GREAT SALT LAKE; SALT, CHEMICAL; CHINA (picture: Salt Recovered from the Yellow Sea).

**Cathedral of Salt Near Bogotá, Colombia,** lies 345 feet underground. Chapel of Our Lady of the Rosary was carved out of an old salt mine. The immense cathedral holds 10,000 people.

*Wide World*

### LEADING SALT PRODUCING COUNTRIES
Tons of salt produced in 1966

|  |  |
|---|---|
| United States | 36,463,000 tons |
| China (Mainland) | 14,300,000 tons |
| Russia | 10,500,000 tons |
| Great Britain | 8,105,000 tons |
| Germany (West) | 7,117,000 tons |
| India | 4,969,000 tons |
| France | 4,630,000 tons |
| Canada | 4,328,000 tons |
| Italy | 3,900,000 tons |
| Poland | 2,651,000 tons |

Source: *Minerals Yearbook 1966*, Bureau of Mines

# SALT, CHEMICAL

**SALT, CHEMICAL,** is a compound that results when a base neutralizes an acid. For example, ordinary table salt, *sodium chloride*, is formed when the base sodium hydroxide neutralizes hydrochloric acid. The salt *calcium carbonate* is formed when the base calcium hydroxide neutralizes carbonic acid. See NEUTRALIZATION.

Salts are among the most important chemical compounds. They are used in making many industrial and agricultural chemicals. For example, sodium chloride is used in making sodium hydroxide, a chemical needed in making rayon, soap, and many other products. The salt ammonium nitrate is used in fertilizers to add nitrogen to soil. Some metals, including sodium and potassium, are extracted from salts. Plants and animals need various salts in order to stay healthy. For example, the salts sodium chloride and potassium chloride supply *ions* (electrically charged atoms) needed by nerve cells.

The earth's crust contains many salts. The most abundant salt, sodium chloride, is found in large land deposits and in the ocean. The salt calcium carbonate is found in limestone and in the shells of sea animals. Well-known natural salt deposits include Great Salt Lake in Utah, beds of borax in Nevada, and large salt beds near Stassfurt, Germany.

The salt formed when a base completely neutralizes an acid is called a *normal salt*. Sodium sulfate ($Na_2SO_4$) is a normal salt. Incomplete neutralization may produce either an *acid salt* or a *basic salt*. These salts act like acids or bases as well as like salts. Acid salts contain hydrogen ions, as in sodium bisulfate ($NaHSO_4$). Basic salts contain hydroxyl radicals, as in basic bismuth chloride ($Bi[OH]Cl_2$ or $Bi[OH]_2Cl$).

A salt crystal contains positive and negative ions in a regular, repeating arrangement. This arrangement is called an *ionic lattice*. When the salt crystal dissolves in water, these ions are released and move about freely in the solution. ESMARCH S. GILREATH

**Related Articles** in WORLD BOOK include:

| | |
|---|---|
| Acetate | Nitrate |
| Carbonate | Nitrites |
| Chloride | Sulfate |
| Halogen | Sulfide |

**SALT LAKE.** See GREAT SALT LAKE.

**SALT LAKE CITY** (pop. 189,454; met. area 447,795; alt. 4,390 ft.) is the capital and largest city in Utah, and the headquarters of the Mormon Church. It lies in the scenic Salt Lake Valley at the foot of the Wasatch Range. The city is about 15 miles east of Great Salt Lake. For location, see UTAH (political map). For monthly rainfall and temperatures in Salt Lake City, see UTAH (Climate).

Mormon pioneers laid out the streets of the city in 1848. Almost all streets run directly north and south or east and west. The state Capitol stands at the northern edge of the city on Capitol Hill. Murals in the Capitol portray events in early Utah. A 285-foot dome towers over the building.

Salt Lake City is the headquarters of the Church of Jesus Christ of Latter-day Saints. Members of this church, or *Mormons*, originally settled the area. About 65 of every 100 of today's residents belong to the Mormon Church. The granite Mormon Temple, with

*Salt Lake Chamber of Commerce*
**Salt Lake City, Utah,** lies in the Salt Lake Valley at the foot of the snow-covered Wasatch Range. The Mormon leader Brigham Young led his followers to the region on July 24, 1847.

its six spires, stands in Temple Square. The Tabernacle has a huge organ and a world-famous choir. A monument to pioneer Brigham Young is in the same area. Nearby is the Sea Gull Monument. Grateful pioneers erected the monument to honor gulls that devoured crop-destroying crickets in the summer of 1848.

**Industry and Trade.** The Salt Lake City area is one of the world centers for processing, or *smelting*, nonferrous ores. Copper, gold, lead, and silver constitute the chief mineral wealth. Salt Lake City also serves as a banking center. The city has candy factories, canneries, dairies, flour and woolen mills, oil refineries, and sugar- and salt-processing plants.

**Education.** Salt Lake City is the home of the University of Utah and Westminster College. It has five public libraries and six museums.

**History.** Explorer Jim Bridger arrived in the area in 1824 and discovered Great Salt Lake. A group of Mormons from Illinois arrived in the region on July 24, 1847. When their leader, Brigham Young, saw the scenic land, he said, "This is the place, drive on." He referred to the site he had seen in a vision. "This is the Place" monument in Pioneer Monument State Park now marks the spot where Young and his party halted. The Mormons planted the first crops on the day they arrived. They soon developed a thriving community. Brigham Young became a civic, as well as a religious, leader. He served as the governor of the Utah territory in the 1850's. Salt Lake City was incorporated in 1851

and reincorporated in 1860. The city has a commission form of government. A. R. MORTENSEN

See also YOUNG, BRIGHAM; MORMONS (pictures); UTAH (pictures).

**SALT LICK.** See SALT (Salt from Mines).

**SALT RIVER** is a stream in south-central Arizona formed by the joining of the White and the Black rivers in Gila County. From there, the Salt River flows west for 200 miles and empties into the Gila River near Phoenix. The Salt River Valley is irrigated by five dams, which form a series of artificial lakes extending for 60 miles along the Salt River. For the location of the Salt River, see ARIZONA (physical map).

**SALT SEA.** See DEAD SEA.

**SALT SPRINGS DAM** ranks among the highest rock-fill type dams in the United States. It makes up part of a power project on the North Fork of the Mokelumne River in central California. The dam, completed in 1931, is 328 feet high and 1,300 feet long. It contains about 3 million cubic yards of rock-fill. Its power plant has a 44,000-kilowatt capacity. T. W. MERMEL

**SALT-WATER FISH.** See FISH (color picture).

**SALTBUSH.** See AUSTRALIA (Plants).

**SALTEN, FELIX** (1869-1945), was the pen name of SIEGMUND SALZMAN, an Austrian novelist, essayist, critic, and journalist. He won international fame for his stories for children about Bambi, a wild deer. Salten's books include *Maximilian I, Emperor of Germany* (1913); *Bambi* (1923); *The Hound of Florence* (1923); *Samson and Delilah* (1928); *Fifteen Rabbits* (1929); *Good Comrades* (1930); *The City Jungle* (1931); *Florian, the Emperor's Stallion* (1933); *Renni, the Rescuer* (1940); and *Bambi's Children* (1940). Walt Disney made a successful motion picture from *Bambi*. Salten was born in Budapest, Hungary, but spent most of his life in Vienna, Austria. He fled to Switzerland after the Nazis took control of Austria in March, 1938. CHARLEMAE ROLLINS

Simon and Schuster
**Felix Salten**

**SALTER, SUSANNA MADORA** (1860-1961), was the first woman mayor in the United States. She was elected mayor of Argonia, Kans., in 1887 and served for one year. Persons who opposed Prohibition put her name on the ballot as a joke. They thought Mrs. Salter would lose. She was a Woman's Christian Temperance Union officer who favored Prohibition. Mrs. Salter was born in Lamira, Ohio. H. E. SOCOLOFSKY

**SALTO,** *SAHL toh* (pop. 57,714; alt. 184 ft.), is the second largest city in Uruguay. It is located 60 miles north of Paysandú. For location, see URUGUAY (color map). The city provides an important trading center for the farmers and ranchers of northern Uruguay. Salto is sometimes called the *City of Oranges* because of its large orange and tangerine groves. JOHN TATE LANNING

**SALTON SEA,** *SAWL t'n*, is a shallow, saline lake in southeastern California. It measures about 30 miles long and from 8 to 10 miles wide. Its surface is about 240 feet below sea level. Salton Sea lies chiefly in Imperial County between the Santa Rosa and Chocolate mountains. The lake is about 80 miles northeast of San Diego. Salton Sea shares an arid trough with the Imperial and Coachella valleys. The trough has been shut off from the Gulf of Lower California by sediment deposited by the Colorado River. Until 1905, the valley area was a salt-covered depression. Between 1905 and

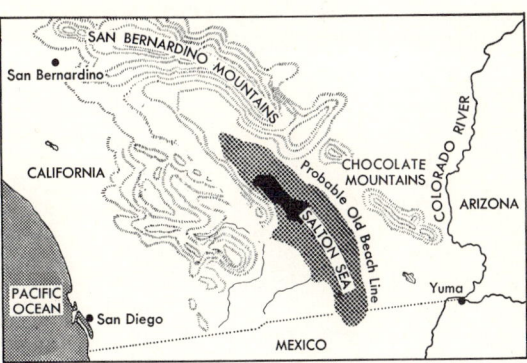

**Outline of the Salton Sea** in California shows the largest area the lake covered before it started to recede.

1907, the Colorado River broke through irrigation head gates and burst into the valley to the west. Then it flowed north into the Salton Basin to form the Salton Sea, a lake that covered about 450 square miles. When the floodwaters were halted, much of the lake evaporated. C. LANGDON WHITE

# SALTONSTALL, LEVERETT

**SALTONSTALL, LEVERETT** (1892-      ), served as U.S. senator from Massachusetts from 1944 to 1967. He was elected to serve out the unexpired term of Henry Cabot Lodge, Jr., who resigned to enter the army. A Republican, Saltonstall served in the state house of representatives from 1923 to 1936. He became governor of Massachusetts in 1939 and served three consecutive terms. He was born in Chestnut Hill, Mass.

**SALTPETER**, also called NITER, is a mineral known to chemists as *potassium nitrate*. It occurs in limestone caves when decaying animal and plant materials *oxidize* (combine with oxygen). Industry uses saltpeter to prepare matches, explosives, and fertilizers. Chemists use it as a reagent in analytical chemistry. It is also used as an oxidizer in liquid rocket fuel propellants.

Saltpeter occurs as colorless or white crystals or crystalline powder that has a cool salty taste. It dissolves readily in water and melts at about 337° C. Saltpeter has the chemical formula, $KNO_3$. Industry manufactures it by reacting potassium chloride with either sodium nitrate or nitric acid.

The name *saltpeter* also refers to two other chemicals. *Chile saltpeter* is impure sodium nitrate ($NaNO_3$). It is used much like potassium nitrate. Purified Chile saltpeter forms white crystals that melt at 308° C. *Lime saltpeter*, or *Norwegian saltpeter*, is calcium nitrate ($CaNO_3$). This chemical is a white solid used to make matches, explosives, and other chemicals.

**SALTS** are saline laxatives. Some common salts include *Epsom salt* (magnesium sulfate), *Glauber's salt* (sodium sulfate), and *Rochelle salt* (sodium and potassium tartrate). Salts act in the intestines by causing water to accumulate and move waste materials. Salts are valuable when used carefully at the correct time, but excessive use may irritate the intestines. See also EPSOM SALT; GLAUBER'S SALT; SEIDLITZ POWDERS. LOUIS D. BOSHES

**SALUDA DAM**, *suh LOO duh*, is among the 30 largest earth-fill dams in the United States. It is part of a hydro-electric power project on the Saluda River, 10 miles upstream from Columbia, S.C. Saluda Dam is 211 feet high and 8,650 feet long at the top. It contains 11 million cubic yards of earth. The dam was completed in 1930 at a cost of $6 million. T. W. MERMEL

**SALUKI**, *suh LOO kee*, or GAZELLE HOUND, is believed to be the oldest purebred dog in the world. It was developed in Syria, and was brought to Egypt by Arab traders about 7000 to 6000 B.C. One of the swiftest dogs, the Saluki was once used in hunting gazelles. It was often teamed with hawks for hunting gazelles. The hawk struck the prey and the Saluki held it down until the hunters arrived. The Saluki resembles the greyhound. It has a smooth, soft coat, with fringes of long hairs on its ears, legs, and thighs. It is 23 to 28 inches high at the shoulder and weighs about 60 pounds. See also DOG (color picture: Hounds). OLGA DAKAN

**SALUTE**, *suh LYOOT*, is a gesture of greeting, courtesy, or recognition, such as a handshake. In the armed forces, men use the military salute to show respect to an officer.

**Military Hand Salutes.** According to U.S. Army regulations, a man must use the hand salute at a distance of not more than 30 paces and not less than six paces. He raises his right hand snappily to his forehead, with his palm down and his index finger at the peak of his cap. He holds his forearm at a 45° angle. Soldiers must look directly at the officer when saluting, and he must return the salute if possible. Soldiers must salute, whether or

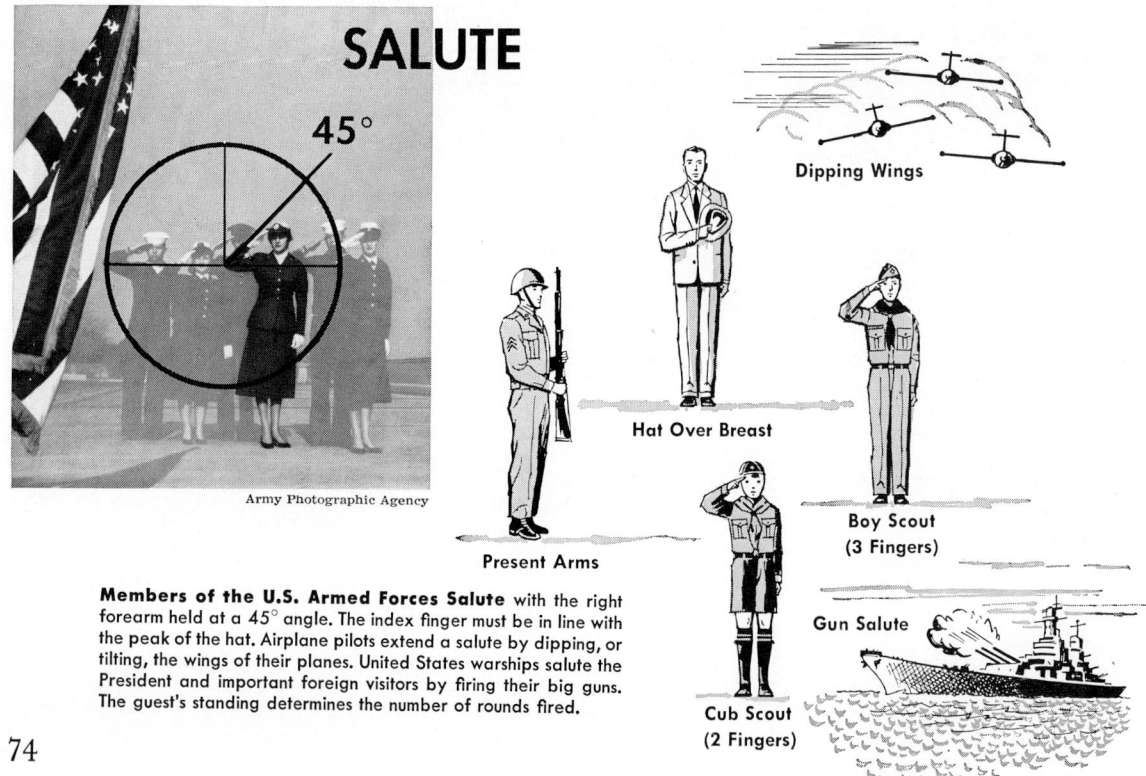

**Members of the U.S. Armed Forces Salute** with the right forearm held at a 45° angle. The index finger must be in line with the peak of the hat. Airplane pilots extend a salute by dipping, or tilting, the wings of their planes. United States warships salute the President and important foreign visitors by firing their big guns. The guest's standing determines the number of rounds fired.

Army Photographic Agency

U.S. Army Photograph
**United States**

Canadian Forces Photo
**Canada**

British Information Service
**Great Britain**

Sovfoto
**Poland**

not they are wearing any head covering. Navy men must be wearing head covering when they salute. Aboard ship, sailors salute an officer only at the first meeting during the day, except when reporting in the course of duty. Officers and enlisted men salute the flag and officer of the deck when boarding or leaving their ship.

Men in uniform must stand at attention and salute while the national anthem is played and while the flag is raised or lowered. They must also salute when they pass the flag or the flag passes them in a parade. A man who is running should slow to a walk before saluting. Only men in good standing may salute. A prisoner may not salute.

**Salutes with Weapons.** Soldiers in formation carrying rifles *present arms* to officers. A man does this by holding the rifle vertically in front of himself, with the trigger forward. Standing sentinels also present arms. Marching soldiers, in formation or singly, give the *rifle salute* by raising their left forearms, with wrists and fingers in a straight line, and touching their rifles at a point just behind the rear sight.

**In Other Countries,** military salutes are similar to those of the United States. British servicemen salute with their palms out, rather than down. Some dictatorships adopted special salutes that all persons had to use. In Fascist Italy and Nazi Germany, civilians and soldiers saluted by holding their right arms out at an angle, palms down. Russian and Spanish soldiers and civilians often used a clenched-fist salute with their right arms. Such salutes were often adopted by political parties for their members.

**Planes and Ships** also exchange salutes. Fliers often dip, or tilt, the wings of their planes. Ships passing on the high seas salute by dipping their flags once. Merchant ships in port outside their own country raise the national flag of the country they are visiting as a salute.

**Other Salutes.** Cannon, drum flourishes, and music are often used to salute visiting dignitaries. The number of rounds fired depends on the importance of the visitor. When a head of state visits a country, armed forces usually give a 21-gun salute, four ruffles and flourishes on the drums, and the visitor's national anthem. Other salutes may be given with as few as five guns. Warships have similar salutes. CHARLES B. MACDONALD

See also FLAG (Saluting the Flag).

## SALVARSAN

**SALVADOR,** SAHL *vuh* DAWR, also called BAHIA, *buh EE uh* (pop. 863,000; alt. 135 ft.), is one of the largest cities in Brazil. Founded in 1549, it is the oldest city in Brazil, though some smaller towns are older. From 1549 to 1763, Salvador was the capital of the Portuguese colony of Brazil. Salvador is an Atlantic port on the Bay of All Saints, about 800 miles northeast of Rio de Janeiro. For location, see BRAZIL (political map). The lower part of the city lies along the bay, and the upper part stands on the bluffs overlooking the bay. Roads and hydraulic elevators connect the two sections of the city.

Salvador has large cotton factories, and exports sugar, cotton, hides, tobacco, and cacao. Bahia cigars and chocolate are famous. The city has many monumental buildings of the past. There are several cultural institutions, including the state and Roman Catholic universities, a gallery of art, and a Foundation for the Development of Science in Bahia. Salvador's medical school is the oldest in Brazil. The Prince Regent of Portugal (later King John VI) founded the school in 1808. MANOEL CARDOZO

**SALVADOR, EL.** See EL SALVADOR.

**SALVAGE,** *SAL vij*, is money or goods paid to those who save ships or cargo abandoned at sea. Help which is given to a vessel in distress or danger is called *salvage service*. In Great Britain, salvage is granted only for acts on the high seas. In the United States, courts allow salvage for saving goods, ships, and life on inland waters as well as on the high seas.

The *salvor* is a person who helps to save a ship other than the one on which he sails. A salvor cannot collect salvage for helping to save his own ship. Salvage can be collected only for saving a ship that sails under its own power, or a moving barge. It is not granted in the case of a barge or other floating structure moored to a shore or dock. The danger from which a ship is salvaged must be real, not something which might happen. The ship saved must be brought to a safe place, ready to be returned to its owner for repair.

Some countries have fixed by law the amounts to be paid in salvage cases. The United States and Great Britain have no such laws. American and British courts grant salvage claims based on conditions under which the act has been performed. It is usual to pay amounts substantially more than those generally paid to seamen for regular work.

Division of salvage among the salvors also rests on the decision of the courts. The master's share is usually double that of the mate. The mate's share is usually double that of a seaman. The share of the men who do the work and sail the salvaged ship back to port is usually double that of those who remain aboard the salvor vessel. The greatest amount that was ever recovered from a sunken ship was the $24,793,540 brought up from the British liner *Laurentic*. The liner had been sunk by a German torpedo off the coast of Northern Ireland in 1917.

The term *salvage* is also used to describe goods recovered from emergencies on land, such as floods or fires. Critically reviewed by TELFORD TAYLOR

See also DIVING, UNDERWATER; FLOTSAM, JETSAM, AND LAGAN.

**SALVARSAN.** See EHRLICH, PAUL.

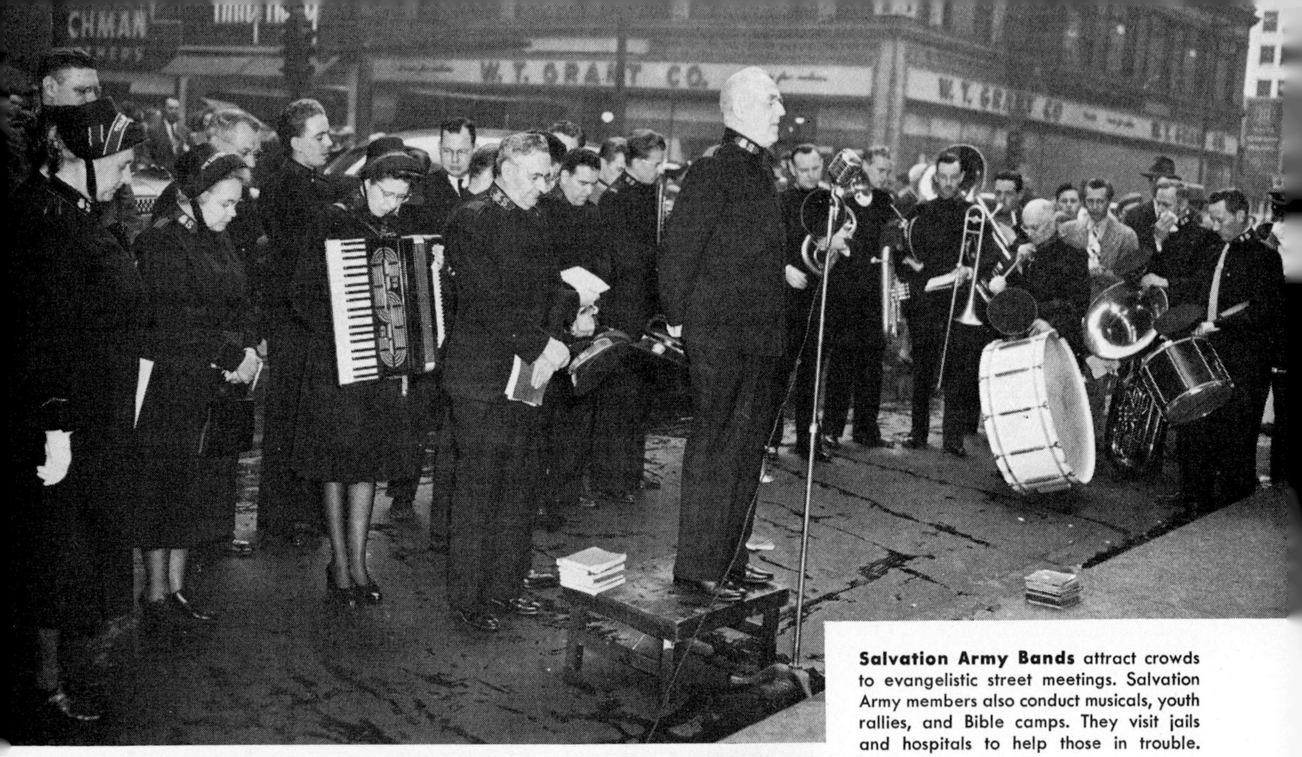

**Salvation Army Bands** attract crowds to evangelistic street meetings. Salvation Army members also conduct musicals, youth rallies, and Bible camps. They visit jails and hospitals to help those in trouble.

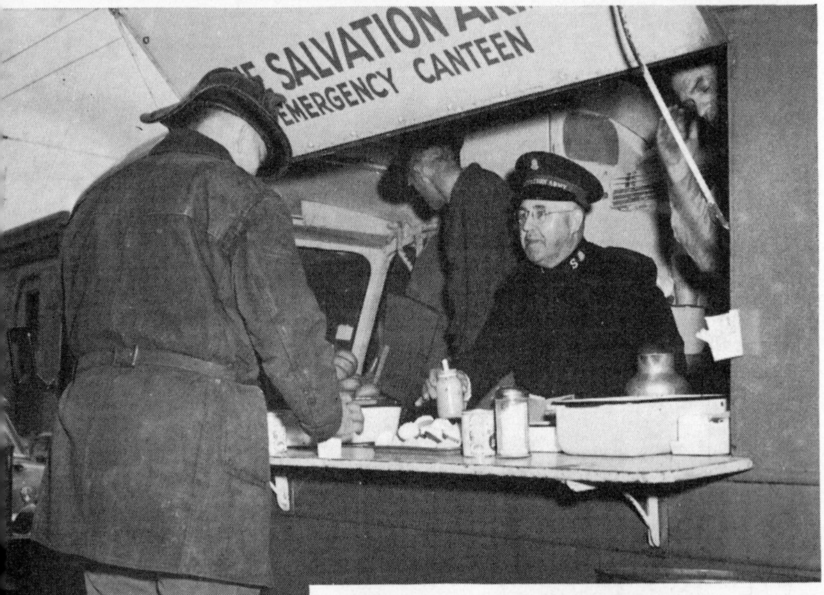

**Mobile Canteens** to serve food are set up by the Salvation Army at the scene of fires, floods, and other disasters. Canteens also are operated at advance military bases during wartime.

**Youth Work and Family Welfare** make up part of the Salvation Army's program. The Army gives food and clothing to those in need. It operates day nurseries and settlement houses.

Salvation Army

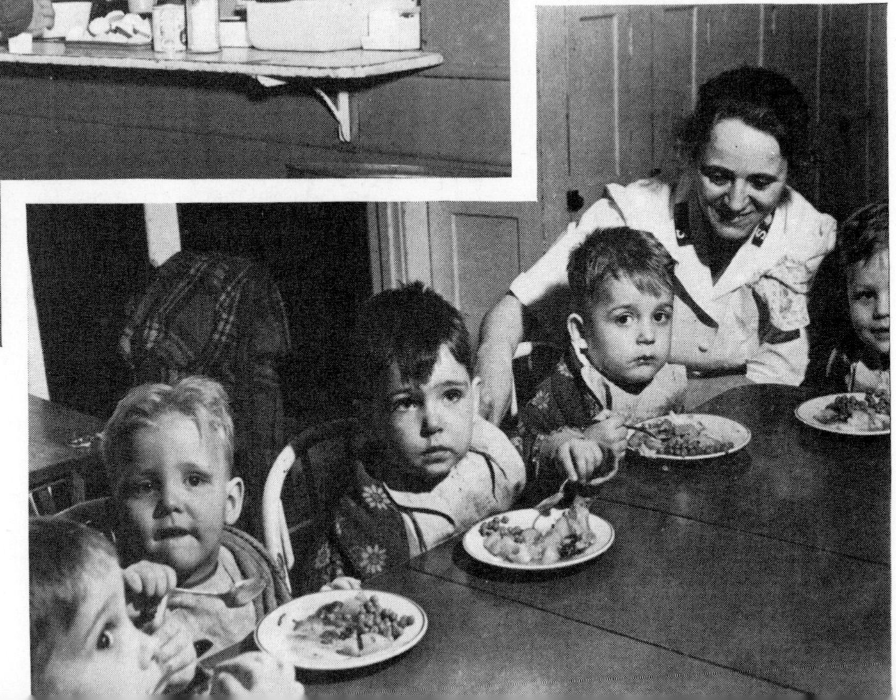

**SALVATION ARMY, THE,** is a world-wide Christian religious body with semimilitary structure. It provides food, shelter, and clothing to the needy, and administers to the spirit by bringing religion to many whom churches never reach.

**Services and Activities.** The Salvation Army maintains hospitals for unwed mothers, industrial homes where men rebuild their characters, low-cost lodging-houses, and nurseries for babies of working mothers. It also maintains fresh-air camps, boys' clubs, family welfare-work programs, and provides aid to prisoners and their families.

A distinctive feature of the army is its street-corner musicians, who play, sing, and preach the glory of God. Indoor religious meetings usually follow. In country after country, this method of spreading the Gospel has succeeded in winning converts.

The Salvation Army has over 26,000 officers, both men and women. During World War I, its mobile canteens were welcome sights on all fronts, and it established more than 2,000 rest and recreation centers for service men and women. The army was partly responsible for the formation of the United Service Organizations (USO). Wherever disaster has struck, the Salvation Army has stepped forward with aid. The organization's official paper is the *War Cry.*

**History.** "General" William Booth, a former Methodist minister, conducted meetings to bring the Gospel to the poor of London's East End slums in 1865. His work was well received, and he organized the Christian Mission. In 1878, the mission changed its name to the Salvation Army, designed uniforms for both men and women officers, and adopted a semimilitary system of leadership. The cause spread, and the army now operates in 86 countries and colonies. It was established in the United States in 1880, and the founder's son, Ballington Booth, took command in 1887. The army has over 8,000 centers in the United States today. For membership in the United States, see RELIGION (table).

William Booth died in 1912. His son Bramwell became general. He was succeeded by Edward J. Higgins. The founder's daughter Evangeline became the next general, and in 1939 George Carpenter succeeded her. Albert Osborn became general in 1946, General Wilfred Kitching in 1954, and Frederick L. Coutts in 1963. The Salvation Army's headquarters are at 101 Queen Victoria Street in London. U.S. headquarters are at 120 W. 14th Street, New York, N.Y. NORMAN S. MARSHALL

See also BOOTH.

**SALVE REGINA COLLEGE.** See UNIVERSITIES AND COLLEGES (table).

**SALVIA,** *SAL vee uh,* is a group of plants that grow in the temperate and warm regions of the world. Salvias have two-lipped flowers that range in color from white and pale yellow to blue, purple, and scarlet. Gardeners use many kinds as ornamentals, including the *scarlet sage,* which has brilliant red flowers. It is native to Brazil, but is grown in other parts of the world. The *garden sage* used to flavor foods is a salvia.

**Scientific Classification.** Salvias belong to the mint family, *Labiatae.* They make up the genus *Salvia.* The scarlet sage is species *S. splendens,* and the garden sage is *S. officinalis.* H. D. HARRINGTON

See also FLOWER (color picture: Fall Garden Flowers); SAGE.

## SAM HOUSTON STATE COLLEGE

**SALVINI,** *sahl VEE nee,* **TOMMASO** (1829-1915), was one of the leading Italian actors of the late 1800's. He gained fame in tragic roles for his intensity, magnificent voice, and boundless energy. His reputation in the United States was firmly established in 1886, when he played the role of Othello. Born in Milan, Salvini became an actor when he was 14. CLIFFORD E. HAMAR

**SALWEEN RIVER,** or SALWIN, is the second most important river in Burma. It rises in eastern Tibet, and flows through eastern Burma to the Bay of Bengal. It empties into the ocean near Moulmein. The 1,750-mile-long river drains eastern Burma and western Thailand. It has little value as a commercial waterway, because much of it flows through a deep gorge. In its lower course it is important for crop irrigation.

The Salween Delta is one of the most fertile sections in Burma. During flood season, the upper Salween River rises nearly 100 feet above its low water level and becomes a raging torrent. A suspension bridge carries the Burma Road over the upper river and is a vital transportation link. J. E. SPENCER

See also RIVER (chart: Longest Rivers).

**SALZBURG,** *ZAHLTS boork* (pop. 115,720; alt. 1,391 ft.), is a city in the mountains of northwestern Austria. It is best known for its annual music festivals, which attract music lovers from all parts of the world. Wolfgang Amadeus Mozart, one of the world's greatest composers, was born in Salzburg. Salzburg is the capital of Salzburg province. See AUSTRIA (map).

**SAM HOUSTON STATE COLLEGE.** See UNIVERSITIES AND COLLEGES (table).

**The Scarlet Sage Is a Salvia.**
J. Horace McFarland

# SAMA-VEDA

**SAMA-VEDA.** See VEDA.
**SAMAR.** See PHILIPPINES (The Islands).
**SAMARA.** See KUYBYSHEV.
**SAMARIA,** *suh MAIR ee uh,* was the name of a city and its surrounding region in ancient Palestine. King Omri built Samaria in about 800 B.C., and made it the capital of the kingdom of Israel. The king named it after Shemer, who owned the land where it was built.

Assyria conquered Samaria in 721 B.C., after a siege of three years. In 331 B.C., the city fell to Alexander the Great. Then Hyrcanus attacked and destroyed it in 120 B.C. It was later rebuilt by Herod the Great, who called it *Sebaste*. Excavations begun in 1909 have yielded many ancient treasures. According to tradition, John the Baptist is buried there. Remains of the Crusaders' church, built in the 1100's, have also been found. The village of Sabasṭiyah, Jordan, now stands on the site of ancient Samaria. See also SAMARITAN.

**SAMARITAN,** *suh MAR uh tun,* was a citizen of ancient Samaria. The Assyrians destroyed Israel in 721 B.C. and took the ablest Israelites to Assyria as captives. The Assyrian ruler then forced people from eastern Assyria to settle in the region of Samaria (see SAMARIA). The new settlers brought their own religious ideas, but also sought to please "the god of the land." Many of them intermarried with the remaining Israelites. People with this mixed ancestry and mixed religion came to be called *Samaritans*.

The Samaritans adopted the *Torah*, the first five books of the Hebrew Bible, as their scripture. But the Hebrews to the south refused to associate with them, and considered their religion inferior. When the Hebrews rebuilt their temple, they refused help that the Samaritans offered. Eventually, the Samaritans built a temple of their own, but it was destroyed in 128 B.C.

Jesus disapproved of the Jews' dislike for the Samaritans. When asked to define the term *neighbor*, He told a story in which a priest and a Levite passed by an opportunity to help a man in need. But a Samaritan helped the needy person (Luke 10:29-37).

There are now about 300 Samaritans. Half of them live near Mt. Gerizim in Nābulus, Jordan. W. W. SLOAN

**SAMARIUM,** *suh MAY rih um* (chemical symbol, Sm), is one of the rare-earth metals. Its atomic number is 62, and its atomic weight is 150.35. It is named after the Russian engineer Colonel Samarski. Paul Émile Lecoq de Boisbaudran of France discovered samarium in 1879. Samarium is best separated from other rare earths by ion-exchange processes. It has a silver color and slowly oxidizes in air. The common oxide, $Sm_2O_3$, has a pale yellow color, and is rapidly soluble in most acids. The metal melts at about 1072° C., and boils at about 1900° C. FRANK H. SPEDDING

See also ELEMENT, CHEMICAL (table); RARE EARTH.

**The Good Samaritan,** painted by Rembrandt, illustrates a parable told by Jesus to show the brotherhood of man. The parable tells of a Jew who was robbed, beaten, and left to die. Two Jews saw him and passed on. But a Samaritan came to his aid.

From a private collection, Paris

Samarkand has many old buildings. The Shahki-Zinda, built in the 1300's and 1400's, holds burial vaults of medieval noblemen.

Y. Bosin, Novosti

A Samoan Basket Weaver patiently twists coconut palm fronds while working on the sand near the blue sea.

U.S. Marine Corps

**SAMARKAND,** *SAM ur kand* (pop. 226,000; alt. 2,050 ft.), is the second largest city and former capital of the Uzbekistan Soviet Socialist Republic. It lies in Turkestan (see RUSSIA [political map]). Samarkand is an educational center. Its factories produce silk goods, superphosphate, and tractor parts.

Samarkand occupies the site of ancient Maracanda. Alexander the Great destroyed Maracanda in 329 B.C. In the 1300's, Tamerlane, the Mongol conqueror, chose the city as his capital. THEODORE SHABAD

**SAMBUKE.** See ELDER.

**SAMFORD UNIVERSITY.** See UNIVERSITIES AND COLLEGES (table).

**SAMNITE** was a member of an ancient tribe in what is now southern Italy. The Samnites are known chiefly for their fierce battles against the Romans. The Romans expanded their empire to Samnite territory during the 300's B.C. The Samnites beat the Romans at the Battle of the Caudine Forks, but the Romans overpowered the Samnites in the 290's B.C. This greatly reduced the Samnite population. In the Social War of the 80's B.C., the Romans crushed the Samnites. Most Samnites adopted the Roman customs and language. HERBERT M. HOWE

**SAMOA,** *suh MOH uh,* is a group of 14 islands in the South Pacific Ocean about 4,800 miles southwest of San Francisco, Calif. The group was once called the Navigators Islands because of the fine canoes built by the Samoans. The islands cover an area of 1,173 square miles and have a population of 184,000. Almost all the people of Samoa are Polynesians.

The seven eastern islands—including Tutuila, the Manua group, Rose Island, and Swains Island—make up American Samoa. American Samoa has been a territory of the United States since 1900. The western islands, including Savai'i and Upolu, make up Western Samoa. Western Samoa was administered by New Zealand for the League of Nations and the United Nations until it became an independent country in 1962.

Tutuila has the only good harbor in the islands. The United States had a naval base there until 1951.

Nearly all the Samoan islands are volcanic formations, and coral reefs surround most of them. Rich forests and flat lands slope gently toward the sea. The climate is hot and rainy.

See also AMERICAN SAMOA; WESTERN SAMOA; SWAINS ISLAND.

# SAMOS

**SAMOS,** *SAY mahs,* is a Greek island in the Aegean Sea. It lies in the Grecian Archipelago, and is separated from the coast of Asia Minor by the Strait of Little Boghaz. Samos once belonged to Turkey. It became a Greek island in 1923, under the terms of the Treaty of Lausanne. Samos covers an area of about 184 square miles, and has a population of 41,124. Farmers of Samos raise olives and grapes. Limín Vathéos is the capital. For location, see GREECE (color map). HARRY N. HOWARD

See also POLYCRATES.

**SAMOSET,** *SAM oh set* (1590?-1655), was one of the early Indian friends of the Pilgrim settlers of the Plymouth Colony. He was a *sagamore* (chief) of the Pemaquid Indians, and apparently first came into contact with Englishmen when he met some fishermen along the coast of Maine. He learned a little English from them. In March, 1621, he startled the Plymouth colonists by appearing on the street and welcoming them in broken English. He later introduced the leaders of the colony to Massasoit, the Indian chief of the Plymouth area. In 1625 Samoset made what is believed to be the first deed of Indian land to English colonists. He transferred 12,000 acres of his tribe's land to John Brown, one of the settlers. E. ADAMSON HOEBEL

See also MASSASOIT.

Historical Pictures

**Samoset's First Appearance in Plymouth Colony** startled the colonists, who thought he was a dangerous savage. But Samoset proved to be a loyal and helpful Indian friend.

**SAMOTHRACE,** *SAM oh thrays,* or SAMOTHRÁKI, is a Greek island in the Aegean Sea, often mentioned in Greek mythology. The island covers 66 square miles and has about 3,800 people. Agriculture, sponge fishing, and sulfur production are leading industries of Samothrace.

Ruins found on the island date from 500 B.C. In 1863, the famous statue of the Winged Victory of Samothrace was found on the island (see WINGED VICTORY). For location, see GREECE (color map).

**SAMOYED,** *SAM oh YED,* is the name of a tribe of Mongol people who live in the arctic region of northern Russia. The Samoyed people are much like the Lapps and the Eskimos.

**SAMOYED** is a dog bred by the Samoyed peoples of northern Siberia. It is one of the dogs called *lupines*, which also include spitz and chow. The Samoyed is used to guard reindeer herds and to pull sleds. It is intelligent, has a pleasant disposition, and is fast. The samoyed has a muscular body covered with long, white hair. It is about 23 inches high at the shoulder and weighs between 35 and 60 pounds. OLGA DAKAN

See also DOG (color picture: Working Dogs).

**SAMPAN,** *SAM pan,* is a small, light boat, which is used chiefly in the rivers and harbors of China, Japan, and nearby islands. The sampan usually has a cabin with a roof made of mats. Many persons use these boats for homes. It is rowed with one or more oars, and some have a single sail. See also SHELTER (picture: Oriental Houseboats). ROBERT H. BURGESS

**SAMPLER** is a small square or strip of cloth covered with sample patterns of needlework. The term *sampler* comes from the Latin word *exemplar*, meaning a *pattern*. Adults first used samplers to record patterns of embroidery or lace. But as early as the 1500's, young girls learning to sew made samplers for practice or to show their skill.

Samplers were made of colored silks stitched on wool or linen canvas, or of lace patterns on closely woven linen. The girls often embroidered letters, numerals, quotations, and verses to gain experience with different techniques. Sometimes a girl would add her name, age, and the date the sampler was made. Many samplers had intricately embroidered birds, flowers, patterns of Bible verses, and even tiny human figures.

Samplers are mentioned in the literature and wills of the early 1500's. Many styles and shapes were produced in Europe and the United States until the end of the 1800's. Today, many museums and private collectors own early samplers. HELEN MARLEY CALAWAY

**A Young Woman Embroiders a Sampler Held in a Frame.** Mottoes are particularly popular as sampler themes.

National Life Insurance Co.

**SAMPLING** is the use of a limited number of cases to gather statistical information. Suppose a doctor wanted to study the effects of a diet. He could not study everyone. The total number of cases that could be studied is called the *universe* or *population*. But the doctor could study a *sample*, or limited number of cases. A statistician would decide how many cases must be studied in order to draw valid conclusions. In theory, a *random sample* gives each case in the universe an equal chance of being included. See also STATISTICS.

**SAMPSON, WILLIAM THOMAS** (1840-1902), an American naval officer, became noted for the part he played in the Battle of Santiago during the Spanish-American War. When the war broke out in 1898, Sampson took command of the North Atlantic Squadron, and tried to stop the Spanish fleet from entering a Cuban port. But the Spaniards slipped into Santiago. Sampson blockaded the port until July 3, 1898, when the Spanish fleet, under Admiral Pascual Cervera y Topete, tried to leave and was destroyed. Sampson was away when the battle began, but quickly returned to his ships. Since Commodore Winfield Schley gave the initial orders, a quarrel developed over which man was responsible for the victory. A naval court of inquiry gave Schley credit, but also criticized his actions and strategy during the entire campaign. See SCHLEY, WINFIELD SCOTT.

Brown Bros.
**William Sampson**

Sampson was born in Palmyra, N.Y. He was graduated from the United States Naval Academy in 1857 at the head of his class. DONALD W. MITCHELL

See also SPANISH-AMERICAN WAR (Chief Events).

**SAMSON** was a hero of ancient Israel, famed for his great strength. His story is told in the Old Testament, Judges 13-16. In it, we see the beginnings of

**Samson Destroyed the Temple of His Enemies** by pulling down two pillars which held up the roof. The avalanche of stone killed the giant Israelite and thousands of Philistines.
Historical Pictures

# SAN ANDREAS FAULT

Israel's struggle with the Philistines in the 1000's B.C.

Consecrated before his birth by his mother's vow, Samson was forbidden to drink wine, eat impure food, or cut his hair. When he was grown, he fell in love with a Philistine woman who was unfaithful to him. So he set fire to the fields of her people. When the Hebrews handed him over for punishment, he broke loose and killed 1,000 Philistines with the jawbone of an ass. Later, the Philistines tried to capture him in the city of Gaza by locking the city gates. But he tore out the gates and carried them away.

Samson's downfall came when he fell in love with a second Philistine woman, Delilah. She learned that the secret of his strength lay in his hair, and she had his head shaved while he slept. Samson was easily taken, blinded, and made to work as a slave. At the festival of the god Dagon, when the temple was filled with people, the Philistines led Samson in so the crowd could make fun of him. But his hair had grown back, and he was strong again. He seized the pillars that supported the roof, and pulled the building down, killing himself and thousands of his enemies. JOHN BRIGHT

See also DELILAH; GAZA; PHILISTINE (picture).

**SAMUEL** was a Hebrew leader during the middle 1000's B.C. He was a prophet, priest, judge, and ruler. At this time, judges ruled the Hebrew tribes. Samuel, a judge, helped unite all the Israelites under a monarchy. He selected Saul, first king of Israel, and also chose David to succeed Saul. Samuel led in the struggle against the Philistines.

Samuel was born into a peasant family. His mother, Hannah, dedicated him at an early age to the service of God at the shrine at Shiloh. Some scholars believe that he not only became a priest, but also organized and led an important order of prophets.

The two books of Samuel in the Old Testament are named after him because of his prominence in I Samuel. They tell the story of the Hebrews from the birth of Samuel to the closing days of King David, a period of about a hundred years. The books are collections of stories written by various authors. They contain the important records of David. WALTER G. WILLIAMS

**SAMUEL S. FELS FUND.** See FELS FUND, SAMUEL S.

**SAMURAI**, *SAM oo rye*, was the hereditary warrior class in feudal Japan. The term originally referred only to the imperial guards. After the coming of a feudal system, it meant the entire military class. This included the samurai warriors, the feudal lords called *daimios*, or *daimyos*, and the shogun (see SHOGUN). About 5 of every 100 Japanese belonged to this group.

A code of unquestioning obedience and loyalty, called *Bushido*, bound the samurai warriors to their lords. The samurai prized honor above wealth or life, and atoned for dishonor by committing hara-kiri, or ceremonial suicide (see HARA-KIRI). They wore two swords and a distinctive headdress. The samurai were graded in military ranks, each with an appropriate income in rice. They lost their privileges when the Japanese abolished feudalism in 1871. MARIUS B. JANSEN

**SAN ANDREAS FAULT** is the most active fault in California. It extends for over 600 miles, from Cape Mendocino to the Colorado Desert. In 1906, horizontal movement of the earth's crust along the fault caused

81

## SAN ANGELO

the great San Francisco earthquake. See also EARTH-QUAKE.

**SAN ANGELO,** Tex. (pop. 58,815; met. area 64,630; alt. 1,845 ft.), is an oil and a sheep and cattle ranch center in west-central Texas (see TEXAS [political map]). The city has the largest market in the U.S. for the purchase of wool from ranchers. The seat of Tom Green County, San Angelo serves as the trading center for 24 surrounding counties. Industries produce building materials, foods and beverages, furniture, leather goods, paint, sheet metal products, and trailers. San Angelo is the home of Angelo State College.

The city developed from a trading post established to serve Fort Concho, which was built in 1867 at the junction of the Concho rivers. It was originally called *Santa Angela*, but was renamed after a post office opened. At first a cattle-raising center, it became a center for raising sheep and Angora goats in the late 1800's. Oil was discovered in the 1920's. San Angelo has a council-manager government. H. BAILEY CARROLL

**SAN ANTONIO,** Tex. (pop. 587,718; met. area 716,168; alt. 650 ft.), became famous in United States history as the scene of the Battle of the Alamo in 1836. The city is now the headquarters of a rich oil district, and a shipping and industrial center. During World Wars I and II, it was one of the largest military supply and training centers in the country.

**Location, Size, and Description.** San Antonio lies on the San Antonio River. The city is about 150 miles north of the Gulf of Mexico and 100 miles south of the geographical center of the state. The San Antonio River winds through the entire downtown district of the city. San Antonio covers about 154 square miles, and has an elevation ranging from 600 to 850 feet above sea level. For location, see TEXAS (political map).

**Industry and Trade.** Four oil refineries and many oil-supply companies have headquarters in San Antonio. The city has over 700 industrial plants. Industries include brewing, flour milling, food processing, and meat packing. Factories produce boxes, brooms, building materials, cement, ceramics, concrete products, clothing, furniture, highway and transportation equipment, jail equipment, refrigerators, and tile.

San Antonio is the trading center for a fertile agricultural region. Farm products include citrus fruits, cotton, forage crops, grain, and vegetables. The area also produces wool, mohair, and pecans.

San Antonio has become a center of military organization. About 60,000 military personnel are assigned to the San Antonio area. Fort Sam Houston, the headquarters for the Fourth Army, stands in the city. Brooke Army Medical Center at Fort Houston is one of the largest army medical installations in the world. Five United States Air Force bases—Brooks, Kelly, Lackland, Medina, and Randolph—are in the area. About 30,000 civilians work at the military installations.

San Antonio also has become one of the Southwest's leading convention cities. Its municipal auditorium seats 6,000 people. A Livestock Exposition and Rodeo is held each February in the Bexar County Coliseum there.

**Transportation.** Three major railroads and five United States highways supply transportation for the San Antonio area. The city also has air service.

**Education.** San Antonio has about 90 public elementary schools and 40 junior and senior high schools. The city is the home of Incarnate Word College, Oblate College of the Southwest, Our Lady of the Lake College, St. Mary's University of San Antonio, and Trinity University. The Southwest Research Institute engages in industrial research. The Southwest Foundation for Research and Education conducts agricultural, biological, and medical research.

**Cultural Life.** San Antonio has a symphony orchestra. Metropolitan Opera stars and other noted singers appear in five performances each season as part of the Grand Opera Festival. The city also has several dramatic groups. Many dramatic productions, lectures, and other cultural events take place in the San Pedro Playhouse. The city has a number of museums and art galleries. The Witte Memorial Museum in Brackenridge Park has historical and fine arts exhibits. Also in Brackenridge Park are the Chinese Sunken Garden and the Sunken Garden Theater. The McNay Art Institute in San Antonio is one of the leading art centers in the Southwest. The public library contains the Harry Herzberg Circus Collection, one of the largest sources of circus lore in the world.

San Antonio serves as the headquarters for the Roman Catholic Archdiocese of San Antonio and the Episcopal Diocese of West Texas.

Much of San Antonio's cultural life is closely linked with its colorful history. The city has many historic sites. The San Antonio Historical Association has encouraged interest in the city's past. San Antonio's Fiesta of San Jacinto, held every April, commemorates the establishment of the Texas republic in 1836.

La Villita, a "Little Spanish Town," occupies a block within the business district of modern San Antonio. Some of the structures of La Villita date from the earliest Spanish settlement. Many artists live in the old

San Antonio Chamber of Commerce

**Skyscrapers in San Antonio, Tex.,** tower above a residential district, *left*. In the heart of the downtown area, an outdoor theater, *above*, stands on a bend of the San Antonio River, with seating space on one bank and a stage on the other.

homes of La Villita. Art schools, a library, and a theatrical workshop are located in the area. The old Spanish Governor's Palace is maintained as a museum there.

The Alamo was originally the chapel of a Spanish mission. It became a fort and was besieged by a Mexican army in 1836. Today the Alamo is a shrine.

During its early days, San Antonio became *Queen City of the Missions* of North America. Several missions are preserved in the city. Some of the finest examples stand on Mission Drive, south of the center of the city. All of these missions were started between 1720 and 1731. Mission San José, the largest, has beautiful sculpture and architecture. Its rose window by Pedro Huizar won a first-place award in the Louisiana Purchase Exposition of 1904. Other missions include Capistrano, Concepcion, and San Francisco de la Espada.

HemisFair '68 opened in San Antonio in 1968, celebrating the city's 250th anniversary. About 25 nations from North and South America had exhibits at the fair.

**Recreation.** San Antonio has more than 50 parks and several polo fields. The Texas Open Golf Tournament takes place in San Antonio each year, usually in February. Many sporting events are held in Alamo Stadium, which seats 23,000 people. The San Antonio Zoo, one of the largest zoos in the nation, is located in Brackenridge Park.

**History.** Captain Domingo Teran of Spain arrived in the San Antonio area on June 13, 1691, the feast day of Saint Anthony of Padua. He named the region *San Antonio* in honor of the saint. However, permanent settlement did not begin until 1718, when the Spanish built the Mission of San Antonio de Valero, now called the *Alamo*. Spanish power began to weaken in the late 1700's, and Mexico gained control of the area around 1820. At about the same time, American pioneer Moses Austin arrived there. Other settlers followed. In 1835-1836, the new settlers fought for freedom from Mexico.

During this struggle, 182 Texas soldiers defended the Alamo against the Mexicans. The siege lasted from Feb. 23 to Mar. 6, 1836. All of the defenders of the Alamo were destroyed by a Mexican army (see ALAMO). About a month later, the Texas forces under General Sam Houston defeated the Mexicans in the Battle of San Jacinto. The city celebrates the anniversary of this battle every April. Mexican rule ended in San Antonio in 1836, when Texas became a republic.

San Antonio is the seat of Bexar County. It has a council-manager form of government. H. BAILEY CARROLL

See also CITY (color picture: City Flags); FORT SAM HOUSTON.

**SAN BERNARDINO,** BUR *nuh* DEE *noh*, Calif. (pop. 91,922; alt. 1,080 ft.), lies at the foot of the San Bernardino Mountains, 58 miles east of Los Angeles (see CALIFORNIA [political map]). It is the chief trading center of a large mining and farming district in southern California. With Riverside and Ontario, it forms a metropolitan area of over 800,000 population.

The city was founded in 1810. A group of Mormons settled there in 1851, and helped lay out the townsite. San Bernardino is the seat of San Bernardino County, the largest county in the United States. The county covers 20,154 square miles. San Bernardino has a mayor-council type of government. GEORGE SHAFTEL

**SAN BLAS INDIANS,** *san BLAS*, is the term for four tribes of Indians that live on the San Blas Islands off the eastern coast of Panama. Most of the 20,000 Indians belong to the Cuna tribe. These Indians live now much as they did before Europeans came to Latin America. Tribal law prohibits marriage with whites. The highest proportion of albino births in the world occurs among these Indians (see ALBINO). Experts estimate that about 7 out of 1,000 San Blas are albinos. The albinos gave rise to the myth that a tribe of "white Indians" lived in Panama. See also PANAMA (picture).

# SAN DIEGO

**SAN DIEGO,** Calif. (pop. 573,224; met. area 1,033,011; alt. 20 ft.), is one of the most important naval and aircraft centers in the United States. It lies in the southwestern corner of the country, 16 miles north of Tijuana, Mexico (see CALIFORNIA [political map]).

San Diego is the headquarters of the Eleventh Naval District, including southern California, Arizona, and Clark County, Nevada. The city has one of the best natural deepwater ports in the country. It serves naval vessels, steamships, and tuna clippers.

**Description.** The San Diego metropolitan area has one of the largest populations in the Western States. San Diego has grown rapidly since 1950, when its population totaled 334,387. It covers 294.7 square miles.

A mild climate has stimulated the city's growth. Temperatures average 55° F. in winter and 67° in summer. About 10 inches of rain falls yearly. The balmy climate lures retired people from other parts of the country.

A popular vacation region, San Diego's fashionable resort areas include Coronado, La Jolla, Mission Bay Aquatic Park, and Oceanside. Balboa Park lies in the heart of the city. Its ornate buildings, left from two international expositions, are cultural centers. The park also contains the famous San Diego Zoological Gardens, one of the world's largest zoos. It has 100 acres of semitropical trees and flowers and more than 4,000 animals. The park also displays the world's largest outdoor organ.

A national monument to Juan Cabrillo, the city's founder, stands on Point Loma west of the city. It is one of the country's smallest national monuments (80.50 acres). San Diego's Old Spanish Lighthouse also stands on Point Loma. See CABRILLO NATIONAL MONUMENT.

Many tourists also visit San Diego's Old Town district, the original center of the city. The area formed the setting for *Ramona*, a novel by Helen Hunt Jackson. Presidio Park, behind Old Town, is the site of Father Junípero Serra's Cross. In 1769, the first mission in California was dedicated there. The mission was later moved six miles up the valley. The restored mission buildings continue to attract many visitors.

**The People.** Many of San Diego's citizens originally came from the East and Midwest. More than 50,000 residents are over 60 years old. About 10 of every 100 retired U.S. Navy officers live in the region. The city has large Japanese and Mexican communities in the Logan Heights section of the south side. Several thousand Portuguese tuna fishermen and their families live in the western (Point Loma) area. They form a distinct group and have preserved their own customs.

**Education.** San Diego has about 100 public elementary schools and about 30 high schools. It is the home of the United States International University, the University of San Diego, San Diego State College, and the University of California at San Diego. The University of California maintains the Scripps Institution of Oceanography in La Jolla. La Jolla also houses the John Jay Hopkins Laboratory for Pure and Applied Science (General Atomics Division of General Dynamics) and the Salk Institute. The Mount Palomar Observatory stands about 40 miles northeast of San Diego. See SCRIPPS INSTITUTION OF OCEANOGRAPHY.

**Recreation.** The city's annual events include the National Shakespeare Festival, the Starlight Opera, and the Summer Symphony. Many tourists take sightseeing tours on land and water through San Diego's scenic and historic areas. San Diego's annual New Year Regatta takes place during the first week in January. The San Diego Chargers play in the National Football League's American Conference, the San Diego Rockets play in the National Basketball Association, and the San Diego Padres play baseball in the National League's Western Division.

**Industry.** San Diego has more than 800 manufacturing plants that employ about 60,000 workers. About 35,000 of them work in the manufacture of commercial and military airplanes, and missiles. Several large aircraft companies have offices in San Diego. Many persons work in the agricultural, fishing, forestry, and shipbuilding industries. The canning of tuna and other fish is another major occupation. Other products include electronic equipment, marine motors, plastic and fiberglass products, and canned and packaged foods such as olives, pimentos, and salt. San Diego County leads the world in the production of avocados.

**Naval Installations.** Most of the area's 26,000 government employees work in the shore installations of the United States Navy. The navy's largest air station on the Pacific Coast is on North Island in San Diego Bay. This island, together with its connections south to the mainland, helps form San Diego's great sheltered harbor. The air station was established in 1917. During

San Diego, Calif., Has One of the Finest Natural Harbors in the World. The City Is Also an Important Defense Center.

*San Diego Union*

**The Historic Old Mission of San Diego de Alcalá on the Outskirts of San Diego, Calif., Was Built in 1769.**

World War II, 31,400 pilots, bombardiers, navigators, and gunners received training there. The air station, the Eleventh Naval District Headquarters, and several other installations make up the San Diego Naval Base (see SAN DIEGO NAVAL BASE).

**Transportation.** Eight airlines and two major railroads serve San Diego. More than 70 motor-freight lines radiate from the city. San Diego is a port for about 50 steamship lines and home base for fleets of tuna clippers.

**History.** San Diego is sometimes called *The Cradle of California Civilization.* Juan Cabrillo, a Portuguese navigator, discovered San Diego Bay in 1542. Father Junípero Serra established California's first mission, San Diego de Alcalá, in 1769. It soon became the center of the Pacific Coast hide trade. San Diego was organized as a town in 1834. It was incorporated as a city in 1850.

Three wealthy men pioneered in the development of San Diego. In the 1860's, Alonzo Horton, a businessman, plotted the New Town section near the city's wharf. New Town eventually replaced Old Town as the center of the city. Industrialist John Spreckels developed the Coronado area during the late 1800's. The newspaper publisher Edward W. Scripps built up the La Jolla area.

San Diego is the seat of San Diego County, and has a council-manager form of government. GEORGE SHAFTEL

See also CITY (color picture: City Flags).

**SAN DIEGO, COLLEGE FOR MEN, UNIVERSITY OF,** is a Roman Catholic university at San Diego, Calif. It offers liberal arts, science, and business administration courses. It was chartered in 1949 and opened for instruction in 1954. For enrollment, see UNIVERSITIES AND COLLEGES (table). JOHN PAUL CADDEN

**SAN DIEGO, COLLEGE FOR WOMEN, UNIVERSITY OF.** See UNIVERSITIES AND COLLEGES (table).

**SAN DIEGO MARINE CORPS RECRUIT DEPOT,** Calif., trains United States Marine Corps recruits generally from west of the Mississippi River. It covers 467 acres and lies three miles north of downtown San Diego. The 544-acre Camp Matthews Rifle Range, 12 miles north of the city, also forms part of the depot. The depot includes a recruit training command and schools. It was commissioned as a marine corps base in 1921.

**SAN DIEGO NAVAL BASE,** Calif., provides headquarters for several United States Pacific Fleet commands. These include the naval air force, cruiser-destroyer, amphibious force, and training commands, and the First Fleet. The base also includes the Eleventh Naval District headquarters, a training center, a hospital, a naval station, a supply center, a recruit depot, and naval air stations on North Island and Miramar. There is also an anti-submarine warfare school, an anti-air warfare training center, and a recruit training command. An amphibious base is at Coronado, on San Diego Bay. San Diego Naval Base covers 46,675 acres and is the largest Pacific Coast naval base. Naval activity began there in 1917. JOHN A. OUDINE

**SAN DIEGO STATE COLLEGE** is a state-supported coeducational college in San Diego, Calif. It grants bachelor's and master's degrees in a wide range of subjects. It grants doctor's degrees in chemistry, ecology, and genetics jointly with the University of California. The San Diego State College library has about 500,000 volumes.

San Diego State College was founded in 1897. For the enrollment of the college, see UNIVERSITIES AND COLLEGES (table). MALCOLM A. LOVE

**SAN DOMINGO,** a variant of Santo Domingo. See SANTO DOMINGO.

**SAN FERNANDO VALLEY STATE COLLEGE** is a state-supported coeducational college located in Los Angeles, Calif. From 1956 to 1958, it formed a part of Los Angeles State College of Applied Arts and Sciences. In 1958, it became a separate institution. Its courses of study lead to bachelor's degrees. For enrollment, see UNIVERSITIES AND COLLEGES (table).

# SAN FRANCISCO

**SAN FRANCISCO,** Calif., the leading seaport of the Pacific Coast, is one of the world's most beautiful and unusual cities. Its mild climate, exciting scenery, fine restaurants, and unusual places to visit give the city a special charm. San Franciscans boast that every visitor ends up wanting to live there.

Built on steep hills, the *City by the Golden Gate* faces water on three sides. The Pacific Ocean lies to the west. On the east is San Francisco Bay, the largest natural harbor in the world. To the north is the Golden Gate, a mile-wide channel that links the ocean and the bay. Ships pass in and out in a steady parade beneath the Golden Gate Bridge, one of the world's largest suspension bridges.

The best view of San Francisco can be seen from Mount Tamalpais, north of the Golden Gate. Early in the morning, the city's skyscrapers seem to float above the fog. Later in the day, white buildings clustered on the hills glisten in the bright sunlight.

In downtown San Francisco, gaily clanging cable cars seem almost to stand on end as they climb Nob Hill. The cars pass large hotels and fashionable shops. They skirt Chinatown, then cross Russian Hill to Fisherman's Wharf on the waterfront. Throughout the downtown area, sidewalk flower stands add spots of bright color all year round. Store windows attract shoppers with displays of goods from many countries. More than 125 parks and recreation areas throughout the city provide green open spaces.

The people of San Francisco represent many nations. People came to the city from other lands after three important events. First was the Gold Rush of 1849 with its promise of sudden wealth. Second was the opening of the Panama Canal in 1914. The canal greatly shortened the sailing time from the eastern United States and Europe. Third was World War II in the 1940's. Thousands of American soldiers and sailors passed through the city and later returned to live there. In addition, many civilians came to help the war effort, and remained as permanent residents.

### Downtown San Francisco

The city is built on and around 42 hills of the coastal mountain range. Much of the business district, however, rests on filled land that was the waterfront of Gold Rush days. San Francisco is almost square, lying

San Francisco Chamber of Commerce

**Bridges and Cable Cars** add to the unique charm of San Francisco. The San Francisco-Oakland Bay Bridge, *left*, is more than 8 miles long. Cable cars, *above*, clang loudly as they climb the steep hills.

on the 7-mile-wide tip of a peninsula.

**The Waterfront** is at the northeast corner of the city. A wide street called the *Embarcadero* runs parallel to the waterfront. Traveling along the Embarcadero, a visitor can see ships from many countries tied up at the docks and wharves.

The famous *Fisherman's Wharf* is at the north end of the waterfront. Here, the visitor can take his choice of nearly 20 restaurants that serve seafood to as many as 5,000 persons an hour. He can buy souvenirs at dozens of shops. Or he can watch dozens of small fishing boats coming into the wharf with loads of fish and crabs.

Moored next to Fisherman's Wharf is the *Balclutha*, a three-masted sailing ship that rounded Cape Horn 17 times during the 1880's and 1890's. Owned by the San Francisco Maritime Museum Association, the *Balclutha* has been completely restored. It is the last surviving ship of the hundreds that once made the dangerous voyages around South America to San Francisco.

Three blocks west of Fisherman's Wharf, the visitor finds *Aquatic Park* and the *Maritime Museum*. The park provides salt-water swimming, fishing, and other outdoor activities. The museum preserves relics of the ships and the sailors that made San Francisco a great port.

In the middle of the waterfront area stands the *Ferry Building* with its clock tower. Large ferryboats used to carry passengers across San Francisco Bay to Oakland, Calif. The building now serves as a world trade center. It houses exhibits of goods from many countries, and has several foreign consulate offices.

**Market Street,** the main street of the downtown area, crosses the city from northeast to southwest. It starts at the Ferry Building and runs about three miles to the *Twin Peaks Tunnel*. The tunnel cuts through the high hills in the city's center to reach the southwest section.

**Montgomery Street,** the financial district, extends off Market Street to the north. It bustles with office workers during the day and is a canyon of deserted buildings at night. Gleaming skyscrapers in this area include the Crown-Zellerbach, Shell, Equitable, and Standard Oil buildings.

**Nob Hill** rises north of Market Street. At the foot of

---------- FACTS IN BRIEF ----------

**Population:** 740,316; met. area (five counties), 2,648,762.

**Area:** 46.6 square miles; metropolitan area, 2,488 square miles.

**Altitude:** 65 feet above sea level; *highest point,* Mount Davidson, 933.6 feet.

**Climate:** *Average temp.,* Jan., 50° F.; July, 59° F. *Average annual rainfall,* 20 inches.

**Government:** Municipal corporation governs county and city; mayor and 11 supervisors elected to four-year terms.

**Founded:** 1776. Incorporated as a city, 1850.

**City Seal:** A shield in the center is supported by a miner to the left and a sailor to the right. Emblems of commerce, navigation, and mining lie at the men's feet. The shield pictures a steamship sailing through the Golden Gate. A phoenix rising from flames is above the shield and the city motto is below it.

**City Flag:** A phoenix rising from flames is in the center of the flag. The phoenix and the city motto below the figure are in a golden hue on a white field. The words "San Francisco" appear in dark blue under the motto. A gold band borders the flag. See CITY (color picture).

**City Motto:** *Oro en Paz—Fierro en Guerra* (Gold in Peace—Iron in War).

86a

GOLDEN GATE BRIDGE

SAN FRANCISCO-OAKLAND BAY BRIDGE

# SAN FRANCISCO

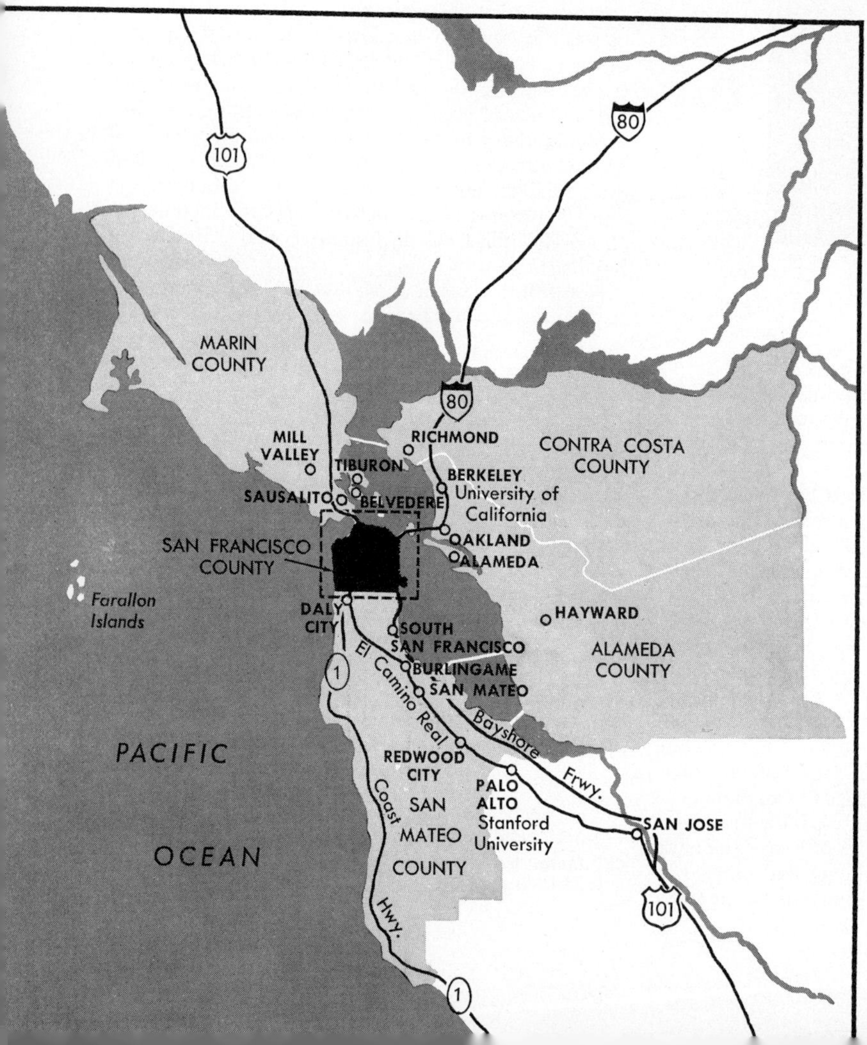

### ◄ METROPOLITAN AREA

The San Francisco-Oakland metropolitan area is shown in gray. It includes five counties—San Francisco, Marin, Contra Costa, Alameda, and San Mateo. The city of San Francisco (San Francisco County) is shown in black. The dotted line encloses the area of the large map, *right*.

### THE CITY ►

The city of San Francisco lies on a peninsula between San Francisco Bay and the Pacific Ocean. The city limits include the entire county of San Francisco.

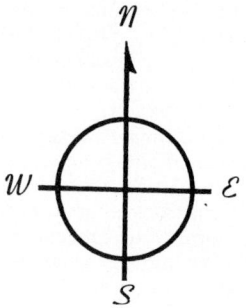

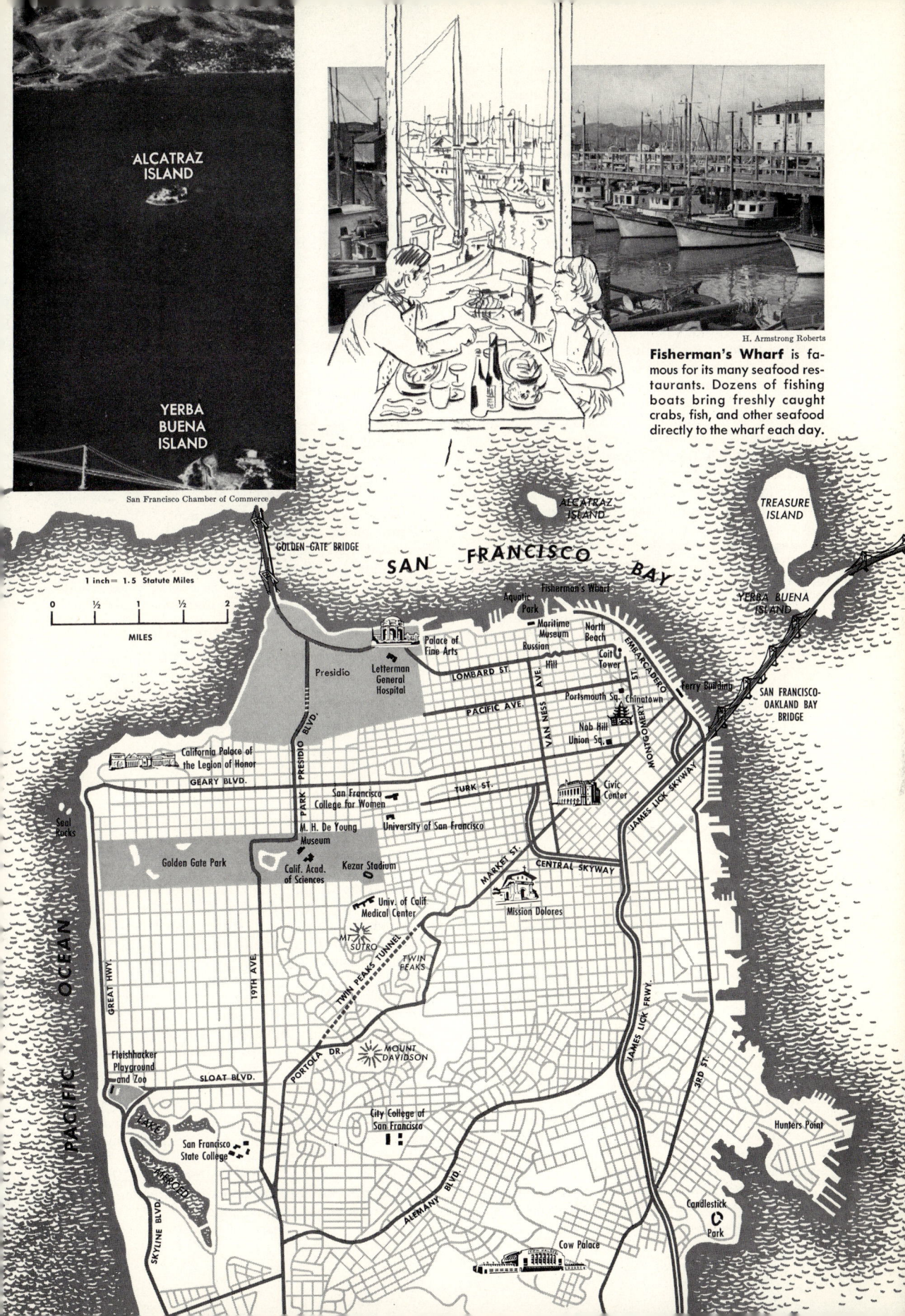

**Fisherman's Wharf** is famous for its many seafood restaurants. Dozens of fishing boats bring freshly caught crabs, fish, and other seafood directly to the wharf each day.

**Coit Memorial Tower,** *center,* stands on top of Telegraph Hill. The tower, built in 1933, honors San Francisco's volunteer firemen of the mid-1800's. It is 210 feet tall.

the hill, the city's main shops, restaurants, and hotels center in a few blocks. The Emporium is the largest department store. The St. Francis Hotel overlooks Union Square. This park lies on the roof of a huge automobile parking garage dug four stories deep. On Nob Hill stand two famous hotels, the Fairmount and the Mark Hopkins. The Mark Hopkins is particularly well-known for the view of San Francisco Bay from its Top of the Mark lounge.

**Chinatown,** one of the largest Chinese settlements outside Asia, lies east of Nob Hill along Grant and Kearny streets. About 36,000 Chinese live there. Shops, restaurants, and even buildings with modern fronts have Chinese-style upturned roofs. Oriental clothing, furniture, porcelain, and toys fill the shops. Strange and exotic Asian foods crowd the windows of grocery stores. A stainless steel statue of Sun Yat-sen by Beniamino Bufano stands in St. Mary's Square.

**Russian Hill** is north of Nob Hill. It received its name because its early residents were Russians. It is famous for Lombard Street, the crookedest street in the city. Flowers and shrubs border the sharp S-curves of this unusual street.

**Telegraph Hill** stands east of Nob and Russian hills. *Coit Tower,* a shining white memorial to San Francisco's firemen, rises on Telegraph Hill. From the east side of the hill to the bay is the section known as *North Beach.* A famous entertainment area, the *Latin Quarter,* is in this section. Most of the people who live there are of Italian descent. Visitors enjoy many-course Italian dinners at the dozens of restaurants in this section.

**The Civic Center** is on Van Ness Avenue just north of Market Street. Important public buildings grouped there include the city hall, the public library, the civic auditorium, state buildings, the modern art museum, and the opera house.

**The Presidio,** originally a Spanish army post, has about 1,500 acres of wooded parkland in the northwest corner of the city. For many years it has been the headquarters of the U.S. Sixth Army. The officers' club is in a long, low adobe building built by the Spaniards in 1776. It is the oldest building in the city. The Presidio is also the site of Letterman General Hospital, the largest military hospital in the western states. The nearby Palace of Fine Arts is the last remaining building of San Francisco's Panama-Pacific International Exposition of 1915.

**Seal Rocks,** in the ocean off the northwest corner of the city, are a playground for sea lions. Visitors can watch the playful animals from Cliff House, a restaurant overlooking the ocean.

**Golden Gate Park,** with more than a thousand acres of woods and lakes, extends from the Pacific shore to the center of the city. It has miles of bridle paths for horsemen. It also has four museums and two stadiums for athletic events. The San Francisco Forty-Niners of the National Football League play their home games in Kezar Stadium. A public beach runs along the western side of the city from Golden Gate Park to Lake Merced.

**Lake Merced,** a large freshwater lake in southwestern San Francisco, provides boating and fishing. It is bordered by a public golf course and two private golf courses. Nearby, *Fleishhacker Playground and Zoo* features a 1,000-foot-long heated salt-water swimming pool. The campus of San Francisco State College lies east of the lake. Northeast is Sigmund Stern Grove, where Sunday concerts are presented.

**Hunters Point,** a large U.S. Navy shipyard, juts into the bay in southeastern San Francisco.

South along the bay shore from Hunters Point is *Candlestick Park,* where the San Francisco Giants of the National League play baseball. Inland and just south of the city limits is the *Cow Palace,* a huge auditorium used for livestock shows and large conventions.

### The San Francisco Bay Region

San Francisco Bay covers about 450 square miles. It is more than 50 miles long and over 10 miles wide in some places. Two peninsulas shelter it from the Pacific Ocean on the west.

The metropolitan area of San Francisco includes five counties. San Francisco and San Mateo counties cover the southern peninsula. Marin County is on the northern peninsula. On the eastern shore of the bay are Contra Costa and Alameda counties.

The population of the metropolitan area divides almost evenly between the southern peninsula and the eastern bay area. The northern peninsula area of Marin County is more sparsely settled.

**San Mateo County,** south along the peninsula, has four main highways. *Bayshore Freeway* carries traffic past San Francisco's busy International Airport and on to San Jose. *El Camino Real* follows an old Spanish trail farther inland through the heart of many residential areas to Palo Alto. Stanford University is located nearby. *Skyline Boulevard* is a scenic drive along the hills that rise in the center of the peninsula. The *Coast Highway* runs along the Pacific Coast side of the peninsula. Leading suburbs of San Mateo County include Daly City, South San Francisco, Burlingame, San Mateo, and Redwood City.

**East of the Bay,** across the $8\frac{1}{4}$-mile San Francisco-Oakland Bay Bridge, is Oakland, the fourth largest city in California. In the center of the city, tall buildings stand near Lake Merritt, a wild duck refuge. Nearby Berkeley is the home of the University of California. Other leading suburbs of the east bay region include Alameda, Hayward, and Richmond.

Corson, Devaney

**Marin County,** north of San Francisco across the Golden Gate Bridge, has only about 150,000 residents. Rugged Mount Tamalpais rises a few miles inland from the bay. Muir Woods, a forest of giant redwoods, stands on the slope of the mountain. Each suburb has special characteristics. Sausalito is an artists' colony. Belvedere has large homes alongside man-made lagoons. Tiburon has dockside restaurants where yachtsmen can tie up their boats to come ashore and eat. Mill Valley is the home of many businessmen and fishermen.

**Islands.** About 30 miles west of the Golden Gate are the *Farallon Islands.* These islands warn incoming ships they are close to San Francisco. In the fog that frequently curtains the Farallons, a number of ships have been wrecked on the islands.

Several famous islands lie in the bay. Tiny *Alcatraz Island* is the site of a former federal prison for dangerous criminals. *Treasure Island,* the largest man-made island in the world, was the setting of the Golden Gate International Exposition in 1939 and 1940. It is now the site of a naval station. Treasure Island is connected to *Yerba Buena Island* by a causeway. Yerba Buena has a coast guard station, and provides an anchor for the center of the long San Francisco-Oakland Bay Bridge. *Angel Island* was once an important immigration station.

### Climate

Few homes in the San Francisco area have air conditioning, because of the ideal climate. September is the warmest month. But even then the temperature rarely rises into the 70's. January is the coldest month. But winter temperatures seldom drop to freezing.

Only about 20 inches of rain fall during the year, mostly in the winter months. But fogs occur frequently. Fog helps keep the temperature even and provides necessary moisture to keep plants green all year. The fog usually lifts by noon. Light snow occasionally falls, but rarely in measurable amounts.

San Francisco has cleaner air than most big cities because almost no coal is burned. Natural gas is the chief fuel. Most homes do not have screens on the windows because there are so few insects.

### The Economy of San Francisco

More than a million persons work in the San Francisco metropolitan area. The city is one of the nation's leading seaports, and even many persons not directly connected with ships owe their jobs to the shipping industry. Almost a fourth of the area's people work in wholesale and retail trade. Manufacturing, service occupations, and government each provide employment for about 200,000 workers. Food processing, printing and publishing, petroleum refining, and the manufacture of metal products make up the leading manufacturing industries. The main exports of the harbor include cotton, grain, lumber, machinery, paper, and petroleum products. Most of these goods go to the Far East.

San Francisco is the insurance and financial capital of the West. The world's largest commercial bank, the Bank of America, has its headquarters and over 50 branches in the city. Other banks, insurance companies, and investment firms employ more than 70,000 persons in the metropolitan area. The San Francisco Stock Exchange has been important since Gold Rush days.

The city ranks with New York City as a world communications center. Telephone and telegraph messages that cross the Pacific go through San Francisco. The city is also headquarters for the U.S. Information Agency's West Coast Voice of America. Daily newspapers include the *Chronicle,* the *Examiner,* and the *News-Call Bulletin.* More than 20 newspapers are published in various languages for people of foreign descent.

### Education

San Francisco's many schools, colleges, universities, libraries, and museums have given the city a reputation for intellectual and artistic leadership. Universities and colleges in the area include the University of California at Berkeley, Stanford University at Stanford, the University of San Francisco, Golden Gate College, San Francisco College for Women, San Francisco State College, and the college of the San Francisco Art Institute.

The city has 130 public schools, with about 100,000 students. Some 30,000 students attend 50 private and parochial schools. About 4,000 Chinese boys and girls study Chinese language and culture in their own schools after public school hours.

**Libraries.** One of San Francisco's noted book collections is the Sutro Library on the campus of the University of San Francisco. It includes Shakespearean folios, early Mexican books, and books printed before 1500. The California Academy of Sciences and the California Historical Society also have important libraries. The

87

# SAN FRANCISCO

Public Library at the Civic Center administers 25 branches and has more than 800,000 books.

**Museums.** San Francisco has a number of museums, devoted to art, science, and history. The M. H. de Young Museum displays San Francisco historical items, and art treasures from ancient Egypt, ancient Rome, and medieval Europe. The California Palace of the Legion of Honor, a memorial to the state's World War I dead, has a fine collection of tapestries, paintings, and sculpture. Works by the Mexican painter Diego Rivera and other modern artists are the special interest of the San Francisco Museum of Modern Art. The California Academy of Sciences in Golden Gate Park includes the Morrison Planetarium, the Steinhart Aquarium, and African and North American halls.

### Government

The city and county of San Francisco have identical boundaries. The two have formed a single municipal corporation since 1856. For some purposes, this corporation operates as a county, for others as a city. In the city limits are the Farallon Islands, Alcatraz Island, Treasure Island, and Yerba Buena Island.

A board of 11 supervisors serves as the legislative body. The mayor, supervisors, and most other elected officials all have four-year terms. Municipal judges serve for six years. The mayor nominates members of the board of education who are then passed on by the voters. The city operates the local transit system, including buses, electric coaches, and cable cars.

### History

**Early Explorers and Settlers.** Fog and the narrow entrance to the Golden Gate delayed the discovery of San Francisco Bay for more than 200 years. The Portuguese explorer Juan Rodríguez Cabrillo discovered the Farallon Islands in 1542. But Cabrillo did not sight the Golden Gate. The English explorer Sir Francis Drake may have seen it when he sailed along the California coast in 1579. He is believed to have anchored in Drake's Bay, a few miles north of San Francisco. In 1595, the Spanish explorer Sebastián Rodríguez Cermeño again found Drake's Bay. He renamed it *Puerto de San Francisco* (Port of St. Francis). This established the name San Francisco for the region.

Almost 200 years later, in 1769, scouts of a Spanish expedition under Gaspar de Portolá became the first white men to see San Francisco Bay. On Sept. 17, 1776, the Spaniards dedicated the *Presidio* (military post) of San Francisco. A mission was built that same year about three miles inland. It was named *Mission San Francisco de Asís*, in honor of St. Francis of Assisi. The original mission was destroyed, but another mission built in 1782 is still preserved. It became known as *Mission Dolores*, from nearby Lake Dolores. A few Mexican families settled near the mission. The settlement was called the *Pueblo of San Francisco*.

California became part of Mexico in the 1820's. In 1835, the Mexican governor appointed a British sailor, William Richardson, as captain of the Port of San Francisco. On the waterfront at the foot of Telegraph Hill, Richardson set up a tent made from a ship's sail. The tiny village that grew there became known as *El Paraje de Yerba Buena* (the little valley of the good herb). Jacob Leese, an American trader, arrived in Yerba Buena in 1836 and built the first wood frame house. Leese celebrated the Fourth of July that year by raising the Stars and Stripes alongside the Mexican flag for the first time in the village. By 1841, about 30 families lived in Yerba Buena and the Pueblo of San Francisco.

On July 9, 1846, during the Mexican War, the U.S.S. *Portsmouth* anchored off Yerba Buena. Sailors and marines rowed ashore. They hauled down the Mexican flag and hoisted the Stars and Stripes over the Custom House. This adobe building stood on the site of Portsmouth Square near today's Chinatown. Lieutenant Washington A. Bartlett was appointed as the first *alcalde* (mayor) under American rule. In 1847, the village of Yerba Buena was officially named San Francisco.

**Gold Rush.** In 1848, San Francisco had 820 residents, 200 houses, 2 wharves, 2 hotels, and 1 newspaper, the *Star*. It was published by an American, Sam Brannen. When Brannen received news of the discovery of gold at Sutter's Mill on the American River, about 100 miles to the northeast, he led the rush for gold. Only seven persons remained in San Francisco.

By 1849, some 40,000 persons had swarmed to the gold fields. As the supply point for the adventurers, San Francisco became a city of tents and shacks filled with gold-hungry men. Ships from throughout the world were abandoned in the harbor as their crews deserted to seek gold.

**Crime and Culture.** The city was incorporated on April 15, 1850. But the government had difficulty keeping law and order. The Barbary Coast, a district around Pacific and Kearny streets, became a center of vice and crime. Crimes went unpunished. Fires broke out repeatedly. Many persons believed the fires were set to make it easier to rob houses while the owners were fighting the fires. Citizens organized vigilance committees to put down crime (see VIGILANTE). The Vigilantes seized, tried, and hanged suspected criminals. After their harsh methods restored order, control of the city returned to the legal authorities.

Fortunes made in the Gold Rush also brought culture to the city. Lavish houses were built on Nob Hill. Theaters opened. Debating societies were established. Leading actors, singers, and opera stars entertained the new millionaires.

Construction of the transcontinental railroad brought hundreds of Chinese to California to work as laborers. When the railroad was completed in 1869, San Francisco became the gateway to the Pacific. In 1873, Andrew S. Hallidie, a local engineer, designed the first cable car to travel up and down the city's steep hills. The cars move by gripping a continuously moving cable under the street.

**Earthquake, Fire, and Dynamite.** By 1900, the population of the city had grown to 342,782. At 5:13 A.M. on April 18, 1906, a heavy earthquake shook San Francisco. The first shock damaged the water system. As a result, the fires that broke out could not be controlled. Firemen and soldiers from the Presidio fought the flames day and night. Finally, on the third day, they used dynamite to destroy entire blocks of buildings to create a fire break. The whole business district and many homes lay in ruins. In three days, earthquake, fire, and dynamite had killed 700 persons and destroyed 497 blocks of buildings covering 4½ square miles.

**Continued Growth.** San Franciscans quickly rebuilt the city. The new San Francisco displayed itself to the world at the Panama-Pacific International Exposition of 1915. The exposition marked the opening of the Panama Canal, which shortened the water route between San Francisco and the East Coast by more than half. This brought expansion in shipbuilding.

The city continued to grow during the 1920's and 1930's. In 1936, the San Francisco-Oakland Bay Bridge was opened to traffic. The next year the Golden Gate Bridge was completed. In 1939 and 1940, the city celebrated its two great bridges with the Golden Gate International Exposition held on Treasure Island.

During World War II, San Francisco became the world's largest shipbuilding center. Thousands of military personnel were stationed in and around the city. U.S. Navy ships streamed in and out of the Golden Gate. From April 25 to June 26, 1945, the city was host to delegates from many nations as they drew up the charter for the United Nations organization.

As the metropolitan area population grew in the 1950's and 1960's, San Francisco faced many problems. These included the need for more schools, housing, and recreation areas. More transportation routes were planned. The 1960's saw tests and construction on the Bay Area Rapid Transit System, which will carry metropolitan area commuters at speeds up to 80 miles an hour. The Golden Gate Development, a renewal project along the Embarcadero, includes housing and 45 acres of parks and plazas.   GERTRUDE M. CORDTS

**Related Articles** in WORLD BOOK include:

| | |
|---|---|
| Alcatraz | Oakland |
| Bank of America | Panama-Pacific International |
| Cable Car | Exposition |
| California (pictures) | San Francisco Conference |
| Farallon Islands | San Francisco-Oakland |
| Gold Rush | Bay Bridge |
| Golden Gate | Treasure Island Naval Station |
| Golden Gate Bridge | Westward Movement |
| Golden Gate International Exposition | (picture: "Gold Fever") |

**Outline**

I. Downtown San Francisco
II. The San Francisco Bay Region
III. Climate
IV. The Economy of San Francisco
V. Education
VI. Government
VII. History

**Questions**

What is the Golden Gate?
What three events brought people of many lands to San Francisco?
Who were the Vigilantes? What did they accomplish?
What means did firemen use to bring fires under control after the earthquake of 1906?
In what ways is the climate of San Francisco unusual?
Where is the oldest building in the city located?
What is the main street of downtown San Francisco?
How is the population of metropolitan San Francisco divided?
What four main roads lead out of the city to the southern peninsula?
What historical event took place on the location of present-day Portsmouth Square?

# SAN FRANCISCO-OAKLAND BAY BRIDGE

**SAN FRANCISCO, UNIVERSITY OF,** is a coeducational school in San Francisco. It is conducted by the Society of Jesus of the Roman Catholic Church. The university has colleges of liberal arts, science, and business administration; schools of law and nursing; and a department of education. Master's degrees are offered in the graduate division. The University of San Francisco also conducts an evening college and a summer session. It began as St. Ignatius College in 1855 and received its present name in 1930. For enrollment, see UNIVERSITIES AND COLLEGES (table).   CHARLES W. DULLEA

**SAN FRANCISCO ART INSTITUTE** is a coeducational private college and an artists' association. The college offers courses in humanities and in ceramics, design, painting, photography, and sculpture. It grants bachelor's and master's degrees in fine arts. It was founded in 1871. The association sponsors exhibits, lectures, and discussions. For the college's enrollment, see UNIVERSITIES AND COLLEGES (table).

**SAN FRANCISCO COLLEGE FOR WOMEN.** See UNIVERSITIES AND COLLEGES (table).

**SAN FRANCISCO CONFERENCE.** Delegates from the United Nations met at San Francisco on April 25, 1945, to form a world organization strong enough to prevent another global war. Representatives of the nations then winning World War II drew up the charter for the United Nations, providing a framework for further cooperation in time of peace.

The United States, Great Britain, Russia, and China sponsored the San Francisco Conference. They originally invited 41 nations to send delegates to the conference. Later, they also invited Syria and Lebanon to attend. When the conference met, it agreed to invite four more nations to send delegates—Argentina, Byelorussian Soviet Socialist Republic, Denmark, and Ukrainian Soviet Socialist Republic. This made a total of 51 nations, but only 50 were actually represented, because Poland's postwar government had not been formed and it could not send a delegation.

After two months of work, the conference drew up the United Nations Charter. The delegates signed it on June 26, 1945. Each nation agreed to fulfill its obligations under the Charter, settle disputes peacefully, cooperate in police actions, and help solve world economic and social problems.   PAYSON S. WILD

See also UNITED NATIONS (picture).

**SAN FRANCISCO CONSERVATORY OF MUSIC.** See UNIVERSITIES AND COLLEGES (table).

**SAN FRANCISCO-OAKLAND BAY BRIDGE** is one of the longest bridges in the world over navigable water. It crosses San Francisco Bay between Oakland and San Francisco, Calif. The Bay Bridge is really a series of bridges. It is more than 8 miles long, including its two approaches. It carries two decks for traffic. Opened in 1936, the bridge cost over $76 million.

One part of the Bay Bridge, consisting of two suspension bridges, reaches from San Francisco to Yerba Buena Island in the bay. The roadway passes through a double deck, 540-foot tunnel on the island. From there, the bridge crosses to Oakland and Berkeley.

The upper deck of the Bay Bridge originally had six lanes—three in each direction—for automobile traffic. The lower deck had three lanes for buses and trucks,

89

# SAN FRANCISCO STATE COLLEGE

and two tracks for interurban trains. Train service stopped in 1958, and the lower deck was converted into a five-lane road for all eastbound traffic. The upper deck became a five-lane westbound, all-traffic road.

Halfway between San Francisco and Yerba Buena the suspension spans are anchored to a concrete anchorage pier. The spans themselves are carried by suspension cables supported by towers extending about 500 feet above the water. The two center spans on each side of the anchorage pier are 2,310 feet long. The California Toll Bridge Authority and the California State Department of Public Works planned and built the bridge.
E. R. FOLEY

**SAN FRANCISCO STATE COLLEGE** is a publicly controlled coeducational school in San Francisco, Calif. Courses include teacher training, nursing, business, social service, language arts, journalism, and the liberal arts. The college was founded in 1899.

San Francisco State College maintains a School of World Business which is sponsored by the San Francisco Chamber of Commerce and firms engaged in international banking, construction, and the export-import business. Its nurses training program leads to the B.A. degree and to the R.N. certificate, with students assigned to hospitals under the direct supervision of the college. The college is the center for work in training teachers for exceptional children. For enrollment, see UNIVERSITIES AND COLLEGES (table).
RAYMOND N. DOYLE

**SAN GABRIEL DAM** is the name of two flood control projects on the San Gabriel River in southern California. The Los Angeles County Flood Control District built both dams.

*San Gabriel Dam No. 1* ranks among the largest and highest rock-fill dams in the United States. It rises 285 feet, and has a crest length of 1,500 feet. The reservoir had an original capacity of 43,928 acre-feet of water. The dam was completed in July, 1937, at a cost of $17,001,132.

*San Gabriel Dam No. 2* is sometimes called *Cogswell Dam*. It is a rock-fill structure, 270 feet high and 620 feet long. Its reservoir originally stored 10,915 acre-feet of water. This dam was completed in 1935, at a cost of $3,127,762.
T. W. MERMEL

See also DAM (Kinds of Dams).

**SAN JACINTO,** *san juh SIN toh*, **BATTLE OF.** The last battle of the war for Texan independence was fought near the San Jacinto River and Buffalo Bayou in Texas. The Mexican general, Antonio López de Santa Anna, commanded a force of over 1,200 men. The Texans, under General Sam Houston, had only about 910 men. Following a long retreat, the Texans took the overconfident Mexicans by surprise on April 21, 1836, and won a complete victory in just 18 minutes. Nearly every man in the Mexican army was killed or captured. Santa Anna himself became a prisoner the following day. The Texan losses at the Battle of San Jacinto were 9 killed and 30 wounded. General Houston was shot in the ankle during the battle. A monument commemorating this battle stands near Houston (see TEXAS [Places to Visit]).
NORMAN A. GRAEBNER

**SAN JOAQUIN RIVER,** *wah KEEN*, is the chief stream in the southern part of the Central Valley of California. It rises on the western slope of the Sierra Nevada in Tulare County. The river flows southwest, then turns northwest to cross the fertile San Joaquin Valley. It joins the Sacramento River to form a delta near San Francisco Bay. For location, see CALIFORNIA (physical map).

The San Joaquin River is about 350 miles long. Deep-draft vessels can go up the stream for about 50 miles to Stockton, Calif. The San Joaquin Valley is one of the richest farming areas in the United States. Friant Dam, a part of the Central Valley Project, stands on the river. See also FRIANT DAM.
C. LANGDON WHITE

**SAN JOSE,** *SAN hoh SAY*, Calif. (pop. 204,196; met. area 642,315; alt. 90 ft.), is the world center of the dried fruit industry. The city's other industries include electronics and missiles. San Jose lies 50 miles south of San Francisco in the Santa Clara Valley. For location, see CALIFORNIA (political map).

San Jose State College is California's oldest state-owned public educational institution. The city was settled in 1777 as Pueblo de San José de Guadalupe. It served briefly as the state's first capital, and was incorporated as a city in 1850. San Jose is the seat of Santa Clara County. It has a mayor-council government.
GEORGE SHAFTEL

**SAN JOSÉ** (pop. 176,219; met. area 335,396; alt. 3,021 ft.) is the capital and largest city of Costa Rica. It lies in a valley near the center of the country (see COSTA RICA [color map]). A transcontinental railroad that links Puntarenas on the Pacific Ocean with Limón on the Atlantic runs through San José.

The city's elevation gives it a pleasant year-round climate. Manufactures include leather goods, textiles, and furniture. In 1924, an earthquake severely damaged San José. In 1963, nearby Irazu volcano began spouting heavy clouds of volcanic ash. The volcanic eruptions damaged crops and threatened the city's economy.
WILLIAM S. STOKES

**SAN JOSE ROSE GARDEN.** See FLOWER (Famous Flower Gardens).

**SAN JOSE SCALE** is an extremely destructive scale insect. It is commonly found on shrubs and fruit trees in all parts of the United States and Canada. The largest are no larger than the head of a pin. The branches of infected trees are literally powdered with their tiny bodies. Because these insects give off a gray scaly wax, the plants look as if they were coated with ashes. The San Jose scale sucks the sap of the host plant through a slender beak composed of several delicate stylets which fit together to form a tube.

The danger of the pest is increased by the great number of kinds of plants on which it can feed. These plants include fruit trees in orchard or nursery, the members of the rose family, the pecan, the English walnut, the elm, and other trees. The fruits of infected apple and pear trees show a reddish discoloration of the skin and are often rough, pitted, and distorted in shape, or cracked. A full-grown apple tree may resist these insects for several years, but a young peach tree is often killed in two seasons.

The pest takes its name from that of the city in California in which it was discovered in 1880. It is believed to have been introduced on trees brought from China. The insect was not found east of the Rocky Mountains until 1893, but by 1895 it had become widespread.

The pest is spread by infected nursery stock. The

# SAN JUAN CAPISTRANO

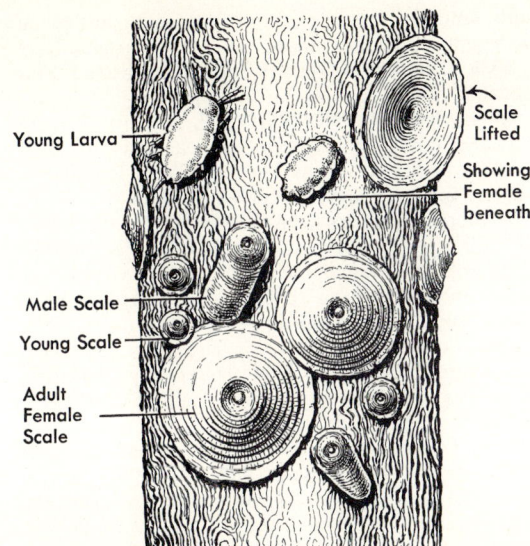

**Enlarged View of the Life Stages of the San Jose Scale** shows the insects on the trunk of a fruit tree.

scales are carried by the wind, and on the feet of birds and flying insects. The Chinese ladybird beetle and the chalcid fly are enemies of scales.

**Scientific Classification.** San Jose scales are in the armored scale family, *Diaspididae*. They are classified as genus *Aspidiotus*, species *A. perniciosus*. H. H. ROSS

**SAN JOSE STATE COLLEGE** is a publicly controlled coeducational school of the liberal arts in San Jose, Calif. Teacher training is the college's main function, but students may major in about 40 subjects. The college offers an experimental two-year humanities course, combining literature, social science, composition, speech, study of values, ideas, and the arts. San Jose State grants bachelor's and master's degrees. Founded in 1857, it was the first public college in California. For enrollment, see UNIVERSITIES (table). JOHN T. WAHLQUIST

**SAN JUAN,** *san HWAHN*, Puerto Rico (pop. 432,377; met. area 647,979; alt. 20 ft.), is the island's capital and chief seaport (see PUERTO RICO [map]). The older part of the city lies on an island off the northern coast of Puerto Rico. Newer residential districts lie on the main island. Four bridges and a highway over the water link these parts of the city. Trade, various manufactures, and government are the chief activities. Some of the Spanish forts and the walls around the older part of the city are over 250 years old. San Juan National Historic Site, covering 40 acres, contains many of these fortifications. Morro Castle, begun in 1539 and completed during the late 1700's, lies on a bluff at the entrance to the bay, one of the best harbors in the West Indies. In 1521, followers of Ponce de León founded the city. It was the seat of the Spanish provincial government. JAIME BENÍTEZ

See also PUERTO RICO (pictures).

**SAN JUAN BAUTISTA.** See PUERTO RICO (picture: Historic Puerto Rico).

**SAN JUAN CAPISTRANO,** *kah pih STRAH noh*, Calif. (pop. 2,551; alt. 20 ft.), is a city 60 miles southeast of Los Angeles (see CALIFORNIA [political map]). It grew up around a mission founded in 1776. The mission is known for the swallows which leave every year about October 23 to winter in the south and return to Capistrano on March 19. GEORGE SHAFTEL

**The Ruins of the Mission San Juan Capistrano** now serve as the summer home for the famous swallows of Capistrano. The statue with upraised hand is of Father Junípero Serra, who founded the first Franciscan mission in Upper California in 1769.

Western Ways

# SAN JUAN HILL, BATTLE OF

**SAN JUAN HILL, BATTLE OF.** See SPANISH-AMERICAN WAR (Land Battles; map).

**SAN JUAN ISLANDS** are a group of over 170 islands bounded by Haro and Rosario straits. They lie between Washington and Vancouver Island, and belong to Washington. Orcas, San Juan, and Lopez are the largest islands. The islands are drier and sunnier than the mainland. Most people work at farming, fishing, or the tourist industry. Friday Harbor is the chief port. Spanish explorers named the islands. The United States acquired them from Britain in 1872. HOWARD J. CRITCHFIELD

**SAN LEANDRO,** *SAN lee AN droh*, Calif. (pop. 65,962; alt. 45 ft.), called the *Cherry City of California*, lies southeast of Oakland. The city stages colorful dahlia and cherry festivals each year. San Leandro was settled in 1854 and incorporated in 1872. It has a council-manager government. For location, see CALIFORNIA (political map).

**SAN LORENZO, TREATY OF.** See ALABAMA (Territorial Days).

**SAN LUIS POTOSÍ,** *sahn LWEES POH toh SEE*, is a state of central Mexico. For location, see MEXICO (political map). The state has a population of 1,234,231, and an area of 24,266 square miles. The Sierra Madre Oriental mountains stretch across San Luis Potosí from north to south. Farmers grow coffee, sugar cane, rice, tobacco, wheat, fruits, and vegetables. The state produces silver, gold, mercury, manganese, antimony, and other minerals. The city of San Luis Potosí is the capital. See also SAN LUIS POTOSÍ (city). CHARLES C. CUMBERLAND

**SAN LUIS POTOSÍ,** *sahn LWEES POH toh SEE* (pop. 185,448; alt. 6,156 ft.), is a farming and mining center in central Mexico. The city stands 225 miles northwest of Mexico City. It is the capital of the state of San Luis Potosí. For location, see MEXICO (political map).

Spanish-style churches, public buildings, and houses from the 1600's stand in San Luis Potosí. Many people work in nearby silver, lead, and gold mines. The city is an important air and rail center. It stands on the highway between Mexico City and Eagle Pass, Tex. Industries include an aircraft plant, flour mills, textile mills, tanneries, breweries, furniture factories, and metal refining and smelting plants. JOHN A. CROW

**SAN LUIS REY COLLEGE.** See UNIVERSITIES AND COLLEGES (table).

**SAN MARCOS, UNIVERSITY OF,** in Lima, Peru, is the oldest university in South America. It is also called the UNIVERSITY OF LIMA. The school was founded in 1551 by Emperor Charles V of Spain. Dominican friars supervised the university until 1571. During the 1600's and 1700's, the University of San Marcos was noted for its schools of law and medicine. The university was closed during the early 1800's and reopened in 1861. It became a government-supported institute in 1874. Today it offers courses in letters and science, journalism, education, law, medicine, pharmacy, dentistry, economics, and veterinary medicine. About 15,000 men and women attend the university. EMILE DELAVENAY

**SAN MARINO,** *muh REE noh*, is the smallest republic in Europe. It covers an area of only 24 square miles. San Marino lies on the eastern slopes of the Apennine Mountains in northern Italy near the Adriatic Sea. The tiny country is completely surrounded by Italian territory. For location, see ITALY (political map). The capital is San Marino, a walled city of 4,000 persons. It is perched on top of Mount Titano.

Two *Captains-Regent*, assisted by a 10-member Congress of State, govern San Marino. The legislature, a 60-member Grand Council, is elected by the people every five years. It elects the Captains-Regent, who serve six-month terms.

The country's 19,000 people speak Italian, and are closely related to the people of northern Italy. They are proud of their independence and their traditions. San Marino's chief sources of income are the tourist trade, postage stamps, and industry. About 2 million tourists visit the republic each year, and its stamps are popular with collectors in many countries.

San Marino was founded in the A.D. 300's by Marinus, a Christian stonemason from Dalmatia, who sought refuge from persecution by the Roman emperor Diocletian. The country has many fine historical buildings, including a church built in the 1300's. The present constitution of the republic was drawn up in the 1600's.

**A Church Built in the 1300's Overlooks the Town of San Marino, Capital of the Tiny Republic of San Marino.**
Wide World

In 1945, San Marino elected a Communist government. In September and October, 1957, it had two rival governments, Communist and anti-Communist, vying for control. The Communists were defeated in the 1959 and 1964 elections. Women were given the right to vote in 1960.   CLARA BOSCAGLIA

See also FLAG (color picture: Flags of Europe).

**SAN MARTÍN,** *SAHN mahr TEEN,* **JOSÉ DE** (1778-1850), was an Argentine general who fought for the independence of South America in the wars with Spain. He and Simón Bolívar were the two great leaders in the cause of South American independence.

San Martín was born on Feb. 25, 1778, at Yapeyú in what is now Argentina. He went to Spain for his education. There he fought with the Spanish forces against Napoleon.

The Spanish colonies in South America began their rebellion against Spain, and in 1812 San Martín sailed for Buenos Aires. He was given command of a patriot army, and he planned a surprise attack against a Spanish army in Chile.

LIBERATOR OF ARGENTINA CHILE AND PERU
Little, Brown & Co.

**José de San Martín** fought for South America's independence from Spanish rule. (From *He Conquered the Andes,* by Mabel Lorenz Ives, illustrated by Forrest Orr.)

After nearly three years of preparation, San Martín undertook the campaign for which he is famous. He joined forces with Bernardo O'Higgins, the *George Washington of Chile.* In spite of terrible hardships, they led their army over the snow-covered Andes. In 1817, they appeared before the astonished Spaniards on the Chilean side of the mountains. The liberation army defeated the Spaniards at Chacabuco and the river Maipo. By the end of 1818, the liberators had driven the Spaniards out of Chile. See CHILE (History).

San Martín later went to Peru and helped that country win its freedom. In 1821 he was made Protector of Peru. In 1822 he and Bolívar met for the first and only time at Guayaquil. San Martín gave up his command and returned to Argentina. He wanted to avoid any struggle for the leadership of the independence forces.

He became discouraged by the quarrels and disputes that disturbed Argentina after the liberation. He was too unselfish to take part in the struggle for power in Buenos Aires, and soon left for Europe. He died at Boulogne-sur-Mer, France.   E. TAYLOR PARKS

See also FLAG (color pictures: Historical Flags); PERU (The Republic); ARGENTINA (color picture).

**SAN MATEO,** *muh TAY oh,* Calif. (pop. 69,870; alt. 25 ft.), is the West Coast center for over 30 national firms. It lies on San Francisco Bay, about 20 miles south of San Francisco (see CALIFORNIA [political map]).

Firms with offices in San Mateo include American Crystal Sugar Company, American-Standard, Holly Sugar Company, and Pacific Telephone Company. San Mateo was founded in 1776 and incorporated in 1894. It has a council-manager government.   GEORGE SHAFTEL

**SAN MIGUEL,** *SAHN mee GEL* (pop. 40,432; alt. 465 ft.), is a trading and manufacturing city in El Salvador (see EL SALVADOR [map]). Its chief products include coffee, sisal fiber, indigo, cotton, gold, and silver.

**SAN PEDRO SULA,** *sahn PAY throh SOO lah* (pop. 58,632; alt. 250 ft.), is the second largest city of Honduras. It stands on the banks of the Chamelecón River (see HONDURAS [map]). It is the center of the banana and sugar-cane industries, and of trade for the northern and western interior. Industries include a brewery, a sugar mill, and the plants producing soap, candles, shoes, and cigarettes.   ROLLIN S. ATWOOD

**SAN SALVADOR** (pop. 281,122; alt. 2,178 ft.) is the capital of El Salvador. The city lies in the valley of Las Hamacas (see EL SALVADOR [color map]). It is a leading business and railroad center. Merchants trade in coffee, tobacco, rubber, sugar, and other farm products.

San Salvador lies in the heart of an earthquake region. An earthquake and volcanic eruption destroyed many of the old buildings in 1917.   CHARLES C. CUMBERLAND

**SAN SALVADOR ISLAND.** See BAHAMAS.

**SAN SEBASTIÁN,** *sahn SAY bahs TYAHN* (pop. 140,893; alt. 10 ft.), is a seaside resort in Spain. The city has a landlocked harbor and a magnificent beach. The city lies on an isthmus in the Bay of Biscay (see SPAIN [color map]). San Sebastián was the summer residence of the Spanish royal family until 1931. The city serves as the official seat of the Spanish government from July 20 to October 1.   WALTER C. LANGSAM

**SAN STEFANO, TREATY OF.** See BERLIN, CONGRESS OF; BULGARIA (Struggle for Independence).

**SAN XAVIER DEL BAC MISSION.** See ARIZONA (Places to Visit).

**ṢAN‘Ā',** *sahn AH* (pop. 89,000, alt. 7,700 ft.), is the capital of Yemen (see YEMEN [map]). The city lies about 100 miles from the Red Sea, in a fertile district where fruits, vegetables, and some grains grow. Wells provide water for irrigation. A wall with eight gates surrounds the city. Most of the people are Moslems. The city is a trading center.   DOUGLAS D. CRARY

**SANATORIUM.** See SANITARIUM.

**SANBORN CONTRACTS.** See UNITED STATES, HISTORY OF ("Let Us Have Peace").

**SÁNCHEZ VILELLA, ROBERTO** (1913-    ), became governor of Puerto Rico in 1965. He is a member of the Popular Democratic party, which favors the continuation of Puerto Rico as a commonwealth of the United States. Before he was elected governor, Sánchez Vilella served as mayor of San Juan, commissioner of the interior, secretary of public works, and secretary of state. He was born in Mayagüez, Puerto Rico.

**SANCHO PANZA.** See DON QUIXOTE.

**SAND** is any earth material that consists of loose grains of minerals or rocks larger than silt but smaller than gravel. Engineers and geologists usually measure sand by shaking it through wire screens. Sand includes those grains less than $\frac{1}{12}$ of an inch, but greater than $\frac{1}{400}$ of an inch, in diameter.

Most grains of sand are parts of solid rocks that have crumbled away. Rocks break down in many ways. Some rocks crumble by the action of the air, rain, or frost. Strong waves wear away rocks by rolling over them and beating against them.

Sand is widely distributed on the earth. It is found at the bottom of the sea and shallow lakes. Sand is also

93

# USES OF SAND

Corning Glass Works
Glassmaking

Casting

Abrasives

Sandblasting

**Sand Is Useful to Man** in many ways. It is an important ingredient in glass, and is used in molds for casting. Sand also acts as an abrasive on grinding wheels and sandpaper. Sandblasting is used to clean the walls of buildings.

Julius Shulman for Anshen and Allen Architects

**Concrete** is made of sand, cement, and other materials. This concrete church stands beside a sandstone cliff.

rolled along the bottom of rivers and may be spread by the rivers over lowland areas. Great quantities are found on beaches and in sand dunes. In desert areas, sand covers thousands of square miles. It is usually piled up by the wind in hills called sand *dunes*. These dunes move with the wind, and have buried ancient towns for hundreds of years.

Geologists find many types of minerals in sand. The most common one is *quartz*. Some sand consists almost entirely of quartz, but usually grains of many other minerals are also present. Other sand, such as that found on the beaches of many Pacific islands, consists of grains of *basalt*. Basalt is a black lava rock that has flowed from or has been blown out of volcanoes on these islands. Some Pacific island beaches have sand that consists of tiny particles of coral and shells of clams and snails, broken up and rolled about by the waves.

Some river sands are rich in precious metals. These mineral deposits are called *placers*. The California pioneers took many millions of dollars' worth of gold from placers. Platinum, diamonds, and other valuable minerals also come from placers. Rare metals for jet engines come from placers in Florida, India, and Australia.

Sand has many practical uses. Manufacturers use quartz sand to make chemicals and glass. They make sandpaper by gluing loose sand onto heavy paper. Sand is also used in mortar and concrete.   RICHARD M. PEARL

**Related Articles** in WORLD BOOK include:
| | | | |
|---|---|---|---|
| Beach | Dune | Loam | Sandstorm |
| Desert | Glass | Sandstone | Silica |

**SAND, GEORGE** (1804-1876) was the pen name of AMANTINE LUCILE AURORE DUPIN, a French novelist whose books were highly popular during the 1800's. She is best known today for her love affairs with the composer Frédéric Chopin and the poet Alfred de Musset. She defied social convention by such acts as smoking cigars and wearing men's clothes.

She was born in Paris and grew up in the tiny village of Nohant, which she later described affectionately in her novels. She went to Paris in 1831 to find a new life, after the failure of her marriage.

George Sand's many works can be divided roughly into four periods. From 1832 to 1837, she wrote novels of romantic passion, notably *Indiana* (1832), *Valentine* (1832), and *Lélia* (1833).

**George Sand**
Chicago Historical Society

These novels reflect her own emotional desires and disappointments. They plead for a woman's right to sincere love and to lead her own life. From 1838 to 1845, she expressed her concern with social problems in such novels as *Consuelo* (1842). She dreamed of a world in which wealth would be abolished and brotherly love would unite all social classes. From 1846 to 1853, she wrote gentle, idealized novels of life in the French provinces. These include what is perhaps her best-known novel, *The Haunted Pool* (1846). Finally, from 1854 to 1876, she wrote simple stories resembling fairy tales.

George Sand's characters are overidealized and her plots very artificial. Her style is poetic, but wordy and unoriginal. Today, her memoirs are her most interesting works, especially *The Story of My Life* (1854-1855) and *She and He* (1859), which concerns her relationship with Musset. IRVING PUTTER

**SAND BAR.** See OCEAN (diagram: How The Ocean Changes Coastlines).

**SAND CHERRY.** See BEACH PLUM.

**SAND DOLLAR** is an animal that lives in the shallow coastal waters of eastern North America. Its thin, flat, circular body is two to four inches wide. The sand dollar looks somewhat like a silver dollar or a cookie. The body of many *species* (kinds) may contain slots, or be notched. The top surface has a set of breathing tubes arranged in the form of a five-point star. The sand dollar's body is covered with tiny movable spines which are used for crawling and digging.

The sand dollar lives slightly buried in the sand. Its food consists of tiny bits of animals and plants found among the sand grains. This food travels along the grooves on the underside of the sand dollar's body to its mouth, in the center of the under surface.

Like the sea urchin and the starfish, the sand dollar is an echinoderm. The sand dollar most nearly resembles the sea urchin.

**Scientific Classification.** Sand dollars belong to the phylum *Echinodermata*. They are classified in the class *Echinoidea*. ROBERT D. BARNES

See also ECHINODERM; SEA URCHIN; STARFISH.

**SAND DUNE.** See DESERT (picture); DUNE.

**SAND FLY** is a hairy, dark-brown insect about $\frac{1}{8}$ inch long. Female sand flies are active at night, and suck blood from man and animals. The *larvae* (young sand flies) live in moist places and feed on decaying material from both plants and animals.

About half a dozen kinds of true sand flies live in the southern United States. But several hundred kinds thrive in the tropics and subtropics. They cause serious diseases, such as kala-azar and verruga peruviana in man.

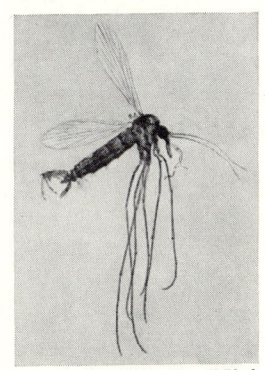

Courtesy of Dr. Carroll Birch
**The Sand Fly**

*Moth flies* are related to sand flies, but they do not suck blood. Their wings fold over the body like a roof. Tiny biting *midges* are sometimes called sand flies. They have two wings that lie flat on the back when the insect rests. In spring and fall, biting midges may appear in swarms. They rank among the smallest blood-sucking insects. Some measure only $\frac{1}{25}$ inch long.

**Scientific Classification.** Sand flies, moth flies, and biting midges are all classified in the true fly order, *Diptera*. E. GORTON LINSLEY

See also DIPTERA; KALA-AZAR.

**SAND MARTIN.** See SWALLOW.

American Museum of Natural History
**Sand Paintings** make up an important part of Navaho Indian healing rites. The paintings are made by sprinkling powdered colored rock on a sand bed, under a medicine man's direction.

**SAND PAINTING** is the name for making pictures in sand. The Navaho Indians of the southwestern United States are noted for their sand painting, also called *dry painting*. The paintings form a part of many ceremonies, especially healing rites. Medicine men usually make sand paintings on the floor of a *hogan* (earth-covered dwelling). They get colored sands by grinding stones from nearby cliffs. They make the designs freehand and from memory, and destroy them after the ceremonies. Colored sand paintings were made in Japan in the A.D. 600's, and in England and France during the 1700's and 1800's. See also INDIAN, AMERICAN (color picture: Sand Paintings). WILLIAM M. MILLIKEN

**SAND VERBENA** is a low summer annual with fragrant pink, white, or yellow flowers. The blossoms resemble those of the verbena, but the two plants are not related. Sand verbenas are native to western North America. The plants grow best in open, sunny places and in light soils. They are used for rock and seaside gardens, and hanging baskets. They adapt well to desert conditions.

**Scientific Classification.** Sand verbenas belong to the four-o'clock family, *Nyctaginaceae*. They make up the genus *Abronia*. One species is *A. umbellata*. ROBERT W. SCHERY

**SANDAKAN** (pop. 28,806; alt. 30 ft.) is the largest city in Sabah (North Borneo). It lies near the Sulu Sea, about 140 miles east of Jesselton. For location, see INDONESIA (color map).

Ships connect Sandakan with Indonesia, the Philippines, and Australia. Rubber plantations and lumber camps spread inland from the city. Sawmills and fisheries form Sandakan's largest industries. Sandakan was once the capital of North Borneo. JUSTUS M. VAN DER KROEF

**SANDAL.** See SHOE (History).

95

# SANDALWOOD

**SANDALWOOD** is a scarce, valuable wood obtained from several related kinds of trees. These trees grow in southern India, Indonesia, and Australia. Sandalwood has a fairly straight grain. The wood also has a fine structure and is so heavy that it will barely float in water. The *heartwood* (center) has a yellowish-brown or orange color. Sandalwood has a fragrant odor from an oil it contains. Most sandalwood is shipped to China, where it is used in funeral ceremonies, for carving, and for incense in temples. It is well suited to making carved boxes, jewel cases, fans, combs, and walking sticks. Sandalwood oil is obtained by pressing it out of the wood. The oil is used in perfumes, cosmetics, and medicines.

**Scientific Classification.** Sandalwood trees make up the family *Santalaceae*, and the genus *Santalum*. The principal species is *S. album* of India.  HARRY E. TROXELL

Frank Fenner
**Sandalwood** makes lovely fans. Intricate designs can be carved in the fine-grained, fragrant wood.

**SANDBLASTING** is a method for engraving glass or for cleaning metal and some buildings. Compressed air forces sand through a hose from the blasting machine. The sand acts as an abrasive to wear away scale on metal, dirt on stone buildings, or to smooth the surface of glass. See SAND (picture: Sandblasting).

Machines that have a rapidly rotating bladed wheel to hurl metal abrasives, particularly steel shot, are also used. Manufacturers prefer this method because it is faster and costs less.  ALDEN E. LENHARD

See also GLASS (How Glass Is Decorated).

**SANDBUR**, or BUR GRASS, is a troublesome prickly weed that originally came from the plains of the western United States. It now grows in sandy places in almost all temperate and tropical countries.

The stem of the sandbur plant grows between 1 and 2 feet high. It bears spikes with 10 to 20 shiny, sharp spined burs that cause painful wounds when they prick the flesh. A species closely related to the sandbur is called the *cockspur*. This plant is common in the South.

**Scientific Classification.** Sandbur is in the grass family, *Gramineae*. Its several species belong to the genus *Cenchrus*.  FRANK THONE

**Sandbur**
The New Britton and Brown Illus. Flora of the Northeastern U.S. and Adjacent Canada by H. A. Gleason, © 1952

Schaal, Pix
**Carl Sandburg**

**SANDBURG, CARL** (1878-1967), was an American poet, biographer, and collector of folk songs. Many consider his *Abraham Lincoln* the great biography of this generation. The biography took Sandburg 20 years of research and writing. The work originally appeared in two parts, *The Prairie Years* (2 vols., 1926) and *The War Years* (4 vols., 1939). Sandburg won the Pulitzer prize for history in 1940 for *The War Years*. In 1954, he published a one-volume edition of *Abraham Lincoln*, to which he added new material.

Sandburg was born on Jan. 6, 1878, in Galesburg, Ill., the son of a Swedish blacksmith. He left school at 13. When the Spanish-American War broke out, he enlisted in the army. After leaving the army, Sandburg entered Lombard College in Galesburg, where he began to write poetry. Later, he became an editorial writer on the *Chicago Daily News*.

At this time, interest in poetry was reviving in Chicago. *Poetry: A Magazine of Verse* led this revival, and, through it, Sandburg soon found an audience for his poems. Along with Edgar Lee Masters, Vachel Lindsay, and others, Sandburg spoke for the Middle West and the West. Up to that time, poetry had been associated with the New England tradition, represented by Henry Wadsworth Longfellow, Ralph Waldo Emerson, and James Russell Lowell. It was proper and often genteel poetry. But Sandburg was a realist, and he used his poetic language and subjects in an effort to catch the primitive vitality of a quickly expanding and often crude society. He frequently quoted a saying of Rudyard Kipling's: "I will be the word of the people. Mine will be the bleeding mouth from which the gag is snatched. I will say everything." In 1951, he received the Pulitzer prize for poetry for his *Complete Poems* (1950).

America was shifting from an agricultural to an industrial way of life, but Sandburg did not write exclusively about industrial Chicago. He also wrote about the prairies and the farms, and especially about the hopes and sufferings of the common people. "I glory," he once said, "in this world of men and women, torn with troubles, yet living on to love and laugh through it all."

Sandburg also became well known as a singer and collector of ballads. He collected some of the folk songs he sings in *The American Songbag* (1927). As a memorial to Sandburg, his birthplace in Galesburg, Ill., has been restored.  WILLIAM VAN O'CONNOR

**SANDE, EARL** (1898-1968), a famous American jockey, rode Kentucky Derby winners in 1923, 1925, and 1930. He gained a reputation as a quarter-mile rider and broncobuster before becoming a jockey in 1918. He went on to win 967 races and purses totaling $3 million. After retiring to become a trainer in 1932, Sande attempted a comeback as a jockey in 1953, but he won only one race. He was elected to racing's Hall of Fame in 1955. Sande was born in Little Falls, Idaho, on Nov. 13, 1898.  RICHARD G. HACKENBERG

Hugh M. Halliday, NAS

**The Sanderling** spends winters in the warmer regions of America. It looks for its food along the seashore.

G. Ronald Austing, NAS

**The Semipalmated Sandpiper** is one of the smallest of the shore birds. It is frequently called the black-legged peep.

**SANDERLING** is a bird that belongs to the same family as the snipes and sandpipers. It differs from these birds by having only three toes. Sanderlings breed on Arctic beaches and tundra, and travel south in the winter. They appear then from California and Texas to South America and also may appear on many of the Pacific islands.

The bird is about 8 inches long. Its feathers are hoary gray on the upper parts, and pure white beneath. It is a true beach bird and usually lives on seashores. Its favorite foods are small shellfish and marine insects that wash up with the tide. The female lays 3 or 4 eggs colored a brownish-olive. The eggs are speckled with darker markings.

**Scientific Classification.** The sanderling belongs to the snipe and sandpiper family, *Scolopacidae*. It is classified as genus *Crocethia*, species *C. alba*.   ALFRED M. BAILEY

**SANDGLASS.** See HOURGLASS.

**SANDIA BASE,** N.Mex., operates as the field headquarters of the United States Defense Atomic Support Agency. Covering 28,192 acres, it lies on the southeastern outskirts of Albuquerque. The post assists the Atomic Energy Commission and the military services in developing and testing atomic weapons, and in training men to handle these weapons. Originally a municipal airport, Sandia Base came under United States Army control in 1942. It takes its name from the nearby Sandia Mountains.   SAMUEL J. ZISKIND

**SANDOW,** *SAN doh,* **EUGENE** (1867-1925), a German strong man, performed great feats of strength in Europe and the United States. His fame helped make physical culture and body-building popular. Sandow was weak and sickly as a child. But he studied anatomy and built up his muscles by scientific methods. Sandow trained British soldiers during World War I. He was born in Königsberg, Germany.   RICHARD G. HACKENBERG

**SANDOZ,** *SAHN dohz,* **MARI SUSETTE** (1901-1966), was an American biographer and novelist. Her first book, *Old Jules* (1935), told of her father's hard farm life.

She also wrote *Crazy Horse* (1942), a biography of an Indian chief; *Cheyenne Autumn* (1953), which treats Indian history; *Buffalo Hunters* (1954), which records the slaughter of the bison; and *Love Song to the Plains* (1961), which describes life on the Plains. She was born in Sheridan County, Nebraska.   JAMES WOODRESS

**SANDPAPER.** See ABRASIVE.

**SANDPIPER.** A large number of birds are sometimes called sandpipers. But the name is usually given to small birds with long, sensitive bills. These birds live on the seashore in all parts of the world, and many *species* (kinds) of sandpipers build their nests north of the Arctic Circle.

Their plumage varies from buff to brown, gray, white, or black. The birds dig in the soft mud or sand in search of insects, worms, shrimps, and soft mollusks. They often follow receding waves, sometimes alone, sometimes in flocks, searching for bits of food. Their graceful movements and cheerful cries have made them popular birds. The female sandpiper lays 3 to 4 eggs that are colored a light gray, buff, or olive, and spotted with dark brown.

One of the best-known American species is the *spotted sandpiper,* which is found throughout the United States and southern Canada. The *Bartramian sandpiper,* also called the *upland plover,* is a useful bird that eats insects. It lives on dry uplands in the United States and Canada. Hunters once killed Bartramian sandpipers in great numbers. A larger species called the *willet* lives in marshes along the warm Atlantic and Gulf coasts, and in many western states. Laws protect all sandpipers from hunters.

**Scientific Classification.** Sandpipers belong to the sandpiper and snipe family, *Scolopacidae*. The spotted sandpiper is genus *Actitis*, species *A. macularia*, the upland plover is *Bartramia longicauda*, and the willet is *Catoptrophorus semipalmatus*.   ALFRED M. BAILEY

See also BIRD (color picture, Color Protects Them); GODWIT; RUFF; SNIPE; WILLET.

# SANDSTONE

**SANDSTONE** is a rock made up of sand grains. The sand grains are cemented together by some substance, usually silica, clay, or carbonate of lime. Some sandstone contains quartz and looks glassy. This variety is used in making glass. Sandstone ranges in color from white to dark gray or brown. The cement gives sandstone its color. For example, carbonate of lime often produces gray sandstone.

Brownstone, a reddish-brown variety of sandstone, was once widely used in building houses in the eastern United States. Before the use of Portland cement and reinforced concrete, sandstone was widely used to build large buildings. Some of the finest cathedrals in Europe were built of sandstone. RICHARD M. PEARL

See also BUILDING STONE; QUARRYING.

**SANDSTORM** is a storm that occurs when a strong wind carries sand through the air. It may result from the heat of the sun beating on broad deserts or plains. The rapid daytime heating of the lower air over deserts makes the heated air rise, and it is quickly replaced by cooler air. The wind that results may be strong and constant or intermittent and turbulent. Sandstorms in the southwestern United States result from strong wind gusts that sometimes accompany a passing cold front.

A desert trip is often a steady struggle against wind and blowing sand. Desert wind may be clouded with fine dust that fills the eyes, nose, and throat. In India, sandstorm winds are called *peesash*, from the Hindu, or *shaitan*, from the Arabic name for devil. Heavy particles hurled about in sandstorms help shape sand dunes and rocky surfaces. JAMES E. MILLER

See also DESERT; SIMOOM; SIROCCO.

**SANDUSKY**, Ohio (pop. 31,989; alt. 595 ft.), is an industrial city on Sandusky Bay of Lake Erie (see OHIO [political map]). Products include ball bearings, crayons, paper boxes, radios, and wines. Sandusky is one of the largest coal-shipping centers and fresh-water fishing ports on the Great Lakes.

**SANDWICH.** See FOOD (Interesting Facts).

**SANDWICH GLASS.** See GLASSWARE.

**SANDWICH ISLANDS.** See HAWAII (Discovery).

**SANDY HOOK** is a low, sandy point of land reaching north from the New Jersey coast into New York Bay. Sandy Hook Bay is on the west of the peninsula, and the Atlantic Ocean lies to the east. The sandy waste is covered with poison ivy, huge holly trees, and beach-plum bushes. The Hook is 18 miles south of Manhattan Island. It is 6 miles long, and a mile wide at its widest point.

Fort Hancock is on the farthest tip of Sandy Hook. Part of the peninsula is used by the United States government as a testing ground for heavy guns. The tip of the Hook is guarded by a beacon, but the first light seen by incoming ships comes from a 90-foot lighthouse about a mile from the tip. This lighthouse, built in 1763, is the oldest one still in service in the Western Hemisphere. ERNEST L. THURSTON

**SANFORD, MARIA L.** (1836-1920), was one of the first woman professors in the United States. She taught at the University of Minnesota for 30 years. She became a leading educator of Negroes, Indians, and exceptional students. Minnesota placed a statue of her in the Statuary Hall collection in the U.S. Capitol, Washington, D.C., in 1958. She was born in Saybrook, Conn.

**SANGAMON RIVER**, *SANG guh mun*, flows for about 250 miles through central Illinois. It rises in Champaign County and runs south to Decatur, where a dam forms Lake Decatur. It enters the Illinois River near Beardstown. For location, see ILLINOIS (physical map).

In 1830, Abraham Lincoln's father built a cabin on the north bank near Decatur. Later, Abraham Lincoln settled at New Salem on the Sangamon. He lived there from 1831 to 1837. PAUL M. ANGLE

**SÄNGER, EUGEN.** See ROCKET (Early Research).

**SANGER, FREDERICK** (1918- ), an English chemist, won the 1958 Nobel prize in chemistry for developing a method of studying the structure of proteins. He helped establish the structure of insulin by working on its chemical constitution in different species of animals. He lived in Cambridge, England. PAUL R. FREY

**SANGER, MARGARET** (1883-1966), led the birth-control movement in America, and founded the Planned Parenthood Federation of America. A trained nurse, she felt that the poor needed to control the size of their families. It was illegal to distribute birth-control information, but she wrote booklets and opened clinics to advise people on the subject. She was arrested several times, but helped get laws passed permitting doctors to give birth-control information for the "cure or prevention of disease." She also worked for birth control in other countries, especially in India. She was born in Corning, N.Y. LOUIS FILLER

See also PLANNED PARENTHOOD.

**SANGRE DE CRISTO MOUNTAINS,** *SANG gree duh KRIS toh*, extend for more than 200 miles from central Colorado to north-central New Mexico. For location, see physical maps with COLORADO; NEW MEXICO. Blanca Peak in Colorado is 14,317 feet high, the highest in the system.

**SANGSTER, CHARLES** (1822-1893), was a Canadian poet. He started writing patriotic verses about 1860, at a time when political conditions in Canada were at their worst. His poems helped arouse national feeling in favor of union of the provinces. His works include *The Saint Lawrence and the Saguenay, and Other Poems* (1856) and *Hesperus and Other Poems and Lyrics* (1860). Sangster was born in Kingston, Ont. PETER VIERECK

**SANHEDRIN,** *SAN hee drin*, was the highest national governing council of the Jews in Roman times. According to some scholars, there were two Sanhedrins. The 23 members of the political and civil Sanhedrin came mostly from among the Sadducees. The 70 members of the religious Sanhedrin, which was presided over by the high priest, came largely from among the Pharisees. Jesus was tried before the religious Sanhedrin. Peter, John, Stephen, and Paul appeared before it on charges of religious error. After the fall of Jerusalem in A.D. 70, the council declined and completely disappeared. See also GAMALIEL; SADDUCEE. LOUIS L. MANN

**SANIDINE.** See FELDSPAR.

**SANITARIUM,** *SAN uh TAIR ee um*, is a place where people go to improve their health. The word comes from the Latin word for health, *sanitas*. It is sometimes used as another word for *sanatorium*.

A *sanatorium* is an establishment where sick people are treated. It is especially used for a place where a particular treatment is given. THOMAS PARRAN

**SANITARY ENGINEERING.** See ENGINEERING (table: Specialized Engineering Fields [Environmental]).

# SANITATION

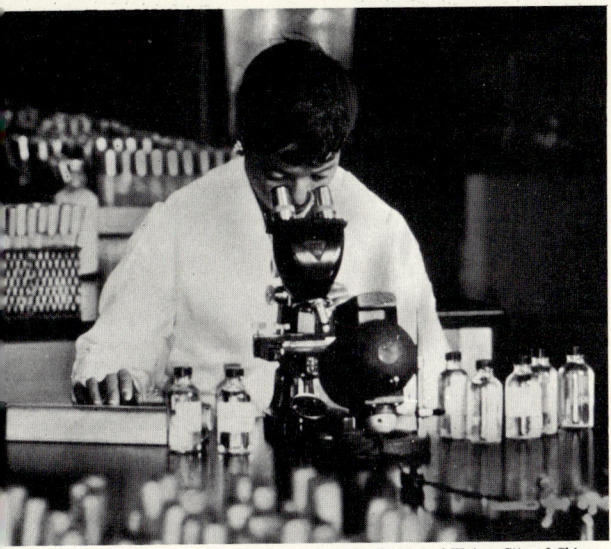

Bureau of Water, City of Chicago
**City Drinking Water Is Examined for Impurities.**

Cook County Dept. of Public Health
**A Water Inspector Checks a Stream for Pollution.**

**SANITATION,** SAN ih TAY shun, is the science of controlling man's surroundings to promote health and comfort. Sanitation includes purifying water, removing wastes, and inspecting foods. These public health activities prevent the loss of countless lives. They are based on the knowledge of how germs develop, are transmitted to people, and cause disease.

Even ancient peoples had methods and rules of sanitation. The Romans built aqueducts that brought fresh, clean water to the cities. They also built sewers to carry refuse away. Jewish laws regulated the sanitary preparation of foods. But no one knew the connection between filth and disease until scientists in the 1800's discovered disease germs and proved that some thrive in filth. Diseases that stem from filth were widespread until the early 1900's. They are still a leading cause of death in many underdeveloped areas where epidemics sometimes kill thousands of people.

**Water Purification.** Perhaps the most important sanitation function is to provide drinking water free from disease germs. Some underground water is safe to drink directly, but all surface water must be purified. Most cities purify their water in large purification plants. Common purification methods include the use of filters, *chlorine* (a germ-killing chemical), and sedimentation. In *sedimentation*, impurities settle to the bottom of tanks. See WATER (City Water Systems).

Piping systems that distribute water to the public must be carefully designed to protect water purity. They must maintain continuous pressure to prevent impure water from being drawn into the system. Most sanitation laws prohibit plumbing connections that make pollution possible. Public distribution systems are usually kept separate from systems not under the constant supervision of official community agencies, such as systems that supply water for use in private industrial processes.

**Sewage Removal.** Modern plumbing systems remove human waste matter from the community. But the wastes from these systems often pollute the soil or water where they are discarded. As a result, sewage must be made safe before disposal. Small disposal systems treat the sewage in septic tanks before it enters the soil. Larger systems pass the sewage through tanks where the solid wastes are removed or broken down. This treated sewage is dumped in a body of water or on land. Land disposal includes allowing the sewage to evaporate and seep into the ground from large ponds.

The solids removed from sewage are often changed into soil conditioners and fertilizers. Manufacturers usually heat-treat these products to destroy infectious germs. See SEWAGE.

**Food Inspection.** Local and federal health officials inspect milk, meat, and other foods to make sure they are safe to use. Milk from diseased cows can spread tuberculosis and undulant fever, and infected pork can cause trichinosis. Both hogs and cattle can spread tapeworm. Most states have laws that require strict meat inspection. The Bureau of Animal Industry of the U.S. Department of Agriculture inspects meat shipped from state to state.

The Public Health Service provides local communi-

**Meat Must Be Inspected Before It Can Be Marketed.**
U.S. Dept. of Agriculture

99

## SANS-CULOTTE

ties with model laws listing requirements for producing, processing, and handling foods. For example, one model law deals with pasteurization, a method of heating milk to kill bacteria in it. The Food and Drug Administration supervises a national inspection program that protects against labeling foods falsely, and sees that pure food laws are obeyed.

**Other Sanitation Measures** include eliminating rats and other rodents that spread plagues. Fleas, flies, lice, mosquitoes, and ticks also carry disease germs. Sanitation measures include draining ponds and marshes where these insects breed, and killing them with insecticides. Garbage should be put into tight containers to keep out insects and rodents so they cannot spread the germs that breed in refuse.

Garbage removal itself is a major sanitary problem, especially in big cities. Chemical, radioactive, and other wastes produced by industry must be disposed of effectively.

Sanitation also includes personal cleanliness, which helps protect against disease. Careful washing and bathing is especially important for those who handle food or have contact with sick people.     C. FRED GURNHAM

**Related Articles** in WORLD BOOK include:

| | |
|---|---|
| Bacteria | Health, Board of |
| Baths and Bathing | Mosquito |
| Disinfectant | Public Health |
| Epidemic | Public Health Service |
| Fly | Pure Food and Drug |
| Garbage Disposal | Laws (Foods) |

**SANS-CULOTTE,** *SANZ kyoo LAHT*, is a French word that means *without breeches*. It refers to the French workers who wore long trousers at the time of the French Revolution (1789-1799). The aristocrats, against whom they had rebelled, wore knee-length breeches.

**SANSKRIT LANGUAGE AND LITERATURE** originated in ancient India. The Sanskrit language is divided into two periods. Old Sanskrit is the language in which the holy *Vedas*, sacred Hindu books, were written. Old Sanskrit is also called *Vedic Sanskrit*, or simply *Vedic*. Most writings of the second, or classical, period deal with nonreligious subjects.

It is not definitely known when Sanskrit was introduced into India, but 1500 B.C. is the date generally accepted. For a period, Sanskrit was the common speech of the people, as well as the literary language. But by the 500's B.C., local dialects had sprung up. Buddha preached his doctrine in one of these. Pāṇini (300's B.C.) was the first and greatest Indian grammarian. He fixed the characteristics of *Sanskrit* ("purified, cultivated") in contrast with the common spoken language *Prakrit* ("natural, unpurified").

*Om* is a sacred syllable in the Sanskrit language, similar in meaning to the English *amen*. It might well be

ᵃ काको वृक्षे वसतः ᵇ देवो वदति
ᶜ किमर्थस्पितरम्पुत्रो न स्मरति

**Sanskrit** was the language spoken in India about 3,000 years ago. Translated, these Sanskrit sentences mean: (a) Two crows dwell in a tree; (b) The God speaks; (c) Why does the son not remember the father?

translated, *So it shall be*. It was supposed to be uttered at the beginning of every Vedic recitation and again at its close. This gave assurance that the understanding of what was spoken should not be lost. Later, the syllable referred to the Hindu Trinity of Vishnu, Brahma, and Siva. It symbolized the abstract unity of the universe: Absolute (a) and Relative (u) are related (m). The three letters, *a-u-m*, are pronounced *om*.

**The Sanskrit Language** became widely known to Europeans in the late 1700's. This knowledge enabled Franz Bopp (1791-1867) and other linguists to develop the comparative study of languages (see LINGUISTICS). Many words in the Greek, Latin, English, German, Persian, and other languages are also found in Sanskrit. The Sanskrit word *mata* became *mater* in Latin, *Mutter* in German, and *mother* in English. The English words *brother*, *sister*, *daughter*, and *son* are directly related to the Sanskrit *bhrātā*, *svasr*, *duhita*, and *sunu*. Scholars study the *Rig-Veda* to compare it with the myths and religions of other lands.

**Sanskrit Literature** began with the *Vedas*. They constitute the oldest work in any Indo-European language. The works of the Vedic period are religious and were long transmitted orally. They consist of the *Rig-Veda* (about 1000 B.C.), the *Sama-Veda*, the *Yajur-Veda*, and the *Atharva-Veda*. The *Brahmanas* (about 800-600 B.C.) discuss the *Vedas*. Religious philosophy is taught in the *Upanishads* (about 600-300 B.C.).

In its second, or classical, period the literature was mostly secular, or nonsacred. The outstanding epics are the *Mahabharata* (200 B.C.?) and the *Ramayana*. Dramas were produced in India as early as in the Western world, first appearing in the 400's B.C. The author Kalidasa appears to be India's Shakespeare. There are also lyric and instructive poems, *Manu* (laws), and philosophical works of various schools, such as the *Vedanta*, *Sankhya*, and *Yoga*. India's chief contributions to Western literature are in the fields of fiction and fable. Indian fairy-tale motifs appear in the *Arabian Nights* and in medieval legends and stories. The *Panchatantra* is the chief Sanskrit collection of fables.     FRANZ ROSENTHAL

See also HINDI; MAHABHARATA; RAMAYANA; VEDA.

**SANTA ANA,** Calif. (pop. 100,350; alt. 121 ft.), is the chief trading center of the rich farm area of Orange County. With nearby Anaheim and Garden Grove, it forms a metropolitan area with a population of 703,925. Santa Ana lies about 33 miles southeast of Los Angeles (see CALIFORNIA [political map]).

The city's 180 factories manufacture a wide variety of products, ranging from electronic components to bowling balls. The surrounding farming region produces oranges, beef cattle, green beans, celery, sugar beets, peppers, and pimentos. Three railroads, an airport, and two heliports serve the city.

Santa Ana was established in 1869 and incorporated in 1886. It is the county seat of Orange County, and has a council-manager government.     GEORGE SHAFTEL

**SANTA ANA,** *SAHN tah AH nah* (pop. 72,839; alt. 2,200 ft.), is the second largest city in El Salvador. It is an important commercial center, especially for the exporting of coffee. Other important industries in Santa Ana include sugar milling, brewing, and the manufacture of cotton textiles, footwear, and furniture. Santa Ana also has a national theater and an art school. For location, see EL SALVADOR (color map).

Ayer Coll., Newberry Library; Bettmann Archive

**Santa Anna,** *above,* led the Mexican army against Texas in the war for Texan independence. He was captured during the Texas victory at San Jacinto, and brought before Gen. Sam Houston on April 23, 1836, *left.*

**SANTA ANNA,** *SAN tuh AN uh,* **ANTONIO LÓPEZ DE** (1795-1876), was a Mexican soldier and politician. He ruled Mexico three times as a dictator-president, but he was always overthrown.

**Young Soldier.** Santa Anna was born in Jalapa, in the province of Veracruz, on Feb. 21, 1795. At 15, he became a cadet in the Spanish army stationed in Mexico. He began his long career by fighting against the Mexicans in the War of Independence. Toward the end of the struggle, he deserted the Spaniards and joined forces with Agustín Iturbide, who won and declared himself emperor (see ITURBIDE, AGUSTÍN DE).

Santa Anna expected the new emperor to make him governor of Veracruz. When Iturbide failed to do so, Santa Anna led a revolt against him and drove him from power. In 1829, Spain attempted to reconquer Mexico. Santa Anna, as commander in chief of the Mexican Army, won several victories, and the Spanish invasion was defeated. In 1833, he became president.

**War With Texas.** Santa Anna had little regard for the law. He abolished the federal constitution and placed the governors of provinces under his own control. These acts caused a revolt in Texas, a part of Mexico which had been settled by persons from the United States.

Santa Anna rushed north to put down the revolt. He attacked San Antonio and stormed the Alamo in March, 1836, with a great army that outnumbered the Texans 30 to 1. All the Texas troops were slain (see ALAMO). Then Santa Anna met the main Texas army under General Sam Houston at San Jacinto. Santa Anna's army was routed, and he was taken prisoner. The Texans forced him to sign a treaty acknowledging the independence of Texas. But the treaty was rejected in Mexico City, and Santa Anna was removed from power.

**The American War.** In 1838, the French attacked Veracruz. Santa Anna took command of the defending troops and beat back the attackers. From 1841 to 1844, he was president of Mexico again. In 1844, there was a revolt against him, and he fled to Jamaica. War broke out with the United States in 1846. Santa Anna returned the next year and took command of the army. The American forces defeated him at Buena Vista, at Cerro Gordo, and at Chapultepec. After the fall of Mexico City, Santa Anna left Mexico for several years.

In 1853, he returned to Mexico and became president again. He declared himself president for life, but within two years was again overthrown and exiled. He tried to return during the French invasion of Mexico in 1864, but was not allowed to enter the country. He returned in 1874 after the death of President Benito Juárez, and died in poverty in Mexico City.   DONALD E. WORCESTER

See also MEXICAN WAR.

**SANTA BARBARA,** Calif. (pop. 58,768; met. area 168,962; alt. 100 ft.), is an old Spanish mission town. It lies on the Pacific Coast, 98 miles northwest of Los Angeles (see CALIFORNIA [color map]).

Santa Barbara preserves much of its Spanish background. Its mission is often called the "Queen of the Missions." Many visitors come to Santa Barbara during the "Old Spanish Days," which are held every August. Electronics research and development and tourism are major sources of income in Santa Barbara.

Father Junípero Serra and Captain José Francisco de Ortega founded Santa Barbara in 1782. It was incorporated as a city in 1850. The city is the seat of Santa Barbara County, and has a mayor-council form of government.   GEORGE SHAFTEL

**SANTA CATALINA.** See CATALINA ISLAND.

**SANTA CLARA,** Calif. (pop. 58,880; alt. 75 ft.), is a rapidly growing city 45 miles southeast of San Francisco. Food processing is the main industry. Santa Clara was founded as a Franciscan mission in 1777 and incorporated in 1866. It has a council-manager government. For location, see CALIFORNIA (color map).

**SANTA CLARA, UNIVERSITY OF,** is a coeducational school at Santa Clara, Calif. It is controlled by the Jesuit order of the Roman Catholic Church, but is open to students of all faiths. Women are admitted to the college of law and the evening and graduate divisions. The university grants degrees in the sciences, engineering, liberal arts, business administration, law, teacher education, and in specified graduate areas. Santa Clara was founded in 1851. For enrollment, see UNIVERSITIES AND COLLEGES (table).   PATRICK A. DONOHOE

# SANTA CLAUS

**SANTA CLAUS** is a mythical old man who brings gifts to children at Christmas. Today's Santa Claus developed from a real person, Saint Nicholas, who lived in the A.D. 300's. He was bishop of Myra, an ancient town of Lycia, now in Turkey. According to legend, he was only a boy when he became a bishop. He was extremely kind, and often went out at night, taking presents to the needy. After his death, his fame spread throughout Europe. During the Middle Ages, Saint Nicholas became the patron saint of schoolboys. Schoolboys in various European towns celebrated his feast day on December 6 by electing a boy-bishop. Dressed in magnificent robes, the boy-bishop led a parade through the streets. There was much feasting, but on the whole the occasion was solemn. Later, this custom died out, although Nicholas still remained the favorite saint with children.

In Belgium and The Netherlands, both young and old still celebrate his feast day. A person representing the saint wears the robes of a bishop and rides through the street on a white donkey. In Germany, Nicholas sometimes appears as a hairy imp, *Pelz Nichol*, meaning *Nicholas in Fur*. Parents tell Pelz Nichol how their children have behaved during the year. Then good children are rewarded with presents, while bad boys and girls receive only a bundle of twigs or switches.

Children were so fond of Saint Nicholas and his habit of bringing gifts that the custom of celebrating his feast day was maintained. Dutch settlers brought the custom with them to New Amsterdam (now New York City), and English settlers eagerly borrowed the legends and festivities surrounding the kindly Saint Nicholas. English-speaking children tried to pronounce the Dutch name for the saint, *Sinter Klaas*. But they said it quickly and excitedly, and soon the name changed to *Santy Claus* or *Santa Claus*.

**Appearance.** Santa's appearance began to change about the same time as his name. For hundreds of years, Europeans had imagined Saint Nicholas as a tall, thin, stately person. But Washington Irving created a new picture of him as a fellow who looked very much like a typical Dutch settler in the state of New York. In his *Knickerbocker's History of New York* (1809), Irving described the saint as the guardian of New York City. He pictured him as a jolly fellow wearing a broad-brimmed hat and huge breeches and smoking a long pipe. Irving's Saint Nicholas rode over the treetops in a wagon, took presents from his pockets, and dropped them down chimneys.

In 1822, Clement C. Moore wrote for his children the poem "A Visit from St. Nicholas," which describes the saint more as we know him today (see MOORE, CLEMENT C.). In this poem, which begins with the familiar line "Twas the night before Christmas," the saint is pictured as a round and jolly figure with twinkling eyes, a "nose like a cherry," and a white beard. He puffs a stump of a pipe and rides in a sleigh pulled by eight reindeer. Like the German *Pelz Nichol*, "he was dressed all in fur, his head to his foot." In 1837, a painting by Robert W. Weir showed Santa as a friendly, tubby fellow, wearing a hood and knee boots, and carrying a bag of toys. He was grinning and, in Moore's words, "laying his finger aside of his nose."

Harold M. Lambert

**Jovial and Kindly Santa Claus** reads a letter from a young admirer, before starting on his Christmas rounds.

Thomas Nast, the famous American cartoonist, further developed the figure of Santa Claus in a cartoon in 1863. Later, his famous drawing "Santa Claus and His Works," which appeared as a Christmas picture in *Harper's Weekly* in 1866, showed Santa Claus in his workshop with his record of the good and bad deeds of all children. The drawing also showed the reindeer-drawn sleigh, the pack of toys, the stockings hung at the fireplace, and the Christmas tree.

**Festivities.** For hundreds of years, people celebrated the feast of Saint Nicholas on December 6, which is the anniversary of the saint's death. After the Protestant Reformation, Saint Nicholas was replaced by the Christ Child, called *Christkindl*, in parts of Germany and Switzerland. From this name came the character *Kris Kringle*, the angel-like figure who brings gifts at Christmastime. Sometimes Pelz Nichol accompanies him.

In England, Saint Nicholas Day festivities were banned when Henry VIII founded the Church of England. They were later resumed when Queen Victoria married a German prince, Albert. Then Saint Nicholas returned as Father Christmas, a gentleman dressed in a long tail coat and square beaver hat. He, too, appeared at Christmastime. But in many European countries, such as The Netherlands, Belgium, Austria, and parts of Germany and Switzerland, Saint Nicholas celebrations still take place on December 6.

In the United States, Santa Claus' activities always occur at Christmastime. The American version of Santa Claus has also become popular in Canada, England, and Australia as a person who brings presents and Christmas cheer. ARTHUR M. SELVI

See also CHRISTMAS; NICHOLAS, SAINT.

**SANTA CLAUS,** Ind. (pop. 250; alt. 440 ft.), is about 10 miles north of the Ohio River, and 30 miles northeast of Evansville, Ind. Every December, thousands of letters addressed to "Dear Santa Claus" pour into this Indiana town. In a typical year, close to four million pieces of mail may come from everywhere to be remailed with the magic postmark. A small park in the town has a statue of Santa Claus dedicated to "The Children of the World."  PAUL E. MILLION, JR.

**SANTA CRUZ, ANDRÉS.** See PERU (The Republic); BOLIVIA (Independence).

**SANTA CRUZ ISLANDS** lie in the Pacific Ocean about 1,800 miles northeast of Sydney, Australia. They have a population of 7,000 and cover 199 square miles. The Santa Cruz island group is east of the Solomon Islands. It is administered as part of the same British Protectorate as the Solomon Islands. The chief islands are Ndeni (or Santa Cruz), Utupua, and Vanikoro. The islands are in Melanesia, but many of the people are of Polynesian ancestry.  EDWIN H. BRYAN, JR.

**SANTA CRUZ Y ESPEJO, FRANCISCO XAVIER DE.** See ECUADOR (Early Days).

**SANTA FE,** *SAHN tah FAY* (pop. 259,560; alt. 75 ft.), is a shipping center in east-central Argentina. On the upper Paraná River, it has facilities for ocean shipping (see ARGENTINA [political map]). Milling and the making of quebracho extract are its main industries.

**SANTA FE,** N.Mex. (pop. 34,676), is the capital of the state. It has served as a seat of government longer than any other state capital in the United States. Santa Fe was founded as the capital of the Spanish province of New Mexico in 1610. Santa Fe lies in north-central New Mexico. The city is located about 6,950 feet above sea level in the Sangre de Cristo Mountains (see NEW MEXICO [political map]).

Santa Fe's major industry is the tourist trade. The

**La Fonda Hotel in Santa Fe, N.Mex.,** background, is on the site of an old inn that marked the end of the Santa Fe Trail.
New Mexico State Tourist Bureau

# SANTA MARTA

Museum of International Folk Art, the New Mexico Museum, the Museum of Navaho Ceremonial Art, the Hall of Ethnology, and the Laboratory of Anthropology contribute to Santa Fe's cultural life. The city has many old churches. The San Miguel Mission, built about 1710, is one of the oldest mission churches in the United States. A campus of Saint John's College (Md.) and the College of Santa Fe are located there. Santa Fe has a council-manager government, and is the seat of Santa Fe County.  FRANK D. REEVE

See also NEW MEXICO (picture: The State Capitol).

**SANTA FE, COLLEGE OF.** See UNIVERSITIES AND COLLEGES (table).

**SANTA FE DAM** is a flood control project on the San Gabriel River, about 29 miles above its mouth in southern California. It is a rolled earth-fill dam, designed to hold back 35,800 acre-feet of water. It is 92 feet high, and 24,100 feet long.  T. W. MERMEL

**SANTA FE RAILROAD.** See RAILROAD (Leading Railroad Companies).

**SANTA FE TRAIL** was one of the longest commercial routes in the United States in the pre-railroad era. It began at Independence, Mo., and ended at Santa Fe, N.Mex., a distance of 780 miles. Caravans of traders traveled to Council Grove, Kans., and on to the Cimarron Crossing of the Arkansas River near Cimarron, Kans. There the route divided. One branch led up the Arkansas to Bent's Fort (near La Junta, Colo.), then turned southwest across Raton Pass to the upper Canadian River in New Mexico. The other route cut from the Arkansas across the Cimarron Desert. This one was shorter, but Indians made it more dangerous.

The early travelers transported their goods by pack horses. William Becknell first used the Santa Fe Trail in 1821. After that, traders took wagons loaded with manufactured goods to Santa Fe to exchange for mules, furs, gold, and silver. Between 1822 and 1843, an average of about 80 wagons and 150 men used the trail each year. Travel westward along the trail increased greatly during the 1850's and 1860's. By the late 1860's, more than 5,000 wagons a year used the trail. An extension of the trail, known as *The Old Spanish Trail*, ran from Santa Fe to Los Angeles in a semicircular route by way of Durango, Colo., the Green and Virgin rivers in Utah, the Colorado River, and across the Mojave Desert in California.  W. TURRENTINE JACKSON

See also TRAILS OF EARLY DAYS (map).

**SANTA GERTRUDIS.** See CATTLE (The Santa Gertrudis; color picture).

**SANTA ISABEL,** *SAHN tah EE sah BEL* (pop. 37,237; alt. 164 ft.), is a seaport and the capital of Equatorial Guinea. It is located on the island of Fernando Póo. The chief export of the city is cacao. The British founded Santa Isabel in the 1820's under the name of Port Clarence. For location, see EQUATORIAL GUINEA (map).

**SANTA MARÍA.** See COLUMBUS, CHRISTOPHER (First Voyage to America); CARAVEL.

**SANTA MARTA** (pop. 89,161; alt. 15 ft.), is a seaport near the northern tip of Colombia. For location, see COLOMBIA (color map). The city is important as a banana-shipping center. Many years ago it was the point from which adventurers started in search of El

103

**SANTA MONICA**

Dorado. Santa Marta was founded in 1525 by Rodrigo de Bastidas, a Spanish navigator and explorer. It is the oldest permanent settlement in South America. Nearby is the *hacienda* (estate) of San Pedro Alejandrino, where the South American liberator Simón Bolívar spent his last days. See also EL DORADO.

**SANTA MONICA,** Calif. (pop. 83,249; alt. 85 ft.), is a city and beach resort about 15 miles west of Los Angeles, on crescent-shaped Santa Monica Bay. For location, see CALIFORNIA (political map).

The city was probably named by Father Crespi, a Spanish missionary who camped on the site on Saint Monica's Day in 1769. The McDonnell-Douglas Corporation, a large aircraft company, is in the city. Pacific Ocean Park, a beach amusement center there, is often called the *Coney Island of the West.* Santa Monica was incorporated in 1886, and has a council-manager government. It extends to Santa Monica Canyon, where there are mansions and estates. GEORGE SHAFTEL

**SANTA ROSA ISLAND** is a long, narrow island outside Pensacola Bay off the northwestern Florida coast. Santa Rosa Sound separates the island from the mainland. Santa Rosa Island is about 50 miles long (from east to west) and averages about a mile in width. Its area is 49 square miles. The island is a popular residential and resort area. Fort Pickens Military Reservation, an important post during the Civil War, stands on the western end. In the 1870's, the fort became a military prison. It served as a coastal defense center in the Spanish-American War and in World Wars I and II. See also FORT PICKENS. KATHRYN ABBEY HANNA

**SANTA SOPHIA.** See SAINT SOPHIA.

**SANTANDER,** *SAHN tahn DAIR,* **FRANCISCO DE PAULA** (1792-1840), was a South American soldier and statesman. From 1822 to 1827 he governed New Granada (now Colombia) as acting president while Simón Bolívar was absent. Later, as president from 1832 to 1837, he encouraged national industry, built up a trained army, and established schools and courts.

Santander was born in Cúcuta. He studied law in Bogotá, but enlisted at 18 in the revolutionary army. At 25, he was promoted to the rank of full general. In 1828 he was exiled for political reasons, but returned after Bolívar's death. DONALD E. WORCESTER

**SANTAYANA,** *SAN tuh YAH nuh,* **GEORGE** (1863-1952), was an American philosopher, essayist, poet, and novelist. He described himself as a materialist, but he did not claim to know what matter is in itself.

He expressed his major ideas in a series of five volumes which he called *The Life of Reason.* Their individual titles are *Reason in Common Sense, Reason in Religion, Reason in Society, Reason in Art* (all 1905), and *Reason in Science* (1906).

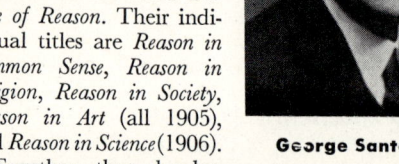
George Santayana

Together, they develop his major thesis that the wise man is the contemplative one, who views his universe with reasonable detachment. The excellence of Santayana's literary style has never failed to impress his readers. It is evident even in his most abstract philosophical works. In poetry, he became distinguished largely for his sonnets. He wrote most of his poetry in early life.

Santayana was born in Madrid, Spain. He was taken to Boston when he was a boy just nine years old. Santayana was graduated from Harvard University in 1886, and then he studied for two years in Berlin. He taught philosophy at Harvard University from 1889 to 1912. Then he moved to England. In 1932, Santayana finally settled in Rome, where he died. His other works include the four-volume *The Realms of Being* (1928-1940), *Character and Opinion in the United States* (1920), and *Persons and Places* (1943). His only novel is *The Last Puritan* (1935). A collection of his poems and two plays were published in 1953 under the title *The Poet's Testament.* EUGENE T. ADAMS

**SANTEE-COOPER PROJECT** is an electric-power and navigation development 36 miles north of Charleston, S.C. The project consists of two dams. The $7\frac{1}{2}$-mile-long Santee Dam forms Lake Marion. Pinopolis Dam and Dikes, about 28 miles long, forms Lake Moultrie. The two lakes are connected by a $7\frac{1}{2}$-mile-long diversion canal. This canal turns the waters of Lake Marion into Lake Moultrie, through an electric powerhouse, and then through the Tailrace Canal into the Cooper River. The $57 million Santee-Cooper Project was built by the South Carolina Public Service Authority. The project was started in 1938 and went into operation in 1941. See also SOUTH CAROLINA (color map: Historic South Carolina). T. W. MERMEL

**SANTEE RIVER.** See SOUTH CAROLINA (Rivers).

**SANTIAGO** (pop. 2,447,741; alt. 1,795 ft.), is the capital and largest city of Chile. It is the commercial, industrial, and cultural center of the nation. The city lies in a valley between the Andes Mountains and the Pacific coastal range, about 70 miles southeast of Valparaiso (see CHILE [political map]).

Santiago's many parks help make it one of the loveliest cities in South America. Santiago produces over half of Chile's manufactured goods, including leather goods, machinery, paper, processed foods, and textiles. Catholic University, the National Institute, and the University of Chile are located there. Pedro de Valdivia founded Santiago in 1541. ROBERT N. BURR

See also CHILE (pictures); LIBRARY (picture: National Library of Chile).

**SANTIAGO** (pop. 83,523; alt. 455 ft.), also called SANTIAGO DE LOS CABALLEROS, is the second largest city in the Dominican Republic. It lies on the Yaque del Norte River, 85 miles northwest of Santo Domingo (see DOMINICAN REPUBLIC [map]). Santiago is a trading center for cacao, rice, and tobacco of the northern lowlands. THOMAS G. MATHEWS

**SANTIAGO, BATTLE OF.** See SPANISH-AMERICAN WAR (Chief Events).

**SANTIAGO CONFERENCE.** See PAN-AMERICAN CONFERENCES.

**SANTIAGO DE CUBA,** *sahn TYAH goh day KOO bah* (pop. 231,000; alt. 20 ft.), lies at the foot of the Sierra Maestra range on the southeast coast of Cuba. It is 460 miles southeast of Havana. For location, see CUBA (color map). Santiago serves as the center of Cuba's mining industry. It is a shipping center for iron, manganese, sugar, coffee, and tobacco. Morro Castle, one of its noted landmarks, was built to defend its harbor from British and French pirates. In 1898, during the Spanish-American War, a United States fleet destroyed most of the Spanish fleet near Santiago harbor.    OTIS P. STARKEY

**SANTO DOMINGO,** *SAHN toh doh MING goh* (pop. 367,053; alt. 85 ft.), is the capital and largest city of the Dominican Republic. It lies at the mouth of the Ozama River on the southern coast of the country (see DOMINICAN REPUBLIC [map]). Santo Domingo is an important seaport and airport. Its factories produce sugar products, textiles, and liquor. Resort hotels and fine beaches make Santo Domingo a popular tourist spot.

Santo Domingo is the oldest European-founded city in the Western Hemisphere. Bartholomew Columbus, a brother of Christopher Columbus, founded it in 1496 as *Nueva Isabela*. The Cathedral of Santo Domingo, completed about 1540, is the oldest church in the West Indies. Some historians say it holds Christopher Columbus' tomb.

A hurricane destroyed most of the city in 1930. It was rebuilt along modern lines, but many of its buildings are in the Spanish colonial style. An impressive example is the Alcazar, the rebuilt palace of Viceroy Diego Columbus, Christopher's son. From 1936 to 1961, under dictator Rafael Trujillo, the city was called CIUDAD TRUJILLO.    THOMAS G. MATHEWS

**SANTO DOMINGO, UNIVERSITY OF,** in Santo Domingo, Dominican Republic, is the oldest university in the Western Hemisphere. It was established by Pope Paul III in 1538 as the University of Saint Thomas Aquinas. The Dominican Order of Preachers operated the school, granting degrees to lay students as well as the clergy. The university became a lay institution in 1815. It has received government support since 1944. About 3,800 men and women study law, philosophy, medicine, business, engineering, agronomy, architecture, and veterinary medicine there.    EMILE DELAVENAY

**SANTO TOMÁS, UNIVERSITY OF.** See PHILIPPINES (Education).

**SANTOS,** *SAN tus* (pop. 300,000; alt. 40 ft.), is the port for the city of São Paulo, Brazil. It lies on the Atlantic Ocean about 200 miles southwest of Rio de Janeiro. For location, see BRAZIL (political map). Santos is the greatest coffee-shipping port in Brazil. Its beaches attract many tourists. It was founded between 1532 and 1536.    MANOEL CARDOZO

**SANTOS-DUMONT,** *SAHN toozh DYOO MAWNG,* **ALBERTO** (1873-1932), was an aviation pioneer in both lighter-than-air and heavier-than-air machines. He used his wealth to promote aviation and to help promising inventors.

Santos-Dumont was born in Brazil of wealthy parents, and was educated mostly in France. In 1898, he flew a cigar-shaped gas bag propelled by two small engines driving a single propeller. He built a box-kite airplane in 1905. Each wing was a box-kite, and a third box-kite was suspended ahead of the aircraft to provide control. In 1906, he flew it for eight seconds in the first heavier-than-air flight in France. The main advantage of the box-kite construction was its light weight, about half that of the first Wright brothers' biplane. One of his most lasting contributions was the use of wheeled undercarriages.    ROBERT B. HOTZ

See also AIRPLANE (Landing Gear).

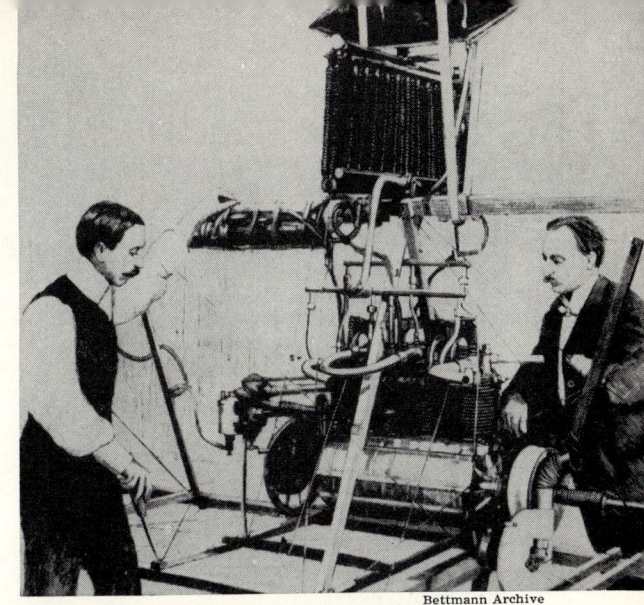

Bettmann Archive

**Alberto Santos-Dumont,** *left,* experimented with motor-powered dirigibles and later built the first successful French airplane.

**SÃO FRANCISCO, RIO,** *sown fran SEESH koo,* also called SAN FRANCISCO, RIO, is a river of eastern Brazil. It rises in the state of Minas Gerais. It flows northeast, then eastward, to form the boundary between the states of Bahia and Pernambuco. Then the river turns to the southeast, and empties into the Atlantic Ocean, about 1,800 miles from its source. As it leaves the mountains in Minas Gerais, it plunges over falls and rapids. Then it is a broad, navigable stream for 1,000 miles of its middle course. But 200 miles from the Atlantic, it again becomes swift and rocky as it tumbles over rapids and a magnificent falls called Paulo Afonso. See also RIVER (chart: Longest Rivers).    MARGUERITE UTTLEY

**SÃO MIGUEL ISLAND,** *sown me GEHL,* is the largest island of the Azores. It covers 292 square miles and has a population of 168,610. Ponta Delgada is the chief city (see PONTA DELGADA). The island produces cereals, fruits, potatoes, tea, tobacco, and wine.

**SÃO PAULO,** *sown POW loo* (pop. 5,383,000), is Brazil's largest city and its greatest industrial center. It is located at 2,545 feet above sea level in southeastern Brazil, about 200 miles southwest of Rio de Janeiro (see BRAZIL [political map]).

The metropolitan area, with its modern skyscrapers, covers 700 square miles. São Paulo sends large quantities of coffee by rail to Santos, Brazil's leading coffee port, 33 miles away. Industries in the city process food, and manufacture appliances, chemicals, footwear, furniture, iron and steel, machinery, motor vehicles, plastics, pottery, and textiles.

Interesting places to visit include the government palace, the University of São Paulo, the Municipal Library, and the Paulista Museum. The Jesuits founded the city in 1554, on the site of an Indian village. The city did not become important commercially until 1885, when coffee cultivation spread throughout São Paulo state. Since 1950, thousands of Europeans and Asians have come to live in São Paulo, making it one of the world's fastest-growing cities.    MANOEL CARDOZO

See also BRAZIL (picture: In the Large Cities).

**SÃO TIAGO.** See CAPE VERDE ISLANDS.

105

## SOME FACTS ABOUT SAP

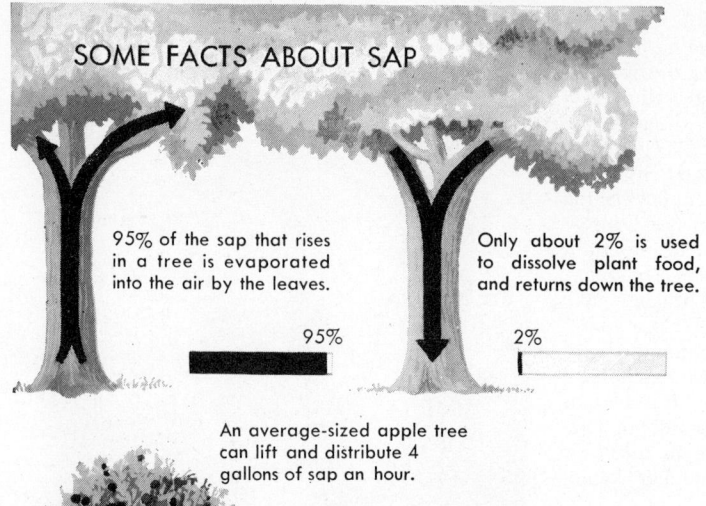

95% of the sap that rises in a tree is evaporated into the air by the leaves.

Only about 2% is used to dissolve plant food, and returns down the tree.

An average-sized apple tree can lift and distribute 4 gallons of sap an hour.

The force that raises the sap is so great that it could lift the fluid to the top of a tree more than 300 feet high.

A tapped maple tree will give more than 100 drops of sap each minute.

**SÃO TOMÉ AND PRÍNCIPE,** *SOWN too MEH, PREEN see pih* (pop. 62,000), is an overseas province of Portugal and a base for trade with West Africa. It lies in the Gulf of Guinea. For location, see AFRICA (political map). The province consists of São Tomé Island and Príncipe Island, and covers 372 square miles. The city of São Tomé is the capital of the province.

See also PRÍNCIPE ISLAND.

**SAÔNE RIVER,** *sohn,* is a waterway in eastern France. It rises near the foothills of the Vosges Mountains and flows for 268 miles. The Saône, most important branch of the Rhône River, joins it at Lyon. Light ships can sail on it for 232 miles. The industrial city, Chalon-sur-Saône, lies on its banks. Canals connect the Saône River to the Moselle, Marne, Yonne, and Loire rivers. For location, see FRANCE (physical map).

**SAP,** in botany, means the liquid in the stems and roots of plants. There are really two kinds of sap. One kind is water, with dissolved minerals, that travels from the roots to the leaves. It moves through a layer in the stem and trunk called the *xylem*. The other kind of sap is water carrying dissolved plant foods. It moves from the leaves to parts of the plant where it is to be used or stored. This sap travels in a special layer called the *phloem*.

**How Sap Moves.** The xylem sap movement begins near the growing tip of the root, where water and minerals enter the plant. From the region of the root hairs, the water with the minerals dissolved in it moves toward the inside of the root by diffusion. When it reaches the xylem layer in the root, it moves up the root into the xylem of the stem. Finally it passes to the leaves. The force that causes the sap to rise is, to a great extent, a pull from above. The pull results from the *transpiration* (evaporation) of the water from the leaves.

In young trees, the water moves through the xylem in all parts of the wood. But in old trees, the only part of the xylem that transports sap is the part near the bark. This part of the wood is called *sapwood*. The part through which the sap does not move is called the *heartwood*. It is usually possible to tell these two kinds of wood from each other by their color. Sapwood is usually light in color, while heartwood is usually much darker.

The leaves are the organs of the plant which manufacture carbohydrates from carbon dioxide and water. The plant then uses the carbohydrates as food. Carbohydrates dissolve in water, and form the other kind of sap. In the stems and trunk of the plant, this stream of sap moves downward. The force which causes the downward movement of phloem sap is probably the high osmotic pressure. This pressure results from the movement of water into the sugar-rich cells of the leaves. The pressure passes to the conducting cells of the phloem, and a column of sap is forced downward. At certain times of the year, in some trees, the stream moving upward may also contain carbohydrates. An example is the sugar maple, whose rising sap contains sugar.

**Uses of Sap.** The sap of many plants is valuable to man. Most sugar sold in stores is made from the sap of sugar cane. The sugar maple is also a source of sugar and syrup. Plants contain other liquids that are not true saps, in the botanical sense. The milky juice of milkweed is an example. Many milky juices have great value. The milky juice of rubber trees becomes the raw material for natural rubber. Gums and resins also are valuable plant juices. ARTHUR W. GALSTON

**Related Articles** in WORLD BOOK include:
Gum            Phloem     Rubber (Natural Rubber)
Maple Sugar    Resin      Turpentine
Osmosis

# SAPPHIRE

The White-Fronted Sapajou Monkey is regarded by some as one of the most intelligent members of the monkey family.

**SAPAJOU,** *SAP uh joo,* is a South American monkey. It is one of a large group of New World monkeys called *capuchins.* The name *sapajou* is sometimes used to mean the whole group of *capuchins.* The *white-fronted sapajou* lives in forests of the Amazon River Basin. It has a white forehead and a light-brown body.

**Scientific Classification.** Sapajous and other capuchins belong to the New World monkey family, *Cebidae.* Capuchins make up the genus *Cebus.* GEORGE B. SCHALLER

See also CAPUCHIN.

**SAPIR,** *suh PEER,* **EDWARD** (1884-1939), was an American anthropologist. He won fame for his studies of American Indian languages and for his development of general linguistics. He taught at the University of Chicago and Yale University, and wrote *Language, an Introduction to the Study of Speech* (1921). Sapir was born at Lauenberg, Germany. DAVID B. STOUT

See also LINGUISTICS (The Structuralists).

**SAPODILLA,** *SAP oh DILL uh,* is an important tropical tree. It produces the chicle used to make chewing gum. It also grows a delicious fruit. The sapodilla is native to tropical America. It now also grows in southern Florida, India, Ceylon, and many other parts of the world.

The sapodilla tree is an evergreen and grows 50 to 60 feet high. The bark contains a milky juice that is boiled down to make chicle. The fruit measures about three inches across, and may be round, oval, or cone-shaped. It has a reddish-brown skin, and black seeds. Its thick, soft, yellowish-brown pulp tastes somewhat like a pear

and smells like flowers. It is an important food in tropical America. The sapodilla tree is sometimes called the *sapota.*

**Scientific Classification.** The sapodilla belongs to the sapodilla family, *Sapotacae.* It is classified as genus *Achras,* species *A. sapota.* JULIAN C. CRANE

See also CHICLE; CHEWING GUM.

**SAPONIN.** See SOAPBERRY.

**SAPOTA TREE.** See CHICLE; SAPODILLA.

**SAPPHIRA.** See ANANIAS.

**SAPPHIRE,** *SAF ire,* is a transparent gem, a variety of the mineral *corundum.* The best-known variety of sapphires has blue tints caused by impurities of iron and titanium, but sapphires exist in all the colors of the rainbow. The colored varieties are known as fancy sapphires, except the red gems, which are rubies.

The best sapphires once came from Kashmir, in northern India. Jewelers consider the typical cornflower blue color of Kashmir sapphires as the measure of fine color in a sapphire. Large stones nearly equal a fine diamond in value. The highly prized *star sapphires* have a crystal structure that reflects light in starlike rays. This effect is called *asterism.* The largest blue star sapphire in the world, called the *Star of India,* is on exhibit in the American Museum of Natural History in New York City. It weighs 563 carats (see CARAT). The gem was stolen in 1964, but was later recovered.

The best sapphires now come from Burma and Thailand. Those from Ceylon are often pale. Australian sapphires have a rich blue color in natural light, but appear black in artificial light. They have less value

**The Sapodilla Tree** is a tropical plant that has leathery evergreen leaves and apple-shaped fruits. The flesh of the fruit is thick, soft, and sweet, and is delicious to eat.

# SAPPHO

than Kashmir stones, which keep their color at night.

Large, heavy sapphires have weighed as much as 2 pounds. The sapphire is second only to the diamond in hardness. For this reason, the stone is often used as an abrasive or polishing agent. It is also used as a needle in playing phonograph records. The sapphire is the birthstone for September. Ancient peoples regarded it as a love charm. FREDERICK H. POUGH

See also CORUNDUM; GEM (color picture); RUBY.

**SAPPHO,** *SAF oh,* a Greek woman poet, lived about 600 B.C. Plato called her the *Tenth Muse,* and she is supposed to be the greatest woman poet the world has known. Little of her poetry has survived. We have only two short lyrics and odd lines quoted by ancient critics and grammarians. These show intense but controlled emotion expressed in language which seems wholly natural. Later poets, especially the Romans Catullus and Horace, imitated her special meter, the Sapphic.

Sappho lived at Mitylene (now Mitilíni) on the island of Lesbos. There, she led a circle of young women who were her disciples. She was married, and had a daughter named Cleis. MOSES HADAS

**SAPPORO,** *sahp POH roh* (pop. 815,000; alt. 245 ft.), is the capital of Hokkaido, Japan's northernmost island. It lies on the western part of the island near Otaru Bay. For the location of Sapporo, see JAPAN (political map).

Sapporo was laid out in 1871, and was patterned after western cities. It is important because it serves as the island's manufacturing and cultural center. Products of the island include hemp cloth and rubber goods, as well as such food products as condensed milk and processed soybeans. Sapporo's chief attractions include Hokkaido University and the botanical gardens, which specialize in alpine flora. Residents and visitors enjoy the ski slopes, located in the suburbs, and Jozānkei hot springs, 11 miles southwest.

**SAPROPHYTE,** *SAP roh fite,* is a living thing that must get its food from dead plants or animals. The saprophytes are chiefly plants that lack the green substance chlorophyll. Plants with chlorophyll can manufacture their food from water and the carbon dioxide of the air, by the process of photosynthesis (see PHOTOSYNTHESIS). Saprophytes must depend on food that has already been made by some other living thing. The best-known saprophytes are the plants known as fungi. They include mushrooms, molds, mildew, bacteria, rusts, and smuts. Partial saprophytes may live part of their lives on dead plants and animals, and part on living plants and animals. Some bacteria are partial saprophytes. Animals or plants that live on living organisms are *parasites.* WILLIAM C. BEAVER

See also CHLOROPHYLL; FUNGI.

**SAPSUCKER** is one of a group of birds of the woodpecker family. It lives only in North America. Sapsuckers are so called because part of their diet includes sap from trees. They get this sap by making holes in the bark. They also feed on ants and wild fruit. The common sapsucker in the East is the *yellow-bellied sapsucker.* The male has a bright scarlet crown and throat, and black upper parts with white markings. This sapsucker nests in the northern United States and Canada. In the winter, it flies as far south as Central America. It builds

John H. Gerard

**The Yellow-Bellied Sapsucker** drills so many holes in the bark of tree trunks that its work often kills small trees.

its nest in holes in trees. The female lays 3 to 7 eggs which are pure white. The western *red-breasted sapsucker* lives on the Pacific Coast. The adults of both sexes have the crown, throat, and breast entirely red. The *Williamson's sapsucker* is found in mountain regions of the western United States.

Sapsuckers have much the same habits as woodpeckers, but are sometimes harmful, as they injure trees and wood. When large numbers of sapsuckers are found in any locality, it may be necessary to drive them away. The Williamson's sapsucker, however, does little damage to trees.

**Scientific Classification.** Sapsuckers are members of the woodpecker family, *Picidae.* The yellow-bellied sapsucker is genus *Sphyrapicus,* species *S. varius.* Williamson's sapsucker is *S. thyroideus.* HERBERT FRIEDMANN

**SAPWOOD.** See SAP; TREE (color diagram: Parts of a Tree; picture: Tree Rings Tell a Story).

**SARABAND.** See DANCING (The Renaissance).

**SARACEN,** *SAR uh sun,* was the name used first in the Middle Ages for the Moslems who invaded and occupied large parts of the Christian world in Asia, Africa, and Europe. This occupation took place during the 600's and 700's. The Saracens included the people of Palestine and Syria, Arab Moors who set up the Spanish kingdom in the 700's, and Seljuk Turks who fought the Crusaders. The Greeks and Romans first used the term *Saracen* to describe the wandering Arab tribes of the Syro-Arabian Desert. WILLIAM C. BARK

**SARAGAT,** *sah rah GAHT,* **GIUSEPPE** (1898-    ), became president of Italy in 1964. Parliament elected Saragat, a Socialist, after a bitter debate between liberal and conservative members.

Saragat joined the Socialist Party in 1922, and was a member of its executive committee by 1925. He represented the party in the cabinet formed in 1944. In 1946, he was named president of the Constituent Assembly that wrote a new constitution. Saragat broke with the Socialist Party in 1947 after it became connected with the Communist Party. He formed his own party, which later became the Democratic Socialist Party. He served as deputy premier from 1946 to 1948 and from 1954 to 1957. Saragat was born and educated in Turin.

**SARAGOSSA,** SAR uh GAHS uh, or ZARAGOZA, SAH rah GOH thah (pop. 343,468; alt. 820 ft.), is a trading center in northeastern Spain. The city has metalworks, sugar refineries, chemical plants, and factories that manufacture electrical equipment, agricultural machinery, and furniture. For location, see SPAIN (map).

The central part of Saragossa is a district of ancient, crowded lanes and dilapidated houses. An attractive newer section has grown up around the old quarter.

The city's name comes from *Caesarea Augusta*, which was the name Emperor Augustus gave to the settlement in 25 B.C., when he made it a Roman colony. Saragossa was the capital of the old kingdom of Aragon from the 1100's to the 1400's. WALTER C. LANGSAM

**SARAH.** See ISHMAEL; ISAAC.

**SARAH LAWRENCE COLLEGE.** See UNIVERSITIES AND COLLEGES (table).

**SARAJEVO,** sah RAH yeh vaw (pop. 206,000; alt. 1,690 ft.), is a trading center in Yugoslavia. For location, see YUGOSLAVIA (color map). On June 28, 1914, the Austrian Archduke Francis Ferdinand and his wife were assassinated in Sarajevo. This was the immediate event that started World War I. See also SERBIA; WORLD WAR I (introduction). HIBBERD V. B. KLINE, JR.

**SARAN** is a synthetic plastic material manufactured as a thin flexible film or sheet, or as a textile fiber. It is also known as VELON and CRYOVAC. Its chemical name is *vinylidene chloride polymer*. Saran film is strong, transparent, and moistureproof.

Because of these characteristics, it is often used as a wrapping for meat, fruit, and vegetables. Saran fibers and yarns make excellent belts, insect screens, and automobile seat covers. Commercial methods for making Saran were developed by the Dow Chemical Company in the 1940's. ERNEST R. KASWELL

**SARANAC LAKES** are the Upper Saranac, Middle Saranac, and Lower Saranac. The lakes lie in the Adirondack Mountains of northeastern New York. The Upper Saranac is the largest. It is about 8 miles long, and nearly 2 miles wide in places. The lake contains brook, lake, and rainbow trout; and whitefish. The Middle Saranac, usually known simply as Lake Saranac, is nearly 3 miles long and over 1 mile wide. The Lower Saranac is over 5 miles long and over a mile wide. These lakes, all within a few miles of each other, total nearly 14 square miles in area. The action of huge glaciers created them thousands of years ago. The rugged beauty of the Adirondack Mountains region attracts tourists and sportsmen. WILLIAM E. YOUNG

See also NEW YORK (Places to Visit).

**SARASOTA,** Fla. (pop. 34,083; alt. 5 ft.), lies on Sarasota Bay in southwestern Florida (see FLORIDA [political map]). Chief industries are agriculture, livestock raising, and tourism. The Ringling Brothers and Barnum & Bailey circus had winter quarters there from 1927 to 1960. Sarasota still has the John and Mable Ringling Art Museum, and the Circus Hall of Fame. It is also the home of New College. Scottish families founded Sarasota in the 1880's. It has a council-manager government. KATHRYN ABBEY HANNA

**SARATOGA.** See AIRCRAFT CARRIER.

**SARATOGA, BATTLE OF.** See REVOLUTIONARY WAR IN AMERICA (Defeat at Saratoga).

**SARATOGA NATIONAL HISTORICAL PARK.** See NATIONAL PARK (National Historical Parks).

**SARATOGA SPRINGS,** N.Y. (pop. 17,288; alt. 569 ft.), is a health resort and horse-racing center. It lies in the southeastern foothills of the Adirondack Mountains. For location, see NEW YORK (political map).

In 1910, the state took over the city's mineral springs. The National Museum of Racing in Saratoga Springs has paintings, trophies, and other horse-racing exhibits. Skidmore College is located in the city. Saratoga National Historical Park is nearby. The city built a $4,100,000 cultural center in the mid-1960's that is a summer home for the Philadelphia Orchestra and the New York City ballet. Saratoga Springs has a commission form of government. WILLIAM E. YOUNG

**SARATOV,** suh RAH tuf (pop. 665,000; alt. 250 ft.), is one of the chief ports on the Volga River. For location, see RUSSIA (political map). It stands about 450 miles southeast of Moscow.

**SARAWAK,** suh RAH wahk, is a state in the Federation of Malaysia. The state lies on the northwestern coast of the island of Borneo. Sarawak has an area of 48,342 square miles, and a population of 990,000. For location, see INDONESIA (color map). Sarawak has a tropical climate. Its products include sago palm, timber, rubber, pepper, coconuts, and camphor. It has valuable coal and oil deposits. Kuching is the capital.

Most of the people of Sarawak are Dyaks, Malays, Melanaus, and Muruts. Many Chinese and a few Europeans also live there.

James Brooke, an Englishman, and his heirs ruled Sarawak as the *white rajahs* for a hundred years. Brooke helped the Sultan of Brunei put down a rebellion in 1839 and 1840. The sultan gave Sarawak, which was part of his land, to Brooke. The Japanese took Sarawak in World War II. In 1946, the ruling rajah ceded Sarawak to England. Sarawak became part of the Federation of Malaysia in 1963. JOHN F. CADY

See also BORNEO; DYAK; KUCHING; MALAYSIA.

**SARAZEN, GENE.** See GOLF (Golf Immortals).

**SARCASM.** See HUMOR (The Types of Humor).

**SARCODINA.** See PROTOZOAN (Kinds).

**SARCOLACTIC ACID.** See LACTIC ACID.

**SARCOPHAGUS,** sahr KAHF uh gus, is a stone coffin. The ancient Egyptians probably first made a sarcophagus for the burial of a king. Some Egyptian sarcophagi were shaped like small houses, others as ovals or oblongs. Many were covered inside and out with inscriptions and figures of gods intended to protect the body from decay. The Etruscans made sarcophagi of terra cotta. The Romans used marble or stone. The Greeks often decorated their coffins with carved bas-reliefs.

The best-known modern sarcophagi include those of George Washington in Mount Vernon, Napoleon Bonaparte in Paris, the Duke of Wellington in London, and the tomb of V. I. Lenin in Moscow. KEITH C. SEELE

See also NAPOLEON I (picture); TOMB; SCULPTURE (picture: The Alexander Sarcophagus).

**Sardine Fishermen** off the coast of California scoop up part of their day's catch, *above*. The abundant California sardine, or Pacific pilchard, *below*, grows about 10 inches long.

United Press Int.

**SARDINE,** *sahr DEEN*, is a small fish of the herring family (see HERRING). It is also known as the *pilchard*. Sardines are found in great numbers along the coasts of Europe and North America. The name *sardine* comes from the fact that this fish was first caught off the island of Sardinia, near Italy. Today, sardines can be found along the coast of the Mediterranean Sea, in the Bay of Biscay near France, and along the coast of the English Channel. Fishermen catch sardines off the coasts of California, Oregon, Washington, Baja California, British Columbia, and Japan. The California, or Pacific Coast, sardine is about 10 inches long and weighs about four ounces. The upper parts of its body appear dark blue and the lower parts silvery.

Sardines eat the tiny one-celled plants and animals that live in the ocean. They usually swim in large groups called *schools*. In the daytime, sardines can be seen in the water as tiny black spots, causing ripples. At night, they may glow in the dark water.

Sardines are important as food and for the oil they contain. Fishermen catch them in large nets. Some of the sardine catch goes to canneries. Industry uses sardine oil in varnish, paint, margarine, and many toilet preparations. Some sardines are dried, pounded into powder, and placed in sacks. Called *fish meal*, this is used for chicken feed and fertilizer. Persons in the southern part of France consider sardines preserved in red wine a delicacy.

The sardine industry ranks as one of the biggest fishing industries in California and British Columbia. Young herring, menhaden, or other small fishes are sometimes sold on the market as sardines.

**Scientific Classification.** Sardines belong to the herring family, *Clupeidae*. The European sardine is genus *Sardina*, species *S. pilchardus*. The Pacific sardine is *Sardinella sagax*.   LEONARD P. SCHULTZ

**SARDINIA,** *sahr DIN ih uh*, or in Italian, SARDEGNA, is an Italian island in the Mediterranean west of the mainland of Italy and over 100 miles from it. The nearest land is the French island of Corsica, nine miles north across the Strait of Bonifacio. Sardinia is second largest of the Mediterranean islands. Only Sicily is larger. Sardinia is about 166 miles long from north to south. It has an area of 9,301 square miles. This island and some small ones nearby form the region of Sardinia, which has a population of 1,448,011. For location, see ITALY (physical map).

**Mountainous Area.** Nine-tenths of Sardinia is mountainous. The only important area of lowlands is the southwestern plain. Human settlement in the mountains is difficult because the steep slopes and heavy rainfall produce landslides and floods. The agricultural improvement of the small areas of level land has been retarded in places by malarial swamps and elsewhere by lack of moisture during the hot, dry summers. These problems are gradually being overcome by drainage projects and by irrigation. In 1957, experts predicted that these projects would increase the land value five or six times and provide employment for many workers. The most important agricultural products include almonds, grapes, herbs, lemons, olives, oranges, and wheat. Many goats and sheep are raised. Tunny and lobster are brought in to local fisheries. Sardinia is also one of Italy's leading cork producers. Ancient mines in the mountains still produce copper, iron, lead, lignite, manganese, silver, zinc, and other minerals.

Sardinia is divided into the provinces of Sassari, Nuorò, and Cagliari. The chief cities bear these same names. The city of Cagliari is also the capital of the region. Even these settlements have little industry. Most of the products, including fish, goatskins, mineral ores, olives, and wine, are exported with a minimum of processing or manufacturing.

**History.** Sardinia has been invaded and ruled by first one power and then another. These have included Carthage, Rome, the Vandals, Byzantium, the Moslems, the city-states of Pisa and Genoa, Aragon, Piedmont, and finally unified Italy. Sardinia preserves many ancient customs, traditions, and costumes.

During World War II, Sardinia became an important airplane and naval base for Fascist Italy. In 1943 American fighter planes smashed two convoys at Sardinia, and destroyed many airfields. American Flying Fortress attacks later damaged more Italian vessels lying in Sardinia's naval base. But the war made little permanent impression on Sardinia.   BENJAMIN WEBB WHEELER

See also CAGLIARI; SARDINIA, KINGDOM OF.

**SARDINIA, KINGDOM OF,** became the nucleus of united Italy. The kingdom was founded in 1720 when the Duchy of Savoy was united with the island of Sardinia, with the Alpine fortresses of Aosta, Fenestrelle, Pinerolo, and Saluzzo, and with Montferrato, a *marquisate*, or area governed by a marquis. Duke Victor Amadeus II of Savoy was made the first monarch of the kingdom of Sardinia.

Pinned between French, Austrian, and Spanish powers, Sardinia inherited the geographic liabilities of old Savoy. The kingdom allied itself with Austria in the 1700's. Napoleon annexed Sardinia to France in 1802. After his defeat in 1815, it was restored, and Genoa and Liguria were added to it. It became the foremost independent state in Italy, but Austria dominated affairs in most of the peninsula.

When Charles Albert became king of Sardinia in 1831, it became the hope of Italy. He granted his people a new constitution in 1848. During the revolution against Austria in that year, Charles tried to drive the enemy from Lombardy and Venetia. Indecision cost him the victory and his throne. His son, Victor Emmanuel II, succeeded him. Through the efforts of his great prime minister, Camillo Benso, Count di Cavour, the movement for unifying Italy succeeded.

Cavour obtained an alliance with France and provoked war with Austria in 1859. After the bloody battles of Magenta and Solferino, Cavour resigned his office when France made a separate peace with Austria at Villafranca before Italy had been liberated. But all was not lost. Popular assemblies in Modena, Parma, and the Romagna voted union with Sardinia in 1860. Giuseppe Garibaldi and his glorious "thousand" volunteers brought southern Italy into the nation. In 1861, Victor Emmanuel II was proclaimed king of a united Italy that included Sardinia. WILLIAM H. MAEHL

See also CAVOUR, COUNT DI; ITALY (History); map: Italy—Late 1800's); SARDINIA; VICTOR EMMANUEL (II).

**SARDIS,** an ancient city near present-day Izmir, Turkey, was capital of the kingdom of Lydia. The oldest remains of Sardis go back to the 1300's B.C., but indicate that the city is older. Persians conquered Sardis in 546 B.C. The city was later destroyed and rebuilt several times, until its final destruction by Sassanian Persians about A.D. 615. JACOB J. FINKELSTEIN

**SARDIS DAM** is one of the largest earth-filled flood-control dams in the United States. About 16,450,000 cubic yards of material went into its construction. Sardis, one of the largest dams in the U.S., stands on the Little Tallahatchie River, in northwestern Mississippi. Sardis Dam chiefly serves flood-control purposes. The dam is 118 feet high, almost a quarter of a mile wide at its base, and 15,300 feet long along the top.

Sardis Reservoir, behind the dam, is over 30 miles long. The United States Army Corps of Engineers completed the Sardis Dam in 1940 at a cost of about $13,300,000. T. W. MERMEL

See also DAM.

**SARDONYX,** *SAHR doh nicks*, is a form of quartz used in rings and other jewelry. It is a variety of agate and is cut from flat layers of banded masses of agate. It is found in Arabia, Brazil, India, Ireland, Israel, Scotland, and Uruguay. Sardonyx is one of the cheaper gem stones. Jewelers cut it flat, convex, or dome-shaped to bring out its full color of brown, golden, or blood red. Sardonyx is one of the birthstones for August. Saint John called it the fifth of the foundation stones in his description of the Holy City (Rev. 21:20). Many ancient myths and legends were built around the sardonyx. See also CAMEO; GEM (color picture); ONYX. FREDERICK H. POUGH

**SARDOU,** *SAHR DOO,* **VICTORIEN** (1831-1908), was one of the most successful French playwrights of his time. His light comedies, such as *Diplomacy* and *A Scrap of Paper*, were popular for years. He was a master of the *well-made play*, which emphasized plot construction.

Sardou was born in Paris. His dramas earned him a large fortune, and election to the French Academy in 1878. His *La Tosca* became the basis of Giacomo Puccini's opera of the same name. JOHN W. GASSNER

**SARGASSO SEA** is an irregular oval-shaped area of the North Atlantic Ocean. Its center is about 2,000 miles west of the Canary Islands. It lies roughly between the 20th and 40th parallels of north latitude, and between the 35th and 75th meridians west of Greenwich. No land boundaries of any kind mark off this body of water from the rest of the open ocean. It is set apart only by the presence of marine plants, or seaweed, which float on its surface. It is also a region of slow ocean currents surrounded by a boundary of rapidly moving currents, such as the Gulf Stream and the North Equatorial Current. The Sargasso Sea derives its name from *sargaço*, one of the Portuguese words for seaweed. The word originally meant grape, because the small floats on some seaweeds resemble grapes. Christopher Columbus is given credit for the first reliable report on this region. He sounded the Sargasso Sea in 1492 to make sure that no rocks lay beneath the weeds.

### The Legends of the Sea

The early navigators who sailed their small ships to North America saw the Sargasso Sea as patches of gulfweed that seemed to form wide-spreading meadows. Soon there were legends and myths about the region which told of large islands of thickly matted seaweed inhabited by huge monsters of the deep. Poets and novelists used their imaginations in describing the sea. They pictured a blanket of netted seaweed from which no ship could escape, once it became entangled in the weed. They described many of the ghost ships of the past as huddled together in a weaving, rotting mass. Shapeless hulks of ancient galleons, covered with weeds and barnacles, were pictured lying beneath the waters of this mysterious sea. The passing years contributed skeletons of slave ships, then of pirate ships, and later of the gallant ships of Revolutionary War days. Wrecks of smart clipper ships and the latest doomed ships completed the legendary collection.

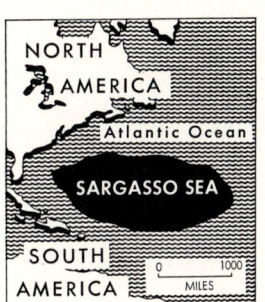

### The Facts About the Sea

Present-day explorers of the ocean have changed the picture of the Sargasso Sea. They have shown that its area is about 2 million square miles, and their study has opened up fascinating research problems.

**Origin of the Seaweed.** Scientists believe that the seaweed originally came from the shores of the West Indies, after it had been torn loose by wind and wave. Parts of it became adapted to living and growing in the open sea. The weeds have developed a strange method of reproduction which enables them to multiply and grow without the production of seeds. Waves break off small sections of the mature plants. These fragments then grow into full-size plants in the same way that a cutting from a grape plant grows into a large grapevine. The weeds are supported by small air sacks which resemble tiny grapes, and grow as a part of the weeds. Sargassum weeds grow in many other ocean regions. One variety is used as food in Japan.

Many small marine animals have adapted themselves to growing on and among the weeds in the Sargasso Sea. These animals include tiny crabs, shrimps,

111

## SARGENT, JOHN SINGER

and barnacles. Fish can see at depths as great as 1,200 feet in the Sargasso Sea, the deepest that fish can see anywhere in the oceans. Sargassum fish are difficult to distinguish from Sargassum weeds, because the fish have taken on the colors and patterns of the weeds.

The greatest quantity of seaweed is found in the central part of the Sargasso Sea. It occurs in scattered masses, some a hundred feet in diameter. Wind action forms long strips of the weed, which follow the general direction of the wind. While patches of the weed may cover an acre or more, there are no islands of weeds which extend for miles. Nowhere is the region so thickly covered that the weeds can interfere with the movements of a ship. Sometimes, unusually strong winds or currents cause some of the weeds to drift into the Gulf Stream, and eventually to New England or even Ireland and Norway.

**Waters of the Sea.** The waters of the Sargasso Sea have many distinctive features. The water has an unusually deep blue color; a high salt content (3.7 per cent); a high temperature (up to 83°F.); and extreme clearness. These features result chiefly from the location of the sea and its great depth, averaging over three miles. Also, there are no islands nearby except for Bermuda. WAYNE V. BURT

See also SEAWEED.

**SARGENT, JOHN SINGER** (1856-1925), was an American painter who did his major work in Europe. He lived much of his adult life in England, and today his works hang in the Tate Gallery in London as examples of English painting of the late 1800's.

Sargent established his reputation as a portrait painter, and is best known for his perceptive portraits of fashionable people. Although he might broadly brush in his subjects' clothing or accessories, he captured with remarkable penetration their personalities. His portrait *Madame X* appears in color in the PAINTING article. Other Sargent paintings appear in the HERCULES; HOSEA; and PROPHET articles.

Sargent was born in Florence, Italy, to American parents. He made the first of many trips to the United States in 1876. He studied in Italy and France and his first major exhibition was at the Paris Salon of 1878. Sargent moved to London in 1884 and made England his permanent home although he never became a British subject. During the last dozen years of his life, he virtually gave up portrait painting to paint other more personally satisfying subjects and murals. The Brooklyn Museum has a large collection of his water colors. His murals may be seen at the Boston Public Library.

Sargent received many awards and honors during his lifetime, but his reputation declined after his death. However, since the mid-1950's interest has slowly revived in his work. GEORGE EHRLICH

**SARGENT, SIR MALCOLM** (1895-1967), a British conductor, was appointed conductor in chief of the British Broadcasting Corporation (B.B.C.) orchestra in 1950. This is one of the most important musical posts in Great Britain. Previously he was principal conductor of the Liverpool Philharmonic. Sargent conducted premières of important works by Ralph Vaughan Williams and Sir William Walton. He was born in Lincolnshire. IRVING KOLODIN

**SARGENT, WINTHROP.** See MISSISSIPPI (Territorial Days).

**SARGON,** *SAHR gawn,* is the Biblical form (Isaiah 20) of a name which was applied to three rulers of ancient Mesopotamia (now approximately Iraq). The name meant *declared king,* and it was chosen by the first and third kings precisely because those kings were usurpers, yet tried to deny it. The second king took his name from the first one.

**Sargon of Akkad** was one of the greatest rulers in all antiquity. His exact birth and death dates are still uncertain, but they must have been not less than 4,300 years ago. We know that he ruled for 61 years.

Starting out from the obscure city of Akkad (or Agade) in what is now Iraq, Sargon first conquered all Sumer. He then extended his empire to Persia in the east and to the Mediterranean Sea and Asia Minor in the west. His was the first great empire in history.

Sargon became the first ruler to raise to prominence the Semitic inhabitants of the country. Sargon himself was a Semite. He displaced the older Sumerians, who were of an entirely different racial background. It was because of his great achievements that the whole region came to be known as Akkad, and its Semitic speech as Akkadian, after the small city in which he rose to power. See BABYLONIA (The Semites).

Sargon's many achievements gave rise to various legends. These have been preserved not only in Sargon's Akkadian, but in the languages of the Hurrians, the Elamites, and the Hittites. One legend describes the infant Sargon as being rescued from a basket that had been left in a river, as Moses was some 1,000 years later. See WORLD, HISTORY OF (picture). JOHN W. SNYDER

**Sargon I of Assyria** ruled about 500 years after Sargon of Akkad. His kingdom maintained profitable business colonies in Cappadocia, an area which contained mostly traders and merchants. Little is known about this ruler.

**Sargon II** was one of the last and greatest kings of Assyria. He ruled from 722 to 705 B.C. His many conquests included Babylonia, Armenia, Philistia, and ancient Israel, which was wiped out by its defeat. Sargon built a new capital. The town of Khorsabad now stands on its site in northeast Iraq. Sargon II died in battle in Persia (now Iran). JACOB J. FINKELSTEIN

See also SENNACHERIB.

**SARI.** See INDIA (Clothing).

**SARK,** *sahrk,* is one of the Channel Islands, about 70 miles south of England and 22 miles off the French coast. Sark is over 3 miles long and over 1½ miles wide. It has a population of 560 and an area of 2 square miles.

Sark is the smallest self-governing unit in the United Kingdom. Many bays and coves cut into the coastline. Cliffs rise on all sides of the island. German troops occupied Sark during World War II. See also CHANNEL ISLANDS. FREDERICK G. MARCHAM

**SARMIENTO, DOMINGO FAUSTINO.** See LATIN-AMERICAN LITERATURE; ARGENTINA (Literature).

**SARNIA** (pop. 54,552; alt. 612 ft.), a city in southwestern Ontario, lies opposite Port Huron, Mich. Bridge and tunnel connections link Sarnia with Port Huron. Sarnia lies on the Saint Clair River, at the southern end of Lake Huron. The center of Canada's petrochemical industry, Sarnia has the country's largest oil refinery and synthetic rubber factory. Englishmen first settled the Sarnia area in the 1830's. The city has a council-manager form of government. See ONTARIO (map). D. M. L. FARR

**SARNOFF,** *SAHR nawf,* **DAVID** (1891- ), was one of the first businessmen to see the full possibilities of using radio and television for entertainment. He served as president of the Radio Corporation of America (RCA) from 1930 through 1948. He became chairman of the board in 1947. Sarnoff was born in Minsk, Russia, and came to the United States in 1900. As a messenger boy in 1906 for the Commercial Cable Company, he learned the Morse code. He later became a wireless operator for the Marconi Wireless Telegraph Company. In 1912, he picked up word that the *Titanic* was sinking, and stayed at his station 72 hours, helping to direct ships to the sinking liner. Other wireless stations shut down to avoid interfering with his work.

Sarnoff operated various stations for the company, and studied electrical engineering. By 1917 he was commercial manager of the Marconi Company, which RCA took over two years later. BARNARD HEWITT

**SARONG.** See BATIK (picture).

**SAROS.** See ECLIPSE (Solar Eclipses).

**SAROYAN,** *sah ROH yahn,* **WILLIAM** (1908- ), is one of the most colorful contemporary American writers. His works include short stories, novels, and plays. His style is loose but rhythmic, and the structure of his writing is rather formless. Genuine humor and a sympathetic understanding of human nature lighten the occasional sentimentality of his writing.

Saroyan was born in Fresno, Calif., the son of Armenian immigrants. He received little formal education. He gained immediate fame in 1934 with the publication of his short story "The Daring Young Man on the Flying Trapeze." A book of short stories, *Love, Here Is My Hat,* was published in 1938. He wrote a book of related sketches, *My Name Is Aram* (1940); and a play, *The Time of Your Life* (1939). The play won a Pulitzer prize in 1940, but Saroyan refused to accept it. His novel *The Human Comedy* was made into a motion picture in 1942. Saroyan's next work was a drama, *The Cave Dwellers* (1957). He also wrote *Not Dying* (1963) and *Boys and Girls Together* (1963). GEORGE FREEDLEY

Jerry Bauer, Pix from Publix
**William Saroyan**

**SARTO, ANDREA DEL.** See DEL SARTO, ANDREA.

**SARTO, GIUSEPPE.** See PIUS (Saint Pius X).

**SARTRE,** *SAHR t'r,* **JEAN-PAUL** (1905- ), is a French existentialist philosopher who has expressed his ideas in novels, plays, and short stories, as well as in theoretical works.

The bare existence of things, especially his own existence, fascinates and horrifies Sartre, because there seems to be no reason why anything should exist. In his first novel, *Nausea* (1938), he describes the horror and mystery which a man experiences when he considers the unexplainable fact of a thing's existence.

In his chief philosophical work, *Being and Nothingness* (1943), Sartre investigates the nature and forms of

# SARTRE, JEAN-PAUL

Wide World
**Jean-Paul Sartre**

*existence* or *being*. He claims that human existence, which he calls "being-for-itself," is radically different from the existence of such inanimate objects as tables, which he calls "being-in-itself." Sartre says that only human existence is conscious of itself and of other things. He argues that inanimate objects simply are what they are; however, a man is whatever he chooses to be. Sartre says that a man is not a coward, for example, in the same simple way that a table is only a table. A man is a coward only if he chooses to be one. Sartre says that a man, unlike a table, has no fixed character or "essence" assigned to him. Primarily, man "exists" as the being who must *choose* his own character or "essence." Thus, in his essay *Existentialism and Humanism* (1946), he defines existentialism as the doctrine that, for man, "existence precedes essence." See EXISTENTIALISM.

Sartre believes that man is completely free, but is afraid to recognize this freedom and to accept full responsibility for his behavior, which such freedom implies. Thus, man tends to deceive himself about his true situation. Throughout his philosophical and literary works, Sartre examines and analyzes the varied and subtle forms of *self-deception*.

Sartre criticizes Sigmund Freud's psychoanalytic theory of human behavior and offers his own "existential psychoanalysis." Sartre says that the ultimate motive for all human behavior is the desire to achieve perfect self-sufficiency by becoming the cause of one's own existence. However, he argues that this goal is actually self-contradictory and impossible to attain. Therefore, he considers all human activity ultimately futile. As Sartre says: "Man is a useless passion." Furthermore, he identifies this idea of a perfectly self-sufficient being who is the cause of his own existence as the traditional idea of God. According to Sartre, man ultimately wants to become God, and God cannot possibly exist. In the *Critique of Dialectical Reason* (1964), Sartre presents his political and sociological theories which he considers to be a form of Marxism.

Sartre's plays include *The Flies* (1943), *No Exit* (1945), *Dirty Hands* (1948), and *The Condemned of Altona* (1959). He wrote *The Roads of Freedom,* a sequence of novels including *The Age of Reason* (1945), *The Reprieve* (1945), and *Troubled Sleep* (1949). He applied his psychoanalytic theories in his biographies, *Baudelaire* (1947) and *Saint Genet* (1953). *Words* (1963) is the first installment of his autobiography.

Sartre was born in Paris where he studied at the École Normale Supérieure. During World War II, he fought in the French army and was active in the French resistance. He has been editor of the monthly review *Les Temps Modernes* since he founded it in 1945. In 1964, Sartre was awarded the Nobel prize for literature, which he refused to accept. IVAN SOLL

113

**Vast Wheat Fields Form a Checkered Pattern on the Prairie near Milestone.**

George Hunter, Publix

# SASKATCHEWAN

SASKATCHEWAN, *sass CATCH uh wahn*, one of the Prairie Provinces of Canada, is the greatest wheat-growing region in North America. Saskatchewan farmers produce about three-fifths of Canada's wheat. The province's vast fields of golden wheat gave it the nickname of *Canada's Breadbasket*. Railroads carry huge loads of the grain to Canadian ports for shipment to all parts of the world. The Saskatchewan Wheat Pool is one of the world's largest marketing cooperatives. Its headquarters are in Regina, the province's capital and largest city.

Saskatchewan has over a third of all the farmland in Canada—more than any other province. Saskatchewan's farms are on its flat southern prairies, where most of the people live. Tall grain elevators rise in the hundreds of towns and villages that dot the fertile plains. More of the land is used to raise wheat than any other crop. In many areas, wheat fields extend to the horizon in all directions. Saskatchewan also ranks among the leading provinces and states in the production of barley, flaxseed, and rye. The farmers of Saskatchewan raise

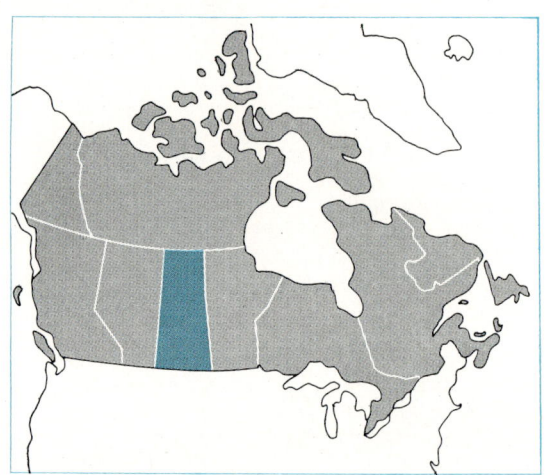

**Saskatchewan (*blue*) is 5th in Size among the Provinces.**

114

large numbers of beef cattle as well as grain crops.

Southern Saskatchewan is much more than a rich farming region. Major oil fields were discovered there during the 1950's. These discoveries brought sudden changes to the prairies. Oil wells and drilling rigs became a common sight in the fields of golden wheat. Today, Saskatchewan produces more than a fourth of Canada's petroleum, and is a leading oil producer of North America. Petroleum refining has become one of Saskatchewan's chief manufacturing industries. Large-scale mining of potash, used in fertilizers, began during the early 1960's. Saskatchewan's potash fields are the largest in the western world. Potash mining is the fastest growing mining industry in the province. By the early 1970's, Saskatchewan is expected to provide more than a third of the world's supply of potash.

Northern Saskatchewan is rocky and covered with forests and lakes. It has the largest lakes in the province. Deposits of copper, gold, uranium, and zinc there help make Saskatchewan a leading producer of these minerals. South of this region are forests of commercially valuable trees, including pines, poplars, and spruces. Caribou, elk, and moose roam the rugged forests. Grayling, pickerel, and trout swim in the sparkling lakes and streams. Many sportsmen from Canada and the United States fly to this rough wilderness to hunt and fish. Indians, *métis* (persons of mixed Indian and white descent), and whites live in small, scattered communities in northern Saskatchewan. They earn their living by fishing, mining, trapping, and woodcutting.

The province took its name from the Saskatchewan River, named by the Cree Indians. They called the winding river *Kisiskadjewan* or *Kis-is-ska-tche-wan*, which means *fast flowing* or *river that turns around when it runs*.

For Saskatchewan's relationship to the other provinces of Canada, see CANADA; CANADA, GOVERNMENT OF; CANADA, HISTORY OF; PRAIRIE PROVINCES.

*The contributors of this article are Stirling King, Political Editor of* The Leader-Post *of Regina; and J. Howard Richards, Professor and Head of the Department of Geography at the University of Saskatchewan.*

---— FACTS IN BRIEF ———

**Capital:** Regina.

**Government:** *Parliament*—Senators, 6; Members of the House of Commons, 13. *Provincial Legislature*—Members of the legislative assembly, 59. *Counties*—none. *Voting Age*—18 (provincial elections); 21 (national elections).

**Area:** 251,700 sq. mi. (including 31,518 sq. mi. of inland water), 5th in size among the provinces. *Greatest Distances*—(north-south) 760 mi.; (east-west) 393 mi.

**Elevation:** *Highest*—4,546 feet above sea level, in the Cypress Hills. *Lowest*—697 feet, at Lake Athabasca.

**Population:** *1966 Census*—955,344, sixth among the provinces; density, 4 persons to the square mile; distribution, 51 per cent rural, 49 per cent urban. *Estimated 1971 Population*—984,000.

**Chief Products:** *Agriculture*—barley, beef cattle, flaxseed, oats, rapeseed, rye, wheat. *Mining*—coal, copper, natural gas, petroleum, potash, sodium sulfate, uranium, zinc. *Manufacturing*—dairy products, flour, meat and meat products, petroleum products. *Forest Products*—lumber, plywood, posts, pulpwood. *Fur Industry*—beavers, minks, muskrats. *Fishing Industry*—lake trout, pickerel, pike, tullibee, whitefish.

**Entered the Dominion** with Alberta on Sept. 1, 1905, as the 8th and 9th provinces.

**Regina Is Saskatchewan's Capital and Largest City.**
Provincial Government of Saskatchewan

# SASKATCHEWAN / Government

**Lieutenant-Governor** of Saskatchewan represents Queen Elizabeth in the province. He is appointed by the governor-general-in-council of Canada. The lieutenant-governor's position is largely honorary, like that of the governor-general.

**Premier** of Saskatchewan is the actual head of the provincial government. The province, like the other provinces and Canada itself, has a *parliamentary* form of government. The premier is a member of the legislative assembly, in which he is the leader of the majority party. The voters elect the premier of Saskatchewan as they do the other members of the assembly. The premier is paid $13,000 a year, in addition to the allowances that he gets as an assembly member. For a list of all the premiers of Saskatchewan, see the *History* section of this article.

The premier presides over the executive council, or cabinet. The council also includes ministers chosen by the premier from among his party's members in the legislative assembly. Each minister directs one or more departments of the provincial government. The executive council, like the premier of Saskatchewan, resigns if it loses the support of a majority of the legislative assembly.

**Legislative Assembly** of Saskatchewan is a one-house legislature that makes the provincial laws. It has 59 members elected from the province's 59 electoral districts. Regina has six districts, Saskatoon has five, and Moose Jaw has two.

The terms of the assembly members may last up to five years. However, the lieutenant-governor, on the advice of the premier, may call for an election before the end of the five-year period. If he does so, all assembly members, including the premier, must run again for office.

**Courts.** The highest court in Saskatchewan is the court of appeal. It consists of the chief justice of Saskatchewan and four *puisne* (associate) judges. The court of queen's bench has a chief justice and seven puisne judges. In addition, 14 district court judges hold sessions in various parts of the province. All these justices and judges are appointed by the governor-general-in-council. They can serve until the age of 75. Provincial authorities appoint the 23 judges of magistrates' courts and the provincial magistrate.

**Local Government.** There are no counties in Saskatchewan. The province has 11 cities and about 120 towns, 360 villages, and 300 rural municipalities. Most of them are governed by councils, elected to terms of one to three years, and headed by a mayor or a *reeve*. These areas make up most of the southern two-fifths of Saskatchewan. The remainder of this southern region consists of 12 unincorporated areas called local improvement districts.

The northern three-fifths of the province has no organized local government. This thinly populated region is called the Northern Administration District of Saskatchewan. The region is administered by the provincial department of natural resources. The department provides a few municipal services to some communities.

**Taxation.** Taxes collected by the provincial government provide about two-thirds of its income. A retail sales tax used for education and health is the greatest source of tax income. Saskatchewan also collects taxes on gasoline, liquor, motor licenses, resources, and tobacco. The other third of Saskatchewan's income comes from federal-provincial tax sharing agreements. By these agreements, the federal government collects individual and corporation income taxes for the province. The province also receives some federal payments, or grants.

**Politics.** The major political parties of Saskatchewan are the Liberal, Co-operative Commonwealth Federation (C.C.F.), and Progressive Conservative parties. The provincial C.C.F. is associated with the New

National Film Board of Canada

**Headquarters** of a division of the Royal Canadian Mounted Police are in Regina. Recruits in the Mounties receive 8 to 10 months of training there.

**The Provincial Coat of Arms**

**Symbols of Saskatchewan.** On the coat of arms, the lion symbolizes the British Crown, and the three wheat sheaves, a resource of the province. Red stands for prairie fires, green for grass, and golden yellow for wheat fields. The arms were adopted in 1906. The province selected a special flag for Saskatchewan's Diamond Jubilee in 1965 and Canada's Centennial of Confederation in 1967. Its symbolism is similar to that of the arms.

**The Provincial Flag**

**The Floral Emblem**
Prairie Lily

**The Provincial Bird**
Prairie Sharp-Tailed Grouse

Democratic party, a national organization. The Progressive Conservative party was formerly named the Conservative party, and today its members are usually called simply Conservatives.

The Liberals controlled the provincial government from 1905, when Saskatchewan became a province, until 1929. The Conservatives then took control, but lost to the Liberals in 1934. The C.C.F., a socialist party, defeated the Liberals in 1944. For a discussion of the 20-year administration of the C.C.F. and of its fall to the Liberals in 1964, see the *History* section of this article.

**Legislative Building** in Regina stands in a 167-acre landscaped park. The building, constructed of Manitoba stone, was completed in 1912. It is 542 feet long and has 265 rooms. The dome reaches a height of 188 feet. Regina has been the capital since Saskatchewan became a province in 1905. The city had previously served as the capital of the North West Territories from 1883 to 1905.

Provincial Government of Saskatchewan

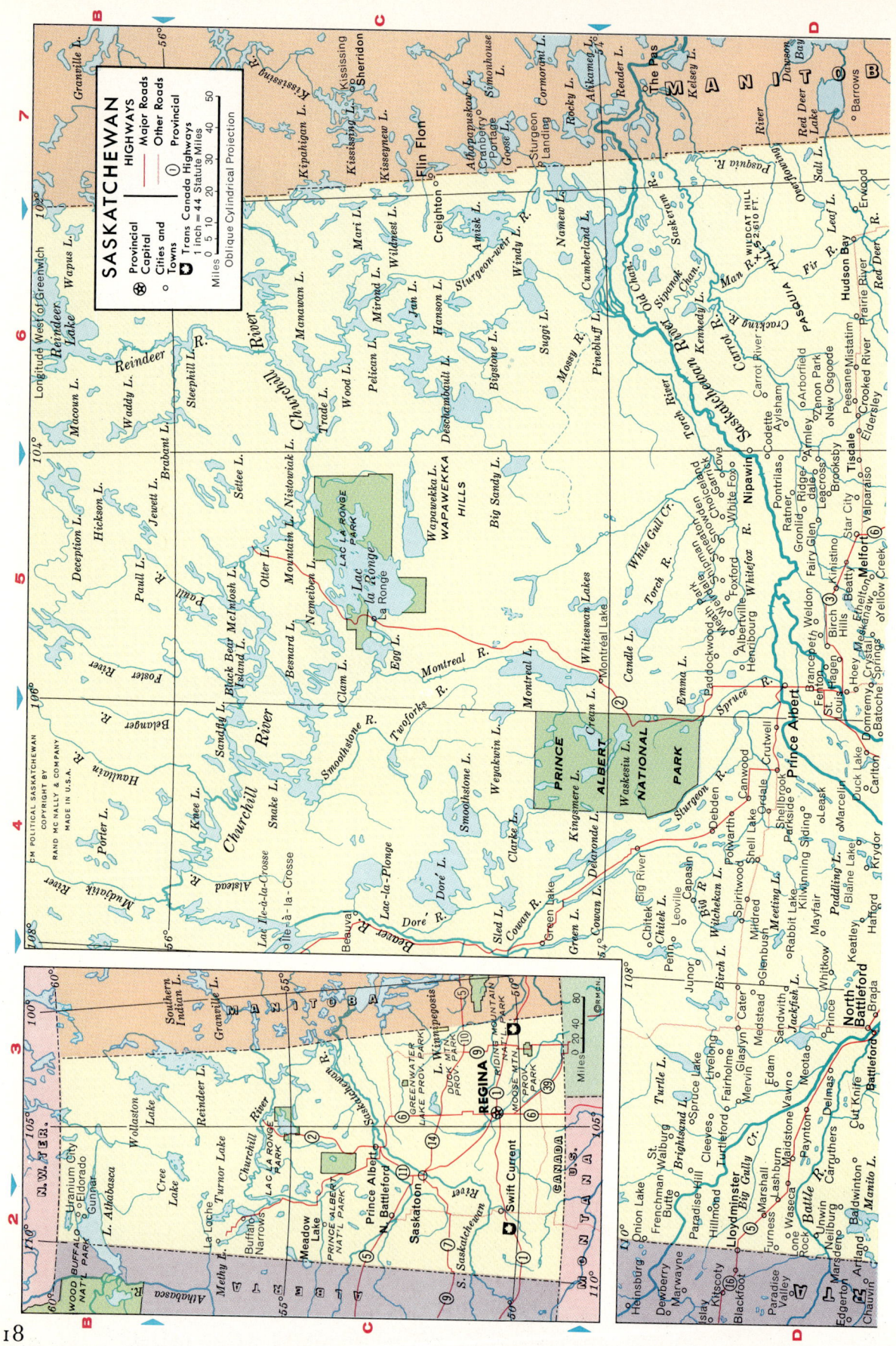

Specially created for **World Book Encyclopedia** by Rand McNally and World Book editors

## Population

984,000 .. Estimate .. 1971
955,344 .... Census .. 1966
925,181 " 1961
831,728 " 1951
895,992 " 1941
921,785 " 1931
757,510 " 1921
492,432 " 1911

## Metropolitan Areas

Regina† 131,127
Saskatoon† 115,892

## Cities and Towns


Abbey 321 E 3
Aberdeen 311 D 4
Abernethy 311 E 6
Adanac 33 D 3
Admiral 122 F 3
Alameda 328 F 6
Albertville 78 D 5
Alida 297 F 7
Allan 676 E 4
Alsask 292 E 3
Alvena 208 D 4
Aneroid 251 F 4
Annaheim* 186 D 5
Antler 126 F 7
Arborfield 494 D 6
Archerwill 321 D 6
Arcola 658 F 6
Ardath 46 E 4
Ardill 28 F 5
Arelee 73 D 4
Arran 139 E 7
Asquith 304 D 4
Assiniboia 2,872 F 5
Atwater 88 E 6
Avonlea 429 E 5
Aylesbury 111 E 5
Aylsham 209 D 6
B-Say-Tah 33 E 6
Balcarres 751 E 6
Baldwinton 66 D 3
Balgonie 446 E 5
Bangor 78 E 6
Bateman 80 E 4
Battleford 1,766 D 3
Beatty 110 D 5
Beauval* 486 C 4
Beechy 428 E 4
Belle Plaine 76 E 5
Bengough 695 F 5
Benson 106 F 6
Bethune 301 E 5
Beverley Station 41 E 4
Bienfait 908 F 6
Big Beaver 116 F 5
Big River 898 D 4
Biggar 2,755 D 3
Birch Hills 663 D 5
Birsay 164 E 4
Bjorkdale* 244 D 6
Black Lake* 378 B 2
Bladworth 186 E 4
Blaine Lake 650 D 4
Blumenhof 64 E 4
Borden 210 D 4
Bounty 81 E 4
Bracken 122 F 3
Bradwell 136 E 4
Bredenbury 569 E 6
Briercrest 171 E 5
Broadacres 48 D 3
Broadview 1,051 E 6
Brock 223 E 3
Broderick 122 E 4
Brooksby 58 D 5
Brownlee 158 E 4
Bruno 736 D 5
Buchanan 446 E 6
Buffalo Narrows* 611 B 2
Bulyea 167 E 5
Burstall 405 E 3
Cabri 733 E 3
Cadillac 248 F 4
Calder 225 E 7
Candiac Station 103 E 6
Cando 219 D 3
Canora 2,734 E 6
Canwood 342 D 4
Carievale 252 F 7
Carlton 47 D 4
Carlyle 1,064 F 6
Carlyle Lake Resort* 8 F 6
Carmel Station 118 D 5
Carmichael 41 E 3
Carnduff 1,194 F 7
Caron 102 E 5
Caronport* 205 E 5
Carragana 160 D 6
Carrot River 1,092 D 6
Cedoux 60 F 6
Central Butte 549 E 4
Ceylon 332 F 5
Chamberlain 201 E 5
Chaplin 443 E 4
Chelan 95 D 6
Choiceland 508 D 5
Christopher Lake* 163 D 5
Churchbridge 914 E 7
Clair 109 D 5
Climax 393 F 3
Coalfields* 189 F 6
Cochin* 159 D 3
Coderre 209 E 4
Codette 187 D 5
Coleville 521 E 3
Colfax 67 F 6
Colgate 96 F 6
Collacott Sub-division* 265 E 6
Colonsay 348 E 5
Congress 74 F 4
Conquest 265 E 4
Consul 227 F 3
Corning 72 F 6
Coronach 474 F 5
Courval 65 E 4
Craik 556 E 5
Crane Valley 117 F 5
Craven 140 E 5
Creelman 191 F 6
Creighton 1,710 C 7
Crooked River 151 D 6
Crystal Springs 69 D 5
Cudworth 755 D 5
Cumberland House* 628 D 6
Cupar 586 E 5
Cutbank* 696 E 4
Cut Knife 567 D 3
Dafoe 52 E 5
Dalmeny 416 D 4
D'Arcy Station 68 E 3
Darmody 38 E 4
Davidson 1,066 E 4
Davin 55 E 5
Debden 401 D 4
Delisle 665 E 4
Delmas 273 D 3
Demaine 118 E 4
Denholm 79 D 3
Denzil 282 D 3
Deschambault Lake* 253 C 6
Dilke 163 E 5
Dinsmore 510 E 4
Disley 52 E 5
Dodsland 388 E 3
Dollard 132 F 3
Domremy 235 D 5
Donavon 55 E 4
Drake 199 E 5
Drinkwater 168 E 5
Dubuc 176 E 6
Duck Lake 704 D 4
Duff 100 E 6
Dunblane 400 E 4
Dundurn 373 E 4
Duval 146 E 5
Dysart 297 E 5
Earl Grey 256 E 5
Eastend 866 F 3
Eatonia 624 E 3
Ebenezer 151 E 6
Edam 310 D 3
Edenwold 147 E 5
Edgeley 57 E 6
Elbow 470 E 4
Eldorado 470 B 2
Elfros 280 E 6
Elrose 619 E 3
Elstow 114 E 4
Endeavour 213 D 6
Englefeld 226 D 5
Ernfold 123 E 4
Erwood 119 D 6
Eskbank E 4
Esterhazy 3,190 E 6
Estevan 9,062 F 6
Estlin E 5
Eston 1,548 E 3
Ethelton 51 D 5
Evesham 81 D 3
Eyebrow 273 E 4
Fairholme 50 D 3
Fairlight 161 F 7
Fairy Glen 38 D 5
Fenwood 127 E 6
Fielding 52 D 4
Fife Lake 119 F 5
Fillmore 385 F 6
Findlater 95 E 5
Fir Mountain 48 F 4
Fiske 120 E 3
Flaxcombe 100 E 3
Fleming 219 E 7
Flin Flon** 527 C 7
Foam Lake 1,165 E 6
Fond du Lac* 229 B 2
Forgan 66 E 4
Forget 139 F 6
Fort Qu'Appelle 1,600 E 6
Fosston 144 D 6
Fox Valley 506 E 3
Foxford 36 D 5
Francis 164 E 6
Frenchman Butte 111 D 3
Frobisher 268 F 6
Frontier 266 F 3
Froude 53 F 6
Furdale* 164 D 4
Gainsborough 414 F 7
Garrick 105 D 5
Gerald 231 E 7
Girvin 127 E 5
Gladmar 107 F 5
Glaslyn 349 D 3
Glen Ewen 260 F 6
Glenavon 358 E 6
Glenbain 33 F 4
Glenbush 55 D 4
Glenside 137 E 4
Glentworth 157 F 4
Glidden 112 E 3
Golden Prairie 153 E 3
Goodeve 218 E 6
Goodsoil* 239 C 2
Goodwater 101 F 6
Govan 367 E 5
Grandview Beach*2 E 5
Gravelbourg 1,626 F 4
Gray 75 E 5
Grayson 284 E 6
Green Lake 635 C 4
Grenfell 1,369 E 6
Griffin 129 F 6
Gronlid 151 D 5
Guernsey 141 E 5
Gull Lake 1,235 E 3
Hafford 587 D 4
Hagen 49 D 5
Hague 439 D 4
Halbrite 142 F 6
Handel 101 D 3
Hanley 461 E 4
Hardy 59 F 5
Harris 287 E 4
Hawarden 267 E 4
Hazenmore 140 F 4
Hazlet 219 E 3
Hearne 43 E 5
Hendon 100 D 6
Henribourg 47 D 5
Hepburn 300 D 4
Herbert 1,040 E 4
Herschel 187 E 3
Heward 119 F 6
Hitchcock 93 F 6
Hodgeville 413 E 4
Hoey 96 D 5
Holdfast 446 E 5
Horizon 47 F 5
Hubbard 180 E 6
Hudson Bay 1,957 D 6
Humboldt 3,979 D 5
Hyas 236 E 6
Île-à-la-crosse 941 C 4
Imperial 564 E 5
Indian Head 1,891 E 6
Insinger 111 E 6
Invermay 444 E 6
Island Falls* 178 C 6
Ituna 975 E 6
Jansen 282 E 5
Jasmin 50 E 6
Jedburgh* 58 C 2
Kamsack 2,982 E 7
Kandahar 107 E 5
Katepwa Beach* 19 E 6
Kayville 118 F 5
Keeler 67 E 5
Kelfield 31 E 3
Kelliher 503 E 6
Kelvington 980 D 6
Kenaston 466 E 4
Kendal 124 E 6
Kennedy 257 E 6
Kerrobert 1,237 E 3
Keystown E 5
Khedive* 121 F 5
Killaly 208 E 6
Kincaid 310 F 4
Kindersley 3,534 E 3
Kinistino 861 D 5
Kinley 91 D 4
Kipabiskau* 4 D 5
Kipling 838 E 6
Kisbey 284 F 6
Kronau 58 E 5
Krydor 157 D 4
Kuroki 225 E 6
Kyle 518 E 3
Lac Vert 105 D 5
Lacadena 138 E 3
Lafleche 742 F 4
Laird 273 D 4
Lajord 96 E 5
Lake Alma 151 F 5
Lake Lenore 459 D 5
La Loche 1,090 C 2
Lampman 763 F 6
Lancer 254 E 3
Landis 266 D 3
Lang 223 F 5
Langbank 67 E 6
Langenburg 1,269 E 7
Langham 433 D 4
Lanigan 911 E 5
Laporte 63 E 3
La Ronge 933 C 5
Lashburn 506 D 3
Laura 65 E 4
Lawson 98 E 3
Leader 1,236 E 3
Leask 497 D 4
Lebret 272 E 6
Leipzig 121 D 3
Lemberg 441 E 6
Lemsford 59 E 3
Leney 23 D 4
Leoville 367 D 4
Leross 91 E 6
Leroy 502 E 5
Leslie 105 E 6
Lestock 448 E 5
Lewvan E 5
Liberty 164 E 5
Limerick 204 F 4
Lintlaw 252 D 6
Lipton 453 E 6
Lisieux 71 F 5
Livelong 165 D 3
Lloyd-minster‡ 3,304 D 3
Lockwood 89 E 5
Lone Rock 138 D 3
Loon Lake* 368 C 2
Loreburn 314 E 4
Lorlie 42 E 6
Love 146 D 5
Loverna 75 E 3
Lucky Lake 429 E 4
Lumsden 846 E 5
Lumsden Beach* 2 E 5
Luseland 826 D 3
Macdowall* 188 D 5
Macklin 824 D 3
MacNutt 204 E 7
Macoun 175 F 6
Macrorie 194 E 4
Madison 107 E 3
Maidstone 658 D 3
Main Centre 57 E 4
Major 175 E 3
Makwa* 156 C 2
Manitou Beach 129 E 5
Mankota 416 F 4
Manor 394 F 6
Mantario 99 E 3
Maple Creek 2,359 F 3
Marcelin 305 D 4
Marchwell 164 E 7
Marengo 135 E 3
Margo 251 E 6
Markinch 125 E 5
Marquis 195 E 5
Marsden 255 D 3
Marshall 191 D 3
Martens-ville* 724 D 4
Maryfield 459 F 7
Mawer 61 E 4
Mayfair 114 D 4
Maymont 191 D 4
Mazenod 98 F 4
McCord 88 F 4
McGee E 3
McKague 110 D 6
McLean 173 E 5
McMahon 36 E 4
McTaggart 100 F 5
Meacham 194 D 5
Meadow Lake 3,375 C 2
Meath Park 198 D 5
Medstead 179 D 3
Melaval 75 F 4
Melfort 4,386 D 5
Melville 5,690 E 6
Mendham 206 E 3
Meota 267 D 3
Mervin 231 D 3
Metinota* 2 D 3
Meyronne 172 F 4
Midale 762 F 6
Middle Lake 252 D 5
Mikado 158 E 6
Milden 288 E 4
Mildred 68 D 4
Milestone 503 F 5
Minton 219 F 5
Mistatim 215 D 6
Molanosa* 214 C 4
Montmartre 566 E 6
Moose Jaw 33,417 E 5
Moosomin 2,141 E 7
Morse 482 E 4
Mortlach 331 E 4
Mossbank 596 F 5
Mozart 75 E 5
Muenster 258 D 5
Naicam 784 D 5
Neidpath 47 E 4
Neilburg 327 D 3
Netherhill 90 E 3
Neudorf 506 E 6
Neville 140 F 4
New Osgoode D 6
Nipawin 3,963 D 5
Nokomis 620 E 5
Norquay 534 E 6
North Battle-ford 12,262 D 3
North Portal 228 F 6
Northgate 42 F 6
Nut Mountain 129 D 6
Odessa 275 E 6
Ogema 427 F 5
Onion Lake D 3
Orkney 77 F 4
Ormiston 220 F 5
Osage 68 F 6
Osler 158 D 4
Outlook 1,499 E 4
Oxbow 1,569 F 6
Paddockwood 227 D 5
Palmer 70 F 4
Pambrun 116 F 4
Pangman 248 F 5
Paradise Hill 313 D 3
Parkbeg 87 E 4
Parkman F 7
Parkside 128 D 4
Parry 120 F 5
Pasqua E 5
Pathlow 110 D 5
Paynton 219 D 3
Peebles E 6
Peesane 72 D 6
Pelly 472 E 7
Pemmican Portage* 208 D 6
Pennant 289 E 3
Pense 342 E 5
Penzance 81 E 5
Perdue 455 D 4
Piapot 203 F 3
Pierceland* 227 C 2
Pilger 117 D 5
Pilot Butte 405 E 5
Pine House* 336 C 5
Plato 102 E 3
Pleasantdale 147 D 5
Plenty 250 E 3
Plunkett 125 E 5
Ponteix 855 F 4
Pontrilas 53 D 5
Porcupine Plain 858 D 6
Portreeve 90 E 3
Prairie River 80 D 6
Preeceville 1,202 E 6
Prelate 572 E 3
Primate 109 D 3
Prince 43 D 3
Prince Albert 26,269 D 5
Prud'homme 321 D 5
Punnichy 436 E 5
Qu'Appelle 550 E 6
Quill Lake 578 D 5
Quinton 227 E 5
Rabbit Lake 218 D 4
Radisson 489 D 4
Radville 1,053 F 5
Rama 267 E 6
Raymore 537 E 5
Readlyn 55 F 5
Redvers 795 F 7
Regina 131,127 E 5
Regina Beach 306 E 5
Renown E 5
Reserve 187 D 6
Revenue 87 D 3
Reynaud D 5
Rhein 332 E 6
Riceton 130 E 5
Richard 53 D 4
Richlea 82 E 3
Richmound 229 E 3
Ridgedale 187 D 5
River Park* 195 F 6
Riverhurst 301 E 4
Riverside* 152 F 5
Robsart 70 F 3
Rocanville 628 E 7
Roche Percee 171 F 6
Rockglen 540 F 5
Rockhaven 60 D 3
Rose Valley 618 D 6
Rosetown 2,658 E 4


†City and metropolitan area have same boundary and population.
**Town on Saskatchewan-Manitoba border; total population, 10,201.
‡City on Saskatchewan-Alberta border; total population, 7,071.

*Not on map; key shows general location.
Source: Latest census (1966); places without population figures are unincorporated and have less than 50 persons.

# SASKATCHEWAN / People

The 1966 Canadian census reported that Saskatchewan had 955,344 persons. The population had increased 3 per cent over the 1961 figure of 925,181. If the annual growth rate continues, Saskatchewan will have about 984,000 persons by 1971.

Almost one-half of the people of Saskatchewan live in cities and towns. Saskatchewan has two Census Metropolitan Areas as defined by the Dominion Bureau of Statistics, Regina and Saskatoon. The province has seven cities with populations of more than 10,000. They are, in order of size, Regina, Saskatoon, Moose Jaw, Prince Albert, Swift Current, Yorkton, and North Battleford. Over a fourth of the province's people live in Regina and Saskatoon. See the separate articles on the cities of Saskatchewan listed in the *Related Articles* at the end of this article.

About 85 per cent of Saskatchewan's people were born in Canada. Most of those born in other countries came from Great Britain, the United States, or Russia. About 40 per cent of the people have English, Irish, or Scottish ancestors. Other groups, in order of size, include those of German, Ukrainian, Scandinavian, or French descent. Saskatchewan has about 30,600 Indians. Most of the province's Indians live on reservations. Several thousand *métis* (persons of mixed Indian and white descent) live in the thinly populated northern part of the province.

More of Saskatchewan's people belong to the United Church of Canada than to any other religious body. Other large church groups, in order of size, include Roman Catholics, Lutherans, and members of the Anglican Church of Canada.

*National Film Board of Canada*

**Downtown Regina** attracts shoppers from surrounding areas. Almost half of Saskatchewan's people live in cities and towns. Over a fourth of the people live in Regina and Saskatoon.

## POPULATION

This map shows the population density of Saskatchewan, and how it varies in different parts of the province. Population density is the average number of persons who live on each square mile.

PERSONS PER SQUARE MILE
- over 50
- 1 to 50
- less than 1

WORLD BOOK map

Source: Latest census (1966); places without population figures are unincorporated and have less than 50 persons.

| | | | |
|---|---|---|---|
| Rosthern | 1,414 | D 4 | |
| Rouleau | 419 | D 5 | |
| Ruddell | 39 | D 4 | |
| Runnymede | 96 | E 7 | |
| Rush Lake | 189 | E 3 | |
| Ruthilda | 85 | D 3 | |
| St. Benedict | 234 | D 5 | |
| St. Brieux | 409 | D 5 | |
| St. Gregor | 398 | D 5 | |
| St. Louis | 100 | D 5 | |
| St. Walburg | 628 | E 2 | |
| St. Victor* | 385 | F 4 | |
| Saltcoats | 604 | E 6 | |
| Salvador | 141 | D 3 | |
| Sandy Bay* | 561 | C 6 | |
| Sandy Beach* | 11 | E 6 | |
| Saskatchewan Beach | 5 | E 5 | |
| Saskatoon | 115,892 | D 4 | |
| Sceptre | 257 | E 2 | |
| Scotsguard | 51 | F 3 | |
| Scott | 290 | D 3 | |
| Scout Lake | 67 | F 4 | |
| Sedley | 321 | E 5 | |
| Semans | 376 | D 5 | |
| Senlac | 116 | D 3 | |
| Shackleton | 88 | E 2 | |
| Shamrock | 157 | E 4 | |
| Shaunavon | 2,318 | F 3 | |
| Shell Lake | 345 | D 4 | |
| Shellbrook | 1,088 | D 4 | |
| Silton | 121 | E 5 | |
| Simmie | 44 | F 3 | |
| Simpson | 307 | D 5 | |
| Sintaluta | 352 | E 6 | |
| Skinnerville* | 167 | D 5 | |
| Smeaton | 335 | D 5 | |
| Smiley | 168 | D 3 | |
| Snowden | 65 | D 5 | |
| Somme* | 152 | D 5 | |
| Sonningdale | 135 | D 4 | |
| Southey | 581 | E 5 | |
| Sovereign | 134 | D 4 | |
| Spalding | 399 | D 5 | |
| Speers | 163 | D 4 | |
| Spiritwood | 622 | D 4 | |
| Spring Valley | 94 | F 5 | |
| Springside | 410 | E 6 | |
| Springwater | 88 | D 3 | |
| Spruce Lake | 98 | D 3 | |
| Spy Hill | 344 | E 7 | |
| Stalwart | 44 | E 5 | |
| Star City | 634 | D 5 | |
| Stenen | 263 | E 6 | |
| Stewart Valley | 128 | E 3 | |
| Stockholm | 372 | E 6 | |
| Stony Beach | 55 | E 5 | |
| Stornoway | 92 | E 6 | |
| Storthoaks | 196 | F 7 | |
| Stoughton | 749 | F 6 | |
| Stranraer | 198 | D 3 | |
| Strasbourg | 739 | E 5 | |
| Strongfield | 159 | D 4 | |
| Sturgis | 705 | E 6 | |
| Success | 91 | E 3 | |
| Summerberry | 62 | E 6 | |
| Superb | | D 3 | |
| Swift Current | 14,485 | E 4 | |
| Sylvania | 115 | D 5 | |
| Talmage | 27 | F 6 | |
| Tantallon | 328 | E 7 | |
| Tarnopol | | D 5 | |
| Tessier | 70 | D 4 | |
| Theodore | 489 | E 6 | |
| Tisdale | 2,914 | D 5 | |
| Togo | 285 | E 7 | |
| Tompkins | 444 | E 3 | |
| Torquay | 443 | F 5 | |
| Tramping Lake | 288 | D 3 | |
| Tribune | 144 | F 6 | |
| Trossachs | 68 | F 5 | |
| Truax | 87 | F 5 | |
| Tuberose | 328 | E 3 | |
| Tugaske | 429 | E 4 | |
| Turtleford | 385 | D 3 | |
| Tuxford | 138 | E 5 | |
| Twan | 101 | D 5 | |
| Unity | 2,154 | D 3 | |
| Uranium City | 1,665 | B 2 | |
| Val Marie | 385 | F 4 | |
| Valley Centre | | E 4 | |
| Valparaiso | 50 | D 5 | |
| Vanguard | 379 | F 4 | |
| Vanscoy | 156 | D 4 | |
| Vantage | | F 4 | |
| Vawn | 137 | D 3 | |
| Venn | 45 | E 5 | |
| Verigin | 231 | E 6 | |
| Verwood | 64 | F 5 | |
| Vibank | 317 | E 5 | |
| Viceroy | 346 | F 5 | |
| Viscount | 322 | D 5 | |
| Vonda | 404 | D 5 | |
| Wadena | 1,404 | E 5 | |
| Wakaw | 1,032 | D 5 | |
| Wakaw Lake* | 5 | D 5 | |
| Waldeck | 224 | E 4 | |
| Waldheim | 596 | D 4 | |
| Waldron | 110 | E 6 | |
| Wapella | 610 | E 7 | |
| Warman | 725 | D 4 | |
| Wartime | 62 | D 3 | |
| Waseca | 103 | D 3 | |
| Waskesiu Lake* | 207 | D 4 | |
| Watrous | 1,459 | E 5 | |
| Watson | 929 | D 5 | |
| Wauchope | 46 | F 7 | |
| Wawota | 452 | E 6 | |
| Webb | 160 | E 3 | |
| Weekes | 121 | D 6 | |
| Weirdale | 256 | D 5 | |
| Welwyn | 186 | E 7 | |
| West Bend | 62 | E 6 | |
| Weyburn | 9,000 | F 6 | |
| White Bear | 128 | E 3 | |
| White Fox | 409 | D 5 | |
| Whitewood | 1,069 | E 6 | |
| Whitkow | 226 | D 4 | |
| Wilcox | 1,603 | E 5 | |
| Wilkie | | D 3 | |
| Willmar Station | 51 | F 6 | |
| Willow Bunch | 631 | F 5 | |
| Willowbrook | 100 | E 6 | |
| Windthorst | 460 | E 6 | |
| Winter | 48 | D 3 | |
| Wiseton | 197 | D 4 | |
| Wishart | 282 | E 5 | |
| Wollaston Lake* | 257 | B 3 | |
| Wolseley | 1,048 | E 6 | |
| Wood Mountain | 124 | F 4 | |
| Woodrow | 111 | F 4 | |
| Wroxton | 127 | E 7 | |
| Wymark | 202 | E 4 | |
| Wynyard | 1,956 | E 5 | |
| Yarbo | 208 | E 7 | |
| Yellow Creek | 191 | D 5 | |
| Yellow Grass | 511 | F 5 | |
| Yorkton | 12,645 | E 6 | |
| Young | 395 | E 5 | |
| Zealandia | 181 | E 4 | |
| Zelma | 79 | E 5 | |
| Zenon Park | 379 | D 6 | |

*Not on map; key shows general location.

# SASKATCHEWAN / Education

**Schools.** Missions and churches provided the only schooling in the Saskatchewan region until 1884. That year, the federal government started a system of public education. By 1892, the region had 249 schools. Attendance was required between the ages of 7 and 12, for at least 12 weeks a year.

In 1907, the legislative assembly provided by law for high schools. Until then, many schools taught both grade and high school subjects. In 1944, the province began to organize public education under the Larger School Units Act. Over 4,800 school districts have been organized into about 60 larger administrative units.

Saskatchewan schools are supervised by the provincial department of education, headed by the minister of education. The province has almost 1,400 public and separate schools. *Separate schools* are tax-supported schools operated by a religious group but controlled by the department of education. Children between the ages of 7 and 16 must attend school. For the number of students and teachers in Saskatchewan, see EDUCATION (table). The University of Saskatchewan, with campuses in Regina and Saskatoon, is the province's only university (see SASKATCHEWAN, UNIVERSITY OF).

**Libraries.** The first public library in Saskatchewan was established in Regina in 1908. Today, the province has over 35 public libraries and over 10 community libraries. There are regional libraries at Prince Albert, Weyburn, and Yorkton. The Legislative Library in Regina and the University Library in Saskatoon have collections on western Canada.

**Museums.** The Saskatchewan Museum of Natural History, established in Regina in 1906, has exhibits on animals and plants of the province, and on archaeology, ethnology, and geology. The Royal Canadian Mounted Police has a historical museum in Regina. The Norman Mackenzie Art Gallery is in Regina. The Western Development Museum in Saskatoon, with branches in North Battleford and Yorkton, has farm equipment exhibits.

**Royal Canadian Mounted Police Museum in Regina**

122

# SASKATCHEWAN / A Visitor's Guide

More than a hundred historic markers honor battlefields, forts, missions, and other reminders of Saskatchewan's colorful past. Many markers identify early trails used by hunters, fur traders, and patrols of the old North West Mounted Police.

The sparkling lakes of the Qu'Appelle Valley have popular summer resorts that feature boating, fishing, golfing, and swimming. Northern Saskatchewan offers some of the best hunting and fishing in North America. Sportsmen fly there to fish for grayling and trout, or to hunt bears and moose. The southern plains attract many duck hunters.

## PLACES TO VISIT

Following are brief descriptions of some of Saskatchewan's many interesting places to visit.

**Moose Jaw Wild Animal Park** is the largest of its kind in Saskatchewan. It has lions, monkeys, and many animals that live in the province.

**North West Territorial Capitol,** in Regina, housed the territorial government from 1883 to 1905, and then the Saskatchewan government until 1911.

**Royal Canadian Mounted Police Barracks,** in Regina, is the Mounties' training headquarters in western Canada. Recruits train there for 8 to 10 months.

**Saskatchewan Landing,** near Stewart Valley on the South Saskatchewan River, was a traditional Indian crossing point. Later, métis buffalo hunters used their carts as boats and paddled them across the river.

**National Parks.** Prince Albert National Park lies in central Saskatchewan, north of Prince Albert. The province also has two national historical parks—Batoche Rectory near Duck Lake, and Battleford near North Battleford. For the area and chief features of these three parks, see CANADA (National Parks).

**Provincial Parks.** Saskatchewan has 14 provincial parks, in the southern and central parts of the province. For information on these parks, write to Director of Parks and Conservation, Department of Natural Resources, Regina, Sask.

**Western Development Museum in Saskatoon**

**Boating in Prince Albert National Park**

## ANNUAL EVENTS

The main event of the fishing season is the Saskatchewan Anglers' Derby, held late in June throughout the province. Many cities and towns hold three-day agricultural and industrial fairs in July and August. Other annual events include the following.

**January-May:** La Ronge Winter Carnival (January or February); Trappers' Festival in Prince Albert (February); Regina Winter Fair (March); International Band Festival in Moose Jaw (May).

**June-August:** Pion-Era in Saskatoon (June and July); Dominion Day, province-wide (July 1); Frontier Day Rodeo in Swift Current (July); Buffalo Days and Provincial Exhibition in Regina (late in July and early in August).

Photos from Provincial Government of Saskatchewan

**Snowshoe Race at the Winter Carnival in La Ronge**

**Battleford National Historic Park**

**Duck Hunting on a Saskatchewan Pond**

123

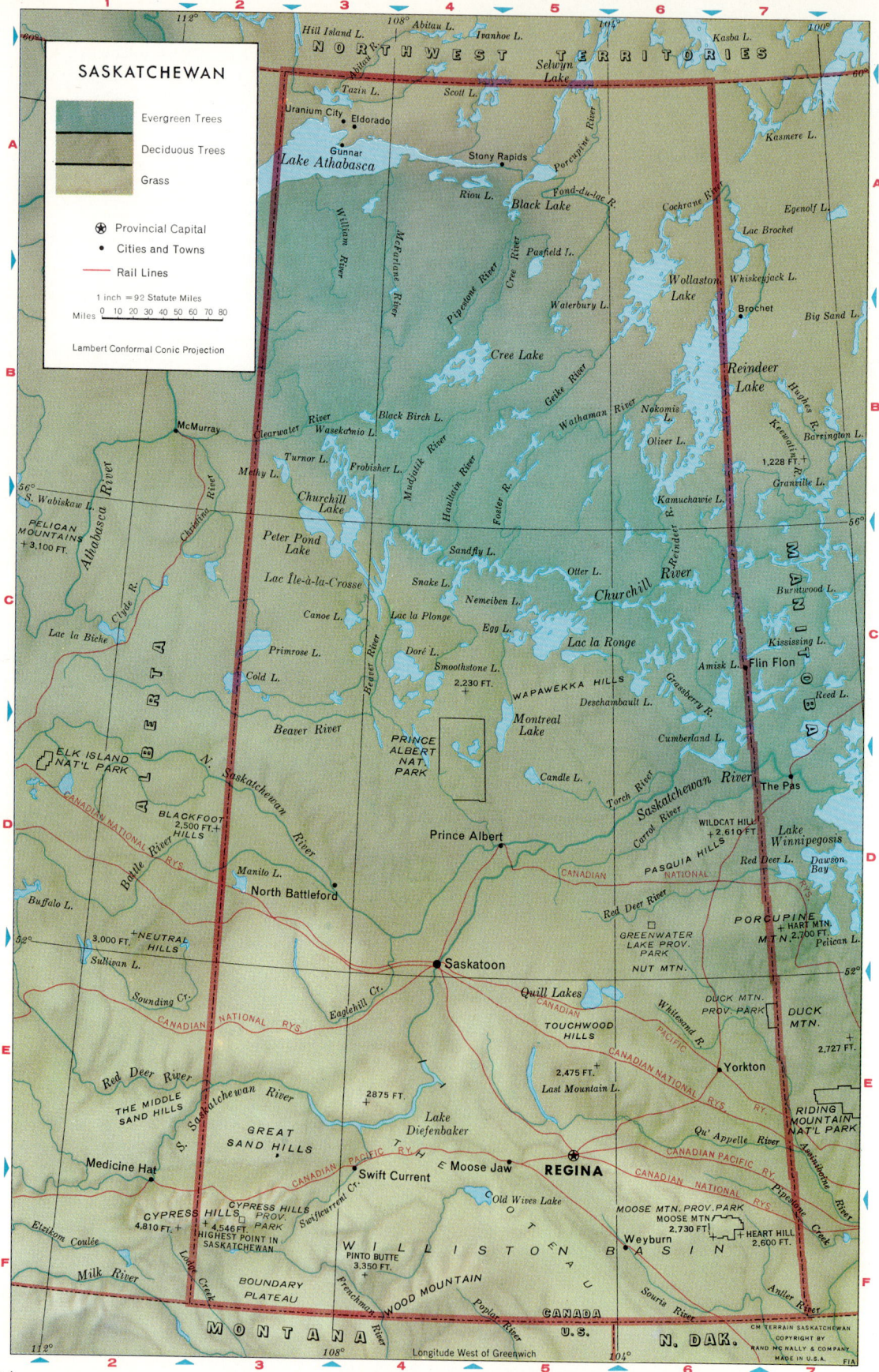

# SASKATCHEWAN / The Land

**Land Regions.** Saskatchewan has four land regions: (1) the Canadian Shield, (2) the Manitoba Lowland, (3) the Saskatchewan Plain, and (4) the Alberta Plain. The lowland and plain regions form part of the Western Interior Plains, the Canadian section of the North American Great Plains.

*The Canadian Shield* is a vast, horseshoe-shaped region that covers almost half of Canada and dips into the United States. This rough area, made up of ancient granites and other rocks, covers most of the northern half of Saskatchewan. It has deposits of copper, uranium, zinc, and many other minerals. The region also has the largest lakes of the province. Pine and spruce forests cover most of the land. An area of *muskegs* (peat bogs) is in the northeast. See CANADIAN SHIELD.

*The Manitoba Lowland* in Saskatchewan extends westward from the Manitoba border for about 90 miles. Rocky soils and poor drainage make the land generally unsuitable for farming. The region has large areas of marshes and forests, and many lakes and rivers.

*The Saskatchewan Plain* is mostly level land, broken by some low hills. Most of the region is between 1,700 and 2,000 feet above sea level. The province's chief commercial forests grow in the northern part of the Saskatchewan Plain. To the south are grasslands with scattered groves of trees that give way to almost treeless plains. Saskatchewan's chief farming area lies in this region.

*The Alberta Plain* is separated from the Saskatchewan Plain by a hilly belt called the *Missouri Coteau* or *Missouri Escarpment*. The rolling, treeless land of most of the region is from 2,000 to 3,000 feet high, and has

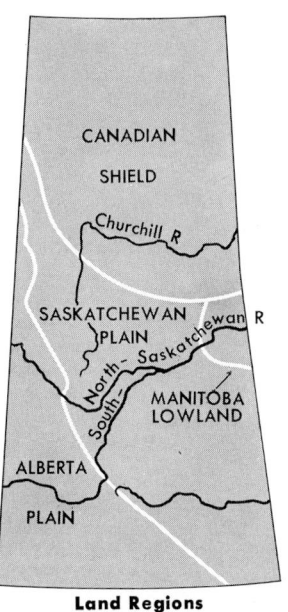

**Land Regions of Saskatchewan**

Dean, Miller Services

**The Qu'Appelle River** winds through southeastern Saskatchewan into Manitoba. This river helps drain the southern part of the province. The river valley has some of Saskatchewan's best farmland.

## Map Index

| | | | | |
|---|---|---|---|---|
| Abitau R. ........A 3 | Cypress Hills (Highest Point in Saskatchewan) ...F 3 | Kamuchawie Lake ..B 6 | Otter Lake .........C 5 | Selwyn Lake .......A 5 |
| Amisk Lake ........C 6 | | Lac Île-à-la-Crosse .C 3 | Pasfield Lake ......A 5 | Smoothstone Lake ..C 4 |
| Antler R. ..........F 7 | | Lac la Plonge ......C 4 | Pasquia Hills ......D 6 | Snake Lake ........C 4 |
| Assiniboine R. .....E 7 | Cypress Hills Prov. Park ............F 3 | Lac la Ronge ......C 5 | Peter Pond Lake ...C 3 | Souris R. ..........F 6 |
| Battle R. ..........D 2 | Deschambault Lake .C 6 | Lake Athabasca ....A 3 | Pinto Butte ........F 4 | South Saskatchewan R. ..............E 3 |
| Beaver R. ..........C 3 | Doré Lake .........C 4 | Last Mountain Lake E 5 | Pipestone Creek ....E 7 | |
| Black Birch Lake ..B 4 | Duck Mountain Prov. Park ......E 7 | Lodge Creek .......F 3 | Pipestone R. .......B 4 | Swiftcurrent Creek ...........F 3 |
| Black Lake ........A 5 | | Manito Lake .......D 3 | Poplar R. ..........F 4 | |
| Boundary Plateau ..F 3 | Eaglehill Creek .....E 3 | McFarlane R. ......A 4 | Porcupine Mtn. ....D 7 | Tazin Lake ........A 3 |
| Candle Lake .......D 5 | Egg Lake ..........C 5 | Methy Lake .......B 3 | Porcupine R. ......A 5 | Torch R. ..........D 6 |
| Canoe Lake ........C 3 | Fond-du-lac R. .....A 5 | Montreal Lake .....C 5 | Primrose Lake .....C 3 | Touchwood Hills ...E 5 |
| Carrot R. ..........D 6 | Foster R. ..........B 5 | Moose Mountain Prov. Park ......F 6 | Prince Albert Nat. Park ............C 4 | Turnor Lake .......B 3 |
| Churchill Lake .....B 3 | Frenchman R. ......F 4 | | | Wapawekka Hills ...C 5 |
| Churchill R. .......C 6 | Frobisher Lake .....B 3 | Mudjatik R. .......B 4 | Qu'Appelle R. ......E 6 | Wasekamio Lake ..B 3 |
| Clearwater R. ......B 3 | Geike R. ..........B 5 | Nemeiben Lake ....C 5 | Quill Lakes ........E 5 | Waterbury Lake ....A 5 |
| Cochrane R. .......A 6 | Grassberry R. ......C 6 | Nistowiak Lake ....C 5 | Red Deer R. .......D 6 | Wathaman R. ......B 5 |
| Cold Lake .........C 3 | Great Sand Hills ...E 3 | Nokomis Lake .....B 6 | Reindeer Lake .....B 6 | Whitesand R. ......E 6 |
| Coteau, The (Plateau) .......E 4 | Greenwater Lake Prov. Park .....D 6 | North Saskatchewan R. ..............D 3 | Reindeer R. .......C 6 | Wildcat Hill .......D 6 |
| Cree Lake .........B 4 | | Nut Mtn. ..........D 6 | Riou Lake .........A 4 | William R. ........A 3 |
| Cree R. ...........A 5 | Haultain R. .......B 4 | Old Wives Lake ....E 4 | Sandfly Lake ......C 4 | Williston Basin ....F 4 |
| Cumberland Lake ...C 6 | Heart Hill ........F 6 | Oliver Lake ........B 6 | Saskatchewan R. ...D 6 | Wollaston Lake ....A 6 |
| | | | Scott Lake ........A 4 | Wood Mtn. ........F 4 |

124a

Provincial Government of Saskatchewan

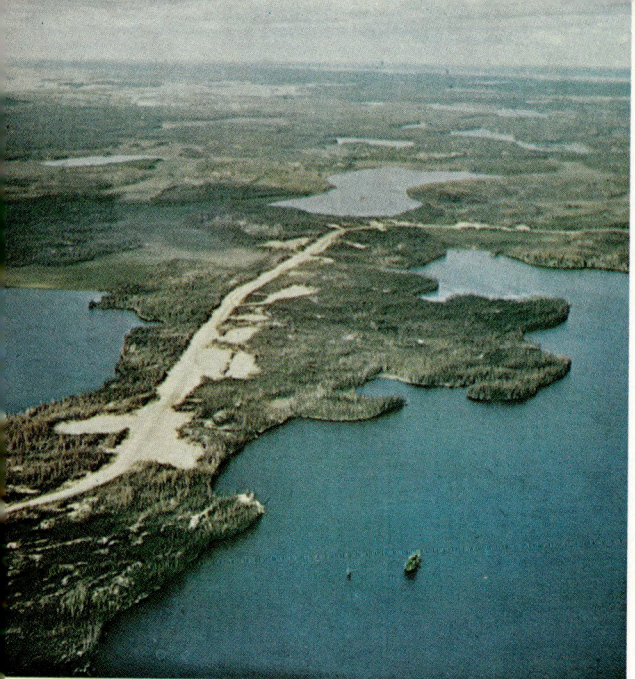

**Peat Bogs** called *muskegs* lie in the far northeastern section of the Canadian Shield. Pine and spruce forests cover most of the shield. The shield has the largest lakes in Saskatchewan.

deep river valleys. The highest hill in the province rises to 4,546 feet in the Cypress Hills, a wooded plateau in the southwest. The region's northern strip extends into the commercial forest belt.

**Rivers and Lakes.** Southern Saskatchewan, which has a dry climate, has few important rivers and lakes. The most important river is the 1,205-mile-long Saskatchewan River. It is fed by waters from Alberta and Montana. Its major branches in the province are the North Saskatchewan and South Saskatchewan rivers. The Assiniboine River and its main branches, the Qu'-Appelle and Souris, drain southeastern Saskatchewan. The largest lakes in the south are Old Wives and Quill lakes, which are shallow and salty, and Last Mountain Lake. Gardiner Dam, built on the South Saskatchewan River near Outlook, created a 170-square-mile reservoir called Diefenbaker Lake. It provides water to irrigate 500,000 acres of farmland.

Northern Saskatchewan is less dry, and has most of the rivers and lakes. The Churchill River system and the rivers flowing into Lake Athabasca drain northern Saskatchewan. Many northern rivers are actually narrow lakes that connect with each other. Lake Athabasca, the largest of Saskatchewan's many thousands of lakes, covers 3,120 square miles. About a third of it extends into Alberta. Other large lakes include Reindeer, Wollaston, La Ronge, and Cree lakes.

**Forests and Farms** surround Batoche Rectory near Duck Lake in the Saskatchewan Plain. The province's most important commercial forests are in the northern part of this region. Almost treeless grasslands in the south provide an excellent farming area.

C.O. Dean, Miller Services

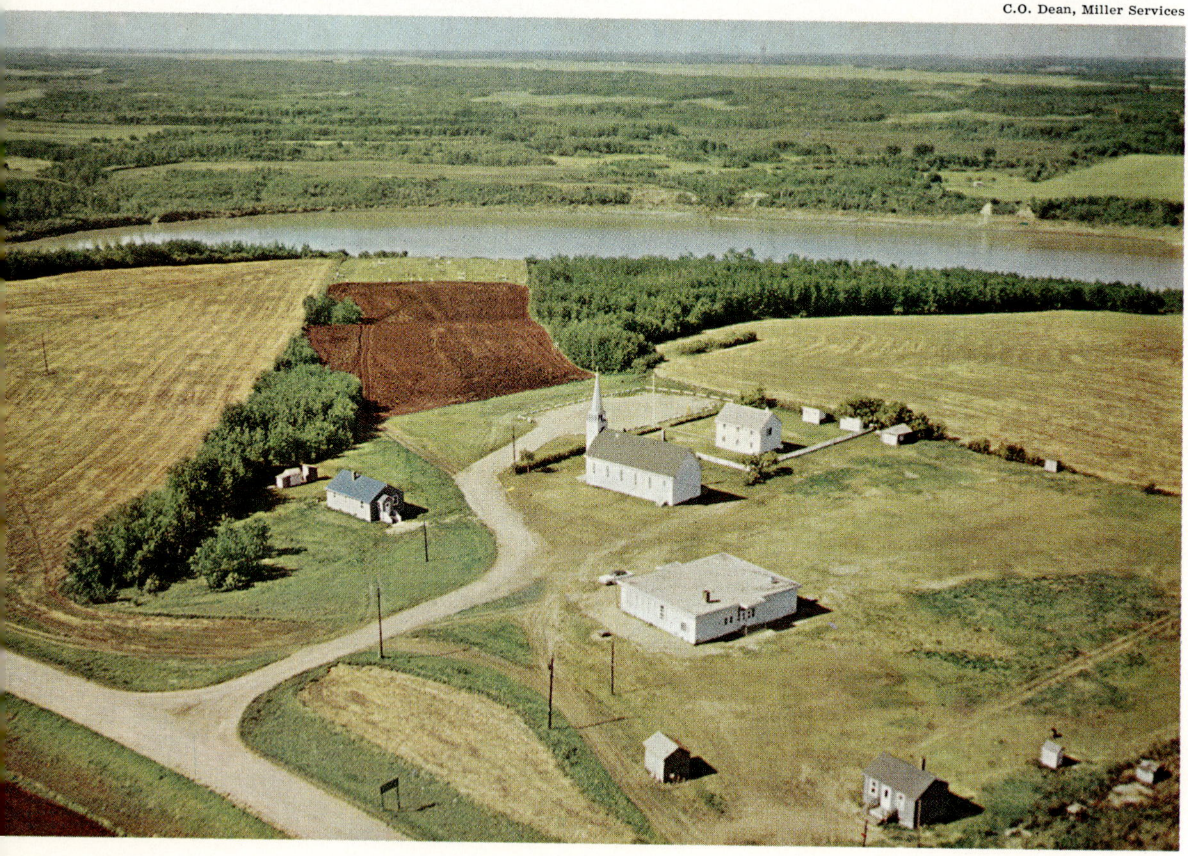

# SASKATCHEWAN /Climate

Saskatchewan has short, warm summers and cold winters. Average January temperatures range from −23° F. in the northeast to 10° F. in the southwest. Warm chinook winds may raise winter temperatures as much as 20° F. within a few hours (see CHINOOK). Average July temperatures vary between 57° F. in the northeast and 67° F. in the southwest. The lowest temperature recorded, −70° F., occurred in Prince Albert on Feb. 1, 1893. Midale and Yellow Grass had the highest temperature, 113° F., on July 5, 1937.

Saskatchewan's annual *precipitation* (rain, melted snow, and other forms of moisture) ranges from 12 to 17 inches. The southwest and far north are the driest regions. Annual snowfall varies from 50 inches in the north to 30 inches in the south.

**Winter Comes Early** in Saskatchewan. Freezing temperatures cause ice even on the largest river, the Saskatchewan.

## SEASONAL TEMPERATURES

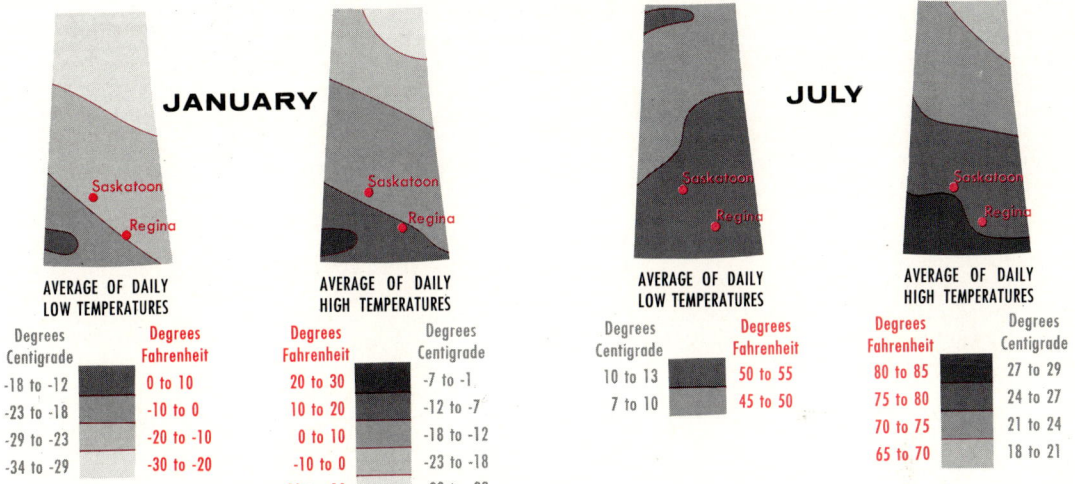

### AVERAGE YEARLY PRECIPITATION
(Rain, Melted Snow, and Other Moisture)

Source: Meteorological Branch, Canadian Department of Transport

WORLD BOOK maps

| | JAN | FEB | MAR | APR | MAY | JUNE | JULY | AUG | SEPT | OCT | NOV | DEC | Average of: |
|---|---|---|---|---|---|---|---|---|---|---|---|---|---|
| **REGINA** | 12 | 16 | 29 | 50 | 66 | 73 | 81 | 78 | 67 | 53 | 31 | 18 | High Temperatures |
| | -7 | -5 | 9 | 27 | 38 | 47 | 52 | 49 | 39 | 29 | 13 | 0 | Low Temperatures |
| | 11 | 10 | 10 | 8 | 8 | 13 | 10 | 9 | 7 | 6 | 10 | 11 | Days of Rain or Snow |
| | 9 | 9 | 7 | 7 | 9 | 12 | 10 | 9 | 8 | 7 | 9 | 9 | Days of Rain or Snow |
| **SASKATOON** | 10 | 14 | 28 | 49 | 65 | 72 | 79 | 76 | 65 | 51 | 29 | 15 | High Temperatures |
| | -8 | -5 | 10 | 28 | 39 | 48 | 54 | 50 | 40 | 30 | 13 | 0 | Low Temperatures |

Temperatures are given in degrees Fahrenheit.

124C

# SASKATCHEWAN / Economy

In early days, the economy of the Saskatchewan region was based on the fur trade. Wheat growing and ranching became important during the late 1800's. Today, farming is the chief source of income. Saskatchewan grows more wheat than any other province or state.

All values given in this section are in Canadian dollars. For the value of Canadian dollars in U.S. money, see MONEY (table).

**Natural Resources** of Saskatchewan include fertile soils, rich mineral deposits, valuable forests, and plentiful wildlife.

*Soil.* The rich grassland soils of southern Saskatchewan are probably the province's chief natural resource. These soils lie in parallel zones that slant from northwest to southeast. The far southwestern zone has brown soils that produce good crops when enough rain falls. But the region is dry, and much of it is used for raising cattle. Rainfall increases to the northeast, where dark brown and black soils are found. These soils are the most fertile in the province. The northern forest region has less fertile, gray soils.

*Minerals.* The Canadian Shield has varied mineral deposits, including copper, gold, silver, uranium, and zinc. The most important deposits are near Amisk, Athabasca, Île-à-la-Crosse, and Reindeer lakes. South of the Canadian Shield, near Choiceland, are deposits of iron ore. Salt and potash occur in a wide belt in south-central Saskatchewan. The potash deposits are the largest in the western world.

Southern Saskatchewan has about 900 million barrels of proved petroleum deposits. This region also has important lignite coal beds, especially near Estevan, and much natural gas. About 200 million tons of sodium sulfate occur in the southern lake beds. The deposits of this salt, used in medicine and manufacturing, are among the richest in the world. Helium is found near Swift Current. Many areas of the province have clay, gravel, and sand.

*Forests* cover about 118,000 square miles in Saskatchewan, or more than half the land area of the province. Commercial forests cover about 41,000 square miles. They extend across the province in an irregular belt about 150 miles wide, most of it north of Prince Albert. The most valuable trees in this belt are spruces, pines, and poplars. Other trees of Saskatchewan include balsam firs, birches, and larches.

*Plant Life.* The provincial flower, the prairie lily, grows throughout the plains regions, as do cacti, crocuses, vetches, and violets. Shrubs such as chokecherries, hazels, and wild roses grow in the woodlands.

*Animal Life.* Elk, moose, and Barren Ground caribou live mainly in woodlands of the central and northern regions. Deer and rabbits may be seen throughout the province. Fur-bearing animals in the forests include bears, beavers, minks, otters, and wolves. Pronghorns and coyotes roam the southwestern plains.

Game birds, especially ducks and geese, nest along the lakes. Partridges, pheasants, and ruffed and sharp-tailed grouse live in the southern Saskatchewan Plain. The lakes and rivers have many kinds of fishes, especially pickerel, pike, trout, tullibee, and whitefish. Grayling live chiefly in the northern waters.

**Agriculture.** Saskatchewan's farm products have an annual value of about $219,388,000. Saskatchewan has about 65,409,000 acres of farmland—more than any other province, and over a third of Canada's total. Much of the farmland is unused each year. This helps the soil store up moisture. The province has about 86,000 farms. They cover most of the land west and south of the Manitoba Lowland, or almost half the total land area. The farms average 763 acres in size.

Saskatchewan raises about three-fifths of Canada's wheat, the province's chief crop. Saskatchewan's wheat production averages about 400 million bushels yearly. More than 19½ million acres of land are devoted to wheat.

The Saskatchewan Wheat Pool, a marketing cooperative, was established in 1924 to sell grain. It grew into one of the largest primary grain-handling organizations in the world. *Primary handling* means that the organization gets wheat directly from the farmers. About 75,000 member farmers deliver their wheat to the pool's elevators for marketing.

Saskatchewan is a leader among the provinces and states in the production of barley, flaxseed, and rye. Farmers also raise large crops of oats and rapeseed. Other farm products include honey and poultry.

The raising of beef cattle is one of the fastest growing

**PRODUCTION IN SASKATCHEWAN**

Total yearly value of goods produced—$517,100,000

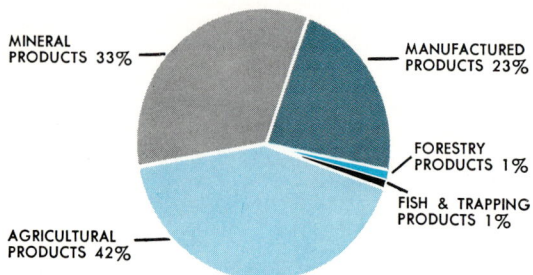

MINERAL PRODUCTS 33%
MANUFACTURED PRODUCTS 23%
FORESTRY PRODUCTS 1%
FISH & TRAPPING PRODUCTS 1%
AGRICULTURAL PRODUCTS 42%

Note: Percentages based on net value of production (total value of shipments less such costs as materials, fuel, electricity, and supplies).

Source: Dominion Bureau of Statistics

**EMPLOYMENT IN SASKATCHEWAN**

Average yearly number of persons employed—193,478

| | Number of Employees |
|---|---|
| Services | 50,527 |
| Wholesale & Retail Trade | 35,935 |
| Transportation, Communications & Utilities | 28,514 |
| Government & Defense | 18,259 |
| Manufacturing | 14,316 |
| Construction | 14,189 |
| Agriculture | 13,450 |
| Finance, Insurance & Real Estate | 6,551 |
| Mining | 3,925 |
| Fishing & Forestry | 959 |
| Other | 6,853 |

Source: 1961 Census of Canada

## FARM, MINERAL, AND FOREST PRODUCTS

This map shows where the province's leading farm, mineral, and forest products are produced. The major urban areas (shown in red) are the province's most important manufacturing centers.

WORLD BOOK map

**Cattle Await Branding** in the Big Muddy Valley. The raising of beef cattle is one of Saskatchewan's fastest-growing farm activities. The province has over a third of Canada's farmland.

**Oil Refinery** spreads across the prairie near Moose Jaw. Saskatchewan provides over a fourth of Canada's petroleum. The province also produces much copper, sodium sulfate, and uranium.

farm activities. Saskatchewan has more than 1,880,000 beef cattle. Its 229,000 dairy cattle produce about 1,300,000,000 pounds of milk each year. The largest cattle-raising areas are near Lloydminster, Moosomin, Swift Current, and Yorkton.

**Mining** is the fastest growing industry in Saskatchewan. The province's mineral products have an annual value of about $170,208,000. Saskatchewan is a leader among the provinces and states in the production of copper, gold, petroleum, potash, uranium, and zinc.

Petroleum is the major mineral product of Saskatchewan. Oil wells in the province pump about 94 million barrels of petroleum a year. Large-scale production began after several major fields were discovered in 1951 and 1952. Saskatchewan produces more than a fourth of Canada's petroleum. Wells in the Coleville-Smiley area and near Lloydminster supply heavy crude oil. Wells near Cantuar, Success, and Swift Current provide medium crude oil. The greatest number of wells are in the southeast, between Gainsborough and Weyburn. They produce light and medium crude oil.

Potash mining is developing rapidly. Major potash mines, completed during the early and middle 1960's, operate near Belle Plaine, Esterhazy, and Saskatoon. Most of the potash is used in fertilizers.

Uranium mining became important after the discovery of deposits in 1950. The uranium ore comes from the Uranium City area in the far northwest. Saskatchewan produces nearly a fourth of Canada's uranium, and world demand is increasing production.

The annual output of copper is about 20,000 tons.

The ore comes chiefly from the Flin Flon Mine on the Saskatchewan-Manitoba border. Annual coal production totals about 2 million tons, about a sixth of Canada's total. Strip mines near Estevan supply most of the coal, which is of the lignite type.

Saskatchewan produces all of Canada's sodium sulfate. Most of it comes from the Chaplin Lake area. Natural-gas fields near Gull Lake, Kindersley, and Swift Current yield about 48 billion cubic feet of gas a year. Pipelines carry the gas to cities and industrial centers. In 1957, Regina became the first city to receive natural gas through the Trans-Canada Pipeline. Other important minerals include cadmium, gold, helium, selenium, silver, tellurium, and zinc.

**Manufacturing.** Goods manufactured in Saskatchewan have a *value added by manufacture* of about $120,-972,000 yearly. This figure represents the value created in products by Saskatchewan's industries, not counting such costs as materials, supplies, and fuels.

Petroleum refining is one of Saskatchewan's most important manufacturing industries. Most oil refineries are in Moose Jaw, Regina, and Saskatoon. Food processing is also important. Many cities, including Prince Albert, Regina, and Saskatoon, have slaughtering and meat-packing plants. Saskatoon and Swift Current have flour mills. Dairy-product centers include Moose Jaw, Prince Albert, Regina, and Saskatoon.

Plants in Saskatchewan process helium, natural gas, potash, sodium sulfate, uranium, and other minerals. Other factories produce cement, chemicals, electric equipment, steel pipe and other steel products, and

124e

# SASKATCHEWAN

wood products such as lumber, plywood, and posts.

**Forestry.** Logs and pulpwood cut in Saskatchewan have an annual value of about $3,556,000. Lumbermen in the commercial forest zone cut about 242,950,000 board feet of lumber yearly. The spruce forests in the north-central section supply the most timber. Prince Albert is the chief center of the forest industry. The province's first pulp mill, one of the largest in the world, started production in Prince Albert in 1968.

**Trapping.** Fur trapping has been an important occupation in the north since about 1750. Today, fur-bearing animals caught in Saskatchewan have an annual value of about $1½ million. Beaver, mink, and muskrat pelts account for most of this income.

**Fishing Industry.** Commercial fishing produces about 14,515,000 pounds of fish a year, with a value of about $1,385,000. Lakes that supply most of the catch are, in order of yield, Athabasca, Reindeer, Peter Pond, Wollaston, and La Ronge. Whitefish account for nearly half the catch, pickerel for about a sixth, and trout for a seventh. Plants in the north freeze some fish for shipment, but much fresh fish is shipped by air.

**Electric Power.** Since 1949, the government-owned Saskatchewan Power Corporation has supplied most of the province's electric power. About three-fourths of the power comes from steam plants. The rest comes from hydroelectric plants at Island Falls, Squaw Rapids, and the Gardiner Dam near Outlook. For the kilowatt-hour production of Saskatchewan, see ELECTRIC POWER (table).

**Transportation.** Saskatchewan has more than a third of Canada's road mileage. The roads and highways stretch mainly over the southern half of the province, where most of the people live. Saskatchewan has about 6,200 miles of hard-surfaced highways, 50,600 miles of gravel roads, and 67,500 miles of earth roads. In 1957, Saskatchewan became the first province to complete its portion of the Trans-Canada Highway, which runs from St. John's, Nfld., to Vancouver, B.C.

The province has more than 10 major airports and about 280 small airfields. Three commercial airlines serve the southern cities, and another airline links the scattered settlements of the north. Saskatchewan has about 8,600 miles of railways, all in the south. The thinly populated north has no railroads. Important terminals operate in Melfort, Moose Jaw, Regina, Saskatoon, and Weyburn.

**Communication.** The first newspaper in the Saskatchewan region was the *Saskatchewan Herald*, established in Battleford in 1878. Today, Saskatchewan has four daily newspapers. They are, in order of size, the *Regina Leader-Post*, the *Saskatoon Star-Phoenix*, the *Moose Jaw Times-Herald*, and the *Prince Albert Herald*. Almost 150 weekly newspapers are published in the province.

Radio broadcasting in Saskatchewan began in 1922 when stations CHAB in Moose Jaw and CKCK in Regina went on the air. The province's first two television stations, CKCK in Regina and CFQC in Saskatoon, began broadcasting in 1954. The province now has over 20 radio stations and 8 major television stations. A number of smaller television stations rebroadcast programs from the major stations to distant areas.

# SASKATCHEWAN / History

**Indian Days.** The first white men in the Saskatchewan region found three Indian tribes roaming the forests and prairies. The Chipewyan lived north of the Churchill River. The Assiniboin lived in the south, in the valleys of the Assiniboine and Saskatchewan rivers. The land of the Plains Cree lay between that of the northern and southern groups. All these Indian tribes lived by hunting.

**Exploration.** In 1670, King Charles II of England granted fur-trading rights in the Saskatchewan region to the Hudson's Bay Company of London. The region was part of a vast territory called Rupert's Land. White men did not enter the Saskatchewan region until 1690. That year, the Hudson's Bay Company sent Henry Kelsey on an expedition to find new sources of fur. After spending two years with the Indians, Kelsey returned to York Factory on Hudson Bay. He brought reports of vast numbers of fur-bearing animals. See HUDSON'S BAY COMPANY; RUPERT'S LAND.

In 1731, a French-Canadian fur trader, Pierre Gaultier de Varennes, Sieur de la Vérendrye, and his sons left Montreal. They sought an overland route to the Pacific Ocean. During their western explorations, La Vérendrye's sons built trading posts on the Saskatchewan River in the early 1740's. Louis François de la Corne later became commander of the French-Canadian trading posts. He was one of the first men to experiment with grain growing in the region. The Hudson's Bay Company did not promote further exploration until 1754, when Anthony Henday crossed the Saskatchewan region on his way to the Rocky Mountain foothills.

**Fur-Trading Settlements.** In 1774, Samuel Hearne of

---
### IMPORTANT DATES IN SASKATCHEWAN

**1670** King Charles II of England granted trading rights in the Saskatchewan region to the Hudson's Bay Company.

**1690-1692** Henry Kelsey of the Hudson's Bay Company explored the Saskatchewan region.

**1740's** The La Vérendrye brothers, French-Canadian fur traders, built trading posts on the Saskatchewan River.

**1774** Cumberland House, Saskatchewan's first permanent settlement, was established.

**1870** Canada acquired Rupert's Land and made it part of the North West Territories.

**1882-1883** The Canadian Pacific Railway was built across the Saskatchewan region.

**1885** The métis rebelled against the Canadian government in the Saskatchewan Rebellion.

**1905** Saskatchewan became a province on September 1.

**1924** Farmers organized the Saskatchewan Wheat Pool.

**1944** The voters of Saskatchewan elected the first socialist government in North America.

**1947** Saskatchewan became the first province to provide all residents with free hospital care financed by taxes.

**1951-1952** Major deposits of petroleum were discovered in Saskatchewan.

**1962** Continuous potash production started in Saskatchewan. The province began a program of tax-supported, free medical care for all residents. In protest, doctors treated only emergency cases for 23 days.

**1964** The Liberals defeated the socialist government.

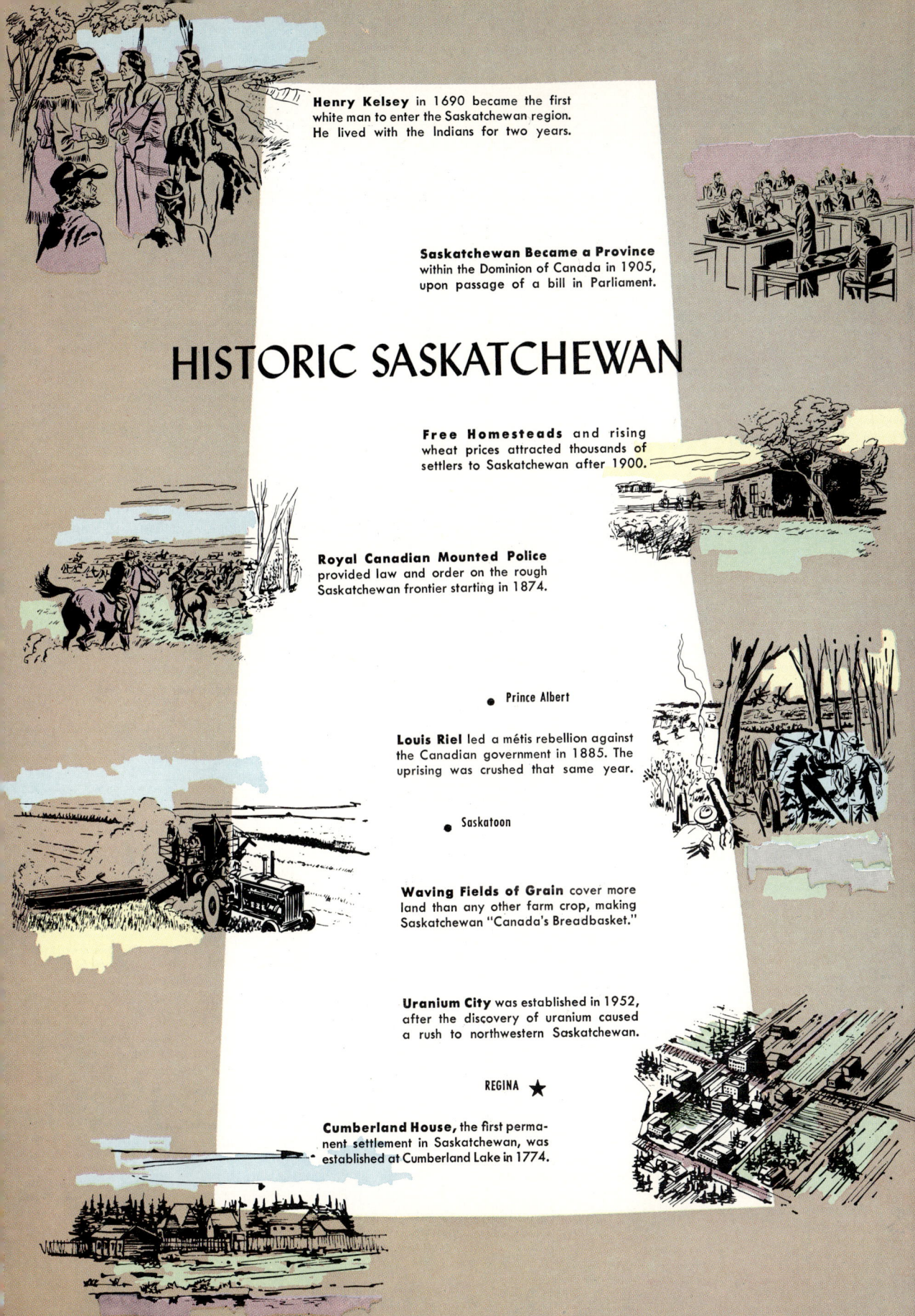

**Cree Indians** joined the famous 1885 rebellion led by Louis Riel against the Canadian government. This picture was taken inside Fort Pitt in western Saskatchewan. A few months later, these Cree chiefs led Indians in looting and burning the fort.

the Hudson's Bay Company built Cumberland House on Cumberland Lake. This trading post was the company's first in the interior of Rupert's Land. The post became the first permanent settlement in the Saskatchewan region. During the following years, other trading posts were established, most of them in the north. In 1783, a group of Canadian fur traders in Montreal formed the North West Company to compete with the Hudson's Bay Company. The two fur-trading firms operated in the Saskatchewan region until 1821, when the North West Company combined with the Hudson's Bay Company. See NORTH WEST COMPANY.

**North West Territories.** In 1870, the newly formed Dominion of Canada purchased Rupert's Land from the Hudson's Bay Company. Canada paid the company $1,500,000 and permitted it to keep large areas of the plains. Later in 1870, Canada established the North West Territories, which included the former Rupert's Land. At first, the lieutenant-governor of Manitoba governed the Territories. But in 1875, the Canadian parliament passed an act that reorganized the territorial government. The Canadian government appointed a territorial lieutenant-governor and council, and provided for elected members to be added gradually to the council. In 1876, the first lieutenant-governor, David Laird, took office. The council met in Fort Livingstone, near what is now Pelly, in 1877. The government moved to Battleford the next year.

In 1882, the Canadian government divided part of the Territories into districts. Two of these districts, Assiniboia and Saskatchewan, made up most of what is now Saskatchewan. Regina became the territorial capital in 1883.

**Métis and Indian Troubles.** The Canadian Pacific Railway was built across the Saskatchewan region in 1882 and 1883. The railroad opened the region to agricultural settlement, and led to the establishment of many towns. *Métis* (persons of mixed Indian and white descent) and Indians feared the settlers would destroy the buffalo herds. These people depended on the buffalo for food and clothing. The métis had no legal titles to their lands, and thought they would lose their homes to the white settlers. In 1885, the métis and some Indians, led by Louis Riel, joined in the Saskatchewan Rebellion against the Canadian government. See RIEL, LOUIS; SASKATCHEWAN REBELLION.

**Territorial Progress.** Agricultural settlement spread slowly during the late 1800's. The raising of wheat near the Canadian Pacific Railway began on a large scale during the 1880's. Ranching became important in the 1890's. Most of the early settlers came from Ontario. They established churches, newspapers, and schools, and asked for a more democratic form of government. In 1888, the settlers gained the right to elect a legislative assembly for the North West Territories.

Settlement was rapid after 1900. Good free land and rising wheat prices attracted thousands of immigrants from Europe and the United States. The larger population required a more efficient government than a territorial administration. In 1905, the Canadian government created the province of Saskatchewan. Walter Scott, a Liberal, became the first premier.

**The Early 1900's.** The Saskatchewan legislature met for the first time in 1906, in Regina. Settlement spread rapidly, railway construction expanded, and cities grew into important trading and supply centers.

During World War I (1914-1918), the province's farmers provided Great Britain and its allies with great amounts of food. Farm production continued to increase after the war. But world wheat prices fell, and a better method of the marketing of grain was needed. This need gave birth in 1924 to the Saskatchewan Wheat Pool, which became a huge farmers' cooperative.

**Between World Wars.** The depression caused by the fall of wheat prices ended after a few years, and Saskatchewan's farmers prospered again. In 1930, the provincial government took control of Saskatchewan's natural resources, including forests and mineral deposits. These resources had been controlled by the federal government since territorial days.

The world-wide depression of the 1930's hit Saskatchewan hard, and farm prices dropped again. Drought, soil drifting, and grasshoppers destroyed crops. The Wheat Pool nearly collapsed early in this period. Thousands of people left Saskatchewan to seek work elsewhere in Canada. The federal government provided some emergency financial aid. After 1935, work programs and land improvement projects of the federal Prairie Farm Rehabilitation Administration also helped the people.

Late in June, 1935, a trainload of unemployed workers arrived in Regina from British Columbia, which was also suffering from the depression. They had been going to Ottawa to complain to the federal government about their living conditions, but federal officials ordered them to stop. The workers resented this order. On July 1, a fight called the Regina Riot occurred between the police and some of the workers. Many on both sides were injured, and the rioters killed one policeman. The workers returned to their homes a few days later.

**The 1940's and 1950's.** Saskatchewan's economy recovered during World War II (1939-1945). The Allies' demand for food led to a great increase in farm production. Many persons found employment in defense and other industries.

In 1944, Saskatchewan voters elected the first socialist government in North America. It was headed by Thomas C. Douglas of the Co-operative Commonwealth Federation (C.C.F.). The C.C.F. government started an extensive program to strengthen the province's economy. It established government-owned companies called *crown corporations*. These included an airline, a bus company, insurance firms, a shoe factory, and other businesses. The C.C.F. government promoted the growth of the northern fishing and fur industries by establishing government marketing services. These services were operated like cooperatives. The province later encouraged industrial growth by lending money to private industries. Between the late 1940's and the late 1950's, the value of manufactured products in Saskatchewan increased 85 per cent.

As provincial income increased, the government expanded and improved its educational, public health, and social welfare services. In 1947, Saskatchewan became the first province to provide hospital care for all its people. This service was financed by hospital-insurance taxes.

In 1951 and 1952, large deposits of petroleum were discovered in Saskatchewan. The development of these and other mineral resources helped make the province less dependent on agriculture. After 1955, microwave telephone and television connections, and rural electrification were greatly expanded.

**Saskatchewan Today.** Agriculture is still Saskatchewan's greatest source of income, but other industries have been gaining rapidly. Between the late 1940's and mid-1960's, farm production increased about 50 per cent. However, mining increased 325 per cent during the same period, and manufacturing expanded 200 per cent. More oil was produced during the mid-1960's than in any other period in Saskatchewan's history. Petroleum refining was the most important manufacturing activity.

But the fastest growth in the province's mining operations is taking place in the vast potash fields. Continuous potash mining began in 1962, at Esterhazy. Potash mines were later developed at other sites, and construction began on still others. These projects resulted from a great worldwide demand for potash,

Miller Services

**Large Potash Mining Operations** began in Saskatchewan near Esterhazy in 1962. By the early 1970's, the province probably will produce more than a third of the world's potash.

which is used in fertilizers. The demand was heaviest in large, underdeveloped countries, which sought to increase farm production to feed their huge populations. Experts estimated that by the early 1970's, Saskatchewan will provide more than a third of the world supply of potash.

On July 1, 1962, Saskatchewan became the only province to provide a tax-supported program of medical aid for all. Under this program, all doctors were to be paid by a government commission. Most Saskatchewan physicians objected to government control, and treated only emergency cases. On July 23, the doctors reached an agreement with the government and returned to work. The physicians were permitted to be paid indirectly by the government through doctor-sponsored insurance agencies, or they could treat private patients outside the program altogether. Most of the province's physicians chose to be paid through the insurance agencies.

Many doctors who originally opposed the plan claimed that it led to poor medical care and great overcrowding in hospitals. For example, Regina General Hospital has had a waiting list of more than a thousand persons. Supporters of the program denied that medical care became worse. They claimed the hospital overcrowding was the result of a heavy population move-

――――― **THE PREMIERS OF SASKATCHEWAN** ―――――

| | Party | Term |
|---|---|---|
| 1. Walter Scott | Liberal | 1905-1916 |
| 2. William M. Martin | Liberal | 1916-1922 |
| 3. Charles A. Dunning | Liberal | 1922-1926 |
| 4. James G. Gardiner | Liberal | 1926-1929 |
| 5. James T. M. Anderson | Conservative | 1929-1934 |
| 6. James G. Gardiner | Liberal | 1934-1935 |
| 7. William J. Patterson | Liberal | 1935-1944 |
| 8. Thomas C. Douglas | Co-operative Commonwealth Federation | 1944-1961 |
| 9. Woodrow S. Lloyd | Co-operative Commonwealth Federation | 1961-1964 |
| 10. W. Ross Thatcher | Liberal | 1964- |

# SASKATCHEWAN

ment from rural areas to the cities. They pointed out that many rural hospitals were half empty. Much new hospital construction has begun in order to expand facilities in the cities.

In 1964, after 20 years in power, the Socialist C.C.F. government was defeated by the Liberal Party. Experts gave several reasons for the C.C.F. defeat. They believed that the younger, newer voters objected to the socialist program of a government-controlled economy.

Many voters opposed the C.C.F. association since 1961 with the New Democratic Party, chiefly a labor party. In addition, many persons felt that 20 years in power was long enough.

The new Liberal government began to attract new lumber and natural-gas companies, and firms in other industries. The government attracted these companies by permitting them to sell their products freely. Under the C.C.F. administration, some firms had to sell only to the provincial government. The Liberals continued the programs of free medical and hospital care.

STIRLING KING and J. HOWARD RICHARDS

## SASKATCHEWAN / Study Aids

**Related Articles** in WORLD BOOK include:

### CITIES AND TOWNS

| | | |
|---|---|---|
| Battleford | Prince Albert | Saskatoon |
| Moose Jaw | Regina | Uranium City |

### HISTORY

| | |
|---|---|
| Canada, History of | Rupert's Land |
| Hudson's Bay Company | Saskatchewan Rebellion |
| North West Company | |

### PHYSICAL FEATURES

| | |
|---|---|
| Assiniboine River | Reindeer Lake |
| Churchill River | Saskatchewan River |
| Lake Athabasca | Wollaston Lake |

### PRODUCTS

For Saskatchewan's rank among the provinces and states in production, see the following articles:

Barley   Rye   Uranium   Wheat

### OTHER RELATED ARTICLES

| | |
|---|---|
| Canadian Shield | Saskatchewan, |
| McNaughton, Andrew G. L. | University of |

### Outline

I. **Government**
  A. Lieutenant-Governor
  B. Premier
  C. Legislative Assembly
  D. Courts
  E. Local Government
  F. Taxation
  G. Politics
II. **People**
III. **Education**
  A. Schools
  B. Libraries
  C. Museums
IV. **A Visitor's Guide**
  A. Places to Visit
  B. Annual Events
V. **The Land**
  A. Land Regions
  B. Rivers and Lakes
VI. **Climate**
VII. **Economy**
  A. Natural Resources
  B. Agriculture
  C. Mining
  D. Manufacturing
  E. Forestry
  F. Trapping
  G. Fishing Industry
  H. Electric Power
  I. Transportation
  J. Communication
VIII. **History**

### Questions

What is the chief farm product of Saskatchewan?
How did Saskatchewan pioneer in public health plans?
In which two cities do a fourth of the people of Saskatchewan live?
What is the fastest growing mining industry in Saskatchewan?
Where is Saskatchewan's chief farming region?
What is the Saskatchewan Wheat Pool?
Why did the métis of Saskatchewan rebel in 1885?
What is Saskatchewan's major manufacturing activity?
Which part of the province has the most rivers and lakes? Why?
How does local government in southern and northern Saskatchewan differ?

### Books for Young Readers

ARCHER, JOHN H., and DERBY, A. M. *The Story of a Province: A Junior History of Saskatchewan.* McClelland (Toronto), 1955.
CASWELL, MARYANNE. *Pioneer Girl.* McGraw (Toronto), 1964.
DICKIE, DONALDA J. *The Great Golden Plain: A History of the Prairie Provinces.* Gage (Toronto), 1962.
HAYES, JOHN F. *Bugles in the Hills.* Copp (Toronto), 1956.
LONG, PHILIP S. *The Great Canadian Range.* Ryerson (Toronto), 1963.
McCOURT, EDWARD A. *Revolt in the West: The Story of the Riel Rebellion.* Macmillan (Toronto), 1959.
MITCHELL, WILLIAM O. *Jake and the Kid.* Macmillan (Toronto), 1961.
MOWAT, FARLEY. *The Dog Who Wouldn't Be.* Little, Brown (Toronto), 1957. *Owls in the Family.* 1961.
REYNOLDS, HELEN D. *Perilous Prairie.* Ryerson (Toronto), 1956.

### Books for Older Readers

CAMPBELL, MARJORIE W. *The Saskatchewan.* Rinehart, 1950.
HIEMSTRA, MARY. *Gully Farm.* McClelland (Toronto), 1955.
HOWARD, JOSEPH K. *Strange Empire: The Story of Louis Riel.* Swan Pub. Co. (Toronto), 1965.
MACEWAN, GRANT. *Between the Red and the Rockies.* Univ. of Toronto Press (Toronto), 1952.
MITCHELL, WILLIAM O. *Who Has Seen the Wind.* Macmillan (Toronto), 1948.
SHEPHERD, GEORGE. *West of Yesterday.* Ed. with a commentary by John H. Archer. McClelland (Toronto), 1965. Recollections of the early history of Saskatchewan.
STANLEY, GEORGE F. G. *The Birth of Western Canada: A History of the Riel Rebellions.* Univ. of Toronto Press (Toronto), 1961. *Louis Riel.* Ryerson (Toronto), 1963.
STEGNER, WALLACE E. *Wolf Willow: A History, a Story, and a Memory of the Last Plains Frontier.* Viking, 1962.
WRIGHT, JAMES F. C. *Saskatchewan: The History of a Province.* McClelland (Toronto), 1955.

**SASKATCHEWAN, UNIVERSITY OF,** is a coeducational university with campuses in Regina and Saskatoon, Sask. It is supported largely by the province.

The Regina campus has *faculties* (colleges) of administration, arts and science, education, engineering, and graduate studies. It grants bachelor's, master's, and doctor's degrees. The Saskatoon campus has colleges of agriculture, arts and science, commerce, dentistry, education, engineering, home economics, law, medicine, pharmacy, and veterinary medicine; and schools of nursing and physical education. It grants bachelor's, master's, and doctor's degrees. Four theological schools—Emmanuel, Lutheran, St. Andrew's, and St. Pius X—are associated with the university.

The university was founded in 1907. The Regina campus was founded in 1911 as Regina College, and became part of the university in 1934. For enrollment, see CANADA (table: Universities). J. W. T. SPINKS

**SASKATCHEWAN REBELLION,** or SECOND RIEL REBELLION, was an uprising of the *métis* (persons of mixed French and Indian descent) in Canada in 1885. Louis Riel led the revolt (see RIEL, LOUIS). In 1869 and 1870, the métis took part in the Red River Rebellion in Manitoba (see RED RIVER REBELLION). After that rebellion, the Canadian government gave 240 acres of Manitoban land to each of the dissatisfied métis. At first, this satisfied the métis.

But Manitoba soon began to fill with settlers from eastern Canada. Many of the restless métis gave up their land grants and drifted westward to the Saskatchewan River Valley. There they were again disturbed by the advance of the settlements. The Indians and the métis were afraid that the settlers would destroy the buffalo herds upon which they depended for food and clothing. They had no legal titles to the lands where they lived, and feared that they would lose their homes. They also disliked the Canadian government's method of surveying and laying out farms. They preferred the old French system by which all farms were narrow strips fronting on the river.

In 1884, the métis asked Riel to come to Saskatchewan to help them uphold their rights. Riel, who was living in Montana at the time, agreed to come. In March, 1885, Riel helped the métis set up a provisional government at Saint Laurent. Riel was moderate at first, and there seemed to be a possibility that the government and the métis would reach a compromise.

This possibility vanished when a skirmish between the métis and the mounted police took place at Duck Lake. An uprising of the Cree Indians followed the trouble at Duck Lake. Led by Chief Big Bear, the Cree attacked a settlement at Frog Lake, where they killed the men and carried off the women and children.

The news of this outbreak aroused the people of eastern Canada. A force of 4,400 men was sent into the Saskatchewan territory. The métis were no match for the troops, and were quickly defeated. Riel surrendered, and was hanged for treason.

The Saskatchewan Rebellion had important results. The Canadian government recognized the claims of the métis, and gave them legal titles to their lands. The rebellion showed the increasing importance of the North West (later Northwest) Territories, and they were given representation in Parliament.

The rebellion also gave the white people living in the west a sense of belonging to Canada. However, the rebellion heightened racial hatred between French and English Canadians in the east, and it has never been entirely forgotten. P. B. WAITE

**SASKATCHEWAN RIVER** begins in Alberta, Canada. Two branches join to make the stream. The river flows across Alberta and Saskatchewan and part of Manitoba.

# SATELLITE

The North Saskatchewan rises west of Edmonton in glaciers in the Rocky Mountains. The South Saskatchewan is formed by the Bow and Oldman rivers near Grassy Lake. The branches flow east, and join near Prince Albert in Saskatchewan. The river then flows east into Manitoba, and empties into the northwest side of Lake Winnipeg. The Nelson River flows from the northeast side of Lake Winnipeg to the Hudson Bay.

The branches of the South Saskatchewan are widely used for irrigation in southern Alberta. The South Saskatchewan River Dam, near Outlook, Sask., provides hydroelectric power, irrigation, and lake recreation facilities. J. BRIAN BIRD

**SASKATOON,** SAS *kuh TOON* (pop. 115,892; alt. 1,590 ft.), is the distributing center for a farming region of central Saskatchewan. It lies on the South Saskatchewan River. It is the second largest city in the province. For location, see SASKATCHEWAN (political map).

A grain elevator in the city can store $5\frac{1}{2}$ million bushels of grain. Saskatoon has stockyards, cold-storage plants, and meat-packing plants. The Dominion Forestry Station and one of the campuses of the University of Saskatchewan are located in the city.

Saskatoon was founded in 1882 by John N. Lake. It received a city charter in 1906. F. C. CRONKITE

For monthly rainfall and temperature information on Saskatoon, see SASKATCHEWAN (Climate).

**SASSAFRAS,** SAS *uh fras*, is a medium-sized tree of the laurel family. It is found in the Eastern United States from Maine west to Iowa and south to Texas and Florida. It also grows as a shrub along roadsides. The peculiar spicy taste and fragrance of its bright green twigs, leaves, and bark identify the sassafras. In autumn, its leaves turn gold and scarlet. Its small flowers are pale yellow. Sassafras tea, once used as a spring tonic, is prepared by boiling the root bark. Oil of sassafras is used to perfume soap. The soft, light wood is used for fence posts and lumber.

*Scientific Classification.* The sassafras tree belongs to the laurel family, *Lauraceae*. It is classified as genus *Sassafras*, species *S. albidum*. ELBERT L. LITTLE, JR.

**SASSARI.** See SARDINIA.
**SATAN.** See DEVIL.
**SATANTA.** See KIOWA INDIANS.
**SATEEN,** sa *TEEN*, is a cotton material made with mercerized yarns. The weave is the same as in satin, except that the lustrous surface is across the goods and not lengthwise as in satin. Sateen is used for linings, pajamas, draperies, and comforters. See also SATIN.

**SATELLITE,** SAT *uh lite* (astronomical), is a body which revolves about a planet. The word *satellite* means *an attendant.* Our moon, which circles the earth in its journey around the sun, is a satellite. The faint or dark bodies which revolve about certain stars and cause their light to dim and brighten are also called satellites. The stars they attend are called eclipsing, or variable, stars. Six planets in our solar system have satellites. These planets are Earth, with 1 satellite; Mars, with 2; Neptune, with 2; Uranus, with 5; Saturn, with 10; and Jupiter, with 12. E. C. SLIPHER

For a description of these satellites see the separate planet articles, such as JUPITER. See also MOON (The Moon's Movements; Other Moons).

127

**SATELLITE, ARTIFICIAL.** See SPACE TRAVEL; COMMUNICATIONS SATELLITE; SPUTNIK.

**SATIE,** *sah tee,* **ERIK** (1866-1925), was a French composer and pianist whose bold harmonies influenced other composers, including Maurice Ravel and *Les Six,* a group of composers such as Darius Milhaud and Francis Poulenc. As a cafe pianist in Paris, he acquired a sensational reputation for his wit and criticism of musical taste. His piano pieces, such as *Three Gymnopédies* (1888), established new, simple textures. With Jean Cocteau and Pablo Picasso, he produced a satirical ballet, *Parade* (1917). He was born in Honfleur. JOYCE MICHELL

**SATIN,** *SAT in,* is a weave in which the *weft* (crosswise yarns) do not cross the *warp* (lengthwise yarns) as often as in a plain weave. The resulting fabric is smooth and shiny. The name *satin* is also used to mean silk, nylon, and rayon or cotton fabrics with a satin weave. See also SATEEN. KENNETH R. FOX

**SATIN GLASS.** See GLASSWARE.

**SATIRE,** *SAT ire,* is a literary composition which ridicules persons or the things that they do. Satire often makes use of irony. One of the best-known satires of current life is Al Capp's comic strip, *Li'l Abner.* One character, General Bullmoose, satirizes business tycoons, and Senator Phogbound satirizes politicians. Satire is often used today in cartoons, plays, motion pictures, and television programs.

The term *satire* was first used by the Romans, but they used it only for some kinds of poetry. The kind of satire that aimed to improve the conditions satirized is known as *Horatian,* after the poet Horace. Other satirists, such as Juvenal, wrote wrathfully, in what is now known as the *Juvenalian* manner.

Elijah's taunts of the prophets of Baal on Mount Carmel are examples of scathing satire. Aristophanes and Lucian were masters of satire in Greece. One of the world's greatest satirists was Desiderius Erasmus of Rotterdam, the author of *Praise of Folly.* William Langland's *Piers Plowman* was the first notable English satire. Langland railed against the clergy and the courts. Alexander Pope's *Dunciad* is among the best satirical poems in English. Jonathan Swift's *Gulliver's Travels,* in prose, is one of the greatest satires. To these names must be added those of Laurence Sterne, Joseph Addison, Robert Burns, G. B. Shaw, and George Orwell. Among the French were Rabelais, Molière, Voltaire, and Anatole France. Germany is represented by Richter and Heine; Spain by Cervantes; Norway by Ibsen; Sweden by Strindberg; and Russia by Gogol. Thomas C. Haliburton, who used the pen name of Sam Slick, was the foremost Canadian satirist. In the United States, James Russell Lowell, Mark Twain, Artemus Ward, Finley Peter Dunne, James Thurber, E. B. White, and Philip Wylie have all written satires. J. N. HOOK

**Related Articles** in WORLD BOOK include:

| | | |
|---|---|---|
| Capp, Al | Molière | Shaw, George B. |
| France, Anatole | Orwell, George | Swift, Jonathan |
| Gogol, Nikolai | Pope, Alexander | Thurber, James G. |
| Juvenal | Rabelais, François | Voltaire |

**SATO,** *sah toe,* **EISAKU,** *ay sah koo* (1901-    ), became premier of Japan in 1964. He had previously held important Cabinet posts. As premier, Sato supported the United States-Japan Security Treaty under which the United States defends Japan. But he wanted Japan to take on more of the responsibility for its own defense.

Sato was born in Tabuse, a small town on the Inland Sea. He received a law degree from Tokyo University, and then went to work in the government's transportation ministry. During World War II, he directed the operation of the railroads. Later, he became vice-minister of transportation.

Sato was elected to the *Diet* (parliament) in 1949. He served in a series of important party and Cabinet offices until 1954 when he and other top government officials were accused of taking bribes. They resigned. Sato returned to the government four years later in the Cabinet of his brother, Premier Kishi. He also served in Premier Ikeda's Cabinet. When Ikeda resigned because of illness, Sato was selected as premier.

See also ASIA (picture: Leaders of Asia).

**SATRAP,** *SAY trap,* was the governor of a *satrapy* (province) in the ancient Persian Empire. The satrap also was tax collector and chief judge of the province. Each satrap kept his own force of bodyguards. Satraps continued to rule after Alexander the Great conquered the empire around 330 B.C. RICHARD N. FRYE

**SATSUMA WARE.** See KOREA (The Arts).

**SATURATION,** *SACH ih RAY shun,* is a term used in chemistry and physics. Chemists say that a solution is *saturated* when no more of a substance will dissolve in it at the same temperature and pressure. A solution in which more of a substance will dissolve is called *unsaturated.* In *saturated organic compounds,* a single bond connects each carbon atom to four other atoms (see BOND [chemical]). Saturated compounds do not have double or triple bonds. A *saturated color* is not mixed with white. See also EVAPORATION. W. NORTON JONES, JR.

**SATURDAY,** called *Saeter-daeg* by the Anglo-Saxons, is the seventh day of the week. It is named for the Roman god Saturn and is the only day named for a Roman god. Saturday is the Sabbath among the Jews and the Seventh-day Adventists. Most employers give their workers a half or full holiday on Saturday. See also WEEK. GRACE HUMPHREY

**SATURN** was the youngest son of Uranus (Heaven) and Gaea (Earth) in Roman mythology. He was a god of the harvest, and ruled the world during its Golden Age. His name probably comes from the Latin verb *serere* (to sow). The Greeks called him *Kronos* or *Cronus.*

Saturn married his sister Rhea and became the father of many gods. He swallowed his first five children because an oracle said that one of his children would overthrow him. Rhea hid their sixth child, Jupiter. After Jupiter grew up, he forced his father to cast up the other children and give up his throne. Jupiter then made Saturn go to Italy.

Saturn taught the Italians how to farm, and made them prosperous. The Saturnalia festival was held in Rome every year from December 17 to 23 in his honor.

The Greek word *chronos* means *time.* Kronos, or Saturn, is usually pictured as a bent old man with a scythe in one hand. In the other hand, he holds a snake that bites its own tail. The story of Saturn's swallowing his children symbolizes the idea that time creates and then destroys what it has created. JAMES F. CRONIN

See also SATURNALIA.

SATURN

Mt. Wilson and Palomar Observatories

**The Three Rings of Saturn** are a spectacular sight when the planet is viewed through a telescope. Only two of the rings are visible in this photograph, because the inner ring is so small.

**SATURN** is the second largest planet. Only Jupiter is larger. Saturn differs from all the other planets because there are three thin, flat rings around it. These rings are made up of swarms of tiny particles that travel around the planet. The gleaming rings make Saturn one of the most beautiful objects in the solar system.

The diameter of Saturn at its equator is about 75,100 miles, almost 10 times that of the earth. Saturn can be seen from the earth with the unaided eye, but its rings are not visible except through a telescope.

Saturn was the farthest planet from the earth that the ancient astronomers knew about. They named it for the Roman god of agriculture.

**Orbit.** Saturn is the sixth closest planet to the sun. Its mean distance from the sun is about 887,500,000 miles, compared with about 93,000,000 miles for the earth. At its closest approach to the earth, Saturn is about 793,000,000 miles away.

Saturn travels around the sun in an *elliptical* (oval-shaped) orbit. Its distance from the sun varies from about 937,000,000 miles at its farthest point to about 838,000,000 miles at its closest point. Saturn takes about 10,759 earth-days, or about $29\frac{1}{2}$ earth-years, to go around the sun, compared with 365 days, or one year, for the earth.

**Rotation.** As Saturn travels around the sun, it spins on its *axis*, an imaginary line drawn through its center. Saturn's axis is not *perpendicular* (at an angle of 90°) to the planet's path around the sun. The axis tilts at an angle of about 27° from the perpendicular position. For an illustration of the tilt of an axis, see PLANET (The Axes of the Planets).

*The contributor of this article is Hyron Spinrad, Associate Professor of Astronomy at the University of California in Berkeley.*

**SATURN AT A GLANCE**
Saturn, shown in blue in the diagram, is the sixth closest planet to the sun. Astronomers still use the ancient symbol for Saturn, *right*.

**Distance from Sun:** *Shortest*—838,000,000 miles; *Greatest*—937,000,000 miles; *Mean*—887,500,000 miles.
**Distance from Earth:** *Shortest*—793,000,000 miles; *Greatest*—1,030,000,000 miles.
**Diameter:** About 75,100 miles.
**Length of Year:** About $29\frac{1}{2}$ earth-years.
**Rotation Period:** 10 hours and 14 minutes.
**Average Temperature:** —240° F. (—151° C.).
**Atmosphere:** Hydrogen, helium, methane, ammonia (?).
**Number of Satellites:** 10.

128a

# SATURN

Saturn rotates faster than any other planet except Jupiter. Saturn spins around once in only 10 hours and 14 minutes, compared to about 24 hours, or one day, for the earth. The rapid rotation of Saturn causes the planet to bulge at its equator and flatten at its poles. The planet's diameter is 8,000 miles larger at the equator than between the poles.

**Surface and Atmosphere.** Astronomers do not know exactly where Saturn's atmosphere ends and where its surface begins. Only the top of a layer of clouds is visible from the earth. Saturn is so far from the earth that little is known about its surface beneath the clouds.

The atmosphere of Saturn appears to consist of about 70 per cent hydrogen and about 25 per cent helium, plus small amounts of methane and perhaps ammonia. The *atmospheric pressure* (force exerted by the weight of the gases) on Saturn has not been accurately measured. Astronomers estimate the pressure near the top of Saturn's clouds to be close to the earth's atmospheric pressure of 14.7 pounds per square inch. Dark lines that sometimes appear on the clouds of Saturn indicate that winds occur in the planet's atmosphere.

The gases that form Saturn's atmosphere also form most of its interior. They are highly compressed in the interior of the planet, and may even be in solid form. In addition to the gases, some rock and other solid material is thought to make up part of Saturn's interior.

The plants and animals that live on the earth could not live on Saturn. Astronomers do not know whether any form of life exists on the planet.

**Temperature.** The tilt of Saturn's axis causes the sun to heat the planet's northern and southern halves unequally, resulting in seasons and temperature changes. Each season on Saturn lasts about $7\frac{1}{2}$ earth-years, because Saturn takes about 29 times as long to go around the sun as the earth does. The temperature on Saturn is always much colder than that on the earth, because Saturn is so far from the sun. The average temperature at the top of Saturn's clouds is about $-240°$ F. ($-151°$ C.).

Astronomers believe the temperatures below Saturn's clouds may be somewhat higher than those at the top of the clouds. They also have found that the planet may give off a little more energy than it receives from the sun. If these ideas prove to be correct, Saturn may be considered to act somewhat like a weak star.

**Density and Mass.** Saturn has a lower *density* than any other planet (see DENSITY). It is only about one-tenth as dense as the earth, and about two-thirds as dense as water. That is, a portion of Saturn would weigh much less than an equal portion of the earth, and would float in water.

Although Saturn has a low density, it has a greater *mass* than any other planet except Jupiter (see MASS). Saturn is 95 times as massive as the earth. The force of gravity on Saturn is only a little higher than that on the earth. A 100-pound object on the earth would weigh about 116 pounds on Saturn.

**Rings.** The rings of Saturn surround the planet at its equator. They do not touch Saturn. As Saturn orbits the sun, the three rings always tilt at the same angle as the equator. Because of this tilt, the rings can be seen at

U.S. Naval Observatory

**Seven of Saturn's 10 Satellites** can be seen in a photograph taken when Janus was discovered in December, 1966. Janus is visible only when the rings "disappear" from view.

### SATELLITES OF SATURN

| Name | Diameter (miles) | Distance from Planet (miles) | Revolution Time (days) | (hours) | Year of Discovery |
|---|---|---|---|---|---|
| Titan | 3,100 | 759,000 | 15 | 23 | 1655 |
| Rhea | 1,150 | 327,000 | 4 | 12 | 1672 |
| Iapetus | 800 | 2,210,000 | 79 | 8 | 1671 |
| Dione | 800 | 234,000 | 2 | 18 | 1684 |
| Tethys | 750 | 183,000 | 1 | 21 | 1684 |
| Enceladus | 370 | 148,000 | 1 | 9 | 1789 |
| Mimas | 320 | 115,000 | | $22\frac{1}{2}$ | 1789 |
| Hyperion | 300 | 920,000 | 21 | $6\frac{1}{2}$ | 1848 |
| Phoebe | 190 | 8,034,000 | 550 | 2 | 1898 |
| Janus | 190 | 95,000 | | 18 | 1966 |

various angles when viewed through a telescope.

The countless tiny particles that make up the rings are too small and too close together to be seen individually. Astronomers estimate their average diameter to be about one-tenth of an inch. The particles appear to be ice crystals or solid objects covered with ice.

Saturn's outermost ring is about 10,000 miles wide. It has a diameter of about 170,000 miles—more than twice the diameter of Saturn itself. Between the outer ring and the middle ring is an empty space about 3,000 miles wide. The middle ring is the brightest of the three rings. It is about 16,000 miles wide. The innermost ring is difficult to see because it is relatively small and almost transparent. Astronomers know little about it. There is an empty space about 7,000 miles wide between the innermost ring and the visible surface of Saturn.

The thickness of the rings appears to be less than 10 miles. This small thickness and extremely large outer diameter can be compared to those of a circular sheet of tissue paper 1 foot in diameter. The rings are so thin that they cannot be seen when they are in direct line with the earth.

Saturn's rings were discovered in the early 1600's by the Italian astronomer Galileo. Galileo could not see

*E. C. Slipher, Lowell Observatory*

**The Position of Saturn's Rings** appears to change as the planet orbits the sun, but the rings are always parallel to Saturn's equator. The three rings are less than 10 miles thick, and seem to vanish when in direct line with the earth (middle photo).

the rings clearly with his small telescope, and thought they were large satellites. In 1655, using a more powerful telescope, Christian Huygens, a Dutch astronomer, described a "thin and flat" ring around Saturn. Huygens thought the ring was a solid sheet of some material. In 1675, Jean Domenique Cassini, a French astronomer, announced the discovery of two separate rings made up of swarms of satellites. Observations since Cassini's discoveries resulted in the discovery of the innermost ring.

**Satellites.** In addition to its rings, Saturn has 10 large *satellites* (moons). All of them travel around the planet beyond the rings. Only Jupiter has more large satellites.

Saturn's largest satellite, Titan, has a diameter of about 3,100 miles, about 940 miles larger than the diameter of the earth's moon. Titan is the only satellite in the solar system that has an atmosphere. It is surrounded by methane gas. Saturn's other satellites are all much smaller than the earth's moon.

Until 1966, astronomers had seen only nine satellites traveling around Saturn. That year, the French astronomer Audouin Dollfus discovered a 10th satellite. This satellite, Janus, travels closer to the rings than any of Saturn's other large satellites.

**Flights to Saturn** will probably not be attempted for many years. Saturn is almost 800 million miles from the earth at its closest approach, and spacecraft will take at least five years to reach the planet. It will be difficult to equip a spacecraft with enough power for such a long time. Energy from the sun will not be available for power, because the spacecraft will be too far from the sun.

When a spacecraft does reach Saturn, it will send back information that will help astronomers answer many questions about the planet. Photographs will show the thickness of the rings and the size of the satellites that make up the rings. Measurements will help determine what materials make up Saturn's clouds, atmosphere, and interior. Other measurements will be used to find out whether the planet gives off any form of energy.                                    HYRON SPINRAD

See also PLANET; SOLAR SYSTEM.

**SATURN ROCKET.** See SPACE TRAVEL (Launch Vehicles).

**SATURNALIA,** *SAT er NAY lih uh*, was the name of an ancient Roman festival given in honor of Saturn, the Roman harvest god. The festival began on December 17, and lasted for seven days. On the first day, public religious ceremonies honoring Saturn took place. On the second day, many families offered sacrifices of young pigs.

The Saturnalia festival was a gay occasion. Schools closed and all public business stopped. Courts of law closed their doors, and no criminals could be punished. Families held banquets. Even slaves were free to attend the festival. The last days of the festival were spent visiting and exchanging presents. Some of the gifts were little clay images called *sigillaria*, from the Latin word *sigilla*, which means *small images*.           THOMAS A. BRADY

See also SATURN (Roman god).

**SATYAGRAHA.** See GANDHI, MOHANDAS K.

**SATYR,** *SAT ur*, was the name given to gods of the woods in Greek mythology. They were thought to be part human and part goat or horse. In art, they are often shown as men with pointed ears, hooves, and short tails. Often their legs were shown as goats' legs. Young satyrs were mischievous and handsome. Old satyrs were ugly and lazy. They followed the greater gods Pan and Dionysus. See also FAUN; PAN; SILENUS.           VAN JOHNSON

**SAUCER, FLYING.** See FLYING SAUCER.

**SAUD,** *sah OOD* (1902-1969), became Saudi Arabia's second king in 1953, after the death of his father, Ibn Saud. King Saud supported policies friendly to the Western nations. He also helped Jordan maintain its independence. Poor health forced him to give up his throne in 1963, in favor of his younger brother, Crown Prince Faisal. Saud remained as a figurehead ruler until 1964.

**King Saud**
*Wide World*

Saud was born in Kuwait. As his father's agent, Saud traveled widely and visited such countries as Great Britain, India, and Egypt.           SYDNEY N. FISHER

# SAUDI ARABIA

Robert Yarnall Richie

**Rich Deposits of Oil** are Saudi Arabia's chief source of wealth. Busy petroleum refineries now lie in a vast desert that was once a wilderness area where only a few Bedouin tribesmen lived.

**SAUDI ARABIA,** *suh OO dee*, is a large kingdom in southwest Asia. This desert country of mountains, plateaus, and rocky plains covers two-thirds of the Arabian Peninsula. It is over three times as large as Texas. The name of the country in Arabic is AL-MAMLAKA AL'ARABIYAH AS-SA'UDIYAH, meaning KINGDOM OF SAUDI ARABIA. *Al-Saud* is the family name of the country's kings. Saudi Arabia's capital is Riyadh.

About two out of three Saudi Arabians are farmers or herders. The farmers raise barley, citrus fruits, dates, wheat, and other crops in *oases* (fertile areas in the desert that have water). The herders are nomads who roam the deserts with camels and other livestock. Less than a third of the people live in cities and towns. The oases farmers live in rural villages. The nomads live in desert camps.

The country was the birthplace of Islam, the Moslem religion. Mecca and Medina are the chief holy cities of the Moslems. Until the 1930's, the people of Saudi Arabia lived just as their ancestors did hundreds of years ago. Then gushing oil wells brought wealth and new ways of life to the country. The government has used some of the profits from the oil industry to

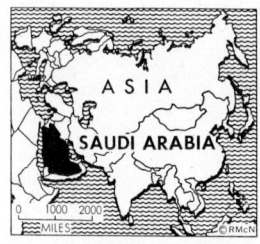

build new roads, airfields, schools, and hospitals. Farm experts have introduced modern methods of agriculture and irrigation. Many desert tribesmen have now settled in the villages where they make their living as farmers.

Saudi Arabia is a leading country among the Arab states of the Middle East. For the relationship of Saudi

───────── **FACTS IN BRIEF** ─────────

**Form of Government:** Monarchy.
**Capital:** Riyadh.
**Official Language:** Arabic.
**Area:** 830,000 square miles. *Greatest Distances*—(north-south) 1,400 miles; (east-west) 1,200 miles. *Coastline*—Red Sea and Gulf of Aqaba, about 1,200 miles; Persian Gulf, about 250 miles.
**Population:** No census available. *Estimated 1970 Population*—7,353,000; distribution, 70 per cent rural, 30 per cent urban; density, 9 persons to the square mile. *Estimated 1975 Population*—7,999,000.
**Chief Products:** *Agriculture*—alfalfa, barley, camels, citrus fruits, dates, goats, horses, millet, sheep, wheat. *Mining*—petroleum. *Fishing*—cod, mackerel, pearls.
**Flag:** The flag is green. It has a white sword below the Arabic inscription, "There is no god but Allah, and Mohammed is the prophet of Allah." Green is a popular Moslem color, the sword is a traditional emblem of the Wahhabi religious group. See FLAG (color picture: Flags of Asia).
**National Anthem:** "As-Salaam Al-Malaki As-Saudi" ("Royal Anthem of Saudi Arabia").
**National Holiday:** Unification of the Kingdom, September 23.
**Money:** *Basic Unit*—riyal. See MONEY (table).

*John R. Randall, the contributor of this article, is Professor of Geography at Ohio State University, and the co-author of* Pattern of Asia.

# SAUDI ARABIA

Arabia to other Asian countries, see ARABIA; ARAB LEAGUE; ASIA; MIDDLE EAST.

## The Land and Its Resources

**Location and Size.** Saudi Arabia covers 830,000 square miles on the Arabian Peninsula. Two neutral zones lie on Saudi Arabia's northern boundary. Separate treaties with Iraq and Kuwait created the neutral zones for the benefit of tribesmen who must cross the boundaries of the three countries in search of grazing land. The boundary between Saudi Arabia and the Trucial States has never been exactly defined because it crosses uninhabited desert.

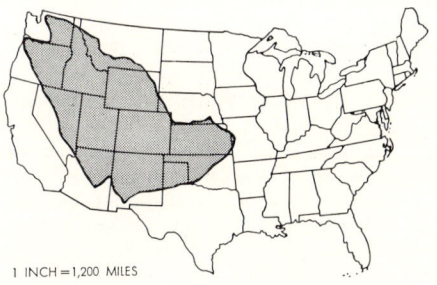

1 INCH = 1,200 MILES

**Saudi Arabia** is more than three times as large as Texas.

**Land Regions.** Saudi Arabia has four land regions: (1) the *tihama* (plain), (2) the western mountains, (3) the interior plateaus, and (4) the eastern coastlands.

*The Tihama* lies along the 1,200-mile-long coastline of the Red Sea and the Gulf of Aqaba. This flat, infertile area reaches a width of 40 miles near Juddah.

*The Western Mountains* rise steeply from the tihama and then slope gently to the east. The jagged red sandstone and black lava peaks of the Hejaz mountain range in the north rise from about 3,000 feet near Juddah to a few peaks of over 5,000 feet near the Gulf of Aqaba. The peaks of the Asir range in the south reach heights of almost 10,000 feet near the Yemen border.

*The Interior Plateaus* extend from the mountains eastward toward the Persian Gulf. This almost barren region of sandy and rocky desert plateaus covers nine-tenths of Saudi Arabia. The region's largest sand deserts are the 250,000-square-mile Rub al Khali and the 25,000-square-mile An Nafud (see ARABIAN DESERT). A few tribesmen live on the waterless Rub al Khali. Some small farm settlements stand at oases in the An Nafud.

*The Eastern Coastlands* lie along the 250-mile-long Persian Gulf coastline. Gravel or sand covers most of this low, rolling plain. Mud flats, lagoons, and sand ridges fringe the Eastern Coastlands on the east. Coral reefs lie offshore in some areas.

**Rivers and Lakes.** The country has no rivers or lakes. However, *wadis* (steep-sided, flat-bottomed valleys) cross many areas. The wadis are dry most of the time. But rainstorms fill them with water that often becomes a torrent until it evaporates or soaks into the ground.

**Natural Resources.** Petroleum is Saudi Arabia's chief natural resource. The country has about one-fifth of the world's oil reserves. The richest deposits are near the Persian Gulf. Western Saudi Arabia has small deposits of gold, copper, and silver. Date palms, and trees and shrubs of the acacia and tamarisk families, grow in the oases. Wood from these trees is used in the oases, but lumber used in cities is imported.

**Climate.** Saudi Arabia is one of the hottest countries in the world. Temperatures in the deserts and coastal

**Mecca Is Islam's Main Holy City.** Moslems all over the world turn toward the Kaaba in Mecca five times a day to pray.
*Arabian American Oil Co.*

**The Mosque of the Prophet in Medina** houses the tomb of Mohammed, who founded the Islamic religion in the A.D. 600's.
*Arabian American Oil Co.*

131

# SAUDI ARABIA

areas may reach 125° F. in summer. Average temperatures at Juddah, on the Red Sea coast, range from 72° F. in January to 87° F. in July. In winter, temperatures sometimes drop to freezing (32° F.) in the mountains and on the interior plateaus.

The coastal regions have a high humidity, but the interior plateaus are extremely dry. About four inches of rain falls on most areas every year. But in some sections, such as the Rub al Khali, several years may pass without any rain.

## Life of the People

**The People and Their Language.** Saudi Arabia has a population of about 7,353,000. An average of about 9 persons live on each square mile. About 70 of every 100 persons live in rural regions, and 30 of every 100 in urban areas. Almost all the people are Arabs. They speak Arabic, the official language. Arabs that roam the deserts are called Bedouins. See ARAB; BEDOUIN.

**Family Life** centers around the Islamic religion. In accordance with Islamic practice, the people usually stop whatever they are doing at sunrise, noon, midafternoon, sunset, and nightfall to bow toward Mecca and pray. Islamic law allows a man to have as many as four wives. However, most men can afford to have only one. The women usually live in one section of the house and the men in another. Saudi Arabian women in cities and villages have little freedom, and seldom leave the house except to shop. Boys and girls play together until the age of 10. Then boys move to the men's section of the house, and the girls move to the women's section.

Until 1962, slavery was legal, and many wealthy persons in Saudi Arabia owned slaves. But the government completely outlawed the slave trade, setting all slaves free in November, 1962.

*Shelter.* Most people in cities and villages live in gray, thick-walled houses from two to six stories high. The houses are made of wood frames and sun-dried clay, mud brick, or stone. High walls surround many of the houses. Following Arab custom, the rooms have no tables or chairs. The people sit on pillows, and eat their meals from bowls placed on cloths spread on the floor. The homes of the wealthy have beautiful rugs. The people sleep on mats rolled out on the floor.

Bedouins live in tents usually made of goat's hair or wool. They divide the tents into sections for the men and for the women. The Bedouins eat and sleep on the mat or rug-covered floors.

*Food.* Dates and grain are the chief foods. The wealthy eat the meat of camels, sheep, and other animals. They consider the hump of a young camel a delicacy. But most Saudi Arabians value their animals too highly for transportation, milk, and other uses to kill them for food. Bedouins seldom bake bread, but city people make flat, leathery loaves. Bedouins enjoy eating locusts, raw or roasted. People along the coasts eat a great deal of fish. Tea, thick coffee, and soured camel's milk are the chief beverages.

*Clothing.* Men wear baggy trousers and *thobs* (loose, ankle-length shirts). They wear *aba'a* (flowing robes of striped camel's-hair cloth) over the thobs. Men cover their heads with round cotton or wool skull caps called *kufiyahs*. Over this they wear *gotras*. A gotra is a red or yellow striped cloth held in place by cords of woven wool wrapped around the head. Women wear loose trousers under long dresses called *gomduras*, and *haiks* (loose veils). Islamic custom requires women to cover their faces in public, although some women go about unveiled in the larger cities.

*Recreation.* Racing fine Arabian horses is a sport of the wealthy in Saudi Arabia. The people also enjoy hunting. Many sheiks hunt with falcons that they train to kill small game. People along the coasts enjoy swimming. Wealthy people in the cities play basketball and soccer, and enjoy other Western sports.

**City Life.** Many of Saudi Arabia's cities have high walls that were built at the time when tribal warfare was common. Most of the larger and newer cities there have been built without walls. Tall *minarets* (towers) and domed *mosques* (Moslem houses of worship) make the drab, dusty cities look different from those in the United States and Canada. Most of the cities serve as trading centers. Mecca is the chief holy city of the Moslems. It was the birthplace of Mohammed, the founder of the Islamic religion. The city's Great Mosque contains a small stone building called the *Kaaba* (see KAABA). The sacred Black Stone is set in the southeast corner of the Kaaba. Moslems believe their sins will be forgiven if they make a *hajj* (pilgrimage) to Mecca. During the *hajj*, the pilgrims march seven times around the Kaaba, kiss the Black Stone, and take part in other religious ceremonies.

After World War II, the cities became more modern, with electric lights, paved streets, and schools and hospitals. The American company that operates the nation's petroleum industry built modern towns with supermarkets and swimming pools for the Saudi Arabians who work in the oil fields and refineries. See HOFUF; MECCA; MEDINA; RIYADH.

**Country Life.** Country people other than the Bedouins live in small villages in the oases. Stone or mud-brick houses crowd together along twisting, unpaved streets. Walls built for protection surround the villages just as they surround the cities.

Every day the Saudi Arabian farmers work in the fields and date gardens around the villages. A village usually has a market place, a few shops, a coffeehouse, and sometimes a mosque. The chief recreation in the villages is telling stories or exchanging gossip over a cup of coffee.

**Bedouin Life.** The Bedouins roam the country with their camels, sheep, and goats. Their desert home has little food or water, and they travel great distances to find grazing land. Each tribe or group of tribes has an area in which it usually lives. The Bedouins often live for months on nothing but dates, cheese, and camel's milk. See ARAB (Nomadic Life); BEDOUIN.

## Work of the People

About 65 of every 100 Saudi Arabians are farmers, and between 20 and 25 of every 100 make their living by raising livestock. Most of the other people are merchants, craftsmen, or workers in the oil industry. Saudi Arabia has no large-scale manufacturing.

**Mining.** Saudi Arabia ranks fourth among the oil-producing nations of the world. Pipelines carry about two-thirds of the petroleum to refineries and shipping centers at Ra's at Tannūrah and on Bahrain Island in the

Specially created for **World Book Encyclopedia** by Rand McNally and World Book editors

## SAUDI ARABIA MAP INDEX

### Cities and Towns

| | | |
|---|---|---|
| Abhā ............E 3 | Al Qaṭīf ............C 4 | Ma'qalā' ............C 4 |
| Abū Hadrīyah ......C 4 | Al Qunfudhah ......E 3 | Masṭūrah ............D 2 |
| Ad Dam- | Al Wajh ............C 2 | Mecca (Mak- |
| mām ....35,408..C 5 | Ar Riyād, | kah) ...185,000..D 2 |
| Afīf ............D 3 | see Riyadh | Medina (Al Ma- |
| Al Ḥamrā' ........D 2 | Aṣ Ṣabyā ........E 3 | dīnah) ..72,291..D 2 |
| Al Ḥillah ........D 4 | As Sulayyil ......D 4 | Qal'at Bīshah ......E 3 |
| Al Hufūf, | Ash Shaqrā' ......C 4 | Qīzān ....15,542..E 3 |
| see Hofuf | Aṭ Ṭā'if ..54,000..D 2 | Rābigh ............D 2 |
| Al Jawf ..........C 2 | Buraydah .43,607..C 3 | Ra's at Tan- |
| Al Khubar .15,688..C 5 | Dhahran ..7,300..C 5 | nūrah ...17,000..C 5 |
| Al Līth ..........D 3 | Ḥā'il ....20,121..C 3 | Riyadh (Ar |
| Al Madīnah, | Hofuf (Al | Riyād) .225,000..C 4 |
| see Medina | Hufūf) .51,837..C 4 | Sakākā ..........C 3 |
| Al Maqnāh ........C 1 | Juddah ..194,000..D 2 | Tabūk ..12,376..C 2 |
| Al Mubarraz ......C 4 | Kāf ............B 2 | Taymā' ............C 2 |
| Al Muwayh ........D 3 | Khaybar ..........C 2 | Turabah ............D 3 |
| Al Muwayliḥ ......C 2 | Majma'ah ..........C 4 | 'Unayzah ..23,455..C 3 |
| Al Qadīmah ......D 2 | Makkah, see Mecca | Yanbu' ............D 2 |

### Physical Features

Ad Dahnā'
  (desert) ........C 4
Al Hasa (region) ...C 4
An Nafūd (desert) ..C 3
Arabian Peninsula .D 4
Asir (region) ......E 3
Farasān Islands ....E 3
Gulf of Aqaba .....C 1
Hejaz (region) ....C 2
Jabal Radwá
  (mountain) ......D 2
Jabal Shār
  (mountain) ......C 2
Nejd (region) .....C 3
Persian Gulf ......C 5
Ra's Abū Madd
  (cape) ..........D 2
Red Sea ..........D 2
Rub' al Khali
  (desert) ........E 4
Syrian Desert .....B 2
Tihama (coastal
  plain) ..........E 3
Tuwayq Mountains .D 4

Source: 1962-63 preliminary census and 1965 official estimates.

132a

**Juddah, a Trade Center,** *left*, is one of Saudi Arabia's most modern cities. It is the major port on the Red Sea. Most Moslem pilgrims stop at Juddah on the way to Mecca.

**Rich Desert Oil Reserves** make Saudi Arabia one of the world's leading oil producers. Pipelines carry petroleum to refineries at Ra's Tannurah, near the Persian Gulf, *below*.

Aramco

Persian Gulf. The 1,068-mile Trans-Arabian pipeline carries about one-third of the oil across the desert to the Mediterranean port of Sidon (Ṣaydā) Lebanon.

Geologists from the United States discovered oil in Saudi Arabia in 1935. The Arabian American Oil Company (Aramco) operates Saudi Arabia's oil industry. Four United States oil companies own Aramco. Aramco pays Saudi Arabia half the value of the crude oil pumped from its wells. This amounts to more than $500 million a year. The money is used to run the government and develop the country.

**Agriculture.** The farmers use crude tools and farming methods on their small farms. Swarms of locusts sometimes destroy crops. But the water shortage and salty soil are the chief agricultural problems. Agricultural experts from the United States have set up farms to teach the farmers improved cultivation methods.

Date palms grow in gardens in almost every oasis. Other important farm products include alfalfa, barley, citrus fruits, millet, and wheat. Some farmers raise cattle. Bedouins have herds of camels, or of sheep and goats. Some rich Saudi Arabians raise Arabian horses.

**Fishing Industry.** Fishermen catch cod, mackerel, and other fishes in the Red Sea and the Persian Gulf. Divers gather pearls from oysters in the Persian Gulf.

**Trade.** Saudi Arabia ships about 600 million barrels of oil a year, mostly to Europe, Asia, and Australia. Other exports include gold and animal hides and skins. Chief imports include automobiles, fruit, lumber, machinery, rice, sugar, and wheat. The United States is the country's largest source of imports. Saudi Arabia usually exports more goods than it imports.

**Transportation.** Camel caravans, donkeys, and automobiles serve as the chief means of transportation. The government-owned Saudi-Arabian Airlines link the chief cities and nearby countries. Airlines from other lands also serve Saudi Arabia. The only railroad runs 350 miles between Riyadh and Ad Dammām. There are over 10,000 miles of road, most of them unpaved. Many international shipping lines serve the ports of Ad Dammām, Juddah, and Ra's at Tannūrah.

**Communication.** Saudi Arabia has four daily newspapers. There are several book and magazine publishers in Mecca and Medina. Mecca has a radio station. A broadcasting station in Riyadh serves Saudi Arabia and neighboring Arab states. Juddah, Ad Dammām, and Riyadh have television stations and motion picture theaters.

## SAUDI ARABIA

### Activities of the People

**Education** is free but not required in Saudi Arabia. There are about 25,000 teachers and 225,000 children in the country's elementary and secondary schools. Saudi Arabia has colleges in Mecca, Medina, and Riyadh. Only about one out of 20 persons in Saudi Arabia can read or write. But the government has opened centers where both adults and children can learn reading and writing.

**The Arts.** Skilled craftsmen make fine jewelry and other objects of gold and silver. See ISLAMIC ART.

### Government

**The King** of Saudi Arabia is hereditary head of state, and he normally is absolute ruler. He also serves as *Imam* (religious leader). A cabinet assists the king (see CABINET). His eldest son or brother often serves as prime minister. The king appoints cabinet members for indefinite terms.

**The Consultative Assembly** advises the ruler, who must approve all laws and acts passed by this body. The assembly has no set number of members. It includes cabinet members, other high-ranking officials, and intellectuals who are appointed for indefinite terms.

**Courts.** The law of Saudi Arabia is based on the *Koran* (the sacred book of Islam) and on the *Sharia* (the Islamic religious law). The Koran and the Sharia cover almost all the people's activities. For example, the Koran forbids Moslems to drink alcoholic beverages. The king is the highest court, except in cases dealing with the interpretation of the Koran and Sharia. The *Ulema* (council of learned men) hands down decisions on these cases. However, the king can ignore the decisions of the Ulema if he desires. Saudi Arabia also has a court system that includes courts of appeal and lower courts.

Ronald Codrai

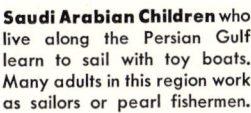

**Saudi Arabian Children** who live along the Persian Gulf learn to sail with toy boats. Many adults in this region work as sailors or pearl fishermen.

133

Aramco

**Endless Waves of Sand Dunes** stretch across Saudi Arabia's deserts. Sandstorms and intense heat sometimes block the movement of trucks to the oil fields. Date palms, *right*, grow in oases in the desert, and provide one of the nation's chief foods.

The government appoints the judges of these courts for indefinite terms.

**Local Government.** The country is divided into Hejaz, Nejd, Eastern, and Asir provinces. These provinces are divided into counties, and then into districts. A governor-general appointed by the king administers each province. The governor-general is assisted by a provincial council of no more than 30 members. Council members serve for two years.

**Politics.** Saudi Arabia is one of the few nations that has no national elections and no political parties.

**Armed Forces.** Saudi Arabia has a small volunteer army and air force, but no navy. United States military advisers have helped train the forces since 1954.

## History

**Early Days.** Scholars know little about the early history of what is now Saudi Arabia. In Biblical days, tribesmen of Arabia roamed the deserts or lived in trading centers such as Mecca and Medina.

Mohammed was born in Mecca in about A.D. 570. He converted most of the people of the Arabian Peninsula to the Islamic religion. The caliphs who succeeded Mohammed as rulers of the Moslems formed Arab armies to spread the Islamic religion (see CALIPH). By the 730's, they controlled an empire that extended from India to Spain.

The Moslem empire began to crumble after the 800's, because of rivalries between several caliphs. By the late 1200's, the Arabian Peninsula had been broken up into many small sheikdoms, under various sheiks.

**The Turkish Conquest.** The Ottoman Turks conquered Hejaz and other sections of western Arabia in the early 1500's. The Nejd area in central Arabia remained under tribal rule. The *Wahhabi* religious group conquered the Nejd and Hejaz regions in the late 1700's and early 1800's. The Wahhabis wanted to reform the Moslems and make them follow Mohammed's teachings more strictly. The Turks sent their allies, the Egyptians, to Saudi Arabia to stop the Wahhabis. The Egyptians defeated the Wahhabis in 1818 and gave the Turks control of much of Arabia. The Turks ruled Hejaz as a province. However, they never gained complete control of Nejd, which was ruled by desert tribes. The Turks forced the Wahhabi leaders to flee to nearby countries.

**Founding a Nation.** Abdul Aziz Ibn Saud, the leader of the Wahhabis, formed an army in the early 1900's and invaded Nejd from Kuwait. Ibn Saud's army conquered all of Nejd and Hejaz between 1902 and 1925. He proclaimed himself *King of Hejaz and Nejd and Its Dependencies* in 1926. The dependencies were Hasa and Asir, provinces of present-day Saudi Arabia. Ibn Saud made Mecca, the chief city of Hejaz, the religious capital; and Riyadh, the home of his family, the political capital of the new kingdom. He changed the country's name to Saudi Arabia in 1932. Ibn Saud founded an army and police force to keep the Bedouins from robbing each other and molesting people in the cities. Geologists discovered vast oil fields in Saudi Arabia in 1935.

Saudi Arabia declared war on Germany and Japan in 1945, but took no part in the fighting. Later that same year, Saudi Arabia became a charter member of both the United Nations and the Arab League. Saudi Arabia fought alongside other Arab nations in 1948 to try to prevent formation of the state of Israel in Palestine. See ISRAEL (History); PALESTINE.

**Recent Events.** Ibn Saud named his oldest son, Saud ibn-Abdul Aziz, prime minister in 1953. When Ibn

134

Saud died later that year, Saud became king and Saud's younger brother, Faisal, became crown prince.

In 1962, Saudi Arabia refused to renew the U.S. Air Force lease to an air base the U.S. built at Dhahran. In April, 1962, Saudi Arabia and Jordan announced plans to merge armed forces and to coordinate economic policies. Late in 1962, Saudi Arabia became involved when a revolt overthrew Yemen's monarchy, replacing it with a republic. Egypt supported the rebels. Saudi Arabia and Jordan aided the royalist forces.

Economic and social reforms in Egypt during the late 1950's and early 1960's started demands for similar changes in Saudi Arabia. The revolt in Yemen and Egyptian President Gamal A. Nasser's campaign for Arab unity caused further unrest in Saudi Arabia in 1963.

Poor health forced King Saud to turn over power in 1963 to Prince Faisal, who immediately started making reforms. He created four provinces for more effective political administration. He also removed King Saud's sons from government positions. A council of the royal family and religious leaders proclaimed Faisal king of Saudi Arabia in November, 1964.

Saudi Arabia sided with Egypt, Jordan, and Syria in the Arab-Israeli war of June, 1967. Saudi Arabia sent troops into Jordan, but the troops did no fighting. The Arab nations were defeated. After the war, Saudi Arabia and Egypt agreed to withdraw their support from the opposing sides in Yemen's civil war. Saudi Arabia also agreed to give $140 million a year to Egypt and Jordan to help their economies because of the losses they suffered during the war.      JOHN R. RANDALL

**Related Articles** in WORLD BOOK include:

| | | |
|---|---|---|
| Arab | Hofuf | Minaret |
| Arab League | Ibn Saud | Mohammed |
| Arabia | Ikhwan | Mosque |
| Arabian Desert | Islam | Petroleum |
| Bedouin | Kaaba | Riyadh |
| Faisal | Mecca | Saud |
| Hejaz | Medina | |

**Outline**

I. **The Land and Its Resources**
   A. Location and Size
   B. Land Regions
   C. Rivers and Lakes
   D. Natural Resources
   E. Climate
II. **Life of the People**
   A. The People and Their Language
   B. Family Life
   C. City Life
   D. Country Life
   E. Bedouin Life
III. **Work of the People**
   A. Mining
   B. Agriculture
   C. Fishing Industry
   D. Trade
   E. Transportation
   F. Communication
IV. **Activities of the People**
   A. Education
   B. The Arts
V. **Government**
VI. **History**

**Questions**

What is Saudi Arabia's chief export?
How is Saudi Arabia's government different from that of the United States or Canada?
What are Hejaz and Nejd?
What part does Mecca play in the Islamic religion?
Why are oases important in Saudi Arabia?
How does family life in Saudi Arabia differ from that in the United States and Canada?
Why is the camel important to Saudi Arabia?
What are some unusual foods eaten in Saudi Arabia?
What role did Abdul Aziz Ibn Saud play in the founding of Saudi Arabia?

## SAULT SAINTE MARIE CANALS

**SAUERKRAUT.** See CABBAGE.

**SAUK INDIANS,** *sawk*, or SAC, belonged to the Algonkian language group of the North American eastern forests tribes. They lived with their close relatives, the Fox Indians. They originally made their home in Canada or Michigan, but the Iroquois drove them out. They then settled in southern Wisconsin, northern Illinois, and Iowa. These Indians had a large village where Rock Island, Ill., now stands. They also set up villages in Iowa along the Mississippi River.

The Sauk and Fox lived in long lodges covered with elm bark. When hunting away from the village in winter, they lived in round houses made of stakes covered with matting. The men wore skin clothing long after cloth was available from white traders.

The Sauk and Fox ceded their Illinois lands to the United States in 1804, and most of them moved across the Mississippi. But a famous warrior, Black Hawk, refused to leave the Rock Island village. This led to the Black Hawk War in 1832, and the defeat of his band (see BLACK HAWK). Most Sauk and Fox now live on reservations in Iowa and Oklahoma.   WAYNE C. TEMPLE

**SAUL** was the first king of Israel and one of the most tragic figures in history. He reigned shortly before 1000 B.C. The dramatic story of his life and times is contained in an unusually vivid section of the Old Testament (I Samuel 9-31).

Israel's existence as a nation was threatened by the Philistines, who had mastered the new technique of fabricating iron, and had a monopoly of iron weapons. Israel's old system of government under casually chosen judges was not equal to the situation. The people clamored for a king, and the old ruling group reluctantly gave in and picked Saul for the task. At this time, he was only a young member of an insignificant clan.

Saul surprised everybody with his ability. He was brave, generous, and modest, and he would not take orders blindly from the old guard. But the mounting pressures and responsibilities of ruling slowly undermined his personality. He became moody and suspicious, and grew jealous of young David's growing popularity.

Saul won many victories, but when the final test came, at the battle of Mount Gilboa, his outnumbered and poorly equipped army was no match for the Philistines. Mortally wounded, he fell on his sword. He was mourned by friend and foe alike.   E. A. SPEISER

See also DAVID.

**SAUL OF TARSUS.** See PAUL, SAINT.

**SAULT SAINTE MARIE,** *SOO saynt muh REE*, Ontario (pop. 74,594; alt. 590 ft.), stands on the Saint Marys River, which connects Lake Superior and Lake Huron (see ONTARIO [political map]). French missionaries named it for the falls in the river. The Old French word *sault* means *falls*. These falls provide hydroelectric power for plants making pulp and paper, chemicals, lumber, and tar. The city has one of the largest iron and steel mills in Canada. Engineers built the International Bridge near the city in 1887, and a canal in 1895 (see SOO CANALS). A highway bridge, completed in 1962, links the city with Sault Ste. Marie, Mich. The French founded a settlement at Sault Sainte Marie in 1668.   D. M. L. FARR

**SAULT SAINTE MARIE CANALS.** See SOO CANALS.

135

# SAUNA

**SAUNA.** See FINLAND (Way of Life).
**SAUNDERS, RICHARD.** See POOR RICHARD'S ALMANAC.
**SAURISCHIAN.** See DINOSAUR.
**SAUROPOD.** See DINOSAUR.
**SAUSAGE,** *SAW sij,* is a food made of chopped and seasoned meat. The meats used in making sausage include beef, game, pork, poultry, veal, and—in some countries—fish. Sausage is seasoned with herbs and spices, including salt, red and black pepper, sage, garlic, onions, sugar, and ginger. Most sausages contain small amounts of curing agents called *nitrates* and *nitrites,* which give sausages their color. Europeans sometimes add gin or red wine to the sausage they make to give it a special flavor.

Most sausage meat is pressed into a long, round *casing* (skin). Natural casings are made from the intestines of farm animals, especially sheep. Before these casings are used, they are carefully cleaned and salted, or soaked in *brine* (salty water). Casings made of cellulose materials are often used today (see CELLULOSE). Skinless frankfurters are sausages that have their casings removed before the sausages are marketed.

Sausage meat and sausages are important products of the packing industry. In many countries, sausage is also made at home. Fresh sausages are sold raw and may be boiled, fried, or broiled. Other sausages are sold cooked or smoked. They are ready to eat.

The frankfurter, named for Frankfurt, Germany, is the most popular sausage in the world. It is made of cured and well-smoked pork and beef. Experts believe frankfurters were first made in Germany during the Middle Ages. Frankfurters are also called *hot dogs, red hots,* and *wienies* in America. Frankfurters served in a bun (usually called hot dogs) are a favorite American food.

Vienna sausage, or *wienerwurst,* looks like a frankfurter but is shorter. It is named for Vienna (Wien), Austria.                                   JOHN C. AYRES

See also MEAT PACKING (picture).
**SAUSAGE TREE.** See TREE (picture: Some Unusual Trees).
**SAUSSURE, FERDINAND DE.** See LINGUISTICS (The Structuralists).
**SAVA RIVER,** *SAH vah,* is a branch of the Danube River in Yugoslavia. The Sava rises in the Carnic Alps, near the southern border of Austria and continues in a southeasterly direction for 450 miles. It flows through Yugoslavia to Belgrade, where it joins the Danube. Three-fourths of the Sava's course can be used for shipping.

**SAVAGE ISLAND.** See NIUE ISLAND.
**SAVAI'I ISLAND.** See WESTERN SAMOA.
**SAVANNA,** *suh VAN uh,* or SAVANNAH, is any large area of land covered with tall, stiff grasses, and clumps of trees. The grass on savannas grows in bunches and tufts and seldom forms a continuous cover of sod. Most savannas make good grazing for cattle. Many savannas lie between forests and deserts. A good example of this is the grasslands of the Sudan in Africa, which lie between the dense growth of the Congo and the great desert expanse of the Sahara region. Other savanna areas of the world include the llanos region of northern South America, the campos of Brazil, and the veld grasslands of South Africa. The great plains of North America and the steppes of Europe may also be called savannas. The prairies of North America are rich agricultural regions. The savannas of central Africa are the homes of the big game of the world. See also LLANOS; PAMPA; PASTURE; PRAIRIE; STEPPE.          ERNEST L. THURSTON

**SAVANNAH,** nuclear ship. See SHIP AND SHIPPING (Nuclear Power for Ships; color picture).

*New York Public Library Picture Collection*
**The *Savannah* Used Both Steam and Sails for Power.**

**SAVANNAH** was the first steamship to cross the Atlantic Ocean. The *Savannah* sailed from Savannah, Ga., on May 22, 1819, and docked in Liverpool, England, on June 20, 1819. The ship was driven by steam for a total of between 80 and 105 hours. Sails were used the rest of the time.

*Armour and Company*

**Many Kinds of Sausages** are made by meat packers. They include, *left to right,* cervelat, capacola, cooked salami, Genoa salami, B.C. salami, and thuringer.

136

**Johnson Square** in Savannah, Ga., was laid out by Georgia colonists in 1733. The Nathanael Greene Monument, *left*, stands in the center of the square. The City Hall, *background*, contains a replica of the S.S. *Savannah*, first steamship to cross the Atlantic.

Al L'Heureux, Savannah Chamber of Commerce

**SAVANNAH,** Ga. (pop. 149,245; met. area pop. 188,299; alt. 20 ft.), the state's second largest city, is one of the chief Southern ports. It has one of the most up-to-date systems of docks and warehouses in the world. Savannah lies about 18 miles inland, across the Savannah River from South Carolina. A 40-foot-deep channel connects the city with the Atlantic Ocean. See GEORGIA (political map). For the monthly weather in Savannah, see GEORGIA (Climate).

Hunter Army Airfield near Savannah and Fort Stewart 40 miles south of the city make up the U.S. Army Flight Training Center for helicopter pilots. Armstrong State College and Savannah State College are in Savannah. The Telfair Academy of Arts and Sciences ranks as one of the leading art galleries in the South. The Rev. George Whitefield opened Bethesda, the nation's oldest orphanage, near Savannah, in 1740. Girl Scouts from all parts of the world come to Savannah to visit the home of Juliette Gordon Low, who founded the Girl Scouts in the United States.

**Industry and Trade.** Savannah is the trading center for a large farming region. Sawmills located nearby ship much lumber through Savannah each year. The city's chief industry is the manufacture of kraft paper, a strong paper used for making bags. Mills make this paper from southern slash pine, which grows around the city. Savannah is an important naval stores center (see NAVAL STORES). Other important products include wood pulp, refined sugar, fertilizer, packaged tea, petroleum products, roofing materials, ships, truck trailers, cement, and aircraft assemblies. Canneries process shrimp, crab meat, and oysters.

**History.** James Oglethorpe founded Savannah on Feb. 12, 1733, as Georgia's first colonial settlement. Because of this, people call it the *Mother City of Georgia*. Savannah was one of the first planned cities in the United States. Settlers built it according to a design by William Bull and Oglethorpe. It was the chief city and capital of the Georgia colony until after the Revolutionary War. Eli Whitney invented the cotton gin near Savannah in 1793. The first steamship to cross an ocean, the S.S. *Savannah*, traveled from Savannah to Liverpool, England, in 1819. General William T. Sherman ended his march to the sea when he captured Savannah in 1864. Savannah is the county seat of Chatham County, and has a council-manager form of government. ALBERT B. SAYE

**SAVANNAH RIVER** is a waterway that forms a large part of the boundary between Georgia and South Carolina. Several small streams unite to form the main stream. The rivers rise near the southern boundary of North Carolina and flow together on the boundary of Georgia and South Carolina, a few miles southwest of Anderson, S.C. From this boundary point, the Savannah River flows southeast, and empties into the Atlantic Ocean at Tybee Roads. The Savannah River is 341 miles long. An 18-mile long channel, dug 30 feet deep, leads from the ocean to the city of Savannah. Large ships can use this channel. Smaller ships can go 230 miles up the river, as far as Augusta, Ga. The Clark Hill Dam above Augusta, Ga., forms a reservoir 38 miles long. It supplies power to the Savannah River Atomic Energy Plant in South Carolina. For location, see GEORGIA (physical map). DAVID J. DE LAUBENFELS

**SAVANNAH STATE COLLEGE** is a state-controlled coeducational school at Savannah, Ga. The college offers liberal arts, technical, and teacher-training courses. Graduates receive B.S. degrees. Savannah State College was founded in 1890. For enrollment, see UNIVERSITIES AND COLLEGES (table).

## SAVE THE CHILDREN FEDERATION

**SAVE THE CHILDREN FEDERATION** is a nonprofit organization. It sponsors needy children and schools, without regard to race, creed, or color. The federation collects clothing for welfare and disaster use, and aids rural communities to help their children. It works in the United States and 12 other countries. Its main office is in Norwalk, Conn.

**SAVINGS** provide a sense of security and independence that cannot be achieved in any other way. This sense of security can be a source of great satisfaction and pride to people. Hoarding money for no useful purpose is miserliness, just as hoarding physical energy, without using it for anything, is laziness. But saving for some definite goal can be a source of real satisfaction.

There are probably as many reasons for saving money as there are ambitions and desires for men and women to have. Some persons who work for others save something from their wages each payday to be able to buy their own businesses some day. Others save in order to buy a home, an automobile, or new furniture; or to take a vacation. Families often save so that their sons and daughters may be able to go to college. A large number of persons save money during their working days so they may have money to live on in addition to their retirement pensions. Almost everyone tries to *save for a rainy day*, putting aside a certain amount of money with which to pay for a sudden illness or some other emergency. Some persons save for these emergencies by buying insurance.

The practice of thrift is largely a matter of habit. The amount saved is less important than the process of saving itself. Andrew Carnegie once said, "The best way to accumulate money is resolutely to bank a fixed portion of your income, no matter how small the amount."

Some persons believe that saving is not so important as it once was. Many things can be bought on the installment plan, paid for with a little money from each month's wages instead of with funds already saved. Installment buying does make it possible to enjoy many things without first having to save money to pay for them. But some persons often buy more than they can afford on the installment plan. Later payments, plus interest payments on this *borrowed* money, must be made with future income. These installment payments can become a financial strain. The availability of easy credit does not in itself reduce the importance of the savings habit.

**Aids to Saving.** Most people once saved cash at home, hiding it under mattresses, in sugar bowls, or in some other special place. Many persons mistrusted banks, and most banks were not interested in handling small savings accounts. Only the wealthy could invest in stocks and bonds.

Hoarding cash at home or hiding it in some place is dangerous, because the funds can be lost or stolen. It is also unprofitable, because the money earns no interest. But invested savings are safe, and they earn interest. There are many ways to invest savings, no matter how small the amount.

*Government Bonds.* The United States government encourages systematic saving on a national basis by selling bonds and savings stamps. Schools encourage students to save part of their allowances and to buy savings stamps every week. This plan starts the savings habit early in life.

*Savings Banks.* Almost all banks encourage people to save, and most banks have savings departments. Savings banks specialize in this work, and many of them will open an account of as little as $1, sometimes even less.

*Credit Unions* are cooperative savings and loan groups that help people save in much the same way as savings banks do. The unions are operated by the members who join them. Many credit unions are organized among employees of companies, in labor unions, among farm groups, and in educational, religious, and social institutions.

*Stocks and Bonds.* A growing number of persons invest their savings in securities, such as common and preferred stocks and corporate bonds. In this way they help furnish capital to industrial companies, and earn interest and dividends for themselves. Since World War II, small stockholders have become an increasingly important factor in industrial financing. Investors in stocks may usually buy as few shares as they like. Some investment firms encourage stockholders to invest a small amount monthly in stocks and bonds. Many companies throughout the United States permit their employees to buy stock in the company at a reduced rate. Another popular form of savings is through investment clubs, in which a group of people agree to pool their money to buy stock in various companies.

**Interest.** Savings made in the ways discussed in this article earn interest or dividends for the investor. Interest and dividends are a major element in the growth of a savings account or an investment in securities. A sum of money deposited in a savings account on which interest is compounded annually at $3\frac{1}{2}$ per cent will double itself in about 20 years. LEONARD C. R. LANGER

**Related Articles** in WORLD BOOK include:

| | |
|---|---|
| Banks and Banking | Investment |
| Bond | Savings and Loan |
| Credit Union | Association |
| Federal Deposit | Savings Bank |
| Insurance Corporation | Stock, Capital |
| Insurance | Stock Exchange |

**SAVINGS AND LOAN ASSOCIATION** is a home-financing and savings organization. It is a *mutual* institution, owned and operated by its shareholders. Its savers, as shareholders, elect a board of directors to manage the organization. Savings and loan associations help individuals pay for the cost of buying, building, repairing, and remodeling homes. They also promote thrift. These organizations are sometimes called *building and loan associations*, *homestead associations*, or *cooperative banks*.

Savings and loan associations receive savings for safekeeping and investment. Technically, the savers buy *shares* of ownership in the associations, but actually their savings are much like deposits in a commercial bank. Associations lend money in the form of first mortgage loans for the purpose of building, buying, or remodeling homes. Borrowers pay off the loan in small monthly amounts, usually over a period of from 12 to 30 years. Savings and loan associations hold about half the mortgages on one- to four-bedroom homes in the United States. These mortgages amount to over $180 billion. Nearly 9 of every 10 dollars of all savings association assets go into home mortgages. Associations also invest some money in government bonds, and maintain some money as a cash balance.

Each association pays its operating costs and other expenses with part of the interest earned on loans and investments. It also invests some money in financial reserves. The rest of the interest, better than one-half of all income, is distributed among the shareholders in the form of dividends.

The first savings and loan association in the United States opened in 1831. Today, more than 6,200 such institutions serve over 35 million savers. The savers hold share accounts worth more than $93 billion. The associations have their own central reserve system, and are controlled by both federal and state laws. In most associations, savings up to $15,000 for each member are insured against loss by the Federal Savings and Loan Insurance Corporation. EDWARD W. REED

**SAVINGS BANK.** The savings of the average wage earner are often too small to be invested. But the total savings of many wage earners can be invested at a profit. Savings banks receive small deposits and are able to pay interest by profitably investing the merged funds.

State laws often limit the types of investments savings banks can make, minimizing the chance that depositors' money will be lost. Federal laws also regulate savings banks.

There are two classes of savings banks, *mutual* savings banks and *stock* savings banks. Depositors own mutual savings banks as a group, and share in the profits of the bank. The bank lends about half of these deposits to individuals and businesses, and invests the rest in bonds. Persons who hold stock in the bank own stock savings banks. They divide the profit.

Daniel Defoe, the English author, is credited with originating the idea of the savings bank in 1697. But a Scot, Henry Duncan, is called the *father of savings banks*. In 1810, he founded a savings bank which took in $5,800 in deposits in four years. The first savings banks in the United States were the Philadelphia Savings Society and the Provident Institution of Boston, both founded in 1816. G. L. BACH

See also BANKS AND BANKING; CREDIT UNION; SAVINGS AND LOAN ASSOCIATION.

**SAVINGS BOND** is a kind of bond issued by the United States government. Through the sale of savings bonds, the federal government borrows billions of dollars in small amounts from many individuals. The person who buys a savings bond agrees to lend his money to the government for a certain length of time. The government agrees to pay interest on the money it borrows. A savings bond is thus a form of government debt.

The best-known savings bond is called the *Series E* bond. This kind of savings bond pays an interest rate of 4.15 per cent when held until it *matures* (comes due) in 7 years. An individual who lends the government $75 will get $100 when the bond matures. This includes $25 interest on his money for the period of the loan. The buyer may cash in the bond after 60 days and get back his original investment. But he receives no interest until the bond is held for 6 months. There are bonds in the *E* series from $25 to $10,000. Each is sold at 75 per cent of

# SAVOY

its *face* (maturity) value. No person is allowed to buy more than $10,000 worth of *Series E* bonds in any single year.

Another type of savings bond is the *Series H* bond, which pays interest at the rate of 4.15 per cent if held for 10 years. Interest payments are made every six months by U.S. government check. No person may buy more than $20,000 worth of *Series H* bonds in any single year.

The United States government first issued savings bonds in the *Liberty Loan* drive during World War I. A new savings bond drive was organized in May, 1941, to help meet the cost of defense. From then until the end of World War II in 1945, more than $54 billion worth of savings bonds were sold. The government has continued to sell savings bonds ever since. The savings bond program is conducted by the Savings Bond Division of the Department of the Treasury. G. L. BACH

See also BOND (picture); NATIONAL DEBT.

**SAVONAROLA,** SAV oh nuh RO luh, **GIROLAMO** (1452-1498), was an Italian friar, a fiery religious reformer, and a preacher. By 1490, he had begun his attempts to reform the city of Florence through preaching. He was a highly emotional, but effective, preacher. His humor, charm, colorful language, and theatrical presentations made him a leading figure. He claimed he had prophetical inspiration, and criticized bitterly the immorality of Pope Alexander VI (see ALEXANDER [VI]). He also predicted punishment of the Roman Catholic Church and Italy.

Pope Alexander VI ordered Savonarola to Rome in 1495 to explain his claim to special revelation, but the friar refused. He said his health and fear of violence on the way made it impossible and stated: "It is not the will of God that I leave Florence." The pope then ordered him to stop preaching.

When Savonarola resumed preaching during Lent in 1496, the pope excommunicated him for disobedience. When he continued his defiance, Alexander VI threatened to place Florence under an *interdict* (ban on worship) unless the city could force him to go to Rome or could force him to be silent until he asked absolution. Savonarola surrendered to the civil authorities. He was tried and condemned by an ecclesiastical court, which turned him over to the civil authorities for punishment. On May 23, 1498, Savonarola was hanged, and his body burned.

Savonarola was born in Ferrara of a noble family. He studied humanism, philosophy, and medicine before he joined the Dominican order in 1474. The English novelist George Eliot portrayed Savonarola's life in her novel *Romola*. JAMES A. CORBETT and FULTON J. SHEEN

**SAVOY,** suh VOY, was, until 1946, the oldest reigning family in Europe. Humbert, count of Savoy, founded the house during the 1000's. The family originally ruled a few small countries on the slopes of the Alps in northwestern Italy. Then it acquired holdings on the plains below the mountains. Genoa was added in 1815. The family extended its rule over all Italy by taking advantage of three wars fought between 1859 and 1871. The House of Savoy lost the Italian throne in 1946. R. JOHN RATH

See also VICTOR EMMANUEL.

139

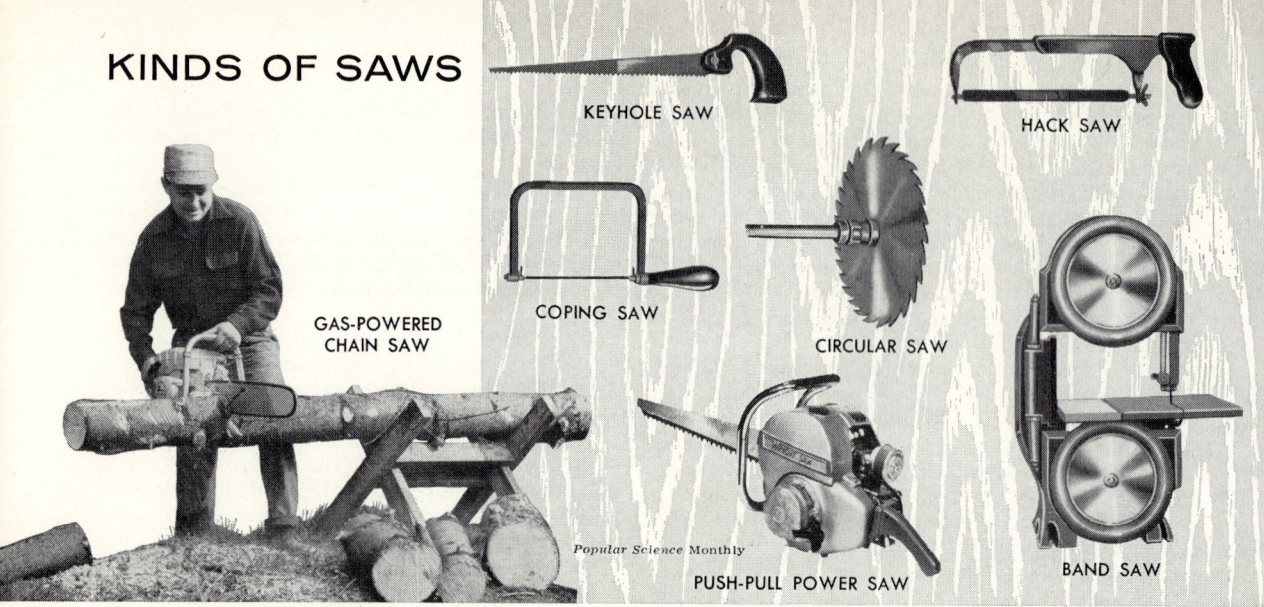

## KINDS OF SAWS

KEYHOLE SAW
HACK SAW
COPING SAW
CIRCULAR SAW
GAS-POWERED CHAIN SAW
PUSH-PULL POWER SAW
BAND SAW

*Popular Science Monthly*

**SAW** is a cutting tool that has a metal blade with teeth set at an angle along one edge. Workmen use saws to cut wood, stone, metal, plastics, and other material.

**Circular Saws** each have a round disk or plate with teeth around the edge. Different sizes and shapes of the teeth enable the saw to cut rough or fine work on many different materials. Sawmills use circular saws as large as 7 feet in diameter for cutting logs into lumber. Smaller sizes, from 6 inches to 2 feet in diameter, cut lumber and plywood for wood products.

**Band Saws** have flexible bands of steel with teeth along one edge. Band saws form an endless belt on a power-driven pulley. They saw straight, curved, or irregular cuts in both wood and metal. Sawmills use large band saws to make lumber.

**Crosscut Saws** are straight saws about 8 feet long, with handles at both ends. The teeth are designed to cut on both the forward and the backward motion of the saw. Crosscut saws are used to cut down trees.

**Chain Saws** serve the same general purposes as crosscut saws. But the teeth fit on an endless chain that is driven by a gasoline engine or electric motor.

**Hack Saws** have a narrow blade of hardened steel, and are used chiefly for cutting metal. The operator may run the saw by hand or use power.

**Scroll Saws,** or *coping saws*, have narrow blades with fine teeth. They cut intricate patterns in thin material. They may be used by hand, or be power driven.

**Friction Saws** may be made in the form of band saws or circular saws. Sometimes they have no teeth. They run at high speeds, and can cut even the hardest steel. The blades move rapidly, and cause the material to become red hot and soft at the point of contact. The blade remains cool because only a part of it touches the material at one time.   ARTHUR C. ANSLEY

See also LUMBER (pictures).

**SAWBILL.** See MERGANSER.

**SAWFISH** is a fish that lives in the warm parts of the oceans and in some fresh coastal waters. It is a relative of the shark and the ray. The sawfish can be recognized by its long, flat snout that looks like a saw. The saw shark has a similar snout, but can be told from the sawfish by the position of the gill openings. In the saw shark, these slits are on the side of the neck. In the sawfish, the gill slits are on the undersurface. The snout is sometimes six feet long. Each side of the snout has many sharp teeth like the teeth of a saw. The sawfish uses its teeth to tear open the body of its victim, and to defend itself against bigger and stronger sea animals. Because of its snout, the sawfish is one of the most dangerous of all fish of the sea. There are several species.

**Scientific Classification.** The sawfish belongs to the sawfish family, *Pristidae*. A common species in the United States is genus *Pristis*, species *P. pectinatus*.   CARL L. HUBBS

**Two Dangerous-Looking Sawfish** came from the Gulf of Mexico near Fort Myers, Fla. These fish have sharklike bodies and long snouts, with a single row of teeth on each edge.

*Ewing Galloway*

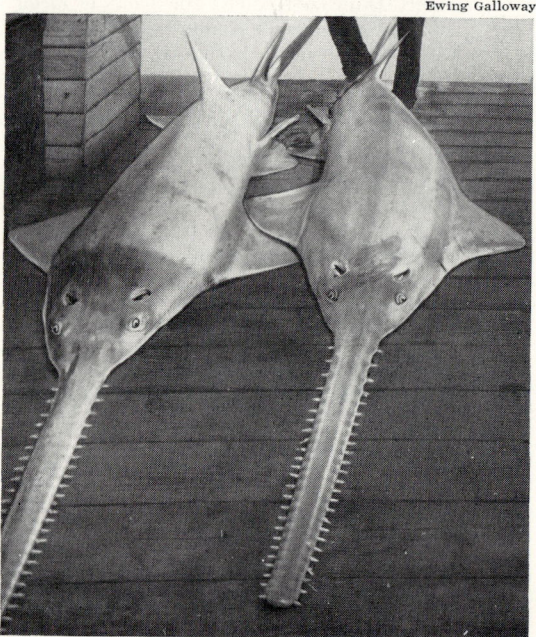

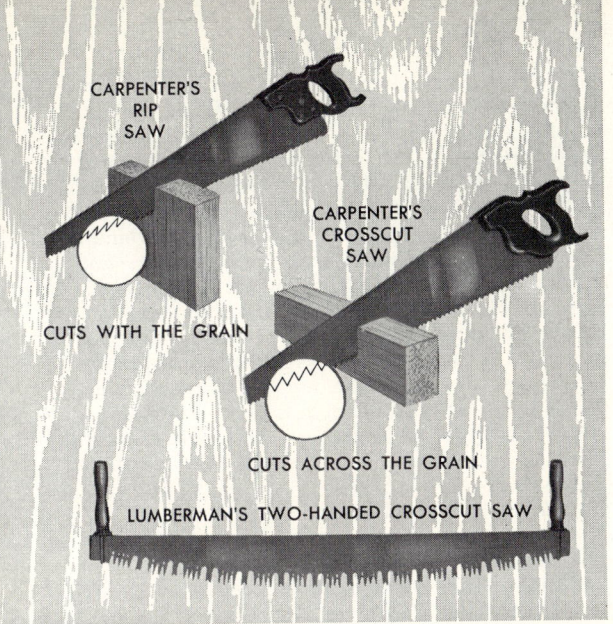

CARPENTER'S RIP SAW
CUTS WITH THE GRAIN
CARPENTER'S CROSSCUT SAW
CUTS ACROSS THE GRAIN
LUMBERMAN'S TWO-HANDED CROSSCUT SAW

**SAWFLY** is an insect related to ants, bees, and wasps. Female sawflies lay their eggs in the leaves and stems of plants and trunks of trees. A sawlike organ slits the leaf and pushes the egg inside. Most young sawflies resemble caterpillars but they have more legs along their abdomens than caterpillars. Some young sawflies make holes in stems, fruit, wood, or leaves. Some form *galls* (swellings) on leaves or stems. Adult sawflies have four thin wings.

The most destructive North American sawflies are those that attack pine, fir, larch, and spruce trees. Other important species damage garden roses, currant bushes, wheat stems, cherry and pear trees, and birch and elm trees.

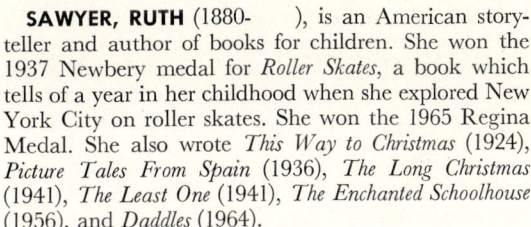

USDA
**The Sawfly**

**Scientific Classification.** Sawflies belong to the ant, bee, and wasp order, *Hymenoptera*, and make up the sawfly family *Tenthredinidae*. E. G. LINSLEY

**SAWMILL.** See LUMBER.

**SAWYER, RUTH** (1880- ), is an American storyteller and author of books for children. She won the 1937 Newbery medal for *Roller Skates*, a book which tells of a year in her childhood when she explored New York City on roller skates. She won the 1965 Regina Medal. She also wrote *This Way to Christmas* (1924), *Picture Tales From Spain* (1936), *The Long Christmas* (1941), *The Least One* (1941), *The Enchanted Schoolhouse* (1956), and *Daddles* (1964).

*The Long Christmas* appeared in Dutch in 1950. *The Least One*, the story of a Mexican boy, was published in German in 1952 for distribution by the U.S. Army.

She was born in Boston, attended the Garland Kindergarten Training School in Boston, and was graduated from Columbia University. EVELYN RAY SICKELS

**SAWYER, TOM.** See TWAIN, MARK; NOVEL.
**SAX, ADOLPHE.** See SAXOPHONE.
**SAXE, COMTE DE** (1696-1750), MAURICE DE SAXE, a German soldier of fortune, led French armies to victory in the War of the Austrian Succession (see SUCCESSION WARS). He was made a Marshal of France for his successes over the British in The Netherlands. Saxe was born at Goslar, Germany, the illegitimate son of King Augustus II of Saxony. RAYMOND O. ROCKWOOD

**SAXE-COBURG-GOTHA.** See WINDSOR (family).
**SAXIFRAGE,** *SACK sah frij*, is any one of a group of small, hardy plants that grow in cold and temperate parts of the northern hemisphere. The word *saxifrage* means *rock-breaker*. The plants were given this name because they usually grow between mountain rocks.

Saxifrages grow from 2 inches to 3 feet high. The thick, fleshy leaves grow near the ground. The flower stalk grows straight upward, and bears clusters of white, pink, purple, or yellow blossoms. The blossoms usually have 5 sepals, 5 petals, and 10 stamens.

The *early saxifrage* is one of the most common species. It has white flowers, and blooms as early as April. It grows from southeastern Canada to Georgia and west to Missouri.

**Scientific Classification.** Saxifrages are in the saxifrage family, *Saxifragaceae*. They make up the genus *Saxifraga*. Early saxifrage is *S. virginiensis*. ROBERT W. HOSHAW

See also CURRANT; DEUTZIA; GOOSEBERRY; HYDRANGEA; MOCK ORANGE.

**Strawberry Saxifrage** is a hardy and attractive plant in the home. Like the strawberry, it sends out long runners which form new roots.

**Early Saxifrage** is among the first spring flowers. It blooms early in April.

J. C. Allen & Son; Devereux Butcher

# SAXON

**SAXON** was a member of a Germanic tribe that invaded the island of Britain about 1,500 years ago. The Angles, another Germanic tribe, invaded Britain about the same time. The two tribal groups mixed and established the Anglo-Saxon kingdom, which lasted until the Norman Conquest of 1066.

The ancient geographer Ptolemy first mentioned the Saxons in a book he wrote during the A.D. 100's. According to Ptolemy, the Saxons lived in an area in southern Denmark called *Saxony* (now Schleswig, in Germany). They were a warlike people who invaded Roman territory in the late 300's, during the reigns of the emperors Julian and Valentinian. By the 500's, the Saxons had settled along the coast of Gaul (now France), between the Elbe and Loire rivers. The Saxons invaded Britain in the mid-400's, conquered the Celts who lived there, and settled in the southern and western parts of the island.

In the 700's, Charlemagne conquered the Saxons still on the continent, forced them to accept Christianity, and made their country part of his empire. The home of the Saxons became part of Germany.   BRYCE LYON

See also ANGLO-SAXON.

**SAXON, LYLE** (1891-1946), an American author, won fame for his books about Southern life. Many of his stories are set in the Louisiana bayou country. His works include *Father Mississippi* (1927), *Fabulous New Orleans* (1928), *Old Louisiana* (1929), *Lafitte, the Pirate* (1930), and *Children of Strangers* (1937). Saxon was born in Baton Rouge, La. He was graduated from Louisiana State University.

**SAXONY,** a region and former state in east-central Germany, covers 6,839 square miles. The East German government abolished it as a political unit in 1952, and divided the region into the districts of Leipzig, Dresden, and Chemnitz (now Karl-Marx-Stadt).

Mountains cover the southern part of Saxony, but more than half the land can be tilled. Farmers grow wheat, rye, barley, oats, potatoes, and fruits on their small farms. Forests cover about a fourth of Saxony. The Fichtelberg, the region's highest peak, rises 4,000 feet in the beautiful Erzgebirge section, in the southeast. Saxony's great waterway, the Elbe, crosses in a northwesterly direction.

The region has deposits of silver, coal, iron, lead, tin, and marble. Saxony produces more textiles than any other section in Germany. Dresden china, made at Meissen, is world famous. The 5½ million people who live in Saxony speak German.

In the 1400's, the eastern part of the Duchy of Saxony came under the rule of the Wettin family, who called it Saxony. Saxony joined the German Empire in 1871. It became a republic after World War I. Russia occupied Saxony after Germany surrendered in World War II.   JAMES K. POLLOCK

See also DRESDEN; SEVEN WEEKS' WAR.

**SAXOPHONE,** *SACK soh fohn,* is a single-reed wind instrument made of brass. It combines the conical tubing of the cornet-type instruments with the single-reed tone principle of the clarinet. Military bands quickly put the saxophone to use. It has taken an important place in concert bands and dance bands. It is a good solo instrument, and has been used in some important orchestral works, such as Bizet's *L'Arlésienne* suite. Saxophones range in size from the little-used E-flat and B-flat sopranos to the contrabass in E-flat. The E-flat alto and the B-flat tenor are most commonly used. Adolphe Sax (1814-1894), a Belgian instrument maker, invented the saxophone about 1840.   CHARLES B. RIGHTER

**SAY, JEAN BAPTISTE** (1767-1832), a French economist, did much to spread the doctrines of Adam Smith. Say's principal work was *Treatise on Political Economy* (1803). He is credited with dividing the subject of economics into production, distribution, and consumption. He also established a *law of markets*, which stated that there can be no general overproduction of goods. He believed that additional supplies create an additional demand. Say was born in Lyon.   H. W. SPIEGEL

**SCAB,** a disease of plants. See APPLE (Diseases and Pests); POTATO (Insect Pests and Diseases); WHEAT (Other Diseases).

**SCAB,** in labor. See LABOR (Terms); STRIKE.

**SCAB,** in medicine. See BLOOD (Blood Clotting).

**SCABLAND.** See WASHINGTON (Land Regions).

**SCAFELL PIKE.** See ENGLAND (Location, Size, and Surface Features).

**SCALAWAG** was a white Southerner who worked with Negroes and northern Republicans to control politics in the South after the Civil War. Southern Democrats, who believed these men were "beasts in men's clothing," called them *scalawags,* a term commonly applied to useless cattle. Most scalawags were businessmen and planters who had opposed *secession* (withdrawal) from the Union before the war. Some sought personal gain, but others believed that the South had to discard its prewar social and racial views in order to survive. Scalawags helped to bring about educational and social reforms and to pass laws that allowed Negroes to vote. They

Bowmar Educational Records

**The Saxophone** is a brass wind instrument with a reed. It is widely used in military and concert bands, and groups that play popular music.

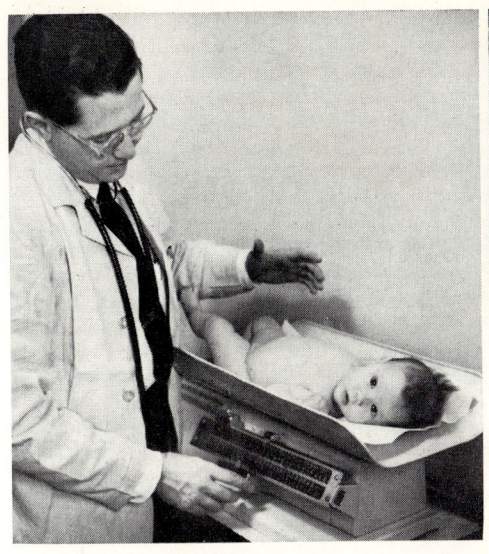

Rie Gaddis Wehrmann; Fairbanks-Morse & Co.

**Scales—Small and Large.** The baby scale, *left*, helps record the growth of tiny infants. The platform scale, *above*, checks the weight of giant trailer trucks to see if they exceed highway weight limits.

gradually disappeared during the 1870's, as Democrats regained control of the South. See also RECONSTRUCTION (Scalawags and Carpetbaggers). FRANK L. KLEMENT

**SCALDS.** See BURNS AND SCALDS.

**SCALE.** See MAP (Scale).

**SCALE,** in music. See MUSIC (Sound in Music).

**SCALE.** Scales are flat plates that form the outer covering of most fishes and of many snakes and lizards. Hardened, horny folds of skin form the scales of reptiles. In most fishes, the scales are bony discs developed from the under skin. But sharks' scales bear enamel on the outer surface and bone on the inner surface. Scales also cover a few mammals, such as the scaly anteater. Scales overlap one another like shingles, and form a protective armor for the softer body beneath. They vary in size, shape, and arrangement, according to the animal they cover. The wings of butterflies and moths have tiny, downy scales.

In botany, scales are little flaky leaves that cover tree buds and woody plants in cold and temperate climates. These scales shield the buds from sudden temperature changes. The regular pieces of a pine cone are called scales. L. B. AREY

See also SCALE INSECT.

**SCALE, WEIGHING,** *WAY ing*, is a mechanical device for finding the weight of any substance. All types of weighing scales are based on the principles of balance. The principle is easy to understand if a horizontal bar is balanced at the top of a vertical bar so that it will tilt at an angle if touched. If a one-pound piece of iron is hung from each end of the balanced rod, the rod will not tilt. If two unequal weights are hung from the ends, the heavier one will pull its end of the rod down, and raise the lighter weight.

Now suppose the horizontal bar were pivoted at a point to one side of the center. It would not be balanced. A heavier weight would be needed at the end of the shorter arm to raise the pound weight hung at the end of the long arm. This is the type of lever on which most scales are based.

The *beam scale* or *balance* probably originated in ancient Egypt. Some historians believe it was invented 5,000 years before the Christian Era. The earliest balances were of the cord-pivot type. The beam was hung at its center by a cord attached to a fixed support. Scale pans hung by cords from the ends of the beam. The object to be weighed was placed on one scale pan. Known weights were placed on the other pan until the two hung in balance.

The balance scale is still commonly used in laboratories, for accurate weighing during experiments. It can precisely weigh extremely light objects.

**The Platform Scale** is one of the more familiar weighing machines. The scales used to weigh persons are usually of this type. It has a hinged platform, set within or above a fixed platform. A weight placed on the hinged platform will cause the platform to press on a lever underneath. The lever is connected with a rod which rises perpendicularly for a certain height (according to the size of the machine). A knife-edge joint in turn connects this to the short end of a horizontal lever. The longer arm of the lever carries a movable counterweight. The arm is marked off into pounds.

The object being weighed presses down the lever under the platform. This pulls down the shorter end of the weighing lever and causes the longer arm with the weights to rise. Then a weight is moved along the lever to a place where the lever is brought into perfect balance. The mark on the lever at the spot where the weight rests indicates how much the object weighs.

In some platform scales, a one-pound weight on the lever will balance 10 pounds or 100 pounds on the platform. If the lever is made longer, the difference will increase until one pound on the lever balances 1,000 pounds or more on the platform. Such a great difference is needed for weighing very heavy objects. Thaddeus Fairbanks patented the platform scale in 1831.

**Other Weighing Machines.** Some weighing machines are so large that they will correctly weigh monster locomotives. Others, used by scientists, have such delicate adjustment that a few words written on a piece of paper with a soft lead pencil can be weighed. Machines for weighing heavy guns in government arsenals may weigh more than 300,000 pounds. Spring scales can be made

## SCALE INSECT

to measure in tons a locomotive's pull. Many weighing machines keep a record of the amounts they weigh.

Retail stores often use a complicated balance scale for weighing groceries and such goods. These machines can also figure the cost. A pointer is set at the price per pound at which the goods are to be sold. The articles are then put on the scale. A lever shows the weight in the ordinary manner, and the price of the products being weighed shows on a dial.    E. A. FESSENDEN

See also BALANCE; CALCULATING MACHINE (picture).

**SCALE INSECT,** or BARK LOUSE, is one of many kinds of sucking insects that feed on plants. Scale insects cluster on plants, sucking out the juices through their tiny, tube-like beaks. They may weaken a plant so much that it dies.

The female scale insect does the damage. The adult male has no mouth and cannot feed. It lives long enough only to fertilize the female's eggs. A typical female scale insect is round or globe-shaped, and is only a fraction of an inch across. It gets its name from the waxy or scaly shell that covers its body. Fully grown females of many kinds of scale insects scarcely look or act like insects at all. They lack legs, eyes, and feelers, and stay in one spot for most of their lives.

Scientists know of more than 2,000 kinds of scale insects, over 400 of which live in the United States. The *San Jose scale,* one of the best known and most harmful kinds, feeds on many types of fruit trees and shrubs. It was first found in the United States near San Jose, Calif., in about 1880 (see SAN JOSE SCALE). Another scale insect that attacks fruit trees, the *cottony cushion scale,* seemed likely at one time to wipe out all the citrus trees in California. But, in 1890, a scientist found an Australian species of ladybird beetle which fed on the cottony cushion scale. The beetles were let loose in California in time to save the citrus growers from ruin.

Some scale insects are useful to man. Shellac, a varnish, comes from the shells of the *lac scale* (see LAC). Cochineal, a crimson dye, comes from the *cochineal scale* (see COCHINEAL). One kind of scale insect is even used as jewelry. It lives on plant roots and covers itself with a lovely, bronze-colored shell. The shells are called *ground pearls* and make pretty beads.

**Scientific Classification.** Scale insects are in the superfamily *Coccoidae,* of the order *Homoptera.*    DONALD J. BORROR

**SCALLION.** See ONION.

**SCALLOP,** *SKAHL up,* is a shellfish that is used for food in many parts of the world. It is a *bivalve mollusk* (animal with a two-pieced shell around its soft, boneless body). Scallops live in shallow waters throughout the world, but some live at depths of $4\frac{1}{2}$ miles.

The scallop shell is made up of two equal rounded valves that usually have fanlike, radiating ribs. At the hinge, where the ligament unites the two valves, there are two winglike projections called *ears.* The inside of the shell is lined with fleshy skin, the *mantle.* The edge

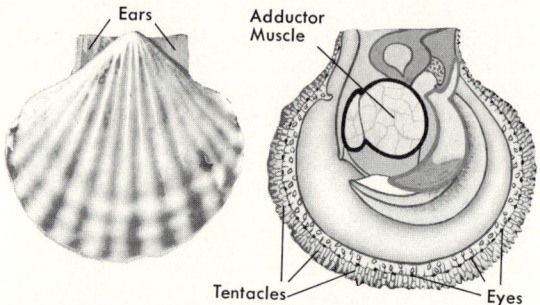

**The Scallop** has a hard shell, *left.* Tentacles and eyes edge the inner lining, *right.* The edible muscle is outlined in black.

of this mantle is folded and fringed with *tentacles* (feelers) and a row of eyes.

Scallops are active, and swim by rapidly opening and closing their valves. When the large adductor muscle closes the valves, the water between them is forced out alternately through openings near the hinge. This action pushes the creature forward in a zigzag fashion.

Several species of scallops live along the Atlantic and Pacific North American coasts. The most important of these is the common bay scallop, which may be found in inlets from Massachusetts to the Gulf of Mexico. The deep-sea scallop may grow to be 8 inches in width. It is found from Labrador to North Carolina and especially along the coasts of Maine and Nova Scotia. Fishermen catch deep-sea scallops at depths of 30 to 90 feet by dragging chain bags over the ocean bottoms.

The large adductor muscle is the only part of the scallop sold for food. The tender meat tastes somewhat like lobster meat, and is considered a delicacy.

Scallop shells have been used widely in designs. In the Middle Ages (about A.D. 400 to 1400) persons wore scallop shells on their hats to show they were on a *pilgrimage* (journey to a holy place).

**Scientific Classification.** Scallops belong to the clam and oyster class, *Pelecypoda* of the phylum *Mollusca.* The common bay scallop of North America is genus *Aequipecten,* species *A. irradians.*    R. TUCKER ABBOTT

**Scale Insects,** such as mealy bugs, *below,* attack fruit plants in large numbers, and often cause tremendous damage.

Cornelia Clarke

**SCALP** is the covering of the skull on which the hair grows. It is formed by the thickest skin of the body. There are layers of fat and connective tissues and many blood vessels under the skin. The scalp muscles, located at the front and back of the skull, are connected by a cap of connective tissue over the top of the skull. When Indians scalped victims, they cut off this loose cap of tissue and its covering skin. The bones of the skull are nourished from below, so they do not die when the scalp is removed. Many persons lived for years after being scalped. Infections which develop between the connective tissues and the skull are difficult to control, and this area of the scalp is often called the "danger zone." See also DANDRUFF; HAIR. WILLIAM V. MAYER

**SCALPEL.** See SURGERY (Instruments); KNIFE.

**SCAMMONY,** *SKAM oh nih*, is a twining, climbing plant which comes from Asia Minor. It has white flowers and thick fleshy roots that are usually 2 to 3 feet long. A white, milky juice is taken from the roots and allowed to dry and harden in the air. This juice forms a gum resin used in medicine. Its principal use is in preparing laxatives, because the resin is a powerful cathartic.

**Scientific Classification.** The scammony belongs to the morning-glory family, *Convolvulaceae*. It is genus *Convolvulus*, species *C. scammonia*. HAROLD NORMAN MOLDENKE

**SCANDINAVIA,** *SKAN duh NAY vih uh*, is the name often given to the peninsula of Norway and Sweden. But the term Scandinavia really refers to the countries where Scandinavian people live. This includes Denmark, Norway, and Sweden. These three countries together with Finland and Iceland form *Norden*. The countries belonging to Norden are often mistakenly referred to as Scandinavia.

*Fennoscandia* is a term that is often used to describe Finland and the Scandinavian Peninsula. Many re-

**The Scandinavian Countries Lie in Northern Europe.**

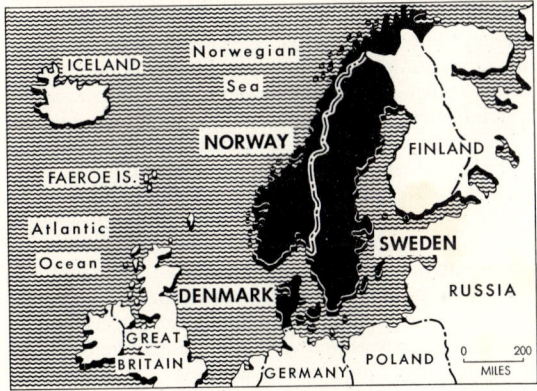

gions near the Baltic Sea are known as *Baltoscandia*, because their climate and customs are much like those of the Scandinavian countries. Southern Sweden is called *Skåne*, or *Scania*, an ancient Roman word for a legendary island north of the Baltic Sea. RICHARD BECK

See also DENMARK; NORWAY; SWEDEN.

**SCANDINAVIAN AIRLINES SYSTEM.** See AIRLINE.

**SCANDINAVIAN LITERATURE** is rich in folk tales. Its history dates back almost a thousand years to the time of the *sagas* (heroic tales) and the two *Eddas*, in prose and verse, from Norway and Iceland. Among the most important of the sagas was the *Volsunga Saga*, the story of the Norse gods and heroes. Ancient poets, called *skalds*, were usually well educated, and composed poems about princes, warriors, and heroes. There were skalds in Norway as early as the 800's. From the time of the sagas to the 1700's, little outstanding literary work appeared in Scandinavia. The best-known figures of recent Scandinavian literature include the great dramatist Henrik Ibsen, the critic Georg Brandes, the poet Bjørnstjerne Bjørnson, and Nobel prizewinners Pär Fabian Lagerkvist, Selma Lagerlöf, Halldór Laxness, Knut Hamsun, and Sigrid Undset. RICHARD BECK

**Related Articles.** See the Arts section of the DENMARK; NORWAY; and SWEDEN articles. Other related articles in WORLD BOOK include:

| | |
|---|---|
| Andersen, Hans C. | Laxness, Halldór K. |
| Asbjørnsen, Peter C. | Mythology |
| Bjørnson, Bjørnstjerne | Pontoppidan, Henrik |
| Dinesen, Isak | Rölvaag, Ole E. |
| Edda | Saga |
| Hamsun, Knut | Sigurd |
| Holberg, Ludvig | Skald |
| Ibsen, Henrik | Snorri Sturluson |
| Jensen, Johannes V. | Strindberg, August |
| Lagerkvist, Pär F. | Undset, Sigrid |
| Lagerlöf, Selma | Wergeland, Henrik A. |

**SCANDIUM** (chemical symbol, Sc), is a soft, silvery-white metal. Its atomic number is 21, and its atomic weight is 44.956. In 1869, Dmitri Mendeleev of Russia predicted its discovery, and described its properties. In 1879, Lars Nilson of Sweden discovered the element. He named it *scandium* after Scandinavia. Scandium occurs mainly in the minerals thortveitite and wiikite, but some also occurs in tin and tungsten ores. Scandium forms colorless salts, melts at 1539° C., and boils at 2832° C. Spectrographic observations show that some stars contain much scandium. See also ELEMENT, CHEMICAL (table). FRANK H. SPEDDING

**SCANNING.** See TELEVISION (Scanning Beam; diagram: How Scanning Works); READING (Survey Reading); POETRY (Scansion).

**SCAPA FLOW,** *SKAP uh*, is a sea basin surrounded by the Orkney Islands off the north coast of Scotland. It is about 15 miles long and 8 miles wide. Scapa Flow became the headquarters of the battleship squadrons of the British Grand Fleet during World War I. On June 21, 1919, the defeated German navy scuttled its remaining ships in the basin. In World War II, a German submarine sank the British battleship *Royal Oak* in Scapa Flow. For location, see GREAT BRITAIN (physical map). JOHN D. ISAACS

See also ORKNEY ISLANDS.

**SCAPEGOAT,** *SKAYP goht*, originally meant one of the two goats received by the Jewish high priest in ancient Jerusalem on the Day of Atonement. One was for Jehovah, the Hebrew God, and was killed as a sacrificial offering. The second was called the scapegoat. This one was for *Azazel*, which may have been the spirit of evil. The priest laid his hands upon the scapegoat as he confessed the people's sins. Then the priest sent the scapegoat into the wilderness. This was a symbol that the sins had been put away, or forgiven.

Today, when someone refers to a person as a scapegoat, it means he has been made to take the blame for something which is the fault of another. LOUIS L. MANN

**SCAPHOPODA.** See SHELL (Kinds of Mollusk Shells).

145

# SCAPULA

**SCAPULA**, in anatomy. See SKELETON.

**SCARAB**, *SKAR ub*, is a beetle once held sacred by the ancient Egyptians. Scarabs are dung beetles. Like some other dung beetles, they have the peculiar habit of breeding in dung. They sometimes roll this dung into small pellets, which they roll to their underground burrows to be used as larval food. Eggs are laid in the pellets. Egyptians regarded the pellets as symbols of the world, and believed that projections on the heads of the beetles were emblems of the rays of the sun. For the Egyptians, the scarab also symbolized the resurrection and immortality. They carved figures of the insects out of stone or metal, and used them as charms. Such figures were called scarabs. Usually, Egyptians removed the heart of a dead person, and put a large carved scarab in its place when the body was embalmed. Many of these carved scarabs were richly jeweled.

**Scientific Classification.** The scarab belongs to the scarab family, *Scarabaeidae*. It is classified as genus *Atenchus*, species *A. sacer*. H. H. ROSS

**Two Scarabs With a Ball of Dung.** The scarab on the right pushes the ball with its hind legs. Sometimes, another scarab tries to steal the ball by pulling it with its front legs, *left*.
Cornelia Clarke

**SCARCITY.** See RATIONING; VALUE.
**SCARIFICATION.** See TATTOOING.
**SCARLATINA.** See SCARLET FEVER.
**SCARLATTI**, *skahr LAHT ee*, is the family name of two Italian composers, father and son.

**Alessandro Scarlatti** (1659-1725), a leading composer of early Italian opera, achieved his greatest success with such works as *La Rosaura*, *Telemaco*, and *Griselda*. These operas stood on a high musical level and influenced composers in other countries, but they were less interesting from a dramatic point of view. His operas had overtures, called *sinfonia*, which usually consisted of a fast, a slow, and second fast movement. This form became of great significance in the development of the later orchestral symphony.

Scarlatti's fertility of mind was staggering. He wrote no less than 115 operas, 150 oratorios, and more than 600 cantatas, as well as instrumental compositions. He was born in Palermo, Sicily. As a young man, he lived in Rome as court composer of the former Swedish queen, Christina. He later moved to Naples.

**Domenico Scarlatti** (1685-1757) was the son of Alessandro Scarlatti. As a composer, he is nearly as famous as his father. He wrote vocal compositions, but became best known for his clavier sonatas. He wrote more than 550 of these bold and imaginative pieces, which display a great variety of expression.

Scarlatti was born in Naples in the same year as George Frideric Handel and Johann Sebastian Bach. He studied music with his father and became a harpsichord player. He taught the Portuguese princesses, and later moved to Madrid when one of them became Queen of Spain. When he was 69, he returned to Naples, where he died. KARL GEIRINGER

**SCARLET FEVER**, sometimes called *scarlatina*, is an infectious disease that chiefly affects children. It is named for the scarlet skin rash that develops. Because of increased knowledge of its cause and treatment, doctors no longer regard it as a grave disease.

**Cause and Spread.** A variety of bacteria called *hemolytic streptococci* cause scarlet fever (see STREPTOCOCCUS). They also cause tonsillitis and septic sore throat. Physicians often group all these diseases together and call them scarlet fever and related diseases. A person with a streptococcal infection may spread scarlet fever even though he has no sign of the disease himself. For example, a person with a sore throat, who coughs and sneezes without covering his nose and mouth, may spread the germs to a child. The child may develop a rash and other symptoms of scarlet fever.

**Symptoms.** The illness develops rapidly, with high fever, rapid pulse, nausea, headache, muscle pain, and general distress. The rash appears about a day after these first symptoms. It consists of red spots that become most pronounced about 48 hours after they first appear. Then they begin to fade. When the rash disappears, the skin starts to peel. If the rash has been extensive, the peeling will also be extensive. *Toxins*, or poisons, given off by the germs cause the rash and the peeling. The toxins may affect other organs. Sometimes they damage the heart and kidneys. A few patients develop other infections such as pneumonia, meningitis, and infections of the middle ear and lymph glands. Scarlet fever is most serious in children less than one year old. But as children grow older, they develop more resistance. Doctors believe that the greatest danger of scarlet fever and its related diseases is that they seem to precede rheumatic fever (see RHEUMATIC FEVER).

**Treatment.** Because scarlet fever is an infectious disease, patients should be kept apart from other persons. This helps keep the disease from spreading. The room should be quiet and well ventilated. The patient should cover his nose and mouth whenever he coughs or sneezes. Paper tissues are best for this purpose because they can be burned after use. All discharges from the patient's ears, nose, and throat should be destroyed. All bedding and clothing used by the patient should be thoroughly disinfected before they are used again.

Doctors prescribe measures that control the patient's fever and make him comfortable. The physician often gives penicillin, which is particularly effective against these germs. But he may give other drugs as well. Sometimes he injects an *antitoxin* to neutralize the poison given off by the germs. But often this is given only in severe cases. The antitoxin used was developed by George F. and Gladys H. Dick, pioneer investigators of infections caused by streptococcal germs. They injected small amounts of scarlet fever toxin into a horse's blood and derived an antitoxin from the animal's blood serum (see ANTITOXIN). The Dicks also developed a skin test designed to show sensitivity to scarlet fever. See also DISEASE (tables). H. WORLEY KENDELL

**SCARLET HAW.** See HAWTHORN.

**SCARLET LETTER, THE.** See HAWTHORNE, NATHANIEL.

**SCARLET TANAGER.** See BIRD (color pictures: Birds' Eggs, Color Makes Them Stand Out); TANAGER.

**SCARRITT COLLEGE FOR CHRISTIAN WORKERS.** See UNIVERSITIES AND COLLEGES (table).

**SCENERY.** See THEATER (Scenery Construction); STAGE DESIGNER.

**SCHACHT,** shahkt, **HJALMAR** (1877- ), was a German financial statesman. As Adolf Hitler's minister of economics, he devised ways to finance Germany's preparations for World War II. He resigned his position in 1937 after disagreeing with Nazi economic and foreign policies. Schacht remained in the government as a minister until 1942. He took part in plots to assassinate Hitler. Schacht was acquitted at the Nuremberg trials (see NUREMBERG TRIALS). He became a banker after the war and advised Asian and African governments.

He was born in Tingleff, Germany (now Tinglev, Denmark) and was a brilliant student at Kiel University. He made banking his career, and received an important position with the Bank of Dresden. He eventually became head of the Reichsbank, Germany's central bank, in 1924. After World War I, Schacht represented Germany on the commissions which settled German war reparations. DONALD L. KEMMERER

**SCHECHTER V. UNITED STATES** was a case in which the Supreme Court of the United States ruled that the National Industrial Recovery Act (NIRA) of 1933 was unconstitutional. The NIRA, a basic part of President Franklin D. Roosevelt's New Deal, empowered the President to set up codes of fair competition for businesses and industries. It was based on the federal government's constitutional power to regulate *interstate commerce* (trade between states). The Schechter Poultry Corporation of New York City was convicted of violating an NIRA code. The Supreme Court found the NIRA unconstitutional because it excessively delegated legislative power to the President, and it involved the federal government in regulating *intrastate commerce* (trade wholly within a state). STANLEY I. KUTLER

See NATIONAL RECOVERY ADMINISTRATION.

**SCHEELE,** SHAY luh, **CARL WILHELM** (1742-1786), was the Swedish pharmacist-chemist who discovered chlorine. He also prepared oxygen. But he did not publish his work in time, and Joseph Priestley, an English scientist, received credit.

In 1770, Scheele discovered tartaric acid. He was also the first to obtain pure lactic, oxalic, citric, and hydrofluoric acids. He discovered Scheele's green (copper arsenite), molybdenum, and scheelite (calcium tungstate). Scheele was born in Stralsund, Germany, and as a boy became a pharmacist's assistant. He later opened his own pharmacy shop in Köping, Sweden, and made most of his discoveries there. K. L. KAUFMAN

See also CHLORINE; CHEMISTRY (The Discovery of Oxygen); MOLYBDENUM.

**SCHEELITE.** See TUNGSTEN.

# SCHENECTADY

**SCHEHERAZADE,** shuh HER uh ZAHD, was the legendary queen who told the stories in the *Arabian Nights*. According to the legend, she married the Sultan Shahriyar of Persia, who made a practice of strangling his wives the morning after each wedding. But he spared Scheherazade because she entertained him with her stories. See also ALADDIN; ARABIAN NIGHTS; RIMSKY-KORSAKOV, NICHOLAS. ARTHUR M. SELVI

**SCHELDE RIVER,** SKEHL duh, is one of the most important commercial waterways of Europe, and is especially important to Belgium. It rises in the northern part of France (where it is called the Escaut), southeast of the city of Lille. From there, the river flows in a northeasterly direction through Belgium. For location, see BELGIUM (color map). At Antwerp, Belgium, the river separates into the *East Schelde* and the *West Schelde*, which flow through The Netherlands to the North Sea. The Schelde is 270 miles long. By means of locks, boats can sail over about 210 miles of its course. Canals link the Schelde, Meuse, and Rhine rivers.

For 200 years the Dutch held the right to close the Schelde to water traffic. When Belgium and The Netherlands drew up the Treaty of London of 1839, The Netherlands received permission to charge a *toll* (tax) for the use of the Schelde River by commercial vessels. These tolls were finally abolished in 1863. During World War I, The Netherlands closed the entrance of the Schelde to warships. In the peace negotiations in 1919, Belgium tried unsuccessfully to gain Dutch territory along the Schelde for full control of the river.

During the German invasion of Belgium and of The Netherlands in 1940, and during the German retreat in 1944, heavy fighting occurred along the Schelde and the Albert Canal. The canal connects the Meuse and the Schelde rivers. DANIEL H. THOMAS

**SCHELLING,** SHEL ing, **FRIEDRICH WILHELM JOSEPH VON** (1775-1854), was a German philosopher. His earlier works are generally understood as an important link between Immanuel Kant and Johann Gottlieb Fichte on the one hand, and G. W. F. Hegel on the other. These works are representative of German idealism and romanticism. Schelling's *System of Transcendental Idealism* (1800) was the major work of his youth. He later criticized his own early works and Hegel's philosophy as "negative philosophy." Schelling attempted to develop a "positive philosophy" which stressed revelation and influenced existentialism (see EXISTENTIALISM).

Schelling was born in Leonberg, near Stuttgart, Germany. He entered the Tübingen theological seminary at 16, and became a friend of G. W. F. Hegel and Friedrich Hölderlin. By 1807, when Hegel published his first book, Schelling had published 10. In the preface to his first book, Hegel criticized Schelling, though not by name, and Schelling never forgave him. Soon Hegel's influence far exceeded Schelling's. WALTER KAUFMANN

**SCHENCK V. UNITED STATES.** See FREEDOM OF SPEECH (Dangerous Speech).

**SCHENECTADY,** skuh NEK tuh dih, N.Y. (pop. 81,682; alt. 245 ft.), is sometimes called the *City that Lights and Hauls the World* because it has a huge electrical-manufacturing industry and an important locomotive concern. The city is also known as the *City of Magic* be-

147

cause of the important scientific work performed at the research laboratory of the General Electric Company. This is the largest industrial establishment in the state (see GENERAL ELECTRIC COMPANY). Factories in the city make gloves, chemical products, and cement products.

*Schenectady* is an Indian name meaning *end of trail*. The city received its name because it lay at the meeting point of Indian trails from the north, south, and east.

**Location, Size, and Description.** Schenectady lies in east-central New York, about 15 miles northwest of Albany, and about 160 miles northwest of New York City. Schenectady faces mountain ranges on three sides. The Adirondacks are on the north. The Green Mountains and the Berkshire Hills lie on the east. On the south are the Helderberg and Catskill mountains. The Mohawk River flows eastward along the northern limits of the city. In the early days of Indian and pioneer life, Schenectady shared the Mohawk River's reputation as the *Gateway to the West*. See NEW YORK (political map).

**Cultural Life and Recreation.** Schenectady is the home of Union College, one of the oldest colleges in the United States, founded in 1795. The city is the site of Schenectady County Historical Society and the Schenectady Museum. Dutch homesteads still stand in some sections of the city. There are 12 parks and 25 recreation areas.

**History.** Arendt van Curler and 14 other Dutch pioneers purchased the site of the city in 1661. The Indians gave up all their claims to this land. Several years later, they received in exchange belts of white wampum, six coats, 20 barrels of lead, and nine bags of gunpowder. The English took possession of Schenectady in 1664. In 1690, the settlement suffered from a terrible French and Indian massacre. It was rebuilt and became an important trading post. Schenectady received its borough charter in 1765, and became a city in 1798. It has a council-manager government.  WILLIAM E. YOUNG

**SCHERZO,** *SKEHR tso*, is a musical term usually applied to the liveliest and happiest movement of a sonata, symphony, or string quartet. The term may also be used for a separate instrumental composition. A scherzo is characterized by marked rhythmic figures and frequent repetitions of themes. The word *scherzo* is Italian, meaning *jest* or *joke*.

**SCHEVENINGEN.** See HAGUE, THE.

**SCHICK,** *shik*, **BÉLA** (1877-1967), was an authority on the diseases of childhood. He became best known for a skin test, developed in 1913, for determining whether or not a person is likely to catch diphtheria (see DIPHTHERIA; SCHICK TEST). He also did important research on such children's diseases as scarlet fever, serum sickness, tuberculosis, and infantile diarrhea.

Schick worked in Vienna with Theodor Escherich and Clemens von Pirquet, and became an authority on scarlet fever. With Von Pirquet, he laid the foundation of our knowledge of serum sickness and allergy. He came to the United States in 1923. Schick was born in Boglár, Hungary.  HENRY J. L. MARRIOTT

**SCHICK TEST** is a test for diphtheria immunity. A very small amount of diphtheria toxin is injected under the skin. There is no effect if the person is immune to the disease, but the area around the injection becomes inflamed if he is not. Children with a positive reaction should receive injections to immunize them. Béla Schick introduced the test in 1913. See also DIPHTHERIA; SCHICK, BÉLA.  PAUL S. RHOADS

**SCHICKLGRUBER.** See HITLER, ADOLF (Boyhood).

**SCHILLER, JOHANN CHRISTOPH FRIEDRICH VON** (1759-1805), ranks second only to Goethe among the leading figures of German literature, and no German compares to him as a playwright. Schiller was a master of dramatic construction and character portrayal. His dramas are pleas for human freedom and dignity. They inspired German liberals in their fight for liberty during the early 1800's and during the Revolution of 1848.

Friedrich Schiller was born in Marbach in the duchy of Württemberg. The duke of Württemberg made him attend a military academy where he studied medicine, but he left his post as an army surgeon in 1782 to devote himself to writing. Schiller's early plays protested against the tyranny of the German aristocracy. His first drama, *The Robbers* (1781), enjoyed sensational success. His other early plays include the political-historical dramas *Fiesco* (1783) and *Don Carlos* (1787), and the middle-class tragedy *Intrigue and Love* (1784).

The period between 1787 and 1796 formed a separate part of Schiller's career. Unsure of his abilities as a dramatist, he turned to historical writing with *The Revolt of The Netherlands* (1788), a work dealing with the same period as *Don Carlos;* and *The History of the Thirty Years' War* (1791-1793). Schiller's literary talents injected a vivid dramatic quality into these works. Schiller's writings in the early 1790's on philosophy and aesthetic theory gave him an important place in the development of German idealism. These writings also established him as the most important theorist of German classicism.

Schiller's friendship with Goethe from 1794 reawakened his interest in drama. His greatest drama, *Wallenstein* (1796-1799), is a tragedy set during the Thirty Years' war. It explores the relationship between a great individual and fate. The drama is a cycle of three parts, written in dignified blank verse. Three other historical plays followed. *Maria Stuart* (1800) deals with the life of the Scottish queen. *The Maid of Orleans* (1801) is the story of Joan of Arc. *William Tell* (1804), Schiller's most popular play, dramatizes Switzerland's struggle for freedom. *The Bride of Messina* (1803) is modeled on classical Greek drama.

Between 1785 and 1800, Schiller edited three literary magazines, to which he contributed many essays, lyrics, and stories. He became known for such philosophical lyrics as "The Song of the Bell." One of his most famous ballads is "The Diver." Two stories, "The Ghostseer" and "The Criminal from Lost Honor," rank among the first German short-story masterpieces.  CORA LEE PRICE

See also GERMAN LITERATURE (Storm and Stress).

**SCHILLING** is the monetary unit of Austria. It is made up of 100 groschen. The schilling was first introduced in Austria in 1924. It was temporarily replaced by the German mark from 1938 to 1945. See MONEY (table).

**SCHIPPERKE,** *SKIP er kih*, is a dog of Belgium. It is also called the *Barge Dog* or *Little Skipper*, because it once guarded canal barges and hurried the horses that pulled them. The dog has a foxlike head with small, pointed ears. It has a heavy black coat with a long frill on its neck and *culottes* (trousers) on its hind legs. Sometimes it is born without a tail. The schipperke weighs about 15 pounds. See also DOG (color picture: Non-sporting Dogs).  JOSEPHINE Z. RINE

**SCHIRRA,** *shur RAH,* **WALTER MARTY, JR.** (1923- ), is one of the first seven United States astronauts. On Oct. 3, 1962, he flew around the earth six times in *Sigma 7,* a Project Mercury spacecraft. On Dec. 15, 1965, Schirra served as command pilot on the *Gemini 6* spacecraft which accomplished man's first *rendezvous* (meeting) in space. With astronaut Thomas Stafford, Schirra guided *Gemini 6* to within a foot of the *Gemini 7* spacecraft piloted by astronauts Frank Borman and James Lovell. Schirra's spacecraft chased *Gemini 7* for more than 105,000 miles until Schirra could maneuver into the orbit of *Gemini 7.* Both spacecraft were traveling at about 17,500 miles per hour.

Schirra was born in Hackensack, N.J. He learned to fly an airplane as a boy. His father, a World War I pilot, and his mother were stunt fliers. Schirra graduated from the U.S. Naval Academy in 1945. He flew 90 combat missions during the Korean War, and received the Distinguished Flying Cross and two air medals. Later, he served as a flight instructor, then as a test pilot before becoming an astronaut. Schirra resigned from the astronaut program and the U.S. Navy in 1969, and entered private business.   JOHN J. PETERSON

See also ASTRONAUT; SPACE TRAVEL.

**SCHISM, GREAT.** See CHRISTIANITY (Heresies and Schisms); POPE (The Troubles of the Papacy).

**SCHIST.** See ROCK (Metamorphic Rock).

**SCHISTOSOMIASIS,** *SHIHS toh soh MY uh sis,* also called bilharziasis, is a disease caused by *schistosomes* (blood flukes). Adult flukes live in the blood of man and animals. Their eggs leave the host's body in waste materials. The eggs hatch into larvae and enter snails. They develop and emerge as minute whip-tailed creatures that burrow into the skin of those who enter the infested water. They damage vital organs such as the liver and spleen. See also FLUKE.   LOIS G. LOBB

**SCHIZOMYCETE,** *SKIZ oh my SEET,* is the name of a group of primitive plant organisms without chlorophyll.

**SCHIZOPHRENIA.** See MENTAL ILLNESS (Kinds).

**SCHLEICHER, AUGUST.** See LINGUISTICS (The Comparativists).

**SCHLEIDEN, MATTHIAS.** See BIOLOGY (The 1800's).

**SCHLESINGER,** *SHLAY zing er,* is the family name of two American historians, father and son.

**Arthur Meier Schlesinger** (1888-1965) became known as the dean of American historians. As a teacher and author, he was a leader in interpreting American history in its economic, social, and cultural aspects in such books as *The Colonial Merchants and the American Revolution* (1918), *The Rise of the City* (1933), and *Prelude to Independence* (1957). He described trends in the manners and morals of America in *Learning How to Behave* (1946) and other works. He also emphasized the importance of the growth of cities in American history. Schlesinger was born in Xenia, Ohio. He taught American history at Harvard University from 1924 to 1954.

**Arthur Meier Schlesinger, Jr.** (1917- ), won

**Arthur Schlesinger, Jr.**
Houghton Mifflin Co.

two Pulitzer prizes. In 1946, he won the history award for *The Age of Jackson.* In 1966, his *A Thousand Days: John F. Kennedy in the White House* won the Pulitzer prize for biography. *The Age of Roosevelt,* Schlesinger's three-volume biography of Franklin D. Roosevelt was published in 1957, 1959, and 1960. Schlesinger taught at Harvard University from 1947 to 1961. From 1961 to 1964, he served as a special assistant to Presidents Kennedy and Lyndon B. Johnson. In 1966, Schlesinger joined the faculty at the City University of New York. He was born in Columbus, Ohio.   MERLE CURTI

**SCHLESWIG-HOLSTEIN,** *SCHLES wig HOHL stine,* or *SHLAYS vik HAWL shtine,* is a state in West Germany. It lies just south of Denmark, in the southern part of the peninsula separating the North and Baltic seas.

Schleswig-Holstein covers an area of 6,046 square miles, and has a population of 2,423,300. The Eider River divides Schleswig from Holstein. The state's chief city is the seaport of Kiel. Most of the people of Schleswig-Holstein are farmers, and dairying is an important industry.

Schleswig and Holstein have belonged at various times to Denmark and to Germany. Prussia took control of them in 1866. After World War I, the northern part of Schleswig united with Denmark. The rest of the state became a part of Germany.   JAMES K. POLLOCK

See also KIEL; KIEL CANAL; DENMARK (The Schleswig Wars); SEVEN WEEKS' WAR.

**SCHLEY,** *sly,* **WINFIELD SCOTT** (1839-1911), an American naval officer, commanded the expedition that rescued the Arctic explorer Adolphus W. Greely in 1884. With James Russell Soley, he published the book *The Rescue of Greely* in 1885. Schley also commanded the American naval forces at the battle of Santiago in 1898, and became involved in a famous dispute with Rear Admiral William Sampson over credit for the victory (see SAMPSON, WILLIAM THOMAS). Schley was born in Frederick County, Maryland.   DONALD W. MITCHELL

**SCHLEYER, JOHANN MARTIN.** See VOLAPÜK.

**SCHLIEFFEN PLAN,** *SHLEEF en,* formed the basis for Germany's strategy to meet threats of war with Russia in the east and France in the west at the same time. The plan was devised between 1895 and 1905 by General Alfred von Schlieffen, chief of the German general staff, after France and Russia allied against Germany.

Schlieffen believed Germany must defeat France before Russia could fully mobilize for war. The entire German Army would march swiftly through neutral Belgium and The Netherlands and destroy the French army. Then it would move east to face the Russians.

When World War I began, however, a modified form of this plan failed. Some German forces were left to defend Alsace-Lorraine, and others went to the Russian front. The rest marched through Belgium, but were met by Belgian, French, and British forces. This shattered German hopes for a quick victory.   GEORGE G. WINDELL

**SCHLIEMANN,** *SHLEE mahn,* **HEINRICH** (1822-1890), a German businessman, became famous as an archaeologist. He discovered and excavated the ruins of ancient Troy and other buried cities mentioned in Homer's *Iliad* (see TROY). These discoveries were important to knowledge of early Greek civilization.

Schliemann's extensive business dealings in Russia

149

## SCHMALKALDIC LEAGUE

during the Crimean War helped make him a wealthy man. He retired in the 1860's, and spent the rest of his life directing the excavation of ancient cities along the eastern Mediterranean Sea.

Schliemann was born at Neu-Buckow, in Mecklenburg-Schwerin, of a poor family. He received little formal education. Schliemann became a United States citizen in 1869.   DAVID B. STOUT

**SCHMALKALDIC LEAGUE,** shmahl KAHL dik, was an alliance formed by the early German Protestants to defend themselves against Emperor Charles V and the Roman Catholic states. The league was formed in 1531, and the War of the Schmalkaldic League followed. The Protestants were defeated in 1547. But the league's aims were partly realized five years later in the Treaty of Passau. Charles V agreed to a temporary peace until a conference could settle matters more definitely. That conference took place in 1555 and is known as the Peace of Augsburg. Under its terms, both Roman Catholic and Lutheran churches were legally permitted for the first time in Western Europe. See also REFORMATION (In Germany).   J. SALWYN SCHAPIRO

**SCHMIDT, "MILT," MILTON.** See HOCKEY (Famous Hockey Players).

**SCHMIDT TELESCOPE.** See PALOMAR OBSERVATORY; TELESCOPE.

**SCHNABEL,** SCHNAH buhl, **ARTUR** (1882-1951), was an Austro-American pianist, composer, writer, and teacher. He gained fame for his interpretations of Ludwig van Beethoven's music. He recorded most of Beethoven's piano works, and edited his piano sonatas. He wrote *Reflections on Music* (1933) and *Music and the Line of Most Resistance* (1942). Artur Schnabel was born in Lipnik, Austria. He became a United States citizen in 1945.   ROBERT U. NELSON

**SCHNAUZER,** SHNOU zer, is a German dog that looks like a terrier. It has shaggy eyebrows and muzzle, like the airedale. There are three separate breeds, based on size. The *miniature* schnauzer is about 12 inches high, the *standard* is 18 to 20 inches high, and the *giant* is 21 to 25 inches high. See also DOG (color pictures: Working Dogs, Terriers); GIANT SCHNAUZER.   OLGA DAKAN

**SCHNITZER, EDUARD.** See EMIN PASHA.

**SCHNITZLER, ARTHUR** (1862-1931), was an Austrian writer whose works reflect the influence of Sigmund Freud's psychoanalytical teachings. Many of Schnitzler's plays and stories deal with middle-class and aristocratic society in Vienna, showing their liberal attitudes and double standards of morality. Schnitzler was a master of characterization and he was fond of his fellow Viennese. But he exposed their weaknesses and shortcomings through subtle psychological probing.

Two main themes appear in Schnitzler's work: love, and the question of what reality actually is. Both appear in his plays *Anatol* (1893), concerning a young man's adventures in love; and *La Ronde* (1900), a cycle of love affairs involving different groups in society. Schnitzler's best-known story is the short novel *Leutnant Gustl* (1901). He was born in Vienna.   WALTHER L. HAHN

**SCHOENBRUNN VILLAGE.** See OHIO (Places to Visit).

**SCHOEPPEL,** SHEP uhl, **ANDREW FRANK** (1894-1962), served as governor of Kansas from 1943 to 1947, and then served in the U.S. Senate. Schoeppel, a Republican, was elected to the Senate in 1948, and was reelected in 1954 and 1960. In the Senate, he supported many measures to reduce government spending. Schoeppel attended Kansas University. When the United States entered World War I, he left school and enlisted in the Naval Air Service. In 1922, he was graduated from the University of Nebraska Law School. Schoeppel was born in Claflin, Kans.   H. E. SOCOLOFSKY

**SCHOFIELD,** SKOH feeld, **JOHN McALLISTER** (1831-1906), commanded the Union forces that captured Wilmington, N.C., during the Civil War. He also successfully defended Franklin, Tenn., in 1864. He was born in Chautauqua County, New York, and was graduated from the United States Military Academy at West Point. After the war he served as secretary of war, and from 1888 to 1895 as U.S. Army commanding general.   H. A. DE WEERD

**SCHOFIELD BARRACKS,** Hawaii, is the largest United States Army outpost outside the continental United States. It houses combat units of the United States Army, Hawaii. The command also includes Tripler General Army Hospital, on the slopes of the Koolau Mountains; and the National Memorial Cemetery of the Pacific, which lies within Punchbowl Crater. The post lies 28 miles north of Honolulu and covers 14,219 acres. It was set up in 1908 and named for Civil War General John M. Schofield.   SAMUEL J. ZISKIND

**SCHOHARIE RESERVOIR.** See CATSKILL MOUNTAINS.

**SCHOLARSHIP** is a grant of money or free tuition awarded to a student on the basis of achievement, ability, or financial need. People usually consider a scholarship an honor in recognition of outstanding academic work, as well as financial aid to those who need it. Scholarships are generally awarded as a means of selecting and training capable young persons so that they may become assets to the community and nation.

Endowed foundations and government agencies often grant funds for advanced study and for research. Such grants are called *fellowships*. Universities and colleges grant *scholarships* for undergraduate study. More and more businesses, industries, labor unions, and government sources provide thousands of scholarships each year for general education or for special fields of study. See FOUNDATIONS (Education).

In _____, educators estimated that about 72,00_ _____ and fellowships were available in the United _____ _____ed in value about $11 million. The number of scholarships increased to an estimated 300,000 with a total value of about $98 million by the mid-1960's. Most individual undergraduate scholarships range in value from $100 to $1,500 a year. They average about $340 a year. In 1965, Congress passed the Higher Education Act. The act includes provisions for cash grants to university and college students. The grants are called "Education Opportunity Grants."

**Private Colleges and Universities** establish scholarships to attract students of outstanding intellectual ability or academic achievement. Scholarships also help promote particular fields of study, such as science, humanities, engineering, and nursing. Many scholarships are founded for personal reasons, and carry the name of the donor. The donor sometimes requires certain qualities of character or achievement for the award.

**State Scholarships** are available in various forms for persons with special abilities, disabilities, or needs. State colleges and universities grant fewer scholarships than private institutions, because they have lower tuitions. Nevertheless, many states establish *legislative scholarships* for students from various regions of the state or for out-of-state residents. Many states also provide special scholarship aid for students with various types of disabilities, through their vocational rehabilitation programs.

**National Merit Scholarships** were established in 1955, and quickly became the largest independently supported scholarship program in the country. The National Merit Scholarship Corporation, of Evanston, Ill., administers this program. The Ford Foundation gave $20 million and the Carnegie Corporation gave $500,000 to finance the administration of the program. The Ford Foundation also granted another $14½ million in 1962 to finance scholarships. Of this money, $8 million was set aside to match grants from business and industry. In the first two years of operation, 2,000 business organizations sponsored merit scholarships.

About 1,500 merit scholars are chosen each year from more than 300,000 high-school seniors throughout the country who take the examinations. Final selections are made by a board of experts and businessmen. The board considers students' test scores, records, participation in school and community activities, character, leadership, financial needs, and recommendations of the high schools. The number of scholarships in each state is based roughly on the number of high-school seniors in the state. A presidential committee, set up in 1964, then awards up to 121 presidential scholarships to the most outstanding scholars.

**Grants to Veterans.** Federal grants were given to veterans of World War II for study in any approved college, university, or vocational or trade school under the amended Servicemen's Readjustment Act, often called the *GI Bill of Rights*. To be eligible, veterans must have had at least 90 days of service and an honorable discharge. Grants were available for a period up to four years, depending on the length of service. The veteran received a monthly maintenance allowance, but the government paid the tuition and fees directly to the institution. Similar grants were made to veterans who served in the Korean War or afterwards, and who were not covered by other bills. The government sent monthly payments for maintenance and fees directly to the veterans. The veterans paid the fees themselves. By the mid-1960's, over 10 million men and women received educational benefits amounting to over $16 billion. See GI BILL OF RIGHTS.

**International Scholarships.** More than 82,000 students from other countries study in the United States every year, many on government or private scholarship funds. Organizations in the United States and in other countries also award a number of scholarships to send American students and teachers overseas. The purpose of such scholarships is to promote better international understanding and cultural relations.

The oldest and most famous of the international scholarships are the *Rhodes scholarships* (see RHODES SCHOLARSHIP). The newest and most numerous are the *Fulbright scholarships*, supported by the federal government (see FULBRIGHT SCHOLARSHIP). The Fulbright awards provide a year's schooling in the United States for students from other countries, and a year of study abroad for U.S. students and teachers. The United States also exchanges several international scholarships with Latin-American countries. The U.S. clearing house for exchange scholarships and fellowships is the Institute of International Education in New York City. A growing number of colleges and universities offer scholarships to returning volunteers from Peace Corps or other government service. R. FREEMAN BUTTS

See also AMERICAN FIELD SERVICE; FELLOWSHIP; PULITZER PRIZES (Scholarship Awards); EDUCATION (Government Financial Support).

**SCHOLASTICISM,** *skoh LAS tuh siz'm*, was a system of philosophy and theology developed during the 1100's and 1200's. It applied ideas of non-Christian thinkers to matters of Christian faith and used *reason* (persuasion by argument) in teaching religion.

The Scholastics inquired into the nature of God and man. They carefully defined their terms and principles. They discussed all aspects of their questions, including ideas of non-Christian thinkers, such as Plato, Aristotle, and the Arabic philosophers. *Summa Theologiae* (also spelled *Theologica*) by Saint Thomas Aquinas ranks as the masterpiece of Scholastic method and doctrine. Other leading Scholastics were Saint Albertus Magnus, John Duns Scotus, and Saint Bonaventure.

Pope Leo XIII urged reconsideration of Scholastic theories in 1879. *Neo-Scholastics* have since studied modern problems in terms of medieval ideas. JAMES COLLINS

See also ALBERTUS MAGNUS, SAINT; AQUINAS, SAINT THOMAS; ARISTOTLE; BACON, ROGER; DUNS SCOTUS, JOHN.

**SCHÖNBEIN, CHRISTIAN F.** See GUNCOTTON.

**SCHÖNBERG,** *SHUN behrg*, **ARNOLD** (1874-1951), was one of the most revolutionary of recent composers. At first strongly influenced by Richard Wagner, he gradually developed a style of writing which he called "the technique of composition with 12 tones." He derived his melodies and harmonies from an arrangement of all 12 chromatic tones. All are of equal importance, and there is no feeling of key. The technique, formulated about 1925, has influenced many later composers.

Schönberg was born in Vienna and studied music there, but he mainly taught himself theory and composition. His association with the "expressionist" painters was influential in forming his musical style. Much of his music aroused hostility, especially *Pierrot Lunaire*, a group of 21 short melodramas for voice and instruments.

Schönberg taught in Berlin until he was ousted when Adolf Hitler came to power in 1933. Then he came to the United States, where he continued to teach. His best-known works include the string sextet, *Transfigured Night;* two chamber symphonies; and four string quartets. HALSEY STEVENS

See also BERG, ALBAN.

**SCHONGAUER,** *SHONE gow ur*, **MARTIN** (1445?-1491), was a German painter and one of the first printmakers to engrave on copper. He was also the first painter-engraver, and greatly influenced Albrecht Dürer. The altarpiece, *Virgin and Child with Hedge of Roses*, is the only painting attributed to him with certainty. Of his 113 known prints, the *Death of the Virgin* is perhaps the best known. Schongauer was born in Colmar, Alsace (now in France). S. W. HAYTER

# SCHOOL

**SCHOOL.** Children and young men and women in every country in the world go to school. One school might be a group of youngsters listening to stories in an Indian village. Another could be part of a great university where men and women gain valuable experience in advanced research.

In the United States and Canada, schools are usually places of organized instruction below the college level, such as nursery schools and kindergartens, elementary schools, and high schools. In universities and colleges, a school may be a branch of instruction in a specialized field. For example, a university might have a school of education that trains future teachers.

Schools aim to develop a person's abilities and talents. They teach many important skills. Schools also provide knowledge that helps make students useful, productive members of society. They help children and young people to become good students, to learn their obligations as citizens, and to understand and interpret national and international events. They also aim at teaching young people the need for respecting the rights of others and living cooperatively with them in the community. In addition, schools teach the importance of personal and community health.

The idea of organized schools has developed through hundreds of years of struggle and experimentation. During the Middle Ages, the church often served as the only organization, outside the home, that concerned itself with teaching. Wealthy parents employed *tutors* (private teachers) for their children. Most other children had little or no formal instruction. In the 1700's and 1800's, statesmen and government leaders realized that the social and economic well-being of a nation depends on educated people. This brought about the development of public school systems in Europe and in the United States and Canada. See EDUCATION, HISTORY OF.

## Kinds of Schools

Schools in the United States and Canada include (1) nursery schools, (2) kindergartens, (3) elementary schools, (4) junior high schools, (5) high schools, (6) junior colleges, and (7) universities and colleges. In the United States, about 51 million boys and girls attend schools below the college level. In Canada, about 5,300,000 boys and girls attend these schools.

**Nursery Schools** teach children 3 and 4 years old. These schools use informal methods, including play, to teach youngsters basic skills and how to get along with others. For example, various mechanical, toylike devices help develop skills, and games encourage the idea of working with others. The United States has about 4,000 nursery schools. Canada has about 800 kindergartens and nursery schools. Most nursery schools in the two countries are private. See NURSERY SCHOOL.

**Kindergartens** teach children about 5 years old. They continue the informal methods used in nursery schools. But, in addition, kindergarten often gives a child his first formal school instruction. In the United States and Canada, a kindergarten frequently forms part of an elementary school. See KINDERGARTEN.

**Elementary Schools** teach children from 5 or 6 to 12 or 14 years old. Most elementary schools have either six or eight grades. A major purpose of the elementary school is to teach the fundamentals of arithmetic, reading, spelling, writing, and other basic subjects. Elementary schools also teach art, citizenship, geography, health, history, music, physical education, recreation, safety, and science. The United States has about 92,000 elementary schools, almost 15,000 of which are private. Canada has about 21,000 elementary and high schools, of which 1,300 are private. See ELEMENTARY SCHOOL.

**Junior High Schools** are an American development. They usually teach boys and girls in grades 7, 8, and 9. Basically, these are the last two years of an eight-grade elementary-school program and the first year of a four-year high-school program. The junior high school aims at giving 12- to 14-year-old students a school program adapted to their maturity and interests. It also serves as a transition from elementary to high school instruction. In many elementary schools, a youngster studies most of the day in the same class. In high school, he attends a number of different classes. Junior high schools offer students some experience in attending different kinds of classes. They also help a student explore his abilities

152

Glenn A. Wagner; Reproduced by special permission of *The Saturday Evening Post* © 1945 Curtis Publishing Company

**The School Opens the Door** to better citizenship, skills in living, and new worlds of knowledge. Modern school buildings feature long, low designs and spacious surroundings.

and interests. The United States has over 7,100 junior high schools. See JUNIOR HIGH SCHOOL.

**High Schools** aim at producing well-rounded citizens. They continue the development of skills and knowledge, and also offer young people training that will help them on the job or in the home. For example, many high schools have courses in such subjects as bookkeeping, homemaking, mechanical drawing, metalworking, and typing. High schools prepare many students for entrance to college by general and special instruction.

Most high schools offer a *general program* consisting of regular school subjects, such as English, history, and mathematics, and a variety of other courses, including art, foreign languages, business education, music, and shop. In many large cities, certain high schools have specialized training to meet students' special abilities, interests, and occupational needs. Specialized high schools include *technical schools*, *trade schools*, *vocational schools*, *business schools*, and *agricultural schools*. Most high schools offer college preparatory programs.

The United States has about 7,200 *four-year high schools* (grades 9 through 12), 5,600 *senior high schools* (grades 10 through 12), and 6,000 *junior-senior high schools* (grades 7 through 12). Some private schools at this level are called *preparatory schools*, because they prepare students for college. See HIGH SCHOOL; PREPARATORY SCHOOL.

**Junior Colleges** usually offer the first two years of a regular college program. Many junior colleges recognize that a number of occupations, such as that of a dietitian, require two years of specialized college training. They have *terminal programs* to help train high school graduates for these jobs. A number of junior colleges are *community colleges*. They offer various courses to serve the educational, recreational, musical, artistic, and other interests of adults in the community. The United States has over 1,000 two-year junior colleges. See JUNIOR COLLEGE.

**Universities and Colleges.** In general, a college is a four-year institution that offers a broad program of studies to high-school graduates. Universities usually include colleges of engineering, law, liberal arts, medicine, and other subjects. Universities and colleges often have divisions for specialized training, called *schools*. For example, a student could earn a bachelor's degree in one of the colleges, then study for an advanced degree in the school of education. Excluding junior colleges, the United States has over 1,600 universities, colleges, and other institutions of higher education, such as theological seminaries. Canada has about 400 universities and colleges. See UNIVERSITIES AND COLLEGES.

## Public-School Systems

**School Boards.** In the United States, each community or group of communities organizes and manages its own schools. These schools are usually under the supervision of a *board of education* and a *superintendent of schools*. Rural counties and townships often develop similar organizations. In either the city or the county, the area managed by a school board is usually called a *school district*. The school board may also be called a *board of trustees* or a *board of school directors*.

In most states, the local school board has considerable independence in employing and paying teachers and providing buildings. It may also develop courses of study within the framework of state law. State laws also outline general academic standards, how teachers are certified, and the use of public funds for schools.

Local boards of education organize and manage pub-

*Harvester World*, International Harvester Co.

**School Begins In Kindergarten** for many boys and girls. Meeting a real hen is one of many vivid experiences that help to combine learning about new things with fun and wonder.

Two or more small rural districts may combine to organize a *consolidated school* (see CONSOLIDATED SCHOOL).

The United States has three major plans of school organization. These plans are often known by a combination of a letter and numbers.

K—6—3—3 {Kindergarten / Elementary School (6 years) / Junior High School (3 years) / Senior High School (3 years)

K—8—4 {Kindergarten / Elementary School (8 years) / High School (4 years)

K—6—6 {Kindergarten / Elementary School (6 years) / Junior-Senior High School (6 years)

There are many local variations of these three major plans of school organization. The K—6—3—3 plan is the most common plan in the largest cities. Smaller communities are gradually adopting it.

Canada has about 11,300 school boards. Of these, about 2,400 are independent local boards. The others operate under larger administrative units.

Canada has two major traditions of school organization. In provinces with a British background, the organization resembles that in the United States. Most schools in these provinces use the plan that calls for an eight-year elementary school and a four-year high school. A number of Canadian boards have adopted plans that include a six-year elementary school, a three-year junior high school, and a three-year senior high school. About 40 per cent of Canada's five-year-old children attend kindergarten, mostly in public schools.

In Quebec, the French-language schools have a plan

lic schools in Canada. Boards of education are subject to the regulations of the provincial Schools Acts.

**Organization.** School districts vary greatly in size and in the range of their school programs. In 1967, the United States had about 20,300 local public school districts. Of these, about 11,400 operated both elementary and high schools, about 7,600 had only elementary schools, and about 700 included only high schools.

**Light, Well-Planned Classrooms** help boys and girls do a good job with lessons. New elementary schools like this one have the most modern lighting, desks, and teaching materials. The pupils study in an atmosphere designed for their work.

World Book photo

E. H. Sheldon Equipment Co.

**Science Lessons in High School** may mark the beginning of a lifelong interest in science. Some of the students in this class may go on to careers in scientific research, or as science teachers. Some of them may become technicians.

that calls for a three-year *pre-primary*, or *infant*, *school*, and a seven-year *primary school*. After completing primary school, a boy or girl may enter an eight-year *collège classique* (pronounced *col LEHZH class SEEK*), or continue a two-year *complementary course* in the primary schools. The collège classique awards bachelor's degrees and prepares students for professional work in a university. The complementary course prepares students for training in a business or trade school.

**Administration.** In most school districts in the United States, the voters elect the members of their school boards. In a few communities, judges or local government officials appoint the board members. Because school board members do not usually have teaching experience, they employ specialists to operate the schools. For example, they usually hire a superintendent of schools to supervise the entire local educational program. The board and superintendent also hire *principals* or *head teachers* to direct the schools, and classroom teachers to do the actual instructing. In addition, the board may employ librarians, nurses, and others.

A large city may have several assistant superintendents in charge of special phases of work. For example, an assistant superintendent may handle instruction, or perhaps finance. School boards sometimes appoint advisory committees of citizens to help study school and community problems. Parent-teacher groups also advise and help with many school problems (see PARENTS AND TEACHERS, NATIONAL CONGRESS OF).

**Finance.** Local and state taxes provide most public-school support. The average local district in the United States supplies about 54 per cent of the money, the state gives around 38 per cent, and the federal government furnishes 8 per cent. Federal aid to schools takes the form of special aid, such as lunchroom programs from farm surpluses and funds for agricultural and home-

**Parents and Teachers Get Together at PTA Meetings** to exchange views on school problems. PTA's have set up vaccination programs, supervised playgrounds, and arranged field trips to help promote the health, safety, and education of children.

*International Harvester Today*

# SCHOOL

making instruction and vocational training in school.

The people of the United States spend about $22\frac{1}{2}$ billion a year on current expenses in public elementary and high schools. *Current expenses* include salaries, supplies, fuel, and other items used during the school year. About $4\frac{1}{2}$ billion a year goes for capital outlays and interest payments. *Capital outlays* include the cost of equipment and of constructing new school buildings. *Interest payments* include interest paid on bonds and on loans.

The average cost in various states for one student for one year in a public school ranges from about $335 to about $912. The average for the United States is about $622 for one student for one year.

## Private and Parochial Schools

In addition to public schools, the United States and Canada have many schools that are not supported by taxes. These schools range from nursery schools, most of which are private, to large universities. In general, the term *private school* refers to an institution that is not supported or controlled by the public. Individuals or groups may organize private schools and operate them for profit or as a service for the people of the community. See PRIVATE SCHOOL.

In general, the term *parochial school* refers to an institution that is owned and operated by a church. Many church groups, such as the Roman Catholics, Episcopalians, Jews, Lutherans, and Seventh-day Adventists, operate elementary and high schools. The number of Roman Catholic schools is by far the largest. Many church groups also operate universities and colleges. See PAROCHIAL SCHOOL.

In Canada, taxes help support Roman Catholic and other parochial schools in Quebec and several other provinces. See CANADA (Education).

Private and parochial schools must maintain certain state and provincial standards regarding courses of study and preparation of teachers. Many private and parochial schools belong to regional accrediting associations. These associations establish various standards and certify the quality of instruction in member schools.

## School Buildings

**Design.** In the early 1800's, most school buildings in the United States had only one room. The room usually had 20 to 40 desks or benches for the students. Equipment consisted of little more than a slate and a few books for each boy and girl. The United States still has about 9,900 one-room schools, but their equipment has improved. As schools in the United States and Canada became larger, they often added rooms in a haphazard way. This practice sometimes led to school buildings that were neither safe nor convenient.

During the 1900's, new school building designs have made instruction easier and better. These new schools have many classrooms, and often include auditoriums, cafeterias, gymnasiums, libraries, offices, and play spaces. Architects and engineers have improved designs and equipment to increase the safety and usefulness of the buildings. Canadian school boards have similar building programs.

**Standards.** Most experts on school building standards agree that each building must be individually planned. Before planning a school, they often study the kind of community, the scope of the school's program, the kind of building site available, and the probable community uses of the building. They estimate the possible size of the future population to be served by the school. They also try to locate the building to avoid traffic on highways, railroads, and other danger spots.

Some experts recommend a minimum site of 5 acres for an elementary school and 10 acres for a high school. In growing communities, additional acreage is provided for the school's estimated final enrollment. For example, an elementary school of 350 that is expected to double in size should have about 10 acres. A high school with 1,000 students should have from about 15 to 20 acres. Experts arrive at these figures from estimates of the school's future enrollment, playground needs, program of studies, community services, and other important factors.

Elementary school classrooms for about 25 to 30 students should have an area of about 900 to 1,000 square feet. Each student should have about 30 to 40 square feet. The additional space is for handicrafts, a library corner, and storage of teaching aids. High school classrooms should have about 25 to 30 square feet for each student. School building standards also include many other features of construction, site, and equipment. In a number of states, the state department of education must approve all building plans. This procedure insures that the building meets the minimum requirements for instruction, health, and safety. Architects for school buildings must observe the local and state building standards required for other types of construction. The Canadian provinces have similar regulations for building schools.

**Uses.** In the 1800's, Americans often used their school buildings for community gatherings. Spelling bees, dances, and important town meetings took place in the schoolhouse. But, in the early 1900's, Americans used their school buildings less for community affairs. Dur-

**Colonial Schools** often met in homes where housewives taught their students reading, writing, and arithmetic. Only about one colonial child in 10 went to school at all.
U.S. Office of Education

156

ing World Wars I and II, the Red Cross, Selective Service, relief programs, and similar activities increased the community use of schools. Since World War II, schools have regained much of the importance in community life that they had in the 1800's. Increasingly, "community schools" provide space and staffs for adult education.   SIDNEY DORROS and FRANK W. HUBBARD

**Related Articles.** See the Education sections of the various state, province, and country articles, such as SOUTH DAKOTA (Education). See also the following articles:

### KINDS OF SCHOOLS

| | |
|---|---|
| Academy | Kindergarten |
| Boarding School | Laboratory School |
| Consolidated School | Night School |
| Correspondence School | Nursery School |
| Elementary School | Parochial School |
| Graduate School | Preparatory School |
| High School | Private School |
| Junior College | Universities and Colleges |
| Junior High School | |

### OTHER RELATED ARTICLES

| | |
|---|---|
| Architecture (How an Architect Designs) | Grading |
| | Library (School Libraries) |
| Education | School Lunch |
| Education, History of | Teaching |

### Outline

I. **Kinds of Schools**
  A. Nursery Schools
  B. Kindergartens
  C. Elementary Schools
  D. Junior High Schools
  E. High Schools
  F. Junior Colleges
  G. Universities and Colleges
II. **Public-School Systems**
  A. School Boards
  B. Organization
  C. Administration
  D. Finance
III. **Private and Parochial Schools**
IV. **School Buildings**
  A. Design
  B. Standards
  C. Uses

### Questions

What are the general purposes of schools?
What are the purposes of the junior high school?
In what ways can a high school help a student?
What are three kinds of high schools? How do they differ?
How can junior colleges help the community?
How is a school district governed?
What are the three major plans of school organization in the United States?
What are the two main sources of financial support for public-school systems?
What uses other than education can a school have in the community?

**SCHOOL** (of water animals). See DOLPHIN; PILOT WHALE; SARDINE; WHALE (Life of the Whale).

**SCHOOL ADMINISTRATORS, AMERICAN ASSOCIATION OF,** is a professional association of about 17,500 school administrators and professors of school administration. It is a department of the National Education Association of the United States.

The association holds important national and regional conferences. These conferences help school administrators discuss practical problems in their work and current issues in education. The association also publishes information on educational issues. It was founded in Harrisburg, Pa., in 1865. Headquarters are at 1201 Sixteenth Street, NW, Washington, D.C. 20036.

Critically reviewed by AMERICAN ASSOCIATION OF SCHOOL ADMINISTRATORS

See also NATIONAL EDUCATION ASSOCIATION OF THE UNITED STATES; TEACHING.

## SCHOPENHAUER, ARTHUR

**SCHOOL LUNCH** is a noon meal served to children in school. In the 1800's, Germany, France, and other European countries began to serve lunches in their public schools. By 1900, New York, Philadelphia, Chicago, and other large cities started the program in the United States, when they began to feed hungry children at school. By 1925, many city and country schools throughout the United States served lunches as hot noon meals. The practice soon spread throughout a great part of the United States.

The value of a hot lunch at school greatly impressed both parents and teachers. Gradually, many schools came to employ lunchroom managers with training in home economics or dietetics. Most teachers now accept lunch programs as important educational devices for teaching good food habits and social skills.

Federal assistance to school lunch operations began in 1933. This support stimulated the program; more children came to participate, and the nutritional quality of the lunches improved. A *Type-A* lunch supplies from one-third to one-half of a child's daily nutritional requirements. It contains foods from all seven of the basic groups (see NUTRITION [The Basic Seven]). In the mid-1960's, over 17 million children ate lunches provided under the National School Lunch Program. Federal, state, and local groups contribute funds that help to support this program's work.   JANICE M. SMITH

**SCHOOL OF FOREIGN SERVICE.** See GEORGETOWN UNIVERSITY.

**SCHOOL OF MONTREAL.** See CANADIAN LITERATURE (Since 1900).

**SCHOOL OF QUEBEC.** See CANADIAN LITERATURE (Literary Expansion).

**SCHOOLCRAFT, HENRY ROWE** (1793-1864), was a noted authority on American Indians. He recorded the Indian myths and legends which provided the source material for such works as Henry Wadsworth Longfellow's *Hiawatha*. One of his best-known works is *Algic Researches* (1839), a collection of Indian legends and myths.

Schoolcraft was born at Watervliet, N.Y. He became a geologist and spent most of his later years on the Indian frontier. He discovered the source of the Mississippi River in 1832.   ARVID SHULENBERGER

**SCHOONER.** See SAILING (Kinds of Sailboats; picture).

**SCHOPENHAUER,** *SHOH pen HOW er*, **ARTHUR** (1788-1860), a German philosopher, became widely known for his fine prose style and his pessimism. His philosophy is atheistic, but the Eastern religions, especially early Hinduism and Buddhism, profoundly influenced him (see BUDDHISTS; HINDUS). He described blind will as the ultimate reality, and he sought release from suffering through the contemplation of works of art and an ethic of sympathy. His main work is *The World as*

**Arthur Schopenhauer**
Brown Bros.

157

# SCHOTTISCHE

*Will and Idea* (1819, 1844). Some of Schopenhauer's essays in the collection *Parerga and Paralipomena* (1851) have also been widely read, especially his bitter discussion "On Women."

Schopenhauer was born in Danzig. He trained for a business career, but turned to philosophy after his father, a banker, died. He denounced Johann G. Fichte, Friedrich Schelling, and G. W. F. Hegel. Schopenhauer's own philosophy became popular in the last 10 years of his life.  WALTER KAUFMANN

**SCHOTTISCHE,** *SHAHT ish*, is the name of a German dance, popular in the 1800's. Its hopping and sliding steps are in $\frac{2}{4}$ time.

**SCHOUTEN, WILLEM CORNELIS.** See ADMIRALTY ISLANDS; TONGA ISLANDS; CAPE HORN.

**SCHOUTEN ISLANDS,** *SKOU tun*, lie north of New Guinea in the South Pacific Ocean. They were once part of Netherlands New Guinea. But in 1963, they were ceded to Indonesia and are now part of West Irian (West New Guinea). They cover an area of 1,236 square miles and have a population of about 37,000. Biak and Soepiori are the largest islands. During World War II, Allied and Japanese forces fought in this area. See also NEW GUINEA (Government).  EDWIN H. BRYAN, JR.

**SCHRICKER, HENRY FREDERICK.** See INDIANA (The 1940's and 1950's).

**SCHRÖDINGER,** *SHRAY ding ur*, **ERWIN** (1887-1961), was an Austrian theoretical physicist and Nobel prize winner. In 1926, he put into mathematical form the revolutionary idea of a French physicist, Louis Victor de Broglie, that the motion of material particles is guided by so-called *pilot waves*. The formulation of the famous "Schrödinger equation" put quantum theory on a strict mathematical basis, and provided the foundation for its further rapid expansion (see QUANTUM THEORY). For this work, Schrödinger shared the 1933 Nobel prize for physics with Paul Dirac of Cambridge, England.

In later years, he concerned himself with the extension of Albert Einstein's theory of gravitation to include electrical and magnetic phenomena. He also became interested in fundamental biology, and published a short popular book, *What Is Life?* (1945). In this book, he attempted to explain the phenomena of life on the basis of purely physical concepts.

Schrödinger was born in Vienna, and received his Ph.D. from the university there. He served as a professor of theoretical physics in several universities in Germany and Switzerland. He was also associated with the Dublin Institute for Advanced Studies.  G. GAMOW

**SCHUBERT,** *SHOO bert*, **FRANZ PETER** (1797-1828), an Austrian composer, wrote an astonishing variety of music in many forms. He was one of the greatest creators of melody, and perhaps the leading composer of *lieder* (German songs).

**His Life.** Schubert was born in Vienna on Jan. 31, 1797. He was the son of a poor schoolmaster. By the time he was 11, he was a choirboy. He attended school at the Imperial and Royal Seminary, and played the violin and sometimes conducted there. Schubert was composing when only 13, and wrote his first song the next year. He began his first symphony in 1813. He was 18 when he wrote the well-known song "Gretchen at the Spinning Wheel." In 1815, he wrote such outstanding *lieder* as "Hedge Roses" and "The Erl King," as well as his second and third symphonies, and several works for the musical stage.

Schubert taught for a time in his father's school, then went to live with his friend Ferdinand Schober in 1816. Schubert's operas failed to earn much money, and he suffered greatly from poverty because he lived a disorganized and easygoing life. In 1826, he tried, but failed, to get a position at the court of the Austrian emperor. Although he composed constantly and gained some recognition, Schubert managed to get only a few of his works published. He never achieved real success.

Schubert foolishly neglected his health. He planned to visit Hungary in 1828, the year in which he composed several of his major works. But he became very ill, and had to abandon the trip. On Nov. 14, 1828, Schubert contracted typhus. He died five days later at the age of 31.

Schubert was the classic example of a man of genius who was so devoted to his art that he never managed to live well or adjust to the world. He never married. His music and his personal charm won him admiring friends, but he gained little public recognition. Schubert heard only a few of his great orchestral works performed, and his great *Symphony in C major* was not performed during his lifetime. Ten years after his death, his brother Ferdinand gave the manuscript to Robert Schumann. Schumann in turn gave it to Felix Mendelssohn, who conducted the work in Leipzig. Ferdinand also made many of Schubert's other works available for publication.

But posterity has made up for the neglect Schubert suffered while he was alive. He never went far beyond his home city of Vienna. But his music, crossing borders throughout the world, has become a lasting international treasure.

**His Works.** Schubert's orchestral works include dances, overtures, and symphonies. The two-movement *Symphony No. 8 in B minor* ("Unfinished") has long been a public favorite. Many regard Schubert's *Symphony in C major* (known either as No. 7 or No. 9), as his greatest masterpiece. His charming chamber music varies from an octet and two quintets to many string quartets and piano trios, as well as sonatas for piano and violin. Schubert also wrote many pieces for solo piano, notably sonatas, *impromptus*, waltzes, and *Moments Musicaux* (Musical Moments). He also composed many works for piano duet.

**Franz Schubert**
Detail of a watercolor portrait (1825) by Wilhelm August Rieder. *Historisches Museum der Stadt Wein* (Art Reference Bureau)

Schubert was especially attracted to the musical possibilities of the human voice. He composed much religious music, including Masses, and choral pieces to nonreligious texts. He wrote several operas and operettas. But these works lacked theatrical effectiveness and failed. However, Schubert's incidental music for the play *Rosamunde, Princess of Cyprus*, is still popular.

Schubert's special contribution to music lies in his

more than 600 solo *lieder*. These include the *cycles* (groups of related songs) called *Die schöne Müllerin* (*The Beautiful Mill-Girl*), *Winterreise* (*Winter Journey*), and *Schwanengesang* (*Swan Song*). Such separate songs as "Ave Maria," "Death and the Maiden," "Serenade," "The Trout," and "Who Is Sylvia?" are among the greatest in song literature. No other composer has written so many expressively beautiful songs of such high quality. See LIEDER.

Schubert was not a man of searching and tough-fibered intellect like Beethoven, a man he admired greatly. Schubert sometimes was unable to sustain his musical ideas once he had presented them in larger forms. As a result, some critics feel that many of his sonatas are simply too long for the musical ideas they contain. But Schubert was especially gifted in creating melody, and his poetic inspirations easily carry the listener through some perhaps needless repetition. This problem does not arise in his astonishing *lieder*, which would place him among the great composers even if he had written nothing more. HERBERT WEINSTOCK

**SCHULBERG,** *SHOOL burg*, **BUDD** (1914-    ), is an American novelist and screen writer. His screen play *On The Waterfront* won many awards in 1954. He wrote the novels *What Makes Sammy Run?* (1941), *The Harder They Fall* (1947), and *The Disenchanted* (1950). Schulberg also wrote a collection of short stories, *Some Faces in the Crowd* (1953). Schulberg was born in New York City. GEORGE J. BECKER

**SCHULZ, CHARLES MONROE.** See COMICS (Peanuts).

**SCHUMAN, WILLIAM** (1910-    ), is an American composer and administrator. His compositions include ballets, such as *Undertow;* six symphonies; and many choral and chamber music works. His music has won several awards, including a 1943 Pulitzer prize, two Guggenheim fellowships, and a grant from the Metropolitan Opera. Schuman was born in New York City. After teaching music at Sarah Lawrence College and Columbia University, he was made president of the Juilliard School of Music in 1944. Schuman served as president of the Lincoln Center for the Performing Arts from 1962 to 1968. HOMER ULRICH

**SCHUMAN PLAN.** See EUROPEAN COMMUNITY (History).

**SCHUMANN,** *SHOO mahn*, **ROBERT** (1810-1856), was a German composer and pianist. With Frédéric Chopin and Franz Liszt, he evolved the literature and techniques of romantic piano music.

His earliest compositions were piano pieces, such as the much-loved *Papillons* (Butterflies), *Carnaval*, and various children's pieces. His wonderful songs rank with those of Franz Schubert, Johannes Brahms, Hugo Wolf, and Richard Strauss, other masters of the German *lieder* (songs). They include the song cycles *Dichterliebe* (Poet's Love) and *Frauenliebe und -leben* (Woman's Love and Life). Schumann's only piano concerto is a favorite of concert audiences. His symphonies, though often criticized, have never lost their popularity. He also wrote choral and chamber music.

**His Life.** Schumann was born at Zwickau, the son of a bookseller and publisher. He began to study music when he was eight years old, and was soon trying to compose. His talent as a pianist developed early. Struck by the intensely romantic writings of Johann Paul Friedrich Richter, Schumann tended to imitate Richter char-

Robert Schumann

acters in his own youthful writings. In 1828 he entered the Leipzig Lyceum to study law. During that year he met Friedrich Wieck, a pianist and teacher, and Wieck's nine-year-old daughter, Clara, who was already a pianist. He married Clara 12 years later.

Schumann neglected his studies of law and spent much time on music. He became a well-known pianist. In 1830 he wrote the first of many piano pieces that are still performed. Shortly afterward, he began writing articles on music. His printed salutes to early compositions by Chopin and Brahms are famous. In 1832, he injured a finger and abandoned his piano studies. He launched an influential music magazine, *The New Music Journal*, in 1833.

In 1836 Friedrich Wieck tried to stop the love developing between his daughter and Schumann. Three years later, the lovers went to court to force his consent to their marriage. They were married in 1840.

**His Illness.** Schumann showed signs of mental illness in 1843, but he was able to teach at the Leipzig Conservatory founded by Mendelssohn. In 1844, he suffered a severe breakdown. When he became conductor at Düsseldorf in 1849, his increasing mental illness caused difficulties with the orchestra. He tried to commit suicide in 1854, but was rescued and placed in an asylum. By the following year, he had become hopelessly insane. He died on July 29, 1856. HERBERT WEINSTOCK

**Clara Schumann** (1819-1896), the wife of Robert Schumann, was a famous German pianist and composer. Following her marriage, she furthered her husband's career by giving the first performances of many of his works, including the *Concerto for Piano and Orchestra* and the *Piano Quintet*. She became the most celebrated woman pianist of her time.

She was born in Leipzig, the daughter of the noted piano teacher, Friedrich Wieck. She received her entire musical training from him, and appeared in public from the age of nine. She later lived in Berlin and Frankfurt, where she taught piano at a conservatory. ROBERT U. NELSON

**SCHUMANN-HEINK,** *SHOO mun HYNK*, **ERNESTINE** (1861-1936), was a greatly admired contralto. During her long and active career as an artist, she appeared in operas, oratorios, concerts, and even motion pictures and vaudeville. She made her debut in Graz, Austria, when she was 15, as contralto soloist in Beethoven's *Symphony No. 9*. Madame Schumann-Heink first sang in opera at Dresden in 1878. Her growing reputation earned her

Madame Schumann-Heink
Brown Bros.

159

## SCHUMPETER, JOSEPH ALOIS

invitations to the Wagner festivals at Bayreuth, Germany, from 1896 to 1903 and in 1905 and 1906. She joined the Metropolitan Opera Company of New York in 1899 after an American debut in Chicago. Later, she toured extensively as an interpreter of *Lieder* (German art songs).

Madame Schumann-Heink was born near Prague, Czechoslovakia. SCOTT GOLDTHWAITE

**SCHUMPETER, JOSEPH ALOIS** (1883-1950), was a noted economist of the first half of the 1900's. Schumpeter gained prominence for his studies of economic growth, business cycles, and the conflict between capitalism and socialism.

In his first major work, *The Theory of Economic Development* (1911), Schumpeter argued that growth in a private enterprise economy was caused by forceful, daring *entrepreneurs* (business organizers) who hope to make large profits. The entrepreneur did something new. His innovation might be a new product, invention, or process that would lead to new industries and markets. In *Business Cycles* (1939), Schumpeter suggested that new developments generally came irregularly and in bunches. He said this condition created cycles of good and bad times.

In *Capitalism, Socialism, and Democracy* (1942), Schumpeter said that government efforts to reduce unequal distribution of income and to eliminate business cycles would destroy the conditions in which entrepreneurs could flourish, and that the growth of big business would eliminate the entrepreneurs from decision-making positions in industry. Capitalism would then lose its ability to grow and develop, and the resulting economic conditions would lead to socialism.

Schumpeter was born near Jihlava, Czechoslovakia, and was educated at the University of Vienna. He taught briefly at Harvard University in the late 1920's, joining Harvard's regular faculty in 1932. Schumpeter became a U.S. citizen in 1939. DANIEL R. FUSFELD

**SCHURZ**, *shoorts*, is the family name of an American statesman and his wife, an educator.

**Carl Schurz** (1829-1906) was an American editor, soldier, and political leader. He has been called the greatest American citizen of German birth. He was born at Liblar, Prussia, and attended the University of Bonn. He fought in the revolution of 1848-1849 against the autocratic rulers of the German states. After the revolution failed, he escaped to Switzerland. Schurz then made his way to the United States.

Schurz settled in Wisconsin, and became a leader in the antislavery fight. He campaigned for Abraham Lincoln in the election of 1860. Lincoln named him minister to Spain. During the early years of the Civil War, Schurz was in Madrid safeguarding the Union cause. Later, he resigned to become a brigadier general in the Union Army. After the war, he established the *Westliche Post*, a German-language newspaper, in St. Louis, Mo. It soon became a powerful influence in the West. In 1869 he was elected a Republican United States senator from Missouri, and soon became a leader of the opposition against the measures of President Ulysses S. Grant. He helped form the Liberal Republican party, which fought Grant in the election of 1872.

**Carl Schurz**
Brown Bros.

President Rutherford B. Hayes appointed Schurz secretary of the interior in 1877, a post he held until 1881. As secretary, he argued for fair treatment of the Indians, and installed a civil-service merit system in his department (see CIVIL SERVICE). Later, he became editor of the New York *Evening Post*, and from 1892 to 1898, he was chief editorial writer for *Harper's Weekly*. W. B. HESSELTINE

**Margaretha Meyer Schurz** (1834-1876) was the wife of Carl Schurz. In Germany, she had been a pupil of Friedrich Froebel, the founder of the kindergarten. She came to the United States with her husband in 1852. In 1856, she established a school at Watertown, Wis., for the young German-speaking children of immigrants. This school was the first kindergarten in the United States. Mrs. Schurz also supported her husband's activities as a leader of German immigrants, and as a United States senator. CLAUDE A. EGGERTSEN

**SCHUSCHNIGG**, *SHOOSH nik*, **KURT VON** (1897- ), was chancellor of Austria until Adolf Hitler forced Austria to unite with Germany in 1938. In the Vienna rebellion of 1934, he played a leading part in suppressing the Socialists, and seized power as chancellor after the assassination of Engelbert Dollfuss. Schuschnigg opposed the Nazi seizure of Austria, and was held prisoner by the Nazis until the Allies freed him in 1945. He was born in Italy, and became a United States citizen in 1956. GABRIEL A. ALMOND

**SCHUYLER**, *SKY lur*, **PHILIP JOHN** (1733-1804), was an American soldier and statesman. At the start of the Revolutionary War in 1775, he was a delegate to the Continental Congress. After the battle of Bunker Hill, he was appointed a major general in the Continental Army.

In 1777, British forces under Generals John Burgoyne and Sir Henry Clinton, and Colonel Barry St. Leger converged on Albany, N.Y., from three directions. Schuyler delayed Burgoyne's advance by felling trees across the road, contributing to General Horatio Gates' famous victory over Burgoyne at Saratoga. From 1789 to 1791 and in 1797 and 1798, Schuyler served as a United States senator from New York. He was born in Albany, N.Y. IAN C. C. GRAHAM

**SCHUYLKILL RIVER**, *SKOOL kil*, is an important river in Pennsylvania. It rises in Schuylkill County and flows southeastward for about 131 miles before it empties into the Delaware River at Philadelphia. The Schuylkill furnishes power, and part of Philadelphia's water supply. Coal barges use the river, which has been improved by dams and locks.

**SCHWA.** See PHONETICS (An International Phonetic Alphabet).

**SCHWAB, CHARLES MICHAEL** (1862-1939), was a founder and president of both the United States Steel Corporation and the Bethlehem Steel Corporation. He started as an engineer's stake driver with the Carnegie Company. He rose rapidly, and became the first president of U.S. Steel in 1901. Resigning in 1903, he took control of Bethlehem Steel Corporation and directed its growth in shipbuilding, munitions, and allied fields (see BETHLEHEM STEEL CORPORATION). He was president of the American Iron and Steel Institute. Schwab was born in Williamsburg, Pa.        W. H. BAUGHN

**SCHWANN, THEODOR.** See BIOLOGY (The 1800's).

**SCHWARZ, BERTHOLD.** See GUNPOWDER (History).

**SCHWARZKOPF,** *SHVAHRTS kawf,* **ELISABETH** (1915-    ), a lyric soprano, won great success in the 1940's and 1950's as a concert and opera singer. She sang at the Salzburg, Bayreuth, and other important festivals. She was born near Poznan, Poland. She studied at the Berlin Hochschule für Musik and in England. Miss Schwarzkopf sang her first operatic role in Richard Wagner's *Parsifal* at Charlottenburg, Germany, on Easter Sunday in 1938. She made her American debut in a song recital at Town Hall, New York City, in 1953. In 1955, she made her American opera debut in San Francisco.        SCOTT GOLDTHWAITE

**SCHWARZWALD.** See BLACK FOREST.

**SCHWEITZER,** *SHVY tsur,* **ALBERT** (1875-1965), was a brilliant German philosopher, physician, musician, clergyman, missionary, and writer on theology. His accomplishments in any one of these fields could be regarded as a full life's work for one man.

Schweitzer has been called one of the greatest Christians of his time. Early in his career, he based his philosophy on what he called "reverence for life" and on a deep feeling of obligation to serve his fellow man through thought and action. Schweitzer's many years of work as a humanitarian won for him the 1952 Nobel peace prize.

**His Life.** Schweitzer was born on Jan. 14, 1875, at Kaysersberg, Alsace, and was educated in both France and Germany. At the age of 21, he decided to spend his next nine years in science, music, and preaching, and then to devote the rest of his life to serving humanity directly. Before he was 30, he had won an international reputation as a writer on theology, as an organist and authority on organ building, as an interpreter of the works of Johann Sebastian Bach, and as an authority on Bach's life.

In 1902, Schweitzer became principal of St. Thomas Theological College at the University of Strasbourg. He was inspired to become a medical missionary, and studied medicine from 1905 to 1913 at the university. He raised money for a hospital at Lambaréné, French Equatorial Africa (now Gabon), from his parishioners and by giving concerts for the Paris Bach Society, which he had helped found. In 1913, he began serving at Lambaréné. His first consulting room at his jungle hospital was a chicken coop. Over the years, he built a large hospital and a medical station where thousands of Africans were treated yearly. He used his $33,000 Nobel prize money to expand the hospital and set up a leper colony.

**His Books.** Schweitzer continued to write on other subjects while in Africa. He completed in 1923 the first two volumes of his monumental work *The Philosophy of Civilization.* These books are *The Decay and Restoration of Civilization* and *Civilization and Ethics.* His other works include *The Quest of the Historical Jesus* (1906), *Out of My Life and Thought* (1931), and *From My African Notebook* (1939).

Schweitzer visited the United States in 1949 to speak at the Goethe Bicentennial Convocation at Aspen, Colo.

Erica Anderson, United Press Int.

**Albert Schweitzer,** a man of many accomplishments, even designed all of the buildings in his hospital and leper colony.

In 1955, Queen Elizabeth II conferred Great Britain's highest civilian award, the Order of Merit, on Schweitzer. In 1957, Schweitzer went on record as opposing further atomic weapons tests because of the danger of radioactive fallout to mankind.        DAVID EWEN

See also FRENCH EQUATORIAL AFRICA (picture).

**SCHWENKFELDERS,** *SHVENGK FEL derz,* is the name of one of the groups of people who went to North America for religious freedom. In 1734, 34 families arrived in North America from Silesia, Germany. Others followed two years later, and organized a settlement in Montgomery and Berks counties in Pennsylvania. The colonists founded an independent denomination in 1782. They named their group in honor of Kaspar Schwenkfeld (1489-1561), a German religious reformer. They have simple church services. The Schwenkfelders have approximately 2,200 members, and five churches in Pennsylvania.        WILBUR C. KRIEBEL

**SCHWINGER, JULIAN SEYMOUR** (1918-    ), of the United States, shared the 1965 Nobel prize in physics with Richard P. Feynman and Shinichiro Tomonaga. Working independently, the three men developed an improved theory of quantum electrodynamics in the late 1940's. *Quantum electrodynamics* is the study of the interaction between electrons and electromagnetic radiation. The theory enables scientists to predict accurately the effects of electrically charged particles on each other in a radiation field. Schwinger was born in New York City. He earned A.B. and Ph.D. degrees from Columbia University. He joined the faculty at Harvard University in 1945.        R. T. ELLICKSON

**SCHWYZ.** See SWITZERLAND (History).

**SCIATICA,** *sy AT ih kuh,* is an inflammation of the *sciatic nerve.* This large nerve runs down the back of each thigh. It originates at the lower end of the spinal cord and runs downward into each leg. It is one of the longest nerves in the body, and is strong enough to suspend 400 pounds. When it becomes injured, inflamed, or infected, it may cause severe pain in the back of the thighs and the legs. In severe cases, sciatica can cause loss of leg reflexes or the wasting of muscles in one or both calves. Treatment of sciatica includes medications to stop pain, bed rest on a hard board, stretching the leg with traction, vitamin preparations, and other physical therapy measures.        LOUIS D. BOSHES

# SCIENCE

**The Science of Astronomy** delves into the mysteries of the universe. It deals with the stars, planets, and other objects that are spread out through the enormous distances of space.

SCIENCE covers the broad field of human knowledge concerned with facts held together by *principles* (rules). Scientists discover and test these facts and principles by the *scientific method*, an orderly system of solving problems. Scientists feel that any subject which man can study by using the scientific method and other special rules of thinking may be called a science.

The sciences include: (1) *mathematics* and *logic;* (2) the *physical sciences,* such as physics and chemistry; (3) the *biological sciences,* such as botany and zoology, and

National Science Foundation; United Press Int.

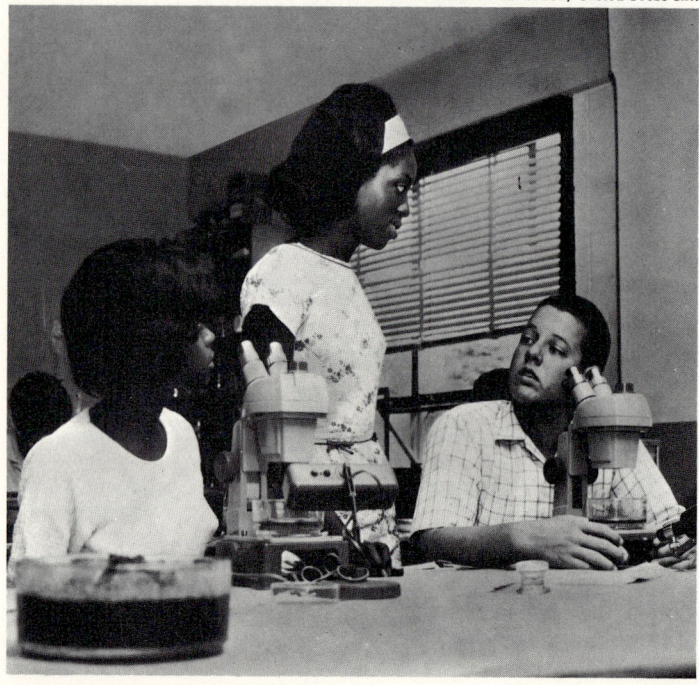

**Biology,** one of the oldest sciences, is the study of all living things—plants, animals, and organisms such as bacteria and viruses. Biologists use instruments to investigate things that cannot be seen with the unaided eye, such as viruses, *above,* seen through an electron microscope. Students, *left,* use simpler types of microscopes to study other kinds of living things.

(4) the *social sciences*, such as sociology and anthropology.

Scientific study may be divided between pure science and applied science. *Pure science* summarizes and explains the facts and principles discovered about the universe and its inhabitants. *Applied science* uses these scientific facts and principles to make things that are useful to man. Both pure science and applied science are necessary to bring the benefits of scientific research to mankind. Most people know more about applied science than about pure science, because they come into contact with the achievements of applied science.

The growth of civilization depends on progress and change brought about by scientific discoveries and their use. The military power and peacetime standard of living of modern nations are closely linked with the ability of their scientists to make new discoveries and learn how to use them.

### Science in Our Daily Lives

Science is important to everyone. Science has given the world such communication devices as the telephone, radio, and television. It has revolutionized transportation by means of the railroad, automobile, airplane, and rocket. It has made it possible for people to live longer through medical discoveries. Science brought about the Industrial Revolution and made possible the mass production of many products. The armed forces use weapons based on scientific knowledge.

**In the Home,** scientific progress has made life easier and more pleasant. A housewife once had to spend almost all her time washing and sewing clothes, cooking and preserving food, cleaning house, and tending fires. Science has provided electric energy to run washing machines, sewing machines, refrigerators, heating equipment, and air conditioners. Electric light has replaced the candles, oil lamps, and gas flames that once lighted homes. Frozen foods and automatic stoves make the preparation of meals more convenient. Detergents have made cleaning and washing easier. These and other advances have given the housewife more time for recreation and community activities.

**In Agriculture,** science has revolutionized the raising of crops and livestock. In colonial times, about 90 of every 100 Americans lived on farms. Today, only about 6 of 100 work in agriculture. This reduction in the number of persons needed to produce food was achieved largely through scientific advances. Years ago, a farmer could keep only about four horses at work at one time. Today, a tractor provides the power of 50 or more horses. Milking machines and other electric machinery do many farm chores automatically. Scientists working in agriculture have developed new types of grain that both resist plant diseases and produce larger yields. New fertilizers have increased the productivity of the soil. Scientifically designed irrigation systems have made the farmer less dependent on the weather. See AGRICULTURE (How Science Helps Agriculture).

**In Manufacturing.** Science has enabled manufac-

**A Laboratory Is a Scientist's Workshop.** Here, scientists conduct careful research and experiments to solve problems and find answers to questions. Delicate scales and other equipment aid the scientist in his unending search for new knowledge.

Ford Motor Co.

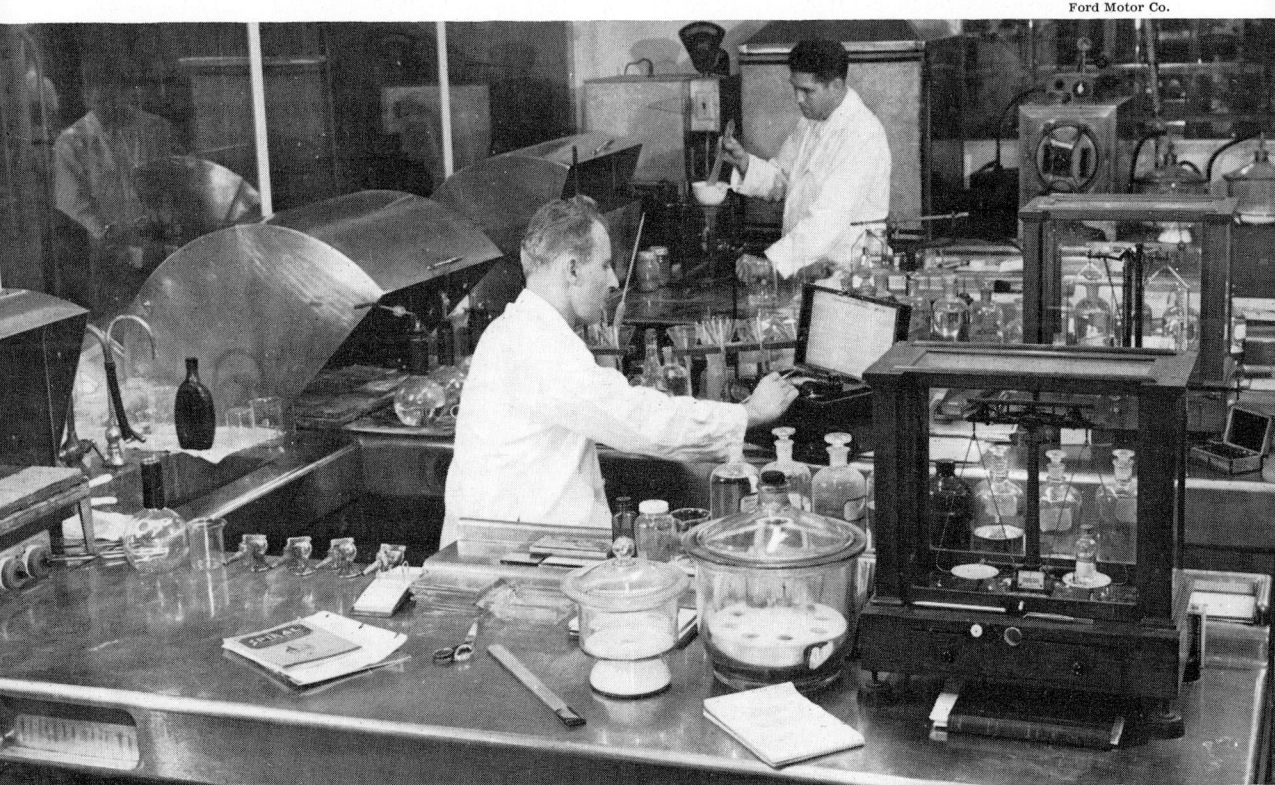

**Chemistry** students, *left*, determine the effects of heat on various substances. Research chemists, *above*, may use complex apparatus to investigate the physical and chemical properties of different materials.

*Better Living;* Shell Oil Co.

turing to move from the home and small shop to the factory. It has also given man the wonders of mass production and automation.

One of the chief advances made in manufacturing has been the development of new sources of power to run machines. In the late 1700's, steam power replaced muscle power. One steam engine could run many large machines. This enabled skilled craftsmen to produce more goods, because they did not get so tired operating their machines. The electric motor, developed in the early 1900's, cost less and was more convenient than the steam engine. Electricity soon largely replaced steam as a source of industrial power.

Also during the early 1900's, scientists and engineers found ways to make large numbers of parts identical in size. This made possible the assembly line, the key to

E. H. Sheldon Equipment Co.; Moody Institute of Science

**Studying the Human Body** may be done by students, *left*, using simple plaster models. A doctor, *below*, may use a complex machine to observe the way a human heart beats.

mass production. Developments in electronics resulted in machines that can receive and give instructions. These "electronic brains" can be put in charge of other machines that produce goods automatically.

Without scientific discoveries, many modern factories would not exist. New developments in science lead to new products that in turn create millions of jobs. These include jobs in industries that make drugs, automobiles, chemicals, electronic equipment, and synthetic fibers—all the result of scientific discovery. See MANUFACTURING (How Science Helps Manufacturing).

**In Medicine,** science has given man a longer, healthier life. As a result of advances in preventing and curing disease, a person born in 1965 can expect to live almost 30 years longer than a person born in 1865.

One of the first great developments in the fight against disease took place in 1795, when Edward Jenner used scientific methods to discover a vaccine that could prevent smallpox. In the late 1800's, Louis Pasteur and Robert Koch found that germs cause many diseases and infections. Joseph Lister, influenced by Pasteur's work, developed the method of antiseptic surgery during the same period. His work made operations safer. The development of sulfa drugs and penicillin and other antibiotics in the 1930's and 1940's gave doctors new tools to cure diseases. Jonas Salk reduced the scourge of infantile paralysis when he produced the first polio vaccine in the 1950's. The development of atomic energy gave doctors radioisotopes with which to investigate and cure a number of diseases.

Studies in physiology and anatomy help surgeons perform new operations. They can repair damaged hearts, remove diseased tissues, and relieve continuous pain. Work in nutrition helps doctors tell us what foods we should eat to keep well. Research in basic science has helped in treating patients suffering from diabetes and other diseases of the glands.

**In the Community,** science plays a larger part than most persons realize. Scientists look into almost every daily activity in order to improve the way we live. They study the family to learn the causes of divorce and other social problems. Other research has revealed how slum conditions breed crime. Social scientists help plan schools so that they can best serve the interests of the community. Political scientists suggest ways to improve government.

Scientific methods that determine and analyze public opinion have a great effect on community life. Public-opinion polls aid advertising men in selling products, help television companies in planning programs, and guide candidates for office in conducting their campaigns.

Science also plays an important part in the business life of a community. Research in economics gives bankers and other businessmen ways to predict the ups and downs of business activity. Manufacturers use electronic computers to predict how much of their products they can expect to sell. This helps them plan how much to produce and how many employees to hire.

**In War,** science has given man terrible new weapons. A guided missile carrying a hydrogen bomb can destroy a city of 10,000 persons. Atomic submarines can cruise beneath the sea for months without coming to the surface. Drops of germs placed in public water supplies could make thousands of persons ill. Nerve gases can cause paralysis and death.

# SCIENCE

But the same atomic reactor that powers a submarine can propel a merchant ship. Knowledge about the effects of deadly radiation produced by atomic bombs helps cure disease. Even knowledge of nerve gases promises to relieve the suffering of the sick. The same rocket that sends a guided missile through the air can launch an artificial satellite and send instruments to outer space to help man learn more about the universe. The jet engine that powers a bomber can power a giant passenger plane. Scientific discoveries can either help or hurt man. It is up to the people of the world to choose how to use them.

## The Branches of Science

Many areas of science overlap, and workers in several fields may study the same problem from different points of view. For example, a psychologist and a physiologist might study the reactions of a man under the conditions present in a space ship. The physiologist would be interested in any changes in the heart rate or respiration, and in other physical reactions. The psychologist would be interested in any hallucinations, errors in seeing, and other mental reactions.

Because the sciences overlap in some areas, it is difficult to make clear-cut definitions of where one science begins and another ends. For example, both chemistry and physics are involved in studying atomic reactions. Both paleontology and geology may study the age of rocks in the earth. In general, the various biological sciences are more closely related than the physical sciences. The distinctions between the social sciences are even less clear.

In some cases, sciences may overlap so much that *interdisciplinary* fields have been established that combine parts of two or more sciences. For example, physical chemistry draws on both physics and chemistry. Biochemistry combines physiology and organic chemistry. Other interdisciplinary fields include mathematical economics, social psychology, astrophysics, and economic geography.

When viewed as a whole, the sciences may be arranged into four main groups: (1) mathematics and logic, (2) the physical sciences, (3) the biological sciences, and (4) the social sciences. Other groupings are sometimes made. For instance, parts of biology, psychology, and anthropology may be grouped as the *behavioral sciences*. Geology, meteorology, oceanography, and astronomy may be grouped as *earth sciences*.

**Mathematics and Logic.** Some persons do not consider mathematics and logic as sciences. But these fields of knowledge are such valuable tools for science that we cannot ignore them. Man's earliest questions were concerned with *how many?* and *what belongs together?* He struggled to count, to classify, to think systematically, and to describe exactly. Mathematics and logic developed as tools that helped in these struggles. Scientists generally feel more certain of their results if they can express them in terms of mathematics. Scientists in many areas make mathematical and statistical analyses of their observations.

The state of development of a science is indicated by the use it makes of mathematics. A science seems to begin with simple mathematics to measure, then works

# SCIENCE

toward more complex mathematics to explain. Most sciences start by naming and describing events. The social sciences are now in this position. Then the scientists try to find explanations, or principles, that hold true throughout the whole group of related sciences. The biological sciences are working on this. After developing satisfactory theories, the scientists study the basic problems of the field. For example, physical scientists do this by studying the nature of the atom. They hope to write mathematical equations and rules of logic to predict its behavior. See MATHEMATICS; LOGIC.

**The Physical Sciences** are concerned mainly with the nature of the universe. They study tiny atoms and vast galaxies. They also study the earth and the physical events that take place on it. Physical sciences include astronomy, chemistry, geology, meteorology, and physics.

*Astronomy* is the study of the heavenly bodies and their motion. Astronomers have discovered and classified stars, planets, and distant galaxies. They try to learn why stars blow up, and what space and the interior of the sun are like. Much remains to be known about the millions of objects that exist far out in space. See ASTRONOMY.

*Chemistry* studies materials found on the earth to determine their atomic and molecular structure and the changes that occur in them. Chemists learn to take molecules apart and put them together in new ways. Some chemists analyze substances to determine what elements and compounds make them up. Chemists in industry work to develop better textiles, paper, rubber, plastics, drugs, metals, and other products. *Chemurgy* involves the use of farm and forest products as raw materials for chemical manufacturing. *Organic* chemistry is the study of compounds containing the element carbon, and *inorganic* chemistry concerns all other compounds. *Physical* chemistry undertakes to explain why and how chemical reactions take place. See CHEMISTRY.

*Geology* studies the shape and structure of the earth and how the earth has changed during its history. Geologists learn how mountains rise up and are worn down, and how rivers and glaciers cut deep valleys out of the earth. They study the location of coal, petroleum, and other minerals beneath the surface of the earth. Geologists have named and classified rocks and minerals. They are concerned with the age of rocks, and with events that occurred millions of years ago and changed the contours of the earth's surface. Branches of geology include *petrology*, the study of rocks; *mineralogy*, the study of minerals; and *seismology*, the study of earthquakes. See GEOLOGY.

*Meteorology* is the study of weather and the air, or atmosphere. Its chief problem involves predicting the weather. Many meteorologists study the stratosphere, or upper atmosphere, above the highest clouds. They try to learn how conditions there affect weather at the earth's surface. They also want to know what conditions will be met in space travel. See METEOROLOGY.

*Physics* is concerned with matter and energy. Physicists study mechanics, heat, light, sound, electricity and magnetism, and the properties of matter. Energy and power of all kinds fall within the scope of physics. This science helps engineers design methods to get energy from one place to another. In *atomic* and *nuclear physics*, scientists study the properties of atoms and their nuclei. They search for new ways to control and use the energy of the atom. Other important areas of physics include *aerodynamics*, the study of the motion of air and the forces acting on objects in air; *electronics*, the study of the behavior of electrons; and *solid state physics*, the study of the properties of solids. See PHYSICS.

**The Biological Sciences,** or life sciences, involve the study of living organisms and their activities. Biological sciences include botany, zoology, paleontology, and psychology. See BIOLOGY.

*Botany and Zoology.* Botany, the study of plants, and zoology, the study of animals, are concerned with collecting, naming, classifying, examining, and describing living things. Biologists do not merely describe how living things look and act. They try to learn *how* and *why* organisms act as they do. Plants and animals have many characteristics in common, so botany and zoology may be combined as *biology*.

Botany and zoology may be divided into several main fields, each of which can be further subdivided. For example, *morphology*, the study of the structure of organisms, includes *anatomy*, the study of structures of living things; *histology*, the study of tissues; *cytology*, the study of cells; and *embryology*, the study of the development of organisms. *Taxonomy* involves the classification of living things. *Physiology* studies how the bodies of plants and animals function. Medical scientists often work in the area of physiology to study what happens when the body does not function properly. Other areas of biology include *genetics*, the study of heredity, and *ecology*, the study of the relation of organisms to their environment. Some botanists and zoologists specialize in only certain kinds of plants or animals. For example, *bacteriology* is the study of bacteria, and *ornithology* is the study of birds. See BOTANY; ZOOLOGY.

*Paleontology* is the study of prehistoric plants and animals. Paleontologists investigate *fossils,* or the remains of prehistoric organisms that have been preserved in rocks. They work with geologists to re-create a picture of the earth in prehistoric times. They have found evidence of the gradual change in the form of animals and plants throughout the earth's history. See PALEONTOLOGY.

*Psychology* is concerned with the behavior of man and animals. Psychologists study how the nerves and the brain work. They may investigate how animals react to certain situations, or how children learn. They try to find the effects conditions in the body have on various mental reactions. They may work with medical scientists to study the causes of mental and nervous diseases. Some psychologists study the behavior of people in groups, and work in areas similar to those covered by some of the social sciences. See PSYCHOLOGY.

**The Social Sciences** are concerned with the study of man and society. This is a difficult area to investigate scientifically. Man is an individual who decides what he will do. Usually, he does not act in exactly the same way twice. Not many persons will take part in a large social experiment. So social scientists must find most experimental situations by accident. It is hard for them to carry on precise research. Social scientists use observations, logic, and statistics to arrive at conclusions. See SOCIAL SCIENCE.

*Anthropology* studies different groups of people. *Social*

*anthropology* is particularly concerned with the development of the various customs and habits of a culture. Anthropologists have made only a few scientific studies of different cultural groups. *Physical anthropology* deals with the development of man's personal characteristics, including his body build and mental traits. It also involves the problem of the evolution of man, and the structure of his ancestors. In this area, anthropologists work closely with paleontologists. *Archaeology* deals with the way ancient men lived. The archaeologist studies the objects made by these people. See ANTHROPOLOGY.

*Economics* seeks to learn how groups of people use various resources to satisfy their wants and needs. Economists try to predict business trends and the demand for products. They investigate the problems of management and labor. They also try to find how economic systems work, and which ones work best. Economists use computers and statistical analysis in their studies. See ECONOMICS.

*Geography* studies the use of the physical earth and the living things it supports. Geographers often furnish information needed by economists to make predictions about an area. They study the mineral and water resources needed for development of cities. They try to learn how people adapt to life in various climates. Areas of geography include *physiogeography*, the study of land forms; *oceanography*, the study of waves, tides, currents, and depths of the oceans; and *biogeography*, the study of how living things affect the earth. See GEOGRAPHY.

*Linguistics*, or philology, involves the similarities and differences between the languages of people in various parts of the world. Linguists try to learn how and why languages change. Some of these experts work on the problem of whether a single language can be developed for all mankind. See LINGUISTICS.

*Political Science* is chiefly the study of government. Political scientists study customs and laws relating to governments, and try to find out what kind of government benefits the individual most. They also investigate and measure public opinion. See POLITICAL SCIENCE.

*Sociology* deals with the relation of individuals to the group, and of one group to another. It studies changes in the size and organization of the family and other groups. Sociologists investigate the effect of automation, atomic energy, and high-speed communication on society. See SOCIOLOGY.

## How Scientists Work

A scientist is interested mainly in events that can happen again. By repeating an experiment, a measurement, or an observation, a scientist helps find the cause of an event. The scientist may change one part of the experiment slightly when repeating it. What happens to the result of the experiment helps him discover more about how the whole experiment works. If other scientists are to believe what one scientist finds out, the

Illinois Education Association

**Mathematics Is an Important Scientific Tool.** Students learn to use numbers and solve simple problems, *right*. In scientific research, electronic computers, *below*, may quickly solve complex problems that would otherwise require years of work.

U.S. Dept. of Health, Education, and Welfare

# SCIENCE

experiment must be so designed that they can repeat it and get the same result.

When a scientist discovers a truth or fact through observations or experiments, he usually makes a written record of it and publishes his discovery. A large number of related facts may be organized to form a scientific principle, sometimes called a *conceptual structure*. The principles help scientists search for and find new facts and principles. The new ideas are linked with the old to make science an organized body of knowledge.

Scientists study a great range of facts and events. For example, a physicist may try to find ways to make atomic energy work for man. A chemist may try to produce new plastics to make life easier. A physician seeks ways to make man healthier. Biologists study how plants and animals grow. The psychologist is interested in how children learn. Scientists try to discover what happens, how it happens, and why it happens.

Although scientists can study many objects and events, there are many things they cannot test. A scientist cannot measure a mother's love for her children. He cannot measure the difference between good and evil. There is no way to tell scientifically what feeling an artist expresses in a painting. Such information has not been scientifically observed and measured.

**The Scientific Method** is a way of thinking about problems and solving them. The general rules used today were worked out by many men during hundreds of years. Scientists find it difficult to tell in what order they actually use the steps of the scientific method. The human mind probably does not actually solve problems in a systematic fashion. But, after the problem is solved, the scientist can use the scientific method to explain the problem and its solution in an orderly way. The formal plan has at least five check points: (1) stating the problem, (2) forming the hypothesis, (3) observing and experimenting, (4) interpreting data, and (5) drawing conclusions.

*Stating the Problem.* The scientific method is not hard to use. Anyone who is curious about nature can use it to try to find answers. For example, a student notices that dew is the same thing as rain but there is less of it. He states the problem by wondering whether there is any connection between the rain, the dew, and the amount of each.

*Forming the Hypothesis.* In forming a possible explanation, or hypothesis, the student considers what he knows of the problem. Both dew and rain are water. Where did the water come from? There are not always clouds when there is dew. Sometimes it rains when it is warm, but it is usually cool when there is dew. Fog leaves water on the ground like dew. From an airplane, a cloud looks like fog. The hypothesis might be that water is carried in the air and condenses into drops when the temperature falls.

*Observing and Experimenting.* The student used observation in stating the problem and in forming the hypothesis. An experiment might consist of placing an ice-filled metal pitcher above a teakettle standing on a stove. A foggy cloud appears above the teakettle. Part of this cloud forms drops of water on the pitcher. A piece of warm, moist grass sod placed under the pitcher will soon have drops of water on top of it.

*Interpreting the Data.* In the experiment, the student realizes, the top of the grass gets colder than the bottom, and the water condenses out of the air onto it. The data of the experiment have been interpreted. Dew and rain have the same source. Water can come out of the air.

*Drawing Conclusions.* The conclusion might be that dew and rain both come from the air. The experiment showed that water can come from the air. Sometimes it is high in the air, sometimes near the ground. Big drops may fall as rain, or small drops may form and make fog or dew.

**Logic and Organization.** The scientific method described above involves mainly *inductive* logic. This kind of logic requires repeated observations of an experiment or of an event. From observing many different examples, the scientists can draw a general conclusion. But scientists may also use *deductive* logic. In using deductive logic, a scientist reasons from known scientific principles or rules to draw a conclusion relating to a specific case. The accuracy of a conclusion reached by deductive logic depends on the accuracy of the principles and rules used. See DEDUCTIVE METHOD; INDUCTIVE METHOD.

Another important tool used in science is *classification*. Scientists in all fields try to classify their facts, so that their information will have more meaning. For example, chemists classify the elements into families or groups in the periodic table of elements. The elements in these groups have similar properties. Biologists classify plants and animals to show how the different organisms are related to each other. See CLASSIFICATION.

Scientists also have rules for drawing up theories or hypotheses. A theory should explain, unify, or organize known facts. It should be able to predict the results that scientists have obtained. It should also predict new events and open new areas of research. See RESEARCH.

## History

Science began thousands of years before man learned to write. No one knows who first discovered fire, invented the wheel, developed the bow and arrow, or tried to explain the rising and the setting of the sun. But all these events ranked as major advances in science. They were among man's first attempts to explain and control the things he saw around him. In general, mathematics was the first of the sciences to develop, followed by the physical sciences, the biological sciences, and the social sciences.

**Ancient Civilizations.** The Egyptians invented many tools and techniques as early as 3000 B.C. They learned some physiology and surgery while embalming their dead. They developed a practical system of geometry to fix property lines, and had a system of mathematics. The Egyptians also studied the stars, named the constellations, and developed a calendar.

In ancient Babylonia, the people developed a calendar, a system of measurement, and a number system. They also developed the pseudoscience of *astrology*. Astrologers tried to foretell the future by interpreting the different positions of the stars and planets. See ASTROLOGY.

The Chinese civilization developed a little later than the Egyptian and Babylonian cultures. The Chinese developed their own system of writing and mathematics, and made advances in astronomy, chemistry, and medicine. But they had little contact with other

# SCIENCE

WORLD BOOK photo

**Geology Students** learn how the earth was formed and how it changes. They study oceans, rocks, and other parts of the earth.

U.S. Geological Survey

**Some Geologists Study Minerals.** They conduct many kinds of tests to discover where various minerals may be found.

civilizations, and did not influence Western science. In India, a number system was developed during the 200's B.C. The Arabs learned this system and later passed it on to the West.

The Aztec, Inca, and Maya Indians of America also had some science. The Maya developed a number system. By the A.D. 600's, they knew more about numbers than the Europeans of that time. They used a highly accurate calendar. The Aztec had a number system and a calendar. The Inca also had a number system. But none of these civilizations contributed to European science.

**The Greeks** left the largest heritage of science of all the ancient peoples. Hippocrates taught that diseases had natural causes and that the body had the power to repair itself. At that time, about 400 B.C., most men thought that the gods caused illness. Aristotle, one of the greatest Greek philosophers, studied all areas of science. He showed the need for classifying knowledge, and recognized the importance of observation, especially in biology. He developed deductive logic as a means of reaching conclusions. Many of his conclusions were false, because Aristotle based them on mistaken "common sense" ideas, instead of on experiments.

Thales, Pythagoras, Euclid, and others had perfected geometry by about 300 B.C. During the 200's B.C., a center of Greek learning grew up in Alexandria, Egypt. Most Greek scholars were interested mainly in *metaphysics*, or philosophy (see METAPHYSICS). But a few had an interest in practical affairs. For example, Archimedes performed experiments and learned how the lever works. He studied floating bodies and understood *density*, or weight compared with size. Other Greeks measured the size of the earth with surprising accuracy. They also mapped the stars. Ptolemy, in the A.D. 100's, developed a unified idea of the universe. He thought that the stars, planets, and sun move around the earth.

Our scientific heritage from the Greeks includes their emphasis on the rules of thinking, the need for classifying, and the desirability of explaining events.

**The Romans** were interested mainly in applied

U.S. Navy

**Oceanography Studies the Sea** and its animals and plants. Here, a scientist uses a special bottle to bring up water samples.

169

# SCIENCE

science. They developed advanced techniques of engineering and government. But they did little work in theoretical science.

The Greek anatomist Galen practiced medicine in Rome during the A.D. 100's. His conclusions on anatomy were based on thoughts rather than observations, and he had many mistaken ideas. Even so, he greatly advanced the anatomical knowledge of his time.

**The Middle Ages.** By the fall of Rome in A.D. 476, scientific advance had ceased. Alexandria fell to the Arabs in A.D. 642. They discovered and preserved some parts of the great library there. The Arabs learned the decimal number system from the people of India, and helped develop algebra. This knowledge joined other scientific knowledge that the Arabs preserved.

In Europe, scholars were more interested in *theology*, or the study of religion, than in the study of nature. They added little new scientific knowledge. Arabic translations of Greek writings began to reach Europe during the A.D. 1000's. But the interpretation of these writings depended on the theology of the times. In the 1200's, theologians organized the knowledge in the Greek writings to agree with their religious views. Scholars saw no need for direct observation of nature. The writings of Aristotle, Galen, and Ptolemy were considered the truth. To disagree with them was considered heresy, punishable by imprisonment or death.

Some scholars of this time were interested in *alchemy*, a mixture of magic and simple chemistry. They tried to produce gold from less costly metals. By their experiments, they laid the basis for later study in chemistry. Some men learned about botany and pharmacology while trying to find magic herbs to lengthen their lives. But a few men were consciously interested in advancing knowledge in the field of science. One of these was the English monk Roger Bacon, who lived during the 1200's. Bacon criticized the deductive method of obtaining knowledge. He saw the need for experiment, measurement, and mathematics. Bacon was imprisoned because he criticized dependence on accepted authority.

**The Renaissance** began earlier in art and literature than in science. Many men of the 1400's developed an

## RED-LETTER DATES IN SCIENCE

| | |
|---|---|
| c. 400 B.C. | Hippocrates taught that diseases have natural, rather than supernatural, causes. |
| 300's B.C. | Aristotle's studies in logic and classification contributed to the foundations of science. |
| c. 300 B.C. | Euclid formulated basic postulates of deductive geometry. |
| 200's B.C. | Archimedes performed experiments and discovered basic physical principles. |
| A.D. 100's | Galen laid the foundation for the study of anatomy and physiology. |
| | Ptolemy developed a theory that the earth is the center of the universe. |
| c. 1500 | Leonardo da Vinci recognized the importance of observation and experimentation in learning. He used experiments to make many discoveries. |
| 1543 | Nicolaus Copernicus' theory that the earth and other planets move around the sun laid the background for modern astronomy. |
| | Andreas Vesalius published a book on the anatomy of man, based on observation. |
| c. 1600 | Galileo emphasized the mathematical interpretation of experiments in science. He discovered many important physical laws. |
| 1609 | Johannes Kepler established astronomy as an exact science. |
| 1628 | William Harvey published his theory on the circulation of the blood. |
| 1660's | Robert Boyle applied the scientific method to chemistry. |
| 1687 | Sir Isaac Newton published the *Principia*, which summarized basic laws of mechanics. |
| c. 1730 | Carolus Linnaeus founded the method of classification of plants and animals. |
| 1774 | Joseph Priestley discovered oxygen. |
| 1776 | Adam Smith published the first systematic formulation of classical economics. |
| c. 1780 | Antoine Lavoisier explained that when an object burns, it unites with oxygen. His research laid the foundation for modern chemistry. |
| c. 1796 | Edward Jenner discovered a method of vaccination against smallpox. |
| 1803 | John Dalton announced the atomic theory. |
| c. 1830 | Charles Lyell founded modern geology. |
| | Auguste Comte started the study of sociology. |
| 1831 | Michael Faraday induced an electric current with a moving magnet. |
| 1839 | Matthias Schleiden and Theodor Schwann theorized that all living things are composed of cells. |
| 1858 | Charles Darwin advanced his theory of evolution of plants and animals. |
| 1860's | James Clerk Maxwell developed his electromagnetic theory. |
| 1866 | Gregor Mendel published his discovery of the laws of heredity. |
| 1869 | Dmitri Mendeleev developed the periodic table, classifying elements by their atomic weights and their properties. |
| c. 1876 | Louis Pasteur found that microorganisms cause fermentation and disease. |
| 1879 | Wilhelm Wundt founded the first laboratory of experimental psychology. |
| 1882 | Robert Koch discovered the bacteria that cause tuberculosis. |
| 1895 | Wilhelm K. Roentgen discovered X rays. |
| 1898 | Marie and Pierre Curie isolated the element radium. |
| 1900 | Max Planck advanced the quantum theory. |
| c. 1900 | Paul Ehrlich originated *chemotherapy*, the treatment of disease with chemicals. |
| | Sigmund Freud developed psychoanalysis. |
| 1905 | Albert Einstein presented his Special Theory of Relativity. |
| 1911 | Ernest Rutherford put forth a theory of atomic structure. He recognized that the mass of the atom is located in a nucleus. |
| 1928 | Alexander Fleming discovered penicillin. |
| 1938 | Otto Hahn and Fritz Strassmann found lightweight atoms, after bombarding uranium with neutrons. |
| 1942 | Enrico Fermi and his associates achieved the first successful nuclear chain reaction. |
| 1953 | Jonas Salk produced the first effective vaccine against polio. It was released for use in 1955. |
| 1957 | Russia launched the first artificial satellite. |
| 1957 | Arthur Kornberg grew DNA, the basic chemical of the gene, in a test tube. |
| 1957-8 | During the International Geophysical Year, scientists of 66 countries studied the earth and its surroundings. |
| 1961 | Yuri Gagarin of Russia and Alan B. Shepard, Jr., of the United States became the first men to fly in space. |

**Studying the Weather** is an important part of science. A meteorologist, *left*, uses a balloon to study the atmosphere. Students, *right*, learn about elements of weather in science classes.

interest in nature. But most of them turned to the Greek writings, rather than trying to add new knowledge. Few questioned the authority of Aristotle and Ptolemy.

Leonardo da Vinci, the Italian artist, represented a new type of thinker. In the late 1400's, he studied anatomy by dissecting bodies, rather than by reading what Galen had written. He found that light and sound follow certain rules. But he did not publish his results, and had little influence on the men of his time. The Swiss physician Philippus Paracelsus also observed nature. He found experience and observation more important than the authority of Aristotle and Galen.

**The Rebirth of Science** began about 1543, with the publication of two books that changed man's ideas about his world and about himself. Nicolaus Copernicus, the Polish astronomer, published *De Revolutionibus Orbium Celestium*, which contradicted Ptolemy's view of the solar system. Andreas Vesalius, the Belgian anatomist, published *De Fabrica Corporis Humani*, which described his own anatomical observations, rather than repeating Galen's statements. Both these books were based on observations. Both broke from the old ideas, but kept portions of the Greek influence.

Copernicus' book revolutionized the thinking of many scholars. Before his work, scholars had accepted Ptolemy's view that the earth was the center of the universe. The Greeks viewed the circle as the perfect shape, so Ptolemy thought that the planets moved in circular paths. But, to agree with observations, Ptolemy had to assume a complicated series of motions for each planet. Copernicus saw that the explanation of the movements would be simpler if the earth traveled around the sun. This required a less complicated arrangement of circles. But it did not predict the motion of all the planets exactly.

Tycho Brahe, the Danish astronomer, made accurate observations of the planets in the late 1500's. Johannes Kepler of Germany used Brahe's observations as a basis to test Copernicus' theory. In 1609, he showed that the theory could explain observed facts if the circular paths of the planets were replaced by elliptical paths. This also made the movements of the planets still simpler. His discovery marked the start of modern astronomy.

The second important book published in 1543, Vesalius' work on anatomy, showed that Galen had made many mistakes. Vesalius based his work on the observation of actual dissections of bodies. But he used the inaccurate physiology presented by Galen. The final break with tradition came in 1628, when William Harvey of England described the circulation of the blood. His work was based on observation, careful experiments, and simple mathematics. Harvey's work marked the beginning of modern physiology.

Men began to turn from the established patterns in areas other than astronomy and physiology. In 1600, William Gilbert of England summarized knowledge about electricity and magnetism. He based his work on observation and experiments. Francis Bacon, the English writer, summarized the theory of the experimental method. He also urged the use of the inductive method of reasoning. Robert Boyle introduced the scientific method in chemistry in the 1660's. He defined a chemical element, and proposed theories on the nature of matter.

**Galileo and Newton.** Galileo, the great Italian physicist of the late 1500's and early 1600's, is recognized as

171

**Scientists Study Plants** to learn about heredity and ways to improve crops. Here, a research worker studies how an insect attacks wheat in order to find ways to prevent crop damage.

the father of modern experimentation. He was one of the first scientists to use the scientific method. Galileo recognized the importance of observation at a time when most scientists referred only to "the authorities." In his research, Galileo set up relationships between events, depending on observation and mathematical analysis. He recognized that experimentation can lead to the discovery of new principles. For example, his observations of falling bodies led him to discard Aristotle's laws. After performing many experiments, he was able to set up a new principle. One of Galileo's greatest contributions to science was his recognition of the importance of observation, exact measurement, and planned experiments.

Galileo discovered many principles of physics, particularly in mechanics. He also improved the instruments of measurement known at the time. In his research with the telescope, he found important evidence supporting Copernicus' view of the universe. See GALILEO.

Sir Isaac Newton of England, in the late 1600's, used the findings of others to develop a unified view of the forces in the universe. His book, the *Principia*, published in 1687, presented a common explanation for many physical events. These included the difficulty of making a heavy object move quickly, the explanation of falling bodies, and the paths of the moon and planets.

A number of scientists had described observations and measurements for physical events. Galileo and those following him also performed many experiments, and obtained various measurements. But the measurements often had little meaning. There were too many of them and they were unrelated. To unite these unrelated observations and measurements, Newton developed a concept that would explain the events. He also set up a mathematical explanation that could predict the measurements accurately. Newton's main idea was *gravitation*. Using this idea, everything fitted together. It not only explained events on earth, but also in the rest of the universe.

Newton demonstrated the application of the rules of the scientific method. He showed their use in making general explanations that covered a wide group of separate events. His writings form the essential basis for the study of much physics today. Without men such as Newton to guide the development of theories in science, the efforts of many workers would be lost in a jumble of isolated facts. Science progresses because its knowledge is *systematized*, or organized, by the development of unifying ideas to explain many events. See NEWTON, SIR ISAAC.

**In the 1700's,** scientists discovered new chemical substances, including chlorine, oxygen, hydrogen, and carbon dioxide. In 1774, Antoine Lavoisier of France discovered the true nature of combustion. He showed that burning results from the rapid union of the burning material with oxygen. He also developed the method of describing chemical reactions by equations.

Great advances also occurred in biology during the 1700's. The Swedish scientist Carolus Linnaeus developed the first successful method for naming and classifying plants and animals. This method, with many modifications, is still used today. In 1757, the Swiss physiologist Albrecht von Haller developed systematic physiology by organizing what biologists had learned about respiration, circulation, embryology, and the nervous system.

**In the 1800's,** physicists carried the work of Newton further. They produced a unified, seemingly complete, view of the laws of nature. James P. Joule of England showed that heat is a form of energy. He also stated the principle of the conservation of energy. This principle states that energy cannot be created or destroyed, but only changed in form.

Michael Faraday of England found in 1831 that a moving magnet can induce an electric current. In the 1860's, James Clerk Maxwell, also of England, used mathematics to describe Faraday's work on the relationship of electricity and magnetism. Maxwell showed that light and other energy waves are fundamentally the same.

Dmitri Mendeleev of Russia simplified and systematized the description of chemical reactions when he published his periodic table of elements in 1869. This table, which groups elements according to their atomic weights and chemical properties, clarified the relations between the various elements. Other chemists explained the nature of organic compounds, and devised new ways to explain chemical reactions mathematically.

In the 1830's, the English geologist Charles Lyell provided evidence that the earth's surface changed slowly and gradually through millions of years by means of processes that are still continuing. Other geologists had believed that the earth reached its present shape as a result only of great *cataclysms*, or violent changes.

In 1858, Charles R. Darwin presented to biology a

unifying idea—the concept of orderly, gradual change, or *evolution*. He presented evidence that plants and animals have changed their characteristics through the ages. Darwin formulated a theory explaining how these changes might take place. This was the idea of natural selection through competition. See EVOLUTION.

Several new sciences had their beginnings during the 1800's. In the mid-1800's, Gregor Mendel, an Austrian monk, discovered basic laws of heredity that laid the foundation for the science of genetics. Louis Pasteur of France started modern microbiology with his studies of fermentation and disease. He found that certain microscopic organisms can produce disease in man and in animals. Many scientists studied the relationship between the physiology of the nervous system and human behavior. In 1879, Wilhelm Wundt founded the first laboratory of experimental psychology in Leipzig, Germany.

**The Early 1900's** brought revolutionary advances in all fields of science. But perhaps the most dramatic discoveries have been made in the field of physics, especially as a result of atomic research.

*In Physics*, several discoveries during the late 1800's showed scientists that the picture of the universe as seen by the followers of Newton was not accurate. In 1900, Max Planck of Germany advanced his celebrated quantum theory to explain certain properties of heat energy (see QUANTUM THEORY). This theory states that energy is not released continuously, but in units, or bundles, called *quanta*. Albert Einstein extended the quantum theory to light energy in 1905. He showed that light rays are streams of energy units which he called *photons*. That same year, Einstein published his famous Special Theory of Relativity (see RELATIVITY). Einstein's theory revised many of Newton's concepts and added new ideas. One of the most important of these was the possibility that mass could change into energy, as expressed in the formula $E=mc^2$.

Research into the structure of the atom led to the discovery of many atomic particles. Soon after 1910, Ernest Rutherford of New Zealand and Niels Bohr of Denmark presented theories of the internal structure of the atom. Rutherford produced the first nuclear reaction in 1919. He bombarded nitrogen atoms with alpha rays and changed some of them into oxygen. During the late 1930's, Otto Hahn and Fritz Strassmann of Germany, and Lise Meitner and Otto Frisch of Austria developed the possibility of releasing energy by splitting atoms of uranium. Enrico Fermi and his coworkers achieved the first controlled nuclear chain reaction in 1942. Intensive research during World War II led to the development of atomic energy in weapons. After the war, scientists directed research toward perfecting it as a source of power and producing still more powerful weapons. See ATOM (Development of the Atomic Theory); ATOMIC ENERGY (Development).

Advances in other areas of physics included studies of the properties of matter at extreme temperatures. Research in electricity led to the development of television, electronic computers and factory controls, and other electronic devices. Further work in the area of the quantum theory produced additional knowledge about the nature of the atom and its particles.

*In Chemistry*, scientists acquired much information about the preparation of new compounds. They developed many plastics, synthetic fibers, and drugs. Linus Pauling of the United States devised accurate models of the molecular structure of many complex compounds.

*In the Biological Sciences*, many advances were made during the 1900's. Paul Ehrlich of Germany founded the now-important field of *chemotherapy*, the treatment of diseases with chemicals. In 1928, Alexander Fleming of Great Britain discovered penicillin, the first of many antibiotics used in the battle against disease. In the field of genetics, the work of the Dutch scientist Hugo de Vries led to a greater understanding of heredity. In 1901, he first extensively described *mutations*, or changes in hereditary material (see MUTATION). Scientists later applied statistics to the study of heredity. This work in genetics resulted in the improvement of breeding techniques with plants and animals.

*In the Social Sciences*, research brought new facts and the development of theories to organize these facts. Great progress has been made in perfecting methods of collecting data and analyzing facts statistically.

**The Mid-1900's** saw continued progress in all fields of science. Medical science developed the Salk and Sabin polio vaccines and introduced new surgical techniques. Surgeons transplanted organs from one person to another. Physicists discovered new subatomic particles and produced new radioactive elements (see TRANSURANIUM ELEMENTS). Anthropologists made new discoveries about man's remote past. Geneticists grew *deoxyribonucleic acid* (chemicals that play a vital part in heredity, known as DNA) in laboratories (see HEREDITY).

During the International Geophysical Year (1957-1958), scientists of 66 nations cooperated in special experiments to increase knowledge about the earth and its surroundings. See INTERNATIONAL GEOPHYSICAL YEAR.

The *Space Age* opened in 1957, when Russia launched artificial satellites that circled the earth. The United States sent up its first artificial satellite in 1958. In 1961, both nations began sending men into space. Unmanned rockets probed the earth's outer atmosphere and the moon's surface, orbited the sun, and came close to nearby planets. See SPACE TRAVEL; ROCKET. The invention of *lasers* (concentrated beams of light) promised great advances in communications, medicine, electronics, and weapons (see LASER).

**Problems of the Future.** Despite the great advances made in science, scientists still have many unsolved problems. Physicists have not yet produced the high temperatures needed for controlled atomic fusion reactions. Botanists still do not know exactly how the process of photosynthesis works. Biologists and biochemists have not yet found the answer to the question of how life originated. Astronomers have not yet developed a satisfactory explanation of the origin of the universe. Medical scientists and physiologists do not know the cause or cure of cancer or how to cure the various virus diseases. Paleontologists and geneticists search for still more evidence on the events and processes of evolution of plants and animals. Psychologists do not know all the causes of mental illness.

### Careers in Science

**Science Education** begins in a general way in elementary school. Even in the early grades, students learn

# SCIENCE

the names of many things. Experiments show how things work. The general ideas of science are used to explain events in nature. For example, children may learn a simple explanation of what causes the differences in the seasons, what makes rain, or what keeps a satellite in the sky. From these general ideas, the students begin to build an understanding of science.

In the later elementary grades, science teaching becomes more formalized. The students receive an understanding of science as a field of knowledge. They learn that science includes many fields, such as biology, chemistry, and physics. Most of their study is general, covering many areas of science, but not in a detailed manner.

*High-School Science* and mathematics are more specialized than in elementary school. Most students take a minimum of one year of science. This may be general science, biology, chemistry, or physics. Many students continue their science education and study more than one field of science. High-school science courses help students learn how the scientific method works and how our industrial society uses science. Some students may study the applied sciences, such as agronomy, aeronautics, or specialized shop courses.

Students who plan professional careers in pure and applied science usually take at least two years of natural science and three years of mathematics in high school. High-school biology, chemistry, and physics courses show students how scientists obtain and organize knowledge in these fields. Experiments illustrate both what happens and how scientists use the scientific method. High-school science projects provide young people with a chance to be creative in science, and to apply known scientific concepts to fields that interest them. They work individually to perform an experiment, to complete a collection, or to build a model. This work helps them gain an idea of what scientific research involves. Many students exhibit their projects in science fairs.

Mathematics courses in high school teach mathematical reasoning, and show how to apply it to scientific problems. Algebra, geometry, trigonometry, and other mathematics courses are highly recommended for students interested in scientific careers.

*College Science* courses appeal chiefly to men and women who plan to become professional scientists. But most college students take some science during the freshman year as part of their general education. Students majoring in biology, chemistry, physics, mathematics, or one of the social sciences take at least four one-year courses in their major subject. The college science major also usually takes three years of courses in a related science or in mathematics.

*Graduate School.* Most students interested in research or in one of the scientific professions take graduate courses after receiving a bachelor's degree. In graduate school, the student studies one or two subjects intensively. He can usually meet the requirements for a master's degree after one year of graduate work. Requirements for the Ph.D. and similar degrees normally take three additional years of graduate study.

*On-the-Job Training.* A college graduate employed by a large corporation may receive still more training. College provides him with a knowledge of scientific principles. Industrial training programs may teach him how to apply these principles to the problems of a particular company. The industrial training program serves both to introduce employees to the company, and to help scientific workers keep up to date.

**Working in Science** is one of the most rewarding careers a young person can choose. The opportunities for jobs are unlimited, because science holds such an important place in modern life. For example, industry hires technicians to control the quality of products. Some companies hire persons trained in science as salesmen. Research scientists work on the frontiers of knowledge to discover new facts. Schools need more and more trained science teachers.

*Research.* The scientist in research and development works where knowledge is fresh. He must know his special field well, and be acquainted with related fields of knowledge. He should be creative, dedicated to his work, and interested in exploring and testing new ideas. Team research in large laboratories may have as many as a dozen men and women working under a group leader on different aspects of the same problem. But the researcher must be able to work individually.

Career opportunities have grown increasingly in scientific research and development. The physical sciences and mathematics have the most critical need for scientists. But the demand for biological scientists and social scientists is growing rapidly. Other career opportunities include science administration and social engineering.

Beginning work in research requires a master's degree. The doctor's degree is desirable for positions of leadership. Generally, industrial work pays better than university, institute, or government employment. Scientific consultants who work independently for manufacturers usually enjoy the highest incomes.

*Teaching.* Good positions are available for many more than the number of science teachers entering the profession each year. Positions include serving as science consultant in elementary school, teaching science in high school, and teaching advanced courses in college and graduate school. The qualifications include a mastery of the field and the ability to transmit interest and understanding to others. Most science teachers earn a master's degree before they become established in the profession. A college teacher having a doctor's degree may be promoted to higher professorial rank. Teaching normally provides time during vacations for travel and further study. Some college teachers have both teaching and research assignments.

*Technicians.* An increasing number of science technicians work in industries and offices. They include medical technicians, dietetic assistants, laboratory assistants, and computer operators. A supervising scientist or engineer directs their work. Generally, some college work is desired for these positions, but a major in science is not always needed. Technicians may also work in university, hospital, and institute laboratories.

*Other Careers.* A great variety of other careers exist in the field of science. These include science writing, abstracting, editing, and reporting; scientific and medical illustrating; science library work; and translation of scientific articles and books. Technical salesmen, trained in science or engineering, call on industries and professional men. Graduates in the social sciences may help administer welfare funds. Naturalists and game-management specialists may work for public parks and forest preserves. Large numbers of students enter the many science-related professions, which include medicine, dentistry, engineering, and dietetics.   H. CRAIG SIPE

**Related Articles** in WORLD BOOK include:

### THE BIOLOGICAL SCIENCES

| | | | |
|---|---|---|---|
| Agronomy | Biophysics | Genetics | Pharmacology |
| Anatomy | Botany | Histology | Physiology |
| Bacteriology | Cytology | Medicine | Taxonomy |
| Biochemistry | Ecology | Morphology | Zoology |
| Biology | Embryology | Paleontology | |

### THE PHYSICAL SCIENCES

| | | |
|---|---|---|
| Acoustics | Electronics | Nuclear Physics |
| Aerodynamics | Engineering | Optics |
| Astronomy | Geochemistry | Physical Chemistry |
| Chemistry | Geology | Physics |
| Chemurgy | Geophysics | Solid State Physics |
| Dynamics | Mechanics | Statics |
| Earth Science | Metallurgy | Thermodynamics |
| Electrochemistry | Meteorology | |

### THE SOCIAL SCIENCES

| | | |
|---|---|---|
| Anthropology | Geography | Political Science |
| Archaeology | Linguistics | Psychology |
| Economics | Philosophy | Sociology |

### MATHEMATICS AND LOGIC

Biomathematics   Logic   Mathematics   Statistics

### ORGANIZATIONS

| | |
|---|---|
| American Association for the Advancement of Science | International Council of Scientific Unions |
| Arts and Sciences, American Academy of | National Academy of Sciences |
| Future Scientists of America | Royal Institution |
| | Royal Society |
| | Science Clubs of America |
| | Sigma Xi |

### SCIENCE PROJECTS

The following articles contain special WORLD BOOK Science Projects:

| | | |
|---|---|---|
| Air | Electric Motor | Metal |
| Antibiotic | Electricity | Microscope |
| Astronomy | Electronics | Nutrition |
| Atom | Energy | Physics |
| Atomic Energy | Eye | Rocket |
| Biology | Heredity | Seed |
| Chemistry | Leaf | Skeleton |
| Color | Light | Weather |
| Dam | Magnet and Magnetism | Zoology |
| Ear | | |

### OTHER RELATED ARTICLES

Experimentation, Scientific
Instrument, Scientific
Research
Technology
Testing

### Outline

I. **Science in Our Daily Lives**
  A. In the Home
  B. In Agriculture
  C. In Manufacturing
  D. In Medicine
  E. In the Community
  F. In War

II. **The Branches of Science**
  A. Mathematics and Logic
  B. The Physical Sciences
  C. The Biological Sciences
  D. The Social Sciences

III. **How Scientists Work**
  A. The Scientific Method
  B. Logic and Organization

IV. **History**

V. **Careers in Science**

## SCIENCE PROJECTS

### Questions

How does the scientific method work?
What is the difference between inductive and deductive logic? Between pure and applied science?
What were the main contributions of the Greek philosophers to science?
What kinds of problems do social scientists try to solve? What techniques do they use?
What is an interdisciplinary science?
How is mathematics valuable to the various sciences?
In general, what was the order in which the four branches of science developed?
What ancient people left the largest heritage of science?

**SCIENCE, AMERICAN ASSOCIATION FOR THE ADVANCEMENT OF.** See AMERICAN ASSOCIATION FOR THE ADVANCEMENT OF SCIENCE.

**SCIENCE AND INDUSTRY, MUSEUM OF.** See MUSEUM OF SCIENCE AND INDUSTRY.

**SCIENCE CLUBS OF AMERICA** is an international organization open to boys and girls of all ages who have a hobby or professional interest in science. About 25,000 science youth groups in the United States and other countries are affiliated with it. These have more than 500,000 members. Each club is sponsored by an interested adult. Science Clubs of America sponsors the National Science Fair-International and the Science Talent Search.

*The National Science Fair-International*, held in a different city each May, is open to high school sophomores, juniors, and seniors. Representatives come from the finalists chosen at annual regional fairs.

*The Science Talent Search* for the Westinghouse Science Scholarships and Awards is open to high school seniors in the continental United States. Each applicant must take a science aptitude test and write a report on his science project. His completed entry includes a personal data form and school records filled out by his teachers and principal. Honors are awarded to about 10 per cent of the students. The top 40 go to Washington, D.C., for the five-day, all-expense paid, Science Talent Institute. They are judged there for five scholarships of $7,500, $6,000, $5,000, $4,000, and $3,000, and 35 cash awards of $250 each.

In an attempt to assist talented science students, State Science Talent Searches are conducted in 37 states and the District of Columbia by special arrangement with Science Clubs of America.

The organization was founded in 1941. It is administered by Science Service with headquarters at 1719 N St., NW, Washington, D.C. 20036.   LESLIE V. WATKINS

**SCIENCE FICTION** is a form of writing based on imaginative adventures in time, space, other worlds, and other dimensions. Some science-fiction stories are based on known or predictable scientific fact, while others have no relation to reality at all. Many ancient works, such as *The Arabian Nights*, contain elements of science fiction. Jules Verne wrote many excellent science-fiction stories, predicting many later scientific and social developments. H. G. Wells also wrote science fiction.

See also VERNE, JULES; WELLS, H. G.

**SCIENCE PROJECTS.** For a list of articles that include special WORLD BOOK Science Projects, see the Related Articles of the SCIENCE article.

## SCIENTIFIC CLASSIFICATION

**SCIENTIFIC CLASSIFICATION.** See CLASSIFICATION.
**SCIENTIFIC EXPEDITION.** See EXPLORATION AND DISCOVERY.
**SCIENTIFIC INSTRUMENT.** See INSTRUMENT, SCIENTIFIC.
**SCIENTIFIC METHOD.** See SCIENCE (The Scientific Method).
**SCILLY ISLANDS,** *SIL lih*, lie in the Atlantic Ocean off the coast of Cornwall, England, about 25 miles from Land's End. The islands belong to Great Britain. They are the first land that travelers see as they approach England from New York City.

The group has about 150 islands, but only five of them are important. The capital of the island group is Hugh Town, which stands on Saint Mary's Island.

The islands cover an area of 6 square miles, and have a population of about 1,940. They are wild and colorful. Because the climate is mild, the Scilly Islands have become a popular tourist center. The islands also supply flowers, vegetables, and fish to British markets. FREDERICK G. MARCHAM

**SCIMITAR.** See SWORD.
**SCINTILLATION COUNTER.** See GEIGER COUNTER.
**SCINTILLOSCOPE.** See SPINTHARISCOPE.
**SCION,** a variant of CION. See GRAFTING (plants).
**SCIOTO RIVER,** *sye O toh*, a branch of the Ohio River, flows 237 miles and drains the rich farming region of central Ohio. The river rises in the west-central part of the state, flows eastward, and then turns south. It empties into the Ohio River at Portsmouth.

**SCIPIO,** *SIP ih oh*, was the name of a branch of the great Roman family, the Cornelii. Two of its members are called AFRICANUS MAJOR and AFRICANUS MINOR.

**Publius Cornelius Scipio,** AFRICANUS MAJOR (236?-184? B.C.) was the Roman general who invaded Africa and defeated Hannibal of Carthage (see HANNIBAL). He is known as AFRICANUS because of this victory. During the Second Punic War, Scipio took Spain away from the Carthaginians. He then invaded Africa, and Hannibal was recalled from Italy to fight Scipio. In 202 B.C., Scipio defeated Hannibal at Zama, the last battle of the Second Punic War. See PUNIC WARS.

Scipio's political party dominated Rome for the next 10 years, but Cato the Censor and other Roman senators were suspicious of his popular appeal. Scipio retired from public life when his brother Lucius was convicted of dishonest practices.

**Publius Cornelius Scipio Aemilianus,** AFRICANUS MINOR (185-129 B.C.) was the son of Lucius Aemilius Paullus, a Roman statesman, and by adoption the grandson of AFRICANUS MAJOR. Scipio Aemilianus is known as AFRICANUS because of his victories in Africa. He was *consul* (chief government official) in 147 B.C., and directed the siege which led to the destruction of Carthage during the Third Punic War. As consul again in 134 B.C., he destroyed Numantia in Spain.

Scipio was a political leader. He also did much to spread Greek learning in Rome, and led a group of intellectuals known as the *Scipionic Circle*. Its members included the dramatist Terence, the Greek historian Polybius, the Greek philosopher Panaetius, and Rome's first great satirist Lucilius. HENRY C. BOREN

**SCISSORBILL.** See SKIMMER.

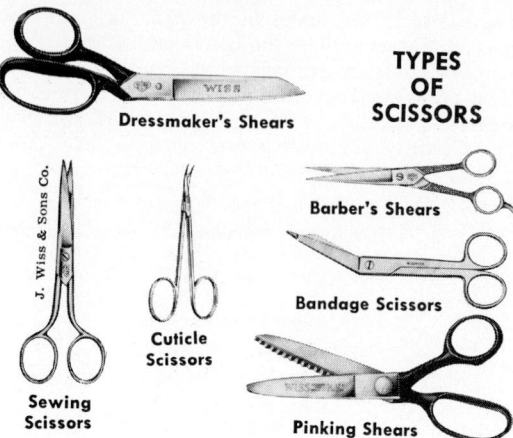

TYPES OF SCISSORS

Dressmaker's Shears
Barber's Shears
Cuticle Scissors
Bandage Scissors
Sewing Scissors
Pinking Shears

**SCISSORS,** *SIHZ urz*. A pair of scissors is really two knife blades joined together to form a double lever. Each blade operates as a lever of the first class (see LEVER). A pin or bolt holds the blades together, and acts as their common fulcrum. The lever action starts by squeezing the open scissors handles together. This applies pressure against both sides of the material, which is cut when both blades come together.

To most persons, scissors and shears refer to the same instrument. But, in the hardware trade, the word *shears* refers to a pair of scissors with blades more than 6 inches long. The handles of scissors usually have rings of equal size. Most shears have a larger ring on one handle to make room for the four fingers of the cutting hand. The thumb of the cutting hand fits through the other ring. Scissors and shears range in size from tiny manicuring scissors to giant, power-operated metal shears that cut scrap metal to size for steel-mill furnaces. *Pinking shears*, or *pinking scissors*, have saw-tooth edges. They give cloth a scalloped edge that keeps the thread in the material from raveling. Scissors developed shortly after man learned to make knives. Sharp, sturdy scissors were developed in the late 1200's. WALTER R. WILLIAMS, JR.

**SCLERA.** See EYE (The Eyeball; color diagram: Parts of the Eye).
**SCLEROMETER.** See HARDNESS.
**SCLEROSIS, MULTIPLE.** See MULTIPLE SCLEROSIS.
**SCOLIOSIS,** *SKOH lih OH sihs*, means a side-to-side curve or bend of the normally straight spine or backbone. Scoliosis may occur in any part of the spine. It may be single (curved like a *C*) or double (curved like an *S*). Scoliosis usually starts in childhood or the teens. It may come from disturbance of growth, paralyzed back muscles, or a short leg. Treatment includes exercises, braces, or surgery. IRVIN STEIN

**SCONE,** *skohn*, **STONE OF,** is a coronation stone on which the kings and queens of Great Britain are crowned. It lies beneath a special coronation chair in Westminster Abbey. It is also called the *Stone of Destiny*. King Edward I took the stone from Scotland and brought it to England in 1296. For hundreds of years before that, the kings of Scotland had been crowned on the stone. See also WESTMINSTER ABBEY (picture).

**SCOOTER.** See MOTORCYCLE.
**SCOPES TRIAL.** See BRYAN (William Jennings); DARROW, CLARENCE S.; TENNESSEE (The Early 1900's).

**SCOPOLAMINE,** *skoh PAHL uh meen*, is a drug used as a sedative, to quiet a person and make him drowsy. It is an alkaloid and is sometimes called *hyoscine* (see ALKALOID). Doctors use scopolamine to control acute excitement, delirium tremens, and tetanus. It increases the quieting effect of morphine. These two drugs were formerly popular to produce "twilight sleep" in childbirth. The combination lessened the pain and erased memory of the event. Scopolamine has also been used in remedies for seasickness and airsickness. The effects of scopolamine resemble those produced by atropine, especially when given in doses large enough to be poisonous (see ATROPINE). However, small doses of scopolamine have a sedative action, whereas atropine causes excitement. AUSTIN EDWARD SMITH

See also HALLUCINATORY DRUG.

**SCORIA.** See NORTH DAKOTA (Land Regions); ROCK (Extrusive Rocks).

**SCORPION,** *SKAWR pih un*, is a small animal with a dangerous poisonous sting in its tail. Most people fear the scorpion because of its sting and ugly appearance. The scorpion is not an insect. It belongs to a class of animals called *arachnids*. Spiders, mites, and ticks also belong to this class. Scorpions live in warm countries in most parts of the world. About 20 different kinds live in the United States. One of these lives as far north as Medicine Hat, Alberta, in Canada.

The body of the scorpion has two parts. Its short and thick forward part is called the *cephalothorax*. This part is made up of the head and chest (thorax), which join together. The hind part is the long abdomen. The last six segments of it form a slender tail. Scorpions usually are black or yellowish, and from $\frac{1}{2}$ to 8 inches long.

The scorpion has six pairs of jointed appendages. The first pair are tiny pincers, not visible in the accompanying illustration. The second pair, also a mouth part, have large claws, used to seize and crush prey. The last four pairs are leg parts. There are 6 to 12 eyes—different kinds of scorpions have different numbers. The breathing pores are on the abdomen.

All mother scorpions produce their young alive. The newly born young stay with the mother several days, and cling to her body with their tiny pincers.

Scorpions eat large insects and spiders, and are most active at night. The scorpion's sting is a curved organ in the end of its tail. Two glands at the base give out a poison that flows from two pores. A scorpion wound is painful, but does not usually cause death. The poison should be sucked or squeezed out of the wound, and the spot should be bathed with ammonia.

**Scientific Classification.** Scorpions belong to the class *Arachnida*, order *Scorpionida*. The families of scorpions include *Buthidae* and *Chactidae*. EDWARD A. CHAPIN

See also ARACHNID.

**SCORPION FLY** is a small insect with long wings. The male has two slender, pincerlike growths on the end of its body. These growths look like the scorpion's stinger. It is not a true fly, for it has four wings instead of two. The scorpion fly is about a half inch or more in length, and its two pairs of wings are netted and as long as its body. The pincers can be used to clasp objects, but they are not a stinging organ. Both adults and larvae feed on dead or dying insects. The adults also eat some vegetable matter. They lay their eggs in cracks in the ground. The larvae, which resemble caterpillars, hatch in about a week and grow rapidly. However, not much is known about the life cycle.

**Scientific Classification.** The scorpion fly is in the scorpion fly family, *Panorpidae*. A common scorpion fly is genus *Panorpa*, species *P. nebulosa*. DALE W. JENKINS

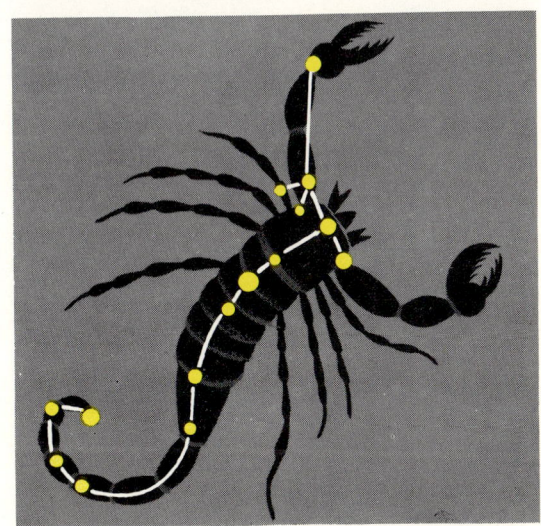

**The Constellation Scorpius, the Scorpion**

**The Scorpion** is common in the southwestern part of the United States. It stings its prey and sucks the body juices.
Cornelia Clarke

**SCORPIUS,** or **THE SCORPION,** is the eighth sign of the zodiac. Its symbol is ♏. The constellation Scorpius appears in the southern part of the sky. It contains the bright star Antares, a giant star which shines with a fiery-red light, and is of the first magnitude of brightness. It has a companion star whose light is greenish. According to Greek mythology, Orion boasted that he would kill every poisonous reptile on earth, and Artemis (Diana) sent the scorpion to kill him. The scorpion was known as a constellation even before the Greeks. It appears in the mythology of the Sumerians. See also ANTARES; ASTRONOMY (Skies of the Seasons); CONSTELLATION; ZODIAC. I. M. LEVITT

**SCOTLAND** is a rugged, mountainous country in the northern part of the island of Great Britain. It is part of the United Kingdom of Great Britain and Northern Ireland. Edinburgh is the capital and Glasgow is the largest city.

Scotland is about the same size as South Carolina, but it has over twice as many people as that state. Most of the people work in shipyards, steel mills, and other large industrial plants.

---
### FACTS IN BRIEF
---

**Form of Government:** Constitutional monarchy.
**Capital:** Edinburgh.
**Official Language:** English.
**Area:** 30,414 square miles. *Greatest Distances*—(north-south) 274 miles; (east-west) 154 miles. *Coastline*—about 2,300 miles.
**Population:** *1961 Census*—5,179,344; distribution, 70 per cent urban, 30 per cent rural. *Estimated 1970 Population*—5,171,000; density, 170 persons to the square mile. *Estimated 1975 Population*—5,146,000.
**Chief Products:** *Manufacturing and Processing*—chemicals, iron and steel products, jam, jute, marmalade, ships, textiles, whisky. *Agriculture*—barley, cattle, eggs, fruits, hay, meat, milk, oats, potatoes, sheep, sugar beets, turnips, wool. *Fishing Industry*—crabs, herring, lobsters, whitefish. *Mining*—clay, coal, granite, iron, oil shale.
**Flag:** Same as Great Britain.
**National Anthem:** "God Save the Queen" (or "King").
**National Holiday:** Celebration of the monarch's official birthday, usually in the spring.
**Money:** *Basic Unit*—pound. Twenty shillings equal one pound. For value, see MONEY (table: Great Britain).

◀ **Kilts and Bagpipes** are national symbols of Scotland. A few Highland Scots wear colorful tartan kilts every day.

Gendreau

## SCOTLAND

Mountains cover much of the country. Dark clouds often blanket the land, bringing heavy rains. Strong winds from the Atlantic Ocean usually clear the skies quickly, revealing bright green moors, heather-covered plateaus, blue lakes, and mountain peaks.

The Scots keep many symbols of their colorful history. Parades at Edinburgh Castle feature troops clad in *kilts* (short pleated skirts), who march to the shrill music of bagpipes. A few Highland Scots still wear kilts every day. Scottish regiments guard the ancient royal crown in Edinburgh Castle. The royal flag of Scotland, with its red lion on a gold background, still flies over the towers of the castle. The country also flies the Union Flag, the national flag of Great Britain, and the Cross of St. Andrew, the national flag of Scotland.

For the relationship of Scotland to the other countries of the United Kingdom, see GREAT BRITAIN.

### The Land and Its Resources

**Location and Size.** Scotland lies in the northern part of Great Britain. It has an area of 30,414 square miles. In the south, the River Tweed, the Cheviot Hills, and a bay called the Solway Firth form the border between Scotland and England. On the southwest, the North Channel separates Scotland from Northern Ireland. The western coast of the country faces the Atlantic Ocean.

*William A. Hance, the contributor of this article, is Professor of Economic Geography at Columbia University.*

A large group of islands called the Hebrides stretches along the west coast of the country (see HEBRIDES). The Orkney and Shetland islands lie north of Scotland, and form the boundary between the Atlantic Ocean and the North Sea (see ORKNEY ISLANDS; SHETLAND ISLANDS). The North Sea lies in the east, and separates Scotland from continental Europe.

**Land Regions.** Scotland has three natural regions: (1) the Highlands in the north, (2) the Central Lowlands, and (3) the Southern Uplands.

*The Highlands* include two mountain ranges, the Northwest Highlands and the Grampian Mountains. Both ranges have parallel rocky ridges running from northeast to southwest. The Highlands have two kinds of valleys: steep, narrow *glens*, and broad, rolling *straths*. A deep valley called *Glen More*, or *the Great Glen*, separates the two mountain ranges. Ben Nevis, the highest peak in Great Britain, rises south of Glen More to a height of 4,406 feet above sea level. The highest mountains in the Highlands rise along the Atlantic Ocean. Deep glens cut between these barren peaks. Most of the area is wasteland overgrown with scattered trees, evergreen shrubs, and purple heather. The coastal plains are narrow along the west side of the Highlands. Wide valleys cut through the low, rolling moors, or grassy plains, in the east. See GREAT BRITAIN (color picture).

*The Central Lowlands* lie between the Highlands and the Southern Uplands. The valleys of the rivers Clyde,

**Scottish Shepherds** drive their flock through a narrow street in Inverness. The alert, well-trained dogs keep the sheep together and drive back any sheep that try to leave the flock. Inverness is the center of trade for Highland sheep and wool.

Tatch, Black Star

179

Gendreau; Cash, Rapho-Guillumette

**Farmhouses** are widely scattered in the fertile but lonely pastures of the Highlands, *above*. The fields of *crofters*, or small farmers, extend to the sea on the Isle of Skye, *right*. Many crofters are skilled, part-time fishermen.

Forth, and Tay contain Scotland's best farmland and most of its minerals. Wide fields of fertile soil and low hills with patches of trees cover the entire region. Both coasts of the Lowlands have *links* (long stretches of sandy ground covered with grass).

*The Southern Uplands* consist of rolling moors and occasional rocky cliffs. Rich pasture lands cover much of this region. Heavy rains keep the countryside green and fresh during most of the year. In the south, the Uplands rise to the Cheviot Hills, along the boundary between Scotland and England.

**Coastline.** Many bays cut into the 2,300-mile-long coast. Cliffs along the western coast rise from the sea in great rock walls, or jut sharply into the water. Narrow bays called *sea lochs* reach far inland. *Stacks* (tall pillars of rock), stand in the coastal waters. Rocky islands lie off the western coast.

Many rivers flow into wide bays called *firths* (see FIRTH). The Firth of Clyde is the most heavily traveled, because all ships bound for the city of Glasgow must pass through it. North of the Firth of Clyde lies the island-filled Firth of Lorne. The firths of Forth and Tay form part of the east coast. North of them, Moray Firth cuts deeply into the Highlands.

**Rivers and Lakes.** The Clyde is the most important river in Scotland. The river was once narrow and shallow, but engineers widened and deepened it during the 1700's so ships could sail to Glasgow from the Atlantic Ocean. The longest rivers in Scotland flow eastward into the North Sea. The River Tay flows 118 miles, and carries more water than any other British river. Small streams tumble through glens in the western Highlands.

Most of Scotland's many lakes, called *lochs*, lie in deep Highland valleys. Picturesque Loch Lomond is the largest lake in Scotland. Many castles stand on the islands and along the shores of Loch Lomond. Loch Katrine, scene of Sir Walter Scott's poem *The Lady of the Lake*, lies in a lovely valley region called *Trossachs*. A series of lakes, including Loch Ness and Loch Lochy, extends through Glen More. These lakes are connected by short canals, and the entire waterway is called the Caledonian Canal.

**Natural Resources.** Scotland has few valuable natural resources. More than three-fourths of the land is used for farming and for grazing cattle and sheep. During the 1950's, the government enlarged the small forests. Fresh- and salt-water fish are an important source of food. Deposits of coal, iron, and oil shale lie in the Lowlands. In the Highlands, rushing river waters provide electric power. Scotland has the largest hydroelectric power plants in the United Kingdom.

**Climate.** Scotland has a fairly mild climate, compared with other countries lying equally far north. Summers are cool, with temperatures averaging about 57°F. Winters are cold, especially in the inland districts where temperatures average about 39°F. Moist winds from the Gulf Stream warm the west coast. As much as 200 inches of rain a year falls in parts of the western Highlands. Along the drier east coast, the annual rainfall ranges from 25 to 60 inches.

### Life of the People

The country has a population of over 5,171,000 persons living in an area of 30,414 square miles. One

# SCOTLAND

**Edinburgh Castle** overlooks Scotland's capital from atop Castle Rock. The great fortress houses the royal jewels, or *regalia*.

Ewing Galloway

third of the people live in farm areas, and the rest live in cities. Four fifths of the Scots live crowded together in the Central Lowlands, an area that makes up only one fifth of the country.

Of every 100 persons in Scotland, 92 are Scottish. About 7 of every 100 are Irish or English. Only 1 person in 100 comes from outside the British Isles.

**Language.** Nearly all Scots speak English, but they make many changes in pronunciation. For example, they pronounce *r* sounds with a trill of the tongue, emphasizing them sharply. They also use many of their own words. Well-known Scottish words include *wee* (small), *bairn* (child), and *bonnie* (lovely). Some people in remote parts of Scotland still speak Gaelic, the old Highland language (see GAELIC LANGUAGE).

**Way of Life.** Family life in the Highlands is based on the *clan*, a group of families related to each other through a common ancestor. The members of each clan elect a chieftain who makes important decisions for the clan. Clans play an important part in the social life of their members, and usually meet once a year. These meetings help renew friendships and knit the families closely together. See CLAN.

Similar tight-knit family groups live in the Southern Uplands, although these groups do not call themselves clans. Family life in the Central Lowlands is more like that in the United States and Canada.

*Shelter.* Typical Scottish houses are built of stone or concrete, and have two stories. They usually have four or five rooms with large windows.

*Food.* Oatmeal forms a basis for many meals in Scotland. *Brose* is made by mixing oatmeal quickly with water or broth. When thickened, the dish becomes *porridge*. Scottish cooks roll fish in oatmeal before cooking it. Fresh herring dipped in oatmeal is considered a delicacy. *Bannocks* are thick, flat cakes made from coarsely ground oatmeal or barley.

The Scots enjoy salmon and trout from their streams and lakes. Scones are rich biscuits usually served at tea. Rich, crumbly cookies, called *shortbread*, are another teatime favorite. Soups and broths form an important part of the diet. Cooks often thicken soups with oatmeal and flavor them with herbs. *Haggis* is another Scottish specialty (see HAGGIS).

*Clothing.* Most people in Scotland wear clothing much like that worn in North America. But each Highland clan has its own special plaid design called a *tartan*. The tartan is a many-colored fabric used for kilts and cloaks. The design of the tartan symbolizes either a clan or district in Scotland. Kilts are usually worn only for special occasions. See TARTAN; TWEED.

*Religion.* Scotland is the birthplace and stronghold of the Presbyterian Church. Most Scots belong to the Presbyterian Church of Scotland, the national church.

*Recreation.* Golf originated in Scotland as early as the 1400's, and almost all Scottish people play the game. Rugby and soccer are popular team sports. In winter, many Scots enjoy *curling* (see CURLING).

On November 30, St. Andrew's Day, banquets honor Scotland's patron saint. The high point comes when a steaming haggis is carried into the banquet hall to the accompaniment of bagpipes.

**Cities.** The largest cities in Scotland are Glasgow (pop. 979,798), Edinburgh (pop. 468,765), Dundee (pop. 183,744), and Aberdeen (pop. 183,463). Other large cities and their populations include Paisley (95,808), Motherwell and Wishaw (75,963), Greenock (72,388), Coatbridge (53,738), Kirkcaldy (51,886), Clydebank (50,640), and Dunfermline (50,138). Most cities lie in the Central Lowlands or along the east coast, because the rest of the country is mountainous.

Ancient castles stand in the centers of most Scottish cities. Wide boulevards pass through green parks and shop districts. For a list of Scottish cities with separate articles, see the *Related Articles* at the end of this article.

**Country Life.** Scotland's farms are large, and most of them lie near large cities. But people in farm regions of the Highlands and Southern Uplands live lonely lives. Villages are small and scattered in these mountainous areas. Large estates cover much of these areas. Sheep grazing is the leading occupation. Small farmers, called *crofters*, raise garden crops here, but often work as fishermen or foresters to make enough money to live.

### Work of the People

About 76 of every 100 Scots make their living from manufacturing and trade. Nearly 14 of every 100 Scots are farmers, and the remaining 10 are miners.

**Manufacturing and Processing.** Most of the manufacturing is done in the Central Lowlands. Glasgow, the center of the metal industries, produces about one-seventh of the iron and steel used in the United Kingdom. The Glasgow region also produces aluminum, carpets, chemicals, industrial machinery, and iron and steel castings. One of the world's greatest shipbuilding centers stands on the banks of the River Clyde in a

181

# SCOTLAND

region called *Clydeside*. Ocean liners built here include the *Queen Mary* and *Queen Elizabeth*.

The textile industry produces large quantities of cotton, linen, silk, and rayon cloth. Tweed mills stand in south-central Scotland and in the Hebrides and Shetland Islands. The jute industry, centered in Dundee, produces burlap and coarse linen for export. Dundee also makes world-famous marmalade and candy. Scotch whisky distilleries are scattered throughout the country. Scotland is the only country that produces Scotch whisky.

**Agriculture.** The Scots use more than three-fourths of their land for farming and grazing. Farming in the Highlands is more difficult than anywhere else in Great Britain. The mountainous plateaus of the Highlands and Southern Uplands are used mainly for sheep grazing. Most of the sheep are black-faced sheep, which live through cold weather better than other breeds. Scottish shepherds developed the collie to serve as an intelligent, sturdy dog to help tend their flocks.

The Central Lowlands have some of the best farmland in Great Britain. Oats grow on more than half the plowed land. Other important crops include barley, fruits, hay, potatoes, tomatoes, turnips, and wheat.

Scottish farmers have developed famous cattle breeds such as Ayrshire, Aberdeen-Angus, Galloway, and Highland. Clydesdale draft horses were originally raised in the Clyde Valley. Scottish breeders developed the hardy Shetland pony, a friend of children in many parts of the world.

**Mining.** Most of Scotland's coal comes from Lothian, Ayr, and Fife counties in the Central Lowlands. Every year West Lothian County supplies about 1,500,000 tons of shale, a source of oil. Highland quarries furnish granite, slate, and diatomite (see DIATOM).

**Fishing Industry.** Fishermen take in their largest catches of herring, whitefish, crabs, and lobsters in the North Sea and along the northern coast. Aberdeen is the center of the fishing industry.

**Trade.** Scotland exports fine marmalade, other jams, and candy. Scotch whisky earns more dollars than any other British product. Other important exports include clothing, tweed cloth, carpets, and burlap. Scotland's chief imports include food, and raw materials and fuel for its industries.

**Transportation.** Highways totaling more than 27,000 miles crisscross most of Scotland. The Caledonian Canal carries small boats through the Highlands between the Atlantic Ocean and the North Sea. The Forth and Clyde Canal carries freight in the industrial area of the Lowlands. In the expression, "You take the low road, and I'll take the high road," the low road refers to the coastal road in western Scotland, and the high road is the hilly route through the Highlands.

Scotland has about 4,000 miles of railroads. Fast trains run between English cities and the chief cities of Scotland. Many transatlantic flights use the important airport of Prestwick, near Ayr.

**Communication.** Telephone and telegraph lines link all parts of Scotland. Most of the radio programs originate in Scottish stations, but many television programs come from England. Edinburgh is Scotland's publishing center. Scotland has six major book-publishing firms and four monthly magazines. The country is served by more than 100 newspapers.

## Education

The Scottish Department of Education, under the British Secretary of State for Scotland, administers Scotland's public-school system. Almost all the schools are coeducational. The country has few private schools. The law requires children between the ages of 5 and 15 to attend school. The University of Strathclyde at Glasgow is the largest engineering school in the Commonwealth. Scotland has universities at Aberdeen, Edinburgh, Glasgow, and St. Andrews.

## The Arts

Artists in Scotland use many artistic symbols and techniques developed by the ancient Celtic peoples. These people used straight lines and geometric forms to decorate their weapons and household articles. They cut zigzag designs and spirals into stone doorways.

The beautiful scenery of Scotland attracts many painters. Important Scottish painters include Sir Henry Raeburn, Sir William Q. Orchardson, Sir James Guthrie, John Pettie, and Sir David Wilkie.

**Literature.** Bards, or poets, wrote the earliest Scottish literature in the Gaelic language (see BARD; GAELIC LITERATURE). During the 1300's, John Barbour composed poetry about Scotland, as did William Dunbar, Gawin Douglas, and Allan Ramsay in later years. In the late 1700's, Robert Burns became the greatest poet to use the everyday language of the Scots. Burns often wrote in the Ayrshire dialect. Many present-day poets, including Hugh McDiarmid, Douglas Young, and Tom Scott, use Scottish dialects.

Most Scottish authors have written in English. James Boswell and Thomas Carlyle made important contributions in history and biography. John Arbuthnot and John Lockhart wrote famed essays and works of literary criticism. Robert Louis Stevenson and Sir Walter Scott wrote popular novels and poetry. Plays by Sir James Barrie, including *Peter Pan*, are favorites in many countries. Scottish philosophers include David Hume, James Mill, and Adam Smith.

**Music.** The bagpipe, with its shrill, high-pitched notes, is a national symbol of Scotland (see BAGPIPE). The Scots divide bagpipe music into "big music" and "little music." *Pibroch*, one kind of "big music," is usually a lament, or song of grief. "Little music" includes marches and reels. The Scottish reel, the Highland fling, the sword dance, and various country dances are performed to the background of "little music."

**Handicrafts** developed early in Scotland. Craftsmen made fine metal jewelry with elaborately curved and twisted designs. The Scots also developed skill in wood carving, needlework, pottery making, and glassmaking. Many Scottish tartans are woven by hand.

## What To See and Do in Scotland

Scotland is famous for the beauty of its mountains and coastal areas. The heather-covered Highlands provide an attractive setting for mountain climbers and hikers. Yachtsmen test their skill along the rugged coastline with its many islands. The streams and moors of Scotland contain many kinds of wildlife to delight the nature lover, the hunter, and the fisherman.

# SCOTLAND

**Shipyards on the River Clyde** built the Queen Mary, Queen Elizabeth, and other famous ships. This industrial area near Glasgow makes up one of the leading shipbuilding centers in the world.

*British Information Services*

Robert Louis Stevenson, in Edinburgh, is maintained as a museum.

### Government

Scotland has 71 representatives in the British Parliament (see GREAT BRITAIN [Government]). The British Cabinet includes a secretary of state for Scotland who is responsible for local administration. The duties of the secretary of state are performed by four main departments in Edinburgh, with representatives in London. These departments direct agriculture, criminal justice, education, fisheries, police and fire protection, prisons, and public health. The London office is called the Scottish Office.

The country is divided into 33 counties. The people elect administrative officials in counties, cities, and towns. The legal system differs from that in the rest of Great Britain. Scottish law is based on Roman *civil law* instead of English *common law* (see CIVIL LAW; COMMON LAW). Under Scottish law, juries can return one of three verdicts: *guilty, innocent,* or *not proven.* All judges are appointed to life terms by the British monarch.

### History

**Early Years.** Historians believe that the first people to live in Scotland were Iberians. They farmed the land, built ships, and made bronze tools and weapons. Celtic invaders entered England after about 600 B.C. and taught the Iberians how to work with iron.

A Roman army, commanded by England's governor, Gnaeus Julius Agricola, invaded Scotland in A.D. 80 from the center of Britain. The Romans called the people of the country *Picts,* or *painted people,* because they painted their bodies. The Romans referred to the country as *Caledonia.* Agricola conquered the Picts and retired to Rome in triumph. The Roman emperor Hadrian built a wall from the Solway Firth to what is now Newcastle-on-Tyne. He built the wall to keep the Picts under control.

A tribe of Celts called the Scots left northern Ireland in the early 500's and established a colony on Scotland's western coast. Columba, the Abbot of Darrow, followed the Scots in 563. The Scots urged Columba

Scotland's fine golf courses are favorites with golfers from many countries.

Many places famous in Scottish history have become monuments and parks. Mary, Queen of Scots, lived at Holyroodhouse in Edinburgh. The ancient royal jewels of Scotland, called the *regalia,* are displayed in Edinburgh Castle on top of Castle Rock in Edinburgh. The scene of the Battle of Bannockburn lies near the town of Stirling. Here, in 1314, Robert Bruce led a Scottish army to a great victory in the war that led to Scotland's independence.

The region where Macbeth lived is near Moray Firth. The "blasted heath" mentioned in Shakespeare's play *Macbeth* lies just outside Forres. The Edinburgh Festival of Music and Drama is presented every year during the last two weeks in August and the first week in September. The Cowal Highland Gathering at Dunoon in August, the Royal Highland Society Gathering at Braemar in September, and the Northern Meeting Highland Gathering at Inverness in September feature contests in dancing, piping, and athletics.

During the second weekend in August, a colorful pageant celebrates the declaration of Scottish independence in 1320. The *Commons Riding* ceremony takes place each year in the *commons,* or border farm lands. A horseman called the *Cornet* sets out at dawn with an escort to make sure that the stones marking the border between Scotland and England have not been moved.

The homes of many Scottish writers are now museums. The two-room cottage where the poet Robert Burns was born stands in the village of Alloway. Sir Walter Scott lived at Abbotsford, near Galashiels. The birthplace of

--- **RED-LETTER DATES IN SCOTLAND** ---

A.D. 80 The Roman general Gnaeus Agricola invaded Scotland and conquered the Picts.
844 Kenneth MacAlpin established Alba, the first united kingdom in Scotland.
1249-1286 Scotland entered a period of peace and social progress under Alexander III.
1314 Robert Bruce routed an English army in the Battle of Bannockburn.
1320 Scotland declared its independence from England.
1328 The English recognized Scottish independence, and Robert Bruce became King of Scotland.
1560 The Scottish Parliament founded the Presbyterian Church as the national church of Scotland.
1707 The Act of Union united Scotland with England and Wales to form the United Kingdom of Great Britain.
1715 The English subdued the first Jacobite rebellion.
1746 The English won the Battle of Culloden Moor, ending the second Jacobite rebellion.
(For later dates, see GREAT BRITAIN [History].)

183

**Tossing the Caber, a Scottish Test of Strength,** is an athletic event designed for only the most muscular men. The caber is a long wooden pole or beam that weighs about 180 pounds. Some contestants have tossed the caber about 40 feet.

and his monks to convert the fierce Picts to Christianity. By the mid-600's, all the Picts were converted.

Kenneth MacAlpin, King of the Scots, claimed the throne of the Picts in 844, and established Alba, the first united kingdom in Scotland. He and his successors waged many wars against the English and the Norsemen who continually raided the coasts. King Duncan I was killed in 1040 by one of his generals, Macbeth. Macbeth died in battle in 1057. His stepson Lulach ruled for only a few months. Then Duncan's son Malcolm III became King. See MACBETH.

**Feudalism.** King Malcolm's wife, Margaret, was an English princess, and influenced him greatly. The king gave charters to the towns, and developed a parliament like that of England. During the Norman conquest of England in 1066, refugees fled to Scotland. These refugees were often given grants of land, and introduced feudalism into Scotland (see FEUDALISM).

During the reign of Alexander III (1241-1286), the Scots made great progress. Peace with England lasted for nearly 100 years, and the two countries established a border for the first time. Agriculture and trade flourished. Many roads and bridges were built.

**Struggle for Independence.** Scottish barons competed for the throne when Queen Margaret died in 1290. Edward I of England declared one baron, John de Baliol, king of Scotland. But Baliol was required to recognize Edward as his superior. This caused the barons to revolt against England, and forced Baliol to form a military alliance with France, England's enemy. Edward stopped the revolt for a time by invading Scotland and winning a great victory at Dunbar in 1296. He then proclaimed himself king of Scotland.

The Scots rallied under William Wallace, the first popular hero of Scottish history. After several victories over the English, Wallace was betrayed and executed. Robert Bruce then took up the struggle. He defeated Edward II at the Battle of Bannockburn in 1314, but Edward still refused to recognize Scottish independence. The Scots declared their independence in 1320. Finally, in 1328, the regents of Edward III recognized Bruce as King Robert I of Scotland.

**The House of Stuart.** David II, son of Bruce, died without an heir in 1371, and several families competed for the Scottish throne. The Stuarts won the struggle, and the first Stuart king, Robert II, was crowned in 1371. Later Stuart kings had to deal with feuds among Scottish barons. They also fought many wars with England. In 1502, James IV tried to form a peaceful union with England by marrying Margaret Tudor, an English princess. However, he soon returned to Scotland's former policy of cooperation with France. The French Queen, Anne of Brittany, urged James to invade England. He did so in 1513, but was defeated and killed in the Battle of Flodden Field. His granddaughter, Mary, Queen of Scots, was brought up in France.

**The Reformation.** Before 1560, the Roman Catholic Church was the official church of both Scotland and France. Many Scottish leaders resented the church's power and French influence, and sought to establish a Protestant church. They drove out French Catholic officials and soldiers in the late 1550's with the secret help of Queen Elizabeth I of England. A Scottish minister, John Knox, led the Scottish Parliament in establishing the Presbyterian Church as the national church of Scotland in 1560. Queen Mary was forced to give up the throne because she was a Catholic. She escaped to England in 1568, but was captured and imprisoned. Elizabeth had her executed in 1587. Mary's infant son, James VI, was made king of Scotland in 1567. He was reared as a Protestant, and the Presbyterian Church became firmly established in Scotland.

**War with the King.** James VI was the great-grandson of Margaret Tudor, an English princess. When Elizabeth I of England died in 1603, James inherited the English throne. He ruled both England and Scotland as James I of England. In order to promote British influence in Ireland, James sent many Scots to northern Ireland to form colonies between 1609 and 1611. They became known as the Scotch-Irish. In the early 1700's, many of the Scotch-Irish came to the United States to seek their fortune. Political and religious institutions in Scotland and England remained separate under James. But his son, Charles I, wanted to reorganize the Presbyterian Church. In 1638, the Scots signed a National Covenant that pledged to keep the Presbyterian Church as it was. English Puritans turned against Charles at the same time (see CHARLES; ENGLAND [The Civil War]). In the civil war that followed, Scottish signers of the Covenant supported Oliver Cromwell and the Puritans against Charles I. Charles was captured and beheaded in 1649. At the Battle of Dunbar in 1650, Cromwell defeated the dead king's son, who later became Charles II. In 1654, Cromwell forced the Scots into union with England. Charles II persecuted the signers of the Covenant when he became king in 1660.

**Union with England.** Scottish and English leaders finally realized that peace could be preserved only if their countries united. The Act of Union joined England and Wales with Scotland in 1707 under the name the United Kingdom of Great Britain. The union left Scottish laws and the Presbyterian Church unchanged. The Scots received representation in the British Parliament, and dissolved their own legislature.

Scotland benefited from increased trade after the union with England. But many Highland Scots remained loyal to the House of Stuart. These Scots were called *Jacobites*, from *Jacobus*, the Latin name of their leader, James Edward Stuart, *The Old Pretender*. In 1715, the Jacobites rebelled against English rule. James was defeated and fled to France.

The Highlanders revolted again in 1745 in support of *The Young Pretender*, Charles Edward Stuart, whom they called *Bonnie Prince Charlie*. The clansmen overwhelmed English troops in Scotland, and Charles marched into England. But English troops forced Charles into battle on Culloden Moor in 1746, and destroyed the Stuart forces. Charles fled into the wild Highlands and escaped to France. The English executed many clan chiefs, disarmed the Highlanders, and outlawed kilts and bagpipes. These restrictions were removed in 1782 when the Jacobite threat to England had passed. After the rebellion of 1745, the history of Scotland became one with that of Great Britain (see GREAT BRITAIN [History]). WILLIAM A. HANCE

**Related Articles** in WORLD BOOK include:

### RULERS

Bruce, Robert
David (kings of Scotland)
Duncan I
James (I, kings of England)
Macbeth
Mary, Queen of Scots

### POLITICAL AND MILITARY LEADERS

Bothwell, Earl of
Campbell-Bannerman, Sir Henry
Henderson, Arthur
Wallace, Sir William

### OTHER BIOGRAPHIES

Adam (brothers)
Black, Joseph
Broom, Robert
Brown, Robert
Burns, Robert
Dunlop, John B.

# SCOTLAND

Frazer, Sir James G.
Geikie, Sir Archibald
Kelvin, Lord
Knox, John
Lauder, Sir Harry
Lipton, Sir Thomas
Macdonald, Flora
Manson, Sir Patrick
Maxwell, James C.
Mill (James)
Napier, John
Nasmyth, James
Rob Roy
Scott, Sir Walter
Selkirk, Alexander
Selkirk, Earl of
Simpson, Sir James Y.
Smith, Adam
Stevenson, Robert
Stevenson, Robert Louis B.
Telford, Thomas
Todd, Lord
Watson-Watt, Sir Robert A.
Watt, James

### CITIES

Aberdeen
Ayr
Dundee
Dunfermline
Edinburgh
Glasgow
Gretna Green
Inverness
Paisley
St. Andrews

### HISTORY

Bannockburn, Battle of
Caledonia
Gael
Pict
Stuart, House of

### ISLANDS

Hebrides
Orkney Islands
Shetland Islands

### PHYSICAL FEATURES

Ben Lomond
Ben Nevis
Clyde, River
Doon, River
Firth
Firth of Clyde
Firth of Forth
Galloway
Inchcape Rock
Loch Katrine
Loch Lomond
Loch Ness
Minch, The
Tay, River
Trossachs
Tweed, River

### OTHER RELATED ARTICLES

Abbotsford
Bagpipe
Clan
Covenanters
Curling
Dancing (picture, The Sword Dance)
Doll (color picture)
Edinburgh, University of
Glasgow, University of
Golf (History)
Haggis
Holyrood
Tartan
Tweed

### Outline

**I. The Land and Its Resources**
   A. Location and Size
   B. Land Regions
   C. Coastline
   D. Rivers and Lakes
   E. Natural Resources
   F. Climate

**II. Life of the People**
   A. Language
   B. Way of Life
   C. Cities
   D. Country Life

**III. Work of the People**
   A. Manufacturing and Processing
   B. Agriculture
   C. Mining
   D. Fishing Industry
   E. Trade
   F. Transportation
   G. Communication

**IV. Education**
**V. The Arts**
   A. Literature
   B. Music
   C. Handicrafts

**VI. What to See and Do in Scotland**
**VII. Government**
**VIII. History** (to 1746)

### Questions

What are Scotland's chief exports?
What are the three main land regions in Scotland?
Where are most Scottish industries located? Why?
Why are there few farms in the Highlands?
Why did the Scots rebel against Charles I of England?
What is a glen? A tartan? A strath? A kilt? A stack?
How does Scottish law differ from that of England?
Who were the Jacobites? How did they get this name? What did they do?
What is the national musical instrument of Scotland?

## SCOTLAND YARD

**SCOTLAND YARD** is the headquarters of the London Metropolitan Police. The name *Scotland Yard* is often used to mean a special department of the force called the *Criminal Investigation Department*, or C.I.D. The C.I.D. is one of the most famous police organizations in the world. Detective story writers have made Scotland Yard men the heroes of many thrilling tales.

Scotland Yard gets its name from the building which housed the London police until 1890. This was an ancient structure where visiting Scottish kings and ambassadors stayed between the 900's and the 1100's. In 1890, the Metropolitan Police moved into offices on the Thames Embankment. These offices were named New Scotland Yard. In 1967, New Scotland Yard moved to the Westminster section of London. JOHN J. FLOHERTY

**SCOTT, BARBARA ANN** (1928-    ), became the first North American girl to win the Olympic, European, and world figure-skating championships. She won the Canadian championship three times, and the North American, European, and world championships twice. She won the 1948 Olympic games title, and then became a professional. Miss Scott was born in Ottawa, Ont., Canada. RICHARD G. HACKENBERG

**SCOTT, DRED.** See DRED SCOTT DECISION.

**SCOTT, DUNCAN CAMPBELL** (1862-1947), was a Canadian poet, biographer, and short-story writer. He was an official of the Canadian Department of Indian Affairs. This connection accounts for the Indians in his poems and stories. Scott published his first volume of poetry, *The Magic House*, in 1893. Eight other volumes followed. He also published two volumes of short stories and biographies of historical figures. He was born in Ottawa, Ont. DESMOND PACEY

**SCOTT, ROBERT FALCON** (1868-1912), an English explorer and naval officer, became the first man to reach the South Polar plateau. He reached it on an expedition that took place from 1901 to 1904.

Scott sailed in 1910 from New Zealand on the *Terra Nova* in an attempt to reach the true South Pole. The party reached Cape Evans on Ross Island, and set up headquarters there. Scott started over the ice with sledges in November, 1911. Snowstorms made his progress slow and difficult, but finally conditions improved. The men reached the Pole on Jan. 18, 1912, but they found that Roald Amundsen, a Norwegian explorer, had already reached it only a month before. On the return trip, all five members of the party died from hunger and cold. Three bodies, as well as the records and diaries the men had kept, were found later in the tent they had set up as their last camping place. Scott had written his journal up to the day of his death. He wrote in it what he considered to be the causes of their disaster, and ended with an appeal to the public to help their families. Scott was born at Devonport. JOHN E. CASWELL

United Press Int.
**Robert Scott**

See also ANTARCTICA (Exploration; map; picture).

**SCOTT, SIR WALTER** (1771-1832), was a Scottish romantic writer. He created and popularized historical novels in a long series of works called the *Waverley* novels. In such novels as *Ivanhoe*, *The Heart of Midlothian*, and *The Talisman*, Scott showed his unique genius for recreating social history. He arranged his plots and characters so the reader can enter into the lives of both great and ordinary people who were caught up in violent, dramatic changes in history.

Scott's art shows the influence of the Enlightenment of the 1700's. He believed every human was basically decent, regardless of his class, religion, politics, or ancestry. Tolerance for different ways of life is a major theme in all of Scott's historical works. The *Waverley* novels express his belief in the need for social progress that does not reject the precious traditions of the past. He was the first novelist to portray peasant characters sympathetically and realistically. He was equally just to provincial businessmen, professional soldiers, and even kings.

Scott's amiability, generosity, and modesty made him popular with his fellow writers. He declined the offer of poet laureate in 1813 and supported Robert Southey, who received the honor. Scott entertained on a grand scale at Abbotsford, his famous estate. A Frenchman visiting Great Britain reported of his travels to the north, "As Scott was not at home, I saw only Scotland."

Scott's influence can be seen in the works of Victor Hugo and Honoré de Balzac of France, James Fenimore Cooper of the United States, and Leo Tolstoy of Russia. But despite his great influence, Scott's reputation declined sharply from the late 1800's to the mid-1900's. His reputation has begun to rise again in the last few years. But it probably will never reach the heights it attained during Scott's lifetime, when Goethe ex-

**Abbotsford, Sir Walter Scott's Home,** stands on the right bank of the River Tweed in Scotland. Scott began building the home in 1812, at the height of his popularity. He died there in 1832.
Rapho Guillumette; Portrait by Sir John Watson Gordon. The National Galleries of Scotland, Edinburgh

claimed, "All is great in the *Waverley* Novels: material, effect, characters, execution." Literary historians regard Scott's death in 1832 as marking the close of the romantic age in English literature.

**His Life.** Scott was born in Edinburgh. His father, a successful lawyer, had young Walter trained for a law career. Scott became an attorney in 1792 and practiced actively for many years.

A childhood illness, probably polio, left Scott lame in his right leg. But he had unusual physical strength, and was an enthusiastic outdoorsman. He enjoyed taking trips into the Scottish countryside. These trips gave him first-hand knowledge of the life of rural people, and provided material for his first major publication *Minstrelsy of the Scottish Border* (1802-1803). This book was one of the great early collections of popular songs and ballads. *Minstrelsy* led to his first long verse poem *The Lay of the Last Minstrel* (1805). The poem tells the legend of a famous goblin, and is filled with information about life along the English-Scottish border in the 1500's.

Scott continued his success at narrative poetry with *Marmion* (1808), which includes his best-known ballad "Lochinvar" (see LOCHINVAR). In 1810, Scott wrote his most popular story-poem, *The Lady of the Lake*. This romantic tale, set in the famous Trossach Mountains, deals with picturesque Highland customs and history.

**The Waverley Novels.** From the publication of his first novel *Waverley* in 1814, Scott devoted himself primarily to fiction. Scott's progress from ballads through narrative verse-romances to historical novels was natural. His talents as a storyteller and as a creator of character, as well as his gift for realistic Scottish dialect, could never find full expression in poetry.

*Waverley* describes a Scottish rebellion against England in 1745. It was published anonymously, and so it did not have the benefit of Scott's famous name. Yet it was an immediate critical and financial success. Between 1814 and 1832, Scott published 27 other novels, as well as four plays and much nonfiction. All of Scott's novels were referred to as part of the *Waverley* series, because the author was identified on the title page simply as "The Author of *Waverley*." Scott's authorship was officially revealed in 1827, but it had been generally known for many years.

Scott wrote frequently about the conflicts between different cultures. *Ivanhoe* (1819) deals with the conflict between Normans and Saxons, and *The Talisman* (1825) describes the conflict between Christians and Moslems. The novels dealing with Scottish history are probably Scott's best. They deal with the conflict between the new commercial English culture and an older Scottish culture. Scott contrasts the earthy vividness of the Scottish peasants with the formal, stilted language of his English-speaking, upper-class characters. Many critics consider *The Heart of Midlothian* (1818) Scott's best novel. It takes place in Edinburgh in the early 1700's. *The Antiquary* (1816) and *Redgauntlet* (1824) are of special interest because of their autobiographical elements. Scott's other novels in the *Waverley* series include *Old Mortality* (1816), *Rob Roy* (1817), *A Legend of Montrose* (1819), and *Quentin Durward* (1823). KARL KROEBER

**SCOTT, WINFIELD** (1786-1866), an American Army officer for more than 50 years, served in the War of 1812,

Culver

**General Winfield Scott** led American forces to victory in a bitter battle at Contreras during the Mexican War.

the Mexican War, and the beginning of the Civil War. His men affectionately called him "Old Fuss and Feathers" because he loved colorful uniforms.

Scott was born on June 13, 1786, near Petersburg, Va. He attended William and Mary College and then studied law. He gave up law in 1808 to join the Army.

When the War of 1812 broke out, he became a lieutenant colonel and went to the Canadian border. Scott was captured at the Battle of Queenston Heights, but he was freed a month later. As a colonel, he carried out a successful attack on Fort George and took charge of that post. He became a brigadier general in March, 1814, and fought at Chippewa and Lundy's Lane. Two horses were shot from under him at Lundy's Lane. He fought on so stubbornly that he had to be carried from the field, severely wounded (see WAR OF 1812 [Chief Battles of the War]). He became a national hero, and Congress and the state of Virginia voted him a medal. He had gained the rank of major general when the war ended.

In 1825, Scott prepared the first complete manual of military tactics in the United States Army. He also reviewed and enlarged *Infantry Tactics* (1835), and wrote his autobiography in 1864. He became general in chief of the Army in 1841, and in 1844, became lieutenant general.

During the Mexican War, in 1847, Scott led an army into Mexico. He won at Veracruz, Cerro Gordo, Contreras, Churubusco, Molino del Rey, and Chapultepec, and he captured Mexico City (see MEXICAN WAR [Scott's Campaign; Principal Battles]). He ran for President of the United States in 1852 on the Whig ticket but lost to the Democratic candidate, Franklin Pierce.

Early in 1861, Scott went to Washington, where he recruited men to defend the capital. When the Civil War began in April, Scott, a Southerner, refused to join the Southern forces, because he believed in the Union. He retired from the Army in 1861. JOHN R. ALDEN

## SCOTT AIR FORCE BASE

**SCOTT AIR FORCE BASE,** Ill., is the headquarters of the U.S. Military Airlift Command (MAC) and the Air Force Communications Service (AFCS). The 2,768-acre base lies about 6 miles east of Belleville. The base was used as a training center during World Wars I and II. It was once the headquarters of the Air Training Command. The base was established in 1917 and named for Corporal Frank S. Scott, the first enlisted man to die in an air accident. RICHARD M. SKINNER

See also MILITARY AIRLIFT COMMAND.

**SCOTTI,** *SKAWT tee,* **ANTONIO** (1866-1936), an Italian operatic baritone, was a member of New York City's Metropolitan Opera Company from 1899 to 1933. His artistry as a singer and actor was superb. His famous roles included Scarpia in Giacomo Puccini's opera *Tosca,* and the title roles in Wolfgang Mozart's *Don Giovanni* and Giuseppe Verdi's *Rigoletto.* Scotti was born in Naples, Italy. He made his opera debut at Malta in 1889. SCOTT GOLDTHWAITE

**SCOTTIE.** See SCOTTISH TERRIER.

**SCOTTISH DEERHOUND** was for hundreds of years a dog of the peerage. In Scotland, only persons with the rank of earl or higher could own deerhounds. The deerhound stands from 30 to 32 inches, or even taller, and weighs from 75 to 110 pounds. It has a rough coat of wiry hair, colored dark blue-gray, light gray, brindle, yellow, sandy red, or fawn red. Scottish lords developed the deerhound for hunting wild deer, but in America it is used for hunting wolves. The deerhound also makes a good companion. OLGA DAKAN

**The Scottish Deerhound Was Bred to Hunt Wild Deer.**
WORLD BOOK photo by Walter Chandoha

**SCOTTISH EPISCOPAL CHURCH.** See CHURCH OF ENGLAND.

**SCOTTISH RITE.** See MASONRY (The Lodges and Degrees of Masonry).

**SCOTTISH TERRIER** is a breed of dogs first raised in the Scottish highlands in the 1800's. Commonly called "Scottie," it is the only breed with the official name of Scottish terrier. But the cairn, Skye, and West Highland white terriers are also native to Scotland. The Scottish terrier is a small dog with short legs and a chunky body, weighing 18-22 pounds. It has a hard wiry coat and a long head with small upright ears. Its coat may be colored black, wheat, sandy, steel gray, or brindle. The Scottish terrier is brave, and likes to hunt rats and other small animals. It is devoted to its master. See also DOG (color picture: Terriers). JOSEPHINE Z. RINE

**SCOTTS BLUFF NATIONAL MONUMENT** is in western Nebraska. Established in 1919, it is a landmark on the Oregon Trail, which passed through the region. It has a museum of historical relics and fossils. The 3,000-acre area rises to an elevation of 4,649 feet. See also NEBRASKA (picture: Mitchell Pass).

**SCOTTSBLUFF,** Nebr. (pop. 13,377; alt. 3,880 ft.), is the trading center for over 500,000 irrigated acres in the North Platte River valley. The city lies along the river at the foot of Scotts Bluff (see SCOTTS BLUFF NATIONAL MONUMENT). Lincoln is about 430 miles to the southeast (see NEBRASKA [political map]). For the weather in Scottsbluff, see NEBRASKA (Climate).

Scottsbluff is an important food processing center. It has dairying, canning, and sugar-processing plants. The major crops in the area are beans, potatoes, and sugar beets, and corn and other small grains.

The city was established in 1900. It has a council-manager form of government. JAMES C. OLSON

**SCOTUS.** See DUNS SCOTUS, JOHN.

**SCOURING RUSH.** See HORSETAIL.

**SCOUT.** See BOY SCOUTS; GIRL SCOUTS.

**SCOUT.** The first explorers of the American frontier were usually fur traders. They knew the Indian tribes, found mountain passes, and located camping places and water holes. These experienced frontiersmen served as scouts to guide colonial armies. The first wagon trains of settlers to Oregon and California also employed fur traders as guides. The U.S. Army used friendly Indians as scouts. One of the best-known scouts was Kit Carson (see CARSON, KIT).

**SCOW.** See BARGE; SAILING (Kinds of Sailboats).

**SCRANTON,** Pa. (pop. 111,443; met. area 234,531; alt. 725 ft.), is the largest city in Pennsylvania's anthracite region, and one of the largest cities in the state. At one time, the economy of the Scranton region depended solely on coal. But mining has declined, and Scranton has become a major center for manufacture of textiles, household appliances, shoes, cigars, and electronic equipment. Its name comes from the Scranton family, which founded an iron works there in 1840.

Scranton lies in northeastern Pennsylvania, 134 miles from New York City. The city stands in a deep valley closely bordered by ridges of the Allegheny Mountains. It is a short distance from the Pocono Mountains resort area. For location, see PENNSYLVANIA (political map).

Scranton is the home of the International Correspondence Schools. Also located in Scranton are the University of Scranton, Marywood College (for girls), and a Pennsylvania State University extension school.

Scranton has a large wholesale and retail trade. Besides coal, the city produces heating and air conditioning equipment, textile machinery, bathtubs, caskets, stokers, plastic products, and paints and varnishes. Other products include books, clothing, lamps, condensers, paper boxes, and phonograph records.

The first settlers came in the 1780's. The first railroad entered Scranton in 1851. Scranton became a borough in 1853, and a city in 1866. It has a mayor-council form of government. S. K. STEVENS

**SCRANTON, UNIVERSITY OF.** See UNIVERSITIES AND COLLEGES (table).

**SCRANTON, WILLIAM WARREN** (1917-    ), was the governor of Pennsylvania from 1963 to 1967. He campaigned for the Republican presidential nomination in 1964, but lost. He did not begin his campaign until most of the states had pledged their convention votes to Senator Barry M. Goldwater.

Scranton was born in Madison, Conn. He studied law at Yale, and served as an Army flier in World War II. After the war, he built a successful business career, and worked to develop Scranton, Pa. The city is named for his family. Scranton served briefly in the U.S. Department of State. He served in the U.S. House of Representatives from 1960 to 1962 as a representative of his home district in Pennsylvania.      ERIC SEVAREID

**SCRAP IRON.** See IRON AND STEEL (The "Recipe" for Making Steel; picture: Why Collecting Scrap Iron Is Important).

**SCRATCH TEST.** See ALLERGY (Search for Allergic Causes).

**SCREW** is an inclined plane wrapped around a cylinder or a cone (see INCLINED PLANE). Scientists and engineers classify the screw as a *simple machine*. A screw has two main parts. The spiral part that sticks out from the cylinder or cone is called the *thread*. The cylinder or cone itself is called the *body*. The center line of the body is called the *axis*. As the screw rotates one full turn, the object in contact with the thread moves along the axis. It travels from crest to crest of the thread. The distance between the crests is called the *pitch*. The movement along the axis per revolution is called the *lead* (pronounced *leed*) of the screw. If the thread consists of only one spiral, the lead and the pitch are identical. If a screw has 10 threads for every inch, both the pitch and the lead will measure $\frac{1}{10}$ of an inch. But some screws have two separate threads that start on opposite sides of the body. Therefore, the screw has two separate spirals. In this case, the lead is twice as large as the pitch.

**The Principle of the Screw.** The main purpose of the screw is to raise a load over the threads of the screw by applying a small force. The distance moved by a point on the screw as it turns is called the *circumference* of the screw. The work done per revolution equals the force applied at a tangent to the screw times the circumference. Therefore work ($W$) equals $F \times 2\pi r$, where $F$ equals the force, and $2\pi r$ equals the circumference.

A screw always offers a certain amount of *resistance* due to friction, since the surfaces of the thread can never be made perfectly smooth. The resistance is a force opposite to the force applied to the machine. The resistance means that a somewhat larger force than the $F$ in the formula must be applied.

Engineers sometimes desire to find out how heavy a load can be raised by a certain amount of force. They figure this by multiplying the force by the circumference of the screw. Then, the engineers divide this product by the lead. The formula for this is $L = \dfrac{F \times 2\pi r}{l'}$, where $L$ stands for load, $F$ for force, $r$ for the radius, and $l'$ for lead.

**Uses of Screws.** Screws have many practical applications. The screws most commonly used are wood screws and machine screws.

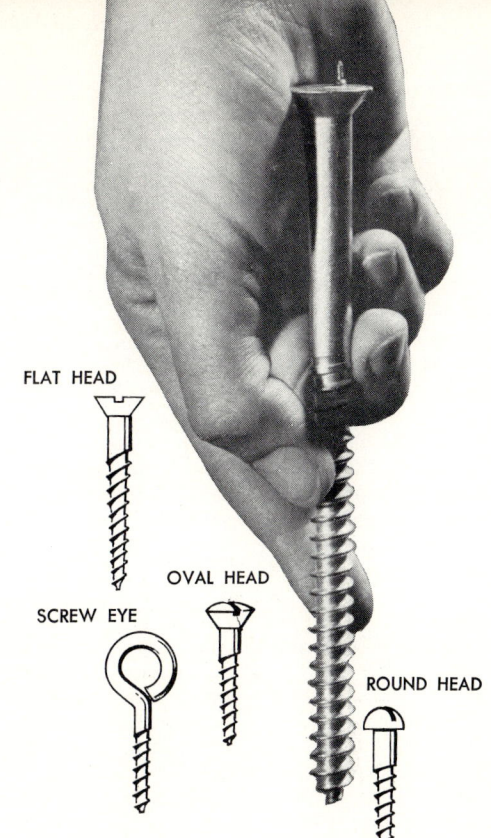

*Popular Science Monthly*

**A Large 6-Inch Screw,** above, is more than 25 times as long as the tiny screw resting on its head. It takes about 10,000 of the small screws, but only 5 large ones, to weigh a pound.

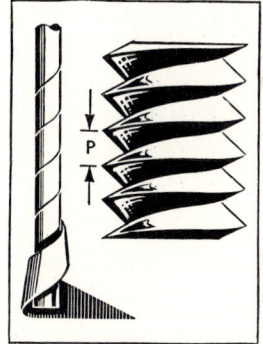

**The Screw** is an inclined plane, spirally wound around a center pole. A strip of paper wrapped around a tube, *left*, illustrates this. The letter *P* shows the screw's pitch (distance between the threads).

**A Supercavitating Propeller,** *below*, will greatly increase a ship's speed. This new screw-type propeller is not slowed by *cavitation* (vacuum pockets that form around conventional propellers). It bites into water just as a screw bites into wood.

U.S. Navy

189

## SCREW, ARCHIMEDEAN

*Wood Screws and Machine Screws* are made of steel, copper, aluminum, and other material that is easy to form. They are usually made by automatic screw machines that make several thousand screws an hour. Screws come in all sizes and shapes, depending on their uses. Screws are often inserted through a hole in a flat disk called a *washer*. The washer keeps the screw from damaging the material on which it is used. Some screws come with the washer attached. *Lockwasher* screws have a washer with a bent or toothed edge. When the screw is driven in, the lockwasher creates friction between the screw and the surface on which it is used. This friction helps to hold the screw in place. Many industries use a large number of *self-tapping* screws, which make a separate small thread inside a hole. The surface of self-tapping screws creates a large amount of friction, and eliminates the need of fastening devices, such as nuts, to hold them in place. Self-tapping screws are used in automobile and truck bodies and in all types of home appliances.

*Other Uses.* Screws also open and close nearly all vises. *Jackscrews* raise heavy buildings and hold heavy weights in position. The *micrometer*, which measures small distances with great accuracy, works by means of a screw that has fine threads (see MICROMETER). Screws also produce motion. An airplane propeller is an *air screw*. A ship propeller is a *water screw*. ALLEN S. HALL, JR.

See also BOLT; PROPELLER.

**SCREW, ARCHIMEDEAN.** See ARCHIMEDEAN SCREW; ARCHIMEDES.

**SCREWWORM.** See BLOWFLY.

**SCRIABIN,** *skree AH bin*, or *SKRYAH byin*, **ALEXANDER** (1872-1915), a Russian composer and pianist, became known for his experiments in using harmony as melody. His last six sonatas for piano, written between 1908 and 1913, are considered masterworks. He was influenced by literary ideas and mystic visions, and he composed *The Divine Poem* (1905), *Poem of Ecstasy* (1907), and *Prometheus, the Poem of Fire* (1909-1910) for large orchestra.

His smaller pieces for piano, including etudes, preludes, and impromptus, show his romanticism. Scriabin won fame as a concert pianist, and toured the United States in 1906. He toured Russia with Serge Koussevitzky between 1908 and 1910. Scriabin was born in Moscow. He studied at the Moscow Conservatory, and later taught piano there. JOYCE MICHELL

**SCRIBE** was an official who wrote books by hand before printing was invented. Kings usually kept scribes at court to copy manuscripts and write official letters and documents.

A scribe's work was slow and painstaking. A nobleman in Florence, Italy, once had 45 scribes copy books for his private library. At the end of two years of copying, the nobleman's scribes had produced only about 200 books.

In many parts of the world today, thousands of people still do not know how to write. They depend on scribes to do all their writing. In Istanbul, Turkey, scribes work in public places, such as the courtyards of mosques. They sit at little tables and write letters or documents that people dictate.

In Biblical times, scribes were called *sopherim*. Early scribes were men who copied the *Torah*, or Law. Later, the scribes developed into a class of learned men who taught and interpreted the Scriptures, and kept charge of official documents. The scribe Ezra became the leader of the Jews who returned to Judea after the Babylonian Exile. In the time of Jesus, the scribes were called *doctors of the law*. Some scribes held classes to train rabbis. Paul's teacher, Gamaliel, was a scribe. In Matthew 23: 13-33 Jesus rebuked the "scribes and pharisees."

Today, trained scribes still write the scrolls of the Torah used in synagogues. They wear special ritual robes while at work. A scribe must be a pious man with a thorough knowledge of Hebrew. WILLIAM F. ROSENBLUM

See also EZRA; HANDWRITING; MANUSCRIPT; PHARISEE.

**Saint Luke Was a Learned Scribe.** He is shown in this Flemish painting at work drawing a picture of the Virgin.
Newberry Library

**SCRIBE,** *skreeb,* **AUGUSTINE EUGÈNE** (1791-1861), was a French dramatist. His name is associated with the phrase "the well-made play," which means a play that is valued more for its plot complications and thrills than for its thought. He wrote *A Glass of Water* (1820), which deals with intrigues at the English court. His best-known serious play was the tragedy *Adrienne Lecouvreur* (1849). He often worked with other writers, and it is believed he wrote more than 400 dramatic pieces. He was born in Paris. JOHN W. GASSNER

**SCRIBNER** was the family name of two American book publishers, father and son. Charles Scribner, Sr. (1854-1930), and Charles Scribner, Jr. (1890-1952), were the second and third members to head the Scribner publishing firm since its founding in New York City in 1846. Charles Scribner, Sr., reorganized his father's company into Charles Scribner's Sons in 1878. Under his direction and that of his son, the firm published works which helped to make many authors famous. Both Scribners were born in New York City.     I. W. COLE

**SCRIMMAGE, LINE OF.** See FOOTBALL (The Players).

**SCRIPPS, EDWARD WYLLIS** (1854-1926), was a famous American journalist. He started the first newspaper chain and founded the United Press Associations, now United Press International. He controlled a large number of newspapers and newspaper services.

Scripps was born on a farm near Rushville, Ill. At the age of 18, he started to work on the *Detroit Tribune* as an office boy. Six years later, he began a newspaper of his own, the *Cleveland Penny Press*. This paper was the first of a chain that included papers from the Middle West to the Pacific Coast. Scripps and his brothers bought the *St. Louis Evening Chronicle* in 1880. Two years later, they purchased the *Cincinnati Penny Post*, which they later renamed the *Cincinnati Post*.

Scripps' health failed in 1917, and he gave control of his newspaper holdings to his son, Robert P. Scripps. In 1922, the chain became known as the Scripps-Howard Newspapers, Inc.     JOHN E. DREWRY

See also UNITED PRESS INTERNATIONAL.

**SCRIPPS COLLEGE** is a privately controlled women's college in Claremont, Calif. The plan of study centers around required courses in the humanities. The college was founded in 1926. For enrollment, see UNIVERSITIES AND COLLEGES (table).

**SCRIPPS INSTITUTION OF OCEANOGRAPHY** is a graduate research institution in La Jolla, Calif., for the study of ocean geography, plant, and animal life. Subjects studied include the topography and composition of the ocean bottom, the properties of water, waves, currents, and tides. The institution is a part of the University of California. It was founded in 1901 as a marine biological station, and became Scripps Institution in 1912.     ROGER REVELLE

**SCRIPT.** See TYPE; WRITING (Scripts).

**SCROD** is a young codfish cut into strips across the grain in preparation for cooking. In the United States, the term *scrod* is sometimes used to mean various other young fish as well as cod. See also COD.

**SCROFULA,** *SKRAHF yoo luh,* is a form of tuberculosis that attacks the lymph glands, and sometimes the bones and joints. Usually, the lymph glands in the neck are affected. Infected bones and joints become swollen and may break down, causing pus to form. The infection usually occurs in young people. Treatment consists of sunlight, fresh air, good food, and warm and suitable clothing. Physicians may prescribe cod-liver oil and similar tonics. An operation may be necessary to provide drainage when an abscess forms.

In England, scrofula was formerly called *the king's evil,* because many people believed that a victim could be healed if the king touched him. The practice is supposed to have originated with the Anglo-Saxon king, Edward the Confessor, and to have died out during the 1800's. See also FIGWORT FAMILY; TUBERCULOSIS; ANNE (picture).     HYMAN S. RUBINSTEIN

**SCROLL** is a roll of paper, parchment, or other material. Many ancient peoples used scrolls as books. The Egyptians used papyrus for writings and illustra-

Barry, Three Lions

**The *Torah* Is Written on a Large Scroll,** *above.* It is made up of the first five books of the Bible.

tions. The Greeks and Romans used papyrus, and parchment or other skins. They rolled these materials around rods of wood, ivory, or bronze to form scrolls. They usually decorated the rods at both ends with small knobs or other ornaments. This protected the scrolls and made them easier to handle. The Hebrews have always used scrolls for their sacred writings.

The Chinese and Japanese use scrolls made from such materials as silk or paper. They use these scrolls both for paintings and for writings. When the scrolls are rolled horizontally, they are called *makemono.* When rolled vertically, they are called *kakemono.*

The design called *scroll* or *scrollwork* is a curving design suggested by the appearance of the end of a loosely wound scroll.     WILLIAM M. MILLIKEN

**Related Articles** in WORLD BOOK include:
Bible (picture)          Dead Sea Scrolls      Manuscript
Book (picture)           Japanese Print        Papyrus

**SCROOGE.** See DICKENS, CHARLES (The First Phase).

**SCRUPLE,** *SKROO p'l,* is a unit of weight used in drug measurement. The scruple is equal to 20 grains, or $\frac{1}{3}$ of a dram. There are 24 scruples in an ounce, and 288 scruples in a pound.

**SCUBA DIVING.** See DIVING, UNDERWATER (Free Diving); SKIN DIVING (Kinds of Skin Diving).

**SCULL.** See ROWING.

**SCULPIN** is a family of fishes that have large mouths, large heads, and bodies that taper sharply to the tail fin. They live in many parts of the world. Most of them live near rocky shores. Some, however, live in deep parts of the ocean, and others live in fresh, inland water.

Most sculpins have spiny heads and fins and warty skins. People in the Arctic regions eat them, although these fish have little flesh and many bones. The sculpins eat small sea animals, and have greedy appetites. They often steal the bait from fishermen's hooks. Sculpins are eaten by larger fish. They are also called *blob, bullhead, miller's-thumb,* and *tide-pool johnny.*

**Scientific Classification.** Sculpins make up the sculpin family, *Cottidae.*     LEONARD P. SCHULTZ

191

# SCULPTURE

Archaeological Museum, Athens; photo by Raymond V. Schoder, S.J.

**A Greek god, either Poseidon or Zeus (detail)**
Greece, about 460 B.C. Bronze. Figure 82 inches high.

Museum of Fine Arts, Boston; WORLD BOOK photo by Robert Crandall

**The Hindu goddess Durga**
India, A.D. 600's. Stone. 59 inches high.

**SCULPTURE** is one of the most interesting and complex of man's arts. It ranges from Michelangelo's powerful carvings to African masks worn in religious ceremonies, and from stone statues that decorate cathedrals to metal mobiles that sway gracefully in the air.

A piece of sculpture can be small enough to stand on a table, or as large as the Statue of Liberty. But whether large or small, sculpture tends to have a *monumental* quality—the quality of grandeur and nobility in a work of art. Large-scale sculpture is often called monumental because of its size. Yet even the smallest sculpture can express noble and grand ideas.

The art of sculpture probably developed in association with religious and magical practices. The oldest known sculptures were created more than 20,000 years ago, during the Paleolithic Period (Old Stone Age). Prehistoric men carved small *amulets* (charms) and idols from such materials as bone or ivory. They probably

---

*The contributors of this article are Mulk Raj Anand, Chairman of the National Academy of Art, New Delhi, India; John Boardman, Reader in Classical Archaeology at Oxford University and author of* Greek Art; *Douglas Fraser, Associate Professor of Art History and Archaeology at Columbia University and author of* Primitive Art; *H. D. Molesworth, author of* European Sculpture *and formerly Keeper of Sculpture and Woodwork at the Victoria and Albert Museum, London; Bernard Myers, Tutor at the School of Industrial Design of the Royal College of Art, London, and author of* Sculpture: Form and Method; *Sir Herbert Read, author of* The Art of Sculpture; *and Allen S. Weller, Dean of the College of Fine and Applied Arts at the University of Illinois. The article was critically reviewed by Sir Herbert Read.*

WORLD BOOK photo by Leonard von Matt

West portals of Chartres Cathedral (detail)
France, about 1150. Stone. Figures 20½ feet high.

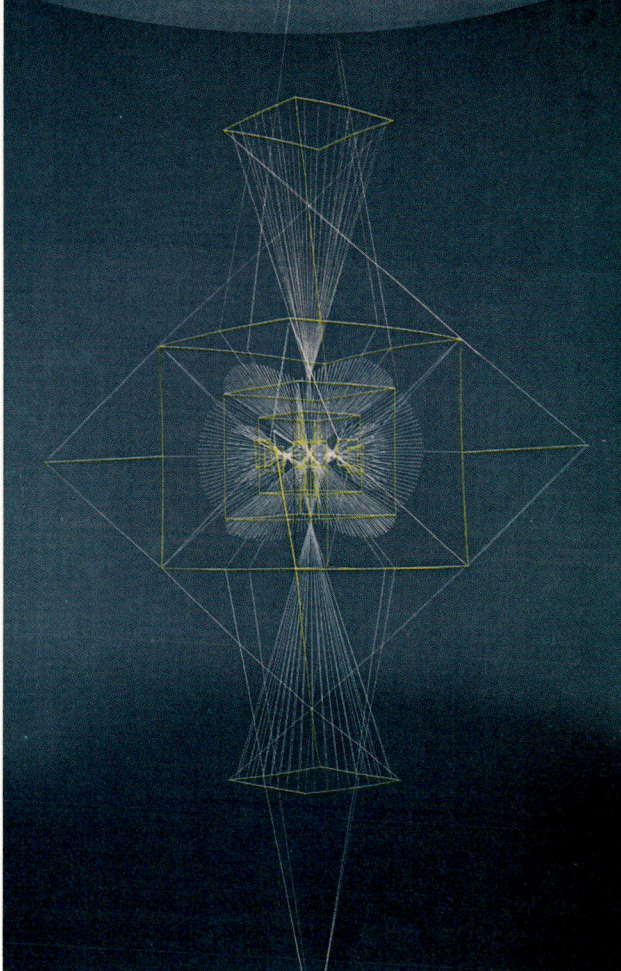

The Museum of Modern Art, New York

*Variation Number 7: Full Moon* by Richard Lippold
1949-1950. Brass rods, nickel-chromium and
stainless steel wire. 10 feet high.

used these carvings in connection with their burial or fertility ceremonies. They modeled similar objects in clay. Although the word *sculpture* originally meant *cut* and implied the technique of carving, modeled objects are also called sculpture.

### The Importance of Sculpture

**As a Record of History.** No art presents a more complete or clearer record of the development of human culture than sculpture. Sculpture can tell us much about the way of life of a particular people or period by physically representing the ideas and ideals of a civilization. For example, the ancient Greeks and the people of the Middle Ages both idealized the human form in their sculptures, and showed the human body as they felt it should look. The Greeks admired man and his works, and they tried to make the human form as perfect as possible in such sculptures as the bronze statue of the *Greek god Poseidon* or *Zeus*, shown on the opposite page. During the Middle Ages, people were more concerned with life after death than with life on earth. Medieval sculptors made the human form longer and thinner than it really is. They did this to represent an ideal view of a spiritual world, as in the long, narrow figures that decorate the *west portals of Chartres cathedral*. These figures, shown on this page, represent characters from the Old Testament.

The Aztecs of Mexico created a grim, sacrificial art dominated by religious ideas. *Xolotl, an Aztec death god*, shown on page 194, appears as a skeletal figure because the Aztecs believed that he, in the form of an evening star, guided the dead through the underworld.

In India, China, and other Oriental civilizations, sculpture is used to aid contemplation. Such Oriental

193

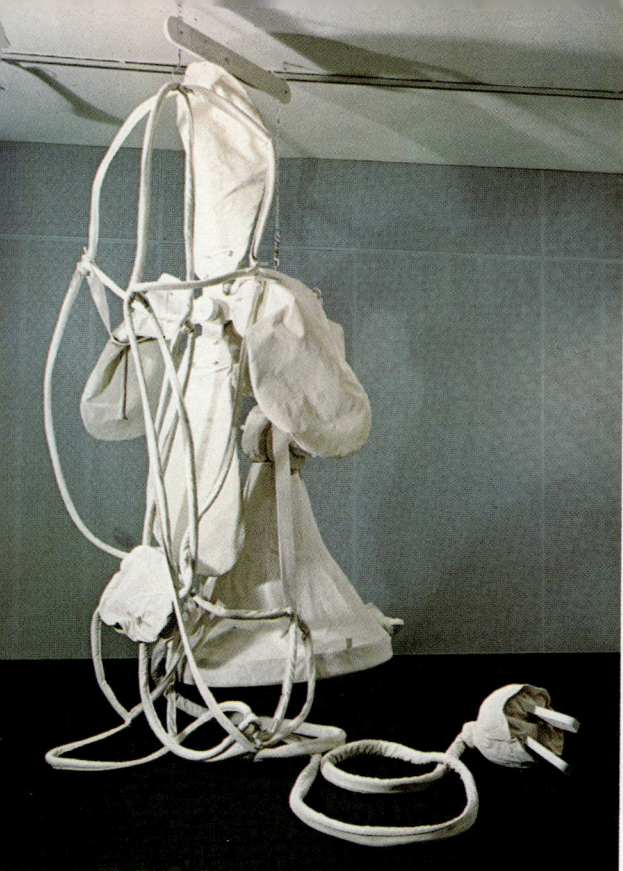

*Giant Soft Fan, Ghost Version* by Claes Oldenburg
1967. Canvas, wood, and foam rubber. 120 inches high.

The University of St. Thomas, Houston; Gift of Mr. and Mrs. John de Menil; Courtesy Sidney Janis Gallery, New York

religions as Buddhism and Hinduism stress the eternal, invisible powers of the universe rather than the temporary, observable realities of the everyday world. Through contemplation of sculptured images, Oriental peoples seek to understand these divine powers and to become united with the eternal. Indian sculptures that decorate Hindu temples show the Indian desire to contemplate the mythical acts of the gods. The stone carving of the *Hindu goddess Durga*, shown on page 192, represents the goddess engaged in a legendary drama that teaches salvation.

Some modern artists create sculptures that comment on the ideas and ideals of their society. The American sculptor Claes Oldenburg seems to satirize present-day society's dependence on machines, mechanical objects, and gadgets. In such works as *Giant Soft Fan, Ghost Version*, he uses electrical fixtures, typewriters, bathroom plumbing, and other mechanical devices. Oldenburg constructs these forms out of canvas or some other limp fabric, which transforms them into mysterious objects that disturb the viewer.

Sculpture does more than reflect the religious, moral, and social values of a society. It can also create a record of the everyday life of a particular era. Much of our knowledge about the ancient cultures of Egypt, Assyria, and America comes from their works of sculpture. The linen clothing portrayed in the sculpture *Egyptian Soldiers Leading Prisoners* tells us that the Egyptians

*Cubi XIX*
by David Smith
1964. Stainless steel.
113 inches high.

The Tate Gallery, London, from Art Reference Bureau

Xolotl, an Aztec death god
Mexico (Aztec style), A.D. 1324-1521. Jade. 11 inches high.
Linden-Museum, Stuttgart, Germany; loan gift of Württembergisches Landesmuseum, Stuttgart, from Art Reference Bureau

194

## SCULPTURE

**Egyptian Soldiers Leading Prisoners**
Fragment of a relief from the tomb of the Egyptian king Horemheb.
Egypt (Dynasty XVIII), about 1330 B.C. Limestone. 24½ inches wide.

**Model of a ball court with spectators**
Western Mexico (Nayarit style), about A.D. 100-600.
Clay. About 12 inches high.

were farmers who grew cotton and flax, rather than herdsmen who produced wool. The artists of western Mexico constructed delightful scenes in clay that illustrate various ceremonies and other aspects of village life. The *model of a ball court with spectators* represents a game known from the Arizona region to the Caribbean. The purpose of the game was not merely entertainment. The ball game was also a ceremony that re-enacted the daily disappearance of the sun into the underworld, and implied the sun's return. Thus, the ball game was a symbol of the renewal of the universe.

**As Monuments and Memorials.** Because sculpture can be created from such long-lasting materials as stone or metal, it is the art most suitable for monuments and memorials. This type of sculpture is called *commemorative* sculpture. In Western civilizations, most commemorative sculpture represents important persons or great events. For example, the Italian Renaissance sculptor Andrea del Verrocchio designed the bronze *equestrian monument of Bartolommeo Colleoni* in honor of a famous Italian general. In Russia, where people of many cultures are under Soviet rule, commemorative sculpture has an additional purpose. The Russian government uses such war memorials as *The Motherland* by Yevgeny Vuchetich as landmarks to give the people a sense of belonging to one culture (page 196).

**As Artistic Expression.** Many artists create sculpture to satisfy their creative need to communicate, to express their own ideas and feelings, or simply to create an object of beauty. When we look at a piece of sculpture, we can ask ourselves: "What is the sculptor saying in this work?" or "Why do I find this work beautiful, profound, or disturbing?"

Much modern sculpture is created partly to satisfy the sculptor's desire to experiment with new forms and

**Equestrian monument of Bartolommeo Colleoni
by Andrea del Verrocchio**
Italy, 1479-1488; pedestal by Alessandro Leopardi, 1496.
Bronze. Figures over life size.

Novosti Press Agency, Moscow

*The Motherland* by Yevgeny Vuchetich
Part of a memorial, made up of several sculptures, in honor of the heroes of the Battle of Stalingrad. Volgograd (formerly Stalingrad), Russia, 1967. Reinforced concrete. About 270 feet high.

WORLD BOOK photo by Dhiraj Chawda

Kailasanatha Temple
Ellora, India, about A.D. 750-850.
Carved out of solid rock.

materials. Many sculptors are more interested in pure form—that is, the physical shapes of sculptured works—than they are in the communicative content of their sculptures. For this reason, many modern sculptures are *abstract* or *non-representational* in style. Modern sculptors often use stainless steel, plastics, aluminum, glass, or other industrial materials. They try to develop the unique qualities and emphasize the beauty of these materials, as the American sculptor Richard Lippold did in *Variation No. 7: Full Moon*, a beautiful geometrical construction of tightly stretched wire (page 193). David Smith, another American sculptor, worked mainly with metals in *Cubi XIX* and other sculptures. He expressed the natural qualities of these materials with imagination and originality (page 194).

**As Part of Architecture.** Throughout history, sculpture has been closely associated with architecture, partly because similar materials and skills are used in both fields. In the temples of the Middle East, India, and ancient Greece and Rome, and in the cathedrals of the Middle Ages, the forms of the buildings blend completely into sculpture. This blending can be seen in the heads and bases of columns, the moldings around doors and along the edges of roofs, and the abstract decorations. In some cases, including the *Kailasanatha temple* at Ellora, India, the temple itself was carved out of solid rock. All these features show that the stonemason's carving skill approached that of a sculptor.

Greek sculptors took particular care in applying sculpture to their temples. They made it blend so well with the architecture that the sculpture was not purely decorative. The Greeks carved their works on panels and *friezes* (horizontal bands) on the sides of buildings, on *metopes* (rectangular areas above columns), and on *pediments* (the triangular ends of a sloping roof).

Some sculpture which is part of the structure of a building also performs a function. Sculptures of the human figure, for example, have been used as columns. Greek sculptors made draped female figures called *caryatids* which support the roof of the south porch of the *Erechtheum* on the Athens Acropolis. Many medieval cathedrals are decorated with grotesque figures called *gargoyles* which serve as water spouts.

Acropolis, Athens; photo by Raymond V. Schoder, S.J.

Caryatids from
the south porch of
the Erechtheum
Greece, about 421-405 B.C.
Marble. Figures 7½ feet high.

# SCULPTURE / The Sculptor at Work

Carving and modeling have been the basic techniques throughout most of the long history of sculpture. In carving, a sculptor works with a solid block of wood, stone, or some other material. He visualizes the finished figure, and then cuts and chips away the material until only the figure as he imagines it remains. In modeling, the artist builds up his sculpture by adding layers of clay, wax, or some other soft, pliable material that will stick to, and blend with, itself.

Because the materials used in modeling are soft, brittle, or otherwise impermanent, most modeled sculpture is turned into a more lasting form. From the earliest times, sculptors have preserved clay figures by baking them until they are hard. Figures made in this way are called *terra cotta*, an Italian term meaning *cooked earth*. Usually, only small figures can be made by this process, and they break easily.

A common way to make a modeled sculpture permanent is to *cast* it in metal or another hard material. First, the artist makes a mold of the modeled work. Into the mold, he pours a more permanent material—cement, bronze, or aluminum, for example—and lets it harden. As long as the mold lasts, he can cast any number of replicas of the original. See CAST AND CASTING.

Sculptors today experiment with new industrial techniques and materials, and no longer create sculpture exclusively by carving or modeling.

**The First Sculptors.** Men of the Stone Age used sharp flint knives to carve wood and bone. On their spearheads they scratched pictures of animals. They also carved little figurines, including the so-called *Venus of Willendorf* (page 204).

Ancient Egyptian sculptors used only simple stone tools to skillfully cut and polish the hardest stones. To make a statue such as the one of *King Mycerinus of Egypt and his queen* (page 198), the sculptor chose a block of stone and trimmed it into a right-angled solid slightly larger than the finished work would be. On each side, he drew an outline of the figure to be carved. He copied the outline from a master drawing on papyrus.

Next, the sculptor removed the excess stone on the corners of the block by crushing it with a stone mallet or a pounding stone. The result was a blocklike figure that needed only to have the edges and corners rounded and details added. The artist rounded off the corners of the figure by slowly chipping away layers of stone. As each layer was removed, the sculptor's technique became more skillful. Finally, the sculptor rubbed and polished the figure until it had the hard, clean-cut look characteristic of Egyptian sculpture. This *finishing* treatment was done with special hard rubbing stones and a mixture of fine, glassy sand and water.

The Egyptians carved wooden figures in the same way, but wood could be carved more quickly because it is softer than stone. The sculptor gave the finished wood figure a thin coat of plaster or *bitumen* (a tarlike material). Then he painted the figure in bright colors and *gilded* it (coated it with a thin layer of gold).

**In the Direct-Metal Technique,** the American sculptor Richard Stankiewicz uses a welding torch to join pieces of metal into a finished piece of sculpture.

Photo courtesy of Henry Moore

**Carving in Wood,** the British sculptor Henry Moore uses a mallet and chisel to trim a block of elmwood to the desired shape. Modern carvers use the same kinds of tools as the ancient Greeks used.

WORLD BOOK photo by Erich Lessing, Magnum

**Modeling in Clay,** the Italian sculptor Giacomo Manzù builds up a figure with small pieces of clay. He then will make a permanent cast of the figure in bronze, similar to the one at his right.

WORLD BOOK photo by Robert Crandall

# SCULPTURE

Egyptian sculptors had workshops that were organized somewhat like the mass-production lines in factories today. Beginner-sculptors and apprentices did the rough work at the early stages of the carving. Skilled sculptors did the final carving, and specialists did the finishing work. The master sculptor probably became more of a studio manager and administrator than an artist as he reached the top of his profession.

The Egyptian method of carving was practiced throughout Mesopotamia, Assyria, and other parts of the ancient Middle East. Middle Eastern sculptors worked with jewelers to make beautiful metal sculpture by the *repoussé* process. First, the sculptor carved a wooden pattern. Then sheets of gold or silver were hammered into shape over the pattern. The shields, helmets, and cups made by this process are small-scale sculptures that made up part of the furnishings of a palace.

**Greek Sculptors** took their stone-working techniques from the Egyptians and from civilizations in Asia Minor. By the 500's B.C., the Greeks were carving most of their statues from white marble. They used hand tools made of hard bronze and iron. The sculptor set up a block of marble and drew an outline of the figure on it. Then he roughed out the figure with a hammer studded with sharp points. He used pointed chisels for the finer work. As the sculptor grew closer to the finished work, he used smaller tools and made lighter blows with his hammer. Finally, he gave a sharp edge to the figure's eyes and lips with a triangular, pointed tool. He used specially shaped tools to cut out folds in drapery, in the same way that *flutes* (grooves) were cut in architectural columns.

The Greeks also modeled many sculptures, ranging from small figures for the home to giant terra-cotta statues that decorated temples. Artists learned to *fire* (bake) the huge terra-cotta sculptures without having them break. They used this knowledge to cast life-sized or larger bronze figures of men and animals.

When casting a sculpture in bronze, the sculptor first modeled his work in wax. He dipped the wax figure in a *refractory mixture* (a kind of clay mixture), and then fired it. As the figure baked hard, the wax melted and drained out, leaving a hollow mold in the shape of the original figure. The sculptor then poured liquid bronze into the mold. This casting process is called *cire-perdue*, a French term meaning *lost-wax*.

Sculptors throughout the world have used the lost-wax casting process. The people of the ancient kingdom of Benin in Nigeria used this process to make such splendid bronzes as the *altarpiece* shown here.

**Roman Sculptors.** The finest work of Roman sculptors was probably their mass-produced portrait sculpture. The *portrait of Lucius Verus* is an example. To meet the large demand for portrait busts, the Romans developed a set of standard symbols for hair, eyes, nose, and mouth. A student learned to carve by reproducing these

**A royal group**
An altarpiece of the Benin people. Nigeria, perhaps dating from the late A.D. 1700's. Bronze. 24 inches high.

Museum für Völkerkunde, Staatliche Museen, Berlin, from Art Reference Bureau

Museum of Fine Arts, Boston; WORLD BOOK photo by Robert Crandall

**King Mycerinus of Egypt and his queen**
Egypt (Dynasty IV), 2600-2500 B.C. Schist. 55 inches high.

details accurately, rather than by copying a living model. After learning to carve the standard symbols, he modified them to produce a likeness of a particular individual. Art schools used this method of teaching—in which sculpture itself is the model—until as recently as the 1940's. The method is still used in Russia.

**Medieval and Renaissance Sculptors** used the same methods and tools as did ancient sculptors. Medieval sculptors also used specially shaped tools for wood carving, which resulted in highly intricate work. These artists worked in organized workshops called *guilds*.

During the 1400's and 1500's, Renaissance sculptors cast such small-scale bronzes as *Hercules and Antaeus* by Antonio del Pollaiuolo of Italy. These sculptors rediscovered the techniques of large-scale bronze casting, and produced giant *equestrian monuments* (figures on horseback). Machines were developed to help enlarge the models. These machines led to the development of carving machines that copied and enlarged stone sculpture entirely mechanically. The carving machines were used for a short time during the 1700's and 1800's.

Sculptors of the 1800's, like Renaissance sculptors, worked in large workshops with student assistants. During this period, the industrially developed technique of sand-mold casting was used to mass-produce bronzes.

**Sculptors Today.** Social and economic changes in the 1900's have forced sculptors to use methods and materials different from those of the past. Most modern sculptors work alone, rather than in workshops. They are trained in schools, not in workshops as apprentices. They must produce works quickly because of the expense of maintaining a large studio and buying tools and materials. Sculptors also must show collections of their work at art galleries at regular intervals, both to sell their output and to attract commissions. Only occasionally are sculptors paid in advance, because few patrons request specific works to be sculptured.

Today, hardly any sculptors carve in wood or stone. Carving is strenuous and time-consuming, and is not finished until the artist makes the last stroke with mallet and chisel. In addition, the sculptor's money is tied up in heavy, expensive materials. Modeling is much faster and more flexible than carving. A modeler can add to or take away from the sculptured form, changing his design as he works. This sense of speed and urgency appeals to modern artists.

A modeler uses soft materials including sculptor's wax, wet plaster, clay, or a synthetic clay called *plasticene*. His main tools are his hands, but he also uses different kinds of trimming and shaping tools. Soft clay and wet plaster fall down because of their own weight when they are drawn into thin shapes. The modeler overcomes this situation by building a framework called an *armature* to support the figure. An armature consists of wire for small figures, and metal tubing or wood for large figures. To give the sculpture permanence, a casting must be made. This is a highly specialized and expensive process that few sculptors are equipped to do themselves. Most of them make a *maquette* (model) and take it to a foundry where an enlarged copy is cast under the artist's supervision.

Because of the difficulties in casting, many sculptors work metal by hand. With such modern industrial equipment as electric arc and gas welding tools, an artist can cut and shape metal and then join it together again. Using this *direct-metal* technique, sculptors build works out of wire, pipe, sheet metal, and even junk metal from wrecked automobiles.

Other modern sculptors choose ready-made materials and assemble them into sculpture. They use a variety of materials, including steel girders, bolts, gear wheels, cardboard, and cloth. The tools used in this *assemblage* technique include power saws, drills, and hammers.

To finish their sculptures, modern artists use such industrial equipment as sandblasting machines and grinding tools driven by power motors. They can produce a *patina* (surface film) on bronze by applying heat and various chemicals to the finished work. This treatment changes the natural shine and golden color of bronze to reddish-brown, green, or black.

Museo Nazionale del Bargello, Florence, from Art Reference Bureau

*Hercules and Antaeus* by Antonio del Pollaiuolo
Italy, about 1475-1480. Bronze. 18 inches high.

Portrait of Lucius Verus
Rome, A.D. 100's. Marble.
Approximately life size.

Ashmolean Museum, Oxford, from Art Reference Bureau

# SCULPTURE / Sculpture as an Art Form

**Kinds of Sculpture.** The most familiar kind of sculpture is called *sculpture in the round* or *free-standing sculpture*. It is modeled or carved on all sides. Such sculpture can have a main view, giving it a "back" and a "front," as in certain sculptures of the human figure. Or it can be completely finished on all sides so that it can be viewed with pleasure from any angle, as can much abstract sculpture. In the past, some sculpture in the round was meant to be seen only from the front. The artist left the back of the figure rough and unpolished, with his tool marks showing. This practice has provided much information about the methods of sculptors of the past.

Sculpture in the round varies greatly in size and scale. Some statues are life size or larger. Statues that are somewhat larger than life size are said to be in *heroic* scale. If they are from several to many times larger than life size, they are in *colossal* scale.

Sculpture that is completely attached to, or absolutely part of, a flat surface is called *sculpture in relief*. There are two kinds of relief work—*true relief* and *intaglio*. In true relief, the figure stands out from the surface, as in *Lion Fighting a Bull* (page 205). In intaglio, the figure is carved into the background, as in the *seal carved with the figure of a unicorn* (page 206). The same technique was highly developed by the ancient Egyptians for decorating the massive outside walls of their temples. As used by the Egyptians, it is usually called *sunk relief*. This kind of relief is best seen in strong light, which makes the outlines of the figures stand out as sharp shadows. *Egyptian Soldiers Leading Prisoners* is an example (page 195).

Relief sculpture can be carved or modeled. Some of the early carved reliefs of the Egyptians are little

*Charioteer of Delphi*
Greece, about 475 B.C. Bronze. 71 inches high.

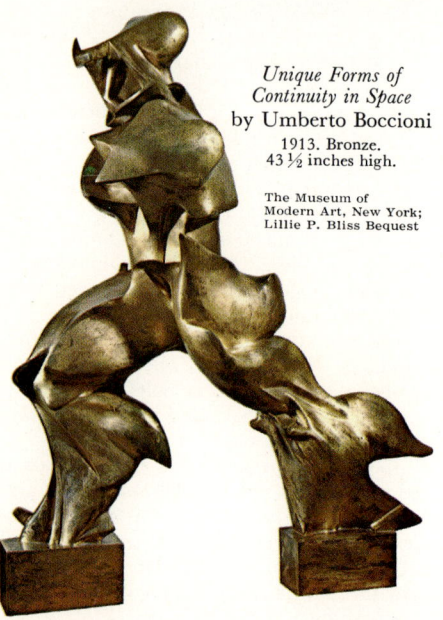

*Unique Forms of Continuity in Space*
by Umberto Boccioni
1913. Bronze.
43½ inches high.

The Museum of Modern Art, New York; Lillie P. Bliss Bequest

*Red Petals* by Alexander Calder
1942. Painted metal and wire. 8½ feet high.
The Arts Club of Chicago; WORLD BOOK photo

more than engraved lines on stone. Many Greek reliefs are shallow, but they stand up from a flat surface in true relief. In some reliefs, the Greeks flattened off the forms nearest the viewer, and deeply undercut and rounded the forms at the back. Later Greek and Roman reliefs tend to have the nearer forms rounded, as in painting. The figures seem almost detached from the background, as in the *Alexander Sarcophagus* (page 206e).

Reliefs can also be modeled in clay or wax and cast in bronze. Two famous examples of cast reliefs are the doors for the Florentine Baptistry by the Italian Renaissance sculptor Lorenzo Ghiberti, and the new doors for Saint Peter's Basilica in Rome by the modern Italian sculptor Giacomo Manzù. See ITALY (color picture: Modern Italian Sculpture).

**Form and Treatment.** Sculptors use many elements found in painting. These elements include space, mass, volume, line, movement, light and shadow, texture, and color. But a painting has only two dimensions—height and width—because it is created on a flat surface. The painter can give only an illusion of depth. By contrast, sculptured forms have three dimensions. They have depth, or solidity, as well as height and width because the sculptor creates his forms in space. The terms *mass* and *volume* are used to describe the way sculptured forms occupy space. Mass describes the amount of bulk, solidity, or weight of a form in space. Volume refers to the amount of space occupied by a sculpture. *Line*, or the edges of a sculpture, encloses or defines the shape of the sculptured form.

*Movement* is one of the most important elements of sculpture. Some sculptures seem to be completely at rest, and suggest little or no movement. For example, the bronze statue of the *Charioteer of Delphi* has a simple outline and little detail. It appears powerful, solid, and calm. It stands firmly on its base, in complete balance. This kind of sculpture is called *static*.

Sculpture that gives an impression of change, movement, and energy is called *dynamic*. Sculptors can create the illusion of movement in several ways. In *Unique Forms of Continuity in Space*, the modern Italian sculptor Umberto Boccioni created rhythms within the statue itself through the repetition of curved shapes. The figure seems to hurl itself through space in successive stages of continuing movement. Antoine Coysevox, a French sculptor, showed a figure in violent action in his statue of *Mercury* (page 206k). When we look at such a figure, our eyes follow the lines of the body and the limbs. These lines lead in many directions in such an arrangement, creating a feeling of movement.

Some sculptures actually do move. These works are called *kinetic* sculpture. The first and most original kinetic sculptures were the *mobiles* invented by the modern American sculptor Alexander Calder. As in *Red Petals*, the various elements of most of Calder's mobiles are made of thin sheet metal. Some of them suggest swimming fish or leaves blowing on a tree. The metal shapes are linked by rods and wires to form a series of balanced pairs which are suspended from one point. They rotate about each other in the lightest breeze.

Some artists build kinetic sculptures in which the various parts move mechanically. The modern French sculptor Jean Tinguely makes elaborately complicated structures out of scrap metal. They have mechanically moving parts which actually break apart, turning the sculpture into scrap once more. The sculpture's "self-destruction" is part of the artist's purpose.

*Light and Shadow*. A painter shows form by using light and dark shades. After this shading is finished, it is unchangeable. A sculptor builds form, and the shading varies with the light that falls on it. In his imagination or in his preparatory drawings, the artist must consider the effect of light and shadow on his forms.

*Texture*. Because of the natural play of light and shadow, the sculptor also must consider the texture of his forms. He must decide whether to leave the surface of his work rough, or how far to go in giving it a smooth, highly polished surface. A rough surface, such as one showing the sculptor's hand marks or tool marks, catches light and gives the sculpture an appearance of dash and liveliness. A smooth, highly polished surface can make a work as impersonal as a piece of machinery.

*Color*. Many sculptors finish their works with color. Colors are naturally lighter and darker in themselves. For example, pure blue tends to be dark, red has a middle tone, and yellow tends to be light. As a result, when the sculptor colors his work, he interferes with the natural process of shading. This matters little to some sculptors. Egyptian and Greek sculptors attempted to color their statues naturalistically by painting the skin, lips, eyes, and hair. However, the colors have faded from most of their works that still survive. Many modern sculptors combine color and sculptural form, as in *Black X* by the American George Sugarman. But such works look like modern painting done in three dimensions.

*Black X* by George Sugarman
1963-1964. Multicolored, laminated wood. 50½ inches high.
Stephen Radich Gallery, New York

## LOOKING AT SCULPTURE
*by Sir Herbert Read*

The first quality to appreciate in sculpture is its volume or mass—the fact that it is three-dimensional. Relief sculpture gives the illusion of objects occupying space, but sculpture as a distinct art is usually in the round. Thus, there is no single point of view from which a piece of sculpture should be seen. Either we should walk around the sculpture, or the sculpture itself should be rotated.

There are many exceptions to the above rule, because of the association of sculpture with architecture. If sculpture is to be incorporated in the front of a building, it can be seen only from a frontal point of view. In this case, most sculptors have not thought it necessary to carve the back of the figure with the same care as the front of the figure. But if a figure stands free and is not necessarily intended to take its place in a particular architectural setting, the artist must visualize his sculpture in the round, and make it equally effective from every point of view.

Before the Renaissance, monumental sculpture (as distinct from small sculpture) was planned and created in association with architecture. In the ancient civilizations of the Middle East and India, almost all sculpture was a basic part of a building. If Greek and Roman sculpture was not actually carved for a position on or in a temple, most of it was part of an architectural scheme—a forum, a palace, a villa, or a tomb. Even most Roman portrait busts were set in a *niche* (hollow in a wall), which itself might be carved. The sculpture of the Gothic period—except for small, portable objects—was planned as part of a building, or of an altar or a pulpit.

When Michelangelo carved his statue of David in the early 1500's, he had no particular site in mind for the work. A committee of artists was appointed to select a site in Florence. The committee decided that the statue was meant to be seen from the front and must be related to a wall surface. This debate made artists and their public aware for the first time of the problem of three-dimensionality in sculpture.

Benvenuto Cellini, who lived at the same time as Michelangelo, was perhaps the first sculptor to think about the free placement of sculpture in space. Cellini claimed that sculpture is seven times as great as any other art because a statue has 8, or even 40, viewpoints, all of which must be reconciled in a single overall unity.

After sculpture became independent of architecture, it grew into a unique art in itself. To fully appreciate the qualities of sculpture, we must develop a special kind of awareness. This awareness enables a person to respond to mass and volume, rather than to the qualities we associate with painting. The art of painting is associated almost exclusively with visual perception,

Warrior on a high-stepping horse (in the style of Leonardo da Vinci). Italy, about 1508. Bronze. Figures about 9½ inches high. Szépművészeti Múzeum, Budapest; WORLD BOOK photo by Erich Lessing, Magnum

We enjoy sculpture most when we can move around it, seeing all sides of the work as the sculptor meant it to be seen. The twisting, spiraling forms of this horse and rider come to life only when we look at the statue from every side.

and involves qualities of linear rhythm, color harmony, and *perspective* (the illusion of deep space). The art of sculpture is associated with *tactile* sensations (sensations of touch), and with those hard-to-define sensations associated with weight and pressure. We should touch and handle a sculpture to sense its three-dimensional shape, as well as its texture. We should also lift, or imagine ourselves lifting, the object to sense its weight.

Great modern sculptors, including Auguste Rodin and Henry Moore, have emphasized the importance of feelings of thrust and pressure. Their works provide these feelings by means of *bosses* (bulges) and hollows. Moore's *Reclining Figure* should be thought of as a tightly packed volume held in tension by the pressure of the surrounding atmosphere. We need some practice or experience to develop this specific approach to sculpture. But when such an approach has been perfected, we can derive greater pleasure from sculpture than from painting.

Today, there is a tendency to abandon the established tradition of sculpture, and to construct objects of steel, iron, concrete, plastics, and other materials that appeal more to the visual senses. Modern sculptors skillfully use their materials to create linear and dynamic effects, as Alexander Calder did in *Red Petals* (page 200). The spectator has no desire to handle these objects, many of which are prickly, and their weight is not important. Most of them are abstract in style. Like architecture, these modern sculptures define or enclose space rather than occupy it.

Sculpture began as architecture. Today, it seems to be returning to its original nature and function.

*Reclining Figure* by Henry Moore
1935. Elmwood. 35 inches long.
Albright-Knox Art Gallery, Buffalo, N.Y.

# SCULPTURE / The Beginnings

**Prehistoric Sculpture.** Men of the Stone Age thought they recognized the forms of living things in such objects as bones, animal horns, and rocks. Prehistoric sculptors carved eyes or arms and legs in these objects to make them look like men or animals.

There were only a few subjects of prehistoric sculpture, and all of them apparently had some magic significance. The figure of *a bison licking itself* and other animal figures probably represented animals killed by hunters. Figures of a plump woman, such as the *Venus of Willendorf,* may have represented the Mother Goddess, who gave life to man and his food.

After prehistoric peoples learned to make pottery vessels by firing clay, they used this technique to make figurines. Terra-cotta figurines have been found in many parts of Egypt, Asia Minor, Mesopotamia, and the Indus Valley. Although few details appear on these figurines, the sculptors obviously did try to emphasize such important physical features as an animal's strong horns or neck, or a goddess's breasts and buttocks.

Beginning about 3000 B.C., ancient civilizations produced many fine sculptures. By this time, artists had gained skill at working with such harder materials as stone and metals.

**Middle Eastern.** Most early Mesopotamian sculpture consists of small-scale figures of kings or priests. For example, the *stele of Ur-Nammu* shows Ur-Nammu, king of the Sumerian city-state Ur, pouring a *libation* (offering) to the goddess Ningal. Mesopotamian sculptors showed their subjects in stiff poses, and did not attempt to suggest movement or to portray actual persons. Livelier scenes of everyday life appear only on minor stone reliefs that decorated furniture or boxes.

During the era of the Assyrian Empire (900's B.C. to 600's B.C.), sculpture was used mainly as architectural decoration. The Assyrians carved colossal stone figures of bulls with human heads to stand beside palace gateways. Palace walls were decorated with reliefs made

Musée des Antiquités Nationales,
St.-Germain-en-Laye, France, from Art Reference Bureau

A bison licking itself
From the cave of La Madeleine in the Dordogne Valley, France, about 9000 B.C. Reindeer antler. About 4 inches high.

Venus of Willendorf
Willendorf, Austria,
30,000-25,000 B.C.
Limestone. 4⅜ inches high.

Naturhistorischen Museum,
Vienna, Austria

University Museum, Philadelphia; WORLD BOOK photo by Robert Crandall

Stele of Ur-Nammu (detail)
Relief showing Ur-Nammu, king of the Sumerian city-state Ur, pouring a libation before the goddess Ningal. Mesopotamia, about 2054-1946 B.C. Limestone. Figure of king about 15 inches high.

Lion Fighting a Bull
Relief from the stairway to the Audience Hall of Darius I at Persepolis. Persia (Achaemenid Empire), about 500 B.C. Stone. Figures over life size.

Cycladic Marble Figurine
Cyclades Islands, Greece, about 3000 B.C. Marble. 30 inches high.

up of many scenes. These scenes told the story of complete military campaigns and other important events. Some of the finest relief carvings are those from Nineveh (now Kuyunjik), showing a royal lion hunt. Assyrian sculptors carved the forms and movements of animals more accurately and realistically than earlier sculptors did. But their human figures were stiff and unemotional, both in relief carvings and in the few large figures that they carved in the round.

Persian sculptors of the Achaemenid Empire (500's B.C. to 300's B.C.) also were interested in the patterns of animal limbs and muscles. An example of their work is the relief *Lion Fighting a Bull*. The Persians decorated buildings with large relief sculpture, but their finest work was on a small scale. Some of it shows clear signs of influence from classical Greece.

The Hittites, who founded a great kingdom in Asia Minor after 2000 B.C., used architectural relief sculpture in a manner similar to the Assyrians. They also carved a number of large monuments from solid rock, showing kings, gods, or religious ceremonies.

**Aegean.** The islanders who inhabited the Cyclades in the Aegean Sea about 3000 B.C. carved figures in white marble. Like the *Cycladic Marble Figurine*, most of these figures were of women. The sculptors had no metal tools, but rubbed the figures smooth with pebbles of emery.

During the 1500's and 1400's B.C., the Minoans of Crete made superb small figures of worshipers, cast solid in bronze. They did not smooth or polish the bronze, so these figures have a rough finish. The figures show a vigor not developed elsewhere at this early date, as can be seen in the bronze figure of a *woman praying*.

The Mycenaean Greeks copied the Minoans, but with little success. Their best attempt is the relief over the Lion Gate at Mycenae.

**Egyptian.** A distinctive style of sculpture developed in Egypt about 3000 B.C., and continued with little major change for more than 3000 years. Egyptian sculpture was made for limited purposes—to commemorate a person or event, or to serve as a substitute for the activities of real persons.

Woman Praying
Crete, Minoan period, 1500's B.C. Bronze. 7½ inches high.

205

# SCULPTURE

Commemorative sculpture includes *King Mycerinus of Egypt and his queen* (page 198) and other great statues of kings and queens, whom the Egyptians regarded as gods. Some of these statues are colossal in scale. The seated statues of Ramses II, cut in rock at Abu Simbel, are more than 65 feet high. Reliefs covering the walls of temples commemorated religious ceremonies or such events as important battles. An excellent example of a battle relief is *Egyptians Leading Prisoners* (page 195).

Egyptian sculptors also carved stone or wooden statues which were placed in tombs to represent the dead. These reliefs and modeled figures showed scenes of daily life similar to the activities the dead were expected to perform in the next world.

In carving the human figure, the Egyptians considered realistic scale unimportant. They showed a king much taller than his subjects or his enemies. Egyptian sculptors followed fixed rules that controlled the proportions of the parts of the body. These rules applied to sculptures ranging from tiny figures to colossal statues carved out of cliffs.

Tradition also required figures to have quiet, restful poses and expressionless faces. The Egyptians considered any vigorous action or realism unnecessary. Only for a short time during the 1300's B.C. did some realism appear in figures and portraits.

**Indus Valley.** The Indus Valley civilization flourished in what is now West Pakistan from about 2500 B.C. to about 1500 B.C. Sculptures have survived from the major areas of this civilization, including such centers as Mohenjo-daro, Harappa, Lothal, Rupar, and Maheshwar. These sculptures include small stone tablets that were used as seals, and figures of animals and human beings that apparently were used in magic ceremonies.

The seals show the rounded forms of bulls, elephants, and rhinoceroses, along with triangular, curved, and vertical signs. Such seals as the *seal carved with the figure of a unicorn* show the ability of the Indus people to carve intaglio in delicate, curved lines.

The limestone *torso of a god* is believed to represent a friendly god. The rhythmic repetition of the curving lines of the torso shows a love of linear rhythm. Indus sculptors also stressed harmonized forms, as shown in the way the torso is unified by the softly swelling curves of the body. The sculptor has carefully rounded these curves, especially the abdomen. This emphasis on harmonized forms appeared later as a dominant characteristic of Indian sculpture.

Linear rhythm is also apparent in the bronze *statuette of a dancer*. The sculptor has captured the dancer at the moment when she is either pausing after a movement or is just about to move. The dynamic quality of this sleek figure is partly due to the rhythmic, angular thrusts of her arms, legs, and torso. The sculptor has also indicated movement by contrasting the linear rhythms of the torso and legs against the triangular right arm and the forward left leg. This contrast of linear rhythm with square and triangular shapes to produce movement characterized later Indian sculpture, both Buddhist and Hindu.

**Statuette of a dancer**
Mohenjo-daro, West Pakistan
(Indus Valley Civilization),
about 2500-2000 B.C.
Bronze. About 4 inches high.

National Museum, New Delhi;
WORLD BOOK photos
by Dhiraj Chawda

**Seal carved with the figure of a unicorn**
Mohenjo-daro, West Pakistan
(Indus Valley Civilization),
about 2500-2000 B.C.
Soapstone. About 2 inches square.

**Torso of a god**
Harappa, West Pakistan
(Indus Valley Civilization),
about 2500-2000 B.C.
Limestone. 3¾ inches high.

# SCULPTURE / Oriental

**India.** During the first thousand years of Indian culture, from the 500's B.C. to the A.D. 500's, Indian sculpture shows the influence of the Buddhist religion. Some of the most magnificent Buddhist sculptures decorate the gateways and stone railings that surround *stupas* (domed mounds). These mounds were built to enshrine the relics of the Buddha. The sculptures are relief carvings that illustrate the life and teachings of the Buddha. The delicate carvings that decorate stupas at Amravati, Barhut, and Sanchi seem to contain the energy of life. In the *fragment of a relief from the stupa at Amravati*, the dense composition of the scenes, with many elements in a small space, shows the skill of Indian relief carvers. These craftsmen were originally trained in ivory carving.

The earliest reliefs were merely lines engraved on a flat surface. They had no depth. After about A.D. 1, Indian sculptors were influenced by the art of the Roman Empire. They produced deeper and more rounded reliefs. Many Indian reliefs are so deeply carved that they give the effect of free-standing sculpture.

The art of medieval India, dating from the A.D. 500's, reflects the influence of Hinduism. Siva, the Hindu god of creation, preservation, and destruction, is portrayed in many sculptures. A number of sculptures show Siva as Nataraja, Lord of the Dance. Most of them portray him as a figure with four arms, trampling the body of a dwarf representing evil. In some sculptures, a ring of fire, representing the universe, surrounds Siva.

The bronze image of *The Hindu god Siva as Nataraja, Lord of the Dance*, shows linear rhythms in their purest form. Indian sculptors were highly skilled in the lost-wax method of casting, as shown in the perfect balance of Siva, poised at the height of his dance. Sculptors of India used this method from the early medieval period on, especially in the southern peninsula.

**China.** The early Chinese, like other ancient peoples, faced the mysteries of the universe by making offerings to unknown spirits. The earliest Chinese sculptures were small figures that were placed in tombs. These tomb sculptures date from sometime before the Shang dynasty (about 1500 B.C. to 1027 B.C.). They were of exquisite workmanship.

From the Shang dynasty through the Han dynasty (206 B.C. to A.D. 221), craftsmen made bronze bells and other metal objects along with ceramic and jade works. All these were used for ancestor worship. The production of such sculptures led to the foundation of guilds of highly skilled craftsmen who produced masterly sculptural works.

Early sculptors bored holes in rounded objects to suggest space relationships. These artists scooped hollows from forms so that light could play over the uneven surfaces, thus creating the effect of energy and movement.

During the Han dynasty, the influence of Buddhist art traveled from India across central Asia to China by way of the silk trade routes. Chinese sculptors began to carve monumental wood and stone figures of the Buddha. Their patient skill and love of finish transformed the foreign Indian tradition into graceful

Government Museum, Madras, India;
WORLD BOOK photo by Dhiraj Chawda

**Fragment of a relief from the stupa at Amravati**
This fragment shows the entire stupa,
a domed mound that enshrined the relics of the Buddha.
India, about A.D. 200. Stone. About 75 inches high.

**The Hindu god Siva as Nataraja, Lord of the Dance**
Southern India, A.D. 1100's. Bronze. 60½ inches high.
Rijksmuseum, Amsterdam, from Art Reference Bureau

206a

# SCULPTURE

rhythms. The unique grace which the Chinese gave to the Buddha's face is shown in the wood carving of the *Head of Buddha*. The suggestion of a mysterious smile gives this work complete tranquillity.

A favorite subject in Oriental sculpture has been the *bodhisattva*, a person potentially capable of becoming a Buddha. In handling the form of the bodhisattva, the Chinese improved upon the rather severe Indian sculptures of the same subject. Chinese sculptors introduced such decorative elements as ropes of pearls, jewelry, and falling scarfs, which added something new to the Asian tradition of carving. These decorative objects can be seen in the figure of *Kuan Yin, goddess of mercy in Chinese Buddhism*, who is called *Bodhisattva Avalokitesvara* in India. The slightly bent posture of the figure reflects the tenderness that Chinese Buddhism introduced into the Indian interpretation of the Buddha's teachings.

Chinese sculptors also made decorative, nonreligious sculpture in ceramic and jade. Their emphasis on pure line and volume and on polished finish of fundamental forms continued until the A.D. 1700's.

**Ceylon and Southeast Asia.** Beginning in the 200's B.C., traders and missionaries carried Indian cultural influences to the nations of the Indian Ocean. These countries included Ceylon, Burma, Thailand, Cambodia, Malaya, Java, and Sumatra. The influence of Indian culture increased after the Christian era began, especially during periods of rule by monarchs of Indian origin.

The peoples of Ceylon and southeast Asia combined their own forceful, primitive beliefs with the soul-centered doctrines of India. As Chinese culture gradually reached these countries, it added another aspect to the contemplation of life and death.

The relief carvings of Angkor Wat and other Hindu temples of Cambodia are of greater size and scale than anything achieved in India. The temple of Borobudur in central Java is one of the three greatest Buddhist monuments in the world. The ruins of the ancient cities of Anuradhapura and Polonnaruwa in northern Ceylon include temples, palaces, monasteries, and stupas that surpass in artistic achievement many similar structures in India.

Kuan Yin, goddess of mercy in Chinese Buddhism
China, about A.D. 580. Painted stone. 98 inches high.

Museum of Fine Arts, Boston, Francis Bartlett Donation of 1912; WORLD BOOK photo by Robert Crandall

Head of Buddha
China, A.D. 600's.
Wood. 20 inches high.

Collection of
Mulk Raj Anand, New Delhi;
WORLD BOOK photo
by Dhiraj Chawda

# SCULPTURE

The seated *Buddha of Anuradhapura* illustrates the portrayal of the perfect yogi. The Buddha radiates both stillness and motion. Sculptors tried to make thought itself liquid and flowing, as in the great Indian tradition of carving. The emphasis of sculpture throughout Ceylon and southeast Asia, as in India, is on swelling, rounded forms, linear rhythm, and the search for balance in space.

**Japan.** The prehistoric peoples of Japan made clay figures intended as funeral sculptures. The figures derive their power from early man's love of monumentality. In this respect, Japanese figures resemble similar works of other Oriental civilizations, especially those of China.

During the medieval period, beginning in the A.D. 600's, Japanese sculptors absorbed the power and intensity of the prehistoric clay figures, and gave a certain resilience to the art of carving. The dramatic aspect of *Aizen Myo-o, god of love in Japanese Buddhism*, is the result of the Japanese talent for portraying psychological moods through the facial expressions and bodily attitudes of sculptured figures.

Japanese sculptors have always been able to absorb foreign techniques. Medieval sculptors took from China a love of rounded forms. The lyrical, cylindrical forms of Korean Buddhist figures also influenced Japanese handling of forms.

The Japanese preferred wood carving with gold coloring, similar to that of the Sui, T'ang, and Sung periods in China. They excelled in simplification of structure and in abstraction of detail to stress severely simple lines.

WORLD BOOK photo by Dhiraj Chawda

Seated Buddha from Anuradhapura
Ceylon, A.D. 500's. Stone. Over life size.

Aizen Myo-o, god of love in Japanese Buddhism
Japan, about A.D. 1300. Painted wood. 3 feet high.

Museum of Fine Arts, Boston; Gift of F. G. Curtis; WORLD BOOK photo by Robert Crandall

# SCULPTURE / Greek

Early Greek sculptors made simple, formal works. They gradually learned to make realistic figures and to indicate emotion by facial expression or bodily pose. This was the style copied by Roman sculptors and relearned by Renaissance sculptors. It served as the basic style for European sculpture until the late 1800's.

There were three major periods in the development of Greek art. The Archaic period dated from about 630 to about 480 B.C. The Classical period lasted until about 323 B.C. The Hellenistic period ended about 146 B.C.

**Archaic Sculpture.** In the 700's B.C., before the Archaic period, artists knew how to make only small figures of clay or bronze. However, they also may have carved wooden statues. During the 600's B.C., they began making clay figures in molds. The Greeks learned this technique from the Phoenicians and other peoples of the East. Archaic sculptors developed a rigid and Eastern-looking style called *Dedalic*, which they also used in carving small limestone figures.

At the end of the 600's B.C., the Greeks learned from the Egyptians how to make larger statues, and how to carve harder stone—their own white marble. From then until about 480 B.C., the Greeks perfected their carving techniques and gradually succeeded in making figures that were more lifelike. They carved many standing figures of naked male youths. These figures, called *kouroi*, served as attendants to the temple of a god, or as memorials over tombs. Similar carvings of clothed maidens were called *korai*. The frontal pose and calm expression of *Kore* shows how much the Greeks improved on Egyptian work. Livelier figures appeared in reliefs on temples and treasuries, as in the *Battle of the Gods and Giants* from the Treasury of the Siphnians at Delphi.

**Classical Sculpture.** After Greek sculptors learned to show the human body accurately, they paid more attention to drapery. In early classical works, drapery hung straight and rather stiffly, as in the *Charioteer of Delphi* (page 200). In later works, it hung in deeply

Kore 675
Greece (island of Chios), about 520 B.C. Marble. 22 inches high.
Acropolis Museum, Athens; photo by Raymond V. Schoder, S.J.

Battle of the Gods and Giants
Detail from the north frieze of the Treasury of the Siphnians at Delphi.
Greece, about 525 B.C. Marble. 26 inches high.
Delphi Museum, Delphi, Greece; photo by Raymond V. Schoder, S.J.

**The Alexander Sarcophagus (detail)**
Relief showing Alexander the Great hunting lions, from a coffin made for a ruler of Sidon. Phoenicia, about 323 B.C. Painted marble. Frieze 23 inches high.

cut folds. Finally, sculptors showed drapery clinging to the body or blowing free from it.

The Greeks thought of their gods as being like men, and sculptors portrayed gods as men in such works as the *Greek god Poseidon* or *Zeus* (page 192). They showed men as godlike beings. Even after sculptors began to make portraits of real persons, they idealized the faces.

The earliest important classical sculpture appeared on the Temple of Zeus at Olympia. The high point of the classical style is generally considered to be the sculptures on the Parthenon in Athens. They were created after the mid-400's B.C.

During the 300's B.C., sculptures of the human figure showed some emotion and vigorous action. Some sculptors showed goddesses nude for the first time. Lysippus made heavily built athlete figures. Praxiteles specialized in a softer, flowing style in his figures of gods and goddesses. Sculptors decorated *sarcophagi* (stone coffins) with reliefs, as in the *Alexander Sarcophagus*. Portrait sculpture also began during this period.

**Hellenistic Sculpture.** The conquests of Alexander the Great carried Greek culture into Egypt and the lands of the East. After Alexander's death in 323 B.C., his empire was split into smaller kingdoms. In these kingdoms, the courts encouraged local schools of art, the most important of which were at Rhodes, Pergamum, and Alexandria. Artists blended local ideas with Greek standards of beauty. The result was a varied and colorful art called *Hellenistic*.

Athenian artists continued to follow a more classical style, but Hellenistic sculptors preferred to create works in active, dramatic poses. In such works as the *Laocoön*, the *Venus de Milo*, and the *Winged Victory*, sculptors portrayed violent feelings and lifelike actions. (For pictures of these famous sculptures, see the articles LAOCOÖN; EUROPE [Arts]; and AVIATION.) Many Hellenistic figures were much less idealized than earlier works. In the *statue of a seated boxer*, for example, the sculptor showed a boxer's broken nose.

**Statue of a seated boxer**
Greece, about 100-70 B.C. Bronze. About 50 inches high.

206e

# SCULPTURE / Etruscan and Roman

**Etruscan Sculpture.** The Etruscans probably came from Asia Minor, and settled in Etruria (present-day Tuscany) in central Italy about 1000 B.C. They learned sculpture from Greek artists who settled in Etruria, and from Greeks living in neighboring colonies in southern Italy and Sicily.

The Etruscans specialized in bronzes and in terra-cotta works which they painted in bright colors. The best examples of their terra-cotta sculptures are the reclining figures on the lids of coffins, and the figure of *Apollo* and three other life-sized statues from the roof of a temple at Veii. Sculptures of this size are seldom achieved in clay, even today.

Etruscan sculptors also carved works from a soft limestone called *tufa*. These works included animals that were used to guard tombs, and reliefs that decorated boxes containing the ashes of the dead. The Etruscans showed a fondness for gruesome figures and for portraiture, particularly of ancestors. However, Etruscan artists gradually adopted classical Greek styles.

**Roman Sculpture.** The earliest Roman sculpture was influenced by the Etruscans to the north of Rome and by Greek colonists to the south. When the Romans conquered Greece and the Hellenistic kingdoms in the 100's B.C., they brought hundreds of Greek statues to Italy. They also encouraged Greek artists to work for Roman patrons.

These Greek artists brought to Italy the fully developed Hellenistic style, especially that of Alexandria. From 100 B.C. to A.D. 100, they produced many works in a Greek style which at the same time expressed Roman ideas.

Portraiture was important in Roman sculpture. Such portraits as the *portrait of Lucius Verus* on page 199 were more realistic than Greek examples, because Greek sculptors still idealized facial features to some degree. Roman sculptors often combined a Roman portrait head with a copy of a Greek statue of a god. They copied and changed famous Greek statues freely at all scales.

The Romans were deeply religious, and many reliefs from altars show ceremonies or symbolic stories. A famous example is the Ara Pacis (Altar of Peace) in Rome.

The Romans also were particularly interested in showing historical events, a theme which the Greeks had avoided. Reliefs on commemorative arches and columns tell the story of complete military campaigns. The best known columns are *Trajan's Column* and the Column of Marcus Aurelius.

Relief decoration on coffins was more Greek than Roman in style and subject matter. But many reliefs symbolized Roman and, later, Christian ideas about death. As time passed, later artists failed to further develop the basically Greek sculptural styles. Nor were these styles replaced by a stronger sculptural tradition.

Apollo
One of four figures from the roof of an Etruscan temple at Veii. Italy, about 500 B.C. Painted terra cotta. 68 inches high.

Villa Giulia Museum, Rome; photo by Raymond V. Schoder, S.J.

Trajan's Column (detail)
Relief showing Trajan's campaign against the Dacians. Rome, A.D. 113. Marble. Relief band about 50 inches high.

Near Trajan's Forum, Rome; WORLD BOOK photo by Leonard von Matt

# SCULPTURE / Medieval

As the Roman Empire declined, monumental sculpture died out almost completely, but the art still persisted in small ivories. In the Byzantine Empire, centered in Constantinople, sculptors developed a stiff, formal style. An artistic tradition was maintained in the courts of the Carolingian and Ottonian emperors in western Europe, as well as in monastery workshops.

Most of these sculptures show active scenes full of figures inspired by late Roman sculpture. In Britain, the Celts and Saxons combined their traditional art forms with Christian subjects. They used a complicated ornamental style of interlaced bands, or of birds and beasts entwined in vine scrolls. They combined this style with crude but expressive figures. This combination was refined and developed later in metalwork or ivories such as the *Cross of Ferdinand I of León*. This style of interlacing continued for a long time in Scandinavian carvings and occasionally in other European sculpture.

About 1100, a revival of monumental sculpture spread along a line from northern Spain to northern Italy, but was centered in southern France. By this time, the Christian church had become a dominant force in Europe. All the new monumental carvings appeared on church property, including church porches and *tympanums* (areas above doorways). The sculptures all showed such religious subjects as Christ enthroned or doomsday scenes. These sculptures may have helped express church doctrines for all classes of people.

At first, monumental sculpture appeared in many styles, apparently based on earlier sarcophagi, ivories, manuscripts, and *frescoes* (wall paintings). By 1135, the *Romanesque* style appeared in a fairly uniform aspect throughout Europe. This style featured elongated fig-

**Cross of Ferdinand I of León**
From the Church of San Isidoro, León, Spain, about 1063.
Ivory. 21 inches high.

**The prophet Isaiah**
Relief from the Church of Sainte-Marie, Souillac, France, about 1130.
Stone. Figure life size.

**Ekkehardt and Uta**
Figures from the choir of Naumburg Cathedral. Germany, about 1250.
Stone. Over life size.

**The Virgin and Child**
France (School of Paris), early 1300's.
Ivory. 14 inches high.

206g

ures with formal, staring faces, and the use of decorative, stylized lines of drapery. These characteristics can be seen in the relief of *the prophet Isaiah* (page 206g).

Sculptors continued to devote most of their work to church decoration during the period when the great Gothic cathedrals were being built, from about 1150 to about 1300. The earliest Gothic sculpture appeared in Chartres, Paris, and other cities of northern France. Sculptors created formal, stylized works in which the vertical lines of drapery seemed to serve as additional pillars for the new, soaring Gothic architecture. An example is the detail from the *west portals of Chartres cathedral* on page 193. The faces of the figures look more natural and human than in Romanesque sculpture. This new naturalism grew until, by the mid-1200's, statues expressed the freedom and naturalism that marked the great flowering of Gothic art. The Gothic style quickly spread throughout western Europe. Such figures as *Ekkehardt and Uta* reflect the dignity and crusading idealism of early Gothic art (page 206g).

During the 1200's, sculptured tombs became numerous. At first, sculptors decorated only the tombs of kings and other great persons with *effigies* (figures) of those persons. Soon, members of the lesser nobility, such as knights, arranged for sculptors to carve figures on their tombs. These effigies lying on tombs created a great new outlet for sculpture.

Sculpture of the 1300's reflects the changed political structure of medieval society. A courtly style developed as sculpture came under the influence of the princes and their courts. The effect of this style on sculpture can be seen in the beautiful ivory carving of *the Virgin and Child* on page 206g. Compared with the early Gothic figure of *Uta*, the Virgin looks like a fashionable court lady with affected gestures. These characteristics of affected poses and sweetly smiling faces appeared in both large and small sculptures of the 1300's.

During the 1400's, church construction declined. Instead of decorating church *façades* (fronts), sculptors turned to furnishing the insides of churches and chapels with altars and statues of saints for worship and decoration. This type of carving dominated the sculpture of the 1400's. Workshops in Flanders and southern Germany mass-produced and exported thousands of figures and altarpieces. Most were made of painted wood, and were carved naturalistically. They were created in small sections so they could be transported easily.

Late Gothic sculpture in northern Europe came to a climax between 1490 and 1510. It centered in the great trading towns of Flanders and southern Germany, including Antwerp, Nuremberg, Ulm, Augsburg, and Munich. Many individual styles developed. This expression of a personal artistic style was influenced by artistic developments of the Renaissance in Italy. Outstanding artists of this late Gothic period included Veit Stoss, Tilman Riemenschneider, and Michael Pacher, who carved the great *St. Wolfgang Altar*. As a group, sculptors in northern Europe still followed medieval traditions. Even sculptors most influenced by the Renaissance, including Conrad Meit and the Vischer family, produced Gothic monuments in the 1530's.

**St. Wolfgang Altar (detail) by Michael Pacher**
Church of St. Wolfgang-am-Abersee, St. Wolfgang, Austria, 1471-1481.
Painted wood, partially gilded. Figures approximately life size.

## SCULPTURE / Italian Renaissance

Figures made by medieval sculptors of northern Europe represented types rather than individuals, such as the concept of a "good man." But Italian Renaissance sculptors portrayed individual persons—for example, a particular man who was good.

Renaissance sculpture reflected the new outlook on life that appeared in Italy during the 1300's. This outlook, which later scholars termed *humanism*, emphasized the importance of man and his activities. Humanism had its roots in the civilizations of ancient Greece and Rome. The Renaissance was given its name, which means *rebirth*, because of the revival of interest in classical art, architecture, and civilization.

In the late 1200's, Nicolo Pisano and his son Giovanni began the revolutionary changes that led up to the Renaissance in Italian sculpture. They were architects and designers as well as sculptors, and are noted for their reliefs and ornamentation on pulpits. *The Massacre of the Innocents* by Giovanni Pisano is an example. The dense composition of this relief shows that the sculptor was inspired by Roman sarcophagi. Its content, in which each person reacts as an individual, shows the new attitude of the Renaissance. The actual carving remains Gothic, however.

During the 1300's, political and economic troubles in Italy limited sculptural activity. But the great revival of art in Florence about 1400 brought two generations of sculptors who were the equals of any artists anywhere at any time. They returned to classical Mediterranean traditions, and turned away from the Gothic style which was more at home in northern Europe.

**Early Renaissance.** The greatest sculptor of the early Renaissance was Donatello. By 1409, he had produced a stone statue of *David* which, though Biblical in subject matter, was entirely new in spirit—the portrait of a proud, triumphant boy. In a bronze statue of David,

Museo Nazionale del Bargello, Florence, from Art Reference Bureau

*David* by Donatello
Italy, about 1408. Marble. Figure about 62 inches high.

Julius Caesar
by Desiderio da Settignano
Italy, about 1450-1453.
Marble relief. 16½ inches high.

*The Massacre of the Innocents* by Giovanni Pisano
Detail from a panel of the pulpit in the Church of Sant'Andrea.
Pistoia, Italy, 1298-1301. Marble. 33 inches high.

206i

# SCULPTURE

completed about 1430, Donatello revived the use of the nude figure. This statue re-established the classical idea of beauty—the naked human body.

The new naturalness quickly affected sculpture throughout Italy. Donatello decorated the pulpits and singing galleries of churches in Florence and Padua with gay *putti* (singing and dancing children). Luca della Robbia made popular colored terra-cotta figures which were copied for generations. Sculptors also began to make figures of the Virgin Mary whose models might have been attractive local Italian girls. These sculptures differed greatly from the formal, impersonal Romanesque and Gothic types.

Other new forms of sculpture developed during the 1400's, including lifelike portrait busts and great monuments in the classical style. Desiderio da Settignano became famous for portraits, including his relief of *Julius Caesar* (page 206i). Among the other brilliant sculptors of the 1400's were Jacopo della Quercia, Michelozzo Michelozzi, Bernardo and Antonio Rossellino, and Agostino di Duccio.

In the mid-1400's, Donatello moved to Padua. His style of modeling became more precise and sharp, and influenced the whole trend of sculpture in northern Italy. Among the sculptors influenced by this new style were the Mantegazza brothers, Giovanni Amadeo, the Lombardi family, and the great bronze worker Andrea Briosco, who was called *Il Riccio*. They all showed rather stylized, flattened planes in their works. Only in later nonreligious works, such as small bronzes and medals, did sculptors return to rounder, classical forms.

Two important sculptors of the late 1400's were Antonio del Pollaiuolo and Andrea del Verrocchio, both of Florence. Pollaiuolo, like Donatello and many other artists of this period, made a careful study of the appearance of muscles while the body is in motion. These artists caught fleeting moments of tense action in their poses. An example is *Hercules and Antaeus* by Pollaiuolo (page 199). Verrocchio designed the powerful, stern *equestrian monument of Bartolommeo Colleoni* (page 195).

**Michelangelo.** The great flood of Italian genius came to a climax in the early 1500's in Michelangelo Buonarroti. Michelangelo's great brooding sculptures, including the figures of *Evening* and *Dawn* on the *tomb of Lorenzo de' Medici* in Florence, carry the observer beyond earthly reality. The deep feeling and emotion of his figures set them apart from all other works of sculpture of that time.

Most other sculptors of the 1500's produced rather forced adaptations of imperial Roman figures and groups. Some monumental dignity can be seen in the works of such Venetian sculptors as Jacopo Sansovino and Alessandro Vittoria. Other sculptors followed Giovanni da Bologna's experiments in composition in which figures turn and twist in complicated poses. Still others, including Benvenuto Cellini and Bartolommeo Ammanti, developed the Mannerist style. This style emphasized grace and elegance, and resulted in the creation of slender, artful figures. An example is Cellini's bronze *statue of Perseus*

Statue of Perseus by Benvenuto Cellini
Italy, 1545-1554. Bronze. Figure 10½ feet high.

Tomb of Lorenzo de' Medici by Michelangelo
Italy, about 1524-1534. Marble. Figures life size.

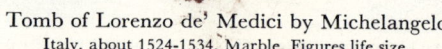
Medici Chapel, Florence; WORLD BOOK photo by Leonard von Matt

Piazza della Signoria, Florence; WORLD BOOK photo by Leonard von Matt

# SCULPTURE / 1600-1900

**European Sculpture.** The greatest master of European sculpture in the 1600's was Giovanni Lorenzo Bernini of Italy. Bernini was a superlative craftsman and also an outstanding architect. His sculpture for the *tomb of Pope Alexander VII* shows the wide range of his talent. The work is typical of the *baroque* style of the period because it was designed to appeal primarily to the emotions and senses. Bernini combined emotional and sensual freedom with theatrical presentation and an almost photographic naturalism. His saints and people seem to sit, stand, and move as living people—and the viewer becomes part of the scene. This involvement of the spectator is a basic characteristic of baroque sculpture.

The sculptors who succeeded Bernini in Rome during the late 1600's softened the dynamic and showy baroque style. They used a more static and restrained classical style. These artists were technically skilled, and made hundreds of monuments that filled the churches of the time. By the early 1700's, they had become more interested in technical skill than in content, and their art reflected the change. But these artists had an important influence on sculptors of France and Flanders who made up the Franco-Flemish school.

Franco-Flemish sculptors were responsible for many church and public monuments built in northern Europe during the 1700's. Their sculptures decorated many royal palaces and gardens, including Versailles in France. These artists all followed the same style. They combined naturalistic details with artificial poses and

St. Peter's Church, Rome; WORLD BOOK photo by Leonard von Matt

*Tomb of Pope Alexander VII* by Giovanni Lorenzo Bernini
Italy, 1671-1678. Marble and gilt bronze.
Figures over life size.

*A Shepherd Boy* by Bertel Thorvaldsen
Denmark, 1817-1825. Marble. 57 inches high.

Thorvaldsens Museum, Copenhagen, from Art Reference Bureau

*Mercury* by Antoine Coysevox
France, 1700-1702. Marble. About 10 feet high.

Gardens of the Tuileries, Paris; WORLD BOOK photo by Leonard von Matt

206k

# SCULPTURE

gestures, as shown in Antoine Coysevox's statue of *Mercury* (page 206k).

A brilliant new movement called *rococo* grew up. In Germany during the early 1700's, it was led by such artists as Ignaz Gunther and Ferdinand Dietz. Dramatic, colorful, and technically superb, its saints and goddesses mingle in architecture with plasterwork and painted ceilings to create an extraordinary world of fantasy.

The *neoclassical* movement arose in the late 1700's. The members of this vast international school restored what they regarded as classical principles of art. They were direct imitators of ancient Greek sculptors. They emphasized classical drapery and the nude. Leading neoclassical sculptors included Antonio Canova of Italy, John Flaxman of England, and Bertel Thorvaldsen of Denmark. Thorvaldsen's delightful marble statue *A Shepherd Boy* is typical of the neoclassical style (page 206k). This style greatly influenced churchyard and public monuments.

The *romantic* movement began in the 1830's, and existed side by side with neoclassicism until about 1900. Romantic sculpture was sentimental and it appealed to the senses. Leading sculptors who worked in the romantic style included François Rude, Jean Baptiste Carpeaux, and Auguste Rodin, all of France. Such works as Rodin's *Orpheus* emphasize the possibilities of the modeler's technique. Rodin's technique greatly influenced sculpture of the 1900's.

**American Sculpture.** North America had no professional sculptors until the late 1700's. However, anonymous craftsmen created fine examples of what is called *folk art*. The *gravestone* by Zerubbabel Collins and other gravestones in New England cemeteries reflect Puritan ideals in crude but vigorous reliefs. Many metal weathervanes were designed with fanciful imagination.

The earliest American sculptors made small wax portraits in relief, and decorative figures in wood. The finest of the early wood carvers was William Rush. His *allegorical* (symbolic) figures show the influence of the elegant European rococo style. Jean Antoine Houdon, the greatest French sculptor of his generation, came to America in 1785 to make a portrait statue of George Washington. Several less important Italian sculptors worked on the decorations of the United States Capitol in Washington, D.C., in the early 1800's.

In the 1820's, American sculptors started to go to Italy, where they were greatly influenced by the classical works they saw. Congress commissioned Horatio Greenough to make a colossal marble statue of George

*Orpheus* by Auguste Rodin
France, 1892. Bronze. 59 inches high.
Musée Rodin, Paris, from Art Reference Bureau

A New England gravestone by Zerubbabel Collins
United States (Columbia, Conn.), 1791. Marble. 31½ inches high.
WORLD BOOK photo by Robert Crandall

# SCULPTURE

*Washington.* Greenough represented his subject seated, semi-nude, in the pose of the Greek god Zeus. Hiram Powers created smooth and impersonal nude mythological figures, and some remarkable realistic portrait busts of public men. William Rimmer made a few dramatic, struggling figures, including *The Dying Centaur.* These figures were more emotional, powerful, and tragic than earlier American works. They showed a great knowledge of anatomy and a strong feeling of tension. John Rogers made small groups of Civil War scenes, and also created works that suggested the pleasant, warmhearted quality of small-town everyday life.

About the mid-1800's, French influence began to be felt more strongly than Italian. The greatest American sculptor of his period was Augustus Saint-Gaudens, best known for his statue of Abraham Lincoln.

Important sculptors of the late 1800's included Daniel Chester French, who made many serene and idealistic compositions, and George Grey Barnard, master of the expressive human figure. Frederick MacMonnies introduced extravagant and rich surface details into the monumental style. Frederic Remington showed another aspect of American life in his small bronzes. He used vivid, dramatic themes from the life of the Far West in such works as *The Cheyenne.*

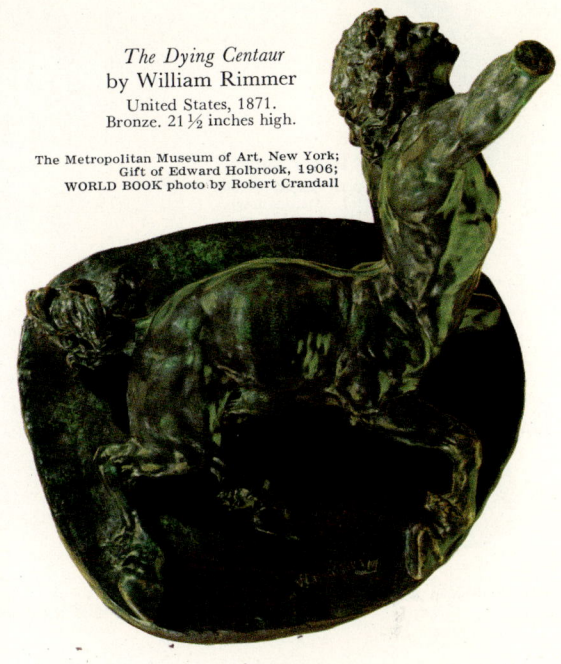

*The Dying Centaur* by William Rimmer
United States, 1871.
Bronze. 21½ inches high.

The Metropolitan Museum of Art, New York;
Gift of Edward Holbrook, 1906;
WORLD BOOK photo by Robert Crandall

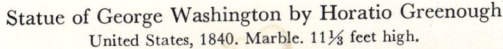

Statue of George Washington by Horatio Greenough
United States, 1840. Marble. 11⅛ feet high.
The Smithsonian Institution, Washington, D.C.;
WORLD BOOK photo by Robert Crandall

*The Cheyenne* by Frederic Remington
United States, 1901. Bronze. 23½ inches high.
Thomas Gilcrease Institute, Tulsa, Okla.;
WORLD BOOK photo by Bob Taylor

206m

# SCULPTURE / African

**A power figure**
Eastern Congo (Songe style), date unknown. Wood with glass beads, metal, horn, snakeskin, and hide. 35⅝ inches high.

Etnografisch Museum, Antwerp, Belgium, from Art Reference Bureau

**A *banda* mask**
Dance mask, Guinea, western Africa (Baga style), early A.D. 1900's. Painted wood. 56 inches high.

Museum Rietberg, Zurich, Switzerland; Wettstein and Kauf Foto, from Art Reference Bureau

**King Shamba Bolongongo**
Portrait of a Kuba king. Central Congo. About A.D. 1650. Wood, partially painted. 22 inches high.

British Museum, London, from Art Reference Bureau

African sculpture consists of figures, masks, and other decorated ceremonial and useful objects. Because most African sculptures were made in perishable materials, such as wood, few of these works are more than 100 or 200 years old. However, works in bronze, ivory, and terra cotta may date back several centuries. The oldest known African sculptures are terra-cotta figures created about 500 B.C. in the Nok culture of Nigeria. Wood carvings, terra-cotta works, and bronze castings still are being made in Africa, but increasingly for the tourist trade.

Figures and masks are found mainly in the western and central parts of Africa. Many figures represent ancestors—either the recently dead or the ancient, mythical tribal founders who watch over the well-being of the living. Most masks represent powerful spirits or legendary tribal ancestors. In the past, Africans believed that these spirits and ancestors would seek out and avenge wrong-doing, sanctify the position of youths just initiated into adult society, or perform other important tasks.

Many African figures are carved with details of costume, body decoration, and hairdo seen in everyday life, as in the portrait statue of *King Shamba Bolongongo* carved by a Kuba sculptor. In masks, on the other hand, African sculptors often use contrasting colors, weird shapes, and strange subject matter to achieve an uncanny appearance. The *banda* mask made by a Baga artist of the west coast of Guinea combines antelope, crocodile, and human forms, illustrating its supposed power to pursue evil forces over land and water.

Artists throughout Africa also carve decorated ceremonial and practical objects. Among the most impressive objects are those made for use at royal courts. They include royal stools, neckrests, ceremonial pipes, fly-whisks, crowns, staffs, bracelets, containers, cosmetic boxes, doors, and wall ornaments. These objects are elaborately carved to increase a king's importance in the eyes of his subjects and to glorify his office.

Most African sculptures perform more than one function. An example is the Kuba statue of *King Shamba Bolongongo*, a ruler in the central Congo in the mid-1600's. In illustrating the king's fleshy appearance, the statue also shows his health and wealth. In addition, the statue serves to house the king's second soul or "spirit double" which remained behind when the king died or was away on a journey. This statue sums up Kuba thinking about fertility, kingship, and the spirit world.

Much African sculpture shows attempts to gain control over human behavior and spiritual forces by the use of various artistic devices. For example, the people of Benin regarded their king as a god living on earth. In the *altarpiece* on page 198, the king is shown greatly enlarged to signify his political and spiritual power. An attendant on each side of the king suggests the balanced character and good judgment required of a monarch. By contrast, figures made by the Songe people of the eastern Congo serve mainly as *fetishes* (objects with magic power). Beads, horns, and skins attached to the Songe *power figure* activate the figure visually and increase its imagined power.

Despite its remarkable variations, African sculpture reveals a few recurring characteristics. Many of its forms have an expressive rhythm because the same shapes are repeated again and again. Various materials, including cloth, metal, raffia, and feathers, are added to these forms to give the art object a composite appearance in which many distinct textures function together as an ensemble. This emphasis on a cumulative effect is similar to the interweaving of varied instrumental and vocal rhythms so typical of traditional African music. See also AFRICA (The Arts).

# SCULPTURE / Pacific Islands

The masks and figures of Oceania are even more varied in appearance than are the sculptures of Africa. The islanders of the South Pacific produced sculptures in such extraordinary materials as bark cloth (Melanesia and Easter Island), feathers (Hawaii and New Guinea), cobwebs (New Hebrides), and pieces of turtle shell (Torres Strait). Giant stone figures, also rare in Africa, appear in Tahiti; Easter Island; the Austral, Marquesas, and Solomon Islands; and in several areas of Indonesia. Because most Oceanic sculptures were made of impermanent materials, most surviving works date from a period no earlier than the 1800's. The oldest known specimens probably date from the period between 1000 and 500 B.C.

The chief themes of Oceanic sculpture involve spirits, ancestors, monsters, and gods important to a local community. For example, the Baining people of New Britain make huge *hariecha* images from bamboo, leaves, and bark cloth—that is, from perishable materials. These images represent friendly spirits which are believed to attend the annual ceremony marking both the harvesting of crops and the initiation of boys into adult society.

The Asmat people of New Guinea carve their enormous *bis* poles as memorials to the recently dead. All these dead are believed to be victims of headhunting or witchcraft. The carvings represent gigantic soul boats that carry the souls of the dead and serve as a pledge of revenge by the living. The rough surfaces and bold, contrasting colors of the poles are characteristic of Melanesian art. Asmat sculptors also were probably influenced by Indonesian art. Soul boats have been an important theme in Indonesia since the beginning of Bronze-Iron Age culture there about 500 B.C.

In the Sepik River area of New Guinea, the people make masks of monsters and images of demons with extended tongues. An example is *drum with mask and hornbill*. The Sepik people believe these masks and figures have the power to drive away evil spirits or to harm enemies. The Sepik art style probably was influenced by ideas coming originally from southeast Asia or southern China, where similar demon images existed before 200 B.C. Sculptures resembling the Sepik faces are found in the arts of central Borneo and northern Sumatra. The Maori sculpture of New Zealand also shows a similar style.

The Baining also make bizarre-looking *owl masks* that appear in ceremonies designed to ensure the health and well-being of children. The colossal size, strange shapes, and perishable construction of these masks and figures typify the art of many other Melanesian peoples.

Color is unimportant in Polynesian sculpture. Instead, artists emphasize dignified, solid forms in space. In a unique image of the Polynesian supreme god *Tangaroa*, the god is shown creating the other gods out of his own body. Tangaroa's calm, motionless posture, contrasting with the active poses of the little figures, expresses his seniority and dignity. The Polynesians consider these qualities to be those of a superior social position. Here, too, in spite of the attention given to religious symbols, Oceanic art reveals a concern with rank or social standing.

**Drum decorated with mask and hornbill**
A dance drum from the Sepik River region of New Guinea. Melanesia, early A.D. 1900's. Wood with skin and string. 2 feet high.

British Museum, London, from Art Reference Bureau

**Tangaroa** *(below)*
Supreme god of Polynesia. Rurutu, Austral Islands. Polynesia, A.D. 1700's or early 1800's. Wood. 45 inches high.

British Museum, London, from Art Reference Bureau

**An owl mask**
A ceremonial mask of the Baining people of New Britain. Melanesia, date unknown. Cane and bark cloth. 31¼ inches high.

Museum für Völkerkunde, Basel, Switzerland; WORLD BOOK photo by Werner Bruggman

**A *bis* pole** *(right)*
A memorial pole of the Asmat people of southwestern New Guinea. Melanesia, date unknown. Wood. About 13 feet high.

Museum für Völkerkunde, Basel, Switzerland; WORLD BOOK photo by Werner Bruggman

# SCULPTURE / American Indian

American Indian cultures can be divided into two broad groups—pre-Columbian and tribal American Indian. Pre-Columbian cultures include the Mexican, Peruvian, and other highly developed civilizations which died out soon after the European discovery of the Americas. Tribal Indian cultures include all the less centralized, native peoples of North and South America except the Eskimos.

Pre-Columbian civilizations differed from tribal Indian cultures in having full-time priests, military leaders, traders, and artisans. This specialization enabled pre-Columbian societies to develop complex religions involving calendars and astronomical observations. These societies conquered and governed neighboring peoples and engaged in widespread trade, including the exchange of luxury goods. Specialization also encouraged their artisans to do elaborate work in such difficult materials as stucco, turquoise, and jade. By contrast, the art of tribal Indian communities scarcely approaches the level of sophistication achieved in the pre-Columbian civilizations.

The earliest pre-Columbian civilization, the Olmec, flourished about 1000 B.C. on the southern Gulf Coast of Mexico. Olmec sculpture consisted primarily of colossal stone heads, rock-cut reliefs, carved boulders, altars, giant stone slabs called *stelae*, and clay and jade figurines. Perhaps the most frequent theme in Olmec art was a half-jaguar, half-baby figure which many scholars identify as a rain god. An example is the jade *figure holding a jaguar-baby*. Olmec sculpture was more monumental in scale and plainer in design than later Mexican art styles. But, like the later styles, Olmec art emphasized ornate costumes and complex arrangements of figures. This emphasis on insignia and spatial organization indicates that the Olmec society was divided into distinct social classes.

After the Olmec culture died out, other major civilizations eventually emerged in Mexico. Among these were: (1) the Teotihuacán civilization, in the central highlands; (2) the Classic Veracruz civilization, on the Gulf Coast; (3) the Monte Alban civilization, centered in the Oaxaca Valley of western Mexico; and (4) the Maya civilizations of southern Mexico, Guatemala, and Honduras. Each of these interrelated cultures produced impressive stone and ceramic sculptures. The Maya made what are probably the finest works, as shown in *Lintel 25 from Yaxchilán*, a relief of a worshiper. The worshiper is offering sacrifices to a serpent-monster that spits out a warlike figure armed with a spear. This relief shows the Maya tendency to combine minute detail with fantastic imagery.

The warlike Toltec, Mixtec, and, later, Aztec cultures end the story of pre-Columbian civilizations in Mexico. The gruesome subject matter and heavy,

**Lintel 25 from Yaxchilán**
Relief showing a worshiper, *lower right*, kneeling before a double-headed serpent god. Mexico (Mayan style), probably A.D. 680. Stone. About 50 inches high.
British Museum, London, from Art Reference Bureau

**Figure holding a jaguar-baby**
Southern Mexico (Olmec style), 1000–300 B.C. Jade. 8⅝ inches high.
Guennol Collection, The Brooklyn Museum, New York

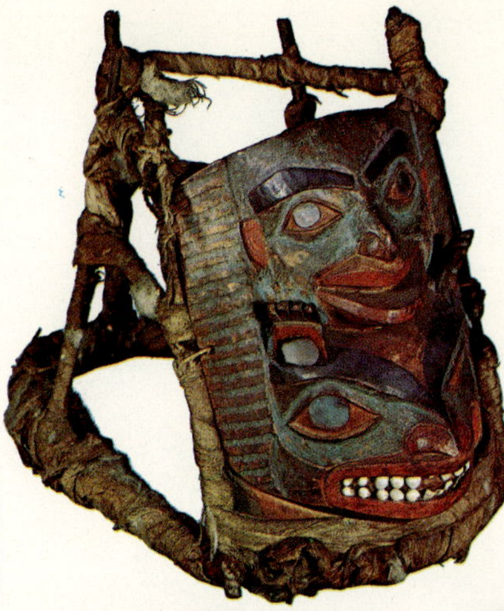

# SCULPTURE

blocky forms of *Xolotl, an Aztec death god*, illustrate the terrifying Aztec style (page 194).

Pre-Columbian civilizations also reached a high level in Peru and the adjacent regions of the central Andes mountains. The earliest major Peruvian art style is associated with the Chavin culture, which began about 800 B.C. Chavin sculpture consisted mostly of fanged human, jaguar, or bird gods created in stone, gold, shell, or ceramic. The stone *bowl in the form of a jaguar* is an example. Chavin art shares numerous traits with Early Chou art of China of the same date. Many scholars regard Chavin sculpture as one of the clearest instances of transpacific influences in the Americas.

The Mochica civilization flourished on the northern coast of Peru from about 100 B.C. to A.D. 800. Mochica artists modeled many funeral vessels that appear to be naturalistic portraits of important persons, as seen in the *Mochica portrait jar*. This realism eventually gave way to mechanical copying and the use of a few stylized forms in the Tiahuanaco, Chimu, and Inca civilizations that followed.

Pre-Columbian and tribal American Indian traditions are mingled together in the sculpture of the Arawak people of the Caribbean islands. In such works as the *zemi* (spirit) *figure*, the use of gold and shell-inlay indicates that these sculptures were produced by a wealthy society divided into social classes. But the simple, nearly nude forms of the body and the lack of insignia of status show that the Arawak culture was not so sophisticated as the pre-Columbian civilizations of Mexico or Peru.

The finest American Indian tribal sculptures are the masks, figures, and totem poles created by the peoples of the Pacific Northwest Coast. Animals, birds, fish, monsters, and spirits appear in such works as the *Nootka Indian headdress*. The animals and spirits are those believed to have given privileges to the founder of a particular family. Scholars have found striking similarities between certain Pacific Northwest Coast themes and the art of ancient China. These similarities suggest contacts between the two civilizations.

**Headdress**
Pacific Northwest Coast (Nootka Indian tribe), late A.D. 1790's or early 1800's. Wood inlaid with abalone shell and bone. 7¼ inches high.

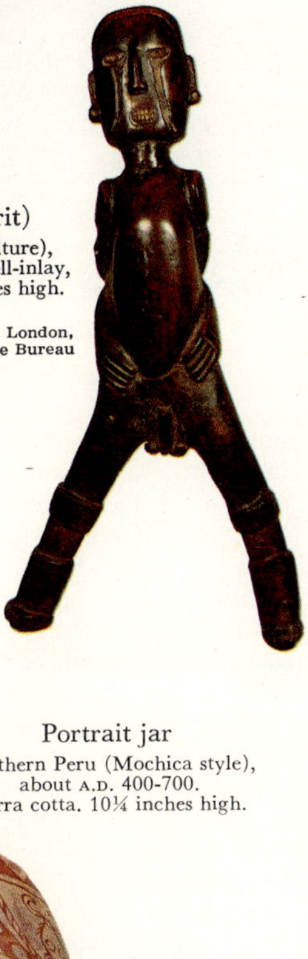

**Figure of a *zemi* (spirit)**
Jamaica (Arawak Indian culture), date unknown. Wood with shell-inlay, gold, and bark cloth. 40 inches high.

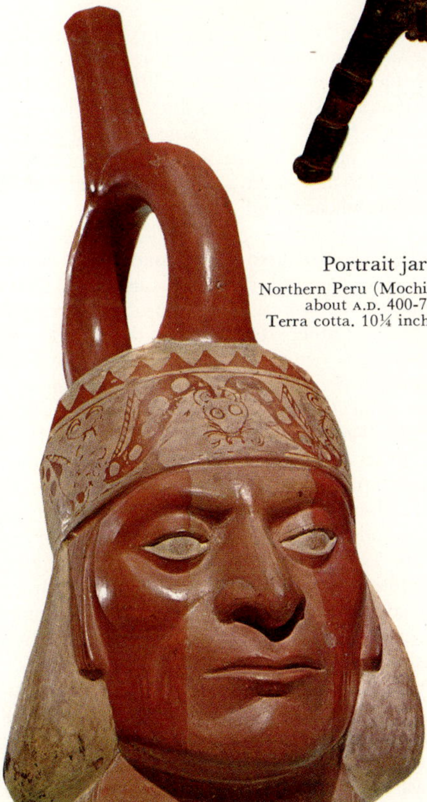

**Portrait jar**
Northern Peru (Mochica style), about A.D. 400-700. Terra cotta. 10¼ inches high.

**Bowl in the form of a jaguar**
Peru (Chavin style), about 1200-400 B.C. Stone. 6½ inches high.

206q

# SCULPTURE / Modern International

Sculpture of the 1900's has become increasingly international in character as national differences in sculpture have disappeared. Sculptors follow many different styles. Some continue in the classic figure traditions. Others distort and exaggerate the human figure for dramatic and expressive reasons. Still others express the human figure in increasingly abstract ways. Some kinds of earlier art, such as African sculpture, which had not previously influenced European and American artists, became a new source of inspiration.

Many sculptors have become more and more interested in problems of pure form, and avoid representational content. As a result, the human figure, which had been the great theme of sculpture for centuries, has become less and less important.

New ways of thinking about sculpture, plus the use of new materials, have resulted in exciting and original developments during the 1900's. A new sense of reality led some artists to introduce actual light and actual movement into their works. New relationships developed between the world of the artist and everyday modern life. One example was the use of fluorescent lights and searchlights in three-dimensional work. Artists also began to use the shapes of modern machines in their works. New materials, many of which were developed for industrial rather than artistic purposes, also had a distinct influence on modern sculpture.

A major influence on all forms of art in the 1900's has been the artist's concern with space. This interest has led to some unusual sculptures because, both historically and technically, sculpture has been an art of mass.

In the early 1900's, the great traditions of classic figure style were upheld by Aristide Maillol of France in such works as *Mediterranean*. His figures, whether in bronze or marble, have a noble tranquility and an almost Greek purity of form. Gaston Lachaise, a French artist who worked in the United States, used generously

*Seated Youth* by Wilhelm Lehmbruck
1918. Bronze. 41 inches high.

*The Mediterranean* by Aristide Maillol
About 1901. Bronze. 41 inches high.
The Museum of Modern Art, New York; Gift of Stephen C. Clark

rounded, classic figures. But he gave them an astonishing lightness—a combination of the robust and the delicate. More recently, beginning in the 1930's, Giacomo Manzù of Italy showed that a deep concern with the human figure is still possible in our time. He combined most of his figures with religious subject matter. There has not been a humanistic relief style of comparable delicacy and power since the Italian Renaissance.

Many sculptors have used the human figure for increasingly expressive and dramatic purposes. These artists often used exaggeration or distortion to increase the intensity and immediate impact of their works. In such works as *The Reunion*, the German woodcarver Ernst Barlach created squat figures whose passion and intensity resemble Gothic sculpture. Wilhelm Lehmbruck, another German sculptor, greatly elongated the human figure in *Seated Youth* and other works. This style created forms of extreme sensitivity. Sir Jacob Epstein of England developed a brilliant style, particularly in such bronzes as *The Visitation*. He presented the human figure, especially the individual portrait head, with great authority and insight. The Swiss sculptor Alberto Giacometti created bronzes of human figures that seem to be increasingly consumed by the active and aggressive space around them. Such works as *Man Pointing* are so thin that they seem to be a kind of painful drawing in space, rather than sculpture in the traditional, three-dimensional sense. Pablo Picasso, the Spanish-born artist who launched many movements in painting, was also a sculptor. He handled figures of animals and humans with abstract and expressive

# SCULPTURE

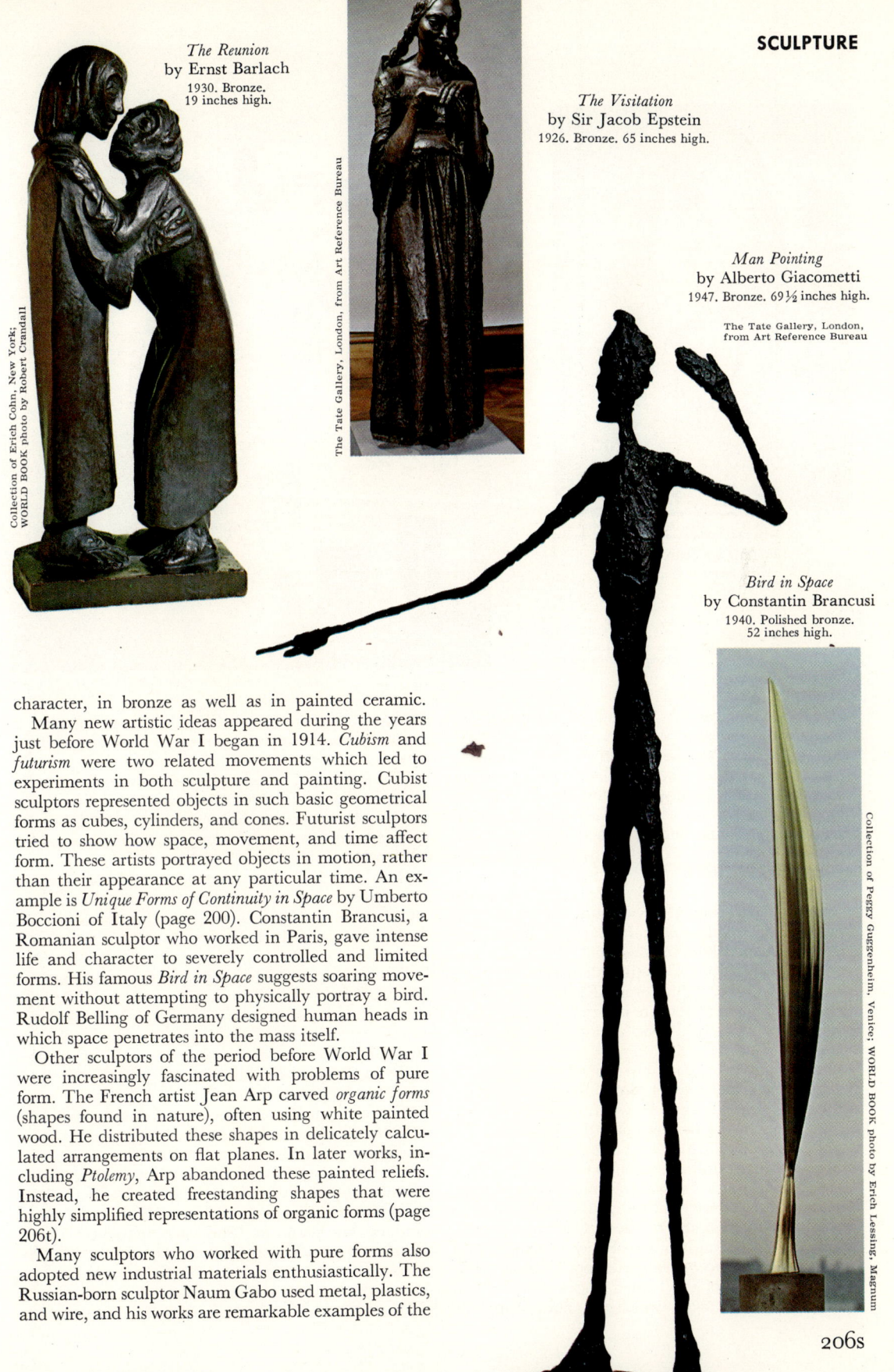

*The Reunion*
by Ernst Barlach
1930. Bronze.
19 inches high.

*The Visitation*
by Sir Jacob Epstein
1926. Bronze. 65 inches high.

*Man Pointing*
by Alberto Giacometti
1947. Bronze. 69½ inches high.

*Bird in Space*
by Constantin Brancusi
1940. Polished bronze.
52 inches high.

character, in bronze as well as in painted ceramic.

Many new artistic ideas appeared during the years just before World War I began in 1914. *Cubism* and *futurism* were two related movements which led to experiments in both sculpture and painting. Cubist sculptors represented objects in such basic geometrical forms as cubes, cylinders, and cones. Futurist sculptors tried to show how space, movement, and time affect form. These artists portrayed objects in motion, rather than their appearance at any particular time. An example is *Unique Forms of Continuity in Space* by Umberto Boccioni of Italy (page 200). Constantin Brancusi, a Romanian sculptor who worked in Paris, gave intense life and character to severely controlled and limited forms. His famous *Bird in Space* suggests soaring movement without attempting to physically portray a bird. Rudolf Belling of Germany designed human heads in which space penetrates into the mass itself.

Other sculptors of the period before World War I were increasingly fascinated with problems of pure form. The French artist Jean Arp carved *organic forms* (shapes found in nature), often using white painted wood. He distributed these shapes in delicately calculated arrangements on flat planes. In later works, including *Ptolemy*, Arp abandoned these painted reliefs. Instead, he created freestanding shapes that were highly simplified representations of organic forms (page 206t).

Many sculptors who worked with pure forms also adopted new industrial materials enthusiastically. The Russian-born sculptor Naum Gabo used metal, plastics, and wire, and his works are remarkable examples of the

206s

# SCULPTURE

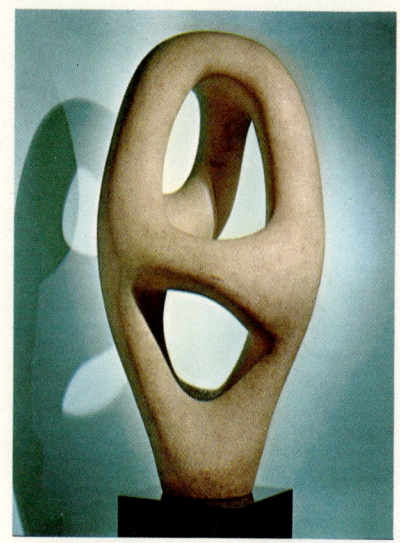

Collection of Mr. and Mrs. William A. M. Burden,
New York; WORLD BOOK photo by Robert Crandall

*Ptolemy* by Jean Arp
1953. Cast limestone. 40 inches high.

*The Family* by Marisol
1962. Painted wood and other
materials. 82⅝ inches high.

The Museum of Modern Art, New York

use of these new materials. Alexander Calder used various metal and wire shapes in such mobiles as *Red Petals* (page 200). Louise Nevelson, an American sculptor born in Russia, assembled machine-made wooden objects into extraordinary sculptures. Many of her works are complex compartments which seem to open into or to suggest eternity. The interest in actual movement in sculpture is brilliantly shown in the work of José de Rivera of the United States. His elegant, twisted steel forms move mechanically and rotate slowly. The works of the American sculptor David Smith are much more dramatic and forceful (page 194). Harry Bertoia, an American sculptor born in Italy, makes vast screens of metal forms with open areas that allow space to move back and forth through the work. Richard Lippold of the United States creates wire designs of refined architectural quality in such works as *Variation Number 7: Full Moon* (page 193).

Other sculptors have not abandoned the representation of human and animal forms, but have handled these forms in significant new ways. Jacques Lipchitz, an American, has worked in many different styles. He is probably best known for his powerful and expressive figures, which are full of symbolic movement. Henry Moore of England makes vast reclining wood or stone figures (page 203). Holes in the figures allow space to move freely through the massive blocks of material. Another British sculptor, Reg Butler, balances thin figures against space in an exciting, unusual way. Theodore Roszak of the United States shapes rough textured forms of metal which are not identifiable images of men or animals. They have a strong sense of organic form, however, and seem to grow physically in space.

The machine, which plays such a basic role in modern life, has become an important influence on artistic developments. Not only have machine forms and industrial materials become part of the present-day art world, but the actual machine is being used as an artistic material. The American sculptor Richard Stankiewicz uses wheels, boilers, chains, bolts, and other actual mechanical parts. He puts them together in new ways and often gives them a dramatically humanistic quality.

Some young artists have avoided the use of machine parts, but have created works that appear to have been produced by machines. These sculptors have produced forms in aluminum, plastics, and other industrial materials which remain severely geometrical, deliberately anonymous, and almost totally impersonal. Such work has been called *minimal art*.

The clear distinction between sculpture and other art forms has become less and less definite. Artists create sculptures from shaped and painted canvas, solid colored forms, and combinations of many materials. In *The Family*, the American sculptor Marisol wittily combined painting and sculpture with objects of actual clothing and furniture. She often introduces plaster casts of her own face and hands in her work. MULK RAJ ANAND, JOHN BOARDMAN, DOUGLAS FRASER, H. D. MOLESWORTH, BERNARD MYERS, SIR HERBERT READ, and ALLEN S. WELLER

Critically reviewed by SIR HERBERT READ

# SCULPTURE / Study Aids

**Related Articles.** See the Arts sections of the various country articles, such as JAPAN (Arts). See also the following articles:

### AMERICAN SCULPTORS

Borglum, Gutzon
Calder, Alexander
Crawford, Thomas
Dallin, Cyrus E.
Davidson, Jo
Fraser, James E.
French, Daniel C.
Greenough, Horatio
Hoffman, Malvina
Lipchitz, Jacques
Manship, Paul
Milles, Carl W. E.
Noguchi, Isamu
Powers, Hiram
Remington, Frederic
Russell, Charles M.
Saint-Gaudens, Augustus
Segal, George
Taft, Lorado
Zorach, William

### FRENCH SCULPTORS

Bartholdi, Frédéric A.
Barye, Antoine L.
Brancusi, Constantin
Coysevox, Antoine
Goujon, Jean
Houdon, Jean A.
Maillol, Aristide
Rodin, Auguste

### GERMAN SCULPTORS

Barlach, Ernst H.
Lehmbruck, Wilhelm
Riemenschneider, Tilman
Stoss, Veit

### ITALIAN SCULPTORS

Bernini, Giovanni L.
Canova, Antonio
Cellini, Benvenuto
Da Vinci, Leonardo
Della Robbia (family)
Donatello
Ghiberti, Lorenzo
Michelangelo
Pollaiuolo, Antonio del
Verrocchio, Andrea del

### OTHER SCULPTORS

Archipenko, Alexander
Epstein, Sir Jacob
Giacometti, Alberto
Lysippus
Mestrovic, Ivan
Moore, Henry
Phidias
Picasso, Pablo
Praxiteles
Thorvaldsen, Bertel

### FAMOUS SCULPTURES

Elgin Marbles
Farnese Bull
Hand (pictures)
Hermes of Praxiteles
Laocoön
Liberty, Statue of
Mount Rushmore National Memorial
Nefertiti
Sphinx
Statuary Hall
Stone Mountain
Tanagra Figurines
Venus de Milo
Winged Bull
Winged Lion
Winged Victory

### HISTORY OF SCULPTURE

Ancient Civilization (The Arts)
Assyria (Art and Architecture; pictures)
Aztec (The Arts)
Babylonia (Art; picture)
Egypt, Ancient (The Arts; pictures)
Etruscan (Language and Culture; pictures)
Greece, Ancient (The Arts)
Indian, American (Sculpture)
Maya (The Arts; pictures)
Persia, Ancient (pictures)
Roman Empire (The Arts)

### KINDS OF SCULPTURE

Bust
Carving
Collage
Gargoyle
Idol
Intaglio
Mask
Mobile
Relief
Sarcophagus

### METHODS AND MATERIALS

Alabaster
Bronze
Cast and Casting
Clay
Ebony
Fiber Glass
Iron and Steel
Ivory
Jade
Lacquer
Marble
Plaster of Paris
Plasticine
Plastics
Terra Cotta
Welding
Wood Carving

### STYLES

Baroque
Byzantine Art
Carolingian Art
Classicism
Cubism
Futurism
Gothic Art
Humanism
Impressionism
Renaissance
Rococo
Romanticism

### OTHER RELATED ARTICLES

Africa (The Arts)
Art and the Arts
Asia (Art)
Australia (Arts)
Design
Europe (Arts)
Latin America (Arts)

### Outline

I. The Importance of Sculpture
II. The Sculptor at Work
III. Sculpture as an Art Form
IV. Looking at Sculpture
V. The Beginnings
VI. Oriental Sculpture
VII. Greek Sculpture
VIII. Etruscan and Roman Sculpture
IX. Medieval Sculpture
X. Italian Renaissance Sculpture
XI. 1600-1900
XII. African Sculpture
XIII. Pacific Islands Sculpture
XIV. American Indian Sculpture
XV. Modern International Sculpture

### Questions

Why did prehistoric peoples create sculpture?
What is the lost-wax method of casting?
In what type of sculpture did the Romans excel?
What is (a) sculpture in the round? (b) relief sculpture? (c) true relief? (d) intaglio?
How can sculptors create the illusion of movement in their works?
What is the purpose of sculpture in Oriental civilizations?
How can we develop an appreciation of the qualities of sculpture?
What rules did Egyptian sculptors follow when carving the human figure?
Why have some modern sculptors avoided representations of human and animal figures?
What is an armature? How and why is it used?

### Books for Young Readers

ALLEN, AGNES. *The Story of Sculpture.* Roy, 1958.
GLUBOCK, SHIRLEY. *The Art of Ancient Egypt.* Atheneum, 1962. *The Art of Ancient Greece.* 1963. *The Art of Lands in the Bible.* 1963. *The Art of Ancient Rome.* Harper, 1965.
RUSKIN, ARIANE. *The Pantheon Story of Art for Young People.* Pantheon, 1964.

### Books for Older Readers

BOARDMAN, JOHN. *Greek Art.* Praeger, 1964.
FRASER, DOUGLAS. *Primitive Art.* Doubleday, 1962.
GARDNER, ALBERT TEN EYCK, comp. *American Sculpture: A Catalogue of the Collection in the Metropolitan Museum.* Metropolitan Museum of Art, 1965.
HAGGAR, REGINALD G. *Sculpture Through the Ages.* Roy, 1962.
MOLESWORTH, H. D. *European Sculpture: From Romanesque to Neoclassic.* Praeger, 1965.
MYERS, BERNARD. *Sculpture: Form and Method.* Reinhold, 1965.
READ, HERBERT. *The Art of Sculpture.* 2nd ed. Pantheon, 1961.
ENCYCLOPEDIA OF WORLD ART. 14 vols. McGraw-Hill, 1959-1967.

## SCUP

**SCUP** is the common name for two kinds of ocean fish. The northern scup ranges from Maine to North Carolina. The southern scup ranges southward from North Carolina. They are about 18 inches long, weigh about 4 pounds, and live on the ocean bottom.

**Scientific Classification.** The northern scup is in the porgy family, *Sparidae*. It is genus *Stenotomus*, species *S. versicolor*. Southern scup is *S. chrysops*. LEONARD P. SCHULTZ

**SCURVY** is a disease caused by lack of *ascorbic acid* (vitamin C) in the diet. Foods especially rich in this vitamin include citrus fruits, tomatoes (raw or cooked), raw cabbage and lettuce, celery and onions, cress, fresh carrots, and potatoes. These foods must be fresh to be useful in supplying vitamin C.

If a person does not get enough vitamin C, any wound he might have heals poorly. He also bruises easily. The walls of the *capillaries* (small blood vessels) become so weak that slight pressure may cause them to break. The mouth and gums become sore. The gums bleed and the teeth may become loose. The patient loses his appetite, his joints become sore, and he becomes restless. Anemia may also develop.

Foods that contain vitamin C prevent scurvy. They will also cure most cases of scurvy. Proper sanitary habits are also important. Treatment may include the use of antiseptic mouth lotions, blood tonics, and ascorbic-acid tablets.

Scurvy was once a common disease among sailors. During long voyages, sailors rarely had fresh fruits and vegetables. They lived on salt beef and *hardtack* (dry biscuits) for weeks at a time. Portuguese navigator Vasco da Gama once lost 100 out of 160 men from scurvy. In 1795, the British Navy began issuing daily rations of lime juice to its men in order to prevent the disease. British sailors got the nickname *limeys* from this practice.

Improved understanding of food requirements has made scurvy rare. Today, scurvy is mainly a disease of babies and elderly persons whose diets are inadequate. Scurvy in infants is called *Barlow's disease*. It usually occurs when breast feeding stops. Bottle-fed babies should drink orange juice or tomato juice after the first month. Mothers should give fruit juices regularly to infants learning to drink from a cup.     J. F. A. MCMANUS

See also VITAMIN (Vitamin C).

**SCUTCHING.** See FLAX (Processing Fiber Flax).

**SCYLLA,** *SIL uh*, in Greek mythology, was at first a beautiful nymph. The sea-god Glaucus fell in love with her when he saw her walking on the shore by the Strait of Messina. She would not love him, and so he went for help to the sorceress, Circe. Circe asked him to love her instead of Scylla, but Glaucus would not. In a jealous rage, Circe turned Scylla into a dreadful sea monster, part woman and part fish, with heads of dogs growing out of her waist.

Scylla then lived in a cave above the Strait of Messina opposite the whirlpool Charybdis. She seized and ate sailors that came too close. When Ulysses passed that way, she seized six of his men (see ODYSSEY; ULYSSES). Sailors who went through the Strait tried to steer a middle course *between Scylla and Charybdis*. This expression is sometimes used when a person speaks of having to take a course between two evils. JOSEPH FONTENROSE

**SCYTHE,** *sithe*, is a hand-harvesting implement with a curved cutting blade. It has a long, bent wood handle, called a *snath*, with a short bar for each hand, distinguishing it from the *sickle*, that has a short handle for one hand. The *cradle scythe* has fingers or light rods which receive the grain and lay it in even *gavels* on the stubble in the field. See REAPING MACHINE.     A. D. LONGHOUSE

**SCYTHIAN,** *SITH ih un*, was a member of an ancient group of nomads that lived in southern and eastern Europe between the 600's B.C. and the A.D. 100's. The Scythians wandered from southern Russia, near the Black Sea, eastward to the Altai Mountains in central Asia. They also went westward into what are now Bulgaria, Romania, Hungary, Poland, and East Germany. They were defeated by the Sarmatians, another nomadic tribe, in the 200's B.C., and were completely wiped out by the Goths in the A.D. 100's.

The Scythians were wealthy and somewhat cultured. They decorated their jewelry and implements with distinctive animal designs, which influenced the arts of other European peoples. Historians do not know if the jewelry and implements were made by Scythians or by the Greeks with whom they traded. Their jewelry, horses, and weapons were buried with them when they died. Each chieftain's grave also included one of his wives and several servants, who were strangled. Graves were covered with mounds of earth.     JACOB J. FINKELSTEIN

**SEA.** See OCEAN.

**SEA ANEMONE,** *uh NEM oh nee*, is a sea animal that looks like a flower called the *anemone*. The shape of the animal's body and its bright color give it a plantlike appearance. Its body may be blue, green, pink, red, or a combination of colors. The sea anemone can move slowly. But it usually remains fixed to a rock or other surface. Sea anemones are *coelenterates*, the group of water animals that also includes the corals, hydras, and jellyfish. The sea anemone's body diameter varies from about $\frac{1}{4}$ inch in some *species* (kinds) to more than 3 feet in the giant sea anemone of Australia.

Like some other coelenterates, sea anemones are *polyps*. One end of the cylinder-shaped body attaches to rocks, shells, or wharf pilings. The other points out from the surface. This end has a mouth surrounded by *tentacles* (tiny arms). Sea anemones capture food with their tentacles. Stinging cells in the tentacles throw out tiny poison threads that paralyze other small sea animals and tiny fish. Then the tentacles drag the prey into the mouth. The mouth leads directly to a large cavity, where the food is digested. When a sea anemone is disturbed, it pulls in its tentacles and shortens its body. It then looks like a round lump on a rock.

A sea anemone reproduces by forming eggs, by dividing in half, or by *budding*. When it buds, a young sea anemone grows out of the base of the parent's body. Eventually, it breaks off and grows by itself.

**Scientific Classification.** Sea anemones belong to the phylum *Coelenterata*. They are classified in the class *Anthozoa*.     ROBERT D. BARNES

See also ANIMAL (color picture: Animals of the Oceans); OCEAN (color picture: Benthos).

**SEA ANIMAL.** See FISH; CORAL; CRUSTACEAN; DUGONG; MOLLUSK; SEA COW; SEAL; SPONGE; TURTLE; WALRUS; WHALE; OCEAN (color pictures).

**SEA BASS.** See BASS; JEWFISH.

**The Sea Anemone Eating a Fish** which has been paralyzed by barbed threads shot from the anemone's tentacles. Now that the fish is helpless, the anemone uses its tentacles to draw its prey slowly toward the small round mouth opening.

Dever, Croy, Unger, Black Star

**The Tentacles of the Sea Anemone** are beautifully colored, but their touch means death to small fishes and other digestible sea animals.

**The Foot of the Sea Anemone** allows it to slide about very slowly on rocks and corals.

# SEA BAT

**SEA BAT** is a fish with a batlike shape and stubby armlike fins. Its snout juts forward and is covered with small sensitive projections. Its body is protected by a bony covering. Sea bats are found in the warm waters of the western Atlantic Ocean. Sea bats are also known as *batfish*.

**Scientific Classification.** Sea bats belong to the batfish family, *Ogcocephalidae*. The common sea bat is classified as genus *Ogcocephalus*. LEONARD P. SCHULTZ

**SEA BIRD.** See BIRD and the separate articles on Oceanic Birds listed in the Related Articles section.

**SEA COW,** or MANATEE (MAN uh TEE), is a large water animal that looks somewhat like a seal. It belongs to the same *order* (group) of mammals as the dugong (see DUGONG). The sea cow is native to the coasts of South America, the West Indies, and Africa. In the United States, it may be found in the warm waters off the coast of Florida. The sea cow lives in both fresh and salt water, where it browses on water plants. It has been hunted much for its flesh, hide, and oil.

The sea cow grows from 8 to 13 feet long and has a

**The Florida Sea Cow** can perform the trick of standing partly out of the water, balanced on its broad tail. Although the front legs can be used as paws, the sea cow is helpless on land.

grayish black skin. It is an awkward animal, with no hind legs. Its front legs are paddle-shaped. The sea cow has a rounded tail, while the dugong's tail is forked.

The sea cow's upper lip is divided into two parts. The halves close on weeds and water grasses like a pair of pliers. On a still night the sea cow's flapping lips and crunching teeth can be heard 200 yards away.

**Scientific Classification.** The sea cow belongs to the family *Trichechidac*. It is genus *Trechichus*. There are three species. *T. manatus* lives in northern the southern United States, the Caribbean, and northeastern South America. *T. inunguis* lives in the Amazon Valley. *T. senegalensis* lives in West Africa. REMINGTON KELLOGG

**SEA CUCUMBER** is a sea animal with a cylinder-shaped body that looks like a cucumber. It belongs to a group that includes sea lilies, sea urchins, and starfish. The sea cucumber either lies on one side on the sea bottom or burrows in the sand. Its mouth is at one end of the body. Ten branching tentacles encircle the mouth. The animal can lengthen and shorten these tentacles, which catch food and sweep it into the mouth. There are five double rows of *tube feet* on the body, and some sea cucumbers use them to crawl. Some can also throw out sticky, threadlike tubes from inside their body when another animal attacks. These tubes block the attacker's movements while the sea cucumber crawls away. The sea cucumber then grows a new set of tubes.

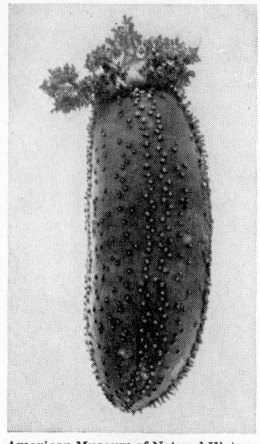

American Museum of Natural History

**The Sea Cucumber** looks as if it came from a garden, instead of the ocean floor.

About 500 *species* (kinds) of sea cucumbers live in the oceans of the world. Those living in tropical waters may grow 2 to 3 feet long. Sea cucumbers in temperate waters are a few inches to a foot long. Many sea cucumbers are caught in Indonesia, where they are dried and sent to Chinese markets as a food called *trepang*.

**Scientific Classification.** Sea cucumbers belong to the phylum *Echinodermata*. They make up the sea cucumber class, *Holothuroidea*. ROBERT D. BARNES

See also ECHINODERM; TREPANG.

**SEA DOG.** During the Elizabethan Age (late 1500's), English pirates and privateers who raided Spanish towns and shipping in America and nearby waters were called *sea dogs*. Their daring attacks threatened Spanish holdings in America and nearly drove the Spanish fleet from the seas. Today, the term is applied to any experienced sailor.

**SEA ELEPHANT,** or ELEPHANT SEAL. See SEAL.

**SEA FAN** is a colorful coral that has a flat, fanlike shape. It is made of a horny material which is called *gorgonin*. The fan has many openings, and grows about 2 feet tall. Sea fans live in shallow water at the bottom of the sea, especially in parts of the Pacific Ocean and along the eastern Atlantic Coast near Florida, Bermuda and the West Indies. They are known for their beautiful yellow, orange, red, and purple colors.

**Lacy Sea Fan Arms** sway gracefully with underwater currents on coral reefs.

D. P. Wilson

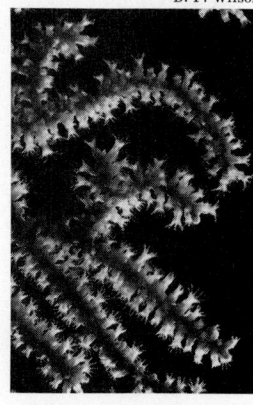

**Scientific Classification.** Sea fans belong to the family *Gorgoniidae*. The sea fan is genus *Gorgonia*, species *G. flabellum*. LEONARD P. SCHULTZ

See also CORAL.

**SEA GULL,** any gull found on or near the sea. See GULL.

**SEA HORSE** is a small, odd-shaped fish that lives in the sea. The sea horse is so named because its head resembles that of a tiny horse. Another name for the sea horse is a scientific term, *Hippocampus*, which comes from Greek words meaning *horse* and *sea monster*. The sea horse is in the same family as pipefishes. Numerous species live in tropical and temperate waters.

The sea horse has a long snout and prominent eyes. The body is about 6 to 10 inches long, and is covered by spiny, bony plates, like armor, that protect it from its enemies. It ends in a long tail, which can coil around objects. A tail of this kind is called *prehensile*. The sea horse uses its tail to cling to rooted plants or growths of floating sea vegetation. It moves about in an upright position, weakly swimming with its dorsal fin. It is usually carried along by the currents.

Sea horses mate in the spring and summer. The female lays about 200 eggs, and the male sea horse keeps them in a pouch located on the underside of his body

# SEA MAMMALS

Geographers use mean, or average, sea level as a starting point for measuring height or depth on earth. For example, Mount McKinley in Alaska is 20,320 feet *above* sea level. Death Valley, in California, is 282 feet *below* sea level. SIGISMOND DE R. DIETTRICH

**SEA LILY** belongs to a class of lovely sea animals called *crinoids*. The animals have arms and stalks that make them look like flowers. They get their name from this appearance. Crinoids were abundant in past ages, but only a few kinds exist today.

Sea lilies usually live in the deep waters of all the seas. A long stalk attaches a typical sea lily to the sea bottom. The main part of the body, called the *calyx*, is at the top of the stalk. The calyx contains the animal's vital organs. Five featherlike arms branch out from the calyx. The arms screen out tiny plants and animals from the water. This food is passed in grooves to the mouth, which is in the center of the

New York Zoological Society

**The Sea Horse** is the only fish that has a grasping tail. The heads of sea horses are sometimes preserved, fitted on wood bases, and then used as knights in the game of chess.

Rochester Museum of Arts and Sciences

**The Sea Lily** is an animal, not a plant. It received its name because it resembles a flower. Its slender stalk ends in a tubelike foot. The sea lily's foot serves as an anchor.

until the eggs hatch. Sea horses live for as long as six years.

**Scientific Classification.** The sea horse belongs to the pipefish family, *Syngnathidae*. The sea horse found along the Atlantic Coast of the United States is genus *Hippocampus*, species *H. hudsonius*. LEONARD P. SCHULTZ

**SEA LEOPARD,** or LEOPARD SEAL. See ANTARCTICA (Seals and Whales; picture: Animal Life).

**SEA LEVEL** is the level of ocean waters. It is not the same in all parts of the world, and it changes with every tide. For purposes of measurement, a definite average of sea levels at various times has been agreed upon by scientists who must use sea level in their studies.

top of the calyx. *Feather stars* are in the same animal class as sea lilies. They have no stalks and are not attached to the sea bottom. They swim by moving their arms. Most feather stars live in tropical seas. There are many more species of feather stars than sea lilies.

**Scientific Classification.** Sea lilies and feather stars belong to the phylum *Echinodermata*. They make up the class *Crinoidea*. ROBERT D. BARNES

See also OCEAN (color picture: Benthos).

**SEA LION.** See SEAL.

**SEA MAMMALS** are mammals that live in the sea. See CETACEAN; DOLPHIN; DUGONG; OTTER; PORPOISE; SEA COW; SEAL; SIRENIA; WALRUS; WHALE.

# SEA NECKLACE

**SEA NECKLACE.** See CONCH.

**SEA OF CORTES.** See GULF OF CALIFORNIA.

**SEA OF GALILEE** is a small fresh-water lake in the northern district of Palestine. It is often mentioned in the Bible. The sea is called the *Sea of Chinnereth* in the Old Testament. The name Galilee is used in the New Testament. This sea is also called *Gennesaret*, for the plain that lies to the northwest, and *Tiberias*, for a city on its shore. The sea is also known as *Lake Kinnereth*.

The Sea of Galilee lies on the Jordan plain in Israel, 30 miles from the Mediterranean. It touches Syria on the northeast. For location, see ISRAEL (color map). The River Jordan flows through the Sea of Galilee on its southward course to the Dead Sea, into which it empties. The Sea of Galilee is 14 miles long and 8 miles across at its broadest point. Many fish live in it. Gently sloping hills lie along the shores, except where the plain of Gennesaret meets the sea. Figs, olives, dates, and pomegranates grow on the southern hills.

The ancient cities of Magdala, Capernaum, and Bethsaida were once situated on the northern shores of Galilee. Today, only ruins of them remain.

It was beside the Sea of Galilee that Jesus performed a miracle to feed loaves and fishes to a large gathering (John 6: 1-14). Another Bible story tells of Jesus' walk along the shore to recruit disciples from among the fishermen (Matt. 4: 17-20).   LOYAL DURAND, JR.

### Sea of Galilee
**Area:** 64 square miles
**Elevation:** 688 feet below sea level
**Deepest Point:** 145 feet

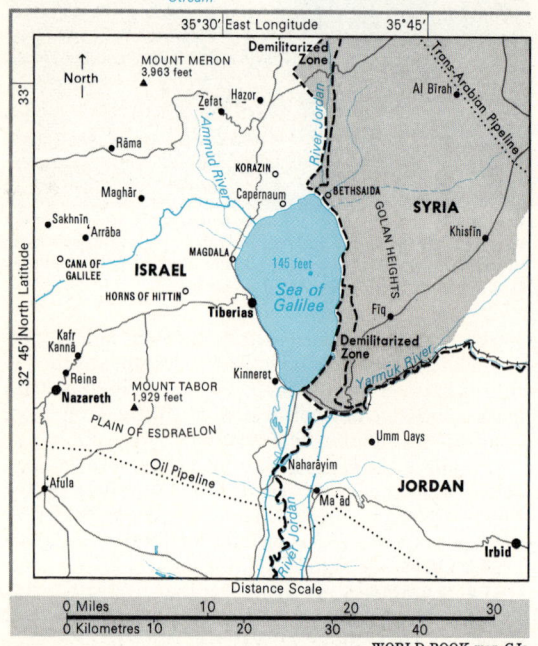

WORLD BOOK map-GJa

**SEA OF JAPAN, BATTLE OF THE.** See RUSSO-JAPANESE WAR (Last Battles).

**SEA ONION.** See SQUILL.

**SEA PARROT.** See PUFFIN.

**SEA PIE.** See OYSTER CATCHER.

**SEA PIGEON.** See GUILLEMOT.

**SEA PLANT.** See MARINE BIOLOGY with its list of Related Articles.

**SEA SERPENT** is an imaginary creature dating from ancient times. It has appeared in the legends of most peoples. In early times, many people believed in sea monsters. Today, reports of such monsters result from imaginative memories, unreliable observations, or deliberately false stories.

Many marine animals have been mistaken for sea serpents, including arctic or basking sharks, whale sharks, large eels, and oarfish. Giant sea squid or cuttlefish have also been called sea serpents.

**SEA SHELLS.** See SHELL.

**SEA SQUIRT** is a name for a group of sea animals which are also called *ascidians*. These animals have a habit of squirting out water through one of two body openings. Adult sea squirts have leathery bottle-shaped bodies. All their adult lives they remain attached to stones, shells, and other fixed objects. Some live together in colonies. The adult animal receives its food from water which it draws into the digestive tract through one of the body openings, the mouth. It squirts out the water from the other opening, the *atriopore*.

Sea squirts go through a larval stage before they become mature. The larva looks like the frog tadpole and can swim about freely. It has a *notochord* (elastic rod), which extends through the tail. Because the larva has this rodlike "backbone," scientists think the sea squirts are relatives of the simplest fishlike animals, *lancelets* and *lampreys*. After a few days, the larval sea squirt loses its tadpole shape and settles on the ocean floor. Soon it develops its adult form.

**Scientific Classification.** The sea squirt is a member of the subphylum *Tunicata*. It makes up the class *Ascidiacea*.   LEONARD P. SCHULTZ

Russ Kinne, Photo Researchers

**A Sea Squirt** is a jellylike animal that lives on the ocean bed. It squirts out water through a hole in the side of its body.

**SEA STAR.** See STARFISH.

**SEA TROUT.** See WEAKFISH.

**SEA URCHIN** is a sea animal. Its body is shaped like a ball and is covered with long, movable spines. Close-fitting limestone plates lie just under the skin and form an internal shell called a *test*. The long spines grow from

212

# SEAFOOD

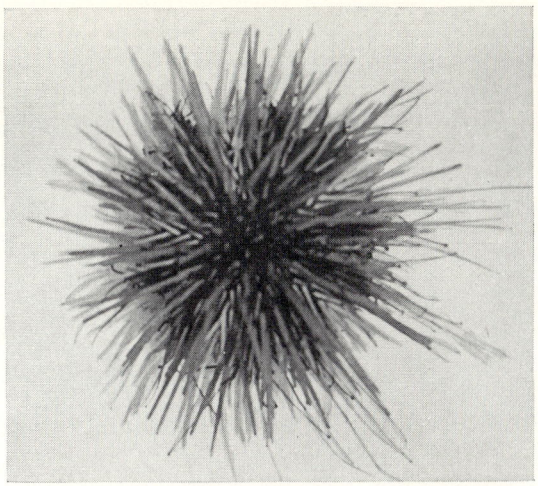

Ralph Buchsbaum

**A Sea Urchin,** *above,* may grow up to 7 inches in diameter. Long, sharp spines stick out from its body in all directions. The spines grow from a hard, limestone shell, *below,* that protects the animal's soft body. Sea urchins' shells make attractive ornaments.

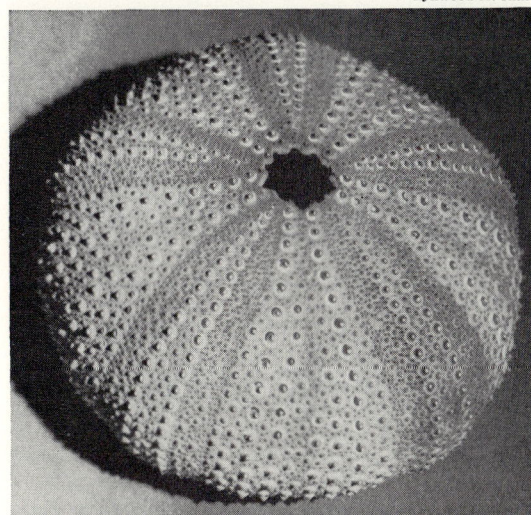

Lynwood M. Chace

these plates and stick out through the skin. The sea urchin is in the same animal group as the starfish, sea lily, sand dollar, and sea cucumber.

Sea urchins are called *scavengers* because they feed on decaying matter. But they also eat seaweed and living animals found on rocks and the sea bottom. The sea urchin's mouth is in the center of its lower surface. The animal chews with its five sharp teeth. Body wastes and eggs leave the animal through openings in the center of its upper surface. Sea urchins move by the pushing action of their spines and tiny *tube feet,* which have sucking disks attached. The tube feet are pushed out through small holes in the test. Some sea urchins can dig holes into rock with their teeth, or by rotating their spines.

**Scientific Classification.** Sea urchins belong to the sea urchin class, *Echinoidea* of the phylum *Echinodermata.*           ROBERT D. BARNES

**SEA WALNUT.** See CTENOPHORE.
**SEA WATER, PURIFICATION OF.** See WATER (Fresh Water from the Sea).
**SEABEES** are members of U.S. Navy construction battalions. The name *Seabees* is taken from the first letter of each word of the official name, Construction Battalion. Seabees build and repair overseas bases to support Navy and Marine Corps forces. They are also trained to defend what they build. They have built bases from the tropics to the North and South polar regions, and their work includes projects such as airfields and waterfront facilities. Most of the World War II Seabees were experienced carpenters, plumbers, electricians, and engineers who left civilian jobs to join the Seabees. They earned their "Can Do" reputation on such islands as Guadalcanal, Tarawa, and Guam.

The first battalion of Seabees was authorized on Jan. 5, 1942. The official birthday of the construction battalions is March 5, the date in 1942 on which they received authorization to call themselves *Seabees.* Since World War II the Seabees have been made a permanent part of the U.S. Navy.           EUGENE J. PELTIER

**SEABORG, GLENN THEODORE** (1912-     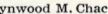     ), is one of the American scientists responsible for the development of the atomic bomb. He shared the 1951 Nobel prize for chemistry with Edwin M. McMillan for the discovery of artificial elements heavier than uranium. Seaborg is a discoverer of elements 94 through 98, and of element 101 of the periodic table. These are *plutonium, americium, curium, berkelium, californium,* and *mendelevium.* Seaborg and his coworkers produced these elements in the cyclotron at the University of California at Berkeley. Seaborg also discovered many radioactive isotopes used in medical therapy and in biological and chemical research. He obtained his Ph.D. degree in 1937 from the University of California. He joined the Manhattan Project in 1942, and worked out on a minute scale the process for separating plutonium from uranium. This process was magnified 10 billion times to produce enough plutonium for the first atomic bomb. Seaborg was chancellor of the University of California from 1958 until 1961, when President John F. Kennedy appointed him chairman of the Atomic Energy Commission. He was born in Ishpeming, Mich.           HERBERT S. RHINESMITH

**Related Articles** in WORLD BOOK include:

| | | |
|---|---|---|
| Americium | Element, Chemical (table) | Mendelevium |
| Atomic Energy Commission | Manhattan Project | Nobel Prizes (picture) |
| Berkelium | | Plutonium |
| Californium | | |
| Curium | | |

**SEABURY, SAMUEL** (1729-1796), became the first American Episcopalian bishop in 1784. He served as the first presiding bishop of the Protestant Episcopal Church from 1789 to 1792. Seabury was born at Groton, Conn. He was ordained in 1753. During the American Revolutionary War, his Tory sympathies cost him his position, and he supported his family by practicing medicine and serving as a regimental chaplain in the British Army.           EARLE E. CAIRNS

**SEAFOOD.** See FISH (Importance to Man). See also FISHING INDUSTRY with its list of Related Articles.

213

# SEAL

Steve McCutcheon
**Many Northern Fur Seals Spend the Summer on Alaskan Islands, and Travel South for the Winter.**

**SEAL** is a sleek sea animal with a body shaped like a torpedo. Seals are excellent swimmers and divers, and spend much time in the water. But they give birth to their young on land.

Most kinds of seals live in the oceans or in inland seas. A few kinds are found in fresh water. The Baikal seal, for example, lives in Lake Baykal in southern Russia.

Some kinds of seals, including harbor seals and ringed seals, spend much of their time on land or on floating chunks of ice. Northern fur seals, on the other hand, stay at sea for six to eight months. Every year these seals *migrate* (travel) about 5,000 miles—farther than any other mammal. They swim south from the Bering Sea almost to the northern border of Mexico, and then return north. During the entire trip, the seals swim from 10 to 100 miles from the coast and never go ashore. No one knows why the seals make their long trip every year.

The largest seal is the southern elephant seal, which lives in the sub-Antarctic waters off South America. The male may grow to be 21 feet long and may weigh up to 8,000 pounds. This seal ranks second in size only to whales among all sea mammals. The smallest seal is the ringed seal of the Arctic. It is about $4\frac{1}{2}$ feet long and weighs up to 200 pounds.

*Karl W. Kenyon, the contributor of this article, is a wildlife research biologist for the U.S. Fish and Wildlife Service.*

Men hunt some kinds of seals chiefly for their soft, silky fur. The fur wears well and makes excellent coats, hats, and trimming for cloth coats. The yearly U.S. catch of northern fur seals is worth about $3\frac{1}{2}$ million. After the fur has been removed, the seal meat may be frozen and sold as animal food. The meat also can be ground into meal for use as fertilizer or poultry feed.

Some Eskimos and other Alaskans eat seal meat. The meat has such a strong flavor that most people in other parts of the world do not like it. Seal blubber is used for cooking, or is burned for light and heat. Eskimos also make hunting clothes from the skins of ringed seals,

---
**FACTS IN BRIEF**

**Names:** *male,* bull; *female,* cow; *young,* calf, pup, or whelp; *group,* herd or pod.

**Gestation Period:** About 8 to 12 months, depending on the species.

**Number of Newborn:** Usually 1, rarely 2.

**Length of Life:** 40 years or more.

**Where Found:** Along the coasts of continents in most parts of the world; a few kinds in fresh-water lakes and inland seas.

**Scientific Classification:** Seals make up the pinniped order, *Pinnipedia.* Fur seals and sea lions belong to the eared seal family, *Otariidae.* Walruses belong to the walrus family, *Odobenidae.* Elephant seals and harbor seals belong to the earless seal family, *Phocidae.*

---

214

## SEAL

and use walrus hides to cover the wooden frames of their boats. They stretch the intestines of seals and sew them together in strips to make raincoats.

Seals make up a group of mammals called *Pinnipedia*. This name comes from Latin words meaning *fin-footed*. A seal's flippers look somewhat like fins.

There are three main groups of pinnipeds: (1) eared seals, which include fur seals and sea lions; (2) earless seals, including harbor seals and elephant seals; and (3) walruses. An earless seal has small ear openings, but no ears on the outside of its body. Walruses also have small ear openings but no outside ears. They are the only pinnipeds with tusks.

### The Body of a Seal

Most kinds of seals have hair on their bodies, but some adult male walruses are almost hairless. Fur seals have thick coats of fine hair. Like all other mammals with fur, seals shed their coats every year and grow new ones. Most species of seals shed a few hairs at a time, much as cats and dogs do. Elephant seals lose large pieces of skin and hair, and the peeling fur makes them look ragged.

All seals have a layer of blubber that may be an inch to six inches thick. It helps keep the animals warm, and gives them energy when they can get no food.

**Head.** Some kinds of seals have small heads with short noses that give their faces a "pushed in" appearance. An elephant seal has a long, curved nose. The male hooded seal's nose joins a pouch that extends over the top of its head. When the animal is annoyed, it blows air into the pouch. The outer skin of the nose and pouch expands like a balloon, and forms a bright red hood on the animal's head. The seal uses its hood to frighten enemies. All seals have slitlike nostrils, which they close when they dive or swim under water.

The eyes of most species of seals are large and shiny, but walruses have small eyes. Most seals can see and hear well, but they have a poor sense of smell.

**Flippers.** Seals have four legs, but the leg bones above the ankles are buried inside the body. The parts that extend outside, including the feet, form the animal's large, paddlelike flippers. The front flippers of fur seals and sea lions are longer and flatter than those of other species. A fur seal's front flippers may be more than 1½ feet long and 6 inches wide, and help make this animal a powerful swimmer. The front flippers of earless seals are smaller and narrower than those of fur seals. Earless seals swim by moving their bodies and rear flippers much as fish move their bodies and tails. A frightened fur seal can swim as fast as 10 miles an hour for about five minutes, but then it tires and slows down.

Fur seals, sea lions, and walruses turn their rear flippers forward and downward to help support their bodies on land. They walk on all four flippers. The rear flippers of earless seals extend straight back, palm to palm. These seals cannot turn their flippers forward. They pull themselves across land or ice by contracting their strong belly muscles.

### The Life of a Seal

Most kinds of seals live in groups and may stay together on long ocean journeys. A few species, including the Ross seals of the Antarctic, live alone or with only two or three other seals. Some species, including grey seals and ringed seals, have lived 40 years or more.

**Seal Rookeries.** Every spring, seals go to their breeding grounds, called *rookeries*, to have young and to find mates. Most rookeries are on islands. Rookeries of northern fur seals are large beach areas, and more than 150,000 seals may gather at one rookery.

The northern fur seal *bulls* (males) are the first to arrive at the rookeries. Late in May their bellows and roars can be heard more than a mile away as they fight for their choice of places, called *territories*, along the beach. The *cows* (females) come ashore in early July and join the *harem* (group of females) of one of the bulls. A bull's harem consists of 3 to more than 40 cows, and a few bulls may have more than 100 cows. Shortly after a cow arrives on shore, she gives birth to the baby she has carried inside her body for about 12 months. The cow mates again a few days after giving birth.

Bull seals fight to get their territories and to protect them, but they do not fight to get cows. Bulls are not strong enough to hold a territory until they are about 10 years old. The young bachelors, and older bulls without harems, live apart from the others. Most cow seals bear their first young when they are about 5 years old, and may give birth each year until they are 13. Some cow seals may bear young until they are 20 or older.

**Young.** A female seal almost always has one *pup* (baby seal) at a time. Twins are rare. A newborn pup has all its teeth, and fine, soft fur covers its body. Sea lion pups have brown fur, and newborn fur seals, elephant seals, and monk seals have black coats. The

## THE SKELETON OF A SEAL

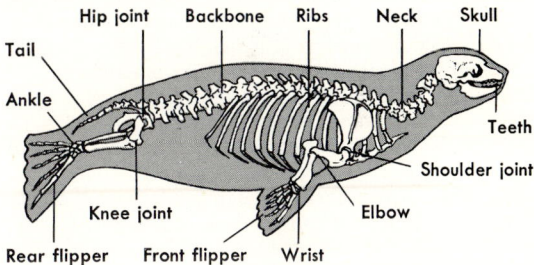

WORLD BOOK illustration by Tom Dolan

## WHERE SEALS LIVE

The black areas of the map show the parts of the world where seals are found. Most seals live in the Northern Hemisphere.

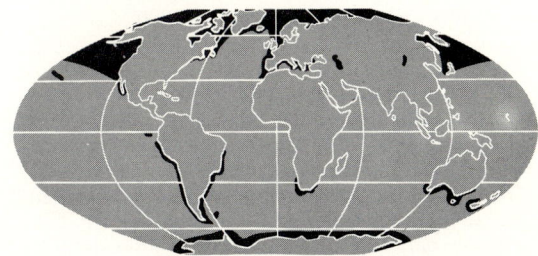

215

**A California Sea Lion** stands on its rear flippers and uses its nose to shoot a ball into the basket. These seals learn tricks easily and are star performers in many zoos and circuses.

**The Elephant Seal,** sometimes called the *sea elephant,* is named for its large nose, which grows about 15 inches long. The animal's tough skin also looks somewhat like an elephant's hide.

pups of harp seals, leopard seals, walruses, and other seals that live on floating islands of ice may be white, grayish, or brown.

Northern fur seal pups can swim and can travel on land as soon as they are born. The mothers divide their time between eating at sea and nursing their pups on land. A mother may stay at sea from seven to nine days. After she returns, she hunts for her pup among the hundreds of others on the beach. Each mother feeds only her own pup, which she recognizes by its cry and its odor. The pup gets enough milk to stay alive until its next feeding. Seal milk is rich, and the pups grow quickly. A fur seal weighs about 10 pounds at birth. The pup weighs from 30 to 35 pounds three or four months later, when its mother leaves it.

**Food.** Seals eat fish, sea birds, and squids. Leopard seals and walruses sometimes eat other seals. Crabeater seals, which live on floating ice in the Antarctic, do not eat crabs. Their food consists of shrimp and small fish.

A seal has sharp, pointed teeth. It cannot chew food because its teeth do not have flat surfaces. Seals grasp and tear most of their prey, but they swallow small fish whole, head first. Walruses are the only seals with tusks. They probably use their tusks somewhat like skis to skid along the ocean bottom. A walrus uses its tongue like a vacuum tube to eat clams, its favorite food.

**Enemies.** The seal's greatest enemy is man. For hundreds of years, hunters have killed seals for blubber, bones, fur, and meat. During the 1800's, so many seals were killed that only a few survived. Several nations, including the United States, quarreled about how northern fur seals should be hunted. In 1911, they agreed to limit the hunting. In 1957, Canada, Japan, Russia, and the United States signed a treaty to protect seals. In 1963, the treaty was extended for six years.

The number of seals has increased because of careful international management of seal hunting. In 1911, there were only about 150,000 northern fur seals on the Pribilof Islands. Today, there are about 1½ million. The yearly harvest of skins averages about 60,000. Under the treaty, seals are hunted commercially only on land. Canada and Japan do not hunt seals because none of the rookeries are in their territory. The Soviet Union and the United States each give 15 per cent of their catch to Canada and 15 per cent to Japan. In this way, the seal catch is shared by all the nations in whose territory the animals live.

All U.S. sealing is done by men employed by the federal government. The sealskins are given to private firms for processing and selling, and the money goes into the U.S. Treasury. Alaska gets 70 per cent of the money under the terms of its statehood act. Congress gives some of the rest to the Bureau of Commercial Fisheries, which manages the fur seal industry.

Seals have few enemies beside man. Large sharks and killer whales attack them in the water, and polar bears hunt seals on ice. A seal has few defenses against its enemies. In the water, it usually tries to escape an attacker. Some species swim swiftly and easily among the strong waves and between the large rocks close to shore where most of their enemies cannot follow. Other species take deep dives when an enemy approaches. A Weddell seal of the Antarctic can dive as deep as 2,360 feet. It can stay underwater as long as 43 minutes before surfacing to breathe.

Many kinds of seals are so slow and clumsy on land or ice that they have little chance of escaping an enemy. The crabeater is one of the fastest seals on land or ice. It can move about 15 miles an hour—almost as fast as a man can run. KARL W. KENYON

**Related Articles** in WORLD BOOK include:

Alaska (Natural Resources; Wildlife Products)
Animal (color picture: Animals and Their Young)
Antarctica (Seals and Whales)
Bering Sea Controversy
Eskimo
Fur
Pribilof Islands
Walrus

**SEAL** is a device with a design or lettering for *impressing* (stamping) on paper, wax, or metal. Seals are often attached to official and important documents to prove that they are trustworthy. Every country in the world and many cities, states, provinces, important officials, and commercial enterprises have seals. They are also used by private citizens.

The *matrix* (mold) of a seal may be made of paper, metal, or gem. It may consist of two pieces, the *baso* (bottom) and *alto* (top). The matrix is used for stamping one design on paper. It can also be used to stamp different designs on the *obverse* (front) and the *reverse* (back) of wax or lead.

In early times, kings and other government officials wore signet rings. They pressed the design of the ring on hot wax to make a seal. ARTHUR E. DuBois

For a description and color picture of each state seal in the United States, see each state article. See also BABYLONIA (Art and Architecture); GREAT SEAL OF THE UNITED STATES; NAPOLEON I (picture); PRIVY SEAL; SEALING WAX.

**SEALING WAX** is used for sealing letters and documents and for taking the impression of seals (see SEAL [a design or lettering]). The wax may be made of rosin, shellac, turpentine, magnesia, chalk, or gypsum. Wax also may be used for sealing bottles and jars.

Before envelopes with gummed flaps were invented, sealing wax was used to seal letters. Wax used for letters and documents is colored with vermilion, a red coloring matter. It is sold in a stick form. An inferior grade of sealing wax used for sealing packages is usually colored with lampblack. An inexpensive wax for sealing fruit bottles and jars may be made by mixing nine parts of rosin with one part beeswax, and heating the mixture until it melts. The necks of the bottles should be dipped in the melted wax. GEORGE R. GREENBANK

**SEALYHAM TERRIER** is a strong, short-legged, white-and-brown dog. It is a good rat catcher, and can be trained to pull animals such as the fox and otter out of burrows. The Sealyham stands 10 inches high, and weighs about 20 pounds. It has a long head, powerful jaws, and a blunt, heavy muzzle. Its wiry coat is white, with brownish patches on the head. It was first bred at Sealyham, Wales, about 1850. See also DOG (color picture, Terriers). JOSEPHINE Z. RINE

**SEAM.** See COAL (Coal Beds); SEWING.
**SEAMANSHIP.** See NAVIGATION.
**SÉANCE.** See SPIRITUALISTS; MESMER, FRANZ.
**SEAPLANE.** See AIRPLANE (Kinds of Airplanes).
**SEAPORT.** See HARBOR; PORT.
**SEARCH, RIGHT OF.** See RIGHT OF SEARCH.
**SEARCH WARRANT** is a paper issued by a court, which permits a law officer to search a house or other building. It is issued if there is reasonable cause to believe that illegal equipment, such as gambling devices, burglar tools, or counterfeiting machinery, is hidden there. A search warrant may also be issued to search for persons. In the United States Constitution, Amendment 4 states that no unreasonable searches or seizures may be made. The cause of search must be supported by oath. The search warrant must describe the place to be searched, and what is to be seized in the search.

Before 1760, search warrants in England and America were issued only for concealed stolen goods. In England, searches and seizures became so great an issue, and were finally so restricted, that it led to the saying that "every man's home is his castle." FRED E. INBAU

**SEARCHLIGHT** is a device that projects a beam of light. Electricity usually provides the power for searchlights. A concave reflector or a lens focuses the light into nearly parallel rays. Automobile headlamps act as small searchlights. They produce beams of light with both a concave mirror and a glass lens. Beacons in lighthouses and along airways are searchlights specially designed for these purposes. Some searchlights used in war to spot enemy airplanes have concave mirrors 60 inches in diameter. MATTHEW LUCKIESH

See also BEACON.

**SEARLES LAKE.** See MOJAVE.
**SEARS, PAUL BIGELOW** (1891-    ), an American botanist, became an authority on pollens, applied ecology, and the history of climate. He taught at the University of Nebraska, the University of Oklahoma, and Oberlin College. Sears became chairman of the Yale University conservation program, and wrote *Deserts on the March* (1935), *Life and Environment* (1939), *This Is Our World* (1939), and *This Useful World* (1941). He was born at Bucyrus, Ohio. ROGERS McVAUGH

**SEARS, ROEBUCK AND COMPANY.** See MAIL-ORDER BUSINESS.

**SEASHORE.** See OCEAN (The Changing Shoreline).
**SEASHORE, CARL EMIL** (1866-1949), an American psychologist, became known for his studies of musical ability. He pioneered in the scientific testing of hearing, and his measures of musical ability have been widely used in guiding and selecting students in music. He was born at Mörlunda, Sweden.

**SEASICKNESS** is a disagreeable illness that comes from the pitching and rolling of a ship at sea. The symptoms include dizziness and headache, nausea, a sinking feeling in the stomach, and vomiting. In a severe attack, the skin becomes pale, almost green, and damp, the pulse is feeble, and the person feels exhausted.

Doctors have given several different explanations of seasickness. The one most widely accepted says that the ailment is caused by disturbance in the semicircular canals of the inner ear. These canals give a person his sense of equilibrium. Some persons get the illness by swaying in a hammock, or from traveling by airplane.

Persons who become seasick easily can make the attacks less severe. During the week before a voyage, they should keep their bowels active, and should eat simple but nourishing food. It is well to eat plenty of fresh fruit and vegetables and avoid heavy, rich foods. Enough sleep and daily exercise in the open air will also help.

On a rough sea, a person can help overcome his nausea by lying quietly in a steamer chair on deck, with his eyes closed. If he has a bad attack, he should stay in his berth in a well-ventilated cabin.

Seasick persons have different reactions to food and drink. Some feel better if they eat no solid food for a day or more. But if the attack continues, the ship's doctor should take charge of the case, to see that the patient does not suffer a collapse. Drugs such as hyoscine and Dramamine help prevent and treat seasickness. They are usually effective with most people. PAUL R. CANNON

See also AIRSICKNESS; DRAMAMINE.

# SEASON

**SEASON.** Changes of temperature and changes in the lengths of the days and nights divide the year into natural periods that we call seasons. These seasons, spring, summer, autumn, and winter, have old names. *Spring* is an Anglo-Saxon word that means *rising; summer* comes from a Sanskrit word for *season. Autumn* is a form of the Latin word for *maturing,* and *winter* is an Anglo-Saxon word for *wet season.*

March, April, and May are the months of spring in the northern part of the world. Spring begins about March 21 and ends on about June 21. In leap years, spring begins slightly earlier than in the three other years. Summer begins on June 21, 22, or 23, and ends on September 22, 23, or 24. Although the earth receives the greatest heat from the sun on June 22, the warmest weather of the year usually comes several weeks later. The autumn season starts on about September 23 and continues until about December 21. The cold, windy, and cloudy days of autumn are interrupted by a period of fair weather and warm days called *Indian Summer.* Winter starts about December 21 or 22, and includes the months of January and February. During the winter season, the days are short and the weather is cold in the northern part of the world.

In the Southern Hemisphere, the seasons are reversed. Spring begins in September, summer in December, autumn in March, and winter in June. The seasons south of the equator are generally milder than those in the Northern Hemisphere.

Changes of season are caused by movement of the earth around the sun. The earth makes one complete revolution around the sun in a year. The earth is always tipped at an angle of about $23\frac{1}{2}°$ from a line perpendicular to its path around the sun. The northern half of the earth receives more sunlight when the axis is tipped toward the sun, and less when the axis is tipped away from it. See WEATHER (Temperature Patterns).

The vertical rays of the sun reach the northernmost point on the earth's surface about June 21. This is called the *summer solstice,* and marks the beginning of summer in the Northern Hemisphere and of winter in the Southern Hemisphere. About December 21 or 22, the sun's vertical rays reach the southernmost point on the earth, and winter begins in the Northern Hemisphere as summer starts in the Southern Hemisphere.

On about March 21, the sun is at its *vernal equinox,* or directly over the equator. Spring begins then in the Northern Hemisphere, and autumn begins in the Southern Hemisphere. Summer lasts from about June 21 until the *autumnal equinox* about September 23. Autumn extends from about September 23 until the *winter solstice* about December 22.

These are the four astronomical seasons. The four seasons of our Temperate Zone occur at almost the same time. Elsewhere, the Torrid Zone generally has only a wet and a dry season. The polar regions also have only two seasons during the year, a light season and a dark season. W. ELMER EKBLAW

**Related Articles** in WORLD BOOK include:

| | | |
|---|---|---|
| Autumn | Mythology | Spring |
| Equinox | (Explanatory Myths) | Summer |
| Indian Summer | Solstice | Winter |

**SEASONING.** See COOKING; SPICE.

**SEATO.** See SOUTHEAST ASIA TREATY ORGANIZATION.

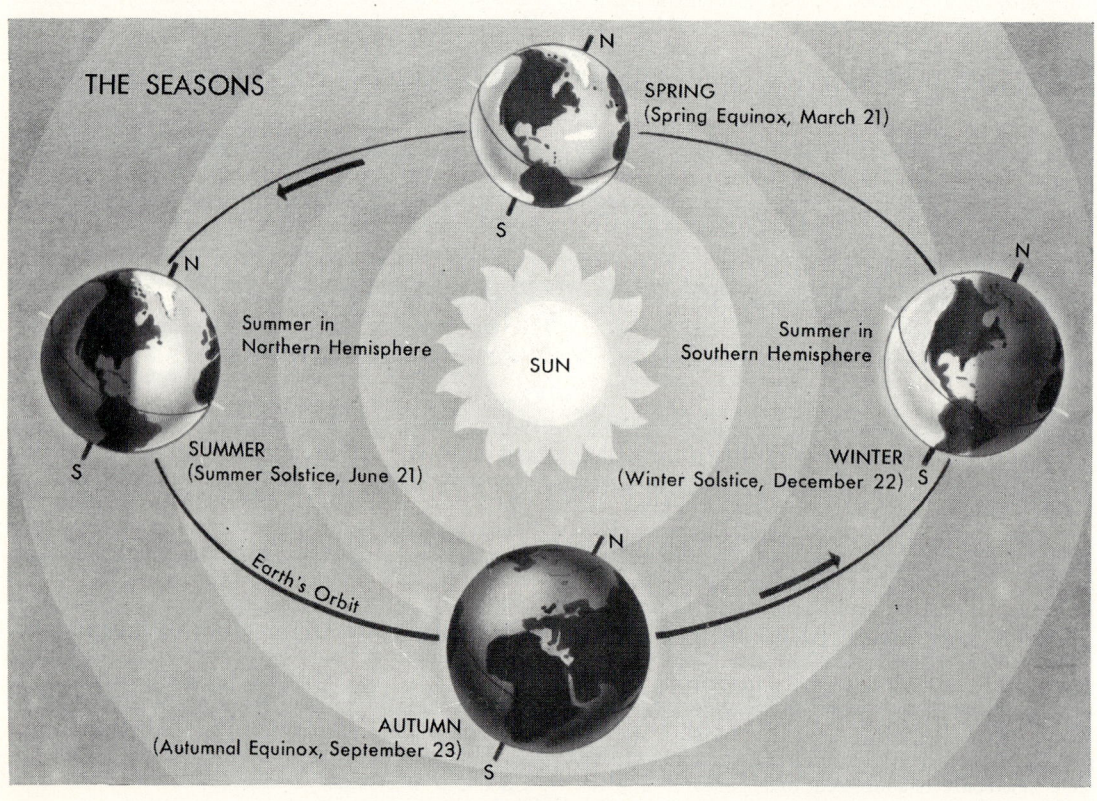

THE SEASONS

Bob and Ira Spring

**Seattle's Space Needle and Mount Rainier** stand as landmarks of the city. The 600-foot-high tower was built for the 1962 Seattle World's Fair.

**SEATTLE,** Wash. (pop. 557,087; met. area, 1,107,-213), is the largest city of the Pacific Northwest. It is the fourth largest seaport of the Pacific Coast. Seattle is the headquarters of the Northwest fishing industry, including the rich Alaska salmon fisheries. The city is the trading and transportation center for a region rich in timber, metals, and fertile farmlands. For location, see WASHINGTON (political map).

During World War II the population of Seattle was almost doubled when the city became an important center of naval shipbuilding and aircraft construction.

Seattle was named for Chief Seattle, a Dwamish Indian who was friendly to early settlers in the 1850's.

### Location, Size, and Description

Seattle lies on Elliott Bay, on the east shore of Puget Sound. It is about 900 miles north of San Francisco, and about 125 miles from the Pacific Ocean.

The city is built on seven hills that rise steeply from the shore of Puget Sound. East of Seattle is Lake Washington, a beautiful body of fresh water that is twenty-four miles long. The lake and the sound are connected by an eight-mile channel through Lake Union, the Hiram Chittenden locks, and a ship canal. These locks rank next in size to those of the Panama Canal. Lakes Washington and Union serve as a fresh-water extension of the Puget Sound water front. A United States Naval Air Station is located on Lake Washington.

Seattle is situated near a scenic wonderland of evergreen forests, clear lakes, and rugged, snow-capped mountains. The hills on which the city is built rise as high as 514 feet above sea level, and give a clear view of this scenery from most parts of the city. Across Puget Sound lie the Olympic Mountains. To the east rise the mountains of the Cascade Range, including Mount Rainier, one of the highest peaks in the United States.

The area of Seattle is about 92 square miles. The central business district of the city extends eastward from the water front for eighteen city blocks. The district covers five blocks on the higher but flatter ground to the north. The residential districts are located on the hillsides. These hills were at one time serious handicaps to the streetcar, bus, and automobile traffic. By using water with great pressure, however, sections of the hills were washed into the bay. This extended the shore line and created new ground covering about 1,400 acres for an industrial area. The height of some streets was cut as much as 130 feet by this operation.

The city is surrounded by residential and industrial suburbs. Many beautiful homes have been built in the residential areas.

### Cultural Life

Seattle is the home of the University of Washington, which is the largest institution of higher learning in the Pacific Northwest, and also of Seattle University. Colleges in the city include Seattle Pacific College, the Academy of the Holy Names, and the Cornish School of Music, Drama, and Dance.

The Seattle library system is made up of a large central library and 18 branches. Excellent collections of paintings and other examples of the fine arts are maintained in the Seattle Art Museum and the Henry Art Gallery on the campus of the University of Washington. The Seattle Center opened in 1962. It consists of the Opera House, Playhouse, and Exhibition Hall.

**Parks and Playgrounds** cover about 3,500 acres in Seattle. The largest parks include Lincoln, Volunteer, and Woodland. Many of the parks are located on hills and have been left in a natural state. The mild climate permits flowers and shrubbery to flourish the year round in Seattle, which adds greatly to the beauty of the parks. The city has 30 miles of scenic boulevard, and 10 public bathing beaches. In the winter, skiers can use six

University of Washington

**The University of Washington Campus** lies on the shore of Union Bay in northern Seattle. It was opened in 1861.

major ski areas near the city. Thousands of visitors come to the Seattle area for water and mountain sports.

### Industry and Trade

The port of Seattle is one of the best equipped in the United States, and ranks high in the amount of tonnage handled during each year. Seattle is a general cargo port, and exchanges goods with practically all of the ports of the world. It is served by over 250 steamship lines and agencies. The port facilities include wharves, transit sheds, cold-storage warehouses, grain elevators, and steam and electric freight-handling equipment.

Seattle has about 1,500 industrial plants which normally employ about 80,000 workers. The city has progressed rapidly as a manufacturing center because the region nearby is rich in water power, coal, lumber, and other raw materials. The products of Seattle industries include aircraft, flour, meat, lumber and wood products, metal products, clay products, cement, textiles, and fishing supplies. Ships and small boats are built in shipyards along the Sound. The processing of canned and frozen fish is an important industry of the city. Fruits, vegetables, tea, coffee, and spices are also prepared for market in Seattle.

**Transportation.** Four transcontinental railroads enter Seattle, and branch lines provide connections with the water front. Federal highways stretch north and south along Puget Sound and eastward through the Cascade Mountains. Two bridges of floating concrete pontoons extend across Lake Washington, providing passage for automobiles and trucks. There is ship service in the summer to Victoria, B.C. Ferries run to Bremerton, Wash., and other Puget Sound ports. Several major airlines use the Seattle-Tacoma International Airport. In 1962, a monorail train began operating between downtown Seattle and the World's Fair grounds.

**Public Services.** Seattle is one of the leading cities of the United States in public ownership of utilities. The city produces its own water supply from the Cedar River. Electricity from the first city-owned hydroelectric power plant in the United States, at Cedar Falls, began to light Seattle streets in 1905. Construction began in 1919 on the first of a series of power projects on the Skagit River. The projects now have a capacity of more than 600,000 kilowatts of electric power. Electricity powers the trolley buses that serve the city transit system.

### History

The founders of Seattle landed at Alki Point in 1851. But this location was not suitable as a harbor for large vessels, and the settlers moved to the shores of Elliott Bay in 1852. Here a small group of houses and stores was clustered around a sawmill built by Henry Yesler in 1853. The settlement was named for the Indian chief Seattle (1786?-1866), who had befriended the first settlers in the region. Chief Seattle, or Seathl, believed that after death his spirit would be troubled every time his name was spoken, and was unwilling that the growing village of Seattle should be named for him. In his later years he often asked for gifts from Seattle residents to repay him in advance for his troubles in the afterlife.

The settlement developed rapidly, and Seattle was incorporated as a city in 1869. In 1875 regular steamship service was begun between Seattle and San Francisco, Calif. A short railroad connected Seattle with the Washington coal fields in 1877, and another was completed to the Puyallup Valley in 1883. In 1884 Seattle became a terminal of the Northern Pacific Railroad. In 1889, a fire destroyed the entire business district.

Seattle experienced its greatest rate of growth during the gold rush to the Yukon and Alaska that began in 1897. Thousands of prospectors outfitted themselves in the city. Steamship service between Seattle and Atlantic ports began when the Panama Canal opened in 1914.

Seattle experienced sharp growths in population and industries during World Wars I and II. In 1962, the city sponsored a world's fair called the *Century 21 Exposition.* HOWARD J. CRITCHFIELD

See also BRIDGE (picture: Pontoon Bridge); DIABLO DAM; PUGET SOUND; ROSS DAM.

**SEATTLE,** or **SEATHL.** See SEATTLE (History).

**SEATTLE PACIFIC COLLEGE** is a liberal arts school in Seattle, Wash. It is controlled by the Free Methodist Church, but admits students of all faiths. It includes separate schools of education, music, religion, missions, recreational leadership, a special department in nursing, and a graduate school. The college was founded in 1891. For enrollment, see UNIVERSITIES AND COLLEGES (table).

**SEATTLE UNIVERSITY** is a coeducational school in Seattle, Wash. It is administered by the Roman Catholic Jesuit Fathers, but admits students of all faiths. Bachelor's degrees are offered by the college of arts and sciences; and by the schools of business, education, engineering, and nursing. The college of sister formation conducts courses for women preparing to become nuns. Graduate programs lead to master's degrees. Seattle University was founded in 1891. For the enrollment of Seattle University, see UNIVERSITIES AND COLLEGES (table). JOHN A. FITTERER

## SOME TYPES OF SEAWEED

**Red Algae** from the coast of California

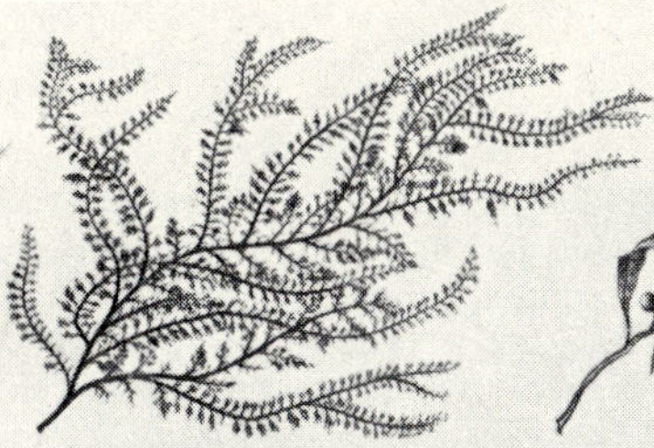

**Beautiful Red Algae** from New York harbor

**Sargassum,** typical of algae in Sargasso Sea

**Brown Algae** from the coast of Massachusetts

**Coral-like Red Algae** from subtropical waters

**The Brown Algae, Kelp,** valuable as a fertilizer, grows to 100 feet

Hoffpauir Studio

**Boatloads of Giant Kelp Seaweed,** a source of the chemical element iodine, dock at the outer harbor in San Pedro, Calif.

**SEAWEED.** Any plant that grows in the sea can be called a seaweed. But when a botanist speaks of seaweed he usually means one of the larger brown or red algae. These seaweeds are relatives of the green pond scums of stagnant water, but not of the higher water plants. The seaweeds of cold waters are chiefly brown algae. Those of the tropics are chiefly red algae.

On Columbus' first voyage to America, his ships passed through masses of seaweed. These weeds were brown algae known as *gulfweeds.* One kind of gulfweed has small air bladders, shaped like berries, and it can float in the water. There is a large mass of these weeds floating in the Atlantic Ocean east of Florida. The area containing these weeds is called the Sargasso Sea.

Giant kelps of the Pacific are another type of brown algae. The "stems" of these giant weeds sometimes grow nearly 200 feet long. During World War I, giant kelp were harvested to make fertilizers and explosives. Chemists extract large amounts of iodine and algin from kelps. Algin has many commercial uses because it has the ability to hold several different liquids together. In ice cream, it keeps the water in the milk from forming crystals. It is also used in salad dressings, chocolate milk, aspirin, and other foods and drugs.

Irish moss and other red algae contain similar substances as *agar* and *carrageenin,* used in food and drugs.

**Scientific Classification.** Seaweeds belong to the seven different phyla of algae in the subkingdom *Thallophyta.* The giant kelp and the gulfweed belong to the phylum *Phaeophyta,* or brown algae. The giant kelp is genus *Macrocystis,* species *pyrifera.* The gulfweed is *Sargassum bacciferum.* Irish moss is in the phylum *Rhodophyta,* or red algae. It is *Chondrus crispus.* LEWIS HANFORD TIFFANY

**Related Articles** in WORLD BOOK include:

| | | |
|---|---|---|
| Agar-Agar | Irish Moss | Sargasso Sea |
| Algae | Kelp | Water Plant |
| Harvey, William H. | Ocean (picture) | |

# SEBACEOUS GLAND

**SEBACEOUS GLAND.** See SKIN (The Work of the Skin).

**SEBASTIAN,** *see BAS chun,* **SAINT** (died A.D. 288), was one of the early defenders of the Christian faith. He entered the Roman army without revealing his intent to assist and protect the Christians. The Emperor Diocletian liked him and made him commander of soldiers at Milan. But Sebastian's religious faith was discovered, and he was condemned to death. A troop of soldiers tied him to a tree and shot him with arrows. They thought him dead and left him. He was cared for by a Christian woman named Irene. Sebastian again declared his faith after he recovered. The emperor then ordered him clubbed to death in the amphitheater, and he was buried in the catacombs. Saint Sebastian tied to the tree was a favorite subject of early Italian painters. His feast day is January 20. FULTON J. SHEEN

**SEBASTOPOL.** See SEVASTOPOL.

**SEBORRHEA.** See DANDRUFF.

**SEC.** See SECURITIES AND EXCHANGE COMMISSION.

**SECESSION.** See CIVIL WAR; NULLIFICATION.

**SECHURA DESERT,** *say CHOO rah,* is the central portion of the Peruvian Coastal Desert. It covers about 10,000 square miles. The desert begins roughly at Paita in the north and includes Lima in the south. Almost half of the people of the Peruvian Coastal Desert live in the urban centers of the Sechura Desert. C. LANGDON WHITE

**SECONAL.** See BARBITURATE.

**SECOND.** See MINUTE.

**SECOND CONTINENTAL CONGRESS.** See CONTINENTAL CONGRESS.

**SECOND EMPIRE.** See FRANCE (The Revolutions of 1830 and 1848); NAPOLEON III.

**SECOND REPUBLIC.** See REVOLUTION OF 1848.

**SECOND SIGHT.** See CLAIRVOYANCE.

**SECOND VATICAN COUNCIL.** See VATICAN COUNCIL.

**SECONDARY EDUCATION.** See EDUCATION (Secondary Education); HIGH SCHOOL; JUNIOR HIGH SCHOOL.

**SECORD,** *SEE kawrd,* **LAURA INGERSOLL** (1775-1868), was a Canadian heroine of the War of 1812. She risked her life crossing the American lines to warn the British of an American attack in 1813.

Mrs. Secord overheard American troops who were quartered in her Queenstown, Ont., house planning an attack on a British detachment at Beaver Dam in southern Ontario. According to the story, she walked through the American lines, driving a cow ahead of her to avoid suspicion, and warned the British commander. In the battle of Beaver Dam on June 23, 1813, the British surrounded the American force and tricked it into surrendering. The story of Mrs. Secord's courage and ingenuity greatly heartened the Canadian people. She was born in Massachusetts. CLINTON ROSSITER

**SECRET BALLOT** refers to the right to vote and mark ballots in private. See BALLOT.

**SECRET POLICE** are used by dictators to control, terrorize, and spy on people. Joseph Fouché, minister of police under Napoleon I, established the modern secret-police system. The political police of the Russian czars was called the *Okhrana.* Since 1917, the Communist dictators in Russia have used the secret police as their main tool for keeping power. This police force has had various names such as OGPU, MVD, and KGB. Hitler developed the German Gestapo to help him keep power. STEFAN T. POSSONY

See also GESTAPO; MVD; POLICE STATE.

**SECRET SERVICE, UNITED STATES,** is a bureau of the Treasury Department. The primary responsibility of the Secret Service is to protect the President of the United States and members of his immediate family, the President-elect, and the Vice-President at his request. The Secret Service also has the important responsibility of suppressing the counterfeiting of government currency and bonds and investigating forgeries of government checks and bonds.

The White House Police Force and the Treasury Guard Force are supervised by the Secret Service. The White House Police protect the White House and its grounds. The Treasury Guard Force protects the Main Treasury Building, its annex, and the billions of dollars in currency and other securities stored in the Treasury vaults.

The White House Detail, a select and well-trained group of special agents, accompanies the President at all times. The Protective Research Section investigates persons who write threatening letters to the President.

The Secret Service captures and destroys from three to four million dollars in counterfeit money each year before it can be passed on the public. It provides instructors for police schools and conducts classes for banks and other money handlers on how to detect counterfeit money. A Secret Service publication entitled *Know Your Money* furnishes information on how to detect counterfeit money and how to report such information to the proper authorities.

Applicants must pass a civil service examination to become Secret Service agents. They should be college graduates or experienced investigators. They are given extensive training in all phases of the protective and investigative functions of the Secret Service.

The origin of the Secret Service may be traced back to 1860 when Congress appropriated funds to be spent by the secretary of the treasury for the suppression of counterfeiting of U.S. coins. The first chief of the Secret Service was appointed in 1865. The service began protecting the President in 1901 after the assassination of President William McKinley.

The chief of the Secret Service has his headquarters in the Main Treasury Building in Washington, D.C. He supervises offices located in 63 cities in the United States and its territories. JAMES J. ROWLEY

See also COUNTERFEITING; FORGERY; PINKERTON, ALLAN; POLICE (Federal Police); PRESIDENT OF THE UNITED STATES (Guarding the President).

**SECRETARIAL WORK.** See OFFICE WORK.

**SECRETARIAT.** See UNITED NATIONS.

**SECRETARY BIRD** is a large African bird that looks like a hawk. Its name comes from the tufts of narrow feathers standing out from the sides and back of its head. The tufts resemble the quill pens that busy secretaries and clerks once carried behind their ears.

The secretary bird makes its home from Ethiopia and the Sudan to the Cape of Good Hope Province. It stands about 4 feet high and has long legs and a long tail. It usually prefers to run instead of fly. It builds a bulky nest in a tree or bush, and lays 2 or 3 eggs at a time. They are dull white, spotted with rust. The secre-

New York Zoological Park

**The Secretary Bird** has long narrow feathers extending from the back of its head, resembling the old quill pens.

tary bird eats frogs, insects, lizards, small tortoises, and snakes. Sometimes it flies with its victim high in the air and kills it by dropping it. Then it lands and eats it.

In the Cape of Good Hope Province, secretary birds destroy many snakes, and there is a fine for killing the birds. South African farmers sometimes tame secretary birds and keep them to kill rats.

**Scientific Classification.** The secretary bird belongs to the secretary bird family, *Sagittariidae*. It is genus *Sagittarius*, species *S. serpentarius*.   OLIN SEWALL PETTINGILL, JR.

**SECRETARY OF ———.** For the secretaries of the executive departments of the U.S. government, see the articles on the departments. For example, see STATE, DEPARTMENT OF; DEFENSE, DEPARTMENT OF.

**SECRETIN.** See GLAND (Hormones of the Stomach and Intestines).

**SECRETION,** *see KREE shun,* is a substance that body cells form from blood. Cells that form a secretion are often grouped into a gland. A duct from the gland may then pour the product into another body part. Secretions from such glands include saliva, tears, mucus, sweat, bile, and digestive juices. The endocrine glands have no ducts. They return their secretions, called *hormones,* to the blood. Important hormones include *insulin, thyroxin,* and *epinephrine*. These help to regulate *metabolism* (body processes). Working with other hormones, they regulate growth and health. EWALD E. SELKURT

**Related Articles** in WORLD BOOK include:
| | | |
|---|---|---|
| Gland | Insulin | Perspiration | Tears |
| Hormone | Mucus | Saliva | |

**SECTION,** land. See PUBLIC LANDS (Management).

# SEDATIVE

**SECULARISM.** See POLITICAL SCIENCE (Secularism).
**SECURITIES.** See INVESTMENT; BOND; STOCK, CAPITAL.
**SECURITIES ACT OF 1933** was passed by Congress to protect the public from buying unsafe securities. It requires a detailed statement from each corporation planning to issue securities and offer them for sale in interstate commerce. These statements must be filed with the Securities and Exchange Commission before the securities are offered for sale. They must give complete details about the purpose and the financial backing of all new security issues.   ROBERT D. PATTON

See also SECURITIES AND EXCHANGE COMMISSION.

**SECURITIES AND EXCHANGE COMMISSION (SEC),** an independent federal agency, administers federal laws governing the purchase and sale of *securities* (stocks and bonds). These laws were passed to protect people who invest money in securities. Companies offering stock for public sale must disclose information on company finances and other matters as long as their securities are offered to the public.

The SEC investigates complaints and possible violations of federal securities laws. It also licenses brokerage firms and investment advisers, and establishes codes of conduct for them. The SEC consists of five commissioners and has a staff of about 1,400. It was established in 1934.   WILLIAM L. CARY

See also INVESTMENT (Government Regulations); INVESTMENT BANKING; SECURITIES ACT OF 1933.

**SECURITY COUNCIL.** See UNITED NATIONS (The Security Council).

**SEDALIA,** *see DAYL yuh,* Mo. (pop. 23,874; alt. 910 ft.), is the trading center of a large farming region. Every year farmers bring their products to the state fair in Sedalia. The city lies in west-central Missouri, about 180 miles west of St. Louis and about 80 miles southeast of Kansas City (see MISSOURI [political map]). Whiteman Air Force Base is located 18 miles west of Sedalia.

Sedalia is an important railway center. It ships corn, oats, wheat, and soybeans to all parts of the Middle West. Its products include shoes, work clothing, beverages, dairy and poultry products, and feed. Sedalia has a mayor-council government.   NOEL P. GIST

**SEDAN, BATTLE OF.** See FRANCO-PRUSSIAN WAR (Progress of the War).

**SEDATIVE,** *SED uh tiv,* is a drug that acts on the nervous system to produce a state of calmness. Most sedatives usually produce sleep when taken in large doses. Drugs called *barbiturates* and *bromides* are commonly used sedatives.

Many drugs used to treat other conditions have a sedative side effect. Psychiatrists and other physicians sometimes prescribe *tranquilizers* for their patients. Tranquilizers produce calmness but do not decrease mental and physical activity. Some tranquilizers also have a sedative effect.

Sedative side effects may be undesirable. For example, some of the *antihistamine* drugs used to control hay fever may have a sedative side effect. Some people who take the drug may get drowsy, making it dangerous for them to drive or work.

Some sedatives are habit-forming and others are *addictive* (create a mental and physical need). When a

223

## SEDDON, JAMES ALEXANDER

person stops taking an addictive drug, he may experience *withdrawal illness.* That is, he may suffer a fever, nausea, or more serious illness. Sedatives should never be used unless they have been prescribed by a doctor or dentist for the person taking them. SOLOMON GARB

See also ANALGESIC; ANODYNE; BARBITURATE; NARCOTIC; TRANQUILIZER.

**SEDDON, JAMES ALEXANDER** (1815-1880), served as Confederate secretary of war from 1862 to 1865. A close friend of Jefferson Davis, Seddon influenced him more than any of the six men who served successively as his secretary of war. Seddon urged an offensive military campaign in the West to save the Confederacy. He was criticized in the Confederate Congress because he enforced such unpopular measures as the conscription act. He was born in Stafford County, Virginia, and was graduated in law from the University of Virginia. Before the Civil War, he was a member of the United States House of Representatives. RICHARD N. CURRENT

**SEDGE,** *sej,* is one of a large family of grasslike plants that grow in wet places throughout the world. Sedges thrive in marshes, swamps, and shallow water. Like grasses, they have long, narrow leaves. But sedges usually have triangular, solid stems. Grasses have round, hollow stems. Sedges have three rows of leaves, but grasses have only two.

The *sheath* (covering) at the base of each sedge leaf is closed around the stem. In grasses, the side of the sheath opposite the leaf blade is split and overlaps.

Sedges have tiny green flowers on small spikes called *spikelets.* These flowers have no petals, but they have small bristles. Farmers sometimes cut sedge for hay.

**Scientific Classification.** Sedges make up the sedge family, *Cyperaceae.* Common genera include *Carex, Cyperus,* and *Scirpus.* RICHARD W. POHL

See also GRASS; BULRUSH.

**SEDGES, JOHN.** See BUCK, PEARL S.
**SEDGMAN, FRANK.** See TENNIS (tables).
**SEDIMENTARY ROCK,** *sed uh MEN tar ee,* is rock formed when mineral matter settles out of water, or, less commonly, out of air or ice. Sedimentary rock covers about three-fourths of the earth's land area. In some places, such as at the mouth of the Mississippi River, sedimentary rocks are more than 40,000 feet thick. Geologists estimate that sedimentary rock has been forming on the earth for at least $3\frac{1}{2}$ billion years. Sedimentary rock is one of three major kinds of rock. The other kinds are igneous rock and metamorphic rock.

The most common sedimentary rock is *shale* or *mudstone.* It is made of compressed mud or silt (fine particles of mineral matter). Other common sedimentary rocks include *limestone,* made of the mineral calcite, and *sandstone,* made of sand. *Conglomerate* is a sedimentary rock made of gravel cemented together. One kind of conglomerate, called *breccia* (pronounced *BRECH ee uh*) contains sharp, rather than smooth, pebbles.

Most sedimentary rock starts forming when silt and grains of sand settle along river beds or on the bottoms of lakes and oceans. Year after year, these minerals collect and form broad, flat layers called *beds* or *strata.* The layers, which differ in color and texture, distinguish sedimentary from most igneous and metamorphic rock. After thousands of years, layers of fine silt and clays are squeezed into compact layers by the weight of other layers above them. Water slowly oozing through coarse, sandy layers deposits mineral matter around the grains, cementing them together to form rock. When the earth's crust changes shape, large areas of sedimentary rock may be exposed.

Some sedimentary rock forms during the evaporation of water. For example, beds of rock salt were formed after ocean inlets were cut off by changes in the earth's surface. As the trapped water evaporated, layers of salt crystals were left behind.

Most fossils are found in sedimentary rock. The fossils formed when sediments covered dead plants and animals. As the sediments changed to rock, either the remains or the outlines of the plants and animals were preserved in the rock. See FOSSIL. SHELDON JUDSON

**Related Articles** in WORLD BOOK include:

| | | |
|---|---|---|
| Chalk | Flint | Rock (pictures; map) |
| Clay | Limestone | Sandstone |
| Concretion | Marl | Shale |
| Coral | Oil Shale | Travertine |

**SEDITION** is an act which stirs up discontent against established government authority. Many countries, including the United States, have tried at times to prevent sedition by law. Americans, however, value the right to criticize government officials and their actions. Therefore, sedition laws are not popular in peacetime.

In time of war, statements which are likely to hinder the successful progress of the war are dealt with as sedition. Sedition is regarded as a step toward treason. But it does not aim at direct, open violence. The Espionage Act of 1917, enforced during World Wars I and II, provided punishment for seditious statements. It was used against enemy agents or other persons who tried to undermine the war effort. FRED E. INBAU

See also ALIEN AND SEDITION ACTS.

**SEDNA.** See ESKIMO (Religion).
**SEDUM,** *SEE dum,* is a *genus* (group) of plants that are decorative and hardy. Most sedums are native to the North Temperate Zone. They are *succulent* plants, or plants that store water in their thick, fleshy leaves (see SUCCULENT). Some sedums have low, creeping stems. Their leaves often grow in clusters near the ground. They are often used to cover rocks and bare ground. Others have tall stems and are used as border plants. Many persons call sedums *live-forevers* because they do not wither easily. They are also called *stonecrops.*

**Sedum Plants** usually do well in rock gardens. One kind of sedum, below, has wavy-edged leaves and flat clusters of starlike, yellow flowers.
J. Horace McFarland

**Scientific Classification.** Sedums belong to the orpine family, *Crassulaceae.* They are classified in the genus *Sedum.* H. D. HARRINGTON

**SEE, ELLIOT McKAY, JR.** See ASTRONAUT (table).
**SEE, HOLY.** See POPE (The Papacy).
**SEEBECK, THOMAS JOHANN.** See THERMOCOUPLE.

224

**SEED.** Seeds are the most important part of a plant. The roots, the leaves, the flowers, all exist so there can be seeds. And because each seed has been given the form that is best suited to produce its own kind of plant, there is great variety in their shapes, sizes, and colors.

Some seeds are round. Others are egg-shaped, triangular, circular, long and slender, curved, or coiled like a snail. Some seeds have horns, others have tails, and many have wings. Some are smooth, others are ridged. The color of the skin of the seeds varies also. It may be red, purple, orange, or any gay or dull color, striped or spotted, black or white. Many seeds look like beetles or pebbles in shape and color. In this way they escape being eaten by seed-eating birds. The carrot seed is shaped like a hairy bug, the chickweed seed looks somewhat like a caterpillar, and the castor-oil seed resembles a shiny beetle.

The sizes of seeds vary almost as much as the different kinds of seeds. Tobacco seeds are so tiny that one seed pod may contain as many as 40,000 seeds. Poppy seeds are only slightly larger. From those tiny particles they range up through almost every size to the large Brazil nut and white walnut. The seed of one kind of coconut tree is so large that it weighs about 22 pounds.

The size of the seed has no bearing on the size of the plant that will grow from it. The tallest tree in the world, the California redwood, grows from a very small seed. The large seed of a watermelon will produce only a low vine.

Some plants, such as ferns and mosses, do not have seeds. They reproduce their kind by means of spores (see SPORE). Many plants which bear seeds also have another method of reproduction. Onions, daffodils, and lilies develop bulbs from which new plants sprout. Strawberries have stems that creep along the ground. A new plant grows from each joint of the creeping stem. Lawn grass is thick because it has stems that creep underground, and new shoots sprout from the many joints. Potatoes have "eyes," and each eye is a plant bud.

Most plants, however, depend upon seeds alone to continue their kind.

### How Seeds Develop

The part of a flower which contains the tiny seed-eggs is the ovary. To develop into healthy seeds the eggs must receive pollen from the same flower or the same kind of flower. Many changes then take place, and continue while the seed is developing.

**Kinds of Seeds.** All seeds are either *gymnosperms*, which are naked seeds (not enclosed in an ovary), or *angiosperms*, enveloped seeds (enclosed in an ovary which ripens as a pod or fleshy fruit). Naked seeds are like those of the pine and all other cone-bearing trees, and of certain fernlike plants of the tropics. The seeds of all plants—trees, shrubs, and herbs—that bear flowers are angiosperms.

Angiosperms that ripen in a dry seed pod are called *dry fruits*. When the seeds are surrounded by pulp, as in apples, peaches, and grapes, they are fleshy fruits.

When a plant has seeds with only *one* cotyledon, or seed leaf, it is called a *monocotyledon*. Iris, tulips, lilies, and corn are monocotyledons. Most plants have seeds with *two* cotyledons, or seed leaves. They are called *dicotyledons*. Beans and peas, and oaks, elms, and willows are dicotyledons. Nearly all cone-bearing trees, such as pine, spruce, and hemlock, are *polycotyledons*, because their seeds have *many* seed leaves.

**Parts.** The seed has three important parts—a protective outer skin, or *seed coat;* an *embryo*, which will become the new plant; and a food supply, or *endosperm*, usually in the form of one, two, or many *cotyledons*, or seed leaves. The cotyledons are stored with plant food —chiefly albumen and starch or oily matter. These nourish the embryo as it develops.

The seed coats of some seeds, such as the bean, have two structures, the *hilum* and the *micropyle*. The hilum is a small scar where the seed was attached to the seed stalk. The micropyle is a tiny hole where the pollen tube that fertilized the seed entered. The *epicotyl* and the *hypocotyl* are tiny parts of the cotyledon. The epicotyl becomes the stem of the young plant. The hypocotyl develops into the plant's first root.

**Germination.** It is interesting to study a Lima bean that has been soaked in water. The two cotyledons, or the two halves of the bean, are attached to one end of the embryo stem, which holds the plant bud, or the growing point. At the other end is the tip that will become the root.

When a bean is planted it swells with moisture so that it bursts its seed coat. Then the embryo begins to grow. The root tip pushes through the eye of the bean. The embryo stem does not lengthen until it has rootlets to anchor it firmly in the earth. It then arches up through the earth crust, and brings up the delicate plant bud protected by the tough cotyledons. As the stem straightens, the cotyledons open wide, and the bud is exposed to the light and air it needs for growth.

In some seeds, as most beans, the cotyledons are raised well above the earth. In others they remain at the earth's surface. When the small plant no longer needs their protection and food, they wither away.

In order to germinate, or sprout, a seed must have air, moisture, and the right temperature. Some seeds need a great deal of moisture, others only a little. Some will sprout in the cold ground of early spring. Others must have the sun-warmed ground of late spring or early summer.

Nearly all seeds thrive best if they are planted less than a year after they have ripened. But most of them will keep for some time. Two-year-old corn germinates readily, but if corn is kept for three or four years its chances of sprouting are slight. A bean may sprout if it is eight years old, but usually a bean embryo dies after the third year. Cucumber seeds may be kept for as long as ten years. And wheat has germinated after thirty years.

Each state in the United States has its testing station to determine the vitality of seeds, their germinating possibilities, and their purity from weed seeds and other undesirable seeds. Gardeners and farmers have learned that if they plant only the very best seeds their crops will be larger, healthier, and of better quality.

### How Seeds Travel

Nature's work is not finished when seeds are ripened. They must have a chance to sprout and grow. If they fell straight to the ground, beneath the plant that bore them, they would be too crowded to thrive. A plant's

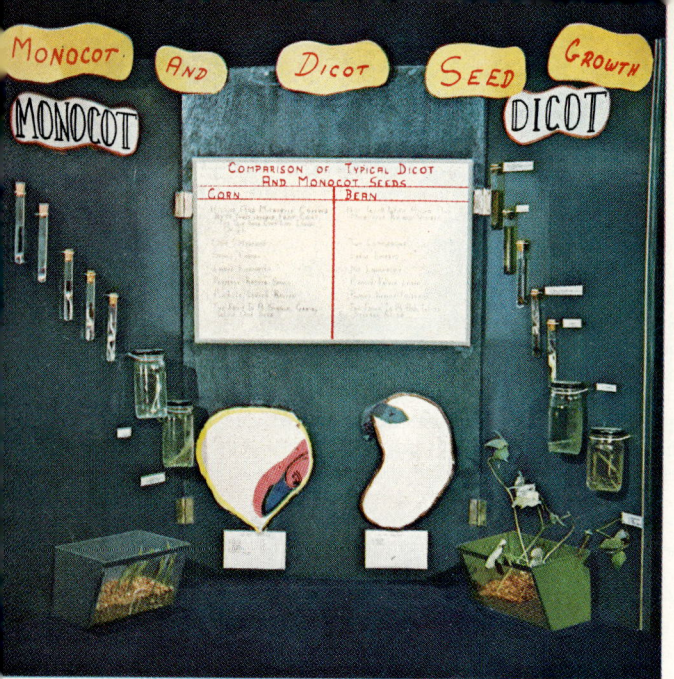

## A WORLD BOOK SCIENCE PROJECT
## HOW SEEDS GROW

The purpose of this project is to learn how monocotyledon seeds differ from dicotyledon seeds at various stages of growth.

**To Study Seed Growth** for this project, the development of monocot and dicot seeds is compared at various stages of growth, *left*. Models of corn and bean seeds are made to show the important parts of each seed. To study plant development, seeds are allowed to sprout and the seedlings are preserved at various stages of growth.

---

### PROCEDURE

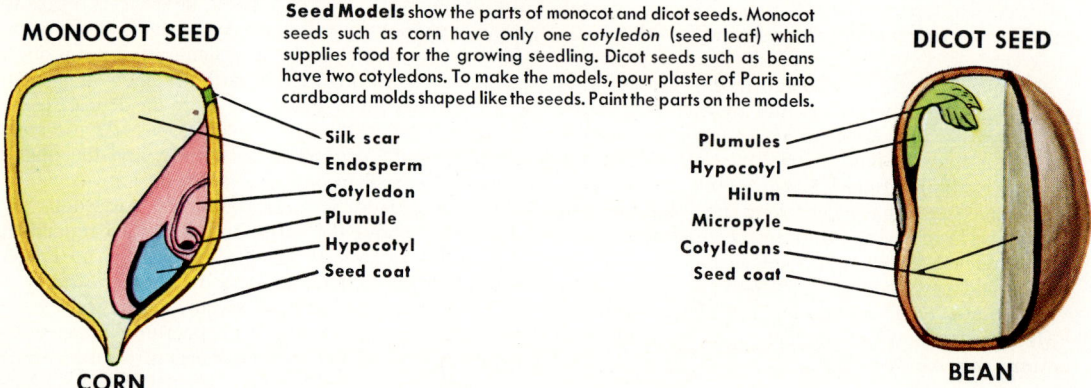

**Seed Models** show the parts of monocot and dicot seeds. Monocot seeds such as corn have only one *cotyledon* (seed leaf) which supplies food for the growing seedling. Dicot seeds such as beans have two cotyledons. To make the models, pour plaster of Paris into cardboard molds shaped like the seeds. Paint the parts on the models.

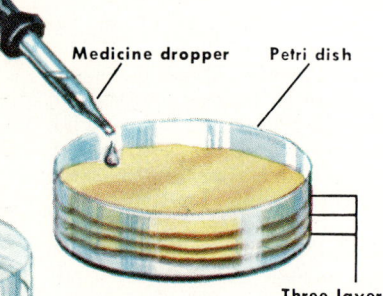

You can buy all the materials you need for this project from local stores. Get four Petri dishes. Cut three layers of paper toweling to fit the bottom of each dish. Dampen the paper toweling with a few drops of water. Place four bean seeds in each of the two Petri dishes, and four corn seeds in each of the remaining dishes. Cover the dishes and put them in a sunny place. The seeds will begin to sprout in about a day.

WORLD BOOK photos

**To Preserve the Seed Sprouts,** fill 10 test tubes three-quarters full of formalin-acetic-alcohol (FAA) solution. When the seeds begin to sprout, remove a corn seed and a bean seed from the Petri dishes. Place each in a test tube and put a cork in the tube. Repeat this procedure at intervals until you have preserved samples of sprouts for each kind of seed at different stages of growth as shown, *right*.

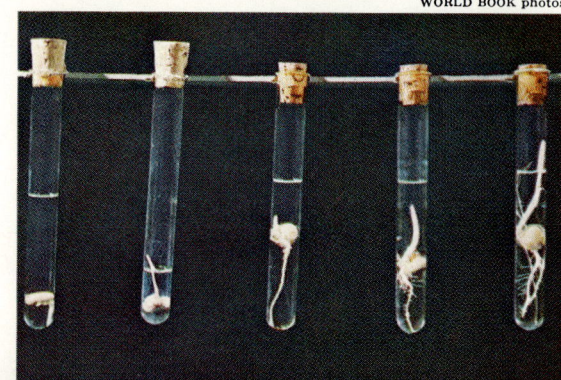

224b

## MATERIALS

**Bean Seeds and Corn Seeds**  **Petri Dishes with Lids**  **Paper Toweling**

**Test Tubes with Corks**  **Glass Jars with Lids**  **Formalin-Acetic-Alcohol Solution**

**To Grow and Preserve the Seedlings,** plant some of the beans and corn in germinating pans that have about 2 inches of Vermiculite (a growing medium) in the bottom. Dampen the Vermiculite and cover the pans. When the seedlings grow, remove them at different stages of growth and preserve them in small jars of FAA solution as shown, *left.*

WORLD BOOK photos

**To Grow the Plants,** plant the bean and corn seeds in germinating pans containing dampened Vermiculite. Cover the pans until seedlings appear. Then place the pans in a sunny place and after the first true leaves develop, add some fertilizer. Water the plants as necessary until they mature as shown, *right.*

Illustrated by Bill Fleming for WORLD BOOK

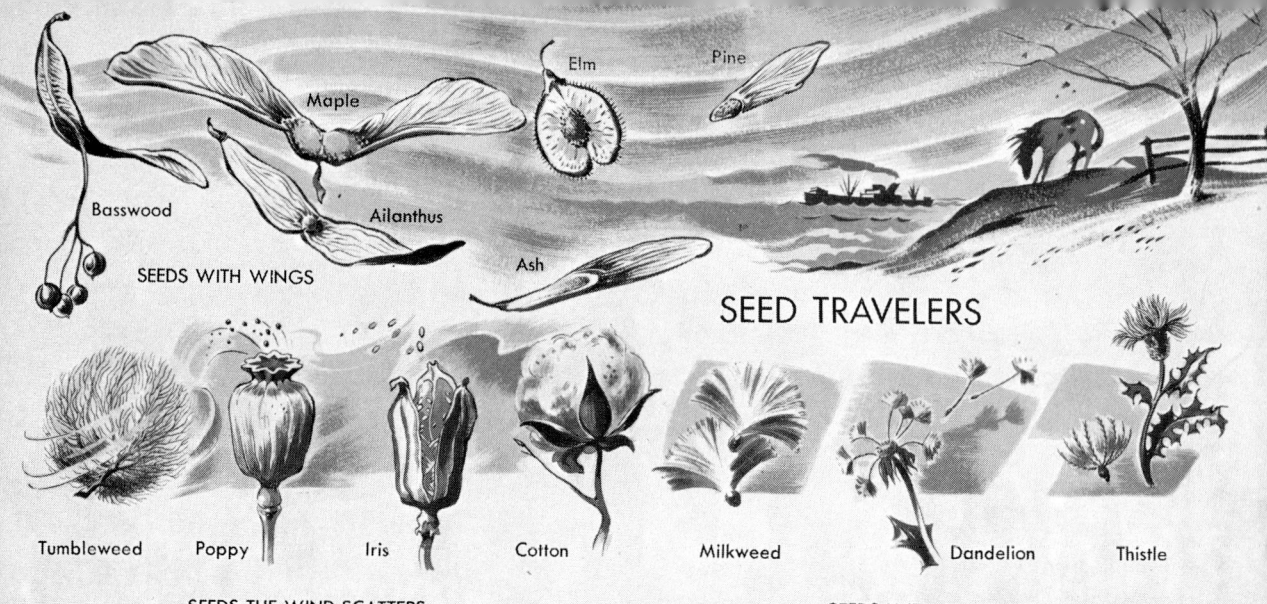

seeds must be scattered, or dispersed. There are many ways in which this is done.

When the seeds of fleshy fruits are ripe, ready for planting, the skin of the fruit turns to a bright color, or even to black or white, to make it easy to see against the green leaves. Birds and other creatures are quickly attracted and eat the fruit. The seeds are not digested. They pass through the animal's body and are scattered in this way. Man helps by shipping fruits to distant points, or by eating them and throwing the seeds away. Most dry-fruit seeds are scattered by the wind.

When a dandelion's blowball head is ripe, each seed has a long tail tipped with a parachute of fluffy hairs. The wind snatches the seeds off and carries them, held up by their parachutes, far away. When they spin to the earth, the seed, which is the heavier end, sinks a little if the ground is soft. The first rain may beat it in, or an animal may tramp it into the earth—and so it is planted.

Milkweed, cotton, kapok, and other seeds are covered with fluffy down to enable them to sail on the wind. The clematis seed trails a long feathery plume.

A great many seeds have downy hairs that help them travel a long distance on the wind.

Other wind-borne seeds have delicate wings instead of down. The most familiar wings are probably those of maple seeds which grow in pairs. The pine seed's long wing is curved like a propeller blade. The wing helps the seed spin in the air, catch currents from all directions, and so travel farther. Ash, elm, and other trees have seeds with similar wings.

Many seeds that depend on the wind to scatter them have neither wings nor down. They ripen in dry pods or capsules. A pod such as a bean or milkweed pod has only one cavity. A capsule is divided into two or more compartments, or carpels.

In a great many cases, the pod or capsule splits open when it is dry. The seeds do not fall out and down. They wait for the wind. In an iris capsule they are packed so firmly they can not dislodge themselves, but when the wind shakes the stalk they are thrown out in every direction.

There are other ways in which the wind is useful in scattering seeds. The tumbleweed of the Western plains rolls itself into a ball when the seeds are ripe, and its roots dry and shrink. The first wind uproots the entire plant and sends it rolling over the prairies, scattering seeds as it goes.

Dry fruits with seeds too heavy for the wind to scatter have other methods. Some "shoot" their seeds out, forcing them to hop far away by an elastic contraction of the inner wall of the pod. When a bean pod dries and splits into two halves, it whirls the beans out in many directions by twisting or curling.

A familiar way for seeds to travel far from the parent plant is by means of hooks and barbs. These grasp and cling to the fur of passing animals. Burs, sticktights, and Spanish needles are very well known for they cling to the clothes of people who brush against them.

A great many of the seeds that are produced each year and are so well scattered never become plants. Many fall where conditions are not suitable for germination and growth. Many are eaten by birds and rodents. In many the embryo is not alive. Because of this tremendous loss of seeds, the plant produces a great number of them so that some will surely survive. One tobacco plant may ripen a million seeds. But when there is so enormous a quantity, the number of them that will sprout is very small. A coconut palm rarely produces more than a hundred seeds, often no more than twenty. Whenever there is a smaller number of seeds, very few can afford to be wasted.

## Uses of Seeds

Seeds are of great importance to man. Their widest use is for food. Among all seed foods, cereals rank first. Rice is the most important. It is the chief food of millions of people in Asia and many in the Pacific Islands. Enormous quantities of wheat are consumed throughout the world. Other important cereals are corn, oats, barley, millet, buckwheat, and rye.

Edible fruits and nuts are seeds and seed coverings. Seed foods in the vegetable garden include beans, peas, tomatoes, eggplants, peppers, okra, cucumbers, squashes, pumpkins, and melons. Coffee, chocolate, and cocoa are beverages made from seeds. Vanilla flavoring comes from seeds. Mustard, black pepper, caraway, and nutmegs are other flavoring substances made from seeds.

Cotton is the fluffy down of seeds. Kapok is the down of similar seeds from a kapok tree.

Even more important in industry are the oils extracted from seeds. Cottonseed oil, linseed oil, castor oil, sunflower oil, soybean oil, coconut oil and palm oil are only a few. Seed oils have a multitude of uses. They are used for food as salad oils and cooking fats, and in making soaps and perfumery, linoleum, printer's ink, artists' colors, paints and varnishes, insecticides, and many other things. When the oil has been extracted from cotton seeds, sunflower seeds, and soybeans, the remaining pulp is used for cattle and poultry feed.

Seeds are used in making industrial alcohol, plastics, synthetic rubber, and medicine. Valuable seed medicines are strychnine and belladonna.   VERNON QUINN

**Related Articles** in WORLD BOOK include:

| | |
|---|---|
| Angiosperm | Germination |
| Cotyledon | Grain |
| Cross-Pollination | Gymnosperm |
| Dicotyledon | Hilum |
| Flower (How Flowers Reproduce) | Nut |
| Fruit | Plant (How Plants Reproduce) |
| Gardening (Planting Seeds) | Pollen and Pollination |
| | Spore |

## Outline

I. **How Seeds Develop**
   A. Kinds of Seeds
   B. Parts
   C. Germination
II. **How Seeds Travel**
III. **Uses of Seeds**

## Questions

Why are seeds the most important part of the plant?
Why do seeds have so many shapes and colors?
What are the two kinds of seeds? How do they differ?
What jobs do the different seed parts perform?
How do seeds get from place to place? How does the rest of the plant help them? How does nature help them?
Why is it necessary for so many seeds to be produced?
How are seeds valuable to man? What are some of their uses?

# SEEDEATER

**SEEDEATER.** See FINCH.

**SEEGER, ALAN** (1888-1916), an American poet, wrote one of the most memorable poems of World War I, "I Have a Rendezvous with Death." A feeling that he was going to die inspired him to write the poem. Later, he was wounded and died on the battlefield. His *Collected Poems* was published in 1916. Seeger was born in New York City. He joined the French Foreign Legion at the start of World War I. WILLIAM VAN O'CONNOR

**SEEING EYE.** The Seeing Eye, Inc., has headquarters near Morristown, N.J., where dogs are trained to guide blind people. Seeing Eye trainers teach the dogs to obey their owners and to disobey any command which would be dangerous to carry out. These dogs learn to guide their masters around such overhanging obstacles as low branches or awnings. The dogs also learn to watch traffic and cross streets only when it is safe. The dog is trained for three months before the master arrives at the school. The master spends a month learning how to use the dog. Most Seeing Eye dogs are German Shepherds. The Seeing Eye was founded in 1929. See also DOG (Famous Dogs [Buddy]). GEORGE WERNTZ, JR.

**A Seeing Eye Dog** guides its blind master. The dog was trained at a special school near Morristown, N.J., to follow orders, but to disobey commands that might be dangerous to its master.

The Seeing Eye, Inc.

**SEERSUCKER** is a cotton or rayon material with crinkled stripes used to make dresses, children's clothes, and men's summer suits. It may be worn without being ironed. It is made in 30 to 36 inch widths.

**SEFERIS, GEORGE** (1900-    ), a Greek poet and diplomat, won the 1963 Nobel prize in literature. He became the first Greek ever to win a Nobel prize. His symbolic, lyric verse shows his strong interest in Greece, its history, and its mythology. Seferis' books of poetry include *The Turning Point* (1931), *Mythistorima* (1935), *The Thrush* (1947), and *Log Book III* (1955). He also wrote essays, and translated into Greek works by T. S. Eliot and other poets.

Seferis was born GEORGE STILIANO SEFERIADHIS in Smyrna (now Izmir, Turkey). He moved to Athens in 1914 and to Paris in 1918. He returned to Greece in 1925, and served in the Greek Foreign Service from 1926 to 1962. He was the Greek Ambassador to Great Britain from 1957 to 1962. Seferis retired from diplomatic work in 1962.

**SEGAL, GEORGE** (1924-    ), is an American sculptor noted for his realistic, life-size plaster figures. Segal uses actual objects of everyday life with these figures. His figures, casts of actual bodies, sit on real chairs, look out of real doorways or windows, and sit behind actual automobile steering wheels.

Segal works in a kind of realism characteristic of many young artists of his day. His work lacks symbolism or obvious emotion. He seems to present the figures as objects, rather than personalities. But they take on a fresh intensity because of their isolation and lack of normal human associations. Segal was born in New York City. ALLEN S. WELLER

See also UNITED STATES (Art and Architecture [color picture]).

**SEGO LILY,** *SEE goh,* is one of the Mariposa lilies, a group of over 40 bright flowering herbs native to western North America. It is the state flower of Utah (see UTAH [color picture]). *Mariposa* is a Spanish word for butterfly, and the petals of the sego lily look like a butterfly's wings. They are white, tinted with yellowish-green or lilac, and have a spot of purple at the base. The sego lily is native from Washington to New Mexico, but can be grown in the Northeastern states if it is protected from frost. The flower grows on a stem about a foot and a half tall, and the leaves are long and thin. The plant has a thick underground stem that looks like a bulb. The early Mormons in Utah cooked and ate these stems.

**Scientific Classification.** The sego lily belongs to the lily family, *Liliaceae*. It is classified as genus *Calochortus*, species *C. nuttallii*. DONALD WYMAN

**SEGOVIA,** *say GOH vyah,* **ANDRÉS** (1893-    ), is one of the world's foremost guitarists. His remarkable virtuosity and musicianship helped elevate the guitar to importance as a solo instrument. His programs contain transcriptions of classic and romantic music and works written for him. Segovia was born in Linares, Spain. See also GUITAR (picture). DAVID EWEN

**SEGRÈ,** *say GRAY,* **EMILIO** (1905-    ), an American physicist, shared the Nobel prize in physics in 1959 with Owen Chamberlain. They won the award for the discovery of the antiproton in 1955 (see ANTIPROTON). The discovery was made at the University of California. Segrè was born in Tivoli, Italy, and came to the United States in 1938. See also TECHNETIUM.

**SEGREGATION** is the separation of groups of people by custom or by law. It is often based on differences of race, religion, wealth, or culture. Whatever the differences may be, many persons consider them highly important.

Segregation can occur in almost any area of life. It is particularly evident in housing, education, and employment, and in the use of eating, sleeping, transportation, and other public facilities. Almost all systems of segregation discourage marriage between persons of different racial, religious, or social groups. In the United States, for example, many states outlawed marriage between Negroes and whites. But in 1967, the Supreme Court of the United States ruled such laws unconstitutional. Segregation almost always involves some kind of discrimination by one group against another.

The term *desegregation* refers to the process of ending group separation. It generally is used to describe efforts to abolish racial segregation in the United States. The people most affected by racial segregation—in the United States and elsewhere—have been Negroes.

During the course of desegregation, two or more separated groups may begin to act toward each other in new, friendlier ways. The process of *integration* goes further, and refers also to the quality of the new relationship. A desegregated situation becomes integrated when it involves acceptance and friendship between persons in different groups. For example, a desegregated school is no longer all-Negro nor all-white—but there may be little friendship between the Negro and white students. After student friendships form across racial lines, the school is truly integrated.

Segregation is not limited to the United States nor to discrimination against racial minorities. It has been practiced in various forms in many countries throughout history.

## Causes and Effects of Segregation

Segregation is usually the result of a long period of group conflict, with one group having more power and influence than another. In time, both groups develop beliefs and attitudes that support the system of separation. Segregation comes to be seen as "right"—particularly by the dominant group—and as the only way society should be organized. When people violate the accepted code of group separation, their action is considered "wrong" and deserving of stern punishment.

Further support for segregation comes from hostile attitudes and feelings between groups. The dominant group typically believes its members are born with superior intelligence, talents, and moral standards. These attitudes help ease the dominant group's guilt for its mistreatment of the *subordinate* (less powerful) group. The subordinate group, in turn, develops fear and extreme dislike toward the dominant group. Such attitudes and actions tend to maintain segregation.

Segregation usually involves favored treatment for the dominant group. Members of this group are expected to have—and usually do have—the best education, homes, jobs, and public services. As a result, their beliefs of superiority are strengthened. They do not

*Thomas F. Pettigrew, the contributor of this article, is Professor of Social Psychology at Harvard University and author of* A Profile of the Negro American.

consider the system unfair, but regard it as the proper way for society to distribute its resources. Likewise, the subordinate group has a sense of inferiority that is reinforced by a system that denies it the social benefits enjoyed by others. Each group naturally views the other as fundamentally "different." Sometimes, subordinated groups try to make up for their low status. They develop intense group loyalty, and make special efforts to overcome the limitations of separation.

A segregated society runs the risk of its groups growing apart and developing highly different values and ways of life. Eventually, the differences may become so great that they cause serious conflicts between the groups. These differences reduce the chances for peaceful desegregation and integration in the future.

## Racial Segregation in the United States

Racial segregation in its modern American form started in the late 1800's. But slavery existed in the United States for more than 200 years before the Civil War (1861-1865). After the war, the freed Negroes suffered widespread discrimination, especially in the South. See CIVIL WAR; RECONSTRUCTION.

**Jim Crow Laws** were adopted by many Southern states in the late 1800's. These segregation laws required that whites and Negroes use separate public facilities. No detail was too small. At one time, for example, Oklahoma required that whites and Negroes use separate telephone booths. Arkansas specified separate gambling tables, and many courts provided separate Bibles for swearing in witnesses. Several Southern states adopted "grandfather clauses" and other Jim Crow laws that deprived Negroes of their voting rights. See GRANDFATHER CLAUSE; JIM CROW.

The rapid spread of segregation laws through the South was supported by a series of decisions by the Supreme Court of the United States. The most influential case was *Plessy v. Ferguson* in 1896. In that case, the court supported the constitutionality of a Louisiana law requiring separate but equal facilities for whites and Negroes in railroad cars. The era of *de jure* (by law) racial segregation in America began with this decision. For over 50 years, many states used the "separate but equal" rule to segregate the races in public schools, and in the use of transportation, recreation, sleeping, and eating facilities.

**The Beginning of Change.** The system of de jure segregation gradually began to crumble in the 1900's. During World War I (1914-1918), orders for military equipment created a great demand for labor. The demand led to mass Negro migration from the South to the manufacturing centers of the North. This migration is still going on. In 1910, only about a tenth of all Negro Americans lived outside the South. Today, about half live outside the South. The majority of Negroes live in the largest metropolitan areas. For example, the New York City metropolitan area has more Negroes than any Southern state.

Starting in the 1930's, Negroes have gained increasing importance in national politics and a fairer hearing in federal courts. The high point was reached in the 1954 case of *Brown v. Board of Education of Topeka*, in which the Supreme Court ruled against de jure segrega-

# SEGREGATION

tion in public schools. The court held that "in the field of public education the doctrine of 'separate but equal' has no place. Separate educational facilities are inherently unequal."

**De Facto Segregation.** In the 1960's, national attention shifted to so-called *de facto* segregation. This type of separation has developed more by custom than by law.

Although many laws supporting de jure segregation have been declared unconstitutional, de facto racial separation has increased. In American cities, Negroes were more residentially segregated in the 1960's than in the 1930's. A larger percentage of Negro children attended predominantly Negro public schools in the late 1960's than at the time of the Supreme Court's desegregation ruling in 1954.

Efforts to eliminate segregation have benefited middle-class Negroes. This group, which accounts for about a fourth of all Negroes, has the education and the skills to take advantage of new opportunities. But the situation has not improved basically for millions of unskilled, low-income Negroes. In many ways, poor Negroes are relatively worse off than they were in the 1930's. Although their standard of living has improved, it has not risen so fast as that of whites and middle-class Negroes. In addition, the gap between their goals and the realization of those goals has widened.

De facto segregation was a basic cause of the race riots that swept American cities in the 1960's. The riots represented, among other things, a mixture of despair, desperation, and defiance. Many social scientists believe that racial unrest will continue until de facto segregation begins to decrease and the living conditions of poor Negroes improve significantly.

Antidiscrimination laws are a major tool for breaking down de facto segregation. For example, the Civil Rights Act of 1968 provides protection against discrimination in the sale or rental of housing. Many sociologists predict that antidiscrimination laws, if enforced and respected, will bring about changes in racial attitudes and lead to improved relations between races.

For more information on discrimination against Negroes, see the article on NEGRO.

## Other Segregation in the United States

The United States has sometimes been described as a huge "melting pot" where different races and cultures intermingle and live together in peace. But the pot has not "boiled" evenly for all groups. Other minorities besides Negroes have been subjected to segregation and discrimination.

Immigrants and nonwhites have been frequent victims of discrimination. In the 1800's, for example, white settlers took vast areas of land from the American Indians and forced them to move onto reservations. Since then, most Indians have been treated as second-class citizens. Orientals also have suffered discrimination. In the late 1800's and early 1900's, Congress passed *exclusion acts* to stop immigration from China and Japan. During World War II, after Japan attacked Pearl Harbor in 1941, thousands of patriotic Japanese-Americans were suspected of being disloyal to the United States. They were placed in detention camps and lost many of their constitutional rights. Immigrants from Mexico, Puerto Rico, and southern and eastern Europe have also suffered discrimination in education, job opportunities, and housing. See also INDIAN, AMERICAN (History); ROOSEVELT, THEODORE (Friction with Japan).

Segregation of other minorities has generally been less forceful and less obvious. Many Jewish Americans, for example, have been excluded from certain residential areas. Many have also been discriminated against in educational and job opportunities by "quotas" that limited Jewish participation. These practices have steadily declined since the 1940's.

Sometimes segregation is voluntary rather than forced. For this reason, sociologists distinguish between a *segregated ghetto* and an *ethnic area of choice*. A ghetto is, in effect, a prison, because forced segregation gives its people little choice of living elsewhere. An ethnic area of choice is a community where members of a group prefer to live, though they could live elsewhere. Ethnic areas of choice are particularly common among groups with a distinctive language and culture. For example, many U.S. cities have large communities of such groups as Germans, Italians, Jews, or Poles.

## Segregation in Other Countries

Segregation has existed since history began. During the Middle Ages, from the 400's to the 1500's, segregation was especially directed against European Jews. In many countries, Jews had to live in city ghettos. Laws prohibited them from owning land, joining labor guilds, or entering medicine, law, or other professions. As a result, these Jews could earn a living only in occupations avoided by Christians, including money lending and tax collecting. In time, people came to think of Jews as a clannish group that dealt dishonestly in trade. Jews were blamed for all types of misfortunes, even the plagues which swept Europe during the Middle Ages. See JEWS (Persecutions of the Jews).

Segregation also can occur within a religion, with sacred approval. An example is the complex Hindu system of separation by *castes* (social classes) in India. For about 2,000 years, the many castes remained strictly separated in almost all areas of life. In 1948, the Indian government began a campaign against the caste system. The government has made progress, but segregation remains in many parts of India. See CASTE; INDIA (Hinduism).

In some countries, segregation and discrimination are based on national and racial differences. For example, Koreans living in Japan are typically segregated, discriminated against, and regarded as inferiors by the Japanese. South Africa has the world's most complete system of racial segregation. The South African government, which is controlled by whites, follows a racial policy called *apartheid* (pronounced *uh PART hayt*). Apartheid aims to separate the races in every walk of life. See SOUTH AFRICA (The People).

Since the early 1940's, segregation has declined steadily throughout the world. Several forces have led to increased contact across class, cultural, racial, religious, and national lines. These forces include the global scale of World War II, the end of colonialism, the expansion of literacy, and the rapid growth of cities. Other forces have been mass migrations and the growth of rapid transportation systems and of mass communication.

THOMAS F. PETTIGREW

**SEGREGATION, LAW OF.** See HEREDITY (Gregor Mendel).

**SEICHE,** *saysh,* is a long wave in the relatively shallow water of a lake, bay, or harbor. It may be anywhere from a few inches to several feet in height. High winds, a small earthquake, or atmospheric changes may cause a seiche. Minor seiches occur daily on Lake Geneva in Switzerland, and on Lake Superior.

Small seiches occurred at San Francisco in 1883, after the Krakatoa volcanic eruption (see KRAKATOA). A more recent seiche struck 25 miles of the Lake Michigan shoreline from Whiting, Ind., to Waukegan, Ill., on June 26, 1954. Eight persons were drowned by the wave, which was 10 feet high. High winds and a sudden rise in air pressure over the lake apparently formed the seiche.

**SEIDL,** *ZYE d'l,* **ANTON** (1850-1898), an orchestra conductor, greatly influenced musical life in the United States with his interpretations of Richard Wagner's operas. He worked with Wagner in copying many of his scores, and helped with arrangements in 1876 for the first Bayreuth festival (see BAYREUTH).

Seidl came to the United States to conduct German opera at the Metropolitan Opera House in New York City in 1885. He conducted the orchestra of the New York Philharmonic Society from 1891 to 1898. He conducted the first performance of Antonín Dvořák's famous *Symphony in E minor: From the New World,* in 1893. Seidl was born in Budapest, Hungary. IRVING KOLODIN

**SEIDLITZ POWDERS,** *SED litz,* also called *Rochelle salt,* are used in a gentle laxative drink. They are named for a Bohemian spring of carbonated water. They are often put up in two packages, one blue and one white. The blue paper contains a sodium and potassium tartrate with sodium bicarbonate. The white contains an acid tartrate. The powders are first dissolved separately in two half-tumblers of water. One solution is then poured into the other. The mixture begins to fizz, and should be drunk at once. The powders give best results when taken on an empty stomach. AUSTIN EDWARD SMITH

See also SALTS; SODA.

**SEIGNEURIAL SYSTEM,** *seen YOO ree uhl,* also spelled SEIGNIORIAL, was a method of landholding the French brought to eastern Canada (New France) in the 1600's. Seigneuries were tracts of land the king of France gave to noblemen or rich merchants called *seigneurs.* Most of the tracts covered between 12 and 100 square miles. The seigneurs rented sections of their land to *habitants.* The habitants were poor peasants who made their living farming the land. In addition, they paid a small rent, performed military service when needed, and worked three to six days a year without pay for the seigneur. About 300 seigneuries were granted between 1598 and 1788. Most of them were located along the Saint Lawrence River. The Canadian legislature abolished the seigneurial system in 1854.

**SEINE RIVER,** *sayn,* and its branches form the chief commercial waterway of France. It rises 18 miles northwest of Dijon. From there, the Seine flows in a winding course about 475 miles northwestward to its mouth in the English Channel near Le Havre. About 235 miles from its source, it becomes the broad river which flows through the heart of Paris. In Paris, its waters move under more than 30 bridges, some of which were built over 300 years ago. On the left bank of the Seine in Paris are the Latin Quarter, the Sorbonne, and the Luxembourg Gardens. On its right bank are the Louvre, the Champs Élysées, and the Trocadero. The Cathedral of Notre Dame stands on an island in the Seine. See PARIS.

Small boats carry people and goods westward from Paris on the Seine past Saint Cloud, which is famous for its horse races, and past Saint Germain with its handsome palaces. The Seine then winds through the pleasant province of Normandy to Rouen, where seagoing ships dock. Southeast of Paris, the river flows through Fontainebleau, past wheat fields, orchards, and vineyards.

The Seine is important to commerce as well as being a beautiful, winding river. It is joined by the Aube, Marne, Yonne, and Oise rivers. Canals connect it with the Loire, Rhône, Rhine, Meuse, and Schelde rivers. Boats can sail about 340 miles of its length. The Seine has flooded its banks seven times. It caused much damage to crops and property when it rose more than 24 feet in a flood in 1910. W. R. MCCONNELL

See also LIBERTY, STATUE OF (picture).

**The Seine River** flows through the heart of Paris. The new Grenelle Bridge, *below,* is one of many that cross it.

French Embassy Press and Information Division

**SEINING.** See FISHING INDUSTRY (How Fish Are Caught).

**SEISMOGRAPH,** *SIZE moh graf,* is an instrument that amplifies and records small movements of the ground. From these records, scientists called *seismologists* can determine the location and size of earthquakes.

Scientists also use seismographs to hunt for oil, to study the earth's crust, and to determine the thickness of glaciers. During these investigations, explosives are set off above, on, or below the surface. This produces sound waves that bounce back from rock *strata* (layers) at various depths below the surface. The seismograph measures travel time of these waves to tell what lies beneath the surface.

The most sensitive seismograph, the *Benioff,* magni-

Fordham University

**The Seismograph at Fordham University** in New York City is embedded in granite, 20 feet below the surface of the campus.

fies ground motion by as much as a million times. It consists of a weight suspended from a frame by a delicate spring. The frame moves with the ground. But the weight, due to its inertia, tends to remain stationary (see INERTIA). The relative motion between the weight and the frame is magnified by using an electromagnetic transducer and a sensitive galvanometer (see GALVANOMETER). The transducer, a coil attached to the weight, moves in the magnetic field created by a magnet attached to the frame. This movement induces an electric current in the coil which passes to the galvanometer. A mirror attached to the galvanometer deflects a beam of light and makes a record on a moving sheet of photographic paper.

Different types of seismographs are used to measure short and long seismic waves. The *Press-Ewing* seismograph records long waves at least 500 miles in length. The *Benioff linear strain* seismograph measures changes in distance between two piers attached to the ground.

Seismographs are used in groups of three to measure separately three types of ground motion: up-down, north-south, and east-west. There are about 500 seismograph stations throughout the world. FRANK PRESS

See also EARTHQUAKE; PETROLEUM (Analyzing Earth Conditions); SEISMOLOGY.

**SEISMOLOGY,** *size MAHL oh jee*, is the study of earthquakes. When an earthquake occurs, the sudden and violent movement beneath the surface causes shock waves, called *seismic waves*, to radiate through the earth. The waves nearest the center of the earthquake may shake the ground so severely that buildings crack and fall. But as the waves travel away from the center, they become weaker and less destructive. The strength and direction of these waves can be measured by a sensitive instrument called a *seismograph* (see SEISMOGRAPH).

*Seismologists,* scientists who study earthquakes, use the seismograph to determine the *epicenter* (site of the earthquake), and the *Richter magnitude* (size). They may also determine the size of the quake by comparing the shock felt by people in the area and the amount of damage with the *Mercalli Scale of Intensity.*

Information gathered in seismology helps engineers construct buildings that can resist shock. Seismic waves from earthquakes and explosions are used to explore the earth's interior. For example, it is known that certain types of waves, called *shear waves,* do not travel through liquids. A seismograph, on the other side of the earth, opposite the epicenter, will not record shear waves. This indicates that the earth may have a liquid core because other waves from the same earthquake are recorded. Seismic waves are also used to measure the thickness of the earth's crust, to find underground oil and water reservoirs and to locate underground nuclear explosions. FRANK PRESS

See also EARTHQUAKE; SEISMOGRAPH.

**SEJANUS.** See TIBERIUS.

**The Seismograph Recording of an Earthquake** which occurred at Helena, Mont. The three records show, from top to bottom, vertical, north-south, and east-west movement. "A" marks the beginning of the quake and "B" marks the end of the run about one minute later. "C" marks the aftershocks. This record was made on photographic paper wound on a drum.

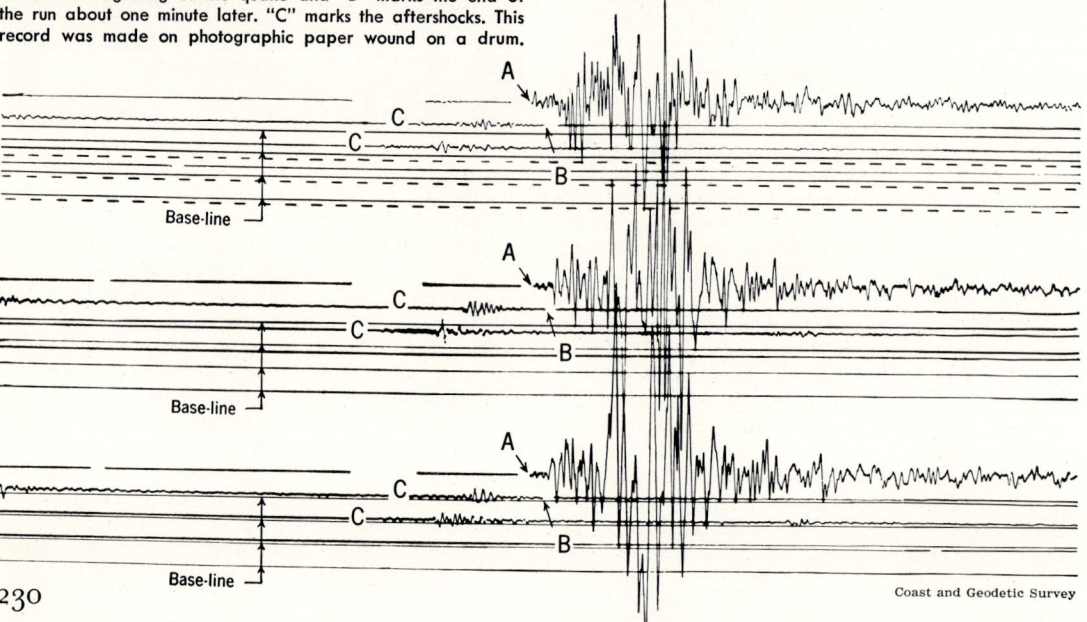

Coast and Geodetic Survey

**SEJM.** See POLAND (National Government).

**SEKONDI-TAKORADI,** SEK un DEE TAH kuh RAH dee (pop. 110,800; met. area pop. 181,000; alt. 25 ft.), is the third largest city of Ghana. It lies on the Gulf of Guinea, about 110 miles west of Accra (see GHANA [map]). The city has a modern harbor and a railroad connects it with other cities in Ghana. Industries include fishing, railroad repair shops, and sawmills. The Dutch founded the city in the 1600's. ALAN P. MERRIAM

**SELDEN, GEORGE.** See AUTOMOBILE (Selden Case).

**SELECTION, NATURAL.** See NATURAL SELECTION.

**SELECTIVE SERVICE SYSTEM (SSS)** is an independent agency of the United States federal government. Its job is to provide enough drafted men to maintain the authorized strength of the armed forces. The SSS consists of a national headquarters, state headquarters, local boards, state appeal boards, and the National Appeal Board. The President, with the Senate's approval, chooses the director of selective service. Young men must register with their local boards within 5 days after their 18th birthday. Each local board is made up of three or more members appointed by the President, on the recommendation of the state governors. The board decides upon the classification of each registrant. Registrants may appeal these decisions. See also DRAFT, MILITARY (Selective Service).

*Critically reviewed by* SELECTIVE SERVICE SYSTEM

**SELENITE.** See GYPSUM.

**SELENIUM,** *seh LEE nee uhm,* is an element related to sulfur. The Swedish chemist Jöns J. Berzelius discovered it in 1817. Selenium is classed as a nonmetal. But it acts like a metal because it conducts electricity when light shines on it. This makes selenium useful in devices that depend on changes in electric current that are produced by changes in light. Such devices include *photoelectric cells* (electric eyes), television cameras, and certain copying equipment.

Industry uses selenium as a semiconductor in solar batteries and rectifiers. It is also used to color glass and ceramics red, and to harden rubber. Selenium is obtained from lead, copper, and nickel refining.

Selenium occurs either as dark-gray, lustrous rods, or as dark-red crystals or powder. It has the symbol Se. Its atomic number is 34, and its atomic weight is 78.96. It melts at 217° C. (422.6° F.) and boils at 684.9° C. ±1.0° C. (1264.8° F. ±1.8° F.) J. GORDON PARR

**SELEUCID DYNASTY,** *see LOO sid,* lasted from 305 B.C. until 64 B.C. Seleucus I, a general under Alexander the Great, started the *dynasty* (series of rulers), which was centered in Syria and Mesopotamia. The Seleucids fought many wars with the Ptolemies, rulers of Egypt. Antiochus III, a Seleucid king, lost much land to the Romans about 190 B.C. Judas Maccabaeus led a Jewish revolt against Antiochus IV in the 160's B.C. By 129 B.C., the Seleucids had lost Mesopotamia, and their power had declined in Syria. Syria became a Roman province in 62 B.C. THOMAS W. AFRICA

See also JUDAS MACCABAEUS.

**SELF-BINDER.** See REAPING MACHINE.

**SELF-DENYING ORDINANCE** was an act passed during the Civil War between the English Parliament and Charles I. It required all members of Parliament to resign from civil or military office. Cromwell and the Independents carried this "self-denying ordinance" through Parliament. It was designed to get rid of inefficient commanders and to give control of the remodeled army to the Independents. J. SALWYN SCHAPIRO

See also CROMWELL, OLIVER; LONG PARLIAMENT.

**SELF-DETERMINATION.** See WORLD WAR I (Results of the War).

**SELF-GOVERNMENT.** See GOVERNMENT; HOME RULE; STUDENT GOVERNMENT.

**SELF-POLLINATION.** See FLOWER (Pollination).

**SELIGMAN,** *SEL ig mun,* **EDWIN ROBERT ANDERSON** (1861-1939), was an American economist and pioneer in public finance. He vigorously opposed the single tax on land value advocated by the reformer Henry George (see GEORGE, HENRY). Instead, Seligman proposed a personal income tax. He justified progressive taxation based on ability to pay. His book *The Income Tax* (1911) discussed principles which Congress put into practice in the new income tax law of 1913. Seligman was born in New York City. DUDLEY DILLARD

**SELJUK,** *sell JOOK,* was the name given Turks who advanced from Turkestan in the middle 1000's and gained control of the Caliphate of Baghdad. They adopted Arabic culture and became the champions of Islam against the Christians in the age of the Crusades.

The unity of Seljuk rule lasted barely 50 years. During the 1100's several independent Seljuk sultans ruled realms in the Near East. Seljuk power was weakened by the Crusaders and by the Mongols under Genghis Khan. The rise of the Ottoman Turks at the end of the 1200's ended Seljuk power. WILLIAM F. MCDONALD

**SELKIRK, ALEXANDER** (1676-1721), was a Scotsman whose experiences as a castaway on a lonely island inspired the story of Robinson Crusoe (see ROBINSON CRUSOE). While sailing in the South Seas in 1704 on a pirate expedition, Selkirk had a quarrel with the captain of the ship. At his own request, he was left on one of the Juan Fernández islands, about 400 miles west of Valparaiso, Chile. Here he remained alone for 52 months, until Captain Woodes Rogers rescued him.

The captain recorded Selkirk's experiences on the island in *A Cruising Voyage Around the World.* Captain Edward Cooke described them in *A Voyage to the South Seas* and *Round the World.* Selkirk was born at Largo, Fifeshire. See also JUAN FERNÁNDEZ. FRANK GOODWYN

**SELKIRK, EARL OF** (1771-1820), THOMAS DOUGLAS, was a British philanthropist and colonizer. A man of warm sympathies, he interested himself in the welfare of the Scottish tenant farmers who were being forced off estates in the Highlands area to make room for sheep runs. In 1803 he placed 800 of these people on Prince Edward Island in Canada. Later, he colonized the Red River Valley of Manitoba. He was born on St. Mary's Isle, Kirkcudbrightshire, Scotland. W. R. WILLOUGHBY

**SELKIRK MOUNTAINS,** a range in southeastern British Columbia, extends north from the United States boundary to the Columbia River. The Columbia River and its tributary, the Kootenay, run almost completely around this range. The Selkirks are not so high as the Rocky Mountains, which lie 70 miles to the east, but they are considered more beautiful. The largest of the many glaciers in the Selkirk range is the Illecillewaet, near the Glacier House station of the Canadian Pacific Railway. Mount Sir Sanford (11,590 feet) is the highest peak in the Selkirks.

## SELLING

The range is about 200 miles long, and about 80 miles wide. Gold was discovered there in 1857, and silver, copper, zinc, mercury, coal, and marble also have been found. The mountains were named for Thomas Douglas, Earl of Selkirk.   RODERICK HAIG-BROWN

**SELLING.** See SALESMANSHIP.

**SELLING SHORT.** See BOARD OF TRADE.

**SELVA** is the thickly forested plain of the Amazon Valley in South America. It is often called the rain forest because the rainfall is so heavy in the region. The selva extends from northern Brazil to southern Venezuela. The plant life of the selva includes such trees as rubber, bamboo, rosewood, Brazil nut, cacao, and wax palm. Thick tangles of tropical plants grow among the trees in the selva.   ERNEST L. THURSTON

**SELYE,** *SEH lyay,* **HANS** (1907-    ), a Canadian scientist, became known for his concept of *stress.* He helped show the nature and effects of disease and the reaction of our bodies to the wear and tear of living. His medical research showed what can be done to adjust ourselves to energy depletion. Selye became director of the Institute of Experimental Medicine and Surgery at the University of Montreal in 1945. He was born in Vienna.   NOAH D. FABRICANT

**SEMANTICS,** *see MAN ticks,* in logic, is the study of the conditions under which signs and symbols, including words, may be said to be meaningful. It is also the study of how human behavior is affected by words, whether spoken by others or to oneself in thought. In philology, the scientific study of languages, semantics used to mean the historical study of changes in the meanings of words.

Semantics may be said to ask such basic questions as: "What are you talking about—if anything?" and "What are the relations between words and the things talked about?" Semantics deals with meaning as a factor in all human relations. Human beings are the only creatures who can talk themselves into trouble, and semantics is concerned with how to avoid doing so.

Modern semantics originated in the early 1900's in what an English philosopher, Lady Viola Welby, called *significs*. She described it as "the science of meaning or the study of significance, provided sufficient recognition is given to its practical aspect as a method of mind." Lady Welby felt that a proper study of meaning should begin with the study of what words are about, namely, experience.

C. K. Ogden, a British psychologist, and I. A. Richards, an English literary critic, contributed insights from psychology, anthropology, and the physical sciences. They showed how emotive utterances are often mistaken for statements of fact; how meaning is determined by context; and how disputes are caused by lack of awareness of verbal traps. The *operationalism* of P. W. Bridgman, an American physicist, added much to semantics. According to this theory, a statement may be said to have meaning only if it can be translated into operations to test it. If a table is said to be 5 feet long, a person can measure it with a ruler. But if one says "Man is born free, but everywhere he is in chains!" what operations could verify this assertion?

Alfred Korzybski, a Polish-American scientist, proposed a system called "general semantics." The basic postulates state that (1) words are not to be confused with things; (2) words can never say all about anything; and (3) words about words about words, and so on, can go on indefinitely.   S. I. HAYAKAWA

See also DICTIONARY; LINGUISTICS.

**SEMAPHORE,** *SEM uh fohr,* is a method of signaling with targets or flags. Each target position has a meaning that trained persons can interpret. Switch mechanisms of railroad signals have semaphore targets that indicate to trainmen how switches are set.

The U.S. Navy uses semaphore flags for short-range

**The Semaphore Code** makes use of two flags for sending messages. The sender holds the flags in various positions to represent the letters of the alphabet and other signals. The first 10 letters of the alphabet, preceded by the numeral signal, become the numbers 1 to 0. Punctuation marks must be spelled out.

signaling. Messages are sent by two flags, each of which has two colors. Boy Scouts once learned how to send messages with semaphore flags. CHARLES B. MACDONALD

See also FLAG (picture: Flags That Talk); RAILROAD (picture: Railroad "Talk"); SIGNALING (Methods of Signaling).

**SEMARANG,** *suh MAH rahng* (pop. 503,153; alt. 10 ft.), is a port in north-central Java. Semarang is one of Indonesia's largest cities. It has textile, machinery, glass, shoe, and electrical equipment industries. For location, see INDONESIA (color map).

**SEMELE,** *SEM uh lee,* was the lovely daughter of King Cadmus of Thebes in Greek mythology. Zeus (Jupiter) changed himself into a man because he wanted to marry her. His wife Hera (Juno) became jealous. She disguised herself, and persuaded Semele to ask Zeus to appear as a god. Semele made Zeus promise to grant her desire, and then told him what it was. Zeus begged Semele not to ask him, but she did.

At last he appeared before her as a god. Semele was burned to death at the sight. Zeus saved their son Dionysus (Bacchus) from being killed in the fire, and made him immortal (see BACCHUS). JAMES F. CRONIN

**SEMENOV,** *SUM uh nuf,* **NIKOLAI N.** (1896-    ), a Russian scientist, shared the 1956 Nobel prize in chemistry with Sir Cyril Hinshelwood. Semenov wrote many publications based on his research work in chemical kinetics and chemical reactions that release large amounts of energy. He proposed theories to account for the mechanism of many complex chain reactions. He was born in Saratov, Russia. PAUL R. FREY

**SEMICIRCULAR CANAL.** See EAR (The Inner Ear).

**SEMICOLON.** See PUNCTUATION.

**SEMICONDUCTOR** is a material that conducts electricity better than insulators like glass, but not as well as conductors like copper. Such materials have made possible important electronic devices. The *transistors* used in tiny pocket radios are semiconductor devices. So are the *solar batteries* that provide electric power in artificial satellites. Germanium and silicon are the two most widely used semiconductor materials. Other semiconductor materials include cuprous oxide, gallium arsenide, gallium phosphide, lead sulfide, selenium, and silicon carbide.

Electronic devices made of semiconductor materials can perform many functions, including those of vacuum and gas-filled tubes. However, semiconductor devices have a number of advantages over these tubes. Semiconductor devices use much less power than tubes, they last longer, and they can be built much smaller. Some semiconductor devices are smaller than a pinhead.

Like tubes, semiconductor devices can *rectify* (change alternating current to direct current). They can also amplify weak electric signals. In addition, these devices can *oscillate* (make alternating current or radio waves) at frequencies from a few hertz to over 100,000 megahertz. Radios, television sets and other electronic devices depend on rectifiers, amplifiers, and oscillators. Some semiconductor devices can make light, and others can detect light. Many television camera tubes are semiconductor devices.

**Basic Principles.** In ordinary copper wire, the copper atoms have electrons that are free to move from atom to atom. Such a flow of electrons makes up an electric current. In an ideal state, semiconductor materials would be insulators because they would have no free electrons. But if very small amounts of certain impurities such as antimony, arsenic or phosphorus are present, a few free electrons are produced that can move and form an electric current. These semiconductors are known as *n-type* semiconductors.

Another type of semiconductor, called *p-type,* is formed by adding small quantities of other impurities such as aluminum, boron, or gallium. These impurities take electrons away from a few atoms of the semiconductor. This lack of an electron in an atom is called a *hole.* A hole can pass from one atom to another. A flow of such holes passing from atom to atom also forms an electric current.

The abbreviation *n* means *negative,* referring to the negative charge of the electrons in n-type materials. Similarly, *p* means *positive,* referring to the positive charge associated with holes in p-type materials.

Semiconductor materials must be exceptionally pure to work properly. Scientists have developed special techniques to obtain pure crystals of semiconductor materials and to add the right amounts of impurities.

**Semiconductor Devices** include semiconductor diodes, semiconductor lamps, semiconductor lasers, solar batteries, and transistors. These devices are formed by making certain regions in a semiconductor either p- or n-type.

**Semiconductor Solar Cells Turn Light into Electricity.**
International Rectifier Corp.

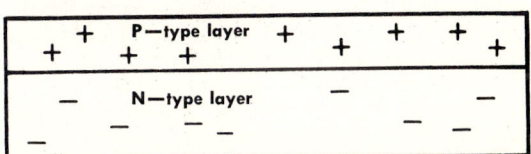

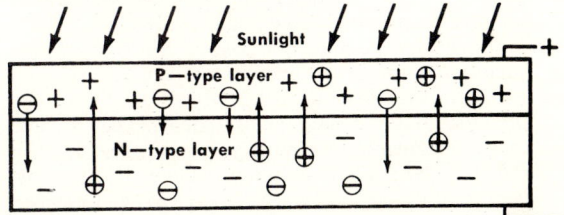

A silicon cell consists of two layers of silicon joined together. An electric field keeps *holes* (positive charges) in the p-type layer and *electrons* (negative charges) in the n-type layer, *above.* Sunlight produces additional charges (circles, *below*) that are driven into the positive and negative layers by the electric field. These charges flow out of the cell as an electric current.

## SEMILUNAR VALVE

*Semiconductor Diodes* allow current to flow in only one direction, and are used as rectifiers. They have a piece of gallium phosphide, germanium, or silicon with an n-type region and a p-type region. The area where the two regions touch is called a *p-n junction*. When the p-type region has a positive charge and the n-type region has a negative charge, the p-type attracts electrons from the n-type and the n-type attracts holes from the p-type. Thus, electric current flows across the p-n junction. If the p-type region is made negative and the n-type region is positive, almost no current will flow across the junction. The p-type then repels electrons in the n-type, and the n-type repels holes in the p-type.

Other semiconductor diodes, such as the Esaki or tunnel, Gunn, IMPATT, and LSA diodes can oscillate. They generate extremely high frequency radio waves used for communications, radar, or other purposes.

*Semiconductor Lamps* are tiny gallium phosphide diodes that produce light with little electric power. These lamps are used in some telephone sets.

*Semiconductor Lasers* produce narrow beams of intense light. They are efficient lasers, but their light covers a wider frequency range than the light from other types of lasers.

*Solar Batteries* change sunlight into electricity. They are made of slabs of silicon with a p-n junction near the surface. Light knocks electrons out of the atoms, producing electrons and holes that flow to make an electric current.

*Transistors* have more than one p-n junction. Many types are used to amplify electrical signals or to oscillate.
JOHN ROBINSON PIERCE
Critically reviewed by WILLIAM SHOCKLEY

See also ELECTRONICS (Solid State Devices; Diode); LASER; SOLID STATE PHYSICS; SOLAR ENERGY (Solar Batteries); TRANSISTOR.

**SEMILUNAR VALVE.** See HEART (Parts of the Heart; How the Heart Works; color picture).

**SEMINARY,** *SEHM uh NEHR ee,* is a school for training clergymen. It is also called a *theological seminary.* Most religions have seminaries of some kind. Seminary students usually take comprehensive courses in the doctrines, history, philosophy, and sacred writings of their religion. Many also study practical subjects, such as pastoral psychology, and academic subjects.

**SEMINARY OF OUR LADY OF PROVIDENCE.** See UNIVERSITIES AND COLLEGES (table).

**SEMINARY OF SAINT PIUS X.** See UNIVERSITIES AND COLLEGES (table).

**SEMINARY OF SAINT VINCENT DE PAUL.** See UNIVERSITIES AND COLLEGES (table).

**SEMINOLE INDIANS,** *SEM ih nohl,* resisted the United States longer than any other tribe in North America. A small fraction of the band held out against the government until peace finally came in the 1930's.

The Seminole originally belonged to the Creek confederation of tribes, and lived in Alabama and Georgia (see CREEK INDIANS). But, in the early 1700's, they moved into Florida, then owned by the Spanish. They became known as *Seminole,* meaning *runaways.* The English took Florida in 1763, and often incited the Seminole against American settlers. Negro slaves who escaped from their masters sometimes found safety with the Seminole. For these reasons, American forces under Andrew Jackson invaded Florida in 1818. This first Seminole War ended in defeat for the Seminole in that year.

The United States bought Florida in 1819, and began urging the Indians there to sell their lands and move to Indian Territory (now Oklahoma), along with other southeastern tribes. Some Seminole leaders signed a treaty in 1832, and part of the tribe moved. They became one of the Five Civilized Tribes (see FIVE CIVILIZED TRIBES). But other members of the tribe refused to recognize the treaty, and fled into the Florida swamps. The Second Seminole War, fought to force the Seminole west, began in 1835 and lasted for seven years. It cost the United States 1,500 men and more than $20 million. Osceola led the Seminole until he was tricked into discussing peace terms under a flag of truce with General Thomas Jesup. Instead, Jesup seized and imprisoned the Seminole Indian chief, who died in prison in 1838 (see OSCEOLA). Although many of the Indians finally agreed to move west to join their fellow tribesmen in Indian Territory, a small group remained unsubdued in the Everglades until 1934, when they finally signed a peace treaty with the United States government.

Today, most Seminole have small farms in Oklahoma, and live like their white neighbors. The few hundred who stayed in Florida make a living as hunters, fishermen, farmers, cattlemen, and curio sellers. They live in palm-thatched *chickees.* These open huts stand on platforms raised above the ground. Many of the Seminole still dress in cotton clothes based on Spanish costumes of the 1700's.
WILLIAM H. GILBERT

See also FLORIDA (Territorial Days; color picture: Seminole Indians Branding a Calf); INDIAN, AMERICAN (color picture).

**Seminole Women in Florida** wear their traditional tribal costumes, but the men usually wear ordinary work clothes.
Jos. J. Steinmetz, Publix

234

**SEMINOLE WARS.** See FLORIDA (Territorial Days); INDIAN WARS (In the South); MONROE, JAMES (War with the Seminole).

**SEMIRAMIS,** *see MIHR uh miss*, was the name of a mythical queen of Assyria. She supposedly founded the ancient city of Babylon, and conquered Persia (Iran) and Egypt.

Semiramis was the daughter of a Syrian youth and a fish goddess. Her mother left her, and she was fed by doves. Semiramis grew to be a beautiful woman and married King Ninus of Assyria. She became queen when he died, and won many battles, but her son overthrew her. Herodotus mentions a Semiramis who was queen of Babylon in the 700's B.C. PADRAIC COLUM

**SEMITE,** *SEM ite*, is a member of a group that speaks one of the Semitic languages. The ancient Hebrews, Assyrians, Phoenicians, and Carthaginians were Semites. The Arabs and some Ethiopians are present-day Semitic-speaking peoples.

Semitic peoples gave the world the idea of One God. They started three great religions, Judaism, Christianity, and Islam, the religion of the Moslems. The world also is indebted to a Semitic people—the Phoenicians—for developing and simplifying the alphabet. The greatest literary achievements of the Semites are the Bible; the Talmud, or code of Jewish law; and the Koran, the sacred book of the Moslems.

Most Semitic-speaking peoples are of the Mediterranean race. Jews were once a subtype of this race, but they have mixed with other peoples until the name Jew has lost all racial meaning. Hebrew, which is the traditional language of the Jews, is a Semitic language, and Jews are sometimes called Semites. The term *anti-Semitism* (hatred of the Jews) comes from this name.

The so-called "Semitic nose" is a trait inherited from people who lived in Armenia and the Iranian Plateau. Typical present-day Semites include such peoples as the Bedouins of Northern Arabia and the Himyarites of South Arabia. WILTON MARION KROGMAN

**Related Articles** in WORLD BOOK include:

| | |
|---|---|
| Assyria | Jews |
| Bedouin | Judaism |
| Carthage | Phoenicia |
| Hebrew Language and Literature | Races of Man Semitic Language |

**SEMITIC LANGUAGE.** The Semitic languages are very old. They are now spoken mainly in Arabia, Palestine, Syria, and Iraq, and in Egypt and the other North African countries. The Semitic languages include Assyrian, Aramaic, Syrian, Canaanitic, Phoenician, Hebrew, Arabic, and Ethiopic. The Aramaic language was spoken by Jesus.

People who spoke the Semitic languages are supposed to have been the first to develop a true alphabet. Their languages are among those which have the longest recorded history. Of the ancient Semitic languages, Hebrew is the only one that has survived as a spoken language. The Assyrian and Babylonian languages have been preserved extensively as literary monuments of the past. They were written in wedge-shaped characters known as *cuneiform*. LEONARD C. MISHKIN

See also ALPHABET; ARABIC LANGUAGE; ARAMAIC; CUNEIFORM; HEBREW LANGUAGE AND LITERATURE; SEMITE.

**SEMLIKI RIVER.** See LAKE ALBERT.

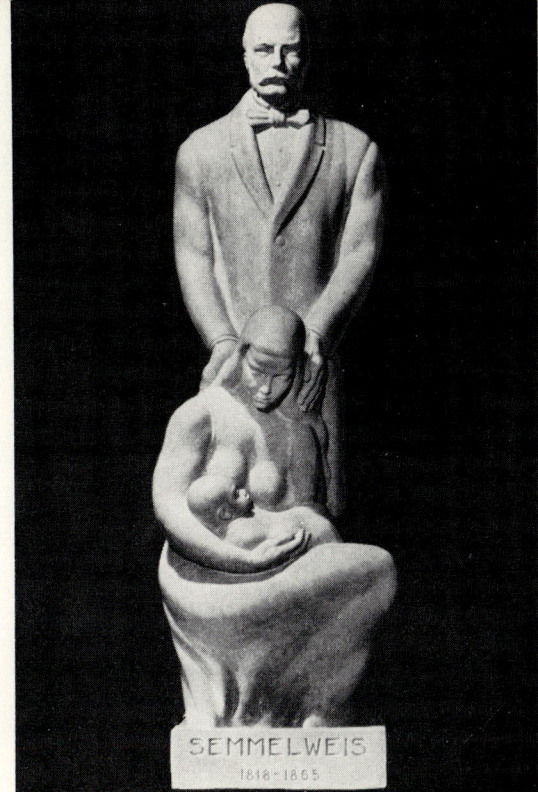

International College of Surgeons, Chicago

**Ignaz Semmelweis,** Hungarian physician, pioneered in the use of antiseptic methods in childbirth. This sculpture by Edouard Chassaing stands in the Hall of Medical Immortals in Chicago.

**SEMMELWEIS,** *ZEM ul vise*, **IGNAZ PHILIPP** (1818-1865), was a Hungarian doctor who first used antiseptic methods extensively in childbirth. At the Vienna General Hospital, he discovered that childbed fever, which then killed about 12 mothers out of every 100, was contagious, and that doctors themselves were spreading the disease by not cleaning their hands. He was ridiculed for this idea. But he maintained his stand, and in 1860 published his classic work on *The Etiology, Concept and Prophylaxis of Childbirth Fever*.

Opponents of his ideas attacked him fiercely. This battle eventually brought on a mental illness. The year of Semmelweis' death, Joseph Lister performed his first antiseptic operation, and soon afterward it was recognized that Semmelweis had been right. Semmelweis was born in Budapest. GEORGE ROSEN

**SEMMES,** *semz*, **RAPHAEL** (1809-1877), a rear admiral in the Confederate Navy, commanded the famous ship *Alabama* in the Civil War. When the *Alabama* was sunk off Cherbourg, France, an English yacht rescued Semmes and took him to England. He returned home and took command of the James River squadron, which he had to destroy during the evacuation of Richmond. Semmes organized his men into a land force, but later surrendered at Greensboro, N.C. He was born on Sept. 27, 1809, in Charles County, Maryland. He joined the Navy when he was about 17. After the Civil War, Semmes practiced law in Mobile, Ala. See also ALABAMA (ship). RICHARD S. WEST, JR.

**SEMPACH, BATTLE OF.** See WINKELRIED, ARNOLD VON.

235

**SENATE** is the upper and usually smaller house of a *bicameral* (two-house) national legislature in some countries. Such countries as Australia, Canada, France, Ireland, Italy, South Africa, and the United States have Senates. The upper houses of state legislatures in the United States are also called *Senates*. Most state Senates convene every two years.

The Senate takes part with the lower house in making laws. It may have only a minor role, as in Ireland, where the Senate serves mainly as an advisory body to the lower house. But it may have a considerable part in lawmaking, as in the United States, where all laws must have the approval of the Senate. The Senate of the United States can initiate any law, except those dealing with revenue. It alone has power to confirm treaties and the President's nominations for major federal offices.

The Romans established the first Senate. The Roman Senate had about 300 to 600 wealthy and prominent men as members. During the Roman Republic, it became one of the most important organs of government (see ROMAN EMPIRE [The Republic]). Modern Senates were set up as a check on the more democratic lower houses. They were considered the superior branch of the legislature, because of their prestige, power, and lack of direct control by the voters. The Senate of the United States now is the only upper house of a national legislature with greater prestige than the lower house.

### The United States Senate

The Constitutional Convention of 1787 reached a deadlock over the problem of representation in Congress. The delegates from the small states insisted on equal representation for each state. Those from the large states wanted representation according to population. A compromise provided for two representatives for each state regardless of population in the Senate, and for representation according to population in the house of representatives. The Senate now has 100 members.

**Qualifications.** The Constitution provides that a senator must be: (1) at least 30 years old, (2) a citizen of the United States for nine years, and (3) a resident of the state from which he is elected. It also provides that senators should receive some payment for their services. Each senator now receives $42,500 a year. He receives an office in the Senate Office Building, and allowances for travel, office upkeep, secretaries' salaries, and similar expenses. The Constitution protects senators from arrest for anything that they say or write in Congress in connection with the business of the Senate. This guarantee frees the senators from fear of offending someone by what they might say.

**Organization.** Senators are elected for six-year terms. Only about one-third of the senators are elected at any one time. This prevents a complete turnover in the Senate. The more experienced senators manage the affairs of the Senate, until they can train the new ones.

The Vice-President of the United States presides over the Senate. He is not a member of the Senate, and votes only in case of a tie. The Senate selects a *president pro tempore*, or temporary president, who presides during the absence of the Vice-President.

The Senate carries on much of its work by means of committees. It has 16 *standing* (permanent) committees, handling aeronautical and space sciences, agriculture, appropriations, armed services, banking, finance, foreign relations, government operations, interior affairs, interstate and foreign commerce, judiciary, labor, post office and civil service, public works, rules, and the District of Columbia. It also has special committees, and joint committees with the house.

The Senate elects the members of the committees. But the party *caucuses* (meetings) actually decide committee assignments before the formal elections. Both parties are represented on each committee. But the

# SENATE

**United States Senate Hearings,** *above,* on affairs that affect the country and its government are an important part of the work carried on by Senate committees. In this picture, John F. Kennedy, then a Senator, serves on the Senate Labor Rackets Committee. His brother, Robert F., was counsel for the committee.

**The Senate Chamber in the Capitol,** *left,* was officially photographed during the vote in September, 1963, on the nuclear test ban treaty. Normally, the Senate does not permit photographers to take pictures of the Senate Chamber.

United Press Int.; Wide World

**An Electric Subway Train,** *above,* carries Senators, their aides, and visitors between the new Senate Office Building and the Capitol.

**The Senate Meets** in the white marble wing of the Capitol on the right, *below.* The House of Representatives meets in the left wing. The Capitol dome, in the center, rises nearly 300 feet high.

Library of Congress

majority party in the Senate has more members on any one committee than the minority party. Committee chairmanship and rank are based on *seniority,* or the number of years of service on a particular committee.

Senators can debate an issue indefinitely, unless they agree to limit discussion. The practice of carrying on unlimited debate in order to block legislation is known as *filibustering* (see also FILIBUSTERING). A move to limit debate, called *cloture,* requires a vote of two-thirds of the Senators present and voting.

**Executive Functions.** The framers of the Constitution intended the Senate to serve as an advisory council to the President. The Constitution states that the *ratification,* or approval, of treaties requires the "advice and consent" of two-thirds of the Senators present. The President nominates more than 25,000 federal officers with the approval of the Senate. These include some of the most important positions in the executive branch of the government. Senators of the President's own party usually suggest candidates in their home states for federal positions. Under the custom called *senatorial courtesy,* the Senate usually refuses to confirm nominations made without the approval of the Senators from the state where the candidate lives.

**Representation.** Each state, regardless of population, is equally represented in the Senate. Some people criticize this practice, because Senators who represent only a minority of the population can stop legislation that the majority wants. The Senate is also criticized as representing an overweighted rural population. But, in some ways, the Senate today actually represents urban and industrial populations better than the house does. In a state-wide senatorial election, every city vote is equal to every rural vote.

**Prestige of the Senate.** Senators are usually men of great influence in their own states, and are often persons of outstanding ability. Their six-year term of office provides them much independence. They do not have to think constantly about re-election. Senate rules are more flexible than those in the House. Full debate is permitted, and Senators are not seriously checked by their leaders. This allows them time and freedom to analyze and discuss problems. In 1963, the Senate gave former U.S. Presidents the right to speak on the Senate floor after notifying the presiding officer.

Portraits of John C. Calhoun; Henry Clay; Robert M. La Follette, Sr.; Robert A. Taft; and Daniel Webster hang in the reception room off the Senate Chamber in the Capitol. The Senate chose these men for its Hall of Fame because they "left a permanent mark on our nation's history and brought distinction to the Senate."

## Senates in Other Countries

The Senates in some countries, such as Canada and Ireland, are not elected directly by the people. In Canada, the *governor-general-in-council* (the governor-general with the advice of the prime minister and the cabinet) appoints Senators for life terms. In Ireland, the prime minister appoints 11 of the 60 senators. Two universities appoint six members, and the rest are appointed by various occupational groups.

Voters in Italy elect members of the Senate. Representation is based on population, with one Senator

**236a**

All Photos Courtesy of the U.S. Capitol Historical Society

**The Senate Reception Room,** *above,* is where senators greet guests. It has portraits of Senators John Calhoun, Henry Clay, Robert La Follette, Robert Taft, and Daniel Webster.

**Congressional Pages,** *left,* run errands for legislators in both the House and the Senate. There are 26 pages assigned to the Senate. The boys attend a special congressional high school.

**The Senate Restaurant,** *below,* is open only to senators and their guests. The restaurant is famous for its Senate Bean Soup and flaky apple pie which are daily menu items.

Library of Congress

**The New Senate Office Building** stands near the Capitol in Washington, D.C. The $25 million building was completed in 1959. It is made of gray-veined marble, and it has about 500 offices and rooms.

elected for every 200,000 persons. Many Latin-American countries, such as Argentina and Brazil, have senates modeled after the Senate of the United States.

The French Third Republic had a Senate. Under the Fourth Republic, the upper house was called the Council of the Republic. The constitution of the Fifth Republic, adopted in 1958, provided for a Senate elected indirectly. Regional and municipal electors in France choose most of the senators. Overseas departments and territories elect the others. WILLIAM G. CARLETON

**Related Articles.** See the Government sections of the articles on each country mentioned, such as IRELAND (Government); also the Legislature section of each state article, such as OHIO (Legislature). Other related articles in WORLD BOOK include:

Address, Form of
Canada, Government of
  (The Senate)
Cloture
Congress of the United
  States
Filibustering
House of Representatives
Impeachment
Parliament
Senator
State Government
  (Legislative Branch)
United States, Government of
United States Constitution
Vice-President of the U.S.

**SENATOR** is a name given to a member of the United States Senate or a state senate. It also refers to national representatives in other countries. See also ADDRESS, FORM OF.

**SENATORIAL COURTESY.** See SENATE (Executive Functions).

**SENDAI,** *SEN dye* (pop. 425,272; alt. 250 ft.), is the largest city in northeastern Japan. For location, see JAPAN (political map). Founded in the 1500's, the city now serves as a manufacturing and cultural center. Products include foodstuffs, chemicals, metal goods, and silk yarns. Tohoku University is located there.

**SENDAK, MAURICE** (1928-   ), is an American illustrator and writer of children's books. He won the Caldecott medal in 1964 for his illustrations in *Where the Wild Things Are* (1963), which he also wrote. His first published illustrations appeared in *The Wonderful Farm* (1951) and *A Hole Is To Dig* (1952). He wrote and illustrated *Kenny's Window* (1956), *Very Far Away* (1957), and *The Sign on Rosie's Door* (1960). Sendak was born in Brooklyn.

**SENECA, LUCIUS ANNAEUS** (4 B.C.?-65 A.D.), was a Roman statesman, author, and Stoic philosopher. His surviving works include 12 philosophic essays, 124 letters, a meteorological essay, a satire, and 9 tragedies. His tragedies adapt subjects used by the Greek playwrights. But they are intense, violent melodramas full of rhetorical language. They focus on the Stoic belief that catastrophe results when passion destroys reason. The plays widely influenced tragic drama in Italy, France, and Elizabethan England.

Seneca was born in Spain into a distinguished Roman family. He became prominent in political and literary life in Rome. Later he became the tutor and adviser of the Emperor Nero. Nero accused Seneca of plotting his death, and forced him to commit suicide. NORMAN T. PRATT

See also GEOLOGY (The Romans).

**SENECA INDIANS.** See IROQUOIS INDIANS.

**SENECA LAKE.** See FINGER LAKES.

**SENEFELDER,** *ZAY nuh FEL der,* **ALOIS** (1771-1834), invented the process of lithography (see LITHOGRAPHY). As a young man, Senefelder wrote plays. Because he could not get them published, he tried to print them himself. While preparing to etch a stone slab, he wrote on it with a wax crayon and found that the marks could be inked and printed. He was born in Munich.

236c

# SENEGAL

- ★ National Capital
- • Other City or Town
- —— Road
- +++ Rail Line
- + Highest Known Elevation
- ~~ River

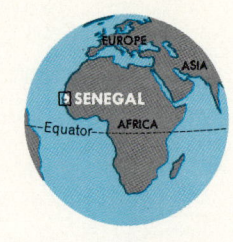

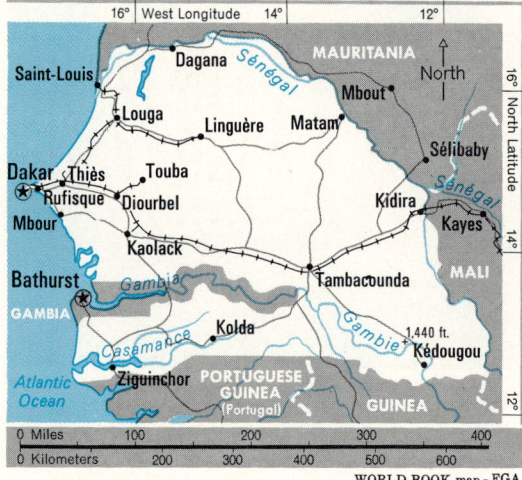

WORLD BOOK map - FGA

**SENEGAL,** *sen eh GAWL*, is farther west than any country in Africa. It lies at the tip of the great bulge of Africa that sticks westward into the Atlantic Ocean. Dakar, the capital and largest city of Senegal, is closer to the American continent than any other city in Africa.

Senegal is slightly smaller than the state of Nebraska, but it has over twice as many people. The country is cut almost in two by the tiny nation of Gambia. A road through Gambia links the northern part of Senegal with the southern part, called the *Casamance*. The country takes its name from the Sénégal River, which forms the northern boundary with Mauritania. Senegal's chief export crop is peanuts, and Dakar is a major port and industrial area.

France ruled what is now Senegal before the African nation gained independence in 1960. French is still the official language and the country's official name in French is RÉPUBLIQUE DU SÉNÉGAL.

**Government.** Senegal is a republic. The people elect the president to a four-year term, and he serves as head of state and the country's chief executive. The National Assembly, the lawmaking body, has 80 members who are elected for four-year terms.

**People.** Senegal has a population of 3,952,000. Most of the people are Negro Africans. About 8 out of 10 are Moslems, and many of the rest are Christians.

Senegal has a rigid caste system that plays an important part in the lives of the people. The caste system divides the people into five groups. These are: (1) nobles, (2) freeborn, (3) *artisans* (skilled workmen), (4) *griots* (musicians and praise singers), and (5) former slaves and their descendants. Members of different tribes often marry. But marriage between members of different castes is extremely rare. See also CASTE.

The six major tribes in Senegal are the (1) Wolof; (2) Serer; (3) Peul, also called the *Fulani* or *Fula;* (4) Tukuler; (5) Diola; and (6) Mandingo. Over a million Wolof tribesmen live in the coastal region from Saint-Louis to Gambia. They are a colorful people who enjoy music and dancing. About 600,000 Serer live next to the Wolof, and are closely related to them. Most of the Wolof and Serer are farmers who raise cattle, goats, and sheep, and crops of millet and peanuts.

More than 200,000 Peul live as nomads who graze their herds mainly in a dry area in the north and east called the *Ferlo*. Most of the more than 400,000 Tukuler tribesmen live along the valley of the Sénégal River. They are closely related to the Peul. The Diola, the largest tribe in the Casamance, are the leading rice growers in Senegal. Most of the more than 200,000 Diola practice tribal religions, but some are Moslems. There are about 200,000 Mandingo. Most are farmers and traders who live in southeastern Senegal.

Most of the older people in Senegal cannot read or write. But the government is trying to make education available to as many people as possible. About 4 out of 10 children attend schools. In the Dakar region, more than 7 out of 10 children go to school. The University of Dakar offers courses leading to several degrees, and has a fine medical school.

**Land.** Senegal covers an area of 75,750 square miles and has a 310-mile coastline along the Atlantic Ocean. Most of the people live in three main areas—(1) the Sénégal River valley; (2) the coastal region, where fishing is among the best in Africa; and (3) the region east and south of Dakar, where the land is watered by such important rivers as the Sine, Saloum, Gambie, and Casamance. The Ferlo, a large area in the northern and eastern sections of Senegal, is extremely dry. Parts of the Ferlo are semidesert.

──────── **FACTS IN BRIEF** ────────

**Capital:** Dakar.
**Official Language:** French.
**Official Name:** Republic of Senegal.
**Form of Government:** Republic. *Head of State*—President.
**Area:** 75,750 square miles. *Coastline*—310 miles.
**Population:** *1960-61 Census*—3,109,840; distribution, 76 per cent rural, 24 per cent urban. *Estimated 1970 Population*—3,952,000; density, 52 persons to the square mile. *Estimated 1975 Population*—4,472,000.
**Chief Products:** *Agriculture*—beans, cassava, corn, livestock (cattle, donkeys, goats, horses, sheep), millet, peanuts, potatoes, rice, sorghum, sweet potatoes. *Mining*—phosphates, zirconium. *Fishing*—tuna. *Manufacturing and Processing*—beer, cement, cotton goods, peanut products.
**Flag:** The flag has green, gold, and red vertical stripes. A green star lies in the center of the gold stripe. See FLAG (color picture: Flags of Africa).
**Money:** *Basic Unit*—franc. See MONEY (table: Values).

*Keith G. Mather, the contributor of this article, is a British expert on Africa and the Middle East. He has lived and traveled in Africa, and written extensively on African countries.*

SENGHOR, LÉOPOLD-SÉDAR

**Dakar Is One of the Leading Ports in Africa. It Stands at the Tip of Cape Verde Peninsula.**

The coastal areas have a pleasant climate for about nine months of the year. Inland areas are very hot most of the year. Rainfall varies sharply in different parts of the country. Ziguinchor, in the Casamance, has an average rainfall of 64 inches a year. Podor, in the extreme north, averages only 12 inches a year.

**Economy.** Senegal's economy is based mainly on its peanut crop. The country produces about 900,000 tons of peanuts a year. Peanuts, peanut products, and phosphates are the main exports. Fishing is an important industry in the coastal areas and near the rivers. Some fish canneries on the Cape Verde peninsula export to France and other countries. Dakar is one of the most important industrial centers in western Africa. Miners in western Senegal dig large quantities of phosphates.

Senegal has about 8,700 miles of roads, but most of them are dirt roads or trails. The most important railroad is the 769-mile rail line that links Dakar with Bamako, the capital of Mali. Dakar is an important stop on air routes between Europe and South America, and between the United States and Africa. It is also one of western Africa's major sea ports.

**History.** In ancient times, Senegal was the site of many important kingdoms. Many of the kingdoms became part of the Sudanic empire of Ghana, which flourished from the A.D. 700's to the 1000's. Parts of what is now Senegal were under the Mali empire during the 1300's, and the Songhai empire during the 1500's. In the 1700's, Fonta Toro, a militant Islamic state, ruled in the Sénégal River valley.

Portuguese sailors, the first Europeans to visit the region, reached the Cape Verde peninsula in the 1400's. They established a settlement at Gorée, a small island off Dakar. France took over Gorée in the 1600's, and also established a settlement in Saint-Louis, at the mouth of the Sénégal River. During this period, Dutch, English, and French traders bought slaves along the coast of Senegal. General Faidherbe became governor of Senegal in 1854. He extended French control in the area, and all of what is now Senegal was under French control by 1895. Senegal then became the headquarters of the French West African Federation.

In 1946, Senegal became a territory in the French Union and elected two deputies to the French National Assembly. It became self-governing within the French Community in 1958. In 1959, Senegal and Sudan (now Mali) formed the Federation of Mali. But Senegal withdrew in 1960, and became an independent republic. Léopold-Sédar Senghor became Senegal's first president. Senegal maintains close ties with Gambia, especially in foreign affairs and defense matters.

Prime Minister Mamadou Dia was arrested for attempting to overthrow the president in 1962. Dia and others were tried, convicted, and imprisoned in 1963. Senegal then adopted a new constitution that gives the president executive authority and abolished the office of prime minister. In 1966, the first World Festival of Negro Arts was held in Dakar.  KEITH G. MATHER

See also CAPE VERDE; DAKAR; FRENCH WEST AFRICA; SENGHOR, LÉOPOLD-SÉDAR.

**SENGHOR, LÉOPOLD-SÉDAR** (1906-    ), was elected the first president of Senegal in 1960. He is a world-famous poet and a leading African thinker.

Senghor was born in Joal, Senegal, in French West Africa, and graduated from the Sorbonne in Paris. In 1948, he founded the party which governs Senegal. Before Senegal gained independence in 1960, Senghor represented the colony in the French National Assembly. He was the first African to hold a seat in the French cabinet. Senghor unsuccessfully urged France to grant independence to its west and central African colonies as a group.  IMMANUEL WALLERSTEIN

237

# SENILITY

**SENILITY** is one of the last steps in the process called *aging*. Senility results when aging causes a fading memory and body defects. Hardening of the blood vessels is one of the major changes in senility. The hardening narrows the blood vessels, the blood supply diminishes, and many organs cannot work as they should.

Senility occurs later in some persons than in others. But those who become senile usually reach this stage after about 65 years of age. They first go through *senescence*, a period when the body ages without becoming weak. See LIFE (Length of Life).  LOUIS D. BOSHES

**SENLAC.** See HASTINGS, BATTLE OF.

**SENNA.** See CASSIA.

**SENNACHERIB,** *seh NACK er ib* (reigned 704-681 B.C.), was king of Assyria, in what is now northern Iraq. He ruled the Assyrian Empire in a period of revolt and war, and fought a long series of battles against Babylonia and its allies from Elam, in what is now Iran.

Sennacherib succeeded his father, Sargon II, as king. In 703 B.C., he ended a revolt of the Babylonians and Elamites led by Merodachbaladan. Merodachbaladan had been king of Babylonia until defeated by Sargon, and was trying to regain his throne. Cities in Syria and Palestine revolted in 701 B.C. Sennacherib regained all except Jerusalem. He crushed a revolt in Babylonia in 689 B.C., and destroyed the city of Babylon as a warning to other rebels. He made Nineveh Assyria's capital and built a city there. In 681 B.C., his sons murdered him. Esarhaddon, a son who claimed to be innocent of the murder, became king.  JACOB J. FINKELSTEIN

See also LIBRARY (Libraries of Clay).

**SENNETT, MACK** (1884-1960), was a pioneer motion-picture director and producer who became famous for his slapstick silent comedies. Almost every silent comedy star worked for him. Sennett's topsy-turvy film world rejected the logical values of everyday life. His famous Keystone Cops seldom arrested anyone. When they did, it was the wrong man. Sennett's bathing beauties fell in love with fat elderly gentlemen instead of youthful suitors. These and other characters were involved in famous chases that climaxed most Sennett films. The chases ended in violent catastrophes in which nobody got hurt. Sennett was born in Danville, Que. His real name was MICHAEL SINNOTT. He directed about 1,000 silent films, beginning in 1910. His career came to a virtual end soon after the arrival of sound films in the late 1920's.  RICHARD GRIFFITH

**SENSATION.** See SENSES.

**SENSES.** The senses of the body bring us our sensations—sights, sounds, tastes, smells, and feelings of hardness, weight, heat, cold, hunger, thirst, weariness, and pain. The senses begin to act when something disturbs one of the sense organs. These organs are connected to sensory nerves. A disturbance in the organ causes a nervous impulse in the sensory nerve which travels along the nerve to the brain, where it is interpreted. The person then becomes conscious of a sensation.

Most people speak of the *five senses*—sight, hearing, smell, taste, and feeling. But scientists have found other kinds of sense organs. For example, the different kinds of feeling that come through the skin have separate organs. The organs that feel pain cannot feel heat. There are still other organs for touch, pressure, and cold.

The senses which bring us knowledge of the world

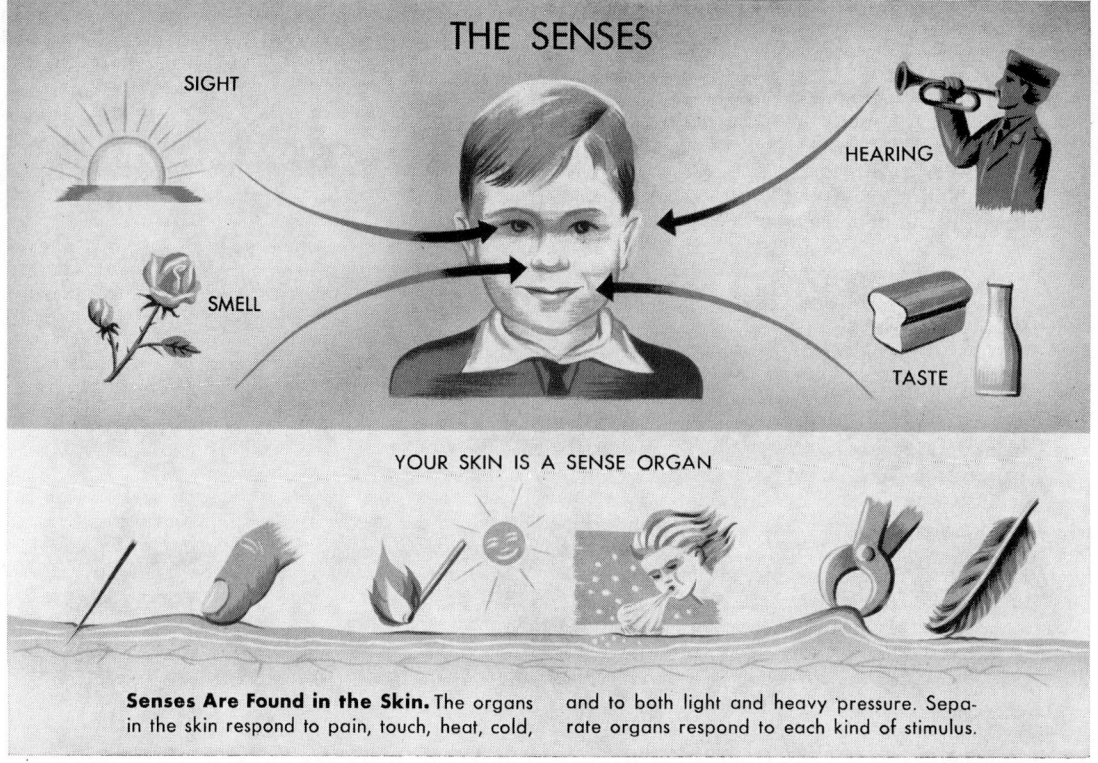

THE SENSES

SIGHT

HEARING

SMELL

TASTE

YOUR SKIN IS A SENSE ORGAN

**Senses Are Found in the Skin.** The organs in the skin respond to pain, touch, heat, cold, and to both light and heavy pressure. Separate organs respond to each kind of stimulus.

around us are called the *special*, or *exterior*, *senses*. They include sight, hearing, smell, taste, touch, and temperature. These are our most delicate and exact senses. The senses that tell us of our body needs are called *general*, or *interior*, senses. Chief among these are hunger, thirst, fatigue, *kinesthesis* (the sense of muscular movement), and pain. Pain may be a warning that some organ is failing to act the way it should.

The senses may also be grouped by the different kinds of sense organs. The *exteroceptors* are organs that report things outside the body. The *interoceptors* report changes in the organs deep inside the body. These senses are sometimes called *organic*. For example, the sense of equilibrium tells our position in space—right side up, or upside down. The sense organs for equilibrium are in the semicircular canals of the inner ear. A third type of sense organs, the *proprioceptors*, are inside our muscles and joints, and make us aware of their activity.                                G. W. BEADLE

**Related Articles** in WORLD BOOK include:
| | | |
|---|---|---|
| Animal | Eye | Perception |
| (Animal Senses) | Hyperesthesia | Sleep |
| Brain | Muscle Sense | Smell |
| Dog (The Body of | Nervous System | Taste |
| the Dog) | Nose | Thirst |
| Ear | Pain | Touch |

**SENSITIVE PLANT** is a small spreading shrub that grows in the tropics of the Western Hemisphere. The plant is called *sensitive* because its small leaflets fold together when touched or exposed to strong fumes. At the same time, the leafstalks bend toward the main stem, as if the plant were shrinking from being touched.

Sensitive plants are sometimes grown in greenhouses as curiosities. Sensitive briars of the southern United

New York Botanical Garden

**Leaves of the Sensitive Plant** react quickly when they are touched or exposed to strong fumes. After a person touches the leaves with his hand, *left*, the leaves fold up tightly, *right*.

States also close when the plants are handled roughly. Leaves of many members of the pea family close at night.

**Scientific Classification.** The sensitive plant belongs to the pea family, *Leguminosae*. It is classified as genus *Mimosa*, species *M. pudica*.         ROBERT W. SCHERY

See also PARTRIDGE PEA; TELEGRAPH PLANT.

**SENSORY NERVE.** See NERVOUS SYSTEM (Kinds of Nerves).

**SENTENCE.** A sentence is a complete thought expressed in words. It may use one word or any number of words. "Stop!" is a clear, complete sentence. There are many other one-word sentences in our language. Sentences may also use many words. In Victor Hugo's novel, *Les Misérables*, there is a sentence containing 823 words. Long sentences may be confusing. But this famous one is clear, because it is well put together.

Every sentence should begin with a capital letter. It should be followed by a punctuation mark to show that it has ended. The punctuation mark may be a period, a question mark, or an exclamation point, depending on the type of sentence. See CAPITALIZATION; PUNCTUATION.

**Parts of the Sentence.** The first part of a sentence usually names a person or thing. This part is called the *subject*. The second part of a sentence is what that person or thing does, some action to be performed, or some thing done. This part is called the *predicate* (see VERB). Even in a one-word sentence, such as "Stop!" there are two parts. The word "you" is understood, even though a person may not say, "You stop!" The word *you* is the subject, and the word *stop* is the predicate.

The subject is always a noun, a pronoun, or something equal to a noun or pronoun. The predicate is always a verb. The verb may be only one word, such as *boils, hurts, dawdles,* or it may contain several words, such as *will go, must have hit, might have been told.*

A subject of more than one word is called a *compound subject*, as in "*Boys, girls, and their noisy pets* crowded through the entrance." When a predicate has more than one verb it is called a *compound predicate*. For example, "The various pets *barked, miaowed, cackled, and squealed.*"

**Purposes of Sentences.** Sentences do one or more of four things. A sentence may state a fact. Such a sentence is called *declarative* and is followed by a period. A sentence may issue an order. Then it is called *imperative* and is followed by a period. If a sentence asks a question, it is called *interrogative* and is followed by a question mark. But if any one of these three types is delivered with strong feeling or emotion, the sentence is then described as *exclamatory* and is followed by an exclamation mark. A declarative sentence would be: *John hit the ball.* An imperative sentence would be: *Hit the ball, John.* An interrogative sentence would be: *Did John hit the ball?* An exclamatory sentence would be: *How hard John hit the ball!*

**Forms of Sentences.** There are three different kinds of sentences according to their forms. The simplest kind is called the *simple* sentence. It expresses only one thought. It has one subject. The subject is a noun or pronoun. It may be a part of speech used as a noun or pronoun. All the words in the subject relate to it. The simple sentence has one predicate. The predicate is the verb with all the words related to it. Complicated ideas can be expressed in simple sentences. Every sentence in this paragraph is a simple sentence. Many great authors in English have been masters of the simple sentence.

The second kind of sentence is a *compound* sentence. This type usually joins two or more simple sentences with a word such as *and, but, or.* "The boys cheered and the girls sang." In this sentence there are two simple sentences joined by the word *and.* In such a sentence, a comma should mark the end of the first part, unless the parts are very short, as they are in the preceding example.

Compound sentences are good for combining closely

## SENTENCE

related ideas. There are some very familiar compound sentences, such as: *I came, I saw, I conquered. Give me liberty or give me death.* The ideas in a compound sentence should always belong together. The sentence, "It is cold out and cats are fine pets," is not a good compound sentence. It is not good writing or speaking to string ideas together with the word *and*, or, worse yet, *and so*. Very young children and careless speakers use too many such compound sentences. Such speaking is annoying to the listener.

The third kind of sentence is called a *complex sentence*. In such a sentence, there are two or more ideas of different importance. *When I went downtown, I saw an attractive suit.* The important idea of the suit is the principal thing in this sentence. The going downtown is not quite so important. It is said to be *subordinate*. In a complex sentence like this there are a *principal clause* and a *subordinate clause*. The principal clause is *I saw an attractive suit*. The subordinate clause is *When I went downtown*. A complex sentence may contain more than one subordinate clause. *When I went downtown, I saw an attractive suit which I should like to buy.* When the subordinate clause comes first in a complex sentence, it is followed by a comma. The preceding sentence is an example.

**Variety.** There is an old saying that "Variety is the spice of life." Variety makes life interesting. In speaking or writing, the careful person does not make all his sentences on the same pattern. He uses many different kinds. He begins and ends differently. Even if he uses only simple sentences, he can vary them. *I have never seen such confusion* may be *Never have I seen such confusion* or *Such confusion I have never seen.* Complex sentences also offer many different patterns for expression. *I stopped spellbound when I saw the car swerve toward the railing. When I saw the car swerve toward the railing, I stopped spellbound. Spellbound when I saw the car swerve toward the railing, I stopped.* See SYNTAX.

**Sentence Fragments.** Ordinary free-and-easy conversation does not always include complete sentences. It uses sentence fragments. *Where did you get that hat? At Harley's.* The answer is a fragment, or piece of a sentence, standing for *I bought it at Harley's*. Sentence fragments are not good for writing or for speech which is intended to give exact information. They are used mostly in conversation.

**Clearness and Accuracy** are important in making a sentence. A person may state something that is clear in its meaning without being accurate. *I worked days on that problem* is quite clear. It may be inaccurate, or untrue, if the person worked only 18 hours. A sentence may be accurate, but not clear. For example, *I worked on that problem for days with the difficult numbers* is unclear because it is poorly organized. Good speech and writing call for both clarity and accuracy. A person uses good *grammar* (the rules of correct English) to achieve sentences that are clear in meaning as well as accurate. (see GRAMMAR).

**Diagram of a Sentence.** The *diagram* of a sentence is merely a way to study it by taking it apart. It is a picture which shows what each part of the sentence does and what its importance is. Some educators believe diagraming is useful in learning grammar and syntax.

The following types of sentences are diagramed and can be used as models for other sentence diagrams.

*Simple Sentence: Travel is a great educator.*

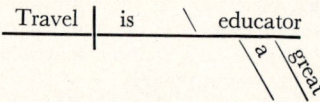

**Explanation:** The principal parts of the sentence, the simple subject and simple predicate, are written on the heavy line. The line is cut by the heavy downward line to mark the division between the two parts. On the lighter slanting lines are the less important parts of the sentence (modifiers). The short, slanting line separating *is* and *educator* shows that the noun is the *complement* of the verb, completing it. When it is a short line straight up and down, it shows the word following it is the *object* of the verb. See diagram under *Complex Sentence*.

*Compound Sentence: Travel, and you possess the world.*

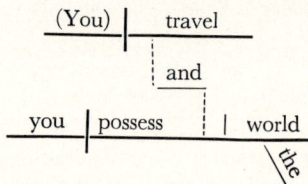

**Explanation:** This sentence has two independent clauses joined by the word *and*. An independent clause is indicated by a heavy line beneath it. The direct object *world* is separated from its verb by a short line.

*Complex Sentence: They who travel widely acquire a broad, practical education.*

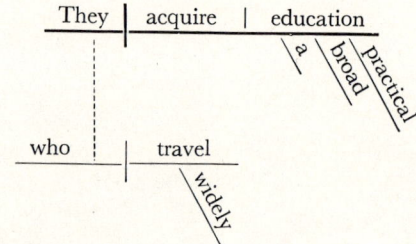

**Explanation:** The independent clause is shown on the heavy line, the subordinate clause on the lighter line. The dotted line indicates that *who* is not only the subject of the subordinate clause but the connecting word between the two clauses.

See also PARSING; CONJUNCTION; CLAUSE.

**SENTENCE,** in law, is the period of prison confinement set by a court after an accused person has been found guilty of a crime for which the law provides punishment. For many years, judges pronounced sentence on convicted criminals according to their own judgment. But now, most laws provide a maximum and a minimum sentence which may be imposed for each particular crime. For instance, a state law may provide that the prison sentence for burglary shall be not less than 6 months and not more than 20 years.

Many criminologists believe that all prison sentences should be *indeterminate* (indefinite). That is, the court merely imposes the minimum and maximum limits of the penalty, and an administrative board determines the prisoner's time of release.    FRED E. INBAU

See also CRIME.

**SEOUL,** *sohl* (pop. 3,470,880; alt. 75 ft.), has been the capital of Korea since 1932 and the capital of the Republic of Korea (South Korea) since 1948. It lies west of the Han River in the south, about 25 miles from the seaport of Inchon. Seoul is the educational and scientific center of the Republic. It contains many palaces and public buildings. The United States maintains Seoul Air Base there. See KOREA (map).

In 1910, Japan occupied Seoul. It was renamed Keijo, which means *capital* in both the Korean and Japanese languages. At the end of World War II, United States troops occupied South Korea, and Russian troops, North Korea. In 1948, separate republics were set up, each claiming Seoul as its capital. North Korean Communists invaded South Korea in June, 1950, and captured Seoul. The city changed hands several times during the war. United Nations forces won final possession in March, 1951. CHARLES Y. HU

See also KOREA (picture); KOREAN WAR.

**SEPAL.** See FLOWER (The Calyx; color pictures).
**SEPARATE SCHOOL.** See EDUCATION (In Canada).
**SEPARATE SYSTEM.** See PRISON (History).
**SEPARATION OF POWERS.** See UNITED STATES, GOVERNMENT OF (Principles); GOVERNMENT (The Organization of Government).
**SEPARATISTS.** See PILGRIM; PURITAN.
**SEPARATOR** is a device that separates cream from milk. The first cream separators were crude wooden spoons that farmers used to skim cream off the top of milk. The farmers would let whole milk stand for several hours until cream, which is lighter than the rest of the milk, rose to the top. Then they would skim off the cream. This method was wasteful, as it left from 30 to 40 per cent of the valuable cream in the milk.

Carl Gustaf de Laval of Sweden invented a mechanical separator in 1877. It took all except a trace of cream from the milk. Present-day separators work on the same principle as De Laval's. They consist mainly of a large storage tank, a rotating bowl with cream and milk outlets, and a crank or electric motor to turn the bowl. Whole milk is poured into the supply tank and drains in small quantities into the bowl below. The bowl begins to turn rapidly. The centrifugal force that the revolving bowl sets up forces the light cream toward the center of the bowl. The heavier ingredients of milk are thrown toward the outer shell of the bowl. The cream at the center of the bowl drains off into one container, and the milk drains off into another.

Separators range in size from small, hand-operated machines that handle only 150 pounds of milk an hour to large, power-driven machines that can handle thousands of pounds of milk each hour. EDWARD T. LEAVITT

See also BUTTER; CENTRIFUGE.

**SEPHARDIM.** See JEWS (Jews in America).
**SEPIA,** *SEE pih uh*, is a dark brown pigment made from an inky fluid found in certain cuttlefish. The fluid is dried, prepared as a powder, and then treated with caustic alkali and acids. Sepia is used to a limited extent to make water colors and drawing ink. The term *sepia* also applies to pigments of similar color made from other materials. See also CUTTLEFISH.

**SEPIOLITE.** See MEERSCHAUM.
**SEPOY REBELLION.** In May, 1857, the *Sepoys* (Indian soldiers) in the Bengal Army revolted against their British officers. (*Sepoy* comes from the Hindi word *sipāhī*, meaning *soldier*.) Before the mutiny was finally suppressed in 1859, it had spread over a large part of northern India and resulted in the end of the British East India Company.

The rebellion was not a mere army revolt or a nationalistic uprising. Before 1857, several Indian mutinies had reflected discontent and distrust among the people. They saw threats to their institutions and beliefs in the gradual reduction of the old Indian aristocracy, new ideas of education, and economic discrimination. An immediate cause of the rebellion was a British order that Sepoys use greased cartridges. Some were greased with cow or hog fat. To use them, the Sepoys had to bite the end patches from the cartridges, and, in doing so, taste the fat. This was prohibited by the Hindu and Moslem religions.

The rebellion broke out at Meerut, near Delhi, on May 10. The mutineers restored the aged Mogul emperor of India to his throne. Conflicts between the rebels soon reduced their chances of success. At first, they seized several cities, including Delhi and Kanpur. But the British soon recaptured Delhi and saved Lucknow. By June, 1858, the British had suppressed the revolt, except for scattered pockets of resistance.

The rebellion had far-reaching consequences. It led to the transfer of power in India from the British East India Company to the British government. More importantly, the shock of the mutiny drove a deeper wedge between the British and the Indians and led to increased segregation. This situation stimulated widespread nationalism. BRIJEN K. GUPTA

See also EAST INDIA COMPANY; INDIA (History); KANPUR; LUCKNOW.

**A Cream Separator** takes cream from whole milk. The cream flows into a small pail, *left*. Milk drains off into the large can.
The DeLaval Separator Co.

# SEPTEMBER

**SEPTEMBER** is the ninth month of the year. It was the seventh month in the old Roman calendar, and its name comes from the Latin *septem*, meaning *seven*. It became the ninth month when Julius Caesar changed the calendar to make the year begin on January 1, instead of March 1. September has always had thirty days.

**Activities.** Summer ends and autumn begins at the autumnal equinox, sometime between September 21 and 23 in the northern half of the world. September is one of the warmest months in the southern United States. States farther north have hot days during September, but nights are likely to be cool, and there are touches of golden haze. September is harvesttime for many crops. It was called the harvest month in Switzerland. The Anglo-Saxons called it the barley month.

**Special Days.** Labor Day, the only legal public holiday in September, comes on the first Monday of the month in Canada and the United States. After Labor Day, most children return to school.

Many peoples have celebrated harvest festivals in September. In Europe, the people hold feasts and games. In America, the Harvest Home supper celebrated the end of harvest. Fairs and exhibitions are often held in September. The Greeks honored Demeter during this month, and the Romans honored Ceres.

Five Jewish holidays are celebrated in September or early October. They are Rosh Hashanah, or New Year; Tzom Gedaliah, a fast day; Yom Kippur, the Day of Atonement; Sukkot, the Feast of Tabernacles; and Simhat Torah, a day of rejoicing.

Hindus begin the 10-day celebration of Durga Puja, or the Festival of the Divine Mother, in September.

## IMPORTANT SEPTEMBER EVENTS

**1** Engelbert Humperdinck, German composer, born 1854.
— Canadian provinces of Alberta and Saskatchewan established, 1905.
— German troops invaded Poland, starting World War II in Europe, 1939.
**2** Great fire of London began, 1666. ▼

— U.S. Department of the Treasury established, 1789.
— Queen Liliuokalani of Hawaii born 1838.
— Henry George, American economist, born 1839.
— Japan formally surrendered on V-J Day, 1945.
**3** Great Britain signed Treaty of Paris, ending the Revolutionary War in America, 1783.
— Sarah Orne Jewett, American author, born 1849.
— Louis H. Sullivan, American architect, born 1856.
— Edward Filene, American businessman, born 1860.
— First Labor Day celebrated as a legal public holiday, 1894.
**4** François René de Chateaubriand, French author, born 1768.
— Marcus Whitman, American missionary, born 1802.
— Anton Bruckner, Austrian composer, born 1824.
— Phoebe Cary, American poet, born 1824.
— Daniel H. Burnham, American architect, born 1846.
— Third Republic declared in France, 1870.
— Transcontinental television service began with a telecast of the Japanese peace conference, 1951.
**5** First Continental Congress assembled in Philadelphia, 1774.
— Jesse James, American desperado, born 1847.
**6** Massachusetts Bay Colony established, 1628.
— Marquis de Lafayette, French statesman, born 1757.
— John Dalton, English scientist, born 1766.
— Jane Addams, founder of Hull-House, born 1860.
— President McKinley shot by an assassin, 1901.
**7** Queen Elizabeth I of England born 1533.
— Brazil proclaimed its independence, 1822.
— American financier J. P. Morgan, Jr., born 1867.
— Blitz of London began, 1940.
**8** Antonín Dvořák, Czech composer, born 1841.

**8** Robert A. Taft, Senator from Ohio, born 1889.
— Italy announced its surrender in World War II, 1943.
**9** Cardinal Richelieu, French statesman, born 1585.
— Luigi Galvani, Italian anatomist, born 1737.
— California became the 31st state, 1850.
**10** Thomas Sydenham, English physician, born 1624.
— Perry won the Battle of Lake Erie, 1813. ▼

— Elias Howe patented his sewing machine, 1846.
— Arthur H. Compton, American physicist, born 1892.
**11** Battle of Brandywine, 1777.
— William Sydney Porter, American short-story writer who used the pseudonym O. Henry, born 1862.
— Sir James Hopwood Jeans, English scientist, born 1877.
**12** Henry Hudson entered the river named for him, 1609. ▼
— Richard Hoe, inventor of rotary press, born 1812.
— Inventor Richard J. Gatling born 1818.
— H. L. Mencken, American editor, born 1880.
— Russians launched first rocket to the moon, 1959.
**13** Walter Reed, American surgeon, born 1851.
— John J. Pershing, American general, born 1860.
— Composer Arnold Schönberg born 1874.
**14** Great Britain and its American colonies adopted the Gregorian calendar, 1752.
— Alexander von Humboldt, German scientist and geographer, born 1769.
— Retreating Russians burned Moscow, 1812.
— Francis Scott Key wrote "The Star-Spangled Banner" during the attack on Fort McHenry, 1814.
— American illustrator Charles Dana Gibson born 1867.
**15** Novelist James Fenimore Cooper born 1789.
— Porfirio Díaz, former president of Mexico, born 1830.
— William Howard Taft, 27th President of the United States, born at Cincinnati, Ohio, 1857. ▶
— Orchestra conductor Bruno Walter born 1876.

# SEPTEMBER

Citizenship Day and Constitution Day are observed on September 17. Constitutional Convention delegates signed the Constitution on that day in 1787.

**September Symbols.** The morning-glory is the flower for September. Sapphire is the gem.  GRACE HUMPHREY

### Quotations for September

By all these lovely tokens
September days are here,
With summer's best of weather
And autumn's best of cheer.
*Helen Hunt Jackson*

The morrow was a bright September morn;
The earth was beautiful as if newborn;
There was nameless splendor everywhere,
That wild exhilaration in the air,
Which makes the passers in the city street
Congratulate each other as they meet.
*Henry Wadsworth Longfellow*

Just after the death of the flowers,
And before they are buried in snow,
There comes a festival season
When Nature is all aglow.
*Author Unknown*

Heap high the farmer's wintry hoard!
Heap high the golden corn!
*John Greenleaf Whittier*

**Related Articles** in WORLD BOOK include:

| | | |
|---|---|---|
| Autumn | Labor Day | Sukkot |
| Calendar | Morning-Glory | Summer |
| Constitution Day | Rosh Hashanah | Yom Kippur |
| Harvest Moon | Sapphire | |

─────── **IMPORTANT SEPTEMBER EVENTS** ───────

**15** British army became the first to use military tanks, 1916.
**16** Pilgrims sailed from England in the *Mayflower*, 1620.

—Francis Parkman, American historian, born 1823.
—James J. Hill, American railroad builder, born 1838.
—Selective Service Act passed, 1940.
**17** Constitution of the United States signed, 1787.
—Friedrich Wilhelm von Steuben, German soldier in the Revolutionary War in America, born 1730.
—Constitution Day and Citizenship Day in the U.S.
**18** Samuel Johnson, English author and dictionary maker, born 1709.
—Quebec surrendered to the English, 1759.
—Washington laid cornerstone of the Capitol, 1793.
—Chile declared its independence from Spain, 1810.
—Jean Foucault, French physicist, born 1819.
—Japanese forces invaded Manchuria, 1931.
**19** Edward, the Black Prince, won the Battle of Poitiers, 1356.
—Andrew Pickens, frontier and Revolutionary War soldier, born 1739.
—Battle of Saratoga began, 1777.
—Washington's Farewell Address published, 1796.
—Lajos Kossuth, Hungarian patriot, born 1802.
—Battle of Chickamauga in Civil War began, 1863.

—President James A. Garfield died of assassin's shot, 1881.
**20** Sister Elizabeth Kenny, Australian nurse who developed a method of treating poliomyelitis, born 1886.
**21** Girolamo Savonarola, Italian reformer, born 1452.
—England abandoned gold standard, 1931.
—Great hurricane swept the Atlantic Coast, 1938.

**22** Earl of Chesterfield, English statesman and author, born 1694.
—Nathan Hale put to death as a spy by British, 1776.
—Michael Faraday, English scientist, born 1791.
—Lincoln issued preliminary emancipation proclamation, 1862.
**23** Augustus, first Roman emperor, born 63 B.C.
—Thomas Osborne, American prison reformer, born 1859.
—John Paul Jones, commanding the *Bonhomme Richard*, defeated the British ship *Serapis*, 1779.
—William McGuffey, publisher of McGuffey readers, born 1800.

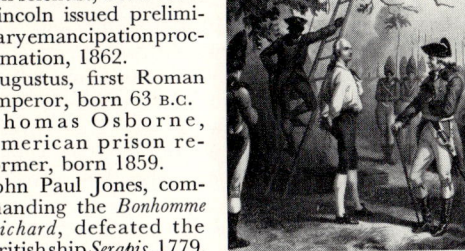

—American writer Walter Lippmann born 1889.
**24** Horace Walpole, English author, born 1717.
—John Marshall, great Chief Justice of the United States, born 1755.
**25** Columbus sailed on second voyage to America, 1493.
—Balboa discovered the Pacific Ocean, 1513.
—*Publick Occurrences*, first American newspaper, appeared in Boston, 1690.
—Amendment 12 to United States Constitution, changing details of presidential elections, proclaimed, 1804.
—Dimitri Shostakovich, Russian composer, born 1906.
**26** George Gershwin, American composer, born 1898.
**27** Samuel Adams, American patriot, born 1722.
—George Cruikshank, English caricaturist, born 1792.
—Alfred T. Mahan, American naval officer and historian, born 1840.
—Thomas Nast, American cartoonist, born 1840.
—The *Queen Elizabeth* launched at Glasgow, 1938.
—Germany, Italy, and Japan signed a mutual military aid pact, 1940.
**28** William the Conqueror landed in England, 1066.
—Frances E. Willard, American temperance leader, born 1839.
—Georges Clemenceau, French premier during World War I, born 1841.
—Kate Douglas Wiggin, American author, born 1856.
—Elmer Rice, American playwright, born 1892.
**29** Robert Clive, British soldier and founder of British rule in India, born 1725.
—Horatio Nelson, British naval hero, born 1758.
—Henry H. Richardson, American architect, born 1838.
—Miguel de Unamuno, Spanish philosopher, born 1864.
—Nuclear physicist Enrico Fermi born 1901.
**30** Pompey, Roman general, born 106 B.C.

# SEPTEMBER MASSACRE

**SEPTEMBER MASSACRE.** See FRENCH REVOLUTION (The Legislative Assembly).

**SEPTIC TANK** is a large, watertight container used to decompose solid particles of sewage. The natural action of bacteria changes the solids so that they will dissolve in liquid and filter into the soil several feet below the ground. They are used in areas without a sewerage removal system. See also SEWAGE (Sewage Treatment in Rural Areas). GEORGE O. PIERCE

**SEPTICEMIA.** See BLOOD (White Blood Cells).

**SEPTILLION,** *sep TILL yun,* in the United States and France, is a number followed by 24 zeros. One septillion is written 1,000,000,000,000,000,000,000,000. In Britain and Germany, it is a number followed by 42 zeros. See also DECIMAL NUMERAL SYSTEM (Larger Numbers).

**SEPTUAGINT,** *SEHP tyoo uh jint,* is the oldest Greek translation of the Old Testament. The name *septuagint* comes from a Latin word meaning *seventy.* A legend says that King Ptolemy II of Egypt had 70 Jewish scholars translate the *Torah,* or Law, the first five books of the Old Testament. Most scholars believe the translation was prepared for Greek-speaking Jews who no longer understood Hebrew, and was not completed at one time. The Law was translated about 250 B.C. The other books were completed during the next 200 years. The most famous manuscripts of the Septuagint are the *Vaticanus,* in the Vatican Library in Rome, and the *Alexandrinus* and *Sinaiticus,* in London. ROBERT GORDIS

**SEPTUM.** See HEART (Parts of the Heart); NOSE.

**SEQUOIA,** *see KWOY uh,* is a tree that ranks among the largest and oldest living things on earth. Millions of years ago these trees grew in large forests throughout much of the world. There were many different kinds. But only two kinds of the true sequoias remain, along with a Chinese tree that is closely related to them. Both kinds of true sequoias, the redwood and the giant sequoia, are found chiefly in California. The name *sequoia* comes from that of a Cherokee Indian who invented a written alphabet for his tribe.

## The Redwood

Redwoods, also called *coast* and *California redwoods,* grow in the mountains on the Pacific Coast from central California into southern Oregon. The trees thrive there in the relatively warm, moist climate that includes fogs, heavy winter rains, and cool summer winds.

Redwoods are the tallest living trees. They grow more than 300 feet high, or about as high as a 30-story building. Their lowest branches may be more than 150 feet from the ground. Many redwoods have trunks that are more than 10 feet in diameter.

The redwood's bark is from 6 to 12 inches thick and is deeply furrowed. It ranges in color from red-brown to cinnamon-brown. The wood of the tree is a light clear red. When it is exposed to the weather, it turns to a dark red. It is extremely durable, and is important in the lumbering industry. A single tree may give as much as 480,000 board feet of lumber. See REDWOOD.

## The Giant Sequoia

The giant sequoia is sometimes called the *big tree* or *Sierra redwood.* It grows only on the western slopes of the Sierra Nevada mountains of California at elevations between 5,000 and 7,800 feet.

The giant sequoias were once distributed over most of the Northern Hemisphere. They now grow in less than 50 groves that are only a few acres to a few square miles in area.

**Size.** Giant sequoias do not grow as tall as redwoods. But their trunks are much larger. Several of them are about 100 feet around at the base. The diameter of the widest trunk is 37.3 feet. The world's largest tree in volume of wood is the General Sherman tree, in Sequoia National Park (see SEQUOIA NATIONAL PARK). It is 272.4 feet high, and the base of its trunk has a circumference of 101.6 feet. It has been estimated that this tree would yield more than 600,000 board feet of lumber. The General Sherman weighs about 6,000 tons. Another of the largest giant sequoias is the Grizzly Giant in the Mariposa Grove in Yosemite National Park.

The wood of giant sequoias is very brittle and therefore of little use in lumbering. Also, because of the great size of the trees, it is not practical to log them.

**Age.** Scientists can tell much about a tree's history and age by looking at the *growth rings.* Each year the tree forms a new layer of wood just inside the bark. The number of rings that make up the trunk show how old the tree is. Sometimes the climate during the year is also shown by the growth ring. Wide rings show that the growing season was good, while narrow rings show that the season was poor. Sometimes lack of rain or moisture will cause a poor growing season. See TREE (illustration: Tree Rings Tell a Story).

Many of the giant sequoias are several thousand years old. It has been estimated that the General Sherman tree is as much as 3,500 years old. Before a law was passed that protected sequoias from being cut, one of the oldest and largest was chopped down. By counting the rings in the trunk, it was found that the tree dated back to 1305 B.C. Therefore, the tree was more than a thousand years old at the time of the birth of Christ.

**Habits.** The giant sequoia is an evergreen. Its scale-like needles are $\frac{1}{4}$ to $\frac{1}{2}$ inch long. They lie more or less parallel to the twig, except for the tip, which is sharp and stands out. The cone is woody and oval-shaped. It grows about 2 to 3 inches long. Each cone contains numerous small seeds, which take two years to mature. The seeds are only $\frac{1}{4}$ inch long. It would take about 50,000 of them to weigh a pound.

The giant sequoias are very durable. They have no known enemies. None of these trees has been known to die from old age, disease, or insect attack. However, lightning has destroyed the tops of most of the largest sequoia trees.

## The Dawn Redwood

The dawn redwood is the only known close relative of the sequoias. Scientists once believed that it had become extinct millions of years ago. They studied it and knew about it only from fossil remains (see FOSSIL). But in 1944, a Chinese botanist, Tsang Wang, discovered the dawn redwood growing in a hidden valley of central China. He compared cones and leaves of the tree with fossil specimens in a museum in Peking and found them to be identical. Thus it was discovered that a tree, believed to have become extinct 20 million

The Present Time

1100 A.D.

At The Time Of The Birth Of Christ

2000 B.C.

Photo © Laval Co., Inc. Drawing and photo used through special permission of Ginn & Co., publishers of Curtis-Caldwell-Sherman's *Everyday Biology*

years before, was still growing in several areas.

Living dawn redwoods have since been found in Szechwan and Hupeh provinces of China. Fossil remains show that it once grew in North America as far south as California, as well as in Greenland, Siberia, and Japan.

Unlike the true sequoias, which are evergreens, the dawn redwood is a *deciduous* tree (see DECIDUOUS TREE). Each fall it sheds its leaves and new ones appear again in the spring. Also, unlike other sequoias, the dawn redwood bears its cones on long naked stalks rather than

**The General Sherman,** *above,* a giant tree in Sequoia National Park, is one of the oldest and largest living things on earth. The huge tree compares in age with the ancient pyramids of Egypt. It may be as much as 3,500 years old. Sequoias grow only on the western coast, *right.*

245

## SEQUOIA NATIONAL PARK

on needle-bearing twigs or branches.

Like the other sequoias, dawn redwoods grow readily from seeds. Scientists brought seedling trees from China and planted them throughout the Pacific Northwest and in southeastern Alaska. Most of the seedlings survived, and have grown.

### Protection of Sequoias

Most of the large sequoias are under protection of the United States government. Only 8 per cent of the trees that are more than 10 feet in diameter are privately owned. Strict provision is made against forest fires and great care is taken to avoid any injury.

**Scientific Classification.** Sequoias belong to the taxodium family, *Taxodiaceae*. The redwood is genus *Sequoia*, species *S. sempervirens*. The giant sequoia is classified as *Sequoia gigantea*. The dawn redwood is *Metasequoia glyptostrobeoides*.  RICHARD J. PRESTON, JR.

See also CONE-BEARING TREES; REDWOOD.

**SEQUOIA NATIONAL PARK** is the home of one of the finest existing stands of giant sequoia trees. In this park are thousands of these big trees, several hundred of which are more than 10 feet in diameter. The world's largest tree is a sequoia known as the General Sherman tree. It is 272.4 feet high and has a circumference of 101.6 feet. The diameter of its trunk at the base, 36.5 feet, is greater than the width of most streets. The tree is about 3,500 years old. See SEQUOIA.

The park is on the western slopes of the Sierra Nevada in central California. It covers about 387,000 acres, most of it mountain wilderness. There is a difference in altitude of over two miles from the lowest point in the park to the highest mountain peak. From the top of Mount Whitney (14,495 feet), one of the highest peaks in the United States, the visitor can look 100 miles east to mountains around Death Valley.

There are more than 900 miles of trails in the park. Mountain streams and lakes offer fine trout fishing. The magnificent Kern River Canyon, Crystal Cave, and rugged crags of the Sierras attract thousands of visitors. The park is popular for winter sports.

Sequoia National Park was established on September 25, 1890, and was the second national park created. Yellowstone National Park, the oldest, was set aside 18 years earlier. It was largely through the efforts of George W. Stewart that the giant sequoia trees were saved from the lumber mills.

Kings Canyon National Park adjoins Sequoia National Park on the north. The National Park Service administers both as one park.  JAMES J. CULLINANE

See also KINGS CANYON NATIONAL PARK.

**SEQUOYA,** see *KWOY uh* (1770?-1843), a Cherokee Indian, invented a system of writing. He has been called the *Cadmus of America* (see CADMUS). The giant sequoia trees and Sequoia National Park in California are named after him.

According to one account, he was born in the Indian town of Taskigi, in Tennessee, to a part-Cherokee mother and a white father, Nathaniel Gist. Sequoya grew up among the Cherokee Indians, and knew no English. But, as an adult, he met many white people and became fascinated with their method of communicating by writing. He set himself the task of inventing a

Culver
**Sequoya Invented a System of Writing** suitable to the Cherokee language. He later became an Indian historian.

system of writing for his own people, and completed it in 1821 after 12 years of work. With this writing system, the Cherokee were able to publish newspapers and books in their own language, and many of them learned to read.

Later, Sequoya became interested in the general advancement of Indians. He went to Washington, D.C., in 1828 as a representative of the western tribes. He died at an unknown location in the Southwest while searching for some lost Cherokee. A statue of Sequoya represents the state of Oklahoma in Statuary Hall, Washington, D.C. Sequoya's home, near Sallislaw, Okla., stands as a memorial to him. A number of authors have written about Sequoya.  WILLIAM H. GILBERT

**SERAGLIO,** see *RAL yoh*, or *seh RAHL yoh*, is the name of the ancient home of the Turkish sultan at Istanbul (formerly Constantinople). The name seraglio comes from the Italian translation of the Persian word *serai*, which means *palace*. The Seraglio stands on a finger of land which sticks out into the sea. Several miles of walls surround the palace. In early days, the walls enclosed many temples, the Museum of Constantinople, the harem, and many large public buildings.

The Turkish sultan did not occupy the palace after 1839. The Seraglio is now open to the public as a museum. It contains treasures from Hittite, ancient Greek, and early Roman and Turkish civilizations. See also SULTAN.  SYDNEY N. FISHER

**SERAJEVO.** See SARAJEVO.

**SERAPE.** See MEXICO (Clothing).

**SERAPHIM.** See CHERUB.

**SERAPIS,** a ship. See JONES, JOHN PAUL.

246

**SERAPIS,** see *RAY pis,* was the name of a god who was worshiped by the Greeks and Romans in Egypt. He was a god of healing, and the protector of sailors. His name comes from the names of Osiris and Apis. Osiris was the most human and kind Egyptian god. He was killed by the god of evil, and became judge of the underworld. Serapis represented Osiris after he had passed into the underworld and had taken the form of Apis, a sacred bull. Many pilgrims came to worship a statue of Serapis in ancient Memphis. JAMES F. CRONIN

**SERBIA,** *SUR bih uh,* was formerly an independent state around which the present-day country of Yugoslavia was formed, following World War I. Today, Serbia is one of the six republics in the federal system of Yugoslavia. It includes the autonomous province of Vojvodina and the autonomous region of Kosovo-Metohija. Its population is 7,642,000.

**The Land.** Serbia covers an area of 34,116 square miles. It lies in the northwestern part of the Balkan Peninsula. The Morava River flows north through the fertile Serbian hills and empties into the Danube. The Vardar River flows through Serbia into the Gulf of Salonika. A chain of mountains rises in western Serbia. See YUGOSLAVIA (color map).

**The People and Their Work.** Most Serbians are Slavs who believe in the Greek Orthodox faith. Some of the people are Moslems. Groups of gypsies and Greeks live in the southern regions of Old Serbia. Most of the Serbian land is used for agriculture, and almost all farms are small. Corn is the most important food for the people of the republic. Serbian plums are in great demand in the markets of Europe.

**History and Government.** As early as 15 B.C., Serbians lived in the Roman province of Moesia. After the barbarian invasions, tribes of Huns, Ostrogoths, and Avars occupied the provinces. In A.D. 637, the Serbs settled in the territory which is now the northwestern corner of the Balkan Peninsula. Serbian regions included Old Serbia, Bosnia, Hercegovina, Montenegro, and northwestern Macedonia.

The first Serbian kingdom rose in 1168, under the reign of Stephan Nemanya. Serbia became a great empire in the 1300's during the reign of Tsar Stephan Dushan. He led the country in successful wars against the Byzantine Empire. But in 1389, the Serbian Empire was destroyed after the disastrous battle of Kosovo

**Serbia Lies in the Southeastern Part of Yugoslavia.**

with the Ottoman Turks. The Turks ruled Serbia for more than 400 years. After the Russo-Turkish War in 1877, Serbia again became a kingdom.

In 1908, Austria annexed the Serbian-speaking province of Bosnia-Hercegovina. This act caused a diplomatic crisis. In June, 1914, the spark that set off World War I flared at Sarajevo in Bosnia when Serbian students assassinated the Austrian Archduke Francis Ferdinand. Austria-Hungary declared war on Serbia on July 28, 1914. The Central Powers crushed Serbian armies. Serbia was occupied until November, 1918. In December, 1918, Serbia helped form the new kingdom of the Serbs, Croats, and Slovenes. In 1929, this kingdom became Yugoslavia. After World War II, Serbia became a republic in Yugoslavia. JOSEPH S. ROUCEK

**Related Articles** in WORLD BOOK include:

| | | |
|---|---|---|
| Balkans | Clothing (color | World War I (The |
| Chetnik | picture: Europe) | War Begins) |
| Christmas (In | Peter I | Yugoslavia |
| Yugoslavia) | Slav | |

**SERBO-CROATIAN LANGUAGE.** See YUGOSLAVIA (The People).

**SERBS, CROATS, AND SLOVENES, KINGDOM OF THE.** See YUGOSLAVIA (After World War I).

**SEREDY,** *SHER uh dih,* **KATE** (1896-    ), wrote and illustrated *The White Stag* (1937), which won the Newbery medal in 1938. The book is based on the legendary account of the founding of Hungary, when Attila, guided by the white stag and the red eagle, led his people to their promised land. The magnificent drawings that are in the book are an integral part of the spirited text.

Kate Seredy was born in Budapest, Hungary. She attended the Academy of Art in that city and studied art in Italy, France, and Germany. During World War I, she was a nurse in military hospitals. She came to the United States in 1922 and learned English in an amazingly short time. Twelve years after coming to America, she wrote and illustrated *The Good Master* (1935), a story based on her own childhood in Hungary. This was followed by a sequel, *The Singing Tree* (1939). Her other books include *A Tree for Peter* (1941), *The Chestry Oak* (1948), and *Gypsy* (1951). EVELYN RAY SICKELS

See also ATTILA (picture); LITERATURE FOR CHILDREN (picture: Attila); DANCING (picture).

**SERENADE,** *SAIR uh NAYD,* is a type of music, or the act of presenting such music, outdoors at night. It is usually an act of gallantry performed under a lady's window. *Serenade* is also the name for a musical composition, such as Mozart's *Eine kleine Nachtmusik.*

**SERF.** The large class of peasants known as serfs developed in the early Middle Ages. The term *serf* comes from the Latin word *servus,* which means *slave.* The status of a serf was midway between that of a freeman and a slave. The serf was a bondman, generally bound to the soil, and required to provide certain payments and services to his lord. In these respects, he was not free. But by custom, the serf enjoyed certain rights of which he could not be justly deprived.

A serf's holdings usually included a crude house, the adjoining plot of ground, a share of surrounding fields, and a few animals. Part of his crop went to the lord of the manor as rent payment. The serf also worked on

# SERGE

the lord's land and made special payments to him.

The institution of serfdom is usually connected with medieval Europe, although it existed elsewhere under corresponding conditions. In the later Middle Ages, the rise of towns weakened the manorial system and caused the gradual decline of serfdom. Many serfs escaped to towns. Others rose in revolt against the lords. In some cases, landlords found it more profitable to give the serfs money for their labor. In the process, the serfs obtained their freedom. Other serfs began to sell their holdings and leave the estates. In time, their liberty was recognized by law. English law declared the end of serfdom in the 1600's. Few serfs were left in France in 1789, the year when the French Revolution began. But there were serfs in Russia and Prussia until the 1800's. BRYCE LYON

See also FEUDALISM.

**SERGE** is a fabric made from wool, rayon, cotton, or silk. It has a twill weave, which appears as diagonal or slanting ribs or lines on the surface of the material. Clothiers use worsted serge to make dresses, suits, coats, and caps. Silk serge is used largely for linings. Serge comes in widths of 44, 50, 54, and 60 inches.

**SERGEANT.** See RANK IN ARMED SERVICES.

**SERGEANT AT ARMS** is an officer who keeps order during the meetings of clubs and deliberative bodies. He also serves legal papers for the assembly. He has the power to compel members to attend sessions when their presence is necessary to make a quorum.

Each branch of the United States Congress has an office for a sergeant at arms. When the sergeant at arms carries the *mace* (staff) down the aisle of the legislature, all disorder must cease (see MACE). Any disorderly member is guilty of contempt.

Historians believe that the office of sergeant at arms was created by Richard I of England, when the king appointed a corps of 24 bodyguards to attend him and guard his person. GEORGE E. MOWRY

**SERGIUS,** *SIR jih us,* was the name of four popes of the Roman Catholic Church. The dates of their reigns were: Sergius I, Saint (687-701), Sergius II (844-847), Sergius III (904-911), and Sergius IV (1009-1012). None achieved great distinction. Sergius III permitted the notorious Roman noblewomen, Theodora, and her daughters, Marozia and Theodora, to dominate the papacy. GUSTAVE WEIGEL and FULTON J. SHEEN

**SERIES,** in mathematics, is the sum of the terms of a sequence. For example, the set of numbers 2, 4, 6, 8, 10 form a *sequence*. If you add these numbers together, they form the *series* $2 + 4 + 6 + 8 + 10$. A sequence can be any set of *terms* (numbers or algebraic expressions) arranged in a specific order. An example of a sequence with algebraic terms is $a, ar, ar^2, ar^3, ar^4$. The related series is $a + ar + ar^2 + ar^3 + ar^4$. A series such as $\frac{1}{2} - \frac{1}{3} + \frac{1}{4} - \frac{1}{5} + \ldots$ contains both positive and negative terms.

Mathematicians name series in a variety of ways to describe how the terms are formed. They call the series $2 + 4 + 6 + 8 + 10$ an *arithmetic series*. Each term of an arithmetic series is formed by adding a certain quantity to the preceding term. In this example, the quantity added is 2. (The sequence 2, 4, 6, 8, 10 is called an *arithmetic progression.*) The series $a + ar + ar^2 + ar^3 + ar^4$ is an example of a *geometric series*. Each term of such a series is formed by multiplying the preceding term by a certain quantity called the *common ratio*. In this example, the common ratio is $r$. (The sequence $a, ar, ar^2, ar^3, ar^4$ is called a *geometric progression*.)

Other common types include power series, trigonometric series, and factorial series. The terms of a *power series* contain some quantity raised to successively higher powers. The simplest power series is $1 + x + x^2 + x^3 + x^4 + x^5$ and so on. The terms of a *trigonometric series* contain such expressions as sines and cosines of angles. A simple *factorial series* has the form $1 + (1 \times 2) + (1 \times 2 \times 3)$ and so on. When written in *factorial notation*, this series appears as follows: $1! + 2! + 3!$.

Series that become important mathematical tools are often named for the men who develop them. Notable among these are *Fourier's Series, Taylor's Series,* and *Maclaurin's Series*.

All series are either *finite* or *infinite*, depending on the number of terms they have. A finite series has a definite number of terms that you can count. For example, the series $2 + 4 + 6 + 8 + 10$ is a finite series because it has only 5 terms. An infinite series goes on indefinitely so that you cannot count the number of terms. For example, the sum of all the numbers used in counting by 2's is an infinite series. It is written:

$$2 + 4 + 6 + 8 + 10 + \ldots$$

The dots at the end of the series indicate that there is no "last" term. Instead, an infinite number of terms follow the ones that are written.

### Working with Finite Series

The most common questions asked about a finite series are: (1) What is the value of a certain term? (2) What is the sum of a certain number of terms? For example, suppose you want to find the 7th term in the sequence of odd numbers (1, 3, 5, 7, 9, and so on). You can find the answer by merely writing out the sequence:

$$1, 3, 5, 7, 9, 11, 13$$

The example shows that the 7th term is 13. In a similar way, you can find the sum of the first 7 terms in the related series:

$$1 + 3 + 5 + 7 + 9 + 11 + 13 = 49$$

Adding the terms shows that the sum is 49.

You can also use mathematical formulas to find terms and sums of many series. The formulas are especially helpful when you must work with a large number of terms. In the formulas, the letter $n$ usually represents the number of a term. For example, the formula for the $n$th term $(U_n)$ in the sequence of odd numbers is

$$U_n = 2n - 1$$

Using this formula, you can calculate the 7th term in the sequence as follows:

$$U_7 = (2 \times 7) - 1 = 14 - 1 = 13$$

This is the same answer you obtain when you write out the sequence. The formula for the sum of the first $n$ terms $(S_n)$ of the odd-number series is

$$S_n = n^2$$

The sum of the first 7 terms is therefore
$$S_7 = 7^2 = 49$$
Again, your answer agrees with the sum you obtain by adding the terms.

Mathematicians have developed similar formulas for finding terms and sums of many kinds of series. For more information about finding terms and sums of progressions, see the article on PROGRESSIONS.

### Working with Infinite Series

Probably the simplest infinite series is a geometric series whose common ratio is less than 1. For example, the following geometric series has a common ratio of $\frac{1}{2}$:
$$1 + \frac{1}{2} + \frac{1}{4} + \frac{1}{8} + \frac{1}{16} + \cdots$$
How do you find the sum of this series if it has an infinite number of terms? You can start by making a table showing the sum of the first two terms, the first three, the first four, and so on.

| Number of Terms ($n$) | Last Term | Sum of $n$ Terms |
|---|---|---|
| 1 | 1 | 1 |
| 2 | $\frac{1}{2}$ | $1\frac{1}{2}$ |
| 3 | $\frac{1}{4}$ | $1\frac{3}{4}$ |
| 4 | $\frac{1}{8}$ | $1\frac{7}{8}$ |
| 10 | $\frac{1}{512}$ | $1\frac{511}{512}$ |

The table shows that the sum gets closer to 2 as you add more terms. If you add enough terms, you can make the sum come as close to 2 as you wish. But the sum never reaches 2. The number 2, then, is called the *limit of the sum of n terms as n increases without bound*. You can express this statement with mathematical symbols as follows:
$$\lim_{n \to \infty} S_n = 2$$
The symbols $n \to \infty$ signify that the number of terms increases without bound. Such a limit may also be called merely the "sum" of the series.

You can use mathematical formulas to prove that the sum of this series is 2. The formula for the sum of $n$ terms ($S_n$) of any geometric progression is:
$$S_n = \frac{a - ar^n}{1 - r}$$
In this formula, $a$ represents the first term of the series, $r$ the common ratio, and $n$ the number of terms. The expression above can also be written as two terms:
$$S_n = \frac{a}{1 - r} - \frac{ar^n}{1 - r}$$

Consider the second term in the above formula. Let the common ratio, $r$, be any number less than 1. Then, as the number of terms, $n$, increases without bound, the factor $r^n$ approaches zero. The limit of the second term is therefore zero. (You may want to tabulate some values for the second term to see why this is so. Make $r$ any value less than 1. Then calculate the value of the second term for several increasing values of $n$.)

The second term of the formula is zero only when $n$ increases without bound. Therefore, we must write:

$$\lim_{n \to \infty} S_n = \frac{a}{1 - r}$$

To put this formula to work, we merely insert the proper values. In our example, $a = 1$, and $r = \frac{1}{2}$:
$$\lim_{n \to \infty} S_n = \frac{1}{1 - \frac{1}{2}} = \frac{1}{\frac{1}{2}} = 2$$
The formula shows that the limit of the sum is 2, the same number arrived at when the series was tabulated.

When the sum of a series approaches a limit as the number of terms increases without bound, the series is said to *converge*. Otherwise, the series is said to *diverge*. Mathematicians can prove that many series converge. However, even though convergence can be proved, it is often difficult or impossible to develop a formula for the sum. In such cases, the sum must be obtained approximately by adding terms in the series. In this way, mathematicians calculate many important quantities. These quantities include the trigonometric functions; logarithms; and mathematical constants such as $\pi$ and $e$ (the base of the natural logarithms).

One of the early expressions for $\pi$ was developed by the Scotch mathematician James Gregory (1638-1675):
$$\pi = 4(1 - \frac{1}{3} + \frac{1}{5} - \frac{1}{7} + \frac{1}{9} - \frac{1}{11} + \cdots)$$
The terms of this series form a *harmonic progression*. Gregory's series converges slowly. This means that you have to add a large number of terms in order to extend the accuracy only a little bit. Today, mathematicians use other series that converge more rapidly to the value of $\pi$. The expression below shows $\pi$ carried out to 20 decimal places:
$$\pi = 3.14159265358979323846\ldots$$
With rapidly converging series and the aid of high speed computers, mathematicians can obtain a value of $\pi$ correct to more than 100,000 decimal places.

For the series used to calculate $e$, see LOGARITHMS (Natural Logarithms).

### Working with Odd Numbers

Consider the formula for the sum of the series of odd numbers $(1 + 3 + 5 + 7 + \cdots)$:
$$S_n = n^2$$
This formula points out a remarkable fact: *the sum of n successive odd numbers is always a perfect square*. The table below illustrates this fact.

| Number of Terms $n$ | Last Term of Series $2n - 1$ | Sum of $n$ Terms $n^2$ |
|---|---|---|
| 1 | 1 | 1 |
| 2 | 3 | 4 |
| 3 | 5 | 9 |
| 4 | 7 | 16 |
| 5 | 9 | 25 |
| 6 | 11 | 36 |
| 7 | 13 | 49 |
| 8 | 15 | 64 |
| 9 | 17 | 81 |
| 10 | 19 | 100 |

**SERIES MOTOR**

The arrows in the table show the relation between the perfect squares and the successive odd numbers. The followers of the Greek mathematician Pythagoras knew this relationship as early as 540 B.C. They discovered it while studying figurate numbers. *Figurate numbers* are arrangements of dots in the form of squares, triangles, and other geometrical figures. For example, the Pythagoreans represented the first 4 perfect squares as follows:

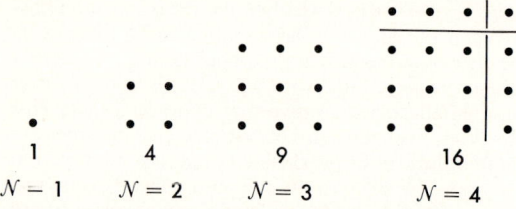

They saw that to form each new perfect square they had to add an odd number of dots to the preceding square. The number of added dots increased by 2 each time. Thus the added dots formed a sequence of odd numbers. To the number 1, the Pythagoreans added *3* dots to make 4, then they added *5* more dots to make 9, and so on. The last diagram shows how the Pythagoreans formed 16 by adding dots to 9. They added (1) 3 dots in a row along the top; (2) 3 more in a column on the right side; and (3) a single dot in the upper right corner. The total number of dots added was $(2 \times 3) + 1 = 7$, an odd number.

In general, $N$ can be used to represent the number of dots in a row or column of any square number. Then, to form the next square, one has to add (1) $N$ dots in a row along the top; (2) $N$ more in a column on the right side; and (3) a single dot in the upper right corner. The total number of dots added would be $(2N + 1)$ which is always an odd number. With each new square, $N$ increases by 1. As a result, the number of added dots $(2N + 1)$ increases by 2. Thus the number of added dots forms a sequence of odd numbers. Also, each perfect square is the sum of a certain number of terms in the odd-number series. PHILLIP S. JONES

**SERIES MOTOR.** See ELECTRIC MOTOR (Kinds).

**SERIF.** See ALPHABET (Capital Letters); LETTERING (Parts of Letters).

**SERIGRAPHY.** See SILK SCREEN PRINTING.

**SERKIN,** *SEHR kin,* **RUDOLF** (1903-      ), is a noted pianist. Born in Eger, Austria (now Cheb, Czechoslovakia), he made his debut at the age of 12. Five years later, he began an active career as a concert pianist in Berlin. Serkin left Germany in 1933 and spent most of his time after 1935 in the United States. He joined the faculty of the Curtis Institute of Music in Philadelphia in 1939. ROBERT U. NELSON

**SERLING, ROD** (1924-      ), an American dramatist, was one of the first writers to reach playwright status solely through performances of his works on radio and television. He began his career writing radio scripts in 1948, and turned to television in 1950. Several of his prize-winning dramas, notably *Patterns* (1955), *The Rack* (1955), and *Requiem for a Heavyweight* (1956), have been included in anthologies and in textbooks. Serling was born in Syracuse, N.Y. PAUL MOLLOY

**SERMON ON THE MOUNT.** See JESUS CHRIST (Ministry).

**SEROTONIN,** *SEE roh TOH nihn,* is a hormone normally present in an inactive form in blood platelets (see BLOOD [Parts of the Blood]). When tissues are damaged, the platelets disintegrate, releasing serotonin. The serotonin constricts the blood vessels and prevents more bleeding.

Serotonin is also present in the brain and intestinal tract. Some drugs affect brain function by preventing the release of serotonin. Other drugs stop nausea by blocking the action of serotonin on the intestinal tract. DAVID P. EARLE

See also HORMONE.

**SERPENT.** See SNAKE; SEA SERPENT.

**SERPENT MOUND.** See OHIO (Places to Visit [Indian Mounds]).

**SERPENTINE,** *SIR pun teen,* is a mineral with the chemical composition $Mg_3Si_2O_5(OH)_4$. It occurs in two distinct forms. *Antigorite,* a flaky variety, is found in massive rocks. These rocks are often mottled in varying shades of green. When polished, these rocks have a marblelike appearance. Such serpentine is used as ornamental stone called *verd antique* or *serpentine marble*. *Chrysotile,* a fibrous variety, is the most important type of asbestos. This form of serpentine is mined in Canada, Russia, and South Africa. CORNELIUS S. HURLBUT, JR.

See also ASBESTOS (Types of Asbestos).

**SERRA, JUNÍPERO** (1713-1784), was a Franciscan missionary. He was born in Petra, Majorca, and joined the San Fernando missionary college in Mexico in 1749. Serra became famous as a preacher, and made long journeys on foot in spite of lameness. In 1767 he became the superior of the Franciscan missions in Lower California (a part of Mexico). He founded the first mission in Upper California (now California) in 1769. Serra's writings include the *Representación* and a *Diario*.

A statue of Junípero Serra represents California in Statuary Hall in the United States Capitol. FULTON J. SHEEN

See also SAN JUAN CAPISTRANO (picture).

**SERTOMA INTERNATIONAL** is a service organization of clubs in the United States, Mexico, and Canada. Its name comes from the motto "Service to Mankind." Sertoma clubs provide scholarships, aid orphanages and other institutions, plan civic improvement, and sponsor a Youth Employment Service. The clubs also sponsor an annual Freedom Week and distribute copies of the Declaration of Independence to school children. The organization has 25,000 members.

Sertoma International has offices at 3200 Broadway, Kansas City, Mo. 64111. RICHARD C. MURRAY

**SERUM,** *SEER um,* is the clear, fluid part of blood that is left after a clot forms. Serum is just like *plasma* (the total liquid part of the blood) except that it does not contain the substance called *fibrinogen* that causes clotting.

Serum contains such substances as salt, proteins, glucose, and fats. Samples of serum are used to help *diagnose* (determine) the medical problems of patients. Tests on the blood serum of a patient are called *serologic tests*.

Serum proteins contain *antibodies* that the body produces to fight certain diseases and *toxins* (poisons). A serum containing antibodies that is taken from a person or animal and injected into a patient is called an *antiserum.* Antiserums work against such diseases as diphtheria and *tetanus* (lockjaw). *Antitoxins* are certain kinds of antiserums.

Serum taken from a person who has recently recovered from a disease usually contains more than the normal amount of antibodies. This serum may help cure or prevent the disease. However, doctors have recently found a more efficient way of providing the antibodies to fight a disease. Instead of using the entire serum, they inject only a part of the serum called *gamma globulin*. Gamma globulin is a kind of protein that contains most of the blood's antibodies. Gamma globulin preparations are used to fight and prevent hepatitis, measles, mumps, and whooping cough.

Serum obtained from animals is easier to obtain and costs less than serum from human beings. But it is often less effective and more dangerous than human serum. A horse is usually used because it has a large amount of blood and produces many antibodies. Horse antiserums are used to prevent rabies and to treat persons bitten by poisonous snakes and black widow spiders. They are also used to treat *botulism* (food poisoning), gas gangrene, and rabies. However, some patients are *allergic* (extremely sensitive) to animal proteins, and may have serious reactions.   SOLOMON GARB

See also ANTIBODY; PLASMA; TRANSFUSION, BLOOD; ANTITOXIN; GAMMA GLOBULIN.

**SERUM SICKNESS** is a nonfatal illness that frequently follows an injection of animal serum (see SERUM). It is caused by a reaction between the protein of the injected serum and specific protective substances produced by the body.

Symptoms include hives, fever, asthma, and painful swollen joints. They usually appear within 5 to 10 days. The symptoms develop sooner and are usually more severe if the person has had a previous injection of a similar serum.   R. B. CAPPS

**SERVAL,** *SUR vul,* is a large wildcat that lives in Africa, from the Cape of Good Hope north to Senegal and the Sudan. Its tawny, black-spotted fur is sold under the trade name of *tiger cat.* The male is from 3 to 4 feet long, and stands 18 to 23 inches tall at the shoulder.

**The Serval** has a head much like that of the domestic cat. The body markings are a combination of dots and stripes.
New York Zoological Society

## SERVICE, ROBERT WILLIAM

It has a 12-inch tail and large ears. These animals are easy to tame if they are captured when young, but they are difficult to raise. They are usually taken in snares or are treed by dogs. They hide in bushes along riverbanks, waiting for their prey. They eat small fowl and other creatures up to the size of small antelopes. They generally hunt on the ground, but are expert climbers and often go into the trees after birds.

**Scientific Classification.** The serval is a member of the cat family, *Felidae.* It is classified as genus *Felis,* species *F. serval.*   ERNEST S. BOOTH

**SERVANT** is an employee who serves in a personal capacity for his employer. He performs such services as preparing food, caring for children, and other domestic duties. At one time, most servants lived in the homes of their employers. Now most servants work for wages at more or less regular hours, just as other employees do. During colonial days in America, indentured servants worked for masters as a means of paying off indebtedness.   JOHN F. CUBER

See also INDENTURED SERVANT.

**SERVETUS,** *sur VEE tus,* **MICHAEL** (1511-1553), was a Spanish physician and theologian. His description of the pulmonary circulation is considered a classic passage in physiology. He was born in Tudela, Spain, and studied medicine in Paris. He lectured in Paris, and then practiced medicine in several French cities. Civil and church authorities condemned Servetus for not conforming to accepted doctrines in his religious writings. John Calvin accused him of being a heretic, and he was burned at the stake.   CAROLINE A. CHANDLER

See also UNITARIAN UNIVERSALIST ASSOCIATION (Beginnings); CALVIN, JOHN (Expelled from Geneva).

**SERVICE, ROBERT WILLIAM** (1874-1958), a Canadian poet, won fame with such rollicking frontier ballads as "The Shooting of Dan McGrew" and "The Cremation of Sam McGee." Service became a productive writer of both prose and verse, but it was his verse that won wide popularity for its vigor and verve. *Songs of a Sourdough* (1907) established his reputation as a poet, and *The Trail of '98* (1910) became his most popular novel.

Service was born in Preston, England, and was educated at Hillhead High School in Glasgow and the University of Glasgow. He worked briefly as a bank clerk in Scotland, and then moved to Canada in 1905. After several years of wandering in the Canadian and American West, he returned to banking. His work as a bank clerk at Whitehorse and Dawson City in the Yukon territory early in the 1900's gave him the material for his poems of the miners, hunters, and trappers of the Northwest. Before World War I, Service was a war correspondent in Europe. After the war broke out, he served as an ambulance driver. He lived in France during most of his later life, although he returned periodically to Canada.   DESMOND PACEY

**Robert Service**
Press Association

249

# SERVICE CLUB

**SERVICE CLUB** is an organization that works to improve the community. Service clubs sponsor community projects, conduct youth activities, support welfare services, and promote good citizenship. Most service clubs are made up of professional and business men or women. Important service clubs include International Association of Lions Clubs, Kiwanis International, Optimist International, and Rotary International. THE WORLD BOOK has a separate article on each of these clubs.

**SERVICE CROSS, DISTINGUISHED.** See DECORATIONS AND MEDALS (Military Awards).

**SERVICE MEDAL, DISTINGUISHED.** See DECORATIONS AND MEDALS (Military Awards).

**SERVICE ORGANIZATIONS, UNITED.** See UNITED SERVICE ORGANIZATIONS.

**SERVICE STATION.** See PETROLEUM (Service Stations).

**SERVING.** See TABLE SETTING; CATERING.

**SERVITES, ORDER OF.** See RELIGIOUS ORDERS.

**SERVIUS TULLIUS,** the sixth of the seven legendary kings of Rome, reigned from 578 to 534 B.C. Many of his deeds are legendary. Legend says his mother was a slave who served the wife of Tarquinius Priscus, a king of Rome. The queen, a prophetess, predicted greatness for Servius. Servius won the favor of the king, and married the king's daughter. He became king when the king died, and held the throne for 44 years.

Servius reorganized the state by placing citizens in *centuries* (voting groups) according to wealth. All people had some power, but the rich were the most powerful. Servius encouraged the *plebeians* (members of the lower class), and built many structures. An early wall and sewer, credited to Servius, were actually built later. Servius was murdered by his daughter and her husband, Tarquinius Superbus. HERBERT M. HOWE

**SERVOMECHANISM,** SUR *voh* MECK *uh nizm*, is a type of control system that detects and corrects errors. Industry uses servomechanisms to control automatic machines. On warships, servomechanisms aim guns, using information received from radar. Servomechanisms are also used to keep guided missiles on course.

In a servomechanism system, a signal from a *controller* is compared to a signal from the controlled mechanism. The difference between the two signals, usually called the *error signal*, is used to operate a *servodevice*. This mechanism moves or changes the controlled device until the difference in signal becomes zero or nearly zero. For example, the automatic pilot used in airplanes has a servomechanism that compares the desired course of the airplane to the actual course. The error signal represents any difference between the two, and is used to operate the airplane's controls until it is back on course. When the airplane is on course, the error signal is zero. See GYROPILOT.

Man also uses the principle of the servomechanism in everyday living. For example, the brain of a driver compares the actual position of his car on the road to the desired position. If the car moves off the road, the eye transmits a signal to the brain. The brain compares the desired position to the actual position seen by the eye. It directs the arms to rotate the steering wheel until the car is back on the road. OTTO A. UYEHARA

See also AUTOMATION.

**SESAME,** SES *uh mee*, is an herb grown in tropical countries. It is grown mainly for the oil obtained from its seeds. It originally grew in China, India, and Japan, and has been cultivated in Mexico and in the southern United States. The plant is an annual, and grows about 2 feet high. Its leaves are oblong. It has tiny flowers that may be pink or white, depending upon the species. Small capsules contain flat seeds that range from white to brown in color.

USDA
**The Sesame Plant** bears capsules that contain seeds.

The oil obtained from sesame seeds is straw-colored, and is similar to olive oil. It is used in salad dressings and in cooking. The seeds have a delicious taste and are used to flavor bread, biscuits, candy, and other delicacies.

**Scientific Classification.** The sesame plant belongs to the pedalium family, *Pedaliaceae*. The scientific name is genus *Sesamum*, species *S. indicum*. HAROLD NORMAN MOLDENKE

**SESAMOID.** See KNEECAP.

**SESQUICENTENNIAL,** SES *kwih sen* TEN *ih ul*, **EXPOSITION** was held in Philadelphia in the summer of 1926, to mark the 150th anniversary of the signing of the Declaration of Independence. Almost 6 million persons visited the 1,000-acre exposition grounds.

**SESSHU,** *ses shoo* (1419-1506), a Buddhist monk, was the greatest Japanese landscape painter in the tradition of Chinese ink drawing. His style is easy to recognize through its bold compositions, forceful drawing, and disregard of subtle modeling. His masterpiece is a long scroll showing Chinese river scenery. One of his landscapes appears in color in the PAINTING article. Sesshu learned his art by studying the works of Chinese ink masters of the 1200's. ALEXANDER C. SOPER

**SESSIONS, ROGER** (1896-    ), is one of the foremost American composers. His music, which is very complex and dissonant, is considered among the most significant work produced in the United States. It includes three symphonies, a piano concerto, an opera entitled *The Trial of Lucullus* (1947), two string quartets, a quintet, and other chamber music. Sessions was born in Brooklyn, N.Y. He lived in Europe from 1925 to 1933. Later, he taught in American universities. HALSEY STEVENS

**SESTET.** See SONNET.

**SET** was the ancient Egyptian god of evil. He was also known by the names Seth and Sutekh. He was a wicked and powerful god who often used witchcraft to achieve his aims. As god of the desert, he was responsible for the storms that blew from the Libyan Desert and damaged the farms and crops.

As the principle of evil, Set was in constant warfare with his brother Osiris, who represented the principle of goodness (see OSIRIS). Set murdered Osiris, but was in turn slain by Horus (see HORUS; ISIS). Set was represented by the head of a strange-looking animal that may have been a cross between a donkey and a pig. His most important center of worship was at Ombos in Upper Egypt. I. J. GELB

Illinois Education Assn.

**SET THEORY** is a way of solving problems in mathematics and in *logic* (reasoning). By studying set theory, you can get a better understanding of arithmetic and of mathematics as a whole.

A *set* is a collection of objects or ideas. A family, a box of crayons, or a flock of sheep is a set of objects. The rules of a game or the even numbers from 10 to 20 are sets of ideas. The items that make up a set are *members* or *elements* of the set. A red crayon is a member of a set of crayons. The number 16 is a member of the set of even numbers from 10 to 20.

Mathematicians use letters to designate sets and the members of sets. Capital letters are used to name sets, and small letters are used to name the members of sets. For example, the letter $C$ may stand for "the set of fifth-grade girls with curly hair." The letters $m$, $s$, and $r$ would stand for the members of this set—Martha, Sara, and Ruth. To show that set $C$ consists of Martha, Sara,

*Charlotte W. Junge, the contributor of this article, is Professor of Education at Wayne State University and Assistant Editor of* The Arithmetic Teacher.

and Ruth, you write: Set $C = \{$Martha, Sara, Ruth$\}$ or simply $C = \{m, s, r\}$. A set is shown by enclosing the members in *braces* $\{\ \}$.

You may want to show that a member belongs to a certain set. For example, to show that Sara belongs to set $C$, you write $s \in C$, which is read: "$s$ is a member of $C$." To show that Jean is not a member of set $C$, you write $j \notin C$, which means: "$j$ is not a member of $C$."

A set may also be defined in terms of its properties. A *property* is something that relates the members to one another. In the example above, $C$ has three properties: (1) its members are girls, (2) its members are in the fifth grade, and (3) its members have curly hair. To show these properties, you write: $C = x|x$ is a fifth-grade girl with curly hair. This statement is read: "$C$ is the set of all members, $x$, such that $x$ is a fifth-grade girl with curly hair." The vertical line between the $x$'s means "such that."

### Kinds of Sets

In working with sets, it is important to be able to compare one set with another. Mathematicians have

250a

# SET THEORY

given names to various kinds of sets to aid in such comparisons. The names refer to the number of members in a set and to relationships between sets. Ten main kinds of sets are (1) finite sets, (2) infinite sets, (3) empty sets, (4) single element sets, (5) equivalent sets, (6) equal sets, (7) overlapping sets, (8) disjoint sets, (9) universal sets, and (10) subsets. Every set can be called by several of these names. For example, equivalent sets can be finite and also disjoint.

**Finite Sets and Infinite Sets.** A *finite* set has a definite number of members. "Three cats" and "three thousand head of cattle" are finite sets. To describe a finite set, you list all the members of the set. For example, if set $W$ is the set of all counting numbers greater than 4 and less than 10, you write: $W = \{5, 6, 7, 8, 9\}$. An *infinite* set has an endless number of members. The numerals you use in counting form an infinite set: 1, 2, 3, 4, 5, and so on without end. It is impossible to list all the members of an infinite set. To describe such a set, you list the first few members and write three dots to show that the number of members is endless:

$$\{1, 2, 3, \ldots\}$$

**Empty Sets** have no members. They also are called *null sets*. The following sets show which students were absent from school on three days. Monday: Paul, Frances. Tuesday: Joe. Wednesday: No one absent.

The Monday set of absentees has two members and the Tuesday set has one member. The Wednesday set has no members, so it is an empty set. You show an empty set by leaving a blank space between a pair of braces, or by writing the symbol $\emptyset$:

Students absent on Wednesday = $\{\ \} = \emptyset$

**Single Element Sets** contain only one member. In the example above, the set of students absent on Tuesday is a single element set.

Students absent on Tuesday = $\{\text{Joe}\} = \{1\}$

**Equivalent Sets** have the same number of members. You can match their members one for one against each other. If the number of desks in a classroom is the same as the number of students, the set of desks is equivalent to the set of students. In the illustration below, the set of dogs is equivalent to the set of doghouses:

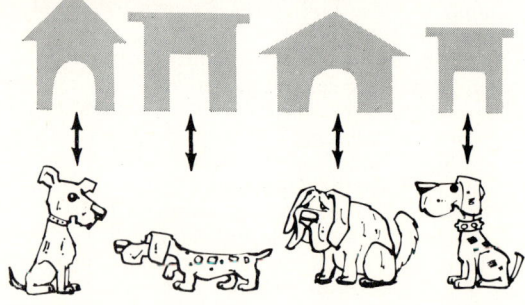

To show that sets $A$ and $B$ are equivalent, you write: $A \leftrightarrow B$. The symbol $\leftrightarrow$ means "is equivalent to." It shows that the members of both sets can be matched one for one, as in the illustration. But if you have a set of five dogs and a set of four dog houses, then the sets are not equivalent and you would write $A \not\leftrightarrow B$, which is read: "$A$ is not equivalent to $B$."

**Equal Sets** have the same members. Suppose that $C$ stands for the set of students who received 100% on a spelling test: $C = \{\text{Steve, Mark, Joan, Tom}\}$. Suppose also that $D$ represents the set of students who received 100% on an arithmetic test: $D = \{\text{Tom, Joan, Mark, Steve}\}$. Then, $C$ is equal to $D$ because both sets have the same members. To show they are equal, you write: $C = D$.

**Overlapping Sets and Disjoint Sets.** *Overlapping* sets have some members in common. Suppose that Dick, Susan, and Betty were class officers last year, and that Mark, Susan, and Tom are class officers this year. Susan belongs to both sets. The sets overlap, as shown in the following diagram:

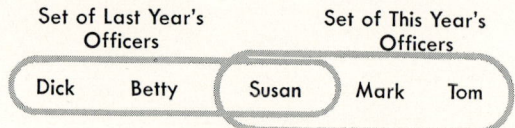

*Disjoint* sets have no members in common. The illustration below shows a pair of disjoint sets:

**Universal Sets** consist of all members being considered at any one time. Such a set may be called a *universe*. It is usually represented by the letter $U$. Suppose that in a certain problem you are working only with the numbers from 1 to 10. The universal set then has the following members: $U = \{1, 2, 3, 4, 5, 6, 7, 8, 9, 10\}$. In another problem, the universe might be "all even numbers," and in still another it might be "all students in sixth grade."

**Subsets** are contained within other sets. For example, the set "all sixth-graders with brown eyes" is a subset contained in the set "all sixth-graders." Two subsets of the set of numbers from 1 to 10 are shown below.

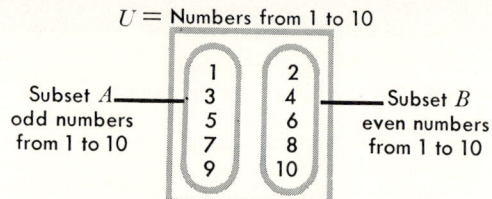

To show that $A$ and $B$ are subsets of $U$, you write $A \subset U$ and $B \subset U$. The symbol $\subset$ means "is included in."

Note that subsets $A$ and $B$ are finite sets because they have a definite number of members. They also are equivalent sets because you can match their members one for one against each other. They also are disjoint sets because no members belong to both $A$ and $B$.

### Diagraming Sets

Mathematicians often use diagrams to show relationships and to solve problems. In the 1700's, Leonhard Euler, a Swiss mathematician, first used circles to represent sets and the relationships between them. In 1894, John Venn, an English scholar, included rectangles in these diagrams.

# SET THEORY

In these diagrams, called *Venn diagrams* or *Euler's circles*, rectangles and circles are used to represent sets. A circle of a certain size may stand for a finite set, an infinite set, or an empty set. Two circles of the same size may represent equivalent sets or sets with different numbers of members. Therefore, there are no specific Venn diagrams for finite sets, infinite sets, empty sets, single element sets, or equivalent sets.

**Diagram for Universal Sets** is a rectangle labeled with the letter $U$. This diagram stands for all the mem-

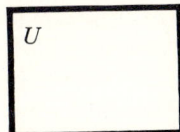

bers you are considering in a particular problem. It may represent "all counting numbers," "the months of the year," or any other such group.

**Diagram for Subsets** is a circle labeled with the letter that represents the set. Suppose that the universal set $U$ stands for all the students in Patrick Henry school, and that the subset $A$ is all the sixth-grade students in Patrick Henry school. You draw the circle for $A$ entirely within the rectangle for $U$ because every member of $A$ is also a member of $U$.

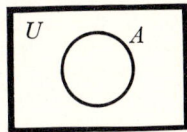

To show a subset of $A$, you draw another circle inside $A$. Suppose $B$ stands for the boys in the sixth grade at Patrick Henry school. Here is the way you would add set $B$ to the Venn diagram above:

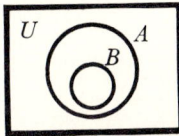

You draw the circle for $B$ entirely within the circle for $A$ because every member of $B$ is also a member of $A$.

**Diagram for Equal Sets** is a single circle labeled with two or more letters. Each letter stands for a set. The

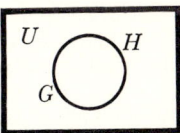

single circle shows that each set has exactly the same members. You can think of the circle as two or more circles that overlap completely. For example, suppose $U$ is the set of numbers from 1 to 10. Let $G$ be the set of numbers used in counting to 10 by 2's. Let $H$ be the set of numbers from 1 to 10 that can be divided evenly by 2. You can list the members of these sets as follows:
$$U = \{1, 2, 3, 4, 5, 6, 7, 8, 9, 10\}$$
$$G = \{2, 4, 6, 8, 10\}$$
$$H = \{2, 4, 6, 8, 10\}$$
Sets $G$ and $H$ have exactly the same members, so you represent both with a single circle in the diagram.

**Diagram for Overlapping Sets** consists of overlapping circles. This diagram shows that some of the

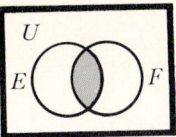

members of $E$ also belong to $F$. Suppose $U$ is the set of all students everywhere. Let $E$ be the set of all girl students, and let $F$ be the set of all students at Patrick Henry school. The shaded portion of the diagram represents the set of girl students who attend Patrick Henry school.

**Diagram for Disjoint Sets** consists of two or more separate circles.

Suppose $U$ stands for all sixth-grade students at Patrick Henry school. Let set $C$ be the boys in sixth grade, and set $D$ the girls in sixth grade. Both $C$ and $D$ are subsets of $U$. But $C$ and $D$ are disjoint sets because no member belongs to both of them.

### Operations with Sets

Three basic operations are used to solve problems involving sets: (1) union, (2) intersection, and (3) complement. These operations resemble arithmetic operations, such as addition and subtraction. In general, you work with two sets at a time, and produce a third set. The terms *union*, *intersection*, and *complement* name the operations and the sets that result from the operations.

**Union of Sets** includes all members of two sets without repeating any members. The symbol for union is $\cup$, which is called "cup." To show the union of sets $A$ and $B$, you write $A \cup B$, which is read: "$A$ union $B$."

*Union of Disjoint Sets:*
$A = \{1, 2, 3\}$
$B = \{4, 5\}$
$A \cup B = \{1, 2, 3, 4, 5\}$

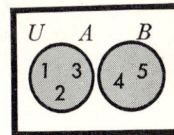

$A \cup B$

The union of sets $A$ and $B$ includes all the members of $A$ and $B$. In the Venn diagram, $A \cup B$ is represented by the shaded portions taken together. Note that $A$ has 3 members, and $B$ has 2. So $A \cup B$ has $3 + 2 = 5$ members. In the union of disjoint sets, the number of members equals the sum of the members in the sets.

*Union of Overlapping Sets:*
$C = \{\text{Dick, Betty, Susan}\}$
$D = \{\text{Susan, Mark, Tom}\}$
$C \cup D = \{\text{Dick, Betty, Susan, Mark, Tom}\}$

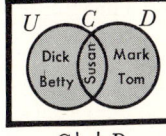

$C \cup D$

The shaded portion of the diagram represents $C \cup D$. If you add the number of members in sets $C$ and $D$, you get 6. But when you list the members of $C \cup D$, you write Susan's name only once. As a result, set $C \cup D$

**250c**

## SET THEORY

has only 5 members. In the union of overlapping sets, the total number of members is always less than the sum of the members in the sets.

*Union of a Set and Its Subset:*
$E = \{3, 6, 9, 12\}$
$F = \{6, 12\}$
$E \cup F = \{3, 6, 9, 12\}$

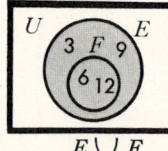

$E \cup F$

When you list the members of $E \cup F$, you write 6 and 12 only once, because these members belong to both sets. So $E \cup F$ has exactly the same members as $E$. The shaded portion of the Venn diagram represents $E \cup F$. This portion lies entirely within the circle for $E$, showing that $E \cup F$ equals $E$. The union of a set and its subset always has exactly the same total number of members as the set itself.

**Intersection of Sets** is a set that includes only those members that belong to both sets. For example, in the sets $G = \{1, 2, 3\}$ and $H = \{2, 3, 4\}$, the intersection of $G$ and $H$ is the set $\{2, 3\}$. These members belong to both $G$ and $H$. The symbol for intersection, $\cap$, is called "cap." To show the intersection of $G$ and $H$, you write $G \cap H$, which is read: "$G$ intersect $H$."

*Intersection of Disjoint Sets* is an empty set:

$A = \{1, 2, 3\}$
$B = \{4, 5\}$
$A \cap B = \{\} = \emptyset$

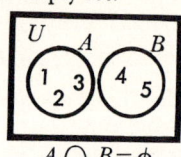

$A \cap B = \phi$

The intersection of $A$ and $B$ is an empty set because the two sets have no members in common.

*Intersection of Overlapping Sets:*

$C = \{\text{Dick, Betty, Susan}\}$
$D = \{\text{Susan, Mark, Tom}\}$
$C \cap D = \{\text{Susan}\}$

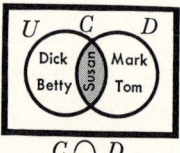

$C \cap D$

Only one member—Susan—belongs to both $C$ and $D$. Therefore, Susan is the intersection of $C$ and $D$, as shown by the shaded area in the Venn diagram.

*Intersection of a Set and Its Subset:*

$E = \{3, 6, 9, 12\}$
$F = \{6, 12\}$
$E \cap F = \{6, 12\}$

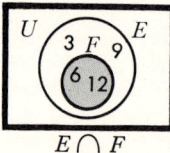

$E \cap F$

Set $F$ is a subset of $E$ because every member of $F$ is also a member of $E$. The intersection of $E$ and $F$ is the set $\{6, 12\}$. The shaded portion of the Venn diagram shows $E \cap F$. This portion lies entirely within the circle for $F$, showing that $E \cap F$ equals $F$.

**Complement of a Set** is represented by the shaded portion of the Venn diagram below.

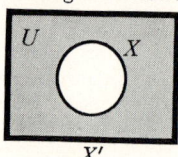

$X'$

In the diagram, $X$ is a subset of the universal set $U$. The shaded portion represents the set of members that belong to $U$, but not to $X$. This set is called the complement of $X$. The symbol $X'$ stands for the complement of $X$. For example:

$U = \{1, 2, 3, 4, 5\}$
$X = \{2, 3, 4\}$
$X' = \{1, 5\}$

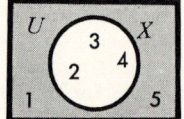

The members 1 and 5 belong to $U$, but not to $X$. Therefore, the complement of $X$ is $\{1, 5\}$, as shown by the shaded portion of the Venn diagram.

### Using Set Theory

**In Arithmetic,** set theory helps you understand some of the basic ideas of working with numbers. For example, you can learn the meaning of *number* by matching the members of two sets against one another.

$A = \{a, b, c, d\}$
$\updownarrow \updownarrow \updownarrow \updownarrow$
$B = \{e, f, g, h\}$

Sets $A$ and $B$ are equivalent. The members are different, but something about the sets is the same. This "something" is the *number* of members in each set. The name you use for any number is called a *numeral*. Thus, the numeral 4 tells you the number of members in either set $A$ or set $B$. Before ancient man learned to count, he used the idea of equivalent sets to keep track of his possessions. See NUMERATION SYSTEMS (History).

Set theory also explains why you can add or multiply numbers in any order and still get the same answer. For example, $2 + 3$ is equivalent to $3 + 2$. Addition in arithmetic is the same as the union of disjoint sets. Here is the way you use set theory to represent the problems $2 + 3$ and $3 + 2$:

$C = \{h, i\}$ (2 members)
$D = \{j, k, l\}$ (3 members)
$C \cup D = \{h, i, j, k, l\}$ ($2 + 3 = 5$ members)
$\updownarrow \updownarrow \updownarrow \updownarrow \updownarrow$
$D \cup C = \{j, k, l, h, i\}$ ($3 + 2 = 5$ members)

The arrows show that $C \cup D$ and $D \cup C$ contain the same number of members. Therefore, $2 + 3$ is equivalent to $3 + 2$. Mathematicians say that addition follows the *commutative law* (meaning *law of order*) because numbers can be added in any order to give the same result. Mathematicians also use set theory to explain other similar laws of working with numbers.

**In Algebra,** sets are helpful in several ways. Suppose that in a certain problem the letter $x$ stands for any number from 1 to 10. You call $x$ a *variable*, and you call the set of numbers from 1 to 10 the *domain of the variable*. The solution of the equation is the set of all numbers in the domain that make a true statement when substituted for $x$. Such a set is called a *solution set*.

Suppose that in a certain problem the domain of $x$ is $U = \{4, 5, 6, 7, 8, 9\}$. You are asked to find the values of $x$ that satisfy the condition: $x$ can be divided evenly by 2. To solve this problem, divide each member of the domain by 2. You find that 4, 6, and 8 can be divided evenly by 2, but 5, 7, and 9 cannot. Therefore, the solution set is $\{4, 6, 8\}$. Depending on the problem, a solution set may be an empty set, or it may have any number of members. See ALGEBRA (Learning Algebra).

250d

# SET THEORY

You can also use set operations, such as union and intersection, to understand and to solve certain algebra problems. For example, suppose the domain of $x$ is $U = \{4, 5, 6, 7, 8, 9\}$. Find the values of $x$ that satisfy the two conditions: (1) $x$ can be divided evenly by 2, or (2) $x$ can be divided evenly by 3. When two conditions are connected by the word *or*, the solution set must include all values of $x$ that satisfy either the first condition or the second. You find that 4, 6, and 8 can be divided evenly by 2. Therefore, the solution set for the first condition is $A = \{4, 6, 8\}$. You can divide 6 and 9 evenly by 3, so the solution set for the second condition is $B = \{6, 9\}$. The solution set for the whole problem is $\{4, 6, 8, 9\}$, because each of these numbers satisfies either the first condition or the second. This solution set is the union of the overlapping sets $A = \{4, 6, 8\}$ and $B = \{6, 9\}$ as shown in the diagram below:

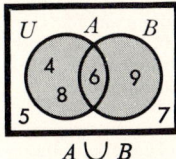

$A \cup B$

When two conditions of a problem are connected by the word *and*, the solution set must include all values of $x$ that satisfy both the first condition and the second condition. For example, let $U = \{4, 5, 6, 7, 8, 9\}$. Find the values of $x$ that satisfy the two conditions: (1) $x$ can be divided evenly by 2, *and* (2) $x$ can be divided evenly by 3. Again, the solution sets are $A = \{4, 6, 8\}$ and $B = \{6, 9\}$. But 6 is the only value that can be divided evenly both by 2 and by 3. The solution set for this problem is $\{6\}$, because only this value of $x$ satisfies both conditions. This solution set is the intersection of the two sets $A = \{4, 6, 8\}$ and $B = \{6, 9\}$, as shown in the following diagram:

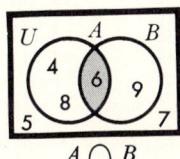

$A \cap B$

**In Geometry**, the sets studied are sets of points. The diagram below shows a set of two points, $A$ and $B$. Each point is represented by a little dot:

•  •
$A$  $B$

When you connect these two points with a straight line, you form a *line segment*. The notation $\overline{AB}$ is used to represent this segment. Points $A$ and $B$ are the *end points* of the segment. But you can imagine many other points, such as $C$, $D$, and $E$, on the same segment. Thus, segment $\overline{AB}$ consists of points $A$ and $B$ and the set of all points that lie between them.

In a similar way, you can think of the set of all points on a sheet of paper, on a wall, or on any other flat surface. Such a set of points makes up a *plane*. On a plane, you can draw simple *closed curves* by starting at any point and returning to that point without lifting your pencil. Examples of simple closed curves include circles, squares, and triangles. A circle is a closed curve, but a half circle is not.

A closed curve separates a plane into three sets of points: (1) those outside the curve, (2) those inside the curve, and (3) those on the curve itself. The interior of any simple closed curve is called a *region*. The curve is the *boundary* of the region. The region and the boundary are called a *closed region*. In the diagram, point $A$ belongs to the set of points on the boundary, $B$ belongs to the set of points inside the circle, and $C$ belongs to the set of points outside the circle.

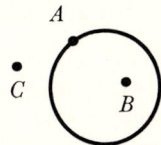

You can use the union and intersection operations to describe the relationship between geometrical figures. In the diagram below, two line segments $\overline{CD}$ and $\overline{EF}$ cross at point $P$. In terms of sets, you would say that $P$ is the intersection of the two sets of points that make up lines $\overline{CD}$ and $\overline{EF}$. You can write: $\overline{CD} \cap \overline{EF} = \{P\}$.

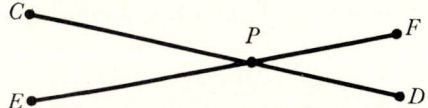

In the next diagram, the segment $\overline{GI}$ is made up of two segments, $\overline{GH}$ and $\overline{HI}$. The set of points in $\overline{GI}$ is the union of the sets of points in $\overline{GH}$ and $\overline{HI}$. You can show this relationship as follows: $\overline{GH} \cup \overline{HI} = \overline{GI}$.

**In Logic**, set theory can help you form conclusions based on statements called *premises*. Here is the way you would use sets to illustrate three simple logical conclusions. In each of these examples, the universal set is the set of all students at Patrick Henry school.

1. *First Premise:* All sixth-grade girls are members of the school glee club. *Second Premise:* Rita is a sixth-grade girl. *Conclusion:* Rita is a member of the school glee club.

Let $A$ be the set of members in the school glee club, and let $B$ be the set of girls in sixth grade. According to the first premise, $B$ is a subset of $A$. That is, every member of $B$ is a member of $A$. According to the second premise, Rita belongs to set $B$. Therefore, Rita must also belong to set $A$.

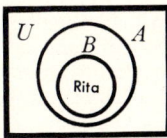

2. *First Premise:* Some fifth-graders take music lessons. *Second Premise:* Bob is a fifth-grader. *Conclusion:* Bob might take music lessons, or he might not.

Let $C$ be the set of students who take music lessons, and let $D$ be the set of fifth-graders. According to the first premise, some members of $C$ are members of $D$. Therefore, the sets overlap. The intersection includes those fifth-graders who take music lessons. According to the second premise, Bob belongs to set $D$. But it is impossible to tell whether Bob belongs to that portion of

250e

# SET THEORY

set $D$ that intersects set $C$. Therefore, the only conclusion you can reach is that Bob might take lessons, or he might not.

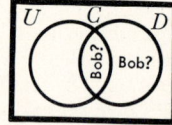

*3. First Premise:* No girls are members of the school baseball team. *Second Premise:* Joan is a girl. *Conclusion:* Joan is not a member of the school baseball team.

Let $F$ be the set of girl students, and let $E$ be the set of players on the school baseball team. According to the first premise, the two sets are disjoint. That is, no mem-

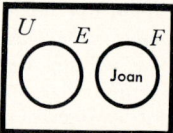

bers of $F$ belong to $E$. According to the second premise, Joan belongs to set $F$. Therefore, Joan cannot be a member of $E$.

### History

The set theory studied in elementary and high schools developed from two mathematical discoveries of the 1800's—*symbolic logic* and *the theory of sets*.

Symbolic logic is a way of using mathematical symbols and operations to solve problems in logic. George Boole (1815-1864), an Irish mathematician, established the basis of this technique in the 1840's.

In the 1870's, the German mathematician Georg Cantor (1845-1918) applied some of the ideas of symbolic logic to sets of numbers. He formed a theory that he called "the theory of sets." Cantor developed this theory because of his interest in infinite quantities. For example, he showed how the members of certain infinite sets could be matched one for one against each other. The set of counting numbers can be matched against the set of even numbers as follows:

$$1, \quad 2, \quad 3, \quad 4, \quad 5, \quad \text{and so on;}$$
$$\updownarrow \quad \updownarrow \quad \updownarrow \quad \updownarrow \quad \updownarrow$$
$$2, \quad 4, \quad 6, \quad 8, \quad 10, \quad \text{and so on.}$$

Both sets are infinite and equivalent, even though the second is a part of the first.

Until the 1950's, the theory of sets was used mostly to solve problems in higher mathematics. Eventually, mathematicians and educators recognized that the ideas of set theory could help students understand the principles of arithmetic and mathematics. The study of sets became an important part of the "new mathematics," a new method of studying mathematics. By studying sets, students learned the meaning of basic ideas such as *number* and *numeral*. They developed a better understanding of operations in arithmetic and algebra. They also learned to apply mathematics to the field of logic. CHARLOTTE W. JUNGE

### Set Theory Problems

1. $A = \{3, 4, 5, 6, 7, 8, 9\}$
   $B = \{4, 6, 8, 10\}$
   List the members of $A \cup B$.

2. List the members of $G = x|x$ is an odd number greater than 11 and less than 22.
3. $C = \{\text{all factors of } 6\}$
   $D = \{\text{all factors of } 12\}$
   List all members of $C \cap D$.
4. Give the union and the intersection of each pair of these sets:
   a. $A = \{\frac{1}{2}, \frac{1}{4}, \frac{1}{6}\}; B = \{\frac{1}{2}, \frac{1}{3}, \frac{1}{4}, \frac{1}{5}\}$
   b. $X = \{1, 3, 5, 7\}; Y = \{2, 4, 6, 8\}$
5. Which of these sets are equal?
   $\{a, b, c, d\}$
   $\{1, 2, 3, 4\}$
   $\{\text{Tom, Bill, Jack}\}$
   $\{4, 2, 3, 1\}$
6. Which of these sets are equivalent?
   $\{\text{Red, White, Blue}\}$
   $\{3, 6, 9\}$
   $\{\text{Red, Yellow, Green, Orange}\}$
   $\{a, b, c, d, e\}$
7. $A = \{\text{The set of counting numbers}\}$. List the members of set $A$.
8. Draw a Venn diagram for the following problem: $U = \{1, 2, 3, 4, 5, 6, 7, 8, 9\}$. Find the values of $x$ that satisfy these two conditions: (1) $x$ is an odd number, *and* (2) $x$ can be evenly divided by 3.
9. Draw a Venn diagram for the following problem: Some insects are social insects and live in colonies. Ants live in colonies. Ants are social insects.
10. $U = \{\text{Square, Rectangle, Circle, Triangle}\}$
    $D = \{\text{Circle}\}$
    List the members of $D'$.

### Answers

1. $A \cup B = \{3, 4, 5, 6, 7, 8, 9, 10\}$
2. $G = \{13, 15, 17, 19, 21\}$
3. $C \cap D = \{1, 2, 3, 6\}$
4. $A \cup B = \{\frac{1}{2}, \frac{1}{3}, \frac{1}{4}, \frac{1}{5}, \frac{1}{6}\}$ $A \cap B = \{\frac{1}{2}, \frac{1}{4}\}$
   $X \cup Y = \{1, 2, 3, 4, 5, 6, 7, 8\}$ $X \cap Y = \{\} = \emptyset$
5. $\{1, 2, 3, 4\} = \{4, 2, 3, 1\}$
6. $\{\text{Red, White, Blue}\}$ and $\{3, 6, 9\}$
7. $\{1, 2, 3, 4 \ldots\}$

8. 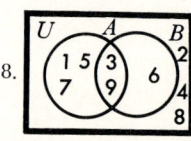   9.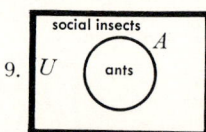

10. $D' = \{\text{Square, Rectangle, Triangle}\}$

**Related Articles** in WORLD BOOK include:

| | |
|---|---|
| Algebra | Logic |
| Arithmetic | Mathematics |
| Boolean Algebra | Numeration Systems |
| Geometry | |

### Outline

**I. Kinds of Sets**
  A. Finite Sets and Infinite Sets
  B. Empty Sets
  C. Single Element Sets
  D. Equivalent Sets
  E. Equal Sets
  F. Overlapping Sets and Disjoint Sets
  G. Universal Sets
  H. Subsets

**II. Diagraming Sets**
  A. Diagram for Universal Sets
  B. Diagram for Subsets
  C. Diagram for Equal Sets
  D. Diagram for Overlapping Sets
  E. Diagram for Disjoint Sets

**III. Operations with Sets**
  A. Union of Sets
  B. Intersection of Sets
  C. Complement of a Set

**IV. Using Set Theory**
  A. In Arithmetic
  B. In Algebra
  C. In Geometry
  D. In Logic

**V. History**

**SETH.** See ADAM AND EVE.

**SETI I,** *SEH tee* (reigned about 1309-1291 B.C.), was a king of ancient Egypt. Early in his reign he conducted two campaigns in Syria in an effort to check the advance of the Hittites and to re-establish the empire of Thutmose III in Palestine and Syria. Seti built the beautiful temple of Abydos, and began the Great Hypostyle Hall (hall of columns) at Karnak, which was completed by his son Ramses II. His tomb, the most splendid one in the Valley of the Tombs of the Kings, was discovered in 1817, and his mummy, together with that of Ramses II, was found in 1881, in another tomb near Dayr al Baḥrī.   RICARDO A. CAMINOS

**SETON, ELIZABETH ANN BAYLEY** (1774-1821), the founder of the Sisters of Charity in the United States, was beatified by the Roman Catholic Church in 1963. She was the first person born in the United States to be beatified, which is the last step before sainthood is conferred.

Mother Seton was born in New York City on Aug. 28, 1774. She married William Magee Seton in 1794. In 1803, she was left a widow with five children. Converted to the Roman Catholic Church in 1805, she went to Baltimore and opened a school for girls. She founded a new religious community there and was elected its first superior. The community was modeled on the Sisters of Charity of Saint Vincent de Paul. Mother Seton and 18 sisters made their vows in 1813.   MATTHEW A. FITZSIMONS

*St. Joseph Provincial House, Emmitsburg, Maryland*
**Elizabeth Ann Seton**

**SETON, ERNEST THOMPSON** (1860-1946), was the pen name of a popular writer and illustrator of animal and woodcraft books for boys. He was active in founding the Boy Scouts of America, wrote the first Scout manual, and was Chief Scout for five years. He founded the Woodcraft Indians, an organization of boys and girls.

Seton was born ERNEST SETON THOMPSON in South Shields, England, and spent his boyhood in Canada. He studied art in England, then returned to Canada as a government naturalist. He went to New York City, where he won fame with *Wild Animals I Have Known* (1898). He also wrote *Animal Heroes* (1905), and *Rolf in the Woods* (1911).   JEAN THOMSON

See also WOODCRAFT LEAGUE OF AMERICA.

**Ernest Thompson Seton**

**SETON HALL UNIVERSITY** is a coeducational Roman Catholic university in South Orange, N.J. The university's schools of arts and sciences, business administration, education, and nursing offer undergraduate and graduate courses. An ROTC unit also operates on the South Orange campus. Seton Hall has undergraduate divisions in Newark, Paterson, and Jersey City.

Seton Hall was founded in 1856 as a liberal arts college and was reorganized as a university in 1950. For enrollment, see UNIVERSITIES AND COLLEGES (table).   JOHN J. DOUGHERTY

**SETON HILL COLLEGE.** See UNIVERSITIES AND COLLEGES (table).

**SETTER** is a long-haired hunting dog. It is used to search for such birds as quail and partridge. There are three recognized breeds in the setter family: *English; Gordon;* and *Irish.* All have silky coats, expressive eyes, and heavy muzzles. They are intelligent and gentle. Breeders in the United States classify setters as sporting dogs. The setter was developed from the old "setting spaniel." Setters are about the same size and shape as pointers, but have the spaniel's long hair.

A setter hunts game in the same way that pointers do (see POINTER). It ranges the field until it smells game. Then it comes to a *point*, with its nose pointing at the game, its body stiff, and its tail out straight or raised a little. Sometimes it lifts one front paw while pointing. The dog holds its point until the hunter *flushes* the game (makes it move from its hiding place). After the shot, the setter brings back the game.   MAXWELL RIDDLE

See also DOG (color pictures: Sporting Dogs); ENGLISH SETTER; GORDON SETTER; IRISH SETTER.

**SETTLEMENT, SOCIAL.** See SOCIAL SETTLEMENT.
**SETTLEMENT HOUSE.** See SOCIAL SETTLEMENT.
**SEURAT,** *suh RAH,* **GEORGES** (1859-1891), a French painter, founded a painting style called *pointillism.* He used dots and dashes rather than brush strokes in building his paintings. He first painted in the Impressionist style, but he became dissatisfied with its lack of discipline in composition and color (see PAINTING [In the 1800's]). He was interested in color and color theory and read scientific treatises on color. He also studied Ferdinand Delacroix's color methods (see DELACROIX, FERDINAND V. E.). As a result of his studies, he devised the pointillist method of painting.

In 1886, Seurat finished his famous painting *Sunday Afternoon on the Island of La Grande Jatte.* This painting, usually called *La Grande Jatte*, appears in color in the PAINTING article. The painting became the outstanding example of the pointillists' style. Seurat showed it and five landscapes at the last Impressionist show in 1886. He used great care in the composition and arrangement of forms in these paintings, because he wanted to combine the classic idea of solidity of form with the Impressionists' use of color. His works aroused great hostility at the time.

*The Art Institute of Chicago*
**Georges Seurat**

Seurat also painted many views of small harbors at the mouth of the Seine River and seven figure paintings, including *The Bathers, The Circus,* and *The Side Show.* When he died at 32, most of his paintings were unsold. Seurat was born in Paris. He entered the École des Beaux Arts in Paris when he was 18.   ROBERT GOLDWATER

251

## SEUSS, DR.

Phyllis Cerf
**Dr. Seuss**

**SEUSS,** *SOOS,* **DR.** (1904- ), is the pen name of THEODOR SEUSS GEISEL, an American cartoonist and writer of humorous verse for children. He wrote delightful nonsense fantasies and accompanied them with his own illustrations. His books for children include *And To Think That I Saw It on Mulberry Street* (1937), *The King's Stilts* (1939), *Horton Hatches the Egg* (1940), and *Green Eggs and Ham* (1960). He also worked as a magazine illustrator and humorist, an advertising artist and writer, and a public relations specialist for the U.S. Department of the Treasury.

He was born in Springfield, Mass. He studied at Dartmouth College and Oxford University. E. HUDSON LONG

**SEVASTOPOL,** *suh VASS tuh pohl* (pop. 184,000; alt. 180 ft.), lies on the Black Sea, in the southwestern part of the Crimean Peninsula in Russia. For location, see RUSSIA (political map). Its large harbor has made it the most important naval base on the Black Sea. The 11-month siege of the city in 1854 and 1855 marked the chief battle of the Crimean War. Sevastopol was attacked again in World War I. An eight-month siege during World War II reduced the city to ruins, but it has been largely rebuilt. THEODORE SHABAD

**ŠEVČÍK,** *SHEF cheek,* **OTAKAR,** *AW tah kahr* (1852-1934), was a Czech virtuoso violinist and an eminent teacher. He taught at the Imperial Russian Music Society in Kiev for 17 years, and then went to the Conservatory at Prague. He moved to Vienna in 1909, and finally came to the United States. He was a dedicated teacher, and his violin method is still widely used. His students included Jan Kubelik and Franz Ondříček. Ševčík was born in Horazdowitz, Bohemia. He served as concertmaster of the Salzburg Mozarteum for three years. DOROTHY DELAY

**SEVEN BASIC FOODS.** See NUTRITION.

**SEVEN CITIES OF CIBOLA.** See CIBOLA, SEVEN CITIES OF.

**SEVEN DAYS, BATTLES OF THE.** See CIVIL WAR (The Peninsular Campaign; table: Major Battles).

**SEVEN PINES, BATTLE OF.** See CIVIL WAR (The Peninsular Campaign; table: Major Battles [Fair Oaks]).

**SEVEN SEAS** is an ancient term describing all the seas and oceans of the world. Many people believe the term means the Arctic, Antarctic, North and South Pacific, North and South Atlantic, and Indian oceans. However, the phrase has no literal meaning, and was used before some of the oceans were known to exist.

**SEVEN SLEEPERS OF EPHESUS** were seven Christian youths in an old legend who were said to have fled to the mountains near Ephesus in Asia Minor to escape the persecution of the Emperor Decius in about A.D. 251. Pursuers discovered their hiding place and blocked the entrance. Two hundred years later, a shepherd stumbled upon the cave and discovered seven youths asleep. When he awakened them, they believed that only a night had passed. One of them went to Ephesus for food and offered to pay for it with coins 200 years old. He was arrested as a thief of hidden treasure. But Emperor Theodosius II believed a miracle had taken place, and led the youth in a triumphant procession to the cave. Later, he had a great church and graveyard built to mark the spot. The seven sleepers lived for only a short time. All died at the same moment, and were buried where they had slept.

In 1928, Franz Miltner, an Austrian archaeologist, found a tomb near Ephesus which shows that the tale of the Seven Sleepers has some basis in fact. Theodosius' ancient church had been covered by other churches, and was discovered only by accident. The legend of the Seven Sleepers began in Syria and appeared in European literature in the A.D. 500's. It was a favorite theme in the art of the Middle Ages, and is told in the Koran, the Moslem holy book. THOMAS A. BRADY

**SEVEN WEEKS' WAR,** also called the AUSTRO-PRUSSIAN WAR, took place between June and August, 1866. Prussia fought against other German states and Austria. Otto von Bismarck, chancellor of Prussia, engineered the war as part of his campaign to force Austria out of the German Confederation and make Prussia the dominant power in Germany.

A dispute over the Danish duchies of Schleswig and Holstein furnished the immediate cause of the war. Austria, joined by the German states of Hesse, Saxony, and Hanover, declared war on Prussia on June 14, 1866. Bismarck secured the help of Italy. He also managed to get France to remain neutral by suggesting vaguely that France would be given new territory if Prussia won the war.

Prussia was outnumbered. But the strategic leadership of General Helmuth von Moltke, the use of the fast-firing "needle gun," and rapid troop maneuvers on the new railroads enabled the Prussians to win a series of quick victories. The greatest of these was the crushing defeat of the Austrians at the Battle of Königgrätz (also called Sadowa) on July 3.

The peace treaty ending the war was signed at Prague on August 23. According to the terms of the treaty, Austria had to give Venetia to the new kingdom of Italy and pay a small amount of money to Prussia. In addition, Austria was excluded from German affairs, and it was never again a power in Germany. The treaty also dissolved the old German Confederation, and permitted Prussia to form a new confederation without Austria. Bismarck organized the North German Confederation in 1867, which was dominated by Prussia. Prussia annexed outright Schleswig-Holstein, the kingdom of Hanover, the duchies of Nassau and Hesse-Cassel, and the free city of Frankfort. ROBERT G. L. WAITE

See also BISMARCK; GERMANY (The Unification of Germany); MOLTKE (Count Helmuth Karl).

**SEVEN WISE MEN OF GREECE** is the name scholars give to various sages who lived in Greece and Asia Minor about 600 B.C. Plato and other Greek philosophers listed the names of the wise men, but not all accounts agree. The usual list of sages is Bias of Priene, Chilon, Cleobulus, Periander, Pittacus, Solon, and Thales. The wise men were active in science and politics. See also SOLON; THALES. C. BRADFORD WELLES

**SEVEN WONDERS OF THE WORLD** is a listing of notable objects in the world. The practice of listing the seven wonders began in ancient times, when Greeks and Romans compiled lists of memorable things that travelers should see. There were many lists compiled that included many different wonders. But all the lists of ancient wonders included only man-made objects that were considered notable because of their size or some other unusual quality.

Since that time, others—usually writers, explorers, and world travelers—have compiled lists of the Seven Natural Wonders and the Seven Modern Wonders. This article lists the most commonly mentioned seven ancient, natural, and modern wonders of the world.

### The Ancient Wonders

**The Pyramids of Egypt,** built as tombs for Egyptian kings, are the oldest and best preserved of all the ancient wonders. The three largest pyramids, at Giza (Al Jizah), were the most famous. The Greeks and Romans marveled at the size of the pyramids, but they considered them foolish extravagances of the Egyptian kings. They made their lists about 2,000 years after the pyramids were built. By that time the religious importance of the pyramids as tombs had been forgotten. See PYRAMIDS.

**The Hanging Gardens of Babylon** were probably built for one of his wives by King Nebuchadnezzar II. He ruled Babylon from 605 to 562 B.C. Babylon was located near modern Baghdad in Iraq. No positive trace of the gardens remains, but scholars know about them from an account by Berosus, a Babylonian priest of the 200's B.C. Berosus described gardens laid out on a brick terrace about 400 feet square and 75 feet above the ground. To irrigate the flowers and trees, slaves worked in shifts turning screws to lift water up to the gardens from the Euphrates River. The massive brick walls that encircled Babylon were also considered notable, because they were so long and so thick. Two chariots could travel side by side on top of the walls.

**The Temple of Artemis at Ephesus,** built about 550 B.C., was one of the largest and most complicated temples built in ancient times. It stood in the Greek city of Ephesus, on the east coast of what is now Turkey. It was made entirely of marble, except for its tile-covered wooden roof. The temple was dedicated to the Greek goddess Artemis (Diana). It was designed by the architect Chersiphron and his son, Metagenes. The temple's foundation measured 377 by 180 feet. It had 106 columns, about 40 feet high, forming a double row around the *cella* (inner space). The wealthy King Croesus of Lydia donated some of the columns.

The temple burned down in 356 B.C., and another one like it was built on the same foundation. Goths burned down the second temple in A.D. 262. Only the foundation and parts of the second temple remain.

**The Statue of Zeus** at Olympia, Greece, was perhaps the most famous statue in the ancient world. The sculptor Phidias made it about 435 B.C., and dedicated it to Zeus (Jupiter), the king of the gods. The 40-foot-high statue showed Zeus on his throne. Zeus's robe and ornaments were made of gold, and his flesh of ivory. He had a wreath around his head, and held a figure of Victory in his right hand and a *scepter* (king's rod) with an eagle in his left.

**The Mausoleum at Halicarnassus,** in what is now southwestern Turkey, was a huge marble building built as a tomb for Mausolos, an official of the Persian Empire. Its size and decorations made it so famous that all large tombs are now called *mausoleums*. The tomb was about 135 feet high. It had a rectangular basement beneath a colonnade formed by 36 columns. A stepped pyramid rested on the colonnade, and a statue of Mausolos in a chariot probably stood on top of the pyramid. The Greek architects Satyros and Pythios designed the tomb. Four famous sculptors—Bryaxis, Leochares, Scopas, and Timotheus—carved the *frieze* (decorated band) on the building. Only pieces of the building and its decorations remain.

**The Colossus of Rhodes** was a huge, bronze statue that stood near the harbor of Rhodes on the Aegean Sea. The statue honored the sun god Helios. It stood about 120 feet tall—about as high as the Statue of Liberty. The sculptor Chares worked 12 years building the statue during the early 200's B.C. He used stone blocks and about $7\frac{1}{2}$ tons of iron bars to support the hollow statue. In 224 B.C., not long after its completion, the statue was destroyed by an earthquake. The metal was sold for scrap in A.D. 653.

**The Lighthouse of Alexandria,** about 440 feet high, stood on the island of Pharos in the harbor of Alexandria, Egypt. It became so famous that the word *pharos* came to mean *lighthouse*. The structure, designed about 270 B.C. by the Greek architect Sostratos, rose from a large stone platform in three sections. The bottom section was square, the middle *octagonal* (eight-sided), and the top circular. A fire on top provided light.

### The Natural Wonders

World travelers and explorers list the following natural wonders: (1) Mount Everest, on the Nepal-Tibet border; (2) Victoria Falls on the Rhodesia-Zambia border; (3) Grand Canyon of the Colorado River; (4) Great Barrier Reef of Australia, the world's largest coral formation; (5) caves in France and Spain with their prehistoric paintings; (6) Parícutin, a young volcano in Mexico; and (7) the harbor at Rio de Janeiro.

Many other natural wonders are often listed, such as the giant sequoia trees of California; Rainbow Natural Bridge of Utah; Yellowstone Falls in Yellowstone National Park; Crater Lake and Wizard Island in Oregon; and the Carlsbad Caverns of New Mexico.

### The Modern Wonders

World travelers and explorers list the following as modern wonders: (1) Suez Canal; (2) Dneproges Dam on the Dnepr River in Russia; (3) Atomic Energy Research Establishment at Harwell, England; (4) Alaska (or Alcan) Highway, connecting Alaska with Canadian and with other United States highways; (5) Golden Gate Bridge in San Francisco; (6) Eiffel Tower in Paris; and (7) Empire State Building in New York City, the

*William P. Donovan, the contributor of this article, is Chairman of the Classics Department at Macalester College, St. Paul, Minn.*

# SEVEN WONDERS OF THE ANCIENT WORLD

**Ancient Greeks and Romans** made up many lists of outstanding man-made wonders. These illustrations show the objects that have been most commonly listed as the seven ancient wonders of the world. The map, *below right*, shows the location of the seven ancient wonders of the world in red.

**The Temple of Artemis** at Ephesus was one of the largest temples built by the Greeks. It was famous for its decoration and extensive use of marble.

**The Statue of Zeus** at Olympia, Greece, was probably the most famous statue made by the Greeks. Thousands who came to Olympia for the Games admired this gold and ivory figure.

**The Pyramids of Egypt** are the only Seven Wonders of the Ancient World still standing. The largest Egyptian pyramids stand outside the present-day city of Cairo.

**The Lighthouse of Alexandria,** Egypt, was the world's first important lighthouse. It guided ships into the city's harbor for over 1,000 years before being toppled by an earthquake.

**The Mausoleum at Halicarnassus** was a great marble tomb. It was built for King Mausolos by some of the most famous Greek sculptors and architects living at that time.

**The Hanging Gardens of Babylon** probably were built by King Nebuchadnezzar after he married a mountain princess. He apparently hoped the gardens would make her feel at home.

WORLD BOOK illustrations by Birney Lettick

**The Colossus of Rhodes** was built in honor of the sun god Helios. It was constructed after the people of Rhodes survived a year-long siege by a large force of Macedonians.

255

# SEVEN YEARS' WAR

world's tallest skyscraper. For engineering achievements of the United States as chosen by the American Society of Civil Engineers, see ENGINEERING (picture: Civil Engineering Achievements). WILLIAM P. DONOVAN

**Related Articles** in WORLD BOOK include:

| | | |
|---|---|---|
| Alaska Highway | Golden Gate Bridge | Parícutin |
| Dneproges Dam | Grand Canyon | Pyramids |
| Eiffel Tower | National Park | Suez Canal |
| Empire State Building | Great Barrier Reef | Victoria Falls |
| | Mount Everest | |

**SEVEN YEARS' WAR** (1756-1763) involved nearly every nation in Europe, and extended to America and India. In America, it was called the French and Indian War. While Prussia and Austria fought for control of Germany, Prussia's ally, England, and Austria's ally, France, battled for control of the seas and of the territories in North America. When it was over, Prussia had become the leader of the German states, and England had driven the French out of North America.

**In Europe.** The Seven Years' War began as a quarrel between Frederick the Great, King of Prussia, and Maria Theresa, Archduchess of Austria, over the possession of Silesia. Frederick had taken Silesia from Austria, but Maria Theresa never gave up hope of regaining her lost province. She allied herself with Czarina Elizabeth of Russia, who bitterly hated and feared the Prussian king. Maria Theresa found it more difficult to make an alliance with France, the ancient enemy of Austria. But she finally succeeded with the aid of her shrewd foreign minister Count Wenzel Anton von Kaunitz. He was aided by an agreement between England and Prussia. This angered the French, who feared England, and made them more sympathetic to Austria.

Meanwhile, Frederick the Great was carefully watching the moves of his enemies. He determined to strike the first blow. In August, 1756, he invaded Saxony, which had sided with Austria. The Austrians sent an army to defend Saxony, but the Prussians quickly defeated it. Frederick soon forced the entire Saxon army to surrender, and made himself master of the country.

In spite of these victories, Prussian hopes for victory were dim early in 1757. Sweden had joined Austria and its allies. Almost all of Europe was now united against the Prussian king. Britain was Prussia's only ally, and England gave but little help.

Frederick invaded Bohemia and won a battle near Prague. He then laid siege to Prague, but was defeated in the battle of Kolin. Frederick was outnumbered, but he moved with great vigor and decision. He attacked and defeated the French in a great battle at Rossbach, and then defeated the Austrians at Leuthen.

At the beginning of operations in the spring of 1758, Frederick's position was much improved. William Pitt came to power in Britain, and began to give more active aid to Prussia. The British organized a new army, which won several victories over Frederick's enemies. But Frederick's resources were limited, and Prussia had been weakened by his costly campaigns. Prussia was near exhaustion, and its ruin seemed almost certain.

Frederick reached his most desperate position in 1762. But in that year Elizabeth of Russia died suddenly and was succeeded by Peter III, an enthusiastic admirer of Frederick. He decided to take Russia out of the war, and began arrangements for a separate peace with Prussia. This turn of fate saved Frederick.

By terms of the peace signed at Hubertusburg early in 1763, Silesia remained under Prussian rule, and other boundaries remained as they had been before the war. There were no territorial changes in Europe. The Treaty of Paris settled disputes between France, Spain, and Great Britain on February 10, 1763.

**In America.** One of the most important results of the Seven Years' War took place far from Europe. Britain finally won its long struggle with France for the control of North America. At the end of the Seven Years' War, France gave up Canada to Britain, and also gave up its empire in America. For a history of the war in America, see FRENCH AND INDIAN WARS. ROBERT G. L. WAITE

**Related Articles** in WORLD BOOK include:

| | |
|---|---|
| Frederick (II) of Prussia | Pitt (family) |
| Maria Theresa | Pompadour, Marquise de |
| Paris, Treaties of | Silesia |

**SEVENTEEN-YEAR LOCUST.** See CICADA.

**SEVENTEENTH AMENDMENT.** See UNITED STATES CONSTITUTION (Amendment 17).

**SEVENTH-DAY ADVENTISTS** are a Christian religious denomination. Members believe that Christ will return in person. They also observe the Sabbath on Saturday, the seventh day.

Adventists originated in the early 1800's, when many people in America and Europe became absorbed in the doctrine of Christ's second coming. References in the Bible that seemed to prophesy the time of Christ's coming aroused their interest. Followers of William Miller, a Baptist minister, predicted a definite time for the coming, but Miller's interpretation of what was to happen proved wrong. One group restudied Bible prophecies and decided that the beginning of the final judgment and Christ's coming were still in the future. This group organized in 1863 as the Seventh-day Adventists.

Adventist headquarters are at 6840 Eastern Ave., Washington, D.C. 20012. For U.S. membership, see RELIGION (table).

*Critically reviewed by the* SEVENTH-DAY ADVENTISTS

**SEVENTY YEARS' CAPTIVITY.** See POPE (The Troubles of the Papacy).

**SEVERN, RIVER,** is one of the chief waterways of Great Britain. It rises in the mountains of Wales and takes a roundabout course through England for 210 miles to the Bristol Channel. A railroad from London to Wales uses a 4-mile tunnel under its mouth. Canals connect the Severn with the Trent, Thames, and Mersey rivers. The banks of the Severn estuary are often flooded by tidal waves. See also BORE. JOHN W. WEBB

**SEVERSKY, ALEXANDER PROCOFIEFF DE.** See DE SEVERSKY, ALEXANDER PROCOFIEFF.

**SEVERUS,** *see VEER us,* **LUCIUS SEPTIMIUS** (A.D. 146-211), a Roman emperor, reorganized the administration of the army and the provinces. He improved conditions for soldiers, and offered new career opportunities to provincial Romans. He also created a new treasury.

Severus was born in North Africa, in what is now Libya. He became an important government official. When the emperor Commodus died in 192, Severus joined a struggle for the throne during which the emperors Pertinax and Didius Julianus were assassinated. Severus seized control in 193. As emperor, he defeated two other claimants to the throne and defended Britain against barbarians. An arch honoring his triumphs stands in the Roman Forum. RAMSAY MACMULLEN

**SEVIER,** *suh VEER,* **JOHN** (1745-1815), was an American soldier, frontiersman, and politician. He served as governor of "The lost state of Franklin," and later became the first governor of Tennessee.

Sevier, the son of a tavern keeper, was born near New Market, Va. He received little education, and as a young man supported himself by farming and trading. Sevier soon grew restless, and became a pioneer. In 1773, he moved to the Holston River Valley, then an unsettled region of the colony of North Carolina. It is now in eastern Tennessee. Here he soon became a leader.

Sevier actively supported the Revolutionary cause, but took little part in the fighting until 1780. In that year he led an expedition over the Smoky Mountains and helped defeat the British at Kings Mountain. Later he led an expedition against the Cherokee Indians. This was the first of many campaigns that brought him fame as an Indian fighter. After the Revolutionary War, the settlers in Tennessee began a movement to make the region a separate state. In 1784, the state of Franklin was organized, and Sevier was elected governor. Indian troubles, land speculation plots, and quarrels with rivals led to his downfall and the practical end of the state of Franklin in 1788. Sevier's career was ended, and he became an outlaw. But, soon after, he was pardoned and elected to the North Carolina Senate. From 1789 to 1791 he served in the federal Congress.

In 1796 "The lost state of Franklin" became part of the new state of Tennessee. Sevier was elected its first governor, and served a total of six terms. In 1796, he quarreled with Andrew Jackson, then one of his associates, over a land speculation Sevier had made. This quarrel embittered the rest of Sevier's life. After the end of his sixth term as governor, Sevier was elected to the state senate for one term and then served again in Congress until his death. A statue of Sevier represents Tennessee in the Statuary Hall Collection in the U.S. Capitol in Washington, D.C. THOMAS D. CLARK

See also FRANKLIN, STATE OF.

**SEVIER RIVER.** See UTAH (Rivers and Lakes).

**SEVILLE,** *suh VIL,* or SEVILLA, *say VEEL yah* (pop. 459,786; alt. 39 ft.) is one of the leading centers of Spanish art, literature, and education. Two of Spain's greatest painters, Diego Velázquez and Bartolomé Murillo, were born in Seville. Two famous operas, *Carmen* and *The Barber of Seville,* have the city as their setting. Legend says that Don Juan lived in Seville. The legend of Don Juan furnished many writers and composers with material for their works. The University of Seville dates back to 1502.

The city lies 60 miles northeast of Cádiz on the Guadalquivir River, in a region of sunny vineyards and orange groves. For location, see SPAIN (color map).

A great wall with 64 towers once surrounded the city, and its remains still stand. The Moors lived in Seville for hundreds of years. Moorish influence shows in the city's network of small, shaded streets, and in the whitewashed, balconied houses built around handsome courtyards and fountains. Fine squares with beautiful fountains lie throughout the city.

Seville's greatest building is its cathedral, started in 1402 and finished in 1519. It stands on the site of a Moorish mosque, and ranks next to St. Peter's in Rome as Europe's largest cathedral. Some people think Christopher Columbus was buried in Seville's cathedral. But the Dominican Republic also claims to be the burial place of the famous explorer. Seville's emblem is the *Giralda,* a Moslem minaret that is part of the city's cathedral. The Giralda stands over 300 feet high. It was built in the 1300's.

Seville's factories produce cigars, pottery, silks, machinery, chocolate, perfume, and iron products. Canals and the Guadalquivir River make the city an important inland port. Exports include wine, olives and other fruit, and cork, mercury, and wool. The city is the capital of Seville province. WALTER C. LANGSAM

**SÈVRES,** *SEH vr',* **TREATY OF.** At the close of World War I, Turkey and the Allies signed the Treaty of Sèvres at Sèvres, France. The treaty was signed on August 10, 1920, and marked a low point in Turkish power and history. It provided that Syria, Palestine, and Mesopotamia (now Iraq) would be "provisionally recognized as independent states to be advised by mandatory powers." Turkey was to give up all its territorial claims in northern Africa, and to cede eastern Thrace to Greece. Smyrna (now Izmir) and the Ionian region were to be under Greek rule for five years. The independence of Armenia was recognized. The waters around Turkey were to be opened to the vessels of all nations, and the Turkish armed forces were to be reduced to a police force. Under the treaty, Turkish finances were to be controlled by an Allied commission.

This treaty was signed by the Turkish government, but it was never ratified by the Turkish nationalists. The Turkish leader, Kemal Atatürk, overthrew the feeble Ottoman government and set up a new, independent Turkey. Ankara was made the new Turkish capital. Kemal Atatürk's government refused to recognize the treaty signed at Sèvres. Turkish forces defeated the Greeks at Afyonkarahisar and Bursa, and later drove the Greeks from Izmir. In 1923, the Turkish government negotiated a new peace treaty with the Allied Powers at Lausanne, Switzerland. DWIGHT E. LEE

See also IZMIR; KEMAL ATATÜRK; LAUSANNE, TREATY OF.

**SÈVRES PORCELAIN.** See PORCELAIN (picture: Decorative Porcelain; Markings on Chinaware).

**SEWAGE,** *SOO ihj,* is water containing waste matter produced by man. Sewage contains such solid waste matter as scraps of food and bits of cloth and paper. It also contains dissolved material that cannot be seen. Bacteria, viruses, and other disease-producing organisms are almost always present in sewage.

The system of pipes that carries sewage from houses, factories, and other buildings is called a *sewerage system.* There are two main types of sewerage systems: (1) disposal systems for cities and towns and (2) disposal systems for rural areas. In city systems, waste matter goes through a network of public sewers. It is usually treated at a special plant to remove undesirable matter and destroy harmful organisms. In rural areas, each sewerage system usually serves one house or building.

### Sewage Disposal in Cities

In heavily populated areas, sewage from homes, offices, and factories flows into a public sewerage system.

# METHODS OF SEWAGE TREATMENT

## SEPTIC TANK

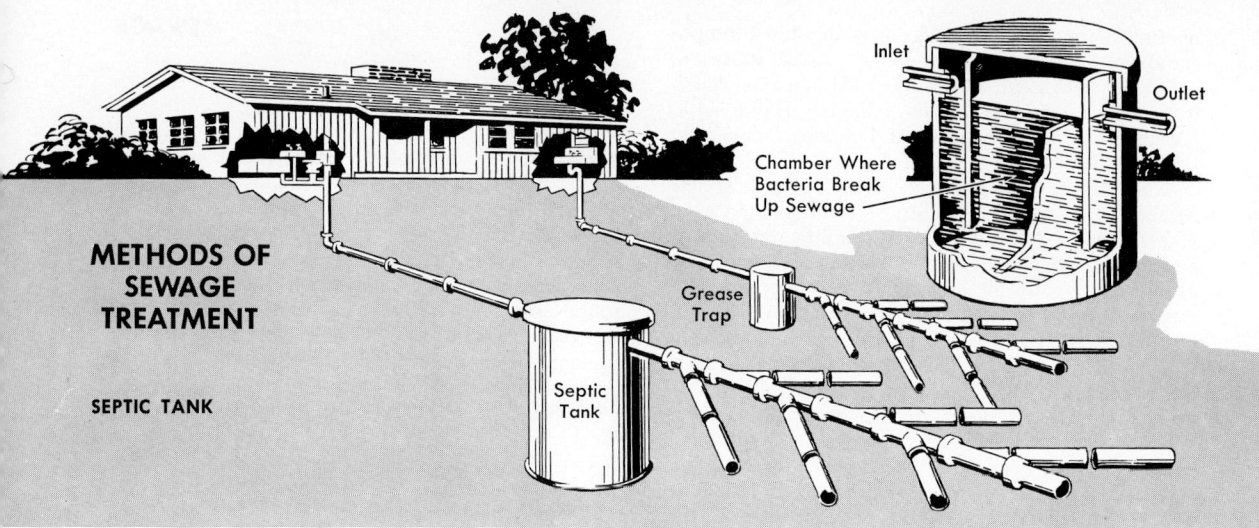

**A Septic Tank** is used for sewage treatment in rural areas. Sewage runs into the tank, where bacteria break it up. Solids settle to the bottom of the tank, while liquids flow through it. Kitchen wastes pass through a trap that removes grease.

## SEDIMENTATION, TRICKLING FILTER, AND SEPARATE SLUDGE DIGESTION

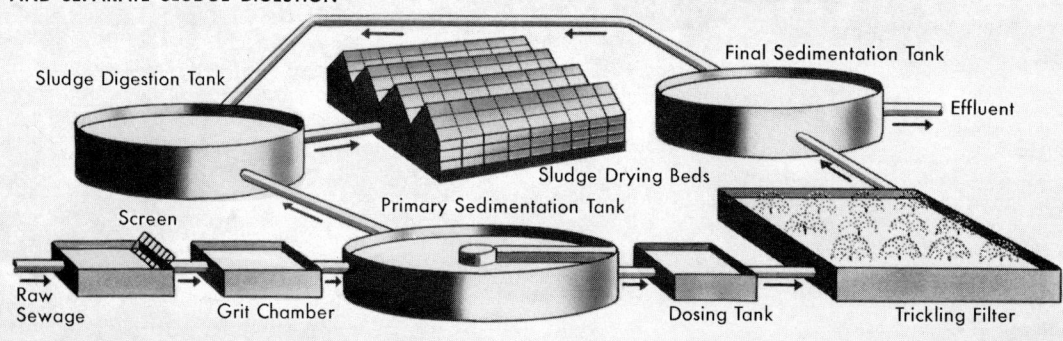

**A Trickling Filter** removes organic matter in one type of city treatment system. Raw sewage first passes through a screen into the grit chamber and primary sedimentation tank, where heavy sludge settles. Remaining waste is treated in a sludge digestion tank.

It is collected, treated, and disposed of safely. Property owners must obtain connections into the system.

**Collecting Sewage.** Waste matter from individual homes and commercial buildings flows into a series of collecting sewers. Smaller sewers carry the sewage into larger ones. The largest sewers, called *interceptors*, carry the sewage to a *treatment plant*. Treatment plants are located at the end of the sewerage system, usually near a river or lake. A treatment plant removes harmful organisms and other matter from the sewage so it can safely be discharged into a river or other body of water. Without treatment, the sewage could create bad odors, contaminate water supplies, and spread disease. Complete sewage treatment requires two main steps: *primary* and *secondary*.

**Primary Treatment** removes the heavier solid material from the sewage. At the treatment plant, the sewage passes through a coarse *screen*, which removes the largest pieces of matter, such as sticks of wood. The sewage then flows slowly through a *grit chamber*. As it passes through this chamber, heavy inorganic matter settles to the bottom. The remaining sewage then flows into a large *primary sedimentation tank*. The sewage remains in this tank from 30 minutes to 3 hours. During this time, most of the remaining heavy solid matter settles to the bottom of the tank and forms a semiliquid called *sludge*. After this primary treatment, the sewage contains only dissolved material, tiny particles, and organisms.

**Secondary Treatment** destroys the harmful organisms and removes part of the remaining dissolved material. This treatment may be accomplished by either the trickling filter method or the activated sludge process.

*Trickling filters* are not really filters, but beds of crushed stone or gravel at least 5 feet deep. Certain organisms form a film on the stone or gravel beds. This organic film combines with oxygen to change the harmful substances in the sewage into solids. The filtered sewage flows from the trickling filter into a *final sedimentation tank*. There, the solid waste settles to the bottom as sludge. After the solids settle, chlorine is added and the clear *effluent* (out-flowing liquid) can be safely discharged.

The sludge is carried into a *sludge digestion tank* for further treatment. From this tank, the sludge is carried to drying beds where it is dried and removed, often to be used as fertilizer.

*The activated sludge* process resembles the trickling filter method. Instead of a crushed-stone bed, an *aeration tank* is used. Certain bacteria live suspended in water in the tank as *activated sludge*. This sludge is mixed with air and the sewage. The combination of bacteria and air moving through the sewage destroys the harmful materials. This treatment forms sludge that is removed in a final sedimentation tank. As in the trickling filter process, the clear effluent is discharged. The sludge is moved to the sludge digestion tank and drying beds.

### Sewage Treatment in Rural Areas

**Cesspools** are sometimes used for sewage disposal for homes in isolated areas. *Cesspools* are holes dug in the ground and loosely lined with either bricks or stone masonry. Liquid waste flows from house drains into the cesspool. The waste then seeps into the soil through spaces in the brick or masonry lining.

Cesspools often overflow, causing bad odors and contaminating water supplies. They can also become breeding places for mosquitoes. As a result, cesspools are considered a poor method of sewage disposal.

**Septic Tanks** are widely used in rural areas where running water is available. The tanks, usually made of concrete or steel, are buried about 1 foot underground. A tank serving a family of 6 would be about 3 feet wide, 7 feet long, and 4 feet deep. Septic tanks serving homes should hold about 100 gallons of liquid for each person.

The sewage flows into the tank through an inlet pipe. Within the tank, the sewage solids separate. They either sink to the bottom to form sludge, or rise to the top to form a floating film called *scum*. A system of baffles and pipes permits only relatively clear liquid to flow out of the tank.

Naturally occurring microorganisms in the sewage attack the sludge and scum in the tank. This process, called *digestion*, changes the sewage into a harmless solid called *humus*, or into gas. The gas escapes from the tank into the outside air. The humus settles to the bottom. The tank should be cleaned every few years to remove extra humus. This humus from the septic tank is often used as fertilizer.

The clear liquid flows through a system of distributing pipes, called *tiles*, into the *irrigation field* outside the tank. The irrigation field is the soil that must absorb the liquid when it flows from the tank. The tiles are usually laid with many small spaces between them. This provides many places where the sewage can escape.

If the soil absorbs the liquid properly, natural bacteria in the soil will combine with air to purify the sewage. It is vital that the ground surrounding a septic tank be able to absorb the waste properly. In heavy clay soils, air cannot reach the waste. This can cause unpleasant odors. A test called the *percolation test* will determine if the soil can properly absorb the sewage. Odors may also occur when the soil contains so much moisture that it cannot properly absorb the sewage. This condition may occur after a heavy rainfall or if too many septic tanks share one irrigation field.

**History.** Important cities of ancient Rome had sewerage systems. In the Middle Ages and later, sewage accumulated in cesspools or was allowed to foul streams and rivers. Most drinking water was taken straight from the streams. The water became contaminated by the impurities and spread diseases, such as cholera and typhoid. In the mid-1800's, the first comprehensive sewerage systems were built in Europe.   C. FRED GURNHAM

See also PLUMBING; SEPTIC TANK.

**SEWALL, ARTHUR** (1835-1900), was the Democratic candidate for Vice-President of the United States in 1896. He and William Jennings Bryan lost to Republicans William McKinley and Garret A. Hobart. Sewall was a Maine shipbuilder, banker, and railroad executive. He owned, built, and operated more sailing vessels than any other American between 1850 and 1900. Sewall was born in Bath, Me.   IRVING G. WILLIAMS

**SEWALL, SAMUEL** (1652-1730), was the presiding judge at the Salem (Mass.) witchcraft trials of 1692. Twenty persons were condemned to death and executed. Five years later, he publicly confessed that he had been wrong. Sewall considered himself more at fault than the other judges. In 1718, he was appointed chief justice of the superior court of judicature. He was born at Bishopstoke, England.   DANIEL J. DYKSTRA

**SEWARD,** *SYOO urd,* **WILLIAM HENRY** (1801-1872), served as United States secretary of state during the Civil War. He was the leading Republican in the nation in 1860, but Abraham Lincoln defeated him for the party's nomination. Seward worked for Lincoln's election, and entered his Cabinet as secretary of state. Because of Seward's able administration of foreign affairs, European countries did not aid the Confederacy. He was wounded by an accomplice of John Wilkes Booth on the night that Lincoln was assassinated. He slowly recovered, and continued as secretary of state under President Andrew Johnson.

Among the important tasks that Seward accomplished was the purchase of Alaska from Russia. Alaska later proved valuable to the United States, and finally became a state in 1959. But at the time it was mockingly called "Seward's Folly" and "Seward's Ice Box." See ALASKA (American Purchase).

Seward was born in Florida, N.Y., and was educated at Union College, New York City. He became a lawyer in 1822, and soon entered politics as a Whig (see WHIG). He served in the state legislature, and was governor of New York from 1839 to 1842. He became a United States senator in 1849. Seward was opposed to slavery, and fought against its spread.   W. B. HESSELTINE

See also JOHNSON, ANDREW (Foreign Relations); LINCOLN, ABRAHAM (Election of 1860; Foreign Relations); TRENT AFFAIR; EMANCIPATION PROCLAMATION (picture: Lincoln Met With His Cabinet).

**SEWARD PENINSULA.** See ALASKA (physical map).

**SEWELL,** *SOO el,* **ANNA** (1820-1878), wrote *Black Beauty* (1877), a story which was a protest against cruelty to horses. It became extremely popular. Anna Sewell was born in Yarmouth, England. A cripple, she could still ride her horse, and her love for it inspired the book.   EVELYN RAY SICKELS

**SEWELLEL.** See MOUNTAIN BEAVER.

**SEWER.** See SEWAGE.

# SEWING

**SEWING** is a useful occupation that many girls enjoy learning. They may make flattering and inexpensive clothing for themselves, or useful household articles. Beginning seamstresses should choose designs that are easy to sew. In that way, they can devote all their attention to good design and flattering lines. They should first work with firm, soft materials, such as gingham or print, which are easy to sew.

## Sewing Tools

**Needles** come in various sizes and kinds. Plain sewing is best done with *sharps*, which are needles of average length. Size 8 sharps are suitable with numbers 50 to 70 thread. Size 9 sharps are suitable with 80 to 100 thread.

**Cotton Thread** is of two general types. *Six-cord* thread comes in white and black. *Mercerized* thread comes in a range of colors. Six-cord thread is stronger than mercerized, because it has more strands and is twisted tighter.

**The Thimble** is a metal or plastic cap which fits over the end of the third finger of the sewing hand. It protects the finger and saves an extra motion in pushing the needle through the cloth.

**Scissors** come in various lengths and kinds. They should be of good steel with sharp cutting edges all the way to the points. Six-inch scissors or shears are suitable for cutting out garments. Shorter scissors are suitable for cutting threads, gashing, and trimming edges.

**Pins** should be of copper or steel, with sharp points. Dressmaker pins in size 5 are good.

**Tape Measures** should be of stitched double cloth with metal tips. They should be reversible, numbering 1 to 60 inches on one side, and 60 to 1 on the other.

**An Iron** is used by every good seamstress to press her work as she goes along. Pressing prevents inaccurate stitching and can frequently take the place of basting.

**The Sewing Machine** is the most used tool of all. In learning to use a machine, the beginner should first practice on ruled paper without a thread. She should learn to stitch on the lines by watching the position of the front of the presser foot. See SEWING MACHINE.

## Basic Stitches

**The Basting Stitch** is a temporary stitch which is used to hold two pieces of material together and to guide the permanent sewing. In *even basting*, the stitches and spaces are of the same length. In *uneven basting*, the stitches and spaces are uneven. The pieces of cloth should be pinned together before they are basted.

**The Running Stitch** is a small regular stitch made by passing the needle over and under an equal amount of material. The cloth should be held straight and taut with the thumb and forefinger of the left hand, about an inch away from the point of the needle. The needle should be woven through the cloth. When the needle is full, the cloth should be pulled off the needle.

When the running stitch is used for gathering, only one end of the thread should be fastened. A long tail of thread should be left at the other end until the material is pulled up. It is best to make two rows of gathering about a quarter of an inch apart.

**The Plain Hemming Stitch** is a slanting stitch used to hold a folded edge down to the material. It is made by placing the needle through the material and the folded edge of the hem. The needle should be slanted slightly, and the stitches kept small and at uniform distances. Starting without a knot, tuck the end of the thread under the fold of the hem. Hold the hem over the forefinger of the left hand. Finish with three little stitches in the fold. Then stitch the needle back through the fold so that the end of the thread is concealed.

**Slip-Stitch Hemming** is used on the bottom of skirts, where stitches should not be seen and the hem should be smooth. Take a very small stitch in the garment parallel with the hem. Slip the needle through the fold of the hem about one-quarter of an inch from this stitch. Then repeat the operation.

**The Overhand Stitch** is a straight stitch used to join edges, hem napkins, or sew lace on a finished edge. Start without a knot, working over the end of the thread. Insert the needle at right angles to the edge of the material. Do not take too deep a stitch; otherwise a ridge will be formed. Fasten by sewing back over the stitches.

**The Overcasting Stitch** is a loose stitch made over raw edges to prevent raveling.

## Simple Construction Processes

**Seams** are used to join two parts of a garment. The *plain seam* is made by placing the right sides of the cloth together, pinning, basting, and then stitching on the seam line. There are several ways to prevent the material in the seams from raveling. Firm material may be trimmed evenly or pinked with pinking shears, and pressed open. Edges which ravel may be pressed open and "self-stitched." Each edge is either turned down by hand or stitched by machine. Another method is to overcast the two edges together. Another is to press both edges to one side and stitch by machine on the right side. This is somewhat like the *flat-felled* and *lapped* seams.

The *lapped seam* is a tailored seam. The seam allowance of the top piece of material is pressed to the wrong side and basted to the seam line of the adjoining piece. It is then machine-stitched. This seam is also used when a ruffle or piping is put into the seam. The folded edge is basted to the ruffle or piping and basted a second time to the adjoining piece. Then it is stitched.

*Flat-felled seams* and *French seams* require more skill to make. They have no raw edges showing.

**Bias** is a line which cuts diagonally across the cloth. Ordinary cuts are made along the line of the thread. To obtain a true bias in cutting, fold the cloth so that the lengthwise threads of the cloth lie parallel with the crosswise threads. Press the fold. Open it out and mark off the number and width of bias strips needed. Cut the ends of the strips along the lengthwise threads of the material and piece together as shown in the illustration.

**Edge Finishes** give a finished appearance to an edge. Common types are hems, facings, bindings, and bands.

The *hem* is made by turning the raw edge of the article down about a quarter inch on the wrong side, then turning it down again the width desired. Curved hems should not be made too wide. The first quarter-inch fold should be gathered to distribute the extra fullness.

A *facing* is a separate piece of material sewed to lie flat on either the right or wrong side of the garment. Narrow facings are usually cut bias and placed on the wrong side. Fitted facings are cut to fit the garment in shape and match the weave or grain of the cloth.

A *binding* is a narrow-edged finish which always

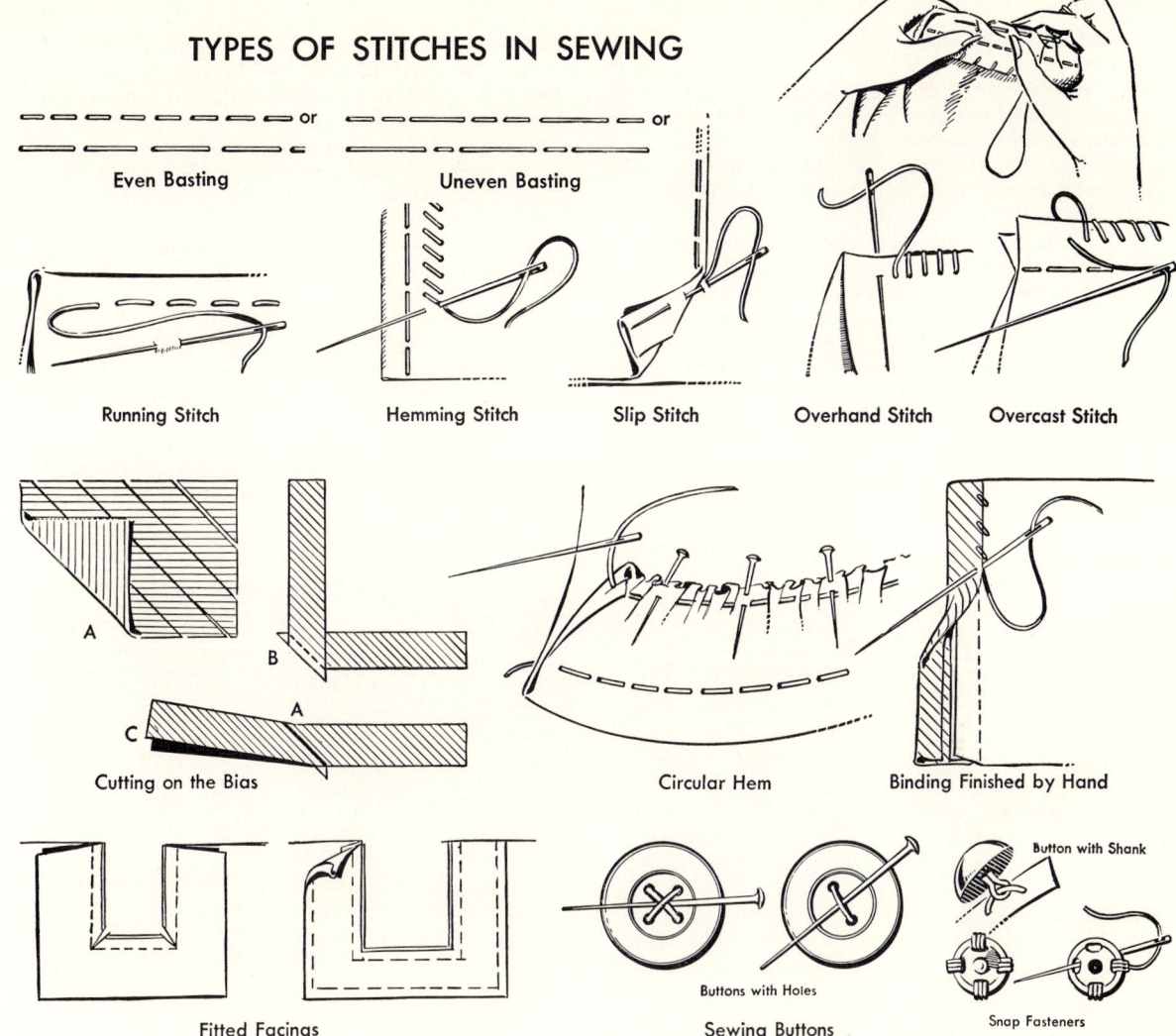

## TYPES OF STITCHES IN SEWING

Even Basting — Uneven Basting
Running Stitch — Hemming Stitch — Slip Stitch — Overhand Stitch — Overcast Stitch
Cutting on the Bias — Circular Hem — Binding Finished by Hand
Fitted Facings — Sewing Buttons (Buttons with Holes) — Snap Fasteners (Button with Shank)

shows. The edge to be bound should be cut without a seam allowance. Strips of bias material are then stitched on the right side of the garment. The binding is pressed against the seam and folded around it. The wrong side can be finished by hand or machine.

*Bands* are used at the waistline or bottom of the sleeve as belts and cuffs to hold in fullness. They are really wide bindings, cut on the lengthwise threads of the material rather than on the bias.

*Plackets* are finished openings in a garment to make it possible to slip the garment over wider parts of the body. Plackets at necklines are usually faced. Plackets in gathered skirts are usually hemmed. Those in fitted skirts or underarm seams are tailored and finished.

### Fastenings

**Buttons** may be used as either decorations or fastenings. Their position on the cloth should be marked carefully. Starting with a knot and double thread, take a small stitch on the right side of the material so the knot will be under the button. Place a pin across the top of buttons with holes or under buttons with shanks and sew over the pin three to five times. Remove the pin. Bring the thread up under the button and wrap it around the threads so there is a strong thread shank. Then fasten the thread on the wrong side of the material.

**Snaps** should also be carefully placed. First sew the ball half of the snap on the front side of the placket. Then rub the ball with chalk and press it into the back side. This will mark the position for the socket half.

**Other Fastenings** include hooks and eyes, and "zippers," or slide fasteners. They must be sewed onto the clothing. Many dresses, particularly house dresses, are fastened only by belts or ties.   JOSEPHINE F. EDDY

**Related Articles** in WORLD BOOK include:

SEWING AND NEEDLEWORK

| | |
|---|---|
| Appliqué | Needle Point |
| Button | Petit Point |
| Clothing | Quilt |
| Crochet | Sampler |
| Dressmaking | Singer, Isaac Merrit |
| Embroidery | Zipper |
| Knitting | |

SEWING TOOLS

Needle    Scissors    Sewing Machine    Thread

## SEWING MACHINE

**SEWING MACHINE** is a machine that uses a needle to bind materials together with thread. It has lightened the household work of women and helped families to have better and less expensive clothing than they might otherwise have had. In factories, it has helped make possible the mass production of clothing.

**Kinds of Sewing Machines.** There are three main types of sewing machines for the home. They have different types of machine heads for sewing: the straight-needle, the swing-needle, and the slant-needle. All three kinds are made in both cabinet and portable models.

*Straight*-needle sewing machines are designed to make sewing as quick and easy as possible for the home seamstress who sews constantly. These machines can be used to do many kinds of decorative stitching, without the use of any special attachment. Various attachments added to the machine assist in such sewing tasks as ruffling, cording, and binding.

The *slant-needle sewing machine* resembles the straight-needle type, but has its needle slanted toward the user so she can see the work more easily.

The *swing-needle sewing machine* is especially suited for use by women who do much decorative or hobby sewing. It does zigzag stitching, as well as many other kinds of decorative stitches, without special attachments. It can even be used to make wired flowers.

Many of the machines on which zigzag stitching can be done are manufactured in Europe. The Anker and

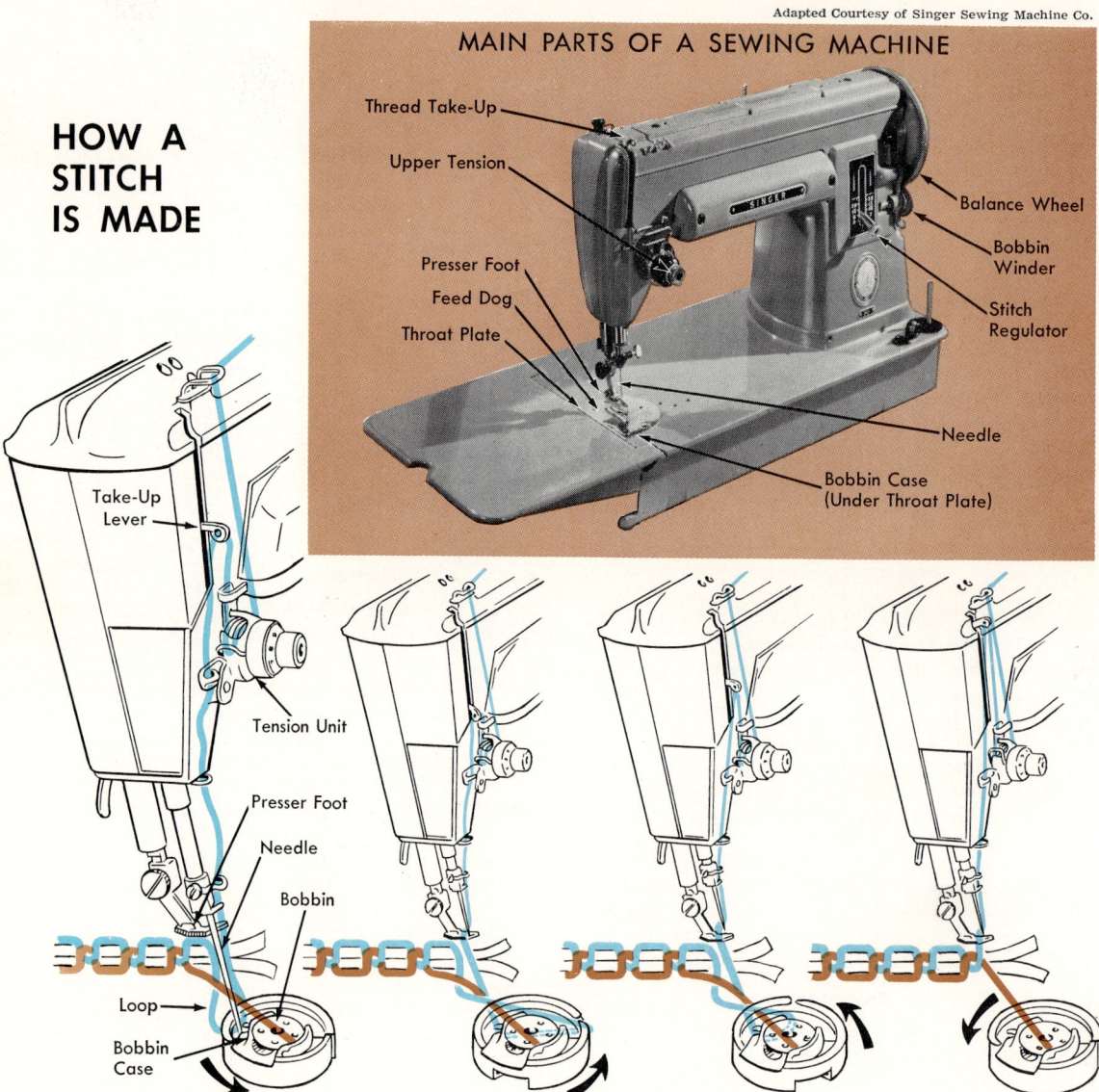

Adapted Courtesy of Singer Sewing Machine Co.

**MAIN PARTS OF A SEWING MACHINE**

Thread Take-Up · Upper Tension · Presser Foot · Feed Dog · Throat Plate · Balance Wheel · Bobbin Winder · Stitch Regulator · Needle · Bobbin Case (Under Throat Plate)

**HOW A STITCH IS MADE**

Take-Up Lever · Tension Unit · Presser Foot · Needle · Bobbin · Loop · Bobbin Case

**1.** The needle moves through the cloth. The take-up lever keeps the thread tight until the needle enters the cloth.

**2.** As the needle rises, the thread forms a loop. The loop passes around the bobbin, and encircles the bobbin thread.

**3.** The bobbin casts off the thread. Then the take-up lever and needle rise, and the stitch tightens around the cloth.

**4.** When the needle point is above the cloth, the feed dog pulls more cloth forward, and another stitch begins.

The *radio sextant* is a device that uses sensitive receiving equipment to locate the sun. It receives constant radio waves from the sun, and automatically tracks the sun in all weather conditions during daylight hours.

The *mirror sextant* was invented independently in 1730 by John Hadley in England and Thomas Godfrey in America. JOHN J. FLOHERTY

See also NAVIGATION.

**SEXTILLION,** *sex TILL yun,* in Canada, France, and the United States, is a number followed by 21 zeros. One sextillion is written 1,000,000,000,000,000,000,000. In England and Germany, sextillion is a number followed by 36 zeros.

**SEXTON BEETLE.** See BURYING BEETLE.

**SEYCHELLES ISLANDS,** *say SHELL* (pop. 50,000), are a British Crown Colony of 92 islands covering 145 square miles. They lie in the Indian Ocean, 700 miles northeast of Madagascar. The capital, Victoria, is on Mahé Island. The people speak French or a Creole dialect. They grow coconuts, cinnamon, patchouli, and vanilla in the fertile volcanic soil. A governor and executive and legislative councils form the government. The governor is also the commissioner of the British Indian Ocean Territory, which was created in 1965. The French held the Seychelles from the middle 1700's until the British captured them in 1794. ROBERT I. CRANE

**SEYMOUR, HORATIO** (1810-1886), an American statesman, was a leading *Peace Democrat,* or *Copperhead,* during the Civil War (see COPPERHEAD). He was six times nominated for the governorship of New York, and was elected twice, in 1852 and in 1862. As governor during the war, he opposed President Lincoln's emancipation policy and the conscription law. He had many disputes with Lincoln over raising troops in New York. He was blamed for the 1863 draft riot in New York City, though he acted promptly to stop it.

He ran for the presidency in 1868 on the Democratic ticket, but was defeated by Ulysses S. Grant. Seymour was born in Onondaga County, New York. He practiced law for many years in Utica, N.Y. RICHARD N. CURRENT

**SEYMOUR, JANE.** See HENRY (VIII) of England.

**SEYSS-INQUART,** *ZYS ING kvahrt,* **ARTHUR VON** (1892-1946), was the leading Austrian Nazi. As the Austrian chancellor's adviser in the 1930's, he betrayed his country and helped Adolf Hitler seize Austria.

When Austria became German territory in 1938, Seyss-Inquart became its governor. He held a similar post in The Netherlands during World War II. After the war, he was tried and hanged in Nuremberg for his repressive policies. He was born in Stannern, in the German fringe of Bohemia. LESTER B. MASON

**SFAX,** *sfahks* (pop. 65,645; alt. 25 ft.), is the second largest city in Tunisia. For location, see TUNISIA (map). It is an important seaport. Its exports include phosphate, olive oil, sponges, almonds, and dates.

**SFORZANDO.** See MUSIC (Terms).

**'S GRAVENHAGE.** See HAGUE, THE.

**SHABUOT,** *shah VOO oht,* or FEAST OF WEEKS, is a Jewish festival that celebrates the day the Ten Commandments were revealed to Moses on Mount Sinai. It falls on the 6th day of the Hebrew month of Sivan. Orthodox and Conservative Jews outside of Israel observe it for two days. The holiday is called *Feast of Weeks* because it comes seven weeks, or "a week of weeks," after the first day of Passover (see PASSOVER).

The ancient Hebrews celebrated Shabuot as a harvest festival. They made pilgrimages to Jerusalem to offer sacrifices at the Temple. During the festival today, Jews read the scroll of Ruth, which describes harvesting in ancient Israel. According to one tradition, the scroll is read because King David, who was a descendant of Ruth, died on Shabuot. LEONARD C. MISHKIN

**SHACKAMAXON, TREATY OF.** See PENNSYLVANIA (Colonial Days).

**SHACKLETON, SIR ERNEST HENRY** (1875-1922), an Irish Antarctic explorer, led a British expedition that came within 97 miles of the true South Pole in 1908 (see ANTARCTICA [Exploration]). In December, 1914, he led an expedition into the Weddell Sea, where ice crushed his ship. His party escaped in small boats to Elephant Island. He went on to South Georgia Island and crossed its icy summit to alert rescuers. He wrote *Heart of the Antarctic* (1909) and *South* (1919). He was born in Kilkee, Ireland. JOHN E. CASWELL

United Press Int.
**Sir Ernest Shackleton**

# SHAD

**SHAD** is an important food fish of the herring family. The American shad lives in the sea from Newfoundland to Florida. The former U.S. Bureau of Fisheries introduced it into the Pacific. The shad goes up fresh-water rivers to spawn. At that time, fishermen catch large numbers of shad in nets. Shad average about 3 pounds in weight, and are about 2 feet long. They are a bluish color above, and have silvery sides.

Shad fisheries, which operate only at spawning time, have been greatly overworked, especially those of the East Coast rivers. So-called "Potomac shad" is shipped from the Pacific Coast to eastern markets. Most shad are eaten fresh, but a few are smoked or salted. Their eggs provide the best substitute for the *roe* (eggs) of sturgeon used in making caviar.

**Scientific Classification.** The common shad belongs to the herring family, *Clupeidae.* It is genus *Alosa,* species *A. sapidissima.* LEONARD P. SCHULTZ

See also HERRING.

**The Shad Is Prized for Its Flesh and Roe (Eggs).**
State of California Department of Fish and Game

# SHAD FLY

**SHAD FLY.** See MAY FLY.
**SHADDOCK.** See GRAPEFRUIT.
**SHADE.** See COLOR (The Color Triangle).
**SHADOOF.** See EGYPT (Agriculture).

**SHADOW,** *SHAD oh*, is the darkness behind an object that is in light. This object must be opaque, or one through which light cannot pass. The east side of an opaque object will be dark if light is shining from the west. Shadows exist all around us, as long as there is light. We see shadows of clouds on meadows and on water. We see shadows of trees and buildings, and shadows of ourselves, on the ground or on other objects. The light of the sun causes the earth to throw a huge shadow into space. The moon may be partly or completely *eclipsed* (shadowed so we cannot see it) if it passes into this darkened space.

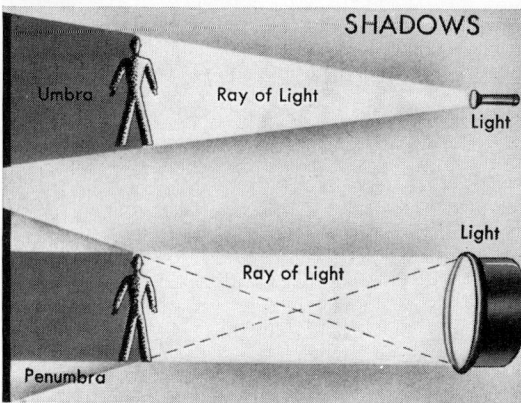

The accompanying diagram shows how shadows are formed. At the top, the source of light is a tiny point, like a flashlight. The opaque figure stops the light rays. No light at all passes the figure, and the space between the figure and the screen is completely darkened. A complete shadow such as this is called an *umbra*. Below, the source of light is larger. In this case the shadow directly behind the figure is darker than the rest of the shadow. This is the umbra. The space where part of the light is cut off is called the *penumbra*.   E. A. FESSENDEN

See also ECLIPSE; PENUMBRA.

**SHADOW MOUNTAIN DAM** is in north-central Colorado. It forms Shadow Mountain Lake which connects with Grand Lake. It is part of the Colorado-Big Thompson Project, designed to furnish a supplementary water supply to 615,000 acres of farmland. It also supplies electric power to cities and towns in Colorado, Nebraska, and Wyoming. This earth dam is 63 feet high and 3,077 feet long. The U.S. Bureau of Reclamation built it in 1946. See also DAM.   T. W. MERMEL

**SHADOW PLAY,** or SHADOW PANTOMIME, is a kind of drama in which the figures of puppets or living actors are thrown in silhouette on a screen. The players or puppets stand behind the screen and a strong light throws their shadows on the screen. The play is usually acted out in *pantomime* (without words).

See also PUPPET.

**The Puppets in a Shadow Play** act out a story in pantomime when they are moved behind the screen. ▶

**SHADWELL, THOMAS.** See POET LAUREATE.
**SHAFT MINE.** See COAL (Mining Methods); IRON AND STEEL (How Iron Is Mined).

**SHAFTER, WILLIAM RUFUS** (1835-1906), an American soldier, served as commander of land operations in Cuba during the Spanish-American War. In a month's fighting his forces captured Santiago and the entire eastern section of the island.

Shafter was born near Galesburg, Mich. He served in the infantry during the Civil War, and remained in the army. Years later, in 1895, Shafter received a Medal of Honor for his gallant fighting at Fair Oaks, Va., in 1862. He was a major general when he retired.   H. A. DEWEERD

**SHAFTESBURY** was the title of two distinguished English statesmen.

**Anthony Ashley Cooper** (1621-1683), EARL OF SHAFTESBURY, an English statesman, secured the passage of the Habeas Corpus Act in 1679. This act is one of the mainstays of English freedom (see HABEAS CORPUS).

Cooper was born in Wimborne in Dorsetshire. He studied at Oxford University and entered Parliament in 1640. He became prominent under Oliver Cromwell during the Civil War and the Commonwealth. After Cromwell's death, he helped plan the restoration of the monarchy (see ENGLAND [The Civil War; The Restoration]). His efforts won him a pardon for his previous actions, when King Charles II came to the throne. The king made him Baron Ashley, earl of Shaftesbury, and lord chancellor. He became a member of the Cabal, worked to establish the Whig party, and supported the Test Acts against the Roman Catholics (see CABAL; TEST ACT; WHIG). His support of the Test Acts cost him his office.

In 1679 he became president of the Privy Council and passed the Habeas Corpus Act. But he became involved in a plot against the king and was arrested. He escaped

R. J. Smith, Black Star

266

Historical Society of Pennsylvania

**Colonial Shakers at Worship** trembled and chanted wordless songs. A church leader said he saw the Hosts of Heaven worshiping in this manner, and he taught the movements to his people. Modern Shakers still tremble and chant at their meetings.

to The Netherlands, where he died on Jan. 21, 1683.

**Anthony Ashley Cooper** (1801-1885), EARL OF SHAFTESBURY, was an English statesman and philanthropist. He served in Parliament from 1826 to 1851. He led a movement to improve the treatment of the insane and the living conditions of the poor in England. He was born in London. WILLARD M. WALLACE

**SHAGBARK.** See HICKORY.

**SHAGREEN.** See SHARK.

**SHAH** is the title of the ruler of certain Middle Eastern countries, such as Iran. See IRAN (Government; History); SHAH JAHAN.

**SHAH JAHAN,** *SHAH juh HAHN* (1592-1666), was the fifth ruler of the Mogul Empire in India. He became ruler in 1627. During his reign, the Moguls reached their golden age, with vaults crammed with treasures and with architecture in magnificent style. Shah Jahan is best remembered for the perfectly proportioned Taj Mahal, an immense tomb of white marble built for his wife in Agra, India (see TAJ MAHAL). He also built a palace of unbelievable splendor in Delhi. These and other buildings still stand as examples of Mogul glory. The dynasty reached its height with Shah Jahan's reign. It began its decline because too much money was spent on luxuries and too much effort was wasted in war. Shah Jahan's reign was a troubled one, and one of his sons took his throne by force. T. WALTER WALLBANK

**SHAHN, BEN** (1898-1969), an American painter, tried through his art to communicate with people and influence their thinking and emotions. His realistic paintings and drawings deal directly and powerfully with such themes as labor movements, race relations, and atomic warfare. His painting *Handball* appears in color in the PAINTING article.

Shahn was born in Lithuania and came to the United States when he was 8. He first attracted attention in the 1930's with a series of paintings about the Sacco-Vanzetti trial (see SACCO-VANZETTI CASE). Shahn saw no difference between fine and commercial art. He accepted many commissions in advertising and commercial art. His style has been influential in these fields, especially in book illustration. ALLEN S. WELLER

**SHAKERS** are members of the religious sect called the United Society of Believers. The sect was started in England about 1706, as an offshoot of the Quakers. In 1758, Ann Lee (1736-1784) joined the society, and in 1770 members recognized her as the leader of the Church of God on earth. Shakers called her *Mother Ann* and made her the head of the society.

In 1774, Mother Ann led a group of Shakers to America and organized a society at Watervliet, N.Y. This was the first communistic organization in the United States. All property belonged to the community as a whole. Members of the society are called *Shakers* because during religious exercises their intense emotions cause them to quiver and shake. Shakers do not marry, and bear no children. The sect is kept alive only through converts. The society now has fewer than 25 members, who live in two New England communities.

The Shakers have made many important contributions to American life. The Shakers were the first producers of commercial seed in the United States. They invented the circular saw, cut nails, a washing machine, flat brooms, and the first metal pen points. The fine furniture early Shaker communities produced is now prized as collector's items. GEORGE R. MONELL

**SHAKERTOWN.** See KENTUCKY (Places to Visit; color picture: Shakertown near Lexington).

267

## SHAKESPEARE'S BIRTHPLACE

**The Half-Timbered Buildings,** *above,* were owned by John Shakespeare, the playwright's father. They are joined together, and stand on Henley Street in Stratford-upon-Avon. William Shakespeare was born in the family home at the left. The house to the right probably served as his father's shop. Thousands visit these buildings every year. Nearby are the lovely fields of Warwickshire, the "heart of England," a region often pictured in the plays of Shakespeare.

## SHAKESPEARE'S SCHOOLHOUSE

**The Stratford Grammar School,** *above,* where Shakespeare is believed to have received his only formal education, is still standing. The stone tower belongs to the Guild Chapel. Troupes of traveling actors performed in the chapel during the poet's youth, and helped turn his attention to the theater.
**The School Library,** *left,* was a classroom when Shakespeare studied there.
Folger Shakespeare Library

# SHAKESPEARE

**SHAKESPEARE, WILLIAM** (1564-1616), is usually considered the greatest dramatist the world has known, as well as the finest poet who has written in the English language. No other writer's plays have been produced so many times in so many countries, and no poet's verse has been so widely read in so many different lands. His works have been translated into more languages than any book in the world except the Bible. Thousands upon thousands of books and articles have been written about Shakespeare and his works. One famous library has more than fifteen thousand volumes of editions of his plays and poems alone. These do not include the thousands of books published *about* the man and his work.

Such unequalled popularity is convincing proof of Shakespeare's influence on millions of theatergoers and readers. Other men of letters have also testified to his greatness. Johann Goethe, the great German writer, said, "I do not remember that any book or any person or event in my life ever made so great an impression on me as the plays of Shakespeare." Thomas Carlyle, the English essayist, once said, "I think the best judgment not of this country alone, but of Europe at large, is slowly pointing to the conclusion that Shakespeare is the chief of all poets hitherto; the greatest intellect who, in our recorded world, has left record of himself in the way of literature."

Among the many literary giants who have testified to the joy and wonder they have felt before Shakespeare's immortal creations are John Milton, John Dryden, Alexander Pope, Joseph Addison, Samuel Johnson, John Keats, Lord Byron, Charles Lamb, Samuel Coleridge, Sir Walter Scott, Robert Browning, Ralph Waldo Emerson, James Russell Lowell, and Walt Whitman. Famous men of different ages and nations have paid so many thousands of tributes to Shakespeare that several anthologies have been prepared to give samplings of them.

One of the reasons for Shakespeare's world-wide appeal is the number and variety of characters he created. They include persons of all types, who came from all walks of life. Shakespeare understood his characters so deeply and presented them so vividly that for many readers they have become more real than some of the living men about them. Pickpockets and kings, fools, country bumpkins and court ladies, drunkards, dandies,

*Folger Shakespeare Library*
**An Engraving of Shakespeare** by Martin Droeshout appeared in the first folio of Shakespeare's plays, published in 1623.

stablemen, generals, lovesick girls, and hired murderers all spring to life in his plays. To many people Hamlet, Falstaff, and King Lear seem far more real than historical characters like Thomas Jefferson and Napoleon. Shakespeare's incomparable creative power is one of the great features of his genius. It cannot be explained, but critics agree that behind it lies a wide acquaintance with men and women of all types in the bustling London of the time of Queen Elizabeth I.

Another characteristic of Shakespeare is his amazing knowledge of a wide variety of subjects — music, the law, seamanship, the Bible, military science, the stage, art, politics, history, psychology, hunting, woodcraft, animal husbandry, and sports. This knowledge is so wide and accurate that lawyers have tried to prove that Shakespeare must have been a lawyer, and sailors have argued that he must have had experience at sea. Yet as far as his life is known, it shows no professional experience in any field other than the theater. Evidently he had a remarkable ability to pick up miscellaneous information and to use it accurately. He could listen to sailors' talk and then write a sea scene as full of detailed information as is Scene I of *The Tempest*.

### Influence on the English Language

Perhaps the most amazing quality of Shakespeare's genius is his unequalled mastery of the English language. From his pen, the words of kings and the talk of thieves flowed with equal ease. Learned men, such as Prospero, and stupid yokels, like William in *As You Like It*, speak as such persons *would* speak. Many lines spoken by Shakespearean characters are such exact statements of the feeling which many men have experienced, that they are quoted again and again. A large number of expressive words and phrases from the plays have passed into the language and are used today by millions of

**Stratford-upon-Avon, Birthplace of the Poet, Is a Small Town About 80 Miles Northwest of London.**

persons who have no idea that Shakespeare created them. Such daily, unconscious tributes to Shakespeare's greatness by persons who speak of the "king's English," of "catching a cold," of "disgraceful conduct," of a "foregone conclusion," of "elbowroom," or of "fair play," prove that he has made a deep impression not only on scholars, authors, and theatergoers, but also on every person who speaks the English language.

One of the most lasting impressions which Shakespeare has made on civilization is one which is usually forgotten. It is his influence on the English language as it is used today. When Shakespeare wrote his plays, there were no English grammars or dictionaries, no accepted standards of spelling or grammar or pronunciation. Well-educated men spelled the same word in different ways, and often pronounced it differently. They used grammatical forms which are not allowed today, such as "more braver," "more hotter," "perfecter," "perfectest," "as tall as me," "to who."

The exact meanings of many words were as unsettled as grammar and spelling, and there were no English words for many ideas which are taken for granted today. New words and new expressions were being taken from other languages or invented for the English language. When the language was in such a state of development, it could be influenced for good or bad more easily than it can now. It is very fortunate that at such a time a writer with Shakespeare's sensitive ear and brilliant gift of phrase was writing plays which became popular.

Many of the common present-day words which can be seen any day in the newspaper or heard over the radio were first used by Shakespeare, so far as scholars have been able to find. He was the most successful of the word inventors of his time. From his works come such words as *assassination, barefaced, baseless, bumps, countless, courtship, critic, critical, denote, disgraceful, dishearten, distrustful, dwindle, eventful, exposure, fitful, fretful, gloomy, hurry, impartial, inauspicious, lonely, misplaced, monumental, recall, suspicious.*

Even more notable than the words Shakespeare invented are the phrases or expressions he put together. No other English writer has ever approached his gift of coining phrases. "Public haunt of men," "fortune's fool," and "pomp and circumstance," are fair samples of phrases which are now used without quotation marks as standard English, although they are really quotations from Shakespeare. A full list of these widely used phrases from the great dramatist would be very long, but some measure of the debt the English language owes Shakespeare is apparent when the number of familiar phrases which come from a single play are noted. *Hamlet* has the phrases "mind's eye," "primrose path," "to the manner born," "making night hideous," "a tale unfold," "shadow of a dream," "caviar to the general," "flesh is heir to," "mortal coil," "sicklied o'er," "glass of fashion," "out-herod Herod," "hold the mirror up to nature," "counterfeit presentment," "flaming youth," "whet thy blunted purpose," "hoist with his own petard," "fellow of infinite jest," "ribband in the cap of youth." How much poorer the English language would be without the words and phrases which were first brought into it by this actor-playwright more than three hundred years ago!

### Shakespeare's Life

In Shakespeare's time, few biographies were written. Most of those recorded the lives of saints, preachers, or kings. None of the literary men of the Elizabethan Age was considered important enough for a full biography until long after his death, and writers of plays were thought to be even less important than poets. Shakespeare himself had been dead nearly a hundred years before anyone tried to write a short account of his life. By then, many of the facts of his life were no longer known. But there were many stories about him, some false, some possibly true. Certain knowledge of Shakespeare's life is, therefore, very scanty, although no more scanty than for other great literary men of the period. Such facts as there are come mostly from church registers, town records, and accounts of business dealings.

**Early Years.** William Shakespeare was born in Stratford-upon-Avon, a fairly important English market town about 80 miles northwest of London, in the year 1564. The registers of Holy Trinity, the parish church in which Shakespeare was buried 52 years later, record his baptism on April 26, 1564, and it is generally thought that he was born on April 23, since babies were sometimes baptized on the third day. But there is no proof of the actual date of his birth.

The poet's father, John Shakespeare, was a fairly prosperous glovemaker and trader in wool, hides, and grain. He owned at least five houses in Stratford, and held various offices in the town. He became mayor when his son William was four years old. Shakespeare's mother was Mary Arden, the daughter of a landowner living near Stratford. John and Mary Shakespeare had eight children. William was the third.

Nothing is known definitely of Shakespeare's boyhood in the town of Stratford, but it is highly probable, considering his father's position, that he went to the Stratford grammar school, which was free to the children of citizens of the town. In grammar schools of the time, the boys studied chiefly Latin, so young William Shakespeare probably read Cicero, Virgil, Ovid, Terence, Plautus, and Seneca. In those days, school began at six or seven in the morning and lasted until five or six in the evening. After the long school day and during holidays, the young Shakespeare certainly became familiar with the beautiful countryside around Stratford, as is shown by the many references to rural sights and sounds in his plays. It was easy for him to go to the country, for his father's home on Henley Street was only about two hundred yards from the open fields. Sometime in his youth, Shakespeare must have acquired an amazing knowledge of field sports, hunting, hawking, and woodcraft, for his plays show a fuller knowledge of sports than the plays of any other dramatist of his time. It is easy to imagine the lad escaping from Stratford and following the neighboring gentry as they roamed the countryside with their hawks and hounds.

**Marriage.** When Shakespeare was thirteen or fourteen, his father began having financial difficulties, which continued the rest of his life. According to Shakespeare's first biographer (who did not write until nearly one hundred years after the poet's death), the boy was taken from school because of these difficulties, and it is said that he was apprenticed to a Stratford tradesman. This story is probable enough, considering the position of the family and the customs of the town, but there is no definite record of Shakespeare until November 27, 1582. On that date, a license was issued for his marriage to Anne Hathaway, the daughter of a farmer who lived about a half mile west of Stratford at Shottery. At the time, William was eighteen and Anne twenty-six.

The only other definite records of William's early life in Stratford are those of the baptism of his children, Susanna on May 26, 1583, and the twins Hamnet and Judith on Feb. 2, 1585. When or why he left Stratford is not definitely known. One story, which was told more than a hundred years later, tells that he was caught *poaching* (stealing) deer, in the deer park of Sir Thomas Lucy, a justice of the peace and member of Parliament, and was prosecuted. In revenge, it is said that he wrote a scandalous ballad about Sir Thomas, was prosecuted further, and had to leave Stratford. Another story, first recorded about fifty years after Shakespeare's death, says that he was a schoolmaster before he went to London. Actually, there is no definite evidence of what happened to him between 1585, when the twins were born, and 1592, when he was acting and writing plays in London. These years are sometimes called "the lost years."

**Actor and Playwright.** Evidently, at some time during this period Shakespeare came to London and became a man of the theater. No one knows how his career began. One legend says that he began as a callboy, still another that he was a minor actor. But all that is definitely known is that by 1592 he was recognized as an actor and a playwright. In that year, the brilliant poet and dramatist, Robert Greene, wrote on his deathbed a sensational pamphlet called *Greene's Groatsworth* (eight cents' worth) *of Wit Bought with a Million of Repentance*. In it, he bitterly attacked Shakespeare as an upstart actor and playwright who thought himself as good as the university-trained dramatists. Soon afterward, Greene died, and the pamphlet was edited by his friend Henry Chettle, who did not know Shakespeare. Two or three months later, Chettle met Shakespeare and heard about him from various friends. He then published an apology. He praised Shakespeare as an actor, writer, and man of "civil" behavior, and expressed regret that he had not suppressed his envious friend's pamphlet. Greene's attack and Chettle's apology make it apparent that by the end of 1592 Shakespeare was fairly well known in London as an actor and playwright, that he had influential friends, and that his success in the theater had been great enough to rouse the envy of at least one of his rivals.

**Poet.** From the summer of 1592 to the summer of 1594, recurrent plague kept the London theaters closed most of the time, so Shakespeare turned to writing nondramatic verse. During this period, he published two long narrative poems, *Venus and Adonis* and *The Rape of Lucrece*. Both of these became very popular and added tremendously to his reputation. They were his first works to be published, and thus the first to reach an audience which could not or would not attend the popular London theaters. In the eyes of many Englishmen of the 1590's, plays had little more claim to literary distinction than motion-picture scenarios do today. Shakespeare himself was probably not entirely free from this strange prejudice, for *Venus and Adonis* and *Lucrece* were the only works whose publication he carefully supervised himself, and the only ones for which he wrote dedications. Both are dedicated to Henry Wriothesley, Earl of Southampton. Because of this fact, the earl is often spoken of as Shakespeare's patron.

**Theater Companies.** Historians do not know definitely to what particular theatrical company Shakespeare belonged in the years before 1594. Plays in Shakespeare's time were performed by permanent repertory companies. The same cast of men and boys pre-

## ANNE HATHAWAY'S COTTAGE

**This Picturesque Cottage,** *above,* is the birthplace of Anne Hathaway, who became Shakespeare's wife. It is located at the village of Shottery, about a mile from Stratford-upon-Avon. It has half-timbered walls, a roof thatched with straw, and small dormer windows. In front is a typical English garden of flowers, shrubs, and vegetables. The Hathaway house, restored and still sturdy and well-preserved, is said to be the most photographed in all England. Today, it is used as a museum.

**The Living Room of the Hathaway Home,** *below,* shows the hooded fireplace, grate, and andirons typical of the times. The cottage is furnished much as it is thought to have been during the poet's courtship, with warming pans hanging on either side of the fireplace, and with chinaware and candlesticks displayed on the mantel. The walls are made of unplastered bricks. In most houses, there was a baking oven set in the wall close to the fireplace.

Folger Shakespeare Library

sented a variety of plays in the same theater week after week. These groups were commercial organizations which depended for their income on the admissions paid by the audiences. The group to which Shakespeare belonged from 1594 to the end of his career was called the Lord Chamberlain's Men until King James I came to the throne in 1603. Later it had the honor of the patronage of the king himself and was known as the King's Men. Shakespeare was one of the leaders and stockholders in this organization, which became the most prosperous theatrical troupe in London. His income was obviously quite a respectable one in the latter part of his life. It apparently came from his share in the profits, for in his time no dramatist received very much money from the sale of either the acting or publishing rights to his plays and poems.

**Financial Success.** Various records show that Shakespeare made a small fortune. In 1596, he owned enough property in the London parish of St. Helen's, Bishopsgate, to have to pay five pounds in taxes, a large sum in those days. The next year, he bought one of the finest houses in Stratford and improved it and the grounds until it became one of the showplaces of the town. It had ten fireplaces and, after his death, while his daughter was living there, it was selected as the residence of Charles I's queen during her visit to Stratford for a few days. In 1598, he bought 10 per cent of the stock in the Globe Theatre and, ten years later, 14 per cent of the stock in the Blackfriars Theatre. In 1602, he bought one hundred acres of land near Stratford, and leased a cottage and another plot of ground in the town. Three years later, he purchased valuable property in the town of Stratford, and in 1613 another house in a fashionable section of London. These real estate dealings are not significant in themselves, but, taken together, they show the prosperity which Shakespeare achieved through his theatrical activities.

The years from 1594 to about 1608 were the most productive years of Shakespeare's career. He must have been a familiar figure about London, but only a few records of his specific activities have survived. In 1596, probably upon Shakespeare's application, the College of Heralds granted his father a coat of arms. This was made up of a gold shield bearing a silver falcon shaking a golden spear.

**Activities.** In the same year, a man named William Wayte claimed that Shakespeare and certain other men had put him in fear of death. Little is known of this particular dispute except that it was part of a long quarrel in which Shakespeare was not personally involved. In 1598 and 1603, Shakespeare acted in two of Ben Jonson's plays which were produced by his company. With his fellow actors, he marched in King James' royal entrance parade into London in 1604. Between 1602 and 1612, he was a fairly close friend of a family of French refugees named Mountjoy, and during some part of this period he lived in their house. When Mary Mountjoy's husband sued her father about Mary's dowry in 1612, Shakespeare, then living at Stratford, was called as a witness and told what he remembered of the arrangements for the marriage.

These few fragmentary records give no real picture of Shakespeare's activities in London. They are merely incidental facts which happen to have been preserved for more than three centuries. Shakespeare's days were

# SHAKESPEARE, WILLIAM

chiefly occupied with affairs of the theater. In addition to the great labor of writing his own plays, he was regularly acting in the company's performances and rewriting and revising old plays. He must have been extremely busy—rehearsing in the mornings, acting in the afternoons, writing and revising plays at night and in odd hours, and attending to his various business affairs whenever he could. It has been suggested that this severe strain led to some kind of breakdown in 1608, and there is evidence that Shakespeare's activities changed in that year. Before then, he seems to have furnished his company with about two plays a year, but after that date not more than five plays can be credited to him in the seven years before his death, and he wrote two or three of them with other dramatists.

**Later Years.** Shakespeare's company bought the fashionable Blackfriars Theatre in 1608 and, from then on, performed there in the winter and at the Globe during the summer. From that time on, Shakespeare probably retired more and more from regular acting and writing for the company. After 1612, he seems to have spent most of his time in Stratford, although he was back in London now and again. Perhaps he was there in 1613 when the Globe burned during a performance of his *Henry VIII*. Certainly he had stock in the new Globe which was built immediately on the old site.

Shakespeare was at Stratford during his last illness. On March 25, 1616, he called in his lawyer, Francis Collins, to revise his will. In it, he remembered various friends, including his old fellow actors of the King's Men in London, John Heminges, Henry Condell, and Richard Burbage, and his Stratford neighbors such as Hamnet Sadler and John Nashe. As was usual at the time, he tried to keep most of his property together to form an estate for his direct descendants. In his case, they were the children of his two daughters. Again, like many Englishmen of the day, he liked to think that his property would serve his descendants for generations. But in this he failed, for all his grandchildren died childless, and his last direct descendant died in 1670.

Shakespeare himself died at the age of 52, on April 23, 1616. As a prominent citizen of the town, he was buried inside the chancel of Holy Trinity Church. On the flat stone over his grave were carved the lines sometimes described as his epitaph, but which are nothing of the kind. They are simply a device to prevent the disturbing of the grave. It is easy to understand that in English churches, where people were buried under the floor of the church year after year for centuries, the space was sooner or later filled. When it was, the sexton removed the bones of those who had long since been forgotten and tossed them unceremoniously into the charnel house where dead bodies and bones were kept. (The one at Stratford opened off the north side of the chancel, only a few feet from Shakespeare's grave.)

**These Lines Are Carved on Shakespeare's Tombstone.**

GOOD FREND FOR IESVS SAKE FORBEARE,
TO DIGG THE DVST ENCLOASED HEARE:
BLESE BE Y MAN Y SPARES THES STONES,
AND CVRST BE HE Y MOVES MY BONES.

Folger Shakespeare Library

**Shakespeare's Tomb Is in Holy Trinity Church,** in the town of Stratford-upon-Avon. He was baptized in this church and now lies under the floor of the chancel. His wife and other members of the family are also buried here.

New burials were then made in the space thus made available. Evidently, Shakespeare, like others, was distressed by this practice, for the lines carved on his gravestone are nicely designed to keep any superstitious sexton from disturbing the grave.

**Portraits.** Some time before 1623, a bust of the dramatist was placed on the wall of the church. It was made after his death by a London tombmaker named Johnson or Janssen, and not by a sculptor, so there is no reason to think that it is a good likeness. The best-known portrait of the playwright is the engraving by Martin Droeshout, which appeared in the first folio of Shakespeare's plays in 1623. Since Droeshout was only fifteen years old when the poet died and Shakespeare could not have sat for the portrait, there can be no complete confidence in its likeness. There is even some evidence that Droeshout made use of the Stratford bust in preparing his engraving. Still, unsatisfactory as the bust and the engraving are, they are the most authentic likenesses we have of Shakespeare.

Besides these two, many so-called portraits of Shakespeare have turned up from time to time, but all are doubtful. In some cases, there is no evidence that they were ever intended to be portraits of Shakespeare. They are simply pictures of unknown men of the time. Others were painted after Shakespeare's death, but not by men such as Droeshout or Johnson, who are known to have been hired by Shakespeare's heirs and friends.

### Shakespeare's Works

Shakespeare was a professional dramatist who made his income directly from the theater, and associated daily with actors. He wrote his plays to suit the tastes of the theater audience. He was not an originator. He did not introduce new types of plays as did Thomas Kyd, Christopher Marlowe, or Ben Jonson. He wrote to meet the demands of the actors for plays of a type that was already popular. Nine of his ten historical dramas were written during a period when such plays were in greatest vogue. All six of his greatest tragedies were written when tragedy was most popular. His dramatic romances, or tragicomedies, were completed when plays of that type were succeeding on the stage. Like so many artists of the greatest genius, he was content to meet the demands of his time. He exercised his genius not in creating new forms but in taking the fullest advantage of the possibilities of whatever form was popular.

**Periods of Development.** In studying the work of any

great artist—painter, sculptor, musician, or writer—his admirers always want to know the order in which his works were created so that they may observe the development of his genius. Scholars have long tried to learn the dates of Shakespeare's various plays so that they might study the development of his genius. They have not yet been completely successful, but it is now possible to be reasonably sure of the approximate dates of most of them. There were four major periods in Shakespeare's development. The first began with his arrival in London and continued until about 1594 or 1595. The second period lasted until about 1600 or 1601, the third until 1608, and the last until he gave up writing for the stage three or four years before his death.

The first period was definitely one of experimentation. Some of these early plays may be revisions of other men's work. All contain experiments in verse forms, in types of situations, and in kinds of dramatic appeal.

The plays of the first period are of various types—tragedy, comedy, history, and farce.

During the second period, Shakespeare used the tools of the playwright and poet much more surely. He seldom failed to get the effect he wanted, and he confined himself mostly to comedies and histories.

In the third period of his development all his greatest tragedies were written—*Hamlet, Othello, King Lear, Macbeth, Antony and Cleopatra,* and *Coriolanus*—as well as the "bitter comedies" or "problem comedies." This is the period of his most mature work. His purpose is deeply serious. His characters are the most profound and subtle creations ever seen on any stage. His blank verse and prose are made into the most effective dramatic instrument ever created. No other writer has produced in the short period of seven or eight years so many works which may truly be called masterpieces.

The fourth period of Shakespeare's work contains the smallest number of plays and shows a sharp falling off from the intensity of his tragedies and "problem comedies." The most representative plays of the fourth period are *The Tempest, The Winter's Tale,* and *Cymbeline.* They combine something of the lightness of *As You Like It* and *Twelfth Night* with more serious situations. In them Shakespeare is still the dramatic master and great poet, but though he seems more eager than ever to pack his lines with meaning, something of his earlier liveliness is gone.

**Types of Plays.** In general, Shakespeare's plays fall into three classes, as was indicated in the first collected edition, the folio of 1623, which was entitled *Mr. William Shakespeare's Comedies, Histories, & Tragedies.*

*Histories.* The histories, which are sometimes called chronicle plays, are the type least familiar today, for they long ago ceased to be written. But they were very popular in Shakespeare's time. More than one hundred and fifty of them appeared, and nearly one third of Shakespeare's own plays were written in this form. They were not simply pictures of heroic figures seen against historic or "period" backgrounds, like the modern play *Abe Lincoln in Illinois.* Rather, they were plays in which the history came first. Their aim was to satisfy the demand of the audience for stories about their own past. These plays were really "pieces out of the story of England dramatized and set on the stage." The audience wanted to see not simply a play with a great king like Henry V in it, but a presentation of what had actually happened when Henry V was king. Thus the chronicle plays tended to include all the well-known events of a reign for the delight of an historical-minded audience. In addition, all such plays took for granted that the audience had a fair knowledge of English history. For this reason the average modern reader does not always understand all of the action.

The Elizabethan historical plays deal with most periods of English history from 950 to 1603, but Shakespeare was interested particularly in the period from about 1397 to 1485. Eight of his ten historical plays are concerned with this period, and picture the reigns of seven successive kings of England—Richard II, Henry IV, Henry V, Henry VI, Edward IV, Edward V, and Richard III.

*Tragedies.* Shakespeare's tragedies belong to a type of play which is fairly familiar today, for not only is tragedy still regularly performed in our theaters, but most modern tragedies have been decidedly influenced by Shakespeare. Confusion about his tragedies occasionally arises because it is easy to forget that the Elizabethans made no distinction between tragedy and melodrama. In those days, any play which involved catastrophes and violent death for the most important character was called a tragedy, regardless of how superficial or melodramatic it was. Thus Shakespeare's *Titus Andronicus* was called a tragedy, although it would generally be labeled melodrama today.

*Comedies.* Shakespeare's comedies show greater variety than his histories and tragedies. Most familiar are *As You Like It, Twelfth Night,* and *A Midsummer Night's Dream.* These were light romantic pieces, highly fanciful and improbable in plot. He also wrote plays which would now be called farces, although the term was not in common use in Elizabethan England. Among these are *The Comedy of Errors* and *The Taming of the Shrew. The Merry Wives of Windsor,* a popular comedy, also has a large element of farce. It would probably be advertised as a farce-comedy if it had been written for the modern stage. Least familiar to most readers are Shakespeare's "bitter comedies," or "problem comedies"—*All's Well that Ends Well, Measure for Measure,* and *Troilus and Cressida.* These plays are more serious and less optimistic, and have unconventional endings. They are the most puzzling of Shakespeare's dramatic works. Still later in his career came the romances, or tragicomedies—*The Tempest, The Winter's Tale,* and *Cymbeline,* each a mixture of romance, melodrama, and near-tragedy.

**Plots.** Regardless of type, most of Shakespeare's plays have plots based upon his own reading of history or fiction. The Elizabethan custom of using old plots instead of inventing new ones often puzzles modern readers who are inclined to consider the plot of a play its most important element. Actually most of the world's greatest dramatists, such as Aeschylus, Sophocles, Euripides, Shakespeare, and Racine, have used secondhand plots. Even in modern times, dramatists like Eugene O'Neill and Maxwell Anderson sometimes deliberately call attention to the fact that their plots are not original. In all ages, the great dramatists portray the eternal realities in the struggles of men with circumstances or fate. To them, plot originality is of little basic importance.

In his search for stories and ideas for effective plays,

## THE FIRST PERIOD

| Probable Date of First Performance* | Title | Date of Publication | Chief Source |
|---|---|---|---|
| 1590-1592 | Henry VI, Part II | 1594 | Holinshed, *Chronicles* |
| 1590-1592 | Henry VI, Part III | 1595 | Holinshed, *Chronicles* |
| 1590-1592 | Henry VI, Part I | 1623 | Holinshed, *Chronicles* |
| 1591-1593 | The Comedy of Errors | 1623 | Plautus, *Menaechmi* and *Amphitruo* |
| 1593-1594 | Titus Andronicus | 1594 | Uncertain |
| 1592-1593 | Richard III | 1597 | Holinshed, *Chronicles* |
| 1594-1595 | Love's Labour's Lost | 1598 | Unknown |
| 1593-1594 | The Taming of the Shrew | 1623 | Anon., *The Taming of a Shrew*; Ariosto, *I Suppositi* |
| 1594-1595 | The Two Gentlemen of Verona | 1623 | Montemayor, *Diana* |

## THE SECOND PERIOD

| | | | |
|---|---|---|---|
| 1594-1595 | Romeo and Juliet | 1597 | Brooke, *The Tragicall Historye of Romeus and Juliet* |
| 1595-1596 | Richard II | 1597 | Holinshed, *Chronicles* |
| 1594-1596 | A Midsummer Night's Dream | 1600 | No single comprehensive source |
| 1596-1597 | King John | 1623 | Anon., *The Troublesome Raigne of John, King of England* |
| 1596-1597 | The Merchant of Venice | 1600 | Fiorentino, *Il Pecorone* |
| 1597-1598 | Henry IV, Part I | 1598 | Holinshed, *Chronicles*; an old play, *The Famous Victories of Henry V* |
| 1600-1601 | The Merry Wives of Windsor | 1602 | Unknown |
| 1597-1598 | Henry IV, Part II | 1600 | Holinshed, *Chronicles*; and *The Famous Victories of Henry V* |
| 1598-1599 | Much Ado About Nothing | 1600 | Belleforest, *Histoires Tragiques*; Ariosto, *Orlando Furioso*, Canto V |
| 1598-1599 | Henry V | 1600 | Holinshed, *Chronicles* |
| 1599-1600 | Julius Caesar | 1623 | Plutarch, *Lives* |
| 1599-1600 | As You Like It | 1623 | Lodge, *Rosalynde* |
| 1599-1600 | Twelfth Night | 1623 | Riche, Apolonius and Silla |

## THE THIRD PERIOD

| | | | |
|---|---|---|---|
| 1600-1601 | Hamlet | 1603 | The early play of *Hamlet*; Belleforest, *Histoires Tragiques* |
| 1601-1602 | Troilus and Cressida | 1609 | Various popular medieval accounts of the story of Troy |
| 1602-1603 | All's Well that Ends Well | 1623 | Painter, *Palace of Pleasure* |
| 1604-1605 | Measure for Measure | 1623 | Whetstone, *Promos and Cassandra* |
| 1604 | Othello | 1622 | Cinthio, *Hecatommithi* |
| 1605-1606 | King Lear | 1608 | Anon., *Chronicle History of King Lear*; various popular accounts, and Sidney's *Arcadia* |
| 1605-1606 | Macbeth | 1623 | Holinshed, *Chronicles* |
| 1606-1608 | Antony and Cleopatra | 1623 | Plutarch, *Lives* |
| 1607-1608 | Coriolanus | 1623 | Plutarch, *Lives* |
| 1607-1608 | Timon of Athens | 1623 | Plutarch, *Lives*; Lucian, *Timon* |

## THE FOURTH PERIOD

| | | | |
|---|---|---|---|
| 1607-1609 | Pericles | 1609 | Gower, *Confessio Amantis* |
| 1609-1610 | Cymbeline | 1623 | Boccaccio, *Decameron*; Holinshed, *Chronicles* |
| 1610-1611 | The Winter's Tale | 1623 | Greene, *Pandosto* |
| 1611-1612 | The Tempest | 1623 | No comprehensive source |
| 1613 | Henry VIII | 1623 | Holinshed, *Chronicles*; Foxe, *Book of Martyrs* |
| 1612-1613 | The Two Noble Kinsmen | 1634 | Chaucer, *The Knight's Tale* |

*Dates are a consensus of leading experts.

Shakespeare used a number of books which were widely read in his time. Chief of these were a popular history by Raphael Holinshed and others called *Chronicles of England, Scotland, and Ireland* and Sir Thomas North's translation of *The Parallel Lives of the Noble Grecians and Romans* by Plutarch. See HOLINSHED'S CHRONICLES.

**Characters.** Whatever the source of his plot, Shakespeare makes the material completely his own. He adds, omits, and changes, until the original source becomes no more than a skeleton about which he has formed a living work of art. This is especially true of Shakespeare's great characters, such as Shylock, Falstaff, Macbeth, Hamlet, Rosalind, Richard II, Beatrice, Brutus, King Lear, Mark Antony, and Iago. In every case Shakespeare's imagination has created a living man or woman from the dry bones found in the source. So vivid are these characters in the minds of educated people that their names have become symbols for types of people and ideas. People often speak of "Falstaffian humor," of a newly-married man as "a Benedick," of a money-grubber as a "Shylock," of a youthful lover as a "young Romeo," and of a small-town policeman as "the local Dogberry."

### Famous Quotations

Not only the names of the characters, but also many of their speeches have passed into general usage. These speeches express so accurately the thoughts and feelings of men and women born long after Shakespeare's day that they have become familiar quotations. Shakespeare is endlessly quoted by writers and speakers of all sorts and in various circumstances. Newspaper editorials are headed by such quotations. Politicians and public speakers use his words constantly. Books carry his lines on their title pages, and novels and plays are given titles taken from his works. In one year seven different books appeared, each with a title taken from one short speech in *Macbeth*. No other writer in the world is so frequently quoted. A standard book of familiar quotations gives five times as much space to Shakespeare as to the next most widely quoted author. Among the most frequently repeated of the lines spoken by Shakespeare's characters are these:

Now is the winter of our discontent
Made glorious summer by this sun of York.
  *King Richard III.   Act I, Sc. 1, 1-2*

I have no other but a woman's reason:
I think him so because I think him so.
  *Two Gentlemen of Verona.   Act I, Sc. 2, 23-24*

He jests at scars, that never felt a wound.
  *Romeo and Juliet.   Act II, Sc. 2, 1*

What's in a name? That which we call a rose
By any other name would smell as sweet.
  *Romeo and Juliet.   Act II, Sc. 2, 43-44*

*Romeo.* Courage, man. The hurt cannot be much.
  *Mercutio.* No, 'tis not so deep as a well, nor so wide as a church door; but 'tis enough, 'twill serve.
  *Romeo and Juliet.   Act III, Sc. 1, 98-100*

A plague o' both your houses!
  *Romeo and Juliet.   Act III, Sc. 1, 103*

This royal throne of kings, this scept'red isle,
This earth of majesty, this seat of Mars,
This other Eden, demi-paradise,
This fortress built by Nature for herself
Against infection and the hand of war,
This happy breed of men, this little world,

## SHAKESPEARE, WILLIAM

This precious stone set in the silver sea,
Which serves it in the office of a wall,
Or as a moat defensive to a house,
Against the envy of less happier lands;
This blessed plot, this earth, this realm, this England.
  *King Richard II.   Act II, Sc. 1, 40-50*

I see thy glory, like a shooting star,
Fall to the base earth from the firmament.
  *King Richard II.   Act II, Sc. 4, 19-20*

Ay me! for aught that I could ever read,
Could ever hear by tale or history,
The course of true love never did run smooth.
  *A Midsummer Night's Dream.   Act I, Sc. 1, 132-134*

Life is as tedious as a twice-told tale
Vexing the dull ear of a drowsy man.
  *King John.   Act III, Sc. 4, 108-109*

Come the three corners of the world in arms,
And we shall shock them. Naught shall make us rue
If England to itself do rest but true.
  *King John.   Act V, Sc. 7, 116-118*

I hold the world but as the world, Gratiano—
A stage, where every man must play a part,
And mine a sad one.
  *The Merchant of Venice.   Act I, Sc. 1, 77-79*

I am Sir Oracle,
And when I ope my lips, let no dog bark!
  *The Merchant of Venice.   Act I, Sc. 1, 93-94*

God made him, and therefore let him pass for a man.
  *The Merchant of Venice.   Act I, Sc. 2, 60-61*

The devil can cite Scripture for his purpose.
  *The Merchant of Venice.   Act I, Sc. 3, 99*

The quality of mercy is not strain'd;
It droppeth as the gentle rain from heaven
Upon the place beneath. It is twice blest—
It blesseth him that gives, and him that takes.
  *The Merchant of Venice.   Act IV, Sc. 1, 184-187*

How far that little candle throws his beams!
So shines a good deed in a naughty world.
  *The Merchant of Venice.   Act V, Sc. 1, 90-91*

By heaven, methinks it were an easy leap
To pluck bright honour from the pale-fac'd moon,
Or dive into the bottom of the deep,
Where fadom line could never touch the ground,
And pluck up drowned honour by the locks.
  *Henry IV, Part I.   Act I, Sc. 3, 201-205*

Uneasy lies the head that wears a crown.
  *Henry IV, Part II.   Act III, Sc. 1, 31*

Every one can master a grief but he that has it.
  *Much Ado about Nothing.   Act III, Sc. 2, 28-29*

Let me have men about me that are fat,
Sleek-headed men, and such as sleep a-nights.
Yond Cassius has a lean and hungry look.
He thinks too much. Such men are dangerous.
  *Julius Caesar.   Act I, Sc. 2, 192-195*

---

**The Illustrations**

Most of the illustrations in this article, taken from books published before 1641, were selected for THE WORLD BOOK ENCYCLOPEDIA with the assistance of the Folger Shakespeare Library, Washington, D.C.

## SHAKESPEARE, WILLIAM

For there was never yet philosopher
That could endure the toothache patiently.
   *Much Ado about Nothing.   Act V, Sc. 1, 35-36*

Men at some time are masters of their fates:
The fault, dear Brutus, is not in our stars,
But in ourselves, that we are underlings.
   *Julius Caesar.   Act I, Sc. 2, 139-141*

Cowards die many times before their deaths;
The valiant never taste of death but once.
   *Julius Caesar.   Act II, Sc. 2, 32-33*

There is a tide in the affairs of men,
Which, taken at the flood, leads on to fortune;
Omitted, all the voyage of their life
Is bound in shallows and in miseries.
   *Julius Caesar.   Act IV, Sc. 3, 218-221*

His life was gentle, and the elements
So mix'd in him that Nature might stand up
And say to all the world, "This was a man!"
   *Julius Caesar.   Act V, Sc. 5, 73-75*

O, how full of briers is this working-day world!
   *As You Like It.   Act I, Sc. 3, 12*

Sweet are the uses of adversity,
Which, like the toad, ugly and venomous,
Wears yet a precious jewel in his head;
And this our life, exempt from public haunt,
Finds tongues in trees, books in the running brooks,
Sermons in stones, and good in everything.
   *As You Like It.   Act II, Sc. 1, 12-17*

Ay, now am I in Arden, the more fool I!
When I was at home, I was in a better place; but travellers must be content.
   *As You Like It.   Act II, Sc. 4, 16-18*

Nay, I shall ne'er be 'ware of mine own wit, till I break my shins against it.
   *As You Like It.   Act II, Sc. 4, 59-60*

If ladies be but young and fair,
They have the gift to know it.
   *As You Like It.   Act II, Sc. 7, 37-38*

True is it that we have seen better days.
   *As You Like It.   Act II, Sc. 7, 120*

All the world's a stage,
And all the men and women merely players.
They have their exits and their entrances;
And one man in his time plays many parts.
   *As You Like It.   Act II, Sc. 7, 139-142*

I had rather have a fool to make me merry than experience to make me sad.
   *As You Like It.   Act IV, Sc. 1, 27-28*

Men have died from time to time, and worms have eaten them, but not for love.
   *As You Like It.   Act IV, Sc. 1, 106-108*

How bitter a thing it is to look into happiness through another man's eyes!
   *As You Like It.   Act V, Sc. 2, 47-49*

Your "If" is the only peacemaker; much virtue in "If."
   *As You Like It.   Act V, Sc. 4, 107-108*

If music be the food of love, play on;
Give me excess of it, that, surfeiting,
The appetite may sicken, and so die.
   *Twelfth Night.   Act I, Sc. 1, 1-3*

Dost thou think, because thou art virtuous, there shall be no more cakes and ale?
   *Twelfth Night.   Act II, Sc. 3, 123-125*

She never told her love,
But let concealment, like a worm i' th' bud,
Feed on her damask cheek: she pin'd in thought,
And, with a green and yellow melancholy
She sat like Patience on a monument,
Smiling at grief.
   *Twelfth Night.   Act II, Sc. 4, 113-118*

Some are born great, some achieve greatness, and some have greatness thrust upon them.
   *Twelfth Night.   Act II, Sc. 5, 157-159*

O! that this too too solid flesh would melt,
Thaw and resolve itself into a dew;
Or that the Everlasting had not fix'd
His canon 'gainst self-slaughter! O God! God!
How weary, stale, flat, and unprofitable
Seem to me all the uses of this world.
   *Hamlet.   Act I, Sc. 2, 129-134*

Neither a borrower, nor a lender be;
For loan oft loses both itself and friend,
And borrowing dulls the edge of husbandry.
   *Hamlet.   Act I, Sc. 3, 75-77*

This above all: to thine own self be true,
And it must follow, as the night the day,
Thou canst not then be false to any man.
   *Hamlet.   Act I, Sc. 3, 78-80*

There are more things in heaven and earth, Horatio,
Than are dreamt of in your philosophy.
   *Hamlet.   Act I, Sc. 5, 166-167*

The time is out of joint; O cursed spite
That ever I was born to set it right!
   *Hamlet.   Act I, Sc. 5, 189-190*

Ay, every inch a king.
   *King Lear.   Act IV, Sc. 6, 109*

Sleep that knits up the ravell'd sleave of care.
   *Macbeth.   Act II, Sc. 2, 37*

To-morrow, and to-morrow, and to-morrow,
Creeps in this petty pace from day to day,
To the last syllable of recorded time;
And all our yesterdays have lighted fools
The way to dusty death. Out, out, brief candle!
Life's but a walking shadow, a poor player
That struts and frets his hour upon the stage
And then is heard no more: it is a tale
Told by an idiot, full of sound and fury,
Signifying nothing.
   *Macbeth.   Act V, Sc. 5, 19-28*

There's beggary in the love that can be reckon'd.
   *Antony and Cleopatra.   Act I, Sc. 1, 15*

In nature's infinite book of secrecy
A little I can read.
   *Antony and Cleopatra.   Act I, Sc. 2, 9*

Age cannot wither her, nor custom stale
Her infinite variety.
   *Antony and Cleopatra.   Act II, Sc. 2, 240-241*

Golden lads and girls all must,
As chimney-sweepers, come to dust.
   *Cymbeline.   Act IV, Sc. 2, 262-263*

We are such stuff
As dreams are made on, and our little life
Is rounded with a sleep.
   *The Tempest.   Act IV, Sc. 1, 156-158*

There's a divinity that shapes our ends,
Rough-hew them how we will.
   *Hamlet.   Act V, Sc. 2, 10-11*

The rest is silence.
   *Hamlet.   Act V, Sc. 2, 369*

**Old London Bridge Was the Only Bridge Over the River Thames Until 1750.**

To be, or not to be: that is the question:
Whether 'tis nobler in the mind to suffer
The slings and arrows of outrageous fortune,
Or to take arms against a sea of troubles,
And by opposing end them. To die: to sleep;
No more; and by a sleep to say we end
The heart-ache, and the thousand natural shocks
That flesh is heir to, 'tis a consummation
Devoutly to be wish'd. To die, to sleep;
To sleep: perchance to dream: ay, there's the rub;
For in that sleep of death what dreams may come,
When we have shuffled off this mortal coil,
Must give us pause: there's the respect
That makes calamity of so long life;
For who would bear the whips and scorns of time,
The oppressor's wrong, the proud man's contumely,
The pangs of despised love, the law's delay,
The insolence of office, and the spurns
That patient merit of the unworthy takes,
When he himself might his quietus make
With a bare bodkin? who would fardels bear,
To grunt and sweat under a weary life,
But that the dread of something after death,
The undiscover'd country from whose bourn
No traveller returns, puzzles the will,
And makes us rather bear those ills we have
Than fly to others that we know not of?
Thus conscience does make cowards of us all,
And thus the native hue of resolution
Is sicklied o'er with the pale cast of thought,
And enterprises of great pitch and moment
With this regard their currents turn awry
And lose the name of action.
    *Hamlet.*    Act III, Sc. 1, 56-88

We burn daylight:
    *The Merry Wives of Windsor.*    Act II, Sc. 1, 54

O, what a world of vile ill-favour'd faults
Looks handsome in three hundred pounds a year!
    *The Merry Wives of Windsor.*    Act III, Sc. 4, 32-33

One touch of nature makes the whole world kin.
    *Troilus and Cressida.*    Act III, Sc. 3, 175

Reputation, reputation, reputation! O, I have lost my
  reputation! I have lost the immortal part of myself,
  and what remains is bestial.
    *Othello.*    Act II, Sc. 3, 262-265

O God, that men should put an enemy in their mouths
  to steal away their brains!
    *Othello.*    Act II, Sc. 3, 291-292

Good name in man and woman, dear my lord,
Is the immediate jewel of their souls:
Who steals my purse steals trash; 'tis something, nothing;
'Twas mine, 'tis his, and has been slave to thousands
But he that filches from me my good name
Robs me of that which not enriches him
And makes me poor indeed.
    *Othello.*    Act III, Sc. 3, 155-161

Then must you speak
Of one that lov'd not wisely, but too well;
Of one not easily jealous, but, being wrought,
Perplex'd in the extreme; of one whose hand,
Like the base Indian, threw a pearl away
Richer than all his tribe.
    *Othello.*    Act V, Sc. 2, 343-348

How sharper than a serpent's tooth it is
To have a thankless child!
    *King Lear.*    Act I, Sc. 4, 310-311

### Nondramatic Works

**Narrative Poems.** Besides his plays, for which he is most famous, Shakespeare left several nondramatic pieces. The first of these were the two long narrative poems, *Venus and Adonis* and *The Rape of Lucrece.*

    *Venus and Adonis* tells the story of Venus' courtship of the indifferent Adonis. The poem is no longer widely read, but in Shakespeare's time it was one of his most

279

# SHAKESPEARE, WILLIAM

popular compositions. It went through more editions in his lifetime than any of his plays. To modern readers one of its most attractive characteristics is the beautiful setting of English fields and woods.

*The Rape of Lucrece* is a more serious piece of work than *Venus and Adonis*, but it is not much more widely read today. It tells the familiar story of the attack on the Roman matron Lucrece by Tarquin, and of Lucrece's suicide. The story itself is less significant than Shakespeare's interest in the conflict in Tarquin's mind.

**Sonnets.** By far the best and most famous of Shakespeare's nondramatic works are his *Sonnets*. They were probably written long before they were published in 1609, for they are referred to in 1598, and two of them were published in 1599. Like *Venus and Adonis* and *The Rape of Lucrece* and most of his plays, the sonnets represent a literary form which was popular during the reign of Queen Elizabeth I. Many English poets who lived during this time, such as Edmund Spenser, Sir Philip Sidney, Samuel Daniel, and Michael Drayton, had written sonnet cycles. These are long series of sonnets generally treating various phases of the poet's love for his mistress. Shakespeare followed other poets in writing his series of 154 sonnets, but his do not form a real cycle, for they deal with more than a single subject. Most of them are written to a young man, probably a nobleman and a beloved friend of the poet. They treat a number of subjects, including a dark lady with whom Shakespeare was in love, but who was unfaithful; a rival poet; advice to the friend to marry; affection for his friend; his long absence (presumably when Shakespeare was traveling with his company on the road); and especially they treat of time and its ravages.

Since there is such world-wide interest in Shakespeare, many attempts have been made to identify the persons he mentioned in the sonnets — the dark lady, the rival poet, and the patron and friend. None of these attempts has been successful, although the dedications of *Venus and Adonis* and *The Rape of Lucrece* to the Earl of Southampton make it possible to think that he was the friend and patron whom Shakespeare addressed.

The fact that we cannot identify the persons of whom Shakespeare speaks in no way affects the greatness of the sonnets as poetry. No other sonnets in the English language are so beautifully made or so deeply moving. No poet has fitted his ideas into the strict sonnet form with so little effort. In reading the finest of the sonnets, such as the seventy-third, which follows, one is almost persuaded that the ideas actually came to the poet in sonnet form, so easily does he fit his thoughts to the structural requirements of the sonnet:

That time of year thou mayst in me behold
When yellow leaves, or none, or few, do hang
Upon those boughs which shake against the cold,
Bare ruin'd choirs, where late the sweet birds sang.
In me thou see'st the twilight of such day
As after sunset fadeth in the West,
Which by-and-by black night doth take away,
Death's second self, that seals up all in rest.
In me thou see'st the glowing of such fire
That on the ashes of his youth doth lie,
As the deathbed whereon it must expire,
Consum'd with that which it was nourish'd by.
This thou perceiv'st, which makes thy love more strong,
To love that well which thou must leave ere long.

## Theories of Authorship

Shakespeare's unequalled accomplishment, and his reputation as the greatest literary genius the world has ever known, have led many to study his life in order to gain a fuller knowledge and understanding of him. But the few facts known about Shakespeare's life do not explain his genius. As a result some ill-informed but ardent admirers of Shakespeare's plays have been bitterly disappointed, and have declared that the actor Shakespeare from the town of Stratford-on-Avon could not have written these masterpieces. They have tried to find some man of Shakespeare's time whose life is better known and whose career better fits their notion of what the life of a literary genius ought to be. Among those to whom the authorship of the plays has been most popularly credited are Edward de Vere, Earl of Oxford; Francis Bacon, Viscount St. Albans; William Stanley, Earl of Derby; and Christopher Marlowe.

All kinds of arguments have been set forth in books and articles to show that one or another of these men wrote the plays. Secret ciphers, curious engravings, revealing portraits, and cryptic allusions have been pointed to as proof that someone other than Shakespeare was the author. The writers who have adopted one or another of these theories, who are known as Baconians, Oxfordians, or anti-Stratfordians, have been sincere admirers of Shakespeare's plays, but not very well informed about Elizabethan life. All have assumed that the literary genius who wrote the plays would surely have excited biographical interest in the 1600's as he does today. Mark Twain, for instance, could not understand why, if Shakespeare wrote the plays, there were not as many stories printed about him in Stratford as there were about Twain in Hannibal, Mo. But close students of Elizabethan life point out that other literary men of genius in Elizabethan times, such as John Webster and Edmund Spenser, left even fewer records of their lives than did Shakespeare. It is noteworthy that no important Shakespearean scholar has ever supported any of these anti-Stratfordian views.

## Shakespeare, a Man of His Own Time

Every man, from the greatest genius to the most lowly beggar, reflects the beliefs and the living conditions of his own time. Shakespeare is no exception to this universal law. Centuries after his death his plays are acted and read in most of the countries of the world, and his comments on men and women are so fitting that today he is quoted more often than any other writer. But he still remains a man of the Elizabethan Age, with the tastes and prejudices common to his time. "Elizabethan" is a confusing word, and is used with various meanings. Elizabethan literature is generally taken to mean not only the literature written when Elizabeth I was on the throne from 1558 to 1603, but also that written between 1579, when Spenser's *Shepheardes Calender* was published, and 1625, when King James I died. Elizabethan drama is the term generally used to refer to plays appearing between Lyly's first comedy in 1584 and the closing of the theaters by law in 1642. Thus, Shakespeare is always called an Elizabethan writer although he actually lived the last quarter of his life under King James I. A full understanding of Shakespeare depends on some knowledge of the conditions under which he lived and worked.

**An Elizabethan Feast.** In Shakespeare's day, tableware was much simpler than it is today. Knives were common, but there were no forks. Even spoons were a luxury. Everyone at the table ate from the serving dishes, and there were no individual plates. The serving woman in the foreground is "mulling" ale—heating and spicing it—over a fireplace.

Shakespeare Lived during the Elizabethan Age, which took its name from Queen Elizabeth I. His writings reflect the beliefs and living conditions of his own time, but many of his comments still fit present-day circumstances.

**Great Elizabethans.** The Elizabethan Age is one of heroic achievement in the history of the English-speaking peoples. Shakespeare was by no means the only great man in his time. In literature, no other period has been more brilliant. Edmund Spenser, Sir Philip Sidney, John Donne, the great poet and preacher, Ben Jonson, Christopher Marlowe, John Webster, and Francis Bacon all lived at the same time as Shakespeare. The period was one of exploration and great expansion on the sea, and Shakespeare may well have known such great captains as Sir Walter Raleigh, Sir Francis Drake, Martin Frobisher, John Hawkins, and Henry Hudson. In government such famous political figures as Francis Walsingham, William and Robert Cecil, and the great lawyer, Edward Coke, were all living in London when Shakespeare did. Queen Elizabeth herself, whom Shakespeare probably saw many times and before whom he acted at court, was one of the most brilliant rulers England ever had. Shakespeare was but one among many great figures of the day.

**London of Shakespeare's Day.** For Shakespeare, London was the heart of England as it was for all Elizabethans, especially for the dramatists. It was a city of about 200,000 people, but all the theaters, all but two of the printers and publishers, and most of the great merchants were established there. The Queen and her court, with their dazzling display, were nearly always in and about London, and their presence not only lent the city such color as is to be found in no modern capital, but it also influenced the daily lives of the citizens. Yet, judged by modern standards, London was a dirty, crowded city, with open sewers and only a few cobblestoned streets. Insanitary conditions led to frequent epidemics of the plague, in which many persons died. Fear of these epidemics was always present, and Shakespeare took for granted a knowledge of the terror which the plague inspired, as is shown in the second scene of Act V of *Romeo and Juliet*.

Crowded conditions in part caused these epidemics, but they gave London an air of bustling activity. Shops generally opened right onto the street, and apprentices shouted their masters' goods to every passerby. Since houses were crowded and the inner rooms tended to be dark and musty, most persons spent more time in the streets than city dwellers do today. The many street meetings and conversations in Shakespeare's plays reflect this tendency of the London populace to spend its leisure time in the market places and out of doors.

**Influence of America.** In Shakespeare's London, the average man was curiously divided in his outlook between the medieval and the modern. The amazing new world of the Americas was very much with him as he listened to the tales told by seamen who had sailed with Frobisher or Hudson, or had raided Spanish ships returning from Mexico and Peru with silver and gold. The famous *Golden Hind*, the very ship in which Drake

Farming during Shakespeare's Time was done with crude tools. This wheat planter is sowing grain in the furrows made by the ox-drawn plow. His grain bag is hanging on the tree. The long stick was used to frighten birds.

282

had sailed around the world, was tied up at Deptford for all Londoners to see. It proved a solid witness to the extraordinary new fact that the world was really round. This background of sailors' stories of wonderful faraway lands is particularly apparent in Shakespeare's *Tempest*. Many details of the wreck and of Prospero's island came from stories about the *Sea Adventurer*, an English ship which had been wrecked in Bermuda on her way to Virginia in 1609. The same interest in seas and ships is evident in *The Merchant of Venice* and *Twelfth Night*.

**Superstitions.** The Elizabethan Englishman, for all his interest in America, new discoveries, and strange facts, still kept many superstitious beliefs which seem odd today. Belief in ghosts, witches, and magicians was common, and Shakespeare used them in such plays as *Julius Caesar*, *Macbeth*, *The Tempest*, *Hamlet*, and *Richard III*. Equally common were beliefs in portents—dreams, supernatural sights, and sounds, which warn men of future catastrophes. Elizabethans accepted such warnings as probable enough when Shakespeare used them, although they seem strange to us today.

**The Audience.** Audiences of Shakespeare's day were both more primitive and more cultivated than they are today. That they were more primitive is shown by their liking for cruelty and bloodshed. One of the most popular sports of the time was bullbaiting, in which the spectators watched a tied bull fight bulldogs. Loud was

**The Upper Classes of Shakespeare's Time** were noted for their lavish dress and elegant manners. This picture from *The Booke of Falconrie* shows that even the horses had beautiful trappings. The nobles hunted with trained falcons.

**The Elizabethan Farmer** used a two-wheeled wooden plow drawn by a yoke of oxen. After he plowed, the farmer broke up the earth with a crude harrow, like the one standing at the edge of the field. Farmers wore a plain and practical costume.
Folger Shakespeare Library

the applause when a bull tossed a dog so high in the air that he was killed by his fall, or when a dog got a firm grip on the bull's lip and held on until his jaws had to be pried apart. Equally popular was bearbaiting, in which dogs fought with a bear, or men stood about and whipped a chained blind bear while he tried to get at them. The same persons who attended these sports at the Bear Garden near Shakespeare's Globe Theatre also flocked to the public executions of traitors at Tower Hill or common criminals at Tyburn. People accustomed to such sights were not shocked when Gloucester's eyes were put out in *King Lear* or Titus' hand was cut off in *Titus Andronicus*.

**Music.** But these same Elizabethans with their tolerance of cruelty had a taste for music and poetry that has seldom been equaled. Their enthusiasm for poetry is shown in the amount of verse published and in the number of plays, most of them written in verse, performed during Shakespeare's lifetime. There are many examples of the popular delight in music. Elizabethan barbershops entertained waiting customers, not as modern shops do with newspapers and magazines, but with *lutes* (guitarlike instruments) on which the customers might play accompaniments for themselves and their friends. The common entertainment in many homes was not cards or books but music. After dinner, songbooks were passed around, and each person was supposed to be able to read his part at sight and join in the singing. A man who could not sing or read music

283

# SHAKESPEARE, WILLIAM

was thought poorly educated. Since music was so popular and so widely understood, it is little wonder that most Elizabethan plays have music in them. Shakespeare used fifty or more songs in his plays and wrote hundreds of stage directions calling for music. Only one of his thirty-seven plays is, like most modern plays, entirely without music. This is *The Comedy of Errors*.

This almost constant use of music shows not only that there was a constant demand for what Shakespeare called the "concord of sweet sounds," but also that the playwrights could count on the presence of singers and musicians among the actors who performed their plays. All London theaters had orchestras, some of them very good indeed. At one time the orchestra at Shakespeare's Blackfriars Theatre was said to be the best in London.

**Innyard Theaters.** The peculiar structure of the theater in which his plays were first acted also influenced Shakespeare's playwriting. Modern readers with little knowledge of the theater often overlook this influence. All good dramatists, from the Greeks to the moderns, have planned their plays to make the most of the peculiarities of the buildings in which their plays would be performed. Consequently, the changing characteristics of theater buildings have always had a great influence on plays.

The first theater in England was built when Shakespeare was twelve years old. For many years before that, the troupes of actors had presented their plays in various halls or innyards. Innyards were convenient and well adapted for the purpose, because of the peculiar structure of the Elizabethan inns. These two- or three-story buildings were built in the form of a hollow square around a paved courtyard where travelers dismounted and wagons were unloaded. Galleries or balconies ran around this courtyard at the second and third stories. These were normally used by the guests of the inn to get to their rooms. When the players came to town, they found it very easy to set up a platform stage at one

**A Butcher in Elizabethan England** scalded slaughtered hogs so that he could scrape off their bristles easily.

*Folger Shakespeare Library*

**Newe Fishe Streete Market in Shakespeare's London** was a bustling trading center. When business began in the morning, shutters were opened outward and used as display stands for various kinds of fish. Sidewalks were unknown and everyone jostled together in the uneven streets. When a carriage approached, the people scattered for safety.

*Folger Shakespeare Library*

## SHAKESPEARE, WILLIAM

The **Baker of Shakespeare's Time** used large brick or clay ovens. He pushed in the bread loaves with a paddle.

end of the innyard. On the afternoon of the performance, one actor stood at the entrance to the courtyard to collect a general admission fee. Another actor at the foot of the stairs leading to the galleries collected a second fee for the reserved seats. The patrons who paid only the general admission fee stood in the courtyard around the platform stage. Those who bought reserved seats went up to the galleries and sat on the stools and benches provided there. All the action of the play took place on the open platform, with no curtain to cut off the view of the stage at any time. The actors had to walk on and off in full view of the audience, and if any character in the play died on the stage, he had to be carried off. This open platform surrounded on three sides by the audience is the basic feature of the Elizabethan stage, both in the innyard and in the later theaters. Its influence is to be seen in nearly all the plays of the time.

**First London Playhouse.** Finally the drama became so popular in London that a permanent theater promised to be a good investment. James Burbage, father of the Richard Burbage who became the greatest actor of the time and the creator of many of the chief roles in Shakespeare's plays, built the first London playhouse and named it "The Theatre." It was located in the suburbs north of the city. There it was beyond the authority of the Lord Mayor and the Council, who were always unfriendly to plays and players and interfered with them whenever they could. All the London public theaters built in Shakespeare's lifetime—the Curtain, the Globe, the Fortune, the Red Bull, the Swan, the Rose—were also located in the suburbs, either north or south of the city. All these public theaters were similar to Burbage's in design. Some had a few minor variations.

James Burbage and the theater builders who came immediately after him patterned their theaters after an innyard, with a few additional conveniences added for the patrons and the actors. Even in the theaters the spectators who paid general admission stood on the bare

The **Grace Churche Market in Elizabethan London** was another of the city's crowded business districts. Despite its high-sounding religious name, the market had much cheating and fraud. The popular rule of the market was "let the buyer beware." After dark, the people carried burning faggots. The women sometimes carried bundles on their heads.

## LINES ASSOCIATED WITH FAMOUS SHAKESPEAREAN CHARACTERS

| Lines | Character | Source |
|---|---|---|
| Lord, what fools these mortals be! | Puck | *A Midsummer Night's Dream* Act III, Sc. 2, 115 |
| Benedick, the married man | Benedick (spoken by Don Pedro) | *Much Ado about Nothing* Act V, Sc. 4, 99 |
| O that he were here to write me down an ass! | Dogberry | *Much Ado about Nothing* Act IV, Sc. 2, 77 |
| Just as high as my heart | Rosalind (spoken by Orlando) | *As You Like It* Act III, Sc. 2, 286 |
| An ill-favour'd thing, sir, but mine own | Audrey (spoken by Touchstone) | *As You Like It* Act V, Sc. 4, 60 |
| Neither a borrower nor a lender be | Polonius | *Hamlet* Act I, Sc. 3, 75 |
| To be, or not to be — that is the question | Hamlet | *Hamlet* Act III, Sc. 1, 56 |
| Frailty, thy name is woman! | Gertrude (spoken by Hamlet) | *Hamlet* Act I, Sc. 2, 146 |
| This was the noblest Roman of them all | Brutus (spoken by Antony) | *Julius Caesar* Act V, Sc. 5, 68 |
| He doth bestride the narrow world like a Colossus | Julius Caesar (spoken by Cassius) | *Julius Caesar* Act I, Sc. 2, 135 |
| One that lov'd not wisely, but too well | Othello | *Othello* Act V, Sc. 2, 344 |
| Her voice was ever soft, Gentle, and low — an excellent thing in woman | Cordelia (spoken by Lear) | *King Lear* Act V, Sc. 3, 272-273 |
| A snapper-up of unconsidered trifles | Autolycus | *The Winter's Tale* Act IV, Sc. 3, 26 |
| Age cannot wither her, nor custom stale Her infinite variety | Cleopatra (spoken by Enobarbus) | *Antony and Cleopatra* Act II, Sc. 2, 240 |
| A horse! a horse! my kingdom for a horse! | King Richard III | *King Richard III* Act V, Sc. 4, 7 |
| A pair of star-crossed lovers | Romeo and Juliet (spoken by the chorus) | *Romeo and Juliet* Prologue, 6 |
| For God's sake, let us sit upon the ground And tell sad stories of the death of kings | King Richard II | *King Richard II* Act III, Sc. 2, 155-156 |
| But screw your courage to the sticking place | Lady Macbeth | *Macbeth* Act I, Sc. 7, 60 |
| I am not only witty in myself, but the cause that wit is in other men | Falstaff | *King Henry IV, Part II* Act I, Sc. 2, 11 |
| Had I but serv'd my God with half the zeal I serv'd my king, he would not in mine age Have left me naked to mine enemies | Cardinal Wolsey | *King Henry VIII* Act III, Sc. 2, 455-457 |
| A pound of flesh | Shylock | *The Merchant of Venice* Act III, Sc. 3, 33 |

Folger Shakespeare Library

**The Innyard Was the Forerunner of the Playhouse.** In such courtyards as this, the early plays of Shakespeare were presented. A stage was set up at one end for the actors. Persons who paid for reserved seats sat on stools and benches on the balconies of the building. Those who paid general admission stood in the courtyard to watch the play.

ground about the stage with only the sky for a roof, just as they had done at the innyard performances. These poorer spectators, who could not pay for seats in the galleries, were called "groundlings" by Shakespeare in some rather insulting remarks he made about them in *Hamlet*. By paying a few pennies extra to go up in the galleries, the well-to-do spectators had somewhat better accommodations than had been available at the inns, for the theater galleries had fairly comfortable benches.

Naturally enough, most of Burbage's improvements were designed for the convenience of the actors. We do not know exactly what The Theatre or its successor, the Globe, looked like because we have no existing pictures of these buildings or detailed descriptions of them. But scholars have been able to piece together certain features from scattered references and from repeated situations in the plays written for these theaters. Behind the platform stage were dressing rooms, which the Elizabethans called the *tiring house*. Above it, a high canopy sheltered the actors from rain and sun. There

287

## SHAKESPEARE, WILLIAM

were trapdoors in the floor, and three separate entrances to the stage. A curtained-off area at the back of the platform provided for sudden appearances. For example, this area was used to reveal Ferdinand and Miranda playing chess in *The Tempest*, and to show Doctor Faustus in his study at the beginning of Christopher Marlowe's *Tragical History of Doctor Faustus*.

The new theaters also included an elevated area behind and above the platform. This area, probably part of the balcony, was used for scenes in which one character on the platform had to carry on a conversation with another standing above him. Juliet stood here while speaking from her balcony to Romeo in the garden below. The governor of Harfleur stood here when he surrendered his city to King Henry in *Henry V*. In the second act of *The Merchant of Venice*, Jessica stood in this raised area when she threw down the casket of jewels to Lorenzo, who then said: "Descend, for you shall be my torch-bearer."

These were the main characteristics of the public theaters in which Shakespeare rehearsed and acted, and for which he wrote his plays. There were private theaters in London at the time, but there is no evidence that Shakespeare ever wrote for them until his company took over the Blackfriars in 1608, when his career as a playwright was nearly over. Many of the Elizabethan plays were acted in both public and private theaters. The private theaters were different from the public ones in that they were smaller, completely enclosed, artificially lighted, and fitted with seats on the main floor as well as in the balcony. They charged much higher prices, and it was not possible for poorer people to attend them. The audiences in private theaters were, therefore, more select.

**Stage Properties.** Elizabethan plays moved much more rapidly than do modern ones. The numerous act and scene divisions in modern versions of Shakespeare's plays (nearly all of which have been added by editors) suggest many curtains and intermissions, but these divisions were scarcely noticeable to the Elizabethan audience. One scene followed another without pause, since there was no curtain to fall and no scenery to be moved. In most scenes there was no reference to the place of action. The spectators simply concentrated on the actors and gave no thought to the place. Such a situation is difficult for modern readers to imagine, for in all modern plays each scene is definitely located and scenery is generally used.

But in spite of the lack of scenery, Shakespeare did not write his plays for a colorless production on a bare, drab platform. The back wall of the stage was hung with bright *arras* (tapestry) behind which characters sometimes hid themselves, as Polonius did before Hamlet plunged his rapier through the arras to kill him. Properties of all kinds were regularly used—tables, benches, beds, chairs, and chests, and even trees, rocks, and walls on occasion.

**Costumes.** The most colorful part of an Elizabethan production was undoubtedly the costumes. These are seldom equaled on the modern stage, for even the most formal gowns and uniforms of today do not offer such a vivid variety of colors and materials as did the everyday dress of Elizabethan ladies and gentlemen. Not only was the costume of any young gentleman likely to display crimson and gray, purple and gold, but the styles were also varied so that no two gentlemen looked alike. Any well-dressed young man, as Orlando, Bassanio, or Romeo, differed as sharply in appearance from a servant, clergyman, or physician as a modern bank president differs in appearance from a circus clown.

Elizabethan costume was thus of great value to the actors and dramatists of Shakespeare's day, who took the fullest possible advantage of it in giving color and variety to their plays. On several occasions one producer is known to have spent twice as much for the costume of one actor as he paid the dramatist for the play in which the costume was worn. In addition, the variety of costumes, haircuts, and beards offered certain possibilities, both in real life and in plays, which have practically disappeared from modern life. The chief of these was disguise, which is almost unknown in modern plays and is rare in modern life. The reason is that most men now shave and cut their hair in the same general style, and their clothes differ only in details. Today a man cannot change his appearance a great deal without making himself conspicuous. But when costumes, beards, and haircuts differed as they did in Shakespeare's day, it was fairly easy for a clever man to deceive even his close friends for a limited time, as did Kent in *King Lear*.

**Women's Parts.** There were no actresses on the London stage when Shakespeare wrote. Boys played the parts of women, as they had done in all English plays for hundreds of years. These boys were apprenticed to become actors. For several years, they lived with the players, heard stage talk all the time, attended hundreds of rehearsals, saw plays nearly every afternoon, took small parts in productions, and practiced female impersonation at every opportunity. It is little wonder that a bright, talented boy could present a convincing portrayal of Rosalind, Viola, or Portia, after several years of such life, with the help of a careful dramatist, a good make-up man, and an intelligent costumer. As a result, the most common disguise used in Shakespeare's plays is often extremely confusing to modern readers and actors. The boys who played the young ladies' parts often disguised themselves as boys or youths. Nothing could be simpler for them than to stop pretending to be Rosalind and be perfectly convincing as Ganymede, drop Viola for Cesario, or change from the dress Portia wore to the formal robes of Balthasar, the young lawyer.

In these ways Shakespeare was not only deeply influenced by the character of Elizabethan life, but he also employed brilliantly the structure of the Elizabethan stage. He constructed his plays to make effective use of the inner, outer, and upper stages. He took full advantage of the swift, continuous action of a curtainless front stage. He used to the fullest degree the variety and color of Elizabethan costume, and even made an asset out of the liability of having no women actors for female roles.

### Editions of Shakespeare

**The First Quartos.** The fact that plays had a low literary reputation in Shakespeare's time is reflected in the early editions of his dramatic works. During his lifetime fewer than half of his plays were ever printed at all, and those that did appear were in the form of cheap pamphlets, now called quartos. Many of them did not

## STAGE AND THEATER

**Shakespeare's London,** *above,* is shown in *View of London* by Visscher, a famous engraver. The Globe Theatre and the Bear Garden are in the foreground.

**The Swan Theatre,** *below,* stood near the Globe, and was built on the same general plan. The titles on this old sketch are written in Latin.

**The Globe Theatre** of Shakespeare's time is known to us through the work of Shakespearean scholars, such as John C. Adams. He spent over 10 years on research before he made models of the exterior, *right,* and the interior, *below.*

Folger Shakespeare Library

Bettmann Archive
**John Drew Played Petruchio in *The Taming of the Shrew*.**

even have the author's name on the title page. Shakespeare did not proofread any of these quartos, and all have numerous mistakes in the printing. Four of them omit at least one fourth of the lines of the play as written by Shakespeare. Such careless printing characterized nearly all plays of the time, and Shakespeare was like many of his fellow dramatists (with the exception of Ben Jonson) in showing little or no concern about the publication of his plays. His whole attention was directed toward the stage.

**The First Folio.** Seven years after Shakespeare's death, when plays had risen somewhat in public esteem, two of his old friends and fellow actors, John Heminges and Henry Condell, collected his plays and had them printed in a large and handsome volume. It contains the famous Droeshout portrait of Shakespeare, a preface by the editors, a list of actors who had roles in Shakespeare's plays, and a dedication to two noblemen. It also included several verses in honor of the playwright, as well as 36 of his plays. Such a book was most unusual in 1623, when this volume of collected works appeared. Only one other collection of English plays had ever been published in England.

This volume, which is now called the *first folio*, is the basis for Shakespeare's text. Even when it first appeared, it was somewhat expensive, and sold for one pound unbound. This was ten to twenty times the price of the average book in 1623. Today, only the wealthy can afford to buy this volume. They sometimes pay as much as $75,000 for a single copy.

The first folio was elaborate for its time. But if we judge it according to today's standards, it is a poorly printed volume. The text is full of mistakes, lines repeated or dropped out, impossible punctuation, and verse printed as prose and prose as verse. Ever since it appeared, editors have been trying to correct its mistakes. Many errors have been caught by comparing the folio passage with the same line in a quarto. Others have been found by applying present-day knowledge of Elizabethan handwriting and obsolete Elizabethan words. Still others have been discovered by using common sense. But many of the errors still exist, for no one has ever been able to puzzle out a satisfactory correction of certain meaningless lines in the first folio.

**Later Editions.** Hundreds of editors and scholars have labored during the last three hundred years to make it easier for modern readers to understand and enjoy Shakespeare's plays. Obviously, the text of a modern edition of Shakespeare is very different from that originally put forth in the 1600's. A few of the mistakes in the first folio were corrected by the anonymous editors of the second folio in 1632, of the third folio (1663-1664), and of the fourth in 1685, but these men made more new mistakes than they corrected old ones. The first editor to make any very great effort to help the reader was the playwright Nicholas Rowe, who edited Shakespeare's plays in six volumes in 1709. He wrote the first life of the dramatist. He made lists of characters for the twenty-eight plays which had never had them before. He divided the plays into acts and scenes, a task which had been only partly done in the folios. He also added many stage directions to the small number contained in the earlier folios. In 1733, Lewis Theobald edited Shakespeare's works in seven volumes, and made more good corrections of bad lines than any other man ever did.

Hundreds of editions of Shakespeare have followed in the last two hundred years. All the best ones make use of the corrections and explanations of the earlier ones and usually contain new additions. Most famous are the editions of Samuel Johnson in 1765; the 21-volume edition of Edmund Malone and James Boswell in 1821; and W. Aldis Wright's Cambridge edition, published from 1863 to 1866.

The most elaborate edition of Shakespeare is the *New Variorum* edition, which was begun by Howard Furness in 1871 but is still incomplete. The vast collection of notes and comments in the bulky volumes of this edition are a monument to an unparalleled piece of Shakespearean scholarship. These volumes are probably the greatest single aid available today to students of Shakespeare.

**Popular Editions.** All these famous editions are useful to scholars, but most people find them more confusing than helpful. Editions that have notes explaining unusual words, historical background, and puzzling situations are usually of greater help to present-day readers. Many such editions exist in a variety of forms. The smallest are the complete editions in one volume. These include *The Complete Works of Shakespeare* edited by George Lyman Kittredge (1936), *The Complete Plays and Poems of William Shakespeare* edited by W. A. Neilson and C. J. Hill (1942), and *The Complete Works of Shakespeare* edited by Hardin Craig (1951). Other more complete editions with fuller notes and introductions are *The New Cambridge* edition, the current *New Arden*

*Edition*, and the current *Pelican Shakespeare*. These are good examples of editions which are issued one play to a volume. Notes are also found in *Twenty-three Plays and the Sonnets*, edited by Thomas Marc Parrott, and *Major Plays and the Sonnets*, edited by George Bagshawe Harrison. These two inexpensive editions contain the more familiar plays, together with comments on Shakespeare's life and background. Holzknecht and McClure's *Selected Plays of Shakespeare* are convenient and inexpensive editions that have five to seven plays bound in each volume, with notes and introductions.

### Shakespeare Through the Ages

Shakespeare was truly a man of his own times, but no man has ever succeeded more completely in passing on his art to other nations and other ages. His own friend, the dramatist Ben Jonson, was one of the first to realize this. Seven years after Shakespeare's death, he wrote, "He was not of an age, but for all time."

The tributes which have been paid to Shakespeare as a playwright would probably have given him the greatest pleasure. Since he began to write, scarcely a year has passed without productions of several of his plays. The plays of Shakespeare have always been in the repertory of the greatest actors of the English and American stage.

**Famous Shakespearean Actors.** Since Richard Burbage performed Hamlet, Othello, Lear, and Richard III during Shakespeare's lifetime, nearly all famous actors have chosen to act in his plays. After the death of Shakespeare and Burbage, Joseph Taylor and John Lowin continued to act in the plays for the King's Men. Following the Restoration in 1660, the greatest English actor of the time, Thomas Betterton, played Hamlet, Brutus, and Othello. Betterton's wife, Mary Saunderson, was one of the first women to act in a Shakespearean play.

In the next generation, the actor-manager Colley Cibber played Iago, Jacques, and Richard III. Samuel Johnson's generation admired one of the most famous of all actors, David Garrick, as Hamlet, Richard III, and Lear. Also popular at that time were Charles Macklin's Shylock, James Quin's Falstaff, and Peg Woffington's Rosalind.

In William Wordsworth's and Samuel Coleridge's day, the late 1700's and early 1800's, John Philip Kemble played in 27 different Shakespearean roles. Sarah Siddons was probably the most noted of all Shakespearean actresses. She was famous as Lady Macbeth, Desdemona, and Ophelia, and as Queen Catherine in *Henry VIII*. Even before she appeared in her greatest role, Lady Macbeth, Samuel Johnson was so impressed that he wrote his name on the hem of her dress in Sir Joshua Reynolds' famous portrait of her as the *Tragic Muse*. Johnson said, "I would not lose the honor this opportunity afforded to me for my name going down to posterity on the hem of your garment."

In the middle 1800's, crowds flocked to see Edmund Kean as Shylock, Hamlet, Othello, Macbeth, and Lear. They also saw William Charles Macready as Richard III, Lear, and Henry V; and Helen Faucit as Juliet, Desdemona, and Lady Macbeth. The favorites of the Victorians were Sir Henry Irving and Ellen Terry. Sir Henry dominated the stage of his time almost as completely as Garrick had a hundred years before. His

Vandamm

**Maurice Evans Played Falstaff in *King Henry IV*.**

*Merchant of Venice* ran for 250 consecutive performances. In North America, Edwin Booth was the greatest Shakespearean actor of the time.

In the early 1900's, some of the best-known Shakespearean actors were Sir Herbert Beerbohm Tree, Robert Mantell, Edward Hugh Sothern and Julia Marlowe (his wife), Sir Robert Benson, Sir Johnston Forbes-Robertson, and Mary Anderson.

Famous performers of Shakespeare are still drawing crowds. In the mid-1900's, Ethel Barrymore, John Barrymore, Katharine Cornell, Maurice Evans, Sir John Gielgud, Walter Hampden, Helen Hayes, Charles Laughton, Alfred Lunt and Lynn Fontanne (his wife), Sir Laurence Olivier, and Orson Welles have performed Shakespeare with great success.

**Recent Performances.** The performances in theaters devoted wholly or chiefly to the production of Shakespearean plays resemble the repertory system of play production in Elizabethan times. One of the most famous of such theaters is the Shakespeare Memorial Theatre in Stratford-upon-Avon, England. An equally famous theater is the Old Vic in London, where the National Theatre Company performs. San Diego began a National Shakespeare Festival in 1949, and Stratford, Ont. began a Stratford Shakespearean Festival in 1953. Stratford, Conn., set up a Shakespeare Festival and Academy in 1955.

Many Shakespearean plays have been made into motion pictures. These include *Romeo and Juliet*, *Henry V*, *A Midsummer Night's Dream*, *Hamlet*, *Richard III*, *Julius Caesar*, and *Othello*. Radio and television have brought Shakespeare's plays to many parts of the world.

# SHAKESPEARE, WILLIAM

Folger Shakespeare Library

**David Garrick and Mrs. Pritchard in *Macbeth***

## Memorials

Memorials to Shakespeare of one kind or another are scattered throughout the world. They include theaters, statues, pictures, and books. Even streets, towns, and commercial products are named for him and his characters. One of the greatest of the memorials, and one of which Americans can be especially proud, is the Folger Shakespeare Library in Washington, D.C. This is the greatest collection that has ever been made of books, manuscripts, and pictures relating to Shakespeare and his time. Scholars from all parts of the world come to the Folger Library to study the material gathered there. Other notable libraries with important Shakespeare collections include the Bodleian Library at Oxford, England; the British Museum; the Horace Howard Furness Memorial at the University of Pennsylvania; and the Henry E. Huntington Library, located at San Marino, Calif.

## Synopses of Plays

**As You Like It.** The scenes of this delightful comedy are laid chiefly in the Forest of Arden, where shepherds lead an easy life and everything is "as you like it." To the forest come an exiled French duke and his followers, leaving at court his daughter Rosalind; his younger brother, Duke Frederick, who has taken his place; and Frederick's daughter Celia, who pleads so eloquently for her cousin's companionship that Frederick allows Rosalind to remain. In a court match, the duke's professional wrestler is overcome by a youth named Orlando, who proves to be the son of an old friend of Rosalind's father. Rosalind and Orlando fall in love, but are soon separated. Rosalind is banished by Frederick. With Celia, who refuses to desert her, and Touchstone, the court jester, she takes refuge in Arden. There the girls buy a farm and live as brother and sister. Celia poses as a shepherdess and the taller Rosalind wears man's clothing and calls herself Ganymede, a young shepherd.

Meanwhile, Orlando flees to Arden with his old servant Adam, to escape the plotting of his murderous brother Oliver, and finds a refuge with the banished duke. His love verses to Rosalind, which he carves on the bark of trees, are read by the disguised Rosalind. When they meet, she tests him by offering to impersonate Rosalind so that he may be cured of his love by meetings and conversations with her. Reluctantly Orlando consents, to Rosalind's delight. Now and then the melancholy Jacques contributes a bit of sour philosophy. One day Orlando kills and is wounded by a lion that is attacking his brother Oliver, who has come to the forest in search of him. The penitent Oliver, sent to Ganymede with a note explaining why Orlando is delayed in keeping a tryst, sees Celia and falls in love with her. The play ends happily with a wedding of four couples. Rosalind resumes her feminine dress and is wed to Orlando. Touchstone is married to the country maid Audrey. Oliver is wed to Celia. The shepherd folk, Phebe and Silvius, complete the party. In the midst of this rejoicing, word comes that Duke Frederick has restored the dukedom to Rosalind's father, and at the end all is well.

**Hamlet,** perhaps the most famous of Shakespeare's plays, is a drama of revenge. Hamlet, a young prince of Denmark, is grieved and mystified by the sudden death of his father; by his beloved mother's hasty marriage with the dead king's evil, plotting brother, Claudius, who has taken the throne; and by the stupidity and (as he thinks) faithlessness of his sweetheart Ophelia, the daughter of Polonius. His friend Horatio tells him that a ghost resembling his father is appearing nightly before the castle, and Hamlet watches for the specter. In a thrilling night scene he is told the story of his father's murder by Claudius. Hamlet's actions have been variously interpreted. Most critics believe he only pretends madness to lull suspicions and to get opportunities for revenge. His course is especially distressing to Ophelia. Shocked and overwhelmed by the evil in his world, Hamlet must await the right moment to act, and broods over the pain of life. He even thinks of suicide. A band of strolling players arrive, and Hamlet traps the king by having the actors speak certain lines about a king's being murdered by his brother. Claudius pretends illness and leaves the hall, thus proving his guilt. Later, in his mother's room, Hamlet scolds her for her conduct. During this interview he thrusts his rapier through a curtain behind which he thinks the king is hiding, but kills old Polonius who is eavesdropping.

The alarmed Claudius sends Hamlet to England under escort of Rosencrantz and Guildenstern. Hamlet finds they carry written orders to have him killed, and secretly substitutes their names for his. He escapes and returns to Denmark. He arrives in time to witness the burial of Ophelia, who has lost her reason and been drowned. At the grave, a meeting between Hamlet and Ophelia's brother Laertes, who plots with Claudius to kill the prince, is followed by a fencing duel between the young men. Laertes uses a poisoned foil with which he wounds Hamlet. In the struggle, the weapons are exchanged and the young prince turns this weapon on Laertes. Before Hamlet dies, he also succeeds in stabbing his treacherous uncle. The guilty mother accidentally drinks the poisoned cup prepared for Hamlet.

**Henry IV, Parts I and II.** The two parts of this historic play form a dramatic whole, and give a vivid picture of England in the early 1400's. The chief characters are King Henry IV, who is conscience-stricken for having taken the throne dishonestly from Richard II; his two sons, the merry Prince Hal and Prince John; Hotspur (Henry Percy), son of the Earl of Northumberland; and Sir John Falstaff, a low-living, fat, and jolly old warrior whose escapades provide most of the humor of the play. Falstaff is Prince Hal's favorite companion. King Henry longs to go on a crusade to make up for his sins, but is delayed by rebellion in Scotland and Wales. He quarrels with Hotspur over the delivery of prisoners taken on the field of Holmedon, and the Percys revolt against him. On the field of Shrewsbury, Hotspur is slain by Prince Hal. In the concluding scenes of Part I, Falstaff pretends death to avoid being killed.

In Part II there is a continuation of the clowning of the Falstaffians, mixed with the story of the tired old king, approaching his end and worried over the Percy rebellion. News comes of the end of the disorder through the hand of Prince John, who has offered the rebels peace with honor, and then had the scattering troops killed and

292

the leaders executed. The death of King Henry follows, and Prince Hal is crowned Henry V. He shows himself a real king, and forbids the Falstaffians to come near him until they reform. See HENRY (IV) of England.

**Henry V.** This play gives an idealized picture of a brave and gallant monarch, Henry V. He gives up the carefree friends of youth, and begins a career of foreign conquest by pushing his claim to the throne of France from the French dauphin. The dauphin responds with the gift of a box of tennis balls, and England prepares for war. In France, the English troops, stirred by their king's eloquent appeal, force the surrender of Harfleur and camp near Agincourt. That night, Henry disguises himself in a long cloak and mingles with his soldiers. In an argument with a private, he accepts the private's glove and challenge for the next day. Though heavily outnumbered, the English win the battle.

Humorous episodes are introduced now and then, including a scene between Henry and the private, who has sworn to box the ears of the man who has his glove. Falstaff, meanwhile, has died, brokenhearted, because the king has cast him off. After the Battle of Agincourt, Henry is graciously received at the French court, and is not only promised the throne of France, but also the hand of the Princess Katharine, with whom he has fallen in love. See HENRY (V) of England.

**Julius Caesar.** The stirring period of the declining Roman republic and a great historic character furnish the background for this magnificent drama. But in spite of its name, the play is the tragedy of Brutus, Caesar's best friend, about whom the drama is built and who has five times as many lines as Caesar. It begins on a high note—victorious Caesar is escorted to the Capitol by enthusiastic admirers and three times refuses the crown offered by Mark Antony. But already storm clouds are gathering. Patriotic, highly respected Brutus, the "lean and hungry" Cassius, and blunt-speaking Casca are plotting Caesar's downfall, for they fear that he is becoming a dictator and that his kingly rule will put an end to the republic and Roman liberty. Caesar is warned by a fortune-teller to "beware the Ides of March," but on that day he goes to the senate house with a group of conspirators and is stabbed to death. He resists until he sees Brutus' dagger. Then he draws his cloak about him and falls with "Et tu, Brute" (Thou, too, Brutus) on his lips.

Brutus persuades the fickle mob that the murder was necessary to save the republic, but unwisely permits Antony to deliver a funeral oration over Caesar's body. The clever Antony turns the people against the plotters, who are forced to flee. Antony, Caesar's grand-nephew Octavius, and Lepidus, form a triumvirate and lead an army against them. On the plains of Philippi, the night before the battle, Brutus is startled by the ghost of Caesar and foresees his own doom. The battle is lost, Cassius orders his servant to kill him, and Brutus falls on his sword, realizing that he had killed a man he both honored and loved and that Antony and Octavius will be worse masters for Rome than Caesar ever could have been. (All the important characters in this play are described under their own names in THE WORLD BOOK ENCYCLOPEDIA.)

**King Lear.** The tragic story of King Lear gives a dramatic presentation of the relationships between parents and children. Lear, king of Britain, prepares to divide his kingdom among his three daughters: Goneril, wife of the Duke of Albany; Regan, wife of the Duke of Cornwall; and Cordelia, youngest and best beloved. The father childishly asks for an expression of their daughterly affection, and is so deceived by the older girls' flowery endearments, and so angered at Cordelia's modest, though sincere, statement, that he disinherits her and arranges to live with the other two in turn. The good Earl of Kent is banished forever because he interfered in Cordelia's behalf, but the girl finds a haven in the love of the king of France, who marries her.

## SHAKESPEARE, WILLIAM

Kent returns in disguise to look after the king and finds Goneril ordering him to reduce his train of followers by half. Angry and hurt by Goneril's ingratitude, Lear meets Regan at the castle of the Earl of Gloucester. She harshly repulses him, and in despair he staggers out into a night storm. With Kent and the faithful court fool, the old king, who is now insane, finds refuge in a hut. He there meets Gloucester's son Edgar, who, disguised as a madman, Tom O'Bedlam, is fleeing from the plots of his wicked half brother Edmund. Gloucester arrives with offers of shelter, and has the old man taken to Dover, where Cordelia has landed an army prepared to restore her father's rights.

In camp the broken old man is tenderly cared for by Cordelia, and thinks himself in Heaven. Meanwhile, Gloucester's eyes are put out by Cornwall, and he is cared for by Edgar. In a battle between the English (commanded by Edmund) and the French, the French are defeated, and Cordelia and Lear are taken prisoners. Edgar discloses his identity to his dying father, and kills Edmund in a trial by combat. But he is too late to save Cordelia, whom Edmund has ordered hanged. Lear dies. Goneril, jealous of her sister's love for Edmund, poisons Regan, and then stabs herself. The tragedy is intensified by the bitter jests of the court fool. His loyal affection for his master shines through his apparent foolery.

**Macbeth** is the story of one who suffered disaster through too much ambition. The scenes are laid in Scotland. On his return from a successful campaign in the north, Macbeth, accompanied by Banquo, meets three witches who hail him as Thane of Glamis, Thane of Cawdor, and King of Scotland, respectively, and prophesy that sons of Banquo will occupy the throne. The first seeds of ambitious design are planted at this time. Macbeth is already Thane of Glamis, and is soon appointed Thane of Cawdor by King Duncan (see DUNCAN I). With the vision of the kingship before him, and urged on by his wife, Lady Macbeth, Macbeth murders the king while he is a guest in Macbeth's home. The two sons of Duncan flee in terror from the castle, and draw suspicion of the murder to themselves. Macbeth is crowned king, but is uneasy concerning the witches' prophecy about Banquo and his sons. Accordingly, he hires assassins to murder Banquo and his son Fleance. At a state banquet, the king is told that Banquo has been slain, but that the son has escaped. Here, Macbeth sees Banquo's ghost and talks so wildly that the feast breaks up in disorder.

He has another interview with the witches, who tell him he must "beware Macduff," but assure him that "none of woman born" can harm him, and that he need not fear until Birnam Wood shall come to Dunsinane Castle. Sinking ever deeper into crime, Macbeth orders Macduff's wife and children slain when he learns of Macduff's flight to England. These crimes so affect the queen that she becomes a sleepwalker and finally dies. Macduff raises a large army and advances toward the castle, with his troops screened by branches from the trees of Birnam. Macbeth is horrified at seeing Birnam Wood really coming to Dunsinane, but relies on the rest of the prophecy. He meets Macduff, and warns him that he will never yield to one of woman born. Macduff replies that he was "from his mother's womb untimely ripped." In the battle that follows, Macbeth is slain and beheaded. Malcolm, son of Duncan, is then proclaimed king of Scotland.

**The Merchant of Venice.** This, one of Shakespeare's most popular plays, is a vivid study of greed and hatred. Shylock, the Jewish moneylender, hates the merchant Antonio, generous friend of Bassanio, because of personal insults, and because Antonio refuses to ask for interest on loans. Bassanio wishes to borrow 3,000 ducats from Antonio, so that he may go to Belmont to ask Portia to marry him. Antonio borrows the money from Shylock,

293

# SHAKESPEARE, WILLIAM

and, remembering that he will soon have several ships in port, agrees to part with a pound of flesh if the money is not repaid in three months. Shylock's hatred of Antonio is increased by the elopement of his daughter Jessica, who runs away with the Christian Lorenzo, another friend of Antonio's, carrying with her much money and many jewels. At Belmont, the beautiful and wealthy Portia is wooed by Bassanio, and both rejoice when he chooses the right one out of three caskets—gold, silver, and lead. According to her father's will, she is to marry the suitor who chooses the lead casket, which contains her picture. Their joy is interrupted by a letter from Antonio telling of the loss of his ships, and of Shylock's determination to carry out the terms of the bond. Bassanio marries Portia, and his friend Gratiano marries Nerissa, her maid. The men return to Venice, but cannot help Antonio in court.

When all seems lost, Portia, disguised as a lawyer, comes to Venice with her clerk (Nerissa, her maid), and argues the case. She reminds Shylock that he can have only the flesh the agreement calls for, and that if a single drop of blood is shed, his property will be confiscated. He is then willing to accept money in lieu of flesh, but the court decrees a punishment for his conspiracy against the life of a citizen, and he is forced to turn Christian and give half his property to Jessica, whom he had renounced. The play ends on a brighter note, with Bassanio and Gratiano being teased by their wives for having given their betrothal rings to the learned "doctor" and his "clerk."

**A Midsummer Night's Dream.** In this fairy play, Theseus, the Duke of Athens, is preparing to marry the lovely Hippolyta, queen of the Amazons. Egeus, a citizen of Athens, comes complaining that his daughter Hermia refuses to marry Demetrius. Hermia is kindly told by the duke that the law orders her to obey her father, so she flees with her lover Lysander to the enchanted wood of the fairies, ruled over by Oberon and Titania. They wander here in company with Hermia's friend Helena, and Demetrius, whose love Helena has lost. King Oberon has quarreled with Titania, and has ordered Puck, his attendant, to get a magic love juice which, when applied to her eyelids, will cause her to love the first person she views on awakening. Oberon sees the unhappy Helena, and in pity he tells Puck to touch the eyelids of Demetrius with the love juice. Puck mistakenly touches Lysander's eyes, and it is Helena whom he first sees on awakening. Then the weaver Bottom and his friends come to the wood to rehearse a play designed for the wedding festivities of Theseus and Hippolyta. Mischievous Puck puts an ass's head on Bottom, and he receives the dainty Titania's affection when she sees him first on awakening.

To add to the complications, Oberon touches the eyes of Demetrius with the love juice, and when he awakens, he begins to quarrel with Lysander, whom he sees making love to Helena. The tangle is straightened out when Puck removes the spell from Lysander's eyes and Oberon releases Titania. Bottom, himself again, is permitted to depart. Theseus and Hippolyta, hunting in the forest, find the happy lovers, and invite them to a wedding feast at the palace. After the feast, the guests are entertained by a performance of *Pyramus and Thisbe*, played by Bottom and his rough companions.

**Othello.** This tragic study is one of Shakespeare's masterpieces. Othello, the Moorish commander of Venetian forces, has won the gentle Desdemona, daughter of a senator of Venice. Othello is ordered to Cyprus to fight the Turkish fleet, and arranges to have his wife brought there by the crafty and evil Iago. Iago is jealous because Othello has made Cassio his chief lieutenant, and resolves to destroy the happiness of the newlyweds. At Cyprus, Iago gets Cassio drunk and involved in a street brawl, and thus brings about his dismissal.

Iago hints that Desdemona and Cassio are in love, and arranges to have Othello overhear Cassio ask Desdemona to intercede for him. Her innocent plea adds color to the evil suggestions planted in Othello's mind, and when he sees Cassio give a street woman a handkerchief he himself had given Desdemona (which Emilia, Iago's wife, had stolen and Iago had dropped in Cassio's room), Othello is tortured by his jealousy and believes the detestable story. Othello orders Iago to get rid of Cassio, and enters his wife's room. After pouring forth his suspicion, he strangles her while she protests her innocence. Too late he learns from Emilia her own innocent part in the tragedy, and the story of her husband's villainy. The furious Iago stabs Emilia, and in turn is wounded by Othello. Then the Moor, who "lov'd not wisely, but too well," kills himself. Cassio, who has escaped with a slight wound, becomes governor of Cyprus, and Iago is led away to well-deserved torture and death.

**Richard III** is the play dealing with the last part of the Wars of the Roses. Richard, Duke of Gloucester, the leading role, has been played by some of the greatest actors of all time. The daring of Richard knows no bounds. He has taken part in the murder of Henry VI and of the late king's son, Prince Edward, and now plots to win the throne occupied by the feeble Edward IV. He has his brother George, Duke of Clarence, imprisoned in the Tower and killed there. He brazenly woos the Lady Anne, widow of the slain Prince Edward, even while she is following the funeral procession of her father-in-law, Henry VI. Though Richard is ugly and deformed, he wins his suit by sheer force of personality. King Edward dies, and Richard manages to get himself crowned king, while the two young sons of Edward are held prisoners in the Tower.

Richard's ally, the Duke of Buckingham, is shocked by the king's cruel command to murder the young princes, and angered by the king's refusal to make him an earl. So he joins Richard's strong enemy, Henry, Earl of Richmond, a member of the House of Lancaster. Richard is seeking the hand of Elizabeth, daughter of Edward IV, having previously arranged for the death of Queen Anne. He is then told of the arrival of Richmond. At Bosworth Field, the night before the battle that decides his fate, Richard dreams that the ghosts of all those he has murdered pass before him and bid him despair. The next day his forces are defeated, his horse is shot from under him, and he is slain by the hand of Richmond, who becomes Henry VII. See EDWARD (IV); HENRY (VI) of England; RICHARD (III); WARS OF THE ROSES.

**Romeo and Juliet.** This story of the most famous of lovers will always be a favorite. In Verona live the Capulet and Montague families, who are bitter enemies. Young Romeo, heir of the Montagues, goes masked to a ball given by Lord Capulet, and there meets and falls in love with Juliet, heiress of the Capulets. Her relative Tybalt would have killed him, but is prevented by Capulet. On her balcony, at night, Juliet tells of her love for Romeo, and is answered by her lover, watching below. The next day they are secretly married in the cell of the friendly Friar Laurence. On his return from the wedding, Romeo meets Tybalt in conversation with his own friends, Benvolio and Mercutio. Tybalt wishes to fight Romeo for having attended the Capulet ball, and when Romeo refuses, Mercutio fights in his place, and is killed. In revenge, Romeo kills Tybalt.

Romeo is banished for killing Tybalt. Juliet's father, who suspects nothing, tries to force her to marry her kinsman Paris. Juliet is advised by Friar Laurence to pretend to agree, and he promises that he will get for her a potion on the wedding day that will give her, for 42 hours, the appearance of death. He further plans to have her placed in the burial vault, from which Romeo will rescue her. But their plans go wrong. Before the friar can communicate with him, Romeo hears that Juliet has died. In his despair, he goes to her tomb, drinks poison, and dies by her side. When she awakens and finds his dead body, she seizes his dagger and plunges it into her breast. The tragedy of the young lovers is followed by a reconciliation between the hostile families.

**The Taming of the Shrew** is one of the broadest of the Shakespearean comedies. It is supposed to be played by strolling actors as an elaborate hoax on a drunken tinsmith, picked out of the street and placed in the luxurious bed of a rich lord, as sport for the household. The shrew with the cutting speech, Katherine, is the daughter of a rich gentleman of Padua, named Baptista. Before her father will consent to the marriage of his gentle daughter Bianca, he insists that someone must marry the daughter with the shrewish temper. Among Bianca's suitors is a student, Lucentio, who disguises himself as a tutor and becomes her teacher.

Meanwhile, Petruchio, a gentleman of Verona, is tempted by Katherine's wealth, and decides to woo her. He wins the father's consent and sets the wedding day, but comes late to the ceremony, appears finally in outrageous clothes, acts like a boor, and refuses to stay for the wedding feast. At home he roars at the servants, beats them without cause, refuses to let Katherine eat the food they prepare, which he claims is not good enough for her, or to wear the new clothes brought by the tailor. In general, he gives a convincing picture of a person with a most villainous temper. So well does he play this part that Kate is utterly subdued, and becomes a model of wifely obedience. In the course of these events, Bianca runs off and marries her tutor, while Lucentio's servant Tranio, masquerading as the real Lucentio, obtains her father's consent to marry her himself. As an added touch, the drunken tinsmith is supposed to find these farcical incidents very dull entertainment.

**The Tempest.** This beautiful fantasy represents the genius of a matured and mellowed Shakespeare. A vessel is tossing in heavy sea near the shore of an enchanted island. On it live Prospero, his beautiful daughter Miranda, the fairy sprite Ariel, and Caliban, a misshapen monster who is Prospero's slave. As they watch the shipwreck, Prospero tells Miranda that twelve years before, as Duke of Milan, he had been deposed by his brother Antonio and his ally, the king of Naples, and cast adrift in a small boat with his three-year-old daughter. A good friend, Gonzalo, put food and water in the boat, together with some books of magic, by aid of which he has been able to command men, spirits, and the weather. Through this power, he had freed Ariel from the spell of the evil hag Sycorax, Caliban's mother, whom he found on the island when their boat reached its shores.

As Prospero and Miranda talk, Ariel comes with news that all on the wrecked ship have been saved, and the play then pictures their adventures on the island. The castaways include Antonio; Alonzo, king of Naples; Alonzo's son Ferdinand; and sailors and courtiers. Ariel's magic brings Ferdinand and Miranda together, discovers a plot hatched by Caliban and two drunken sailors, and brings before Prospero his former enemies and their companions. In the end, Prospero graciously forgives them, is promised the restoration of his dukedom, and, giving up magic, plans to return to Naples. There, he tells Miranda, she and Ferdinand will be married. The faithful Ariel is made joyful by news of his freedom.

**Twelfth Night.** The gay spirit of the twelfth night after Christmas, from which the play gets its name, fills this delightful comedy. It tells the adventures of the identical twins, Sebastian and Viola, who become separated in a shipwreck. In a seaport city of Illyria, Viola, disguised as a page, enters the service of Duke Orsino. He sends her to plead his suit before the wealthy Olivia, but the lady falls in love with the page, called Cesario. The page, meanwhile, learns to love Orsino. The comic scenes, which make this play hilariously entertaining, are carried on by Olivia's uncle, Sir Toby Belch; Sir Andrew Aguecheek; Malvolio the pompous steward, and other servants. Sir Toby, Sir Andrew, and Maria, Olivia's

# SHAKESPEARE, WILLIAM

maid, cause Malvolio to make a fool of himself by sending him a love letter containing ridiculous directions, which he thinks Olivia has written. He follows these directions so conscientiously that Olivia has him shut up as a madman. Sir Andrew, who desires Olivia for himself, is disturbed by the lady's attentions to the page, and, urged on by the fun-loving Sir Toby, challenges Viola to a duel.

The combat is ridiculous because of the terror of both of the duelists. It is interrupted by the entrance of Captain Antonio, who has come to Illyria with Sebastian. Captain Antonio supposes it is Sebastian himself who is in trouble, and interferes. Viola runs away, and the fight is later continued by the real Sebastian, who soon drives off Sir Andrew. Olivia presently marries Sebastian (thinking him the page), and there is a subsequent mix-up when Olivia calls Viola her husband. The appearance of Sebastian and explanations all around clear up matters. The duke discovers his page is a woman, and realizes that he loves her. Malvolio is released, and swears revenge on the "whole pack" of them. G. E. BENTLEY

**Related Articles** in WORLD BOOK include:

SHAKESPEAREAN ACTORS AND ACTRESSES

| | |
|---|---|
| Barrymore (family) | Hampden, Walter |
| Bernhardt, Sarah | Irving, Sir Henry |
| Booth (family) | Kean (family) |
| Evans, Maurice | Olivier, Sir Laurence |
| Forrest, Edwin | Siddons, Sarah Kemble |
| Garrick, David | Terry, Ellen Alicia |
| Gielgud, Sir John | Welles, Orson |

OTHER RELATED ARTICLES

| | |
|---|---|
| Avon, River | Folger Shakespeare Library |
| Blank Verse | Globe Theatre |
| Canada (picture: Theater) | Hathaway, Anne |
| Connecticut (Annual Events; picture) | Kittredge, George L. |
| Denmark (color picture: The East-Central Hills) | Macbeth |
| Elizabeth I | Oregon (Annual Events) |
| English Literature (Elizabethan Drama) | Poetry (What Makes a Poem Great?) |
| | Stratford-upon-Avon |

**Outline**

I. **Influence on the English Language**
II. **Shakespeare's Life**
   A. Early Years
   B. Marriage
   C. Actor and Playwright
   D. Poet
   E. Theater Companies
   F. Financial Success
   G. Activities
   H. Later Years
   I. Portraits
III. **Shakespeare's Works**
   A. Periods of Development
   B. Types of Plays
      1. Histories
      2. Tragedies
      3. Comedies
   C. Plots
   D. Characters
IV. **Famous Quotations**
V. **Nondramatic Works**
   A. Narrative Poems
   B. Sonnets
VI. **Theories of Authorship**
VII. **Shakespeare, A Man of His Own Time**
   A. Great Elizabethans
   B. London of Shakespeare's Day
   C. Influence of America
   D. Superstitions

# SHAKESPEARE, WILLIAM

    E. The Audience
    F. Music
    G. Innyard Theaters
    H. First London Playhouse
    I. Stage Properties
    J. Costumes
    K. Women's Parts
VIII. Editions of Shakespeare
    A. The First Quartos
    B. The First Folio
    C. Later Editions
    D. Popular Editions
IX. Shakespeare Through the Ages
    A. Famous Shakespearean Actors
    B. Recent Performances
X. Memorials
XI. Synopses of Plays

### Questions

What is the only work that has been translated into more languages than Shakespeare's writings?

In what way did Shakespeare have an important influence on the English language?

How was Shakespeare able to portray such a wide range of characters with fitting emotions, speech, and conduct for each?

Why did Shakespeare turn to poetry writing in 1592?

Into what groups are Shakespeare's plays usually divided? What is an example of each type?

In what ways may the great dramatist be described as a man of his own time?

Why has there been any argument about the authorship of the plays?

What other great men lived in England during Shakespeare's lifetime?

Why was so much music used in Shakespeare's plays?

Which are usually considered the greatest of Shakespeare's nondramatic works?

How many sonnets did Shakespeare write?

How did the playhouse of Shakespeare's day differ from a modern theater? What effect did this have on the playwright as he wrote the play?

Why was costuming especially important in Shakespeare's time?

Who are some Shakespearean actors of modern times?

### Books About Shakespeare

Thousands of books deal entirely or partly with Shakespeare, as already noted. Many of them are written for scholars, and assume that the reader already has a wide knowledge of Shakespeare and his work. But hundreds of books are written for general readers. The lists which follow record some of the books which will be most helpful to young people, average adult readers, and teachers who expect to teach some of Shakespeare's plays.

### Books for Young Readers

BENNETT, JOHN. *Master Skylark: A Story of Shakespeare's Time.* Grosset, 1947. This is one of the best-known fictional works about William Shakespeare.

HODGES, C. WALTER. *Shakespeare's Theatre.* Coward-McCann, 1964.

LAMB, CHARLES and MARY. *Tales from Shakespeare.* Several editions. First published in 1807, this book contains the 20 best plays retold for young readers.

WHITE, ANNE T. *Will Shakespeare and the Globe Theater.* Random House, 1955. This fictional biography serves as an introduction to Shakespeare.

### Books for Older Readers

CHUTE, MARCHETTE G. *An Introduction to Shakespeare.* Dutton, 1951. This book gives both a biography of Shakespeare and information on the London of the 1500's for high school students. *Stories from Shakespeare.* World Publishing Co., 1956. The author retells the 36 plays which appear in the first folio.

HALLIDAY, FRANK E. *Shakespeare.* Yoseloff, 1961.

HAZLITT, WILLIAM. *Characters of Shakespeare's Plays.* Several editions. A classic of Shakespearean criticism which was first published in 1817.

HODGES, C. WALTER. *Shakespeare and the Players.* Coward-McCann, 1949. This presentation will help young persons to relive the age of Shakespeare.

HORIZON. *Shakespeare's England.* American Heritage, 1964.

NORMAN, CHARLES. *Playmaker of Avon.* McKay, 1949. A life of Shakespeare which also gives a picture of the London of his time.

SHAKESPEARE, WILLIAM. *The Complete Works.* Ed. by G. B. Harrison. Harcourt, 1952. *The Complete Works.* Ed. by George L. Kittredge. Ginn, 1957. Two recent standard editions which make use of all the findings of modern scholarship.

### Books for Teachers

BECKERMAN, BERNARD. *Shakespeare at the Globe, 1599-1609.* Macmillan, 1962.

BENTLEY, GERALD EADES. *Shakespeare: A Biographical Handbook.* Yale Univ. Press, 1961.

BRADLEY, ANDREW CECIL. *Shakespearean Tragedy: Lectures on Hamlet, Othello, King Lear, Macbeth.* 2nd ed. St. Martins, 1956.

CHAMBERS, EDMUND K. *William Shakespeare: A Study of Facts and Problems.* 2 vols. Oxford, 1930.

CHARLTON, HENRY B. *Shakespearean Comedy.* Barnes & Noble, 1963.

CHUTE, MARCHETTE G. *Shakespeare of London.* Dutton, 1949. The author describes the life and times of Shakespeare, with emphasis on the London of his period.

GODDARD, HAROLD C. *The Meaning of Shakespeare.* Univ. of Chicago Press, 1951. This book gives insights into the meaning of Shakespeare's genius.

GRANVILLE-BARKER, HARLEY, and HARRISON, G. B. *A Companion to Shakespeare Studies.* Doubleday, 1960.

GRANVILLE-BARKER, HARLEY. *Prefaces to Shakespeare.* 2 vols. Princeton Univ. Press, 1946-1947. These books have outstanding studies of Shakespeare's plays and their staging.

HOLZKNECHT, KARL J. *The Backgrounds of Shakespeare's Plays.* American Book Co., 1950.

NICOLL, ALLARDYCE. *Shakespeare: An Introduction.* Oxford, 1953. A general discussion of modern criticism and interpretation of Shakespeare's plays and sonnets.

ROWSE, ALFRED L. *William Shakespeare: A Biography.* Harper, 1963.

SHAKESPEARE, WILLIAM. *A New Variorum Edition of the Works.* Lippincott, various dates. This set includes most of the plays. It gives various versions of the texts of the plays and the notes of editors.

SMITH, IRWIN. *Shakespeare's Globe Playhouse: A Modern Reconstruction in Text and Scale Drawings.* Scribner, 1957.

TRAVERSI, DEREK. *An Approach to Shakespeare; A Study of the Plays Through Analysis of Their Imagery.* Doubleday, 1956.

VAN DOREN, MARK. *Shakespeare.* Doubleday, 1953. This book contains essays on each of Shakespeare's plays and a chapter on his poems.

WADSWORTH, FRANK W. *The Poacher from Stratford; A Partial Account of the Controversy Over the Authorship of Shakespeare's Plays.* Univ. of California Press, 1958.

WAIN, JOHN. *The Living World of Shakespeare: A Playgoer's Guide.* St. Martin's, 1964.

WEBSTER, MARGARET. *Shakespeare Without Tears.* Rev. ed. World Publishing Co., 1955. A producer-director of Shakespeare's plays discusses the Elizabethan theater and the staging of Shakespeare's plays.

**SHAKESPEARE GARDEN** is any garden designed to include the features of gardens in Shakespeare's time. All the outdoor plants mentioned in his plays and poetry grow in such a garden. Many public parks, such as Central Park in New York City and Golden Gate Park in San Francisco, have Shakespeare gardens.

**SHALE,** *shayl,* is a sedimentary rock found in layers, often with layers of sandstone or limestone. It is formed from clay under heat and pressure. It is easily broken. When a slab is broken off, the split lies roughly parallel to the layer. Sometimes, heat and pressure change the shale to slate.

Like clay, shale is ground up to use in manufacturing bricks and portland cement. Bituminous shale is rich in petroleum and related substances. It burns with a flame, and the petroleum can be extracted. WALTER H. BUCHER

See also OIL SHALE; PETROLEUM (Oil Shale); SLATE.

**SHALIMAR GARDENS** cover about 80 acres near Lahore, Pakistan. The gardens were laid out in 1637 by order of Shah Jahan for the enjoyment of his court and the royal family, and have become famous for their beauty (see SHAH JAHAN). A wall surrounds the lawns and flower beds. Huge, ancient trees shade much of the area. The Shalimar Gardens consist of three parts, laid out on different levels. Beautiful pavilions stand at the four corners of the area. About 100 fountains spout in the garden, and 200 in the pool in its center.

**SHALLENBERGER, OLIVER B.** See ELECTRIC METER.

**SHALLOT** is a plant similar to the onion. It is smaller than the onion plant and has long slender leaves. The bulbs grow in clusters. The bulbs may be red, brown, or gray. Shallots have a fine flavor that is stronger than that of onions but not as sharp. For this reason, they are often used in flavoring cooked foods. Nearly all of the commercial crop grows in Louisiana.

**Scientific Classification.** The shallot belongs to the amaryllis family, *Amaryllidaceae*. It is classified as genus *Allium*, species *A. ascalonicum*. ARTHUR JOHN PRATT

See also LEEK.

**SHALMANESER III.** See ASSYRIA (History).

**SHAMAN,** *SHAH mun,* is a medicine man or priest among certain peoples. The term came from a Mongolian word, but peoples in many parts of the world have shamans who supposedly cast out evil spirits or bring good. They may use dances, feasts, and chants. Shamans may be found among the Eskimos, Maoris, Mongolians, Polynesians, and others. American Indians had similar beliefs. See also INDIAN, AMERICAN (Shamans and Priests).

**SHAMROCK** is the national flower of Ireland (Eire). According to legend, St. Patrick planted the little plant in Ireland because its three small leaves represented the Holy Trinity. All loyal sons of Eire still wear a shamrock in their lapels on St. Patrick's Day. The name *shamrock* is anglicized from *Seamrog*, which means trefoil (three-leaved). It is given to a number of plants, but a small clover is usually considered the true shamrock. Its leaves have a blue-green color. *Black medic, nonesuch, yellow trefoil,* and *hop clover* all have been called shamrocks. The shamrock appears with the thistle and the rose on the British coat of arms, because these are the national flowers of Ireland, Scotland, and England. Some authorities say that the wood sorrel is the true shamrock. Its leaves are much like those of the white clover. DONALD WYMAN

**SHANG DYNASTY.** See CHINA (History).

**SHANGHAI,** *SHANG high* (pop. 6,900,000; alt. 20 ft.), is the largest city in China and one of the largest cities in the world. Shanghai was a small fishing port until foreign businessmen made the village a thriving center of trade and industry after the Treaty of Shanghai in 1842. Before World War II, almost half of China's foreign trade passed through Shanghai's harbor.

**Location, Size, and Description.** The word *Shanghai*, which means *up from the sea*, describes the city's location. Shanghai lies on the Whangpoo River, about 14 miles from the meeting place of the Whangpoo and the Yangtze rivers. It is an independent city in Kiangsu Province of China. For location, see CHINA (political map). Constant dredging keeps the harbor deep enough for ocean vessels. Docks and warehouses stand along the Whangpoo River. China's largest banks lined the city's famous water front, called the *Bund*, before the communists conquered China in 1949.

Shanghai developed as three cities. These were the International Settlement, the French Concession ("Frenchtown"), and the Chinese City. After World War II, these areas were united into the city of Shanghai. The International Settlement was built along the Whangpoo River bank. The area's skyscraper banks, hotels, and office buildings give Shanghai a modern skyline. Several buildings rise more than 20 stories. The former French Concession has smaller office buildings and shops and many fine residences. The municipality of Greater Shanghai, incorporated in 1928, surrounded the International Settlement and the French Concession. The municipality area covered several

**The True Irish Shamrock,** according to many people, is a small clover plant with green leaves consisting of three leaflets.
J. Horace McFarland

**Nanking Road Separates Skyscrapers in the International Settlement Section From the Shanghai Peoples' Park.**

suburban towns. It included the old walled city of Shanghai; Nantao to the south; Chapei, Hongkew, and Yangtzepoo to the north; and Pootung across the river. The former international areas have wide streets and modern buildings. The Chinese City areas combine modern sections and narrow streets.

Shanghai was the home of the National Chiao-tung, Tung Chi, Fuh Tan and Chi-nan universities, the University of Shanghai, and St. John's University, before they were reorganized or merged by the communists.

**Industry and Trade.** Shanghai's location near the great Yangtze River makes it the trading center of central China. Textiles account for about two fifths of the city's manufactures. Other industries include the manufacture of cement and soap, publishing, shipbuilding, and sugar refining. Imports include chemicals, metal goods, petroleum products, raw cotton, and sugar. From Shanghai, China exports animal hides, cloth, eggs, and silk. The Chinese have taken over most of Shanghai's industries, originally financed by persons from other countries.

**History and Government.** Shanghai was first settled about A.D. 960. It was an insignificant market village until 1842. That year, the Treaty of Nanking ended the first war between Great Britain and China and made Shanghai a treaty port. Great Britain, and later France and the United States, received *concessions* (areas outside Shanghai) for businesses and homes. In 1863, the British and American sections were combined into the International Settlement. No single nation controlled the International Settlement. It was open to persons of all nationalities. A 13-member council, elected by taxpayers in Shanghai, governed the Settlement. Troops of different countries guarded the area. A French consul general administered the French Concession. A Chinese mayor governed the Chinese City.

Rebels attacked Shanghai during the Taiping Rebellion of 1850 to 1864 and again during the Boxer Rebellion of 1900 (see BOXER REBELLION). Chiang Kai-shek's troops besieged the city in 1927. The Japanese fought the Chinese at Shanghai in 1932 and destroyed large parts of the Chinese City. These areas were rebuilt but were destroyed again by the Japanese in 1937. In 1941, Japan occupied Shanghai. The Japanese held the city until the end of World War II. During the war, the United States and Britain gave up their privileges in China. After the Japanese surrendered in 1945, the Chinese took over the International Settlement. The French gave up their concession in 1946. The importance of Shanghai declined after the Communist conquest of China in 1949.          THEODORE H. E. CHEN

**SHANNON, MONICA** ( ? -   ), an American author, received the Newbery medal in 1935 for *Dobry*, the story of a Bulgarian boy who longed to be an artist. Miss Shannon was born in Belleville, Ont., Canada, but grew up on a California ranch. She made friends with Bulgarian immigrants who worked on the ranch, and stories she heard from them became the basis for her book *Dobry*. She also wrote *California Fairy Tales* (1926) and *Goose-Grass Rhymes* (1930). She was a librarian in the Los Angeles Public Library from 1916 to 1925.          EVELYN RAY SICKELS

**SHANNON RIVER** is the main waterway of Ireland, and the longest river in the British Isles. The Shannon rises in Cavan County in upper Leinster, and flows 250 miles southwest to the Atlantic Ocean. The river flows through many beautiful *loughs*, or lakes. The mouth of the Shannon is 50 miles long. Limerick is the chief city on the river. An electrical power project on the Shannon was completed in 1929.

**SHANTEY,** or **SHANTY.** See CHANTEY.

**SHANTUNG,** *shan TUNG*, is a heavy grade of *pongee*, or wild silk, woven in China. Shantung made of cotton, rayon, or cotton and silk mixtures imitates the silk shantung fabric. Rough-spun yarns of these fibers give the same effect as wild silk. Shantung has a plain weave, and is used in making curtains, sportswear, pajamas, robes, and women's summer suits.          KENNETH R. FOX

**SHAPE** stands for Supreme Headquarters Allied Powers Europe. See NORTH ATLANTIC TREATY ORGANIZATION.

**SHAPIRO, KARL JAY** (1913-    ), is an American poet. In *Person, Place and Thing* (1942), he defends the blessings of individuality (*person*) against conformity; the searching examination of society (*place*) in contrast to uncritical allegiance; and the richness of the created *thing* as opposed to destruction.

Shapiro won the 1945 Pulitzer prize for poetry with *V-Letter and Other Poems*. His essays often express rebellion against rules for making or judging art. *The Bourgeois Poet* (1964) denounces the style of life and poetry, including his own, that lies within the safety of middle-class attitudes and formal verse.

Shapiro was born in Baltimore. He has taught in several colleges and he has edited two literary magazines, *Poetry* from 1950 to 1956 and *The Prairie Schooner* from 1956 to 1963. Shapiro published his *Selected Poems* in 1968. MONA VAN DUYN

**SHAPLEY,** *SHAP lee,* **HARLOW** (1885-    ), an American astronomer, studied clusters of stars called *globular clusters*. These clusters lie far out at the edge of the Milky Way, the galaxy to which our solar system belongs. He concluded from his studies that the diameter of the Milky Way is about 100,000 light-years and that its center lies near the constellation Sagittarius.

Shapley served as astronomer at the Mount Wilson (Calif.) Observatory from 1914 to 1921. He was professor of astronomy at Harvard University and director of the Harvard Observatory from 1921 to 1952. He worked to organize science on an international, as well as national, scale. He was born in Nashville, Mo., and studied at the University of Missouri. HELEN WRIGHT

**SHARAKU TOSHUSAI,** the most individual Japanese print artist of the late 1700's, was also a dancer employed by one of the great feudal families. These two sides of his career belonged to separate worlds. One was the conservative, formal, and severely disciplined society of the aristocrats; the other, the pleasure-seeking world of city merchants and workers.

The details of Sharaku's life are not known. To make the break so successfully he must have been unusually bored and reckless. His prints, by their brilliant impudence, suggest a strange, harsh personality. All his dated works fall within one year, 1794. His best-known actor portraits are drawn almost like caricatures in awkward, forceful poses. ALEXANDER C. SOPER

See also JAPANESE PRINT (picture: Portraits of Actors).

**SHARE.** See STOCK, CAPITAL.

**SHARECROPPER** is a farmer who grows crops on another person's land. He usually shares the crops equally with the owner. The sharecropper usually supplies all the labor. The landowner supplies the land, a house and garden, farming equipment, and machinery or work animals. He may also supply fertilizer, insecticides, and cash or credit for family living.

Sharecropping was once widespread in the southern United States, mainly on cotton and tobacco farms. It has nearly disappeared in recent years. MARSHALL HARRIS

See also AGRICULTURE (The United States).

**SHARIA,** *shah REE uh,* is the sacred law of Islam. The word *sharia* means *the road to the watering place,* or *the clear path to be followed.* The Sharia is made up of all Allah's commandments relating to man's activities. It prescribes regulations for worship and ritual, and for political and legal activities. A. H. ABDEL KADER

**SHARK** is one of the greediest eaters and killers of the sea animals. Sharks live in all parts of the ocean, but are most numerous in warm seas. Sharks have rounded bodies which may be 40 feet long. They are covered with scales which give the skin a rough feeling when the hand is rubbed forward along the fish.

The shark's mouth is on the underside of its head. Some persons believe that sharks have to turn over on their backs to bite, but this is not true. Some kinds of sharks have several rows of long, sharp teeth, with all the rows except one or two folded back on the jaws. As they lose each tooth, another grows in its place. Other sharks have broad, flat teeth, and, in a few varieties, the teeth are small. Shark's gills are on the sides of the head and have five to seven openings on the surface. The tail is usually notched. The upper part of the tail is longer than the lower part.

Sharks swim rapidly. They often follow ships for days at a time to get the food and waste matter that is thrown overboard. They eat small fish of all kinds and do great damage to man's supply of food fish.

Certain sharks are vicious and greedy. Some authorities say that they are not as "mean" as they seem, but suffer from continual hunger. Their stomachs will not let them rest. Almost as soon as they eat they must be off after more food. These sharks have been known to swim close to beaches, where they wait for bathers.

**Kinds of Sharks.** The largest shark is the harmless *whale shark*, which is often more than 50 feet long. Fortunately for bathers and sailors in southern waters, it feeds only on small sea animals and plants. This shark is the largest known fish. The whale, which is larger and resembles members of the fish family, is not a fish but a mammal. The next largest shark is the *basking shark*,

**The Common Sandbar, or Brown, Shark** lives along the Atlantic coast of the United States and in the Mediterranean Sea.

Marine Studios, Marineland, Florida

**The Whale Shark,** the largest shark, is also the largest known fish. This baby, caught in Florida, measured 33 feet long and weighed over 15 tons. Whale sharks have jaws wide enough to swallow a man, but they lead quiet lives in the warm sea, eating seaweed and small surface fish.

*American Museum of Natural History*

the *dusky, porbeagle, bullhead, Mako,* and *dog* sharks. The *leopard* shark has spots like a leopard.

Some sharks have their young by laying eggs which are protected by a horny shell. But most sharks bear live young, from three to six or more in a brood. Some of the young are born quite large, considering the size of their parents. For example, the female *black-tip shark* is usually 5 feet long. Her young measure about $1\frac{1}{2}$ feet long at birth.

**The Shark Industry.** The Norwegians have long been specialists in shark fishing. These fish form the basis of several thriving industries in Norway. Men use the heads of the sharks in making glue. They use the flesh to make an excellent fertilizer. Leather is made from the hides, and "cod-liver" oil from the livers.

Shark fisheries have been established in Florida, along the Gulf Coast, in the Virgin Islands, and along the Pacific Coast of North America. Fishermen catch sharks on strong hooks fastened to chain leaders with a heavy line. They also use rope nets.

The flesh of some species of shark is used as food. Much shark flesh is salted and exported to parts of Africa. But shark flesh has not come into general use in America, where fish of much finer flavor are plentiful. The Chinese consider dried shark fins a great delicacy. The skin is marketed for shoes, pocketbooks, and other articles under the name of *shagreen.* It is sometimes used like sandpaper for polishing.

**Scientific Classification.** All the shark families are in the order *Selachii.* LEONARD P. SCHULTZ

another harmless fish. It is found mainly in the Arctic Ocean, and gets its name because it likes to come to the surface and bask in the sun. One of the best-known species is the *white shark,* which is a man-eater. It lives in the tropical seas, and sometimes along the southern coasts of the United States. Another shark which preys on man is the *blue shark,* named for its color.

Some sharks are called *hammerheads* because of their hammer-shaped heads. The many other species include

See also DOGFISH; FISHING (table); OCEAN (color picture, Life in the Ocean); REMORA.

**SHARK SUCKER.** See REMORA.

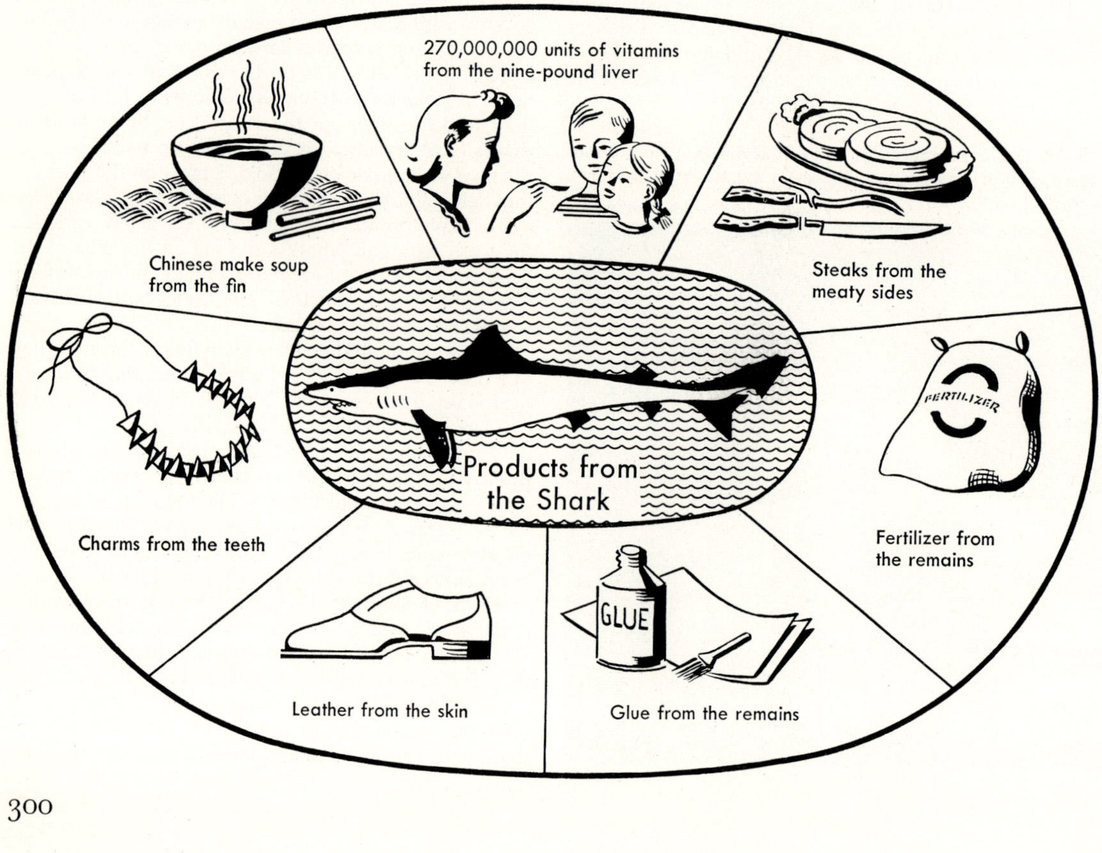

270,000,000 units of vitamins from the nine-pound liver

Chinese make soup from the fin

Steaks from the meaty sides

Charms from the teeth

Products from the Shark

Fertilizer from the remains

Leather from the skin

Glue from the remains

300

**SHARON,** *SHAIR un,* **PLAIN OF,** is part of the coastal plain of Israel. Averaging about 10 miles in width, it stretches 50 miles between Mount Carmel and Tel Aviv-Yafo (Jaffa). The plain contains rich farming land, and is the most densely populated area in Israel.

**SHARON, ROSE OF.** See HIBISCUS.

**SHARPS AND FLATS.** See MUSIC (Sound in Music).

**SHASTA, MOUNT.** See MOUNT SHASTA.

**SHASTA DAISY.** See BURBANK, LUTHER (His Achievements); DAISY (picture).

**SHASTA DAM,** located on the Sacramento River about 12 miles north of Redding, Calif., is the second highest concrete dam in the United States. It is a feature of the Central Valley Project in California (see CENTRAL VALLEY PROJECT). Its spillway drops 480 feet, making it the highest overflow dam in the world. The reservoir created by Shasta Dam provides irrigation water and electric power. The dam is 602 feet high, 3,460 feet long, and contains 8,711,000 cubic yards of concrete. The reservoir extends 35 miles from the dam up the Sacramento, Pit, and McCloud rivers. It has a capacity of $4\frac{1}{2}$ million acre-feet. The United States Bureau of Reclamation built the dam in 1945.   T. W. MERMEL

**SHASTINA.** See MOUNT SHASTA.

**SHASTRI, LAL BAHADUR** (1904-1966), became prime minister of India in June, 1964, after the death of Jawaharlal Nehru. Shastri won a reputation as a mild-mannered, efficient, political moderate, and as a man skilled at compromise.

Shastri was born in the Banaras district of eastern India. He graduated from Kashi Vidyapith, which is a Hindu nationalist university. He entered politics and joined the Indian National Congress in the 1920's. Shastri took an active part in Mahatma Gandhi's movement for Indian independence and was arrested several times in the 1930's and 1940's.

After India gained independence in 1947, Shastri became minister for police and transport of the state of Uttar Pradesh. In 1951, he became general secretary of the Indian National Congress. He directed the national ministries of transport and railways, communication, commerce and industry, and home affairs before becoming prime minister of India. Shastri died in Tashkent, Russia, in January, 1966, just a few hours after signing a nonaggression pact with Pakistan (see INDIA [Recent Developments]).   RICHARD L. PARK

**SHATT AL ARAB** is a river in Iraq and Iran. It is formed by the meeting of the Tigris and Euphrates rivers at Al Qurnah, Iraq, and flows 120 miles to the Persian Gulf. The Karun River of Iran also joins the Shatt al Arab. The oil port of Abadan, Iran, and the city of Basra, Iraq, are on the river.

**SHAW, ANNA HOWARD** (1847-1919), was an American preacher, physician, and woman's rights advocate. She was ordained a Methodist minister in 1880, and received her medical degree from Boston University in 1886.

Anna Shaw began to work closely in 1888 with Susan B. Anthony in the National Woman Suffrage Association, and became its president in 1904. By 1915, when she became honorary president, she had raised the membership from 17,000 to 200,000. During World War I, she served as chairman of the Women's Division of the Council of National Defense. She was born in Newcastle upon Tyne, England.   LOUIS FILLER

## SHAW, GEORGE BERNARD

**SHAW, GEORGE BERNARD** (1856-1950), an Irish-born dramatist, critic, and essayist, ranks as one of the most important literary figures of the 1900's. He won the Nobel prize for literature in 1925.

Shaw disliked the romantic and sentimental Victorian theater of the late 1800's. Influenced by the revolutionary social dramas of the Norwegian playwright Henrik Ibsen, he viewed the theater as a platform for supporting social reform. In a remarkable career that covered nearly 60 years, he wrote over 50 plays. Most of them are comedies in which a debate on ethics is as important as traditional dramatic values such as character and appeals to the emotions of an audience.

Shaw was a mischievous and original thinker. He defended women's rights, became a vegetarian, and promoted a simplified alphabet. He defended his opinions in a series of admirable essays, many published as prefaces to his plays. Like the plays, the essays are charming for their verbal brilliance and wit, even when the causes they argue no longer seem daring or even unconventional.

**Early Life.** Shaw was born in Dublin on July 26, 1856. He moved to London in 1876, and became a successful music critic. In 1884, he helped found the Fabian Society, an organization of socialists who believed that political and economic change could be gained through reform. It was for the Fabian Society that Shaw prepared a famous lecture on Ibsen, later published as *The Quintessence of Ibsenism* (1891).

Because of their radical subject matter, Shaw's early plays did not become popular immediately in London. His first play, *Widower's Houses* (1892), attacked slum landlords. *Mrs. Warren's Profession*, which deals with the causes of prostitution, was written in 1893. But it was not produced until 1902, and then was immediately banned. *Arms and the Man* (1894), an entertaining antiwar comedy, was only mildly successful when it first opened.

**Mature Period.** Public hostility to Shaw began to disappear after 1904, when his friend Harley Granville-Barker produced 11 of his plays in less than three years at the Royal Court Theatre. These included *Candida* (1895), *The Devil's Disciple* (1897), *Caesar and Cleopatra* (1898), and *Man and Superman* (1903). This last play contains the celebrated scene "Don Juan in Hell," which is often performed as a separate work.

*Man and Superman* introduced Shaw's theory of what he called the "life force." To Shaw, the "life force" was the energy that dominates man biologically. However, when harnessed by man's will, the "life force" can lead to a higher, more creative existence. This concept is central to Shaw's most ambitious play, the five-part *Back to Methuselah* (1918-1920), a fable that traces the entire history of mankind. It foresees a curious future for the human race as a new, more

**George Bernard Shaw**
Culver

## SHAW, HENRY WHEELER

intelligent species, but predictable and unexciting.

*Saint Joan* (1923), a drama about the individual in conflict with historical necessity, is widely regarded as Shaw's masterpiece. But some critics prefer *Pygmalion* (1912). This ironic Cinderella story describes how a professor of *phonetics* (speech sounds) demonstrates the absurdity of class distinctions by changing an ignorant Cockney flower girl into a counterfeit aristocrat simply by changing her speech (see PYGMALION). The play was adapted into the musical *My Fair Lady* (1955). Shaw's other major plays include *Major Barbara* (1905), *The Doctor's Dilemma* (1906), *Androcles and the Lion* (1913), and *Heartbreak House* (1919). RALPH G. ALLEN

**SHAW, HENRY WHEELER.** See BILLINGS, JOSH.

**SHAW, IRWIN** (1913-    ), an American dramatist, short-story writer, and novelist, pictured the threats to free men embodied in fascism and other restrictive forces. He showed his sympathy with common men in his first play, *Bury the Dead* (1936). His novel *The Young Lions* (1948) tells about the lives and development of three soldiers fighting in World War II. He also wrote *Voices of a Summer Day* (1965). Shaw was born in New York City. HARRY R. WARFEL

**SHAW, ROBERT** (1916-    ), an American conductor, became music director of the Atlanta Symphony Orchestra in 1967. He was an associate conductor with the Cleveland Symphony Orchestra from 1956 until his Atlanta appointment. Shaw founded the Robert Shaw Chorale in 1948 and directed it until 1953. He was born in Red Bluff, Calif. DAVID EWEN

**SHAW, WILBUR** (1902-1954), was an American racing car driver. He won the annual Indianapolis 500-mile race three times and finished second three times, a record performance. He won in 1937, 1939, and 1940, and was second in 1933, 1935, and 1938. He retired from racing in 1941, and worked for a rubber company. He became president and general manager of the Indianapolis Speedway, site of the race, in 1946. Shaw was born in Shelbyville, Ind. He was killed in an airplane crash at Decatur, Ind., in 1954. PAT HARMON

**SHAW UNIVERSITY.** See UNIVERSITIES AND COLLEGES (table).

**SHAWINIGAN,** *shuh WIN ih gun,* Quebec (pop. 30,777; alt. 306 ft.), is an important industrial center on the St. Maurice River. It lies about 20 miles north of Trois-Rivières (see QUEBEC [political map]).

A waterfall north of Shawinigan provides electric power for the city's industries. The Shawinigan Water and Power Company, formed in 1898, is one of the world's largest privately owned electric-power companies. Products of Shawinigan include abrasive materials, aluminum, carbide, chemicals, lumber, paper, pulp, resins, and stainless steel products. Shawinigan was founded in 1901. M. G. BALLANTYNE

**SHAWN, TED** (1891-    ), was a pioneer in establishing the role of the male dancer in America. Shawn developed his own method for training male dancers. He also created dances for men based on American Indian and Western folklore and on modern themes.

EDWIN M. SHAWN was born in Kansas City, Mo. In 1915, he and his wife, Ruth St. Denis, formed the Denishawn dance company. He trained dancers and toured with his wife and the company until 1931 (see SAINT DENIS, RUTH). From 1933 until 1940, Shawn headed his own performing group of male dancers. He created and starred in several ballets, including *Invocation to the Thunderbird, Gnossienne,* and *St. Francis.* In 1941, Shawn established a summer dance school and festival at Jacob's Pillow, in Lee, Mass. The festival has provided a showcase for both established and young dancers, and for notable foreign companies. SELMA JEANNE COHEN

**SHAWNEE INDIANS** lived in the eastern forests of North America. They spoke an Algonkian language, and were closely related to the Sauk and Fox Indians. We know little about their way of life, because they split into many wandering groups and lived away from well-traveled routes. The Shawnee built wigwam villages along riverbanks in such states as Ohio, West Virginia, Pennsylvania, and Tennessee.

In the middle 1700's, many groups of Shawnee settled together on the banks of the Ohio River in Pennsylvania, Ohio, Virginia, and West Virginia. For 40 years they fought against settlers in these regions, and became known as the most hostile tribe in the area. In 1774, under the leadership of their chief, Cornstalk, the Shawnee met defeat at the Battle of Point Pleasant, which ended Lord Dunmore's War.

After their defeat, many of the Shawnee moved across the Mississippi River. Those who remained behind included Chief Tecumseh and his brother Tenskwatawa, the Shawnee Prophet. They tried to unite all the Indians of the Mississippi Valley against the whites, but were defeated by William Henry Harrison at the Battle of Tippecanoe in 1811. Most Shawnee now live on reservations in Oklahoma. WAYNE C. TEMPLE

See also INDIAN WARS (Along the Frontier); SHAWNEE PROPHET; TECUMSEH; CORNSTALK; KANSAS (Communication).

**SHAWNEE PROPHET** (1768?-1837?) was the twin brother of the great Shawnee Indian chief, Tecumseh. He was known by the Indian name of TENSKWATAWA. He once fell as though dead. Just as his friends were ready to bury him, he came back to life. He claimed he had been lifted to heaven and shown all about the past and future. In 1806 he predicted an eclipse of the sun. After that, Indians believed what he said. He said Indians should give up everything that came from the white man. He gave hope to the eastern tribes, who were trying to keep the whites out of their territory. He lost the Battle of Tippecanoe, however, and his tribe was disbanded. He was born near the present-day city of Springfield, Ohio. See also TECUMSEH. E. ADAMSON HOEBEL

**SHAWNEE TRAIL.** See WESTERN FRONTIER LIFE (The Cattle Boom).

**SHAYS' REBELLION** was a revolt by debtor farmers against their creditors and against the high taxes collected in Massachusetts during the 1780's. The rebellion was part of widespread discontent among small property owners and farmers in the United States after the Revolutionary War. Many of these persons faced imprisonment because they could not pay their debts.

Daniel Shays was one of several men who became leaders of the rebellion. Shays had served in the Revolutionary War, and after 1780 he held political offices at Pelham, Mass. His sympathy for the farmers led him to take an active part in their protests, and the movement was named for him. In 1786, unrest among farmers and debtors grew into revolt. Shays led a mob of about 600 persons that gathered in front of the courthouse at Springfield, Mass. The mob threatened the supreme court, and hoped to prevent the court from allowing the foreclosure of farms and imprisonment of debtors.

Skirmishes took place between the rebels and the state militia. Major General Benjamin Lincoln finally subdued the rebels on Feb. 2, 1787. Shays escaped to Vermont with a death penalty on his head. He was later pardoned.

The fears that were aroused by the rebellion helped to produce a stronger central government in the United States. As a result of the rebellion, the Annapolis Convention's call for a revision of the Articles of Confederation gained strength throughout the nation (see ANNAPOLIS CONVENTION). This eventually led to the adoption of the United States Constitution. MERRILL JENSEN

**SHAZAR, SCHNEOR ZALMAN,** *shah ZAHR* (1889- ), became president of Israel in 1963. He devoted much of his life to the cause of *Zionism* (formation of a Jewish state).

Shazar was born SCHNEOR ZALMAN RUBASHOV in Minsk, Russia. He formed *Shazar* from letters in his name. He became a Zionist in 1905, and started a German Zionist movement in 1916, while studying in Germany. Shazar settled in Palestine in 1924. As cofounder and editor of *Davar*, a Labor Zionist daily newspaper, he helped build the power of the Israeli labor movement. Israel became a state in 1948. Shazar held several government posts and helped shape Israel into a modern nation. He wrote on history, literature, politics, religion, and other subjects. ELLIS RIVKIN

**SHEARER, THOMAS.** See FURNITURE (Thomas Shearer).

**SHEARING STRESS.** See STRENGTH OF MATERIALS.

**SHEARS.** See SCISSORS.

**SHEARWATER** is the name of a group of sea birds that live in the oceans. They vary in length from 12 to 20 inches. Shearwaters have long slender wings and soar over the waves, flapping their wings only occasionally. Some fly alone, other kinds gather in flocks that may include thousands. They feed on fish, squids, and small crustaceans. When fishermen clean fish, shearwaters come to feed on the waste. Some shearwaters are grayish black above and white underneath.

The shearwater comes to shore only to reproduce, usually on an island. Here it lays one large white or yellowish-white egg in a hole dug in the ground, or concealed under rocks. There are many species of shearwater. One of the best known is the *greater shearwater*, which lives in the Atlantic Ocean from near the Arctic Circle to southern South America and South Africa. Fishermen in the north call it hag or hagdon. Other species that live in North American waters are the *black-vented shearwater*, the *pink-footed shearwater*, the *New Zealand shearwater*, and the *sooty shearwater*.

**Scientific Classification.** Shearwaters belong to the order *Procellariiformes* and the Shearwater family, *Procellariidae*. The greater shearwater is genus *Puffinus*, species *P. gravis*; the black-vented is *P. opisthomelas*; the pink-footed is *P. creatopus*; the New Zealand is *P. bulleri*; and the sooty shearwater is *P. griseus*. ALEXANDER WETMORE

**SHEATHING.** See HOUSE (Terms; The Frame).

**SHEBA, QUEEN OF.** See SOLOMON (His Wisdom).

**SHEBOYGAN,** Wis. (pop. 45,747; alt. 590 ft.), is a Lake Michigan port at the mouth of the Sheboygan River. It has been called *the City of Cheese, Chairs, Children, and Churches*. It lies in the heart of a rich dairy-farming region. For location, see WISCONSIN (political map). Furniture factories, plastics firms, and woodworking plants employ many people of Sheboygan. Warehouses line the city's port. Sheboygan's first settlement was established in 1834. The city was chartered in 1853. It has a mayor-council government. JAMES I. CLARK

**SHECHEM.** See CITIES OF REFUGE.

**SHEE.** See FAIRY (Leprechauns).

**SHEELER, CHARLES** (1883-1965), was an American painter and photographer. He was among the first American artists whose work shows the influence of cubism. Sheeler is best known for paintings that blend realism with the geometric forms associated with cubism. This style can best be seen in Sheeler's paintings of architectural forms, both interior and exterior.

Sheeler was born in Philadelphia. The style of his early paintings shows the influence of his art teacher, William Merritt Chase. Sheeler's paintings took on cubistic characteristics, especially after he exhibited in the Armory Show of 1913. In the late 1920's, Sheeler's work in industrial and architectural photography influenced his art. His paintings became precise and realistic while retaining the influence of cubism. GEORGE EHRLICH

**SHEEN, FULTON JOHN** (1895- ), is one of the best-known spokesmen for the teachings of the Roman Catholic Church in the world. His more than 50 books, along with his articles, have brought Catholic doctrine to millions of people around the world.

In 1950, he resigned as professor at the Catholic University of America to direct the Society for the Propagation of the Faith in the United States. This is an international mission aid society which raises and distributes money for the support of Roman Catholic missionaries throughout the world. The year after his appointment to that post, he was named titular bishop of Cesariana. In 1966, he was named the bishop of the diocese of Rochester, N.Y., by Pope Paul VI.

As early as the 1920's, he was a vigorous opponent of Communism in his writings and radio talks on "The Catholic Hour," a national program. During the 1950's, he became widely known as a television personality for his "Life Is Worth Living" series.

Bishop Sheen was born in El Paso, Ill., and studied for the priesthood at St. Paul Seminary. After his ordination in 1919, he took graduate work in philosophy at universities in the United States and Europe. In 1926, he began teaching at the Catholic University of America, and published his first book, *God and Intelligence in Modern Philosophy*. Bishop Sheen also wrote *Communism and the Conscience of the West* (1948), *Peace of Soul* (1949), *Life Is Worth Living* (1953), and *The Priest Is Not His Own* (1963). JOHN TRACY ELLIS

**Fulton J. Sheen**

**Feeding the Sheep** is important during the winter when pasture land is barren. Sheep eat grain and hay grown on the farm.

U.S. Indian Service

**SHEEP** are among the most important animals that man has tamed because they provide both food and clothing. Long before man began to write history, shepherds watched the flocks in the fields to guard them against wild animals. Today sheep are raised in all parts of the world. Australia is the world's leading sheep-producing country, raising about one-sixth of the world's sheep. In Australia, there are about 14 sheep for every person. In New Zealand, there are about 20 sheep for every person. Some states in the western United States also have more sheep than people. Sheep yield wool, meat, and leather. They also furnish the raw materials for many byproducts, such as glue, tallow, suet, soap, fertilizer, cosmetics, and the catgut used in stringing tennis rackets.

### The Body of the Sheep

Domestic sheep vary greatly in size. The *ewes* (females) of some breeds may weigh as little as 100 pounds. Other ewes may weigh more than 225 pounds. The *rams* (males) are larger. Their weight, including a heavy coat of wool, ranges from 150 to 350 pounds.

Sheep are different from goats in many ways. They do not have the familiar beard of the billy goat, nor the well-known "goaty" odor. Sheep have a gland between their toes which is not found among the goats. The horns of a ram usually curve outward. In some breeds, both rams and ewes have horns. In other kinds, only the rams have horns, or the breed is hornless.

Sheep walk upon hoofs that are divided into two toes. Their ankles are slim. The upper part of their legs is muscular, helping them to move quickly and easily.

Sheep have no incisor, or cutting, teeth on their upper jaws, though they have eight on their lower jaws. They have six grinding teeth on the back part of each jaw. Sheep can bite off grass much closer to the ground than cattle can. In fact, where sheep have eaten their fill, there is little plant life left. Most sheep have tails, but these are cut off for reasons of cleanliness.

Sheep live for about 13 years. They begin breeding at the age of about two years, and have young every year after that. The mother carries the young sheep inside her body about five months before it is born.

### Wild Sheep

Sheep are supposed to have come originally from the lofty plateaus and mountains of Central Asia. The largest of all the wild sheep, the *argali*, is found in the Altai Mountains of Siberia and Mongolia. The male argali stands four feet high at the shoulders, and his massive horns curve into a spiral twenty inches around.

The great Marco Polo sheep of Asia live on the plateaus of Pamir, the "roof of the world," three miles above sea level. This sheep was first described by Marco Polo. The Marco Polo sheep is a little smaller than the argali, but it is remarkable for the wide spread of its horns. The *blue sheep*, or *bharal*, which is closely related to the goat, lives in Tibet. About half a dozen other kinds of wild sheep live in Asia.

Wild sheep look much like wild goats. Some kinds of wild sheep are thought to be halfway between sheep and goats. Wild sheep are high-spirited, daring, and self-reliant. They brave the fiercest storms of winter and climb to great heights that no other animals but mountain goats dare ascend. They live in bands among the mountains and plateaus of the Northern Hemisphere.

All the domestic breeds of sheep are descended from two different kinds of wild sheep. These are the *urial* that lives in Southern Asia, and the *mouflon*, which is the only wild sheep still living in Southern Europe. Both of these sheep probably resemble their original ancestors. Many kinds of bighorn sheep live in North America.

### Breeds of Domestic Sheep

Domestic sheep have been slowly and carefully changed from their wild ancestors. Originally, the wild sheep were tamed for the sake of their hides and milk. They were also used to carry burdens. Very early they became important for their fleece. The coarse hair that covered the wild sheep was replaced by a soft coat of wool through breeding. Only in the last 200 years have

**At Two Days Old, Lambs Already Are Sure-Footed**
Newton H. Hartman

# IMPORTANT BREEDS

**Rambouillet Ram**

**Dorset Horn Ram**

**Lincoln Ram**

**Southdown Ram**

**Cotswold Ram**

**Shropshire Ram**

**Hampshire Ewe**

**Merino Ram**

Amer. Delaine-Merino Record Assn.; Live Stock Photo Co.; U.S.D.A.
**Leicester Ram**

# SHEEP

breeders developed sheep primarily for their meat.

Sheep are classified into five groups, depending upon their fleece. These are *fine wool, long wool, crossbred wool, medium wool,* and *coarse wool.* The coarse wool group is of little importance.

**Fine-Wooled Sheep.** Most of our fine-wooled sheep originated from the Spanish Merino. These sheep were raised in Spain as far back as history has been written. Spanish Merino sheep were greatly prized, and the Spanish government forbade taking the sheep out of the country. But many sheep were smuggled into Germany, France, and England. Spaniards had improved the breed very little. It was in these other countries that the Merino was developed into the modern type of sheep.

There are more sheep with Merino blood than any other breed. American Merino sheep are considered the best in the world. They have white faces and legs, and are thickly covered with fine wool down to their toes and noses. Rams usually have horns.

The *Rambouillet* is another important breed which is descended from the Spanish Merino. It is named after a town in France, but it was largely developed in Germany, and, later, in the United States. The breed began more than a hundred and fifty years ago. This breed is very hardy. The *Debouillet* breed was developed in New Mexico about 1920. This breed was developed to produce wool and mutton under difficult range conditions.

**Long-Wooled Sheep.** Four of the most important long-wooled breeds come from England. They are the *Lincoln, Leicester, Cotswold,* and *Romney.* Lincoln sheep are among the largest of domestic sheep, and produce the longest fleece. The Leicester sheep is especially valuable to stock breeders for crossing with other sheep. It is the ancestor of most of the other long-wooled breeds of sheep. American ranchmen have also used the Cotswold in improving quality, crossing the rams with Merino ewes. Romney sheep, which originated in southeastern England, are popular in New Zealand and in Oregon and California.

**Crossbred-Wooled Sheep.** Crossing two or more of the accepted domestic breeds to produce a new breed has become very common in developing modern types of sheep. Except for the Merino and Rambouillet types, probably all modern breeds are the result of such crossing. The *Corriedale* is a cross-bred sheep that has become popular throughout Australia, New Zealand, South America, and the United States. In the Corriedale, the breeders have attempted to combine the maximum wool and mutton production, to develop what is known as the dual purpose sheep. The Corriedale was bred from fine-wool and long-wool sheep in Australia and New Zealand. The breed was first imported into the United States in 1914. Similar crosses have also been made. They have resulted in the *Columbia, Romeldale, Panama, Montadale, Polwarth,* and *Targhee* breeds.

**Medium-Wooled Sheep.** These sheep are grown primarily for the meat they produce, but they also are a source of wool. The most important breeds are the *Hampshire, Shropshire, Southdown,* and *Suffolk.* Most farmers raise these sheep as purebreds. But in the West, they are used for breeding with the ewes of native sheep in order to produce lambs for the market.

The Shropshires are extremely popular on farms. Together with the Hampshire and Southdown, they are largely raised east of the Missouri River. The Hampshire and the Suffolk are extremely popular west of the Missouri. These breeds came from England. The face, ears, and legs of the Hampshire range in color from dark brown to black. The black face, ears, and legs of the Suffolk contrast sharply with its white wool body. The Southdown is a rather small sheep with a square-shaped body. The *Dorset* sheep is raised along the Atlantic Coast. This breed produces lambs at any season of the year, and therefore is valuable for producing lambs for the winter market. Other important medium-wool breeds are the *Cheviot, No-Tail, Oxford, Tunis,* and *Ryeland.*

## LEADING SHEEP RAISING STATES
Number of sheep in the state in 1968

|  |  |
|---|---|
| Texas | 4,206,000 |
| Wyoming | 1,847,000 |
| California | 1,535,000 |
| Colorado | 1,384,000 |
| South Dakota | 1,382,000 |
| Montana | 1,275,000 |
| Utah | 1,074,000 |
| Iowa | 947,000 |
| New Mexico | 873,000 |
| Idaho | 834,000 |

Source: *Livestock and Poultry Inventory, Jan. 1, 1968,* U.S. Department of Agriculture

## LEADING SHEEP RAISING COUNTRIES
Number of sheep in the country in 1968 and earlier years

|  |  |
|---|---|
| Australia | 165,000,000 |
| Russia | 138,300,000 |
| China (Mainland) | 68,400,000 |
| New Zealand | 60,100,000 |
| Argentina | 48,000,000 |
| India | 44,410,000 |
| South Africa | 42,172,000 |
| Turkey | 35,000,000 |
| Ethiopia | 25,275,000 |
| United States | 22,122,000 |

Sources: U.S. Department of Agriculture; FAO

**Coarse-Wooled Sheep.** *Karakul* lambs have a glossy fur that is used to make women's fur coats. Lambs are usually killed and pelted when they are 3 to 10 days old, when the fur is most valuable. The *Scottish Blackface*, called *Blackface Highland* in the United States, produces a wool that is valuable for tweeds, carpets, and mattresses. *Navajo* sheep also produce a coarse wool for rugs and blankets.

### Raising Sheep

There are two distinctly different ways of raising sheep in the United States. The most important way is on the range. Here sheep are herded about in large bands containing from 1,000 to 2,000 or more sheep. The herds are moved about on large tracts of land which may be owned by the sheep owner, or may be leased from another owner or from the government. The sheep eat grass in the pasture.

The other important way of raising sheep is on farms. The farmer raises from thirty to a few hundred head of sheep. He keeps them in fenced pastures and in the winter he feeds them grain and hay grown on the farm.

Throughout history, sheep have generally been raised in places that are far from cities and other thickly populated areas. There are two main reasons for this. Compared to most products, wool is very valuable in proportion to its bulk. Furthermore, it does not spoil. Therefore, it can be stored and shipped over long distances. In the second place, sheep tend to herd together, and therefore they can be handled in large bands in open country with very little labor. Sheep like to eat woods and shrubs. They can live without water for long periods of time. This permits farmers to raise sheep on dry plains all over the world.

In the United States, most sheep are raised west of the Mississippi. Wool sheep predominate in the West, in Ohio, and in a few other sections. Mutton sheep are raised in practically all parts of the country. The United States can produce nearly all the lamb and mutton it needs. But it imports much of the wool it uses, because of the demand for special types of wool.

### Enemies of Sheep

Sheep are attacked by various parasites and diseases. Foot rot and sore mouth are common diseases. Sheep suffer from internal parasites, and also from a disease called *sheep scab* caused by mites and ticks. Meat-eating wild animals often attack sheep, and dogs sometimes kill sheep. The kea parrot of New Zealand sinks its sharp, hooked bill into the sheep's back and eats the sheep's flesh and fat.

**Scientific Classification.** Sheep, together with cattle, goats, and buffaloes, belong to the bovid family, *Bovidae*. The urial sheep is genus *Ovis*, species *O. vignei*. The mouflon sheep is *O. musimon*. Domesticated sheep are genus *Ovis*, species *O. aries*. TONY J. CUNHA

**Related Articles** in WORLD BOOK include:

| | |
|---|---|
| Animal (color pictures: Animals of the Mountains) | Mange |
| | Mutton |
| Australia (Agriculture; color picture) | New Zealand (picture) |
| Bighorn | Ranching |
| Foot-and-Mouth Disease | Ruminant |
| Karakul | Scotland (picture) |
| Lamb | Uruguay (picture) |
| Lanolin | Wool |
| Livestock | |

# SHELL

**SHEEP DOG.** Almost everywhere that sheep have been raised, a type of dog has been developed to herd and watch the sheep. The dogs turn wandering sheep back to the flock, and keep the flock together. They also defend the flock from attacks by wolves and other animals. Sheep dogs are loyal, gentle, and intelligent.

The American Kennel Club recognizes 10 breeds of sheep dogs. They are (1) *Belgian sheep dog*, (2) *Briard*, (3) *collie*, (4) *German shepherd dog*, (5) *Great Pyrenees*, (6) *komondor*, (7) *old English sheep dog*, (8) *puli*, (9) *Shetland sheep dog*, and (10) *Schnauzer* (*standard*). See the articles on these breeds in WORLD BOOK. Many countries have breeds not recognized in the U.S. OLGA DAKAN

See also DOG (color picture: Working Dogs).

**SHEEPSHEAD.** See DRUMFISH (picture).

**SHEFFIELD** (pop. 534,100; alt. 325 ft.) is a city in Yorkshire, England. It lies about 160 miles northwest of London on pleasant wooded slopes overlooking the Sheaf and Don rivers. For location, see GREAT BRITAIN (political map). Sheffield University was founded in 1905. German bombers damaged the medieval Cathedral of Saints Peter and Paul during World War II, but it was repaired after the war.

The city has been known for its fine cutlery since the 1300's. Candlesticks and teapots of *Sheffield plate* (silver on copper) are treasured possessions. During World War II, Sheffield's steel foundries and mills made armor plate and weapons. FREDERICK G. MARCHAM

**SHEHAN, LAWRENCE JOSEPH CARDINAL** (1898-    ), is an American religious leader. He was named a cardinal of the Roman Catholic Church in 1965 by Pope Paul VI. He also received the honorary title of primate of the United States because his Baltimore diocese is the oldest in the country. Cardinal Shehan was ordained a priest in 1922, and served at St. Patrick's Church in Washington, D.C., from 1923 to 1941. He became a bishop in 1945 and was appointed first bishop of Bridgeport, Conn., in 1953. He became archbishop of the Baltimore diocese in 1961. Cardinal Shehan was born in Baltimore. THOMAS P. NEILL

**SHEIK**, *sheek*, or *shayk*, is an Arabic title referring either to an old and respected man or to the chief of a tribe or village. Sometimes a sheik is the leader of a religious society. Only Moslems use the title of sheik. A sheik's power usually depends upon his own will and character. Songs and stories have pictured the sheik as a romantic figure.

**SHEKEL**, *SHEK ul*, is an ancient term that meant a unit of weight. Later it was used to mean a gold or silver coin. The shekel was used as a weight by the Babylonians, Phoenicians, and Hebrews. The Bible often refers to the Hebrew shekel. It weighed about 218 grains, or one and a half ounces. It was first used as money in the form of uncoined gold and silver. The Hebrews coined their first metal money about 139-138 B.C. Half and quarter silver shekels also were coined. Today, the word *shekel* is a slang term referring to money. FRED REINFELD

**SHELBURNE MUSEUM.** See VERMONT (Places to Visit).

**SHELBY, ISAAC.** See KENTUCKY (History).

**SHELDRAKE.** See MERGANSER.

**SHELL** is a projectile. See AMMUNITION.

307

Coiled Shell of Land Snail

Brittle Bird's Egg Shells

Leathery Shell of Sea Turtle

Huge Shell of Giant Clam

Tough Shell of Stag Beetle

Plated Shell of Armadillo

# SHELL

**SHELL.** Many kinds of animals and plants have shells. Clams, lobsters, oysters, shrimps, snails, and turtles all grow shells. Shells also hold the seeds and nuts of the coconut, peach, walnut, and other plants.

Most shells grow on the outside of an animal or plant. These shells are like strong suits of armor that protect the bodies they cover. Some shells grow inside the bodies of cuttlefish and many kinds of squids. These shells, called *cuttlebones* in cuttlefish or *pens* in squids, help support the bodies of the animals.

Some kinds of shells have beautiful shapes and bright colors. Others are plain and colorless. Among the smallest kinds are the shells of the Vitrinellid, a sea snail found in many parts of the world. Some Vitrinellid shells grow only about as big as a grain of sand. The largest shell is that of the giant clam of the South Pacific Ocean. This huge shellfish has a shell that may measure up to 4 feet long and weigh up to 500 pounds.

Some kinds of animals begin their lives inside egg shells. Thin, brittle shells cover the eggs of birds. Thick, leathery shells protect the eggs of alligators, snakes, and many other reptiles. Strong, rubbery shells hold the eggs of the platypus and echidna. Many other animals spend all their lives in shells that are important parts of their bodies. The shells of clams and oysters are really the skeletons of these animals. The shells of turtles and tortoises include part of their backbone and ribs.

Many persons collect shells as a hobby. Most shells in these collections belong to *mollusks*, a group of animals that includes clams, conchs, cowries, oysters, and snails. This article provides general information about mollusk shells. For information about the animals that grow these shells, see the separate WORLD BOOK article on MOLLUSK and its list of Related Articles. For information about other kinds of shells, see the WORLD BOOK articles on EGG and SEED, and articles on individual plants and animals, such as WALNUT and TURTLE.

*R. Tucker Abbott, the contributor of this article, is a staff member of the Academy of Natural Sciences of Philadelphia, and the author of* American Seashells *and* Sea Shells of the World.

## SHELL / How Shells Are Formed

There are about 100,000 kinds of mollusk shells. Each kind has its own special design and shape, but all are formed in much the same way. Some mollusks that grow the shells live in the ocean, some in fresh water, and others on land.

Most shells consist of three layers—an outer, middle, and inner layer. These layers are also called the *prismatic layer* (outer layer), the *lamellar layer* (middle layer), and the *nacreous layer* (inner layer). Each layer contains a form of calcium carbonate, a kind of limestone also found in marble and other kinds of rocks. In most shells, the mineral in these layers provides a hard covering for the shell. In the outer layer, the mineral may be in the form of small particles called *prisms*. In the inner layer, the mineral is often produced as a smooth, shiny substance called *nacre* or *mother-of-pearl*. The nacre of certain kinds of shells, including those of clams and scallops, has a dull appearance.

The food eaten by a mollusk provides the minerals that form the shell and give it color. The blood stream of the animal carries the minerals to the *mantle*, a fleshy skinlike tissue inside the shell. Special glands in the mantle produce the substances that make the shell in the form of a liquid. Other glands in the mantle add a hardening material so that the liquid quickly becomes firm and strong. Still other glands produce the color. The pattern of the color depends on (1) whether color is added continuously, and (2) the number of places in the mantle from which color is added. For example, if color is added continuously from only one place in the mantle, the shell will have one stripe. If color is added continuously from four places, the shell will have four stripes. If the color flow is interrupted from time to time, spots or bars will form on the shell.

Most kinds of mollusks add material to their shells throughout their lives. As long as the animal grows, its shell also grows. Clams and snails begin to grow shells before they hatch. After they leave the egg, their bodies rapidly increase in size. A sea snail that is only $\frac{1}{10}$ of an inch long when it hatches may grow 5 or 6 inches in six months. Most clams and sea snails grow for about six years.

## SHELL / Kinds of Mollusk Shells

Mollusk shells can be divided into five main groups, each with a common name and a scientific name. These groups are (1) univalves or *Gastropoda*, (2) bivalves or *Pelecypoda*, (3) tooth shells or *Scaphopoda*, (4) octopuses and squids or *Cephalopoda*, and (5) chitons or *Amphineura*. A sixth group, the *Monoplacophora*, is extremely rare. Scientists have found these shells only as fossils or in the deepest waters of the Pacific Ocean.

**Univalves.** The word *univalve* means *one shell*. Snail shells are univalves. Most snails have a tubelike shell that winds around itself as it grows. The soft body of the snail is in the open part of the tube. Most snail shells grow by winding to the right in a clockwise direction, and are called *right-handed shells*. A few kinds of snails have *left-handed shells*.

The shells of univalves have an opening at one end. Most of them have a hard lidlike part called an *operculum* at the opening. The animal can pull the operculum over the entrance of the shell to keep out such enemies as fish and crabs.

Univalves are found in almost every part of the world except on the highest mountain peaks. Some live in the ocean, some in fresh water, and some on land. Many ocean univalves have smooth, glossy shells. Others have shells with deep ridges, rough surfaces, and long, sharp spines. The carrier shell snail attaches bits of shells, stones, and other objects to its soft shell substance as it grows. The shell substance acts as cement, and when the shell hardens, the objects are held firmly in place. Most univalves that live in fresh water or on land have thin, smooth shells. Many tree snails, particularly those of the tropics, have brightly colored shells.

Limpet shells are also univalves. These shells grow almost flat and form a point in the center. The shells of keyhole limpets have a hole at the top, and look like miniature volcanoes.

Scientists have identified more than 60,000 species of

**THE PARTS OF A UNIVALVE SHELL**

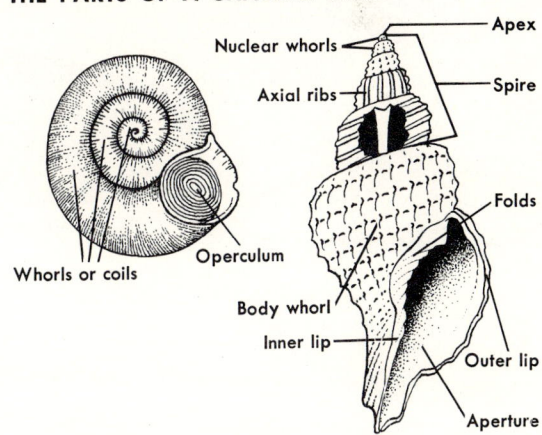

**THE PARTS OF A BIVALVE SHELL**

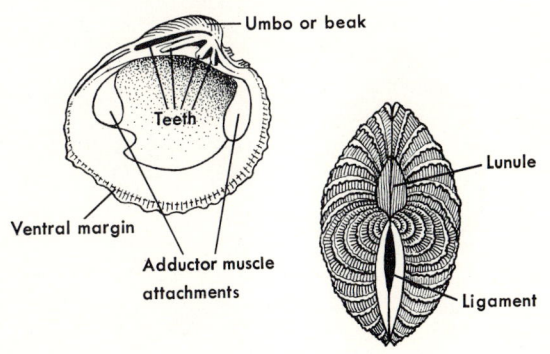

WORLD BOOK illustration by Tom Dolan

# UNIVALVE SHELLS

**Commercial Top Shell**
*Trochus niloticus*
Indian and S.W. Pacific Oceans
½ actual size

**Delphinula Shell**
*Angaria delphinus*
S.W. Pacific Ocean
Actual size

**Oriente Tree Snail**
*Polymita picta*
Cuba
Actual size

**Eastern Moon Snail**
*Polinices duplicatus*
U.S. Atlantic Coast
½ actual size

**Limpet**
*Patella lugubris*
Azores
⅔ actual size

**Tiger Cowrie**
*Cypraea tigris*
Indian and S.W. Pacific Oceans
½ actual size

(top)

(underside)

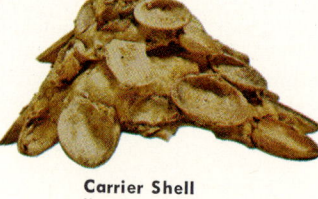

**Carrier Shell**
*Xenophora neozelanica*
New Zealand Coast
½ actual size

**Left-Handed Whelk**
*Busycon contrarium*
U.S. Atlantic Coast
½ actual size

**Tent Olive Shell**
*Oliva porphyria*
Pacific Coast of Panama
½ actual size

**Regal Murex**
*Murex regius*
Pacific Coast, Mexico to Panama
½ actual size

**Textile Cone**
*Conus textile*
Indian and S.W. Pacific Oceans
⅔ actual size

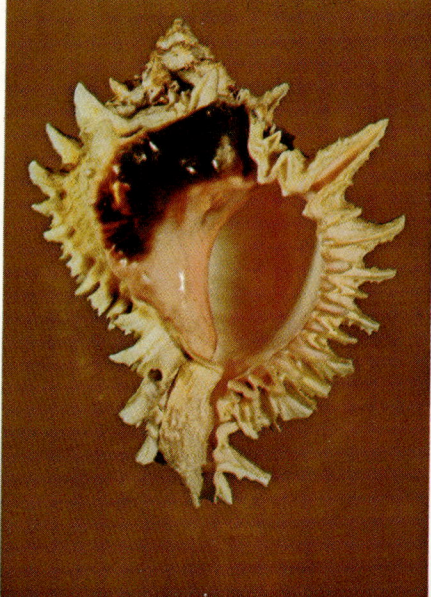

**Crown Conch**
*Melongena corona*
West Florida Coast
Actual size

310

# BIVALVE SHELLS

**Fragile River Mussel**
*Leptodea fragilis*
Fox River, Illinois
½ actual size

**Pacific Thorny Oyster**
*Spondylus pictorum*
Pacific Coast of Mexico
⅓ actual size

**Mantle Scallop**
*Gloripallium pallium*
S.W. Pacific Ocean
½ actual size

**Sunrise Tellin**
*Tellina radiata*
West Indies
⅔ actual size

**Blue Mussel**
*Mytilus edulis*
North Atlantic Ocean
½ actual size

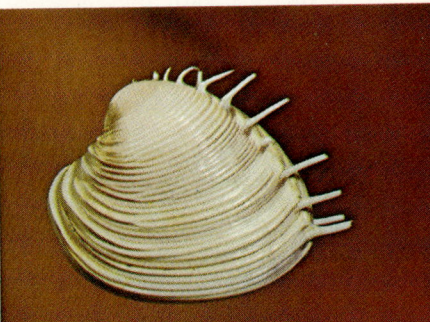

**Royal Comb Venus**
*Pitar dione*
Caribbean Sea
⅔ actual size

# NAUTILUS SHELL

(Whole)

**Chambered Nautilus**
*Nautilus pompilius*
S.W. Pacific Ocean
¼ actual size

(Cutaway)

# CHITON SHELL

**West Indian Chiton**
*Chiton tuberculata*
West Indies
⅔ actual size

# TOOTH SHELL

**Elephant's Tusk Shell**
*Dentalium elephantinum*
Japan and Philippine Islands
Actual size

WORLD BOOK photos; specimens courtesy the Academy of Natural Sciences of Philadelphia and Albert Lindar.

# SHELL

univalve shells. The largest are the horse conch of Florida and the baler of Australia. Both grow about 2 feet long. The giant African snail has a larger shell than any other land snail. It is about 8 inches long. Many kinds of univalves have shells so small they can hardly be seen. For example, a row of 30 Barlia snail shells covers less than an inch.

**Bivalves** have two matching shells. The shells move on hinges that look like small teeth. Clams, oysters, and scallops are bivalves. Bivalves keep their shells open when resting and undisturbed. A broad band of elastic tissue acts like a prop to hold the shells apart. If an enemy comes near, a strong muscle attached to both shells acts like a spring. It snaps the shells shut and keeps them closed. If the muscle gets tired and relaxes, the shells open again. An enemy usually does not wait this long.

Bivalves are found almost everywhere except on dry land. There are about 11,000 kinds of bivalves. Most of them live in shallow ocean waters near land, but a few species live in the beds of large rivers. Perhaps the best known of these are the fresh-water clams of the Mississippi River valley. Occasionally, a pearl is found in these shells. But most pearls valued as gems come from the pearl oyster of the sea.

The giant clam of the South Pacific, whose shell may grow up to 4 feet long, is the largest bivalve. Among the smallest are the turton clams of the North Atlantic. They grow about half as large as a grain of rice.

**Tooth Shells** look like long needles or like miniature elephant tusks. They are sometimes called *tusk shells*. The shells are hollow tubes that curve slightly and become smaller at one end. Both ends are open.

Tooth shells are found in the sand or mud of the ocean bottom in many parts of the world. Some kinds live close to shore. Others burrow in the ocean floor thousands of feet below the surface of the water. The small end of the shell sticks up into the water.

Scientists have identified about 500 kinds of tooth shells. The shells vary in length from $\frac{1}{2}$ inch to 5 inches. Most of them are white, but some have green, red, or yellow tints. The most colorful tooth shell is the elephant's tusk of the Philippines, which is dark green with bluish ribs.

**Octopuses and Squids.** In this group of sea animals, the cuttlefish and squids have shells inside their bodies. The cuttlefish, also called the Sepia squid, has a chalky cuttlebone inside its body. This shell is light and spongy, but it serves as a strong support for the animal's body. The Spirula squid has a shell about an inch long under the skin at the rear of its body. The tightly coiled Spirula shell looks somewhat like a ram's horn. In tropical countries, waves often wash these curled shells ashore. Octopuses have no shells at all.

Perhaps the best known shell of this group is the chambered nautilus, also called the pearly nautilus. It consists of a series of inside chambers, each larger than the one before. Thin walls seal off every chamber except the outer one, where the soft body of the nautilus is found. The coiled shell is cream colored with brown stripes, and the chambers are lined with shiny pearl. Nautilus shells may grow up to 10 inches in diameter. They are found mostly in the South Pacific Ocean.

The paper nautilus or argonaut has a single, paper-thin shell much like that of the chambered nautilus. The paper nautilus never lives in its shell, which serves only as an egg case and nest. The female builds the thin, fragile shell, and carries it about until the eggs hatch. Then she lets it float away. The paper nautilus lives at the surface of warm tropical seas.

**Chitons.** A chiton shell consists of eight separate, movable pieces called *plates* that are held together by a leathery *girdle* (belt). The girdle acts like a series of hinges between the plates, and allows the animal to bend and move about easily. Chiton shells are also called coat-of-mail shells because they look like tiny suits of armor. Chitons attach themselves to rocks in the sea. Some kinds are less than an inch long. The largest chiton, Steller's chiton of the California coast, grows up to 8 inches long.

## SHELL / Collecting Shells

Many persons find shell collecting a fascinating hobby. They spend leisure time hunting and cleaning shells, and mounting them in attractive displays. Some collectors become so interested in their hobby that they begin the scientific study of shells, which is called *conchology*. Hundreds of amateur and professional shell collectors exchange ideas, information, and shells. This exchange often takes place through shell clubs in cities in almost every country.

Beginning collectors gather all the shells they can find, even broken and discolored ones. Serious collectors replace poor shells with those of the finest quality as soon as they can. The best quality of shells are *live shells* —those taken with the live animal still inside. These shells have their natural color and luster because they have not been bleached by the sun or scratched by the sand. The next best quality are *recently dead shells*. Storm waves or outgoing tides leave them on the beach. The poorest shells are *dead shells*. Most shells found on beaches are dead shells. The sun has faded the colors, and sand and water have dulled the luster.

**Searching for Shells.** You can find the best sea shells during the night or in the early morning hours at low tide. Use a strong flashlight or lantern to light your way. Wear a bathing suit and soft canvas shoes, and take a small bag or bucket to hold the shells. Look for clams buried in the sand, for snails sheltered under rocks, and for scallops hiding in eelgrass. Never hunt for sea shells alone. Always go with a companion who can help in case of an accident.

Many kinds of fresh-water mussels and snail shells can be found in rivers, streams, lakes, ditches, and ponds. Use a dip net to sweep along the grassy edges of ponds. To find the shells of land snails, roll logs over, scrape away the leaves and soil, and look in the cracks of the bark.

As you gather shells, write down the date and the exact location where you find each one. Keep these notes with the shells until you add them to your collection. Then put the information on labels that identify the shells.

**Cleaning Shells.** The best and simplest way to clean live mollusk shells is to boil them. Put the shells in a pan of water, bring the water slowly to a boil, and boil for 5 to 10 minutes. Then let the water cool slowly. The meat of the clams will fall out. Use a twisted safety pin to pull out snail meat. Save the snail's operculum because it is part of the shell. Wash the shells with soap and water, and place them on paper to dry in the sun. Very small live shells can be soaked in alcohol for several days, and then dried in the sun.

**Displaying Shells.** You can mount your shells on cardboard, or you can put them on cotton in flat boxes with glass or plastic covers. Some collectors use a cabinet with large drawers to store their shells. A square cardboard tray holds each kind of shell. A label bears the name of the shell and tells where, when, and by whom it was collected. The label also gives information about the shell's surroundings, such as grass, mud, sand, or depth of water. A logbook serves as an index to the shells in the collection and gives further information about them.

Every part of a shell helps identify it. For example, the number and location of the teeth in a shell hinge show that the mollusk belongs to a certain family of clams. The color, ridges, and shape of a snail shell identify the group to which it belongs. Each part of a shell has a special name, such as lip, ribs, or shoulders. Drawings with this article show the parts of shells and name them.

A shell collection should be arranged so that it begins with the shells of the simplest kinds of mollusks. Many shells have popular names, such as mouse cone or Florida cone. These names may vary from one country to another, and even from one area to another. For this reason, collectors identify shells by their scientific names. These names are in Latin and are understood in all parts of the world. The Latin name of the mouse cone is *Conus mus,* and that of the Florida cone is *Conus floridanus.*

## PREPARING A SHELL COLLECTION

Most shell collectors like to find and prepare their own shells. They hunt for shells along the shores of oceans, lakes, or rivers. Then they clean the shells, identify and label them, and arrange them in attractive displays. Some collectors buy special shells for their collections.

**A Shell-Collecting Expedition**

WORLD BOOK photos by Don Stebbing

**Cleaning the Shells**

**Identifying the Day's Catch**

**Labeling the Shells**

**An Interesting Shell Display**

"Madonna of the Sea," courtesy of Edward Waldo Forbes, Director Emeritus, Fogg Art Museum, Cambridge, Mass.

**Shell Mosaic,** by Edward Waldo Forbes and associates, is made from pieces of clam shells carefully fitted to form the design.

The Metropolitan Museum of Art, New York. Bequest of Benjamin Altman, 1913.

**A Graceful Shell,** *above,* provides the basic design of the famous Rospigliosi cup by the artist Benvenuto Cellini.

**A Butterfly Pin,** *below,* combines gleaming mother-of-pearl with silver to make the insect's colorful wings.

Walter Dawn

## SHELL / Uses of Shells

The color and luster of shells make them especially useful as decorations and for jewelry. Manufacturers cut the shells of fresh-water mussels to make pearl buttons. Craftsmen use mother-of-pearl from abalone and oyster shells to decorate fancy boxes, jewelry, and musical instruments. Artists carve raised designs called *cameos* in many kinds of shells to make ornamental pins and other kinds of jewelry. Conchs and some other large shells can be polished and used as lamp bases or paperweights. Many kinds of small shells are fastened together in the shape of animals or dolls, or to form attractive designs.

Scientists sometimes use shells to help them in their work. Atomic scientists may expose shells to atomic rays to test the effects of radiation. Oil prospectors search for certain kinds of fossil shells in deserts and prairies. The shells show that the area was an ocean bed in ancient times. Large oil pools formed in many of these ancient ocean beds.

In prehistoric times, cowrie shells and tooth shells were used as money. The Phoenicians and Romans made a purple dye from Murex sea snails. They believed that cloth colored with this dye was more valuable than gold.

The Indians of North and South America also used shells as money. North American Indians carved wampum beads from large clam shells and parts of the knobbed whelk of the Atlantic Coast.

In the Philippines, the thin, almost transparent shells of the Placuna oyster serve as window "glass." The shells are cut into small squares and put into narrow wooden frames. The frames are then fastened together to make a large window.

R. TUCKER ABBOTT

## SHELL / Study Aids

**Related Articles.** See MOLLUSK with its list of Related Articles. See also the following articles:

| | | |
|---|---|---|
| Armadillo | Fossil | Pearl |
| Button | Mother-of-Pearl | Turtle |
| Crustacean | Nummulite | Wampum |

### Outline

I. **How Shells Are Formed**
II. **Kinds of Mollusk Shells**
    A. Univalves
    B. Bivalves
    C. Tooth Shells
    D. Octopuses and Squids
    E. Chitons
III. **Collecting Shells**
    A. Searching for Shells
    B. Cleaning Shells
    C. Displaying Shells
IV. **Uses of Shells**

### Questions

What is a univalve shell?
When are the best times to hunt for sea shells?
What is the largest shell?
How many layers do most mollusk shells have?
What is *conchology?*
When do clams and snails begin to grow shells?
Where do mollusks get the minerals for their shells?
What do keyhole limpet shells look like?
Why are tooth shells sometimes called *tusk shells?*
How does the paper nautilus use its shell?

**SHELLABARGER, SAMUEL** (1888-1954), a popular novelist, won success as a writer when he published *Captain from Castile*, a historical romance, in 1945. He had been a professional educator, and had published a number of romances and detective stories before then. His other literary works include *Prince of Foxes* (1947), *The King's Cavalier* (1950), and *Lord Vanity* (1953). Shellabarger was born in Washington, D.C. He wrote several of his earlier works under the pen names of John Esteven and Peter Loring. BERNARD DUFFEY

**SHELLAC**, *shuh LACK*, is the liquid formed of resin flakes which have been dissolved in alcohol. It is used as a varnish. The flakes are the dried form of a sticky substance called *lac resin* (see LAC). When shellac is applied to a surface, the alcohol in the solution evaporates, leaving a shiny finish. Shellac resin flakes are yellow, orange, or reddish, but can be bleached white. Shellac is also used in sealing wax, insulating materials, phonograph records, and as a stiffener. GEORGE L. BUSH

See also LACQUER; RESIN; VARNISH.

**SHELLEY, MARY WOLLSTONECRAFT** (1797-1851), an English author, wrote the famous horror novel *Frankenstein* (1818). She was born in London, the daughter of philosopher William Godwin. When she was 16, she met the poet Percy Bysshe Shelley. Although Shelley was married, Mary ran away with him. They were married after Shelley's first wife died in 1816, and settled in the Italian coastal village of Lerici. Mary wrote *Frankenstein* there at the suggestion of her husband and the poet Lord Byron. Shelley drowned in Lerici in 1822.

Shelley's death changed Mary's life from one of adventure and excitement to one of loneliness and failure. She wrote a few novels after her husband's death, including the autobiographical *Lodore* (1835). But she was forced to write much low-quality material to support herself and her children. JAMES D. MERRITT

See also FRANKENSTEIN; SHELLEY, PERCY BYSSHE; GODWIN.

**SHELLEY, PERCY BYSSHE** (1792-1822), was one of the great English lyric poets. He experimented with many literary styles and had a lasting influence on many later writers, particularly Robert Browning, Algernon Charles Swinburne, William Butler Yeats, George Bernard Shaw, and Thomas Hardy.

**His Life.** Shelley was born on Aug. 4, 1792, in Sussex into a wealthy and politically prominent family. He had a stormy career at Eton College and Oxford University, from which he was expelled in 1811 for writing a pamphlet called *The Necessity of Atheism*.

In August, 1811, Shelley eloped with 16-year-old Harriet Westbrook, the daughter of a former coffeehouse owner. He abandoned her in 1814 and ran away with Mary Wollstonecraft Godwin. Although both said they did not believe in marriage, Shelley and Mary Godwin were married in 1816, after Harriet drowned herself. See SHELLEY, MARY WOLLSTONECRAFT.

Shelley believed the Irish were being oppressed by their English rulers, and tried to rouse the Irish to rebel against England. He wrote *Queen Mab* (1812-1813), a revolutionary poem which attacked both political tyranny and orthodox Christianity. In 1816, Shelley and his wife formed a close friendship with the poet Lord Byron in Geneva, Switzerland. After March, 1818, Shelley went into permanent exile in Italy. There he wrote a sequence of important poems, including *Prome-*

Portrait by Amelia Curran. National Portrait Gallery, London
**Percy Bysshe Shelley**

*theus Unbound* (1818-1819), *The Witch of Atlas* (1820), *Epipsychidion* (1821), and *Hellas* (1821). The death of an acquaintance, the English poet John Keats, inspired Shelley's important elegy *Adonais* (1821). On July 8, 1822, Shelley drowned during a storm while sailing near Leghorn, Italy.

**His Writings.** Shelley's poems are emotionally direct, but difficult to understand intellectually. Much of his poetry is autobiographical, including his most famous lyric "Ode to the West Wind" (1819). Shelley's spiritual attitudes were intensely personal and tended to oppose traditional Christian views. Shelley felt that spiritual truth was not based on either supernatural revelation or natural experience. Instead, he thought truth could be understood by the imagination alone. The role of the imagination as a spiritual guide is the subject of "Mont Blanc" (1816). This powerful meditative poem first revealed Shelley's mature style.

In his most ambitious long poem, the lyrical drama *Prometheus Unbound*, Shelley attempted to combine his imaginative faith with his hopes for mankind. Like much of Shelley's work, this play is based on classical Greek models. Prometheus, the creative power in Man, is liberated by Demogorgon, a mythical figure who stands for inevitable change in human events. At the end of the play, earthly rulers and government institutions are defeated, and love and beauty reign over mankind, but perhaps not forever.

Shelley's poetry became somber after the revolutionary hope expressed in *Prometheus Unbound*. The Irish poet William Butler Yeats described Shelley's themes as an increasing conflict between infinite desire and the inability fully to realize such desire. *Epipsychidion* expresses Shelley's love for an Italian noblewoman, Emilia Viviani. This poem tries to achieve a vision of ideal love finding its lasting home in an earthly paradise. The poem ends in despair of its own quest.

In 1821, Shelley wrote his famous essay *A Defence of Poetry*. The work is valuable for its insights into every poet's general ideas and Shelley's views on the role of imagination in poetry.

Whether Shelley had begun to find some definite faith, philosophical or otherwise, we do not know, but his final poems are as grim and sorrowful as any he wrote. His final love lyrics are serene only in their hopelessness. According to his powerful unfinished poem on human defeat, *The Triumph of Life*, good and the means of accomplishing good cannot be reconciled. However grim his final vision, he always looks toward the hope of inspiration, as in the "Ode to the West Wind":

Scatter, as from an unextinguished hearth
Ashes and sparks, my words among mankind!
Be through my lips to unawakened earth
The trumpet of a prophecy! HAROLD BLOOM

**SHELLFISH.** See CRUSTACEAN; MOLLUSK.

# SHELTER

**A Skyscraper Apartment Building** provides shelter for Chicago children and their families. The glass-enclosed structure stands in the Lake Meadows housing development.
*Stephen Lewellyn*

**An Ancient "Skyscraper"** still provides shelter for Turkish farmers. Early Christians hacked out the rooms in volcanic cones.
*Marc Riboud, Magnum*

**SHELTER** is a place for protection. It is one of man's three most important needs. The others are food and clothing. Shelter protects man from wind and rain, and from the heat and cold. It shields him against insects and wild animals, and helps protect him from other dangers. Man could not live long without shelter, except in a few places where the climate is always mild.

Natural shelter, such as a cave, may provide protection from the weather. But man-made shelter, such as tents, houses, and apartments, provides comfortable homes for the enjoyment of family life.

### Why All Shelters Are Not Alike

Three factors affect the kinds of shelter that men build: (1) the climate in which they live, (2) the kind of building materials they can use, and (3) the dangers that might threaten them.

**Climate.** People in hot, dry countries build houses with thick walls to keep out the heat. The walls have only a few narrow windows, or none at all, to prevent the sun's rays from pouring into the house. In many regions, if there is not much rain, the houses have flat roofs, where families can sleep in the cool night air.

People who live in rainy climates usually live in houses with steep, pointed roofs, so the rain will run off easily. They sometimes lay bundles of grasses, rushes, or leaves in rows on the roof, so that rain water runs off without leaking into the house. People also use thin strips of stone or wood called *shingles* to keep water out.

In Borneo, the Philippines, New Guinea, and India, people often build houses on stilts or high posts to protect them from dampness. The posts raise the house several feet off the ground. In Borneo, the average home holds 40 to 50 families. The people of Borneo also live in one-family stilt houses. The side walls slant outward to join the peaked roofs.

314

# SHELTER

People of snowy climates build strong, warm shelters to keep out the cold. They make their roofs strong so they will not fall in under the weight of heavy snows. They also slant the roofs steeply so the snow can slide off. The roofs usually hang far out over the sides of the houses. This keeps snow from piling up around the windows and doors.

In some countries, people need protection from high winds. They build their shelters low to the ground. On windy slopes in Switzerland, the people pile heavy stones on top of their houses to keep the roofs from blowing away.

**Materials.** People usually build shelters with materials they can get easily. Eskimos, for example, cannot build wooden houses. The region where they live has no trees. They make their homes of stone, grass, or earth. When Eskimos go hunting in icy regions, they cannot find these materials. So they cut snow into blocks to make igloos (see IGLOO). In Mexico and the southwestern United States, many people mix clay and dirt or mud with water to make *adobe*, or sun-dried bricks, for their thick walled homes (see ADOBE). Some people in India and other countries live in clay shelters.

In Northern Europe, wood is scarce and clay would melt away under the heavy rains. The people make their homes out of stone, which they find nearby.

In some parts of Africa, the grass grows as tall as a man's head, and is very strong. The people weave the grass into huts that look like wicker baskets turned upside down. One of these huts may be large enough for only one person to sleep in. The people of many Pacific islands also weave strong stems of grass together for their shelters. The Sakai tribe of Malaya builds huts in the forked branches of trees for protection. These people make walls of thick stems called *rattan*, and use palm leaves from 6 to 10 feet long for the roof. The floor is made of bamboo poles. See RATTAN.

**Dangers.** In countries such as Japan, where earthquakes occur frequently, people make their homes of light materials. They are safer in such homes if an earthquake shakes down their shelters. Japanese homes have roofs of light bamboo sticks. The walls that separate the rooms are light sliding screens made of bamboo frames covered with paper. The houses usually have wooden frames, and walls of wood, slate, tile, or plaster.

Many people in New Guinea and other South Pacific islands build homes on stilts in the water of lakes and lagoons. They have little to fear from wild animals or human enemies. When these dangers threaten them, they pull up the bridges that connect their houses to the shore. For the same reason, some people in Borneo, the Philippines, and Malaya build tree houses that are reached by ladders which can be drawn up.

## Shelter Around the World

**In the United States,** shelter varies widely according to income and surroundings. City families may live in apartments or houses. Farmers and most people in small towns live in houses. Wood, brick, stone, stucco, and concrete are the common building materials.

Most apartments consist of one, two, or three rooms. But the finest apartments may be as large as a big private home. The building owner usually provides janitor service and heat. The rent may include the cost of gas, electricity, and telephone, or the tenant may pay for these separately.

The usual one-family house is one or two stories high. Often it has a basement and an attic. The living room is usually the largest room in the house. Many houses have central heating provided by coal, oil, or gas furnaces. The windows are fairly large and the ceilings rather low. Many modern homes are air-conditioned.

City houses usually have smaller yards than those in small towns or suburbs, because city land is scarce and costly. A farmer's house may vary little from a house in a small town or suburb. But it generally has a larger kitchen. Most farmhouses are comfortable structures of two or three stories, usually built of wood. More

## HOW CLIMATE AFFECTS SHELTER

**In Warm Climates,** such as tropical islands, only a light shelter is needed to protect inhabitants from sun and rain.

**In Wet Climates,** a tight roof is needed to protect persons from rain. The house must be high where drainage is a problem.

**In Cold Climates,** the walls of the shelter must be of thick material to keep the inhabitants warm.

# SHELTER

**Many European Houses** retain the charm of medieval times. Their high-pitched roofs and elaborate outside decorations were typical of the homes of the wealthy.

**Japanese Houses** are famed for their simplicity of design and construction. They feature opaque paper windows and sliding doors. The gabled roofs shed heavy rains.

**Oriental Houseboats** provide shelter for many families. Many persons live in boats for a lifetime, cooking their meals, eating them, and sleeping in the same small quarters.

Japan Tourist Assn.; Black Star

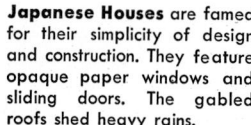

**Shelter in Modern Athens** stands below the Acropolis, the fortified hill that was the center of the city in ancient times. The ruins of the Parthenon, an ancient temple, still exist as a reminder of the glory of Greece 2,400 years ago.

and more farm homes have bathrooms and electricity.

Houses and apartment buildings in the United States may be of any style of architecture. The style depends on tastes, climate, and local tradition. In New England, people often cover the outside walls of their houses with overlapping boards, called *clapboards*. These keep out cold winds. Clapboard houses are common in many parts of the United States.

In the South, many houses have no basements. Instead, the houses are set on brick or stone pillars 2 to 4 feet high. This lets air circulate beneath the floor, which helps keep the house cool in summer.

Many persons in the Southwest build cool, sprawling Spanish-type houses of stucco or adobe. Spacious rooms and cool patios make these houses pleasant. In many larger houses, the rooms surround the patio, which usually has a fountain.

**In Canada,** there is a large lumber supply from the vast forest areas. Most of the houses are made of wood, but builders also use brick and stone. Some people in the north woods build log cabins. They build great stone fireplaces to keep the cabins warm during the cold winters, and stop the chinks in the logs with clay or grass to keep out the wind.

**In Latin America,** homes show the influence of the early Spanish and Portuguese settlers. Like many homes in the southwestern United States, these homes are built of stucco or adobe, and have tiled roofs. Larger houses often have cool, comfortable patios. In Mexico, the people usually build thick walls of adobe.

Many huts in the South American jungles resemble those in other tropical countries that have much grass and trees. The people build these huts by making frames of tree branches and covering them with grass or leaves. The Telhuelche Indians, who live near the chilly Strait of Magellan, have shelters that serve chiefly as windbreaks. They build a semicircular frame out of tree branches and cover it with animal skins.

**In Europe** the people usually build wooden houses if forests grow nearby. Where there is clay, they make bricks for their homes. If there is no clay or forest, the people build stone houses.

The Scandinavian countries have plenty of lumber. The people there build colorful wooden houses, with large beams and attractive balconies. They carve decorations on the beams and paint them bright colors. Sometimes they plaster the outside walls of their homes and paint large pictures on them.

Farmers in southern Italy often use loose stones to build their houses. These round "beehive" shelters look like dome-shaped Eskimo igloos, and often have walls 7 feet thick. The narrow windows let in only a little light. The farmers build their beds into the walls and make the floors of large, flat pieces of stone. In the Dordogne Valley of southern France, people still live in caves, as men did thousands of years ago. A dry cave can be quite comfortable in both winter and summer.

German farmers usually build houses of wood or stone, depending on which material is more plentiful. They make roofs of tile, shingles, or straw. Thatched roofs are common in both Eastern and Western Europe.

Austrians who live in the Tyrolean Alps often build two-story houses with the upper floor extending out over the ground floor. They store their firewood under the overhanging floors. Usually they make the upper story of wood and the lower story of stucco or cement. In southern Austria, the farmers often decorate their stone houses with carved posts. Many farmers in northern Austria decorate the outside walls of their houses with paintings of religious scenes.

Most houses in Poland are one-story cottages, with large windows. Farmers in the Ukraine build adobe houses which they cover with thatched roofs. Many people in Russia build small houses of logs or rough lumber with straw-thatched roofs.

**In Asia.** People usually build shelter on land, but thousands of Chinese live in houseboats that float on the rivers of central and southern China. These boats are only about 20 feet long, but entire families are born on them and live aboard all their lives. Parents tie ropes

317

**Canadian Farm Buildings** provide shelter for a farm family, their domestic animals, and harvested crops. The high-pitched roofs on the frame buildings allow snow to slide off freely during the winter months.

*Canadian Geographical Journal*

around children to keep them from falling overboard.

Most Chinese live in houses made of brick, tile, adobe, or bamboo. The country has no large forest areas. The people generally make roofs of tile and floors of wood or tile, or simply the ground itself.

Some Chinese houses have a wall around them, with a shorter wall inside the entrance gate. Visitors go through the entrance gate, then must walk around the shorter wall before entering the house. Many Chinese once believed that this kept out evil spirits. An old Chinese belief held that spirits cannot go around a corner.

In Tibet, many people live in tentlike structures called *yurts*. They make these dwellings by covering a framework of tree branches with felt. Wool for felt comes from the yak, a long-haired animal that looks somewhat like a cow. The felt-covered shelters keep the people warm during the cold winters.

The stilt houses of Borneo, the Philippines, and India sometimes have running water. Water flows to the houses through bamboo pipes from nearby hillside springs. Under the houses, the people build fences between the stilts, and keep their animals in the enclosures to protect them from wild beasts.

**In Africa.** In many parts of Africa, the people live in grass shelters, because the trees produce wood that is hard to shape into boards. The Swazi tribe of southeast Africa builds entire villages of dome-shaped grass huts. The tribesmen weave basketlike frames out of young trees and reeds that bend easily. Then they cover the frames with long, slender blades of grass, weaving the grass through the frames. A Swazi hut is so light and strong that its owner can pick it up and carry it wherever he pleases.

In areas with little rainfall, the people often build mud houses. They make a framework of wood and set a grass roof on top. They pat mud into little cakes that look like mud pies, and press them against the sticks of the frame. Then they smooth the mud with wet hands, and let the hot sun bake the mud dry. Mud houses may last 10 years or more. See AFRICA (picture: Shilluk Village in Sudan).

The Egyptians also build shelters of mud bricks, as they have done for thousands of years. They mix mud with straw, mold it into bricks, and lay the bricks in the sun to dry. Egyptian houses have flat roofs and only a few windows. Stairs lead up the outside of the houses to the roofs where the people sleep. Egyptian houses look much like the adobe dwellings of the Indians of the southwestern United States.

### History

**The First Shelters.** Before men knew how to build shelters, they may have lived in trees. Trees kept off some of the rain, and protected men from animals that could not climb. Later, they learned to pile branches and make crude shelters from the wind. Still later, men found caves to live in (see CAVE DWELLERS).

Man slowly learned to make simple tools, first of stone and much later of metal. Tools helped him build better shelters. He built his shelter from the best material he could find to suit his needs. Where there were few trees, man learned to pile stones together to make a shelter. In some places, he found that he could build shelters from the earth itself. He learned how to form clay into small blocks that could be dried in the sun. He built shelters by piling these blocks on each other.

Sometime before 4000 B.C., lake-dwelling peoples learned how to make their homes over water. They drove heavy logs into the lake bottom near the shore and built platforms on the logs. Then they built shelters on the platforms. See LAKE DWELLING.

**Homes in Ancient Civilizations.** The ancient Egyptians began building their flat-topped homes of sun-dried brick around 3100 B.C. About 2500 B.C., the Assyrians adopted this method of building. The Assyrians discovered that putting bricks into fire made them harder and stronger. They also learned how to burn a glasslike coating on their bricks. We call this *glazing*.

The ancient Greeks lived in well-made stone houses with slanted roofs that carried off snow and rain. The Greeks left the wall facing the street blank, except for a door, so they would not have to look at the narrow, dirty streets. In some places, fresh water was brought into the city through clay pipes. See GREECE, ANCIENT (Family Life).

The Romans copied many of the Greek ideas about building, and added a few of their own, such as central heating. The Romans laid rows of earthenware pipes under the floors and ran hot air or hot water through them to heat the floors. The Egyptians probably first used lead pipes to carry water, but the Romans were the first to use them widely. In fact, the word *plumbing* comes from the Latin word *plumbum*, meaning *lead*. The Romans built their houses around an *atrium*, or central court, with rooms opening off the court. Sometimes they left the court entirely open, but generally they roofed the sides and left only the center open. They made roofs of tile, and often planted lovely gardens around the houses. The Romans had only a few small windows in their walls, but they were the first people to use glass windowpanes. See ROMAN EMPIRE (Family Life).

**Shelter in the Middle Ages.** The Roman Empire collapsed in the A.D. 400's, and the improvements that the Romans had made in shelter were lost for several hundred years. German and Scandinavian tribes overran Europe. These Northmen constructed a set of buildings called a *ham*, from which the word *home* comes. The principal building of the ham was a long hall called the *heal*. The Northmen supported their buildings with frameworks of heavy wooden timbers, and filled the spaces between the timbers with clay. They covered the high-peaked roof with a layer of bark and a layer of grass sod. They also dug ditches and built earthen walls around their homes, to help protect them from attacks.

Some of these homes developed into the fortified castles of the Middle Ages, with thick stone walls, water-filled moats, and drawbridges. Inside the walls, people built stables for horses, barracks for soldiers, shops for making tools and weapons, kitchens, dining halls, and even a prison for captured enemies. Around 1300, European nobles began building fireplaces in their castles. Townspeople built walls around their towns to protect them from roving bands of warriors or robbers. Inside the walls, they built their houses several stories high and close together. Many families lived in one building.

About 1400, Europeans began to build half-timbered houses, with brick or stone foundations. They placed a tree trunk at each corner of the house, and set upright wooden beams between the trunks. Then they fastened crossbeams at the tops and bottoms of the upright beams, and added slanting braces. They covered the walls with lath, or thin wooden strips, plastered with a mixture of clay and straw.

By the 1500's, people were building their half-timbered houses three or four stories high. They added bay windows and elaborate fireplaces and stairways.

**The Influence of the Renaissance.** The Renaissance revived interest in the art and learning of ancient times (see RENAISSANCE). Details of Roman architecture were studied and adapted to form new styles. Kings and nobles hired architects to design elaborate palaces for them. These styles also influenced the houses of the

Hedrich-Blessing

**An Ultramodern Apartment Building,** such as Chicago's famous "Glass House" by Ludwig Mies van der Rohe, provides shelter for many persons. With glass walls on all sides, it is supported by steel.

**A Modern Single-Family Dwelling** provides shelter for a Santa Barbara (Calif.) family. The long, low lines of the house, stretched along the side of a hill, blend in nicely with the surrounding terrain.

Julius Shulman for *Architectural Record*

**Tree Dwellers in the Philippines** build their houses high above the ground. They can then pull up their entry ladder in order to protect themselves from their enemies.

**Pueblo Indians in the Southwest** built houses many stories high, using ladders to get to the upper floors. They also drew up the ladders to keep out their enemies.

**Castles in the Middle Ages** used moats and stone walls to give their inhabitants protection. The high towers afforded a view of any approaching danger.

## HOW SHELTER PROVIDES PROTECTION

wealthy and middle-class people. Brick became a common building material. Furniture became more plentiful, comfortable, and decorative. Hallways were built so that a person did not have to go through one room to reach another. Water was first piped into London houses about 1619.

In the 1700's, decoration became more dignified. Many wealthy people began to use wallpaper, and sash windows of glass came into common use. Fine furniture designs appeared, such as the Adam, Chippendale, Hepplewhite, and Sheraton, which were named for their makers. The styles of this period are still used.

**Indian Shelter.** Before the white men came to North America, the Indians built several kinds of shelter from the materials they found in different parts of the continent. The eastern woodland tribes made wigwams by tying wide strips of bark to frames made of young trees bent to form arches. The Iroquois sometimes built bark houses 150 feet long and 20 feet wide.

The Plains Indians had few trees, but they lived among great buffalo herds. These tribes made their tepees by tying a few poles together at the top, spreading them at the bottom like an umbrella, and covering them with buffalo skins.

Indians of the northern Pacific Coast built houses as large as 50 by 60 feet. These houses had frames of heavy beams and posts, and walls and roofs of split cedar planks. The Pueblo Indians of the Southwest often built their homes in the sides of cliffs. They reached their homes by ladders which they drew up in times of danger from wild animals or hostile tribes. Some of their houses were five stories high, with ladders between the floors. For descriptions of the different kinds of shelters that various Indian tribes built, see INDIAN, AMERICAN (Shelter).

Before the Spaniards came to Peru, the Inca made unusual stone shelters. One of these ancient Inca villages still stands at Machu Picchu, Peru. Every house is made of stone blocks cut by hand with stone tools. The Inca built their houses on several levels with stone stairways connecting the different floors. Stone aqueducts carried water to pools outside the houses where the people drank and bathed.

**Pioneer and Colonial Shelter.** The first European colonists in North America made crude homes by driving pointed logs side by side into the ground and making roofs of thatch or bunches of dried grass. Later, when the pioneers had more time, they built more elaborate log cabins out of timber from the great forests of North America.

On the vast plains west of the Mississippi River, the pioneers found grassy sod which they used to build shelters. They also dug cellars or caves in the earth, roofed them over with the little lumber they had, and lived in them through the bitter winters.

After they were settled, many of the American colonists built fine homes. Many of these homes resembled houses that the settlers remembered from England and Holland. But the American climate forced the colonists to develop a warmer kind of house. They grouped the rooms around a chimney in the middle of the house for central heating. They made the floors of planks. The New Englanders devised overlapping clapboard walls to keep out the cold winds.

The early Dutch settlers of New York and Pennsylvania brought boatloads of brick from Holland. They made their homes with Dutch roofs, some shaped like stairsteps, and some like the decorations on top of an old-fashioned clock. Such roofs are called "step-roofs" and "clock-roofs." Many of these houses still stand in the northeastern United States.

In the South, wealthy planters built beautiful homes with long porches and two-story columns. Some of these southern homes were made of brick or stone, but most of them were wooden. High ceilings helped keep the rooms cool in summer, and the long porches provided shade for part of the house, usually along the front.

**The Industrial Revolution.** During the late 1700's, the period called the Industrial Revolution began (see INDUSTRIAL REVOLUTION). Many products, including homes, became cheaper and more abundant. Homes became more comfortable in the 1800's as iron stoves replaced fireplaces. Kerosene lamps often took the place of candles, and gaslight later replaced both. Indoor toilets also became common in the late 1800's.

At the same time, factories needed more and more workers. People who worked in the factories had to live nearby, because they had no automobiles or other means of rapid transportation. Factory owners often built hundreds of small houses close together, and rented them to their employees. Many of these homes were ugly and unsanitary, and slums developed where people lived in poverty and filth. After 1850, tremendous efforts were made to clear up these conditions.

**Shelter in the 1900's.** Many changes have taken place in shelter during the 1900's. With the development of inexpensive, convenient transportation, people need not live near their jobs. They can live in the suburbs of cities or even in country areas, and still drive to work or take buses and trains.

Today, a house must supply comfort and satisfaction as well as protection. A modern home usually has a washing machine, clothes drier, dishwasher, vacuum cleaner, heating and cooling system, refrigeration, and good lighting. All these comforts make the modern home more luxurious than the most elegant palace of an ancient king.           WILLIAM A. BURNS

**Related Articles.** Many WORLD BOOK articles on countries have a section on shelter. See, for example, CHINA (Shelter). For modern shelter, see HOUSE; HOUSING. See also the following articles:

### KINDS OF SHELTER

| | | | |
|---|---|---|---|
| Castle | Igloo | Quonset Hut | Tepee |
| Hogan | Lake Dwelling | Sod House | Trailer |
| Houseboat | Log Cabin | Tent | Wigwam |

### OTHER RELATED ARTICLES

Architecture
Cave Dweller
Climate
Colonial Life in America (Houses)
Eskimo (Family Life)
Fallout Shelter
Furniture
Indian, American (Shelter)
Pioneer Life in America (A Pioneer Home)
Western Frontier Life (Frontier Towns; Life in the Country)

### Outline

I. **Why All Shelters Are Not Alike**
  A. Climate  B. Materials  C. Dangers
II. **Shelter Around the World**
  A. In the United States    D. In Europe
  B. In Canada               E. In Asia
  C. In Latin America        F. In Africa
III. **History**

### Questions

How does the amount of rainfall and snow affect the building of roofs?
Who were the first people to use central heating?
Why do some people build shelters on stilts?
What usually determines the choice of materials in building a shelter?
Where are stone "beehive" houses found?
Why do Japanese build houses of lightweight materials?
Why do people in hot, dry climates build houses with thick walls and narrow windows?
What people build shelter to protect them from spirits as well as from natural dangers?

**SHELTER BELT** is a line of trees or shrubs which are planted to protect the soil of a region from wind and erosion. The Shelter Belt Project, which later became the Prairie States Forestry Project, was created by the United States government in 1934. It was set up under the Forest Service to develop wind barriers on farms in the plains states which had suffered from erosion and dust storms. By the time it was transferred to the Soil Conservation Service in 1942, about 220 million trees had been planted on more than 30,000 farms in the Dakotas, Nebraska, Kansas, Oklahoma, and Texas. The project has since extended its work into other areas of the country.           CARL D. DUNCAN

**SHEM,** a son of Noah. See NOAH.

**SHENANDOAH.** See AIRSHIP (United States Airships).

**SHENANDOAH NATIONAL PARK,** *shen uhn DOH uh,* lies in the heart of the Blue Ridge Mountains of Virginia. Established in 1935, the park covers 193,538.66 acres. Most of it is wilderness. Nearly all of the park is at least 2,000 feet above sea level, and it has about 60 wooded mountain peaks. The highest is Hawksbill (4,049 feet). The Skyline Drive runs 105 miles through the park along the crest of the mountains. Trails lead from the drive into the mountains.

Azaleas, mountain laurel, dogwood, and other wild flowers grow abundantly there. Wildlife includes red and gray foxes, squirrels, opossums, skunks, minks, weasels, and ground hogs.

Shenandoah National Park is rich in history. George Washington passed through the area during the French and Indian Wars. Battlefields of the Civil War lie on both sides of the mountains.           JAMES J. CULLINANE

**SHENANDOAH RIVER** rises in Augusta County, Virginia, and flows northeast for 170 miles through a beautiful valley between the Blue Ridge and Allegheny mountains. This largest tributary of the Potomac River joins the main stream at Harpers Ferry, W.Va. For location, see VIRGINIA (physical map). The river is not navigable. The Shenandoah furnishes electric power to the surrounding country.           RAUS M. HANSON

**SHENANDOAH VALLEY** is a beautiful rolling area in northwestern Virginia. It includes the seven counties drained by the Shenandoah River, and much of the area drained by the James River west of the Blue Ridge Mountains. The Massanutten Ridge and other prominent hills rise above the valley. For the location of the Shenandoah Valley, see VIRGINIA (physical map).

Livestock and animal products account for three-fourths of the valley's farm income. The region has many springs, caverns, and other tourist sites. During the Civil War, the Shenandoah Valley saw heavy fighting during General "Stonewall" Jackson's Valley Campaign of 1862 and in cavalry maneuvers involving generals Philip Sheridan and Jubal Early in 1864. Civil War troops used the Valley Pike, now U.S. Route 11. Other highways run from the valley through gaps in the Blue Ridge Mountains.

The valley has several well-known preparatory schools and colleges, including Staunton Military Academy in Staunton and the Virginia Military Institute in Lexington.           RAUS M. HANSON

**SHENYANG.** See MUKDEN.

**Astronaut Alan B. Shepard** wore a 20-pound aluminized nylon pressure suit on the United States' first manned space flight.

**SHEPARD, ALAN B., JR.** (1923-   ), became the United States' first man in space on May 5, 1961. While the nation watched on television, astronaut Shepard rocketed 116 miles into space from a launching pad at Cape Canaveral (now Cape Kennedy), Fla. He landed 15 minutes later, 302 miles out in the Atlantic Ocean. He made his historic flight less than a month after Major Yuri Gagarin of Russia orbited the earth in the world's first manned space trip.

Shepard rode lying on a padded fiber glass couch in a capsule mounted on a Redstone rocket. The capsule, named *Freedom 7*, weighed more than 2,000 pounds and was shaped much like a TV picture tube. Unlike Gagarin, whose flight was controlled from the ground, Shepard manually operated controls to change the altitude of his spacecraft during the 15-minute flight. Shepard reached a top speed of 5,180 miles an hour during his flight, and endured forces 12 times the force of gravity while re-entering the earth's atmosphere.

Shepard was born on Nov. 15, 1923, in East Derry, N.H. He graduated from the United States Naval Academy in 1944. After serving on a destroyer in World War II, he took flight training and became a Navy test pilot. Shepard was one of seven men picked in 1959 to be trained as the United States' first astronauts. He received the Distinguished Flying Cross and the Distinguished Service Medal of the National Aeronautics and Space Administration (NASA) for his historic space flight. In April, 1964, Shepard became chief of the astronaut office at the Manned Spacecraft Center near Houston, Tex.   WILLIAM J. CROMIE

See also ASTRONAUT (pictures); SPACE TRAVEL.

**SHEPARD, ERNEST** (1879-   ), is a British painter and illustrator. His illustrations for the *Pooh* stories and poems by A. A. Milne are particularly well known. He also illustrated *Dream Days*, *The Reluctant Dragon*, and other stories by Kenneth Grahame, as well as many books of interest to older readers. His autobiography, *Drawn from Memory* (1957), contains his own illustrations. Shepard was born and educated in London. Early in his career, he worked as a staff cartoonist for the magazine *Punch*.   NORMAN RICE

See also LITERATURE FOR CHILDREN (picture: Christopher Robin).

**SHEPARD, HELEN MILLER GOULD.** See GOULD (Helen Miller).

**SHEPHERD COLLEGE** is a state-controlled coeducational school of liberal arts and teacher education in Shepherdstown, W.Va. The college features educational tours in Europe and the United States, and holds a political science seminar in Washington, D.C. It grants A.B. and B.S. degrees. It was founded in 1871. For enrollment, see UNIVERSITIES AND COLLEGES (table).

**SHEPHERD DOG.** See SHEEP DOG.

**SHEPHERD LIFE.** See ARAB (Nomadic Life); BEDOUIN; IRAN (Agriculture); NOMAD; SHEEP (Raising Sheep).

**SHEPILOV,** *sheh pee LOHV,* **DMITRI TROFIMOVICH** (1905-   ), was the Russian foreign minister in 1956 and 1957. He became the Communist Party's chief of propaganda in 1949, and editor of *Pravda*, the party's main newspaper, in 1952. Shepilov entered the party's Presidium in 1956, but he was expelled in 1957. He was born in the Krasnodar area near the Sea of Azov.

**SHERATON,** *SHER uh tun,* **THOMAS** (1751-1806), was the last of the great English furniture designers of the 1700's. He combined a highly developed sense of proportion with an elegance and originality of treatment in his pieces. They were severely simple in form but light and perfectly balanced with decorative details.

Sheraton was born in Stockton-on-Tees, and went to London about 1790 as a journeyman cabinetmaker. He never had a shop of his own. Besides being a furniture maker, he was an author, publisher, bookseller, teacher of drawing, and preacher. He died a poor man. See also FURNITURE (Sheraton).   OTTO V. HULA

**SHERBROOKE,** Que. (pop. 75,690; alt. 521 ft.), is the trading center of a rich agricultural and industrial region. It lies at the juncture of the Saint Francis and Magog rivers, about 80 miles east of Montreal and about 30 miles north of the United States border (see QUEBEC [political map]). Sherbrooke factories make clothing, silk and artificial silk products, machine tools, rubber goods, jewelry, boats, iron and steel products, building materials, paper products, and plastics.

Gilbert Hyatt, the first settler, built a homestead in 1796. The settlement was known as Hyatt's Mills until 1818, when it was renamed in honor of a former governor-general of Canada, Lord Sherbrooke. The city was incorporated in 1875. A large number of people of both French and English descent live there, and it has become the custom to elect alternately French- and English-speaking mayors. Sherbrooke has a mayor-council form of government.   M. G. BALLANTYNE

**SHERBROOKE, UNIVERSITY OF,** is a coeducational Roman Catholic school in Sherbrooke, Quebec. It offers bachelor's, master's, and doctor's degrees. It was started in 1875 as the Seminary of Sherbrooke, and became a degree-granting university in 1954. For enrollment, see CANADA (table: Universities).   ROGER MALTAIS

**SHERIDAN,** Wyo. (pop. 11,651; alt. 3,740 ft.), is the largest city in the northern part of the state. It lies in the fertile Goose Creek Valley, about 15 miles east of the Bighorn Mountains (see WYOMING [political map]). Sheridan is the seat of Sheridan County.

Vacationists enjoy nearby dude ranches. The Eaton brothers, Howard, Alden, and Willis, established the West's first dude ranch near Sheridan in 1904. Coal, livestock, and agriculture contribute to Sheridan's economy. The city was founded in 1882.         T. A. LARSON

**SHERIDAN, PHILIP HENRY** (1831-1888), was a Union general during the Civil War. A captain at the outbreak of the war, "Little Phil," as he became known, rose rapidly in rank. He commanded a division at the battles of Perryville and Stones River, and became a major general of volunteers. In 1863, he became a corps commander in the Army of the Cumberland. He fought at Chickamauga, and in the Battle of Chattanooga his corps broke the Confederate line on Missionary Ridge. Grant named Sheridan to lead the cavalry of the Army of the Potomac in 1864.

Brown Bros.
**Philip H. Sheridan**

Sheridan guarded the flanks of the Union Army in Virginia, and attacked General Robert E. Lee's communications. When Confederate forces appeared in the Shenandoah Valley, General Ulysses S. Grant gave Sheridan command of all Union forces in that area. Sheridan was instructed to drive the enemy from the valley and to destroy the region's economic resources. He defeated the Confederates, under General Jubal A. Early, at Winchester, Fisher's Hill, and Cedar Creek.

Sheridan was at Winchester when fighting broke out at Cedar Creek. He rode 11 miles to take command of his men, who had been driven back 4 miles from Cedar Creek. Thomas B. Read's stirring poem, "Sheridan's Ride" (1865), wrongly indicates that Sheridan rode 20 miles. Returning to Grant's command, Sheridan broke Lee's right flank at Five Forks, and helped force the evacuation of Petersburg and Richmond. In 1864, he became a major general in the Regular Army.

There is a mystery surrounding Sheridan's birthplace. His parents came from County Cavan, Ireland, and he was reared at Somerset, Ohio. He was graduated from the United States Military Academy.

After the Civil War, Sheridan was commander of the Division of the Gulf, where he worked to force the French out of Mexico. During Reconstruction, he commanded the Fifth Military District (Louisiana and Texas). Later, he headed the Department of the Missouri, and conducted operations against hostile Indians. He became a lieutenant general in 1869, and the following year he went to Europe to observe the Franco-Prussian War. He succeeded General William T. Sherman in 1884 as army commander, and in 1888 he became a full general.

In the closing months of his life, Sheridan wrote his recollections, *Personal Memoirs*. He was buried in the National Cemetery at Arlington, Va.   T. HARRY WILLIAMS

See also CIVIL WAR (picture: Sheridan's Ride).

**SHERIDAN, RICHARD BRINSLEY** (1751-1816), was an Irish dramatist and politician. During his brief writing career, he produced several sparkling comedies. In later life, he was a brilliant speaker in the British Parliament.

While in his early 20's, Sheridan wrote *The Rivals* (1775). This comedy has a memorable character named Mrs. Malaprop who is a genius at using words incorrectly, as when she says, "Illiterate him, I say, quite from your memory." *The School for Scandal* (1777), Sheridan's finest play, is one of the great comedies of English drama. With glittering wit, the play exposes society people who love malicious gossip. It also contrasts a careless but kind young man, Charles Surface, with his scheming and selfish brother Joseph. *The Critic* (1779), a short satiric play, attacked theatrical fashions in a witty manner. Sheridan's other plays include the farce *St. Patrick's Day* (1775) and a comic opera *The Duenna* (1775). He also adapted Sir John Vanbrugh's comedy *The Relapse* into *A Trip to Scarborough* (1777).

Sheridan was born in Dublin, the son of an actor-manager, and grew up in England. Sheridan eloped with a beautiful singer in 1772, and fought two duels because of her. In 1776, he became manager of the Drury Lane theater, and it was his chief source of income for many years.

In 1780, Sheridan was elected to Parliament. From that date until 1812, he devoted himself to politics. A gifted orator, Sheridan made a memorable speech in the trial of Warren Hastings (see HASTINGS, WARREN). A man of great charm and wit, Sheridan lived a busy social life among the rich and the powerful. He is best remembered for his witty plays, but he spent little of his life as a writer.        THOMAS H. FUJIMURA

**SHERIFF,** in the United States, is one of the chief administrative officers of a county. It is his duty to take charge of prisoners, to oversee juries, and to prevent breaches of the peace. He also carries out the judgments of the county court. For example, if the court gives a judgment against a debtor, the sheriff seizes his property and sells it to satisfy the claims of creditors. The sheriff may perform these duties himself, or he may give other persons the power to act in his name. These persons are called *deputy sheriffs*. In most states, the voters elect the sheriff. In Canada, sheriffs are appointed.

The word *sheriff* comes from old England. Each *shire*, or county, had a headman known as a *reeve*. The title *shire reeve* gradually came to be run together in the single word *sheriff*.          H. F. ALDERFER

See also COUNTY; LAW ENFORCEMENT; SHIRE.

**SHERMAN** is the family name of two American brothers, a military leader and a statesman.

**William Tecumseh Sherman** (1820-1891) was a Union general in the Civil War and the commanding general of the United States Army for 14 years. His greatest feat in the war was to march an army across Georgia, "from Atlanta to the sea," and then through South Carolina. On the way, he destroyed the South's last economic resources. Because he waged economic warfare against a civilian society, Sherman has been called the first modern general. He is supposed to have said, "War is hell."

Sherman commanded a brigade at the first battle of Bull Run. He was promoted to brigadier general of

323

## SHERMAN, FORREST PERCIVAL

volunteers, and took command of the Department of Kentucky. His anxiety over the safety of his position caused him to be relieved. Early in 1862, he came under Ulysses S. Grant's command, and fought with Grant at Shiloh. As major general and corps commander, he took part in the capture of Vicksburg in 1863. Later he helped relieve the Union army at Chattanooga.

In 1864 Grant appointed Sherman commander of Union forces in the West. With three armies totaling about 100,000 men, Sherman captured Atlanta, and then started his famous march to the sea. After Savannah fell, he moved north through the Carolinas. In April, General Joseph E. Johnston surrendered to him.

Sherman was born in Lancaster, Ohio. His father died when Sherman was young, and Thomas Ewing, an Ohio political figure, adopted him. Sherman was graduated from the United States Military Academy. He served at various posts in the South, and fought in the Mexican War. In 1853 he resigned from the army.

Brown Bros.
**William Tecumseh Sherman**

Everything Sherman tried as a civilian seemed to end in failure. He became a banker in San Francisco, and the bank collapsed in the panic of 1857. He practiced law in Kansas, and lost the only case he ever tried. He became superintendent of a military academy in Louisiana (later Louisiana State University), but resigned when the state seceded. Then he became president of a St. Louis street railway company.

Sherman was a major general in the regular army at the end of the war. He succeeded Grant in 1869 as commanding general of the army with the rank of full general. Many people tried to induce him to run for President, but he refused. He said, "I will not accept if nominated and will not serve if elected." He wrote *Memoirs of General W. T. Sherman*.   T. HARRY WILLIAMS

**John Sherman** (1823-1900) was an American statesman. He became noted for introducing the silver and antitrust laws that bear his name (see TRUST [Trust Legislation]). For almost 50 years Sherman held office in Washington, D.C., either as a Republican member of Congress or in the Cabinet. He was elected to the House of Representatives from Ohio in 1854, and seven years later was elected to the Senate. Sherman served as secretary of the treasury from 1877 to 1881, and then returned to the Senate. His last public office was as secretary of state in 1897 and 1898. He was born in Lancaster, Ohio.   ARTHUR A. EKIRCH, JR.

**SHERMAN, FORREST PERCIVAL** (1896-1951), was the youngest man up to that time to hold the United States Navy's top post, chief of naval operations. He assumed this post in 1949, when the navy was deeply disturbed by technological changes and conflicts within the Department of Defense. By his ability and knowledge, he guided the service through a difficult period.

Sherman was born in Merrimack, N.H. During World War II, he commanded the aircraft carrier *Wasp*, until it was sunk in the Solomon Islands. Later, as deputy chief of staff to Fleet Admiral Chester W. Nimitz, he prepared plans for most of the navy's Central Pacific campaigns. He took part in the Japanese surrender talks, and became a vice-admiral in 1945.   DONALD W. MITCHELL

**SHERMAN, JAMES SCHOOLCRAFT** (1855-1912), served as Vice-President of the United States from 1909 to 1912 under President William Howard Taft. He became the first Vice-President to be renominated in the history of the Republican party, but he died during the election campaign. His death created a unique situation in American politics. It was too late to replace him on the ballot, and over 3 million people voted for Taft and Sherman. Sherman's eight electoral votes were cast for Columbia University president Nicholas Murray Butler.

Sherman was born in Utica, N.Y. He started practicing law in 1880, and served as mayor of Utica in 1884. He served in the U.S. House of Representatives from 1887 to 1891 and from 1893 to 1909.   IRVING G. WILLIAMS

See also VICE-PRESIDENT OF THE UNITED STATES (picture).

**SHERMAN, ROGER** (1721-1793), was the only man who signed all four of these great documents: the Articles of Association (1774), the Declaration of Independence (1776), the Articles of Confederation (1777), and the United States Constitution (1787). Sherman was born in Newton, Mass., but in 1743 he moved to Connecticut where he became prominent in business and politics. He served as judge of the Connecticut Superior Court from 1766 to 1789.

U&U
**Roger Sherman**

Sherman feared excesses when the revolutionary movement began, but he was among the first to deny the supremacy of the British Parliament over the colonies. He was influential in the Continental Congress, where John Adams said he was "as firm in the cause of American Independence as Mount Atlas." During the Constitutional Convention of 1787, Sherman presented the famous Connecticut Compromise that resolved the differences between the large and small states on representation in the national legislature (see UNITED STATES CONSTITUTION [The Compromises]). He served his state in the U.S. Congress as representative from 1789 to 1791, and as a senator from 1791 to 1793.   CLARENCE L. VER STEEG

**SHERMAN ANTITRUST ACT.** See HARRISON, BENJAMIN (Domestic Affairs); TRUST (Trust Legislation).

**SHERMAN SILVER PURCHASE ACT.** See CLEVELAND, GROVER (Saving the Gold Standard); HARRISON, BENJAMIN (Domestic Affairs).

**SHERPA.** See NEPAL (The People).

**SHERRINGTON, SIR CHARLES SCOTT** (1861-1952), a British scientist, shared the 1932 Nobel prize for physiology and medicine with Edgar D. Adrian. His researches contributed greatly to understanding how the nerves coordinate and control body functions. He wrote *The Integrative Action of the Nervous System* (1906). This book explained the plan of the brain and spinal cord, based on numerous reflex pathways by which the activities of the body are adjusted to the environment. Sherrington was born in London. MORDECAI L. GABRIEL

**SHERWOOD, ROBERT EMMET** (1896-1955), was an American playwright, journalist, and biographer who stressed the evils of war in his writings. His play *Idiot's Delight* (1936) lamented the approaching outbreak of war in Europe. *Abe Lincoln in Illinois* (1938) used Lincoln's own words to show the necessity of firm action in the face of war. *There Shall Be No Night* (1940) opposed Russia's invasion of Finland. It was also Sherwood's stand against what he called mankind's hysterical desire to escape from reality. All three of these plays won Pulitzer prizes.

Sherwood was born in New Rochelle, N.Y. In 1920, he joined *Life* magazine. He became a nationally-known film critic at *Life*, and was the magazine's associate editor from 1924 to 1928.

Sherwood's first produced play, *The Road To Rome* (1927), was a satire on Hannibal's campaign against Rome. It said every sacrifice in the name of war is wasted. *The Petrified Forest* (1935) showed criminal morality triumphing in the world. During World War II, Sherwood wrote speeches for President Roosevelt. He won a Pulitzer prize for his biography *Roosevelt and Hopkins: An Intimate History* (1948). THOMAS A. ERHARD

**SHERWOOD FOREST.** See ROBIN HOOD.

**SHETLAND ISLANDS** lie in the Atlantic Ocean near the North Sea. The islands, Great Britain's most northerly European possession, make up a county of Scotland. The county's official name is *Zetland*. They lie about 50 miles northeast of Scotland's Orkney Islands, and 210 miles west of Norway. For location, see EUROPE (color map).

More than a hundred islands make up the group, but people live on fewer than 20 of them. Some islands have only lighthouse keepers and a few shepherds. The islands have an area of 551 square miles, and a population of about 17,400. These people are of Scandinavian origin and their language still contains many Icelandic words. Many Norse customs still survive. Ancient stone towers stand on the islands. The county seat, Lerwick, is on Mainland, the largest island.

The Shetland Islands have a wild, colorful beauty. Their rugged coasts rise from the ocean in deeply cut cliffs. Lonely lighthouses stand on hills which overlook the sea. Many tourists visit the islands in summer, when daylight remains almost around the clock. In winter, there is little daylight. The famous small, shaggy Shetland ponies, the long-wooled Shetland sheep, and an unusually small breed of cattle inhabit the islands. The islands contain peat, copper, and iron deposits.

The main occupations of the Shetland people are weaving, knitting, fishing, and raising cattle, sheep, and ponies. Farmers raise oats, barley, and vegetables. Knitting hosiery and shawls is an important home industry. There once was considerable whale hunting off the Shetland Islands. FREDERICK G. MARCHAM

**SHETLAND PONY** is the smallest of all horses. It stands from 32 to 46 inches high. The original Shetlands came from the Shetland Islands of Great Britain. They were short and stocky. People used Shetlands to pull coal carts in the mines, because they were strong and required little food. Shetlands were imported to the United States as children's pets. However, horse breed-

Frank C. Zak

**Riding a Shetland Pony Thrills Most Youngsters.**

ers decided that a lighter, flashier type of pony would be more popular. To gain these characteristics, they bred the Shetland with the Hackney pony. Today, many Shetlands have so much Hackney blood that they are no longer suitable for children. But their slender legs; fine, delicate heads; and silken manes and tails make them popular show animals.

Some Shetlands still make excellent pets for children. However, they are intelligent and crafty animals, and must be trained by an expert. MARGARET CABELL SELF

**SHETLAND SHEEP DOG** is considered one of the most beautiful of all herding dogs. It is short, standing only from 13 to 16 inches high. It was bred to herd the small livestock of the Shetland Islands. The Shetland looks dainty and fragile, but it is actually a rugged dog, capable of many hours of hard work. Sheep raisers in the western United States use the Shetland because it can cover large areas without getting sore feet. The Shetland looks somewhat like a miniature collie. It is more gentle than some of the heavier types of herding breeds. It makes a good pet and an excellent watchdog. See also DOG (color picture: Working Dogs). OLGA DAKAN

**SHEVCHENKO,** *shehf CHAYN koh,* **TARAS** (1814-1861), was a leading Ukrainian patriot and the Ukraine's most famous poet. Shevchenko and other Ukrainians organized the Society of Saints Cyril and Methodius in 1843. The society led an unsuccessful movement to win the Ukraine's independence from Russia. To punish Shevchenko, the Russian government sent him to serve at an army post in the Ural Mountains in 1847. Shevchenko's poems include *Katerina* (1840), *Haydamaki* (1841), and *The Dream* (1844). His poems describe the hard life of the Ukrainian people and express their desire for freedom. He was born in Kiev. GEORGE KISH

**SHEVOUT.** See SHABUOT.

**SHEYENNE RIVER.** See NORTH DAKOTA (Rivers and Lakes).

**SHIAH** or SHIITE. See ISLAM (Sects); IRAN (People).

325

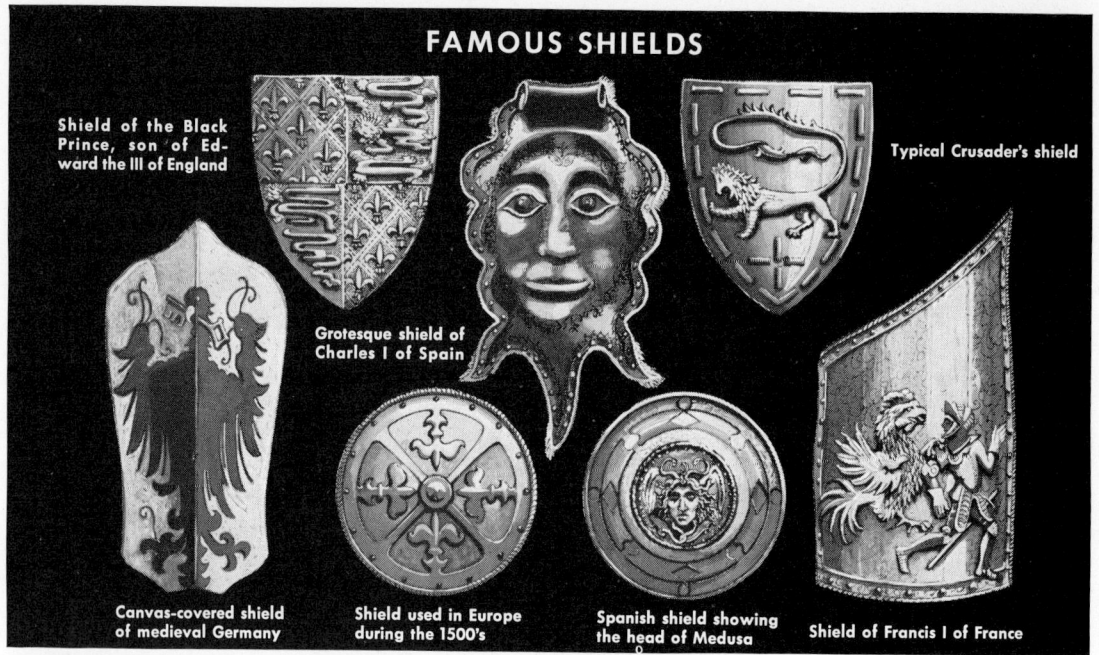

**SHIELD,** *sheeld,* was the chief means of protection in war from earliest times until the invention of firearms. Shields of wood, sometimes covered with animal hide, could be held in one hand to ward off blows of an enemy, while the other hand was free to use a club, sword, or spear. Later, metal shields were used.

Shields were of many sizes and shapes. The Greeks used both round and oval shields which were heavy and almost covered the body. A large shield called the *clipeus,* at first circular, was used by Greeks and Romans. The Romans introduced the rectangular shield. They also used a large, oblong shield called a *scutum.*

During the Middle Ages, both armored knights and common foot soldiers used the shield. The knights' shields were decorated with their coats of arms, so they could be recognized even when in full armor. If the shield was to be held at arm's length, it was called a *buckler.* If fastened to the arm, and held across the body in combat, the shield was called a *target.*

Many tribes still carry shields to war or when hunting wild animals. These shields are usually made of wood covered with hide. *Shield,* in modern warfare, is the armor-plate covering installed around a gun to protect the gun's crew from enemy fire. THEODORE ROPP

See also ARMOR.

**SHIELDS, JAMES** (1806-1879), served as governor of the Oregon Territory and as a brigadier general of volunteers in the Mexican and Civil wars. A Democrat, he also served as a U.S. Senator from Illinois, Minnesota, and Missouri. Shields was born in County Tyrone, Ireland, and came to the United States in 1826. Illinois placed a statue of Shields in the Statuary Hall collection in the U.S. Capitol in 1893. T. HARRY WILLIAMS

**SHIITE.** See ISLAM (Sects).

## SHIELDS OF ANCIENT AND MEDIEVAL TIMES

A foot soldier ready for battle. He is holding a target shield.

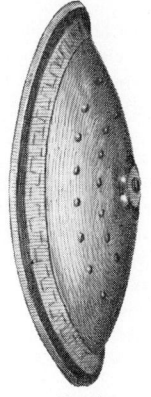

Greek

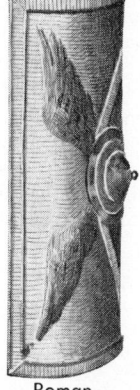

Roman

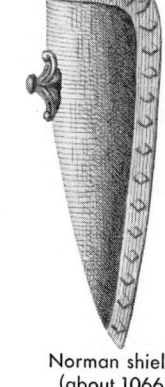

Norman shield (about 1066)

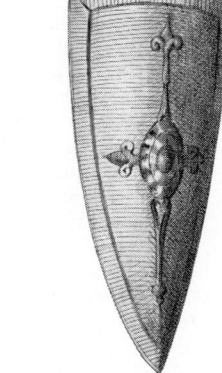

English Crusader's shield during the Third Crusade (1189-1192)

326

**SHIKELLAMY,** SHICK el LAH mih, or SWATANEY, swah TAH nih ( ? -1748), was an Oneida Indian chief. He represented the Iroquois Confederacy to the colonial government of Pennsylvania, and attended most treaty meetings between whites and Indians. He was born in Montreal. See also IROQUOIS INDIANS.

**SHIKOKU.** See JAPAN (Land Regions).

**SHILLING** is a coin in the English money system. It is equal to 12 pence, and is $\frac{1}{20}$ of an English pound sterling. For the value of the pound in dollars, see MONEY (table, Values). One shilling equals 12 U.S. cents. See also PINE-TREE SHILLING.

**Face and Reverse Side of a Shilling of 1723**
Chase Manhattan Bank Money Museum

**SHILOH, BATTLE OF.** See CIVIL WAR (The War in the West; table: Major Battles).

**SHILOH NATIONAL MILITARY PARK.** See NATIONAL PARK (National Military Parks).

**SHIMER COLLEGE.** See UNIVERSITIES AND COLLEGES (table).

**SHIMMY.** See DANCING (The 1900's).

**SHIMONOSEKI, TREATY OF.** See CHINESE-JAPANESE WARS.

**SHINGLES** is a painful disease in which small clusters of blisters form on the skin of the face, neck, chest, stomach, or limbs. These blisters usually follow the path taken by a *sensory* (feeling) nerve. Doctors call shingles *herpes zoster*. It is believed that shingles results from a virus infection of the nervous system.

Shingles often starts with intense pain in the area where the blisters form later. The blisters are usually pink or white. At first, they contain a colorless liquid, but pus may form later. After about a week, the blisters dry up and disappear. The diseased area may feel irritated after the blisters dry up.

Children usually recover quickly from shingles. The disease is more serious for adults. They recover slowly and the pain lasts longer. Doctors treat shingles with pain-relieving drugs, and when pain is intense, may inject nerve areas with an anesthetic (pain-blocker). Other treatments include ultraviolet rays, X rays, and antibiotics. See also CHICKEN POX. LOUIS D. BOSHES

**SHINGLES** are thin pieces of wood, asbestos, slate, or other materials that are used to cover the roofs and outer walls of buildings. Wooden roof shingles are usually 16 inches long. They are cut thicker at one end, and taper from about $\frac{1}{2}$ an inch to less than $\frac{1}{8}$ of an inch.

Shingles laid on a roof should overlap so that there are at least three layers at all points. On walls, however, only two layers need be nailed over each other.

*Flat-grain* shingles are made by sawing wood parallel to the annual growth rings. *Edge-grain* shingles are sawed more or less at right angles to the rings. A roof laid with good edge-grain shingles will last many years longer than a roof laid with flat-grain shingles. Most shingles produced in North America are made of western red cedar. ARTHUR KOEHLER

See also HOUSE.

**SHINN, EVERETT** (1876-1953), was an American painter and illustrator. Most of his works portray theater life, with its changing moods and lively movement. Shinn also designed sets for the theater and for films.

Shinn was born in Woodstown, N.J. He began his career in 1893 as a newspaper illustrator and cartoonist. He worked in Philadelphia and New York City, and illustrated for magazines in his later years. The influence of his work as an illustrator can be seen in the brilliant draftsmanship in his paintings. In 1908, Shinn joined a group of realistic painters organized by Robert Henri, and called *The Eight* (later the *Ashcan School*). Within this group, Shinn showed the lightest and most delicate touch in his paintings. For more information on *The Eight*, see HENRI, ROBERT. E. MAURICE BLOCH

**SHINNY,** or SHINTY. See FIELD HOCKEY (History).

**SHINTOISTS,** SHIN toh ists, are followers of Shinto, a religion of Japan. Shinto, which means *the Way of the Gods*, was originally a form of nature worship. Its gods were those of forests, waterfalls, rivers, and the sea. People still worship such gods in many Shinto shrines. Confucian influence raised standards of conduct and culture in Shinto, and Buddhist influence brought deeper thought into it. The religion later had two distinct phases, Sect Shinto and State Shinto.

*Sect Shinto* centers around the teachings of a particular leader or group. Individual sects carry out programs of religious education and worship. *State Shinto*, developed in the late 1800's, centered around the history of the Japanese people. It aimed to instill patriotism built around the emperor, who was thought to be a descendant of the sun goddess, highest of the Shinto deities. The government supported State Shinto, and the emperor took a leading part in ceremonies at the Grand Imperial Shrine at Ise and other shrines.

After World War II, the Japanese government withdrew its support of State Shinto, and the emperor denied his divinity. But large numbers of Japanese continued to practice Sect Shinto. GEORGE NOEL MAYHEW

See also JAPAN (Religion); RELIGION (Religions of the World); TORII.

**A Shinto Priest** at the Ise Shrine in Japan twirls a stick in a notched board to make a pure ceremonial fire by friction.
H. Haga, Fuji Service & Trading

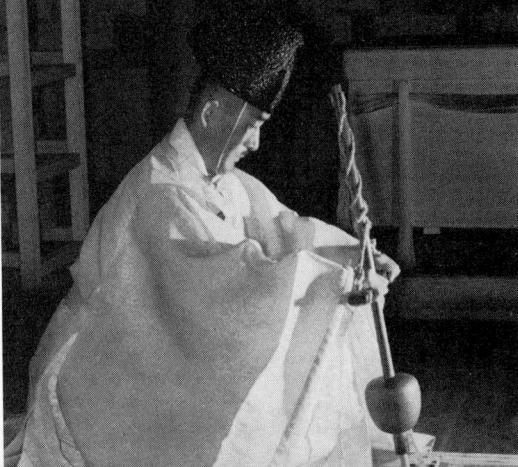

**A Giant Ocean Liner** overshadows a toy tugboat as it steams slowly past the shore of Staten Island, N.Y. Some ocean liners can carry more than 2,000 passengers.

# SHIP & SHIPPING

Ship's figurehead made in Boston probably before 1832. Photo courtesy National Gallery of Art, Index of American Design.

*Robert S. Burns, the contributor of this article, is Assistant Marine News Editor for the New York* Herald Tribune. *Edouard A. Stackpole, who critically reviewed this article, is President of the Nantucket Historical Association.*

**SHIP AND SHIPPING.** Every day, hundreds of ships enter and leave ports throughout the world. They cross the oceans carrying passengers and cargo from country to country. The ships that sail the seas provide man with one of his most important kinds of transportation.

For hundreds of years, ships gave man his best means of exploring coasts of the unknown world. Ancient sailors first crossed the Mediterranean Sea in vessels propelled by oars and sails. Three tiny sailing ships—the *Santa María,* the *Pinta,* and the *Niña*—brought Christopher Columbus and his men to the Western Hemisphere. Graceful, speedy packet and clipper ships carried cargoes around the world in the 1800's. Today, few thrills can match a voyage on such modern liners as the *United States* and the *France.*

No matter what kind of ships men have used, they have always answered the call of the sea. Sailors have battled weather and waves for thousands of years. The courage of seamen and the beauty of their ships have inspired artists and writers of every nation and time. The vessel might be a slow-moving galley propelled by oars, a sleek sailing ship with wind-filled sails, or a powerful liner driven by whirring turbines. But a ship has always meant excitement and adventure.

In sailing days, a ship was a three-masted, square-rigged vessel such as the famous "Old Ironsides," the *Constitution.* Smaller vessels with different sail arrangements included schooners and sloops. Today, the word *ship* usually means any large, seagoing vessel driven by engines. Small craft not equipped to cross large bodies of water are usually called *boats.* But some larger vessels, such as Great Lakes freighters, are also called boats. See BOATS AND BOATING.

This article chiefly describes *merchant* ships, those that carry cargo and passengers. For a description of the many kinds of warships, see WARSHIP.

### Kinds of Ships

**Passenger Ships,** or *ocean liners,* are luxurious, seagoing hotels. These fast, graceful vessels are the queens of the sea. They range in size from the *France,* the world's largest ocean liner, down to the combination passenger-cargo ships. The *France* is 1,035 feet long, and can carry 2,047 passengers. Some passenger-cargo ships carry only 40 to 50 travelers. Most liners sail at average speeds of between 20 and 25 knots. But the *United States,* the world's fastest merchant ship, has a *cruising* (normal) speed of 30 knots. Ocean liners normally cross the Atlantic Ocean in about five days, sailing from New York City or Montreal to England or France. The voyage across the Pacific Ocean is longer. It takes about 15 days for a liner to sail from San Francisco to Yokohama, Japan.

In a busy port, the long, sleek ocean liners can easily be distinguished from other ships. The liners have hulls topped by three or more *decks* (stories) of cabins that extend most of the length of the vessels. A liner also has one or more tall smokestacks, and a long row of lifeboats hung along each side of the ship.

**Freighters,** or cargo ships, are the workhorses of the sea. They carry cargo across the oceans and along the coasts of the world. The hull of a freighter is usually shorter than that of an ocean liner, but has the same general appearance. The upper part of a freighter differs greatly from the top of an ocean liner. The cabins of a

### NAUTICAL MEASUREMENTS

**Deadweight Tonnage** is the actual carrying capacity of a freighter or tanker expressed in long tons (2,240 pounds each). It includes cargo, crew, fuel, supplies, and spare parts.

**Displacement** is the quantity used to measure naval ships. It is the weight of the volume of water *displaced* (occupied) by a ship, measured in long tons.

**Gross Tonnage** is the measurement used for passenger ships. It is based on the number of cubic feet of enclosed space. Each 100 cubic feet equals a gross ton.

**Knot** is one nautical mile an hour. The *International Nautical Mile* equals 6,076 feet. Navigators usually round this off to 6,080 feet. A land mile is 5,280 feet.

**Net Tonnage** is a measure of the revenue-producing spaces of ships. It is figured by deducting from the gross tonnage cabins, engine rooms, and other spaces that have no cargo-carrying capacity. It is used to determine taxes, canal tolls, and port charges.

## SHIP AND SHIPPING

freighter are usually amidships. But more cargo ships are being built with their engines and cabins at the narrow, tapering stern. This enables the ship to carry more cargo, because the widest part of the hull can be used as a cargo hold.

Long poles called *booms* are attached to the bottom of vertical *masts*. Steel cables running from the masts and booms raise and lower cargo through *hatchways* (openings in the deck). The hatchways lead to the *holds* (storage places for cargo). Freighters carry from 1,000 to 13,000 tons of cargo, depending on their type and the route they travel. They have speeds ranging from 10 to 24 knots.

Dock workers called *longshoremen* load most cargo aboard freighters. The cargo is usually swung aboard in rope nets or on *pallets* (flat wooden platforms) that are lifted into the air and lowered into holds. On some freighters, called *roll-on, roll-off* ships, trucks and railroad boxcars can be rolled through openings in the sides or stern. *Lift-on, lift-off* freighters carry loaded truck trailers or metal containers that are lifted on board by cranes. Ships that carry bulk cargoes such as coal, wheat, or iron ore are loaded by means of shore equipment that pours the material directly into the holds. This reduces the time needed to load cargo.

Freighters in *liner service* or *berth service* carry general cargo on a regular schedule along a definite route, just as passenger ships or railroad trains do. *Tramp* freighters do not follow a regular schedule. They carry cargo as they find it. For example, a tramp ship may load coal at Norfolk, Va., and unload it at Bergen, Norway. Then the vessel might take Norwegian ore to Baltimore, Md., go to Philadelphia to pick up grain for India, and then return to Baltimore with another cargo.

**Tankers** carry oil, chemicals, and other liquids. The hull of a tanker contains huge tanks that give the vessels their name. The engine rooms and some cabins are located at the stern. The location of the machinery at the stern keeps sparks and heat from engines and boilers from causing an explosion of escaping gases. Some cabins and the tanker's *bridge* (control center) are also located amidships.

**Bulk Carriers** resemble tankers from afar, but they are more like self-propelled boxcars. They carry coal,

**The Crew of a Luxury Liner** works smoothly as a team for the comfort, safety, health, and enjoyment of the passengers. This picture shows almost all the 583-member crew of the American liner S.S. **Constitution** assembled on the ship's upper decks.

DECK STAFF   ENGINEERING STAFF   ASSISTANT COOKS

STEWARDS AND BAGGAGEMEN

CAPTAIN AND EXECUTIVE STAFF

CHEFS

STEWARDESSES   NURSES, SOCIAL DIRECTOR, SHIP'S OFFICERS

American Export Lines

330

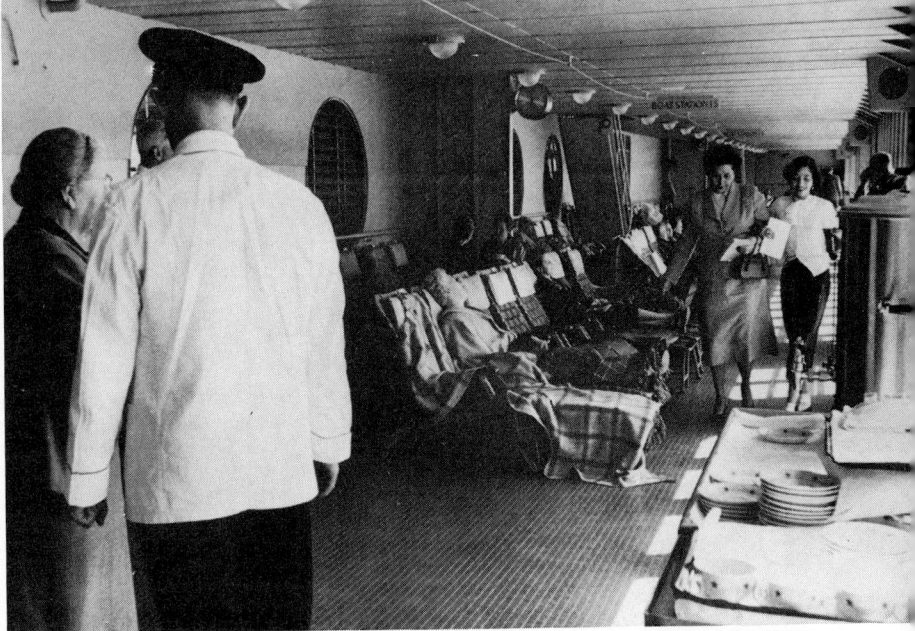

**Promenade Deck** of an ocean liner where passengers can relax in deck chairs or take part in games such as shuffleboard. Here, stewards serve between-meals refreshments to the passengers.

United States Lines

grain, ore, cement, and wood chips. Some bulk carriers are called *self-unloaders*, because they are fitted with conveyors that automatically unload cargo.

**Refrigerator Ships** have cargo holds that are large refrigerators. These holds keep meat, fruits, and vegetables fresh during long ocean voyages. Refrigerator ships carry bananas from the tropics to every major port of the world. These vessels also carry meat and dairy products from Australia and New Zealand to Great Britain, transport beef from Argentina to the United States, and provide other services.

**Great Lakes Ore Boats** are special ships that carry iron ore, limestone, and coal to steel production centers along the Great Lakes. The long, low ore boats have their engines aft, their cabins at the bow and stern, and their holds in between. These ships can be loaded and unloaded quickly, so they can make as many trips as possible during the ice-free months.

### A Trip on an Ocean Liner

**The Crew** of an ocean liner works as a team to make the voyage as pleasant as possible for the passengers. A

---------- INTERESTING FACTS ABOUT SHIPS ----------

**Fastest Merchant Ship** is the American liner *United States*, with a cruising speed of 30 knots.

**Fastest Sailing Ships** were the American *clipper* ships of the 1800's. They could travel 20 knots. Two of them, the *Flying Cloud* and the *Andrew Jackson*, sailed from New York City, around the tip of South America, to San Francisco in 89 days.

**Fastest Transatlantic Crossing** by a merchant ship was made in July, 1952, by the *United States*. The vessel sailed 2,942 miles from Ambrose Lightship at the entrance to New York Harbor to Bishop Rock Lighthouse at the western end of the English Channel in 3 days 10 hours 40 minutes. The *United States* traveled at an average speed of 35.59 knots, or about 41 land miles an hour.

**Greatest Peacetime Ship Disaster** occurred in 1912 when the British liner *Titanic* struck an iceberg and sank with a loss of 1,517 lives.

**Largest Great Lakes Boat** is the 712-foot-long *Edward L. Ryerson*. This boat and four other boats of its class can carry 26,000 long tons of iron ore each.

**Largest and Longest Passenger Ship** is the French liner *France*. It is 1,035 feet long, and can carry 2,047 passengers.

**The Brain and the Brawn of a Ship.** Deep in the hull, pulsating engines, *below*, turn the propellers, while high in the wheelhouse, *right*, sailors steer the ship.

United States Lines

33I

## SHIP AND SHIPPING

large liner, such as the *United States*, carries a crew of about a thousand men. This means that the ship has about one crewman for every two passengers. The personnel of a passenger ship is divided into three departments. These are (1) the deck department, (2) the engine department, and (3) the steward's department. Radio operators and pursers are in the deck department. A passenger ship also has doctors, nurses, musicians, barbers, and other personnel who provide services for the passengers.

*The Officers* are in charge of the ship. They give orders to the sailors and keep discipline aboard the vessel. The *captain* is the highest-ranking officer. He has full command of the vessel and everyone on it, including the passengers. He also has full responsibility for the safety of the ship and the people it carries. Various officers assist the captain. The *deck* officers stand four-hour *watches* on the ship's bridge. While on watch, the deck officers *navigate* the ship, or keep it on course. Deck officers are also in charge of the cargo and of keeping the ship clean and in good repair. The highest-ranking deck officer is the *staff captain*, the captain's right-hand man. Below him, in order of rank, are the *chief mate*, the *second mate*, the *third mate*, and, on some ships, a *fourth mate*, also called a *junior third mate*. The *chief engineer* has charge of the ship's *engineering* department. He has the final say in matters concerning the ship's machinery. The chief engineer is aided by the first, second, third, and fourth *assistant engineers*, who stand watches in the engine room.

Other officers on an ocean liner include the *radio officer* and his assistants who have charge of the ship's radios, and the *purser* and his assistants who keep the ship's records. Pursers pay the crew, keep cargo and passenger records, and perform hundreds of other clerical jobs.

*The Crewmen* are known by the jobs they do in the different departments. Members of the deck department are often considered the real "sailors" on a ship. The *ordinary* seamen, who do painting and other maintenance work, and the *able-bodied* seamen, who stand watches as lookouts, make up the majority of the deck department. The *boatswain* (pronounced *BOH s'n*) is the ship's foreman and the highest-ranking man in the deck department. Other men in the department include the *carpenter* who has charge of nonengineering repairs, and the *quartermasters* who steer the ship.

The crewmen of the engineering department include *electricians*, *oilers*, *firemen*, *wipers*, and other men with special jobs. The members of the engineering department are often called the "black gang." This name came from the days when coal furnished power for most ships. The firemen usually had blackened faces from the coal dust. The *chief steward* and his assistants are in charge of feeding the crew and passengers and attending to their personal needs. On a large liner, members of the steward's department may include nurses, laundrymen, waitresses, cooks, bakers, bartenders, and many other workers.

**Leaving Port** is one of the most exciting parts of a trip on an ocean liner. The ship is a beehive of activity long before the first passengers come on board. Longshoremen load the vessel with supplies and cargo. The deck officers check their charts and navigating equip-

## THE MODERN LUXURY LINER... a floating city

The S.S. *United States* is the world's fastest ocean liner. This 990-foot-long giant can steam 10,000 miles without stopping for fuel or supplies. Its galleys can prepare 9,000 meals a day for about 1,090 crewmen and 1,930 passengers.

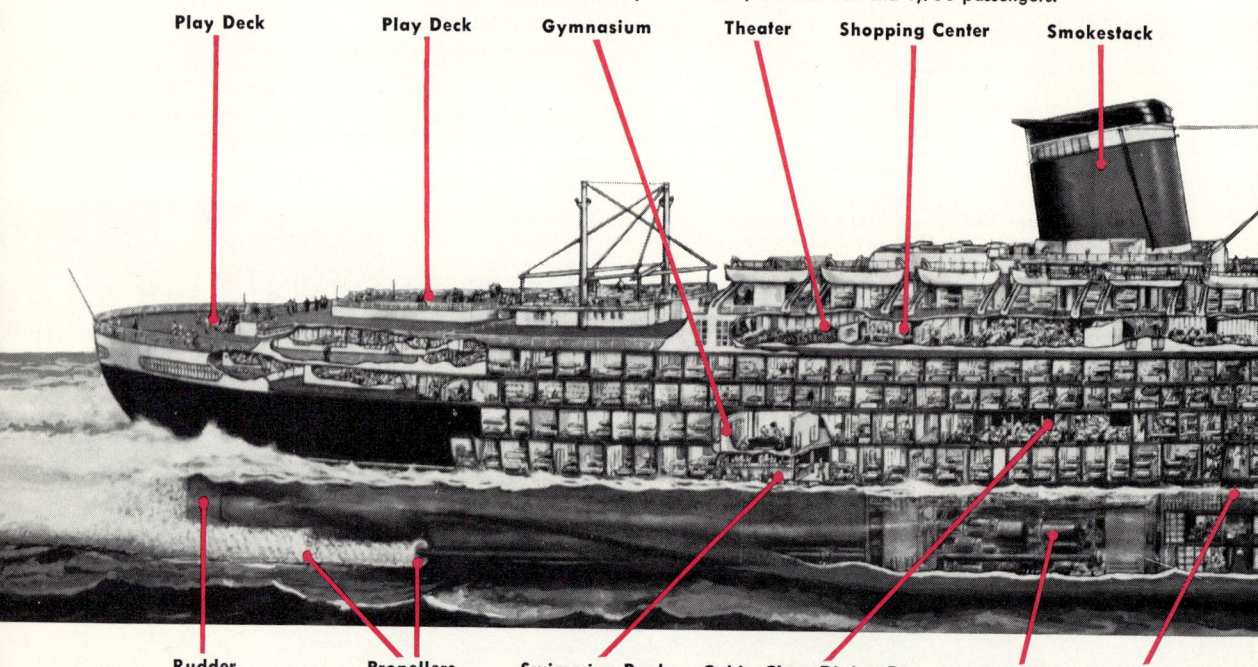

Play Deck · Play Deck · Gymnasium · Theater · Shopping Center · Smokestack

Rudder · Propellers · Swimming Pool · Cabin-Class Dining Room · Engines · Storerooms

ment. The engineers take thousands of gallons of fuel oil on board and test the engines and steering gear. Members of the steward's department store everything from caviar and milk to soap and matches.

Passengers begin to arrive about three hours before the ship *sails*, or leaves port. Longshoremen carry their luggage aboard and pursers check their tickets and passports. Stewards show the passengers to their cabins.

Finally, sailing time arrives. Longshoremen cast off the mooring lines that hold the vessel to the pier, and the ship slowly moves out into the harbor. As the ship leaves the pier, a band plays and friends of the passengers wave good-by and shout "bon voyage" (pleasant trip) above the blast of the ship's whistle.

Three or four small, powerful tugboats pull the liner away from the pier and into the harbor. A *docking pilot* directs the tugs and the ship until the vessel clears the pier and is under way in the harbor, headed for the open sea. Then the docking pilot turns the vessel over to the *harbor pilot*, who guides it from the harbor after the tugs have left.

Taking a large ship out of a crowded harbor requires skill, experience, and expert knowledge of the harbor. The pilot must know every channel, turn, and sand bar or other obstacle that might endanger the vessel. The channel that the ship follows is marked by buoys (see BUOY). Black buoys mark the *starboard*, or right, side of the channel as the ship heads for sea. The *port*, or left, side is marked by red buoys. Ships travel on the right side of the channel, just as automobiles travel on the right side of a highway. Red or black bell buoys mark turns or intersections. Lightships or lighthouses are located at the harbor entrance (see LIGHTHOUSE; LIGHT-

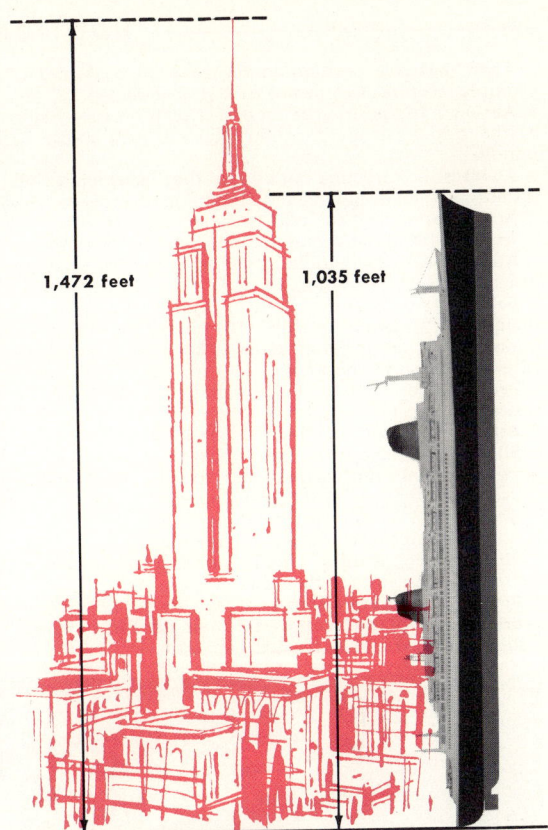

French Line

**The Giant Merchant Ship,** the *France,* if placed on end would almost reach the top of the Empire State Building.

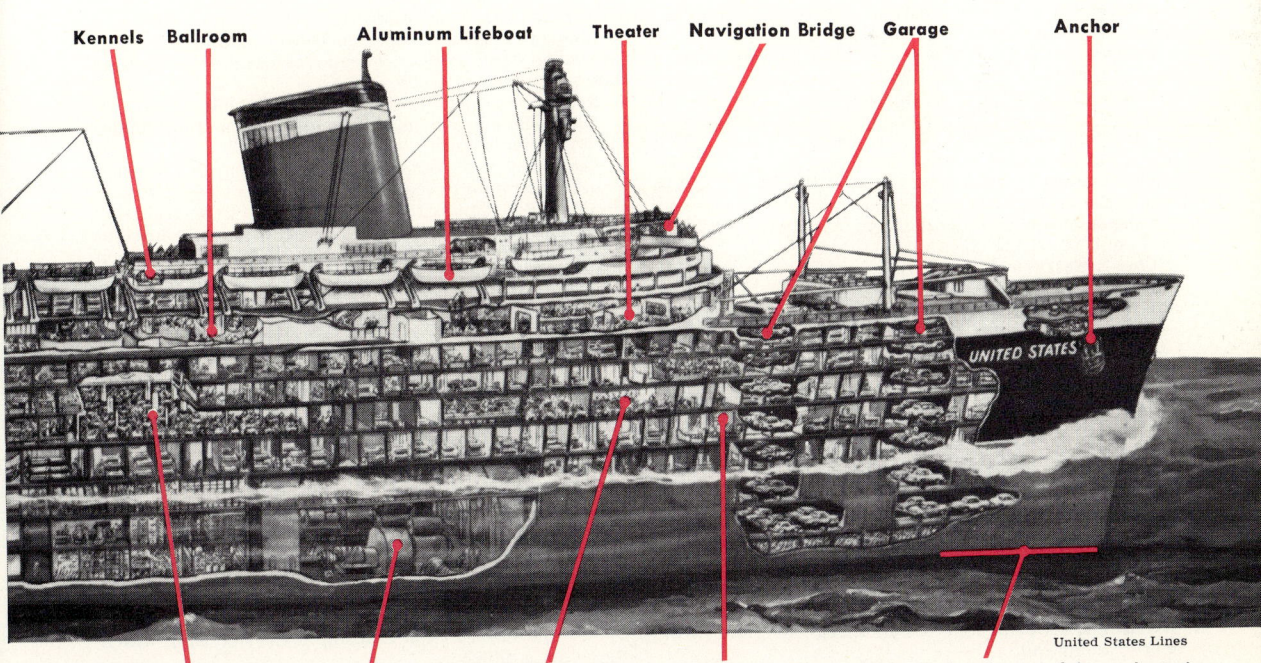

United States Lines

333

# NAUTICAL TERMS

**Abaft** means a position to the rear on a ship. For example, *abaft the bow* means *back of the bow*.

**Abeam** is the position of an object seen on either side of the ship near an imaginary line drawn across its middle.

**About** is the direction opposite to that in which a ship is sailing. When a ship "comes about," it reverses course.

**Aft** means toward the rear or stern of a ship.

**Aloft** means above the main or top deck of a vessel.

**Amidships** is the middle of a vessel, referring either to its length or its width.

**Ballast** is any material used to keep a ship *stable*, or steady. For example, a ship with no cargo will carry tanks of water in its ballast tanks to keep the vessel from riding too high in the water.

**Beam** is the width of a ship's hull measured at the widest point.

**Below** means beneath the main deck.

**Bilgewell** or **Bilge** is the lowest part of a hold or compartment, generally where the rounded side of a ship curves from the keel to the vertical sides.

**Binnacle** is a stand near the steering wheel that holds a magnetic compass, compensating magnets, and a light.

**Bitts** are deck fittings, usually found in pairs, used to secure mooring lines to the ship.

**Bow** is the front of a ship.

**Bridge** is the platform above the main deck from which a ship is steered and navigated.

**Hatchway** is an opening in the deck through which cargo is lowered into or raised out of a hold. A hatchway is closed by a *hatch cover*.

**Hawsepipe** is a pipe or channel in each side of the bow through which anchor chains run from the chain locker to the anchors.

**Hold** is the space below decks where cargo is stored.

**Hull** is the body of a ship, not including superstructure, mast, and machinery.

**Inboard** means toward the center of a ship.

**Keel** is the steel backbone of a ship. It runs along the lowest part of the hull from the bow to the stern.

**Lee** or **Leeward** means the direction toward which the wind is blowing across a ship. The *lee side* of a ship is the side away from the wind.

**List** occurs when a vessel leans to one side.

**Mooring** means tying a ship to a pier, to a buoy, or to another vessel.

**Pitching** is the fore-and-aft rocking of a ship.

**Poop Deck** is a short deck raised above the main deck at the stern.

**Port** is the left side of the ship facing forward.

**Porthole** is a round window in a ship's side, fitted with glass and metal covers.

**Quarter** is either side of a ship near the stern.

**Quarterdeck** is the part of the upper deck that extends from the mainmast aft, between the amidships *house*, or cabin, and the poop deck. On naval ships, it is the part

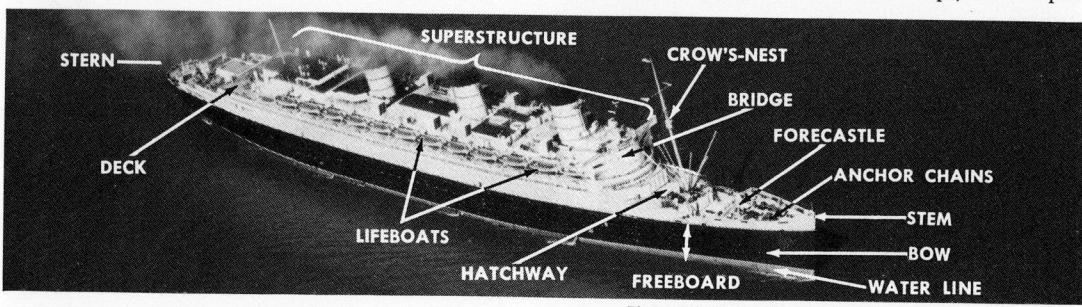

Photo of the *Queen Mary* courtesy The Port of New York Authority

**Bulkhead** is a wall or partition that separates rooms, holds, or tanks within the hull of a ship.

**Bulwark** is the part of a ship's side that extends fore and aft above the main deck to form a rail.

**Bunker** is a compartment for storing coal or fuel oil.

**Capstan** is a revolving wooden or steel drum mounted on a vertical axle on deck. Sailors use capstans as pulleys to help move heavy objects with ropes.

**Chain Locker** is the compartment in the hull of a ship where the anchor chain is stored.

**Companionway** includes the steps leading from deck to deck, and the space taken up by the steps.

**Crow's-Nest** is a lookout's platform on a mast.

**Davit** is one of a pair of cranes used to hold lifeboats and to lower them over the side of a ship.

**Deck** is one of the floorlike horizontal surfaces of a ship.

**Draft** is the depth of water that a ship needs to float. It is also the distance from the keel to the water line.

**Forecastle**, *FOHK s'l*, is the forward part of a ship, usually in the bow.

**Forepeak** is the space below the forecastle in the bow.

**Forward** means toward the front of an object on a ship. It is the opposite of abaft.

**Freeboard** is the distance from the water line to the main deck.

**Gangway** is an opening in the rail or bulwarks of a ship through which people walk on and off.

**Gear** is a ship's ropes, blocks, and tackles, or a sailor's personal belongings.

**Gunwale**, *GUN el*, is the upper edge of a ship's or boat's side or rail.

of the main deck set aside for ceremonies.

**Rigging.** The fixed ropes and wires holding the masts are called *standing rigging*. The movable ropes that operate booms are *running rigging*.

**Rolling** is the side-to-side motion of a ship.

**Scuttle Butt** is a drinking fountain on a ship. It also means a ship's gossip.

**Seaworthy** describes a vessel that can meet the usual conditions found at sea.

**Ship's Bell** signals the time on a vessel. A ship's day consists of six four-hour *watches*. Watches change at eight bells, or 12, 4, and 8 o'clock. The bell sounds at each half-hour of a watch. For example, during the 12 to 4 watch, the bell rings once at 12:30, twice at 1:00, three times at 1:30, and so on until eight bells are rung again at 4 o'clock.

**Shipshape** means neat, or in proper order.

**Starboard** is the right side of a ship facing forward.

**Stay** is a wire or rope used to support a mast or spar of a ship.

**Stem** is the extreme forward end of the bow.

**Stern** is the rear of a ship.

**Superstructure** is the part of a ship that extends above the main deck.

**Taffrail** is the bulwark around a ship's stern.

**Topside** means on or above the main deck.

**Water Line** is the point on the hull that the water reaches when a ship is floating normally.

**Windward** is the direction toward the wind, or opposite to lee. The *windward side* of a ship is the side from which the wind is blowing.

ship). Other beacons mark reefs and sand bars.

The ship slows down when it reaches the open sea, and the pilot climbs down a ladder into a small launch. The launch usually takes the pilot to a pilot boat, where he may wait to guide another ship into the harbor.

**At Sea,** the passengers can enjoy the pleasant routine of shipboard life. Once the ship is at sea, they go to their staterooms to unpack their luggage. Then they go to the dining room, where a steward assigns each to a table for the voyage. Next, the passengers usually go to the purser's office, where they deposit any important papers or other valuables for safekeeping. The passengers then go on deck, where the deck steward puts their names on the deck chairs assigned to them.

Each passenger must learn the location of the lifeboat he will use in case of an accident or other emergency. The second day out, the captain orders an *abandon-ship drill,* or a rehearsal of what to do in case the passengers and crew must leave the vessel at sea. A loud alarm rings to tell everyone to get his life preserver and go on deck to his assigned lifeboat or station.

Life aboard an ocean liner is like one holiday after another. Daytime hours can be spent in the swimming pool or playing deck games such as shuffleboard. Night life aboard ship is even gayer. After dinner, movies are shown. Costume balls and dances for children and adults are held. On the next to last night at sea, the captain holds his traditional dinner. This formal affair is the gayest event of the trip.

While the passengers enjoy the voyage, the crew is busy at work. On the navigating bridge, the officers use radar, sextants, and other navigating equipment to locate the ship's position (see NAVIGATION). In the radio shack, the radio officers send and receive messages and take news for the ship's newspaper. The telephone operator handles calls between the staterooms and all parts of the world.

In the *galley,* or ship's kitchen, a small army of butchers, bakers, and salad makers prepare food 24 hours a day. Down in the noisy but clean engine room, the engineers, electricians, firemen, and oilers watch over the complicated machinery that powers the liner across the ocean.

**Arriving in Port.** On the day before the ship arrives in port, the crewmen prepare the mooring lines and bring the passengers' baggage out of the hold. The pursers type the necessary papers and documents for the officials at the destination port, and the passengers start to pack.

On the day of arrival, everyone is excited and up earlier than usual. As the passengers line the rails watching the scenery, they feel the ship slow down to pick up the harbor pilot. Next, immigration and customs officers climb on board to begin checking the passengers.

The arrival of a large ocean liner at busy ports such as Southampton, England, and Cherbourg, France, is hardly noticed. The ship ties up, the passengers leave, and the crew begins preparations for the next voyage. But in some ports a ship arrival is a holiday event. Probably the most exciting welcome is extended to incoming ships at Honolulu, Hawaii. A Hawaiian band and hula-dancing girls greet each liner. The girls, wearing colorful Hawaiian dresses, hang *leis,* or flower necklaces, around the passengers' necks and extend the traditional Hawaiian greeting, "aloha."

### Parts of a Ship

A ship is one of the most complicated objects made by man. It is actually a floating city that must generate its own power, heat, and electricity. It carries its own fuel, provisions, and spare parts; makes its own fresh water; and disposes of its own garbage. The chief parts of a ship include (1) the hull and superstructure, (2) the engines, (3) the propellers, and (4) the rudder.

**The Hull and Superstructure.** The *hull* is the watertight body of a ship. *Bulkheads,* or walls, divide the hull into several watertight compartments that form the holds and the engine room. Each compartment must have *watertight integrity.* This means that water cannot enter it even if the adjoining compartment is flooded as the result of an accident. Watertight integrity enables a ship to float even though a hole may be pierced in the ship's hull.

Each of the ship's watertight compartments may have one or several decks that divide it from top to bottom. The top of the hull is usually called the *main deck.* The *superstructure,* or section of the ship above the main deck, is also divided into several decks.

The Greek mathematician Archimedes discovered the principle that explains why a ship floats. He found that an object placed in water is held up by a force equal to the weight of the water that the object *displaces,* or occupies. This upward force is called the *buoyant* force. Thus, if an object weighs less than the water it displaces, it will float, because the downward force, or weight, of the object, will be less than the upward, or buoyant, force. Shipbuilders design ships so that they weigh less than the water they will displace. See GRAVITY, SPECIFIC (Archimedes' Principle).

But a hull must do more than float. It must also speed through the water. A ship's hull has a pointed bow that pushes the water aside as it knifes through it, just as a snowplow pushes snow from its path. The rounded stern of most hulls helps the water close in around the propellers and rudder.

Ever since sailors first became seasick, they have tried to keep their ships from rolling and pitching. After World War II, ship designers developed an effective *stabilizing* system to prevent rolling. This system has a horizontal underwater fin attached to each side of the hull. Machinery moves the fins up or down so that they act against the waves and reduce the ship's roll.

**The Engines.** Most ships are driven by steam or diesel engines. Diesel engines are large and complicated, but they cost less to operate than steam engines. However, most diesel-driven ships are slower than steamships.

*Steamships.* There are two types of steam engines used on ships, reciprocating and turbine. *Reciprocating* steam engines (known as up-and-down engines) operate much as an automobile engine. However, the pressure of expanding steam, rather than of exploding gas, pushes the three pistons that turn a crankshaft attached to the propeller shaft of the ship. Reciprocating steam engines are slow and inefficient, and modern ships rarely use them. See RECIPROCATING ENGINE.

The most powerful steam engines used on ships are

## SHIP AND SHIPPING

*steam turbines*. Steam from a boiler spins a turbine that drives the propeller. On *turboelectric* ships, the turbine drives a generator that supplies electricity for a motor. The motor turns the propeller. On nuclear-powered ships, the heat that turns the water into steam comes from an atomic reactor rather than from an oil furnace. Engineers are also designing gas turbines for ships. See ATOMIC ENERGY; STEAM ENGINE; TURBINE.

*Diesel Ships*, also called *motor ships*, have either geared-drive or diesel-electric machinery. On a *geared-drive* ship, the diesel engine works through reduction gears to turn the propeller. On a *diesel-electric* ship, the engine turns an electric generator which supplies current to operate an electric motor that is connected to the propeller shaft. See DIESEL ENGINE.

**The Propellers**, or *screws*, move the ship through the water. Bolts hold the propellers to a long shaft that juts from the stern. The engine turns the shaft, which turns the propeller. Each propeller has from three to five curved blades that suck the water in ahead of them and force it out behind them. The pressure of this stream of water as it presses against surrounding water drives the ship forward.

Most small ships have only one propeller. But most larger ships have at least two, and often four propellers. The additional propellers increase the ship's power and make the vessel easier to maneuver.

A propeller's *pitch* is the distance it would advance with each revolution if it were cutting through a solid (see PITCH). *Variable-pitch* propellers can be reset from one pitch to another only when the ship is in dry dock. *Controllable-pitch* propellers can be changed while the ship is at sea. They permit a moving ship to go from *full-speed ahead* to *full-speed astern* without reversing the engines. A motor inside the ship changes the pitch by moving gears in the propeller hub. See PROPELLER (Marine Propellers).

**The Rudder** is a steel structure hinged to a post at the stern of the ship. The rudder turns the vessel. Cables, electric wires, or oil-filled tubes connect the rudder to the *helm*, or steering wheel, in the *pilot house*. This is the room on the bridge that houses the ship's controls. When the helmsman turns the wheel to port, the rudder shifts so that the water presses against its left side. As a result, the stern moves to the right and the bow swings to the left. When the helmsman turns the wheel to starboard, the rudder shifts so that the water presses against its right side. The bow then swings to the right.

A ship can also be steered automatically by a gyropilot, called an *Iron Mike*, which is controlled by a gyrocompass (see GYROCOMPASS; GYROPILOT). If the vessel strays from a set course, the gyrocompass starts an electric motor that turns the steering wheel of the Iron Mike and brings the ship back on course.

**Other Equipment.** The *funnel* (smokestack) is an exhaust pipe in a streamlined casing. Funnels rise from the top deck of the ship and discharge smoke or exhaust fumes high enough above the vessel to keep them from coming down on the decks.

Every ship has a port and a starboard anchor (see ANCHOR). The *flukes*, or hook-shaped ends of the anchors, dig into the ocean bottom like a pickax and

## BUILDING A SHIP

Newport News Shipbuilding and Dry Dock Co.

**Designing a Ship** requires the work of skilled architects who prepare the plans from which the vessel is built. The plans include every detail down to the last nut and bolt. The actual construction takes place at the shipyard. Here, workers prepare *templates*, or patterns, from the plans for the various sections of the ship. After the *keel*, or backbone, of the ship is put in place, workers begin assembling the hull. As the hull plates are welded or riveted into place, boilers and other machinery are also added inside the hull.

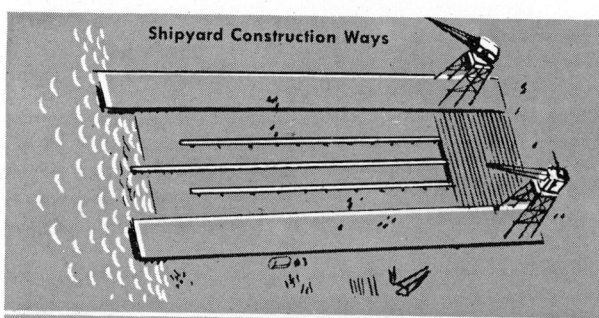

Shipyard Construction Ways

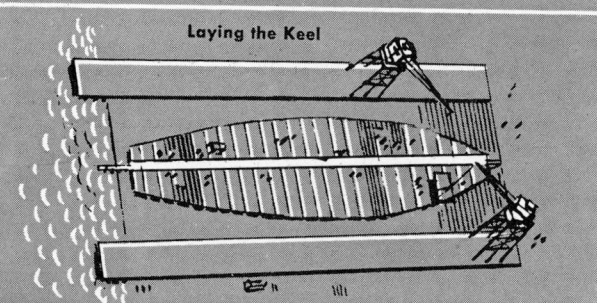

Laying the Keel

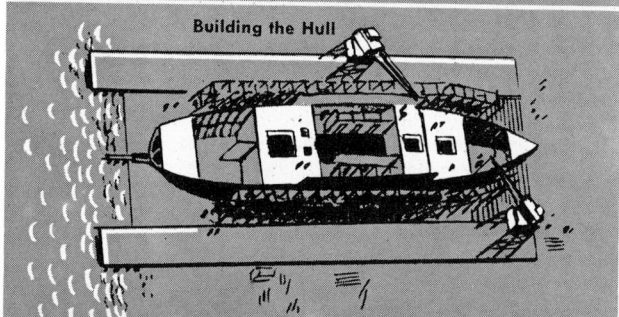

Building the Hull

336

## SHIP AND SHIPPING

keep the ship from drifting when it is stopped. Anchors do not have to be used when a ship is tied with mooring lines at a pier. Each anchor of the liner *United States* weighs 29,050 pounds.

*Maritime*, or sea, law requires every ship to carry enough lifeboats to hold all persons on board. Lifeboats are usually made of a light metal such as aluminum. They may be propelled by oar, motor, or sail. They range in number from two lifeboats on a freighter to 24 on the *United States*. The number of persons a lifeboat carries depends on its size, seating capacity, and number of air tanks installed to keep it afloat.

### Building a Ship

**Design.** Before a shipping company orders a ship to be built, the firm makes a careful study of the route the vessel will travel and the cargo it will carry. It then decides what type of ship to order and what its size and speed will be. The firm also specifies what type of machinery the ship should have, and how much space will be needed for passengers, cargo, or both.

Naval architects and marine engineers design a ship that meets the company's specifications. The ship must also comply with strict government safety regulations. A major concern of any marine architect is to design a ship that will be both economical to build and profitable to operate.

**The Shipyard** builds and repairs ships. It has drafting rooms, workshops, and construction ways that spread over many acres. The *construction ways*, also called *building slips*, are sloping floors that extend to the edge of the water. Ways form the end of the shipyard assembly line. Here, workers join large, assembled sections of the hull, and prepare the ship for launching. A row of wooden blocks, called *keel blocks*, stretches down the center of each slip to support the bottom of the ship's hull. Workers add curved wooden supports, called *bilge cradles*, as construction proceeds. The bilge cradles support the sides of the hull.

**Construction** on a new ship begins in the *mold loft*, a large room where draftsmen make blueprints and *templates*, or patterns, from the architect's design. The templates serve as patterns for steel plates and parts. Workers lay them out on steel, much as dressmakers place dress patterns on cloth. They mark the steel, then cut, bend, or roll it into the desired shapes. Next, the steel parts go to subassembly shops to be joined to make larger parts, or go directly to the slip to be put into position.

The actual assembly of the ship itself begins with *laying the keel*. The workers form the *keel*, or backbone, of the ship first. Then they build the middle section by adding the *frames*, or ribs, that support the hull and give it shape. Next, they rivet or weld the metal plates that actually form the hull. As the workers build the middle section, they add the various compartments, the necessary machinery, and the boilers.

Workers make the bow and stern separately in subassembly shops. When they complete these sections, they bring them to the slip, and rivet and weld them to the center section of the hull. When the hull is completed, the shipbuilders add the cabins deck by deck,

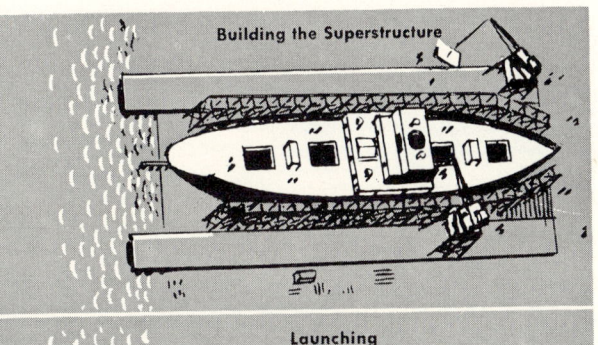
Building the Superstructure

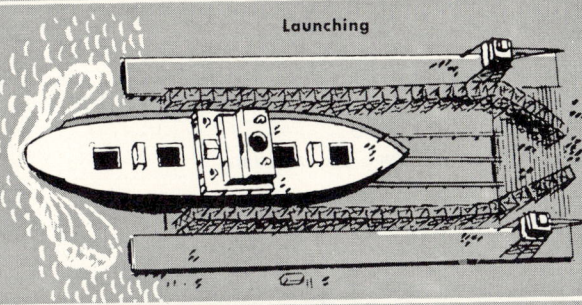
Launching

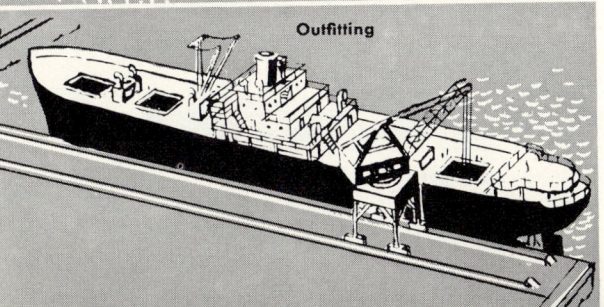
Outfitting

**Christening and Launching a Ship** takes place after the hull has been made watertight and parts of the superstructure have been added. At the christening ceremony, the ship's sponsor breaks a bottle of champagne across the bow and names the vessel. At that instant, the ship begins to slide into the water. Workers put the finishing touches on the vessel during its outfitting, and then the ship is ready for its *builder's trials*, or tests. When these are completed, the ship is ready for service.

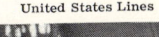
United States Lines

# SHIP AND SHIPPING

and install the smokestacks and lifeboats. If the ship is a freighter, they add the masts and cargo booms.

**Launching and Outfitting.** The launching of a ship is the first actual test of the vessel's buoyancy and stability, and of the designers' and builders' workmanship. Shipbuilders launch a ship when it is 70 to 80 per cent completed. Just before launching, workers lay *ground ways*, or *slipways*, on either side of the keel blocks. Ground ways are long, greased pieces of wood that extend the entire length of the vessel and into the water. They look like railroad tracks down which the ship will slide into the water. *Launching timbers*, or *sliding ways*, are laid on the greased slipways and built up to the bottom of the ship. The workers then build strong supports called *poppets* on the launching timbers at the bow and the stern. The built-up timbers and poppets form the *launching cradle*. The cradle supports the weight of the ship on the ground ways after the keel blocks are removed. The ship usually slides down the ground ways due to its own weight. If it should stick, a ram at the bow gives the vessel a push. The ship rides on the cradle into the water until it floats.

Ocean vessels are usually launched stern first. Great Lakes boats are sometimes launched sideways, if they are built along narrow rivers. Some large passenger ships are built in graving docks (see DRY DOCK [Graving Docks]). These vessels are floated off the keel blocks by flooding the dock with water.

The christening takes place just before the ship is launched. The builder designates a woman as the ship's *sponsor*. She breaks a bottle of champagne over the bow and the vessel is released down the ground ways.

After a ship is launched, a tug pulls it to an *outfitting dock* or *wet basin*. There, workers complete the hull and superstructure, add the interior fittings and tune up the machinery for the *builder's trials* (tests). If the ship returns from its trial runs with a broom tied to the mast, it has made a "clean sweep" of its tests.

### The Shipping Industry

The world's merchant fleet totals about 45,000 ships, with carrying capacity of over 180 million gross tons. More than 14 million gross tons of new shipping are built every year. Japan, West Germany, and Sweden lead the world in shipbuilding.

**In the United States.** About 55,000 seamen are employed aboard ocean-going merchant ships. The United States has more than 3,000 merchant ships, including Great Lakes and other inland-water vessels. Its ocean-going merchant fleet can carry more than 30 million dead weight tons of cargo. Besides seamen, the shipping industry employs about 95,000 longshoremen and over 50,000 shipyard workers. It also provides jobs for thousands of tugboat crewmen, office workers, government employees, and members of banks, insurance companies, and manufacturers who are connected with the shipping industry.

Building and operating ships costs over 50 per cent more in the United States than it does in other countries, because of the high costs of labor and materials. The government pays the industry *subsidies* (grants of money) to help it meet competition (see SUBSIDY). The Maritime Administration exercises control over subsidized shipping lines (see MARITIME ADMINISTRATION).

All vessels registered in the United States must be built and operated under the most rigid safety rules in the world. The Coast Guard, Public Health Service, and private agencies, including the American Bureau of Shipping, set and enforce standards.

**In Other Countries.** Shipping is an important industry in many countries. Several European nations have long traditions of shipping leadership. These include Great Britain, Norway, Italy, The Netherlands, France, Sweden, and Denmark. Great Britain ranks second to Liberia in gross tonnage of its ships, but has a larger number of vessels. Norway, Sweden, and Denmark are famous for their sleek motor ships. The ocean liners of France and Italy have luxurious interiors.

Japan ranks as the leading shipping nation in Asia. The Japanese have a long tradition of skillful

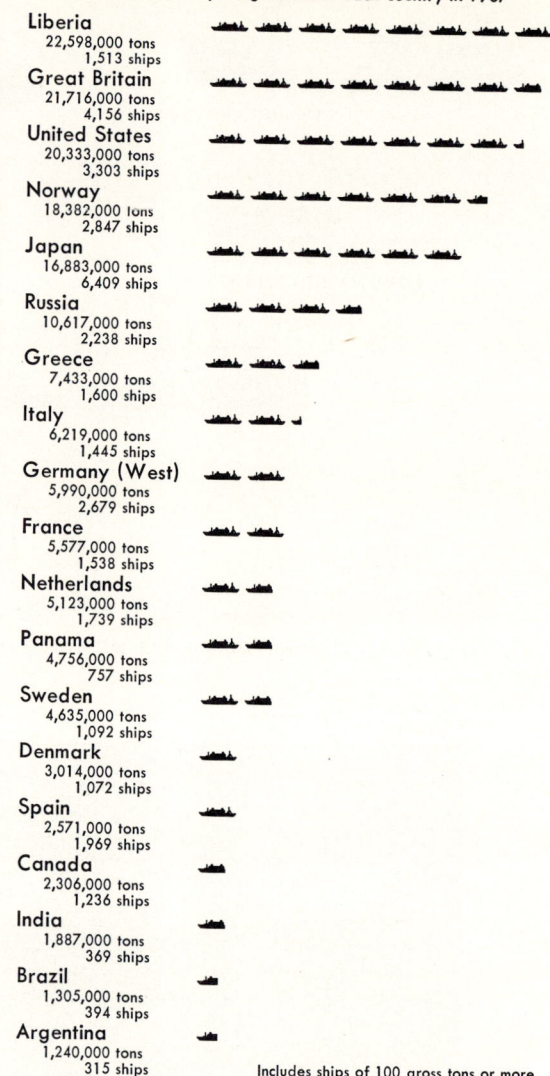

**LEADING MERCHANT FLEETS OF THE WORLD**
Gross tons of ships registered in each country in 1967

Liberia — 22,598,000 tons — 1,513 ships
Great Britain — 21,716,000 tons — 4,156 ships
United States — 20,333,000 tons — 3,303 ships
Norway — 18,382,000 tons — 2,847 ships
Japan — 16,883,000 tons — 6,409 ships
Russia — 10,617,000 tons — 2,238 ships
Greece — 7,433,000 tons — 1,600 ships
Italy — 6,219,000 tons — 1,445 ships
Germany (West) — 5,990,000 tons — 2,679 ships
France — 5,577,000 tons — 1,538 ships
Netherlands — 5,123,000 tons — 1,739 ships
Panama — 4,756,000 tons — 757 ships
Sweden — 4,635,000 tons — 1,092 ships
Denmark — 3,014,000 tons — 1,072 ships
Spain — 2,571,000 tons — 1,969 ships
Canada — 2,306,000 tons — 1,236 ships
India — 1,887,000 tons — 369 ships
Brazil — 1,305,000 tons — 394 ships
Argentina — 1,240,000 tons — 315 ships

Includes ships of 100 gross tons or more.

Source: *Lloyd's Register of Shipping, Statistical Tables, 1967*

seamanship, chiefly because of their island location.

About 2,300 merchant ships fly the flags of Liberia, Panama, and Honduras. Almost all of these ships are owned by companies located in other countries. The ships are registered in these countries because the countries levy no taxes on ships, allow the owners to pay lower wages, and do not require as many costly safety features as do some other nations.

For a description of shipping throughout the world, see the Transportation sections of the country and continent articles, such as SOUTH AMERICA (Transportation).

**International Agreements.** Hundreds of treaties regulate and promote international shipping. They involve safety requirements, salvage agreements, and provisions for operating the International Ice Patrol. This patrol is an international movement to track and report the movements of icebergs that might endanger North Atlantic shipping routes. The U.S. Coast Guard operates the patrol which is paid for by 11 nations.

### Leading Shipping Companies in the U.S.

American shipping companies operate vessels on nearly every trade route in the world. The following are the largest shipping firms in the United States.

**American Export Isbrandtsen Lines** began with one freighter in 1919, under the name of the Export Steamship Corporation. In 1924, it became the first United States line in more than a hundred years to provide passenger service to Mediterranean ports. The company became the American Export Lines in 1944. It put the *Independence* and the *Constitution*, both 1,000-passenger liners, into service in 1951. American Export Lines merged with the Isbrandtsen Company in 1962. The line has about 30 freighters that travel from the Atlantic Coast of the United States to India, Pakistan, Ceylon, Burma, and to the Mediterranean and Red seas. These freighters also make trips around the world. The company has headquarters in New York City.

**American President Lines,** with headquarters in San Francisco, was organized in 1929 as the Dollar Steamship Lines. It adopted its present name in 1938. It operates the round-the-world passenger ships *President Polk* and *President Monroe*; three trans-Pacific liners, the Presidents *Wilson*, *Cleveland*, and *Roosevelt*; and more than 25 freighters. Its ships operate from United States Atlantic and Pacific coast ports and travel to the Pacific Islands, Asia, and the Caribbean and Mediterranean seas.

**Lykes Bros. Steamship Company** was founded by James Lykes in 1922 to handle cattle shipments to Cuba. Today, the line is owned by more than 80 members of the Lykes family. It has over 50 freighters that sail from ports in the Gulf of Mexico to ports in the Caribbean Sea, Europe, Africa, and Asia. The company has headquarters in New Orleans.

**Matson Navigation Company** has linked the U.S. Pacific Coast with Hawaii and the South Pacific Islands since 1882. Captain William Matson founded the line, which provides both passenger and freight service. The company operates three passenger lines—the *Lurline*, the *Matsonia*, and the *Monterey*—and eight freighters. It has headquarters in San Francisco.

**Moore-McCormack Lines** was founded in 1913 by Emmet J. McCormack and Albert V. Moore. It operates about 45 ships of various types, including the liners *Argentina* and *Brasil*, from the West and East coasts of the United States. It serves Scandinavia, south and east Africa, and eastern and western South America. The company's headquarters are in New York City.

**United States Lines** was organized in 1871 by the Pennsylvania Railroad under the name of American Steamship Lines. The International Mercantile Marine Corporation took it over in 1903, and reorganized the firm

# SHIP AND SHIPPING

in 1943 as the United States Lines. Its home offices are in New York City. The company's passenger liner *United States* travels from New York City to Great Britain, France, and Germany. The line pioneered *tourist-class*, or *economy-class*, transportation in 1921 when it converted its *steerage* (third-class) quarters into tourist accommodations. Its 50 freighters travel to ports in Great Britain, Western Europe, the Far East, and Japan.

### History

The first ships were probably floating logs that carried prehistoric men across lakes and rivers. During the Old Stone Age, from about 1,500,000 B.C. to 8000 B.C., men learned how to hollow out logs with stone axes and fire (see STONE AGE). They used poles or paddles to move their boats. Sometime during the Stone Age, men developed the *canoe*, a light, swift boat made of skin or bark stretched over a wooden or bone frame.

The first people to sail the seas may have been Arabs who traveled across the Indian Ocean in small sailing vessels called *dhows* thousands of years ago. Or they may have been sailors who ventured onto the Mediterranean Sea as early as 5000 B.C. From about 3000 to 1000 B.C., the island of Crete became one of the world's first important seagoing communities. It maintained a large fleet of *galleys* (open vessels propelled by oars) for trade with Egypt and other nations on the shores of the Mediterranean (see GALLEY).

**Early Egyptian Ships.** As early as 5000 B.C., Egyptian sailors navigated the Nile River. They used flimsy boats made of reeds that they tied together. They also tied a rope from the bow to the stern to keep the curved

### RED-LETTER DATES IN SHIP DEVELOPMENT

c. 1500 B.C. The Egyptians built deep-sea sailing vessels.
c. 1000 B.C. The Phoenicians developed the *bireme*, a galley with two rows of oars on each side.
c. 200 B.C. The Romans built galleys with as many as 200 oars.
c. A.D. 1000 Leif Ericson led a band of vikings in open boats from Greenland to North America.
1500's The galleon became the standard merchant and naval vessel.
1607 The first ship built in North America, the *Virginia*, was launched at present-day Kennebec, Me.
1790's Iron hulls began to be used on sailing ships.
1807 Robert Fulton's *Clermont* began the world's first regular steamship passenger service.
1819 The American ship *Savannah* became the first ship with a steam engine to cross the Atlantic Ocean.
1838 The British *Sirius* became the first ship to cross the Atlantic Ocean entirely under steam power.
1839 A screw propeller was first used successfully on the British steamer *Archimedes*.
1845 The first true clipper ship, the *Rainbow*, was launched.
1853 The American ship *Monumental City* became the first steamship to cross the Pacific Ocean.
1894 Charles Parson's *Turbinia* became the first ship equipped with a steam turbine.
1912 The first ocean-going diesel entered service. It was the Dutch tanker *Vulcanus*.
1954 The U.S. Navy launched the world's first nuclear-powered ship, the submarine *Nautilus*.
1956 The American ship *John Sergeant* became the world's first merchant ship powered only by a gas turbine.
1962 The first nuclear-powered merchant ship, the American *Savannah*, completed trials for sea service.

341

# EARLY Ships

LOG

DUGOUT CANOE

EGYPTIAN GALLEY—1500 B.C.

ROMAN GALLEY—A.D. 200

VIKING LONG SHIP—A.D. 1000

ROMAN CORN SHIP—A.D. 300

CARGO SHIP—MIDDLE AGES

CARAVEL—1500

SPANISH GALLEON—1550

BRITISH EAST INDIAMAN—1700'S

ROBERT FULTON'S *CLERMONT*—1807

SAVANNAH—1819

AMERICAN WHALING SHIP—1840'S

AMERICAN CLIPPER SHIP—MID-1800'S

PADDLE-WHEEL STEAMER—1850'S

SCREW-PROPELLER STEAMSHIP—1860'S

TRANSATLANTIC LINER—1870'S

STEAMSHIP WITH EMERGENCY SAILS—1880'S

FREIGHTER—EARLY 1900'S

PASSENGER SHIP—EARLY 1900'S

BRITISH LUXURY LINER *TITANIC*—1912

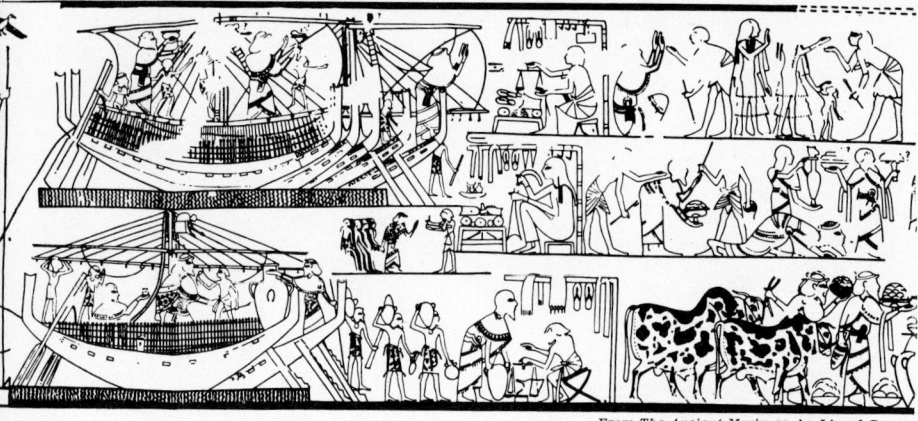

**An Ancient Port** was an exciting place. This drawing shows workmen unloading cargo from Phoenician vessels newly arrived at a port in Egypt.

From *The Ancient Mariners*, by Lionel Casson

ends of the ship from drooping into the water.

By about 1500 B.C., Egyptian sailors navigated seagoing vessels. Their ships carried one sail, about 15 oars on each side, and two oars at the stern for steering. Most of these ships measured about 70 feet long, 17 feet wide, and 4 or 5 feet deep. Like the boats that traveled the Nile, the deep-sea boats used a rope to support the curved bow and stern.

During the 1400's B.C., the Egyptians made their ships much more seaworthy by building them of planks imported from Phoenicia, a country that Egypt had conquered. Drawings found in ancient Egyptian tombs show ships whose hulls strongly resemble the bodies of ducks and swans. Some archaeologists believe the Egyptians may have patterned their ships after the shapes of waterfowl.

**Mediterranean Sailing Ships.** The Phoenicians dominated Mediterranean trade from around 1000 B.C. until about the time of Christ. They carried their goods to all known parts of the world in *biremes*, or large galleys with two *banks*, or rows, of oars on each side. Phoenician galleys provided the models for the vessels the Greeks and Romans later used to travel throughout the Mediterranean Sea and beyond.

Phoenician sailors traveled all parts of the Mediterranean Sea, through the Strait of Gibraltar, and perhaps as far as the British Isles. They also journeyed far southward along the east coast of Africa.

Greece has an extensive coast line and many small islands. The Greeks became expert sailors early in their history. Their *long ships*, which were long, narrow warships, carried a large sail but depended mainly on oars for power. According to Homer's epic poems, the ships carried the Greeks to the shores of Troy during the Trojan War about 1200 B.C. These wooden warships were from 60 to 100 feet long and from 10 to 16 feet wide. They had a curved stern and a tall, curved bow tipped with a *figurehead*, or carved decorative figure. The ships had rowers' benches on each side of the hull and a deck between the benches. Each ship had about 50 oars for power. A large oar that hung over the stern served as a rudder. Castlelike platforms, from which missiles were hurled at the enemy, stood at the bow and the stern. Long poles, used to ram enemy ships, jutted from the front of the bow. See GREECE, ANCIENT (color picture, Legend and History).

Besides the long warships, the Greeks also built broader cargo ships. These freighters, called *round ships*, depended primarily on sails for power. They did not need the speed and maneuverability of warships.

The Romans also had rounded cargo ships. St. Paul described the shipwreck of one of these round ships in the New Testament. The type of ship he sailed on had a hull 90 feet long and from 26 to 28 feet wide. It carried 250 tons of cargo, and 276 passengers and crew members. Judging from St. Paul's description of the ship, it probably had no keel and the square sail could not be shifted. For this reason, it could sail only with the wind (see SAILING [Why a Boat Sails]).

Roman warships, like those of the Greeks, used both sails and oars. By the 400's B.C., the Roman ships had become the most powerful on the seas. These *triremes* measured as long as 140 feet, with three banks of 20 oars each on both sides.

**The Vikings** were Scandinavian warriors and sailors who traveled the North Atlantic Ocean and the Baltic and Mediterranean seas. They used open ships that carried one sail and also used oars for power. A viking ship built about A.D. 1000 was unearthed near Gogstad, Norway, in 1880. It is $79\frac{1}{2}$ feet long and $16\frac{1}{2}$ feet wide. It has a hull with no keel, and an upswept bow and stern. A dragon figurehead adorns the tip of the bow. The hull is *clinker-built*, or constructed with overlapping planks like the side of a house, instead of *carvel-built*, or built with planks that butt together like floor boards. Shields along the sides of the hull protected the oarsmen on viking ships. The Gogstad ship carried 32 oarsmen and was steered by a long oar or side rudder. Historians believe that Leif Ericson, a seaman from Greenland, may have led a band of vikings from Greenland to the mainland of North America in ships of this type. See ERICSON, LEIF; VIKING.

**Ships of Trade and Exploration.** Single-masted ships continued to be used during the Crusades (1096-1291), and served until the end of the Middle Ages, about 1400. Moorish sailors from North Africa began using *lateen* sails on their ships in the Mediterranean area about 1000. The lateen sail has a triangular shape. It is hung from a long, tapered *yard*, or pole, that is suspended from near the top of the mast at an angle of about 45 degrees. The lateen sails made it easier for ships to sail in light winds than they could with square sails. The Arabs were the first to use lateen sails when they put them on their dhows in the Mediterranean

Sea, the Red Sea, and the Persian Gulf. English sailors began using lateen sails on their ships after seeing them on Moorish vessels.

After the Crusades, ships became wider and deeper. They had square sterns with rudders in the center of the stern. But they still had curved bows and flat bottoms similar to viking ships.

From about 1400 to around 1527, sailors began using lateen sails in addition to square sails to help in steering their ships. A second mast called a *mizzenmast* carried the lateen sail behind the mainmast. Soon, they added a third mast, the *foremast*, in front of the mainmast in order to add power to the ship. Both the foremasts and mainmasts carried square sails. Christopher Columbus used ships with square sails on his first voyage to the Western Hemisphere in 1492. Two, and possibly three, of Columbus' ships were *caravels*. These light, fast ships usually had both square and lateen sails arranged in different patterns. Columbus' *Niña* had square sails on the foremast and mainmast, and a lateen sail on the mizzenmast. The Spanish *galleon* was a bigger, more advanced version of the caravel. A galleon carried more sail and more armament. It became the standard naval and merchant ship throughout Europe in the 1500's. See CARAVEL; COLUMBUS, CHRISTOPHER; GALLEON.

The sail and hull patterns of ships remained basically unchanged from the 1500's until the 1700's. But the battle castles on the bow and stern became closed structures. The stern castle was changed on British ships, and gradually became the high poop used in the 1500's. The hull lines of the stern were continued upwards so that the stern castle became not only an additional structure for defense on deck, but cabins and quarters for the steersmen. The forecastle was lowered from its location well over the *stem*, the extreme forward part of the bow. Eventually, the forecastle was placed on the main deck at the bow. This type of vessel was widely used in the 1500's in both war and commerce. During the 1600's, shipbuilders increased the seaworthiness of the hull and the area of the sails.

## SHIP AND SHIPPING

During the early 1800's, the British attempted to increase the speed of their sailing cargo ships. Until that time, their biggest cargo vessels, the cumbersome *East Indiamen* operated by the East India Company, carried guns. But the British built new cargo ships called *Blackwall frigates*, which were unarmed and faster than the East Indiamen. See EAST INDIA COMPANY.

Swift American *clipper* ships appeared on the seas during the 1830's. They had long, narrow hulls and sharp, gracefully curved bows. They carried rectangular sails on three masts that slanted backward slightly. The fastest sailing ships ever built, some clipper ships could travel 20 knots. They carried both passengers and cargo. See CLIPPER SHIP.

By 1875, when steamships were threatening to replace sailing vessels, sailing-ship designers produced a new type of cargo ship, the *windjammer*. This was a slow, square-hulled ship built of iron and steel. Their sturdier design enabled them to sail around Cape Horn with up to 3,000 tons of cargo. Windjammers remained in operation in fewer and fewer numbers in the early 1900's.

**From Sail to Steam.** In the 1700's, James Watt of Scotland made improvements on the steam engine that made it possible to run ships with this new source of power (see STEAM ENGINE). In 1783 a French boat owned by the Marquis d'Abbans made a 15-minute trip under its own power on the Saône River near Lyon. In 1787 John Fitch built the first workable steamboat in

**In the 1860's,** whaling ships were a common sight in American ports. Barrels of whale oil unloaded from this ship line the edge of the wharf.
The Whaling Museum, New Bedford

## SHIP AND SHIPPING

the United States. By 1790, Fitch had begun operating a steamboat line on the Delaware River between Philadelphia and Trenton, N.J.

In 1807, Robert Fulton's famous steamboat, the *North River* (usually called the *Clermont*), launched the first commercially successful steamboat passenger service. His boat traveled the Hudson River between Albany and New York City. Two years later, John Stevens' *Phoenix* became the first steamboat to make an ocean voyage when it traveled from Hoboken, N.J., to Philadelphia.

An American vessel, the *Savannah*, was the first ship equipped with a steam engine to cross the Atlantic Ocean. The *Savannah* was a sailing ship fitted with a 90-horsepower auxiliary steam engine and collapsible paddle wheels. She sailed from Savannah, Ga., on May 22, 1819, and arrived at Liverpool, England, on June 20. It is believed that the *Savannah* used its engines from 80 to 105 hours during the trip. In 1838, the British steamer *Sirius* became the first ship to cross the Atlantic under continuous steam power.

Inventors in the United States, France, and England began experimenting with screw propellers for ships in the late 1700's and early 1800's. In the late 1700's, John Fitch and John Stevens of the United States worked with propellers shaped like wood screws. But most historians credit the Swedish-American inventor John Ericsson with developing a successful bladed propeller similar to those used today. In 1839, Ericsson installed a propeller on his boat *Robert F. Stockton*. In 1845, the *Great Britain* became the first propeller-driven ship to cross the Atlantic. By 1855, propellers had replaced paddle wheels on most ships. But sails were kept for emergencies on transatlantic liners as late as 1884.

**Ships of Iron and Steel.** Shipbuilders began constructing iron vessels in the late 1700's, because good shipbuilding wood was becoming scarce. Iron ships also provided more cargo space than wooden vessels. Iron ships needed only half-inch iron plates, and wooden ones used 12-inch planks. Iron ships were stronger, safer, more economical, and easier to repair.

The British ship *Vulcan*, built in 1818, was the first all-iron sailing ship of which a record exists. Another British vessel, the *Aaron Manby*, was probably the first iron steamship. It entered service in 1821. By the late 1800's, shipbuilders had begun to use steel for ships. One of the earliest steel ships was the *Servia* of Great Britain. It began operations in 1881.

**Power and Speed.** New sources of power were developed as steamships changed from wood to steel and from paddle wheels to propellers. In 1854, the *compound* engine was introduced. In these engines, the steam pushed a piston in one cylinder, then passed on to a second cylinder. Thus, it developed more power from the same amount of steam. *The City of Paris*, built in 1888, had three-stage engines and twin propellers.

The development of the marine steam turbine by Charles Parsons of England in the late 1800's brought a new source of propulsion for ships. The first turbine-driven vessel was Parsons' *Turbinia*, built in 1894. After 1907, any vessel designed for speed was driven by steam turbines. Steam propulsion was also greatly advanced by the change from coal to oil as fuel for furnaces after World War I. Oil also provided fuel for the marine diesel engine developed by Rudolf Diesel of Germany in the late 1800's. The first seagoing motor ship was the tanker *Vulcanus*, launched in 1913.

**Nuclear Power for Ships.** The tremendous advances in all branches of ship construction since World War II have been overshadowed by the harnessing of nuclear power for ship propulsion. In 1954, the United States launched the first nuclear-powered ship, the submarine *Nautilus*. This started the navy's change-over from steam to nuclear power. But the great expense of nuclear power for ships slowed its use for merchant vessels. The keel for the *Savannah*, the first nuclear-powered merchant ship, was laid in 1958. The ship went into operation in 1962. It was named for the original *Savannah*, the first steamship to cross the Atlantic. The new *Savannah* resembles a conventional steamship in design. It is 595 feet long, has a top speed of 23 knots, and can carry 60 passengers and about 10,000 tons of cargo. Another nuclear-powered merchant ship, West Germany's 15,000-ton ore carrier *Otto Hahn*, was launched in 1964.

The Port of New York Authority

**A Modern Port,** left, is a beehive of activity. Here, tugboats nudge the *United States* into its berth at New York City.

**Automation.** Several U.S. lines are building freighters that are partially *automated* (self-regulating). For example, electronic equipment regulates the flow of fuel oil and air to the furnace, and water to the boilers. It records temperatures and pressures. Many valves are operated hydraulically by pushbutton control. Electronic equipment reduces the number of crewmen required by about 25 per cent. In 1965, more than 30 partially automated 24-knot freighters were being built in the United States.

### Careers in Shipping

**On Ships.** Persons interested in seagoing careers can find a wide variety of jobs in the United States Merchant Marine. In addition to jobs as seamen and engineers, men can find employment as cooks, radio operators, pursers, and stewards. Passenger ships also employ medical staffs, musicians, barbers, beauticians, printers, and waitresses. See MERCHANT MARINE.

Most companies—except some Great Lakes lines, tanker companies, and the U.S. Navy's Military Sea Transportation Service—hire seamen, engineers, and members of the steward's department through *hiring halls* in the major ports of the United States. Engineers belong to the Marine Engineers' Beneficial Association; deck officers to the International Organization of Masters, Mates, and Pilots; radio operators to the American Radio Association or the Radio Officers Union; and pursers to the Staff Officers' Association. Almost all the sailors who find jobs aboard ship are union members. Federal law requires that the unions also allow nonmembers to find jobs through the halls. But these men usually can do so only when there are more jobs available than there are union members to fill them. A person going to sea for the first time must also get a Merchant Mariner's Document from the United States Coast Guard. This card, commonly called "seaman's papers," gives the holder the official position of seaman. Before an inexperienced person can get these papers, he must prove to the Coast Guard that he has a job on a ship.

Many ship's officers work their way up through the ranks from seaman to mate. But many more are graduated from federal and state maritime academies. These include the United States Merchant Marine Academy, Kings Point, N.Y.; the New York State Maritime College, Fort Schuyler, N.Y.; the Maine Maritime Academy, Castine, Me.; the Massachusetts Maritime Academy, Hyannis, Mass.; the California Maritime Academy, Vallejo, Calif.; and the Texas Maritime Academy, a division of Texas A&M University at College Station, Tex.

**In Shipyards.** Shipyards offer a great variety of positions to college-trained specialists. They employ metallurgists (metal specialists), chemists, physicists, nuclear engineers, statisticians, and librarians. They also need many skilled tradesmen, including metalworkers, welders, and riveters.

ROBERT S. BURNS

Critically reviewed by EDOUARD A. STACKPOLE

**Related Articles** in WORLD BOOK include:

#### BIOGRAPHIES

| | | |
|---|---|---|
| Ericsson, John | Kaiser, Henry J. | Sperry, Elmer A. |
| Fitch, John | Maury, Matthew F. | Stevens (family) |
| Fulton, Robert | McKay, Donald | |

## SHIP AND SHIPPING

#### FAMOUS SHIPS

| | | |
|---|---|---|
| Alabama | Graf Spee | Monitor and |
| Bismarck | Great Eastern | Merrimack |
| Clermont | Lusitania | Savannah |
| Constellation | Maine | Titanic |
| Constitution | Mayflower | |

#### KINDS OF SHIPS

| | | |
|---|---|---|
| Barge | Galleon | Submarine |
| Brig | Galley | Tanker |
| Caravel | Lightship | Trireme |
| Clipper Ship | Rotor Ship | Tugboat |
| Dreadnought | Steamboat | Warship |
| Frigate | | |

#### PARTS OF A SHIP

| | | |
|---|---|---|
| Anchor | Gyrostabilizer | Plimsoll Mark |
| Gyrocompass | Hydrofoil | Propeller |
| Gyropilot | | |

#### OTHER RELATED ARTICLES

| | | |
|---|---|---|
| Barnacle | Insurance | Naval Stores |
| Boats and Boating | (Marine) | Navigation |
| Coast Guard, | Japan (picture: | Navy |
| United States | Shipbuilding) | Port |
| Customs, Bureau of | Knot | Sailing |
| Dock | Log | Salvage |
| Dry Dock | Logbook | Ship Model |
| Federal Maritime | Maritime | Shipwreck |
| Commission | Administration | Signaling |
| Flag | Maritime Law | Transportation |
| Harbor | Merchant Marine | Waterway |
| Inland Waterway | Naval Shipyard | |

#### Outline

I. **Kinds of Ships**
   A. Passenger Ships    E. Refrigerator Ships
   B. Freighters    F. Great Lakes Ore
   C. Tankers                Boats
   D. Bulk Carriers
II. **A Trip on an Ocean Liner**
   A. The Crew    C. At Sea
   B. Leaving Port    D. Arriving in Port
III. **Parts of a Ship**
   A. The Hull    C. The Propellers
        and Superstructure    D. The Rudder
   B. The Engines    E. Other Equipment
IV. **Building a Ship**
   A. Design    D. Launching and
   B. The Shipyard         Outfitting
   C. Construction
V. **The Shipping Industry**
   A. In the United States    C. International Agree-
   B. In Other Countries        ments
VI. **Leading Shipping Companies in the U.S.**
VII. **History**
VIII. **Careers in Shipping**

#### Questions

What is the world's largest ocean liner? The fastest?
Why does a ship float?
In what respect does part of shipbuilding resemble making a dress?
How does an "Iron Mike" keep a ship on course?
Even though they are small countries, why do Liberia and Panama have a large number of merchant ships sailing under their flags?
What was the first steam-powered vessel to cross the Atlantic? What other famous ship has the same name?
What were the fastest sailing ships ever built?
A broom has what meaning when tied to the mast of a new ship completing its test run?
What device designed after World War II helps prevent a ship from rolling at sea?
What are the three leading shipbuilding countries?

347

Herbert Smit

**A Ship Model in a Bottle** is first completely constructed outside the bottle. The builder then folds the masts down, slides the ship down the bottle's neck, and pulls up the masts.

**SHIP MODEL** is a small copy of a full-sized ship or boat. Making ship models can be a fascinating hobby for both children and adults. Some hobbyists carve models by hand. Others make boats and ships from accurate kits sold by hobby shops. These models are made of plastic or wood. Some sailboat modelmakers belong to clubs that sponsor races.

Sailors on long voyages often made ship models in narrow-necked bottles. These make interesting collectors' items. Putting them together took careful workmanship. The spars and rigging were made in fine detail. When the model was finished, the sailor inserted it in the bottle with the spars and rigging lying down. A pull of one thread drew the rigging upright.

Ship models also play an important part in the shipbuilding industry. Old-time shipbuilders carved models to guide the workmen. They used no blueprints or plans. Today, preliminary models help designers select the final form of a ship's hull before they draw the design. These models are tested in a towing tank to provide information on how the hull of a full-sized ship will act at sea and at various speeds. All important commercial and naval ship designers tank-test preliminary models before finally deciding on a design.

**A Ship Model Takes Form** under the steady hands and watchful eyes of a young craftsman. The model is an 18-inch replica of a 110-foot subchaser used by the U.S. Navy in World War I.

ITC Modelcraft

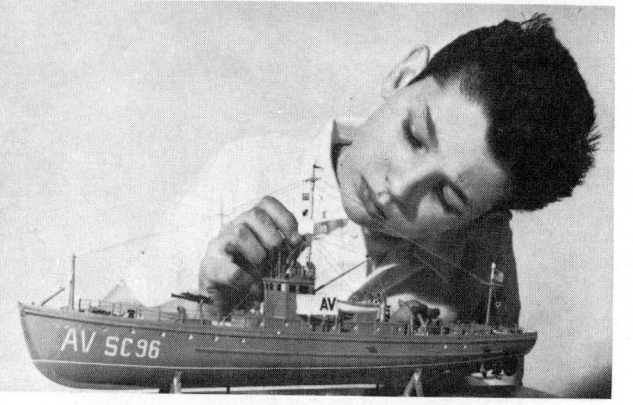

**A Prized Ship Model** in the French Naval Museum is a 124-cannon man-of-war, built more than 200 years ago for the nautical instruction of Louis XV. The fully-rigged ship is 1/36 actual size.

Museums display models of vessels of former times. Many steamship companies use large elaborate models of their ships to decorate their offices and travel bureaus. These models sometimes cost thousands of dollars. The New York Yacht Club, in New York City, owns one of the largest collections of model sailing and power yachts.  WILLIAM W. ROBINSON

See also MAINE (Places to Visit [Penobscot Marine Museum]); FROUDE (William).

**SHIP OF THE DESERT.** See CAMEL (Legs and Feet).
**SHIPPENSBURG STATE COLLEGE.** See UNIVERSITIES AND COLLEGES (table).
**SHIPPING.** See SHIP AND SHIPPING.
**SHIPROCK.** See NEW MEXICO (Land Regions).
**SHIP'S BELL.** See SHIP AND SHIPPING (Terms).
**SHIP'S LOG.** See LOGBOOK.
**SHIP'S STORE.** See POST EXCHANGE.
**SHIPWORM** is one of a group of sea animals that bores in wood. Certain kinds of shipworms can make tunnels more than 3 feet long. They bore downward and inward

*Popular Mechanics* Magazine

348

with two clamlike shells. They line the tunnel with a white shelly material.

Shipworms are *bivalves* (animals with a two-pieced shell). Young shipworms look like tiny clams and can swim about freely. But they soon attach themselves to wood and begin to bore a hole in it. Shipworms have been known to bore $\frac{3}{4}$ inch in a day and to honeycomb lumber within six months.

**Scientific Classification.** Shipworms are in the shipworm family, *Teredinidae*. They make up the genera *Bankia* and *Teredo*. The common teredo of the United States, Europe, and Africa is genus *Teredo*, species *T. navalis*. R. TUCKER ABBOTT

**SHIPWRECK** is a disaster at sea. It may take the form of a grounding, collision, or storm. Causes of some shipwrecks are unknown. Some ships just vanish. Following are some of the world's worst ship disasters:

| Year | Ship | Dead | Disaster |
|---|---|---|---|
| 1831 | Lady Sherbrooke | 273 | wrecked off Newfoundland |
| 1833 | Lady of the Lake | 215 | struck iceberg in N. Atlantic |
| 1854 | City of Glasgow | 480 | vanished out of Liverpool |
| 1857 | Central America | 400 | sank on Havana-New York run |
| 1858 | Austria | 471 | burned in N. Atlantic |
| 1859 | Pomona | 400 | wrecked in N. Atlantic |
| 1860 | Lady Elgin | 300 | collision on Lake Michigan |
| 1865 | Sultana | 1,450 | exploded on Mississippi R. |
| 1867 | 50 vessels | 1,000 | hurricane in West Indies |
| 1873 | Atlantic | 547 | wrecked off Nova Scotia |
| 1891 | Utopia | 574 | collision off Gibraltar |
| 1892 | Namchow | 414 | wrecked in China Sea |
| 1893 | Victoria | 350 | collision off Tripoli |
| 1894 | Norge | 600 | wrecked on Atlantic reef |
| 1895 | Reina Regenta | 400 | foundered in Atlantic |
| 1904 | General Slocum | 1,030 | burned in East River, N.Y. |
| 1908 | Matsu Maru | 300 | collision off Japan |
| 1912 | Titanic | 1,517 | struck iceberg in N. Atlantic |
| | Kickermaru | 1,000 | sank off Japanese coast |
| 1914 | Empress of Ireland | 1,029 | collision in St. Lawrence R. |
| 1915 | Eastland | 812 | overturned in Chicago R. |
| 1916 | Hsin Yu | 1,000 | sank off China coast |
| 1917 | Mont Blanc | 1,635 | collision in Halifax harbor |
| 1918 | Kiang-Kwan | 500 | collided near China coast |
| 1921 | Hongkong | 1,000 | hit rock near China coast |
| 1926 | Troopship | 1,200 | exploded in Yangtze River |
| 1928 | Vestris | 113 | sank off Virginia coast |
| 1931 | St. Philibert | 450 | overturned off France |
| 1934 | Morro Castle | 125 | burned off New Jersey |
| 1948 | Kiangya | 1,100 | exploded in China Sea |
| 1954 | Toya Maru | 1,172 | sank in Tsugaru Strait, Japan |
| 1956 | Andrea Doria | 51 | collided with *Stockholm* off New York |
| 1957 | Eshghabad | 270 | grounded off Caspian Sea |
| 1958 | Uskudar | 351 | capsized off Izmit, Turkey |
| 1961 | Dara | 212 | burned in Persian Gulf |
| 1963 | Lakonia | 125 | burned in N. Atlantic |
| 1963 | U.S.S. Thresher | 129 | sank off New England coast |
| 1965 | Yarmouth Castle | 90 | burned and sank in Atlantic, east of Miami |
| 1966 | Heraklion | 250 | sank in Aegean Sea |
| 1968 | U.S.S. Scorpion | 99 | lost in Atlantic |

The International Ice Patrol is one of the chief agencies that helps prevent shipwrecks (see ICE PATROL, INTERNATIONAL). It furnishes information on drifting ice and icebergs. Safety devices used to help prevent shipwrecks include *electronic depth finders* to keep ships from going aground and *radar* to make navigation safer at night (see FATHOMETER; RADAR [Ships]).

See also NAVIGATION; SALVAGE; TITANIC.

**SHIRAZ,** *shee RAHZ* (pop. 229,761; alt. 5,020 ft.), one of Iran's largest cities, is the capital of the southwestern province of Fars (see IRAN [map]). It has many mosques and public buildings. Shiraz is famous as the birthplace of the poets Hafiz and Saadi (see HAFIZ; SAADI). The city's products include Persian rugs, hand-woven textiles, and silverwork. Historians think Shiraz was founded in the A.D. 600's. RICHARD N. FRYE

**SHIRE,** *shyr,* was an early geographical division of England. Shires had about the same boundaries as modern counties. They were first formed in the early Anglo-Saxon states, and were made up of a number of smaller districts called *hundreds*.

See also ENGLAND (Anglo-Saxon Period; map: The 38 Counties).

**SHIRE RIVER.** See LAKE NYASA.

**SHIRLEY, WILLIAM** (1694-1771), served as colonial governor of Massachusetts from 1741 to 1756. For a short time, he commanded all British forces in North America. He was responsible for the important capture of the French stronghold of Louisbourg in 1745, during the French and Indian Wars. When England paid Massachusetts for its part in the war, Shirley redeemed the colony's paper money and built a sound currency. Shirley was born in Sussex, England. BRADFORD SMITH

**SHIVA.** See JUDAISM (Special Occasions); SIVA.

**SHOAT.** See HOG (Hog Terms).

**SHOCK.** A blow, a wound, a burn, or some other accident can cause a severe shock to the entire body. Shock stuns and weakens the vital processes of the body. Control of blood-flow through the body is upset. Blood vessels near the skin *dilate* (enlarge). The patient's skin becomes warm, and he perspires and feels faint. The blood pressure decreases, and the pulse grows weak.

About an hour later, *secondary shock* occurs. The patient loses color and grows weaker. His blood pressure falls, and his pulse becomes feeble. His breathing becomes shallow and weak, his perspiration turns cold, and blood vessels near the surface of the skin collapse. Some accident victims seem unaware of their serious condition, and want to go on their way as if nothing had happened. But if the condition is not corrected, the victim may lose consciousness or even die.

Secondary shock is common in severe wounds and operations. It is best treated by placing the patient in the *shock position,* with his feet higher than his head. This helps blood reach his vital organs. Further treatment with complete rest, warmth, stimulating drugs, and blood plasma should follow. JOHN B. MIALE

**SHOCK, ELECTRIC.** See FIRST AID (Stoppage of Breathing); SAFETY (Safety with Electricity); SHOCK TREATMENT.

**SHOCK ABSORBER** is a device that reduces shock or concussion. It is used on automobiles, airplane landing gears, and doors. Most shock absorbers consist of a piston inside a cylinder that contains air or oil. Automobile shock absorbers consist of a piston inside an oil-filled cylinder. When the car wheel hits a bump, the piston pushes upward. But the oil resists the piston. This resistance to the motion of the piston offsets the force of the bump and absorbs the shock. See also SPRING (metal); TORSION BAR SUSPENSION. WILLARD L. ROGERS

349

# SHOCK TREATMENT

**SHOCK TREATMENT** is a term applied to several different treatments for patients with serious mental illnesses, usually the psychoses (see PSYCHOSIS). These treatments are alike in that they make the patient temporarily unconscious, or put him in *shock*. Doctors use shock treatment alone or together with psychotherapy (see PSYCHOTHERAPY).

The most widely used forms of shock treatment are *insulin* treatment and *convulsive* treatment. Both were first used equally for treating psychotic patients in the 1930's. By 1950, however, doctors used convulsive treatment far more frequently.

When doctors first used insulin to produce shock, they hoped it would effectively cure schizophrenia. Unfortunately, the treatment helped only to a limited degree and only in some cases. It often produced only temporary improvement. For these reasons, and because it is difficult to use insulin treatment safely, many doctors gave up using it. See INSULIN.

Convulsive treatment was introduced a few years after insulin treatment. Its name comes from the fact that the treatment produces convulsions in a patient. The simplest and most usual method for this treatment consists of passing an electric current through a patient's brain for a fraction of a second. This form of treatment is often called *electroshock*.

The technique used in electroshock treatment is quite simple, but it must be adjusted to the individual case. The number of treatments varies, but it is usually three times a week. Doctors determine the amount and the duration of the electric shock by estimating the voltage and amperage of the current beforehand. A preshock medication is often given to reduce the anxiety of the patient. Often, a complete anesthetic is given. In the standard electric shock, the patient does not feel the electric current.

Doctors use electroshock to some extent to treat schizophrenia. But its most important use is in treating patients with manic-depressive psychosis. Electroshock treatment is often successful in restoring depressed patients to a normal or healthy mental state. The way it does this is not known. Doctors also use drugs, such as Metrazol, to induce shock. CHARLES BRENNER

See also MENTAL ILLNESS (Shock Treatment).

**SHOCK WAVE.** See AERODYNAMICS (Supersonic Flight).

**SHOCKLEY, WILLIAM** (1910-    ), an American physicist, was one of the discoverers of the transistor. With John Bardeen and Walter Brattain, he received the 1956 Nobel prize in physics for discovering the principles of electrical conduction in solids that make the transistor possible (see TRANSISTOR). Shockley directed operations research on antisubmarine warfare in 1944 and 1945. He became Director of Research for the Weapons Systems Evaluation Group in the Department of Defense of the United States government in 1954. He was born in London. CHALMERS W. SHERWIN

**SHODDY** is a woolen cloth made of yarn that has been used before. The Federal Wool Products Labeling Act, adopted in 1939, requires that shoddy be labeled in such a way that a purchaser will know that the goods are made of used yarn. The name *shoddy* has come to mean any cloth of poor quality.

**SHOE.** Early man made shoes long before he made records of what he thought or did. He made shoes to protect his feet against rough stones, hot sand, and cold weather. Shoes are so important in man's life that he has for years given them magic powers in stories and legends. The tales of Puss in Boots, Cinderella, the Seven League Boots, and the winged sandals of Mercury are examples of stories of magic or unusual shoes.

## Making Shoes

There are more than 200 operations for the making of a single shoe today. The shoe factory usually has eight departments, each of which has a different part of the manufacturing process.

In the *cutting room*, machines cut most of the leather or fabric used in the upper part of a shoe into the proper shape and size. The shoe linings are also cut in this room. When fancy shoes are made in small quantities, they are sometimes cut by hand.

The second operation takes place in the *stitching room*. Here the different parts of the upper shoe and lining are stitched together to make a finished *shoe upper*. In making this finished shoe upper, all the other operations needed are done here, such as making designs in the toes, punching eyelets for the laces, and making buttonholes.

The third job takes place in the *stock-fitting* or *sole-leather* room. Here, all the lower parts of the shoe are made and put together. These include insoles, outsoles, counters, and box toes. *Counters* are pieces made to fit into and shape the heel of the shoe. *Box toes* do the same thing for the toe.

In the *lasting room*, the different shoe parts are assembled and shaped on the last. The *last* is a wooden or metal form that gives shape to the entire shoe. Lasting is highly skilled work, because the shoe must be shaped evenly all around so it can stand an even strain in all parts when it is worn.

The fifth operation, called *bottoming*, is one of the most important in shoemaking. Here the outsole is attached to the rest of the shoe by sewing, cementing, or nailing.

In the sixth operation, in the *making room*, the heel is attached to the shoe, and trimmed.

In the *finishing room*, the bottoms of the shoes are scoured lightly, a finishing wax or gum is applied, and the bottoms are polished.

In the eighth and last operation, called *treeing and packing*, the shoe gets its final cleaning and dressing. Laces, bows, or buckles are put on, and the shoes are packed after a final inspection.

## The Shoe Industry

The United States leads the world in making shoes. St. Louis, Mo., is the leading shoe-producing city in the United States. But Salem, Mass., and the surrounding cities have ranked as leading shoe-producers since the mid-1600's. Leading shoemaking states include Massachusetts, Pennsylvania, New York, Missouri, Maine, New Hampshire, Tennessee, and Illinois. The shoe industry produces about 600,000,000 pairs of shoes yearly.

The shoe-manufacturing industry employs about 250,000 persons. Thousands of others are engaged in the wholesale distribution and retail selling of shoes. There are excellent opportunities for advancement in the

# SHOE

**High Laced Sandals** made of leather carried Roman soldiers on to world conquests.

**Jeweled Platform Slippers** called *chopines* were worn by the Sultana of Zanzibar.
Traphagen School of Fashion

Metropolitan Museum of Art

**Leather Slippers** worn by French women in the late 1700's had high, tapered heels.

Metropolitan Museum of Art

**A Simple Leather Sandal** was worn by Egyptian children.

**The Hand-Tooled Boot** of a Moslem's favorite wife is made of fine morocco leather.
Ewing Galloway

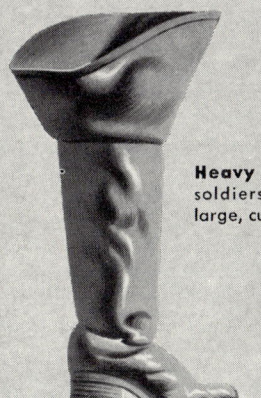

**Heavy Jack Boots,** worn by soldiers in the 1500's, had large, cufflike tops.

**A Classic Opera Pump** with a pointed toe and aluminum heel became popular in the 1950's.
O'Connor & Goldberg

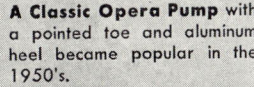

**A Fancy Fur-Topped Boot** with a thick sole protected a Russian woman from ice and snow.
Ewing Galloway

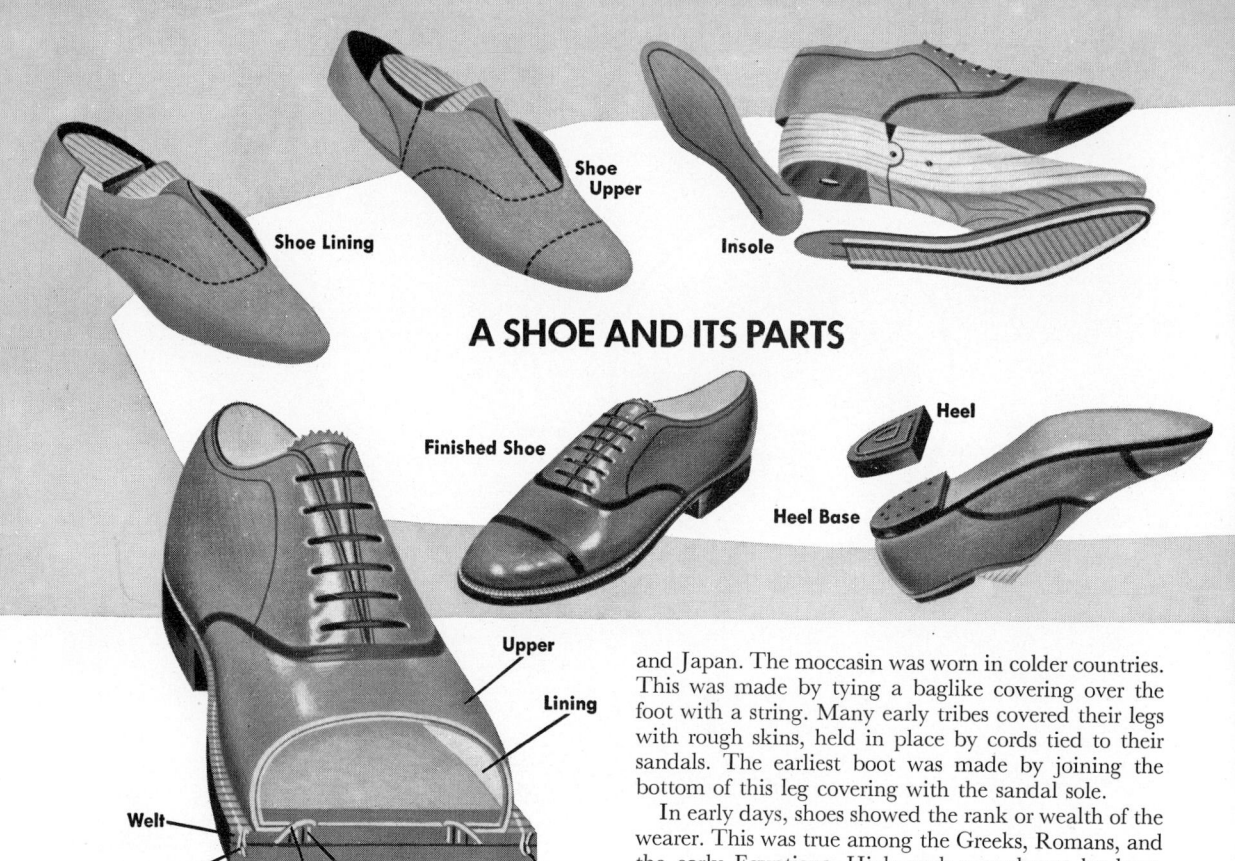

## A SHOE AND ITS PARTS

industry for factory workers, office employees, salesmen, accountants, and shoe-style designers.

### Shoes and Health

Shoes should be bought with the idea that they are made to protect and support the feet. They should be chosen for shape, fit, and quality of material. Size is no sign that shoes will fit, and wearers should learn to pick shoes that follow the shape of the foot. Heels for women's shoes should be from $\frac{3}{4}$ inch to $1\frac{1}{2}$ inches high for best daytime wear. Only with properly fitted shoes will the wearer avoid the pain of having small foot bones pushed out of place.

Outgrown shoes cause about three fourths of the foot trouble found in children. In children from 2 to 6 years old, shoe sizes change every 4 to 8 weeks. From 6 to 10 years, sizes change every 2 or 3 months. Children from 12 to 15 should have their shoe sizes checked every 4 months. Children over 15 years old should have shoe sizes checked about every 6 months until their feet are fully developed.

### History

The first shoes were probably pieces of hide or braided grass held to the foot by leather cords. This shoe, the simplest kind of sandal, is still worn in warm countries. The *pampootie* of the island fishermen of western Ireland is an example. Sandals like this are also worn in China and Japan. The moccasin was worn in colder countries. This was made by tying a baglike covering over the foot with a string. Many early tribes covered their legs with rough skins, held in place by cords tied to their sandals. The earliest boot was made by joining the bottom of this leg covering with the sandal sole.

In early days, shoes showed the rank or wealth of the wearer. This was true among the Greeks, Romans, and the early Egyptians. High rank was shown by long, pointed toes and different kinds of decoration. In the 1300's, a shoe called the *crackowe* had a pointed toe so long that a chain had to be used to hold it up so its wearer could walk. In the reign of Queen Mary of England, the *duckbill* shoe was made so wide that a law was finally passed limiting the width of its toe to 6 inches. The *chopine* was a wooden shoe with an iron ring to help its wearer lift his feet from the mud. The *jack boot* had a large cufflike top high on the thigh. It was worn by gentlemen and soldiers from about 1650 until 1775. Jack boots were so heavy and fitted so tightly that men had to be helped in and out of them.

**The Early Shoemaker.** Although many changes took place in types of shoes throughout the years, little care was given to fitting them properly. The shoemakers of the Middle Ages paid little attention to the shape of the foot. Their art was directed more to fancy decoration. As late as the middle 1800's, shoemakers still used practically the same tools as those used by the ancient Egyptian sandal maker. These included a simple awl, a scraper, and a few other hand tools.

The first American shoemaker was Thomas Beard, who came to Salem, Mass., in 1629. The shoemakers of early American days traveled from house to house, making shoes for each family. Elias Howe's sewing machine, patented in 1846, was adapted for sewing shoes by John Nichols of Lynn, Mass., in 1851. This was the first time that machines were used for making shoes.

In 1858, Lyman Reed Blake of Abington, Mass., invented a machine for sewing soles to shoes. Gordon McKay, a financier, introduced Blake's invention to the shoemaking industry. Then came the Civil War, and shoes in great numbers were needed for soldiers. To

meet the heavy demands, shoe manufacturers had to install new machines in their factories. The year 1900 marks the beginning of modern shoemaking. By then, machines performed almost every shoemaking operation.

**Modern Shoes.** Some people in The Netherlands still wear wooden shoes. In parts of France, a shoe with a wooden sole is used. Many people in the Orient still wear shoes made entirely of fabric.

The upper parts of a modern shoe are usually leather. But the sole is often a composition of rubber, cork, and leather and wood fibers. Composition soles account for two-thirds of the soles for shoes that are produced in the United States. LYNN FARNOL

See also CLOTHING (Interesting Facts about Clothing); LEATHER; MOCCASIN; WOODEN SHOE; CORFAM.

**SHOEBILL.** The shoebill is a large, strange-looking bird related to the stork. It is sometimes called the *whale-headed stork*. The shoebill was once thought to be the rarest of birds. But a number of them live in Africa on marshes from the Upper Nile to Uganda and Congo. The bird stands about 4 feet high. It is ashy gray in color, and has an enormous bill from which it gets its name. When the bird is disturbed, it snaps its bill open and shut rapidly, making a loud rattling sound.

The shoebill has long legs. It wades in shallow water, where it feeds on fish. It flies with its neck in the shape of an *S*, its long legs trailing behind. Shoebills live in pairs and sometimes prey on small animals. They do not nest in trees. They make a large platform of reeds lined with grass for nesting. The female shoebill lays one or two rough-shelled white eggs.

**The African Shoebill**
N. Y. Zoological Society

**Scientific Classification.** The shoebill belongs to the shoebill family, *Balaenicipitidae*. It is classified as genus *Balaeniceps*, species *B. rex*. RODOLPHE MEYER DE SCHAUENSEE

**SHOEMAKER, WILLIE** (1931-    ), an American jockey, became horse racing's all-time leading money-winner in 1964. He won purses totaling over $30 million. He set a record by winning 485 races in 1953. In 1956, he became the first of two jockeys to win more than $2 million in purses in one year. In the 1957 Kentucky Derby, Shoemaker led throughout, but misjudged the finish line and lost. Born WILLIAM LEE SHOEMAKER in El Paso, Tex., he became a jockey in 1949. RICHARD G. HACKENBERG

**SHOGUN,** *SHOH GOON*, was the title of the greatest of the Japanese feudal lords. The term *shogun* means *great general* in Japanese, and is an abbreviation of a title meaning *Barbarian-Subduing Generalissimo*. This official had originally received emergency military powers from the Japanese emperor to fight against the Ainu tribe in the A.D. 800's. After 1192 the power of the imperial court decreased, and the shogun also assumed civil power. In theory, the emperor appointed each new shogun, but the shogun was the real ruler of Japan. After 1600, his capital, Edo (now Tokyo), was Japan's administrative center. The Minamoto, the Ashikaga, and the Tokugawa families carried the shogun title. The shogun's power reached its peak under the Tokugawa family, from 1600 to 1867. In 1867, the shogun resigned and returned his powers to the emperor. MARIUS B. JANSEN

See also JAPAN (The Shoguns); SAMURAI.

**SHOLES,** *shohlz*, **CHRISTOPHER LATHAM** (1819-1890), an American inventor and journalist, helped develop the first practical typewriter. Sholes, Carlos Glidden, and Samuel W. Soulé designed the typewriter in 1867, and patented it in 1868. Glidden and Soulé sold their interests to Sholes and his new partner, James Densmore, who began to manufacture the typewriter. But they were unable to make it and sell it, so in 1873 they gave E. Remington and Sons a contract to make it. Sholes later sold almost all of his interests.

Sholes was born near Danville, Pa. He was a successful Wisconsin newspaper editor and served in the Wisconsin state legislature before turning to inventing. Sholes and Soulé invented a page-numbering machine in 1866. MONTE A. CALVERT

**SHOLOKHOV, MIKHAIL ALEXANDROVICH** (1905-    ), is a Russian author. Sholokhov won fame for his novels and stories about the Don Cossacks, a group of people who lived near the Don River in southern Russia (see COSSACKS, DON). In 1965, Sholokhov was awarded the Nobel prize for literature.

Sholokhov's best-known work is the four-volume historical novel *The Quiet Don* (1928-1940). This novel deals with the way the Russian Revolution and civil war from 1917 to the early 1920's caused

**Mikhail A. Sholokhov**
Tass from Sovfoto

SHOLOKHOV, MIKHAIL A.

353

## SHOLOM ALEICHEM

conflicts among the Don Cossacks. Sholokhov also wrote *Virgin Soil Upturned* (1932, 1960), a two-volume novel about the problems Don Cossack farmers faced when the government set up collective farms. His first works were two books of stories about the Don Cossacks, *Don Tales* (1925) and *The Azure Steppe* (1926). He was born in Veshenskaya, a Don Cossack village.

**SHOLOM ALEICHEM,** *SHOH luhm ah LAY hehm* (1859-1916), was the pen name of SOLOMON RABINOWITZ, the most widely read of all Yiddish writers. He wrote humorous novels, short stories, and plays about Jewish life in western Russia and Jewish immigration to the United States. His technique of "laughter through tears" emphasized the dignity, generosity, and shrewd self-appraisal of his poverty-stricken characters. His writings have been translated into many languages. Major works include the novels *Tevye the Dairyman, Menakhem-Mendl,* and *Motl the Cantor's Son,* and the play *It's Hard to Be a Jew.* He was born near Kiev, Russia, and came to the United States in 1914. URIEL WEINREICH

**SHOOTING.** See ARCHERY; FIREARM; GUN; HUNTING.

**SHOOTING STAR.** See METEOR.

**SHOOTING STAR.** See COWSLIP.

**SHOPPING.** See CONSUMER EDUCATION; HOMEMAKING.

**SHORAN,** an abbreviation for **SHO**rt **RA**nge **N**avigation, is the name of an electronic system used for short-range aerial navigation, aerial photography, and aerial surveying. An airplane using shoran sends out radio signals to two ground stations, which rebroadcast the signals to the airplane. Electronic instruments record the time interval between sending and receiving the signals. Shoran calculates the distance to the ground stations by means of the time intervals. Shoran was developed during World War II by the United States Army Air Forces and private industry. See also LORAN; NAVIGATION. G. D. DUNLAP

**SHORE PATROL** is the police department of the United States Navy. It is made up of selected officers and enlisted men with ratings of petty officers. They patrol shore areas that are occupied or visited by members of the navy. In some cases, the Shore Patrol has authority over all servicemen. Shore Patrol members receive special training. They can arrest navy men and enforce discipline, but cannot punish anyone. An offender is turned over to his commanding officer for trial. See also MILITARY POLICE. JOHN W. WADE

**SHORT, WALTER CAMPBELL.** See WORLD WAR II (The Attack on Pearl Harbor).

**SHORT BALLOT.** See BALLOT.

**SHORT CIRCUIT.** See FUSE, ELECTRIC.

**SHORT-HORNED GRASSHOPPER.** See LOCUST.

**SHORT STORY** is a form of fiction writing. We often tell our friends stories about events in our daily lives. We may tell *jokes* to make our friends laugh, or use *anecdotes* to help explain what we mean. These forms are closely related to the short story. But the short story has three important elements that are lacking in the stories we tell. A short story is carefully created, it is compact, and it is unified. All the details in a short story have a purpose, and add to its effect.

The short story is also related to the novel. Both deal with events in the lives of real or imaginary persons, and with almost any subject. But a short story generally develops only a single incident or crisis in human relations. Its characters are usually described quickly, with little detail.

A short story can run from about 3,000 to about 10,000 words in length. Some magazines specialize in so-called *short-short* stories, only about 1,000 to 1,500 words long. Longer prose works are sometimes called *novelettes* or *short novels.*

Authors interested in selling their stories should consult literary market lists to find which magazines accept their kinds of stories. These lists also give information on how manuscripts should be prepared for publication, the length of articles individual publishers will consider, and addresses of magazine and other publishing offices.

In the United States, Washington Irving developed the setting, Nathaniel Hawthorne added characterization, and Edgar Allan Poe brought in plot and helped establish the short story as a form. Some of Poe's famous stories, such as "The Gold Bug" and "The Cask of Amontillado," helped make the short story popular. Guy de Maupassant in France aided its development. Another American author, O. Henry, developed the surprise ending, sometimes in the last sentence, or even the last word. Two Russian authors, Anton Chekhov and Ivan Turgenev, specialized in realistic stories centered on characters rather than events.

Many kinds of short stories have been created by short-story writers. Poe's mystery stories led the way for A. Conan Doyle's detective stories about Sherlock Holmes; and the adventure stories of Robert Louis Stevenson, Rudyard Kipling, Jack London, and Bret Harte. Joseph Conrad and Katherine Mansfield wrote character studies. P. G. Wodehouse and Dorothy Parker produced humorous short stories based on comic situations. Damon Runyon and Octavus Roy Cohen wrote stories in unusual local dialects. DONALD H. LUDGIN

See also FICTION; JOKE; NOVEL; PARABLE.

**SHORT TON.** See TON.

**SHORT WAVE** is a radio term for wave lengths that represent higher frequencies than those used for ordinary broadcast transmissions. The classification of the different frequency bands above 3,000 kilohertz (abbreviated kHz.) is as follows:

| Frequency in Kilohertz | Frequency Designation | Wave Length in Meters |
|---|---|---|
| 3,000- 30,000 | High (abbrev. HF) | 100-10 |
| 30,000- 300,000 | Very high (VHF) | 10-1 |
| 300,000- 3,000,000 | Ultra high (UHF) | 1-0.1 |
| 3,000,000-30,000,000 | Super high (SHF) | 0.1-0.01 |

Short waves carry farther without weakening than do regular broadcasting waves. Short waves are generally used to broadcast to foreign countries and other distant places. They are also used by amateurs, and in FM (frequency modulation) broadcasting, in television programs, and for transoceanic telephone conversations. Special equipment is needed to receive short-wave broadcasts. Short waves exhibit such peculiarities as *skip distances* (areas they skip over). PALMER H. CRAIG

See also RADIO (Radio Waves).

**SHORTENING.** See BUTTER; LARD; MARGARINE; VEGETABLE OIL.

**SHORTER COLLEGE.** See UNIVERSITIES AND COLLEGES (table).

354

# SHORTHAND

Gregg Publishing Div., McGraw-Hill Book Co., Inc.

**SHORTHAND** is a method of writing rapidly in symbols or letters instead of in words. Shorthand is used mostly to *take dictation*, or record what someone says. A person can write shorthand much faster than longhand because he writes symbols only for *sounds*. Many words contain letters that are not pronounced. In shorthand, a person writes only what he actually *hears*. For example, the word *people* becomes *pepl* in shorthand. Other short cuts include using one or two symbols or letters to represent whole words or entire phrases of several words.

There are many systems of shorthand, but all belong to three major classes. These are: (1) those that use symbols, (2) those that use regular longhand letters, and (3) those that use shorthand machines.

Hundreds of shorthand systems have been devised. The *Gregg* and *Pitman* methods are the best-known systems using symbols. The *Thomas Natural* system, a newer symbol method, is not used as much as the other methods. *Speedwriting* is the most common system that uses longhand letters (see SPEEDWRITING). The *Stenograph* is the most widely used shorthand machine.

Most persons speak at an average rate of about 140 words a minute. A stenographer can take most dictation by writing shorthand at a rate of only 80 words a minute. But some stenographic jobs require speeds of up to 120 words a minute. Court reporters must be able to take down conversation at a rate of 200 words a minute. In a contest, one court reporter set a record of taking down testimony at a rate of 282 words a minute.

## Gregg Shorthand

The Gregg method was invented by John Robert Gregg, an educator born in Ireland. It is the most widely used shorthand system in the world. Gregg published his first book, *Light-Line Phonography*, in England in 1888. Gregg later promoted his system in the United States. The symbols are based on longhand strokes and flow along in the same smooth style as longhand writing.

**Consonants.** Many characters in the Gregg system appear in pairs and differ only in length.
Written forward:

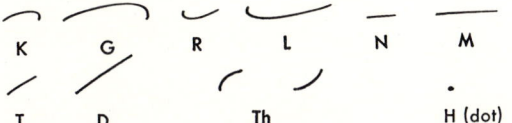

Written downward:

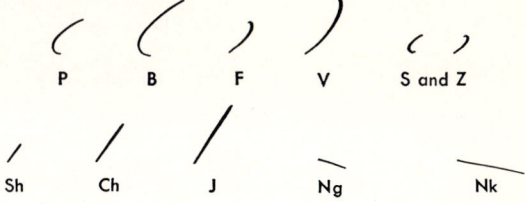

**Vowels.** A large circle, ⃝, represents the several sounds of *a*: ă as in *cat;* ä as in *calm;* ā as in *cane*.

A small circle, ᴏ, is used for the following sounds: ĭ as in *hit*, ĕ as in *hen*, and ē as in *greet*.

A hook, ⌣, is used to indicate the following sounds: ŏ as in *rot*, aw as in *raw* and *bought*, and ō as in *wrote*.

A different hook, ⌢, is used for these sounds: ŭ as in *duck;* oo as in *took;* oo as in *pool*.

**Diphthongs:**

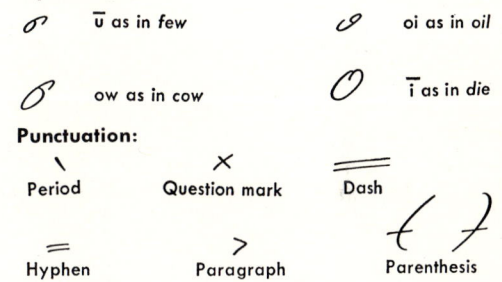

**Punctuation:**

| \ | × | = |
|---|---|---|
| Period | Question mark | Dash |

| = | > | ⊂ ⊃ |
|---|---|---|
| Hyphen | Paragraph | Parenthesis |

**Brief Forms.** The student of Gregg shorthand learns the symbols, and also memorizes 184 *brief forms* representing commonly used words and phrases. Before the 1949 revision of the system, there were several hundred of these brief forms. The Gregg writer learns to write many long words by writing just enough of each word to suggest the entire word. Examples: *prelim* for *preliminary* and *reluc* for *reluctant*.

| can | ⌒ | be, by | ( |
|---|---|---|---|
| go, good | ⌒ | but | ) |
| are, our, hour | ⌒ | have | ) |
| will, well | ⌒ | please | C |
| in, not | — | could | ⌒ |
| am, more | — | should | ⌒ |
| at, it | / | some | ⌒ |
| the | ⌒ | with | ᴏ |

**Phrasing.** There are many standard phrases in all shorthand systems. The shorthand student usually learns these from a textbook. In addition, most writers work out their own phrases for expressions that are used frequently by their employers.

355

# SHORTHAND

**Examples of Phrases:**

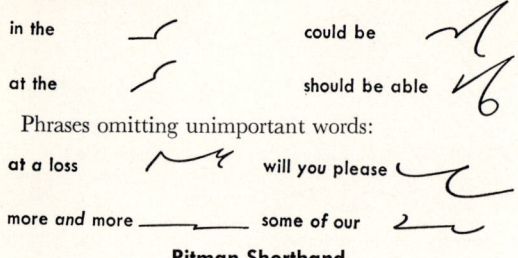

Phrases omitting unimportant words:

**Diphthongs:**

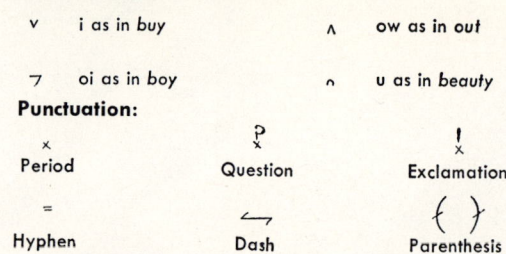

## Pitman Shorthand

The Pitman method was invented by Isaac Pitman, an Englishman, in the 1830's. His first shorthand book was published in England in 1837. Pitman shorthand is characterized by the *shading* of strokes. Some strokes are light and others are heavy or dark. In Pitman shorthand, the position of the symbol *above*, *on*, or *through* the line further determines the meaning of the word.

**Consonants.** Similar-sounding consonants are often represented by the same symbol. The shading of the symbol indicates differences in sound.

Written downward:

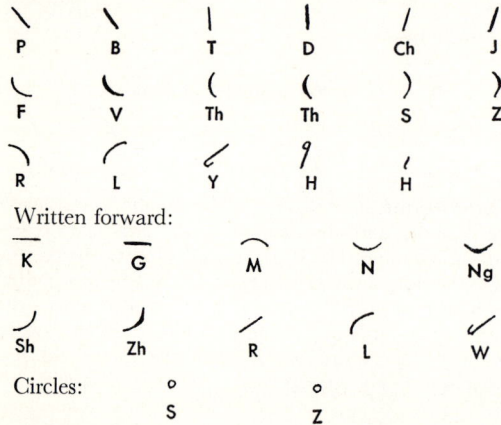

**Vowels.** When the first vowel in a word has the sound of ă, ah, ŏ, or aw, the outline is written *above* the line. When the first vowel has the sound of ĕ, ā, ŭ, or ō, the outline is written *on* the line. When the first vowel in a word has the sound of ĭ, ē, o͝o, or o͞o, the outline is generally written *through* the line. But there are some exceptions to this rule for writing outlines through the line.

When placed near the beginning of a consonant stroke, a light dot expresses the sound of ă as in *sat*, a heavy dot expresses the sound of ah as in *car*, a light dash expresses the sound of ŏ as in *got*, and a heavy dash expresses the sound of aw as in *talk*.

When placed close to the middle of a consonant stroke, a light dot expresses the sound of ĕ as in *get*, a heavy dot expresses the sound of ā as in *mate*, a light dash expresses the sound of ŭ as in *trust*, and a heavy dash expresses the sound of ō as in *low*.

When placed close to the end of a stroke, the sound of ĭ as in *sit* is shown by a light dot, the sound of ē as in *tea* by a heavy dot, the sound of o͝o as in *foot* by a light dash, and o͞o as in *food* by a heavy dash.

**Short Forms.** Pitman shorthand has 214 *short forms*. Like the Gregg brief forms, these represent frequently-used words and phrases.

## Thomas Natural Shorthand

The Thomas Natural system was invented in the 1930's by Charles A. Thomas, an American shorthand teacher. His first textbook appeared in 1935. It was designed to provide a simpler symbol system. However, the Thomas Natural system never became a widely used system of shorthand. It has only 12 word forms. They correspond to brief forms and short forms. All other words may be shortened by writing the first consonant and one or more other major sounds.

**Consonants** have definite symbols.
Written counterclockwise:

Written clockwise:

Straight-line strokes:

**Vowels.** The vowel following the first consonant of a word is expressed automatically by placing the base of the consonant stroke above the line to express *a*, *on* the line to express *e* and short *i*, and *below* the line to express *o*, *oo*, and *u*. At the beginning of words, vowels are written as follows:

(Long *i* is always written in this manner).

**Punctuation:**

356

**Word Signs.** These are the 12 memory forms:

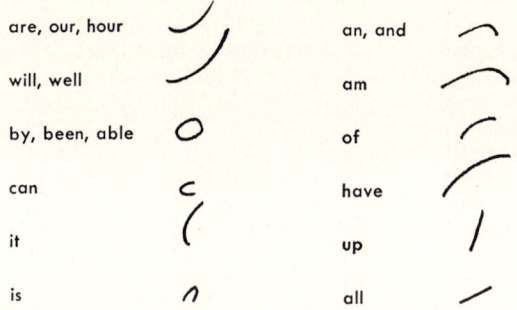

Here is a letter written in the two leading systems of symbol shorthand.

Gentlemen:
   The back issue of your publication, which I recently requested, arrived this morning. Please accept my thanks for your promptness.
   Cordially yours,

**Gregg:**

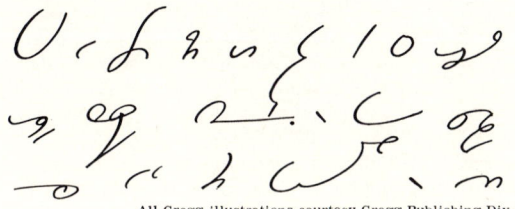

All Gregg illustrations courtesy Gregg Publishing Div., McGraw-Hill Book Co., Inc.

**Pitman:**

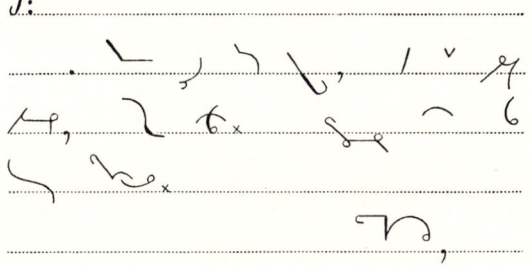

All Pitman illustrations courtesy Pitman Publishing Corp.

### History

Marcus Tullius Tiro, a secretary to the Roman orator Cicero, invented a shorthand system about 50 B.C. During the A.D. 700's, the art of shorthand seemed to disappear. It was revived in England in 1588, when Timothy Bright published his *Characterie: an Art of Short, Swift, and Secret Writing by Character.* This was followed by Peter Bale's *Brachygraphy.* In 1602, John Willis published *The Art of Stenography*, the first attempt at a genuine alphabetical system. Pitman's book in 1837 brought shorthand into world-wide use. Gregg published his book in 1888. Gregg shorthand has been adapted to many languages.   EDWIN R. BOWMAN

**Related Articles** in WORLD BOOK include:

| | |
|---|---|
| Court Reporter | Pitman, Sir Isaac |
| Gregg, John Robert | Shorthand Machine |
| Office Work | Speedwriting |

## SHOSHONI INDIANS

**SHORTHAND MACHINE** is used to record speech rapidly and accurately. The machine has 21 lettered keys. Any number of letters may be struck at one time. The operator writes numbers by striking a numeral bar and a key bearing the desired number. The numeral bar corresponds to the shift key of a typewriter.

The keyboard is arranged so that the fingers of the left hand print the beginning consonants of a word, the right hand prints the concluding consonants, and the thumbs print the vowels. The letters, C, I, J, M, N, Q, V, X, Y, Z, are omitted. These letters are represented by combinations of other letters that are printed by a single stroke. For example, *M* is represented by the letters *PH*. The letters, P, R, S, and T are in both the left-hand and the right-hand positions on the keyboard.

A shorthand machine operator writes by sounds, much like writers using other shorthand systems. He omits all letters of a word that are not actually pronounced. Many words and phrases can be written with single strokes. He writes multi-stroke words one syllable at a time. The letters are printed on a narrow paper pad that moves automatically, a line with each stroke. Each letter or number is always printed in the same position on the tape. Anyone familiar with this method of shorthand can easily transcribe the notes. The sentence: *She was at our house* would be written like this:

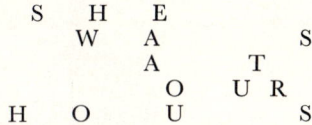

There are several different types of shorthand machines in use, such as the Stenograph, Stenotype, and Brevitype. These machines differ in about the same way that a typewriter made by one company differs from that made by another. They are often used for recording speeches and court testimony.

Ward Stone Ireland, a stenographer and court reporter from Dallas, Tex., invented the first shorthand machine, the Stenotype, in 1910.   EDWIN R. BOWMAN

See also SHORTHAND; COURT REPORTER.

**SHORTHORN.** See CATTLE (Beef Cattle; color picture, Shorthorn).

**SHORTSIGHTEDNESS.** See NEARSIGHTEDNESS.

**SHOSHONE DAM.** See BUFFALO BILL DAM.

**SHOSHONE FALLS.** See IDAHO (Places to Visit; picture).

**SHOSHONI INDIANS,** *show SHOW nee,* also spelled SHOSHONE, once lived in the desert area of what is now eastern Nevada, southern Idaho, and western Utah. The first white settlers in this region sometimes called the Shoshoni "Snake" or "Digger" Indians. Sacagawea, one of the most famous Indians in American history, belonged to the Shoshoni tribe (see SACAGAWEA).

The Shoshoni lived on some of the most barren land in the United States. They formed small, isolated family groups of eight to ten persons. These groups constantly moved from place to place in search of seeds, roots, fish, birds, and small animals such as rabbits. The Shoshoni planned their journeys so that they could collect each type of plant as it ripened, and visit each

357

## SHOSTAKOVICH, DIMITRI

animal's favorite haunt. They returned to the same areas once each year. One family referred to another according to the main food of a region. There were Seed Eaters, Rabbit Eaters, and so on. If people had an abundance of food in the fall, several families gathered together where the winter was mild to form a camp. They spent much of the time singing, dancing, and telling stories. If the winter was severe and food was scarce, they often abandoned the sick, the aged, and the newborn babies to die of exposure.

Some of the Shoshoni acquired horses from the Spaniards, and became buffalo hunters like the Plains tribes. Well-known leaders of these Shoshoni included the chieftains Pocatello and Washakie (see WASHAKIE). The Shoshoni now live as ranchers and farmers in Wyoming, Nevada, and Idaho.   CHARLES E. DIBBLE

**SHOSTAKOVICH,** SHAHS *tuh* KOH *vich*, **DIMITRI** (1906-   ), is a leading Russian composer. His "Polka" from the ballet, *Age of Gold* (1930), shows a satirical style reminiscent of Igor Stravinsky's *Petrouchka*. Shostakovich's tendency to be daring and experimental was responsible for his being frequently in and out of government favor. His early symphonies, ballets, and the opera *Lady Macbeth of Mtsensk* (1934), won popularity, but were condemned as being in conflict with "socialistic realism." Shostakovich's brilliant *Symphony No. 5* (1937), frequently played in the United States, was subtitled "A Soviet Artist's Reply to Just Criticism." His *Quintet for Piano and Strings*

Sovfoto
**Dimitri Shostakovich**

(1940) won the Stalin prize. But he again lost favor with the Russian government with *Symphony No. 9* (1945), which was considered too light and humorous. His *Symphony No. 10* (1953), two violin concertos (1955, 1956), and *Symphony No. 11* (1957), restored him to favor and won international acclaim. He was born in Leningrad.   WILLIAM FLEMING

**SHOT.** See SHOTGUN.

**SHOT-PUT** is a test of strength in track and field meets. In ancient days, athletes used a heavy stone in the shot-put. Present-day athletes use an iron ball. Senior athletes use one weighing 16 pounds, high-school boys use one of 12 pounds, and beginners use 8-pound balls.

Success in shot-putting depends upon ability to get the whole force of the body behind the heave. The put is made from a circle seven feet in diameter. An arc-shaped wooden stopboard usually forms the front of the circle. Standing at the back of the circle, the shot-putter balances the shot in his fingers. Then he hops, or *glides*, forward until his leading foot is near the stopboard. He propels the shot, and as he does so, the momentum forces him to turn his body so that the positions of his two feet are reversed and so that his weight is well forward on the other foot. His arm thrusts out in a long follow-through. The shot can be sent into the air most effectively at an angle of 40 degrees. The measurement is made from the nearest edge of the first break of ground to the nearest point on the inside edge of the shot-put circle.   FRED RUSSELL

See also TRACK AND FIELD.

**SHOT TOWER** was a structure used by colonists to make small shot for their muzzle-loading firearms. They were wooden or brick towers from 50 to 100 feet high. The men poured melted lead through a vessel at the top of the tower that had holes in it. As each piece of lead dropped, it formed a round ball. It cooled in this shape when it landed at the bottom of the tower in a vessel containing cold water.   JOHN D. BILLINGSLEY

**SHOTE.** See HOG (Hog Terms).

## HOW TO PUT THE SHOT

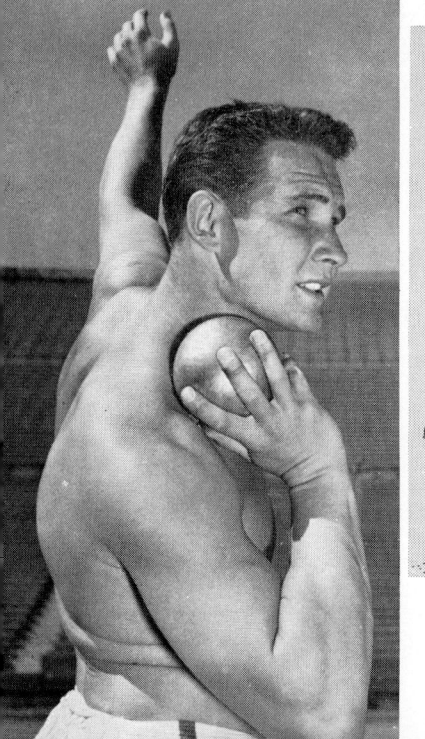

Wide World

The shot-putter cradles the shot against his neck with one hand, and extends the other arm to maintain his balance, *left.* The drawings, *above,* show how he swings one leg for balance and momentum, then glides across the ring, and pushes the shot away.

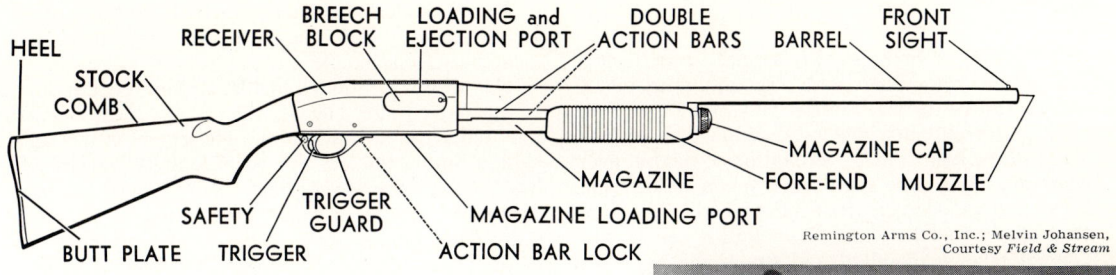

Remington Arms Co., Inc.; Melvin Johansen, Courtesy *Field & Stream*

**MAIN PARTS OF A PUMP ACTION SHOTGUN**

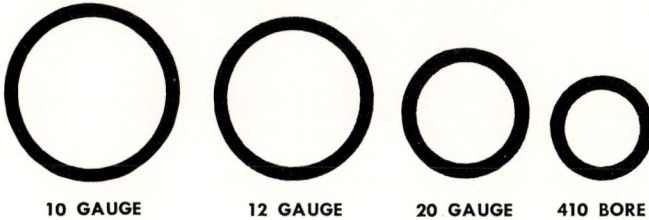

10 GAUGE   12 GAUGE   20 GAUGE   410 BORE

**The Shotgun** is the favorite weapon of duck hunters, *right*. The size of a shotgun's bore is its *gauge*. This is determined by the number of round lead balls, each the size of the bore, that are needed to weigh a pound. If 10 are needed, the shotgun is a 10 gauge. The only exception is the 410 bore, which is .410 inch in diameter and 67.5 gauge.

**SHOTGUN** is a shoulder gun that fires a cartridge that contains a powder charge and a load of lead pellets, called *shot*. The shot spreads over a wide area. This makes it easier to hit a moving target with a shotgun than with the single bullet from a rifle or a pistol. Sportsmen prefer shotguns for hunting flying and running game, and the modern shotgun is chiefly a hunting gun. Small pellets used in shotguns are called *bird shot*. Larger ones, called *buckshot*, are used to shoot deer.

The size of a shotgun is measured by *bore*, or *gauge*. The weight of the lead ball required to fit the muzzle of the gun is the standard of measurement for the bore. If a bullet weighing one-twelfth of a pound fits the bore, the shotgun is called a 12-bore, or a 12-gauge, gun. Popular gauges are 10, 12, 16, 20, 28, and .410.

The amount of spread in the shot is controlled by the *choke*. If a barrel will put 70 per cent of its shot charge in a 30-inch circle at 40 yards, it is called *full choke*. *Modified choke* will deliver about 60 per cent; *improved cylinder* about 50 per cent. A full choke 12-gauge gun will kill ducks that are about 60 to 65 yards away.

The first shotgun, developed in 1537, was loaded with small shot instead of one round ball. In 1831, Augustus Demondion patented a cartridge that held small shot. Modern shotguns are single barrels, double barrels, or single barrels with automatic repeating magazines that hold several cartridges. Repeating shotguns are popular in the United States. JACK O'CONNOR

See also FIREARM; HARQUEBUS; SHOT TOWER; SKEET.

**SHOTOKU, PRINCE.** See JAPAN (Early History).

**SHOULDER** is the part of the body that lies between the trunk and the arm. In human beings it consists of two bones: (1) a broad, flat shoulder blade (or *scapula*) in the back, and (2) a slender collarbone (or *clavicle*) in front. The large bone of the arm, the *humerus*, has a round head that fits into a shallow depression of the scapula to form a ball-and-socket joint, which allows great freedom of movement. Seventeen muscles serve to move the joint. The shoulder joint, because of its great mobility, is the most frequently dislocated joint of the human body. The clavicle, lying very close to the surface, is the most frequently fractured bone.

Fishes, amphibians, and reptiles have simpler and fewer shoulder bones. Aquatic mammals and other animals—for example, the horse, deer, and pig—have only one bone, the scapula, in the shoulder. WILLIAM V. MAYER

See also HUMAN BODY (Trans-Vision three-dimensional color picture); COLLARBONE (picture).

**SHOUP,** *shoop,* **GEORGE LAIRD** (1836-1904), was the first governor of Idaho. He volunteered for the Union Army during the Civil War, and rose to the rank of colonel. He helped found Salmon, Idaho, in 1866, and was successful as a merchant there. He served in the territorial legislature, and was appointed territorial governor by President Benjamin Harrison. When Idaho was admitted to the Union in 1890, Shoup was elected governor. But he resigned to serve as a Republican in the United States Senate from 1890 to 1901. He was born at Kittanning, Pa., and worked as a young man on the family farm in Illinois. NELSON M. BLAKE

**SHOVELBOARD.** See SHUFFLEBOARD.

# SHOVELER

**SHOVELER,** or SPOONBILL, is a small river duck of the Northern Hemisphere with a spoon-shaped bill. It lives in North America, Europe, and Asia in summer, and migrates south in winter to Colombia, North Africa, and southern Asia. The upper portion of the bill overhangs the lower. The male has a green head, white breast, and blue-and-chestnut-colored body. The shoveler feeds in shallow water on mollusks, insects, and roots. It takes a mouthful and strains the mud and water out through "gutters" in the sides of its bill, leaving the food trapped inside. Shovelers nest on the ground. They sometimes build their nests quite a distance from water. The female lays from 6 to 14 pale greenish to bluish-white eggs.

**Scientific Classification.** The shoveler belongs to the duck family, *Anatidae*. It is classified as genus *Spatula*, species *S. clypeata*. JOSEPH J. HICKEY

See also BIRD (color picture: Wild Ducks and Wild Geese).

**SHOW.** See CIRCUS; DOG (Dog Shows); FAIRS AND EXPOSITIONS; FLOWER (Flower Shows); INTERNATIONAL LIVE STOCK EXPOSITION; MOTION PICTURE; THEATER.

**SHOW ME STATE.** See MISSOURI.

**SHOWA.** See HIROHITO.

**SHOWBOAT** is a floating theater. It has become an American contribution to theatrical history. The showboat is a flat-bottomed boat with a theater. It travels along rivers, especially the Ohio and Mississippi, and stops at towns to present stage productions. Noah Ludlow built the first showboat in 1817. There are still a few in existence, but they were especially popular in the 1800's.

Many books and articles have been written about the colorful life of showboats. They describe the life of the versatile performers, and the excitement in river towns at the time of performances. The novel *Show Boat* by Edna Ferber gave the setting for Jerome Kern's popular operetta of the same name. GLENN HUGHES

**SHRAPNEL** is a form of artillery shell invented by Lieutenant (later, Lieutenant General) Henry Shrapnel (1761-1842). The shell contained a number of balls and a charge of powder that burst the shell. The British Army used the first shell of this type in Surinam in 1804. During World War I, shrapnel was considered one of the most reliable and effective antipersonnel shells. Since World War II, the word commonly refers to the steel fragments of the shell casing hurled by an explosive charge, although some types of shells filled with metal fragments are still used. Infantry soldiers usually have steel helmets to protect their heads from shrapnel. See also AMMUNITION; ARTILLERY. JOHN D. BILLINGSLEY

**SHREVEPORT,** La. (pop. 160,535; met. area 281,481; alt. 204 ft.), is an industrial center and Louisiana's second largest city. It is on the Red River in the northwestern part of the state. It is about 310 miles northwest of New Orleans and 190 miles east of Dallas, Tex. (see LOUISIANA [political map]). For the monthly weather in Shreveport, see LOUISIANA (Climate).

Shreveport developed rapidly after the Caddo oil field was discovered in 1906. Today, the natural gas in this region furnishes fuel for the city's factories. Shreveport has cotton gins, cottonseed-oil mills, glass plants, oil refineries, iron and steel foundries, railroad shops, and wood-products factories. The city is the home of the Louisiana State Fair, Barksdale Air Force Base, and Centenary College.

The town was founded in 1835 as Shreve's Landing. It was named after Henry Miller Shreve, who opened the Red River to navigation. The city was the state capital during the last two years of the Civil War. It has a commission government. EDWIN A. DAVIS

**SHREW,** *shroo*, is a small animal that looks like a sharp-nosed mouse. Some shrews are among the smallest known mammals, weighing as little as an American

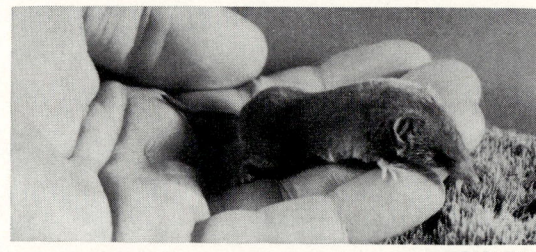
Cy La Tour

**The Tiny Shrew** can fit in the palm of the hand, but it is a big eater. It eats about three times its own weight each day.

penny. Shrews live in both the Eastern and Western hemispheres. They make their homes in fields, woodlands, gardens, and marshes.

Shrews are often mistaken for mice because of their small size. Shrews have long, slender snouts which they can move to explore small holes and crevices for food. Their eyes and ears are tiny, and their bodies are covered with short, dark hair. One of the largest shrews in America is the *water shrew*, which is 6 inches long, including its tail. The smallest, the *pygmy shrew*, is about 3½ inches long.

Shrews eat insects and worms chiefly, but they sometimes kill and eat birds and other small creatures. They even attack mice larger than themselves. They are fierce fighters. The bite of some shrews is poisonous to their prey. Shrews must eat almost continually during the day to satisfy their high energy requirements.

Weasels, foxes, and owls prey upon the shrews. But the shrew's strong musky odor is a good protection against enemies. One of the species in the United States is the *short-tailed shrew* of the East. This tiny animal has a taste for snails. Another, the *masked shrew*, is found in the northern United States and in Canada. It usually lives near marshes and streams.

Shrews are harmless to man. They are useful in gardens, for they eat insects and grubs.

**Scientific Classification.** The shrew belongs to the shrew family, *Soricidae*. The water shrew is classified as genus *Sorex*, species *S. palustris*. The short-tailed shrew is *Blarina brevicauda*. FRANK B. GOLLEY

See also TREE SHREW.

**SHREWSBURY SCHOOL,** *SHROOZ ber ih*, founded by King Edward VI in 1552, ranks as one of England's famous public schools. It is in Shrewsbury. After a period of decline in the 1700's, two great headmasters restored the school to a leading position. Samuel Butler, who served from 1798 to 1836, raised the standards of scholarship. Benjamin Kennedy, headmaster from 1836 to 1866, added modern studies and encouraged interest in music and sports. R. W. MORRIS

**SHRIKE** is a bird that can be recognized by its strong, slightly hooked beak, and by its habit of thrusting grasshoppers, mice, and smaller birds onto thorns, barbs, or twigs, much as a butcher hangs meat. The shrike then tears its prey to pieces and eats it. From this habit comes its common name of *butcherbird*.

A Young Northern Shrike
Charles W. Schwartz

There are two species in North America: the *northern shrike*, or *butcherbird*, and the *loggerhead shrike*. The northern shrike ranges from the far north in summer to Kansas and Virginia in the winter. The loggerhead shrike nests in Mexico and northward to southern Canada, and travels south for the winter. Both species have feathers of gray, black, and white. Their nests are built of grass and small sticks in bushes or low trees. Both adult and young shrikes are often seen in summer on bushes, wires, and fences along country roads. The female lays 4 to 8 eggs. They are dull or grayish white, and are thickly marked with brown and lavender. The northern shrike is about 10 inches long, and the loggerhead shrike is about 9.

The shrike's name may be an imitation of its harsh call notes, which are screeches or shrieks. But its song is a sweet warble. Shrikes are protected by law, because they destroy insects and predatory mammals.

**Scientific Classification.** The shrike belongs to the family *Laniidae*. The northern shrike is classified as genus *Lanius*, species *L. borealis*; the loggerhead shrike is *L. ludovicianus*.
LEON A. HAUSMAN

See also BIRD (color picture: Birds That Help Us).

**SHRIMP** is a sea animal distantly related to the lobster. But shrimps do not have claws, and are much smaller and more slender than lobsters. Shrimps have long feelers and five pairs of delicate legs. They swim backward by fast strokes of their fanlike tails. Powerful muscles in the back move the tail. These muscles make the shrimp's back look "humped." The shrimp's body is covered by a thin, translucent shell that is jointed to allow the animal to move. But as the shrimp grows, it must shed the shell and form a new one. Some shrimps grow 9 inches long. Large shrimps are sometimes called *prawns*. Shrimps feed on tiny ocean life.

Shrimps vary in color from white to a brilliant red. Deep-sea shrimps are bright red. But those that live near the coasts have pale colors that match the sandy shore bottoms over which they swim. The three most valuable species of shrimps for commerce are the white, brown, and pink ones.

The common shrimp spawns early in spring in offshore coastal waters. The female lays her round eggs directly into the water. It has been estimated that about 500,000 to 1,000,000 eggs are laid at a single spawning. The eggs drop to the sea bottom and hatch in about 24 hours. Shrimps must go through 10 *larval* (developmental) stages before they reach adulthood. During most of this time, they look like tiny mites and are barely visible to the naked eye. It takes many weeks for shrimps to mature. Almost all of this time they are capable of very little movement and are carried about by the currents. Once they reach adulthood, they grow very rapidly and soon swim out to the deeper and warmer sea waters.

Shrimps are fished from Alaska and Maine southward along the seacoasts to Argentina. The waters off Alaska have some excellent shrimp-fishing grounds. Shrimps are also fished in the coastal waters of Africa, Asia, and Europe. The shrimp fishery is one of the most valuable fisheries in the United States. The annual catch is worth more than $113 million.

Fishermen catch shrimps by dragging nets on the bottom of the bay or ocean. The *otter trawl* net is most often used (see FISHING INDUSTRY). This net is bag-shaped, with two winglike boards attached to its open end. The pressure of the water against these boards as the ship moves along spreads the net's mouth. When the net is filled, power winches draw the net and catch

**Shrimps** are used in preparing many tasty dishes. These sea animals vary in color from bright red to white. Some grow as long as 9 inches. Florida fishermen, *right*, provide about a sixth of the North American shrimp supply. They catch shrimps in the waters off the west coast of Florida.

New York Zoological Society

Florida State News Bureau

# SHRINE

into the vessel. Fresh, canned, or frozen shrimps may be bought in stores. They are sources of vitamins A and D.

**Scientific Classification.** The shrimp belongs to the class *Crustaceae*.                              GEORGE A. ROUNSEFELL

See also CRUSTACEAN; LOBSTER.

**SHRINE** is an object or place considered sacred for its associations. All major religions have sacred places to which the devout make pilgrimages to give thanks or to ask divine favors. See also KAABA; LOURDES; OUR LADY OF FATIMA; SAINTE ANNE DE BEAUPRÉ.

**SHRIVER, SARGENT** (1915-    ), helped organize the Peace Corps and served from 1961 to 1966 as its first director. From 1964 to 1968, he served as special assistant to President Lyndon B. Johnson, in charge of organizing and directing the *war on poverty* program. President Johnson appointed him United States ambassador to France in 1968.

Shriver was born ROBERT SARGENT SHRIVER, JR., in Westminster, Md. He was graduated from Yale in 1938, and became assistant general manager of the Merchandise Mart in Chicago in 1946. Shriver served as president of the Chicago Board of Education from 1955 to 1960. He was a campaign adviser for his brother-in-law John F. Kennedy during the 1960 presidential campaign.

Peace Corps

**Sargent Shriver**

See also PEACE CORPS.

**SHROPSHIRE.** See ENGLAND (color map: The 38 Counties of England).

**SHROUD OF TURIN,** *TOO rin*, is a cloth 14 feet long by 3½ feet wide, kept at Turin, Italy. Tradition claims that it wrapped Jesus' body in the tomb after His crucifixion. Photographic reversal of the lights and shadows of the stains on the shroud (which are largely negative) reveals a life-size front and back figure of a man who was crucified, scourged, lanced, and bloodily crowned.                                           FRANCIS L. FILAS

**SHROVE TUESDAY** is the day before Ash Wednesday, the beginning of Lent. Its name came from the old custom of confessing (being *shriven*) on that day. Shrove Tuesday is a time of rejoicing in many countries and communities. It is the last day of the *carnival* season of southern Europe, and corresponds to the *Mardi Gras* of the French and the *Pancake Tuesday* of the English. See also CARNIVAL; MARDI GRAS.       FULTON J. SHEEN

**SHRUB** is one of the four main groups of plants in terms of size and form. A shrub is a perennial with woody stems that is smaller than a tree. Shrubs usually have several low stems branched near the ground. They also are called *bushes*, especially if they have many branches (see BUSH). Trees have one large stem, the trunk. Shrubs differ from vines because they stand up without support, and do not climb. They differ from herbs because they have hard, woody, long-lived stems. Shrubs grow in almost all lands. They provide cover and food for birds and game, and protect the soil from erosion. Shrubs are popular for ornamental planting along foundations of houses, in gardens, and as hedges around the borders of lawns. Many shrubs produce fragrant blossoms, or decorative leaves, twigs, and fruits.

Most shrubs will grow in well-drained soil, spaded to a depth of 1½ to 2 feet. Smaller plants may be spaced 2 to 3 feet apart, the larger ones 6 feet apart. Transplanting may be done in either fall or spring. For best growth, prune old branches.           ELBERT L. LITTLE, JR.

**Related Articles** in WORLD BOOK include:

| | | |
|---|---|---|
| Acanthus | Deutzia | Plumbago |
| Azalea | Dogwood | Privet |
| Bayberry | Eglantine | Pussy Willow |
| Beach Plum | Forsythia | Rhododendron |
| Begonia | Furze | Rose of Sharon |
| Black Haw | Hawthorn | Saint John's-Wort |
| Bougainvillea | Hydrangea | Snowball |
| Box | Hyssop | Spiraea |
| Bridal Wreath | Lilac | Sumac |
| Broom | Magnolia | Viburnum |
| Buckthorn | Manzanita | Wax Myrtle |
| Cascara Sagrada | Mock Orange | Winterberry |
| Crape Myrtle | Oleander | Yucca |
| Datura | | |

**SHRUBBY ALTHEA.** See ROSE OF SHARON.

**SHUFFLEBOARD,** or SHOVELBOARD, is a game played on smooth surfaces, such as pavements, gymnasium floors, and ship decks. The object of the game is to push wooden or metal disks into scoring areas, and to knock the opponent's disks out of scoring areas. A player pushes the disks with a *cue* (a stick with a wide end).

Two persons can play shuffleboard against each other, or four persons can form two opposing teams. Each side has four disks. The players take turns shooting from the 10-off space. A player scores 10 points for each disk in the 10-area; eight points for the 8-area; and seven points for the 7-area. Ten points are subtracted for each disk in the 10-off space. After all the disks have been pushed, the players add up their scores and move to the other end of the court and continue play. The winning score may be 50, 75, or 100 points. The

**Shuffleboard Can Be Played on a Smooth, Narrow Surface, Such as a Ship's Deck.**

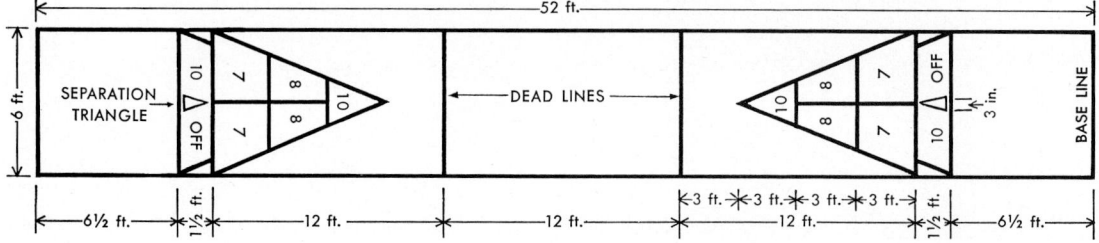

362

winner is the team with the highest scores in two out of three games.

A shuffleboard disk is six inches in diameter. The cue may be no longer than 6'3". The head of the cue is shaped like a half-moon. An official court is 52 feet long and 6 feet wide. The two triangles that form the scoring areas are 18 feet apart. DOROTHY DONALDSON

**SHULEVITZ, URI** (1935-    ), a book illustrator, won the 1969 Caldecott medal for his illustrations for *The Fool of the World and the Flying Ship*. This story is based on an old Russian folk tale.

Shulevitz was born in Warsaw, Poland. He fled Poland with his family in 1939, soon after the German invasion. After wandering through Europe for eight years, the family settled in Paris in 1947. Shulevitz lived in Israel from 1949 to 1959, when he moved to New York City. He published his first children's book, *The Moon in My Room*, in 1963.

**SHULL, GEORGE H.** See CORN (Improving Corn).

**SHUMAN, CHARLES BAKER** (1907-    ), became president of the American Farm Bureau Federation—the nation's largest general farm organization—in 1954. He favors a free market for farm products and opposes all government programs that control farm prices and production.

A central Illinois farmer, Shuman never takes part in government farm programs. He has said that taking government farm checks was like taking narcotics. Once farmers got the habit, they were "hooked." He believes that farmer marketing associations can do more to boost farm income than government programs. Under Shuman, the farm bureau has set up organizations to help sell such crops as tomatoes, apples, and asparagus.

Shuman was born on a farm near Sullivan, Ill. He received a master's degree in agriculture from the University of Illinois in 1929. He served as director of the Moultrie County (Ill.) Farm Bureau from 1931 to 1933, and became its president in 1934. Shuman was elected president of the Illinois Agriculture Association in 1945. DON C. MUHM

**SHUNT.** See AMMETER.

**SHUNT MOTOR.** See ELECTRIC MOTOR (Kinds of Electric Motors).

**SHUSH.** See SUSA.

**Shuffleboard** is a popular game among passengers on ships. Each player uses a long stick called a cue to push the disks.
Swedish American Line

**SHUTTER.** See CAMERA (How a Camera Works).
**SHUTTLE.** See WEAVING (How Cloth Is Woven).
**SHUTTLECOCK.** See BADMINTON (Battledore and Shuttlecock; picture).
**SHYLOCK.** See SHAKESPEARE, WILLIAM (Synopses of Plays [The Merchant of Venice]).

**SI KIANG,** *SHE jih AHNG,* or WEST RIVER, is the most important stream of southern China. The Si Kiang rises on the border of Yunnan and Kweichow provinces and flows southeast for about 1,650 miles. It empties into the South China Sea. Canton, one of China's largest cities, is on the delta formed by the Si Kiang and smaller rivers. Steamships can sail 230 miles up the Si Kiang to Wuchow. L. CARRINGTON GOODRICH

**SI LING-SHI.** See SILK.

**SIALKOT,** *see AHL koht* (pop. 164,346; alt. 1,015 ft.), or SEALKOTE, is an industrial and trading center in West Pakistan (see PAKISTAN [color map]). Factories in the city make sporting goods, surgical instruments, and metal products. Cotton ginning, weaving, tanning, flour milling, and food processing are also important industries in Sialkot. The city is a distribution center for the wheat, rice, millet, sugar cane, and other crops produced nearby. Sialkot has a technical institute. The city has grown up on the site of a fortress that was built in 1181.

**SIAM.** See THAILAND.
**SIAMESE CAT.** See CAT (Siamese Cats; color picture).
**SIAMESE FIGHTING FISH.** See FIGHTING FISH.
**SIAMESE TWINS.** See TWINS.

**SIBELIUS,** *sih BAY lih us,* **JAN,** or JEAN (1865-1957), was a Finnish composer who became the best known of his nation's musicians. Although he wrote music in many categories, he is remembered chiefly for his seven symphonies. His other works include the symphonic poem *Tapiola;* a concerto for violin and orchestra; and a string quartet, *Intimate Voices*. He also wrote many songs, choral works, and short compositions for piano.

Sibelius, the son of an army doctor, was born in Hameenlinna. He began piano lessons at the age of nine, and was soon composing. When he was 20, he entered the University of Helsingfors (now Helsinki) to study law, but continued to study violin and composition at the conservatory there.

Sibelius went to Berlin in 1889 for further study, and the following year he studied in Vienna. There he began an opera based on the Finnish national epic poem, *Kalevala*. He never completed the opera, but its music was used in four symphonic poems, of which *The Swan of Tuonela* is the best known. In those works, as well as in *A Saga* and *Finlandia*, Sibelius interpreted the spirit of Finland. The Finnish government granted him funds in 1897 so that he could spend all his time composing.

In 1899, performances of his *Symphony No. 1 in E minor* established Sibelius' reputation. He toured Europe in 1900 with the Helsingfors Philharmonic Orchestra. Later, he made several trips to England, and visited the United States in 1914. His last significant compositions appeared in 1925. Sibelius was the first to receive the Sibelius Award for international composing achievements. It was established as an annual award in 1953 in his honor. Sibelius lived in Helsingfors. HOMER ULRICH

363

# SIBERIA

**SIBERIA,** *sy BEER ih ah,* is the name of most of the Asian part of Russia. It is called SIBIR in the Russian language. Siberia is not an official region of Russia and it has no official boundaries. Most large centers of population are along the route of the original Trans-Siberian Railroad. Thousands of square miles of Siberia are forested plains, where few people live.

For hundreds of years, Siberia has been a place to send exiles and criminals. The czars and dictators of Russia have sent millions of their enemies and criminals to cold and isolated parts of Siberia. Many of these people have been used to develop mining, agricultural, and manufacturing industries there. Since World War II, many Russians have been sent to Siberia to work in industry and to develop new farm areas.

## The Land and Its Resources

**Location and Surface Features.** Siberia lies in northern Asia. It is bordered by the Arctic Ocean, the Bering and Okhotsk seas, Mongolia and Soviet Middle Asia, and the Ural Mountains. See RUSSIA (physical map).

There are three geographic regions in Siberia: West Siberian Plain, Central Siberian Plateau, and East Siberian Highlands. The *West Siberian Plain,* an area of forests in the north and *steppes* (grasslands) in the south, stretches from the Ural Mountains to the Yenisey River. The high plateaus of the *Central Siberian Plateau* extend from the Yenisey to the Lena River. The southern part of the region contains the Altai and Sayan mountains, and Lake Baykal. The lake has an area of 12,162 square miles. It is the largest fresh-water lake in northern Asia, and the deepest lake in the world. The *East Siberian Highlands* extend from the Lena River to the Bering and Okhotsk seas. The region contains 15,584-foot Mount Klyuchevskaya, an active volcano on the Kamchatka Peninsula.

**Climate.** Siberia is famous for its long, cold winters. The temperature falls lower than at the North Pole. The climate generally is dry as well as cold. The dryness makes the cold seem less severe. Average summer temperatures are between 50 and 65°F.

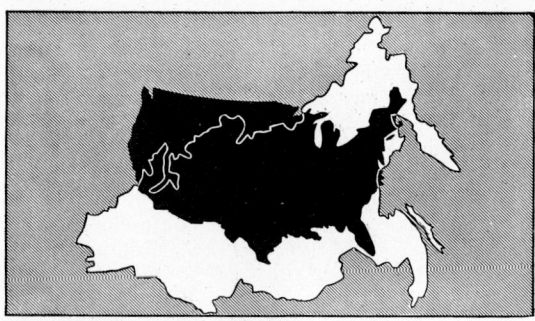

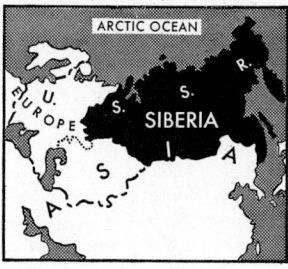

**Siberia** is about 1 ⅔ times as large as the United States. It lies in Asia in the eastern part of the state of Russia in the U.S.S.R.

**Natural Resources.** Siberia is rich in minerals, including coal, oil, natural gas, iron, and gold. Animals such as the bear, lynx, wolf, fox, sable, and ermine are trapped for fur. Forests cover over one million square miles. Fishing is important, especially in the area of the Sea of Okhotsk. Lobsters, crabs, salmon, cod, and herring are the principal fish caught for sale.

## The People and Their Work

**The People** of Siberia are chiefly Russians. Since the 1700's, Russia has moved many white settlers into the region. However, descendants of the original Mongoloid peoples still live in remote areas.

**Way of Life.** Living conditions are often harsh, due to the climate and rugged land. The people dress as warmly as possible. Their food consists largely of fish dishes, cabbage soup, and black bread. Many people live in small houses on collective farms. Those who live in the cities are usually crowded into small apartments.

**Cities.** Novosibirsk is the largest city in Siberia. Omsk and Sverdlovsk are important transportation centers. Irkutsk has a university. See the separate articles on cities listed in the *Related Articles* section of this article.

**Agriculture.** The best farming is in southwestern Siberia. All the farming is under government supervision, and much of it is done by machinery. Wheat, oats, and rye are the chief crops.

Livestock raising is important in the steppes. Cattle, horses, goats, and reindeer are raised. Dairying also is an important industry.

--- **FACTS IN BRIEF** ---

**Type of Government:** Part of Russia.
**Area:** About 4,000,000 square miles. *Greatest distance*—(east-west) 4,000 miles; (north-south) 2,000 miles.
**Elevation:** *Highest*—Mount Klyuchevskaya, 15,584 feet; *Lowest*—sea level.
**Population:** About 30,000,000; density, 8 persons to the square mile.
**Chief Products:** *Agriculture*—butter, cattle, horses, oats, rye, wheat. *Manufacturing and Processing*—flour, leather, machinery, vehicles, weapons. *Mining*—coal, gold, iron, lead, oil, natural gas, silver, tungsten, zinc.

**Siberian Hunters Sell Fox Pelts** at one of the government's delivery centers. Siberia produces many fur-bearing animals.
Sovfoto

**City Buses and Government Buildings in Irkutsk** are similar to those in many cities in the United States.

Sovfoto

**"The Chicago of Siberia"** is a name given to Novosibirsk, because of its rapid growth and its many industries.

**Mining.** Siberia has some of the world's largest coal deposits. Russia has linked the iron fields of the Urals and the coal of the Kuznetsk Basin into a system of mines and factories known as the *Ural-Kuznetsk Combine*. West-central Siberia contains large iron deposits. Russia ranks second only to South Africa among gold-producing countries. Most Russian gold is mined in Siberia along the Kolyma, Aldan, and Yenisey rivers. Oil and natural gas deposits in the West Siberian Lowlands began to be developed in the mid-1960's. A large diamond field was discovered in eastern Siberia in 1956 and another in 1959.

**Manufactures.** Home industries, such as flour mills and tanneries, used to be the most important plants. But the Communists have built up many new industries, such as aluminum, iron and steel, and the manufacture of heavy machinery, vehicles, and weapons. There also are atomic and hydrogen-bomb plants near Lake Baykal, which has large reserves of water power.

**Transportation and Communication.** The railroad once known as the Trans-Siberian Railroad is the main railway in Siberia. It connects Siberian cities with European Russia. Many Siberian highways follow ancient caravan routes which led from the chief Siberian cities to Manchuria and Mongolia.

The chief rivers of Siberia flow north, but their branches form interlocking east-west waterways. By making short overland journeys between rivers, it is possible to go by water from the Volga River in Russian Europe to the Amur River on the Asiatic coast. Ships can navigate in the Arctic Ocean in August and September. Aviation has grown in importance in Siberia since World War II.

The Russian government has built a network of radio stations across Siberia. Telegraph lines connect all the major areas of Siberia.

## Government

Siberia forms the eastern two-thirds of the Russian Soviet Federated Socialist Republic (R.S.F.S.R.), one of the divisions of Russia. Within Siberia are three so-called "republics," or states, and several administrative regions. The states are the Yakut, Buryat, and Tuva Autonomous Soviet Socialist Republics. They are governed by their own *Presidium* and *Council of Ministers*. All Siberia is under the Russian government at Moscow. See RUSSIA (Government).

## History

**Early History.** People lived in Siberia as far back as the Stone Age. The Mongols, or Tartars, of central Asia drove many tribes into Siberia. Turkish tribes invaded Siberia through the years. In the early 1200's, the Mongol warrior Genghis Khan conquered many of the Siberian peoples.

**Beginning of Russian Control.** The first movement of Russian power into Siberia was made by the Cossack adventurer Yermak. In 1581, he and his band defeated the Tartars and captured their capital city of Sibir, which was then abandoned. By about 1630, the Russians had reached parts of the Siberian Pacific Coast. Peter the Great sent the first political prisoners to Siberia in 1710. In 1860, Russia forced China to give up its territory from the Amur River to the Pacific.

**In the 1900's.** After the Communist revolution of 1917, there was a strong movement to separate Siberia from the Moscow government. But the movement was put down and, by 1922, all Siberia was part of the Russian S.F.S.R.

During World War II, Russia moved entire factories to Siberia to protect them from enemy attack. Russia has continued to build industrial plants in Siberia, and dams have been constructed there to supply electric power. In 1961, one of the world's largest hydroelectric plants went into operation on the Angara River near Bratsk. By the late 1960's it had a capacity of $4\frac{1}{2}$ million kilowatts.   THEODORE SHABAD

**Related Articles** in WORLD BOOK include:

### CITIES

| | | |
|---|---|---|
| Irkutsk | Omsk | Vladivostok |
| Novosibirsk | Sverdlovsk | |

### PHYSICAL FEATURES

| | | |
|---|---|---|
| Amur River | Okhotsk, Sea of | Ural Mountains |
| Kamchatka Peninsula | Sakhalin | Yablonovyy |
| Lake Baykal | Stanovoy | Mountains |
| Novaya Zemlya | Mountains | Yenisey River |

### OTHER RELATED ARTICLES

| | | |
|---|---|---|
| Aquamarine | Russia | Trans-Siberian |
| Arctic | (pictures) | Railroad |
| Eskimo | Steppe | Tundra |

# SIBERIAN HUSKY

**SIBERIAN HUSKY** is an Arctic sled dog. It is related to the Alaskan malamute, the Eskimo dog, and the Samoyed. Some authorities believe it originated in Siberia. A graceful, quick dog, the husky is also alert and strong. It has a thick, soft, double coat, with a smooth outer coat and a downy under coat. It is usually colored some shade of gray, often with white markings. The husky stands about 23 inches high, and weighs 35 to 60 pounds. OLGA DAKAN

See also DOG (color picture: Working Dogs).

**SIBLEY, HENRY HASTINGS.** See MINNESOTA (Places to Visit; History).

**SIBYL,** *SIB il,* was the name ancient Romans gave to any aged woman who could supposedly foretell the future. The best known was the Cumaean Sibyl. According to legend, the god Apollo promised that she would live one year for each grain of sand she could hold in her hands. But Apollo did not give her eternal youth, and she continued to age. Her shrunken body was eventually kept in a bottle. Sybil guided Aeneas, the Trojan warrior, to the lower world to learn the future of Rome. Later, she offered to sell nine books of prophecy for a high price to a king of Rome. When the king refused twice, the Cumaean Sibyl burned three books each time. The king finally paid the original price for only three. These books of prophecy were consulted in times of danger until they were destroyed by fire in 83 B.C. HERBERT M. HOWE

**SICILIES,** *SIS uh liz,* **KINGDOM OF THE TWO,** was the name of an early kingdom of Italy. It consisted of the Kingdom of Naples in southern Italy, and the Kingdom of Sicily on the island of Sicily. At times, they were united as the *Two Sicilies* (see ITALY [map: Italy—Late 1800's]). The kingdom was formed in the early 1100's by Normans, who conquered the region during the 1000's. See MIDDLE AGES (map [Feudal States of Europe]).

In 1266, the Two Sicilies came under French rule. In 1282, an uprising known as the Sicilian Vespers took place in Sicily. It resulted in the massacre of nearly all the French on the island. Sicily was later separated from Naples and ruled by the Spanish. In the War of the Spanish Succession in 1713, Austria seized Naples, and Sicily was given to Savoy. Savoy turned Sicily over to Austria in 1719, in exchange for Sardinia.

In 1734, Spain conquered the Two Sicilies, and the Spanish Bourbon family ruled them until the time of Napoleon. King Ferdinand I joined the allies against France and lost Naples as a result. The two parts of the kingdom were reunited after Napoleon's downfall.

The Kingdom of the Two Sicilies played an important part in the movement for a united Italy. In 1820, there was an uprising in Naples of the Carbonari, a secret nationalist society. King Ferdinand was forced to grant the Neapolitans a constitution. An Austrian army invaded Naples, and restored Ferdinand to power.

In 1860, Giuseppe Garibaldi landed at Marsala, on the Sicilian coast, and conquered all Sicily. Garibaldi then invaded the mainland and marched on Naples. King Francis II fled, leaving the kingdom in the hands of the patriots. In a plebiscite, the people approved the unification of Italy. In 1860, the Kingdom of the Two Sicilies became part of the domain of Victor Emmanuel, who became King of Italy in 1861. J. SALWYN SCHAPIRO

**SICILY,** or, in Italian, SICILIA, is a large Italian island in the Mediterranean Sea. It is one of Italy's *political regions* (states). Palermo is the capital and chief city of the region. Sicily is separated from the toe of the Italian boot by the narrow strip of water called the Strait of Messina. In prehistoric times, Sicily was part of the mainland of Italy.

Because of the strait, Sicily had an early history separate from that of Italy. Early Carthaginians, Greeks, Romans, and Saracens invaded the island and added their share to Sicilian civilization. But the Strait of Messina kept the barbarian hordes from overrunning Sicily when they destroyed the Roman Empire.

**Location, Size, and Description.** Sicily covers an area of 9,926 square miles, to form the largest island in the Mediterranean Sea. It is a little larger than New Hampshire. For location, see ITALY (political map).

The Apennine Mountains run the length of the Italian mainland and cross Sicily from east to west. Most of the island is mountainous. Its highest point is Mount Etna (11,122 feet). See MOUNT ETNA.

Sicily has many earthquakes. These are especially severe near the Strait of Messina. Geologists believe that the earthquakes are connected with volcanic activity in Mount Etna. Earthquakes have twice destroyed the city of Messina.

Sicily may be divided into three natural areas. These slope to the sea north, east, and south of the mountains. The richest section of the island is the interior upland which makes up part of the northern slope. Palermo lies on a shallow harbor along the northern coast. The eastern shore has been famous for its beautiful cities since the days of the ancient Greeks. Catania, Syracuse, and Taormina are there (see ITALY [picture: Taormina]). The southern coast is a broad plain which is flat near the coast and hilly as it rises toward the uplands. It is sandy and has no good harbors. It is the driest and least productive part of Sicily.

The rivers of Sicily rise in the mountains and flow southward and eastward toward the sea. They fill their beds for only a short season in the winter, and are almost dry in the summer. The Salso and Simeto rivers are the largest.

**Climate.** During the winter, the coasts of Sicily have a mild climate that attracts many tourists. Temperatures average 45°F. in the winter and 79°F. in the summer. The highlands in the winter are rainy. In the summer, the highlands are pleasant, but the coastal plains are dusty and hot. The *sirocco*, a hot, damp wind which blows from the Libyan Desert of Africa, is especially severe on the southern coast of Sicily.

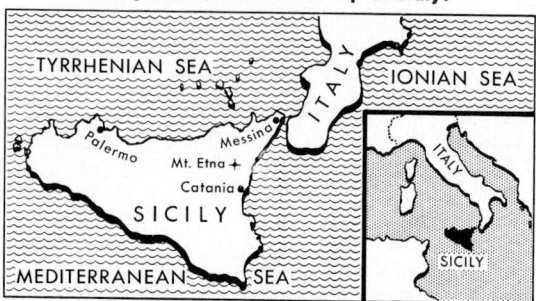

**Sicily Lies at the Lower Tip of Italy.**

Mondadori Press

**Reminders of Ancient Sicily** include the ruins of a large Greek theater in Taormina, *left*. The Romans replaced Greek plays with gladiator contests there. A Sicilian cart, *above*, combines the arts of the cartmaker, the wood carver, and the painter. Delicately carved figurines decorate the cart body.

K. W. Gullers, Rapho-Guillumette

**Natural Resources.** Volcanic ash makes the land of eastern Sicily very fertile, and many people live in that region. Sicily's mountains have deposits of several minerals. The most important of these is sulfur. The waters off the coast are rich in fish of many kinds. The Ragusa oil field in southeastern Sicily produces about a million tons of oil annually. A $4 million pipeline, which was opened in 1957, links this oil field with the port of Augusta. The island also produces much of Italy's asphalt and marine salt.

**The People.** Sicily has a population of about 4,809,-130. About 485 persons live on each square mile. The Sicilians are often described as fierce, emotional, and independent. They use the Sicilian dialect, one of the many Italian dialects. Sicily has many colorful religious festivals.

Greek, Roman, and Renaissance ruins have been found in numerous places in Sicily. These ancient ruins draw tourists to the island. Sicily has many historical cathedrals, palaces, and temples that house works of art. Taormina has a Greek theater and other monuments. The remains of a villa have been unearthed near the village of Piazza Armerina in central Sicily. The villa was built by Emperor Maximilian in the A.D. 200's. It contains precious mosaics.

**Farming and Fishing.** Most of the people earn their living by farming and fishing. The seas around Sicily yield great quantities of tunny, sardines, coral, and sponges. The chief agricultural products of the island are olives, oranges, lemons, grapes, wheat, and winter vegetables. Southern Sicily requires irrigation to produce crops. For years, most of the land in Sicily was owned by great landlords. But small farmers were given some plots of their own under land reforms enacted in 1953. The people of Sicily, however, are poor, partly because there is not enough rainfall to grow good crops.

**History and Government.** Sicily lies between Europe and Africa. For many years, it has been a battlefield for the continents. Early settlers, probably related to those in southern Italy, were conquered by the Greeks who founded the colonies of Syracuse, Agrigentum, Naxos, and others. The Greeks brought their culture to the island. The Athenian Navy was defeated in the Syracuse harbor around 415 B.C.

Sicily was in turn invaded by forces from Phoenicia, Carthage, and Rome. The Goths and Vandals from the north drove the Romans out of Sicily around A.D. 440. The island became part of the Byzantine Empire around 535. Saracens from North Africa replaced the Byzantine rulers in the 870's.

The Normans became rulers of the island in the 1000's. They joined Sicily with southern Italy to form the Kingdom of the Two Sicilies. In 1266, Charles of Anjou, a French ruler, became king of the Two Sicilies. In 1282, an uprising against the French took place in Palermo. The massacre, called the *Sicilian Vespers*, ended French rule. Sicily was ruled by kings of the Spanish house of Aragon, and by Spain, Savoy, and Austria during the next 400 years. In the 1730's, Spain again conquered the region. In 1860, the Italian hero Garibaldi freed Sicily from the rule of the Spanish Bourbon kings. Sicily then became part of the newly united Italy.

During World War II, American, British, and Canadian troops landed on the southeastern coast of Sicily. Air and naval bases on the island were heavily bombed during the war. Messina fell to Allied troops on Aug. 8, 1943. Sicily then became a springboard for the Allied invasion of southern Italy.

Sicily is a political part of Italy, but is a semi-autonomous region. The island is divided into nine provinces, and it elects its own 90-member parliament. Sicilians elect representatives to the federal government in Rome.         BENJAMIN WEBB WHEELER

**Related Articles** in WORLD BOOK include:

Catania
Garibaldi, Giuseppe
Italy
Mafia
Messina
Messina, Strait of
Palermo
Sicilies, Kingdom of the Two
Syracuse

## SICK MAN OF EUROPE

**SICK MAN OF EUROPE.** See TURKEY (History).
**SICKLE.** See KNIFE (picture); SCYTHE.
**SIDDHARTHA GAUTAMA.** See BUDDHA.
**SIDDONS,** *SID'nz,* **SARAH KEMBLE** (1755-1831), was a British actress who enchanted audiences and critics with her rich voice, striking beauty, and powerful presence. She became a subject of poets and painters.

Sarah Siddons was born in Brecon, Wales. She acted in her father's touring company, and married actor William Siddons when she was 18. In 1775 and 1776, she failed as an actress in David Garrick's Drury Lane Theatre in London. She gained more experience, rejoined Garrick's company in 1782, and succeeded. Her great roles include the Shakespearean tragic heroines Lady Macbeth, Desdemona, and Ophelia. Sarah Siddons retired in 1819. MARSTON BALCH

Portrait by Thomas Gainsborough, The National Gallery, London
**Sarah Siddons**

See also SHAKESPEARE, WILLIAM (Famous Actors).

**SIDEREAL TIME,** *sye DEER ee ul,* is star time. It is measured by the rotation of the earth in relation to the stars. Sidereal time measures the actual spin of the earth, separate and apart from its orbital rotation about the sun. Our familiar sun time, generally used on clocks, measures the time from noon to noon. Because of the earth's revolution in its orbit, the sun rises nearly four minutes later each day as measured by the stars. A sidereal day equals 23 hours, 56 minutes, and 4.09054 seconds of *mean* (average) solar time. Conversely, a mean solar day equals 24 hours, 3 minutes, and 56.55536 seconds of sidereal time. The result is that there are approximately $366\frac{1}{4}$ sidereal days in a year.

Sidereal time is observed with an instrument called a *transit telescope.* Every star in the sky has a position number, called its *right ascension.* When that star touches the central wire position in the transit telescope, its right ascension number is the time on the sidereal clock. "Noon" of sidereal time is the place where the sun crosses the equator coming north. It is called the "first point of Aries," and its symbol is ♈. OLIVER J. LEE
**SIDERITE.** See IRON AND STEEL (Kinds of Iron Ore).
**SIDESADDLE FLOWER.** See PITCHER PLANT.
**SIDING.** See HOUSE (House-Building Terms).
**SIDJAKOV,** *SID jah kahv,* **NICOLAS** (1924- ), is a Latvian-born artist and illustrator. He won the Caldecott medal in 1961 for illustrating *Baboushka and the Three Kings,* an old Russian Christmas folk tale adapted by Ruth Robbins. He also illustrated *The Friendly Beasts* (1957) by Laura N. Baker.

Sidjakov was born in Riga, Latvia. He studied painting at the École des Beaux Arts in Paris. He came to the United States in 1952 and became a leading commercial artist. ELOISE RUE
**SIDNEY, ALGERNON.** See RYE HOUSE PLOT.
**SIDNEY, SIR PHILIP** (1554-1586), was an author, courtier, and soldier during the reign of Queen Elizabeth I of England. He became famous for his literary criticism, prose fiction, and poetry.

Sidney was born at Penshurst in Kent. He traveled widely and was popular at court. In *The Defense of Poesy* (1580?), Sidney championed the poet as more important than the philosopher or the historian. This was the first major literary criticism in English.

Sidney opposed Queen Elizabeth's proposed marriage to the Duke of Anjou in 1580. He went into temporary retirement at Wilton, home of his sister Mary, Countess of Pembroke. For her amusement, he wrote a romantic prose and verse narrative *Arcadia.* Sidney later made major revisions, but the work was edited in its final form by the countess. *Arcadia* provided source material for many later writers.

Sidney's greatest work is *Astrophel and Stella*—108 sonnets and 11 songs. This sequence—written in the early 1580's out of his unreturned love for Penelope Devereux—is one of the world's great love poems. Sincere and dramatic, it ranks with the poems of Shakespeare.

Sidney ended his retirement in 1583. In 1585, he became governor of Flushing in The Netherlands. He died of a wound in a battle there in 1586. THOMAS A. ERHARD
**SIDON,** *SY'd'n,* was an important manufacturing and port city in ancient Phoenicia. The present-day town of Ṣaydā, Lebanon, occupies its site. Sidon was most famous for its purple dye and blown-glass industries. The Greek poet Homer mentioned silver bowls of Sidon. Sidon was usually overshadowed in importance by the nearby Phoenician city of Tyre (now Ṣūr, Lebanon), its chief commercial rival. But Sidon enjoyed a brief period of supremacy and independent prosperity after Babylonia defeated Tyre in 573 B.C. LOUIS L. ORLIN
**SIEGBAHN,** *SEEG bahn,* **KARL MANNE GEORG** (1886- ), a Swedish physicist, became noted for his work with X rays and X-ray spectroscopy. He turned from an early interest in electricity and magnetism to the study of X rays in 1914. To overcome difficulties in this field of research, he developed new types of X-ray spectrographs, and improved X-ray tubes. With this more accurate equipment, he could make more precise measurements than had previously been possible, and he investigated the internal structure of atoms through the study of their X-ray spectra. He received the 1924 Nobel prize in physics. Siegbahn was born in Örebro, Sweden, and studied in Sweden and Germany. In 1937, he became director of the Nobel Institute for Physics at the Stockholm Academy of Sciences. G. GAMOW
**SIEGE,** *seej,* takes place when a military force surrounds a defended position in order to capture it by assaults or by starving it into surrender. The besieging army first *invests* (stations forces around) the enemy position. It hopes to keep outside help from reaching the besieged. Then it places artillery at important and commanding positions to bombard the enemy defenses. It may attack the defenses openly or from trench to trench. The digging of trenches is usually difficult and dangerous. It must be carried on under the cover of artillery or rifle fire, or at night. The word *siege* comes from the Latin *sedere, to sit.*

When a defending force succeeds in beating off an attack, the siege is said to have *held.* A siege is *relieved,* or *raised,* if outside reinforcements rescue the besieged forces. The position under siege is considered *fallen* if

### SOME FAMOUS SIEGES

| | |
|---|---|
| 1200 B.C. | Troy, 10 years. Fell. |
| A.D. 1428-1429 | Orléans, 7 months. Relieved by Saint Joan of Arc. |
| 1779-1783 | Gibraltar, 3 years, 7 months, 15 days. Held. |
| 1854-1855 | Sevastopol, 316 days. Fell. |
| 1857 | Delhi, 132 days. Fell. |
| 1857 | Lucknow, Siege of the Residency, 141 days. Relieved. |
| 1863 | Vicksburg, 47 days. Fell. |
| 1864-1865 | Petersburg, 287 days. Evacuated. |
| 1870 | Metz, 70 days. Fell. |
| 1870-1871 | Paris, 130 days. Fell. |
| 1877 | Plevna, 144 days. Fell. |
| 1884-1885 | Khartoum, 321 days. Fell. |
| 1899-1900 | Ladysmith, 118 days. Relieved. |
| 1900 | Peking, Siege of the Legations, 55 days. Relieved. |
| 1904-1905 | Port Arthur, 241 days. Fell. |
| 1912-1913 | Adrianople (now Edirne), 155 days. Fell. |
| 1914-1915 | Przemysl, 185 days. Fell. |
| 1936 | Alcazar, 71 days. Relieved. |
| 1941-1942 | Leningrad, 455 days. Relieved. |
| 1942-1943 | Stalingrad, 166 days. Relieved. |
| 1954 | Dien Bien Phu, 55 days. Fell. |

the attacking force breaks through and is victorious.

During World War II, modern cities, with their strong buildings and underground shelters and passages, proved that they could resist sieges. But the development of atomic weapons and guided missiles drastically changed the ability of cities to resist. HUGH M. COLE

**Related Articles** in WORLD BOOK include:

| | |
|---|---|
| Army | Roman Empire (color picture: The Roman Army [When Besieging City Walls]) |
| Battering-Ram | |
| Catapult | |
| Civil War | |
| Crimean War | Russo-Japanese War |
| Crossbow (picture) | Sepoy Rebellion |
| Franco-Prussian War | Spain (Civil War) |
| Gibraltar | Troy, or Ilium |
| Hundred Years' War | World War I |
| | World War II |

**SIEGE PERILOUS.** See ROUND TABLE.

**SIEGEL, JERRY.** See COMICS (Superman).

**SIEGFRIED,** SEEG freed, is the hero of several German legends. We know his story best from the music-dramas of Richard Wagner. Siegfried is the hero of two of these, *Siegfried* and *Die Götterdämmerung*. In Wagner's operas, Siegfried forges a great sword from the broken one of his father, Siegmund. He kills a dragon with this powerful weapon. He then wins the magic ring and the cloak of Tarnhelm. This makes him unbeatable in battle. He frees Brunhilde, the Valkyrie daughter of Wotan, from enchantment, and they fall in love.

Siegfried is cast into a spell by the plotting of Hagen, and aids Gunther in marrying Brunhilde. Siegfried marries Gutrune (Gudrun), Gunther's beautiful sister, while still under the spell. Siegfried is killed by Hagen while he is off guard after coming out of the enchantment. EINAR HAUGEN

See also NIBELUNGENLIED; OPERA (Some of the Famous Operas [Nibelungen Ring; Siegfried]); SIGURD.

**SIEGFRIED LINE,** or WESTWALL, was a German chain of steel forts and concrete tank barriers that extended along the border between Germany and France. It was opposite the Maginot Line, a similar fortification built by France. The Siegfried Line was completed in 1938 under the supervision of Adolf Hitler, the Nazi dictator. The Siegfried Line, like the Maginot Line, was supposed to be impossible for attacking forces to get through. But the Allied forces assaulted and broke through the line in many places during World War II. Parts of the line still stand. THEODORE ROPP

See also MAGINOT LINE.

**SIEMENS,** ZEE munz, is the family name of two brothers from Germany who were inventors and industrialists.

**Werner von Siemens** (1816-1892) built telegraph lines in Germany, Russia, and other European countries. With his brother, he developed electric railways and lighting, and helped lay the early deep-sea telegraphic cables. While in the Prussian army's engineering service, Siemens developed an improved electroplating process. Later, he invented a dynamo which his brother used to run railways. ERNST WERNER VON SIEMENS was born in Lenthe near Hannover, Germany.

**Wilhelm Siemens** (1823-1883) invented a regenerative gas-fired furnace in 1856 that led to the open-hearth steelmaking process. He took his brother's electroplating process to England to sell in 1843, and settled there. He was knighted as Sir Charles William in 1883, shortly before his death. Siemens was born in Lenthe and studied at technical schools. JOHN B. MCFERRIN

**SIENA,** see EN uh (pop. 61,453; alt. 1,056 ft.), lies in the hills of Tuscany near Florence, Italy (see ITALY [color map]). Its central square, the Piazza del Campo, is internationally famous. The City Hall overlooks it. Horses sponsored by various districts in the city run the colorful races known as the *Palio* in this square each year.

Siena's Gothic cathedral is made of black and white marble, and is one of Europe's most famous medieval cathedrals. Siena has a university which dates from the 1200's. The city is the home of Saint Catherine, the patron saint of Italy. SHEPARD B. CLOUGH

**SIENA COLLEGE.** See UNIVERSITIES AND COLLEGES (table).

**SIENA HEIGHTS COLLEGE.** See UNIVERSITIES AND COLLEGES (table).

**SIENKIEWICZ,** *shen KYEH veech*, **HENRYK** (1846-1916) was a popular Polish novelist. He won the Nobel prize for literature in 1905. His first novel, *A Prophet in His Own Country*, appeared in 1872. Translations of his novels made him well known to American readers.

Sienkiewicz' most celebrated romance is *Quo Vadis?* (Whither Goest Thou?, 1895). A story of Roman society under Nero, it was dramatized and made into motion pictures in a number of countries.

The novel *With Fire and Sword* (1890) gained almost as much popularity in America. This book is the first part of a *trilogy* (three-part work) that describes society in Poland during the wars of the 1600's against the Cossacks, Turks, and Swedes.

Sienkiewicz was born in Siedlce, Russian Poland. He studied at Warsaw University. He traveled much, and visited the United States in 1876. After his return to Poland, he became a leader of patriots working for Polish independence. ERNEST J. SIMMONS

# SIERRA LEONE

- ★ National Capital
- • Other City or Town
- —— Road
- +++ Rail Line
- ~~ River
- ▲ Mountain

WORLD BOOK map—FGA

**SIERRA LEONE,** *sih AIR uh lee OHN*, is a small country on Africa's western "bulge," north of the equator. It is slightly larger than the state of West Virginia, and has about as many people as Iowa.

Sierra Leone provides a large portion of one of the world's most valuable treasures—diamonds. It ranks as the world's third largest producer of gem stones and the sixth largest producer of industrial diamonds. The country's diamonds lie in gravel deposits along river beds and in swamps in eastern parts of the country. About half of the diamonds make gem stones, and the rest are less expensive industrial diamonds.

Sierra Leone, a former British colonial possession, became independent in 1961. It remained a member of the Commonwealth of Nations. Freetown is the country's capital, only large town, and main port. The city was founded in 1787 as a settlement for freed slaves.

**Government.** Sierra Leone is a constitutional monarchy. Queen Elizabeth of Great Britain is also queen of Sierra Leone. A governor-general represents the British monarch. The law-making body, the house of representatives, has 62 elected members. All adults are eligible to vote. The house of representatives also has 12 members who are tribal chiefs elected by district councils of chiefs. Members of the house choose the prime minister, who serves as the head of government.

**People.** Sierra Leone has a population of 2,550,000. Most of the men are farmers. But many grow only enough food for their families, and work during the dry season mining diamonds. Many of the women run profitable businesses selling goods in local markets. Freetown has many modern buildings (see FREETOWN). Many people in villages live in concrete block houses, and many poor people in rural areas live in houses made of mud with corrugated iron or thatched roofs.

Most of Sierra Leone's people are Africans who form 12 main tribes. About a third of the people belong to the Mende tribe. They live in the southern part of the country. About a fourth of the people belong to the Temne tribe, and live in western Sierra Leone. About 130,000 *Creoles* (descendants of freed slaves) live in or near Freetown. English is the official language, but most of the people speak tribal languages. The Creoles speak *Krio*, a local form of English.

Most of the people practice local religions. For example, Mende tribesmen believe *Ngewo* (God) created the world and everything in it. They worship small human images called *nomoli*, which they find in the soil. No one knows who made the figures. The Mende believe Ngewo made them. Some of the people practice Christianity and Islam. The creoles are Christians.

Education is developing rapidly. Illiteracy, once widespread, is disappearing. More than 100,000 boys and girls attend about 700 elementary schools, and about 10,000 attend secondary schools. More than 2,000 students receive higher education. Sierra Leone also has two university colleges.

**Land.** The country covers an area of 27,699 square miles. Freetown lies at the end of the Sierra Leone Peninsula. The Sierra Leone mountains rise to about 3,000 feet above sea level there. Swampland covers most of the coastal region, and extends about 20 miles inland.

Inland from the coastal swamps, a coastal plain extends as far as 100 miles in the northern part of the country. This plain slopes up to a region of plateaus and mountains in the northeast that covers about half of the country. The mountains rise to more than 6,000 feet near the eastern border with Guinea. Loma Mansa, 6,390 feet, is the country's highest point. Gravel or sandy soil, on which only short grass grows, covers more than half the country. The government is clearing

─────── FACTS IN BRIEF ───────

**Capital:** Freetown.

**Official Language:** English.

**Form of Government:** Constitutional monarchy.

**Area:** 27,699 square miles. *Greatest Distances*—(north-south) 220 miles; (east-west) 190 miles. *Coastline*—210 miles.

**Population:** *1963 Census*—2,289,373. *Estimated 1970 Population*—2,550,000; density, 92 persons to the square mile. *Estimated 1975 Population*—2,748,000.

**Chief Products:** *Agriculture*—bananas, cassava, cattle, cocoa, coffee, ginger, millet, palm products, peanuts, piassava, rice, sorghum. *Fishing*—tuna. *Mining*—chrome ore, diamonds, iron ore, rutile.

**Flag:** Three horizontal stripes—green, white, and blue. See FLAG (color picture: Flags of Africa).

**Money:** *Basic Unit*—leone. See MONEY (table: Values).

*W. E. F. Ward, the contributor of this article, is the author of several books on Africa, and former Deputy Educational Advisor in the British Colonial Office.*

370

## SIERRA LEONE

coastal mangrove swamps to convert them into rice fields. It has also planted new forests.

Sierra Leone has a rainy, tropical climate. The dry season lasts through January and February in the south, and from December through March in the north. Freetown receives about 144 inches of rainfall a year, and some high places receive more. Only a narrow strip in the north has less than 80 inches a year. Temperatures average between 77° and 81° F. except in the extreme north, where greater variation occurs.

**Economy.** Farmers of Sierra Leone produce a wide variety of crops. But poor soil, the dry season, and the use of traditional farming methods keep crop yields low. Little effort is made to keep the soil fertile. As soon as the soil wears out on one plot, a farmer moves to a new area, clears the land, and plants a food crop.

Rice is the main food crop. Palm kernels are the chief export crop. The country is the world's leading exporter of *piassava*, a fiber from the raffia palm used in making brushes (see RAFFIA). There is also some tuna fishing off the coast near Freetown.

Diamonds make up about two-thirds of the total value of Sierra Leone's exports. Diamonds are mined by a British company, Sierra Leone Selection Trust, Ltd., and by over 3,000 licensed Sierra Leone diggers. The British firm can work in only a small part of the field, an area of about 310 square miles. The diggers can work in areas covering about 9,500 square miles. The government controls the quantities of diamonds mined, but many persons mine diamonds illegally and smuggle them out of the country. The government made an agreement with a U.S. company in 1965 to establish a diamond-cutting industry in Sierra Leone.

Diamonds were discovered in 1930. Since then, deposits of iron ore, bauxite, and rutile have been discovered. Bauxite is used in making aluminum, and rutile contains the important metal titanium. Iron ore is the second most important export from Sierra Leone.

Sierra Leone has 358 miles of railroads. One line links the seacoast with iron ore deposits at Marampa. Another connects Freetown with Makeni and Pendembu. There are over 3,000 miles of roads. About 500 miles of rivers are navigable by small craft for three months each year. Freetown has an international airport.

**History.** Historians know little about Sierra Leone before 1460, when Portuguese seamen visited the area. In the 1500's, European trading ships began stopping there. The Europeans shipped many of the people from this area to America as slaves.

About 1725, Fulani people who lived east of present-day Sierra Leone began a holy war to convert their neighbors to the Islamic religion. As the Fulani moved westward, many other peoples also migrated toward the coast and settled in what is now Sierra Leone.

In 1787, Granville Sharp, an Englishman opposed to slavery, settled about 400 freed American Negro slaves on land where Freetown now stands. The settlers suffered from hunger, disease, and warfare, and the settlement almost died out. Great Britain made the slave trade illegal in 1807. The next year, the British government made the Sierra Leone Peninsula a colony. The British freed slaves from the slave ships of many nations, and settled them in the colony. British influence gradually spread inland. In 1896, the British established a protectorate over an area that, with the colony, had almost the same borders as present-day Sierra Leone.

Between 1896 and 1961, Sierra Leone moved gradually toward self-government. In 1961, it became completely independent, but remained a member of the Commonwealth of Nations. Sir Milton Margai, the first prime minister, died in 1964. His brother, Sir Albert Margai, succeeded him, and in March, 1966, tried unsuccessfully to make Sierra Leone into a one-party state. Political leaders struggled for power after indecisive parliamentary elections in 1967. Young army officers then took over the government. Colonel Andrew Juxon-Smith became its head. In April, 1968, a group of non-commissioned officers overthrew Smith's military government. Siaka Stevens became prime minister and head of a new civilian government. W. E. F. WARD

United Nations

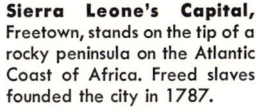

**Sierra Leone's Capital,** Freetown, stands on the tip of a rocky peninsula on the Atlantic Coast of Africa. Freed slaves founded the city in 1787.

**SIERRA MADRE,** *MAD ray*, a name often used for mountain ranges, is Spanish for *Mother Range*. Sierra Madre is the name of mountain ranges in Spain, Mexico, and on Luzon Island in the Philippines. The Sierra Madre mountains in Mexico form the edge of a wide central plateau.

The Sierra Madre Oriental (east) lies on the east side of the plateau, toward the Gulf of Mexico. The Sierra Madre Occidental (west) borders the plateau on the west. Canyons and deep deposits of volcanic material make it difficult to cross. Part of the Sierra Madre Occidental extends north into Arizona and New Mexico. The mountain range is 2,000 miles long and over 100 miles wide.                              MARGUERITE UTTLEY

See also MEXICO (physical map).

**SIERRA NEVADA.** See SPAIN (Land Regions).

**SIERRA NEVADA** is a huge uplifted and tilted granite mountain range which extends north and south for 400 miles in eastern California. Its highest point is Mount Whitney (14,495 feet). The Sierra Nevada is about 70 miles wide. It covers 31,000 square miles between the Great Basin and the Central Valley of California.                              JOHN H. GARLAND

See also CALIFORNIA (Land Regions; physical map); LAKE TAHOE; SEQUOIA NATIONAL PARK; YOSEMITE NATIONAL PARK.

**SIESTA.** See LATIN AMERICA (Customs).

**SIEVE OF ERATOSTHENES** is a method developed by the Greek mathematician Eratosthenes for identifying *prime numbers*. These are numbers other than 1 that can only be divided evenly by 1 and themselves. Today, electronic computers can be used to identify prime numbers, but the system still resembles the method used by Eratosthenes.

The first step in finding prime numbers with a sieve of Eratosthenes is to write a series of whole numbers, beginning with the number 2. Next, counting from 2, underline every second number to mark it off. You can imagine that the numbers not underlined have passed through a wire sieve. This eliminates numbers that can be divided evenly by 2, except for 2 itself.

Starting again with 3, the next number after 2 not underlined, cross off every third number. Count numbers which have not passed through the sieve as well as those which have. This eliminates numbers that can be divided evenly by 3, except for 3 itself. By continuing this process with the next larger unmarked number, only prime numbers remain.

The beginning of a sieve of Eratosthenes is shown below. It shows that 2, 3, and 5 are the first three prime numbers.

2 3 4̸ 5 6̸ 7 8̸ 9̸ 10 11 12̸ 13 14̸ 15̸ 16 17 18̸ 19 20̸ . . .

In the next step, start with 5 and cross off every fifth number. The process is endless, because there is no last prime number.                              PHILLIP S. JONES

**SIEVE TUBE.** See BARK.

**SIEYÈS,** *syay YES*, **EMMANUEL JOSEPH** (1748-1836), popularly known as ABBÉ SIEYÈS helped start the French Revolution with his booklet, *What Is the Third Estate?* In this booklet, published in 1789, Sieyès insisted that the people should have a voice in government.

Born in Fréjus, France, Sieyès became a priest. He was elected to the Estates-General in 1789 and served as president of the Assembly in 1790. Sieyès was a moderate and an expert on constitutions. He was a member of the Convention during the Reign of Terror. Robespierre called him the *cunning fox* for his silent opposition to the Jacobins.

Sieyès served as ambassador to Berlin in 1798, and a year later joined the French executive, the Directory. From 1815 to 1830, Sieyès was exiled by the restored Bourbon kings.                              RAYMOND O. ROCKWOOD

**SIF.** See THOR.

**SIFTON** is the family name of two Canadian political leaders who were brothers. Both were born in Middlesex County, Upper Canada (now Ontario).

**Arthur Lewis Sifton** (1858-1921) served as chief justice of the supreme court of the Northwest Territories from 1903 to 1905, and of Alberta from 1905 to 1910. As leader of the Liberal Party, he became premier of Alberta in 1910 and served until 1917. In 1917, he entered the Canadian federal government as minister of customs.

Sifton served as a Canadian delegate to the peace conference at Versailles in 1919 following World War I. He was secretary of state for Canada from 1920 until his death.

**Sir Clifford Sifton** (1861-1929) served as Canadian minister of the interior from 1896 to 1905. He played a leading part in settling western Canada by launching a vigorous immigration campaign in Great Britain and continental Europe. In 1909, he became chairman of the Canadian Conservation Commission, a post he held until 1918.

**SIGH,** *sy*, is a single long breath. It may be a long inhalation followed by a long exhalation. It may also be a long inhalation followed by a hard short exhalation. The sigh may vibrate the vocal cords and sound the voice, or it may not. No one really knows why people sigh or what it does for the body. A person may sigh from boredom, weariness, in times of extreme pleasure, or in times of stress. A sigh might be thought of as expressing something for which no words can be found.                              GORDON FARRELL

**SIGHT.** See EYE.

**SIGHT BILL.** See BILL OF EXCHANGE; DRAFT.

**SIGILLARIA.** See SATURNALIA.

**SIGISMUND,** *SIJ is mund* (1368-1437), was a Holy Roman emperor and a king of Bohemia and Hungary. His chief concern was to end the Great Schism which split the Roman Catholic Church. In 1414, he forced John XXIII (an antipope) to call the Council of Constance, which resulted in the election of Martin V as pope. The council also ended the schism and burned the religious leader John Huss. Following the council's action, the Hussites rose in a rebellion which Sigismund could not crush.                              ROBERT G. L. WAITE

See also POPE (The Troubles of the Papacy); HUSS, JOHN.

**SIGMA 7.** See SPACE TRAVEL (table: Manned Space Flights); SCHIRRA, WALTER M., JR.

**SIGMA XI,** *SIG muh ZI*, is an honorary scientific society. It was founded at Cornell University in 1886 to encourage study in the pure and applied sciences. Members include men and women who have done important scientific work. University students who are qualified

# SIGNALING

WORLD BOOK photo

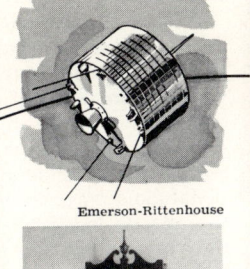
Emerson-Rittenhouse

Hedrich-Blessing

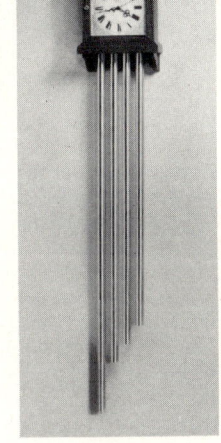

Jet Propulsion Laboratory

WORLD BOOK photo

**Signals** are used in many ways to send various types of information. Some signals are warnings of danger, some are used to transmit messages long distances, and others are used to explain actions when direct voice communication is impossible.

may be elected to associate membership in the society.

Sigma Xi has about 160 chapters and 175 local clubs in the leading universities of the United States. There are about 110,000 members who are actively associated with the society. Sigma Xi publishes a magazine called *American Scientist*, and *Science in Progress*, which contains articles by leading scientists of Sigma Xi. The society has headquarters at 51 Prospect St., New Haven, Conn. 06520. T. T. HOLME

**SIGN, ELECTRIC.** See ELECTRIC SIGN.

**SIGN LANGUAGE** is a system of hand signs and gestures that persons may use in order to communicate with one another. Primitive men talked in sign language. Early monks who took vows of silence used sign language. Some South American Indians use sign language to communicate with tribes who speak a different language.

The Abbe de l'Epee, who founded the first school for the deaf in Paris about 1760, used sign language and finger spelling to teach the deaf. Deaf persons use as many as 1,500 signs as well as finger spelling. In finger spelling, a person places his fingers in certain positions to indicate each letter of the alphabet (see DEAFNESS).

Sign language is also used in sports. For pictures of some of the signals used in sports, see the BASKETBALL, CRICKET, and FOOTBALL articles. E. B. BOATNER

See also INDIAN, AMERICAN (illustration: Indian Sign Language); SIGNALING.

**SIGNAL CORPS.** See ARMY, UNITED STATES (Communications); SIGNALING (Military Signaling).

**SIGNALING** is one way of passing information from one person or place to another. Signals are used when direct and unaided voice or direct written communication is impossible or undesirable.

There are three main forms of signals: (1) electrical, (2) visual, and (3) sound. Various electrical, mechanical, and hand devices are used to transmit signals. International codes—such as the International Morse Code and the International Flag Code—have been developed for some kinds of signals. Such signals are the same throughout the world and can be understood anywhere. For more information on these, see FLAG (The International Flag Code); MORSE CODE.

### Methods of Signaling

Visual and sound signals of one kind or another have been used since ancient times. Early methods included smoke signals, drum signals, and beacon fires. Electrical signals were first used in the early 1800's.

**Visual and Sound Signals** still have many uses today. Sound signals are made with such devices as bells, gongs, guns, horns, sirens, and whistles.

Visual signals are often made with flags. *Semaphore signaling* is done with two hand flags. The sender holds the flags in various positions to represent the letters of the alphabet and to give several other meanings. *Flaghoist signals* are made by hanging colored flags from crosspieces on the masts of ships. Both four-cornered flags and *pennants* (triangular flags) are used. Sailors often send messages with flaghoists by following the International Flag Code.

373

# SIGNALING

**Military Signaling.** Soldiers often use radiotelephones to relay strategic information quickly from the battlefield.

WORLD BOOK photo

Visual signaling can be done with lights. Light signals can be made with colored lights, with each light having a different meaning. Lights are often flashed or blinked according to some code. Signals may be passed by reflecting sunlight with mirrors. *Pyrotechnics* (fireworks) provide signals in which color is important. Pyrotechnic signals are made with various devices, including rockets, flares, smoke, and cartridges or shells fired from guns. Visual signals can also be made by hand and body movements, or by cloth *panels* (strips) laid flat on the ground or some other surface.

**Electrical Signals** can be transmitted in various ways. These include radio, radar, television, telephone, teletypewriter, and facsimile. Messages are often transmitted by a combination of these methods.

Objects can be found and accurately located by radar signals. A telegram or other message can be sent by teletypewriter. Computer information coded on magnetic tape or on punched cards or paper tape can be transmitted at high speeds by teletypewriters. Facsimile machines can transmit copies of maps, pictures, and printed materials. Communications satellites are used to carry electrical communication to any part of the world. Coaxial cables are also used to carry several types of electrical communication. Each of these means of electrical communication has a separate article in WORLD BOOK.

## Important Uses of Signals

Throughout history, signals have been used in a wide range of activities. This article discusses only a few important uses. For information on other uses of signals, read the separate articles listed in the *Related Articles* at the end of this article.

**Military Signaling.** Armies use such modern electrical communications as radio, radar, telephone, teletypewriter, and television. Radio is used most often, but it is also the least secure means of communication. Radio can reveal the sender's position to the enemy. When secrecy is vital, radio messages are often sent in code.

The U.S. Army relies mainly on electrical communications. However, it also uses messengers and visual and sound signals. Visual signals include arm and hand signals, hand flags, panels, lights, and fireworks. Sound signals that are used include horns, gunshots, and whistles.

**Aircraft Signaling.** Radio signals are passed between ground stations and aircraft concerning take-off and landing instructions, the position of other planes, and weather information. In the Air Force, radio communication between pilots flying in the same group or formation is important. Some airplanes also have an *automatic direction finder*, or radio compass, and use omnidirectional radio range equipment. This equipment enables the pilot to locate his position at all times. Radar is used to guide aircraft to safe landings in any kind of weather, to help airplanes land on aircraft carriers, and to guide military aircraft to their targets. Visual signals that are used to aid pilots include beacons, running lights, wind socks, and approach light systems located at airports.

**Marine Signaling.** Various means of electrical communication are used by both commercial and naval vessels. Radio is used extensively in ship-to-ship communication, and for controlling naval aircraft. Radio and teletypewriter circuits connect ships at sea with stations ashore. Radar helps reveal the position of ships. Enemy submarines and explosive mines can also be detected by an echo-sounding device called *sonar*.

Lights, semaphore flags, and flaghoists are the most common means of visual signaling at sea. Sound signals include electrical sound-producing devices and such devices as bells, gongs, and whistles on *buoys* (floating markers) that are operated by the motion of the sea. Lights and fog signals on lighthouses, lightships, and buoys warn that ships are approaching land or dangerous hidden objects. Lights are also used as running lights on ships, and as signal searchlights. They are flashed or blinked to signal for help. Sailors use semaphore and flaghoists to relay information to nearby ships.

**Distress Signals.** A ship or aircraft in need of help can send several internationally agreed upon distress signals. Two of the best known are the radio signal *SOS* in code, which is used at sea, and the aircraft call of *Mayday* sent over voice radio. Other well-known distress signals include a gun fired at short intervals; a continuous sounding of fog signals; colored flares thrown from shells or rockets; the international flag signal *NC*; and flying the national flag upside down. These signals may be used either separately or in combination. Persons on land who are in urgent need of help sometimes make up signals or use variations of these standard signals.   PAUL J. SCHEIPS

**Related Articles** in WORLD BOOK include:

ILLUSTRATIONS OF SIGNALS

The following articles include illustrations of various methods of signaling:

| | | |
|---|---|---|
| Basketball | Communication | Football |
| Board of Trade | Deafness | Indian, American |
| Boats and Boating | Flag | Railroad |

OTHER RELATED ARTICLES

| | | |
|---|---|---|
| Beacon | Morse Code | SOS |
| Codes and Ciphers | Radio (Uses) | Traffic |
| Fireworks | Semaphore | Weather |
| Heliograph | Sign Language | Whistle |
| Lighthouse | Siren | Wigwagging |
| Lightship | | |

374

**SIGNATURE, LEGAL.** A legal signature identifies a person and indicates his intention to stand by a signed document as written. It is usually his name, handwritten by himself or by another with his authority. If he is physically unable to write, his hand may be guided at his request. A person who has not learned to write may make an identifying mark, such as an X. In such cases, the conditions of signing must be described and witnessed according to law.

Courts have held that a signature written by any means is lawful. Properly witnessed wills have been held legal when the name of the person making the will appeared only in the phrase "I, John Doe, . . . ." But some states require the signature at the end.

The first and last names make up a person's legal signature. Prefixes, titles, and middle names or initials are not legally necessary parts of a signature. But they may help to identify the individual. The United States government usually requests the middle name or initial for its records, because of the danger of confusing one person with others who have the same first and last names. A married woman's given name followed by her husband's surname is her lawful signature even if she becomes a widow. But if she wishes to do so, she may sign with her husband's name preceded by "Mrs.," as "Mrs. John Doe." A divorced woman may also sign in these ways until the court permits her to take her maiden name again. A married woman may legally use her maiden name as her signature in connection with property which she owns independently of her husband.

Anyone can legally establish a new name and signature merely by using it all the time. State laws usually permit a person to have his name legally changed by a court if no fraud is intended. FRED E. INBAU

**SIGNET RING.** See SEAL (design).

**SIGNORELLI,** *SEEN yoh REL ee,* **LUCA DI EGIDIO DI VENTURA DE'** (1450?-1523), was one of the great Italian painters during the Renaissance. He is best known for his frescoes in the Cathedral of Orvieto. These wall paintings, *The Resurrection of the Dead* and *The Last Judgment,* show many powerful figures. He is admired for the clarity of his design. Signorelli was born in Cortona. WOLFGANG LOTZ

**SIGNS OF THE ZODIAC.** See ZODIAC.

**SIGSBEE, CHARLES DWIGHT** (1845-1923), was an American naval officer. He was in command of the battleship *Maine* when it was blown up in Havana harbor in 1898. After the disaster to the *Maine,* he took command of the cruiser *Saint Paul.* Sigsbee was born in Albany, N.Y. He was graduated from the United States Naval Academy in 1863, and fought in the battle of Mobile Bay during the Civil War. In 1903, Sigsbee was appointed to the rank of rear admiral. He retired in 1907. See also SPANISH-AMERICAN WAR (American Intervention). DONALD W. MITCHELL

**SIGURD,** *SIHG urd,* is the Scandinavian name for the mythical German hero, Siegfried. The stories about him probably originated in the A.D. 400's, and soon found their way to Scandinavia. They were given poetic treatment in the *Elder Edda,* a collection of poems composed in Iceland during the 1000's and 1100's. The prose *Saga of the Volsungs,* written in Iceland during the 1100's or 1200's, tells the stories more fully. See also EDDA; FAFNIR; NIBELUNGENLIED; SIEGFRIED; VOLSUNGA SAGA. KENNETH CHAPMAN

**SIHANOUK, NORODOM.** See NORODOM SIHANOUK.

**SIKHS,** *seeks,* are followers of Sikhism, a religion of the Punjab region of northwestern India. The term *Sikh* means *disciple.* There are more than 8 million Sikhs, and almost all of them live in India. They are chiefly farmers and soldiers.

Sikhism was founded by Guru Nanak (1469-1538). He tried to unite the Moslems and all *castes* (classes) of Hindus into one brotherhood. He taught that there is one true, universal God. The central shrine of the Sikhs is in Amritsar. There, the *Granth* (holy book of the Sikhs) is read aloud every day.

The political state of the Sikhs was established by Govind Singh (1666-1708). He built up their military power, to protect them from the Moslems and other religious groups. But after Singh's death, the Sikhs were overcome by the Moslems. A few Sikhs escaped to the

Pix

**The Sikh Golden Temple** stands in a pool of fresh water in Amritsar, the holy city of the Sikhs in India.

mountains. They returned a few years later and captured Lahore. The Sikh communities were united from 1799 to 1824 by Ranjit Singh, a skillful ruler who gave himself the title of *maharajah.* By 1824, Ranjit Singh's military talent brought most of India north of the Sutlej River under his control. After his death, the Sikhs fought the British in India. In the First Sikh War (1845-1846), they lost Lahore. In the Second Sikh War (1848), they were conquered by the British.

The Sikhs were afraid that Moslem power might be restored in India, and for this reason they backed the British during the Sepoy Rebellion (1857). The Sikhs supported Britain in World Wars I and II. In 1966, the Indian government, in response to Sikh demands, created Punjab, a separate Punjabi-speaking state in the Punjab region. GEORGE NOEL MAYHEW

See also INDIA (Religion); PUNJAB; RANJIT SINGH.

**SIKINNIS.** See DANCING (Greek Dancing).

# SIKKIM

- ⊛ Capital
- • Other City or Town
- — Road
- ---- Trail
- ⊢⊢⊢ Rail Line
- ▲ MOUNTAIN
- ‖ MOUNTAIN PASS
- ~ River

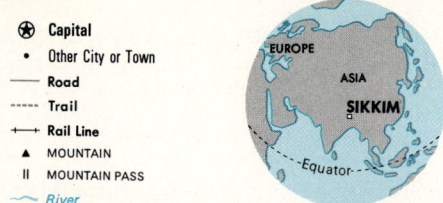

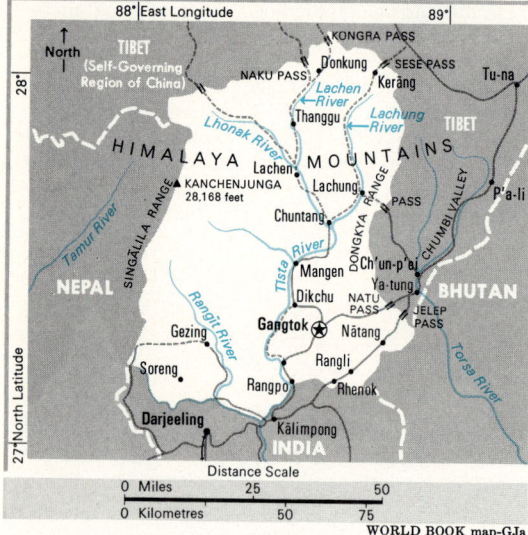

WORLD BOOK map-GJa

**SIKKIM,** *SIH kim*, is a small kingdom tucked away in the towering mountains of south-central Asia. It lies in the heart of the high Himalaya. Mount Kanchenjunga, the third highest mountain in the world, lies on Sikkim's western border with Nepal. China lies to the north. An arc of great mountain peaks in the east separates Sikkim from China and Bhutan.

Sikkim is only about as big as the state of Delaware. Its geography ranges from snow-covered mountains more than 28,000 feet high to a thick, tropical rain forest that lies at sea level. Sikkim is a protectorate of India. Gangtok, a city of about 7,000 persons, is the capital and only city (see GANGTOK).

**Government.** A maharaja rules as king of Sikkim, but he shares power with an administrator appointed by

---
**FACTS IN BRIEF**
---

**Form of Government:** Monarchy.
**Capital:** Gangtok.
**Official Language:** English.
**Area:** 2,744 square miles. *Greatest Distances*—(north-south) about 70 miles; (east-west) about 55 miles.
**Population:** *1961 Census*—162,189; distribution, 96 per cent rural, 4 per cent urban. *Estimated 1970 Population*—194,000; density, 71 persons to the square mile.
**Chief Products:** *Agriculture*—rice, corn, cardamom. *Mining*—copper, lead, zinc.
**Flag:** White background (for the country) with a red border (for the mountains). In the center is a golden *Khorlo*, a wheel (for the Buddhist priesthood). See FLAG (color picture: Flags of Asia and the Pacific).
**Money:** *Basic Unit*—Indian rupee.

India. The maharaja controls internal matters, with the help of an executive council, an advisory group. The administrator controls foreign affairs, defense, and communications. Sikkim has no constitution.

Maharaja Palden Thondup Namgyal, crowned in 1965, has supported political reforms, the development of political parties, and a legislature largely elected by the people. But a government elected by the people has been slow to develop, because of racial and cultural differences and lack of political experience.

**People.** Nepalese, Lepchas, Bhutias, and Indians live in Sikkim. Many Nepalese have moved to Sikkim since 1890. Today, about 7 out of 10 persons are Nepalese. Most of the Nepalese live on small farms in the middle altitudes in the south. They cultivate the fields with simple hand tools.

The Lepchas, first settlers in Sikkim, were pushed aside by later settlers. Today, they live in distant valleys. Many hunt and fish for food, and others farm or raise livestock. In some areas, Nepalese farmers have cleared many forests to plant crops. This has destroyed the hunting grounds of the Lepchas and has caused trouble between the two groups.

The Bhutias came to Sikkim from Bhutan and Tibet in the 1600's. Today, they herd cattle and *yaks* (Asian oxen). In the summer, they live in tents and graze their herds in high mountain meadows. In the winter, they live in wooden houses in the highlands. A few Indian administrators, clerks, and merchants have moved to Sikkim since 1950.

Lepchas and Bhutias practice Tibetan Buddhism, the state religion. Over half of the people, including most Nepalese, are Hindus. But their Hinduism has been influenced by Buddhism.

English is the official language. However, most Nepalese speak Gurkhali, and most Lepchas and Bhutias speak Sikkimese. Education is free in the first two grades. About 2 out of 10 persons can read and write.

**Land.** People cannot live in many parts of Sikkim, because the mountain land is too rocky and barren. Over thousands of years, the streams flowing down the mountains into the Tīsta river have cut into the mountain sides, and formed a basin in south-central Sikkim. This 40-mile-wide basin is the heart of the country.

The highest mountain peaks are covered with snow all year. The lower mountain slopes have cool, grassy meadows. Still farther down are warm forests and hot, rainy areas. Lush tropical rain forests grow in the southern river valley bottoms, where heavy rains fall. Some parts of Sikkim receive 200 inches of rain a year. Other areas receive less than 40 inches.

**Economy.** Sikkim's economy is based on agriculture, and most of the people are farmers. Some farmers raise rice, corn, and other cereal crops to feed the people. Others raise apples, *cardamom* (a spice), citrus fruits, pineapples, and potatoes to sell to India.

Handicrafts provide the chief industry. Craftsmen weave cloth, blankets, and rugs, and make copperware and woodcarvings. Since the early 1960's, the government has tried to develop other industries. The first hydroelectric power project was finished in 1961, and others are being built. Most of Sikkim's trade is with India. Poor roads often hamper trading. Since 1963, the government has built about 300 miles of roads to link India and Sikkim. Sikkim has no railroads or airports.

Forests cover almost a third of Sikkim. The country has some copper, lead, and zinc deposits.

**History.** Sikkim became a separate state about 1640, when Penchu Namgyal was crowned maharaja. Sikkim then controlled lands that are now part of Bhutan, Communist China, India, and Nepal. In 1780, warriors from Nepal and Bhutan invaded Sikkim and seized much of the land. Britain defeated the Nepalese in 1814 and restored some land to Sikkim.

In 1861, Britain made Sikkim a protectorate, and a British official later took over much of the maharaja's power. By 1918, the maharaja had regained control of internal matters. Britain gave India control over Sikkim in 1947. In 1950, Sikkim agreed to Indian control of its defense, foreign relations, and vital communications. In 1963, Maharaja Palden Thondup Namgyal married Hope Cooke, an American.     ROBERT I. CRANE

**SIKORSKY,** sih KAWR skih, **IGOR IVANOVICH** (1889-    ), an aircraft designer and manufacturer, pioneered in multiengine airplanes, helicopters, and transoceanic flying boats. He designed the world's first four-engine aircraft in 1913. He produced a successful single-rotor helicopter in 1939 (see HELICOPTER).

Sikorsky was born in Kiev, Russia. He was educated at the Petrograd Naval College and at engineering schools in Paris and Kiev. He first attempted to build helicopters, but failed because he lacked suitable engines. He then concentrated on fixed-wing aircraft and rose to a prominent position in Russian aviation, designing one of the most successful bombers of World War I. Sikorsky came to the United States in 1919 after abandoning a personal fortune in Russia during the Bolshevik Revolution. He founded a company in 1923 which produced a line of outstanding flying boats. His company became part of the United Aircraft Corporation in 1929. From that time on, he concentrated on designing and building helicopters.     ROBERT B. HOTZ

**SILAGE.** See SILO.

**SILENCE, TOWER OF.** See TOWER OF SILENCE.

# SILHOUETTE

**SILENUS,** sy LE nus, was a minor god in Greek mythology. He was a wise old satyr, fat and bald. Silenus nursed and taught Dionysus (Bacchus). Silenus could foretell the future, and charm all living things with his songs. See also MIDAS; SATYR.

**SILESIA,** sy LEE zhuh, is a region in southwestern Poland and north-central Czechoslovakia that includes the upper Oder River Valley. Silesia covers an area of 20,000 square miles, and has a population of about 6,250,000. The main city is Wrocław. For location, see POLAND (color map).

The Sudetes Mountains are on the border between Polish Silesia and Czechoslovakia. Silesia has many mineral springs. Over half of the land is fertile. The region produces rye, oats, barley, wheat, and flax. Silesia also contains rich coal and zinc deposits, and is one of Europe's great industrial areas.

Before World War I, most of Silesia was a province of Prussia, but the southern end was one of the crownlands of the Austrian Empire. This southern section became part of the Republic of Czechoslovakia at the end of World War I.     JAMES K. POLLOCK

**SILHOUETTE,** SIL oo ET, is an outline drawing filled in with solid color to resemble a shadow. The term usually refers to a profile, or side, view of the human head. Étienne de Silhouette (1709-1767), French minister of finance, is responsible for the name of this kind of portrait.

The easiest way to make a silhouette is to place a small object, such as a leaf, a shell, or a key, on a piece of paper. Draw a line around the edge of the object with a pencil, and fill in the outline with a dark color.

A silhouette portrait may be made by drawing an outline around a person's shadow. The person should sit between a lighted candle and a piece of paper on the wall. Another method is to photograph a person against the light of a window.     HARRY MUIR KURTZWORTH

**Igor Sikorsky,** *right,* built and piloted the first successful four-engined airplane in 1913. It weighed only 9,000 pounds.
Brown Bros.

**Animal Silhouettes** and a detailed background can be cut out of a black sheet of paper by using a special knife.
William Sumits, *Life,* © 1953 Time, Inc.

# SILICA

**SILICA,** *SIL ih kuh* (chemical formula, $SiO_2$), is the name given to silicon dioxide. It is the most abundant material in the earth's crust, and the most widely distributed. About 60 per cent of the earth's crust is silica. In the form of quartz, it makes up the largest part of sand. It is a necessary material in the formation of most crystalline rocks. Silica enters into chemical combinations with other substances to form part of many minerals, which are called *silicates*. It gives strength and toughness to some plant stalks, the quills of bird feathers, and some living sponges. It also makes up the shells of some microscopic forms of life.

Silica occurs in both crystalline form and amorphous form, which means without a definite structure. It will not dissolve in water or in any mineral acid except hydrofluoric acid. Crystalline silica forms the common mineral, quartz, and the rare minerals tridymite and cristobalite. Opal, amethyst, and jasper are varieties of quartz.  A. PABST

**Related Articles** in WORLD BOOK include:
| | | |
|---|---|---|
| Hornblende | Quartz | Silica Gel |
| Opal | Sand | Sillimanite |

**SILICA GEL** is a colloidal form of silica that has a powerful affinity for water. This material, when dried, removes water vapor and other gases from air. Silica does not react with many materials and therefore it is a safe substance to insert into a pipe as a filter. When the filter is saturated, it can be cleaned merely by heating the silica.

When water is removed from silicic acid, a gel of silicon dioxide, or *silica gel*, is precipitated. The silica in this gel is porous. Silica gel is therefore valuable as a gas filter.  GEORGE L. BUSH

**SILICATE.** See CERAMICS; SILICA.

**SILICON** (chemical symbol, Si) is the most abundant nonmetallic element in nature, except oxygen. Its atomic number is 14 and its atomic weight is 28.086. It is never found in a pure state, but always combined with other elements. Crystalline silicon has been made from quartz in electric furnaces. Fine-grained silicon, called *amorphous*, is a dark-brown powder which will burn in air and chlorine and can be dissolved in alkalies. One of the principal compounds of silicon is the dioxide, or silica, which occurs chiefly as the common mineral quartz. See also SILICA.  A. PABST

**SILICONE,** *SIL ih kohn*, is the name given to a family of man-made materials. They are unlike anything found in nature or made before by man. Silicones are a cross between organic materials such as oil, rubber, and plastics, and inorganic materials such as sand, glass, and quartz. Their key material is silicon, the most abundant material in the earth's crust (see SILICON).

**Uses.** Silicones, which come in solid, liquid, and gaseous forms, are now in use in thousands of industries. Scientists are discovering new applications almost daily. As release agents, silicones keep bread from sticking to pans in commercial bakeries. Clean and smokeless, they work better than the grease that was once used. They also keep tires and other rubber and plastic parts from sticking in the molds. Silicone fluids are used as polishing agents for automobiles, furniture, and eyeglasses. They keep instrument pointers on automobile dashboards from wobbling.

Fabric and leather treated with silicone will not absorb water or water-based products such as ink and tomato juice. Repeated washing or dry cleaning will not remove the effect of the silicone. Yet silicone will not stiffen the fabric.

Silicone oils and greases serve as permanent lubricants for clocks and ball bearings. Silicone water repellents keep brick and concrete walls dry in the rain. Some hand lotions contain silicone. Paints made with silicone resins do not blister and peel off at temperatures of 500 to 1,000 degrees Fahrenheit. Outdoor weathering does not make them lose their gloss and color. Silicone paints are often used on ships.

As electrical insulating materials, silicones make hard-working motors, generators, and transformers last 10 to 100 times as long as they ever did before. They make it possible for a 10-horsepower motor to do as much work as a 15-horsepower motor.

Silicone rubber does not melt at oven temperatures or become hard and brittle at temperatures from $-70°$ to $-110°F$. It is used therefore to seal oven doors and rocker boxes on aircraft and tank engines. It stays flexible enough to seal bomb-bay doors when they open and close on high altitude bombers. Silicone rubber is used to insulate communications cables on naval vessels and motor coils in diesel-electric locomotive motors.

**Composition.** The amount of heat, weathering, and aging a material can stand is determined by the strength of the bond that holds the atoms together. Silicones are several times as heat-stable and weather-resistant as organic materials. Like sand, glass, and quartz, silicones have a molecular skeleton of alternate silicon and oxygen atoms. And the links in this silicon-oxygen chain are strong. The linkage, or bond strength, between silicon and oxygen is about one and a half times as great as the carbon-to-carbon bond that holds organic molecules together.

In making silicone products, "flesh" is put on the silicon-oxygen skeleton with certain organic groups. These organic groups give the silicones such useful properties as water repellency, lubricating properties, flexibility, and ease of handling.

Silicones can be made in the form of fluids, resins, and varnishes or gums. Silicone greases and compounds are made by adding fillers. Silicone rubber is made by adding fillers and vulcanizing agents.  W. R. COLLINGS

**SILICOSIS,** *SIL ih KO sis*, is a disease of the lungs that is caused by breathing in dust that contains silica (see SILICA). Granite cutters, road builders, glassmakers, blasters, and workers in the abrasive and grinding industries are especially in danger of getting this disease.

If a person regularly inhales silica dust for a year or more, the dust may begin to lodge in the lung and irritate the lung tissues. The lung may become inflamed and tiny swellings may begin to develop all over the lung. In the midst of each swelling, or *nodule*, there is a speck of silica dust. This silica dust has a bad chemical effect upon the body. Silicosis usually causes short breath, coughing, and pains in the chest. As time goes on, the body becomes weaker and the person may not be able to work. He may finally get tuberculosis.

Silicosis has caused the death of many workers every year. Preventing the disease involves supplying workers with masks, respirators, or nose filters. Ventilating systems help prevent the disease.  MARK D. ALTSCHULE

# SILK

René Burri, Magnum

**Silk, the Queen of Fibers,** has a radiance and beauty that few other fibers can equal. The silk worker, above, is folding silk cloth that will be made into dresses. Women wear silk dresses for both daytime and evening wear. Much silk is also used in curtains, upholstery materials, and neckties.

**SILK** is a strong, shiny *fiber* (threadlike substance) that is used to make cloth. Silk comes from worms called *silkworms*. Silk has a natural beauty that few other fibers can equal. Because of its beauty, silk is often called the *Queen of Fibers*.

Silk is the strongest of all natural fibers. A thread of silk is stronger than the same size thread of some kinds of steel. Silk is highly elastic. It can be stretched and will still return to its original shape. Silk garments are extremely light in weight, and are warmer than cotton, linen, or rayon clothing. Dyed silk cloth has a deeper, richer appearance than most other dyed fabrics. Silk can be ironed easily, and it resists wrinkling.

Silk is used widely in making women's fashionable clothing and men's high quality neckties. It is also used in upholstery and curtain materials, especially in mixed fabrics.

Japan produces more raw silk than any other country. Mainland China ranks second. Other leading silk producers include Russia, India, Italy, and South Korea. The United States is the world's leading manufacturer of silk products.

### Sources of Silk

**Cultivated Silk** is spun by silkworms that are raised on silk farms. Almost all commercial silk is cultivated. Most high quality cultivated silk is produced by the caterpillars, or larvae, of a moth called *Bombyx mori*. The first part of its name comes from *Bombycidae*, the family of moths to which it belongs. The last part comes from *Morus multicaulis*, the scientific name of the mulberry tree, on which it feeds.

The *Bombyx mori* is a rather large white moth, with black-lined wings. From wing tip to wing tip, the moth measures a little more than 2 inches. Its body is short and thick, and its legs are stout.

**Wild Silk** comes from silkworms that feed chiefly on oak leaves. These worms grow wild, chiefly in China and India. Wild silk is also called *tussah*. Tussah is difficult to bleach because its natural color is tan or brown. It is less shiny than cultivated silk. Tussah is used as a filling in fabrics and is often blended with other fibers.

### Raising Silkworms

The raising of silkworms requires a great deal of care and patience. Silk farmers treat the *Bombyx mori* as carefully as they would a newborn baby. They raise it in their own homes under carefully controlled temperatures. They protect it from mosquitoes, flies, and other insects.

**Production of Silkworms.** In early summer, a female *Bombyx mori* lays from 300 to 500 eggs. It deposits them on specially prepared strips of paper provided by the silk farmer. The moth dies soon after it lays its eggs. The eggs undergo many tests to make sure that they contain perfect, disease-free worms. Then they are put in cold storage. Early the next spring, the silk farmer takes the eggs out of cold storage and puts them in an incubator. An *incubator* is a device for keeping the eggs at a suitable temperature for hatching. About 20 days later, the eggs hatch out into tiny silkworms.

**Development of Silkworms.** The young silkworms are put on trays that are kept spotlessly clean to prevent disease. At first, the silkworms have enormous appetites. They eat almost continually, both night and day. The silk farmer supplies them with fresh mulberry leaves every two or three hours. During this time, the worms grow to about 70 times their original size, and they shed their skins four times. After four to five weeks, the silkworm is about three inches long and nearly an inch thick. Its body has 12 sections and three pairs of legs.

**Spinning the Cocoon.** When fully grown, the silkworm stops eating and is ready to spin its *cocoon* (outer wrapping). The worm creeps into a tiny wooden compartment containing twigs or stems of straw that the

---

*Hans Vaterlaus*, the contributor of this article, is Executive Vice-President of the International Silk Association (U.S.A.), Inc.

379

# SILK

**Thousands of Cocoons** are piled high on the floor of a silk factory. Workers use machines to unwind the long, delicate threads from the cocoons. The threads of several cocoons are drawn together to form a strand strong enough for commercial use.

Eastfoto

their covering. Silk farmers usually kill the insects by placing the cocoons in a hot oven.

## Processing Silk

**Reeling.** After the pupa has been killed, silk workers are ready to *reel* (unwind) the long delicate threads of the cocoon. This is done in a reeling factory called a *filature*.

The cocoons are soaked in basins of hot water to dissolve the gummy sericin that holds the threads together. Threads from several cocoons are unwound at the same time, because a single *filament* (slender thread) is far too fine to be reeled separately. As the cocoons bob about in the basin, their filaments are drawn together and pulled by pulleys through a tiny porcelain *guide*. The guide is much like the eye of a needle.

The melted sericin glues several silk filaments into a single thread, which is wound onto a reel. Later, the silk is removed from the reel and twisted into *skeins* (small coiled bundles). Fifteen double skeins or 30 small skeins are bound into a larger bundle called a *book*. A bale of raw silk ready to be shipped to a mill for weaving contains about 30 books and weighs about 135 pounds.

**Throwing.** The raw silk is now much stronger than it was when it left the cocoon. But it is still not strong

**Laboratory Workers Examine Silkworms** under a microscope to see if they are healthy. The industry produces top quality silk by permitting only healthy worms to live and spin cocoons.

Eastfoto

farmer has prepared. The worm spins a net or web to hold itself to a twig or stem. It then forms a cocoon, which is the silk. To do this, it swings its head from side to side in a series of figure-eight movements. Two glands near the silkworm's lower jaw give off a fluid that hardens into fine silk threads as it hits the air. At the same time, it gives off a gum called *sericin*. The sericin firmly cements the two threads of silk together.

The silkworm spins the silk around and around its body. It does not stop until all the fluid has been used. Finally, after about three days of spinning, the cocoon is completed. The worm then changes into a *pupa*, the third stage of its life cycle. If permitted to live, the pupa becomes a moth in about three weeks. This would complete the life cycle, or *metamorphosis*, of the *Bombyx mori*—egg, silkworm (caterpillar), pupa, and moth (see METAMORPHOSIS).

When a pupa changes into a moth, it bursts the cocoon and breaks the one long silk thread into many short ones. For this reason, silk farmers allow only a small percentage of pupas to develop into moths. These moths are kept to lay the next batch of eggs. To save the silk, the other insects are killed before they break

## THE SILK CYCLE

1. Moth coming out of cocoon

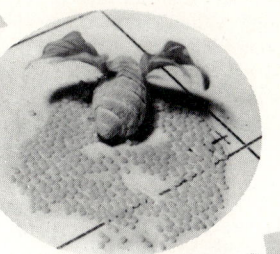
2. Moth laying eggs

8. Finished silk garments

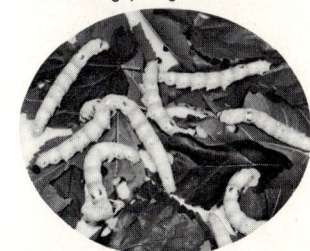
3. Feeding young silkworms

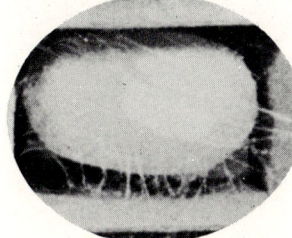
7. Cones of silk thread

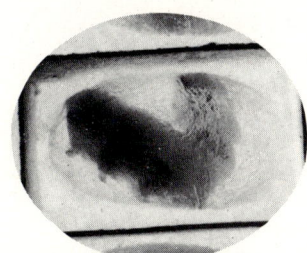
5. Silkworm making cocoon

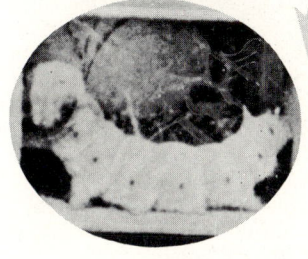
4. Full-grown silkworm

6. Completed silk cocoon

Japan Silk Association; Japan National Tourist Organization

enough to be woven into anything except the sheerest material. It is strengthened by a series of processes called *throwing*. The term comes from the Anglo-Saxon word *thraw* (twist). Throwing is increasing the twist or adding strands and twisting them together.

The number of threads thrown together depends on the fabric to be woven. Most raw silk used to make the *woof* (crosswise threads) is thrown with a certain twist. But much silk used for the *warp* (lengthwise threads) is reeled in heavier sizes, and need not be thrown.

**Boiling Off and Weighting.** When the silk comes from the throwing machines, there is still too much sericin on it. Workmen boil the silk in a solution of hot soap to remove the sericin. This process is called *boiling off*. The removal of the sericin uncovers the natural beauty of the silk. Boiled-off silk is usually milky white. The sericin can be removed either before or after weaving, depending on the type of fabric. Boiling off causes the silk to lose about 25 per cent of its weight. Before World War II, silk fabrics were often *weighted* (loaded) with mineral salts to make up for this loss in weight. But heavily weighted silk cracks and tears much more easily than *pure-dye* silk. In 1938, the U.S. Federal Trade Commission established strict trade-practice rules for the silk industry. Today, U.S. manufacturers do not weight silk. Most European silk fabrics are still weighted. But the amount of weighting must be stated on a label attached to the garment.

**Dyeing.** Brilliant dyes may be applied to silk yarn before it is woven. This type of dyeing is called *skein dyeing*. Some silk fabrics are dyed after they are woven. This process is called *piece dyeing*.

**Weaving.** Silk yarns are woven on looms much like those used for cotton and wool. Automatic power looms have replaced hand-weaving methods in almost all countries. Many silk fabrics, including damasks and heavy evening wear fabrics, are woven on Jacquard looms. Beautiful designs or patterns can be woven on these looms. See JACQUARD.

**Douppioni** are uneven, double silk threads. They come from two silkworms that have nested together and spun one cocoon around the two of them. In processing, the double threads are not separated. Fabrics woven from douppioni thread have a knotted or twisted appearance. Douppioni are used for the filling in shantungs and other rough weaves (see SHANTUNG).

381

# SILK

**Spun Silk.** Not all silk can be reeled and thrown for weaving. When a moth bursts its cocoon, it breaks the one long filament into several short ones. These pierced cocoons and the beginnings and ends of reeled-off cocoons are silk *wastes*. These fibers are spun into silk yarn. Spun silk is used for the filling in some silk, woolen, and cotton fabrics.

## History

**Discovery of Silk.** No one knows for sure when silk was discovered. According to a Chinese legend, it was discovered about 2700 B.C. in the garden of Emperor Huang-Ti. The emperor ordered his wife, Si-Ling-Shi, to find out what was damaging his mulberry trees.

Si-Ling-Shi found white worms eating the mulberry leaves and spinning shiny cocoons. She accidentally dropped a cocoon into hot water. As she played with the cocoon in the water, a delicate, cobwebby tangle separated itself from the cocoon. Si-Ling-Shi drew it out and found that one slender thread was unwinding itself from the cocoon. She had discovered silk.

Si-Ling-Shi persuaded her husband to give her a grove of mulberry trees, where she could grow thousands of worms that spun such beautiful cocoons. It is said that Si-Ling-Shi invented the silk reel, which joined these fine filaments into a thread thick and strong enough for weaving. Some stories also credit her with inventing the first silk loom.

No one knows how much, if any, of this story is true. But historians do know that silk was first used in China. The Chinese guarded the secret of the silkworm. Disgrace and death faced the traitor who disclosed the origin of silk to the outside world. Only the Chinese knew how to make silk for about 3,000 years.

**Silk Making Spreads.** China carried on a profitable silk trade with Western nations in the days of the Han Dynasty (founded in 206 B.C.). Traders from ancient Persia (now Iran) bought richly colored silks from Chinese merchants. Camel caravans blazed routes across Asia, transporting silk from China to Damascus, the market place at which East and West met. From Damascus, silk was taken to the Roman Empire, where there were riches to exchange for it.

As early as the 300's B.C., the Western world heard rumors of the strange worm that spun silk threads. But no one in the West saw the worm until about A.D. 550. At that time, Persia controlled all silk that came out of China. Persians sold it at fabulously high prices.

The Roman, or Byzantine, emperor Justinian objected to paying high prices to the Persians. In about 550, he tried unsuccessfully to find a trade route from Constantinople (now Istanbul) to China that would bypass Persia. He later sent two monks to China as spies. Risking death, they smuggled out silkworm eggs and mulberry seeds in hollow bamboo canes. This adventure ended the Chinese and Persian silk monopolies.

During the next few hundred years, various peoples learned how to raise silkworms and take silk from the cocoons. The Moslems brought silkworms to Spain and Sicily in the 800's and 900's. By the 1200's, Italy had become the silk center of the West. Silk weaving began in France in the late 1400's. The French soon rivaled the Italians as silk manufacturers.

New York Public Library
**Ancient Silk Farming.** Japanese women of long ago sliced mulberry leaves and fed them to hungry silkworms.

Silk weaving became an important industry in England after a large number of skilled Flemish weavers entered the country in 1585. The first silk factory in the United States was built in Mansfield, Conn., in 1810.

**Silk Making Today.** Before World War II, the hosiery industry was by far the biggest user of raw silk. But almost all stockings are now made of nylon. At one time, there was also a great demand for silk lingerie and ribbons. Now these products are usually made of nylon, rayon, or other synthetic fibers. See SYNTHETICS.

Most silk produced today is used in making fashionable clothing, neckwear, curtains, and upholstery. Silk is being used more and more in combination with other natural and man-made fibers to achieve new effects in fabrics. For such mixed fabrics, the Federal Trade Commission requires that the exact fiber composition be stated on a label attached to the fabric.

For many years, Paterson, N.J., was the center of silk manufacturing in the United States. But today most of the large silk mills are in Pennsylvania, Virginia, South Carolina, and North Carolina. HANS VATERLAUS

See also COCOON; MOTH; MULBERRY; PATERSON.

**SILK SCREEN PRINTING** is a means of printing with stencils. The process is used in making fine art pictures and in commercial printing. Silk screen printing may be used to print on almost any surface. It is unique because any kind of ink or paint may be used. Silk screen printing has many uses. Labels on bottles; prints on textiles; and decorations on toys, glass, china, earthenware, and furniture are printed in this way.

The equipment for silk screen printing consists of a piece of stencil silk, called *bolting cloth*, stretched across a wooden frame. The stencil pattern can be applied to the silk in many ways. Some patterns are painted directly on the silk with glue or shellac. More complicated stencils may be cut from special stencil sheets called *pro-film*. Most frequently, photographic stencils, much like the negative film in cameras, are used.

The stencil is placed on the silk screen, which acts as its support. A *squeegee*, similar in principle to the kind used for cleaning windows, is used to force the ink or paint through the open areas of the stencil.

One or more colors may be used in silk screen printing, as in other types of printing. There is a new stencil pattern for each distinct color, and each new color is applied only after the preceding color has dried. As a result, a four-color print may take several days to complete.

In fine art printing, silk screen printing is called *serigraphy*, from the Latin *seri*, meaning *silk*, and the Greek *graphein*, meaning *to draw*. Stencil printing is one of man's oldest arts. It developed into a fine art in the Orient, and gradually spread to Europe. In 1907, Samuel Simon in England received the first patent granted for silk screen stencil printing.   HARRY STERNBERG

**SILKWORM.** See SILK.

WORLD BOOK photo by E. F. Hoppe
**The Silky Terrier**

**SILKY TERRIER** is a toy dog developed about 1900 in Sydney, Australia. It is descended from a cross between the Australian and Yorkshire terrier. Australians keep the dogs as pets and once used them on farms to kill rats and snakes. Silky terriers have erect ears; *docked*, or cut off, tails; and long silky hair with tan markings. They weigh about 8 to 10 pounds.   JOSEPHINE Z. RINE

**SILL.** See HOUSE (The Frame).

**SILLIMANITE,** *SILL ih mun ite* (chemical formula, $Al_2SiO_5$), is an uncommon substance that belongs to the large class of minerals known as silicates (see SILICA). It is sometimes called *fibrolite*. It may be brown, pale green, or white, and it has a glassy luster. It occurs in central Europe, in Brazil, and also in the United States.

## SILURIAN PERIOD

**SILO,** *SI loh*, is a storage bin for chopped green plants used as livestock feed. Silos make it possible for farmers to supply livestock with juicy, tasty feed all year. Before silos were invented, cows gave less milk during winter because they had no green grass to eat.

Farmers use machines to chop up the plants. The chopped material is called *silage*. Machines blow the silage in at the top of the silo. It is removed from the bottom. Most American farmers use corn and juicy grasses called *sorghums* for silage.

If silage is packed properly, all air is forced out. Feed does not spoil in a silo, because molds that cause feed to spoil cannot survive without air. Chemical changes that occur in the silage called *fermentation* also help prevent rotting. Acids produced by fermentation help to prevent the growth of molds. If a feed does not have enough starch or sugar for fermentation, farmers may add hydrochloric acid, sulfur dioxide, sodium metabisulfite, or other acids to the feed to keep it from spoiling. Farmers may use molasses or ground grains to make *legumes* (pea plants) into silage. Molasses and ground grains contain starches and sugars that help to start fermentation.

Americans learned how to make silos from Europeans in the 1870's. The first silos were pits covered with boards. Then Fred L. Hatch, an Illinois farmer, built a square, wooden silo above ground in 1873. But its square corners made it impossible to pack feed tightly in all parts of the silo. Air got in, and much of the feed spoiled. In 1882, Franklin H. King, an agricultural scientist in Wisconsin, built a round silo. Farmers now know that round silos resist the pressure of tightly packed feed best. Today, round silos are built high above the ground throughout the world. They are made of stone, brick, clay tile, sheet metal, concrete, or wood blocks. Airtight, glass-lined steel silos are widely used in areas where farmers use silage all year.

Other types of silos include *trench*, *bunker*, and *box* silos. The trench silo is made by digging a shallow, narrow ditch in the ground, filling it with silage, and then covering it with a sheet of heavy plastic. The bunker silo is built above ground, and usually has wood or concrete sides. One or both ends may be left open. The box silo also is built above ground with poles and wood siding. Livestock can take feed from these types themselves. Temporary *plastic silos* can be made by piling silage on a sheet of plastic placed on the ground, then covering the pile with a second sheet of plastic. After a vacuum pump removes all the air, the two sheets of plastic are sealed.   ALLEN D. TILLMAN

**SILONE, IGNAZIO.** See ITALIAN LITERATURE (The 1900's).

**SILT** is a fine-grained or muddy material which is made up of tiny particles of rock that settle at the bottom of rivers and other bodies of water. A material which sinks in water or air is known as *sediment*. Common examples of sediment are silt, sand, gravel, mud, and dust, or soil. Silt is made up of tiny particles which are anywhere from .01 to .1 mm. (.0004 to .004 inches) in diameter. The larger grains are called *coarse silt*, and the smaller grains are called *fine silt*. Lands on which silt has been deposited are usually fertile.   ELDRED D. WILSON

**SILURIAN PERIOD.** See EARTH (table).

383

# SILVER

**SILVER** (chemical symbol, Ag). Some of the most useful and beautiful objects of the world are made from this lustrous, moonbeam-colored metallic element. Silver was known and used by primitive men. The ancient Hebrews knew it by a name meaning *pale*. The Greeks called it a name meaning *shining*. The chemical symbol for silver, Ag, comes from its Latin name, *argent*.

The gleaming sterling tableware treasured in many homes is made from silver. Ornaments and jewel settings of great value also are made from the precious metal. Silver is widely used in surgery and dentistry. The photographic industry, the world's largest silver consumer, uses it for purposes ranging from coating the film to developing it.

**Properties of Silver.** Silver is harder than gold, but softer than copper. It can be hammered out into sheets so thin that it would take 100,000 of them to make a stack an inch high. These sheets are so thin that light shines through them. Silver also may be drawn out into wires finer than human hair. It is the best conductor of heat and electricity among the metals. But its high cost usually prohibits its use in electrical conductors.

The atomic weight of silver is 107.870 and its atomic number is 47. Silver melts at a temperature of about 1761° F., or 960° C. When melted, silver can absorb as much as 20 times its own volume of oxygen.

One of the most interesting experiments of the chemical laboratory is to expose molten silver to the air. As the silver absorbs oxygen, it swells larger and larger. Then, when the metal cools and becomes solid again, it gives up the oxygen and slowly shrinks back to its original size. If the silver cools too fast, a crust forms on top of the mass before all the oxygen gets out, and bubbles of oxygen form in the metal. The bubbles grow larger and finally explode through the crust, driving out balls of silver with soft, swooshing noises. This action is known as *spitting*. It takes place only in pure silver. In working silver for commercial purposes, spitting is prevented by adding a small amount of some other metal to molten silver. Silver is not changed by moisture, dryness, alkalies, or vegetable acids. But sulfur, or air that contains sulfur, will cause silver to turn black. For this reason silver tarnishes very quickly in places where coal gas, which contains sulfur, is likely to creep in.

**Sources of Silver.** Pure silver is mined chiefly in Mexico and Peru; the provinces of British Columbia and Ontario in Canada; the state of New South Wales in Australia; and Arizona, Idaho, and Montana in the United States. The most important silver ores are *sulfides*, or ores containing sulfur. The richest ore mineral of silver is called *argentite*. It is classified as a simple sulfide because it contains pure silver and sulfur. Argentite is made up of two parts silver to one part sulfur.

The other sulfides are more complex and are found chiefly in Mexico, Peru, Bolivia, Chile, and Idaho. *Light ruby silver* contains arsenic, sulfur, and silver. *Dark ruby silver* contains antimony, sulfur, and silver. *Brittle silver* is made up of the same combining elements as dark ruby silver. Other important silver ores include *horn silver*, which contains chlorine and silver, and *hessite*, a compound of silver and tellurium. Galena, the chief ore of lead, often carries silver. In most of the silver-producing countries of Europe, silver is found in lead ores. There is a valuable lead mine in the Coeur d'Alene district of Idaho, where silver is mined in large quantities. Silver occurs with copper in the Butte (Mont.) district. A famous silver-copper mine is in Mansfeld, East Germany (near Halle). Sometimes silver is found alloyed with other metals, such as gold, mercury, and copper.

**Silver Production.** The world's richest silver mines are in North America. Canada, Mexico, Peru, and the United States produce over half the world's supply of silver. Canada, Mexico, and the United States com-

## LEADING SILVER MINING COUNTRIES
Troy ounces of silver mined in 1966

|  |  |
|---|---|
| United States | 43,669,000 oz. |
| Mexico | 41,984,000 oz. |
| Canada | 33,342,000 oz. |
| Peru | 32,841,000 oz. |
| Russia | 27,000,000 oz. |
| Australia | 18,278,000 oz. |
| Bolivia | 5,125,000 oz. |
| Germany (East) | 4,800,000 oz. |
| Sweden | 4,495,000 oz. |
| Honduras | 3,734,000 oz. |

Source: *Minerals Yearbook, 1966*, U.S. Bureau of Mines.

## LEADING SILVER MINING STATES, PROVINCES, AND TERRITORIES
Troy ounces of silver mined in 1966

|  |  |
|---|---|
| Idaho | 19,777,000 oz. |
| Ontario | 10,318,000 oz. |
| Utah | 7,755,000 oz. |
| Arizona | 6,339,000 oz. |
| Quebec | 5,780,000 oz. |
| British Columbia | 5,412,000 oz. |
| Montana | 5,320,000 oz. |
| Yukon Territory | 4,078,000 oz. |
| New Brunswick | 3,025,000 oz. |
| Colorado | 2,086,000 oz. |

Sources: Bureau of Mines, Washington, D.C.; Department of Energy, Mines, & Resources, Ottawa.

# THE SILVERSMITH AT WORK

A wax model is made from the artist's design.

Circular designs are shaped on a wheel or lathe.

**This Beautiful Chocolate Pot** is a masterpiece of the silversmith's art. It was made in London in 1697 by the English craftsman, Isaac Dighton.

Some parts are shaped by hand hammering.

Embossed designs are made by hammering.

**A Covered Dish and Plate.** This intricate design was done by the French silversmith, L. Landes, in Toulouse, about 1773.

Covers for vessels are stamped out on a hand press.

Solid parts and figures of the piece are cast.

**A Coffeepot** made in New England by the American silversmith, Samuel Edwards, during the early 1700's.

Photos: Metropolitan Museum of Art

Chased designs are added by skilled engravers.

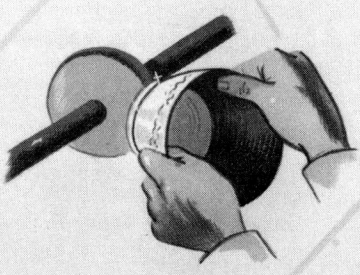

The finished piece is cleaned and polished on buffing wheels.

## SILVER

pete for first place among the world's silver producing countries.

The leading silver-producing states of the United States include Arizona, Colorado, Idaho, Montana, and Utah. The chief silver mining areas of Canada are in British Columbia, Ontario, and Quebec.

Silver mines may be close to the surface, or they may go down for thousands of feet. The metal is mined in the same way as other underground deposits of metal.

After they are mined, silver ores are usually reduced to a rich concentrate which in turn is *smelted* (a heat process). The product of the smelting is further refined in various ways which remove the metals associated with the silver.

**Uses of Silver.** Pure silver is too soft to stand up under constant wear. It is usually mixed with copper to form an *alloy* before it is made into commercial articles. This alloy is used to make coins, jewelry, and tableware. Silver coins in the United States used to be made of 90 per cent silver and 10 per cent copper. But in 1965, Congress passed a bill to eliminate all silver from new dimes and quarters, and to reduce the silver in new half dollars from 90 per cent to 40 per cent. Until the Coinage Act of 1920, British coins were $92\frac{1}{2}$ per cent silver and $7\frac{1}{2}$ per cent copper. The 1920 act reduced the silver content to 50 per cent. The 1946 Coinage Act eliminated all silver in British coins. They are now made of a copper-nickel alloy.

*Sterling* silver contains as much or more silver as British coins did. The word *sterling* has been used to mean high-quality silver since the 1200's. At that time, the coins of England had decreased in value and contained little silver. The only coins that contained large proportions of silver were those coined by the merchants of the Hanseatic League in northern Germany. These coins were called *Easterlings* to distinguish them from the low-silver alloy coins of England. English speech quickly turned Easterling to *sterling*.

*Silver plate* is made by coating base metals with pure silver or silver alloy by electrolysis (see ELECTROLYSIS). Silver plate does not wear so well as solid silver alloy, because the base metal shows through as the plate wears off. But silver plate is a good deal less expensive than solid silver, and is more widely used for tableware.

In the laboratory, silver has many uses. One of its most important chemical compounds is called *silver nitrate* or *lunar caustic*. This compound is made by dissolving silver in nitric acid. Silver nitrate is widely used in photography, silver plating, and indelible ink. *Silver chloride* is made by adding hydrochloric acid to a solution of silver. It is then combined with silver bromide for use in various chemical processes of photography.

*Silver fulminate*—which contains nitrogen, carbon, hydrogen, and oxygen in addition to silver—is a violent explosive. But its use in explosives has been largely displaced by mercury fulminate and other cheaper compounds.   HARRISON ASHLEY SCHMITT

**Related Articles** in WORLD BOOK include:

| | | |
|---|---|---|
| Alloy | Dollar (picture) | Silver Nitrate |
| Amalgam | Ductility | Western Frontier |
| Bullion | England (picture: | Life (The |
| Colonial Life | Sheffield Silver) | Search for Gold |
| in America | Money | and Silver) |
| (Crafts) | | |

**SILVER, ABBA HILLEL** (1893-1963), was an American rabbi and Zionist leader. In 1917, he became rabbi of The Temple in Cleveland, Ohio, one of the largest Jewish Reform congregations in the United States. He helped promote the first unemployment insurance law in Ohio, as well as child-labor laws. In 1940, he lectured at Harvard University.

Silver's principal writings include *Messianic Speculations in Israel* (1927), *The Democratic Impulse in Jewish History* (1928), *Religion in a Changing World* (1930), *The World Crisis and Jewish Survival* (1941), and *Vision and Victory* (1949). He was born in Neinstadt, Lithuania, and settled in the United States in 1902. He was graduated from the University of Cincinnati and Hebrew Union College.   CLIFTON E. OLMSTEAD

**SILVER CERTIFICATE.** See MONEY (U.S. Money Today).

**SILVER FISH** is a small silver-colored insect with no wings. It is sometimes called a *silver fish moth*. This house pest is one of the most primitive insects. It has two long feelers, and three long appendages at the "tail" end. The silver fish eats anything with starch, paste, or glue on it. It can be controlled by dusting with pyrethrum powder (see PYRETHRUM).

**Scientific Classification.** Silver fish belong to the firebrat and silver fish family, *Lepismatidae*. They are genus *Lepisma*, species *L. saccharina*.   ANTHONY STANDEN

**SILVER FOX** is a red fox whose fur is dark instead of the usual red, and has a silvery appearance. It may have normal red brothers and sisters. The silver fox looks like a small collie dog. It is slender and usually weighs no more than 10 pounds. Its fur is long and soft, and is black with more or less white-tipped hair. This gives the fur a silvery appearance. The silver fox has a long sharp nose and small piercing eyes. It has keen senses of smell, sight, and hearing.

The silver fox lives in forests, in mountains, and in flat countries where there is a great deal of plant life. It can be found throughout most of the United States and Canada, but is most numerous in Alaska and western Canada. It may make its own den in a rocky ledge, in the earth, or in a hollow log. It also may take over the home of another animal, such as the badger, coyote, marmot, or woodchuck, because its legs are not good for digging homes. The silver fox eats birds, rabbits, mice, ground squirrels, and other small animals, as well as birds' eggs, fruits, and insects.

The silver fox is a valuable animal because of its fur. There are many "farms" in the United States and Canada that raise nothing but silver foxes. The furs are made into expensive coats, scarfs, and trimmings for coats.

**Scientific Classification.** The silver fox is a member of the dog family, *Canidae*. It is classified as genus *Vulpes*, species *V. fulva*.   E. LENDELL COCKRUM

See also Fox; FUR.

**SILVER NITRATE** is a chemical used in medicine and industry. Silver nitrate burns the skin, and can cause severe poisoning or even death if swallowed. Doctors use silver nitrate to *cauterize* (burn) wounds to prevent bleeding or infection, and to remove warts. They use a mild solution of silver nitrate to treat certain eye and skin diseases, and as an antiseptic. Some states require that the eyes of all newborn infants be treated with silver nitrate solution to prevent possible blindness (see BLINDNESS [Diseases]).

The photographic industry uses silver nitrate in making film. Most silver salts used in film are manufactured from silver nitrate. For example, silver bromide photographic film is made from silver nitrate and a potassium bromide solution. Gelatin, a protein substance, is then added to the silver salt solution to form an *emulsion* which coats the film (see PHOTOGRAPHY [Developing Film]). Silver nitrate is also used to make mirrors and indelible ink, and in silver plating.

Silver can be purified by dissolving it in nitric acid and passing electricity through the silver nitrate solution. Pure silver forms at one electric terminal. Chemists use silver nitrate to help prepare other silver compounds, and also to identify chemicals in solution.

Manufacturers make silver nitrate by dissolving silver in nitric acid, and then evaporating the solution. They sometimes melt silver nitrate and allow it to harden into a crystalline mass. Silver nitrate in this form is also known as *lunar caustic.*

Silver nitrate has the chemical formula $AgNO_3$. It dissolves easily in water, and changes back into silver when it reacts with many metal and organic compounds. OTTO THEODOR BENFEY

**SILVER PURCHASE ACT OF 1934.** See MONEY (U.S. Monetary Standards).

**SILVER STAR.** See DECORATIONS AND MEDALS (United States Decorations and Medals).

**SILVER STATE.** See NEVADA.

**SILVERED GLASS.** See GLASSWARE (Mercury Glass).

**SILVERSMITH.** See COLONIAL LIFE IN AMERICA (Crafts); REVERE, PAUL; SILVER.

**SILVERWARE.** See NICKEL SILVER; SILVER (Uses).

**SILVICULTURE.** See FOREST AND FOREST PRODUCTS (Forest Management).

**SIMCOE, JOHN GRAVES** (1752-1806), was a British soldier and the first lieutenant governor of Upper Canada. He served from 1791 to 1797. During the Revolutionary War, he raised and commanded a corps of loyalists called the Queen's Rangers. Later, as lieutenant governor of Upper Canada, he helped found Toronto and settle loyalists who had fled from the United States. He was born in Cotterstock, England. W. B. WILLCOX

See also TORONTO (History).

**SIMEON II.** See BULGARIA (In World War II).

**SIMEON STYLITES,** *sty LIE teez* (388?-459), was the famous saint who lived on top of a stone pillar for 36 years. He fasted rigorously, and became the spiritual guide of great numbers of pilgrims. He believed that the severity of his life was necessary to call attention to the evil habits of the people of his time. He was born in Syria. See also ASCETIC.

**SIMHAT TORAH,** *sim KAHT toh RAH*, is a Jewish festival of rejoicing in the Torah, or Law. It is the ninth day of Sukkot, and falls on the 23rd day of the Hebrew month of Tishri. Jews in Israel and Reform Jews observe it as the eighth day of Sukkot. Simhat Torah marks the end of the annual cycle of reading the Pentateuch in the synagogue. The cycle begins again on the first Sabbath after Sukkot. See also SUKKOT. LEONARD C. MISHKIN

**SIMILE,** *SIM uh lee*, is a figure of speech used in describing or explaining something. It points out a likeness between two different objects or ideas by using a connective word. This connective word is usually *like* or *as*. An example of a simile would be, "He is as cross *as* a bear today," or "She ran *like* a deer."

Often a simile becomes so compact that we drop the connecting word. Then the simile becomes a *metaphor*. For example, the simile "He is *like* a fox" becomes a metaphor in "He *is* a fox." JOSEPHINE MILES

See also FIGURE OF SPEECH; METAPHOR.

**SIMMONS COLLEGE.** See UNIVERSITIES AND COLLEGES (table).

**SIMON FRASER UNIVERSITY** is a coeducational university located on top of Burnaby Mountain in Burnaby, B.C., a town east of Vancouver. It offers courses leading to bachelor's, master's, and doctor's degrees in arts, education, and science. The university was founded in 1963, and opened in 1965. It receives support from the provincial and federal governments, and private gifts. For enrollment, see CANADA (table: Universities and Colleges). PATRICK McTAGGART-COWAN

**SIMON PETER.** See PETER, SAINT.

**SIMON THE CANAANITE, SAINT,** was one of the more obscure apostles of Christ. The word *Canaanite* does not mean *belonging to the land of Canaan*, but is the Hebrew or Aramaic word for the Greek *Zelotes*, or Zealot. He is called *Simon called Zelotes* in Luke 6:15. This name distinguishes him from Simon Peter.

Many authorities believe that Simon was called the Zealot because of his zeal for his work. But some believe the name might have indicated Simon belonged to a Jewish political party called *The Zealots*. This party advocated overthrow of the Roman government by violence and re-establishment of the independent Jewish state. Nothing certain is known of Simon's career after the beginning of the church, recorded in Acts 1:13. His feast day is generally celebrated as the feast of Saints Simon and Jude on October 28. However, the Eastern Orthodox Church celebrates the feast of Saint Simon on May 10. FULTON J. SHEEN and MERRILL C. TENNEY

**SIMONIDES OF CEOS,** *sy MAHN ih deez* (556?-469? B.C.), was a Greek lyric poet. He wrote lyrics of many kinds, from majestic choral odes to short epigrams to be inscribed on devotional offerings or monuments. His most famous epigram is an epitaph for the heroes of Thermopylae: "Tell them in Lacedaemon, passer-by, That here obedient to their word we lie."

Simonides could be thoughtful, but also gay or sad. His elegy on the heroes of Marathon is perhaps his best. Simonides was born in Ceos (Kéa). MOSES HADAS

**SIMONS, MENNO.** See MENNONITES.

**SIMONT, MARC** (1915-    ), is an American artist. He won a Caldecott award in 1957 for his illustrations in the book *A Tree Is Nice*, by Janice May Udry.

Simont was born in Paris, and grew up in France, Spain, and the United States. In 1948, he illustrated a new edition of Andrew Lang's *Red Fairy Book*. In 1950, Simont was a runner-up for a Caldecott award for his pictures in Ruth Krauss's book *Happy Day*. He also has done illustrations for newspapers, magazines, and folk tales. ELOISE RUE

**SIMONY.** See BARRATRY.

**SIMOOM,** *sih MOOM*, or SIMOON, is a hot dry wind that blows in the Sahara and the Arabian Desert. The simoom carries great clouds of sand and dust. It rises suddenly. Men and animals may suffer from heatstroke when they are exposed to a simoom. The simoom may pass in 10 minutes, or it may last for days. It leaves

## SIMPLON PASS AND TUNNEL

the desert in great drifts like snow after a blizzard. Simooms are caused by the overheating of the soil and the layers of air next to it. JAMES E. MILLER

**SIMPLON PASS AND TUNNEL** are important gateways through the Swiss Alps. Napoleon built a military road over the pass in the early 1800's. The present improved road leading to the pass begins at Brig in the Rhône Valley. It reaches an elevation of 6,592 feet, then descends into the Lake District of northern Italy. The Simplon Tunnel, completed in 1905, is the longest railroad tunnel in the world. It is 12.3 miles long, and has a maximum elevation of 2,312 feet. For location, see SWITZERLAND (color map). FRANKLIN C. ERICKSON

**SIMPSON, SIR JAMES YOUNG** (1811-1870), a Scottish doctor, specialized in the problems of childbirth, or obstetrics. In 1847, he found in chloroform a substitute for ether, and was the first to suggest the use of this drug to relieve the pain of childbirth (see ANESTHESIA; CHLOROFORM). An argument followed the discovery. It ended in Simpson's favor when Queen Victoria gave birth to her eighth child, Prince Leopold, under chloroform. Simpson was born in Bathgate, Scotland. GEORGE ROSEN

**SIMPSON BIBLE COLLEGE.** See UNIVERSITIES AND COLLEGES (table).

**SIMPSON COLLEGE.** See UNIVERSITIES AND COLLEGES (table).

**SIMS, WILLIAM SOWDEN** (1858-1936), was an American naval officer who introduced reforms in naval gunnery and became a noted writer on naval subjects. Sims commanded United States naval forces in European waters during World War I.

Sims was graduated from the U.S. Naval Academy in 1880, and served as naval attaché at the U.S. embassies in France and Russia. Later, Sims became inspector of target practice for the Asiatic squadron. He suggested a new system which greatly improved American naval gunnery. This system kept gunsights on target despite the rolling of a firing ship. Sims became a rear admiral when the United States entered World War I, and rose to admiral in 1918. He retired in 1922.

Sims won a Pulitzer prize in 1921 for *The Victory at Sea*, which he wrote with Burton J. Hendrick. Sims was born in Port Hope, Canada. DONALD W. MITCHELL

**SINAI,** SIGH *nigh,* is the mountain on which Moses received the *Decalogue* (Ten Commandments) and learned much of the Hebraic law. Mt. Sinai, also called *Horeb*, is located somewhere in the mountain district of the Sinai Peninsula, a triangle between the two north arms of the Red Sea. For the past 1,500 years, scholars have considered Mt. Sinai to be an 8,000-foot peak in the southern tip of the triangle. But today, many experts think it may be in the northeastern part of the peninsula. See also DECALOGUE; MOSES. W. W. SLOAN

**SINALOA,** *SEE nah LOH ah*, is a long, narrow Mexican state along the Gulf of California and the Pacific Ocean. For location, see MEXICO (political map). Sinaloa covers 22,429 square miles from a broad coastal plain to the Sierra Madre Occidental Mountains in the interior. It has a population of 1,047,972. It is one of the chief agricultural states in Mexico. Cattle graze in the mountainous section. Culiacán is the capital and Mazatlán is a leading port (see MAZATLÁN). Sinaloa became a state in 1830. CHARLES C. CUMBERLAND

**SINATRA, FRANK** (1915-    ), ranks among the most famous singers in the history of popular music. Nicknamed "The Voice," he became well known for both his soulful ballad singing and his interpretations of rhythm songs. He also appeared in about 50 motion pictures, and won the 1953 Academy Award as best male supporting actor for his work in *From Here to Eternity*.

FRANCIS ALBERT SINATRA was born in Hoboken, N.J., the son of a fireman. He sang with local bands and won an amateur show prize in 1937 before joining trumpeter Harry James' band in 1939. While touring with the band of trombonist Tommy Dorsey from 1940 to 1942, he gained great popularity with teen-agers throughout the United States. Sinatra began his career as a solo singer in 1943, and later gained popularity with audiences of all ages. LEONARD FEATHER

See also NEVADA (picture: Night Clubs).

**SINBAD THE SAILOR.** See ARABIAN NIGHTS; ROC; BASRA.

**SINCLAIR, HARRY FORD** (1876-1956), was an American oil producer and refiner. His vast holdings became the Sinclair Oil Corporation. He was involved in the *Teapot Dome* oil scandal of 1923, but was found innocent of fraud (see TEAPOT DOME). He went to prison briefly in 1927 for contempt of the United States Senate during an investigation. Sinclair was born in Wheeling, W.Va., on July 6, 1876. W. H. BAUGHN

**SINCLAIR, UPTON BEALL** (1878-1968), a much discussed American writer, tried to expose the evils in various industries. *The Jungle* (1906) revealed unsanitary conditions in the Chicago meat-packing industry. It helped arouse public opinion for investigation which led to pure-food laws (see PURE FOOD AND DRUG LAWS). Sinclair also wrote *King Coal* (1917), *Oil!* (1927), *Boston* (1928), *The Wet Parade* (1931), and *Little Steel* (1938).

Two of Sinclair's books, *The Goose-Step* (1923) and *The Goslings* (1924), attacked the American educational system. *The Profits of Religion* (1918) sought to show that churches were used by capitalists to make poorly paid people resigned to their hard lot. He received the Pulitzer prize in 1943 for *Dragon's Teeth* (1942), one of the "Lanny Budd" novels. His later works include the biographical *My Lifetime in Letters* (1960) and *The Autobiography of Upton Sinclair* (1962).

Sinclair was born on Sept. 20, 1878, in Baltimore, Md. He studied at The City College in New York and at Columbia University. Sinclair ran unsuccessfully for public office as a Socialist. He also ran for governor of California as a Democrat in 1934. HARRY H. CLARK

See also ROOSEVELT, THEODORE (Domestic Problems).

**SINE.** See TRIGONOMETRY.

**SINEW.** See TENDON.

**SINFONIA.** See SYMPHONY.

**SING SING** is a state prison in Ossining, N.Y. It is almost a city in itself, with its own school and factories. Whenever possible, the convicts are given jobs in Sing Sing for which they are suited by their training and experience. This follows modern prison methods. The prison originally had a building for women. But now the only women housed in the prison are those who have been condemned to death. The construction of the prison buildings was started in 1825 with convict labor. Later the entire prison was reorganized, and a number of new buildings were put up. W. L. DENNO

# SINGAPORE

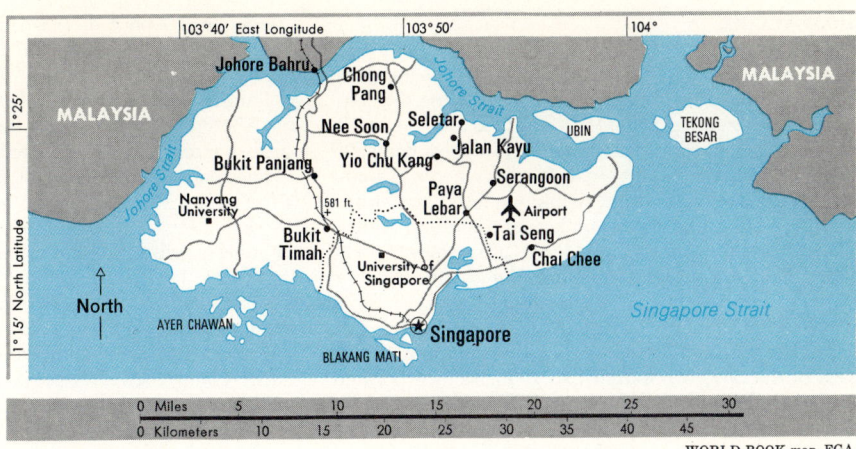

* ★ National Capital
* • Other City or Town
* — Road
* +++ Rail Line
* ...... City Limits
* + Highest Known Elevation

WORLD BOOK map-FGA

**SINGAPORE,** *SING guh pohr,* is a small island country in Southeast Asia. It is about as big as the city of Chicago, and only one-fifth as big as Rhode Island—the smallest state in the Union. The country lies at the southern end of the Malay Peninsula. Singapore is separated from the island of Sumatra in Indonesia by the Strait of Malacca. The name of the country in Malay, the official language, is SINGAPURA.

The bustling, crowded city of Singapore, on the southern end of the island, is the heart of the country. Most of the people live there, and the country's thriving economy is based on the city's business. Singapore city is a business and banking center, and one of the world's busiest ports. Ships from many countries stop there to load and unload cargo. Many Asian countries send copra, lumber, rubber, spices, and other goods to Singapore to be sorted, graded, and packed. Ships then carry the goods to other countries.

---

*John F. Cady, the contributor of this article, is Professor of History at Ohio University and the author of* Southeast Asia: Its Historical Development.

---

Great Britain controlled the island from 1824 to the mid-1900's. Singapore became part of the independent Federation of Malaysia in 1963, but was excluded from the federation and became an independent country in 1965. It joined the Commonwealth of Nations and the United Nations in 1965.

**Government.** Singapore is a republic. The president is elected to a four-year term by the Legislative Assembly (parliament). The president is head of state, and appoints the prime minister. The prime minister actually directs the government. The prime minister directs foreign and domestic policy and selects the 14 members of the *Council of Ministers* (cabinet). The people elect the 51 members of parliament.

**The People.** About three out of four Singaporeans are Chinese. The Chinese of Singapore are noted as good businessmen. They run most of the import trade and much of the country's other business. Some Chinese work on farms. About 15 out of 100 persons are Malays. Many Malays work as fishermen, policemen, plantation laborers, or taxicab drivers. Most of the other people are Indians, Pakistanis, and Europeans. The Europeans work mainly in trade and commerce. Malay is the official language of Singapore. English, Chinese, and Tamil are also spoken there.

**The City.** About 1,820,000 persons, or nine out of ten persons in the country, live in the city of Singapore. This crowded city lies along the southern shore. It was built over hills that were leveled and marshes that had to be filled with earth.

The city's location and port facilities make it the major commercial and shipping center in Southeast Asia. Singapore is a gateway from India to the Far East. Ships sailing from India to China, Japan, and Australia stop at Singapore to load and unload cargo. The 36-square-mile harbor boasts the best facilities in Southeast Asia. Singapore is built around the harbor. Warehouses and concrete docks line the port. Singapore is a *free port,* which means that goods can be unloaded, stored, and reshipped without paying duty fees.

Much of Singapore city resembles large cities in the United States. Raffles Square and nearby streets in the eastern part lie near the water front. Five-story department stores and many one-room shops carry on a lively trade. Some buildings rise as high as 15 stories, tall by Asian standards. A monument to Sir Stamford Raffles, founder of Singapore, stands on Empress Place.

Most of the people live in the western part of the

---

### FACTS IN BRIEF

**Capital:** Singapore.
**Official Language:** Malay.
**Form of Government:** Republic.
**Area:** 224 square miles. *Greatest Distances*—(north-south) 14 miles; (east-west) 27 miles. *Coastline*—60 miles.
**Population:** *1957 Census*—1,476,694. *Estimated 1970 Population*—2,106,000; density, 9,402 persons to the square mile. *Estimated 1975 Population*—2,383,000.
**Chief Products:** *Agriculture*—coconuts, fruits, tobacco, vegetables. *Manufacturing and Processing*—copra products, rubber products, sawmilling, shipbuilding and repairing, spices, tin products.
**National Anthem:** "Majullah Singapura" ("Forward Singapore").
**Flag:** There are two horizontal stripes, red on top (for equality and brotherhood), white below (for purity and virtue). A white crescent and five white stars (for democracy, peace, progress, justice, and equality) lie in the upper left corner. See FLAG (color picture: Flags of Asia and the Pacific).
**Money:** *Basic Unit*—Singapore dollar.

# SINGAPORE

city. Crowded tenement houses stand next to modern, luxurious apartment buildings. Large housing developments have replaced many of the tenements.

The Botanical Gardens are among the most beautiful sights of Singapore. They include many acres of plant life, and a wild jungle where monkeys play. The Padang sports field features soccer, cricket, and football games. The Chinese operate three large amusement parks called the *Great World*, the *Happy World*, and the *New World* in the eastern part of the city.

**Education.** Singapore has about 650 primary and secondary schools. The University of Singapore, northwest of the city, was founded in 1949. It incorporated Raffles College and King Edward VII College of Medicine. Chinese residents financed and built the Nanyang University in the western part of the island. It opened in 1956.

**Land.** Singapore covers 224 square miles. Except for a plateau in the center of the island, most of the land is low. The western and central sections of the island are hilly, and the east is flat.

Singapore Strait forms the island's southern coastline. In the north, the Johore Strait, only three-quarters of a mile wide, separates the island from Johore, a state in Malaysia. A stone and cement *causeway* (bridge) carries railway tracks, a highway, and a pipeline across the Johore Strait. The pipeline carries fresh water to the island.

Singapore has a hot, moist climate. The average annual temperature is about 80° F. The island receives about 95 inches of rainfall a year. The rainfall is fairly equally distributed throughout the year.

**Economy.** About 40,000 ships enter and leave the port each year. Loading and unloading ships provide work for many Singaporeans. Some of the goods, such as natural rubber received from Malaysia, Thailand, and Vietnam, are processed there. Copra, lumber, and spices are also processed there.

Singapore has about 2,400 manufacturing firms. It is the largest ship repair port in Southeast Asia, and it has one of the world's largest centers for storing, blending, and distributing oil. Products of Singapore include aluminum, beer, biscuits, coconut oil, household utensils, paint, and soap. A large industrial district is being developed along the southwest coast. The city of Singapore is an important financial center. It has 35 banks.

The country imports most of its rice. Only a small portion of the land there is used for farming. Singapore produces about one-half of the fish and vegetables that its people eat. But it produces nearly all of the pigs and poultry used for food. Chinese gardeners raise fruits and vegetables on most of the cultivated land. Some rubber plantations lie in the northern section of the island, and coconuts grow in the sandy eastern part.

Singapore's 16 miles of railroad are linked to Kuala Lumpur, Malaysia; and Bangkok, Thailand. Most of the 525 miles of roads on the island are paved. Airlines use the Paya Lebor airport, east of the city.

**History.** Historians know little of the early history of Singapore. In the 1200's and 1300's, Singapore harbor (then called Tumasik) was a fairly important trading center. Invaders from the island of Java (now part of Indonesia) destroyed Tumasik in 1377. The port of Malacca was founded north of Singapore about 1409. Singapore then lost its commercial importance.

In the early 1800's, Singapore was a jungle-covered

**Dock Workers Unload Rubber From Barges On the Crowded Singapore River, Which Flows Through the City.**

island, with only a fishing village on the southern coast. Sir Stamford Raffles, an agent for the British trading organization called the East India Company, recognized the potential importance of the island to British trade. In 1819, he gained possession of Singapore harbor for Britain through an agreement with a sultan of Johore. The entire island came under British control in 1824 by agreement with the Dutch. In 1826, Singapore became part of the Straits Settlements, a British colony (see STRAITS SETTLEMENTS). Emigrants from China poured in to become traders and workers.

The British built a huge naval and air base on the northern shore of the island during the 1930's. They installed strong defenses, cut airfields out of the jungle, and placed submarine nets across the harbor entrance. Singapore was called the *Gibraltar of the East*. But the British prepared only for attack from the sea. Early in World War II, Japanese troops marched down the Malay Peninsula from Thailand and easily took Singapore. They occupied the city from 1942 to 1945.

The British dissolved the Straits Settlements in 1946, and made Singapore a separate crown colony. Small islands surrounding the main island, and Great Britain's Christmas Island south of Java, were administered from Singapore. Christmas Island was transferred to Australia in 1958.

The people of Singapore elected their first representative legislature in 1955, and some of them began to ask for complete independence about the same time. In October, 1957, the Legislative Assembly passed a bill which made all people who had lived in the colony eight years citizens of Singapore. Singapore gained internal self-government on June 3, 1959. Britain was responsible for Singapore's defense and foreign affairs.

Brian Brake—Magnum

# SINGER, ISAAC MERRIT

The territories of Singapore, *Sabah* (formerly North Borneo), and Sarawak (also in Borneo) joined Malaya in forming the Federation of Malaysia on Sept. 16, 1963. Many social and political differences existed among the peoples in the federation. When Singapore's Chinese leadership threatened to upset the balance in the federation, the Malaysian government excluded Singapore in 1965. Singapore became an independent country.

The island controls its own defense and foreign affairs, but Britain still maintains its naval base on the island. Lee Kuan Yew, a lawyer, became the first prime minister of the country. JOHN F. CADY

See also MALAYSIA (History).

**SINGAPORE** (pop. 1,820,000; alt. 25 ft.) is the capital of the country of Singapore. The city has one of the busiest ports in the world. The city is described under SINGAPORE (the country). JOHN F. CADY

Singer Manufacturing Co.

**Isaac Singer** developed a better sewing machine in 1851 and later took out 20 patents for additional improvements.

**SINGER, ISAAC MERRIT** (1811-1875), more than any other man, made the sewing machine a universal household appliance. When a crude sewing machine was brought to him for repairs in 1851, his skill as a machinist led him to see how it could be made an efficient, versatile, and salable device. Unaware of Walter Hunt's and Elias Howe's work on the sewing machine, Singer hit on solutions similar to theirs (see HOWE, ELIAS).

In 1854, the courts awarded basic patent rights to Howe, after a hard-fought trial. Then Singer organized sewing-machine manufacturers into the first patent pool in American industry. It permitted seven leading companies to share the best features of the machine.

By his energetic promotion and keen business sense, Singer acquired $13 million. He was the first man to spend a million dollars a year on advertising. Singer was born in Oswego, N.Y. He became a mechanic at the age of 12. RICHARD D. HUMPHREY

See also SEWING MACHINE.

391

# SINGING

**SINGING** is as much a natural function of the human voice as speaking is. We speak for practical purposes, in order to convey our thoughts. We sing for joy from early childhood and, through the songs we learn later, to express emotions. The spontaneous singing of young children and the humming of adults may occur without any cultivation of the voice or technical training. But the singing of songs and of more elaborate music in front of an audience is a different matter, and requires study and training.

**How We Sing.** When we want to sing, nerve centers near the brain cause the vocal cords to start vibrating. The energy of the air stored in our lungs amplifies this vibration to make it audible. Small modifications in the length and width of the vocal cords produce different pitches and also musical phrases.

An average untrained voice can sing 12 notes, which is the range of most popular songs. Well-trained voices can cover two octaves, or 16 notes. Some unusual voices, after much training, have been able to cover three octaves.

**Voice Classification.** Voices are classified by their range and by their *timbre* (tone color). The highest woman's voice is the *soprano*. Below it is the *mezzo-soprano*, and next the *contralto* (or *alto*). The highest man's voice is the *tenor*, then the *baritone*, and below it the *bass*.

**Training the Voice.** Most people can be taught to sing at least simple melodies. With the help of microphones, talented singers of popular songs have made successful careers with voices of average power and range. But to become an opera star or a concert recitalist requires a voice of unusual power, range, and quality. Some arias include very high and very low notes; the performer may have to sing many words without taking a breath; the voice may have to rise above powerful orchestrations; or perhaps the performer must sing quite softly for a long time. An opera singer must be able to sing through the entire length of an opera (sometimes for more than three hours) and to sing another opera two days later. Many young persons try to become singers, but only a few succeed in achieving the excellency necessary to become a successful opera and concert singer.

The training of the voice for professional singing takes patience and practice. A voice student must learn to know and discipline many things in himself, including the way he stands, the posture of his body, the depth and ease of his air intake, and the relaxation of his neck and upper chest. The singer must also control the energy created by the large quantities of air in his lungs, and must use this for sending tones into the resonances of the head without making his throat tense and tired. Low notes should sound near the lips; high notes, in the cavities above the bone of the palate. The breath support must be able to back low tones or spin soft ones. The singer does this by regulating smoothly the muscles of his lower chest and upper abdomen. The singer must learn to express the gamut of human feelings. He must not neglect musical studies, because the human voice at its best is a beautiful musical instrument.

Song sheets often indicate how to sing. For example, they sometimes have *mezza di voce* printed in certain places. This means that, at such a point, the voice must increase the tone gradually from *pianissimo* (very soft) to *fortissimo* (very loud), and then back again. Another term, *legato*, means to sing smoothly.

The student usually begins by singing scales on pure vowels. Then he switches to words and phrases, and finally to entire songs. The singer must remember that the words he sings must be clearly understood. Singing clear and precise vowels, and connecting them with crisp, light consonants will improve the enunciation more than any exaggerated effort of the mouth to project the diction. Persons training for public singing are advised to work on Italian songs and arias, because the precision of Italian vowels helps the voice attain beauty and freedom.   MARTIAL SINGHER

**Related Articles** in WORLD BOOK include:

### AMERICAN OPERA SINGERS

| | |
|---|---|
| Anderson, Marian | Pons, Lily |
| Callas, Maria | Ponselle, Rosa Melba |
| Farrar, Geraldine | Price, Leontyne |
| Garden, Mary | Raisa, Rosa |
| Hayes, Roland | Robeson, Paul |
| London, George | Swarthout, Gladys |
| Maynor, Dorothy | Tibbett, Lawrence M. |
| Melton, James | Tucker, Richard |
| Peerce, Jan | |

**Choral Singing** adds to the beauty of the religious services in many churches. Church singing includes hymns, anthems, chorales, and chants.

*Oilways* Magazine, Esso Standard Oil Co.

### Italian Opera Singers
- Caruso, Enrico
- Galli-Curci, Amelita
- Martinelli, Giovanni
- Pinza, Ezio
- Scotti, Antonio
- Tebaldi, Renata
- Tetrazzini, Luisa

### Scandinavian Opera Singers
- Bjoerling, Jussi
- Flagstad, Kirsten
- Lind, Jenny
- Melchior, Lauritz L. H.
- Nilsson, Birgit

### Other Opera Singers
- Bori, Lucrezia
- Calvé, Emma
- Chaliapin, Feodor I.
- Fischer-Dieskau, Dietrich
- García (family)
- Lehmann, Lilli
- Lehmann, Lotte
- Malibran, Maria Felicita
- McCormack, John
- Melba, Nellie
- Patti, Adelina
- Reszke (family)
- Schumann-Heink, Ernestine
- Schwarzkopf, Elisabeth
- Sutherland, Joan

### Popular Singers
- Burleigh, Harry Thacker
- Cantor, Eddie
- Cohan, George M.
- Crosby, Bing
- Durante, Jimmy
- Hopper, De Wolf
- Ives, Burl
- Jolson, Al
- Lauder, Sir Harry
- Russell, Lillian
- Sinatra, Frank
- Waters, Ethel

### Other Related Articles
- A Cappella
- Alto
- Aria
- Barbershop Quartet Singing
- Cantata
- Chorus
- Folk Music
- Glee Club
- Hymn
- Minnesinger
- Monophony
- Music
- Musical Comedy
- National Anthems
- Opera
- Operetta
- Oratorio
- Song
- Voice
- Westminster Choir
- Yodel

**SINGING GAMES.** See GAME.

**SINGING TOWER** is a beautiful tower, 205 feet high, which stands in a 50-acre park at Mountain Lake, Fla. It contains one of the biggest sets of *carillons* (bell chimes) in the world. Edward Bok built it as a gift to the American people. The park is a bird refuge. Milton B. Medary designed the tower, and Samuel Yellin made the brass doors and iron railings. Two marble bridges span the moat around the tower. Mountain Lake is near Lake Wales, in central Florida. G. HOLMES PERKINS

See also BOK, EDWARD W.

**SINGLE-ENTRY BOOKKEEPING.** See BOOKKEEPING (Kinds of Bookkeeping).

**SINGLE TAX** is a type of property tax. The term is usually applied to a system of land taxation supported in the late 1800's by Henry George, an American social reformer. The system was never put into general use.

Henry George said that a tax on land should be the only source of money for the government. He believed that landowners receive all the wealth from the use of their land. But the landowners do nothing to earn the wealth. A few square feet of rocky soil on the point of Manhattan Island are worth a fortune solely because millions of people are crowded into a small area in New York City. This increased value of land is due not to the owner's effort but to population growth and other factors beyond his control. It is called *unearned increment*.

Single taxers argue that since the whole population gives the land its value, the whole population should share it. They urge that the government should, by taxation, take the entire unearned increment from land and use it for the public good. CHARLES J. GAA

See also GEORGE, HENRY.

**SINGMASTER, ELSIE** (1879-1958), an American author, wrote gently realistic stories of "Pennsylvania-Dutch" life. Her best-known books for young people include *A Boy at Gettysburg* (1924) and *"Sewing Susie"* (1927). She also wrote *Ellen Levis* (1921) and *The Magic Mirror* (1934). She was born in Schuylkill Haven, Pa., and was graduated from Radcliffe College. HERBERT R. BROWN

**SINHALESE.** See CEYLON (People).

**SINK,** in geology, means a large sunken place in the earth, especially a lake which has no outlet.

**SINKIANG.** See TURKESTAN (Chinese Turkestan); CHINA (political map).

**SINN FÉIN,** *shin fayn,* was an Irish nationalist society that favored an independent Irish republic, and played an important part in achieving it. The Gaelic words mean *we ourselves* or *ourselves alone.* Arthur Griffith formed the society in 1905. The Sinn Féin urged that the Irish refuse to pay taxes, to sit in Parliament, to serve in the armed forces, or to abide by court decisions. By 1915, Sinn Féin had won support among the Irish people. In 1916, the society led an uprising in Dublin during the Easter season. The British suppressed the so-called "Easter Rebellion," but this added to the popularity of the Sinn Féin. Two years later, it organized an Irish national assembly, the Dáil Éireann (pronounced *dawl AIR un*). The leaders of the assembly were Michael Collins and Eamon de Valera.

In 1922, the British Parliament established the Irish Free State in southern Ireland as a dominion within the British Commonwealth. In 1926, a majority of Sinn Féin followed De Valera in the formation of a separate party, the *Fianna Fáil* (Soldiers of Destiny), which entered the British-controlled assembly (*Dáil Éireann*). The Sinn Féin, as a separate party, lost much political influence. Fianna Fáil won government control in 1932. By 1948, Ireland was established as an independent republic (Éire). CHARLES F. MULLETT

See also DE VALERA, EAMON; IRELAND (History).

**SINO-JAPANESE WARS.** See CHINESE-JAPANESE WARS.

**SINO-TIBETAN LANGUAGES.** See LANGUAGE (Other Language Families).

**SINTERING** is the process of making metal parts from powdered metals. The powdered metals are pressed together in a die. Sintering gives parts special characteristics, such as heat resistance, heaviness, and hardness, that cannot be obtained by other methods. It is used to make bearings, gears, and similar parts.

**SINUIJU,** *SHIN ee joo* (pop. 118,414; alt. 20 ft.), is a city in Korea and the capital of Pyongyang province. For location, see KOREA (color map). Trade began to flourish in 1910 with the opening of the international bridge across the Yalu River, linking Sinuiju with Tan-tung, Manchuria. Sinuiju industries include sawmilling, paper milling, and soybean processing.

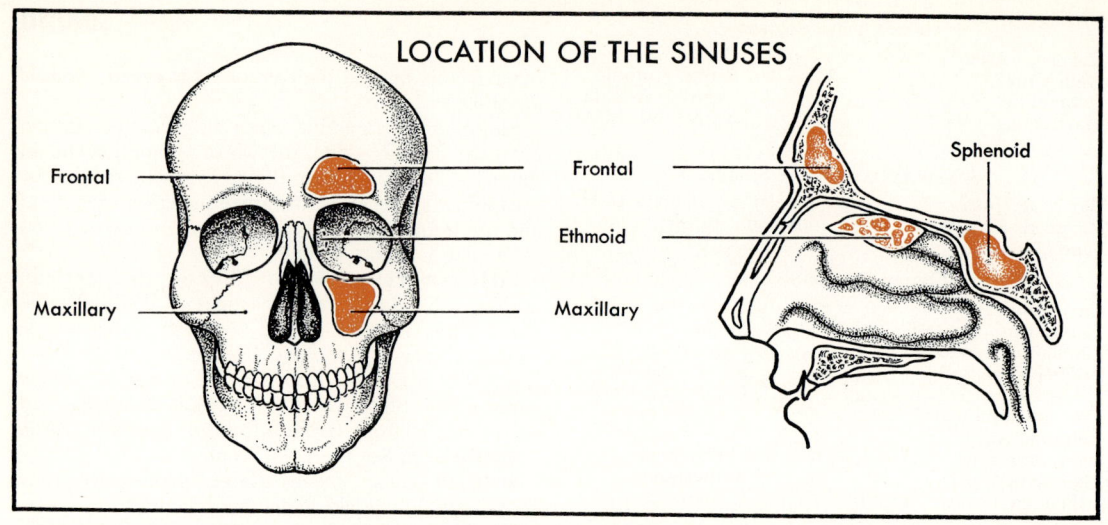
LOCATION OF THE SINUSES

**SINUS,** *SYE nus,* is a cavity in the front of the skull. Humans have four groups of sinuses. Doctors sometimes call these groups the *paranasal* sinuses, because they all connect with the nasal cavity. Each group takes its name from the bones of the skull in which it is found (see HEAD).

The *frontal* sinuses are in the frontal bone of the forehead just above the eyes. The *maxillary* sinuses, largest of the paranasal sinuses, are located in the cheekbones on each side of the nose. The *ethmoid* sinuses lie just above the nasal cavity, and the *sphenoid* sinuses are behind them. If the front of the skull were solid bone, the face would be very heavy and would tend to rest on the chest. The sinuses lighten the weight of the skull, and make it easier to hold up the head and to balance it on the neck.

The sinuses are lined with the same kind of membranes as those that line the nose (see MEMBRANE). Infections of the nose spread easily to the sinuses. There, the infection causes a disease commonly called *sinus trouble,* or *sinusitis.* In sinusitis, the inflamed mucous membranes in the sinuses become swollen, closing the opening and preventing infected material from draining out. When this happens, painful pressure builds up in the sinuses. This pain may occur at the same time every day. Other symptoms of a sinus ailment may include dizziness and a running nose. Allergies, colds, influenza, and many other diseases often result in sinus trouble. Other factors that may make certain individuals more susceptible to sinusitis include climate, dampness, drafts, and smoking.

The treatment of sinus trouble includes rest and liquid diet. Pain-relieving drugs are helpful. Sometimes surgery may be used to puncture a maxillary sinus and permit proper drainage. Sinus trouble is dangerous because it may serve as a center of infection that spreads to other parts of the body, such as the eye or brain.

Sinuses occur only in mammals, birds, and crocodiles. The huge sphenoid sinus of the elephant extends to the very back of the skull. WILLIAM V. MAYER

See also COLD, COMMON.

**SINUSOIDAL PROJECTION.** See MAP (picture, Kinds of Map Distortion).

**SIOUAN.** See INDIAN, AMERICAN (Hokan-Siouan).

**SIOUX CITY,** Iowa (pop. 89,159; met. area 120,017; alt. 1,110 ft.), is a livestock market and an important wholesale distributing center for northwestern Iowa, northern Nebraska, and South Dakota. Sioux City lies on the east side of the Missouri River below the mouth of the Big Sioux River. It lies about 100 miles northwest of Omaha (see IOWA [political map]).

Sioux City covers an area of about 45 square miles. It has many attractive streets lined with well-built homes. The city has 42 parks. Morningside College and Briar Cliff College are among the city's schools.

**Industry.** Sioux City claims to have the largest creamery in the United States, the largest honey-packing plant, the largest popcorn company, and the largest manufacturer of wind-propelled electric generators. Other products that come from Sioux City include meat products, automobile parts, building materials, furniture, leather goods, farm machinery and tools, livestock serums, and electrical and television supplies.

**History.** John K. Cook, who surveyed northwestern Iowa for the federal government, laid out the town in 1854 and named it for the Sioux Indians who lived in the region. During its early years, the town served as an outfitting place for prospectors hunting gold in the Black Hills. It was also a government post from which expeditions were sent out against hostile Indians.

In 1880, when the population was 7,360, Sioux City began to grow at a faster rate than any other city in the United States. By 1890, the population numbered 37,800. Sioux City has a council-manager form of government. WILLIAM J. PETERSEN

**SIOUX FALLS** (pop. 65,466; met. area 86,575; alt. 1,395 ft.), is the largest city and leading commercial and livestock center in South Dakota. Sioux Falls lies at the falls of the Big Sioux River. Its products include packaged meats, processed dairy foods, fabricated steel, millwork, high-altitude balloons, crushed rock, and electromagnetic equipment. Sioux Falls was first settled in 1856. Indians drove the settlers out in 1862, but the site was soon settled again. Sioux Falls is the home of Augustana College, Sioux Falls College, Johnson Memorial Hospital for Veterans, a state school for the deaf, and the state prison. It has a commission government. EVERETT W. STERLING

**SIOUX FALLS COLLEGE.** See UNIVERSITIES AND COLLEGES (table).

**SIOUX INDIANS,** *soo,* once roamed through the northern plains of North America. They became famous for their bravery and their fighting ability. The Sioux called themselves *Dakota* or *Lakota,* meaning *allies.* The Sioux had many divisions. The *Santee* Sioux lived in what is now Minnesota. The *Yankton* Sioux made their homes in eastern North and South Dakota. Both groups farmed and hunted. The *Teton* Sioux hunted buffalo west of the Missouri River.

During the middle and late 1800's, white settlers and gold seekers overran Sioux hunting grounds and killed many buffalo. The Santee rebelled in 1862 and fled westward. In 1868, the Teton agreed to live on reservations. But they had no experience in farming, and their land was poor. Crazy Horse and Sitting Bull led groups that broke out in 1876. When Colonel George Custer marched against them, they killed every man in his immediate command in "Custer's Last Stand." Troops forced them to return to their reservations. In 1890, the Ghost Dance cult, introduced by Wovoka, brought new hope to the Sioux (see WOVOKA). Army leaders thought that the Indians meant to revolt, and attacked them. See INDIAN WARS (The Sioux Wars).

Most Sioux now live on reservations, and make a living as farmers and cattlemen. JOHN C. EWERS

See also CRAZY HORSE; RED CLOUD; SITTING BULL.

**SIPHON.** See CLAM; GOEDUCK; OCTOPUS.

**SIPHON,** *SY fahn,* is a bent tube with unequal arms which is used to carry a liquid from a higher level to a lower level. As shown in the accompanying figure, the tube is entirely filled with liquid. When the short arm is inserted in the container at the higher level, the liquid *(m)* in this container will then flow through the tube *(t)* to the container at the lower level. It flows because the pressure on surface *a* is greater than the pressure on surface *d.* The pressure on each surface is equal to the air pressure (about 15 pounds per square inch) minus the pressure caused by the liquid in the tube. This liquid pressure is proportional to the height of the liquid above the surface. The pressure on surface *a* is greater than that on surface *d* because distance *ab* is less than distance *cd.* As soon as surface *d* rises to the level of surface *a,* the flow stops, because *cd* then equals *ab,* and the same pressure acts on both surfaces. If the

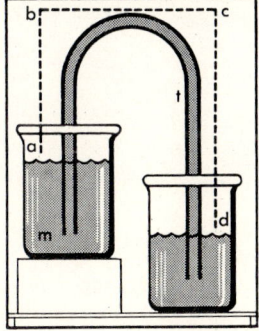

level of *d* is raised above *a,* the liquid will flow from *d* to *a.* A water siphon depends on air pressure and will not work at sea level if the top of the bend is more than 34 feet above level *a.* The best height is 26 feet or less. E. A. FESSENDEN

**SIPHONAPTERA** is an order of wingless insects that live as parasites on man and animals. This group includes fleas, chigoes, and chiggers. All insects of this order have mouth parts that can pierce the skin and suck blood. Many transmit serious diseases such as bubonic plague and typhus fever. See also FLEA; CHIGOE; CHIGGER; INSECT (table).

**SIPLE,** *SYE p'l,* **PAUL ALLMAN** (1908-1968), was an American Antarctic explorer and geographer. While a Boy Scout, Siple was a member of Richard E. Byrd's first Antarctic expedition in 1928. He headed the biology department on the second Byrd expedition from 1933 to 1935, and was geographer for the United States expedition from 1939 to 1941. In 1942, he joined the Department of War (now the Department of the Army). Siple went on major U.S. expeditions from 1946 to 1957, and was scientific leader of the South Polar Station in 1956 and 1957. He was scientific attaché at the U.S. embassy in Australia from 1963 to 1966. Siple was born in Montpelier, Ohio. JOHN E. CASWELL

See also ANTARCTICA (picture: The Geographic South Pole).

**SIQUEIROS, DAVID.** See LATIN AMERICA (Painting; color picture: Huge Murals); MEXICO (color picture: The Story of the Mexican Revolution).

**SIR GEORGE WILLIAMS UNIVERSITY,** a private, co-educational school in Montreal, has the largest evening college program in Canada. Courses lead to bachelor's degrees in arts, science, commerce, and engineering; and to master's degrees in arts and science. Classes were first held at the university in 1929. For enrollment of the university, see CANADA (table: Universities and Colleges). ROBERT C. RAE

**SIRACUSA.** See SYRACUSE.

# SIREN

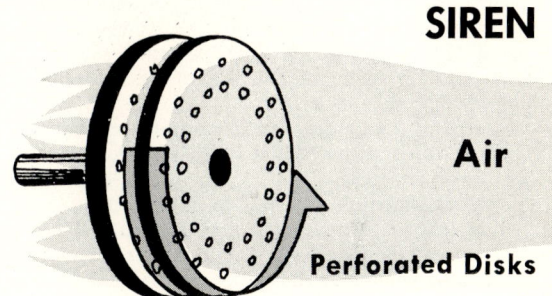

**SIREN** is a device used to sound warning signals. Ambulances, fire trucks, and police cars use sirens to alert traffic. Sirens called *foghorns* are used on lighthouses and ships to warn other ships away during foggy and other bad weather. Sirens are also used for air-raid warnings.

One type of siren has two cylinders, one inside the other. The cylinders are *perforated* (punched with holes). This type of siren makes its sound when the outside cylinder revolves around the inner cylinder, and air is forced through the holes. An electric motor turns the cylinder in sirens on police cars, fire trucks, and other vehicles. When the holes in the cylinders are lined up, puffs of air escape and cause vibrations. As the cylinder is turned faster, the puffs become more frequent and produce a wailing sound. Some sirens have perforated disks instead of cylinders, and some of these can be turned by hand.

A newer type of siren produces its wailing sound

# SIREN

electronically. It has no moving parts, and does not wear out as quickly as older types. PAUL J. SCHEIPS

See also CIVIL DEFENSE (picture: Air-Raid Sirens).

**SIREN** was the name given to some sea nymphs who lived on an island. According to Greek mythology, their singing drew sailors to their shores. The men would forget home and friends, and at last starve to death. In some stories, the Sirens would die if someone sailed past unmoved by their song. Ulysses put wax in his sailors' ears so they could not hear the song. Then he had them tie him to the mast. Ulysses listened to the Sirens, but could not go to them. The Sirens killed themselves because they had failed. PADRAIC COLUM

See also ODYSSEY (picture); ULYSSES; CAPRI.

**SIRENIA,** *sy RE nih uh*, is the name of an order of mammals that live in the water. The only living species are the dugongs and manatees, or sea cows (see DUGONG; SEA COW). The name *Sirenia* came from the belief of mariners that dugongs and manatees were sirens or mermaids. Sirenians feed on grasses along banks of streams or on bottom-growing plants in shallow water two or more miles offshore. They are found in bayous, estuaries, lagoons, swamps, and rivers. They never swim far out in the ocean. At times, some are cast on land by the tide. Scientists know little of their origin and their relation to other mammals. REMINGTON KELLOGG

**SIRHAN, SIRHAN B.** See KENNEDY, ROBERT F.

**SIRIUS.** See SHIP AND SHIPPING (From Sail to Steam).

**SIRIUS,** or the DOG STAR, is the brightest star in the heavens excluding the sun. It is one of the stars nearest to earth, but is still so far that its light takes nearly 9 years to reach earth. The Dog Star can be seen by looking along an imaginary line pointing southward through Orion's belt. It is the head of the constellation Canis Major, the Great Dog.

Sirius is a star of the first magnitude and radiates about 30 times as much light as the sun. Astronomers discovered its companion star in 1862. This star's gravity explained the fact that Sirius seemed to move in a wavy line. The two stars move around each other as they travel through space. The companion star is one of the most remarkable stars in the sky because the material in it is 50,000 times as heavy as water. A cubic foot of material from this star would weigh about 1,500 tons if brought to the earth's surface. The Dog Star's companion was the first *white dwarf* star discovered. Many more have since been found, some with densities 500,000 times that of water. The great density of Sirius' companion is believed to be caused by the stripping of electrons from its atoms, which are packed tightly. CHARLES ANTHONY FEDERER, JR.

See also CANIS MAJOR; DOG DAYS.

**SIROCCO,** *sih RAHK oh*, is the Italian name for two different types of southeast winds. They occur frequently in countries on the north side of the Mediterranean Sea. Both winds are warm because they come from warm regions. But one is a damp wind that usually comes before a rain, while the other is dry and carries desert dust from the Sahara. When the dry sirocco blows, fine sand darkens the sky. It burns the skin and parches the throat. It is similar to, but less violent than, the simoom of the desert. The term *sirocco* is now applied to certain other unseasonably warm winds. VANCE E. MOYER

**SIRUP.** See CORN (Uses); MAPLE SUGAR; MOLASSES; SORGHUM; SUGAR (Corn Sugar and Sirup).

**SISAL,** *SY sul*, or *SIHS ul*, is the name for two tropical plants with swordlike leaves that yield a valuable fiber. These plants, *henequen* and *sisalana*, produce fibers 20 to 50 inches long, which are used chiefly to make binding twine. Sisalana produces much stronger fiber than henequen. Henequen has thorns on its leaf edges. Sisalana leaves do not have thorns. Henequen is raised in Cuba and Mexico, and sisalana in eastern Africa, Brazil, Haiti, and Java. Sisal is also called *sisal hemp*.

Workers harvest sisal once or twice a year. They cut the leaves at the base and feed them into a machine called a *decorticator*. This machine removes the pulp from the fiber. About 100 pounds of leaves are needed to produce 4 pounds of fiber. Eastern Africa is the leading producer of sisal.

**Scientific Classification.** Sisal is in the agave family, *Agavaceae*. Henequen is genus *Agave*, species *A. fourcroydes*. Sisalana is *A. sisalana*. EDWIN O. COGAN

See also ROPE.

**Workmen Cut the Agave Plant to Get Sisal Fiber.** It remains after the pulp is removed. The people of the Kikuyu tribe in eastern Africa cultivate the plant for export.

Ewing Galloway

**SISERA.** See MOUNT TABOR.

**SISKIN, PINE.** See PINE SISKIN.

**SISLEY, ALFRED** (1839-1899), was the only British member of the French Impressionist movement in painting (see PAINTING [In the 1800's]). Sisley painted many views of the Seine and Loing rivers with great delicacy of feeling. He was born in Paris of English parents. He was educated in England, but returned to France in 1862 and joined the painters who developed Impressionism. ROBERT GOLDWATER

**SISTER OF CHARITY.** A number of communities of women in the Roman Catholic Church are called *Sisters of Charity*. All are devoted to the care and education of the sick, the poor, the aged, or the orphaned. Each group is known by its special gown or habit. Usually this is a loose robe of black, relieved at the throat and about the face by a touch of white. The first organization was established in France by Saint Vincent de Paul (1581?-1660) in 1629. Members have been spared during religious conflicts because of their self-sacrificing lives and their care of the needy.

The American Sisters of Charity was founded in 1813 by Elizabeth Ann Bayley Seton, better known as Mother Seton. She has been given the title of patroness of the American parochial schools. Since 1931, steps have been taken toward her canonization. FULTON J. SHEEN

See also SETON, ELIZABETH ANN BAYLEY.

**SISTER OF MERCY** is a member of a Roman Catholic order of nuns. The main mission of the Sisters of Mercy is to care for the poor and sick and to educate the young. The name belongs especially to the congregation of Our Lady of Mercy. This Roman Catholic society was founded in Dublin in 1827. Its founder and first mother superior was Catherine McAuley (Mother Mary Catherine). The first house of the institute in North America was established in Pittsburgh, Pa., in 1843. Now there are communities of these Sisters in all parts of the world. Each convent was at first a separate foundation subject to the bishop of the locality. In the United States, there has been since 1929 a more centralized organization with a superior general. Foundations are free to enter this new arrangement if they choose. The religious habit of the Sisters of Mercy is a black robe with long, loose outer sleeves, and a white hood with a black veil. FULTON J. SHEEN

**SISTERS OF THE POOR, LITTLE.** See LITTLE SISTERS OF THE POOR.

**SISTINE CHAPEL** is a famous chapel in the palace of the Vatican at Rome. It was erected by Pope Sixtus IV in 1473. The chief papal ceremonies take place in this chapel. The chapel also is used by the cardinals for the voting by which they elect a new pope. Canonizations and other public church ceremonies are held in St. Peter's Church.

The Sistine Chapel is a simple building, 134 feet long by 44 feet wide, and 85 feet high. But it has on its walls and ceiling some of the greatest art ever produced in the Western world. Brilliant artists of the early Renaissance decorated the walls with paintings that tell the stories of Moses and Christ. On the ceiling are magnificent Biblical stories painted by the great artist, Michelangelo, in the 1500's. It took him four and a half years to complete this ceiling. Its stories tell the history of the creation of the world, the fall of man, and the flood. On the wall above the altar is the *Last Judgement*, a painting 60 feet high and 30 feet broad. Michelangelo began it when he was 60 and worked on it eight years. Its beauty has been damaged by dust.

The most famous of all the paintings in the Sistine Chapel is in the center of the ceiling. It is called *The Creation of Adam*, and it appears in color in the PAINTING article. CARL K. HERSEY

See also MICHELANGELO (pictures).

**SISTINE MADONNA.** See MADONNA AND CHILD.

**SISYPHUS**, *SIS uh fus*, was a king of Corinth in Greek mythology. He was tricky, and his schemes puzzled even the gods.

Once he outwitted Death, whom Zeus had sent to punish him for meddling. Sisyphus tricked Death and tied him with chains. No man died while Death was bound.

Ares (Mars) freed Death and gave him power over Sisyphus. Sisyphus secretly told his wife to bury him without the usual funeral rites. When he died and went to the Lower World, he complained to Pluto that he had not been buried properly. He begged to return to earth to punish his wife. When Pluto let him go, Sisyphus planned not to go back to Hades.

Hermes (Mercury) captured him at last. As eternal punishment, Pluto ordered Sisyphus to roll a huge stone to the top of a high hill. But each time he reached the top, the stone rolled back down. G. M. KIRKWOOD

**SITKA**, Alaska (pop. 3,237; alt. 25 ft.), a fishing and lumbering center, is the second oldest town in Alaska. It lies on the west coast of Baranof Island, about 1,000 miles by sea from Seattle, Wash. For location, see ALASKA (color map).

Fishing and lumbering are of equal importance to Sitka's economy. The coastal and inland waters provide quantities of salmon and halibut. The commercially valuable Sitka spruce takes its name from the town. Sitka also has a pulp mill.

Sitka was founded by Alexander Baranof, a Russian trader, in 1799. It served as headquarters for the fur-gathering enterprises of the Russian-American Company. Originally named *New Archangel*, Sitka became the capital of Russian America in 1807. It was called *The New World Paris*, because it was the Pacific Coast's most important and cosmopolitan city for over a century. When the United States bought Alaska in 1867, the formal transfer took place at Sitka. The town was the capital of Alaska from 1884 to 1906.

Sitka has many tourist attractions. They include the Sitka National Monument, with its 18 large totems and a replica of a Russian blockhouse. Sitka is also the site of the Alaska Pioneers' Home. The Sheldon Jackson High School and Junior College is the oldest educational institution in Alaska. It offers secondary education to children of all races. Sitka has a council-manager form of government. LYMAN E. ALLEN

**SITKA NATIONAL MONUMENT,** in southeastern Alaska, marks the site of the Indian stockade where Kik-Siti Indians made their last stand in 1804 against Russian settlers. The 54.3-acre monument was established in 1910.

**Sitka, Alaska,** lies on the western shore of Baranof Island, on the Pacific Ocean. Mount Edgecumbe rises in the background.
Alaska Department of Economic Development and Planning

**Sitting Bull,** *left,* sketched some of his battles with Crow Indians. His drawing, *above,* shows him fighting another Indian. The black buffalo seated on the horse is a symbol of his name.

**SITTING BULL** (1834?-1890) was a famous medicine man and leader of the Hunkpapa Teton Sioux Indians. Many people think that he was the leader of the Indians at the battle of the Little Bighorn, on June 25, 1876, in which General George Custer lost his life. Actually, Sitting Bull acted only as the leading medicine man in the preparations for the battle. The year before, he had received a vision that all his enemies would be delivered into his hands. In the spring of 1876, he led a sun dance at which he told the Indians to change their way of fighting. Instead of showing off to prove their bravery, they should fight to kill, or they would lose all their lands to the whites. This new tactic led to the annihilation of Custer and his men.

After the battle of the Little Bighorn, Sitting Bull and his followers were driven into Canada. He returned to the United States in 1881. After two years in confinement at Fort Randall in South Dakota, he lived on the Standing Rock Reservation in that state. There, in 1890, he helped start the Ghost Dance. The government thought this was an attempt to renew the Indian wars, and sent Indian policemen to arrest Sitting Bull. In the process, he and his son were killed.

Sitting Bull was born in what is now South Dakota. As a boy, he was known as *Jumping Badger,* but he was honored by receiving his father's own name when he showed great bravery in a fight against the Crow Indians. E. ADAMSON HOEBEL

See also CUSTER, GEORGE A.; SIOUX INDIANS.

**SITWELL** is the family name of three British writers, two of them brothers and one a sister.

**Edith Sitwell**

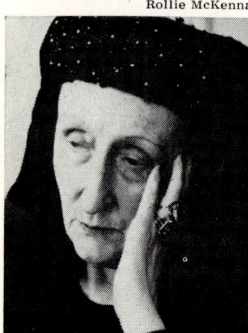
Rollie McKenna

**Dame Edith Sitwell** (1887-1964) wrote poetry and literary criticism. Her books of poetry include the satirical *Façade* (1922), *Collected Poems* (1930, 1954), and *Music and Ceremonies* (1963). She often gave public readings of her verse. Her critical works include *The Pleasures of Poetry* (1930-1932). From 1916 to 1921, she edited *Wheels,* an annual poetry anthology. She was born in Scarborough, England, and made her home there.

**Sir Osbert Sitwell** (1892-1969) recounted the life of English aristocratic and literary groups in the prose works *Left Hand, Right Hand* (1945), *The Scarlet Tree* (1946), *Great Morning* (1948), *Laughter in the Next Room* (1949), and *Noble Essences* (1950). He also wrote short stories. He was born in London.

**Sacheverell Sitwell** (1897-    ) wrote many books of art history and poetry. They include *Southern Baroque Art* (1924) and *The Hunters and the Hunted* (1948). He was born in Scarborough, England. JOSEPH E. BAKER

**SIVA,** SEE *vuh,* or SHIVA is the second god in the Hindu triad of Brahma, Siva, and Vishnu. The name *Siva* means *kind.* Siva was originally the god of storms, but today his wife, Kali, has these powers. It is believed that Siva restores what he destroys so that man may live again. He looks toward eternal truths, and ignores fleeting aspects of physical life. He has become the god of happiness, and represents the freedom and joy which inspire artists. Siva has more worshipers than any other Hindu god. See also BRAHMAN; SCULPTURE (picture: The Hindu God Siva); VISHNU. CLIFTON E. OLMSTEAD

**SIX, LES.** See MUSIC (The 1900's); MILHAUD, DARIUS; HONEGGER, ARTHUR; POULENC, FRANCIS; SATIE, ERIK.

**SIX-DAY WAR.** See ISRAEL (History).

**SIX NATIONS.** See IROQUOIS INDIANS.

**SIX PER-CENT METHOD.** See INTEREST.

**SIX-SHOOTER.** See REVOLVER.

**SIXPENCE** is a British coin made of copper-nickel alloy. It is worth one-fortieth of a pound sterling.

**SIXTEENTH AMENDMENT.** See UNITED STATES CONSTITUTION (Amendment 16).

**SIXTUS** was the name of five popes of the Roman Catholic Church. The dates of their reigns were:

| | |
|---|---|
| Sixtus I, Saint | (115-125) |
| Sixtus II, Saint | (257-258) |
| Sixtus III, Saint | (432-440) |
| Sixtus IV | (1471-1484) |
| Sixtus V | (1585-1590) |

**Sixtus IV** (1414-1484) became a Franciscan at the age of nine. He later became provincial superior of the order of the Friars Minor, and in 1467 became a cardinal of the Roman Catholic Church. Sixtus was elected pope on the death of Pope Paul II in 1471. His first concern as pope was to overcome the Turks, and he energetically tried to achieve alliances with the Christian nations of Europe for this project. But he failed to accomplish this. He then tried to consolidate the power of the papal states in Italy, but was again unsuccessful.

Sixtus' lasting accomplishments included the opening of the Vatican Library and the establishment of the Sistine Choir and the great hospital of Santo Spirito. He also sponsored the development of the Sistine Chapel (see SISTINE CHAPEL). His weakness was his tendency to favor his friends and relatives. Sixtus was born FRANCESCO DELLA ROVERE at Celle, Italy.

**Sixtus V** (1521-1590) entered the order of the Friars Minor at the age of nine. He rose in the order and was made a cardinal in 1570. When Pope Gregory XIII died in 1585, Sixtus was elected pope.

Sixtus was one of the great reforming popes. He strenuously attacked abuses everywhere, and was an able administrator. He fixed the number of cardinals at 70, a number which was not abandoned until 1958. He gave a definite form to papal administration by establishing 15 secretariates, which he called Congregations. He established the Vatican Press, and also urged Philip of Spain to launch the Armada against England. Sixtus was born FELICE PERETTI in Grottamare, Italy, on Dec. 13, 1521.  GUSTAVE WEIGEL and FULTON J. SHEEN

**SIZING.** See PAPER (Special Kinds); DEXTRIN.

**SJAELLAND.** See DENMARK (The Land).

**SKAGERRAK,** *SKAG er ak*, is an arm of the North Sea. The Skagerrak divides Norway and Sweden to the north, and separates them from Denmark on the south. The name is often spelled *Skager-Rak* or *Skagerrack*. The Skagerrak is about 130 miles long. The Skagerrak is important because it is the connecting link between the North Sea and the Kattegat. The two channels form the entrance into the Baltic Sea. Along the shores of Jutland, no good harbors for ships exist. This coast is lined with dangerous sand banks. But along Norway, 80 miles away, good harbors are plentiful. For location, see EUROPE (color map).  ROBERT O. REID

**SKAGIT RIVER.** See WASHINGTON (Rivers, Waterfalls, and Lakes).

**SKALD,** the Icelandic word for *poet,* refers to the Scandinavian poets of the Middle Ages. From the 900's through the 1200's, most court poets in Scandinavia came from Iceland. Most skaldic poetry honored the kings whom the skalds served. Many of these poems, or parts of them, are preserved in the Icelandic *sagas* written in the 1100's and 1200's. Skaldic poetry was very complex in form. It employed involved patterns of *alliteration* (repeating the first sound of each word) and *assonance* (similar sounds), and a type of extended metaphor called a *kenning*.  KENNETH G. CHAPMAN

See also EDDA; SAGA.

**SKATE** is the name of a family of *rays.* It is related to the shark. The skate may grow from 1 to 4 feet long and may weigh as much as 100 pounds. It has two large fins on the sides of its body. These fins are so large that the fish is almost as broad as it is long. The fins have a round edge and form a sort of a disk with the body. The skate has a slender tail which is used as a rudder. It eats snails, mussels, clams, crabs, and other fish. This fish makes its home on the sandy and muddy bottoms along shores, in bays, or in deep water. The skate usually lays egg cases, often called *mermaids' purses,* on these bottoms.

Most kinds of skate are sold as food. One of the best-known species is the *common,* or *summer,* skate,

American Museum of Natural History
**Common Skate**

which is found along the Atlantic Coast of North America. The common skate is 1 to 2 feet long. A larger skate which lives along the Atlantic Coast is the *barn-door* skate. The *big skate* is another species which is found along the Pacific Coast.

**Scientific Classification.** The skate is a member of the skate family, *Rajidae*. The common skate is genus *Raja*, species *R. erinacea*; the barn-door skate is *R. laevis*; and the big skate is *R. binoculata*.  LEONARD P. SCHULTZ

**SKATING.** See ICE SKATING; ROLLER SKATING.

**SKEAT,** *skeet,* **WALTER WILLIAM** (1835-1912), an English scholar, edited many works in Anglo-Saxon and Middle English literature. His edition of the works of Geoffrey Chaucer is generally regarded as the standard edition of Chaucer's writings. Skeat taught at Cambridge University from 1860 until his death.

**SKEENA RIVER** is one of the most valuable salmon fishing grounds in the world. The river rises in north-central British Columbia and flows southwest to the Pacific Ocean. It is about 335 miles long, and drains an area of about 19,300 square miles. The Skeena empties into Hecate Strait about 10 miles south of the city of Prince Rupert.  RODERICK HAIG-BROWN

**SKEET** is an American form of clay target shooting. As in trapshooting, the target is thrown from a metal-sprung trap, and flies through the air like a bird. Two target houses are located 42 yards apart. The targets spring from each house over the center post between the two houses, and at different angles of flight so as to approximate closely the effect of shooting at winged game.

Seven shooting stations, corresponding to the half face of a clock, are located on a 21-yard radius. Another is in the center of the circle, half way between the two target houses. Shooters, using shotguns, fire from each station. Most targets are thrown as single shots, alternating from each house. But some targets spring out in pairs, one from each target house, at different levels. The shooter tries to bring both down.

The name *skeet* comes from a Scandinavian form of the word *shoot*.  CAROLA MANDEL

See also TRAPSHOOTING.

**SKELETON** is the flexible, bony framework of any vertebrate animal. It gives the body shape, protects vital organs, and provides a system of levers, operated by muscles, that enables the body to move. The skeleton houses *bone marrow*, the blood-forming tissues. It stores elements such as sodium, calcium, and phosphorus, and releases them to the blood. It also holds reserves of protein that the body uses during fasting.

### The Human Skeleton

The human skeleton has about 206 separate bones. That is, a human being generally forms that many bones

399

A WORLD BOOK
SCIENCE PROJECT

# COMPARING ANIMAL SKELETONS

The purpose of this project is to learn how the skeletons of four kinds of animals compare with one another.

**Comparing Animal Skeletons,** *left,* shows that each kind of animal has a special kind of bony framework. In this project, the skeletons represent four major groups of animals—bony fishes, amphibians, birds, and mammals. You can study skeletons of other animal groups in the same way.

WORLD BOOK photos

## PREPARING A FISH SKELETON

Get a fish at least 12 inches long for this project. Use great care in stripping the tissue from the bones because the skeleton breaks apart easily. Make a cardboard or wood mold about 4 inches longer and 3 inches wider than the skeleton. Pour plaster of Paris into the mold and let it harden. Remove the plaster block and cover it with colored construction paper. Carefully glue the fish skeleton in place in the center of the covered plaster block.

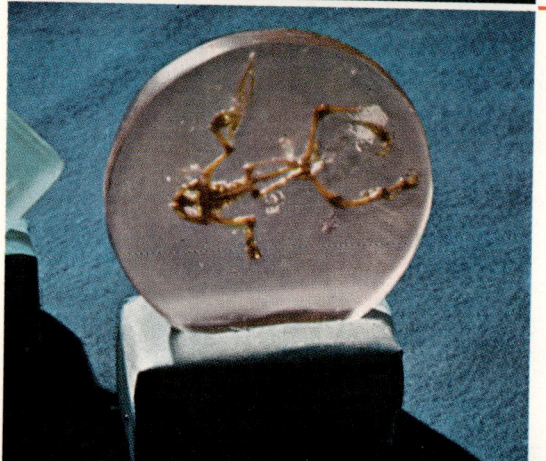

## PREPARING A FROG SKELETON

Use a round or square mold of plastic, metal, or heavy cardboard. It should be at least 1 inch larger than the frog skeleton. Place the skeleton in the mold. Pour melted plastic slowly down the side of the mold to prevent bubbling. Let the plastic dry completely, then take it out of the mold. Smooth the plastic with sandpaper and polish it with a soft cloth. Set the molded skeleton in a plaster of Paris stand covered with colored kraft paper.

## MATERIALS AND PROCEDURE

You can get most of the materials for this project from local stores. For example, many local markets sell whole fowl and fish. Pet shops have guinea pigs. But you can capture a frog near a pond. Hardware stores stock the rods, stiff wire, and plaster of Paris needed to mount the bird, fish, and guinea pig skeletons. Most hobby shops sell the plastic used for the frog skeleton.

Illustrated by Bill Fleming for WORLD BOOK

**To Prepare the Skeletons,** remove as much flesh as possible from the bones. For all animals except the fish, soak the bones for about 2 hours in soapy water. Keep the water hot, but not boiling. Scrub the bones with a stiff brush, then rinse them well. Soak the fish bones for only about 15 minutes, then scrub them. To position the skeletons, arrange the bones in proper order. Let them dry thoroughly. Use stiff wire wherever necessary to support the skeleton. Glue all loose bones together with an all-purpose glue.

WORLD BOOK photos

### PREPARING A BIRD SKELETON

Bleach the bones of the bird skeleton before you begin to put them together. You can bleach the bones of any of the skeletons used for this project by soaking them in a 10 per cent hydrogen peroxide solution. Let the bones dry thoroughly before assembling them. Use stiff wire to reinforce the bird skeleton and to hold it in the position you want for display. Sink metal rods into a plaster of Paris stand and wire the skeleton securely to the rods.

### PREPARING A GUINEA PIG SKELETON

Skin the pelt off the guinea pig and remove as much flesh as possible from the bones. Soak and scrub them carefully so most of the ligaments will stay in place and hold the bones together. Bleach the bones. Place the skeleton in the position you want for display and let the bones dry thoroughly. Glue or wire any loose bones in place. Reinforce the whole skeleton with wire and mount it on a plaster of Paris block covered with construction paper.

400a

# SKELETON

out of cartilage as he develops to maturity. Sixty-four of these bones are in the hands and arms alone.

Bones are joined to neighboring bones by joints. Joints are either immovable, as in the skull, or movable, as in the arms and legs. The bones fit together and are held in place by strong bands of flexible tissue called *ligaments*. The human skeleton is divided into two main parts, the *axial skeleton*, and the *appendicular skeleton*.

**The Axial Skeleton** is made up of the bones of the head, neck, and trunk. The spine (*spinal column* or *backbone*) forms an axis that supports the other parts of the body. The skull is at the top of the spine. The spine consists of separate bones, called *vertebrae*, with fibrous discs between them. Seven bones make up the *cervical vertebrae* (neck bones). The 12 *thoracic* vertebrae are at the back of the chest.

The ribs are attached to the thoracic vertebrae. Each side usually has 12 ribs. The upper ribs fasten in front to the *sternum* (breastbone). The ribs protect the heart and lungs, and act as a bellows box for the breathing process.

The five *lumbar* vertebrae lie in the lower part of the back. Below the last lumbar vertebra is the *sacrum*. In babies, five separate bones make up the sacrum. In adults, these bones have grown together into one solid structure. The pelvis is attached to the sacral segment of the spine by *sacroiliac joints*. The coccyx is at the bottom of the spine. In children, four separate bones make up the coccyx. But these bones have fused by the time a person is about 25. The point where the sacrum and coccyx meet remains fibrous throughout life.

**The Appendicular Skeleton** consists of bones of the arms and legs. The *shoulder girdle* consists of the *scapula*, *humerus*, and *clavicle* (collarbone). The skeleton of the arm is divided into the *scapula* (shoulder blade); *humerus* (upper arm); *radius* and *ulna* (forearm); *carpus* (wrist bones); *metacarpus* (hand); and *phalanges* (fingers). The bones of the leg include the *pelvic girdle* (pelvis and sacrum); *femur* (thigh); *tibia* and *fibula* (leg); *tarsus* (back of the foot); *metatarsus* (forefoot); and *phalanges* (toes).

## Animal Skeletons

The skeletons of all backboned animals are basically alike. There are two pairs of limbs, front and hind limbs. A giraffe's neck has the same number of bones as a mouse's neck, although the giraffe's bones are longer and larger. Most backboned animals are *quadrupeds*. That is, they run on all four legs. Man is a *biped* because he walks on only two legs. Many animals without backbones, such as insects and lobsters have hard body coverings. This *exoskeleton* (external framework) provides support and protection for the soft parts of their bodies.

MARSHALL R. URIST

**Related Articles.** See the Trans-Vision three-dimensional color picture with HUMAN BODY. See also the following articles:

| | | | | |
|---|---|---|---|---|
| Arm | Foot | Joint | Rib | Spine |
| Bone | Hand | Leg | Shoulder | Vertebra |
| Collarbone | Hip | Pelvis | Skull | |

### Outline
I. **The Human Skeleton**
  A. The Axial Skeleton
  B. The Appendicular Skeleton
II. **Animal Skeletons**

### Questions
What are the two main parts of the human skeleton?
What groups of bones make up each part?

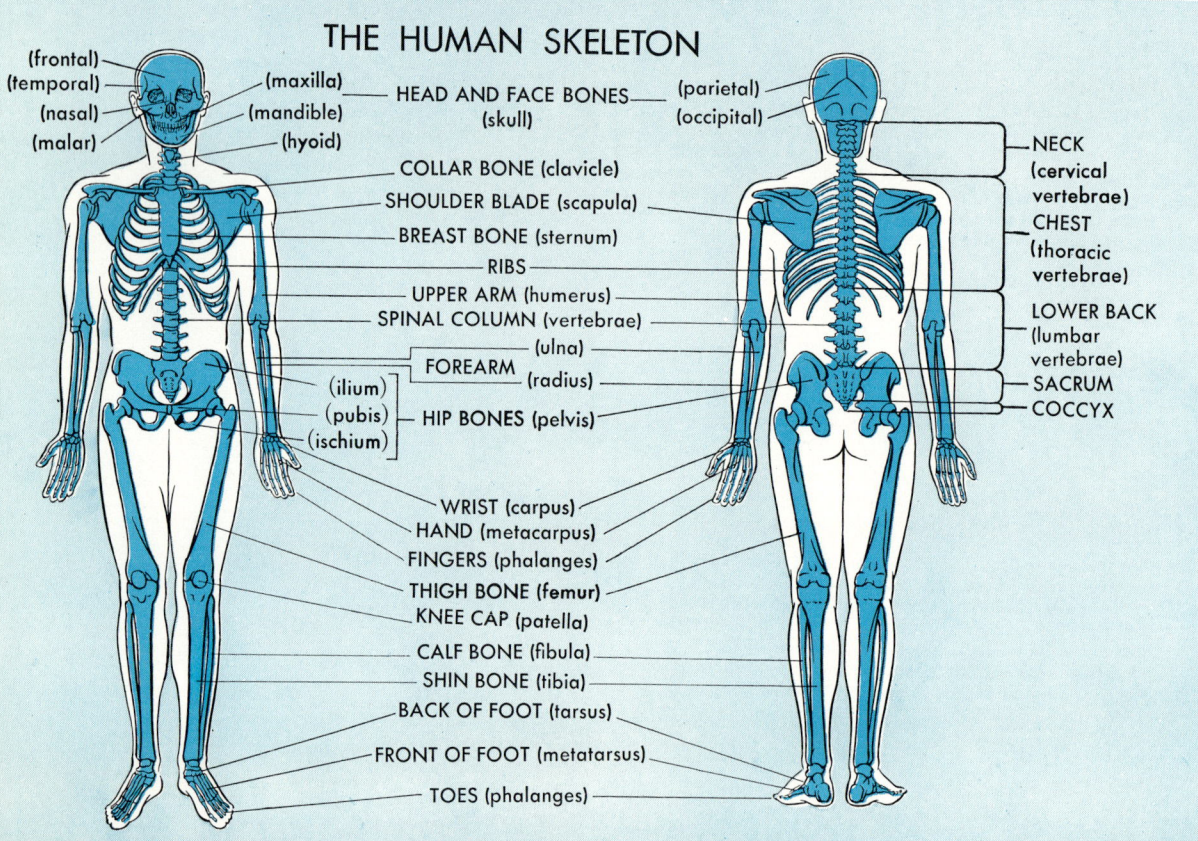

# TYPES OF SKELETONS

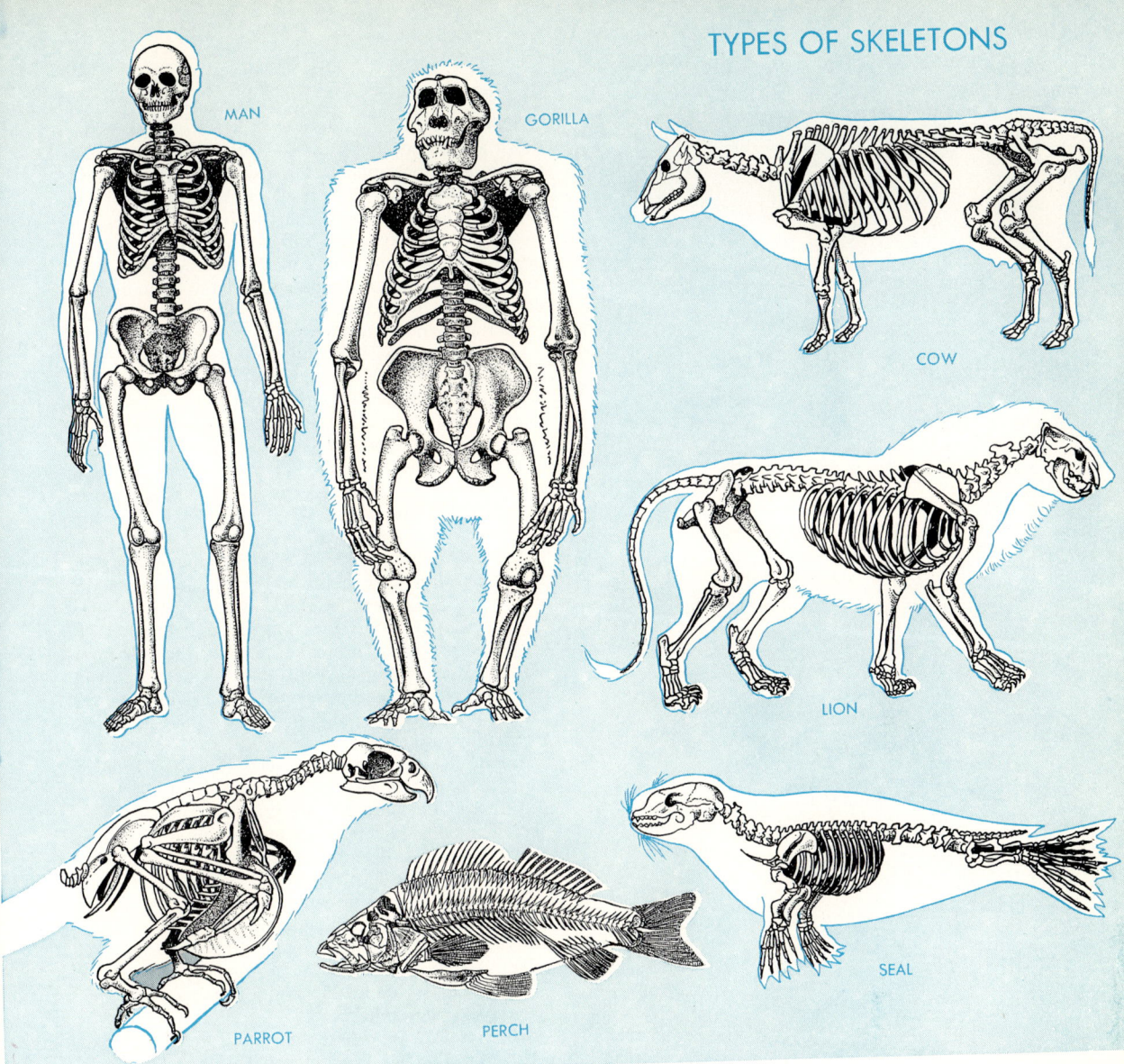

What kind of animals have skeletons?
How many bones are in a human skeleton?
How are the bones of the skeleton held together?
What are some of the jobs of the skeleton?
What are the vertebrae? How many are there? What is their function?
How does the skeleton develop?
How are the skeletons of backboned animals alike? How are they different?
What is an exoskeleton?
What are two functions of the ribs?

**SKEP.** See BEE (Beekeeping).

**SKEPTICISM** is a philosophy which states that no knowledge is certain. Some skeptics doubt everything which cannot be proved by the evidence of the senses. The first skeptics were the Sophists of ancient Greece. More recent skeptics include the Scottish philosopher, David Hume.

See also SOPHIST PHILOSOPHY.

**SKERRIES.** See NORWAY (Coast and Islands).

**SKETCHING.** See DRAWING.

**SKEW LINE**, in advanced geometry, is a line in space that neither runs parallel to another line nor intersects another line. The word *skew* means *slanting* or *indirect*. In statistics, a normal distribution has a mound-shaped curve. A curve that tapers off to the right or left is said to be *skewed*.

See also STATISTICS (Frequency Distributions).

**SKEWBACK.** See BRIDGE (The Arch Principle).

**SKIDMORE COLLEGE** is a privately controlled liberal arts school for women in Saratoga Springs, N.Y. It offers courses in liberal arts, business, drama, home economics, music, nursing, and physical education. The college grants B.S. and B.A. degrees. Skidmore has a College Government Association, a community government system in which all students and faculty members work together. The college was chartered in 1911. For enrollment, see UNIVERSITIES (table).

**SKIFF.** See BOATS AND BOATING (Unusual Boats).

401

# SKIING

Margaret Durrance, Photo Researchers

**SKIING,** *SKEE ing*, is the exciting sport of speeding down a snow-covered slope or soaring through the air on two slats, or runners, called skis. People of almost every country enjoy the thrill of skimming over the snow on skis. In recent years, skiing has gained increasing popularity in the United States. Machines that produce artificial snow have made it possible for people to ski when no natural snow is available. Hundreds of ski resorts provide facilities to make the sport more comfortable and convenient.

**Equipment.** A *ski* is a long, narrow, flat runner that is turned up at the front end. Skis are made of wood, metal, or sometimes fiber glass that is reinforced with *epoxy* (a strong plastic). Most skis have a plastic running surface and metal edges. Skis are about 3 to 4 inches wide. Most experts use skis that are stiff and more than a foot longer than the skier is tall. Other skiers use more flexible, shorter skis. Skis 8 feet long or longer are used for cross-country racing.

The skier carries two *poles*. These are made of metal, cane, fiber glass, or bamboo, and are shaped to a point at one end. Several inches above the point is a circular *basket*, about 3 inches in diameter and attached to the pole by spokes. The basket prevents the pole from plunging too deeply into the snow. When a person skis downhill, he uses the poles to help keep his balance. They are also used as walking sticks on flat land and for uphill climbing.

Among the most important safety items for the skier are the *boots*. They are made of stout, pliable leather, and have thick soles that are usually reinforced with steel. The boots fit snugly around the ankles and support the ankles so that they do not tire. The boots can be attached to the skis by several methods. One of the safest methods requires metal attachments, called *safety-release bindings*, on the skis and boots. These clamp the boot firmly to the ski, but allow the ski to come off when pressure is exerted in an emergency. This release of the ski helps prevent skiers from twisting, spraining, or breaking their ankles.

**Where to Ski.** Almost any hill that is free from rocks, trees, and other obstructions can be a good place to learn to ski. Special *ski areas* provide many kinds of skiing for persons with all degrees of ability. Such ski areas as Aspen and Vail, Colo., Sun Valley, Ida., Stowe, Vt., Banff, Alta., and Mont Tremblant, Que., attract thousands of skiers every winter. A ski area has one or more *slopes*, the steep sides of hills or mountains. In some areas, the slopes are more than 3,000 feet high.

Most ski areas offer the advantage of *lifts*. These mechanically operated devices transport the skier to the top of the slope. The *rope tow* is a rope attached to two pulleys, one at the top of the slope and one at the bottom, and driven by a motor. The skier hangs on to the rope and it pulls him up the slope. The *T-bar* con-

---

*Bob Beattie, the contributor of this article, is Head Alpine Coach of the United States Ski Team.*

---

**Skiers Skim Through the Snow** at speeds as high as 80 miles per hour. They turn and twist to control their speed and to avoid trees and rocks. This slope is one of several at Aspen, Colo.

sists of a motor-driven cable from which metal bars shaped like upside-down letter T's are suspended. The skier leans against the crossbar and holds on to the upright as he goes up the slope. The *chair* lift is a series of chairs hung from a high motor-driven cable. *Gondola* and *cable car* lifts operate in a similar manner, but skiers ride in enclosed cars.

### Types of Skiing

Skiing may be divided roughly into two general categories, noncompetitive and competitive. Noncompetitive skiing is recreational. Competitive skiing includes specialized and regulated events.

**Noncompetitive Skiing.** The most common kind of noncompetitive skiing is the downhill run. When a skier points straight down a slope without trying to turn or slow down, he is said to be *schussing*. A skier *traverses* a slope when he skis at an angle to the *fall line* (a straight line from the skier to the bottom of the slope). He must learn to traverse properly and turn by edging. A skier edges by shifting his weight to the edges of his skis, causing the skis to dig into the snow.

The *snowplow* is usually the first turn a skier learns. It is also used to stop or slow down. To stop or turn, a skier forces out his heels and brings the tips of his skis almost together to form a *V*. At the same time, he shifts his weight to the inside edges of his skis. This helps slow down for his forward motion. A turn occurs when the skier shifts his weight to the ski that is opposite to the direction of the turn.

The *stem christie*, sometimes called a *stem turn*, is more difficult than the snowplow. To turn right, a skier *stems* when, by pushing out his left heel, he places his left ski at an angle to the direction of motion. This puts his weight on the left ski and causes it to turn toward the fall line. At the end of the turn, the skis are parallel. The skier reverses the procedure to turn left.

A *parallel christie* is a difficult turn usually done at high speeds. It is sometimes called a *full christiana* or *parallel turn*. To turn right, the skier keeps his skis parallel and shifts his weight to the right edges of his skis by turning his body. To turn left, the skier reverses the procedure. A *wedeln* is a series of short, connected parallel turns.

A skier must also know how to climb the slope. Two common methods are the *herringbone* and *sidestepping*. Both of these methods require edging at an angle to the slope.

**Competitive Skiing.** One of the most exciting competitive races is the *downhill*. The object of this event is to start from the top of a 1,500- or 2,500-foot slope and ski down by the straightest, fastest route possible. *Moguls* (snow mounds), ruts, and other obstacles are added to make many downhill courses more difficult.

The *slalom* is an obstacle course with a vertical drop of 400 to 700 feet. Pairs of closely spaced flag poles mark the edges of the path, which winds about in a snakelike fashion. The skier must weave his way between each pair of poles. The *giant slalom* has a drop of 1,000 to 1,300 feet. The sets of flags are farther apart, and the course is studded with steep pitches, moguls, and ruts. Competitors in the downhill and slalom are judged on the basis of speed.

**A Snowplow** is a beginner's way to stop, slow down, or turn. He places his weight on the inside edges of the skis.

**A Stem Christie** is a more advanced method of turning. At the end of the turn, the skis are parallel.

WORLD BOOK illustrations by William Gorman

**A Parallel Christie** requires great coordination. The skier's feet remain close together and parallel throughout the turn. Skiers try to keep their feet together throughout a run.

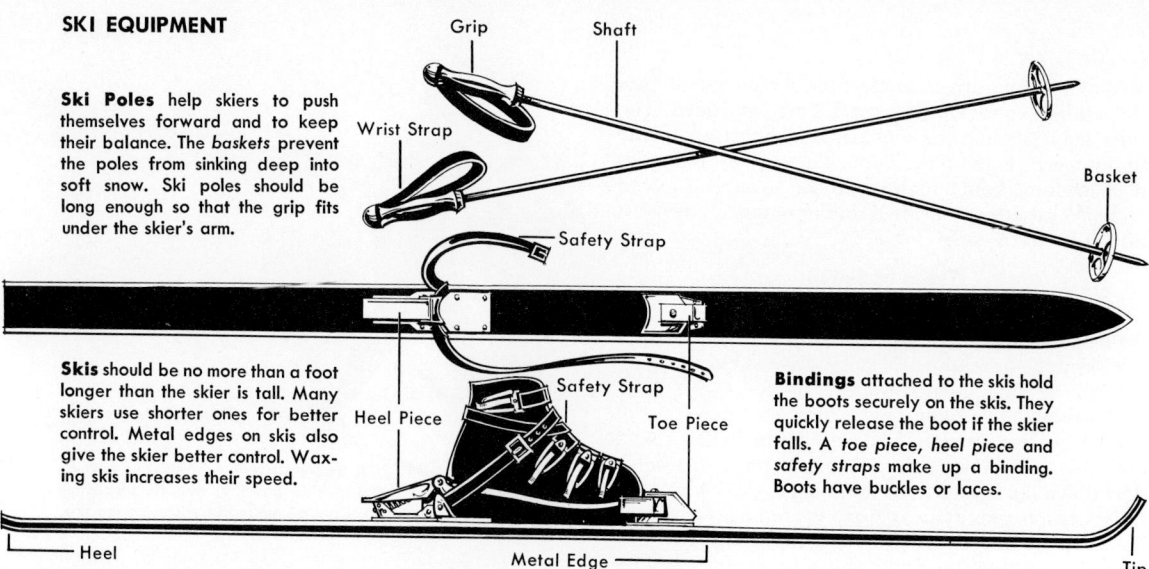

**SKI EQUIPMENT**

**Ski Poles** help skiers to push themselves forward and to keep their balance. The *baskets* prevent the poles from sinking deep into soft snow. Ski poles should be long enough so that the grip fits under the skier's arm.

**Skis** should be no more than a foot longer than the skier is tall. Many skiers use shorter ones for better control. Metal edges on skis also give the skier better control. Waxing skis increases their speed.

**Bindings** attached to the skis hold the boots securely on the skis. They quickly release the boot if the skier falls. A *toe piece, heel piece* and *safety straps* make up a binding. Boots have buckles or laces.

In *ski-jumping*, the skier speeds down a long, steep take-off that levels off for a few feet before ending suddenly, high above the ground. He is judged on the basis of the distance of his jump, and on his control and style in the air and in his landing.

The fourth competitive event is the *cross-country race*. This event tests the stamina, endurance, and all-around technique of the skier. The course consists of natural terrain, and includes uphill, downhill, and flat-land skiing. There are no artificial obstacles, but many trees and rugged trails provide challenges. The Olympic Games include all four of these competitive events.

### History

Skiing was developed as a method of transportation by peoples who lived in regions with heavy snowfall. Originally, skis were probably made from the bones of large animals. A pair of skis on exhibit in Stockholm, Sweden, is about 5,000 years old.

Skis later came into use for military purposes. During the battle of Oslo between Norway and Sweden in 1200, the Norwegians used skiers as scouts. Sweden used ski troops in 1521 against Denmark. United States ski troops fought in the Alps during World War II.

Skiing as a sport probably began about the early 1800's. Norwegian immigrants brought it to the United States in the mid-1800's. Fédération Internationale de Ski (FIS) was founded by 26 countries in 1924. This organization convinced the Olympic Games committee to add competition in the winter sports to the program. The first winter games took place in France in 1924.

Outstanding U.S. skiers of the 1940's and 1950's included Arthur Devlin, Alf Engen, and Torger Tokle. All three achieved fame as ski jumpers, but Devlin and Engen also excelled in other events. In the 1960's, outstanding skiers in the slalom and downhill events included Gordon Eaton, Charles Ferries, Jim Heuga, Billy Kidd, Jean Saubert, and Bud Werner. Gene Kotlarek excelled in jumping. BOB BEATTIE

See also MICHIGAN (Places to Visit [American Ski Hall of Fame]); WATER SKIING.

**SKIM MILK.** See MILK (Other Processes).

**SKIMMER,** or SCISSORBILL, is a bird related to the gulls and terns. The name *skimmer* comes from its habit of skimming rapidly along the surface of the water. It holds its beak open and keeps the lower part of it beneath the surface, scooping up insects, small fish, shrimp, and other small animals. The name *scissorbill* comes from its thin, bladelike bill, which has the lower part much longer than the upper.

The skimmer holds its body at an angle while flying, to keep its wings from touching the water. There are three species, the one found in America being called the *black skimmer*, or *black scissorbill*. It is black above, and white underneath its body. It makes its nest in a hollow in the sand, and lays three to five eggs.

**Scientific Classification.** Skimmers make up the skimmer family, *Rynchopidae*. The black skimmer is genus *Rynchops*, species *R. nigra*. ALEXANDER WETMORE

See also BIRD (color picture: Water Birds).

**SKIN.** The skin is one of the largest organs of the human body. If the skin of an adult were spread out flat, it would cover about eighteen square feet. The skin of an adult weighs about six pounds. It is an organ of the body because it performs many essential functions. Perspiration is given off through the skin. The skin also helps the body regulate its own temperature. A piece of skin the size of a quarter contains a yard of blood vessels, 4 yards of nerves, 25 nerve ends, 100 sweat glands, and more than 3 million cells.

There are two basic parts to the skin. The surface is called the *epidermis, corneum,* or *cuticle*. This is the part that gets rubbed off when we skin a knuckle. Below this layer lies the *dermis*, or the *corium*. The word *dermis* is taken from the original Greek word for skin. The Greek word *epi*, meaning over, is added to the word *dermis* to form the word *epidermis* for the outer skin.

**Epidermis.** The top layer of the skin is made up of numerous cells that are placed side by side like the paving stones in a street. There are twelve to fifteen of these rows, arranged one above the other. The cells of the skin grow from the bottom up. In the lowest row they are shaped like columns, or posts, and are perpendicular to the cells of the under skin. Above this lowest row of epidermis cells are several rows of round cells. These cells grow flatter and flatter toward the surface of the skin. They also become drier as they are pushed upward and outward by the new cells below them. When they finally reach the surface they are shed as thin flakes. These flakes are the dead skin a person often rubs off with a towel after taking a bath.

Some nerves are located in the lower cells of the epidermis, but there are no blood vessels in the epidermis. Any cut which draws blood must be deep enough to reach the dermis. The epidermis also is responsible for the color of the skin. Dark races have a great deal of pigment called *melanin* in the lower layers of their epidermis. The freckles which appear on the skins of the lighter races also are caused by melanin, and may result from exposure to the sun. The hair and nails are parts of the epidermis which have special functions.

**The Dermis** is made up of a closely woven network of connective tissue. It is from one-sixteenth of an inch to one-eighth of an inch thick. It is thickest on the back and thinnest on the eyelids. In the dermis there are blood vessels, vessels for carrying the lymph, nerve glands, and hair follicles.

On the outer surface of the dermis are a great many tiny elevations about one two-hundredth of an inch high. These are called *papillae*. Their name was taken from the Latin word for pimple. The papillae fit into tiny pits on the undersurface of the epidermis, and help connect the two layers of the skin. The papillae contain the nerves that are sensitive to touch. They are especially well developed on the inside of the hands, where they are arranged in rows. The fine ridges on the balls of the fingers and the thumb show the pattern of the papillae. When a small group of papillae becomes overdeveloped, it sticks out above the surface of the epidermis, and forms a wart.

Wrinkles in the skin occur when fat and other soft parts beneath the dermis are absorbed into the body and the skin itself does not shrink at the same rate.

**The Work of the Skin.** There are two kinds of glands in the skin. Some pour out sweat, others discharge oil. The sweat glands are tiny tubes that open up on the surface of the body. There are about two million sweat glands distributed over the surface of the body. They are most abundant on the palms of the hands, the soles of the feet, and the forehead. The sweat glands give off small amounts of liquid waste matter. But their most important function is to regulate body heat. As the sweat evaporates, it cools the surface. The oil glands, or *sebaceous glands*, generally open into the hair follicles. They give off an oily substance which makes the hair smooth and glossy, and keeps the skin from becoming too dry. A blackhead forms when a hard fatty material from an oil gland blocks the gland's opening.

The amount of blood that flows through the skin varies greatly. Blood in the skin helps regulate body heat. If the body needs to give off heat, the blood vessels in the skin expand, and place the blood closer to the outside air. When the body needs to conserve heat, the blood vessels in the skin tend to contract. This slows the rate of heat loss from the body.

**Care of the Skin.** The most important care that can be given to the skin is to keep it clean. This keeps the tiny pores, or mouths of glands, in the skin from becoming clogged. It also hinders the spread of infection in the skin. Any kind of inflammation or infection in the skin is called *dermatitis*. There are many germs which can infect the skin. The skin also is subject to various rashes which may result from allergies. In some cases, such as in pellagra, the skin may show symptoms of vitamin deficiencies.      W. B. YOUMANS

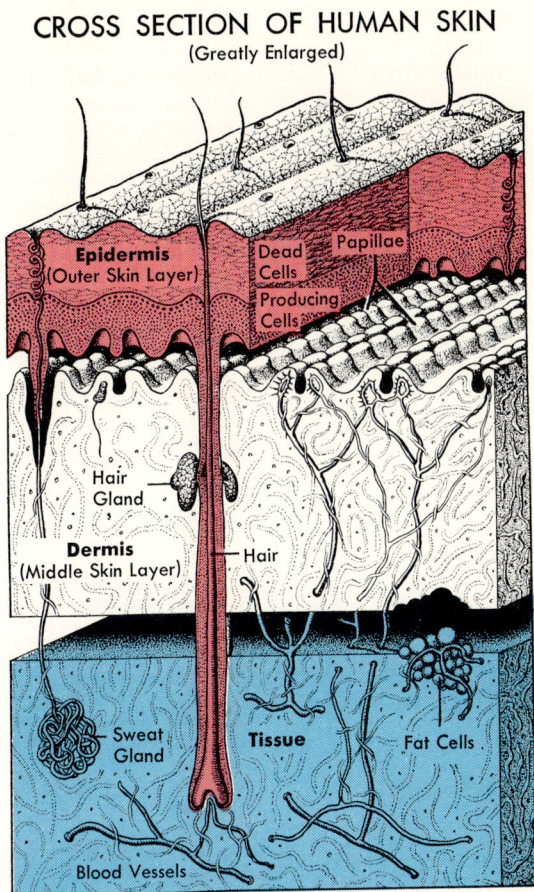

## CROSS SECTION OF HUMAN SKIN
(Greatly Enlarged)

Adapted from *Man in Structure and Function* by Fritz Kahn, by permission of and special arrangement with Alfred A. Knopf, Inc.

**Related Articles** in WORLD BOOK include:

SKIN DISEASES AND CONDITIONS

| | | |
|---|---|---|
| Acne | Erysipelas | Pimple |
| Athlete's Foot | Erythema | Prickly Heat |
| Birthmark | Hives | Psoriasis |
| Boil | Hyperesthesia | Ringworm |
| Callus | Impetigo | Shingles |
| Corn | Jungle Rot | Tumor |
| Dermatitis | Leprosy | Wart |
| Eczema | Lupus | Wen |
| Elephantiasis | Pellagra | |

OTHER RELATED ARTICLES

| | |
|---|---|
| Beard | Perspiration |
| Dermatology | Pore |
| Epithelium | Races of Man |
| Freckles | Scalp |
| Hair | Tissue |
| Nail | |

**SKIN DISEASE.** See DERMATOLOGY.

405

# SKIN DIVING

**SKIN DIVING** is a popular name for *free diving*. Skin divers, or *free divers*, go under water with no air supply, or with metal tanks from which they breathe compressed air.

Skin divers explore the world beneath the surface of rivers, lakes, and oceans. They hunt fish, study nature, and take pictures. Skin divers also search for crime and disaster evidence, repair ships, and do other important work under water.

Skin divers are able to move about under water more freely than *helmet divers*. A helmet diver wears a large helmet that is bolted to a bulky canvas suit. He breathes through a hose that runs from his helmet to pumps or tanks above the water. The air hose and clumsy equipment limits the range and enjoyment of diving. Most of the work that helmet divers once did is now done by skin divers.

## Kinds of Skin Diving

The simplest form of skin diving is to go under water while holding one's breath. This can be done without any equipment. But most skin divers who hold their breath under water swim with rubber foot fins and see through a *face mask*. A face mask consists of a glass plate mounted on rubber. It covers both the eyes and nose. *Mask divers* usually use *snorkels* (short breathing tubes). A snorkel allows a diver to breathe while holding his face down in the water. The best snorkel consists of a tube that is open at the top and is fitted with a mouthpiece at the bottom.

A mask diver with a snorkel swims face down on the surface looking for something of interest under water. Spotting an object, he takes a deep breath and bends sharply from the waist. In this position, he snaps his legs straight into the air and dives head down, toward the bottom.

Divers who hold their breath under water cannot dive very deep or stay under water very long. Therefore, the most common use of this kind of diving is for recreation, such as hunting for fish.

Longer, deeper dives can be made by divers who use independent breathing devices such as the *Aqua-Lung*. An Aqua-Lung diver breathes compressed air through a hose that is attached to metal tanks. The tanks are usually strapped on the diver's back. A valve, called a *demand regulator*, responds to the diver's breathing, and feeds him the exact volume of air that his lungs need to withstand the increased pressure under water. The

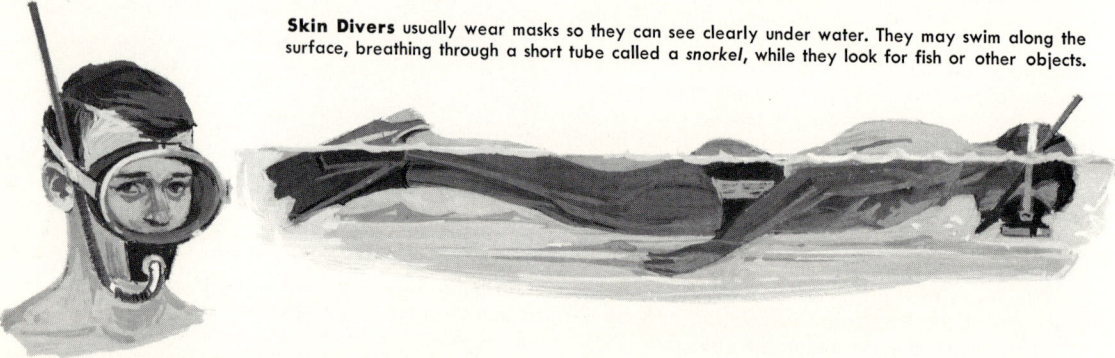

**Skin Divers** usually wear masks so they can see clearly under water. They may swim along the surface, breathing through a short tube called a *snorkel*, while they look for fish or other objects.

**Hunters Spearfish** in all areas of the world. This underwater hunter has speared a fish in the waters of the Black Sea.
Leonid Dorensky, Sovfoto

**Underwater Treasure** lures skin divers to sunken ships. The diver, *below*, is recovering a limestone-covered piece of copper.
Peter Throckmorton, Nancy Palmer

406

# SKIN DIVING

Aqua-Lung and similar devices are popularly and incorrectly called *SCUBA* (Self-Contained Underwater Breathing Apparatus).

Many skin divers wear rubber suits to protect their bodies from cold water. The most common type, the *wet suit*, is a tight-fitting coverall of foam rubber or fabric. It is worn over long, woolen underwear that has been soaked with water. The water adds to the suit's ability to retain body heat.

Skin diving instruction by qualified teachers is available at most YMCA and other community center swimming pools. A student diver should be aware of the dangers found under water. Some of these dangers are discussed under DIVING, UNDERWATER (Dangers).

## History of Skin Diving

Through the ages, divers have used a great variety of equipment to swim under water. Early divers, called *naked divers*, used no equipment to aid their breathing or sight. They dived for pleasure and in search of pearls, sponges, and shells. In A.D. 1300, divers in the Persian Gulf of the Arabian Sea used clear tortoise shell goggles to help them see under water. Divers began using rubber goggles with glass lenses and face masks in the 1930's.

Devices similar to the Aqua-Lung had been designed before 1943, but the Aqua-Lung was the first to use a demand regulator. Developed by Jacques-Yves Cousteau and Émile Gagnan, the Aqua-Lung was first successfully tested by Cousteau in 1943.

The popularity of diving has led to the formation of the Underwater Society of America. The society consists of regional councils representing hundreds of diving clubs. It regulates diving competitions and provides diving information to its members. The society has headquarters in the Bourse Building, Philadelphia, Pa. 19106. It is the largest of 40 organizations in the world that belong to the World Underwater Federation, which is headquartered in Paris.                JAMES DUGAN

See also DIVING, UNDERWATER; SPEARFISHING; AQUA-LUNG.

---

**SAFE DIVING LIMITS**

Divers wearing an Aqua-Lung independent breathing device may go safely to the following depths.

**100 feet**    A trained amateur without experience.
**150 feet**    A trained amateur with experience.
**200 feet and below**    A professional diver under full safety controls.

---

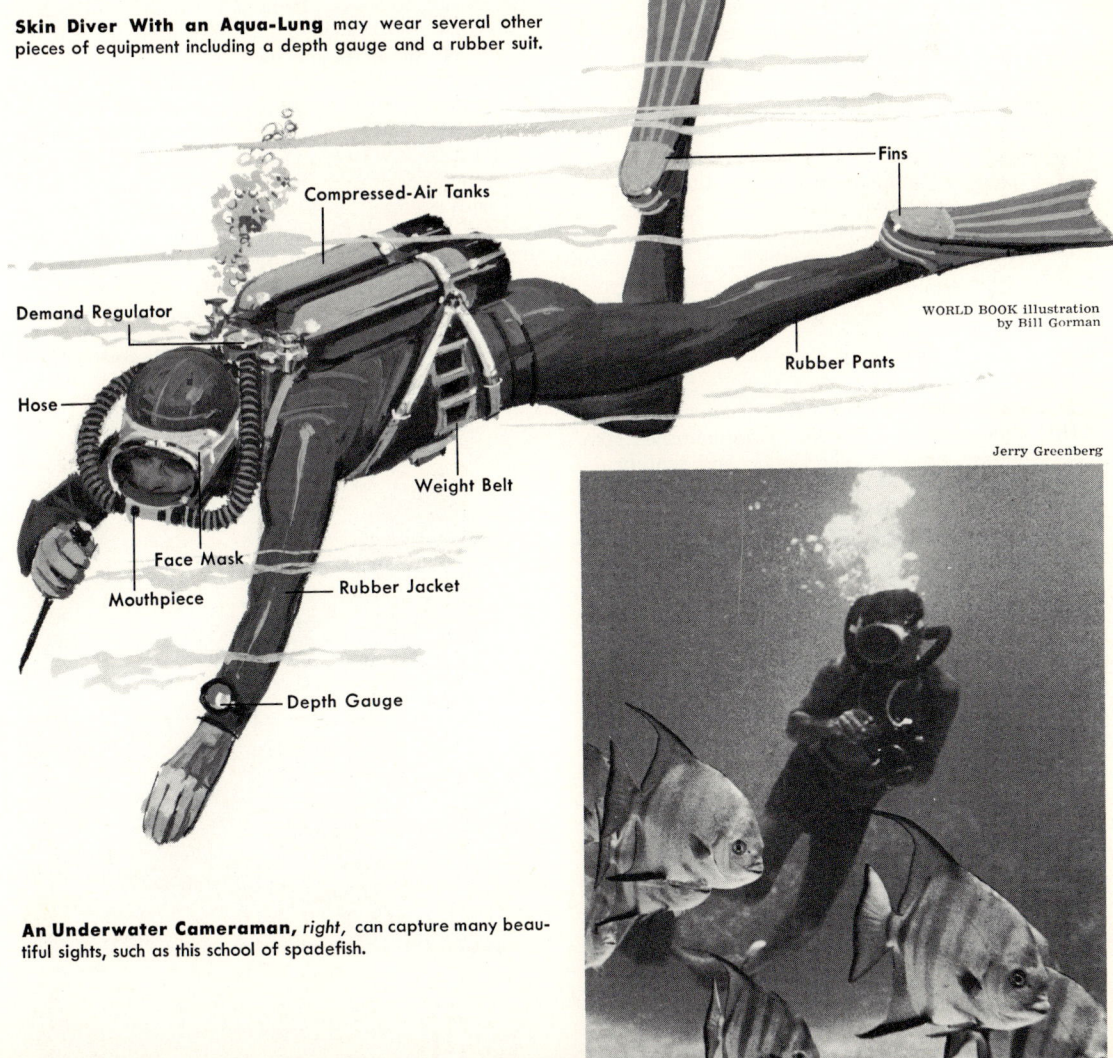

**Skin Diver With an Aqua-Lung** may wear several other pieces of equipment including a depth gauge and a rubber suit.

WORLD BOOK illustration by Bill Gorman

Jerry Greenberg

**An Underwater Cameraman,** *right,* can capture many beautiful sights, such as this school of spadefish.

# SKIN GRAFTING

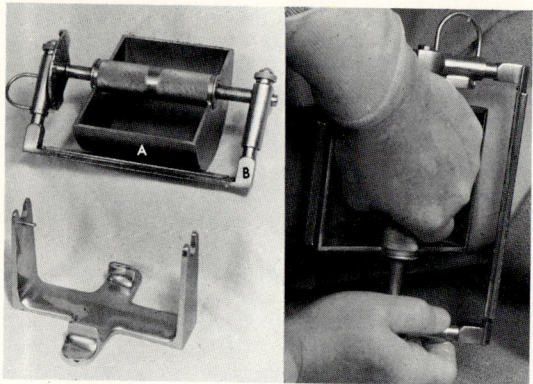

Bernard G. Sarnat, M.D., Beverly Hills, Calif.

The **Dermatome**, above, is a surgical instrument that cuts slices of skin for skin grafts. As the drum, (A), rolls over the skin, the arm with attached blade, (B), can cut different thicknesses.

**SKIN GRAFTING** is the transfer of skin from one part of a body to another. When skin is moved to another part of the same body, the graft is called an *autograft*. When the skin is moved from one body to another, the graft is called a *homograft*. Autografts are more successful and are used more often than homografts.

A thin skin graft is about eight one-thousandths of an inch thick and includes all of the *epidermis* (top layer of skin) and a little of the *dermis*. The dermis includes the blood vessels, sweat glands, and *hair follicles* (sacs that hairs grow out of). A full thickness graft includes all of the dermis and epidermis (see SKIN [illustration: Cross Section of Human Skin]). A split thickness graft includes part of the dermis, but does not include the deeper parts of the tubelike sweat glands and hair follicles. Thin and split thickness grafts grow more readily in the new site. Also, the skin grows back more readily at the donor site in thin and split thickness grafts. WILLIAM B. YOUMANS

See also PLASTIC SURGERY.

**SKINK.** See LIZARD.

**SKINNER** is the family name of two American actors.

**Otis Skinner** (1858-1942) was a distinguished actor who skillfully portrayed both comic and sentimental roles. He gained fame as Falstaff, and as Hajj in *Kismet*. His other successes were in the plays *The Duel, Mr. Antonio, Blood and Sand, Cock of the Walk,* and *Sancho Panza*. He was born in Cambridge, Mass. He made his first performance in 1877.

**Cornelia Otis Skinner**

Friedman-Abeles

**Cornelia Otis Skinner** (1901-    ), the daughter of Otis Skinner, is an actress and writer. She won great popularity for her interpretations in monologues, such as "The Wives of Henry VIII," "The Empress Eugénie," and "Edna His Wife." With Emily Kimbrough, she wrote *Our Hearts Were Young and Gay* (1942), an account of their trip to Europe as girls.

Miss Skinner has played leading roles in *Candida, Theatre, Lady Windermere's Fan,* and *The Pleasure of His Company.* She also wrote several popular books, including *Elegant Wits and Grand Horizontals* (1962) and *Madame Sarah* (1967), a biography of actress Sarah Bernhardt. Miss Skinner was born in Chicago. She made her first stage appearance in 1921. MARY VIRGINIA HEINLEIN

**SKINNER, B. F.** See TEACHING MACHINE (History); LEARNING (Instrumental Conditioning).

**SKITTLES.** See BOWLING (History).

**SKJAEGGEDALS,** *SHEG uh dahls,* also SKJAEGGEDALSFOSS, is a 525-foot-high waterfall in Norway.

**SKLODOWSKA, MARIE.** See CURIE (Marie).

**SKOKIE,** Ill. (pop. 67,865; alt. 625 ft.), is a suburb northwest of Chicago. Its industries include publishing, food processing, and the manufacture of light machinery. Skokie's population increased by 50,000 between 1945 and 1960. It was incorporated as the village of Niles Center in 1888, and took its present name in 1940. It has a mayor-council government. For location, see ILLINOIS (political map). PAUL M. ANGLE

**SKOPJE,** *SKOH pyeh,* or SKOPLJE, *SKOHP lyeh* (pop. 172,000; alt. 787 ft.), is the capital of Macedonia, one of the republics of the Socialist Federal Republic of Yugoslavia. It lies on the Vardar River. For location, see YUGOSLAVIA (map). Skopje's products include antimony, chrome and other metals, opium, saltpeter, textiles, and tobacco. Skopje is the home of Macedonian University. During the 1200's, the city was the capital of the Serbian kingdom. In July, 1963, a devastating earthquake leveled about 80 per cent of Skopje and killed 1,100 persons. More than half of the city's residents were left homeless. GEORGE KISH

**SKUA,** *SKYOO uh,* is a bird of prey that lives for much of the year over the ocean. The skua is a fierce bird with a strong, hooked beak and brown-and-white feathers. Skuas are found far out over the sea, where they attack gulls and terns, taking the fish which these birds have caught. On land, they also eat smaller birds

The **Skua** is a robber bird that may be found in almost all parts of the world. It is a solitary bird and never travels in a flock.

Alfred M. Bailey

408

and their eggs. They are related to the hunting gulls, or jaegers, but are larger. Skuas build their nests of sticks and grasses on the ground or on bare rocks. They do not conceal their nests, but they fight to protect them.

**Scientific Classification.** The skua belongs to the skua and jaeger family, *Stercorariidae*. The skua is classified as genus *Catharacta*, species *C. skua*.   ALEXANDER WETMORE

See also ANTARCTICA (Birds).

**SKULD.** See NORNS.

**SKULL** is the bony frame of the head of man and other animals with backbones. It is a case made up of bones that enclose and protect the brain, and bones that form the face. The human skull has 22 bones. Eight bones enclose the brain and make up what is called the *cranium*. These eight bones are called the *cranial bones*. The cranial bones are the *occipital*, at the back of the skull; the *sphenoid*, at the base of the skull; two *parietal* bones, at the top and sides; two *temporal* bones, above the ears; the *frontal*, at the forehead; and the *ethmoid*, at the nose. The other 14 bones of the skull form the face and the jaw. They are called *facial bones*.

The skull bones of an adult form a rigid, united structure. But the skull bones of babies are still in the process of growing, and are soft in areas where the bones join. After a few years, the bones grow together in a hard, firm, zigzag joint called a *suture*.

Animal skulls are shaped in ways that help the animal feed according to its way of life. For example, a wolf or cat has long jaws and strong, sharp teeth to grasp and tear its prey. But a horse's broad jaw and flat-edged teeth are shaped for cutting and grinding grasses and plants. The whale has a streamlined skull suited to its life in the water.   GORDON FARRELL

See also the Trans-Vision three-dimensional color picture with HUMAN BODY; also HEAD; MANDIBLE; MASTOID; SINUS.

**SKULL AND CROSSBONES.** See SYMBOL.

# SKUNK

John Gerard

**A Frightened Skunk Gives off a Disagreeable Odor.**

**SKUNK** is a small mammal famous for its unpleasant odor and its distinctive black and white markings. These members of the weasel family live only in North and South America.

About the size of a large house cat, the skunk has a broad forehead, an arched back, and short legs. Its tail is long and bushy, and a white patch of fur covers its forehead. The skunk is slow and deliberate, and walks like a person whose shoes are too tight.

A skunk has a pair of scent glands near its tail. These glands give out a vile-smelling fluid that serves as a defense against human and animal enemies. A frightened skunk can squirt the fluid up to 10 feet with good aim. With their scent glands removed, skunks make friendly, and sometimes playful, pets.

Skunks are active at night and sleep during the day. They make their *dens* (homes) in hollow trees, burrows, or under buildings. In winter, several skunks may share the same den. They sleep through much of the winter, but skunks do not really hibernate (see HIBERNATION).

Skunks help farmers by killing and eating insects, rats, mice, and other small animals that damage crops. But they also eat eggs, and sometimes raid hen roosts.

## SIZES OF SKULLS

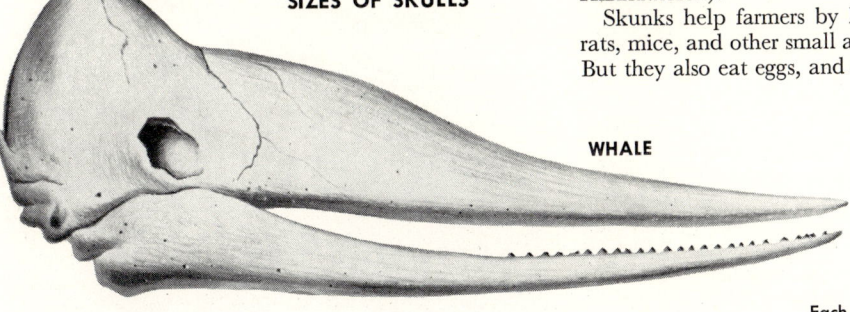

WHALE

MOUSE (Actual size)

Each Square = One Square Inch

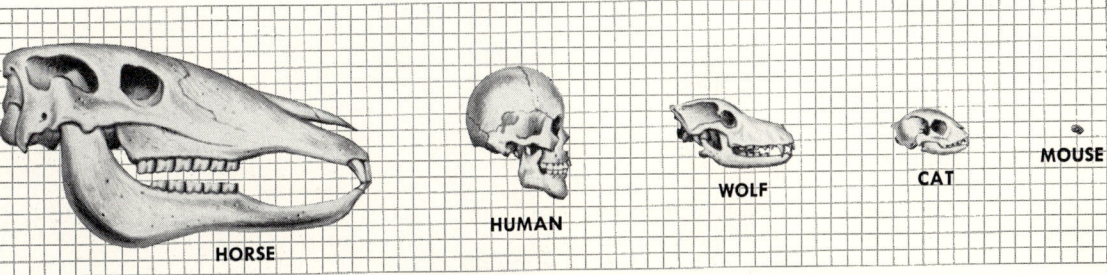

HORSE   HUMAN   WOLF   CAT   MOUSE

409

## SKUNK CABBAGE

Because of their abundance, skunks are among the most valuable fur-producing animals in North America. They are easy to trap. Their long, thick, and shiny fur makes attractive garments that wear well. But skunk fur is not as valuable as the pelts of such animals as minks. Skunk fur was called "black marten" or "Alaska sable" before the law required that all fur be sold under the name of the animal from which the pelt came.

**Scientific Classification.** Skunks belong to the weasel family, *Mustelidae*. Scientists classify the common skunk of North America as genus *Mephitis*, species *M. mephitis*. ROBERT K. ENDERS

See also ANIMAL (color picture, Animals of the Woodlands); FUR; PET (picture); POLECAT.

**SKUNK CABBAGE** is a soft-stemmed plant which is found in low swamps in eastern and central North America. It is known for its heavy, skunklike odor. Skunk cabbage is called a *perennial* because its roots send up new stems each year. The roots are heavy and coarse. The small flowers grow in a thick spike, which is surrounded by a brown leaflike organ called a *spathe*. The spathe gives off an unpleasant odor. The leaves of the skunk cabbage are broad and 1 to 3 feet long. The leaves grow in tufts.

Occasionally, skunk cabbage is planted in gardens because of the attractive appearance of the flowers and leaves.

**Scientific Classification.** The skunk cabbage belongs to the Arum family, *Araceae*. It is genus *Symplocarpus*, species *S. foetidus*. JULIAN A. STEYERMARK

See also ARUM.

**SKY** is the name we give to the great dome of the heavens we see above us. To astronomers, the sky is the *celestial sphere*, where celestial objects such as the stars, planets, moon, and sun are fixed. The expression "high in the sky" implies all space from the earth outward. The lower portion of this space is the earth's atmosphere and is the region of wind, rain, and cloud.

The word *sky* is generally thought to have come from the Anglo-Saxon language. In ancient literature the word appears as *skewes*, *skye*, *skiwes*, and *skie*.

The color of the sky results from the air within less than 100 miles of the earth. This belt of atmosphere is composed of nitrogen, oxygen, carbon dioxide, water vapor, certain rare gases, and suspended particles. When sunlight passes through the atmosphere, molecules scatter different colors. The shorter the wave length of the light, the more it is scattered. Blue light is scattered the most and red the least. The greatest part of the sky appears blue on a clear day, because these rays are reflected back to us from all parts of the sky. If there were no atmosphere around the earth, part of the sunlight would hit us directly and the rest would go on past. The sky would always look black, with the sun, moon, and stars shining on a great black dome. Scientists believe that this situation exists on the moon, because it has very little atmosphere.

If there are only a few dust particles in the air, more blue light is reflected to us. Therefore, the sky appears bluer on a clear day. When the sun rises or sets, the light passes through much more atmosphere than it does when the sun is overhead. Most of the blue light is lost, and we see red or pink colors in the sky and from clouds nearly in front of the sun. The sky is dull in rainy weather because clouds of moisture hide the light that comes from the sun.

Poetry and literature often refer to the sky. The expression "praise him to the sky" means to give high praise to a person. The word *firmament* is sometimes used for the sky. An example of this is in Psalms 19: 1, where it is written that "the firmament showeth His handiwork." R. WILLIAM SHAW

See also ASTRONOMY; HORIZON; LIGHT.

**SKYDIVING** is the sport of parachute-jumping. Skydiving refers to the technique of maintaining absolute control of one's body during a free-fall before the parachute is opened. The skydiver tries to land as near as possible to the center of a target, a 1,000-foot circle. The skydiver leaves the airplane at heights up to 13,000 feet in a familiar diver's position. Some skydivers hold their legs apart, and some use the regular swan dive. The skydivers use certain body movements to change direction, maintain balance, and drop on a target. Some divers amuse themselves with turns and spins. The diver opens his parachute at 1,600 to 2,000 feet above the ground, and then floats to earth at about 12 mph. An international meet is held annually. In 1957, several colleges in the eastern United States held an informal skydiving meet. The sport developed in France after World War II. RICHARD G. HACKENBERG

**Daring Skydivers** parachute from an airplane, then try to land on a target in the center of a 1,000-foot circle.
United Press Int.

**SKYE TERRIER.** This bushy-faced dog is one of the oldest terrier breeds. It originated during the 1600's on the island of Skye, off Scotland, and is kept as a house pet. It is a good rat hunter. The Skye is only 8 to 10 inches high, but its body is about 22 inches long. Its ears may be either erect or hanging. Its coat is about 5 inches long, and may be dark or light blue, gray, or fawn. The dog has a black muzzle. See also Dog (color picture: Terriers); TERRIER. JOSEPHINE Z. RINE

**SKYKJE FALLS,** or SKYKJEDALS, is a waterfall about 820 feet high on the Simoa River in southern Norway.

**SKYLARK.** See BIRD (color picture: Birds of Other Lands); LARK.

**SKYLINES.** See pictures with various city articles.

**SKYROCKET.** See ROCKET.

**SKYSCRAPER** is the name given to the tallest buildings in big cities. These giant structures were first built in Chicago and New York City, because the high price of land and the limited space made it necessary to build upwards. The development of iron girders capable of supporting many floors made the skyscraper possible.

William Le Baron Jenney designed the first skyscraper, the Home Insurance Building, Chicago. It was built with an iron frame in 1884, and torn down in 1931. Skyscrapers are now made of steel and concrete.

**Related Articles.** See the pictures in the articles for such cities as CHICAGO; NEW YORK CITY. See also:

Architecture
Building Construction
 (Constructing a
 Skyscraper)
Burnham, Daniel H.
Elevator
Empire State Building
Jenney, William Le Baron
Mies van der Rohe, Ludwig
Sullivan, Louis Henri

--- THE WORLD'S TALLEST SKYSCRAPERS ---

| Name of Building | City | Stories | Height to Roof (Feet) | *Total Height (Feet) |
|---|---|---|---|---|
| Empire State | New York | 102 | 1,250 | 1,472 |
| John Hancock Center | Chicago | 100 | 1,107 | 1,451 |
| Chrysler | New York | 77 | 865⅔ | 1,046 |
| 40 Wall Street | New York | 71 | 851 | 927 |
| RCA | New York | 70 | 850 | 885 |
| First National Bank | Chicago | 60 | 844 | 864 |
| 60 Wall Tower | New York | 66 | 825½ | 950 |
| 1 Chase Manhattan Plaza | New York | 60 | 813 | 813 |
| Pan Am | New York | 59 | 808 | 808 |
| Woolworth | New York | 60 | 792 | 792 |
| Bank of America World Headquarters | San Francisco | 52 | 778 | 778 |
| Prudential Tower | Boston | 52 | 749 | 820 |
| 20 Exchange Place | New York | 57 | 741 | 753 |
| 500 Fifth Avenue | New York | 58 | 727 | 741 |
| One Shell Plaza | Houston | 50 | 714 | 837½ |
| Terminal Tower | Cleveland | 52 | 708 | 768 |
| Union Carbide | New York | 52 | 707⅔ | 755 |
| Metropolitan Life | New York | 51 | 688 | 702 |
| Chemical Bank New York Trust Co. | New York | 52 | 687⅓ | 707⅓ |
| American Tobacco Co. | New York | 45 | 663 | 700 |
| Lincoln | New York | 55 | 656 | 681 |
| Irving Trust Co. | New York | 50 | 654 | 654 |
| Marine Midland Grace | New York | 52 | 648⅔ | 673⅔ |
| Chicago Civic Center | Chicago | 31 | 648 | 648 |

*Includes flagpole, TV antenna, statue, or other structures on roof.

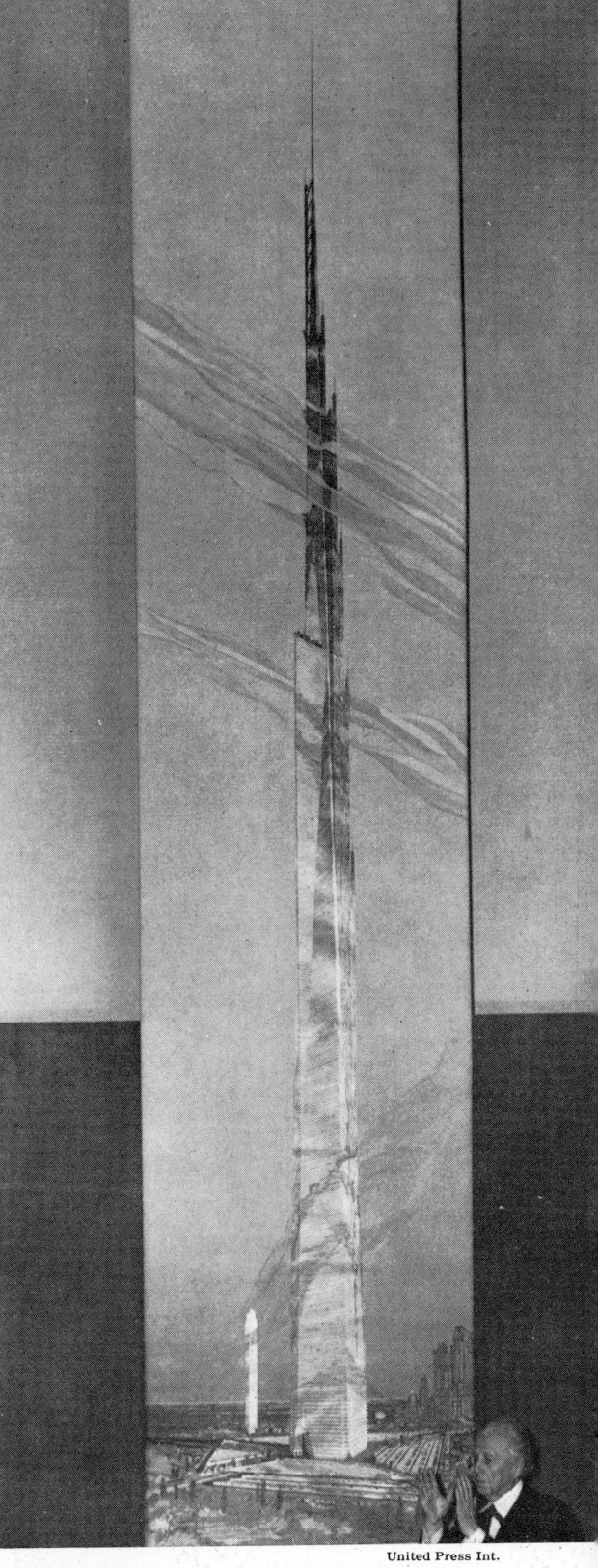

United Press Int.

**Frank Lloyd Wright,** *right*, won fame for his architectural designs. He proposed building this mile-high skyscraper in Chicago.

411

# SKYWRITING

**SKYWRITING** is a method of writing in the sky with an airplane. A trail of smoke traces the letters. A special preparation mixed with the fuel of the plane produces the smoke. People can see the gigantic letters for many miles. Some advertisers use skywriting to promote their products.

**SLAB.** See IRON AND STEEL (How Steel Is Shaped).

**SLAG** is the impure material removed in the process of making pig iron, and in smelting copper, lead, and other metals. The slag from steel blast furnaces is called *cinder*. It contains silicate of calcium, magnesium, and aluminum. The slag from copper and lead-smelting furnaces contains iron silicate, and other metals in small amounts. Slag from open-hearth steel furnaces contains lime and some iron. Often it is smelted again. Slag is sometimes used under pavement in building roads.

**SLAM.** See BRIDGE (Contract Bridge; Scoring).

**SLANDER.** A person who tells an untruth likely to injure the reputation or good name of another person may be charged with *slander*. Writing or printing a similar statement is called *libel*. The person responsible for a slanderous statement may be subject to criminal action. The person he has injured may file a civil suit. See also LIBEL.     F. S. SIEBERT and FRED E. INBAU

**SLANG** is a kind of language in which words and phrases are used in unconventional ways. It may violate basic rules of good speech, yet effectively convey the thoughts of the speaker. Slang may be vivid, grotesque, expressive, and sometimes vulgar. It has been an important part of everyday speech since men first began to talk to each other.

Slang words and phrases almost always meet with some disapproval when they are first introduced to polite language. Ben Jonson in 1601 attacked the word *strenuous*, then a slang expression, as uncouth and vulgar. Ambrose Bierce, an American journalist, described slang as "the speech of him who robs the literary garbage cans on their way to the dump."

Other people have welcomed slang. The English essayist, Gilbert K. Chesterton, wrote, "All slang is a metaphor, and all metaphor is poetry." Carl Sandburg called it "language that takes off its coat, spits on its hands, and goes to work." William Shakespeare drew heavily upon the slang of his day for the dialogue of his plays.

**Types of Slang.** Many, perhaps most, slang expressions are popular for a short time, then die out and are forgotten. *Gib* once meant *pout*, a *cake-eater* was a young man interested in girls. *Do* was once a slang noun meaning fraud, and *mump* a verb meaning to cheat. Other short-lived words were *skiddoo*, *blustiferous*, and *peedoodles*. *Tell it to Sweeney* was briefly a popular slang expression, as were *goo-goo eyes* and *Oh, you kid!* A person using expressions like these today would be considered old-fashioned, or perhaps, would not even be understood.

Another type of slang is that which has enjoyed a long and useful life and appears to be a permanent part of the *slanguage*. Some slang expressions of this sort have been in use for hundreds of years. *Lousy* is such a word. People have spoken it for more than 250 years. Yet *lousy* has never been able to break into polite language. More than 500 years ago, people described a boastful man as one inclined to *blow* and today he may be called a *blowhard*. About 1400, Chaucer referred to a pair of dice as the *bones*. *Booze* was slang even earlier. *Grub* (for food) has been traced back to the 1650's, and *frisk* (for search) to 1781. *Swell* (for excellent) was used in 1888. These words began as slang, have remained slang for many years, and perhaps may never become standard English.

A third type of slang provides standard language with many of its good new words. Some of these words fill an important need and move quickly into polite speech. Others remain on the fringes of polite language for many years and then finally become accepted. *Strenuous* was such a word. It carried Ben Jonson's stigma for centuries. Not until the 1900's did it finally find a secure place in standard English. *Hoax* (for falsehood) was slang in George Washington's day, but was a full member of polite language 50 years later. About 1920, women first arranged their hair in *hairdo's* (a slang term for coiffure). *Hairdo* was standard English in less than 20 years.

Some slang terms express ideas so clearly that one can almost predict their future acceptance as good speech. Such terms include *cold feet*, *wisecrack*, *blurb*, *razz*, *ghost writer*, *hard-boiled*, *double cross*, *stuffed shirt*, *haywire*, *ritzy*, *scab*, *rubberneck*, *easy mark*, *scram*, and *in the doghouse*. Dictionaries disagree today on the status of *skyscraper*, *bootleg*, *bunk*, *gadget*, *vamp*, *jazz*, *hoodlum*, and *highbrow*.

The term *O.K.* (sometimes spelled *okey* or *okay*) has not been accepted as standard English, except when used as a sign of approval on documents. Then it is. The origin of the term, incidentally, is in dispute. Some experts believe it developed from the *O.K. Club*, a group that supported Martin Van Buren for President of the United States in 1840. The club letters stood for Old Kinderhook, N.Y., Van Buren's birthplace. The *O.K. Club* touted Van Buren as "all right." Other authorities believe *O.K.* originally stood for *orl k'rect*, a frontier misspelling of *all correct* that was used by President Andrew Jackson.

Slang is not confined to any one language. French is particularly rich in slang. As in English, much French slang has found its way into the standard language. The word *tête*, for example, is a perfectly good French word meaning head. But it originated as *testa*, meaning pot. Soldiers of the Roman Empire used *testa* as slang for *head*. England and America have developed their own slang expressions, and these have been freely loaned back and forth across the Atlantic. New Zealand and Australia have distinctive slang vocabularies.

**Sources of Slang.** As the dispute over *O.K.* indicates, the sources of slang are often obscure. H. L. Mencken, an American journalist, explained that slang is a "kind of linguistic exuberance, an excess of word-making energy" (see MENCKEN, HENRY L.). Others have pointed out that slang does not necessarily fill any particular need. It may simply be a new and different way of saying what can be said perfectly well in standard English.

*Criminal Cant.* The criminal world has long had a slang language almost its own. This slang, or *cant*, developed partly in a deliberate effort to keep outsiders from knowing what the criminals were talking about. It was almost like a code. Thus *bull* came to mean policeman, and *dip* a thief who robbed the pockets of others. *Skirt* and *broad* (meaning woman) began in this way, as did *moonshine* (for illegal liquor). *Joint* (meaning a place of low repute) is another word that was graduated from cant to slang. Other colorful words that began as cant are *eye* (for detective), *third degree* (for questioning), *gyp* (for cheat), *shakedown* (for search) and *fence* (for receiver of stolen goods).

The *underworld* of large cities produced many slang terms during the gangster period of the 1920's. *Racket* became slang for a dishonest but profitable business. A bomb came to be called a *pineapple* because of the shape of bombs used by gangsters. When a gangster kidnaped a rival gangster and murdered him, it was said the victim was *taken for a ride*. *Moll* (for woman), *heater* and *rod* (for gun), and *needle* (for adding alcohol to liquor) were other slang terms that developed in this period.

*Jargon*, the vocabulary of special groups, may work its way into the common language as slang. Theater jargon has produced many such words. Among them are *ham* (for bad actor), *turkey* (for failure), *dead-pan* (for a comedian without facial expression), *hoofer* (for dancer), and *the sticks* (for small towns). The amusement journal *Variety* once headed a story "Stix Nix Hix Pix." It meant that motion pictures which made fun of farmers as "hicks" were unpopular in rural areas.

Musicians and their fans have produced much rich slang. Jazz music has given the language *hepcat*, *rat race*, *killer-diller*, *jerk*, *blow one's top*, and *jitterbug*. Radio and television produced *stand by* (meaning to wait), *sign off*, *static* (for any disagreeable noise), *disk jockey*, and *Zilch* (for anyone whose name is not known). The publishing world added *deadline*, *handout*, *slug*, and *scoop*.

It is easy to see why the jargon of the theater, radio, and television, is likely to spread rapidly to general use. Performers need only to speak their jargon before audiences. People in the audience pick up the expressions and adapt them to their own use.

Farmers, bakers, architects, barbers, bartenders, and carpenters all have words that relate particularly to their work and may be picked up by other people as slang. Aviation has produced many terms, among them *bail out*, *socked-in* (meaning fog-bound), and *flying blind*. Railroads added *highball*, *caboose*, and *sidetrack*.

University students refer to an invitation to a college affair as a *bid*, a sudden thought as a *brain storm*, and a general discussion as a *bull session*. The armed forces during World War II produced *snafu* (situation normal, all fouled up), *blockbuster*, *black market*, *blitz*, *flak*, *Quisling*, *task force*, and *DP* (for displaced person).

Any large organization is likely to produce jargon that may become general slang. One of the big contributors in this way is the United States Department of Defense, whose headquarters are located in the Pentagon in Arlington, Va. This particular slang vocabulary is sometimes called *Pentagonese*, itself a slang word. Pentagonese includes *finalize* (for complete), *flap* (for state of tension or excitement), *bind* (for a prolonged flap), and *File 13* (for wastebasket). In the Navy Department, however, the wastebasket is referred to as *Deep Six*.

Sailors have always been ready inventors of slang. This is perhaps the result of the colorful jargon of the sea, which lends itself to general use. A few examples are *above-board*, *overboard*, *three sheets in the wind*, *Davy Jones' locker*, *pipe down*, *run afoul*, and *keel over*.

Each of the major sports has added to slang. From golf have come *par*, *divot*, and *stymie*. Baseball has produced *home run*, *charley horse*, *bunt*, *fan*, *peg* (a throw), and *seventh-inning stretch*.

*Invented Slang.* Mencken points out that entertainers and writers produce much of our slang deliberately, as a means of adding freshness to their work. Just as Chaucer may have invented the use of *bones* for dice, Jack Conway, a theatrical writer, produced *palooka* (meaning a person of little ability), *belly laugh*, and *pushover*. Walter Winchell, a newspaper columnist, added *whoopee* to the slang vocabulary. Winchell also is credited with *middle-aisled* and *lohengrined* (for married) and *Reno-vated* (for divorced). T. A. Dorgan, a cartoonist, scored on *dumbbell*, *apple sauce*, and *You said it!* But he missed on *cake-eater* and *Twenty-three, skiddoo!*

**Fads in Slang** change so fast that some expressions no sooner become known than they pass out of style. Someone might be described one year as *out of this world*, but *real gone* the next. Still later, he may be *the greatest*, or even *the most*. Something might be *real hot* during one slang fad and *real cool* during the next. Then it might be *far out*.

Overuse of a slang word robs it of the freshness and novelty upon which slang thrives. There was a period in the 1950's, for example, when *crazy* meant wonderful. Later *crazy* began to mean almost anything. It might even be used as a casual and nonsensical goodby. When this happened, *crazy* quickly passed out of use as a slang expression.

**Dangers of Slang.** There have been periods in history when any use of slang marked a person as ill-bred or unrefined. It gave him a stigma that handicapped him in polite society. This is not necessarily true today. Educated people often use some slang terms as a relief from formal speech. Slang may add to the zest and fun of conversation. The danger of slang is mainly in its overuse. A slang term becomes tiresome when it is too often repeated. Slang also tends to identify its user with a specific group in society. This is because different groups tend to use different styles of slang. A frequent user of slang, therefore, may find himself handicapped when he moves outside his own circle of friends. His speech will mark him as different and, perhaps, of a limited background of experience.

The user of slang also runs the risk of being misunderstood. The meanings of slang terms are not always written down. And they change rapidly. Because of this, a slang term may mean different things to different people.

Experience has shown also that heavy use of slang tends to restrict one's use of standard English. Standard English words have been developed through years of experience to cover almost every shade of meaning. By discriminating use of standard English, a person can convey the most subtle differences of thought. When slang words can contribute to this process, they are usually absorbed into standard English. Then they are no longer slang.

See also Dialect; Idiom.

**SLAPSTICK COMEDY.** See Humor; Sennett, Mack.

# SLATE

**SLATE** is a fairly hard rock which can be split into thin, smooth layers. It is made up of tiny crystals of micalike minerals. These crystals are closely packed together and arranged in layers. Slate is a metamorphic rock (see METAMORPHISM). It is produced from clay and shale which have been compressed and deformed by earth pressures. A great deal of pressure rearranges the tiny clay minerals into thin layers, which then can be split into sheets as thin as paper. These layers of rock are slate, and the way in which the rock splits is known as *slaty cleavage*.

Slate is useful to man, particularly in roofing. Slate shingles are durable and fireproof. Workmen split the slate into thin layers with chisels, and then cut the layers into various sizes for shingles. Slate is usually gray, but red, brown, and green shades sometimes occur. These shades are more valuable, because they make attractive roofing shingles.

Wales is the most important slate-producing center in the world. Europe produces slate in great quantities. The largest slate quarries in the United States are located in Pennsylvania, Vermont, New York, Maine, and Maryland. A. J. EARDLEY

See also BUILDING STONE.

**SLATER,** *SLAY ter*, **SAMUEL** (1768-1835), an Englishman, founded the American cotton industry. Born at Belper, Derbyshire, England, Slater was apprenticed at 14 to a former partner of Sir Richard Arkwright, an inventor of cotton-spinning machinery (see ARKWRIGHT, SIR RICHARD). England tried to monopolize the textile industry by forbidding textile machinery, plans, and workers to leave the country. Slater, now skilled in improved textile machinery, left England in 1789 disguised as a farm boy.

He entered the firm of Almy and Brown in Providence, R.I., agreeing to build and operate the cotton-spinning machinery invented by Arkwright. In 1790, the firm opened a 72-spindle mill in Pawtucket, R.I., the first successful spinning mill in the United States (see COTTON [In America]). Slater began manufacturing woolen cloth in 1815. In 1796, he established a Sunday school for the improvement of his workers. This was one of the first institutions of its kind to be established in the United States. KENNETH W. PORTER

**SLATER FUND.** See SOUTHERN EDUCATION FOUNDATION.

**SLAV,** *slahv*, or *slav*. The Slavs, or Slavonians, are a group of people who live in Eastern Europe and Siberia. There are about 200,000,000 Slavs. Most Russians, Poles, Ruthenians, Czechs, Slovaks, Croats, Serbs, Slovenes, Ukrainians, Bulgars, and Montenegrins are Slavs.

The original Slav people were probably a division of the old Aryan-speaking or Indo-European peoples. The early Slavs lived in regions of northwestern Ukraine and southeastern Poland. Most of them were farmers and herdsmen. Between A.D. 200 and 500, the Slavs began to migrate to other parts of Europe. They went into regions of Germany, Montenegro, Albania, and Russia.

Slavs form a language group, rather than a race. They vary in appearance according to the region in which they live. Slavs who live near the Mediterranean Sea are much darker than the fair-skinned Slavs of White Russia. Some Slavs are blond, and others have brown hair. Ruthenians have long heads and dark skin, while Poles are roundheaded and light-skinned.

**Culture.** Slavs have contributed much to the world in education and art. The Charles University at Prague, founded in 1348, was for many years one of the finest schools in Europe. The University of Kraków was the school of the Polish astronomer, Nicolaus Copernicus. Marie Sklodowska Curie, the renowned scientist, was born in Warsaw, Poland. Many outstanding artists and musicians have come from Bohemia. Polish music is world-famous, and Russian music ranks high. Bedřich Smetana and Antonín Dvořák were famous musicians from Bohemia. Polish composers include Frédéric Chopin and Ignace Paderewski. Russia produced such composers as Peter Ilich Tchaikovsky, Nicholas Rimsky-Korsakov, Igor Stravinsky, Sergei Prokofiev, Dimitri Shostakovich, Sergei Rachmaninoff, and Modest Mussorgsky. Russian writers include Fyodor Dostoevsky, Maxim Gorki, and Leo Tolstoy.

**History.** Every Slav nation has had its national tragedy. The savage tribes of Genghis Khan invaded Russia. Serbia lost its power after the Battle of Kossovo, and the Czechs suffered cruel defeat at the Battle of White Mountain. Polish territory was divided among its enemies three different times. Still the Slavs carried on their struggle for freedom.

About 1830, a Slavic nationalist movement began to arise throughout Europe. The movement was led by Russia and was known as *Panslavism*. The scattered Slavic peoples of Europe began to awaken to the hope of national independence. Panslav congresses were held in Prague, Moscow, and Vienna. Inspired by the thought of unity, the oppressed Slavs grew restless and dissatisfied. They began to demand freedom from foreign control, and discontent reached a boiling point throughout the Balkans. But the movement met with failure because Slav national groups could not cooperate.

After World War I, Poland, Czechoslovakia, and Yugoslavia became independent Slav nations. The Slavs in the Ukraine formed a state in the Soviet Union. Germany destroyed Czechoslovakia in 1939, and divided Poland with Russia. German armies invaded Yugoslavia in 1941. Russian troops drove them out of Poland, Czechoslovakia, and parts of Yugoslavia at the end of World War II. Communist puppet governments imposed their own rule. WILTON MARION KROGMAN

See also CZECH; RUTHENIAN; SLOVAK.

**SLAVE LAKE, GREAT.** See GREAT SLAVE LAKE.

**SLAVE RIVER,** or **GREAT SLAVE RIVER,** is an important link in the great Mackenzie River system of Canada. The Slave River is about 258 miles long. It flows out of Lake Athabasca in the province of Alberta, and winds in a northerly direction across the Northwest Territories to empty into Great Slave Lake. The Mackenzie River flows out of the western end of Great Slave Lake. Just as the Slave leaves Lake Athabasca, it gets the waters of the Peace River, which also is a part of the Mackenzie system. Midway in its course the smooth flow of the Slave River is interrupted by the 13-mile Rapids of the Drowned. Fort Smith, the administrative center of the Mackenzie District, stands at the northern end of the rapids. The river's transportation value has dwindled with the increase of air, truck, and rail service in the area. W. D. MCDOUGALL

From a sketch in *Harper's Weekly*, January 24, 1863, Culver

**In a Slave Warehouse, Slaves for Sale as Domestic Servants Wore Their Best Clothes to Attract Buyers.**

**SLAVERY** is a practice in which human beings are owned by other human beings. A slave works for his *master*, or owner, without pay, although he receives food, clothing, and shelter. Slavery has existed for thousands of years. The earliest slaves included debtors and people captured in warfare. Some historians consider early slavery a forward step toward civilization, because at one time conquerors simply killed their prisoners. Early slaves belonged to many races. Most later slaves were Negroes.

### In Ancient Times

Most ancient peoples had slaves. Among the Hebrews, the laws of Moses provided that a slave of their own people should be set free after six years, and foreign slaves should be liberated twice in each hundred years. Among the ancient Greeks, people often purchased slaves from pirates. Poor men sometimes sold their children into slavery, and debtors were sometimes sold into slavery to satisfy their debts. In Rome, slavery flourished as long as the armies continued their conquests.

### Later Revival

Slavery in Europe slowly changed into serfdom, and had almost disappeared by the 1300's (see SERF). But, during the 1400's, Portuguese explorers in Africa allowed several captured Moors to free themselves by giving the conquerors black slaves. Soon the Portuguese began capturing African Negroes and bringing them into Europe as slaves.

**The Slave Trade.** In 1516, King Charles I of Spain gave colonists and slave traders permission to take slaves into the Spanish colonies in America. This trade was formalized through the *assiento*, a contract between Spain and another country for furnishing Negro slaves. Slavery soon developed into a profitable industry. By the late 1770's, British ships were carrying about half the slaves brought to America.

Persons who opposed slavery, called *abolitionists*, agitated to do away with the slave trade. In England, the Society of Friends (Quakers) started an antislavery movement in 1671. American Quakers took up the fight in 1696. Rhode Island, in 1652, passed a law providing that no man should be held in service for more than 10 years, and that no man should be sold. The law was probably not enforced. In 1792, Denmark became the first nation to put a stop to the slave trade. Thomas Clarkson and William Wilberforce persuaded the British government to pass a bill against the slave trade in 1807. Slavery was abolished in all British colonies in 1833.

In March, 1807, the United States prohibited further importation of slaves after Jan. 1, 1808. This act legally ended the overseas trade in slaves, but slavery itself continued until the end of the Civil War.

Most Latin-American countries abolished slavery as soon as they had won independence. But Brazil did not entirely give up slavery until 1888.

**Slavery in the United States** began in the early 1600's. Because of the nature of farming in the North, slavery was not profitable there. It became concentrated in the South, where farming on large plantations formed the main industry (see PLANTATION). By 1860, there were about 3,954,000 Negro slaves in the United States, nearly one third of the total population of the 15 Southern slave states. See NEGRO (The Slave Trade; Slavery in America).

415

# SLAVIC COUNTRIES

Most slaves worked as *field hands* in gangs. They planted, weeded, and harvested tobacco, rice, sugar, and especially cotton. Their hours were long, like those of white laborers at the time, generally lasting from sunrise to sunset. *House slaves* worked as servants in the master's home, and had more privileges. An adult slave usually received a peck of corn and three or four pounds of salt pork or bacon as his weekly food allowance. His master housed and clothed him. If the slave did not work, or tried to run away, he might be punished.

Both contemporary observers and later historians have disagreed bitterly over nearly every aspect of American Negro slavery. Abolitionists branded it as an evil system that led to the ruthless exploitation of labor and the moral degradation of both slaves and masters. Southerners defended slavery as a necessary but kindly labor system which served as a civilizing force for the allegedly barbarous Negro. There is no reliable evidence to indicate that, as late as the outbreak of the Civil War, slavery was a dying institution in the United States. Lincoln's Emancipation Proclamation of 1863 declared slaves free in all areas of the Confederate States still in rebellion. But slavery was not entirely abolished until the states had ratified Amendment 13 to the United States Constitution in 1865. Amendments 14 and 15, passed after the war, gave former slaves citizenship and civil rights.

## Slavery Today

Despite new attitudes and the abolishment of a widespread slave trade, slavery still exists in the world. During World War II, Nazi Germany followed the old practice of making slaves of conquered people. Russia and other Communist countries began using political prisoners for forced labor, a form of slavery. The Anti-Slavery Society, a British organization, has reported that the slave trade still flourishes in Africa, the Middle East, the Far East, and parts of South America.

DAVID DONALD

**Related Articles** in WORLD BOOK include:

IN ANCIENT TIMES

Aesop's Fables
Egypt, Ancient
Greece, Ancient (The People; Manufacturing)
Roman Empire (The People)

IN AMERICA

Abolitionist
Buchanan, James (The Struggle Over Slavery)
Civil War
Colonial Life in America
Compromise of 1850
Confederate States of America
Crittenden Compromise
Dred Scott Decision
Emancipation Proclamation
Free Soil Party
Fugitive Slave Law
Hawkins, Sir John

Kansas-Nebraska Act
Liberty Party
Lincoln, Abraham
Mason and Dixon's Line
Missouri Compromise
Negro
Proslavery Movement
Reconstruction
Russwurm, John Brown
Squatter Sovereignty
Truth, Sojourner
Uncle Tom's Cabin
Underground Railroad
Wilberforce (William)
Wilmot Proviso

OTHER RELATED ARTICLES

Saudi Arabia (Family Life)    Toussaint L'Ouverture

**SLAVIC COUNTRIES** are nations where most of the people are Slavs (see SLAV). These countries include Czechoslovakia and Poland in central Europe, Bulgaria and Yugoslavia in southern Europe, and Russia, which lies partly in eastern Europe and partly in Asia.

**SLAVONIA.** See CROATIA AND SLAVONIA.

**SLAYTON, DONALD KENT** (1924-    ), was one of the first U.S. astronauts. However, Slayton was restricted to ground duty when doctors discovered he had a slight heart problem. In 1963, Slayton became director of flight crew operations for the National Aeronautics and Space Administration (NASA) at the Manned Spacecraft Center, near Houston, Tex. He is responsible for directing astronaut activities and evaluating their performances. He was awarded the NASA Distinguished Service Medal in 1965.

Slayton was born in Sparta, Wis. He entered the U.S. Air Force in 1942, and flew 63 combat missions in World War II. He was graduated from the University of Minnesota in 1949, and worked as an aeronautical engineer for the Boeing Aircraft Company until recalled to active duty in 1951. From 1956 until 1959, he served as a test pilot.

WILLIAM J. CROMIE

See also ASTRONAUT.

**SLED** is a vehicle that has parallel runners instead of wheels, so that it can move easily over snow or ice. Sleds can be used for sport, but in some parts of the world they are important means of transportation. In the Far North, where snow and ice cover the ground for many months, sleds are the chief means of transportation. People in parts of Alaska and the Yukon travel on sleds pulled by teams of huskies.

Alaskan sleds are built to stand the roughest travel.

**Sledding Is a Popular Winter Sport** in many regions. The coaster sled, *below*, has steel runners and a wood frame.

H. Armstrong Roberts

The most common Alaskan sled is the *Nome sledge*, a long, narrow type with basketlike sides. A good team of dogs, hitched to a Nome sledge, can haul a thousand pounds of cargo. The *Nansen* sled, made of wood and lashed with rawhide, is wider and lighter than the Nome sledge. However, a 30-pound Nansen sled can carry a 600-pound load. Sleighs called *troikas* are used in Russia. They are drawn by horses or reindeer. In Lapland, reindeer pull sledges carrying heavy goods.

Early man made crude sledges from logs. He tied these together and dragged them along the ground. Later, men found that the sled would move more easily and quickly if thin slats of wood, called *runners*, were fastened beneath the logs.

The North American Indians used a *toboggan* sled that looked like a canoe on runners. The Pilgrims made sleds of a box set on a pair of runners.

After 1870, the *coasting* sled came into use in the United States. The original coasting sled was the "clipper" type. It was built low, with long, pointed sides and runners of round steel rods. The "girl's sled" was a light, short box, with high, cutout or skeleton sides, and wide, flat runners.

The *double-runner* or *bobsled* was formed of two clipper sleds joined end to end by a board. The rider steered the sled by means of ropes, a wheel, or a crossbar. Four to ten persons rode in the bobsled. Sleds used in bobsled racing are more complex.   FRANKLIN M. RECK

See also BOBSLEDDING; DOG SLED; TOBOGGANING; TRANSPORTATION (picture: Land Transportation Without Wheels); TROIKA.

**SLEDGE.** See SLED.

**SLEEP** is a period of rest in which most conscious mental and physical activity is suspended. It is a normal part of the behavior of human beings and many animals. Sleep is essential to maintain life and health.

Falling asleep is a complicated process that takes place gradually. All activity decreases and the muscles relax. A person becomes less and less aware of his surroundings. Eventually sensation leaves—first sight, then taste, smell, hearing, and touch.

### What Happens During Sleep

The essential body processes continue during sleep. But the heart beats less rapidly and breathing is slower. The body produces less heat and the sleeping person must be protected from cold.

It is not important to assume a "good" position in going to sleep, because the first position will not be maintained throughout the night. The stillness of a sleeping person is interrupted many times by minor movements of his head, arms, and legs. A person may make a dozen or more complete changes in position during a single night's sleep. Such changes allow more complete relaxation of different muscles.

The depth of sleep varies. In the course of a night's sleep, there is a succession of five to six cycles that alternate from deep to light sleep. During 15 to 20 minutes of each cycle, the sleeper dreams. Only about two to four hours of the time spent sleeping is deep sleep. The remainder of the sleep is *superficial*, or light.

### How Sleep Patterns Develop

The time spent in sleep is different for adults than it is for babies. Adults spend only about a third of their time sleeping. But newborn babies sleep about two-thirds of the time. They interrupt their sleep every three or four hours, day and night, to be fed, bathed, or comforted. The change from the baby's inborn need for short periods of wakefulness to the adult's learned ability to remain awake for long periods depends on growth. The change requires normal development of various organ systems of the body, but particularly of the *cerebral cortex*, the part of the brain involved in learning and thinking.

An infant adapts to adult patterns of sleeping and wakefulness in several stages. By the time a baby is 6 to 10 weeks old, he learns to sleep through the whole night, some 10 hours at a stretch. Naps in the morning and afternoon supplement the night sleep. Later, the morning nap is omitted. By the time the child is 3 to 6 years old, the afternoon nap is omitted as well. From this time on, the hours of sleep are gradually shortened until the average adult requirement of seven to eight hours of sleep is met. Thus, a person's ability to remain awake increases four times as he grows up. A baby needs two hours of sleep for every hour of wakefulness. Older children and adults learn to supply 30 minutes of sleep for every hour that they are awake.

### Sleep Habits

Every person does not need seven to eight hours of sleep each night. Some persons get along quite well on less sleep. Others require more. Generally, a person has had enough sleep if he wakes up in the morning without being called, and if he is not drowsy during waking hours, especially in the afternoon.

A person's daily schedule usually involves a fixed time for getting up, but not for going to bed. Good sleep habits are established by following a regular daily schedule. There should be regular amounts of time set aside for work, meals, recreation, and sleep. Such a routine, even with occasional exceptions, allows the body to develop a 24-hour rhythm of activity and rest. When an individual has established such a rhythm, he is able to sleep more soundly and to awake refreshed.

### Difficulty in Sleeping

*Insomnia* is a condition in which a person has difficulty in falling asleep, or in sleeping the customary number of hours. Such sleeplessness is often associated with pain. But worry or discomfort can also keep a person awake. All these factors tend to increase muscle tension and make falling asleep difficult. It is important for relaxation that night clothes be loose and that bedding be comfortable. A dark, quiet room that is well ventilated and cool will help a person to relax.

### Experiments with Sleep

Investigators have studied sleeping persons to find out how the body functions during sleep. Instruments have been used to record the activity of the brain, the heart rate, blood pressure, and the degree of disturbance needed to awaken a sleeping person. Changes in body temperature also have been studied. It has been found that the lowest body temperature occurs at about 2 to 4 A.M., during sleep. The highest occurs in the afternoon or early evening. This variation probably results from

# SLEEPING BAG

changes in muscle tenseness. Tense muscles give off more heat than relaxed muscles. In laboratory experiments, persons deprived of sleep for several days have difficulty thinking and easily become angry. What they want most to do is to lie down and relax their muscles. The 24-hour sleep-wakefulness pattern persists. For example, it is more difficult for them to stay awake in the middle of the second night than it is during the afternoon of the third day.   NATHANIEL KLEITMAN

**Related Articles** in WORLD BOOK include:
Dream
Hibernation
Insomnia
Nightmare
Sleeping Sickness
Sleepwalking
Snoring

**SLEEPING BAG.** See CAMPING (Sleeping Bags).

**SLEEPING CAR.** See PULLMAN, GEORGE MORTIMER.

**SLEEPING SICKNESS** is the common name for any one of several diseases that result in a deep sleep from which the patient cannot be aroused. But the term usually refers to African sleeping sickness, a disease confined to Africa.

**African Sleeping Sickness** is technically known as *trypanosomiasis*, because it is caused by a parasite called a *trypanosome* (see TRYPANOSOME). This long, rather thin organism consists of a single cell. A fin-like fold, called the *undulating membrane*, grows along the length of the body and ends in a thin, whiplike growth in front. The organism moves by waving or whipping this membrane. When doctors suspect that a person has sleeping sickness, they remove a drop of blood, spinal fluid, or tissue fluid from a swollen gland of the victim. They place this material under a microscope for examination. If the person has sleeping sickness, the investigator can see the wiggling parasite.

Sleeping sickness occurs widely throughout tropical Africa. The disease parasites may live in certain game animals and domestic livestock as well as in man. A particular kind of fly, called the *tsetse fly*, transmits these parasites from animal to man or from man to man (see TSETSE FLY). The fly becomes infected by sucking the blood of a man or animal that has the disease. The disease germs thus enter the insect's body, where they grow and multiply. As they develop, they move into the salivary glands and mouth parts of the fly. When this fly bites a man, it injects some of these parasites into the man's body. The speed with which the disease develops varies.

The kind of sleeping sickness found in East Africa is known as the *Rhodesian* type. It is more severe than the kind found in West Africa.

The first symptoms of sleeping sickness usually are fever, headache, and chills. The patient's lymph glands swell, and a skin rash develops. Soon he becomes quite weak. As the disease progresses, the parasites attack the victim's brain, causing deep sleep

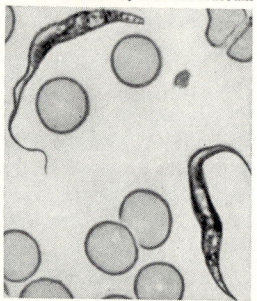

**Sleeping Sickness** is caused by long wormlike parasites named *trypanosomes*.
U. S. Army Medical Museum

and coma (see COMA). Unless he receives treatment, he will usually die. To be effective, treatment must be given before there is severe damage to the patient's nervous system. Once his nervous system has been damaged, complete cure is impossible. Scientists have developed a variety of complex drugs, some of which contain arsenic, to treat sleeping sickness.

Sleeping sickness has caused a serious health problem in Africa. Many African species of trypanosomes produce fatal illness in cattle and horses making it almost impossible to raise livestock there. As a result, sleeping sickness both of man and of animals has slowed down the development of Africa. Scientists have done much work on measures to control the disease and its carriers. Sometimes they give small doses of drugs to try to prevent the disease. They also try to destroy the breeding and resting places of the tsetse fly.

**Encephalitis Lethargica** is another disease people often call sleeping sickness. This epidemic disease occurred in many parts of the world during and after World War I (1914-1918). The name *encephalitis lethargica* means *an inflammation of the brain that causes lethargy*, or sleepiness. Some investigators believe that a filterable virus may cause the disease. Researchers during the 1940's and 1950's discovered a large number of insect-transmitted viruses that cause encephalitis in men and animals. The diseases produced by these organisms, however, do not resemble those seen in the early 1920's. Therefore, the cause of encephalitis lethargica is still a scientific mystery.   THOMAS H. WELLER

**SLEEPLESSNESS.** See INSOMNIA.

**SLEEPWALKING,** or SOMNAMBULISM, is a condition in which a person carries out physical actions while he is asleep. Everybody dreams during sleep. But few persons act out their dreams in real physical motion. Some sleepwalkers, or somnambulists, simply get out of bed and walk around. Other somnambulists perform many more difficult acts.

Tests have shown that most sleepwalkers cannot hear ordinary sounds. The somnambulist cannot see, taste, or smell. But generally he has excellent control over his muscles. Many sleepwalkers have performed acts which they could not do if they were awake. Upon awakening, sleepwalkers may remember what they have done, but they remember it only as a dream.

Psychologists describe somnambulism as an extreme form of absent-mindedness. Something in the subconscious mind forces the sleepwalker to follow a single line of action. Many psychologists believe that sleepwalkers have really hypnotized themselves.

Sleepwalkers usually are nervous persons. Sleepwalking is fairly common in childhood, but tends to disappear as children grow older. Good health care and the avoidance of strain and excitement help many cases of somnambulism. It is not harmful to awaken a sleepwalker abruptly.   NATHANIEL KLEITMAN

**SLEET** consists of round, hard balls of ice about the size of raindrops. Sleet usually occurs with showery conditions in unstable air. It is formed in the upper air when droplets of *supercooled* water, water cooled below the 32° F. freezing point, come in contact with small ice crystals or snowflakes. The mixture of supercooled water and ice freezes almost instantly. Each little pellet may grow still larger if it comes in contact with another supercooled water drop. If a sleet particle falls through

418

a layer of warm air, it may melt and form raindrops.

Sleet pellets rebound when they strike hard surfaces. Sleet and hail are formed in much the same way. But sleet occurs only in winter, because sleet particles are so small they quickly melt in warm weather. Hailstones, which fall mostly in the spring and summer, may last a fairly long time. GEORGE F. TAYLOR

See also HAIL.

**SLEIGH.** See SLED.

**SLEIGHT OF HAND.** See MAGIC; TRICKS AND PUZZLES.

**SLICK, SAM.** See CANADIAN LITERATURE (The Early 1800's).

**SLIDE.** See BACTERIOLOGY (Studying Bacteria); MICROTOMY.

**SLIDE,** in photography. See PHOTOGRAPHY (Color [Color Film]).

**SLIDE RULE** is a device used for rapid numerical calculations that involve mainly multiplication and division. It is usually in the form of a ruler. Circular slide rules, with a movable disk attached, are also used. They operate on the same principle. Basically, a slide rule is an addition or subtraction device. For example, arrange two equally divided rulers with the zero of the lower

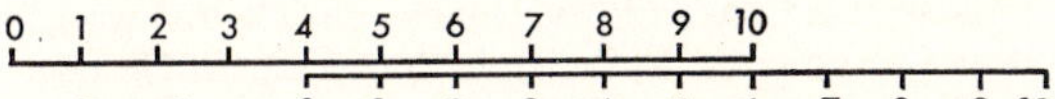

Figure 1

scale below, say, 4 of the upper (as in Figure 1). The numbers on the upper scale are 4 larger than those on the lower. These scales can be used for addition or subtraction simply by sliding the lower scale to different positions.

To use rulers for multiplying numbers, logarithmic scales are used (see LOGARITHMS). Mark off the logarithms of numbers and label the marks with the num-

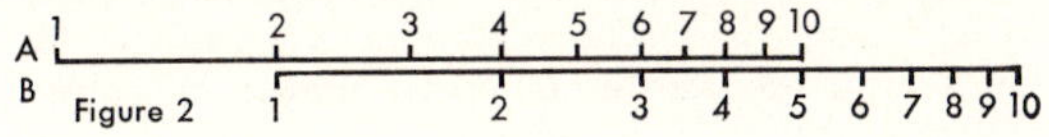

Figure 2

bers. Figure 2 shows two such scales. Every number on the A scale is twice the number on the B scale immediately below it. If 1 on the B scale had been placed under 3 on the A scale, the multiplier would have been 3. Also in the figure, every number of the A scale divided by the number below it on the B scale gives 2, which illustrates how these scales are used for division. In its perfected form, a slide rule consists of a ruler with a sliding middle section. Both ruler and the slide have similar logarithmic scales printed on their corresponding edges. A runner or indicator made of transparent material, with a vertical line down the middle, is used to fix coinciding points on the scales. The slide rule in everyday use solves problems that involve multiplying, dividing, squaring, cubing, and extracting square and cube root. Some slide rules have additional scales for working out more complicated operations or problems. T. H. HILDEBRANDT

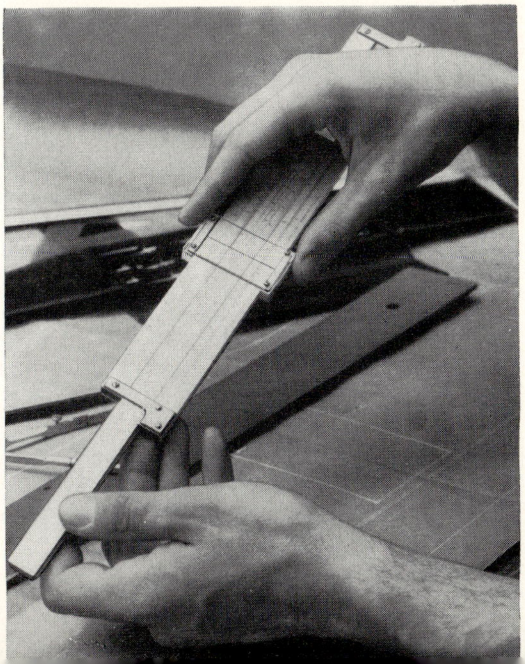

**SLIDELL, JOHN.** See MASON AND SLIDELL.

**SLIME MOLD** is a tiny plant of simple structure. It usually grows on decaying wood, and moist soil which contains a large amount of humus. Some slime molds live as parasites on cultivated plants. They cause clubroot of cabbage and powdery scab of potato.

Slime molds have been classed as both animals and plants. In some respects, they resemble tiny animals. The spores are distributed by the wind. Then they germinate and form a simple cell with a single, hairlike attachment called the *flagellum*. With this attachment, the organism swims about. Later it loses the attachment and several cells unite in a jellylike mass which has the power of slow, creeping movement. This mass, called the *plasmodium*, is sometimes a foot wide. This forms the vegetable body of slime molds. Finally, the plasmodium develops into masses of moldlike spores which have many forms. The masses are often found on stumps and bark, varying in color from white to orange and red. The masses may grow to several inches square.

**Scientific Classification.** Slime molds make up the plant phylum *Myxomycophyta*. They are also sometimes classed as the order *Mycetozoa* in the animal phylum *Protozoa.* WILLIAM F. HANNA

**SLING** is one of the most ancient weapons. It was probably the first weapon designed to hurl a stone with more force than a man could deliver with his hand and arm. In its oldest form, the sling is a leather or hide strap, with a string fastened to each end. A stone or other object is placed on the strap, and the operator holds the two cords in his hand. He whirls the sling above his head, and then lets go of one end of the cord to hurl the stone. Slings are mentioned many times in the Bible. A most familiar reference is to the slaying of Goliath by David with a stone (I Sam. 17:49-50).

The ancient people of the Balearic Islands became famous for their skill with the sling. The sling was of great use to the armies of Egypt, Greece, and Rome. During the Middle Ages, soldiers used slings attached to a staff. They hurled big stones against fortifications.

In America, a small hand catapult is called a *slingshot*, or *sling*. It is made by fastening an elastic band on each prong of a forked stick, and connecting the elastics by a leather pouch. The pouch holds a stone or small metal bullet. The fork is held in one hand, and the elastic is stretched with the other hand. The thumb and first finger hold the stone or bullet in place. The shot is hurled with great force when the elastic is released. Such

**The Slide Rule** makes it possible for the draftsman to make mathematical calculations easily and rapidly.
H. Armstrong Roberts

419

# SLIP

SOME TYPES OF SLINGS
Roman Sling
Modern Slingshot
South American Bola

slings also can cause serious injury. Most cities forbid the use of slingshots.

*Bolas* are weapons used on the pampas of many South American countries and by the Eskimos. Bolas are made of stone or balls of clay, fastened to the ends of lengths of rope or cowhide. The free ends are tied or braided together and used as a handle. The thrower hurls it at a running animal or flying bird. The stones or balls wind the ropes around the animal's legs and throw it to the ground.  JACK O'CONNOR

**SLIP.** See PORCELAIN (The Making of Chinaware); POTTERY (Making Pottery; pictures: How Pottery Is Made).

**SLIPPERWORT** is the name of several evergreen plants whose blossoms are shaped somewhat like slippers. They are native to tropical America, but several are grown in hothouses and gardens in temperate parts of North America. Slipperworts have many flowers. Popular species include the *common* slipperwort, with spotted yellow flowers, the *bush* slipperwort, which has small yellow flowers, and the *violet-flowered* slipperwort.

**Scientific Classification.** Slipperworts belong to the figwort family, *Scrophulariaceae*. The common slipperwort is genus *Calceolaria*, species *C. crenatiflora*. The bush slipperwort is *C. integrifolia*. The violet-flowered slipperwort is *C. purpurea*.  PAUL C. STANDLEY

**SLIPPERY ROCK STATE COLLEGE.** See UNIVERSITIES AND COLLEGES (table).

**SLIVER.** See SPINNING.

**SLOAN, ALFRED PRITCHARD, JR.** (1875-1966), an American industrialist, pioneered the development of roller bearings for automobiles. He was president and general manager of the Hyatt Roller Bearing Company from 1901 to 1916. After serving as president of General Motors Corporation for 14 years, he became chairman of its board of directors in 1937. He retired in 1956. He also served on the board of directors of several other companies. Sloan was born in New Haven, Conn., on May 23, 1875.  V. E. CANGELOSI and R. E. WESTMEYER

**SLOAN, JOHN** (1871-1951), was an American artist. In 1907, Sloan, Robert Henri, and others formed an informal association of painters called *The Eight* (later the *Ashcan School*). In his paintings, etchings, and illustrations, Sloan honestly and sympathetically portrayed scenes from everyday life. In this way, he came closest to the artistic philosophy of *The Eight*.

Sloan was born in Lock Haven, Pa. He first worked as an illustrator for Philadelphia newspapers. He never traveled abroad, but Henri introduced him to the works of the Europeans Frans Hals, Edouard Manet, and Diego Velázquez. These painters became major influences on Sloan's style. Sloan's favorite subjects include city streets, tenements, cafes, and barrooms. His painting *South Beach Bathers* appears in color in the article UNITED STATES (Art and Architecture).  E. MAURICE BLOCH

**SLOAN FOUNDATION, ALFRED P.,** is a trust fund established in 1934 by Alfred P. Sloan, Jr., with an original gift of $500,000. The foundation makes grants to universities and other nonprofit organizations. Its funds support scholarship programs in about 35 colleges and universities. It emphasizes support to education and research projects in mathematics, engineering, science, economics, industrial management, and cancer. It has offices at 630 Fifth Ave., New York, N.Y. 10020. For its assets, see FOUNDATIONS (table).

Critically reviewed by the ALFRED P. SLOAN FOUNDATION

**Blossoms of the Common Slipperwort**
J. Horace McFarland

420

**SLOANE, SIR HANS** (1660-1753), was a British physician and botanist. His private collections and library provided the beginning of the British Museum. Throughout his life, he collected plants. The plants he gathered in Jamaica in 1687 and 1688 were the first brought to England from the West Indies. He succeeded Sir Isaac Newton as president of the Royal Society of London. Sloane became a baronet in 1716, the first medical man to receive a hereditary title. He was born in Ireland on April 16, 1660.　　　　　LORUS J. MILNE and MARGERY MILNE

**SLOBODKIN,** *sloh BAHD kin,* **LOUIS** (1903-　　), is an American sculptor and author-illustrator of children's books. He received the Caldecott medal in 1944 for his illustrations for James Thurber's book *Many Moons.* The first children's books he wrote and illustrated were *Friendly Animals* (1944) and *Magic Michael* (1944). Others include *Bixxy and the Secret Message* (1949) and *Amiable Giant* (1955). His sculpture decorates many public buildings. He wrote *Sculpture: Principles and Practice* (1949). He was born in Albany, N.Y.　RUTH HILL VIGUERS

**SLOE,** *sloh,* is the name of a spiny, branching shrub related to the plum. It grows in Europe, Central Asia, and the mountains of North America. It has white blossoms which appear before the leaves do. Small black fruits about the size of a pea develop from the flowers. People use these fruits to make wine, jelly, preserves, and dyes. The branches of the shrub are used to make canes and tool handles. Sloe is also called *blackthorn.*

**Scientific Classification.** The sloe is in the rose family, *Rosaceae.* It is genus *Prunus,* species *P. spinosa.*　J. J. LEVISON

**SLOOP.** See SAILING (Kinds of Sailboats).
**SLOPE MINE.** See COAL (Mining Methods).
**SLOT CAR RACING.** See AUTOMOBILE MODEL (picture).

**SLOT MACHINE** is a gambling device that has been outlawed in many states. It is sometimes called the *one-armed bandit.* A player drops a coin into a slot and pulls a lever on the side of the machine. This causes a group of reels to spin. When the reels stop, various combinations show in a small window. The combinations determine if a player wins, or loses his coin. A machine pays a maximum of 20 coins, plus the *jackpot* (all the money showing through another window in the machine). Jackpots are rare, and the player loses more often than he wins. Charles Fey of San Francisco invented the slot machine in 1895.

A pinball machine is an amusement device similar to the slot machine. A player inserts a coin into the machine and operates a plunger. The plunger propels a metal ball onto an inclined playing surface that is studded with holes, nails, and electrical devices. In one kind of pinball game, the player tries to guide the ball against the posts and into the holes.　JOHN SCARNE

**SLOT MINING.** See DIAMOND (Where Diamonds Are Found).

**SLOTH,** *slohth,* or *slawth,* is the common name of a family of South American animals which have a slow and peculiar way of moving about. When moving in the trees, they walk upside down, hanging from branches. Sloths can hang so securely from the branches with their hooklike claws that they even fall asleep in this position. A sloth may even stay suspended in the trees for some time after it dies.

These strange animals have an odd appearance. They have almost no tails or ears, and their noses are blunt.

# SLOTH BEAR

Dr. Bernhard Grzimek, from Publix

**Sloths Use Claws to Walk Upside Down on Branches.**

They have well-developed peglike teeth. Their hair is long and coarse. In some species, it is grayish in color, which makes them hard to see among the branches. A sloth asleep looks much like the stump of a bough, especially when it has a growth of green algae on the hair, as many sloths do. Sloths seldom come down to the ground. They feed on leaves, buds, and young twigs. They sleep by day and usually move about slowly.

People use the expression "slothful" to describe lazy people. Scientists say that the sloth's sluggishness is, at least partly, caused by its extremely low body temperature. It moves about one-third of a mile an hour, when it moves at all. Scientists have discovered that the sloth's speed increases 50 per cent when its temperature is raised 5 or 6 degrees.

There are two main species. One, called the *Unau,* has two toes on the front feet. The other, called the *Ai,* has three toes on the front feet.

**Scientific Classification.** The sloth makes up the sloth family, *Bradypodidae.* The common two-toed sloth is genus *Choloepus,* species *C. didactylus.* The common three-toed sloth is *Bradypus tridactylus.*　FRANK B. GOLLEY

See also ANIMAL (color picture: Animals of the Tropical Forests); GROUND SLOTH.

**SLOTH BEAR** is a big, shaggy animal with a mane of fur around its neck and shoulders. It is also called a *honey bear* because honey is one of its favorite foods. Sloth bears live in the rocky canyons and hills of India and Ceylon. They have a short temper, and can be dangerous when approached.

The sloth bear is about 5 feet long and weighs up to 250 pounds. It has long black fur with a light-colored U-, V-, or Y-shaped patch on the chest. Its face is gray and almost hairless.

Sloth bears usually eat *termites* (white ants) and the *larvae* (grubs) of bees. They also eat flowers, leaves, fruits, and grain. They will climb anywhere to get at nests of termites or bees. They use their big feet and long claws to rip open termite nests and to open tree trunks and branches that hold honeycombs. At a termite nest, they blow away the dust and expose the termites. Then they draw the termites into their mouths with loud sucking noises. The sloth bear's lips, tongue, and teeth are well suited to its feeding habits. It has a long snout, flexible lips, and a long sticky tongue.

421

Ylla, Rapho-Guillumette
**Sloth Bear Cubs** grow up to be champion climbers. Sloth bears climb tall trees in India and Ceylon in search of food. Their food includes termites and the *larvae* (grubs) of bees.

**Slovakia Lies North of Hungary.**

Sloth bears hunt for food at night. During the day they sleep in protected places, usually in caves along river banks. They do not sleep for long periods in the winter as some other bears do.

Most female sloth bears give birth to one or two *cubs* (young bears) at a time. The cubs often ride around on their mother's back.

**Scientific Classification.** Sloth bears belong to the bear family, *Ursidae*. They make up the genus *Melursus*, and are species *M. ursinus*. CHARLES M. KIRKPATRICK

**SLOVAK,** *SLO vak*, is the name given about 4 million people living in Czechoslovakia. They are Slavs. The Slovaks look somewhat like the Czechs, but most of them look more like eastern Slavs than like the people of Bohemia. The Slovaks are shorter and smaller-headed than the Czechs. Most Slovaks have snub noses, broad faces, and blond hair.

Early Slovakia, Moravia, and Bohemia made up a mighty kingdom until the death of King Svatopluk in A.D. 894. Then the Slovaks came under the rule of the Magyars of Hungary. The Magyars abused and mistreated the Slovaks, but the Slovaks managed to keep their spirit alive.

In 1867, the new government of Austria-Hungary passed laws to protect all nationalities. But the government did not enforce the laws, and the Slovaks continued to suffer. After World War I, the Slovaks and Czechs formed Czechoslovakia. In 1939, the Nazis destroyed the republic. But, after World War II, the Slovaks and Czechs reunited. WILTON MARION KROGMAN

See also CZECHOSLOVAKIA (The People); SLAV.

**SLOVAKIA,** *sloh VAH kih uh*, is a territory which makes up the eastern part of Czechoslovakia. It is called SLOVENSKO in the Slovak language. For almost a thousand years, Slovakia suffered under the harsh rule of the Magyars of Hungary. In 1918, the Slovaks united with the Czechs to form the independent republic of Czechoslovakia. In 1939, Slovakia became an "independent" state under German domination. Much Slovak territory was transferred to Hungary. After World War II, Slovakia again became part of Czechoslovakia, and the land lost to Hungary was recovered. Until recently, Slovakia had a largely agricultural economy. But the Communist government has built many factories in the area, and the economy has become more industrialized. See CZECHOSLOVAKIA (color map).

Slovakia covers an area of 18,918 square miles, and has a population of about 4,175,000. Bratislava was the capital of the state of Slovakia. S. HARRISON THOMSON

See also BRATISLAVA; CZECHOSLOVAKIA.

**SLOVENIA.** See YUGOSLAVIA.

**SLOW-MOTION PICTURE.** See MOTION PICTURE (Camera).

**SLOWWORM.** See BLINDWORM.

**SLUG** is a kind of snail. Most snails have a shell on the outside of their bodies. Some slugs have a small, flat shell under the skin, but most of them have no shell at all. The slug has two pairs of *tentacles* (feelers) with eyes on the outer end of the longer pair. The great gray slug is a pest because it has a huge appetite and eats plants. It is about 4 inches long.

**Scientific Classification.** Slugs are in the slug family, *Limacidae*. The great gray slug is genus *Limax*, species *L. maximus*. R. TUCKER ABBOTT

See also SNAIL.

**The Slug Leaves a Wake of Slime** when it crawls. This slime comes out of its body to lubricate sliding and to protect its underparts. If a razor blade were placed edge up in a slug's path, the slime would allow the slug to crawl over it unhurt.

L. W. Brownell

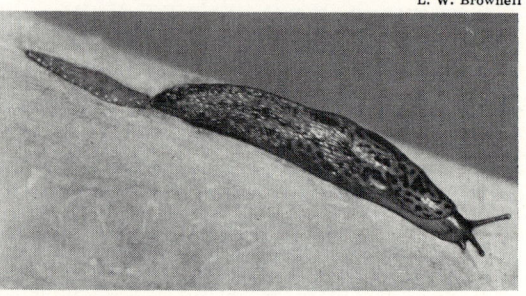

422

**SLUM.** See BLIGHTED AREA; CITY (Slums); POVERTY.

**SLURRY.** See CEMENT AND CONCRETE (Crushing and Grinding).

**SMALL BUSINESS ADMINISTRATION,** a U.S. government agency, assists and protects the interests of small businesses. It insures that small businesses receive a fair share of government purchases and contracts. It also makes loans to small business concerns and to victims of catastrophes. It was established in 1953.

**SMALL GAME.** See BIG GAME.

**SMALLPOX** is one of the most contagious of known diseases. It attacks persons of all ages. In severe epidemics, 30 of 100 persons attacked may die, while in mild epidemics the death rate may be less than 1 in 100. For hundreds of years, smallpox killed many people every year, and scarred others for life. Now it can be prevented almost entirely by vaccination. Because an outsider may introduce smallpox into a community, all visitors to the United States must be vaccinated.

Smallpox is caused by a small germ, of the group known as *filtrable viruses*. Like many other diseases, smallpox probably is carried by the tiny droplets that are shot out into the air in coughing, sneezing, and even talking. These germ-carrying droplets from an infected person find their way to the mucous lining of the nose and throat of another person. From there, they invade the rest of the body. The germ also is present in skin eruptions. Transmission may take place indirectly through clothing, bedclothes, and utensils.

**Smallpox Symptoms.** The smallpox *incubation period* (time when germs develop) is usually 7 to 12 days. The first symptoms often are chills, headache, backache, nausea, vomiting, and fever. Red spots appear on the skin about three or four days after the disease begins. These spots become raised, and in a few days change to blisters that fill with pus. They reach their largest size on about the 14th day. The spots usually appear first on the face and arms, then on the trunk and legs. The location of these spots helps physicians tell smallpox from similar diseases. If necessary, laboratory tests may be used for diagnosis. If the patient lives, the blisters dry up, the fever drops, and improvement begins. Scabs are formed which eventually drop off. They leave red or brown discolorations underneath. If the skin eruption was severe, pockmarks may always remain in the skin.

**Preventing Smallpox.** Edward Jenner, an English physician who developed vaccination in 1796, used cowpox germs as a method of preventing smallpox. People had tried inoculation with smallpox germs before, but until then it was not safe or dependable.

There is no specific cure for smallpox. The only sure way to combat smallpox is vaccination, combined with quarantine of infected persons. When the disease occurs, the sick person should be isolated and all articles of clothing and eating utensils should be sterilized.

Smallpox may attack a person who has been vaccinated more than five years previous to exposure. A single vaccination usually protects for some years, and limits the severity of infection. But doctors today usually vaccinate all children when they are only a few months old, and then every five years. AUSTIN EDWARD SMITH

See also DISEASE (table); FINSEN, NIELS RYBERG; JENNER, EDWARD; VACCINATION; VIRUS.

**SMALLS, ROBERT** (1839-1915), was a Negro American who became a Union hero during the Civil War

# SMELL

(1861-1865). He later had a successful political career.

Smalls was born into slavery in Beaufort, S.C. He became an expert pilot on boats in and around Charleston (S.C.) Harbor. The outbreak of the Civil War gave him the chance to win his freedom. In 1861, the Confederacy forced Smalls to pilot the *Planter*, a messenger and transport steamer. In 1862, Smalls guided the ship out of Charleston Harbor and delivered it to Union officials. After this daring act, he piloted the *Planter* for the Union. Smalls served in the South Carolina legislature from 1868 to 1875, and in the U.S. House of Representatives from 1875 to 1879 and from 1882 to 1887. RICHARD BARDOLPH

**SMALT.** See COBALT (Uses).

**SMARTWEED** is an annual plant that grows as a weed in North America. Its flowers are pink or greenish and it may grow 5 feet high. It grows in low places and sometimes in water. The *lady's-thumb* is one of the most common smartweeds.

*Scientific Classification.* Smartweeds belong to the buckwheat family, *Polygonaceae*. They make up the genus *Polygonum*. Lady's-thumb is *P. persicaria*. EARL L. CORE

**SMELL** is one of the most important senses in man and animals. However, it is less important in man than in some animals. Like sight and hearing, smell gives information about the surroundings. Many lower animals probably get most sensory information through smell. The scientific term for smell is *olfaction*.

**How Smells Are Produced.** Smells are caused by tiny particles in the air called *molecules*. They exist in the form of gases and vapors. These molecules spread rapidly, and can be carried long distances. Man and animals that breathe in air have their organs of smell in the lining of the nose.

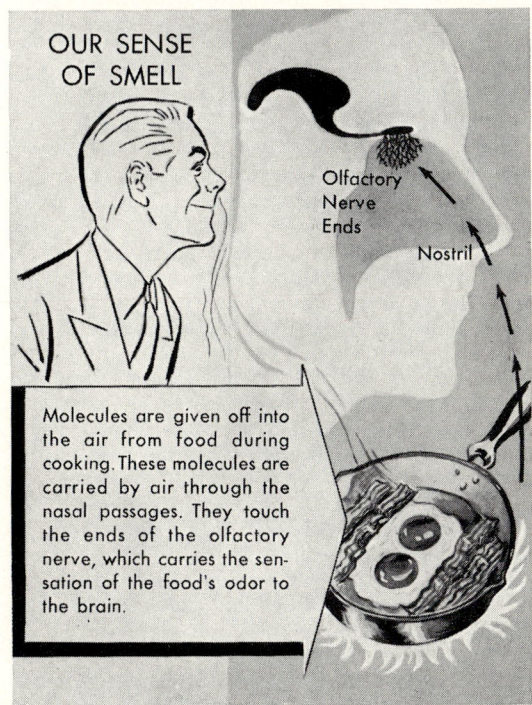

OUR SENSE OF SMELL

Olfactory Nerve Ends

Nostril

Molecules are given off into the air from food during cooking. These molecules are carried by air through the nasal passages. They touch the ends of the olfactory nerve, which carries the sensation of the food's odor to the brain.

423

# SMELLING SALTS

Some fishes and other water animals have olfactory organs, but they are often more like the organs of taste. Insects have their olfactory organs in their antennae.

In man, the olfactory organs are at the top of the nasal cavity. They take up about 2.5 square centimeters in each nostril. Liquid from the lining of the nose keeps the organs damp, and the vapors dissolve in this liquid. The chemicals of the solution then stimulate the organs. The olfactory organs themselves are nerve cells that end in hairlike cilia at the surface of the mucous membrane. These cells lead to the olfactory nerves, which end on each side in an olfactory bulb. The bulb forms the front part of one of the olfactory lobes of the brain. The olfactory lobes are in the front of the brain on each side of the central cleft. They take up much more of the brain in animals than in man.

Many tastes are really blends of tastes and smells. If a person holds his nose, he may find it difficult to tell the difference between a piece of onion and a piece of apple. Scientists have also found that some smells consist largely of feelings, since the lower part of the nasal lining has organs of feeling. For example, a camphor smell is partly a feeling of cold, and the sharp odor of ammonia or chlorine is partly a feeling of pain.

**Kinds of Smells.** Scientists are not sure how to classify the different smells. They usually name the odor by the object it comes from, such as an odor of rose or tar. One such classification includes the following: spicy (clove, cinnamon), flowery (heliotrope, vanilla), fruity (orange oil, ether), resinous (pine needles), putrid (decay, hydrogen sulfide), and burnt (tar). Other odors can usually be fitted between some two of these six. For example, roasted coffee is placed between resinous and burnt. Other scientists have found that organic substances of similar chemical make-up have similar smells.

While smell is not the most highly developed sense in man, it is very sensitive. The organs can react to some vapors when there is only one part in one million parts of air. Artificial musk can be smelled when there are only .00004 milligrams per liter of air. The organs of smell easily become tired, and grow insensitive to a smell after being with it a few minutes. But they are sensitive to a new smell. There also are *complementary* smells that cancel each other. Gardenia acts this way against orange blossom. G. W. BEADLE

See also DOG (Nose); INSECT (Smell); NOSE; TASTE.

**SMELLING SALTS** are used to relieve faintness and headaches. They are made up of ammonium carbonate mixed with perfume. This drug is known as a stimulant.

The ammonia fumes from the salts irritate the membranes of the nose. They also cause the muscles controlling breathing to work faster. AUSTIN EDWARD SMITH

See also AMMONIA.

**SMELT** is a family of fishes much like the salmon, but smelts are smaller and have larger scales. Their stomachs also are different from those of the salmon. All smelts live in the cool waters of the Northern Hemisphere. Although they are salt-water fish, some species swim up rivers to spawn. A few stay permanently in fresh water.

The common *American smelt* swims along the Atlantic Coast between the Gulf of Saint Lawrence and New York. Fishermen trap them in several northern lakes. Men have brought these fish to the Great Lakes, where they have thrived. They are also found in the Pacific Ocean. Smelts enter the streams and rivers to spawn in spring, and can be caught easily with hooks or nets.

The upper part of the smelt's body is a transparent greenish color, and its sides are silvery. The average length of the fish is 8 to 10 inches. Some smelts have been caught that are over a foot long and weigh about a pound.

Smelts are valuable food fish, and large numbers are marketed as frozen fish. The unfrozen, or "green," fish are considered a delicacy.

**Scientific Classification.** The American smelt is in the smelt family, *Osmeridae*. It is classified as genus *Osmerus*, species *mordax*. CARL L. HUBBS

See also CANDLEFISH.

**The Smelt** lives on crustaceans, insects, and smaller fishes. The female often lays her eggs on the gravel bottoms of river beds.
State of Calif. Dept. of Fish and Game

**SMELTING** is a method by which metals are taken from their original ore. Smelting is done in specially built furnaces. The blast furnace for making pig iron is as tall as a 10-story building. It operates continuously, day and night. Iron ore, coke, and limestone are fed through the top of the furnace. Hot blast (preheated air) is delivered at the bottom. This burns the coke and generates the gases and heat required to reduce iron from its oxide minerals in the ore, and to melt limestone and unwanted materials in the ore to form *slag*. Molten slag and iron are removed through bottom openings. Furnace gas is removed at the top.

Another type of smelter is the *reverberatory* furnace, which refines copper. In this smelter, the copper sinks to the bottom in a form called *matte*, which contains iron sulfide and sometimes small amounts of other metals. The matte is refined to get copper. GEORGE S. ROSE

See also METALLURGY; BLAST FURNACE; FLUX; IRON AND STEEL (How Iron Is Made); SLAG.

**SMETANA,** *SMEH tah nah,* **BEDŘICH** (1824-1884), was a leading composer of Bohemia. He tried to produce a Bohemian (Czech) national music based on folk songs and folk dances. He expressed his tendency most clearly in *The Bartered Bride* (1866), one of the greatest of all comic operas. His other operas include *Two Widows* (1873), *The Kiss* (1875-1876), and *The Secret* (1877-1878). Smetana also composed symphonies. His cycle of six symphonic poems called *My Country* ranks foremost among his orchestral works. *My Country* contains one of Smetana's best-known works, *The Moldau*.

Smetana was born in Litomyšl, Bohemia. He conducted the Göteborg, Sweden, orchestra from 1856 to 1861, and became conductor of the National Theater in Prague in 1866. He resigned the position in 1874 when he suddenly became deaf. He soon suffered a mental breakdown and was committed to an asylum, where he died. HANS ROSENWALD

**SMILAX,** *SMI lacks,* is a group of woody or herbaceous vines with hardy, tuberous roots and veined evergreen leaves. The stems end in tendrils by which the plants climb. The vines grow in temperate and tropical climates, and bear small clusters of red, blue, or black berries. A well-known American species is the *common greenbrier.* Some species yield *sarsaparilla,* and others have stems that can be worked into baskets. In the South, the roots are sometimes used to make beer and to fatten hogs. See also GREENBRIER.

**Scientific Classification.** Smilax belongs to the lily family, *Liliaceae.* The common greenbrier is genus *Smilax,* species *S. rotundifolia.* J. J. LEVISON

**Smilax Plants Have Clusters of Small Berries.**
J. Horace McFarland

**SMILODON.** See PREHISTORIC ANIMAL (The Age of Mammals; color picture).

**SMITH, ADAM** (1723-1790), is generally regarded as the founder of modern economics. Smith's major book was *The Wealth of Nations* (full title *An Inquiry into the Nature and Cause of the Wealth of Nations*). Published in 1776, it was the first complete work on political economy. The book discusses the relationship between freedom and order, analyzes economic processes, and attacks the British mercantile system's limits on free trade (see MERCANTILISM). All three aspects are woven together to create a unified social theory.

The book dealt with the basic problem of how social order and human progress can be possible in a society where individuals follow their own self-interests. Smith argued that this individualism led to order and progress. In order to make money, people produce things that other people are willing to buy. Buyers spend money for those things that they need or want most. When buyers and sellers meet in the market, a pattern of production develops that results in social harmony. Smith said all this would happen without any conscious control or direction, "as if by an invisible hand."

## SMITH, ALFRED EMANUEL

Smith also believed that labor—not land or money—was both the source and the final measure of value. He said that wages depended on the basic needs of workers, and rent on the productivity of land. Profits, he said, were the difference between selling prices and the cost of labor and rent. Smith said profits would be used to expand production. This expansion would in turn create more jobs, and the national income would grow.

Smith believed that free trade and a self-regulating economy would result in social progress. He criticized the British government's tariffs and other limits on individual freedom in trade. He preached that government need only preserve law and order, enforce justice, defend the nation, and provide for a few social needs that could not be met through the market. Smith's argument for a "hands off" government policy toward business and his analysis of economic forces laid down the basic ideas of *economic liberalism.* See LIBERALISM; FREE ENTERPRISE SYSTEM.

Smith was born in Kirkcaldy, Scotland. He studied at the University of Glasgow and Oxford University. In 1751, he became a professor at Glasgow. While there, he became a close friend of Scottish philosopher David Hume (see HUME, DAVID). He wrote *The Theory of Moral Sentiment* (1759) there. This philosophical work gained Smith an appointment in 1764 as tutor of the young duke of Buccleuch. The tutoring took Smith to France, where he started writing *The Wealth of Nations.* When Smith returned to England in 1766, the duke's stepfather provided Smith with a regular income. The money enabled Smith to retire from teaching and devote the next 10 years to writing. *The Wealth of Nations* went through five editions during Smith's lifetime. But it had little major influence on economic policy until the beginning of the 1800's. DANIEL R. FUSFELD

**SMITH, ALFRED EMANUEL** (1873-1944), was an American political leader. He was elected governor of New York four times, and in 1928 was an unsuccessful candidate for President of the United States.

Smith became active in politics at the age of 22. He worked his way up in the Tammany Hall machine to become one of the leaders of the Democratic party. He was elected to the state legislature in 1903, and became governor of New York in 1919.

Smith failed to win the Democratic party's nomination for President in 1924. But four years later he won the nomination with the help of his friend and associate, Franklin D. Roosevelt. The *Happy Warrior,* as Roosevelt called him, lost the election to Herbert Hoover (see HOOVER, HERBERT CLARK [Election of 1928]). Some people opposed Smith because he was a Roman Catholic and because he opposed prohibition. At the start of the depression of the 1930's, Smith supported federal spending. Later, he broke with Roosevelt, and be-

**Alfred E. Smith**
Wide World

425

## SMITH, BESSIE

came critical of New Deal policies (see NEW DEAL).

Smith was born in New York City. He left school at the age of 12, and worked first as a newsboy. Later he worked seven years in the Fulton Fish Market of New York City. GEORGE M. WALLER

**SMITH, BESSIE** (1894-1937), became one of the finest blues singers in the history of jazz. A series of recordings she made from 1923 to 1933 rank among the best in jazz. In them, she applied the strength and beauty of her voice to simple songs. Louis Armstrong, Fletcher Henderson, Joe Smith, and James P. Johnson were among the jazz musicians who played on her records.

Bessie Smith was born in Chattanooga, Tenn., into extreme poverty. She left home when she was a teen-ager to tour with a minstrel show. A recording director discovered her and brought her to New York City. The Negro public bought millions of her records during the years of her greatest fame from 1923 to 1928. Her work was almost unknown to white audiences until shortly before her death. Miss Smith died of injuries suffered in an automobile accident in Mississippi. LEONARD FEATHER

**SMITH, DAVID** (1906-1965), was an American sculptor who worked with metals in many forms. His most typical works are muscular metaphors resembling hieroglyphics in wrought iron. His work has influenced sculptors who create their work out of junk materials. His sculpture *Cubi XIX* appears in the SCULPTURE article.

Smith was born in Decatur, Ind. While working on a Studebaker automobile plant assembly line, he learned the metal techniques he used in his later work. In 1926, Smith went to New York City to study at the Art Students League. He began to create welded iron works after seeing Picasso's welded sculpture and the forged iron constructions of Julio González of Spain in the early 1930's. DOUGLAS GEORGE

**SMITH, DONALD ALEXANDER.** See STRATHCONA AND MOUNT ROYAL, BARON OF.

**SMITH, EDMUND KIRBY.** See KIRBY-SMITH, EDMUND.

**SMITH, FRANCIS HOPKINSON** (1838-1915), gained fame in his chosen profession of engineering. But he also became well-known for his hobbies of painting and writing. As an engineer, he built the foundation for the Statue of Liberty. He also built the sea walls around Governors Island, N.Y., and Tompkinsville, Staten Island, N.Y., and constructed the Race Rock Lighthouse off New London, Conn.

Smith won many medals as an artist for his water-color landscapes and charcoal drawings. He also lectured extensively on art. Smith wrote some 30 novels and books of short stories. His books include *Colonel Carter of Cartersville* (1891), *Gentleman Vagabond and Some Others* (1895), and *The Fortunes of Oliver Horn* (1902).

Smith was born in Baltimore, Md. He learned civil engineering working in foundries. ROBERT W. ABBETT

**SMITH, FREDERICK M.** See LATTER DAY SAINTS, REORGANIZED CHURCH OF JESUS CHRIST OF.

**SMITH, HOLLAND MCTYEIRE** (1882-1967), a general in the United States Marine Corps, commanded some of the most hard-fought Pacific campaigns during World War II. He led the landings on Makin and Tarawa atolls and on Kwajalein. In July, 1944, he became commander of the Fleet Marine Force and directed the battles for Saipan and Iwo Jima (see WORLD WAR II [Saipan; Iwo Jima]). His toughness in combat earned him the nickname of *Howlin' Mad*. An expert on amphibious warfare, Smith helped design many of the landing craft used in the war. In 1940 and 1941, he established a training program in ship-to-shore warfare that both the marines and the army used. Smith was born in Seale, Ala. He retired from military service in 1946. DONALD W. MITCHELL

**SMITH, IAN DOUGLAS** (1919-    ), became prime minister of Rhodesia in 1964. He sought independence from Great Britain under a constitution that would allow Rhodesia's white minority to govern the African majority indefinitely. Britain refused to grant independence on these terms, and Smith declared Rhodesia independent without Britain's consent on Nov. 11, 1965 (see RHODESIA).

Born in Selukwe, Rhodesia, Smith graduated from South Africa's Rhodes University. He was a member of Southern Rhodesia's parliament from 1948 to 1953, and of the Federation of Rhodesia and Nyasaland federal assembly from 1953 to 1961. Elected to the Rhodesian parliament in 1962, Smith was deputy prime minister and treasury minister until 1964. KENNETH KIRKWOOD

**SMITH, JAMES** (1719?-1806), was a Pennsylvania signer of the Declaration of Independence. He urged a boycott of British goods and a general congress of colonies when he was a delegate to a conference in Philadelphia in 1774. He helped draft a resolution for independence at the provincial conference in June, 1776. He served in the Continental Congress from 1776 to 1778 and as judge of the Pennsylvania High Court of Errors and Appeals in 1781. He was born in Ireland, and came to Pennsylvania as a boy. RICHARD B. MORRIS

**SMITH, JAMES, JR.** See WILSON, WOODROW (Governor of New Jersey).

**SMITH, JEDEDIAH STRONG** (1798-1831), was an American trader and explorer. As a young man, he entered the fur trade in the West. He set out in 1826 to find trade routes to California and the Northwest. From the Great Salt Lake, he crossed Ute and Paiute Indian territories, the Mojave Desert, and the High Sierras, until he reached Mission San Gabriel in California. But the Spaniards ordered him out. He started north to find a pass across the Sierra Nevada. While returning to California the next year, Indians killed 10 of his party. Smith escaped. In 1828, he led an expedition to Fort Vancouver (now Vancouver, Wash.), but an Indian attack along the way wiped out most of his party. Smith was born in Bainbridge, N.Y. He was killed by Indians on the Santa Fe Trail. RICHARD F. DEMPEWOLFF

**SMITH, JOHN** (1580-1631), was an English soldier and adventurer. He played a vital role in founding Virginia and New England (see VIRGINIA [History]).

Smith sailed in the squadron of three ships that established the first permanent English colony in America in 1607 at Jamestown, Va. He was accused of mutiny, but later was admitted to the ruling council. Largely because of his energy, the colony built up its defenses against hostile Indians and gathered enough corn from trading to survive the first desperate winter (see JAMESTOWN). Smith explored the nearby rivers and made a fine map that was used later to determine the boundaries of the colonies. According to a story Smith told, Indians captured him while he was on an expedi-

# SMITH, JOSEPH

**SMITH, JOSEPH** (1805-1844), was the founder and first president of the Mormon Church, officially called the CHURCH OF JESUS CHRIST OF LATTER-DAY SAINTS. Several other churches recognize him as their founder. The largest of these is the Reorganized Church of Jesus Christ of Latter Day Saints. Those who follow Smith's teachings regard Smith as a prophet of God.

**Early Life.** Smith was born in Sharon, Vt., on Dec. 23, 1805, the fourth of ten children. The Smiths met with hard times in Vermont. When Joseph was 11, his parents, Joseph and Lucy Mack Smith, moved the family to Manchester, N.Y., near Palmyra.

Young Joseph Smith was troubled by the counterclaims made by religious groups of his day. He could not decide which to join. In 1820, he went alone into the woods to seek God's guidance. According to his account, God the Father and His Son (Jesus Christ) appeared to him. They told him not to join any existing church and to prepare for important tasks.

Smith said the angel Moroni visited him in 1823, and told him he would receive gold plates on which he would find a book engraved in a strange language. Smith said he received the plates in 1827. His translation of the writings, called the *Book of Mormon*, was published in 1830. The book is a history of early peoples of the Western Hemisphere. Mormons and other followers of Joseph Smith believe the book was divinely inspired. They regard it as holy scripture.

**Organizing the Church.** On April 6, 1830, Smith and five associates founded the Church of Jesus Christ of Latter-day Saints at Fayette, N.Y., with Joseph Smith as its leader. Smith moved to Kirtland, Ohio, in 1831, and made many converts there. The Mormons also established communities in Mentor, Ohio, and Independence, Mo.

Smith instituted many of the church's present doctrines and its basic organization at Kirtland. He organized the *quorums* (groups) of the priesthood, which gave most male church members priestly authority. Later, in Missouri in 1838, he introduced *tithing* (giving one-tenth of one's income to the church).

In Kirtland, the church faced many problems. A bank established by the Mormons failed in 1837, a year of national economic depression. The bank failure, opposition from persons who had left the church, and conflict with non-Mormons led to the breakup of the Kirtland community. Smith joined the Mormons in Missouri in 1838. There, hostilities arose between Mormons and non-Mormons. Non-Mormons feared the increasing size of the Mormon community and opposed their antislavery beliefs. The hostilities led to the outbreak of an armed conflict. Smith led the Mormons in their effort to defend themselves. The outnumbered Mormons surrendered, and Smith was imprisoned on what the Mormons regard as false charges. He escaped a few months later and joined his people who had fled from Missouri to Illinois.

**Life at Nauvoo.** Joseph Smith and the Mormons founded the city of Nauvoo (*the plantation beautiful*) in Illinois. Nauvoo's population reached 20,000 in the early 1840's, making it the largest city in the state. By that time, Smith headed a church with thousands of members. He was mayor of Nauvoo, and a successful

Culver

**Captain John Smith** won the friendship of Pocahontas, the daughter of an Indian chief, after the Indians captured him.

tion, and condemned him to death. But Pocahontas, the daughter of an Indian chief, saved him (see POCAHONTAS; POWHATAN).

Smith became president of the colony in 1608. He forced his men to work to save themselves from starvation. Gravely wounded in a gunpowder accident and opposed by enemies within the colony, Smith sailed for England in 1609.

He returned to America in 1614 and explored and named New England. He described the region in his book, *A Description of New England*. Smith hoped to establish a permanent colony in Massachusetts Bay, but bad luck prevented him.

Smith was born in Willoughby, Lincolnshire. He attended grammar school and was apprenticed to a merchant. But his thirst for adventure sent him to The Netherlands to fight the Spaniards. He returned to England only long enough to master the art of military horsemanship, and then went to fight the Turks in Hungary. He was left for dead on a battlefield, and then taken as a slave to Turkey. He later escaped.

Smith spent his later years writing in London. He wrote about his exploits in *The True Travels, Adventures, and Observations of Captaine John Smith, in Europe, Asia, Africa, and America* (1630). These adventures, though once doubted, were confirmed by careful research. His principal work is *The Generall Historie of Virginia, New England and the Summer Isles* (1624). He is called *Admiral of New England* on the title page, but authority for the title never has been found. He was one of the first men to understand that a great nation would arise in North America. BRADFORD SMITH

**SMITH, JOHN,** British clergyman. See BAPTISTS.

**SMITH, JOHN MERLIN POWIS.** See BIBLE (Other Modern Versions).

427

Bettmann Archive

**Joseph Smith** claimed that the angel Moroni appeared to him in a vision and told him where to find the *Book of Mormon* plates.

businessman. He headed the *Nauvoo Legion*, a small army authorized by the state to protect the community. The rapid growth of the Mormon church had political significance. In 1844, the year he was killed, Joseph Smith declared himself a candidate for President of the United States to rally public opinion for their defense.

Smith instituted the doctrine of *polygamy* at Nauvoo in 1843. Polygamy is the practice of a man having more than one wife at the same time. Most non-Mormons and many Mormons disagreed with this practice. The church finally outlawed polygamy in 1890. Some members who did not agree with the doctrine of polygamy broke away in 1844. They set up a newspaper that criticized Smith. The paper was destroyed, and Smith was blamed for it. This caused a wave of hostility against him in Illinois. He and his brother Hyrum were jailed at Carthage, Ill., on charges of rioting and treason which the Mormons felt were false. A mob attacked the jail and killed the brothers on June 27, 1844. But the church continued to grow after Joseph Smith's death. Brigham Young led the main body of Mormons to present-day Utah, where they prospered.

In addition to the *Book of Mormon*, Smith wrote the *Pearl of Great Price* (1830, 1835) and *Doctrine and Covenants* (1835) based on his revelations. He wrote an autobiography in 1842.  MARK E. PETERSEN

See also MORMONS; LATTER DAY SAINTS, REORGANIZED CHURCH OF JESUS CHRIST OF; UTAH (History); BRIGHAM YOUNG UNIVERSITY (picture: The Joseph Smith Memorial Building).

**SMITH, JOSEPH F.** (1838-1918), was the sixth president of the Church of Jesus Christ of Latter-day Saints (the Mormon Church). His uncle Joseph Smith founded the church (see SMITH, JOSEPH). Joseph F. Smith became church president in 1901. He showed little interest in theology and doctrine. But he helped the Mormons by paying off their debts and by starting a building program. He was born in Far West, Mo. Smith's early life was tragic. His father, Hyrum, and his uncle Joseph were murdered when he was 5. Several years later, he went to Utah with the Mormons. His full name was JOSEPH FIELDING SMITH.  NORMAN F. FURNISS

**SMITH, MARGARET CHASE** (1897-    ), was the first woman to be elected to both houses of the United States Congress. Her husband was a Republican congressman from Maine. When he died in 1940, Mrs. Smith replaced him in the U.S. House of Representatives. She served four full 2-year terms. She was elected to the U.S. Senate in 1948. Maine voters re-elected her to the Senate in 1954, 1960, and 1966. In 1950, she gained fame by becoming one of the first senators to oppose tactics used by Wisconsin Senator Joseph R. McCarthy. In 1964, Mrs. Smith campaigned for the Republican presidential nomination, the first woman ever to do so for a major party. She was born MARGARET MADELINE CHASE in Skowhegan, Maine.  ERIC SEVAREID

**SMITH, ROBERT SIDNEY.** See CARTOON.

**SMITH, SAMUEL FRANCIS** (1808-1895), an American clergyman, editor, and poet, wrote the words to the patriotic hymn "America" (1831). He was born in Boston, Mass., and was graduated from Harvard University in 1829, and Andover Theological Seminary in 1832. He was ordained a Baptist minister in 1834. Smith served as pastor at Waterville, Me., and as a professor of modern languages at Waterville College until 1842. He edited *The Christian Review* magazine from 1842 to 1854.  EARLE E. CAIRNS

See also AMERICA.

**SMITH, THEOBALD** (1859-1934), was an American investigator of diseases in both human beings and domestic animals. In 1886 he separated the microbes of swine plague from those of hog cholera and showed how to prevent hog cholera. He helped discover the cause of Texas fever in cattle by proving that microbes were carried by ticks. These findings saved the southern beef-cattle industry and established the science of insect-borne diseases (see CATTLE TICK). Smith also announced that tuberculosis in cattle is caused by an organism that differs from the one that afflicts humans. Smith was born in Albany, N.Y., and was educated at Cornell University and Albany Medical College. He was head of animal pathology at the Rockefeller Institute for Medical Research (now Rockefeller Institute) until 1929.  STANLEY E. WEDBERG

**SMITH, WALTER BEDELL** (1895-1961), served the United States as a general, statesman, and industrial leader. He was Dwight D. Eisenhower's chief of staff in Europe during World War II, and headed the Allied delegation that accepted Germany's surrender in 1945. He served as ambassador to Russia from 1946 to 1949, director of the Central Intelligence Agency from 1950 to 1953, and under secretary of state in 1953 and 1954. Smith wrote *My Three Years in Moscow* (1950) and *Eisenhower's Six Great Decisions: Europe, 1944-1945* (1956). He was born in Indianapolis, Ind.  MAURICE MATLOFF

**SMITH ACT,** or ALIEN REGISTRATION ACT OF 1940, makes it a crime to advocate the violent overthrow of the United States government or to belong knowingly to a group advocating it. In 1951, the Supreme Court upheld the act in the case of 11 convicted leaders of the Communist Party. But in 1957, it ruled that Communist Party membership was not, in itself, grounds for conviction. Proof was required that a defendant himself had urged violent revolution. In 1961, the Supreme Court again upheld the conviction of a member of the Communist Party under the act. The court maintained that in this case the person had been an active party member and had intended to overthrow the government of the United States.

**SMITH COLLEGE** is a privately controlled college in Northampton, Mass. Its undergraduate school admits only women, but its graduate school is coeducational. Smith grants bachelor's, master's, and doctor's degrees. Undergraduates take liberal arts programs. Graduate students may take programs in arts, education, education of the deaf, fine arts, philosophy, physical education, or social work. Smith also participates in a cooperative doctoral degree program with the University of Massachusetts and Amherst, Hampshire, and Mount Holyoke colleges. At Smith, qualified juniors and seniors may participate in an honors program of specialized study. Juniors may study abroad.

Smith was founded in 1871. For enrollment, see UNIVERSITIES AND COLLEGES (table). RUSSELL F. CARPENTER

**SMITH-HUGHES ACT,** also known as the VOCATIONAL EDUCATIONAL ACT, provides federal funds to the states for vocational education. The payments are used for training in agriculture, home economics, and trades and industries. To be eligible, states must submit plans to the federal government for approval. The act was adopted by the U.S. Congress in 1917. Since then, Congress has passed additional acts for vocational rehabilitation programs. THOMAS J. MCLERNON

See also AGRICULTURAL EDUCATION; FUTURE FARMERS OF AMERICA (History).

**SMITH-LEVER ACT.** See AGRICULTURAL EDUCATION (Cooperative Extension Work).

**SMITHSON, JAMES** (1765-1829), a British scientist, founded the Smithsonian Institution. In his will he gave $550,000 to the United States for the establishment of a scientific institution. Congress accepted this gift and in 1846 created the Smithsonian Institution at Washington, D.C. See SMITHSONIAN INSTITUTION.

Smithson was born in France, and was educated at Oxford University. Smithson became known for his researches in chemistry and mineralogy. One of the many minerals that he studied was named *smithsonite* (zinc carbonate) in his honor. HENRY M. LEICESTER

**SMITHSONIAN INSTITUTION** is an institution of learning and research located in Washington, D.C. James Smithson, an Englishman who had never visited the United States, left $550,000 to the country in 1829 to establish an institution for the "increase and diffusion of knowledge among men." Congress accepted the gift in trust, and established the Smithsonian Institution on Aug. 10, 1846.

**Administration.** A board of regents governs the Institution. It consists of the Vice-President, the Chief Justice of the United States, three senators, three representatives, and six private citizens. Congress appoints all members except the Vice-President and the Chief Justice. The board selects a secretary to serve as executive officer. Joseph Henry, the first secretary, outlined a policy of administration that has guided later secretaries. The Institution is not a federal agency.

**Activities** of the Institution include scientific research, exploration, publication, museum exhibition, and care of collections. It administers several government agencies for which Congress grants funds. Bureaus and programs under the Institution, or connected with it, include the following:

The *National Gallery of Art*, *National Collection of Fine Arts*, *National Portrait Gallery*, and *Freer Gallery of Art* contain art objects owned by the U.S. government. These include paintings, prints, sculptures, antique furniture, jewels, and oriental art objects.

The *United States National Museum* has two departments. The *Museum of History and Technology* houses its collection of historical objects and technological inventions. For example, the gowns of Presidents' wives and early telephones of Alexander Graham Bell and Thomas

**The Smithsonian Institution** in Washington, D.C., attracts millions of visitors yearly. Its Museum of History and Technology includes an exhibit of gowns worn by wives of U.S. Presidents.

The Smithsonian Institution

# SMITHSONITE

Edison are preserved there. The *Museum of Natural History* exhibits animal and plant life, fossils, and other natural science items.

The *Bureau of American Ethnology* collects and publishes information on the American Indians. It has the largest collection of photographic negatives on American Indians. A unit of the bureau is the *River Basin Surveys*, a program for saving and recording archaeological remains that might otherwise be destroyed by irrigation, hydroelectric, and other river projects.

The *National Zoological Park* houses about 3,000 living animals. Among the first animals shown was a herd of American bison. The park covers 175 acres in Washington's Rock Creek Valley.

The *Astrophysical Observatory*, located in Cambridge, Mass., carries on research on the physical aspects of the heavenly bodies, especially the sun. The observatory maintains stations throughout the world to track artificial satellites. A unit of the observatory is the *Division of Radiation and Organisms*, which has laboratories in Washington, D.C. It carries on basic research on the role of sunlight in maintaining life.

The *National Air Museum* preserves and exhibits historic aircraft, engines, scale models, rockets, space vehicles, and items used by famous airmen.

The *Canal Zone Biological Area* is located on Barro Colorado Island in Gatun Lake, Panama Canal Zone. This island, left in its natural state, is the only tropical research station of its kind in the Western Hemisphere.

The *International Exchange Service* is the official United States agency for the free exchange of various publications with other countries.

A plan for building the *John F. Kennedy Center for the Performing Arts* was approved by Congress in 1964. When completed, this national cultural center in Washington, D.C., will stand as a memorial to the late President Kennedy. It will be under the nominal administration of the Smithsonian Institution.

Critically reviewed by SMITHSONIAN INSTITUTION

**Related Articles** in WORLD BOOK include:

| | |
|---|---|
| Ethnology, Bureau of American | National Gallery of Art |
| Freer Gallery of Art | National Zoological Park |
| Henry, Joseph | Smithson, James |
| National Air Museum | United States National Museum |
| National Collection of Fine Arts | Washington, D.C. (color picture) |

**SMITHSONITE.** See ZINC.

**SMOG** is the name given to fogs composed of smoke, dust, gasoline vapors, and other fumes that collect over some industrial areas. The fogs occur when a stationary air mass prevents the fumes from blowing away. Some smogs contain harmful chemical compounds that can cause death, illness, and much damage to textiles and plants. In 1948, 20 persons died and nearly 6,000 became ill when a smog covered Donora, Pa. Many cities, including Tokyo, Los Angeles, and Rio de Janeiro, have serious smog problems.

See also AIR POLLUTION; SMOKE PREVENTION; GREAT BRITAIN (Climate).

**SMOKE** occurs when finely divided solid particles become *suspended* (mixed) in a gas. A mixture of fog and smoke is *smog* (see SMOG). Most smoke is caused by particles of carbon from the burning of fuels. Smoke is bad for the health. The most dangerous accumulation of smoke occurs with a weather condition called *inversion*. In this type of weather, no vertical air currents exist to remove the smoke or smog. Smoke causes huge economic losses by blackening buildings, corroding metals, and damaging plants. The annual loss because of smoke in the United States is about $1 billion. A few helpful uses for smoke include colored military signals, curing meats, and protection of orchards with smudge pots during freezes (see SMUDGE POT). WALTER J. MOORE

**SMOKE PREVENTION** is a task many communities face. They try to keep the air free from smoke. Smoke is a great nuisance in cities, where there are many furnaces, incinerators, and other smoke-producing devices. Smoke is harmful both to man and to plant life.

Smoke is a mixture that comes from burning any kind of material, such as coal, wood, or petroleum. Smoke is made up of water vapor, carbon dioxide, and other gases that cannot be seen. Yet smoke itself can be seen clearly. This is because smoke contains many tiny particles of carbon that have not been burned. These particles are black and are known as *soot*. In some cities, 100,000 tons of soot comes from chimneys each year.

**Smoke Harms Health** because of its effect on the nose, throat, and lungs. Smoke-filled air increases sinus trouble, nose trouble, tuberculosis, and pneumonia. Smoke also makes cities look dark and cuts out much sunlight. Sulfuric acid, a chemical in smoke, poisons plant life. Smoke harms the outside of buildings and causes metals to wear away. People spend millions of dollars each year to clean smoke stains and soot smudges from clothes, curtains, and furniture.

Burning soft coal causes much of the smoke problem. To remedy this, many cities have changed to burning hard coal, fuel oil, natural gas, and coke. Engineers have designed better furnaces. They also have tried to teach people how to make a fire properly. These steps reduce the amount of soot. Engineers have developed an automatic stoker that feeds fires no faster than the coal is burned. Special fans and flues have been made to give furnaces the right kind of drafts.

**Preventive Measures.** Smoke once formed by incomplete combustion cannot be consumed. The only effective way to prevent the formation of sooty smoke is by improving the ways of burning fuel.

Many cities have laws intended to reduce the amount of smoke. In some cities, such as New York City, all railway trains within the city limits must use electricity. Some other cities permit only certain types of coal to be burned. The California legislature has passed a law requiring that each new automobile registered in the state must use an approved smoke-reducing device on its exhaust system. Four such devices were approved in 1964.

E. A. FESSENDEN

See also COLLOID; SOOT; SMOG.

**SMOKE SCREEN.** See BOMB (Other Types of Bombs).

**SMOKE SIGNAL.** See INDIAN, AMERICAN (Signs and Signals).

**SMOKED FOOD.** See FOOD PRESERVATION (Curing; picture: Curing); FISHING INDUSTRY (Processing).

**SMOKELESS POWDER.** See GUNPOWDER (History).

**SMOKING.** See TOBACCO (Effects of Using Tobacco); NICOTINE.

**SMOKY MOUNTAINS, GREAT.** See GREAT SMOKY MOUNTAINS.

**SMOLENSK,** *smoh LENSK* (pop. 177,000; alt. 600 ft.), is one of the oldest cities of western Russia. It lies on the Dnepr River, about 275 miles southwest of Moscow. For location, see RUSSIA (political map). It is a railroad junction on the main east-west line across Russia. It produces linen goods, textile machines, and road-building equipment. During World War II, Smolensk was severely damaged. THEODORE SHABAD

**SMOLLETT,** *SMAHL et,* **TOBIAS GEORGE** (1721-1771), was one of the great early English novelists. He was born near Dumbarton, Scotland, and became a doctor. After an adventurous life at sea as a ship's doctor, he settled in London. Smollett's first two novels, *The Adventures of Roderick Random* (1748) and *The Adventures of Peregrine Pickle* (1751), draw heavily on his sea experiences. *The Expedition of Humphry Clinker* (1771) is generally considered his best novel. Told in letters, it gives a vivid picture of a family traveling through England and Scotland.

Smollett's novels are loosely-constructed accounts of amusing and sometimes vulgar incidents in the hero's life. They are read for their eccentric characters, for their bitter social satire, and for their broadly comic high spirits. IAN WATT

**SMOOT, REED** (1862-1941), served as a Republican United States senator from Utah from 1903 to 1933. For many years, he was chairman of the Senate Finance Committee. Tax and tariff problems were his special assignments, and he was coauthor of the Smoot-Hawley tariff law in 1930. American protectionists liked the high rates of the law, but many economists criticized it. Smoot strongly supported programs to promote economy and efficiency in government.

Smoot also was one of the leaders of the Church of Jesus Christ of Latter-day Saints (Mormons). He became an apostle in that church in 1900. Smoot was born in Salt Lake City, Utah. He was graduated from Brigham Young Academy in Provo, Utah. NELSON M. BLAKE

**SMOOT-HAWLEY TARIFF LAW.** See SMOOT, REED; HOOVER, HERBERT CLARK (Champion of Prosperity).

**SMOOTH-COATED FOX TERRIER.** See FOX TERRIER.

**SMÖRGÅSBORD,** *SMAWRgus BOARD,* or *SMUR gohs BAWRD,* is an informal Scandinavian meal noted for its variety. It includes many kinds of smoked and pickled fish, tongue, sweetmeats, spiced fruits, appetizers, vegetables, and salads. The food is spread on a table, and each person fills his plate. See also SWEDEN (Food).

**SMUDGE POT** contains a smoldering fire used to protect plants and early-blooming fruit trees from killing frosts. Smoke does not spread heat readily. Therefore, commercial growers place a layer of smoke over vegetation when frost is forming. Smoke from nearly any fuel can be used for a smudge pot. Hay, damp leaves, old rubber, and oil waste may be burned in it.

Oil-burning heaters, which warm the air directly, have almost entirely replaced smudge pots. These heaters raise the air temperature about eight degrees. To protect citrus fruits on cold nights, 20 to 100 heaters per acre are needed. HENRY T. NORTHEN

**SMUGGLING** is the illegal transportation of people or goods into or out of a country or area. People who smuggle goods are usually trying to avoid the payment of *customs duties,* or taxes (see TARIFF). Most countries have customs officers stationed at seaports and at various points on their borders. These officers examine shipments of merchandise and the personal baggage of travelers to make sure that customs duties are paid.

Sometimes a country may have laws prohibiting the importation of a particular article. For example, the United States once prohibited the importing of alcoholic liquors. Violation of such laws also is called smuggling. During prohibition in the United States, people sometimes referred to the illegal manufacture, sale, or transportation of alcoholic liquors as *bootlegging.*

Persons who are guilty of smuggling may be punished by fines, imprisonment, or by having the goods taken, according to the seriousness of the offense. In the United States, no one is held guilty of smuggling unless he has acted intentionally. FRED E. INBAU

**SMUT** is a fungus that lives as a parasite in certain plants and causes diseases in them. Smut gets its name from the fact that it produces tiny black spores that look like particles of soot. Smuts are dangerous to both cultivated and wild plants. They are particularly harmful to agricultural crops such as wheat, oats, barley, corn, and rice. Smuts usually destroy the seeds or entire clusters of flowers. This may result in the plant's becoming completely useless or unable to produce seeds.

One of the most common of all smuts is the *corn smut.* This smut causes the loss of millions of bushels of corn each year. Corn smut usually grows on the ears of corn plants, causing large growths which resemble boils. Sometimes these growths also occur on the tassels. The spores of corn smut may live in the soil, or in manure which has come from animals fed with infected corn stalks. These spores may later infect plants with which they come in contact. As the corn plant develops, the tiny threads of smut grow within the tissues of the plant. These threads produce large blotches of dark-brown spores in the ears, the tassels, and sometimes in the leaves of the corn plant.

The best way to prevent corn smut is by *rotation of crops.* This means to change the location of the crops planted each year. This helps to prevent smut because the spores do not usually live in the soil for more than a year. It also is desirable that all plants that are affected with smut be destroyed in order to prevent the transfer of the infection.

The *oat smuts, stinking smut* of wheat, and the *covered smut* of barley are three common smuts which are dan-

**Corn Smut**  **Wheat Stinking Smut**
Hugh Spencer; USDA

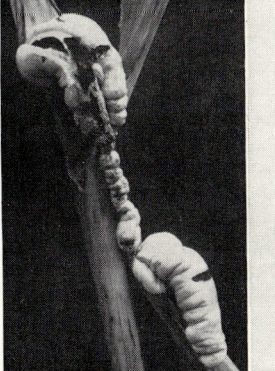 

## SMUTS, JAN CHRISTIAAN

gerous to cereal crops. The spores of these smuts are dusted on the outside of the seeds when the crop is threshed. *Threshing* means the separation of the seed from the straw. When seeds carrying smut spores are sown, the spores sprout and infect the young seedlings. The spores can be destroyed by treating the seeds with a disinfecting solution, such as *copper sulfate* or *formalin*. Some mercury dusts also destroy smut spores on seeds.

Although most of the best-known smuts cause serious damage to agricultural crops, there are a few kinds of smuts that improve the taste of certain edible plants. Some smuts can be grown in culture in the laboratory in the same way as yeast cultures. WILLIAM F. HANNA

**SMUTS, JAN CHRISTIAAN** (1870-1950), was a South African soldier, scholar, and statesman. He fought against Great Britain in the Boer War, but he later followed a policy of reconciling the Boers (Dutch settlers) and the British.

Smuts was born in Cape Town of an old Dutch family. He studied law at Cambridge University. He returned to Cape Town to study law, and became state attorney of the Transvaal Republic. When war broke out with Great Britain in 1899, Smuts received a command in the Boer Army and became a skillful military leader (see BOER WAR). He rose to the rank of general in that war.

Rosenthal, Pix
**Jan Christiaan Smuts**

In 1906, Great Britain gave the Transvaal self-rule, and Smuts worked hard for the union of the South African colonies. When the Union of South Africa was formed in 1910, Smuts became minister of the interior under Prime Minister Louis Botha (see BOTHA, LOUIS). Smuts later served as minister of defense, minister of finance, and minister of justice.

During World War I, Smuts fought for Great Britain, and served in London as a member of the British War Cabinet. At the Paris Peace Conference, Smuts became one of the authors of the Covenant of the League of Nations. When Botha died in 1919, Smuts became prime minister of the Union of South Africa.

The Nationalist party defeated Smuts in 1924. James Hertzog, the Nationalist leader, formed a coalition in 1933, with Smuts second in command. Smuts again became prime minister in 1939 on the platform of aiding Great Britain against Nazi Germany. During World War II, he became a British field marshal. In 1945, Smuts was mainly responsible for drafting the Preamble to the Charter of the United Nations.

Smuts was a champion of internationalism. He was an intellectual known for philosophic writings and profound speeches. He favored a more liberal policy for the Negroes of his nation. Smuts resigned in 1948 after the Nationalists defeated his party. T. WALTER WALLBANK

See also SOUTH AFRICA (History); UNITED NATIONS (The Preamble).

**SMYRNA.** See IZMIR.

**SMYTH, JOHN.** See BAPTISTS (History).

Hugh Spencer, N.A.S.
**The Marine Snail's Shell,** above, protects it from other animals. Certain colorful shells are prized among *conchologists* (people who study shells and shellfish).

Robert Hermes, N.A.S.
**Fresh-Water Snails Lay Eggs** in clumps either on the bottom of the body of water or on the stems of water plants. These snails are common prey of certain fish, frogs, toads, and birds.

**SNAIL** is an animal whose soft body is usually covered with a coiled shell. A snail creeps along on a strong muscular organ called a *foot*. Its body has a head with *tentacles* (feelers), eyes, a mouth, and tiny teeth. There are more than 80,000 kinds of snails. Some are as small as a pinhead. Others grow 2 feet long.

Snails live almost everywhere—in forests, deserts, rivers, ponds, and all parts of the ocean. They eat many kinds of food. Many snails that live on land eat rotting plants. Snails that live in rivers and lakes feed on water plants and dead animals. Some ocean snails feed on seaweeds, and some eat other sea animals. A few ocean snails are *parasites*, and live in the flesh of starfish or inside living sea animals called corals. Snails may live from 2 to 20 years.

Snails that live on land have both male and female sex organs in the same animal. Most of those that live in water are either male or female.

L. W. Brownell

**The Foot of the White-Lipped Snail** shows plainly, as the little mollusk crawls forward slowly on the branch of a bush.

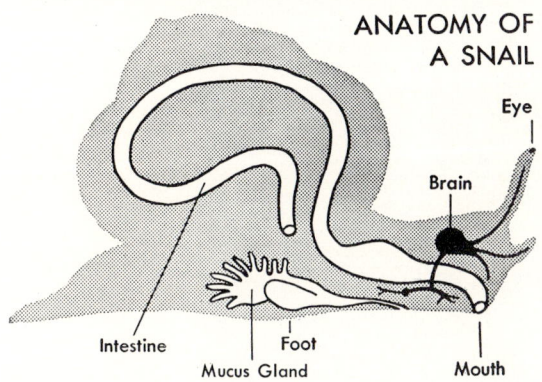

ANATOMY OF A SNAIL

Ralph Buchsbaum

**The Tree Snail's Shell Has Barber-Pole Stripes.**

**Groups of Snails.** Snails can be divided into three groups, according to where they live: on *land*, in *fresh water*, or in *salt water*.

Land snails are found in damp, shady places—under logs and stones, at the edges of ponds and rivers, and in woods. Most land snails live on the ground. But in tropical forests, many large, colorful kinds are found in the trees. Most land snails have lungs.

The land snail uses its muscular foot to crawl about. The muscles of its foot move in a backward, wavelike motion that causes the snail to inch forward. As the snail crawls, it pours out a sticky liquid called *mucus*, which serves as a path. The snail's enemies, beetles and ants, sometimes get caught in the mucus. During dry weather, the snail seals itself inside its shell with a "door" of dried mucus, called an *epiphragm*. It rests in this inactive condition, called *estivation*, until the dry spell ends.

Fresh-water snails live in rivers, ponds, lakes, and hot springs. There are about 5,000 kinds of fresh-water snails. Some of them have lungs, and must come to the surface to breathe the oxygen in the air. Others have gills, which take in oxygen from the water.

Salt-water or marine snails are the largest group of snails. There are about 55,000 kinds. Some kinds live along the seashore. Some live on the ocean floor in the deepest parts of the ocean. Most marine snails have gills. Many of these snails have a shelly lid, called an *operculum*, which seals the animal in whenever it draws itself into its shell. People who collect shells as a hobby prize the colorful shells of various salt-water snails.

**Useful and Harmful Snails.** Many snails are an important food for fish and birds. Many people consider the *Helix* garden snail, which is known as *escargot*, a great delicacy. The *turban snail* of Australia is used to make pearly shirt buttons.

Certain fresh-water snails in China and Egypt carry a disease that causes thousands of deaths each year. The 6-inch-long *giant African snail* destroys flowers, vegetables, and young rubber plants. Some kinds of *cone snails* of the Indian and southwest Pacific oceans have a poisonous, half-inch-long stinger. The poison is used to kill small fish, but it has also caused the death of several human beings. The sea snails that people eat can carry such diseases as typhoid fever and hepatitis, if they are taken from polluted water near sewers.

**Scientific Classification.** Snails belong to the class *Gastropoda*, in the phylum *Mollusca*. Snails with gills are members of the order *Prosobranchiata*. Those with lungs are in the order *Pulmonata*.   R. TUCKER ABBOTT

**Related Articles** in WORLD BOOK include:

| | | |
|---|---|---|
| Abalone | Mollusk | Shell (with |
| Conch | (Gastropods) | color pictures) |
| Cowrie | Periwinkle | Slug |
| Limpet | | Whelk |

433

Roy Pinney

**The Sonora Mountain Kingsnake** forms a colorful red, white, and black pattern as it coils around a pine cone. This snake looks like the poisonous coral snake, but it is harmless.

**Hognose Snake**
(nonpoisonous)

**Eastern Ribbon Snake** (nonpoisonous)

**Pine Snake** (nonpoisonous)
(eastern form of bull snake)

**Banded Water Snake** (nonpoisonous)

# Snake

**SNAKE** is a legless animal that crawls. Many persons fear snakes. But this fact only makes snakes more interesting to persons who have either never had this fear or who have overcome it.

The snakes are the best-known legless reptiles. They form a large division of reptiles, rivaled in size only by the lizards. Their other relatives are the turtles, tortoises, alligators, crocodiles, and the tuatara.

More snakes live in the tropics than anywhere else, and that is where the largest ones are. The giant anaconda of South America and the reticulate python of Asia may grow to be thirty feet long. But there are very small snakes, not over five inches long, and others of various sizes. There are no snakes in New Zealand, the Azores, or Ireland, and there are few on most remote islands in the ocean.

### Appearance and Habits

Many persons group snakes, earthworms, and eels together in their minds. About the only things these animals have in common are their shape and cold-bloodedness. The snake is not slimy like the worm and eel, but dry and smooth. It is covered with scales (see SCALE). The snake is deaf to sound carried by air. It hears by sensing vibrations from the ground. A snake's eyes are protected by a transparent cap that is shed with the skin. This cap keeps a snake's eyes always open, which makes it difficult to prove scientifically that a snake sleeps.

A snake's tongue is long, slender, and forked. The popular belief that a snake can sting with its tongue is untrue. Actually, the tongue is harmless. A snake keeps flicking out its tongue while moving along the ground, because it is the snake's organ of touch. A snake also uses its tongue to pick up particles and put them into two tiny cavities in the roof of its mouth. The cavities, known as *Jacobson's organ*, are linked with the snake's sense of smell. By picking up the particles, the tongue helps the snake to smell.

The snake has a backbone, like the eel. The snake's backbone is a very long chain of as many as 300 small bones, or vertebrae. A man has only 33 or 34 vertebrae.

**Emerald Tree Boa** (nonpoisonous)

**Corn Snake** (nonpoisonous)

# FACTS ABOUT SNAKES

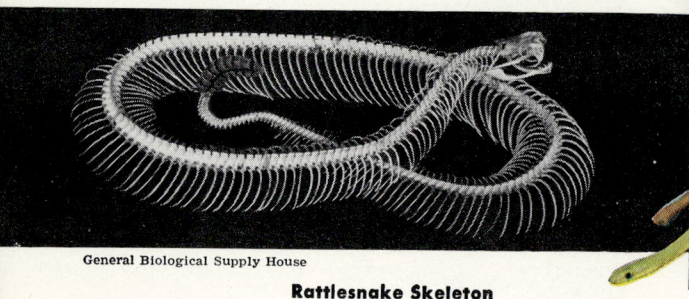

General Biological Supply House
**Rattlesnake Skeleton**

Hal H. Harrison
**Rough Green Snake**

**The Backbone of a Snake,** *left,* may have 300 bones, or vertebrae. This flexible backbone makes it possible for a legless snake to crawl by wriggling its body, *right.* Most snakes travel very slowly, but some can go as fast as 3 mph.

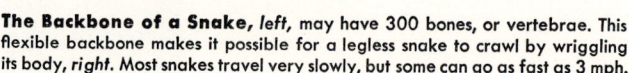

**Indigo Snake**

**Tongue.** A snake uses its forked tongue to touch or feel objects.

**Garter Snake and Young**

**Birth of a Snake.** Most newly born snakes hatch from eggs, but some are born alive. The average female produces about 10 offspring at a time. But the python may lay as many as 100 eggs. The garter snake usually gives live birth to a brood of 20 or more.

**Baby Blacksnakes and eggs**

Lynwood M. Chace

With this long string of bones, the snake can crawl, climb, and swim. The snake can bend easily because it has so many joints.

A person can tell the number of vertebrae in a snake's body if he counts the scales across the belly. There is about one scale for each vertebra, with its pair of ribs.

It is hard for a snake to crawl on a smooth, flat surface. Each curve of its body must have something on the ground to push against. When the curves all push at the right time, the snake can crawl with a rapid and beautiful motion. When it moves, it does not raise its body off the ground, but only bends it from side to side.

Snakes are cold-blooded, like all other animals except mammals and birds. This is the reason they feel cool to the touch. A man's body is always warm, but a snake's body is always about the same temperature as its surroundings. A snake taking a sun bath feels warm because its body takes up heat. Snakes and men can stand about the same degree of fever. But a snake can stand much greater chill. It does not die until its temperature goes below the freezing point.

Snakes thrive in the tropics, like other animals that cannot control their own temperature. They have great trouble avoiding the severe cold of winter, and there are almost no snakes in the Arctic regions. In temperate zones, they pass the winter deep in the ground, or in some other place where it is warm enough. This way of spending the winter is called *hibernation*. The dense foliage of the tropics usually gives them enough protection from the sun. Very dry spells in some regions give the snakes too much heat. Then they hide themselves the way snakes of the temperate zones do in the

**Fox Snake**

**Shedding Skin.** Snakes grow a complete new skin several times each year. They discard the old skin in a process called molting.

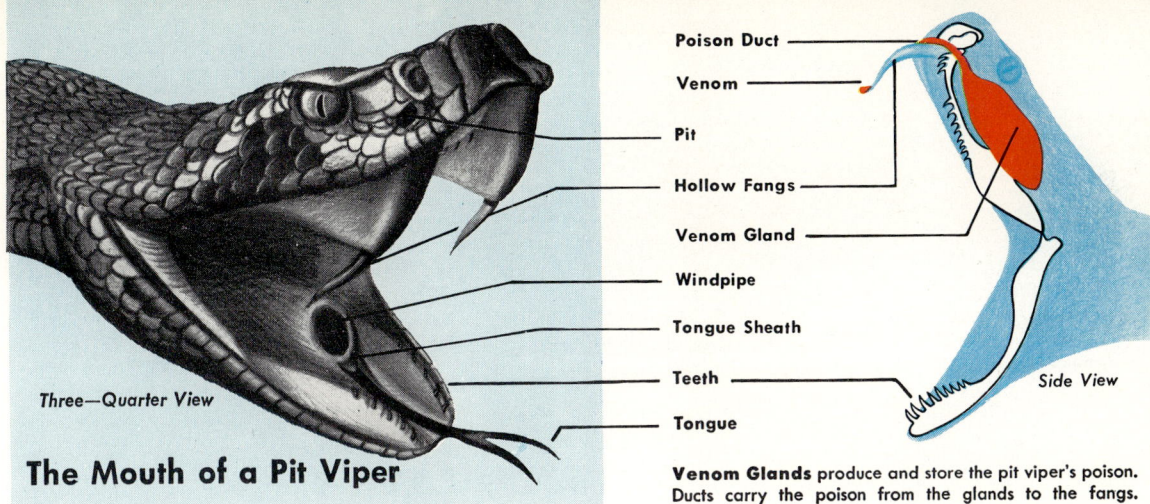

**The Mouth of a Pit Viper**

**Venom Glands** produce and store the pit viper's poison. Ducts carry the poison from the glands to the fangs.

winter. A snake hibernates in winter, and, when necessary, *estivates*, or passes the summer in inactivity.

It is not unusual to find almost perfect snakeskins in rocky or bushy places. Snakes grow a complete new skin several times a year. They slip out of the old one, turning it inside out, and leave it behind like a hollow tube. This process is called *molting*. See MOLTING (picture, A Molting Snake).

One of the more remarkable actions of a snake is the way that it feeds. It must swallow its food whole because its teeth are sharp like needles, and not good for chewing. They are curved toward the throat to give a better grip, and help make up for the lack of legs. The bones of a snake's lower jaw are loosely connected to each other and to the skull. The snake can separate them and swallow an animal two or three times as thick as its head. Its powerful stomach juices then digest all the animal except feathers and hairs.

A healthy snake can do without food for a year or more. But snakes usually eat regularly and often, storing up extra food as fat. Since the snake can swallow large objects, it can eat many different kinds of animals. The big pythons sometimes eat mammals weighing more than 100 pounds. But animals with long bodies are the easiest to swallow. Lizards and other snakes are favorite foods of snakes. This does not mean that snakes eat their own kind. Zoologists say different kinds of snakes are no more closely related to each other than men are to the cows they eat. Some tropical snakes as small as worms eat tiny insects with soft bodies.

Most snakes hatch from eggs, but others are born alive, like mammals. In either case, the young snakes

**Reticulate Python**

**Largest Snake.** The reticulate python of Asia, *above*, and the anaconda of South America are the largest snakes. Both may grow 30 feet long, about the length of six bicycles placed end to end. Many snakes are small. Some kinds of snakes, *left*, may be only 5 inches long when they are born.

Lewis D. Ober

**Black Swamp Snake**

437

Lewis D. Ober

**Eastern Diamondback Rattlesnake**

# POISONOUS SNAKES IN

Hal H. Harrison

**Timber Rattlesnake**

can take care of themselves. They can live without food for months if they have to. The number of young in a brood is different for different kinds of snakes. Some kinds have only a few at a time, whereas many others have dozens and a few even have scores.

### Growth of Snakes

Zoologists have found it difficult to learn about the growth of snakes, because they can be studied only in captivity. The kinds of snakes that have been studied grow quickly, and reach maturity in about two years. Common snakes, such as the garter snake, are about 6 inches long at birth. At maturity, they measure about 18 inches. The reticulate python, one of the largest snakes, is about 3 feet long at birth. When fully-grown, it may be some 30 feet long, and weigh about 200 pounds. Scientists believe that most snakes live for a period of from 20 to 30 years. See LIFE (table, Length).

### Poisonous Snakes

In most cases there is little reason to fear snakes. About 2,400 kinds of snakes are known, but only about 8 out of 100 are dangerous to man. Many places are entirely free of poisonous snakes. Some snakes are helpful. They kill many rats, mice, and other rodents that destroy crops. Scientists estimate that one snake will eat nearly 150 mice in six months.

Poisonous snakes are easy to recognize in the United States. Here, every poisonous snake is either a pit viper or a coral snake. Pit vipers have a deep hollow, or pit, in front of each eye and below it, on the side of the head. Rattlesnakes are pit vipers and are easy to know by their rattles. The only other pit vipers are the water moccasin and the copperhead.

# POISONOUS SNAKES IN OTHER LANDS

Ylla, Rapho-Guillumette

**Indian Cobra** has a pattern on the back of its hood, or flattened neck. The pattern looks like eyeglasses. In preparing to strike an enemy, cobras rear up without looping their bodies. Fully-grown Indian cobras are nearly 6 feet long.

**Indian Snake Charmer** may fool his audience, but he does not charm the snake. The cobra cannot hear the music of the flute. It sways merely to follow the movements of the charmer.

# THE UNITED STATES

↑ Water Moccasin or Cottonmouth
P. W. Smith

Lewis D. Ober
**Eastern Coral Snake**

**Western Coral Snake**

**Copperhead**
Hal H. Harrison

Coral snakes have bright bands of red, yellow, and black. They live in tropical South America and in some warm regions of the United States and Mexico. Some harmless snakes look much like coral snakes. Two facts will help to identify them. In coral snakes, the snout is usually black, and the red and yellow bands are next to each other. In harmless snakes, the snout is red, and the red and yellow bands are separated.

**Scientific Classification.** Snakes belong to the class *Reptilia*. Many scientists group them together with the lizards, in the order *Squamata*, and call them the suborder *Serpentes* (formerly *Ophidia*). CLIFFORD H. POPE

**Related Articles** in WORLD BOOK include:

KINDS OF SNAKES

| | | |
|---|---|---|
| Adder | Asp | Boa Constrictor |
| Anaconda | Blacksnake | Bushmaster |
| Cobra | Garter Snake | Python |
| Copperhead | King Snake | Rattlesnake |
| Coral Snake | Mamba | Viper |
| Fer-de-Lance | Milk Snake | Water Moccasin |

UNCLASSIFIED

Brazil  Snake Bite  Snake Charming
(Health and Science)

Outline

I. Appearance and Habits
II. Growth of Snakes
III. Poisonous Snakes

Questions

How does the snake use its tongue?
Why does a snake move so easily?
What kinds of poisonous snakes live in the U.S.?
Why are there only a few snakes in the arctic regions?
How do snakes help man?

Gates Priest

**Fer-de-Lance**
(Latin America)

**Gaboon Viper**
(Africa)

J. C. Couffer

**Yellow-and-Black Sea Snake**
(Latin America)

# SNAKE BITE

**SNAKE BITE.** The fangs of a rattlesnake or copperhead snake are like hollow hypodermic needles, which inject poison into the victim's body. The bite of a poisonous snake can be recognized by one or more punctures caused by the fangs. The poison quickly causes severe stinging. Soon the area around the bite begins to swell and turn purple. The victim may then become pale, weak, and sick at the stomach. His pulse becomes weak and rapid.

The coral snake leaves a different bite. It does not strike, but hangs on and chews. There is little pain at first, but later the breathing organs are partly paralyzed, and the patient becomes sleepy.

If the snake is not poisonous it leaves only a group of surface bites, sometimes shaped like a horseshoe.

If possible, the first thing to do in case of snake bite is to call a doctor. If the doctor's office or a hospital is near, take the patient there. Keep him motionless and quiet because activity causes poison to spread.

If there is no doctor near, use first aid. A first-aid kit may contain the proper serum. The following measures are also necessary:

1. Apply a tight bandage above the wound.
2. Paint the wound with iodine or alcohol. Sterilize a knife or razor blade (this can be done with a flame), and make an X-shaped cut through each fang mark.
3. Apply suction to the cuts to remove the poison. Many first-aid kits contain a suction or bulb syringe. If there is none, suck the wound by mouth, and spit out the poison. Be sure you have no open sores or cuts in your mouth. A hot bottle or glass with its mouth tight over the wound also will create a suction as it cools. Apply suction about 15 minutes in each hour for several hours if necessary. Between these periods, cover the wound with hot Epsom-salt or with table-salt compresses.
4. If the poison spreads, move the bandage higher, and make other cuts where the swelling is bad.
5. Give the victim plenty of water to drink. Whiskey should *not* be given, but in case of collapse, the patient may take strong, hot coffee or aromatic spirits of ammonia ($\frac{1}{2}$ teaspoon in cold water every half hour).

**SNAKE CHARMING** is an ancient form of entertainment in northern Africa, and in India, Pakistan, and other parts of southern Asia. A charmer usually uses a cobra in his act. He sits before the snake, playing a flute-like instrument and swaying to and fro. The cobra slowly raises its head and neck and follows the charmer's swaying movements to stay in front of him. The music has nothing to do with charming the snake. The snake has no external ears or eardrums, and cannot hear sound waves in the air. The snake is fascinated by the charmer's rhythmic movements. A snake charmer must understand thoroughly the habits of his snakes. Snake charmers sometimes cut out the fangs of poisonous snakes to make them harmless. Some circuses have "snake charmers," who merely handle harmless boas or pythons. CLIFFORD H. POPE

**SNAKE DANCE** is a sacred ceremony of the Hopi Indians of northeastern Arizona. The Indians dance and pray for rain and good crops. The snake dance is held each August, and lasts nine days. Near the end of the ceremony, Indians called Snake priests dance with live rattlesnakes in their mouths. As far as is known, no Snake priest has ever been killed while handling the rattlesnakes. Some persons believe the snakes' fangs are taken out or the snakes' *venom* (poison) is removed before the public dance begins. JOHN C. EWERS

**SNAKE KILLER.** See ROAD RUNNER.

**SNAKE RIVER** is the chief branch of the Columbia River. It rises in Wyoming near the Continental Divide in Yellowstone National Park. It then flows southward through Grand Teton National Park. Near southern Idaho, it bends westward and enters the Snake River Plains. Irrigation projects, dams, and many falls provide water for power and irrigation for the cities and potato fields of the plains. For location, see IDAHO (physical map).

The Snake River turns northward at the Oregon border, and forms 170 miles of the boundary between Idaho and Oregon. For about 40 miles, the Snake flows through Hells Canyon. Parts of the canyon are deeper than the Grand Canyon. The Idaho Power Company maintains three power dams in the canyon.

At Lewiston, Ida., the Snake turns westward and flows through a valley in southeastern Washington. Boats sail the Snake and Columbia rivers inland as far as Lewiston. The Snake joins the Columbia near Pasco, Wash., 1,038 miles from its source. JOHN H. GARLAND

See also IDAHO (Rivers); LEWISTON (picture).

**SNAKEBIRD.** See DARTER; WRYNECK.

**SNAKEROOT** is the name given to a large number of plants whose roots look like snakes. The plants grow throughout the United States and in many parts of Canada. Some kinds have medicinal value. *Black snakeroot*, or *cohosh*, yields a drug used to treat St. Vitus's Dance. The roots of *Virginia snakeroot*, or *birthwort*, have tonic properties. Another species, *Canada snakeroot*, or *wild ginger*, has stimulating qualities. An emetic is prepared from *senega snakeroot*. An alkaloid called *reserpine* is made from a snakeroot, *Rauwolfia*, and is sometimes used to treat high blood pressure (see RAUWOLFIA SERPENTINA).

**Scientific Classification.** Black snakeroot belongs to the crowfoot family, *Ranunculaceae*. It is genus *Cimicifuga*, species *C. racemosa*. Virginia snakeroot and Canada snakeroot belong to the birthwort family, *Aristolochiaceae*. Virginia snakeroot is genus *Aristolochia*, species *A.*

**White Snakeroot** is found in woods and clearings throughout eastern North America. It has clusters of small white flowers.
N.Y. Botanical Garden

*serpentaria.* Canada snakeroot is genus *Asarum,* species *A. canadense.* Senega snakeroot is in the milkwort family, *Polygalaceae.* It is genus *Polygala,* species *P. senega.* White snakeroot: composite family, *Compositae;* genus *Eupatorium,* species *E. rugosum.* HAROLD NORMAN MOLDENKE

**SNAPDRAGON** is a group of hardy, colorful plants with flowers that look like an animal's head. Each blossom has two lips. The lips open like jaws when the sides of the blossom are pressed. When the pressure is

**Caribbean Red Snappers** rank among the tastiest and most important food fishes caught off the coast of Florida.

Ferry-Morse Seed Co.

**The Snapdragon Is a Favorite Flower with Children,** who enjoy snapping the blossoms open by gentle pressure.

released, the lips snap shut again. The velvety flowers come in many colors. Tall varieties of snapdragons often grow 4 feet high. Dwarf varieties may reach a height of 9 inches. The best varieties of snapdragons resist *rust,* a plant-killing disease that is caused by a virus.

The *common snapdragon* is a popular garden flower. It must usually be grown from seeds each year, but sometimes lives through the winter.

**Scientific Classification.** Snapdragons belong to the figwort family, *Scrophulariaceae.* They make up the genus *Antirrhinum.* The common snapdragon is classified as *A. majus.* H. D. HARRINGTON

See also FLOWER (color picture: Summer Garden Flowers); BEARDTONGUE.

**SNAPHAUNCE.** See PISTOL.

**SNAPPER** is one of the important food fishes of southern waters. It lives in both the Pacific and Atlantic. The snappers of the Western Hemisphere are most common around Florida, the West Indies and the shores of the Gulf of Mexico, and the Caribbean region. In the Pacific, they live chiefly around the tropical coral atolls and the East Indies and Philippines. They live rather close to shore, usually in rocky places.

The snapper grows as long as 2 or 3 feet. It has a high, almost humped, back, and is rather flat from side to side. The mouth is large, with strong teeth. Its tail is slightly forked. Snappers may be red, greenish, or striped. They often have a black spot on each side of their bodies.

**Scientific Classification.** The snappers make up the snapper family, *Lutjanidae.* The Caribbean red snapper is genus *Lutjanus,* species *L. campechanus.* LEONARD P. SCHULTZ

**SNARE FISHING.** See FISHING INDUSTRY (Snaring).

**SNCC.** See STUDENT NATIONAL COORDINATING COMMITTEE.

**SNEAD, SAM.** See GOLF (Golf Immortals).

**SNEEZEWORT** is a hardy perennial plant that grows in damp fields and along roadsides in Europe, Asia, and North America. It is called sneezewort because its strong odor causes some people to sneeze. The plant grows from 1 to 2 feet high. It has loose clusters of small white flowers.

**Scientific Classification.** The sneezewort belongs to the composite family, *Compositae.* It is classified as genus *Achillea,* species *A. ptarmica.* ROBERT W. HOSHAW

**SNEEZING** is a sudden and violent rush of air out through the nose and mouth. A person has no control over sneezing. The body takes this action to get rid of irritating or harmful objects in the nose. Sensitive nerve endings that line the nose react to these objects by causing the sneeze. Sneezing occurs often in an ailment called *hay fever.* Plant pollen lodges in the nose of sufferers and causes the sneeze. Bright sunlight can also cause sneezing because the eye nerves are closely connected with nerve endings in the nose.

Sneezing aids the body, but can be harmful to other persons. For example, a person's nose fills with congestion that contains germs when he has a cold. Sneezing helps clear the nose. But unless the sneezer

**High-Speed Photograph of a Sneeze** shows how the thousands of droplets are violently ejected from the nose and mouth.
M. W. Jennison

## SNELLING, JOSIAH

covers his mouth and nose, the germs escape into the air and may infect others. ALBERT P. SELTZER

See also DISEASE (How Diseases Spread); COLD, COMMON; NOSE; HAY FEVER.

**SNELLING, JOSIAH.** See MINNESOTA (History).

**SNICK.** See STUDENT NATIONAL COORDINATING COMMITTEE.

G. Ronald Austing

**Wilson's Snipe** is called the jacksnipe by sportsmen. Because it lives in bogs, and is a fast flier, it is a difficult bird to shoot.

**SNIPE** is the name of a group of shore birds related to sandpipers, curlews, and plovers. The common snipe, also called *Wilson's snipe*, is about 11 inches long. It has a short tail and a long bill. It uses the flexible, sensitive tip of its bill to poke about for worms and grubs. This bird performs acrobatics in the air during the mating season. It also makes a strange "bleating" or "drumming" sound by flying to great heights and descending in a series of quick swoops as air rushes through its feathers. Wilson's snipe spends its summers from the northern United States to Hudson Bay and Labrador. It winters from Illinois and South Carolina southward. The snipe is more timid than the sandpiper about being seen in the open by day. It nests in low places in the ground on the edge of marshes. The female lays four olive brown or grayish drab eggs thickly spotted with chocolate color.

**Scientific Classification.** The snipe belongs to the sandpiper family, *Scolopacidae*. Wilson's snipe is genus *Capella*, species *C. gallinago*, subspecies *delicata;* European snipe is species *C. gallinago*, subspecies *gallinago*. ALFRED M. BAILEY

See also BIRD (How Birds Protect Themselves); CURLEW; YELLOWLEGS.

**SNIPERSCOPE** is an electronic infrared device that enables a person to see objects in the dark without the aid of visible light. It can be mounted on M-1 and M-14 rifles. The sniperscope consists of a telescopic image tube and an infrared source attached to the weapon. A small battery cartridge strapped to the person's belt provides power for the device. The sniperscope looks like a fog

442

Raytheon Co.

**The Sniperscope** enables a rifleman to see targets in the dark. It is powered by an electric battery worn at the shooter's waist.

light with a glass face painted black. Troops equipped with sniperscopes can fight effectively in the dark. They first used the instruments during World War II.

The sniperscope depends upon the reflection of invisible infrared rays from the object being viewed. The infrared source sends out rays that are reflected by objects in their path. The telescopic image tube picks up the reflected image and converts it into a visible one.

**SNO-CAT.** See FLOODS AND FLOOD CONTROL (picture: Predictions of Flood Stages in Rivers).

**SNOOK.** See FISHING (table: Game-Fishing World Records).

**SNORING,** *SNOHR ing*, is a rough, broken sound made during sleep. Almost everyone snores occasionally, but men usually snore more often than women and children. Snoring takes place when a sleeper breathes through his mouth. Air rushing out through the mouth vibrates the *soft palate*, the soft tissue in the roof of the mouth near the throat. This vibration produces the sound. As the soft palate vibrates, the lips and other mouth tissue, cheeks, and nostrils also may vibrate. The rushing air dries the soft mouth tissues, causing them to vibrate faster. This makes the snoring louder.

Many remedies have been tried to stop snoring. Bandages have been tied around the chin to the top of the sleeper's head so that his mouth would remain closed. A hundred years ago doctors removed the *uvula*, a tab of soft tissue hanging from the roof of the mouth near the throat. Attendants at an English hospital even tried dropping tiny soap pellets into a snorer's mouth whenever he made the sound. But doctors have never discovered a sure way to prevent snoring. ALBERT P. SELTZER

**SNORKEL.** See SKIN DIVING; SUBMARINE (Power).

**SNORRI STURLUSON** (1179-1241) was a great medieval Icelandic poet and historian. His major work was the *Heimskringla*, a history of the kings of Norway up to his time. He probably also wrote *The Saga of Egill Skallagrimsson*, one of the best Icelandic sagas about a great poet of the 900's who was one of Snorri's forefathers. Snorri wrote an *Edda* as a textbook to instruct the young poets of his day in *skaldic* poetry. Snorri was a wealthy and powerful man in Iceland. He became involved in a power struggle in Norway between Hákon Hákonsson and Skule Bardsson. Snorri supported Skule, who was defeated by Hákon. Snorri disobeyed Hákon's orders not to leave Norway in 1240, and Hákon ordered him killed in Iceland. KENNETH G. CHAPMAN

Photomicrographs by Vincent J. Schaefer

**These Types of Snowflakes** are shown in "casts." The flake falls into a plastic solution which coats the snowflake and hardens quickly. As the flake melts, it leaves a hollow shell, or cast, which retains the exact shape of the flake.

**SNOW** is the name for the shimmering ice crystals that form when the water vapor in clouds freezes. If the falling snowflakes pass through warm air, they melt and appear as raindrops. But if the falling snowflakes come in contact with cold raindrops at a temperature below 32°F., the *supercooled* raindrops instantly freeze over the snowflakes. They form small bits of ice called *sleet*. This form of snow occurs when the air has vertical currents. The currents hold the snowflakes in the air until the sleet forms. If the currents are especially strong, *hail* may form. Sleet and hail need a strong vertical air current to keep them in the air until they form.

Many people have never seen snow, because it falls on only about a third of the earth's surface. In the polar regions, it falls in all seasons. But in the temperate zone, snow falls in winter. The heaviest snowfalls occur in the mountainous areas of the temperate zone, such as the Rocky Mountains and the Sierra Nevada Mountain range in the United States, and in the Alps in Italy and Switzerland.

**Properties of Snow.** Snow always appears as tiny six-sided crystals. But no two snow crystals are exactly alike. Sometimes the crystals are flat. At other times they form long needles. Snow crystals often cling together to form snow pellets over an inch thick.

When mountain snow melts, it provides water for streams, electric-power plants, and irrigation reservoirs. There is much less water in snow than in rain. It takes a 6-inch layer of moist snow or a 30-inch layer of dry snow to equal the water in a 1-inch rainfall.

The tiny crystal surfaces of fresh snow reflect light and make the snow appear white. However, microscopic plants may change the color of snow after it has fallen. Greenland and other places in the Arctic sometimes have red and green snow on the ground.

**Record Snowfalls.** Weather records show that the average annual snowfall has remained about the same since the last half of the 1800's. In some years, it snows only a little, but in others it snows a great deal. Some persons believe that it snows less today than it did years ago. Yet, new snowfall records are set almost every year. In January, 1957, Grand Junction, Colo., had a record monthly snowfall of 33.7 inches. On Thanksgiving Day, 1956, a 27-inch snowfall buried the city of Erie, Pa. In January, 1958, snow fell as far south as Lakeland, Fla. Single snowfalls of over 30 inches are not unusual. In the hills southeast of Lake Erie and Lake Ontario, the average winter snowfall is over 150 inches.

The all-time United States record for snowfall in one season was set from July, 1955, to June, 1956, when 1000.3 inches of snow fell at the 5,500-foot level of Mt. Rainier, Wash. In 1921, at Silver Lake, Colo., a 76-inch snowfall set a record for the largest snowfall during a 24-hour period. The greatest four-day snowfall occurred at Tahoe, Calif., which had 108 inches of snow from Jan. 12 to 15, 1952.

The record snowfall for a calendar month occurred at Tamarack, Calif., where 390 inches of snow fell in January, 1911. In the same year, a record depth of snow accumulated at Tamarack, where 454 inches of snow covered the ground.

**Artificial Snow.** Man has produced artificial snow both in the laboratory and outdoors. In 1946, Vincent J. Schaefer of Schenectady, N.Y., produced the first artificial snow. The moist air of his breath condensed into supercooled water clouds when he breathed into a deep-freeze. He changed the clouds into snowflakes by inserting an extremely cold rod into the cloud. Since then, Schaefer and other research scientists have caused snow to fall from the water clouds in the sky by using various chemicals.          GEORGE F. TAYLOR

**Related Articles** in WORLD BOOK include:

| | | |
|---|---|---|
| Avalanche | Rain Making | Snowplow |
| Climate | Sleet | Snowshoe |
| Glacier | Snow Blindness | Weather |
| Hail | Snow Line | |

**The Rare Stud Snowflake** comes from a great height. It is formed only in very cold temperatures. The model of the stud snowflake shows its two hexagonal plates, which are arranged one above the other, and attached by a hexagonal column.

E. H. Reiber, Buffalo Museum of Science

## SNOW, C. P.

**SNOW, C. P.** (1905-    ), is an Englishman of many talents who is most famous as a novelist. He is also a scientist, government official, and lecturer.

Snow's series of novels *Strangers and Brothers* is a study of England's professional class. Lewis Eliot is an important character and the narrator in all the novels. Like Snow, Eliot is a man of lower class birth who works his way into professional life. Eliot appears in many jobs in the series, a device that allows Snow to present a panoramic view of English life. Eliot is a lawyer in *Strangers and Brothers* (1940) and *Time of Hope* (1949), a university teacher in *The Light and the Dark* (1947) and *The Masters* (1951), and a government official in *The New Men* (1954). In *The Sleep of Reason* (1968), Eliot serves as an observer at a sensational murder trial. Colorless, almost stodgy, Eliot is nevertheless an impartial, selfless man. To Snow, he is the kind of man needed to make responsible professional decisions.

CHARLES PERCY SNOW was born in Leicester and earned a doctor's degree in physics from Cambridge University. As a civil service commissioner from 1945 to 1960, Snow selected scientists for government projects. He was knighted in 1957. Snow served as parliamentary secretary to the minister of technology from October, 1964, to April, 1966. *The Two Cultures and the Scientific Revolution* (1960) is a published lecture in which Snow deplores the lack of communication and understanding between scientists and nonscientists.    FREDERICK R. KARL

**SNOW BLINDNESS** is a temporary loss of sight caused by bright sunlight reflected from snow. It usually lasts from several days to a week. Occasionally a person has trouble distinguishing between colors after snow blindness, and "sees red" for a long time. Snow blindness disappears when a person rests his eyes and remains indoors. Wearing dark-colored glasses helps avoid snow blindness. Eskimos living in arctic areas avoid it by wearing gogglelike bone shields with long, narrow slits over their eyes.    LOUIS D. BOSHES

**SNOW BUNTING**, or SNOWFLAKE, is a sparrow-like bird of northern North America. It is mostly white on its head and breast, but its back, wings, and tail are partially black. During the fall and winter, the head and back feathers are edged with brown. These edges wear off as the winter passes on. The bird turns black and white before it reaches its nesting ground on the tundra plains in Canada and Alaska. Snow buntings are among the most familiar winter birds in Canada. They come as far south as the United States only when the snow is heavy. They spend their summers in the arctic regions.

**Scientific Classification.** The snow bunting belongs to the finch family, *Fringillidae*. It is genus *Plectrophenax*, species *P. nivalis*.    LEONARD W. WING

**SNOW LEOPARD.** See OUNCE.

**SNOW LINE** is the lower edge of the permanent snow fields found on upper mountain slopes. The location of the snow line depends upon the height of the sun, winds, temperature, and moisture. Sometimes the snow line on the same mountain range may change from year to year. In the tropics, the snow line is about three miles above sea level. The snow line of the Rocky Mountains is about two miles above sea level. In the Alps, the snow line is about a mile and two-thirds above sea level. It is less than a half mile above sea level in Greenland. It is at sea level in polar lands.    SIGISMOND DER. DIETTRICH

**SNOW-ON-THE-MOUNTAIN** is a popular garden plant grown for its attractive white flowers and white-edged upper leaves. It is found mostly in the western and midwestern parts of the United States. It must be replanted each year. The plant has a soft stem and may grow to be 2 feet high. The flowers are small and shaped somewhat like umbrellas. Each flower is enclosed by white parts, known as bracts, that look like petals.

**Scientific Classification.** Snow-on-the-mountain belongs to the spurge family, *Euphorbiaceae*. It is genus *Euphorbia*, species *E. marginata*.    MARCUS MAXON

**SNOW PLANT.** See FLOWER (color picture: Mountain Flowers [Bright-Red Snow Plants]).

**SNOW REMOVAL.** See ROADS AND HIGHWAYS (Clearing Ice and Snow); SNOWPLOW.

**SNOWBALL**, or GUELDER-ROSE, *GEL der ROHZ*, is a handsome shrub of the honeysuckle family which produces large, ball-shaped white flowers. The plant is believed to have originated in the Dutch province of Gelderland. The snowball is often grown in parks and lawns of the United States today. It is a cultivated form of high-bush cranberry, and grows from 7 to 12 feet high. The flowers of the cultivated species do not produce fruit, but a wild guelder-rose bears juicy, red berries. It is also called *European cranberry bush*.

**The Snowball**
J. Horace McFarland

**Scientific Classification.** The snowball is in the honeysuckle family, *Caprifoliaceae*. It is classified as genus *Viburnum*, species *V. opulus*.    J. J. LEVISON

**SNOWBIRD.** See JUNCO.

**SNOWDON** is the highest mountain in Wales. This peak rises to a height of 3,560 feet above sea level. The mountain is in Caernarvon, in northwest Wales. It is a background for many Welsh legends.

**SNOWDROP** is the name of a plant in the amaryllis family. It gets its name from its many delicate white blossoms which seem to be made out of snow. Snowdrops grow in many parts of the world. They bloom in March or April in northern countries. The snowdrop is

**The Snow Bunting**
Mitchell Campbell, NAS

one of the special flowers for the month of January.

The plant grows from a small bulb which produces 2 or 3 narrow green leaves and a flower stalk without leaves. The nodding, bell-shaped flowers grow alone, one on top of each stalk. The *common snowdrop* of the gardens is one of the hardiest outdoor plants. It sometimes blooms in midwinter when a sudden warm spell causes the surface of the ground to thaw. In England, the people call the plant the *Fair Maid of February*. Snowdrops are easy to cultivate, for the bulbs can be planted in a sheltered place in early fall and left to themselves. They require little attention.

**Scientific Classification.** The common snowdrop belongs to the amaryllis family, *Amaryllidaceae*. It is genus *Galanthus*, species *G. nivalis*. ALFRED C. HOTTES

**The Snowdrop Is One of the First Heralds of Spring.**
J. Horace McFarland

**SNOWFLAKE.** See SNOW.

**SNOWFLAKE**, a bird. See SNOW BUNTING.

**SNOWMOBILE** is a motorized sled that carries from one to four persons over ice and snow. Joseph-Armand Bombardier of Valcourt, Quebec, built the first sled-sized snowmobiles for mass production in the late 1950's. Snowmobile driving has become a popular winter sport in Canada and the northern United States.

Most snowmobiles are from 5 to 10 feet long, and from 2 to 4 feet wide. They ride on two short skis on the front of the vehicle, and a wide rubber *track* (belt) toward the rear. An engine of from 8 to 45 horsepower moves the track, propelling the snowmobile forward. The operator uses handlebars to steer the skis. Most snowmobiles can go up to 50 miles per hour, and some more than 90 miles per hour. Some models are powerful enough to pull loads of up to 1,000 pounds. J. L. BOMBARDIER

**SNOWPLOW** is an implement used to clear snow from streets, highways, railroad tracks, and airport runways. A type commonly used to clear streets consists of a V-shaped metal blade mounted on the front of a truck or road grader. For light snows, trucks may be equipped with a single, horizontal curved blade that throws the snow to one side. Rotary plows are used to clear deep snowdrifts. A common type of rotary plow consists of a horizontal, spiral rotor that resembles an auger. The rotor breaks up the snow and forces it to the center of the plow where a fan blows it out of a spout. Small rotary plows about the size of power lawn mowers have been developed for homeowners. Railroads often use powerful fan-type plows mounted on the front of locomotives. F. H. KELLOGG

# SOAP

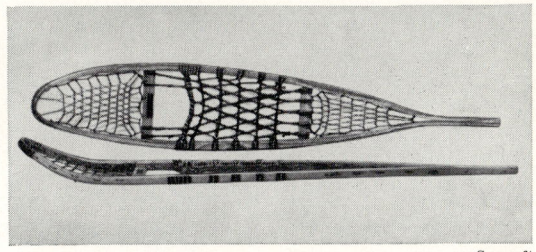

Snocraft

**Snowshoes** look like oddly shaped tennis rackets. They are made of strings of animal hide stretched over a wood frame.

**SNOWSHOE** is a device that enables a person to walk over deep snow without sinking into it. This is possible because snowshoes distribute a person's weight over a large area. Most snowshoes are at least three feet long, and from a foot to a foot and a half wide. They are made of a light wooden frame, bent into a long oval. Strings of animal hide are stretched across the frame.

In walking with snowshoes, the wearer moves his feet so that the snowshoes slide along the surface of the snow. He gives an outward motion to the snowshoes with each step. Experts on snowshoes can walk for hours at the rate of five or six miles an hour, and many can run on them in a sort of dogtrot at 10 miles an hour.

Snowshoes were first used by the North American Indians. Today, they are used in regions of deep snow by hunters, trappers, loggers, and farmers. In some parts of Canada, there are snowshoe clubs organized for recreation. FRANKLIN M. RECK

See also SASKATCHEWAN (picture: Snowshoe Race at the Winter Carnival in La Ronge).

**SNOWSTORM.** See BLIZZARD.

**SNOWY MOUNTAINS SCHEME** is a big irrigation and hydroelectric power project in southeastern Australia. Its generators will provide electric power for the Australian Capital Territory and the states of New South Wales and Victoria. The dams will store water from the Snowy River, on the southern slopes of the Snowy Mountains, and send it through the mountains to irrigate farmlands in the Murray and Murrumbidgee river valleys, north of the mountains. The project is one of the largest power and irrigation schemes in the world. It includes 17 large dams and several small ones, 9 power stations, about 100 miles of tunnels, 80 miles of aqueducts, and many miles of high-voltage electricity transmission lines. Work is to be completed in 1975.

**SNOWY OWL.** See OWL (with picture).

**SNUFF** is a fine powder made from the stems and leaves of the tobacco plant. The tobacco is first fermented by heat and moisture, and then dried and ground. Snuff may be sniffed in through the nostrils, chewed, or rubbed on the gums. Various mixtures of flavors or scents are added to make the powder pleasant. At one time, each person carried a snuffbox and it was considered a matter of etiquette to offer a pinch of snuff upon meeting a friend. This practice is still carried on in southern Europe. The habit of taking snuff is considered harmful. It irritates the nerves of smell and lessens the ability to distinguish odors.

**SOAP.** See DETERGENT AND SOAP.

445

**Soap Box Derby** entries speed down a long course before thousands of spectators each August in the All-American and International Soap Box Derby at Akron, Ohio. Contestants come from the United States and other countries.

General Motors

**SOAP BOX DERBY** is a coasting race for small motorless racing cars. The derby received its name because the cars sometimes are made from wooden soap boxes. In many cities, newspapers sponsor soap box derbies. The winners of these local races then attend the All-American and International Soap Box Derby, held every August in Akron, Ohio. The contestants, who are boys between the ages of 11 and 15, build the racing cars. Rules govern the size and weight of the racer, how it is built, and how much money it may cost. The Chevrolet Motor Division offers a $7,500 college scholarship to the winner of the All-American and International Soap Box Derby. The event attracts contestants from the United States, Canada, South America, and Europe.

**SOAP PLANT** is a tall herb of California which reaches a height of about 5 feet. It grows from a bulb and has tufted leaves and white flowers streaked with purple. The leaves may be about 1½ feet long. The flowers spread open in the afternoon. The bulb was formerly used by the Indians as a kind of soap.

**Scientific Classification.** Soap plants belong to the lily family, *Liliaceae*. They are genus *Chlorogalum*, species *C. pomeridianum*. JULIAN A. STEYERMARK

**SOAP SCULPTURE** is the art of carving figures from soap. It is best to use a large bar of soft white soap—the larger the better, especially for the beginner. When you start to carve the soap, you want plenty of room for trial and error and shaky hands. A hard soap chips and leaves rough edges.

Scrape off all lettering or raised designs on the soap. Then, on paper, draw an outline of the shape that will appear on each side of the bar. Transfer the outline onto each side, using carbon paper under the design you drew on paper. Cut through the soap about one-quarter inch outside the outline. It is best to start at the top and work downward. When you have cut away the excess soap, you have a flat piece in the general shape of your design. Work carefully, taking a little soap with each

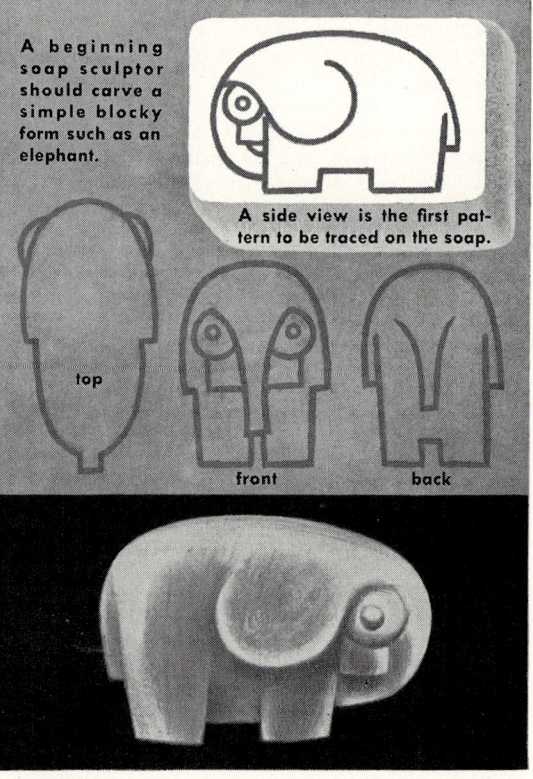

446

cut, until you reach the outline, molding and shaping the figure as you work. An orange stick, used in fingernail care, makes a good tool for scraping out small areas and shaping angles and curves, such as those in an animal's body or in facial features. You can also use your thumb or fingers to smooth rough surfaces.

Set the finished carving aside for several days to dry. Then polish it with a soft paper tissue or napkin, and use your finger tips and the palm of your hand to bring out highlights.

Soap sculpture can take on the lovely look of old ivory. You can preserve the carving with a coat of transparent lacquer, or you may paint it with colors. This also adds a more realistic appearance.

The beginner should start off with simple designs and should practice cutting the soap until he becomes acquainted with this art medium. Then he can try more ambitious designs.
JACK WAX

Western Ways

**The Fruit of Soapberry** yields a soapy substance called *saponin* which is used by people in the tropics for cleaning purposes.

National Soap Sculpture Committee

**This Soap Sculpture, "Siesta,"** won first prize in a national amateur contest. Soap sculpture is both simple and cheap. A knife and a bar of soap are the only materials needed.

**SOAPBERRY,** or **CHINABERRY,** is the name of a group, or genus, of trees and shrubs that bear fruit containing a soapy substance called *saponin*. Soapberry trees and shrubs grow in tropical regions, and as ornamental plants in the southern part of the United States. The fruit has a fleshy or leathery berry. People in the tropics use the saponin from the berries for cleaning purposes. Soapberry plants are reproduced either by seeds or by cuttings in early spring. They grow well in dry, sandy soil.

One type of soapberry is an evergreen tree that grows in India and Japan. This tree is about 60 feet in height. It has an orange-brown fruit which contains much saponin. Another species grown in the tropical regions of the United States is known as the *chinaberry*. It has small white flowers with orange-brown fruit, and grows to a height of about 30 feet. A third species grows in the U.S. from Missouri to Mexico. It has yellowish-white flowers and sheds its leaves in winter.

**Scientific Classification.** Soapberries belong to the soapberry family, *Sapindaceae*. It makes up the genus *Sapindus*. The evergreen trees are species *S. mukorossi*, and *S. saponaria*. The deciduous tree is *S. drummondii*. J. J. LEVISON

**SOAPSTONE,** also known as *steatite*, is a soft rock made up mostly of *talc* (see TALC). The soapy or oily feeling of soapstone gives it its name. Soapstone can be cut more easily than most other rocks. It varies in color from white through gray to green. It is generally impure and contains small amounts of other minerals like chlorite and magnetite.

The United States provides more than half the talc and soapstone produced in the world each year. Virginia has the largest soapstone deposits in the United States. These deposits lie in a belt 30 miles long near Schuyler, Va. Soapstone is found in sheetlike form. These sheets are 180 to 330 feet thick and 1,500 to 2,000 feet long. Soapstone is quarried in large blocks. Workmen then saw the soft mineral into smaller blocks and slabs for commercial use.

Soapstone is not affected by high temperature or by acid, and is a good electrical insulator. It is used to make fireless cookers, laboratory table tops, and switchboards. It has also been used to line laundry tubs and sinks. Tailors use pieces of light-colored, soft soapstone, called "French chalk," to mark cloth. Soapstone has many uses in powdered form. It is used as "filler" for paper, for some grades of face powder, and for certain paints.
A. J. EARDLEY

**SOARING SOCIETY OF AMERICA.** See GLIDER (How Gliders Are Used).

**SOBIESKI, JOHN.** See JOHN III SOBIESKI.

**SOBRERO, ASCANIO.** See NITROGLYCERIN.

447

# SOCCER

*Pictorial Parade*

**Soccer Is One of the World's Most Popular and Exciting Sports.** In many countries, huge crowds pack big stadiums to watch soccer teams play. Soccer players move the ball quickly and cleverly with the feet, head, or body, and try to knock it into the opposing team's goal.

**SOCCER** is one of the most popular sports in the world. It is the "national sport" of several European and South American countries, and of many countries in Asia. Soccer games often attract huge crowds of up to 200,000 persons. Soccer's most famous international competition, the World Cup matches, pits national teams from many countries against each other every four years. World Cup matches arouse as much interest and excitement in many countries as the World Series does in the United States each October.

In a soccer game, two teams of 11 men each try to knock a round ball through the opponent's goal. The speedy, muscular players wear only shirts and shorts, heavy knee-length socks, and cleated soccer shoes. Some players wear shin guards. The team that scores the most goals wins the game.

Only the goalkeepers, playing within a certain area, can touch the ball with their hands. Other players must kick it with their feet or hit it with their heads or bodies. Acrobatic soccer players leap high to bounce the ball away with their heads or turn in midair to kick the ball back over their heads.

Soccer is a tough, fast, exciting game that requires great physical endurance. Play rarely stops once the game begins, and the players move up and down the field almost continuously. Play is stopped only when a goal is scored, a foul occurs, or if a player is seriously injured. A player taken out of a game cannot play again in that game. So soccer players often stay on the field in spite of painful injuries.

In Great Britain, soccer is called *football* or *association football*. The word soccer comes from *assoc.*, an abbreviation for *association*. American and Canadian football and rugby developed from soccer.

## Soccer Field and Equipment

**The Field.** Most adult teams play on fields that are from 100 to 130 yards long and from 50 to 100 yards wide. Children may play on fields that are about 80 by 60 yards.

The boundary lines on the long sides of the field are called *touch lines*. Those on the short sides are called *goal lines*. When a player knocks the ball out of bounds, play stops until a player from the opposing team kicks or throws the ball into the playing area. The *halfway line* runs across the center of the field, halfway between the two goal lines.

**The Goals** stand in the center of the goal lines. Each goal consists of two wooden posts 24 feet apart and joined at the top by a crossbar that is 8 feet above the ground. A net is usually attached to the back of the crossbar and posts and pegged to the ground behind them. The net is helpful, because it stops the ball when it goes in the goal. In this way everyone can be sure that the ball has passed between the posts and under the crossbar to score a goal.

---

*George E. Fishwick, the contributor of this article, is Director of Promotion and Publicity of the United States Soccer Football Association.*

# SOCCER

Two rectangles are marked in front of each goal. The smaller rectangle is called the *goal area*. It is 60 feet wide and extends 18 feet in front of the goal. The larger rectangle is called the *penalty area*. The penalty area is 132 feet wide and extends 54 feet in front of the goal.

The goalkeeper cannot be charged by an opponent in the goal area, unless he is holding the ball and has both feet on the ground. The penalty area is important, because defenders are seriously penalized if they break certain rules in that area. In such cases, a member of the offensive team gets a kick from the *penalty spot* 12 yards in front of the goal. Only the goalkeeper can attempt to block the shot.

**The Ball** is a leather casing inflated by a rubber bladder. A ball about 27-28 inches in circumference is used for adult games and one about 25 inches is generally used for children's games.

### Soccer Rules

**The Officials** are the *referee* and two *linesmen*. The referee acts as the timekeeper and enforces the rules. He blows a whistle to stop and start play whenever (1) a goal is scored, (2) the ball goes out of bounds, (3) a player commits a foul, and (4) play is stopped for an injury. He may put a player out of the game for repeated fouling.

A linesman stands on each touch line and decides which team throws the ball in when it goes out of bounds. The linesmen also call fouls.

**Time.** Most games last 90 minutes. Games are divided into two halves, and there is usually a short rest period between the two halves. Sometimes, the teams play an overtime period to determine a winner if the score is tied at the end of the second half.

**Starting Play.** Before a game starts, the team captains flip a coin to decide which team will kick off and to choose the goals their teams will defend. The teams change goals at the beginning of the second half, and the team that did not kick off to start the game kicks off for the second half.

Teams kick off from the *center spot*, a point in the middle of the halfway line. Players line up on their own half of the field with three players on the kicking team generally standing close to the ball. Opponents must be at least 10 yards away from the ball. One of the attackers kicks the ball forward to a teammate to start play again. Play resumes with a kickoff after each goal.

**Fouls.** The referee may penalize a team for a foul by sending the offending player off the field for the rest of the game, and perhaps awarding a free kick to the opponents. The kick may be a *direct free kick*, a *penalty kick*, or an *indirect free kick*.

A direct free kick is taken toward the opponent's goal from the spot where the foul occurred. Opponents must stay at least 10 yards from the ball. A direct free kick may be awarded for (1) deliberately kicking or attempting to kick an opponent; (2) tripping, striking, holding, or pushing an opponent; (3) deliberately running into an opponent, and (4) jumping so as to endanger another player while trying to get the ball. If a player other than the goalkeeper touches the ball with his hands, the other team gets a direct free kick.

A penalty kick is awarded if a defender commits one of these fouls within his own penalty area. The offended team takes the penalty kick from the *penalty spot*, 12 yards directly in front of the goal. All players, except the opposing goalkeeper and the kicker, must stand outside of the penalty area.

The referee awards indirect free kicks for less serious fouls. The kicker must kick the ball so that it touches another player before it enters the opponent's goal. All opponents must stay at least 10 feet from the ball. Indirect free kicks are awarded for (1) dangerous play such as kicking the ball when the goalkeeper is holding it, (2) blocking an opponent, (3) pushing an opponent when the ball is not nearby, and (4) running into the goalkeeper when he is not holding the ball, when he is in his goal area, or when he is not blocking an opponent. The referee awards an indirect free kick against the goalkeeper if the goalkeeper takes more than four steps with the ball without bouncing it.

The referee also awards an indirect free kick if a

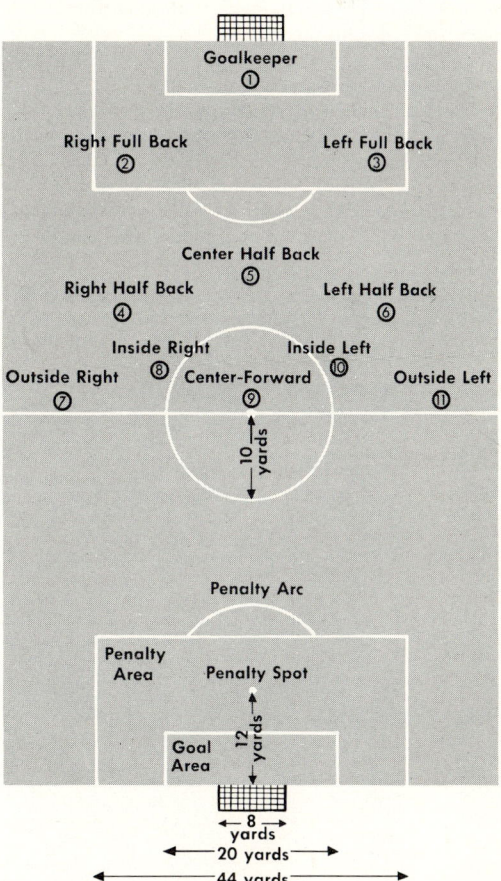

**A Soccer Field** is a rectangular area divided by the halfway line, which runs across the center of the field. The diagram, *below*, shows how the soccer players line up for the kickoff.

448a

# SOCCER

player is offside. Generally, an attacking player who is in his opponent's half of the field is offside if he is between the ball and the goal line. But he is not offside if (1) two opponents are closer to their goal line than he is, (2) he moved between the ball and goal line after a teammate kicked the ball, (3) the ball touched an opponent, or (4) he received the ball from a *goal kick*, a *throw-in*, a *corner kick*, or a *dropped ball*. These terms are explained in the table: *Soccer Terms* elsewhere on this page.

### Soccer Players

A soccer team is divided almost equally into attackers and defenders. As the teams line up on either side of the halfway line to start a game, the first line for each team has five forwards. They are the left and right outside (*wing*) players; a center forward; and left and right inside players. The second line consists of the left, center, and right halfbacks. The left and right fullbacks play in front of the goalkeeper.

The forwards are offensive players, and they try to score goals. They must be fast, agile, and able to move the ball accurately and quickly with their feet or their heads. The *center forward* plays close to his opponent's goal and usually has the most opportunity to score. The *wing forwards* must be able to *center* the ball accurately. That is, they kick it in front of the opponent's goal from the sides of the field so that one of their teammates can knock the ball into the goal.

The *inside forwards* must be able to *dribble* (run while moving the ball along with one foot to the other), pass accurately, and receive passes from their own defenders.

The defense consists of the goalkeeper and the five *backs*. The backs on a soccer team are generally bigger than the forwards. The *left* and *right fullbacks* and the *center halfback* form the main defensive barrier in front of the goalkeeper. The center halfback plays near his own goal. He is the most important back, because he often stops attacks by *clearing* the ball (pushing it away from his own goal area) with his head. He stays very close to the opposing center forward to prevent him from scoring.

The *wing halfbacks* play both defense and offense. They try to stop opponents' attacks on their own goal, and then they pass the ball out to teammates to start moving the ball toward the opponent's goal. Wing halfbacks occasionally score goals from 20 to 30 yards out in front of the goal.

The goalkeeper stands between the goal posts and moves quickly to all parts of the penalty area to stop shots. He is the only player that can use his hands and arms to stop the ball.

### Soccer Skills

Kicking includes those kicks that (1) attempt to score a goal, (2) put the ball in play, or (3) put the ball into a particular area of the field. Good players should be able

---
#### SOCCER TERMS
---

**Goal Kick** is made by a defender when a ball last touched by a member of the attacking team passes over the goal line without going into the goal. He must kick the ball from inside his team's goal area, and it must go beyond his team's penalty area.

**Corner Kick** is made by an offensive player when a ball last touched by a defensive player over the goal line without going into the goal. The player kicks the ball from the nearest corner of the field.

**Throw-In** takes place after a player knocks the ball over one of the touch lines. A member of the other team throws the ball back into play. The thrower must have both feet on the ground either on the touch line or outside the playing area and he must throw the ball with both hands from above his head.

**Dropped Ball.** The referee drops the ball onto the ground between opposing players. This starts play again after the referee has stopped it for some reason other than foul, such as injury to a player.

---

**A Soccer Player Tries to Score a Goal with a Header.** He dove through the air, *right*, and hit the ball with his forehead, trying to knock it past the goalkeeper, *left*. Skilled soccer players can hit the ball in almost any direction quickly and accurately with a header.

Pictorial Parade

# SOCCER

to kick the ball well with either foot. A player who can kick best with his right foot generally plays on the right side of the field, and a left-footed kicker will play on the left side. For example, a left wing forward must be able to kick the ball well with his left foot.

A player may kick the ball with (1) his *instep* (top of the foot), (2) the outer or inner sides of his foot, or (3) his heel. The instep is perhaps the most effective kick. A player can control the length, accuracy, and power of his kick much better with the instep.

Players kick with greater accuracy if they kick the ball so that it travels close to the ground. A player about to kick the ball along the ground should place his nonkicking foot near the ball. He should keep his head down and his eyes on the ball. He swings the kicking leg so that his foot hits the ball squarely. After his foot hits the ball, it should *follow through* (continue to move forward) to make the ball travel in the right direction and to keep the ball low.

To *chip* the ball, a player kicks it with his instep or the inside of his foot, lifting the ball over the head of an opponent. A player who chips cannot always be sure that the ball will travel the right distance and in the right direction. Also, an opponent may anticipate the chip, back up quickly, and intercept the ball with his head or his body.

Other common kicks are the *volley* and the *half volley*. A player volleys when he kicks hard, just as the ball bounces off the ground. Volleys make powerful shots, but the ball is likely to sail high and go over the goal's crossbar.

*Passing* the ball to teammates is one of the most important skills in soccer. For accuracy, especially for quick, short passes, a player usually passes with the inside of his foot. Quick passes often fool opponents who are unable to recover in time to get the ball or get into the proper defensive position. Most passing is done to the right or left, but soccer players also pass the ball forward to a teammate.

A player sometimes passes the ball 20 yards or more with the inside of his foot. But if he wants to make a long pass, he is much more likely to reach a teammate by kicking the ball with his instep. The ball travels much faster this way and it is much more difficult for opponents to intercept it.

Players occasionally *back-heel* (pass the ball backwards by kicking it with the heel). Players sometimes use the back heel to send the ball to a teammate in one direction after getting the opposing player's moving in the opposite direction.

*Dribbling* means to move the ball down the field by kicking it gently or nudging it with one foot to the other. Dribbling allows the player to keep the ball in his possession as he runs. By faking with his head or body to go one way, then actually going in another direction, a player may dribble quickly past several opponents. The ball will never be more than a few inches from the player's feet as he moves down the field.

*Trapping* occurs when a player uses his chest, thigh, foot, or his head to stop a ball and gain control of it. He may wedge it between his foot and the ground, or he may allow it to hit his chest, thigh, or head and drop to the ground at his feet. If the ball bounces even a foot away from him, he is likely to lose possession of it to an opponent.

*Heading* means hitting the ball with the head. Forwards score many goals by running into the goal area as the ball is kicked there, and heading it into the goal. Good players can head the ball long distances. Goalkeepers seldom head the ball, because the rules allow them to use their hands.

Players head the ball with their foreheads. A player may head the ball directly from the front, or flick it with his head. If a player heads the ball with the top or back of his head, he cannot control the ball as well, and

**A Soccer Player Kicks the Ball** with the instep or inside of his foot. He kicks with his instep when trying for a goal, *top*. He uses the inside of his foot to pass to a teammate, *bottom*.
*The New York Times*

**A Soccer Player Tackles an Opponent** to knock the ball away from him. He usually slides one leg in front of his opponent's feet to kick the ball away from him, *below*.
*Wide World*

448c

# SOCCER

the impact of the ball as it hits may stun him.

*Tackling* is hooking or kicking the ball away from an opponent with the feet. In the most common type of tackle, a player faces his opponent and lunges at the ball, reaching with one foot to take it away from his opponent. In the *sliding tackle*, the player slides along the ground with one leg extended to kick the ball away from his opponent. In the shoulder charge, the player meets shoulder to shoulder with his opponent and tries to move him away from the ball. Players must never push with their elbows or arms, or deliberately kick or trip an opponent.

### Soccer History

A game similar to soccer was probably played as early as 400 B.C. by the Chinese. In the A.D. 200's, the Romans played a game in which two teams tried to move a ball across a line on the field. During the 1100's, London children played a form of soccer in the streets.

During the early 1800's, many English schools played a game similar to soccer. The players made a number of rules that changed and developed the game. But each school interpreted the rules differently. In 1848, an association of school representatives met at Trinity College, Cambridge, to draw up the first set of rules.

### WORLD CUP FINALS

| 1930 | Uruguay 4, Argentina 2 | (in Montevideo) |
| 1934 | Italy 2, Czechoslovakia 1 | (in Rome) |
| 1938 | Italy 4, Hungary 2 | (in Paris) |
| 1950 | Uruguay 2, Brazil 1 | (in Rio de Janeiro) |
| 1954 | West Germany 3, Hungary 2 | (in Bern) |
| 1958 | Brazil 5, Sweden 2 | (in Stockholm) |
| 1962 | Brazil 3, Czechoslovakia 1 | (in Santiago, Chile) |
| 1966 | England 4, West Germany 2 | (in London) |

In 1863, representatives of English football clubs founded the Football Association. In 1871, the association introduced the Football Association Challenge Cup Competition. This competition is still one of the most famous in soccer. Professional soccer began in 1885 in England, and three years later 12 clubs formed the Football League of England.

Soccer began to spread throughout the world in the late 1800's. By 1900, associations were founded in Belgium, Chile, Denmark, Italy, The Netherlands, and Switzerland. In 1904, the national associations founded the *Federation Internationale de Football Association* (FIFA). Soccer rules are made by a 20-man board made up of equal numbers of representatives from the FIFA, England, Northern Ireland, Scotland, and Wales. Board members have a total of eight votes, with the FIFA representatives having four of them. The over 130-member FIFA supervises international matches, which have become an important part of soccer.

In 1930, Jules Rimet, a Frenchman who was president of the FIFA, presented a cup for the winner of an international competition. This competition is now called the World Cup, and its winner is determined in a famous series between national teams from many countries. The World Cup games are held every four years.

Soccer was the only form of football played in the United States until the mid-1800's, when American football became popular. Many U.S. and Canadian universities and colleges still have soccer teams.

The United States Soccer Football Association (U.S.S.F.A.), founded in 1913, is a member of the FIFA. Until the mid-1960's, it was mainly concerned with amateur soccer. In 1967, professional teams began play in the United States. GEORGE E. FISHWICK

See also RUGBY FOOTBALL; WORLD (color picture); CHILE (picture); PELÉ.

**Maracanã Stadium in Rio de Janeiro,** Brazil, is one of the largest soccer stadiums in the world. It seats about 150,000 persons. The 1950 World Cup games were played there.
Wide World

448d

**SOCHE,** *SWAH CHUH,* or YARKAND, *yahr KAND* (pop. 80,000; alt. 4,430 ft.), is a trading center in southwestern Sinkiang, an autonomous region of China. It lies about 700 miles north of New Delhi, India. The city has been a station on the trade routes of Asia since ancient times. Factories in the city produce carpets and embroideries and weave cotton, silk, and wool. For location, see CHINA (political map).

**SOCIAL AND REHABILITATION SERVICE (SRS)** is an agency of the United States Department of Health, Education, and Welfare. It was formed in 1967 to bring together in a single organization the department's social service and rehabilitation programs and its income support programs for needy Americans. The agency has five major divisions. (1) The *Rehabilitation Services Administration* administers programs that aid physically and mentally handicapped persons. (2) The *Children's Bureau* administers child welfare and maternal and child health programs, and crippled children's services. (3) The *Administration on Aging* administers programs that help aged persons. It also gathers and distributes information on the problems of old age. (4) The *Medical Services Administration* is responsible for Medicaid and other medical assistance programs for needy persons administered by states and local communities. (5) The *Assistance Payments Administration* handles payments involved in federal-state aid programs for the needy.

Critically reviewed by the SOCIAL AND REHABILITATION SERVICE

**SOCIAL CHANGE.** See SOCIOLOGY; CULTURAL LAG.

**SOCIAL CLASS** is a group of persons in a society that have about the same social standing. Social classes exist because people usually classify one another into more or less distinct groups based on such factors as wealth, power, prestige, ancestry, religion, and occupation. Often, people rank these groups in their minds, considering some "better" than others. Social scientists call the groups *social classes* and describe the process of social ranking as *social stratification.*

All societies seem to have some system of social stratification. That is, there are no "classless" societies. In the United States and other Western democracies, the class system is usually informal, and social scientists disagree on how to classify the groups that seem to exist. Some arbitrarily divide the American people into three classes—upper, middle, and lower. Other social scientists add a fourth class—the working class—between the middle and lower groups, while others merely substitute the term *working class* for *lower class.*

In the late 1940's, social anthropologist W. Lloyd Warner identified six social classes in a New England community he studied. He called them (1) upper-upper class, (2) lower-upper class, (3) upper-middle class, (4) lower-middle class, (5) upper-lower class, and (6) lower-lower class. The characteristics of each group are described in *Yankee City Series*. Although some sociologists disagree with Warner's findings, his classifications have been widely used by scholars and the general public.

In most Western democracies, persons can move from one category to another and there are few clear-cut signs as to which group a person belongs. But in some societies, people are born into a certain social class, and change to another class is difficult if not impossible. A class with such rigid barriers is called a *caste.* A person belongs to the caste of his parents. Laws and traditions severely limit the social contacts he may have with members of other castes. India has a more firmly established caste system than any other country. See CASTE; INDIA (Hinduism).

Communism has long had the goal of achieving a "classless" society without distinctions based on rank or birth. But in the Soviet Union and other Communist countries—just as in the non-Communist world—some groups of persons, such as government officials, have much more power, wealth, and prestige than others. See COMMUNISM (Marxism); RUSSIA (Way of Life).

**How Persons Are Ranked.** Various methods are used to compare and rank individuals and groups. A social scientist may use such objective measures as how much money a person earns. Or members of a group may rank one another, or place themselves on the class ladder. Surveys show that the way persons rank themselves depends on the categories that are used. If they are told to place themselves in either the upper, middle, or lower class, most place themselves in the middle class. But when the working-class category is included, the majority rank themselves in that class. Almost all are unwilling to say they are members of the lower class.

Occupation is one of the best indicators of class, because people tend to agree on the relative prestige they attach to similar jobs. Those at or near the top rung of the prestige ladder usually have the highest incomes, the best education, and the most power. In general, persons who hold positions of leadership and responsibility—such as heads of government and industry—rank at the top. Persons whose jobs require long training and superior intelligence—such as physicians, scientists, college professors, and university-trained professional people—rank next in order of prestige. Persons with low-paying positions that require little training or formal education—such as unskilled laborers—rate at the bottom. People in both capitalist and Communist countries, as well as those in both economically developed and underdeveloped countries, rank these jobs almost exactly the same way.

**Class Differences.** A person's social status affects his behavior, values, and style of life. Upper-class members, for example, are aware of their privileged position and try to preserve it by encouraging marriage within their own class. Persons with higher status usually back conservative political parties and candidates, because they wish to maintain the existing system of inequality. Socially, the upper class is noted for its elegant and refined style of living.

Most members of the middle class enjoy a better-than-average education and standard of living. Middle-class values are usually the dominant values in a society. In the United States, the middle class stresses thrift, self-improvement, and economic success and job advancement. This group also believes it is important to own property and to conform to the community's standards on morality and respectability. Members of the middle class frequently send their children to college, and they are generally prominent in civic and governmental affairs.

Members of the lower class usually have less formal

**SOCIAL CLASS**

448e

# SOCIAL CONTRACT

education and training than those of the middle- and upper-classes, and have unskilled or semiskilled jobs. Because many lower-class members live in poverty or near-poverty, they are more concerned with immediate needs than with long-range goals.

**Why Social Classes Exist.** Most sociologists who study stratification believe a society must have a system of rewards to encourage some men to undertake the key jobs. Persons who hold these positions usually need much education and training, and often work under great strain. For men to seek out and to work efficiently in such socially crucial occupations, society must see that they are well rewarded. Therefore, these sociologists argue, stratification and unequal reward are necessary if there is to be a division of labor with some persons taking greater responsibility than others.

A group of sociologists influenced by the teachings of Karl Marx rejects this interpretation. This group argues that differing rewards are due to variations in power positions. For example, the people who control the resources that men value or who control the police or other instruments of force have the highest income and status. This group suggests that stratification exists in any social organization that involves a chain of command. SEYMOUR MARTIN LIPSET

**SOCIAL CONTRACT.** See ROUSSEAU, JEAN JACQUES.

**SOCIAL CREDIT PARTY.** See ALBERTA (Depression and Recovery; Industrial Expansion).

**SOCIAL INSECTS** are insects that live and work with others of their kind in organized groups. The groups are usually called *colonies* or *communities*. See ANIMAL (Animals That Live Together); ANT (The Ant Colony); BEE (The Honeybee Colony; Kinds of Bees); TERMITE; WASP.

**SOCIAL LEGISLATION.** See CHILD LABOR; HOUSING; LABOR (The Federal Government); PUBLIC HEALTH (Health Laws); SOCIAL SECURITY; WOMAN; MEDICARE.

**SOCIAL PSYCHOLOGY** is the study of social behavior, including its origins and effects. Social psychologists study the influence that persons have on one another individually and within groups. They also study relationships between groups. All these relationships are part of the process of *social influence*. The effects of social influence can be seen in conformity, leadership, prejudice, morale, attitude change, and child-rearing. Social psychology includes all these areas of study.

Social psychologists also study learning, adjustment, and other psychological processes that are affected by social factors. These psychologists examine the part played by *culture* and *society* as sources of social influence. A culture is a way of life that is transmitted to children from generation to generation. It dictates various social practices, including education, language, family relationships, child-rearing customs, and economic and political forms (see CULTURE). A society is made up of people who are organized to live according to their own culture. The study of culture and society reveals much about the learning and adjustment processes which lead to both normal and abnormal social behavior.

Through research, social psychologists try to understand problems of intergroup tensions and prejudice, industrial morale, and international relations. Social psychology is therefore both a basic field of social science and an area of applied activity.

Social psychologists use various research techniques, including observing and interviewing people in their own surroundings. A technique of growing importance is experimentation in a *social psychology laboratory*. Here, psychologists can control and alter certain social conditions and measure the effects produced. For example, to study conformity in group situations, a psychologist might ask five persons to make a simple judgment, such as judging which of two lines is longer. If four members of the group are told beforehand to give the wrong answer, the fifth person often will give that response, too. However, if the procedure is varied slightly so that the fourth person is instructed to give the correct judgment, then the fifth person usually does not attempt to conform to the majority opinion.

Social psychologists concentrate on three general problem areas: (1) social interaction in groups and organizations, including the study of conformity and leadership; (2) the effects of propaganda and other forms of communication on attitude change; and (3) social learning and personality development.

## Social Interaction

The term *social interaction* refers particularly to contact between persons who depend on each other. There are formal and informal social interactions.

In formal interaction, behavior is dictated by cultural forms, particularly by *social roles*. For example, society determines certain patterns of social behavior in relationships between parent and child, husband and wife, teacher and student, and employer and employee. In informal interaction, the form of the relationship depends more on the satisfactions of the persons themselves. Examples of informal interaction include friendships among strangers who meet while traveling.

Whether or not we continue a relationship depends on *interpersonal attraction* (liking or disliking a person). This is especially true in informal interaction. Researchers have found that most of us like a person if his attitudes are similar to ours. The satisfying continuance of interaction depends on a process of *social exchange*. That is, we usually expect that the rewards we give another person will be exchanged for rewards from him. Such an exchange occurs, for example, when we approve of a person and he approves of us. When we give a favor to a friend, we often receive the same kind of favor in return. Sometimes the reward received (tickets to a play) is not the same as the reward given (the loan of a football). The important factor is that the reward be important to the recipient.

In groups, social interaction usually involves the relationships of many people with one another. The study of these relationships is called *group dynamics*, and makes up a major area of laboratory experimentation.

Experiments have provided much information about factors affecting group performance and satisfaction. The most important of these factors is *group cohesiveness*, the attraction of a group for its members. If the members are strongly motivated to belong to a group, they are more likely to conform to its *norms* (standards of conduct). In groups that are more cohesive, the members are inclined to interact and communicate more.

The members also tend to have higher morale, in the sense of greater shared enthusiasm for the group and its activities. Morale is not necessarily a direct gauge of good performance. But morale and good performance have been found to be associated with each other and with cohesiveness. See MORALE.

Several factors help determine who will succeed as leader of a group. These factors include the task the group performs and the nature of the group's situation—its size, the composition of its membership, its history, and its resources. A leader's ability to influence his followers depends on how they regard him in the light of their situation. A leader's status and influence rise when the members believe he is providing resources which help the group in its task and the attainment of its goals. The leader then has a greater opportunity to introduce changes through actions that might be considered nonconformity for others in the group.

### Attitudes and Attitude Change

A *social attitude* is a view of people, things, or events. It can be either favorable or unfavorable, and influences a person to respond in a particular way. Every person has many attitudes, some of which are more important than others in determining responses. Some attitudes are also more likely to change than others. A person may change one of his attitudes because it conflicts with another one. He also may change attitudes that conflict with his behavior or with new information he has acquired.

Some social psychologists study *cognitive dissonance*, which arises, for example, when a person is required to do something even though an attitude prompts him to do the opposite. In such a situation, the person may change his attitude to fit his behavior, especially if he does not feel too greatly pressured to do so.

Other researchers study attitude change through research on *communication effects* from a communicator, such as a propagandist. They examine the relationship between how a person evaluates the new information and the way he perceives the communicator.

### Social Learning and Personality Development

Another area of social psychology is *socialization*, the child-rearing process. Most social psychologists emphasize learning as the central feature of socialization. They examine the ways in which socialization affects a child's personality, including his attitudes and social behavior. Their findings show that an important aspect of socialization lies in the child's identification with his parents and his friends.

The way a child imitates others is determined partly by his dependence on his parents, especially during early childhood. In general, the closer the relationship between parent and child, the more the child adopts characteristics from his parents. The child's pattern of identification is also determined by the balance of discipline and affection from his parents. This balance influences the development of the child's conscience, his attitudes toward himself, and his relations with his friends.

Personality development is also affected by the interaction between the child and certain groups. These groups include his friends, his school, his church, and other community organizations. Groups in which a person values his membership highly are called *reference groups*. They have a greater influence on his personality than other groups.    EDWIN P. HOLLANDER

**Related Articles** in WORLD BOOK include:

| Developmental | Human Relations | Personality |
| Psychology | Industrial Psychology | Prejudice |
| Group Dynamics | Learning | Psychology |

**SOCIAL SCIENCE.** Scholars generally identify three categories of knowledge: (1) the natural sciences and mathematics, (2) the humanities, and (3) the social sciences. The natural sciences concern nature and the physical world. The humanities try to interpret the meaning of man's life on earth rather than to describe his physical world or society. The social sciences focus on man's life with other men in groups. They include anthropology, economics, history, political science, sociology, criminology, and the science of law. Some scholars also regard education, ethics, philosophy, and psychology as social sciences. Certain studies in other fields, such as biology, geography, medicine, art, and linguistics, may be said to fall within the broad category of the social sciences.

**Relationship to Natural Sciences.** Scholars in the social sciences have developed certain ways of studying people and their institutions. Generally these scholars have borrowed from the natural sciences the methods they use to study, simplify, and classify the observed behavior of human society. Their observations of the regularity of human behavior lead them to form *hypotheses* (propositions) and then to test their validity.

The social sciences are still a comparatively new field of learning. History and geography have existed as separate disciplines for a long time. But attempts to organize man's endeavors into systems of economics, sociology, and political science are so new that many scholars doubt that the scientific method can be used with complete success to know and control any aspect of society. They see a wide gulf between the clear and exact nature of the natural sciences and the inexact nature of the social sciences. One of the most powerful tools of the natural sciences is the controlled experiment. Such a method is difficult to use in experiments involving human beings.

**Relationship to Humanities.** The interdependence of the social sciences and the humanities is important. In a social science, the scholar must note the underlying values of a society, which are stated by the scholars of the humanities. For instance, suppose a political scientist wishes to determine scientifically whether a particular community should have an authoritarian or a representative form of political organization and control. He must first learn the importance which that community attaches to such values as the right of the individual to differ with authority, or to have a voice in policy and laws. Then he can formulate the principles that govern its political action.    PAUL R. HANNA

**Related Articles** in WORLD BOOK include:

| Anthropology | Geography | Political Science |
| Archaeology | Geopolitics | Psychology |
| Civics | Government | Social Psychology |
| Criminology | History | Social Studies |
| Economics | Law | Sociology |
| Education | Linguistics | |
| Ethics | Philosophy | |

# SOCIAL SECURITY

**SOCIAL SECURITY** is a governmental program that provides cash payments or medical care to individuals. Social security includes three basic types of payments: (1) social insurance, (2) subsidized voluntary insurance, and (3) public assistance. *Social insurance* payments are financed by taxes paid by workers and employers. Payments are made to persons after they have fulfilled certain conditions. *Subsidized voluntary insurance* is a program under which a person buys a policy and the government pays part of the cost. *Public assistance* includes government payments financed by general taxes and based on the individual's needs.

Most persons in the United States receive their social-security protection from the provisions of the Social Security Act of 1935. But payments from the government do not provide the only form of security for most people. Private savings, home ownership, life insurance, annuities, hospitalization and health insurance, employer- and union-sponsored benefit programs, and other plans offer additional protection.

Every major country has a social-security program. In the 1880's, Germany became the first country to adopt workmen's compensation and old-age pension laws. In the United States, the first trade-union unem-

*Robert J. Myers, the contributor of this article, is Chief Actuary of the Social Security Administration, and author of* Social Insurance and Allied Government Programs.

ployment insurance plan was adopted in 1831, and the first private pension plan in American industry went into effect in 1875. Wisconsin in 1911 passed the first state workmen's compensation law to go into effect and be held constitutional. Great Britain passed its workmen's compensation act in 1897, and an old-age pension law in 1908. The Scandinavian countries began social-security programs in the 1900's. Canada's first social-insurance programs began in the 1940's.

## Social Insurance

The social-insurance program in the United States covers (1) old-age, survivors, and disability benefits; (2) hospital insurance; (3) unemployment insurance; (4) workmen's compensation; and (5) sickness insurance.

In 1935, Congress passed the Social Security Act sponsored by Senator Robert F. Wagner of New York. Before then, social-security laws included only workmen's compensation, old-age and mothers' assistance, and general relief. The new law provided for federally administered old-age insurance. Monthly payments began in 1940. Later laws widened coverage, liberalized qualifications, and added and increased benefits.

Congress passed a law in 1954 requiring state unemployment-insurance plans to cover persons in any business that employed four or more workers, rather than eight or more as before. In 1965, Congress established a system of hospital and related social-insurance benefits under the Social Security Act. A voluntary system of insurance to pay doctor bills also was set up. Both programs apply only to persons 65 or older and are called *Medicare*.

**Old-Age, Survivors, and Disability Insurance** is administered entirely by the federal government. The Social Security Administration, an agency of the De-

**A Social Security Card** bears a worker's name and account number. The first three digits identify the office issuing the card.

partment of Health, Education, and Welfare, directs these programs.

*Coverage.* The plan covers about 87 of every 100 workers in the United States. Of those not covered, about half come under special plans for railroad workers and for federal, state, and local government employees. Coverage is compulsory for most persons. Those without coverage include some government employees, farm and domestic workers who are not regularly employed, and self-employed persons with earnings that amount to less than $400 a year.

*Benefits* are paid to retired workers and their dependents, to disabled workers and their dependents, and to survivors of workers who have died. They are paid in monthly checks, except for lump-sum death payments.

A worker may receive old-age benefits if he is 62 or older, and substantially retired from gainful work. The government considers him substantially retired if he earns $1,680 or less annually, or $140 or less in any month. He becomes eligible at the age of 72, regardless of his earnings. If he retires at 65, he receives full benefits. But he may retire at 62 and get 80 per cent of the benefit he would get at 65. He then receives a lower benefit for the rest of his life. The amount of a person's benefits depends only on his average earnings in work covered by the law, not on his length of coverage or contributions to the program. Lower-paid workers receive a larger benefit in proportion to earnings than higher-paid workers do. The smallest benefit a worker can get at age 65 is $55 a month, and the largest is $218. A worker draws additional benefits if he has a wife of 62 or older, or if he has a child who is disabled or under 18, or age 18 to 21 and in school. The normal benefit for each dependent is half the worker's benefit. But a wife who claims benefits between 62 and 65 receives less. The maximum that a family can receive is 80 per cent of the worker's average wage, but the highest payment cannot exceed $434.40 a month.

*Eligibility.* A person qualifies for old-age benefits if he has worked a certain length of time after 1936 on a job covered by social security. This employment does not have to be continuous. Generally, 10 years' employment is required. But persons now above or near the minimum retirement age do not need to have been covered for this length of time.

A totally disabled worker may receive monthly benefits for himself and dependents after six months of disability and if he is likely to be disabled for at least six

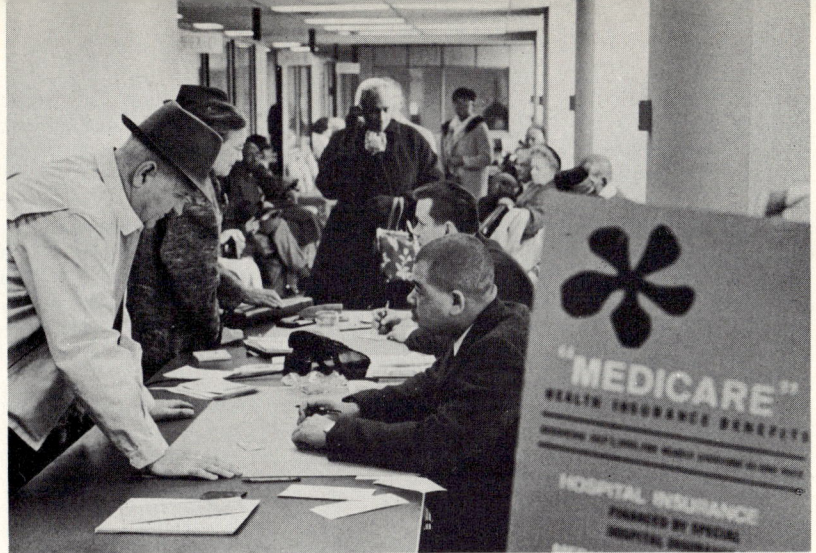

**Social Security** funds provide many benefits, such as cash payments or medical care. Medicare, a hospital and voluntary medical insurance plan, is financed through Social Security program funds.

U. S. News & World Report

more months. Additional amounts are paid for his wife if she is 62 or older, and for eligible children. A mother of eligible children receives benefits regardless of her age, if the children are under 18 or disabled. The disabled worker must have been in work covered by social security for 5 of the last 10 years. If he is under 31, lower requirements apply.

If an insured worker dies before or after his retirement, his dependents are eligible for monthly survivor benefits. Payments may go to his widow if she is 62; to his dependent parents if age 62; and to children and their mother just as in the case of a disabled worker. The widow can claim benefits at a permanently reduced rate between 60 and 62, or between 50 and 60 if she is disabled. Payments are based on the benefits the worker was receiving (or would have been receiving if he had been old enough to retire) when he died. A widow or dependent parent aged 62 or older receives $82\frac{1}{2}$ per cent of the worker's benefit. A widow aged 60 receives $71\frac{1}{2}$ per cent, and one aged 50 receives 50 per cent. A child or widowed mother receives 75 per cent. To be eligible, the worker must have been receiving old-age or disability benefits, or must have been eligible to receive old-age benefits if he had been old enough. Or, for benefits for children or their mother, he must have had a job covered by social security for half the time during the three years before his death. Dependents of women workers, including their husbands, may draw dependent and survivor benefits under the same conditions that apply for men workers.

*Payments.* The government does not automatically pay social-security benefits when a worker retires, becomes disabled, or dies. He or his survivors must file a claim at one of the over 600 district offices of the Social Security Administration. If the qualified person does not file promptly, he may lose money. The number of back payments possible for retirement or survivor benefits is limited to 12 months. If he is not satisfied with his benefit, he may appeal to referees and the appeals council of the Social Security Administration. He may also take his case to a federal court.

*Payments to Uninsured Persons.* Special benefits of $40 a month ($60 for married couples) apply for certain uninsured persons 72 or older who became 72 before 1968. General requirements are that they be ineligible for a governmental pension and not be getting public assistance payments. Benefits are paid by the Old-Age, Survivors, and Disability Insurance system. The money comes from general revenues.

*Financing.* A payroll tax in the form of a contribution shared equally by the employer and employee finances the Old-Age, Survivors, and Disability Insurance program. The tax is paid only on annual earnings up to $7,800. The employer and employee together pay the tax. The rate was set at 8.4 per cent for 1969 and 1970, 9.2 per cent for 1971 and 1972, and 10 per cent for 1973 and after. A self-employed person pays about three-fourths of this rate.

Each payday, the employer deducts the tax from the worker's pay, adds an equal contribution, and sends it monthly or quarterly to the Department of the Treasury. A self-employed person pays quarterly. The tax for hospital insurance is paid with the Old-Age, Survivors, and Disability Insurance tax. The government puts all payments in the Disability Insurance Trust Fund and the Old-Age and Survivors Insurance Trust Fund.

*Administration.* Every person covered has an account number. The worker's employer reports his number and earnings to the Social Security Administration. By 1969, this agency had records on about 131 million persons. It does not keep a record of the contributions each person has paid, because these deductions do not accumulate with interest, as they would in a savings bank. A person's benefits have no direct relationship to the contributions he has made.

In 1968, about 72 million persons held jobs covered by social security on an average day. They worked for about $5\frac{1}{2}$ million employers. About 24,600,000 persons were receiving monthly benefits at the end of 1968.

A total of $12\frac{1}{2}$ million retired workers had 3 million eligible dependents receiving benefits. There were 1,300,000 disability beneficiaries with 1,000,000 eligible dependents. Survivor beneficiaries totaled 6,000,000 including 2,900,000 aged widows, 2,500,000 orphaned children, and 500,000 mothers of such children. About 700,000 uninsured persons 72 or over received special payments.

*Amounts Paid.* The average retired worker received a monthly benefit of about $98 in 1968, excluding any

## SOCIAL SECURITY

benefits for dependents. The average benefit for a retired worker with an eligible wife was about $165 a month. An aged widow received an average of $86, and a widow with two children got about $255. Disability beneficiaries had an average payment of $111, excluding benefits for dependents. Total benefit payments for 1968 were $25 billion, and total contributions were $27 billion. Assets of the trust funds totaled $29 billion at the end of 1968.

**Railroad Retirement** is a separate system of social security for railroad workers. The Railroad Retirement Board, an independent agency of the government, administers this program of old-age, survivors, and disability benefits (see RAILROAD RETIREMENT BOARD).

Railroad employers and workers share equally in financing the program. Together they contributed, in 1969, 19.1 per cent on earnings up to $650 a month. A worker with less than 10 years' railroad service has his wage credits transferred to the general social-security system, and receives benefits from it. But, even though he has more than 10 years' railroad service, survivor benefits are based on his combined earnings in railroad and other work, and are generally paid by the Railroad Retirement Board. A railroad worker can receive two retirement payments.

**Hospital and Supplementary Medical Insurance.** The *hospital insurance* is for all persons under the Old-Age, Survivors, and Disability Insurance system, and railroad pensioners. It pays the cost for the first 60 days of hospital care (excluding the first $44). It also pays all except $11 a day for the next 30 days. It also includes skilled nursing home care after the hospital. It does not pay doctors' fees. The *supplementary medical insurance* is a voluntary plan. It pays 80 per cent of doctor bills and certain other related costs in excess of $50 a year. It costs $4 a month (which the government matches) and covers anyone 65 or older who signs up for the plan. See MEDICARE.

**Unemployment Insurance** makes weekly payments to workers who have been unemployed or released from their jobs for more than one week. Benefits are paid for as long as 39 weeks. Each state administers its own program. Railroad workers qualify under a separate federal plan. The federal government requires businesses with four or more workers to pay a 3.1 per cent tax on wages up to $3,000 a year. But it excuses 2.7 per cent of this tax if the employer's state has an acceptable unemployment-insurance system. The federal government uses the 0.4 per cent tax actually collected to pay grants to states for administering their insurance systems, and to build up a fund from which states may borrow. Each state sets its own tax rate on employers. A few require a small contribution from workers. The state tax rates average about $2\frac{1}{2}$ per cent. In many states, benefits amount to about half a worker's earnings, with a maximum weekly payment of $30 to $45. See UNEMPLOYMENT INSURANCE.

**Workmen's Compensation.** Persons suffering from industrial injuries or diseases may receive workmen's compensation. In some states, the state government administers the program. In others, private insurance companies provide the payments, or compete with state funds. Coverage usually applies only to industrial and commercial workers. Benefits include medical care, cash benefits during temporary or permanent disability, and lump-sum or continuous benefits for survivors. The employer generally pays the entire cost of workmen's compensation. The amount he pays varies with the size of his payroll and the type of work his employees do. The average rate is about 1 per cent of the payroll. See WORKMEN'S COMPENSATION.

**Sickness Insurance** provides weekly cash payments to persons unable to work because of illness due to disease or injury. The Railroad Retirement Board and four states—California, New Jersey, New York, and Rhode Island—sponsor such programs. Each plan resembles unemployment insurance or workmen's compensation as to duration and amount of payments. In some systems, benefits are paid for maternity as well as for sickness. California also pays additional cash benefits for hospitalization. The employer, the employee, or both contribute to the sickness-insurance plan. The total contribution rate varies from about $\frac{1}{2}$ to 1 per cent. See INSURANCE (Health Insurance).

### Public Assistance

Some state and local governments had their own public-assistance programs before 1935. But most of these

### EXAMPLES OF SOCIAL SECURITY PAYMENTS

|  | $74 or less | $150 | $300 | $400 | $550 | $650 |
|---|---|---|---|---|---|---|
| **Retirement and Disability Benefits** | | | | | | |
| Monthly payment to retired worker at age 65 or disabled worker | $ 55.00 | $ 88.40 | $127.10 | $153.60 | $189.90 | $218.00 |
| Monthly payment to retired worker at age 62 | 44.00 | 70.80 | 101.70 | 122.90 | 152.00 | 174.40 |
| Monthly payment to wife at age 65, or under age 65 with a child in her care | 27.50 | 44.20 | 63.60 | 76.80 | 95.00 | 105.00 |
| Monthly payment to wife at age 62 | 20.70 | 33.20 | 47.70 | 57.60 | 71.30 | 78.80 |
| **Survivors Benefits** | | | | | | |
| Monthly payment to widow at 62 | 55.00 | 73.00 | 104.90 | 126.80 | 156.70 | 179.90 |
| Monthly payment to widow at 60, no child | 47.70 | 63.30 | 91.00 | 109.90 | 135.90 | 156.00 |
| Monthly payment to disabled widow at 50, no child | 33.40 | 44.50 | 63.60 | 76.90 | 95.00 | 109.10 |
| Monthly payment to widow under 62, 1 child | 82.50 | 132.60 | 190.80 | 230.40 | 285.00 | 327.00 |
| Maximum monthly family benefit | 82.50 | 132.60 | 240.00 | 322.40 | 395.60 | 434.40 |
| Lump-sum death payment | 165.00 | 255.00 | 255.00 | 255.00 | 255.00 | 255.00 |

Workers Average Monthly Earnings After 1950

# SOCIAL SECURITY

plans were poorly organized or had strict residence requirements. The Social Security Act provides federal grants-in-aid to states that establish certain special categories of public aid and meet certain standards. The 1935 law created three categories: (1) old-age assistance, or aid to the aged; (2) aid to the blind; and (3) aid to dependent children. In 1950, Congress added aid to persons who are permanently and totally disabled. Almost all states have programs in each category. In 1960, Congress gave added funds to states to encourage better medical care for old-age assistance recipients. It also established a federal-state program of medical care to help aged persons meet unusually heavy medical bills. In 1965, the medical assistance program was extended to needy persons of all ages. Persons receiving public assistance are generally allowed to earn small amounts of money without having their payments reduced. The Social and Rehabilitation Service carries out the federal government's responsibilities for joint federal-state public assistance programs. See SOCIAL AND REHABILITATION SERVICE.

**Old-Age Assistance.** The states make direct payments to needy persons of 65 or older who are not in public institutions. In addition, the states may pay their medical and hospital expenses. Persons receiving old-age insurance benefits may also receive state old-age assistance in case of need. Some states have requirements for applicants, such as residence in the state for at least five of the last nine years. Federal financial aid to each state is based on the average payment to every person receiving old-age assistance. For example, if the average is $65 a month, the federal government pays from $45 to $49.20 of this amount. The remainder may come from the state, or the state and local governments.

At the end of 1968, about 2 million persons were receiving old-age assistance. Of these, about half also received old-age insurance benefits. Individual payments vary widely because they depend on the needs in each case. Payments by states range from about $40 a month in some states to over $100 in others. The average payment is about $70. Assistance payments total about $1,700,000,000 a year, of which the federal government pays about two-thirds.

**Aid to the Blind** resembles old-age assistance. The basis for federal aid to the states is the same. However, blind persons of all ages may receive payments. In 1968, about 80,000 blind persons received an average of $93 a month. Annual payments to the blind totaled $90 million, of which the federal government paid about 57 per cent.

**Aid to Dependent Children** provides payments to needy children and to the parents or other adults taking care of them. Children may become needy because their father died, deserted the home, is unemployed, or has become too disabled to support them. Federal aid is based on the average payment of a state to each child and adult caretaker.

In the late 1960's, more than 4½ million children in 1½ million families received payments. The average monthly payment was about $172 for each family and $56 for each child. Average state payments for individuals ranged from about $10 to about $50 a month. Total payments for 1968 amounted to $2,800,000,000, with the federal government paying more than half. See AID TO DEPENDENT CHILDREN.

**Aid to the Permanently and Totally Disabled** resembles old-age assistance. At the end of 1968, about 700,000 disabled persons received aid. Their payments averaged about $80 a month. Annual payments totaled about $650 million, of which the federal government paid about 59 per cent.

**Medical Assistance** provides care for public assistance recipients and others who do not have enough money to pay for such care. Payments in 1968 amounted to about $4 billion, of which the federal government paid about half.

**Other Public Assistance Programs** include *General Assistance*, or *Relief;* and *Veterans' Welfare* programs. See RELIEF; VETERANS ADMINISTRATION.

**Other Public Aid** under the federal Social Security Act includes state-administered programs that are partly financed by federal grants. These programs cover maternal and child-health services, crippled children's services, and child-welfare services.

## Social Security in Canada

Canada has a social-insurance program that is administered by the national government. A public-assistance program is shared by the national government and the provinces. It began in 1927. Unemployment insurance began in 1940, family allowances in 1944, old-age insurance in 1951, and hospitalization insurance in 1957.

**Social Insurance.** In Canada, one part of the program is called *old age security pensions*. Applicants must be 65 or older, and must have lived in Canada at least 10 years. They do not have to stop working to qualify. Special taxes pay for the program. All benefits are $77 a month, but will be adjusted to changes in the cost of living in the future.

The other part of the old-age program is the *Canada Pension Plan*. It operates on contributions from earnings much like the United States plan. The Canadian plan provides monthly benefits for retirement, disability, and survivors. It covers almost all employed persons who earn over $600 a year. Employer and worker each contribute at a rate of 1.8 per cent on wages between $600 and $5,200 a year.

The *Guaranteed Income Supplement* program provides up to $31.20 a month additional income to old-age security pensioners who have no sizable income from the Canada Pension Plan or other sources.

*Unemployment Insurance* is for workers in business and industry who earn less than $5,460 a year. Employers and workers contribute equally. The national government pays the administrative cost of the program, and also provides one-fifth of the combined contributions from employers and workers. Benefits range from about 40 per cent of earnings for workers without dependents to 50 per cent for those with dependents. Payments may extend to a maximum of 52 weeks.

*Hospitalization Insurance* is paid in all Canadian provinces. Each province receives grants from the national government that cover about half the cost of hospital services. The insured person and the province pay the remainder of the cost in a manner determined by each province. The province also establishes the benefit provisions. There is a similar program for physicians'

453

## SOCIAL SECURITY ADMINISTRATION

services, but not all provinces participate in it.

*Family Allowances* are paid by the government to children under 18 who meet certain residence requirements. Children aged 16 and 17 must be in school or disabled. Payments are $6 a month for children aged 9 or under, $8 for those 10 to 15, and $10 for those 16 and 17.

**Public Assistance.** Nearly all public assistance is provided through the Canada Assistance Plan, enacted in 1966. This plan is designed to provide cash assistance to all needy persons. The cost of the program is shared equally by the national and provincial governments. The provinces administer the plan, which largely replaced previous programs that provided help only to the aged, the blind, the disabled, and widowed mothers. Several Canadian provinces kept parts of the older programs while switching to the Canada Assistance Plan.                                    ROBERT J. MYERS

**Related Articles** in WORLD BOOK include:

| | |
|---|---|
| Aid to Dependent Children | Relief |
| Annuity | Townsend Plan |
| Beveridge, William H. | Unemployment |
| Insurance | Insurance |
| Medicare | Veterans Administration |
| Pension | Workmen's Compensation |

**SOCIAL SECURITY ADMINISTRATION (SSA)** was created in 1953 as a division of the Department of Health, Education, and Welfare of the United States government. It took over most of the social security duties of the former Federal Security Agency. The work of the SSA is directed by the commissioner of social security.

See also SOCIAL SECURITY; FEDERAL CREDIT UNIONS, BUREAU OF.

**SOCIAL SETTLEMENT.** Social settlements are institutions which grew up in many crowded cities during the late 1800's and the 1900's. They try to educate people to better citizenship. Social settlements, or *settlement houses*, carry on many activities. These include nurseries, clubs for all ages, adult-education classes, libraries, baths, and savings banks. Many settlements have halls where community groups may hold social, political, or religious meetings. Sports and recreational programs are often scheduled.

Men of Oxford University founded the first social settlement in London in 1884. It was known as Toynbee Hall. It grew out of the work begun by Arnold Toynbee in the crowded Whitechapel district of London. In 1887, Stanton Coit founded the University Settlement in New York City. Two years later, Jane Addams and Ellen Gates Starr opened Hull House in Chicago.

The National Federation of Settlements and Neighborhood Centers encourages local programs through its more than 240 affiliated groups.           EMORY S. BOGARDUS

See also ADDAMS, JANE; HULL HOUSE; SOCIAL WORK; TOYNBEE (Arnold); WALD, LILLIAN D.

**SOCIAL STRATIFICATION.** See SOCIAL CLASS.

**SOCIAL STUDIES** is the program of citizenship education provided by the elementary and secondary schools. The social studies program organizes the subject matter of the social sciences for presentation to children and young people. At the higher education levels, students generally study and specialize in one or more of the separate social sciences, such as history, geography, economics, political science, sociology, or anthropology.

In the lower schools, particularly in the elementary grades, educators usually combine materials from these separate fields into one plan of work. Sometimes, scholars use the terms *social sciences* and *social studies* interchangeably.

**In the Elementary Grades,** a social studies course tries to help children understand and carry on the basic human activities: producing and exchanging goods and services, protecting and conserving life and resources, transporting goods and people, communicating facts and feelings, providing education and recreation, expressing spiritual and aesthetic impulses, and organizing and governing.

The social studies program also tries to develop competent membership in each of the communities of men: the family, the school, the neighborhood, the town or city, the state, the region, the nation, the region of nations, and the world. A pupil studies each of these.

A coordinated social studies program in the elementary school has a close relationship to history and values. Each of the communities of men has always carried on the basic human activities, but in different ways and at different times. The historical changes that have come about in the tools and techniques for carrying on these activities are important aspects of the social studies program. The values which a community holds affect the way in which people conduct these activities. For example, the Puritans placed great emphasis on orderliness, and this value pervaded most of their enterprises.

Subject matter drawn from the social sciences fills out the story of how men have carried on the basic human activities in various settings.

**In the Secondary Schools,** the study pattern usually shifts to a series of social science subjects taught separately. For example, schools may offer civics in grade 9, world history or world geography in grade 10, United States history in grade 11, and contemporary problems in grade 12. Many high schools also offer economics, anthropology, sociology, or other social sciences as electives.                                               PAUL R. HANNA

**Related Articles.** See the separate articles in WORLD BOOK on each state, province, country, and continent. Other related articles include:

| | |
|---|---|
| Anthropology | Geography |
| Citizenship | Government |
| Civics | History |
| Civilization | Human Relations |
| Communication | Political Science |
| Community | Social Science |
| Conservation | Sociology |
| Culture | Transportation |
| Economics | World |
| Family | |

**SOCIAL SURVEY.** See SOCIOLOGY (Surveying).

**SOCIAL WAR.** See ROMAN EMPIRE (A Century of Revolution).

**SOCIAL WELFARE.** See SOCIAL WORK; GREAT BRITAIN (Social Welfare).

**SOCIAL WELFARE, NATIONAL CONFERENCE ON,** promotes discussion of the problems and methods of practical human improvement. It has about 6,500 members, about 1,200 of them agencies or social-welfare organizations. It holds an annual forum and publishes a quarterly *Conference Bulletin.* Conference headquarters are located at 22 W. Gay Street, Columbus, Ohio 43215.                                              JOE R. HOFFER

# SOCIAL WORK

**SOCIAL WORK** refers to the services of trained persons called *social workers* who help and guide individuals, families, or groups. Social workers may be connected with public or private agencies. They work in children's homes, churches, clinics, clubs, community centers, courts, employment offices, family-aid bureaus, hospitals, schools, and settlement houses. They participate in delinquency programs, craft and recreation projects, and youth services.

The term *social work* was first used in the early 1900's. In a broad sense, anyone who performs good works is doing social work. The roots of social work lie deep in mankind. The desire to help people and to share with those in need is the basis of all social work, professional and volunteer. The professional social worker is trained to help people through a scientific knowledge of human behavior and society. This training helps the social worker handle the many complex problems and situations of modern life.

## The Need for Social Work

People vary in abilities and ambitions. They differ in their needs and in the circumstances in which they find themselves. The needs of people do not always balance with the means to obtain them. The young and the aged are less able to pay for what they need than are the middle-aged. The sick are less able to pay than the well, and the poor less able than those with average or high incomes. This relation of needs to means, where services are scarce, justifies thoughtful action in behalf of those in need.

The moral values and attitudes that underlie organized social work have changed in the past few decades. Originally, many people felt that every individual should be able to take care of himself. If an individual, except in extreme circumstances, did not work, make money, and get ahead, it was his own fault. He was scolded for his condition and given some charity. Charities were a type of "tax" levied by the poor on the rich, the nonworker on the worker, the weak on the strong, and the lawbreaker on the law-abiding.

This attitude began to change in the 1930's when it became clear that every family could not be expected to take care of itself in economic hard times. Government provided more aid for social work. People became interested in finding ways to prevent social problems from occurring. They began to feel that all citizens were entitled to minimum standards of health, decency, and opportunity, regardless of their economic means. They based their belief on a deepening recognition of the rights of individuals. They believed that such minimum standards were necessary for national security, progress, and well-being.

Since World War II, the public attitude toward social work has shifted from minimum standards of service to very favorable standards in health, education, recreation, and welfare. Individuals often turn to government agencies when their incomes do not permit a high level of social well-being. They may also organize into groups to provide the services they need, as, for example, a nursery school for which parents pay dues.

## Professional Training

Throughout history, many men and women have worked to help those in need. Most of these people contributed their services on a voluntary basis. They did not receive any formal training to prepare them for the work. They learned to deal with people and their problems in a trial-and-error fashion while on the job.

The problems of modern society became more complicated with the growth of population and industry, and the movement of people from rural areas to the cities. These new circumstances made it necessary to establish social agencies on a more organized basis and

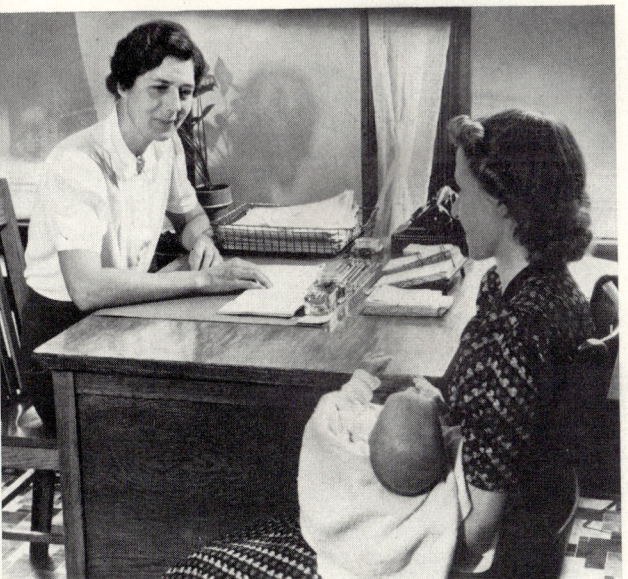

**Family Counseling,** advice on child care, and vocational guidance are all part of the professional social worker's job.

**Social Work Programs** provide assistance for the underprivileged in many ways, such as by giving free medical services.
Community Fund of Chicago

# SOCIAL WORK

to employ full-time staffs. People soon realized that these agencies needed trained personnel in order to do the work effectively. The first schools of philanthropy, now known as *schools of social work*, were established in the 1900's to provide this training. The United States and Canada now have about 60 accredited schools of social work.

Schools of social work recognize at least five major areas of social work. These include: (1) case work, (2) group work, (3) area organization, (4) national programs and legislation, and (5) research. Each area has its own set of guiding values, its own body of facts, principles, and theories, and its own methods of operation. This does not mean that the areas are completely separate and distinct. All share a common body of values, knowledge, and practice that is the core of professional social work.

**Case Work** involves direct contacts between the social worker and individuals and families. It deals with problems of relations within the family, such as parent-child tensions; personal relations outside the family, such as relations with neighbors and friends; and various other activities, such as household management, health care, and public relief when it is needed.

As a student, the prospective case worker receives supervised field experience, and training in methods of work such as interviewing, motivating persons, budgeting, and the use of community resources.

**Group Work** refers to programs for groups of all ages. It includes activities in the arts, crafts, and recreation. The group worker tries to develop the individual capacities and to fulfill the needs of each member of the group. He also tries to interest the group in other community projects so as to develop civic responsibility.

The group worker's training includes the principles of group dynamics and planning, assessment of group activities, and leadership training. This training prepares the group worker to serve in social settlements, churches, schools, and institutions for the aged, delinquents, and the physically handicapped.

**Area Work,** or community organization, is an activity in social work that deals with area-wide efforts to plan programs, coordinate agencies and resources, and administer community health and welfare services. It includes working with community councils and councils of social agencies. Chief emphasis is placed on the training of local leaders. The social worker provides indirect leadership to help citizen groups work out their problems. For example, the social worker can direct community resources to achieve a desired goal by helping in slum clearance and area redevelopment.

**National Programs** constantly increase in number and complexity. Keeping up to date on state and federal social programs requires a great deal of time. This special area of study provides important information to social workers in the other areas, so that they may direct their clients' activities to the proper channels. Such knowledge helps the individual obtain those benefits that are rightly his. Proper knowledge of existing legislation also helps to plan future developments in social legislation.

**Research.** Fact-finding forms a vital part of social work. Such surveys add to existing knowledge by systematic study. The everyday observations of the social worker are important. But this information must be analyzed and studied systematically to provide a complete picture of the goals and methods of the profession. Social work research centers on studies of service agencies and their programs, on persons as individuals and in groups, and on changing conditions and trends in society at large. Knowledge in social work depends also on the research in such other areas as sociology, psychology, and psychiatry.

### Careers in Social Work

Social work is an area of great activity and growth. Many new specialties are developing to meet the problems created by social and technological changes in modern life. Many people now realize the valuable contribution that the social worker makes to the community. As a result, the demand for social services and for trained social workers has increased.

Most social workers deal directly with people. They try to help the individual work out his problems. They work with individuals, families, or groups. Social workers also administer various community programs. Some social workers devote their time to research.

Most social work is rather exacting in its demands, because the social worker must deal with people at their worst as well as at their best. Changes in individuals may be slow or none at all. The social worker must learn to take this in his stride. But the social worker gains much personal satisfaction from the knowledge that he is doing something basic and essential. He feels that he is helping individuals develop, and thus helping the community solve its problems.

The educational requirements for a professional social worker include a bachelor's degree and two years professional training leading to a master's degree in social work. The program includes class work and field work. The starting salary ranges from $3,500 to $4,500. Men and women with professional training and experience can work up to administrative positions that pay from $10,000 to $25,000. Other benefits include good working conditions, paid vacations, sick leaves, retirement programs, and modern personnel standards. Vocational information on social work may be obtained from the Council on Social Work Education, 345 E. 46th St., New York, N.Y. 10017.   LLOYD ALLEN COOK

**Related Articles** in WORLD BOOK include:

ORGANIZATIONS

Big Brothers of America
Children, Societies for
Family Service, Association of America
Jewish Welfare Board, National
Junior Leagues of America, Inc., Association of the
Public Welfare Association, American
Red Cross
Salvation Army, The
Social Welfare, National Conference on
Social Workers, National Associations of
Travelers Aid
United Funds

OTHER RELATED ARTICLES

Addams, Jane
Child Welfare
Hull-House
Lathrop, Julia C.
Service Club
Social Settlement
Wald, Lillian D.

**SOCIAL WORKERS, NATIONAL ASSOCIATION OF,** is a professional organization devoted to the improvement of social work practices. It tries to raise the standards of services to individuals, groups, and the community. The association was formed in 1955 by the merger of seven organizations. It has 50,000 members in 170 chapters in the United States, Puerto Rico, and Europe. Its publications include a quarterly journal, *Social Work;* a membership news bulletin; and *The Encyclopedia of Social Work.* It has headquarters at 2 Park Avenue, New York, N.Y. 10016. JOSEPH P. ANDERSON

**SOCIALISM,** *SO shul iz'm,* is both a doctrine and a movement which seeks to place in the hands of the people, either directly or through their government, the ownership and control of the principal means of production and distribution. Ownership may be by national or local government, or by cooperatives. For example, the city ownership of an electric power plant is no less an example of socialism than is the ownership of railroads by a national government.

Democratic socialists insist that control must be democratic. They urge that socialized industries should be controlled by public corporations governed by directors representing both the consumers in general, and the workers who invest their labor in the particular industry. Cooperative associations, common in many parts of the world, are much like socialism, because they extend ownership to many members of the community.

Socialism is a much-abused term. It does not mean equal income for everyone, but it does imply more equality in income than is now common. It does not mean collective ownership of personal belongings, such as shoes or toothbrushes. Instead, it proposes collective ownership of the principal means of production and distribution. Nor does it mean political dictatorship, although some dictatorships have practiced it. Socialism is an economic system, not a political one. Many persons believe in both democracy, a political idea, and socialism, an economic one. They are called democratic socialists.

**The World-wide Socialist Movement.** Most persons think of Karl Marx (1818-1883) as the founder of modern socialist principles. But other persons had advanced socialist ideas at an earlier period. The term *socialist* was first used in its modern sense in Great Britain in 1827. A few years later it was used in both France and Great Britain to describe the social ideals of François Marie Charles Fourier, Comte de Saint-Simon, and Robert Owen. Louis Blanc (1811-1882) worked to have the French adopt many socialist principles during the late 1840's. In 1861, the first Socialist Party was founded in Germany. The movement rapidly gained strength and spread to other countries. World War I resulted in a temporary setback in socialist strength in most countries. But in Russia, socialists took part in the revolution which deposed the czar, and in the later revolution which overthrew the Kerensky government. Moderate socialists soon lost any influence they might have had in the new Communist government, which claimed to follow the principles of Karl Marx. See COMMUNISM; RUSSIA (History).

After World War I, socialism picked up new strength in many countries. It continued to grow through the 1920's and 1930's. The Fascist governments in Italy, Germany, Spain, and other countries during this period had the destruction of the socialist movement as one of their major purposes. Fascist dictatorships reached a peak in World War II. Socialist groups emerged from World War II with renewed strength and increased membership. Today, almost every country of Europe and North and South America, as well as some countries of Asia, has socialist political organizations. Some of these organizations have great strength.

**Socialism and Communism.** There has been a long history in the development of differences between socialism and Communism. Today, the major Communist parties maintain that socialism has already been achieved in Russia. In their definition, socialism is a step on the road to Communism. They defend dictatorship and the denial of all civil liberties. They still hold to the teachings of Marx and Engels that first the dictatorship and then the state itself will wither away once capitalism has been abolished.

Democratic socialists say that the present economic system in Russia could best be described as state capitalism, that there is none of the democracy of control which is essential to socialism, and that obviously neither the dictatorship nor the state is withering away. Socialists oppose dictatorship and the abolition of civil liberties, and seek to bring about a peaceful transition to the new society. Socialists and Communists disagree bitterly, and have seldom been able to work together.

**In the United States,** the Socialist Party was organized in the 1890's. By 1904, its membership had increased to more than 400,000. By 1912, the socialist vote approached 900,000. Socialist votes increased to about 920,000 in 1920. By 1924, when the Socialists supported the Progressive candidate for President, Robert M. LaFollette, their voting strength was probably about a million. Since then, Socialist votes have varied greatly in number. The number of persons who accept Socialist principles may have gradually increased, but if this is true, these persons have generally voted with one of the major parties. In the 1948 national elections, the Socialist vote was 139,521. The Socialist vote fell to 20,189 in 1952, and to 2,192 in 1956.

The Socialist Party platforms have commonly included demands for (1) the socialization and democratic control of natural resources, money, banking and credit, and monopolies and semimonopolies; (2) better protection for workers and their families, such as higher wages and shorter hours, health and accident insurance, and old-age and mothers' pensions; (3) the extension of free public education; and (4) various political changes, including the direct election of the President and Vice-President, and some device by which, in case of deadlock between Congress and the President, an appeal can be taken to the voters.

The Socialist Party has advanced many proposals for political reforms. Most of these are designed to make the national government more flexible and more responsive to the will of the people. Since the Civil War, the United States has adopted much social legislation and established many controls over industry. But the major parties have avoided the term *socialism* for fear of arousing possible prejudice.

Socialists claim that socialism holds the answer to many problems of modern industrial society, such as

## SOCIALIZATION

unemployment, poverty, business cycles, and conflicts between capital and labor. But it is also clear that socialization is likely to bring new problems with it.

The Tennessee Valley Authority might be considered an example of modern socialist practice, although the Socialist Party would make various changes in its administration. This vast enterprise is controlled by a board of experts who have been freed from political influence. The citizens of local communities in the region carry on much of the detailed administration. This gives the undertaking a certain democratic character (see TENNESSEE VALLEY AUTHORITY). But the Socialist Party would like to see consumers and workers take more direct part in the management of the authority than they are now able to do.

NORMAN THOMAS

**Related Articles** in WORLD BOOK include:
| | |
|---|---|
| Bebel, August | Marx, Karl H. |
| Berger, Victor L. | Owen (family) |
| Communism | Proudhon, Pierre J. |
| Cooperative | Saint-Simon, Comte de |
| Debs, Eugene V. | Thomas, Norman M. |
| Fabian Society | Webb (family) |

**SOCIALIZATION.** See SOCIAL PSYCHOLOGY (Social Learning).

**SOCIALIZED MEDICINE** usually refers to compulsory health insurance in which the law compels citizens to join a government health program. It sometimes describes a system of health care in which a government owns and operates all medical and hospital services. The government employs all health personnel, including doctors, dentists, and nurses. Russia and other Communist nations have this type of health program.

More than 50 countries have government-sponsored health insurance. Usually, the people contribute either a flat sum or a percentage of their wages. Sometimes the employer matches this amount. Often, the government also makes a contribution. When a person needs medical care, the government uses the money collected to pay for the doctor, dental, hospital, or nursing bills. Some compulsory health programs provide eyeglasses, artificial limbs, false teeth, and other aids.

Under compulsory health insurance, hospitals may be privately owned. The doctors, nurses, and dentists are not necessarily hired by the government. Usually, the patient may select his own hospital and doctor.

Many persons oppose compulsory health insurance because they believe it restricts the freedom of the medical profession, results in inadequate medical care, and becomes the tool of politicians. But others argue that compulsory health insurance provides medical care for more people, and thereby improves the health of a nation. They also contend it keeps patients from worrying about medical costs.

C. S. MIHANOVICH

See also MEDICARE.

**SOCIETY.** See CULTURE; SOCIOLOGY.

**SOCIETY FOR THE ADVANCEMENT OF EDUCATION, INC.,** was organized in 1939 to purchase and publish the journal *School and Society*. The journal publishes information on problems and trends in education. The society has over 1,000 members. Headquarters are at 1860 Broadway, New York, N.Y. 10023.

**SOCIETY FOR THE PRESERVATION AND ENCOURAGEMENT OF BARBER SHOP QUARTET SINGING IN AMERICA.** See BARBERSHOP QUARTET SINGING.

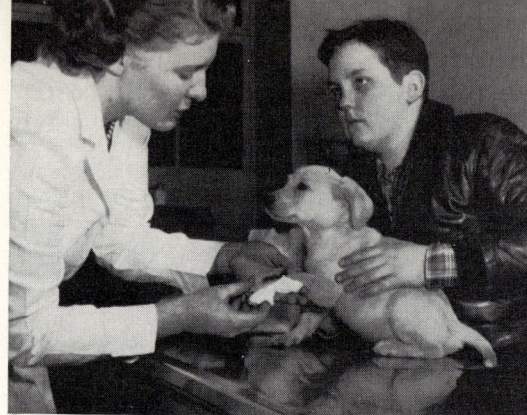

Elliott Robinson, Chicago Anti-Cruelty Society

**The Society for the Prevention of Cruelty to Animals** helps animals that have been hurt, mistreated, or abandoned.

**SOCIETY FOR THE PREVENTION OF CRUELTY TO ANIMALS (SPCA)** is the name for many groups which do important work in preventing the mistreatment of animals. These anticruelty societies influence governments to pass laws providing for the punishment of persons who mistreat animals.

The first humane society was founded in 1824 in England. The first in the United States was the American Society for the Prevention of Cruelty to Animals (ASPCA), organized in New York by Henry Bergh and chartered by the state legislature in 1866. It is limited to that state.

Although there is no national organization, there are about 600 similar societies in the United States. One of the main functions of such societies is to enforce the laws by investigating cases of cruelty and by regular inspection of places where many animals are kept. Some societies, such as the ASPCA, maintain animal hospitals and shelters. The American Humane Education Society sponsors an annual Be Kind to Animals Week to promote better treatment of animals.

JUNE ELIOT

**SOCIETY ISLANDS** is a group of islands in the Pacific Ocean. The islands lie slightly northeast of the Cook Islands, about 4,200 miles southwest of San Francisco. Samuel Wallis claimed the islands for Great Britain in 1767. But Louis Antoine de Bougainville claimed them for France in 1768. The group became a French protectorate in 1843, and a colony in 1880.

The Society Islands group consists of 14 islands. Tahiti and Raiatea are the largest islands of the group. The Society Islands cover an area of 646 square miles, and have a population of about 82,000. For location, see PACIFIC ISLANDS (color map).

Ancient volcanoes on the Society Islands form many high peaks, making the land rough and mountainous. Some of the islands are low atolls, and are used as fishing centers. The capital of the island group is the busy seaport of Papeete, on Tahiti.

The people of the islands are Polynesians. Many of them fish and dive for pearls.

EDWIN H. BRYAN, JR.

See also TAHITI.

**SOCIETY OF FRIENDS.** See QUAKERS.

**SOCIETY OF JESUS.** See JESUIT.

**SOCIETY OF THE CINCINNATI.** See CINCINNATI, SOCIETY OF THE.

**SOCIETY OF THE SACRED HEART OF JESUS.** See SACRED HEART OF JESUS, SOCIETY OF THE.

**SOCIODRAMA.** See ROLE PLAYING.

**SOCIOLOGY,** *so see AHL oh jee,* is the study of human relationships. Sociologists try to find out how people live and work together. They study what happens when people take jobs, get married, join organizations, or deal with each other in countless other ways.

Sociology adds to man's knowledge of his society. Sociologists try to learn the causes of individual or group problems. After sociologists have learned the causes of social problems, they try to find ways of solving the difficulties. They also try to predict where similar problems will arise.

The sociologist uses scientific methods to study human behavior. Therefore, sociology is classified as a behavioral or social science, along with history, economics, political science, psychology, and anthropology.

### The Main Divisions of Sociology

Sociologists use different methods to divide or classify the subjects they study. But the field may be divided into six main areas: (1) general sociology, (2) social psychology, (3) demography, (4) the community, (5) social organization, and (6) social change.

**General Sociology** studies the ways people associate with one another in groups of all kinds and sizes. Such groups include the family, the church, the school, labor unions, trade associations, and athletic teams. The most general group of all is a *society* (all the people who have any sort of contact with each other and have common traditions and history). The people of your hometown make up a society. All the people of the United States make up a larger society. The people of the United States, Canada, and western Europe together make up an even larger society.

On the broadest scale, general sociology studies a society's *culture* (attitudes, possessions, and ways of life). Such ideas and attitudes enable people to live together in a society without making deliberate agreements whenever they come in contact with each other. For example, we seldom bump into people walking toward us on a sidewalk. We have a common understanding that we should move to the right to avoid them.

Individuals can form groups only by *communicating* (exchanging ideas and information). For this reason, sociologists believe that communication is the most important group activity. They study how people communicate in face-to-face conversation or by such means as letters, radio, television, and newspapers.

General sociology also studies such group activities as *cooperation* (the ways people work together) and *conflict* (the ways people resist each other).

**Social Psychology** studies the ways society affects a person's behavior and personality. A person belongs to many groups in a society. Each group has somewhat different standards of behavior. Generally, these standards set limits on the range of behavior. But a person often must decide how he should act within these limits. Social psychology studies the person's actions as related to the standards set by groups and society.

Three areas of study are especially important in social psychology: (1) the *processes* by which a person learns how he is expected to act in the various groups to which he belongs, (2) the *roles* (actions) he is expected to perform in society, and (3) the *models* (individuals) a person chooses to imitate in forming his behavior.

**Demography** studies changes, movements, and distribution of populations. Demography is also concerned with the sizes of populations, and with the groups that make up these populations.

As the population of a society increases, decreases, or remains the same, it can influence the society in several ways. It may change the members' outlook on life. It may affect the stability of the culture. Or it may affect the society's relationships with other societies.

The sociologist studies the *distribution of population* to learn how it affects relations between societies or groups. Demographic studies help the sociologist learn how *population density* (the number of persons per square mile) makes one society different from another.

Demographic information is also useful in many other ways. The sociologist may use it to show how different communities have different needs. One community may have an unusually high number of old people. The needs of such a community differ from those of a community of younger people. Demographic studies may show why a population is growing or decreasing. A population grows through births and immigration. A population decreases because of deaths and emigration.

**The Community.** The study of the community refers, basically, to the relationship between man and his environment. Sociologists study the community to learn

---
#### SOCIOLOGICAL TERMS

**Case Study** is a research method in which a person or group is studied in detail.

**Caste** is a class or group of people distinguished from other members of a society by their birth, marriage, or occupation. See CASTE.

**Class** refers to a social group whose members have nearly the same possessions and characteristics valued by a culture.

**Culture** includes all the attitudes, possessions, and ways of life of a group of people. See CULTURE.

**Disorganization** refers to the state of a person or group that violates social rules.

**Ethnocentrism** is a belief in the superiority of one's own culture. It involves judging other individuals and groups by the standards of one's own group. See ETHNOCENTRISM.

**Folkway** is a custom or habit commonly followed by the members of a society. See FOLKWAY.

**Group** is a number of persons who have some customs, standards, or purposes in common.

**Institution** is a social organization or activity that uses a set of customs to achieve a goal.

**Interaction** means contact or movement by persons or groups that affects other persons or groups.

**Mobility,** or **Social Mobility,** usually refers to the movement of a person or group from one class or social group to another.

**Mores** are important customs that a society considers essential to its organization and welfare. See MORES.

**Personality** is the sum total of everything a person is and does. See PERSONALITY.

**Prejudice** is an idea formed without considering all the facts. Prejudice usually refers to unfavorable opinions toward racial, religious, or minority groups. See PREJUDICE.

**Role** refers to the actions that an individual in a group is expected to perform.

**Society** is a group of people who have direct or indirect communication with one another and share a culture.

---

*Arnold M. Rose, the contributor of this article, is Professor of Sociology at the University of Minnesota.*

# A Study in Sociology

After the State of Israel was established in 1948, thousands of immigrants began pouring into Israel from countries throughout the world. Sociologists worked with government officials in planning communities and teaching people of various backgrounds to live and work together. As the communities grew, the sociologists studied them to see how the people were adjusting to their surroundings. A typical Israeli settlement is Kiryat Gat, in the southwest. Its residents came from more than 50 countries. Many had no education at all. Few could speak Hebrew, Israel's national language. All had to learn a new way of life in an unfamiliar land.

Leni Sonnenfeld, Pix

**Community Life** in Kiryat Gat was carefully planned so that the people would quickly learn to know and trust one another. Villages were built around a main community center. Families of similar national backgrounds live close to each other in the villages. But all the people mingle as they shop, work, and study in the common center. Social workers make house calls on every family to discuss community affairs and help solve problems that arise.

how people adjust to the geographical areas or neighborhoods in which they live. For example, facts about man's environment may be used to explain why people in a certain area form particular groups.

Two types of communities have especial interest for the sociologist. In *urban sociology*, he studies city communities. For example, he may try to find out why some neighborhoods grow and change while others decline or remain the same. In *rural sociology*, the sociologist studies farm or small town communities. For example, he may try to find out why people living in rural areas form communities in certain places and not in others.

**Social Organization** is the study of institutions. Sociologists define an *institution* as a social organization or activity that uses a set of customs to accomplish a specific purpose. These customs are always closely related. Most of the chief institutions in a society are connected with the family, the economy, the school, the church, and the government. Family institutions include marriage and parenthood. Government institutions include elections, laws, and the jury system.

Sociologists study institutions to learn (1) why they were established, (2) how they function, (3) how persons carry out their roles in institutions, and (4) how institutions serve the needs of individuals.

**Social Change** may be regarded as an essential part of all the fields of sociology. But many sociologists believe it deserves special attention. In speaking of change, a sociologist usually refers to basic forces that cause social change. In particular, he studies social changes caused by (1) inventions, (2) the spread of culture, (3) culture conflicts, (4) fashions, (5) social movements, and (6) war and revolution.

Sociologists believe some changes help men form a better or more efficient society. For example, a change in fashions may produce more comfortable clothing. But change also can lead to difficulty or unhappiness for many people, and may create *social problems*. Such problems include juvenile delinquency, crime, divorce, alcoholism, desertion, prejudice, slums, unemployment, and corruption in government.

### How a Sociologist Works

A sociologist begins most projects with an idea or a theory. For example, he may want to show that a new college in a small town makes the townspeople more aware of the benefits of higher education. He has two main tasks: (1) *surveying* (collecting information), and (2) *evaluating* (using the data to reach a conclusion).

**Surveying.** The sociologist may conduct his own interviews or research projects to obtain information. Or he may use sources of information provided by the society or group being surveyed.

In studying small-town attitudes toward higher education, the sociologist would probably begin surveying before the college is built. He would try to find out what people in the town think of college education. After the school has operated for some time, he would conduct further research. He might use letters, diaries, or other documents to show how particular townspeople have changed their attitudes. The second survey could indicate that book circulation from the town library has increased greatly. Perhaps interviews show that more young people became interested in a college education after the school was built.

In conducting his own surveys in any field, a sociologist can use many different techniques. He could interview individuals or whole groups. He might ask only a few questions, or he could make a wide variety of inquiries. In studying an institution, the sociologist

Leni Sonnenfeld, Pix

**Work and Education** in the community of Kiryat Gat bring together adults and children from many lands. Settlers may choose the kind of work they want to do. Experts teach them how to use tools and equipment. The community's school enrollments are set up so that each school includes children from several villages.

would probably observe certain phases of its operations. To learn how an organization works, he could attend its meetings.

Societies and groups provide many kinds of official and unofficial sources of information. One official source in the United States is the national census taken every 10 years. Other government reports are also useful. In industrial research, the sociologist uses such sources as personnel records. In studying crime, he can examine records of arrests, convictions, and imprisonment.

**Evaluating.** The sociologist might collect hundreds, or even thousands, of facts and opinions. Then he must decide what all this information means. He must also state his conclusion.

Comparison of data is a basic process in most sociological research. The sociologist may compare earlier information with later findings, as in the project on college education. Or he might compare his facts with those gathered by other researchers. He could observe two groups and compare the different actions of the members of each group.

The sociologist usually expresses his conclusion as a general statement. In the study of attitudes toward college education, the sociologist may conclude that the college raised the cultural level of the town. The college aroused the interest of the townspeople. It provided a greater opportunity for young people in the region to earn college degrees. Perhaps the sociologist would predict that other towns would also benefit if they could attract colleges.

### The Development of Sociology

**Beginnings.** Auguste Comte (1798-1857), a French philosopher, gave sociology its name. He combined the Latin word *socius* (meaning relationship) and the Greek word *logos* (meaning study). In his book *The Course of Positive Philosophy* (1830-1842), Comte declared that sociology would explain man to himself.

Interest in sociology spread rapidly. Frédéric Le Play (1806-1882) of France developed the *case study* method of research. He studied a single person or group in great detail. In England, Herbert Spencer (1820-1903) collected information from travelers and missionaries. His *Principles of Sociology* (1882) tried to show that all human societies develop, change, and grow in the same ways. An American, Lester Ward (1841-1913), declared in *Dynamic Sociology* (1883) that man could improve society after learning more about human behavior.

**Sociology Becomes a Science.** During the 1800's and early 1900's, physical sciences such as chemistry and physics made great progress. Many sociologists decided that sociology should also be recognized as a science. But they had difficulties because they were trying to measure human behavior. They could not conduct experiments as chemists could. They could not measure social events exactly because they could not control the conditions that influenced these events.

Émile Durkheim (1858-1917) of France published the first truly scientific study in the field of sociology. In this work, *Le Suicide* (1897), Durkheim investigated the causes of suicide. He presented theories about these causes and tried to test them scientifically. To do this, he obtained data from all countries that had statistics on suicide. Soon sociologists in Europe, China, India, and the United States made similar studies of cultural contacts, religion, and other subjects.

**Modern Sociology.** After World War I, a number of "schools" of sociology developed. They differed both on the methods sociologists should use, and on the purposes of sociology. Leading theorists included the Ital-

461

# SOCIOLOGY

ian Vilfredo Pareto (1848-1923), the author of *Mind and Society* (1916), and the German Max Weber (1864-1920).

American sociologists took the lead in developing new ideas. Gradually, many turned away from social problems and concentrated more on normal aspects of human society. Three major trends developed.

One group of sociologists called for emphasis on collecting facts. Leaders of this group were William F. Ogburn (1886-1959) of the University of Chicago and F. Stuart Chapin (1888-    ) of the University of Minnesota. Ogburn and Chapin thought sociologists should use the research methods of other sciences to gather facts. They emphasized the use of statistics.

A second group of sociologists stressed the necessity of finding out how individuals interpreted social facts. To obtain information, they often studied personal documents such as letters and diaries. The leaders of this group included W. I. Thomas (1863-1947), Robert E. Park (1864-1944), and Ernest W. Burgess (1886-1966), all of the University of Chicago.

A third group believed that the various parts of a society fitted together and functioned to maintain the stability of the society. These men followed the ideas of Talcott Parsons (1902-    ) of Harvard University. Pitirim A. Sorokin (1889-1968), also of Harvard, was another leading sociologist who believed that different parts of society worked together. Sorokin's books include *Social Mobility* (1927) and *Social and Cultural Dynamics* (1937-1941).

During the 1950's and 1960's, American sociologists specialized more and more. They published many books and articles. Some writers not originally trained in sociology wrote popular books on sociological subjects. For example, *The Lonely Crowd* (1950), by David Riesman (1909-    ), tells how modern life changes people. *The Organization Man* (1957), by William H. Whyte (1917-    ), describes how working for large corporations affects individuals.

## Careers in Sociology

Sociology offers a variety of career opportunities. They include teaching, research, and social work with governmental or private agencies. Usually, advanced study is necessary for men or women who want to work in sociology. But some high school graduates who have studied sociology can find employment as interviewers or research assistants.

At most colleges, students begin to study sociology in their junior year. Sociology courses are usually offered as part of a liberal arts curriculum that includes such courses as history, literature, and philosophy. Students who find general courses in sociology interesting may take courses in special fields such as social problems, the family, or social planning. At the same time, they can study anthropology, biology, government, psychology, and other related subjects. Many sociology students attend meetings of the American Sociological Association, the Rural Sociological Society, or the Society for the Study of Social Problems. In addition to books, the student can read professional journals such as the *American Journal of Sociology* and the *American Sociological Review*.

College graduates who major in sociology sometimes find teaching careers in adult education. For example, some may teach race relations to policemen. Others teach human relations to management and union officials in business firms. College teachers of sociology need a Master of Arts (M.A.) or a Doctor of Philosophy (Ph.D.) degree. Most jobs for sociologists in industry and government also require advanced degrees.

Sociological research is an increasingly broad field. In the U.S. government, the Departments of Agriculture and the Interior employ specialists on communities. The Department of Health, Education, and Welfare has sociologists who study such subjects as juvenile delinquency, problems of the aged, and mental and physical illness. State governments hire sociologists to work primarily in the fields of crime and juvenile delinquency.

Sociologists in business and industry study public relations, personnel counseling, public attitudes, and labor problems. One large mail order company has sociologists who help decide which customers make good credit risks. In associations or other private groups, the sociologist might study propaganda, health and disease, housing needs, consumer relations, city planning, and other problems.

Many organizations and publications offer information on careers in sociology. The *Occupational Outlook Handbook*, issued yearly by the U.S. Department of Labor, provides data on job opportunities in sociology as well as in other professions. Information may also be obtained from the American Sociological Association, New York University, Washington Square, New York, N.Y. 10003.

ARNOLD M. ROSE

**Related Articles** in WORLD BOOK include:

### BIOGRAPHIES

| | |
|---|---|
| Addams, Jane | Owen (family) |
| Booth (family) | Pareto, Vilfredo |
| Comte, Auguste | Riis, Jacob August |
| Du Bois, William Edward Burghardt | Spencer, Herbert |
| | Wald, Lillian D. |
| Lathrop, Julia Clifford | Weber, Max |

### RELATED STUDIES

| | | |
|---|---|---|
| Anthropology | Ecology | Social Psychology |
| Criminology | Psychology | Social Science |
| Demography | | |

### AGENCIES, ORGANIZATIONS, AND INSTITUTIONS

| | |
|---|---|
| Child Study Association of America | Reformatory |
| | Sage Foundation, Russell |
| Children's Bureau | Salvation Army, The |
| Family Service Association of America | Social Workers, National Association of |
| Hull House | United Funds |
| Junior Leagues of America | United Jewish Appeal |
| Juvenile Court | United Service Organizations |
| Prison | |
| Public Welfare Association, American | |

### OTHER RELATED ARTICLES

| | | |
|---|---|---|
| Aid to Dependent Children | Custom | Population |
| | Family | Poverty |
| Behavior | Folkway | Public Opinion |
| City | Human Relations | Research |
| Community | Juvenile Delinquency | Social Work |
| Crime | | Statistics |
| Cultural Deprivation | Mores | Unemployment |
| Cultural Lag | Poll of Public Opinion | Vital Statistics |
| Culture | | |

**SOCRATES**, *SAHK ruh teez* (469?-399 B.C.), was a Greek philosopher and teacher. His noble life and courageous death, together with his teachings, have made him one of the most admired figures in history. He believed that man's nature leads him to act correctly and in agreement with knowledge. Socrates felt that man's evil and wrong actions arise from ignorance and the failure to investigate why people act as they do. Socrates is credited with saying "the unexamined life is not worth living" and "no man knowingly does evil." Socrates devoted himself completely to seeking truth and goodness.

**Socrates' Life.** Socrates wrote nothing of his own. Most of our information about his life and teachings comes from *Memorabilia* and *Symposium* by the historian Xenophon; dialogues by the philosopher Plato; *Clouds*, a comedy by Aristophanes; and writings by the philosopher Aristotle. Xenophon and Plato were Socrates'

simply and was known for moderation in eating and drinking. He was married to Xanthippe, who, according to tradition, was ill-tempered and difficult to live with. They probably had at least two children.

Socrates taught in the streets, market place, and gymnasiums. He taught by questioning his listeners, and showing them how inadequate their answers were. Socrates had an enthusiastic following among the young men of Athens, but the general public mistrusted him because of his unorthodox views on religion and his disregard of public opinion.

Inevitably, Socrates made enemies among influential Athenians. He was brought to trial, charged with corrupting the young and showing disrespect for religious traditions. Socrates defended himself by stating that clear knowledge of the truth is essential for the cor-

Metropolitan Museum of Art, N.Y., Wolfe Fund, 1931

**Socrates Drinks the Cup of Hemlock** to carry out the sentence of death imposed on him by the rulers of ancient Athens. This painting, *Death of Socrates* (1787) by Jacques Louis David, shows Socrates' followers in great despair. Socrates made a toast to the gods and drank the bitter poison. He met death with the same calm and self-control with which he had lived.

pupils, and Aristotle was a pupil of Plato's. Aristophanes was a leading playwright in Socrates' time.

According to Xenophon, Socrates was a highly respected teacher chiefly interested in helping men become good. Plato's dialogues tell us that Socrates cared not only about ethics, but also about logic and a theory of *forms*. This theory tried to identify the quality in an object or idea that remains constant and unchangeable. Plato's dialogues contain the most probable account of Socrates' life and teachings. Aristotle seemed to agree generally with Plato's view of Socrates. However, Aristotle claimed that the theory of forms was more characteristic of Plato's philosophy than that of Socrates. In Aristophanes' *Clouds*, Socrates appears as a bumbling, foolish man who supports fantastic theories.

Socrates was born and lived in Athens. He dressed

rect conduct of life. Action, he said, equals knowledge. Thus, virtue can be taught because correct action involves thought. Socrates implied that rulers should be men who know how to rule—not necessarily those who have been elected. Socrates may have appeared dangerous to Athenian democracy, but what he defended were the foundations of that democracy. Plato described Socrates' defense in his dialogue, the *Apology*.

The jury found Socrates guilty and sentenced him to death. The jury may have given Socrates the severe sentence because it resented the unbending pride with which he conducted his defense. He refused several opportunities to escape from prison, and carried out the sentence by calmly drinking a cup of hemlock poison. A moving account of Socrates' death appears in Plato's *Phaedo*.

463

# SOD HOUSE

**The Socratic Method.** Socrates introduced the idea of *universal* (standard) definitions. He believed that although individual men or things vary and are constructed differently, the definitions of how they are similar or vary remain constant. For example, individual dogs differ in shape, color, and size. Yet there are some common characteristics by which we identify these animals as dogs, not as cats or camels. These common characteristics are the universal, to which man must turn when he judges anything.

Socrates believed that the correct method of discovering the common characteristics was by *inductive* means—that is, by reasoning from particular facts to a general idea. This process took the form of *dialectic* (philosophic) conversation, which became known as the *Socratic method*. Two or more men would begin a discussion with the assumption that each knew the definition of some key term. The conversation first showed that their assumptions were different, and then that the assumptions were inadequate to claim true knowledge. In this way, the men proceeded from less adequate to more adequate definitions. They also progressed from definitions that applied to only a few particular examples to a universal definition that applied to all examples. Although the men often reached no satisfactory conclusion, their goal was always the same —to gain a true and universal definition.

The Socratic method tended to expose men's ignorance. It showed that many things they assumed to be true were false. Socrates also used *irony* to expose men's ignorance of key concepts—that is, he claimed to differ from other men only in knowing that he was ignorant. Socrates' insistence on his ignorance reminded others of their own ignorance.  JASON L. SAUNDERS

**SOD HOUSE** is a house with walls built of sod or turf in horizontal layers. Sod houses were constructed by early settlers on open plains where there were no trees to supply lumber.

For a description of sod houses and how they were built, see WESTERN FRONTIER LIFE (Life in the Country); NEBRASKA (Territorial Days; picture: Homesteading Families).

**SODA** is the common name for a group of compounds that contain sodium. These sodium compounds are manufactured from common salt (NaCl), which is made up of sodium and chlorine.

One common sodium compound is *sodium carbonate* ($Na_2CO_3$), known as *sal soda*, *washing soda*, and *soda ash*. Sodium carbonate comes in crystals or white powder and has a strong alkaline reaction. This means that it neutralizes acids. Sodium carbonate is used in the manufacture of glass, soap, and paper. The compound is also used as a disinfectant, a cleaning agent, and a water softener.

Sodium bicarbonate ($NaHCO_3$) is a popular soda used in cooking and in medicines. It is also known as *baking soda* or *saleratus*. Baking powder contains sodium bicarbonate, which acts as a leavening agent because it causes bread, biscuits, or pastries to rise in baking. Seidlitz powders also contain sodium bicarbonate. They relieve excess stomach acid.

Sodium hydroxide (NaOH) is a sodium compound known as *caustic soda*. Sodium hydroxide is used in the making of hard soap, paper, and dyestuffs. It is also used in making bleaching compounds and in refining petroleum.

See also SODIUM; BAKING POWDER; GLASS (Recipes); LEBLANC, NICOLAS.

**SODA WATER.** See SOFT DRINK.

**SODDY, FREDERICK** (1877-1956), was a British chemist who worked on atomic structure. He received the 1921 Nobel prize in chemistry for his research. He and Ernest Rutherford showed that radium breaks down by itself and gives off electrons, helium nuclei, and gamma rays, which are like X rays. Soddy gave the name *isotopes* to atoms of the same element which have different weights (see ISOTOPE). He was born in Eastbourne, Sussex, and studied at Oxford University. He also taught at Oxford.  HENRY M. LEICESTER

Brown Bros.
**Frederick Soddy**

**SÖDERBLOM,** *SUH der bloom,* **NATHAN** (1866-1931), a Swedish archbishop and professor, was a leader of the ecumenical movement among the churches of the world. He won the 1930 Nobel peace prize for his work for war relief and peace during and after World War I. Söderblom was born in Trönö, near Uppsala, Sweden. He was educated at the University of Uppsala. In 1901 he became a professor in Uppsala, and in 1912, in Leipzig, Germany. He became archbishop of the Church of Sweden (Lutheran) in 1914.  L. J. TRINTERUD

**SODIUM** is a silvery-white metallic element that has many important uses. It is a soft metal, and can easily be molded or cut with a knife. Sodium belongs to a group of chemical elements called the *alkali metals*.

**Where Sodium Is Found.** Sodium is the sixth most common chemical element in the earth's crust. It makes up about 2.8 per cent of the crust. Sodium never occurs *pure*—that is, as a separate element—in nature. It combines with many other elements, forming *compounds*. To obtain pure sodium, the metal must be *extracted* (removed) from its compounds.

One of the most familiar sodium compounds is *sodium chloride*, which is common table salt. Sodium chloride can be found in dry lake beds, underground, and in seawater. Countries with the largest deposits of sodium chloride include China, France, Great Britain, India, Russia, the United States, and West Germany.

Such minerals as borax and cryolite contain sodium. Many plants and the bodies of animals contain small amounts of sodium salts. The human body must have a certain amount of sodium for the cells to live and work.

**Uses.** Sodium compounds have many uses in industry, medicine, agriculture, and photography. Manufacturers use *sodium borate* (borax) in making ceramics, soaps, water softeners, and many other products (see BORAX). *Sodium hydroxide* (caustic soda) is an important industrial alkali used in refining petroleum and in making paper, soaps, and textiles. A lead-sodium *alloy* (combination of metals) produces tetraethyl lead, a gasoline compound that improves the performance of automobile engines. *Sodium carbonate* (soda ash or washing

464

**Bricks of Pure Sodium** must be stored and shipped in airtight, watertight containers because sodium quickly unites with other elements.

E. I. duPont deNemours & Company

soda) is used in the manufacture of *sodium bicarbonate* (baking soda). Many people take sodium bicarbonate to relieve an overly acid stomach. Doctors sometimes prescribe *sodium bromide* as a sedative for tense patients. *Sodium nitrate* (Chile saltpeter) is a valuable fertilizer. Photographers use *sodium thiosulfate* (hypo) to fix photographic images on paper.

Pure sodium also has industrial uses. Some nuclear power plants use it in liquid form to cool atomic reactors. A few electric power cables have been made of pure sodium metal. Special insulation around the sodium keeps it from combining with air, water, or other substances.

**Extracting Sodium.** In 1807, the English chemist Sir Humphry Davy became the first man to obtain pure sodium. He used electricity to extract the metal from sodium hydroxide. Manufacturers still use electricity to obtain sodium. The process is called *electrolysis*. In this process, an electric current is passed through a molten sodium compound, such as sodium chloride. The current separates the compound into chlorine gas and sodium metal. See ELECTROLYSIS.

**Chemical Properties.** Pure sodium is extremely active chemically. Sodium immediately combines with oxygen when it is exposed to the air. As a result, the element loses its shiny appearance and becomes dull. Sodium's bright surface can be seen only after it has been newly cut or extracted.

Sodium weighs less than water. It *decomposes* (breaks up) water, producing hydrogen gas and sodium hydroxide. This reaction is very violent. It produces much heat that often causes the hydrogen to burst into flame.

The element also reacts quickly with such other nonmetals as chlorine and fluorine, and it forms alloys with many metals. Liquid ammonia dissolves sodium, forming a dark-blue solution. A common test for determining whether a material contains sodium is to hold it in a flame. If sodium is present, the flame will be bright yellow.

Sodium must be handled and stored with extreme care. In laboratories, small amounts are stored under kerosene in airtight bottles. The kerosene prevents air or moisture from reaching the metal. Large quantities of sodium in brick form are stored and shipped in airtight, moisture-free barrels. Sodium is also shipped in sealed tank cars. The metal is melted and poured into the tanks. The sodium hardens during shipping, and must be melted again before it can be removed.

Sodium has the chemical symbol Na. Its atomic number is 11, and its atomic weight is 22.9898. The melting point of sodium is 97.8° C. (208° F.), and its boiling point is 892° C. (1638° F.). OTTO THEODOR BENFEY

See also ALKALI; SALT; SALT, CHEMICAL; SALTPETER; SODA.

**SODIUM AMYTAL.** See BARBITURATE.
**SODIUM BICARBONATE.** See BICARBONATE OF SODA.
**SODIUM BORATE.** See BORAX.
**SODIUM CARBONATE.** See SODA; CARBONATE.
**SODIUM CHLORIDE.** See CHLORIDE; SALT.
**SODIUM HYDROXIDE.** See CAUSTIC; LYE; SODA.
**SODIUM METASILICATE.** See WATER GLASS.
**SODIUM NITRATE.** See SALTPETER; NITRATE.
**SODIUM PENTOTHAL.** See PENTOTHAL SODIUM.
**SODIUM SULFATE.** See SALT, CHEMICAL.
**SODIUM TETRABORATE.** See BORAX.
**SODIUM THIOSULFATE.** See HYPO.
**SODIUM-VAPOR LAMP.** See ELECTRIC LIGHT (Neon Lights).

**SODOM,** *SAHD um,* was one of the ancient cities on the plain around the Dead Sea. It is believed that the place where the city stood now lies beneath the waters near the south end of the sea. During early Bible times, the region was so fertile it was compared to the "garden of the Lord" (Gen. 13:10). But later, according to the Old Testament, God destroyed Sodom and the neighboring city of Gomorrah, because the people were wicked.

The Old Testament also tells how Lot, the nephew of Abraham, escaped from Sodom just before it was destroyed. Lot and his wife had been warned by two angels to flee the city and not look back. Lot obeyed, but his wife took a last glance at Sodom. She was immediately turned into a pillar of salt as punishment for her disobedience. WILLIAM A. IRWIN

See also LOT.

**SODOM, APPLE OF.** See APPLE OF SODOM.

465

# SOFIA

**SOFIA,** *SOH fee uh* (pop. 800,953; met. area 894,487; alt. 332 ft.), is Bulgaria's capital and largest city. It is also the chief trading center of Bulgaria. Sofia stands on a high plain between the Vitosha Mountains and the main Balkan mountain ranges. It is about 180 miles southwest of Bucharest. The city's many factories produce such items as machinery, textiles, food products, and electrical equipment. For location, see BULGARIA (color map).

Important buildings include the former royal palace, the Cathedral of Saint Alexander, the House of Parliament, the opera house, Communist Party headquarters, and the Kliment Ochridski University (formerly Sofia University), founded in 1888. The ancient ruins of the Mosque of Buyuk lie in the old section of the city.

Early Sofia was a Roman city. The Huns invaded the city during the 400's, and the Bulgarians occupied it 400 years later. Sofia was under Turkish rule from 1382 to 1878. IRWIN T. SANDERS

**SOFT DRINK** has become as typically American as the hot dog and chewing gum. Soft drinks are called *soft* to distinguish them from *hard* (alcoholic) beverages. Soft drinks are often called *pop*, because of the noise they made when the caps were removed from the bottles. Caps used since the mid-1890's do not make this noise when they are removed.

**Ingredients.** Almost all soft drinks consist of soda water, flavorings, and sugar. A small part of the flavoring of the most popular soft drinks in the United States comes from the extract of the kola, or cola, nut (see KOLA NUT). Soft drink manufacturers also use various fruit flavorings, such as raspberry, lime, strawberry, orange, and lemon.

Soda water, the most important ingredient of soft drinks, actually contains no soda. Water charged with carbon dioxide gas causes the water to *effervesce* (bubble) as the gas escapes. Soda water is stored in metal tanks under pressure. It is drawn off and mixed with flavorings to make the finished drink. Most soft drinks are bottled, but they are also made at soda fountains. Soft drinks in cans were introduced in 1953.

**Leading Soft Drink Companies.** The soft drink industry has become one of the most profitable American industries. The wholesale value of soft drinks is about $3½ billion a year. The four leading soft drink companies in sales are listed below. Other large companies in the soft drink field include 7-Up and the Dr. Pepper Company.

*Coca-Cola Company* is the largest soft drink company in the world. It has over 24,000 employees, and annual sales of over $1 billion. It sells and distributes soft drinks in the United States and many other countries. Coca-Cola was first sold in 1886. Its headquarters are in New York City.

*PepsiCo, Inc.* is the second largest soft drink company, with annual sales of about $665 million. The company has about 25,000 employees. Company headquarters are in New York City.

*Canada Dry Corporation* ranks as the third largest soft drink company, with annual sales of more than $162 million. It makes ginger ale and other carbonated beverages. Headquarters are in New York City.

*Royal Crown Cola Company*, the fourth largest soft drink company, has annual sales of about $74 million. It makes flavored beverages and concentrated bases for use in carbonated beverages. Its headquarters are in Columbus, Ga.

**History.** In 1772, Joseph Priestley of England made the first soda water. He was trying to imitate the natural bubbling water of some mineral springs. The first artificial mineral water contained soda.

In 1806, Benjamin Silliman, a chemistry professor at Yale College in Connecticut, made and bottled the first artificial soda water in the United States. But drug stores and soda fountains later prepared and dispensed most soda water.

Flavored soda water, especially lemon, became popular after 1830. Ginger ale and root beer became popular later. After 1850, the soft drink industry sold bottled soda water with flavoring.

In 1900, an annual average of about 12 bottles of soft drinks a person was consumed in the U.S. By the late 1960's, yearly U.S. consumption rose to about 290 bottles a person. Diet drinks with reduced sugar content became popular in the 1960's. CHARLES W. ADAMS

**SOFT-SHELLED CRAB.** See BLUE CRAB.

Courtesy the Coca-Cola Company

**Soft Drink Bottlers** operate fast-moving assembly lines. Machines feed syrup and carbonated water into the bottles at the same time. Other machines then cap the bottles.

# SOFTBALL

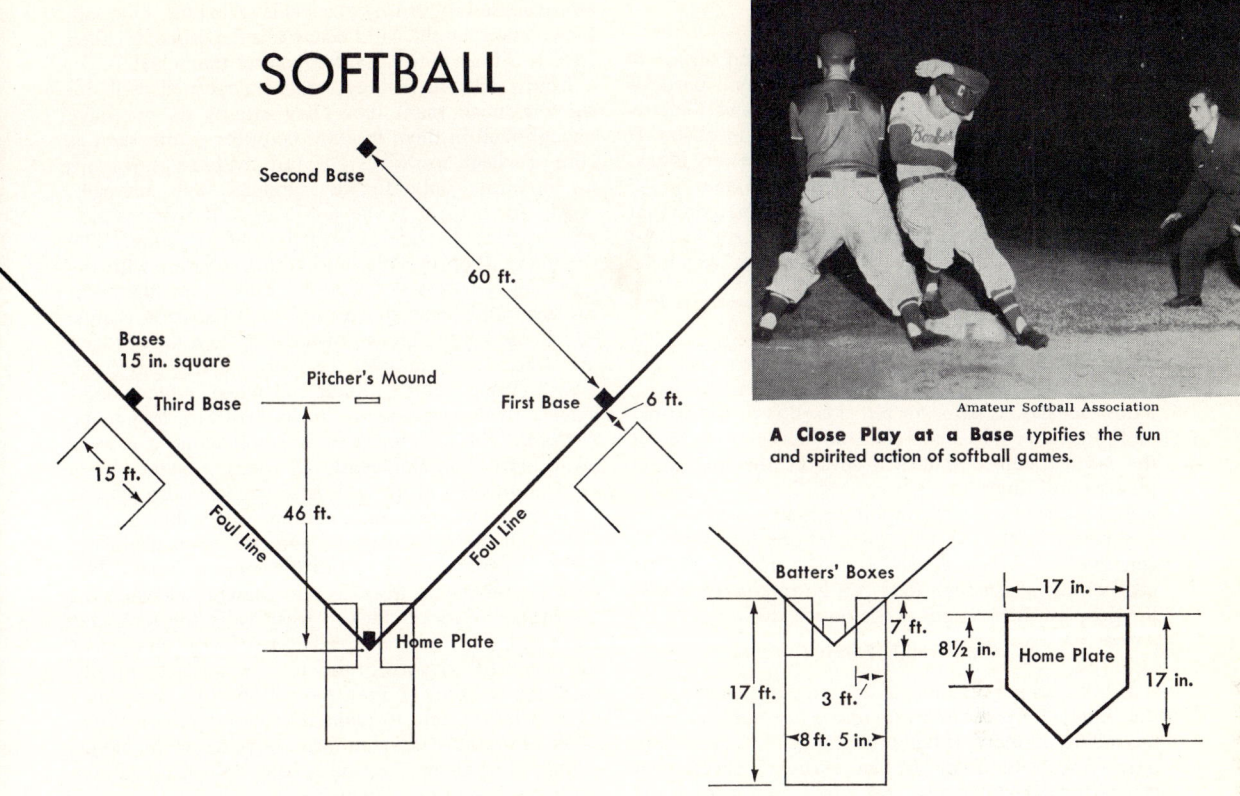

A Close Play at a Base typifies the fun and spirited action of softball games.

**SOFTBALL** is a game similar to baseball. It is played on a smaller field than baseball, and a larger ball is used. Softball teams, like baseball teams, have nine players (see BASEBALL). Softball began in Chicago as an indoor version of baseball. It became especially popular for school and public recreation programs, because it requires less room and equipment than baseball. By the mid-1960's, more than 20 million persons in over 30 countries were playing softball.

The bases are closer together in softball than in baseball. They are 60 feet apart in softball, and 90 feet apart in baseball. A softball's circumference is 12 inches; a baseball's is 9 to $9\frac{1}{4}$ inches. The softball pitcher stands 46 feet from home plate instead of $60\frac{1}{2}$ feet as in baseball. The base runner cannot leave his base in softball until the ball has left the pitcher's hand. Baseball players can *lead off* (leave) a base.

All softball pitching must be underhand. A regulation softball game lasts seven innings. Except for these differences, softball is played like baseball. Women play softball by the same rules as men except that the pitcher stands 40 feet from home plate instead of 46 feet.

**Types of Softball.** Every year, men's and women's teams compete in regional, national, and international tournaments. There are two classes of competition, *fast-pitch* and *slow-pitch*.

Fast-pitch softball teams play on an infield with the bases 60 feet apart, and the pitcher 46 feet from home plate. The players use a 12-inch ball, and a bat that cannot be thicker than $2\frac{3}{4}$ inches. All pitching must be underhand, in a motion similar to bowling.

In a common type of slow-pitch softball, the same size infield and ball are used, but the ball must be pitched so that it arches on its way to the batter. Unlike fast-pitch softball, slow-pitch rules do not allow bunting or base stealing. Many persons play a slow-pitch game with a 14- or 16-inch ball. Slow-pitch softball is popular in many large cities.

**History.** Softball was developed in 1887 by George W. Hancock of the Farragut Boat Club in Chicago. Hancock designed the game for indoor play with a 16-inch ball that had the seams turned out. In 1895, Lewis Rober of the Minneapolis Fire Department adapted the game for outdoor play. He used a 12-inch ball that had the same type of cover as that used in baseball. Rober's version is considered the forerunner of the present game. For many years, 10 players were used instead of nine. The extra player was short-fielder.

Softball spread to all parts of the United States. In 1923, the National Recreation Association appointed a committee of recreation executives to study the variety of rules used in different parts of the United States so that they could be standardized. Many of the rules were later changed by a joint rules committee formed in 1933. The Amateur Softball Association, founded in 1933, is the governing body of the sport in the United States. It has aided the development of softball in the U.S. and other countries. International softball competition is governed by the International Softball Federation, founded in 1952.  DON E. PORTER

**SOFTWOOD.** See LUMBER (Softwood Lumber); WOOD.
**SOGDIANA.** See ALEXANDER THE GREAT (The Battle of Arbela).
**SOGLOW, OTTO.** See CARTOON (Leading Cartoonists).

# SOIL

**SOIL** is the covering over most of the land surface of the earth. It is made up of rock and mineral particles of many sizes mixed with living things and their remains. It is shallow in some places, deep in others. It may be red, as it is in Georgia, or it may be very black, as it is in North Dakota. It may be sand or clay.

A geologist thinks of soil as the loose material that covers the solid rocks below the earth's surface. An engineer thinks of soil as the material on which he

*Ernest E. Wahlstrom, the contributor of this article, is Professor of Geology at the University of Colorado.*

erects buildings and other heavy structures. He also regards it as material from which to build roads, earth dams, or landing strips for airfields. But to the farmer and to most people, soil is the thin layer of material at the earth's surface that will support the growth of plants of all kinds.

Soil is one of the most important natural resources of any country. That is why great efforts are made to conserve soil. When the soil becomes unable to grow good crops, not enough food can be produced to feed the people. The strength of the nation declines.

## How Soil Is Formed

It takes a long time for soil to form. In places where the climate is moist and warm and is just right for making soil out of rocks, it takes thousands of years to form only a few inches of soil. In places where it is very cold or in dry desert regions, soil forms only with great difficulty, or not at all.

Soil is formed in two general ways. The action of weather on rocks causes them to decompose, or break down. Little by little the surface of the rock becomes softer and decays to become soil. Such soil is called *residual soil*. Soil surfaces may also be formed when wind, water, or glaciers carry soil from one place to another. Soil deposited by rivers and streams is called *alluvium*. Soil moved by glaciers is called *till*. Fine soil, blown about by the wind before it is deposited, is called *loess*. It is finer than sand, but coarser than clay.

Many soils, when they are first deposited, will not support much plant life. They usually do not have enough food in them to allow complex plants, such as corn or wheat, to thrive. They are ready to grow crops for the farmer only after they undergo many changes.

**Air.** Air helps to make soil because it contains oxygen, carbon dioxide, nitrogen, and moisture. The oxygen, carbon dioxide, and water combine with the chemical elements in the rocks. This causes the rocks to decay and break down into small particles. Plants, which also help to break down rocks, need the nitrogen and water. For example, the root of a tree can crack a rock. Wind helps to make soil when it blows sand against rocks, wearing the rocks into tiny fragments.

**Water.** The force of running water alone can wear away hard rock. But nearly all running water carries sand or gravel with it, and these particles also help to wear the rock away. Rain and snow help break rocks into small pieces. When water freezes in cracks in the rocks, it expands and causes the rock to break. The constant process of freezing and thawing of water on the surface of rocks helps to wear away the rock and make soil. This process is called *weathering*. Oxygen in the water, like oxygen in the air, combines chemically with the substances that have been dissolved from rocks. Glaciers help to make soil by scraping up loose rocks from the earth's surface, carrying them along, and grinding them into small pieces. When the glacier melts, the soil remains behind.

**Plants** increase the value of the soil in two ways. They send their roots through the soil, which breaks it up and makes it better for growing things. When plants die, they decay and form *humus*, an organic material that makes the soil more fertile (see HUMUS). The roots of plants, although tiny, are very strong. They have been known to split hard rocks. Small plants called bacteria help the green plants to decay.

HOW SOIL IS MADE

Moving air, or wind, blows sand against rock and wears it away.

Rain wears away rocks, and soaks decayed plant and animal matter into the soil.

Running water wears down rocks with the help of particles of sand and gravel.

Glaciers help to make soil by grinding and breaking loose rocks.

Water splits and chips rocks by freezing and expanding in cracks, like a powerful wedge.

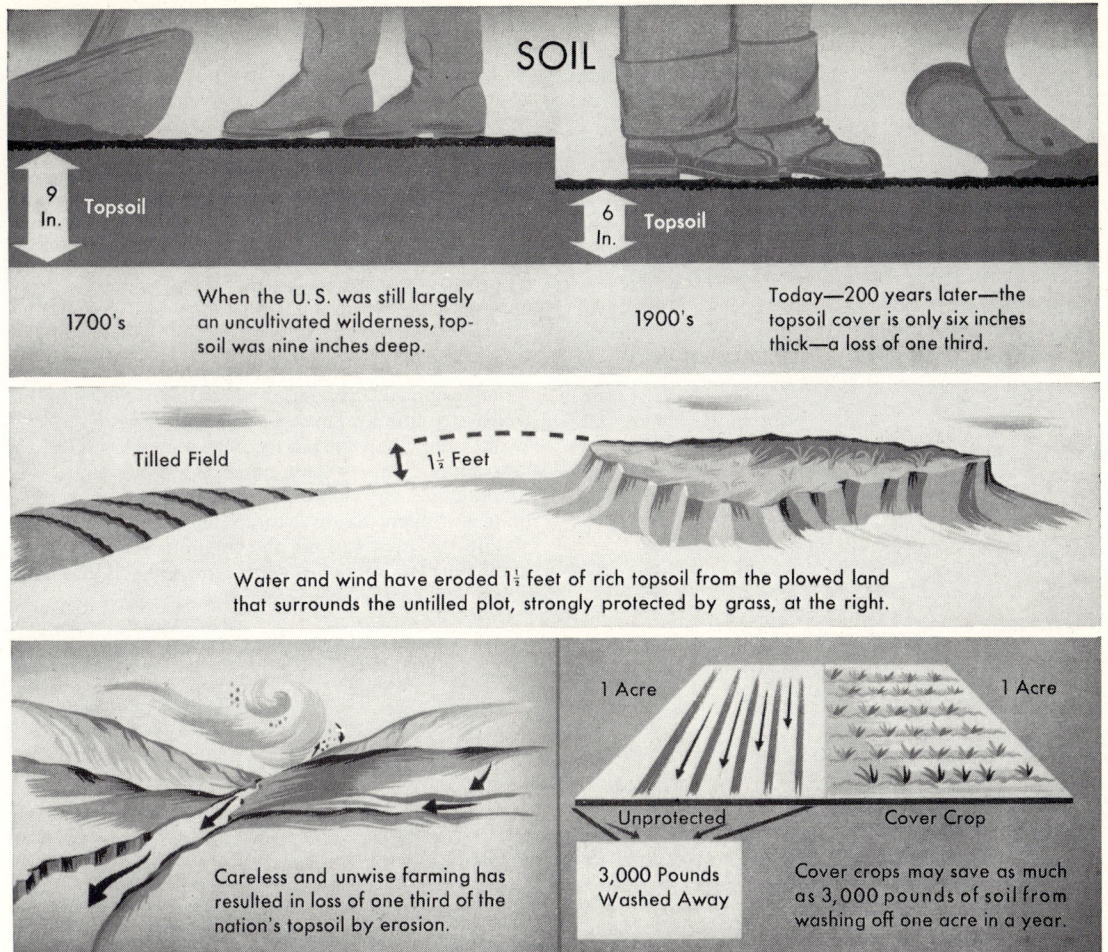

Animals also help to keep the soil fertile. Body wastes of many animals enrich the soil. When an animal dies, its body decays and adds important materials to the soil. Animals that burrow beneath the soil surface help to mix the soil. Perhaps the most valuable of all these animals are the earthworms. To obtain food, earthworms take soil into their bodies and pass it out again in a finely pulverized state (see EARTHWORM).

### How Soil Is Destroyed

Cultivated land can be seriously damaged by soil erosion (see EROSION). It takes hundreds of years to build up an inch of topsoil. But all the topsoil on a farm can be washed away by rains in less than 20 years. When the first colonists came to North America, they found rich soil. The early settlers quickly exhausted their soil by not fertilizing it and by failing to take measures that would prevent erosion.

As the pioneers pushed westward across the continent, they left worn-out soils behind them. When they cut down trees to clear the land for farms, they increased the amount of open soil that could be carried away by rain water. Rain not only washes away the soil itself, but also dissolves important chemicals in the soil and carries them away. Scientists believe that almost six times as much of the plant food in the soil is washed away by rain as is taken out of the soil by growing crops.

Water is not the only thing that destroys soil through erosion. During and immediately after World War I, many acres of grasslands were plowed up and planted with wheat because of the importance of wheat on the world market. When this land lost the covering of grass that had protected it, winds easily swept up the topsoil and carried it away. The dust storms that occurred during the middle 1930's ruined many farmlands in the Middle West. This area was called the *Dust Bowl*. See DUST BOWL; DUST STORM.

Various methods were used to prevent further erosion by the elements. Trees were planted along a shelter belt to check wind erosion. Farmers planted crops such as kudzu and lespedeza, which grow quickly and send out vast networks of roots. The roots hold the soil in place and keep the rain from washing it away. Terraces, which also help to hold the soil in place or catch the soil as it washes down, were built on hillsides. Contour plowing, in which the plow runs across the slope of the land rather than with it, was adopted to keep the water from running off the field too quickly.

Soil erosion is also an important problem in other countries. Palestine (now Israel) was once a fertile country, but erosion washed off so much soil that most of the land became barren. Similar erosion took

**Most Soil Needs Fertilizer** to help it produce a sturdy crop, and also to keep it healthy for the next planting. Tractor-drawn fertilizer distributors spread the fertilizer evenly, efficiently, and quickly over all the soil in a field.

*International Harvester Co.*

place in Greece and North Africa. See CONSERVATION (Soil Conservation).

### Characteristics of Soil

To the farmer, soil has four important characteristics. These are (1) depth, (2) structure, (3) texture, and (4) the chemical elements that are found in it.

**Depth.** *Topsoil* is the essential part of the soil for agriculture. It seldom lies deeper than the depth of a spade over any part of the earth's surface. Topsoil is generally deepest in valleys. It is thinnest near the tops of hills and mountains. Beneath the topsoil is another layer of soil that may be 2 or 3 feet deep. This is called the *subsoil*.

**Structure** of the soil is important because it shows how well the various grains that make up the soil cling together. In the ideal plant soil, each grain is not entirely separate. Rather, it tends to form small crumbs with other grains. Humus is valuable in soil because it tends to help the particles cling together.

**Texture** of the soil depends entirely upon the size of the grains or particles that make it up. The largest particles are the pebbles and small rocks that we call gravel. The smallest particles are found in clay soil. Between these two in size are the particles that make up silt and sand. Particles of sand are large enough to feel gritty when the soil is rubbed between the fingers. Particles of silt are just large enough to be seen. Decayed animal or plant matter in the soil is called humus.

Most soils are not pure sand, clay, or silt. Rather, they are mixtures of all the particles found in the soil. Such mixtures are called *loam*. To be considered a sandy soil, the soil must be at least half sand. Clay soil must be at least half clay. Clay soils are called *heavy* soils because their particles are packed tightly together. Sandy soils are considered *light* because the particles are loose.

The texture of the soil often helps to determine its fertility. Sandy soil, for example, is not good for growing plants. It does not hold water well. Clay soil is not good either, for it is packed so tightly that not enough air can reach the plant roots. A fine loam, with a large amount of silt and humus, is usually the best kind of soil.

**Chemical Make-Up.** Plants obtain much of their food from the soil. For this reason it is necessary that the chemicals that provide these foods be found in the soil. If these foods do not exist in the soil, they must be added. Fertilizers are used for this purpose. Sodium, potassium, calcium, phosphorus, magnesium, iron, and chlorine are essential for the growth of all living substances. If one crop takes too much of these substances from the soil, the farmer must replace them. Phosphorus, the nitrates that contain nitrogen, and calcium must often be replaced. But some of the substances rarely need replacement. For example, most soils contain enough iron so that it is usually not used up. Some soils contain too much acid. In this case the farmer adds lime to make the soil more alkaline.

The chemical composition of soil also influences the health of animals. Plants obtain minerals from the soil. As the animals eat the plants, these minerals are passed on to them. Some of these minerals are poisonous. For example, in some western states the soil contains selenium, a mineral harmful to animals. The plants that grow in this area can use the selenium without much harm. But if animals eat plants grown in soil that contains selenium, they are poisoned.

### Kinds of Soil

Scientists who specialize in the study of soil are called *pedologists*. They have developed many ways of classifying soil other than on the basis of the particles that make it up.

As soils develop from solid rock, alluvium, till, or loess, several changes take place that depend on the climate. In the eastern United States, where there is abundant rainfall, moisture seeps downward through the top layer, called the *zone of leaching*, or the *A horizon*. This moisture dissolves the chemical elements such as sodium, calcium, and magnesium, and carries them away to the rivers and the sea. Below the top layer of soil, insoluble iron oxides and clay minerals are deposited in another layer. This is called the *zone of accumulation*, or the *B horizon*. The B horizon grades downward into the *C horizon*, which contains a mixture of decomposed rock and unchanged materials from which soil has not yet begun to form.

In the western United States, where there is little rainfall, calcium carbonate is formed and remains in the soil, especially in the B horizon. Deposits of calcium carbonate in such soils form a whitish material called *caliche*. Soils that are poor in calcium are called *pedalfers*. Soils that contain much calcium are called *pedocals*. In tropical regions, soils become rich in aluminum and red-colored iron oxides. These soils are called *laterites*.

There are many varieties of each of the major kinds of soils and many gradations between them. Exact classification of soils can be made only by experts who specialize in the study of soils.    ERNEST E. WAHLSTROM

**Related Articles.** See the Natural Resources sections of the various country, state, and province articles. See also the following articles:

| | | |
|---|---|---|
| Agronomy | Erosion | Loam |
| Alkali | Farm and | Loess |
| Clay |   Farming | Soil Bank |
| Conservation | Fertilizer | Soil Conditioner |
| Drainage | Gardening | Soil Conservation Service |
| Dust Bowl | Humus | Topsoil |
| Earthworm | Irrigation | |

470

Adding a Soil Conditioner improves the structure of cracked, crusty soil, and enables seeds to germinate.

A Soil Conservationist helps farmers and ranchers put their land and water resources to the best possible use.

**SOIL BANK** was a United States federal government program designed to reduce crop surpluses by taking croplands out of production. The program consisted of a short-term *acreage reserve plan* and a long-term *conservation reserve plan*. It was adopted in 1956, but was replaced by other programs in the early 1960's.

The acreage reserve plan provided government payments to farmers who agreed to take designated cropland out of production for a year. Farmers put about 50,800,000 acres of land under this program from 1956 to 1958.

The conservation reserve plan provided for annual government payments to farmers who agreed to keep land out of production for from three to ten years. About 28 million acres were under this program at its peak.

Critically reviewed by the DEPARTMENT OF AGRICULTURE

**SOIL CONDITIONER** is a synthetic chemical or natural substance that improves soil structure. Good soil structure helps plants grow by bringing air and water to the roots. It also lessens erosion and prevents soil from crusting. Manure, peat, leaf mold, and other natural substances are more effective and less expensive than synthetic chemicals such as Krilium. Natural conditioners also provide plant food, but synthetic ones do not. See also SOIL (Texture).   HENRY T. NORTHEN

**SOIL CONSERVATION.** See CONSERVATION (Soil Conservation); EROSION.

**SOIL CONSERVATION SERVICE** is an agency of the United States Department of Agriculture. Its main purpose is to help farmers and ranchers use their land and water resources to reduce loss by flood or erosion. The service gives assistance through soil-conservation districts and other state and federal agencies. It makes soil surveys, develops technical plans for individual farms, and lends special equipment to carry out the conservation practices. This agency also manages a national program of flood prevention, drainage and irrigation, and watershed protection. The Soil Conservation Service was established in 1935.   JOHN C. BOLLENS

**SOILLESS AGRICULTURE.** See HYDROPONICS.

**SOKOL,** *SO kohl,* is a gymnastic organization with local societies in eastern Europe, particularly in Poland and Czechoslovakia, and in the United States. The Sokol movement stresses the physical development of young people, and also promotes patriotism and character development. Sokol was founded in Prague in 1862. The United States branch of the society was founded in 1865. Sokol activities in Europe are now controlled by Communist governments. See also CZECHOSLOVAKIA (picture: The Sokol Movement).

**SOL.** See CALENDAR (Calendar Reform).

**SOL,** *sohl,* is a standard silver coin used in Peru. One hundred centavos equal one sol. The radiant sun pictured on the coin gives the sol its name. Sol also is the name of a coin formerly used in France. For the value of the sol, see MONEY (table: Values).

**SOLANACEAE.** See NIGHTSHADE.

**SOLANUM,** *soh LAY num,* is an important group of plants that belong to the nightshade family. More than 1,000 different kinds of herbs and shrubs are included in the group. They grow in many parts of the world, but are especially abundant in tropical regions of North and South America. Some of the plants are cultivated for their showy flowers, others for their edible parts.

The most common species of solanum is the *potato*. Another is the *eggplant*. A few of the other species of the temperate regions are *bittersweet* and *common nightshade*. The *horse-nettle* and other spiny troublesome weeds are native to the United States. Several species were once used as medicine, and are still used in China. The fruits of many Indonesian varieties are eaten. The *kangaroo-apple* is a common food in Australia and New Zealand.

**Scientific Classification.** Solanums are genus *Solanum* in the nightshade family, *Solanaceae*.   GEORGE H. M. LAWRENCE

**Related Articles** in WORLD BOOK include:

| | | |
|---|---|---|
| Bittersweet | Flowering Tobacco | Painted-Tongue |
| Eggplant | Nightshade | Potato |

**SOLAR CELL.** See SEMICONDUCTOR.

**SOLAR DAY.** See DAY.

471

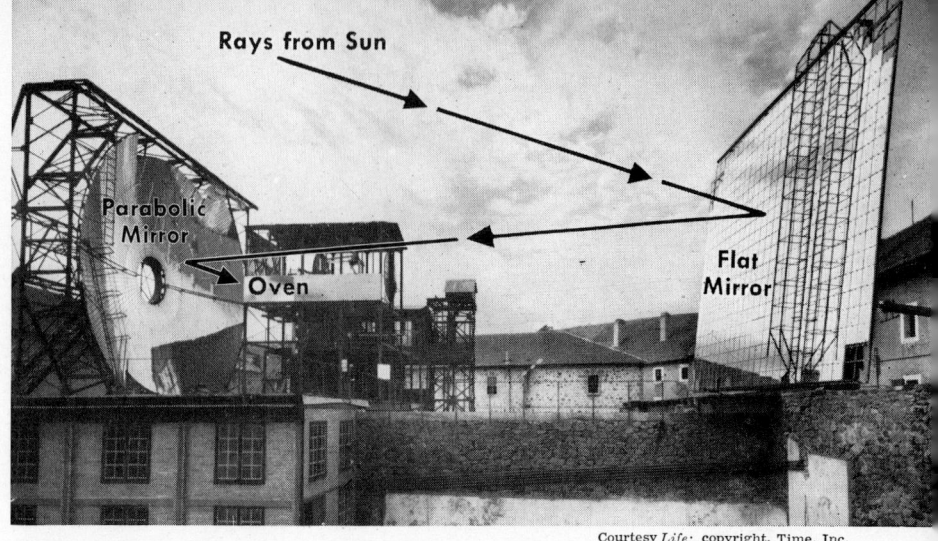

**Solar Furnace** creates high temperatures for industrial uses such as testing metals. Rays from the sun strike the flat mirror, which is made up of hundreds of small plate-glass mirrors. The rays are reflected to the parabolic mirror, which focuses them onto a single hot spot in the oven. A solar furnace may build up temperatures of more than 8,000°F.

*Courtesy Life; copyright, Time, Inc.*

**SOLAR ENERGY.** The sun sends out a never-ending stream of radiant energy. Most of this energy we call sunlight. The amount of solar energy streaming toward the earth in only one day equals the energy that could be produced by burning 550 billion tons of coal. This is as much coal as would be dug in the United States in 1,000 years at the present rate of mining. Enough solar energy falls on the United States every 20 minutes to fill the country's entire power needs for one year.

In the past 100 years, the world has used increasing amounts of coal, oil, electricity, and atomic energy to produce power and energy. Scientists have been hard at work to find ways of using the sun's energy more directly and more efficiently. But it is not easy to put the sun to work. The total amount of the sun's energy is large, but it is spread thinly over the surface of the earth.

In order to be used as an effective source of power, solar energy will have to be collected and, depending on its use, perhaps concentrated and stored. Scientists have conducted experiments with solar energy to heat and air-condition homes. They also have used it to cook food, to purify water, to irrigate land, and to furnish power for telephone lines. Huge solar furnaces have provided heat for testing metals. But further research is needed before these uses of the sun can become important practically, or before the sun can be used directly as a major source of power.

**Collecting and Concentrating** solar energy has been done by two chief methods. In one method, *parabolic* (bowl-like) *mirrors* capture the sun's rays to build up heat. The other method uses a *flat-plate collector*.

The parabolic mirrors concentrate the sun's rays by focusing them onto a black receiving surface, such as a tube. Water circulates through the tube, and the heat from the sun turns the water into steam. The steam then can run a turbine that produces mechanical power.

*Courtesy Newsweek; Howard Dewald*

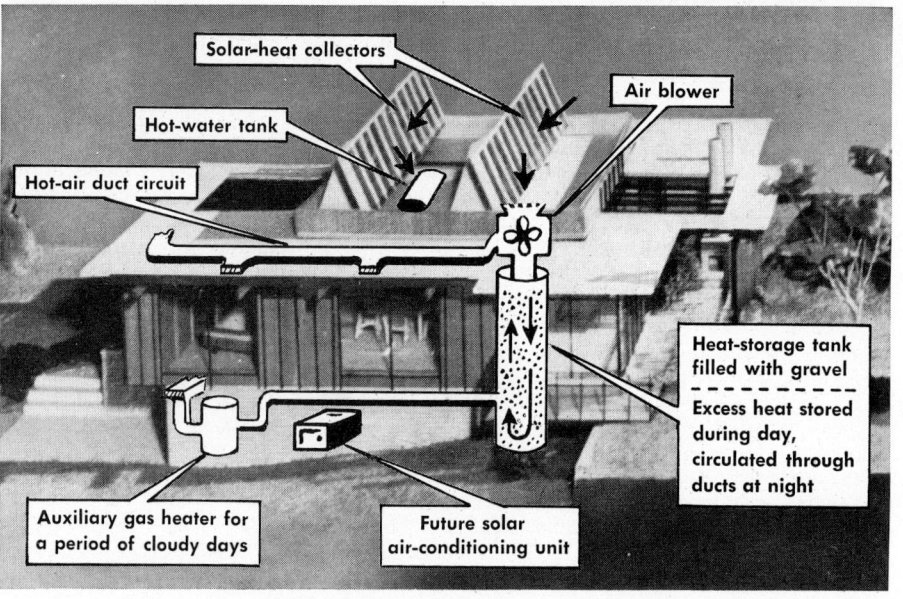

**Solar House-Heating** would take the load off conventional sources of heat such as coal, gas, and oil. To heat a house, flat-plate collectors trap the sun's rays. The heat is carried to a heat-storage tank containing gravel. A fan blows the heat through hot-air ducts when needed.

472

Parabolic mirrors are sometimes made of glass. But scientists also have used mirrors of aluminum foil or aluminized plastic sheets. The mirrors are rotated by machine or by hand to keep them facing the sun. They work best in areas where the sun shines brightly most of the time, such as in Arizona.

The flat-plate collector is made of metal and glass. One or more layers of glass are laid over a blackened metal plate, with an air space between each layer. Air or water circulates through tubes or over fins attached to the metal plate. The layers of glass act as a *heat trap.* They let in the sun's rays, but keep most of the heat from escaping. The heated air or water can be used to operate engines, to warm homes, or to cool them in the way a gas refrigerator cools by the use of heat. Much more study is required to determine the conditions under which flat-plate collectors are more effective than mirror systems.

**Solar House-Heating.** Scientists believe one of the first widespread uses of solar energy will be to heat homes and other buildings. To heat a home, a flat-plate collector is mounted on the part of the roof that slopes south, so that the maximum solar energy is received. In the Southern Hemisphere, the collector would be mounted on the part of the roof that slopes north. The collector is tilted at an angle to receive the largest amount of sunlight throughout the day or the season in which it is to be used.

The sun heats water or air circulating through the collector. The heated water is stored in an insulated tank, then pumped to the house through pipes and radiators. If air is used in the collector, the heat is stored in a bin containing crushed rock, which is heated by the hot air. When the house requires heat, air is blown through the rocks and into the house through hot-air ducts.

Storing the sun's heat is one of the problems in solar house-heating. In areas that have many cloudy days, it costs too much to store enough heat for more than 5 days. Consequently, an auxiliary heating system of the usual kind is provided, and the solar system is designed to do only a part (perhaps two-thirds) of the winter heating job. Solar house-heating collectors have been used experimentally to provide energy for air-conditioning systems, as well as for heating.

**Solar Engines** are run by solar boilers that generate steam which can be used to produce mechanical power. Turbines powered by solar-produced steam have generated electricity and pumped water for irrigation systems, but at present the cost is too great for widespread use of solar energy in this way. By using mirror collectors, solar boilers can convert about three-fifths of the collected solar energy into steam energy.

**Solar Furnaces** can develop high temperatures for industrial uses. A solar furnace in San Diego, Calif., builds up a temperature of 8,500° F. It is used by an aircraft company to test metals. A 40-foot solar furnace in the French Pyrenees has been used to make ceramic materials. A parabolic mirror, or set of mirrors, provides the heat for a solar furnace.

**Solar Batteries** are devices that convert sunlight directly into electricity. Solar batteries have been used to operate portable radios and to provide power for telephone circuits. A solar battery developed by the Bell Telephone Laboratories is made of specially-

United Press Int.
**Solar Battery.** Silicon disks atop a pole convert sunlight into electricity for a telephone circuit. Electricity that is not used immediately goes to a storage battery at the foot of the pole.

**Solar Cooker** uses the sun as its fuel. Aluminum mirrors focus the sun's rays on the food to be cooked. Some solar stoves can boil water in 20 minutes. Such devices are used in India and Japan where other fuels are scarce.

Stanford Research Institute

treated silicon crystals. An electric current is generated when light falls on the silicon crystals. On a bright day, a solar battery can produce electricity at the rate of almost 100 watts per square yard of its silicon-crystal surface. In this process, it converts about one-tenth of the solar energy received into electric energy. In 1958, the electronics equipment in the Vanguard I satellite was powered by a solar battery. See SEMICONDUCTOR.

Scientists are now testing flashlights that store solar energy for use as highway warning lamps. Many stores sell portable radios powered by the sun's energy. The great advantage of these devices is that the silicon disks, or crystals, never wear out.

**Solar Distillation.** Solar energy can be used to distill, or purify, water. A solar-distillation device consists of a

## SOLAR ENERGY

triangular roof of glass over a blackened pan filled with salty or impure water. The pan rests on an insulated pad. The sun evaporates the water, and air circulation carries the resulting water vapor to the glass roof, where it condenses. The condensed vapor, or distilled water, runs into troughs along the edge of the pan. Solar distillation has been used experimentally to remove salt from ocean water. The method may prove useful for some purposes in places that do not have large supplies of pure water, such as sheep-grazing lands in Australia.

**Photochemistry.** Scientists hope someday to put the sun to work in the same way that green plants use solar energy. In a process called *photosynthesis*, green plants use the sun's energy to make *carbohydrates* (sugars and starches) out of carbon dioxide and water. Scientists believe it is possible to use sunlight in a similar way to carry out other chemical reactions. For example, the sun might be used to break down water into its two parts, hydrogen and oxygen. The hydrogen then could be used as fuel. Such a process is called a *photochemical* reaction. See PHOTOSYNTHESIS.

**History.** For hundreds of years, man has regarded the sun as a possible source of power. In 1615, Salomon de Caux, a French engineer, conducted simple experiments in solar energy. Antoine Lavoisier, a French chemist, used solar energy to melt iron in 1774. John Ericsson, an American engineer and inventor, built the first solar steam engine in 1870.

Modern research on the use of solar energy started in the 1930's with the invention of a solar boiler by Charles G. Abbot, the initiation of the Godfrey Cabot solar programs at Harvard University and the Massachusetts Institute of Technology, and the establishment of the Heliotechnic Institute in Russia. The Bell Telephone Laboratories developed a solar battery in 1954. In the same year, the National Physical Laboratory of India devised an aluminum solar cooker, or stove, that will be valuable in areas with little fuel of any kind. The solar stove boils a kettle containing three quarts of water in less than an hour.

Solar-energy scientists formed the Association for Applied Solar Energy in 1954. Scientists from 35 countries met in Arizona in 1955 for the Association's first world symposium on applied solar energy. Plans have been announced for several large solar energy projects. Many of the world's scientists and engineers are trying to help harness the sun more effectively.    HOYT C. HOTTEL

See also RADIATION; SUN.

**SOLAR FURNACE.** See SOLAR ENERGY.

**SOLAR PLEXUS** is a large network of nerves back of the stomach. It is part of the autonomic nervous system. This system controls all the abdominal *viscera* (internal organs). The nerve threads of this system connect by numerous branches with the organs of the abdominal cavity.

A blow on a spot between the navel and breastbone, a little to the right, is called the solar plexus punch. A fighter can be knocked out by this punch if it is hard enough. The exact manner in which this occurs has not been determined. The solar plexus first became well known in 1897 as a result of the championship boxing match between James Corbett and Robert Fitzsimmons. Fitzsimmons knocked out Corbett with a blow to the solar plexus.    W. B. YOUMANS

See also NERVOUS SYSTEM.

**SOLAR SPECTRUM.** See LIGHT (color picture: Spectrum and Spectrum Analysis).

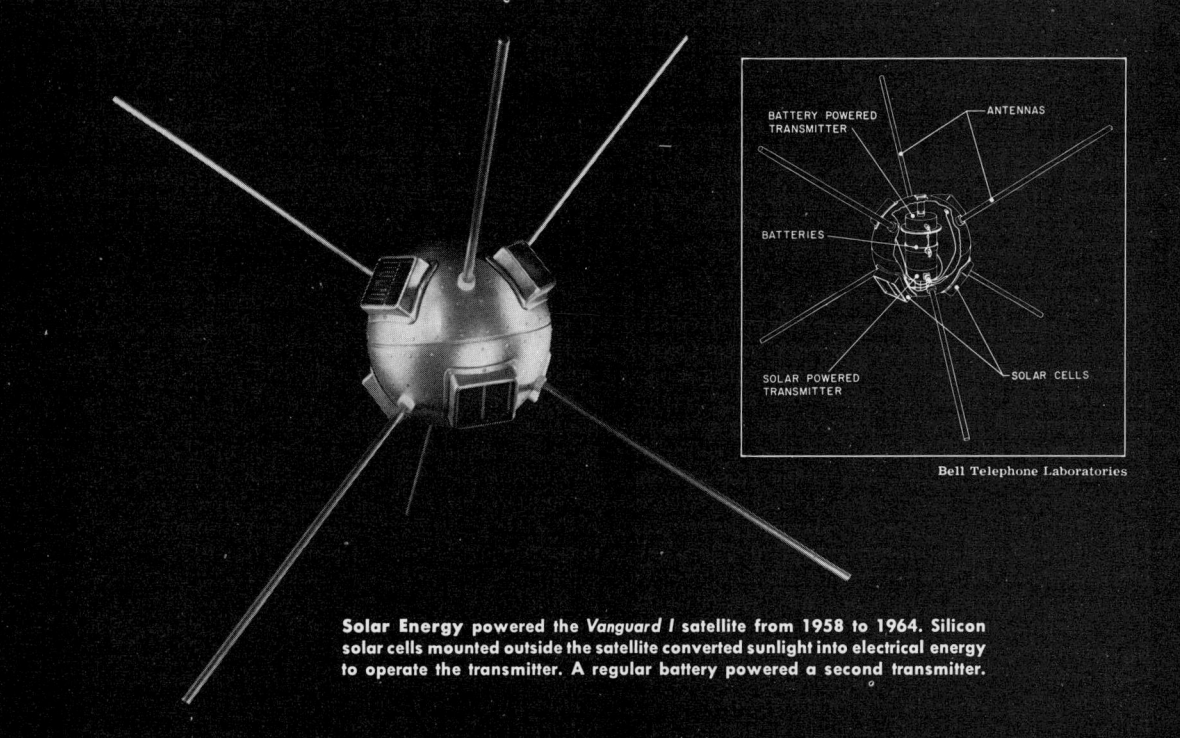

**Solar Energy** powered the *Vanguard I* satellite from 1958 to 1964. Silicon solar cells mounted outside the satellite converted sunlight into electrical energy to operate the transmitter. A regular battery powered a second transmitter.

Bell Telephone Laboratories

# SOLAR SYSTEM

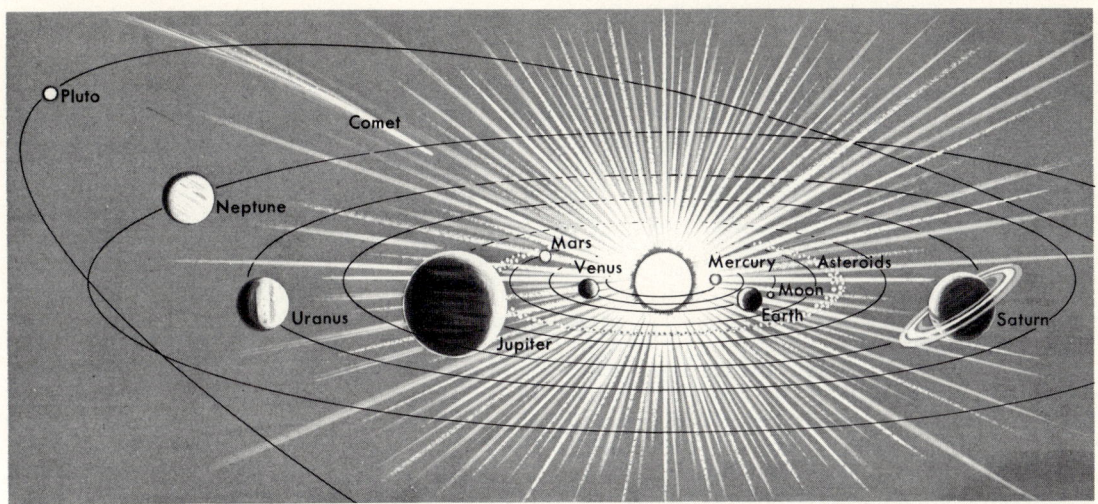

WORLD BOOK illustration by Dick Larson

**The Solar System Includes Many Different Objects** that travel around the sun. These objects vary from planets with diameters of thousands of miles, to tiny meteoroids and dust particles.

**SOLAR SYSTEM** is the sun and all the objects that travel around it. The solar system includes (1) the earth and eight other *planets*, along with the *satellites* (moons) that travel around most of them; (2) planetlike objects called *asteroids;* (3) chunks of iron and stone called *meteoroids;* (4) bodies of dust and frozen gases called *comets;* and (5) drifting particles called *interplanetary dust*, and a drifting gas called *interplanetary plasma*.

The solar system has a circular shape. It is only a tiny part of a *galaxy* (family of stars) called the *Milky Way*. The Milky Way consists of more than 100 billion stars that are somewhat similar to the sun. The Milky Way, which also has a circular shape, is about 100,000 light-years across, and about 16,000 light-years thick at its center. A *light-year* is the distance light travels in one year at a speed of 186,282 miles per second. The solar system itself is less than one *light-day* (the distance light travels in one day) across. It is about 30,000 light-years from the center of the Milky Way. The galaxy turns, and the solar system travels around the center of the Milky Way about every 200 million years.

Many stars in the Milky Way are the centers of solar systems. Some astronomers think many of these systems may have some form of life. The nearest solar system that might have intelligent life is about 100 light-years away. It would take 100 years for a radio message sent from the earth at the speed of light to reach this solar system, and another 100 years for a reply to reach the earth.

### Parts of the Solar System

**The Sun** is the center of the solar system. Its *mass* is more than 750 times as great as that of all the planets combined (see MASS). The huge mass of the sun creates the gravitation that keeps the other objects traveling around the sun in an orderly manner.

The sun continuously gives off energy in several forms—visible light; invisible *infrared*, *ultraviolet*, *X*, and *gamma* rays; radio waves; and *plasma* (hot, electrically charged gas). The flow of plasma, which becomes interplanetary plasma and drifts throughout the solar system, is called the *solar wind*.

The surface of the sun changes continuously. Bright spots called *plages* and dark spots called *sunspots*, frequently form and disappear. Gases often shoot up violently from the surface. For a complete description of the sun, see the article SUN.

**Planets** are the second largest objects in the solar system. The four planets nearest the sun—Mercury, Venus, Earth, and Mars—are the smallest planets, although Pluto's size has not been accurately determined. Those four planets are called *terrestrial* (earthlike) planets, and appear to consist chiefly of iron and rock. The earth has one satellite, and Mars has two. Mercury and Venus have no satellites.

The four largest planets—Jupiter, Saturn, Uranus, and Neptune—are called the *major* planets. They are probably made up chiefly of hydrogen, helium, ammonia, and methane. Compared to the terrestrial

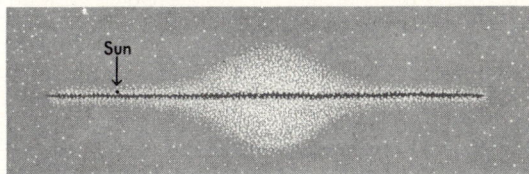

**The Milky Way** is made up of more than 100 billion stars similar to the sun. Many stars have their own solar systems. This side view of the Milky Way shows the position of the sun in the galaxy.

*The contributor of this article is A. G. W. Cameron, Professor of Space Physics at the Belfer Graduate School of Science of Yeshiva University.*

474a

# SOLAR SYSTEM

planets, they contain little iron and rock. Each of the major planets has several satellites. Pluto, the farthest planet from the sun, appears to be somewhat like the terrestrial planets. But because Pluto is so far away, astronomers know little about it and do not include it in either group.

All the planets except Pluto are surrounded by varying kinds and amounts of gases. The earth is the only planet that has enough oxygen surrounding it and enough water on its surface for life as we know it. For a more complete description of the planets, see the article PLANET and the separate articles on each planet.

**Asteroids,** also called *planetoids*, are small, irregularly shaped objects. Most asteroids are between the orbits of Mars and Jupiter. Astronomers have figured out the sizes and orbits of about 1,600 of the largest asteroids. Only a few are larger than 100 miles across, and many are less than 1 mile across. Astronomers believe the asteroid belt includes large amounts of dust created by collisions between asteroids. See ASTEROID.

**Meteoroids** are small chunks of iron and rock that also are thought to result from collisions between asteroids. Many meteoroids fall into the earth's atmosphere, but most are burned up by friction before they reach the surface of the earth. Meteoroids are called *meteors* while falling through the atmosphere, and *meteorites* if they are found on the earth's surface. See METEOR.

**Comets.** Most comets have three parts: (1) a solid *nucleus*, or center; (2) a round *coma*, or head, that surrounds the nucleus and consists of dust particles mixed with frozen water, frozen methane, and frozen ammonia; and (3) a long *tail* of dust and gases that escape from the head. Most comets stay near the outside of the solar system. Some come near the sun, where their bright heads and long, shining tails provide a rare and spectacular sight. See COMET.

### Formation of the Solar System

Astronomers do not have enough information to describe the formation of the solar system completely. Many ideas have been suggested, but parts of all of them have been proved wrong.

Until the mid-1900's, theories of how the solar system was formed could be based on only five important observations. (1) The sun and most other parts of the solar system spin in the same direction on their *axes* (imaginary lines drawn through their centers). (2) Most parts of the solar system travel around the sun in the same direction that the sun spins. (3) Most satellites travel around their planets in the same direction that the planets travel around the sun. (4) Going outward from the sun, the distance between the orbits of the planets increases. (5) The solar system has a circular shape.

The theories that have been suggested to explain the above observations can be divided into two general groups—*monistic theories* and *dualistic theories*. Most astronomers believe that some form of monistic theory will someday be proved correct.

**Monistic Theories** are based on the belief that the solar system was formed from a single flat cloud of gas. According to some monistic theories, all parts of the solar system were formed from the gas at the same time. Other monistic theories suggest that the sun was formed first, and the planets and other objects came later from the remaining gas. The first monistic theory was proposed in the early 1600's by the French scientist and philosopher René Descartes. In the late 1700's, Pierre Simon de Laplace, also of France, suggested another monistic theory which was called the *nebular hypothesis*.

**Dualistic Theories** are based on the belief that the solar system was formed when some huge object passed near the sun. According to these theories, the force of gravity of the passing object pulled a long stream of gas out from the sun. The planets and other objects were formed from this gas. The first dualistic theory was proposed in the 1700's by the French scientist Compte de Buffon. Buffon believed the passing object was a large comet, which he incorrectly thought was as large as a star. In the early 1900's, Thomas Chamberlin and Forest Moulton, both of the University of Chicago, offered a dualistic theory called the *planetesimal hypothesis*.

**Theories Since the Mid-1900's** are helping scientists come closer to learning how the solar system was formed. For example, astronomers have discovered that the Milky Way is at least twice as old as the solar system. For that reason, the processes of star formation seen in the galaxy today are probably similar to the processes that formed the sun.

The study of meteorites is producing new information about temperatures, pressures, and other conditions that probably existed during the formation of the solar system. Measurements of the radioactivity of meteorites indicate that they were formed at about the same time as the solar system, about $4\frac{1}{2}$ billion years ago.

Information gathered by artificial satellites and space probes indicates that the atmospheres and interiors of the other planets differ greatly from those of the earth. A complete theory of the formation of the solar system probably cannot be developed from studies of the earth alone.

By studying the sun, astronomers hope to learn how the center of the sun heats its outer atmosphere. Astronomers also want to find why the formation of sunspots reaches a peak about every 11 years.

By studying the planets, astronomers hope to discover how various chemical elements are spread throughout the solar system. They hope to learn whether the planets have liquid centers, and why some planets have large amounts of carbon dioxide in their atmospheres.

Exploration of the moon is expected to provide knowledge of how and when the moon was formed. Astronomers also want to know whether there are volcanoes on the moon, and whether the interior of the moon is similar to that of the earth.  A. G. W. CAMERON

**Related Articles** in WORLD BOOK include:

| | | |
|---|---|---|
| Asteroid | Jupiter | Planet |
| Astronomy | Mars | Pluto |
| Comet | Mercury | Saturn |
| Earth (The Birth of | Meteor | Star |
| the Solar System) | Milky Way | Sun |
| Galaxy | Moon | Uranus |
| Gravitation | Neptune | Venus |

**SOLDER,** *SAHD er,* is a metal alloy used to join metal surfaces together (see ALLOY). It is also used to mend metal objects. To be effective, the solder must melt more easily than the metals to which it is applied.

There are two types of solder, hard and soft. Hard solders will melt only at high temperatures. The advantage of hard solders is their strength and the fact that they can be pressed or hammered into various shapes without breaking. Some hard solders are drawn out into long threads and others are pressed into sheets. The most common hard solder is silver solder, which consists of silver, copper, and zinc. Other common solders include brasses made up mainly of copper and zinc. Many copper alloys are also used as hard solders.

Soft solders will melt at low temperatures. But they are brittle and cannot be hammered without breaking. The most common soft solders include various alloys that consist mainly of tin and lead. These alloys also contain other metals such as antimony, cadmium, bismuth, and silver.     WILLIAM W. MULLINS

See also BRAZING.

**SOLDIER.** See ARMY; ARMY, UNITED STATES; RANK IN ARMED SERVICES.

**SOLDIERS' BONUS.** See BONUS.

**SOLDIERS' HOMES.** See VETERANS ADMINISTRATION.

**SOLDIER'S MEDAL.** See DECORATIONS AND MEDALS (Military Awards).

**SOLE** is the name of a family of flatfishes which have twisted skulls so that both eyes are on the same side of the body. Soles live in warm seas near shores. Their eyes are small and set close together. The mouth is crooked,

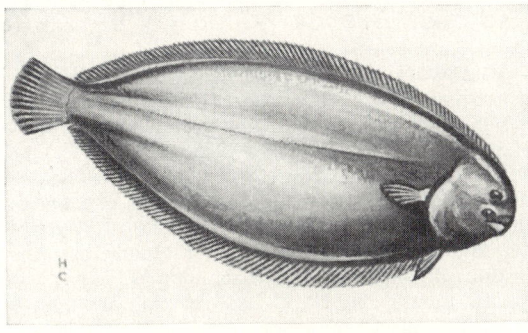

**The European Sole Is a Famed Food Delicacy.**

and the body flat and oval shaped.

The *European sole* grows from 10 to 20 inches long, and usually weighs about a pound. The *common American sole,* also called *hogchoker,* lives along the eastern coast of North America. This sole sometimes travels up rivers for some distance. The American sole is often used as food.

Some kinds of flounder that live along seacoasts are also called soles (see FLOUNDER).

**Scientific Classification.** Soles make up the sole family, *Soleidae.* The American sole is genus *Achirus,* species *A. fasciatus.* The European sole is classified as genus *Solea,* species *S. vulgaris.*     LEONARD P. SCHULTZ

See also BELGIUM (picture: A Fisherman).

**SOLENODON,** *soh LEE nuh dahn,* is a rare animal that looks like a long-nosed rat. The *yellow-headed solenodon*

New York Zoological Society

**The Rare Solenodon** looks like a long-nosed rat. It is a shy animal, and rarely comes above ground in daylight hours.

lives in Cuba and the *brown solenodon* makes its home in Haiti. The solenodon lives in hollow logs and rocky dens, and comes out for food only at night. It scratches for insects with its long claws. The solenodon weighs about 2½ pounds and grows about 2 feet long, including its stiff, scaly, 10-inch-long tail. It has a long, pointed snout and short, coarse hair. The solenodon is bad tempered, and zoologists believe its saliva may be poisonous.

**Scientific Classification.** The solenodon is in the solenodon family, *Solenodontidae.* The Haitian solenodon is genus *Solenodon,* species *S. paradoxus.* The Cuban solenodon is *S. cubanus.*

**SOLENOID,** *SOH luh noid,* is a coil of wire wound on a hollow cylinder. The cylinder is made of a material that permits a magnetic force to pass through it. When a direct current passes through the wire, the magnetic field that develops inside the solenoid pulls a magnetic plunger into the cylinder.

Solenoids are used where an electric impulse must be changed into a pushing or pulling action. They make up part of the equipment in mechanical sorting and grading devices, and are used in many electrical relays, contactors, and circuit breakers.     PALMER H. CRAIG

See also ELECTRIC EYE.

**SOLFATARA.** See VOLCANO (Products of Volcanic Eruption); FUMAROLE.

**SOLICITOR.** See LAWYER.

**SOLICITOR GENERAL.** See JUSTICE, DEPARTMENT OF.

**SOLID,** in mathematics, is a term used to describe a geometric figure with the three dimensions of length, breadth, and thickness. Some solids are named from the shapes of the surfaces that bound them, such as cubes, cylinders, cones, and spheres. In physics, solid refers to one of the three possible *states* (forms) in which matter may exist. The other two states are *liquid* and *gaseous.* The state of each body of matter is classified according to the power of its molecules to resist outside forces that tend to change its shape. A solid has a fixed shape, weight, and volume.     HOWARD S. KALTENBORN

**Related Articles** in WORLD BOOK include:

| Cone | Gas | Prism |
| Cube | Liquid | Pyramid |
| Cylinder | Mensuration | Sphere |

**SOLID GEOMETRY.** See GEOMETRY.

475

# SOLID SOUTH

**SOLID SOUTH.** The bitter feelings aroused by the Civil War and the Reconstruction Period caused many Southerners to feel that the Republican Party opposed most Southern principles. As a result, the Democratic Party came to control most of the local government in the South, and to command overwhelming majorities of the Southern vote in national elections. The almost solid Democratic control caused the Southern States to be called the *Solid South*.

See also SOUTHERN STATES.

**SOLID STATE PHYSICS** deals with the physical properties of solid materials. These properties include magnetism, *luminescence* (giving off light), mechanical strength, and the conduction of electricity and heat. Solid state physicists try to understand the properties of solids by studying the arrangement and motion of the atoms and electrons that make them up.

The atoms or molecules of most solids are arranged in a repeated pattern called *crystals* (see CRYSTAL and CRYSTALLIZATION). The basic building block of a crystal is the *unit cell*, which is repeated over and over again. Physicists beam electrons, X rays, or neutrons at crystals to learn how the atoms or molecules in the crystals are arranged.

Much of the progress in solid state physics has been made by preparing extremely pure single crystals of various substances and studying their properties. The detailed structure of the electron distribution of a solid can be determined in this way. The information learned from such relatively ideal materials provides a better understanding of common materials and helps man create new materials with superior properties.

The field of solid state physics has grown rapidly since about 1946 because of its importance to industry and its scientific interest. More people are involved in it than in any other area of physics. Achievements of solid state physics include the development of transistors and other devices used in electronic circuits. Solid state physicists have also made *ferrites* (magnets that do not conduct electricity) used in the memory cores of computers, solid lasers, solar batteries, solid *luminescent sources* (devices that change electricity directly into light), and sensitive detectors for many types of radiation. The electrical, computer, communications, and space industries particularly make use of solid state technology.

A knowledge of the *quantum theory* is essential in studying solid state physics. The quantum theory forms the basis of understanding the structure of atoms and molecules and the forces that bind them together to form crystals. See QUANTUM THEORY.

Quantum theory has given an understanding of one of the most remarkable properties to be studied in solid state physics, *superconductivity*. In normal metals, voltage must be applied and power used to keep an electric current flowing. But in a superconductor, a current will flow indefinitely with no applied voltage. Superconductivity is exhibited by many metals and alloys at extremely low temperatures—for example, a few degrees above absolute zero ($-273.15°$ C. or $-459.67°$ F.). Scientists are seeking materials which will be superconducting at higher temperatures. See CRYOGENICS.

Solid state physics is an expanding field of research with many other challenging problems. Some of the problems being studied involve the interaction of light from intense laser beams with matter. Other areas of research include the conversion of electrical energy into light, and improving materials for solid lasers and light sources. Methods of solid state physics are also being applied to the transfer of energy and electrical charge in organic systems important in biology. JOHN BARDEEN

See also SEMICONDUCTOR; TRANSISTOR.

**SOLÍS, JUAN DÍAZ DE.** See RÍO DE LA PLATA; URUGUAY (Early Years).

**SOLITAIRE**, a bird. See DODO.

**SOLITAIRE**, SAHL uh TAIR, is the name given to many card games that are played by only one person. Solitaire is usually played with 52 cards. Kings usually rank highest and aces lowest.

In one kind of solitaire, the player deals seven cards in a row, the first one face up and the rest face down. Then he deals a card face up on the second card, and a card face down on each of the remaining five. He continues until all seven piles have a card facing up.

One card may be placed on a second card if it is one lower in rank and is the opposite color of the second card. Aces are put in a row above the main piles. The object is to stack the cards by suits and in order in the top piles, from ace to king. The top card in any lower pile may be moved to this row if the card before it in the same suit is the last card in a pile. A face-down card that becomes the top card in a lower pile may be turned face up. The cards that were not dealt into piles are kept face down. Every third card is turned face up. LILLIAN FRANKEL

**SOLITARY INSECT.** See BEE (Solitary Bees); WASP.

**SOLOGUB, FYODOR.** See RUSSIAN LITERATURE (New Approaches).

**SOLOMON**, the son of David, was the king under whom Israel reached its greatest prosperity and glory. Significantly enough, his name comes from *shalom*, a Hebrew word which means *peace*. His mother was Bathsheba, the woman whom King David fell in love with and married after her husband, Uriah, had died on the field of battle (see BATHSHEBA; DAVID). In the closing days of David's life, an older son, Adonijah, unsuccessfully attempted to gain recognition as his successor on the throne. But David had Solomon anointed as king in his place, and Adonijah had to flee for refuge.

**Builds Temple.** When Solomon felt secure upon his throne, he set out to accomplish the great task his father had not been allowed to perform, that of building the Temple of Jehovah. He went about this undertaking with a spirit of reverence, desiring to set up a worthy sanctuary for the one true God. He wanted it to surpass in glory the idolatrous temples of the heathen. In the fourth year of his reign, about 966 B.C., he began building the temple (I Kings 6:1). He finished it in seven or eight years. He used gold and silver worth as much as $4 billion in building the temple.

**Solomon**
Detail from bronze relief by Lorenzo Ghiberti. Brogi from Art Reference Bureau

The greatest day in Solomon's life was the day of the service of worship when this magnificent temple was dedicated to the Lord (I Kings 8). Solomon stood on a great platform before the altar of the Lord, and led his people in a long and eloquent prayer of dedication, begging God to meet with mercy and blessing all who should come to worship and present sacrifice there. The Lord miraculously answered by sending down fire to enkindle the sacrifice on the altar, and by forming a brilliant "glory" cloud which signified His presence (II Chronicles 7:1).

**His Wisdom.** Solomon thus began his reign under most favorable circumstances and with the noblest of intentions. Soon after he had become king and before work started on the temple, he went up to the sanctuary at Gibeon to pray. When the Lord appeared to him in a dream and asked him to name whatever blessing he most desired, Solomon modestly requested only one thing: wisdom to know how best to govern his people and encourage them to lead a godly life, in obedience to the Law of Moses. God bestowed upon him not only the wisdom he asked for, but also great wealth and power, and victory over his enemies. He became so renowned that he excited the admiration of other countries. Some of their rulers, like the Queen of Sheba, came to see with their own eyes the glory and magnificence of which they had heard so much.

Solomon composed remarkable works on natural history and practical philosophy. He also wrote beautiful poetry, such as the Biblical book, Song of Solomon (see SONG OF SOLOMON). The book of Ecclesiastes and a large part of Proverbs are also attributed to Solomon.

**His Downfall.** Unfortunately for Solomon, the very greatness of his success and prosperity led to his undoing. His unlimited power led to unlimited pride and self-indulgence. He filled his harem with an almost incredible number of wives and concubines. The Bible gives the total as about 1,000. He indulged their religious preferences by building pagan shrines at which they might carry on their idolatrous worship. Starting with the Egyptian princess whom he honored above all his other wives, he allowed their image-worship. This paved the way for the deadly influence of idolatry upon the Hebrew nation. Solomon was also very proud of his chariotry and built huge stables in which to quarter his horses. One of his stables was discovered at the site of Megiddo. His ships brought goods from such far-off places as India, southern Arabia, and Ethiopia.

But after a few decades the prosperity of Israel dwindled greatly. Economic hardship became widespread, despite an almost complete freedom from war and despite friendly relations with all the neighboring peoples. This economic hardship finally led to a revolt against high taxes and the system of forced labor which supported Solomon's extravagant building projects. His last years were embittered by personal disillusionment and by hostility at home and abroad. When Solomon died, his incompetent son, Rehoboam, could not hold the Hebrew empire together. The Ten Tribes broke away in successful rebellion and set up the Northern Kingdom of Ephraim, or Israel.   GLEASON L. ARCHER, JR.

**SOLOMON ISLANDS** lie east of New Guinea in the southwestern Pacific Ocean. The northern Solomons include Bougainville, Buka, and a few smaller islands. Australia governs them as part of a United Nations trust territory. They cover 4,100 square miles and have a population of 72,490. The southern Solomons make up the British Solomon Islands Protectorate. They include Guadalcanal, Santa Isabel, San Cristóbal, Malaita, New Georgia, and Choiseul. They cover an area of 11,500 square miles and have a population of 153,000.

The islands' climate is hot, damp, and unhealthful. Some of the soil is fertile, especially the soil formed by lava. The islands are largely mountainous, heavily wooded, and well watered. They have many active volcanoes. The highest peak is Mt. Balbi (10,170 ft.) on Bougainville. The islands' crops include bananas, coconuts, pineapples, rubber, sweet potatoes, and taro. Exports include copra, ivory nuts, shells, and timber.

Most of the people are dark-skinned Melanesians. Several thousand Polynesians, and hundreds of Chinese and Europeans also live there. Most of the people can speak some Pidgin English (see PIDGIN ENGLISH).

Álvaro de Mendaña of Spain discovered the Solomons in 1568. He named them in the belief that he had found the source of the gold that had been used for Solomon's Temple at Jerusalem. Later expeditions were unable to locate the islands. The English navigator Philip Carteret finally found them again in 1767.

Germany occupied the northern Solomons from the 1880's until 1900, when it transferred all but Bougainville to Britain. The southern Solomons became a British protectorate in 1893. Early in 1942, the Japanese seized most of the islands, and they became a bitterly contested area of World War II. United States troops finally took the islands from the Japanese after heavy fighting in 1942 and 1943.   GEORGE F. DEASY

See also BOUGAINVILLE; GUADALCANAL ISLAND; PACIFIC ISLANDS (picture; map).

**SOLOMON'S-SEAL** is a hardy plant that belongs to the lily family. Several closely related plants have this name. Solomon's-seal grows in the temperate zones of North America, Europe, and Asia. It gets its name from its thick, creeping rootstalks which bear growth scars that resemble the mystic seal of Solomon.

J. Horace McFarland
**Solomon's-Seal Flowers**

The plant has a long, arching stem that gives it a graceful appearance. It bears round berries that may be blue or black. Greenish, bell-shaped flowers grow at the bases of the leaves. Solomon's-seal grows best in shady places and rich, moist soil.

**Scientific Classification.** Solomon's-seal belongs to the lily family, *Liliaceae*. It is genus *Polygonatum*.   EARL L. CORE

See also PLANT (color picture: Some Members of the Lily Family).

**SOLON,** *SOH lahn* (639?-559? B.C.), was a famous lawmaker. He was known as one of the *seven wise men of Greece* (see SEVEN WISE MEN OF GREECE).

Solon was born in Athens of a noble family. He first

became known as a poet. His poems played a great part in urging the Athenians to regain the island of Salamis, which had long been in foreign hands. He was given command of the forces sent to take back the island, and he quickly conquered it. Afterward, Solon was elected an *archon* (chief government official) of Athens and was given authority to change the laws (see ARCHON).

Athens was badly in need of political and economic reforms. Most of the wealth was in the hands of a few powerful citizens. The farmers had been forced to mortgage their lands and to borrow money, offering themselves and their families as security. Solon immediately passed a law which canceled all these debts and mortgages, and freed those who had become slaves. He also changed the monetary system so that foreign trade was made easier. The only change he made in foreign trade was a law prohibiting grain exports.

Solon's constitutional reforms redivided the citizens into four classes, according to income. Citizens of all classes were allowed to become members of the assembly and the public law courts. Solon established a council of 400 to take over the political powers of the Areopagus, and set up popular courts in which citizens could appeal the decisions of the officials (see AREOPAGUS). He kept the old provisions that allowed only the three higher classes to hold public office, and only the highest class to hold the archonship. These provisions continued the oligarchy, but his reforms were a definite step toward democracy.

Solon is said to have made the Athenians promise to keep his laws for 10 years. He then left the state. When he returned 10 years later, he found the country fighting a civil war. Soon afterward Pisistratus seized control. After opposing Pisistratus, Solon retired from public life. DONALD KAGAN

**SOLSTICE,** *SAHL stis,* is the point at which the sun appears to be farthest from the equator. As the earth travels in its orbit around the sun, the sun seems to move. The earth is tilted about $23\frac{1}{2}$ degrees on its axis, so that the sun does not always seem to be in the same position. During summer in the Northern Hemisphere, the northern half of the world is tilted toward the sun. During winter, the Northern Hemisphere is tilted away from the sun. The sun seems to rise high in summer and much lower in winter. The solstice is the point at which the sun seems to start back in the opposite direction. The summer solstice comes about June 21. The sun seems to stand still for several days, and then start back toward the equator. It crosses the equator about September 23 and reaches the winter solstice about December 22. The summer solstice is the longest period of daylight in the Northern Hemisphere, and the winter solstice is the shortest period of daylight. See also SEASON; EQUINOX. E. C. SLIPHER

**SOLUBLE GLASS.** See WATER GLASS.

**SOLUTION** is a mixture of substances that cannot be separated by mechanical methods, such as filtration. Blood plasma, a mixture of water, salts, and proteins, is a solution in the body. Salt water is a natural solution that fills the oceans. A solution may be a liquid, a solid, or a gas.

*Liquid solutions* result when a liquid dissolves another liquid, or a solid or a gas. Two liquids that can form a solution are said to be *miscible*. This ability depends on the chemical properties of the liquids, and on such physical conditions as temperature and pressure. For example, most oils are only slightly miscible with water at room temperature. But they become more miscible when heated.

Gases and solids that dissolve in a liquid are said to be *soluble*. This ability also depends on the chemical properties of the substances, and on physical conditions. As the temperature of a liquid solution rises, dissolved gases usually become less soluble. But dissolved solids usually become more soluble. Soft-drink manufacturers dissolve carbon dioxide gas in water under pressure. When a soft-drink bottle is opened, this pressure is released. The carbon dioxide then becomes less soluble, and part of it bubbles away. Pressure changes usually have little effect on the solubility of a solid.

*Solid solutions* are formed when liquid solutions freeze. For example, when a solution of melted copper and zinc freezes, it forms a solid solution called *brass*. Steel is a solid solution that results when various metals and nonmetals are dissolved in iron. The melting point of a solid solution usually differs from the melting points of its parts.

*Gaseous solutions* can be made from any combination of gases. Air is a gaseous solution. The most abundant gases in air are nitrogen, oxygen, argon, carbon dioxide, and water vapor. The ability of gases to form a solution is not affected by their chemical properties or by physical conditions. JOHN P. FACKLER, JR.

See also SOLVENT.

**SOLUTION SET.** See SET THEORY (In Algebra).

**SOLVENT** is a liquid that dissolves another substance and forms a solution. Water is the most common solvent. It dissolves a great many substances. Substances that dissolve in water include sugar, salt, alcohol, and air. Turpentine, another common solvent, is used to wash oil-base paints out of paint brushes. Carbon tetrachloride is a solvent used to remove oily spots from clothing. Each year, chemists develop many new solvents to meet specific needs.

The substance that dissolves in a solvent is called the *solute*. A solute may be a solid such as salt, a liquid such as alcohol, or a gas such as oxygen.

In a solution of two or more liquids, the most abundant liquid is called the solvent. For example, vinegar consists mainly of water and acetic acid. This solution contains more water than acetic acid, so water is called the solvent. The acetic acid is called the solute.

A solvent that has dissolved as much solute as possible is said to be *saturated*. For example, when water has dissolved so much salt that additional salt cannot be dissolved, the water is said to be saturated with salt. The amount of solute that a solvent can dissolve depends on the chemical properties of both substances. It also depends on such conditions as temperature and pressure. JOHN P. FACKLER, JR.

Related Articles in WORLD BOOK include:

| | | |
|---|---|---|
| Acetone | Carbon Tetrachloride | Paint |
| Alcohol | Chloroform | Solution |
| Carbon Disulfide | Furfural | |

**SOLYMAN.** See SULEIMAN I.
**SOMA.** See GERM CELL.

# SOMALIA

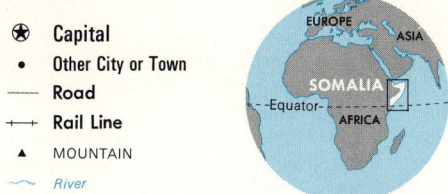

- ★ Capital
- • Other City or Town
- — Road
- +++ Rail Line
- ▲ MOUNTAIN
- ~ River

WORLD BOOK map–FIa

**SOMALIA,** *soh MAH lee uh,* is the easternmost country in Africa. It stretches along Africa's "horn," facing the Gulf of Aden and the Indian Ocean. Somalia is a little smaller than Texas, and has only about one-fourth as many people as that state. Most Somalis are herdsmen who wander over the hot, dry land in search of water and pasture. Somalia has few towns. Mogadiscio, which has about 141,770 persons, is the capital and largest town.

Wild animals are plentiful in Somalia. Antelope, cheetahs, and lions roam the grasslands. Crocodiles swim in the country's main rivers, and elephants and hippopotamuses live in the forests along the riverbanks.

Somalia consists of two regions that were once called British Somaliland and Italian Somaliland. These colonies became independent in 1960, and combined to form the SOMALI REPUBLIC.

*I. M. Lewis, the contributor of this article, is Reader and Tutor in Anthropology at University College, London, England. He is the author of* The Modern History of Somaliland *and* Peoples of the Horn of Africa.

**Government.** Somalia has a democratic government based on a constitution approved by the people in 1961. The prime minister and his cabinet are responsible to the parliament, and may be dismissed by the president. The president may also dissolve the parliament, but not during his first or last year of office. The Somali Youth League is the largest political party.

**People.** More than 80 per cent of the Somalis are nomads who raise herds of camels, cattle, goats, and sheep. The others live on farms or in Somalia's few towns. Almost all the people are Moslems of the Sunnite branch of Islam. They claim Mohammed, the founder of Islam, as their ancestor. See ISLAM.

The nomads roam over vast stretches of their hot, dry land in search of water and pasture for their herds. Their hard life leaves little time for relaxation. When water and pasture are plentiful, however, they enjoy telling stories and holding poetry contests in the evening around a campfire. They recite long poems about major events, such as battles and victories, or in praise of prized possessions such as camels and horses.

The nomads live in small, collapsible, beehive-shaped huts that have arched wooden braces covered with skins and grass mats. When the grass and water are used up in one spot, they pack their huts and move to a new spot. Their chief food is milk, especially camel's milk. They eat rice and other grains, and mutton. In southern parts of Somalia, the people roast coffee beans in butter oil and eat them boiling hot with milk. They believe that it is healthful to inhale the hot fumes of the oil and to rub the oil over their arms and hair.

---
### FACTS IN BRIEF
---

**Form of Government:** Republic.
**Political Divisions:** 8 regions, each headed by an elected council and a governor appointed by the minister of the interior.
**Capital:** Mogadiscio.
**Head of State:** President, elected to a 6-year term by the parliament.
**Head of Government:** Prime minister, appointed by the president. He chooses his cabinet (Council of Ministers), which is officially appointed by the president.
**Parliament:** *National Assembly*—124 deputies, elected by the people to 5-year terms.
**Voting Age:** 18 (men and women).
**Courts:** *Highest*—Supreme Court (5 judges appointed by president). Moslem judges called *cadis* handle civil matters between Moslems.
**Official Languages:** Arabic, English, Italian.
**Area:** 246,200 square miles. *Greatest Distances*—(north-south) 950 miles; (east-west) 730 miles. *Coastline*—1,837 miles.
**Elevation:** *Highest*—Mount Surud Ad, 7,894 feet above sea level. *Lowest*—sea level along the coast.
**Population:** *Estimated 1970 Population*—2,941,000; density, 12 persons to the square mile. *Estimated 1975 Population*—3,476,000.
**Chief Products:** *Agriculture*—bananas, grains, hides and skins, livestock, milk, sugar cane. *Manufacturing*—processed foods.
**Flag:** The light blue flag has a large white star in the center. The colors come from the United Nations flag. See FLAG (color picture: Flags of Africa).
**Money:** *Basic Unit*—shilling. For its value in dollars, see MONEY (table: Values).

479

# SOMALIA

The men and women wrap brightly colored cloth or cotton sheeting around their bodies like a toga. Many of the men wear the *lungi*, a kind of kilt. Many who live in the towns wear trousers and shirts.

Most of the people speak Somali, an unwritten language. Arabic, English, and Italian are used in the schools. Children are not required by law to go to school, and few of the nomads' children receive any education. Less than a tenth of the Somalis can read and write. There are fewer than 300 public elementary and high schools in the country. Mogadiscio has a small university, the University Institute of Somalia.

The Somalis band together in large groups of relatives whose relationships are traced through the men. If members of one group kill or injure a member of another, the attackers' group must pay the victim's group. A man's life is valued at 100 camels, and a woman's at 50. Payment may also be in money.

**Land.** Narrow plains line the coast in the northern half of Somalia. Behind them, mountains rise nearly 8,000 feet above sea level. Farther inland lie a series of high plateaus covered with rich pasture after rainy seasons, and dry plains of thorn bush and tall grasses.

Wide coastal plains in the southern half of Somalia rise gradually toward the west to a plateau cut by plains and valleys. The most important valleys are those of the Giuba and Scebeli rivers, the only rivers in Somalia that have water all year. Forests line the river banks. Somalia's richest farmland lies between the two rivers. Dry plains cover the rest of the southern region.

Somalia has an average year-round temperature of slightly more than 80° F. In June and July, the temperature rises to 115° F. on the northern coastal plains. That region, the driest in Somalia, receives 2 or 3 inches of rain a year. The southern farmlands receive about 20 inches of rainfall a year.

**Economy.** Somalia is an underdeveloped agricultural country. Bananas, hides and skins, and livestock are its chief products, and make up about 90 per cent of the exports. Some sorghum and other grains are grown, but large amounts must be imported. There is little manufacturing. Somalia's mineral resources, including rich deposits of iron ore and gypsum, have not been mined.

Somalia has no railroads, and only about 450 miles of its 9,000 miles of roads are surfaced. Somali Airlines flies between Mogadiscio and other Somali towns.

The government operates radio stations in Mogadiscio and in Hargeisa. Many nomads listen to the programs on transistor radios. Somalia also has a few small newspapers.

**History.** Ancestors of the Somalis began migrating from what is now northern Somalia to the south in the 800's and 900's. They were converted to Islam by Arabs who had settled on the coast. The Arabs and Somalis fought many religious wars against the Christian kingdom of Ethiopia to the west between the 1300's and 1500's.

Europeans began to colonize the Somali regions during the mid-1800's. France developed a colony in what is now the French Territory of Afars and Issas in the 1860's. The British took over what later became British Somaliland (now northern Somalia) in 1884. In 1889, Italy established control in what is now southern Somalia. During the 1890's, Ethiopian armies seized the Ogaden, a Somali territory west of the British and Italian colonies. The Somalis revolted in 1900, but the British crushed the revolt in 1920.

Italian forces conquered Ethiopia in 1936, and joined it to Italian Somaliland. In 1940, during World War II, Italy also seized British Somaliland. But the British drove the Italians from eastern Africa in 1941. The British returned the Ogaden to Ethiopia in 1948. In 1950, the United Nations gave Italy its former colony as a trust territory for 10 years, during which Italy agreed to prepare it for independence. By that time, the Somali movement to unite all Somali regions was well established. But in 1955, the British turned over another part of its colony, a huge grazing region called the Haud, to Ethiopia.

The British granted British Somaliland independence on June 26, 1960. On July 1, Italian Somalia also became independent, and the two regions combined to form the Somali Republic. But many Somali people were living in eastern Ethiopia, northern Kenya, and French Somaliland (now the French Territory of Afars and Issas). Somali leaders claimed that these Somalis should also have the right to decide what form of government they wanted. As a result, Somalia's relations with its neighbors have usually been tense. Border fighting with both Ethiopia and Kenya has broken out frequently.   I. M. Lewis

See also Hargeisa; Mogadiscio.

**Bananas, Somalia's Chief Export,** are grown on irrigated land in southern regions. Most bananas are shipped to Italy.
United Nations

**SOMALILAND,** *soh MAH lee LAND,* is the name of a large region along the eastern coast of Africa, inhabited by Somali tribes. These tribes live in Somalia, the French Territory of Afars and Issas, northeastern Kenya, and eastern Ethiopia. The region covers 500,000 square miles. Somaliland has a population of 4,302,000. See also SOMALIA; FRENCH TERRITORY OF AFARS AND ISSAS.  R. J. HARRISON CHURCH

**SOMALILAND, FRENCH.** See FRENCH TERRITORY OF AFARS AND ISSAS.

**SOMBRERO.** See MEXICO (Clothing).

**SOMERSET.** See ENGLAND (color map: The 38 Counties of England).

**SOMERSET, DUKE OF.** See EDWARD (VI).

**SOMERVILLE,** Mass. (pop. 94,697; alt. 15 ft.), is an industrial suburb of Boston. For location, see MASSACHUSETTS (political map). It was first settled in 1630 as part of Charlestown. Prospect Hill, one of the city's seven hills, became an important observation post during the American siege of Boston in the Revolutionary War. The first United States flag with 13 stripes was raised on Prospect Hill in 1776.

Somerville became a town in 1842, and a city in 1871. It has a mayor-council government.  WILLIAM J. REID

**SOMME RIVER,** *sawm.* Great battles of World Wars I and II were fought along this stream in northern France. The river rises near the Belgian border, and follows a westerly course for 140 miles to the English Channel. For location, see FRANCE (physical map). Ocean steamers enter the port of Saint Valéry through the mouth of the Somme. A canal runs beside the Somme from Saint Valéry to Saint Quentin. From Saint Quentin, canals connect with the Oise and Schelde rivers.  EDWARD W. FOX

**SOMNAMBULISM.** See SLEEPWALKING.

**SOMNUS** was the god of sleep in Roman mythology. The Greeks called him HYPNOS. He was the son of Erebus and Nox, the goddess of night. His brother was Mors, the god of death, whom the Greeks called Thanatos. Somnus' son was Morpheus, god of dreams (see MORPHEUS). Somnus and Mors lived in a great cave. The river Lethe flowed nearby, and its gentle murmuring invited sleep. The light was dim in the cave, and everything slept. The forms of pleasant dreams floated about. Dark nightmares were also believed to hide in the cave.  JAMES F. CRONIN

**SOMOZA,** *suh MOH zuh,* is the family name of three Nicaraguan dictators, a father and his two sons. The Somozas have dominated the social, economic, and political life of Nicaragua since the 1930's.

**Anastasio Somoza García** (1896-1956) ruled Nicaragua for 20 years before he was killed by an assassin. He crushed all opposition and did not allow freedom of expression. He also used his power to become rich.

Somoza was born in San Marcos, Nicaragua, the son of a small rancher. He studied at Peirce Union Business College (now Peirce Junior College) in Philadelphia, then returned to Nicaragua, and became a tax collector in León. Somoza soon joined a revolutionary movement led by his wife's uncle, Juan Batista Sacasa. Somoza became an officer in Nicaragua's newly organized National Guard in 1926. He became minister of war in 1932, after Sacasa was elected president.

In 1934, Somoza gained a reputation as a feared and ruthless man when he ordered Augusto Sandino, a popular guerrilla fighter, killed by the National Guard.

In 1936, Somoza drove Sacasa from power. Somoza was elected president later that year in an election controlled by his troops. In 1939, he changed the constitution, extending his term of office to eight years. He also appointed himself head of the National Guard. Somoza resigned as president in 1947, but he forced his successors to rule as he wished. He was elected president again in 1950.

Somoza improved Nicaragua's agriculture, cattle raising, and mining. He balanced the budget and introduced easier credit for farmers. He also expanded port facilities and built new highways, houses, hospitals, power plants, railroads, and schools.

**Luis Somoza Debayle** (1922-1967) became president of Nicaragua after his father was killed, and served until 1963. He tried to bring about social reforms and loosen the tight military control of Nicaragua. One of his reform laws prevented any member of his family from succeeding him. But the Somoza family hand-picked the man who was elected to succeed him as president. Luis Somoza Debayle was born in León, Nicaragua.

**Anastasio Somoza Debayle** (1925-    ) was elected president in 1967. He rules as a dictator, controlling the military services and the economy as his father did. He was born in León. He graduated from the U.S. Military Academy, and headed the National Guard during his father's second term and during his brother's administration.  THOMAS G. MATHEWS

See also NICARAGUA.

**SONAR** is a detecting device that uses sound. The term sonar is made up from the words **so**und **n**avigation **a**nd **r**anging. There are two types of sonars. One type is used in navigation to find the depth of water under a ship. Warships and military aircraft use the other type of sonar to find submarines, and then attack and destroy them.

Both types of sonars operate on the same principle. They send out a sound wave into the water. When the wave meets an object, it reflects back. The distance to the object is found by measuring the time taken by the sound wave to return. This is called *echo ranging.* Sonars and radars are echo-ranging devices. See RADAR.

**How Sonar Works.** Sonars generally use sound frequencies of 5,000 to 25,000 hertz. The signals are gen-

Raytheon Manufacturing Co.

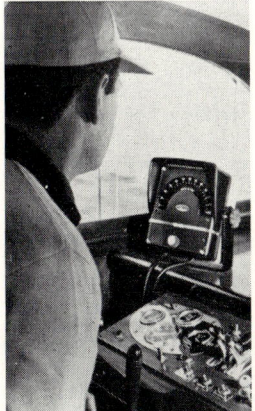
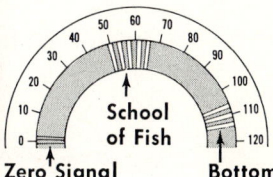

**Sonar** is a depth-sounding instrument. It beams short bursts of sonic energy toward the ocean bottom. As the sonic receiver picks up echoes, different kinds of flashes on the indicator, *below,* tell if they are reflected from the ocean bottom, reefs or obstructions, a school of fish, or other objects.

# SONATA

erated in a *transmitter* within the ship. They are sent to a *transducer*, an antennalike device in the water under the ship. The transducer changes the electrical signals to sound waves and sends them through the water. The waves travel outward or downward until they strike an object and reflect back to the transducer. As the signal is sent out, part of it is routed within the ship to a *receiver* and *indicator*, which resembles an electric stop watch. It marks zero time as it receives a signal that sound waves are being sent out. It then begins to keep time. As the waves return from an object, they are changed by the transducer to electric signals, which again are sent to the indicator. When it receives these signals, it indicates the range. Since sound travels in water at about 1,600 yards each second, the indicator can be marked to give the distance in yards. In depth-finding equipment, the distance is given in fathoms.

**History.** At first, all ranging devices were built on a "searchlight" principle. The transducer was moved back and forth like a searchlight to catch the sound waves. As the "searchlight" crossed the target, the bearing could be measured and ranges recorded. But it takes a long time to search through a circle with such a device. During World War II, it was learned that a cylinder could be built of *staves* (sections), each of which was a transducer. Sound waves could be sent in all directions. The electronic circuits were devised to scan two or more sections of the transducer, forming their signals into a beam. The result was a scanning sonar with electronic beam rotation which can be used for rapid search.

**Natural Sonar.** Some animals find direction by means of echo sounding. For example, bats make *ultrasonic* (high-frequency) squeaks that bounce back from obstacles. See BAT; DOLPHIN.   RAWSON BENNETT

**SONATA,** *soh NAH tuh,* is an instrumental composition with three or four movements with contrasts both in tempo and key, but related in thought. The usual four-movement sonata begins with a brilliant *allegro,* and the second movement is slow, rhythmic, and lyrical (*andante, adagio,* or *largo*). The third movement is usually light and graceful, and may be in dance form, or a *scherzo.* The *finale* (last movement) is in quick, bright tempo. Symphonies, string quartets, and long works for solo instruments use this sonata form. The first movement of the sonata is called the *sonata-allegro* form. It has three sections called the *exposition,* the *development,* and the *recapitulation,* which is almost a repetition of the exposition, but usually shorter.   RAYMOND KENDALL

**SONG.** In music, there are two types of song: *folk songs* by unknown artists, and *art songs,* musical settings of poetic texts. In the Middle Ages, English bards, German minnesingers, Scandinavian skalds, and French troubadours sang of brave deeds, the gods, and love. Later, composers set beautiful poems to music. The rise of opera in the 1600's tended to slow the development of the more lyric song. The lyric song persisted in Germany, and was developed in the 1800's by Franz Schubert, Robert Schumann, and Johannes Brahms.

**Related Articles.** See SINGING with its list of Related Articles. See also the following articles in WORLD BOOK:

| | | | |
|---|---|---|---|
| Berceuse | Chantey | Lieder | Popular Music |
| Canon | Folk Music | Lullaby | Round |
| Carol | Hymn | Madrigal | Spiritual |

**SONG OF BIRDS.** See BIRD (Bird Songs); also names of specific birds such as BLACKBIRD; ROBIN.

**SONG OF DEBORAH.** See DEBORAH.

**SONG OF ROLAND.** See ROLAND.

**SONG OF SOLOMON** is the name of a poetic book in the Old Testament. The book is also called the *Song of Songs* and *Canticles.* For hundreds of years, most persons considered it an allegory that showed God's love for His children by means of a description of human love. Many Jews saw in it the love of God for the people of Israel. Many Christians found in it the love of Christ for the church. Some persons still accept these allegorical interpretations. But most scholars today interpret the book literally. Some consider it a poetic drama whose characters include a girl, her shepherd lover, and King Solomon. Others suggest that the songs were originally part of a pagan spring festival, and were later changed so that they could be included in the Bible. Many scholars regard the book as a collection of love and nature songs written in ancient Israel.   ROBERT GORDIS

**SONG OF THE LARK.** See BRETON, JULES ADOLPHE.

**SONIC BARRIER** is the sharp increase in resistance met by an object moving through the air at a speed of about 765 miles an hour. This is the speed of sound in air at a temperature of about 32° F. An object moving through air pushes aside the air to make room for itself. This movement creates ripples in the air like the ripples made on a pond's surface when a stone is thrown into it. The air ripples move at the speed of sound. An object

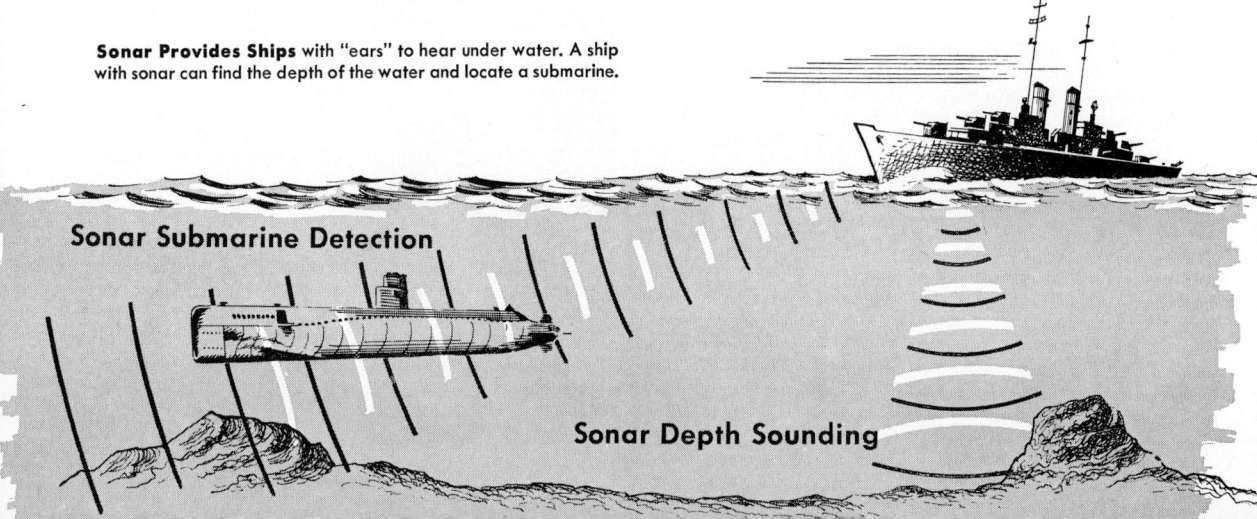

**Sonar Provides Ships** with "ears" to hear under water. A ship with sonar can find the depth of the water and locate a submarine.

Sonar Submarine Detection

Sonar Depth Sounding

moving at the same speed literally collides with the air and finds it hard to go forward. See also AERODYNAMICS (Supersonic Flight).  C. B. SMITH

**SONNET** is a poem of 14 lines with a fixed pattern of meter and rhyme. Its name is an Italian word meaning *a little song*. In the Italian sonnet, the *octave* (the first eight lines) states a theme or experience and the *sestet* (the final six lines) responds to or comments on the theme. The octave rhyme scheme is *abbaabba*. That is, lines one, four, five, and eight rhyme; as do lines two, three, six, and seven. The sestet often rhymes *cdecde*.

During the Italian Renaissance (the A.D. 1200's and 1300's), poets wrote groups of love poems called *sonnet sequences* in this form. Dante addressed sonnets to Beatrice, Petrarch to Laura. The French court poet, Pierre de Ronsard, wrote *Sonnets to Hélène* (1578).

English poets brought back this form from their travels abroad. Sonnets by Sir Thomas Wyatt and Henry Howard, Earl of Surrey, were published in *Tottel's Miscellany* (1557). For his *Amoretti* (1595), Edmund Spenser invented his own rhyme scheme. But the form used by William Shakespeare has been accepted as typically English. It consists of three *quatrains* (four-line stanzas) followed by a *couplet* (two-line stanza), rhyming *abab cdcd efef gg*. By the time Shakespeare's *Sonnets* was published in 1609, the writing of sonnet sequences already was out of fashion.

Few sonnets were written in English during the next 200 years. But in the mid-1600's, John Milton wrote a few great sonnets, including "On His Blindness" (1655). The form was revived during the Romantic period (1798-1832). An example is John Keats' "On First Looking into Chapman's Homer" (1816). Later in the 1800's, Elizabeth Barrett Browning wrote love poems to her husband in the sequence *Sonnets from the Portuguese*. Edna St. Vincent Millay is the best known of recent American poets to write in this exacting and compressed poetic form.  CHARLES W. COOPER

See also SHAKESPEARE, WILLIAM (Sonnets); POETRY (What Makes a Poem Great?).

**SONOMA STATE COLLEGE.** See UNIVERSITIES AND COLLEGES (table).

**SONOMETER,** *so NAHM ee ter,* is an instrument used to study the mathematical relations of musical tones. The sonometer, sometimes known as the *monochord*, consists of a tightly stretched string, one end of which passes over a pulley wheel. When plucked, the string vibrates and thus produces sound. The *frequency* (number of vibrations a second) of the tone is increased if the string is made shorter or tighter.  RICHARD H. BOLT

**SONORA,** *soh NOH ruh,* a state in northwestern Mexico, borders the United States. For location, see MEXICO (political map). Sonora has an area of 71,403 square miles, and a population of 1,106,114. The rough, dry land resembles that of Arizona and New Mexico. Its mountains contain rich deposits of copper, lead, graphite, and some silver. Farmers in the river valleys grow rice, wheat, chick-peas, tomatoes, vegetables, and cotton. Sonora became a state in 1830. Hermosillo is the capital and largest city.  CHARLES C. CUMBERLAND

**SONS OF LIBERTY** was a group of patriotic societies which sprang up in the American colonies before the Revolutionary War. The Sons of Liberty groups began as secret societies, but later came into the open. They fought against the Stamp Tax of 1765. They opposed the importation of British goods after the passage of the Townshend Acts, and later began to demand national independence. They helped other independence moves, including the calling of the Continental Congress.

During the Civil War, a group of men known as *Copperheads* began to call themselves the *Sons of Liberty*. They were Northern sympathizers with the South, and planned to overthrow the Lincoln Government. Their plots were discovered and suppressed.  JOHN R. ALDEN

See also COPPERHEAD (nickname).

**SONS OF SAINT GEORGE.** See GEORGE, SAINT.

**SONS OF THE AMERICAN REVOLUTION** is a patriotic organization. Its members are male descendants of persons who served in the Revolutionary War, or who contributed toward establishing the independence of the United States. The society is dedicated to perpetuating American ideals and traditions, and to protecting the Constitution. Constitution Day, Flag Day, I Am an American Day, and Bill of Rights Day were established through its efforts. The society was founded on April 30, 1889. Its official name is National Society of the Sons of the American Revolution. It has about 20,000 members in the United States and France. The society has national headquarters at 2412 Massachusetts Ave. NW, Washington, D.C. 20008.  HAROLD L. PUTNAM

**SONS OF UNION VETERANS OF THE CIVIL WAR** is an American patriotic society. It was founded in 1881, and incorporated in 1954. Its 3,000 members are men 16 years of age or older who are descendants of Union veterans of the Civil War. Headquarters are in Gettysburg, Pa. The Daughters of Union Veterans of the Civil War is a similar organization for women. It has headquarters at 503 S. Walnut Street, Springfield, Ill. 62704.  H. H. HAMMER

**SOO CANALS,** also called SAULT SAINTE MARIE CANALS, permit ships to pass between Lakes Superior and Huron. These canals are located on the United States-Canadian border. For location, see MICHIGAN (political map).

About 85 to 90 per cent of the tonnage on the canals is eastbound. Iron ore and grain make up most of the eastbound cargo. Coal, stone, and oil are the chief products carried on westbound ships. About 90 million tons of cargo pass through these canals annually. In the late 1960's, the total tonnage shipped through them was about three-fourths of the cargo tonnage shipped through the Panama Canal. Ice closes the Soo Canals from about mid-November to early April.

The Saint Marys River forms a natural connection between lakes Superior and Huron. Early trappers sometimes "ran the rapids" to cross from one lake to the other. However, they usually carried their canoes and furs around the rough water. In 1798, the Hudson's Bay Company completed a canal with a single lock that permitted canoes and flat-bottomed boats to pass up the river. American troops destroyed the lock during the War of 1812. After 1839, ships were moved around the rapids on rollers. A railroad was built in 1850.

**The American Canals.** Increasing shipments of iron and copper during the late 1800's created a need for better transportation between lakes Superior and Huron. A federal grant enabled Michigan to complete a canal with a lock in 1855. The U.S. government took over the

483

# SOO CANALS

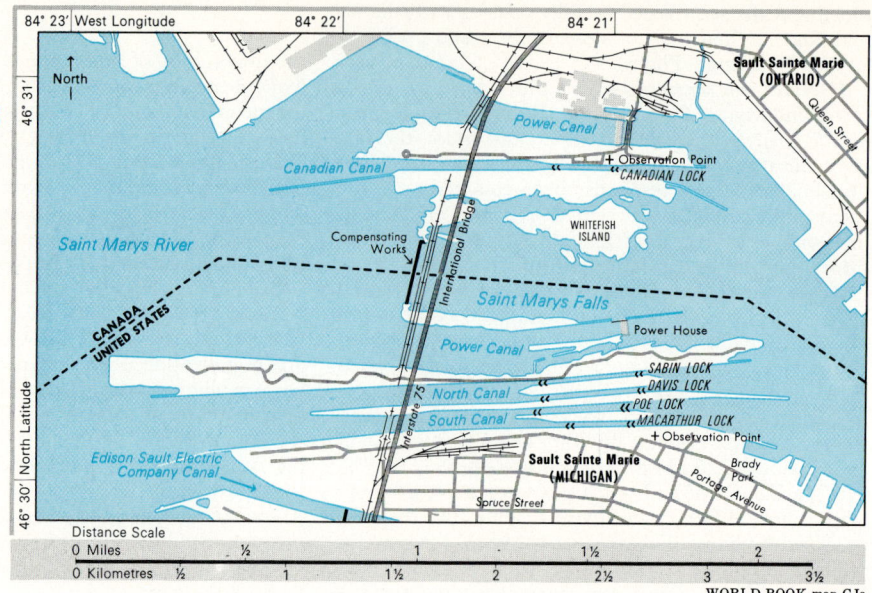

WORLD BOOK map-GJa

canal's administration in 1881, and abolished tolls.

The American canals are about one and three-quarters miles long. Davis lock, opened in 1914, and Sabin lock, opened in 1919, are in the North Canal, which is 280 feet wide and 23 feet deep. Each lock is 1,350 feet long, 80 feet wide, and 23.5 feet deep. The South Canal is 304 feet wide and 27 feet deep. MacArthur lock, opened in 1943, is 800 feet long, 80 feet wide, and 31 feet deep. The new Poe lock, opened in 1969, is 1,200 feet long, 110 feet wide, and 32 feet deep. This lock replaced the smaller Poe lock, torn down in 1962.

**The Canadian Canal.** Canada completed its canal in 1895. It cost $4,935,809. Until the Davis lock was built, the larger lake ships used the Canadian canal. It is one and three-tenths miles long, 150 feet wide, and 25 feet deep. The lock is 900 feet long, 60 feet wide, and 18.3 feet deep. The two-mile International Bridge, opened in 1962, carries traffic across the Saint Marys River at Sault Ste. Marie.   WILLIS F. DUNBAR

**SOOCHOW** (pop. 633,000; alt. 30 ft.), also called SUCHOU and WUHSIEN, lies in Kiangsu Province, China, between Nanking and the port of Shanghai. It has many canals and pagodas. A 10-mile wall surrounds the center of Soochow. The city lies in a rich agricultural area. Industries include jade carving, rice processing, and the production of cotton and silk textiles. The city's history dates back to the A.D. 400's. For location, see CHINA (political map).   L. CARRINGTON GOODRICH

**SOONER STATE.** See OKLAHOMA.

**SOONG CHING-LING** (1890-    ), MADAME SUN YAT-SEN, is a prominent figure in the Chinese Communist government. In 1949, she was elected one of six vice-chairmen in the government. She served as head of a national woman's organization and of the Sino-Soviet Friendship Association after the Communist victory in China. She won the 1951 Stalin peace prize.

Soong Ching-ling was the second wife of Sun Yat-sen, the founder of the Chinese Republic (see SUN YAT-SEN). She worked with him in Japan and later married him there. After his death in 1925, Soong Ching-ling rose to a high position in the Chinese government. When Chiang Kai-shek, the president of the Chinese Nationalist government, broke with the Chinese Communists in 1927, she left China and lived in Moscow (see CHIANG KAI-SHEK). She remained in exile until Communist leaders joined the Kuomintang, the Nationalist Party, in a common front against the Japanese forces that invaded China in 1937.

Soong Ching-ling, the daughter of Charles Jones Soong, was born in K'un-shan, Kiangsu. She attended high school in Shanghai and graduated from Wesleyan College in Macon, Ga.   IMMANUEL C. Y. HSU

**SOOT** is a black substance found in smoke. Soot is made up of tiny particles of fuel, such as coal, wood, or oil, that have not been burned. These particles are usually considered harmful to man and plant life, but they also have a certain value. Soot contains a great deal of carbon and ammonium salts. The ammonium salts contain a large amount of nitrogen, which is an excellent fertilizer. Soot is therefore useful as a fertilizer.

Soot is used as a *pigment* (coloring matter). The soot found nearest the fire is usually a shining brown powder containing dried tar. This soot is used as a pigment which is called *bister*. The soot found farther from the fire and up higher in the chimney is usually black. It is used as a pigment which is called *lampblack*.

Soot sticks to anything it touches. For this reason, smoke which blows through a city leaves its soot upon buildings and makes them look dingy. In London, it is said that the damage from soot is several million dollars each year. In some cities, about 3 per cent of the coal that is burned is converted into soot. This soot formation is a serious waste and has added to the problem of smoke prevention.   RALPH G. OWENS

See also SMOKE PREVENTION.

**SOPHIST PHILOSOPHY** was an educational movement in the city-states of Greece during the second half of the 400's B.C. The Sophists were migrant teachers who taught grammar and public speaking, which was vital in such ancient democracies as Athens. They were

484

not interested in philosophical thoughts about the nature of the physical universe. Instead, they criticized conventional morality and religion, and described virtue as being successful in the world.

The Sophists believed that law is not part of the nature of things, but is merely custom. Thus, they said, men who are clever enough to evade laws have no moral obligation to obey them. Plato described Socrates as opposing the Sophists because their ideas were vague and contradictory, and especially because their teachings could destroy the social order.

The best-known Sophists included Protagoras, Gorgias, and Antiphon. Protagoras believed that old customs and ceremonies should be followed so society could be held together (see PROTAGORAS). Gorgias became known for his intellectually stimulating and skeptical ideas. Antiphon emphasized the difference between civil law and man's natural search for pleasure in life. He believed man could often serve his own advantage by evading the law and following his natural desires, if he could get away with it. JOSIAH B. GOULD

**SOPHOCLES**, *SAHF oh klees* (496?-406? B.C.), was the second in time of the three great Greek writers of tragedy. The others were Aeschylus and Euripides. His tragedies were not concerned with abstract problems of guilt and punishment over several generations, like those of Aeschylus. Instead they dealt with a specific struggle of a strong individual against fate. Where Aeschylus required whole *trilogies* (three plays) to cover one subject, Sophocles wrote single plays.

Sophocles' usual pattern is to show a powerful figure who chooses a course which the chorus and lesser characters may not approve. This course costs him suffering or death, but it makes him more noble and somehow benefits mankind. Sophocles did not make his figures ordinary in order to criticize conventional morality, as Euripides did. That is why Aristotle said that Sophocles pictured men as they should be, Euripides as they are.

Bettmann Archive
**Sophocles**

Artistically and in their dramatic construction, Sophocles' plays are more finished than those of Aeschylus or Euripides, and Aristotle regarded his works as models. Sophocles added a third actor, fixed the size of the chorus at 15, and used scene-painting. His plays show intrigue and suspense. Of the 100 or more plays Sophocles wrote, seven complete ones have survived. These are *Ajax, Antigone, Trachinian Women, Oedipus Tyrannus, Electra, Philoctetes,* and *Oedipus at Colonus*. Part of one of Sophocles' plays, called *The Trackers*, was found in 1907.

Sophocles was a fortunate man. He lived during Athens' greatest period. He won many prizes for his tragedies, and was universally loved. One of his greatest plays, *Oedipus at Colonus*, was written when he was nearly 90. He was born near Athens, and remained there all his life. MOSES HADAS

See also ANTIGONE; GREEK LITERATURE; OEDIPUS.

**SOPRANO**, *soh PRAH noh*, is a term describing a type of voice. It may also mean a voice part in compositions for mixed voices. The soprano voice is the highest of four voices. It usually covers more than two octaves above middle C. A woman or a young boy may sing it. A soprano part is the upper voice part in a harmonic arrangement to be sung by mixed voices. See also OPERA. RAYMOND KENDALL

**SORATA** is another name for Illampu, a peak of the Andes Mountains in Bolivia. See ILLAMPU.

**SORBONNE**, *sawr BAHN*, is the name of a famous institution of learning in Paris, the outgrowth of a medieval college of theology. It is a part of the state-owned University of Paris. One of the finest university buildings in the world houses the present-day Sorbonne. It dates from 1889, and is known as *La Nouvelle Sorbonne* (The New Sorbonne). The institution maintains faculties of science, law, literature, and medicine. The Sorbonne has well-equipped laboratories, lecture rooms, and libraries.

Robert of Sorbon founded the old Sorbonne in the 1200's. Originally it was a residence hall for poor theological students. It gradually became one of the strongest theological schools in Europe. In the 1600's, Cardinal Richelieu rebuilt it and provided a magnificent chapel for the students. In 1885, the faculty of theology was abolished.

Students from many parts of the world study at the Sorbonne. As many as 35,000 foreign students have enrolled there in one year. I. L. KANDEL

**SORCERY.** See MAGIC (Black Magic).

**SOREL**, *saw REL*, Quebec (pop. 19,021; alt. 48 ft.), is an industrial and shipping center at the junction of the Richelieu and St. Lawrence rivers. A good port with a deepwater front, it is on the Canadian National Railways. Sorel's industries include shipbuilding and ship-repair plants, steel foundries, lumber mills, and clothing and shirt factories. Sorel has a mayor-council form of government. M. G. BALLANTYNE

**SORENSEN, VIRGINIA** (1912-    ), is an American author. She won the 1957 Newbery medal for her children's book *Miracles on Maple Hill*, the story of a 10-year-old girl in the farmland of Pennsylvania. Her story *Plain Girl*, about the life of a small Amish girl, won the Children's Book Award of the Child Study Association of America in 1955. Mrs. Sorensen also wrote *Curious Missie* (1953), *The House Next Door* (1954), *Lotte's Locket* (1964), a number of adult novels, and a collection of short stories. She was born in Provo, Utah. ELOISE RUE

**SORET, J. LOUIS.** See HOLMIUM.

**SORGHUM**, *SAWR gum*, is the name of a group of tropical grasses from Africa and Asia. In regions of warm summer climate, farmers grow some of them for forage, syrup, grain, and broom fiber. The common varieties of sorghum have thick, solid stalks and look like corn plants. But their flowers grow in branched clusters at the tips of the stems. Farmers plant and grow sorghums in much the same manner as they do corn. About 20 million acres of sorghum are planted on farms in the United States each year, especially in the Great Plains region. All the kinds of sorghum fall into four main groups: (1) grain sorghums, (2) sweet sorghums, (3) grassy sorghums, and (4) broomcorn.

485

J. Horace McFarland

**Sorghums** furnish sap to make syrup and feed for livestock. Two kinds are Red Top African, *left,* and Milo Maize, *right.*

**Grain Sorghums** are grown especially for their rounded, starchy seeds. The grain serves as a substitute for corn in feeding animals. Some grain sorghums grow as much as 15 feet tall. Plant breeders have produced varieties 2 to 4 feet tall that can be harvested with a grain combine. Farmers feed the grain to livestock, or make the entire plant into silage. In India, Africa, and China, the grain is ground and made into pancakes or mush as food for man. Common types of grain sorghum include durra, milo, and kafir.

**Sweet Sorghums,** or *sorgos,* have sweet, juicy stems. They are grown especially for the production of sorghum syrup. This syrup is made by pressing the juice out of the stems with rollers and boiling it down to the proper thickness. Animal feed and silage can also be made from sweet sorghums.

**Grassy Sorghums** are used for green feed and hay. *Sudan grass* is a tall annual sorghum with thin stalks. It grows quickly and may reach 10 feet in height. It serves as excellent summer pasturage. Johnson grass, a perennial sorghum, grows as a weed in the southern United States. It resembles Sudan grass, but it spreads by creeping rootstocks. Johnson grass is a pest on land needed for cotton or other row crops. But it makes excellent cattle feed or hay.

**Broomcorn** is a kind of sorghum grown for the *brush* (branches) of the seed cluster.

**Scientific Classification.** The sorghums belong to the grass family, *Gramineae.* Grain, sweet, and broomcorn sorghums are classified as genus *Sorghum,* species *S. vulgare.* Sudan grass is *S. sudanense.* Johnson grass is *S. halepense.*    WAYNE W. HUFFINE

See also KAFIR; SUDAN GRASS.

**SOROKIN, PITIRIM A.** See SOCIOLOGY (Modern Sociology).

**SOROPTIMIST INTERNATIONAL ASSOCIATION** is an organization of service clubs for professional and executive businesswomen. Soroptimist clubs have been organized in 30 countries and have a world membership of about 45,000 women. Each member of a Soroptimist club must represent a different profession or business. The purposes of the clubs include the advancement of world peace and of the status of women. Soroptimist clubs are divided into three federations: Soroptimist Federation of the Americas, Inc.; European Federation of Soroptimist Clubs; and Federation of Soroptimist Clubs of Great Britain and Ireland. The Americas federation has headquarters at 1616 Walnut St., Philadelphia, Pa. 19103. The first Soroptimist club was founded in Oakland, Calif., in 1921.    MARTHA R. SERVIS

**SORORITY,** *suh ROAR uh tee,* is a women's society of college or university students and graduates. Sororities, like fraternities, are often called *Greek-letter societies.* Most sororities form their names by combining two or three letters of the Greek alphabet. The word *sorority* comes from the Latin word *soror,* which means *sister.*

There are three kinds of sororities: (1) *general,* or *social,* (2) *professional,* and (3) *honor societies.* General sororities, the most common of the three, encourage high academic standards, carry on charitable and educational programs, and sponsor social activities for their members. On many campuses, they also provide room and board for members in sorority houses. Professional sororities consist of women with the same academic interest, such as education or journalism. Honor societies are for women with exceptional academic records.

There are 34 national general sororities in the United States. They have a total of more than 2,600 collegiate *chapters* (local units) and about 5,000 alumnae chapters. Membership totals more than 1,400,000. Twenty-seven of the national sororities belong to the National Panhellenic Conference. It and similar organizations promote cooperation among national sororities. Most university and college campuses have an intersorority council, which regulates general sorority activity.

There are 35 U.S. professional sororities and honor societies. They have more than 3,300 chapters and about 540,000 members. Some groups admit men.

Many school clubs, the forerunners of sororities, were formed during the 1800's. *Adelphean* began as a literary society at Wesleyan College, in Macon, Ga., in 1851. It adopted the name *Alpha Delta Pi* in 1905. *Pi Beta Phi* was organized as I.C. Sorosis at Monmouth College in Monmouth, Ill., in 1867. It was the first organization of college women to be established on a national basis.

*Kappa Alpha Theta* was the first group founded as a women's Greek-letter society. It began at DePauw University in 1870. *Gamma Phi Beta,* founded at Syracuse University in 1874, was the first group to use the name *sorority.*

Critically reviewed by NATIONAL PANHELLENIC CONFERENCE

**SORREL,** *SAHR ul,* is a name given to several plants of the buckwheat family. All the sorrels have juicy leaves and stems which contain oxalic acid. This gives them a sour taste.

The common American sorrel is a low-growing plant with three-lobed, arrow-shaped leaves, and spikes of small white, pink, or yellow flowers. *Sheep sorrel, sour sorrel,* and *red sorrel* are some of the names for this plant. The name "red sorrel" comes from the masses of triangular reddish seeds the plant bears.

The common American sorrel is a weed that grows well in acid soil, and its presence in a meadow indicates that the land needs lime.

**Scientific Classification.** The common American sorrel belongs to the buckwheat family, *Polygonaceae.* It is genus *Rumex,* species *R. acetosella.*    HAROLD NORMAN MOLDENKE

**SORREL TREE,** or SOURWOOD, is a beautiful tree of the heath family. It grows in the woods of the southern United States, and as far north as Pennsylvania, Indiana, and Ohio. The name *sourwood* comes from the

## SORORITIES IN THE UNITED STATES

### GENERAL SORORITIES

| Name | Undergraduate Chapters | Graduate Chapters | Year Founded | Where Founded | National Headquarters |
|---|---|---|---|---|---|
| Alpha Chi Omega | 109 | 82 | 1885 | DePauw University | Indianapolis |
| Alpha Delta Pi | 119 | 363 | 1851 | Wesleyan College | Atlanta |
| Alpha Epsilon Phi | 53 | 43 | 1909 | Barnard College | Pittsburgh |
| Alpha Gamma Delta | 92 | 98 | 1904 | Syracuse University | Indianapolis |
| Alpha Kappa Alpha | 111 | 206 | 1908 | Howard University | Chicago |
| Alpha Omicron Pi | 87 | 102 | 1897 | Barnard College | Indianapolis |
| Alpha Phi | 90 | 215 | 1872 | Syracuse University | Evanston, Ill. |
| Alpha Sigma Alpha | 47 | 111 | 1901 | Longwood College | Springfield, Mo. |
| Alpha Sigma Tau | 30 | 44 | 1899 | Eastern Michigan University | St. Louis |
| Alpha Xi Delta | 115 | 175 | 1893 | Knox College | Indianapolis |
| Chi Omega | 150 | 172 | 1895 | University of Arkansas | Cincinnati |
| Delta Delta Delta | 111 | 330 | 1888 | Boston University | Chicago |
| Delta Gamma | 93 | 145 | 1873 | University of Mississippi | Columbus, Ohio |
| Delta Phi Epsilon | 32 | 42 | 1917 | New York University | Flushing, N.Y. |
| Delta Sigma Theta | 104 | 214 | 1913 | Howard University | Washington, D.C. |
| Delta Zeta | 174 | 272 | 1902 | Miami University | Indianapolis |
| Eta Upsilon Gamma | 5 | 8 | 1901 | Christian College (Mo.) | None |
| Gamma Phi Beta | 85 | 211 | 1874 | Syracuse University | Kenilworth, Ill. |
| Iota Alpha Pi | 11 | 15 | 1903 | Hunter College | Valley Stream, N.Y. |
| Kappa Alpha Theta | 93 | 74 | 1870 | DePauw University | Evanston, Ill. |
| Kappa Delta | 104 | 360 | 1897 | Longwood College | Springfield, Mo. |
| Kappa Kappa Gamma | 94 | 362 | 1870 | Monmouth College (Ill.) | Columbus, Ohio |
| Phi Mu | 97 | 186 | 1852 | Wesleyan College | Memphis, Tenn. |
| Phi Sigma Sigma | 29 | 30 | 1913 | Hunter College | Coral Gables, Fla. |
| Pi Beta Phi | 111 | 340 | 1867 | Monmouth College (Ill.) | St. Louis |
| Sigma Delta Tau | 50 | 51 | 1917 | Cornell University | Kenilworth, Ill. |
| Sigma Gamma Rho | 44 | 85 | 1922 | Butler University | None |
| Sigma Iota Chi | 10 | 5 | 1903 | Alexandria, La. | Encinitas, Calif. |
| Sigma Kappa | 106 | 216 | 1874 | Colby College | Indianapolis |
| Sigma Sigma Sigma | 66 | 140 | 1898 | Longwood College | Woodstock, Va. |
| Theta Phi Alpha | 17 | 26 | 1912 | University of Michigan | Cincinnati |
| Zeta Mu Epsilon | 3 | 3 | 1921 | Stephens College | None |
| Zeta Phi Beta | 84 | 170 | 1920 | Howard University | Washington, D.C. |
| Zeta Tau Alpha | 110 | 224 | 1898 | Longwood College | Evanston, Ill. |

### LARGEST PROFESSIONAL SORORITIES AND HONOR SOCIETIES

| Name | Undergraduate Chapters | Graduate Chapters | Year Founded | Where Founded | National Headquarters |
|---|---|---|---|---|---|
| Alpha Lambda Delta (Freshmen)** | 143 | None | 1924 | University of Illinois | South Miami, Fla. |
| Pi Lambda Theta (Education)* | 55 | 35 | 1910 | Columbia, Mo. | Washington, D.C. |
| Sigma Alpha Iota (Music)* | 148 | 105 | 1903 | University of Michigan | Des Moines |
| Mortar Board (Leadership)** | 124 | 44 | 1918 | Syracuse, N.Y. | None |
| Mu Phi Epsilon (Music)* | 108 | 83 | 1903 | Cincinnati | Wichita, Kans. |
| Alpha Delta Kappa (Education)* | None | 1,200 | 1947 | Kansas City, Mo. | Kansas City, Mo. |
| Phi Upsilon Omicron (Home Economics)* | 53 | 22 | 1909 | University of Minnesota | Fargo, N.Dak. |
| Omicron Nu (Home Economics)** | 43 | 3 | 1912 | Michigan State University | East Lansing, Mich. |
| Theta Sigma Phi (Journalism)* | 68 | 46 | 1909 | University of Washington | Austin, Tex. |
| Kappa Delta Epsilon (Education)* | 39 | None | 1933 | Washington, D.C. | Decatur, Ga. |
| Phi Beta (Music & Speech)* | 31 | 29 | 1912 | Northwestern University | Chicago |

*Professional Sorority  **Honor Society

taste of its leaves and twigs, which hunters and woodsmen sometimes chew when they are thirsty. The name *sorrel* comes from an Old French word which means *sour.*

The sorrel tree may reach a height of 50 to 60 feet. It has reddish-gray bark and smooth, oblong leaves. In summer it bears graceful clusters of small, bell-shaped, white flowers, which are soon followed by little downy capsules. In spring the foliage is bronze-green, but in autumn it turns a brilliant scarlet. The wood is sometimes used to make handles for tools. Leaves of the sorrel tree furnish a black dye.

**Scientific Classification.** The sorrel tree belongs to the heath family, *Ericaceae*. It is classified as genus *Oxydendrum,* species *O. arboreum.*　　　THEODORE W. BRETZ

**S O S** is the accepted call for help from a ship in distress. It does not stand for anything. It was chosen because it was convenient to send by wireless. It consists of three dots, three dashes, and three dots.

**SOTO, HERNANDO DE.** See DE SOTO, HERNANDO.

**SOU** was a small coin in the French money system. It was worth 5 *centimes* (hundredths of a franc). It has not been used since World War II.

**SOUDAN.** See SUDAN.

**SOUL.** See RELIGION (Life and Death); MIND (The Nature of Mind); TRANSMIGRATION OF THE SOUL.

**SOULE, JOHN,** originated the phrase, "Go West, young man." See GREELEY, HORACE.

**SOULÉ, PIERRE.** See OSTEND MANIFESTO.

**SOULÉ, SAMUEL W.** See TYPEWRITER (with picture).

# SOUND

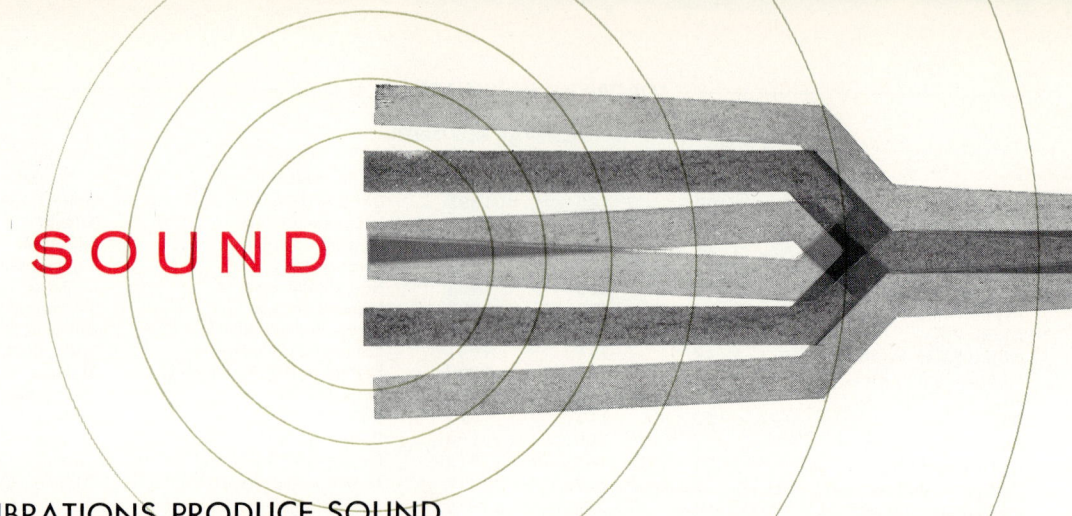

## VIBRATIONS PRODUCE SOUND

**Vibrating Strings** produce the violin's sound by making the surrounding air vibrate.

**Pneumatic Hammers** make a deafening noise. The vibrations of the hammer striking the concrete cause the sound.

**Alarm Clocks** ring when a tiny hammer strikes a bell. You can feel the bell vibrate.

**The Screech** of chalk is caused when it vibrates on a chalkboard.

**SOUND** is all around us. The whispering wind may lull you to sleep at night. A jingling alarm clock may awaken you in the morning. The voices of friends, the roar of machinery, the rustle of papers, the clatter of pans, and countless other sounds surround us.

All these sounds have one thing in common. Each is caused when something moves back and forth in quivering motions called *vibrations*. These vibrations travel through the air to our ears, and we hear them as sounds. If you gently put your fingers on a ringing bell, you can feel it vibrating. If you press harder, you will stop both the vibrations and the sound.

The air can carry many vibrations at the same time, and the vibrations can travel in many different directions. You may sit in a room and hear a radio playing, a bird singing, a friend talking, and an airplane passing overhead, all at the same time.

A world without sound would be unpleasant and even dangerous. It is the world of a deaf person. We would be unable to chat with our families and friends, either in the same room or by telephone. We would not be protected by such warning devices as automobile horns.

### What Is Sound?

A famous riddle asks whether sound is produced when a tree crashes to earth in a distant forest and no one hears it. This question is a riddle because there are two ways to define sound. One way is to define it as something that is heard. According to this definition, the tree makes no sound because no one hears it. The second way is to define sound as vibrations produced by an object. According to this definition, the tree makes sound because it produces vibrations when it crashes.

Most scientists use the second definition. This definition describes events that occur in nature rather than the act of hearing these events.

**Producing Sound.** When an object vibrates, it makes the surrounding air vibrate. This vibration of the air has two causes. First, as the vibrating object moves outward, it *compresses* the surrounding air. Second, the air *expands*, or rushes into the space formerly occupied by the vibrating object, when the object moves inward. Each succeeding vibration of the object again causes the surrounding air to compress and expand.

Scientists call these compressions and expansions *condensations* and *rarefactions*. The compressions and expansions of the air near the source of the sound also compress and expand the air farther away. In this way, a vibration travels through the air until it weakens and dies away. These vibrations are known as *sound waves*.

You can demonstrate sound vibrations with a tuning fork. Strike the fork and dip the prongs of the fork into a glass of water. The vibrations of the prongs will make the water splatter. See TUNING FORK; VIBRATION.

**Sound Waves** travel along the back-and-forth movement of the vibrating object that produces them. Scientists call these waves *longitudinal waves* or *compressional waves*. You can see longitudinal waves by attaching one end of a long spiral spring to a hook or some other

## SOUND TRAVELS IN WAVES

If you throw a rock in a pool of water, you will see small ripples, or waves, travel outward from the point where the rock struck the surface. Sound also travels in waves. When an object vibrates and produces sound, it makes the surrounding air vibrate. These vibrations ripple outward in waves in all directions from the object. When the waves reach our ears, we hear them as sounds.

support. Allow the other end of the spring to hang free. Pull apart and then release several turns of the spring near its free end. You will see a stretching motion travel up to the attached end of the spring and return to the free end. If you pinch together and then release several turns of the spring at its free end, a wave of compression will travel up to the attached end and return. Sound waves travel through the air in a similar fashion. They consist of compressed and expanded air that moves back and forth in the same direction that the wave is traveling. See WAVES.

**How Sound Travels.** You may have read how Indians once put their ears to the ground to detect the approach of an enemy. This shows that sound travels through a *medium*, or substance, such as the ground or the air.

The *speed of sound* depends upon two factors: (1) the density of the medium through which sound waves travel, and (2) the elasticity of the medium (see DENSITY; ELASTICITY). The more elastic a medium, the greater the speed of sound. The denser a medium, the slower the speed of sound. Steel is 6,000 times denser than air. But it is also two million times more elastic. Therefore, sound travels more swiftly through steel than through air. Sound travels about 16,400 feet a second in steel, 4,700 feet a second in water, and 1,100 feet a second (about 750 miles an hour) in air at freezing temperature, 32° F.

The density and elasticity of air change as the temperature changes. For this reason the speed of sound in air changes with the temperature. It increases by about 1 foot a second for each increase of 1° F.

The speed of sound is much slower than the speed of light, which is 186,282 miles a second. You may have noticed that you almost always see the flash of lightning before you hear the sound of thunder. Another example would be the firing of a gun. You usually see the puff of smoke from the gun barrel before you hear the sound of the shot. If you know the time in seconds between a flash of lightning and the sound of thunder, you can tell how far away the lightning is. At the normal temperature range in the United States and Canada, the lightning will be about a mile away for every five seconds between flash and thunder. Jet airplanes often fly at *supersonic speeds* (faster than the speed of sound). The ratio of the speed of an airplane to the speed of sound in the air through which it is flying is called the *Mach number*. See AERODYNAMICS (Mach Number).

**Hearing Sound.** The construction of the ear enables it to catch sound waves that come to it through the air. The waves enter your ears and travel along tubes to the eardrums and other delicate organs in the head. These organs send the vibrations over sensitive nerves to the brain, which interprets what we hear. See EAR.

Some sounds do not vibrate with enough energy to make the eardrums vibrate. These sounds are not loud enough to be heard. They are said to be below the *threshold of audibility*, the point at which we can hear sounds. Some sounds have so much energy that they hurt the ear. These sounds are above the *threshold of feeling*. Sounds made by violent explosions, such as the firing of a large cannon, often reach the threshold of feeling. A sound at the threshold of feeling has about five billion times as much energy as the sound of a whispering voice. Sounds must be made more and more intense to reach the threshold of audibility of a person who is becoming deaf. When the sounds must be so intense that the threshold of feeling is reached, the person is deaf. See DEAFNESS.

### Characteristics of Sound

Sound waves must have different characteristics, because we can distinguish one kind of sound from another. For example, musical sounds have three dis-

489

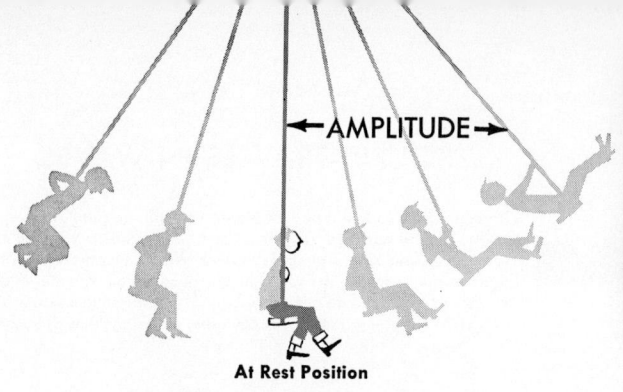

At Rest Position

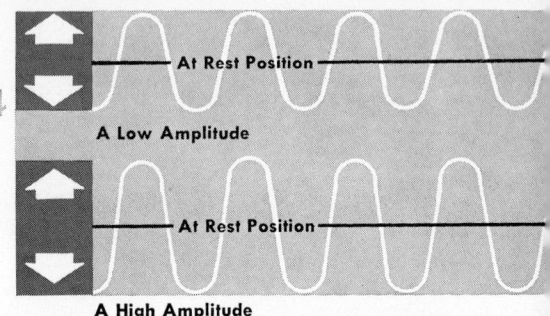

Amplitude can be compared to a boy on a swing. It is the distance a vibrating object moves from its position of rest as it vibrates. The larger the amplitude of sound vibrations, the more intense the sound.

## THE IMPORTANT DIMENSIONS OF SOUND
### ...Amplitude and Pitch

tinguishing characteristics: pitch, loudness, and quality. Beats, echoes, resonance, and sympathetic vibrations also affect the character of sound.

**Pitch** is determined by how rapidly an object vibrates, or by its frequency. *Frequency* is the number of times that an object, or the sound wave it produces, vibrates in a second. The higher the frequency, the higher the pitch. You can demonstrate this by fastening a piece of cardboard so it touches the spokes of a bicycle wheel. The faster you turn the wheel, the more rapidly the cardboard vibrates, and the higher the pitch of the sound you hear. You also may have noticed how the pitch of the sounds made by an electric fan or by a phonograph record rises and falls as their speed of rotation is increased or decreased. See PITCH.

*Audible Range of Frequencies.* The normal human ear can hear sounds with frequencies between about 20 and 20,000 vibrations a second. The lowest tone on a piano has a frequency of 27 vibrations a second. Some organs have tones with frequencies as low as 15 vibrations a second. The highest tone on a piano has a frequency of about 4,000 vibrations a second. Different persons can hear different ranges of sound frequencies. One person may be able to hear a sound of a certain frequency that his friend cannot hear at all. Some animals can hear sounds above or below the frequencies that humans can hear. Dogs and bats, for example, can hear sounds with frequencies far above those heard by the human ear. See BAT (How Bats Navigate); DOG (Ears).

*The Doppler Effect.* You may have noticed the difference in pitch of a locomotive's whistle as a train approaches and then passes you. When the locomotive approaches, the pitch of its whistle appears to rise. After the locomotive passes, the pitch of its whistle drops. More sound vibrations reach your ear each second as the locomotive approaches, because the sound waves are crowded together. You hear fewer vibrations after the locomotive passes, because the sound waves are stretched apart. Actually, the sound of the whistle has only one pitch. The apparent change in the pitch of sounds made by moving objects is called the *Doppler effect* (see DOPPLER EFFECT).

**Loudness and Intensity.** People often use the words *loudness* and *intensity* as if they mean the same thing. But the words have different meanings.

The *intensity* of sound refers to the amount of energy flowing in the sound waves (see ENERGY). The *loudness* of sound is the apparent strength of the sensation received by the eardrum and sent to the brain. The same intensity of sound may produce different degrees of loudness for different people. For example, one person may barely hear a sound that seems clear to another. But for any one person, both the intensity and loudness of a sound depend on four factors: (1) the distance from the source of the sound, (2) the amplitude of vibration, (3) the density of the medium through which the sound travels, and (4) the area of the vibrating object.

The intensity and loudness of a sound decrease as the *distance* increases between a person and the source of the sound. This happens because sound waves move out from their source in all directions. The energy flowing in the sound waves spreads over a greater area and decreases the farther away the sound travels. That is why cheerleaders use megaphones when shouting to a crowd at a football game. The megaphone prevents the sudden spreading of the sound waves, and directs more of the sound energy toward the crowd.

The *amplitude of vibration* is the distance that a vibrating object moves as it vibrates. For example, the amplitude of vibration of a boy on a swing is the distance he moves front and back as he swings. It takes

## WHAT SOUND WAVES LOOK LIKE

Sound waves consist of alternate condensed and expanded particles of air, and are called *compressional waves*. The length of such waves is measured from condensation to condensation. Attach one end of a coil spring to a wall and pinch several coils in the free end. A wave of compression will flow up and down the spring.

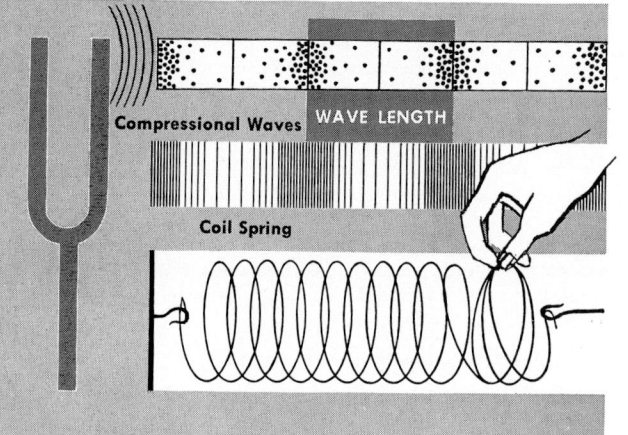

490

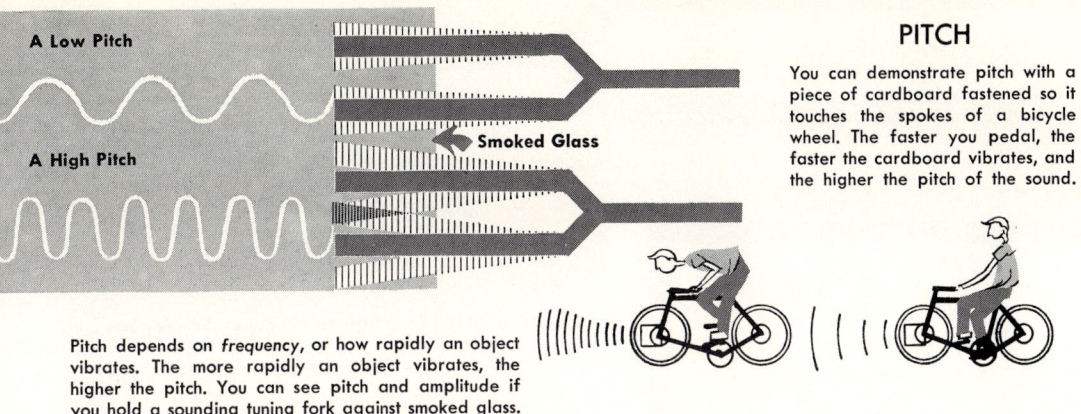

## PITCH

You can demonstrate pitch with a piece of cardboard fastened so it touches the spokes of a bicycle wheel. The faster you pedal, the faster the cardboard vibrates, and the higher the pitch of the sound.

Pitch depends on *frequency*, or how rapidly an object vibrates. The more rapidly an object vibrates, the higher the pitch. You can see pitch and amplitude if you hold a sounding tuning fork against smoked glass.

more energy for a swing to have a large amplitude of vibration than a small amplitude. For the same reason, it requires more energy for an object such as a tuning fork or a violin string to have a large amplitude of vibration than a small amplitude. The larger the amplitude of vibration of a sounding body, the louder and more intense the sound. The amplitudes of sound waves are measured from condensation to condensation.

The loudness and intensity of a sound decrease as the *density* of the medium decreases. For example, compare the loudness of a sound made by striking two stones together under water with the loudness produced when you strike them together in air. The sound is much louder under water, because water is denser than air.

The *area*, or size, of a vibrating object also affects the loudness and intensity of a sound. You can prove this by hitting a table fork so that its prongs vibrate. Then quickly put the handle of the fork against the top of a table. The loudness of the sound made by the vibrating fork immediately increases, because the fork makes the table top vibrate. This increases the area of vibration. Notice how much louder a ticking clock sounds if you place it so the frame of the clock rests against a table top.

Pitch affects the loudness, but not the intensity, of a sound. The sensitivity of the ear varies with the pitch of a sound. The ear has low sensitivity to low pitches. But its sensitivity increases as the pitch increases, until the pitch reaches about 1,000 vibrations a second. After this point, its sensitivity to sound decreases again.

**Quality of Sound** is a characteristic of a musical tone. It distinguishes a tone produced by one musical instrument from a tone of the same pitch and intensity produced by another instrument. For example, quality makes the difference between the same tones from a violin and a banjo, even though both tones have the same pitch and intensity.

The quality of a musical tone generally results from the blending of many frequencies. A vibrating object produces many frequencies by vibrating both as a whole and in parts at the same time. For example, a violin string may vibrate as a whole 256 times a second. This produces the string's *fundamental tone*, and is middle C on the musical scale. At the same time, the string may also vibrate in several parts. That is, each half of the string, each third of the string, and each fourth of the string may vibrate separately. These vibrations of the parts of a string produce *overtones*. Overtones are also called *harmonics* of the fundamental frequency. The overtones produced by each half of the string vibrate at a frequency of 512 times a second, or twice the frequency of the fundamental tone. Therefore, these overtones are known as the *second harmonic*. The overtones produced by each third of the string (the *third harmonic*) vibrate at a frequency of 768 times a second, or three times the frequency of the fundamental tone. The overtones produced by each fourth of the string (the *fourth harmonic*) vibrate at a frequency four times that of the fundamental tone, and so on. The number and relative strength of the overtones determine the quality of a tone. See HARMONICS; TONE.

**Beats.** When two tuning forks that vibrate at the same frequency are sounded together, their tones blend and strengthen each other. But if the forks vibrate at different frequencies, the sounds they produce will swell and fade at regular intervals. The swellings, or *pulsations*, of loudness are called *beats*. They occur because the vibrations of the forks are "out of step" with each other. The number of beats a second equals the number of vibrations that differ from each other in a second. If one tuning fork has a frequency of 256 vibrations a second and another fork has a frequency of 257 vibra-

## SOUND TRAVELS AT DIFFERENT SPEEDS

The speed of sound depends on the density and elasticity of the substance through which the sound travels. The denser the substance, the slower the speed. The more elastic the substance, the higher the speed. Dense substances are often many times more elastic than less dense ones, and sound travels faster through them. Sound will not travel if there is no substance, as in a vacuum.

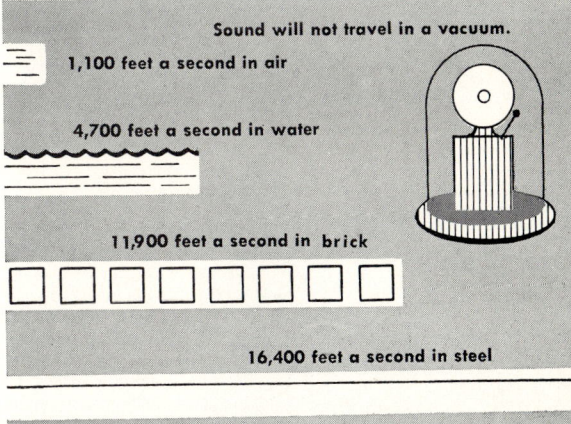

Sound will not travel in a vacuum.
1,100 feet a second in air
4,700 feet a second in water
11,900 feet a second in brick
16,400 feet a second in steel

49I

# INTERESTING FACTS ABOUT SOUND

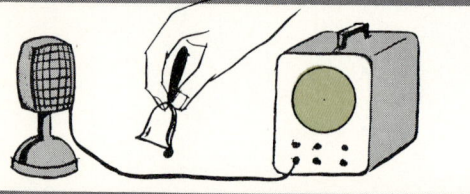

## SEEING SOUND

Scientists and engineers often must know the pattern, or shape, of sound waves. They find this with an electronic device called an *oscilloscope, right above*. A microphone feeds the sound into the oscilloscope. The oscilloscope shows the sound waves on a fluorescent screen similar to a television screen.

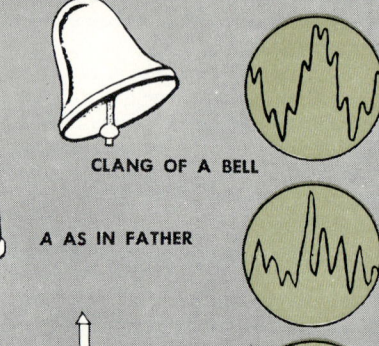
CLANG OF A BELL

A AS IN FATHER

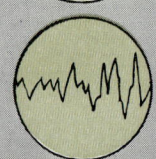

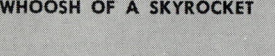
WHOOSH OF A SKYROCKET

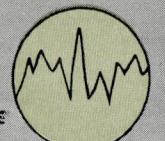
SOUND OF AN OBOE

Acoustica Associates, Inc.; The Sheffield Corp.

**An Object Vibrates When It Produces Sound.** You can show this by striking a tuning fork so it makes a sound. Then dip the fork into water. The vibrating prongs will splatter the water.

**A Megaphone** makes a shout sound louder, because it keeps the sound waves from spreading and sends them in one direction. For the same reason, cupping a hand to the ear helps to hear sound.

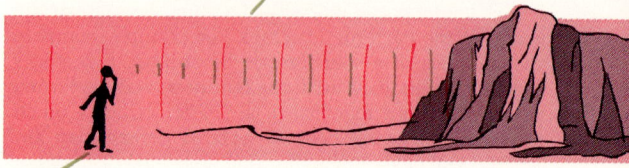

**Echoes Can Measure Distance.** Shout at a cliff and measure the time it takes to hear the echo. If you multiply the seconds by 544, you will arrive at the distance to the cliff in feet.

**Sound Can Make Objects Vibrate.** For example, the sound made when a glass is struck may make another glass vibrate. The vibrations of the second object are called *sympathetic vibrations*.

**Animals Have Sensitive Hearing.** Some animals, including bats, dogs, and various insects, can hear sounds with such high pitches that humans cannot hear them.

**Ultrasound,** or sound that vibrates at frequencies too high to be heard by humans, has many uses. Ultrasound can be used to sterilize instruments, *left,* and to drill metal, *right.* It can also be used to drill teeth, to pasteurize milk, and to detect submarines.

## THE DOPPLER EFFECT
The pitch of a train whistle seems to drop as the train passes by. This apparent change in pitch is called the *Doppler effect*. More sound waves strike your ear each second as the train approaches, because the sound waves are crowded together. You hear fewer sound waves each second after the train passes, because the waves are farther apart. Actually, the whistle has only one pitch.

tions a second, there will be one beat every second.

Most persons pay little attention if the number of beats produced by two vibrating objects is not more than five or six a second. But if the number of beats increases to 30 a second, the sound becomes unpleasant. Scientists call these sounds *dissonance*. As the number of beats increases above 30 a second, we no longer hear the separate beats, and the sensation of unpleasantness decreases. Musical instruments are tuned by changing their pitches to the same frequency to eliminate beats.

**Echoes.** We can produce echoes by shouting while standing some distance from a cliff or large building. In order to produce an echo, the sound waves we send out must strike some surface that has a density different from that of the surrounding air. The sound bounces back to us from this surface much as a rubber ball bounces back from a concrete wall. However, if we stand too close to the reflecting surface, we do not hear an echo. This is because a sound sensation lasts only about one tenth of a second. If a second sound is made within one tenth of a second, our ears cannot distinguish between the two sounds. An echo that returns before one tenth of a second has passed strengthens the original sound wave, but we hear no separate echo. See ECHO.

**Resonance** occurs when a small repeated force produces large vibrations in an object. For example, a series of small pushes can make a swing move in a bigger and bigger arc. But resonance occurs only if the force takes place at the same frequency as the natural frequency of the object. *Natural frequency* is the frequency at which the object would vibrate naturally if it were disturbed in some way. In the case of the swing, you must push with the same frequency at which the swing moves to keep it in motion. Resonance plays an important part in all musical instruments by increasing the loudness of the sounds they produce.

You can demonstrate resonance by holding a vibrating tuning fork over a tube that is open at one end and closed at the other end. If the tube is one fourth as long as the sound wave that comes from the fork, it will make the fork sound much louder. This increase in loudness is caused by resonance. A sound wave from the fork goes down the tube, hits the bottom, and bounces back to the fork just in time to cause it to vibrate with a larger amplitude. If the tube is not the proper length, the reflected sound wave will act against the vibration of the fork. This tends to make the fork stop vibrating, and is called *destructive interference*. See INTERFERENCE.

**Sympathetic Vibrations** are related to resonance. They can be demonstrated by hanging two rope swings of equal length from the same horizontal branch of a tree. If you set one swing in motion, the other swing will also start to move. Small impulses carried through the tree branch from the first swing to the second swing cause the motion of the second swing. These vibrations of the second swing are due to resonance and are called *sympathetic vibrations*. They would not occur if one swing were much longer than the other one—that is, if the natural frequencies of the two swings were greatly different from each other. The sound made when a certain note is hit on a piano may cause sympathetic vibrations among the dishes in a cupboard. Soldiers marching in step can cause sympathetic vibrations in a bridge and even make it fall. This is why troops break step while marching across bridges.

### Kinds of Sound
Sounds can be classed as either noisy or musical. A *noise* is produced by a vibrating object, such as a rattling window, that sends out irregular vibrations at irregular intervals. *Music* is made by a vibrating body that sends out regular vibrations at regular intervals, such as a piano played by a skilled musician. Some other kinds of sound include the sounds made by people and animals, and stereophonic sound and ultrasound.

**Noise** can harm people in two ways. Intense noise may produce actual deafness. Boilermakers, steelworkers, and others who are exposed to intense noise for long periods sometimes become deaf. Jet airliners often make such loud, disturbing sounds that they are not allowed to use some airports. Continuous or periodic noise may cause people to become tired or irritable, even if it is not extremely loud. The steady whine of a saw or the periodic ringing of a telephone can cut a worker's production in half. Builders often cover the inside walls of offices and factories with felt, cork, and other materials that absorb sound. This reduces the noise and improves the efficiency of the workers. See INSULATION (Soundproofing).

**Musical Sounds** are made by three types of instruments: (1) stringed, (2) wind, and (3) percussion.

*Stringed Instruments* have strings stretched over some kind of *resonance box* or *board*. Violins and guitars, for example, have resonance boxes. Pianos have resonance boards. The *tension* (tightness) of a string controls the frequency at which it vibrates and, therefore, the pitch of the sound it makes. An increase in the tension of a string increases its frequency. However, the longer the string, the lower the frequency. The frequency of a string also decreases as its *mass per unit length* increases

493

## SOUND LABORATORY

Scientists and engineers who study sound need special laboratories designed to eliminate unwanted sounds. The sound laboratory, *right*, is the world's largest *anechoic*, or echoless, chamber. Special materials that absorb sound line the floor, ceiling, and walls of the chamber.
General Electric Co.

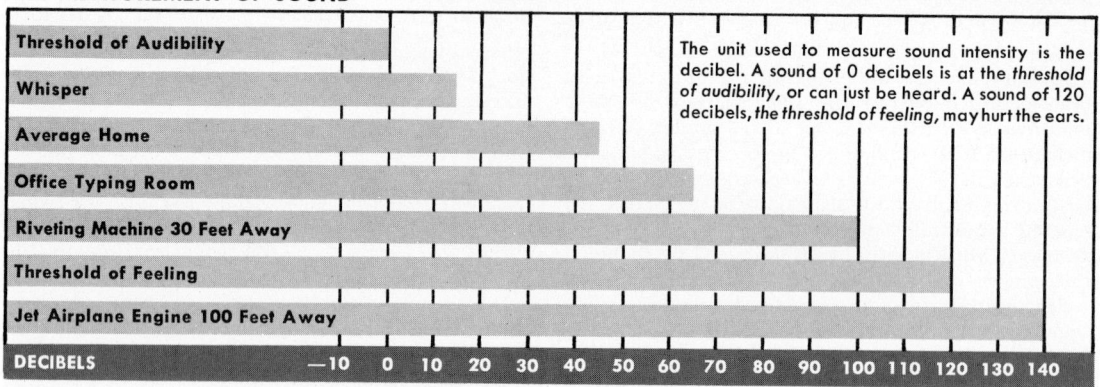

**THE MEASUREMENT OF SOUND**

The unit used to measure sound intensity is the decibel. A sound of 0 decibels is at the *threshold of audibility*, or can just be heard. A sound of 120 decibels, *the threshold of feeling*, may hurt the ears.

(see Mass). For example, a tight, heavy string has a lower pitch than an equally tight, light string. But a tight, heavy string has a higher pitch than a loose, heavy string.

A musician controls the length of the vibrating part of a string on a violin, or any similar instrument, by pressing his fingers on the string at different places. One end of the strings on these instruments is attached to the resonance box, and the other is wound about small pegs. The musician controls the tension of the strings by turning the pegs so that they loosen or tighten the strings. The mass per unit length is controlled by having strings with different masses. This provides a wide range of tones.

*Wind Instruments.* You may have produced a musical tone by blowing across the open top of a bottle. A musician plays a wind instrument in much the same way. He blows a stream of air across the opening of a tube or a pipe. The stream of air makes the air column inside the tube or pipe vibrate. The frequency of the vibration of this air column depends on the length of the tube or pipe. If the tube or pipe is closed at the bottom, the note produced has a wave length four times the length of the tube or pipe. If the tube or pipe is open at both ends, the note has a wave length twice the length of the tube or pipe.

All wind instruments work on this principle. A pipe organ, for example, has pipes of different lengths to produce different notes. Musicians press valves to regulate the length of the column of air that produces sounds in other wind instruments. Clarinets, saxophones, flutes, and horns have such valves to shorten or lengthen the air column. A musician controls the length of the air column in a slide trombone with a slide.

A reed helps make the air columns vibrate in wind instruments such as the saxophone, clarinet, oboe, and bassoon. In brass instruments, such as the trumpet and French horn, the vibrating lips of the musician make the air columns vibrate.

*Percussion Instruments* include drums, cymbals, bells, and gongs. A drum has a membrane stretched tightly across the open ends of a cylinder made of metal or wood. The musician beats the membrane with sticks or his hands. This makes the membrane vibrate and produce sound. Musicians also beat solid metal instruments such as cymbals, bells, and chimes to make them vibrate. These instruments, like the drum, create musical effects when used with other instruments, but often produce unpleasant sounds when used alone. See Music.

**The Human Voice** is an example of sound produced by air columns vibrated by membranes. A pair of membranes called *vocal cords* are located on each side of the *larynx*, or *voice box*, in the throat. You make these cords vibrate and produce sounds by forcing air past them. Changing the muscular tension of the cords produces sounds of different pitches. See Larynx.

**Animal Sounds.** Animals make and use sounds in many ways. For example, lions roar, birds sing, dogs bark, and cats meow. These and many other animals have vocal cords, and make their sounds the same way that humans do.

The cricket rubs the rough surfaces of its wings together to make its cheery chirp. The buzzing of flies, bees, and some other insects is caused by the vibration of their wings as they beat against the air.

One of the most interesting animal sounds is one that people cannot hear: the high-pitched twittering of bats. The pitch of these sounds is far above the frequency that humans can hear. But bats can hear them. The bat makes these sounds as it flies in the dark, and listens for

# SOUND

echoes. The echoes warn the bat when it approaches a tree, house, or some other obstacle. See BAT.

**Stereophonic Sound.** Perhaps you have heard the big difference between "live" music at a concert and the same music on an ordinary recording. In a concert hall, the music reaches you from many points. Your ears hear separate instruments or groups of instruments. At the same time, the sounds of the orchestra blend and fill the air. An ordinary recording lacks brilliance, because the music comes from only one point, often only a single loudspeaker.

Stereophonic sound tries to reproduce the feeling of depth, or of sounds coming from many points, that a listener would receive if he heard the sounds in person. To create this effect, engineers make two or more separate recordings from microphones placed at various points around an orchestra. In the home, these separate recordings, combined on one tape or disk, are played back, each through its own loudspeaker system. The loudspeakers are located at various places in the room, so that the music comes to the listener from different points. This gives the music a feeling of depth.

**Ultrasound** vibrates at frequencies too high to be heard by humans, more than 20,000 vibrations per second. Commonly used ultrasonic waves may have frequencies that range as high as 500 million vibrations per second. The M.I.T. Laboratory at Lexington, Mass., has produced sound waves that have a frequency of 70 billion vibrations per second.

Ultrasonic waves have many uses, because they can be focused much like the beam of light from a searchlight. An obstacle strongly reflects a beam of ultrasonic waves. An ultrasonic device detects objects by sending out a beam of ultrasonic waves and listening for echoes reflected from the objects. For example, naval vessels have ultrasonic devices called *sonar* to detect submarines under water (see SONAR). Scientists measure the depth of the ocean with similar devices, and fishermen use them to locate schools of fish. Factories use ultrasonic waves in much the same way to detect flaws in metals, wood, and other materials. Railroads regularly check their tracks with ultrasonic waves to locate weaknesses that might cause the tracks to break. Ultrasonic waves can also kill insects, pasteurize milk, sterilize surgical instruments, and treat diseases such as arthritis. Many dentists use ultrasonic drills that lessen the patient's discomfort.

Ultrasonic waves can be produced by sirens, and in several other ways (see SIREN). In one method, an alternating current of electricity is sent through a quartz crystal. The electrical variations of the current make the crystal expand and contract rapidly so that it produces ultrasonic vibrations in the surrounding medium. Certain ceramic materials such as barium titanate produce ultrasonic waves in the same way that quartz crystals do, and are more useful than quartz. Devices that use these materials are called *transducers*. An iron or nickel rod vibrated by an alternating magnetic field

## SIMPLE EXPERIMENTS WITH SOUND

### HOW SOUND TRAVELS

Place a clock on its side on one end of a table, and press your ear to the other end. You will hear the tick of the clock. This shows that sound travels through a substance.

### TIN-CAN TELEPHONE

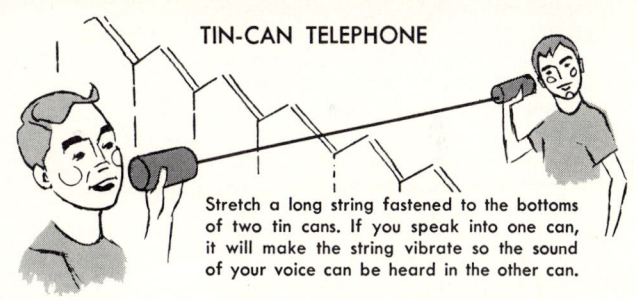

Stretch a long string fastened to the bottoms of two tin cans. If you speak into one can, it will make the string vibrate so the sound of your voice can be heard in the other can.

### AMPLIFYING SOUND

Tie a string to a fork and strike the fork so that it rings. Now tie the string to the handle of a pan on a table and strike the fork again. Notice that the ringing sound is much louder.

### DEADENING SOUND

You can *mute*, or deaden, the sound of the fork, *left*, if you insert toothpicks or paper between the prongs.

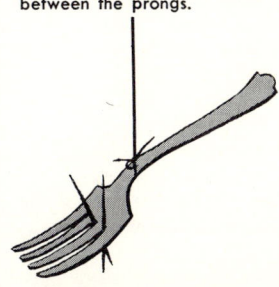

### SPOON BELL

Tie a string to a spoon and hold the string to your ear. Hit the spoon and hear it ring.

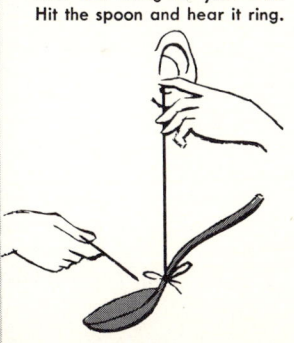

# SOUND

can also produce ultrasonic waves. This method is known as *magnetostriction*.

## Working with Sound

**Measuring Sound.** The unit commonly used to measure the intensity of sound is the *decibel*. The decibel system is a *compressed scale* of measurement. Under this system, a sound intensity of 0 decibels is at the threshold of audibility for the normal human ear. A sound of 10 decibels has an intensity 10 times greater than a sound of 0 decibels. A sound of 20 decibels is 100 times more intense than 0 decibels, 30 decibels is 1,000 times more intense, and so on. A whisper amounts to only about 20 decibels. The ordinary speaking voice has an intensity of about 60 decibels. Automobile horns may reach an intensity of 90 decibels, and a jet airplane 100 feet away produces about 140 decibels. See DECIBEL.

The unit used to measure the loudness of sound is the *phon*. Sounds have different degrees of loudness at different frequencies. For example, a sound with an intensity of 60 decibels sounds louder at a frequency of 1,000 vibrations a second than at 500 vibrations a second. Therefore, to provide a loudness measure, the number of phons is said to be the same as the number of decibels for sounds produced at frequencies of 1,000 vibrations a second. Thus, a 60-decibel sound with a frequency of 1,000 vibrations a second has a loudness of 60 phons. A 60-decibel sound with a frequency of 500 vibrations a second has a smaller number of phons. A 60-decibel sound with a frequency of 2,000 vibrations a second also has less than 60 phons of loudness. This is because the sensitivity of the ear to loudness increases up to 1,000 vibrations a second. After this point, the sensitivity of the ear falls off again.

**Sound Instruments** enable scientists to study sound and put it to work in phonograph recordings, telephones, radio, television, and public address systems. The most important of these instruments include the microphone, the amplifier, the loudspeaker, and the oscilloscope.

A *microphone* changes sound waves into an electric current. A *loudspeaker* changes an electric current, such as the one produced by a microphone, back into sound. Usually, the currents from a microphone are too weak to make a loudspeaker work. Therefore, most sound systems have an *amplifier* that changes weak electric currents into stronger ones. Every radio, television set, phonograph, and public address system has at least one amplifier. See MICROPHONE; LOUDSPEAKER; ELECTRONICS.

In order to study sound, scientists and engineers must know the shape, or pattern, of sound waves. They can get such information from an *oscilloscope*, an electronic device similar to a television picture tube. For example, current from a microphone is fed into an oscilloscope. The oscilloscope shows the pattern of the sound waves that produced the current on a fluorescent glass screen. See OSCILLOSCOPE.

**Controlling Sound.** The science of *acoustics* deals with the problem of controlling sound. Scientists and acoustical engineers design theaters, schools, and other buildings to add clarity to useful sounds, such as a speaker's voice and an orchestra's music. The designs of these buildings, and the materials used, reduce noises by absorbing or reflecting unwanted sounds. See ACOUSTICS.

**Recording Sound.** Until the late 1800's, people had no way of preserving sound. Speeches, plays, and concerts were lost forever. About the 1870's, Thomas A. Edison and other scientists began developing ways of recording and reproducing sound. Edison invented the phonograph in 1877. Today we have three main ways of recording sound: (1) on disks or cylinders made of wax or plastics, (2) on film, and (3) on magnetic tape or wire. For articles describing these methods of recording sounds, see Sound Instruments and Devices in the *Related Articles* listed below.

ROBERT T. BEYER

**Related Articles** in WORLD BOOK include:

### PRINCIPLES OF SOUND

| | | |
|---|---|---|
| Acoustics | Harmonics | Tone |
| Decibel | Interference | Ultrasonic Waves |
| Doppler Effect | Larynx | Vibration |
| Ear | Noise | Voice |
| Echo | Pitch | Waves |

### SOUND INSTRUMENTS AND DEVICES

| | | |
|---|---|---|
| Dictating Machine | Phonograph | Stethoscope |
| Electronics | Public Address | Tape Recorder |
| Fathometer | System | Telephone (How |
| Hearing Aids | Radio | the Telephone |
| High Fidelity | Resonator | Works) |
| Loudspeaker | Siren | Television |
| Megaphone | Sonar | Tuning Fork |
| Microphone | Sonometer | Voder |
| Motion Picture | Sound-Powered | |
| Oscilloscope | Telephone | |

### OTHER RELATED ARTICLES

| | | |
|---|---|---|
| Aerodynamics | Edison, Thomas A. | Music (The |
| (Supersonic Flight) | Frequency Modulation | Elements |
| Bell, Alexander G. | Helmholtz, Hermann | of Music) |
| Berliner, Emile | Insulation | Phonetics |
| Deaf-Mute | (Soundproofing) | Singing |
| Deafness | Mach, Ernst | |

### Outline

**I. What Is Sound?**
  A. Producing Sound
  B. Sound Waves
  C. How Sound Travels
  D. Hearing Sound

**II. Characteristics of Sound**
  A. Pitch
  B. Loudness and Intensity
  C. Quality of Sound
  D. Beats
  E. Echoes
  F. Resonance
  G. Sympathetic Vibrations

**III. Kinds of Sound**
  A. Noise
  B. Musical Sounds
  C. The Human Voice
  D. Animal Sounds
  E. Stereophonic Sound
  F. Ultrasound

**IV. Working with Sound**
  A. Measuring Sound
  B. Sound Instruments
  C. Controlling Sound
  D. Recording Sound

### Questions

What causes sound?
Does sound travel faster in steel or air? Why?
What do engineers mean when they say an airplane is supersonic?
How is sound used to measure ocean depths?
What is meant by a person's threshold of audibility?
What do scientists call sounds that vibrate more than 20,000 times a second?
What is the difference between music and noise?
How can a table increase the loudness of the sound made by a vibrating fork?
What characteristic of sound can you demonstrate with a piece of cardboard and a bicycle wheel?
Why does the pitch of a train whistle rise when the train comes toward you and drop when it moves away?

**SOUND** is a narrow stretch of water. There are several different kinds of such bodies of water. The word *sound* often describes a fiord or submerged glaciated valley, such as Howe Sound in British Columbia, or Doubtful Sound on South Island in New Zealand. The word sometimes denotes a deep, protected bay formed by the submergence of nonglaciated hilly land below sea level like Hingwha Sound on the southeastern coast of China. *Sound* is also used as a synonym for a strait, or narrow passage of water, between two broad areas of sea. Such straits include Kalmar Sound, separating the island of Öland from Sweden, and The Sound, or Øresund, which separates the Danish island of Sjaelland from Sweden. The word *sund* in the Danish, Norwegian, and Swedish languages means *sound*.     J. ROWLAND ILLICK

See also BAY; FIORD; STRAIT.

**SOUND BARRIER.** See SONIC BARRIER.

**SOUND EFFECT.** See RADIO (Sound Effects); MOTION PICTURE (Sound).

**SOUND-POWERED TELEPHONE** is a communication device that operates only on the power of the sound that enters it. Telephones and most other communication systems operate on electrical power supplied by batteries or electric-power lines. However, the sound-powered telephone has no outside source of power other than that supplied by sound waves.

A sound-powered telephone system consists of two or more identical phone units connected by wires. Each phone consists of a metal diaphragm and a permanent magnet around which a coil is wound. The magnet is placed close to the diaphragm. This forms a type of microphone. When a person speaks into the microphone his voice causes sound waves that make the metal diaphragm vibrate. The coil and magnet transform the waves of sound into electrical impulses. These impulses are carried by wires to the other phone units in the system. There the coils and magnets pass on the electrical variations to the receiving diaphragms, causing them to vibrate and thus produce sound.

These telephones can work only over short distances, usually not more than a few thousand feet. Because no amplification is used, the speaker must talk very close to the telephone and in a loud voice. But the sound-powered telephone is rugged, reliable, and inexpensive.

It is easy to build a private telephone system between rooms or homes if the distance is not great. Ordinary telephone receivers or headphones from radio receivers may be used. These are already equipped with magnet, wire, and diaphragm. However, the magnet must be strong to work efficiently. If the receivers have been stored for a long time, the magnets will have lost their power. They can be remagnetized easily at a radio supply shop. Or a strong horseshoe magnet fastened to the outside of the receiver will work very well. Two copper wires are then strung between each of the receivers and attached to them, and the private telephone system is complete.     RICHARD H. BOLT

**SOUNDING.** See FATHOMETER; SONAR.
**SOUNDING LEAD.** See LEAD, SOUNDING.
**SOUNDING ROCKET.** See SPACE TRAVEL (Space Probes).
**SOUNDPROOFING.** See ACOUSTICS; INSULATION.
**SOUR DOCK.** See DOCK.
**SOUR GUM.** See BLACK TUPELO.

**SOURIS RIVER.** See ASSINIBOINE RIVER.
**SOURWOOD.** See SORREL TREE.
**SOUSA, JOHN PHILIP** (1854-1932), was a famous American composer and bandmaster. Sousa wrote many kinds of music, including operettas, orchestral suites, songs, waltzes, and a symphonic poem. But his fame rests on his marches, and he became known throughout the world as the "March King."

Sousa took the rather simple form of the military march and gave it a personal style and new rhythmic and melodic vitality. The best-known of his more than a hundred marches include "Semper Fidelis," "The Washington Post," "El Capitan," "Thunderer," "The High School Cadets," "Liberty Bell," "Manhattan Beach," "Hands Across the Sea," and "The Stars and Stripes Forever." A man of many gifts, he also wrote five novels and an autobiography, *Marching Along* (1928).

Sousa was born in Washington, D.C. His parents could not afford to send him to Europe to study music. But Sousa later said, "I feel I am better off as it is . . . for I may therefore consider myself a truly American composer." After studying violin and harmony, he began his professional career at the age of 17, playing in theater and dance orchestras and touring with a variety show. In 1877, he played in Jacques Offenbach's orchestra when the famous French composer toured the United States. Soon afterward, Sousa wrote an operetta, *The Smugglers*, the first of many that he wrote in the next 35 years. He was one of the first Americans to compose operettas. He wrote the words as well as the music for these. The most successful of Sousa's operettas was *El Capitan* (1896).

**John Philip Sousa** composed many famous marches.

U&U

Sousa was appointed leader of the U.S. Marine Band in 1880, and made the band into one of the finest in the world. He wrote some of the marches that made him famous for the band. In 1892, Sousa obtained his discharge from the Marine Corps and formed his own band. He gave concerts in America and Europe, playing arrangements of the classics as well as military marches. He was honored wherever he traveled. In England, King Edward VII decorated him with the Victorian Order. In 1900, the American writer Rupert Hughes wrote, "There is probably no other composer in the world with a popularity equal to that of Sousa." In 1910 and 1911, "Sousa's Band" made a triumphal world tour. From 1917 to 1919, Sousa served as bandmaster for the United States Navy.     GILBERT CHASE

**SOUSAPHONE.** See TUBA.
**SOUTH, THE.** See SOUTHERN STATES.
**SOUTH, UNIVERSITY OF THE,** is a liberal arts and theological school for men in Sewanee, Tenn. It is controlled by the Protestant Episcopal Church. Courses lead to bachelor's degrees in the arts and sciences and to master's degrees in theology. For enrollment, see UNIVERSITIES AND COLLEGES (table).

**Pretoria, One of South Africa's Two Capitals,** lies on a plateau in the northwestern part of the country. The president lives there, and all government departments have their headquarters in Pretoria. The parliament meets in Cape Town.

SOUTH AFRICA, or, officially, the REPUBLIC OF SOUTH AFRICA, is an independent country that occupies the southern tip of Africa. As the Union of South Africa, it was a member of the Commonwealth of Nations from 1910 until 1961. On May 31, 1961, it withdrew from the Commonwealth and changed its form of government. South Africa has two official languages, English and *Afrikaans,* a tongue developed by Dutch settlers. In Afrikaans, the name of the country is SUID-AFRIKA. The country has two capitals. The parliament meets in Cape Town, the legislative capital and South Africa's oldest city. All government departments maintain headquarters at Pretoria, the administrative capital. Johannesburg is the largest city.

The country is slightly larger than California, Arizona, Utah, and Nevada combined. Most of South Africa lies on broad plateaus covered by vast grasslands and sweeping plains. Barren mountain ranges rise from a narrow, rugged coast. These mountain ranges form a massive wall along the southern and eastern edges of the country's plateaus.

South Africa is the world's greatest gold producer. It has the richest yield of gem diamonds, and is also a leading producer of uranium concentrates. Factories have been developed near the mines and harbors. Almost one-half of the people live in cities and

*Hibberd V. B. Kline, Jr., the contributor of this article, is Chairman of the Department of Geography and of the African Studies Program at the University of Pittsburgh.*

--- **FACTS IN BRIEF** ---

**Capitals:** Cape Town (legislative) and Pretoria (administrative).

**Official Languages:** English and Afrikaans.

**Form of Government:** Republic.

**Area:** 471,445 square miles (excluding the enclave of Walvis Bay, 434 square miles). *Greatest Distances*—(northeast-southwest) 925 miles; (northwest-southeast) 675 miles. *Coastline*—1,800 miles.

**Population:** *1960 Census*—16,002,797 (excluding the enclave of Walvis Bay, 12,648); distribution, 53 per cent rural; 47 per cent urban. *Estimated 1970 Population*—20,114,000; density, 43 persons to the square mile. *Estimated 1975 Population*—22,647,000.

**Chief Products:** *Agriculture*—cattle, corn, cotton, dairy products, fruit, goats, hogs, mohair, peanuts, potatoes, poultry, sheep, sugar cane, tobacco, wattle bark, wheat, wine, wool. *Manufacturing and Processing*—chemicals, clothing, food products, leather, metals, textiles. *Mining*—asbestos, chromite, coal, copper, diamonds, gold, iron, manganese, platinum, tin, uranium.

**Flag:** Horizontal orange, white, and blue stripes (top to bottom) honor the old Dutch flag. Three miniature flags in the center stand for the four provinces of South Africa. The flag was adopted in 1927. See FLAG (color picture: Flags of Africa).

**National Anthem:** "Die Stem van Suid-Afrika" ("The Call of South Africa").

**National Holiday:** Republic Day, May 31.

**Money:** *Basic Unit*—rand. One hundred cents equal one rand. For its value, see MONEY (table: Values).

# SOUTH AFRICA

towns. The rest of the people live in rural areas.

People of both Dutch and British descent govern the country, but Negro and other nonwhite peoples make up four-fifths of the population. Since 1948, the government has followed a racial policy called *apartheid* (*uh PART hayt*). Apartheid aims at the separate development of the races. It calls for separate institutions, jobs, and residences for whites and nonwhites.

## The Land and Its Resources

**Location and Size.** The *Color Map* shows that South Africa occupies the southern tip of Africa. The country administers South West Africa, a territory on the northwest border. Lesotho (formerly Basutoland) lies entirely inside South Africa. The enclave of Walvis Bay, a separate part of the country, covers 434 square miles on the coast of South West Africa. South Africa covers 471,445 square miles.

**Land Regions.** Broad, flat plateaus that rise 2,000 to 6,000 feet above sea level cover most of the country. Cliffs and mountains separate the plateaus from a narrow coastal strip. The plateaus, mountains, and coastal strip form the country's three land regions.

*The Plateaus* form the vast north-central region of the country. Large plateaus called *karroos* make up the dry western half of this region. The eastern half contains the highest and most fertile plateau, the *Northern Karroo*, also called the *High Veld*. Veld is the Afrikaans word for *grassland*. Much of this plateau lies a mile above sea level. Sheep graze among the bushes on the karroo plateaus. Farms and mining and industrial cities lie on the green grasslands of the Northern Karroo, which is flat or gently rolling.

*The Namaqua Highlands* border the plateaus along the west coast. The *Kalahari Desert* lies on the northwest. To the northeast, the Northern Karroo descends to another plateau, the *Transvaal Low Veld*, which is grassy, hot, and humid.

*The Mountains.* The chief mountain ranges form a rocky wall along the eastern and southern edges of the plateaus. Mont aux Sources, the country's highest point, towers 10,822 feet above sea level. It stands in the Drakensberg range along the southeastern edge of the plateaus. Two lowlands, the *Little Karroo* and *Great Karroo*, lie among the mountains along the southern edge of the plateaus. Few plants grow on the dry mountains, but farms dot the valleys and lowlands.

*The Coastal Strip.* The narrow coastal strip rises from the Atlantic and Indian oceans to an average height of 500 to 600 feet. It varies in width from 30 miles in the northeast to as little as 3 miles in the southeast. The southwestern coast has little rainfall, and the west coast is a part of the Namib Desert. Northeast of Port Elizabeth, the coast becomes increasingly hot and humid.

**Rivers and Lakes.** The few large rivers include the Orange, the Vaal, and the Limpopo, or Crocodile. Several rivers have dams that provide water for irrigation. The mountains and the low rainfall prevent ships from sailing more than a few miles inland on the rivers. There are few lakes, but marshy areas called *vleis* collect in low places during rainy seasons.

**Natural Resources.** Great mineral deposits provide a major source of wealth for the nation. South Africa produces almost two-thirds of the world's gold and over one-fourth of the gem diamonds. Some scientists regard Transvaal Province as the richest mineral area in the world. This region and the Orange Free State contain the gold fields, as well as deposits of asbestos, chromite, coal, iron, platinum, tin, and uranium.

The country's greatest natural handicap is lack of water, due to low rainfall and a high rate of evaporation. The dryness makes much of the land suitable only for grazing. South Africa has few good forests, but it supplies much of the world's wattle bark, the source of

---

## SOUTH AFRICA MAP INDEX

### Provinces

| | | |
|---|---|---|
| CAPE OF GOOD HOPE | 5,362,853 | D 2 |
| NATAL | 2,979,920 | C 5 |
| ORANGE FREE STATE | 1,386,547 | C 4 |
| TRANSVAAL | 6,273,477 | B 4 |

### Cities and Towns

| Aliwal North | 10,762 | D 4 |
|---|---|---|
| Barberton | 11,075 | C 5 |
| Beaufort West | 16,467 | D 3 |
| Benoni | 122,502 | |
| *140,790 | | C 4 |
| Bethal | 11,988 | C 4 |
| Bethlehem | 24,125 | C 4 |
| Bloemfontein | 112,606 | |
| *145,273 | | C 4 |
| Boksburg* | 71,029 | C 4 |
| Brakpan | 77,777 | C 4 |
| Brits* | 9,407 | C 4 |
| Burgersdorp | 7,165 | D 4 |
| Cape Town | 508,341 | |
| *807,211 | | D 2 |
| Carletonville* | 56,246 | C 4 |
| Ceres | 6,195 | D 2 |
| Cradock | 19,561 | D 4 |
| De Aar | 14,510 | D 3 |
| Despatch* | 9,992 | D 4 |
| Dundee | 10,939 | C 5 |
| Durban | 560,010 | |
| *681,492 | | C 5 |
| East London | 113,746 | |
| *116,056 | | D 4 |
| Ermelo | 17,025 | C 4 |
| Estcourt | 9,027 | C 4 |
| Ficksburg | 8,146 | C 4 |
| Fort Beaufort | 9,750 | D 4 |
| George | 14,759 | D 3 |
| Germiston | 148,102 | |
| *214,393 | | C 4 |
| Glencoe | 8,334 | C 5 |
| Graaff-Reinet | 16,936 | D 3 |
| Grahamstown | 32,611 | D 4 |
| Greytown* | 7,743 | C 5 |
| Harrismith | 13,924 | C 4 |
| Heidelberg* | 9,295 | C 4 |
| Heilbron | 7,216 | C 4 |
| Hennenman* | 6,446 | C 4 |
| Johannesburg | 595,083 | |
| *1,152,525 | | C 4 |
| Kempton Park* | 17,763 | C 4 |
| Kimberley | 75,376 | |
| *79,031 | | C 3 |
| King William's Town | 14,678 | D 4 |
| Klerksdorp | 43,726 | C 4 |
| Knysna | 11,045 | D 3 |
| Kokstad | 7,902 | D 4 |
| Kroonstad | 42,438 | C 4 |
| Krugersdorp | 89,947 | C 4 |
| Kuruman | 6,505 | C 3 |
| Ladybrand* | 7,049 | C 4 |
| Ladysmith | 22,955 | C 4 |
| Lichtenburg* | 14,271 | C 4 |
| Louis Trichardt | 9,890 | B 4 |
| Lydenburg | 7,587 | C 5 |
| Mafeking | 8,362 | C 4 |
| Malmesbury | 8,267 | D 2 |
| Messina | 10,295 | B 5 |
| Meyerton* | 8,256 | C 4 |
| Middelburg | 8,681 | C 4 |
| Middelburg* | 12,941 | C 4 |
| Mosselbaai | 12,225 | D 3 |
| Nelspruit | 15,498 | C 5 |
| Newcastle | 17,554 | C 4 |
| Nigel* | 34,008 | C 4 |
| Noupoort | 6,322 | D 3 |
| Nylstroom | 6,669 | B 4 |
| Odendaalsrus | 21,268 | C 4 |
| Orkney* | 22,425 | C 4 |
| Oudtshoorn | 22,229 | D 3 |
| Paarl | 41,540 | D 2 |
| Parys* | 12,683 | C 4 |
| Pietermaritzburg | 91,988 | |
| *128,598 | | C 5 |
| Pietersburg | 28,071 | B 4 |
| Piet Retief | 8,696 | C 5 |
| Port Alfred | 6,184 | D 4 |
| Port Elizabeth | 249,211 | |
| *290,693 | | D 4 |
| Potchefstroom | 41,927 | C 4 |
| Potgietersrus | 11,491 | B 4 |
| Pretoria | 303,684 | |
| *422,590 | | C 4 |
| Prieska | 6,485 | C 3 |
| Queenstown | 33,182 | D 4 |
| Randfontein* | 41,499 | C 4 |
| Robertson | 8,195 | D 2 |
| Roodepoort-Maraisburg | 95,211 | C 4 |
| Rustenburg | 21,016 | C 4 |
| Sasolburg* | 11,890 | C 4 |
| Senekal* | 7,415 | C 4 |
| Somerset East | 9,801 | D 4 |
| Somerset West* | 8,437 | D 2 |
| Springs | 137,253 | |
| *141,943 | | C 4 |
| Standerton | 16,897 | C 4 |
| Stanger | 9,619 | C 5 |
| Stellenbosch* | 22,333 | D 2 |
| Strand | 13,389 | D 2 |
| Stutterheim | 9,025 | D 4 |
| Uitenhage | 48,755 | D 4 |
| Umtata | 12,221 | D 4 |
| Upington | 20,366 | C 3 |
| Vanderbijlpark* | 41,415 | C 4 |
| Vereeniging | 78,835 | C 4 |
| Virginia | 18,273 | |
| *41,057 | | C 4 |
| Volksrust | 8,243 | C 4 |
| Vrede* | 6,778 | C 4 |
| Vryburg | 14,659 | C 3 |
| Vryheid | 10,782 | C 5 |
| Walvis Bay | 12,165 | B 1 |
| Warmbad | 6,354 | B 4 |
| Welkom | 48,069 | |
| *97,614 | | C 4 |
| Wellington* | 11,658 | D 2 |
| Westonaria* | 26,640 | C 4 |
| Witbank | 25,881 | C 4 |
| Wolmaransstad* | 6,054 | C 4 |
| Worcester | 32,274 | D 2 |
| Zeerust | 6,934 | C 4 |

### Physical Features

| Algoa Bay | D 4 |
|---|---|
| Cape Agulhas | D 3 |
| Cape of Good Hope | D 2 |
| Drakensberg (Mountains) | D 4 |
| Great Karroo (Plateau) | D 3 |
| Grootvloer | C 3 |
| Kalahari Desert | B 3 |
| Kruger National Park | B 5 |
| Little Karroo (Plateau) | D 3 |
| Molopo River | C 3 |
| Mont aux Sources (Mountain) | C 4 |
| Namaqua Highlands | C 2 |
| Northern Karroo (Plateau) | C 4 |
| Olifants River | B 5 |
| Orange River | C 2 |
| Saint Helena Bay | D 2 |
| Transvaal Low Veld | B 5 |
| Vaal River | C 4 |
| Verneukpan | D 3 |
| Witwatersrand | C 4 |

*Population of metropolitan area, including suburbs.
*Does not appear on the map; key shows general location.

Source: Latest census figures (1960).

498b

# SOUTH AFRICA

Mörath, Magnum

**Basuto Women** often carry children in colorful, woolen blankets, and return from shopping with purchases balanced on their heads.

a tanning material. Atlantic coastal waters contain lobsters (crayfish) and such fishes as sole, snoek, and pilchard. Elephants, lions, giraffes, zebras, rhinoceroses, and other animals live in wildlife parks.

**Climate.** South Africa has a mild, sunny climate similar to that of the southwestern United States. Temperatures average 55° F. to 65° F., but reach as high as 90° F. in the summer, October to March. Most of the rain falls in summer except in the southwest. Only about a third of the country receives more than the 25 inches of rain a year needed to raise crops. The eastern half generally has more rain than the western half.

## Life of the People

**The People** of South Africa include two basic groups, the *whites* and the *nonwhites*. About four-fifths of the people are nonwhites, and about one-fifth are whites. About half of the people, including one-sixth of the whites, live in farm areas. The rest live in cities and towns. The people have an average yearly income of about $400 a person. This figure is low because of the large number of very poor nonwhites who live in primitive tribal conditions. The whites enjoy a standard of living similar to the British.

*The Whites* are also called Europeans. Their ancestors came from such European countries as The Netherlands, Great Britain, France, and Germany. The Boers, the first white settlers in South Africa, came from The Netherlands starting in the mid-1600's. *Boer* is the Dutch word for *farmer*. The descendants of the Boers are called *Afrikaners*.

*The Nonwhites* are classified by the government into three main groups: *Bantus, Coloureds,* and *Asians*. Special laws apply to each group.

The 11 million Bantus are also called Natives or Africans. They are divided according to their tribes, which are officially known as *nationalities*. The main tribal groups include the Zulus, Basutos, Xhosas, Pondos, and other Bantu-speaking peoples. About 3½ million Bantus live on tracts of land the government has set aside for them. Another 3½ million Bantus work on farms owned by whites. The rest live in parts of cities and towns reserved for them.

The 1½ million Coloureds are the mixed-blood descendants of the Hottentots and other peoples who mingled with the first white settlers. The Hottentots lived in South Africa when the whites arrived in 1652. They have almost died out as a distinct group. A few thousand Cape Malays live in the Cape Town area. Some of the ancestors of these Coloured peoples were imported as slaves from southeast Asia.

Most of the 475,000 *Asians* are descendants of laborers brought from India in the 1860's to work on sugar plantations. Most of them live in Natal Province.

The various Dutch Reformed sects are the largest religious group. They have nearly 2 million members, including most of the Afrikaans-speaking whites. The next largest denominations are the Methodists, with 1,300,000 members, and the Anglicans, with 1,200,000. Other religious groups include about 600,000 Roman Catholics, 500,000 Lutherans, 270,000 Presbyterians, 230,000 Congregationalists, 180,000 Hindus, 110,000 Jews, 100,000 Moslems, and 100,000 Baptists.

**Languages.** Most whites speak both English and Afrikaans. *Afrikaans* developed through the years from the Dutch spoken by the Boers.

Most of the Coloureds and Cape Malays speak Afrikaans. The Asians speak either Afrikaans or English. Many also speak Hindi and other tongues of their former homeland in India. Most of the Natives speak one of the Bantu group of languages.

**Family Life.** White families live much as people do in North America and Eu-

**Location Map**

**South Africa Is ⅛ the Size of the U.S.**

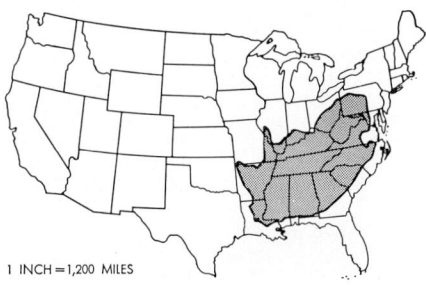

1 INCH = 1,200 MILES

498c

## SOUTH AFRICA

rope. The whites live in the same types of brick homes, eat similar foods, and wear the same kinds of clothing. The Coloureds and Cape Malays have adopted the whites' ways of life, but their homes, food, and clothing are poorer. Asian families still observe many customs of India. See INDIA (Ways of Life).

Many Bantus live with their families in the cities. About 100,000 Bantu men work in the mines. They leave their families at home in the tribal areas and live in bachelor compounds near the mines. In rural areas, the Bantus live much as they did before white men came to the country. There, family life centers on the *kraal*, a cluster of huts. Cattle are the most prized possession of the Bantus.

The Bantus usually live in huts made of sod or of grass and straw. Many of the huts look like cone-shaped beehives, or huge baskets turned upside down. Some tribes decorate their huts with colorful paintings on the walls. The main food of the Bantus is corn. They call the corn *mealies*, and usually eat it as porridge.

Many Bantus wear blankets and skins decorated with colorful beads and ornaments. They sometimes insert bone and metal ornaments in their ears and noses. Recreation in Bantu villages consists largely of dances held to celebrate coming-of-age ceremonies, weddings, harvests, and other special events.

**City Life.** South Africa has 10 cities with more than 100,000 persons each. They look much like cities in North America, with fine shops, tall office buildings, busy factories, and beautiful homes. The farm areas have many smaller towns and villages. See the separate articles on the cities listed in the *Related Articles* at the end of this article.

Large numbers of nonwhites live in *townships* (locations) on the outskirts of the cities. These areas once consisted mainly of slums. But government rebuilding programs have eliminated the worst of the slums. Many of the nonwhites in the townships are young Bantu men who have been drawn to the cities by the wages paid by the mines and industries.

**Country Life.** Most white farmers in the country are hardy Afrikaners of Dutch descent. They live either in large homes on their farms or in country villages.

The Bantus live on government-supplied lands called the Bantu National Homelands. Covering more than 30 million acres, the homelands include the Transkei and Ciskei areas in Cape Province, parts of western and northern Transvaal, and much of Zululand, a district of Natal. Many old people and children live on the homelands. Most of the young people leave to work in the

**Cape Town, South Africa's Leading Port, Nestles Between Table Mountain and the Cape of Good Hope.**
South African Dept. of Information

**Elephants Are "Hunted"** by tourists armed with cameras in Kruger National Park, the largest animal sanctuary in the world. Lions, giraffes, zebras, rhinoceroses and other wild animals roam freely over its 8,000 square miles.

Satour

cities. Overcrowding, soil erosion, and the lack of young men have led to poverty and caused a breakdown in tribal organization. The government has tried to re-establish the tribal form of life, and to improve Bantu farming methods. It has a program to develop light industries, such as sugar and hemp. In 1963, the Transkei Territory achieved internal self-government.

### Work of the People

In the mid-1950's, manufacturing became the biggest industry, surpassing gold mining and wool production.

**Agriculture.** The nation raises most of its own food, but farmers cultivate only about 6 per cent of the land. Drought, poor soil, and soil erosion make much of the country suitable only for grazing livestock.

Over half the farms cover more than 600 acres each, and over one-fourth cover more than 1,000 acres. The average farm has machinery similar to that used in Canada or the United States. Much handwork is done by Coloured or Bantu families who live on white-owned farms. Whites own four-fifths of the cultivated land.

Large flocks of sheep graze on the plateaus. Wool is the most important farm product, ranking second only to gold in export value. Farmers also raise cattle and goats. About half of the cattle are owned by Bantus. Other leading livestock products include skins, hides, and mohair. Dairy farms support a thriving industry.

The chief crop is corn. Farmers also raise barley, cotton, oats, peanuts, potatoes, rye, tobacco, and wheat. Orchards on the broad plateaus produce apples, grapes, and peaches. Citrus fruits come from the warm lowlands of the Transvaal. Coastal plantations in Natal raise bananas, mangoes, papayas, and sugar cane. The southwestern Cape has a flourishing wine industry.

**Manufacturing and Processing.** About a million South Africans work in factories. Many new industries developed during the 1940's and 1950's. Most of them were built to process local raw materials, especially fibers, foods, metals, and coal. Most manufactured products are sold in local markets. But some manufactured goods are exported to Asian markets and Rhodesia. The country ships tinned and frozen foods to European countries, Japan, and the United States.

The city of Virginia has one of the world's largest sulfuric acid plants outside the United States. Plants at Pretoria and Vereeniging produce nearly 2 million tons of iron and steel a year. The world's largest oil-from-coal plant operates at Sasolburg. It supplies about one-seventh of South Africa's gasoline needs, and produces important chemical by-products. Factories in the Transvaal Low Veld turn out phosphate fertilizers. Rayon pulp comes from a plant at Umkomaas, near Durban. Manufacturers from the United States and Europe assemble automobiles and make rubber tires at some of the port cities of South Africa.

The industrial area in southern Transvaal is larger than all the other industrial regions in the country combined. It has one-third of the industrial plants, more than half the metal and engineering factories, and over a third of the furniture, chemical, and construction firms.

**Mining.** South Africa produces almost two-thirds of the world's new gold. Most of it comes from mines in the

498e

# SOUTH AFRICA

Witwatersrand, in the southern Transvaal, and in the Orange Free State. More than 50,000 whites and nearly 350,000 nonwhites work in the gold mines. Rich amounts of uranium found in the gold ores have greatly increased the value of the gold deposits. The waste rock from these gold mines is one of the cheapest sources of uranium. Only Canada and the United States produce more uranium concentrates than South Africa.

Mines in northeastern Cape of Good Hope produce most of the country's diamonds. South Africa produces 27 per cent of the world's supply of gem diamonds. Until 1908, when diamonds were found elsewhere in Africa, nearly all the world's diamonds came from mines at Kimberley and Pretoria. Coal deposits in the southern Transvaal and northern Natal are the largest in the Southern Hemisphere. South Africa is a leading producer of nickel and copper. Miners also dig large amounts of asbestos, chrome, iron ore, limestone, manganese, platinum, and tin.

**Electric Power.** The coal mines supply fuel for most of the country's electric-power plants. The government controls and operates most of the power plants through the Electricity Supply Commission. A few industries have their own power plants. South Africa generates about 32 billion kilowatt-hours of electricity a year.

**Trade.** South Africa imports more than it exports. But the government does not include the value of gold bullion exports in computing the balance of trade. Such items as corn, fish, fruit, hides and skins, sugar, wattle bark, and wool account for nearly half the exports. Asbestos, chrome, copper, diamonds, lead, manganese, and uranium make up a third of the exports. Imports include automobiles, clothing, machinery, and textiles.

**Transportation.** The government-owned South African Airways provides regular service between all major cities in South Africa, and between Johannesburg and London. International airlines connect South Africa with all parts of the world. The government-owned South African Railways operates more than 14,000 miles of narrow-gauge track. The country has 50,000 miles of primary and secondary roads and highways. Cape Town and Durban are the largest and best-equipped ports. Other ports include Port Elizabeth and East London. Some of South Africa's trade passes through the port of Lourenço Marques, Mozambique. South Africa's merchant fleet has 230 vessels.

**Communication.** South Africa has about 170 newspapers, and many magazine- and book-publishing firms. The leading English-language newspapers include the Johannesburg *Star* and the Cape Town *Cape Times*. *Die Burger* of Cape Town and *Die Transvaler* of Johannesburg are prominent Afrikaans dailies. The government operates four radio networks. Telephone and telegraph service links all sections of the country.

### Education

White and Coloured children go to free elementary and high schools provided by the national and provincial governments. The law requires that all white boys and girls between the ages of 7 and 16 attend school. White and nonwhite children attend separate schools. South Africa has about 7,000 schools for the exclusive use of Bantu children. These schools also are free.

In 1953, the Bantu Education Act gave the government control over most nonwhite schools. Until that year, government-aided missionary groups taught most nonwhite children.

South Africa has nine universities for whites: The University of Cape Town, the University of Stellenbosch, the University of Witwatersrand (Johannesburg), the University of Pretoria, the University of Natal (Pietermaritzburg and Durban), Rhodes University (Grahamstown), the University of South Africa (Pretoria), the University of the Orange Free State (Bloemfontein), and the University of Potchefstroom. There are three university colleges for Bantus: Fort Hare, Zululand, and North. Coloured students attend the University College of the Western Cape. Indians attend the University College for Indians in Durban.

### The Arts

South Africa has produced some noted painters, musicians, and writers. The recordings of Joseph Marais and his wife, Miranda, have popularized "Tante Koba," "Stellenbosch Boys," and other Boer folk songs. Alan Paton, author of *Cry, The Beloved Country*, is one of the better-known writers. Nadine Gordimer has written *World of Strangers* and other novels and many short stories. Laurens van der Post has written *Flamingo Feather*, and Stuart Cloete wrote *Turning Wheels*.

### What to See and Do in South Africa

Fine resorts and hotels dot the mountains, coast, and other scenic areas. Guides conduct *safaris* (tours) through wildlife parks, where tourists can "hunt" wild animals with cameras. Many visitors enjoy watching tribal activities of the Bantu tribesmen in the reserves.

Kruger National Park in northeastern Transvaal is the world's largest animal sanctuary and the biggest tourist attraction in South Africa. Here lions, elephants, and many other wild animals roam freely over 8,000 square miles of wild grasslands. Table Mountain, a great flat-topped peak that confronts visitors arriving at Cape Town, is another famed scenic attraction. Many tourists visit the mile-deep Witwatersrand gold mines and the *Big Hole* diamond mine near Kimberley.

### Government

South Africa is a republic with a president as the head of state. But a prime minister actually heads the executive branch of the government. The leader of the majority party in parliament usually serves as prime minister. He administers laws with the help of a cabinet of 18 ministers. Cabinet ministers also are members of parliament (see CABINET).

Parliament meets every year in Cape Town. It has a house of assembly and a senate. Only whites who qualify as registered voters may serve in parliament.

The assembly is the more powerful house. For example, all money legislation must originate in the assembly. All white persons over 18 years of age may vote. They elect 166 members of the assembly in the following proportions: 54 from Cape Province, 18 from Natal, 73 from the Transvaal, 15 from the Orange Free State, and 6 from South West Africa. Coloured voters of Cape Province elect 4 whites to represent them.

The senate has 54 members. National and provincial legislative groups elect them. Eleven are from Cape

**Bantu Tribal Life** centers on the Kraal, a group of sod huts that look like baskets that have been turned upside down.

**Cattle Inspection** by a Veld farmer follows a disinfectant bath. The *Afrikander* breed was introduced to the United States in 1931.

United Nations; Mörath, Magnum

Province, 8 from Natal, 14 from the Transvaal, 8 from the Orange Free State, and 2 from South West Africa. There are 11 additional senators who are nominated by the president. He chooses 2 senators for each of the 4 provinces, 2 for South West Africa, and 1 to represent the Coloureds of Cape Province. All of the members of parliament hold their seats for five years, unless the parliament is dissolved before that time. Since 1960, the Bantu people have had no direct representation in parliament.

**Courts.** A supreme court and a system of lower courts administer justice. The appellate division, a branch of the supreme court, is the highest court of the land. It consists of 11 justices and a chief justice. The laws are based partly on English law and partly on Roman-Dutch law. Courts of Bantu Affairs commissioners administer laws among the tribal people.

**Local Government.** Elected provincial councils enact the laws in each province. Each council must have at least 25 members, but most have more than this minimum. Administrators named by the president, and executive committees of four persons selected by the provincial councils, govern the provinces. The administrators, executive committees, and council members serve five-year terms. The provincial governments handle all matters not under the authority of the national government, such as lower education.

**Taxation.** Income taxes provide about half the government's revenue. All the people are subject to income taxes. The Bantus also pay a personal tax, known as the *General Tax*.

**Politics.** All whites over the age of 18 can vote in national elections. The Coloureds have separate elections for their members of parliament.

The country has two major political parties, the National and the United. The Nationalists led a drive that resulted in South Africa withdrawing from the Commonwealth of Nations in 1961. They also promote a white supremacy program involving complete separation of the races. Nearly all Nationalists are Afrikaners. The United party stands for partial integration of the races, and wants to give the nonwhites a greater voice in the government. It includes whites of British descent and about a fifth of the Afrikaners.

**Armed Forces.** South Africa maintains a permanent army, air force, and navy. The country operates a military, air force, and naval academy, and three military gymnasiums. The law makes all whites over the age of 17 liable for four years of military training.

### History

**Exploration and Settlement.** Colorful rock drawings and other relics indicate that tribes of Bushmen and Hottentots were the first inhabitants of South Africa. In 1487 and 1488, the Portuguese navigator Bartolomeu Dias became the first white man to round the Cape of Good Hope, while seeking a water route from Europe to India. Nine years later, Vasco da Gama, another

498g

**Jinrikisha Boys** wear charms and amulets as protection from city dangers when pulling cargo through the streets of Johannesburg.

**Schoolchildren** in Johannesburg often attend schools as modern as those in the United States. Holiday pageants of the two countries also are alike.
Mörath, Magnum

Portuguese navigator, sailed around the Cape and found the long-sought route.

Control of the Cape meant control of trade with India. In 1652, the Dutch East India Company sent Jan van Riebeeck (1619-1677), a naval surgeon, to establish a settlement. He brought Dutch settlers to the present site of Cape Town. In succeeding years, several thousand British, French, and Germans joined the Boer settlers. The colonists brought Malay slaves from southeast Asia to serve as laborers.

As the colonists spread inland during the 1700's, they encountered powerful tribes of Bantu, such as the Xhosa, which had drifted south from central Africa. Beginning in 1779, and continuing for nearly 100 years,

---------- **IMPORTANT DATES** ----------

1487-1488 Bartolomeu Dias discovered the Cape of Good Hope.
1652 Jan van Riebeeck founded the first white settlement at the present site of Cape Town.
1806 Great Britain seized the Cape of Good Hope from The Netherlands.
1836-1852 The Boers made their Great Trek into the interior of the country. They founded the Orange Free State and the South African Republic.
1866-1867 Diamonds were discovered near Hopetown.
1886 Gold was discovered in Transvaal.
1899-1902 British defeated the Boers in the Boer War.
1910 The four colonies of Cape of Good Hope, Natal, Orange Free State, and Transvaal formed the Union of South Africa.
1914-1918 The country joined Great Britain in fighting Germany in World War I.
1939-1945 The Union fought in World War II on the side of the Allies.
1948 The National party won the general elections and began a program of white supremacy.
1955 The Nationalists increased their power by expanding the size of the senate.
1960 The people voted to make South Africa a republic.
1961 South Africa became a republic on May 31, and left the Commonwealth of Nations.
1966 The Nationalist party increased its power again by a sweeping victory in the general elections.

the colonists fought wars with the Bantu, and eventually subdued them and confined them to reservations.

**British Occupation.** Great Britain seized the Cape from the Dutch in 1806, in order to protect its sea route to India. Eight years later, the Dutch signed a treaty giving Great Britain official ownership of the territory. A depression occurred in England about this time, and the British government encouraged people to migrate to the Cape. The first large group of English settlers landed at Algoa Bay in 1820.

The Boers bitterly resented British control. Starting in 1836, hundreds of Boers departed on their historic Great Trek, or journey, to the interior. They were determined to live outside British rule. When they reached the Orange River, the *Voortrekkers* (advance pioneers) founded the Orange Free State. Some of the Voortrekkers continued northward across the Vaal River to establish the South African Republic, now Transvaal Province. Great Britain recognized the independence of the South African Republic in 1852, and of the Orange Free State in 1854. While the Boers moved inland, the British took control of Natal in 1843, and made this territory a separate British colony in 1856.

**Boer Wars.** About 1866, a Boer family discovered diamonds in an area claimed by the Orange Free State.

498h

Great Britain angered the Boers by seizing the area in 1871. Six years later, it annexed the South African Republic. The Boers fought back in the first Boer War (1880-1881). They won, and the South African Republic, called the Transvaal, again won freedom.

The Witwatersrand gold field was discovered in 1886, and prospectors rushed into the Transvaal from the British colonies and elsewhere. Growing tensions between the Boers and the British resulted in the second Boer War (1899-1902). Great Britain won the war, and the Boer regions became British colonies. See BOER WAR.

**Union.** In 1906, Great Britain granted self-government to the Orange Free State and Transvaal. The two Boer states and the two British colonies of Cape of Good Hope and Natal agreed to unite in 1909. In 1910, the four colonies formed the Union of South Africa. In 1931, the British Parliament passed the Statute of Westminster, which made South Africa fully independent.

During World War I, two Boer generals led South African forces against Germany. Louis Botha seized South West Africa from Germany in 1915, and Jan Christiaan Smuts defeated German East Africa in 1917. In 1920, the country took control of South West Africa under a League of Nations mandate. Industry began developing after the war.

Smuts, of the United Party, became prime minister in 1939. At the start of World War II, a lengthy debate in the South African parliament ended in a vote to enter the war on the side of the Allies. South African troops fought in Ethiopia, northern Africa, and Europe.

South Africa requested permission in 1946 to annex South West Africa. The United Nations Trusteeship Council turned down the request because one of the South West African tribes objected. In 1949, the government allowed South West Africa to send elected representatives to parliament. This virtually made South West Africa a province of South Africa.

**Nationalism.** Daniel François Malan became prime minister in 1948 when the National party won the general elections. Under Malan's guidance, the Nationalists began a widespread apartheid program. The Group Areas Act of 1950 provided for separate white and nonwhite residential areas. The Bantu Education Act of 1953 gave the government control over Bantu education. Other laws gave the government far-reaching police powers.

The Nationalists kept control of the government in the 1953 general elections. Johannes Gerhardus Strijdom became prime minister after Malan retired in 1954. In 1955, Strijdom's government increased the size of the senate. Nearly all the new members of the senate were Nationalists. The government then changed the constitution to limit the Coloureds' voting rights.

The government's chief delegate to the United Nations walked out in 1956 in protest against UN discussion of South Africa's race problem. The government ended its UN boycott in 1958. In 1958, the Nationalists chose apartheid-backer Hendrik F. Verwoerd as prime minister. Verwoerd stiffened segregation policies. Riots raged throughout 1959 because of these policies. Racial tensions reached a critical point in March, 1960, when 69 Africans were killed by police.

In April, 1960, a white farmer shot Prime Minister Verwoerd in the head. But Verwoerd recovered. The emergency arising from racial tensions and the attempted

# SOUTH ALABAMA, UNIVERSITY OF

assassination finally ended on Aug. 31, 1960. About 10,500 persons were released from prisons on that day.

**The Republic.** South Africans voted on Oct. 5, 1960, to change their government from a constitutional monarchy to a republic. South Africa withdrew from the Commonwealth on May 31, 1961, after other Commonwealth nations criticized its racial policies. In 1961, Verwoerd was re-elected prime minister.

In 1961, the United Nations condemned South Africa's racial policies. The UN General Assembly adopted a resolution in 1962, asking member nations to impose economic sanctions on South Africa to force it to end racial segregation. The UN Security Council recommended an embargo on arms in 1963. Later the United States and other countries ended arms shipments to South Africa.

Prime Minister Verwoerd won his third term in March, 1966. In September, a parliamentary messenger assassinated Verwoerd during a session of parliament. Balthazar J. Vorster became prime minister.

In October, 1966, the United Nations voted to end South Africa's mandate over South West Africa. But South Africa refused to recognize the UN action, calling it illegal.

HIBBERD V. B. KLINE, JR.

**Related Articles** in WORLD BOOK include:

### BIOGRAPHIES

| | | |
|---|---|---|
| Barnard, Christiaan N. | Kruger, Paulus | Roberts, Frederick |
| Botha, Louis | Luthuli, Albert J. | Smuts, Jan C. |
| Broom, Robert | Pretorius (family) | Theiler, Max |
| | Rhodes, Cecil J. | Vorster, Balthazar |

### CITIES

| | | |
|---|---|---|
| Bloemfontein | Johannesburg | Port Elizabeth |
| Cape Town | Kimberley | Pretoria |
| Durban | Mafeking | Springs |
| Germiston | Pietermaritzburg | |

### PROVINCES

| | |
|---|---|
| Cape of Good Hope | Orange Free State |
| Natal | Transvaal |

### OTHER RELATED ARTICLES

| | | |
|---|---|---|
| Africa | Diamond | Orange River |
| Afrikaans | Gold | Platinum |
| Bantu | Hottentot | Sheep |
| Boer | Lesotho | South West Africa |
| Boer War | Limpopo River | |
| Bushman | Manganese | Vaal River |
| Copper (table) | Mining | Zululand |

### Outline

I. The Land and Its Resources
II. Life of the People
III. Work of the People
IV. Education
V. The Arts
VI. What to See and Do in South Africa
VII. Government
VIII. History

### Questions

Why has South Africa become the most important industrial nation in Africa?
What is the country's greatest natural handicap? Why?
What different kinds of people live in the country?
For what minerals is the country most famous?
Why has the gold ore taken on new significance?
What is the country's most important industry?
How do the two major political parties differ on the treatment of nonwhites?
What kind of government does the country have?

**SOUTH AFRICAN WAR.** See BOER WAR.

**SOUTH ALABAMA, UNIVERSITY OF.** See UNIVERSITIES AND COLLEGES (table).

499

# SOUTH AMERICA

**SOUTH AMERICA,** the fourth largest continent, is almost twice as large as the United States, but it has fewer people. Almost half of South America is a wilderness made up of high mountains, empty plains, and tropical forests. Most of the continent's large modern cities are near the coasts.

The continent has some of the world's largest deposits of minerals, rich farmlands, and vast timberlands. However, South America is one of the large areas of the world that has been slow in developing its natural resources. Millions of South Americans live much as their ancestors did hundreds of years ago. Oxcarts are more common than automobiles in country areas. They are more useful because most roads are unpaved.

*Preston E. James, the contributor of this article, is Chairman of the Department of Geography of Syracuse University, and the author of* Introduction to Latin America.

Machu Picchu, an Ancient Inca City in Peru

Three Lions

## FACTS IN BRIEF

**Area:** 6,889,000 square miles. *Greatest Distances*—(north-south) 4,750 miles; (east-west) 3,200 miles. *Coastline*—24,783 miles.

**Physical Features:** *Elevation—highest*, Mount Aconcagua (22,834 feet); Ojos del Salado (22,590 feet); Pissis (22,546 feet); Tupungato (22,310 feet); Mercedario (22,211); *lowest*, 131 feet below sea level in the Península Valdés in Argentina. *Chief Mountain Ranges*—Andes, Brazilian Highlands, Guiana Highlands. *Chief Rivers*—Amazon, Madeira, Magdalena, Orinoco, Paraguay, Paraná, Pilcomayo, Purús, São Francisco, Uruguay. *Chief Lakes*—Maracaibo, Mirim, Poopó, Titicaca. *Chief Islands*—Falkland Islands, Galapagos Islands, Marajó, Tierra del Fuego. *Chief Gulfs*—Darien, Guayaquil, San Jorge, San Matías, Venezuela. *Highest Waterfalls*—Angel (3,212 feet); Kukenaam (2,000 feet). *Largest Deserts*—Atacama, Patagonia.

**Population:** *Estimated 1970 Population*—190,000,000. *Density*—28 persons to the square mile.

**Chief Products:** *Agriculture*—bananas, beef, cacao, coffee, corn, cotton, sugar cane, wheat, wool. *Mining*—bauxite, copper, emeralds, gold, iron ore, lead, manganese, nitrate, petroleum, silver, tin, tungsten, zinc. *Manufacturing and Processing*—automobiles, beverages, canned meats, cement, chemicals, electrical appliances, flour, packaged foods, paper, textiles.

Christ of the Andes, on the Argentina-Chile border    J. Barnell, Shostal

More than half the people of South America work on farms, plantations, and ranches. But most of the small farmers cannot raise enough food to feed their families from their small plots of poor land. At the same time, a relatively few wealthy families own huge areas of fertile land that lies idle. How to put this idle land to use is probably South America's greatest problem. The governments of most South American countries have started or are planning land reform programs. Under these programs, some large estates are being broken up, and the land is given to small farmers.

Manufacturing is growing rapidly in South America. But South American countries still must import many manufactured products. They pay for these goods by exporting agricultural products and minerals. South America exports such agricultural products as bananas, beef, coffee, cotton, sugar, wheat, and wool. The chief mineral exports of South America are bauxite, copper, iron ore, manganese, petroleum, silver, and tin.

Brazil, the largest of the 11 independent South American countries, covers almost half the continent. The other countries in order of size are Argentina, Peru, Colombia, Bolivia, Venezuela, Chile, Paraguay, Ecuador, Guyana, and Uruguay. Two small possessions of European countries occupy the northeastern edge of South America. They are Surinam, an overseas territory of The Netherlands, and French Guiana, an overseas department of France. The Falkland Islands, a British crown colony, lie in the South Atlantic Ocean, about 300 miles southeast of the tip of the South American continent.

South America is part of the cultural region called *Latin America* that also includes Mexico, Central America, and the islands of the Caribbean Sea. For information on the way of life of the people and their education, arts, and history, see LATIN AMERICA.

### INDEPENDENT COUNTRIES OF SOUTH AMERICA

| Map Key | Name | Area (sq. mi.) | Population | Capital | Government | Date of Independence | Official Language |
|---|---|---|---|---|---|---|---|
| L-5 | Argentina | 1,072,073 | 24,083,000 | Buenos Aires | Republic | 1816 | Spanish |
| I-5 | Bolivia | 424,165 | 3,963,000 | La Paz; Sucre | Republic | 1825 | Spanish |
| H-7 | Brazil | 3,286,488 | 95,305,000 | Brasília | Republic | 1822 | Portuguese |
| L-5 | Chile | 292,258 | 9,510,000 | Santiago | Republic | 1818 | Spanish |
| F-4 | Colombia | 439,737 | 21,093,000 | Bogotá | Republic | 1819 | Spanish |
| G-3 | Ecuador | 109,484 | 6,089,000 | Quito | Republic | 1822 | Spanish |
| E-6 | Guyana | 83,000 | 737,000 | Georgetown | Sovereign Democratic State | 1966 | English |
| J-6 | Paraguay | 157,048 | 2,368,000 | Asunción | Republic | 1811 | Spanish |
| H-4 | Peru | 496,225 | 13,573,000 | Lima | Republic | 1821 | Spanish |
| L-7 | Uruguay | 72,173 | 2,884,000 | Montevideo | Republic | 1828 | Spanish |
| E-5 | Venezuela | 352,145 | 10,401,000 | Caracas | Republic | 1830 | Spanish |

### OTHER POLITICAL UNITS IN SOUTH AMERICA

| Map Key | Name | Area (sq. mi.) | Population | Capital | Status |
|---|---|---|---|---|---|
| O-6 | Falkland Islands | 4,618 | 2,172 | Port Stanley | British crown colony |
| E-7 | French Guiana | 35,135 | 41,000 | Cayenne | Overseas department of France |
| E-7 | Surinam (Dutch Guiana) | 63,039 | 402,000 | Paramaribo | Overseas territory of The Netherlands |

Each country and political unit has a separate article in WORLD BOOK.    Populations are 1970 estimates based on the latest official figures.

501

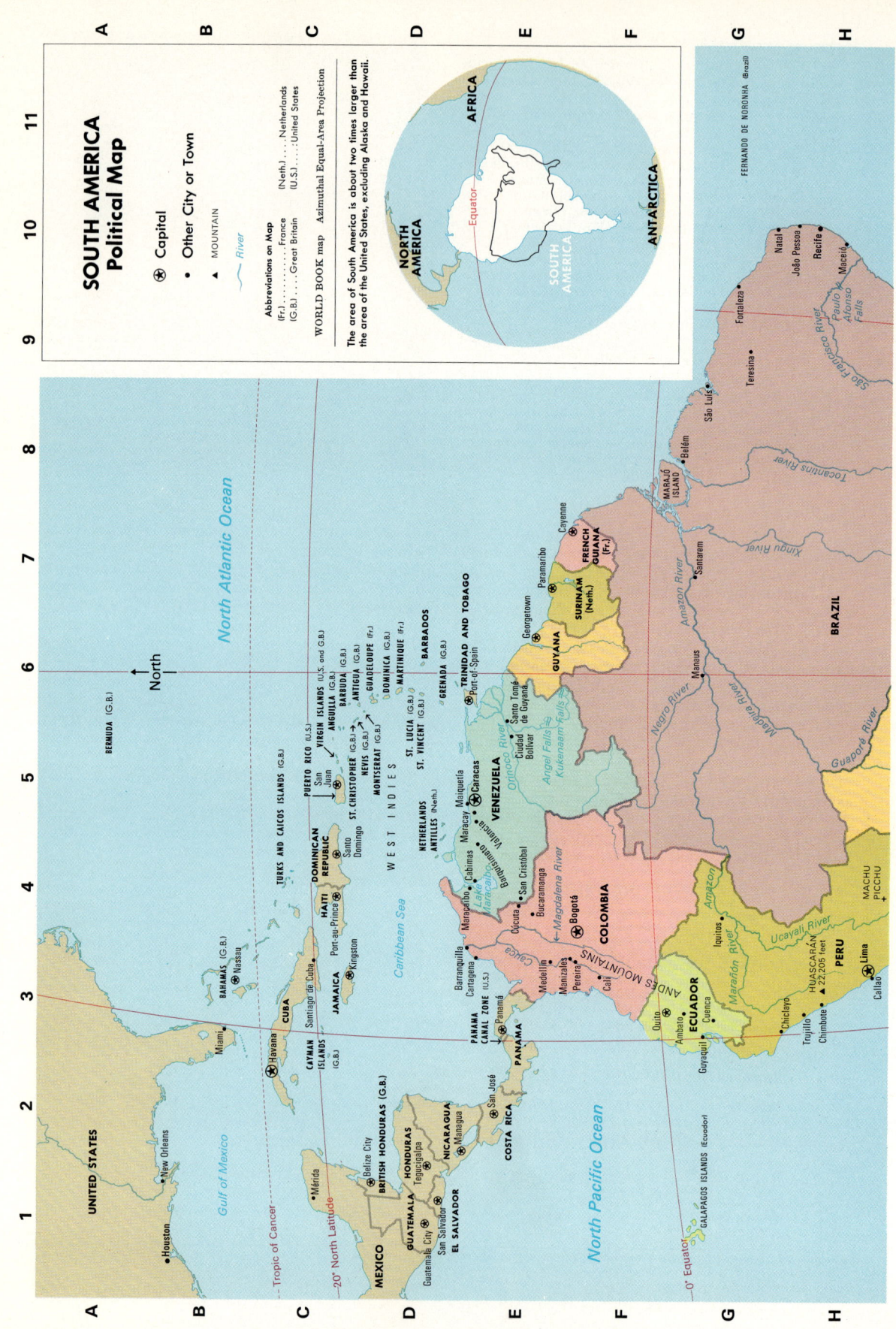

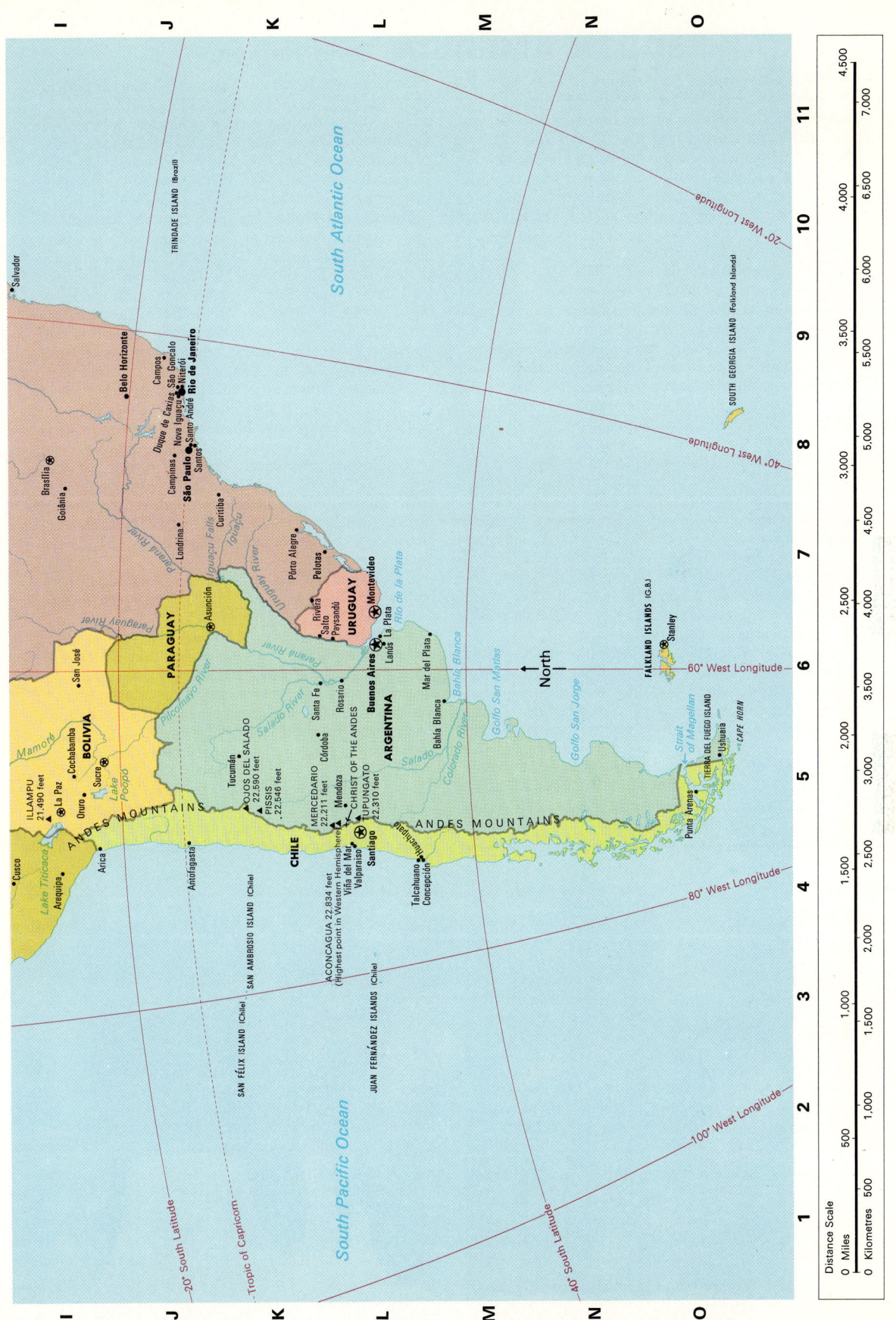

# SOUTH AMERICA / Land Regions

The equator crosses South America near the continent's widest point. More than three-fourths of South America lies in the tropics. From the equator southward, the continent narrows sharply. The southern tip of South America is only about 600 miles from Antarctica.

Oceans surround South America except at its northwest corner, where the narrow Isthmus of Panama links the continent to North America. The Pacific Ocean washes South America's western shores, and the Atlantic Ocean borders the continent on the east. The Caribbean Sea is on the north. The Drake Passage separates South America from Antarctica.

The land surface of South America is much like that of North America. High mountains tower in the west, and low mountains form highlands in the east. Great plains cover most of the central area. South America has four main land regions: (1) the Pacific Coastlands, (2) the Andes Mountains, (3) the Central Plains, and (4) the Eastern Highlands.

**The Pacific Coastlands** lie along the Pacific Ocean, west of the Andes Mountains. Most of the coastlands are less than 50 miles wide, and in some places they are only 5 miles wide. The northern coastlands in Colombia and Ecuador are swampy and covered by tropical forests. In Peru and northern Chile, the coastlands form a desert. In central Chile, the Pacific Coastlands are a fertile area of farms, grazing lands, and forests. Farther south, the seas flow into the valleys to form the Chilean archipelago, a 1,000-mile stretch of stormy fiords and cold, rainy islands.

**The Andes Mountains** rise along the entire western coast of South America. They form the longest mountain range in the world, and only the Himalaya mountains in Asia are higher. More than 50 Andean peaks are higher than 20,000 feet. These include 22,834-foot Mount Aconcagua in Argentina, the highest peak in the Western Hemisphere. Earthquakes often shake parts of the Andes region, and some Andean peaks are active volcanoes. Glaciers move slowly toward the sea in many valleys, especially in the south.

In most places, the Andes region is not more than 200 miles wide. It widens to about 450 miles in Bolivia, and narrows to less than 20 miles in Chile.

In addition to snow-capped peaks and rocky cliffs, the Andes region also has thickly forested slopes, grassy plateaus, and valleys. Andean valleys make up much of Colombia and Venezuela. In Bolivia, a 400-mile-long plateau lies about 12,500 feet above sea level.

**The Central Plains,** east of the Andes Mountains, cover about three-fifths of South America. The plains consist of four large areas: (1) grassy plains called *llanos* in the Orinoco River basin of Colombia and Venezuela; (2) tropical rain forests called *selvas* in the Amazon River basin of Brazil; (3) partly forested scrublands in the Gran Chaco region that lies largely in Argentina and Paraguay; and (4) productive farmlands and ranch lands of Argentina called the *Pampa*.

The South American central plains, unlike those of North America, are largely unproductive. However, the rich soil and temperate climate of the Pampa make it one of the world's largest food-producing regions.

**The Eastern Highlands** consist of mountains that are much lower than the Andes. They resemble the Appalachian Mountains of North America. The Eastern Highlands make up three separate areas: (1) the Guiana Highlands, (2) the Brazilian Highlands, and (3) the Patagonian Plateau.

*The Guiana Highlands* rise along Brazil's northern boundary. They are covered mainly by tropical forests, and are less than 5,000 feet high.

*The Brazilian Highlands,* largest of the three areas, cover eastern Brazil. The mountains that rise steeply along the Atlantic coast include 9,462-foot Pico da Bandeira, the highest point east of the Andes. Inland, the Brazilian Highlands area is generally one of tablelands and rolling hills, sloping away from the coast. Rich mines, coffee plantations, cattle ranches, and two of South America's largest industrial centers—Rio de Janeiro and São Paulo—are located in this area.

*The Patagonian Plateau* forms flat, rocky tablelands in southern Argentina. These tablelands make up one of the world's largest sheep-grazing areas.

Eastern Highlands — Harald Schultz

Pacific Coastlands — Leon V. Kofod

Andes Mountains — Three Lions

Central Plains — FPG

Lake Titicaca — Tom Hollyman, Photo Researchers

Upper Amazon River — Shostal

# SOUTH AMERICA/
## Natural Features

**Rivers.** Five great river systems drain the South American continent: (1) the Amazon; (2) the Río de la Plata system, formed by the Paraná, Paraguay, and Uruguay rivers; (3) the Magdalena-Cauca; (4) the Orinoco; and (5) the São Francisco.

The Amazon drains an area of about 2,400,000 square miles, the largest drainage basin in the world. It rises in the Peruvian Andes and flows 3,900 miles into the Atlantic Ocean. Only the Nile River is longer.

The Río de la Plata system forms the most important inland waterway system in Latin America. It serves Argentina, Bolivia, Brazil, Paraguay, and Uruguay.

The Magdalena and Cauca rivers flow through two long Andean valleys in Colombia. They join, and empty into the Caribbean Sea.

The Orinoco flows along the Colombia-Venezuela border and through the middle of Venezuela to the Atlantic Ocean. More than 400 tributaries give the Orinoco a huge volume of water.

The 1,800-mile-long São Francisco drains the eastern Brazilian highlands.

**Waterfalls.** South America's many waterfalls include two of the highest in the world. Angel Falls, on one of the headwaters of the Caroní River in southeastern Venezuela, drops 3,212 feet. The other great waterfall, Kukenaam Falls in Venezuela, falls about 2,000 feet. Brazil has many smaller waterfalls, including Paulo Afonso Falls on the São Francisco River and Iguaçu Falls on the Brazil-Argentina border. See BRAZIL (color picture).

**Lakes.** South America has few large lakes. The largest is Lake Maracaibo, which covers 6,300 square miles in Venezuela. Lake Titicaca on the Bolivia-Peru border is the highest body of water in the world on which steamships operate. It lies in the Andes, 12,507 feet above sea level, and covers 3,261 square miles.

**Islands.** Several major island groups lie off the coasts of South America. The largest is the Tierra del Fuego group. It is separated from the southern end of the mainland by the stormy Strait of Magellan. Argentina and Chile own these islands. Chile also owns the Juan Fernández Islands, about 400 miles west of the mainland in the Pacific Ocean. The Falkland Islands, about 300 miles east of the Strait of Magellan in the Atlantic Ocean, are a British crown colony. Both Tierra del Fuego and the Falklands have valuable sheep-grazing lands. The Galapagos Islands are South America's principal islands in the Pacific Ocean. They lie 650 miles off Ecuador, which owns them. The Galapagos Islands, once a pirate hideout, have large colonies of lizards, huge turtles, and strange birds. Marajó, a flat, grassy island about the size of Denmark, lies at the mouth of the Amazon River. It is owned by Brazil.

Ushuaia, Tierra del Fuego — Harrison Forman

Angel Falls — Ewing Krainin, Photo Researchers

# SOUTH AMERICA/Climate

Most of South America is warm the year around, except high in the Andes Mountains where the climate is always cold. The lowland area in the widest part of the continent, near the equator, is always hot and humid. The narrow southern part of the continent has cool summers and mild winters. Both the summers and winters are much milder than those of most of North America. The seasons south of the equator are opposite to those of North America—summers last from December to March, and winters are from June to September.

Although South America's climate is warm, temperatures usually do not rise as high as summer temperatures in North America. Even in the tropical lowlands of the Amazon River valley, the temperature generally ranges between 70° and 90° F., and rarely reaches 100° F. South America's hottest weather occurs in the Argentine Gran Chaco. The temperature there climbs above 110° F. at least once a year.

South America has four regions where rainfall averages more than 60 inches a year: (1) the Amazon River valley, (2) the coastal lands of Guyana, French Guiana, and Surinam, (3) the coasts of Colombia and Ecuador, and (4) southwestern Chile.

Rain-bearing winds sweep into South America from both the Atlantic and the Pacific oceans. East of the Andes Mountains, the Atlantic trade winds bring rains to the northern two-thirds of the continent (see TRADE WIND). West of the Andes, in the north, heavy rains drench the coast of Colombia. In the south, the Pacific's moist westerlies keep Chile's central valley well watered in winter. They bring heavy rain to the Chilean archipelago during most of the year.

The cold Peru Current of the Pacific Ocean flows near the continent's southwest coast. It cools the air that blows onto shore at a low level. This cooling of the lower air prevents rain from forming. As a result, the coastal lands in Peru and northern Chile are dry. Cold Atlantic Ocean currents act the same way on the breezes that blow over southeastern South America. As a result the Patagonian Plateau gets little rainfall.

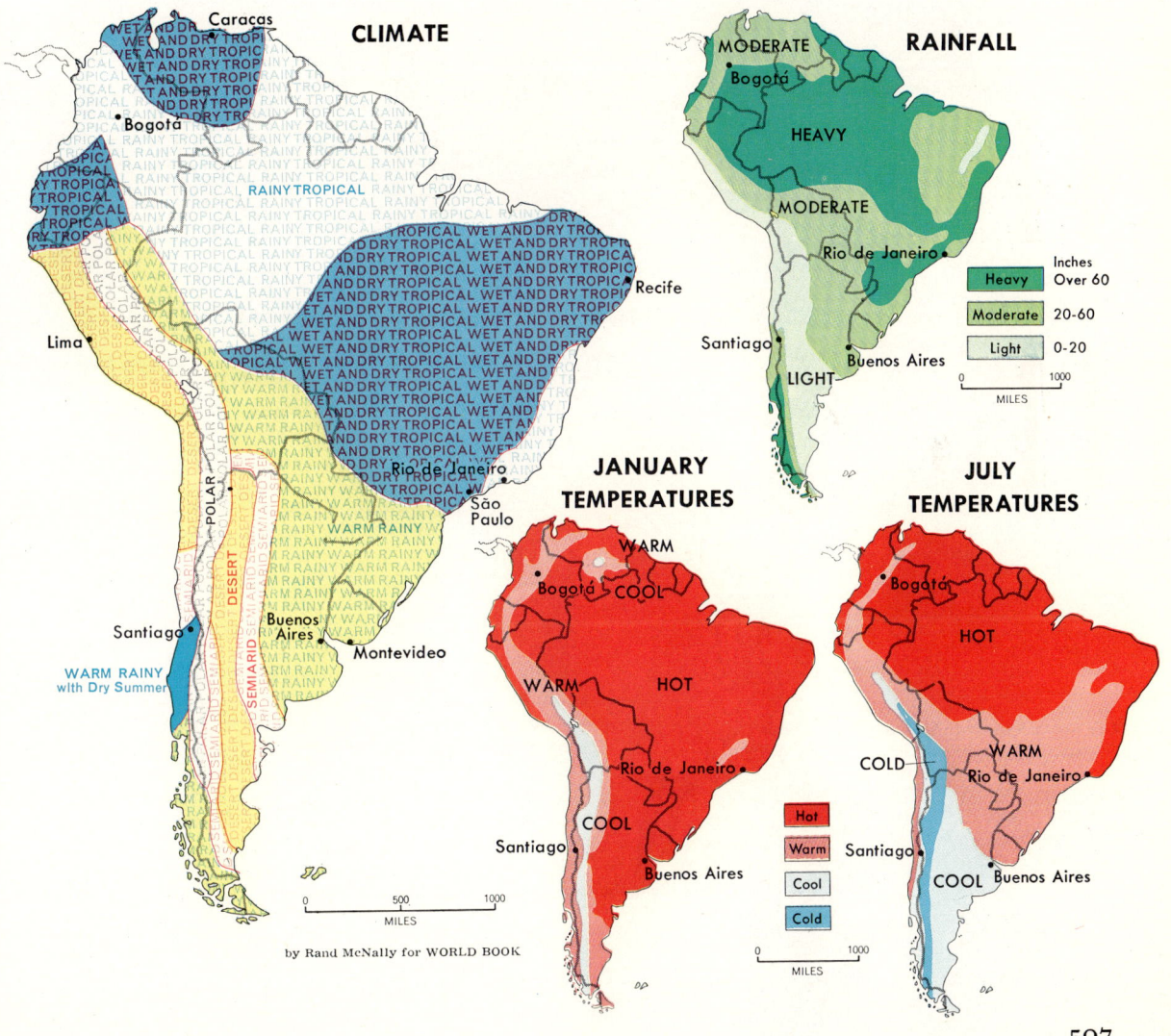

by Rand McNally for WORLD BOOK

507

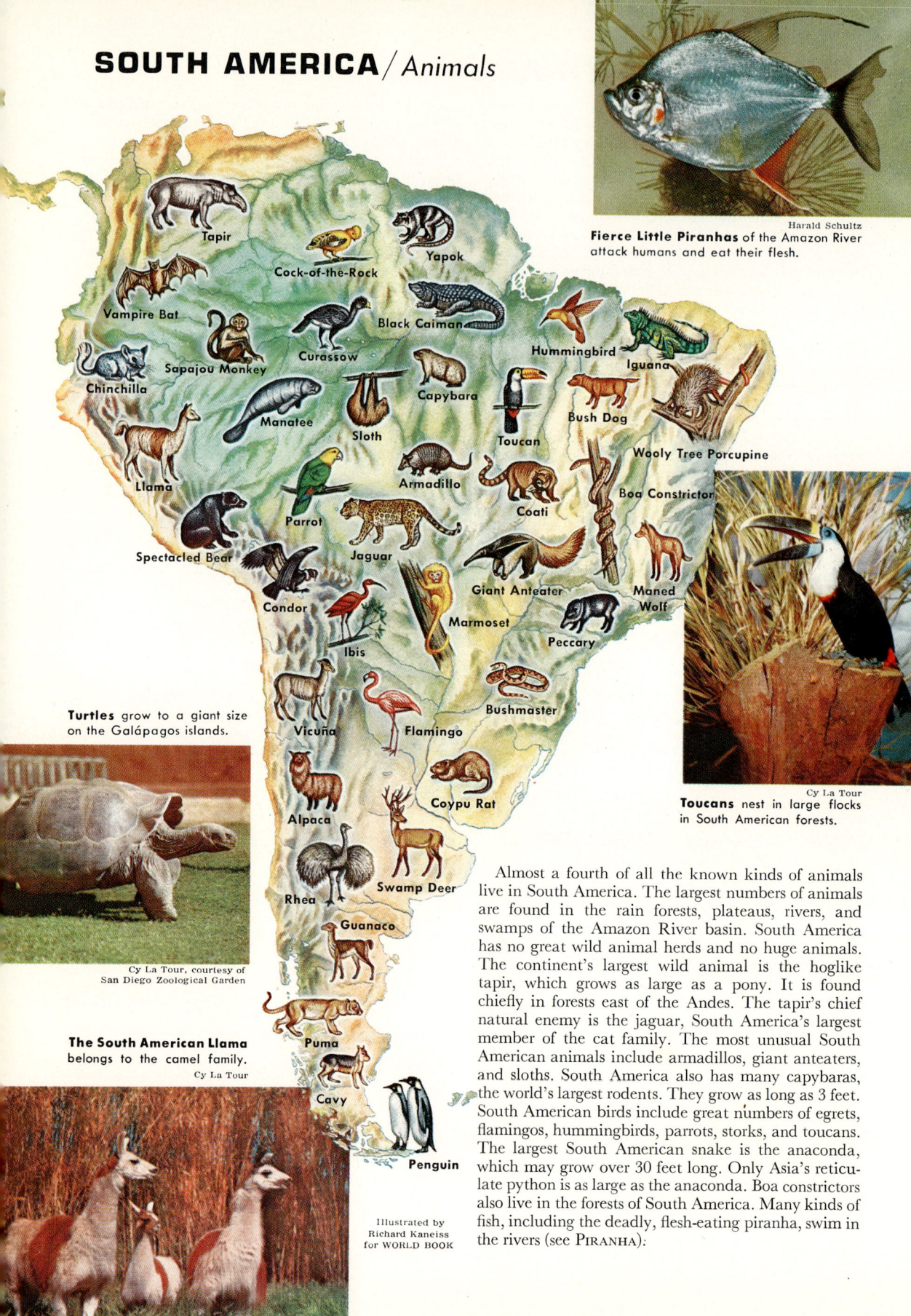

# SOUTH AMERICA/Plants

Orchids of rare beauty grow wild in the South American rain forests.

Tall Tree Ferns are common in the tropical mountain areas.

Brazil-nut Trees grow to 150 feet in height.

Illustrated by Richard Kaneiss for WORLD BOOK

Some kinds of plants that grow in South America cannot be found on any other continent. More than 2,500 kinds of trees grow in the rain forests, and so many varieties of orchids bloom there that they have never been fully counted. The carnauba palm provides valuable lubricating and polishing waxes. The quebracho tree supplies one of the hardest of all woods, a chief source of tannin, used to tan hides and to make inks and dyes. The bark of the cinchona tree is the chief natural source of quinine, a drug used to treat malaria. Many rubber trees grow wild, and South American Indians were the first to discover the use of rubber. The giant among South American plants is the Brazil-nut tree in the Amazon River forests. It grows up to 150 feet tall. Balsa, one of the lightest woods, grows on the northwest coast, mainly in Ecuador. Other important South American trees include mahogany, pine, and rosewood.

# SOUTH AMERICA/Agriculture

More than half the people of South America earn their living on farms or ranches. The average South American farm is small, and barely provides a living for the farm family. Most of the farms produce simple food crops such as beans, cassava, and corn. Most South American farmers still plow the land with ox-drawn plows, plant seeds by hand, and reap small harvests. As a result, food shortages occur frequently.

South America also has some of the world's largest farms, plantations, and ranches. They are owned by wealthy families, and produce such important exports as bananas, beef, coffee, sugar, wheat, and wool. Sharecroppers and hired laborers do the work. The owners let much good farmland lie idle as meadows or as pastures for their riding horses. The largest farms and ranches spread over the plains, plateaus, and valleys of Argentina, Brazil, and Chile. On the broad Pampa in central Argentina, cattle graze on many ranches larger than 100,000 acres each. In southern Argentina's Patagonia region, some sheep ranches cover more than a million acres. Brazil has some plantations as large as the state of Oregon. In Chile's fertile central valley, most of the rich farmland is part of estates that cover about 250,000 acres each.

In most South American countries, government programs have been started to break up large estates into small farms. These land reform programs aim to put much idle land to use and increase food production. However, the landowners must be paid for the land, and the new owners need money to buy seed, fertilizer, and modern machinery. The governments do not have enough money to pay for large-scale land reform programs. The United States has made loans to assist land reform programs in such countries as Argentina, Brazil, Chile, and Venezuela.

A major problem of South America is to find ways of increasing food production to meet the needs of growing populations. Some countries, such as Brazil and Venezuela, operate model farms to show farmers how modern methods can be used to raise larger crops.

B. Newman, Photo Researchers

**Sheep Raising** is a major agricultural industry of South America. Some Argentine ranches in the vast sheep raising region of Patagonia cover more than a million acres. The Peruvian Indians graze their small flocks on many grassy slopes high in the Andes Mountains.

**Bananas** rank among the chief agricultural products of South America. Ecuador exports more bananas than any other country in the world, and Brazil and Colombia are also leading banana exporters. Many of Colombia's bananas are carried in small boats from the plantations to the port of Barranquilla for shipment abroad.
Robert Leahy, Shostal

510

Three Lions

**Modern Machinery** and ancient oxcarts often work side by side on the large farms that produce grains for the world market.

Joe Barnell, Shostal

**Growing Coffee** requires much hand labor. These plantation workers are cultivating trees in the state of São Paulo, Brazil, one of the world's chief coffee-producing areas.

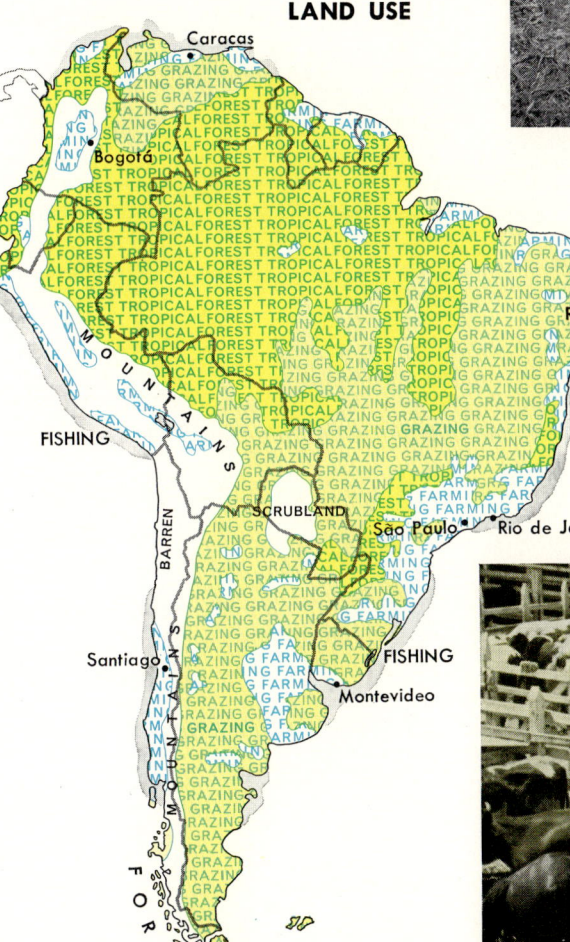

## LAND USE

by Rand McNally for WORLD BOOK

**South American Cattle** are raised on ranches that cover some of the largest grazing lands in the world. Chilled beef is a major export of Argentina and Uruguay.

Authenticated News Int.

# SOUTH AMERICA / Mining

South America has some of the world's largest deposits of minerals. These minerals have made possible the development of important manufacturing industries in Brazil, Chile, Colombia, Peru, Uruguay, and Venezuela. Argentina has relatively few minerals except for petroleum. The large Argentine manufacturing industry is built chiefly around factories that process farm and ranch products. Much of South America's mineral wealth remains untouched in mountainous and tropical regions that are hard to reach. However, mining is the most important industry of Bolivia, Chile, and Venezuela. These countries earn most of their income by selling minerals on the world market.

Petroleum is South America's most valuable export. Most of the petroleum that is exported comes from Venezuela, one of the world's leading petroleum-producing countries. Colombia, Ecuador, and Peru also export some petroleum.

Chile is the world's largest copper-exporting country, and ranks as a leader in total copper production. Chile also exports much iron ore and nitrate. It has the world's only deposits of natural sodium nitrate, used largely for fertilizer.

Some of the world's largest iron ore deposits are in Brazil and Venezuela. Brazilian mines also produce large amounts of bauxite and manganese. Bolivia ranks among the world's leading suppliers of tin, and also exports lead, silver, tungsten, and zinc. Peru is a leading silver producer. Colombia is the largest producer of emeralds in the world. Large bauxite deposits are mined in Surinam and Guyana.

South America, like Africa and Australia, has only small deposits of coal. The only country on the continent in which coal is a chief mining product is Colombia, although Brazil and Chile mine some coal. Most South American countries must import coal to power many of their manufacturing industries. To make up for their small supplies of coal, the larger countries, such as Argentina, Brazil, and Chile, are expanding oil production. They also are building hydroelectric projects.

Fritz Henle, Photo Researchers

**Petroleum** is South America's most valuable export, and Venezuela produces almost all of it. Many oil-pumping derricks operate in Lake Maracaibo.

**Mining** helps support several South American countries. Bolivia supplies the world market with many minerals, such as tin from this mine at San José.

Thorlichen, Black Star

### MINING AND MANUFACTURING

by Rand McNally for WORLD BOOK

510b

# SOUTH AMERICA / Manufacturing

Manufacturing has become an important industry in South America, largely since the 1920's. Its most rapid growth came after World War II. When the war ended, the demand for South America's farm and mine exports fell sharply. The governments of several South American countries, especially Argentina, Brazil, and Chile, helped businessmen start factories to make use of locally produced raw materials. Large American and European companies also were invited to open manufacturing branches in South America. As a result, hundreds of factories now operate, and manufacturing centers have been built in several countries. South America's chief manufactured products are textiles and processed foods, such as canned meats, flour, and refined sugar. However, the output also includes many products which previously were imported from Europe or the United States. Among these products are automobiles, cement, chemicals, drugs, electrical appliances, furniture, glassware, machinery, and paper.

Most South American countries aim to build self-supporting economic systems by further expansion of their manufacturing industries. All the South American countries have large resources of manpower. They are handicapped by a lack of the large amounts of money needed for such development. However, the United States is assisting South America's economic development, largely through the long-range program of the Alliance for Progress (see ALLIANCE FOR PROGRESS).

Authenticated News Int.

**Hydroelectric Dams** supply industrial power in several South American countries that lack large supplies of coal or oil. The Itulinga Dam generates electricity near Rio de Janeiro.

**Manufacturing** has grown rapidly in many South American countries since the end of World War II. Textiles and processed foods make up the chief products of the factories. Chile's Huachipato steel mill is one of the giants of South American heavy industry.

Authenticated News Int.

# SOUTH AMERICA/Transportation and Communication

Both airplanes and oxcarts are common means of transportation in South America. Railroads and good highways serve the large cities. But in most country areas, horses and oxen pull high-wheeled carts over dirt roads. Millions of South Americans who live in those areas have never ridden in an automobile or even seen a railroad train. In fact, most South Americans are accustomed to traveling on foot and carrying heavy burdens on their backs. Vast forest regions of the continent have no roads at all. Where rivers flow in those regions, small boats carry people and goods between the villages. Elsewhere, especially in mountainous areas, pack animals, such as mules or llamas, are used for travel on the rugged trails.

The development of commercial aviation has greatly improved long-distance travel in South America. The airplane solved the problem of crossing high mountains and tropical rain forests that made railroad construction difficult. More than 50 international airlines and many domestic airlines crisscross the continent.

Most of South America's railroads are in Argentina and southeastern Brazil, where many people live. Argentina, with over 27,000 miles of railroads, and Brazil, with over 20,000 miles of railroads, rank among the 10 countries of the world with the greatest railroad mileage. Chile, Colombia, and Uruguay have railroads that connect their important cities. However, much of the equipment on South America's railroads is old and worn, and service on some lines is poor.

Many South American countries are building new highways to keep pace with their growing automobile and truck manufacturing industries. The continent has about 500,000 miles of roads. Only about 30,000 miles of these roads are paved, compared with more than 2 million miles of paved highways in the United States. The Pan American Highway links the countries of South America (see PAN AMERICAN HIGHWAY).

Steamships provide the most important means of commerce between South American countries and the rest of the world. The largest merchant fleets belong to Brazil, which has about 390 ships, and Argentina, with about 320 ships. Chile also has a large merchant marine, and Colombia, Ecuador, Peru, and Venezuela have many ships in coastal trade.

Communication is one of the basic problems in South America. More than half the people cannot read, and most South Americans cannot afford a telephone, radio, or television set. A majority of South Americans must depend for information on what they hear from friends or members of their families. In country areas, the town market place serves as a major communication center. There, the people gather

**Steamships** provide South American countries with their most important means of commerce. Argentina and Brazil operate South America's largest merchant fleets. Many of the continent's major cities are seaports, such as Valparaiso, Chile.

Joe Barnell, Shostal

**The Pan American Highway** links the countries of South America, often slicing through miles of thick forests or swamps. This section of the highway is in Chile.

Pan American Union

510d

George Holton, Photo Researchers

**Small Boats** are common means of transportation in many South American areas where rivers serve as roads. Villagers on the upper Amazon River use boats such as these Peruvian craft at Iquitos.

to talk about local happenings, and to pick up news about national and world events. In the cities, wealthy and middle class people have telephones, radios, and television sets. But even in the cities, many South Americans are too poor to have modern communication devices in their homes.

Argentina and Brazil together publish more books and magazines than all the other countries of South America combined. In most countries, the publications are in Spanish, but those in Brazil are in Portuguese. All the South American countries have radio stations, but there are only about eight radio receivers for every hundred people. Television stations broadcast in Argentina, Brazil, Chile, Colombia, Peru, Uruguay, and Venezuela. But there is only one television set for about every hundred South Americans. PRESTON E. JAMES

Authenticated News Int.

**Railroads** of South America often operate with out-of-date equipment. The old-fashioned trains of this Peruvian line climb more than 15,000 feet to towns nestled in the Andes Mountains.

**Air Transport** has greatly improved long-distance travel in South America. Many airlines crisscross the continent, and all the large cities have modern airports.

Pan American World Airways

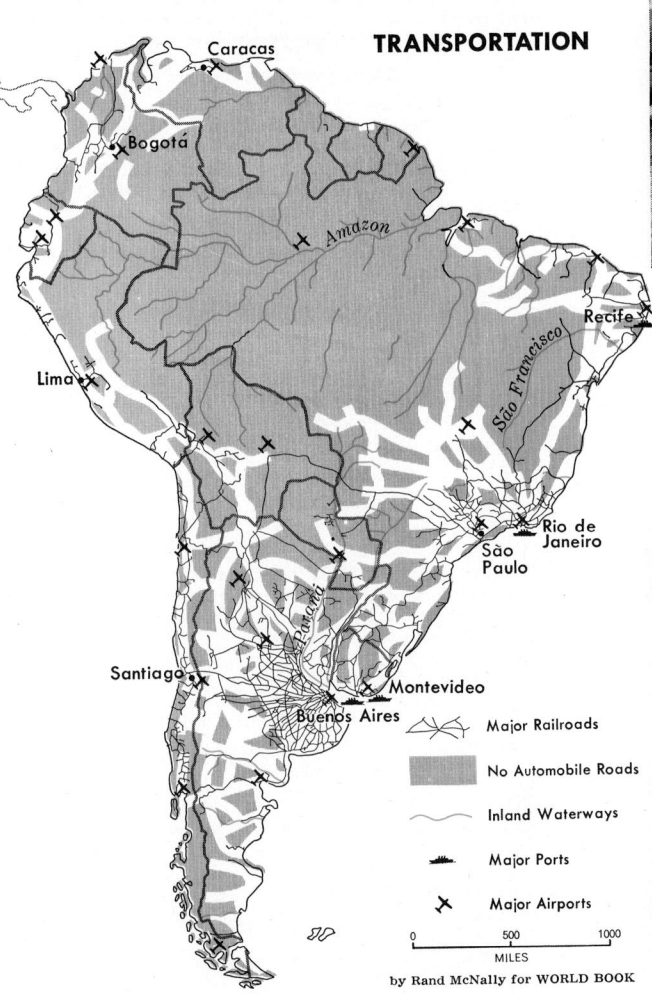

by Rand McNally for WORLD BOOK

510e

# SOUTH AMERICA/Study Aids

**Related Articles** in WORLD BOOK include:

### COUNTRIES

| | | |
|---|---|---|
| Argentina | Colombia | Peru |
| Bolivia | Ecuador | Uruguay |
| Brazil | Guyana | Venezuela |
| Chile | Paraguay | |

### COLONIES AND TERRITORIES

Falkland Islands  
French Guiana  
Surinam

### CITIES

See the following articles on the 12 largest cities of South America:

| | | |
|---|---|---|
| Belo Horizonte | Lima | Rio de Janeiro |
| Bogotá | Montevideo | Salvador |
| Buenos Aires | Pôrto Alegre | Santiago |
| Caracas | Recife | São Paulo |

### ISLANDS

Galapagos Islands  
Juan Fernández  
Marajó  
Tierra del Fuego

### MOUNTAINS

| | | |
|---|---|---|
| Aconcagua | Cotopaxi | Illimani |
| Andes Mountains | El Misti | Ojos del Salado |
| Chimborazo | Huascarán | Pichincha |
| Cordillera | Illampu | |

### PLAINS AND DESERTS

| | | |
|---|---|---|
| Atacama Desert | Llanos | Patagonia |
| Gran Chaco | Pampa | |

### PRODUCTS

| | | | |
|---|---|---|---|
| Balsa | Copper | Maté | Silver |
| Banana | Corn | Nitrate | Sugar |
| Bauxite | Cotton | Petroleum | Tin |
| Cacao | Emerald | Quebracho | Wheat |
| Cattle | Guano | Rubber | Wool |
| Coffee | Manganese | | |

### RIVERS, LAKES, AND WATERFALLS

| | | |
|---|---|---|
| Amazon River | Lake Titicaca | Río de la Plata |
| Angel Falls | Madeira River | Rio Negro |
| Araguaia River | Magdalena River | Roraima Falls |
| Iguaçu River | Marina Falls | São Francisco, Rio |
| King George VI Falls | Orinoco River | Tapajós River |
| | Paraguay River | Tocantins River |
| Kukenaam Falls | Paraná River | Uruguay River |
| Lake Maracaibo | Purús River | |

### OTHER RELATED ARTICLES

Alliance for Progress  
Cape Horn  
Clothing (color pictures: Latin America)  
El Dorado  
Gaucho  
Indian, American  
Latin America  
Magellan, Strait of  
Pan American Conferences  
Pan American Highway  
Pan American Union  
Pan Americanism  
Panama, Isthmus of  
Selva  
Woman (In South America)

### Outline

**I. Land Regions**
  A. The Pacific Coastlands
  B. The Andes Mountains
  C. The Central Plains
  D. The Eastern Highlands

**II. Natural Features**
  A. Rivers
  B. Waterfalls
  C. Lakes
  D. Islands

**III. Climate**

**IV. Animals**

**V. Plants**

**VI. Agriculture**

**VII. Mining**

**VIII. Manufacturing**

**IX. Transportation and Communication**

### Questions

What are the major causes of food shortages in South American countries?

What South American plain is one of the world's largest food-producing regions? Why?

How is the land surface of South America like that of North America?

What is South America's most valuable export? Which country leads in its production?

How are Argentina, Brazil, and Chile making up for their lack of extensive coal deposits?

Where are most South American railroads?

How do most South Americans in country areas learn about world events?

Why is there little rainfall on the coasts of Peru and northern Chile? What are some of the areas of South America that have heavy rainfall?

Which South American country has the largest area? The smallest area?

When did manufacturing in South America have its most rapid growth? How did the governments of South America aid manufacturing development?

### Books for Young Readers

BRO, MARGUERITTE H. *Three, and Domingo.* Doubleday, 1953. A beautifully written tale of a dog, a goat, and a burro that go to church with their young master on Christmas Eve in a little Brazilian village.

CARTER, WILLIAM E. *The First Book of South America.* Watts, 1961. Brief history, geography, and present-day life of each country.

CLARK, ANN N. *The Secret of the Andes.* Viking, 1952. Story of an Indian boy of Peru. Newbery medal winner.

FIDELER, RAYMOND and KVANDE, CAROL. *South America.* Fideler, 1963.

GOETZ, DELIA. *Neighbors to the South,* Rev. ed. Harcourt, 1956. Describes the customs, geography, and people of each Central and South American country.

QUINN, VERNON. *Picture Map Geography of South America.* Lippincott, 1941.

### Books for Older Readers

BAKER, NINA B. *He Wouldn't Be King: The Story of Simón Bolívar.* Vanguard, 1941.

FAWCETT, PERCY H. *Lost Trails, Lost Cities.* Funk, 1953. Photographs illustrate this realistic journal of exploration in South American jungles.

JAMES, PRESTON E. *Latin America.* 3rd ed. Odyssey, 1959.

KANE, ROBERT S. *South America, A to Z.* Doubleday, 1962. Practical information on each of the South American countries, colonies, and territories.

NEVINS, ALBERT J. *Away to the Lands of the Andes; Colombia, Ecuador, Peru, Bolivia, Chile.* Dodd, 1962. Descriptions of the countries in terms of climate, geography, government, history, and people.

PECK, ANNE M. *The Pageant of South American History.* 3rd ed. McKay, 1962.

SHIPPEN, KATHARINE B. *New Found World.* Viking, 1945.

*The South American Handbook.* Rand McNally, published annually. Information and travel guide.

VON HAGEN, VICTOR W. *Sun Kingdom of the Aztecs.* World Publishing Co., 1958. *Maya, Land of the Turkey and the Deer.* 1960. *The Incas, People of the Sun.* 1961. A trilogy of cultures in the Americas before the white man came to the region.

**SOUTH AMERICAN OSTRICH.** See Rhea (bird).

**SOUTH ARABIA, FEDERATION OF,** was a union of 17 small states at the southern tip of the Arabian Peninsula. It included the British-protected state of Aden; the state of Dathina; the emirates of Beihan and Dhala; the sultanates of Audhali, Fadhli, Haushabi, Lahej, Lower Aulaqi, Lower Yafa, Upper Aulaqi, and Wahidi; and the sheikdoms of Alawi, Aqrabi, Mufhahi, Shaibi, and Upper Aulaqi. The federation covered 60,000 square miles. Great Britain controlled the federation's foreign affairs and defense, and provided economic assistance.

The union was once called the Federation of the Arab Emirates of the South. It was formed in 1959 by six of the states. By 1965, the other 11 states had joined. On Nov. 30, 1967, the federation gained independence as the People's Republic of Southern Yemen (see Southern Yemen).

**SOUTH AUSTRALIA** is a state in south-central Australia. It faces the Indian Ocean and the Great Australian Bight. South Australia extends about 800 miles into the continent. For detailed maps, see Australia.

The state covers an area of 380,070 square miles. Much of its land lies from 1,000 to 2,000 feet above sea level. The Gawler and Flinders mountain ranges rise in the south. The Adelaide and southeastern coastal regions include fertile lands. The Musgrave mountain ranges are in the north. Wheat farms and rolling plains stretch between the northern ranges. The north also has flat sheep-grazing lands. Sandy deserts extend into the center of the state from the north. The *Nullarbor* (treeless) Plain covers much of the western section.

The Murray River is the continent's largest waterway. The Murray rises near the eastern border of Victoria and flows for 1,520 miles before it empties into the Indian Ocean near Adelaide (see Murray River). A number of smaller rivers flow into Lake Eyre, which lies in the northeastern section of South Australia.

South Australia's yearly temperature averages around 70° F. Less than 10 inches of rain falls annually in all but the southern part of the state.

The state has excellent farming and grazing lands. Shallow lakes produce great quantities of salt. The eastern mountains have deposits of gypsum, ironstone, limestone, manganese ore, opals, and phosphate rock.

**The People.** South Australia has a population of 1,125,212, including about 5,500 aborigines. Two out of three persons live in the Adelaide metropolitan area. Other cities and towns include Elizabeth, Mount Gambier, Port Augusta, Port Lincoln, Port Pirie, Reynella-Port Noarlunga, Salisbury, and Whyalla. Most of the people are of British descent.

Education is free and compulsory for children under 14 years of age. Adelaide has a state university and a state school of mines and industries. Flinders University at Bedford Park opened in 1966.

In the southern and eastern sections, people produce large crops of barley, hay, oats, potatoes, and wheat. The Murray River irrigates miles of orchards, orange groves, and vineyards. About $16\frac{1}{2}$ million sheep and 660,000 cattle graze there. The state produces over 173 million pounds of wool annually. Exports include butter, copper, flour, fruits, meats, wheat, wine, and wool.

Industrial products include automobile bodies, chemicals, cotton and woolen goods, electrical equipment, and sheet metal. Mining and quarrying are important. Uranium mining began during World War II.

The state has about 3,900 miles of railroads and over 62,000 miles of roads. Port Pirie is the chief port.

**Government.** The British ruler appoints a governor for the state on the recommendation of the South Australian Parliament. But a premier actually heads the government. The South Australian legislature consists of a 20-member upper house and a 39-member lower house. The voters elect members of the upper house to six-year terms, and members of the lower house to three-year terms. They also elect 22 members to the Australian Parliament in Canberra. All adult British subjects who live in the state must vote in elections.

**History.** Matthew Flinders, a British navigator, made the first extensive explorations along the South Australian coast about 1802. In 1836, British settlers founded the first settlement in the area at Adelaide. The discovery of gold in the neighboring colony of Victoria in 1851 brought many new settlers to South Australia. In 1856, South Australians won the right to govern themselves. South Australia joined with five other Australian colonies to form the Commonwealth of Australia in 1901.  C. M. H. Clark

See also Adelaide; Great Australian Bight; Lake Eyre.

**SOUTH BEND,** Ind. (pop. 132,445; met. area 271,057; alt. 710 ft.), is one of the largest cities in the state. This industrial center lies in north-central Indiana, 90 miles east and slightly south of Chicago. It is named for its location at the southernmost point of the Indiana bend in the St. Joseph River (see Indiana [political map]). South Bend factories make farm machinery and tools, and automobile and airplane brakes and equipment.

The University of Notre Dame and Saint Mary's College are located near South Bend. Bethel College and a branch of Indiana University are also nearby.

In 1823, Alexis Coquillard, a fur trader, founded South Bend. He called it Big St. Joseph Station. The name was later changed to South Bend. The village was incorporated in 1835, and became a city in 1865. It has a mayor-council government.  Paul E. Million, Jr.

See also Notre Dame, University of.

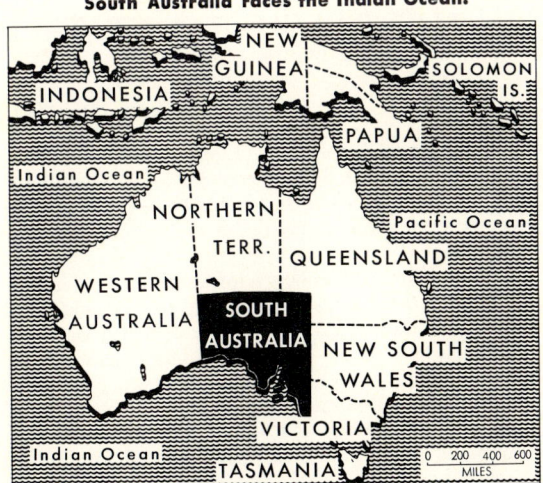

**South Australia Faces the Indian Ocean.**

511

Louis Schwartz
**Stately Homes in Historic Charleston**

# SOUTH CAROLINA  THE PALMETTO STATE

**SOUTH CAROLINA** is the smallest state in the Deep South. In spite of its size, South Carolina is an important manufacturing and farming state. South Carolina factories produce large amounts of a wide variety of textiles. Among all the states, only North Carolina makes more textiles than South Carolina. South Carolina raises one of the nation's largest tobacco crops, and only California grows more peaches. Columbia is the capital and largest city of South Carolina.

More than half the people of South Carolina live in farm areas, even though manufacturing is the state's chief economic activity. South Carolina still has many features of the South of pre-Civil War days. Graceful buildings erected before the war stand in Beaufort, Charleston, and other cities. Large plantations, once the backbone of the South's economy, remain in parts of South Carolina. The state's many beautiful flower gardens recall the leisurely life of the South before the Civil War.

Eastern South Carolina is a lowland that borders the Atlantic Ocean. In the west, the land rises to sand hills, and then to mountains. The people of South Carolina call the eastern part of the state the *Low Country*. They call the western section the *Up Country*.

South Carolina was named for King Charles I of England, in 1629. *Carolina* is a Latin form of *Charles*. The word *South* was added in 1730, when North and South Carolina became separate colonies.

512

Lake and Table Rock near the Blue Ridge Mountains
*Tom Hollyman, Photo Researchers*

Palmetto Trees Along the Atlantic Coast
*Louis Schwartz*

## FACTS IN BRIEF

**Capital:** Columbia.

**Government:** *Congress*—U.S. Senators, 2; U.S. Representatives, 6. *Electoral Votes*—8. *State Legislature*—senators, 46; representatives, 124. *Counties*—46. *Voting Age*—21 years.

**Area:** 31,055 square miles (including 783 square miles of inland water), 40th in size among the states. *Greatest Distances*—(east-west), 273 miles; (north-south), 210 miles. *Coastline*—187 miles.

**Elevation:** *Highest*—Sassafras Mountain, 3,560 feet above sea level. *Lowest*—sea level along the Atlantic Coast.

**Population:** *1960 Census*—2,382,594, 26th among the states; density, 77 persons to the square mile; distribution, 59 per cent rural, 41 per cent urban. *Estimated 1965 Population*—2,494,000.

**Chief Products:** *Manufacturing*—chemicals, clothing, paper and paper products, textiles. *Agriculture*—beef cattle, chickens, corn, cotton, dairy products, eggs, hogs, peaches, soybeans, tobacco. *Mining*—kaolin and other clays, sand and gravel, stone. *Fishing Industry*—crabs, oysters, shrimps.

**Statehood:** May 23, 1788, the eighth state.

**State Mottoes:** *Animis opibusque parati* (Prepared in mind and resources); *Dum spiro spero* (While I breathe, I hope).

**State Song:** "Carolina." Words by Henry Timrod; music by Anne Custis Burgess.

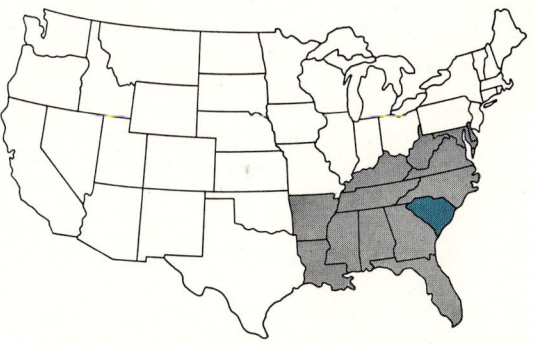

**South Carolina** (blue) ranks 40th in size among all the states and 11th in size among the Southern States (gray).

Many important Revolutionary War battles were fought in South Carolina. Colonial victories in the Battle of Kings Mountain and the Battle of Cowpens were turning points of the war in the South. South Carolina may have earned its nickname, the *Palmetto State*, during the war. In 1776, colonists in a small fort built of palmetto logs defeated a British fleet that tried to capture Charleston Harbor. The next day, William Moultrie, the colonial commander, saw a column of smoke rising from a burning British ship. The shape of the smoke reminded Moultrie of the palmetto tree, which grows widely in South Carolina. These events supposedly gave South Carolina its nickname.

South Carolina was the first state to *secede* (withdraw) from the Union before the Civil War. It did so on Dec. 20, 1860. Confederate troops fired the first shot of the Civil War when they attacked Fort Sumter in Charleston Harbor on April 12, 1861.

For the relationship of South Carolina to other states in its region, see SOUTHERN STATES.

---

*The contributors of this article are Donald O. Bushman, Associate Professor of Geography at the University of South Carolina; Ernest M. Lander, Jr., Professor of History and Government at Clemson University; and William D. Workman, Jr., Editor of* The State *of Columbia, and author of* The Case for the South.

# SOUTH CAROLINA / Government

**Constitution** of South Carolina was adopted in 1895. The state's six earlier constitutions were adopted in 1776, 1778, 1790, 1861, 1865, and 1868.

The constitution has been *amended* (changed) about 350 times. The state legislature or a constitutional convention may propose an amendment. An amendment proposed by the legislature requires approval by two-thirds of the members of both the Senate and House of Representatives. Next, it needs the approval of a majority of the persons voting on it in a state-wide election. To become law, the amendment must then be approved by a majority of members of the state legislature.

A two-thirds vote in each house of the legislature is required to call a constitutional convention. The convention also must be approved by a majority of the persons voting on the issue in a state-wide election.

**Executive.** The governor of South Carolina is elected to a four-year term. He receives a $25,000 yearly salary. The governor may not serve two terms in a row. He is the state's only elected executive official who cannot serve consecutive terms. For a list of all the governors of South Carolina, see the *History* section of this article.

South Carolina voters also elect the lieutenant governor, adjutant general, attorney general, commissioner of agriculture, comptroller general, secretary of state, state treasurer, and superintendent of education. All these officials serve four-year terms.

**Legislature,** called the *General Assembly*, consists of a 46-member Senate and a 124-member House of Representatives. Voters in 20 senatorial districts elect from 1 to 5 senators, depending on population. Voters in each of the state's 46 counties elect from 1 to 11 representatives, depending on population. Senators serve four-year terms, and representatives two-year terms.

Until the mid-1960's, one senator was elected from each of the state's 46 counties. In 1965, a special federal court ordered the legislature to *reapportion* (redivide) the Senate to provide equal representation based on population. The court approved a temporary plan for the 1966 elections, and all senators were elected to two-year terms. In 1968, the court approved the legislature's plan of electing 46 senators from 20 districts. The plan went into effect in the 1968 elections.

The legislature meets each year, starting on the second Tuesday in January. Sessions have no time limit, but the legislators are paid for only 40 working days. The governor may call special sessions.

**Courts.** The Supreme Court is South Carolina's highest court. It is a court of appeals, and has a chief justice and four associate justices. The justices are elected by the legislature to 10-year terms. Circuit courts of common pleas and general sessions are the chief trial courts. The legislature elects the state's 16 circuit court judges to four-year terms. Supreme court and circuit court members are usually chosen from the legislature.

Magistrates' courts hear minor civil and criminal cases. The magistrates who head the courts are appointed by the governor. Voters elect probate court judges. Twelve counties have special courts that hear circuit court cases. These courts lighten the workload of the circuit courts. Nine counties have juvenile courts.

**Local Government.** In theory, boards of county commissioners or similar local boards head each county government. In practice, *county delegations* usually control the governments. A county delegation consists of the legislators who represent the county in the legislature. It makes laws for the county, but the legislature must approve the laws. County commissioners and their assistants carry out government functions such as enforcing laws and regulating taxes. County officials include the county attorney, auditor, court clerk, coroner, sheriff, supervisor, and treasurer.

South Carolina cities and towns operate under charters granted by the state legislature. They cannot change their charters without the legislature's approval. Most of the cities have the mayor-council form of government, but some have the city-manager form.

**Taxation** provides about three-fourths of the state government's income. Almost all the rest comes from federal grants and other U.S. government programs. A 3 per cent general sales and use tax provides more than 30 per cent of the state's tax income. A *use tax* is a tax on goods brought into the state from another state. An individual income tax brings in about 20 per cent of

**Governor's House,** built in 1856, was once part of a state military school. It has been the governor's residence since 1879.
South Carolina State Development Board

**Statue of John C. Calhoun,** Vice-President and U.S. senator, stands in the lobby of the South Carolina Capitol.
South Carolina State Development Board

514

**The State Seal**

**Symbols of South Carolina.** On the seal, a palmetto tree towers over an uprooted oak. The palmetto symbolizes the successful defense in 1776 of the palmetto-log fort on Sullivan's Island against the oaken ships of the British. The figure of Hope carrying a laurel branch across a sword-covered beach represents the wish to remain forever independent. The seal was authorized in 1776. The state flag, adopted in 1777, also bears a palmetto, the state tree.

Flag, bird, and flower illustrations, courtesy Eli Lilly and Company

**The State Flag**

**The State Bird**
Carolina Wren

South Carolina's tax income. A gasoline tax also accounts for about 20 per cent. Funds from the gasoline tax are used to build and maintain highways.

**Politics.** The Democratic party has controlled South Carolina politics throughout most of the state's history. South Carolina's only Republican governors served during the Reconstruction period, from 1868 to 1877. In presidential elections since 1880, only three non-Democratic presidential candidates have won South Carolina's electoral votes. They were Strom Thurmond of South Carolina, the States' Rights Democratic (Dixiecrat) Party candidate in 1948; Senator Barry M. Goldwater of Arizona, a Republican, in 1964; and Richard M. Nixon, a Republican, in 1968. For South Carolina's voting record in presidential elections, see ELECTORAL COLLEGE (table).

The Republican party gained much strength in South Carolina during the 1950's and 1960's. In 1964, Senator Strom Thurmond of South Carolina resigned from the Democratic party and became a Republican.

**The State Flower**
Carolina Jessamine

**State Capitol** is in Columbia, which has been South Carolina's capital since 1790. Charleston was the capital from 1670 to 1790.

Ellis Sawyer, FPG

**The State Tree**
Palmetto

# SOUTH CAROLINA MAP INDEX

## Population

| | |
|---|---|
| 2,494,000 | Estimate 1965 |
| 2,382,594 | 1960 |
| 2,117,027 | 1950 |
| 1,899,804 | 1940 |
| 1,738,765 | 1930 |
| 1,683,724 | 1920 |
| 1,515,400 | 1910 |
| 1,340,316 | 1900 |
| 1,151,149 | 1890 |
| 995,577 | 1880 |
| 705,606 | 1870 |
| 703,708 | 1860 |
| 668,507 | 1850 |
| 594,398 | 1840 |
| 581,185 | 1830 |
| 502,741 | 1820 |
| 415,115 | 1810 |
| 345,591 | 1800 |
| 249,073 | 1790 |

## Metropolitan Areas

Charleston ......254,578
Columbia ......260,828
Greenville ......255,806

## Counties

Abbeville ..21,417..C 3
Aiken ..81,038..D 5
Allendale ..11,362..E 6
Anderson ..98,478..B 3
Bamberg ..16,274..E 6
Barnwell ..17,659..E 6
Beaufort ..44,187..G 7
Berkeley ..38,196..E 9
Calhoun ..12,256..D 7
Charleston 216,382..F 9
Cherokee ..35,205..A 5
Chester ..30,888..B 5
Chesterfield 33,717..B 8
Clarendon ..29,490..D 8
Colleton ..27,816..F 7
Darlington ..52,928..C 9
Dillon ..30,584..C 10
Dorchester ..24,383..E 8
Edgefield ..15,735..D 5
Fairfield ..20,713..C 6
Florence ..84,438..C 9
Georgetown 34,798..E 10
Greenville 209,776..B 4
Greenwood ..44,346..C 4
Hampton ..17,425..F 7
Horry ..68,247..D 10
Jasper ..12,237..F 6
Kershaw ..33,585..C 7
Lancaster ..39,352..B 7
Laurens ..47,609..C 4
Lee ..21,832..C 8
Lexington ..60,726..D 6
Marion ..32,014..C 10
Marlboro ..28,529..B 9
McCormick ..8,629..D 4
Newberry ..29,416..C 5
Oconee ..36,238..B 2
Orangeburg 68,559..E 7
Pickens ..49,996..B 3
Richland ..200,102..D 7
Saluda ..14,554..C 5
Spartan-
burg ..156,830..B 4
Sumter ..74,941..D 8
Union ..30,015..B 5
Williams-
burg ..40,932..D 9
York ..78,760..A 6

## Cities and Towns

Abbeville ..5,436.°C 4
Adams Run ..350..G 8
Adamsburg ..150..B 5
Aiken ..11,243.°D 5
Aiken South* ..2,980..D 5
Aiken West* ..2,602..D 5
Alcolu ..600..D 8
Allendale ..3,114.°E 6
Alvin ..100..E 9
Anderson ..41,316.°B 3
Andrews ..2,995..E 9
Angelus ..40..B 8
Appleton ..50..E 6
Aragon Mills* ..650..B 6
Arcadia ..2,000..B 5
Arcadia Lakes* ..316..C 6
Ardincaple* ..729..C 6
Arial (Ariail) ..950..B 3
Arkwright* ..1,656..B 6
Arlington ..500..B 4
Arthur ..D 6
Arthurtown* ..200..D 7
Ashepoo ..200..F 7
Ashley
Phosphate ..100..F 8
Ashton ..75..F 7
Atlantic Beach ..40..D 11
Awendaw ..150..E 9
Aynor ..635..D 10
Baldwin Mills
(Baldwin) ..1,201..B 6

Ballentine ..350..C 6
Bamberg ..3,081.°E 6
Barksdale ..45..B 4
Barnwell ..4,568.°E 6
Batesburg ..3,806..D 5
Bath ..1,419..C 5
Bay View* ..600..C 6
Beaufort ..6,298.°G 7
Beckhamville ..325..B 6
Beech Island ..900..E 5
Belton ..5,106..B 3
Belvedere ..2,000..D 5
Ben Avon* ..200..B 5
Bendale ..1,544..E 7
Bennettsville 6,963.°B 9
Bennettsville
Southwest* 1,022..B 9
Berea ..1,000..B 3
Bethera ..165..E 9
Bethune ..579..C 8
Bingham ..95..C 9
Bishopville ..3,586.°C 8
Blacksburg ..2,174..A 5
Blackstock ..100..B 6
Blackville ..1,901..E 6
Blair ..50..C 6
Blair Mills ..80..B 3
Blaney ..329..C 7
Blenheim ..185..B 9
Bluffton ..356..G 7
Blythewood ..250..C 7
Bon Air
Terrace ..150..D 8
Bonneau ..402..E 9
Borden ..50..C 7
Bowling Green 700..A 6
Bowman ..1,106..E 7
Boykin ..50..C 7
Bradley ..140..C 4
Branchville ..1,182..E 7
Brandon ..2,200..B 4
Brunson ..603..F 6
Bucksport ..600..D 10
Buffalo ..1,209..B 5
Burgess ..25..D 10
Burnettown ..510..D 5
Burton ..300..G 7
Cades ..150..D 9
Calhoun
Falls ..2,525..C 3
Callison ..60..C 4
Camden ..6,842.°C 7
Cameron ..607..D 7
Campobello ..420..A 4
Canadys ..200..E 7
Carlisle ..390..B 6
Cartersville ..160..C 8
Cassatt ..100..C 8
Cateechee ..450..B 3
Cayce ..9,490..D 6
Cedar
Terrace* ..1,000..C 6
Celriver ..255..B 7
Centenary ..150..C 10
Centerville ..1,000..F 4
Central ..1,473..B 3
Central
Pacolet* ..333..B 5
Chapin ..358..C 6
Chappells ..128..C 5
Charleston ..75,940.°F 9
Charleston
Heights ..25,000..F 9
Cheddar ..500..B 3
Cheraw ..5,171..B 9
Cherokee Falls 325..A 5
Cherry Grove
Beach ..208..D 11
Chesnee ..1,045..A 5
Chester ..6,906.°B 6
Chesterfield ..1,532.°B 8
City View* ..2,475..B 3
Claremont ..D 7
Clarks Hill ..25..D 4
Clearwater ..1,450..D 5
Clemson ..1,587..B 3
Clemson
College ..4,600..B 3
Cleveland ..200..A 3
Clifton ..1,249..B 5
Clinton ..7,937..C 5
Clio ..847..B 9
Clover ..3,500..A 6
Cokesbury ..100..C 4
College
Heights ..1,330..C 8
Columbia ..97,433.°C 6
Conestee ..750..B 4
Converse ..300..B 5
Conway ..8,563.°D 10
Coosawhatchie 400..F 7
Cope ..227..E 6
Cordesville ..500..E 9
Cordova ..209..E 7
Cornwell ..100..B 6
Coronaca ..200..C 4
Cottageville ..520..F 8
Coward ..552..D 9
Cowpens ..2,038..A 5
Crescent
Beach ..440..D 11
Creston ..40..D 7
Crocketville ..75..F 6
Cross ..100..E 8

Cross Anchor ..300..B 5
Cross Hill ..441..C 5
Cummings ..150..F 6
Dacusville ..25..B 3
Dale ..100..F 7
Dalzell ..300..C 8
Darlington ..6,710.°C 9
Daufuskie
Island ..130..G 7
Davis Station 150..D 8
Delphia ..B 5
Delta ..50..B 9
Denmark ..3,221..E 6
Denny
Terrace* ..3,000..D 6
Dents ..C 7
Dillon ..6,173.°C 10
Dinkins ..70..D 8
Dixiana ..150..D 6
Donalds ..416..C 4
Doneraile ..1,043..C 8
Dorchester ..350..E 8
Douglass ..C 6
Dovesville ..250..C 9
Drake ..C 9
Drayton ..1,128..B 5
Du Bose Park* 760..C 7
Due West ..1,166..C 4
Dunbar ..50..B 9
Duncan ..1,186..B 4
Dunean* ..3,000..B 4
Dunwegan ..160..D 10
Dupont ..4,000..F 3
Dutch Fork* ..900..C 6
Early Branch ..50..F 7
Easley ..8,283..B 3
East Gaffney 4,779..A 5
Eastover ..713..D 7
Edgefield ..2,876.°D 5
Edgemoor ..275..B 6
Edisto
Island ..30..F 8
Effingham ..200..C 9
Ehrhardt ..482..E 6
Elgin ..300..B 7
Elko ..194..E 6
Elliott ..475..C 8
Elloree ..1,031..D 7
Enoree ..825..B 5
Estill ..1,865..F 6
Eureka ..75..D 5
Eureka, see
Hemlock
Eutawville ..468..E 8
Evergreen ..150..C 9
Fair Play ..260..B 3
Fairfax ..1,814..F 6
Fairforest* ..950..B 4
Fairmont ..350..B 4
Filbert ..225..A 6
Fingerville ..300..A 5
Florence ..27,208.°C 9
Floyd Dale ..200..C 10
Folly Beach ..1,137..F 9
Forest Acres 5,894..C 7
Forest Lake* ..243..C 7
Forest View* 1,000..B 4
Foreston ..200..D 8
Fork ..100..C 10
Fork Shoals ..250..B 4
Fort Fremont ..200..G 7
Fort Lawn ..192..B 7
Fort Mill ..3,315..A 7
Fort Motte ..150..D 7
Fountain Inn 2,385..B 4
Four Holes ..150..E 8
Frogmore ..30..G 7
Furman ..244..F 6
Furman
University* 2,000..B 4
Gable ..120..D 8
Gadsden ..200..D 7
Gaffney ..11,448.°A 5
Galivants ..100..C 10
Gantt ..900..B 4
Garnett ..100..F 6
Gaston ..250..D 6
Georgetown 12,261.°E 10
Gifford ..300..F 6
Gilbert ..171..D 6
Gillisonville ..50..F 7
Givhans ..200..E 8
Glendale ..175..B 5
Glenn Springs* 300..B 5
Gloverville ..1,551..D 5
Gluck (part of
Anderson) ..C 3
Golden Grove ..200..B 4
Goose Creek ..830..F 9
Gourdin ..E 9
Govan ..138..E 6
Grace ..800..B 7
Grahamville ..350..G 7
Gramling ..150..A 4
Graniteville ..3,000..D 5
Graves ..300..E 10
Gray Court ..473..B 4
Grays ..100..F 6
Great Falls ..3,030..B 7
Greeleyville ..504..D 9
Green Pond ..500..F 7
Green Sea ..120..C 11
Greenville ..66,188.°B 4
Greenwood 21,042.°C 4

Greer ..8,967..B 4
Gresham ..150..D 10
Guthries ..75..B 5
Hagood ..40..C 7
Hamburg ..200..E 5
Hamer ..200..C 10
Hampton ..2,486.°F 6
Hanahan ..7,000..F 9
Hardeeville ..700..G 6
Harleyville ..561..E 8
Harris ..850..C 4
Hartsville ..8,762..C 8
Harveytown* ..150..B 4
Heath Springs 832..B 7
Helena ..350..C 5
Hemingway ..951..D 10
Hemlock
(Eureka) ..1,423..B 6
Hendersonville 100..F 7
Heriot ..100..C 8
Hickory Grove 287..B 6
Hilda ..259..E 6
Hiltonhead 200..G 7
Hodges ..209..C 4
Holly Hill ..1,235..E 8
Hollywood ..334..F 8
Homewood ..50..D 10
Honea Path 3,453..C 4
Hopkins ..300..D 7
Horatio ..200..C 7
Horrel Hill ..125..D 7
Horsegall ..115..F 6
Huger ..100..E 9
Hyman ..40..C 9
Industrial ..1,000..B 7
Inman ..1,714..A 4
Inman Mills 1,769..A 4
Irby ..B 9
Irmo ..359..C 6
Irwin* ..1,113..B 7
Islandton ..30..F 7
Isle
of Palms ..1,186..F 9
Iva ..1,357..C 3
Jackson ..1,746..E 5
Jackson Mill* 500..B 4
Jacksonboro ..600..F 8
Jamestown ..184..E 9
Jamison ..25..D 7
Jedburg ..25..E 8
Jefferson ..493..B 8
Jenkinsville ..500..C 6
Jericho ..125..F 2
Joanna ..1,831..C 5
Johns Island ..500..F 8
Johnson City* 500..B 5
Johnsonville 2,810..D 10
Johnston ..2,119..D 5
Johnstown* ..400..B 5
Jonesville ..1,439..B 5
Judson* ..4,000..B 4
Kathwood ..2,000..D 5
Kellytown ..450..C 8
Kelton ..75..B 5
Kensington ..900..E 10
Kershaw ..1,567..B 7
Killian ..800..C 7
Kinards ..234..C 5
Kings Creek 100..A 5
Kingstree ..3,847.°D 9
Kirksey ..60..C 4
Kirkwood ..275..C 7
Kline ..213..E 6
Ladson ..250..F 8
La France ..800..B 3
Lake City ..6,059..D 9
Lake
Forest* ..1,200..B 4
Lake View ..865..C 10
Lamar ..1,121..C 8
Lancaster ..7,999.°B 7
Lancaster
Mills* ..6,255..B 7
Lando ..700..B 7
Landrum ..1,930..A 4
Lane ..497..D 9
Lanford ..100..B 4
Langley ..1,300..D 5
Latta ..1,901..C 10
Laurens ..10,138.°B 4
Leeds ..40..B 6
Leesville ..1,619..D 5
Lena ..200..F 6
Leo ..D 9
Lesslie ..200..B 7
Level Land ..C 4
Lexington ..1,127.°D 6
Liberty ..2,657..B 3
Liberty Hill ..250..C 7
Lincolnville ..420..E 3
Little
Mountain ..238..C 6
Little River ..250..D 11
Little Rock ..300..C 10
Livingston ..208..D 6
Lobeco ..100..F 7
Lockhart ..128..B 6
Lodge ..151..E 7
Lone Oaks, see
Southern
Shops
Lone Star ..150..D 7
Longcreek ..70..B 2
Longs ..100..D 11

Lonsdale Mill,
see Utica
Loris ..1,702..C 11
Lowndesville ..274..C 3
Lowrys ..298..B 6
Lucknow ..50..C 8
Lugoff ..800..C 7
Luray ..102..F 6
Lydia ..300..C 8
Lydia Mills* 1,177..C 5
Lykesland ..50..D 7
Lyman ..1,261..B 4
Lynchburg ..544..C 8
Lyndhurst ..100..E 6
Macbee ..80..E 9
Madison (part of
Graniteville) ..B 2
Manning ..3,917.°D 8
Marietta ..900..A 3
Marion ..7,174.°C 10
Martin ..25..E 6
Maryville ..F 3
Mauldin ..2,577..B 4
Mayesville ..750..D 8
Mayfair ..4,000..B 4
Mayo ..500..A 5
Mayo Mills* ..200..A 5
McBee ..512..C 8
McClellanville 354..E 9
McColl ..2,479..B 9
McConnells ..266..B 6
McCormick ..1,998.°D 4
McPhersonville 40..F 7
Meggett ..188..F 8
Meriwether ..150..D 4
Midland Park 600..F 9
Midway ..25..E 7
Miley ..450..F 6
Millett ..180..E 5
Millwood
Gardens ..350..D 8
Modoc ..100..D 4
Monaghan ..750..B 4
Monarch (Monarch
Mills) ..1,990..B 5
Monarch Mills,
see Monarch
Moncks
Corner ..2,030.°E 8
Monetta ..300..D 5
Mont Clare ..C 9
Monticello ..200..C 6
Montmorenci ..900..D 5
Moore ..200..B 5
Morgana ..122..D 4
Mount Carmel 109..C 4
Mount Croghan 145..B 8
Mount Holly ..150..E 8
Mount
Pleasant ..5,116..F 9
Mountville ..120..C 5
Mullins ..6,229..C 10
Murrells Inlet 500..D 10
Myers ..1,000..F 4
Myrtle Beach 7,834..D 11
Neeses ..347..D 6
Nesmith ..85..D 9
New Ellenton 2,309..E 5
New Holland
Crossroads ..130..D 6
New Port ..50..B 6
New Zion ..200..D 8
Newberry ..9,405.°C 5
Newry ..700..B 3
Nichols ..617..C 10
Ninety Six ..2,038..C 4
Norris ..594..B 3
North ..1,047..D 6
North
Augusta ..10,348..D 5
North Charles-
ton ..24,000..F 9
North Harts-
ville* ..1,899..C 8
Norway ..525..E 6
Oakland Mill* 550..C 5
Oakley ..C 8
Oakway ..150..B 2
Oats ..75..C 9
Ocean Drive
Beach ..313..D 11
Olanta ..568..D 9
Olar ..467..E 6
Olympia Mills* 900..C 6
Ora ..125..B 5
Orangeburg 13,852.°E 7
Osborn ..60..F 7
Oswego ..50..C 8
Owings ..230..B 4
Pacolet ..1,252..B 5
Pacolet Mills 1,476..B 5
Pacolet Park* 117..B 5
Pageland ..2,020..B 8
Pamplico ..988..C 9
Paris* ..1,000..B 4
Park Place* ..2,500..B 4
Parksville ..164..D 4
Patrick ..393..B 8
Pauline ..200..B 5
Pawleys
Island ..500..E 10
Paxville ..216..D 8
Peak ..86..C 6
Peedee ..225..C 10

°County Seat.
Source: Latest census (1960) and special censuses.

*Does not appear on the map; key shows general location.

518

# SOUTH CAROLINA

Louis Schwartz

**Seaport at Charleston** is a principal U.S. port on the South Atlantic coast. Cargo passing through the port includes bananas, oil, ore, fertilizer, jute, coal, and tobacco. Georgetown and Port Royal are also important South Carolina port cities.

| | | | | |
|---|---|---|---|---|
| Pelham ........500..B 4 | Riverland | Silverstreet ...181..C 5 | Switzerland ....50..G 6 | Wattsville (Watts |
| Pelion ........233..D 6 | Terrace ...3,000..F 3 | Simpson ......100..C 7 | Sycamore ....401..E 6 | Mills) ....1,438..B 5 |
| Pelzer ........106..B 4 | Riverside* ..2,200..B 4 | Simpsonville 2,282..B 4 | Tamassee ....300..B 2 | Wedgefield ...150..D 7 |
| Pelzer* .....2,300..B 4 | Rock Hill .31,110..B 6 | Slater ........900..A 4 | Tatum ........132..B 9 | Welcome* ..1,500..B 4 |
| Pendleton ..2,358..B 3 | Rockville .....150..G 3 | Smallwood .....75..C 7 | Taylors | Wellford ...1,040..B 4 |
| Perry .........196..D 6 | Rodman .......125..B 6 | Smoaks .......145..E 7 | (Taylor) ..1,100..B 4 | West |
| Pickens ....2,198.°B 3 | Roebuck ......300..B 5 | Smyrna ........52..A 6 | Tigerville ....105..A 4 | Columbia .7,221..D 6 |
| Piedmont ..2,108..B 4 | Round-O .....150..F 7 | Snelling ......100..E 6 | Tillman .......100..G 6 | West |
| Pinehurst* ...200..E 8 | Rowesville ...398..E 7 | Society Hill ..677..B 9 | Timmonsville 2,178..C 9 | Hartsville* 2,427..C 9 |
| Pineland .......82..F 6 | Ruby ..........284..B 8 | South Bennetts- | Toddville ......100..D 10 | West Marion ..45..C 10 |
| Pineridge* ...329..D 6 | Ruffin .........250..E 7 | ville* ......1,025..B 9 | Townville .....200..B 3 | West Pelzer ..687..B 4 |
| Pineville .....900..E 8 | Russellville ..100..C 8 | South | Tradesville ....75..B 7 | West Union ..443..B 2 |
| Pinewood .....570..D 8 | St. Andrews 5,500..F 3 | Congaree* ..650..D 6 | Travelers | Westminster 2,413..B 2 |
| Pinopolis .....300..E 8 | St. Charles ..100..C 8 | South Green- | Rest ......1,973..B 4 | Westville .....250..C 7 |
| Plantersville .100..D 10 | St. George .1,833.°E 7 | wood .....2,520..C 4 | Trenton .......314..D 5 | Whetstone .....60..B 2 |
| Pleasant Hill .100..B 4 | St. Matthews 2,433.°D 7 | South Lynch- | Trio ............50..E 9 | White Hall ....45..F 7 |
| Plum Branch .139..D 4 | St. Paul .......50..D 8 | burg .........50..C 8 | Troy ..........260..D 4 | White Oak ...100..C 6 |
| Pocataligo ....65..F 7 | St. Stephen .1,462..E 9 | Southern | Turbeville ....355..D 8 | White Pond ..200..E 6 |
| Poe* .........900..B 4 | Salem .........206..B 3 | Shops (Lone | Ulmers ........168..E 6 | White Rock ..200..C 6 |
| Pomaria ......230..C 6 | Salem Road ...30..B 6 | Oak)* ....1,435..B 5 | Una .........1,500..B 5 | White Stone* .150..B 5 |
| Port Royal ...686..G 7 | Salley ........403..D 6 | Spartan- | Union ....10,191.°B 5 | Whitmire ...2,663..B 5 |
| Poston ........250..D 10 | Salters .......100..D 9 | burg ....44,352.°B 5 | Utica | Whitney ...1,600..B 5 |
| Pregnall .......75..E 8 | Saluda ......2,089.°C 5 | Spring Mills* 1,069..B 7 | (Lonsdale | Williams .....194..E 7 |
| Princeton .....200..B 4 | Saluda | Springdale* .2,144..D 6 | Mill) .....1,294..B 3 | Williamston 3,721..B 4 |
| Pritchardville .100..G 7 | Gardens* .2,500..D 6 | Springfield ...787..D 6 | Valley Falls* .900..B 5 | Willington .....40..C 4 |
| Prosperity ....757..C 5 | Sandy Springs 174..B 3 | Starr ..........243..C 3 | Van Wyck ...150..B 7 | Williston ...2,722..C 6 |
| Rains .........400..C 10 | Sans Souci .4,500..B 4 | Startex .......950..B 4 | Vance ..........85..E 8 | Wilson .........50..D 8 |
| Rantowles ....300..F 3 | Santee ........105..D 8 | State Park* ..250..C 7 | Varnville ...1,461..F 6 | Windsor ......200..E 5 |
| Ravenel .......527..F 2 | Sardinia ......100..D 8 | Stateburg .......D 7 | Vaucluse .....500..D 5 | Windy Hill .2,201..C 9 |
| Red Bank ....350..D 6 | Saxon .......1,700..B 5 | Stockman ......50..C 5 | Verdery ......100..C 4 | Windy Hill |
| Reevesville ...268..E 7 | Schofield ......60..E 6 | Stoneboro .....40..B 7 | Victor Mills* 2,018..B 6 | Beach ......273..D 11 |
| Reidville .....242..B 4 | Scotia .........102..F 6 | Stuckey* .....199..D 10 | Wadmalaw | Winnsboro .3,479.°C 6 |
| Rembert ......200..C 7 | Scranton ......613..D 9 | Sullivans | Island .......100..G 2 | Winnsboro |
| Renfrew ......360..B 4 | Seabrook .......75..F 7 | Island ....1,358..F 4 | Wagener ......614..D 6 | Mills .....2,411..C 6 |
| Renno ..........50..C 5 | Sellers ........431..C 10 | Summerton .1,504..D 8 | Walhalla ...3,431.°B 2 | Wisacky .......150..C 8 |
| Richburg .....235..B 6 | Seneca ......5,547..B 3 | Summerville .3,633..E 8 | Wallace .......150..B 9 | Witherbee .....60..E 9 |
| Richland .....150..B 2 | Shannontown 7,064..D 8 | Summit .......108..D 6 | Walterboro .5,417.°F 7 | Woodford ....172..D 6 |
| Ridge Spring .649..D 5 | Sharon ........280..B 6 | Sumter ....23,062.°D 8 | Wando ........150..F 9 | Woodruff ...3,679..B 4 |
| Ridgeland ...1,192.°G 6 | Sheldon .......200..F 7 | Sunset ...........5..A 3 | Ward ..........162..D 5 | Woodside* ...196..B 4 |
| Ridgeville ....611..E 8 | Shelton .........95..C 6 | Surfside | Ware Shoals 2,671..C 4 | Yemassee .....473..F 7 |
| Ridgeway .....417..C 7 | Shoals Junction 75..C 4 | Beach* .....933..D 11 | Warrenville .1,128..D 5 | Yonges Island 100..F 8 |
| Rimini ........200..D 7 | Shulerville ...250..E 9 | Swansea ......776..D 6 | Wateree ........30..D 7 | York ........4,758.°B 6 |
| Rion ..........400..C 6 | Silver ..........30..D 8 | Switzer ........85..B 4 | Waterloo .....148..C 4 | Zion ..........100..C 10 |

*Does not appear on the map; key shows general location.

°County Seat.
Source: Latest census figures.

519

## SOUTH CAROLINA / People

The 1960 United States census reported that South Carolina had 2,382,594 persons. The population had increased by about 13 per cent over the 1950 figure, 2,117,027. The U.S. Bureau of the Census estimated that by 1965 South Carolina's population had reached 2,494,000.

Almost 60 per cent of South Carolina's people live in farm areas. The state has three Standard Metropolitan Statistical Areas as defined by the U.S. Bureau of the Budget (see METROPOLITAN AREA). More than 770,000 persons, or about a third of the population, live in these areas—Charleston, Columbia, and Greenville. For the populations of the three areas, see the *Index* to the political map of South Carolina. Part of the Augusta, Ga., Standard Metropolitan Statistical Area extends into Aiken County, South Carolina. About 80,000 South Carolinians live in this metropolitan area.

South Carolina's largest cities, in order of size, are Columbia, Greenville, and Charleston. They are the only cities in the state with more than 50,000 persons. See the separate articles on South Carolina cities listed in the *Related Articles* at the end of this article.

More than 80 of every 100 South Carolinians were born in the state, and many are descendants of early settlers. About 99 of every 100 persons in the state were born in the United States. Britons and Germans make up the largest groups born in other countries. About 35 of every 100 persons who live in South Carolina are Negroes.

Most South Carolinians are Protestants. Baptists outnumber all other religious groups. Other large religious groups include Episcopalians, Lutherans, Methodists, Presbyterians, and Roman Catholics. South Carolina has a higher percentage of church members in proportion to population than any other state except Utah.

Louis Schwartz

**Textile Worker** inspects yarn. About half the persons employed in manufacturing in South Carolina work in the textile industry. The state rebuilt its economy around this industry after the Civil War, and is now one of the nation's leading textile producers.

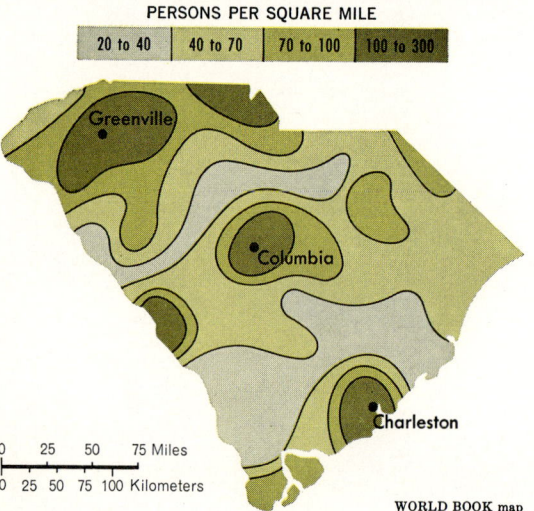

### POPULATION
This map shows the *population density* of South Carolina, and how it varies in different parts of the state. Population density is the average number of persons who live on each square mile.

PERSONS PER SQUARE MILE
20 to 40 | 40 to 70 | 70 to 100 | 100 to 300

WORLD BOOK map

**Paraders and Spectators** enjoy the annual Sun-Fun Festival in Myrtle Beach. Other annual events in South Carolina include a steeplechase, a jazz festival, and peach and flower festivals.
South Carolina State Development Board

520

# SOUTH CAROLINA / Education

**Schools.** In colonial times, most South Carolina children were educated at home or in private schools. In 1710, the colonial government established semipublic schools called *free schools*. These schools were free to poor children, but other youngsters paid tuition. The colonial government and individuals helped pay school costs.

In 1811, the state legislature approved a plan to set up free schools in all parts of South Carolina. But not enough money was put aside to run the schools. There were few free schools except in the largest towns. The 1868 constitution called for free public schools for all children. The legislature failed to provide enough money for the schools. Finally, the 1895 constitution provided enough tax support for statewide public schools.

Like other Southern states, South Carolina had separate schools for Negroes and whites for many years. In 1954, the Supreme Court of the United States ruled that public school segregation on the basis of race is unconstitutional. In 1955, the state legislature repealed the law that required children to attend school. But in 1967, it reversed the repeal, and required all children from ages 7 to 16 to attend school. The first racial integration in South Carolina public schools took place in Charleston in 1963. For the number of students and teachers in the state, see EDUCATION (table).

A superintendent of education and a state board of education head the South Carolina public school system. The board of education has 16 members, one from each *judicial* (court) district. The board members are elected by the state legislators from the counties in each district. The superintendent is elected by the people of South Carolina.

**Libraries.** South Carolina had the first government-supported lending library in the 13 original colonies. The library opened in Charleston in 1698, but closed a few years later. In 1840, the University of South Carolina built the nation's first separate college library building. Today, the state has about 40 public county and *multicounty* (regional) libraries. There are about 20 city and town public libraries, and many school libraries.

**Museums.** The Charleston Museum, founded in 1773, ranks among the oldest museums in the United States. It has natural history and colonial history exhibits, and a planetarium. The Columbia Museum of Art and Science and the Gibbes Gallery in Charleston are large art museums. Other art museums are in Florence and Greenville. One of President Woodrow Wilson's boyhood homes is a museum in Columbia.

---
### UNIVERSITIES AND COLLEGES
---

South Carolina has 19 universities and colleges accredited by the Southern Association of Colleges and Schools. For enrollments and further information, see UNIVERSITIES AND COLLEGES (table).

| Name | Location | Founded |
|---|---|---|
| Benedict College | Columbia | 1870 |
| Charleston, College of | Charleston | 1770 |
| Citadel, The | Charleston | 1842 |
| Claflin College | Orangeburg | 1869 |
| Clemson University | Clemson | 1889 |
| Coker College | Hartsville | 1908 |
| Columbia College | Columbia | 1854 |
| Converse College | Spartanburg | 1889 |
| Erskine College | Due West | 1839 |
| Furman University | Greenville | 1826 |
| Lander College | Greenwood | 1872 |
| Limestone College | Gaffney | 1845 |
| Newberry College | Newberry | 1856 |
| Presbyterian College | Clinton | 1880 |
| South Carolina, University of | Columbia | 1801 |
| South Carolina State College | Orangeburg | 1895 |
| Voorhees College | Denmark | 1897 |
| Winthrop College | Rock Hill | 1886 |
| Wofford College | Spartanburg | 1854 |

**University of South Carolina's** McKissick Memorial Library is on the campus at Columbia. The campus also includes the nation's oldest separate college library building, built in 1840.
Shostal

**Woodrow Wilson's Boyhood Home** in Columbia was bought by the state in 1929. It is now a museum. The President lived in the house with his parents from 1870 to 1874.
South Carolina State Development Board

521

# SOUTH CAROLINA / A Visitor's Guide

South Carolina's mountains, seashore, and historic sites make the state a favorite vacationland. Abundant wildlife in the fields and streams provide exciting action for hunters and fishermen. Visitors also enjoy the state's many beautiful flower gardens.

Louis Schwartz
**Fort Sumter, Site of the Opening Battle of the Civil War**

Tom Hollyman, Photo Researchers
**Monument at Kings Mountain Battlefield**

## PLACES TO VISIT

Following are brief descriptions of some of South Carolina's many interesting places to visit.

**Battlegrounds** recall South Carolina's part in the Revolutionary War. *Kings Mountain National Military Park* near Kings Creek, and *Cowpens National Battlefield Site* mark the sites of major Revolutionary War battles. Other battlefields are marked at *Camden* and at *Eutaw Springs*, near St. Matthews.

**Beaches** along South Carolina's northern Atlantic Coast offer swimming and sunbathing. Myrtle Beach is probably the state's most famous seaside resort. Other beaches, from north to south, include Cherry Grove, Ocean Drive, Crescent, Atlantic, Windy Hill, Isle of Palms, Folly, Edisto Island, Hunting Island, and Hilton Head Island.

**Forts** are among South Carolina's most interesting historic sites. *Fort Sumter*, in Charleston Harbor, is the place where the Civil War began. The fort is now a national monument. *Fort Moultrie*, also in Charleston Harbor, is the site of a brave defense by the colonists against the British during the Revolutionary War. Other forts include *Fort Johnson* in Charleston Harbor and *Windmill Point* near Charleston. Fort Johnson is the place where Americans seized tax stamps from the British in 1765 in opposition to the Stamp Act. Windmill Point is the fort from which Governor Sir Nathaniel Johnson turned back French and Spanish fleets in 1706, during Queen Anne's War (see FRENCH AND INDIAN WARS)

**Gardens** are among South Carolina's most beautiful attractions. Near Charleston are the famous *Cypress Gardens*, *Magnolia Gardens*, and *Middleton Place Gardens*. Cypress Gardens include a variety of colorful flowers and several lagoons flanked by cypress trees. Magnolia Gardens feature more than 500 varieties of flowers and trees from many lands. The English novelist John Galsworthy called Magnolia Gardens "the most beautiful in the world." Middleton Place Gardens are the oldest landscaped gardens in the United States. They were begun in 1741, and feature azaleas, camellias, and ancient oak trees. *Brookgreen Gardens*, north of Georgetown, cover parts of Brookgreen and three other former rice plantations. These gardens feature South Carolina plants and trees, a zoo of U.S. animals, and an excellent collection of statues. *Edisto Gardens*, in Orangeburg, is a city-owned display of azaleas, camellias, roses, and many other flowering plants.

**National Forests.** South Carolina has two National Forests—Francis Marion near Charleston, and Sumter, which covers three areas in the Piedmont. For details, see NATIONAL FOREST (table).

**State Parks and Forests.** South Carolina has 31 state parks and historic sites, and 4 state forests. For information, write to State Park Director, Division of State Parks, Box 357, Columbia, S.C. 29202.

**Middleton Place Gardens near Charleston**

## ANNUAL EVENTS

Favorite annual events in South Carolina include the Carolina Cup Steeplechase, held in Camden in spring, and the Southern 500 stock car race, held in Darlington on Labor Day.

Other annual events in South Carolina include the following.

**January-June:** Polo Games in Aiken (each Sunday from the beginning of February through the end of April); Garden Tours, state-wide (mid-February through May); Intercollegiate Track Meet in Columbia (March, no fixed date); Plantation Tours, state-wide (March, April); Rebel 400 Stock Car Race in Darlington (May 10); Iris Festival in Sumter (last week in May); South Carolina Folk Music Festival in Myrtle Beach (first week in June); Sun-Fun Festival in Myrtle Beach, featuring parades, contests, and the crowning of Miss Sun-Fun, U.S.A. (second week in June); Hampton County Watermelon Festival in Estill (end of June).

**July-November:** Historical Drama, *The Liberty Tree*, in Sesquicentennial State Park near Columbia (nightly from the end of June through August); Carolina Summer Jazz Festival in Columbia (July 4); Water Festival in Beaufort (mid-July); Watermelon Festival in Pageland (early August); State Fair in Columbia (third week in October); Clemson University-South Carolina University football game (Saturday before Thanksgiving Day).

**Polo Players Compete in Aiken**
W. D. Madewell

**Colorful Garden and Mansions near Beaufort**
Shostal

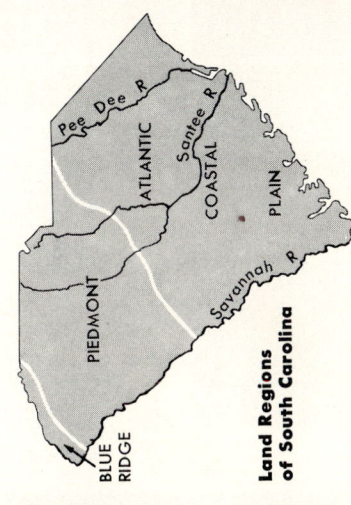

**Barge Transports Goods** near Beaufort, a seacoast town. Harbors line the Atlantic Coastal Plain region and provide shipping facilities for agricultural and industrial products.

Tom Hollyman, Photo Researchers

## Map Index

| | | | | | | |
|---|---|---|---|---|---|---|
| Bird Isl. | D11 | Fort Sumter | F 9 | Palms, Isle of | F 9 |
| Black Creek | C 8 | Hartwell Dam | C 3 | Pee Dee R. | B 9 |
| Black R. | D 9 | Hartwell Reservoir | C 2 | Piedmont | |
| Blue Ridge Mts. | A 2 | Hilton Head Isl. | G 7 | Plateau | C 3 |
| Braddock Pt. | G 7 | Hunting Isl. | G 8 | Pinopolis Dam | G 7 |
| Broad R. | C 6 | Intracoastal Waterway | D11 | Port Royal Sound | G 7 |
| Bull Bay | E10 | James Isl. | F 9 | Pritchard Isl. | G 8 |
| Cape Isl. | E10 | Johns Isl. | F 8 | Red Hills | E 7 |
| Cape Romain | E10 | Keowee River | B 3 | Reedy R. | B 4 |
| Catawba Reservoir | A 6 | Kiawah Isl. | F 8 | St. Helena Isl. | G 7 |
| Charleston Harbor | F 9 | Ladies Isl. | G 7 | St. Helena Sound | G 8 |
| Chattooga Ridge | B 2 | Lake Greenwood | C 5 | Salkehatchie R. | E 6 |
| Chattooga R. | A 2 | Lake Marion | D 8 | Saluda R. | B 4 |
| Clark Hill Reservoir | D 4 | Lake Moultrie | E 8 | Sand Hills | D 6 |
| Coastal Plain | E 8 | Lake Murray | D 5 | Santee Dam | E 9 |
| Combahee R. | F 7 | Little Lynches R. | C 6 | Santee R. | E 9 |
| Congaree R. | D 7 | Little Pee Dee R. | C10 | Sassafras Mtn. (Highest | |
| Cooper R. | E 9 | Little R. | D 3 | Point in South | |
| Coosawhatchie R. | F 6 | Little River Inlet | D11 | Carolina) | A 3 |
| Daufuskie Isl. | G 7 | Long Bay | D10 | Savannah R. | C 3 |
| Edisto Isl. | F 8 | Lynches R. | D 9 | Secession Lake | B10 |
| Edisto R. | E 7 | Mingo Creek | D 6 | Shoeheel Creek | B10 |
| Enoree R. | D 6 | Morris Isl. | F 9 | Tugaloo Lake | B 2 |
| Fishing Creek | B 4 | Murrells Inlet | E10 | Tyger R. | B 5 |
| North Fork | | North Inlet | E10 | Waccamaw R. | D11 |
| South Fork | B 6 | North Isl. | E10 | Wando R. | F 9 |
| Fort Pulaski | | Paoleet R. | B 7 | Wateree Reservoir | C 7 |
| Nat. Mon. | G 7 | | | Wateree R. | D 7 |

**Land Regions of South Carolina**

# SOUTH CAROLINA / The Land

**Land Regions.** South Carolina has three main land regions: (1) the Atlantic Coastal Plain, (2) the Piedmont, and (3) the Blue Ridge. South Carolinians call the Atlantic Coastal Plain the *Low Country*, and the Piedmont and Blue Ridge the *Up Country*.

*The Atlantic Coastal Plain* is a lowland that covers the southeastern two-thirds of South Carolina. It is part of the plain of the same name that stretches from New York to Florida. In South Carolina, the land rises gradually from southeast to northwest. Near the Atlantic Coast, the plain is flat and broken by wide bays and rivers. Swamps cover much of the land near the coast and extend far inland along the rivers. A belt of forest called the *Pine Barrens* covers part of the central Atlantic Coastal Plain. A series of sand hills runs through Aiken, Camden, Cheraw, and Columbia, marking the western edge of the plain. These sand hills form part of an ancient beach, and indicate that the Atlantic Coastal Plain once lay under the ocean.

*The Piedmont* covers most of northwestern South Carolina. It is part of a land region that extends from New York to Alabama. The *Fall Line* forms the eastern edge of the Piedmont in South Carolina. The Fall Line is a zone where rivers tumble from higher land to the lowlying Atlantic Coastal Plain (see FALL LINE). In the southeast, the South Carolina Piedmont is a rolling upland with elevations from 400 to 1,000 feet above sea level. The region rises to a hilly area 1,500 feet above sea level at its western edge.

The Piedmont slopes from northwest to southeast, which causes rivers in the region to flow rapidly. The swift-running rivers are a major source of hydroelectric power. This power helps make the Piedmont an important manufacturing area.

*The Blue Ridge* covers the northwestern corner of South Carolina. It is part of a larger region of the same name that runs from southern Pennsylvania to northern Georgia. The famous Blue Ridge Mountains, part of the Appalachian Mountain system, give the region its name. The Blue Ridge Mountains of South Carolina are less rugged and more easily crossed than those of North Carolina. Few Blue Ridge peaks in South Carolina rise more than 3,000 feet, and all are topped with forests. Sassafras Mountain, the highest point in the state, rises 3,560 feet above sea level in the Blue Ridge.

**Coastline** of South Carolina has many bays and inlets. Measured in a straight line, the coastline totals 187 miles. If all the coastal area washed by water were measured, the coastline would total 2,876 miles. Important bays and harbors along the coast include, from north to south, Little River Inlet, Winyah Bay, Bull Bay, Charleston Harbor, St. Helena Sound, and Port Royal Sound. The northern part of the coastline, from North Carolina to Winyah Bay, has an almost unbroken beach. South of Winyah Bay, salt-water marshes cover much of the coastal area, and tidal rivers cut far inland. Many islands lie along the coast. They include, from

**Contour Farming,** above, in the hilly Piedmont region of South Carolina helps prevent soil erosion. By planting alternate strips of crops that are harvested at different times, the farmer always has a soil-holding crop on the land. Agriculture has been an important activity in South Carolina since the first permanent settlers arrived in 1670. Tobacco is the leading crop. The state also ranks high in the production of cotton, peaches, and soybeans.

**Blue Ridge Mountains,** left, cover the northwestern corner of South Carolina and give the Blue Ridge region its name. These mountains are less rugged than the Blue Ridge of North Carolina, and are capped with pine and hemlock forests. The region's scenic beauty makes it popular with vacationers. The Blue Ridge region is too mountainous for farming, and most of the people earn their living in manufacturing.

Photos, Tom Hollyman, Photo Researchers

**Rivers, Waterfalls, and Lakes.** Many large rivers cross South Carolina from northwest to southeast. The largest is the Pee Dee River, which drains an area of 16,320 square miles in North and South Carolina. The Santee River is a close second in size, and the Savannah River is third. Other rivers include the Broad and the Saluda. Every South Carolina river that crosses the Fall Line has a series of rapids or waterfalls. Larger and more beautiful waterfalls may be seen in the Blue Ridge Mountains. South Carolina has no large natural lakes. Dams form many large man-made lakes or reservoirs. The largest is Lake Marion. Other man-made lakes include Catawba, Greenwood, Moultrie, Murray, and Wateree. Clark Hill and Hartwell lakes, on the Savannah River, are shared by South Carolina and Georgia.

north to south, Pawley's Island, Bull Island, Isle of Palms, Sullivan Island, Edisto Island, Hunting Island, Fripps Island, and Hilton Head Island. Parris Island, near Beaufort, is a major U.S. Marine training center.

# SEASONAL TEMPERATURES

## JANUARY

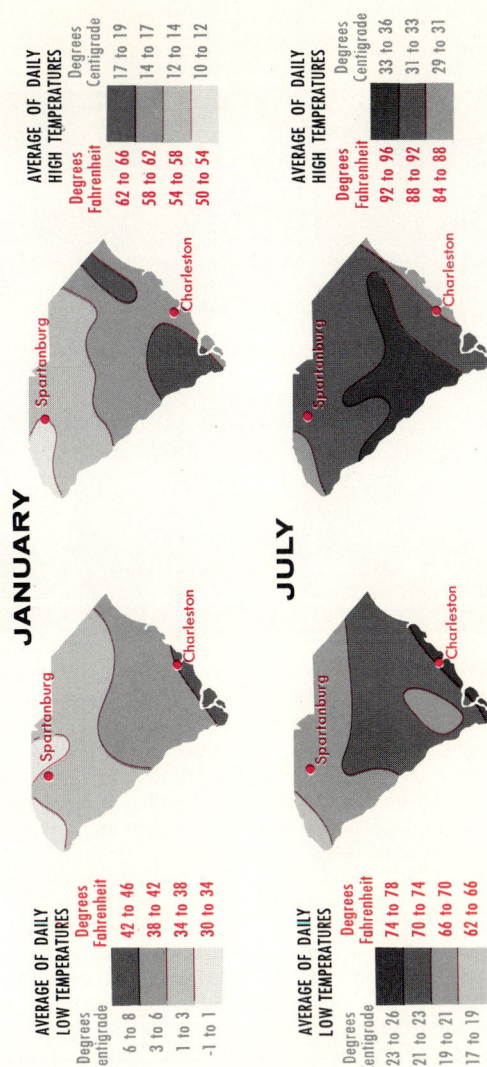

**AVERAGE OF DAILY LOW TEMPERATURES**

| Degrees Centigrade | Degrees Fahrenheit |
|---|---|
| 6 to 8 | 42 to 46 |
| 3 to 6 | 38 to 42 |
| 1 to 3 | 34 to 38 |
| -1 to 1 | 30 to 34 |

**AVERAGE OF DAILY HIGH TEMPERATURES**

| Degrees Fahrenheit | Degrees Centigrade |
|---|---|
| 62 to 66 | 17 to 19 |
| 58 to 62 | 14 to 17 |
| 54 to 58 | 12 to 14 |
| 50 to 54 | 10 to 12 |

## JULY

**AVERAGE OF DAILY LOW TEMPERATURES**

| Degrees Centigrade | Degrees Fahrenheit |
|---|---|
| 23 to 26 | 74 to 78 |
| 21 to 23 | 70 to 74 |
| 19 to 21 | 66 to 70 |
| 17 to 19 | 62 to 66 |

**AVERAGE OF DAILY HIGH TEMPERATURES**

| Degrees Fahrenheit | Degrees Centigrade |
|---|---|
| 92 to 96 | 33 to 36 |
| 88 to 92 | 31 to 33 |
| 84 to 88 | 29 to 31 |

## AVERAGE YEARLY PRECIPITATION
(Rain, Melted Snow, and Other Moisture)

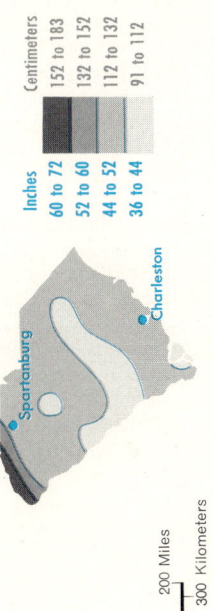

| Inches | Centimeters |
|---|---|
| 60 to 72 | 152 to 183 |
| 52 to 60 | 132 to 152 |
| 44 to 52 | 112 to 132 |
| 36 to 44 | 91 to 112 |

**MONTHLY WEATHER IN CHARLESTON AND SPARTANBURG**

|  | JAN | FEB | MAR | APR | MAY | JUNE | JULY | AUG | SEPT | OCT | NOV | DEC |
|---|---|---|---|---|---|---|---|---|---|---|---|---|
| **CHARLESTON** Average of: | | | | | | | | | | | | |
| High Temperatures | 59 | 60 | 66 | 73 | 80 | 86 | 88 | 87 | 84 | 75 | 66 | 60 |
| Low Temperatures | 44 | 45 | 50 | 58 | 66 | 73 | 75 | 75 | 71 | 61 | 51 | 44 |
| Days of Rain or Snow | 9 | 9 | 9 | 7 | 8 | 11 | 13 | 12 | 10 | 6 | 7 | 9 |
| **SPARTANBURG** | | | | | | | | | | | | |
| Days of Rain or Snow | 11 | 10 | 11 | 9 | 9 | 8 | 12 | 10 | 7 | 6 | 8 | 10 |
| High Temperatures | 52 | 55 | 62 | 71 | 80 | 88 | 89 | 87 | 83 | 73 | 61 | 53 |
| Low Temperatures | 35 | 36 | 41 | 50 | 58 | 67 | 69 | 68 | 64 | 52 | 41 | 35 |

Temperatures are given in degrees Fahrenheit.

WORLD BOOK maps
Source: U.S. Weather Bureau

**Warm Summer Weather** attracts sunbathers and horseback riders to Myrtle Beach, South Carolina's largest seashore resort. The 312-acre Myrtle Beach State Park is a year-round vacation spot.

Tom Hollyman, Photo Researchers

## SOUTH CAROLINA / Climate

South Carolina has a warm climate. July temperatures average about 81° F. in the south and about 72° F. in the northwest. January temperatures average about 51° F. in the south and about 41° F. in the northwest. The state's record high temperature, 111° F., was recorded in Blackville on Sept. 4, 1925; in Calhoun Falls on Sept. 8, 1925; and in Camden on June 28, 1954. The record low temperature, −13° F., was recorded in Longcreek on Jan. 26, 1940.

Yearly *precipitation* (rain, melted snow, and other forms of moisture) in most parts of South Carolina averages about 45 inches. The mountains receive over 70 inches of precipitation annually. South Carolina gets little snow. Annual snowfall ranges from about 7 inches in the mountains to light traces of snow in the south.

# SOUTH CAROLINA / Economy

Manufacturing is South Carolina's chief economic activity. Agriculture ranks second, followed by the tourist industry. The Piedmont has long been South Carolina's most important manufacturing region. Manufacturing is also important in the Atlantic Coastal Plain. Farms and the tourist trade thrive in many parts of the state.

**Natural Resources.** South Carolina's most important natural resource is its plentiful water supply. The state also has large forests and abundant wildlife.

*Soil.* The Atlantic Coastal Plain has some of South Carolina's best soils. Deposits of silt from rivers have left a black loam along the river valleys. A lighter loam covers other parts of the plain. A red soil covers the Piedmont and Blue Ridge.

*Minerals.* Large deposits of kaolin and other clays lie scattered throughout the Atlantic Coastal Plain and the eastern Piedmont. The Piedmont also has granite deposits, and limestone is found in the Piedmont and Atlantic Coastal Plain. Almost every South Carolina county has deposits of sand and gravel. Ores containing titanium and radioactive thorium are found in stream beds near the Georgia border.

*Forests* cover almost two-thirds of South Carolina. The Low Country has thick forests of gums, hickories, live oaks, magnolias, pines, and red and white oaks. Bald

**Worker Inspects Felt** at a factory in St. Stephen. South Carolina textile mills also make cotton and synthetic fabrics.

cypresses, cottonwoods, and tupelo gums grow in the swamps. Longleaf pines and scrubby oaks grow in the sand hills. Piedmont forests have beeches, maples, pines, tulip poplars, and white oaks. Pines and hemlocks cover the Blue Ridge Mountains.

*Plant Life.* Palmettos, yuccas, and other subtropical plants grow along the South Carolina coast. Thick growths of dwarf white honeysuckle and sweet bay spread over large areas in the Low Country. Spanish moss hangs from many live oak and cypress trees. Other South Carolina plants include Carolina jessamine and the Venus's-flytrap, a rare insect-trapping plant that grows wild only in North and South Carolina. Brilliant patches of azaleas, mountain laurels, and rhododendrons blanket the South Carolina mountains in spring.

*Animal Life.* White-tailed deer live in the forests near the coast. A few black bears roam the swamps, where alligators sometimes can be seen lying in the sun. Fox squirrels, foxes, and wildcats live in the state's inland forests. Opossums, raccoons, and cottontail rabbits may be seen throughout the state. Short-eared marsh rabbits live along the coast. More than 360 kinds of birds, including wild turkeys, live in South Carolina. Few other states have so many kinds of birds.

People often see bottle-nosed dolphins, sharks, and sperm whales along the South Carolina coast. About 180 kinds of salt-water fishes live in the state's coastal waters and salt marshes. Fresh-water streams and lakes have bass, bream, rockfish, and trout.

**Manufacturing** accounts for about 80 per cent of the value of goods produced in South Carolina. Goods manufactured there have a *value added by manufacture* of about $1,977,000,000 annually. This figure represents the value created in products by South Carolina industries, not counting such costs as materials, supplies, and fuel. South Carolina's chief manufactured goods, in or-

### PRODUCTION IN SOUTH CAROLINA
Total yearly value of goods produced—$2,480,730,000

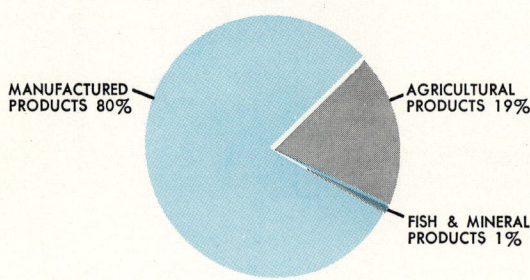

MANUFACTURED PRODUCTS 80%
AGRICULTURAL PRODUCTS 19%
FISH & MINERAL PRODUCTS 1%

Note: Manufacturing percentage based on value added by manufacture. Other percentages based on value of production.
Source: Latest available U.S. Government statistics

### EMPLOYMENT IN SOUTH CAROLINA
Average yearly number of persons employed—810,683

| | Number of Employees |
|---|---|
| Manufacturing | 266,500 |
| Agriculture | 178,000 |
| Wholesale & Retail Trade | 104,800 |
| Government | 93,600 |
| Services | 60,000 |
| Construction | 37,300 |
| Transportation & Public Utilities | 26,700 |
| Finance, Insurance & Real Estate | 24,400 |
| Fishing, Forestry & Mining | 19,383 |

Source: Employment statistics supplied by employers to government agencies

der of importance, are (1) textiles, (2) chemicals and chemical products, and (3) clothing.

*Textiles* have a value added of about $1,234,160,000 yearly. South Carolina ranks second only to North Carolina in textile production. Cotton fabrics are the most important products made in South Carolina's more than 340 textile mills. These mills use about 2½ million bales of cotton yearly. The state's textile mills also make dacron, orlon, rayon, silk, wool, plastic and glass fiber yarns; plastic-coated cottons; and rayon and nylon tire cord.

Most of South Carolina's textile mills are in the northwestern part of the state. Spartanburg County ranks as the leading textile-producing county, and Greenville (in Greenville County) is the leading textile city. Other important textile-manufacturing centers include Anderson, Gaffney, Greenwood, Lancaster, Rock Hill, and the Horse Creek Valley in Aiken County.

*Chemicals and Chemical Products* have an annual value added of about $343,000,000. Chemical factories in Charleston, Columbia, Spartanburg, and more than 30 other South Carolina cities and towns produce over 7½ million tons of fertilizers yearly. Factories in Aiken, Anderson, Camden, Irmo, and Rock Hill make synthetic fibers. These fibers are later woven or knitted in other mills throughout South Carolina. The Atomic Energy Commission operates a large chemical plant near the Savannah River, south of Aiken. Workers at the plant produce plutonium, and take deuterium from the river.

*Clothing* has a yearly value added of about $141 million. More than a hundred South Carolina factories make clothing from the textiles woven in the state's mills. Greenville and Spartanburg are the leading clothes-making centers.

*Other Products.* South Carolina has more than 20 pulp and paper mills. Paper and paper products rank fourth in value among the state's manufactured goods. Other products made or processed in South Carolina are, in order of importance, processed foods; stone, clay, and glass products; lumber; electric machinery; and furniture.

**Agriculture** accounts for about 19 per cent of the value of goods produced in South Carolina. The state's farmers earn about $465,300,000 a year. South Carolina's 56,000 farms average 144 acres in size. Farmland occupies about two-fifths of the state, but only about two-fifths of that is used to grow crops. Most of the rest of the farmland is covered by forests. South Carolina farmers sell much timber from the forests.

*Tobacco* is the state's leading cash crop. It has a yearly value of about $107 million. South Carolina grows about 83,000 tons of tobacco annually, and is a top tobacco-producing state. Bright-leaf tobacco is raised in the Low Country and the Pee Dee River area. Aromatic tobacco grows in the Piedmont.

*Cotton* is South Carolina's second leading cash crop. The state produces about 250,000 bales of cotton annually. This crop earns about $57 million. Farmers sell about 200,000 tons of cottonseed yearly to cottonseed oil mills. The seed yields an oil used in food. Cotton is grown in every South Carolina county.

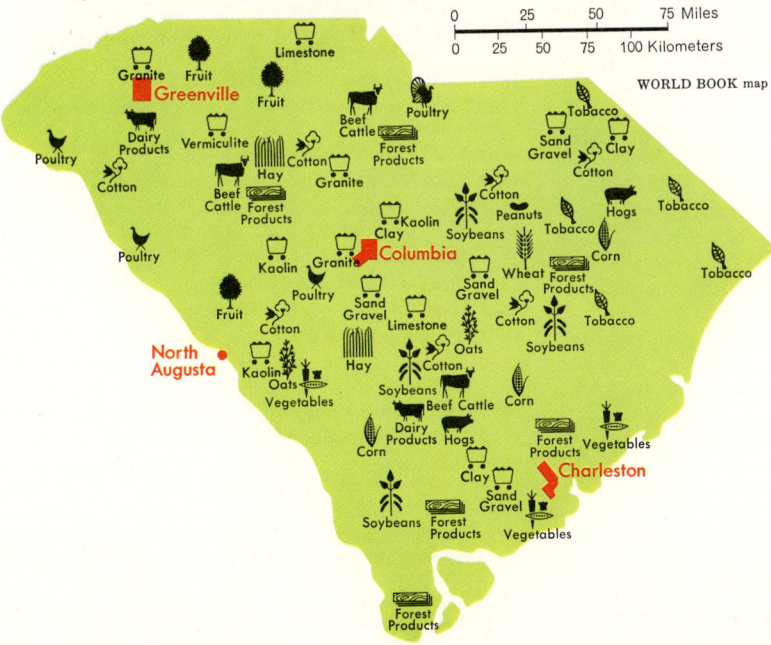

**FARM, MINERAL, AND FOREST PRODUCTS**
This map shows where the state's leading farm, mineral, and forest products are produced. The major urban areas (shown in red) are the state's important manufacturing centers.

WORLD BOOK map

Shostal

**Woodsmen Cut Trees** for pulp. One of the largest U.S. pulp mills is in Georgetown. Lumber mills operate in every section of South Carolina. Many plants in the swamp areas along the coast produce crates and boxes.

# SOUTH CAROLINA / History

Orangeburg and Sumter are the leading cotton counties.

*Other Crops.* Soybeans, peaches, and corn are other important South Carolina farm crops. More South Carolina farmland is used for soybeans than for any other crop. South Carolina ranks second only to California in peach production. Most of the corn grown in the state is used to feed animals, or in making corn meal, corn syrup, and grits. Other farm crops include cabbage, cucumbers, oats, peanuts, snap beans, sweet potatoes, tomatoes, watermelons, and wheat.

*Livestock and Poultry.* South Carolina farmers raise more hogs than any other animal. But beef cattle bring in more money than hogs. Eggs are the state's chief poultry product. South Carolina chickens lay more than a billion eggs yearly.

**Mining** contributes about $33,901,000 annually to the value of goods produced in South Carolina. Granite is the state's most valuable mineral. Limestone and clay are also important. The granite comes chiefly from the Piedmont. Limestone is mined in the Atlantic Coastal Plain, and *kaolin* (a kind of clay) is mined in Aiken and Lexington counties. Sand and gravel are mined in most South Carolina counties.

**Fishing Industry** of South Carolina earns about $4,720,000 yearly. The state's fishermen catch about 23 million pounds of seafood annually. South Carolina ranks among the leading states in the number of shrimps caught. Other valuable catches include crabs, mullets, oysters, and spots.

**Electric Power.** Hydroelectric plants generate about a fourth of South Carolina's electric power. Most of the rest comes from steam-generating plants. In 1951, the Atomic Energy Commission opened its Savannah River Plant in Aiken, Allendale, and Barnwell counties. Scientists at this plant experiment with methods of producing atomic power for commercial use. An experimental atomic energy plant at Parr produced electricity for privately-owned public utility companies of South Carolina, North Carolina, and Virginia until it was closed in 1967. For South Carolina's kilowatt-hour production, see ELECTRIC POWER (table).

**Transportation.** South Carolina has about 57,000 miles of roads and highways, about three-fifths of which are paved. Railroads operate on about 3,200 miles of track in the state. About 85 airports serve South Carolina. The state has three seaports—Charleston, Georgetown, and Port Royal. The Atlantic Intracoastal Waterway is South Carolina's chief inland shipping route (see ATLANTIC INTRACOASTAL WATERWAY).

**Communication.** More than 15 daily newspapers and 75 semiweeklies and weeklies are published in South Carolina. The *South Carolina Weekly Journal,* the state's first newspaper, was published for only six months, sometime between 1730 and 1732. Today, the state's largest daily newspapers include the *Anderson Independent,* the *State* of Columbia, the *Greenville News,* and the *Charleston News and Courier.*

South Carolina's first radio station, WSPA, began broadcasting in Spartanburg in 1930. The first television station, WCOS-TV, opened in Columbia in 1953. South Carolina now has about 100 radio stations and 15 television stations.

**Indian Days.** More than 30 Indian tribes lived in what is now South Carolina before the white man came. The chief tribes were the Catawba, the Cherokee, and the Yamasee (or Yemasee). The Catawba belonged to the Siouan Indian language family, the Cherokee to the Iroquoian language family, and the Yamasee to the Muskhogean language family. The Indians lived in semipermanent log shelters. Most of them raised crops.

**Exploration and Settlement.** In 1521, Francisco Gordillo led a Spanish expedition that explored the Carolina coast. Gordillo came from Spanish-held Santo Domingo in the Dominican Republic. In 1526, Lucas Vásquez de Ayllón, a judge from Santo Domingo Island, tried to establish a colony in what is now South Carolina. He led about 500 men, women, and children from Santo Domingo to the Winyah Bay region. But the colony failed because of disease and bad weather, and the settlers soon returned to Santo Domingo. Between 1562 and 1565, French explorers tried to settle at Port Royal and at another place farther south. They failed, partly because they lacked food.

England claimed the entire North American mainland in the early 1600's. The English based their claim on John Cabot's voyage to America in 1497 (see CABOT). In 1629, King Charles I of England granted North American land to Sir Robert Heath. Part of the grant was a strip of land that included what are now the states of South Carolina and North Carolina. The strip extended to the Pacific Ocean. The land was named *Province of Carolana* (land of Charles). The spelling was changed to *Carolina* in 1663. Heath made no attempts

--- **IMPORTANT DATES IN SOUTH CAROLINA** ---

**1521** Francisco Gordillo of Spain explored the Carolina coast.

**1526** Lucas Vásquez de Ayllón established a temporary settlement at Winyah Bay.

**1670** Englishmen established the first permanent white settlement in South Carolina, at Albemarle Point.

**1719** South Carolina became a separate royal province.

**1780** American forces won the Battle of Kings Mountain, a turning point in the Revolutionary War.

**1788** South Carolina became the 8th state on May 23.

**1832** South Carolina passed the Ordinance of Nullification.

**1860** South Carolina seceded from the Union on Dec. 20.

**1861** The Civil War began on April 12 when Confederate forces fired on Fort Sumter.

**1865** Union soldiers burned Columbia.

**1868** South Carolina was readmitted to the Union on June 25.

**1877** Reconstruction ended in South Carolina.

**1890** Benjamin Tillman, a leader of small farmers, became governor.

**1895** South Carolina adopted its present constitution.

**1942** The Santee-Cooper Project was completed.

**1955** The Atomic Energy Commission completed a plant near Aiken to produce fissionable materials.

**1964** South Carolina voted for Barry M. Goldwater, the first Republican presidential candidate to carry the state since the Reconstruction. Senator Strom Thurmond resigned from the Democratic party and became a Republican.

**1968** South Carolina reapportioned its Senate to provide representation based on population.

**Andrew Jackson** born in Lancaster County

# HISTORIC SOUTH CAROLINA

**Battle of Kings Mountain,** in which the British were defeated, was fought Oct. 7, 1780. It was the turning point of the Revolutionary War in the South.

**Blackbeard** and other pirates preyed along the South Carolina coast in the early 1700's. Many were hanged from the gallows on Charleston's Execution Dock.

**Santee Dam,** completed in 1942, harnessed the Santee River to provide hydroelectric power. The dam also made an abandoned canal navigable.

**Rice Was First Raised** successfully in North America near Charleston about 1685 by H. H. Woodward, from seed given to him by a ship's captain.

**H-Bomb Plant,** covering 315 square miles along the Savannah River, began operating in 1956. It uses 1,000,000,000 gallons of water each day.

**The Civil War Began** on April 12, 1861, when Confederate batteries bombed Fort Sumter in Charleston Harbor. Federal troops evacuated the fort on April 14.

Charleston Water Front in 1760

One of the Nation's First Museums

First Fireproof Building

First Theater
First Opera Performance

**Charleston's Early Achievements** include one of the first museums, founded in 1773; the first fireproof structure, built in 1822; the first opera performance, given about 1702; and the first steam engine in service, in 1830.

Best Friend of Charleston

# SOUTH CAROLINA

to establish settlements in the area of Carolina.

In 1663, King Charles II granted Carolina to eight English noblemen called *lords proprietors*. In 1670, the proprietors sent settlers to America. The settlers established South Carolina's first permanent white settlement at Albemarle Point, near what is now Charleston. The colonists moved to Oyster Point in 1680, and named the settlement Charles Town. The spelling was changed to *Charleston* in 1783.

**Colonial Days.** The proprietors wanted to limit self-government in Carolina. They also failed to protect the settlers when enemies threatened the colony. During Queen Anne's War (1702-1713), the colonists turned back French and Spanish forces at Charleston. They successfully defended themselves against attacks by the Yamasee Indians and against several pirate raids between 1715 and 1718. During these battles, the colonists received little help from the powerful proprietors. In 1719, the proprietors rejected laws requested by the colonists. As a result, the colonists rebelled against the proprietors that same year.

The South Carolina region was Great Britain's southern line of defense against French and Spanish attacks. Partly for this reason, King George I bought the South Carolina region from the proprietors in 1719, and made it a royal colony. Britain ruled the colony, but the people were allowed self-government. In 1729, the king bought the North Carolina region, and in 1730 he divided Carolina into two royal provinces—South Carolina and North Carolina. In 1732, the southern part of South Carolina became the colony of Georgia.

During the mid-1700's, many South Carolinians moved from coastal settlements to the Up Country. The Up Country population was also increased by waves of settlers from Pennsylvania and Virginia. By 1775, about 70,000 white persons and about 100,000 Negroes lived in South Carolina. Most of the Negroes were slaves.

**The Revolutionary War.** During the 1760's, Great Britain passed a series of laws that caused unrest in South Carolina and the other American colonies. Most of these laws set up new taxes or restricted colonial trade. Some South Carolinians, called *Tories*, urged loyalty to Britain in spite of the laws. But the majority of the people, called *Whigs*, favored independence.

The Revolutionary War began in Massachusetts in 1775. South Carolina became the scene of many important battles. In June, 1776, British land and sea forces tried to capture Charleston. But the colonists defeated the British in the Battle of Fort Moultrie. A second British attack on Charleston was turned back in 1779. The British finally captured the city in 1780. In August of that year, the British defeated colonial troops under General Horatio Gates at Camden. The British and their Tory allies then controlled most of South Carolina. Colonial victories in the Battle of Kings Mountain (Oct. 7, 1780) and at Cowpens (Jan. 17, 1781) turned the tide of war in the South. In 1781, colonial troops under General Nathanael Greene drove the main British army from South Carolina to Virginia. The South Carolina militia forced smaller British units from the area. Famous leaders of the militia included Francis Marion, called the *Swamp Fox;* Thomas Sumter, called the *Gamecock;* and Andrew Pickens. The British evacuated Charleston in 1782. During the war, 137 battles or smaller fights took place in South Carolina. Most of them were fought between bands of Whigs and Tories.

On July 9, 1778, South Carolina *ratified* (approved) the Articles of Confederation, the forerunner of the United States Constitution. South Carolina became the eighth state of the Union on May 23, 1788, when it ratified the U.S. Constitution.

**Nullification.** South Carolina strongly supported state's rights and free trade. The state's people opposed federal tariffs because South Carolina's economy depended heavily on trade with European nations. Tariffs, of course, discouraged this trade. A depression hit the United States in 1819, and South Carolinians blamed federal tariffs for their economic problems. In 1828, Congress passed a law that raised tariffs even higher than before. This law was called the "tariff of abominations." Reaction against the federal government spread throughout the state. In 1828, Vice-President John C. Calhoun, a South Carolinian, wrote the *Exposition and Protest*. This document declared that no state was bound by a federal law which the state regarded as unconstitutional. After another high tariff law was passed in 1832, South Carolina adopted an *Ordinance of Nullification*. This ordinance declared the tariff acts of 1828 and 1832 "null and void." President Andrew Jackson threatened to send troops to South Carolina to enforce the law. But Congress passed a compromise tariff bill in 1833, and South Carolina repealed the Ordinance of Nullification. See NULLIFICATION.

**The Civil War.** Shortly after the nullification crisis, an antislavery movement gained strength in the North. In 1850, a dispute between the North and South arose over whether slavery should be allowed in parts of the West. South Carolina threatened to *secede* (withdraw) from the Union. But little support came from other Southern states, and South Carolina took no further action. On Nov. 6, 1860, Abraham Lincoln, a Northern Republican, was elected President. South Carolina feared Lincoln would use federal power to abolish slavery. On Dec. 20, 1860, South Carolina became the first state to secede from the Union. By the spring of 1861, ten other Southern states had joined the secession movement and had formed the Confederate States of America (see CONFEDERATE STATES OF AMERICA).

The Civil War began on April 12, 1861, when Confederate troops fired on Fort Sumter in Charleston Harbor. Fighting raged along the South Carolina coast throughout the war. A blockade of Charleston Harbor by the Union fleet ruined South Carolina's economy. In 1865, Union troops led by William T. Sherman destroyed many plantations in the state. They also burned Columbia, the capital. About a fourth of the 63,000 troops from South Carolina died during the war.

**Reconstruction.** During the Reconstruction period after the Civil War, Union troops occupied South Carolina and the other Southern states. The Republican party in the state was made up chiefly of Negroes, southern Union sympathizers called *scalawags*, and northern adventurers called *carpetbaggers*. The Republicans controlled the South Carolina government during part of the Reconstruction period, and had the support of the Union troops. In 1868, South Carolina adopted a new state constitution. The new constitution gave Negroes

526f

# SOUTH CAROLINA

the right to vote. Congress readmitted South Carolina to the Union on June 25, 1868.

In 1876, Wade Hampton, a Democrat and a Confederate cavalry hero, defeated the Republican candidate for governor. The Republicans challenged the election results, and South Carolina had rival state governments for several months. President Rutherford B. Hayes withdrew the federal troops from South Carolina in March, 1877. Republican power then collapsed, and the Democrats gained control of the state.

**Industrial Growth** began in South Carolina during the late 1800's. Profits from agriculture had declined greatly after the Civil War. The decline was caused chiefly by competition from many new farms in the western United States. About 1880, South Carolina businessmen began expanding the textile industry. Hydroelectric power, rather than direct water power, became the source of energy for many textile mills. Thousands of poor farmers welcomed the chance to work in the textile mills, even at low wages. A number of textile companies moved from Northern states to South Carolina, partly to take advantage of this inexpensive labor.

During the late 1800's, a group of Democrats called *Tillmanites* gained control of South Carolina politics. The group was led by Benjamin R. Tillman. Before 1890, a group called the Bourbon Democrats ran South Carolina politics. The Bourbon Democrats were lawyers, planters, and businessmen whose strength was in the Low Country. Owners of small farms, especially those in the Up Country, protested the Bourbon rule after farm prices dropped. Tillman campaigned for widespread reforms in state government, and was elected governor in 1890. The Tillmanites rewrote the state constitution, and all but eliminated Negro voting rights. Tillman became a U.S. Senator in 1895, and remained a powerful force in South Carolina politics until his death in 1918.

After the United States entered World War I in 1917, South Carolina's textile mills produced large quantities of cloth for the armed forces. By 1920, the state's textile industry employed about 54,600 workers and was still growing.

## THE GOVERNORS OF SOUTH CAROLINA

| | Party | Term |
|---|---|---|
| **Under the Articles of Confederation** | | |
| 1. John Rutledge | None | 1779-1782 |
| 2. John Mathews | None | 1782-1783 |
| 3. Benjamin Guerard | None | 1783-1785 |
| 4. William Moultrie | None | 1785-1787 |
| 5. Thomas Pinckney | None | 1787-1789 |
| **Under the United States Constitution** | | |
| 1. Thomas Pinckney | None | 1787-1789 |
| 2. Charles Pinckney | None | 1789-1792 |
| 3. William Moultrie | Federalist | 1792-1794 |
| 4. Arnoldus Vander Horst | Federalist | 1794-1796 |
| 5. Charles Pinckney | *Dem.-Rep. | 1796-1798 |
| 6. Edward Rutledge | Dem.-Rep. | 1798-1800 |
| 7. John Drayton | Dem.-Rep. | 1800-1802 |
| 8. James B. Richardson | Dem.-Rep. | 1802-1804 |
| 9. Paul Hamilton | Dem.-Rep. | 1804-1806 |
| 10. Charles Pinckney | Dem.-Rep. | 1806-1808 |
| 11. John Drayton | Dem.-Rep. | 1808-1810 |
| 12. Henry Middleton | Dem.-Rep. | 1810-1812 |
| 13. Joseph Alston | Dem.-Rep. | 1812-1814 |
| 14. David R. Williams | Dem.-Rep. | 1814-1816 |
| 15. Andrew Pickens | Dem.-Rep. | 1816-1818 |
| 16. John Geddes | Dem.-Rep. | 1818-1820 |
| 17. Thomas Bennett | Dem.-Rep. | 1820-1822 |
| 18. John L. Wilson | Dem.-Rep. | 1822-1824 |
| 19. Richard I. Manning | Dem.-Rep. | 1824-1826 |
| 20. John Taylor | Dem.-Rep. | 1826-1828 |
| 21. Stephen D. Miller | Democratic | 1828-1830 |
| 22. James Hamilton, Jr. | Democratic | 1830-1832 |
| 23. Robert Y. Hayne | Democratic | 1832-1834 |
| 24. George McDuffie | Democratic | 1834-1836 |
| 25. Pierce M. Butler | Democratic | 1836-1838 |
| 26. Patrick Noble | Democratic | 1838-1840 |
| 27. B. K. Henagan | Democratic | 1840 |
| 28. John P. Richardson | Democratic | 1840-1842 |
| 29. James H. Hammond | Democratic | 1842-1844 |
| 30. William Aiken | Democratic | 1844-1846 |
| 31. David Johnson | Democratic | 1846-1848 |
| 32. Whitemarsh B. Seabrook | Democratic | 1848-1850 |
| 33. John H. Means | Democratic | 1850-1852 |
| 34. John L. Manning | Democratic | 1852-1854 |
| 35. James H. Adams | Democratic | 1854-1856 |
| 36. Robert F. W. Allston | Democratic | 1856-1858 |
| 37. William H. Gist | Democratic | 1858-1860 |
| 38. Francis W. Pickens | Democratic | 1860-1862 |
| 39. Milledge L. Bonham | Democratic | 1862-1864 |
| 40. Andrew G. Magrath | Democratic | 1864-1865 |
| 41. Benjamin F. Perry | Democratic | 1865 |
| 42. James L. Orr | Democratic | 1865-1868 |
| 43. Robert K. Scott | Republican | 1868-1872 |
| 44. Franklin J. Moses, Jr. | Republican | 1872-1874 |
| 45. Daniel H. Chamberlain | Republican | 1874-1876 |
| 46. Wade Hampton | Democratic | 1876-1879 |
| 47. William D. Simpson | Democratic | 1879-1880 |
| 48. Thomas B. Jeter | Democratic | 1880 |
| 49. Johnson Hagood | Democratic | 1880-1882 |
| 50. Hugh S. Thompson | Democratic | 1882-1886 |
| 51. John C. Sheppard | Democratic | 1886 |
| 52. John P. Richardson | Democratic | 1886-1890 |
| 53. Benjamin R. Tillman | Democratic | 1890-1894 |
| 54. John G. Evans | Democratic | 1894-1897 |
| 55. William H. Ellerbe | Democratic | 1897-1899 |
| 56. Miles B. McSweeney | Democratic | 1899-1903 |
| 57. Duncan C. Heyward | Democratic | 1903-1907 |
| 58. Martin F. Ansel | Democratic | 1907-1911 |
| 59. Coleman L. Blease | Democratic | 1911-1915 |
| 60. Charles A. Smith | Democratic | 1915 |
| 61. Richard I. Manning | Democratic | 1915-1919 |
| 62. Robert A. Cooper | Democratic | 1919-1922 |
| 63. Wilson G. Harvey | Democratic | 1922-1923 |
| 64. Thomas G. McLeod | Democratic | 1923-1927 |
| 65. John G. Richards | Democratic | 1927-1931 |
| 66. Ibra C. Blackwood | Democratic | 1931-1935 |
| 67. Olin D. Johnston | Democratic | 1935-1939 |
| 68. Burnet R. Maybank | Democratic | 1939-1941 |
| 69. J. Emile Harley | Democratic | 1941-1942 |
| 70. Richard M. Jefferies | Democratic | 1942-1943 |
| 71. Olin D. Johnston | Democratic | 1943-1945 |
| 72. Ransome J. Williams | Democratic | 1945-1947 |
| 73. Strom Thurmond | Democratic | 1947-1951 |
| 74. James F. Byrnes | Democratic | 1951-1955 |
| 75. George B. Timmerman, Jr. | Democratic | 1955-1959 |
| 76. Ernest F. Hollings | Democratic | 1959-1963 |
| 77. Donald S. Russell | Democratic | 1963-1965 |
| 78. Robert E. McNair | Democratic | 1965- |

*Democratic-Republican

# SOUTH CAROLINA

Nylon Industries, Inc.
**Huge Nylon Manufacturing Plant** was built in Greenville in 1963. Industry expanded in South Carolina after World War II. Today, almost every county has one or more factories built since 1945.

The boll weevil damaged much cotton in South Carolina during the 1920's. Many farmers began raising other crops, including fruits, tobacco, and wheat. But cotton remained the main farm product. As in other states, the Great Depression of the 1930's caused widespread unemployment in South Carolina. Economic conditions improved as the depression eased in the late 1930's.

**The 1940's and 1950's.** World War II (1939-1945) brought a great demand for South Carolina farm products and textiles. In 1942, the South Carolina Public Service Authority completed the Santee-Cooper navigation canal and power dam between the Santee and Cooper rivers. This $57 million project created Lakes Marion and Moultrie, supplied electric power, and helped South Carolina industry (see SANTEE-COOPER PROJECT). In 1945, the state legislature established the Research, Planning, and Development Board (now the State Development Board). This agency works to improve industry in South Carolina and to attract new industries to the state.

In 1948, Governor Strom Thurmond of South Carolina was nominated for President by the States' Rights Democratic (Dixiecrat) party. Thurmond received the electoral votes of four states—Alabama, Louisiana, Mississippi, and South Carolina.

In 1955, the Atomic Energy Commission completed its $1,400,000,000 Savannah River Plant near Aiken. Workers at this plant manufacture fissionable materials that can be used in atomic and hydrogen bombs. Also in 1955, many other factories were begun in South Carolina. Twenty-five of them represented an investment of $1 million or more, or were designed to employ at least a hundred workers.

**South Carolina Today** continues its industrial expansion while keeping its agricultural importance. The state's economy has changed greatly since the early 1900's. At that time, the economy depended chiefly on one crop—cotton—and on one kind of manufactured product—cotton textiles. Today, cotton still has great importance. But other farm products, including peaches, soybeans, and tobacco, are also produced in large quantities.

A variety of manufactured products have joined cotton textiles among South Carolina's important manufactured goods. These products include chemicals, clothing, electrical machinery, and paper products. Almost every South Carolina county now has one or more factories that were built after World War II. To keep pace with industrial growth, South Carolina sponsors a widespread technical education program. It trains men and women in the skills required to work with today's modern manufacturing methods.

Like many northern and southern states, South Carolina faces racial problems. Many white South Carolinians want to keep the state's pattern of life that separates Negroes and whites. But a number of schools, libraries, and restaurants in South Carolina have become integrated in response to federal laws prohibiting segregation.

During the 1960's, the Republican party gained considerable strength in traditionally Democratic South Carolina. About 75,000 South Carolinians voted for President Dwight D. Eisenhower, the Republican presidential candidate in 1956. About 188,000 of the state's voters supported Vice-President Richard M. Nixon, the Republican candidate in 1960. In 1964, the Republican presidential candidate, Senator Barry M. Goldwater of Arizona, won South Carolina's electoral votes, and received over 300,000 popular votes in the state. Republican candidate Nixon also won the state in 1968. The only other times voters there supported Republican presidential candidates were during Reconstruction.

Senator Strom Thurmond resigned from the Democratic party in 1964 and joined the Republican party. He supported Nixon in the 1968 campaign. South Carolina Republicans also won state and local offices and General Assembly seats during the 1960's. DONALD O. BUSHMAN, ERNEST M. LANDER, JR., and WILLIAM D. WORKMAN, JR.

## SOUTH CAROLINA/Study Aids

**Related Articles** in WORLD BOOK include:

### BIOGRAPHIES

| | |
|---|---|
| Allston, Washington | Marion, Francis |
| Butler, Pierce | Middleton, Arthur |
| Byrnes, James F. | Moultrie, William |
| Calhoun, John C. | Pinckney (family) |
| Gadsden (family) | Pinckney, Charles |
| Hampton, Wade | Rutledge (family) |
| Hayne, Robert Y. | Smalls, Robert |
| Heyward, Thomas, Jr. | Thurmond, Strom |
| Jackson, Andrew | Watson, John B. |
| Longstreet, James | Westmoreland, |
| Lynch, Thomas, Jr. | William Childs |

### CITIES

| | | | |
|---|---|---|---|
| Beaufort | Columbia | Greenville | Sumter |
| Charleston | Florence | Spartanburg | |

526h

### History

Civil War
Confederate States of America
Fort Moultrie
Fort Sumter
Nullification
Reconstruction
Revolutionary War in America

### Physical Features

Atlantic Intracoastal Waterway
Blue Ridge Mountains
Pee Dee River
Piedmont Region
Saluda Dam
Savannah River

### Products

For South Carolina's rank among the states in production, see the following articles:

Peach   Textile   Tobacco

### Other Related Articles

Charleston Naval Base
Fort Sumter National Monument
Parris Island Marine Corps Recruit Depot
Santee-Cooper Project
Southern States

### Outline

I. **Government**
  A. Constitution
  B. Executive
  C. Legislature
  D. Courts
  E. Local Government
  F. Taxation
  G. Politics
II. **People**
III. **Education**
  A. Schools
  B. Libraries
  C. Museums
IV. **A Visitor's Guide**
  A. Places to Visit
  B. Annual Events
V. **The Land**
  A. Land Regions
  B. Coastline
  C. Rivers, Waterfalls, and Lakes
VI. **Climate**
VII. **Economy**
  A. Natural Resources
  B. Manufacturing
  C. Agriculture
  D. Mining
  E. Fishing Industry
  F. Electric Power
  G. Transportation
  H. Communication
VIII. **History**

### Questions

What percentage of South Carolina's people live in rural areas?
Where did the Civil War begin?
Who have been the only non-Democratic presidential candidates to win South Carolina's electoral votes since Reconstruction?
What is a *county delegation* in South Carolina? What political importance does it have?
What school built the first separate college library building in the United States?
When was the Santee-Cooper Project completed?
Who were the *lords proprietors*?
What is South Carolina's chief economic activity?
What South Carolina garden has been called "the most beautiful in the world"?
What are South Carolina's three main land regions?

### Books for Young Readers

BAILEY, BERNADINE F. *Picture Book of South Carolina*. Whitman, 1956.
COMMAGER, EVAN C. *Tenth Birthday*. Bobbs, 1954. How little girls of five generations of one family spent their 10th birthdays.
GRAY, ELIZABETH J. *Beppy Marlowe of Charles Town*. Viking, 1936. Beppy leaves London with her brother to live on their Carolina plantation in 1715.
LATTIMORE, ELEANOR F. *The Fig Tree*. Morrow, 1951. *Diana in the China Shop*. 1955. *Fair Bay*. 1958. Stories of South Carolina.
OLIPHANT, MARY C. S., and FURMAN, MARY S. O. *Gateway to South Carolina*. M. C. S. Oliphant, Greenville, S.C., 1947.

### Books for Older Readers

BASS, ROBERT D. *Swamp Fox: The Life and Campaigns of Francis Marion*. Holt, 1959. *Gamecock: The Life and Campaigns of General Thomas Sumter*. 1961.
DABBS, JAMES M. *Pee Dee Panorama*. Univ. of South Carolina Press, 1951.
ELEAZER, JAMES M. *Dutch Fork Farm Boy*. Univ. of South Carolina Press, 1952.
EPSTEIN, BERYL W. and SAMUEL. *Francis Marion: Swamp Fox of the Revolution*. Messner, 1956. A story of the Revolutionary War general who helped defeat the British in the South.
JULIEN, CARL T. *Beneath So Kind a Sky: The Scenic and Architectural Beauty of South Carolina*. Univ. of South Carolina Press, 1947. *Sea Islands to Sand Hills*. 1954.
LANDER, ERNEST M., JR. *A History of South Carolina, 1865-1960*. Univ. of North Carolina Press, 1960.
ROBERTSON, BEN. *Red Hills and Cotton: An Upcountry Memory*. Univ. of South Carolina Press, 1960.
*South Carolina: A Guide to the Palmetto State*. Oxford, 1946.
WALLACE, DAVID D. *South Carolina: A Short History, 1520-1948*. Univ. of South Carolina Press, 1961.

**SOUTH CAROLINA, UNIVERSITY OF,** is a state-controlled coeducational school at Columbia, S.C. Its divisions include the college of arts and sciences; the graduate school; the schools of law, engineering, journalism, pharmacy, education, and business administration; and an extension division. It grants B.A., B.S., M.A., M.S., and Ph.D. degrees. The university has AFROTC and NROTC programs.

In 1801, the school was chartered as South Carolina College. It is one of the oldest state-supported schools in the United States. Its library building contains the largest and most valuable collection of South Carolina historical material in existence.

The University of South Carolina operates four off-campus centers, in Beaufort, Conway, Florence, and Lancaster. These four centers offer the first two years of college work. For enrollment, see UNIVERSITIES AND COLLEGES (table).           WILLIAM H. PATTERSON

**SOUTH CAROLINA STATE COLLEGE** is a state-supported coeducational college in Orangeburg, S.C. It has schools of arts and sciences, agriculture, education, home economics, industrial education, law, and graduate studies. Courses lead to bachelor's and master's degrees. There is a summer session and a graduate extension division. The college library has a special collection of material written about the American Negro. South Carolina State College was founded in 1895, and took its present name in 1954. For enrollment, see UNIVERSITIES AND COLLEGES (table).     J. D. MCGHEE

**SOUTH CENTRAL STATES.** See SOUTHERN STATES; ALABAMA; ARKANSAS; KENTUCKY; LOUISIANA; MISSISSIPPI; OKLAHOMA; TENNESSEE; TEXAS.

South Dakota Dept. of Highways
**Tending Cattle on the Plains of South Dakota**

# SOUTH DAKOTA  The Sunshine State

**SOUTH DAKOTA** is a midwestern state of many startling and beautiful contrasts. The wide Missouri River flows southward through the middle of the state. Low hills, lakes formed by ancient glaciers, and vast stretches of fertile cropland lie east of the river. West of the river are deep canyons and rolling plains. The enchanting Black Hills rise abruptly in the southwest. Southeast of the Black Hills are the weirdly beautiful Badlands. South Dakota is often called the *Land of Infinite Variety* because of the many great differences in its landscape.

South Dakota is mainly a farm state. Farms and ranches cover about nine-tenths of the state, and more South Dakotans are employed in farming than in any other occupation. Sheep and cattle graze on the sprawling ranches of the western plains, and on smaller farms in the east. Crops are grown on the rich soil of eastern South Dakota. The state is a top producer of beef cattle, hogs, and sheep. It also ranks high in growing corn, flaxseed, rye, spring wheat, and other crops.

Millions of tourists visit South Dakota every year. The tourist trade ranks second only to agriculture in importance. The Black Hills are one of the nation's most popular vacationlands. Attractions there include Mount Rushmore National Memorial, also called the *Shrine of Democracy.* Sixty-foot-high heads of George Washington, Thomas Jefferson, Theodore Roosevelt, and Abraham Lincoln have been carved out of a granite mountain. The memorial is the world's largest sculpture. Nearby, an even larger statue of the great Sioux chief Crazy Horse is being blasted out of a mountain.

Most of South Dakota's mineral wealth lies in the Black Hills. Gold was discovered there in 1874. Two years later, the rich Homestake *lode* (deposit) was discovered. The Homestake Mine is still the greatest gold producer in the Western Hemisphere.

The history of South Dakota reads like an adventure story. It is a tale of daring fur traders, battles between Indians and white settlers, and stampedes for gold. Included in the story are such colorful names as Calamity Jane, George A. Custer, Sitting Bull, and Wild Bill Hickok. But the most important figure in the state's history has been the farmer. The courageous South Dakota farmer has clung to his land through droughts, depressions, and blizzards. He has made South Dakota one of the nation's great agricultural states.

South Dakota was named for the Sioux Indians who once roamed the region. The Sioux called themselves *Dakota* or *Lakota,* meaning *allies* or *friends.* South Dakota's sunny climate earned it the nickname of the *Sunshine State.* The many coyotes that once lived in South Dakota gave it another nickname, the *Coyote State.*

The geographic center of the United States is in South Dakota, 17 miles west of Castle Rock. Pierre is the capital of South Dakota, and Sioux Falls is the largest city. For the relationship of South Dakota to other states in its region, see MIDWESTERN STATES.

Mount Rushmore National Memorial near Rapid City
H. Armstrong Roberts

## FACTS IN BRIEF

**Capital:** Pierre.
**Government:** *Congress*—U.S. Senators, 2; U.S. Representatives, 2. *Electoral Votes,* 4. *State Legislature*—senators, 35; representatives, 75. *Counties,* 67. *Voting Age,* 21 years.
**Area:** 77,047 square miles (including inland water); 16th in size among the states. *Greatest Distances:* (east-west) 380 miles; (north-south) 245 miles.
**Elevation:** *Highest,* Harney Peak, 7,242 feet above sea level in Pennington County; *Lowest,* Big Stone Lake, 962 feet above sea level in Roberts County.
**Population:** 680,514 (1960 census), 40th among the states. *Density,* 8 persons to the square mile. *Distribution,* rural, 61 per cent; urban, 39 per cent. *Estimated 1965 Population,* 682,000.
**Chief Products:** *Agriculture,* alfalfa seed and grass seeds, beef and dairy cattle, barley, corn, flaxseed, hay, hogs, oats, rye, sheep, spring wheat. *Manufacturing,* clay products, dairy products, flour and feed, lumber and wood products, meat products, printed materials. *Mining,* clay, gold, sand and gravel, stone.
**Statehood:** Nov. 2, 1889, the 40th state.
**State Motto:** *Under God the People Rule.*
**State Song:** "Hail, South Dakota." Words and music by Deecort Hammitt.

*The contributors of this article are Duncan J. McGregor, State Geologist and Professor of Geology at the University of South Dakota; Everett W. Sterling, Professor of History at the University of South Dakota; and Anson A. Yeager, Executive Editor of the* Sioux Falls Argus-Leader.

**Days of '76 Parade in Deadwood**
South Dakota Dept. of Highways

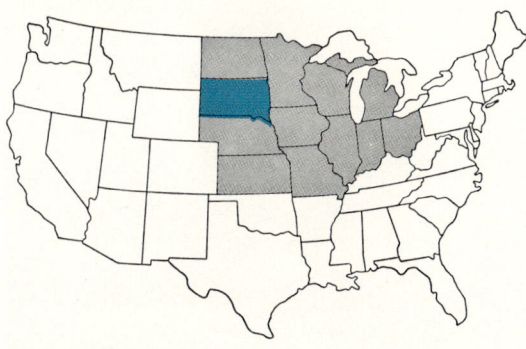

**South Dakota** (blue) ranks 16th in size among all the states, and 4th in size among the Midwestern States (gray).

529

# SOUTH DAKOTA / Government

**Constitution.** South Dakota is still governed under its original constitution, adopted in 1889. *Amendments* (changes) to the constitution may be proposed in the legislature or by a constitutional convention. An amendment proposed in the legislature must be approved by a majority of both houses of the legislature. Then approval is required by a majority of voters casting ballots on the amendment.

A proposal to call a constitutional convention must first be approved by two-thirds of both houses of the legislature. Then a majority of voters in an election must approve the convention. An amendment proposed by a convention becomes law after approval by a majority of citizens voting on the issue.

**Executive.** The governor of South Dakota is elected to a two-year term. He may not serve more than two terms in a row. The governor receives a yearly salary of $18,000. For a list of South Dakota's governors, see the *History* section of this article.

Other executive officials include the lieutenant governor, secretary of state, attorney general, commissioner of school and public lands, treasurer, and auditor. They are also elected to two-year terms. All except the treasurer may serve an unlimited number of terms. The treasurer may not serve more than two terms in a row.

**Legislature** consists of a 35-member senate and a 75-member house of representatives. Voters in 29 senatorial districts elect from one to four senators, depending on population. Voters in 39 representative districts elect from one to nine representatives, depending on population. Members of both houses serve two-year terms. In even-numbered years, the legislature meets on the Tuesday after the first Monday in January. In odd-numbered years, it meets on the Tuesday after the third Monday in January. Sessions last 30 days in even-numbered years, and 45 days in odd-numbered years. The governor may call special sessions.

In 1898, South Dakota became the first state to adopt the initiative and referendum. The *initiative* gives voters the right to propose laws directly. If 5 per cent of the state's voters sign a *petition* (formal request) for the adoption of a law, the legislature must pass the measure. It is then put on a statewide ballot. The *referendum* allows voters to accept or reject measures approved by the legislature. Any law passed by the legislature must be submitted to the people if 5 per cent of the voters sign a petition asking that a vote on the law be taken. See INITIATIVE AND REFERENDUM.

In 1965, the legislature *reapportioned* (redivided) the senate and house of representatives to provide equal representation based on population.

**Courts.** The state supreme court is the highest court. It has five judges elected to six-year terms. Each year, the judges select one of their number to be the presiding judge. Voters in each of the 12 judicial districts elect from one to three circuit court judges to four-year terms. The number of judges depends on district population. The state has 19 county district courts. Each of these courts is presided over by a judge who is elected to a four-year term.

**Local Government.** South Dakota has 67 counties. Three of these counties—Shannon, Todd, and Washabaugh—do not have an organized county government. Their county functions are administered by adjoining counties. Each organized county is governed by a board of commissioners of three to five members elected to four-year terms. Other elected county officials include the attorney, auditor, clerk of the court, register of deeds, sheriff, and treasurer.

South Dakota has more than 300 cities and towns. The state constitution gives them the power of *home rule*. That is, cities and towns may operate under their own charters and adopt their own form of government. Most cities have the mayor-council form of government.

**Taxation.** Taxes and licenses bring in about three-fifths of the state government's income. Almost all the rest comes from federal grants and other U.S. government programs. Motor vehicle license fees, and taxes on sales and motor fuels provide most of the state's tax revenue. South Dakota also collects taxes on alcoholic beverages, tobacco, and other items. The state does not tax property, or personal or corporation incomes.

**The Governor's Mansion** is in Pierre. The house, surrounded by landscaped grounds, was built in 1936. A basement room serves as a museum of Indian relics.

South Dakota Dept. of Highways

"Great Seal of South Dakota"

**The State Seal**

**The State Flag**

**Symbols of South Dakota.** On the seal, the smelter chimney represents mining, the plowman stands for farming, and the riverboat symbolizes transportation. The seal was adopted in 1889. The state flag, adopted in 1963, has the seal in the center. The gold circle around the seal represents the blazing rays of the sun. The blue field symbolizes South Dakota's clear skies.

Flower illustration, courtesy of Eli Lilly and Company

**Politics.** South Dakota voters have strongly favored the Republican party throughout most of the state's history. In 1889, the people elected a Republican as the first governor of their state. Since then, South Dakota has had only three Democratic governors. The state has voted for the Democratic presidential candidate in only four elections—1896, 1932, 1936, and 1964. For South Dakota's electoral votes and voting record in presidential elections, see ELECTORAL COLLEGE (table).

South Dakota shows no real signs of becoming a two-party state, although a few Democrats were elected to high office in the 1950's and 1960's. In 1958, for the first time since 1934, the voters elected a Democratic governor, Ralph Herseth. But in 1960, the voters returned the governorship to a Republican, Archie Gubbrud. In 1962, for the first time since 1936, South Dakota elected a Democrat, George McGovern, to the U.S. Senate.

**The State Bird**
Ring-Necked Pheasant

**The State Capitol** stands near the Missouri River in Pierre. The limestone and white marble building was begun in 1905. Pierre has been South Dakota's capital since 1889. Earlier capitals were Yankton (1861-1883) and Bismarck, N.Dak. (1883-1889).

South Dakota Dept. of Highways

**The State Flower**
American Pasqueflower

**The State Tree**
Black Hills Spruce

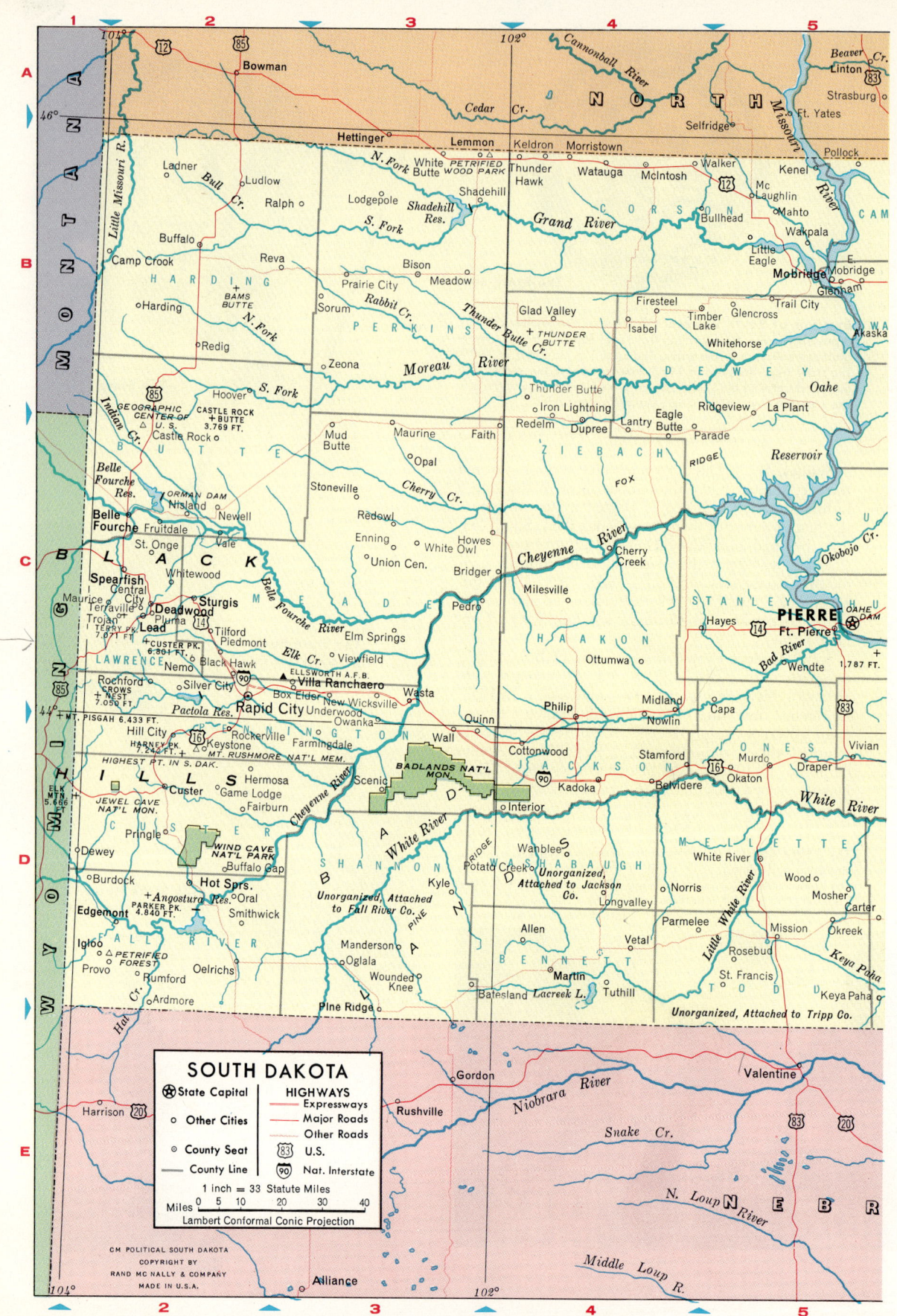

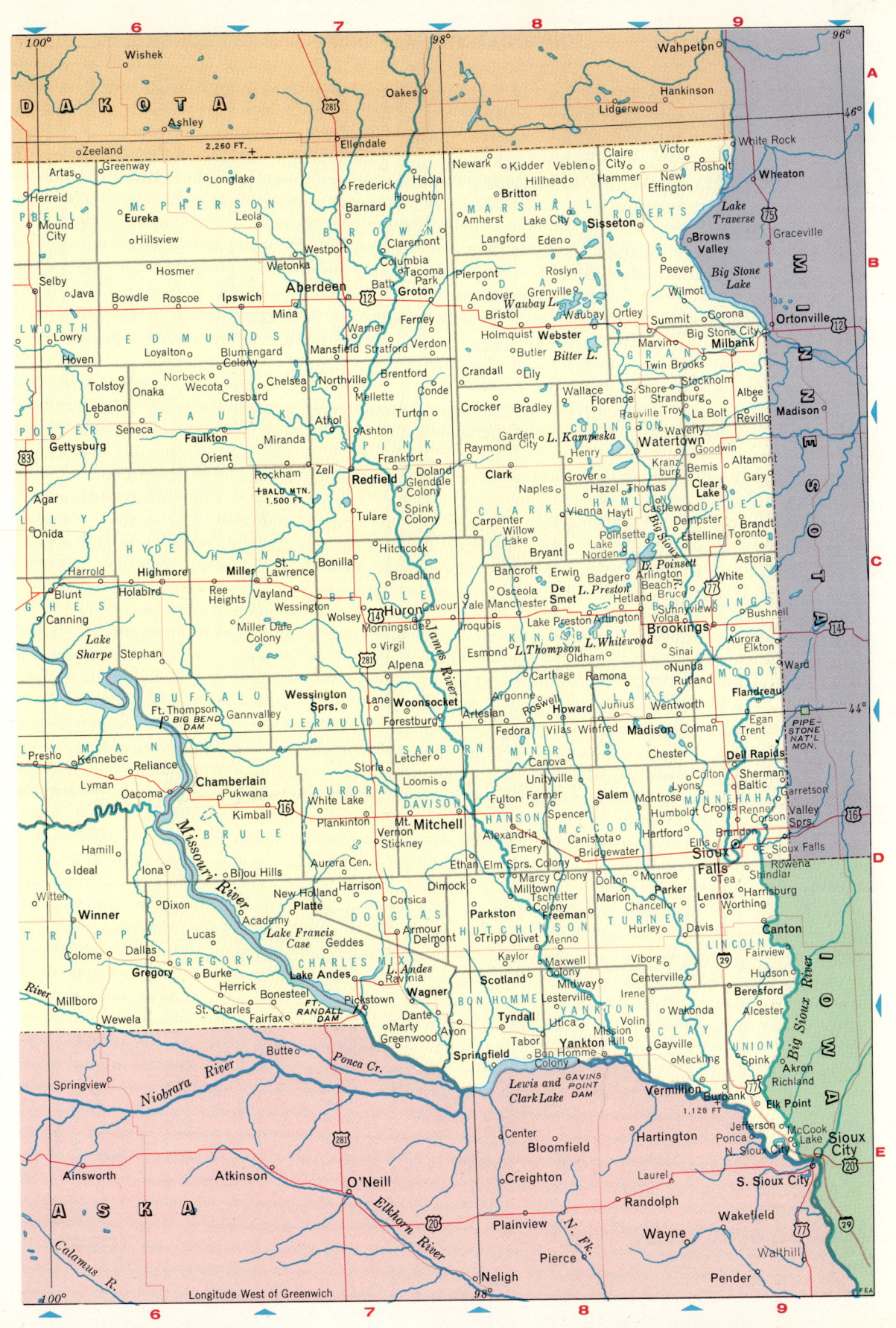

SOUTH DAKOTA MAP INDEX

## Population

682,000 ..Estimate 1965
680,514 ............1960
652,740 ............1950
642,961 ............1940
692,849 ............1930
636,547 ............1920
583,888 ............1910
401,570 ............1900
348,600 ............1890
98,268 ............1880
11,776 ............1870

## Metropolitan Area

Sioux Falls.......86,575

## Counties

Aurora ......4,749..D 7
Beadle .....21,682..C 7
Bennett ....3,053..D 4
Bon Homme .9,229..D 7
Brookings ..20,046..C 8
Brown .....34,106..B 7
Brule .......6,319..D 6
Buffalo .....1,547..C 6
Butte .......8,592..C 2
Campbell ....3,531..B 5
Charles Mix 11,785..D 7
Clark .......7,134..C 8
Clay .......10,810..E 8
Codington ..20,220..C 8
Corson ......5,798..B 4
Custer ......4,906..D 2
Davison ....16,681..D 7
Day .......10,516..B 8
Deuel .......6,782..C 9
Dewey ......5,257..B 4
Douglas .....5,113..D 7
Edmunds ....6,079..B 6
Fall River .10,688..D 2
Faulk .......4,397..B 6
Grant .......9,913..B 9
Gregory .....7,399..D 6
Haakon .....3,303..C 4
Hamlin .....6,303..C 8
Hand .......6,712..C 6
Hanson .....4,584..D 8
Harding .....2,371..B 2
Hughes ....12,725..C 5
Hutchinson .11,085..D 8
Hyde .......2,602..C 6
Jackson .....1,985..D 4
Jerauld .....4,048..C 7
Jones .......2,066..D 5
Kingsbury ...9,227..C 8
Lake .......11,764..C 8
Lawrence ..17,075..C 2
Lincoln ....12,371..D 9
Lyman ......4,428..D 5
Marshall ....6,663..B 8
McCook .....8,268..D 8
McPherson ..5,821..B 6
Meade .....12,044..C 3
Mellette ....2,664..D 5
Miner .......5,398..D 8
Minnehaha .86,575..D 9
Moody .......8,810..C 9
Pennington 58,195..D 2
Perkins .....5,977..B 3
Potter ......4,926..B 6
Roberts ....13,190..B 8
Sanborn ....4,641..D 7
Shannon ....6,000..D 3
Spink ......11,706..C 7
Stanley .....4,085..C 5
Sully .......2,607..C 5
Todd .......4,661..D 5
Tripp .......8,761..D 5
Turner .....11,159..D 8
Union .....10,197..E 9
Walworth ...8,097..B 5
Washabaugh 1,042..D 4
Yankton ....17,551..D 8
Ziebach .....2,495..C 4

## Cities and Towns

Aberdeen ..23,073.°B 7
Agar .........139..C 5
Akaska ........90..B 5
Albee ..........42..B 9
Alcester ......479..D 9
Alexandria ...614.°D 8
Allen .........100..D 4
Alpena .......407..C 7
Altamont .......77..C 9
Amherst .......75..B 8
Andover ......224..B 8
Ardmore .......73..D 2
Arlington .....996..C 8
Arlington Beach 20..C 8
Armour .......875.°D 7
Artas ..........87..B 6
Artesian ......330..C 8
Ashton .......182..B 7
Astoria .......176..C 9
Athol .........100..B 7
Aurora ........232..C 9
Aurora Center ..25..D 7
Avon .........637..E 7
Badger .......117..C 8
Baltic ........278..D 9
Bancroft ......86..C 8
Barnard ......100..B 7
Batesland ....100..D 3
Bath .........100..B 7
Belle Fourche ..4,087.°C 2
Belvidere .....232..D 4
Bemis .........50..C 9
Beresford ...1,794..D 9
Big Stone City 718..B 9
Bison ........457.°B 3
Black Hawk ..350..C 2
Blumengard Colony ......70..B 6
Blunt ........532..C 6
Bon Homme Colony .....100..E 8
Bonesteel ....452..D 7
Bonilla ........50..C 7
Bowdle .......673..B 6
Box Elder .....150..C 3
Bradley ......188..B 8
Brandon ......600..D 9
Brandt .......148..C 9
Brentford ......96..B 7
Bridgewater ...694..D 8
Bristol .......562..B 8
Britton .....1,442.°B 8
Broadland .....33..C 7
Brookings ..10,558.°C 9
Bruce ........272..C 9
Bryant .......522..C 8
Buffalo .......652.°B 2
Buffalo Gap ..194..D 2
Bullhead .....300..B 4
Burbank .......125..E 9
Burke ........811.°D 6
Bushnell .......92..C 9
Butler .........62..B 8
Camp Crook ...90..B 2
Canistota .....627..D 8
Canning ........25..C 5
Canova .......247..D 8
Canton ......2,511.°D 9
Carpenter ......50..C 8
Carthage ......368..C 8
Castle Rock ...28..C 2
Castlewood ...500..C 8
Cavour .......140..C 7
Centerville ....887..D 9
Central City ..247..C 2
Chamberlain 2,598.°D 6
Chancellor ....214..D 9
Chelsea ........53..B 7
Cherry Creek ..200..C 4
Chester .......200..D 9
Claire City .....86..B 8
Claremont ....247..B 7
Clark ......1,484.°C 8
Clear Lake ..1,137.°C 9
Colman .......505..D 9
Colome .......398..D 6
Colton ........593..D 9
Columbia .....272..B 7
Conde ........388..B 7
Corona .......150..B 9
Corsica .......479..D 7
Corson .........75..D 9
Cottonwood ....38..D 4
Cresbard ......229..B 7
Crocker ........65..B 8
Crooks ........160..D 9
Custer ......2,105.°D 2
Dallas ........212..D 6
Dante ........102..D 7
Davis .........124..D 9
Deadwood ...3,045.°C 2
Dell Rapids .1,863..D 9
Delmont ......363..D 7
Dempster .....100..C 9
De Smet ....1,324.°C 8
Dewey ..........25..D 2
Dimock .......160..D 8
Dixon ..........15..D 6
Doland ........481..C 7
Dolton ..........71..D 8
Draper ........215..D 5
Dupree .......548.°B 4
Eagle Butte ...495..B 4
Eden ..........136..B 8
Edgemont ...1,772..D 2
Egan .........310..C 9
Elk Point ...1,378.°E 9
Elkton ........621..C 9
Ellis ............75..D 9
Elm Springs Colony .....100..D 8
Emery ........502..D 8
Erwin .........157..C 8
Estelline ......722..C 9
Ethan ........297..D 8
Eureka .....1,555..B 6
Fairburn .......47..D 2
Fairfax ......253..D 7
Fairview ......101..D 9
Faith ........591..B 3
Farmer ........95..D 8
Farmingdale ...15..D 3
Faulkton ...1,051.°C 6
Fedora .......100..C 8
Ferney ........85..B 7
Firesteel .......50..B 4
Flandreau ..2,129.°C 9
Florence ......216..B 8
Forestburg ...200..C 7
Fort Pierre .2,649.°C 5
Fort Thompson 150..C 6
Frankfort .....240..C 7
Frederick .....381..B 7
Freeman ....1,140..D 8
Fruitdale ......79..C 2
Fulton ........135..D 8
Game Lodge ...85..D 2
Gannvalley ....95.°C 7
Garden City ..226..C 8
Garretson .....850..D 9
Gary ..........471..C 9
Gayville .......261..E 8
Geddes .......380..D 7
Gettysburg ..1,950.°C 6
Glad Valley ...20..B 4
Glendale Colony ......100..C 7
Glenham ......171..B 5
Goodwin ......113..C 9
Greenway .....101..B 6
Greenwood .....200..E 7
Gregory .....1,478..D 6
Grenville ......151..B 8
Groton ......1,063..B 7
Grover .........35..C 8
Hamill .........75..D 6
Hammer ........45..B 8
Harrisburg ....313..D 9
Harrison .......65..D 7
Harrold .......255..C 6
Hartford ......688..D 9
Hayti .........425.°C 8
Hazel .........128..C 8
Hecla .........444..B 7
Henry .........276..C 8
Hermosa ......126..D 2
Herreid .......767..B 5
Herrick .......160..D 6
Hetland .......107..C 8
Highmore ...1,078.°C 6
Hill City ......419..D 2
Hillhead ........30..B 8
Hillsview ......44..B 6
Hitchcock .....193..C 7
Holabird .......40..C 6
Holmquist .....35..B 8
Hosmer .......433..B 6
Hot Springs .4,943.°D 2
Houghton ......90..B 7
Hoven .........568..B 6
Howard .....1,208.°C 8
Hudson ........455..D 9
Humboldt .....446..D 8
Hurley ........450..D 8
Huron .....14,180.°C 7
Igloo .......1,000..D 2
Interior .......179..D 4
Ipswich .....1,131.°B 6
Irene .........399..D 8
Iron Lightning .60..B 4
Iroquois ......385..C 8
Isabel ........488..B 4
Java ..........406..B 6
Jefferson ......443..E 9
Junius .........60..C 8
Kadoka .......840.°D 4
Kaylor ........150..D 8
Keldron ........25..B 4
Kenel .........150..B 5
Kennebec ....372.°D 6
Keystone ......500..D 2
Kidder ........120..B 8
Kimball .......912..D 7
Kranzburg ....156..C 9
Kyle ............70..D 3
La Bolt .......125..B 9
Lake Andes .1,097.°D 7
Lake City .......81..B 8
Lake Norden ..390..C 8
Lake Preston .955..C 8
Lane ............99..C 7
Langford ......397..B 8
Lantry ..........40..B 4
La Plant ......175..B 5
Lead .......6,211..C 2
Lebanon ......198..B 6
Lemmon .....2,412..B 3
Lennox .....1,353..D 9
Leola ........833.°B 7
Lesterville ....173..D 8
Letcher .......296..D 7
Lily ...........119..B 8
Little Eagle ..200..B 5
Longlake .....109..B 6
Loomis ........45..D 7
Lowry .........44..B 6
Loyalton ......34..B 6
Lyons .........95..D 9
Madison ....5,420.°C 8
Manchester ....20..C 8
Manderson ...100..D 3
Mansfield ....150..B 7
Marion .......843..D 8
Marcy Colony ..45..D 8
Martin .....1,184.°D 4
Marty .......135..E 7
Marvin ........93..B 9
Maxwell Colony ......200..D 8
McCook Lake .300..E 9
McIntosh .....568.°B 4
McLaughlin ...983..B 5
Meadow ........25..B 3
Meckling .......93..E 8
Mellette .......208..B 7
Menno .......837..D 8
Midland ......401..C 4
Milbank ....3,500.°B 9
Milesville ......20..C 4
Millboro ........20..D 6
Miller ......2,081.°C 7
Miller Dale Colony ......50..C 6
Miltown ........25..D 8
Mina ..........35..B 7
Miranda .......55..C 7
Mission ......611..D 5
Mission Hill ..165..E 8
Mitchell ...12,555.°D 7
Mobridge ....4,391..B 5
Monroe .......156..D 8
Montrose .....430..D 8
Moreau ............B 5
Morningside ..150..C 7
Morristown ...219..B 4
Mound City ...144.°B 5
Mount Vernon 379..D 7
Murdo ........783.°D 5
Naples .........36..C 8
Nemo ..........65..C 2
New Effington 280..B 9
New Holland .110..D 7
New Underwood .......462..C 3
New Witten (Witten) ....146..D 5
Newark ........39..B 8
Newell ........797..C 2
Nisland .......211..C 2
Norris .........40..D 4
North Sioux City .........736..E 9
Northville ....153..B 7
Nowlin ........25..C 4
Nunda ........106..C 9
Oacoma .......312..D 6
Oelrichs ......132..D 2
Oglala ........50..D 3
Okaton ........65..D 5
Okreek .......150..D 5
Oldham .......291..C 8
Olivet .......135.°D 8
Onaka .........65..B 6
Onida ........843.°C 5
Oral ...........60..D 2
Orient ........133..C 6
Ortley ........127..B 8
Osceola ........20..C 8
Owanka .........50..C 3
Parker .....1,142.°D 8
Parkston ....1,514..D 8
Parmelee .....150..D 4
Peever .......208..B 9
Philip ......1,114.°C 4
Pickstown ....400..D 7
Piedmont .....200..C 2
Pierpont .....258..B 8
Pierre .....10,088.°C 5
Pine Ridge ..1,300..D 3
Plankinton ...644.°D 7
Platte ......1,167..D 7
Poinsette ......50..C 8
Pollock .......417..B 5
Potato Creek ..40..D 4
Presho .......881..D 5
Pringle .......145..D 2
Provo ........175..D 2
Pukwana .....247..D 6
Quinn ........162..D 3
Ramona .......247..C 8
Rapid City .42,399.°C 2
Ravinia ......164..D 7
Raymond ......168..C 8
Redfield ....2,952.°C 7
Ree Heights ..188..C 6
Reliance ......201..D 6
Renner .......150..D 9
Revillo .......202..B 9
Richland .......65..E 9
Ridgeview .....40..B 5
Rochford ......90..C 2
Rockerville ....20..D 2
Rockham .....197..C 7
Roscoe .......532..B 6
Rosebud ......500..D 5
Rosholt ......423..B 9
Roslyn ........256..B 8
Roswell ........39..C 8
Rowena ........80..D 9
Rutland ......100..C 9
St. Charles ....50..D 6
St. Francis ...421..D 5
St. Lawrence .290..C 7
St. Onge ......80..C 2
Salem ......1,188.°D 8
Scenic .........40..D 3
Scotland ....1,077..D 8
Selby ........979.°B 5
Seneca ........161..B 6
Sherman .....116..D 9
Silver City .....50..C 2
Sinai .........166..C 9
Sioux Falls 65,466.°D 9
Sisseton ...3,218.°B 8
Smithwick .....40..D 2
South Shore ..259..B 9
Spearfish ...3,682..C 2
Spencer ......460..D 8
Spink Colony ..100..C 7
Springfield .1,194..E 8
Stickney ......456..D 7
Stockholm ....155..B 9
Storla ..........50..D 7
Strandburg ...105..B 9
Stratford ....109..B 7
Sturgis .....4,639.°C 2
Summit .......283..B 9
Sunnyview .....75..C 9
Tabor ........378..E 8
Tea* ..........188..D 9
Terraville .....200..C 2
Thunder Butte .50..B 4
Thunder Hawk .60..B 4
Tilford ..........60..C 2
Timber Lake ..624.°B 4
Tolstoy .......142..B 6
Toronto ......268..C 9
Trail City .....75..B 5
Trent .........232..D 9
Tripp .........837..D 8
Tschetter Colony ......75..D 8
Tulare ........225..C 7
Turton ........140..B 7
Tuthill ........40..D 4
Twin Brooks ...86..B 9
Tyndall .....1,262.°E 8
Union Center ..35..C 3
Unityville ......40..D 8
Utica ..........70..E 8
Vale ..........115..C 2
Valley Springs 472..D 9
Veblen ........437..B 8
Vermillion ..6,102.°E 9
Viborg ........699..D 8
Victor .........40..B 9
Vienna ........191..C 8
Vilas ...........49..C 8
Villa Ranchaero 3,000..C 3
Virgil ...........81..C 7
Vivian ........250..D 5
Volga .........780..C 9
Volin .........171..E 8
Wagner .....1,586..D 7
Wakonda .....382..D 8
Wakpala ......325..B 5
Wall ..........629..D 3
Wallace ......132..B 8
Wanblee ......300..D 4
Ward ...........74..C 9
Warner .......150..B 7
Wasta .........196..C 3
Watauga .......85..B 4
Watertown .14,077.°C 9
Waubay .......851..B 8
Waverly .......40..C 9
Webster .....2,409.°B 8
Wentworth ....211..C 8
Wessington ....378..C 7
Wessington Springs ...1,488.°C 7
Westport ......100..B 7
White .........417..C 9
White Lake ...397..D 7
White River ..583.°D 5
White Rock ....76..B 9
Whitehorse .....80..B 5
Whitewood ....470..C 2
Willow Lake ..467..C 8
Wilmot .......545..B 9
Winfred .......137..C 8
Winner .....3,705.°D 6
Wolsey ........354..C 7
Wood .........267..D 5
Woonsocket .1,035.°C 7
Worthing .....304..D 9
Wounded Knee ........50..D 3
Yale ..........171..C 8
Yankton ....9,279.°E 8
Zell ..........100..C 7

*Does not appear on the map; key shows general location.

°County Seat.
Source: Latest census figures.

## SOUTH DAKOTA / People

The 1960 United States census reported that South Dakota had 680,514 persons. The population had increased 4 per cent over the 1950 figure, 652,740. The U.S. Bureau of the Census estimated that by 1965 the population had reached about 682,000.

South Dakota's percentage of city dwellers ranks among the lowest in the nation. Only about two-fifths of the people live in cities and towns. The state has only one Standard Metropolitan Statistical Area as defined by the U.S. Bureau of the Budget (see METROPOLITAN AREA). This is the Sioux Falls metropolitan area. It has 86,575 persons, including 65,466 in Sioux Falls.

South Dakota has no great manufacturing industries to prompt the growth of large cities. Only eight cities in the state have populations of more than 10,000. Only two cities—Sioux Falls and Rapid City—have more than 25,000 persons. Most South Dakota towns were established to serve the surrounding agricultural regions. A majority of these towns lie east of the Missouri River, in the state's chief farming area. Many towns have also grown up in the Black Hills, where mining and the tourist industry prosper. See the separate articles on the cities of South Dakota listed in the *Related Articles* at the end of this article.

About 97 of every 100 South Dakotans were born in the United States. Most of those born in other countries came from Denmark, Germany, Norway, Russia, and Sweden.

Lutherans make up the largest single religious group in South Dakota. Roman Catholics are the second largest group, followed by Methodists, Presbyterians, and members of the United Church of Christ.

### POPULATION

This map shows the *population density* of South Dakota, and how it varies in different parts of the state. Population density is the average number of persons who live on each square mile.

PERSONS PER SQUARE MILE
- 20 to 110
- 10 to 20
- 5 to 10
- 1 to 5

WORLD BOOK map

## SOUTH DAKOTA / Education

**Schools.** The first schoolhouse in the South Dakota region opened in 1860 in Bon Homme. The building was torn down after three months, and its logs were used in a stockade built for protection against Indian attacks. The first territorial legislature authorized a public school system in 1862. In 1864, a superintendent of public instruction was appointed.

Today, the state board of education controls the public school system. The board consists of the superintendent of public instruction and seven other members. The superintendent is elected to a two-year term. The other board members are appointed by the governor with the approval of the state senate. They serve for five years. Children must attend school between the ages of 7 and 16. For the number of students and teachers in South Dakota, see EDUCATION (table).

**Libraries and Museums.** South Dakota's first library, the Alexander Mitchell Library, was established in Aberdeen in 1884. This library still exists. In 1913, the state legislature established a commission, now called the South Dakota State Library Commission, to improve library services. Today, the state has about 90 public libraries and several bookmobiles.

The University of South Dakota in Vermillion has the largest library in the state. It owns over 200,000 books. The Sioux Falls Carnegie Library has fine collections on art, biography, history, and music. The State Historical Library in Pierre has excellent materials on South Dakota history.

Museums are operated by the University of South Dakota, the South Dakota School of Mines and Technology in Rapid City, and the State Historical Society in Pierre. Other museums in Rapid City and Sioux Falls exhibit Indian arts and crafts, and historic items. Adams Memorial Hall in Deadwood has many interesting pioneer items on display.

### UNIVERSITIES AND COLLEGES

South Dakota has 13 regionally accredited universities and colleges. For enrollments and further information, see UNIVERSITIES AND COLLEGES (table).

| Name | Location | Founded |
|---|---|---|
| Augustana College | Sioux Falls | 1860 |
| Black Hills State College | Spearfish | 1883 |
| Dakota Wesleyan University | Mitchell | 1885 |
| General Beadle State College | Madison | 1881 |
| Huron College | Huron | 1883 |
| Mount Marty College | Yankton | 1936 |
| Northern State College | Aberdeen | 1901 |
| Sioux Falls College | Sioux Falls | 1883 |
| South Dakota, University of | Vermillion | 1882 |
| South Dakota School of Mines and Technology | Rapid City | 1885 |
| South Dakota State University | Brookings | 1881 |
| Southern State College | Springfield | 1881 |
| Yankton College | Yankton | 1881 |

# SOUTH DAKOTA / A Visitor's Guide

More than 4 million tourists visit South Dakota yearly. Most of them tour the famous Black Hills. Great numbers of hunters shoot many kinds of game birds and animals in the state each autumn. South Dakota offers visitors breath-taking scenery, and swimming, fishing, and other recreational facilities.

### PLACES TO VISIT

Following are brief descriptions of some of South Dakota's many interesting places to visit.

**Corn Palace,** in Mitchell, is redecorated every fall with murals made of different colors of corn and other grains. Concerts, dances, and many other events are held in the building.

**Crazy Horse Memorial,** near Custer, is a gigantic sculpture of the great Sioux chief being carved out of a granite mountain by Korczak Ziolkowski.

**Deadwood,** in the Black Hills, was a brawling mining town of the Old West. It has many reminders of its wild early days. Wild Bill Hickok, Calamity Jane, Preacher Smith, and other famous characters are buried in Deadwood's Boot Hill Cemetery.

**"Great Lakes of South Dakota"** are formed by four huge dams on the Missouri River. These lakes—Francis Case, Lewis and Clark, Oahe, and Sharpe—offer fishing, boating, and other water sports. Visitors may tour the power plants of the dams.

**National Forests, Parks, Memorials, and Monuments.** South Dakota shares Black Hills National Forest with Wyoming, and Custer National Forest with Montana. For the areas and chief features of these forests, see NATIONAL FOREST (table). The federal government also administers Wind Cave National Park, Mount Rushmore National Memorial, and Jewel Cave and Badlands national monuments. All are in the Black Hills except Badlands National Monument, which is just southeast of this region. Each has a separate article in WORLD BOOK.

**State Parks.** South Dakota has 11 state parks. For information, write to Assistant State Forester; Department of Game, Fish and Parks; State Office Building; Pierre, S.Dak. 57501.

**Corn Palace in Mitchell**

**Pheasant Hunting in Eastern South Dakota**

**Czech Days Festival in Tabor**

All photos from South Dakota Department of Highways unless otherwise indicated

Model of Crazy Horse Memorial and Sculptor Korczak Ziolkowski near Custer

Judging the Snow Queen at the Festival in Aberdeen
Aberdeen Junior Chamber of Commerce

Racing Wild Horses at a Rodeo in Belle Fourche

Sioux Festival Dancers in Fort Sisseton State Park

## ANNUAL EVENTS

Many South Dakota communities stage pioneer celebrations, rodeos, stagecoach races, and fairs. Plays and pageants are presented in summer at Custer State Park and Black Hills towns. The famous Black Hills Passion Play is staged at Spearfish (see PASSION PLAY [picture]). Other annual events include:

**January-March:** Snow Queen Festival in Aberdeen (January); Ski Meets at Terry Peak near Lead (February); Winter Carnival in Deadwood (March); Little International Stock Show in Brookings (March).

**April-June:** Miss South Dakota Beauty Pageant in Hot Springs (June); Czech Days Festival in Tabor (June); Crazy Horse Pageant in Hot Springs (June-August).

**July-September:** Oglala Sioux Sun Dance in Pine Ridge (July); Gold Discovery Days in Custer (July); Days of '76 in Deadwood (August); Black Hills Motorcycle Classic in Sturgis (August); Prairie Village Threshing Jamboree in Madison (August); Sioux Empire Fair in Sioux Falls (August); State Fair in Huron (September); Corn Palace Festival in Mitchell (September).

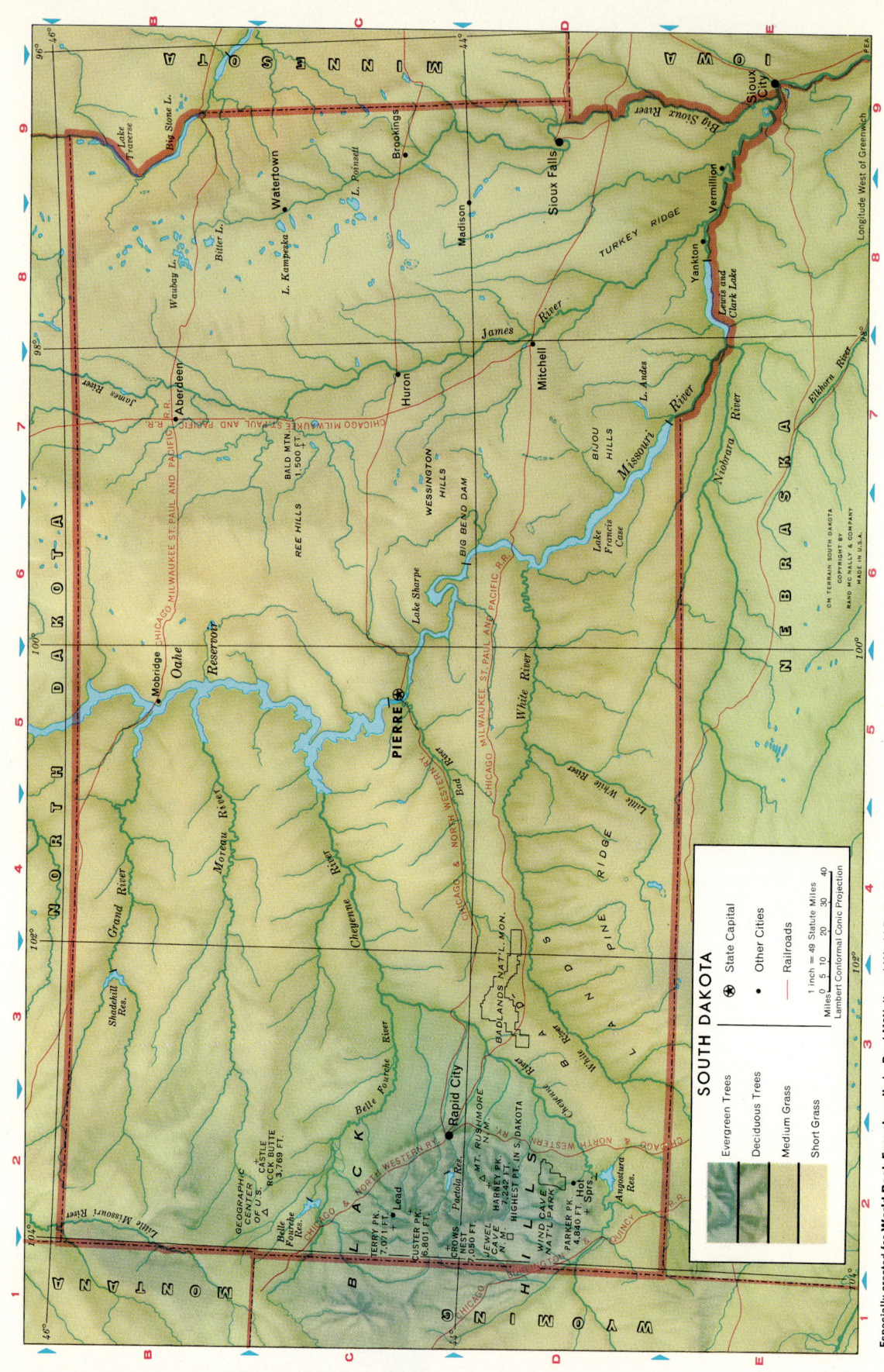

Especially created for World Book Encyclopedia by Rand McNally and World Book editors

## SOUTH DAKOTA / The Land

The Missouri River flows through the middle of South Dakota from north to south. The river marks the western edge of a series of glaciers that crossed eastern South Dakota during the Ice Age. The glaciers leveled off high places, filled in valleys, and created lakes. As the glaciers spread across the region, they dragged or pushed boulders, rocks, and other materials. When the glaciers melted, they left these materials behind. All the materials deposited by the glaciers or by their melted waters are called *drift*. These materials are either unsorted or laid down in layers. Materials deposited directly by the glaciers are unsorted, and are called *till*.

**Land Regions.** South Dakota has four major land regions: (1) the Young Drift Plains, (2) the Dissected Till Plains, (3) the Great Plains, and (4) the Black Hills. The Young Drift Plains and the Dissected Till Plains together are known as the *Prairies* or *Central Lowlands*.

*The Young Drift Plains* extend across most of eastern South Dakota. This region is marked by low, rolling hills and glacial lakes. The roughest part of the region is near its eastern edge. Most of the region's lakes are in this area. Early French fur traders called the area the *Coteau des Prairies* (Prairie Hills). The northeastern corner of the Prairie Hills ends abruptly at a 600-foot *escarpment* (steep slope) along the Minnesota River Valley. A 300-foot escarpment marks the western end of the Prairie Hills along the James Basin. The James Basin occupies the western part of the Young Drift Plains. The basin is a flat to slightly rolling lowland. It extends in a wide belt down the width of the state. The James River winds through the basin. A 300-foot escarpment rises along the basin's western edge.

*The Dissected Till Plains* cover the southeastern corner of South Dakota. Glaciers left large deposits of till over the region. A deep cover of wind-blown soil particles called *loess* then settled on the till. Streams have *dissected* (cut up) the region, giving it a rolling surface.

*The Great Plains* cover most of the western two-thirds of South Dakota. The Missouri Hills form the eastern edge of the Great Plains. These hills are between the James Basin and the Missouri River. Rolling hills formed by glaciers mark the eastern part of the area. Rugged ridges and valleys mark the western part. The chief features of the land west of the Missouri are rolling plains, canyons, and *buttes* (steep, flat-topped hills that stand alone). Many of the buttes rise from 400 to 600 feet above the surrounding plains.

Badlands are common in the Great Plains. Wind and water have worn the soft rocks of these regions into steep hills and deep gullies. The nation's most famous badlands lie southeast of the Black Hills. This area has little plant or animal life. See BADLANDS.

*The Black Hills* are a low, isolated mountain group in west-central South Dakota. The region has great scenic beauty, with deep canyons and towering, rugged rock formations. The Black Hills also have rich mineral deposits, and thick forests of tall pines, spruces, and other trees. The state's highest point—7,242-foot Harney Peak—rises in the Black Hills. See BLACK HILLS.

**Rivers and Lakes.** The Missouri River is the state's most important river. The Missouri and its branches drain all the state except the northeastern corner. The Missouri's western branches include the Cheyenne, Grand, Moreau, and White rivers. The Big Sioux, James, and other rivers join the Missouri in the east.

Most of South Dakota's lakes were formed during the Ice Age by glaciers. A series of such glacial lakes

### Land Regions of South Dakota

### Map Index

| | | | |
|---|---|---|---|
| Angostura Reservoir | D 2 | Lake Andes | D 7 |
| Bad R. | C 5 | Lake Francis Case | D 6 |
| Badlands | D 3 | Lake Kampeska | C 8 |
| Badlands Nat. Mon. | C 3 | Lake Poinsett | C 8 |
| Bald Mtn. | C 7 | Lake Sharpe | C 6 |
| Belle Fourche Reservoir | | Lewis and Clark Lake | E 8 |
| Belle Fourche R. | C 2 | Little Missouri R. | B 2 |
| Big Bend Dam | C 6 | Little White R. | D 6 |
| Big Sioux R. | E 9 | Missouri R. | B 4 |
| Bijou Hills | D 7 | Mount Rushmore Nat. Mem. | D 2 |
| Bitter Lake | B 8 | Pactola Reservoir | D 2 |
| Black Hills | C 2 | Parker Peak | D 2 |
| Castle Rock Butte | B 2 | Pine Ridge | D 4 |
| Cheyenne R. | C 4 | Ree Hills | C 6 |
| Crows Nest | C 2 | Shadehill Reservoir | B 3 |
| Custer Peak | C 2 | Terry Peak | C 2 |
| Grand R. | B 4 | Turkey Ridge | D 8 |
| Harney Peak (Highest Point in South Dakota) | D 2 | Waubay Lake | B 8 |
| James R. | D 8 | Wessington Hills | C 7 |
| Jewel Cave Nat. Mon. | D 2 | White R. | D 5 |
| | | Wind Cave Nat. Park | D 2 |

**Flocks of Sheep** graze in the Great Plains region of western South Dakota. Large-scale ranching in this "short grass country" makes the state a leader in the production of sheep and wool.

Grant Heilman

# SOUTH DAKOTA

stretches across eastern South Dakota. The state's biggest lakes are man-made, created by four dams on the Missouri River. The largest lake is Oahe Reservoir, 250 miles long. It was created by Oahe Dam. Fort Randall Dam created Lake Francis Case, 140 miles long. The 80-mile-long reservoir formed by Big Bend Dam is named Lake Sharpe. Gavins Point Dam forms a 25-mile-long reservoir called Lewis and Clark Lake.

One of South Dakota's most interesting lakes is Medicine Lake, near Florence in Codington County. Medicine Lake has a salt content of more than 4 per cent, compared with about 3½ per cent for seawater. Its water was once believed to have medicinal qualities.

H. Armstrong Roberts

**Badlands National Monument,** *right,* is a desolate area in southwestern South Dakota. Water and wind have worn away the land, leaving deep ravines, steep ridges, and colorful cliffs. The area is part of the Great Plains region.

**Falls of the Big Sioux River** are near the city of Sioux Falls. The river flows through the Dissected Till Plains region.

**Lake Kampeska,** below, lies near the center of a broad belt of lakes in South Dakota's Young Drift Plains region.

South Dakota Department of Highways

**Towering Granite Boulders,** *right,* form the tops of rugged mountains in the Black Hills. This region has many rich mineral deposits.

# SOUTH DAKOTA/Climate

South Dakota is far from any large body of water. For this reason, the state has great ranges in temperatures. Temperatures of 100° F. and above occur every summer. But even the hottest days are seldom uncomfortable, because the humidity is low. Below-zero temperatures are common on midwinter mornings. Average July temperatures range from 78° F. in south-central South Dakota to 68° F. in the Black Hills. The state's record high temperature, 120° F., was set at Gann valley (or Gann Valley) on July 5, 1936. Average January temperatures range from 10° F. in the northeast to 22° F. in the southwest. The state's record low, −58° F., was set at McIntosh on Feb. 17, 1936.

South Dakota's annual *precipitation* (rain, melted snow, and other forms of moisture) ranges from about 13 inches in the northwest to about 25 inches in the southeast. Most of the rain falls during the growing season, from April through September. The heaviest snowfalls occur in February and early March.

**Early Winter Snow** covers a pasture near Hermosa. Cattle can dig through the light snow to get grass. But ranchers must bring food to the herds when heavy snow falls in midwinter.

H. Armstrong Roberts

## SEASONAL TEMPERATURES

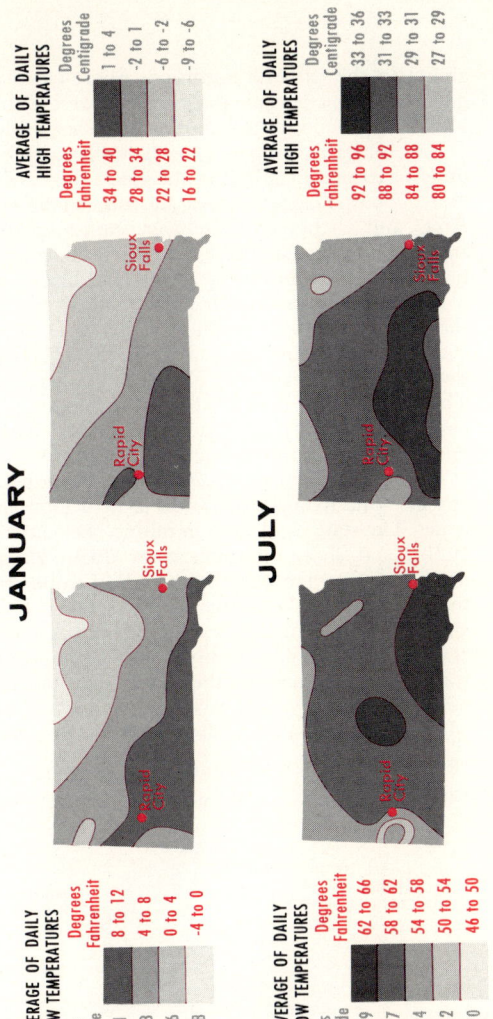

### JANUARY

**AVERAGE OF DAILY LOW TEMPERATURES**

| Degrees Centigrade | Degrees Fahrenheit |
|---|---|
| −13 to −11 | 8 to 12 |
| −16 to −13 | 4 to 8 |
| −18 to −16 | 0 to 4 |
| −20 to −18 | −4 to 0 |

**AVERAGE OF DAILY HIGH TEMPERATURES**

| Degrees Fahrenheit | Degrees Centigrade |
|---|---|
| 34 to 40 | 1 to 4 |
| 28 to 34 | −2 to 1 |
| 22 to 28 | −6 to −2 |
| 16 to 22 | −9 to −6 |

### JULY

**AVERAGE OF DAILY LOW TEMPERATURES**

| Degrees Centigrade | Degrees Fahrenheit |
|---|---|
| 17 to 19 | 62 to 66 |
| 14 to 17 | 58 to 62 |
| 12 to 14 | 54 to 58 |
| 10 to 12 | 50 to 54 |
| 8 to 10 | 46 to 50 |

**AVERAGE OF DAILY HIGH TEMPERATURES**

| Degrees Fahrenheit | Degrees Centigrade |
|---|---|
| 92 to 96 | 33 to 36 |
| 88 to 92 | 31 to 33 |
| 84 to 88 | 29 to 31 |
| 80 to 84 | 27 to 29 |

## AVERAGE YEARLY PRECIPITATION
(Rain, Melted Snow, and Other Moisture)

| Inches | Centimeters |
|---|---|
| 24 to 28 | 61 to 71 |
| 20 to 24 | 51 to 61 |
| 16 to 20 | 41 to 51 |
| 12 to 16 | 30 to 41 |

0  100  200 Miles
0 100 200 300 Kilometers

WORLD BOOK maps

| MONTHLY WEATHER IN RAPID CITY AND SIOUX FALLS | | JAN | FEB | MAR | APR | MAY | JUNE | JULY | AUG | SEPT | OCT | NOV | DEC |
|---|---|---|---|---|---|---|---|---|---|---|---|---|---|
| **RAPID CITY** | Average of: High Temperatures | 33 | 36 | 43 | 57 | 67 | 76 | 86 | 85 | 74 | 62 | 47 | 37 |
| | Low Temperatures | 9 | 12 | 20 | 32 | 43 | 52 | 59 | 57 | 47 | 36 | 24 | 14 |
| | Days of Rain or Snow | 7 | 6 | 9 | 8 | 12 | 13 | 9 | 8 | 6 | 5 | 5 | 5 |
| **SIOUX FALLS** | Days of Rain or Snow | 5 | 6 | 8 | 9 | 10 | 11 | 10 | 10 | 7 | 5 | 5 | 6 |
| | High Temperatures | 24 | 30 | 42 | 59 | 71 | 80 | 88 | 85 | 75 | 63 | 43 | 29 |
| | Low Temperatures | 4 | 9 | 22 | 34 | 45 | 56 | 62 | 60 | 49 | 37 | 21 | 9 |

Temperatures are given in degrees Fahrenheit.

Source: U.S. Weather Bureau

# SOUTH DAKOTA / Economy

**Natural Resources.** South Dakota's most precious natural resource is its fertile soil, the basis of its great agricultural economy. The state also has rich mineral resources. Most of the forest reserves are in the Black Hills. Other plant life and animal life are abundant.

*Soil.* The soils that cover most of eastern South Dakota developed from glacial materials. These soils are loamy, and range in color from dark brown to black. A belt of loess stretches along the east bank of the Missouri River. A deep deposit of loess also covers southeastern South Dakota. The soils of eastern South Dakota are good for growing corn, wheat, and other crops. Most of the soils west of the Missouri were formed from the weathering of various shales. These soils make good grazing lands.

*Minerals.* South Dakota's most important metallic mineral is gold. It is found in the Black Hills. A rich vein of gold ore, the Homestake lode, was discovered at Lead in 1876. This vein has yielded millions of tons of gold ore, and it still has reserves of about 14 million tons. The gold ore contains some silver. Other metallic minerals in the Black Hills include antimony, arsenic, bismuth, iron, lead, manganese, tellurium, tungsten, and zinc. Molybdenum, uranium, and vanadium occur in southwestern and northwestern South Dakota. The northwestern counties have nearly 2 billion tons of *lignite*, a low-grade coal. Much of western South Dakota lies in the great Williston Basin. This basin is a rich petroleum reservoir that extends across North Dakota and eastern Montana into southern Canada. Most South Dakota counties have sand and gravel deposits of commercial value. Granite is quarried in the northeast, and limestone in the Black Hills area. Manganese ore deposits are found in south-central South Dakota. Other minerals, found chiefly in the Black Hills, include beryl, clays, feldspar, gypsum, and mica.

*Forests* cover only about 2 million acres, or about 4 per cent of South Dakota. Most of the forests lie in the Black Hills. These forests contain chiefly cone-bearing trees, including junipers, ponderosa pines, and spruces. Ashes, cottonwoods, oaks, and other hardwoods are scattered over the rest of the state, especially in river valleys.

*Other Plant Life.* The American pasqueflower, South Dakota's state flower, blooms on hillsides in early spring. Black-eyed Susans, goldenrod, Mariposa lilies, poppies, sunflowers, wild orange geraniums, and other flowers grow on the eastern prairies. Cactus plants are common in western South Dakota. Bluebells, forget-me-nots, lady's-slippers, larkspurs, and many other kinds of flowers blossom in the Black Hills.

*Animal Life.* White-tailed deer live in all parts of South Dakota. They are most numerous in the Black Hills and in the woodlands of the Missouri River Valley. Pronghorns (antelopes) roam the land west of the Missouri. Mule deer graze in the rocky butte and canyon areas of the northwest. Bighorn sheep, elks, and Rocky Mountain goats live in the Black Hills. About 2,000 buffaloes, the nation's largest herd, roam Custer State Park in the Black Hills.

The ring-necked pheasant, the state bird, is found throughout eastern South Dakota. Hungarian partridges nest in northern parts of the state, and sage grouse in the extreme northwest. Sharp-tailed grouse and prairie chickens are found chiefly west of the Missouri River. Wild turkeys feed in the Black Hills.

Bass, bluegills, crappies, perch, walleyed pike, and other fishes are abundant in the glacial lakes of northeastern South Dakota. Among the fishes in the Missouri River and its branches are bass, catfish, paddlefish, sauger, and sturgeon. Fishermen catch brook and rainbow trout in the rivers and lakes of the Black Hills.

**Agriculture** accounts for more than 80 per cent of the value of all goods produced in South Dakota. The state's farm income totals about $753,500,000 yearly. South Dakota has about 55,000 farms and ranches. They range in size from less than 100 acres in the southeast to more than 100,000 acres in the west. The farms and ranches cover an average of 818 acres.

*Livestock and Livestock Products* provide South Dakota farmers with about three-fourths of their total farm income. The state is a leader in raising beef cattle, hogs, lambs, and sheep. Pastures cover about 25 million acres, or more than half the state. Beef cattle graze on the enormous ranches of the western section. The ranchers often ship their calves and yearlings to cattlemen called *feeders* in eastern South Dakota or in neighboring states. The feeders fatten the young cattle on corn and other grains. They then send the livestock to market. Most of South Dakota's sheep and lambs come from

## PRODUCTION IN SOUTH DAKOTA
Total yearly value of goods produced—$930,171,000

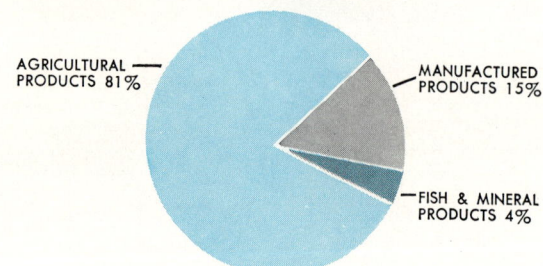

AGRICULTURAL PRODUCTS 81%
MANUFACTURED PRODUCTS 15%
FISH & MINERAL PRODUCTS 4%

Note: Manufacturing percentage based on value added by manufacture. Other percentages based on value of production. Fish Products are less than 1 per cent.

Source: Latest available U.S. Government statistics

## EMPLOYMENT IN SOUTH DAKOTA
Average yearly number of persons employed—244,789

|  | Number of Employees |
|---|---|
| Agriculture | 88,000 |
| Government | 41,500 |
| Wholesale & Retail Trade | 40,500 |
| Services | 24,900 |
| Manufacturing | 15,600 |
| Construction | 13,700 |
| Transportation & Public Utilities | 10,100 |
| Finance, Insurance & Real Estate | 6,700 |
| Fishing, Forestry & Mining | 3,789 |

Source: Employment statistics supplied by employers to government agencies

the northwest area. The state is a leader in wool production. Hogs are raised in the southeast. Most of the state's chickens and eggs are also produced in this section. Farmers raise dairy cattle throughout the eastern part of the state.

*Field Crops* are raised on about a third of South Dakota's land area. Most of the crops are grown east of the Missouri River. South Dakota is a leading state in the production of alfalfa seed, corn, flaxseed, hay, oats, rye, spring wheat, sweet clover seed, and various grass seeds. The southeastern and south-central sections harvest the most corn and oats. Soybeans are also grown in these sections. The northeast leads in barley and flaxseed production. Rye and wheat are raised chiefly in the northern half of the state, and in counties just east of the Missouri River. Irrigation projects built by the federal government have made the land in some western areas suitable for growing crops. Crops grown on this irrigated land include corn and sugar beets.

**Manufacturing** accounts for only about 15 per cent of the value of all goods produced in South Dakota. Goods manufactured in the state have a *value added by manufacture* of about $137½ million yearly. This figure represents the value created in products by South Dakota's industries, not counting such costs as materials, supplies, and fuels.

South Dakota has about 575 manufacturing and processing plants. Most of them employ fewer than 50 persons. Food processing is by far the leading manufacturing activity, with an annual value added by manufacture of $98,139,000. Meat processing and packing is the single most important industry. The largest plant is in Sioux Falls. Other plants are in Huron, Madison, Mitchell, and Watertown. Poultry is dressed and packed in Madison, Rapid City, Sioux Falls, Watertown, and other cities. Creameries and dairy-processing plants operate in Mitchell, Rapid City, Sioux Falls, and many other towns. Rapid City has flour and feed mills. Feed mills also operate in Sioux Falls.

A state-owned plant near Rapid City manufactures cement, and a number of cities make concrete products. Factories in Belle Fourche process *bentonite* (a type of clay), and make bricks, tiles, and other clay products. Lumber mills operate in Custer, Rapid City, Spearfish, and other towns in the Black Hills. Rapid City also makes products of clay, glass, and stone.

**Mining** accounts for about 4 per cent of the value of all goods produced in South Dakota, or about $39 million yearly. About half this total comes from gold. South Dakota is the most important gold-producing state, and supplies about two-fifths of the nation's output. The Homestake Mine at Lead is the largest gold-producing mine in the Western Hemisphere. It has produced many millions of ounces of gold since the first ore was mined and milled in 1878. The mine still yields more than 500,000 ounces annually.

Almost every South Dakota county produces sand and gravel, which rank second in value to gold. Sand and gravel are used chiefly by the construction industry. Quarries in Grant County are the state's chief sources of granite, which is used as building and monument stone. Uranium is mined in southwestern and northwestern South Dakota.

In 1954, South Dakota drilled its first oil-producing well, in Harding County in the northwestern part of the state. Today, the county has about 20 producing wells. In 1955, a second oil field was discovered in Custer County in southwestern South Dakota. This county now has several producing wells.

Other minerals produced in South Dakota include beryl, clays, feldspar, gypsum, iron ore, lignite, limestone, mica, and silver.

**Electric Power.** About 70 per cent of South Dakota's electric power comes from hydroelectric projects. The rest is generated by fuel-burning plants. In 1964, the Pathfinder Atomic Power Plant was dedicated near Sioux Falls. The power plant started commercial production of electricity in 1966. Four huge Missouri River dams—Big Bend, Fort Randall, Gavins Point, and Oahe—supply most of South Dakota's hydroelec-

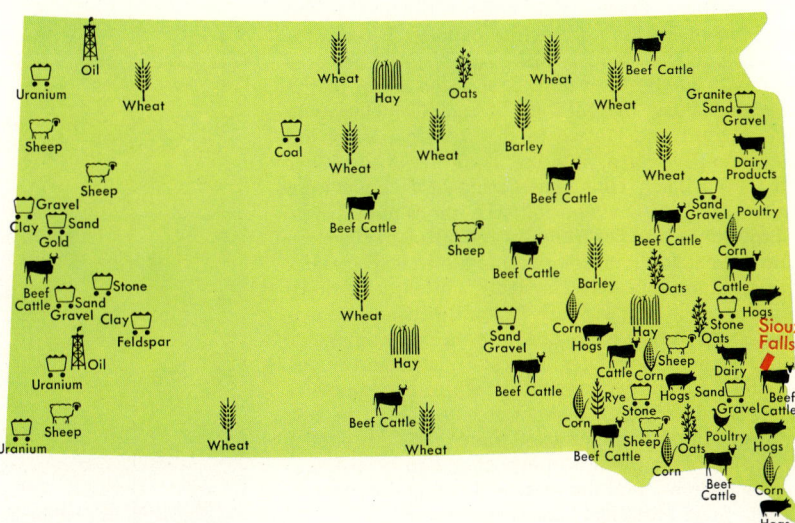

**FARM AND MINERAL PRODUCTS**

This map shows where the state's leading farm and mineral products are produced. The major urban area (shown on the map in red) is the state's important manufacturing center.

WORLD BOOK map

# SOUTH DAKOTA

tric power. The swift streams of the Black Hills are also used to generate electric power. For South Dakota's kilowatt-hour production, see ELECTRIC POWER (table: Electric-Power Production in the United States).

**Transportation.** The wide Missouri River provided the first great highway into South Dakota. Early explorers, fur traders, and missionaries sailed up the river in canoes or flat-bottomed boats. In 1831, the first steamboat reached the site of what is now Fort Pierre. During the 1870's, gold was discovered in the Black Hills. Prospectors carved trails into the region as they rushed to the gold fields in stagecoaches and oxcarts. In 1872, the first railroad to enter South Dakota reached Yankton. By 1880, two rail lines crossed eastern South Dakota to the Missouri River. A railroad reached the Black Hills in 1886.

Today, five railroads serve the state on about 3,900 miles of track. More than 90,000 miles of roads and highways cross South Dakota. Over half of them are surfaced. Commercial airlines serve about 10 cities and towns. South Dakota has about 90 airports and airfields.

**Communication.** South Dakota's first newspaper, the *Dakota Democrat*, was established in Sioux Falls in 1859. The oldest newspaper still published in the state is the *Yankton Press and Dakotan*. It was founded as the *Weekly Dakotian* in 1861, and became a daily in 1875. South Dakota has more than 10 daily newspapers, about 150 weeklies, and over 30 periodicals. Daily newspapers with the largest circulations include the *Rapid City Journal* and the *Sioux Falls Argus-Leader*.

The South Dakota School of Mines and Technology established the state's first radio station, WCAT. The station was licensed in Rapid City in 1922. The first television station, KELO, began operating in Sioux Falls in 1953. Today, 40 radio stations and 10 television stations serve the state.

## SOUTH DAKOTA / History

**Indian Days.** Three major Indian tribes lived in the South Dakota region before white explorers first arrived. The Arikara were farmers who made their homes near the mouth of the Cheyenne River, and north of the Cheyenne along the Missouri River. The Cheyenne Indians lived and hunted in the western part of the Cheyenne River area, and also along the White River and in the Black Hills. The Sioux, or Dakota, were hunters and warriors who followed the buffalo herds.

**Exploration and Fur Trade.** In 1682, Robert Cavelier, Sieur de la Salle, claimed for France all the land drained by the Mississippi River system. This vast territory included what is now South Dakota, because the waters of the Missouri River flow into the Mississippi.

The French-Canadian explorers François and Louis-Joseph La Vérendryc were the first white men known to have visited the South Dakota area. In 1743, the two brothers buried a small lead plate near the site of present-day Fort Pierre to prove they had been there. Schoolchildren found the plate in 1913, and the South Dakota State Historical Society now owns it.

540d

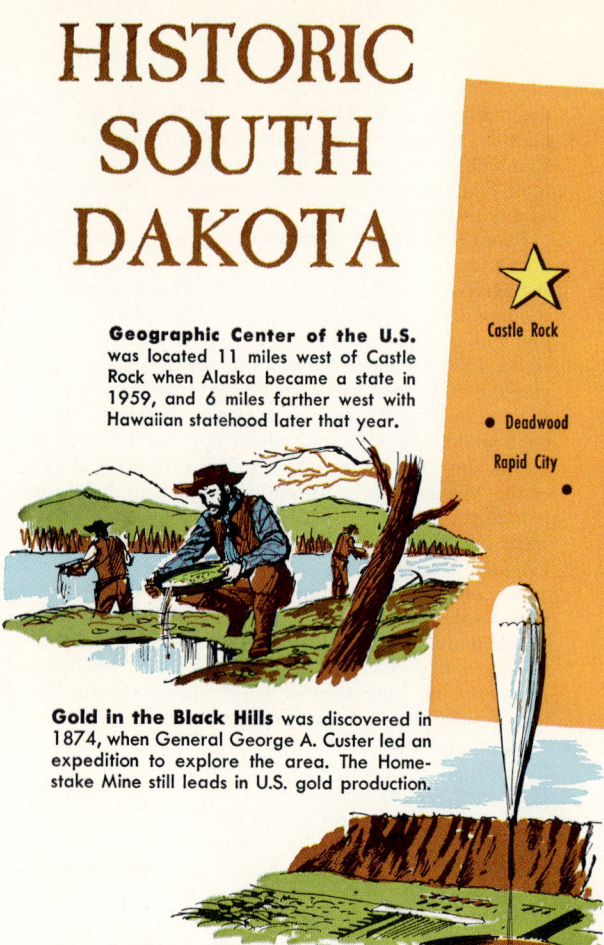

# HISTORIC SOUTH DAKOTA

★ Castle Rock

● Deadwood

Rapid City ●

**Geographic Center of the U.S.** was located 11 miles west of Castle Rock when Alaska became a state in 1959, and 6 miles farther west with Hawaiian statehood later that year.

**Gold in the Black Hills** was discovered in 1874, when General George A. Custer led an expedition to explore the area. The Homestake Mine still leads in U.S. gold production.

**The Balloon *Explorer II*,** which cast off near Rapid City in 1935, soared to a height of 72,395 feet. This record stood for 21 years, but has since been broken several times.

**Fort Randall Dam,** completed in 1956, crosses the Missouri River near Lake Andes. It is 165 feet high and 10,700 feet long.

South Dakota Dept. of Highways

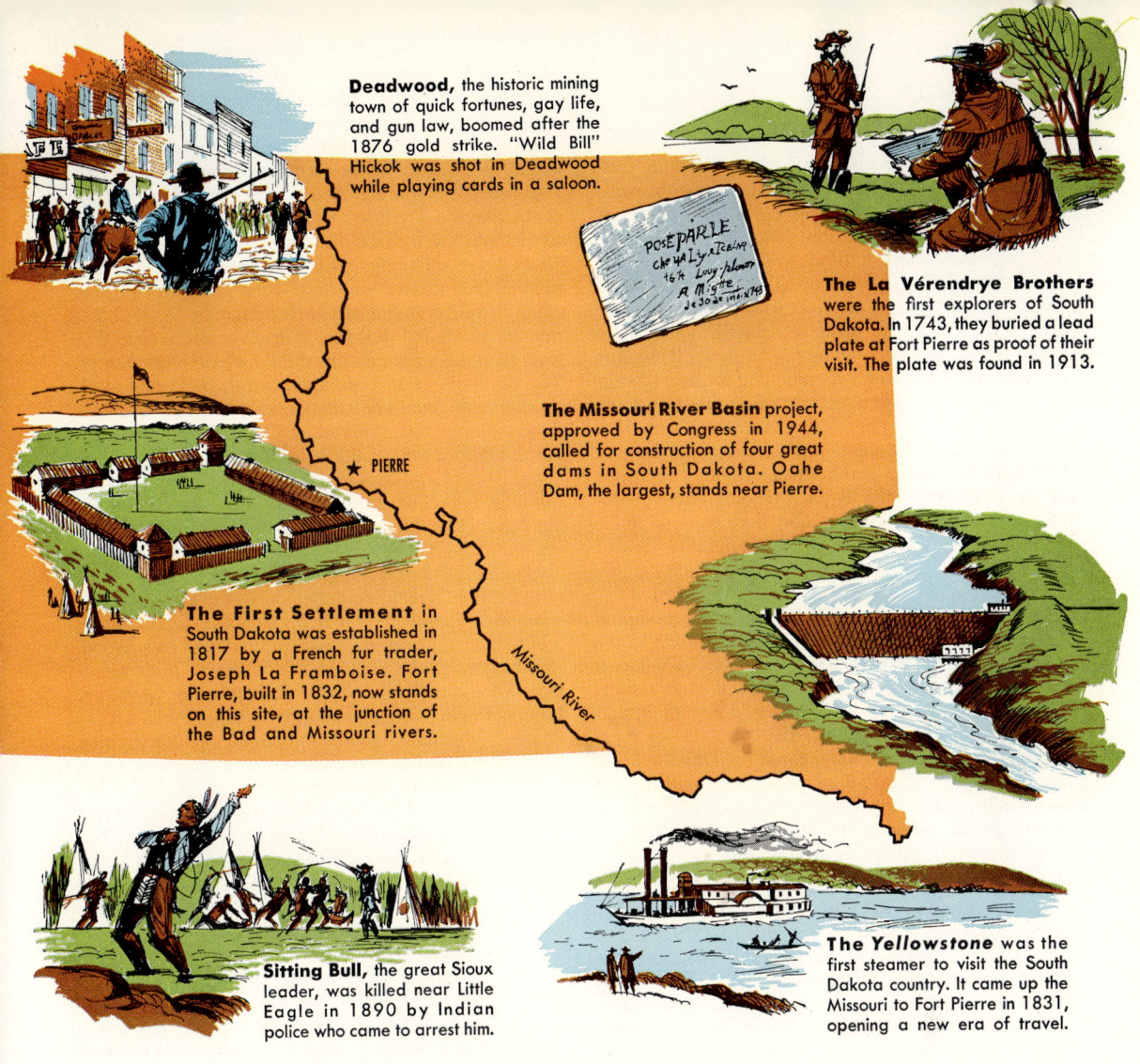

In 1762, France gave its land west of the Mississippi River to Spain. Spain returned it to France in 1800. In 1803, the United States bought this territory, called Louisiana, from France (see LOUISIANA PURCHASE).

About 1785, Pierre Dorion, a French fur trader, arrived in the lower James River Valley, near what is now Yankton. He became the first white man to settle permanently in the South Dakota region.

In 1804, President Thomas Jefferson sent Meriwether Lewis and William Clark to explore the Louisiana Territory and to blaze a trail to the Pacific Ocean. In August, the explorers camped in the South Dakota region for the first time, near what is now Elk Point. They followed the Missouri River through the region. Lewis and Clark passed through again in 1806 on their return from the Pacific. Their reports of the abundant fur-bearing animals in the region attracted an increased number of fur traders. The explorers had also established friendly relations with many Indian tribes.

The most important trading post was built in 1817 at the mouth of the Bad River, on the site of present-day Fort Pierre. This lonely post became the first permanent settlement in the South Dakota region. It was established by Joseph La Framboise, a French trader.

The first large-scale military action against South Dakota Indians took place in 1823. The Arikara tribe attacked a fur-trading party led by General William Ashley, lieutenant governor of Missouri. The federal government sent troops under Colonel Henry Leavenworth to punish the tribe. The Sioux, traditional enemies of the Arikara, joined in fighting them.

In 1831, the steamboat *Yellowstone* sailed up the Missouri River from St. Louis to Fort Tecumseh (now Fort Pierre). The *Yellowstone* proved that steamboats could travel the upper Missouri. This development further spurred the fur trade in South Dakota. Large cargoes could be shipped in far less time than it took for flat-bottomed boats that were moved by the river currents. The fur trade thrived for several years, but began to decline by 1850. The number of fur-bearing animals had started to decrease, and the demand for furs fell as silk became more fashionable.

540e

# SOUTH DAKOTA

**Agricultural Settlement.** The land that became North Dakota and South Dakota was part of the Missouri Territory between 1812 and 1834. The eastern section later belonged, in turn, to the Michigan, Wisconsin, Iowa, and Minnesota territories. The western section remained part of the Missouri Territory until 1854, when it became part of the Nebraska Territory.

Before the 1850's, all white settlement in the South Dakota region had been along the Missouri River and had been related to the fur trade. Agricultural settlement began in the eastern section during the late 1850's.

In 1857, Congress passed the Minnesota statehood bill. This bill set the new state's western border east of the Big Sioux River. But nothing was done about the rich farmland westward to the Missouri River. Some businessmen and politicians saw a chance to make money. They quickly formed land companies, gained control of choice locations, and laid out townsites. Settlements were established at Sioux Falls, Medary, Flandreau, and other points. In 1858, the Sioux signed a treaty with the government giving up their land in the southeastern corner between the Big Sioux and Missouri rivers. The opening of this land attracted more settlers to the South Dakota region. Yankton, Vermillion, and Bon Homme were founded in 1859.

**Territorial Days.** Congress created the Dakota Territory in 1861. It consisted of present-day North and South Dakota, and much of Montana and Wyoming. William Jayne was the first governor of the Dakota Territory, and Yankton was the capital.

Indian wars prevented rapid settlement of the territory during the 1860's. One of the most important wars was the Red Cloud War, named for Chief Red Cloud of the Sioux. The government planned to build a road across the Powder River country to newly discovered gold fields in Wyoming. At the time, Wyoming was part of the Dakota Territory. Red Cloud believed the road would ruin the Indians' hunting grounds. In 1866, the Sioux attacked troops sent to make a survey for the road. The Indians continued their raids until 1868, when the government met their demands. In the Laramie Treaty signed that year, the government agreed to give up its military posts in the Powder River country. The government also promised not to build any roads through the area. The treaty created the Great Sioux Reservation, which covered all the land in present-day South Dakota west of the Missouri River.

In 1874, General George A. Custer violated the Laramie Treaty when he led a military expedition into the Black Hills. The government had ordered him to investigate reports of gold in the mountains. The soldiers discovered gold near the present town of Custer. The news brought a rush of prospectors to the area. In 1876, prospectors discovered far richer deposits of gold in the area between the present towns of Lead and Deadwood. Another stampede of gold seekers followed. The town of Deadwood sprang up as the center of mining operations. It became a brawling, wide-open town, and won a reputation as the most lawless settlement on the frontier. Wild Bill Hickok, Calamity Jane, and other citizens of Deadwood became legends.

The invasion of the Black Hills by white men caused a series of Indian uprisings led by Crazy Horse and Sitting Bull. But in 1876, the Indians signed a new treaty giving up their claims to the Black Hills. Most of the Sioux surrendered and settled on reservations west of the Missouri River. Sitting Bull fled to Canada.

In 1881, Sitting Bull returned to the South Dakota region. He settled on Standing Rock Reservation in 1883. In 1890, a religious movement spread among the Sioux. This movement, called the Ghost Dance, was started by an Indian named Wovoka (see WOVOKA). Army leaders feared the Ghost Dance would lead to another Sioux uprising. They sent Indian police to arrest Sitting Bull, but he resisted and was killed. Some of Sitting Bull's followers fled the reservation and joined Chief Big Foot's band of Sioux on the Cheyenne River. Federal troops caught up with the Indians and took them to a cavalry camp on Wounded Knee Creek. There, the soldiers began to disarm the Sioux. A bloody battle began when someone fired a rifle. The soldiers massacred about 200 Indian men, women, and children. The Battle of Wounded Knee was the last big fight between Indians and white men on the northern plains. See INDIAN WARS (The Sioux Wars).

**Statehood.** A great land boom followed the discovery of gold in the Black Hills. Thousands came to seek gold. But many more came to farm in other sections of South Dakota. An enormous land rush began in 1878. Between 1878 and 1887, waves of farmers and speculators poured into South Dakota. They acquired more than 24 million acres of public lands offered by the government. In 1870, the South Dakota region had a population of less than 12,000. By 1890, the population had soared to 348,600. Most of the settlers came from neighboring states, but many came from Germany, Great

### IMPORTANT DATES IN SOUTH DAKOTA

**1682** Robert Cavelier, Sieur de la Salle, claimed for France all the land drained by the Mississippi River. This land included the South Dakota region.

**1743** The brothers François and Louis-Joseph La Vérendrye were the first white men known to have visited the region.

**1803** The United States acquired South Dakota through the Louisiana Purchase.

**1804, 1806** Meriwether Lewis and William Clark passed through South Dakota on their expedition to and from the Pacific Ocean.

**1817** Joseph La Framboise established the first permanent settlement in South Dakota, at what is now Fort Pierre.

**1831** The first steamboat reached Fort Tecumseh (now Fort Pierre).

**1861** Congress created the Dakota Territory.

**1868** The Laramie Treaty ended the Red Cloud War.

**1874** Gold was discovered in the Black Hills.

**1889** South Dakota became the 40th state on November 2.

**1927** Gutzon Borglum began work on Mount Rushmore National Memorial.

**1930's** South Dakota suffered its worst drought.

**1944** Congress authorized the Missouri River Basin Project, including construction of Fort Randall, Oahe, Gavins Point, and Big Bend dams in South Dakota.

**1962** Titan missiles became operational in South Dakota.

**1963** Minutemen missiles became operational in South Dakota.

**1966** The Pathfinder Atomic Power Plant near Sioux Falls started to produce electricity. The powerhouse of Big Bend Dam, the last of South Dakota's huge dams on the Missouri River, was completed.

**Boom Town of Deadwood** sprang up in 1876 after rich gold deposits were found in the Black Hills. The Homestake Mine, the richest gold mine in the Western Hemisphere, was established near Lead at that time. It is still in operation.

Bettman Archive

Britain, Norway, Russia, and other European countries.

Railroad building also boomed during this period. By 1880, two railroads had crossed eastern South Dakota to the Missouri River. In 1886, a railroad reached the Black Hills. Many towns sprang up along the rail lines. During the late 1870's and the 1880's, cattlemen entered the open rangeland west of the Missouri. The rush of miners and merchants to the Black Hills and the needs of the Indian agencies and military posts had created a heavy demand for meat.

During the 1870's, a movement began to divide the Dakota Territory into two parts. The major population centers had grown up far apart—in the northeastern and southeastern corners of the territory. The two groups of settlers wanted to develop separate governments. In February, 1889, Congress set the present boundary between South Dakota and North Dakota. It also passed an *enabling act*, which allowed the two regions to set up the machinery to become states (see ENABLING ACT). On Nov. 2, 1889, North Dakota and South Dakota entered the Union as the 39th and 40th states. South Dakotans elected Arthur C. Mellette, a Republican, as their first governor. Pierre became the state capital in 1889, shortly after South Dakota gained statehood.

**The Early 1900's.** The population of South Dakota had climbed to almost 350,000 by the time it became a state. But little growth occurred during the first 10 years of statehood. A severe drought began in 1889, and lasted until 1897. In 1890, part of the Great Sioux Reservation between the White and Cheyenne rivers was opened to settlement. But few settlers came.

Prosperity returned to South Dakota in the early 1900's. The drought had ended, and prices for farm crops were good. The government opened more new Indian lands in the west, and thousands of settlers poured into the state. Some of this land was offered through great land lotteries. People registered for land and received claims if they were lucky in the lottery drawings. Special trains brought people from all parts of the United States to take part in the lotteries.

By 1910, South Dakota's population had soared to almost 584,000. Between 1900 and 1910, the railroads added more than 1,100 miles of track in the state. Most of this new track was laid west of the Missouri River to serve the growing sheep and cattle ranches.

**State Experiments.** The prosperity and population growth of the first 10 years of the 1900's ended in 1911. Drought again hit the state. In 1915, South Dakota had about the same number of persons it had in 1910.

In 1915, a state law was passed guaranteeing the safety of bank deposits. This law was the first step in a program designed to promote the social and economic welfare of South Dakota's people. Later, the state loaned millions of dollars to farmers. The state also bought a coal mine, built a cement-making plant, and operated an insurance program against damage by hail. By 1932, all except the cement plant had failed because of mismanagement.

The prices of South Dakota's farm products increased after the United States entered World War I in 1917. The value of the state's farmland doubled. The 1920's were years of good rainfall and fine crops. But the state's economy suffered after 1925 because of lower farm prices and bank failures. Then, in 1930, the worst drought and grasshopper plague in South Dakota's history began. Except for some relief in 1932 and 1935, the drought lasted for 10 years. It was accompanied by great dust storms called *black blizzards*. In addition, the entire nation was hit by the Great Depression. Prices for South Dakota's farm products sank lower and lower.

540g

# SOUTH DAKOTA

The population of the state also began to decline. In 1930, South Dakota's population had reached a record 692,849. By 1965, it had still not returned to that level.

The federal government provided money and jobs to help the distressed farmers. The Civilian Conservation Corps (CCC) gave thousands of young men jobs in the forests of the Black Hills. The Works Progress Administration (WPA) provided money to construct bridges, buildings, and other projects. The government also helped farmers plant wheatlands with grasses whose roots reach deep for moisture and hold the soil in place.

**The 1940's and 1950's.** South Dakota's economy recovered during World War II (1939-1945). Farmers broke their production records in supplying food for the armed forces. In 1944, Congress authorized the Missouri River Basin Project. This vast program is designed to provide flood control, electric power, and irrigation throughout the basin. Part of the project called for the construction of four huge hydroelectric dams on the Missouri River in South Dakota. Work began on Fort Randall Dam in 1946, on Oahe Dam in 1948, on Gavins Point Dam in 1952, and on Big Bend Dam in 1959. By 1966, the four dams were completed and producing hydroelectric power. These projects brought thousands of workers into the state, and contributed greatly to South Dakota's economic progress.

**South Dakota Today** is waging a determined drive to broaden its economy. The state is working especially hard to expand its industry. About 35 per cent of South Dakota's workers are employed in agriculture—one of the highest percentages in the nation. But fewer and fewer workers are needed on farms because of the ever-increasing use of machinery and scientific farming meth-

## THE GOVERNORS OF SOUTH DAKOTA

|    | Name | Party | Term |
|----|------|-------|------|
| 1. | Arthur C. Mellette | Republican | 1889-1893 |
| 2. | Charles H. Sheldon | Republican | 1893-1897 |
| 3. | Andrew E. Lee | Populist | 1897-1901 |
| 4. | Charles N. Herreid | Republican | 1901-1905 |
| 5. | Samuel H. Elrod | Republican | 1905-1907 |
| 6. | Coe I. Crawford | Republican | 1907-1909 |
| 7. | Robert S. Vessey | Republican | 1909-1913 |
| 8. | Frank M. Byrne | Republican | 1913-1917 |
| 9. | Peter Norbeck | Republican | 1917-1921 |
| 10. | W. H. McMaster | Republican | 1921-1925 |
| 11. | Carl Gunderson | Republican | 1925-1927 |
| 12. | W. J. Bulow | Democratic | 1927-1931 |
| 13. | Warren Green | Republican | 1931-1933 |
| 14. | Thomas "Tom" Berry | Democratic | 1933-1937 |
| 15. | Leslie Jensen | Republican | 1937-1939 |
| 16. | Harlan J. Bushfield | Republican | 1939-1943 |
| 17. | M. Q. Sharpe | Republican | 1943-1947 |
| 18. | George T. Mickelson | Republican | 1947-1951 |
| 19. | Sigurd Anderson | Republican | 1951-1955 |
| 20. | Joseph J. Foss | Republican | 1955-1959 |
| 21. | Ralph Herseth | Democratic | 1959-1961 |
| 22. | Archie Gubbrud | Republican | 1961-1965 |
| 23. | Nils Boe | Republican | 1965-1969 |
| 24. | Frank L. Farrar | Republican | 1969- |

ods. More and more farmworkers have moved to the larger towns and cities in search of jobs. But the towns and cities have been unable to meet the demand. As a result, thousands of South Dakotans—mostly young people—have had to leave the state.

The state government has established an Industrial Development Expansion Agency (IDEA) to attract new industry to the state. In addition, development corporations have been organized in about 40 South Dakota communities. These corporations are also designed to attract new businesses, and to help existing ones expand. They provide industrial sites and funds for new or expanding plants. To attract new industry, South Dakota points out that it does not collect taxes on corporation or personal incomes. It also calls attention to its abundant water supplies and low electric power rates.

As another means of broadening its economy, South Dakota is actively promoting its tourist trade. Tourism ranks second only to agriculture in importance. The state hopes to develop its "Great Lakes," formed by the four huge dams on the Missouri River, into one of the nation's major water playgrounds. South Dakota also plans to build a network of highways to border the 2,350-mile total shoreline of these lakes.

South Dakota also hopes for increased development of its mineral resources, especially in the Black Hills. The state's location in the Williston Basin holds great promise for the future. South Dakota has two small oil-producing fields. The State Geological Survey provides oil companies with information to help them conduct explorations to discover new fields. New oil fields would help decrease the state's dependence on agriculture.

Today, western South Dakota is dotted with missile sites. In 1962, the first Titan intercontinental ballistic missiles in South Dakota became operational. The next year, Minuteman missiles in South Dakota became operational. The state's missile complex is directed from Ellsworth Air Force Base near Rapid City. The missile sites and the air force jets streaking across the sky symbolize South Dakota's goals for future progress.

DUNCAN J. MCGREGOR, EVERETT W. STERLING, and ANSON A. YEAGER

**Unloading a Minuteman Missile** at a launch site near Newell requires special machinery. Shafts tilt the boxlike container upright. Then the huge missile is lowered into a pit.

U.S. Air Force

# SOUTH DAKOTA / Study Aids

**Related Articles** in WORLD BOOK include:

### BIOGRAPHIES

| | |
|---|---|
| Beadle, William H. H. | Hansen, Alvin H. |
| Calamity Jane | Hickok, "Wild Bill" |
| Case, Francis H. | Lawrence, Ernest O. |
| Crazy Horse | Mundt, Karl E. |
| Custer, George A. | Sitting Bull |
| Deadwood Dick | Ward, Joseph |
| Foss, Joseph J. | |

### CITIES

| | | |
|---|---|---|
| Aberdeen | Pierre | Sioux Falls |
| Lead | Rapid City | Yankton |

### HISTORY

| | |
|---|---|
| Indian Wars | Missouri River Basin Project |
| Lewis and Clark Expedition | Sioux Indians |
| Louisiana Purchase | Western Frontier Life |

### PHYSICAL FEATURES

| | | |
|---|---|---|
| Badlands | Black Hills | Minnesota River |
| Belle Fourche Dam | Fort Randall Dam | Missouri River |
| | Great Plains | |

### PRODUCTS

For South Dakota's rank amoung the states in production, see:

| | | | |
|---|---|---|---|
| Alfalfa | Flax | Oats | Sheep |
| Cattle | Gold | Rye | |

### Outline

I. **Government**
  A. Constitution
  B. Executive
  C. Legislature
  D. Courts
  E. Local Government
  F. Taxation
  G. Politics
II. **People**
III. **Education**
  A. Schools
  B. Libraries and Museums
IV. **A Visitor's Guide**
  A. Places to Visit
  B. Annual Events
V. **The Land**
  A. Land Regions
  B. Rivers and Lakes
VI. **Climate**
VII. **Economy**
  A. Natural Resources
  B. Agriculture
  C. Manufacturing
  D. Mining
  E. Electric Power
  F. Transportation
  G. Communication
VIII. **History**

### Questions

What are the "Great Lakes of South Dakota"?
Why is South Dakota called the *Land of Infinite Variety?*
Why is it so important for South Dakota to expand its industry?
What part of South Dakota was covered by glaciers during the Ice Age?
Where is the nation's largest buffalo herd?
What is South Dakota's most precious natural resource? Why?
How does the Homestake Mine compare with other gold mines in the Western Hemisphere?
What was the first country to claim the South Dakota region? How did the United States acquire this land?
What was the last big fight between Indians and whites on the northern plains?
What were the *black blizzards?*

### Books for Young Readers

LENSKI, LOIS. *Prairie School*. Lippincott, 1951. *Little Sioux Girl.* 1958.
ROUNDS, GLEN. *Blind Colt*. Holiday, 1941. *Stolen Pony.* 1948.
SCHELL, HERBERT S. *South Dakota: Its Beginnings and Growth.* American Book Co., 1955.
WILDER, LAURA I. *Long Winter*. Harper, 1953. *Little Town on the Prairie.* 1953. *These Happy Golden Years.* 1953.

### Books for Older Readers

CASEY, ROBERT J. *The Black Hills and Their Incredible Characters: A Chronicle and a Guide.* Bobbs, 1949. With Mary M. Borglum: *Give the Man Room: The Story of Gutzon Borglum.* 1952.
FITE, GILBERT C. *Peter Norbeck: Prairie Statesman.* Univ. of Missouri Press, 1952. *Mount Rushmore.* Univ. of Oklahoma Press, 1952.
LAMAR, HOWARD R. *Dakota Territory, 1861-1889: A Study of Frontier Politics.* Yale Univ. Press, 1956.
OVER, WILLIAM H. *Flora of South Dakota.* New ed. Univ. of South Dakota Press, 1932. *Wild Flowers of South Dakota: Describing and Illustrating Fifty-Two Common Wild Flowers of South Dakota.* 1942.
REEVES, GEORGE S. *A Man from South Dakota.* Dutton, 1950.
RÖLVAAG, OLE E. *Giants in the Earth: A Saga of the Prairie.* Harper, 1927. *Peder Victorious.* 1928. *Their Fathers' God.* 1931.
SCHELL, HERBERT S. *History of South Dakota.* Univ. of Nebraska Press, 1961.
SINCLAIR, HAROLD. *The Cavalryman.* Harper, 1958.
VAN NUYS, LAURA B. *The Family Band: From the Missouri to the Black Hills, 1881-1900.* Univ. of Nebraska Press, 1962.

---

**SOUTH DAKOTA, UNIVERSITY OF,** is a state-supported coeducational school at Vermillion, S.Dak. The university includes the college of arts and sciences; the college of fine arts; the schools of business administration, education, law, and medicine; and a graduate school. The university was first opened in 1882.

The school colors are red and white. The nickname of the athletic teams is the Coyotes. For the enrollment of the University of South Dakota, see UNIVERSITIES AND COLLEGES (table). I. D. WEEKS

**SOUTH DAKOTA SCHOOL OF MINES AND TECHNOLOGY.** See UNIVERSITIES AND COLLEGES (table).

**SOUTH DAKOTA STATE UNIVERSITY** is a state-controlled, coeducational, technological college at Brookings, S.Dak. It is a land-grant school, and offers courses in agriculture, engineering, home economics, pharmacy, nursing, chemistry, journalism, and science and the applied arts. It was founded in 1881. For enrollment, see UNIVERSITIES AND COLLEGES (table). HILTON M. BRIGGS

**SOUTH EQUATORIAL CURRENT.** See OCEAN (map: Major Ocean Currents).

**SOUTH FLORIDA, UNIVERSITY OF.** See UNIVERSITIES AND COLLEGES (table).

**SOUTH GATE,** Calif. (pop. 53,831; alt. 110 ft.), is a manufacturing city 8 miles southeast of Los Angeles. Products include automobiles, containers, and pipe, and rubber, cork, fiberboard, and gypsum products. South Gate was established in 1917 and incorporated as a city in 1923. It has a mayor-council government. For location, see CALIFORNIA (political map). GEORGE SHAFTEL

# SOUTH GEORGIA

**SOUTH GEORGIA.** See FALKLAND ISLANDS (Dependencies).

**SOUTH ISLAND.** See NEW ZEALAND (Location and Size).

**SOUTH KOREA.** See KOREA.

**SOUTH MAGNETIC POLE.** See EARTH (The Earth's Magnetism); SOUTH POLE.

**SOUTH ORKNEY ISLANDS.** See FALKLAND ISLANDS (Dependencies); ATLANTIC OCEAN (map).

**SOUTH PLATTE RIVER.** See COLORADO (Rivers and Lakes).

**SOUTH POLE** is a term used for several invisible surface points in the Antarctic region. The best known is the *South Geographic Pole*. But other important south poles include the *Instantaneous South Pole*, the *South Pole of Balance*, the *South Magnetic Pole*, and the *Geomagnetic South Pole*.

*The South Geographic Pole* lies near the center of Antarctica at the point where all the earth's lines of longitude meet. Explorer Roald Amundsen of Norway beat Robert Scott of England to the South Geographic Pole in 1911 by one month. In 1956, the United States established a permanent scientific base at the pole called the Amundsen-Scott South Pole Station.

*The Instantaneous South Pole* lies at the point where the earth's *axis* (an imaginary line through the earth) meets the surface. The earth wobbles slowly as it turns on its axis, causing the Instantaneous South Pole to move. This pole takes about 14 months to move counterclockwise around an irregular path called the *Chandler circle*. The diameter of the Chandler circle varies from a few inches to about 70 feet.

*The South Pole of Balance* lies at the center of the Chandler circle. Its position locates the South Geographic Pole. The South Pole of Balance has moved about 6 inches toward Australia each year since 1900. This motion has caused tiny changes in the latitude and longitude of points around the earth.

*The South Magnetic Pole* is the point toward which south-seeking compass needles point. This pole may move many miles in a few years. In 1960, it was located south of Australia near the Adelie Land Coast of Antarctica.

*The Geomagnetic South Pole* lies about 900 miles from the South Geographic Pole, toward Vincennes Bay. In the upper atmosphere, the earth's magnetic field is directed upward and away from this point. PAUL A. SIPLE

**Related Articles** in WORLD BOOK include:
Amundsen, Roald
Antarctica (Exploration)
Byrd, Richard E.
Earth (The Earth's Magnetism)
Exploration and Discovery (Polar Exploration)
Scott, Robert F.
Siple, Paul A.

**SOUTH SANDWICH ISLANDS.** See FALKLAND ISLANDS (Dependencies); ATLANTIC OCEAN (map).

**SOUTH SEA** was the name that Vasco Núñez de Balboa, governor of Darien, gave to the Pacific Ocean.

**SOUTH SEA COMPANY.** See WALPOLE (Sir Robert).

**SOUTH SEA ISLANDS.** See PACIFIC ISLANDS.

**SOUTH SHETLAND ISLANDS.** See FALKLAND ISLANDS (Dependencies); ATLANTIC OCEAN (map).

**SOUTH VIETNAM.** See VIETNAM.

**SOUTH WEST AFRICA** is the territory formerly known as German Southwest Africa. The League of Nations placed it under the control of South Africa after World War I. The United Nations now calls the territory NAMIBIA. South West Africa covers 318,261 square miles. On its borders are Angola to the north, Botswana to the east, South Africa to the south, and the Atlantic Ocean to the west. Windhoek is the capital of South West Africa.

**The Land and Its Resources.** South West Africa is a dry country. The only important rivers, the Kunene and the Orange, form the northern and southern boundaries, respectively. The coastal desert area, called the *Namib*, is from 60 to 100 miles wide. Except for coastal towns, it is practically uninhabited and uninhabitable. Walvis Bay is the only important port.

Inland from the Namib lies the region called *Namaqualand*, which is higher and receives more rain. Poor grass and scrub vegetation cover it. Underground water is available in places. Northern Namaqualand receives sufficient rainfall to support grasses for cattle and wild game such as gazelle. Most of the Europeans live here and operate cattle ranches and farms.

*Ovamboland* occupies northern South West Africa. Its dry land of rough bushes, coarse grass, and thorn trees supports some dry farming and livestock-raising. The *Kalahari*, a desert region, lies to the east. The central part of South West Africa is called *Damaraland*.

Diamonds and copper are the important mineral deposits in South West Africa. Diamonds are obtained from the gravel of the Orange River and the coast, and by large-scale dredging of the Atlantic Ocean floor.

**The People and Their Work.** South West Africa's population of 627,000 includes about 38,000 Europeans. Bushmen and Ovambos live in Ovamboland. Hereros, Hottentots, and Ovambos live in Namaqualand. The Hereros were once warlike, cattle-raising

**Herero Women Shop in Windhoek,** the territorial capital, *below.* Most Herero tribesmen are cattle raisers in the interior.
South African Information Service

# SOUTH WEST AFRICA

nomads. They ruled most of the territory when the first Europeans arrived. The Rehoboths, of mixed African and European ancestry, are an important group. All these peoples—except the Bushmen—farm, raise cattle, or work in mines, on railroads, and for the Europeans.

**Government.** South West Africa is governed by South Africa. Its government consists of an administrator appointed by South Africa and an 18-member elected Legislative Assembly. It also sends six assembly members and four senators to the South African parliament.

**History.** In 1883, a German company set up a trading post in South West Africa at Lüderitz. Germany annexed the area in 1884. During World War I, South African troops drove out the Germans. The League of Nations mandated the territory to South Africa in 1920.

In 1946, South Africa applied to the United Nations to annex South West Africa. The UN turned down the application, and asked South Africa to place the territory under UN trusteeship. South Africa denied that the UN had any jurisdiction, and rejected the request. In 1950, the International Court of Justice ruled that South Africa's mandate in South West Africa was legal, but that South Africa must submit annual reports of its administration to the UN. South Africa has refused to submit these annual reports.

In 1960, Ethiopia and Liberia asked the International Court of Justice to rule that South Africa's practice of *apartheid* (complete separation of races) in South West Africa violates its mandate. In 1966, the court rejected the case. Since 1961, the United Nations has sought South West Africa's independence. In 1966 and 1967, the UN voted to end South Africa's mandate and set up a commission to try to bring South West Africa under UN control.  HIBBERD V. B. KLINE, JR.

See also KALAHARI DESERT; WINDHOEK.

**SOUTHAMPTON,** *sou THAMP tun* (pop. 209,790; alt. 45 ft.), is England's leading ocean passenger port. It lies near the head of Southampton Water on the Channel coast, north of the Isle of Wight. See GREAT BRITAIN (map). The island shelters Southampton's harbor, which has the advantage of tides twice a day. The city is a shipping center, with piers and a dry dock that can service the largest ocean steamers. The *Mayflower* sailed from Southampton in 1620. Southampton University was founded in 1952.  JOHN W. WEBB

**SOUTHAMPTON ISLAND** is an ice covered island in Canada's Northwest Territories. It lies in northern Hudson Bay. It is 210 miles long and 150 miles wide, and covers about 15,700 square miles. About 300 persons live on the island. See CANADA (physical map).

543

# SOUTHEAST ASIA

**SOUTHEAST ASIA** includes the peninsular projection of Asia and the islands that lie east of India and Pakistan and south of China. Most people consider that the following areas make up Southeast Asia: Brunei, Burma, Cambodia, Indonesia, Laos, Malaysia, North and South Vietnam, the Philippines, Portuguese Timor, Singapore, and Thailand.

Much of Southeast Asia is mountainous. Six important rivers cut through the continental region of Southeast Asia. They are the Irrawaddy, Salween, and Sittang in Burma; the Menam in Thailand; the Mekong on the north and east boundaries of Thailand; and the Red in Vietnam.

**Natural Resources.** Southeast Asia produces more natural rubber than any other region in the world. It is also rich in minerals, precious stones, and spices. Rich forests cover the mountains of Southeast Asia, and the coastal waters abound with many kinds of fish. Tropical plants support much wild life in many regions. Such animals as boars, carabaos, elephants, monkeys, panthers, and tigers live in various areas.

**Climate.** Southeast Asia has an unusually uniform climate for so large an area. Most of the region has an average annual temperature of 80°F., and an average annual rainfall of 40 inches. Typhoons and monsoons frequently increase the amount of rain in Southeast Asia. Monsoons sometimes bring the annual rainfall to as much as 200 inches a year in some places.

**The People.** Southeast Asia has about 284 million people. Most mainlanders have Mongoloid ancestors. The islanders are descended chiefly from Malay peoples. Many Southeast Asians live in small villages, often in wooden and bamboo huts. Rice is the chief food, and the people also eat fish caught in nearby waters. They enjoy religious festivals and have beautiful temples and shrines. Tribal religions, Buddhism, and Islam predominate. The Philippines is the only Christian country in Asia. Over half of the Southeast Asians cannot read or write, but education is developing rapidly.

**Cities.** Djakarta, Indonesia (pop. 2,906,533) is the largest city in Southeast Asia. Other important cities include Bandung, Indonesia; Bangkok, Thailand; Hanoi, North Vietnam; Kuala Lumpur, Malaysia; Manila, Philippines; Phnom Penh, Cambodia; Rangoon, Burma; Saigon, South Vietnam; Singapore (city), Singapore; and Surabaja, Indonesia.

**Agriculture** is the most important industry in Southeast Asia. Cambodia, Indonesia, Malaysia, and Thailand rank among the leading producers of natural rubber. Rice is grown for domestic use in all of the countries. Indonesia stands among the world's chief suppliers of tea. Spices come from Malaysia and the Moluccas, and Burma produces peanuts. Other products of Southeast Asia include copra, livestock, sugar cane, tobacco, and vegetables.

**Forest Industry** also has a major part in Southeast Asia's economy. The area is one of the world's most important teak producers. Other forest products include bamboo, cedar, ebony, mahogany, pine, and sandalwood.

**Mining.** Malaysia, Indonesia, and Thailand are among the world's leading producers of tin. About half

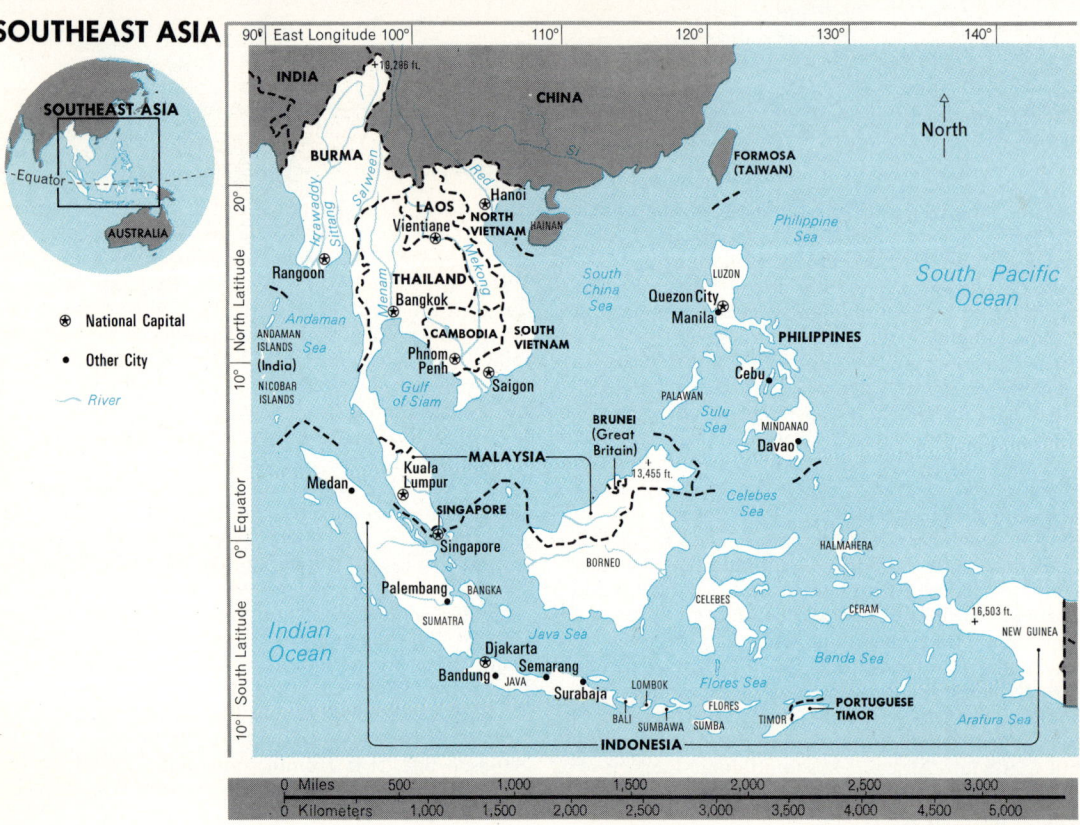

WORLD BOOK map-FGA

the world's sapphires come from Thailand, and Malaysia is a leading producer of diamonds. Malaysia, Burma, and Sumatra have rich petroleum deposits, and Burma is also rich in precious stones. Other minerals include coal, copper, iron, lead, manganese, silver, and zinc.

**Fishing Industry.** The people of Southeast Asia eat large quantities of fish and other sea food from the coastal waters. These include anchovies, bass, mackerel, mollusks, shellfish, and tuna. The waters also provide mother-of-pearl and sponges.

**Manufacturing** remains largely undeveloped in Southeast Asia. Much of the industry centers around the processing of raw materials. Products of the region include beverages, cement, chemicals, glass, leather, rubber products, textiles, and tobacco. Many craftsmen in Southeast Asia make beautiful pottery and other types of handicrafts.

**Transportation** between the regions of Southeast Asia is chiefly by sea and air. On the mainland, mountains prevent easy land transportation. Thailand and the Philippines have well-developed rail and highway systems. Singapore is one of the most important ports in the world. Manila also has an excellent harbor.

**History.** Europeans first entered Southeast Asia in the 1500's. Portuguese forces captured Malacca in Malaya in 1511, and Spain gained control of the Philippines in 1565. The Dutch arrived in the 1600's, replacing the Portuguese as colonial leaders. Dutch power centered chiefly in Java. Great Britain took over Singapore, Lower Burma, and part of Borneo in the early 1800's. The United States acquired the Philippines from Spain after the Spanish-American War in 1898. During the late 1800's, France took over the area which is now Cambodia, Laos, North Vietnam, and South Vietnam. Only Thailand escaped colonial rule. Colonial rule ended quickly after World War II. Most territories gained independence peacefully, but fighting broke out in Java and Vietnam.

In December, 1946, Communists and other Vietnamese attacked the French at Hanoi (now in North Vietnam), and the Indochina War began. Fighting ended in 1954 when the Geneva Conference on Indochina divided Vietnam into North Vietnam and South Vietnam. In 1954, eight nations, including the Philippines and Thailand, formed an alliance to oppose Communist aggression in Southeast Asia (see SOUTHEAST ASIA TREATY ORGANIZATION).

Civil war broke out in Laos in 1960. The *Pathet Lao* (Communist rebels) seized most of northern Laos and had overrun half the country by 1962. In July, 1962, a 14-nation Geneva (Switzerland) Conference agreed to establish Laos as a neutral nation.

After the division of Vietnam, the *Viet Cong* (Communist Vietnamese forces) continued attacks on South Vietnam. Late in 1961, the United States sent military advisers to assist in the defense of South Vietnam. Later, the United States sent in thousands of fighting troops. For further information on the conflict in Vietnam, see VIETNAM WAR.

Malaya, North Borneo (Sarawak), Sabah, and Singapore formed the Federation of Malaysia in 1963. Singapore was excluded from the federation in 1965. JOHN F. CADY

See also the separate articles in WORLD BOOK for each country in Southeast Asia.

Werner Bischof, Magnum

**Flooded Rice Fields** surround a Vietnamese village in Southeast Asia. The tower is one of four gates to the walled village.

**Oriental Paintings and Sculpture** are displayed in a museum in Phnom Penh, the capital of Cambodia in Southeast Asia.

Werner Bischof, Magnum

545

## SOUTHEAST ASIA TREATY ORGANIZATION

**SOUTHEAST ASIA TREATY ORGANIZATION (SEATO)** is an alliance of eight nations that signed the Southeast Asia Collective Defense Treaty in Manila, the Philippines, on Sept. 8, 1954. The member nations are Australia, France, Great Britain, New Zealand, Pakistan, the Philippines, Thailand, and the United States.

The treaty was proposed by the United States after Communist forces defeated France in Indochina (present-day Vietnam, Laos, and Cambodia). It was intended to prevent the further expansion of Communist influence in Southeast Asia. The SEATO nations agreed to help defend each other—as well as other designated nations—against military aggression in Southeast Asia. In the event of threats other than armed attack, the members agreed to "consult immediately" regarding action to be taken. The United States signed the treaty with the understanding that "aggression" meant only Communist aggression.

SEATO headquarters are in Bangkok, Thailand. The organization maintains no military forces. SEATO has a council that meets once a year, a military advisory group that meets twice a year, and a small permanent staff. Through these groups, members attempt to coordinate their defense plans for Southeast Asia.

SEATO did not develop into a strong alliance, partly because India, Indonesia, and Japan—three of the largest non-Communist nations in Asia—did not join. The SEATO members themselves divided on the extent of the Communist threat and how to meet it. Only four of the SEATO nations—the United States, Thailand, New Zealand, and Australia—sent combat troops in the 1960's when forces supported by Communist North Vietnam tried to take over South Vietnam.

**SOUTHEAST MISSOURI STATE COLLEGE.** See UNIVERSITIES AND COLLEGES (table).

**SOUTHEASTERN LOUISIANA COLLEGE.** See UNIVERSITIES AND COLLEGES (table).

**SOUTHEASTERN MASSACHUSETTS TECHNOLOGICAL INSTITUTE.** See UNIVERSITIES AND COLLEGES (table).

**SOUTHEASTERN STATE COLLEGE.** See UNIVERSITIES AND COLLEGES (table).

**SOUTHERN BAPTIST CONVENTION** is the largest Baptist organization in the world. The convention has more than 34,000 churches in 50 states, but most of its members live in the South and Southwest.

The Southern Baptist Convention has 29 state conventions that operate 38 senior colleges, 15 junior colleges, 7 academies, 6 seminaries, and 4 Bible schools. The state conventions also operate hospitals, children's homes, and homes for the aging. The convention supports about 2,300 missionaries in other countries and about the same number in the United States. Many of the denomination's offices are located at 460 James Robertson Parkway, Nashville, Tenn. 37219.

The Southern Baptist Convention was organized in Augusta, Ga., in 1845, after a split among the country's Baptists over whether slaveholders should be appointed as missionaries. For more information about Baptist doctrine and history, see BAPTISTS. For the convention's membership in the United States, see RELIGION (table).

Critically reviewed by the SOUTHERN BAPTIST CONVENTION

**SOUTHERN BAPTIST THEOLOGICAL SEMINARY.** See UNIVERSITIES AND COLLEGES (table).

**SOUTHERN CALIFORNIA, UNIVERSITY OF,** is a coeducational private university in Los Angeles. It is the largest private university in the western United States. The university grants degrees in architecture and fine arts; business administration; dentistry; education; engineering; international relations; journalism; law; letters, arts, and sciences; library science; medicine; music; performing arts; pharmacy; philosophy; public administration; religion; and social work. It has a full graduate program, a summer session, and evening and extension programs. It requires students majoring in the natural sciences or studying in the professional schools to have a strong background in letters, arts, and social sciences. The university has Air Force and Naval Reserve Officers Training Corps programs.

The university conducts major research programs in many fields. It is especially famous for its science, engineering, and world affairs programs and facilities. The university operates a center on Catalina Island for studying marine biology, and it has a materials science center and an international and public affairs center on its Los Angeles campus.

The University of Southern California was founded in 1880. Its School of Music is housed in a building that was constructed in 1880. It is the oldest university building in southern California. For enrollment, see UNIVERSITIES AND COLLEGES (table). NORMAN TOPPING

**SOUTHERN CALIFORNIA COLLEGE.** See UNIVERSITIES AND COLLEGES (table).

**SOUTHERN CHRISTIAN LEADERSHIP CONFERENCE (SCLC)** is a civil rights organization in the United States. It works to gain equal rights for black Americans and other minority groups through nonviolent civil protest and community development programs. Most SCLC affiliates are church and civil rights groups. Staff membership is open to all, but most SCLC leaders are black Protestant ministers. The SCLC is financed by contributions from individuals and organizations, and by grants from foundations.

Martin Luther King, Jr., and other civil rights leaders founded SCLC in 1957 to coordinate civil rights work in the South. King headed SCLC from 1957 until his assassination in 1968. Ralph D. Abernathy followed King as president. Headquarters are at 334 Auburn Avenue N.E., Atlanta, Ga. 30303. C. ERIC LINCOLN

See also KING, MARTIN LUTHER, JR.

**The U.S.C. Campus** lies about three miles southwest of downtown Los Angeles. The campus covers 95 acres.

SC Photo

**The Southern Cross Is Seen Below the Equator.**

**SOUTHERN COLLEGE OF OPTOMETRY.** See Universities and Colleges (table).

**SOUTHERN COLORADO STATE COLLEGE.** See Universities and Colleges (table).

**SOUTHERN CONNECTICUT STATE COLLEGE.** See Universities and Colleges (table).

**SOUTHERN CROSS** is a famous *constellation* (group of stars) in the Southern Hemisphere. It is also called the *Crux*, which is Latin for *cross*. The constellation gets its name from the outline of a cross formed by its four brightest stars. The star farthest to the south is a star of the first magnitude. The eastern and northern stars are of the second magnitude, and the western star is of the third magnitude. The four stars are not arranged in the exact form of a cross, and the constellation is sometimes difficult to pick out if one has not seen it before. The upper and lower stars, which form the "upright" of the cross, point to the South Pole of the sky.

The Southern Cross appears too far south to be seen in the United States, except for a few places. The cross was visible in ancient Babylonia and Greece, where people considered it a part of the constellation Centaurus (see CENTAURUS). The Southern Cross has gradually shifted southward in the sky as a result of the earth's *precession* (circular motion of the earth's axis). I. M. LEVITT

**SOUTHERN EDUCATION FOUNDATION** is an organization that works to improve the educational conditions of Negroes in the southern United States. In 1937, the foundation was formed from the funds of George Peabody, John F. Slater, and Anna T. Jeanes. In 1938, the Virginia Randolph fund was added. A board of directors cooperates with school officials to help pay the salaries of Negro teachers in 14 southern states. The foundation has headquarters at 811 Cypress St. N.E., Atlanta, Ga. 30308.

See also PEABODY EDUCATION FUND.

**SOUTHERN HEMISPHERE.** See HEMISPHERE.

**SOUTHERN ILLINOIS UNIVERSITY** is a state-supported, coeducational university with campuses in Carbondale and Edwardsville, Ill.

The Carbondale campus grants bachelor's, master's, and doctor's degrees. It has colleges of education and liberal arts and sciences, and schools of agriculture, business, communications, fine arts, home economics, and technology. The Edwardsville campus grants bachelor's, and master's degrees. It has divisions of business, education, fine arts, humanities, nursing, science and technology, and social sciences. It also offers courses in Alton and East St. Louis.

The university was founded in 1869, and became a four-year school in 1907. The Edwardsville campus was established in 1957. For enrollments, see UNIVERSITIES AND COLLEGES (table). DELYTE W. MORRIS

**SOUTHERN METHODIST UNIVERSITY** is a coeducational school in Dallas, Tex. It is controlled by the United Methodist Church. The university has a college of arts and sciences, schools of business administration, engineering, law, music, and theology, and a graduate school. Dallas College is an extension division. The school was chartered in 1911, and opened in 1915. For enrollment, see UNIVERSITIES AND COLLEGES (table). R. C. KNICKERBOCKER

**SOUTHERN MISSIONARY COLLEGE.** See UNIVERSITIES AND COLLEGES (table).

**SOUTHERN MISSISSIPPI, UNIVERSITY OF.** See UNIVERSITIES AND COLLEGES (table).

**SOUTHERN OREGON COLLEGE.** See UNIVERSITIES AND COLLEGES (table).

**SOUTHERN PACIFIC COMPANY.** See RAILROAD (Leading Railroad Companies).

**SOUTHERN RHODESIA.** See RHODESIA (History).

**SOUTHERN STATE COLLEGE** in Arkansas. See UNIVERSITIES AND COLLEGES (table).

**SOUTHERN STATE COLLEGE** in South Dakota. See UNIVERSITIES AND COLLEGES (table).

*Southern Methodist University*

**Southern Methodist's** central quadrangle has many crisscrossed walks leading to important campus buildings. The dome-topped Dallas Hall faces the quadrangle.

# SOUTHERN STATES

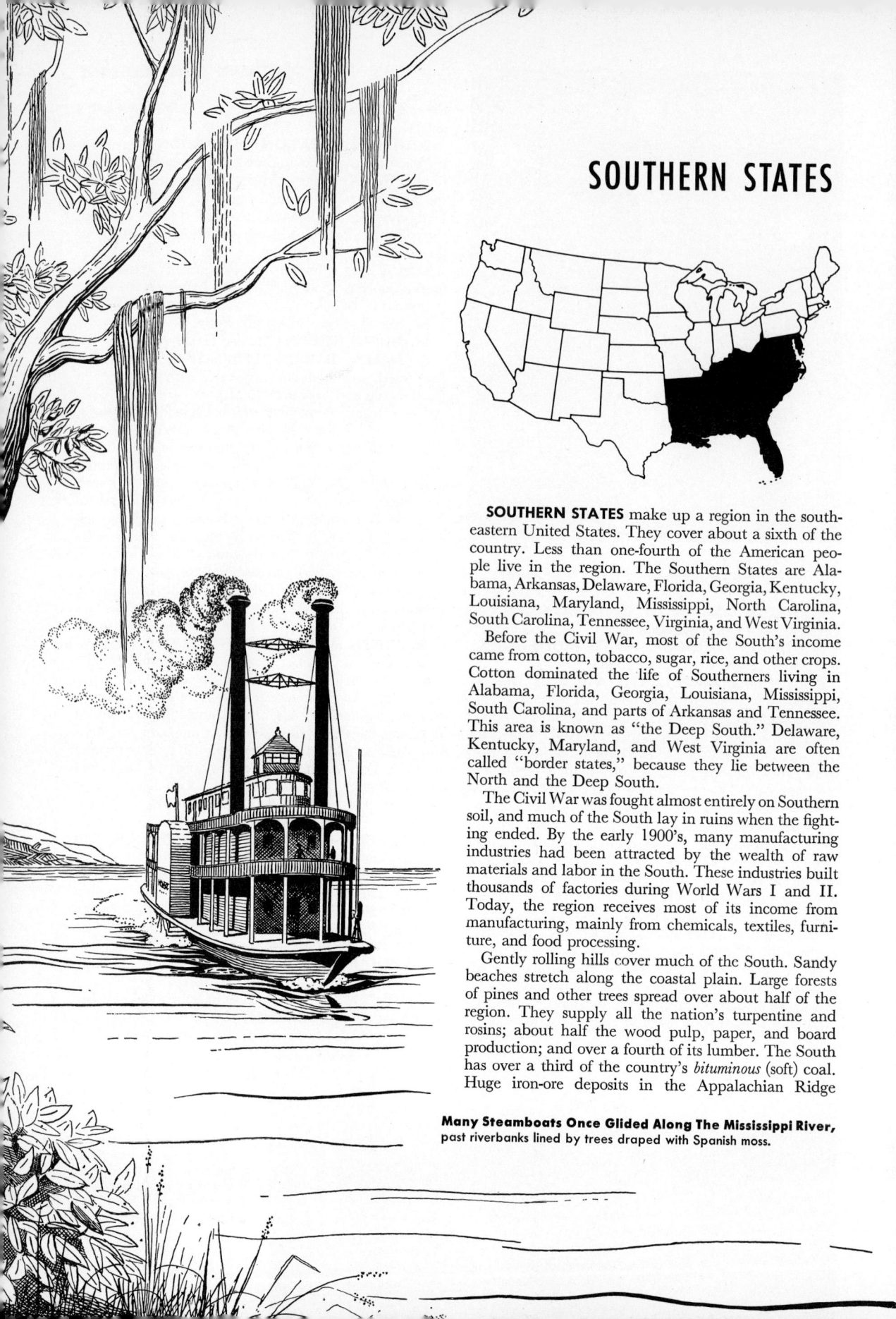

**SOUTHERN STATES** make up a region in the southeastern United States. They cover about a sixth of the country. Less than one-fourth of the American people live in the region. The Southern States are Alabama, Arkansas, Delaware, Florida, Georgia, Kentucky, Louisiana, Maryland, Mississippi, North Carolina, South Carolina, Tennessee, Virginia, and West Virginia.

Before the Civil War, most of the South's income came from cotton, tobacco, sugar, rice, and other crops. Cotton dominated the life of Southerners living in Alabama, Florida, Georgia, Louisiana, Mississippi, South Carolina, and parts of Arkansas and Tennessee. This area is known as "the Deep South." Delaware, Kentucky, Maryland, and West Virginia are often called "border states," because they lie between the North and the Deep South.

The Civil War was fought almost entirely on Southern soil, and much of the South lay in ruins when the fighting ended. By the early 1900's, many manufacturing industries had been attracted by the wealth of raw materials and labor in the South. These industries built thousands of factories during World Wars I and II. Today, the region receives most of its income from manufacturing, mainly from chemicals, textiles, furniture, and food processing.

Gently rolling hills cover much of the South. Sandy beaches stretch along the coastal plain. Large forests of pines and other trees spread over about half of the region. They supply all the nation's turpentine and rosins; about half the wood pulp, paper, and board production; and over a fourth of its lumber. The South has over a third of the country's *bituminous* (soft) coal. Huge iron-ore deposits in the Appalachian Ridge

**Many Steamboats Once Glided Along The Mississippi River,**
past riverbanks lined by trees draped with Spanish moss.

Florida Citrus Commission

**Citrus Fruits, Peaches, and Apples** are raised in Southern orchards for U.S. markets.

Rod Heinrichs, Grant Heilman

**Cotton Is the Chief Farm Crop** in the South. Seven of the leading cotton states are in the region.

American Electric Power Service Corp.

**Electric Power Plants** aid industrial growth in the South. This plant is at Louisa, Ky., on the West Virginia border.

and Valley Region provide raw materials for Birmingham, one of the nation's major iron- and steel-manufacturing centers.

Southern farmers harvest huge quantities of cotton, tobacco, soybeans, corn, rice, sweet potatoes, pecans, peanuts, and watermelons. Florida ranks first in the growing of oranges and grapefruit. Louisiana stands third, after Hawaii and California, in sugar production. Kentucky is world famous for its race horses.

Famous Southerners include four of the first five U.S. Presidents—George Washington, Thomas Jefferson, James Madison, and James Monroe. The fiery champion of states' rights, John C. Calhoun, served as Vice-President from 1825 to 1832. Confederate General Robert E. Lee led his outnumbered troops to victory after victory during the Civil War until finally forced to surrender. George Washington Carver, the son of Negro slaves, won world fame as a chemist who helped revolutionize farming methods through his work with peanuts, pecans, and sweet potatoes. William Faulkner, internationally known novelist, won the Nobel prize for literature in 1949. The Reverend Martin Luther King, Jr., a noted leader of the U.S. Negro civil rights movement, won the Nobel prize for peace in 1964.

### The Land and Its Resources

**Land Regions** of the Southern States have great variety. These five regions are: (1) the Coastal Plain, (2) the Piedmont, (3) the Blue Ridge Mountains, (4) the Appalachian Ridge and Valley Region, and (5) the Appalachian Plateau.

*The Coastal Plain* stretches from Delaware on the Atlantic Ocean to Louisiana on the Gulf of Mexico. In some sections of this region, beaches with high sand dunes give way to marshes with thick beds of peat. Islands and sand bars lie off the coast. A smaller plain extends along the banks of the Mississippi River in Tennessee, Arkansas, Mississippi, and Louisiana. Here, farmers grow cotton, rice, and other crops.

*The Piedmont*, an area of low hills and upland plains, extends from Delaware southwestward into Alabama. Swift streams flow southeasterly across the Piedmont. Rapids and falls provide power to generate electricity for industry. An area known as the Piedmont Industrial

North Carolina Dept. of Conservation & Development
**Craftsmen in the Mountain Regions** of the South make furniture and other products to sell to tourists.

Howard O. Allen
**Traditional Steeplechases** are held on such courses as Glenwood Race Course, near Middleburg, Va.

Delaware State Development Dept.
**A Famous Vacationland,** the South has beautiful, sandy beaches and recreation areas. They have become increasingly popular with people from all over the U.S.

Crescent, stretching from Virginia to east-central Alabama, has most of the South's manufacturing plants, as well as large deposits of marble, and large stands of forests. About 40 of every 100 Southerners live in the Piedmont. See PIEDMONT REGION.

*The Blue Ridge Mountains,* west of the Piedmont, form part of the Appalachian system. They stretch from Maryland to northern Georgia. From a distance, the forested slopes have a blue haze. The mountain area of eastern Kentucky is also part of the Appalachian system. Most of the state's coal comes from this area, where the "mountain people" live. See APPALACHIAN MOUNTAINS; BLUE RIDGE MOUNTAINS.

*The Appalachian Ridge and Valley Region,* between the Blue Ridge and the Appalachian Plateau, reaches from Maryland through Alabama. Rich soil covers the river valleys, which are separated by ridges and plateaus.

*The Appalachian Plateau* covers parts of Maryland, Virginia, West Virginia, Tennessee, and Georgia. Rivers have cut through the uplands, carving scenic gorges.

**Climate** of the Southern States is usually uniformly mild and humid. Extremes of temperatures occur, but only for brief periods. This mild climate helps farmers raise a large variety of field crops and pasture grasses. Average January temperatures range from 30° F. in West Virginia to around 70° F. in the Miami area. In winter, vacationers from the North find the warm, sunny climate of the South a welcome relief from the cold. The tourist industry provides Florida with about half of its income. Average July temperatures range from between 75° and 80° F. along the Gulf Coast to slightly lower in the northern and central parts of the South.

The most abundant rainfall generally comes in late winter and early spring, but no season is dry. An average of about 35 inches of rain falls in northern Virginia. The Appalachian Mountains in the Asheville, N.C., area receive around 80 inches a year.

### Activities of the People

**The People** are mostly of English, Irish, or Scottish descent. During the early 1700's, many French settled along the coast in Mississippi and Louisiana.

Large numbers of Scandinavians, Germans, Slavs, and Italians emigrated to the United States in the late

549

# SOUTHERN STATES

1800's and early 1900's. But they were attracted to jobs in factories in the industrial North, and did not settle in the Southern States. The white population of the South is unique in the nation, because the people have generally similar backgrounds.

Dutch traders brought Negro slaves to Virginia in 1619. Plantation slavery in America began on South Carolina rice plantations. By 1808, when Congress prohibited importation of slaves, about 450,000 had been brought into the country. After the Civil War, thousands of Negroes sought work in the North.

Until the middle 1900's, most of the South's income came from agriculture. After 1940, machines replaced thousands of farmers in the fields. Many northern industries moved south, attracted by the climate, the raw materials, and the great numbers of markets and workers. By the time World War II ended, the South had a healthy economy for the first time since the Civil War.

**Manufacturing and Processing** began about 1875, when New England cotton industrialists began moving their textile mills to the Southern States. Today, textiles rank second in importance only to chemicals, the chief manufactured product of the South. Most manufactured products come from the Piedmont Industrial Crescent, the South's largest manufacturing area.

Chemical industries have been attracted to the Louisiana-Texas coastal plain since the early 1900's, because of its great petroleum and natural-gas fields. Plants there produce more than 700 chemical products, including synthetic fibers, glycols, and carbon black.

Textile and clothing manufacturing in the Carolinas, Virginia, and Georgia employs about a fourth of the industrial workers in the South. Many clothing factories have been built since 1940, especially in small towns in Georgia and North Carolina. These plants concentrate on making sports and work clothes, shirts, and children's apparel.

Florida, Maryland, North Carolina, South Carolina, and Virginia produce about one-third of the wooden furniture sold in the United States.

Only Hawaii and California produce more sugar than Louisiana. A variety of cheeses comes from plants in Tennessee and Kentucky. Factories throughout the South produce cooking oils and peanut butter, as well as other processed foods. Tobacco-processing plants operate in all the Southern States.

Iron-ore deposits in the Appalachian Ridge and Valley Region supply raw materials for the Birmingham iron and steel district.

Thousands of pine trees in southern forests yield sap, used to make turpentine sold in the United States. About one-half of the country's pulp, paper, and board; and more than a fourth of its lumber come from southern forests. The Mobile Bay area in Alabama, northern Florida, and southeastern Georgia have most of the paper and pulp mills.

**Agriculture.** The South has about 1,324,000 farms, more than one-third of the total in the United States. The size of the average farm in the South ranges from 83 acres in North Carolina to about 340 acres in Florida.

Cotton ranks as the chief income-producing crop. Of the 10 leading cotton-growing states, 7 are in the South. The chief cotton areas include the Mississippi Valley, the Tennessee Valley in northern Alabama, the inner coastal plains in Georgia and the Carolinas, and the lower Georgia-South Carolina Piedmont.

Most American tobacco comes from the Southern States, led by North Carolina. Tobacco also grows well in Florida, Georgia, Kentucky, Maryland, South Carolina, Tennessee, and Virginia.

Alabama, Georgia, North Carolina, and Virginia rank among the leading peanut producing states. Alabama, Georgia, and Louisiana are among the leading pecan producing states. Louisiana, North Carolina, and Virginia grow about half of the country's sweet potatoes. Southern farmers also harvest corn, rice, soybeans, tomatoes, and watermelons. Florida has more than 500,000 acres of citrus groves. Farmers in Georgia and South Carolina raise large peach crops. Apples flourish in Virginia and West Virginia.

Seven of the top 10 broiler chicken states are in the South. Central Alabama and northwestern Mississippi have fine grazing land for beef and dairy cattle. Kentucky's bluegrass pastures are excellent for raising thoroughbred race horses.

**Mining.** West Virginia stands first among the states in coal mining. Kentucky, Alabama, Tennessee, and western Virginia also have valuable coal deposits. About 11 billion tons of known iron-ore reserves lie in northern Alabama, northwestern Georgia, and eastern Tennessee.

The South has important petroleum reserves, especially in the Gulf coastal area. Here also are large underground deposits of sulfur and salt-bearing rock. Only Texas supplies more natural gas than Louisiana. Georgia and South Carolina produce much of the country's kaolin, a clay used in making pottery. Miners take phosphates from Tennessee and Florida. Brick clays are found in every Southern State. Georgia leads all the states in the quarrying of granite, and Tennessee is one of the leading marble producing states.

**Transportation.** The South's natural harbors on the Atlantic Ocean and the Gulf of Mexico serve passenger liners and freighters from all parts of the world. Every year, thousands of tons of cargo pass through Hampton Roads, Va., one of the world's busiest ports. Since pioneer days, the Mississippi River has been a great natural waterway for travelers and freight.

**Regional Cooperation.** Worn-out soil, caused by a one-crop farming system, has been a major problem throughout the South. Until 1930, cotton or tobacco furnished the chief source of income in most farming areas. Year after year, farmers planted these crops on the best soils, robbing the land of valuable minerals.

Most of the cotton and tobacco were grown by tenant farmers or sharecroppers, who rented the land from the owner. They usually received half of the income from the crop sold. But sometimes disease attacked the plants or market prices dropped, and the tenant farmer earned little. The breakup of the one-crop, share-tenant pattern began in the 1930's. The federal Agricultural Adjustment Act of 1933 fixed prices for basic farm commodities at a certain level, in keeping with prices of manufactured goods. Southern farmers could then count on improved incomes every season, which had not been possible before that time. The government also restricted acreages that could be planted in cotton and tobacco. Farmers began planting many kinds of crops on the freed acres, or developed them as grazing land to feed livestock. These practices increased income.

Soil erosion also resulted from the one-crop system. Since 1945, reforestation commissions have planted vast tracts with pine trees to help anchor the soil and prevent it from being washed down hillsides.

The Tennessee Valley Authority has built 21 dams on the Tennessee River and its branches for irrigation and industry. The Southern States have also created interstate agencies to manage sanitation, transportation, and parks. Kentucky and Virginia, for example, each supply three commissioners to the Breaks Interstate Park Commission. It collects fees and issues bonds for the use and upkeep of the Breaks of the Sandy River Park, shared by both states.    MERLE PRUNTY, JR.

**Related Articles.** See the separate article on each of the states in this region with its list of Related Articles. Other related articles in WORLD BOOK include:

HISTORY AND GOVERNMENT

| | |
|---|---|
| Border State | Pioneer Life in America |
| Carpetbagger | Reconstruction |
| City and Local Governments | Revolutionary War in America |
| Civil War | Scalawag |
| Colonial Life in America | Solid South |
| Confederate States of America | State Government |
| | States' Rights |
| French and Indian Wars | Tennessee Valley Authority |
| Indian, American | |
| Louisiana Purchase | United States, Government of |
| Mason and Dixon's Line | |
| Negro | United States, History of |

PHYSICAL FEATURES

| | |
|---|---|
| Allegheny Mountains | Everglades |
| Cumberland Mountains | Great Smoky Mountains |
| Delaware River | Gulf of Mexico |
| Delmarva Peninsula | Hampton Roads |
| Delta | Mississippi River |
| Dismal Swamp | Ohio River |

Outline

I. **The Land and Its Resources**
  A. Land Regions     B. Climate
II. **Activities of the People**
  A. The People     D. Mining
  B. Manufacturing and     E. Transportation
    Processing     F. Regional Cooperation
  C. Agriculture

Questions

When was manufacturing introduced into the South?
How did the Agricultural Adjustment Act of 1933 help raise farm income in the South?
How is the South's population unique in the country?
Where are most of the South's manufacturing plants?
What is the South's largest manufacturing industry?
What is the South's chief income-producing crop?

**SOUTHERN UNIVERSITY** is a state-supported coeducational school at Baton Rouge, La. It offers courses in liberal arts, agriculture, technical education, home economics, music, law, and education. It also offers graduate work in education. The school was founded in New Orleans in 1880. For enrollment, see UNIVERSITIES AND COLLEGES (table).    F. G. CLARK

**SOUTHERN UTAH, COLLEGE OF.** See UNIVERSITIES AND COLLEGES (table).

## SOUTHERN YEMEN

⊛ Capital
• Other city or town
─── Road
---- Trail
▲ Highest Known Elevation
~~ Seasonal Stream

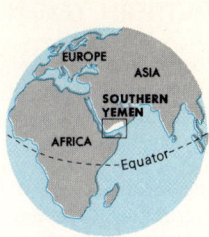

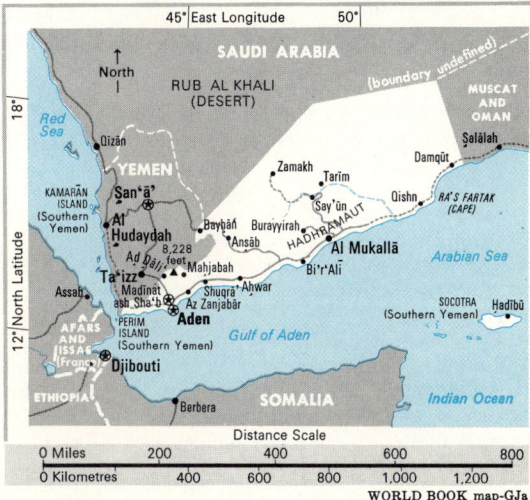

WORLD BOOK map-GJa

**SOUTHERN YEMEN** is an independent country on the southern edge of the Arabian Peninsula. It extends from the mouth of the Red Sea eastward along the Indian Ocean about 740 miles to the boundary of Muscat and Oman. Three islands—Socotra in the Indian Ocean, and Kamaran and Perim in the Red Sea—are part of the country. About 90 per cent of Southern Yemen's people are Arabs. The rest are Indians, Pakistanis, or East Africans.

Most of Southern Yemen is hot and dry. There are only a few fertile areas where the land can be farmed. Southern Yemen has two capitals—Aden and Madīnat ash Shaʻb. Aden, the nation's largest city, is an important port and oil center. Most of Southern Yemen's government offices are there, but some are in Madīnat ash Shaʻb.

─────────── **FACTS IN BRIEF** ───────────

**Form of Government:** Republic.

**Capitals:** Aden and Madīnat ash Shaʻb.

**Official Language:** Arabic.

**Area:** 111,075 square miles. *Coastline*—about 740 miles.

**Elevation:** *Highest*—8,000 feet. *Lowest*—sea level.

**Population:** No census available. *Estimated 1970 Population*—1,249,000. *Estimated 1975 Population*—1,392,000; density, 11 persons to the square mile.

**Chief Products:** *Agriculture*—barley, cotton, dates, millet, sorghum, wheat. *Industry*—dyeing, fishing, oil refining, ship refueling, tanning, weaving.

**Flag:** Red, white, and black horizontal stripes with a red star on a blue triangle at the mast. See FLAG (color picture: Flags of Asia and the Pacific).

550a

## SOUTHERN YEMEN

Southern Yemen gained independence from Great Britain on Nov. 30, 1967. The country's name in Arabic, the official language, is *Jumhuriyah al-Yaman al-Janubiyah ash-Sha'biyah* (People's Republic of Southern Yemen).

**Government.** Southern Yemen is a republic. It is governed by a five-man presidential council. The high command of the National Liberation Front (NLF), a nationalist group that signed the treaty of independence with Britain, serves as a legislature. It has 41 members.

The country is divided into 22 *directorates* (states). Each is governed by a director selected by the president and the cabinet. Southern Yemen is a member of the United Nations and the Arab League (see ARAB LEAGUE).

**People.** About 1,250,000 people live in Southern Yemen. About 90 per cent are Arabs of various tribes. The rest are Indians, Pakistanis, or East Africans. Almost all the people of Southern Yemen are Moslems of the Shafii sect.

The British brought Western ways of life to Aden, and some of the people there live much as Europeans do. They wear Western-style clothing, live in modern houses or apartments along broad streets, and shop in supermarkets. Others follow an older way of life. They live in thick-walled houses along narrow, twisting alleys, and they shop in open-air markets. Most of the men wear the striped *futa* (kilt) of Yemen. On their heads, the men wear skullcaps, turbans, or tall round hats called *tarbooshes*. Most of the women wear veils and shapeless clothing in public.

Each street in Aden's market district has its own trade. For example, all jewelers are on one street, and all woodcarvers are on another. Craftsmen work in small one-room shops.

Aden has many cafes where the men sit and drink strong coffee. In the afternoon, the men meet in the cafes or in homes to chew the leaves of the qat plant. These leaves contain a drug that gives people a feeling of contentment.

Outside of Aden, most of the people belong to tribes that follow various ancient customs. There are four classes of men: (1) tribal rulers, (2) *sayids* (holy men), (3) tribesmen, and (4) townspeople. The sayids are respected for their wisdom, and are called on to settle many disputes. Only rulers and tribesmen may carry arms.

On the coast and on Socotra Island, the people live by fishing. The men spear fish near the shore from dugout canoes called *sambuqs*, or in deeper water from single-sail *dhows*. Inland are several oases where the people farm the land. Some farm families live in towns that have mud brick houses standing three or four stories high. Others live in small villages close to the land they farm. Most farm families have at least one member working as a trader or merchant in some other country. This relative sends money back to his family in Southern Yemen.

In the desert, the people are herdsmen. They travel constantly in search of water and food for their sheep and goats. Most of the men own nothing but their clothes and their curved *jambiya* (dagger). Women are

WORLD BOOK photo by Henry Gill
**In Aden, Southern Yemen's Most Important City,** Arab hillside houses overlook European-style buildings below.

unveiled. Many are tattooed on their faces and arms with tribal marks.

Rice, bread, lamb, and fish are the chief foods in Southern Yemen. But most of the desert people live on bread and on ilb nuts gathered from wild thorn trees.

The British established the first public schools in Southern Yemen. In the mid-1960's, the nation had 195 elementary schools, 38 intermediate schools, 16 high schools, and 3 teacher training colleges. The law requires all children to go to school for seven years. But some areas have no schools, and many children receive little or no education. About 10 per cent of the people can read and write.

**Land.** Southern Yemen covers 111,075 square miles, an area a little larger than that of Nevada. The mainland part of the country has three regions: (1) the coastal plain, which is mostly sand but has a few fertile areas; (2) a dry, hilly plateau cut by deep valleys called *wadis* that have some rich farmland; and (3) the Empty Quarter, a stony desert that extends into Saudi Arabia. Socotra has a narrow coastal plain and a steep, rugged interior.

Southern Yemen is hot most of the year. Temperatures range from 61° F. to 106° F. in Aden and climb to 130° F. in the desert. Rainfall averages 3 inches a year.

**Economy.** Aden's oil refinery and port provide Southern Yemen with most of its income. The oil refinery can process about 50 million barrels of oil a year. Ships of many nations use the port for refueling, repairs, and transferring cargoes. In 1965, 6,000 ships stopped at Aden. Most of these ships traveled between Europe and Asia through the Suez Canal. But since the closing

## SOUTHWESTERN STATE COLLEGE

An Open-Air Shop in Aden sells a wide variety of goods. The clerks are wearing the *futa* (kilt) of Southern Yemen.

WORLD BOOK photo by Henry Gill

of the canal in 1967, fewer ships use the port and Southern Yemen's income has dropped.

Outside of Aden, the economy is largely undeveloped. The country has no known mineral resources. Agriculture is limited to the few areas that have underground water for irrigation. Farmers grow three or four crops a year of millet, sorghum, sesame, wheat, and barley.

**History.** In ancient times, southern Arabia grew rich because it lay along important trade routes between Europe, Asia, and Africa. Cities were built and the land was irrigated. But fighting among local leaders and invasions from the north and east brought widespread destruction. During the 600's, the Prophet Mohammed's son-in-law, Ali, introduced Islam to the people (see YEMEN [History]).

Great Britain seized Aden in 1839, after people from the town robbed a wrecked British ship. Aden became an important refueling stop for British ships going to India by way of the Suez Canal and the Red Sea. Aden was a part of British India until 1937, when it became a British crown colony.

To protect Aden from Yemen, which claimed the town, Britain extended its control to the tribal states in the region around Aden. Britain signed treaties with the tribal leaders, promising protection and aid in return for loyalty. The region came to be known as the Aden Protectorate.

In 1959, six of the tribal states in the protectorate formed the Federation of Arab Amirates of the South. Britain signed a treaty with the federation, promising to grant independence. The date for independence was later set for 1967. Meanwhile, the British controlled the federation's foreign policy and provided military protection and economic aid. In 1962, the name of the federation was changed to the Federation of South Arabia. By 1965, Aden and all but four of the tribal states that made up the protectorate had joined the federation.

In the early 1960's, Britain tried to form a representative government that would rule the federation after independence. But Arab nationalist leaders in Aden and tribal leaders in the protectorate both wanted to rule. The nationalists began a terror campaign against the British and the tribal leaders. Two nationalist groups, the National Liberation Front (NLF) and the Front for the Liberation of Occupied South Yemen (FLOSY), also fought each other.

In late 1967, the federation government collapsed. Britain announced that it would withdraw its troops and give power to any group that could set up a government. The National Liberation Front emerged from the internal struggle as the most powerful group in the federation. NLF leaders then met with the British in Geneva, Switzerland. On Nov. 30, 1967, the federation gained independence and was renamed the People's Republic of Southern Yemen.

See also ADEN; ARAB LEAGUE; SOUTH ARABIA, FEDERATION OF; MADĪNAT ASH SHAʻB.

**SOUTHEY,** *SUTH ee,* **ROBERT** (1774-1843), was poet laureate of England from 1813 until his death. He is chiefly remembered for a few ballads, including "The Battle of Blenheim" (1798), and for his association with William Wordsworth and Samuel Taylor Coleridge (see LAKE POETS).

Critics consider Southey a better prose writer than poet. He wrote much history and biography, including the *Life of Nelson* (1813). His prose collection *The Doctor* (1834-1847) popularized the fairy tale "The Three Bears." Southey also wrote two long free verse romances, *Thalaba, the Destroyer* (1801) and *The Curse of Kehama* (1810). These works use Moslem and Hindu mythologies, and influenced several poets, including Percy Shelley and Sir Walter Scott.

Southey was born in Bristol. He and Coleridge supported ideals that inspired the American and French revolutions. They planned to establish a utopian community in the United States, but the project failed because of lack of money. Southey later became conservative and supported the English monarchy. KARL KROEBER

**SOUTHWEST BAPTIST COLLEGE.** See UNIVERSITIES AND COLLEGES (table).

**SOUTHWEST MISSOURI STATE COLLEGE.** See UNIVERSITIES AND COLLEGES (table).

**SOUTHWEST TEXAS STATE COLLEGE.** See UNIVERSITIES AND COLLEGES (table).

**SOUTHWESTERN ARBORETUM.** See ARIZONA (Places to Visit).

**SOUTHWESTERN AT MEMPHIS.** See UNIVERSITIES AND COLLEGES (table).

**SOUTHWESTERN COLLEGE.** See UNIVERSITIES AND COLLEGES (table).

**SOUTHWESTERN LOUISIANA, UNIVERSITY OF.** See UNIVERSITIES AND COLLEGES (table).

**SOUTHWESTERN STATE COLLEGE.** See UNIVERSITIES AND COLLEGES (table).

551

# SOUTHWESTERN STATES

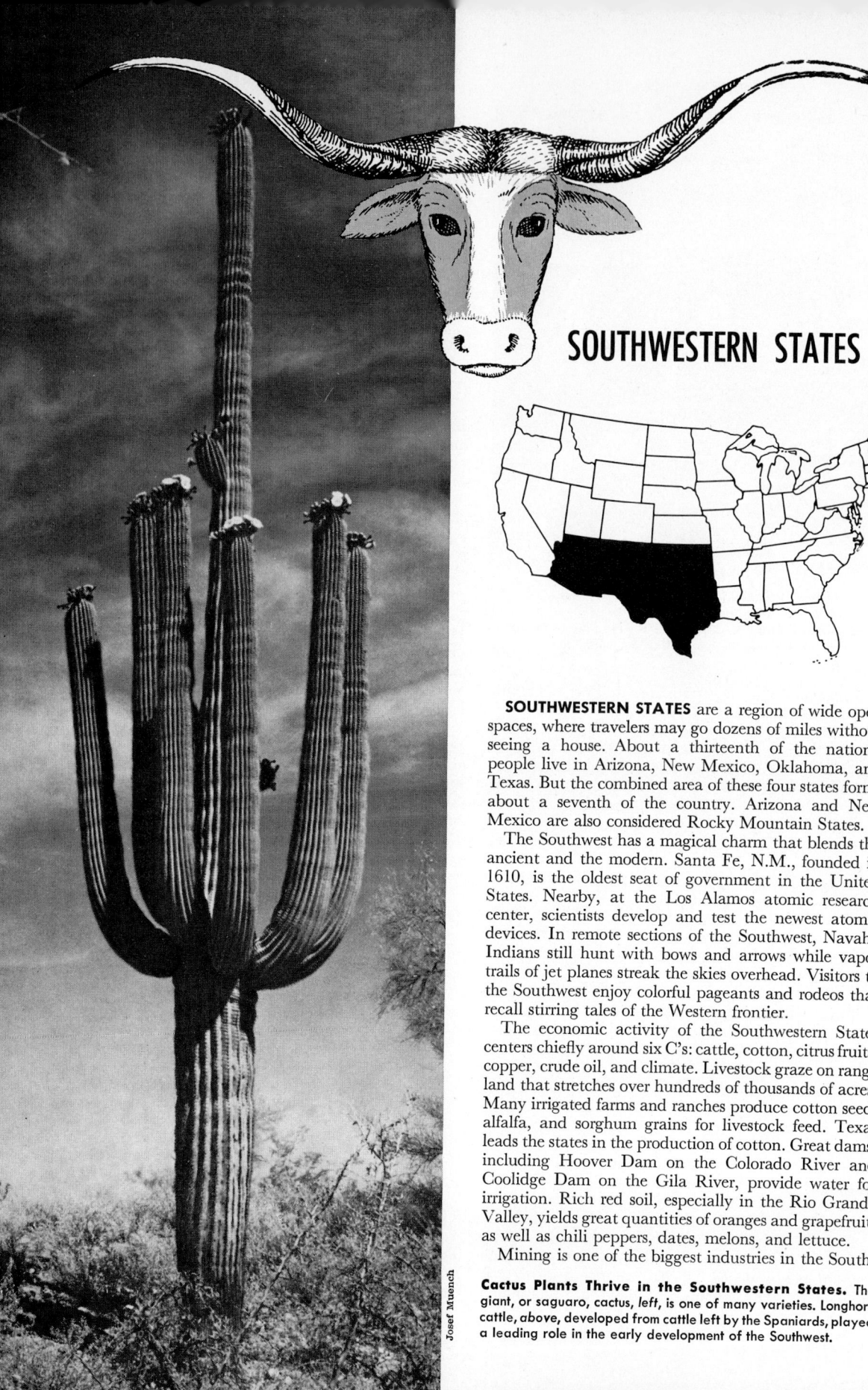

**SOUTHWESTERN STATES** are a region of wide open spaces, where travelers may go dozens of miles without seeing a house. About a thirteenth of the nation's people live in Arizona, New Mexico, Oklahoma, and Texas. But the combined area of these four states forms about a seventh of the country. Arizona and New Mexico are also considered Rocky Mountain States.

The Southwest has a magical charm that blends the ancient and the modern. Santa Fe, N.M., founded in 1610, is the oldest seat of government in the United States. Nearby, at the Los Alamos atomic research center, scientists develop and test the newest atomic devices. In remote sections of the Southwest, Navaho Indians still hunt with bows and arrows while vapor trails of jet planes streak the skies overhead. Visitors to the Southwest enjoy colorful pageants and rodeos that recall stirring tales of the Western frontier.

The economic activity of the Southwestern States centers chiefly around six C's: cattle, cotton, citrus fruits, copper, crude oil, and climate. Livestock graze on range land that stretches over hundreds of thousands of acres. Many irrigated farms and ranches produce cotton seed, alfalfa, and sorghum grains for livestock feed. Texas leads the states in the production of cotton. Great dams, including Hoover Dam on the Colorado River and Coolidge Dam on the Gila River, provide water for irrigation. Rich red soil, especially in the Rio Grande Valley, yields great quantities of oranges and grapefruit, as well as chili peppers, dates, melons, and lettuce.

Mining is one of the biggest industries in the South-

**Cactus Plants Thrive in the Southwestern States.** The giant, or saguaro, cactus, *left*, is one of many varieties. Longhorn cattle, *above*, developed from cattle left by the Spaniards, played a leading role in the early development of the Southwest.

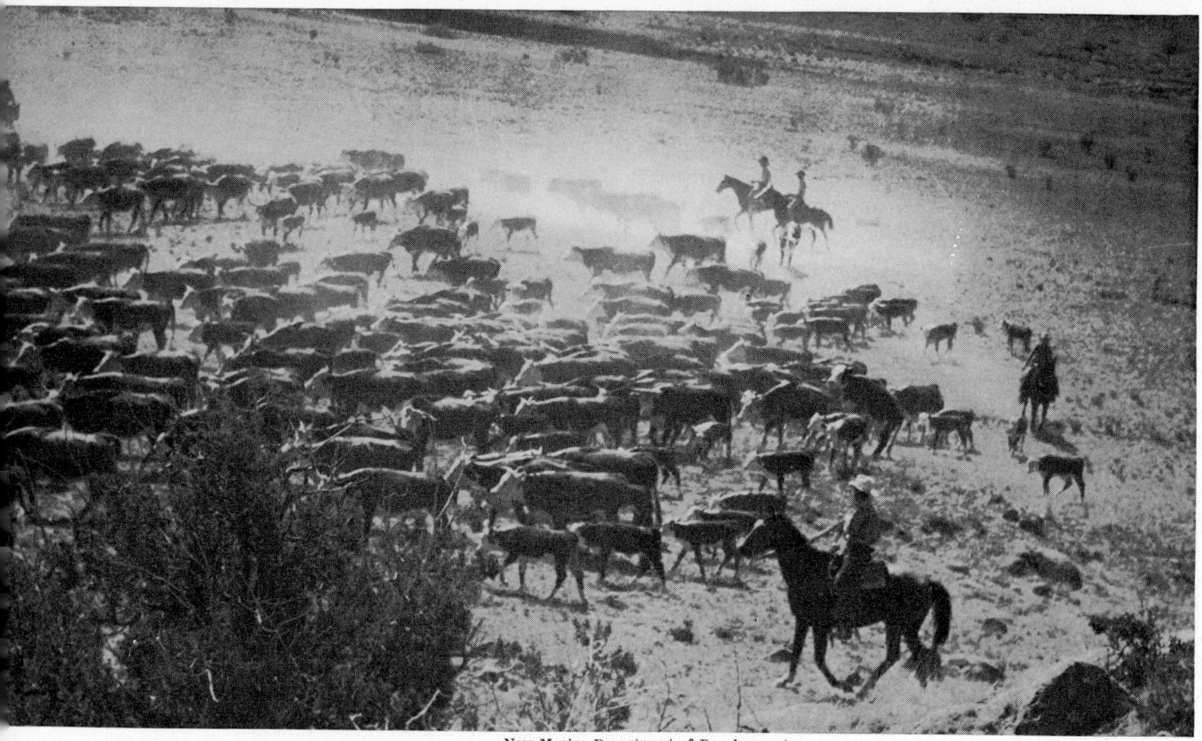

New Mexico Department of Development

**The Cattle Ranches of the Southwest** produce most of the nation's beef. Arizona, New Mexico, Oklahoma, and Texas also produce sheep and other livestock.

El Paso Chamber of Commerce

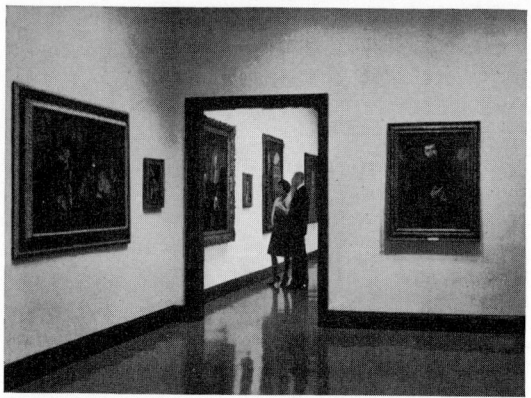

**Cultural Life in the Southwest** includes theaters and excellent museums, such as the El Paso Museum of Art.

**Rich Oil Fields** have produced great wealth. The Southwest is one of the world's greatest petroleum producers.

Humble Oil & Refining Co.

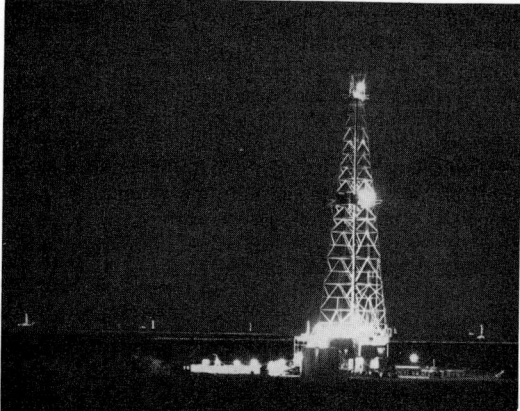

west. Drillers tap vast pools of petroleum and natural gas underground. Giant tanks store refined oil, and pipelines carry gas to many parts of the United States and Canada. Texas supplies about a tenth of the petroleum produced in the world.

The year-round warm, dry climate attracts visitors to resorts and dude ranches scattered throughout much of the region. Cactus plants thrive in the Southwest, providing a vivid contrast between their beautiful flowers and their sharp spines. Some of the world's most spectacular sights may be seen in the region. These include the Grand Canyon, Carlsbad Caverns, and the Petrified Forest.

Prehistoric Indians lived in the Southwest as long as 25,000 years ago. Later, Cliff Dwellers built their homes high and safe in the sides of cliffs. They developed a civilization that reached its peak between A.D. 1100 and 1300. The Hopi, Zuñi, Acoma, Taos, and other Pueblo Indians who live there today are probably descendants of these early Cliff Dwellers. See CLIFF DWELLERS.

More than 210,000 Indians, or about 40 per cent of the Indian population of the United States, live in the Southwestern States, mostly on reservations. Some Spanish-Americans in the region are descendants of settlers who followed the route pioneered by the expedition of Francisco Coronado in 1540.

### The Land and Its Resources

The Treaty of Guadalupe Hidalgo, which ended the Mexican War in 1848, fixed the boundary between Texas and Mexico at the Rio Grande. Texas, New Mexico, and Arizona lie along most of the border.

# SOUTHWESTERN STATES

New Mexico Department of Development

**Big Fruit and Vegetable Crops** now grow on once-barren land. This pecan orchard is near Las Cruces, N.Mex.

Bob Taylor

**Farmers in Oklahoma** rank among the world's leading wheat producers. They also produce big cotton crops.

**Land Regions** of the Southwest include almost every kind of terrain. There are mountains, plains, steep valleys, flat valleys with alkali flats, mesas, spectacular gorges, and desert basins with no sea outlets.

*The Basin and Range Region* covers about a third of the Southwest. It extends from northwestern Arizona to southwestern Texas. Southwestern Arizona has both mountains and plains. The plains consist of ancient valleys that have filled with rock and soil washed down from mountains. Broad plains, mountains, and valleys characterize the region in New Mexico and Texas.

*The Colorado Plateau* is a vast upland area that extends across northeastern Arizona and northwestern New Mexico. Thick pine forests cover the slopes of isolated mountain ranges. Hematite, an iron-ore mineral, glows red, purple, and yellow in Arizona's Painted Desert, coloring the landscape. The country's most famous petrified forest lies near Holbrook, Ariz.

*Great Plains* cover eastern New Mexico and north-central Texas. Farmers plant alfalfa and other crops in New Mexico's irrigated Pecos Valley. The *Llano Estacado*, or *Staked Plains*, of western Texas stretch over a vast, dry, treeless area. The irrigated soil provides one of the richest farming belts in the region. Herds of cattle and sheep graze on grasses that cover a large plateau to the south. Mining areas yield building stone, potassium, and petroleum. Plains also spread over a wide belt running north-south through Oklahoma where farmers raise cotton and sorghums.

*West Gulf Coastal Plains* in Texas extend along the Gulf of Mexico. Narrow sand bars and coastal islands enclose shallow lagoons. Rice is grown in this humid, subtropical section. Dense forests of pines and cypresses cover rolling hills in the northeastern part. Petroleum and other minerals lie beneath the region's sandy soil.

**Climate** of the Southwestern States is generally dry, with little humidity. The driest sections, in western and northern Arizona, south-central New Mexico, and a tip of western Texas, attract vacationers and health seekers from all parts of the country. Phoenix and Tucson have long been famous winter resorts.

Average January temperatures range from about 30° F. in western New Mexico to about 60° F. in the southern tip of Texas. The southern desert regions have generally warm, sunny, winter days, but night temperatures may drop to freezing. July temperatures average about 73° F. in northeastern New Mexico, and about 85° F. in southwestern Texas. Along the Mexican border, summer temperatures often reach 115° F.

The average yearly rainfall varies from about 5 inches in southwestern Arizona to about 50 inches in the Beaumont-Port Arthur, Tex., area. Cloudbursts occur frequently during the summer (see CLOUDBURST). The hard, parched, desert ground cannot absorb the torrents of water quickly, and dry gullies, called *arroyos*, become flooded in a few minutes. Severe droughts may come in spring and fall. During these seasons, blinding dust storms may blow up suddenly. The annual average snowfall ranges from 1 inch in the mountains of southwestern Arizona and southern Texas to about 200 inches in the north-central mountains of New Mexico.

The Southwest has about 340 frost-free days in the eastern Gulf region. This year around warm weather helps farmers grow a variety of crops.

## Activities of the People

**The People.** The first white man to enter the Southwest was a Spaniard, Alonso Álvarez de Piñeda, who explored and mapped the Gulf Coast of Texas in 1519. In 1540, Francisco Coronado, a Spanish explorer from Mexico, led an expedition into the region. In 1610, 10 years before the Pilgrims landed at Plymouth Rock, Spaniards founded Santa Fe. But Spain made little effort to colonize the vast, dry region.

Westward migration began during the 1800's. Prospectors, miners, trappers, railroad workers, and cowboys sought adventure and wealth in the vast, sunny land. The United States and Mexico fought the Mexican War of 1846-1848 for control of the Southwest (see MEXICAN WAR). After the war, Mexico ceded the United States more than 525,000 square miles of land.

Today, three distinct cultures—Indian, Spanish-American, and Anglo-American—are represented among the people of the Southwestern States. American Indian tribes include the Hopi, Mohave, Navaho, Papago, Pima, and Yuma in Arizona; the Pueblo of the Rio Grande Valley of New Mexico; the Apache, Comanche, and other groups in eastern New Mexico and Texas; and the Cherokee, Cheyenne, and other groups in Oklahoma. Many Indians remain on reservations where, as herdsmen and farmers, they live much as their ancestors did hundreds of years ago. Their exquisite silver and turquoise jewelry, pottery, blankets, rugs and other arts and crafts products are sold at hotels, curio shops, and trading posts. Many Indians in Oklahoma

553

**The Southwest Supplies Sulfur and Gas** to most of the nation. Sulfur is being put into cars for shipment, *above*. Tanks, *right*, hold butadiene, a gas used to make synthetic rubber.

Houston Chamber of Commerce; Standard Oil Co. (N.J.)

do not dwell on reservations, but live and work throughout the state. See INDIAN, AMERICAN (table, Indian Tribes).

The Spanish-Americans live mainly in small farming communities, many in secluded foothill valleys. Others make up segments of the populations of big cities. People in villages raise sheep, goats, and poultry, as well as fruits and vegetables. Spanish-American farmers grow large quantities of chili peppers. Following the autumn harvest, they hang *ristras* (strings) of the scarlet peppers over the walls of their houses and barns to cure in the hot sun.

Thousands of Anglo-Americans, many of whose ancestors came from Europe and Canada, work in various industries in southwestern cities and farming areas.

**Mining.** Texas ranks first among the mining states in production, and in output of petroleum and natural gas. It supplies about a tenth of the world's petroleum. Oil refineries and smelters reduce some of the ore and crude oil, but much of it is shipped from the region for refining. In 1899, Edward Byrd dug a shallow oil well near Chelsea, Okla. Since then, more than 100,000 oil wells have been dug in the Red Fork-Tulsa, Glenn Pool, Cushing, and other Oklahoma fields. The first important petroleum discovery came with the exploration and drilling of the Spindletop field near Beaumont, Tex., in 1901. The famous East Texas oil field, which opened in 1930, has about 20,000 producing wells.

About two-fifths of the nation's natural gas comes from Texas. This state also supplies about one-half of the country's sulfur. Natural gas fields located in Oklahoma and Texas contain much of the world's supply of helium.

Arizona and New Mexico have huge copper and silver reserves. Miners take lead and zinc from valuable deposits in New Mexico and Arizona. Salt mining centers around the Texas cities of Grand Saline, Palestine, and Corpus Christi. New Mexico and Arizona are leading uranium-ore mining states. New Mexico produces about $9\frac{1}{2}$ million pounds a year. Southwestern stone quarries produce beautiful building stone. Asbestos, beryllium, manganese, mica, molybdenum, and vanadium are other minerals found in this area.

**Manufacturing and Processing** is the largest source of income in value of production. Since World War II, many leading chemical firms have built plants in the Southwest, close to the abundant supplies of raw materials. Chemical products, including synthetic rubber and petrochemicals, rank as the leading manufactures. Chemical production centers mainly in the Texas cities of Beaumont, Brownsville, Corpus Christi, Houston, San Antonio, Texarkana, and Wichita Falls.

Visitors easily recognize the presence of carbon black factories that operate throughout the region. The wind carries black, oily smoke from their chimneys and deposits it across the countryside, leaving plant life greasy and black. Carbon black is used as a pigment in paints and enamels, manufactured chiefly in Tucson, Tulsa, and Corpus Christi.

Several southwestern cities have meat-packing plants and factories that pack or process fruits and vegetables.

Almost every major oil company has petroleum refineries in the Southwest. Some of the large cities manufacture oil-field machinery and supplies, such as drilling supplies, derricks, and pipe. Furniture and other wood products made principally of ponderosa pine come from the Southwest. Other important manufactures include cotton textiles, cement and clay products, metal products, electronics equipment, and airplane parts.

During World War II, the U.S. government began developing new defense materials in New Mexico. Today, scientists conduct atomic experiments in the Los Alamos Scientific Laboratory. The Atomic Energy Commission develops and assembles atomic weapons at Albuquerque.

**Agriculture.** Large herds of beef and dairy cattle, sheep, and horses graze on grasslands that cover hundreds of thousands of acres. Stock raising has been an important industry in the Southwest since the early 1800's, when settlers found herds of Longhorn cattle roaming the plains. These cattle were descendants of the stock introduced by the Spaniards in the 1500's. Today, Texas stands first in the production of beef cattle, sheep and wool, and horses. Ranchers in Okla-

**Window Rock Is a Natural Formation** in Arizona, *left*. Through its opening, visitors see miles of open land where cowboys, such as the one shown above, ride southwestern ranges.

Josef Muench; Meisel, Monkmeyer

homa, New Mexico, and Arizona also have large livestock herds.

The famous King Ranch, the largest in Texas, covers 823,403 acres near Kingsville, Tex. It was founded in the 1850's by Richard King, a steamboat captain. In the early 1900's, this ranch began breeding Santa Gertrudis cattle, the first distinct breed to be perfected in the United States.

The rewards of cotton raising brought many of the earliest settlers south of the Red River and west of the Sabine River. Cotton was first planted in the Brazos Valley during the early 1800's. Texas now leads the states in cotton production. Other leading field crops of the Southwest include alfalfa, barley, corn, flaxseed, oats, rice, rye, sorghums, and wheat. Ranchers use many field crops for winterfeeding livestock.

Farmers grow vegetables and fruits in many sections, but most of the land must be irrigated or dry farmed (see DRY FARMING). Southwestern farmers harvest large crops of pinto beans, chili peppers, lettuce, onions, sugar beets, and sweet potatoes. Texas and Arizona rank among the leading states in the growing of cantaloupes, grapefruit, honeydew melons, oranges, and watermelons. Irrigation has turned the once unproductive soil of the Rio Grande area into one of the finest fruit belts in the United States. Other semitropical fruits, including dates and figs, also grow well in the Southwest.

**Transportation.** The Spaniards built the first road in the Southwest in 1581, between the Santa Fe area and Mexico City. They named it *El Camino Real*, or The Royal Road. This old route parallels present-day U.S. 85. The first railroad did not penetrate the region until 1869, because the mountains and deserts hampered construction. Until that time, travelers came by stagecoaches that lumbered over the rugged terrain. Today, the Southwest has wide, paved highways, hundreds of miles of railroads, and large ports on the Gulf Coast. The Gulf Intracoastal Waterway provides cheap barge service between all Texas ports and the Mississippi Valley (see GULF INTRACOASTAL WATERWAY).

Large southwestern cities have modern airports that serve the major domestic airlines. Private landing fields lie scattered throughout the region. Many ranch owners use planes to oversee their property.

**Regional Cooperation.** New England, the Middle Atlantic States, and the South had become thriving centers of trade and culture long before the opening of the Southwest. Settlers did not begin to move southwestward in great numbers until the early 1900's. Until this time, lack of good transportation, great distances between settlements, and hostile Indians delayed development of the region. Arizona and New Mexico, which became states in 1912, were the last territories to achieve statehood until Alaska and Hawaii joined the Union in 1959.

The Southwestern States entered a period of rapid growth in the mid-1900's, after mass production of automobiles and the expansion of paved highways. The widespread use of air conditioning and evaporative cooling equipment also helped the region's economy by providing comfort from the extreme heat. Activity increased in mining, agriculture, and manufacturing. The population of the Southwest more than doubled between 1900 and 1930.

The population increased at a much slower rate between 1930 and 1960. The region's chief problem, lack of water, contributed to this slower rate of growth. Water is in short supply because streams in the Southwest are comparatively small, and most areas have slight rainfall. In the continuing search for water, all the Southwestern States dammed rivers and tapped great underground water-storage basins with deep-well pumps. Groups of citizens formed organizations, such as the Aqualantes, to persuade Congress to set aside funds for a systematic program of developing the Colorado, the region's largest river. In 1949, New Mexico joined Utah, Colorado, and Wyoming in establishing the Upper Colorado River Basin Pact to provide more water for irrigation and industrial use.

Through the years, many herds of livestock have fed on the prairie grasslands, exhausting these grazing areas. Erosion by cloudbursts also wore away the rich topsoil. Today, soil-conservation commissions of Arizona,

555

## SOUTHWESTERN STATES

New Mexico, Oklahoma, and Texas work together to restore and conserve the vast grazing regions in these states.   Critically reviewed by NATT N. DODGE

**Related Articles.** For additional information on the Southwestern States, see the separate article on each of the states in this region with its list of Related Articles. Other related articles in WORLD BOOK include:

### HISTORY AND GOVERNMENT

| | |
|---|---|
| Alamo | Pony Express |
| City and Local Governments | San Jacinto, Battle of |
| | Santa Fe Trail |
| Cliff Dwellers | State Government |
| Guadalupe Hidalgo, Treaty of | Texas Rangers |
| | Trails of Early Days |
| Indian, American | United States, Government of |
| Indian Territory | |
| Indian Wars | United States, History of |
| Mexican War | Western Frontier Life |
| Pioneer Life in America | Westward Movement |

### PHYSICAL FEATURES

| | |
|---|---|
| Canadian River | Gulf of Mexico |
| Carlsbad Caverns National Park | Mesa |
| | National Park |
| Colorado River | Painted Desert |
| Dam | Pecos River |
| Desert | Petrified Forest |
| Dust Bowl | Red River |
| Gila River | Rio Grande |
| Grand Canyon National Park | |

### Outline

I. **The Land and Its Resources**
   A. Land Regions
   B. Climate
II. **Activities of the People**
   A. The People
   B. Mining
   C. Manufacturing and Processing
   D. Agriculture
   E. Transportation
   F. Regional Cooperation

### Questions

What industry brings the Southwest the largest part of its income?

Why is the Spindletop field in Texas important? Where is it located?

What are the six C's around which most of the Southwest's economic activity centers?

What are three factors that retarded development of the Southwestern States?

How did the United States acquire much of the Southwestern region?

Who was the first white man to enter the Southwestern region?

What famous canyon lies in the Southwest? What other tourist attractions lie in this region?

What are the leading manufactured products of the Southwest?

What Southwestern city is the oldest seat of government in the United States?

What two Southwestern States lead in uranium-ore mining?

What Southwestern ranch is the largest in the United States?

What are the main cultures represented in the Southwestern States?

What two cities in New Mexico are important to national defense? Why?

556

**SOUTHWESTERN UNIVERSITY** is a coeducational liberal arts school at Georgetown, Tex. It is controlled by the United Methodist Church. It has a college of arts and sciences and a school of fine arts. In 1840, the Republic of Texas chartered Southwestern. It is the oldest university in Texas. For enrollment, see UNIVERSITIES AND COLLEGES (table).

**SOVEREIGN.** See POUND STERLING.

**SOVEREIGNTY.** The name "sovereign" was first applied to kings. Everyone in a kingdom was a subject of the king. The king himself was usually *sovereign*, which means *subject to no one*.

Few kings are left in the world, but the idea of sovereignty remains. Today, many countries are considered subject to no one, and therefore sovereign. A sovereign country can conduct its own affairs, enter into treaties, declare war, or adopt any other course of action without another country's consent. Small countries are often sovereign in name only. They shape their policies and conduct their affairs to suit the desires or needs of a stronger country.

The United States of America is a sovereign nation, but the 50 states which compose it do not have full sovereignty.   PAYSON S. WILD, JR.

**SOVIET**, SOH vih ET, or SO vih et, is a Russian word which means *council*. Russian revolutionary groups were known as soviets. The first soviets were formed during the Russian workers' revolution in 1905. Soviets were formed throughout Russia after the downfall of the Czar in March, 1917. These soviets were councils made up of workers, peasants, and soldiers. These councils rallied groups of people to support the Socialist plan for setting up a Russian government. In 1917, the Bolsheviks (Lenin faction) gained control of the soviets. Since 1924, Russia has been officially known as the Union of Soviet Socialist Republics. Since 1946, the Russian army and navy have been officially known as the Soviet Army and Soviet Navy.   WILLIAM B. BALLIS

**SOVIET UNION.** See RUSSIA.

**SOVKHOZY.** See RUSSIA (Agriculture).

**SOW.** See HOG.

**SOW BUG.** See WOOD LOUSE.

**SOW THISTLE,** *sou*, is the name of a group of weeds. These weeds grow wild in Europe, and several species have been introduced into the United States, where they have become a nuisance in gardens and fields. The *annual sow thistle*, one of the best known, grows 2 to 3 feet high and has a branching stem. It contains a milky juice and its flower heads resemble dandelions. Another type of sow thistle is the *perennial sow thistle*. The sow thistle is one of the most troublesome weeds.

**Scientific Classification.** Sow thistles belong to the composite family, *Compositae*. The annual sow thistle is classified as genus *Sonchus*, species *S. oleraceus*. The perennial sow thistle is *S. arvensis*.   LOUIS PYENSON

**SOWING MACHINE.** See DRILL (seeder).

**Sow Thistles** have yellow flowers and prickly leaves.
USDA

**SOYBEAN.** The soybean is a farm crop that supplies animal feed, food for human beings, and many raw materials for industry. The soybean plant is a relative of peas and beans. It is an annual, and belongs to the pea family. Plants in this family are sometimes called *legumes*.

Soybeans have been part of the history of China for about 5,000 years. The ancient Chinese used the soybean as food, and made medicines from it. Soybeans have been grown in the United States for more than 150 years. But, during the early years, the soybean was grown chiefly to be mowed as hay, which was used as livestock feed. When chemists and manufacturers recognized the importance of the bean itself, the great new soybean-processing industry was born. Today, the soybean is the nation's largest single source of vegetable oil, and of protein meal for livestock feeding.

### Uses of the Soybean

**The Plant** is used widely as hay, *silage* (winter food for stock), and *pasturage* (green food for stock). It compares favorably with other leguminous plants used as forage, such as alfalfa and the clovers.

**The Bean** is rich in food values. It has more protein than beef, more calcium than milk, and more of a fatty substance called *lecithin* than eggs. Lecithin from soybeans is used in candy, breads, and drugs. Soybeans also are rich in vitamins, minerals, and acids.

Most soybeans are processed for oil. About one-fifth of the bean is oil. In the 1960's, over 90 per cent of the soybean oil produced in the United States was used in edible products. These products included margarine, shortening, and salad and cooking oils. Industry also uses soybean oil to make such products as paints and lacquers, soap, and ink.

Soybean meal is made from the beans and bean hulls after the oil is extracted. The meal is an important livestock feed. It provides necessary proteins for hogs, chickens, cattle, and other farm animals. Soybeans probably supply more than half of all the protein meals fed to livestock in the United States. The steak we eat may owe its fine flavor and nourishing qualities to soybean meal. Even honeybees are fed a soybean-meal diet.

Soybeans may be ground into soy flour, which is used to make breads, pancakes, and other foods. The marshmallow on your marshmallow sundae may have been made with soybean flour. Commercial soups and puddings are examples of the many foods that contain high-protein soy flour.

Soybean meal is used in the manufacture of many chemical products, from paints to fire-extinguisher fluid. The important germ-killer *streptomycin* is made by growing a certain organism in broth containing soybean meal. This meal also is used in making paper coatings, adhesives, sizing for cloth, fertilizer, linoleum backing, insect sprays, and dozens of other products. Finding new uses for the soybean has been one of the achievements of the science of *chemurgy*. See CHEMURGY.

### Description and Varieties

The soybean is derived from a wild plant of eastern Asia. As it grows, it branches out in all directions and produces thick leaves. The plant grows from two to three-and-a-half or more feet high. The stems, leaves, and pods are covered with short, fine, brown or gray hairs. Small white or purple flowers appear where the leaf joins the stem. The bean pods range in color from very light yellow to shades of gray, brown, and black. Each contains from two to four round or oval seeds. The seeds themselves may be colored in shades of yellow, green, brown, black, or may be speckled.

More than a hundred useful varieties of soybeans have been developed in the United States. Many important new varieties have been produced by *hybridization* (crossing varieties of the plant). The characteristics of both plant and bean vary with the soil, methods of cultivation, seasonal conditions, and locality.

The yellow-seeded varieties have the most oil. When the oil has been pressed out, the meal that is left can be used in foods and other products. Usually the varieties that are used for bean production are fine for stock feed. Most soybeans now grown for their beans have a strong, unpleasant taste to humans, although they are edible and have high food values. Farmers in certain areas grow small-seeded, fine-stemmed, trailing varieties for hay and green manure.

### Culture

Soybeans grow best in areas where corn grows best. They need almost the same soil, fertility, and climate. A well-drained, warm, fertile loam soil is excellent for soybeans. Reasonably good crops can be grown on drained swamplands and muck soils. Soils of low fertility can be used if they are limed, fertilized, and inoculated. Soybeans should always be grown where the soil contains the nitrogen-fixing organism which can produce nodules on the plant's roots. Without this organism, the

---

## LEADING SOYBEAN GROWING STATES
Bushels (60 pounds) of soybeans grown for beans in 1967

| State | Bushels |
|---|---|
| Illinois | 184,171,000 bu. |
| Iowa | 145,692,000 bu. |
| Arkansas | 91,747,000 bu. |
| Missouri | 73,832,000 bu. |
| Indiana | 70,315,000 bu. |
| Minnesota | 70,024,000 bu. |
| Ohio | 50,198,000 bu. |
| Mississippi | 49,820,000 bu. |
| Louisiana | 30,038,000 bu. |
| Tennessee | 27,875,000 bu. |

Source: *Field and Seed Crops, By States, 1966-1967*, May, 1968, U.S. Department of Agriculture

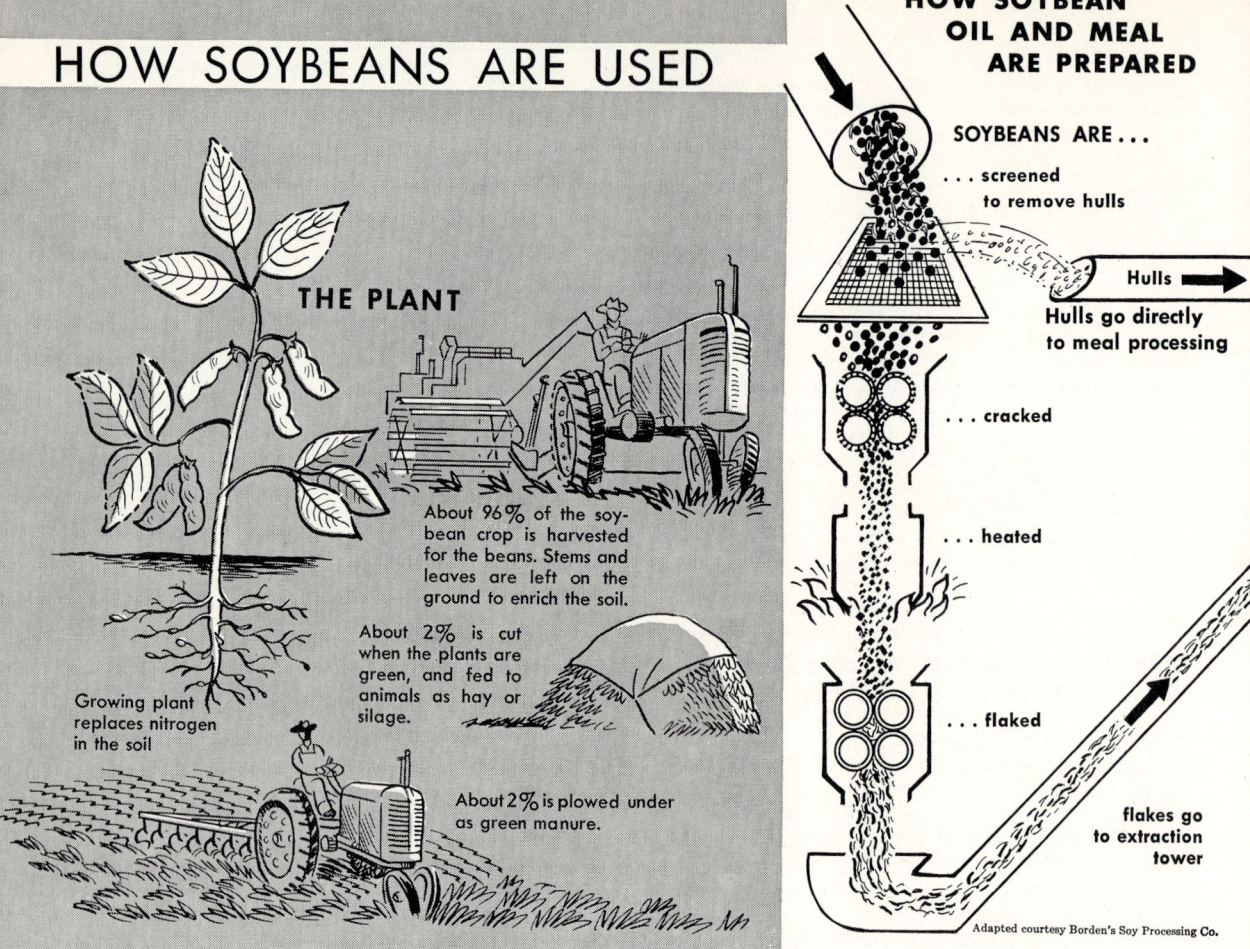

crop yield is less and the nitrogen-fixing benefit of the legume will not be realized.

The soybean is grown in widely spaced rows like corn and closely spaced like small grains. Whichever method is used, weeds should be controlled with a rotary hoe, spike-tooth harrow, or heavy weeder.

The soybean has few enemies in the United States, although in the Orient it is attacked by serious plant diseases. Some fungus, bacterial, and virus diseases exist in the United States. Among the insect enemies are grasshoppers, blister beetles, leafhoppers, the green clover worm, and the velvet-bean caterpillar. However, these insects seldom spoil a crop. Woodchucks and rabbits can cause serious damage.

### Development of the Soybean

The soybean is one of the oldest crops grown by man. In 2838 B.C., the Emperor Shung Nung of China wrote a description of the soybean plant. This is said to be the earliest record of the plant. The ancient Chinese considered the soybean their most important crop, and one of the five sacred grains necessary for living. By the 1600's, soybeans had been tried in Germany, England, France, and Hungary. But the crop was not large in any part of Europe until recent years.

It was not until 1804 that the soybean found its way into American records. At that time, James Mease wrote, "The soybean is adapted to Pennsylvania and should be cultivated." In 1854 the Perry expedition to Japan brought back a few varieties. Several more varieties and seeds were brought across the Pacific in 1889 and 1890. The United States Department of Agriculture, in cooperation with 22 state agronomy departments, has introduced many varieties and types for various growing regions and for special uses, and thus has boosted the commercial growth of the soybean. The greatest acreage and total production are found in the Middle West. Successful soybean processing began in the early 1920's.

The United States produces about three-fourths of the world's soybean crop. In the late 1960's, it grew about 975 million bushels a year on about 40 million acres. The annual crop is worth about $2½ billion.

Besides the United States, the countries that are the leading soybean growers include Brazil, China, Indonesia, and Russia. The crop is also grown in Argentina, Cambodia, Canada, Colombia, Formosa, Japan, Mexico, Nigeria, Paraguay, South Korea, and Thailand.

**Scientific Classification.** The soybean is in the pea family, *Leguminosae*. It is classified as genus *Glycine*, species *G. max*.

ROBERT G. HOUGHTLIN
Critically reviewed by A. E. STALEY, JR.

See also BEAN; PLANT (color picture: Vegetables Unknown to Our Forefathers).

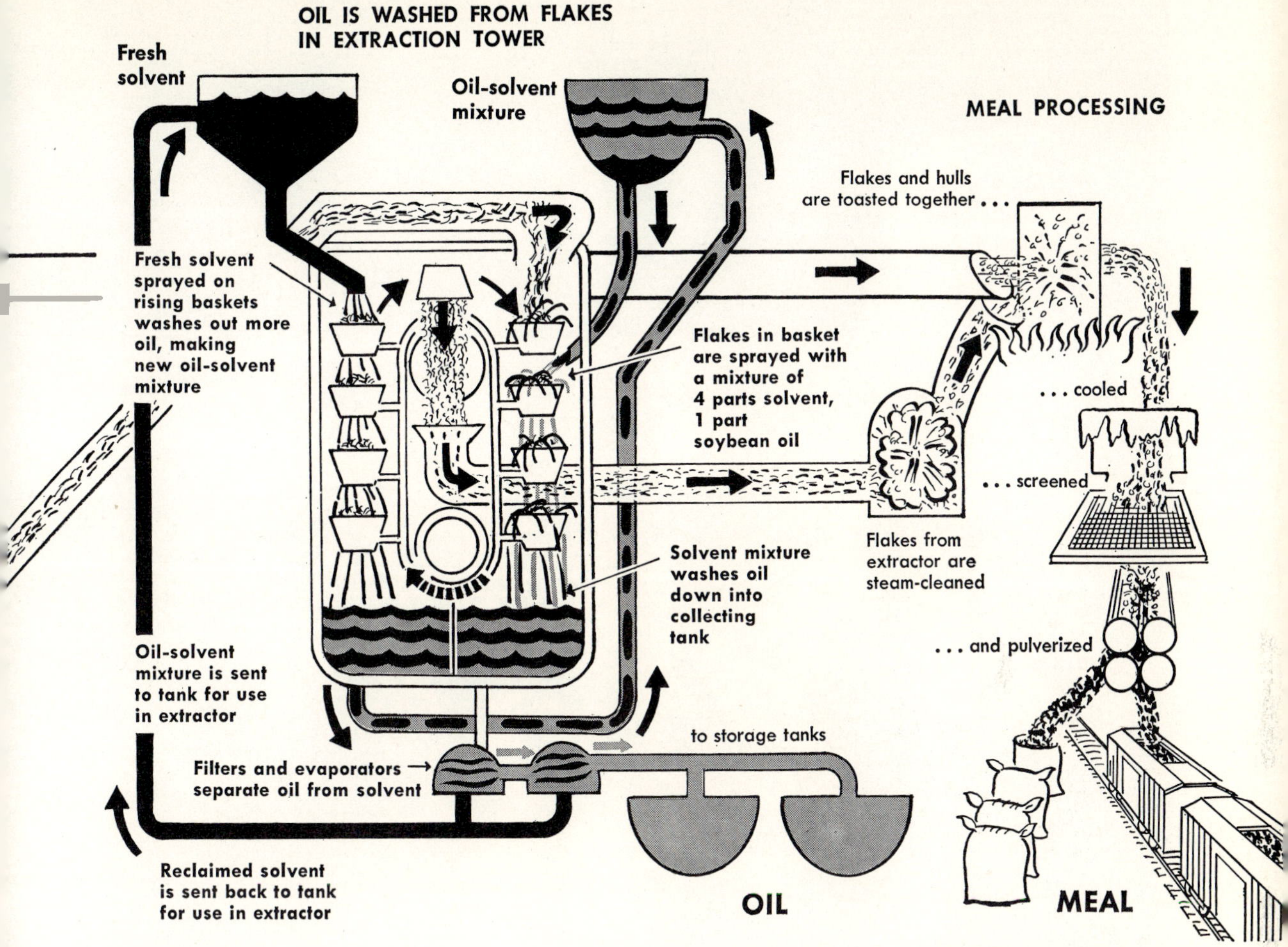

## OIL IS WASHED FROM FLAKES IN EXTRACTION TOWER

- Fresh solvent
- Oil-solvent mixture
- Fresh solvent sprayed on rising baskets washes out more oil, making new oil-solvent mixture
- Flakes in basket are sprayed with a mixture of 4 parts solvent, 1 part soybean oil
- Solvent mixture washes oil down into collecting tank
- Oil-solvent mixture is sent to tank for use in extractor
- Filters and evaporators separate oil from solvent
- Reclaimed solvent is sent back to tank for use in extractor
- to storage tanks
- **OIL**

## MEAL PROCESSING

- Flakes and hulls are toasted together...
- Flakes from extractor are steam-cleaned
- ...cooled
- ...screened
- ...and pulverized
- **MEAL**

---

**SPA.** See BATHS AND BATHING; MINERAL WATER.

**SPAAK,** *spahk,* **PAUL-HENRI** (1899-    ), is a European statesman and a leader of the Socialist party in Belgium. He was elected to Belgium's Chamber of Representatives in 1932. Later, he served in various cabinet posts. He was prime minister of Belgium in 1938 and 1939 and from 1946 to 1949. He became the first president of the General Assembly of the United Nations in 1946. He helped form the Council of Europe in 1949, and was its first president. Spaak became the Belgian Minister of Foreign Affairs in 1954, and worked in that position to bring about a union of Western European countries. He was a planner of the European Common Market and Euratom. He was secretary-general of the North Atlantic Treaty Organization (NATO) from 1957 to 1961. Spaak was born in Brussels.     JANE K. MILLER

**SPAATZ,** *spahts,* **CARL** (1891-    ), was the first Chief of Staff of the United States Air Force. He won this post because of his record as a distinguished combat leader of the Army Air Forces during World War II.

In 1942, he became commander of the Eighth Air Force in England. He commanded the Northwest African Air Forces in 1943. This combined American-British force supported the conquest of Tunisia and the invasions of Sicily and Italy. Spaatz then led the U.S. Strategic Air Forces in Europe for the final air and ground assault on Germany in 1944 and 1945. See WORLD WAR II (The Air War in Europe).

After the victory in Europe, Spaatz went to the Pacific, where his air forces included the B-29's that bombed Japan. He commanded the Army Air Forces in 1946, and was Chief of Staff of the newly independent U.S. Air Force in 1947. Born at Boyertown, Pa., Spaatz was graduated from the U.S. Military Academy.     ALFRED GOLDBERG

U.S. Signal Corps
**Carl Spaatz**

**SPACE.** See SPACE TRAVEL (What Is Space?).

**SPACE COMMUNICATIONS.** See COMMUNICATIONS SATELLITE; SPACE TRAVEL (Artificial Satellites).

**SPACE MEDICINE.** See AVIATION MEDICINE (Space Medicine); SPACE TRAVEL (Problems of Space Travel).

**SPACE NEEDLE.** See SEATTLE (picture).

**SPACE STATION.** See SPACE TRAVEL.

**SPACE SUIT.** See SPACE TRAVEL (picture, Astronaut's Space Suit).

**SPACE SURVEILLANCE.** See RADAR (Radar Warning Systems); DEW LINE.

**SPACE TIME.** See GRAVITATION.

**The First Men on the Moon** were astronauts Neil A. Armstrong, who took this picture, and Edwin E. Aldrin, Jr., above, next to a seismometer. Beyond is a laser reflector. A TV camera and an American flag are in the background. The lunar module *Eagle* stands at the right.

# SPACE TRAVEL

**SPACE TRAVEL** is man's greatest adventure—the chance to explore the moon, the planets, and the stars. Giant rockets carry explorers into space. A roaring blast of orange flame lifts the rocket from the ground. Climbing into the blue sky, the rocket leaves a white trail. Then it speeds out of sight into space, where the sky is always black and the stars always shine. The rocket may carry men on their way to explore the moon, or it may carry instruments to explore a distant planet.

The Space Age began on Oct. 4, 1957. On that day, Russia launched *Sputnik I*, the first artificial satellite to circle the earth. The first manned space flight was made on April 12, 1961, when a Russian cosmonaut, Yuri A. Gagarin, orbited the earth in a spaceship. The next month, U.S. astronaut Alan B. Shepard, Jr., made a 15-minute space flight, but he did not go into orbit. On Feb. 20, 1962, John H. Glenn, Jr., became the first American to orbit the earth. He made three revolutions. During the years that followed, many space flights carried men into orbit around the earth. Then, on Dec. 24 and 25, 1968, astronauts Frank Borman, William A. Anders, and James A. Lovell, Jr., orbited the moon 10 times in their Apollo 8 spacecraft.

Man first set foot on the moon on July 20, 1969. Astronaut Neil A. Armstrong stepped out of the Apollo 11 lunar module, named *Eagle,* and climbed backward down a metal ladder. At 10:56 P.M. E.D.S.T., Armstrong put his left foot on a rocky lunar plain called the Sea of Tranquility. After Armstrong had walked around for 18 minutes, astronaut Edwin E. Aldrin, Jr., joined him. For about two hours, the two Americans

---

*Harold L. Goodwin, the contributor of this article, is a program director of the National Science Foundation, and author of* The Images of Space *and other books on space travel. The article was critically reviewed by Wernher von Braun, the world's foremost rocket engineer and director of the Marshall Space Flight Center near Huntsville, Ala.*

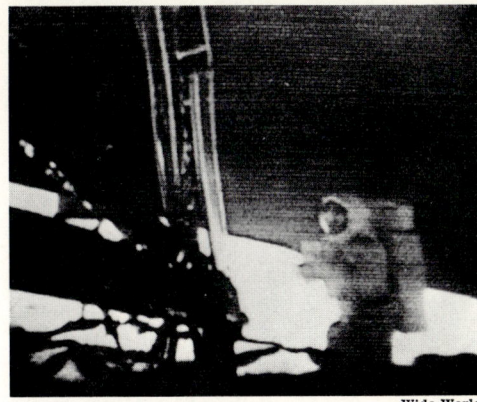

**Man's First Step on the Moon.** As astronaut Neil A. Armstrong, *above*, took the historic step on July 20, 1969, he said: "That's one small step for a man, one giant leap for mankind." The event was televised to the earth, and seen by millions. A plaque, *below*, was attached to the landing craft's descent stage, which was left on the moon.

explored near the lunar module and set up several scientific experiments. *Eagle* was on the moon almost 22 hours before Armstrong and Aldrin lifted off to rejoin the command module *Columbia*, piloted by astronaut Michael Collins.

During the years since the Space Age began, man has found many uses for space travel. The Space Age developed a huge industry called the aerospace industry to design and build space equipment. A new field of medicine called space medicine came into being to study the problems of living and working in space. Weathermen receive warning of storms with pictures taken by weather satellites. Telephone calls and television pictures are sent around the world by communications satellites. Navigators can map the positions of ships using signals broadcast from navigation satellites. Scientific satellites and space probes discovered the Van Allen radiation belt around the earth and made many other discoveries.

Success in space travel has become a measure of a nation's leadership in science, engineering, and national defense. Russia's early superiority in space travel caused criticism of American schools for not training enough scientists and engineers. Americans also feared the Russians had won an important military advantage, because rockets used in space travel could also be used as guided missiles in warfare (see GUIDED MISSILE). Many persons believed the United States should race with Russia to see which nation can become more powerful in space. Others believed the two nations should work together on peaceful uses for space travel.

Man has always wanted to explore the unknown. Many persons believe man *should* go to the moon and beyond simply because he *can* go. Scientists hope that space travel will answer many questions about the universe—how the sun, the planets, and the stars were formed, and whether life exists elsewhere in space. As more powerful rockets are designed and built, men will be able to travel to other planets and perhaps even to the stars to challenge the unknown.

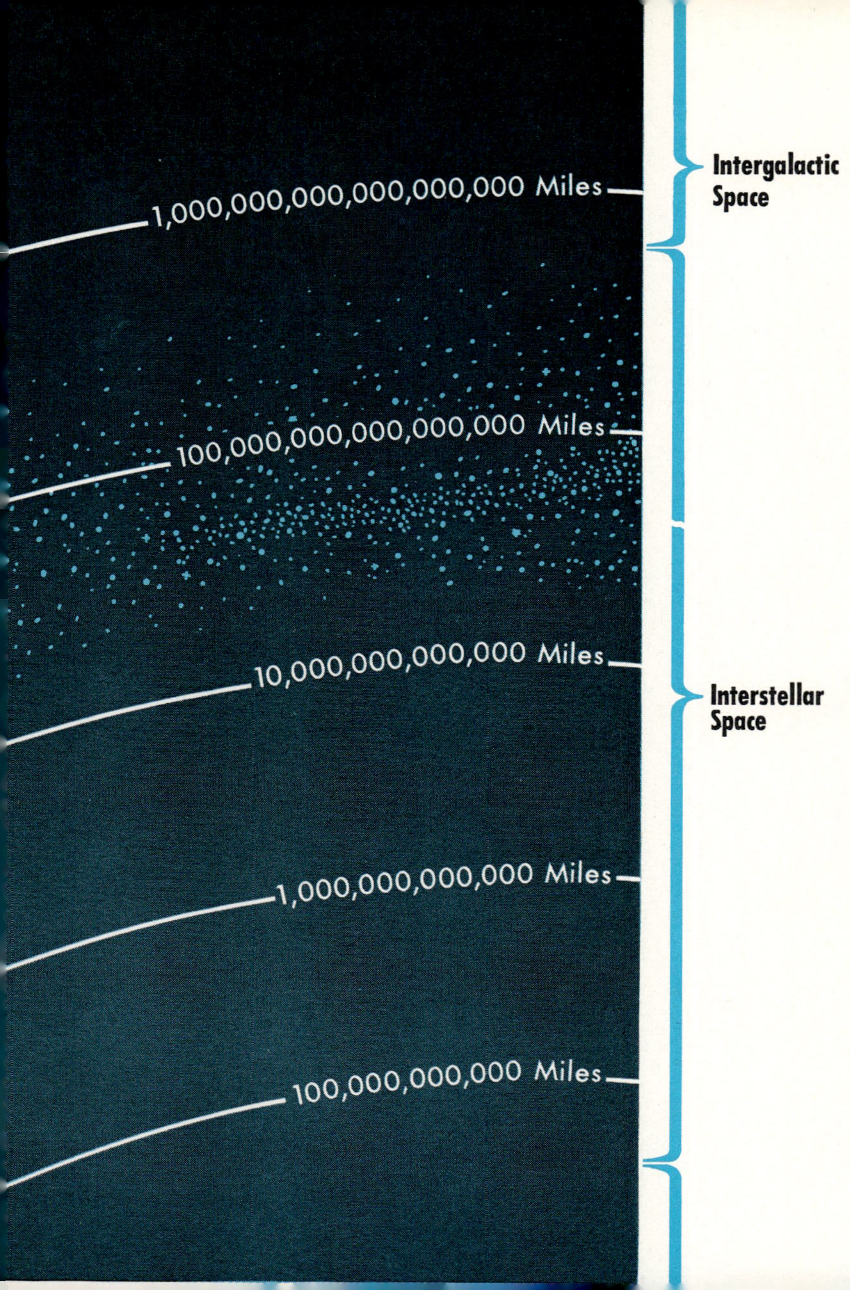

# SPACE TRAVEL / WHAT IS SPACE?

Space continues in all directions, and has no known limits. The moon moves through space around the earth. The earth and the other planets circle in space around the sun. The sun and billions of other stars make up a giant *galaxy* whirling through space. Countless other galaxies are scattered throughout space as far as man can see with the largest telescopes.

**The Beginning of Space.** Space begins where the earth's *atmosphere* (air) is too thin to affect objects moving through it. Near the earth's surface, air is plentiful. But higher above the earth, the air becomes thinner and thinner. Little by little, the atmosphere fades to almost nothing, and space begins.

Space usually is said to begin about 100 miles above the earth. At this height, a satellite may continue circling the earth for months. But, even there, enough air is still present to slow a satellite and finally cause it to fall.

**From Earth to the Moon.** The atmosphere continues beyond 100 miles above the earth. But it is not like the air near earth. It consists of widely scattered atoms and molecules of gas, and radiation. The radiation consists mostly of electrons, protons, and other subatomic particles. The particles carry electric charges. They are "trapped" in space by the earth's magnetic field. Scientists call the part of the atmosphere that contains these particles the *magnetosphere*.

Space between the earth and moon is called *cislunar* space (*cis* means *on this side*, and *lunar* means *of the moon*). As the moon is approached through cislunar space, earth's gravity becomes weaker and the moon's gravity becomes stronger. The combined gravities of earth and moon are effective to about a million miles from earth. Space to this distance is sometimes called *translunar space*.

**Space Among the Planets** Space between the planets is called *interplanetary space*. The sun's gravity controls interplanetary space. But each planet and moon also has its own gravity. Vast distances separate the bodies that move in interplanetary space. The sun is about 93 million miles from earth. Venus, the closest planet to the earth, approaches only to within about 25 million miles of earth. Mars, the planet most likely to be explored first, comes as close as about 35 million miles to the earth. A trip to Mars and back could take about 17 months. Interplanetary space reaches far beyond Pluto, the most distant planet. It ends where the sun's gravity is no longer effective—perhaps 50 billion miles from earth.

**To the Stars and Beyond.** We find even greater distances in the next region, *interstellar space* (space between the stars). *Proxima Centauri*, the star nearest our solar system, is more than 25 trillion miles away. To cover such a great distance, man would have to travel almost as fast as light. Even then, a round trip could take a whole lifetime. Interstellar space reaches distances impossible to imagine. Then *intergalactic space* (space between the galaxies) begins and never ends.

**Intergalactic Space**

**Interstellar Space**

1,000,000,000,000,000,000 Miles

100,000,000,000,000,000 Miles

10,000,000,000,000 Miles

1,000,000,000,000 Miles

100,000,000,000 Miles

## SPACE TRAVEL TERMS

**Ablation** is the melting away of a heat shield during re-entry.

**Aerospace** includes the atmosphere and the regions of space beyond it.

**Aphelion** is the point farthest from the sun in the path of a solar satellite.

**Apocynthion** is the point farthest from the moon in the orbit of a lunar satellite.

**Apogee** is the point farthest from earth in the orbit of an earth satellite.

**Artificial Satellite** is a spacecraft that circles the earth or other celestial body. The term is usually shortened to *satellite*, but it then also applies to natural moons.

**Astro** is a prefix meaning *star*. It also means *space* in such words as *astronautics* (the science of space flight).

**Astronaut** is a United States space pilot.

**Attitude** is the position of a spacecraft in relation to its direction of flight.

**Biosatellite** is an artificial satellite that carries animals or plants.

**Booster** is a launch vehicle's first stage.

**Burnout** is the point in the flight of a rocket when its propellant is used up.

**Capsule** is a manned spacecraft or a small package of instruments carried by a larger spacecraft.

**Cosmonaut** is a Russian space pilot.

**Eccentricity** is the variation of a satellite's path from a perfect circle.

**Escape Velocity** is the speed a spacecraft must reach to coast away from the pull of gravity.

**Exhaust Velocity** is the speed at which the burning gases leave a rocket.

**Gantry** is a special crane or movable tower used to service launch vehicles.

**Heat Shield** is a covering on a spacecraft to protect the craft and astronaut from high temperatures of re-entry.

**Hypergol** is a rocket fuel that ignites upon contact with an oxidizer.

**LOX** or **Liquid Oxygen** is a common oxidizer. It is made by cooling oxygen to −183° C. (−297° F.).

**Module** is a single section of a spacecraft that can be disconnected and separated from other sections.

**Orbit** is the path of a satellite.

**Oxidizer** is a substance that mixes with the fuel in a rocket, furnishing oxygen that permits the fuel to burn.

**Pericynthion** is the point closest to the moon in the orbit of a lunar satellite.

**Perigee** is the point closest to earth in the orbit of an earth satellite.

**Perihelion** is the point closest to the sun in the path of a solar satellite.

**Period** is the time it takes for a satellite to make one revolution.

**Propellant** is a substance burned in a rocket to produce thrust. Propellants include fuels and oxidizers.

**Re-entry** is that part of a flight when a returning spacecraft begins to descend through the atmosphere.

**Rendezvous** is a space maneuver in which two or more spacecraft meet.

**Retrorocket** is a rocket that fires in the direction a spacecraft is moving to slow it down or land it.

**Spacecraft** is a man-made object that travels through space.

**Stage** is one of two or more rockets combined to form a launch vehicle.

**Thrust** is the push given to a rocket by its engines.

---

**Vast Distances in Space** separate the earth from the moon, the planets, and the stars. In the illustration, left, these bodies appear much closer to the earth than they actually are, because the scale of the drawing changes toward the top. But if the diagram had been drawn with each inch equaling 1,000 miles, the picture representing the planet Pluto would have to be placed 40 miles from the drawing of the earth.

Art Lutz for WORLD BOOK

Interplanetary Space

Translunar Space

Cislunar Space

Atmosphere

10,000,000,000 Miles
Neptune
Pluto  Uranus
1,000,000,000 Miles
Saturn  Jupiter
100,000,000 Miles
Venus
Mercury  Mars
10,000,000 Miles
1,000,000 Miles
Moon
100,000 Miles
10,000 Miles
1,000 Miles
100 Miles
Earth

# SPACE TRAVEL / GETTING INTO SPACE AND BACK

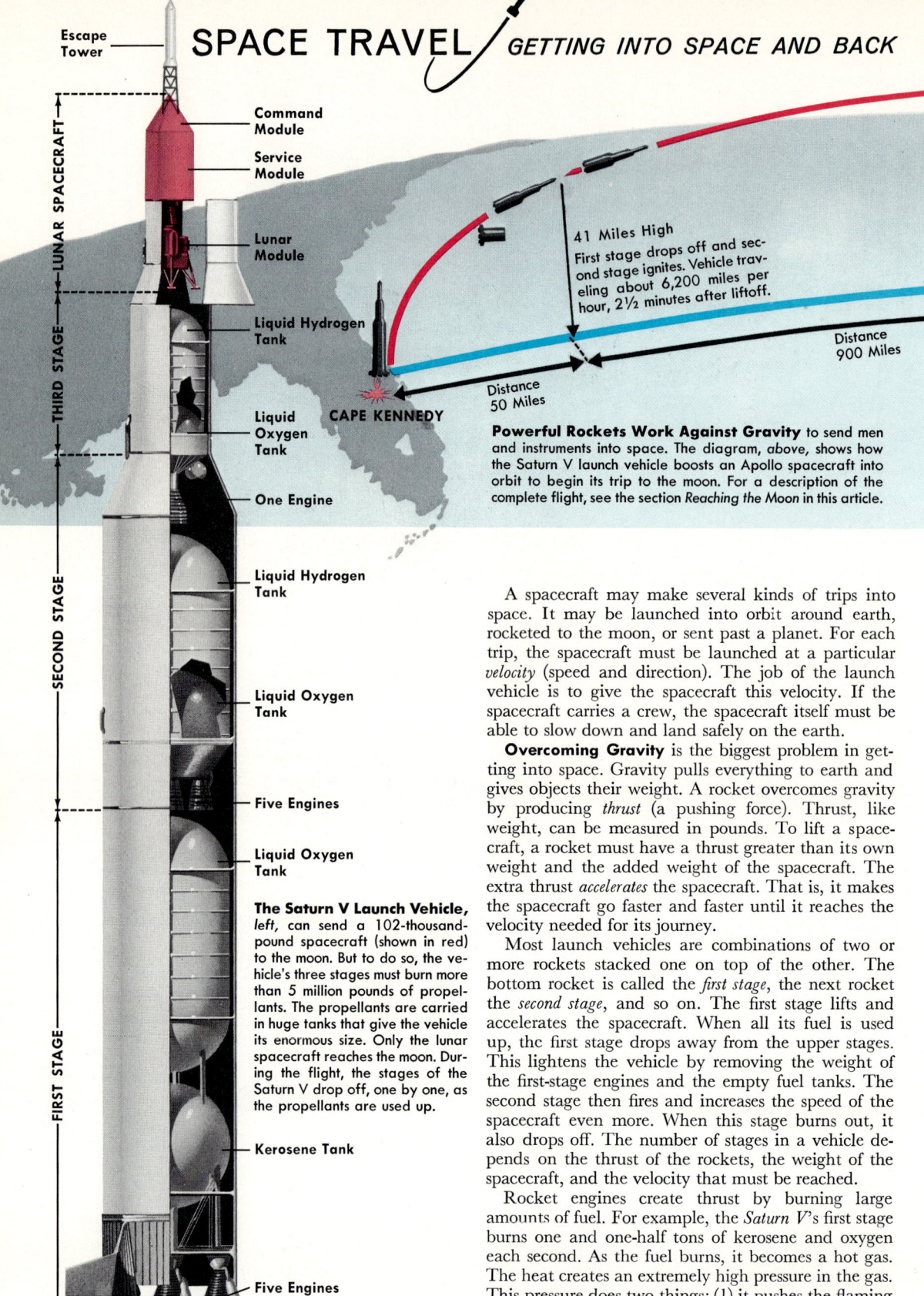

**Powerful Rockets Work Against Gravity** to send men and instruments into space. The diagram, above, shows how the Saturn V launch vehicle boosts an Apollo spacecraft into orbit to begin its trip to the moon. For a description of the complete flight, see the section *Reaching the Moon* in this article.

**The Saturn V Launch Vehicle,** *left,* can send a 102-thousand-pound spacecraft (shown in red) to the moon. But to do so, the vehicle's three stages must burn more than 5 million pounds of propellants. The propellants are carried in huge tanks that give the vehicle its enormous size. Only the lunar spacecraft reaches the moon. During the flight, the stages of the Saturn V drop off, one by one, as the propellants are used up.

A spacecraft may make several kinds of trips into space. It may be launched into orbit around earth, rocketed to the moon, or sent past a planet. For each trip, the spacecraft must be launched at a particular *velocity* (speed and direction). The job of the launch vehicle is to give the spacecraft this velocity. If the spacecraft carries a crew, the spacecraft itself must be able to slow down and land safely on the earth.

**Overcoming Gravity** is the biggest problem in getting into space. Gravity pulls everything to earth and gives objects their weight. A rocket overcomes gravity by producing *thrust* (a pushing force). Thrust, like weight, can be measured in pounds. To lift a spacecraft, a rocket must have a thrust greater than its own weight and the added weight of the spacecraft. The extra thrust *accelerates* the spacecraft. That is, it makes the spacecraft go faster and faster until it reaches the velocity needed for its journey.

Most launch vehicles are combinations of two or more rockets stacked one on top of the other. The bottom rocket is called the *first stage,* the next rocket the *second stage,* and so on. The first stage lifts and accelerates the spacecraft. When all its fuel is used up, the first stage drops away from the upper stages. This lightens the vehicle by removing the weight of the first-stage engines and the empty fuel tanks. The second stage then fires and increases the speed of the spacecraft even more. When this stage burns out, it also drops off. The number of stages in a vehicle depends on the thrust of the rockets, the weight of the spacecraft, and the velocity that must be reached.

Rocket engines create thrust by burning large amounts of fuel. For example, the *Saturn V*'s first stage burns one and one-half tons of kerosene and oxygen each second. As the fuel burns, it becomes a hot gas. The heat creates an extremely high pressure in the gas. This pressure does two things: (1) it pushes the flaming

Illustrated by Herbert Herrick for WORLD BOOK

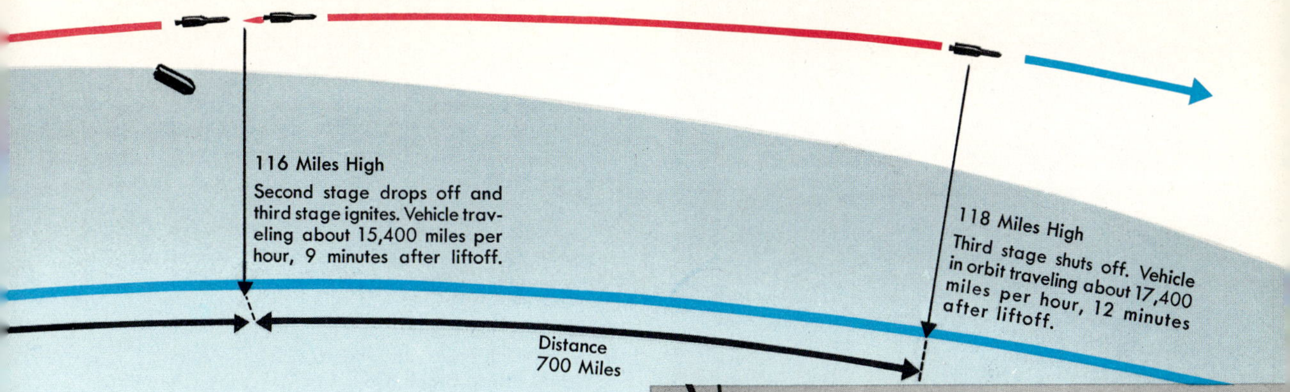

**116 Miles High**
Second stage drops off and third stage ignites. Vehicle traveling about 15,400 miles per hour, 9 minutes after liftoff.

**118 Miles High**
Third stage shuts off. Vehicle in orbit traveling about 17,400 miles per hour, 12 minutes after liftoff.

Distance 700 Miles

**To Return to Earth,** a manned spacecraft must gradually lose speed until it is moving slowly enough to land safely. First, friction with the air begins to slow the spacecraft as soon as it enters the atmosphere. Then, parachutes can be used to lower the spacecraft gently to earth, as shown in the illustration, *right.*

gas backward and out through the rocket nozzle; (2) it pushes the rocket forward. This forward push on the rocket is the thrust.

Rocket fuels are called *propellants.* Liquid-fuel rockets work by combining a fuel, such as kerosene or liquid hydrogen, with an *oxidizer,* such as liquid oxygen. The fuel and oxidizer burn violently when mixed. Solid-fuel rockets use dry chemicals as propellants.

Engineers rate the efficiency of propellants in terms of the thrust that one pound of fuel can produce in one second. This measurement is known as the propellant's *specific impulse.* Liquid propellants have a higher specific impulse than most solid propellants. But some, including LOX and liquid hydrogen, are difficult and dangerous to handle. They must be loaded into the rocket just before launching. Solid propellants are loaded into the rocket at the factory, and are ready for use at all times. Large solid-propellant rockets are extremely heavy when loaded with fuel. Because of this, they are difficult to move from the factory to the rocket launch site.

**Returning to Earth** involves problems opposite to those of getting into space. The spacecraft must lose speed instead of gaining it. For example, a spacecraft returning from the moon may be traveling at a speed of up to 25,000 miles per hour as it enters the atmosphere. The spacecraft loses most of this speed as it falls through the air. As friction with the air slows the spacecraft, it also produces a large amount of heat. So, the spacecraft must be able to withstand this heat without burning up. A special plastic *heat shield* protects the craft by melting and vaporizing slowly to carry away excess heat.

At about 40,000 feet, a special parachute called a *drogue* is released. This chute slows down the spacecraft and straightens out the craft if it is wobbling. At about 10,000 feet, one or more large parachutes open and lower the craft the rest of the way to earth.

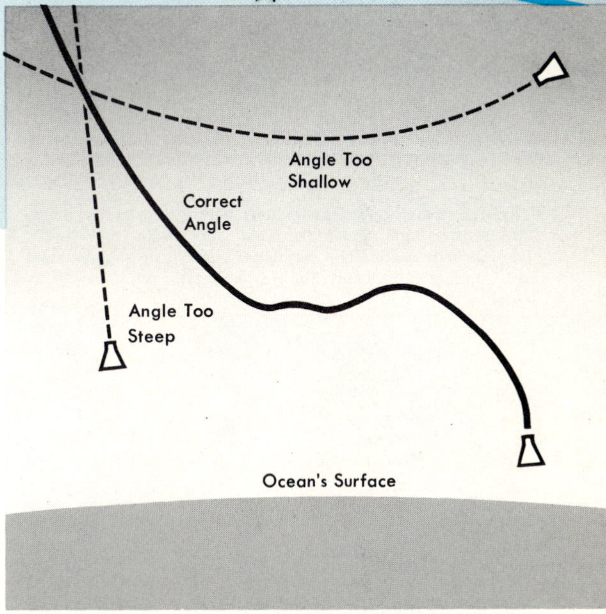

Angle Too Shallow
Correct Angle
Angle Too Steep
Ocean's Surface

WORLD BOOK illustration

**An Apollo Spacecraft Returning from the Moon** must enter the earth's atmosphere at a certain angle to make a safe landing, *above.* If the angle is too shallow, the spacecraft will not reach earth, but will go back into space. If the angle is too steep, the craft will burn up. Once it is sufficiently slowed down, giant parachutes, *below,* are used to lower the craft to a soft landing.

NASA

564a

Courtesy Pratt & Whitney Aircraft

**A Second-Stage Rocket Blasts Away** from its first stage, or booster, high above the earth. The rocket then heads deeper into space while the heavy booster, its engines silent and its fuel tanks empty, falls toward earth.

# SPACE TRAVEL / LAUNCH VEHICLES

A launch vehicle is a rocket or a combination of rockets used to launch satellites, space probes, and other *spacecraft*. The United States uses several launch vehicles with a wide range of lifting power. These vehicles can launch many kinds of spacecraft to various distances in space. Some of the rocket engines use solid fuels and others use liquid fuels (see ROCKET).

To launch a spacecraft, a rocket must burn a large amount of fuel. For this reason, a launch vehicle consists mostly of fuel tanks. The more powerful the vehicle, the larger it must be to hold the needed fuel.

**The Building Block Idea.** Engineers use a few basic rockets and rocket engines to build a family of launch vehicles. They call this method the "building block" idea. Here is how it works.

The Delta launch vehicle sent *Telstar*, *Echo*, *Tiros*, *Syncom*, *Early Bird*, and other satellites into orbit. Delta consists of three sections called *stages*. The first stage, called the *booster*, is a Thor ballistic missile. The second stage is a rocket called AJ-10. The third stage is called Altair. This combination of rockets can launch an 800-pound spacecraft into a low orbit. Or, it can send a 100-pound craft to the moon.

## LAUNCH VEHICLES

| Launch Vehicle | Stages | Takeoff Thrust | Payload |
|---|---|---|---|
| Vanguard | 3 | 28,000 lbs. | 50 lbs. in earth orbit |
| Jupiter C | 4 | 82,000 lbs. | 30 lbs. in earth orbit |
| Scout | 4 | 100,000 lbs. | 300 lbs. in earth orbit |
| Juno II | 4 | 150,000 lbs. | 100 lbs. in earth orbit |
| Mercury-Redstone | 1 | 82,000 lbs. | 2,000 lbs. suborbital |
| Delta | 3 | 172,000 lbs. | 800 lbs. in earth orbit; 100 lbs. to moon |
| Mercury-Atlas | 1½* | 367,000 lbs. | 2,000 lbs. in earth orbit |
| Atlas-Agena | 2½* | 367,000 lbs. | 5,000 lbs. in earth orbit; 750 lbs. to moon; 400 lbs. to Mars or Venus |
| Atlas-Centaur | 2½* | 367,000 lbs. | 8,500 lbs. in earth orbit; 2,300 lbs. to moon; 1,300 lbs. to Mars or Venus |
| Titan II | 2 | 430,000 lbs. | 7,000 lbs. in earth orbit |
| Titan III | 3 | 2,000,000 lbs. | 25,000 lbs. in earth orbit |
| Saturn I | 2 | 1,500,000 lbs. | 21,000 lbs. in earth orbit |
| Uprated Saturn I | 2 | 1,500,000 lbs. | 40,000 lbs. in earth orbit |
| Saturn V | 3 | 7,500,000 lbs. | 260,000 lbs. in earth orbit; 102,000 lbs. to moon; 70,000 lbs. to Mars or Venus |

(*Half stage is droppable booster engine.)

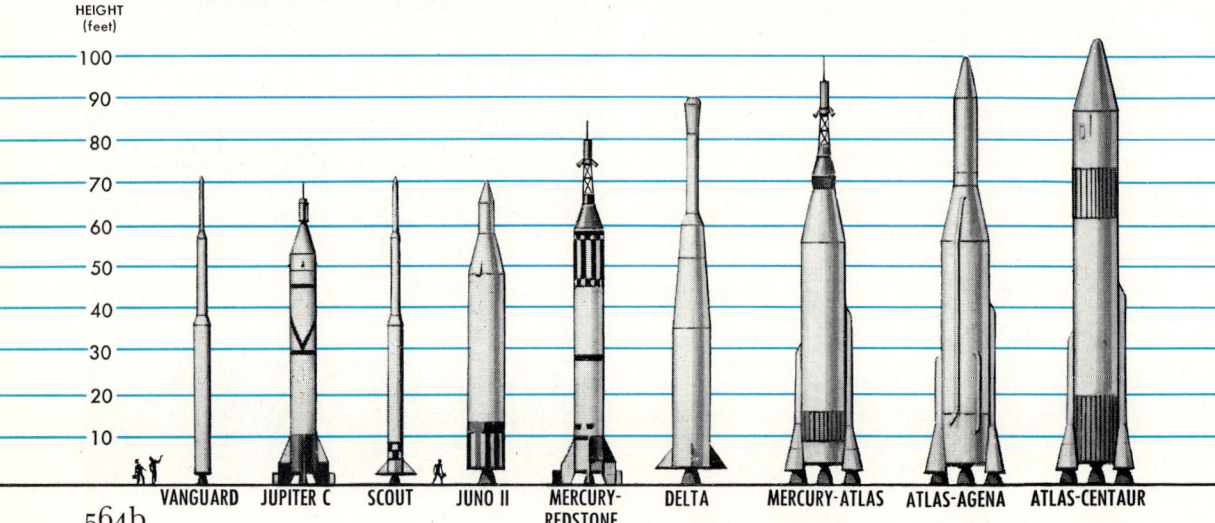

Delta's booster, Thor, is also the booster in a more powerful vehicle called Thor-Agena. The second stage of this vehicle is the Agena rocket, which can be stopped and started again in space.

When a satellite is too heavy for Thor-Agena, the Agena can be placed atop an Atlas booster. Atlas-Agena can lift 5,000 pounds into a 300-mile-high orbit. This vehicle launched the *Mariner* spacecraft to Mars and Venus, and *Ranger* to the moon.

The Atlas rocket can also boost a second stage called Centaur, even more powerful than Agena. The Atlas-Centaur combination can lift 8,500 pounds into a 300-mile-high orbit. The Atlas itself is a powerful launch vehicle. It was used to launch the Mercury program astronauts into orbit.

Engineers use rocket engines as well as whole rockets for building blocks. For example, an engine called the H-1 powered the Jupiter, one of the earliest missiles. Eight H-1 engines now power the Saturn I booster. Saturn I's second stage uses three A-3 engines—the same engine used in the Centaur.

**Piggyback Boosters.** Sometimes engineers attach solid-fuel rockets to the sides of a liquid-fuel launch vehicle to give it extra power. For example, the Titan II liquid-fuel vehicle can lift 6,000 pounds into a low orbit. But with two great solid-fuel boosters strapped to its sides, Titan can lift 25,000 pounds. This piggyback combination is known as Titan III.

**Apollo Program Launch Vehicles** are part of the United States program to land men on the moon. These vehicles are called Saturn. Saturn I and Saturn IB can be used to launch spacecraft into orbit around earth. Saturn V carries the Apollo spacecraft to the moon. This giant launch vehicle stands 33 feet wide and 363 feet tall with its spacecraft. It can carry 130 tons into orbit around earth, or launch 51 tons as far as the moon.

**Nuclear Rockets** will be put to work in the 1970's. These rockets get much more power from each pound of fuel than any rocket used now. Power comes from a nuclear reactor inside the rocket. The reactor creates intense heat that changes liquid hydrogen to a gas. The gas shoots from the tail of the rocket and drives the rocket forward. Engineers will first use nuclear rockets as upper stages of such launch vehicles as the Saturn V.

TITAN II    TITAN III    SATURN I    SATURN IB    SATURN V

564c

# SPACE TRAVEL / MANNED SPACECRAFT

Manned spacecraft are lifted into space atop huge launch vehicles. The spacecraft's upper end is usually somewhat streamlined to reduce air resistance during the flight through the atmosphere. For example, *Mercury*, *Gemini*, and *Apollo* spacecraft have the general shape of a cone. They are launched with the narrow end pointing up. They descend through the atmosphere backwards—with the broad end pointing in the direction of flight. In this way, they lose speed quickly, because the broad end offers great resistance to the air. Spacecraft like the Apollo *lunar module* are not streamlined at all. This spacecraft is designed to operate only near the moon, where there is no air.

All manned spacecraft carry special equipment to protect the astronauts and bring them safely back to earth. This equipment includes (1) life-support systems, (2) communications and navigation equipment, (3) control systems, and (4) re-entry and landing equipment.

**Life-Support Systems** supply the astronauts with oxygen, food, and water. Oxygen and water are carried in tanks. Food is freeze-dried and stored in meal-size packages. Solid body wastes are sealed into plastic bags and stored aboard the spacecraft. Liquid wastes are released into space.

**Communications and Navigation Equipment.** The astronauts need a radio to report to scientists and engineers on the ground. They can answer their questions and ask for directions in an emergency. Some spacecraft carry a television camera so that pictures from space or the moon can be sent to earth during the flight. Navigation equipment includes sextants, gyroscopes, and small electronic computers. The astronauts use this equipment to find their position in space and to check their course. *Telemetry* equipment sends information about all spacecraft systems to ground stations.

**Control Systems** enable the astronauts to put the spacecraft in any position. They do this by firing tiny rocket motors located at various places on the outside of the craft. By operating these motors, the astronauts can tilt the craft, point it to either side, and roll it right or left. To re-enter the atmosphere, the craft must point a certain way, or else it might skip away from earth or descend too fast and burn up.

**Re-Entry and Landing Equipment** includes retrorockets, heat shield, and parachutes. *Retrorockets* are small rockets that fire in the direction the craft is moving. They slow the craft down and cause it to fall out of orbit. The *heat shield* protects the astronauts from the intense heat generated when the craft plunges through the atmosphere. It is a thick layer of material covering the broad end of the spacecraft. The material partly melts and partly vaporizes during re-entry. Air flowing around the spacecraft removes this material, carrying away most of the heat. When the spacecraft has lost enough speed and altitude, parachutes open and lower it gently to the earth.

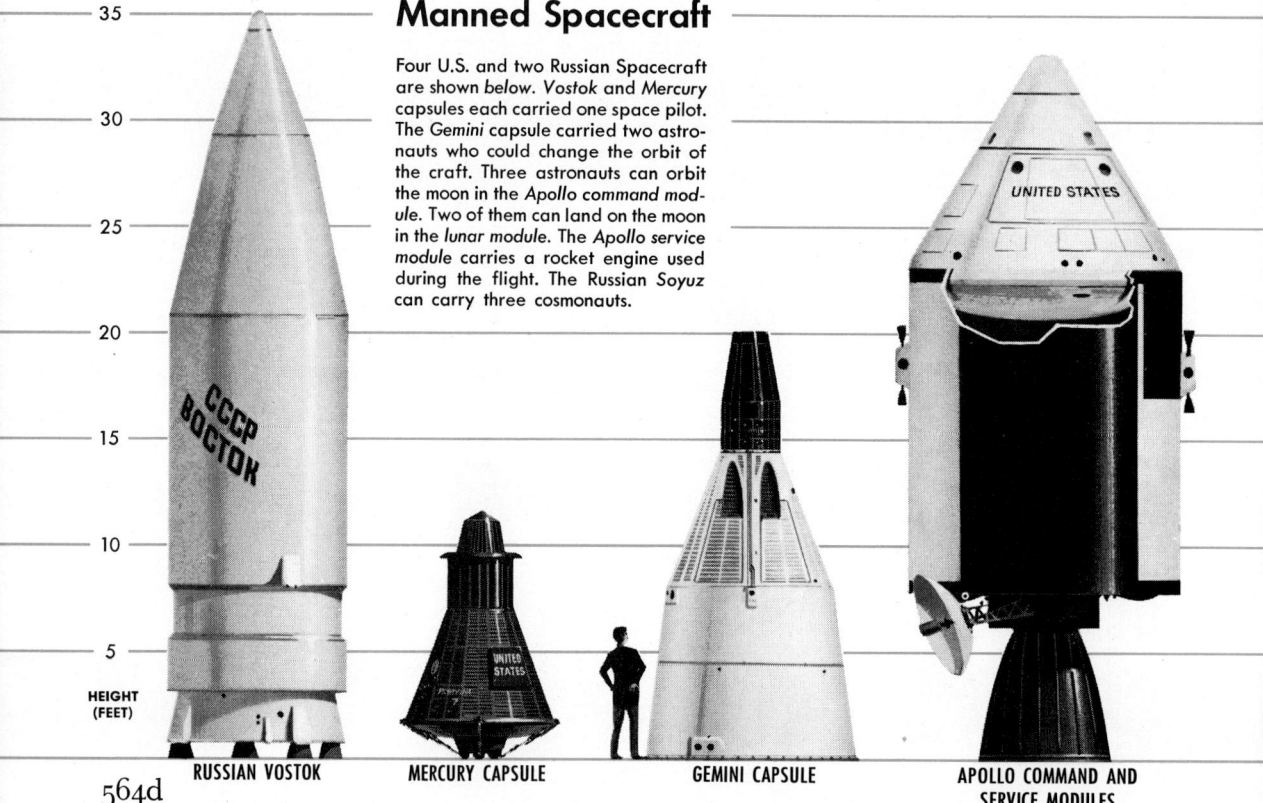

## Manned Spacecraft

Four U.S. and two Russian Spacecraft are shown *below*. *Vostok* and *Mercury* capsules each carried one space pilot. The *Gemini* capsule carried two astronauts who could change the orbit of the craft. Three astronauts can orbit the moon in the *Apollo command module*. Two of them can land on the moon in the *lunar module*. The *Apollo service module* carries a rocket engine used during the flight. The Russian *Soyuz* can carry three cosmonauts.

RUSSIAN VOSTOK — MERCURY CAPSULE — GEMINI CAPSULE — APOLLO COMMAND AND SERVICE MODULES

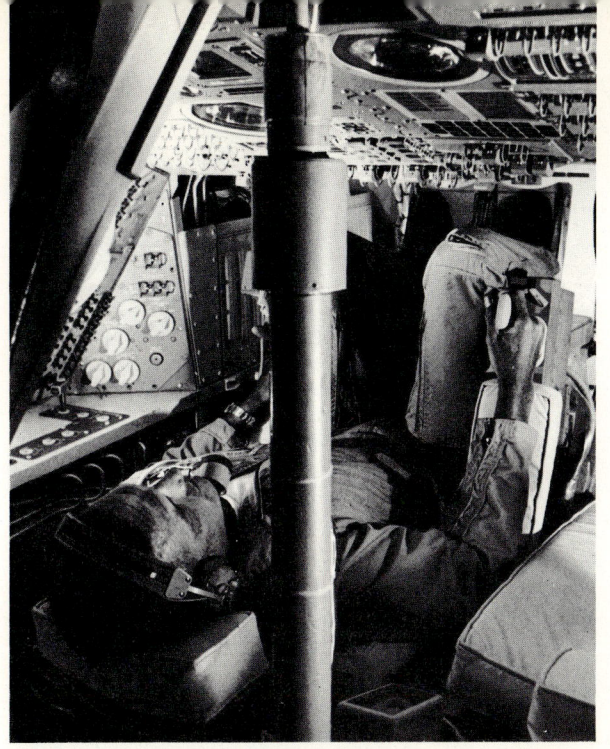

NASA

**Inside an Apollo Command Module,** the pilot moves a control stick to turn the spacecraft. Astronaut Frank Borman is shown lying on his couch during a ground test.

© 1969, World Book Science Service

**Inside an Apollo Lunar Module Simulator,** astronaut Neil A. Armstrong practices a moon landing. Through a window to his left, he sees a simulated moonscape.

APOLLO LUNAR MODULE

RUSSIAN SOYUZ

HEIGHT (FEET)

564e

# SPACE TRAVEL / LAUNCH OPERATIONS

## JOHN F. KENNEDY SPACE CENTER

At Cape Kennedy, Fla., spacecraft launch vehicles are fired from launch complexes, shown on the map, *below*. Each launch complex is designed to fire a particular type of launch vehicle.

The equipment needed to launch a space vehicle depends on the vehicle's size. A small sounding rocket, for example, can be launched from a simple stand that has a rail for guiding the rocket. But a huge vehicle such as the Saturn V needs a special *launch complex*.

The Saturn V is a three-stage launch vehicle used in the Apollo program. The rocket launches the Apollo spacecraft and its crew of three astronauts into orbit around the earth. Once in orbit, the third stage fires again to send the spacecraft to the moon. After the Apollo program, Saturn V launch vehicles may lift space stations or large telescopes into orbit around the earth. The pictures on these pages show the equipment used to launch the Saturn V at Cape Kennedy, Fla.

The three stages of the Saturn V and the Apollo spacecraft are connected together inside the 52-story Vehicle Assembly Building. Then a giant tractorlike machine called a *crawler* carries the rocket and its *mobile launching tower* to one of two launch pads. The crawler sets the tower and rocket on the pad and then moves a *service tower* next to the rocket. From the service tower, technicians put kerosene fuel (called RP-1) and liquid oxygen (called LOX) into the first stage. They then fill the second and third stages with liquid hydrogen and LOX. The tanks in the spacecraft are also filled. Engineers and technicians, with the aid of electronic equipment, constantly observe the vehicle to make sure it will work properly. When all is ready, the crawler moves the service tower away from the pad.

Before the launch, rocket engineers follow a *countdown* (schedule) to be sure that all preparations for the launch are completed at their proper times. As the countdown nears its end, a computer often takes control. But technicians in the safety of the *launch control center* several miles away can resume control of the countdown if necessary. They watch the pad with television cameras. Finally, the first stage engines ignite. A set of arms holds the vehicle until its engines build up enough thrust to lift it off the pad. Then the vehicle roars into the air.

**Crawler Takes Saturn V From Assembly Building.**

**On the Launch Pad**

**The Apollo Spaceport** includes the Vehicle Assembly Building, where the Apollo spacecraft and the Saturn V launch vehicle are connected. The Saturn V is brought to the spaceport on barges. After assembly, the spacecraft and launch vehicle are carried by a crawler to the launch pad. A service tower, from which technicians work, stands next to the spacecraft and launch vehicle until just before launch.

WORLD BOOK diagram

Atlantic Ocean
Launch Pad 39B
Saturn V Vehicle
Launch Pad 39A
Mobile Launching Tower
Vehicle Assembly Building
Mobile Service Tower
Launch Control Center
Crawler
Crawlerway
Barge Canal

**Technicians Wait in Launch Control Center.**

**Liftoff!**

NASA

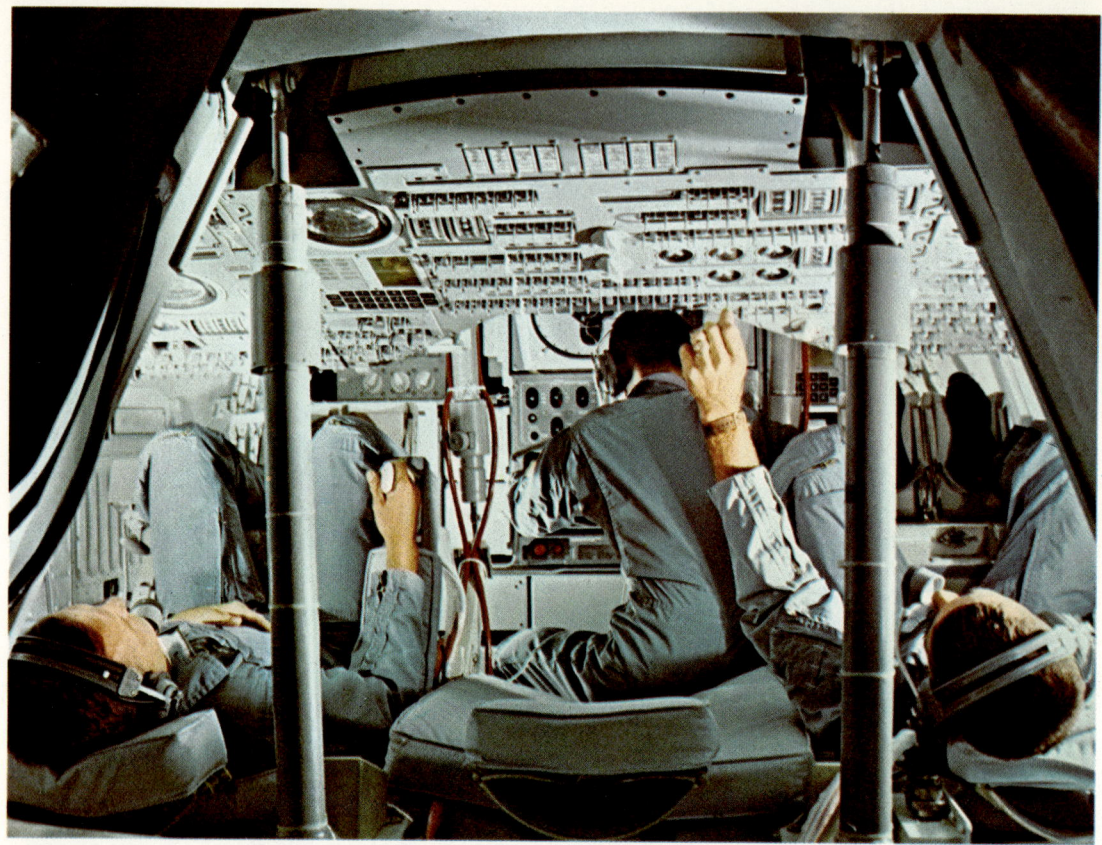

**The Interior of an Apollo Spacecraft** is lined with instrument panels and control switches. Each of the three astronauts in the command module operates the equipment located near his couch.

# SPACE TRAVEL / FLYING A SPACECRAFT

**Before the Flight.** The astronauts start to get ready for a space flight many hours before the launch vehicle lifts off the pad. First, they get a physical examination to make sure they are in shape for the flight. Then they put on their space suits. The suits supply oxygen and protect them from the deadly vacuum of space if the air pressure inside the spacecraft drops. Astronauts wear their suits during lift-off for extra safety, and must wear them to "walk" in space or explore the moon's surface. They usually remove the space suits while they are sealed in the spacecraft and fly in the less bulky flight coveralls.

About two hours before the countdown ends, the astronauts ride in a special truck to the launch pad. An elevator in the mobile launch tower lifts them to the spacecraft poised atop the launch vehicle. Technicians help them into the craft and connect their suits to the oxygen supply, cooling system, and electrical equipment. The astronauts use the time before lift-off to check spacecraft instruments.

**Piloting a Spacecraft.** In the launch control center at Cape Kennedy and the Manned Spacecraft Center near Houston, tension mounts as *T-zero* (lift-off time) approaches. A few seconds before the countdown ends, the rocket's first stage engines roar to life. At T-zero, the vehicle lifts off. It rises slowly at first, then gains speed and streaks into the sky. The flight has begun, but the astronauts are not yet piloting their spacecraft. The launch vehicle's own guidance system controls the engines that lift and steer the rocket.

As the spacecraft gains altitude, the force of the accelerating rocket pushes the astronauts back in their couches. Because of the acceleration, they now weigh 4 to 5 times as much as they do on the earth. About 6 minutes after lift-off, the spacecraft is in orbit. It is about 100 miles above the earth and traveling about 17 thousand miles an hour.

The rocket's first and second stages have fallen back to earth. On some flights, the third stage remains attached to the spacecraft. On other flights, it separates, but orbits near the spacecraft for a time. Now, no force at all pushes the astronauts into their couches. They are weightless and orbiting freely through space along the same path as their spacecraft. Unless they

564h

strap themselves to their couches, they will float inside the cabin.

For the first time during the flight, the astronauts can fly the spacecraft themselves. They steer the craft by moving a small control stick, similar to that in an airplane. Moving the stick fires small rocket motors. The motors rotate the craft in the direction the stick is moved. With a second stick, the astronauts steer the craft to *rendezvous* (meet) with other spacecraft or to change the spacecraft's course. On flights to the moon, the Apollo command module must rendezvous and *dock* (link together) with the Apollo lunar module twice.

The small rocket motors are not powerful enough to send a spacecraft to the moon or to bring it back to the earth. To make large changes in speed and direction, the astronauts need a larger rocket engine. They use either the engine in the attached third stage, or the engine in the service module.

The astronauts must know the spacecraft's position at all times. In flights around the earth, the navigator receives radio information from tracking stations concerning his position. He also sights landmarks on the earth. On flights to the moon or planets, astronauts will miss their target unless they know which way and how fast they are traveling. The navigator uses special telescopes in the spacecraft to determine the position of certain stars in relation to landmarks on the moon. He puts this information into a computer that finds the spacecraft's position.

**Scientific Duties.** Astronauts are scientific explorers as well as pilots. In the early 1960's, almost everything the astronauts did in orbit told scientists something new about manned space travel. For example, no one knew how well men could work when they were weightless. The early flights proved that men could work in space.

Scientists ask astronauts to perform experiments so they can learn more about man's ability to live and work in space. In one test, astronauts pulled rubber exercise ropes to test methods of keeping physically fit during long periods of weightlessness. Astronauts also do experiments to learn more about space and our solar system. On the moon, they set up scientific equipment and bring back rock samples for more study.

**Living in a Spacecraft.** Food the astronauts eat is either *freeze-dried* (frozen and the water removed) or concentrated to save space and weight. The freeze-dried food—chicken and gravy or chocolate pudding, for example—comes in tube-shaped plastic bags. The astronaut injects hot or cold water into one end of the bag from a water supply gun in the spacecraft. He mixes the food and water in the bag for several minutes, then cuts off one end of the bag and squeezes the food into his mouth. Concentrated food—sugar cookies, for example—needs no water. It comes in bite-size pieces. The astronaut drinks water through a tube connected to the spacecraft water supply. Astronauts must eat and drink this way to keep crumbs and drops of liquids from floating inside the spacecraft.

Astronauts can sleep strapped to their couches. But in the Apollo spacecraft, they have special sleeping bags under their couches. They can sleep in the bags without floating. Some astronauts say they have trouble going to sleep on their first night in space. But sleeping pills are provided for them.

**An Astronaut's Space Suit** has layers of protective fabric. While outside the spacecraft, he wears more protective garments and a backpack containing all equipment needed to support life.

Special systems in the craft dispose of body wastes. Liquid wastes are pumped outside. Solid wastes are disinfected and stored in plastic bags.

**Re-Entry.** A spacecraft returning to the earth from the moon must slow down before entering the atmosphere or it will burn up. It must also be in a certain *attitude* (position) with its blunt end pointing forward before firing its retrorockets. These rockets slow the craft to a safe speed for re-entry. The astronauts sit with their backs toward the blunt end and feel the push of the retrorockets as the spacecraft slows down. The spacecraft falls closer to the earth and enters the atmosphere. The astronauts' bodies begin to feel heavy again. The craft is still moving so fast it needs a heat shield to protect the astronauts from the intense heat. The heat *ionizes* (electrically charges) the air around the craft and blocks all radio communications with the astronauts for several minutes. Then the spacecraft releases big parachutes that carry it gently to the earth.

NASA photo taken during rendezvous of Gemini 6 and Gemini 7.

**One Hundred Miles Above the Earth,** an orbiting astronaut can see blankets of clouds over the ocean, the blue band of the atmosphere curving around the horizon, and the ever-black sky of space.

# SPACE TRAVEL / ORBITING THE EARTH

**Selecting the Orbit** is one of the first steps in planning the launch of an earth-orbiting spacecraft. The orbit selected depends on the job to be done. For example, a communications satellite may orbit at a distance of thousands of miles where it can serve many ground stations. Early manned spacecraft usually orbited less than 200 miles high. In this way, they avoided the radiation in the Van Allen belts.

Most orbiting spacecraft do not stay the same distance from the earth all the time. Their orbits have the shape of a flattened circle called an *ellipse*. One end of the ellipse comes closer to the earth than the other. The point closest to the earth is called the orbiting spacecraft's *perigee*. The farthest point is called the *apogee*. Many scientific satellites follow orbits that have a low perigee and a very high apogee. These satellites can explore a wide range of space.

Satellites may also be launched in various directions around earth. They may circle in an east-west direction, in line with the equator. Or, they may travel north and south, passing over the earth's poles. Most satellites travel in a direction between these extremes.

**Launching a Spacecraft.** When the launch vehicle blasts off, it lifts the spacecraft straight up for about a minute. Then the vehicle arches into the proper direction for the selected orbit. Finally, the vehicle's last stage fires to give the spacecraft the velocity it needs to go into orbit. The higher the orbit, the lower the speed needed to stay in orbit. For example, a spacecraft in a circular orbit 200 miles high must travel more than 17 thousand miles an hour. But to orbit at 22 thousand miles, a spacecraft needs a speed of only about 6,900 miles an hour. However, a more powerful launch vehicle is needed to put a spacecraft in the higher orbit.

To place a spacecraft in orbit, the launching rockets must be carefully controlled. Each stage must burn for the exact length of time to give the spacecraft the right speed. Sensitive gyroscopes and other special devices guide the vehicle to keep it on course. Some vehicles are controlled by clockwork or magnetic tape devices. These devices can start and stop the rocket engines according to a carefully laid plan. Many launch vehicles are controlled electronically from the ground. Signals from the vehicle tell a computer on the ground how the vehicle is working. The computer compares this information with the planned operation. It then sends signals back to the vehicle to make the necessary corrections in speed or direction.

**How a Spacecraft Stays in Orbit.** Nothing "holds up" an orbiting spacecraft. Gravity keeps the spacecraft in orbit by pulling down on it. Without gravity, the spacecraft would shoot off into space in a straight line. But gravity pulls the spacecraft out of the straight path and causes it to curve around the earth.

The force of gravity weakens as the distance from earth is increased. Near the earth, a strong gravitational force pulls a spacecraft and causes it to curve. There, the spacecraft must have a high speed. Otherwise it would curve too much and come closer and closer to earth. But at higher altitudes, gravity is not so strong. There, a spacecraft can travel more slowly and still keep from being pulled closer to earth.

# Kinds of Earth Orbits

**Circular and Elliptical Orbits.** The diagram, *right*, shows the difference between circular and elliptical orbits. In a circular orbit, a spacecraft always travels at the same speed and stays the same distance from earth. In an elliptical orbit, a spacecraft's speed and distance from earth change continually. The spacecraft goes fastest at perigee and then slows down as it swings farther from earth. It travels slowest at apogee, but speeds up as it curves back closer to earth.

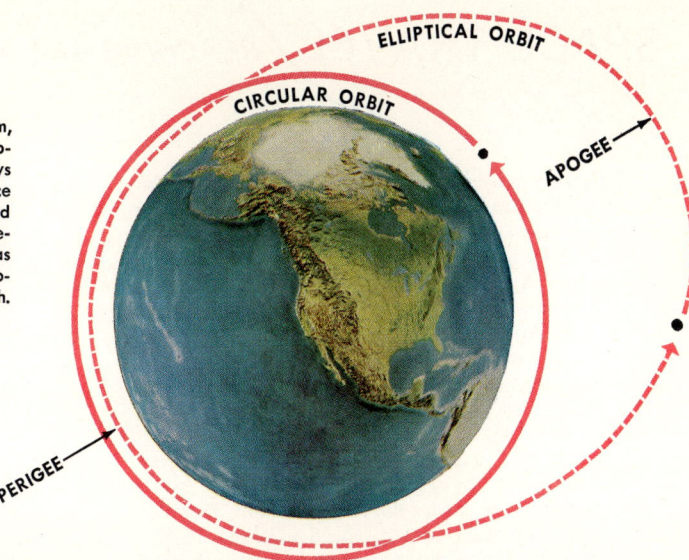

**An Inclined Orbit** forms an angle with the equator, *below, left*. In the diagrams, the red lines show the orbit, and the blue lines represent the spacecraft's path as mapped on the earth. Because the earth rotates, the spacecraft does not pass over the same points on earth during each orbit. As a result, the path of the spacecraft appears as crisscrossed lines on the earth, *right*.

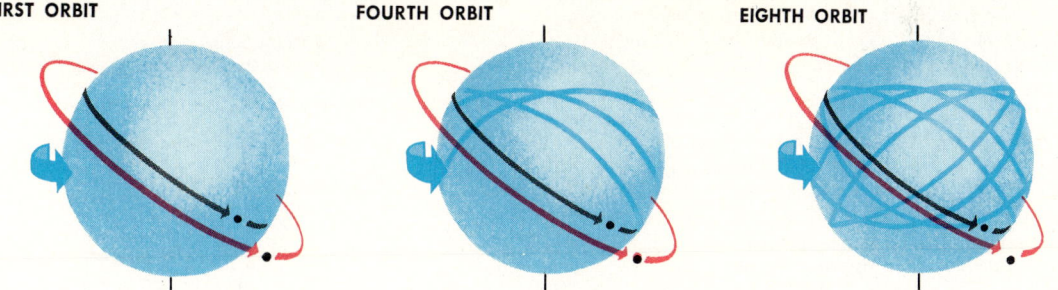

**A Polar Orbit** carries a spacecraft over the north and south poles, as shown in the diagram, *below, left*. As the earth rotates, the spacecraft passes over different points on earth during each orbit, as shown *below, right*. A polar orbit is especially useful in weather satellites such as Nimbus. By orbiting almost directly over the poles, Nimbus can photograph the entire earth once a day.

**A Synchronous Orbit** carries a spacecraft around the earth once every day. The diagram, *below*, shows the path of a Syncom communications satellite. As mapped on earth, the satellite's path is a figure eight, because the orbit is slightly inclined. If the spacecraft were launched directly in line with the equator, it would stay above one spot on earth without moving north or south.

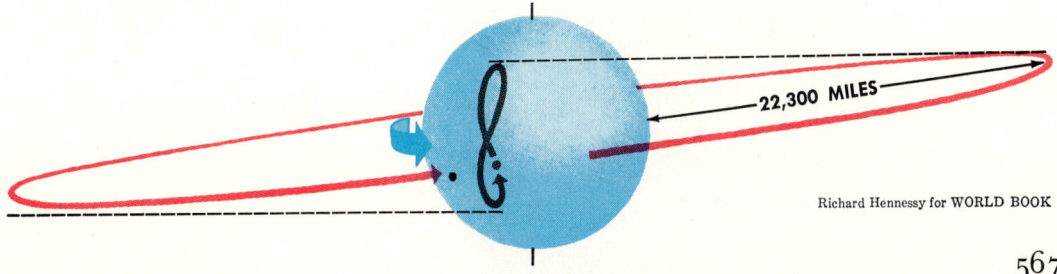

Richard Hennessy for WORLD BOOK

# SPACE TRAVEL / REACHING THE MOON

Much more power is required to send a spacecraft to the moon than to put it in orbit around the earth. To reach the moon, a spacecraft must reach a speed of about 24,300 miles per hour. To reach this speed, a moon-bound Apollo spacecraft is boosted into the sky by a giant Saturn V rocket.

The three Apollo astronauts, riding in the command module near the top of the vehicle, are forced back on their couches as five huge engines lift them from the earth. About $2\frac{1}{2}$ minutes after liftoff, the vehicle is traveling about 6,200 miles per hour and is about 41 miles high. The first stage then separates from the rest of the vehicle, and the second stage ignites.

The second stage carries the vehicle about 116 miles above the earth and boosts its speed to about 15,400 miles per hour. Then the second stage separates and the third stage ignites, sending the vehicle into a 118-mile-high, near-circular "parking" orbit around the earth. While the astronauts are in earth orbit, they check the spacecraft to make certain it was not damaged during liftoff. The third stage then ignites again, and the astronauts leave earth orbit and head for the moon.

**Aiming at the Moon.** The moon is a moving target. It travels around the earth at more than 2,000 miles per hour. During the spacecraft's three-day journey, the moon moves more than 165,000 miles. Therefore, the spacecraft must be aimed at a spot in space 165,000 miles ahead of the moon—and it must reach this spot at exactly the same time that the moon does.

North American Rockwell Corp.

**Apollo Spacecraft Lifts Off for the Moon**

**FROM EARTH TO MOON**

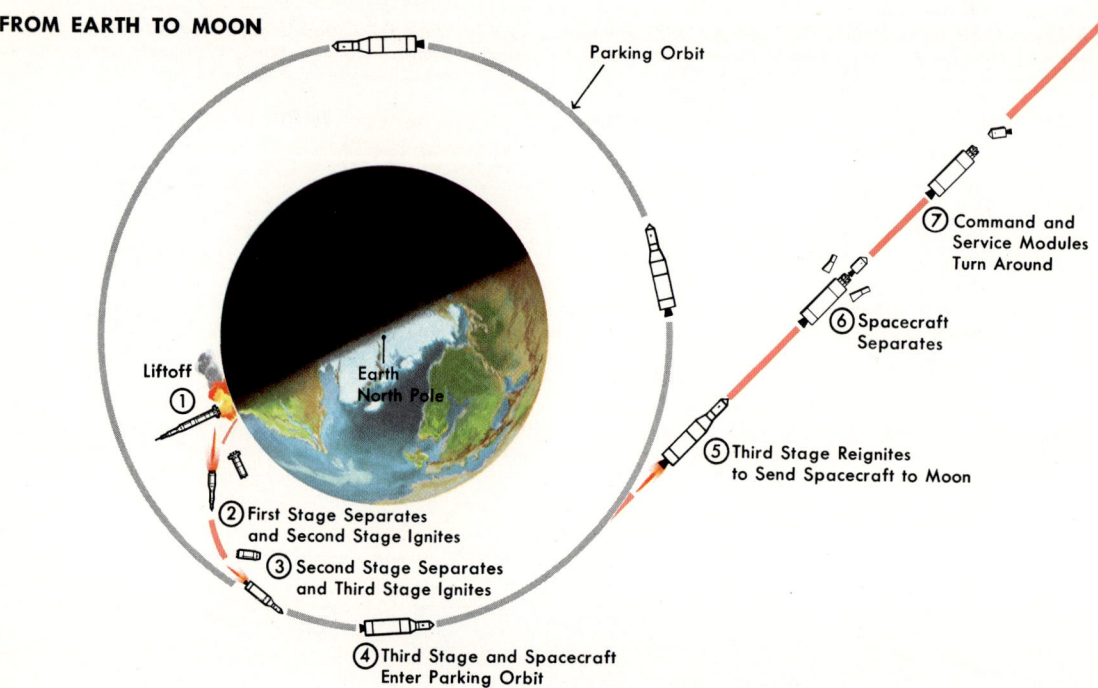

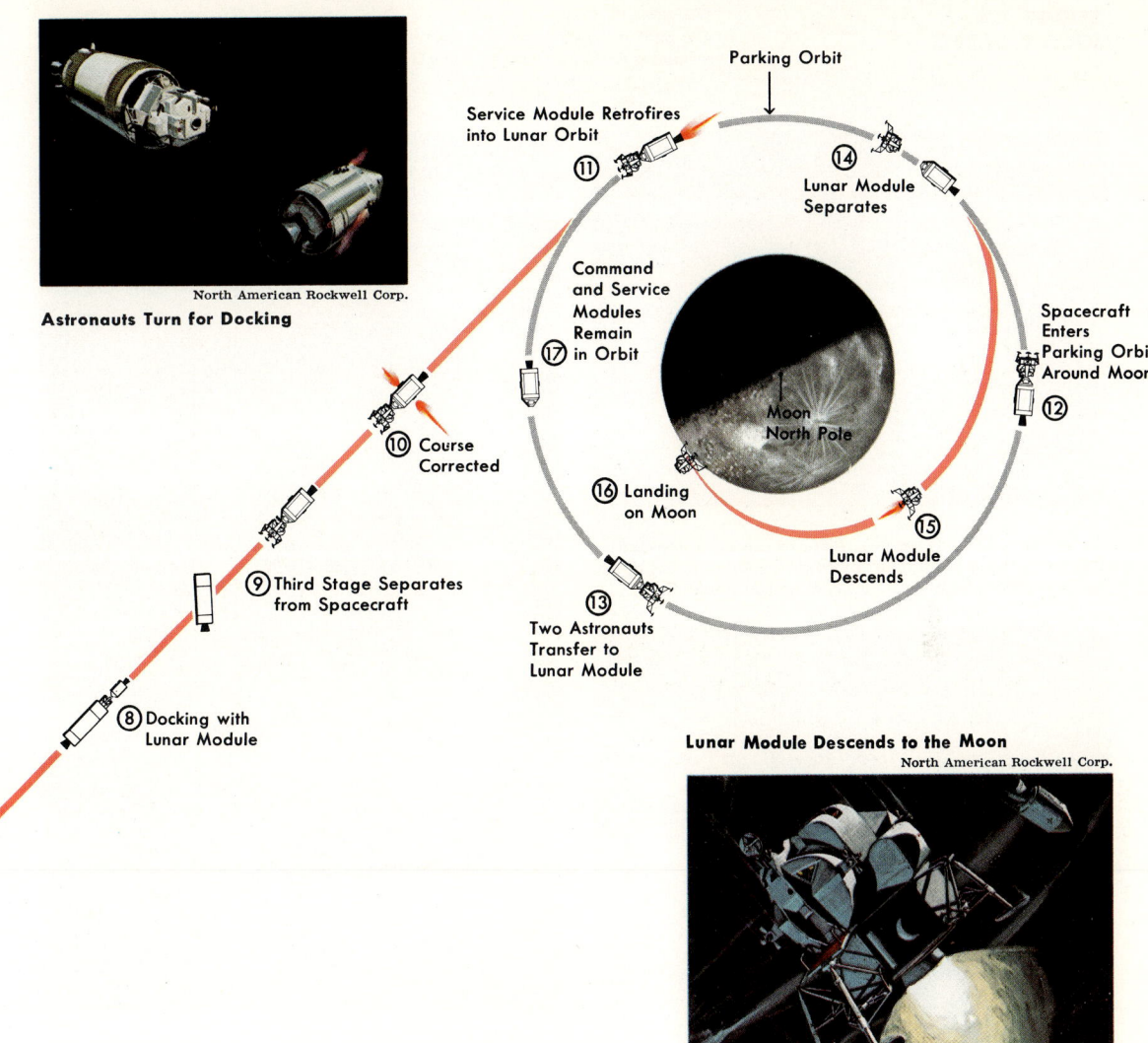

**Astronauts Turn for Docking**
North American Rockwell Corp.

**Lunar Module Descends to the Moon**
North American Rockwell Corp.

The third stage of the Apollo burns for about 5½ minutes, pushing the spacecraft toward the moon at about 24,300 miles per hour. After the third-stage burn is completed, the astronauts turn the command and service modules around. Then they dock with the lunar module (LM), which is atop the third stage. Later, the third stage is disconnected from the LM.

As the spacecraft speeds toward the moon, the navigator determines if the craft is on course. Using a *sextant* and a telescope, he measures the angle between a star and some landmark on the earth, or between a star and the moon's horizon. After measuring the angles to three stars, the navigator uses a computer to determine the spacecraft's position in space. If the craft is off course, the crew can make one or more *mid-course corrections*. Small rocket motors are fired to bring the spacecraft back on course.

As the spacecraft travels toward the moon, the earth's gravity slows it down continuously. When the spacecraft reaches a point about 215,000 miles from the earth, it has slowed to about 2,000 miles an hour. But at this point—only about 30,000 miles from the moon—the moon's gravity is stronger than that of the earth, and the spacecraft begins to pick up speed.

**Orbiting the Moon** follows the same principles as orbiting the earth. The spacecraft needs a certain speed to orbit at a certain altitude. The Apollo spacecraft has more speed than it needs to go into lunar orbit. Therefore, a rocket engine in the service module fires to slow the spacecraft and put it in orbit. Then two of the three astronauts leave the command module and enter the LM through a hatch.

**Landing on the Moon.** After the lunar module has been carefully checked by the astronauts, it is separated from the command module. The command module, manned by the third astronaut, stays in lunar orbit. The LM then fires its engine and begins its descent to the moon. Parachutes and wings cannot be used to lower the craft. These devices need air to work, and there is no air on the moon. The LM carries a rocket engine that

568a

# SEEKING THE MOON'S SECRETS

Scientific experiments on the moon were set up by Apollo astronauts. The astronauts also photographed the moon, collected samples of the lunar surface, and brought the samples back to the earth for study by scientists.

**Lunar Seismometer,** *above,* which measures earthquakelike vibrations of the moon, is set up by Edwin E. Aldrin, Jr. This device was so sensitive that it detected the astronauts' footsteps.

**Laser Reflector,** set up by Apollo 11 astronauts, reflects laser beam pulses back to the earth. Scientists use it to determine within inches the distance of the moon from the earth.

**Solar Wind Experiment,** being put in place by Aldrin, captured 10 trillion atoms cast out by the sun in 1 hour and 17 minutes. The astronauts brought the apparatus back with them.

slows the descent as the craft nears the moon's surface.

Computers normally guide the LM, but the pilot can guide the craft if he wishes. The astronauts can hover above the landing site for about a minute while they make certain that they can land safely. Probes extending from the legs of the LM indicate when the craft is 5 feet above the surface. The men shut off the engine, and the craft lands on the moon.

The astronauts would be stranded on the moon if the LM has been damaged beyond repair while landing. The LM must lift them off the moon because the command module is not designed to land on the moon. If the LM cannot leave the lunar surface, the command module pilot must return to earth alone.

**Exploring the Moon.** After the Apollo lunar module lands on the moon, the two astronauts inside are still several hours away from walking on the surface. They must first check the LM to be sure it will get them back to the command module in lunar orbit.

Before leaving the LM, each lunar explorer puts on

additional garments for protection against the moon's airless environment. A backpack worn outside the LM contains all the systems needed to support life.

The first men to set foot on the moon were U.S. astronauts Neil A. Armstrong and Edwin E. Aldrin, Jr. Their Apollo 11 lunar module, called *Eagle,* touched down on the rocky plain called the Sea of Tranquility on July 20, 1969. First Armstrong and then Aldrin stepped on the moon's surface. The next two astronauts to land on the moon were Charles (Pete) Conrad, Jr. and Alan L. Bean. They landed their Apollo 12 module, *Intrepid,* on the waterless Ocean of Storms on Nov. 19, 1969.

Aldrin described the view of the moon from the surface as "magnificent desolation," and the color of the moon as light gray. The astronauts quickly became adjusted to the gravity of the moon, which is only one-sixth as strong as the earth's. Another difference to which they had to adjust was the lack of gray shadows. The moon has no atmosphere to *diffuse* (scatter) light rays, and so all shadows are completely black. The hu-

**Surveyor 3 Spacecraft Parts** were removed and returned to earth by Apollo 12 astronauts Alan L. Bean and Charles Conrad, Jr. Scientists examined the parts to learn how conditions on the moon had affected them. The Apollo 12 module landed about 600 feet from *Surveyor 3*.

man eye can see nothing that is standing in complete shadow on the moon. The lack of an atmosphere also means that sound waves will not travel across the moon's surface. If the astronauts had not had radios, they could not have talked to each other.

An important scientific task of the Apollo astronauts was the recovery of samples from the lunar surface. Scientists hoped to learn from the lunar samples about the moon's composition, how old it is, and how it formed. Apollo 11 astronauts collected about 48 pounds of surface material on their one journey from *Eagle*. Apollo 12 astronauts made two trips outside *Intrepid*. On their second trip, Conrad and Bean walked to the unmanned *Surveyor 3* lunar probe that had landed in April, 1967. The *Surveyor 3* was about 600 feet from the *Intrepid*. Conrad and Bean removed parts of it so scientists could study how the harsh lunar environment had affected a man-made object.

Armstrong and Aldrin set up a screen of aluminum foil a foot wide and a yard long to capture particles of the solar wind shot out from the sun. They also erected a *seismometer*, an instrument to detect earthquakelike disturbances in the moon. They left this device on the moon, and it reported many vibrations. At least one set of vibrations was thought to have been caused by a moonquake, indicating that the moon may have a molten core and volcanoes. Apollo 12 astronauts Conrad and Bean also set up a seismometer and other experiments. Later, after they were safely aboard their command module, *Yankee Clipper*, they crashed *Intrepid* into the moon to create vibrations for the seismometer to detect. The seismometer reported that the crash produced long-lasting vibrations which surprised scientists on the earth.

Another device left on the moon by Apollo 11 astronauts was a reflector for a *laser beam* (an extremely intense beam of light). With this reflector, scientists can measure the distance to the moon to within a few inches by measuring the time needed for pulses of light from the earth to be reflected back to the earth. See LASER.

568c

# FROM MOON TO EARTH

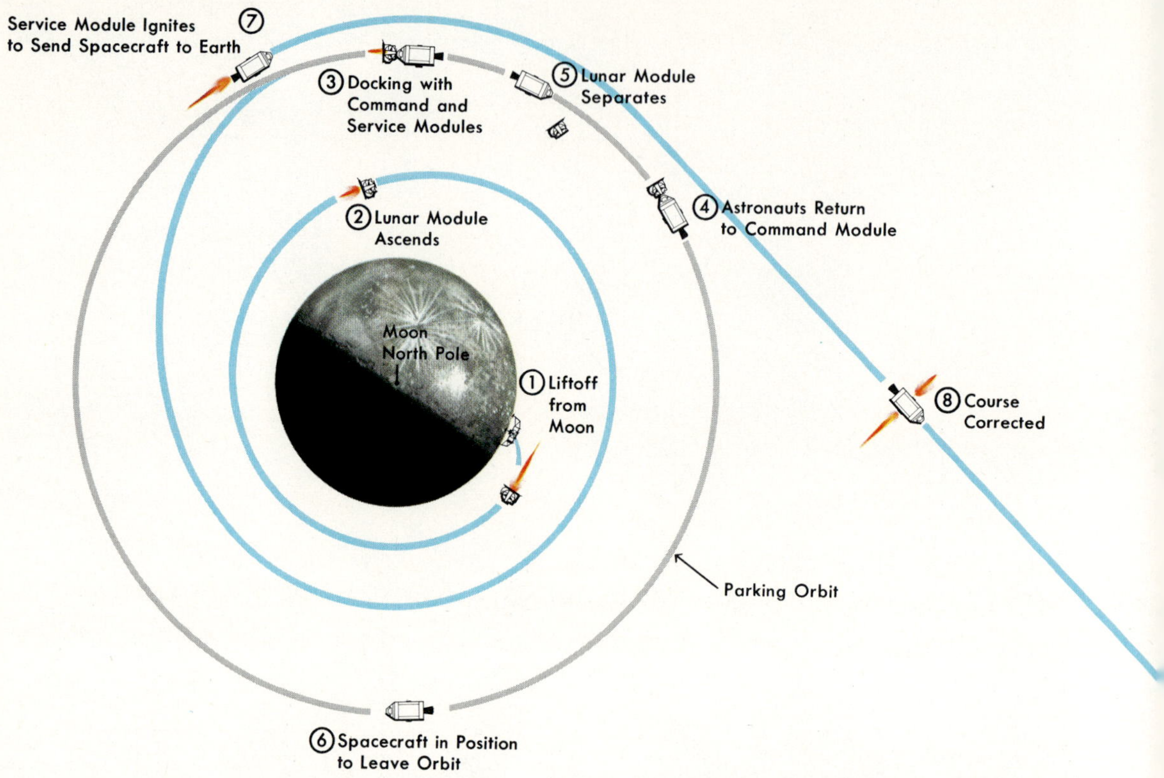

⑦ Service Module Ignites to Send Spacecraft to Earth
③ Docking with Command and Service Modules
⑤ Lunar Module Separates
② Lunar Module Ascends
Moon North Pole
① Liftoff from Moon
④ Astronauts Return to Command Module
⑧ Course Corrected
Parking Orbit
⑥ Spacecraft in Position to Leave Orbit

North American Rockwell Corp.
**Liftoff from the Moon**

North American Rockwell Corp.

**Returning to Earth**

568d

When the astronauts lift off from the moon, they leave behind their backpacks, walking boots, and other equipment that is no longer necessary. Leaving these items lightens the load of the LM ascent stage for its trip back up to the command module.

**Returning to Earth.** The ascent stage of the lunar module lifts off the moon using the descent stage as a launching platform. The LM first goes into an orbit that is lower than that of the command module. When the distance and angle between the two spacecraft are just right, the LM engine is fired and the craft soars into the same orbit as the command module, about 69 miles above the moon.

The command module pilot maneuvers to dock with the LM. After docking, the pressures in the two craft are equalized, and the hatch between them is opened. The moon samples and the equipment to be returned to the earth are transferred to the command module. All equipment that is not to be returned to the earth is placed in the lunar module. The LM crew then moves into the command module, and the LM is disconnected.

The engine of the service module is fired to push the astronauts out of lunar orbit and send them toward the earth. The trip home resembles the trip to the moon. Mid-course corrections are made if necessary. Shortly before the command module enters the earth's atmosphere, the service module is disconnected.

The command module turns around before it enters the atmosphere. The pressure of the atmosphere against the blunt end helps slow the craft.

The command module must first begin to meet the pressure of the earth's atmosphere at a certain angle to make a safe landing. If the angle is too shallow, the craft will bounce off the atmosphere and go back into space. If the angle is too steep, the friction between the atmosphere and the spacecraft will generate too much heat, and the craft will burn up. During a normal re-entry, the special plastic heat shield on the command module may reach a temperature of 4200° F. The temperature inside the cabin remains at about 80° F.

At about 23,300 feet, special parachutes called *drogues* are released. The drogues slow the spacecraft and steady it if it is wobbling. At about 10,500 feet, the main parachutes are released. The main parachutes let the craft hit the water at about 22 miles per hour.

After Apollo 11 returned to the earth, the lunar material, the astronauts, and the equipment that was exposed to the lunar atmosphere were placed in isolation. The purpose of the isolation period, which lasted about 17 days for the astronauts, was to determine whether any germs or other harmful material had been brought back from the moon. No germs or harmful material were found.

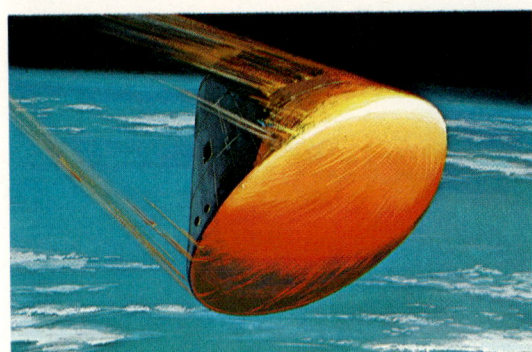

North American Rockwell Corp.

**Heading for Splashdown**

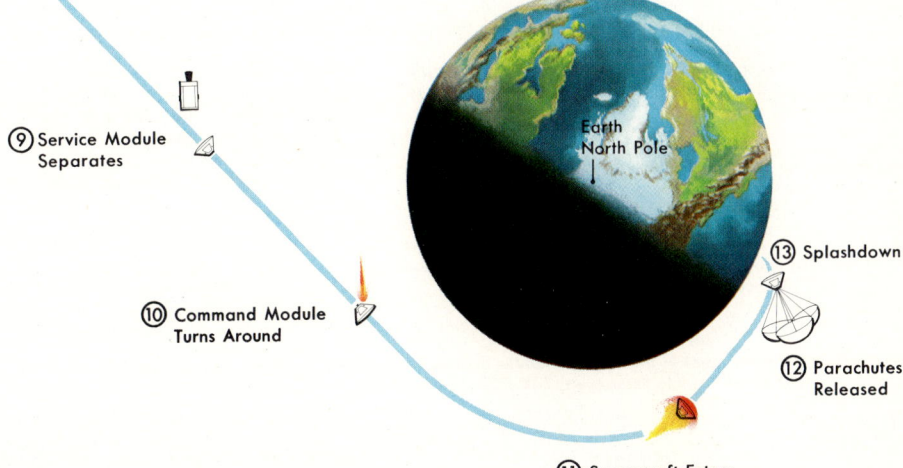

⑨ Service Module Separates

⑩ Command Module Turns Around

⑪ Spacecraft Enters Earth's Atmosphere

⑫ Parachutes Released

⑬ Splashdown

Earth North Pole

568e

**After Splashdown,** the Apollo 11 astronauts were scrubbed with disinfectant to kill possible moon germs. The air bags righted the spacecraft in the water, and the collar helped keep it afloat.

---

## THE LOG OF APOLLO 11

### July 16, 1969

9:32 A.M.† Apollo 11 lifts off launch pad 39A at Cape Kennedy.
9:35 A.M. The first stage of the Saturn V launch vehicle separates, and the second stage ignites.
9:41 A.M. The second stage separates and the third stage ignites.
12:16 P.M. The third stage engine reignites to send the spacecraft to the moon.
12:49 P.M. The command module, called *Columbia,* and the service module separate from the lunar module, called *Eagle,* and the third stage.
12:57 P.M. *Columbia* and the service module dock with *Eagle.*
1:49 P.M. The third stage separates from the spacecraft.

### July 17, 1969

12:16 P.M. The astronauts make a minor correction in their course.

### July 18, 1969

11:11 P.M. Apollo 11 enters the moon's sphere of gravitational influence, 214,102 miles from the earth.

### July 19, 1969

1:21 P.M. The retrorocket in the service module fires to slow the spacecraft into lunar orbit, 244,930 miles from the earth.

### July 20, 1969

1:45 P.M. *Eagle,* with Armstrong and Aldrin aboard, separates from *Columbia.*
4:17 P.M. *Eagle* lands on the moon on the rocky plain called the Sea of Tranquility.
10:39 P.M. The hatch of *Eagle* is opened.
10:56 P.M. Armstrong sets foot on the moon.
11:14 P.M. Aldrin joins Armstrong on the moon. The two astronauts collect lunar samples and set up scientific experiments.

### July 21, 1969

12:57 A.M. Aldrin climbs back into *Eagle* and helps Armstrong load the lunar samples.
1:09 A.M. Armstrong re-enters *Eagle.*
1:11 A.M. *Eagle's* hatch is closed.
1:54 P.M. *Eagle* lifts off the moon.
5:35 P.M. *Eagle* docks with *Columbia,* and Armstrong and Aldrin rejoin Collins.
7:41 P.M. *Eagle* is separated from *Columbia.*

### July 22, 1969

12:55 A.M. The rocket engine in the service module fires to send the spacecraft back to the earth, 235,000 miles away.
4:01 P.M. The astronauts make a minor course correction.

### July 24, 1969

12:20 P.M. The service module separates from *Columbia* shortly before re-entering the earth's atmosphere.
12:35 P.M. *Columbia* re-enters the earth's atmosphere.
12:44 P.M. Parachutes are released to slow the spacecraft.
12:50 P.M. Splashdown! The journey of Apollo 11 ends.

†All times are Eastern Daylight-Saving Time.

# MANNED SPACE FLIGHTS

| Date Launched | Astronaut or Cosmonaut | Spacecraft | Country | Number of Revolutions | Time of Flight |
|---|---|---|---|---|---|
| **1961** Apr. 12 | Y. Gagarin | Vostok I | Russia | 1 | 1 hr. 48 min. |
| May 5 | A. Shepard, Jr. | Freedom 7 | U.S.A. | Suborbital | 15 min. |
| July 21 | V. Grissom | Liberty Bell 7 | U.S.A. | Suborbital | 16 min. |
| Aug. 6 | G. Titov | Vostok II | Russia | 16 | 25 hr. 18 min. |
| **1962** Feb. 20 | J. Glenn, Jr. | Friendship 7 | U.S.A. | 3 | 4 hr. 55 min. |
| May 24 | S. Carpenter | Aurora 7 | U.S.A. | 3 | 4 hr. 56 min. |
| Aug. 11 | A. Nikolayev | Vostok III | Russia | 60 | 94 hr. 22 min. |
| Aug. 12 | P. Popovich | Vostok IV | Russia | 45 | 70 hr. 57 min. |
| Oct. 3 | W. Schirra, Jr. | Sigma 7 | U.S.A. | 6 | 9 hr. 13 min. |
| **1963** May 15 | G. Cooper, Jr. | Faith 7 | U.S.A. | 22 | 34 hr. 20 min. |
| June 14 | V. Bykovsky | Vostok V | Russia | 76 | 119 hr. 6 min. |
| June 16 | V. Tereshkova | Vostok VI | Russia | 45 | 70 hr. 50 min. |
| **1964** Oct. 12 | V. Komarov, K. Feoktistov, B. Yegorov | Voskhod I | Russia | 15 | 24 hr. 17 min. |
| **1965** Mar. 18 | P. Belyayev, A. Leonov | Voskhod II | Russia | 16 | 26 hr. 2 min. |
| Mar. 23 | V. Grissom, J. Young | Molly Brown | U.S.A. | 3 | 4 hr. 53 min. |
| June 3 | J. McDivitt, E. White II | Gemini 4 | U.S.A. | 62 | 97 hr. 56 min. |
| Aug. 21 | G. Cooper, Jr., C. Conrad, Jr. | Gemini 5 | U.S.A. | 120 | 190 hr. 56 min. |
| Dec. 4 | F. Borman, J. Lovell, Jr. | Gemini 7 | U.S.A. | 206 | 330 hr. 35 min. |
| Dec. 15 | W. Schirra, Jr., T. Stafford | Gemini 6 | U.S.A. | 16 | 25 hr. 51 min. |
| **1966** Mar. 16 | N. Armstrong, D. Scott | Gemini 8 | U.S.A. | 7 | 10 hr. 41 min. |
| June 3 | T. Stafford, E. Cernan | Gemini 9 | U.S.A. | 44 | 72 hr. 21 min. |
| July 18 | J. Young, M. Collins | Gemini 10 | U.S.A. | 43 | 70 hr. 47 min. |
| Sept. 12 | C. Conrad, Jr., R. Gordon, Jr. | Gemini 11 | U.S.A. | 44 | 71 hr. 17 min. |
| Nov. 11 | J. Lovell, Jr., E. Aldrin, Jr. | Gemini 12 | U.S.A. | 59 | 94 hr. 35 min. |
| **1967** Apr. 23 | V. Komarov | Soyuz I | Russia | 17 | 26 hr. 40 min. |
| **1968** Oct. 11 | W. Schirra, Jr., D. Eisele, W. Cunningham | Apollo 7 | U.S.A. | 163 | 260 hr. 9 min. |
| Oct. 26 | G. Beregovoi | Soyuz III | Russia | 60 | 94 hr. 51 min. |
| Dec. 21 | F. Borman, W. Anders, J. Lovell, Jr. | Apollo 8 | U.S.A. | Lunar flight | 147 hr. 0 min. |
| **1969** Jan. 14 | V. Shatalov | Soyuz IV | Russia | 45 | 71 hr. 14 min. |
| Jan. 15 | B. Volynov, Y. Khrunov,* A. Yeliseyev* | Soyuz V | Russia | 46 | 72 hr. 46 min. |
| Mar. 3 | J. McDivitt, R. Schweickart, D. Scott | Apollo 9 | U.S.A. | 151 | 241 hr. 1 min. |
| May 18 | T. Stafford, E. Cernan, J. Young | Apollo 10 | U.S.A. | Lunar flight | 192 hr. 3 min. |
| July 16 | N. Armstrong, E. Aldrin, Jr., M. Collins | Apollo 11 | U.S.A. | Lunar landing | 195 hr. 18 min. |
| Oct. 11 | V. Kubasov, G. Shonin | Soyuz VI | Russia | 75 | 118 hr. 42 min. |
| Oct. 12 | A. Filipchenko, V. Gorbatko, V. Volkov | Soyuz VII | Russia | 75 | 118 hr. 41 min. |
| Oct. 13 | V. Shatalov, A. Yeliseyev | Soyuz VIII | Russia | 75 | 118 hr. 50 min. |
| Nov. 14 | C. Conrad, Jr., A. Bean, R. Gordon, Jr. | Apollo 12 | U.S.A. | Lunar landing | 244 hr. 36 min. |

*Transferred to Soyuz IV in orbit

NASA

**Apollo 11 Astronauts** Neil A. Armstrong, Michael Collins, and Edwin E. Aldrin, Jr., *left to right,* smile from quarantine aboard the U.S.S. *Hornet* after their moon landing mission.

Courtesy Pratt & Whitney Aircraft

# SPACE TRAVEL / SPACE STATIONS

A space station is a special kind of earth satellite. It might look like a wheel, a cylinder, or the vanes of a windmill. Whatever its shape, a space station would carry tons of equipment. It would have living quarters for many people, and enough air, food, and water to last them for weeks or months. The station might be a laboratory for scientists and engineers. Or it might be a stopping-off place where space travelers could transfer from a "local" rocket from earth and board an "express" to Jupiter.

Engineers are still studying the problems of building and launching space stations. One idea is to build a station inside the third stage of a rocket, such as the *Saturn V*. The first two stages would place the third stage in orbit. Another method would launch several spacecraft separately and *dock* (connect them together) in orbit to make a station. Still other plans call for the separate launching of many parts of a station. Astronauts would then assemble the parts in space.

**Space Station Laboratories** would be used to study the stars, the sun, the solar wind, and the earth's upper atmosphere and magnetic field. Telescopes in the station would reveal much more about the universe than telescopes on earth. There would be no atmosphere to dim an astronomer's view of the stars and galaxies.

Physicists would perform experiments to check the laws of nature and to test scientific theories. For example, they could compare the time kept by atomic clocks in the station to clocks on earth. This experiment would test Einstein's theory of relativity.

Biologists could use the space laboratory to learn more about the growth of plants and animals. On earth, all living things are affected by gravity, by the regular changes of day and night, and even by the attraction of the moon. Such forces may produce *biological rhythms* in plants and animals. But many of these forces would not affect living things in a space station. As a result, plants and animals might develop differently.

# An Orbiting Scientific Laboratory

A space laboratory, such as the one shown, *left,* would be more useful than a laboratory on earth for solving the problems of space flight and for studying the universe. Scientists would rocket from earth to the space station in small capsules. In the laboratory, they would test fuels and materials, perform biological experiments, and make astronomical observations. The diagram, *right,* shows the station's main sections.

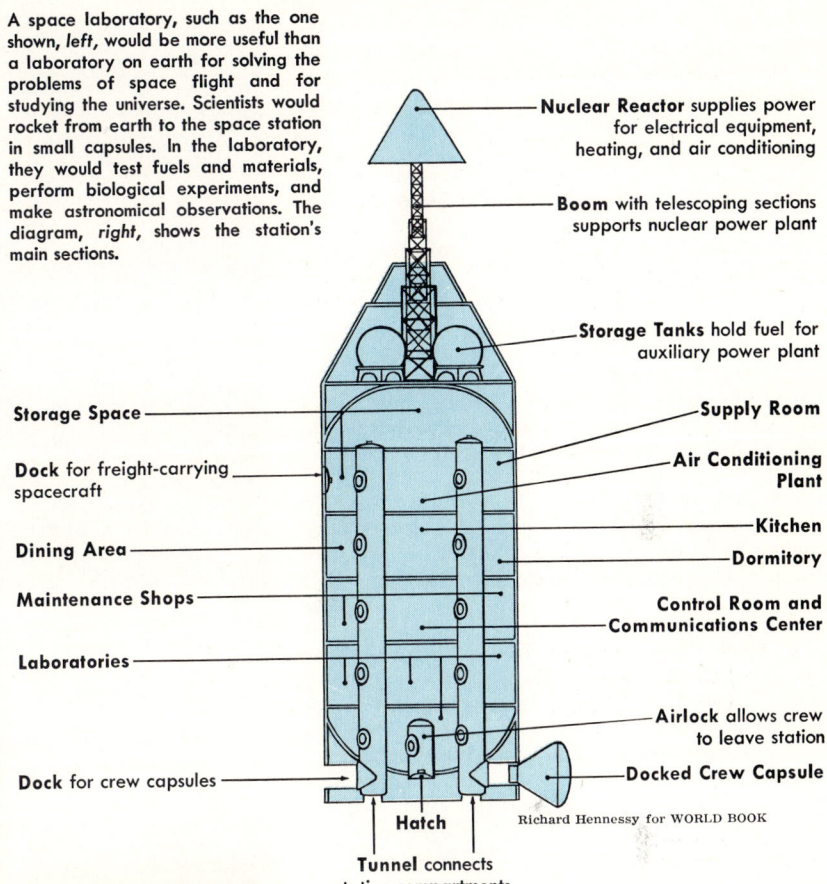

**Nuclear Reactor** supplies power for electrical equipment, heating, and air conditioning

**Boom** with telescoping sections supports nuclear power plant

**Storage Tanks** hold fuel for auxiliary power plant

**Storage Space**

**Dock** for freight-carrying spacecraft

**Dining Area**

**Maintenance Shops**

**Laboratories**

**Dock** for crew capsules

**Hatch**

**Tunnel** connects station compartments

**Supply Room**

**Air Conditioning Plant**

**Kitchen**

**Dormitory**

**Control Room and Communications Center**

**Airlock** allows crew to leave station

**Docked Crew Capsule**

Richard Hennessy for WORLD BOOK

NASA

**Two Kinds of Space Stations.** The *manned orbiting research laboratory* (MORL), above, may consist of a Saturn upper stage with ports for Gemini spacecraft. The rotating station, *below,* would create centrifugal force to give the crew the feeling of weight.
NASA

**Stopping-Off Places for Spaceships.** The launch into orbit is the most difficult part of a space voyage. This part of the journey uses up most of the spacecraft's fuel. After reaching orbit, a spaceship could stop at a space station and pick up more fuel. It could then continue its journey deeper into space. It would be a difficult and costly job to keep a space station stocked with fuel. However, it might make possible some trips that otherwise could not be made. For example, a direct flight to Jupiter needs an extremely powerful launch vehicle that can lift all the fuel needed for the entire trip. But a much less powerful vehicle can be used if it is refueled at a space station.

**Military Space Stations** would serve as orbiting observation posts. They could relay messages and act as communications centers. Operators in the station could keep track of ships and planes, and also of other spacecraft. The space station would be an ideal place to train astronauts and other specialists.

569

# SPACE TRAVEL / REACHING THE PLANETS AND THE STARS

**Escaping Earth's Gravity.** The moon lies within earth's gravity. But at the moon's distance, the force of gravity is very weak. A spacecraft launched at 25,000 miles an hour—just 700 miles an hour greater than that necessary to reach the moon—can escape the influence of earth's gravity. This speed of 25,000 miles an hour (about 7 miles a second) is called *escape velocity*. It sends the spacecraft into interplanetary space. The craft then comes under the influence of the sun's gravity and goes into an orbit around the sun close to earth's orbit.

The earth itself circles the sun with a speed of 18.5 miles a second. A spacecraft launched from earth also travels this fast in relation to the sun. The craft's escape velocity is used up in getting away from earth. It does not affect the speed of the spacecraft around the sun. Escape velocity can send the spacecraft into orbit around the sun. But it cannot send the craft to a planet.

**Traveling to the Planets.** To reach a planet, a spacecraft must be launched from earth at a velocity greater than escape velocity. This extra velocity changes the speed of the spacecraft around the sun. Given the proper velocity, the craft goes into a solar orbit that carries it to the target planet.

To reach Mars, a spacecraft must be launched at 7.4 miles a second—0.4 miles a second faster than escape velocity. Also, the craft must be launched in the same direction the earth moves around the sun. The extra 0.4 miles a second then adds to the 18.5 miles a second the craft has because of the earth's motion. The craft's final speed around the sun is 18.9 miles a second. At this speed, the spacecraft moves too fast to stay near the orbit of earth. It coasts outward from the sun until it crosses the orbit of Mars.

To reach Venus, a spacecraft must also be launched at 7.4 miles a second. But in this case the craft is launched in a direction opposite to the direction the earth moves around the sun. The extra 0.4 miles a second is therefore subtracted from the 18.5 miles a second, giving the craft a final speed of 18.1 miles a second. At this speed, the spacecraft moves too slowly to stay near the orbit of earth. It is pulled closer to the sun until it crosses the orbit of Venus.

A spacecraft launched at the minimum velocity necessary to reach a planet travels along a path called a *minimum energy flight trajectory*. This is the course that requires the least amount of rocket power to reach a particular planet. In practice, planetary spacecraft are usually launched with a velocity greater than the minimum. With the increased speed, they can reach the planet in a shorter time.

**Reaching the Stars.** Present rocket engines do not have enough power to send spacecraft to even the nearest star. Just to escape from the sun's gravity, a spacecraft must be launched from earth at 14.5 miles a second. To travel to a star in a reasonable time, the spacecraft must go at an unimaginable speed close to the speed of light. In the future, such speeds may be reached by advanced rockets using nuclear power.

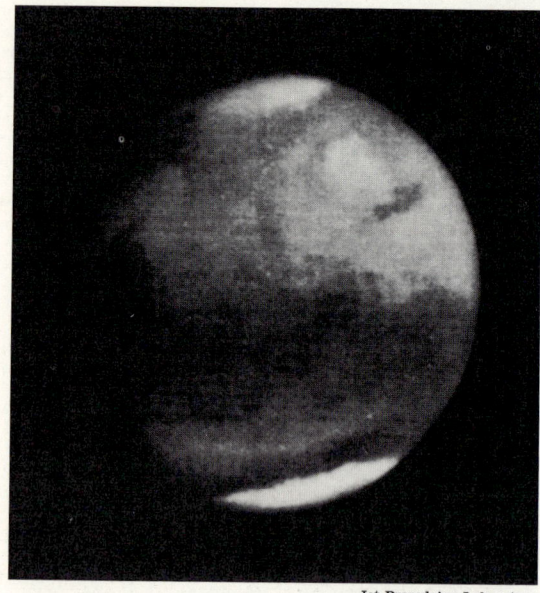

*Jet Propulsion Laboratory*

**The Unmanned Spacecraft *Mariner VII*** took this photograph of Mars from a distance of 535,650 miles on Aug. 3, 1969. The south polar cap of Mars is the white area at the bottom. *Mariner VII* later traveled within 2,190 miles of the planet.

**A Future Mars Spaceship,** *below,* consists of three sections. The *mission module* carries six men into orbit around Mars. The men use the *excursion module* to land on Mars and to return to the orbiting mission module. They ride back to earth in the mission module and use the *re-entry module* to descend through the atmosphere.

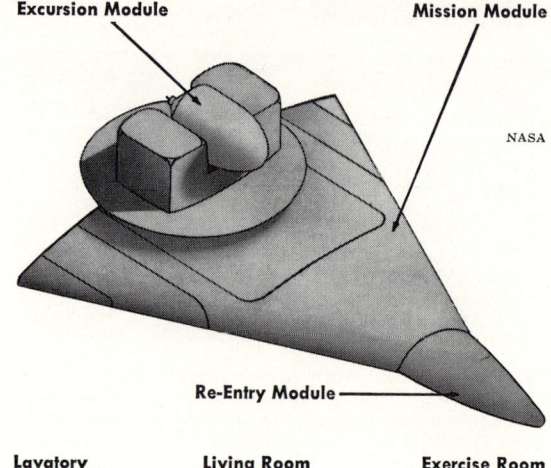

NASA

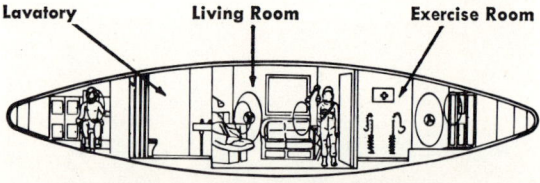

**CROSS SECTION OF MISSION MODULE**

570

# A ROCKET FLIGHT TO MARS

- Position of Earth at Landing
- Position of Mars at Landing
- MERCURY
- SUN
- VENUS
- Launching Direction
- Position of Earth at Launch
- Position of Mars at Launch
- Flight Path

A spacecraft destined for Mars must be launched in the direction the earth moves around the sun. The spacecraft is given a velocity slightly greater than that required to escape gravity. It slowly coasts outward from the sun until it reaches the orbit of Mars.

# A ROCKET FLIGHT TO VENUS

- Position of Venus at Launch
- Position of Venus at Landing
- MARS
- MERCURY
- SUN
- Launching Direction
- Position of Earth at Launch
- Position of Earth at Landing
- Flight Path

A spacecraft destined for Venus must be launched in a direction opposite to that of the earth's motion around the sun. This makes the craft move too slowly to stay in the earth's orbit. The spacecraft coasts toward the sun until it reaches the orbit of Venus.

Richard Hennessy for WORLD BOOK

# A MANNED TRIP TO MARS AND BACK

**EARTH TO MARS FLIGHT PATH**

1. Spacecraft and Rocket Assembled in Orbit
2. Rocket Fires and Launches Spacecraft Toward Mars
3. Rocket Separates
4. Spacecraft Extends Boom and Spins to Produce Artificial Gravity
5. Spacecraft Stops Spinning and Retracts Boom
6. Mission Module Enters Mars Orbit and Excursion Module Separates
7. Excursion Module Descends
8. Landing on Mars
9. Excursion Module Ascends
10. Excursion Module Connects with Mission Module and Crew Transfers
11. Rockets Fire and Spacecraft Heads for Earth
12. Fuel Tanks Separate
13. Spacecraft Extends Boom and Spins
14. Spacecraft Stops Spinning and Retracts Boom
15. Mission Module Separates
16. Re-Entry Module Enters Atmosphere
17. Landing on Earth

**Spinning the Ship** produces a centrifugal force that acts like gravity to give the crew "weight."

**MARS TO EARTH FLIGHT PATH**

In the flight plan shown *above*, the huge Mars spaceship and its rocket are first launched separately into orbit around earth, and then assembled. With a powerful rocket, the round trip could be made in 400 days, including 40 days spent in exploring the planet.

# SPACE TRAVEL / PROBLEMS OF SPACE FLIGHT

**Dangers in Space.** The chief danger to men in space is that they depend entirely on the spacecraft that carries them. Men cannot live in space unless they have oxygen to breathe. They must also be protected from the extreme high and low temperatures and the vacuum of space. The machinery that gives them air, proper temperature, and control of the ship must operate perfectly under all conditions. In the future, pilots on long journeys may have to depend on closed *ecological systems*. These systems dispose of body wastes by using them to produce air, food, and water. They use chemical, electrical, and biological processes, including the growing of plants to produce oxygen and food.

*Meteors*, even those the size of pebbles, could tear holes in a steel spacecraft. But information gathered by United States *Explorer* and *Pegasus* satellites indicates that meteors are not a major danger in space travel. *Pegasus II* reported an average of about one *micrometeoroid* (particle of space dust) per day hitting a "wing" 96 feet long and 14 feet wide hard enough to penetrate it. A smaller spacecraft would be hit less often. Scientists have calculated that the chance of a meteor the size of a cigarette ash hitting the Apollo spacecraft on an eight-day moon flight is about 1 in 1,230.

*Radiation* in space includes atomic particles such as electrons and protons, and high energy gamma rays. This radiation comes from the sun and from outside our solar system. The earth's magnetic field creates a shield in space called the *magnetosphere* that protects the earth from solar radiation. In addition, areas of radiation

## ASTRONAUTS FACE DANGER FROM RADIATION IN SPACE

Dangerous solar radiation streams through space when violent flares occur on the sun. But the earth's magnetic field forms a shield called the *magnetosphere*. It protects the earth, and also contains radiation trapped in the Van Allen belts. Astronauts in the Gemini program orbited safely below the belts. Apollo astronauts have to pass through the belts and leave the magnetosphere to reach the moon. Their spacecraft must be designed to protect them from radiation even if a large solar flare occurs.

WORLD BOOK diagram

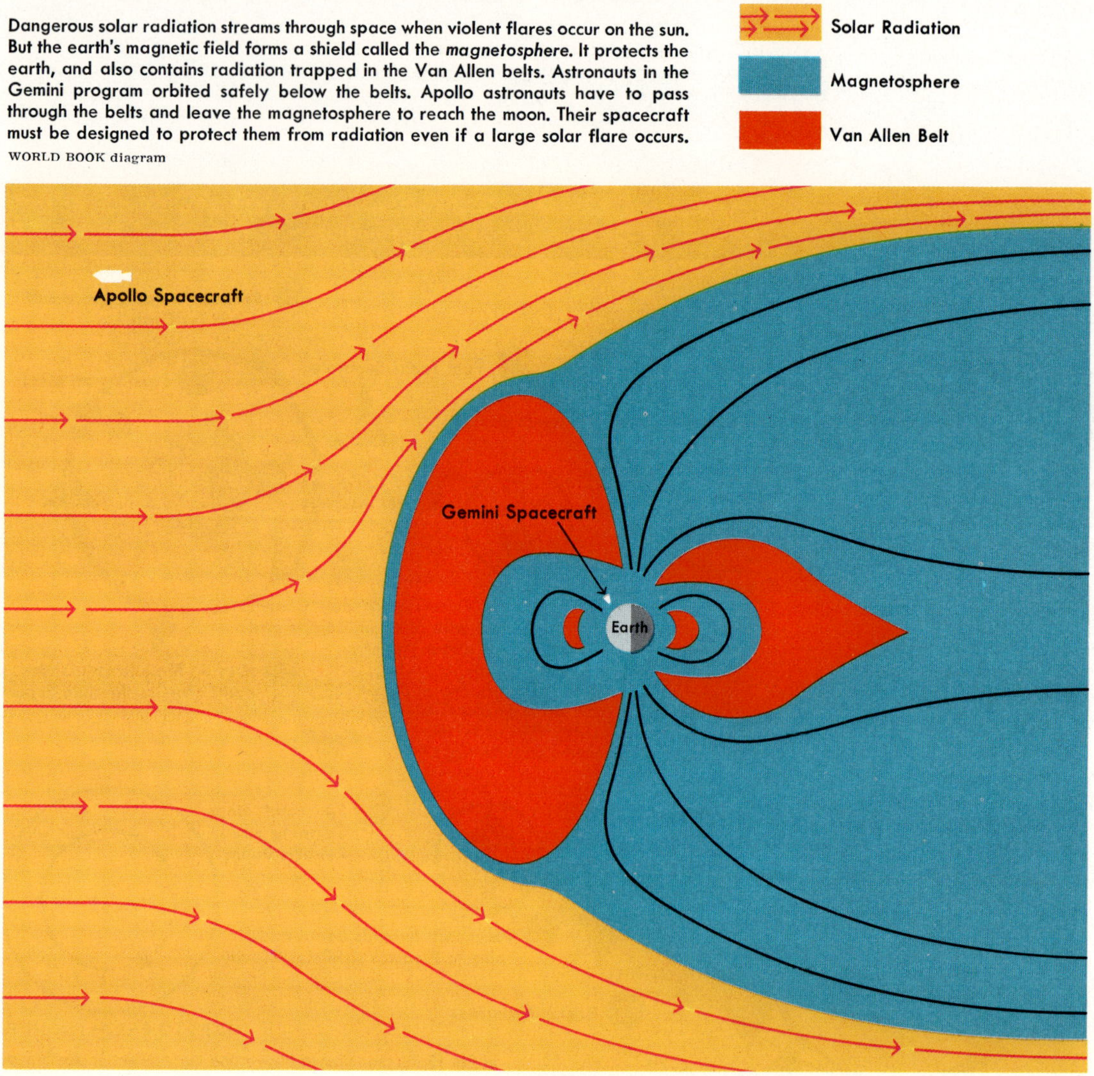

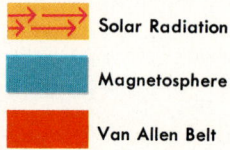
Solar Radiation
Magnetosphere
Van Allen Belt

572

within the magnetosphere called the Van Allen radiation belts circle the earth.

Astronauts in orbit up to several hundred miles from the earth are not exposed to much danger from radiation. But when they travel to the moon or other planets, they are exposed to the radiation in space. First, they travel through the Van Allen belts. After they leave the magnetosphere, they are exposed to solar radiation. Normally, this radiation is not too dangerous. But sometimes storms on the sun's surface send out dangerous amounts of radiation. Astronauts far from the earth could receive enough radiation to kill them unless their spacecraft protects them. The metal walls and heat shield provide protection. For example, Apollo astronauts receive about as much radiation in the Van Allen belts as they would from having their teeth X-rayed by a dentist. Scientists are trying to find ways to predict dangerous solar storms. Flights could then be launched when the danger of a storm was low.

**Tracking a Spacecraft.** The United States has a group of stations around the world to track both manned and unmanned spacecraft. Specially equipped ships track spacecraft when they are out of range of land stations. These stations receive radio signals from the spacecraft. The signals may carry astronauts' voices, information about the spacecraft's operation, or television pictures from space. The controllers of manned flights use radio transmitters at the tracking stations to talk to the astronauts. The stations also send tracking information about the spacecraft to a computer in the Goddard Space Flight Center in Greenbelt, Md. The computer calculates the position and orbit of the spacecraft.

Different tracking networks are needed to follow various kinds of space flights. For example, the orbital space flight network tracks manned flights that orbit the earth. When spacecraft leave earth orbit on a flight to the moon, the deep space network takes over the tracking and communications job. Another network of stations tracks unmanned satellites.

**Space Medicine** is the study of how space flight affects man's body and his ability to work. Space medicine grew from aviation medicine, and it uses many of the same testing methods. The astronaut himself is the main source of information. He carries special devices that measure his heart beat, breath rate, and the amount of radiation he has received. Medical specialists study him carefully before, during, and after a space flight to learn the body's strength and weakness in space. They can then suggest ways of giving astronauts better protection.

Doctors have learned that an astronaut can withstand the forces that act on his body during the launching and the return to earth. He can eat, sleep, and work while his body is weightless during flight. But the astronaut's legs and ankles may swell slightly if he stays in one position too long without exercise. Some astronauts have developed minor illness in flight, and doctors on earth have prescribed medicine for them. Each spacecraft carries a medical kit.

U.S. Air Force

**Tracking Ships,** *left,* maintain contact with spacecraft over the ocean beyond the range of land stations.

**Tracking Antennas,** *right,* point at the spacecraft and follow it across the sky as long as it flies above the horizon.

**Worldwide Networks** of U.S. tracking stations, *below,* send flight information to a central computer in Greenbelt, Md.

NASA

## MANNED SPACE FLIGHT TRACKING STATIONS

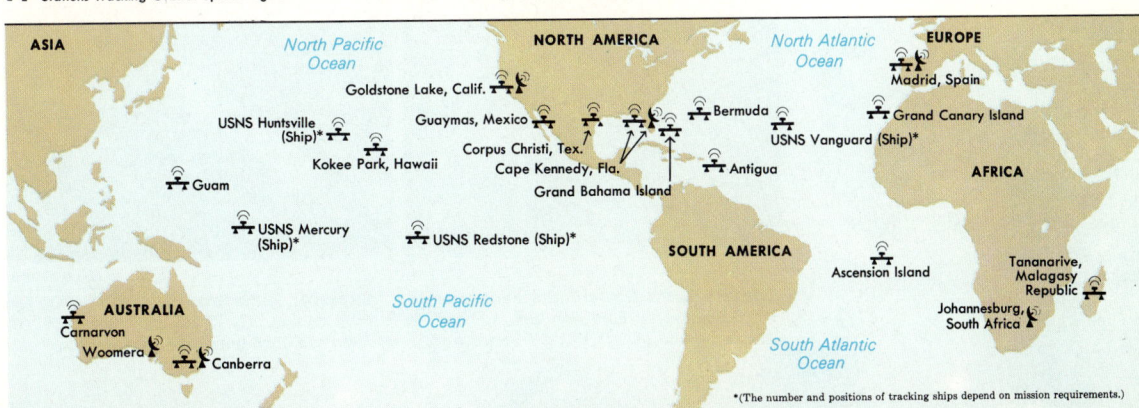

*(The number and positions of tracking ships depend on mission requirements.)

# SPACE TRAVEL / ARTIFICIAL SATELLITES

An artificial satellite is a man-made "moon." It circles the earth in space along a path called an *orbit*. An artificial satellite may be designed in almost any shape, such as a ball, a drum, or a box. It does not have to be streamlined, because there is little or no air where it travels in space. Most satellites measure only a few inches or a few feet across. But some, like the *Echo* balloons, may be 100 feet or more in diameter. A satellite's size and shape depend on its job.

Artificial satellites stay in space for varying lengths of time. The lifetime of each satellite depends on its size and its distance from earth. Whenever a satellite swings close to earth, it runs into many air particles that slow it down. To stay in orbit, a satellite must keep a certain speed. If it slows below this speed, it plunges into the atmosphere and burns up because of friction with the air. The gradual slowing of a satellite by air particles is called *decay*. Large satellites in low orbits decay rapidly. Small ones in high orbits decay slowly. For example, the six-inch *Vanguard I* satellite orbits more than 400 miles above the earth. It will orbit for hundreds of years.

Every satellite carries some kind of radio transmitter. One kind of transmitter is called a *radio beacon*. It sends signals that enable engineers to track the satellite. *Tracking* means finding the satellite's exact position in space. Another kind of transmitter sends to earth the scientific information gathered by the satellite's instruments. This sending of information is called *telemetry*. Telemetry transmitters usually serve also as beacons. Some satellites carry equipment to receive signals. Engineers beam signals to these satellites to turn the instruments on and off.

Most satellites stop working long before they fall to earth. Their batteries finally go dead, or their electronic equipment breaks down. They become "silent" and of no further use. Dozens of silent satellites are now circling the earth.

Artificial satellites may be classified according to the jobs they do as (1) weather satellites, (2) communications satellites, (3) navigation satellites, (4) scientific satellites, and (5) military satellites.

Fairchild Stratos Corp.

**Pegasus Meteoroid Detection Satellite,** *above,* has a "wing" 96 feet long. As meteoroids pierce the wing, instruments record the number of hits and send the information to the earth.

Sovfoto

**Sputnik I,** the first artificial earth satellite, was launched by Russia on Oct. 4, 1957. Its launch marked the start of the Space Age.

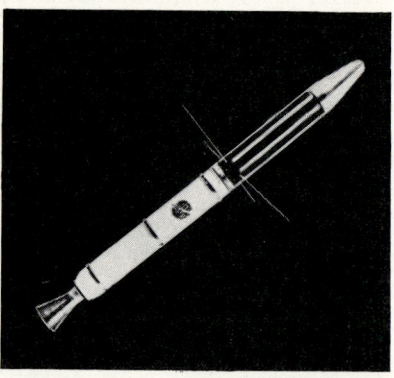

United Press Int.

**Explorer I,** the first U.S. satellite, went into orbit on Jan. 31, 1958, and discovered Van Allen radiation surrounding the earth.

572b

# IMPORTANT SATELLITES

## Communications Satellites

| Date Launched | Name | Accomplishments |
|---|---|---|
| 1958 Dec. 18 | Project Score | Broadcast first voice message from space. |
| 1960 Aug. 12 | Echo I | First passive communications satellite. |
| Oct. 4 | Courier | First active communications satellite. |
| 1961 Dec. 12 | Oscar I | Broadcast practice signals for amateur radio operators. |
| 1962 July 10 | Telstar I | First satellite to relay television programs between United States and Europe. |
| 1963 July 26 | Syncom II | First synchronous satellite. |
| 1964 Jan. 25 | Echo II | Used in joint Russian-U.S. experiments. |
| Aug. 19 | Syncom III | Relayed telecasts of Olympic Games from Tokyo to the United States. |
| 1965 Apr. 6 | Early Bird | First commercial communications satellite; linked Europe and United States. |
| Apr. 23 | Molniya I | First Russian communications satellite. |
| 1967 Jan. 11 | Intelsat 2B | First of a series of satellites in stationary orbit; used for television, data, or voice. |
| 1969 Feb. 9 | TacSatCom | Relayed communications between small ground stations for the military. |

## Weather Satellites

| Date Launched | Name | Accomplishments |
|---|---|---|
| 1959 Feb. 17 | Vanguard II | First satellite to send weather information back to earth. |
| 1960 Apr. 1 | Tiros I | Took the first detailed weather pictures. |
| Nov. 23 | Tiros II | Took weather pictures and measured infrared rays given off by earth. |
| 1961 July 12 | Tiros III | Discovered Hurricane Esther over Atlantic. |
| 1962 Sept. 18 | Tiros VI | Photographed weather over flight path of astronaut Walter Schirra. |
| 1963 Dec. 21 | Tiros VIII | Carried special camera system that transmitted cloud pictures automatically. |
| 1964 Aug. 28 | Nimbus I | Tracked Hurricane Dora off Florida coast. |
| 1966 Feb. 3 | ESSA I | First nonexperimental weather satellite; part of a worldwide weather system. |
| 1969 Apr. 14 | Nimbus III | Measured temperature, water vapor content, and ozone in earth's atmosphere. |

## Navigation Satellites

| Date Launched | Name | Accomplishments |
|---|---|---|
| 1960 Apr. 13 | Transit IB | First navigation satellite. |
| June 22 | Transit IIA | Carried Canadian-built instruments to measure radio interference in space. |
| 1961 Feb. 21 | Transit IIIB | First satellite to broadcast precise information on its own position. |
| June 29 | Transit IVA | First satellite to use nuclear power. |
| Nov. 15 | Transit IVB | Tested method of using earth's gravity to keep satellites in proper position. |

## Scientific Satellites

| Date Launched | Name | Accomplishments |
|---|---|---|
| 1958 Jan. 31 | Explorer I | First U.S. satellite; discovered Van Allen radiation in space. |
| Mar. 17 | Vanguard I | Discovered that earth is pear-shaped. |
| 1959 Aug. 7 | Explorer VI | Mapped Van Allen radiation. |
| 1961 Aug. 16 | Explorer XII | Explored space between 180 and 47,800 miles from earth. |
| 1962 Mar. 7 | OSO-I | First orbiting solar observatory. |
| Apr. 26 | Ariel (U.K. No. 1) | First international satellite; carried U.S. and British instruments. |
| Sept. 28 | Alouette | First Canadian satellite. |
| 1963 Apr. 2 | Explorer XVII | First satellite to study the atmosphere. |
| 1964 Sept. 4 | OGO-I | First orbiting geophysical observatory. |
| 1965 Feb. 16 | Pegasus I | Measured meteoroid density in space. |
| Apr. 3 | Snap 10A | Carried nuclear-powered rocket motor. |
| 1966 Feb. 22 | Cosmos 110 | Orbited 2 dogs for 22 days; cared for their biological needs automatically. |
| 1967 Sept. 7 | Biosatellite II | Carried living cells, plants, and animals into space and returned them to earth. |
| 1968 Dec. 7 | OAO-II | First successful orbiting astronomical observatory. |

Telstar — A.T.&T. Co.
Wide World

Tiros — NASA
Wide World

Transit — U.S. Navy
General Dynamics Corp.

Orbiting Solar Observatory — NASA
Mount Wilson and Palomar Observatories

# The Nimbus Weather Satellite

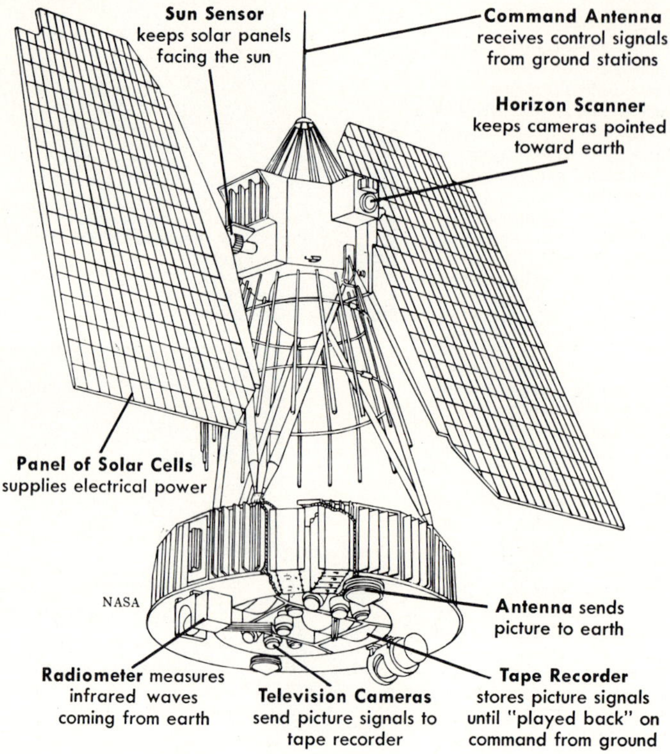

Nimbus watches the weather from a height of more than 500 miles. As shown *below*, the satellite orbits in a north-south direction and takes a band of pictures during each orbit. But as the earth rotates, each orbit carries Nimbus over a different strip of the earth's surface. In this way, the satellite photographs the entire earth once every day.

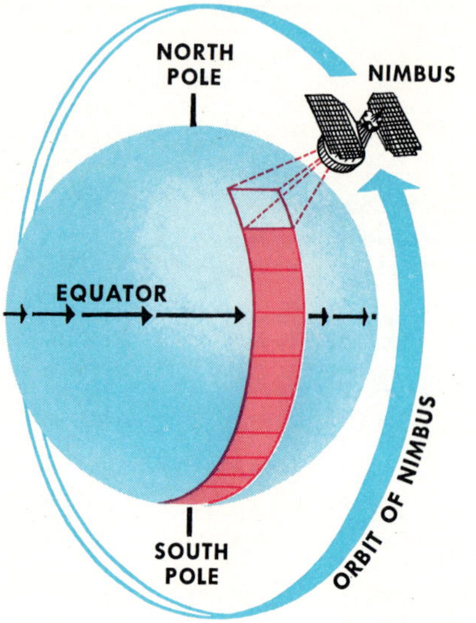

**Sun Sensor** keeps solar panels facing the sun

**Command Antenna** receives control signals from ground stations

**Horizon Scanner** keeps cameras pointed toward earth

**Panel of Solar Cells** supplies electrical power

**Radiometer** measures infrared waves coming from earth

**Television Cameras** send picture signals to tape recorder

**Antenna** sends picture to earth

**Tape Recorder** stores picture signals until "played back" on command from ground

NORTH POLE — NIMBUS — EQUATOR — SOUTH POLE — ORBIT OF NIMBUS

**Weather Satellites**, or *meteorological satellites*, help scientists forecast weather and study how weather is made. The first satellites to do this job were called *Tiros*. These satellites carry television cameras that take pictures of the earth's surface. The pictures show how clouds move through the atmosphere. They also show snow and ice on the earth's surface. By studying the pictures, weathermen can discover dangerous storms forming over the ocean. They can then warn people to prepare for the storms.

Weather satellites also carry instruments called *infrared detectors*. These instruments measure the heat

**Receiving Weather Pictures from Space** requires special equipment, *below*. As the weather satellite passes over a ground station, it beams picture signals and other information down to sensitive antennas, *left*. The signals are sorted out and strengthened by electronic equipment in a "readout room," *center*, and sent to a facsimile recorder that makes the cloud photograph, *right*.

572d

coming from the earth and the clouds. This information helps scientists learn how weather is related to the heating and cooling of the earth.

A Tiros satellite "sees" the earth only part of the time because it always points to a certain spot in space. An advanced weather satellite called *Nimbus* points its camera toward earth all the time.

**Communications Satellites** make it possible to send radio messages, telephone calls, and television programs between distant parts of earth. Communications satellites are called *passive* or *active*, depending on the way they work.

The *Echo* balloon is an example of a passive communications satellite. It acts as a mirror for radio waves. A sending station on earth beams waves to the satellite. The waves "bounce" off the satellite and return to earth. They then reach a receiving station perhaps thousands of miles from the sending station.

*Telstar*, *Relay*, *Syncom*, and *Early Bird* are active communications satellites. They carry radio receivers and transmitters. Active satellites receive signals from sending stations, *amplify* (strengthen) them, and send them back to earth. See COMMUNICATIONS SATELLITE.

**Navigation Satellites** help pilots and sailors find their exact positions in all kinds of weather. The United States Navy's navigation satellite is called *Transit*. Navigators can use it to find their position much as they would use a star. But instead of looking at the satellite, they listen to its radio signals.

**Scientific Satellites** include several types. *Explorer* and *Monitor* satellites carry a variety of instruments around earth. Some instruments measure radiation, such as that found in the Van Allen belt. Other instruments called *magnetometers* measure the earth's magnetic field. Satellites called *topside sounders* explore the upper parts of the atmosphere. These satellites beam radio waves down into the atmosphere and then measure the reflected signals.

*Orbiting observatories* are the largest and most complicated of all scientific satellites. The United States uses three types—geophysical, solar, and astronomical. Each type has a standard size and shape. Many kinds of instruments can be built into each one. The *orbiting geophysical observatory* (OGO) explores space near the earth. Scientists use it to study how the earth's magnetic field affects energy coming from the sun. The sun itself is studied with the *orbiting solar observatory* (OSO). This satellite measures radiations that cannot get through the atmosphere to be measured on earth. The *orbiting astronomical observatory* (OAO) looks deep into space at the stars and galaxies. It too measures rays that never reach the earth.

The United States builds and launches some scientific satellites in cooperation with other countries. The first international satellite, called *Ariel*, carried instruments built by British scientists. The topside sounder *Alouette* was designed and built by Canadian engineers, and then launched by the United States.

**Military Satellites.** The armed forces can use artificial satellites for communications and for navigation. But satellites also have been designed for strictly military purposes. *Reconnaissance satellites*, sometimes called "spy" satellites, can photograph enemy ground forces. *Warning satellites* can guard against surprise missile attacks. They can discover the launching of a missile by measuring the heat of the missile's rocket exhaust. Since 1963, the United States has kept *Vela* satellites in space to detect any "sneak testing" of nuclear bombs in space by other nations. Many military space activities are kept secret.

NASA

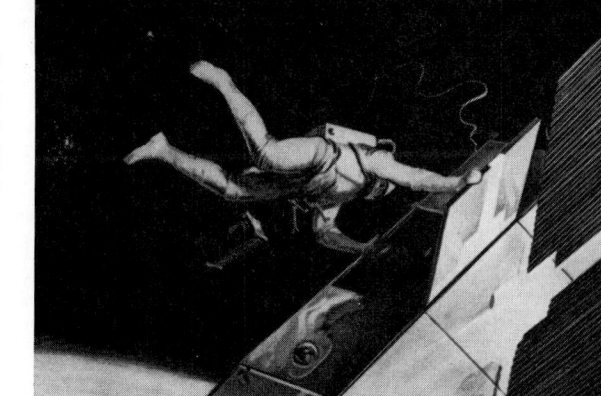

**Satellite Repairmen** of the future may fix damaged satellites as they orbit the earth in space. A repairman would ride into orbit in a small spaceship, "park" near the satellite, and then use a small rocket belt to travel to the satellite.

# SPACE TRAVEL / SPACE PROBES

Space probes are used to explore space at various distances from earth. Four main kinds of probes are: (1) sounding rockets, (2) lunar spacecraft, (3) interplanetary probes, and (4) planetary probes.

**Sounding Rockets** carry instruments into the upper atmosphere and into space near earth. They are the chief means of exploring regions too close for satellites to orbit. Their instruments may measure the temperature and pressure of the atmosphere as well as radiations from space.

**Lunar Spacecraft** explored the moon to prepare the way for man to land there. Engineers needed to know what the surface of the moon is like.

United States lunar spacecraft include *Ranger*, *Surveyor*, and *Lunar Orbiter*. In 1964 and 1965, three Rangers sent more than 17,000 close-up pictures of the moon back to the earth before crashing into the moon. The first Surveyor spacecraft landed softly on the moon in 1966 and sent back over 11,000 pictures of the lunar soil and landscape. The first Lunar Orbiter orbited the moon in 1966 and photographed landing sites for astronauts. Scientists learned from the Lunar Orbiters that the moon's gravitational field is irregular.

Russian lunar spacecraft include *Luna* and *Zond*. The moon's hidden side was photographed by *Luna 3* in 1959 and by *Zond 3* in 1965. In 1966, *Luna 9* landed on the moon and sent back pictures of the surface. *Zond 5* orbited the moon and returned to earth in 1968.

**Interplanetary Probes** go on one-way journeys into interplanetary space. These probes do not reach a particular body in space. They travel among the planets in orbit around the sun. Interplanetary probes measure the changes in solar radiations over millions of miles of space. Scientists use the probes also to

WORLD BOOK Illustration
*Mariner IV Flew Past Mars In 1965.*

## IMPORTANT SPACE PROBES

| Date Launched | Name | Country | Accomplishments |
|---|---|---|---|
| 1959 Jan. 2 | Luna 1 | Russia | Lunar probe; missed moon and became the first spacecraft to orbit the sun. |
| Mar. 3 | Pioneer IV | United States | Lunar probe; first U.S. probe to orbit the sun. |
| Sept. 12 | Luna 2 | Russia | First probe to strike the moon. |
| Oct. 4 | Luna 3 | Russia | Photographed the hidden side of the moon on Oct. 7, 1959. |
| 1960 Mar. 11 | Pioneer V | United States | Transmitted information on conditions more than 22,000,000 miles in space. |
| 1962 Apr. 23 | Ranger IV | United States | First U.S. probe to strike moon; failed to televise pictures to earth. |
| Aug. 27 | Mariner II | United States | Passed near Venus on Dec. 14, 1962; sent scientific information to earth. |
| 1964 July 28 | Ranger VII | United States | Televised 4,316 pictures of moon to the earth on July 31, 1964. |
| Nov. 28 | Mariner IV | United States | Photographed Mars on July 14, 1965; measured conditions in space. |
| 1965 July 18 | Zond 3 | Russia | Photographed the hidden side of the moon on July 20, 1965. |
| Nov. 16 | Venera 3 | Russia | First spacecraft to hit Venus; crashed on March 1, 1966. |
| 1966 Jan. 31 | Luna 9 | Russia | Made first soft landing on the moon on Feb. 3; sent 27 pictures to the earth. |
| Mar. 31 | Luna 10 | Russia | First spacecraft to orbit the moon; began orbiting on April 3. |
| May 30 | Surveyor I | United States | Landed on the moon June 2; sent 11,237 pictures to the earth. |
| Aug. 10 | Lunar Orbiter I | United States | Began orbiting the moon on Aug. 14. Photographed future landing sites. |
| Dec. 21 | Luna 13 | Russia | Landed on the moon; made soil density tests; took photographs. |
| 1967 April 17 | Surveyor 3 | United States | Landed on the moon; dug up lunar soil sample for tests. |
| June 12 | Venera 4 | Russia | Made first soft landing on Venus; landed Oct. 18, 1967. Radioed data on Venus' surface temperature. |
| June 14 | Mariner V | United States | Flew within 2,500 miles of Venus and sent information on Venus' atmosphere. |
| Sept. 8 | Surveyor 5 | United States | Landed on the moon; sent information on lunar soil back to earth for analysis. |
| 1968 Sept. 14 | Zond 5 | Russia | First probe to orbit the moon and return to a soft landing on earth. |
| 1969 Jan. 10 | Venera 6 | Russia | Landed on Venus on May 17, 1969; sent data on Venus' atmosphere. |
| Mar. 27 | Mariner VII | United States | Returned high quality pictures of Mars' south polar cap. |

study *meteoroids*, fast-moving rocklike particles that may be able to damage a spacecraft.

Interplanetary probes explore space in the disc-shaped area formed by the paths of the planets around the sun. This area is called *the plane of the ecliptic*. Future probes will be able to explore space above and below this plane.

**Planetary Probes** are sent mainly to the nearby planets Venus and Mars. Future probes will go to Jupiter and other planets. Planetary probes travel in orbits around the sun. They generally do not land on the target planet. Instead, they fly past at distances of several thousand miles. Even at such distances, a probe's instruments can collect much information about the planet. In 1962, the United States *Mariner II* passed within 22 thousand miles of Venus. It reported that the planet's temperature is about 800 degrees Fahrenheit—too hot for any known animal or plant. In 1965, *Mariner IV* flew within 6,000 miles of Mars. The spacecraft took 22 pictures of Mars, and measured conditions near the planet and in space. The pictures showed many craters, but few other features. The spacecraft reported Mars has a thin atmosphere, no magnetic field, and no radiation belt (see MARS). In 1966, the Russian spacecraft *Venera 3* crashed on Venus. In 1967, Russia's *Venera 4* made a soft landing on Venus and radioed back information to scientists about the planet's atmosphere and surface temperature.

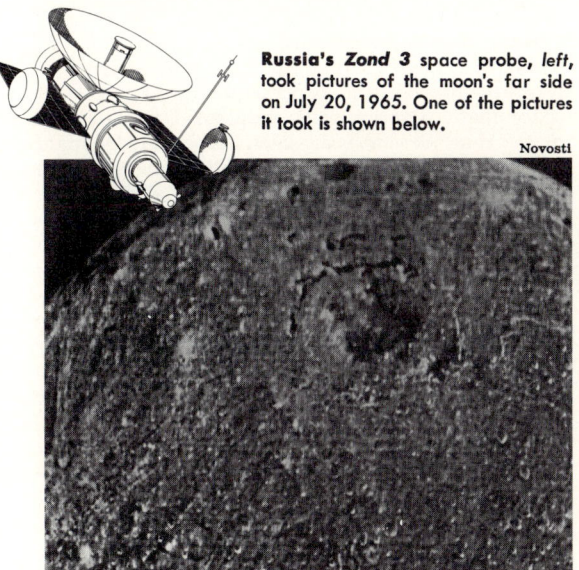

**Russia's *Zond 3*** space probe, *left*, took pictures of the moon's far side on July 20, 1965. One of the pictures it took is shown below.

Novosti

***Surveyor I***, *left*, landed softly on the moon June 2, 1966. It took more than 11,000 pictures of the lunar surface, including the one below.

Jet Propulsion Laboratory

**Mariner Spacecraft**, *left*, took pictures of Mars from distances as close as 2,150 miles during July and August, 1969. On July 30, *Mariner VI* took the photo shown at the left. The large crater at the bottom, with a smaller crater inside it, is about 15 miles across. A few days later, *Mariner VII* passed close to the planet and took a series of photos of the south polar ice cap, including the one at the right.

Jet Propulsion Laboratory

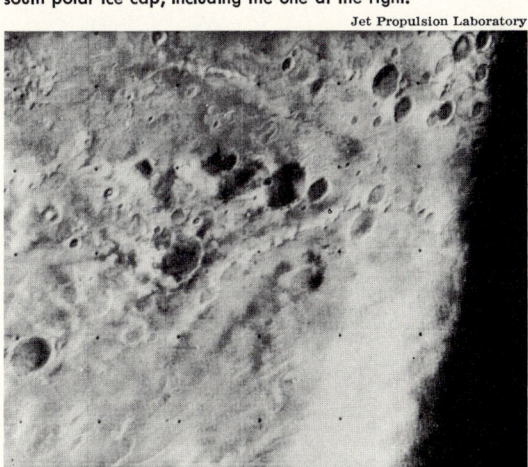

Jet Propulsion Laboratory

# SPACE TRAVEL / STEPS IN THE CONQUEST OF SPACE

The history of space travel could be said to begin more than 300 years ago. In the early 1600's, Johannes Kepler, a German scientist, developed the laws of planetary motion that describe the orbits of bodies in space. Today, these laws are used to determine the orbits of artificial satellites and to plan the flights of spacecraft. See KEPLER, JOHANNES.

In 1687, Sir Isaac Newton published his *Laws of Motion*, which used Kepler's work as a base. Newton's laws, like Kepler's, form a cornerstone of space-flight planning. For example, his third law states that for every action there is an equal and opposite reaction. This law describes why a rocket works. See MOTION (Newton's Laws of Motion); NEWTON, SIR ISAAC.

**Early Developments.** In 1903, Konstantin E. Tsiolkovsky (1857-1935), a Russian schoolteacher, published the first scientific paper on the use of rockets for space flight. But his work attracted little attention at the time. Several years later, Robert H. Goddard (1882-1945), of the United States, and Hermann Oberth (1894-    ), of Germany, succeeded in awakening a scientific interest in space travel. Working independently, these men attacked the technical problems of rocketry and high-altitude research. They earned the title "the fathers of space flight."

In 1919, Goddard explained how rockets could be used to explore the upper atmosphere in his paper "A Method of Reaching Extreme Altitudes." The paper also described a way of firing a rocket to the moon. See GODDARD, ROBERT H.

Oberth published *The Rocket into Interplanetary Space* in 1923. In this book, Oberth discussed many technical problems of space flight. He even described what a spaceship would be like. Interest in Oberth's work in Germany led to the formation of the German Society for Space Travel. The members of this society helped develop the first successful guided missiles during World War II. See GUIDED MISSILE (In World War II).

New York Public Library

**Man's Dream of Space Travel** has led him to design strange spaceships. About 1780, a Frenchman thought a spaceship, *above*, might use a balloon, a parachute, and movable wings. In 1865, the French novelist Jules Verne described a "moon train," *below*.

Bettmann Archive

**First Liquid-Fuel Rocket** was launched by Robert H. Goddard in 1926. It burned gasoline and liquid oxygen and traveled 184 feet at about 60 miles an hour.

United Press Int.

**A Captured German V-2,** like those shown *above,* was used to launch a U.S. WAC *Corporal* rocket to a height of 250 miles in 1949. The WAC Corporal looked like a spike atop the V-2, *right.*

**Jupiter C** launch vehicle sent the first U.S. satellite, *Explorer I,* into orbit in 1958.

**Aerobee,** a research rocket of the 1940's and 1950's, is still used as a sounding rocket.

In the United States, experimenters formed the American Interplanetary Society in 1930. British scientists founded the British Interplanetary Society in 1933. Members of these groups designed and launched experimental rockets, and promoted the idea of space travel.

**High-Altitude Rockets.** During the 1930's, rocket research went forward in the United States, Germany, and Russia. Goddard was the chief American researcher, while Oberth led the German experimenters. Leading Russian scientists included F. A. Tsander (1887-1933) and I. A. Merkulov (1913-    ). By the early 1930's, both the German and Russian governments were conducting rocket research programs. The United States government did not become interested in high-altitude rockets until the early 1940's.

During World War II, German rocketeers under the direction of Wernher von Braun (1912-    ) developed the powerful *V-2* guided missile. A number of these missiles were captured by American forces and sent to the United States to be used in research. After the war, Von Braun and some of the other German scientists came to the United States to continue their work on rockets. Others went to Russia.

In the late 1940's, Americans developed two important research rockets, the *Viking* and the *Aerobee.* In 1949, a small rocket called the *WAC Corporal* soared to what was then a record height of 250 miles. It was launched as a second stage atop a V-2 missile.

**Man-Made Moons.** In 1955, both the United States and Russia announced plans to launch artificial satellites. The "moons" were to be launched during the International Geophysical Year beginning in 1957.

Then, on Oct. 4, 1957, the Russians launched *Sputnik I,* man's first artificial satellite. On Nov. 3, 1957, they launched a second satellite, *Sputnik II.* It carried a dog named Laika, the first animal to soar into space. The United States launched its first satellite, *Explorer I,* on Jan. 31, 1958, and its second, *Vanguard I,* on March 17, 1958. These satellites were much smaller than the Sputniks, because the American launch vehicles were not as powerful as those used by the Russians.

The United States launched many more scientific satellites into orbit and began to make practical use of space. In December of 1958, the United States launched the first communications satellite in a flight called *Project Score.* In February, 1959, the first weather satellite, *Vanguard II,* sent pictures of clouds to earth. Russia launched far fewer satellites than the United States. But the Russian spacecraft continued to be much larger and heavier than U.S. craft.

**Rockets into Outer Space.** Early in 1959, first Russia and then the United States launched probes that escaped earth's gravity. Russia's *Luna 1* and the U.S. *Pioneer IV* were aimed at the moon. They zoomed past the moon and went into orbit around the sun as the first man-made *planetoids.* In the following years, both the United States and Russia sent many spacecraft to the moon and the planets, and around the sun.

**Man in Space.** In the early 1960's, man himself began to travel in space. On April 12, 1961, Russian cosmonaut Yuri Gagarin made a single orbit around the earth. The American astronauts Alan Shepard, on May 5, 1961, and Virgil Grissom, on July 21, rocketed to a height of 118 miles in 300-mile-long flights. Cosmonaut Gherman Titov made 16 revolutions of the earth

572i

*Sovfoto*

**Laika, the Russian Space Dog,** was the first animal sent into orbit. Laika rode in *Sputnik II* in 1957. Studies of animals in space helped pave the way for manned space travel.

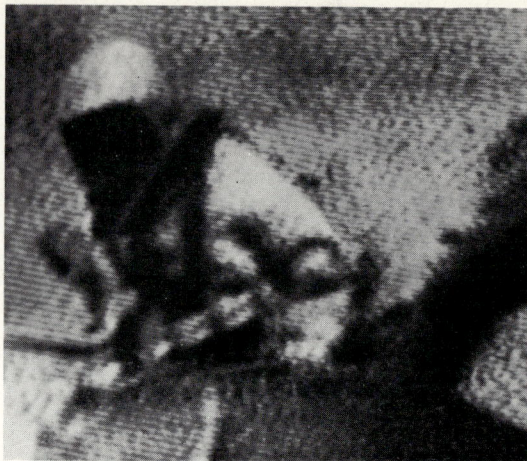

*Wide World*

**First Man to Leave a Spacecraft** was Russian cosmonaut Alexei Leonov. A television camera mounted on *Voskhod II* showed Leonov climbing out of the open hatch on March 18, 1965.

on Aug. 6-7, 1961. John H. Glenn, Jr., first American astronaut to orbit the earth, made three revolutions on Feb. 20, 1962. These men were followed by an ever increasing number of astronauts and cosmonauts.

Russian manned flights of the early 1960's maintained an edge over those of the United States. With its powerful launching rockets, Russia could orbit large spacecraft carrying enough life-support equipment to keep a man in space for several days. Several cosmonauts made *group flights* in which two pilots orbited earth at the same time in separate spacecraft. In such a flight, Valentina Tereshkova, the first woman to fly in space, orbited earth for almost three days, June 16-18, 1963, during Valery Bykovsky's flight. On Oct. 12, 1964, Russia achieved another first in space by orbiting three cosmonauts in one spacecraft, the *Voskhod I*.

Tragedy struck the U.S. space program on Jan. 27, 1967, when three Apollo astronauts were killed in a test of their spacecraft. Virgil I. Grissom, Edward H. White II, and Roger B. Chaffee died when fire and smoke swept their command module during a ground checkout at Cape Kennedy. The three men had been scheduled to fly the first manned Apollo spacecraft on Feb. 21, 1967.

The fire probably began with a spark from faulty electrical wiring. The spark ignited items in the cabin of the module, and the fire broke out. The flames were fed by pure oxygen, used to pressurize the cabin. The tragedy caused a 20-month delay in the first manned Apollo flight. Many safety features were added to the spacecraft to prevent a similar accident.

The first known space flight death occurred in April,

**A Walk in Space** by Edward H. White II was the first of several space walks in the Gemini program. The astronauts practiced maneuvering to prepare for future work in space.

*World Book Science Service*

1967. Cosmonaut Vladimir Komarov was killed when his spacecraft's parachute failed.

America's first man-in-space project, the Mercury program, ended with Gordon Cooper's 22-revolution flight of May 15-16, 1963. The United States' next steps into space were the Gemini and Apollo programs. The first manned flight in the Gemini program was made on March 23, 1965. The *Molly Brown* spacecraft carried Virgil Grissom and John Young on three revolutions around the earth. The first manned Apollo program flight, Apollo 7, carried Walter M. Schirra, Jr., Walter Cunningham, and Donn Eisele in earth orbit on Oct. 11-22, 1968. Astronauts Frank Borman, James A. Lovell, Jr., and William A. Anders orbited the moon aboard the Apollo 8 on Dec. 24-25, 1968.

The first men on the moon were astronauts Neil A. Armstrong and Edwin E. Aldrin, Jr. Their Apollo 11 lunar module landed on July 20, 1969. Armstrong, Aldrin, and command module pilot Michael Collins left the earth on July 16 and returned on July 24.

**The Space Race.** While Russia and the United States made more advanced flights into space, many persons tried to compare the two countries to see which was "ahead." But differences in the purposes of the two space programs made comparisons difficult.

In the early 1960's, Russia was still clearly ahead in rocket power used to launch large manned spacecraft on long journeys. Russian propaganda claimed that the flights showed Russia's military strength and the superiority of Communism.

On the other hand, the United States led in the number of scientific spacecraft it had launched, and in such practical fields as communications, navigation, and weather-reporting by satellite. Also, the main national space program of the United States was a civilian activity. Unlike the Russian program, it was open to extensive news coverage.

Early in 1964, the United States took a giant step in developing a Saturn I rocket that placed over 19,000 pounds in orbit. The powerful Saturn V rocket used in the Apollo program placed 280,000 pounds in orbit in late 1967. By that time, the United States had spent about $37\frac{1}{2}$ billion on space flights.

**Activities in Other Countries.** Many countries cooperate with the United States in the exploration and the practical use of space. Great Britain, Canada, and Italy build satellites and satellite instruments to be launched by American rockets. A number of countries use U.S. sounding rockets for space research. These countries include Argentina, Australia, Canada, Denmark, France, Germany, India, Italy, Japan, New Zealand, Norway, Pakistan, and Sweden.

In 1962, representatives of the United States and Russia agreed that the two countries would cooperate on a limited number of space programs. This cooperation involves mainly the exchange of weather information and of findings on the earth's magnetic field.

Special organizations have been formed in Europe to help create independent European space programs. The European Space Research Organization (ESRO) was established in 1962 to coordinate the activities of European researchers. The European Launch Development Organization (ELDO), also founded in 1962, works to develop launch vehicles for satellites.

The International Astronautical Federation (IAF) was established in 1950 to encourage space research and to promote space flight as a peaceful project. This organization includes 30 rocket societies of more than 20 countries. The Committee on Space Research (COSPAR) of the International Council of Scientific Unions was formed in 1958 to further international scientific investigations which use rockets.

In 1967, the United States, Russia, and many other countries signed a treaty providing for the peaceful exploration and use of outer space. The treaty banned the use of nuclear weapons in outer space.

**How the Earth Looks from the Moon.** The Apollo 8 astronauts took this picture shortly after they began orbiting the moon. They were less than 100 miles from the moon and more than 240,000 miles from the earth at the time. Africa is at the bottom of the lighted area of the earth.

NASA

# SPACE TRAVEL / THE AEROSPACE INDUSTRY

North American Rockwell Corp.

**Huge F-1 Rocket Engines** are shown during manufacturing. Each engine provides 1½ million pounds of thrust. Five F-1's are used to power the first stage of the Saturn V rocket.

**Electrical Harnesses for Service Modules** of Apollo spacecraft are assembled by skilled technicians. The service modules, *background*, carry support systems for the spacecraft.

North American Rockwell Corp.

The aerospace industry includes many kinds of companies. Some firms design and build aircraft, missiles, and space vehicles. Others manufacture systems, such as life-support and navigational equipment. Still others furnish consulting and research services on space problems. Aerospace firms range in size from a small machine shop working on a single part to a great industrial organization with thousands of workers building giant rocket stages. Many electronics firms are also considered part of the aerospace industry.

The aerospace industry began as an extension of the aviation industry. The word *aerospace* is a combination of *aero* (meaning *air*) and the word *space*. In general, an aerospace company is one whose products or services are related to air travel and to space travel.

In the United States, about 10,000 firms work on aerospace projects. The firms are located primarily along the West Coast and in the northern Atlantic states. A secondary grouping lies in the industrial Midwest. Other aerospace centers are also growing in the Gulf states and in the middle-Atlantic and southeastern states. By the mid-1960's, the aerospace industry employed more than 700 thousand workers and topped 15 billion dollars in sales. Production and employment depend largely on government funds appropriated by Congress for space and missile programs.

The total production of the aerospace industry involves many products used in industry and the home. Such products include miniature electronic devices for television receivers, and special ceramic materials used to make frypans. These products are not the direct result of space programs, but they are made possible by aerospace research and development projects.

In the United States, the National Aeronautics and Space Administration (NASA) directs the main national space activities such as the Mercury, Gemini, and Apollo programs. This agency selects space programs and manages the research and development of spacecraft and launch vehicles. It operates the Launch Operations Center at Cape Kennedy, the Manned Spacecraft Center near Houston, and several research and development installations such as the Marshall Space Flight Center in Huntsville, Ala., and the Lewis Research Center in Cleveland. The Department of Defense (DOD) also conducts space programs through the Air Force, Army, and Navy. These programs include the development of missiles such as Polaris and Titan II, military communications satellites, and navigational satellites such as Transit.

**Making Aerospace Equipment.** Most companies do not manufacture an entire spacecraft or launch vehicle for a space program. Usually, a single company is chosen to manage the production of the vehicle. This firm is called the *prime contractor*. It breaks down the main task into smaller jobs, and assigns many of these jobs to other firms called *subcontractors*. For example, in the manufacture of a launch rocket, one firm might manufacture the engine, another the fuel tanks, and a third the guidance system. In some cases, several hundred firms may supply the prime contractor with various items. The subcontractors themselves often divide up their own portions of the task and contract with still more firms for parts and equipment. After the parts have been made, they are delivered to the prime contractor for final assembly.

To select a contractor for a project, a government agency, such as the Department of Defense, first sends out invitations to various companies for bids on the job. Each company can then make its bid in a detailed *proposal*. The proposal usually contains preliminary designs, time schedules, cost figures, and a brief account of the company's experience and abilities in the particular field. The government agency then carefully reviews the proposals. It awards the contract to a particular company on the basis of the company's bid and on its qualifications.

In special cases, a single firm may be exceptionally qualified for a particular job. The government agency then arranges the terms of the contract with this firm without requesting bids. Such a company is known as a *sole source*.

The manufacture of a space vehicle differs greatly from the building of an airplane. Spacecraft cannot be built on an assembly line. Highly trained engineers and technicians must make and assemble the complicated parts with the utmost precision. For example, certain vehicles and space equipment must be manufactured and assembled in a special area called a *clean room*. This room is carefully conditioned with filtered air to prevent even the smallest particles of dust from reaching the equipment. Technicians working in the room wear special lint-free clothing, and look much like doctors in an operating room.

**Space-Age Careers** include perhaps the most exciting career of all—exploring space as an astronaut. But at present only a few persons can enter and enjoy this career. See ASTRONAUT.

However, a great number of persons can share in the exploration of space by working in the aerospace industry. Opportunities are open to almost every kind of scientist and engineer, and to business administrators, doctors, and technicians.

*Scientists* play a major role in designing experiments to be performed by satellites and space probes. They also do basic research on new materials for building spacecraft and on new forms of rocket propulsion.

**The First Stage of a Giant Saturn V Launch Vehicle** is inspected by technicians at an assembly plant. The first stage is 33 feet in diameter and 138 feet tall. It will boost an Apollo spacecraft on the first leg of a journey to the moon.

NASA

## SPACE TRAVEL

Biologists and biochemists devise tests to show whether life may exist on a planet such as Mars. Physicists plan experiments to study radiation in space, the earth's magnetic field, and the conditions on distant planets. Meteorologists and geophysicists work out ways to study the speed and direction of the solar wind, the temperature and pressure of earth's atmosphere, and the size and shape of the earth.

Specialists in nuclear physics and plasma physics work on propulsion systems such as nuclear rockets and ion rockets. Chemists and metallurgists conduct research on new materials that withstand the heat of a rocket exhaust or the impact of meteorites. Mathematicians analyze the information radioed back from instruments speeding through space. They use computers to find a launch vehicle's *reliability* (its chances of making a successful launch). Psychologists measure the astronaut's performance during a space flight. Even economists and sociologists take part in the space program by studying the effect of space travel on education and employment. Political scientists work out solutions to space problems in international law.

*Engineers* of all kinds carry the greatest responsibility in the space program. Engineers design and launch the space vehicles and develop the equipment used in tracking and telemetry. They plan and build the instruments that explore in space, and find the best way of sending the instruments to their destination. They design and build the launch pads, gantries, control rooms, and other ground equipment needed to launch men and instruments into space.

Specialists in human engineering plan manned spacecraft so that the astronaut can work comfortably and efficiently. Mechanical engineers design and build machines that can land on the moon and dig out samples of the moon's surface for analysis. Electronics and communications engineers work on radio transmitters and receivers for tracking and controlling spacecraft. Hydraulic engineers and specialists in low-temperature physics design pumping systems to handle new fuels discovered by research chemists. Metallurgical engineers and specialists in ceramics develop protective coverings for manned spacecraft.

*Technicians* include trained specialists who manufacture, install, maintain, repair, and operate the complicated equipment used in launching a spacecraft. Technicians may specialize in working with metals, plastics, ceramics, and various other materials. They put together the complicated electronics equipment used in spacecraft guidance and control systems. They also inspect manufactured parts and test assembled equipment to see that it works properly.

Students interested in aerospace careers should take as much science and mathematics as possible in high school. For professional positions, the aerospace worker must have at least a bachelor's degree in science or engineering. Students who wish to become technicians can take their training at technical institutes. Information on space age careers can be obtained from the United States Office of Education, Division for Aerospace Education, Washington, D.C.; the Aerospace Industries Association of America, Inc., Washington, D.C.; the National Aeronautics and Space Administration, Washington, D.C.; and the American Institute of Aeronautics and Astronautics, 1290 Avenue of the Americas, New York, N.Y. 10019.   HAROLD L. GOODWIN

Critically reviewed by WERNHER VON BRAUN

**Related Articles.** For information on the astronauts and cosmonauts themselves and on how they are selected and trained, see the ASTRONAUT article. See also the following articles:

### BIOGRAPHIES

Aldrin, Edwin E., Jr.
Anders, William A.
Armstrong, Neil A.
Borman, Frank
Carpenter, M. Scott
Collins, Michael
Cooper, Leroy G., Jr.
Gagarin, Yuri A.
Glenn, John H., Jr.
Goddard, Robert H.
Grissom, Virgil I.
Lovell, James A., Jr.
Schirra, Walter M., Jr.
Shepard, Alan B., Jr.
Slayton, Donald Kent
Tereshkova, Valentina V.
Von Braun, Wernher
White, Edward H., II
Young, John W.

**A Rocket Carried by Barge** is the first stage of a Saturn V moon rocket. This stage, which delivers 7½ million pounds of thrust, is too large to be carried by trucks or train.

NASA

ORGANIZATIONS

American Institute of Aeronautics and Astronautics
Communications Satellite Corporation
European Space Research Organization
National Aeronautics and Space Administration

OTHER RELATED ARTICLES

Astronautics
Aviation Medicine
Brooks Air Force Base
Cape Kennedy
Centrifugal Force
Communications Satellite
Cosmic Rays
Exobiology
Gravitation
Guided Missile
Heat Shield
International Years of the Quiet Sun
Jet Propulsion
Manned Spacecraft Center
Meteor
Moon
Orbit
Planet
Radiation
Relativity
Rocket
Solar Energy
Solar System
Telemetering

**Outline**

I. **What Is Space**
   A. The Beginning of Space
   B. From Earth to the Moon
   C. Space Among the Planets
   D. To the Stars and Beyond
II. **Getting into Space and Back**
   A. Overcoming Gravity    B. Returning to Earth
III. **Launch Vehicles**
   A. The Building Block Idea
   B. Piggyback Boosters
   C. Apollo Program Launch Vehicles
   D. Nuclear Rockets
IV. **Manned Spacecraft**
   A. Life-Support Systems
   B. Communications and Navigation Equipment
   C. Control Systems
   D. Re-Entry and Landing Equipment
V. **Launch Operations**
VI. **Flying a Spacecraft**
   A. Before the Flight
   B. Piloting a Spacecraft
   C. Scientific Duties
   D. Living in a Spacecraft
   E. Re-Entry
VII. **Orbiting the Earth**
   A. Selecting the Orbit
   B. Launching a Spacecraft
   C. How a Spacecraft Stays in Orbit
VIII. **Reaching the Moon**
   A. Aiming at the Moon
   B. Orbiting the Moon
   C. Landing on the Moon
   D. Exploring the Moon
   E. Returning to Earth
IX. **Space Stations**
   A. Space Station Laboratories
   B. Stopping-Off Places for Spaceships
   C. Military Space Stations
X. **Reaching the Planets and the Stars**
   A. Escaping Earth's Gravity
   B. Traveling to the Planets
   C. Reaching the Stars
XI. **Problems of Space Flight**
   A. Dangers in Space
   B. Tracking a Spacecraft
   C. Space Medicine
XII. **Artificial Satellites**
   A. Weather Satellites
   B. Communications Satellites
   C. Navigation Satellites
   D. Scientific Satellites
   E. Military Satellites
XIII. **Space Probes**
   A. Sounding Rockets
   B. Lunar Spacecraft
   C. Interplanetary Probes
   D. Planetary Probes
XIV. **Steps in the Conquest of Space**
   A. Early Developments
   B. High-Altitude Rockets
   C. Man-Made Moons
   D. Rockets into Outer Space
   E. Man in Space
   F. The Space Race
   G. Activities in Other Countries
XV. **The Aerospace Industry**
   A. Making Aerospace Equipment
   B. Space-Age Careers

## SPAIGHT, RICHARD DOBBS

**Questions**

What men are called "the fathers of space flight"?
What is a retrorocket? A heat shield?
How far above earth does space begin?
How does a rocket engine produce thrust?
What is a *clean room?*
What was the first international satellite?
At what speed must a spacecraft be launched to reach the moon? To escape earth's gravity?
How do engineers use the "building block idea" to design launch vehicles?
What holds a satellite up?
What space probes photographed the far side of the moon?
What probe measured the temperature of the planet Venus?

**Books for Young Readers**

CAIDIN, MARTIN. *By Apollo to the Moon.* Dutton, 1963.
DIETZ, DAVID. *All About Satellites and Space Ships.* Rev. ed. Random House, 1962.
GOODWIN, HAROLD L. *All About Rockets and Space Flight.* Random House, 1964.
NEWLON, CLARKE. *Famous Pioneers in Space.* Dodd, Mead, 1963.

**Books for Older Readers**

AMERICAN HERITAGE. *Americans in Space.* American Heritage, 1965. A history of American exploration of space beginning in 1914.
GOODWIN, HAROLD L. *The Images of Space.* Holt, Rinehart, and Winston, 1965.
LIFE (Periodical). *Man and Space,* by Arthur C. Clarke, and the editors of *Life.* Time, Inc. 1964.
SHELTON, WILLIAM R. *Flights of the Astronauts.* Little, Brown, 1963.
VON BRAUN, WERNHER. *First Men to the Moon.* Illus. by Fred Freeman. Holt, 1960. *Space Frontier.* Holt, 1967.
VON BRAUN, WERNHER. *Space Frontier.* Holt, 1967.
*We Seven,* by the Astronauts Themselves. Simon & Schuster, 1962.

**SPACESHIP.** See SPACE TRAVEL (Manned Spacecraft).

**S.P.A.D.** See AIR FORCE (picture: Fighting Planes of Three Wars).

**SPAGHETTI.** See MACARONI.

**SPAGNOLETTO, LO.** See RIBERA, JUSEPE DE.

**SPAHN, WARREN EDWARD** (1921-    ), became one of the greatest pitchers in baseball history. During his major league career, he won 363 games, more than any other left-handed pitcher. Spahn won 20 or more games in one season 13 times, and he led the National League in games-won eight times. He holds the National League record for the most *shutouts* (scoreless games) by a left-hander, 63. Spahn was born in Buffalo, N.Y., and began his major-league career with the Boston (later Milwaukee) Braves in 1942. In 1964, he was traded to the New York Mets. He retired in 1965 from the San Francisco Giants.    JOSEPH P. SPOHN

**SPAIGHT,** *spate,* **RICHARD DOBBS** (1758-1802), was a North Carolina signer of the United States Constitution. He was a delegate to the Continental Congress from 1783 to 1785. In the Constitutional Convention, he favored election of the President by Congress. Later, he worked for the ratification of the Constitution in North Carolina. He was governor of North Carolina from 1792 to 1795. He served in the U.S. House of Representatives from 1798 to 1801. Spaight was born in New Bern, N.C.    ROBERT J. TAYLOR

**A Storybook Castle in Old Castile,** the Alcazar, rises atop a steep hill at Segovia. Built in 1358 and rebuilt later, the castle was the scene of Isabella's coronation as Queen of Castile in 1474.

**SPAIN** is a sunny land famous for bullfights and for more than 1,400 beautiful castles and palaces. The snow-capped Pyrenees Mountains separate Spain from the rest of Europe. The country has a history tied closely to northern Africa, which includes the Spanish province of Spanish Sahara. Spaniards call their country ESPAÑA. Madrid is the capital and largest city.

Many peoples have conquered and lived in Spain and have contributed to its traditions and customs. More than 3,000 years ago the ancient Phoenicians set up colonies there. Then the Carthaginians of Africa ruled Spain as a colony. Next the Romans seized it and made it one of the most valuable provinces of the Roman Empire. Fierce Germanic tribes swept into Spain after the fall of Rome. About 200 years later, they were followed by the Moors of Africa. For about 500 years before 1200, Spain was the center of the brilliant Moslem civilization of the Moors. After 1200, the Spanish people gradually expelled the Moors. Christopher Columbus, sailing in Spanish ships, discovered America and claimed it for Spain. Spanish soldiers and colonists followed him and sent back gold and jewels. By the 1500's, Spain had become the most powerful country in the world. During the years that followed, however, wars with other countries and civil wars used up Spain's wealth and the nation lost most of its overseas colonies.

Despite advances in industry, the country still presents a sharp contrast in the richness of its past and its present poverty. About 40 per cent of the Spanish families now have television sets, but generally the people still are poor and earn their living by tending vineyards, orchards, and small farms. Farm women carry crops to market in huge bundles balanced on their heads. The colorful bullfights, refined by the Moors, show the love of Spanish people for a spectacle that combines courage and elaborate ceremony.

Spain shares the Iberian Peninsula of southwestern Europe with the smaller nation of Portugal. At the southern tip of Spain lies Britain's fortified Gibraltar, which controls the western approaches to the Mediterranean Sea. Including overseas provinces, Spain has an area more than twice the size of Oregon. But it has more than 17 times as many people as that state. A high, almost treeless plateau covers three-fourths of the mainland. Along the seacoasts the fertile soil produces fine crops and the weather remains mild throughout the year. Most of the people live in the coastal regions. Their chief crops include wheat, grapes, olives, oranges, lemons, and nuts.

Spain's many regions differ in geography, customs, and language. For example, the vigorous Basque people

---

*Walter C. Langsam, the contributor of this article, is the President of the University of Cincinnati and author of* World History Since 1870.

live in a forested, mountainous region on the northern coast. Their language has no relationship to any other known tongue. Castile, in central Spain, is a land of gray-brown plains separated by barren ravines. Andalusia in southern Spain typifies the country to most tourists. It is a region famous for bullfights, and for dances with castanets.

For Spain's relationship to the rest of Europe, see EUROPE.

### The Land and Its Resources

**Location and Size.** Spain has an area of 194,884 square miles, including the Balearic Islands (1,936 square miles) and the Canary Islands (2,808 square miles). Spain covers four-fifths of the Iberian Peninsula, at the southwestern end of Europe. The Canary Islands in the Atlantic, the Balearic Islands in the Mediterranean, and Spanish Sahara in Africa are Spanish provinces (see BALEARIC ISLANDS; CANARY ISLANDS; SPANISH SAHARA).

**Land Regions.** Spain's land regions are: (1) the Meseta plateau, (2) the coastal plains, and (3) the mountains.

*The Meseta Plateau.* Three-fourths of Spain is a barren plateau that lies an average of 1,000 to 3,000 feet above sea level. Its central plain is 2,000 to 6,000 feet above sea level. The region is enclosed by lofty mountains and broken by high, rocky hills. The Meseta stretches from the Cantabrian Mountains in the north to the Sierra Morena in the south. A coastal plain lies on the east. On the west, the plateau extends into Portugal. Most of the plateau has dry reddish or yellow soil. The most fertile areas lie along its edges and in the central mountains.

*The Coastal Plains.* The eastern coastal plain extends south from Barcelona to the Gulf of Almería. A spur of the Sierra Nevada Mountains near Cape Nao divides the plain into two almost equal parts. Many streams flow across the plain to the Mediterranean Sea, and provide water to irrigate the region's farms.

Soil that has been washed down from the mountains for hundreds of years forms another coastal plain in the Guadalquivir Valley of southwestern Spain. *Las Marismas* (The Marshes) make up the central part of this plain. Excellent grapes and most of Spain's olives come from this low, warm area.

In most parts of the northwest, rugged mountains separate a narrow coastal plain from the rest of Spain. Vacationers enjoy the famous resorts and bathing beaches along the Bay of Biscay and the Atlantic Ocean.

*The Mountains.* Spain has three main lines of mountains. The Pyrenees, Cantabrian, and Galician mountains in the north form one line. The rugged Pyrenees make up the boundary between France and Spain. This mountain range has only two good passes along its entire 270-mile length. Roads and railroads run through them. One pass is at the western end, near the city of San Sebastián. The other cuts through the mountains at the eastern end. The great Carthaginian general, Hannibal, marched through this eastern pass on his way

---

### FACTS IN BRIEF

**Capital:** Madrid.

**Official Language:** Castilian Spanish.

**Form of Government:** Dictatorship (Officially a kingdom).

**Area:** 194,884 sq. mi. including the Balearic Islands (1,936 sq. mi.) and Canary Islands (2,808 sq. mi.). *Greatest Distances:* (east-west) 668 mi.; (north-south) 538 mi. *Coastline*—1,698 mi.; Bay of Biscay, 416 mi.; Mediterranean Sea, 898 mi.; Atlantic Ocean, 384 mi.

**Elevation:** *Highest*—Mount Mulhacén, 11,424 feet above sea level. *Lowest*—along the coast, sea level.

**Population:** *1960 Census*—30,430,698 (including the Balearic and Canary islands); distribution, 65 per cent rural, 35 per cent urban. *Estimated 1970 Population*—32,918,000; density, 169 persons to the square mile. *Estimated 1975 Population*—34,255,000.

**Chief Products:** *Agriculture*—almonds, bananas, barley, beans, cattle, chestnuts, cork trees, corn, esparto fiber grass, figs, goats, grapes, hazelnuts, lemons, melons, oats, olives, onions, oranges, poultry, rice, rye, sheep, sweet peppers, tomatoes, wheat. *Manufacturing*—automobiles, cement, cork products, cotton and woolen goods, glass, iron and steel, laces, olive oil, paper, silk, sugar, tobacco products, wine. *Mining*—coal, iron, lead, lignite, mercury, potash, pyrites, salt, silver, tin, tungsten, zinc. *Fishing Industry*—cod, herring, tuna.

**National Anthem:** Himno Nacional (National Anthem).

**Flag:** The *national flag*, flown by the people, has a yellow horizontal stripe between two red stripes. Its yellow center stripe is twice as wide as each of the red outer stripes. The colors come from the coats of arms of five old kingdoms. First used in 1785, the flag was readopted in 1936. Spain's coat of arms was added in 1938 to form the *state flag*, used by the government. See FLAG (color picture: Flags of Europe).

**Money:** *Basic Unit*—peseta. See MONEY (table); PESETA.

---

**Bullfighting Ranks as Spain's Best-Known Spectacle.** Outstanding matadors are national heroes in Spain.
Spanish Tourist Office

SPAIN MAP INDEX

## Historic Regions and Provinces

ANDALUSIA (ANDALUCÍA) ....5,893,396......D 4
Almería* ....360,777......D 5
Cádiz* ....818,847......D 4
Córdoba* ....798,437......D 4
Granada* ....769,408......D 5
Huelva* ....399,934......D 3
Jaén* ....736,391......D 5
Málaga* ....775,167......D 4
Sevilla* ....1,234,435......D 4
ARAGON (ARAGÓN) ....1,105,498......B 6
Huesca* ....233,543......A 6
Teruel* ....215,183......B 6
Zaragoza* ....656,772......B 6
ASTURIAS ....989,344......A 3
Oviedo* ....989,344......A 3
BALEARIC ISLANDS (BALEARES) 443,327......C 8
Baleares* ....443,327......C 8
BASQUE PROVINCES (VASCONGADAS) ....1,371,654......A 5
Alava* ....138,934......A 5
Guipúzcoa* ....478,337......A 5
Vizcaya* ....754,383......A 5
CANARY ISLANDS (CANARIAS) ..944,448......F 12
Las Palmas* ....453,793......F 12
Santa Cruz de Tenerife* ....490,655......F 11
CATALONIA (CATALUÑA) ......3,925,779......B 7
Barcelona* ....2,877,966......B 8
Gerona* ....351,369......A 8
Lérida* ....333,765......A 7
Tarragona* ....362,679......B 7
ESTREMADURA (EXTREMADURA) ....1,378,777......C 3
Badajoz* ....834,370......C 3
Cáceres* ....544,407......C 3
GALICIA ....2,602,962......A 3
La Coruña* ....991,729......A 2
Lugo* ....479,530......A 3
Orense* ....451,474......A 3
Pontevedra* ....680,229......A 2
LEON (LEÓN) ....1,291,452......B 4
León* ....584,594......A 4
Salamanca* ....405,729......B 4
Zamora* ....301,129......B 4
MURCIA ....1,171,439......C 6
Albacete* ....370,976......C 6
Murcia* ....800,463......D 6
NAVARRE (NAVARRA) ....402,042......A 6
Navarra* ....402,042......A 6
NEW CASTILE (CASTILLA LA NUEVA) ....4,210,817......C 5
Ciudad Real* ....583,948......C 5
Cuenca* ....315,433......B 5
Guadalajara* ....183,545......B 5
Madrid* ....2,606,254......B 5
Toledo* ....521,637......C 4
OLD CASTILE (CASTILLA LA VIEJA) ....2,218,884......B 5
Avila* ....238,372......B 4
Burgos* ....380,791......A 5
Logroño* ....229,852......A 5
Palencia* ....231,977......A 4
Santander* ....432,132......A 4
Segovia* ....195,602......B 4
Soria* ....147,052......B 5
Valladolid* ....363,106......B 4
VALENCIA ....2,480,879......C 6
Alicante* ....711,942......C 6
Castellón* ....339,229......B 6
Valencia* ....1,429,708......C 6

## Cities and Towns

Abanilla ....8,594..C 6
Abanto y Ciérvana* 11,513..A 5
Abarán* ....8,808..C 6
Adra ......15,669..D 5
Aguilar ....16,409..D 4
Águilas ....15,250..D 6
Agüimes* ..10,476..G 12
Alacuás* ....8,116..C 6
Albacete ...74,417..C 6
Alberique* ..7,945..C 6
Alboraya* ..8,073..C 6
Albox .......9,049..D 5
Alburquerque ......10,054..C 3
Alcalá de Guadaira 31,004..D 4
Alcalá de Henares .25,123..B 5
Alcalá de los Gazules ..11,221..D 4
Alcalá del Río* ......8,707..D 4
Alcalá la Real .....23,314..D 5
Alcañiz ....10,035..B 6
Alcantarilla 15,748..D 6
Alcaudete ..17,403..D 4
Alcázar de San Juan 24,963..C 5
Alcira ......26,669..C 6
Alcoy ......51,096..C 6
Aldaya* ....9,579..C 6
Alfaro ......8,570..A 6
Algarinejo* .8,054..D 4
Algeciras ..66,317..D 4
Algemesí ...19,057..C 6
Alginet .....8,421..C 6
Algodonales .8,018..D 4
Alhama de Granada ..9,950..D 5
Alhama de Murcia ..11,736..D 6
Alhaurín el Grande ..11,525..D 4
Alicante ..126,107..C 6
Allariz ......9,241..A 3
Almadén ...13,443..C 4
Almagro ....9,681..C 5
Almansa ...15,391..C 6
Almazora* .10,178..C 6
Almendralejo ...20,884..C 3
Almería ....86,808..D 5
Almodóvar del Campo 15,618..C 4
Almodóvar del Río* ..8,239..D 4
Almogía ....8,865..D 4
Almonte ....11,538..D 3
Almoradí ..11,141..C 6
Almuñécar .14,603..D 5
Álora .......15,152..D 4
Alosno ......8,089..D 3
Amés* .......9,597..A 2
Amorebieta* .8,346..A 5
Amposta ...12,507..B 7
Andorra .....7,795..B 6
Andújar ...32,185..C 4
Antequera ..42,327..D 4
Aracena .....7,643..D 3
Aranda de Duero ...13,454..B 5
Aranjuez ..27,251..B 5
Archena* ....8,829..C 6
Archidona .11,594..D 4
Arcos de la Frontera .24,197..D 4
Argamasilla de Alba ..7,529..C 5
Arjona .....8,154..D 4
Arnedo .....7,958..A 5
Arrecife ...12,886..F 13
Arrigorriaga* 8,142..A 5
Arroyo de la Luz ....9,781..C 3
Arteijo ....10,887..A 2
Arucas ....25,986..F 12
Arzúa .....10,470..A 2
Aspe .......10,279..C 6
Astorga ....10,101..A 3
Atarfe ......8,036..D 5
Ávila ......26,807..B 4
Avilés ......48,503..A 4
Ayamonte ..13,230..D 3
Azcoitia* ....8,384..A 5
Azpeitia* ...9,400..A 5
Azuaga ....16,306..C 4
Badajoz ..100,974..C 2
Badalona ..92,257..B 8
Baena .....21,976..D 4
Baeza .....15,461..D 5
Bailén .....11,245..C 5
Balaguer ....8,342..B 7
Bañolas ....8,075..A 8
Baños de Cerrato ...7,519..B 4
Barbastro ..10,227..A 7
Barbate ...18,411..D 4
Barcarrota ..7,898..C 3
Barcelona ..1,633,921..B 8
Basauri* ...23,030..A 5
Baza .......20,440..D 5
Baztán .....8,887..A 6
Beasain .....7,610..A 5
Beas de Segura ...14,957..C 5
Becerreá ....7,753..A 3
Béjar .......16,357..B 4
Belalcázar ..8,793..C 4
Bélmez .....9,202..C 4
Benaguacil* .7,690..C 6
Benavente ..11,080..A 4
Benicarló ..10,627..B 7
Benifayó* ...8,095..C 6
Berga .......9,822..A 7
Berja ......12,732..D 5
Bermeo ....13,781..A 5
Betanzos ...10,223..A 2
Bilbao ....317,639..A 5
Blanes ......9,492..B 8
Boiro .......12,661..A 2
Bolaños ....8,501..C 5
Bollullos par del Condado .10,947..D 3
Bornos ......8,697..D 4
Bueu* .......10,317..A 2
Bujalance ..11,475..D 4
Bullas .......9,441..C 6
Burgos .....82,177..A 5
Burguillos del Cerro .8,099..C 3
Burjasot ..17,624..C 6
Burriana ..18,616. C 6
Cabañaquinta ....28,689..A 4
Cabeza del Buey .11,737..C 4
Cabra ......20,739..D 4
Cáceres ....48,005..C 3
Cádiz ......122,568..D 3
Calahorra ..14,462..A 6
Calañas ....11,444..D 3
Calasparra ..9,597..C 6
Calatayud ..17,940..B 6
Caldas de Reyes* ...8,983..A 2
Calella ......7,947..B 8
Callosa de Segura ...12,966..C 6
Camargo ...12,822..A 5
Camas* ....16,047..D 4
Cambados* ..9,971..A 2
Cambre* ....7,748..A 2
Campanario 9,660..C 4
Campillos ...8,791..D 4
Campo de Criptana .14,608..C 5
Candás* ....11,128..A 4
Cangas .....17,115..A 2
Cangas de Narcea ..20,980..A 3
Cangas de Onís .....10,261..A 4
Caniles ......8,643..D 5
Cantillana* .8,850..D 4
Caravaca ...20,735..C 6
Carballedo* .9,778..A 3
Carballino ..9,752..A 2
Carballo ...22,131..A 2
Carcagente .17,937..C 6
Cardona ....7,885..B 7
Carlet .......9,554..C 6
Carmona ..28,216..D 4
Cartagena .123,630..D 6
Cártama .....9,626..D 4
Cartaya ....13,041..D 3
Caspe .......9,507..B 6
Castellón de la Plana ...62,493..C 6
Castillo de Locubín* ..8,079..D 5
Castrillón ..12,382..A 3
Castro de Rey ......7,667..A 3
Castro del Río .....11,842..D 4
Castro-Urdiales .11,988..A 5
Castroverde .8,054..A 3
Castuera ...10,166..C 4
Catarroja ..11,680..C 6
Caudete .....7,544..C 6
Cazalla de la Sierra ...10,109..D 4
Cazorla ....12,232..D 5
Cedeira .....8,411..A 2
Cehegín ....15,928..C 6
Celanova ....8,127..A 3
Cerceda .....7,929..A 2
Chantada ..14,116..A 3
Chiclana de la Frontera .21,524..D 3
Chipiona* ...8,182..D 3
Chirivella* ..9,250..C 6
Ciempozuelos 9,042..B 5
Cieza .......22,438..C 6
Ciudadela .12,228..B 8
Ciudad Real 37,081..C 5
Ciudad-Rodrigo ..12,981..B 3
Cocentaina ..8,688..C 6
Coín .......20,557..D 4
Colmenar Viejo .....8,375..B 5
Conil ........9,861..D 3
Constantina 13,488..D 4
Consuegra ..10,572..C 5
Córdoba ..207,009..D 4
Coria ........8,204..B 3
Coria del Río* ....15,083..D 4
Coristanco ..9,609..A 2
Cornellá ...24,714..B 8
Corral de Almaguer .8,261..C 5
Cortegana ..8,344..D 3
Corvera de Asturias* .9,813..A 4
Cospeito ....8,090..A 3
Crevillente .14,047..C 6
Cuart de Poblet* ..10,571..C 6
Cudillero ...9,566..A 3
Cuenca ....27,007..B 5
Cuevas del Almanzora 9,073..D 6
Cúllar de Baza .....8,883..D 5
Cullera .....14,103..C 6
Culleredo* ..8,520..A 2
Cuntis* .....7,689..A 2
Daimiel ...19,625..C 5
Dalías .....14,409..D 5
Denia ......12,185..C 7
Don Benito 25,248..C 4
Dos Hermanas 27,696..D 4
Durango ...14,417..A 5
Écija ......49,762..D 4
Eibar ......31,725..A 5
Ejea de los Caballeros 10,988..A 6
El Arahal .17,361..D 4
El Barco ...7,695..A 3
Elche .......73,320..C 6
El Coronil* .7,986..D 4
Elda ........28,151..C 6
El Ferrol del Caudillo .74,799..A 2
Elgóibar ...10,847..A 5
El Puerto de Santa María ...35,505..D 3
El Rosario* 8,118..F 11
El Viso del Alcor* ....9,774..D 4
Espejo* .....8,006..D 4
Esplugas* ..12,393..B 8
Estella ......8,236..A 5
Estepa ......9,476..D 4
Estepona ..13,231..D 4
Fabero ......8,141..A 3
Felanitx ...11,797..C 8
Fene .......9,267..A 2
Fernán-Núñez ...11,796..D 4
Figueras ...17,548..A 8
Fonsagrada 12,423..A 3
Forcarey* ...8,079..A 2
Foz ..........8,369..A 3
Fraga .......8,691..B 7
Fregenal de la Sierra .10,498..C 3
Friol .......9,110..A 3
Fuengirola* .8,492..D 4
Fuente-Alamo ....9,506..D 6
Fuente de Cantos ....8,941..C 3
Fuente del Maestre ...8,068..C 3
Fuenteovejuna .....14,887..C 4
Fuente Palmera* .9,002..D 4
Fuenterrabía* ......8,581..A 6
Fuentes de Andalucía* 9,969..D 4
Galdácano* 10,431..A 5
Gáldar ....16,160..F 12
Gandía ....20,340..C 6
Gavá* .....15,725..B 8
Gerona ....32,784..B 8
Getafe .....21,895..B 5
Gibraleón ...8,865..D 3
Gijón .....124,714..A 4
Ginzo de Limia .....9,680..A 3
Gondomar* ..8,133..A 2
Grado ......16,343..A 3
Granada ..157,663..D 5
Granadilla* .8,552..F 11
Granollers .20,194..B 8
Guadalajara 21,230..B 5
Guadix ....24,704..D 5
Guardo .....7,531..A 4
Guareña ....9,742..C 3
Guecho ....22,951..A 5
Guernica y Luno .....7,847..A 5
Guía de Gran Canaria* .11,963..F 12
Guía de Isora* ....7,858..F 11
Güímar* ...10,972..F 11
Guitiriz ....10,406..A 3
Haro .......8,554..A 5
Hellín .....27,242..C 6
Herencia ....8,606..C 5
Hernani ....13,080..A 6
Hinojosa del Duque ...14,767..C 4
Hornachuelos* ......7,894..D 4
Hospitalet .122,813..B 8
Huelma ....7,608..D 5
Huelva ....74,384..D 3
Huércal-Overa ....14,302..D 6
Huesca ....24,377..A 6
Huéscar ...11,198..D 5
Ibiza .......11,259..C 7
Icod* ......15,042..F 11
Igualada ..19,866..B 7
Illora ......14,179..D 5
Inca ........13,816..C 8
Infantes ....9,909..C 5
Ingenio ....10,899..G 12
Irún .........29,814..A 6
Isla-Cristina 12,330..D 3
Iznájar* ....11,711..D 4
Iznalloz ....7,964..D 5
Jaca .........9,856..A 6
Jaén .......64,917..D 5
Jaraiz .......8,130..B 4
Játiva ......19,896..C 6
Jerez de la Frontera 130,900..D 3
Jerez de los Caballeros ....19,268..C 3
Jimena de la Frontera .11,056..D 4
Jódar .......14,424..D 5
Jumilla ....21,590..C 6
La Algaba* .8,507..D 4
La Bañeza ..8,325..A 4
La Calzada de Calatrava ......8,513..C 5
La Cañiza* .8,221..A 2
La Carlota* 10,611..D 4
La Carolina 12,854..C 5
La Coruña 190,213..A 2
La Estrada 28,716..A 2
La Guardia .7,727..B 2
La Laguna 57,344..F 11
Lalín ......19,627..A 2
La Línea ..59,456..D 4
La Orotava 22,371..F 11
La Palma ...8,669..D 3
La Pola de Gordón ...8,607..A 4
La Puebla ..9,931..C 8
La Puebla de Cazalla* .11,374..D 4
La Puebla del Río* .12,612..D 3
La Puebla de Montalbán 7,700..C 4
Laracha ....12,708..A 2
La Rambla* 8,799..D 4
Laredo .....7,520..A 5
La Rinconada* ...13,757..D 4
La Roda ...12,190..C 5
Las Cabezas de San Juan* 8,463..D 4
La Solana .14,948..C 5
Las Palmas de Gran Canaria .205,302..F 12
La Unión ..11,687..D 6
Laviana ....14,946..A 4
Lebrija ....20,937..D 3
Leganés ....8,539..B 5
Lejona ......7,553..A 5
León .......73,483..A 4
Lepe ......10,038..D 3
Lérida .....63,850..B 7



*Does not appear on map; key shows general location.

Source: Latest census figures and official estimates.

# SPAIN MAP INDEX


Linares ....60,068..C 5
Liria .......9,723..C 6
Llanera* ...10,174..A 4
Llanes .....17,451..A 4
Llerena .....8,699..C 3
Llivia ........755..A 7
Lluchmayor 10,664..C 8
Logroño ...61,292..A 5
Loja .......25,976..D 4
Lora del Río 20,914..D 4
Lorca ......58,641..D 6
Los Barrios .8,844..D 4
Los Corrales* 8,111..A 4
Los Llanos* .9,886..F 11
Los Palacios y Villafranca ...12,524..D 4
Los Realejos* 17,777..F 11
Los Santos de Maimona ..9,565..C 3
Luanco ....12,426..A 4
Luarca .....25,211..A 3
Lucena .....28,287..D 4
Lugo ......58,264..A 3
Madrid ..2,443,152..B 5
Madridejos ..9,795..C 5
Mahón .....16,619..C 9
Mairena del Alcor .....8,665..D 4
Málaga ...307,162..D 4
Malagón ...11,208..C 5
Malpartida de Plasencia .8,114..C 3
Malpica* ....7,827..A 2
Manacor ...19,224..C 8
Mancha Real 7,855..D 5
Manises ....13,097..C 6
Manlleu ....9,410..A 8
Manresá ...52,216..B 7
Manzanares 17,847..C 5
Marbella ...12,069..D 4
Marchena ..20,600..D 4
Marín .....18,515..A 2
Marmolejo ..8,439..C 4
Martorell ...7,926..B 7
Martos .....23,990..D 5
Mataró ....41,128..B 8
Mazaricos* ..7,920..A 2
Mazarrón ...9,865..D 6
Medina del Campo ...14,327..B 4
Medina Sidonia ..16,190..D 4
Mellid* .....8,659..A 2
Mérida .....34,297..C 3
Miajadas ....8,632..C 4
Mieres .....70,871..A 4
Minas de Ríotinto ..8,436..D 3
Miranda de Ebro .....27,881..A 5
Mislata* ...10,931..C 6
Moaña .....12,736..A 2
Molina de Segura ...16,308..C 6
Molins de Rey* .....10,191..B 8
Mollet* .....8,303..B 8
Moncada* ...8,667..C 6
Moncada y Reixach* 13,295..B 8
Mondoñedo ..8,010..A 3
Mondragón .14,148..A 5
Monesterio ..8,163..C 3
Monforte ..20,741..A 3
Monóvar ...10,393..C 6
Montefrío ..13,874..D 4
Montellano ..9,334..D 4
Montijo ....14,961..C 3
Montilla ...23,896..D 4
Montoro ....14,950..C 4
Monzón .....9,020..B 7
Mora .......10,657..C 5
Moral de Calatrava* 7,883..C 5
Moraleja ....8,248..B 3
Moratalla ..14,029..C 6
Morón ......35,248..D 4
Mos* ......10,014..A 2
Motril .....24,734..D 5
Moya* ......8,809..F 12
Mula ......14,721..C 6
Murcia ...257,895..D 6
Muros .....10,029..A 2
Narón .....16,436..A 2
Navalmoral de la Mata ...9,073..C 4
Navia .......8,150..A 3
Neda* ......8,865..A 2
Negreira ....8,538..A 2
Nerva ......12,686..D 3
Nigrán* .....8,085..A 2
Níjar ......11,559..D 5
Nogueira ...7,518..A 3
Novelda ....12,911..C 6
Noya ......12,241..A 2
Nules .......8,460..C 6
Oleiros ....10,310..A 2
Olesa de Montserrat* ....7,717..B 7
Oliva ......14,579..C 6
Oliva de la Frontera 11,312..C 3
Olivenza ...12,956..C 3
Olot .......17,185..A 8
Olvera .....10,982..D 4
Oñate* .....8,432..A 5
Onda ......12,414..C 6
Onteniente .18,787..C 6
Ordenes ....11,770..A 2
Orense .....64,153..A 3
Orihuela ...44,830..C 6
Ortigueira ..20,391..A 3
Ortuella* ...7,611..A 5
Osuna .....20,775..D 4
Outes ......10,734..A 2
Oviedo ....132,759..A 4
Padrón* ....8,170..A 2
Palafrugell ..9,123..B 8
Palamós ....7,639..B 8
Palas de Rey 8,674..A 3
Palencia ...48,216..A 4
Palma del Río ......18,757..D 4
Palma de Mallorca 164,963..C 8
Pamplona .105,397..A 6
Pantón* ....8,439..A 3
Paradas* ...9,940..D 4
Pasajes ....15,036..A 6
Paterna ....16,951..C 6
Pedro Muñoz 8,155..C 5
Pego .......8,291..C 6
Peñarroya-Pueblonuevo ....24,152..C 4
Petrel .....10,615..C 6
Picasent ....8,433..C 6
Piélagos ....9,710..A 5
Pilas* ......8,604..D 3
Piloña ....14,707..A 4
Pinos Puente 13,915..D 5
Plasencia ..21,297..B 3
Pola de Allande ...7,862..A 3
Pola de Lena ....16,457..A 4
Pola de Siero ....34,574..A 4
Pollensa ....8,975..C 8
Ponferrada 37,053..A 3
Pontevedra .50,483..A 2
Porcuna ...10,516..D 4
Porriño* ....9,128..A 2
Portugalete .22,584..A 5
Porzuna .....8,189..C 4
Posadas .....8,999..D 4
Pozo Alcón ..8,148..D 5
Pozoblanco .16,020..C 4
Pozuelo de Alarcón ..9,412..B 5
Prat del Llobregat* ..14,131..B 8
Pravia .....11,421..A 3
Priego de Córdoba .25,168..D 4
Puenteáreas 14,552..A 2
Puente Ceso .8,480..A 2
Puentedeume 8,201..A 2
Puente-Genil ....30,185..D 4
Puentes de García Rodríguez .8,317..A 3
Puerto de la Cruz .....15,248..F 11
Puerto del Son .....10,598..A 2
Puertollano 53,136..C 4
Puerto Real 18,138..D 3
Quesada ...10,997..D 5
Quintana de la Serena .7,861..C 4
Quintanar de la Orden ..9,483..C 5
Redondela .17,206..A 2
Reinosa ....10,044..A 4
Rentería ...18,642..A 6
Requena ...18,933..C 6
Reus .......41,014..B 7
Rianjo .....10,484..A 2
Ribadavia ...7,571..A 2
Ribadeo .....9,138..A 3
Ribadesella .7,845..A 4
Ripoll ......9,034..A 8
Ronda .....28,831..D 4
Rota .......16,856..D 3
Rubí* .......9,907..B 8
Rute .......13,106..D 4
Sabadell ..105,152..B 8
Sagunto ...40,293..C 6
Salamanca .90,498..B 4
Salas ......11,977..A 3
Sallent .....9,227..B 7
Salobreña ...8,319..D 5
Salvatierra de Miño .....9,266..A 2
Sama .......65,860..A 4
San Adrián de Besós* 15,801..B 8
San Andrés del Rabanedo .......7,680..A 4
San Bartolomé .....13,384..G 12
San Baudilio de Llobregat* ...19,968..B 8
San Cugat* 11,884..B 8
San Felíu de Guixols ..10,307..B 8
San Felíu de Llobregat* 10,201..B 8
San Fernando 52,389..D 3
San Javier .10,284..D 6
San Juan de Aznalfarache* ...10,533..D 3
San Lorenzo de el Escorial ..7,965..B 4
San Martin del Rey Aurelio ...28,258..A 4
San Mateo* .8,538..F 12
San Nicolás* 8,546..G 12
San Roque .17,126..D 4
San Salvador del Valle* .9,477..A 5
San Sebastián ....140,893..A 6
San Sebastián de la Gomera ...7,577..F 11
San Vicente de Alcántara ......9,652..C 3
San Vicente de Baracaldo ....77,802..A 5
San Vicente del Raspeig ...8,951..C 6
Sangenjo ...11,027..A 2
Sanlúcar de Barrameda ..40,335..D 3
Santa Brígida* ..8,814..F 12
Santa Coloma de Gramanet 32,590..B 8
Santa Comba ...12,115..A 2
Santa Cruz de la Palma 12,967..F 11
Santa Cruz de Mudela ...8,740..C 5
Santa Cruz de Tenerife .....141,557..F 11
Santa Eugenia de Ribeira ....20,697..A 2
Santa Lucía 11,081..G 12
Santafé .....9,803..D 5
Santander .122,630..A 5
Santiago ...57,165..A 2
Santiago de la Espada* ..8,386..C 5
Santisteban del Puerto 7,851..C 5
Santoña ....9,082..A 5
Santurce-Antiguo .25,570..A 5
Saragossa (Zaragoza) ...343,468..B 6
Sarria .....14,759..A 3
Saviñao ....12,083..A 3
Segorbe .....7,538..C 6
Segovia ....33,360..B 4
Sestao* ....24,992..A 5
Seville (Sevilla) 459,786..D 4
Silla .......7,768..C 6
Silleda .....11,758..A 2
Sitges .....10,491..B 7
Sober* .....8,064..A 3
Socuéllamos 14,828..C 5
Sóller ......9,473..C 8
Soria ......19,301..B 5
Sueca ......20,612..C 6
Tabernes de Valldigna 12,890..C 6
Tacoronte ..10,282..F 11
Talavera de la Reina ...31,900..C 4
Tarancón ...7,714..B 5
Tarazona de Aragón ..12,059..B 6
Tarifa .....18,042..D 4
Tarragona .43,519..B 7
Tarrasa ....92,234..B 8
Telde ......32,177..F 12
Teo* ........9,848..A 2
Teror* .......8,545..F 12
Teruel .....19,776..B 6
Tineo ......20,347..A 3
Tobarra ....11,114..C 6
Tocina* .....8,553..D 4
Toledo .....40,651..C 4
Tolosa .....16,281..A 5
Tomelloso ..27,815..C 5
Tomiño ......9,817..B 2
Toro .......10,218..B 4
Torre del Campo* ..10,584..D 5
Torredonjimeno ...14,204..D 5
Torrejón de Ardoz ...10,794..B 5
Torrelavega 31,021..A 4
Torrente ...24,042..C 6
Torre-Pacheco .11,184..D 6
Torreperogil* 9,606..C 5
Torrevieja ...9,234..D 6
Torrox .....8,069..D 5
Tortosa ....43,267..B 7
Totana .....14,281..D 6
Touro* ......7,774..A 2
Trujillo ....13,326..C 4
Tudela .....16,456..A 6
Túy .......12,671..A 2
Úbeda .....28,956..C 5
Ubrique .....9,669..D 4
Utiel ......12,542..C 6
Utrera .....41,126..D 4
Valdepeñas 25,706..C 5
Valdoviño ...7,982..A 2
Valencia ..503,358..C 6
Valencia de Alcántara 13,159..C 3
Valladolid 159,135..B 4
Vall de Uxó 18,596..C 6
Valls ......11,886..B 7
Valverde del Camino ..10,843..D 3
Vejer de la Frontera .13,553..D 4
Vélez-Málaga .35,061..D 4
Vélez Rubio 8,415..D 5
Vergara ....13,162..A 5
Verín .......9,063..B 3
Viana del Bollo .....9,062..A 3
Vich ......20,303..B 8
Vigo ......144,914..A 2
Viladecáns* .7,508..B 8
Villablino ..15,529..A 3
Villacañas .10,113..C 5
Villacarrillo 15,683..C 5
Villa de Cruces ...11,223..A 2
Villa del Río* 8,290..D 4
Villafranca de los Barros ...15,447..C 3
Villafranca del Panadés .11,985..B 7
Villagarcía de Arosa .20,771..A 2
Villajoyosa 11,006..C 6
Villalba ...20,264..A 3
Villamartín 11,069..D 4
Villanueva de Arosa* 12,163..A 2
Villanueva de Córdoba .15,719..C 4
Villanueva del Arzobispo 12,451..C 5
Villanueva de la Serena ...20,812..C 4
Villanueva del Río y Minas ...14,313..D 4
Villanueva y Geltrú ...25,669..B 7
Villarreal de los Infantes .24,516..C 6
Villarrobledo ....21,356..C 5
Villarrubia de los Ojos 9,043..C 5
Villaviciosa 20,333..A 4
Villena ....21,934..C 6
Vimianzo ...9,803..A 2
Vinaroz ....10,968..B 7
Vitoria ....73,701..A 5
Vivero .....13,274..A 3
Yecla ......20,999..C 6
Yeste .......8,992..C 5
Zafra ......10,723..C 3
Zalamea de la Serena .8,543..C 4
Zamora ....42,060..B 4
Zaragoza, see Saragossa
Zarauz ......8,272..A 5
Zas .........8,098..A 2
Zújar .......8,778..D 5


## Physical Features


Agueda R. .........B 3
Alagón R. .........B 3
Alberche R. .......B 4
Alborán, Isla del (Isl.) ...........E 5
Albuferan Lagoon ...C 6
Alcanadre R. ......B 6
Almanzora R. ......D 5
Almería R. ........D 5
Almonte R. ........C 4
Araduey R. ........B 4
Aragón R. .........A 6
Arga R. ...........A 6
Arlanza R. ........A 5
Arlanzón R. .......A 4
Bay of Biscay .....A 4
Bay of Gibraltar ....D 4
Biscay, Bay of .....A 4
Bullaque R. ........C 4
Cabrera Isl. ........C 8
Cabriel R. .........C 6
Cape Creus .........A 8
Cape de Gata ......D 5
Cape Finisterre ....A 2
Cape Nao ..........C 7
Cape Ortegal .......A 3
Cape Palos .........D 6
Cape Peñas .........A 4
Cape Salinas .......C 8
Cape Tortosa .......B 7
Cape Trafalgar .....D 3
Carrión R. .........A 4
Céa R. .............A 4
Cega R. ............B 5
Cordillera Cantábrica (Mts.) .A 4
Duero (Douro) R. ..B 4
Duratón R. ........B 5
Ebro R. ...........B 6
Ega R. ............A 5
Ería R. ...........A 3
Esgueva R. ........B 4
Esla R. ...........B 4
Finisterre, Cape ....A 2
Formentera (Isl.) ....C 7
Fuerteventura (Isl.) F 12
Gallego R. ..........A 6
Gallo R. ............B 6
Genil R. ............D 4
Gibraltar, Strait of .E 4
Giguela R. ........C 5
Gomera (Isl.) .....F 11
Gran Canaria (Isl.) G 12
Guadalhorce R. ....D 4
Guadalope R. ......B 6
Guadalquivir R. ....D 3
Guadiana R. .......C 4
Guadiana Menor R. D 5
Guadiela R. .......B 5
Gulf of Alicante .....C 6
Gulf of Almería .....D 5
Gulf of Cádiz ......D 3
Gulf of Mazarron ..D 6
Gulf of San Jorge ...B 7
Henares R. ........B 5
Hierro (Isl.) .......G 10
Huerva R. .........B 6
Ibiza (Isl.) .........C 7
Jabalón R. .........C 5
Jalón R. ...........B 6
Jandula R. ........C 5
Jarama R. .........B 5
Jiloca R. ..........B 6
Júcar R. ...........C 5
Lago Nava (Lake) ..A 4
Laguna de la Janda D 4
La Mancha (Region) C 5
Lanzarote (Isl.) ....F 12
La Sagra (Mtn.) ...D 5
Las Marismas (Mts.) D 3
Llobregat R. .......B 7
Málaga Bay ........D 4
Mallorca (Isl.) .....C 8
Mar Menor (Lagoon) D 6
Menorca (Isl.) ......C 9
Mijares R. .........B 6
Miño R. ...........A 3
Moncayo (Mtn.) ....B 6
Montes de Toledo (Mts.) ............C 4
Montes Universales .B 6
Montserrat (Mtn.) ..B 7
Mulhacén (Mtn.) ...D 5
Nalón R. ..........A 3
Navia R. ..........A 3
Odiel R. ..........D 3
Orbigo R. .........A 4
Palma (Isl.) .......F 11
Peña Roya (Mtn.) .B 6
Peñalara (Mtn.) ....B 5
Perdido (Mtn.) .....A 7
Pico de Aneto (Peak) A 7
Pico de Teide (Peak) F 11
Pisuerga R. ........A 4
Plaza del Moro Almanzor (Mtn.) ..B 4
Punta Marroqui (Pt.) ...........D 4
Pyrenees (Mts.) ....A 6
Riaza R. ..........B 5
Río Tinto .........D 3
Sangonera R. ......D 5
Segre R. ..........B 7
Segura R. .........C 5
Serranía de Cuenca (Mts.) ..........B 5
Sierra de Gata (Mts.) B 3
Sierra de Gredos (Mts.) ..........B 4
Sierra de Guadalupe C 4
Sierra de Guadarrama (Mts.) B 5
Sierra de Guara ....A 6
Sierra de Gúdar ....B 6
Sierra de la Demanda (Mts.) ..A 5
Sierra de Peña Negra (Mts.) .....A 3
Sierra Morena (Mts.) D 4
Sierra Nevada ......D 5
Sil R. ............A 3
Tajo (Tagus) R. .....C 4
Tajuna R. .........B 5
Tambre R. .........A 2
Tejo R. ...........C 3
Teleño (Mtn.) ......A 3
Tenerife (Isl.) .....F 11
Ter R. ............A 8
Tietar R. ..........C 4
Tórmes R. .........B 3
Torre de Cerredo (Mtn.) ..........A 4
Trabancos R. ......B 4
Turia R. ..........C 6
Ulla R. ...........A 2
Yéltes R. .........B 3


*Does not appear on map; key shows general location.

Source: Latest census figures and official estimates.

**Spain's Location** in southwestern Europe's warm, sunny climate has made outdoor activities popular. Many towns, including Málaga, *left*, have large bullfighting arenas.

Silberstein, Monkmeyer

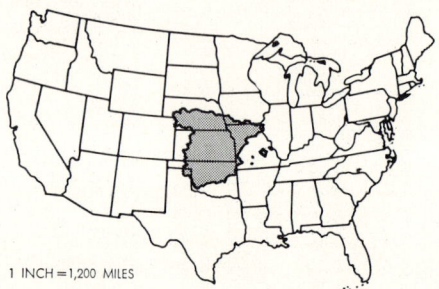

**The United States Is Over 12 Times as Large as Spain.**

from Spain to Italy in 218 B.C. The Spanish village of Llivia lies near the pass, but is entirely surrounded by France. An error in the Treaty of the Pyrenees between France and Spain in 1659 left the village north of the Spanish border. The Cantabrian Mountains extend 300 miles westward from the Pyrenees to the Galician Mountains. The Galicians border the rest of the northern coast.

The second line of mountains runs west to east through central Spain. It includes the Sierra de Gata, Sierra de Gredos, and Sierra de Guadarrama.

The third line of mountains is the steep Sierra Nevada, which borders the southern Mediterranean Coast. It includes 11,424-foot Mulhacén, the tallest peak in Spain. In the east, the range sinks beneath the Mediterranean. The Balearic Islands, farther east, are peaks of this same range.

**Coastline.** Steep cliffs jut from the sea along much of Spain's 1,698-mile coastline. The coast has few natural harbors except in the northwest. The chief gulfs include Cádiz in the southwest, Alicante in the southeast, and Valencia on the east coast.

**Rivers and Lakes.** Four of Spain's great rivers rise in the Meseta plateau and flow into the Atlantic Ocean.

The Duero and Tagus rivers flow west through Portugal. The Guadiana River turns south when it reaches the Portuguese border and then flows into the Atlantic. The Guadalquivir River flows south through the olive-producing region of Andalusia on its way to the ocean. It is the deepest river in Spain, and the only one on which large ships can sail. The prefix *Guad* appears in the names of several Spanish rivers. It comes from the Arabic word *wadi*, which means a stream bed that is dry except during the rainy season.

The Ebro River rises in the Cantabrian Mountains and flows east to the Mediterranean Sea. Melting snows of the nearby Pyrenees provide water that helps irrigate the Ebro Valley and make its soil fertile.

Spain has a number of small mountain lakes, and many salt ponds on the Meseta. The only large bodies of water are three lagoons. The Laguna de la Janda lies near Cádiz, the Albufera near Valencia, and the Mar Menor near Murcia.

**Natural Resources.** The soil is the country's greatest natural resource, but much topsoil has been lost through erosion. Farmers irrigate their land to increase its productivity. The finest forests grow in the western Pyrenees and in the Cantabrian Mountains. The most valuable trees include the cork oak and the Spanish chestnut. Central Spain has few trees. Thick forests once covered much of the country, but wasteful use of the timber destroyed them. The government began a reforestation program in the 1950's. It has supervised the planting of several hundred thousand acres of trees, and built about 150 irrigation dams.

The Cantabrian Mountains yield high-grade iron ore. Spain also has large deposits of high-grade coal, potash, mercury, and wolframite (a source of tungsten).

576d

Other minerals include cobalt, copper, lead, lignite, manganese, phosphorus, pyrites, salt, silver, sulfur, tin, and zinc.

**Climate.** Northern Spain has bleak, damp winters with great storms and many cloudy days. In January, the temperatures average about 49° F. The cool summers have ample rainfall that keeps the northern valleys green. July temperatures average around 64° F. About 60 inches of rain falls annually in the north.

Few parts of Europe have greater extremes of weather than the Meseta, largely because of the height of its central plain. Winters are dry and windy, with an average January temperature of 41° F. In summer, the blazing sun makes the Meseta hot and dusty, and the July temperatures average 78° F. The Meseta has an average annual rainfall of 18 inches.

The southern and eastern coasts have mild winters, with January temperatures averaging about 50° F. The coastal plains of this region are the warmest sections of the country. July temperatures average about 80°F. A withering, scorching wind called the *solano* may blow over the coastal plains for two weeks at a time. Rainfall seldom totals more than 14 inches a year on these plains, and farmers must irrigate most of their land.

### Life of the People

Spain has a population of about 32,918,000. The country has an average of 169 persons to the square mile. The provinces of Barcelona, Madrid, and Valencia have the most people. About 65 of every 100 persons in Spain live on farms or in towns that have no more than 50,000 population.

The first people to live in Spain were Iberians, a European people who were probably related to early tribes of France, Italy, and the British Isles. They mixed with the later invaders of Spain, including Celts, Carthaginians, Romans, Teutons, and Moors.

**Language.** The people speak Castilian Spanish. There are three chief regions where the people also speak a second language or dialect. The people of the Catalonia region speak *Catalan*, a language that resembles the Provençal tongue of southern France. In the region of Galicia, the people speak *Galician*, a dialect of Portuguese. The Basque language, spoken in the Basque provinces, is not known to be related to any other language.

Many common English words come from Spanish, including *cigar*, *cork*, *embargo*, *mosquito*, and *ranch*. Colorado, Florida, Los Angeles, and many other places in the United States have Spanish names. In Latin America, Spanish is the official language of 18 republics, and many places have Spanish names. See SPANISH LANGUAGE.

**Way of Life.** The Spanish mother usually manages the home and family affairs. But in recent years, women have also entered the business and professional fields. Many Spaniards still eat lunch at about 2 or 3 P.M., and then take a nap. But this napping custom, called *siesta*, is gradually disappearing. Dinner may be served any time between 10 P.M. and midnight.

Spanish law requires companies to pay their employees 14-months' salary every year. However, the average annual income is only about $517. The extra salary is paid for summer vacations, and for the New Year's holiday and *Reyes* (January 6), when Spanish children receive their Christmas presents. This feast day honors *Los Reyes Magos*, the three wise men.

*Shelter.* The people usually build their homes of brick or stone, and often whitewash the outside walls. Many houses rise straight from the street, or from a narrow sidewalk, and have iron grillwork over the windows. Courtyards with beautiful trees, fountains, and flowers add beauty to many homes. Gently sloping tile roofs cover most of the houses in northern Spain. The flat roofs on many southern homes provide places where the people can spend the cooler hours after hot days. People of southern Spain sometimes make their homes in caves. These caves are cool in summer and warm in winter. Some of the caves are well furnished and have electricity.

*Food.* Spaniards enjoy seafood, and serve it in a variety of ways. One favorite dish, *paella valenciana*, combines rice, saffron, lobster or shrimp, chicken, and vegetables. Other dishes include eels, skates, squids, crabs, and sardines. Veal appears on Spanish menus more often than beef. There is so little pasture land that it is too expensive to feed steers. Other popular meats include rabbit, chicken, lamb, pork, and goat.

A spicy, cold soup called *gazpacho* includes strained tomatoes, cucumbers, olive oil, and spices. Dried legumes, such as beans, peas, lentils, and chick-peas, form a basic part of the Spanish diet. Bakers make bread from white wheat flour, and prepare it in a round or oval shape. The people often eat goat's-milk cheese with bread. They enjoy oranges, figs, grapes, apples, peaches, strawberries, melons, and other fruits. Spanish cooks use olive oil rather than butter or other fats. They sometimes flavor foods with garlic, onions, and pimentos.

Every region produces wine. The area around the city of Jerez de la Frontera is the producer of the original sherry wine. Favorite beverages include strong, black coffee and thick, hot chocolate, usually served with fried strips of dough called *churros*. Spanish children enjoy *helado* (ice cream) in various flavors.

*Clothing* in the cities and towns resembles that worn in North America. Few persons wear hats. A Spanish woman wears a square veil of black lace called a *mantilla* on her head when she goes to church. Women often carry lace or paper fans in warm weather. They also like to wear flowers in their hair.

In country districts, women usually wear plain, black dresses or loose, full skirts and blouses made of dark cotton. They may wear squares of cotton cloth tied around their heads. Woolen shawls are worn in cool weather. Men wear cotton trousers and shirts, and dark, wool berets or straw hats. They use sashes called *fajas* instead of belts. Men, women, and children in small towns and on farms often go barefooted, or wear *alpargatas*. These are cheap canvas sandals with braided rope soles.

On fiesta days and holidays, people often wear the traditional, gay-colored costumes worn in Spain hundreds of years ago (see CLOTHING [color picture: Europe]).

*Religion.* About 95 of every 100 persons in Spain belong to the Roman Catholic Church. It is the state church, and receives financial aid from the government. According to the 1966 Organic Law, the state assumes the protection of religious freedom. The 1967 Relig-

Silberstein, Monkmeyer

**Sheep Raising Is an Important Occupation** in the flat Mancha region south of Madrid and on the high plain of Estremadura near Portugal. Windmills often supply water for the livestock.

ious Liberty Law grants non-Catholic religious groups such rights as holding public services and owning their church property. But they cannot do missionary work in Spain, and only Roman Catholic marriages are legal.

*Recreation.* Spaniards spend much of their leisure time outdoors. They like to sit for hours visiting or doing business at sidewalk cafés, or in *plazas* (town squares). Almost everyone takes a *paseo*, or walk, every evening before dinner. In small villages, so many people crowd the narrow streets at this time that they often block traffic. On the wide, tree-lined city streets, vendors sell flowers, candy, pastries, soft drinks, ices, or lottery tickets as they stroll among the crowds.

The excitement of the bullfight makes it the best-known spectacle in Spain. Most cities have bull rings, and leading matadors are national heroes. See BULLFIGHTING.

Many colorful Roman Catholic festivals take place during the year. Night celebrations called *verbenas* are held on the evenings before religious holidays. They include fireworks, music, and all-night dancing. Ornamental tapestries, flowers, and ribbons decorate the houses and streets on these occasions.

Hundreds of persons may go on a *romería* (excursion) to a religious shrine or scenic area. They ride in carts drawn by donkeys, and may spend several days picnicking and merrymaking. Religious celebrations called *fallas* take place in cities. They honor patron saints, and include parades, bonfires, street dancing, beauty contests, and battles of flowers. During fallas, which last several days, some city streets are closed to traffic and filled with huge papier-mâché figures. At the end of a falla, the townspeople set the paper figures afire.

Almost all Spaniards celebrate Holy Week at Easter time. The processions in Seville are especially colorful. At the feast of Corpus Christi, usually celebrated in June, some towns collect millions of flower petals of various colors. They use the petals to make a beautifully patterned carpet leading from the local church into the street. Some of these carpets stretch more than a quarter of a mile. A procession, headed by a priest carrying a consecrated wafer, passes over the carpet. Behind come giant figures mounted on wagons. After the procession, the people gather in the square for dancing. At the fiesta of San Fermín, in July, the people of Pamplona turn bulls loose in the streets during part of the festivities. The young men of the town then act as amateur bullfighters.

Spain's many historic and beautiful places attract thousands of visitors every year. The government operates inns called *paradores* and *albergues* for travelers. Paradores are usually in out-of-the-way, scenic spots, and frequently are remodeled parts of ancient castles and monasteries. Albergues resemble American motels, and stand along the main highways.

San Sebastián, one of the finest seaside resorts, is on the Bay of Biscay. This city also serves as Spain's summer capital during August and September, the hottest months in Madrid. The Costa Brava, another popular resort area, stretches along the Mediterranean Coast from 40 miles north of Barcelona to the French border. Torremolinos, south of Málaga, offers swimming and other warm weather sports during the winter months.

Favorite sports include soccer and jai alai (see JAI ALAI). People enjoy skiing in the Pyrenees, skin diving off the coast of Majorca in the Balearic Islands, hunting wild boar and deer in the southwest, and fishing in the inland rivers.

**Cities.** Spain has about 60 cities with populations of over 50,000. Most of them lie within 50 miles of the coast. Narrow streets, lined with buildings that stand close together, wind through the older sections of the cities. The newer sections have broad, tree-shaded streets, parks, and modern buildings.

The usual office hours in Spain are from 10 A.M. to 2 P.M. and from 6 P.M. to 9 P.M. During July, August, and September, many offices are open only from 8 A.M. to 2 P.M., because of the great heat.

The cities of the south, such as Córdoba, Granada, and Seville, show the influence of the Moors who once lived in this region. The stone buildings have iron balconies that overlook narrow streets. Some buildings surround beautiful courtyards and fountains. The northern cities generally have more manufacturing than those in the south. See the separate articles on Spanish cities listed in the *Related Articles* at the end of this article.

**Country Life.** Spanish farmers usually live in neat, clean villages and small towns, rather than on their farms. Every morning and evening farm workers crowd the dirt roads between the farm and towns. They travel on foot or in donkey carts.

Activity in the towns centers in a town square where a Roman Catholic church usually stands. Farmers have open-air markets several days every week, spreading their produce on the ground. Houses usually are one story high, and many stand in long rows with no spaces between them. Village women gather at the community water wells to draw their supplies of water, or at irrigation ditches to wash their families' clothes. Water is so scarce in many places that men take cartloads of water-filled kegs and jugs from house to house for sale.

### Work of the People

About 45 of every 100 workers make their living from agriculture. About 35 of every 100 persons work in manufacturing plants.

**Agriculture** in Spain varies with the climate. Northwestern Spain, for example, has much rain and not much sunshine. Meadows and pastures suitable for cattle raising lie in this region. Goats graze on the higher slopes. The rest of the country has too much sunshine and not enough rain for growing crops without irrigation. The Moors first irrigated the Ebro Valley in the 800's, and it has been productive ever since. The rich Guadalquivir Valley near Seville, and the plain of Vega, south of Granada, have excellent irrigation systems. Streams furnish water for irrigation in the Valencia and Murcia regions. These regions have few crop failures.

Almost two-thirds of the cultivated land is tilled by the owner, either by himself or with the aid of hired day labor. Tenants and sharecroppers work the rest. In Andalusia, the *cortijos*, or plantations, often employ landless day laborers. These workers live in huts along the roads and sometimes try to make a living on as little as a hundred days of work a year.

Many farms have tractors, threshing machines, combines, binders, and, in some areas, mowing machines. But many farmers still cut their grain with scythes and sickles, and bind the bundles by hand. They drive horses or oxen around and around to tread out the grain from the straw on the threshing floor, then remove the straw with wooden pitchforks. Finally, they let the breeze separate the chaff from the heavier grain as they toss the mixture of the two into the air with wooden shovels. Work animals include mules, donkeys, oxen, and even cows in northern Spain. Fine saddle horses are found in the south, and some powerful work horses in Catalonia.

# SPAIN

Wheat is Spain's chief crop. It grows on more than 10 million acres, mostly on the plains of Aragon, Old Castile, Estremadura, and Andalusia. New Castile also is an excellent wheat area, except for a few dry sections. In these areas, farmers raise the famous Merino sheep (see SHEEP [Fine-Wooled Sheep]).

Rye and oats are often grown in the mountain areas. Rice comes chiefly from the lowlands of Valencia and the fertile Andalusian plain near Seville. Farmers grow much corn in northern Spain, where heavy rains fall. Barley thrives in sections with little rain. Cotton is raised in the south and southeast.

Farmers grow olives on about 5 million acres. Olives grow south of the Cantabrian Mountains in areas where the soil is too poor or the land too hilly for other crops. Spain produces some of the finest olives in the world, and is a leader in the production of olive oil. See OLIVE; OLIVE OIL.

Vineyards cover about 4 million acres, mostly in the south. Orange and lemon groves are found in eastern and southern Spain. Almonds and hazelnuts come from southern Spain and the Balearic Islands, and sweet chestnuts are raised in the mountains. Onions, tomatoes, beans, and sweet peppers grow in the regions of Valencia and Murcia. This area also produces delicious melons and figs. Silkworms are raised in southern Spain. Bananas and other tropical fruits come from the Canary Islands.

Many hillsides that would be useless for any other crops are planted in cork trees and produce a valuable export crop. Spain produces about a third of the world's cork supply. Esparto grass grows widely throughout the south. Its fibers are woven into rope. Other farm products include flax, hemp, silk, sugar, and tobacco.

The donkey is the best farm animal in the hot, dry regions. Goats are the chief milk-producing animals, because they are less expensive to keep than cows. The high plain of Estremadura makes a fine sheep-raising region. Farmers in Andalusia use some of their best pastures to raise bulls for bullfighting.

**Manufacturing and Processing.** Spain's largest manufacturing industries are in the northern provinces, which have the richest deposits of coal and iron. The principal manufactures include cotton goods, woolens, and laces. The textile industry centers in Barcelona, but about 3,000 textile mills are located throughout the country. Other mills in northern Spain produce linen, paper, leather, and tobacco products. Spain also produces many automobiles.

Silk weaving is important in the south, where silkworms are raised. Southern Spain also has glassmaking factories, sugar refineries, cement factories, aluminum plants, and iron and steel mills. Andalusia is the center of the olive-oil industry. Seville makes many of the cork products. Spain ranks third among the world's

# SPAIN

wine-producing countries. Wine is made throughout the country.

**Mining.** Spain produces about a third of the world's mercury. Most of it comes from mines near Almadén in south-central Spain. These mines have been worked for more than 2,000 years. Spanish miners produce more than 5,700,000 tons of iron ore a year, mainly from deposits in the Cantabrian Mountains. The country also produces about 17 million tons of coal a year. Pyrites, mined chiefly in the southwest, provide a source of copper and sulfur. Companies of other countries developed a large part of the mining in Spain. But the Spanish government owns and operates the mercury and salt-mining industries and a number of other mining interests. Salt is mined near Santander, and obtained from the salt marshes of Cádiz and along the Mediterranean Coast.

**Fishing Industry.** Spain ranks among the leading European countries in the amount of fish caught. The average annual catch of more than 1,200,000 tons consists chiefly of cod, herring, and tuna. Thousands of persons work in fish-canning factories.

**Electric Power.** Spain has harnessed the water power of many of its mountain streams to produce electricity. The country has more than 1,200 hydroelectric stations. Spain's annual production of electric energy is more than 31 billion kilowatt-hours.

**Trade.** Spain trades mostly with the United States, Great Britain, West Germany, France, Argentina, and Cuba. It exports about the same value of goods that it imports. Principal imports include foodstuffs, livestock, machinery, coal, raw cotton, linen, motor vehicles, and drugs and chemicals. Wine is an important export. Other products shipped from the country include cork, metals, olives, grapes, citrus fruits, rice, sugar, glassware, pottery, wool, and cotton goods.

**Transportation.** Spain has more than 10,000 miles of railroads, all controlled by the government. The country has about 74,000 miles of roads, about two-thirds of which are paved. Spain has about 1½ million motor vehicles. Carts drawn by donkeys and wagons pulled by oxen still provide the most common means of transportation. Commercial airlines link the larger cities, and connect Spain with many other countries. Spain has about 2,000 freight-carrying ships. It has not developed a large merchant fleet, because the rugged coast has few good harbors and the rivers are shallow.

**Communication.** More than 25,000 miles of telegraph lines and over 2 million telephones serve the people. The country has about 90 radio stations. The first television station started operating in Madrid in 1956.

Spain has about 130 daily newspapers, published in 55 cities. They do not publish on Sunday evenings or Monday mornings. In about 30 cities, *Hojas del Lunes* (Monday Leaflets) are published. Spain's more than 170 magazines and journals are published chiefly in Madrid and Barcelona. These cities are also the main book-publishing centers.

## Education

**Schools.** The Roman Catholic Church exerts a powerful influence over Spanish education. The govern-

Pietzsch, Black Star

**Folk Dancers from Aragon** wear traditional costumes. Popular Spanish dances include the *bolero, fandango,* and *saraband.*

Three Lions

**Guitar Music** often accompanies Spanish dancers. Here a university student plays for dancers at a night festival in Seville.

ment requires all schools to offer courses of instruction in the Roman Catholic faith. Non-Catholics may be excused from religious classes in the public schools. But the law forbids any other faith to operate schools.

The law requires all Spanish children between the ages of 6 and 12 to attend school. But this law is only partially enforced because of the lack of schools and teachers, and poor transportation facilities. In spite of these handicaps, Spain has made progress in its battle against illiteracy. In 1900, about 63 of every 100 persons could not read or write. This figure was about 6 of every 100 by the late 1960's.

In 1955 the government ruled that every agricultural, industrial, and mining firm must set up a school for the children of its employees, if the number of children totals more than 30. The government ordered companies to organize night schools to teach illiterate employees how to read and write. Local taxes support the public schools, which are supervised by the government. The government supports special schools of engineering, agriculture, music, and fine arts.

About 60,000 students attend the 12 state universities. Leading universities include the University of Barcelona, founded in 1450; the University of Granada (1525); the University of Madrid (1499); the University of Salamanca (1223); and the University of Valencia (1245). The buildings of the University of Madrid were destroyed during the Spanish Civil War in the late 1930's, but they have been rebuilt.

**Libraries.** Spain has a number of important libraries and archives. Madrid has the National Library, the Library of the Athenaeum of Madrid, and the libraries of the Royal Academies of the Spanish Language, of History, of Jurisprudence (law), and of Moral and Political Sciences. The Hemeroteca Municipal of Madrid owns one of the most complete collections of periodicals in the world. Many records and important documents of Spain and Spanish America are preserved in the National Historical Archive of Madrid, in the Simancas Archive near Valladolid, and in the Archive of the Indies in Seville.

**Museums.** The *Museo del Prado* in Madrid has one of the world's greatest art collections. This museum includes paintings by the great Spanish artists Goya, Murillo, and Velázquez, and by many masters of other countries. The Duke of Alva Museum, also in Madrid, has portraits of the Duke of Alva and his relatives painted by Titian. In addition, it owns other paintings by Italian, Flemish, and Spanish artists. Madrid has the galleries of the Academy of San Fernando, the Museum of Modern Art, and the Galdiano Museum. In addition to its art museums, Madrid is the home of the Archaeological Museum, the Royal Armory (medieval armor and weapons), Museum of the Americas (archaeological), Army Museum, Naval Museum, Municipal Museum, and the Museum of Bullfighting.

In Seville, the art museum known as the *Casa Grande de la Merced* is one of the nation's finest. It has examples of the work of Zurbarán and Murillo. In the house and museum of El Greco in Toledo are 20 of his pictures.

### The Arts

**Painting.** Francisco Goya, Bartolomé Murillo, and Diego Velázquez gained world-wide fame as painters. El Greco was born in Greece, but he ranks as an important Spanish painter because he worked in Spain. Noted contemporary painters born in Spain include Salvador Dali, Juan Gris, Joan Miró, Pablo Picasso, and Tonio Tápies.

**Literature.** The first great Spanish writings were the *Cantar de Mio Cid* (*Poem of the Cid*) and *El Auto de los Reyes Magos* (*The Play of the Wise Men*). Scholars believe both date from the 1100's. But no one knows who wrote them. *Cantar de Mio Cid* tells the deeds of Spain's national hero *El Cid* (see CID, THE). Only part of *El Auto de los Reyes Magos* has been preserved. It tells of the visit of the three wise men, or Magi, to the Christ Child, and their report of Christ's birth to King Herod. Great literature came from Spain between 1550

Wide World

**Huge Papier-Mâché Figures** depicting Spanish life are common at festivals. This figure comments on the housing shortage.

and 1680. Lope de Vega wrote numerous plays, and Miguel de Cervantes wrote *Don Quixote*. In more recent times, Spain has produced many other famous writers and playwrights. See SPANISH LITERATURE.

**Music.** People in all parts of the world enjoy the vitality and rhythm of Spanish music. The early music was influenced by the rise of Christianity, and later by the Moors. In the 1600's, the *zarzuela* was introduced into the country. This is a type of opera in which the performers mix songs with spoken words. The name comes from the Palace of La Zarzuela near Madrid, where fiestas were held to entertain the royal court. Spain's national dances include the *bolero*, *flamenco*, *jota*, *fandango*, *saraband*, and *seguidilla*. The main musical instruments are the guitar, tambourine, castanets, and *gaita* (Spanish bagpipes). Spanish musicians include the

Three Lions

**World-Famous Lace** is made in Valencia and sold in the market place, *left.* A Basque fisherman, *below,* of north-central Spain, carries his fishing gear and boat oars.

Pazovski, Monkmeyer

composer Manuel de Falla, the cellist Pablo Casals, and the guitarist Andrés Segovia.

**Architecture** shows the influence of the various conquests of Spain by other peoples. Bridges and aqueducts built by the Romans can still be seen. The Moors also left their mark on Spanish architecture. The cathedral at Córdoba was built as a Moslem house of worship in the 700's, but became a Roman Catholic cathedral in 1238. More than 1,000 pillars of granite, marble, onyx, and jasper support its arches. It has a ceiling of carved cedar. Mosques built by the Moors still stand in many cities of southern Spain. Most of them are now Roman Catholic churches. The Moors also built fortified palaces called alcazars, in Spanish cities (see ALHAMBRA).

During the 1200's, Gothic architecture was introduced from France into Spain. The cathedral at Seville is one of the largest Gothic buildings in the world. It is 380 feet long and 250 feet wide, and its tower, called the Giralda, is 305 feet high. Some persons believe it contains the tomb of Christopher Columbus. However, the Dominican Republic claims that the body of Columbus rests in the Cathedral of Santo Domingo at Santo Domingo. Toledo's magnificent Gothic cathedral, built between 1227 and 1493, has paintings by El Greco, Goya, Raphael, Rubens, Titian, Velázquez, and Van Dyke. The cathedral has a chapel in which Mass is celebrated daily in accordance with the primitive Mozarabic ritual of Christians who lived for centuries under Moorish rule. The famous monastery of Montserrat stands on the side of a mountain about 2,400 feet above sea level near Barcelona (see MONTSERRAT).

Among Spain's other interesting buildings and monuments are about 1,400 castles. El Escorial, one of the world's largest buildings, stands 25 miles northwest of Madrid. This gray granite structure covers 396,782 square feet. It has 300 rooms, 86 staircases, 88 fountains, 16 interior courts, and 3 chapels. King Philip II built El Escorial in the 1500's as a combination palace, monastery, and burial place. The tombs of many Spanish monarchs are in El Escorial (see ESCORIAL). Four miles away is another burial place and monastery, the Valley of the Fallen. It lies on a granite mountain overlooking a deep, isolated valley. The government completed this memorial in 1956 after 15 years of construction work. Here are buried 150,000 men who died fighting for General Francisco Franco in the Spanish Civil War. A 500-foot-high cross, chiseled from a single piece of stone, stands atop the mountain. More than 250,000 cubic yards of granite had to be blasted out of the mountainside to form the underground sanctuary. Tunnels lead from the sanctuary to the burial chambers. Only the façade, or face of the structure, and plaza of the monument are outside the mountain.

### Government

The Spanish government is a fascist dictatorship (see FASCISM). The executive branch of the government, unlike that of most democratic countries, has the only real power. The *Cortes* (legislature) and the courts follow the dictator's wishes. Instead of a constitution, Spain has groups of basic laws. These include the Charter of the Privileges of the Spanish People, the Labor Charter, the Law of Succession, and the Organic Law of the Spanish State of 1966.

The Charter of the Privileges of the Spanish People includes a bill of rights. But one article specifies that the government may abolish freedom of speech, movement, residence, association, and other rights. The aim of the Labor Charter is to maintain and increase production by setting up a state-controlled trade-union plan. Under this system, industrial "unions" of owners, management, and workers (all within the same industry, and not according to type of job as in the unions of the United States) try to regulate competition and prevent strikes and slowdowns.

Spain has an important treaty with the Vatican. This treaty, called a *concordat*, states that Roman Catholicism shall be the only official religion, and that Roman Catholicism shall be taught in all the schools.

**Chief of State** of Spain is General Francisco Franco. His followers gave him the title of *El Caudillo*, or "The Leader," three years before he took office in 1939. Franco is also the head of the Falange Española, the only "political entity" permitted by the government. A cabinet of 19 members helps Franco direct the various departments of the government.

Franco declared in 1947 that Spain was to become a monarchy upon his death. The people voted approval of this Law of Succession in the same year. The Law of Succession, amended by the Organic Law in 1966, gave Franco the power to name his successor with the approval of the Cortes. In 1969, Franco nominated Prince Juan Carlos Bourbon to become king and chief of state when Franco dies or retires. The prince is the grandson of King Alfonso XIII, who abdicated in 1931. The Cortes approved the nomination.

**Cortes.** About 100 of the 563 members of the Cortes are elected by heads of families and married women. Over 100 are chosen by town, municipal, or provincial councils, and 150 are chosen by the nation's labor unions. The chief of state appoints 25 distinguished citizens. The remainder are members of the cabinet, members of the Falange National Council, heads of universities, representatives of professions, and officials of various cities and provinces. The Cortes does not have great power, and is subject to Franco's orders. A member is called a *procurador* (attorney).

Spain was the second European nation to have a parliament. A Cortes representing the nobility, the Roman Catholic Church, and elected delegates from the free towns met in León in 1188. This was 258 years after Iceland's first parliament met.

**Courts.** Spain's supreme tribunal meets in Madrid. It includes a president appointed by the government, and consists of eight high courts. Spain has 15 territorial courts that meet in the capitals of the country's 15 judicial districts. The capital of each province has a provincial court. There are 1,000 lower courts.

**Local Government.** Fifty of the 51 provinces have *Diputaciones Provinciales* (assemblies) which administer local matters. Spanish Sahara is under military rule. Councils are elected from three groups to govern cities and towns. These three groups are heads of families, the labor organizations, and economic, cultural, and professional organizations. Half the representatives of each group are elected to the councils every six years. Each of the Canary Islands has a governing body called a *Cabildo Insular*, which administers the island's affairs.

**Politics.** Spain has only one legal political organization, the Falange Española. A national council of about 150 members, headed by Franco, directs this "National Movement." Some of the members are elected, and the rest serve because of the offices they hold.

**National Defense.** All qualified men over the age of 21 must serve two years in the armed forces. Spain has an army of more than 300,000 men, a navy of about 40,000 men, and an air force of about 30,000 men.

**Taxation.** Spain receives about half its income from taxes on sales, personal incomes, and business profits. The government taxes the incomes of only the wealthier citizens. Most other revenue comes from government lotteries, and from the government-owned tobacco and gasoline industries.

### History

**Early Days.** The ancestors of present-day Spaniards probably lived in the region as long ago as the Old Stone Age. Paintings in caves at Altamira, in northern Spain, may be from 10,000 to 20,000 years old (see PAINTING [Prehistoric Painting]).

Spain's recorded history dates back to about 1100 B.C., when the Phoenicians began to establish colonies in the area. Many Phoenician cities still survive. Cádiz, believed to be the oldest city in Europe, was founded in 1130 B.C. Starting in 480 B.C., the Carthaginians conquered much of Spain. They used the country as a steppingstone to invade Italy. See ROMAN EMPIRE (Overseas Expansion).

**Roman Conquest.** During the Second Punic War (218-201 B.C.), the Romans drove the Carthaginians out of Spain and made the first complete conquest of the Iberian Peninsula. Roman legions conquered region after region, and stationed garrisons throughout the peninsula. Spain, then called *Hispania*, became Rome's first overseas colony. But the people were rebellious, and the Romans had continuous trouble with them. Even so, Spain became one of the most flourishing provinces of the Roman Empire. Great Roman cities developed, and many Romans spent their lives in Spain. The province became a center of Roman culture, and produced many of Rome's greatest writers, including Lucius Annaeus Seneca, Martial (Marcus Valerius Martialis), and Quintilian (Marcus Fabius Quintilianus). The Roman emperors Trajan, Hadrian, and Theodosius came from Spain.

**Germanic Era.** The Germanic tribes that invaded Italy and destroyed the Roman Empire also seized Spain. Three powerful Germanic tribes got through the northern mountain passes about A.D. 400, and burst into the peninsula. Two tribes, the Suevi from Germany and the Alans from southern Russia, conquered and settled Galicia and Portugal. King Gunderic led his Vandals down into central and southern Spain, and built a Vandal kingdom that reached from the Ebro River to Gibraltar. The Vandals named it *Vandalusia*. Southern Spain is still called *Andalusia*. See VANDAL.

Soon after the Vandals established a Spanish kingdom, the Germanic chieftain Wallia led a powerful Visigoth invasion of Spain in the early 400's. By 573, the Visigoths had conquered the entire peninsula, and had driven the Vandals into Africa. The Gothic conquerors became the chiefs and barons of Spain. The province of *Catalonia* was once called *Gatalonia*, or *Country of the Goths*. See GOTH.

**Moorish Control.** The Goths ruled Spain until the early 700's, when they were overwhelmed by a great Moorish invasion from Africa (see MOOR). Spain became a Moslem country except for the small Visigoth

# SPAIN

kingdoms of Aragon, Castile, Galicia, León, Murcia, and Navarre, which remained Christian.

The Moslem Moors had a far more advanced culture than most of feudal Europe. Under the Moors, Spain became more civilized than most other European countries. They made great changes in Spanish ways of life. For example, the Moors introduced an efficient irrigation system that still serves Spanish farmers.

The Moors gave the Moorish arch to Spanish architecture. Magnificent Moorish cities arose at Córdoba, Toledo, and Valencia. The Moors built some of the most beautiful buildings in the world at Granada. Under the Moors, the people of Toledo became famous for their flawless steel swords, inlaid with gold designs. Craftsmen in Córdoba gained fame throughout Europe for their beautiful leatherwork.

**Union of the Independent Kingdoms.** Ballads tell of the legendary deeds of *El Cid,* Spain's national hero, who lived during the 1000's. El Cid fought on both sides, for the Moors and for the Christian kings. While serving the Moorish king of Zaragoza, El Cid defeated the forces of several Christian noblemen. He conquered Valencia in 1094 for the Christians. El Cid became a symbol of the Christian reconquest of Spain.

In the late 1100's and early 1200's, most of Christian Spain joined in fighting the Moors. By 1276, the Moorish kingdom in Spain consisted only of the southern state of Granada. During the late 1300's and early 1400's, Castile became the most powerful kingdom in Spain. Aragon was another important Spanish kingdom. In 1469, Ferdinand of Aragon married Isabella, the Castilian king's half sister. In 1479, Ferdinand's father, the king of Aragon, died and Ferdinand became king. Isabella became the unquestioned queen of Castile that year. Castile and Aragon united, starting a process that continued until all the independent kingdoms in Spain had united as a single, powerful country.

Ferdinand and Isabella, who were Roman Catholics, wanted to make Spain a wholly Catholic country. Their determination started the Spanish Inquisition in 1480 (see INQUISITION). The Inquisition hunted down and imprisoned persons who were even remotely suspected of not believing Roman Catholic doctrine. It treated Jews and Moslems especially harshly. The Spaniards persecuted the Jews and drove them out of Spain. Spanish troops defeated the Moors at Granada in 1492, and Spain became an entirely Christian nation.

**"Mistress of the World."** In 1492, Ferdinand and Isabella gave Christopher Columbus the money to make the voyage on which he discovered America. Soon afterward, Spanish explorers claimed the territories that now include Mexico, Central America, Cuba, Jamaica, and the Dominican Republic. They also established claims to the land that became the states of California, New Mexico, and Texas, and all South America except Brazil, a Portuguese colony. Hernando Cortes conquered Mexico, Vasco Núñez de Balboa became the first European to see the eastern shores of the Pacific Ocean, and Hernando de Soto discovered the Mississippi River. For more information on these Spanish conquests and explorations, see the history sections of CENTRAL AMERICA; LATIN AMERICA.

Spanish troops extended Spanish conquests to North Africa in the early 1500's, and to Naples and Parma in Italy. Through the marriage of Juana of Castile (1479-1555) and Philip, Archduke of Austria (1478-1506), Spain inherited The Netherlands in 1506. Spain claimed the Philippines in 1521, and conquered Portugal in 1580. It also seized the present Spanish province of Navarre, the French province of Roussillon, and Naples, Sicily, Sardinia, and the Canary and Balearic islands. During this period, Spain was called "the mistress of the world and the queen of the ocean."

**The Spanish Decline.** Spain enjoyed only a short period of glory. The errors of the proud Philip II marked the beginning of the nation's downfall. The people of The Netherlands revolted against Spain in 1568, and declared their independence in 1581. See NETHERLANDS (Freedom from Spain).

In 1588, Philip launched his great Spanish Armada of 130 warships in an attempt to conquer England. Spain's prestige suffered greatly when the British defeated the Armada (see ARMADA).

Spanish power declined steadily during the 1600's. Revolts, religious persecutions, bankruptcy, and civil war weakened the kingdom. The Portuguese drove the Spaniards out of Portugal in 1640. Spain lost the War of the Spanish Succession in 1714, and had to surrender Naples, Parma, Sardinia, and Milan to Austria. The kingdom of Savoy took Sicily, and England seized Gibraltar and the island of Minorca in the Balearic Islands. See SUCCESSION WARS.

**Wars with Great Britain.** In 1779, Spain declared war against Great Britain as an ally of France. Spain gave financial aid to the American colonies in order to

---
### RED-LETTER DATES IN SPAIN
---

1100's B.C. The Phoenicians began colonizing Spain.
480 B.C. The Carthaginians conquered Spain.
201 B.C. The Romans seized Spain.
A.D. 573 Germanic tribes took Spain from the Romans.
711 The Moors invaded and conquered Spain.
1200's Spain's Christian kingdoms took control of Moorish Spain except for Granada.
1479 Castile and Aragon united as a single kingdom.
1480-1834 The Inquisition persecuted non-Catholics.
1492 The Spaniards conquered Granada, the last Moorish stronghold in Spain. Christopher Columbus discovered America and claimed it for Spain.
1500's The Spanish Empire expanded to include the Philippines, most of South America, and parts of North America and Africa.
1588 English ships defeated the Spanish Armada.
1808 Napoleon invaded and conquered Spain.
1813 England and Spain drove the French out of Spain.
1810-1824 Spain's colonies in the Americas revolted and declared their independence.
1898 Spain lost Cuba, Puerto Rico, and the Philippines in the Spanish-American War.
1923 Primo de Rivera declared himself dictator, and ruled the country until 1930.
1936-1939 The Spanish Civil War raged, ending in victory for the rebels. Francisco Franco became dictator.
1953 The United States began building military bases in Spain and providing economic and military aid.
1955 Spain joined the United Nations.
1956 Spain granted Spanish Morocco its freedom.
1958 Spain changed the colonies of Ifni and Spanish Sahara into provinces.
1962 Floods in Barcelona killed over 600 persons; property damage totaled more than $30 million.
1966 The Organic Law of the Spanish State was adopted.
1969 Spain returned Ifni to Morocco.

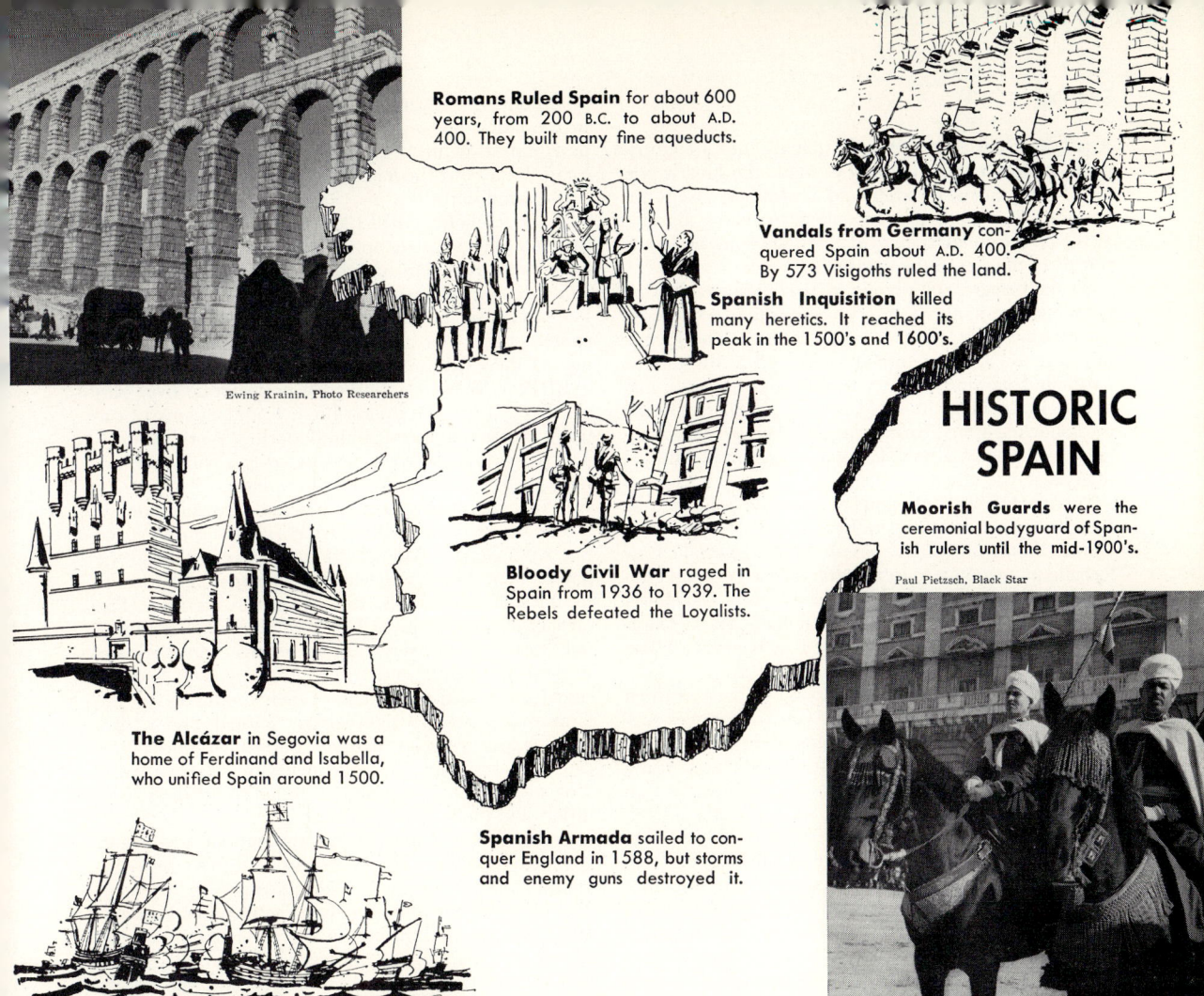

# HISTORIC SPAIN

**Romans Ruled Spain** for about 600 years, from 200 B.C. to about A.D. 400. They built many fine aqueducts.

**Vandals from Germany** conquered Spain about A.D. 400. By 573 Visigoths ruled the land.

**Spanish Inquisition** killed many heretics. It reached its peak in the 1500's and 1600's.

**Moorish Guards** were the ceremonial bodyguard of Spanish rulers until the mid-1900's.

**Bloody Civil War** raged in Spain from 1936 to 1939. The Rebels defeated the Loyalists.

**The Alcázar** in Segovia was a home of Ferdinand and Isabella, who unified Spain around 1500.

**Spanish Armada** sailed to conquer England in 1588, but storms and enemy guns destroyed it.

weaken Great Britain during the American Revolutionary War. Spain seized parts of Florida in 1782, and gained control of all Florida in 1783. It held Florida until the region came under United States control in 1821. Spain prospered after the War of Spanish Succession, but the Napoleonic Wars brought the country back to the edge of ruin. In 1805, Spain joined Napoleon to fight the War of the Third Coalition. The French and Spanish fleets met the British fleet at Trafalgar, on the southern coast of Spain, on Oct. 21, 1805. Spanish sea power was destroyed in the battle. See NAPOLEON I (Dominates Europe); TRAFALGAR.

**French Conquest.** In March, 1808, 100,000 French troops invaded Spain under the pretense of protecting the country's coast line from the British. Napoleon I quickly defeated the Spanish and entered Madrid in triumph. Then he turned his command over to his generals and returned to Paris. The Spanish people resisted the French occupation bitterly, and carried on guerrilla warfare. This guerrilla fighting became the early part of the Peninsular War, in which Spain, Portugal, and Great Britain all fought against France. In 1808, Napoleon forced King Charles IV and his son, King Ferdinand VII (1784-1833), to abdicate. He put his own brother, Joseph Bonaparte, on the throne. While French garrisons held the principal Spanish cities,

Napoleon kept the Spanish royal family as hostages in France. Spanish resistance leaders convened the Cortes of Cádiz in 1810. This assembly drew up the liberal Constitution of 1812. Although the new constitution declared Spain to be a Roman Catholic country, it put certain church lands under control of the government and curbed the power of the Roman Catholic Church. It also abolished feudal rights (see FEUDALISM).

Spain submitted quietly to these reforms. Spanish supporters of absolute monarchy disliked them, but they believed that the French would soon be driven out and the new constitution discarded. They were correct in this belief. In 1809, the Duke of Wellington had taken command of British forces on the peninsula, and had begun a vigorous campaign against the large French Army in Spain. Aided by Spanish troops, Wellington defeated the French by 1813.

**Dissatisfaction and Revolt.** The Spanish people restored Ferdinand VII to the throne in 1814. He speedily repealed the Constitution of 1812, and tried to return the country to prewar conditions. But the Spanish colonies of Chile, Paraguay, Uruguay, and Venezuela had revolted during the Napoleonic Wars. Losing them deprived Spain of one of its chief sources of income, so Ferdinand decided to reconquer them. But, in 1820, Spanish troops at Cádiz refused to embark for South

585

# SPAIN

America. Their mutiny spread quickly into a country-wide military revolt. The troops made the king a prisoner, and general disorder and lawlessness swept the nation. Other European monarchies became alarmed at the civil strife in Spain, because they feared it would spread to the rest of the continent.

At the Congress of Verona in 1822, France received permission from other European countries to send troops into Spain to restore order to the country. The French did so in 1823, and returned Ferdinand to the throne. Ferdinand promptly repealed all liberal measures, and again tried to set up the old feudal order of Spain. During the following years, Spain was torn between the king and the Roman Catholic Church on one hand, and the liberals on the other.

In June, 1833, Ferdinand set aside the Salic Law so that his infant daughter, rather than his brother Don Carlos, would inherit the Spanish throne. The Salic Law forbade any woman to inherit the throne. When Ferdinand died in September, 1833, his daughter Isabella II (1830-1904) succeeded him. Her mother, María Christina de Borbón (1806-1878), acted as regent (see REGENT).

The Carlist, or Roman Catholic Church party, wanted Don Carlos to be king. This forced Christina to seek support from the liberals in order to maintain her position. The plots of the Carlists against Isabella and María Christina became so distasteful to María Christina that in 1840 she resigned the regency in favor of a liberal, General Baldomero Espartero (1792-1879). He served as regent from 1841 until 1843, when Isabella's reign began. Disorder and unrest disrupted Queen Isabella's reign, and the people forced her to abdicate in 1868. Spain then established a provisional government under two generals, Francisco Serrano, who became regent, and Juan Prim, who served as premier.

**The New Spanish Monarchy.** Conditions did not improve, and two years later the Cortes voted to make Spain a monarchy again. The royal family had been banished, so the Spaniards sought a ruler in other countries. They selected an Italian, Amadeo, Duke of Aosta (1845-1890). He ruled only two years, and resigned in 1873 because he refused to be an absolute monarch. A short period of republican government followed. Then Spain set up a new constitutional monarchy. Alfonso XII, the son of Queen Isabella II, received the crown in 1874. He ruled until his death in 1885.

**The Reign of Alfonso XIII.** King Alfonso XII died six months before the birth of his son, Alfonso XIII, in 1886. María Christina of Habsburg-Lorraine (1858-1929), mother of Alfonso XIII, acted as regent until he came of age in 1902. The chief event of her regency was the Spanish-American War in 1898, in which Spain suffered a swift and terrible defeat. The war began in April, 1898, and lasted about four months. It grew out of American sympathy for the oppressed people of Cuba, a Spanish possession. The war ended in American victory, and Spain surrendered the Philippines, Puerto Rico and Guam—the remains of a once mighty empire—to the United States. By the terms of the Treaty of Paris, Cuba received independence from Spanish rule. See SPANISH-AMERICAN WAR.

Defeat abroad and poverty at home caused unrest in Spain during the early 1900's. Trade-unions developed in the cities, and anarchists and union leaders organized protests against low wages and other hardships of Spanish life. But the feudal ruling class did little to improve conditions.

Francisco Ferrer (1859-1909) led a revolt in Barcelona in 1909. He was an anarchist leader who preached against the monarchy and the Roman Catholic Church. The government put down the uprising and executed Ferrer, but the revolutionary movement continued. Discontent with the monarchy remained strong, even among the wealthy.

In 1912, Spain established a protectorate over part of Morocco (see MOROCCO [French and Spanish Control]). Spain remained neutral during World War I. The demands of warring nations led to a wide development of its electrical, textile, iron, and coal industries. In 1921, the Spanish Army suffered a crushing defeat at the hands of the Riffian tribes of Spanish Morocco (see RIF). General Miguel Primo de Rivera blamed the government for the defeat in Morocco and for the troubles of the farmers and industrial workers. The owners of more than half of Spain's land represented only about 1 of every 500 Spaniards. Most farmers worked as tenants and earned little money, because they had to turn over much of their production to the farm owners. Industrial workers earned low wages, and the loss of foreign markets following World War I caused widespread unemployment. In 1923, with the king's approval, Primo de Rivera led a bloodless revolution and made himself dictator.

Primo declared martial law throughout Spain and governed by decree. He promised to return soon to constitutional government, but kept postponing this step. The king and the army finally turned against Primo in 1930 and forced him out of office. General Dámaso Berenguer (1873-1953) succeeded Primo. In 1931, Berenguer announced that the 1876 constitution was restored. During this time, King Alfonso became increasingly unpopular, and the antimonarchists continually demanded a republican form of government. In a final attempt to save the Spanish monarchy, Alfonso chose Admiral Juan Aznar (1860-1933), a monarchist, to succeed Berenguer as premier. The government called for municipal and provincial elections, to be followed by a general election.

**The Spanish Republic.** The people voted overwhelmingly for republican candidates on Apr. 12, 1931. Alfonso refused to abdicate formally, but he and the royal family left the country. Little violence marked the change of government.

The country soon held elections for a constitutional convention, and the Socialists became the largest single party. The newly elected convention drew up a republican constitution, which was adopted in December, 1931. The constitution provided for a one-house legislature and a president to be elected by the people. In December, 1931, Spain elected Niceto Alcalá Zamora (1877-1948), a staunch Roman Catholic, as its first president. However, the people elected an anticlerical parliament, because many of them believed the church was too closely tied to the monarchy. The new government drove the Jesuits from Spain, and suppressed other religious orders or brought them under close state control. The government also closed all Roman Catholic schools. The Spanish Republic broke up many of the great estates, which the aristocracy and Roman Catholic Church had owned and rented at high prices. The estates were divided and sold to small farmers.

This new government won the fierce hatred of the conservatives. An unsuccessful monarchist uprising took place. The government imprisoned the monarchist leaders and exiled many members of the nobility. In 1932, the government yielded to the persistent demands of Catalonia and granted home rule to that province. Other provinces then demanded similar rights.

The situation throughout Spain became especially troubled during the worldwide depression of the 1930's. Exports fell off, and many of the people became desperately poor. In October, 1933, the government dissolved the Cortes and called for a new election. The conservatives won, and the pro-Catholic parties received greater power in the government. Chaos then broke out. A general strike in 1934 led to a workers' revolt in Asturias and other provinces. But the government had enough power to restore order.

The division in Spain grew wider. Army leaders, monarchists, great landowners, and the Roman Catholic parties united in opposition to the republic. They were opposed by Socialists, Communists, Republicans, trade-unionists, and most of the liberal groups. The Right (conservative) groups aligned against the Left (liberal) groups, and hatred became intense. Civil War approached rapidly. The conservatives wanted to destroy the republic and restore the monarchy. President Alcalá dismissed the Cortes in order to save his government, and held elections in February, 1936. For this election, all the radical and republican elements banded together in an organization called the Popular Front. This combination won the election and gained control of the Cortes. Alcalá was too moderate for the Popular Front, and the party removed him from office on April 7, 1936. His former premier, Manuel Azaña (1880-1940), became the new president.

The election touched off an armed conflict between Right and Left, and violence flared from February to July in 1936. Monarchists and Socialists fought each other in the streets. Armed bands dragged people from both sides out of their homes and murdered them.

The government knew that certain army leaders were plotting to overthrow the republic. But the republican officials were afraid to arrest even generals whom they knew to be disloyal. They merely ordered the more dangerous military commanders to duty at remote outposts. General Francisco Franco, the future leader of the revolution, became the military governor of the Canary Islands. The government's policy gave the generals more time to perfect their plans.

**Civil War.** On July 17, 1936, the military leaders suddenly proclaimed a revolution against the Spanish government in Morocco. Troops in army garrisons rose in revolt throughout Spain and its colonies. General Franco became the leader of the revolt after General José Sanjurjo died in a plane crash. Franco flew from the Canary Islands to Morocco and took command of the revolt there.

With Morocco under control, Franco flew to Spain on July 18, and set up a fascist government at Burgos on July 30. Franco called his government the *Junta de Defensa Nacional*, or *Council of National Defense*.

# SPAIN

A violent, bloody civil war followed between Franco's Rebel forces and the *Loyalists*, who remained loyal to the Republic. Both sides killed civilians and massacred prisoners. Moroccan troops brought to Spain by Franco were particularly guilty of atrocities. The war raged back and forth across Spain for 32 months.

The Spanish Civil War has been called the opening battle and the testing ground of World War II. At first, the rest of the world agreed not to intervene in Spain. The League of Nations established a neutrality border patrol to keep foreign aid from reaching either side. But many nations did not stay neutral. Italy and Germany, which were both fascist countries, began to support Franco openly. Pope Pius XI declared his sympathy for Franco's government. Before many months passed, 50,000 Italian troops had joined Franco's armies in the field. Germany sent technicians, military advisers, and aviators. Mexico favored the republic, but most Latin-American countries sympathized with Franco. Most wealthy Spaniards backed Franco. Juan March, the richest man in Spain, was his most influential supporter.

Loyalist sympathizers from the United States and many other countries organized the International Brigade to fight against the Rebels. Aid also reached the Spanish Republic from France and Russia. The Russians helped the Loyalists more than any other country by sending weapons, ammunition, planes, technicians, and military advisers. As a result, the Communists became increasingly powerful in Spain. Communist police agents used their powers to settle old conflicts, and committed thousands of political murders.

The Loyalists were both aided and hindered by a desire for independence in certain regions. Catalonia, which had won self-rule in 1932, supported the republic halfheartedly, because many Catalonians desired complete and immediate independence. On the other hand, the Roman Catholic Basques set up the Basque Republic and allied themselves with the Loyalists.

New types of tanks, artillery, planes, and other weapons had their first tryouts on the battlefields of Spain. The better-armed Rebels held the military advantage from the beginning. They soon drove the Loyalists into the eastern half of Spain. In September, 1936, Franco's forces captured Toledo and relieved the 71-day Loyalist siege of Toledo's alcázar, or fortress. On October 1, the Rebels named Franco as Chief of the Spanish State. Franco reached Madrid on October 21, and laid siege to the city. The Loyalists put up a stiff resistance in spite of heavy air bombardments. The battle for the city ended in a deadlock. The Loyalists moved the seat of the government to Valencia on November 6. Although Madrid held out, the republic's position gradually grew worse. By October, 1937, the Loyalists had to move the capital again, this time to Barcelona.

In April, 1938, Franco's troops reached the sea at Vinaroz, and separated the Republican forces in Castile from those in Catalonia. Franco launched a strong offensive against the republic in December. Within a month, Barcelona had fallen and the Republican armies started to crumble. The president of the Spanish Republic, Manuel Azaña, resigned and fled to France in February, 1939. Great Britain and France recognized Franco as the head of the Spanish government just be-

587

## SPAIN

fore Azaña fled. On March 28, Franco entered Madrid. More than a million Spaniards had died in the war, and Spain lay ravaged and desolate.

**Dictatorship.** Franco set up a fascist dictatorship. He stated that his first aim was to bring unity and order to the country as quickly as possible by establishing a strong, centralized government.

Spain, exhausted by the Civil War, remained neutral during World War II. But "volunteer" Spanish forces fought beside the Germans on the Russian front, and Spain supplied Germany with mercury and other important minerals. Toward the end of the war, Spain began to show more sympathy for the Allied countries.

In 1947, Franco announced the Law of Succession. This law, amended by the 1966 Organic Law, declared that Spain was traditionally a kingdom. It declared that after Franco's death, or at his request, a regency council would nominate—for the Cortes' approval—a king or regent to succeed Franco.

**Alignment with the West.** The Western Powers gradually realized that Franco's opposition to Russia and Communism might help the defense of Europe. In the early 1950's, the United States made loans and gave technical aid to Spain. In 1953, Spain allowed the United States to establish a naval base at Cádiz, and air bases near Seville, Madrid, and Saragossa. The United States then gave Spain $1 billion in loans, grants, and gifts.

Spain became a member of the United Nations in 1955. The government gave Spanish Morocco its independence on April 7, 1956. The colonies of Ifni and Spanish Sahara revolted in 1957. Franco converted them into provinces under military rule in 1958.

**The 1960's.** Spain completed a three-year financial reform program in 1961. This enabled Spain to join the Organization for European Economic Cooperation (now the Organization for Economic Cooperation and Development). Opposition to Franco rose in 1962. Miners struck in defiance of a law banning strikes. The strikes were the first in 25 years. The government finally granted pay raises and other concessions.

In June, 1962, Franco reorganized the government. Captain-General Agustin Munoz Grandes, chief of staff of the armed forces, became vice-president of the national council of ministers (deputy premier).

The government showed signs of relaxing some restrictions in the mid-1960's. In 1965, the Cortes reestablished the right of labor to strike for higher wages. In 1966, a new law relaxed the strict press censorship laws and declared an *amnesty* (pardon) for persons convicted of crimes connected with the Civil War.

In the mid-1960's, Spain renewed its periodic efforts to obtain possession of British-held Gibraltar. Talks between Spain and Great Britain to decide Gibraltar's future status began in 1966, but they broke off in March, 1968. In September, 1967, the people of Gibraltar voted to remain under British control. But Spain and the United Nations did not consider the vote legal. In May, 1968, Spain began allowing only Spanish workers to travel to Gibraltar. In June, 1969, Spain stopped all Spanish workers from crossing the border into Gibraltar. Spain returned Ifni to Morocco in January, 1969.

WALTER C. LANGSAM

**Related Articles.** See SPANISH LITERATURE with its list of Related Articles. See also:

### RULERS

| | | |
|---|---|---|
| Alfonso XIII | Ferdinand V | Philip (kings |
| Boabdil | Isabella I | of Spain) |

### POLITICAL AND MILITARY LEADERS

Alva, Duke of
Franco, Francisco
Gonzalo de Córdoba, Hernández
Jiménez de Cisneros, Francisco
Primo de Rivera, Miguel
Torquemada, Tomás de
Weyler y Nicolau, Valeriano

### EXPLORERS AND DISCOVERERS

Alvarado, Pedro de
Balboa, Vasco N. de
Cabeza de Vaca, Álvar N.
Columbus, Christopher
Coronado, Francisco V. de
Cortes, Hernando
De Soto, Hernando
Jiménez de Quesada, Gonzalo
Narváez, Pánfilo de
Oñate, Juan de
Orellana, Francisco de
Pizarro (brothers)
Ponce de León, Juan

### CITIES

| | | | |
|---|---|---|---|
| Barcelona | Cartagena | Málaga | Seville |
| Bilbao | Córdoba | San Sebastián | Toledo |
| Burgos | Granada | Saragossa | Valencia |
| Cádiz | Madrid | | |

### HISTORY

Aix-la-Chapelle, Treaties of
Armada
Bourbon
Castile and Aragon
Cid, The
Equatorial Guinea
Exploration and Discovery
Falange Española
Granada
Iberia
Inquisition
Loyola, Saint Ignatius
Spanish-American War
Spanish Main
Succession Wars
Trafalgar

### PHYSICAL FEATURES

Bay of Biscay
Cape Finisterre
Douro River
Ebro River
Guadalquivir River
Majorca
Mediterranean Sea
Minorca
Pyrenees
Río Tinto
Tagus River

### POLITICAL DIVISIONS

Andalusia
Balearic Islands
Canary Islands
Navarre
Spanish Sahara

### PRODUCTS AND INDUSTRIES

For Spain's rank among other countries in production, see the following articles:

| | | | |
|---|---|---|---|
| Fishing Industry | Lemon Olive | Orange Ship and Shipping | Tuna Wine |

### OTHER RELATED ARTICLES

Alcazar
Alhambra
Andorra
Basque
Bullfighting
Castanets
Castle (picture)
Christmas
Cork
Doll (picture)
Don Juan
Don Quixote
Easter (In Spain)
Escorial
Fiesta
Flag (color picture: Historical Flags of the World)
Grandee
Montserrat
Peseta
Piaster
Spanish Language

### Outline

**I. The Land and Its Resources**
  A. Location and Size
  B. Land Regions
  C. Coastline
  D. Rivers and Lakes
  E. Natural Resources
  F. Climate

**II. Life of the People**
  A. Language
  B. Way of Life
  C. Cities
  D. Country Life

**III. Work of the People**
  A. Agriculture
  B. Manufacturing and Processing
  C. Mining
  D. Fishing Industry
  E. Electric Power
  F. Trade
  G. Transportation
  H. Communication

**The Cocker Spaniel** makes a fine companion, and is also an excellent dog for hunting in the field.

Evelyn M. Shafer

IV. Education
  A. Schools   B. Libraries   C. Museums
V. The Arts
VI. Government
VII. History

**Questions**

What different peoples have controlled Spain?
What Spanish village is surrounded by France?
What is the official tongue of Spain?
What are some common English words that were derived from Spanish?
Why are there wide differences between the ways of life in various parts of Spain?
Why do the Spaniards eat more veal than beef?
How do the daily schedules of American and Spanish office workers differ?
Why do Spanish workers receive two extra months' pay each year?
How does the Roman Catholic Church influence the life of the Spanish people?
Why is the Spanish Civil War called a testing ground for World War II?

**SPALATO.** See SPLIT.

**SPALDING, ALBERT** (1888-1953), was an American violinist. His world-wide concert tours were highly successful. He taught violin at the Juilliard Graduate School of Music in New York City. Spalding was born in Chicago. At the age of seven, he began to study violin with Ulpiano Chiti in Florence, Italy. He also studied at the conservatory in Bologna, and in Paris, where he made his debut in 1905.   DOROTHY DELAY

**SPALDING, HENRY HARMON.** See IDAHO (History).

**SPALLANZANI,** SPAHL *lahn* TSAH *nee*, **LAZZARO** (1729-1799), an Italian experimental biologist, showed that the air carries microscopic life. He also showed that microscopic life in food can be killed by boiling. Spallanzani was the first to watch isolated bacterial cells divide. He discovered that bats can dodge strings even when blind, and that salamanders can replace damaged limbs. Spallanzani was born in Scandiano, and took orders in the Roman Catholic Church. He taught at the University of Padua.   LORUS J. MILNE and MARGERY MILNE

**SPAN.** See BRIDGE (The Arch Principle).

**SPANIEL,** *SPAN yul*, is a large family of dogs. It contains more breeds than any other. The American Kennel Club recognizes 10 spaniel breeds, including the *American water, Brittany, clumber, cocker, English cocker, English springer, field, Irish water, Sussex,* and *Welsh springer* spaniels. One toy dog, the *English toy spaniel,* may be related to the others. But another toy dog, the *Japanese spaniel,* is probably not related to these spaniels.

The spaniel family probably descended from a Spanish dog, and its name comes from the word *Spain.* All spaniels except the toys are sporting dogs. The spaniel has a gentle and friendly disposition, and likes to hunt in the fields. Spaniels are fine companions as well as good hunters. They make excellent pets. All spaniels except the Brittany have long, silky coats. In general, they have long ears; rather large, round eyes; broad, domed skulls; and sturdy bodies and legs. For a description of the unusual Brittany, see BRITTANY SPANIEL.

All the spaniel breeds except the Brittany hunt game in much the same way. They search the ground within gun range of the hunter. When a spaniel smells game, it rushes in to *flush* it, or make it fly or run. When the game is flushed and the hunter shoots, the spaniel waits for the command, finds the game, and then brings it back to the hunter.   MAXWELL RIDDLE

For a list of the separate articles in WORLD BOOK on each spaniel breed, see DOG (table; color pictures: Sporting Dogs).

**SPANISH AMERICA** is the name sometimes given to the Spanish-speaking parts of Latin America. It includes Central America, except British Honduras; South America, except Brazil and the Guianas; Mexico; Cuba; Puerto Rico; the Dominican Republic; and certain islands of the West Indies. See also LATIN AMERICA.

589

# SPANISH-AMERICAN WAR

**SPANISH-AMERICAN WAR** marked the emergence of the United States as a world power. This brief conflict between the United States and Spain took place between April and August, 1898, over the issue of the liberation of Cuba. In the course of the war, the U.S. won Guam, Puerto Rico, and the Philippine Islands.

## Background of the War

**Spanish Misrule.** Until about 1860, American expansionists had hoped to acquire Cuba. After the Civil War, interest in annexation dwindled, but Americans continued to be displeased by Spanish misrule. A long and exhausting uprising took place in the 1870's. In 1895, during a depression that made conditions worse, a revolution broke out again and threatened to go on endlessly. The Spanish forces were not powerful enough to put down the insurrection and the rebels were not strong enough to win. Large areas of the island were desolated. The Spanish governor, Valeriano Weyler y Nicolau, tried to crush the revolt.

**American Intervention.** American newspapers, especially the "yellow press" of William Randolph Hearst and Joseph Pulitzer, printed sensational accounts of Spanish oppression, and carried seriously exaggerated reports that a quarter of the population had died. They continually agitated for intervention. Many Americans regarded conditions in Cuba as intolerable and began to demand that the United States intervene. A few felt that the United States should also acquire naval and military bases and become an imperial power.

In November, 1897, President McKinley pressured Spain into granting Cuba limited self-government within the Spanish empire. The rebels wanted nothing less than independence, and continued to fight. Meanwhile, pro-Spanish mobs in Havana rioted in protest against self-government. To protect Americans from the rioters, the battleship *Maine* arrived in Havana harbor January 25, 1898. On February 15, an explosion blew up the ship and killed 260 persons on board. Although the cause of the explosion was never definitely determined, the outraged American public instantly blamed Spain. "Remember the Maine" became a popular slogan, but forces already in operation did more to bring about actual war. In March, President McKinley sent three notes to Spain, demanding full independence for Cuba. Spain granted an armistice. On April 19, Congress passed overwhelmingly a joint resolution asserting that Cuba was independent. The resolution also disavowed any American intention to acquire the island, and authorized the use of the army and navy to force Spanish withdrawal. On April 25, the U.S. formally declared that a state of war existed with Spain as of April 21.

## Chief Events

**Manila Bay.** The first important battle of the war took place in the Philippines. The Asiatic Squadron of six ships under Commodore George Dewey sailed from Hong Kong to Manila Bay. On May 1, 1898, it destroyed the entire Spanish fleet of 10 vessels without the loss of an American life or serious damage to any American ship. Then Dewey blockaded Manila harbor while he waited for U.S. troops to arrive.

**Cuban Blockade.** Meanwhile, the North Atlantic Squadron under Rear Admiral William T. Sampson, had begun a partial blockade of Cuba while scouting in the Caribbean Sea for a fleet that had left Spain under Admiral Pascual Cervera y Topete. Finally, on May 28, American ships located Cervera's fleet, which had successfully eluded them and had anchored in the landlocked harbor of Santiago in eastern Cuba. While the navy placed a strong blockading force outside the harbor, the army hastily prepared to send an expeditionary force to assault Santiago by land.

**Land Battles.** On June 22, Major General William R. Shafter began landing 15,000 troops at Daiquirí and Siboney, near Santiago. The Spaniards offered little resistance during the landing and deploying of troops. Joyful newspaper reports of this helped make celebrities of the Rough Rider Regiment and its commanders, Colonel Leonard Wood and Lieutenant Colonel Theodore Roosevelt.

General Shafter launched a full-scale two-pronged assault against Santiago on July 1. He sent nearly half of his men against a small Spanish force strongly defending a stone fort at El Caney. The remainder made a frontal assault on the main Spanish defenses at Kettle Hill and San Juan Hill. The obsolete American artillery could not lay a proper barrage to prepare for infantry charges. By nightfall, the Americans were precariously entrenched on the ridges commanding Santiago, but they had sustained 1,600 casualties.

As soon as Santiago came under siege, the governor of Cuba ordered Admiral Cervera to run the naval blockade to try to save his ships. Cervera led them out on July 3, heading in single file eastward along the Cuban coast. The pursuing American naval vessels, commanded by Commodore Winfield S. Schley, sank or forced the beaching of every one of them. Again no serious damage occurred to any American vessel, and only one man was killed.

After days of negotiations, Santiago surrendered on July 17. On July 25, Major General Nelson A. Miles began an invasion of Puerto Rico which met almost no opposition. Several contingents of U.S. troops arrived

**The Landing of United States Troops** in Cuba during the Spanish-American War is shown in this painting by Joseph Boggs Beale. The fighting men are American Marines.

Joseph Boggs Beale, Modern Enterprise

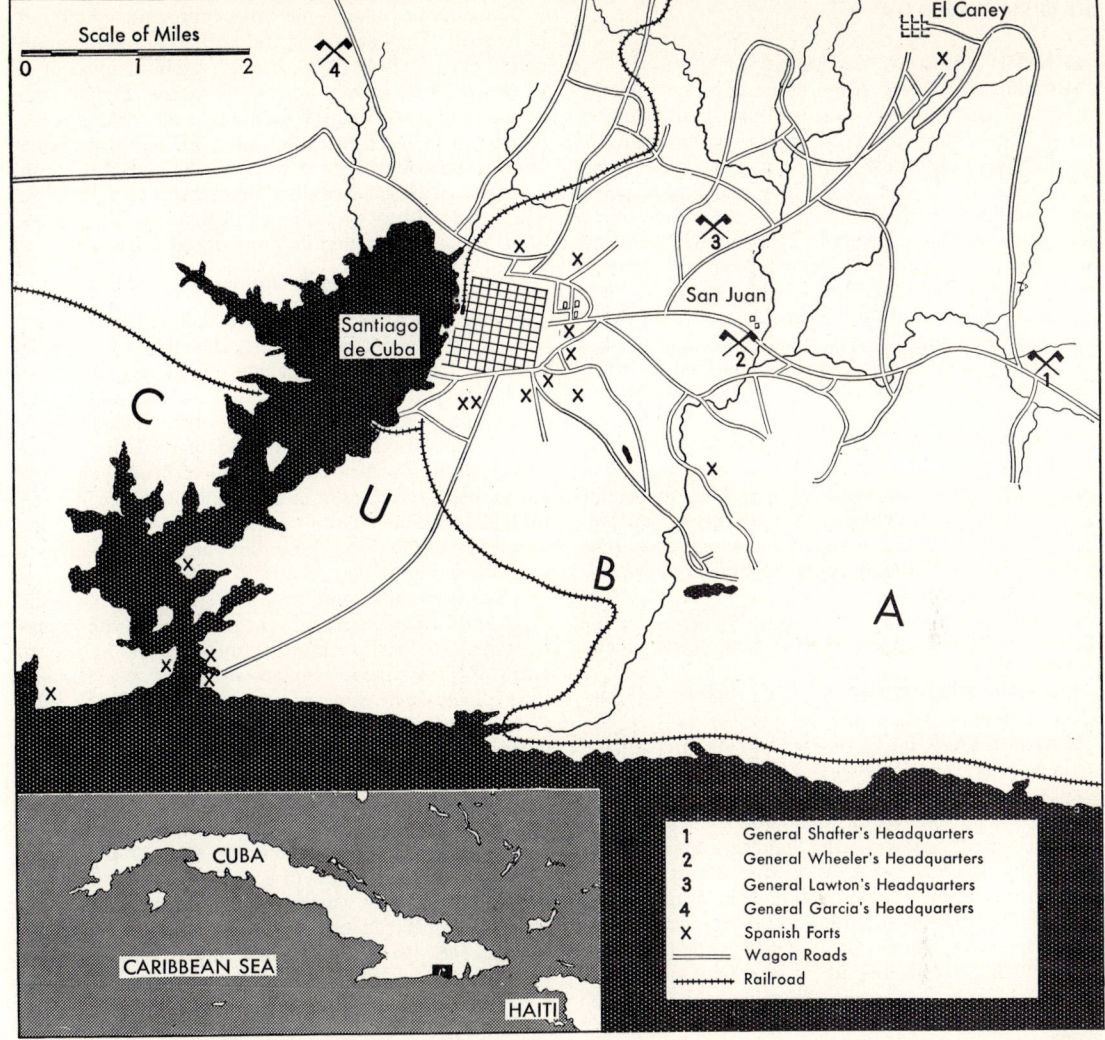

**The Chief Campaign of the Spanish-American War** was fought both at sea and on land in the area shown in the detailed map, *above*. The Americans defeated the Spaniards at El Caney and San Juan, and finally forced their surrender at Santiago. At sea off Santiago, American ships under Commodores Sampson and Schley sank or beached the Spanish fleet under Admiral Cervera. The insert map shows the Santiago region of the larger map in black. The area was backward and disease-ridden.

in the Philippines. On August 13, they entered and occupied Manila, thus keeping the Filipino patriots out. The cables had been cut, and Dewey did not realize that an armistice had been signed the previous day.

### Results of the War

**The Peace Treaty.** Sentiment grew within the United States to keep the spoils of war, except for Cuba. In the Treaty of Paris, signed Dec. 10, 1898, Spain granted Cuba its freedom. Spain ceded Guam, Puerto Rico, and the Philippines to the United States. The United States, in turn, paid Spain $20,000,000 for public property in the Philippine Islands.

**Anti-Imperialism.** Many people in the United States did not like their nation's new position as a colonial power. These *anti-imperialists* opposed the annexations. They did not wish to hold subject peoples by force, run the risk of becoming involved in further wars, or face competition from colonial products or workers. Their forces were so strong in the Senate that it ratified the peace treaty by only one vote on Feb. 6, 1899.

**Other Results.** The United States had to put down a long and bloody insurrection in the Philippines, strengthen its defenses, build more powerful battleships, and reorganize the army to remedy serious weaknesses revealed by the war. The war also showed the need for a canal through the isthmus that separated the Caribbean Sea from the Pacific Ocean, and thus led to the building of the Panama Canal.   FRANK FREIDEL

**Related Articles** in WORLD BOOK include:

| | | |
|---|---|---|
| Cuba | Miles, Nelson A. | Sampson, William T. |
| Dewey, George | Paris, Treaties | Schley, Winfield S. |
| Evans, Robley D. | of | Shafter, William R. |
| McKinley, William (Spanish-American War) | Philippines | Sigsbee, Charles D. |
| | Puerto Rico | Spanish War |
| | Roosevelt, | Veterans, United |
| Maine (ship) | Theodore | Wood, Leonard |

# SPANISH ARMADA

**SPANISH ARMADA.** See ARMADA.

**SPANISH BAYONET** is the name of a low, slender yucca tree which grows in the southern United States and in Mexico and the West Indies. It may grow to about 25 feet but usually is much smaller. It has long, flat, bayonetlike leaves, 2½ feet long and 2 to 3 inches wide. It bears cream-white flowers, sometimes tinted green or purple. They are about 2½ inches wide. Several subspecies have leaves with yellow margins or centers. The flowers, shaped like deep bowls, grow on erect branched stems about 2 feet long.

**Scientific Classification.** The Spanish bayonet belongs to the agave family, *Agavaceae*. It is classified as genus *Yucca*, species *Y. aloifolia*. EDMUND C. JAEGER

See also YUCCA.

**SPANISH CIVIL WAR.** See SPAIN (History).

**SPANISH FLY** is a beetle, not a true fly. Most Spanish flies live in southern Europe. They are about three-quarters of an inch long. A substance called *cantharidin* can be extracted from their wing cases. It is used as a *vesicant* (blistering agent) to increase a person's blood circulation and relieve pain.

**Scientific Classification.** The Spanish fly belongs to the blister beetle family, *Meloidae*. It is genus *Lytta*, species *L. vesicatrix*.

**SPANISH INQUISITION.** See INQUISITION; TORQUEMADA, TOMÁS DE.

**SPANISH LANGUAGE** is the official language of Spain and its overseas provinces. It is also the official language of 18 Latin-American republics, and one of the two official tongues of Puerto Rico. Many people in the United States speak Spanish, especially in Florida and the Southwest. Altogether, about 150 million persons speak Spanish, the most widely used Romance language (see ROMANCE LANGUAGE).

The Spanish spoken in Spain is often called *Castilian Spanish*. The Spanish used in Latin America is known as *American Spanish*. Castilian Spanish and American Spanish are basically the same. But these two forms of Spanish have a few differences in pronunciation and vocabulary.

Many English words come from Spanish. They include *alfalfa, alligator, armada, cargo, cork, lariat, lasso, mosquito, potato, ranch, rodeo, tobacco, tomato, tornado,* and *vanilla*. Some states and many cities in the United States have Spanish names. Among them are *California, Florida, Nevada, Los Angeles, San Antonio, San Francisco,* and *Santa Fe*.

## Spanish Pronunciation

Spanish is one of the most phonetic of all languages. That is, its pronunciation follows its spelling closely. See PHONETICS (The Phonetic Ideal).

**Vowels.** Spanish has only five basic vowel sounds. These sounds are represented by the letters *a, e, i* or *y, o,* and *u*. The following table gives the approximate English sound for each Spanish vowel:

| Spanish Vowel | Approximate Sound in English |
| --- | --- |
| a | a in *father* |
| e | e in *they* |
| i or y | i in *machine* |
| o | o in *owe* |
| u | oo in *moon* |

**Consonants.** Spanish has three consonants not found in English. They are *ch, ll,* and *ñ*. Their pronunciation corresponds roughly to the English pronunciation of *ch* in *church, lli* in *million,* and *ny* in *canyon*. People who speak American Spanish pronounce the consonants *c* (when it is followed by *e* or *i*) and *z* as English-speaking persons pronounce the *s* in *sink*. People who speak Castilian Spanish pronounce them like the *th* in *think*. The letter *h* is not pronounced in Spanish. The consonants *b* and *v* are generally pronounced the same.

## Spanish Grammar

**Nouns and Adjectives.** All Spanish nouns are either masculine or feminine. Most nouns that name male humans or male animals, or that end in *-o, -l,* or *-r,* are masculine. Most nouns that name female humans or female animals, or that end in *-a, -d,* or *-ión,* are feminine. For example, *padre* (father), *libro* (book), *papel* (paper), and *calor* (heat) are masculine. *Madre* (mother), *pluma* (pen), *felicidad* (happiness), and *revolución* (revolution) are feminine. Plurals of nouns and adjectives are formed by adding *-s* to those that end in vowels and *-es* to those ending in consonants.

Adjectives must agree in *gender* (masculine or feminine) and in *number* (singular or plural) with the nouns they modify. For this reason, many adjectives have four forms. *Sombrero pequeño* means *small hat, casa pequeña* means *small house, sombreros pequeños* means *small hats,* and *casas pequeñas* means *small houses*.

**Verbs.** Spanish has eight simple tenses that are regularly used. They are formed by adding endings to the stem of the verb or to the infinitive. Each simple tense has a corresponding *perfect* (compound) tense. The perfect tenses are formed by using the appropriate simple tense of *haber* (to have) with a past participle.

Spanish verbs are classified according to the endings of their infinitives. They fall into three groups: *-ar* verbs, such as *andar* (to walk); *-er* verbs, such as *correr* (to run); and *-ir* verbs, such as *vivir* (to live).

### SPANISH WORDS AND PHRASES

**¿adónde va usted?** *ah DOHN day VAH oo STAYD,* where are you going?
**ayer,** *ah YEHR,* yesterday
**bien,** *BYEHN,* well
**bueno,** *BWAY noh,* good
**buenos días,** *BWAY nohs DEE ahs,* good morning
**¿cómo está usted?** *KOH moheh STAH oo STAYD,* how are you?
**¿cómo se llama usted?** *KOH moh sayl YAH mah oo STAYD,* what is your name?
**gracias,** *GRAH syahs,* thanks, thank you
**hasta luego,** *AH stahl WAY goh,* good-by (until later)
**hombre,** *OHM bray,* man
**hoy,** *oi,* today
**mañana,** *mahn YAH nah,* morning, tomorrow
**me llamo Juan,** *mayl YAH moh HWAHN,* my name is John
**mucho,** *MOO choh,* much, a lot
**mujer,** *moo HEHR,* woman
**muy bien,** *MWEE BYEHN,* very well
**pequeño,** *pay KAYN yoh,* small
**por favor,** *POHR fah BOHR,* please
**¿qué hora es?** *kay OHR ah EHS,* what time is it?
**señor,** *sayn YOHR,* sir, Mr.
**señora,** *sayn YOH rah,* lady, Mrs.
**señorita,** *sayn yoh REE tah,* young lady, Miss
**sí,** *SEE,* yes
**son las dos,** *SOHN lahs DOHS,* it is two o'clock
**tengo hambre,** *TEHNG go AHM bray,* I am hungry

**Word Order** in Spanish is similar to that of English. Two exceptions are the positions of object pronouns and descriptive adjectives in Spanish sentences. Object pronouns usually come before the verb in Spanish. In the English sentence *She greeted us,* the verb (*greeted*) comes before the object pronoun (*us*). In Spanish, this sentence becomes *Ella nos saludó* (*She us greeted*). Descriptive adjectives in Spanish usually follow the nouns they modify. In the English sentence *We live in a white house,* the descriptive adjective (*white*) comes before the noun (*house*). In Spanish, this sentence becomes *Vivimos en una casa blanca* (*We live in a house white*).

A Spanish sentence is made negative by placing *no* before the verb. An *interrogative sentence* (one which asks a question) is formed by placing the subject after the verb. A Spanish interrogative sentence has an inverted question mark before the first word, and a regular question mark after the last word. This construction enables readers to recognize an interrogative sentence as soon as they begin reading it. The following are the affirmative, negative, and interrogative forms of the sentence *Charles lives here:* Affirmative—*Carlos vive aquí;* Negative—*Carlos no vive aquí;* Interrogative—*¿Vive Carlos aquí?*

### Development

**Beginnings.** The Spanish language developed from Latin. During the 200's and 100's B.C., Roman armies conquered the *Iberian Peninsula* (present-day Spain and Portugal). The Iberians gradually adopted the language of their conquerors. This language was called *vernacular* (common) Latin. The Iberians changed the language continually. By the A.D. 400's or 500's, vernacular Latin had become Spanish. Few Iberian words remained.

In the early 400's, Germanic tribes invaded the Iberian Peninsula. These tribes controlled the peninsula until 711, but they had little influence on the Spanish language. In 711, the Arabic-speaking Moors conquered all but a small part of the peninsula. They ruled most of the region until the mid-1200's. The Moors added about 700 Arabic words to Spanish. But Spanish remained basically Latin in vocabulary, and changed little in sound and structure.

**Castilian Spanish.** Like other languages, Spanish developed several dialects. During the 1200's, the Spanish province of Castile became an important literary, military, and political center. The influence of Castile spread, and the Castilian dialect was soon the accepted form of Spanish in most parts of the Iberian Peninsula.

Two other dialects became separate languages during this period. The *Galician-Portuguese* dialect had developed in the western part of the peninsula. This dialect was the basis of the Portuguese language, which began in the 1200's (see PORTUGUESE LANGUAGE). The *Catalan* dialect lived on in northeastern Spain and grew into the Catalan language.

**American Spanish.** Beginning in the 1500's, Spanish colonists, conquerors, and missionaries brought their language to Latin America. Spanish gradually replaced many Indian languages, including those of the Aztec, Inca, and Maya. Today, Spanish is the official language of all Latin-American republics except Brazil and Haiti.                       JOHN A. THOMPSON

See also SPAIN (Language); MEXICO (physical map index [Spanish-English Glossary]).

# SPANISH LITERATURE

**SPANISH LITERATURE** is one of the richest and most varied of all European literatures. The poetry, prose, and drama of Spain are noted for their realism, color, humor, and lyricism.

The geography of Spain helps give special characteristics to the nation's literature. The Pyrenees Mountains and the Mediterranean Sea separate Spain from the rest of Europe. As a result, Spanish writers have kept an individuality somewhat apart from the main currents of European literature. Great rivers and mountain ranges within Spain divide the country into regions. As a result, *regionalism* (concern with a particular area) strongly flavors Spanish literature.

History has also given special features to Spanish literature. The Romans occupied Spain for about 600 years, beginning in the 200's B.C. The main heritage they left to Spain was the Latin language, particularly *vernacular* (spoken) Latin. Vernacular Latin gave birth to three Romance languages that became the most common Spanish dialects—Castilian, Galician-Portuguese, and Catalan (see SPANISH LANGUAGE [Development]). From the A.D. 700's through the 1400's, Christians fought Moslem Moors for control of Spain. This long struggle created a strongly religious patriotism that inspired some of the world's finest religious poetry and prose.

The greatest period of Spanish literature began about the mid-1500's and lasted until the late 1600's. This period, called the Golden Age, brought a flowering of Spanish fiction, poetry, and drama. Spain's greatest and best-known writer, Miguel de Cervantes, the author of *Don Quixote,* lived during this period.

### The Middle Ages

**Early Medieval Literature.** Lyric poetry existed in Spain as early as A.D. 1040. These poems, called *jarchas,* are short refrains added to an Arabic poem called the *muwashaha.* Jarchas were written in Hebrew or Arabic alphabet characters, but the language was a Mozarabic dialect of Spanish (the Mozarabs were Spaniards living under Moslem rule). Jarchas are the oldest form of lyric poetry in a Romance language. Their theme is the sadness of a maiden in the absence of her lover, or simply her longing for love.

Almost all the early Spanish epic poems have been lost. The only one that has survived in nearly complete form is the *Poem of The Cid,* written about 1140. It tells of the adventures of the Castilian hero Rodrigo Díaz. This epic contains stylistic devices similar to those of the *Song of Roland,* a French epic of about 1100. But *The Cid* is more realistic than epics written in other countries during the Middle Ages. It was written only 40 years after the hero's death, so the action of the poem is closer to the actual events that occurred. See CID, THE.

Minstrels called *juglares* who recited epic poems also performed satirical plays called *juegos de escarnio.* Early medieval Spanish drama is not well known. The only play that has survived is a short fragment of a religious

---

*Germán Bleiberg, the contributor of this article, is a leading Spanish poet and critic, and Professor of Hispanic Studies at Vassar College.*

# SPANISH LITERATURE

drama called *The Play of the Wise Men*, from the middle 1100's.

During the 1200's and 1300's, Spanish lyric poetry came under the influence of the poems of the Provençal troubadours of southern France. The early poetry of two related dialects, Galician and Portuguese, was modeled on Provençal poetry. The Galician-Portuguese works, consisting of short *cantigas* (songs) and longer poems, were collected and preserved in three famous medieval *cancioneros* (anthologies). Gonzalo de Berceo was the first Spanish poet known by his name. In the early 1200's, he wrote a series of poems on the *Miracles of Our Lady* in the tradition of other European poets.

The Castilian king Alfonso X, called *the Learned*, helped promote early Spanish prose. In the mid-1200's, he edited the first collection of Castilian laws, *Las Siete Partidas*. Two long historical works were composed under Alfonso's direction—*Crónica General de España*, a history of Spain; and *Grande e General Historia*, a world history. The king also supported the scientific and philosophical interests of the School of Translators of Toledo, which introduced Ptolemy, Aristotle, and other ancient writers to western Europe. In addition, Alfonso is remembered for his Galician cantigas that were dedicated to the Virgin Mary.

The earliest known prose fiction in Spain included a collection of *apologues* (short stories) in Latin. They were collected in 1100 by Pedro Alfonso under the title *Scholar's Guide*. During the 1200's, several series of tales were translated into Spanish from Arabic and other languages. These works included *Calila e Dimna* (1251) and *Sendebar* (1253). In the early 1300's, Spanish prose began to take on a more distinctive character with the writings of Don Juan Manuel, nephew of Alfonso the Learned. Don Juan Manuel wrote many political and historical works. His greatest achievement was *Count Lucanor*, a collection of *exempla* (tales with a moral).

The poetry of the scholars began to decline during the 1300's. Juan Ruiz, archpriest of the town of Hita in Castile, preserved the verse form of the clerics to some extent in his unique and only work, *The Book of Good Love*. This original poetry offers a picture of many details of Spanish life in the 1300's. The poems tell about food, musical instruments, songs, monastic and tavern customs, and love affairs. Ruiz invented the character of Trotaconventos, a go-between of lovers. The poet's elaboration of the fight between Sir Flesh and Lady Lent is the liveliest development of this topic in all medieval literature.

**The 1400's.** A panoramic view of the lyric poetry of the 1400's appeared in two cancioneros compiled by Juan Alfonso de Baena and Lope de Stúñiga. The Italian poets Dante, Petrarch, and Giovanni Boccaccio influenced the poetry. The spirit of the Middle Ages survived, however, in many anonymous *romances* (ballads). These romances were lyrical fragments of epic songs, and were meant to be sung or recited. They have been preserved through oral tradition in Spain, South America, and Morocco, and among Sephardic Jews.

Three great poets belong to the 1400's: (1) Iñigo López de Mendoza, better known as the Marquis of Santillana; (2) Juan de Mena; and (3) Jorge Manrique. Santillana wrote sonnets in the Italian style, and elaborate, courtly *serranillas* (pastoral poems). He also wrote an important letter about the poetry of the times. Mena wrote *El Laberinto de Fortuna*, an allegorical work of 300 stanzas inspired by Dante and Petrarch. In the second half of the 1400's, Manrique wrote the *Coplas*, an inspired and artistically structured elegy on the death of his father.

Several events of literary importance took place during the late 1400's. Printing was introduced in Spain, probably in Saragossa in 1473. The first book known to have been printed in Spain was dated 1474 in Valencia. In 1492, Antonio de Nebrija published his *Grammar of the Castilian Language*, the first grammar ever written on the rules of a modern European language. The theater took its first steps toward secularization before 1500. Juan del Encina and Lucas Fernández wrote not only Christmas and Easter plays, but also drama with pastoral and folk dialogue. Other new trends in Spanish literature appeared in such novels as Diego de San Pedro's *Cárcel de Amor* (1492) and the Catalan book of chivalry, *Tirant lo Blanch* (1490). The long novel *Amadís de Gaula*, well known since the 1300's, was printed for the first time in 1508. It was probably written by Garci Ordóñez de Montalvo. See AMADÍS OF GAUL.

The masterpiece generally known as *La Celestina* appeared in the late 1400's. It was first published as an anonymous drama in 16 acts under the title *Comedia de Calisto y Melibea* (1499, although there may have been an earlier edition). This great work was later expanded to 21 acts and titled *Tragicomedia de Calisto y Melibea*. The author of at least 15 acts—and probably of the whole work—was Fernando de Rojas. The work was immediately translated into the main European languages. The classic English version became that of James Mabbe (*The Spanish Bawd*, 1631).

The central character of the famous drama is Celestina, a witchlike go-between who brings together two lovers, Calisto and Melibea. The drama combines medieval theology with a Renaissance conception of life. Much of the book's fascination centers on the character of Celestina. The main characters lose their lives one by one. Melibea's father closes the work with a tragic lament that has Biblical overtones. In this lament, he questions even the nothingness of his empty world.

## The Golden Age (1500-1681)

The spirit of the Italian Renaissance spread through Spanish literature of the 1500's. Beginning in 1530, literary expression was at constant odds with the Inquisition, an effort by the Roman Catholic Church to punish people who opposed church teachings. Many Spaniards were influenced by the Dutch scholar Erasmus of Rotterdam, who worked for reform of the church. His ideas were clearly present in the philosophical writings of Juan Luis Vives and the brothers Alfonso and Juan de Valdes. The beliefs of Erasmus were even in the work of St. Ignatius Loyola, founder of the Society of Jesus (Jesuits).

**Poetry.** During the early 1500's, Juan Boscán and Garcilaso de la Vega introduced the meters, verse forms, and themes of Italian Renaissance poetry. The Italian influence soon dominated Spanish poetry. But Cristóbal de Castillejo and Gregorio Silvestre, among others, preserved the Castilian tradition of short lines. Spanish poetry is indebted not only to such other Spaniards as Hernando de Acuña and Gutierre de Cetina, but also to the Portuguese Francisco Sá de Miranda and Luiz de Camões. Camões' great epic poem *Os Lusíadas* is a masterpiece in the style of Italian epics.

There were two main poetic schools after the mid-1500's—the Castilian school of Salamanca and the Andalusian school of Seville. Poets of both schools wrote in the style of Petrarch. But a certain serenity and a more cautious use of metaphor characterized the school of Salamanca and its representatives—Fray (Brother) Luis de León, Francisco de Figueroa, and Francisco de la Torre. Poets of the school of Seville included Fernando de Herrera, Francisco de Medrano, Francisco de Rioja, Juan de Jáuregui, and Juan de Arguijo. Through the use of colorful images, they developed a refined artistry in the formal possibilities of language that led to the baroque style of the 1600's.

Another important aspect of Spanish poetry of the 1500's was the lyrical expression of mystics—people who seek union with God through constant meditation. St. John of the Cross was the major mystic poet. Santa Teresa de Jesús contributed several prose works, including her autobiography, to mystical literature. Two similar writers were Fray Luis de Granada, author of *The Sinners' Guide* (1567), and Fray Luis de León, a professor at the University of Salamanca who was persecuted by the Inquisition. León wrote religious poetry and the prose masterpiece *The Names of Christ* (1583).

Medieval epics survived in the 1500's, not only in the romances but also in books of chivalry. The epic glorification of men and events also continued in long poems by Luis de Zapata, Luis Barahona de Soto, and Bernardo de Balbuena, and in Alonso de Ercilla y Zúñiga's *La Araucana*. This epic poem told of the conflicts between the Indians of Chile and the Spaniards. All these poets wrote in the Italian narrative style.

**Prose.** The *pastoral novel* became popular among Renaissance writers, and Spanish novelists produced fashionable works that idealized simple, rural life. *La Diana* (1559?) by Jorge de Montemayor and *La Diana enamorada* (1564) by Gaspar Gil Polo are still well-known Spanish pastoral novels. Cervantes in his first work, *La Galatea* (1585), and Lope de Vega in *La Arcadia* (1598) later followed the vogue of pastoral fiction.

The *picaresque novel* was by far the most important contribution of Spanish Golden Age fiction to world literature. This type of novel presented a picture of society as seen through the eyes of a *pícaro* (rogue). The first important picaresque novel was *Lazarillo de Tormes* (1554), written as the short, anonymous autobiography of a young boy of humble and doubtful birth. Lázaro makes his way by cunning and treachery while serving a blind beggar, then a greedy priest, and later a starving squire and other representatives of Spanish society. During his account of his wandering life, Lázaro moralizes on the episodes of his struggle. *Lazarillo* became a famous character and inspired many sequels.

The peak of the picaresque novel was attained by Mateo Alemán with *Guzmán de Alfarache* (first part, 1599; second part, 1604). *Guzmán*, another autobiography of a pícaro, is more detailed than *Lazarillo*. Alemán presented a more bitter, pessimistic view of life by showing that neither human nature nor conditions of life can be changed.

# SPANISH LITERATURE

The picaresque novel quickly became a tradition. Vicente Espinel wrote *Marcos de Obregón* (1618). López de Ubeda created a female rogue in *La Pícara Justina* (1605). The poet and satirist Francisco de Quevedo wrote the aggressive, skeptical, and sad novel *Life of the Swindler* (1626). Quevedo also became famous for his satire *Visions* (1627) and his moral essays on politics and history.

The counterpart of the realism of the picaresque novel was the idealism of Cervantes' masterpiece, *Don Quixote* (part I, 1605; part II, 1615). This story of a country landowner who considers himself a knight is filled with humor and sadness. Cervantes believed in the heroic ideals of his leading character and the dream-reality aspect of human life. But he went beyond his times, and gave his characters and themes a quality that extends beyond Spain to all mankind (see DON QUIXOTE). The writings of Cervantes that were most typical of the period were his dramas. But they failed to please audiences of the time, which favored the works of Lope de Vega.

**Drama.** The Spanish theater developed slowly during most of the 1500's. In 1517, Bartolomé de Torres Naharro published a collection of plays with a prologue on dramatic theory, *Propalladia*. Gil Vicente of Portugal wrote plays in Spanish—*Don Duardos*, *Amadís de Gaula*, and *La comedia del viudo*. The actor-playwright Lope de Rueda created the *paso*, a short farce that ridiculed the daily life of his time. Juan de la Cueva was the first author to take his plots from Spanish history or from popular narrative songs called ballads.

Lope de Vega emerged in the late 1500's as a unique literary figure of the Golden Age. He wrote for popular audiences, mixing tragic and comic elements. The topics of Lope's dramas had various origins. As the creator of a national drama, he drew on historical events. He also glorified national heroes. Lope filled many of his plays with the greatness of the spirit of the common people. But he also created rulers who had divine attributes and were concerned with justice. Some of Lope's plays were cloak-and-sword comedies, with love and honor the sources of dramatic conflict. Others were light plays with complicated plots in which his qualities of poet and dramatist stand out. The *bobo* (fool) of earlier comedies became a constant character in Lope's plays in the form of the *gracioso*, the witty counterpart of the hero.

Other dramatists of Lope's school included Tirso de Molina, whose *The Deceiver of Seville* (1630) was the first staging of the Don Juan legend; Guillén de Castro; the Mexican-born Juan Ruiz de Alarcón; Lope's biographer, Juan Pérez de Montalván; Francisco de Rojas Zorrilla; and Agustín Moreto.

**The 1600's.** At the beginning of the 1600's, the world of art sought new forms of expression. Artists tended toward greater ornamentation and complication in their works. The resulting style was called *baroque* (see BAROQUE). In Spain, there were two literary indications of this trend—*conceptismo* and *culteranismo*.

Conceptismo featured a subtle and ambiguous use of figures of speech, including antithesis, parallelism, and metaphor (see FIGURE OF SPEECH). The use of an elaborate metaphor called *concepto* (conceit) was the

592c

## SPANISH LITERATURE

best example of this trend. Many works of Quevedo and Baltasar Gracián were also examples.

Luis de Góngora led the culteranismo movement, which later became known as *gongorismo*. Góngora created lyric poetry full of color, imagery, and richness in musical linguistic effects. His long and complex poems *Polifemo and Galatea* (1612) and *Las Soledades* (1613), as well as his sonnets, ballads, and short compositions, became models for new developments in literature. Other poets who cultivated culteranismo included Pedro Soto de Rojas; Juan de Tarsis, the count of Villamediana; Luis de Carrillo y Sotomayor; and Sor (Sister) Juana Inéz de la Cruz, a Mexican nun.

Drama was also influenced by the baroque style. Pedro Calderón de la Barca succeeded Lope de Vega as the leading Spanish dramatist. He was more profound than his predecessor in the creation of character and the presentation of human problems. Calderón dramatized the dreams and realities of life in a singular work, *Life Is a Dream* (1635). The theme of honor and the conflict between love and jealousy were topics frequently staged by Calderón. His historical comedies and religious dramas showed his versatility. Calderón's work was full of examples of the baroque style. But his *autos sacramentales* (religious plays about the Eucharist) reflected culteranismo combined with the spirit of the Counter Reformation. The Counter Reformation was a reform movement within the Roman Catholic Church following the Protestant Reformation. Calderón used symbolism to express in solemn verse philosophical explorations of life and death, original sin, and free will.

Calderón's best-known autos included *The Great Theatre of the World* and *The Feast of Belshezzar*.

### The 1700's and 1800's

**Neoclassicism.** By the end of the 1600's, Spain had declined politically, economically, and artistically. Philip V, a Frenchman, became king of Spain in 1700 and began the Bourbon dynasty of rulers. With French rulers in Spain and the beginning of the Age of Reason (Enlightenment) in the rest of Europe, it was inevitable that Spanish literature would assume new directions.

Many writers tried to refine Spanish literature along the lines of French classicism (see CLASSICISM). Benito Jerónimo Feijóo, a Benedictine friar, wrote on almost every branch of learning in his *Teatro Crítico Universal* (8 volumes, 1726-1739) and *Cartas Eruditas y Curiosas* (5 volumes, 1742-1760). Ignacio Luzán also wrote within the framework of the Enlightenment. He supported the new ideas of reason, simplicity, and common sense in his book of literary criticism, *La Poética* (1737). Few Spanish writers of the time wrote novels. The only novel of note was *The History of the famous preacher, Friar Gerund de Campazas* (1758) by the Jesuit José Francisco de Isla. Two of the most important writers in Spain during the 1700's were José Cadalso and Gaspar Melchor de Jovellanos. Cadalso criticized the defects he saw in his countrymen in his best-known collection of essays, *Cartas marruecas* (1789). Jovellanos was a liberal poet, essayist, and economist.

The spirit of the 1700's did not favor lyrical expression. Neoclassicism, a style strongly influenced by Greek and Roman literature, was the most popular trend of the day. However, two of the best poets, Juan

### SPANISH LITERATURE FROM THE 1100'S

Masters of Spanish literature from the 1100's to the present rank among the greatest literary figures in the world. Spain's Golden Age, a period during the 1500's and 1600's, produced some of the finest drama, poetry, and fiction ever written.

Pedro Calderón de la Barca

Luis de Góngora (1561-1627)

Lope de Vega (1562-1635)

Miguel de Cervantes (1547-1616)

Lazarillo de Tormes (1554)

St. John of the Cross (1542-1591)

Amadís of Gaul (1508)

La Celestina (late 1400's)

Marquis of Santillana (1398-1458)

Miguel de Cervantes

Juan Ruiz (1283?-1350?)

Alfonso X (1221-1284)

Poem of the Cid (about 1140)

1150   1200   1250   1300   1350   1400   1450   1500   1550

# SPANISH LITERATURE

Meléndez Valdés and Nicasio Álvarez de Cienfuegos, wrote sentimental works under the influence of the French philosopher Jean Jacques Rousseau and other romantics. These poets were examples of a pre-romantic taste becoming prevalent in Spain. Manuel José Quintana clearly belonged to the neoclassical school. His odes and long poems had a patriotic sentiment that reflected ideas more than emotions. The works of Juan Nicasio Gallego resembled those of Quintana.

**Romanticism** came late to Spain. It was mainly a response to the more intense romantic impulses in the rest of Europe, and represented little more than a literary fashion (see ROMANTICISM). Spanish liberals brought the new philosophy of art and life with them when they returned from exile in the 1830's after the death of Ferdinand VII.

Ángel de Saavedra, the Duke of Rivas, assured the success of the romantic theater when he staged his drama *Don Álvaro, o La fuerza del sino* in 1835. Antonio García Gutiérrez pleased the public with *El Trovador* (1836). Juan Eugenio Hartzenbusch and Francisco Martínez de la Rosa also wrote for audiences that enjoyed romanticism. The peak of the romantic theater was reached by José Zorrilla. In 1844, he revived the Don Juan myth in *Don Juan Tenorio*, one of the long-lasting successes of the Spanish stage. Manuel Tamayo y Baus showed the influence of the high passion typical of romanticism in his historical tragedy *The Madness of Love* (1855) and in *Un drama nuevo* (1867). Manuel Bretón de los Herreros wrote satirical, realistic comedies. Adelardo López de Ayala took his plots from the life of the Spanish middle class. In the late 1800's, romanticism returned in the dramas of José Echegaray, who received the 1904 Nobel prize for literature. His best-known work was *The Great Galeoto* (1881). A concern for social justice, obvious in *Juan José* (1895) by Joaquín Dicenta, highlighted the Spanish stage in the late 1800's.

Spain's most distinguished poets of the 1800's were José de Espronceda and Gustavo Adolfo Bécquer. Espronceda's long poems *El Diablo Mundo* (1841) and *El estudiante de Salamanca* (on the Don Juan theme) included the richest expression of vibrant Spanish romantic poetry. Bécquer could be called the last of the romantics, but he lived when romanticism as a literary school was already outdated. His collection *Rimas* (1871) shows he was the most sensitive poet of the 1800's.

Two poets, Ramón de Campoamor and Gaspar Núñez de Arce, represented a reaction to romantic sentimentality. Campoamor composed short poems which were philosophical and skeptical. He called them *doloras* and *humoradas*. Núñez de Arce expressed an aggressive patriotism in *Gritos del combate* (1875). Rosalía de Castro wrote delicate lyrics, and her one book in Castilian made her one of the most respected poets of the 1800's.

Romanticism in Catalonia led to a revival of literature in the Catalan language during the last half of the 1800's. It produced such excellent poets as Jacinto Verdaguer and Juan Maragall, and such dramatists as Ángel Guimerá.

Short prose sketches of regional customs and manners developed from romantic literature picturing regional customs and folklore. This type of literature was called *costumbrismo*. Writers who created costumbrista articles

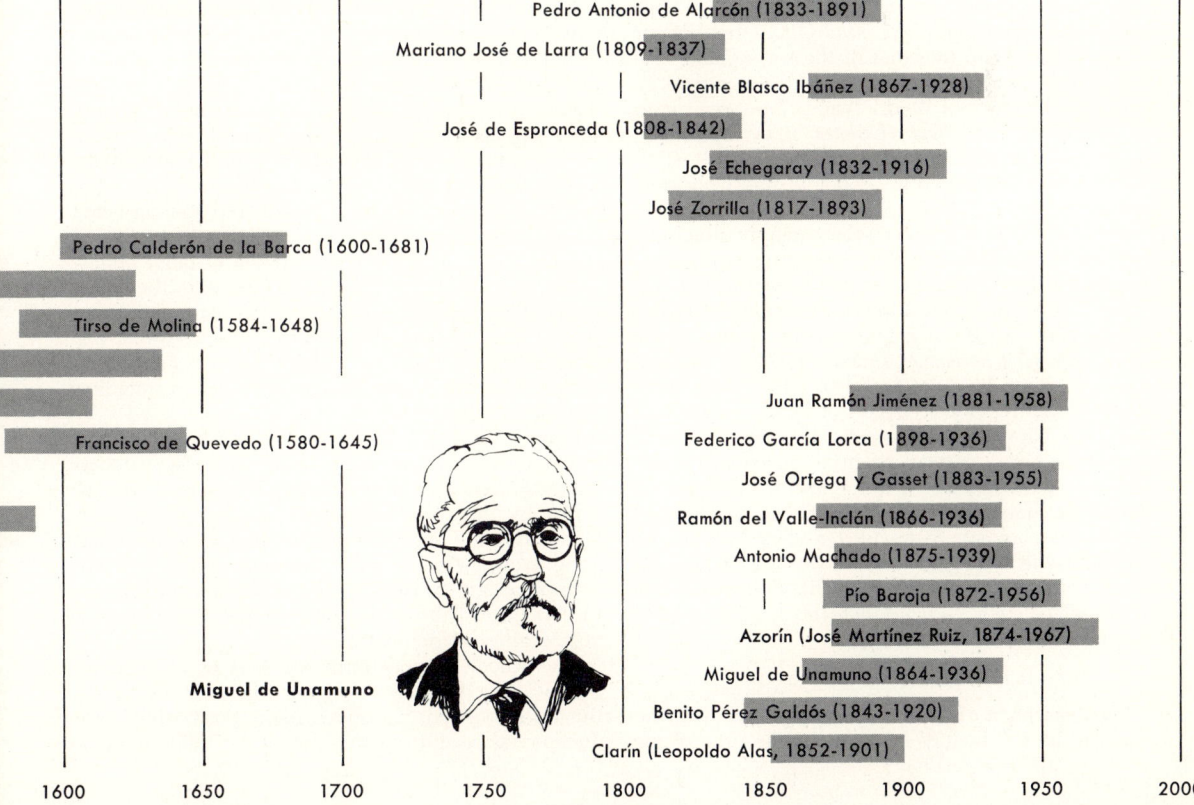

Miguel de Unamuno

# SPANISH LITERATURE

included Serafín Estébanez Calderón, known as *El Solitario*. He described typical scenes and people from the province of Andalusia in articles published as *Escenas andaluzas* (1847). Ramón de Mesonero Romanos, who called himself *El Curioso Parlante*, wrote articles about Madrid and published them in three volumes, *Panorama Matritense*. Mariano José de Larra, one of the best prose writers of the 1800's, was similar but more romantic in his attitude. His costumbrista articles, written in the tradition of Quevedo and Cadalso, showed deep concern for Spain. In his critical essays and journalism, often violent, he tried to awaken the nation to its possibilities.

The costumbrista articles gave rise to the Spanish realistic novel which developed in the mid-1800's. Cecilia Böhl de Faber, who wrote under the name of Fernán Caballero, brought costumbrismo to the novel in *La gaviota* (1849). Pedro Antonio de Alarcón wrote about Andalusian characters in his charming story *The Three-Cornered Hat* (1874) and in *The Infant with the Globe* (1880). Juan Valera, one of the most cultured writers of the 1800's, wrote *Pepita Jiménez* (1874) and *Juanita la Larga* (1895). These novels, as well as his literary criticism, reflected his worldly and sophisticated spirit.

Realistic regional novels dominated the second half of the 1800's. José Mariá de Pereda's *Sotileza* (1884) and *Peñas arriba* (1895) were costumbrista novels about life on Spain's northern coast. *Marta y María* (1883) by Armando Palacio Valdés dealt with the conflict of mystic and domestic virtues set against the detailed description of an Asturian city. Emilia Pardo Bazán wrote *Los pazos de Ulloa* (1886), a sparkling narrative of local traditions and politics of the interior of Galicia. *The Cabin* (1898) and *Reeds and Mud* (1902) by Vicente Blasco Ibáñez were tragedies of the swampland near Valencia. Ibáñez is also known for his two novels inspired by the terror of World War I, *Los cuatro jinetes del Apolcalipsis* (*The Four Horsemen of the Apocalypse*, 1916) and *Mare Nostrum* (1918).

The famous literary critic Leopoldo Alas, who wrote under the name of Clarín, created perhaps the best Spanish novel of the 1800's—the carefully structured and sensitive *La Regenta* (1885). But Spain's truly great novelist of the 1800's, and probably of the last 300 years, was Benito Pérez Galdós. He wrote 80 novels and 24 plays. In the five series of novels that make up the *Episodios nacionales*, Galdós novelized Spanish history from the Battle of Trafalgar (1805) until 1900. Many of his works were novels of ideas in which he dealt with religion and economics. He created profound characterizations—particularly his main female characters—and showed unusual awareness of the depth of human psychology. Galdós wrote about all levels of society, and his novels provided a clear insight into life in Madrid during the last half of the 1800's. His best novels were *Doña Perfecta* (1876), *El amigo Manso* (1882), *Fortunata y Jacinta* (1886-1887), *Miau* (1888), and *Misericordia* (1897).

## The 1900's

**The Generation of 1898** was a group of writers who appeared on the literary scene about the time of the Spanish-American War. These writers played an important part in the history of Spanish literature.

In the Spanish-American War, fought in 1898, Spain lost the last parts of its once mighty empire. The corruption of Spain's ruling class and the loss of its overseas colonies led many Spaniards to examine the nation's culture and civilization. The problem was whether Spain's cultural heritage could be adapted to the progress of modern Europe, and if it was original and creative enough to survive. From this examination of the Spanish character and past came a philosophical, historical, and artistic awakening that produced rich artistic expression.

Many types of writers contributed to the national renaissance of creative genius that dominated Spanish letters during the early 1900's. Miguel de Unamuno expressed romantic and existential grief in such essays as *The Tragic Sense of Life* (1912); poetry; and such novels as *Mist* (1914). Unamuno is often considered a forerunner of the philosophical movement called existentialism. The unique prose of Azorín (José Martínez Ruiz) included delicate and melancholic descriptions of Spanish landscape and history (*Castilla*, 1912; and *Doña Inés*, 1925). Pío Baroja became the leading Spanish novelist of the early 1900's. He showed sensitive heroes fluctuating between failure and triumph in such works as *The Tree of Knowledge* (1911) and *Zalacaín el aventurero* (1909). The poetry of Antonio Machado portrayed the severe spirit and landscape of Castile. Ramiro de Maeztu expressed himself in biting journalism. The beautiful prose style of Ramón del Valle-Inclán appeared in such novels as *Sonata de otoño* (1902) and *Divinas palabras* (1920). In such *esperpentos* (satires) as *Luces de bohemia* (1924), Valle-Inclán saw Spain as a grotesque distortion of normalcy.

Spain's literary past was rediscovered, interpreted, and edited and published by a group of scholars at the Center of Historical Studies in Madrid. These scholars included Ramón Menéndez Pidal, Américo Castro, Tomás Navarro Tomás, and José Fernandez Montesinos. They continued the work of Marcelino Menéndez y Pelayo, the great scholar and critic of the late 1800's.

Two fine novelists succeeded the Generation of 1898. Gabriel Miró was extremely lyrical, and Ramón Pérez de Ayala was one of the most intellectual novelists of his day. Noted essayists included the Catalan philosopher and art critic Eugenio d'Ors, and the internationally famous philosopher, historian, and critic José Ortega y Gasset. Among Ortega's works were *The Dehumanization of Art* (1925) and *The Revolt of the Masses* (1930). He and Unamuno became the outstanding Spanish intellectuals of the 1900's.

**Poetry.** While the Generation of 1898 was trying to discover the spirit of Spain, lyric poetry was undergoing the renewals of *modernism*. This school was inspired by the work of the Nicaraguan poet Rubén Darío and the French Symbolists (see LATIN-AMERICAN LITERATURE [Modernism]). The modernists joined the richness of form, musicality, and expression of the Spanish language with new poetic concepts, and created a new wealth of lyric poetry.

The school of modernism was best represented by Manuel Machado and Gregorio Martínez Sierra. Although short-lived, it inspired many poets whose production has been unequaled during the 1900's in quality and intensity. These writers included Juan Ramón Jiménez, winner of the 1957 Nobel prize for literature.

During the 1920's and 1930's, a number of poets turned to the traditional ballad or to the complex, colorful *gongorismo* for inspiration. Among those who wrote original and expressive lyric poetry were Pedro Salinas, Jorge Guillén, Léon Felipe, Gerardo Diego, Federico García Lorca, Dámaso Alonso, Vicente Aleixandre, Luis Cernuda, and Rafael Alberti. Lorca was also one of the great playwrights of the 1900's.

In the 1930's, Miguel Hernández, Leopoldo Panero, Luis Rosales, Luis Felipe Vivanco, and Germán Bleiberg represented a return to the formal poetry of the Renaissance. But their works reveal the anguish often present in love poetry. Prose writers of note included Ramón Gómez de la Serna and Benjamín Jarnés.

**The Spanish Stage** during the early 1900's was dominated by Jacinto Benavente, winner of the Nobel prize for literature in 1922. His plays *Bonds of Interest* (1907) and *The Passion Flower* (1913) received international praise. Two brothers, Serafín and Joaquín Alvarez Quintero, wrote amusing and delightful plays on Andalusian life. The plays of José María Pemán and the verse dramas of Eduardo Marquina dealt patriotically with Spanish national themes. The *costumbrista* plays of Carlos Arniches and the farces of Pedro Muñoz Seca pleased audiences of the time. The drama of this period reached a peak in the lyrical rural tragedies of Federico García Lorca. His plays included *Blood Wedding* (1933) and *The House of Bernarda Alba* (1936).

**Spanish Literature Today.** The Spanish Civil War (1936-1939) caused a break in Spanish literature. Some writers were killed and others were exiled, and the world of letters took some time to recover. But then came Camilo José Cela's novel *The Family of Pascual Duarte* (1942), followed by Carmen Laforet's *Nada* (1944) and Cela's *The Hive* (1951).

The 1940's and 1950's were productive, with some pre-Civil War writers still dominating the scene. But the new talent, characterized by social realism, was extraordinary. The novels of Miguel Delibes, Rafael Sánchez Ferlosio, José María Gironella, and Juan Goytisolo won international recognition. The theater was represented by the philosophical plays of Antonio Buero Vallejo and Alfonso Sastre, and the social comedies of Alfonso Paso.

Poetry since 1939 first followed a direction toward simpler forms of expression with Dionisio Ridruejo and José Luis Cano. Then poetry changed to a nonconformist attitude with Gabriel Celaya, Blas de Otero, and such younger writers as Claudio Rodríguez. Some writers, including the novelists Francisco Ayala and Ramón Sender and the playwright Alejandro Casona, developed their work in exile. Julián Marías, José Luis Aranguren, and José M. Ferrater Mora wrote philosophical and social essays. GERMÁN BLEIBERG

**Related Articles** in WORLD BOOK include:

| | |
|---|---|
| Alarcón, Pedro A. de | Echegaray y Eizaguirre, José |
| Benavente, Jacinto | García Lorca, Federico |
| Blasco Ibáñez, Vicente | Gongora, Luis de |
| Calderón de la Barca, Pedro | Jiménez, Juan Ramón |
| | Latin-American Literature |
| Cervantes, Miguel de | Molina, Tirso de |
| Cid, The | Ortega y Gasset, José |
| Don Juan | Quevedo, Francisco de |
| Don Quixote | Ruiz, Juan |
| Drama (The Golden Age of Spanish Drama) | Unamuno, Miguel de |
| | Vega, Lope de |

# SPANISH SAHARA

## Outline

I. **The Middle Ages**
   A. Early Medieval Literature
   B. The 1400's
II. **The Golden Age (1500-1681)**
   A. Poetry           C. Drama
   B. Prose            D. The 1600's
III. **The 1700's and 1800's**
   A. Neoclassicism
   B. Romanticism
IV. **The 1900's**
   A. The Generation of 1898    C. The Spanish Stage
                            D. Spanish Literature Today
   B. Poetry

## Questions

What effect did *costumbrismo* have on the novel of the mid-1800's?

What was the Generation of 1898?

What is the significance of the *jarchas* in the history of literature?

Who were the two most important dramatists of Spain's Golden Age?

Why is *The Cid* more realistic than other medieval epic poems?

What are the characteristics of the *picaresque* novel?

What were the contributions of Benito Pérez Galdós to Spanish literature?

How does *conceptismo* differ from *culteranismo*? Why are both characteristic of the baroque style?

Who was Spain's greatest and best-known writer?

**SPANISH MAIN** was the name English buccaneers and pirates gave to the northern coast of South America. By 1550, Spain controlled the Caribbean Sea, the West Indies, and large areas of the South American mainland. *Spanish Mainland* referred to what are now Colombia and Venezuela. English seamen shortened the name to *Spanish Main*.

**SPANISH MOSS** is a flowering plant that hangs from trees in the southeastern United States and in tropical South America. Its long, slender, grayish stems look like hair hanging from the trees. It is neither a true moss nor a parasite. The plant has no roots, and absorbs water directly from the air. It has long, narrow leaves and small yellow flowers. Its stems are dried and used to stuff upholstery.

**Scientific Classification.** Spanish moss belongs to the pineapple family, *Bromeliaceae*. It is genus *Tillandsia*, species *T. usneoides*. ROBERT W. HOSHAW

See also AIR PLANT; TREE (picture: Bald Cypress).

**SPANISH PHALANX.** See FALANGE ESPAÑOLA.

**SPANISH SAHARA** is a province of Spain that lies on the northwest coast of Africa. It is divided into two parts—Southern Region (formerly Río de Oro) and Northern Region (formerly Saguia el Hamra). El Aiún is the provincial capital and capital of Northern Region. Villa Cisneros is the capital of Southern Region.

Most of the 48,000 people in Spanish Sahara are Arabs and Berbers. These people move about constantly, seeking water and grass for their herds of camels, goats, and sheep. Some work as fishermen near El Aiún. Most of the people are Moslems. They are related to the people of neighboring Morocco and Mauritania, and they wander back and forth across the borders of these countries freely.

Most of Spanish Sahara's 102,703 square miles is barren, rocky desert. The province gets little rainfall.

593

## SPANISH SUCCESSION, WAR OF THE

Vegetation is scanty except for patches of coarse grass and low bushes near the coast. Iron ore deposits have been discovered inland, but they have not been developed because there are no roads to the region.

Spain claimed Spanish Sahara in 1509. Morocco ruled it from 1524 until Spain regained control in 1860. Spanish Sahara became a province of Spain in 1958.
JAMES W. FERNANDEZ

See also EL AIÚN.

## SPANISH SAHARA

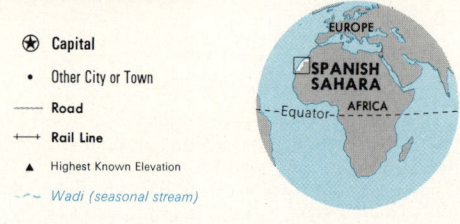

**SPANISH SUCCESSION, WAR OF THE.** See SUCCESSION WARS.

**SPANISH WAR VETERANS, UNITED,** is an organization founded in 1898 by some of the men who took part in the Spanish-American War. The United Spanish War Veterans has over 3,000 members in more than 600 local groups throughout the United States and its possessions. The organization works to gain government benefits for its members, and to help needy veterans and their families. Its headquarters are at 810 Vermont Avenue NW, Washington, D.C. 20005. HARRY E. WILLIAMS

**SPANISH WEST AFRICA** was a group of territories held by Spain on the northwest coast of Africa. It consisted of Ifni, Spanish Sahara, and Morocco Southern Zone. Ifni and Spanish Sahara became provinces of Spain in January, 1958. Spain ceded Morocco Southern Zone, a strip of land along the Dra River, to Morocco in 1958, and the province of Ifni to Morocco in 1969. See also IFNI; SPANISH SAHARA.

**SPARK CHAMBER** is a device which makes visible the paths followed by electrically charged atomic particles. Nuclear physicists use spark chambers to study these particles, which are too small and travel too fast to be seen by the naked eye. Two Japanese physicists, S. Fukui and S. Miyamoto, built the first practical spark chamber in 1959. Since 1960, the spark chamber has become an important research tool for high energy nuclear physicists. Physicists use it with similar devices called the Wilson cloud chamber and the bubble chamber. But unlike these devices, the spark chamber can be made sensitive for just the short interval that a particle a physicist wants to study is in the chamber.

A spark chamber is made of a series of thin metal plates set parallel in an airtight box that is filled with neon gas. A gap of from 3 to 400 millimeters separates the plates, depending upon the design of the chamber. A typical chamber about 3 feet long has 150 plates spaced 6 millimeters apart. Electrical equipment powers the chamber.

The spark chamber is most often used with an *atom smasher* (atomic particle accelerator). The accelerator makes high energy particles that can be studied in the chamber. When a charged atomic particle enters the chamber, it *ionizes* (electrically charges) the neon gas atoms in its path. The particle simply penetrates the thin metal plates. The ionized gas atoms will conduct electricity but the atoms that have not ionized will not. An electrical field of 1,000 volts per millimeter of plate separation is applied to alternate plates immediately after the particle ionizes the neon. This field makes a lightninglike spark between the plates along the ionized path of the particle. The sparks can easily be seen and photographed.

Special electronic circuits apply the high voltage to the plates only after a selected particle enters the chamber. Physicists can select the particle they wish to study in the chamber. By eliminating unwanted particle *tracks* (paths), the physicist can spend more time studying the important tracks. By studying the tracks made by atomic particles, physicists learn more about the atom and atomic particles. Several previously unknown particles have been discovered by experiments with spark chambers.
GERARD K. O'NEILL

See also ATOM; ATOM SMASHER; BUBBLE CHAMBER; WILSON CLOUD CHAMBER.

**Sparks Show Up in a Spark Chamber,** tracing the paths charged atomic particles followed through the chamber. Photographs of these paths help physicists study the particles.

Brookhaven National Laboratory

**SPARK COIL.** See IGNITION.
**SPARK PLUG.** See IGNITION.
**SPARKMAN, JOHN JACKSON** (1899- ), a United States senator from Alabama, was the Democratic nominee for Vice-President of the United States in 1952. He served as a U.S. representative from 1937 to 1947. In 1946, Sparkman won an election to finish the unexpired term of Senator John Bankhead. He entered the Senate in 1947.

In Congress, Sparkman generally supported the policies of the Democratic Presidents except in civil rights policies. He usually backed Republican President Dwight D. Eisenhower on foreign policy, but opposed his domestic policies. Sparkman was born near Hartselle, Ala., on Dec. 20, 1899. He attended the University of Alabama. F. JAY TAYLOR

Chicago Historical Society
**John J. Sparkman**

**SPARKS, JARED** (1789-1866), was an American historian and biographer who pioneered in collecting original documents on American history. His works include the 12-volume *The Writings of George Washington* (1834-1838), *The Library of American Biography* (1834-1838), and the 10-volume *The Works of Benjamin Franklin* (1836-1840). Sparks was born in Willington, Conn. He served as a Unitarian minister from 1819 to 1823. He also held the position as editor for the *North American Review* from 1824 to 1831. He became president of Harvard University in 1849. MERLE CURTI

**SPARROW** is the name of many small, common birds. The name comes from the Anglo-Saxon word *spearwa*, which probably was a general term for all small birds. Today, it applies especially to many members of the finch family, which are found throughout the world except in Australia. In America, about 35 species of this family are called *sparrows*. Other sparrows include the *hedge sparrows* of Europe and Asia and European *house* and *tree sparrows*.

Most American sparrows are plain-looking, brownish birds. Many sparrows are noted for their musical songs. Among these are the *song sparrow, vesper sparrow, lark sparrow, white-crowned sparrow, white-throated sparrow, fox sparrow,* and *Lincoln's sparrow*.

Sparrows usually eat seeds, but during the nesting season they also eat insects. The birds build nests on the ground, in clumps of grass, in bushes, or in low trees, but seldom far from the ground. The *chipping sparrow*, or *chippy*, builds its nest in a higher place than other sparrows do. Sometimes the nest may be found in evergreens 25 feet above the ground. The sparrow's nest is a compact, well-built, open structure made of grasses, plant fibers, and sometimes small twigs. The female lays four or five white eggs that are marked with reddish brown.

American sparrows live almost everywhere. For example, song sparrows live in bushy areas, fox sparrows in forests, swamp sparrows in marshes, vesper sparrows in prairies and sage sparrows in deserts. Those that live in cold regions usually migrate southward in winter. Some of them go to Mexico, others to Central America.

The common house sparrow, often called the *English sparrow* in America, originally lived throughout Europe. It was brought to America in 1850 and now lives in most of the populated regions of Canada, the United States, and northern Mexico.

**Scientific Classification.** American sparrows belong to the finch family, *Fringillidae*. The song sparrow is genus *Melospiza*, species *M. melodia*. Lincoln's sparrow is *M. lincolnii*, and the swamp sparrow is *M. georgiana*. The white-throated sparrow is *Zonotrichia albicollis*, and the white-crowned sparrow is *Z. leucophrys*. The chipping sparrow is *Spizella passerina*, the fox sparrow *Passerella iliaca*, and the vesper sparrow *Pooecetes gramineus*. The sage sparrow is *Amphispiza belli*, and the lark sparrow is *Chondestes grammacus*. Hedge sparrows are in the accentor family, *Prunellidae*. European house and tree sparrows are in the weaver finch family, *Ploceidae*. The house, or English, sparrow is genus *Passer*, species *P. domesticus*. LEONARD W. WING

See also BIRD (Building the Nest; Eggs; color pictures: Birds' Eggs, Birds That Help Us); ENGLISH SPARROW; LIFE (table: Length of Life of Animals).

**SPARROW HAWK** is the smallest falcon in North America. It is a *bird of prey* (one that eats living animals). It is different in both appearance and habits from the sparrow hawk of the Eastern Hemisphere, which resembles the American Cooper's hawk. The sparrow hawk breeds from northern Canada to northern

**Sparrows Are Noted for Their Beautiful Singing.** Among the most musical types in the United States are the song sparrow, left, which lives in bushy areas; the white-crowned sparrow, center, which lives in northern woods; and the house sparrow.

Karl H. Maslowski, NAS
Allan D. Cruickshank, NAS
Leonard Lee Rue, NAS

**The Little Sparrow Hawk** is only slightly larger than a robin. It is a swift flier, and eats rodents and insects.

George M. Bradt

Mexico. It winters in the southern United States and south to Panama. The male has a reddish-brown back with black bars, a plain reddish-brown tail tipped with a band of black and white, and bluish-gray wings spotted with black. The female's back, tail, and wings are reddish brown marked with black bars. The bird eats insects, small rodents, reptiles, and sometimes smaller birds. It is about the size of a mourning dove. The sparrow hawk will nest almost anywhere. It will nest in the hollow of a tree, or even in a crack in the wall of a building. The female sparrow hawk lays from four to six white to brown eggs.

**Scientific Classification.** The North American sparrow hawk belongs to the falcon family, *Falconidae*. It is genus *Falco*, species *F. sparverius*. The European sparrow hawk belongs to the hawk family, *Accipitridae*. It is genus *Accipiter*, species *A. nisus*. OLIN SEWALL PETTINGILL, JR.

See also FALCON AND FALCONRY.

**SPARS** is the popular name for members of the United States Coast Guard Women's Reserve. The name *SPAR* is taken from the first letters of the coast guard motto and its English translation, **S**emper **P**aratus (**A**lways **R**eady). Unlike women in other branches of the armed forces, all SPARS are in the military reserve. SPARS come under the command of the coast guard, which is part of the Department of Transportation.

SPARS have no active duty enlistment program, but women may enlist in reserve units. There are about 120 SPAR officers and 50 enlisted women in the inactive reserve program. Fewer than 20 officers and enlisted women serve on active duty.

The group was formed in November, 1942, to free coast guardsmen for sea duty in World War II. By the war's end, the SPARS had 10,000 enlisted women and 1,000 officers. All were discharged or placed on inactive duty by June, 1946. The group was then dissolved, but it was reactivated in November, 1949.

Critically reviewed by the U.S. COAST GUARD

**SPARTA**, or LACEDAEMON, *LASS ee DEE mohn*, the capital of Laconia, was at one time the most powerful city-state of ancient Greece. It was famous for its military power and its loyal soldiers. The greatest honor that could come to a Spartan was to die in defense of his country. Endurance, a scorn of luxuries, and unyielding firmness are still spoken of as Spartan virtues.

**The Land.** Sparta was situated in a lovely, sheltered valley on the bank of the Eurotas River. For location, see GREECE, ANCIENT (color map). It was protected on three sides by mountains. The climate was mild, and the soil was fertile and well watered. Sparta had few mineral resources. Spartans obtained marble and a little iron from nearby Mount Taygetus.

**The People** belonged to three classes. The Spartans themselves were descended from the Dorians, a people who invaded the Greek peninsula about 1000 B.C. They were the ruling class of Sparta and were the only ones who had full rights of citizenship. They enslaved the earlier Greek peoples of Laconia, the Achaeans and Ionians. These enslaved Greeks, called *helots* (pronounced *HELL ut*) outnumbered the Spartans. Some of the non-Spartan Greeks escaped enslavement. They were not citizens, but they lived in Sparta as free men. This group was known as the *perioeci* (pronounced *PAIR ih EE sigh*). The numbers of the three classes varied widely during Sparta's long history. Some authorities estimate that at the height of Spartan power there were about 25,000 citizens, an unknown number of perioeci, and as many as 500,000 helots.

**Way of Life.** Spartan citizens could engage only in agriculture. A few aristocrats owned their land, but most citizens held state-owned plots. A citizen who could not make enough from his estate to support his family and pay the taxes lost his land to someone who could make it pay. He also lost his citizenship. It was therefore dangerous to try to rear a large family. The Spartans sometimes left unwanted children in a deep cavern in the mountains to die.

Because citizens were not allowed to carry on manufacturing or trade, these pursuits were taken over by the perioeci. Some of them grew wealthy.

The helots farmed the soil, and each had to give a fixed amount of produce to his master. The rest, which was often little, went to the helot himself. The helots bitterly resented their lot, and revolts were not unusual. Once a year the Spartans officially declared war on the helots, so that they could kill any who seemed rebellious without breaking the law against murder.

Every Spartan belonged to the state from the time of his birth. A boy was left to the care of his mother until he was seven years of age, when he was enrolled in a company of 15 members, all of whom were kept under strict discipline. From the age of seven, every Spartan had to take his meals with his company in a public dining hall. The bravest boy in a company was made captain. The others obeyed his commands and bore such punishments as he decided they should have.

When the boys were 12, their undergarments were taken away and only one outer garment a year was allowed them. Their beds consisted of the tops of reeds, which they gathered with their own hands and without knives. Spartans did not consider the arts of reading and writing necessary. Boys learned the *Iliad* and songs of war and religion, but leaping, running, wrestling, and wielding a weapon with grace and accuracy were held much more important. Between the ages of 20 and 30 Spartan youths served as cadets, who policed the country, kept the helots in order, and exacted disciplined obedience from the enslaved people.

At the age of 30, a Spartan attained full maturity and enjoyed the rights and duties of citizenship. He might marry, attend meetings of the assembly, and hold public office. At 60, his military career ended, and he worked either in public affairs or in training the young.

As a result of this system, the Spartan men became tough, proud, disciplined, and noted for obstinate conservatism and for brevity and directness of speech. From childhood, life was one continuous trial of endurance. All the gentler feelings were suppressed.

Spartan women, on the other hand, lived the freest life of any women in Greece. As girls, they engaged in athletics, and as women ran their own households. They engaged in business, and many became wealthy and influential. Aristotle tells us that women owned two-fifths of the land in Sparta.

**History.** The Dorians who settled in Sparta extended their control over all Laconia at an early date. In the 700's B.C., they conquered Messenia, the rich farming region to the west of Mount Taygetus. Sparta failed to conquer the cities of Arcadia, but forced them to enter the Peloponnesian League. The members of the league were obliged to follow Sparta in war. By the middle of the 500's B.C., this league included most of the cities in southern and central Greece.

Sparta conquered Athens, the leader of the powerful Athenian Empire, in the hard-fought Peloponnesian War. In 404 B.C. the Athenians were forced to accept a humiliating peace treaty. But the leadership won by Sparta was short-lived. The Spartans ruled over the other Greek states so cruelly that they revolted and threw off the Spartan yoke. At the battle of Leuctra, in 371 B.C., Sparta lost forever its claim to supremacy in Greece. But it remained a powerful city for the next 200 years. In 146 B.C. it came under the rule of Rome.

There is a modern town of Sparta (pop. about 10,500) near the site of the ancient city. It was laid out about 1835 and made the capital of the modern political division of Laconia. Excavations have been made on the old site, and much valuable material has been discovered from the early city's history. DONALD KAGAN

**Related Articles** in WORLD BOOK include:
Dorians
Education, History of
(In Ancient Greece)
Greece, Ancient (The
Government of Sparta)
Laconia
Leonidas I
Lycurgus
Lysander
Messenia
Peloponnesian War

**SPARTACUS** ( ? -71 B.C.), was the most famous of all Roman gladiators. But he won his fame as the leader of a great slave uprising, rather than in the arena.

Spartacus was born in Thrace. He was captured by the Romans while serving as a soldier, and was sold as a slave to be made a gladiator (see GLADIATOR). With 70 comrades, he escaped, hid on Mount Vesuvius, and raised a large army of rebel slaves from the farms of Italy.

His forces conquered most of southern Italy and defeated two Roman armies. Spartacus wanted to lead his men over the Alps and out of Italy back to their homes, but the slaves forced him to lead them in a march on Rome. They lost their courage, however, and quarreled among themselves. A fresh Roman army under Marcus Licinius Crassus finally defeated them (see CRASSUS, MARCUS LICINIUS). Many were crucified as a warning to other slaves. Spartacus himself fought courageously until he was killed. CHESTER G. STARR

**SPARTANBURG,** S.C. (pop. 44,352; alt. 875 ft.), is an important cotton-textile-manufacturing city. It is also the trading center of a fertile peach-orchard region. Spartanburg lies in northwestern South Carolina, 15 miles from the North Carolina border (see SOUTH CAROLINA [political map]). It is the home of Converse and Wofford colleges. Spartanburg was chosen as the seat of Spartanburg County in 1785. Both county and town were named for the Spartan Regiment, a South Carolina militia group which fought in the Revolutionary War. Spartanburg has a council-manager government. For Spartanburg's monthly temperature and rainfall, see SOUTH CAROLINA (Climate). JULIAN J. PETTY

**SPASM.** See CRAMP; TETANY.

**SPASTIC PARALYSIS** is a form of *cerebral palsy*, a condition in which damage to the brain has resulted in poor control over the muscles. The brain damage usually occurs at birth, although it can happen before birth. Spastic paralysis can also develop after birth if an infection such as meningitis damages the brain, or if damage results from strokes, skull fractures, or other injuries.

The part of the brain that is damaged and the amount of damage done determine which muscles are affected and how severely. Sometimes the damage is so slight that the individual may have only a little clumsiness, a slight loss of balance, or perhaps a slight speech difficulty. In severe cases, the individual cannot walk. Or he may walk on his toes with his feet turned inward, his knees together, and with one leg crossing over in front of the other, in the typical "scissors gait" of the spastic. Because spastic paralysis can affect all the muscles, the face, the tongue, and even the muscles that control breathing may be affected. This may result in uncontrollable grimacing, drooling, and great difficulty in speaking.

Many persons suffering from spastic paralysis are completely normal, except for their difficulties in controlling the affected muscles. But in some cases, brain injury does affect the individual's intelligence. Even mental retardation may occur. Nevertheless, thousands of spastic paralysis cases have above average intelligence.

The brain damage cannot be cured, but the use of the muscles can be improved through surgery, training, and the use of crutches and braces. Spastics can be taught to speak more effectively, to care for themselves, and to earn their own living.

The spastic patient should be treated as a normal person, except for the special training that may be required. Spastic children should be encouraged to play with other children, and live as normal a life as possible while their muscle use is being improved. It is important, too, for people to understand that spastic paralysis is not a communicable disease, that it is not inherited, and that it is not a form of mental illness. A person should not be ashamed of spastic paralysis any more than he should be ashamed of wearing glasses. M. A. PERLSTEIN

See also CEREBRAL PALSY.

**SPATHE.** See LEAF (Leaves That Keep the Plant Warm).

597

# SPAVIN

**SPAVIN,** *SPAV in*, is a common name for two unrelated diseases which affect the hocks of horses. The hock is the ankle joint of the hind leg. *Bone spavin*, or true spavin, is a bony growth usually on the inner and lower part of the joint. The disease is caused by a lack of certain minerals in the bones. *Bog spavin* is a swelling of a capsule of tissue of the main joint. It is believed to exist at birth and seldom causes any trouble. Both are seldom curable. Bone spavin, however, can be treated to end lameness and to keep the growth from enlarging.

**SPAWN** is the eggs of fishes, mollusks, frogs, and other animals. Usually such eggs are produced in great numbers, particularly by sea animals that are eaten by larger species, or that leave eggs and young to hatch and develop alone. These water animals must produce thousands or millions of eggs to keep from dying out. The eggs of certain fish, particularly the sturgeon, are often used in making the delicacy known as *caviar*. The eggs of fishes are also called *roe*, particularly when used as human food. Shad roe is particularly favored. See also CAVIAR; FISH (Reproduction); SALMON (Life History); STURGEON.   CARL L. HUBBS

**SPEAKER.** See LOUDSPEAKER.

**SPEAKER** is the title of the presiding officer in the lower house of several national, state, and provincial legislatures. The duties of the office differ in various legislative bodies.

**In the United States,** the speaker of the House of Representatives can wield great power. He is the recognized leader of his political party in the House, as well as the presiding officer. He is expected to use his office to promote his party. He ranks next after the Vice-President in order of presidential succession. He receives a yearly salary of $43,000 and $10,000 for expenses.

The early speakers considered themselves simply as presiding officers, and tried to be impartial. Henry Clay, elected speaker in 1811, began the practice of using the office for party purposes. The office reached its height as a political force under the strong personalities of Thomas B. Reed, who served as speaker from 1889 to 1891 and again from 1895 to 1899, and Joseph G. Cannon, speaker from 1903 to 1911.

For a time the speaker was considered almost as important as the President. In 1910 he was removed from the Committee on Rules, and his control over the appointment of committees was taken away. But the speaker is still important in national legislation. For the powers, duties, and methods of selection of the speaker of the House, see HOUSE OF REPRESENTATIVES.

**In Great Britain,** a speaker has presided over the House of Commons since at least 1377. The speaker of Commons should be a model of impartiality. He must rule in accordance with the will of the majority, but never permit the minority to be abused. The House elects each new speaker. It is the custom to re-elect the same speaker in all Parliaments until he dies or is ready to retire.

The office of speaker in the House of Commons has great dignity. It carries a salary of 5,000 pounds (about $14,000) a year, and an official residence in the Palace of Westminster. When the speaker retires, he becomes a peer, or nobleman.   GEORGE E. MOWRY

See also MACE.

**SPEAKER, TRIS E.** (1888-1958), a great American baseball player, was known as the *Gray Eagle* because of his gray hair and his speed in playing the outfield. He won fame with the Cleveland Indians and played in the American League from 1907 to 1928. His lifetime batting average of .344 places him in an all-time outfield with "Babe" Ruth and "Ty" Cobb. Speaker's top batting mark was .389 in 1925. He managed the Indians from 1919 to 1926, winning the world championship in 1920. Speaker was born in Hubbard, Texas.   ED FITZGERALD

**SPEAR** has played an important part in history from earliest times. It ranked as the chief weapon used in the battles of ancient Asia and Europe. The famous Greek poet, Homer, tells how Achilles speared Hector through the neck with a "pole heavy with bronze." The early Persians added a sharp spike to the back end of the spear so that both ends could be used. The Romans used a short, heavy spear called a *pilum*. The Gauls fought with a huge, clublike spear. Illyrian soldiers carried a fine, light javelin. In India, soldiers mounted on charging horses threw the lance, a weapon similar to the javelin. The Bedouins of Arabia were famous for their skill in using the lance on horseback.

Today, the spear is used chiefly in fishing. Eskimos kill seals and fish with spears through holes in the ice. Persons who enjoy underwater swimming often use spearguns with great accuracy. These spearguns shoot spears by means of springs, rubber bands, or compressed gas.   JACK O'CONNOR

See also JAVELIN.

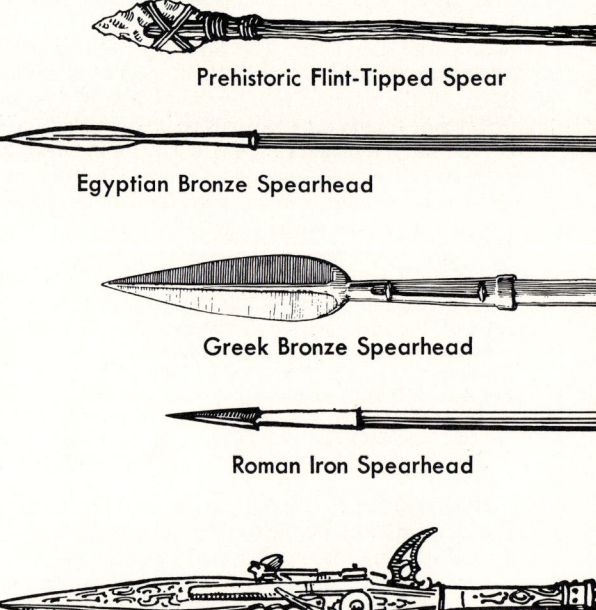

Prehistoric Flint-Tipped Spear

Egyptian Bronze Spearhead

Greek Bronze Spearhead

Roman Iron Spearhead

Medieval Hunting Spearhead

**Spearheads Changed** as men learned to make them of new materials. Early men tied jagged pieces of stone onto their throwing sticks. Then they learned to shape pointed spearheads from pieces of flint. Metals made the best spearheads of all.

## PARTS OF A SPEARGUN

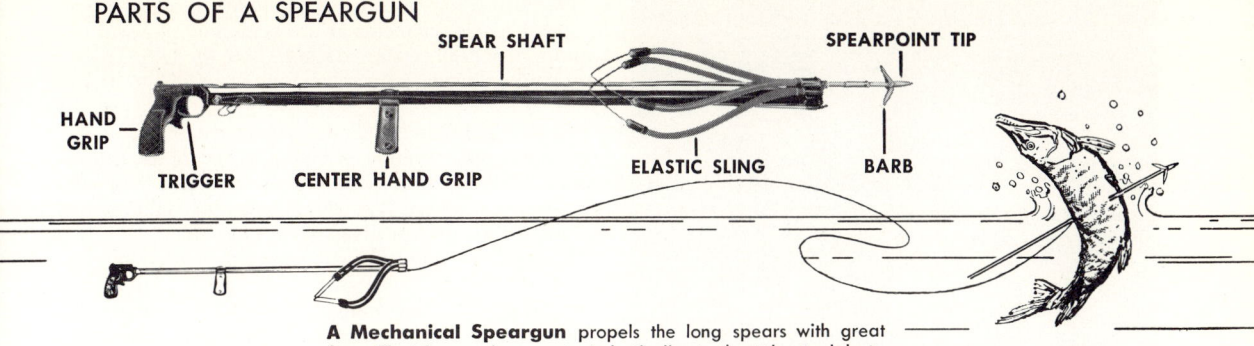

**A Mechanical Speargun** propels the long spears with great force. The trigger releases a taut elastic sling to shoot the steel darts.

U.S. Divers Co.

**SPEARE, ELIZABETH GEORGE** (1908-    ), an American author, won the Newbery medal in 1959 for *The Witch of Blackbird Pond* and in 1962 for *The Bronze Bow*. She also wrote *Calico Captive* (1957). Mrs. Speare was born in Melrose, Mass., and was graduated from Boston University.

**SPEARFISH.** See MARLIN.

**SPEARFISH,** S.Dak. See SOUTH DAKOTA (Annual Events in South Dakota).

**SPEARFISHING,** or UNDERWATER HUNTING, is the sport of shooting fish under water. Some spearfishermen shoot spears to kill fish. Others shoot a harmless dart with a narrow strip of plastic attached to it. The plastic strip sticks to the fish, and can be useful in studying the migration and growth of fish.

Spearfishermen usually shoot fish with a speargun. Most spearguns are built like crossbows. A small bow is mounted on a long shaft. The spearfisherman draws the *bowstring* (large rubber band) back and hooks it on a catch. By pulling a trigger, the hunter releases the catch and shoots a small spear that is attached to a line about 15 feet long. Other spearguns are powered by compressed gas, springs, or rubber slings. Arrowheads that explode may be used to drive the spear into the fish. But most spearfishermen consider exploding arrowheads unsportsmanlike and dangerous to the spearfisherman.

Spearfishing equipment includes a mask that goes over the nose and eyes, foot fins to aid in swimming, and a *snorkel* (short breathing tube). Most spearfishermen consider it unsportsmanlike to hunt using an independent breathing device such as an Aqua-Lung. The use of such equipment is illegal in many places.

The spearfisherman swims along the surface, face down. When he sights a fish, he takes a breath and executes a *coup de reins*. A *coup de reins* is a quick dive in which the diver bends from the waist, snaps his legs straight into the air, and dives toward the fish. If the spearfisherman is hunting to kill, he shoots the fish, rises to the surface, and then pulls in the fish.

Many hunters prefer not to kill fish. Instead, they shoot the fish with the dart. These fishermen belong to a research group. The strip of plastic attached to the dart carries the number of the diver, which has been assigned by his research group. After the spearfisherman shoots a fish, he files a card with his group that tells the size and location of the fish. If the fish is caught later, the card furnishes information that may be compared with the present size and location of the fish.

Expert spearfishermen may dive from 60 to 100 feet to find fish. Some fish hunters have tried to hold their breath longer than they normally can by taking several deep breaths or by breathing pure oxygen before diving. This *hyperventilates* (increases the amount of oxygen in) the lungs, and may cause the diver to faint or even to die. Overwork while holding the breath under water is also dangerous. Overwork raises the level of carbon dioxide in the diver's blood stream and has an effect similar to hyperventilation.

Spearfishing for food probably began thousands of years ago. Spearfishing became a popular sport during the 1900's. Shooting darts for scientific research began in the 1950's.

JAMES DUGAN

See also SKIN DIVING; DIVING, UNDERWATER.

**A Spearfisherman Stalks Fish Underwater** in the Caribbean Sea. He alertly holds his gun in the firing position.

Bahamas News Bureau

L. W. Brownell

**Spearmint Plants Have Spear-Shaped Flowers.**

**SPEARMINT** is a type of mint plant that grows in most of the temperate regions of the world. It yields an oil used in making perfumes, medicine, chewing gum, candies, and mint jelly or sauce. It has smooth, erect stems 1 to 2 feet high, topped with spikes of lavender or white flowers. Most spearmints in the United States grow in Indiana, Michigan, and Washington state.

**Scientific Classification.** The spearmint belongs to the mint family, *Labiatae*. It is classified as genus *Mentha*, species *M. spicata*. HAROLD NORMAN MOLDENKE

**SPEBSQSA.** See BARBERSHOP QUARTET SINGING.
**SPECIAL DELIVERY.** See POST OFFICE (Services).
**SPECIAL FORCES.** See ARMY, UNITED STATES (Special Forces).
**SPECIAL HANDLING.** See POST OFFICE (Special Handling).
**SPECIAL LIBRARIES ASSOCIATION** was founded in 1909 to help special libraries in business and industry. It has more than 6,000 members in the United States, Canada, and other countries. These members represent banking, advertising, insurance, finance, publishing, and manufacturing firms, as well as museums, specialized departments of colleges and universities, business branches of public libraries, and scientific and technical libraries. The association holds an annual convention in May or June. It publishes an official journal, *Special Libraries*; *Technical Book Review Index*; *Translation Monthly*; and handbooks and bibliographic aids in the special library field. It has headquarters at 31 E. 10th Street, New York, N.Y. 10003. MARIAN E. LUCIUS

**SPECIAL SESSION.** See CONGRESS OF THE UNITED STATES (When Congress Meets).
**SPECIE CIRCULAR.** See JACKSON, ANDREW (The Money Surplus).
**SPECIE PAYMENTS, RESUMPTION OF,** refers especially to the redeeming of paper money with gold by the United States Treasury. This action started on Jan. 1, 1879. *Specie* means *coin*, usually gold or silver coin.

Nations using metals as standard money often suspend specie payments at the beginning of a war or during periods of economic strain. Both the U.S. Treasury and commercial banks stopped payments from 1861 to 1879.

Between 1862 and 1865, the Department of the Treasury issued $450 million of United States notes, called *greenbacks*. The government used these notes to help pay the costs of the Civil War. But greenbacks could not be exchanged for gold or silver, so they lost value.

Various government and banking policies gradually reduced the amount of greenbacks in circulation. By the end of 1878, the value of greenbacks was equal to that of gold, and specie payments were resumed. Greenbacks were redeemable in gold from then until 1933, when the United States formally abandoned the gold standard (see GREENBACK). ARTHUR A. WICHMANN

**SPECIES,** *SPEE shiz*, or *SPEE sheez*, is the basic unit of scientific classification. Animals and plants are classified in groups called kingdoms, phyla, classes, orders, families, genera, and species. Members of a single species are more closely related than are members of any other group. Members of a species breed with one another, but one species usually does not breed with another under natural conditions. The name of a species always has two parts. The first part is the name of the genus to which the species belongs. The second word is an adjective. Together they form the name of a particular animal or plant. For example, the lion is named *Felis leo*. WILLIAM V. MAYER

See also CLASSIFICATION (table).

**SPECIFIC GRAVITY.** See GRAVITY, SPECIFIC.
**SPECIFIC HEAT** of a substance is the amount of heat needed to raise the temperature of a unit mass of the substance (1 pound or 1 gram) by 1 degree. The unit of heat energy in the metric system is the *calorie*, the amount of heat that will raise the temperature of 1 gram of water 1 degree Centigrade. The unit in the English system is the British Thermal Unit (B.T.U.). A B.T.U. will raise 1 pound of water 1 degree Fahrenheit. See also BRITISH THERMAL UNIT; CALORIE; HEAT; TEMPERATURE. ROBERT LINDSAY

**SPECIFICATION.** See ARCHITECTURE (Preparing Final Plans).
**SPECTACLES.** See GLASSES.
**SPECTATOR, THE.** See ADDISON, JOSEPH.
**SPECTROGRAM.** See ASTRONOMY (table: Terms).
**SPECTROGRAPH** is an instrument for photographing a *spectrum*, the pattern of colors formed by light passing through a prism. A light source is placed behind a very narrow slit, to eliminate overlapping of colors in the spectrum. A band of images from the light source is focused on a photographic film. Each image is formed by one of the wave lengths in the light from the source. A spectrograph is a spectroscope with a camera instead of a telescope. See also LIGHT; SPECTROSCOPE. JOSEPH VALASEK

**SPECTROHELIOGRAPH,** *SPECK troh HE lih oh GRAHF*, is an apparatus that allows one color of the sun's spectrum to be photographed. An image of the sun, obtained through a telescope, is allowed to pass through the slit of a spectrograph. The spectrum thus obtained is transmitted through a second slit that allows only light of a selected wave length to pass to a film behind it. See also LIGHT (Spectrum Analysis); SPECTROGRAPH; SPECTROSCOPE. JOSEPH VALASEK

## SPEECH, FREEDOM OF

Bausch & Lomb

**Young Joseph Fraunhofer,** Bavarian optician, explains the spectroscope he has invented to one of his friends.

### THE SPECTROSCOPE—AN INSTRUMENT FOR SPECTRUM ANALYSIS

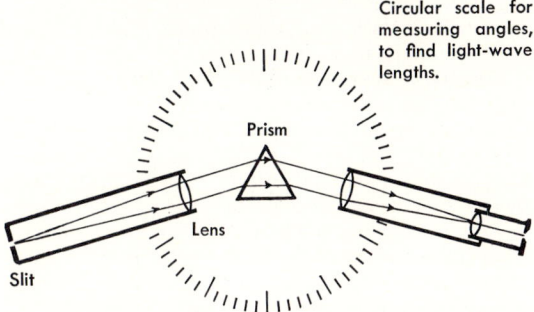

Lens of collimator tube bends light rays from slit to parallel position before they reach the prism.

Telescope gives sharp image of spectrum produced by prism. Hairlines can be focused on colors for wave-length readings.

**SPECTROSCOPE,** SPECK troh skohp. Substances heated to a high temperature give off light. This light may be separated into a pattern of colors by passing it through a prism (see PRISM). The pattern is the *spectrum* for that substance. No two materials have the same spectrum. For this reason, an expert can identify any substance by its spectrum. Any instrument he uses to examine spectra is called a *spectroscope*.

The simplest spectroscope is a triangular glass prism. A person who looks through a prism, preferably with the aid of a small telescope, sees a band of colored images of the light source. These tend to overlap and blend into each other. Less overlapping occurs if the source is narrow and its images are sharply focused. For the best possible separation of the colored images, the light source is placed behind a narrow slit. The slit is attached to one end of a tube, and a lens is attached to the other end, so that a beam of parallel light rays emerges from the lens. This part of the spectroscope is the *collimator*. The light from the collimator passes through the prism and then through a telescope to the eye of the observer.

Spectra of heavenly bodies are often obtained with a compound spectroscope. This consists of a series of prisms arranged in the arc of a circle. The spectroscope is attached to the eyepiece end of a large telescope that forms an image of the heavenly body on the slit of the spectroscope. By using spectra obtained in this way, an astronomer can determine the chemical composition of the sun and the stars, and of the atmosphere of planets. The astronomer can also determine the speed at which the body is moving toward or away from him by measuring small shifts in the spectrum lines.

A spectroscope may use a diffraction grating instead of a prism to separate light into different colors (see DIFFRACTION). Modern gratings are made by ruling straight grooves with a diamond on a glass surface or on a metal mirror. The gratings resemble the grooves on a long-playing phonograph record, but are much closer together. About 15,000 grooves to an inch are common. The spectrum formed by a glass grating is seen by looking through it.    JOSEPH VALASEK

See also GEISSLER TUBE; LIGHT; MASS SPECTROSCOPY; SIEGBAHN, KARL MANNE GEORG; SPECTROGRAPH.

**SPECTRUM.** See COLOR (Color in Light); LIGHT; SPECTROSCOPE.

**SPECTRUM, DIFFRACTION.** See DIFFRACTION; LIGHT.

**SPECULAR IRON.** See HEMATITE.

**SPECULATION.** See BOARD OF TRADE (Speculative Trading).

**SPEECH** has several definitions. It may mean the act of speaking, the result of speaking or what is spoken, the language of a nation or group of nations, or the dialect peculiar to a region or locality.

*The act of speaking* includes conversation, public speaking, debating, forum discussion, reading aloud, storytelling, and acting. It uses the *audible code* and the *visible code*, which are the sounds used by the speaker and the movements or gestures of his face, arms, and other parts of his body that are used for emphasis.

*The result of speaking* is the content and ideas expressed by the act of speaking. In formal speech, it includes the speech at the time it is given, and any written or printed form in which it may appear.

*Language or dialect* differs among peoples of various nations and groups of nations, and also within a nation. In the United States, the chief dialects are: (1) eastern (roughly, the New England states and New York City); (2) southern (roughly, the regions south of the Potomac and Ohio rivers [except West Virginia], most of Louisiana, and parts of Texas and Arkansas); and (3) general American (roughly, the rest of the United States).

The average child learns to speak by imitating the people around him. It is important that he hear proper speech. Parents should note any speech difficulties, such as lisping or stuttering, in their children. If such difficulties occur, parents should take the child to a competent authority on speech problems. A number of speech clinics throughout the country can offer helpful advice.    W. HAYES YEAGER

**Related Articles** in WORLD BOOK include:

| | |
|---|---|
| Communication | Pronunciation |
| Conversation | Public Speaking |
| Dialect | Speech Therapy |
| Handicapped (The Deaf) | Stuttering and Stammering |
| Language | |
| Lisping | |

**SPEECH, FREEDOM OF.** See FREEDOM OF SPEECH.

United Press Int.

**A Speech Therapist** uses a mirror to teach a student the exact mouth formation required to pronounce a certain word.

**SPEECH THERAPY,** *THER uh pih*, helps to correct common speech disorders, such as stuttering and lisping. It also helps to correct other physical or psychological speech defects, such as those caused by cleft palate and cerebral palsy. Speech therapists have special training that equips them to treat most types of speech disorders.

**Types of Speech Therapy.** *Speech defectives,* or persons who have a speech disorder, receive therapy either in groups or individually.

*Group Speech Therapy* is used to treat less severe speech disorders. It helps speech defectives by bringing them together with others with the same or similar problem. In these surroundings, the peculiarities of speech do not stand out as much as they do in a group of persons who speak normally. This usually makes the speech defective feel more at home and less self-conscious. The defectives receive encouragement by listening to others and hearing the improvement of the group.

*Individual Speech Therapy.* Usually, complex cases of speech defects receive therapy individually in a specialized clinic. Both individual and group therapy have a definite importance. But individual therapy concentrates on only one individual at a time. As a result, speech specialists believe that the speech defect is remedied much faster than by group treatment.

**Treatment of Speech Defects.** The speech therapist first examines the speech defective to determine the type and extent of the speech difficulty. By using various interview techniques and examining instruments, the therapist tries to discover the cause of the defect. Gradually, he builds up a case history on the individual being treated. If the patient needs medical treatment, he is sent to a doctor or a medical clinic. Other defects are treated by an appropriate professional, such as a psychologist or dentist. He works with the therapist.

*Common Defects.* If a person has difficulty *articulating,* or expressing words correctly, the speech therapist listens to the quality, the inflections, and the rate of the defective's speech. Often, the therapist uses a recording machine so that the patient can learn to hear the difference between his own speech and normal speech. By such instruction, the defective learns to understand and imitate normal speech. Throughout the treatment, the therapist determines the patient's over-all problem of communication, such as the range of his vocabulary and his ability to use and improve his vocabulary.

*Complex Cases* call for more highly specialized therapy. A good example of a complex case is *aphasia,* or the loss or partial loss of the ability to understand or use speech. Aphasia may be caused by a brain injury or by some other functional or emotional disturbance. In aphasia caused by brain injury, the rest of the brain is not affected. The individual may still have the ability to speak, even though he makes no efforts at speech. In complex cases such as this, the defect is like a highway with the bridge out. The speech therapist must either repair the bridge or create a detour. Since he cannot repair the damaged area of the brain, he must create a detour. He tries to restore the speech of the defective with techniques that are known to help create a detour.

**Careers in Speech Therapy.** Many universities now offer professional training in speech therapy as a part of the regular undergraduate and graduate training. The person who intends to make a career of speech therapy should have at least a master's degree, and preferably a doctor's degree. He receives training in the anatomy of the human body as it relates to speech. He takes courses in psychology and physics, particularly in relation to the study of sound. He also takes courses in language, communications, education, and clinical psychology.

After completing the basic program, the student decides whether he will work in speech or hearing. The speech therapist studies the disorders of expression. The hearing expert studies the special anatomy of the ear and the psychology of hearing. He also learns how to detect hearing losses, to fit hearing aids, and to teach lip reading. He must be able to instruct persons who are deaf and hard of hearing.

About three fourths of the speech therapists work in special educational divisions of the public schools. The remainder work on staffs of hospitals, medical schools, psychology clinics, and university speech and hearing clinics. Speech therapists receive a somewhat higher salary than regular teachers, because of the highly specialized training involved.   MARTIN F. PALMER

See also CLEFT PALATE; HARELIP; LISPING; SPEECH; STUTTERING AND STAMMERING.

**SPEED.** See MOTION; SPEEDOMETER; VELOCITY.

**SPEEDBALL** is a team game that combines elements of soccer and basketball. It is usually played by 11-man teams on an outdoor field. The players advance the ball down the field by kicking it or passing it. They may also take one step while bouncing the ball, but they cannot run with it. Points are scored when a player kicks or drives the ball with his body through a goal post, when a player kicks the ball over the crossbar of the goal post, or when a player catches a pass behind the goal line. See also BASKETBALL; SOCCER.

**SPEEDOMETER,** *speed AHM ee ter,* is an instrument that indicates the speed of a vehicle in miles an hour. It also records the distance traveled by the vehicle. The dial of the speedometer has numbers, usually from 0 to 100, and a pointer that indicates the speed at which the vehicle is moving.

A speedometer is powered by a flexible shaft that connects to a set of gears in the vehicle's transmission (see TRANSMISSION). The gears take into account the tire size and the axle ratio. When the vehicle moves, the gears in the transmission turn a core inside the shaft. The core is attached directly to a permanent magnet that lies near a *speedcup*. The revolving magnet sets up a rotating magnetic field that pulls the speedcup and its attached pointer in the same direction that the magnetic field is turning. A hairspring keeps the speedcup steady. The pointer on the speedcup comes to rest where the hairspring balances the force of the revolving magnet. When the vehicle stops, the hairspring pulls the pointer to zero. When the vehicle speeds up, the magnet increases its pull on the speedcup. This causes the speedometer to register a higher speed.

A device called an *odometer* registers the total miles traveled by a vehicle. Many speedometers have a *trip odometer* that can be reset to zero at the beginning of a trip. Manufacturers design all speedometers so that 1,000 revolutions of the flexible shaft will register one mile on the odometer, and 1,000 revolutions a minute will indicate a speed of 60 miles an hour. Some speedometers run from a small electric generator. Speedometers require little care. But dirt and excess grease will make them inaccurate. They should be lubricated about every 10,000 miles.   HERBERT O. VOGEL

See also PEDOMETER; TACHOMETER.

**SPEEDWELL,** the ship. See PLYMOUTH COLONY.

**SPEEDWELL,** weed. See FIGWORT FAMILY.

# SPEEDOMETER

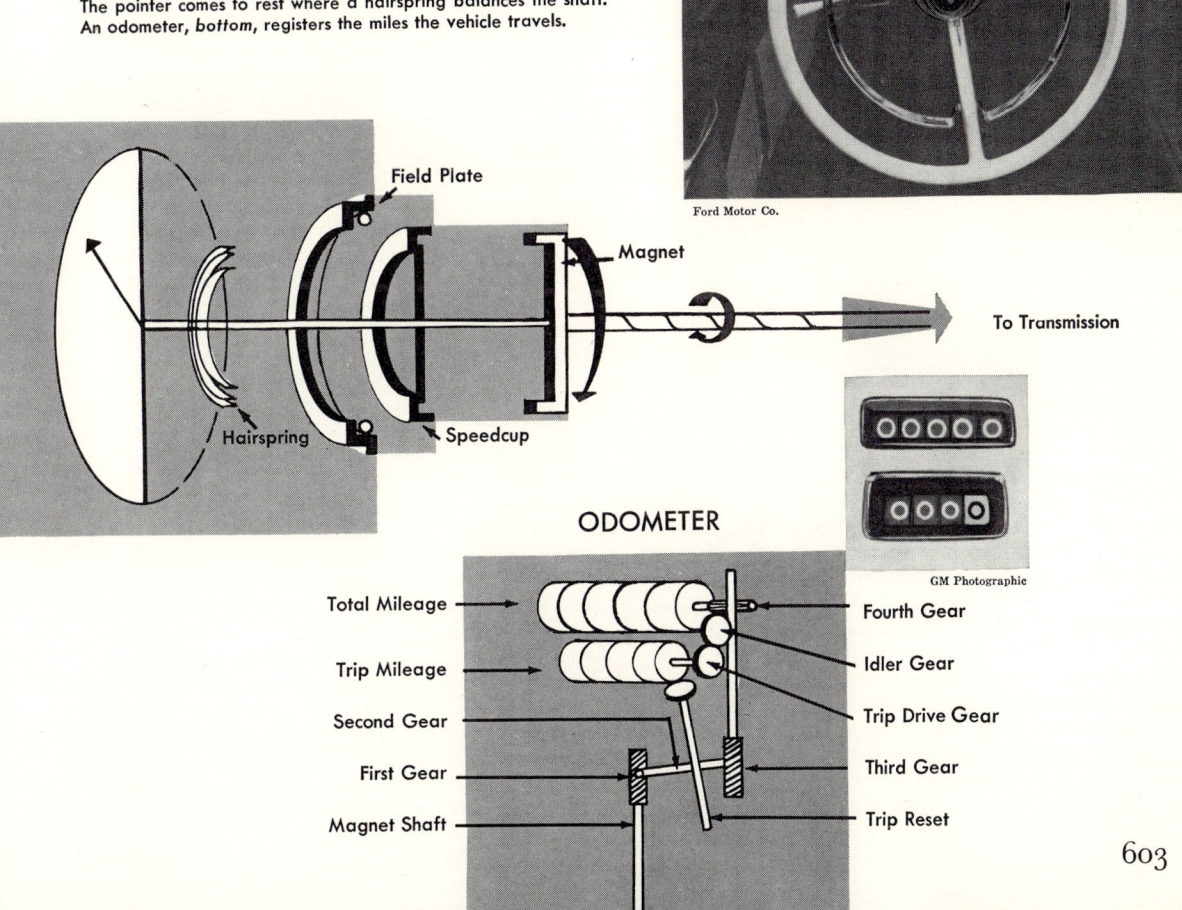

**An Automobile Speedometer Tells the Speed** of the vehicle. A flexible shaft runs between the magnet and the transmission. When the vehicle moves, gears in the transmission turn a core inside the shaft. The core turns a magnet, which sets up a magnetic field that pulls a speedcup and the pointer on the dial. The pointer comes to rest where a hairspring balances the shaft. An odometer, *bottom*, registers the miles the vehicle travels.

603

# SPEEDWRITING

**SPEEDWRITING** is the registered trademark for a widely used shorthand system. It employs letters of the alphabet instead of symbols.

In Speedwriting shorthand, all words are written as they sound. Thus, *you* is written *u*; *are* is *r*; *eye* is *i*. In addition, a whole syllable may be represented by a letter or a punctuation mark. For example, the letter *a* expresses the sound of *ate*. Thus, *late* is *la*; *bait* is *ba*. The letter *r* expresses the sound *re*. Thus, *relate* is *rla*; *rebate* is *rba*. A hyphen represents the final sound of *ment*. Thus, *pigment* is *pg-*. Basement is *bs-*.

Brief forms or abbreviations represent 218 frequently used words. All other words are written according to principle. For example, a secretary using Speedwriting writes the sentence, "*Your rebate check will reach you in a few days,*" as:

u rba ck l rec u n a fu ds\

The main advantage of Speedwriting shorthand is that the student need not learn any new symbols. Therefore, he can take dictation at the rate of about 120 words per minute after only six to eight weeks of training. He can transcribe his notes rapidly and accurately because they are in his regular handwriting.

Emma B. Dearborn, a shorthand teacher of Darien, Conn., originated Speedwriting in 1923.   PAUL M. PAIR

See also SHORTHAND; SHORTHAND MACHINE.

**Speedwriting Uses the Alphabet and Standard Symbols.**

**SPEIDEL,** *SPY dul,* **HANS** (1895-   ), a German general, served in World War II and became a leader in the postwar West German Army. As chief of staff to Field Marshal Erwin Rommel in France in 1944, he united the efforts of the German officers fighting against Adolf Hitler. He was important in the series of unsuccessful plots to rid Germany of Hitler. He became commander of the North Atlantic Treaty Organization (NATO) ground forces in Central Europe in 1957. Speidel was born in Metzingen, Württemberg.   LESTER B. MASON

**SPEKE, JOHN HANNING.** See EXPLORATION AND DISCOVERY (table: Explorers of Africa).

**SPELEOLOGY** is the scientific study of caves. Scientists who make such studies are called *speleologists*. Persons who explore and map caves as a hobby are called *spelunkers*. Many cave explorers belong to the National Speleological Society. See also CAVE.

**SPELL.** See MAGIC (Communicating with Spirits).

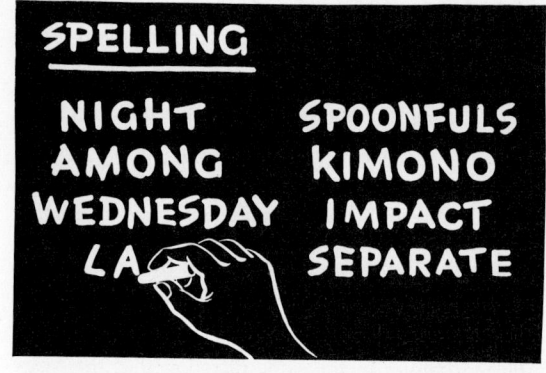

**SPELLING** is the way we combine letters to write words. Learning to spell correctly is part of learning a language. The English language has only 26 letters. But the several hundred thousand words of the English language can all be spelled with these 26 letters. Correct spelling, like correct speaking, is more than a sign of a person's education. It helps him communicate his thoughts in writing so others will know quickly and easily what he means to say.

To understand how the alphabet works, say out loud the word *bat*. Say the word again, and listen carefully for the three sounds that blend together to make up the spoken word. Now, write the word instead of saying it. First, write the letter that stands for the beginning sound of the word, *b*. Next, write the letter that stands for the middle sound, *a*. Last, write the letter that stands for the final sound, *t*. The letters *b-a-t* repeat in the same order the three original sounds of the spoken word. This is the *spelling* of the word *bat*. Spelling is simply the method of writing letters for spoken sounds. But the historical development of the English language has resulted in many spellings that do not follow the way the words are pronounced.

### Learning to Spell

Many persons make spelling more difficult than is necessary. They try to learn their spelling by speaking, as in spelldowns, and forget that writing is the only place in which spelling can possibly matter. They spend time and effort on words that they are unlikely ever to write and whose meanings are vague to them. They emphasize spelling drill and spelling rules, but neglect to work out an effective method of learning to spell new words. They try to learn spelling without developing any interest in the magic of words and the ways people use language to communicate ideas.

**Base Words.** The first problem in learning to spell is to decide which words are the most important. The average person uses fewer than 25,000 words in speaking. He uses even fewer in writing. About 2,000 *base words* will satisfy over 90 per cent of the writing needs of the average eighth-grade student. An additional 1,000 base words, or 3,000 in all, will take care of 95 per cent of the writing needs of the average adult. An example of a base word is *danger*. Some words that come from this base include *dangerous* and *endanger*.

The student should first learn to spell the 3,000 base words. Then he can add the spellings of words that he uses for personal or business reasons. There are two

604

main sources for base words. One is the writing of adults and the other is the writing of children. Many words occur in both groups. Most spelling textbooks include lists of words of both groups.

Thousands of words have been studied to make up the lists of base words. For example, *about* is used by adults and by children as early as the first grade. *Absorb* is used by adults, but is seldom used by children until the eighth grade. *Abrupt* is often used by adults, but is seldom used by young people before high school.

**Methods of Study.** The difference between good spellers and poor spellers can often be traced to one problem: finding an effective *method* of learning to spell. Good spellers have some method for studying words they want to spell. Poor spellers are frequently helpless with a new word. When they try to learn a new spelling, they usually use poor methods. Here are 10 common steps used by good spellers:

1. Looking at the word.
2. Copying the word.
3. Remembering how the word looks.
4. Listening to the pronunciation of the word.
5. Pronouncing the word.
6. Dividing the word into syllables.
7. Saying the letters of the word in order.
8. Writing the word to get its "feel."
9. Studying the difficult parts of the word.
10. Using the word in a meaningful sentence.

Remembering trick phrases, such as "the princi*pal* is a *pal*," is not a good substitute for an effective learning method. A few spelling tricks, such as remembering "station*ery*" with "pap*er*," may be helpful with some particularly hard word. But too many special tricks can be confusing.

A person who wants to improve his spelling can make a combination of the steps listed above that suits him. Few people would use all 10 steps. Once the combination has been selected, it should be tested and changed if necessary. Then the combination can become a regular part of a person's learning habits. Visualizing the word, or remembering how it looks, should probably be part of everyone's combination. Here is a combination suggested by an authority on spelling:

1. Understand the use, meaning, and pronunciation of the word.
2. Visualize the word.
3. Note the spelling of the word.
4. Write the word carefully and neatly.
5. Check the spelling of the word.
6. Use the word as often as possible in writing.

This combination may not be best for some persons, but it should be useful for most beginners.

**Spelling Rules** can help improve a person's spelling. Use these rules with great care, because there are often many exceptions.

Many words come from a base word. For example, the words derived from *develop* include *develops*, *developed*, *development*, *developing*, and *developer*. Each of these new forms is made with a *suffix* added at the end of a word. Here are some rules that help people spell suffixes correctly:

1. Drop the final *e* in a word before a suffix beginning with a vowel. For example, *love + ing* is *loving*. An exception is *dyeing*.
2. Keep the final *e* in a word before a suffix beginning with a consonant. For example, *sure + ly* is *surely*.

Clair Reid

**Spelling Bees** are annual events in many communities. The National Spelling Bee in Washington, D.C., matches the best spellers in each state to determine the national spelling champion. Newspapers throughout the United States sponsor contestants. A boy or girl must be under 16 years old to enter the National Spelling Bee.

3. When a word ends in *y* preceded by a consonant, change the *y* to *i* before adding a suffix (unless the suffix begins with *i*). For example, *plenty + ful* is *plentiful*.
4. When a one-syllable word ends in a consonant preceded by a single vowel, double the consonant before a suffix beginning with a vowel. For example, *run + er* becomes *runner*.
5. When a word has more than one syllable, double the consonant only if the accent of the word is on the last syllable. For example, *admit' + ed* is *admitted*.

*Prefixes* are added to the beginning of words. Three common prefixes are *dis-*, *mis-*, and *un-*. When they are added to a word beginning with the same letter, there will be two *s*'s or *n*'s. For example, *mis + spell* is *misspell*. When they are added to a word beginning with a different letter, there will be only one *n* or *s*. For example, *un + willing* is *unwilling*.

One of the biggest spelling problems comes from the use of *ei* and *ie*. Some words are spelled with *ei*, such as *receive*. Some words are spelled with *ie*, such as *believe*. A spelling rule to remember is: "Use *i* before *e* except after *c* or when it is sounded like *a*, as in *neighbor* and *weigh*." Some exceptions to this rule include *either*, *leisure*, and *seize*.

**Adding New Words**

One way a person can increase the number of words he can spell is to learn the spelling of words derived from a base word. For example, *trust* is a base word. A number of words, such as *mistrust*, *trusting*, and *trustee*, come from this base word. A similar method is to learn the *root meanings* of words. The root of a word is its basic form. For example, the root *port* means *carry*. Knowing this helps to learn the spelling and meaning of such words as *portage*, *import*, *export*, *report*, *porter*, *deport*, *portable*, *comportment*, and *portfolio*.

A more important way of adding new words is to learn the habit of using a dictionary. On seeing a new word, look it up in the dictionary and study its spelling and pronunciation. The dictionary also gives root meanings of words. See DICTIONARY.

Sometimes a word has two or more different spellings. For example, *enrollment* and *enrolment* are both correct spellings. Usually, a dictionary gives the *preferred spelling*

605

## 200 SPELLING DEMONS

| | | | | | | |
|---|---|---|---|---|---|---|
| absence | bicycle | eminent | heinous | neighbor | raise | surgeon |
| absorption | boundary | endeavor | history | night | receipt | sympathize |
| ache | bulletin | enough | hoarse | ninth | receive | temperament |
| acquaintance | burglar | envelope | hour | noticeable | referred | temporary |
| acquitted | business | everything | illiterate | occasion | reign | therefore |
| across | cafeteria | exceed | immediately | occurrence | repeat | tragedy |
| affidavit | ceiling | existence | indictment | often | repetition | typical |
| again | cemetery | expedition | indispensable | omitted | rescind | until |
| aggravate | chauffeur | expense | innocent | optimistic | reservoir | vacuum |
| aghast | chocolate | extraordinary | interfere | origin | restaurant | vegetable |
| all right | colonel | familiar | introduce | original | rheumatism | vengeance |
| ally | column | fascinate | laboratory | pageant | rhyme | warrant |
| already | coming | fasten | legitimate | parliament | ridiculous | wear |
| always | commercial | February | leisure | perform | sacrifice | week |
| among | committee | forfeit | library | permanent | schedule | weird |
| analysis | confidence | forty | license | perseverance | secretary | whether |
| analyze | control | friend | literature | picnicking | seize | which |
| angel | controversy | fulfill | magnificent | pleasant | semester | whole |
| angle | convertible | genius | maneuver | pneumonia | separate | women |
| annual | counterfeit | government | mathematics | possessive | siege | won't |
| answer | courteous | governor | meant | prairie | skein | would |
| appetite | curiosity | grammar | medal | prejudice | sophomore | writer |
| arctic | dealt | gratified | millionaire | principal | specimen | writing |
| ascent | desperate | guarantee | miniature | principle | stationery | written |
| awkward | despise | guess | minute | professor | statistics | wrote |
| bachelor | develop | handsome | mortgage | pursue | strictly | yacht |
| beggar | discipline | hangar | muscle | quantity | succeed | |
| believe | doctor | harass | mystery | quiet | sugar | |
| benefit | eighth | height | necessary | quite | superintendent | |

first. But this does not mean that the alternate spelling is wrong. There are also many differences between American and British spellings. For example, the American *labor* is the British *labour*. The American *center* is the British *centre*. And the American spelling *connection* is the British *connexion*.

### Spelling Demons

Words that people find unusually difficult to spell are called *spelling demons*. They often have an irregular arrangement of letters and need special study. The word *fasten* is a typical spelling demon. Many people who misspell this word write it *fasen*, because the *t* is silent. That is, a person does not sound the *t* in *fasten* when he speaks the word. Another demon is *friend*. People often write it *freind*, because the word has the sound of *e*.

Many spelling demons are *homonyms*, or words that sound alike but have different meanings. For example, *pray* and *prey* are often misspelled because they sound alike. Other homonyms include *bare* and *bear*, *principal* and *principle*, *read* and *red*, and *to*, *too*, and *two*. Failing to pronounce a word accurately and distinctly is a frequent cause of error. The word *government* is an example. If a person says *gov-er-ment*, he may spell the word without the first *n*. Two other examples are *preform* for *perform* and *quanity* for *quantity*.

### Simplified Spelling

Many attempts have been made to simplify the spelling of the English language. The aim of most of these plans is to spell a word exactly as it is pronounced. For example, under these plans the word *though* would be spelled *tho*, and the word *knock* would be spelled *nok*.

There have been two chief arguments against such changes. The first is that simplified spelling would destroy the familiar pattern of words and cause confusion. The second is that the pronunciation of words changes continuously. Changes in pronunciation can occur rapidly or slowly. Words would soon become unrecognizable if the spelling were changed to meet each new change in pronunciation. WALTER LOBAN

See also ABBREVIATION; ALPHABET.

**SPELLMAN, FRANCIS CARDINAL** (1889-1967), was one of the outstanding leaders of the Roman Catholic Church in the United States. His wide acquaintance among church officials throughout the world made his services valuable in special missions for both Presidents Franklin D. Roosevelt and Harry S. Truman. Spellman served as apostolic vicar to the United States armed forces, and made several trips to various battle areas during time of war. Pope Pius XII named him a cardinal in 1946.

United Press Int.
**Cardinal Spellman**

Spellman was born at Whitman, Mass. He took his college degree at Fordham University, and was ordained a priest in 1916 after studying at the North American College in Rome. His first post was in Boston. From 1925 to 1932 he was in the service of the Papal Secretariat in Rome. He was consecrated a bishop in Rome, and returned to serve as auxiliary bishop of Boston. In 1939, Pope Pius XI named him archbishop of the see of New York. FULTON J. SHEEN

**SPELMAN COLLEGE.** See UNIVERSITIES AND COLLEGES (table).

**SPELUNKER.** See SPELEOLOGY.

**SPEMANN,** *SHPAY mahn,* **HANS** (1869-1941), a German biologist, pioneered in the analysis of embryonic development. Through novel, delicate grafting experiments performed on frog and newt embryos, Spemann discovered *organizers*. These are organ-forming influences exerted on tissues by neighboring embryo parts. He showed that the lens of the eye, for example, is induced to develop by the underlying eye-cup. He won the 1935 Nobel prize for physiology and medicine. Spemann was born at Stuttgart. MORDECAI L. GABRIEL

**SPENCER, ANNA GARLIN** (1851-1931), was an American reformer, minister, and educator. She supported women's rights, and became active in groups that worked to give women the right to vote (see WOMAN SUFFRAGE). Her book *Woman's Share in Social Culture* (1913) helped call public attention to the ways society can benefit from men and women working together. She also worked to promote world peace, to ban the sale of liquor, and to strengthen family life.

Anna Garlin was born in Attleboro, Mass. She married William H. Spencer, a Unitarian minister, in 1878. In 1891, she became minister of the Bell Street Chapel in Providence, R.I. She was the state's first woman minister. She later served as associate director of the New York School of Philanthropy, and taught sociology at several universities. LOUIS FILLER

**SPENCER, HERBERT** (1820-1903), was a British philosopher. He is noted for his attempt to work out a philosophy, based on the scientific discoveries of his day, which could be applied to all subjects. In his great work *Programme of a System of Synthetic Philosophy* (1862-1896), Spencer applied his fundamental law—the idea of *evolution* (gradual development)—to biology, psychology, sociology, and other fields.

In his work on biology, Spencer traced the development of life from its lowest recognizable form up to man. He believed that the great law of nature is the constant action of forces which tend to change all forms from the simple to the complex. Spencer explained that the mind of man has developed in this same way, advancing from the simple automatic responses of lower animals to the reasoning processes of thinking man. He claimed that knowledge was of two kinds: (1) knowledge gained by the individual, and (2) knowledge gained by the race. He said that intuition, or knowledge learned unconsciously, was the inherited knowledge or experience of the race.

Spencer was born at Derby on April 27, 1820. He was a delicate child. His first interest was biology, but he later turned to engineering. From 1837 to 1846, he worked as an engineer for the London and Birmingham Railway. Later he served as editor of the *Economist*. Spencer left the *Economist* in 1853 to write *Synthetic Philosophy*. He gained a wide reputation as a philosopher, but scientists later proved many of his theories wrong. EUGENE T. ADAMS

**SPENCERIAN WRITING.** See HANDWRITING (Later Writing Styles).

**SPENDER, STEPHEN** (1909-    ), is an English poet. His best-known poetry is a blend of traditional romanticism and thoroughly modern subject matter and attitudes. Thus, he finds in an express train the sort of beauty earlier romantic poets found in waterfalls and sunsets. In "The Express," he wrote:

Ah, like a comet through flame, she moves entranced,
Wrapt in her music no bird song, no, nor bough
Breaking with honey buds, shall ever equal.*

Much of Spender's poetry expresses his radical political views and his compassion for what he sees as the victims of capitalism, such as the children of the poor.

Spender was born in London. He attended Oxford University, and there gained recognition in the 1930's as one of a group of poets led by his friend W. H. Auden. Spender's *Collected Poems* were published in 1954. He also wrote criticism, drama, fiction, translations, and the autobiography *World Within World* (1951). TIM REYNOLDS

* Lines from "The Express" from COLLECTED POEMS 1928-1953 STEPHEN SPENDER, copyright 1955 by Stephen Spender, courtesy Random House, Inc., and Faber & Faber, Ltd.

**SPENGLER,** *SHPENG lur,* **OSWALD** (1880-1936), was a German philosopher of history. In *The Decline of the West* (1918-1922), he held that the key to history is the law of societies and civilizations, which rise and fall in cycles. Using speculation and insight rather than rigid historical method, he concluded that Western civilization was in a period of decay. Spengler was born at Blankenburg. MERLE CURTI

See also CIVILIZATION (Theories About Civilization).

**SPENSER, EDMUND** (1552?-1599), was a great Elizabethan poet. His epic poem, *The Faerie Queene*, though never finished, is a masterpiece of English literature. Spenser completed only 6 of the 12 books (sections) he planned for this work.

Detail of oil portrait by Benjamin Wilson, Pembroke College, Cambridge, England

**Edmund Spenser**

**Spenser's Life.** Spenser was born in London. He entered Cambridge University in 1569, and received a B.A. degree in 1573 and an M.A. degree in 1576. At Cambridge, he received a strong background in the classics. He also was influenced there by the anti-Roman Catholic feelings and stern moral beliefs of the Puritans. These influences were later reflected in Spenser's poems. In all his works, he effectively blended themes of paganism with moralistic teachings, and revealed his strong English patriotic feelings. At Cambridge, Spenser became the friend of Gabriel Harvey, one of England's intellectual leaders. Harvey introduced Spenser to the author and courtier Sir Philip Sidney, and both encouraged Spenser in his early writings. Most of these works have disappeared.

In 1580, Spenser became secretary to Lord Grey of Wilton, the governor of Ireland. From 1580 until a month before his death, Spenser visited England only twice, to supervise publication of *The Faerie Queene*.

Frequent Irish insurrections against English rule kept Spenser so busy that he needed 10 years to write the first three books of *The Faerie Queene*. These books were published in 1590. Spenser dedicated them to Queen Elizabeth, who awarded him a yearly pension.

In 1594, Spenser married Elizabeth Boyle, the daughter of an Irish landowner. They had four children. The second three books of *The Faerie Queene* appeared in 1596. Spenser was appointed sheriff of Cork in 1598, and late that year was sent to England with reports

# SPERM

on the Irish uprisings. He became ill in London and died on Jan. 13, 1599.

**The Faerie Queene** is set in a fairyland, but the characters are realistic. This *allegorical* (symbolic) work is filled with interesting events and scenes of rural Irish life. In writing *The Faerie Queene*, Spenser was influenced by the works of the English poet Geoffrey Chaucer and two Italian epics of the 1500's, Ludovico Ariosto's *Orlando Furioso* and Torquato Tasso's *Jerusalem Delivered*. *The Faerie Queene* also shows the qualities a gentleman should have, reflecting the tradition of the *courtesy book*. The main character in each of the six books gradually develops a desired virtue—holiness, temperance, chastity, friendship, justice, or courtesy. Spenser included both moral and political allegory in *The Faerie Queene*. He wrote in a distinctive pattern, now called the *Spenserian stanza*, consisting of eight pentameter lines followed by an alexandrine (see POETRY [table: Terms Used in Poetry]).

**Spenser's Other Poems.** Spenser's first major poem, *The Shepheardes Calender* (1579), immediately made his reputation. It consists of 12 *eclogues* (short poems about country life written as dialogues between shepherds). *Colin Clouts Come Home Againe* (1595) shows Spenser's disillusionment with London court life after a visit to England. *Amoretti* (1595) is Spenser's famous *cycle* (series) of 89 love sonnets. *Epithalamion* (1595) has been called literature's greatest poem about marriage. It describes 20 hours in an Irish wedding day, and is a blend of classical and Christian traditions and Irish folklore.   THOMAS A. ERHARD

**SPERM.** See REPRODUCTION.

**SPERM WHALE,** or CACHALOT, is probably the best known kind of whale. It became famous in the novel *Moby Dick* by Herman Melville. During the greatest period of U.S. whaling, from the 1830's to the 1860's, Americans hunted sperm whales more than any other kind.

The sperm whale is found in all the oceans. It grows as long as 65 feet and weighs up to 60 tons. The huge head makes up a third of the sperm whale's body. The head contains a reservoir of *spermaceti*, a valuable waxy material. *Sperm oil* comes from the head and from the blubber. Another waxy substance, *ambergris*, is found in the intestines of some sperm whales.

**Scientific Classification.** The sperm whale belongs to the sperm-whale family, *Physeteridae*. It is genus *Physeter*, species *P. catodon*.   RAYMOND M. GILMORE

See also WHALE; SPERMACETI; AMBERGRIS.

**SPERMACETI,** SPUR muh SEE tee, is a waxy material obtained from the enormous head of the sperm whale. The blubber of the sperm whale also contains some of this substance. Spermaceti is used as an ingredient of some salves and face creams. It once was used to make candles. Manufacturers use sperm oil to lubricate machinery and to soften leather. Some spermaceti comes from the bottle-nosed whale and the giant bottle-nosed whale. Spermaceti probably has a function for whales, but no one knows what it is. See also SPERM WHALE.   RAYMOND M. GILMORE

**SPERMATOPHYTE.** See BOTANY (How Plants Are Classified [The Names of Plants]).

**SPERMATOZOA.** See FERTILIZATION.

**SPERRY, ARMSTRONG** (1897-    ), is an American author and illustrator of children's books. Sperry's interest in the sea began in boyhood, and his great-grandfather told him yarns of his adventures as a sea captain in the South Seas. In 1941, Sperry won the Newbery medal for *Call It Courage* (1940).

Sperry was born in New Haven, Conn., and attended the Yale Art School. He joined the United States Navy during World War I. After the war, Sperry studied art in New York City and then spent two years in the South Pacific.   EVELYN RAY SICKELS

**SPERRY, ELMER AMBROSE** (1860-1930), was an American scientist, inventor, and manufacturer. He is best known for his development of the gyroscope for use in navigation (see GYROSCOPE). Sperry's enterprises included the manufacture of arc lamps in Chicago, of electric railways in Cleveland, Ohio, and gyroscopes in New York City.

Sperry was born in Cortland, N.Y. He studied at the State Normal and Training School and at Cornell University. While still in college, he attracted attention by building an arc lamp with a dynamo to run it. The lamp was much more efficient than any other then used for street lighting, and at the age of 19 Sperry set up his first factory in the city of Chicago where he produced his lamps. Forty years later he returned to the field of lighting and developed the powerful beacon and searchlights later used by many armies and navies. In the meantime, he also developed electrically driven mining equipment, automobiles, and streetcars.

Sperry Rand Corp.
**Elmer Sperry**

Sperry first used the gyroscope in 1911 to develop a new kind of compass for ships. The increase in the amount of steel used in shipbuilding had made magnetic compasses unreliable. Sperry's gyrocompass successfully solved this problem (see GYROCOMPASS). The gyroscopic stabilizer for aircraft, devised with his son Lawrence, was successfully demonstrated in 1914. From his gyrocompass, Sperry developed the gyropilot which steers a ship automatically (see GYROPILOT). Later he installed giant gyroscopes which could steady the rolling motions of ships. After the United States entered World War I, Sperry developed a number of important instruments for gun control. These inventions increased the effectiveness and range of gunfire and torpedoes. He also produced an aerial torpedo controlled by a gyroscope.

Today's naval gunnery methods would be impossible without the inventions which grew out of Sperry's original gyroscope. During World War II it was adapted for use in many complex military instruments, such as naval gunsights. His inventions were equally important for use in navigating aircraft (see AIRCRAFT INSTRUMENTS; GUIDED MISSILE).   RICHARD D. HUMPHREY

**SPEYER, DIET OF.** See PROTESTANT.

**SPHAGNUM MOSS.** See PEAT MOSS.

**SPHALERITE.** See ZINC.

**SPHENOID BONE.** See HEAD.

608

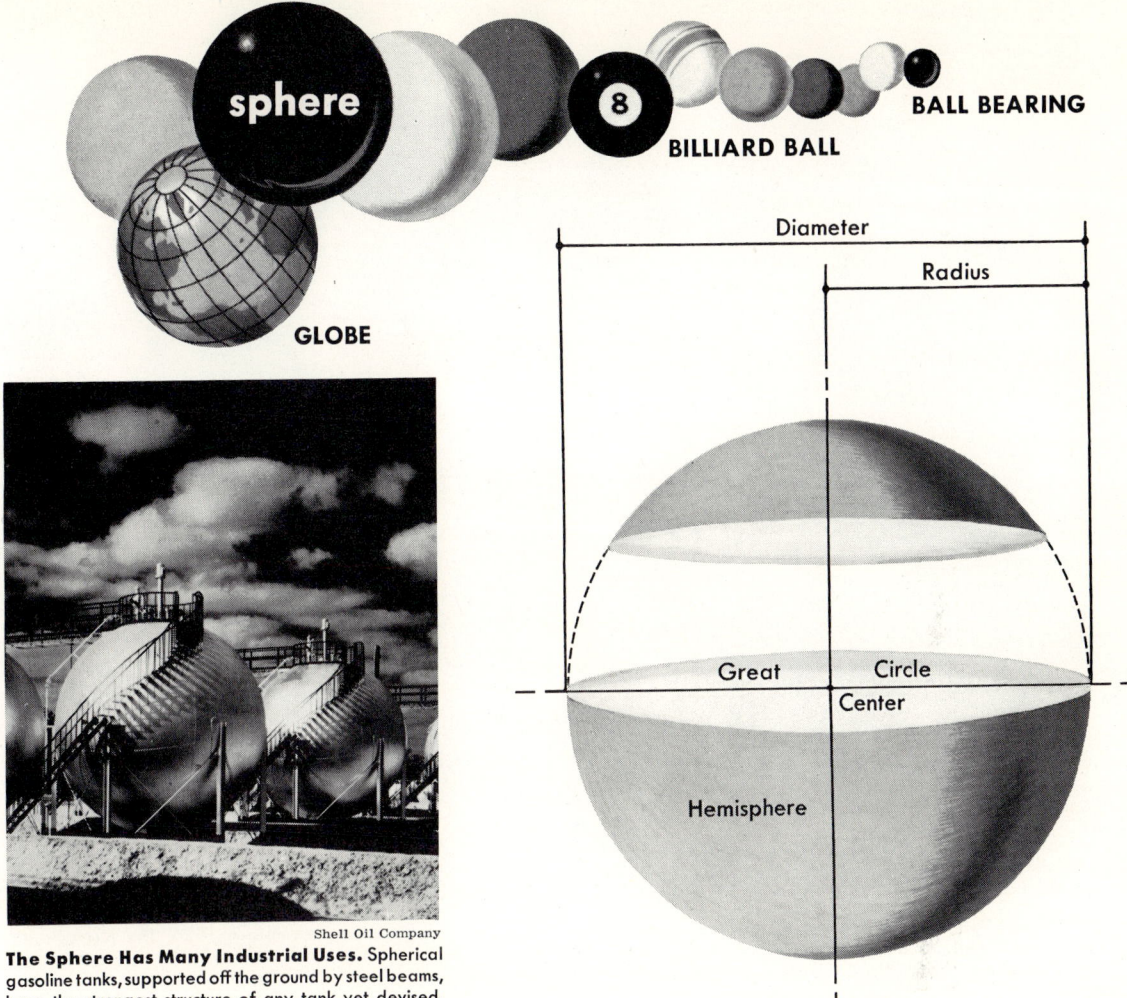

The Sphere Has Many Industrial Uses. Spherical gasoline tanks, supported off the ground by steel beams, have the strongest structure of any tank yet devised.

**SPHERE,** *sfeer,* is a solid figure that resembles a ball or globe. The name *sphere* comes from a Greek word that means *ball.* In geometry, mathematicians define a sphere as the location in space of all points a certain distance from a fixed point called the *center.* This means that a sphere is a solid figure bounded by a single surface. The surface itself does not have any edges or boundaries. Each point on the surface is the same distance from the center.

**Parts.** The *radius* of a sphere is the distance from the center to the surface. Or, the radius is any straight line drawn from the center to the surface. The *diameter* of a sphere is twice the radius. Or, the diameter is any straight line, drawn through the center, whose ends stop at the surface. A *secant* is any line that cuts through a sphere. A *chord* is any line that joins two points on the sphere.

If a *plane,* or flat surface, passes through the center of a sphere, the plane produces a *great circle* of the sphere. The radius and diameter of a great circle are the same as the radius and diameter of the sphere. A great circle cuts a sphere in half. Each half of the sphere is called a *hemisphere.*

**Finding the Surface.** Here is a formula which you can use for finding the area of the surface of a sphere:

$$\text{Surface} = 4\pi r^2$$

In the formula, the letter $r$ stands for the radius. A convenient value for $\pi$ is 3.1416. The surface computed with this formula will appear in square units of measure; for example, in square inches.

**Finding the Volume.** Here is the formula for finding the volume of a sphere:

$$\text{Volume} = \tfrac{4}{3}\pi r^3$$

The letter $r$ stands for the radius. The volume computed with this formula will appear in cubic units; for example, in cubic inches.

See also CIRCLE; GEOMETRY (Solid Geometry).

**SPHEROID** is a solid figure that resembles a sphere. It is not perfectly round. The earth is an *oblate* spheroid. It is wider than it is long. A football is a *prolate* spheroid. It is longer than it is wide.

**SPHINCTER,** *SFINGK tur,* is a circle of muscle surrounding a body tube. The muscle usually is found near the outlet of the tube. It may be a voluntary or involuntary muscle. The *pyloric sphincter* regulates the flow of food from the stomach into the small intestine. See also MUSCLE.

CARL C. FRANCIS

609

**The Great Sphinx at Giza, Egypt,** stares with sightless eyes across the desert, as it has for more than 4,800 years. The photograph was made after the lower part of the great statue had been uncovered by scientists in 1926. The forefeet are made of huge pieces of stone masonry. In the background are three pyramids—once tombs of Egyptian rulers.

Ewing Galloway

**SPHINX,** *sfinks,* is an imaginary creature of ancient myths. The Egyptians, the Greeks, and peoples of the Near East all had stories about such a creature. According to some stories, the sphinx had a human head, the body of a lion, the tail of a serpent, and the wings of a bird.

**The Egyptian Sphinx** usually had the head of a man, and the body, legs, feet, and tail of a lion. It had no wings. The sphinx was supposed to represent the god Horus, who guarded temples and tombs. Egyptians made many statues of sphinxes. When Egyptian sculptors made such a statue, they usually made its face resemble the Pharaoh of the time. But some of the statues had heads resembling those of rams and hawks. The Egyptians often lined both sides of avenues with sphinx statues, as in the great temple at Karnak.

**The Greek Sphinx** usually had the head of a woman. In Greek literature, the sphinx lived on a high rock outside the city of Thebes. When anyone passed by, she asked him a riddle: What has one voice and yet becomes four-footed and two-footed and three-footed? If the traveler could not give the right answer, the sphinx ate him.

When Oedipus passed by on his way to Thebes, the sphinx asked him the riddle. Oedipus replied that the answer was man, because man walks on his hands and feet when he is young, on two feet in the middle of his life, and with a cane or staff in his old age. The sphinx became furious because Oedipus had given the right answer. She howled with rage, and finally threw herself from the rock to her death.

**The Great Sphinx** that stands at Giza, near the Great Pyramid in Egypt, is one of the most famous monuments in the world. Its head and body are carved from solid rock, and the paws and legs are built of stone blocks. The face is believed to be a portrait of the Egyptian king who built it. No one knows exactly which king built the Sphinx.

The Great Sphinx is 240 feet long and about 66 feet high. The width of its face measures 13 feet 8 inches. The head has been used as a gunnery target, and desert sands have worn away part of the stone.

Sand covers the base of the Sphinx, and buries it most of the time. Thutmose IV of Egypt cleared it away in the 1400's B.C., and one of the Ptolemies cleared it during Roman times. The sand was cleared away again in 1818, 1886, and 1926.   HOWARD M. DAVIS

See also OEDIPUS.

**SPHINX MOTH.** See HAWK MOTH.
**SPHYGMOMANOMETER.** See BLOOD PRESSURE.

**SPICA,** *SPY kuh,* is a star of the first magnitude in the constellation Virgo. This blue star gives off the light of 2,440 suns. However, Spica is so far away from earth that it takes this light 300 years to reach us. The name *Spica* means *ear of wheat.*

See also VIRGO.

**SPICE** is the name given to food seasonings made from plants. Spices have a sharp taste and odor. Some spices are valued for their taste, and others for their smell. Common spices include pepper, nutmeg, cloves, ginger, allspice, mace, mustard, and cinnamon.

Spices have little in common except their use. They come from different parts of the various spice plants. For example, cloves come from the bud, cinnamon from the bark, and pepper and nutmeg from the fruit of each plant. Ginger comes from the root and mustard from the seed. Curry, a seasoning made from a combination of spices, is widely used in India.

Spice plants grow in many tropical countries. The Moluccas, or Spice Islands, are a famous source of spices (see MOLUCCAS). Many persons prefer to grow spice plants such as sage, marjoram, thyme, and others in their own gardens. They then dry the plants for later use. Some common spice plants grow indoors if they are placed in pots in sunny windows.

Spices have little food value. But they do increase the appetite and stimulate the organs of digestion. Spices must not be used too generously, for they can sometimes be harmful to the body. Before foods were refrigerated or canned, spices were used to make tainted foods taste better.

Spices have played an important part in history. The cities of Genoa and Venice became powerful because they were at the center of the spice trade with the East. When Columbus and the early explorers set sail across unknown seas, they were interested in discovering an all-water route to the spice lands of the East. Merchants made great profits in the early days of the spice trade. Even in modern times, spices are important to us. During World War II, for example, many of the East Indian sources of spice were temporarily destroyed. As a result, pepper supplies in the U.S. dwindled sharply, and many Americans often had to do without food seasoning. HAROLD NORMAN MOLDENKE

Indonesian Information Office

**A Javanese Spice Seller** offers a basket of dried mace at the marketplace.

**Related Articles** in WORLD BOOK include:

| | | |
|---|---|---|
| Allspice | Clove | Marjoram |
| Anise | Coriander | Mustard |
| Caper | Cubeb | Nutmeg |
| Capsicum | Curry | Paprika |
| Caraway | Dill | Pepper |
| Cardamom | Fennel | Sage |
| Cayenne Pepper | Ginger | Thyme |
| Cinnamon | Mace | Turmeric |

**SPICE ISLANDS.** See MOLUCCAS.
**SPICULE.** See SPONGE (The Body of the Sponge).

**Avenue of Sphinxes** leads to the Great Temple of Amon-Re at Karnak, on the east bank of the Nile River near what is now Luxor, Egypt. King Amenhotep III built the sphinxes about 1400 B.C.

Ewing Galloway

# SPIDER

**SPIDER** is a small, eight-legged animal that spins silk. Spiders are best known for the silk webs they spin. They use their webs to catch insects for food. Even insects that are larger and stronger than spiders cannot escape from the threads of a spider's web.

All spiders spin silk, but some kinds of spiders do not make webs. The bolas spider, for example, spins a single line of silk with a drop of sticky silk at the end. When an insect flies near, this spider swings the line at it and traps the insect in the sticky ball.

All spiders have fangs, and most kinds of spiders have poison glands. A spider's bite can kill insects and other small animals, but few kinds of spiders are harmful to man. In North America, only six kinds of spiders have bites that can harm man. These spiders are the brown recluse spider, the sack spider, the black widow, the brown widow, the red-legged widow, and the varied widow. Of the four "widow" spiders, only the females are known to bite man. Many persons are afraid of spiders. But only hurt or frightened spiders bite human beings.

Spiders are helpful to man because they eat harmful insects. Spiders eat grasshoppers and locusts, which destroy man's crops, and flies and mosquitoes, which carry diseases. Some large spiders eat such animals as mice, birds, lizards, frogs, and fish. Spiders even eat each other. Most female spiders are larger and stronger than male spiders, and often eat the males.

Spiders live anywhere they can find food. They can be seen in fields, woods, swamps, caves, and deserts.

**The Color, Shape, and Size of Spiders** vary greatly. Some crab spiders slowly change color from white to yellow to match the flowers in which they hide. The spiny-bodied spider, hanging from its dragline, looks like a chip of wood. Some kinds of comb-footed spiders are less than 1/50 of an inch long, and are among the world's smallest spiders. South American tarantulas are the world's largest spiders. One tarantula was 10 inches long with its legs extended.

Spiders shown other than natural size are accompanied by a drawing showing natural size. All spiders shown are females except where noted.

Crab Spider

Spiny-Bodied Spider

Comb-Footed Spider

Tarantula

612

One kind of spider spends most of its life under water. Another kind lives near the top of Mount Everest, the world's highest mountain. Some spiders live in houses, barns, or other buildings. Others live on the outside of buildings—on walls, on window screens, or in the corners of doors and windows.

There are more than 29,000 known kinds of spiders, but scientists believe there may be as many as 50,000 kinds. Some kinds are smaller than the head of a pin. Others are as large as a man's hand. One spider, a South American tarantula, measured 10 inches long with its legs extended.

Many persons think spiders are insects. But scientists classify spiders as *arachnids*, which differ from insects in many ways. Spiders have eight legs. Ants, bees, beetles, and other insects have six legs. Most insects have wings and *antennae* (feelers), but spiders do not. Other arachnids include daddy longlegs, scorpions, and mites and ticks.

Scientists classify spiders as either *true spiders* or *tarantulas* according to certain differences in their bodies. Spiders can also be divided according to their way of life. *Web-spinning spiders* spin webs to trap insects. *Hunting spiders* run after insects or lie in wait for them. For the scientific classification of spiders, see the table *Common Kinds of Spiders* at the end of this article.

---

*H. K. Wallace, the contributor of this article, is Chairman of the Department of Zoology at the University of Florida. Willis J. Gertsch, the critical reviewer, is Curator of Arachnids at the American Museum of Natural History, and author of American Spiders. The illustrations throughout this article were prepared for* WORLD BOOK *by Jack J. Kunz unless otherwise credited.*

---

Wolf Spider

Jumping Spider

**Spiderlings Travel in Interesting Ways.** Baby wolf spiders ride on their mother's back. A young jumping spider travels by *ballooning*. It raises its abdomen so that the wind can pull silk threads from its spinnerets. The wind lifts the spiderling into the air like a balloon on a string.

Black Widow

**The Female Black Widow** is one of the few spiders that can harm man. It has a red or yellow patch, shaped like an hourglass, on its abdomen.

**The Bolas Spider** does not trap insects in a web. Instead, it spins a line of silk with a drop of sticky silk at the end. The spider swings the line at an insect and traps it in the sticky ball.

Bolas Spider

**The Ogre-Faced Stick Spider** traps flying insects in a web of sticky silk. With its four front legs, this spider stretches the web to several times its normal size and captures the insect.

Ogre-Faced Stick Spider

**The Purse-Web Spider** extends the silk lining of its burrow up the side of a tree to make a tube-shaped web. The spider bites through the tube to seize insects crawling over its web.

Purse-Web Spider

# SPIDER / The Spider's Body

Spiders may be short and fat, long and thin, round, oblong, or flat. Their legs are short and stubby, or long and thin. Most spiders are brown, gray, or black. But some are as beautifully colored as the loveliest butterflies. Many of these spiders are so small that their colors can be seen only with a microscope.

A spider has no bones. Its tough skin serves as a protective outer skeleton. Hairs, humps, and *spines* (bristles of skin) cover the bodies of most spiders.

A spider's body has two main sections: (1) the *cephalothorax*, which consists of the head joined to the *thorax* (chest); and (2) the *abdomen*. Each of these sections has *appendages* (attached parts). A thin waist called the *pedicel* connects the cephalothorax and the abdomen.

**Eyes.** A spider's eyes are on top and near the front of its head. The size, number, and position of the eyes vary among different species. Most species have eight eyes, arranged in two rows of four each. Other kinds have six, four, or two eyes. Some species of spiders that live in caves or other dark places have no eyes at all.

**Mouth.** A spider's mouth opening is below its eyes. Spiders do not have chewing mouth parts, and they eat only liquids. Various appendages around the mouth opening form a short "straw" through which the spider sucks the body fluid of its victim. The spider can eat some of the solid tissue of its prey by *predigesting* it. To do this, the spider sprays digestive juices on the tissue. The powerful juices dissolve the tissue. By predigestion and sucking, a large tarantula can reduce a mouse to a small pile of hair and bones in about 36 hours.

**Chelicerae** are a pair of appendages that the spider uses to seize and kill its prey. The chelicerae are above the mouth opening and just below the spider's eyes. Each chelicera ends in a hard, hollow, pointed claw, and these claws are the spider's fangs. An opening in the tip of the fang connects with the poison glands. When a spider stabs an insect with its chelicerae, poison flows into the wound and paralyzes or kills the victim.

The fangs of tarantulas point straight down from the head, and the poison glands are in the chelicerae. In

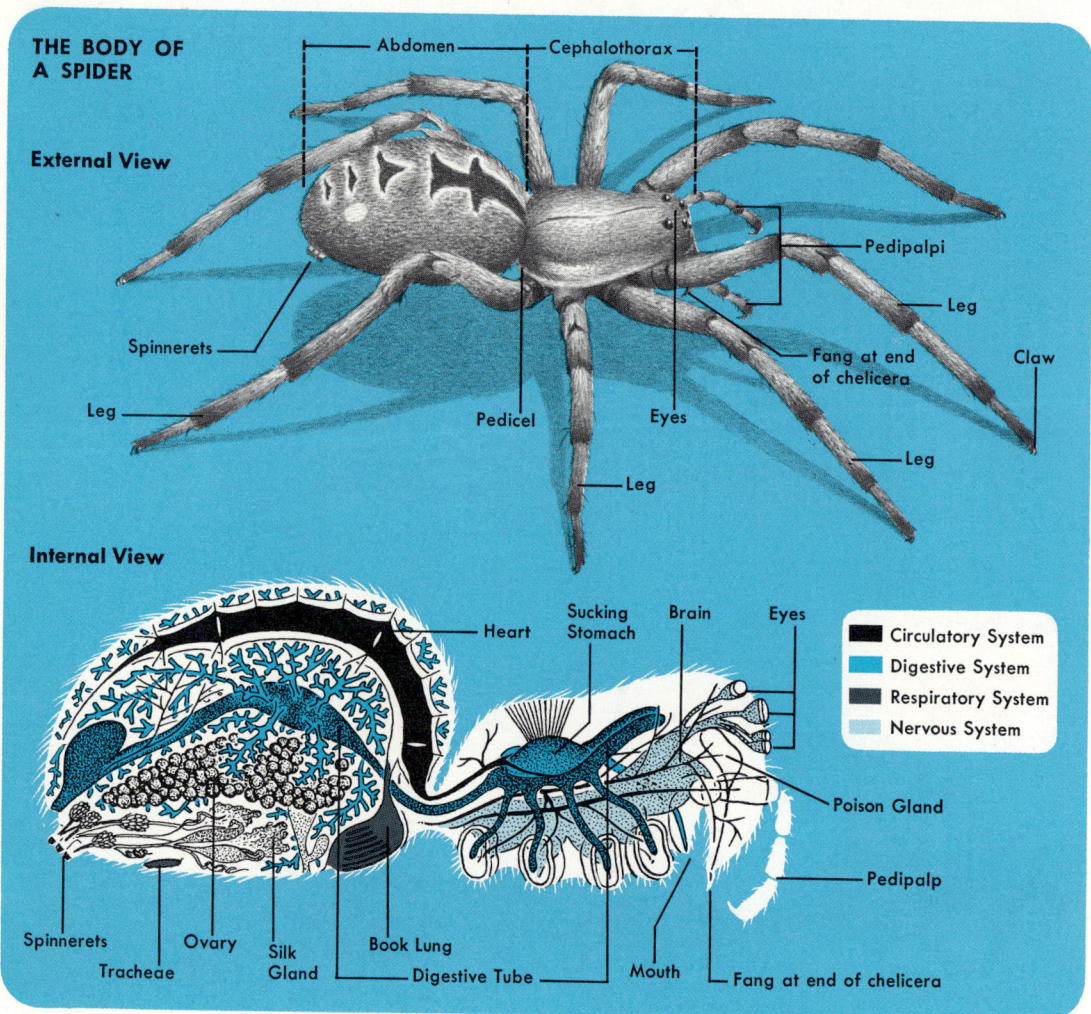

THE BODY OF A SPIDER

614

true spiders, the fangs point crosswise, and the poison glands extend back into the cephalothorax.

Spiders also crush their prey with their chelicerae. Some species use their chelicerae to dig burrows in the ground as nests.

**Pedipalpi** are a pair of appendages that look like small legs. One pedipalp is attached to each side of the spider's mouth, and they form the sides of the mouth opening. Each pedipalp has six *segments* (parts). In most kinds of spiders, the segment closest to the body bears a sharp plate with jagged edges. The spider uses this plate to cut and crush its food. In male spiders, the last segment of each pedipalp bears a reproductive organ.

**Legs.** A spider has four pairs of legs, which are attached to its cephalothorax. Each leg has seven segments. In most kinds of spiders, the last segment has two or three claws at the tip. A pad of hairs called a *scopula* may surround the claws. The scopula helps the spider cling to such surfaces as ceilings or walls.

When a spider walks, the first and third leg on one side of its body move with the second and fourth leg on the other side. Muscles in the legs make the legs bend at the joints. But spiders have no muscles to extend their legs. The pressure of the blood in their bodies makes their legs extend. If a spider's body does not contain enough fluids, its blood pressure drops. The legs draw up under the body, and the animal cannot walk.

**Spinnerets** are short, fingerlike organs with which the spider spins silk. They are attached to the rear of the abdomen. Most kinds of spiders have six spinnerets, but some have four or two. The tip of a spinneret is called the *spinning field*. The surface of each spinning field is covered by as many as a hundred *spinning tubes*. Through these tubes, liquid silk flows from silk glands in the spider's abdomen to the outside of its body. The silk then hardens into a thread.

**Respiratory System.** Spiders as a group have two kinds of breathing organs—*tracheae* and *book lungs*. Tracheae, found in almost all kinds of true spiders, are small tubes which carry air throughout the body. Air enters the tubes through the *spiracle*, an opening in front of the spinnerets in most kinds of true spiders.

Book lungs are in cavities in the spider's abdomen. Air enters the cavities through a tiny slit on each side and near the front of the abdomen. Each lung consists of 15 or more thin, flat folds of tissue arranged like the pages of a book. The sheets of tissue contain many blood vessels. As air circulates between the sheets, oxygen passes into the blood. Tarantulas have two pairs of book lungs. Most true spiders have one pair.

**Circulatory System.** The blood of spiders contains many pale blood cells and is transparent. The heart, a long, slender tube in the abdomen, pumps the blood to all parts of the body. As the blood circulates, it flows through open passages instead of closed tubes, such as those of the human body. If the spider's skin is broken, the blood quickly drains from its body. The animal's tough skin often prevents this from happening.

**Digestive System.** A digestive tube extends the length of the spider's body. In the cephalothorax, the tube is larger and forms a *sucking stomach*. When the stomach's powerful muscles contract, the size of the stomach increases. This causes a strong sucking action that pulls the food through the stomach into the intestine. Juices in the digestive tube break the liquid food into particles small enough to pass through the walls of the intestine into the blood. The food is then distributed to all parts of the body.

**Nervous System.** The central nervous system of a spider is in the cephalothorax. It includes the brain, and controls the activities of all other parts of the body.

A spider gains knowledge of its surroundings through its sense organs. Most kinds of hunting spiders can see better than web-spinning spiders. But all spiders can see only a short distance. The sense of touch is the most highly developed of the animal's senses. Special hairs on its body serve as organs of touch and perhaps as organs of hearing and smell. Each hair contains a nerve. These nerves send messages to the brain that tell the spider how to respond to changes in its surroundings. Spiders can easily sense vibrations and the presence of certain chemicals.

WORLD BOOK illustrations by Tom Dolan

**SPIDER FACES**

Wolf Spider — *Lycosa carolinensis* (Eyes, Chelicera, Fang)

Tarantula — *Aphonopelma eutylenum*

Jumping Spider — *Phidippus variegatus* (Eyes, Chelicera, Fang)

Ogre-Faced Stick Spider — *Deinopis spinosus*

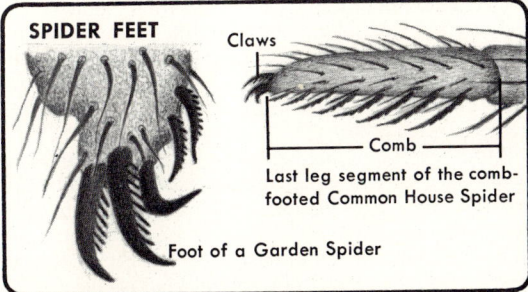

**SPIDER FEET**

Foot of a Garden Spider

Last leg segment of the comb-footed Common House Spider (Claws, Comb)

# SPIDER / The Spider's Silk

*Jerome Wexler, NAS*

**Many Kinds of Spiders Spin Bands of Silk** to tie up insects caught in webs. The orange garden spider turns its victim over and over, wrapping it in silk from the spider's spinnerets.

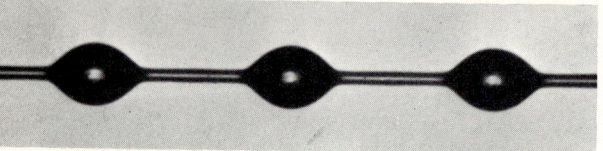

*T. Eisner, © 1967 American Assoc. for the Advancement of Science*

**A Thread of Sticky Silk,** enlarged more than 20 times, looks like a beaded necklace. Insects stick to the thread. Oil on the spider's body prevents the silk from sticking to the spider.

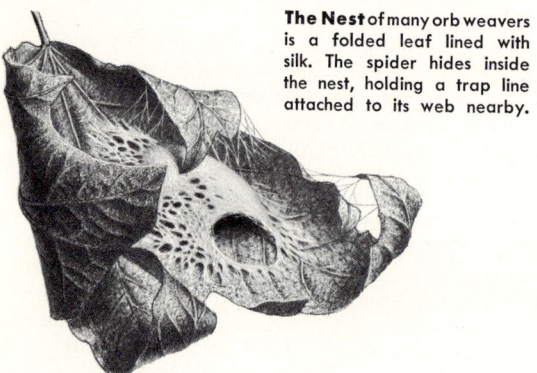

**The Nest** of many orb weavers is a folded leaf lined with silk. The spider hides inside the nest, holding a trap line attached to its web nearby.

**How Spiders Make Silk.** Spiders as a group have seven kinds of silk glands. No species of spider has all seven kinds. All spiders have at least three kinds of silk glands, and most species have five. Each kind of gland produces a different type of silk that the spider uses for a particular purpose.

Some silk glands produce a liquid silk that becomes dry outside the body. Other glands produce a sticky silk that stays sticky.

The spinnerets, which spin the silk, work somewhat like the fingers of a hand. A spider can stretch out each spinneret, pull it back in, and even squeeze them all together. Using different spinnerets, a spider can combine silk from different silk glands and produce a very thin thread or a thick, wide band.

The animal also can make a sticky thread that looks like a beaded necklace. To do this, the spider pulls out a dry thread that is heavily coated with sticky silk. Using the claws of one of its hind legs, the spider stretches this thread and lets go of it with a snap. This action causes the liquid silk to form a series of tiny beads along the thread. A spider uses beaded threads in its web to trap jumping or flying insects.

Some kinds of spiders have another spinning organ called the *cribellum*. It is an oval plate that lies almost flat against the abdomen, in front of the spinnerets. Hundreds of spinning tubes cover the spinning field of the cribellum. These tubes produce extremely thin threads of sticky silk.

Spiders with a cribellum also have a special row of curved hairs called a *calamistrum* on their hind legs. Spiders use the calamistrum to comb together dry silk from the spinnerets and sticky silk from the cribellum. This combination forms a flat, ribbonlike silk structure called a *hackled band*. Spiders use hackled bands in their webs, along with the other silk they spin.

**How Spiders Use Silk.** Spiders, including those that do not spin webs, depend on silk in so many ways that they could not live without it. Wherever a spider goes, it spins a silk thread behind itself. This thread is called a *dragline*. The dragline is sometimes called the spider's "lifeline" because the animal often uses it to escape from enemies. If danger threatens a spider in its web, it can drop from the web on its dragline and hide in the grass. Or the spider can simply hang in the air until the danger has passed. Then it climbs back up the dragline into its web. Hunting spiders use their draglines to swing down to the ground from high places.

Spiders also use silk to spin tiny masses of sticky threads called *attachment discs*. They use the discs to attach their draglines and webs to various surfaces.

Each kind of spider builds a different type of silk nest as its home. Some spiders line a folded leaf with silk to make a nest. Others dig burrows in the ground and line them with silk. Still others build nests in the center of their webs.

Many web-spinning spiders spin sticky bands or wide sheets of silk while capturing their prey. The orb weavers wrap their victims in sheets like mummies so they cannot escape.

The female spider of most species encloses her eggs in an *egg sac*, a bag made of a special kind of silk.

# SPIDER / Hunting Spiders

Hunting spiders creep up on their prey or lie in wait and pounce on it. Most kinds of hunters have large eyes and can see their prey from a distance. The powerful chelicerae of hunting spiders help them overpower their victims. Some hunting spiders spin simple webs that stretch out along the ground and stop insects. These spiders are grouped as hunters because they run after the insects that land in their webs.

**Jumping Spiders** creep up and pounce on their prey. They have short legs, but they can jump more than 40 times the length of their bodies. Jumping spiders are the most colorful of all spiders. Many thick, colored hairs cover their bodies. Most of the males have bunches of brightly colored hairs on their first pair of legs.

**Water Spiders** are the only spiders that live most of their life underwater. This spider breathes underwater from air bubbles that it holds close to its body. Its underwater nest is a silk web shaped like a small bell. The spider fills the web with air bubbles, which gradually push all the water out of the bell. The animal can live on this air for several months. Water spiders are found only in Europe and parts of Asia. See ANIMAL (How Animals Breathe [picture]).

**Tarantulas** are the world's largest spiders. The biggest ones live in the South American jungles. Great numbers of tarantulas also are found in the southwestern United States.

Many kinds of tarantulas dig burrows as nests. The *trap-door spider* covers the entrance to its burrow with a lid (see TRAP-DOOR SPIDER). A California tarantula builds a *turret* (small tower) of grass and twigs at the entrance to its burrow. It sits on the tower and watches for insects moving in the nearby grass. See ANIMAL (Animals of the Tropical Forests [picture]); TARANTULA.

**Fisher Spiders** live near water and hunt water insects, small fish, and tadpoles. These spiders have large bodies and long, thin legs. But because of their light weight, they can walk on the water without sinking. They are sometimes called *nursery-web weavers* because the female builds a special web for her young.

**Crab Spiders** have short, wide bodies and look like small crabs. They can walk backwards and sidewards as easily as crabs do. Some brightly colored crab spiders hide in flowers and capture bees and butterflies. A few kinds of crab spiders can disguise themselves by changing the color of their bodies to match the color of the flower blossom. *Huntsman spiders* are large, tan crab spiders of the southern United States.

**Funnel-Web Spiders** hunt only within large webs that they spin in tall grass or under rocks or logs. The bottom of the web is shaped like a funnel and serves as the spider's hiding place. The top part of the web forms a large sheet of silk spread out over grass or soil. When an insect lands on the sheet, the spider runs out of the funnel and pounces on the victim.

**Wolf Spiders** are excellent hunters. Many kinds have large, hairy bodies, and run swiftly in search of food. Others look and act like other types of spiders. For example, some live near water and resemble fisher spiders in appearance and habits. Others live in burrows, or spin funnel-webs. See ANIMAL (Animals of the Mountains [picture]).

**A Jumping Spider** leaps into space after its prey, and floats to the ground on a dragline.

**Water Spiders** live underwater in airtight silk nests. There they eat, molt, mate, and raise families.

**Many Tarantulas** dig burrows as nests. This male tarantula of the southwestern United States is shown half its actual size.

**A Female Fisher Spider** stands guard over her egg sac after enclosing it in a special nursery web.

**A Grass Spider** spends its life spinning one funnel web. The female leaves the web only to build an egg sac.

## SPIDER / Web-Spinning Spiders

Web-spinning spiders, like hunting spiders, live in caves, in grass or shrubs, or high in trees. Their poor vision makes it almost impossible for them to catch food by hunting. Instead, they spin webs in the air to trap flying insects. A web-spinning spider does not become caught in its own web. When walking across the web, it grasps the silk lines with a special hooked claw on each foot.

**Tangled-Web Weavers** spin the simplest type of web. It consists of a shapeless jumble of threads attached to a support, such as the corner of a ceiling. The *cobwebs* found in houses are tangled webs that have collected dust and dirt.

The *cellar spiders* spin tangled webs in dark, empty parts of buildings. One cellar spider that looks like a daddy longlegs has thin legs more than 2 inches long.

The *comb-footed spiders* spin a tangled web with a tightly woven sheet of silk in the middle. The sheet serves as an insect trap and as the spider's hideout. These spiders get their name from the comb of hairs on their fourth pair of legs. They use the comb to throw liquid silk over an insect and trap it. The *black widow* is a comb-footed spider (see BLACK WIDOW).

Some spiders spin a tangled web containing a hackled band of dry and sticky silk. The *ogre-faced stick spider*

**The Common House Spider** spins a loosely-woven tangled web of dry silk, held in place by long threads attached to walls or other supports. The center of the web forms a large insect trap.

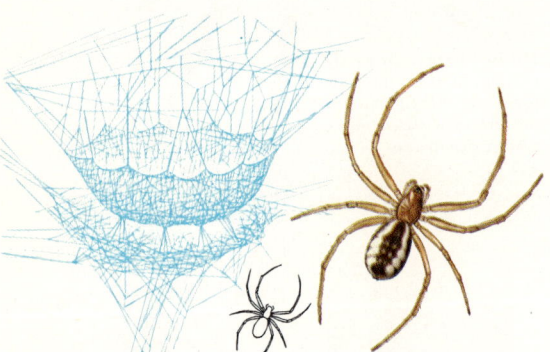

**The Platform Spider** spins a silk sheet below a net of criss-crossed threads. Flying insects hit the net and fall onto the sheet.

**The Bowl-and-Doily Spider** spins a bowl-shaped sheet above a flat sheet of silk. Threads above the bowl stop flying insects.

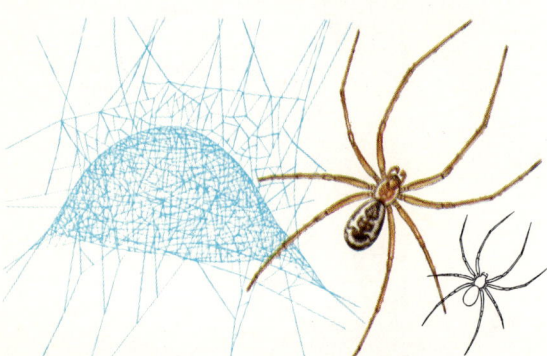

**The Triangle Spider** spins a triangular web between two twigs. The web's *hackled bands* of dry and sticky silk trap insects.

**The Filmy Dome Spider** spins a tangle of threads around a dome-shaped silk sheet, and hangs under the dome. Insects that drop onto the dome are pulled through the webbing by the spider.

**The Labyrinth Spider** spins a tangled web as its hiding place and an orb web as an insect trap. Several trap lines extend from the center of the orb web to the tangled web.

614d

spins a web that is made up largely of hackled bands. The web is only about as large as a postage stamp. This spider spins a structure of dry silk to hold the sticky web in place. With its four rear legs, the spider hangs upside down from the dry silk. It holds the sticky web with its four front legs. When an insect flies near, the spider stretches the sticky web to several times its normal size and captures the insect.

**Sheet-Web Weavers** weave flat sheets of silk between blades of grass or branches of shrubs or trees. These spiders also spin a net of crisscrossed threads above the sheet web. When a flying insect hits the net, it bounces into the sheet web. The spider, which hangs upside down beneath the web, quickly runs to the insect and pulls it through the webbing. Sheet webs last a long time because the spider repairs any damaged parts. *Dwarf spiders*, which are less than $\frac{1}{20}$ of an inch long, spin small, square sheet webs near rivers and lakes.

Some sheet-web weavers spin two separate sheets as a web. The spider hangs upside down under the top sheet. The sheet beneath the spider probably protects it from attack from below.

**Orb Weavers** build the most beautiful and complicated of all webs. They weave their round webs in open areas, often between tree branches or flower stems. An orb web consists of threads of dry silk that extend from the web's center like the spokes of a wheel. Coiling lines of sticky silk connect the spokes, and serve as an insect trap.

Some orb weavers lie in wait for their prey in the center of the web. Others attach a *trap line* to the center of the web. The spider hides in its nest near the web, and holds on to the trap line. When an insect lands in the web, the line vibrates. The spider darts out and captures the insect. Many orb weavers spin a new web every night. It takes them about an hour. Other orb weavers repair or replace damaged parts of their webs.

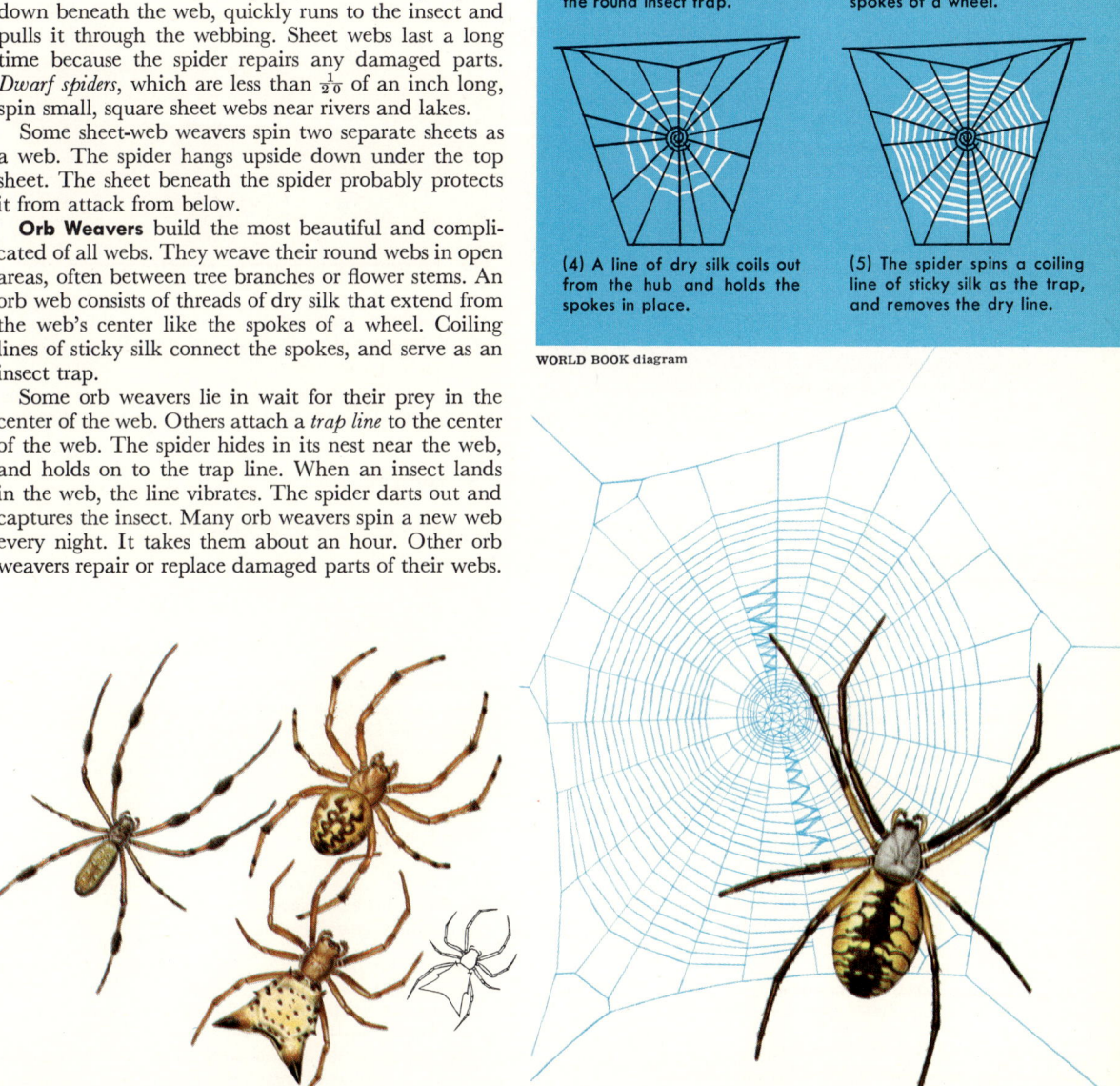

**SPINNING AN ORB WEB**

(1) The web hangs from a thread called a *bridge line*.

(2) *Foundation lines* limit the area in which the spider spins the round insect trap.

(3) Threads extend from the web's *hub* (center) like the spokes of a wheel.

(4) A line of dry silk coils out from the hub and holds the spokes in place.

(5) The spider spins a coiling line of sticky silk as the trap, and removes the dry line.

WORLD BOOK diagram

**Beautiful Orb Weavers** include the silk spider, shown half its actual size at the left; the marbled spider, *above right;* and the arrowhead-shaped micrathena, *below right.*

**The Orange Garden Spider** spins a large orb web that may measure more than 2 feet across. The spider spins a zigzagging band of silk across the middle of the web.

614e

# SPIDER / The Life of a Spider

Each species of spider has a different life story. Many kinds of spiders live only about a year. Large wolf spiders live several years. Certain kinds of tarantulas live the longest—more than 20 years. Spiders become adults at different times of the year. Some mature in the fall, and then mate and die during the winter. Others live through the winter, mate in the spring, and then die.

**Courtship and Mating.** As soon as a male spider matures, it seeks a mate. The female spider may mistake the male for prey and eat him. But most male spiders perform courtship activities that identify themselves and attract the females. The male of some species vibrates the threads of the female's web. Some male hunting spiders wave their legs and bodies in an unusual courtship dance.

Before mating, a male spider spins a silk platform. He deposits a drop of sperm from his abdomen onto the platform. Then he fills each of his pedipalpi with sperm. After mating, the female stores the sperm in her body. When she lays her eggs, several weeks or even months later, the eggs are fertilized by the sperm.

**Eggs.** The number of eggs that a spider lays at one time varies with the size of the animal. A female of average size lays about 100 eggs. Some of the largest spiders lay more than 2,000 eggs. One tiny female cave spider lays only one egg at a time. It is about a fourth the size of her body.

In most species, the mother spider encloses the eggs in a silken egg sac. The sac of each species differs in

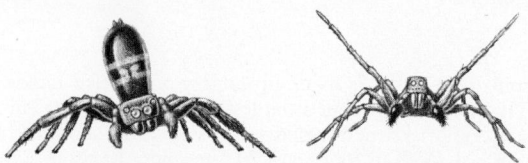

**Courtship Dances** are performed by many male hunting spiders to attract mates. The jumping spider *Peckhamia noxiosa*, left, raises its abdomen into the air and sways from side to side. The wolf spider *Pardosa milvina*, right, waves its front pair of legs.

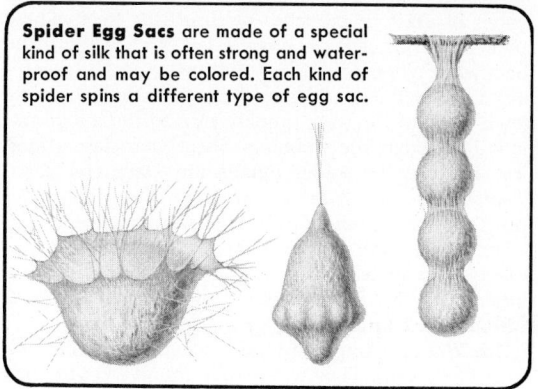

**Spider Egg Sacs** are made of a special kind of silk that is often strong and waterproof and may be colored. Each kind of spider spins a different type of egg sac.

size and shape. Some species that lay large numbers of eggs make several sacs, and some spin them together into a long chain.

In many species, the mother dies soon after making the egg sac. In other species, she stays with the eggs

---
## COMMON KINDS OF SPIDERS

Each of the spiders listed in this table is shown in the pictures with this article.

**TRUE SPIDERS**

**Comb-Footed Spiders** (*Theridiidae*)
  Black Widow (*Latrodectus mactans*)
  Comb-Footed Spider (*Mysmena incredula*)
  Common House Spider (*Achaearanea tepidariorum*)

**Crab Spiders** (*Thomisidae*)
  Crab Spider (*Misumena vatia*)

**Fisher Spiders** (*Pisauridae*)
  Fisher Spider (*Pisaurina mira*)

**Funnel-Web Spiders** (*Agelenidae*)
  Grass Spider (*Agelena naevia*)
  Water Spider (*Argyroneta aquatica*)

**Hackled-Band Orb Weavers** (*Uloboridae*)
  Triangle Spider (*Hyptiotes cavatus*)

**Jumping Spiders** (*Salticidae*)
  Jumping Spider (*Peckhamia noxiosa*)
  Jumping Spider (*Phidippus variegatus*)

**Ogre-Faced Stick Spiders** (*Deinopidae*)
  Ogre-Faced Stick Spider (*Deinopis spinosus*)

**Orb Weavers** (*Argiopidae*)
  Arrowhead-Shaped Micrathena (*Micrathena sagittata*)
  Bolas Spider (*Mastophora cornigera*)
  Labyrinth Spider (*Metepeira labyrinthea*)
  Marbled Spider (*Araneus marmoreus*)
  Orange Garden Spider (*Argiope aurantia*)
  Silk Spider (*Nephila clavipes*)
  Spiny-Bodied Spider (*Gasteracantha cancriformis*)

**Sheet-Web Weavers** (*Linyphiidae*)
  Bowl-and-Doily Spider (*Frontinella pyramitela*)
  Filmy Dome Spider (*Linyphia marginata*)
  Platform Spider (*Microlinyphia mandibulata*)

**Wolf Spiders** (*Lycosidae*)
  Wolf Spider (*Lycosa punctulata*)
  Wolf Spider (*Pardosa milvina*)

**TARANTULAS**

**Purse-Web Spiders** (*Atypidae*)
  Purse-Web Spider (*Atypus abboti*)

**Tarantulas** (*Theraphosidae*)
  Tarantula of South America (*Lasiodora*)
  Tarantula of the United States (*Aphonopelma chalcodes*)

---

Spiders belong to the phylum *Arthropoda*, and to the class *Arachnida*. They make up the spider order *Araneae*. True spiders belong to the suborder *Labidognatha*. Tarantulas belong to the suborder *Orthognatha*.

To learn how spiders fit into the animal kingdom, see ANIMAL (table: A Classification of the Animal Kingdom).

# SPIDERWORT

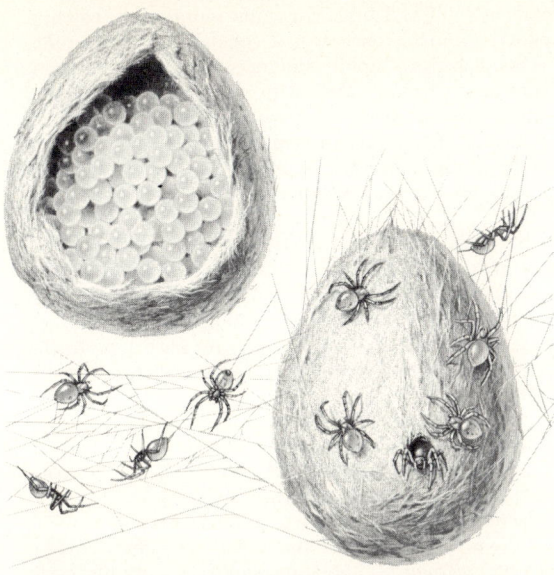

**Spiderlings** hatch from pearly white eggs inside the egg sac. One by one, they leave the egg sac through a tiny hole that they tear in its side. They immediately begin spinning draglines. Many spiderlings then travel to other areas, usually by ballooning.

**Spiderlings** hatch inside the egg sac and remain there until warm weather arrives. If the eggs are laid in autumn, the spiderlings stay quietly inside their egg sac until spring. After leaving the egg sac, the spiderlings immediately begin spinning draglines.

Many spiderlings travel to other areas. To do this, a spiderling climbs to the top of a fence post or some other tall object and tilts its spinnerets up into the air. The moving air pulls silk threads out of the spinnerets. Then the wind catches the threads and carries the spiderling into the air like a balloon on a string. This unusual way of traveling is called *ballooning*. A spider may travel a few feet or many miles by ballooning. Sailors more than 200 miles from land have seen ballooning spiders floating through the air.

Spiderlings *molt* (shed their outer skin) several times while they are growing. A new, larger skin replaces the skin that has grown too tight. Most kinds of spiders molt from five to nine times before they reach adulthood. Tarantulas molt more than 20 times, but dwarf spiders molt only a few times.

**Enemies** of spiders include snakes, frogs, toads, lizards, birds, fish, and many other animals that also eat insects. Even some insects eat spiders. The wasp, for example, is one of the spider's worst enemies (see WASP [Solitary Wasps]). One group of spiders called *pirate spiders* eats only other spiders. Pirate spiders do not spin webs, but creep into the webs of other spiders and kill them.

until they hatch. Some spiders hang the sac in a web. Others attach the sac to leaves or plants. Still others carry it with them. The female wolf spider attaches the sac to her spinnerets, and drags it behind her wherever she goes.

H. K. WALLACE
Critically reviewed by WILLIS J. GERTSCH

## SPIDER / Study Aids

**Related Articles** in WORLD BOOK include:

| | | |
|---|---|---|
| Arachne | Black Widow | Tarantula |
| Arachnid | Bruce, Robert | Trap-Door Spider |
| Arthropod | | |

### Outline

I. **The Spider's Body**
  A. Eyes
  B. Mouth
  C. Chelicerae
  D. Pedipalpi
  E. Legs
  F. Spinnerets
  G. Respiratory System
  H. Circulatory System
  I. Digestive System
  J. Nervous System

II. **The Spider's Silk**
  A. How Spiders Make Silk
  B. How Spiders Use Silk

III. **Hunting Spiders**
  A. Jumping Spiders
  B. Water Spiders
  C. Tarantulas
  D. Fisher Spiders
  E. Crab Spiders
  F. Funnel-Web Spiders
  G. Wolf Spiders

IV. **Web-Spinning Spiders**
  A. Tangled-Web Weavers
  B. Sheet-Web Weavers
  C. Orb Weavers

V. **The Life of a Spider**
  A. Courtship and Mating
  B. Eggs
  C. Spiderlings
  D. Enemies

### Questions

What is ballooning?
What are some of the ways in which spiders use silk?
How do tarantulas differ from true spiders?
How does an orb weaver know that an insect has landed in its web?
How do spiders differ from insects?
How many kinds of spiders in the United States can harm man?
How does a female wolf spider carry her egg sac?
What is the only food of pirate spiders?
Why are spiders valuable to man?
Why is a dragline often called a spider's "lifeline"?

**SPIDERWORT,** *SPI der wurt,* is the common name for a group of mostly tropical plants. Some of them are ornamental plants. The leaves of the spiderworts are often grasslike and sometimes striped. The flowers may be blue, purple, or white. They are fragile and may

**Spiderwort Is a Favorite Perennial Plant** because of its sturdiness and its lovely flowers, which grow in several colors.
J. Horace McFarland

## SPIEGELEISEN

dissolve into watery jelly. They have weak stems.

Some kinds of spiderworts grow erect, and some run along the ground. The *common spiderwort* is the best-known of the erect plants. An example of creeping spiderwort is the *wandering Jew*. It often grows under benches in greenhouses.

The spiderworts are perennials. Gardeners usually propagate them by taking cuttings from an old plant.

**Scientific Classification.** Spiderworts belong to the spiderwort family, *Commelinaceae*. The common spider-wort is genus *Tradescantia*, species *T. virginiana*. The wandering Jew is *Zebrina pendula*. PAUL C. STANDLEY

See also WANDERING JEW.

**SPIEGELEISEN,** *SPEE gul I zun*, is a whitish pig iron that contains manganese and carbon. Steelworkers add it to melted steel to increase strength and remove oxygen. It raises the manganese content of steel when added to scrap steel and pig iron. See also IRON AND STEEL (The Open-Hearth Furnace); MANGANESE; MUSHET, ROBERT FORESTER.

**SPIKE.** See INFLORESCENCE.

**SPIKENARD,** *SPIKE nerd*, or NARD, is a plant related to the valerians. It comes from India and yields a costly perfume. The root is shaped like an ear of corn. A cluster of thick stems about 2 inches long grows from the top of the root. This part is the main source of the perfume. The Bible often mentions the precious ointment of spikenard. The odor is not particularly pleasing to Western peoples. The *American spikenard*, or *Indian root*, is an aromatic herb of the ginseng family. It grows in southern Canada and the northern United States.

**Scientific Classification.** The oriental, or "true," spike-nard belongs to the valerian family, *Valerianaceae*. It is genus *Nardostachys*, species *N. jatamansi*. The American spikenard belongs to the ginseng family, *Araliaceae*. It is *Aralia racemosa*. HAROLD NORMAN MOLDENKE

**SPILLWAY.** See DAM (How Men Build Dams).

**SPINACH,** *SPIN ich*, is a popular garden vegetable. It is a low-growing annual plant that produces a thick cluster of wide, succulent leaves. People eat the leaves raw or cooked. Spinach is related to beets, Swiss chard, and the common weed lamb's-quarters.

Spinach comes from southwest Asia. The Persians once used it as medicine. Englishmen cultivated it as early as 1500, and Americans grew it during the colonial period. Spinach once was a special dish in Europe.

Spinach grows rapidly and matures in the cool season. It is easy to grow. The plant grows best in a fertile, sandy loam. It does not grow well in an acid soil. It withstands frost, but not heat. Gardeners sow the seeds in the spring. In about three months, the spinach crop is ready for harvest. Another crop can be grown in the fall.

Spinach is high in vitamin value and in minerals. It is an excellent source of vitamins A and C, and a fair source of vitamins of the B complex. It also has a large amount of fiber, and acts as a mild laxative.

**Scientific Classification.** Spinach plants belong to the goosefoot family, *Chenopodiaceae*. They are genus *Spinacea*, species *S. oleracea*. ERVIN L. DENISEN

See also LAMB'S-QUARTERS.

**SPINAL ANESTHESIA.** See ANESTHESIA.

**SPINAL CORD AND SPINAL NERVES.** See NERVOUS SYSTEM (Parts of the Nervous System); SPINE.

**SPINAL MENINGITIS.** See MENINGITIS.

**SPINE** is the popular name for the *spinal column*, or *vertebral column*. The spine helps support the body of vertebrate animals. It is made up of a column of bones called *vertebrae*. The vertebrae are held in place by strong connective tissue called *ligaments*. There are 33 vertebrae, but some of them grow together in adults. There are 7 *cervical* (neck), 12 *thoracic* (chest region), 5 *lumbar* (lower back), 5 fused *sacral* (hip region), and 4 fused *coccygeal* (tailbone region). The first cervical vertebra, the *atlas*, supports the skull. The sacral vertebrae unite with the pelvis (see PELVIS).

Each vertebra has two bony arches that form an opening called the *vertebral foramen*. The openings lie directly over one another, forming a continuous canal called the *vertebral canal*. The spinal cord extends from the lower part of the brain and passes through the canal. A pair of nerves branch off between each vertebra. They provide communication between the brain and all parts of the body.

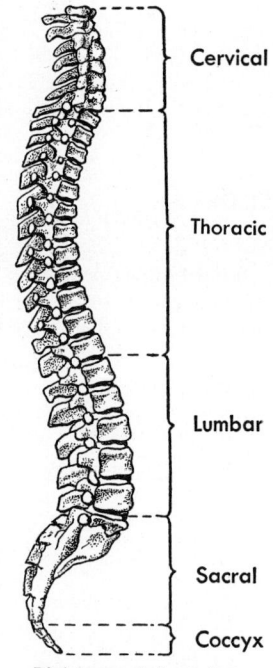

**Divisions of the Spine**

The design of the spine provides strength and freedom of motion, yet the delicate spinal cord is protected. Sometimes vertebrae that are fractured in an accident may injure the spinal cord and cause *paralysis* (loss of muscle movement). GORDON FARRELL

**Related Articles.** See the Trans-Vision three-dimensional color picture with HUMAN BODY. See also:

| | | |
|---|---|---|
| Cerebrospinal Fluid | Myelitis | Skeleton |
| Hunchback | Nervous System | Vertebra |
| Meningitis | Scoliosis | |

William M. Harlow

**Spinach Leaves Are Rich in Minerals and Vitamins.**

616

**SPINET,** *SPIN eht,* was an early keyboard musical instrument. It is now a term used for modern upright pianos. The early spinet looked like a miniature grand piano. Its wire strings were plucked by quill, ivory, or wooden pieces called *plectra.* These were attached to the keys and made a weak, tinkling sound much like that of a music box. The spinet was probably named after Giovanni Spinetti of Venice, Italy, who made important changes in the design of the instrument in the 1500's. The *virginal* and *harpsichord* are modified forms of the spinet. See also PIANO. CHARLES B. RIGHTER

**SPINGARN, JOEL ELIAS** (1875-1939), was an American publisher and literary critic who introduced the works of European writers to American audiences.

He was born in New York City and studied at Columbia College (now Columbia University). After his graduation, he taught English literature at Columbia, but was dismissed in 1911 after a disagreement with President Nicholas Murray Butler. During World War I, he served in France, and returned to join the staff of a publishing firm. His works include *A History of Literary Criticism in the Renaissance* and *Poetry: A Religion.*

After 1913, Spingarn was a leader in the National Association for the Advancement of Colored People. He established the Spingarn medal. HENRY LEE MOON

See also NATIONAL ASSOCIATION FOR THE ADVANCEMENT OF COLORED PEOPLE.

NAACP

**The Spingarn Medal** has a figure of justice on its face, *left.* The winner's name is engraved on the back, *right.*

**SPINGARN MEDAL** awards were instituted by Joel Elias Spingarn, chairman of the board of the National Association for the Advancement of Colored People, in 1914. The awards are gold medals given each year to the Negro who, according to a committee appointed by the board, has reached the highest achievement in his field in that year, or over a period of time. See also NATIONAL ASSOCIATION FOR THE ADVANCEMENT OF COLORED PEOPLE; SPINGARN, JOEL E. HENRY LEE MOON

**SPINNERET.** See SPIDER (The Spider's Body).
**SPINNING.** See FISHING.

## WINNERS OF SPINGARN MEDAL

| Year | Medal Winners | Field of Achievement |
|------|---------------|----------------------|
| 1915 | Ernest E. Just | Research in biology |
| 1916 | Charles Young | Organization of the Liberian constabulary |
| 1917 | *Harry T. Burleigh | Creative music |
| 1918 | W. S. Braithwaite | Literature |
| 1919 | Archibald H. Grimke | Politics and literature |
| 1920 | *William E. B. Du Bois | Founding of Pan-African Congress |
| 1921 | Charles S. Gilpin | Drama |
| 1922 | Mary B. Talbert | Helped create Frederick Douglass Shrine |
| 1923 | *George W. Carver | Agricultural chemistry |
| 1924 | *Roland Hayes | Concert singing |
| 1925 | *James Weldon Johnson | Literature |
| 1926 | *Carter G. Woodson | History |
| 1927 | Anthony Overton | Life insurance |
| 1928 | Charles W. Chestnutt | Literature |
| 1929 | Mordecai W. Johnson | Education, Howard U. |
| 1930 | Henry A. Hunt | Education in the South |
| 1931 | Richard B. Harrison | Drama |
| 1932 | *Robert R. Moton | Educational work |
| 1933 | Max Yergan | Interracial work in South Africa |
| 1934 | William T. B. Williams | Education, Tuskegee Institute |
| 1935 | *Mary McLeod Bethune | Education |
| 1936 | John Hope | Education, Atlanta U. |
| 1937 | *Walter F. White | Civil rights |
| 1938 | No award given. | |
| 1939 | *Marian Anderson | Concert singing |
| 1940 | Louis T. Wright | Surgery and civic affairs |
| 1941 | *Richard Wright | Literature |
| 1942 | *A. Philip Randolph | Labor and civic affairs |
| 1943 | *William H. Hastie | Equal justice for Negroes |
| 1944 | *Charles R. Drew | Medicine |
| 1945 | *Paul Robeson | Singing and acting |
| 1946 | *Thurgood Marshall | Equality before the law |
| 1947 | *Percy L. Julian | Commercial chemistry |
| 1948 | Channing H. Tobias | Civil liberties |
| 1949 | *Ralph J. Bunche | UN mediator, Palestine |
| 1950 | Charles H. Houston | Law; education |
| 1951 | Mabel K. Staupers | Equal rights for Negro nurses |
| 1952 | Harry T. Moore | Civil liberties |
| 1953 | Paul R. Williams | Architecture |
| 1954 | *Theodore K. Lawless | Dermatology |
| 1955 | Carl Murphy | Publishing; equal rights for Negroes |
| 1956 | *Jackie Robinson | First Negro in modern major league baseball |
| 1957 | *Martin Luther King | Led Montgomery, Ala., Negroes' bus boycott |
| 1958 | Mrs. Daisy Bates Minnijean Brown Elizabeth Eckford Ernest Green Thelma Mothershed Melba Patillo Gloria Ray Terrence Roberts Jefferson Thomas Carlotta Walls | Arkansas NAACP First Negro students to attend Little Rock (Ark.) Central High School |
| 1959 | *Duke Ellington | Creative music |
| 1960 | *Langston Hughes | Literature |
| 1961 | Kenneth B. Clark | Psychology; school integration |
| 1962 | *Robert C. Weaver | Government |
| 1963 | *Medgar W. Evers (posthumously) | Equal rights for Negroes in Mississippi |
| 1964 | *Roy Wilkins | Civil rights |
| 1965 | *Leontyne Price | Opera singing |
| 1966 | *John H. Johnson | Publishing |
| 1967 | *Edward W. Brooke | Government |
| 1968 | Sammy Davis, Jr. | Entertainment |
| 1969 | Clarence Mitchell | Fair housing legislation |

*Has a separate biography in WORLD BOOK.

# SPINNING

**SPINNING** is the process of making threads by twisting together plant or animal fibers. It is one of the most ancient arts. For thousands of years, yarn was spun by means of a *spindle*. This consisted of little more than a smooth stick from 9 to 15 inches long. It had a notch at one end for catching the thread, and a stone or baked clay bowl, called a *whorl*, to help make the spindle spin somewhat like a top. The spinner turned the spindle by rolling it against the thigh. Ancient Egyptians used such spindles to make thread for cloth of fine quality.

Ancient spinners in India and South America used finer spindles, usually in a bowl or on the ground. They spun cotton from combed rolls. Wool or flax fibers were wound around a stick called the *distaff*.

**The Spinning Wheel,** used in Europe as far back as the 1200's, was the first device to give the spindle a

National Gallery of Art, Index of American Design; National Cotton Council
**The Old Spinning Wheel,** above, so common to colonial houses, could make only one thread at a time. It could not compare with a modern spinning machine, *right*, which makes hundreds at a time, and gives threads firmness and strength.

spinning movement. The principle was the same as the hand spindle, but the spindle was mounted horizontally. A band or small belt connected to a large wheel passed over a groove in the spindle and turned it. A foot pedal turned the wheel. A distaff carried the material to be spun. The material was drawn off the distaff by hand, and the fineness of the thread depended on the speed with which the twisting thread was drawn out. For very fine thread, two spinnings were necessary. New England housewives used this early type of spinning wheel in colonial times. It was as common then as the sewing machine is today.

**The Spinning Jenny** was invented by James Hargreaves in about 1764. This machine could spin more than one thread at a time. But it produced coarse thread rather than fine thread. The name *jenny* came from *gin*, the local word for *engine*. See SPINNING JENNY.

**The Water Frame** was a cotton-spinning machine patented by Richard Arkwright in 1769. Until then, all cloth had been woven with a linen *warp* (lengthwise threads) since no way had been found to spin cotton for the warp threads. Arkwright's frame drew cotton from the carding machine in a fine, hard-twisted thread suitable for the warp.

**The Spinning Mule,** invented by Samuel Crompton in 1779, combined the principles of the spinning wheel and the water frame. It was also called the muslin wheel because it was widely used to produce this material. The spinning mule had 48 spindles, and produced unusually fine and uniform yarn.

New spinning machines helped bring about that change in history known as the Industrial Revolution, when machines began to take the place of hand workers. The spinning machines created a demand for more cotton. This need brought about Eli Whitney's invention, the cotton gin. With more thread to weave, the weavers developed better and faster power looms. Then came machines to knit, to make lace, to embroider, to cut out patterns, and finally to sew cloth into finished ready-to-wear garments in large quantities.

Cotton spinning in a present-day factory is a typical example of most spinning. After the raw cotton has been

cleaned and arranged into *laps* (bunches) of uniform size, it goes to the carding machines. These machines have huge rollers covered with wire teeth. Here the tangled fibers are straightened out and made to lie in straight, even rows. Then the fibers are rolled over and over one another to form *slivers*, which look like loose ropes of soft cotton yarn. A sliver goes through the processes of *drawing*, *slubbing*, and *roving*, by which it is twisted and retwisted and made continually finer and stronger. Spinning machines carry out these fine operations and give the thread the required twist, firmness, and strength.

New machines have been invented to spin the old natural fibers, such as flax and hemp, and new machines are being made for other fibers, such as kapok and ramie. Machines may some day be developed which will make cloth directly without first spinning thread, but until that time inventors will continue their efforts to improve spinning machines. ELIZABETH CHESLEY BAITY

**Related Articles** in WORLD BOOK include:
Arkwright, Sir Richard
Colonial Life in America
  (Clothing; pictures)
Cotton (Spinning; pictures)
Crompton, Samuel
Dyak (picture)
Hargreaves, James
Industrial Revolution
  (Spinning Machines)
Thread

**SPINNING JENNY** is a machine for spinning yarn. Like the spinning wheel, it may be operated by a foot treadle or by hand. But the spinning jenny can spin more than one yarn at a time. The idea for multiple-yarn spinning was conceived about 1764 by James Hargreaves, an English spinner. He noticed that the upright spindle of an overturned spinning wheel continued to revolve. In 1770, Hargreaves patented a machine that was capable of spinning 16 yarns at one time. ERNEST R. KASWELL

See also HARGREAVES, JAMES (with picture).

**SPINOZA,** *spih NOH zuh,* **BARUCH,** or BENEDICT (1632-1677), was a Dutch philosopher. He accepted René Descartes' idea that the universe is divided into mind and matter (see DESCARTES, RENÉ). But he saw, as Descartes did not, that if mind and matter are separate substances, they cannot interact. Spinoza decided that they are "attributes" of one substance, God. God, being infinite, has many attributes, but mind and matter are the only two that human minds can know.

Among the consequences of this view is the following: everything that exists, including individual men and women, is a part of God; in God, quite literally, we live and move and have our being. This view upset Spinoza's orthodox contemporaries, both Christian and Jewish, because it was so different from their own. The Jews denounced him and forced him to leave Amsterdam. Spinoza actually was deeply religious, and in many respects was a mystic. He held that man's highest happiness consists in coming to understand and appreciate the truth that he is a tiny part of an all-inclusive, pantheistic God (see PANTHEISM).

Culver
**Baruch Spinoza**

Spinoza was born in Amsterdam of Jewish parents who had sought refuge there from persecution. He broke with the Jewish faith after studying Descartes and Giordano Bruno. He prized independence and freedom of thought so much that he preferred to support himself by grinding lenses rather than accept a university professorship or financial aid. W. T. JONES

See also PHILOSOPHY (The Appeal to Reason).

**SPINTHARISCOPE,** or SCINTILLOSCOPE, is an instrument used to observe the flashes of alpha particles emitted from radioactive substances. The instrument consists of a brass tube with a zinc sulfide screen at one end, a lens at the other end, and a speck of radioactive material one millimeter from the screen. Sir William Crookes, an English chemist, developed the instrument in 1903 (see CROOKES, SIR WILLIAM).

**SPINY ANTEATER.** See ECHIDNA.

**SPINY LOBSTER.** See LOBSTER (The Body of a Lobster).

**SPIRACLE.** See FLY (Abdomen); INSECT (Internal Organs).

**SPIRAEA,** *spy RE uh,* is the name of a genus of herbs and shrubs in the rose family which bear white, pink, or rose-colored flowers. Spiraea grows in the temperate and cold regions of the Northern Hemisphere. Gardeners cultivate numerous species as ornamental plants.

Walter Singer
**Plum-Leaved Spiraea,** commonly called bridal wreath, bears small clusters of dainty white flowers on slender stalks.

One of the best known is *Van Houtt's spiraea,* a hardy shrub with thick, deep green foliage. Another is *Thunberg's spiraea,* which has more delicate leaves. The *hardhack,* or *steeplebush,* can be planted in masses. Its flowers grow in narrow, crowded clusters. The *plum-leaved spiraea* is the well-known *bridal wreath* (see BRIDAL WREATH). It may grow more than 6 feet high, and has white flowers. Another well-known species is a troublesome weed called *meadowsweet.* It grows in New England. Spiraeas grow well in good land, but need much water and sunlight.

**Scientific Classification.** Spiraea belongs to the rose family, *Rosaceae.* Van Houtt's spiraea is genus *Spiraea,* species *S. vanhouttei.* Thunberg's is *S. thunbergii.* Hardhack is *S. tomentosa.* Bridal wreath is *S. prunifolia.* Meadowsweet is *S. latifolia.* J. J. LEVISON

See also PLANT (color picture: Some Members of the Rose Family).

**SPIRAL NEBULAE.** See NEBULA.

**SPIRE** is a term used in architecture to describe the pointed top of a tower or steeple. Most spires narrow to a sharp point high above the roofs of their towers. Many of them have eight sides. The spire developed from the *turret,* a small tower.

In early Christian times, tall peaked turrets were placed on many roofs. In the Middle Ages, it became customary to build turrets on top of large church towers. These turrets gradually became taller and more slender. Some of the greatest spires in the world rise above cathedrals in Europe. The spire of the cathedral of Ulm, Germany, rises 528 feet and is the highest in Europe. The spire of the cathedral at Cologne, Germany, rises 525 feet. The spire of Salisbury Cathedral in England rises 404 feet. Many famous skyscrapers in New York City and Chicago, especially those built between 1910 and 1930, are topped with spires. ALAN GOWANS

See also COLOGNE (picture); CATHEDRAL (pictures).

619

# SPIRILLUM

**SPIRILLUM.** See BACTERIA (Kinds; picture).
**SPIRIT LEVEL.** See LEVEL.
**SPIRIT OF ST. LOUIS.** See LINDBERGH, CHARLES A.
**SPIRIT OF '76** is a famous painting by Archibald M. Willard (1837-1918), a carriage painter of Wellington, Ohio. It began as a humorous sketch called "Yankee Doodle," which Willard made in 1874 or 1875 for a Fourth of July celebration. Later, he changed the sketch to a painting with a serious theme for the Philadelphia Centennial Exposition of 1876. His father, a Baptist minister, was the model for the central figure; Hugh Mosher, a soldier friend, posed for the fife-player; and the son of John H. Devereux, pioneer railroad executive, became the drummer boy. The painting was exhibited in cities from coast to coast. Devereux bought it in 1880 and gave it to Marblehead, Mass., where it hangs in Abbot Hall, the town hall. See also REVOLUTIONARY WAR IN AMERICA (picture).

**SPIRIT WRESTLERS.** See DOUKHOBORS.
**SPIRITS OF HARTSHORN.** See AMMONIA.
**SPIRITUAL** is a type of religious song made famous by the Negroes of the Southern United States. The spirituals have a strong rhythm and are emotional. They are especially moving when sung by a group. A leader sometimes sings one or two lines alone, and a chorus comes in with the refrain. Spiritual singers often emphasize the rhythm by clapping their hands. Spirituals have been called the only truly American folk songs.

The melodies used in spirituals are sometimes said to have come from Africa. But there are spirituals which have no relation whatever to African songs. These spirituals show a direct relation to the results of evangelistic preaching among the poor whites in the South. These "revivals" also encouraged "white spirituals." The Negroes' love for rhythm and song led them to put their feelings and memories into their singing. Much of the ship loading and plantation work was accompanied by singing of spirituals.

The slaves based most of their spirituals upon characters and stories from the Bible. The manner in which these stories are told in Negro spirituals shows a colorful imagination and a simple faith. Many slaves thought of themselves as modern children of Israel and looked for a black Moses to deliver them from their bondage. Their songs were warmly appealing and sincere. Among the well-known spirituals are "Go Down, Moses," "Weeping Mary," "Deep River," "Swing Low, Sweet Chariot," and "Nobody Knows the Trouble I've Seen."

Spirituals were little known outside the Southern States until after the Negro was freed from slavery. In 1867, William Francis Allen and Lucy McKim Garrison published a collection of Negro music called *Slave Songs*. The songs included "Climb Jacob's Ladder," "Give Me Jesus," and "I'll Take the Wings of the Morning."

In 1871, spirituals were introduced to other parts of the United States by a group of Negroes called the Jubilee Singers, of Fisk University, Nashville, Tenn. They traveled throughout the United States, and to England and Germany, giving concerts to raise money for their school. Within three years they collected $150,000. Other Negro schools followed their example. The Negro quartets from Hampton Institute in Virginia and Tuskegee Institute in Alabama, became famous.

Spirituals are now one of the best-known forms of American music. Such famous singers as Marian Anderson and Roland Hayes have helped to accomplish this. Their influence can be heard in the opera *Porgy and Bess* by George Gershwin.   RAYMOND KENDALL

See also FOLK MUSIC (picture).

**SPIRITUAL VALUES.** See PHILOSOPHY (What Is Good and What Is Evil?); ETHICS.

**SPIRITUALISM,** in religious philosophy, teaches the existence of a being or reality distinct from matter. This being may be called mind or spirit. Some persons of this philosophy believe that the mind, or spirit, is the only reality. This belief is called *spiritual idealism*. See also IDEALISM.

**SPIRITUALISTS** believe that the spirits of the dead can communicate with living persons. Believers of spiritualism are sometimes called *spiritualists*. They believe that the existence and personal identity of an individual continue after death.

According to the teachings of spiritualism, persons known as *mediums* have special powers and sensitivity. These powers enable a medium to establish communication between living and dead persons. Spiritualists believe that living persons can receive messages or demonstrations from the spirits of the dead at public or private gatherings called séances.

**The Séance.** Spiritualists believe that a dead person's spirit returns and makes known its presence at a séance, sometimes by rapping loudly on a wall or table. At séances, several persons often sit around a small table and hold their hands lightly on its top. Sometimes the table tips back and forth. At other times, it slides around the room. Spiritualists believe a dead person's spirit moves the table.

Spiritualists look for other occurrences at séances. Some spirits are believed to throw things about the room and to cause objects to float, and to appear and disappear. Such actions, as well as occasions when the spirits can be seen, are called physical *manifestations*. The mediums who conduct such meetings are called *physical* mediums.

In another type of séance, conducted by a *mental* medium, no physical action occurs. But the spirits are supposed to take possession of the medium's body. At these séances, the medium may write or speak a message that he says comes from the spirit of a dead person. Other mediums do not claim to be possessed, but they say they hear voices of the spirits.

**Public Services,** sometimes called *message services*, are attended by larger groups than those at séances. These services are open to the public, and sometimes are advertised. The groups usually gather at public meeting places such as hotels or halls.

**Disbelievers.** Many scientists and other persons have challenged the claims put forth by spiritualists. Disbelievers have charged that persons attending séances are tricked into believing that spirits can communicate with the living. Scientists say that explanations can often be given for the strange happenings. Some psychologists, for example, believe that a table in a séance room may be moved by the unconscious hand pressure of persons sitting around it, and not by a dead person's spirit.

Many mediums believe sincerely in spiritualism. They consider spiritualism an authentic religion, based on philosophical, scientific, and moral principles.

**Spiritualist Churches.** Spiritualist churches in the United States are organized into three bodies. These are (1) the International General Assembly of Spiritualists, (2) the National Spiritual Alliance of the U.S.A., and (3) the National Spiritualist Association of Churches. The International General Assembly has headquarters in Norfolk, Va., the National Spiritual Alliance, in Lake Pleasant, Mass., and the National Spiritualist Association of Churches, in Milwaukee, Wis. For membership of the International General Assembly and the National Spiritualist Association of Churches in the United States, see RELIGION (table). The National Spiritual Alliance has more than 3,100 members.

**History.** The Spiritualist movement began in the United States at Hydesville, N.Y., in 1848. The mediums were two little sisters named Margaret and Katherine Fox. The story is that a man was murdered in their house. The girls said the spirit of this man returned at night and rapped on the walls and furniture of their room. The children said the spirit agreed to answer questions by giving a certain number of raps for "yes" and a different number for "no." The story about this spirit spread. The children were taken to Rochester, N.Y. According to the story, the spirit went along with them. More and more persons claimed to hear the spirit. Within a few months, the rappings stirred interest in many countries. Soon other persons said they were mediums, and that spirits came to rap for them.

Famous persons have been active in spiritualism and in *psychical research*, the study of supernatural things. They include Sir Arthur Conan Doyle, the British author; Sir James H. Jeans and Sir Oliver Lodge, British scientists; and William James, the American psychologist.

See also ECTOPLASM; GHOST; HYPNOTISM; MAGIC (Communication with Spirits); PSYCHICAL RESEARCH.

**SPIROCHETE.** See RELAPSING FEVER; VENEREAL DISEASE.

**SPIROGYRA** is the name of a group of fresh-water green algae that form slimy scum in still water.

**SPIROMETER,** *spy RAHM ee ter*, is a device that doctors use to measure how much oxygen a person's body uses. It also measures how much air the lungs can hold, how well the lungs are working, and the number of times a person breathes each minute.

A spirometer is made up of two cylinders. One cylinder is upside down and rests inside a larger cylinder that is filled with water. The patient breathes through a rubber tube into the inner cylinder. The added air causes the cylinder to rise in the water. When the patient inhales, he removes air from the cylinder and it sinks. A writing arm records these movements on a piece of paper. This record is called a *spirogram*.

The spirometer is most often used to measure a person's *basal metabolic rate* (the amount of oxygen the body uses while at rest). Certain diseases, especially those of the thyroid gland, cause the basal metabolic rate to change. To measure how much air the lungs can hold, the patient first breathes in as deeply as possible, and then exhales as much air as possible into the spirometer. The amount of air that was exhaled is called the *vital capacity*. The vital capacity is less than normal if a person has such disorders as asthma or certain heart diseases.  E. CLINTON TEXTER, JR.

See also METABOLISM (Basal Metabolism).

**SPITSBERGEN.** See SVALBARD.

**SPITTELER,** *SHPIT uh ler*, **CARL** (1845-1924), a Swiss poet and writer, won the 1919 Nobel prize for literature. His main concern and theme in the epic poem *Olympic Spring* (1900-1910), and in his other writings, is the suffering of man in this world. He believed that suffering cannot be overcome, but that it can be reduced by the kindhearted acts of truly noble men. Spitteler was born in Liestal.  G. F. MERKEL

**SPITZ** is a name given to several breeds of small dogs. The American spitz is a member of the spitz family of arctic dogs, which includes the chow chow, pomeranian, and samoyed. The spitz weighs about 25 pounds, and has a thick white coat, pointed ears, and a sturdy body. It carries its tail curled up over its back. The spitz is not recognized as a breed by the American Kennel Club.  OLGA DAKAN

See also SAMOYED; POMERANIAN.

**SPLEEN** is a large, glandlike organ in the body. It helps filter the blood. The spleen lies below the diaphragm, to the left of the stomach and a little behind it. In adults it is about 5 inches long and 3 to 4 inches wide, and weighs about 7 ounces. It is soft and spongy, crumbles easily, and has a deep violet-red color. The organ is covered by a fold of the *peritoneum*, the membrane that lines the abdominal cavity. The principal cells of the spleen are similar to those in the lymph glands.

The spleen helps filter foreign substances from the blood, much as a lymph gland filters foreign substances from the lymph. Various kinds of cells in the spleen *engulf* (surround and destroy) these foreign substances. The spleen also serves as a "graveyard" for injured red blood cells. When the body needs extra blood during exercise or hemorrhage, the spleen contracts and squeezes out some of the blood cells it has stored. It may

**The Spirometer Test** shows how much air can be held in the patient's lungs. After he has inhaled as much as possible, he exhales the air through the tube. The lung capacity is determined by the distance the inside cylinder rises.

Army Medical Center

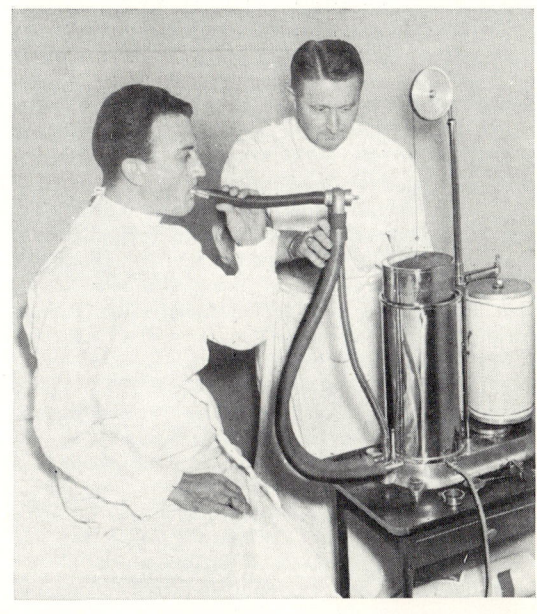

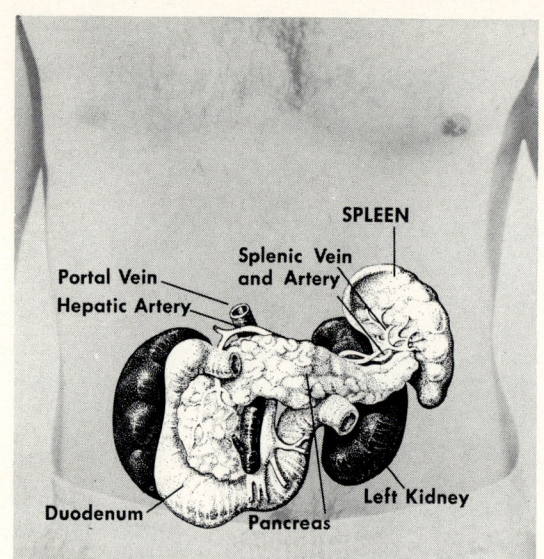

**The Spleen** aids the human body by acting as a blood filter. It also stores up blood cells that can be used in emergencies.

form red blood cells in unborn babies, but it does not do so after birth.

The spleen is thought to be only a helper of other glands and organs, for it may be removed from the body without any noticeable ill effects. It is often necessary to remove the spleen. Sometimes, a disease centers in the spleen and causes it to enlarge. In certain other diseases, the spleen works so hard at destroying worn-out red blood cells that it also destroys healthy red cells and causes anemia. Sometimes, it destroys blood platelets, which help in the clotting of blood. When too many platelets are destroyed, the patient may bleed into the tissues. In all these cases, the spleen has to be removed by a surgical operation. TERENCE A. ROGERS

See also HUMAN BODY (Trans-Vision three-dimensional color picture); IRON.

**SPLICING** is a method of joining two ends of rope or wire together without forming a knot. The strands of the ends are unraveled several turns. Then, the strands of one end are twisted around the strands of the other end. See also KNOTS, HITCHES, AND SPLICES (picture).

**SPLIT**, or SPALATO (pop. 101,000; alt. 400 ft.), is a seaport in Yugoslavia (see YUGOSLAVIA [color map]). It is a commercial and industrial center, and the chief city of the Dalmatian coastal area. Split is an ancient Roman town. Part of it was originally built about A.D. 295, within the walls of the palace of Emperor Diocletian. The palace is one of the finest examples of Roman architecture still standing. GEORGE KISH

**SPLIT INFINITIVE.** See INFINITIVE.

**SPOCK, BENJAMIN McLANE** (1903-    ), an American doctor, became famous for his books on child care. His best-known book, *Common Sense Book of Baby and Child Care* (1946), was translated into more than 25 languages. His other books include *Feeding Your Baby and Child* (1955), *Baby's First Year* (1955), *Dr. Spock Talks with Mothers* (1961), *Problems of Parents* (1962), and *Caring for Your Disabled Child* (1965).

In the 1960's, Spock became an active opponent of United States involvement in the Vietnam War. In 1968, he was convicted on charges of conspiring to counsel young men to avoid the military draft. He appealed the verdict. In 1969, the U.S. First Circuit Court of Appeals reversed his conviction.

Spock was born in New Haven, Conn. He graduated from Yale University and received his medical degree from Columbia University. JOHN A. BARBOUR

**SPODE** was the family name of three famous English pottery makers, father, son, and grandson.

**Josiah Spode** (1733-1797), the father, produced blue and white earthenware and transfer-printed willowware. He was apprenticed to Thomas Wheildon, became a master potter, and started his own shop.

**Josiah Spode** (1754-1827), the son, perfected the formula for bone china (see PORCELAIN [Kinds of Porcelain]). He also designed blue and gold tableware pottery in the style of Oriental porcelains. He was born in Stoke-on-Trent.

**Josiah Spode** (1776-1829), was the grandson. In 1827, he and William Copeland managed the Spode works, which fell to Copeland at Spode's death. Spode was born in London. EUGENE F. BUNKER, JR.

**SPOHR,** *shpohr,* **LOUIS** (1784-1859), was a German violinist, composer, and conductor. His works include the *Violin School* and the opera *Jessonda*. Spohr was born in Brunswick, Germany, and began to study the violin at the age of five. The Duke of Brunswick became his patron eight years later, and Spohr soon became a violin soloist. He started conducting in 1809, and later became court conductor for life in Kassel, Germany. IRVING KOLODIN

**SPOILS SYSTEM** uses public offices as political rewards for party services. The system is used in many countries. When a new political party comes to power, its leaders place many of their faithful followers in important government offices. Many people consider this justifiable when a party places able persons in high offices where policy is to be made. They feel the victorious party must shape policies to satisfy its supporters. It is unjustifiable when political leaders dismiss able persons from positions not of a policy-making type. They do this to make room for others whose chief or only merit consists of their having demonstrated they are "good party men." This makes government less efficient.

It was once widely thought that the spoils system in the United States first came into general use during the presidency of Andrew Jackson. Recent studies show that President Thomas Jefferson, a Democratic-Republican, followed a policy of not appointing Federalists to government offices. However, Jackson's friend, William L. Marcy, popularized the slogan "to the victor belong the spoils of the enemy."

By 1840, the spoils system was widely used in federal, state, and local governments. In 1883, a civil service law made it illegal to fill some federal offices by the spoils system. Since then, much has been done to avoid the evils of the system. Federal civil service legislation has been greatly expanded. Many cities and states have made education and experience the basis of appointment to public office. ROBERT A. DAHL

See also CIVIL SERVICE (History); GRANT, ULYSSES S. (Political Corruption); JACKSON, ANDREW (The Spoils System).

**Spokane, Wash., Lies in the Level Spokane River Valley at the Foot of Steep, Pine-Covered Hills.**

**SPOKANE,** *spoh KAN*, Wash. (pop. 181,608; met. area 278,333), is the trade, rail, and manufacturing center for the *Inland Empire*, an area covering 81,000 square miles in eastern Washington, northeastern Oregon, northern Idaho, and western Montana. Spokane is one of the largest inland cities and railroad centers west of the Mississippi River. Its woodworking plants produce nearly half of the sashes and doors made in the United States. Spokane is an important trade center, with many large wholesale and retail outlets.

**Location, Size, and Description.** Spokane lies on both banks of the Spokane River, near the eastern border of Washington. It is about 15 miles west of the Idaho border. For location, see WASHINGTON (political map). Two waterfalls in the middle of the city furnish hydroelectric power and add to the scenic beauty. Long Lake Dam, which has a power plant with a capacity of 70,000 kilowatts, is near the city.

The city covers 44 square miles of high land. Elevations range from 1,890 feet to more than 2,400 feet above sea level. The downtown section is built on a valley plain. The residential districts of Spokane lie on higher land. South of the falls are the deep gorges of the Spokane River and a river branch, Latah Creek. The chief mills and factories stand in the eastern and northeastern parts of the city.

Spokane International Airport, a municipal airport, lies a few miles southwest of Spokane. Military installations near Spokane include Fairchild Air Force Base and Geiger Air Force Base. Five major railroads serve the city. For Spokane's monthly temperature and rainfall, see WASHINGTON (Climate).

**Cultural Life and Education.** Spokane is the home of Gonzaga University, Fort Wright College, and Whitworth College. The Cheney Cowles and the Grace Campbell memorial museums, and a library system with many branch libraries serve the city.

**Recreation.** Spokane has 60 parks which cover over 2,900 acres. More than 70 lakes lie among thick forests and high mountains within a short distance of the city. The largest lakes are Pend Oreille and Coeur d'Alene, both in Idaho. A highway stretches 25 miles from the city to Mount Spokane State Park, a popular winter sports recreation area. Grand Coulee Dam, located about 90 miles west of Spokane, is a leading tourist attraction. See GRAND COULEE DAM.

**Industry and Trade.** Spokane is the market place and shipping center for a large farming, mining, and lumbering region. It has meat- and poultry-packing plants, flour mills, creameries, bakeries, and sawmills. Leading products of the city include brick and tile, cement, electronic equipment, machinery and metal equipment, paper, and aluminum trailer bodies and other fabricated aluminum products.

**History and Government.** Fur traders entered the area in the early 1800's. The first permanent settlers came to the site of the present city in 1871. The town of Spokane Falls was officially laid out in 1878. It became the seat of Spokane County in 1882. The name Spokane was adopted in 1890. The Northern Pacific Railroad first reached Spokane in 1881. In 1889, the business section of the city was destroyed by fire. Residents soon rebuilt the city. Spokane has a council-manager form of government. HOWARD J. CRITCHFIELD

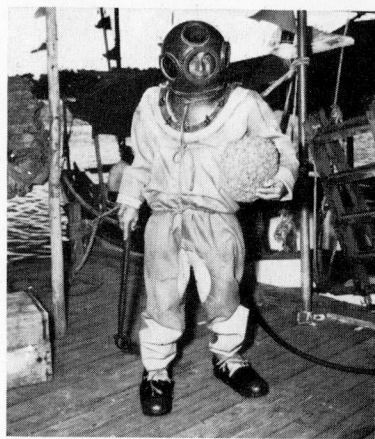

20th Century-Fox; Tarpon Springs C. of C.

**Sponge Fishermen** hang their "catch" in the ship's rigging to dry, *left*. A diver, *above*, uses a grappling hook to pull up sponges.

**SPONGE,** *spunj*, is a water animal. At one time, people thought sponges were plants, because sponges are attached to the bottom of the ocean and do not move around. Many sponges look like a type of plant. But zoologists classify sponges as animals.

Sponges make up the animal phylum *Porifera*, which means *pore-bearers*. The surface of the sponge's body is covered with tiny pores.

Most sponges live in the ocean. But there are a few fresh-water *species* (kinds). Sponges can be found both in shallow and in deep water. They inhabit all the seas, but more kinds and numbers of sponges live in the warm

---

*Robert D. Barnes, the contributor of this article, is Professor of Biology at Gettysburg College; and the author of* Invertebrate Zoology.

---

temperate and tropical waters than anywhere else. The largest sponges, including the well-known commercial sponges that people use for cleaning, grow in these warmer waters.

Sponges have lived from the earliest ages. Scientists have found remains of sponges in the oldest rocks that bear fossils.

### The Body of the Sponge

A sponge does not look like any other animal. Some sponges are shaped like vases or goblets, but most species of sponges have no definite shapes. Some may be thin and flat, while others become round masses. Still others may look like branching shrubbery or treelike bushes. Sponges vary greatly in size. Some grow to only a fraction of an inch, while others grow to more than 4 feet.

A sponge has no head, mouth, or internal organs. It depends on a system of water canals in its body to bring in food and oxygen. This system also carries away waste products.

Tiny pores in the surface of the sponge's body lead to the tiny canals. Food and oxygen enter the body through the pores, and are carried through the canals into small chambers. These are called *flagellated chambers*, because each cell that lines them contains a *flagellum* (long thread that whips around to aid movement). The flagellated chambers drain into other small canals. These canals join a network of small canals that eventually lead to the outside through a large opening in the sponge's body called the *osculum*.

A piece of sponge as small as a marble contains thousands of flagellated chambers and canals. Symmetrical sponges with vase-shaped or goblet-shaped bodies have only one osculum. Sponges with bodies that are not symmetrical have many oscula, each providing an exit from the thousands of flagellated chambers and canals. Many zoologists believe that a sponge with many oscula is not a single animal, but a colony made up of many sponges.

The beating, whiplike movements of the flagella circulate water through the sponge. Water enters through the sponge's surface pores. It flows through the flagellated chambers and canals and moves out through the osculum. The water sweeps tiny plants and animals into the sponge and through its body. When these food particles reach the flagellated chambers of the sponge, the cells that line the chambers *engulf* (surround) and digest them.

Sponges have several types of skeletons. Some sponge skeletons consist of tiny needles, called *spicules*. Other skeletons are made of fibers, called *spongin*. Some sponges have skeletons that consist of both spicules and spongin. There are two kinds of spicules in sponge skeletons. Some skeletons have spicules made of *cal-*

624

# SPONGE

**Sheepswool and Grass Sponges** grow from the same base, *above*. They grow side by side but they are quite different.

**The Horny Sponge, or Elephant-Ear,** from the Mediterranean Sea has a very fine texture. It is used commercially.

**The Glassrope Sponge** is a native of the Indian Ocean.

**The Velvet Sponge** lacks the finer texture of the sheepswool sponge, but it is satisfactory for rougher cleaning work.

**Venus's-Flower-Basket** has a skeleton of fine lacework.

Fish and Wildlife Service; Ralph Buchsbaum; Visual Education Service; American Museum of Natural History

**This Section of a Growing Sponge** shows the strange branchlike formation the sponge follows as it enlarges.

**This Sponge Growth** is like closely twined branches of a gnarled tree.

# SPONGE

*cium carbonate* (limestone). Others have spicules made of *silica* (glass).

All sponge skeletons form a supporting meshwork throughout the sponge's body. *Glass sponges* contain skeletons made of evenly arranged glass spicules. After the sponge cells are removed these beautiful skeletons look like glass wool. The delicate *Venus's-flower-basket* is a glass sponge. Other less attractive sponges leave only the rough spongin fibers after the cells have been removed.

Living ocean sponges may be black, brown, gray, or brilliant shades of red, blue, purple, and yellow. Freshwater sponges are green in color, because *algae* (microscopic plants) live in some of the sponges' cells.

## Life Story of the Sponge

The sponge may begin life as a single cell, an egg. This egg divides inside the body of the parent, and keeps dividing until it forms a tiny *larva* (undeveloped animal form) covered with flagellated cells. Then the water circulating through the parent's body sweeps the larva outside the body. The tiny larva is on its own. Its beating, lashing flagella move the larva through the water until it finally settles to the bottom of the ocean and attaches itself to a hard surface. The larva develops into an adult sponge there.

Sponges may also reproduce *asexually* (without eggs). They do this by growing buds and branches that eventually break away from the parent sponge and grow into new sponges on their own.

Sponges have remarkable powers of *regeneration* (regrowth of body parts). Even if much of the body breaks or is cut away, the sponge can replace the broken parts. To test these powers of regeneration, zoologists have pressed sponges through extremely fine cloths so that all the cells of the sponge separate or divide into small groups. When the zoologists put the cells back into water again, the cells rearrange themselves to form a new sponge.

## Commercial Sponges

Most of the so-called *sponges* sold in stores today are not true sponges. They are synthetic materials made to look and to clean like true animal sponges. Skeletons used as true commercial sponges consist of soft, elastic spongin fibers. They are free from impurities and can absorb large amounts of water. These qualities make sponges excellent cleaning tools.

True commercial sponges come from Tarpon Springs off Florida's west coast, and from waters off Key West, the Bahamas, and Cuba. Sponges are also taken from the Mediterranean Sea off the coasts of Egypt, Greece, Tunisia, and Turkey. The silk cup sponge, found off Egypt and Greece, ranks as the most valuable of all commercial animal sponges. Other valuable commercial animal sponges include the elephant-ear, the honeycomb, and the Rock Island wools.

Sponge fishermen use several different methods to get sponges. In the deeper waters of the Mediterranean Sea, fishermen in diving suits go down after the sponges. Sometimes they use dredges to bring them up. In the shallow waters off the coast of Florida, fishermen use the *hooking* method. Two men go out in a glass-bottom boat. One man manages the boat while the other does the fishing. The men look through the glass bottom of the boat and can see 50 feet or more below the surface. A fisherman lowers a long pole with a pronged hook to where the sponges are. He uses the hook to loosen the sponges and bring them to the surface. In the deeper waters of the Gulf of Mexico, sponge fishermen use diving suits. Sometimes they go down 100 feet or deeper to reach the sponges.

Fishermen spread the sponges out on deck until the flesh decays. After all the decaying substances are removed, the fishermen hang the skeletons in the rigging of the ship to dry. Shallow-water fishermen keep their catch in *kraals* (pens) along the shore. The high tide fills these pens with water, removing the flesh and leaving the skeleton.

**Scientific Classification.** Sponges make up the animal phylum *Porifera*. There are three classes of sponges. Sponges with limestone spicules belong to the class *Calcarea*. Glass sponges belong to the class *Hexactinellida*. The largest class is the class *Demospongiae*. These fibers can have glass spicules, spongin fibers, or both types of skeletal materials. ROBERT D. BARNES

See also FLORIDA (color picture: Diving for Sponges); OCEAN (color picture: Benthos).

**SPONGE RUBBER.** See RUBBER (Sponge Rubber).

**SPONSOR,** in baptism. See BAPTISM.

**SPONTANEOUS COMBUSTION** is burning that begins without the application of a flame. It takes place when oxygen in the air unites with coal, oil, or other inflammable substances. This reaction raises the temperature of the material until it gets so hot that it bursts into flame. See also COMBUSTION (Spontaneous Combustion).

**SPONTANEOUS GENERATION,** or ABIOGENESIS, *AB ee oh GEN uh sis*, is a theory that certain low forms of living matter came into being from nonliving material. This theory started among the ancient peoples, who believed that such living things as insects and mice came to life from the mud where they were found in large numbers. They also believed that worms came from cheese and wood, and maggots from the juices of decaying meat. Later, scientific experiments disproved this theory. In 1668, an Italian biologist, Francesco Redi, proved that maggots would not breed in meat in which flies were kept from laying eggs. He showed that complex creatures were produced only by others like themselves. Later, when scientists discovered bacteria and other microorganisms, the problem of their beginnings came up again. In the middle of the 1800's, Louis Pasteur completely disproved the theory of spontaneous generation. He showed that bacteria would not grow in materials which were sterilized. Today, biologists believe that all complex living matter comes from other living matter.

Some biologists also believe that it is possible that the very lowest forms may have developed through chemical processes from nonliving matter. But no one has ever demonstrated or proved this development under satisfactorily controlled conditions. G. W. BEADLE

See also LIFE (The Origin of Life [Early Theories]); BIOGENESIS.

**SPOOL FURNITURE.** See FURNITURE (American Furniture [Spool]).

**SPOON.** See KNIFE, FORK, AND SPOON.

**SPOON-BILLED CATFISH.** See PADDLEFISH.
**SPOON RIVER.** See ILLINOIS (Rivers and Lakes).
**SPOONBILL.** See SHOVELER.
**SPOONBILL** is a wading bird which looks like an ibis. It has an odd, spoon-shaped bill, which it swings from side to side in the water in search of shellfish, water insects, and small crabs. The *roseate spoonbill* lives in the warmer regions of the Americas. The neck and the upper back of this bird are white. The other feathers are rosy pink, turning to red on the outer part of the wings. The roseate spoonbill nests in colonies, and returns year after year to the same place. The nest is a platform of sticks, placed in low trees or shrubs. The female lays 5 to 7 eggs, which are spotted and blotched with olive brown. The finest colonies in the United States are on islands in the Gulf of Mexico.

**Scientific Classification.** The spoonbills belong to the ibis family, *Threskiornithidea*. The roseate spoonbill is genus *Ajaia*, species *A. ajaja*. ALFRED M. BAILEY

See also BIRD (picture: Types of Beaks; color picture: Water Birds).

**SPORE** is a tiny one-celled body that is able to grow into a new organism. It takes the place of the seed of higher plants. Spores are produced primarily by lower plants, such as the algae, fungi, and bacteria. They may be produced by certain green plants that do not bear seeds, such as ferns and mosses. Certain *protozoa* (one-celled animals) of the class *Sporozoa* also form spores.

The spore is so tiny that it can be seen only through a microscope. It is made up of one cell which contains living matter known as *protoplasm*. The cell contains food materials which aid it to grow into a new organism.

There are two types of spores. One type of spore is known as the *sexual*, or *perfect*, spore because it is formed by the union of the so-called male and female sex cells. The second type of spore is formed in various ways without the use of the so-called sex cells. This type of spore is known as the *asexual*, or *imperfect*, spore. The spores of many fungus plants cause disease in crops. There are spores which cause corn smut, cotton wilt, wheat rust, and apple blight. Certain spore-producing, one-celled animals may also cause diseases in human beings. WILLIAM C. BEAVER

**SPOROPHORE.** See MUSHROOM (Parts).
**SPOROPHYTE.** See BRYOPHYTE; LIVERWORT.
**SPOROZOA.** See PROTOZOAN.
**SPORT** is a term applied to the sudden appearance of certain new hereditary types in plants and animals. Sports are caused by changes in the cells called *mutations* (see MUTATION). The new types are often used as parents to produce new varieties or breeds.

Many plant mutations affect the whole plant. But sometimes the new mutation affects only one branch of the plant. This is known as a *bud sport*. The *variegated* (many-colored) foliage of some plants originated from bud mutations. The navel orange was developed from a bud mutation on an ordinary orange tree. Plant growers have used sports to produce many new plants. Among the new types are the Shirley poppy and the Cupid sweet pea. J. HERBERT TAYLOR

See also FLOWER (Flower Breeding); BREEDING; HEREDITY (Heredity and Evolution).

**SPORTING DOGS.** See DOG (table: Recognized Breeds; color picture: Sporting Dogs).

Hy Peskin, *Sports Illustrated*

**Excited Cheerleaders** symbolize the thrills that come from watching sports and taking part in them. Cheerleading demands the physical skill, enthusiasm, and teamwork found in many sports.

**SPORTS AND SPORTSMANSHIP.** Almost everyone likes sports. Next to the weather, people probably talk more about sports than about any other topic. We discuss a coming game, and after it is over we "replay" the excitement of a winning goal, a touchdown, or a home run. The wide appeal of sports is shown by the large amount of space given them in newspapers and magazines, and on television and radio.

Sports demand a combination of physical skill and strength, an alert mind, enthusiasm, purpose, and usually teamwork. They represent accomplishment for which the body must be trained, and for which a person must work to become skillful.

Many friendships are formed through sports. The ability of people to get along with each other receives one of its greatest tests in sports competition. But perhaps even more important are the qualities that sports develop in making a person well-adjusted to daily life. The term *sportsmanship* may be applied to life in general. We like persons who can win without boasting, and lose without offering excuses.

> Year Book Close-Up
> **SPORTS**
> 1972 Year on File (Sports)

> Special Report
> **SPORTS**
> 1972 Year Book, p. 118

627

Marvin E. Newman

**The Spirit of Good Sportsmanship** is demonstrated by two tennis champions shaking hands across the net after a hard-fought game. Sportsmanship means being modest in victory as well as accepting defeat gracefully after trying your best.

Persons of all ages enjoy watching and taking part in sports. They crowd into stadiums to watch skilled athletes compete on teams sponsored by schools, colleges, recreation departments, and professional and private clubs. Other millions watch sports on television and listen to play-by-play reports on radio. Still others enjoy sports in back yards and vacant lots.

Almost any pleasant activity aimed at exercising the body may be called a sport. What is sport for one person may be just hard work for another. A city resident may find it sport to chop wood for a day. But such activity is merely daily work for a woodsman.

Sports become *athletics* when a person or a team competes against another, or when a team or person competes against a record or some other goal. The most popular athletic sports are baseball, basketball, boxing, football, golf, gymnastics, soccer, swimming, tennis, track and field, volleyball, and wrestling. Other sports include boating, bowling, camping, fishing, hiking, hunting, sailing, and skating.

Sports have provided a common meeting ground for boys and girls, and men and women, from all parts of the world. Every four years, athletes from many nations compete in the Olympic Games. In a spirit of peace and friendship, they battle for honors in all sports.

Sports are also an important business. Americans spend more than $4,000,000,000 each year to buy sporting equipment and to attend sports events.

### Sportsmanship

Sportsmanship demands honesty, fair play, cooperation, competitive spirit, respect for authority and rules, acceptance of responsibility, and respect for others. The true sportsman plays hard in order to win, but respects his opponent and accepts defeat gracefully. A hunter who is a true sportsman observes game regulations and gives his quarry a fair chance.

A person does not have to be a skilled athlete or sportsman to practice sportsmanship. In fact, a less skilled athlete often has the best chance to show sportsmanship. A person can show good sportsmanship in many ways not connected with sports, because sportsmanship is an important part of good citizenship. A student who loses a class election shows good sportsmanship by congratulating the winner.

Perhaps one of the best definitions of sportsmanship is the code of sportsmanship of the Sportsmanship Brotherhood. Here are its rules.

1. Keep the rules.
2. Keep faith with your comrade.
3. Keep your temper.
4. Keep yourself fit.
5. Keep a stout heart in defeat.
6. Keep your pride under in victory.
7. Keep a sound soul, a clean mind, and a healthy body.
8. Play the game.

### Types of Sports

**Individual Sports** are perhaps the oldest and most popular sports. They do not require a group or team of players. These sports include archery, bowling, golf, and swimming. Some individual sports, such as boxing, fencing, tennis, and wrestling, require an opponent. They are *dual*, or *combative*, sports. But in each case, the player competes as an individual. Nearly all individual sports can also be played by a team.

**Combative Sports** set one person against another in the keenest type of competition. Men and boys like to box, fence, and wrestle. School combative sports must be carefully planned and supervised, because young people cannot play combative sports in the same way as grown people.

**Water Sports.** Millions of people of all ages like to hunt, swim, dive, fish, go boating and sailing, try water skiing or skin diving, or just wade in the water. Public and private beaches and pools attract swimmers in the summer. Many schools have their own swimming pools.

**Outdoor Sports** are as old as civilization itself. Every member of the family can enjoy a camping trip, and more and more people are finding a renewed interest in this activity. Boys and girls can learn many things about nature and life from camping and hiking trips.

**Team Sports.** Thousands of men, women, boys, and girls enjoy playing baseball and basketball every year. Men and boys enjoy playing football, soccer, and ice hockey. Each of these sports requires close teamwork.

### Amateur Sports

Amateur athletics are organized for most sports. They have rules for competition and standards that an athlete must follow in order to keep his amateur status. Amateur athletes do not receive pay for performing. In some contests, they receive money for expenses. Winners may also receive such prizes as medals, ribbons, trophies, and watches. Amateur athletic organizations include the United States Golf Association (USGA), the United States Lawn Tennis Association (USLTA), and the Bicycle Association of America.

Amateur sports outside schools and colleges are regulated by the Amateur Athletic Union of the United States (AAU), which was founded in 1888. The United States Olympic Committee, organized in 1896, selects the United States Olympic team. The Canadian Amateur Sports and Physical Fitness Development Services is a program designed to increase interest in sports.

### Professional Sports

Professional sports are played for financial profit. They developed when men decided to make a business of the more popular sports. Teams in professional baseball, basketball, football, and ice hockey spend large amounts of money for players. A few outstanding baseball players earn as much as $100,000 a year. Professionals also perform in bowling, golf, and tennis.

Most professional sports are regulated by associations of owners or promoters. A commissioner appointed by club owners governs professional baseball. Other professional groups include the Professional Golfers Association (PGA), the International Boxing Commission (IBC), and the Thoroughbred Racing Association (TRA).

### Sports in the School

**Elementary-School Sports.** School sports programs usually start in the elementary grades. Most children become interested in competitive sports in about the fifth grade. They learn the fundamentals of team and individual sports. Many schools have organized teams in the higher elementary grades that compete against teams from other schools. Such athletic programs promote good health, sportsmanship, good personal habits, body development, and competitive spirit.

**High-School Sports.** Almost every state has a state high-school athletic association. These groups regulate all contests between high schools, and set the eligibility standards for all players. They also classify schools according to enrollment, to insure fair competition. When necessary, the association changes the rules of games so they may be played by students of high-school age. The state association also lists approved officials, and sets their fees. It decides on codes of conduct for coaches, players, and officials. The National Federation

## SPORTS AND SPORTSMANSHIP

of State High-School Athletic Associations, organized in 1920, operates throughout the United States.

Four Canadian provinces—New Brunswick, Nova Scotia, Ontario, and Saskatchewan—have interscholastic athletic associations. All are affiliated with the U.S. national high school federation.

**Intercollegiate Sports** involve competition between students of two different schools. These sports enjoy great popularity with students, alumni, and millions of other enthusiasts. Football attracts more interest than any other college sport. Huge crowds jam stadiums in every part of the U.S. on fall weekends to watch college football teams play. Receipts from college football games help finance college teams in other sports.

College athletes must be amateurs. The National Collegiate Athletic Association (NCAA) provides national leadership in conducting intercollegiate sports.

**Intramural Sports** provide competition among students of the same school or college. A student usually does not have to be highly skilled to compete. Intramural sports provide spirited competition and recreation in such games as badminton, basketball, bowling, handball, softball, swimming, tennis, touch football, volleyball, and wrestling. Intramural teams are generally formed by classes, dormitories, fraternities, student clubs, and other student groups.

### History of Sports

History shows that man played even in the earliest times. He gradually organized his play into games, and, as civilization developed, his games or sports developed. Early societies used sports to train people for survival and for war. Then, as people learned to live together more peacefully, sports festivals developed.

The Olympic Games became the most outstanding of the early sports festivals. These Grecian games started in

*Friends* Magazine

**Water Sports** combine gleeful fun with healthy exercise. Outdoor and indoor pools make water sports possible the year around.

*Chicago American*

**Team Sports** like baseball provide a valuable lesson in teamwork—the ability to work with others toward a common goal.

629

# SPORTS CAR

776 B.C., and included many events such as the javelin throw that are still part of the Olympics. Sports developed slowly during the Middle Ages, but interest in them grew during the Renaissance and Reformation periods.

James A. Naismith, seeking a sport that could be played indoors and was not too rough, invented basketball. British soldiers developed ice hockey when they played field hockey on the frozen ponds of Canada. Youngsters in Boston and New York changed the rules of cricket and a game called *rounders* to suit themselves. Their game eventually became baseball.

Students led in developing many sports. They organized rugby, cricket, and soccer teams, and had rowing contests in early American colleges. Educators finally recognized the importance of sports in the total education of boys and girls, and play and exercise became part of the school program. WALTER H. GREGG

**Related Articles** in WORLD BOOK include:

### BALL GAMES

| | | |
|---|---|---|
| Baseball | Handball | Rugby Football |
| Basketball | Jai Alai | Soccer |
| Billiards | Lacrosse | Softball |
| Bowling | Lawn Bowling | Speedball |
| Cricket | Little League | Squash |
| Croquet | Baseball | Table Tennis |
| Field Hockey | Pall-Mall | Tennis |
| Football | Polo | Volleyball |
| Golf | | |

### ICE AND SNOW SPORTS

| | | |
|---|---|---|
| Bobsledding | Ice Skating | Snowmobile |
| Curling | Iceboating | Tobogganing |
| Hockey | Skiing | |

### WATER SPORTS

| | | |
|---|---|---|
| Aquaplaning | Diving | Swimming |
| Birling | Rowing | Water Polo |
| Boats and | Sailing | Water Skiing |
| Boating | Skin Diving | Water Sports |
| Canoeing | Surfing | Yacht |

### OTHER SPORTS

| | | |
|---|---|---|
| Acrobatics | Horse Racing | Roller-Skating |
| Archery | Horseshoe | Hockey |
| Automobile Racing | Pitching | Shuffleboard |
| Badminton | Hot Rod | Skeet |
| Bicycle Racing | Hunting | Skydiving |
| Boxing | Judo | Spearfishing |
| Deck Tennis | Mountain | Track and Field |
| Falcon and Falconry | Climbing | Trapping |
| Fencing | Quoits | Trapshooting |
| Glider | Racing | Weight Lifting |
| Hiking | Roller Skating | Wrestling |

### SPORTS ORGANIZATIONS

| | |
|---|---|
| Amateur Athletic Union of the United States | National Collegiate Athletic Association |
| American Bowling Congress | Sokol |
| Helms Athletic Foundation | Turnverein |

### OTHER RELATED ARTICLES

| | | |
|---|---|---|
| Ball | Handicap | Physical |
| Coach | Intramural Sports | Education |
| Court | Madison Square Garden | Physical Fitness |
| Game | Olympic Games | Recreation |
| Gymnasium | Pan American Games | Stadium |

**SPORTS CAR.** See AUTOMOBILE (pictures: Sports Cars).

**SPOT** is a popular sport fish ranging from 6 to 10 inches long and weighing about half a pound. Spots are silvery above, bluish below, and have a small dark spot on the shoulder. The upper side has from 12 to 15 yellowish stripes. Fishermen catch spots along the Atlantic and Gulf of Mexico coasts. The spot has great commercial value as a food.

**Scientific Classification.** The spot belongs to the croaker family, *Sciaenidae*. It is genus *Leiostomus*, species *L. xanthurus*. LEONARD P. SCHULTZ

**SPOT MARKET.** See COTTON (Selling).

**SPOT REMOVING.** See DRY CLEANING; CLEANING FLUID.

**SPOTSWOOD, ALEXANDER** (1676-1740), was a lieutenant governor of colonial Virginia. He took office in 1710. He tried to regulate the fur trade with the Indians, and favored the inspection of tobacco to prevent the export of inferior goods. Spotswood tried to protect the colony from Indian raids. He encouraged settlement along the colony's western frontier and led several expeditions over the Blue Ridge Mountains.

Spotswood quarreled with the council of the Virginia colony over many of his policies. He acquired an estate of about 85,000 acres in Spotsylvania County, and retired there after being removed as lieutenant governor in 1722. He was appointed deputy postmaster general for the colonies in 1730. Spotswood was born in Tangiers, Morocco. J. CARLYLE SITTERSON

**SPOTSYLVANIA COURT HOUSE, BATTLE OF.** See CIVIL WAR (Spotsylvania Court House).

**SPOTTED ALDER.** See WITCH HAZEL.

**SPOTTED FEVER.** See ROCKY MOUNTAIN SPOTTED FEVER.

**SPRAGUE, FRANK JULIAN** (1857-1934), was an American electrical engineer and inventor. His inventions ranged from applications of electric power to theoretical problems of motors and generator design. His work on electric-elevator and railroad motors, power supply, and *multiunit* control systems won him the title, "Father of Electric Traction." Sprague was born at Milford, Conn. See also ELECTRIC RAILROAD (History). ROBERT E. SCHOFIELD

**SPRAIN** is an injury to a ligament or to the tissue that covers a joint. Ligaments are bands of stringy fibers that hold the bones of a joint in proper position (see LIGAMENT). The tissue that covers the joint is called the *capsule*. Most sprains result from a sudden wrench that stretches or tears the tissues of the ligaments or capsule. Sprains of the ankle and wrist are most common, but a person may sprain any joint.

A sprain is usually extremely painful. The injured part often swells and turns black and blue. Doctors usually prescribe rest and elevation of the injured part. They may also apply cold compresses first, then warm compresses. They often use elastic bandages to reduce swelling and to provide support for the injured joint. BENJAMIN F. MILLER

**SPRAT** is one of the smallest sea fish in the herring family. It is only 3 to 6 inches long, and lives in shoals along the Atlantic and Mediterranean coasts of Europe. Sprats are often mistaken for young herring. But sprats can be recognized by the notched edge on the abdomen. They are a wholesome food. See also HERRING.

**Scientific Classification.** The European sprat is genus *Clupea*, species *C. sprattus*. LEONARD P. SCHULTZ

**SPRAY GUN.** See AIRBRUSH; PAINT (Spray Guns).

**SPRAYING** is a method of killing garden pests by means of a poisonous mist. Insect poisons are of two sorts, those that kill on contact, and those that the insect must eat in order to die.

Pyrethrum, nicotine sulfate, and DDT are familiar contact poisons, and are often used on sucking insects. Arsenic salts, such as lead arsenate and calcium arsenate, are familiar stomach poisons used on caterpillars and beetles. Kerosene mixed with soapsuds is effective against some insects because it stops up their breathing pores.

Whatever the poison used for spraying, it must be made into a fine mist before it reaches the insects. This is done with a special kind of pump called a sprayer or with an *aerosol* (pressurized) container.

There should be little wind at the time when the spraying is done, for wind will blow the poison mist away before it can settle on the insects and their food. Spraying should not be done when there is a likelihood of rain within the next day or two because rain washes off the poison before it can do its work. W. V. MILLER

See also AEROSOL; FRUIT (Spraying); FUNGICIDE; INSECTICIDE.

**SPREAD-EAGLEISM.** See JINGO.

**SPREE RIVER** is a German waterway that passes through Berlin. It rises near New Salza in the state of Saxony, and flows across eastern Germany in a northerly direction for 220 miles. It empties into the Havel River. About 50 miles upstream from Berlin, the Spree divides into many small streams, and cuts the land into hundreds of islands. Although the Spree is small, its water traffic is extensive. It is connected with the Oder River by a canal. GEORGE KISH

**SPRING** is a natural source of water that flows from the ground. Water from rain and melting snow seeps into the ground. It filters through the pores and cracks

**Springs Form** when *underground water*, or water from rain or snow that collects in the ground, finds a way to the surface. If the water finds a crack or channel in the rock, it rushes through. When it reaches ground level, the water bubbles forth.

in the soil into the layers of rock. The water finally reaches a layer through which it cannot pass. This water held underground is called *ground water* (see GROUND WATER). Gravity may force the water to rise until it finds a way out to the surface to form a spring.

Springs are found in mountains, hills, and valleys. They are often found at the foot of a cliff or slope or where a crack or fault reaches the surface (see FAULT). Hundreds of springs pour from the walls of the famous Snake River Canyon in Idaho.

## SPRING

The largest springs are found in limestone regions where the water flows underground in cavelike channels. Where such channels reach the surface, great quantities of water may pour from the ground. Famous limestone springs are found in Florida and Missouri, for example.

The temperature of a spring depends on the temperature of the soil or rocks through which its water flows. Ground water that travels close to the surface may produce springs that are warmer in summer than in winter. Springs that come from farther down are always cold. However, deep down in the earth all rocks are hot. In volcanic regions hot rock may even lie close to the surface. As a result, spring water that has traveled from thousands of feet down, or has originated in volcanic regions, is often hot.

Many springs contain minerals dissolved from the rock by the moving water. They are known as *mineral springs*. The belief that these springs relieve ailments has popularized them as health resorts. Examples of such health springs can be found in Mount Clemens, Mich., Saratoga Springs, N.Y.; Hot Springs National Park, Ark.; and in France. ELDRED D. WILSON

**Related Articles** in WORLD BOOK include:

| | |
|---|---|
| Florida (Rivers, Lakes, and Springs) | Indiana (Natural Resources) |
| Geyser | Mineral Water |
| Hot Springs | Missouri (Springs and Lakes) |
| Idaho (Rivers, Waterfalls, Springs, and Lakes) | |

**SPRING** is the quality of a material that causes it to "spring" back after being moved. A metal piece that resumes its shape after it has been bent is called a spring. Nearly all springs are made in the shape of a flat or cylindrical spiral, or are otherwise curved. The common materials used for springs are steel and bronze. Most materials have the quality of elasticity, which is the ability to resume a shape after being bent or pulled by an outside force. Although elasticity can be exerted in many ways, springs are usually made to take advantage of the elasticity of torsion, or twist. When a length of wire is coiled, annealed, and hardened in that position, any effort to elongate or compress the coil causes a twist in its material. The spring promptly resists the compressing or stretching motions.

Springs are extensively used in machinery. We have watch springs, shock-absorber springs, door springs, and valve springs. Some springs react slowly in assuming their normal position after being compressed. Others, like the springs in a rifle, move out quickly when they are released. The rate of the return of a spring depends upon the force of return and the amount of material to be moved. Valve springs are the heart of a piston engine. They must retain their elasticity while hot and work for a long time without failure.

Adding alloys such as chromium, nickel, tungsten, and cobalt to steel wire used in springs increases their ability to withstand heat. Stainless-steel springs will perform well at temperatures up to about 500° F. An alloy of nickel and chromium has been used at 900° F. Jet and gas-turbine engines need springs that withstand even greater heat. LOUIS MARICK

See also ELASTICITY; UPHOLSTERY (Springs).

# SPRING

**SPRING** is the season of the year between winter and summer. In the Northern Hemisphere, spring begins on the day the center of the sun is directly over the equator. This is usually March 21. On this day the sun crosses the equator and starts northward. As it travels north, its rays strike the northern countries more directly each day. Spring lasts till about June 21. In the Southern Hemisphere, spring begins in September and ends in December. In Leap Year, spring begins a few hours earlier. Spring is the time of year when life begins again in nature. In many countries, the people have festivals celebrating spring. GRACE HUMPHREY

**Related Articles** in WORLD BOOK include:

| April | Equinox | May |
|---|---|---|
| Bird (Why Birds Migrate) | June | May Day |
| | March | |

**SPRING ARBOR COLLEGE.** See UNIVERSITIES AND COLLEGES (table).

**SPRING BALANCE.** See BALANCE.

**SPRING BEAUTY** is the name of a wild flower which grows in forests from Nova Scotia to Georgia and from Saskatchewan to Texas. Its long, narrow leaves grow from a stem 6 to 12 inches high. It has two species. The more common Virginia type bears a delicate white and pink flower with bright red veins. It blooms so early that many people call it Mayflower or good-morning-spring. The Carolina type has white blossoms.

**Scientific Classification.** The spring beauty belongs to the purslane family, *Portulacaceae*. The Virginia spring beauty is genus *Claytonia*, species *C. virginica*. The Carolina is *C. caroliniana*. GEORGE H. M. LAWRENCE

See also FLOWER (picture: Alaskan Spring Beauty).

**SPRING HILL COLLEGE.** See UNIVERSITIES AND COLLEGES (table).

**SPRINGBOK,** or **SPRINGBUCK,** is an antelope that lives on the grassy and shrubby open plains of southern Africa. It gets its name from its habit of repeatedly springing from 8 to 10 feet into the air when frightened, and then racing off at high speed. The springbok resembles the gazelle. A fringe of long white hairs in the middle of its back stands erect when the animal is frightened. Because of this trait, the Portuguese in Angola call this antelope the *goat of the fan*.

Slender and graceful, the springbok stands about 2½ feet high, and weighs from 70 to 80 pounds. It is pale brownish-red, with a white face and white on its underparts and on the inner edges of its legs. Both male and female springboks have curved, lyre-shaped horns. The male horns may be from 14 to 17 inches long.

Wandering herds of springboks at times have ruined crops while seeking food and water. They have even lured whole herds of farm animals away with them. The Dutch settlers of South Africa called them *trekbokken* (traveling bucks). Hunters killed so many of them that large wild herds today can be found only in remote regions of Angola and Botswana. The springbok is the national emblem of the Republic of South Africa.

**Scientific Classification.** Springboks belong to the cattle family, *Bovid*. They are classified as genus *Antidorcas*, species *A. marsupialis*. VICTOR H. CAHALANE

**SPRINGER.** See ARCH (picture).

**SPRINGER SPANIEL.** See SPANIEL; DOG (color picture: Sporting Dogs).

**SPRINGFIELD.** See RIFLE.

**SPRINGFIELD,** Ill. (pop. 83,271; met. area 146,539; alt. 610 ft.), is the state capital and the center of a rich farming region. It lies near a central Illinois coal field, 200 miles southwest of Chicago and 100 miles northeast of St. Louis (see ILLINOIS [political map]).

**Industry.** Springfield's products include boilers, earth-moving equipment, electric meters and electronic equipment, farm equipment, flour and cereal products, house and industrial paints, industrial tractors, mattresses, and soybean oil and meal. Springfield has been a mining center since 1865.

Lake Springfield, a large artificial lake, furnishes an adequate supply of water for industrial purposes and for electric power. It also provides recreation.

**History.** Springfield was founded in 1818, and in 1821 was chosen as the county seat of Sangamon County. In 1837, it was designated the capital of Illinois, but the state offices were not moved there from Vandalia until 1839. It has a commission form of government.

The original statehouse, associated with Lincoln, Douglas, Grant, and other famous Illinoisans, is now a museum. It has been restored by the state of Illinois, and houses the Illinois State Historical Society. The cornerstone of the present Capitol was laid in 1868.

Abraham Lincoln lived in Springfield from 1837 to 1861. His home still stands at Eighth and Jackson streets, near the city's center. The Lincoln family lived in the two-story frame house from 1844 to 1861. Lincoln is buried in Springfield's Oak Ridge cemetery. Larkin G. Meade designed Lincoln's tomb. It was dedicated in 1874. The state maintains both the home and the tomb. Thousands of persons visit them yearly.

The state also maintains an outstanding Lincoln collection in the Illinois State Historical Library. In New Salem State Park, 20 miles northwest of Springfield, the pioneer village in which Lincoln lived from 1831 to 1837 has been reconstructed. PAUL M. ANGLE

See also ILLINOIS (picture: Illinois' Capitol); LINCOLN, ABRAHAM (pictures: Lincoln's Tomb, Lincoln's Home).

**The Springbok of Southern Africa** is one of the most graceful and nimble members of the antelope family.

N.Y. Zoological Society

**SPRINGFIELD,** Mass. (pop. 174,463; met. area 493,-999; alt. 85 ft.), is the third largest city in the state and the metropolis of western Massachusetts. It lies on the east bank of the Connecticut River, near the southern boundary of the state (see MASSACHUSETTS [political map]). Springfield's city buildings stand in the Municipal Group. A 300-foot tower rises above the group. Springfield's park system covers about 2,000 acres.

**Industry and Trade.** Springfield has more than 300 factories. They produce adhesives and plastics, books, book matches, children's clothing, diesel fuel injectors, envelopes, firearms, forgings, games and toys, jet aircraft parts, machine tools, master clock systems, school supplies, and toasters and food mixers. The Springfield rifle of World War I, and the M-1 of World War II, were developed in Springfield. Several large insurance companies have headquarters there.

The city is a transportation center for western New England. It serves as the Connecticut Valley's transshipment point for goods bound for New York City and the western parts of the United States.

**Education and Culture.** Springfield has about 30 public elementary schools and about 10 public junior and senior high schools. The city is the home of Springfield College, American International College, and Western New England College.

Springfield's cultural attractions are grouped in a city block called the *Quadrangle*. Included in the Quadrangle are the Springfield Museum of Fine Arts and the Museum of Natural History. The George Walter Vincent Smith Art Museum in the Quadrangle features Chinese porcelain and jade. The William Pynchon Memorial Building of the Connecticut Valley Historical Society displays colonial exhibits.

The Springfield Symphony Orchestra and the Young People's Symphony present many music programs throughout the year in Springfield. The Naismith Memorial Basketball Hall of Fame is located at Springfield College.

**History and Government.** Pioneer William Pynchon led a group of settlers from Roxbury, near Boston, to the Connecticut Valley in 1636. The group settled first at Agawam on the western bank of the Connecticut River. Later, they moved across the Connecticut and settled on its eastern bank at the present site of Springfield. Indians attacked and burned the settlement during King Philip's War (1675-76).

Firearms were manufactured in Springfield during the Revolutionary War. In 1794, the Springfield arsenal became the first United States Armory. In 1786, Daniel Shays led other discontented settlers in an attempt to capture the arsenal. The attempt was unsuccessful, and Shays' Rebellion was halted. See SHAYS' REBELLION.

Samuel Bowles founded the *Springfield Republican* in 1824. The paper's excellent style and liberal editorials made it nationally famous. Abolitionist John Brown lived in Springfield from 1846 until 1849, and helped organize the Underground Railroad. The first successful gasoline-powered automobile in the United States made its trial run in Springfield in 1893. Charles E. and J. Frank Duryea built this automobile. See DURYEA (brothers).

Springfield received its city charter in 1852. The seat of Hampden County, it has a mayor-council type of government. WILLIAM J. REID

**SPRINGFIELD,** Mo. (pop. 98,679; met. area 126,276; alt. 1,300 ft.), is the commercial center for a large farming, lumbering, and mining district. It is the third largest city in Missouri. Springfield lies at the edge of the Ozark Mountains in southwestern Missouri, about 175 miles southeast of Kansas City and 220 miles southwest of St. Louis (see MISSOURI [political map]). It is the gateway to the scenic White River region.

Fruit grows in the large orchards nearby. The city also is an important poultry market. It has flour and lumber mills, machine shops, ironworks, trailer factories, and meat-packing plants. It has one of the largest dairy processing plants in the United States. The two main lines of the Frisco Railroad intersect in Springfield, and have large shops there.

Springfield was settled about 1830. It became a town in 1838, and a city in 1847. It has a council-manager form of government. Springfield is the home of Southwest Missouri State College, Drury College, the Central Bible Institute, and Elfindale Academy. Hospitals in Springfield include Burge Hospital, which is one of the largest in the nation, St. John's Hospital, and the Federal Medical Center. NOEL P. GIST

**SPRINGFIELD,** Ohio (pop. 82,723; met. area 131,440; alt. 980 ft.), is a manufacturing city in west-central Ohio. It lies at the meeting place of Buck, or Lagonda, Creek and the Mad River, about 25 miles northeast of Dayton (see OHIO [political map]). Springfield is on the old National Road, now U.S. Route 40, which extends from Atlantic City, N.J., to San Francisco. The city was named for the springs in nearby cliffs.

Industry in Springfield is highly diversified. Factories in the city produce aircraft-engineering products, awnings, chemicals, diesel engines, electric fans, hoists, incubators, lawnmowers, and lawn sweepers. Other products made in Springfield include leather goods, machine tools, metal caskets, paper-pulp machinery, piano plates, pumps, rigs for drilling wells, road-building machinery, thermometers, trucks, and wire products. These industries have replaced the agricultural-implement plants which made Springfield a world center of farm-machinery production during the last half of the 1800's.

Springfield is the home of Wittenberg University, founded in 1845. It also has a symphony orchestra and an art center. Three railroads serve the city, and several airlines operate from the municipal airport.

The first settler of the Springfield area was James Demint, who arrived from Kentucky in 1799. Springfield became the seat of Clark County in 1818, and received its city charter in 1850. The city has a commission form of government. JAMES H. RODABAUGH

**SPRINGFIELD COLLEGE.** See UNIVERSITIES AND COLLEGES (table).

**SPRINGS** (pop. 137,253; met. area 141,943; alt. 5,280 ft.) is an important gold-mining and manufacturing center in the northern part of South Africa (see SOUTH AFRICA [color map]). The city also serves as a farm-marketing center. Ten gold mines are within the city limits, and other gold and coal mines lie nearby. Springs has uranium- and food-processing plants, and factories that make machinery, electrical products, and glass.

**SPRINGTAIL.** See COLLEMBOLA.

633

# SPRINKLER SYSTEM

**SPRINKLER SYSTEM** is a network of pipes that carries water under high pressure and sprinkles it over a certain area. Automatic sprinkler systems have put out thousands of fires before they could become dangerous. Soft metal plugs are placed in sprinkler heads along pipes at intervals of about 8 feet. The plugs melt at about 165° F. As soon as a fire creates enough heat in a room to melt the plugs, water from the sprinkler heads sprays the surrounding area. At the same time, a bell rings until the water is shut off. Some sprinkler systems have small stoppers made of quartz, which are lifted out by the heat of the fire, releasing sprays of water. One type of sprinkler system sends out SOS calls by telegraph when a fire starts.

The first sprinkler system was patented in 1872 by Philip W. Pratt of Abington, Mass. His system used cords and fuses attached to a valve. When a fire started, the heat melted the valve, which released water.

The cost of fire insurance may be reduced 60 to 90 per cent if a building is equipped with a sprinkler system.                                JOHN J. FLOHERTY

**SPROUTING.** See GERMINATION.

**SPRUANCE, RAYMOND AMES** (1886-   ), was one of the most successful American naval commanders in the Pacific in World War II. Naval forces under his leadership caused greater damage to the Japanese with less loss to themselves than did any other American fleet units in the war.

Many have rated Spruance as the best American naval combat commander of the war. He earned a large share of the credit for working out the circular battle formation which made American carrier groups the most effective fighting fleets in naval history. He won wide praise for his calmness and deliberation in action.

**At Midway.** Shortly before the United States entered World War II, Spruance took command of a cruiser division of the Pacific Fleet. It was part of the force sent out in June, 1942, to stop a Japanese attempt to invade Midway Island. Shortly after the battle began, the force commander's flagship, the *Yorktown*, was put out of action, and Spruance took charge of the battle operations. The victory at Midway, which many historians consider the turning point of the Pacific war, established Spruance's reputation as a combat commander (see WORLD WAR II [The Battle of Midway]). Admiral Chester W. Nimitz, the Pacific Fleet's commander in chief, made him his chief of staff. In this position, Spruance planned many campaigns.

In the fall of 1943, Spruance returned to sea in charge of the assault on Tarawa in the Gilbert Islands. Three months later, as commander of the Central Pacific Force, he directed the successful attacks against the Marshall Islands. In February, 1944, he directed an aerial attack on the great Japanese naval base at Truk in what he called "a partial settlement" for Pearl Harbor. Later that year, he won an overwhelming victory in the Battle of the Philippine Sea and commanded the naval forces in the capture of Saipan and Guam.

**Other Service.** In February, 1945, Spruance led the Fifth Fleet in the first carrier strike on Tokyo and directed the capture of Iwo Jima. He was planning the naval phase of American landings in Japan when World War II ended. After the war, Spruance served for a time as commander in chief of the Pacific Fleet and he later became president of the Naval War College.

Spruance was born in Baltimore, Md., and was graduated from the United States Naval Academy in 1907. By 1914 he had become a recognized expert on the complicated mechanisms of warships. He served as electrical superintendent at the New York Navy Yard during most of World War I. Spruance retired from the Navy in 1948.                        DONALD W. MITCHELL

**SPRUCE** is the common name of a genus of cone-bearing evergreen trees in the pine family. About 40 kinds of spruce trees are native to the Northern Hemisphere. Some spruces grow beyond the Arctic Circle. Others grow as far south as the Pyrenees Mountains in Europe. In North America, they grow as far south as North Carolina and Arizona.

Spruces are more closely related to the firs than to any other cone-bearing tree. But spruces have cones that hang straight downward. Fir trees have cones that stand straight up. The scales on spruce cones remain on the cones. The scales on fir cones fall off when the cones become ripe.

Spruce foliage is also different from that of other cone bearers. Most spruce tree needles are four-sided and grow less than an inch long. Woody, peglike projections join the needles to the twig. Fir trees do not have these projections. Spruce trees grow tall. Usually, they are shaped like pyramids. In old trees, the drooping lower branches may brush the ground.

**Kinds.** The *white, black,* and *red* spruces of the East and the *Sitka* and *Engelmann* spruces of the West are the most important commercial spruces in North America. The white and black spruces are named for the general color of the bark and foliage. These spruces are more widely distributed than any other. They grow between Bering Strait on the north, and Maine, New York, and Michigan on the south. The black spruce also grows in high altitudes in Virginia. The trees grow west to British Columbia and Montana.

The white spruce may reach a height of 150 feet. The black is a little smaller. The red spruce grows between Nova Scotia and North Carolina, and as far west as Tennessee. The Sitka spruce grows on the Pacific Coast between northern California and Alaska. It sometimes reaches a great height, especially in the swamps or tidewater regions. A number of giant Sitkas are over 300 feet high. The Engelmann spruce grows from British Columbia to New Mexico.

The most important spruce in Europe is the *Norway* spruce. This handsome tree is planted in eastern North America as an ornamental. The so-called *Douglas spruce* (Douglas fir) of Washington, Oregon, and British Columbia, belongs to a different genus, but is related to the spruces. It produces more lumber than any other tree in the world.

**Raymond A. Spruance**
U.S. Navy

634

# SPY

The Cones of spruces like the red spruce, *above*, are *pendant* (hang downward). The needles of spruce trees grow in thick spirals around the branches and point in all directions.

The Silvery-Blue Foliage of the Blue Spruce makes it one of the most admired of all the American evergreen trees.

**Uses.** Spruce wood is widely used for wood pulp in the papermaking industry. The timber is strong, light, and flexible, and is well suited for masts and spars of ships. Spruce is also used to make boxes, and forms sounding boards for musical instruments such as pianos.

Spruce wood is also used for interior finishing in houses. Resin, tannin, and turpentine are products of spruce bark. Beer is sometimes made from young twigs. The gum of the black spruce, which is hardened resin, is another product. Dyes have been made from turpentine, which is derived as a by-product in papermaking.

**Scientific Classification.** Spruces belong to the pine family, *Pinaceae*. They form the genus *Picea*. The white spruce is species *P. glauca;* the black, *P. mariana;* the red, *P. rubens.* The Douglas spruce, or fir, is genus *Pseudotsuga*, species *P. menziesii*.     K. A. ARMSON

See also CONE-BEARING TREES; LEAF (picture: Kinds of Leaves); TREE (color picture: Evergreen Trees).

**SPRUCE PARTRIDGE.** See GROUSE.

**SPURGE FAMILY,** or EUPHORBIACEAE, *yoo FAWR-bih AY see ee*, is a family of herbs, shrubs, and trees. Many of the plants give us useful products such as castor oil, croton oil, cassava, and rubber. There are about 7,300 different *species* (kinds) in the spurge family. They grow in many regions, especially in the tropics.

Members of the spurge family bear small, inconspicuous flowers, but they sometimes have brilliantly colored flower *bracts* (leaves that look like flower petals). A biting, milky juice is usually found in the plants. Some species in Africa look almost exactly like a cactus when they are not in bloom. The family also includes ornamentals such as the poinsettia.     EARL L. CORE

**Related Articles** in WORLD BOOK include:
| | | | |
|---|---|---|---|
| Cassava | Croton | Poinsettia | Snow-on-the- |
| Castor Oil | Jumping Bean | Rubber | Mountain |

**SPURGEON, CHARLES HADDON** (1834-1892), was one of the greatest British preachers of his time. He joined the Baptist Church in 1850, and began preaching near Cambridge. He moved to London in 1854. His clear voice, rich command of language, and dramatic abilities attracted crowds. But his strict and narrow religious ideas alienated others. The Metropolitan Tabernacle, with 6,000 seats, was built for his huge audiences. He was born at Kelvedon, Essex, the son of an Independent preacher.     F. A. NORWOOD

**SPUTNIK,** *SPOOT nick*, is the Russian name of the earth satellites launched into space by Russia. *Sputnik* is a Russian word meaning *traveler*. Sputnik I, launched Oct. 4, 1957, circled the earth once about every 95 minutes at a speed of 18,000 mph, until it fell to earth on Jan. 4, 1958. Later, Russia launched other sputniks much larger than Sputnik I. See also SPACE TRAVEL.

**SPUYTEN DUYVIL CREEK.** See NEW YORK CITY (Location, Size, and Description).

**SPY** is anyone who abandons the uniform or distinctive badge of his service and mingles with the enemy in order to obtain information of value to the country he is serving. The international rules of war provide that a soldier in uniform cannot be considered a spy, even if he is attempting to obtain information within enemy lines. Civilians openly carrying messages through enemy lines are not considered spies if they do not attempt to disguise their identity. To be condemned as a spy, a person must be captured within the lines of the enemy *in disguise*, or while representing to be other than what he really is. Suspected spies must receive a trial. The punishment for wartime spying is death.     KARL DETZER

**Related Articles** in WORLD BOOK include:
| | | |
|---|---|---|
| André, John | Fifth Column | Rosenberg, Ethel |
| Boyd, Belle | Hale, Nathan | and Julius |
| Espionage | Mata Hari | |

635

## SPY WEDNESDAY

**SPY WEDNESDAY.** See HOLY WEEK.

**SPYRI,** *SHPEE ree,* **JOHANNA** (1827-1901), was a Swiss author of children's stories. Her best-known book is *Heidi* (1881), a story of child life in the Swiss Alps. *Heidi's* success encouraged Mrs. Spyri to write more books for and about children. She used the background of her childhood in Switzerland for these books. Her other books include *Cornelli* (1890) and *Vinzi* (1894). She was born at Hirzel.   JEAN THOMSON

**SQUAB.** See PIGEON.

**SQUAD.** See ARMY, UNITED STATES (table: Army Levels of Command).

**SQUALL,** *skwawl,* is a sudden rise in the wind, often with a marked change in wind direction. Rain and hail may accompany the wind. A squall may be caused by an advancing mass of cold air that violently lifts the warm air in front of it. See also WEATHER (map: How to Read a Weather Map).

**SQUANTO** ( ? -1622), also called TISQUANTUM, was an American Indian of the Pawtuxet tribe and a friend of the Pilgrims. He was taken to England in 1605. He lived in London until 1614, when he was returned to America. Later, Squanto was kidnaped and sold in Spain as a slave, but he escaped to England. In 1619, an English sea captain returned him to Cape Cod.

Squanto met the Pilgrims in 1621. He acted as their interpreter in the conclusion of the treaty of Plymouth with Massasoit (see MASSASOIT). He stayed with the Pilgrims and showed them how to plant corn and where to fish. Squanto died from a fever while guiding an expedition around Cape Cod. Plymouth Colony might have failed, if not for Squanto's help.   WILLIAM H. GILBERT

See also PLYMOUTH COLONY (The First Year).

**SQUARE,** in geometry, is a plane figure that has four equal straight sides and four right (90°) angles. If each side of a square is 4 inches long, the square can be cut into $4 \times 4$, or 16, smaller squares that have sides 1 inch long. The *area* of this square equals 16 square inches. In general, the area of a square is expressed in square units. It is found by multiplying by itself the number that represents the length of one side of the square. A square that has a side 3 inches long has an area of $3 \times 3$, or 9, square inches.

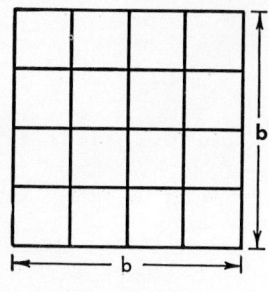

In arithmetic and algebra, the *square* of a quantity is the product of a quantity by itself. For example, 16 is the square of 4, because $4 \times 4 = 16$. If $b$ represents any quantity, the square of $b$, or $b \times b$, is written $b^2$. The small 2 that appears to the right of and above the $b$ is called an *exponent*. The exponent 2 indicates that the quantity $b$ is to be taken twice as a factor.

The term *square* also refers to a tool or instrument for measuring and constructing right angles. Carpenters often use a square made in the shape of an L and draftsmen use a square in the shape of a T.   HOWARD W. EVES

See also POWER; QUADRILATERAL; SQUARE ROOT.

**SQUARE DANCE** is an American form of folk dance done by four couples in a square formation. They perform a variety of patterns as directed by a *caller.* Many basic *calls,* such as "promenade," "form a star," "grand right and left," "swing your partner," and "ladies chain," are common throughout the country. There are also regional differences. The call "do-si-do" means one pattern in the East and a different figure in the West.

The caller is the most important figure at a square dance. The success of the dance depends on his skill in combining the calls into interesting patterns. He often makes up rhymes on the spur of the moment as he calls, such as "swing her high, swing her low, don't step on that pretty little toe."   MICHAEL HERMAN

Dorothy Reed

**Square Dancing** is perhaps the most popular form of American folk dancing. In quadrille formation, the couples salute, swing, curtsey, and change partners as they move through interesting patterns.

# SQUARE ROOT

**SQUARE DEAL** originally referred to fair treatment in dealing playing cards and in handling other transactions. President Theodore Roosevelt used the slogan repeatedly. "When I say 'square deal,'" he wrote, "I mean a square deal to everyone..." He declared that he would use his powers as President to safeguard the rights of both capital and labor (see ROOSEVELT, THEODORE [Friend of Labor]).

**SQUARE MEASURE** is the system used in the measurement of surfaces. The unit for the *area* of a surface is the square whose sides are of equal length. Hence the name of the system. We can describe a table top as being 12 inches long and 10 inches wide, or 12 by 10 inches. But these figures represent only lines, which have just one dimension—that of length.

A plane surface has two dimensions—length and width. They must somehow be combined into a single expression in order to tell how much the table will hold. Thus we describe the area of the same table top as 120 square inches.

Square measure of any square or rectangular plane surface is obtained by multiplying length by width. The reason for this is easily seen if we draw a picture of the table top and mark off its inches. A line should be drawn at every inch along the length and at every inch along the width. The two sets of lines will cross each other. This will give us 120 little squares, each measuring one inch in length and one inch in width. The measure of each is called a square inch. The areas in square inches, feet, yards, and so on, of other geometrical figures are found by special rules. These rules are all based on the one stated above.     E. G. STRAUS

See also WEIGHTS AND MEASURES (Square Measure).

**SQUARE ROOT** of a number is a second number whose product with itself gives the original number. For example, a square root of 4 is 2, because $2 \times 2 = 4$. The symbol for a square root, called a *radical sign*, is $\sqrt{\phantom{x}}$. For example, $\sqrt{25} = 5$ and $\sqrt{4} = 2$. The negative number $-2$ is also a square root of 4, because $-2 \times -2 = 4$. Each positive number has both a positive and negative square root. These two square roots always have the same numerical value.

## Finding Square Roots

**By Tables and Slide Rule.** An easy method for finding a square root of a number is to use a *table of square roots*, a *table of squares*, or a *table of logarithms*. If available, these tables give a square root quickly and make long and tiresome calculations unnecessary. You can easily learn to use these tables in a short time. An even quicker way of finding a square root consists of using a *slide rule*. But a slide rule can usually give a square root in only three digits. See LOGARITHMS; SLIDE RULE.

**By Dividing and Averaging.** If you lack tables, or need greater accuracy than the tables can offer, you must actually compute a square root. You can easily learn, apply, and understand the following method.

Suppose you want to find the square root of 40. Because $6 \times 6 = 36$ and $7 \times 7 = 49$, you can see that 6 is closest to $\sqrt{40}$ in whole numbers. So you begin the square root of 40 with 6. First, divide 40 by 6: $40 \div 6 = 6.6$ (to the nearest tenth). You can see that $6 \times 6.6 = 39.6$, or about 40. Now find the average of 6 and 6.6: $\frac{1}{2} \times (6+6.6) = 6.3$. And $6.3 \times 6.3 = 39.69$, which is even closer to 40.

To obtain greater accuracy, repeat the procedure. First, divide 40 by 6.3: $40 \div 6.3 = 6.349$. Next, find the average of 6.3 and 6.349: $\frac{1}{2} \times (6.3 + 6.349) = 6.325$. Repeating the procedure a third time, you find that $40 \div 6.325 = 6.3241106$, and that $\frac{1}{2} \times (6.325 + 6.3241106) = 6.3245553$.

You may continue this process as long as you wish. In general, in each approximation to the square root you usually keep twice as many digits as in the previous approximation.

Notice that 40 lies between 1 and 100. If you want to find the square root of a number that is not in the 1 to 100 range, you must first divide or multiply it by 100 to bring it within this range. Suppose you want to find the square root of 400,000, or $\sqrt{400,000}$. You must divide 400,000 *twice* by 100. This gives you 40, a number within the 1 to 100 range. You know how to find the square root of 40: $\sqrt{40} = 6.3245553$. Now you must multiply the square root of 40 *twice* by 10 (the square root of 100) to obtain the square root of 400,000: $6.3245553 \times 10 \times 10 = 632.45553$. In the same way, $\sqrt{0.4} = 0.63245553$. You find the square root of 0.4 by multiplying by 100, finding the square root of 40, and dividing by 10.

### A Method Often Used in School

Besides the above, you can use other processes for finding square roots. Here is a method often taught in schools.

### Find $\sqrt{1248.4}$

**Step 1.** Using little marks, separate 1,248.4 into two-digit *periods*, or units, in each direction from the decimal point. One digit of the square root will correspond to each two-digit period.

$$\sqrt{12'48.40'}$$

Now determine the largest *square*, or number multiplied once by itself, in 12, the leading two-digit period. The largest square in 12 is $3 \times 3$, or 9. Write 3 as the first digit of the square root, subtract 9 from 12, and bring down the next period to form the remainder 348:

$$\begin{array}{r} 3 \phantom{00000} \\ \sqrt{12'48.40'} \\ 9 \phantom{0000} \\ \hline 3\,48 \phantom{00} \end{array}$$

**Step 2.** Multiply the partial square root, 3, by 2, and place the product, 6, to the left of 348. Determine the next digit of the square root by dividing 348 by $10 \times 6$, or 60: $348 \div 60 = 5$. Write 5 as the next digit of the square root and annex 5 to the 6 to form the divisor 65. Now multiply 65 by 5, subtract the product from 348, and bring down the next period to form the remainder 2,340:

$$\begin{array}{r} 3\;5 \phantom{0000} \\ \sqrt{12'48.40'} \\ 9 \phantom{000000} \\ 65 \phantom{0} \bigg| \; 3\,48 \phantom{00} \\ 3\,25 \phantom{00} \\ \hline 23\,40 \end{array}$$

637

# SQUASH

**Step 3.** Multiply the partial square root, 35, by 2, and place the product, 70, to the left of 2,340. Determine the third digit of the square root by dividing 2,340 by 10×70, or 700: 2,340÷700=3. Write 3 as the third digit of the square root and annex 3 to the 70 to form the divisor 703. Multiply 703 by 3, subtract the product from 2,340, and bring down the next period to form the remainder 23,100:

```
              3 5. 3
          √12'48.40'
              9
       65   │ 3 48
            │ 3 25
       703  │  23 40
            │  21 09
            │   2 31 00
```

You may continue this process as long as you wish. Place the decimal point in the square root over the decimal point in the given number.

### Square Roots of Negative Numbers

What is the square root of −4? Or, what number multiplied by itself gives a product of −4? If there is such a number, it certainly cannot be positive, negative, or zero. None of these multiplied by itself can give a negative number. But, for convenience in solving certain problems, mathematicians have invented a system of *pure imaginary numbers* whose squares are negative numbers. HOWARD W. EVES

See also CUBE ROOT; ROOT; SQUARE.

**SQUASH** is the name given to three groups of vine vegetables. All three are warm-weather crops, but their growth periods vary. One group includes summer squash and orange-colored winter pumpkins. The second group includes straw-colored *cheese pumpkins* and *cushaw* squashes. The third group includes squashes which can be stored over winter.

Summer squashes grow rapidly. The fruits are harvested while still immature. The autumn squashes produce small fruits. They are harvested when almost mature. The autumn squashes can be stored for a few months, but they rapidly lose their quality. The winter squashes are harvested as soon as they mature. They have hard shells and may be stored through the winter. The Hubbard squash is perhaps the best-known winter variety. Each of these groups has several types and varieties.

Seeds are planted in *hills* (groups of about three plants) about two weeks before the last frost of spring. Several insects attack squashes. Squash bugs are hard to control. The adults, called *stink bugs*, may be picked by hand and killed, or dusted with insecticides such as nicotine, rotenone, or chlordane. The squashvine borer may be controlled by cutting the stem where the insect enters the squash, and covering it with soil.

Squashes provide a good source of vitamin A. They also have a fair degree of energy value.

The history of squashes and pumpkins runs together. Both were first raised in North, Central, and South America. After the Americas were discovered, squash were taken to France and England. Summer squashes thrive in England, where they are called *marrows*. But fall and winter squashes do not grow well in England.

**Scientific Classification.** Squashes and pumpkins belong to the gourd family, *Cucurbitaceae*. Pumpkins are genus *Cucurbita*, species *C. pepo*. Summer squashes are *C. pepo*, variety *melopepo*. Winter squashes are *C. maxima*; cheese pumpkins, *C. moschata*. ERVIN L. DENISEN

See also CHAYOTE; GOURD; PLANT (color picture: Vegetables Unknown to Our Forefathers); PUMPKIN.

**Hubbard Squash,** *above,* is a popular winter variety of squash. It has rich, dry flesh.

J. Horace McFarland; USDA

**White Bush Scallop,** *above,* is a summer squash. Because of its shape, it is sometimes called a "pattypan."

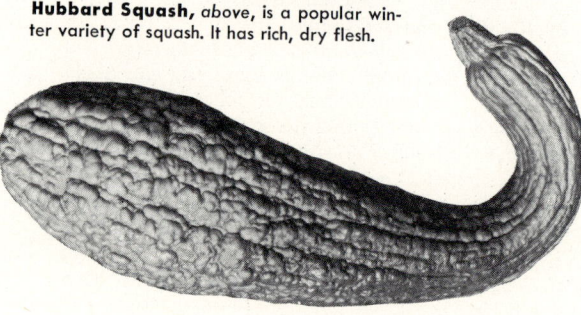

**The Giant Yellow Crookneck,** *right,* has a warty yellow skin and fine-textured, cream-colored flesh.

**SQUASH** is an indoor game similar to handball. But squash is played with rackets and a hard rubber ball about the size of a golf ball. Players use the rackets to hit the ball against the four walls of a court. A player may hit the ball against any wall so long as it reaches the front wall before it touches the floor. His opponent must then hit the ball before it bounces twice. A variety of shots is possible, and the ball travels quickly.

*Singles* squash is played by two men in a cement or wood court 32 feet long and $18\frac{1}{2}$ feet wide. The front and side walls are 16 feet high, and the back wall is $6\frac{1}{2}$ feet high. *Doubles* squash is played by four men on a larger court. At the bottom of the front wall is a 17-inch-high *telltale* made of metal. If a player hits the telltale with the ball, his opponent wins the point. The opponent also wins the point when the player misses the ball, hits it after the second bounce, or hits it out of the court. The game ends when a player or team has scored 15 points.

Squash originated at Harrow School in England about 1850, and was introduced into the United States from Canada in the 1880's. The United States now has about 1,500 squash courts and about 50,000 squash players. The sport, particularly popular in Australia, is also played in about 30 other nations throughout the world.  THOMAS H. LINEAWEAVER, III

**SQUATTER** is a person who lives on land to which he has no deed or other evidence of title. Usually he may make a valid claim to the land if there is no other person with a legal claim. During the period of the westward movement in the United States, many people moved to lands which had not yet been surveyed and which were not yet for sale. Congress passed special laws which allowed squatters to gain title to the lands they occupied. These laws culminated in the Pre-emption Act of 1841 (see PRE-EMPTION).

## SQUATTER SOVEREIGNTY

From 1854 to 1861, the term *squatter* in American politics had a special meaning in connection with *squatter*, or popular, sovereignty (see SQUATTER SOVEREIGNTY).  HAROLD W. BRADLEY

See also HOMESTEAD ACT; SQUATTER'S RIGHTS.

**SQUATTER SOVEREIGNTY,** or POPULAR SOVEREIGNTY, was the doctrine that the people of a territory could decide for themselves whether or not they wanted slavery, even before the territory became a state. This theory developed during the controversy over slavery that is part of the history of the early United States.

The North, as a whole, opposed extension of slavery into any of the land acquired from Mexico after the war with Mexico. The South, even more unanimously, favored it. Many persons on both sides found the theory of squatter sovereignty a happy solution. It relieved both the states and the Congress of a difficult problem. Lewis Cass probably originated the theory of squatter sovereignty, but Stephen A. Douglas was its most prominent advocate. Douglas renamed it *popular sovereignty*.

The Kansas-Nebraska Act of 1854 permitted the people of the Kansas and Nebraska territories to decide for or against slavery within their respective borders. The authors of the law took for granted that Nebraska would vote free, and Kansas, slave. But antislavery advocates sent many free-state settlers into Kansas, while many proslavery residents of Missouri crossed into Kansas, sometimes to settle, but often only to vote. The violence and bloodshed that resulted showed that the principle of popular sovereignty would not work.

After the Civil War, when slavery was abolished, popular sovereignty lost its significance.  JOHN D. HICKS

See also DOUGLAS, STEPHEN ARNOLD; KANSAS-NEBRASKA ACT.

# SQUASH

**The Squash Court,** below, is shown in a cut-away view with the left side wall missing. A player, right, makes a backhand return near the back wall.

Union League Club

## SQUATTER'S RIGHTS

**SQUATTER'S RIGHTS.** During the westward movement in the United States, many *squatters* settled on unsurveyed public land with no title. They did so to avoid buying land or because there was not enough surveyed land to meet the demand. They generally built homes and cleared the land. They believed they had thus earned the right to buy the land at the minimum price when the government sold it. This claim is known as *squatter's rights*. Squatters formed *claim associations* to protect their land before public sales were held. Most Westerners supported the squatters, and Western congressmen backed bills to protect their interests. The Pre-emption Act of 1841 recognized squatter's rights. See also PRE-EMPTION; SQUATTER. HAROLD W. BRADLEY

**SQUETEAGUE.** See WEAKFISH.

**SQUIB.** See NEWSPAPER (Newspaper Terms).

**SQUID** is a sea *mollusk* (animal with a soft, boneless body) that is similar to the octopus, nautilus, and cuttlefish. Squids live throughout the world. They range in size from a few inches to nearly 40 feet in length. The giant squid may measure 55 feet long. Squids frequently swim in large groups called *shoals*. These animals are also called SEA ARROWS.

Squids have dark gray bodies with red spots. The squid's long, slender body has two fins at the tail end. It has a large head surrounded by 10 arms, two of which are longer than the others. Each arm has rows of round sucking discs which it uses to catch and hold its prey. It has a horny *pen* (shell) inside its body. The large head has two well-developed eyes, a pair of powerful jaws, and a rough *radula* (tongue). A muscular tube, or funnel, lies beneath the head.

The squid swims by filling the folds in its body walls with water and forcing the water through the tube. This makes it move backward. Squids have an "ink sac" that spurts a dark fluid or underwater "smoke screen" when they flee from their enemies. They can also change their color to blend with the environment.

Some people eat squid. Fishermen use them for bait. Squids are serious pests to the mackerel and herring fishing industry because they eat large numbers of these and other small fish. The common squid is found from Nova Scotia to Florida. Giant squids swim in Pacific waters near New Zealand and in the North Atlantic.

**Scientific Classification.** The common squid belongs to the squid family, *Loliginidae*. It is genus *Loligo*, species *L. pealeii*. R. TUCKER ABBOTT

See also ARGONAUT; CUTTLEFISH; NAUTILUS; OCTOPUS; OCEAN (color pictures).

**The Ten Arms of the Squid Are Used to Catch Fish.**
American Museum of Natural History

USDA
**The Big Bulblike Root of Squill Is Used in Medicine.**

**SQUILL** is the name of several plants with bulbous roots. They belong to the lily family. One kind of squill, called the *sea onion*, grows around the Mediterranean Sea. It produces bulbs that sometimes weigh as much as four pounds. The bulbs of this squill have medicinal value.

Gardeners collect the bulbs of the sea onion in August. They remove the outer husk, slice the bulb, and dry it in the sun. People make a drug from the bulbs. Usually they use it in syrup form or in "tincture of squill." It stimulates the heart and is rather irritating. It particularly affects the stomach, intestines, and bronchial tracts. Sometimes doctors use squill as an expectorant and diuretic. They also treat chronic bronchitis with it, but never when the disease is acute. Red squill is used as a rat poison.

*Squill* is also the name given the genus *Scilla* in the lily family. It includes 80 or more species that are found in the temperate regions of Europe.

**Scientific Classification.** The sea onion belongs to the lily family, *Liliaceae*. It is classified as genus *Urginea*, species *U. maritima*. HAROLD NORMAN MOLDENKE

**SQUINT** is an abnormal condition of the eyes in which one eye is fixed on one object, and the other eye is fixed on another object. This condition is also known as *strabismus* and *cross-eye*. Normally, the eyes are so located that both eyes see the same object at the same time and in the same place. In strabismus, one eye turns away from its normal position. If this eye turns inward the condition is known as *convergent strabismus*, and if the eye turns outward the condition is known as *divergent strabismus*. If the crossed eye turns upward or downward, the condition is known as *supravergent strabismus*.

The cause of strabismus is not known, except in rare cases where the condition is due to an injury or fall. The tendency to have strabismus is inherited. Strabismus can be corrected in children, especially if the treatment is started early. Treatment of strabismus usually consists of wearing glasses, forced development of the weaker eye, and training in the use of both eyes at the same time. Only 15 per cent of all cases require a surgical operation. HARRY S. GRADLE

See also CROSS-EYE.

**SQUIRE,** or **ESQUIRE.** See KNIGHTS AND KNIGHTHOOD.

**Douglas Squirrel and Young**

**Eastern Gray Squirrel**

**SQUIRREL** is a furry-tailed animal with large, black eyes and rounded ears. Many squirrels are lively animals with long, bushy tails. They scamper about the ground or in trees, and leap from branch to branch. These *tree squirrels* are often seen in parks and woodlands. They include gray squirrels, red squirrels, and flying squirrels. But many kinds of squirrels have short tails and never climb trees. They are called *ground squirrels*, and include chipmunks, marmots, prairie dogs, and woodchucks.

Squirrels live throughout the world except in Australia, Madagascar, and southern South America. One of the smallest squirrels is the African pygmy squirrel, found in western Africa. It weighs about half an ounce and is 3 inches long without the tail, which is about 2 inches long. The marmot is the largest member of the squirrel family. It weighs up to 20 pounds and grows as long as 30 inches, including a 10-inch tail.

There are more than 300 kinds of squirrels, and they make up the squirrel family, *Sciuridae*. Squirrels are one of the largest families of *rodents* (gnawing animals). Like other rodents, all squirrels have chisel-like front teeth that are useful for gnawing.

*Daniel H. Brant, the contributor of this article, is Professor of Zoology at Humboldt State College.*

Many kinds of squirrels, especially tree squirrels and chipmunks, are easy to tame. They may learn to take nuts and other food from a person's hand. But many squirrels, like most other furry animals, carry the germs of a disease called *rabies*. Even a tame squirrel may bite or scratch a person and give him rabies.

The word *squirrel* comes from two Greek words that mean *shadow tail*. At first, the word may have been used only for tree squirrels. The large, bushy tails of these animals curl over their backs and seem to keep them in the shade.

The rest of this article is about tree squirrels only. To learn more about the various kinds of ground squirrels, see the WORLD BOOK articles on CHIPMUNK; MARMOT; PRAIRIE DOG; and WOODCHUCK.

**Homes.** Most kinds of tree squirrels are active, noisy animals. They seem to scold one another continually in a variety of loud chirps, whistles, and noises that sound somewhat like *chirrrr*.

---
**FACTS IN BRIEF**

| Common Name | Scientific Name | Gestation Period | Number of Young | Life Span (in captivity) |
|---|---|---|---|---|
| **Flying Squirrel** | *Glaucomys* | 40 days | 2-6 | 7-13 years |
| **Fox Squirrel** | *Sciurus* | 45 days | 2-4 | 9 years |
| **Gray Squirrel** | *Sciurus* | 44 days | 2-5 | 8-15 years |
| **Red Squirrel** | *Tamiasciurus* | 40 days | 4 | 8-9 years |

Squirrels make up the squirrel family, *Sciuridae*.

641

# SQUIRREL

Many squirrels have two homes—a warm, permanent one, and a temporary one that is cool enough for hot days. The permanent home may be a den in a hollow tree trunk, or a sturdy nest built on a branch. A squirrel's den is lined with dry leaves and strips of bark. During the winter, several squirrels may share one den. A squirrel's permanent nest is made of layers of twigs and leaves packed together tightly to keep out rain, snow, and wind. A temporary nest is only a loose pile of twigs and leaves. It soon falls apart, and a squirrel may have to build several during a summer.

Squirrels move about easily in trees or on rooftops or telephone wires. They spread their legs straight out and leap from place to place. Squirrels use their bushy tails to keep their balance when they jump.

**Food.** Squirrels eat berries, corn, fruits, nuts, mushrooms, and seeds. They spend much of their time searching for food. A squirrel is especially busy in autumn, when it gathers food and hides it to eat during winter. Squirrels store food in holes in the ground, in trees, or in their dens.

Red squirrels are famous for the many pine cones they cut and store for food. A red squirrel may cut more than a hundred cones from a tree in an hour. Then the animal rushes down to the ground, gathers the cones, and hides them. The hiding place may be a hollow tree stump. Or the squirrel may pile the cones around a stone or a log and cover them with leaves. When winter comes, the squirrel may have 3 to 10 bushels of cones.

**Young.** A female squirrel carries her young in her body for 36 to 45 days before birth. She may give birth twice a year, and usually from two to six young are born at a time. Newborn squirrels have no fur, and their eyes are closed. Red squirrels and flying squirrels may open their eyes 26 to 28 days after birth, but gray squirrels may take as long as 37 days. When squirrels are 5 to 8 weeks old, they have all their fur and begin to search for their own food. They start to have their own families when they are about a year old.

## THE BODY OF A SQUIRREL

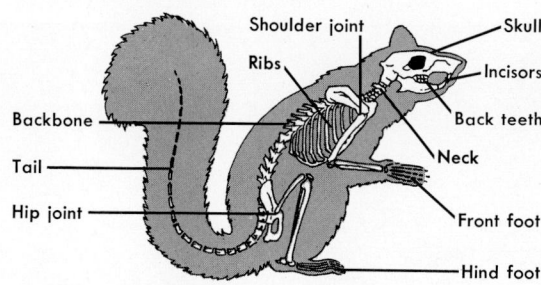

## SQUIRREL TRACKS

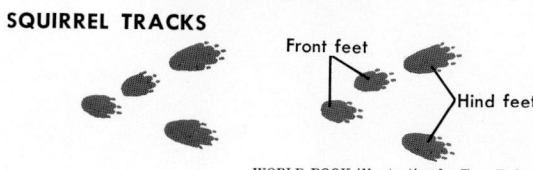

WORLD BOOK illustration by Tom Dolan

**Enemies.** Man is the greatest enemy of squirrels. Men hunt most kinds of squirrels for sport, but they hunt tree squirrels especially for meat and fur. Other enemies of squirrels include bobcats, cats, coyotes, dogs, and foxes. Tree squirrels race for the nearest tree when an enemy comes near. Squirrels may live for 2 to 6 years in the wild, but some have lived as long as 15 years in captivity.

**Kinds of Tree Squirrels.** There are three chief groups of tree squirrels in the United States and Canada: (1) gray squirrels, (2) red squirrels, and (3) flying squirrels.

*Gray Squirrels.* Fox squirrels are the largest gray squirrels. Some grow 28 inches long, including a 12-inch tail. They weigh as much as 3 pounds. Their fur is gray, reddish brown, or black. Fox squirrels are slower and tamer than most other kinds of tree squirrels. They live in the United States east of the Rocky Mountains.

Eastern gray squirrels and western gray squirrels are 16 to 24 inches long, including their tails. They weigh

**Kaibab Squirrels,** or tassel-eared squirrels, have tufts of fur on their ears. They live in pine forests near the Grand Canyon.
Willis Peterson

**Giant Squirrel,** the largest tree squirrel, grows up to 18 inches long, with a tail of the same length. It lives in India and Malaysia.
San Diego Zoo Photo

**WHERE SQUIRRELS LIVE**
The black areas on this map show where squirrels are found.

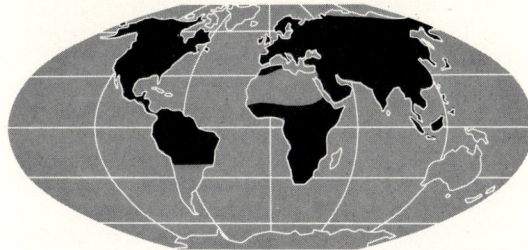

from ¾ to 1½ pounds. These squirrels have gray fur on their backs, and whitish fur on their underparts. Eastern gray squirrels live east of the Rocky Mountains, and western gray squirrels are found along the Pacific Coast.

*Red Squirrels* are the noisiest and most active of all the squirrels. They always seem to be busy cutting down pine cones and hiding them, scolding one another while they work. Few red squirrels are more than 12 inches long, including the tail. They weigh 5 to 11 ounces. These squirrels have reddish fur on their backs. Some have a line of dark fur that separates the red fur from the white fur on the underparts. One kind of red squirrel, the Kaibab squirrel, has a white tail and long hairs on its ears. This squirrel lives in the pine forests north of the Grand Canyon, but is rarely seen. Red squirrels are found in most parts of the United States and Canada except in the Great Plains.

*Flying Squirrels* are the smallest kind of tree squirrels. Few grow more than 10 inches long, including the tail. The flying squirrel has a fold of skin that stretches from its front leg to its rear leg on each side of its body. This skin acts like the wings of a glider, and gives the animal "lift." Some flying squirrels can glide as far as 150 feet, but 50 to 60 feet is a more usual distance.

Unlike other kinds of tree squirrels, flying squirrels are usually active only at night. They live throughout the United States and Canada.        DANIEL H. BRANT

See also CHIPMUNK; FLYING SQUIRREL; MARMOT; PRAIRIE DOG; WOODCHUCK.

**SQUIRREL CORN.** See DICENTRA.

**STADIUM**

**SQUIRREL HAKE.** See HAKE.
**SQUIRRELFISH.** See FISH (color picture: Tropical Salt-Water Fishes).
**SQUIRRELTAIL GRASS.** See WILD BARLEY.
**SRINAGAR,** *sree NUG er* (pop. 325,284; alt. 5,130 ft.), is the capital of India's state of Jammu and Kashmir. The city lies approximately 170 miles northeast of Amritsar in the Vale of Kashmir (see INDIA [political map]). High mountains rise behind the city. Nearby are the Shalimar Gardens, which were built by the Moguls. British and Indian residents enjoy vacations in houseboats on the nearby lakes or on the Jhelum River, which flows through Srinagar. The city's chief products include rugs, silver articles, wood carvings, paper, and leather goods.        ROBERT I. CRANE
**SS TROOPS.** See HITLER, ADOLF (Rise of the Nazis).
**ST. ———.** See SAINT ———.
**STABILE.** See CALDER, ALEXANDER.
**STABILIZER.** See AERODYNAMICS (Rotation); AIRPLANE (Tail Assembly); GYROPILOT; GYROSCOPE; GYROSTABILIZER.
**STABLE EQUILIBRIUM.** See GRAVITY, CENTER OF.
**STADACONA** was an Indian town where the city of Quebec now stands. See QUEBEC (The French Period).
**STADHOLDER.** See NETHERLANDS (Wars with England and France).
**STADIUM,** *STAY dih um,* is a large structure for spectators built around a playing field or arena.

One of the first stadiums was the foot-race course at Olympia in ancient Greece. Other famous stadiums were at Delphi, Athens, and Epidaurus in Greece and at Ephesus in Asia Minor. Usually terraces shaped like horseshoes enclosed the stadiums to give the spectators a clear view of the field. Seats were often built on the terraces. The famous stadium at Athens was rebuilt and used for the Olympic Games in 1896.

Today's stadium has seats arranged in *tiers* (rows) from which spectators view football and baseball games, track meets, boxing matches, and other public events. Universities have built many stadiums for athletic games. Students and alumni have often paid for memorial stadiums. Some cities have built municipal stadiums

All Rights Reserved. © 1965, Houston Sports Association, Inc., Houston, Texas

**Houston's Astrodome Stadium** covers 9½ acres of land. Its plastic dome is 208 feet above the floor at its highest point. It seats 45,000 for baseball, 52,000 for football, over 60,000 for conventions, and 66,000 for boxing. The Houston Astros of the National Baseball League and the Houston Oilers of the National Football League play there.

## STAËL, MADAME DE

where both civic events and sports events are held.

The domed stadium at Houston can be used for baseball, football, circuses, conventions, and other events.

The word *stadium* comes from the Greek word *stadion*,

### 25 LARGEST STADIUMS IN THE UNITED STATES

| Name and Location | Seating Capacity |
|---|---|
| Memorial Coliseum, Los Angeles | *104,573 |
| University of Michigan Stadium, Ann Arbor | 101,000 |
| Rose Bowl, Pasadena, Calif. | *100,423 |
| Soldier Field, Chicago | *100,000 |
| John F. Kennedy Stadium, Philadelphia | 98,604 |
| Stanford University Stadium, Palo Alto, Calif. | 89,000 |
| Ohio (State University) Stadium, Columbus | *81,000 |
| Tulane Stadium, New Orleans | 80,985 |
| Municipal Stadium, Cleveland | 78,516 |
| Camp Randall Stadium, Madison, Wis. | *77,248 |
| California (University of) Memorial Stadium, Berkeley | 76,780 |
| Spartan Stadium (Michigan State University), East Lansing | 76,000 |
| Cotton Bowl Stadium, Dallas | 75,504 |
| Orange Bowl Stadium, Miami | *72,880 |
| Rice Stadium (Rice University), Houston | *72,000 |
| Illinois Memorial Stadium, Champaign | *71,119 |
| Yale (University) Bowl, New Haven, Conn. | 71,000 |
| Gator Bowl, Jacksonville, Fla. | 70,000 |
| Legion Field, Birmingham, Ala. | *68,821 |
| Ross-Ade Stadium (Purdue University), Lafayette, Ind. | *68,000 |
| Louisiana State University Stadium, Baton Rouge | 67,500 |
| Yankee Stadium, New York City | 67,000 |
| Astrodome Stadium, Houston | *66,000 |
| Texas Memorial Stadium, Austin | *65,810 |
| Franklin Field, Philadelphia | *64,767 |

*Includes temporary seats.

which meant the distance between the end pillars of the stadium at Olympia (about 630 feet). ELMER D. MITCHELL

See also COLOSSEUM; HIPPODROME; OLYMPIC GAMES.

**STAËL**, *stahl*, **MADAME DE** (1766-1817), was a prominent French critic and novelist of the early 1800's. Her literary work influenced the growth of romanticism in French literature.

Madame de Staël was one of the first to apply the notion of progress to literature. She felt literature was an extension of society and should reflect social change. In her critical works, such as *On Literature* (1800) and *On Germany* (1810), she emphasized that judgment should be relative, not absolute. *On Germany* introduced the German culture and such great thinkers as Friedrich von Schiller to Europe as a model to imitate.

Her two novels, *Delphine* (1802) and *Corinne* (1807), reflect her own life. They deal with women who disregard public opinion. Their theme, the conflict between the superior person and society, became popular in the romantic movement.

Madame de Staël was born ANNE LOUISE GERMAINE NECKER in Paris. She married Baron Staël-Holstein, Swedish ambassador to France, in 1786, but the marriage ended unhappily. She had a famous love affair with novelist Benjamin Constant. In 1811 she married Albert de Rocca, a Swiss military officer. She traveled extensively in Germany, Italy, and many other countries. She was exiled from Paris several times by Napoleon, who opposed her political beliefs. IRVING PUTTER

**STAFF.** See MUSIC (The Language of Music).

**STAFF** is an inexpensive material resembling plaster. Builders use it as an exterior and interior finish for temporary structures, such as exposition buildings and statuary. They make it chiefly of plaster of Paris and hydraulic cement, mixed in water with dextrine and glycerin. Staff is applied like plaster. See also PLASTERING.

**STAFF, GENERAL.** See GENERAL STAFF.

**STAFF OF LIFE.** See BREAD.

**STAFFORD, THOMAS.** See ASTRONAUT (picture; table).

**STAFFORDSHIRE.** See ENGLAND (color map: The 38 Counties of England).

**STAFFORDSHIRE TERRIER** is a dog that looks like a colored bull terrier. Miners of Staffordshire, England, developed the breed in the 1800's. At first, they called it *half and half*, because it was half bulldog and half Old English terrier. The Staffordshire is a faithful guard and watchdog. It has a broad head and well-rounded cheeks. Its chest is big, and it stands with its legs wide apart. It has large brindle patches on its white coat. The Staffordshire weighs 35 to 50 pounds. JOSEPHINE Z. RINE

See also DOG (color picture: Terriers).

**STAG.** See DEER.

**STAG BEETLE** is the name of a family of beetles in which certain of the males have oddly enlarged jaws. These jaws look somewhat like the horns of a male deer and have given the beetle its name. In some cases, these "horns" are nearly as long as the body of the insect. Common American species include the *giant stag beetle* of the southern states. It has *mandibles* (jaws) an inch long and a body $1\frac{1}{2}$ to 2 inches long. The *pinching bug* of the eastern states is a stag beetle that flies by night. The adult stag beetles may feed on sap and honeydew. The eggs are laid in cracks in the bark of dead, decaying trees. They hatch into soft white grubs called larvae.

**Scientific Classification.** The stag beetle belongs to the stag beetle family, *Lucanidae*. The giant stag beetle is genus *Lucanus*, species *L. elaphus*. H. H. ROSS

See also BEETLE (pictures).

**STAGBUSH.** See BLACK HAW.

**STAGE.** See THEATER; MOTION PICTURE.

**STAGE,** in turbines. See TURBINE (Turbine Terms).

**STAGE DESIGNER** is an artist who designs the stage setting for plays, operas, motion pictures, and television programs. He sets the stage for the players and sets the mood for the audience. His set gives an emotional impression of the production as a whole. Theaters in ancient Greece, Rome, and medieval Europe used only a few pieces of scenery. In the 1700's, Italian painters designed elaborate settings, and the trend spread. See also THEATER. GLENN HUGHES

**STAGECOACH** was a horse-drawn coach which was used to carry passengers and mail on a regular route. Sometimes it also carried freight. The first long stage line was established about 1670 between London, England, and Edinburgh, Scotland, a distance of 392 miles.

Stagecoach lines were established in colonial America about 1756. They operated chiefly between Boston, New York, and Philadelphia. In 1785, Congress began mail service by stagecoach. Greater comforts were added to the coaches, such as springs and cushions. Many of the finest stagecoaches were made at Concord, N.H.

Early in the 1800's, travelers from Philadelphia, Baltimore, and Washington traveled to Ohio by the National Road. In elaborate Concord coaches drawn by six

**Stagecoaches** provided the best transportation for passengers and mail between American cities in the 1700's and early 1800's.

horses, they bounced along at a brisk ten miles an hour, taking two and one-half days for the journey. Horses were changed at relay stations every 15 or 20 miles. Later, stagecoach lines operated in the West. But the railroads gradually took over the job of transportation, except in remote regions. FRANKLIN M. RECK

See also WESTERN FRONTIER LIFE (Transportation).

**STAGG, AMOS ALONZO** (1862-1965), called *Football's Grand Old Man*, gained fame as the oldest active coach in the United States and the man with the greatest number of coaching seasons to his credit. He coached at the University of Chicago for 41 years. After he retired at the age of 70, he coached at College of the Pacific from 1933 to 1946, and at Susquehanna (Pa.) University from 1947 to 1952. He devised many new football developments, including the tackling dummy. Stagg was born at West Orange, N.J. LYALL SMITH

**STAHL, GEORG.** See CHEMISTRY (The Discovery of Oxygen).

**STAIN** is a special type of dye used to bring out the grain in wood. Stains are named according to the type of solvent used to dissolve the dye. Water, oil, and alcohol are the chief solvents of stain. Alcohol is considered the best solvent for wood stain because it does not cause the grain to rise above the surface of the wood, as water does. Oil penetrates the wood deeply and produces a lustrous finish, but has a tendency to smear into coats of varnish that may be applied over it.

**STAIN REMOVING.** See DRY CLEANING; CLEANING FLUID.

**STAINED GLASS** is colored glass that is assembled into pictures or decorative designs in religious and public buildings. Stained-glass windows are made up of many small pieces of colored glass.

**Making Stained-Glass Windows.** An artist designing a stained-glass window must take into consideration the style of architecture of the building in which the window will be set. He must know the amount of light the window will receive. And he must know the distance and direction the viewers will be from the window.

The artist first paints a small colored sketch of the window. He takes care that the lead divisions between the colored sections do not chop up the design. Next the artist makes a full-scale drawing, called a *cartoon*. The cartoon is used as a blueprint for making the window. Each tiny section is numbered to show where the various pieces of colored glass fit.

## STAINED GLASS

The glass used in the window is colored throughout its thickness by chemicals or dyes when the glass is manufactured (see GLASS [Colored Glass]). The thinness or thickness of each piece of glass determines how bright the color will be, and how much or how little light will come through that part of the window.

Workmen using diamonds or hardened-steel wheels cut the pieces of colored glass to fit each of the numbered parts of the cartoon. The jigsaw puzzle of glass pieces is then fitted together on a sheet of glass on top of the cartoon. Melted wax is used to fill the spaces between the colored glass pieces where the lead will be, and to hold the pieces on the sheet of glass. The artist can then make sure that the design is complete and correct.

The artist paints details of his design on the pieces of glass with colored opaque enamels (see ENAMEL). The glass pieces are then placed in a furnace and baked at a temperature of about 2,000°F. so that the enamel becomes part of the surface of the glass. The less enamel the artist uses on the glass, the more light the window will admit. The artist again puts the pieces together and studies the window. He may use acid to cut away parts of the surface of the glass, to let more light through at the highlights of his design.

Finally, the workmen fit the bits of glass together with H-shaped strips of lead, called *cames*. Cracks between the lead and the glass are filled with putty to make the window waterproof. Workmen solder the joints of the lead strips and fit the window in place.

**Early Stained-Glass Windows.** The earliest known fragments of glass windows decorated with figures date from the 1000's. The oldest stained-glass windows still to be seen in their original setting are The Prophets, five larger-than-life-sized figures in the windows of the Cathedral of Augsburg, Germany. These windows were made about 1100 to 1130. The windows at St. Denis, in Paris, were created only a little later. The large stained-glass windows in the west front of the Cathedral of Chartres, France, date from about 1150.

In the late 1200's, more and more stained-glass window space was used in the great cathedrals of France. This form of decoration of churches was followed in England and Germany, but only rarely in Italy. Stained-glass windows were regarded as picture books to tell the story of mankind and of man's salvation. One of the greatest existing series of windows dates from 1200-1240 in the Cathedral of Chartres. These windows show scenes from the Old and New Testaments, the Virgin and Christ, Apostles and Saints. All are represented in the deep colors of the period, particularly the blues and the reds which glow and sparkle in the rays of the setting sun. The color picture with this article shows one window from the Cathedral of Chartres.

In the following years, through the 1500's, the demand for stained-glass windows continued, but the style changed. The early stained-glass windows used only a few colors and expressive designs. But as time went on, glass painters began to imitate oil painting by using flesh tones and perspective. As a result, stained-glass art lost much of the color and design values that had been so important. Finally, stained-glass windows fell into complete disregard.

## STAINLESS STEEL

**Contemporary Stained-Glass Windows.** Interest in stained-glass windows began to revive in the 1800's. Art lovers collected old stained-glass windowpanes and their fragments. Making stained-glass windows became a large business. Commercially this new start was successful, but artistically the new windows proved unsuccessful, because the artists were not creative. They either adopted the methods of oil painters or copied old Gothic designs.

In the late 1800's, changes for the better began to be seen in stained glass. In the United States, Louis Comfort Tiffany began to experiment with new kinds of glass, and John La Farge created original designs and color schemes. In England, the William Morris movement kindled new interest in stained glass. In Holland and Germany, Jan Thorn Pricker established a new school of design for stained glass.

Following these new trends, artists such as Charles J. Connick and Wilbur Herbert Burnham became known. They designed colorful windows for the Cathedrals of St. John the Divine and St. Patrick in New York City, Grace Cathedral in San Francisco, and other churches throughout the United States. Emil Frei became recognized for his progressive design of such windows as those of St. Ann's Church in St. Louis, Mo. In France, Georges Rouault, Henri Matisse, and Fernand Léger designed windows for churches in Assy and other places. Reconstruction of churches damaged during World War II in England and Germany resulted in other outstanding stained-glass windows in contemporary designs. Marc Chagall's 12 windows showing the tribes of Israel are examples of outstanding recent stained-glass art. Completed in the early 1960's, the windows adorn the synagogue of the Hadassah-Hebrew University Medical Center in Jerusalem.  HANS HUTH

See also RELIGION (color picture); TRACERY.

**STAINLESS STEEL** is the name of a family of alloy steels that resist *corrosion* (rust). As a family, the stainless steels have an easily-maintained, attractive appearance. They show remarkable strength and ductility and are unique in their general resistance to the elements and to most corrosives. Some 30 grades of stainless steels have been developed that have different combinations of strength, ductility, and resistance to corrosion and heat. Most stainless steels used in the home are highly polished, with a silvery appearance, but they do not need this finish to resist corrosion. *Stainless-clad steel* is commonly ordinary steel to which a thin layer of stainless steel has been bonded on one or both sides.

The most familiar use of stainless steel in the home is in kitchen knives, flatware, sinks, pots and pans, and other places where cleanliness and easy maintenance are essential. Stainless-steel equipment is used in hospitals, restaurants, chemical industries, dairies, and food-processing plants. Engineers use stainless steel parts for automobiles, aircraft, and railroad passenger cars. Scientists use microporous stainless steel, made with a nickel alloy, to filter gases, liquids, and small particles.

Chromium is the chief metal alloyed with iron, carbon, manganese, and silicon in making stainless steel. The more common stainless steels usually contain about 8 per cent nickel. One or more of the following elements also may be added to iron to make stainless steel: molybdenum, titanium, columbium, aluminum, nitrogen, phosphorus, sulfur, and selenium. Each of these elements modifies stainless steel so it can be used for a specific purpose.  MAX D. HOWELL

See also HAYNES, ELWOOD.

**STAINS, REMOVAL OF.** See DRY CLEANING.

**STAKE DRIVER.** See BITTERN.

**STAKED PLAIN.** See TEXAS (Land Regions).

**STALACTITE,** *stuh LAK tite*. The beautiful stone formations that hang down from the walls and roofs of some caves are called *stalactites*. Most stalactites look somewhat like icicles. They usually form in limestone caves. They are caused when water drips through cracks in the roof of the cave and carries the mineral called *calcite* (calcium carbonate) with it. As the water evaporates, it leaves formations of the calcite hanging. Stalactites of basalt rock hang from the roofs of some lava caverns. Similar formations of ice have been found in the ice caves of Arctic regions.

Formations which build up from the floor of a cave are called *stalagmites* (see STALAGMITE). In the United States, excellent examples of stalactites and stalagmites exist in Carlsbad Caverns National Park in New Mexico, in Luray Caverns in Virginia, in Mammoth Cave in Kentucky, and also in Wyandotte Cave in southern Indiana.  ELDRED D. WILSON

See also CALCITE; CAVE.

**STALAGMITE,** *stuh LAG mite*. Stalagmites are stone formations which rise up from the floors of caves, especially in limestone caverns. They form when water, dripping on the floor from the walls and roofs of the cave, carries with it deposits of calcium carbonate, or calcite. As the water evaporates, the calcite builds up into colorful formations which look like icicles upside down. Similar formations, which hang from the roof, are called stalactites (see STALACTITE). Sometimes stalagmites and stalactites join to form columns or stone curtains against the walls of the cave.  ELDRED D. WILSON

See also CALCITE; CAVE; MAMMOTH CAVE NATIONAL PARK (picture).

**Stalactites Hang from the Roof of Luray Caverns** in Virginia's Shenandoah Valley limestone belt. This tomblike room is called "The Cathedral" because of the beautifully colored rock formations, which look like a pipe organ.

Luray Caverns Corp.

**THE THREE WISE MEN IN STAINED GLASS**

This scene shows the three wise men, or Magi, from the East, who brought gifts to the baby Jesus. It is one of twenty-seven stained-glass panels that make up a window picturing the early life of Christ. This window was designed and installed in the west front of the Cathedral of Chartres, France, nearly 800 years ago. The richly colored glass contains many bubbles and imperfections because it was crudely made. But these make the sunlight coming through the window seem to vibrate or dance.

# JOSEPH STALIN

*Stalin's Signature*

**Joseph Stalin Ruled the U.S.S.R. as Dictator from 1929 until 1953.**

**STALIN,** *STAH lin,* **JOSEPH** (1879-1953), was dictator of the Union of Soviet Socialist Republics (U.S.S.R.) from 1929 until 1953. He rose from bitter poverty to become ruler of a country that covers about a sixth of the world's land area.

Stalin ruled by terror during most of his years as dictator. He allowed no one to oppose his decisions. Stalin executed or jailed most of those who had helped him rise to power because he feared they might threaten his rule. He also was responsible for the deaths of millions of Soviet peasants who opposed his program of *collective agriculture* (government control of farms). Under Stalin, the Soviet Union operated a worldwide network of Communist parties. By the time he died, Communism had spread to 11 other countries.

The Soviet people had cause to hate Stalin, and much of the world feared him. But he changed the Soviet Union from an undeveloped country into one of the world's great industrial and military powers. During World War II, the U.S.S.R. was an ally of the United States and Great Britain against Germany. However,

*Myron Rush, the critical reviewer of this article, is Professor of Government at Cornell University and the author of* Political Succession in the U.S.S.R. *and* The Rise of Khrushchev.

Stalin sharply opposed and, on occasion, betrayed his allies even before the war was over. His last years of power were marked by the Cold War in which the nations of the Free World banded together to halt the spread of Communism.

Stalin had little personal charm, and could be brutal to even his closest friends. He seemed unable to feel pity. He could not take criticism, and he never forgave an opponent. Few dictators have demanded such terrible sacrifices from their own people.

After Stalin became dictator, he had Soviet histories rewritten to make his role in past events appear far greater than it really was. In 1938, he helped write an official history of the Communist party. Stalin had not played a leading part in the revolution of October, 1917 (November by the present Soviet calendar), which brought Communism to Russia. Lenin led the revolution and set up the world's first Communist government. But in his history, Stalin pictured himself as Lenin's chief assistant in the revolution.

Stalin died in 1953. He was honored by having his body placed beside that of Lenin in a huge tomb in Red Square in Moscow. In 1956, Nikita S. Khrushchev strongly criticized Stalin for his terrible crimes against loyal Communists. Later, in 1961, the government renamed many cities, towns, and factories that had been named for Stalin. Stalin's body was taken from the tomb and buried in a simple grave nearby.

### Early Life

**Boyhood and Education.** Joseph Stalin was born on Dec. 21, 1879, in Gori, a town near Tiflis (now Tbilisi) in Georgia, a mountainous area of southwestern Russia. His real name was IOSIF VISSARIONOVICH DJUGASHVILI. In 1913, he adopted the name *Stalin* from a Russian word meaning *man of steel*.

Little is known about Stalin's early life. His father, Vissarion Ivanovich Djugashvili, was an unsuccessful village shoemaker. He is said to have been a drunkard who was cruel to his young son. Stalin's mother, Ekaterina Gheladze Djugashvili, became a washerwoman to help support the family. The Djugashvilis lived in a small shack. The first three children of the family died shortly after birth, and Stalin grew up as an only child. When Stalin was young, his father left the family and went to nearby Tiflis to work in a shoe factory. The boy had smallpox when he was 6 or 7, and the disease scarred his face for life.

In 1888, at great sacrifice, Stalin's mother sent him to a little church school in Gori. He spent five years there and was a bright student. He then received a scholarship at the religious seminary in Tiflis. Stalin entered this school in 1894 at the age of 14. He soon became known among his classmates for reading, debate, and good schoolwork. Some of his classmates later remembered that Stalin held grudges and seldom forgave persons who opposed him.

Stalin studied for the priesthood in the Georgian Orthodox Church. But he was repeatedly punished at the seminary for reading forbidden books. These books included Victor Hugo's novels about social conditions in France, and about French revolutionary movements. Stalin also became interested in the ideas of Karl Marx, a German social philosopher. The people of Tiflis knew little of Marx and his theories about revolution. But political exiles from Moscow and St. Petersburg (now Leningrad) were beginning to bring Marxist pamphlets to Tiflis and other smaller cities.

Czar Alexander III died in 1894, and his son, Nicholas II, became czar. Alexander had ruled Russia with complete power. He closely controlled the press, restricted education, and forbade student organizations. Nicholas continued his father's policies, and Russia made important economic and social progress. However, it was difficult to solve the country's social problems. The peasants were demanding more land. They could not raise enough food for the country on their small farms, and, at times, millions of persons faced starvation. The growing class of factory workers was discontented because of long hours and low wages. For a discussion of conditions in Russia at this time, see RUSSIA (History).

In 1898, Stalin joined a secret Marxist revolutionary group. The Tiflis seminary, like many Russian schools, was a center for the circulation of forbidden revolutionary ideas. In May, 1899, Stalin was expelled for not appearing for an examination. His interest in Marxism probably played a part in his dismissal.

**Young Revolutionist.** After Stalin left the seminary, he got a job as a clerk at the Tiflis Geophysical Ob-

Sovfoto

**Stalin's Birthplace** was a two-room shack in Gori, a town in Georgia in southwestern Russia. A Soviet artist painted this picture of the shack. As a boy, Stalin studied to be a priest.

### IMPORTANT DATES IN STALIN'S LIFE

**1879** (Dec. 21) Born in Gori, Russia.
**1899** Expelled from Tiflis Seminary.
**1901** Joined the Russian Social Democratic Labor party.
**1903** Exiled for the first of six times before the October revolution of 1917.
**c. 1904** Married Ekaterina Svanidze.
**1905** Met Lenin for the first time.
**1912** Named by Lenin to Bolshevik party Central Committee.
**1917** Named commissar of nationalities after Bolshevik revolution.
**c. 1918** Married Nadezhda Alliluyeva.
**1922** Appointed general secretary of Communist party.
**1928** Began five-year plans to industrialize the U.S.S.R.
**1929** Became dictator of the Soviet Union.
**1935** Began great purge of Communist party members.
**1939** The U.S.S.R. signed a nonaggression pact with Germany.
**1941** Named himself premier of the Soviet Union.
**1941** Germany attacked the U.S.S.R. during World War II.
**1953** (March 5) Died in Moscow.

**WORLD LEADERS OF STALIN'S TIME**

Chiang
China

Churchill
Great Britain

Hitler
Germany

Mussolini
Italy

Roosevelt
United States

Tito
Yugoslavia

648a

# STALIN, JOSEPH

servatory. Within a year, he began his career as an active revolutionist. In 1900, Stalin helped organize a small May Day demonstration near Tiflis. He made his first public speech at the demonstration, which was held to protest working conditions.

In March, 1901, the czar's secret police arrested a number of socialists in Tiflis. The police searched Stalin's room, but he was not there and escaped arrest. He left his job and joined the Marxist revolutionary underground movement that was springing up in Russia. To confuse the police, he changed his name to *Koba*, the name of a hero in a Georgian legend.

In September, 1901, Stalin began to write for a Georgian Marxist journal called *Brdzola* (The Struggle). By this time, he had read revolutionary articles written by Lenin. Stalin's first writings closely imitated the views of Lenin, but lacked Lenin's style or force. In November, 1901, Stalin was formally accepted into the Russian Social Democratic Labor (Marxist) party.

Using various false names, Stalin carried on underground activity in the Caucasus Mountains region. He organized strikes among workers in the Batum oil fields. He helped start a Social Democratic group in Batum and set up a secret press there.

In 1902, Stalin was arrested and jailed for his revolutionary activities. In March, 1903, the several Social Democratic groups of the Caucasus united to form an All-Caucasian Federation. Although Stalin was in prison, the federation elected him to its governing body. In November, 1903, he was transferred from prison and exiled to Siberia. Also in 1903, the Russian Social Democratic Labor party, which included many Social Democratic organizations, split into two major groups. Lenin headed the *Bolsheviks*, who demanded that party membership be limited to a small body of devoted revolutionists. The other group, called the *Mensheviks*, wanted a wider membership.

Stalin escaped from Siberia in January, 1904. He returned to Tiflis and joined the Bolsheviks. Stalin met Lenin in Finland in 1905. Shortly before this time, Stalin married Ekaterina Svanidze, the sister of a schoolmate at the Tiflis seminary. She died of tuberculosis in 1907. They had one son, Jacob, who died during World War II after being captured by the Germans. In 1918 or 1919, Stalin married Nadezhda Alliluyeva, a girl in her late teens who had been his secretary. She died mysteriously in 1932, either a suicide or a victim of Stalin's anger. Stalin and his second wife had a son, Vasily, and a daughter, Svetlana. Vasily, a Soviet air force general, died in an automobile crash after Stalin's death in 1953. Svetlana became a teacher and translator of English. She moved to the United States in 1967.

Between 1906 and 1913, Stalin was arrested and exiled a number of times. He spent 7 of the 10 years between 1907 and 1917 in prison or in exile. In 1912, Stalin was suddenly elevated by Lenin into the small but powerful Central Committee of the Bolshevik party.

In 1913, with Lenin's help, Stalin wrote a long article called "The National Question and Social Democracy." Iosif Djugashvili signed the article *Stalin*, a name he had just begun to use. Also in 1913, Stalin was arrested and exiled for the last time. Before his arrest, he served briefly as an editor of *Pravda* (Truth), the Bolshevik party newspaper.

Germany declared war on Russia in 1914 at the beginning of World War I. Stalin was in exile in Siberia, where he remained until 1917. He was turned down by the army in 1916 because a boyhood blood infection made it difficult for him to bend his left elbow.

By the end of 1916, Russia faced defeat in the war against Germany. Conditions became steadily worse at home. Food shortages in the capital, Petrograd (now Leningrad), led to riots and strikes. Finally, on March 15, 1917, Czar Nicholas II gave up his throne. A *provisional* (temporary) government, run mostly by liberals, was formed the next day. The government released Stalin and other Bolsheviks from exile. They returned to Petrograd on March 25. Stalin took over the editorship of *Pravda* from Vyacheslav Molotov. Lenin became concerned that Stalin did not strongly oppose the provisional government in *Pravda*. Lenin arrived in Petrograd from exile three weeks later and criticized Stalin for not taking a strong Bolshevik stand. Lenin launched a radical program for overthrowing the provisional government. This action led to the Bolshevik seizure of power in the October revolution of 1917.

## Rise to Power

**The Bolshevik Revolution.** During the period before the October revolution, Stalin was not, as he later claimed, Lenin's right-hand man. He played an important, but not vital, part in the revolution. Lenin worked most closely with Leon Trotsky in the Bolshevik takeover of the government. After Stalin became dictator of the Soviet Union, he had history books rewritten to say that he had led the revolution with Lenin.

Lenin became head of the new government after the revolution, and named Stalin commissar of nationalities. Within a few months, opposition to the new government developed in many parts of the country. Armed uprisings broke out and grew into civil war. Stalin was active on the southern military front. In Stalin's version of history, he repeatedly corrected the mistakes of others. Stalin took credit for a victory at Tsaritsyn, the city later named Stalingrad (now Volgograd). Actually, Stalin's military role there was exaggerated.

During the civil war, the Russian Social Democratic Labor party was renamed the All-Russian Communist party (Bolshevik). Stalin became one of the five members of the newly formed *Politburo* (Political Bureau), the policy-making body of the party's Central Committee. He also became the leading figure in the *Orgburo* (Organizational Bureau), which carried out party policy. In 1922, the Communist party's Central Committee elected Stalin as its general secretary.

**Stalin Takes Over.** The Bolsheviks won the civil war in 1920. They then began the task of rebuilding the war-torn country. At first, Lenin and the others were unaware of Stalin's quiet plotting. By the end of 1922, however, Stalin's growing power began to disturb Lenin. Before a series of strokes prevented Lenin from working, he wrote a secret note warning that Stalin must be removed as general secretary. He wrote that Stalin was too "rude" in personal relations and abused the power of his office. Because of his illness, Lenin was unable to carry out his plan to remove Stalin.

# STALIN, JOSEPH

**Soviet Farm Workers** had to work on government-controlled farms after Stalin began to end private farming in 1929.

Lenin died in 1924. The leading Bolsheviks finally learned of the secret note warning against Stalin, but they ignored it. They accepted Stalin's promise that he would improve his behavior. Instead, Stalin continued to build his own power. He cleverly used this power to destroy his rivals. In December, 1929, the party praised Stalin on his 50th birthday. He had become a dictator.

## Dictator of the Soviet Union

**The Five-Year Plan.** In 1928, Stalin started the first of the Soviet Union's five-year plans for economic development. The government began to eliminate private businesses. Production of industrial machinery and farm equipment became more important, and production of clothing and household goods was neglected.

In 1929, Stalin began to *collectivize* Soviet agriculture. He ended private farming and transferred the control of farms, farm equipment, and livestock to the government. But the farmers resisted his order and destroyed about half of the U.S.S.R.'s livestock and much of its produce. As punishment, Stalin sent about a million families into exile. The destruction of livestock and grain caused widespread starvation. The economy moved forward, but at the cost of millions of lives.

During the 1930's, Stalin adopted a policy of *Russification*. The minority nationalities in the Soviet Union were subject to increasingly strict control by the government. In 1939, the Soviet Union seized a large part of Poland. In 1940, Soviet troops invaded the Baltic countries—Estonia, Latvia, and Lithuania. Stalin tried to destroy the middle classes in these countries. He set up Communist governments and joined them to the Soviet Union. See BALTIC STATES.

**The U.S.S.R. and Germany Divided Poland** by a treaty signed in September, 1939. Soviet foreign minister Vyacheslav Molotov, *seated*, and German foreign minister Joachim von Ribbentrop, *left*, signed the treaty as Stalin and an aide looked on.

**Rule by Terror.** Under the czars, the Russian secret police had often arrested revolutionists and sent them into exile without trial. Stalin set up a police system that was far more terrible. Millions of persons were executed or sent to labor camps. Stalin also turned over many industries to the secret police, who forced prisoners to work in them. Fear spread through the U.S.S.R. as neighbors were ordered to spy on one another. The government broke up families and urged children to inform on their parents to the police.

In 1935, Stalin started a *purge* (elimination) of most of the old Bolsheviks associated with Lenin. During the next few years, he killed anyone who might have threatened his power. He also executed thousands of other Communist party members, including the chiefs and countless officers of the Soviet army. Stalin achieved his purpose. When he decided to cooperate with the German dictator Adolf Hitler in 1939, there was no one left to oppose his policies. Even when the Soviet Union later suffered terrible military defeats from Hitler's army, no political opposition to Stalin was possible.

After World War II ended in 1945, Lavrenti P. Beria, chief of the secret police, became a leading figure in Stalin's government. Police control grew tighter. The bloody purges went on, but in secret rather than in public. No one was safe. Even Politburo members and Communist party leaders were purged and shot in 1949 and 1950. Anti-Semitism, which had been encouraged by Stalin during the 1930's, was now practiced throughout the country.

**World War II.** By the late 1930's, Adolf Hitler was ready to conquer Europe. Soviet leaders bargained unsuccessfully with the French and the British for a defense agreement against Germany. Then, on Aug. 23, 1939, the U.S.S.R. and Germany suddenly signed a treaty agreeing not to go to war against each other. In a secret part of the treaty, Stalin and Hitler also agreed to divide Poland between themselves.

On Sept. 1, 1939, German troops marched into Poland. On September 3, France and Great Britain declared war on Germany. World War II had begun. Germany quickly conquered western Poland, and the Soviet Union seized the eastern part. On September 28, Germany and the U.S.S.R. signed a treaty which set the boundaries for the division of Poland. The Soviet Union invaded Finland on Nov. 30, 1939, and, after a bitter struggle, took a large portion of that country.

By December, 1940, Hitler began planning an attack on the U.S.S.R. Prime Minister Winston Churchill of Great Britain and President Franklin D. Roosevelt of the United States told Stalin that their secret agents warned of a coming invasion. But Stalin ignored the warnings, as well as those of his own secret service.

In May, 1941, Stalin named himself premier of the Soviet Union. Germany invaded the Soviet Union the next month. In spite of the two extra years that Stalin had to get ready for a war, the country was not prepared. Because of Stalin's purge of the army, the U.S.S.R. did not have enough experienced officers. The country also lacked up-to-date weapons and equipment. The German army approached Moscow, the capital, in October, 1941, and many government offi-

648c

John Bryson, Rapho Guillumette

**Stalin's Grave** lies behind Lenin's tomb. After Stalin died in 1953, his body was placed in Lenin's tomb. It was removed in 1961.

cials were moved to Kuybyshev. Stalin remained in Moscow to give hope and courage to the Soviet people. The army finally beat back German attacks on Moscow and Leningrad in the winter of 1941-1942. Stalin reached the height of his popularity during the war.

In March, 1943, Stalin took the military title of Marshal of the Soviet Union. Later in 1943, Churchill, Roosevelt, and Stalin met at Teheran, Iran. The "Big Three" agreed that the United States, Great Britain, and the U.S.S.R. would work together until Germany was defeated. The three leaders met again early in 1945 at Yalta in the Crimea to discuss the military occupation of Germany after the war. For the story of the Soviet Union in the war, see WORLD WAR II.

**The Cold War.** After the Allies defeated Germany in 1945, Stalin gradually cut off almost all contact between the U.S.S.R. and the West. Stalin used the Soviet army's presence in Eastern Europe to set up Communist governments in Albania, Bulgaria, Czechoslovakia, East Germany, Hungary, Poland, Romania, and Yugoslavia. He also tried unsuccessfully to take over Greece, Iran, and Turkey. The nations of the Free World joined against the Soviet Union and its *satellites* (countries controlled by the U.S.S.R.) to halt the spread of Communism. This struggle became known as the Cold War (see COLD WAR).

Following World War II, Germany was divided into four zones, each occupied by American, British, French, or Soviet troops. Berlin, which lay deep in the Soviet zone, was also divided among the four powers. Stalin refused to cooperate in administering Germany, and in 1948, France, Great Britain, and the United States announced plans to combine their zones into the West German Federal Republic (West Germany). To prevent this action, Stalin tried to drive the Allies out of West Berlin by blockading the city. He hoped the blockade would prevent food and supplies from reaching West Berlin. But the Allies set up the Berlin airlift and supplied the city by airplanes for 11 months. Stalin was defeated, and ended the blockade in May, 1949.

In 1948, Stalin expelled the Yugoslav Communist party from the *Cominform* (Communist Information Bureau), an organization of Communist parties in Europe. Marshal Tito, the Communist dictator of Yugoslavia, had refused to allow the Soviet Union to run his country. In 1949, Tito declared Yugoslavia's independence of control by Stalin and the Soviet Union.

Stalin's aggressive policies led the West in 1949 to form the North Atlantic Treaty Organization (NATO), a mutual defense organization (see NORTH ATLANTIC TREATY ORGANIZATION).

During the Korean War (1950-1953), Stalin supported the Communist North Korean forces that invaded South Korea. Korea had been divided into two parts after World War II. At first, Soviet troops occupied the northern half, and American troops occupied the southern half, but both sides later withdrew their forces. North Korean troops then launched a surprise attack on South Korea in an attempt to unite the divided country by force. As a result, U.S. troops had to be sent back to Korea. The war ended a few months after Stalin's death. See KOREAN WAR.

**Death.** Early in 1953, Stalin prepared to replace the top men in the Soviet government. Apparently he was planning another great purge. Then, on March 4, 1953, the Central Committee of the Communist party announced that Stalin had suffered a brain hemorrhage the night of March 1. Stalin died in Moscow on March 5, 1953.

Critically reviewed by MYRON RUSH

**Related Articles** in WORLD BOOK include:

| | |
|---|---|
| Beria, Lavrenti P. | Potsdam Conference |
| Bolshevik | Russia |
| Cold War | Teheran Conference |
| Khrushchev, Nikita S. | Tito |
| Lenin | Trotsky, Leon |
| Marx, Karl H. | World War II |
| Molotov, Vyacheslav M. | Yalta Conference |
| Politburo | |

### Outline

I. **Early Life**
   A. Boyhood and Education
   B. Young Revolutionist
II. **Rise to Power**
   A. The Bolshevik Revolution
   B. Stalin Takes Over
III. **Dictator of the Soviet Union**
   A. The Five-Year Plan   D. The Cold War
   B. Rule by Terror   E. Death
   C. World War II

### Questions

Why did Stalin have Soviet history books rewritten after he became dictator?
What does the word *Stalin* mean in Russian?
What were the Five-Year Plans?
Why was Stalin expelled from the Tiflis seminary?
When Stalin was editor of *Pravda*, why did Lenin severely criticize him?
What position did Stalin receive in the Bolshevik government after the October revolution?
Why did Lenin plan to remove Stalin as general secretary of the Communist party?
Why was Stalin rejected for military service during World War I?
Why did the U.S.S.R. have difficulty meeting the attack by Germany in World War II?
Why did the Western powers set up the North Atlantic Treaty Organization (NATO)?

**STALINABAD.** See DUSHANBE.
**STALINGRAD.** See VOLGOGRAD.
**STALINGRAD, BATTLE OF,** one of the most important battles of history, marked a turning point in World War II. During the five-month struggle, the Russians kept German troops from capturing Stalingrad (now Volgograd), an important Russian industrial city on the Volga River. The German defeat at Stalingrad ended the Nazis' eastward advance into Russia. The invading German troops had to retreat from the Caucasus oil fields and the lower Don River regions. During the battle, the German army lost about 350,000 soldiers, including about 90,000 prisoners. The prisoners included 24 German generals. Snow and bitter cold took a heavy toll of German troops.

The German Sixth Army launched its drive on Stalingrad on Aug. 21, 1942, from positions about 40 miles away on the Don River. By August 23, German tanks had reached the Volga River, north of Stalingrad. Gradually, they forced their way into the city. By November, German forces had isolated Russian troops in four "pockets" along the river bank in the city. German and Russian units fought hand-to-hand for control of single streets, houses, and factories. When the Volga froze over, Russian troops pushed supplies across on the ice at night.

Russian armies north and south of Stalingrad counterattacked on November 19. The Russians met west of Stalingrad on November 23, completely surrounding the German units in and near the city.

Parimage from P.I.P.

**The Russians Raised a Flag at Stalingrad** after the Germans surrendered on Jan. 31, 1943, following a five-month battle.

Nazi dictator Adolf Hitler ordered his generals to continue the battle for Stalingrad. He sent other German units to help the troops in the city, but the relief forces could not break through the Russian lines. The Russians hammered away at the hungry, half-frozen German troops. Finally, German Field Marshal Friedrich von Paulus, Sixth Army commander, surrendered on Jan. 31, 1943. WILLIAM A. JENKS

See also RUSSIA (World War II); VOLGOGRAD; WORLD WAR II (On the Russian Front).

**STALINO.** See DONETSK.
**STALINOGRÓD.** See KATOWICE.

# STAMP

**STALL.** See AERODYNAMICS (Stall).
**STALLION.** See HORSE (Horse Terms).
**STALWARTS.** See GARFIELD, JAMES ABRAM (Political Career).
**STAMBOLISKI, ALEXANDR.** See BULGARIA (After World War I).
**STAMBOUL.** See ISTANBUL (Location).
**STAMEN.** See FLOWER (The Parts of a Flower; color diagrams: Parts of a Flower).
**STAMFORD,** Conn. (pop. 92,713; met. area 178,409; alt. 35 ft.), lies about 35 miles northeast of New York City, on Long Island Sound. For location, see CONNECTICUT (political map). Many of Stamford's citizens work in New York City. Stamford produces bearings, drugs, electrical equipment, furniture, locks, and plastics. The city has a museum, a public library, a civic music society, and several choral groups.

Stamford was settled in 1641 and incorporated as a city in 1893. In 1949, the township and city of Stamford merged under one government. Stamford has a mayor-council government. ALBERT E. VAN DUSEN

**STAMFORD BRIDGE, BATTLE OF.** See HAROLD, or HARALD (III).
**STAMMERING.** See STUTTERING AND STAMMERING.
**STAMP** is an official mark or seal or a small printed piece of paper with one glued surface. Many documents are not legal until they carry a government stamp. For example, the government may require the payment of a one-dollar tax on a real-estate deed. The collector pastes a revenue stamp of one dollar in value on the deed, as proof that the tax was paid.

The Dutch levied the first stamp taxes in 1624. In 1694, the English used the stamp plan to raise money for carrying on a war with France. The British Stamp Act of 1765 was one of the direct causes of the American colonial revolt against Great Britain.

In 1814, stamp taxes became a part of the fiscal system of the United States. In 1862, the American Congress passed an important stamp law. The law required that legal papers and certain kinds of packages carry government stamps. The purpose of the law was to raise funds to pay some of the expenses of the Civil War. The law was repealed when revenue was no longer needed to pay war expenses. New stamp laws, passed during the Spanish-American War and World War I, helped raise money to pay the costs of war.

Government stamps for raising money are known as internal revenue stamps. Until 1959, the United States government required that such stamps be placed on luxuries such as tobacco and liquor. Some states also tax these luxuries, and require that they be stamped.

During World War II, the United States government offered war savings stamps for sale to citizens. These stamps raised funds for the war. Savings stamps are still sold. Another kind of stamp, the ration stamp, came into use during World War II. The purpose of the ration stamp was to divide food and clothing equally among civilians. However, people throughout the world are probably most familiar with the postage stamp. PAYSON S. WILD

See also INTERNAL REVENUE; POST OFFICE (Postage Stamps); STAMP ACT; STAMP COLLECTING; TRADING STAMPS.

649

Colonists Demonstrated Against the Stamp Act in New York City in 1765. The man carrying the sign is being cheered on by other colonists, except by the one at the right.

**STAMP ACT.** The British Parliament passed the Stamp Act in March, 1765. Its purpose was to raise funds to help support the British army stationed in America after 1763. The act specified that Americans must buy stamps for deeds, mortgages, liquor licenses, law licenses, playing cards, and almanacs. Even newspaper owners and publishers had to purchase stamps for their publications.

The Stamp Act was unpopular throughout the colonies. Societies organized to protest the sale of stamps. In cities and towns the slogan became "no taxation without representation."

The Virginia Assembly declared that the act was illegal and unjust. The assembly passed resolutions against taxation by the British Parliament. The Massachusetts House of Representatives invited all colonies to send delegates to a general congress. The colonies which accepted the invitation were New York, New Jersey, Rhode Island, Pennsylvania, Delaware, Connecticut, Maryland, South Carolina, and Massachusetts.

The Stamp Act Congress met in New York in October, 1765. It declared that stamp taxes could not be collected without the people's consent. American resistance forced the British Parliament to repeal the Stamp Act in 1766.   JOHN R. ALDEN

See also ADAMS, JOHN (In New England); REVOLUTIONARY WAR IN AMERICA (The Quartering and Stamp Acts).

**These Three Stamps** were used by the British government under the Stamp Act it imposed upon the American colonies.

**STAMP COLLECTING** is one of the most popular collecting hobbies in the world. Young persons, old persons, rich persons, and poor persons in every country collect stamps. Stamp collecting has been called "the hobby of kings and the king of hobbies." King George V of England, Franklin D. Roosevelt, and many other famous persons have collected stamps. Students of stamps are called *philatelists*. The name comes from two Greek words, *philos*, meaning *loving*, and *atelos*, meaning *free of tax*, or *paid*. Stamps are signs that the postage, or tax, has been paid.

### Origins

Great Britain issued the first stamps to prepay postage on letters on May 6, 1840. These first stamps were a one-penny stamp (now known as "The Penny Black") and a two-pence stamp. Complete envelopes designed by William Mulready were also sold in the same values. But these were discontinued.

The United States did not issue any stamps until 1847. By that time several other countries had already tried the newly invented stamp. Among them were Brazil, Mauritius, and the *cantons* (states) of Switzerland. By 1860 almost every country had adopted stamps as a method of paying postage.

No one knows exactly when stamp collecting started. It probably occurred right after the first stamp was issued. We do know that the first stamp catalog was published in 1864 by an Englishman named Mount Brown. Since then catalogs of stamps have been published in almost every country. A great many books and magazines about stamps have also been published.

People soon discovered that some stamps were harder to find than others, because smaller quantities of them were printed. Collectors traded rare stamps and soon began selling them to each other. Prices rose as more people began collecting stamps. A one-penny 1856 British Guiana stamp is now valued between $50,000 and $100,000. A two-penny Hawaiian Missionary stamp sold for $41,000 in 1963. In the same year, two 1847 Mauritius stamps (a one-penny and a two-penny) sold for $78,400, and a pair of two-penny British Guiana "cotton reels" brought $71,000. Sometimes errors are made in printing stamps. For example, the center may be upside down, or the wrong ink or paper used. Such stamps are usually rare, and become very valuable.

### Ways in Which Stamps Differ

Small differences in stamps mean a great deal to the stamp collector. Stamps which look the same to the beginner might seem entirely different to the expert.

Philatelists study many things, such as the paper and inks used, the way the stamps are separated, the printing process, and postal history.

**Paper.** The surface of paper may be finished in various ways. Paper with a plain finish is called *wove*. Paper which looks as though it has bars in it when it is held up to the light is known as *laid*. Tiny pieces of colored silk like those in a dollar bill are used in *silk paper*. Pieces of silk so small they can hardly be seen are used in *granite paper*, which is grayish in color.

Sometimes paper is made with a design called a *watermark*, which is pressed into the wet paper with wire. The wire can be laid in any shape wanted. Stamps may look the same on the surface, but have different

# STAMP COLLECTING

**French Air-Mail Stamp,** used in French Equatorial Africa, commemorates the end of World War II with a victory design.

**Cape of Good Hope Triangle Stamp** of 1853 was the first oddly shaped stamp.

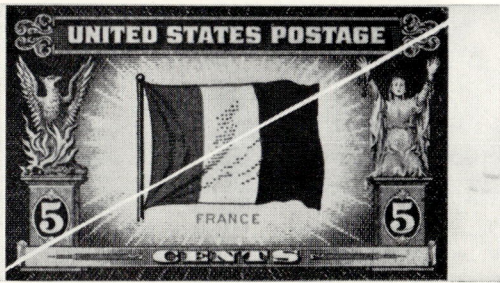

**The United States Honored France** in this stamp, issued during 1943 as a tribute to the war-torn nation's fight against Nazism.

**United States Commemorative Stamp of 1946** honors the Smithsonian Institution. It is typical of United States commemorative stamps.

**United States Miniature Sheet,** issued in 1937. Such sheets are made usually for collectors.

**President Franklin D. Roosevelt** is shown studying his stamp collection, in this memorial stamp issued by Nicaragua in 1946.

**U.S. Newspaper Stamp** was discontinued in 1900's.

**Rare U.S. Air-Mail Stamp** has center upside down.

**Poland's Government-in-Exile Issued This Stamp** during World War II. It honored Polish soldiers who fought at Monte Cassino, Italy.

**German Overprinted** stamp of World War I

Charless Hahn

**Mexican Commemorative** honors 1946 exposition.

# STAMP COLLECTING

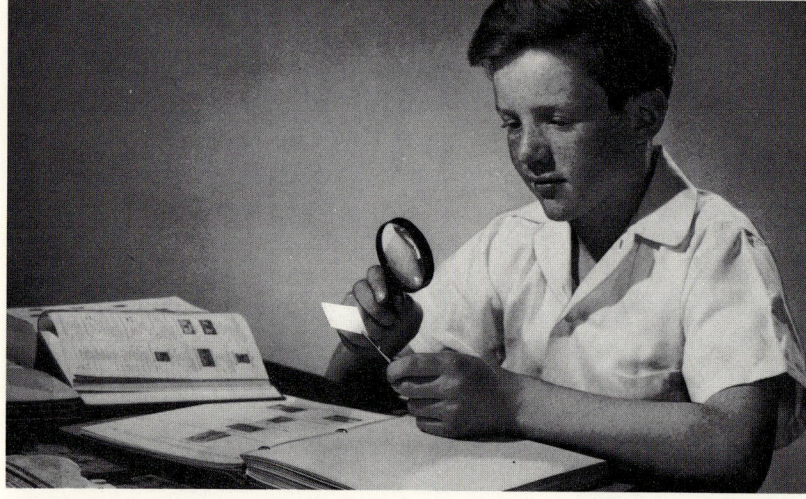

**A Youthful Collector** examines a stamp with a magnifying glass, and consults a stamp catalog as he adds new items to his growing collection. He holds the stamp with tweezers to prevent it from being soiled as he puts it into his album.

*Ewing Galloway*

watermarks. Philatelists consider these as different stamps. The watermark can be seen by holding the stamp up to the light, or by placing it face down in a black dish and pouring watermark fluid on it.

**Ink.** Stamps are printed with different colored inks. Variations of the color of the basic ink make the stamps different for the collector. For example, a blue stamp differs from an ultramarine stamp.

**Printing.** A stamp may be printed by one of three methods—*relief*, *planographic*, and *intaglio*. Relief printing is made from a raised design. Planographic printing is made from a design level with the surface, and intaglio is printed from a design cut lower than the surface. The most common forms of planographic printing are *offset* and *lithography*. One form of intaglio printing used for stamps is called *engraving*. The ink is slightly raised, just as it is on an engraved calling card. Another intaglio process is *gravure*. See PRINTING.

**Separations.** The first stamps had to be cut apart with scissors. Such stamps are called *imperforate*. Soon *perforations* (little holes) were punched between the rows of stamps. Stamps which have a different number of holes per inch along any edge are also considered as different stamps. Sometimes the separations are slits cut with a knife between the stamps, but with no paper punched out. This form is referred to as a *roulette*.

**Cancellations.** The lines printed on a stamp to show that it has been used are called a *cancellation*. Cancellations show postal history. Used stamps are often left on the envelopes, and early stamps are much more valuable that way. Envelopes with a stamp canceled the first day it was used are called *first-day covers*. Collectors now prize such cancellations.

**Surcharged Stamps.** Countries often change stamps by overprinting (surcharging) something new on an old stamp, instead of issuing a new one. A new value may be printed on an old stamp. When a country is overrun in war, the conquerors often print their names on the stamps of the fallen country.

**Special Stamps.** Many special types of stamps are issued, in addition to plain postage stamps. A country may honor or commemorate some event or famous person by issuing *commemorative* stamps. The United States issued its first commemorative stamp in 1893. It was called the Columbian issue, in honor of the four-hundredth anniversary of the discovery of America. A stamp which is sold for more than the cost of postage is called a *semipostal*. Such stamps have been issued by many countries, but not by the United States. Extra funds obtained from such stamps have been given to charity, and to help finance fairs, youth clubs, and the rebuilding of a cathedral.

Many types of special stamps are issued by various countries of the world. Among such stamps are air mail,

**A One-Penny Stamp** issued by British Guiana in 1856 is the world's rarest stamp. Only one of its kind is known to exist, and its value is estimated between $50,000 and $100,000. At the right is a drawing of the original design. Its color was black on magenta.

*United Press Int.*

652

Charless Hahn

**The First Stamps of the U.S. Post Office** were issued in 1847. The 10-cent stamp bears the likeness of George Washington, and was used for letters weighing over a half-ounce. The 5-cent Franklin stamp was for letters under a half-ounce.

**Commemorative Stamps** are issued to honor some special event, such as the 1962 space flight of Project Mercury astronaut John Glenn, or the admission of Hawaii as the Union's 50th state.

parcel post, official, postage due, provisional stamps for emergencies, pneumatic tube, special delivery, and personal delivery. Other types include registration, occupation during war, postal savings, newspaper, special handling, and combinations of special services.

**Other Reasons for Collecting.** Not all people collect stamps because they are rare or special, or have certain markings. Many people like to collect them just for the pictures of odd and out-of-the-way places and things. Some people collect stamps of one country only. Others collect only stamps showing birds, or railroads, or ships. Still others collect stamps of only one color, such as purple stamps. Specialists may collect only one issue or the varieties of one issue. The reason for collecting does not matter as long as the collector has fun. CHARLESS HAHN

See also POST OFFICE; STAMP.

**STAMP WEED.** See INDIAN MALLOW.

**STANDARD.** See FLAG (table: Flag Terms).

**STANDARD BOOK NUMBER** is a group of nine numbers identifying a book and its publisher. Standard book numbers simplify book ordering processes. Booksellers, librarians, and others who handle large numbers of books can send and receive orders faster and more efficiently, using standard book numbers.

A standard book number has three parts, separated by hyphens or spaces. The first four numbers are called the publisher prefix. They represent the publisher of a book. The second four numbers, called the title prefix, represent the book title. The last number is a check *digit* (number under 10). As the standard book number goes through a computer, the check digit indicates errors that may have been made when the number was handwritten.

The standard book number system was first used in Great Britain in 1967. Following general agreement among publishers, the United States adopted the sys-

653

## STANDARD CANDLE

tem later that year. The developers hope that eventually all countries will use standard book numbering.

**STANDARD CANDLE.** See CANDELA.

**STANDARD GAUGE.** See RAILROAD (Gauge).

**STANDARD MONEY.** See MONEY (table: Terms).

**STANDARD OF LIVING** may be defined as the degree to which wants and needs are satisfied, or, as the level of consumption of goods and services. Under either definition, the United States has the highest standard of living of any country in the history of the world. The average American family enjoys a standard of living that is the envy of peoples in all parts of the world. This standard includes healthier foods, better clothing and housing, advanced medical services, educational opportunities, and other comforts.

**Needs and Wants.** Human beings have many needs and wants. Their basic needs have always included food, clothing, and shelter. To these may be added a number of other needs, depending upon the society in which a person happens to live. In many parts of the world, artificial light and artificial heat have become basic needs. In the United States, transportation, leisure, schooling, recreation, and a sense of belonging to something, are generally held to be needs. Throughout the world, a *necessity* is anything without which one cannot live the life that is expected of him. Wants are even less definite than needs. So far as anyone knows, there is no limit to the range of human wants.

The Greek philosopher Epictetus pointed out long ago that unhappiness comes from unsatisfied desires. He could see no way for the ordinary man to increase his satisfactions. So he proposed that people ought to cut down on their desires.

But the world, as we know it, cannot run unless wants are stimulated and appetites whetted. One of the tasks of industry is to create ever greater desires for its products. If standard of living is considered as the satisfaction of wants, it is doubtful whether the standard of living is any higher today than it was in Europe during the Middle Ages. The people of medieval times had less than we have today, but they were more easily satisfied.

When we talk about the standard of living of a country, it is a little like talking about the "average man." No country has a general standard of living for everyone, any more than it has an average citizen. We speak of China and India as having very low living standards, but many Chinese live in great luxury, and some of the world's richest men live in India. The size of the average pay check is no indication of a country's standard of living. The cost of living varies over the world. The man who earns $100 a month in one part of the world may live better than one who is paid $100 a week in another place, because his lower wages buy more goods and services to satisfy his needs. About the best we can do in estimating national living standards is to divide the total of goods and services available by the total population, and assume that everything is equally distributed. On this basis, the world's average standard of living is quite unsatisfactory.

**Area Differences.** At present the world supports more than $3\frac{1}{2}$ billion people. At the American standard of grain consumption, only half this number could live. On the other hand, the world could support an additional billion people at present production if everyone went on the Asiatic standard of living. The whole world, with its present population, could be supplied with grain at the European standard of grain consumption before World War II. This would put an end to starvation and misery in Asia, but it would sharply cut the American standard of grain consumption.

The situation is even more striking when it comes to various other foods, such as meat or dairy products. The North American standard of living calls for about three pounds of meat per person per week. In normal times, Europe gets about two pounds, and South America about a pound and a half. Asia and Africa use only a third of a pound per person a week. If the world's animal foods were equally distributed at the present rate of livestock production, each person would get about a pound of meat per week.

The United States is said to have the highest standard in comparison with living standards in other parts of the world, because it produces more goods per person than any other country in the world. The differences in standards of living in the United States are emphasized by comparing two areas. In some rural regions, the standards are considered lower than in many cities. Such areas may lack some of the comforts that city dwellers consider necessary. But often these rural areas have fresh fruits, vegetables, milk, and meat when such foods are high-priced in the city. LLOYD ALLEN COOK

Related Articles in WORLD BOOK include:

| | |
|---|---|
| Automobile | Income |
| Communication | Industrial Revolution |
| Consumer Education | Mass Production |
| Cost of Living | Technology (with picture) |
| Gross National Product | Wages and Hours |
| Housing | |

**STANDARD OIL COMPANY.** In 1859, Edwin L. Drake, a retired railroad conductor, drilled the first commercial oil well near Titusville, Pa. Four years later, John D. Rockefeller and his partners organized the firm of Andrews, Clark, and Co., and began to develop a vast oil industry that later became the Standard Oil Company. The new firm built a large oil refinery in Cleveland, and began to sell oil at home and abroad.

---

### A MEASURE OF STANDARDS OF LIVING

The standard of living for a country can be measured by dividing its *personal consumption expenditures* by its population. These expenditures represent the value of goods and services purchased by individuals and nonprofit institutions during a year. Such expenditures are a major item in a country's *gross national product* (total value of all goods and services produced). This table lists the 20 leading non-Communist countries in personal consumption expenditures per person in 1966.

| | | | |
|---|---|---|---|
| United States | $2,376 | Great Britain | $1,235 |
| Iceland | $1,786 | Belgium | $1,228 |
| Canada | $1,609 | Kuwait | $1,198 |
| Sweden | $1,537 | Germany (West) | $1,195 |
| Denmark | $1,462 | Norway | $1,109 |
| Switzerland | $1,433 | Finland | $1,090 |
| Australia | $1,341 | Israel | $1,014 |
| France | $1,307 | Netherlands | $964 |
| New Zealand | $1,269 | Austria | $809 |
| Luxembourg | $1,267 | Italy | $745 |

Source: *Monthly Bulletin of Statistics*, July, 1968, United Nations.

The new business expanded rapidly. In 1870, Rockefeller and his associates formed the Standard Oil Company of Ohio and began to buy other refineries.

From 1870 to 1882, Rockefeller and his associates bought practically all the refineries in Cleveland, and acquired refineries in other cities. They developed a pipeline system, purchased new oil-producing lands, and created an efficient organization to market their products. To unify the management of the companies and to overcome certain legal difficulties, they transferred the stock of all companies to the newly formed Standard Oil Trust in 1882 (see TRUST). This made Standard Oil the biggest company in the oil industry. The trust controlled about 90 per cent of the country's refining capacity, and almost as much of its pipelines.

After 1870, Rockefeller and the business practices of Standard Oil came under bitter attacks from newspapers, magazines, books, state and federal investigating agencies, and many courts. In 1892, the supreme court of Ohio dissolved the trust under the provisions of the Sherman Antitrust Act. All the companies in the trust had to operate almost separately, as they did before the trust was formed in 1882. In 1889, the Standard Oil Company of New Jersey amended its charter in an attempt to preserve the vast oil empire and to provide centralized direction for all the companies in the empire. The new company gave its stock in exchange for certificates in the dissolved trust. It also held stock in 20 other constituent companies.

The reorganization of Standard Oil of New Jersey made the company one of the richest and most powerful holding companies in the world. In 1906, the federal government, under the Sherman Antitrust Act, brought suit against the combination. In 1911, the Supreme Court of the United States ordered the company to dissolve under the provisions of the Sherman Antitrust Act. This action forced 34 companies of Standard Oil of New Jersey to operate as independent units.

Today, the largest of the old Standard Oil companies include Atlantic Richfield Company, Mobil Oil Corporation, Standard Oil of California, Standard Oil (Indiana), Standard Oil (New Jersey), and Standard Oil (Ohio). For the sales, assets, and employees of all the above companies, except Standard Oil (Ohio), see MANUFACTURING (table: 100 Leading U.S. Manufacturers).

**Standard Oil of California** produces, refines, and markets oil in the West, the Southwest, the Southeast, and in 12 eastern states. It has 50 subsidiaries in the United States and abroad. Arabian American Company, Trans-Arabian Pipe Line Company, and the Caltex Companies are affiliated with Standard Oil of California.

**Standard Oil (Indiana)** is a major international oil company. At the end of 1960, it became entirely a parent company for domestic and foreign activities. The American Oil Company is its United States refining and marketing subsidiary. Pan American Petroleum is its exploration and production subsidiary.

**Standard Oil (New Jersey)** ranks as the world's largest petroleum company. It is essentially a holding company, with world-wide interests. Its subsidiaries conduct business in all branches of the oil industry in the United States and other countries. Important subsidiaries include Imperial Oil, Ltd.; Esso Standard Oil, and the Ethyl Corporation.

**Standard Oil (Ohio)** is the oldest of the Standard companies. It markets its products in Ohio and surrounding states. It produces oil in Illinois, the Southwest, Canada, Venezuela, and Iran.   PAUL H. GIDDENS

See also PETROLEUM; ROCKEFELLER (family).

**STANDARD SCHNAUZER.** See SCHNAUZER.

**STANDARD TIME** is a world-wide system of uniform time zones. This system divides the world into 24 zones, each about 15° wide in longitude (see LONGITUDE). The difference in time between that of any zone and its neighbor is exactly one hour. Within each zone, all clocks keep the same time, except for some local variations.

**Time Zones.** The *local*, or *sun*, time for any specific location depends on its longitude. There is a difference of 4 minutes for each degree of longitude, or a difference of an hour for every 15°. Under standard time, the time kept in each zone is that of the central *meridian*, or longitude line (see MERIDIAN). The central meridians are those 15°, 30°, 45°, and so on, east or west of the prime meridian. In theory, the zone boundaries should extend $7\frac{1}{2}°$ on either side of the central meridian. In practice, the boundaries are irregular lines. This is to avoid inconvenient changes in time. For example, in the United States, zone boundaries often are changed so that a state will lie entirely within one time zone.

In the United States, the Interstate Commerce Commission (ICC) has the authority to set zone boundaries. However, the law does not require that local areas use the time of their zone. Many communities go off standard time every year when they adopt daylight saving time. In 1966, however, Congress declared that all communities must change to daylight saving time and drop it at the same date each year (see DAYLIGHT SAVING). Canada does not have a federal standard time law. Its time zones generally have the same names as those used in the United States.

The time zones of the United States and Canada are (from east to west) Atlantic Standard, Newfoundland Standard, Eastern Standard, Central Standard, Mountain Standard, Pacific Standard, Yukon Standard, Alaska Standard, and Bering Standard. Hawaii uses the same time as Alaska. For the boundaries of these zones, see TIME (map).

**History.** Before the adoption of standard time, each city in the United States kept the local time of its own meridian. With the growth of railroads, these differences caused difficulties. Railroads that met in the same city sometimes ran on different times. In 1883, the railroads of the United States and Canada adopted a system for standard time. In 1884, an international conference met in Washington, D.C., to consider a world-wide system of standard time. The meridian passing through Greenwich, England, was chosen as the prime meridian. No formal agreement took place, but countries gradually adopted the time zone system. Congress gave the ICC authority to establish limits for time zones in the United States in 1918.

Today, nearly all nations of the world keep standard time. Only a few small countries keep time that differs by a half hour or by some minutes and seconds from standard time.   WILLIAM MARKOWITZ

See also FLEMING, SIR SANDFORD; TIME.

Library of Congress

**Captain Miles Standish** led an attack on Merry Mount in 1628. The Pilgrims destroyed the settlement and captured Thomas Morton, who had been selling guns to the Indians. Standish also led expeditions against the Indians, and helped explore Cape Cod.

**STANDARDBRED.** See HORSE (Light Harness Horses; color picture); HARNESS RACING.

**STANDARDS, BUREAU OF.** See NATIONAL BUREAU OF STANDARDS.

**STANDISH, MILES,** or **MYLES** (1584?-1656), came to America with the Pilgrims in the *Mayflower*. He was not a Separatist, and never joined the Pilgrim Church. But he helped the Pilgrims in their plans and in training a militia. See PILGRIM; PLYMOUTH COLONY.

Short but stocky, Standish had red hair and a florid complexion which turned livid when he grew angry. "A little chimney is soon fired," commented one of his enemies. But no one questioned his bravery. Singlehanded, he attacked a threatening Indian chief, Wituwamat, and brought his head back to Plymouth. His watchfulness probably saved the colony from destruction by Indians in its early years.

In 1625, the colonists sent him to England to get a more favorable agreement with the merchants who were financing the colony. He could not accomplish much, partly because of the plague then raging in London. Standish was one of the leaders who assumed the colony's debts. He served as assistant governor from 1624 or perhaps from 1633 on, and as Plymouth's treasurer from 1652 to 1655.

He helped found Duxbury, Mass., and moved there about 1632. His statue overlooks the town and Plymouth Bay.

Standish was born in Lancashire, and fought as a young man against the Spaniards in The Netherlands. Henry W. Longfellow's account of him in *The Courtship of Miles Standish* is entirely fictitious (see COURTSHIP OF MILES STANDISH, THE). BRADFORD SMITH

**STANDPIPE.** See RESERVOIR.

**STANFIELD, ROBERT LORNE** (1914-    ), became leader of Canada's Progressive Conservative Party in September, 1967. He succeeded John Diefenbaker. Stanfield was premier of Nova Scotia from 1956 until he became the national leader of his party.

Stanfield was born in Truro, N.S. He received a B.A. degree from Dalhousie University in 1936 and an LL.B. degree from Harvard University in 1939. In 1948, he became leader of the Nova Scotia Progressive Conservative Party. He was elected to the Nova Scotia Legislature in 1949. His efforts in encouraging the establishment of new industry in the province helped him win reelection in 1953, 1956, 1960, 1963, and in 1967. He won election to the national House of Commons after the Progressive Conservatives made him their leader.

**STANFORD, LELAND** (1824-1893), was a railroad builder, a governor of California, and a United States Senator. In 1885, he founded Stanford University in memory of his son, with a gift of land and securities. Stanford was born in Watervliet, N.Y. He studied law and started his practice in 1848 at Port Washington, Wis. In 1852, Stanford moved to California and opened a general store. He entered politics and became governor of California in 1862. He helped keep the state loyal to the Union during the Civil War. After his term as governor ended in 1863, Stanford joined others in building the Central Pacific and Southern Pacific railroads. He was president of both railroads. Stanford was a Republican U.S. senator from California from 1885 until his death. W. H. BAUGHN

**STANFORD-BINET TEST.** See INTELLIGENCE QUOTIENT (History).

**STANFORD RESEARCH INSTITUTE** is a contract research organization affiliated with Stanford University. The institute performs both basic and applied research for industry, government, and the public. A staff of about 1,000 scientists provides research services in economics, engineering, the physical and biological sciences, and explosives technology.

Headquarters of the Stanford Research Institute are in Menlo Park, Calif., but it has facilities in several cities throughout the world. The institute was founded in 1946. E. FINLEY CARTER

**STANFORD UNIVERSITY** is a coeducational, privately controlled university in Stanford, Calif., 30 miles southeast of San Francisco. In 1885, Leland and Jane Lathrop Stanford founded the school in memory of their son, Leland Stanford, Jr. The legal name is Leland

Stanford Junior University. Stanford University was opened to students in 1891.

Stanford's divisions include schools of law, medicine, education, business, engineering, humanities and sciences, and mineral sciences; a food research institute; and study centers in France, Germany, Italy, and Japan. Courses lead to bachelor's, master's, and Ph.D. degrees.

The Hopkins Marine Station, at Pacific Grove, specializes in marine biology. The School of Medicine carries on advanced and clinical work. The university has many libraries, including the Hoover Institution on War, Revolution, and Peace.

For the enrollment of Stanford University, see UNIVERSITIES AND COLLEGES (table). PETER C. ALLEN

**STANHOPE, PHILIP D.** See CHESTERFIELD, EARL OF.

**STANISLAS,** *STAN is lus,* **SAINT** (1030-1079), is the patron saint of Poland and the city of Kraków, where he served as bishop. He became a saint of the Roman Catholic Church in 1253, and is honored as a martyr. His name is also spelled STANISLAUS.

Saint Stanislas was born at Szczepanowski, Poland. As a priest he took charge of a parish near Kraków. He was named bishop of Kraków by Pope Alexander II. His outspoken attacks against sin in both low and high places earned him the hatred of King Boleslaw II of Poland. Boleslaw ordered Stanislas killed. The king accompanied the guards who had been ordered to kill Stanislas. When the guards would not obey, the king killed the bishop himself. Saint Stanislas' feast day is celebrated on May 7. FULTON J. SHEEN

**STANISLAUS STATE COLLEGE.** See UNIVERSITIES AND COLLEGES (table).

**Stanford University** is the home of the Hoover Institution on War, Revolution, and Peace. Scholars study a collection of historical materials assembled there to help the world strive for peace. The idea for such a collection came to Herbert Hoover while he was directing relief work in World War I.

Stanford University

## STANLEY AND LIVINGSTONE

**STANISLAVSKI, KONSTANTIN,** (1863-1938), was the stage name of a well-known Russian director and actor. He tried to create truthful performances by having his actors study the inner lives of the characters as if they were real people. The actor's attempt to live the life of the character became known as the "Stanislavski method."

KONSTANTIN SERGEYEVICH ALEXEYEV was born in Moscow. In 1898, with Vladimir Nemirovich-Danchenko, he established the Moscow Art Theater. The theater became famous for its realistic performances of plays by Chekhov, Gorki, and others. Stanislavski's direction of *The Seagull* in 1898 gave Chekhov his first success. Stanislavski's fame increased with his writings describing the methods he used in teaching actors and directing plays. His works include *An Actor Prepares* (in English, 1936) and *Building a Character* (in English, 1949). FREDERICK J. HUNTER

**STANISLAW PONIATOWSKI.** See POLAND (Partitioning of Poland).

**STANLEY** is the family name of identical twin brothers who were inventors. They built the Stanley steam automobile. **Francis E. Stanley** (1849-1918) and **Freelan O. Stanley** (1849-1940) organized businesses and invented products together. They even cut their beards and dressed alike.

The Stanleys invented dry plate film and organized the Stanley Dry Plate Company in 1883. They sold out to Eastman Kodak in 1905. They experimented with steam engines, and in 1897 built the first Stanley steamer automobile (officially called the Stanley). They sold the car company to the Locomobile Company in 1899. But in 1902, they bought back their patents and organized the Stanley Motor Carriage Company. The Stanley brothers retired in 1917, and Francis was killed in an automobile accident in 1918. Freelan built a hotel in Estes Park, Colo., and lived there until he died in 1940. The Stanley brothers were born in Kingfield, Me. SMITH HEMPSTONE OLIVER

See also AUTOMOBILE (picture).

**STANLEY, FREDERICK A.** See STANLEY OF PRESTON, BARON.

**STANLEY, WENDELL MEREDITH** (1904-    ), an American biochemist, did outstanding research on viruses. In 1935, he isolated the *tobacco mosaic virus* in crystalline form, and showed it to be a protein molecule. Before this discovery, scientists had assumed that viruses were submicroscopic living organisms. Stanley shared the 1946 Nobel prize for chemistry for preparing enzymes and virus proteins in pure form. He was born in Ridgeville, Ind. MORDECAI L. GABRIEL

**STANLEY AND LIVINGSTONE,** two famous British explorers, made the African continent known to the world. But they are probably known to most people for the search Stanley conducted to find Livingstone, and for Stanley's famous greeting when they met: "Dr. Livingstone, I presume?"

**David Livingstone** (1813-1873) received a degree in medicine from Glasgow University in 1840, and then became connected with the London Missionary Society. He went to South Africa to begin his missionary work. Livingstone wanted to convert the peoples of Africa to Christianity, to try to put a stop to the slave

657

# LIVINGSTONE'S EXPLORATION OF AFRICA

David Livingstone, *far right*, explored Africa and made the "Dark Continent" known to the world. The map of southern Africa, *right*, shows the routes he followed on his expeditions. Sir Henry M. Stanley, *below*, found Livingstone near Lake Tanganyika in 1871.

·········· **Missionary Travels and 1st Expedition**
–·–·– **2nd Expedition**
– – – **3rd Expedition**

Brown Bros.

trade, and also to explore the mysterious African continent.

Livingstone began working in Bechuanaland (now Botswana) in 1841. He made a number of journeys into the interior of southern Africa, and discovered Lake Ngami in 1849. He reached the Zambezi River in 1851, and began to explore it in 1852. He discovered the Victoria Falls on the Zambezi in 1855. In 1856, he returned to England.

In 1858, Livingstone returned to Africa as British Consul at Quelimane, Mozambique. He explored the Lake Nyasa region and the Shire River, and discovered Lake Shirwa. He went to England again in 1864, but returned to Africa in 1866, and set out to find the source of the Nile River. He reached the southern end of Lake Tanganyika in 1867, and moved on into the interior of central Africa. Concern over his safety led to the expedition of Sir Henry Morton Stanley. Their names became forever linked as "Stanley and Livingstone."

Livingstone refused to return to the coast with Stanley in 1872, and continued his travels for another year. Weakened by illness, he reached Lake Bangweulu, which he had discovered in July, 1868. There he died on Apr. 30, 1873. Livingstone was later buried at Westminster Abbey in London. He was born at Blantyre, Scotland.

**Sir Henry Morton Stanley** (1841-1904) was born at Denbigh, Wales, and was baptized John Rowlands. His father died when the boy was two, and he spent most of his youth in a workhouse. At 18, he sailed as a cabin boy on a ship to New Orleans, La., where a merchant, Henry Morton Stanley, adopted him and gave him his name. When the Civil War began in 1861, Stanley joined the Confederate Army but was soon captured. He later joined the Union Navy. After the war, he became a newspaper reporter, and, in 1869, the *New York Herald* sent him to find Livingstone.

In March, 1871, Stanley started his search from Zanzibar. After many hardships, he reached the town of Ujiji on Lake Tanganyika. There, on Oct. 28, 1871, he met Livingstone, who had been exploring the Lake Tanganyika region. Stanley gave Livingstone some supplies and stayed with him until March, 1872.

In 1874, Stanley heard of Livingstone's death and returned to Africa to carry on his work. In November, 1874, he left Zanzibar with three white men and more than 300 Africans. He pushed into the interior of Africa and sailed about Lake Victoria and other lakes. Then he started the dangerous trip down the Congo River from its sources to its mouth. All his white companions and about 150 of the Africans died before he came to the Atlantic Coast in August, 1877.

The Congo region was rich in rubber and ivory, and Stanley tried to interest the British in the area. But he did not succeed and, instead, the Belgians colonized the region as the Congo Free State. Stanley led another expedition for the Belgians. In 1887, he made his last trip to Africa, to rescue Emin Pasha, who was cut off from civilization after an African uprising (see Emin Pasha). Stanley then returned to Great Britain, where he became a naturalized citizen. He served in parliament until 1900.

James G. Allen

See also Ruwenzori Range.

**STANLEY CUP** is an ice-hockey trophy. Baron Stanley of Preston, a governor-general of Canada, presented it in 1893. It goes to the National Hockey League playoff winner. For Cup winners, see Hockey (table).

**STANLEY FALLS** is a group of seven cataracts on the middle part of the Congo River in Congo (Kinshasa). They drop about 200 feet in 60 miles. They were named after Sir Henry Morton Stanley, the African explorer. To move river traffic around the cataracts, a bypass railway runs from Kisangani to Ponthierville, at the head of the cataracts. Their hydroelectric potential has been estimated at between 10 million and 15 million horsepower, about 5 times the horsepower developed at Niagara Falls.

George H. T. Kimble

**STANLEY OF PRESTON, BARON** (1841-1908), FREDERICK ARTHUR STANLEY, a British statesman, received his first government appointment as lord of the admiralty under Prime Minister Benjamin Disraeli. He served as governor-general of Canada from 1888 to 1893. He gained popularity, and encouraged imperial sentiment. When he returned to England, he became a prominent figure in Liverpool, and was elected mayor. He became president of the British Empire League in 1904. Stanley was born in England. LUCIEN BRAULT

**STANLEY POOL.** See CONGO RIVER.

**STANLEY STEAMER.** See AUTOMOBILE (The First Automobiles [picture]); STANLEY (family).

**STANOVOY MOUNTAINS,** *STAN oh voy*, is a mountain range in Siberia. It extends for about 1,000 miles from the northern end of Lake Baykal northeast to the Sea of Okhotsk. Most of it is like a rugged plateau. The region is rich in minerals, especially gold.

**STANTON, EDWIN McMASTERS** (1814-1869), was an American statesman. He served as secretary of war in President Abraham Lincoln's Cabinet, and later played an important part in the impeachment of President Andrew Johnson.

Stanton was born in Steubenville, Ohio, and was educated at Kenyon College. He studied law and was admitted to the bar in 1836. He practiced law in Pittsburgh from 1847 to 1856, and then moved to Washington, D.C., where much of his practice was before the Supreme Court. President James Buchanan appointed Stanton attorney general in 1860, and Lincoln made him secretary of war two years later.

Brown Bros.
**Edwin M. Stanton**

Stanton was not popular in the war office, and Lincoln did not like him very well. Stanton was outspoken, and made many enemies. But he was an able manager, and gained a reputation for efficiency.

When Andrew Johnson became President, he and Stanton clashed repeatedly over the treatment of the South. Stanton cooperated with Johnson's enemies in Congress, and when Johnson removed Stanton from office, the House of Representatives impeached the President. Johnson was acquitted by one vote, and Stanton left office in May, 1868 (see JOHNSON, ANDREW [Increased Tension]). The next year, President Ulysses S. Grant appointed Stanton to the Supreme Court. But Stanton died four days later. W. B. HESSELTINE

See also TENURE OF OFFICE ACT.

**STANTON, ELIZABETH CADY** (1815-1902), advocated votes and equal rights before the law for women. In 1840 she married Henry B. Stanton, an abolitionist, and went with him to the World Anti-Slavery Convention in London. But women were not permitted to attend. In 1848, she and Lucretia Mott, another rejected delegate, called the first Woman's Rights Convention. Mrs. Stanton was the first president of the National Woman Suffrage Association, which she organized with Susan B. Anthony in 1869. She was born in Johnstown, N.Y. See also WOMAN SUFFRAGE. LOUIS FILLER

**STAPES.** See EAR (The Middle Ear).

**STAPHYLOCOCCUS,** *STAFF ih loh KAHK us,* is a common bacterium belonging to a group of round, or spherical, bacteria called *cocci*. Under a microscope, groups of these tiny organisms look like bunches of grapes. Staphylococci live in the air, in water, and on the bodies of human beings and animals. They cause boils and are responsible for a skin infection known as *impetigo*.

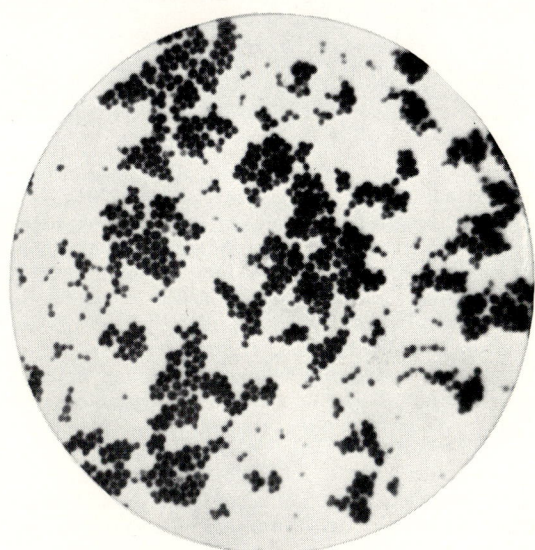

© General Biological Supply House, Inc., Chicago
**Staphylococcal Bacteria** grow in small clusters that look like bunches of grapes when seen through a powerful microscope.

Some staphylococci grow in foods and cause a type of food poisoning. Others cause pneumonia and blood poisoning. Because of differences in their growth habits, staphylococci have been separated into species and strains. Doctors may use antibiotics to treat diseases caused by staphylococci, but some strains have become resistant to these drugs. LOIS G. LOBB

See also ANTIBIOTIC; BACTERIA; BOIL; IMPETIGO; TOXIN.

**STAPLE** is a term used in the textile industry. It is applied to the qualities of a fiber or to its length. Cotton is often said to have good *staple*. This means that choice fiber can easily be worked into a certain size during spinning. The *staple length* for cotton is the average length of the bulk of its fibers. *Short-staple cotton* has fibers that average less than $1\frac{1}{8}$ inches in length. *Long-staple cotton* has fibers that average more than $1\frac{1}{8}$ inches.

See also COTTON (Classing).

**STAPP** is a unit of measure used in aviation medicine to express the combination of time and force that a pilot endures in rapid acceleration or deceleration. The force needed to pull a pilot out of a dive is measured in *G's* (see G). One stapp is the force exerted by one G acting on the human body for one second. Thus, a pilot who is exposed to three G's for 12 seconds is said to have endured 36 stapps. The stapp was named for John P. Stapp of the U.S. Air Force, who pioneered in aviation medicine experiments with rocket sleds.

# STAR

**STAR.** The stars are suns. Some of the stars are bigger and brighter than our own sun, and some are smaller and fainter. Our sun seems so much brighter and larger than all other stars simply because it is much nearer to us than any of the rest. Our sun is only about 93 million miles away. Yet it is far enough away that a rocket from the earth, traveling 25,000 miles an hour, or 7 miles a second, would take 152 days and 8 hours, or about five months, to reach the sun. But the nearest star except for our sun is so far away that our 7-miles-a-second rocket would take almost 115,000 years to reach it. Even this star is a close neighbor, as stars go. Others are millions of times farther away.

We see two kinds of starlike objects in the sky. One is the stars themselves. The other is the sun's "family" of planets that circle the sun as the earth does. See PLANET.

Since very early times man has looked up at the stars and wondered about these diamondlike points of light that shimmer above him. Some ancient carvings show that men who lived 5,000 years ago studied the heavens.

But ancient men probably had no idea what the stars are really like. They did not dream that the stars are other suns, far out in space. They thought that the stars made the outlines of animals or persons in the sky, and they called these shapes *constellations*. The ancient Greeks thought that one group of stars looked like a winged horse, which they named Pegasus. Other groups of stars were named after other animals or persons, and these animals and persons became part of the legends and folk tales that have come down to us through thousands of years. See CONSTELLATION.

It was only in fairly recent times that *astronomers*, the scientists who study the heavens, developed instruments and methods of study which gave us our present knowledge of the stars.

Why do men study the stars? They want to know what the stars are like, where they came from, why they behave as they do, and where they are going. Out of this thirst for knowledge have come many highly practical understandings and facts. Some of these are so important that they have changed the course of history. Our lives today are much different from what they would have been if man had never studied the stars.

## How Man Makes Use of the Stars

**Measuring Time.** Probably the first practical use man made of the stars was in telling time. The stars

**You Can Watch the Stars Go By.** Sit in a comfortable chair facing north or south, with the corner of your house to your left or right. As you watch, you will see the stars "move," appearing or disappearing around the corner of the house. The spinning of the earth makes them seem to move.

and all heavenly bodies seem to make a daily trip across the sky as the earth spins around on its axis. This precise movement of the stars gave man a kind of great heavenly clock by which he could keep a check on the passage of time. Calendars are based on the way the stars seem to move as the earth travels around the sun. See CALENDAR.

**Telling Directions.** The stars have always been used as guiding beacons in the sky. Since earliest times the North Star has helped sailors find their way across the trackless seas. Desert travelers have used stars to guide them. The Bible tells the beautiful story of the Star of Bethlehem that guided the Wise Men to the stable in Bethlehem where the baby Jesus lay in a manger. Even today, we use the stars to help guide our ships and airplanes. See NAVIGATION (illustration, How Stars Help a Navigator).

**Surveying.** All our streets, lots, and highways are laid out by *surveying*, which is a method of finding the exact position of things on the earth. Surveying today, as in the days of ancient Egypt, is based upon careful measurements of the positions of the stars above. See SURVEYING.

**Atomic Energy.** The study of the stars, including our sun, taught men the basic facts about how to make the powerful hydrogen bomb. Astronomers wondered how the stars could continue to shoot out such a tremendous amount of light and heat, and not burn up in just a few years. They found that the stars seem to change atoms of hydrogen into atoms of helium. In the process, some of the atomic material is changed into the energy of light and heat. Other scientists discovered how to work out much the same process here on the earth.

The stars have been put to other important uses, too. But the value of star study cannot be measured only in terms of practical uses. Today, as always, man marvels at the skies above him, dreams his dreams, and thirsts for a better understanding of his universe. There will always be more to learn, and there will always be men who want to learn. A good way to start studying the stars is to learn how to recognize the main constellations and to read about how astronomers have learned what they know. The WORLD BOOK articles on CONSTELLATION and ASTRONOMY will help you start.

### How Many Stars Are There?

Nobody knows how many stars there are. Even on a clear night, you probably can see only about 2,000 stars with the naked eye. That is partly because you can see only the stars that are overhead in your part of the earth. The curve of the earth and the thickness of the atmosphere above you both cut down the number of stars that you can see. But the main reason you cannot see more is that many of the stars are so far away that their light is too dim to be seen with the naked eye. With a powerful telescope, you could see thousands of stars for every one you can see with the naked eye. The great glass "eyes" of the telescopes can see much dimmer light than your eyes can see. A telescope with a mirror "eye" that is 100 inches across could "see" a burning candle about 6,800 miles away.

The great Hale telescope at Mount Palomar in California collects starlight on a mirror that is 200 inches across. It can gather a million times more light than your eyes can. With such large telescopes, astronomers can photograph over thirty billion stars. And we think that there must be billions more beyond the reach of our most powerful telescopes.

### How Far Away Are the Stars?

Imagine that our sun is the size of the dot at the end of this sentence. Then the next nearest star to us (Proxima Centauri) would be another small dot about 10 miles away. Other stars would be hundreds, thousands, and hundreds of thousands of miles away.

Of the billions of stars in the heavens, about twenty are within twelve *light-years* of the earth. (A light-year is the distance that light, traveling 186,282 miles a second, will go in a year's time.) The big Hale telescope on Mount Palomar, California, has photographed star-like objects believed to be about 6,000 million light-years away. A more powerful telescope might find stars even farther away. See PARALLAX (diagram, How Far Is That Star?).

### How Large Are the Stars?

Most of the stars seem to be about the size of our sun, which has a diameter of about 865,000 miles. But there are tiny stars, called *white dwarfs*, that are only about 1,100 miles in diameter. And one supergiant, Alpha Herculis, is more than 2,400,000,000 miles across. It is so big that our sun, together with the earth at its distance of about 93 million miles from the sun, could be placed twenty-five times in a row across the middle of the supergiant.

Stars differ as greatly in weight as they do in size. The white dwarfs are so compact that each cubic inch may contain several tons of matter. On the other hand, supergiants are so spread out that each cubic inch may contain only a millionth of an ounce of matter.

### What Are Stars Made of?

The stars are very hot masses of gas. They seem to be made of about the same elements as those we find in the earth. But these elements are not in the same pro-

FOR AGES, MAN HAS USED THE STARS TO GUIDE HIM

ACROSS THE DESERT

OVER THE SEA

THROUGH THE AIR

An airplane navigator "shoots the stars" to check the plane's position.

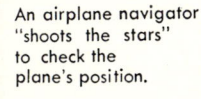

U.S. Navy

## YOUR POSITION ON EARTH DETERMINES WHICH STARS YOU SEE

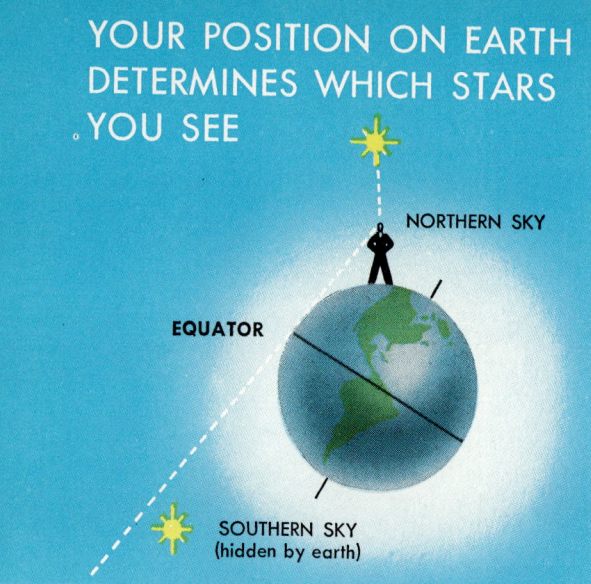

If you are north of the equator, you cannot see all stars of the southern sky.

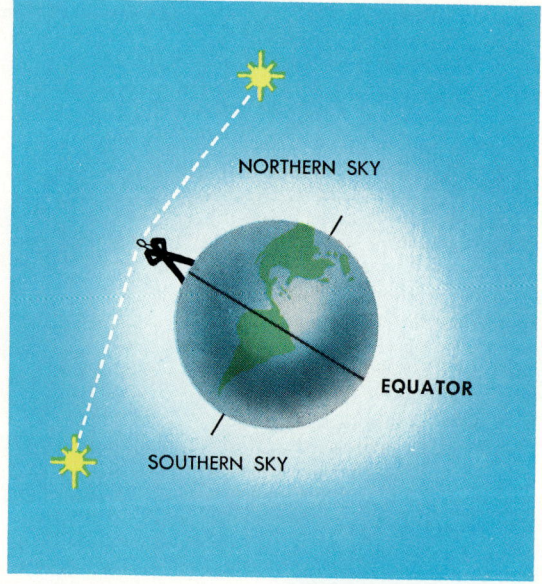

From the equator you can see stars of both northern and southern skies.

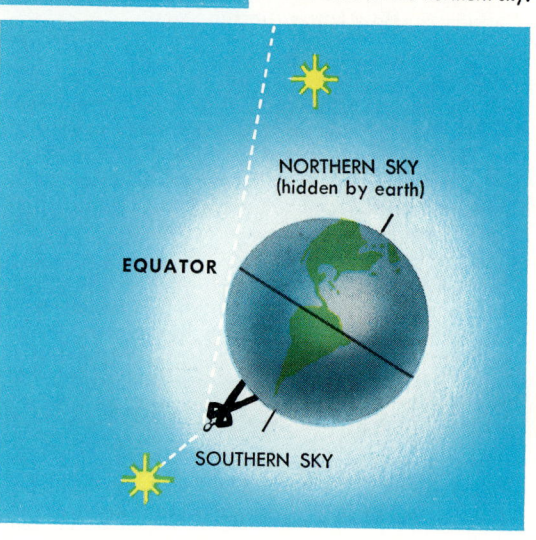

If you are south of the equator, you cannot see all stars of the northern sky.

the stars by the changing of hydrogen into helium. When this happens, a small amount of matter is destroyed. But the matter reappears as a tremendous amount of energy—the energy of light, and of kinds of radiation that cannot be seen. All these radiations act partly like waves and partly like streams of particles called *photons*. The radiations stream away from the star in all directions at the speed of light. They differ in their wave length and in the energy of their photons. Photon energies that affect human eyes range from red light through violet light. A star is visible if photons in this energy range enter the eye at a rate that is fast enough to stimulate nerves in the retina. See RADIATION.

**Will the Stars Keep Shining Forever?** Scientists believe that our sun will go on shining in much the same way it does now for about 5 billion years more. Then the amount of light and heat it shoots out will get less and less, as it finishes "burning" up its fuel. Even so, it will probably keep shining with lessening portions as they are in the earth. Stars differ in the proportions of the elements they contain, too, but, in general, the lighter elements are the most common in all the stars. Hydrogen, helium, calcium, and iron are the most common, and a large amount of carbon is found in some stars.

We study the light from a star to find what it is made of. This light tells us only about the elements that are at or near the surface. We do not know much about what stars are like inside.

### Why the Stars Shine

Starlight comes to us from almost unbelievable distances. If your eyes are sharp, you can see the faint haze of a great group of stars, the Andromeda Nebula. This group is so far away that its light, which you now see, started from the stars almost two million years ago.

How can light travel for two million years to reach our eyes? Scientists think that the light is produced in

STAR

## WHY THE NORTH STAR DOES NOT RISE OR SET

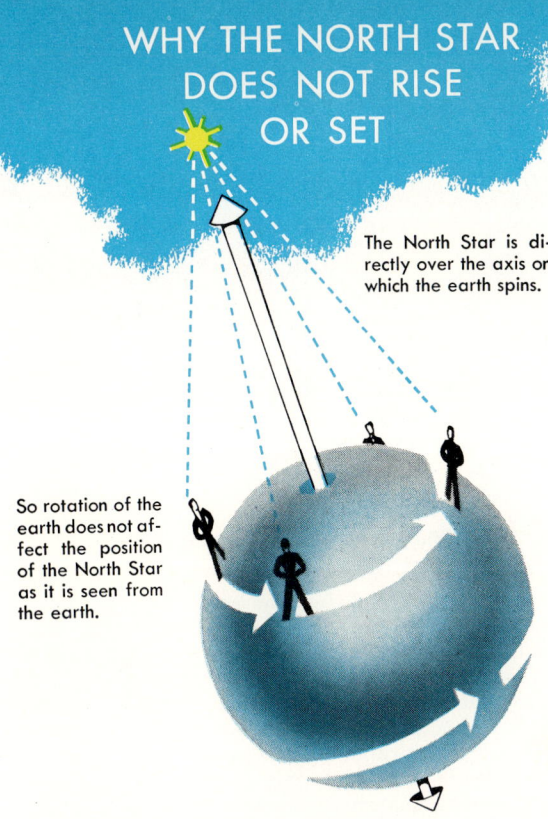

The North Star is directly over the axis on which the earth spins.

So rotation of the earth does not affect the position of the North Star as it is seen from the earth.

brilliance for another 100 billion years or so.

But our sun is a rather slow "atomic furnace." Other stars seem to be using up their hydrogen fuel much more rapidly. Most of the really brilliant stars pour out energy about 5,000 times faster than our sun does. These stars seem to be burning up faster, too, and they probably will quit shining billions of years before our sun dies out.

**Why the Stars Shine Only at Night.** The sun is so near the earth, and its light is so bright, that we cannot see the light from the stars in the daytime. The stars are still out there, of course, and their light keeps streaming to earth. But the sun's light is many thousands of times brighter than starlight and it spreads out through the atmosphere, coloring it blue. In all this brightness, the light from the stars is lost.

### The Movements of the Stars

It is the motion of air that makes the stars seem to twinkle, and it is the motion of the earth that makes the stars seem to rise in the east, move across the heavens, and set in the west. This seeming daily motion of the stars is the result of the earth's spinning around on its axis. See DAY.

What seems to be another motion of the stars is also the result of the earth's movements. You may have noticed that different star groups, or constellations, appear overhead at different seasons of the year. This is because the earth is rushing along in a great circle around the sun. So, at one time of the year, we look out at nighttime on one part of the heavens. Six months later, our earth has moved to the other side of the sun. Then we look out at nighttime on the other part of the heavens. See ASTRONOMY (Skies of the Seasons).

The stars, themselves, do move. Even our sun is rushing through space at a speed of about 43,000 miles an hour. We cannot see it go, however, because our earth and all the other planets are being carried right along with it.

All the stars in the universe seem to be rushing through space. And they all seem to be rushing away from each other, much as if they were dots of paint on a balloon that was being blown up. The farther away they are, the faster they seem to be moving.

### The Changing, or Variable, Stars

**Pulsating Stars.** Some stars have the peculiar habit of *pulsating*, changing in brightness every few days. The North Star (Polaris) is one of these. In a little less than four days it changes from bright to dim, and then back to bright again. The change is too slight for you to see with your naked eyes, but it can easily be noticed through a telescope.

There are many such pulsating stars. Astronomers believe that they expand very rapidly and grow in brilliance as they do so. But, in a short period of time, the expanding gases cave in with a rush. As they collapse and become smaller in size, such stars grow dimmer again.

**Twin Stars and Eclipsing Stars.** In addition to the pulsating stars, there are millions of twin stars, called *binaries*. These are double stars that revolve around each other something like a spinning dumbbell. Most of these double stars are so far away and so dim that only *spectroscopes* (instruments that spread light rays apart so they can be studied) can show that they are really twins. Others can be seen through telescopes. Some of them appear to dim and brighten like the pulsating stars. But this is simply because they *eclipse* each other, getting in the way of each other's light, as they revolve around each other. When they are side by side in relation to the earth, their combined light makes them look like a single bright star. Later, when

## WHY THE STARS SEEM TO TWINKLE

In space, starlight does not twinkle.

Moving layers of the atmosphere break up and scatter the starlight so that it seems to change in brightness.

SPACE

ATMOSPHERE

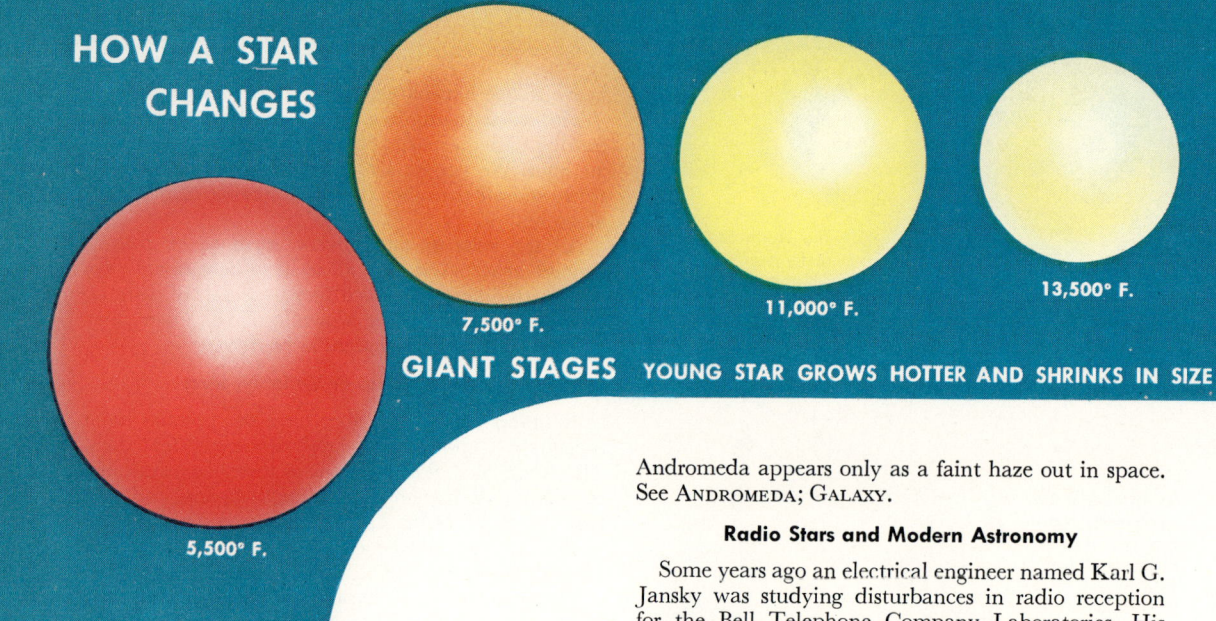

**HOW A STAR CHANGES**

5,500° F. 7,500° F. 11,000° F. 13,500° F.

**GIANT STAGES** YOUNG STAR GROWS HOTTER AND SHRINKS IN SIZE

one moves in front of the other and blocks out its light, the observer seems to see a single star that has suddenly dimmed.

**Exploding Stars.** Once in a few hundred years a new and unusually bright star seems to appear in the heavens. It is called a *supernova*. When astronomers study such supernovae they find that they are really stars which already existed, but which suddenly have increased greatly in brightness. Astronomers think that these supernovae are caused by gigantic explosions. Some astronomers believe that a star bursts into a supernova when it has run out of the hydrogen which had kept it going, and when its spinning has slowed down enough. When these two things happen, the star may "cave in" because of its strong gravitational pull. The great mass of material rushing into the center of the star would produce a gigantic lump of heavy stuff under tremendous pressure. This might blow up in one great blast of energy. See NOVA.

**The Star Islands in Space**

The stars are not equally spaced throughout the heavens. They are grouped together in great starry "islands" in the sky. Our own sun is part of one of these islands, or *galaxies*. We call our galaxy the Milky Way. Every star that you can see as a separate star with your naked eye is part of this great system of stars. The individual stars we see in the sky are those in that part of the Milky Way which is nearest our sun. The fuzzy streak in the sky, which we often call the Milky Way, is made up of stars in this galaxy which are farther from the sun. See MILKY WAY.

The Milky Way is only one of millions of galaxies in the universe. Only the nearest of these—the great spiralling galaxy called the *Andromeda Nebula*—can be seen with the naked eye. Even when the sky is clearest, Andromeda appears only as a faint haze out in space. See ANDROMEDA; GALAXY.

**Radio Stars and Modern Astronomy**

Some years ago an electrical engineer named Karl G. Jansky was studying disturbances in radio reception for the Bell Telephone Company Laboratories. His equipment picked up some strange noises that Jansky decided could come from nowhere but outer space. Since that time, many scientists have made a study of these strange radio noises and have developed huge antennas which capture the signals better.

Where do the strange radio signals come from? Scientists have found that our own sun and other visible stars shoot out some of them. But the most powerful signals seem to come from small spots in the Milky Way where there are no bright stars. These spots are just about the right size to be stars—but no stars can be seen. Scientists think that these spots are places where there are "radio stars"—powerful masses of energy that send out radio waves instead of light waves.

**How Bright Are the Stars?**

The ancient astronomer Claudius Ptolemy drew up the earliest list of the brightness of the stars about A.D. 150. He called about twenty-five of the brightest ones stars of the first magnitude. The stars that were just visible to the naked eye were called stars of the sixth magnitude. The remaining stars were grouped into stars of the second, third, fourth, and fifth magnitude.

This general scheme of measuring the brightness of the stars is still followed, although it has been improved upon. On Ptolemy's scale of magnitude, not all stars in the same group are of the same brightness. Some stars in the same magnitude are brighter than others. The lower the number, the brighter the star. We indicate the brightest stars by writing a minus sign in front of their numbers, or by means of decimal points for figures of less than one. Sirius, the brightest star, has a magnitude of −1.6. The magnitude of Canopus is −0.9, that of Vega 0.1, and Altair 0.9. On such a scale, the magnitude of the sun is −27. The full moon has a magnitude of approximately −11.2.

A first-magnitude star, such as Sirius, may be almost 16 times as bright as another first-magnitude star such as Regulus, on Ptolemy's scale. On the modern scale, a star of any magnitude is 2.512 times as bright as a star one magnitude fainter. This means that a first-magni-

| 35,000 to 60,000° F. Maximum Heat Star Stops Shrinking | 13,500° F. | 11,000° F. Our sun is a yellow dwarf | 7,500° F. | 5,500° F. | Cooling Star Finally Fades Out |

**DWARF STAGES** — STAR NO LONGER SHRINKS AND GRADUALLY LOSES HEAT

tude star is exactly 100 times as bright as a sixth-magnitude star. The 200-inch telescope at the Mount Palomar observatory, on a mountain in California, can photograph stars to the magnitude of 22.5.

The magnitudes considered in these tables are called *apparent* magnitudes, because they deal only with the brightness of the stars as they appear to us. But a faint star near at hand might appear much brighter than a brighter star at a greater distance from the earth. To measure their real brightness, a scale of *absolute magnitudes* has been devised. The absolute magnitude of a star is its apparent magnitude, if it were 33 light-years away from the earth. The sun's absolute magnitude is +4.85. A few stars are known whose absolute magnitudes are about −6, while the brightest star known is about −9. The absolute magnitudes of the stars range from about 100,000,000 times brighter than the sun to about one millionth as bright.

### The Stars in the Arts and Religion

To man, the stars have always been a symbol of high ideals and great hopes. They are often used in mottoes and expressions of hope, in poetry, and in emblems and flags. "Hitch your wagon to a star" is an often-used expression that means a person should set high ideals and work to reach them.

Poetry and music show how the mystery and beauty of the stars have influenced literature, from the jingle "Twinkle, twinkle, little star, how I wonder what you are—" to Wagner's beautiful "Evening Star" from the opera *Tannhäuser*. The Bible speaks of Christ as "the bright and morning star."

Stars are much used as religious symbols. The star of Bethlehem is a symbol of Christianity, and no Christmas would seem complete without a shiny star on the top of the tree or above the fireplace. For thousands of years, the six-pointed Star of David has been a symbol of the Jewish faith. See DAVID, STAR OF.

Stars actually are round, but they are pictured in many ways. The five-pointed star is most commonly used, but stars appear with six, seven, eight, and even more points in flags and other forms of art.

The stars often appear in the folklore, legends, and religions of primitive people and the ancients. Some of the most beautiful of these legends came from the American Indians. The Blackfoot Indians believed that every star was once a human being, and that when a person died his spirit rose to the heavens and became a new star. One of their legends tells how the North Star came to be. The Morning Star came to earth and chose an Indian girl as his bride. He took her back to the heavens, where they lived happily. His wife was allowed to do almost anything she wanted, but was warned against digging a certain turnip. She disobeyed, and the turnip she pulled up made a hole in the heavens. She was returned to the earth and her child became a star that was used to fill up the hole that she had made. This star-child must always stay in

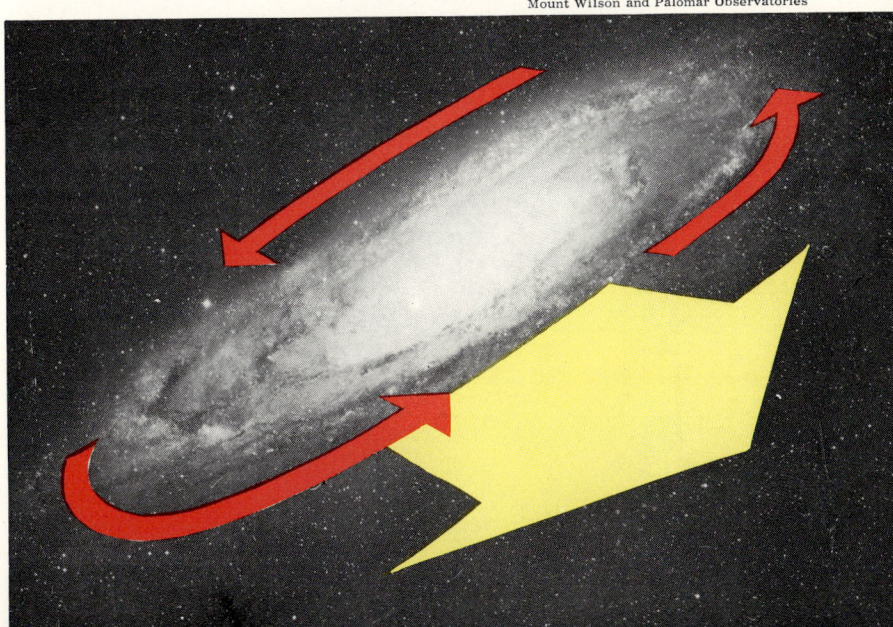

Mount Wilson and Palomar Observatories

Islands of stars, called galaxies, spin around like phonograph records. They also move out through space. This galaxy is Andromeda, the star island nearest the galaxy we live in.

# STAR

place to fill the hole, and can never move about as the others do. And that is why the North Star never moves, according to this legend.

Ancient peoples sometimes worshiped the stars as gods. In Babylonia, the gods were closely related to the stars, and the word-picture Babylonians used for a star was repeated three times to indicate a god. In Egypt, the stars themselves were not considered as gods, but the ancient Egyptians believed that separate gods controlled the many stars. In China, ancient writings show that the constellations and the starry heavens as a whole were among the many objects worshiped. In Japan there was a star-god named *Amatsu mike hoshi* (dread star of heaven). Another Japanese star-god named Ame no Kagase wo (scarecrow man of heaven) was supposed to be extremely evil. In a battle for the control of men, he was beaten by other gods who were good and kindly.

Even today, some of the Berbers of North Africa worship the constellations known as the Great Bear (Big Dipper), the Little Bear (Little Dipper), the Pleiades, and Orion.

E. A. FATH and R. WILL BURNETT

**Related Articles** in WORLD BOOK include:

| | | |
|---|---|---|
| Algol | Comet | Mira |
| Antares | Constellation | Nebula |
| Arcturus | Deneb | North Star |
| Astrology | Double Star | Nova |
| Astronomy (Science Project, Making a Star Chart) | Fixed Star | Parallax |
| | Galaxy | Planet |
| | Magnitude | Sidereal Time |
| | Meteor | Sirius |
| Betelgeuse | Milky Way | Sun |
| Cepheus | | Vega |

## Outline

I. **What Stars Are**
II. **How Man Makes Use of the Stars**
   A. Measuring Time
   B. Telling Directions
   C. Surveying
   D. Atomic Energy
III. **How Many Stars Are There?**
IV. **How Far Away Are the Stars?**
V. **How Large Are the Stars?**
VI. **What Are Stars Made of?**
VII. **Why the Stars Shine**
   A. Will the Stars Keep Shining Forever?
   B. Why the Stars Shine Only at Night
VIII. **The Movements of the Stars**
IX. **The Changing, or Variable, Stars**
   A. Pulsating Stars
   B. Twin Stars and Eclipsing Stars
   C. Exploding Stars
X. **The Star Islands in Space**
XI. **Radio Stars and Modern Astronomy**
XII. **How Bright Are the Stars?**
XIII. **The Stars in the Arts and Religion**

## Questions

What is a star?
What do we call a person who studies stars?
What is meant by a "light year"?
How can stars continue to give off light and heat without burning up?
How far away are the farthest stars that have been photographed?
What might be the weight of a cubic inch of one of the heaviest stars?
What makes stars shine? Why do they seem to twinkle?
Why do twin stars seem to change in brightness from time to time?
How long would it take to reach the sun from the earth, if you could travel at the rate of 2,000 miles an hour?

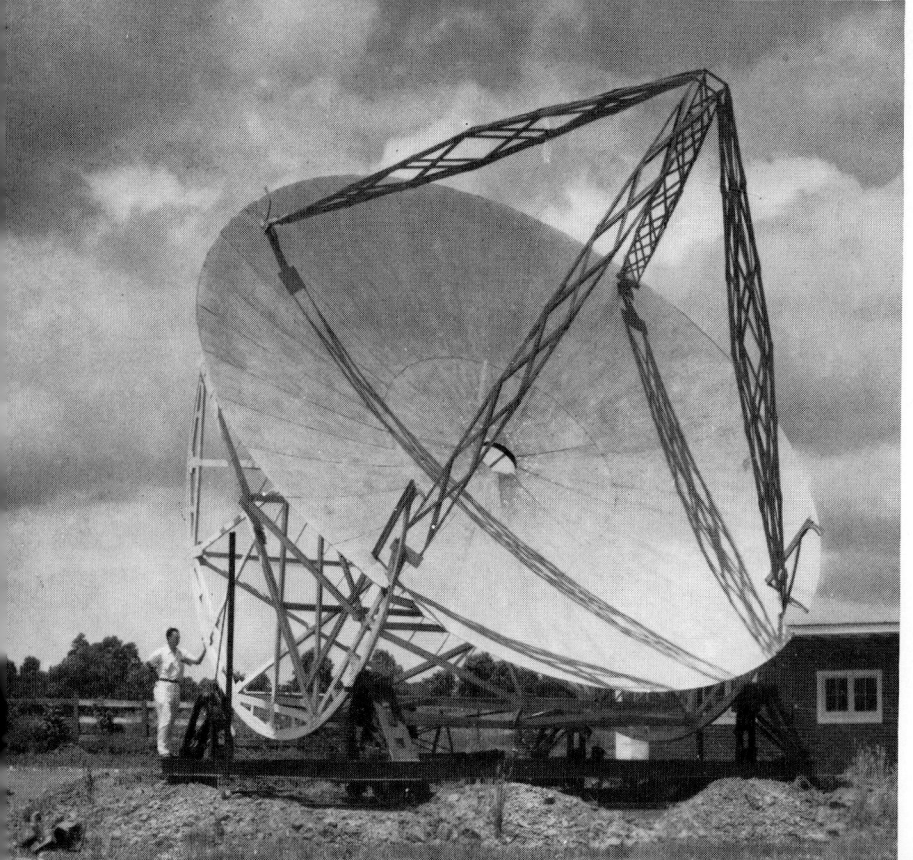

National Bureau of Standards

**A Radio Telescope** is used by astronomers to listen to strange sounds from outer space. They believe many of these sounds are made by radio stars, which send out radio waves instead of light waves. Our sun and other visible stars also broadcast "star music."

**STAR, FIVE-POINTED,** is the star most widely pictured as a symbol and in art. The five-pointed stars in the Flag of the United States symbolize the Union of the states. Here are directions for drawing a five-pointed star, and for cutting it out of paper.

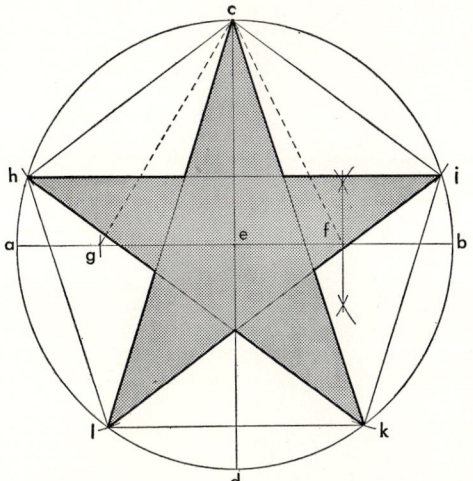

**How to Draw a Star.** This geometric drawing can be made by drawing a four-inch circle. Draw the horizontal and vertical diameter *ab* and *cd*. Mark the point of intersection *e*. Bisect *eb* and mark the point of intersection *f*. With *f* as a center, and *cf* as a radius, describe an arc cutting *ae*. Mark the point of intersection *g*. With *gc* as a radius and *c* as a center, describe two arcs cutting the circumference at *h* and *j*. With *h* and *j* as centers and the same radius, describe arcs cutting the circumference at *k* and *l*. Form a star by connecting *c* and *l*, *c* and *k*, *h* and *k*, *l* and *j*, and *h* and *j*.

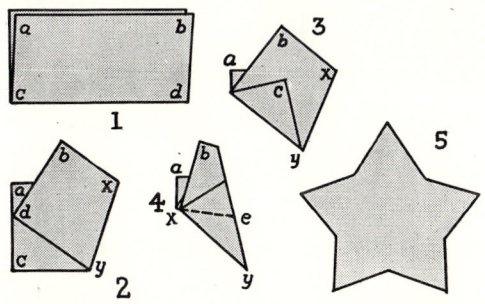

**How to Cut a Star.** The drawings show how a star may be cut quickly by folding paper. Cut on the dotted line, *x* to *e*.

**STAR ANISE.** See ILLICIUM.

**STAR CHAMBER** was an English court of law during the 1500's and 1600's. It tried men too powerful to be brought before the ordinary, common-law courts. The Star Chamber consisted of men from the King's Council, a group of advisers to the king. It passed judgment without trial by jury.

The court was so named because it met in the Star Chamber of Westminster Palace. Today, the term *star chamber* refers to an unregulated, secret meeting of any court of justice or official body.

The Star Chamber was popular for a long time because it protected ordinary men from their oppressors. But eventually it abused its powers. Unlike the common-law courts, which protected the accused, it used torture to obtain confessions. King Charles I used the Star Chamber to crush opposition to his policies. In 1641, the Long Parliament abolished the court (see LONG PARLIAMENT). W. M. SOUTHGATE

**STAR FINDER.** See NAVIGATION (Instruments).

**STAR GRASS** is a flower with six starlike blossoms and yellow-green petals. Star grass grows in Kansas, Florida, and Texas, and from Maine to Ontario.

**Scientific Classification.** The common star grass belongs to the amaryllis family, *Amaryllidaceae*. It is genus *Hypoxis*, species *H. hirsuta*.

**STAR MAPS.** See ASTRONOMY.

**STAR-OF-BETHLEHEM** is a small, hardy plant that belongs to the lily family. It grew first in Italy, but now has become a common garden plant in America. Its flowers form the shape of a six-pointed star. The petal-like parts are white, but have green stripes on the outside.

J. Horace McFarland
**The Star-of-Bethlehem Has Delicate White Flowers.**

The leaves are green with white stripes. The flower stalk rises from a coated bulb.

People grow the star-of-Bethlehem in gardens, greenhouses, and window boxes. Its flowers bloom in May and June, and tend to close before nightfall.

**Scientific Classification.** The star-of-Bethlehem belongs to the lily family, *Liliaceae*. It is genus *Ornithogalum*, species *O. umbellatum*. ALFRED C. HOTTES

**STAR OF DAVID.** See DAVID, STAR OF.

**STAR OF THE SOUTH.** See DIAMOND (Famous Diamonds).

**STAR ROUTE** is a United States postal service. The postal transportation service of the United States Post Office Department makes contracts with agents to carry mail to post offices that are not served by railroads. The routes which these private agents cover are called *star routes*. The mail is usually carried in trucks. An incidental service on some star routes is the delivery and collection of mail in roadside mailboxes of families

667

**The Star-Spangled Banner,** the flag that inspired Francis Scott Key to write the national anthem, hangs in the Museum of History and Technology in Washington, D.C. Key saw the 50-foot-long flag flying over Fort McHenry in Baltimore while he was held prisoner by the British during the War of 1812. The flag covers an entire wall.

D. Jordan Wilson, Pix from Publix

living along the star route. There are over 12,000 star routes. They have an average one-way length of a little over 22 miles a day. Star-route service is not the same as Rural Delivery, which is a direct service of the post office (see RURAL DELIVERY).

The term *star route* comes from the use of three stars, or asterisks, to indicate such a route. The stars replaced the words "Celerity, Certainty, and Security" which were used in Post Office Department records relating to the transportation of mails before 1859.

The development of highway transportation and reduction in railroad operations have brought an increase in star-route service in recent years. They have also resulted in a change from the "horse and buggy" type of transportation to trailer truck operations.

Critically reviewed by the POST OFFICE DEPARTMENT

**STAR-SPANGLED BANNER** is the national anthem of the United States. It was written by Francis Scott Key and is sung to music composed by John Stafford Smith. In March, 1931, Congress officially approved the song as the national anthem. But the Army and Navy had recognized "The Star-Spangled Banner" as the national anthem long before Congress adopted it.

**How the Song Came to Be Written.** During the War of 1812, the British forces took prisoner William Beanes of Upper Marlborough, Md., and held him aboard a warship in Chesapeake Bay. Two Americans received permission from President James Madison to communicate with the British in an effort to have Beanes released. The men were Francis Scott Key, a lawyer, and John S. Skinner, both of Washington, D.C. Key and Skinner boarded the warship just as the vessel was preparing to bombard Fort McHenry, which protected the city of Baltimore. The British agreed to release Beanes. But they held all three Americans on a U.S. prisoner-exchange boat at the rear of the British fleet until after the battle ended, so they could not reveal plans of the attack to patriots on shore.

The bombardment started on Tuesday, Sept. 13, 1814, and continued all that day and almost all night. Key and his friends knew that Fort McHenry had little defense. The prisoners paced the deck all night. Even when dawn came, they did not know who had won the battle because the smoke and haze was so thick.

Suddenly, at 7 o'clock, a break in the mist cleared the view for a moment, and they saw the American flag still flying over the walls of the fort. Key was so excited that he wanted to express his feelings. He pulled an unfinished letter from his pocket and started writing verses. He wrote most of the words of the song in a few

## THE STAR-SPANGLED BANNER

Oh! say, can you see, by the dawn's early light,
What so proudly we hailed at the twilight's last gleaming?
Whose broad stripes and bright stars, thro' the perilous fight,
O'er the ramparts we watched were so gallantly streaming?
And the rockets' red glare, the bombs bursting in air,
Gave proof thro' the night that our flag was still there.
Oh! say, does that star-spangled banner yet wave
O'er the land of the free and the home of the brave?

On the shore, dimly seen thro' the mist of the deep,
Where the foe's haughty host in dread silence reposes,
What is that which the breeze, o'er the towering steep,
As it fitfully blows, half conceals, half discloses?
Now it catches the gleam of the morning's first beam,
In full glory reflected, now shines on the stream.
'Tis the star-spangled banner. Oh! long may it wave
O'er the land of the free and the home of the brave!

And where is that band who so vauntingly swore
That the havoc of war and the battle's confusion
A home and a country should leave us no more?
Their blood has washed out their foul footstep's pollution.
No refuge could save the hireling and slave
From the terror of flight or the gloom of the grave,
And the star-spangled banner in triumph doth wave
O'er the land of the free and the home of the brave.

Oh! thus be it ever when freemen shall stand
Between their loved home and the war's desolation,
Blest with vict'ry and peace, may the Heav'n-rescued land
Praise the Pow'r that hath made and preserved us a nation.
Then conquer we must, when our cause it is just,
And this be our motto, "In God is our trust."
And the star-spangled banner in triumph shall wave
O'er the land of the free and the home of the brave.

---

minutes. Later that day, the British released the Americans, and Key returned to Baltimore, where he finished the other stanzas.

**How the Song Became Famous.** The poem was printed on handbills the next morning and distributed in the city. A few days later, actor Ferdinand Durang sang "The Star-Spangled Banner" in Baltimore to the tune of an old English drinking song called "To Anacreon in Heaven." Americans knew the melody as that of a military march of the 1700's, and as a political song named "Adams and Liberty." Durang's performance marked the first time the anthem was sung in public. It became popular immediately, and three months later it was played during the Battle of New Orleans.

By government permission, the United States flag flies continuously over Key's grave at Frederick, Md., and over Fort McHenry.  RAYMOND KENDALL

See also ANACREON; CONGREVE, SIR WILLIAM; FLAG (Saluting the Flag); KEY, FRANCIS SCOTT.

**STARBOARD.** See SHIP AND SHIPPING (Nautical Terms).

**STARBUCK ISLAND** is an uninhabited coral island in the South Pacific Ocean. It covers about one square mile. At one time, Starbuck Island was an important source of guano, which is used for fertilizer. However, the guano deposits have been depleted. The island was discovered in 1823. Britain maintains a beacon there to guide ships. Both the United States and Great Britain claim Starbuck. For location, see PACIFIC ISLANDS (map).  NEAL M. BOWERS

See also LINE ISLANDS.

**STARCH** is a white, powdery substance found in the living cells of green plants. It can be found in the seeds of corn, wheat, rice, and beans and in the stems, roots, and *tubers* (underground stems) of the potato, arrowroot or cassava (tapioca) plants. Starch is a carbohydrate, one of the most important foods. Starchy foods are an important source of energy for man and animals. When starch is digested in the body, energy is directly obtained from it.

During *photosynthesis* (the food-making process) in green plants, the energy of sunlight changes water and carbon dioxide into glucose and oxygen. Plant cells can quickly convert glucose into starch. Tiny starch *granules* (grains) are formed in most green leaves during the day. At night, the starch is converted back to sugars, which then move to the root, stem, seeds, fruit, and other parts of the plant. The sugar may be used for growth, or stored again as starch.

**Use in Foods.** Starch or flour that contains starch are often used in cooking to thicken mixtures. The mixtures usually become pasty or jellylike. When starchy foods such as rice or macaroni are cooked, the starch granules swell and absorb water. Starch does not dissolve in water. Cooked starch is easily broken down in the body by digestive *enzymes* (chemicals). But uncooked starch is too insoluble to be digested easily.

During the cooking of some foods, the starch may change into other substances. For example, slightly scorched starch becomes *dextrin*, a sticky carbohydrate that is used as glue on stamps and envelopes. During bread making a small amount of starch becomes the sugar *maltose*. Maltose is fermented by yeast and changed into carbon dioxide and alcohol. The carbon dioxide forms bubbles in the bread dough and makes it rise.

Chemists use iodine to test for the presence of starch in food. When a small amount of iodine is added to a starch solution, it becomes blue-black. Under the microscope, starch appears as tiny granules. Cornstarch granules are rounded, irregular *polygons* (many-sided) about 10 to 20 microns in diameter. Potato starch granules are oval with *concentric* (common center) rings and may be more than 100 microns in diameter. Rice starch has tiny granules about 3 to 5 microns in diameter. With experience, a person can identify a certain kind of starch by the way it looks under a microscope.

**Industrial Uses.** Industry manufactures over 5 billion pounds of starch in the United States each year. About half is sold as starch and dextrin, and $1\frac{1}{2}$ billion pounds are converted into starch syrup. Most of the starch is used to *size* (stiffen) weaving yarn and to finish the cloth. Starch gives high-quality paper strength and a smooth, glossy finish. Starches are also used in making paste-

Russ Kinne, Photo Researchers; Bart Cadbury, NAS

**Most Starfishes Have Five Arms,** *above left*, although some kinds have as many as 50 arms. There are many tube feet on the underside of each arm, *above right*. Each of the tube feet has a tiny suction disk at its tip. The starfish uses its tube feet and suction disks to crawl over the seabed.

board, corrugated board, plywood, and wallboard. A starch called *Amioca* is produced from *waxy maize* (a kind of corn). Amioca produces pastes that are clear and fluid, unlike cornstarch.

To manufacture cornstarch, corn is soaked in warm water and sulfur dioxide for two days. The softened kernels are torn apart and the *germ* (part of the inside) is removed. The kernel fragments are then ground and *screened* (sifted) down to starch and *gluten* (proteins). The starch is then filtered, washed, dried, and packaged. Similar processes are used for starch from waxy maize and sorghum.

To make potato starch, the potatoes are washed and ground, and the starch is separated from potato fibers by screening. After further separation, the starch is washed and dried. Arrowroot and tapioca starch may be produced by similar methods.

Wheat starch can be manufactured by *kneading* (mixing) wheat flour into a dough. The starch is washed out of the sticky mass by a stream of water. Rice starch is made by soaking the grain in an alkaline chemical, which dissolves the gluten but not the starch. The starch is then separated and washed.   DEXTER FRENCH

**Related Articles** in WORLD BOOK include:

| | | |
|---|---|---|
| Arrowroot | Cornstarch | Sago |
| Carbohydrate | Dextrin | Tapioca |
| Cellulose | | |

**STARFISH,** or SEA STAR, is a sea animal that has armlike extensions on its body. Most *species* (kinds) have five "arms" and look somewhat like five-pointed stars. However, not all starfish look like stars. Some have such short arms that their body looks like a *pentagon* (five-sided shape). Others have many arms. They are called *sun stars* because their shape resembles the sun and its rays.

Starfish live in all of the world's oceans. But they are not fish. They are members of a group of animals called *echinoderms*. The echinoderm group also includes the brittle star, sea cucumber, sea lily, and sea urchin. See ECHINODERM.

The starfish body has a *central disk* and *arms*. Its mouth, in the middle of the underside of the central disk, leads directly into a large, baglike stomach. On the outside of the body, a groove extends from the mouth to the tip of each arm. Rows of slender tubes, called *tube feet*, line these grooves. The animal uses the suction disk at the end of each tube foot for crawling. These disks grip hard surfaces. The starfish "sees" with a small colored *eyespot* located at the tip of each arm. The eyespot senses light, but cannot form images. The starfish uses its tube feet and a tiny, sensitive *tentacle* located at the tip of each arm to "feel."

Starfish release eggs into the sea through small holes between their arms. The eggs form into tiny swimming larvae. After a while, each larva settles down on the sea bottom and develops into a starfish. Starfish can *regenerate* (grow again) new arms when the old ones are broken off. Even if a starfish is cut in two, each of the pieces will regenerate into a new animal. Most starfish live for three to five years, but some may live as long as seven years.

Many starfish feed on shelled animals such as mussels, clams, and oysters. The starfish can push its stomach out through its mouth. When it feeds on an oyster, it attaches its tube feet to the two halves of the oyster's shell and pulls the shell halves apart, opening a tiny crack between them. Then the starfish pushes its stomach, turned inside out, through the crack. A starfish can slide its stomach through a crack no larger than the thickness of a piece of cardboard. The stomach surrounds the oyster's soft body, slowly digests it, and absorbs the food into the starfish's body. Such starfish are serious pests in the oyster-breeding grounds of the eastern coast of the United States.

**Scientific Classification.** Starfish belong to the phylum *Echinodermata*. They are classified in the class *Asteroidea*.   ROBERT D. BARNES

See also ANIMAL (color picture: Animals of the Oceans; picture: How Animals Eat).

**STARK, JOHANNES** (1874-1957), a German physicist, was noted for his discovery of the *Stark effect*. This discovery, the splitting of spectral lines when an emitting atom is in an electrical field, won for him the 1919 Nobel prize in physics. He also noted the change in frequency of light from moving atoms in a gas-discharge tube. This was the first observation of the optical *Doppler effect* from a source other than the stars (see RELATIVITY [General Relativity Theory]).

Stark was born at Schickenhof, Bavaria. He attended schools in Bayreuth and Regensburg. At the University of Munich, he studied physics, chemistry, mathematics, and crystallography. After graduation, he taught in technical high schools at Hannover and Aachen.

In 1917, Stark went as a professor of physics to the University of Greifswald. From there, he went as a professor to the University of Würzburg in 1920. He served as president of a technical institute in Charlottenburg from 1933 to 1939.   CARL T. CHASE

**STARK, JOHN** (1728-1822), was a leading American general in the Revolutionary War. His crushing defeat of Colonel Friedrich Baum's raiding party of Germans, Tories, Canadians, and Indians near Bennington, Vt., on Aug. 16, 1777, was a turning point of the war. It was a severe setback to General John Burgoyne's campaign to cut the American colonies in half.

Stark's New Hampshire regiment defended the American left wing at Bunker Hill in 1775. He helped cover the 1776 retreat from Canada, commanded units at the battles of Trenton and Princeton, and served in the Rhode Island campaign of 1779. Stark was born in Londonderry, N.H. He served with Rogers' Rangers in the French and Indian War from 1754 to 1763. A statue of Stark represents New Hampshire in the U.S. Capitol in Washington, D.C.      CLINTON ROSSITER

**STARLING** is a black songbird with pointed wings, a short tail, and a long, sharp bill. Its feathers have a greenish-purple or lilac gloss, and are tipped with buff during the winter. Starlings live in large flocks, sometimes even during the nesting season. The birds make nests in hollow trees, in birdhouses, or in holes in cliffs. The female starling lays from 4 to 6 light-blue eggs.

The starling is helpful to farmers because it eats great numbers of harmful insects. But in the fruit season it is a pest because it also eats many berries, cherries, and even apples and pears. Starlings that roost in trees and on buildings are a nuisance to city-dwellers.

The starling came originally from the British Isles and other parts of Europe. In 1890, about 60 starlings were set free in Central Park in New York City. About 40 more were set free in 1891. Millions of starlings now live in the United States. The starlings in Norway and Sweden fly to Southern Europe when winter arrives.

**Scientific Classification.** Starlings are members of the starling family, *Sturnidae*. The starling of North America and much of Europe is classified as genus *Sturnus*, species *S. vulgaris*.      ALBERT WOLFSON

See also BIRD (color picture: Birds' Eggs).
**STARR, ELLEN.** See HULL HOUSE.
**STARR, RINGO.** See BEATLES.
**STARS AND BARS.** See FLAG (color picture: Flags in American History [Confederate Flags]).
**STARS AND STRIPES.** See FLAG (Flags of the U.S.).
**STARS AND STRIPES** is the name of an official army newspaper published during World Wars I and II, and in the occupied countries of Germany and Japan. The name was first used for a weekly newspaper which was published by the American Expeditionary Forces of World War I. The *Stars and Stripes* of World War II was published in London, Paris, the Mediterranean area, the Middle East, Tokyo, Manila, Honolulu, and other places.

The World War II publication began on April 17, 1942, as a weekly in London. Later, as the American forces in England grew, it was published daily. The staff was usually made up of soldiers with civilian newspaper training. Their object was to present war news and information of interest to army men.      EARL FRANKLIN ENGLISH

**STARTER** is a device that sets an engine in motion. Starters use various kinds of power, including human muscle, electricity, compressed air, and even exploding cartridges.

**Automobile Starters.** The gasoline engines in early automobiles had to be started with a crank. A driver had to pull or spin the crank to make the crankshaft revolve and start the engine. Cranking a car was hard work, especially in cold weather when the oil in the engine was stiff. The engine sometimes backfired and spun the hand crank in the wrong direction. This spin could break a man's arm.

Charles F. Kettering developed the first successful electric starter for automobiles. It was first installed in a Cadillac in February, 1911. The chief parts of this starter are the motor and the drive. When the driver turns on the ignition and presses the starter switch, a heavy current from the car's storage battery turns the starter motor. A drive shaft and gear connect the starter motor to the engine's flywheel. The crankshaft revolves, the pistons and rods go up and down, and the engine starts firing. An automatic device then disconnects the starter motor from the engine. Without this device, the engine would turn the starter too fast and ruin it.

**Diesel Starters.** Diesel engines require more starting power than gasoline engines because they work at much higher compression. Some Diesel engines use powerful electric starters similar to those for automobile gasoline engines. Railroad locomotive Diesels use their generators as electric starters. Many Diesels are started by pumping compressed air directly to some of the cylinders. The air drives the pistons until the engine fires of its own accord. A small auxiliary, or helper, engine starts other Diesels.

**The Aggressive Starling** often steals the nests of other birds for its home. The male has glossy black plumage.      John Gerard

# STARTER

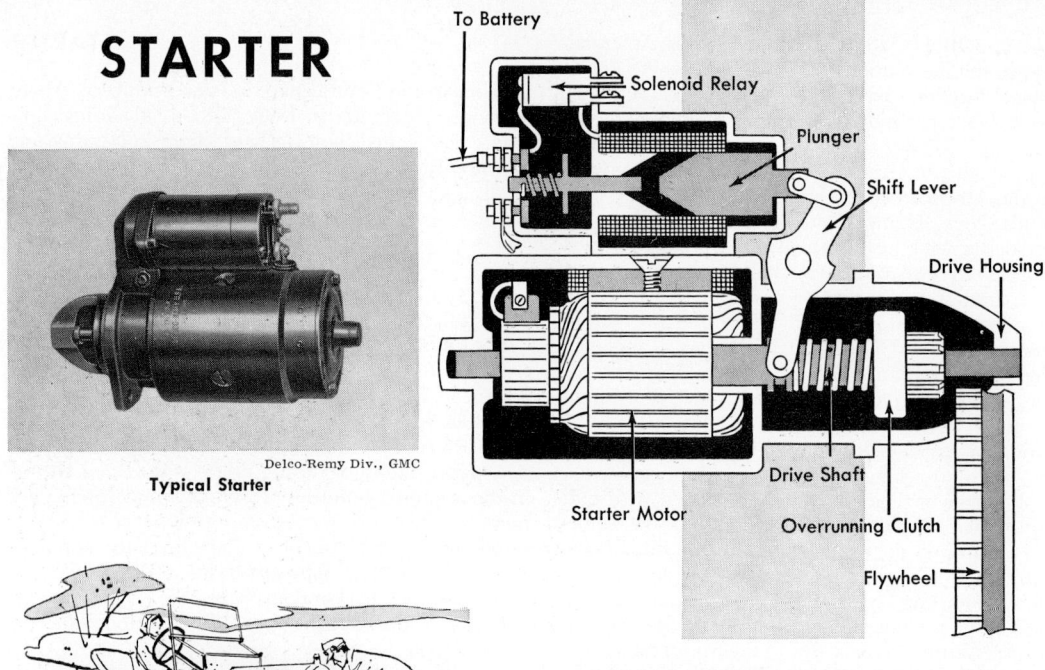

**Typical Starter** — Delco-Remy Div., GMC

**An Automobile Starter** is an electric motor that receives its power from a battery. When a driver engages the starter, the relay connects the motor to the battery. The plunger moves the clutch into position with the engine's flywheel. The revolving starter shaft turns the flywheel, which turns over the engine. The starter then disconnects automatically.

**Airplane Starters.** Mechanics started the first airplanes by pulling the propeller by hand. Then aircraft engineers developed the *inertia starter*. This has a small flywheel that is set spinning by hand or by an electric motor. When gears engage this flywheel with the engine crankshaft, it turns the engine. Aircraft also use compressed-air starters, exploding cartridges, special hand cranks, and electric-motor starters.   FRANKLIN M. RECK

See also DIESEL ENGINE; GASOLINE ENGINE.

**STARVATION** occurs when a living thing dies from lack of food or certain kinds of food. Most plants need water, sunlight, and chemicals from the soil. If any of these foods is removed, the plant eventually dies. Man needs minerals, vitamins, water, and foods such as carbohydrates, fats, and proteins. If he does not receive enough of each, his body wastes away, and he finally starves.

Man needs certain foods because his body cells do not work properly without them. Without food, a cell must use up its own parts to keep working. During its first few days without food, the body uses *glycogen* (also called animal starch) that has been kept in the liver as reserve food. But the main reserves of the body are fat and, later, muscle. As the time without food goes on, the vital cells become so weakened that death occurs.

If man has enough water, he can fast from 40 to 50 days without suffering permanent injury. He will drop to about half his normal weight during that period, however.   EWALD E. SELKURT

See also FAST; NUTRITION.

**STARVED ROCK STATE PARK.** See LA SALLE, SIEUR DE.

**STASSEN, HAROLD EDWARD** (1907-    ), former governor of Minnesota, served as Special Assistant for Disarmament to President Dwight D. Eisenhower from 1955 to 1958. He was a candidate for the Republican nomination for President in 1948 and 1952.

Stassen was born near St. Paul, Minn., and was graduated from the University of Minnesota. After serving as attorney of Dakota County, he was elected governor in 1938 and was re-elected twice. While governor, Stassen revised the civil-service laws and lowered the costs of state government. He supported a labor law that provided a "cooling-off" period before strikes. This brought him national recognition. Early in his third term, he resigned to serve in the navy.

In 1945, Stassen became a delegate to the San Francisco Conference which founded the United Nations. He was appointed president of the University of Pennsylvania in 1948. Stassen resigned in 1953 to serve as Mutual Security Administrator, and then as Foreign Operations Administrator, a position which controlled American aid to many countries. Stassen resigned as Special Assistant for Disarmament to President Eisenhower in 1958 to seek the nomination for governor of Pennsylvania, but lost.   RICHARD L. WATSON, JR.

**Harold Stassen**
Rosenthal, Pix

**STATE.** See STATE GOVERNMENT; UNITED STATES.

672

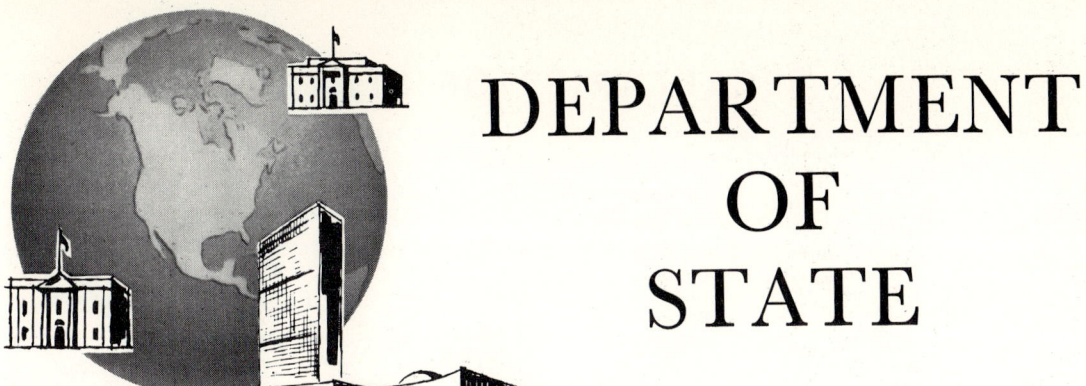

# DEPARTMENT OF STATE

**STATE, DEPARTMENT OF,** is the executive department of the United States government that handles U.S. relations with other governments. The head of the department is the *secretary of state*, the senior member of the President's Cabinet. The secretary and his department advise the President on foreign relations and provide him with information about conditions in other countries.

The department, with advice from the U.S. Congress, plans United States actions in dealing with other governments. When the President approves these plans, they become the official *foreign policy* of the United States. The department is responsible for carrying out foreign policy. It also coordinates the actions of other executive departments that affect foreign policy.

The department negotiates treaties and agreements with other governments; handles official business with foreign embassies in Washington; speaks for the United States in the United Nations and other international organizations; and arranges for U.S. participation in international conferences. The Department of State is also the official custodian of the Great Seal of the United States, which is affixed to all presidential proclamations (see GREAT SEAL OF THE UNITED STATES).

Members of the Foreign Service, the operating arm of the department in other countries, represent the United States throughout the world. They deal with officials of other governments and report to the department on developments that affect the United States. These reports give the President and the secretary of state much of the information on which U.S. foreign policy is based. Members of the Foreign Service also issue passports; grant visas to persons visiting or emigrating to the United States; protect U.S. citizens and their property in other countries; and help businessmen promote U.S. trade and investment.

The Department of State carries on educational and cultural exchanges with other countries. It arranges for students, teachers, and leaders to visit the United States, and for U.S. citizens to study and teach abroad. It promotes public understanding of U.S. foreign policy through information services and publications.

Four other government agencies responsible for foreign-affairs programs receive special guidance from the Department of State. Two—the Agency for International Development (AID) and the Peace Corps—are part of the department. AID administers the U.S. foreign aid program. Peace Corps volunteers train persons in underdeveloped nations.

The Department of State also works closely with the United States Information Agency (USIA) and the United States Arms Control and Disarmament Agency (ACDA), although both are independent agencies. USIA explains U.S. foreign policy and life in the United States to persons in other countries. ACDA formulates United States policy on the control of weapons and disarmament.

## Secretary of State

**Responsibilities.** The secretary of state is appointed by the President with the approval of the Senate. He is the highest-ranking member of the Cabinet and comes after the Vice-President, the speaker of the House, and the president *pro tempore* of the Senate in order of succession to the presidency.

The secretary is the President's chief adviser on foreign affairs. He is responsible for operating the Department of State and carrying out foreign policy. He must identify the major international problems that the United States faces and develop the strategy to deal with them. The secretary serves on the National Security Council and the National Aeronautics and Space Council.

**Relationship with the President and Congress.** The role of the secretary depends on his relationship with the President. Some Presidents have had strong opinions concerning foreign policy and have formulated their own policy. Therefore, they have been, in effect, their own secretaries of state. Secretaries serving such Presidents have had less influence and prestige than those who have served Presidents who were primarily interested in domestic affairs.

The secretary's relationship to Congress is also vital because congressional actions often affect foreign affairs. For example, treaties arranged by the secretary must be approved by the Senate. The Senate also passes on the appointment of ambassadors and other officials. The Congress controls the money that the secretary needs to carry out his policies. In fact, nearly every committee of Congress affects foreign policy. To gain congressional support, the secretary must present the administration's foreign policies effectively. His success with Congress depends mainly on the President's political strength in the country. But the secretary must try to keep partisan politics out of his dealings with Congress. Generally, Congress tries to take a *bipartisan* (nonpolitical) attitude in dealing with foreign affairs.

The type of man appointed secretary of state has changed over the years. In the late 1700's and early 1800's, the post often served as a stepping stone to the presidency. Thomas Jefferson, James Madison, James

673

# SECRETARIES OF STATE

The post of secretary of state was a stepping stone to the presidency during the early years of the United States. Six secretaries have become President. But none has become President since James Buchanan was elected in 1856.

Thomas Jefferson

James Madison

James Monroe

John Quincy Adams

Martin Van Buren

James Buchanan

| Name | Year Appointed | Under President |
|------|----------------|-----------------|
| *Thomas Jefferson | 1789 | Washington |
| *Edmund Randolph | 1794 | Washington |
| *Timothy Pickering | 1795 | Washington, J. Adams |
| *John Marshall | 1800 | J. Adams |
| *James Madison | 1801 | Jefferson |
| Robert Smith | 1809 | Madison |
| *James Monroe | 1811 | Madison |
| *John Quincy Adams | 1817 | Monroe |
| *Henry Clay | 1825 | J. Q. Adams |
| *Martin Van Buren | 1829 | Jackson |
| Edward Livingston | 1831 | Jackson |
| Louis McLane | 1833 | Jackson |
| John Forsyth | 1834 | Jackson, Van Buren |
| *Daniel Webster | 1841 | W. H. Harrison, Tyler |
| Abel P. Upshur | 1843 | Tyler |
| *John C. Calhoun | 1844 | Tyler |
| *James Buchanan | 1845 | Polk |
| *John M. Clayton | 1849 | Taylor |
| *Daniel Webster | 1850 | Fillmore |
| *Edward Everett | 1852 | Fillmore |
| William L. Marcy | 1853 | Pierce |
| *Lewis Cass | 1857 | Buchanan |
| Jeremiah S. Black | 1860 | Buchanan |
| *William H. Seward | 1861 | Lincoln, A. Johnson |
| *Elihu B. Washburne | 1869 | Grant |
| *Hamilton Fish | 1869 | Grant |
| *William M. Evarts | 1877 | Hayes |
| *James G. Blaine | 1881 | Garfield, Arthur |

| Name | Year Appointed | Under President |
|------|----------------|-----------------|
| F. T. Frelinghuysen | 1881 | Arthur |
| *Thomas F. Bayard | 1885 | Cleveland |
| *James G. Blaine | 1889 | B. Harrison |
| John W. Foster | 1892 | B. Harrison |
| Walter Q. Gresham | 1893 | Cleveland |
| *Richard Olney | 1895 | Cleveland |
| *John Sherman | 1897 | McKinley |
| William R. Day | 1898 | McKinley |
| *John M. Hay | 1898 | McKinley, T. Roosevelt |
| *Elihu Root | 1905 | T. Roosevelt |
| Robert Bacon | 1909 | T. Roosevelt |
| *Philander C. Knox | 1909 | Taft |
| *William J. Bryan | 1913 | Wilson |
| *Robert Lansing | 1915 | Wilson |
| Bainbridge Colby | 1920 | Wilson |
| *Charles E. Hughes | 1921 | Harding, Coolidge |
| *Frank B. Kellogg | 1925 | Coolidge |
| *Henry L. Stimson | 1929 | Hoover |
| *Cordell Hull | 1933 | F. D. Roosevelt |
| *Edward R. Stettinius, Jr. | 1944 | F. D. Roosevelt, Truman |
| *James F. Byrnes | 1945 | Truman |
| *George C. Marshall | 1947 | Truman |
| *Dean G. Acheson | 1949 | Truman |
| *John Foster Dulles | 1953 | Eisenhower |
| *Christian A. Herter | 1959 | Eisenhower |
| *Dean Rusk | 1961 | Kennedy, L. B. Johnson |
| *William P. Rogers | 1969 | Nixon |

*Has a separate biography in WORLD BOOK.

Monroe, John Quincy Adams, Martin Van Buren, and James Buchanan all served in the office before being elected President. Other secretaries, such as Henry Clay, Daniel Webster, John C. Calhoun, William H. Seward, and James G. Blaine, were appointed secretary of state mainly because they were political leaders.

In the 1900's, secretaries have been selected mainly for their experience and ability in foreign affairs. John Hay was a career diplomat. Cordell Hull, who won the Nobel peace prize while secretary of state, had served in both the Senate and the House of Representatives. John Foster Dulles, who specialized in "personal diplomacy," had been a UN delegate and a senator. Both Christian Herter and Dean Rusk served in high State Department posts before becoming secretaries of state.

### Organization of the Department

The department's employees work both in the United States and in many countries overseas.

**American Headquarters** are in Washington, D.C. About 7,000 persons work there in the Department of State Building. Dedicated in 1961, the building covers four city blocks.

The secretary of state has five main assistants—four *undersecretaries* and a *counselor*. The undersecretary of state directs the department in the secretary's absence. The undersecretary for political affairs is the secretary's chief adviser on foreign policy. He is assisted by the

674

# STATE, DEPARTMENT OF

Department of State

PRESIDENT

The Department of State acts as the President's chief adviser in forming and carrying out U.S. foreign policy. The department's headquarters, *left,* are on C Street, Washington, D.C.

SECRETARY OF STATE

UNDERSECRETARY OF STATE

UNDERSECRETARY FOR POLITICAL AFFAIRS

- Inspector General Foreign Assistance
- Protocol
- Executive Secretariat

- Arms Control and Disarmament Agency
- Agency for International Development
- Peace Corps

**Deputy Undersecretary for Political Affairs**

- Legal Adviser
- Counselor
- Policy Planning Council
- Congressional Relations
- International Scientific and Technological Affairs
- Public Affairs
- Educational and Cultural Affairs
- East Asian and Pacific Affairs
- Near Eastern and South Asian Affairs

**Deputy Undersecretary for Administration**
**Director General Foreign Service**

- Security and Consular Affairs
- Foreign Service Institute
- Administrative Offices and Programs
- Foreign Service Inspection Corps
- Intelligence and Research
- Economic Affairs
- African Affairs
- European Affairs
- Inter-American Affairs
- International Organization Affairs

Diplomatic Missions and Delegations to International Organizations

674a

**United States Embassies** serve as headquarters for American Foreign Service officials in most countries of the world. The United States embassy in Athens, *left*, houses the State Department delegation to Greece.

U.S. Dept. of State

deputy undersecretary for political affairs, and the deputy undersecretary for administration. The counselor also serves as a senior adviser to the secretary.

The *Policy Planning Council* is made up of a small group of experts who have no regular administrative duties, but devote themselves to planning. They analyze long-range international relations problems and their probable effect on U.S. foreign policy.

*Specialized Bureaus*, usually headed by assistant secretaries, do the day-to-day work of the department. Five bureaus, organized on a geographic basis, handle U.S. foreign relations. They are (1) European Affairs (which includes Russia), (2) Inter-American Affairs, (3) African Affairs, (4) Near Eastern and South Asian Affairs, and (5) East Asian and Pacific Affairs.

The Bureau of International Organization Affairs conducts U.S. relations with the United Nations and other international organizations. The Bureau of Economic Affairs deals with international finance, trade, tariffs, shipping, aviation, and telecommunication matters. The Bureau of Intelligence and Research analyzes the information coming into the department and reports on important international situations.

The Bureau of Educational and Cultural Affairs directs programs for student and cultural exchanges and for grants to educational institutions in other countries. The Bureau of Public affairs informs the public on foreign affairs, publishes periodicals and pamphlets on current U.S. foreign policy, and keeps the official historical record of U.S. foreign relations. The Bureau of Security and Consular Affairs supervises such duties as issuing passports and visas and protecting U.S. citizens abroad. It also protects *classified* (secret) information. The deputy undersecretary for administration manages the budget, personnel, and operations.

The assistant secretary for congressional relations

**The American Embassy in Dublin** houses the State Department delegation which represents the U.S. government in Ireland.
U.S. Dept. of State

**The Embassy in Buenos Aires** is the home of the American Ambassador to Argentina. American flags fly over U.S. embassies.
U.S. Dept. of State

674b

handles affairs between the department and Congress. His office directs the presentation of the department's legislative programs to Congress.

The *Executive Secretariat* of the department coordinates recommendations for actions that come to the secretary and other senior department officials for decision. It directs the Operations Center, which maintains a round-the-clock watch on world affairs and keeps top department officials informed of world developments.

The *chief of protocol* advises the secretary in matters of national and international *protocol* (traditional courtesies shown to officials). For example, the chief of protocol handles the arrangements when the ruler of another country visits the President.

The *U.S. Mission to the United Nations*, in New York City, is part of the department's home organization. The *Mission of the U.S. Representative to the Council of the Organization of American States* (OAS), in Washington, D.C., is also under the department.

**Overseas Missions.** The department has about 275 diplomatic and consular offices in other countries. In the late 1960's, over 7,000 Americans worked at overseas posts. The Foreign Service also employed about 10,000 citizens of other countries.

### History of the Department

**Establishment.** The Department of State is the oldest executive department of the United States government. During the Revolutionary War, the Continental Congress dealt with other countries through its Committee on Secret Correspondence. This committee was established in 1775 with Benjamin Franklin as its first chairman. In 1777, the group was renamed the Committee for Foreign Affairs.

On Jan. 10, 1781, the Continental Congress created a *Department of Foreign Affairs*. Robert Livingston became the first secretary of foreign affairs, and John Jay succeeded him in 1784. After the adoption of the Constitution, Congress set up the Department of Foreign Affairs on July 27, 1789, as an executive agency under the President. Congress changed its name to the *Department of State* on Sept. 15, 1789. The department originally performed such domestic duties as operating the mint, issuing patents, and taking the census. Most of the department's domestic duties have since been transferred to other departments.

President George Washington appointed Thomas Jefferson as the first secretary of state in 1789. But Jay continued as temporary secretary until Jefferson assumed the office in 1790. Under Jefferson, the department had a staff of eight persons. The Foreign Service consisted of legations in London and Paris, an agency at The Hague, and 10 consular offices.

**Growth.** Before World War II, the department grew slowly. The interests of the United States then centered on domestic matters. Foreign affairs became important only during such crises as the Civil War and World War I. The U.S. shunned alliances with other countries, and the department received scant attention from the public and little support from Congress.

In 1833, separate bureaus were set up to supervise the work of U.S. diplomatic and consular representatives. In 1870, the department's work was spread among nine bureaus and two agencies. The Civil Service Act of 1883 and introduction of the merit system enabled the department to hire more highly qualified employees (see CIVIL SERVICE). In 1909 and 1910, the department added four geographic divisions to handle U.S. relations with the rest of the world.

The department's work increased greatly in World War I. Its Washington staff rose to more than 400 in 1918. After World War I, American foreign relations became more important and complex. Congress passed the Rogers Act in 1924 to strengthen the department's overseas organization. In 1939, the Foreign Service absorbed the separate overseas services of the Commerce and Agriculture departments.

**World War II and the Cold War** expanded department activities still more. The war showed that U.S. security depended on affairs in the rest of the world. Americans felt they must cooperate with other nations to maintain peace. The department took over various war agencies that had gathered information and dispensed aid abroad, and assumed new administrative duties in occupied Germany and Japan. It adopted new economic and military aid programs and set up security arrangements with over 40 nations.

In 1946, the Foreign Service was reorganized. The Policy Planning Staff and the Executive Secretariat were set up in 1947. In 1949 and 1950, the department adopted many of the Hoover Commission's recommendations (see HOOVER COMMISSION).

Between 1954 and 1957, the department integrated its home and foreign services. The office of the Inspector General, Foreign Assistance; the Peace Corps; and the Agency for International Development were established as agencies within the department in 1961.

*Critically reviewed by the* DEPARTMENT OF STATE

Related Articles in WORLD BOOK include:
Agency for International Development
Diplomacy
Diplomatic Corps
Disarmament Agency, United States
Flag (picture: Flags of the U.S. Government)
Foreign Aid
Foreign Policy
Foreign Service
International Relations
Peace Corps
Presidential Succession
United States Information Agency

**STATE AND CHURCH.** See CHURCH AND STATE.

**STATE BANKS.** See BANKS AND BANKING (Commercial Banks).

**STATE BIRDS.** See BIRD (table: State and Provincial Birds) and the color pictures with state articles, such as SOUTH CAROLINA (color picture: The State Bird).

**STATE CAPITALS.** See UNITED STATES (table); and the picture with each state article.

**STATE COLLEGES.** See the Education section in each state article, such as ALABAMA (Education).

**STATE FAIR.** For the date and place of state fairs in the United States, see the Annual Events sections in the various state articles, such as ALABAMA (Annual Events).

**STATE FLAGS.** For a description and color picture of the flag of each state of the United States, see the color picture in each state article, such as ALABAMA (color picture: The State Flag). For color pictures of all the state flags together, see the FLAG article.

**STATE FLOWERS.** See FLOWER (table: Flowers of the States); UNITED STATES (table: Facts in Brief About the States); also color picture in each state article.

# STATE GOVERNMENT

**STATE GOVERNMENT** provides many services and regulates many activities for the people of a state. In the United States, a state government maintains law and order and enforces criminal law. It protects property rights and regulates corporations. It supervises public education, including schools and state universities. It operates public-welfare programs, builds and maintains most highways, operates state parks and forests, and regulates the use of state-owned land. It has direct authority over local governments—counties, cities, towns, townships, villages, and school districts.

The national government in some countries, such as Great Britain, operates under the *unitary system*. That is, it defines and establishes the powers of the local governments. But in the United States, a state government has independent powers of its own that are authorized by the Constitution. In such a *federal system*, the national government cannot change these powers formally without the agreement of the state government. The national government has its powers specified in the Constitution, and the state governments retain all the remaining powers, except where the Constitution restricts them. See STATES' RIGHTS.

The independent powers of state governments arose during the colonial period. After the Declaration of Independence in 1776, each former British colony quite properly called itself a *state* to indicate its sovereign position. The term generally means a group of persons who live in a definite territory, and who are organized under a sovereign government.

Each state gave up some of its powers when the Constitution became the supreme law of the land in 1789. The state governments, like the federal government, have three main branches: (1) executive, (2) legislative, and (3) judicial.

Through the years, a strong tendency has developed toward enlarging the activities of the national government in the United States. Often a state must agree to accept some federal regulation in order to share in federal funds for particular purposes. An increasing centralization of functions within each state has also occurred. At the same time, cooperation among all levels of government—national, state, and local—has become an increasingly important development.

## State Constitutions

Each state has a constitution that sets forth the principles and framework of its government. Every state constitution includes a bill of rights. Many have provisions on finance, public welfare, education, and the regulation of business. State constitutions range in length from fewer than 5,000 words for Vermont to more than 250,000 words for Louisiana.

A few states drew up constitutions before the United States Constitution was adopted. But the only one of these early constitutions still in use is that of Massachusetts. Constitutional conventions prepared most of the constitutions now in use.

A state constitution may be amended in several ways. The state legislature may propose an amendment and submit it to the people for approval. Some legislatures may ratify the amendment without a popular vote. In some states, the people may suggest an amendment and vote on it in a state-wide election. Constitutional conventions or commissions may also adopt amendments.

## Executive Branch

**The Governor** elected by the people heads the executive branch in each state. He has the power to appoint, direct, and remove from office a large number of state officials. The state constitution authorizes him to see that the laws are faithfully executed. The governor commands the state militia, grants pardons, and may call the state legislature into special session. He directs the preparation of the state budget. He may veto bills, and, in most states, may even veto parts of a bill. As the state leader of his political party, he gives the legislature much of its political leadership.

Most state governors serve four-year terms. The others hold office for two years. Some state constitutions provide that the governor cannot serve two terms in succession. In a few states, the governor cannot serve *more* than two terms in succession. In all states, he may be removed from office by impeachment. Upon the death of the governor, the lieutenant governor succeeds him in most states.

The powers of state governors in the United States have steadily increased. In colonial times, governors had only limited authority, because the people had learned to distrust the royal governors appointed by the kings of England. The office of governor has grown in stature since 1776. Some governors have more power than others. That is, they have more authority to appoint and control subordinate officials. See GOVERNOR.

**Other Officers.** In most states, the people elect several other executive officials. These officers usually include a lieutenant governor, secretary of state, treasurer, auditor, and attorney general. In some states, the governor or legislature appoints one or more of these officials. In about half the states, a state board of education or the governor appoints a superintendent of public instruction or education. In the other states, the voters elect this official.

In most states, the lieutenant governor presides over the state senate. The secretary of state administers election laws, publishes legislative acts, and directs the state archives. The attorney general advises the governor and his staff on legal matters. He prosecutes or defends cases that involve the state. The superintendent of public instruction administers state schools and distributes school funds. The treasurer collects and maintains state funds. The auditor receives claims against the state and decides which should be paid. He also examines the financial records of state agencies.

## Legislative Branch

The legislature of a state passes laws, levies taxes, and approves money to be spent by the state government. It takes part in amending the state constitution, and has the power to impeach officials.

**Organization.** Every state except Nebraska follows the example of Congress and has a *bicameral*, or two-house, legislature. Every upper house is called *the senate*. In almost all states, the lower house is called *the house of representatives*. A *speaker* presides over the house of representatives. Its members usually represent counties. A lieutenant governor presides over the senate in most states. Its members usually represent counties, towns,

# ORGANIZATION OF A TYPICAL STATE GOVERNMENT

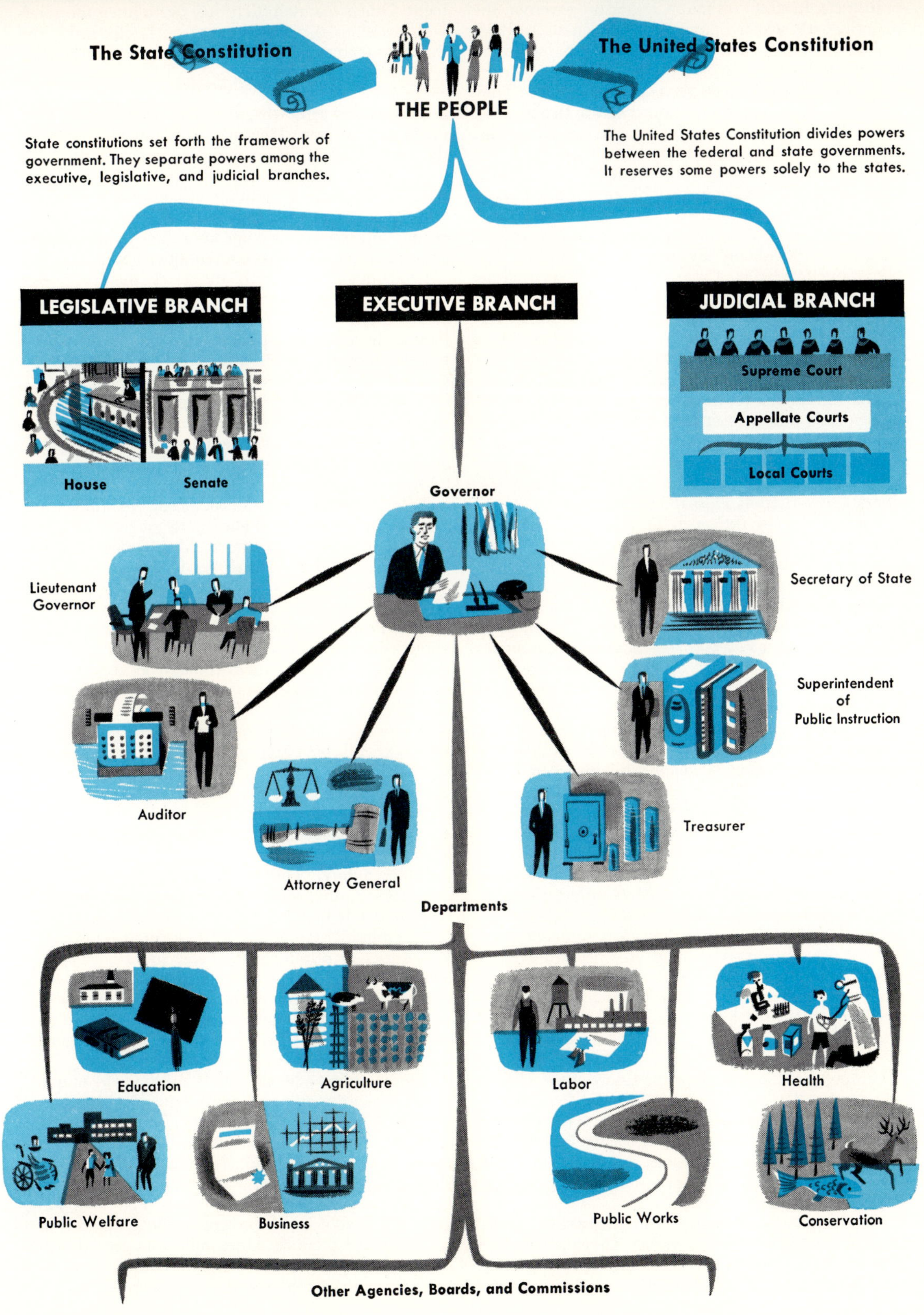

**The State Constitution**

**THE PEOPLE**

**The United States Constitution**

State constitutions set forth the framework of government. They separate powers among the executive, legislative, and judicial branches.

The United States Constitution divides powers between the federal and state governments. It reserves some powers solely to the states.

## LEGISLATIVE BRANCH

House · Senate

## EXECUTIVE BRANCH

Governor

- Lieutenant Governor
- Auditor
- Attorney General
- Secretary of State
- Superintendent of Public Instruction
- Treasurer

**Departments**

- Education
- Agriculture
- Labor
- Health
- Public Welfare
- Business
- Public Works
- Conservation

**Other Agencies, Boards, and Commissions**

## JUDICIAL BRANCH

Supreme Court

Appellate Courts

Local Courts

# STATE GOVERNMENT

or districts. In states without a lieutenant governor, the majority party selects a president of the senate. In 1934, Nebraska adopted a *unicameral* (one-house) legislature to simplify lawmaking.

Senators in most states serve four-year terms. They hold office for two years in the other states. In almost all states, members of the lower house serve two-year terms. In a few states, they serve four-year terms.

State senates range in size from 19 members in Delaware to 67 in Minnesota. The lower houses range from 39 members in Delaware to 400 in New Hampshire.

Salaries of legislators vary from $100 a year in New Hampshire to $10,000 a year in New York. Legislators in some states receive daily payments while the legislature is in session, rather than yearly salaries. The payments vary from $5 a day in North Dakota and Rhode Island to $30 a day in Iowa. All states give legislators travel allowances, and many give other allowances.

The legislatures of about half the states meet annually. The others meet in regular session *biennially* (every other year). Every legislature may be called into special session by the governor. The constitutions of most states limit the length of regular sessions. These limitations vary from 30 to 195 calendar days.

The legislatures do much of their work through *standing*, or *permanent*, *committees*. The typical legislative chamber has about 22 such committees. A few states have joint committees instead of standing committees. A joint committee includes members from both houses. It considers proposed bills and reports to both houses. Many states set up *ad interim* (temporary) committees to study a particular problem during the period when the legislature is not in session. Almost all states also have legislative councils. These councils are permanent joint legislative committees that meet between sessions to study problems that may arise when the next legislative session opens. Council membership ranges from 5 in South Carolina to 260 in Pennsylvania. Legislative work has been speeded up greatly by such mechanical devices as electric roll-call machines. Many legislatures have legislative reference services to do research work, prepare reports, and help draft bills. See LEGISLATURE.

**Problems of Representation.** Most state legislatures have over-represented rural areas and under-represented the more heavily populated urban areas for many years. Most states leave apportioning of representatives to their legislatures. The legislatures often failed to reapportion regularly. For this reason, urban voters could elect only about one-fourth of the state legislators, although almost three-fourths of all U.S. citizens lived in urban areas.

However, in 1962 the Supreme Court of the United States ruled that individuals could bring questions of unfair districting before federal courts. This decision was reached in the case of *Baker vs. Carr*. In 1964, the Supreme Court ruled in decisions against several states that districts in both houses of a state legislature must be substantially equal in population.

The people in 20 states share legislative power through the *initiative* and *referendum*. They may propose bills by petition and adopt them through referendum votes (see INITIATIVE AND REFERENDUM). Some persons believe that these procedures give the voters a check on their legislature, and increase public interest in government. Others maintain that they overburden the voters with decisions they cannot vote on intelligently, and that they tend to weaken the legislature's responsibility.

## Judicial Branch

State courts settle disputes that come before them under various laws. They handle about nine-tenths of the criminal and civil cases in the United States.

A supreme court heads the judicial system of each state. In some states, the supreme court is called by another name, such as *court of appeals*. The memberships of state supreme courts range from three to nine judges. About half the states have seven-judge courts.

In about three-fourths of the states, the voters elect supreme-court judges. In a few states, the governor or legislature appoints them. In others, such as California, the governor appoints the judges, who must then be approved by the voters. Judges hold office for specified terms. These terms range from 2 years in Vermont to 21 in Pennsylvania. Judges serve 6- or 8-year terms in many states, and life terms in a few states.

Some states have intermediate appellate courts to handle some of the supreme court's cases. Each state has general trial courts. County and municipal courts include probate, juvenile, domestic relations, and small-claims courts, and the courts of justices of the peace and police magistrates. Most judges in these courts serve four-year terms. See COURT.

## State Services

**Education.** State governments have always controlled public education. They support public schools through taxes, and administer them through local school districts. A district supervises its public elementary and secondary schools under a school board elected by the people or appointed by the mayor. State governments set up general standards for schools and their courses of study. The state funds supplement local property taxes that help pay for education. Every state has at least one state university. It also maintains such institutions as agricultural colleges, teacher-training schools, junior colleges, trade and vocational schools, and public libraries.

**Public Safety.** The state legislatures enact most criminal laws that protect persons and property. State police promote highway safety, preserve the peace, and enforce criminal laws. Each state maintains prisons, reformatories, or prison camps. Some states have special commissions to investigate the management and affairs of other state agencies. Others have departments that promote safety and enforce laws in such fields as mining and sanitation. Each state has a civil-defense organization to cooperate with the federal government. The governor commands the state militia, or national guard, which he may call out in emergencies (see NATIONAL GUARD).

**Public Works.** Each state has a highway or public-works department that builds and maintains highways. This department may also supervise the construction of bridges, grade separations, canals, and waterways, and take care of beach protection, flood control, and buildings and grounds. Many toll roads are built and operated by special state turnpike authorities elected by the people or appointed by the governor. All states erect and maintain large numbers of public buildings. Since 1931, the states have built many public works with the aid of federal subsidies.

**Recreation.** Departments or agencies in the various states manage more than 2,100 state parks and recreation areas. These parks and areas cover more than 5,170,000 acres of land and water. Many parks and recreation areas have been established in state-owned forests. Other areas have been set up as historical monuments. State highway departments may operate roadside parks for motorists.

**Health.** State departments of health, or boards of health, were first set up in the late 1800's. They supervise local public-health agencies. These agencies are responsible for such activities as keeping vital statistics, controlling communicable diseases, and promoting health education, maternal and infant care, sanitation, and hygiene. They have general control over hospitals, nursing, research, and laboratory facilities. Public-health work by the states also includes improvement of substandard housing and slum clearance.

**Welfare.** Aid from the federal government has stimulated state government activities in welfare programs. Each state operates programs that help the poor, aged, physically handicapped, mentally defective, blind, delinquent, deaf, mute, and unemployed. States also provide institutional care in hospitals, asylums, reformatories, and various types of homes. Public-welfare boards administer the welfare programs in most of the states.

**Conservation** activities include protection of water resources through special drainage, irrigation, water-supply, and sanitation districts, and soil and forest conservation. State governments carry out their responsibilities through education, extension services, and research on water resources, fish and wildlife, forests, soils, and mineral resources. A director or board usually heads the state department of conservation. Some states have fish and game commissions and forest services.

**Agriculture.** The states aid agriculture through county agents, soil-conservation districts, agriculture-extension services, and agricultural colleges. All the states except New Mexico have departments or boards of agriculture. In most states, the governor appoints the director or board members. In others, the voters elect them. Annual state fairs are held in many states.

**Business and Labor.** Each state government grants corporations the charters that allow them to do business. It regulates insurance companies and state banks. It supervises public-utility companies that provide public power, communications, and transportation. Most states have workmen's compensation laws that provide payments to workers who are injured on the job (see WORKMEN'S COMPENSATION). All states regulate child labor and the employment of women (see CHILD LABOR).

### State Finances

State governments must have money to pay for the services they provide. Most of a state's budget goes into payments for education, highways, public welfare, health and hospitals, insurance trusts for retirement of employees, prisons, public safety, natural resources, interest and debt redemption, and veterans' services.

In most of the states, the governor receives the financial requests of the state agencies, and submits a total budget to the legislature. The legislature must approve all appropriations. Almost all state constitutions impose debt limitations upon the states.

Grants-in-aid from the federal government rank as the largest single source of state income. Other major sources of income include taxes on property, general sales, motor fuel, liquor, beer, tobacco, motor-vehicle licenses, individual and corporate incomes, inheritance and gifts, and the use of natural resources.

Local authorities usually collect property taxes, and turn over a share to the state government. Central state agencies collect such state levies as income, motor-vehicle, and business taxes. Most states have a tax commission that supervises tax administration.

Local governments rely heavily upon grants-in-aid from the states. They receive these grants upon agreeing to certain conditions, such as meeting standards imposed by the state. State governments also place debt limits upon local governments. See TAXATION.

### Relations with Other Governments

The federal government has certain constitutional obligations toward the states. It must respect their territorial unity, and cannot divide or break up a state without its consent. It must protect the states against invasion and domestic violence. It must guarantee each state a republican form of government.

The United States Constitution also places certain limitations on the states. They may not interfere in foreign relations, or make compacts among themselves without the consent of Congress. They may not directly burden or discriminate against interstate commerce. They may not levy import or export taxes. They may not issue paper money or pass laws impairing the obligation of contracts.

The Constitution also places certain obligations on the states in their relations with each other. Each state must give "full faith and credit" to the legal processes and acts of every other state. No state may discriminate in favor of its own citizens against persons coming from other states. The Supreme Court of the United States can ultimately decide disputes between states that cannot be settled by negotiation and agreement. For a more complete description of the provisions, meaning, and interpretation of the Constitution, see UNITED STATES CONSTITUTION. DAVID FELLMAN

**Related Articles.** See the Government and History sections of each state article, such as ALABAMA (Government; History). See also the following articles:

| | | |
|---|---|---|
| Canada, Government of | Government | Public Utility |
| Charter | Governor | Recreation |
| City and Local Governments | Health, Board of | Roads and Highways |
| Conservation | Initiative and Referendum | School |
| Corporation | Legislature | Social Work |
| County | Lieutenant Governor | States' Rights |
| Court | Metropolitan Area | Taxation |
| District Attorney | National Guard | Transportation |
| Education | Police | United States, Government of |
| Franchise | Prison | |

# STATE MOTTOES

**STATE MOTTOES.** See the Facts in Brief table in each state article, such as ALABAMA (Facts in Brief).

**STATE PARKS.** See the Places to Visit section of each state article.

**STATE POLICE.** See POLICE (State Police).

**STATE POPULAR NAMES.** See UNITED STATES (table: Facts in Brief about the States of the Union).

**STATE PRESS** is a system of publishing operated by a government or a government-controlled political party. It is the opposite of a *free press*, where individuals publish newspapers and magazines. Freedom of the press is an important element in political freedom. Dictatorships rely on state presses to control public opinion.

See also FREEDOM OF THE PRESS.

**STATE SEALS.** See the color picture in each state article.

**STATE SONGS.** See the Facts in Brief table in each state article, such as ALABAMA (Facts in Brief). See also UNITED STATES (table: Facts in Brief about the States of the Union).

**STATE TREES.** See the color picture in each state article; also UNITED STATES (table: Facts in Brief about the States of the Union).

**STATEMENT.** See BILL; CHECK.

**STATEN ISLAND** forms New York City's borough of Richmond. It has a population of 221,991 and lies in New York Bay, about five miles southwest of Manhattan Island (see NEW YORK [political map]).

Ferries link Staten Island with Manhattan. The Verrazano-Narrows Bridge connects Fort Wadsworth on Staten Island with Fort Hamilton in Brooklyn. Three other bridges connect the island with New Jersey. Staten Island covers 64 square miles. It is about 14 miles long and $7\frac{1}{2}$ miles across at its widest point.

Fort Wadsworth, together with Brooklyn's Fort Hamilton, commands the entrance through the Narrows. Like Manhattan Island, Staten Island was purchased by the Dutch from the Indians in the 1600's. WILLIAM E. YOUNG

See also RICHMONDTOWN.

**STATER.** See MONEY (The First Coins).

**Staten Island,** foreground, and Brooklyn are connected by the Verrazano-Narrows Bridge. The bridge was completed in 1964.

Triborough Bridge and Tunnel Authority

**STATES-GENERAL,** often called ESTATES-GENERAL, was the French representative assembly from 1302 to 1789. It was divided into three *estates* (classes). The first estate represented the clergy, the second the noblemen, and the third the commoners. In the later Middle Ages, the kings began to invite leaders from each of the three estates to meet and discuss legislative or financial matters. These assemblies did not win the power to make laws for many years.

France's states-general never gained the power that England's parliament held. Its influence was limited because each estate met separately and voted as a unit. By the time of Louis XI, in the late 1400's, the states-general asked the king to govern without it. It never even met during the reign of Henry IV, from 1589 to 1610, and only for a short time under his son, Louis XIII. When he dismissed the states-general, it was not called again until the eve of the French Revolution in 1789, 175 years later.

When the states-general met in 1789, members of the third estate insisted on voting individually, instead of allowing each house to cast one vote. The first and second estates resisted this demand. Then, on June 17, 1789, the third estate declared itself to be the national assembly of France. Three days later, its members swore in the Tennis Court Oath that they would not disband until they had written a constitution for France. Under threats of violence, Louis XVI recognized the national assembly as France's representative government.

The name *states-general* was also used in The Netherlands from 1593 to 1796 for an assembly where each province had one representative and one vote. It became the National Assembly in 1796. The Dutch parliament is now called States-General. EDWIN J. WESTERMANN

See also FRENCH REVOLUTION.

**STATES OF THE CHURCH.** See PAPAL STATES.

**STATES' RIGHTS** is a doctrine aimed at protecting the rights and powers of the states against those of the federal government. The 13 American states gave up many powers to the federal government when they ratified the United States Constitution. Only those powers that the Constitution did not grant to the national government were left to the states.

Everyone agrees that the states have rights that the federal government cannot lawfully touch. But the Constitution says that the federal government can make any laws that are "necessary and proper" for carrying its specific powers into effect. This provision makes it difficult to determine exactly what rights the states possess. Therefore, the major issue is not whether the states have rights, but rather who is to decide when these rights are abused.

**Early History.** Today, most people connect the support of states' rights with the South's position on racial segregation. But historically, the doctrine has been invoked by states in every section of the country whenever they have felt their jurisdiction threatened. One of the earliest instances was the Kentucky and Virginia Resolutions, which made a strong claim for the right of each state to decide this issue for itself. This idea gave rise to the doctrine of *nullification*, which asserts that within its own borders, a state can *nullify* (declare illegal) those acts of the federal government which it considers an invasion of its own rights. The doctrine of nullification was developed by John Calhoun and officially adopted by South Carolina in 1832. See NULLIFICATION.

In 1860 and 1861, 11 Southern states carried the states' rights idea to its most extreme point by seceding from the Union. Their defeat in the Civil War put an end to this particular interpretation of states' rights. But it is still generally agreed that the states have a jurisdiction which the federal government has no right to invade. The task of drawing the exact line of state jurisdiction and deciding whether the federal government has overstepped it is now left to the federal courts. The decisions of the courts can be changed only by the courts themselves, or by an amendment to the United States Constitution.

**Later Developments.** In the 1950's, supporters of states' rights claimed that decisions of the federal courts weakened the powers of the states. The Supreme Court of the United States declared that state laws ordering segregation in public schools, in public parks, and on public transportation systems violated provisions of the Constitution. It also set aside state antisedition laws and "right to work" legislation. But states' rights supporters claimed that these decisions violated the police powers of the state.

In the controversy over segregation, advocates of states' rights insisted that each state has the right of *interposition*. This doctrine resembles nullification. It asserts that a state has the right to "interpose the sovereignty of a state against the encroachment upon the reserved power of the state." Under this doctrine, a state has the power to overrule a decision of a federal agency if it conflicts with a state law, and all persons in the state must obey the state, not the federal, law.

Congress set up a Commission on Intergovernmental Relations in 1953 to study the extent of federal aid to the states, and the constitutional limits of federal and state powers. In 1955, the commission made its recommendations to the President and Congress. The recommendations covered such fields as agriculture, education, and housing. The commission noted that the Constitution forbids the states to legislate in such fields as interstate commerce, admiralty laws, and currency. It pointed out that the problem of maintaining a federal system arises where both the federal and state governments have a choice of how to act.

States' rights parties have run candidates in most presidential elections since 1948. The core of these parties came from conservative Democrats and Republicans who opposed the civil-rights policies of their own parties. One of these groups, the States' Rights Democratic Party (nicknamed the Dixiecrat Party), carried four Southern states in 1948. In 1968, the American Independent Party's presidential candidate, former Alabama Governor George C. Wallace, also stressed states' rights and carried five Southern states.     DAVID DONALD

See also ALABAMA (Early Statehood); CALHOUN, JOHN CALDWELL; DIXIECRAT PARTY; KENTUCKY AND VIRGINIA RESOLUTIONS; WALLACE, GEORGE C.

**STATES' RIGHTS DEMOCRATIC PARTY.** See DIXIECRAT PARTY.

**STATESMAN** is a person with a broad general knowledge of government and politics, who takes a leading part in public affairs. Most persons think of statesmen as being concerned with the needs and interests of their country as a whole. In contrast, they think of *politicians* as having only party or political aims. *Elder statesmen*, usually retired from active government, continue to give advice on important issues. Japan developed this system in the *genro*, a council of former government leaders who advise the current government. See also the list of biographies of statesmen at the end of most country articles.

**STATIC,** *STAT ik*, is a broad term covering any electrical atmospheric disturbance. People hear it as a crashing or grating noise over the radio. Usually lightning or some other electrical disturbance in the air causes it. Motors or other electrical devices, especially those devices with a rotating or vibrating contact, also may cause static.

Every water droplet in a cloud carries a tiny charge of electricity. As droplets combine to make bigger drops, and finally to make rain, the electricity on the drops collects. Then the voltage rises so high that a spark jumps, either to another cloud or to the ground.

There are two sorts of static sounds. Small clouds or isolated water drops give a hissing noise like escaping steam, but large electric sparks give a loud snap or crash. Weather observers, using a kind of radio compass called a radio storm detector, can tell the direction and intensity of a storm by listening to the sound of its static, even when the storm is hundreds of miles away.

Static eliminators have been tried in radio sets, but without much success. One of the great advantages of frequency modulation (FM) radio is that it does not have static.     PALMER H. CRAIG

See also FREQUENCY MODULATION.

**STATIC ELECTRICITY.** See ELECTRICITY (Static).

**STATICE,** *STAT ih see*, is a group of colorful plants used in rock gardens and flower-bed borders. It includes the *thrift* (or *sea pink*) and the *sea lavender*. The thrift has narrow, evergreen leaves that grow in large bunches. Its small pink or white flowers grow in dense, globe-shaped clusters. The sea lavender has wider leaves and purple, rose, white, or yellow flowers. These flowers are often dried and made into bouquets for winter use. Statices are hardy and grow well in most garden soils. They usually reproduce by seed. Started in a greenhouse in early spring and then planted outside, they have flowers all summer.

**Scientific Classification.** The statice belongs to the leadwort family, *Plumbaginaceae*. Two common thrifts are classified as genus *Armeria*, species *A. maritima* and *A. pseud-armeria*. Other common statices include *Limonium sinuatum* and *L. latifolium*.     ROBERT W. SCHERY

**STATICS** is a branch of the science of dynamics. Dynamics deals with the properties of matter and forces. It is divided into two branches—*statics* and *kinetics*. Statics deals with conditions under which material bodies do not change motion when acted upon by various forces. That is, a body at rest will remain at rest, and a body in motion will not change direction or speed of motion. When two or more forces act upon a body so as to produce no change of motion, the forces are said to be in *equilibrium*. Kinetics deals with the changes of motion. See also DYNAMICS.     ROBERT F. PATON

**STATION, RAILWAY.** See RAILROAD (Railway Stations).

# STATISTICS

**STATISTICS,** *stuh TISS ticks.* Suppose someone handed you records containing the weights of 13,000 newborn babies. Then he asked you to make some conclusions about the weights. Many persons could be puzzled by page after page of nothing but numbers. Great masses of *data* (facts) usually tend to be confusing. But statistics, a branch of mathematics, has ways of simplifying masses of numbers and facts and of presenting them in an understandable form. For example, a statistician could find that the average weight of the newborn boys is 7.35 pounds and that of the girls is 7.13 pounds. Now you have some easily understood conclusions about the weights. In ways such as this, statistics can help you solve many problems.

The word *statistics* appears sometimes as a singular and sometimes as a plural noun. As a plural noun, *statistics* refers to numbers or numerical facts. For example, you can say that "there *are* many statistics in THE WORLD BOOK." As a singular noun, *statistics* refers to the methods used to analyze numerical data, and to draw conclusions from them. You can say that "statistics *is* the art and science of analyzing numerical data."

## Uses of Statistics

As a science, statistics began in Germany in the 1700's and 1800's. Governments used statistics to count their citizens and to collect taxes. Governments still use statistics for these and many other purposes, such as planning farm production.

Scientists know that it is unsafe to draw conclusions from small numbers of observations. So they find it necessary to study thousands and even millions of cases. Statistics helps all the sciences—physical, biological, and social—to deal with masses of facts.

Statistics makes vital contributions to business and industry. Statistical methods help to organize business and industrial facts, and uncover the principles and trends at work behind the facts. Advertising, finance, insurance, manufacturing, retailing, and many other fields depend on statistics. Statistics helps politicians plan their campaigns, and the use of statistics forms the basis of public-opinion polls.

## How Statistics Works

Solving any problem in statistics involves three steps: (1) definition of the problem, (2) collection of data, and (3) analysis of data.

**Definition of the Problem.** Beginners in statistics usually learn with surprise that even the simplest problem requires careful definition. Suppose someone asks you to count the words on a printed page. You will discover immediately that you must answer questions about this simple problem. For example, how many words are there in the sentence, "The Civil War (1861-1865) created a new public-school shortage in the U.S."? Do you count abbreviated words? How about hyphenated words and numbers? You must define what you mean by *words* before you begin. Similar questions appear in statistics. Suppose you want to count the population of the United States on Apr. 15, 1960. Whom do you count? Do you include a baby born late that afternoon? A man who died early that morning? A person from another country visiting the United States? A United States citizen visiting another country? You must define your terms with great care.

**Collection of Data.** After defining his terms, a statistician proceeds to collect his data. Sometimes he can use data collected by others, such as census figures or school records. This kind of data is called *derived data.* Sometimes a statistician has to obtain his own data. His own data might consist of such things as laboratory experiments, questionnaires sent to housewives, or personal interviews. This kind of data is called *original data.*

**Analysis of Data.** Defining the problem and collecting data have fundamental importance. But a statistician spends most of his time analyzing the data. That is, he tries to find out what the data mean and how they may be interpreted. In some cases, this involves nothing more complicated than computing an average or finding a percentage. In other cases, analyzing the data may require months of labor and the use of giant electronic computers.

### Averages

Suppose a statistician received the records of the number of eggs laid in one year by each of 3,131 White Leghorn hens. He usually arranges values such as these in a *table:*

| NUMBER OF EGGS | NUMBER OF HENS |
|---|---|
| 0- 29 | 30 |
| 30- 59 | 36 |
| 60- 89 | 125 |
| 90-119 | 327 |
| 120-149 | 686 |
| 150-179 | 925 |
| 180-209 | 697 |
| 210-239 | 271 |
| 240-269 | 32 |
| 270-299 | 2 |
| TOTAL | 3,131 |

Just a glance at the table makes the pattern clear. You can see that there is a bunching near the middle of the table. The most common egg production lies somewhere between 150 and 179 eggs. It looks as if the most common or most "popular" production is about 165 eggs, or halfway between 150 and 179. Statisticians call this kind of average the *mode.* A study of the actual data from which the table was prepared shows that as many hens laid more than 162 eggs as laid fewer than 162 eggs. This kind of average is the *median.* The median in the table is 162 eggs. If you add together the numbers of all the eggs and divide by 3,131, the number of hens, you will find the *arithmetic average* or *arithmetic mean.* The mean number of eggs is 157. See AVERAGE; MEAN; MEDIAN; MODE.

### Frequency Distributions

The egg-production table is called a *frequency table,* because it shows the frequency with which various values occur. A frequency table makes it possible for statisticians to gather thousands of cases into a small space. It also shows immediately the general characteristics of the data. Methods exist for the rapid computation of the mean, median, mode, and other useful numbers from frequency tables.

The values themselves, arranged in a table, form a *frequency distribution.* Many, although by no means all, frequency distributions show the same basic pattern

| Two | Three | Four | Five | One |
|---|---|---|---|---|
| 15-Year-Olds | 16-Year-Olds | 17-Year-Olds | 18-Year-Olds | 19-Year-Old |

**Statistics Can Tell a Great Deal** about the ages of the members of this basketball squad. First, you can find the squad's *mean*, or average, age by adding together all the members' ages and dividing by the number of players on the squad. The mean age for the squad is 17 years. Second, you can find the *median* age by listing the ages of all the players from youngest to oldest and finding the age in the middle. The median age for the squad is 17. You can also use statistics to find the *mode* or the age that occurs the most number of times. The mode for the squad is 18, because there are more 18-year-olds than members of any other age.

that appears in the egg-production table. This distribution consists of small frequencies at both ends of the table and large frequencies in the middle. The distribution can be charted, by showing the numbers of cases vertically and the sizes of values horizontally. Here is the chart:

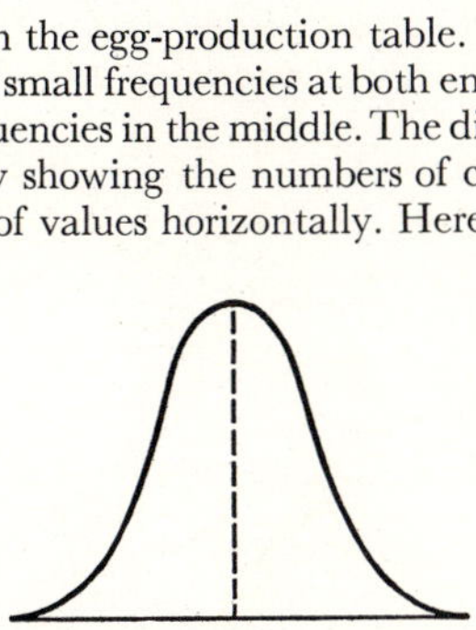

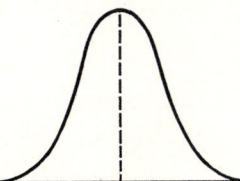

This bell-shaped distribution is called a *normal distribution* or *normal curve*.

### Probability

With certain kinds of data, a statistician can tell in advance what values will occur, and how frequently. Suppose you toss a penny over and over again. You expect it to show "heads" half the time and "tails" half the time. If you toss it only three or four times, this may not happen. But as you increase the number of throws, the proportion of "heads" tends to draw more and more closely to the expected value of one half. Suppose you toss four pennies over and over again. Suppose you toss a very large number of pennies a great number of times. You may be surprised to find that the distribution of "heads" and "tails" draws closer and closer to the bell-shaped normal distribution. *Probability*, in statistics, is the measurement of the likelihood of events in numerical terms. The normal distribution, based on pure chance, helps statisticians to make these measurements.

Sometimes a statistician can reason out in advance the relative frequency with which events will occur, such as tossing coins or throwing dice. This is called *a priori probability* (probability *from the first*). But, in many cases, a statistician cannot reason out probability in advance; for example, whether or not a certain patient will recover from diphtheria. But he can reach fairly reliable conclusions as to these probabilities from a study of actual cases. For example, he might find

683

# STATISTICS

that the probability of recovering in diphtheria cases is 78 out of 100. This is called *statistical probability*.

In a normal distribution, the distance you must go above and below the arithmetic mean to include half of the cases is called the *probable error* of the distribution. In any normal distribution, 50 per cent of the cases lie within one probable error of the mean, 82 per cent lie within two probable errors, 96 per cent within three probable errors, 99.3 per cent within four probable errors, and 99.92 per cent within five probable errors.

Statisticians now use a similar measure called the *standard error* more than the probable error. The standard error has certain mathematical advantages. In a normal distribution, 68.27 per cent of the cases lie within one standard error of the mean, 95.5 per cent lie within two standard errors, and practically all the cases (99.7 per cent) lie within three standard errors.

## Sampling

Statisticians know that it is risky to draw conclusions from small numbers of observations. Yet usually it is impossible to study all the cases. A statistician must study a group of a hundred, a thousand, or some other limited number of cases. Statisticians call the group they actually study the *sample*. They draw their conclusions from this group. The total number of cases from which they select the sample is called the *universe* or the *population*.

A statistician can never be completely certain that his sample accurately reflects the total number of cases. But, in general, the larger the sample, the more reliable it is in reflecting the total number of cases. The reliability of the sample increases, not in proportion to the number of cases, but in proportion to the square root of the number of cases. To double the reliability, a statistician studies four times as many cases. To treble the reliability, he studies nine times as many cases.

A statistician must decide how many cases to study, and which individual cases. He tries to select the individual cases carefully. Often he uses a *random sample*. A random sample consists of cases selected so that each case in the total number has an equal chance of being included.

ALBERT E. WAUGH

**Related Articles** in WORLD BOOK include:

| | | |
|---|---|---|
| Average | Pearson, Karl | Probability |
| Graph | Permutations | Sampling |
| Mean | and Combinations | Skew Line |
| Median | Poll of Public Opinion | Vital Statistics |
| Mode | | |

**STATISTICS, VITAL.** See VITAL STATISTICS.

**STATLER, ELLSWORTH MILTON** (1863-1928), was an American hotel owner and operator. He built a hotel for the Buffalo Exposition in 1901, and operated one at the St. Louis Exposition in 1904. He opened a permanent hotel in Buffalo in 1908, advertising it as the first in the country to have a bath with every room. He later owned hotels in Cleveland, Detroit, and St. Louis, and operated the Pennsylvania in New York City. He was born on Oct. 26, 1863, in Somerset County, Pennsylvania.

DONALD L. KEMMERER

**STATOR.** See ELECTRIC GENERATOR (Parts).

**STATUARY HALL** is one of the large rooms in the United States Capitol at Washington, D.C. It is set aside to house the statues of outstanding citizens of each state. The hall itself is in the form of a half circle under a half dome. It lies near the rotunda, on the side of the Capitol leading to the chamber of the House of Representatives.

**Purpose.** In 1864, Congress authorized the President to invite each state to send two marble or bronze statues to be displayed in the Capitol. The states were asked to

**Statuary Hall** in the U.S. Capitol in Washington, D.C., contains statues of distinguished citizens of the United States. Each state may place one marble or bronze statue in the hall. The first statue honored Nathanael Greene of Rhode Island in 1870.

Architect of the Capitol

choose citizens who had performed distinguished civic or military services and who were "worthy of this national commemoration." Congress set aside the old House of Representatives chamber to hold the statues.

The collection of statues grew over the years. In 1933, architects discovered that the hall was overloaded. Congress amended the law in 1933, providing that one statue from each state would stand in Statuary Hall, and a second statue from each state would be placed in some other part of the Capitol.

**The Statues.** By the mid-1960's, 48 states had sent statues to Statuary Hall. Forty of the 50 states had also sent a second statue to stand elsewhere in the Capitol. Many of the leaders honored were statesmen, governors, members of Congress, or senators. But a number of pioneers, religious leaders, reformers, educators, and physicians have also been honored. For many years, Frances E. Willard of Illinois was the only woman represented in the collection. Her statue was presented in 1905. In 1958, Minnesota sent a statue of Maria L. Sanford.

# STATUE OF LIBERTY

**The Hall** that now stands as a memorial was the scene of many exciting events in the history of the United States. The House of Representatives met in the chamber for 50 years, from 1807 to 1857, with the exception of the period from 1814 to 1819. The Capitol was then being repaired after British soldiers burned it during the War of 1812. Many famous Americans, including John C. Calhoun, Stephen A. Douglas, Abraham Lincoln, and Daniel Webster, won their first national prominence in the House chamber. Henry Clay presided over many bitter debates. The House of Representatives met there in 1825 to choose the President in the contested election of 1824, and elected John Quincy Adams. In 1848, while serving as a representative, Adams suffered a stroke in the chamber, and died soon afterward. Millard Fillmore took the oath as President in Statuary Hall in 1850.

**STATUE.** See SCULPTURE.
**STATUE OF LIBERTY.** See LIBERTY, STATUE OF.

## STATUES IN THE CAPITOL

| State | In Statuary Hall | Date Presented | Elsewhere In the Capitol | Date Presented |
|---|---|---|---|---|
| Alabama | Joseph Wheeler | 1925 | J. L. M. Curry | 1908 |
| Arizona | John C. Greenway | 1930 | Eusebio Francisco Kino | 1965 |
| Arkansas | Uriah M. Rose | 1917 | James P. Clarke | 1921 |
| California | Junípero Serra | 1931 | Thomas S. King | 1931 |
| Colorado | Florence Rena Sabin | 1959 | | |
| Connecticut | Roger Sherman | 1872 | Jonathan Trumbull | 1871 |
| Delaware | Caesar Rodney | 1934 | John M. Clayton | 1934 |
| Florida | John Gorrie | 1914 | Edmund Kirby-Smith | 1922 |
| Georgia | Alexander H. Stephens | 1927 | Crawford W. Long | 1926 |
| Idaho | George L. Shoup | 1910 | William E. Borah | 1947 |
| Illinois | Frances E. Willard | 1905 | James Shields | 1893 |
| Indiana | Lew Wallace | 1910 | Oliver P. Morton | 1900 |
| Iowa | Samuel J. Kirkwood | 1913 | James Harlan | 1910 |
| Kansas | John J. Ingalls | 1905 | George W. Glick | 1914 |
| Kentucky | Henry Clay | 1929 | Ephraim McDowell | 1929 |
| Louisiana | Huey P. Long | 1941 | Edward Douglass White | 1955 |
| Maine | Hannibal Hamlin | 1935 | William King | 1878 |
| Maryland | Charles Carroll of Carrollton | 1903 | John Hanson | 1903 |
| Massachusetts | Samuel Adams | 1876 | John Winthrop | 1876 |
| Michigan | Lewis Cass | 1889 | Zachariah Chandler | 1913 |
| Minnesota | Henry Mower Rice | 1916 | Maria L. Sanford | 1958 |
| Mississippi | Jefferson Davis | 1931 | James Z. George | 1931 |
| Missouri | Thomas H. Benton | 1899 | Francis P. Blair, Jr. | 1899 |
| Montana | Charles M. Russell | 1959 | | |
| Nebraska | William Jennings Bryan | 1937 | J. Sterling Morton | 1937 |
| Nevada | Patrick A. McCarran | 1960 | | |
| New Hampshire | Daniel Webster | 1894 | John Stark | 1894 |
| New Jersey | Richard Stockton | 1888 | Philip Kearny | 1888 |
| New Mexico | | | Dennis Chavez | 1966 |
| New York | Robert R. Livingston | 1875 | George Clinton | 1873 |
| North Carolina | Zebulon Baird Vance | 1916 | Charles B. Aycock | 1932 |
| North Dakota | John Burke | 1963 | | |
| Ohio | William Allen | 1887 | James A. Garfield | 1886 |
| Oklahoma | Sequoya | 1917 | Will Rogers | 1939 |
| Oregon | Jason Lee | 1953 | John McLoughlin | 1953 |
| Pennsylvania | Robert Fulton | 1889 | John Peter G. Muhlenberg | 1889 |
| Rhode Island | Roger Williams | 1872 | Nathanael Greene | 1870 |
| South Carolina | John C. Calhoun | 1910 | Wade Hampton | 1929 |
| South Dakota | William H. H. Beadle | 1938 | Joseph Ward | 1963 |
| Tennessee | John Sevier | 1931 | Andrew Jackson | 1928 |
| Texas | Samuel Houston | 1905 | Stephen F. Austin | 1905 |
| Utah | Brigham Young | 1950 | | |
| Vermont | Ethan Allen | 1876 | Jacob Collamer | 1881 |
| Virginia | Robert E. Lee | 1934 | George Washington | 1934 |
| Washington | Marcus Whitman | 1953 | | |
| West Virginia | Francis H. Pierpont | 1910 | John E. Kenna | 1901 |
| Wisconsin | Robert M. La Follette, Sr. | 1929 | Jacques Marquette | 1896 |
| Wyoming | Esther Hobart Morris | 1960 | | |

Each person listed in the table has a biography in WORLD BOOK.

### STATUE OF LIBERTY NAT. MONUMENT

**STATUE OF LIBERTY NATIONAL MONUMENT** is on Ellis and Liberty islands in New York harbor. The colossal statue by Frédéric Bartholdi stands on Liberty Island. The people of France presented it to the United States on July 4, 1884. Ellis Island was a U.S. immigration station until 1954. It became part of the national monument in 1965. See also ELLIS ISLAND; LIBERTY, STATUE OF; NATIONAL MONUMENT.

**STATUTE,** *STAT yoot*, is a rule of law passed by a law-making body such as the Congress of the United States. *Statute law* is another term for *written law*. The term distinguishes written law from *unwritten* or *common law*, which is based upon custom and upon previous court decisions.

See also COMMON LAW.

**STATUTE MILE.** See MILE.

**STATUTE OF FRAUDS.** See FRAUD.

**STATUTE OF LIMITATIONS** is a law that sets a time limit for the filing of lawsuits. Suits filed after the statute of limitations has passed are barred, no matter how just they may be. Statutes of limitations prevent lawsuits in which the true situation is clouded because of a long lapse of time.

Each state as well as the federal government has its own statute of limitations for different kinds of claims. For example, Illinois has over 20 statutes of limitations. These statutes include limits of one year for libel and slander cases, two years for personal injury lawsuits, 10 years for cases involving written contracts, and 20 years for actions to recover land.

Statutes of limitations also apply to most crimes, limiting the time in which prosecutions must be brought. But serious crimes such as murder are not subject to statutes of limitations. HARRY KALVEN, JR.

**STATUTE OF WESTMINSTER.** See CANADA, GOVERNMENT OF (International Relations); COMMONWEALTH OF NATIONS (History).

**STATUTORY LAW.** See LAW (Statutes).

**STAUBBACH** is the highest waterfall in Switzerland and one of the highest in the world. It is 980 feet high. Staubbach is formed from racing torrents of melted snow that cascade into Lauterbrunnen Valley. Staubbach is outside the city of Lauterbrunnen. See also WATERFALL (picture chart). FRANKLIN C. ERICKSON

**STAUDINGER,** *SHTOU ding ur*, **HERMANN** (1881-1965), a German chemist, pioneered in organic chemistry. He won the 1953 Nobel prize in chemistry for his study of "giant molecules." He developed and proved the idea that the atoms in many complex molecules are hooked together in long chains forming definite patterns. This opened the door to high-polymer chemistry and the development of plastics and synthetic fibers. Staudinger developed many synthetic materials, including artificial pepper and coffee aroma. He was born in Worms, Germany.

**STAVANGER,** *stah VAHNG ur* (pop. 78,435; alt. 151 ft.), is an important seaport on the southwest coast of Norway. It lies at the mouth of Bokna Fiord, which empties into the North Sea. For location, see NORWAY (color map).

Stavanger is noted for its merchant fleet, shipbuilding industry, and fish canneries. It was established about A.D. 1000. ARNE HAUGLAND

**STAY OF EXECUTION.** See REPRIEVE.

**STE.** _____. See SAINTE _____.

**STEAK.** See BEEF; MEAT.

**STEAM,** *steem*, is water which has been changed into a gas. Steam cannot be seen, for it is colorless. The cloud of vapor which we see beginning about an inch from the spout of a teakettle is not steam. The real steam is in the space that seems vacant, just outside the spout. The cloud we see is water that the cooler air has changed from gas form back into tiny water particles.

Steam can be formed by boiling or by evaporation. At sea level, water boils when it is heated to 100° C., the *boiling point*. Water will evaporate at lower temperatures. The steam caused by boiling is as hot as the boiling water. The steam caused by evaporation is not hot. Usually the word steam refers to hot steam.

When water reaches the boiling point, bubbles of steam begin to rise through it and escape into the air. The temperature will remain at the boiling point until all the liquid has become gas. It requires 100 calories of heat to raise one gram of water from the freezing point (0° C.) to the boiling point. To change the same gram of boiling water into steam, without raising its temperature, takes 540 calories of heat. This heat is called the steam's *latent heat*. It is released when the steam changes back to liquid water. Steam can cause more severe burns than boiling water because the steam condenses and releases its latent heat.

Steam fills more space than the water from which it comes. At the moment when boiling stops, the gas is 1,670 times as great in volume as the former liquid. At this stage it is called *saturated steam*. If heated more, it takes up even more space. Then it is known as *superheated steam*. The steam engine is built around this principle. *Wet steam* supports particles of water still in liquid form. *Dry steam*, however, contains only gas. LOUIS MARICK

**Related Articles** in WORLD BOOK include:

| | | |
|---|---|---|
| Boiling Point | Steam Hammer | Turbine |
| Evaporation | Steam Shovel | (Steam |
| Steam Engine | Steamboat | Turbines) |

**Steam Has Many Uses** other than providing power. A steam jet cleans the stonework of buildings, *below*. Steam operates the whistle of a tugboat, *center right*, lifts the cover of a teakettle, *center*, and turns a railroad locomotive's wheels, *far right*.

Press Syndicate

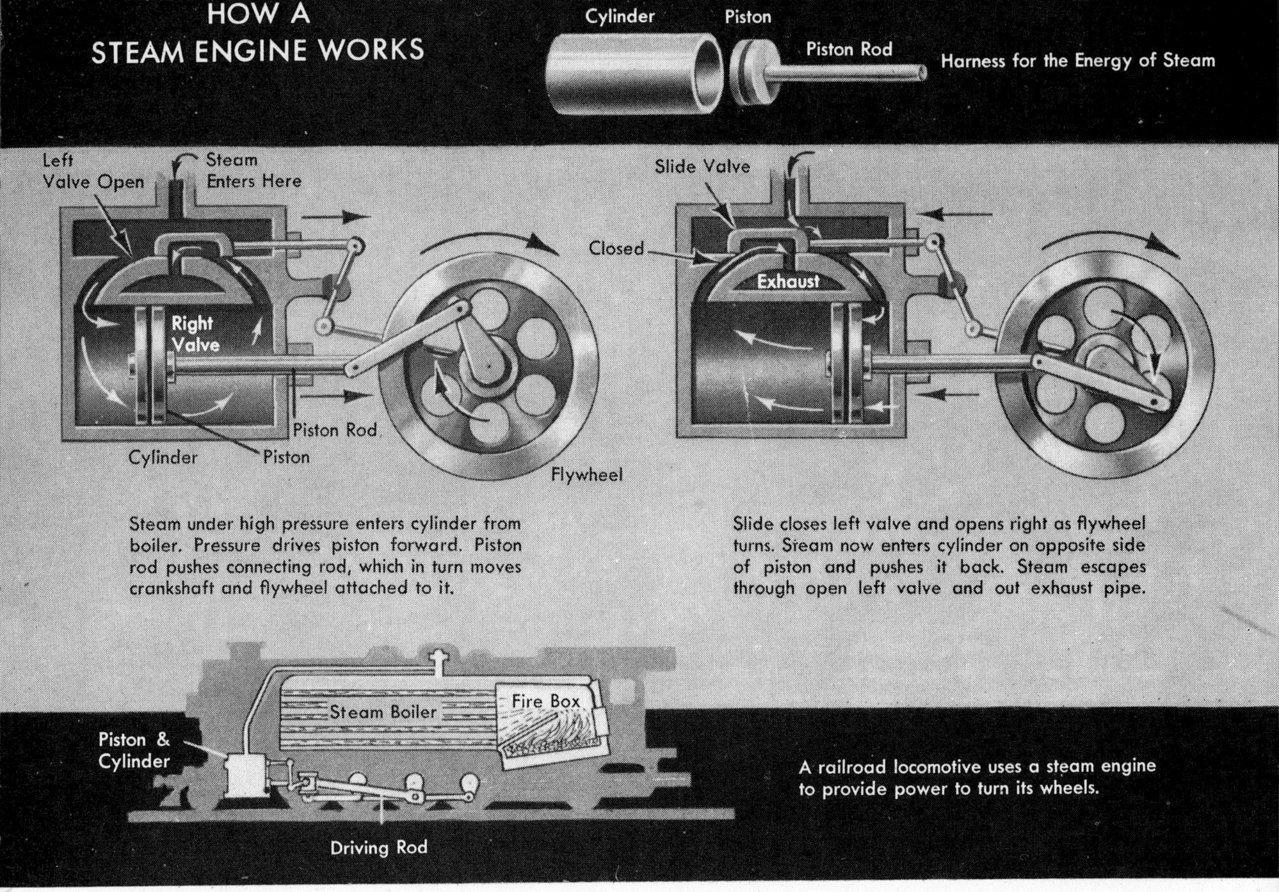
HOW A
STEAM ENGINE WORKS
Cylinder
Piston
Piston Rod
Harness for the Energy of Steam
Left Valve Open
Steam Enters Here
Right Valve
Piston Rod
Cylinder
Piston
Flywheel
Slide Valve
Closed
Exhaust
Steam under high pressure enters cylinder from boiler. Pressure drives piston forward. Piston rod pushes connecting rod, which in turn moves crankshaft and flywheel attached to it.
Slide closes left valve and opens right as flywheel turns. Steam now enters cylinder on opposite side of piston and pushes it back. Steam escapes through open left valve and out exhaust pipe.
Steam Boiler
Fire Box
Piston & Cylinder
Driving Rod
A railroad locomotive uses a steam engine to provide power to turn its wheels.

**STEAM ENGINE** is any engine that is operated by the energy of expanding steam. The steam may be used to push pistons that turn the wheels of powerful locomotives. Or it may be used to spin huge turbines that drive electric generators and giant ocean liners. Large pumps, pile drivers, and many other kinds of powerful machines may also be driven by steam engines.

The development of the steam engine in the 1700's made modern industry possible. Until then, men had to depend on the power of their own muscles or on animal, wind, and water power. One steam engine could do the work of hundreds of horses. It could supply the power needed to run all the machines in a factory. A steam locomotive could haul thousands of tons of freight hundreds of miles in a single day. Steamships provided safe, fast, dependable water transportation.

### How Steam Engines Work

A steam engine does not create power. It uses steam to change the heat energy released by burning fuel into

Gendreau; Ewing Galloway

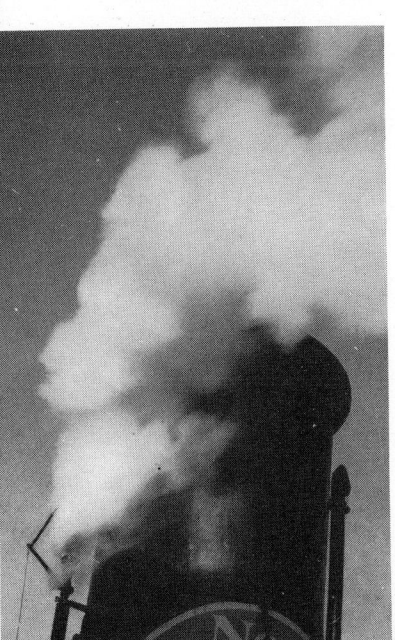

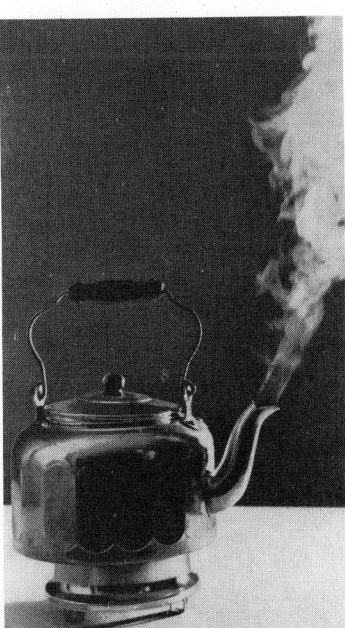

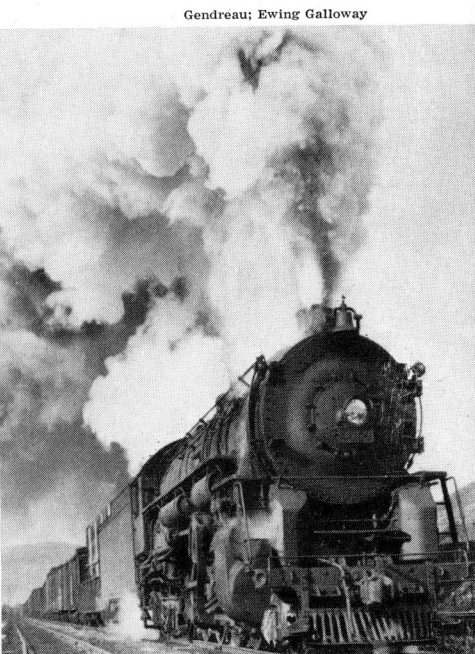

# STEAM ENGINE

rotary or back-and-forth motion that can do work. Each steam engine has a *furnace* in which coal, oil, wood, or some other fuel is burned to produce heat energy. In atomic power plants, a reactor serves as the furnace and splitting atoms produce the heat (see ATOMIC REACTOR). Each steam engine also has a *boiler*. The heat from the burning fuel changes water into steam inside the boiler. The steam expands, or takes up many times the space of the original water. This energy of expansion can be used in two ways: (1) to push a piston back and forth, or (2) to spin a turbine.

**Piston Steam Engines** have pistons that slide back and forth in cylinders (see PISTON). Various systems of valves allow the steam to enter a cylinder and drive a piston first in one direction and then the other, and to exhaust the used steam. These engines are often called *reciprocating* engines, because of the back-and-forth, or reciprocating, motion of their pistons. Steam hammers used to drive piles and to forge metal require this kind of motion (see FORGING; STEAM HAMMER). A locomotive, however, requires rotary motion to turn its wheels. This is done by attaching a crankshaft to the ends of the pistons. In some types of reciprocating steam engines, called *compound engines*, the steam may flow through as many as four cylinders and operate four pistons before it is finally exhausted.

**Steam Turbines** produce a rotary motion. A steam turbine has many sets of bladed wheels mounted on a long shaft. The steam enters at one end of the turbine and spins the bladed wheels as it gushes past them. Steam turbines are used chiefly to turn electric generators and the propellers of ships.

### History

Hero, a scientist who lived in Alexandria, Egypt, described the first known steam engine in 120 B.C. The engine consisted of a small, hollow globe mounted on a pipe running to a steam kettle. Two L-shaped pipes were fastened to opposite sides of the globe. When steam rushed out of the two L-shaped pipes, it caused the globe to whirl (see JET PROPULSION [picture, The First Jet Engine]). This engine, however, performed no useful work, and hundreds of years passed before the first successful steam engines were developed in the 1600's.

**The First Steam Engines** operated on the ability of steam *to condense* back into a liquid rather than on its ability to expand. When steam condenses, the liquid takes up far less space than the steam. If this condensing action takes place in a sealed *vessel*, or container, a partial *vacuum*, or sucking action, is created that can be put to useful work.

In 1698, Thomas Savery (1650-1715), an Englishman, patented the first practical steam engine, a pump to drain water from mines. Savery's pump had no moving parts other than valves operated by hand. These were turned to let steam enter a sealed vessel. Cold water was poured on the vessel to chill it and condense the steam. Then a valve was opened so the vacuum in the vessel could suck water up a pipe.

In 1712, Thomas Newcomen (1663-1729), an English blacksmith, invented another steam-engine pump for mines. Newcomen's engine had a large horizontal beam balanced in the middle like a seesaw. A piston which fitted into a cylinder hung from one end of the beam. When steam was let into the cylinder, it forced the piston up, lowering the other end of the beam. Cold water was then sprayed into the cylinder, the steam condensed, and the vacuum sucked the piston down again. This raised the other end of the horizontal beam. This end of the beam was attached to the piston of a pump in a mine.

**Watt's Engine.** When James Watt began his experiments in 1763, the Newcomen engine was the best known. It set Watt to thinking, because it used an enormous quantity of steam and therefore a large amount of fuel. Watt saw that the alternate heating and cooling of the cylinder wasted much heat. He invented an engine in which the condenser and the cylinder were separate. The cylinder always remained hot. This saved three fourths of the fuel cost, because none of the steam was lost through condensation by entering a cold cylinder.

Watt took out his first patent on a steam engine in 1769, and continued to make improvements in his engines. Perhaps his most important improvement was the use of the *double-action* principle. In engines based on this principle, the steam is used first on one side of the piston, then on the other side. Watt also learned to shut off the steam when the cylinder was only partly filled. This allowed the expansion of the steam already in the cylinder to complete the piston's stroke. Many persons mistakenly believe that Watt invented the steam engine. But he only improved it. He reduced the cost of operating *condensing* engines and made it practical to use these engines for other kinds of work than pumping.

**Modern Steam Engines.** The main improvement in the years after Newcomen and Watt was to develop engines capable of using high-pressure steam. Watt never experimented in the use of high-pressure steam, because he feared the danger of an explosion. The steam pressures in his engines were not much greater than air pressure, or about 15 pounds to the square inch. Then, in the late 1700's and early 1800's, an Englishman named Richard Trevithick designed and built the first high-pressure steam engines. One of the first Trevithick engines operated under 30 pounds of steam pressure. By 1815, Oliver Evans (1755-1819), an American, had built an engine that used 200 pounds of steam pressure. Today, many steam engines use steam under a pressure of more than 1,000 pounds to the square inch.

Other improvements made in steam engines included the development of the compound engine, and the use of *superheated* steam. In superheating, the temperature of the steam is raised above 700° F. without increasing the pressure. This helps keep the incoming steam from condensing on the surfaces of the piston cylinder, because superheated steam does not cool so quickly as ordinary steam. In the late 1800's, the invention of steam turbines marked another big improvement in steam engines. Steam turbines provided an economical source of power to turn electric generators, and to drive the propellers of steamships.

OTTO A. UYEHARA

**Related Articles** in WORLD BOOK include:
Governor
Evans, Oliver
Industrial Revolution
 (The Steam Engine)
Locomotive
Newcomen, Thomas
Ship and Shipping
Steam
Trevithick, Richard
Turbine (Steam Turbines)
Watt, James

**STEAM FITTER** is a worker who installs and repairs the network of pipes needed in heating, air conditioning, refrigeration, and similar systems. He works with pipes made of various materials, and connects them to such equipment as furnaces, radiators, boilers, and cooling devices. Installing large systems requires precise measurements and the steam fitter may use blueprints to guide him in his work. In smaller installation jobs and repair work, the steam fitter frequently relies on his experience to place the pipes. Candidates usually serve a five-year apprenticeship or attend a trade school to become *journeymen* (experienced) steam fitters.

**STEAM HAMMER** is a power-driven hammer which is used to make heavy forgings. The hammer head is raised by the pressure of steam which is admitted into the lower part of the cylinder. When the hammer reaches the desired height, the steam is released and the hammer falls. Steam admitted into the upper part can be used to increase the speed of the fall. The speed with which the hammer is released also determines its force.

Steam hammers vary in weight from 100 pounds to 100 tons. They can be controlled so perfectly that a giant hammer head can descend with crushing force, or crack a nut without harming the kernel.

*Steam drop hammers* are raised like ordinary steam hammers. But they differ from other steam hammers in that they fall by their own weight. The steam hammer was invented by the Scottish engineer and manufacturer James Nasmyth in 1839. ARTHUR C. ANSLEY

See also FORGING; NASMYTH, JAMES; TRIP HAMMER.

**STEAM HEATING.** See HEATING (Central Heating).

**STEAM SHOVEL** is a large *excavating* (digging) machine that is powered by steam. It has a large iron or steel scoop with teeth along the front edge. The bottom of the scoop has a hinge, so it can swing open and release its load. The scoop works from a beam that can be moved in any direction. An operator lowers the scoop to the ground and drives it forward and upward, scooping up earth and rock.

In 1838, William S. Otis of Massachusetts developed the first steam shovel. It dug the roadbed for the Western Railroad in Massachusetts. Engineers used steam shovels for projects such as the Panama Canal. Diesel power shovels have now replaced them. R. G. HENNES

See also BUILDING AND WRECKING MACHINES.

**STEAM TURBINE.** See TURBINE.

**STEAMBOAT** is a term used for steam-driven vessels that sail on rivers. It also refers to the smaller vessels on lakes or in the coastal waters of the sea. *Steamship* is used for large vessels such as those sailing on the open sea. John Fitch built the first workable steamboat in 1787. The first financially successful steamboat was Robert Fulton's *Clermont*. In 1807, it steamed the 150 miles up the Hudson from New York City to Albany in 32 hours. Steamboats carried passengers on the great rivers before the development of railroad systems and other faster or more efficient means of transportation. Steamships are still used along the U.S. coasts and in many other parts of the world. ROBERT H. BURGESS

**Related Articles** in WORLD BOOK include:
Clermont
Fitch, John
Fulton, Robert
Roosevelt, Nicholas J.
Ship and Shipping
Twain, Mark
   (picture: Mississippi
   Steamboats)
Yukon River (picture)

**STEAMING.** See COOKING (Methods).
**STEAMSHIP.** See SHIP AND SHIPPING; STEAMBOAT.
**STEARIC ACID,** *stee AR ik,* is a valuable organic "fatty" acid that comes from many animal and vegetable fats and oils. The acid gets its name from the Greek word *stear,* which means *tallow*.

Stearic acid is prepared commercially by treating animal fats with water at high temperature and at high pressure. Stearic acid is used for softening rubber, and also in manufacturing wax candles, cosmetics, and soaps.

Stearic acid is a waxy solid that melts at a temperature of about 70° C. (158° F.). Its chemical formula is $CH_3(CH_2)_{16}COOH$. JOHN E. LEFFLER

See also FAT; ACID.

**STEARIN,** *STE uh rin,* is a combination of stearic acid and glycerin. Chemically, stearin is an intricate compound of carbon, hydrogen, and oxygen. It is the chief ingredient of mutton and beef fat, and certain vegetable fats such as palm oil. When these substances are boiled, the stearin is crystallized into pearly, waxlike scales which have neither taste nor odor. Stearin is boiled with alkali to form soap. The stearic acid combines with the alkali, and the glycerin is separated as a by-product of the soapmaking. Stearin also yields an oil which is used in the manufacture of some margarines. LEONE RUTLEDGE CARROLL

See also GLYCERIN; STEARIC ACID.

**STEATITE.** See SOAPSTONE.

**STEDMAN, EDMUND CLARENCE** (1833-1908), was an American poet and journalist. He became a respected literary critic for such books as *Victorian Poets* (1875), *Poets of America* (1885), and *The Nature and Elements of Poetry* (1892).

Stedman was coeditor of Edgar Allan Poe's works in 10 volumes (1894-1895) and of the 11-volume *Library of American Literature* (1889-1890). Stedman encouraged the American public's taste for the genteel and idealistic. His work also promoted a greater interest in American literature.

Stedman was born in Hartford, Conn. He entered Yale University, but left school to serve as a war correspondent for the *New York World* during the Civil War. Stedman also operated a prosperous brokerage business in New York City. HARRY H. CLARK

**STEEL.** See IRON AND STEEL; ALLOY.

**STEEL GUITAR.** See HAWAII (Dancing and Music).

**STEELE, SIR RICHARD** (1672-1729), a British writer, created a new kind of essay which mirrored the manners of his day. His essays became as popular as present-day gossip columns.

For his services to the Whig political party, he was appointed *gazetteer,* or editor of the government newspaper, in 1707. He founded the *Tatler* in 1709, which contained essays about society, literature,

**Sir Richard Steele**
Brown Bros.

## STEELE, WILBUR DANIEL

women's affairs, and politics. Joseph Addison contributed several essays, and helped Steele write others (see ADDISON, JOSEPH). Steele had more understanding of character, but Addison was a more polished writer. The two men founded the *Spectator*, another paper, in 1711, and later the *Guardian*.

Steele was born in Dublin. He was educated at Charterhouse School and at Oxford University. He left Oxford to join the army. Steele served in Parliament from 1713 to 1722. ARNOLD WILLIAMS

**STEELE, WILBUR DANIEL** (1886- ), an American writer, became best known for his carefully constructed, workmanlike short stories. He has written such novels as *That Girl from Memphis* (1945). But his reputation rests on the solid body of short stories he has written since his first story, "A White Horse Winter," was accepted by the *Atlantic Monthly* in 1912. His stories have received six O. Henry Memorial awards. Steele was born in Greensboro, N.C. ARTHUR MIZENER

**STEELHEAD.** See TROUT.

**STEELWORKERS OF AMERICA, UNITED (USWA),** is a labor union affiliated with the American Federation of Labor and Congress of Industrial Organizations (AFL-CIO). It has locals throughout North America. Its members work in most occupations that are related to the iron, steel, aluminum, and nonferrous metal industries. For membership, see LABOR (table).

The union was founded in 1936 as the Steel Workers Organizing Committee (SWOC) of the CIO. The Amalgamated Association of Iron, Steel, and Tin Workers became part of the SWOC in 1936. The present name was adopted in 1942. The International Union of Mine, Mill and Smelter Workers merged with the USWA in 1967. The USWA publishes a monthly newspaper, *Steel Labor*. Headquarters are at 1500 Commonwealth Building, Pittsburgh, Pa. 15222.

Critically reviewed by UNITED STEELWORKERS OF AMERICA

See also MCDONALD, DAVID J.

**STEENBOK.** See STEINBOK.

**STEEPLE** is a spire, or spire and tower, usually placed atop such buildings as a church or temple. The tower often contains bells, and is sometimes called a *campanile*.

See also CAMPANILE; CATHEDRAL (pictures); MASSACHUSETTS INSTITUTE OF TECHNOLOGY (picture); SPIRE.

**STEEPLECHASING** is the sport of horse racing over obstacles. Races are described as being *over brush*, *over timber*, or *over hurdles*, depending on the obstacles used. Jockeys ride thoroughbred horses at breakneck speed in steeplechases. Steeplechasing originated in England, and is the outgrowth of fox-hunting on horseback. The name comes from races hunters staged across country to "yonder church steeple." Organized U.S. steeplechasing began shortly after the Civil War. In addition to races at the major tracks, steeplechase meetings are held by fox-hunting clubs. JOHN E. COOPER

**STEER.** See CATTLE.

**STEERING.** See AIRPLANE (Controls); AUTOMOBILE (The Steering System); NAVIGATION.

**STEFAN-BOLTZMANN LAW.** See BOLTZMANN, LUDWIG.

**STEFANSSON,** *STEF'n s'n,* **VILHJALMUR** (1879-1962), an arctic explorer and author, emphasized that the arctic region is of great military and strategic importance. He argued that the region is "warm and friendly," and should be settled and developed.

Stefansson was born in Arnes, Manitoba, Canada, on Nov. 3, 1879, and was educated at the University of North Dakota, the University of Iowa, and Harvard University. In 1905 he became a member of an archaeological expedition to Iceland. Between 1913 and 1918, he led an expedition which explored Canadian and Alaskan arctic regions.

Macmillan
**Vilhjalmur Stefansson**

During World War II, Stefansson served as an advisor to the United States Army and Navy. He became arctic and antarctic consultant to Dartmouth College in 1947. Later, he moved his 35,000-volume polar library to Dartmouth. He wrote many books, including *The Arctic in Fact and Fable* (1945), *Not by Bread Alone* (1946), and *The Fat of the Land* (1956). W. R. WILLOUGHBY

**STEFFENS, LINCOLN** (1866-1936), was an American author, editor, lecturer, and reformer. He was one of a group of writers known as *muckrakers* because their magazine articles from about 1902 to 1909 exposed corruption in government, business, and labor. Starting in 1902 with an exposé of crooked political practices in St. Louis, Steffens went on to study and write about conditions in many U.S. cities and states.

Steffens was born in San Francisco, and studied at the University of California and in Europe. He began his career with the *New York Commercial Advertiser*. He soon joined *McClure's Magazine*, and there wrote the articles that made him famous. Later, he wrote for the *American Magazine* and *Everybody's Magazine*. He published his famous *Autobiography* in 1931. JOHN TEBBEL

Brown Bros.
**Lincoln Steffens**

**STEGOSAURUS.** See DINOSAUR (Bird-Hipped Dinosaurs).

**STEICHEN,** *STY kun,* **EDWARD** (1879- ), is an American photographer. He studied painting, but became interested in photography as an art. In World War I, he took charge of aerial photography for the American Expeditionary Force. In World War II, he headed a Navy aviation photographic unit. Steichen was director of the photographic department of the Museum of Modern Art in New York City from 1947 to 1962. In 1955, he organized the well-known photographic exhibit, *The Family of Man*, at the museum. Steichen received the Presidential Medal of Freedom in 1963. He was born in Luxembourg, and moved to the United States in 1882. See also PHOTOGRAPHY (Photography for Everyone). BEAUMONT NEWHALL

**STEIG, WILLIAM.** See CARTOON (Leading Cartoonists).

**STEIN, GERTRUDE** (1874-1946), an American author, was as important for her influence on other writers as for her own work. She influenced every well-known American writer who worked in Paris during the 1920's, including Ernest Hemingway. Of her own works, the best-known is *Three Lives* (1908), and the most entertaining are her two autobiographies, *The Autobiography of Alice B. Toklas* (1933) and *Everybody's Autobiography* (1937). In her own work, she said, she was "always... possessed by the intellectual passion for exactitude in the description of inner and outer reality."

Miss Stein was born in Allegheny, Pa. She studied at Radcliffe College, where she was a pupil of William James, and at Johns Hopkins University. In 1903 she went to live in Paris with her lifelong friend, Alice Toklas. Miss Stein was a large, plain woman with close-cropped hair, an authoritative manner, and a talent for friendship. She was close to artists Pablo Picasso and Henri Matisse before they were famous. ARTHUR MIZENER

**STEINBECK, JOHN** (1902-1968), was an American novelist. He won the 1962 Nobel prize for literature, primarily for his novel *The Winter of Our Discontent* (1961). His novel, *The Grapes of Wrath* (1939), is one of the most famous books of our time. It describes the "Okie" migration to California during the depression of the 1930's. It has been called the "twentieth-century *Uncle Tom's Cabin*." Steinbeck won the Pulitzer prize in 1940 for this work.

Steinbeck was born in Salinas, Calif., and studied at Stanford University. Most of his novels are set in California, and nearly all deal with the poor and downtrodden. His first works were unsuccessful, but in 1937 his sixth novel, *Of Mice and Men*, became a best seller. Later it was made into a play and a motion picture. Three of his books, *Tortilla Flat* (1935), *Cannery Row* (1944), and *Sweet Thursday* (1954), portray the life of happy-go-lucky ne'er-do-wells in a town on the Monterey (Calif.) peninsula.

In later years, Steinbeck returned to reporting, a career he once followed as a young man. In 1943, he became European correspondent for the *New York Herald Tribune*. He wrote *Russian Journal* (1948), an account of a trip to Russia.

He also wrote *In Dubious Battle* (1936), which tells of a strike in a California valley; *The Moon Is Down* (1942), about the Nazi occupation of Norway; and *East of Eden* (1952), a story of a California family; *The Short Reign of Pippin IV* (1957), a satire on contemporary French life; and *Travels with Charley* (1962), a diary of a trip through the United States. GEORGE J. BECKER

Field Enterprises Educational Corp. Collection

**Steinberg's *Sam's Art*** shows how the artist uses sharp line and an unusual combination of images to make witty comments about modern life. Much of his work appears in *The New Yorker* magazine.

**STEINBERG, SAUL** (1914-    ), is an artist noted for his small-scale pen-and-ink drawings. His work is satirical and full of unexpected images and ideas. He became noted for funny drawings that had no captions or explanations. In many of his drawings, figures utter "words" indicated by fantastic forms coming out of their mouths.

Steinberg likes to draw parades, city crowds, strange animals, railroad stations, and drum majorettes. Some of his drawings of musicians are on music paper. He sometimes uses graph paper as a background and also makes documents resembling diplomas or certificates in which the writing is decorative but illegible. Steinberg was born in Rîmnicu Sărat, Romania. He came to the United States at the age of 28. ALLEN S. WELLER

**STEINBOK**, *STINE bahk*, or STEENBOK, is a small antelope that lives in southern and east-central Africa. Its name, taken from the Dutch, means *stone buck*. It has a reddish or pale brownish coat above, and is almost white below. The animals stand about 22 inches high. Both sexes have straight slender horns that are seldom more than 4 to 5 inches long. Steinboks prefer to live in grassland, but they can sometimes be found in open woodland. Hunters often hunt them with hounds. These antelope hide flat on the ground until the last minute of danger, and then dash away.

**Scientific Classification.** The steinbok is a member of the bovid family, *Bovidae*. The most common steinbok is classified as genus *Raphicerus*, species *R. campestris*. VICTOR H. CAHALANE

**STEINMETZ, CHARLES PROTEUS** (1865-1923), was a German-born mathematician and engineer. He is best known for his development of the theory of alternating currents and for his experiments with "man-made lightning." The disadvantages of poverty, political misfortune, and a physical deformity which

**John Steinbeck**
Philippe Halsman

**Gertrude Stein**
Carl Van Vechten

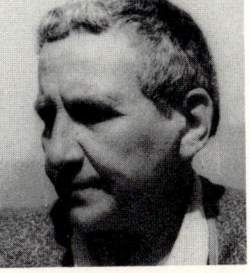

**Charles Steinmetz**
Brown Bros.

691

# STELLA

made him a lifelong cripple, did not prevent him from becoming a scientific genius.

Steinmetz established his reputation in the American scientific community in 1892. He wrote a paper which contained an analysis of *hysteresis loss*, a magnetic effect peculiar to alternating current. He was soon invited to join the newly founded General Electric Company, where he spent the remainder of his career in research on electricity. Out of his laboratory, where for some years he lived as well as worked, came many experimental discoveries and inventions.

Steinmetz was born in Breslau, Germany. He fled the country in 1888, just before receiving a Ph.D. from Breslau University. He had been threatened with arrest for student socialist activity. He came to the United States in 1889. He taught electricity at Union College, Schenectady, N.Y., and wrote books on the theory of alternating current.

ROBERT P. MULTHAUF

**STELLA** was the name used by Swift for Esther Johnson. See SWIFT, JONATHAN.

**STELLITE.** See COBALT.

**STEM** is the central part of a plant. It supports the leaves, flowers, and fruits. The largest stems are the trunks of the sequoia trees of California.

Most stems have special structures which make them semirigid frameworks. In annual herbs, the ordinary cells of the stem usually fill with watery sap. When the stem loses its water, it wilts and is much less rigid. All woody stems and the stems of some herbs have special supporting cells besides the ordinary cell walls of cellulose. These special cells are known as tracheids, bast fibers, and wood fibers.

The stem also furnishes channels for carrying sap between the roots and leaves. The roots absorb minerals and water from the soil, and the leaves manufacture food. Conducting cells and the supporting cells make up a great part of the stem. Sometimes the same cells carry on both functions.

There are special cells that carry water and minerals, and others for dissolved food such as sugar and proteins. The water-carrying cells are known as vessels and tracheids. They form the tissue called *xylem*. The food-conducting cells are known as sieve tubes, and form the *phloem* tissue.

Many plants have a third tissue, the *cambium*. It is located between the xylem and phloem. The cambium produces new layers of xylem and phloem, usually each year.

**Cross Section of the Stem.** There are two common arrangements of xylem and phloem in the stem. One type is found in monocotyledonous plants, such as corn, bamboo, and grass. These plants have no cambium. The xylem and phloem form bundles in the shape of strands running the length of the stem. The second type occurs in dicotyledonous plants, such as oaks, elms, roses, and fruit trees. If a young stem of one of these plants is cut across, it shows bundles of cells, like the spokes of a wheel. In each bundle, all the phloem is on the outside, and the xylem inside. Older stems and trunks have a layer of phloem just inside the bark, and the rest of the stem is all xylem. The stem grows a new layer of xylem each year, thus forming the annual rings. The stems of full-grown dicotyledonous plants have an outer protective covering of bark, which contains cork layers. These layers protect the tree, and keep it from losing water.

**Special Functions.** Besides supporting the plant and carrying sap, some stems manufacture food. Others store food, and still others help produce new plants. In the case of perennial plants, food manufacture stops when the bark grows thick and corky, thus shutting out the light.

Leafless plants, like the cacti, have thick green stems that expose a broad surface to the light and air, and serve as leaves. The fleshy stem also holds water for the plant to use in time of drought. Many a thirsty traveler has drunk this reserve water to save his life.

**Underground Stems.** Some plants have underground stems. If these are long and slender they are called rootstocks. Examples are the May apple, Solomon's-seal, and mints. Other underground stems are the bulbs of the hyacinth and lily, and the tuber of the white potato.

**CROSS SECTION OF A STEM** A cross section of a stem of a monocotyledonous plant, *left*, shows scattered vascular bundles. In a dicotyledonous plant, *right*, the bundles lie in a circle.

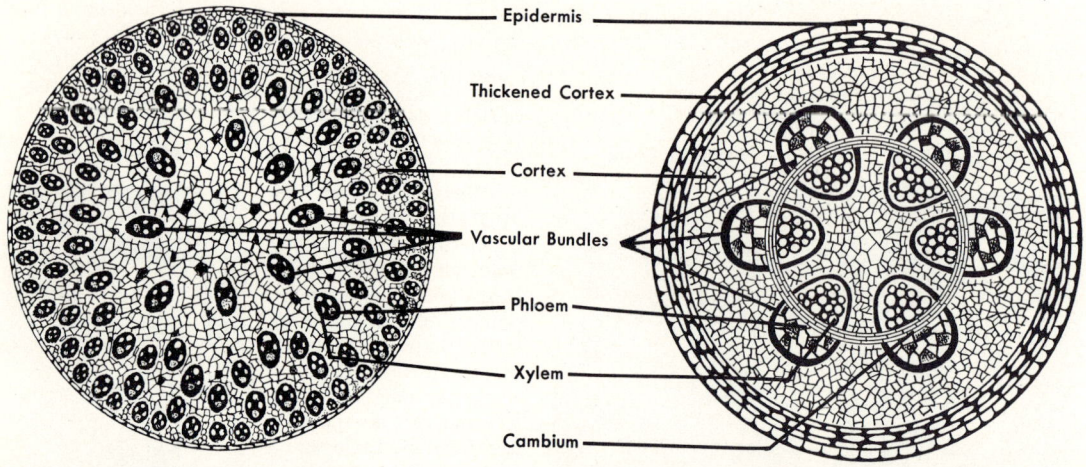

Monocotyledonous Plant            Dicotyledonous Plant

Stems like these hold large reserves of food, and keep the plant alive when it cannot make new food.

**Reproduction by Stems.** Many plants reproduce from portions of the stem. The most troublesome weeds are those which can grow again from their underground stems or rootstocks. The runners of the strawberry, lily bulbs, and potato tubers also produce new plants. A branch of the black raspberry will take root and form a new bush. Many plants, including the grapevine and currant, grow from stems that are broken off and planted. Such stems are called *cuttings*, or *slips*.

**Life and Growth.** In some plants, the stem lives a single year. In others, it may live indefinitely.

Different stems also have different rates of growth. The stalks of the sunflower and the giant ragweed may grow 10 to 12 feet in a season. Slender climbing stems often grow 40 feet in a single summer. Trees in dense forests get light and air by having most of their branches arranged at the tops of their very long trunks.

**Uses of Stems.** Man and the animals get much of their food from plant stems. Sugar, molasses, and syrup come from the sap in the stems of the sugar cane and the maple tree. The edible parts of potatoes and onions are underground stems. Asparagus, celery, and other vegetables are aerial shoots. Corn syrup is made from cornstalks. Common starch is often made from the potato, and sago is made from the starchy pith of the palm trunk. Perhaps most important of all is the use of woody stems as a building material. ARTHUR W. GALSTON

Related Articles in WORLD BOOK include:

| Bark | Leaf (The Petiole) | Root |
| Bulb | Phloem | Sap |
| Corm | Plant (Stems) | Tuber |
| Grafting | Rhizome | |

**STEM.** See SHIP AND SHIPPING (table: Nautical Terms).

**STENCIL,** *STEN sul*, is a thin sheet of metal or other material, with lines and dots cut in it for the purpose of reproducing designs or letters. The stencil is placed on the surface of the material to be decorated or lettered. A brush or sponge is then wet with ink or paint and passed over the stencil. The stencil process serves as a quick method of marking packing boxes. It is also widely used to decorate curtains, bedspreads, furniture, and other household articles, as well as clothes and uniforms. Stencil designs also are used to decorate walls and for various types of signs. See also DUPLICATOR (Stencil Duplicator). ARTHUR ZAIDENBERG

**STENDHAL** (1783-1842) is the pen name of MARIE HENRI BEYLE, one of the chief figures in the history of the French psychological novel. Stendhal was born in Grenoble. He served in the Napoleonic Wars, and Napoleon I became his great hero. Julien Sorel, the hero of Stendhal's masterpiece *The Red and the Black* (1831), lives a life of action and has great ambition, as Napoleon did (see RED AND THE BLACK, THE). Stendhal's other great novel, *The Charterhouse of Parma* (1839), begins with Napoleon's defeat at the Battle of Waterloo, and tells a story of political intrigue in Italy.

In his writings, Stendhal was concerned basically with the search for happiness, which he believed could be achieved by the exercise of physical energy and will. Elements of realism and romanticism can be found in his work. He usually neglected other aspects of his novels in favor of analyses of the minute, changing emotional states of his characters.

# STEPHEN

Stendhal left three partly autobiographical novels unfinished at his death. They are *The Life of Henri Brulard*, *Lamiel*, and *Lucien Leuwen*. ROBERT J. NIESS

**STENGEL, CASEY** (1890?-    ), was one of baseball's great managers. He led the New York Yankees to seven world championships, including five straight from 1949 to 1953, and again in 1956 and 1958. Stengel's Yankees were also American League champions from 1955 through 1958, and in 1960. In 1962, Stengel became manager of the New York Mets. A hip fracture forced him to retire in 1965. He was elected to baseball's Hall of Fame in 1966. Born CHARLES DILLON STENGEL in Kansas City, Mo., he became a professional ballplayer in 1910. During his long career, he also managed the Brooklyn Dodgers and Boston Braves. ED FITZGERALD

**STENOGRAPHY.** See OFFICE WORK; SHORTHAND; SHORTHAND MACHINE.

**STENOSIS.** See RHEUMATIC FEVER.

**STENOTYPE.** See SHORTHAND MACHINE.

**STEPHEN,** *STEE vun* (1097?-1154), was an English king whose reign was so full of strife that it is called "The Anarchy." The cause was a disputed succession. Stephen was the son of Adela, daughter of William the Conqueror. The other claimant to the throne was Matilda, daughter of Henry I. Henry had persuaded his barons to pledge allegiance to her before he died in 1135. In 1153, Stephen was finally forced to recognize as his successor Matilda's son, Henry II, the first Plantagenet king. ROBERT S. HOYT

**STEPHEN** is the name of nine popes of the Roman Catholic Church. The church once listed 10 popes named Stephen. But in 1961 it dropped Stephen II from its list of popes. The numbers of the other Stephens were then moved up accordingly. The dates of their reigns are given below. The Roman numerals in parentheses are the old numbers used to name the popes.

Stephen I, Saint (254-257)  Stephen VI (VII) (896-897)
Stephen II (III) (752-757)  Stephen VII (VIII) (928-931)
Stephen III (IV) (768-772)  Stephen VIII (IX) (939-942)
Stephen IV (V) (816-817)   Stephen IX (X) (1057-1058)
Stephen V (VI) (885-891)

**Saint Stephen I** ( ? -257) became famous because of his controversy with Saint Cyprian, bishop of Carthage. Cyprian insisted on rebaptizing converts who had received baptism from heretical ministers. Stephen opposed this practice, and established the enduring principle that baptism when correctly given, even by a non-Catholic, is valid and cannot be repeated. Stephen was born in Rome.

**Stephen II (III)** ( ? -757) was the first pope to travel to France. There, he sought the help of the Franks against the Lombards, who wanted to conquer Italy. He consecrated Pepin the Short and his sons as kings of the Franks in 754. In return, they became the protectors of the papacy. In 756, Pepin gave land in central Italy to Stephen that established the Papal States.

**Stephen III (IV)** (720?-772) excluded laymen from the election of the pope because of political interference by the Italian princes. He was born in Sicily.

**Stephen IX (X)** (1000?-1058) tried unsuccessfully to prevent the separation of the Eastern and Western churches. He succeeded Victor II as pope in 1057. Stephen was born in Lorraine. GUSTAVE WEIGEL and FULTON J. SHEEN

693

# STEPHEN, GEORGE

**STEPHEN, GEORGE** (1829-1921), BARON MOUNT STEPHEN, was a Canadian financier. He was one of the founders, as well as the first president, of the Canadian Pacific Railway. Stephen was born at Dufftown, Scotland. He went to Canada in 1850 and became a cloth manufacturer in Montreal. In 1876 he became president of the Bank of Montreal. In 1880, he became a leading member of the company that built the Canadian Pacific, Canada's first transcontinental railway. He moved to England in 1888.  W. R. WILLOUGHBY

**STEPHEN, SAINT,** was the first Christian martyr. He was stoned to death outside Jerusalem some time after the Crucifixion (Acts 7:59).

Stephen was one of the seven church officers, or deacons, appointed by the apostles. The deacons were to look after the poor. Stephen was a deeply religious man, known for the miracles he performed and for his preaching. Stephen's enemies accused him of teaching disobedience to the customs and rules associated with the law of Moses. He was brought to trial before the high council of the Sanhedrin. Here he made a great speech in his own defense (Acts 7). He said he was not speaking against the sacred Law, but that instead those who attacked him were failing to obey the Law themselves. The mob became so furious that they attacked Stephen. One witness to his death was Saint Paul, who was not yet converted to Christianity (Acts 8:1). Saint Stephen's Day is observed on December 26, both in the Roman Catholic Church and also in the Church of England.  FREDERICK C. GRANT

**STEPHEN F. AUSTIN STATE COLLEGE.** See UNIVERSITIES AND COLLEGES (table).

**STEPHENS, ALEXANDER HAMILTON** (1812-1883), was vice-president of the Confederate States of America during the Civil War. He was opposed to secession, but he remained loyal to Georgia when the state left the Union in 1861. He served as a delegate to the Montgomery Convention which formed the Confederacy, and he was chosen vice-president of the new government. During the war, he often disagreed with Jefferson Davis, president of the Confederacy, on questions of states' rights.

In February, 1865, Stephens led an unsuccessful peace commission which met with President Abraham Lincoln at Hampton Roads (see HAMPTON ROADS CONFERENCE). After the war, he was arrested and imprisoned for six months at Fort Warren in Boston Harbor. Georgia elected him to the United States Senate in 1866, but Congress refused him his seat. He then devoted his time to writing *A Constitutional View of the Late War Between the States* (1867-1870). Later, he wrote other books, and became editor of the Atlanta *Southern Sun* in 1871.

Stephens was again elected to Congress in 1872, and served 10 years. He was elected governor of Georgia in 1883, but he died a few months after taking office.

**Alexander H. Stephens**
Brown Bros.

Stephens was born near Crawfordville, Ga., and was educated at the University of Georgia. He had originally intended to become a minister, but he changed his mind, and studied law instead. In 1834, he was admitted to the bar, and two years later became a member of the Georgia state legislature. He opposed vigilance committees, and the "slicking clubs," which were the parent of the Ku Klux Klan. From 1843 to 1859, he served as a congressman from Georgia. Alexander Hamilton Stephens represents Georgia in Statuary Hall in Washington, D.C.  W. B. HESSELTINE

See also CIVIL WAR (Secession).

**STEPHENS, JAMES** (1882-1950), was an Irish poet, novelist, and short-story writer. His work is sometimes humorous and playful and sometimes serious, but it is always imaginative and unusual. *The Crock of Gold*, a fantasy-novel, is probably his best-known book. It was first published in 1912. Stephens' interest in Irish folklore is apparent in much of his work, such as his *Irish Fairy Tales* (1920), a book for young people. He also wrote the books of verse *The Hill of Vision* (1912), *Strict Joy* (1931), and *Kings and the Moon* (1938). Stephens was born in Dublin.  JOSEPH E. BAKER

**STEPHENS COLLEGE** is a private college for women at Columbia, Mo. It offers liberal arts and science courses as well as work in selected vocational areas. It grants an Associate in Arts degree upon completion of two years of work. A Bachelor of Fine Arts degree is offered in music, theater, fashion, and dance. The college was founded in 1833 as the Columbia Female Academy. For enrollment, see UNIVERSITIES AND COLLEGES (table).  SEYMOUR A. SMITH

**STEPHENSON** is the family name of two British engineers, father and son. Their inventions helped create the British railway system.

**George Stephenson** (1781-1848) was called the *Founder of Railways*. His skill in repairing coal-hauling engines in the mines earned him the title of *Engine Doctor*. He finally decided to build a locomotive of his own. His second engine, *Puffing Billy* (1814), embodied his invention, the steam blast. This device increased the draft in the boiler. In turn, the fire became hotter and made steam of a higher pressure. His engine was so successful that it pulled heavy loads of coal for years. His locomotive, *The Rocket* (1829), traveled at the then unheard-of speed of 30 mph. It served as a model for later steam locomotives.

Stephenson invented many useful things besides engines, including a miner's lamp, a fisherman's lamp, and an alarm clock. He became well known for building the Stockton and Darlington Railway from 1821 to 1825. Then he built the difficult Liverpool and Manchester Railway. Here Stephenson used his original ideas for tunnels, grading, and bridges to make a level roadbed.

Stephenson was born on June 9, 1781, in Wylam, near Newcastle. At the age of eight he worked as a herdboy. In his spare time as a boy, Stephenson made

**George Stephenson**
Brown Bros.

little models of engines of clay and sticks which later helped him work out some of his great projects. He was consulted on major railway projects in many countries, and spread his original ideas for safety and passenger comfort. With the wealth from his inventions and locomotive factory, he became a philanthropist. His night schools for miners, and libraries, music clubs, recreation rooms, and schools for miners' children, were as original in his day as were his inventions.

**Robert Stephenson** (1803-1859), the son of George Stephenson, was chiefly noted for the great bridges and viaducts he built. He invented the tubular bridge, and introduced the use of tubular girders in the construction of iron bridges. Stephenson built railways in Germany, Switzerland, Canada, Egypt, and India. Later, he became interested in politics, and served in the House of Commons from 1847 until 1859.

Stephenson was born on Oct. 16, 1803, near the coal mines at Willington Quay. He started his partnership with his father by teaching him in the evenings. Afterwards, he studied at the University of Edinburgh and went to South America as a mining engineer. He returned in 1827, and helped his father build *The Rocket*. From 1833 to 1838, Stephenson was chief engineer for the construction of the London and Birmingham Railway. This railway was the first to enter London. He lived in London. JOHN H. KEMBLE

See also LOCOMOTIVE (picture); ROCKET, THE.

**STEPINAC**, *STEP ih nack*, **ALOYSIUS CARDINAL** (1898-1960), a Yugoslavian cardinal of the Roman Catholic Church, became a symbol of resistance to Communism after World War II. At that time, the Communist government of Marshal Tito determined to restrict organized religion in Yugoslavia. Stepinac was charged with aiding Germany and Italy during the war. He was tried in October, 1946, and sentenced to 16 years of hard labor.

*Wide World*
**Cardinal Stepinac**

He was offered freedom if he would leave the country, but he refused. In 1951, he was released. Pope Pius XII made him a cardinal in 1953. Stepinac was born in Zagreb, Yugoslavia. He worked for the rights of the Croatian people in Yugoslavia. Stepinac became an archbishop in 1937. JOHN T. FARRELL and FULTON J. SHEEN

**STEPPE**, *step*, is the Russian word for *plain*. The steppes of Russia stretch throughout the Ukraine, eastward to the Caspian Sea, and to the Altai Mountains in central Asia. These are great stretches of level grassy land with few trees. Cattle, sheep, and horses are grazed on the Asiatic steppes in spring. Farmers lead the animals to other pastures in summer because dry weather scorches the steppe grass. North America's Great Plains resemble the Russian steppes. ERNEST L. THURSTON

**STERE.** See METRIC SYSTEM (table).

**STEREO CAMERA.** See CAMERA (Stereo Cameras; picture).

**STEREOCHEMISTRY.** See PLASTICS (table: Plastics Terms).

# STEREOTYPING

**STEREOPHONIC SOUND.** See PHONOGRAPH (picture: Stereophonic Sound); HIGH FIDELITY (Stereophonic Hi-Fi Systems); SOUND (Stereophonic Sound).

**STEREOPTICON.** See PROJECTION MACHINE.

**STEREOSCOPE**, *STER ee oh SKOHP*, is an optical viewing device that makes photographs seem to have three dimensions. An ordinary camera sees things only in a flat plane, and never in the round, the way our eyes usually see things. But two cameras can work like our eyes. Set several inches apart, they can photograph the same object at the same time. These two photographs are then mounted side by side and viewed through a combination of lenses and prisms called a *stereoscope*. The two views then enter the eyes without strain, and the resulting mental image appears to have three dimensions. Everything is seen in the round.

A stereoscope with a cabinet of pictures was once a common item. The old-style stereoscope consisted of a rack and handle, a slide, and a pair of screened lens-prisms. The present-day stereoscope is a plastic box with two viewing holes. One popular type has picture slides mounted in a cardboard or plastic disk.

Today, stereoscopes are employed extensively in aerial surveys to map out land elevations. Astronomers use a special type of stereoscope for finding small planets. It is possible to mount two stereophotographs side by side and view them without prisms. The effect is a good picture, but it causes considerable eyestrain.

In 1952, producers introduced "three-dimensional" motion-picture projection. Some types used a large, curved screen and a new kind of sound projection to produce a three-dimensional effect. Others used a stereoscopic principle. Persons watching the film wore special eyeglasses so that each eye saw only the view meant for it. The mental image that resulted had three dimensions. EDITH LILLIAN SMITH WEBSTER

See also EYE (Stereoscopic Vision); CAMERA (Stereo Cameras); POLARIZED LIGHT.

**STEREOTYPING** is the method of making metal plates for use in printing. In the process, workmen set the type and lock it into a steel *chase* (frame). Others brush the face of the type with a thin coating of oil. A prepared sheet of thick, composite paper, called *flong*, is laid on the type and beaten or pressed tightly against it, using up to 1,000 tons of pressure. This sheet takes an impression of the face of the type or *cut* (picture) in the frame. The paper mold thus formed then goes into an oven and bakes until it becomes hard and dry. This mold, which is known as a *matrix*, or *mat*, is placed in a box face up. A workman pours melted stereotype metal, made up of tin, antimony, and lead, over it. This hardens at once, forming a solid plate of metal, and the page is printed from this.

Introduction of the stereotype process helped speed up newspaper printing. The stereotype plates used on small presses are flat. Those used on rotary presses for newspapers are in the form of half cylinders. It takes only about 15 minutes to make stereotype plates, and they are inexpensive compared to other printing plates. One matrix can produce a number of plates. Country newspapers get some of their subject matter from plants in cities which specialize in making plates and "mats." "Boilerplate" is the slang term for this

695

# STERILITY

material. Stereotyping is used mostly in printing newspapers, but it is also used to print magazines, catalogs, and inexpensive books. EUGENE M. ETTENBERG

See also ELECTROTYPING; TYPE.

**STERILITY,** *stuh RILL uh tih,* refers to the inability to reproduce. It applies to all forms of life, from microorganisms to higher plants, animals, and man.

Some antibiotics, such as penicillin, interfere with the reproductive powers of disease-producing bacteria. This keeps the number of bacteria low, and enables the body to overcome disease.

A plant may be sterile because of imperfectly developed reproductive organs. If the stamens and pistils are imperfect or absent, the plant cannot reproduce. Sterility in animals results if the reproductive organs do not develop properly. Certain hybrid animals, such as the mule, cannot reproduce.

Sterility in human beings may have several causes. It may result from defects in the structure of the reproductive organs. Certain diseases affect the reproductive organs and may cause sterility. Improper balance of the hormones produced by the pituitary gland, the thyroid gland, the adrenal glands, and the sex glands may result in failure to produce eggs or sperm. STUART ABEL

**STERILIZATION,** *STER uh lih ZAY shun,* in medicine and bacteriology, means the killing of bacteria. Germ killing helps to prevent infection and the spread of disease. Doctors and dentists sterilize their tools before they touch the human body. The bandages we buy, as well as many of the medicines, are sterilized before they are packed. Sterilization has been practiced only since the late 1800's. The noted English surgeon, Joseph Lister, introduced antiseptic, germ-killing methods into surgery.

Proper sterilization is done by fire, steam, heated air, or certain chemicals. Steam and heated air are the best, for they leave no foreign matter on the sterilized object. Fire is commonly used in the home to sterilize a needle with which to prick a blister or remove a splinter. Steam cabinets are often used to sterilize instruments in hospitals and doctors' and dentists' offices. Heated dry air is used to sterilize oily medicines. GEORGE L. BUSH

See also AUTOCLAVE; DISINFECTANT; GERMICIDAL LAMP; PASTEURIZATION; SOUND (Ultrasound).

**STERLET.** See STURGEON.

**STERLING COLLEGE.** See UNIVERSITIES AND COLLEGES (table).

**STERLING SILVER.** See SILVER (Uses of Silver).

**STERN.** See SHIP AND SHIPPING (table: Nautical Terms).

**STERN, ISAAC** (1920- ), is an American violinist, known for his fine artistry. He made his debut with the San Francisco Symphony Orchestra when he was 11 years old. Following this, he appeared with the Los Angeles Philharmonic Orchestra and toured the Pacific Coast in a concert series. Stern

Isaac Stern
S. Hurok

made his New York City debut in Town Hall in 1937 and played at Carnegie Hall in 1943. He was born in Kreminiecz, Russia, and was brought to the United States when he was a year old. DOROTHY DELAY

**STERN, OTTO** (1888- ), an American physicist, received the 1943 Nobel prize in physics. He showed that Louis Victor de Broglie's theory (that moving particles behave like waves) is also true of molecules, by observing their diffraction when a beam of hydrogen or helium struck a crystal. With Walther Gerlach, he developed a method of measuring the magnetic moments of atoms and then refined it to measure those of atomic nuclei. He was born in Sohrau, Germany (now Żary, Poland), and came to the United States in 1933. G. GAMOW

**STERNE, LAURENCE** (1713-1768), was an English clergyman who suddenly became famous as the author of *The Life and Opinions of Tristram Shandy, Gentleman* (1760-1767).

*Tristram Shandy* is an unconventional novel of conversations and reminiscences rather than action. Tristram is only about five years old when the story ends. This is partly because the work was never finished, but mainly because Sterne was more interested in other characters —Tristram's family, their friends and servants. The book is lively and extremely witty. Its popularity reflects the growing regard for humor and laughter and for feeling and sentiment during that period. Tristram's Uncle Toby, the simple and good-hearted soldier, climaxed a long line of lovable but comic eccentrics in the literature of the 1700's.

The novel's conversations and incidents do not follow the usual time sequence. Sterne was influenced by the philosopher John Locke. Locke thought that at birth the mind is a blank tablet upon which ideas take form only through the association of experiences gained through our senses. Locke observed that we may sometimes associate ideas that are logically unrelated. These erroneous chains of ideas form the basis of the narrative development in *Tristram Shandy*. Although readers may at first be confused by the way Sterne jumps from one idea to another, the book eventually may seem closer to our own experience of life than more conventional novels. Its method anticipates the stream-of-consciousness novels of James Joyce and Virginia Woolf.

Sterne was born in Clonmel, Ireland. He suffered from tuberculosis, and made trips to the milder climate of southern France for his health. These trips inspired *A Sentimental Journey Through France and Italy* (1768). This is an unconventional travel book that tells more about Sterne's love affairs and passing reflections than about the places he visited. IAN WATT

**STERNUM.** See SKELETON.

**STEROID,** *STER oyd* or *STE royd,* is a class of chemical compounds that are important in chemistry, biology, and medicine. They play a very important part in the body processes of living things. Steroids are produced naturally by plants and animals. They are also made commercially. Steroids include sterols, such as cholesterol; bile acids from the liver; adrenal hormones; sex hormones; and poisons in certain toads (see CHOLESTEROL; LIVER; GLAND).

All steroids are alike in basic chemical structure. But each steroid has a slightly different arrangement of molecules. Because of this difference, steroids have different effects on living things. In addition, individual organisms may react in different ways to the same steroid.

Steroids influence body *metabolism*, the process by which the body changes food into energy and living tissue. In plants, they help form certain vitamins and other important substances. Some steroids are used in medicine to treat diseases. *Digitalis* is one of the plant steroids, and is often used to treat heart failure (see DIGITALIS).

**The Sex Steroids** *estrogen* and *progesterone* are given off by the *ovaries* (female sex organs). They are responsible for the female's smooth, soft skin; high-pitched voice; rounded hips; and the development of the breasts. *Contraceptive pills* (pills that help prevent pregnancy) are powerful man-made forms of progesterone (see BIRTH CONTROL).

*Androgens* are sex steroids that are produced by the *testes* (male sex glands). Androgens are responsible for the male's beard, large muscles, and deep voice. These steroids may even influence certain personality traits such as aggressiveness, which is considered a male characteristic.

**The Adrenal Steroids** are present in both sexes. *Hydrocortisone* is produced by the adrenal glands and a small amount of it is *converted* (changed) into *cortisone* (see ADRENAL GLAND; CORTISONE). These steroids help regulate protein and carbohydrate metabolism. Adrenal steroids also influence mineral and water balance of the body.

Doctors use adrenal steroids to reduce *inflammation* (redness and swelling from injury) and to treat arthritis, skin diseases, allergies, and many other diseases. If the adrenal glands are surgically removed, a person will die unless he receives treatments with steroids.

Scientists first obtained cortisone for commercial use from adrenal glands. Today, most of it is produced in laboratories by chemical methods. Many other kinds of steroids are made for different commercial uses in medicine.

The normal steroid secretion of the ovaries, testes, and adrenal glands is regulated by a small part of the brain called the *hypothalamus*. The hypothalamus controls the release of the powerful protein hormones *gonadotrophins* and *adrenocorticotrophic hormone* (ACTH) from the pituitary gland. These hormones cause the ovaries, testes, and adrenal glands to release their steroids. The steroids then affect other body parts and characteristics. GORDON FARRELL

See also HORMONE.

**STEROL.** See LIPID.

**STEROPE.** See PLEIADES.

**STETHOSCOPE** is a device physicians use to hear the sounds produced by certain organs of the body, such as the heart, lungs, intestines, veins, and arteries. The stethoscope picks up the sounds made by these organs and excludes other sounds.

The stethoscope consists of a body contact piece, which is placed against the body of the patient, and earpieces, which are placed in the ears of the physician. Hollow rubber tubing connects the body contact piece to the earpieces. Physicians use either a bell, diaphragm, or bell-diaphragm combination body contact piece. The bell type of contact piece picks up low sounds. The diaphragm type allows the listener to hear higher sounds.

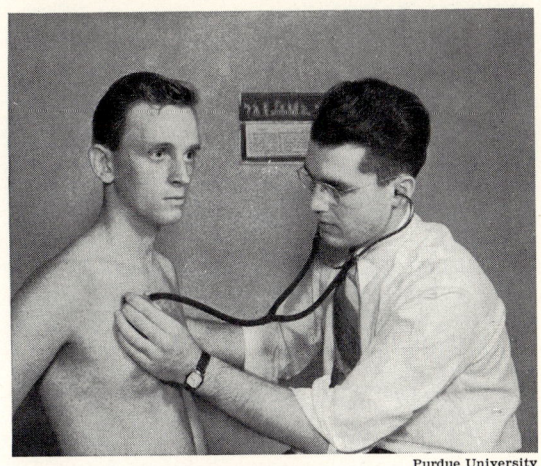

Purdue University

**A Physician Listens** to the action of heart and lungs with a stethoscope, as part of a patient's physical examination.

Before the invention of the stethoscope, the physician placed his ear next to the patient's body to hear the sounds made by the organs. René Laënnec, a French physician, made the first stethoscope from a hollow wooden tube in 1816. E. CLINTON TEXTER, JR.

See also LAËNNEC, RENÉ T. H.

**STETSON, JOHN BATTERSON** (1830-1906), was an American hat manufacturer and philanthropist. He went west in the early 1860's to regain his health, and used his knowledge of western tastes and hatmaking to design his famous ten-gallon hat. He established a factory in Philadelphia in 1865, and became the leading hat manufacturer in America. Though he had no formal education, Stetson endowed a small academy in De Land, Fla., which later became Stetson University. He was born in Orange, N.J. JOHN B. MCFERRIN

**STETSON UNIVERSITY.** See UNIVERSITIES AND COLLEGES (table).

**STETTIN,** *shteh TEEN*, or in Polish, SZCZECIN (pop. 299,200; alt. 50 ft.), is a Baltic Sea port at the mouth of the Oder River (see POLAND [color map]). Ships from Poland, Czechoslovakia, East Germany, and Hungary use its harbor. Stettin is the capital of the Szczecin district of Poland, and a shipbuilding and ship-repairing center. Its factories produce iron, paper, and textiles. In 1945, the Potsdam Conference awarded the city, once in Germany, to Poland. M. KAMIL DZIEWANOWSKI

**STETTINIUS,** *stuh TIN ih us,* **EDWARD RILEY, JR.** (1900-1949), was secretary of state under Presidents Franklin Delano Roosevelt and Harry S. Truman. When the national defense program was set up in 1940, Stettinius held key posts. From 1941 to 1943, he was the lend-lease administrator (see LEND-LEASE). As secretary of state in 1944 and 1945, he joined President Roosevelt at the Yalta Conference. He led the U.S. delegation to the 1945

Edward R. Stettinius, Jr.
University of Virginia

697

## STEUBEN, BARON VON

San Francisco Conference, which organized the United Nations. He became rector of the University of Virginia in 1946.

Stettinius was born in Chicago, and attended the University of Virginia. He became vice-president of the General Motors Corporation in 1931. In 1938, he took the post of chairman of the board of the United States Steel Corporation. HARVEY WISH

**STEUBEN,** *STOO bun,* or *SHTOY bun,* **BARON VON** (1730-1794), FRIEDRICH WILHELM LUDOLPH GERHARD AUGUSTIN, was a German soldier who helped the American colonists against England during the Revolutionary War.

Von Steuben sailed to America in 1777. On Benjamin Franklin's recommendation, General George Washington sent him to Valley Forge to train the raw colonial troops. Appointed inspector general, he reorganized and drilled the Continental Army. As a major general, he led troops against the British at Monmouth and Yorktown. After the war, he became a United States citizen.

Von Steuben was born in Magdeburg, Germany. He joined the Prussian Army and later became aide-de-camp to King Frederick the Great. ROBERT G. L. WAITE

**STEUBEN GLASS.** See GLASSWARE (Present-Day Art Glass).

**STEUBENVILLE, COLLEGE OF.** See UNIVERSITIES AND COLLEGES (table).

**STEUNENBERG, FRANK.** See IDAHO (Early Statehood).

**STEVENS** was the family name of two American engineers, father and son, who helped to develop the steam engines.

**John Cox Stevens** (1749-1838) pioneered in developing steam transportation in the United States. His boat *Phoenix*, which operated on the Delaware River to Philadelphia in 1809, became the world's first seagoing steamboat.

Stevens experimented in the use of steam engines on railways. A railway on his estate carried the first American-built steam locomotive. Stevens was born in New York City. ROBERT W. ABBETT

**Robert Livingston Stevens** (1787-1856) became a leader in steamship design and construction. Stevens invented protective devices and was among the first to use high-pressure steam engines in ships. For railroads, he invented the T-shaped rail and the hook-headed railroad spike.

Stevens was born in Hoboken, N.J. He first worked with his father, a rival of Robert Fulton in steamship construction. He also designed an armored ship for the U.S. government. ROBERT E. SCHOFIELD

**STEVENS, ISAAC INGALLS.** See WASHINGTON (History).

**STEVENS, THADDEUS** (1792-1868), was an American statesman. He was one of the Republican leaders in the United States Congress who favored harsh treatment for the defeated South after the Civil War.

From 1859 to 1868, Stevens was the dominant figure in the House of Representatives. He urged emancipation of the slaves and confiscation of the planters' lands. He favored tariffs, banking laws, and railroad subsidies for Northern businessmen. He led the movement to impeach President Andrew Johnson.

Brown Bros.
**Thaddeus Stevens**

Stevens was born at Danville, Vt., and was graduated from Dartmouth College. He practiced law for many years in Pennsylvania. In the state legislature, he championed public schools. He served from 1849 to 1853 in the U.S. House of Representatives, and opposed fugitive slave laws and other measures favorable to Southern interests. RICHARD N. CURRENT

**STEVENS, WALLACE** (1879-1955), was an American poet. He portrayed man as an earthbound creature without hope of an afterlife. As viewed by Stevens, man faces at every turn the seeming indifference of nature, the certainty of his own death, and his sense of the moral and physical decay occurring around him. Man is rescued from this potentially tragic situation through the use of imagination. Imagination can give meaning to the confusion of reality. It can also discover beauty in indifferent nature and ease the thought of death by marveling at the feeling of being alive. Stevens explored the virtues of the imaginative life in such relatively simple poems as "Sunday Morning" and "The Emperor of Ice Cream," and in such longer, more complex works as "The Man with the Blue Guitar" and "Esthetique du Mal."

Stevens had a unique writing style. His meaning and many of his words are difficult to understand. But his poems are also characterized by an extraordinary richness of language.

Stevens was born in Reading, Pa. His career was unusual in that he turned out his poetry while also succeeding as a lawyer and insurance executive. He was little known as a poet during his lifetime, but became a major influence on other poets after his death. His craftsmanship and his recognition of the moral responsibilities of poetry have been models to younger writers. His *Collected Poems* won the 1955 Pulitzer prize for poetry. CLARK GRIFFITH

**STEVENS DAM.** See MUD MOUNTAIN DAM.

**STEVENS INSTITUTE OF TECHNOLOGY.** See UNIVERSITIES AND COLLEGES (table).

**STEVENSON, ADLAI EWING** (1835-1914), was Vice-President of the United States from 1893 to 1897 under President Grover Cleveland. He was the grandfather of Adlai E. Stevenson, the Democratic presidential nominee in 1952 and 1956. Stevenson was an inflationist in a sound-money administration. Largely for this reason, the public was never informed when Cleveland underwent an emergency operation during the business panic of 1893. His advisers feared the panic might increase if there seemed to be any possibility of Stevenson succeeding to the presidency.

Stevenson was nominated for the vice-presidency again in 1900 as the running mate of William Jennings Bryan. But the Democrats lost to William McKinley and Theodore Roosevelt. Stevenson also ran for governor of Illinois in 1908, but was defeated.

Stevenson served in a variety of appointive and elec-

Adlai E. Stevenson
(1835-1914)

Adlai E. Stevenson
(1900-1965)

tive offices. He was a member of the House of Representatives for two terms. As the first assistant postmaster general of the U.S. from 1885 to 1889, he angered Republicans because he shifted jobs to Democrats. He was born in Christian County, Kentucky, and attended Illinois Wesleyan University.   IRVING G. WILLIAMS

**STEVENSON, ADLAI EWING** (1900-1965), was the Democratic nominee for President of the United States in 1952 and 1956. Dwight D. Eisenhower defeated him both times. Stevenson served as U.S. ambassador to the United Nations from 1961 until his death.

Stevenson was a grandson of Vice-President Adlai E. Stevenson. He was born in Los Angeles, Calif., on Feb. 5, 1900. After graduating from Princeton University, he studied law at Harvard and Northwestern universities. He worked on his family newspaper, the *Bloomington (Ill.) Daily Pantagraph*, and practiced law in Chicago. In 1933 and 1934, Stevenson held his first public office, serving as special counsel to the Agricultural Adjustment Administration. Later, during World War II, he was a special assistant to Secretary of the Navy Frank Knox, and led a United States mission on occupation policies in Italy. After the war, he became an alternate delegate to the United Nations.

In 1948, Stevenson was elected governor of Illinois by the largest plurality in the state's history. He was considered by many for his party's 1952 presidential nomination, but he refused to campaign. Nevertheless, the party nominated him after a dramatic convention struggle. During his campaigns, Stevenson became noted for his wit, speaking ability, and the high literary quality of his speeches. In 1952, his book *Major Campaign Speeches* was published. Stevenson also wrote and published *Call to Greatness* (1954), *What I Think* (1956), *Friends and Enemies* (1959), *Putting First Things First* (1960), and *Looking Outward: Years of Crisis at the United Nations* (1963).   ARTHUR SCHLESINGER, JR.

**STEVENSON, ROBERT** (1772-1850), was a Scottish civil engineer noted as a builder of lighthouses. He built 23 lighthouses along the coast of Great Britain, and invented the flashing light now used in lighthouses throughout the world (see LIGHTHOUSE [The Light]). His most noted work was the Bell Rock Lighthouse, which he designed and built with John Rennie. The poet Robert Southey immortalized Bell Rock in his "Inchcape Bell." The lighthouse still stands in the North Sea 11 miles from Dundee, Scotland. Stevenson was born in Glasgow. The author Robert Louis Stevenson was his grandson.   ROBERT W. ABBETT

## STEVENSON, ROBERT LOUIS

**STEVENSON, ROBERT LOUIS** (1850-1894), was a Scottish novelist, essayist, and poet who became one of the world's most popular writers. His exciting adventure stories *Treasure Island* and *Kidnapped* have long appealed to both children and adults. His essays and travel books are considered models of sophisticated English prose style, while the tender, simple poems collected in *A Child's Garden of Verses* are masterpieces of children's literature.

Stevenson's life was as varied and fascinating as his work. He fought illness constantly, writing many of his best books from a sickbed. He traveled widely for his health and to learn about people. He spent his last years on the South Sea island of Samoa, and the Samoans honored him with the title *Tusitala* (Teller of Tales).

### Stevenson's Life

**Early Life.** Stevenson was born on Nov. 13, 1850, in Edinburgh, Scotland. His full name was ROBERT LEWIS BALFOUR STEVENSON. He was a sickly boy who suffered from a lung disease that later developed into tuberculosis. Young Stevenson loved the open air, the sea, and adventure, but he also loved to read. He preferred literature and history, especially Scottish history which supplied the background for many of his novels.

When he was 17, Stevenson entered Edinburgh University to study engineering, his father's profession. However, he soon gave up engineering for law. He passed his bar examination in 1875, but he did not enjoy law and never practiced it. Stevenson's real love was writing.

Stevenson began publishing short stories and essays in the mid-1870's. His first book, *An Inland Voyage*, appeared in 1878. It relates his experiences during a canoeing trip through France and Belgium. In *Travels with a Donkey in the Cévennes* (1879), Stevenson describes a walking tour through part of France. Although both books reveal Stevenson's inexperience as a writer, they give signs of the graceful, charming essay style for which he was to become famous.

**Marriage.** In 1876, Stevenson met Mrs. Fanny Osbourne, a married American woman who was studying art in Paris. Although she was 11 years older than Stevenson and had a son and daughter, Stevenson fell in love with her. In 1879, he followed her to San Francisco in spite of the opposition of his parents. They were married in Oakland in 1880, after her divorce. The long journey from Europe to California severely affected Stevenson's frail health. To speed his recovery, he moved his family to a rough mining camp in the mountains near St. Helena, Calif. Stevenson described his experiences there in *The Silverado Squatters* (1883).

The Stevensons returned to Scotland in 1880. For the next seven years, they moved through Europe from one resort to another, hoping that a change of air would improve Stevenson's health. In 1887, Stevenson returned with his family to the United States, where he entered a sanitarium at Saranac Lake, N.Y.

**The South Seas.** For Stevenson, the sea had always been bracing. When his health improved, he boldly decided to sail a yacht to the South Seas. He left San Francisco with his wife, widowed mother, and stepson in June, 1888, and for the next six years traveled through

699

**Robert Louis Stevenson** settled with his family near Apia on the South Sea island of Upolu in Western Samoa. There he built a large house which he called *Vailima*. This picture shows Stevenson seated next to his wife Fanny. Stevenson's mother and stepson Lloyd Osbourne (standing) are shown on the author's right.

the South Sea islands. He came to know the life of the islanders better than any writer of his time.

Eventually, Stevenson decided to settle in the South Seas, the one place that seemed to promise some lasting improvement in his health. He bought some forest land near Apia, Samoa, and built a large house, which he called *Vailima* (Five Rivers). He became a planter and took an active part in island affairs. Stevenson's kindness, understanding, and tolerance gained the affection of the Samoans, who built a road to his house which they called *The Road of the Loving Heart*.

Tragedy clouded Stevenson's last years when his wife suffered a nervous breakdown. This misfortune moved him deeply, affecting his ability to complete his last books. Stevenson's life was beginning to brighten when his wife partially recovered, but he died suddenly of a stroke on Dec. 3, 1894. Local chiefs buried him on top of Mount Vaea, where his gravestone is inscribed with his own poem, "Requiem." Its concluding lines make a fitting epitaph for a gallant adventurer:

> Here he lies where he longed to be;
> Home is the sailor, home from the sea,
> And the hunter, home from the hill.

### Stevenson's Writings

**Novels.** In 1881, Stevenson amused his stepson, Lloyd Osbourne, with a little tale about pirates and the buried treasure of Captain Kidd. It grew into *Treasure Island*, Stevenson's first and most famous novel. The story, first published in a boy's magazine, was revised for book publication in 1883. The boy hero Jim Hawkins, the two villains Long John Silver and blind Pew, and the hair-raising search for the buried treasure have become familiar to millions of readers.

With the publication of Stevenson's second major novel, *The Strange Case of Dr. Jekyll and Mr. Hyde* (1886), his reputation was assured. The story tells of a doctor who takes a drug that changes him into a new person, physically ugly and spiritually evil. As a psychological inquiry into the nature of the evil that exists in all men, the novel brilliantly anticipates much modern psychological fiction and is one of the most fascinating horror stories ever written.

Stevenson also published *Kidnapped*, his best long novel, in 1886. Based on considerable historical research, it weaves an exciting fictional story around an actual Scottish murder in 1745. The novel displays Stevenson's matchless ability to create adult entertainment out of the materials of children's adventure stories. Because of its length, Stevenson ended *Kidnapped* before the plot was completed. He finally finished the story in 1893 with a sequel, *David Balfour* (published in England as *Catriona*).

*The Master of Ballantrae* (1889) is set against the background of Scotland's revolt against England in the 1740's. The novel, which tells a story of bitter hatred between two brothers, begins as a promising psychological study, but suffers from its melodramatic ending.

Stevenson's later novels, far different from his early light-hearted romances, are often bitter in tone. Less popular, they still have merit. The short novel *The Beach of Falesá* (1892), which Stevenson described as "the first realistic South Sea story," was called "art brought to a perfection" by novelist Henry James.

Stevenson wrote three other novels, in collaboration with Lloyd Osbourne—*The Wrong Box* (1889), *The Wrecker* (1892), and *The Ebb Tide* (1894). Stevenson also left two novels unfinished at his death. *St. Ives*, which was completed by Sir Arthur Quiller-Couch, describes the adventures of a French prisoner in Britain in 1813. *Weir of Hermiston*, a story of Scotland in the 1700's, promised to be Stevenson's finest novel.

**Other Writings.** Stevenson wrote many short stories, some of which were collected into *New Arabian Nights* (1882) and *More New Arabian Nights* (1885). Many of the stories are rich in imagination and fantasy, although the early ones are often written in an artificial style.

Stevenson's concern with prose style is most apparent in his essays, which are among the finest in the language. His observations on men and manners are marked by a delicate fancy. For charm and perceptiveness, they can be compared only to the essays of Charles Lamb and William Hazlitt. Stevenson's most memorable essays were collected in *Virginibus Puerisque and Other Papers* (1881), *Familiar Studies of Men and Books* (1882), and *Memories and Portraits* (1887).

Stevenson wrote several travel books later in his career. The *Amateur Emigrant* (1880, 1895) describes his voyages to the United States; *Across the Plains* (1892) tells of his trip from New York to San Francisco; *In the South Seas* (1890) contains his reflections on his Pacific voyages. All demonstrate Stevenson's extraordinary stylistic quality—the sudden word or phrase that lights a page with meaning.

Stevenson also composed some delightful letters, wrote several volumes of poetry, and collaborated with William Ernest Henley on some unsuccessful dramas. *A Child's Garden of Verses* (1885) reveals the world of a child's imagination with a deceptive simplicity that still appeals to readers young and old. His adult poetry, however, is almost totally ignored today, in spite of occasional pieces of considerable merit.

### Stevenson's Place in Literature

Stevenson was both the most popular and the most successful among writers of the late 1800's who developed romance as a reaction to the literary movements of realism and naturalism. If his influence has declined today, it is not necessarily because modern writers are more skillful, but rather that Stevenson's optimistic view of life has become unfashionable.

Stevenson insisted that novels are to adults what play is to children, and that one of the legitimate and necessary functions of literature is to supply adventure for people who lead unexciting lives. A theory of fiction seemingly so limited and naïve might well have produced literary trifles. In fact, it resulted in art of such high quality that the disciplined Henry James once praised Stevenson as "the only man in England who can write a decent English sentence."

Stevenson's faults are obvious. His plots are a bit melodramatic, his pirates rather stagy, and, as he readily admitted, his heroines entirely unreal. But his sure handling of narrative pace, his strong sense of atmosphere, and above all his masterly command of style give his novels and stories enduring vitality. The reading public has never lost its admiration for Stevenson, and it appears likely that as long as there is a taste for romance written with artistry, he will continue to have an audience. Furthermore, there are signs that critics are re-evaluating his works, finding more fine shades of meaning in his writings than they had suspected.

Critically reviewed by FRANK W. WADSWORTH

**STEWARDESS.** See AIRLINE STEWARDESS.

**STEWART, MICHAEL** (1906-    ), became British secretary of state for foreign and Commonwealth affairs in 1968. Prime Minister Harold Wilson had named Stewart to the cabinet in 1964.

Stewart was born in London and graduated from Oxford University. He taught school for 12 years, and then joined the Army Intelligence Corps in 1942. Stewart was elected to Parliament in 1945, and was undersecretary of war from 1947 to 1951. In 1951, he served as parliamentary secretary to the minister of supply until the Labour Party lost the election held five months after his appointment. In 1964, when the party returned to power, Stewart was named secretary of state for education and science. He served as secretary of state for foreign affairs from 1965 to 1966 and for seven months in 1968. He also was first secretary of state from 1966 to 1968.

**STEWART, POTTER** (1915-    ), was appointed an associate justice of the Supreme Court of the United States in 1958. He became the second youngest justice in 105 years. Stewart was born in Jackson, Mich. His father, James Garfield Stewart, became an Ohio supreme court judge. Potter Stewart attended Yale University, Yale University Law School, and Cambridge University. He practiced law in Cincinnati, and was elected to the Cincinnati city council in 1949. He served as a judge of the federal court of appeals from 1954 to 1958. See also SUPREME COURT OF THE UNITED STATES (picture).    MERLO J. PUSEY

**STEWART ISLAND.** See NEW ZEALAND (Location and Size).

**STEWING.** See COOKING (Boiling and Simmering).

**STIBNITE.** See ANTIMONY; MINERAL (color picture).

**STICK,** a term used in printing. See TYPE (How Type Is Set; pictures).

**STICK-BUTTON.** See BURDOCK.

**STICK INSECT.** See WALKING STICK.

**STICKLEBACK,** *STIK'l BACK*, is a name given to a family of small fishes of the Northern Hemisphere. They are called sticklebacks because some of their fins are made of strong, sharp, separated spines. Instead of having scales, the body is usually covered by hard plates. There are both fresh-water and ocean sticklebacks. The fresh-water ones reach a length of 1 to 3 inches. The ocean sticklebacks grow to be not more than 7 inches long. The *brook stickleback* is common in the interior parts of Canada and in the Great Lakes states. These fish, like other sticklebacks, build muff-shaped nests of sticks and roots for receiving the spawn. The male carefully guards the spawn. He also watches over the young for several days after the eggs are hatched. Sticklebacks eat the young of other fish.

**Scientific Classification.** Sticklebacks make up the stickleback family, *Gasterosteidae*. The three-spined, or *common* stickleback is classified as genus *Gasterosteus*, species *G. aculeatus*. The brook stickleback is classified as genus *Eucalia*, species *E. inconstans*.    CARL L. HUBBS

See also FISH (Reproduction; picture: Brook Stickleback).

**STICKSEED** is a weedy plant that grows wild in dry soils throughout most of North America. It is named stickseed because its small, nutlike fruit has barbed prickles that stick to clothing and to the fur or hair of animals. Stickseed has a slender hairy stem, grayish-green leaves, and small blue, lavender or white flowers. Gardeners sometimes use it in rock gardens.

**Scientific Classification.** Stickseed is in the borage family, *Boraginaceae*. Annual species are genus *Lappula*. Perennials and biennials are genus *Hackelia*.    ARTHUR CRONQUIST

## STIEGEL, HENRY WILLIAM

**STIEGEL,** *STEE gel,* **HENRY WILLIAM** (1729-1785), was an early American iron and glass manufacturer. Among his iron products were tin-plate wood stoves that were used widely for many years, and iron castings used by sugar planters and refiners in the West Indies.

In 1762 Stiegel and two associates established the town of Manheim, Pa. There he conducted experiments in glassmaking and soon produced his "Stiegel glass." Some experts regard "Stiegel glass" as the most beautiful glass ever blown, and collectors prize it highly (see GLASSWARE [Stiegel Glass]).

Stiegel was born near Cologne, Germany, and came to Philadelphia in 1750. He had a substantial fortune when he arrived, and he became a prominent landowner and ironmaker. He lived in great style and assumed the title of baron. His extravagant personal spending, coupled with disturbed economic conditions in the American colonies, brought financial disaster. He was imprisoned for debt in 1774.       JOHN B. MCFERRIN

See also ANTIQUE (picture: Glass Saltcellar); COLONIAL LIFE IN AMERICA (color picture: Stiegel Glass).

**STIEGLITZ,** *STEEG lits,* **ALFRED** (1864-1946), pioneered in photography as a creative art. His photographs are among the greatest ever produced. In 1902, he founded, with Edward Steichen, the Photo-Secession, an organization to promote photography as an art form. From 1905 until 1946, he operated a gallery in New York City, where he showed paintings as well as photographs. Stieglitz was the first in the United States to exhibit French postimpressionist paintings. He was born in Hoboken, N.J., and studied at the City College of New York. In 1924, Stieglitz married Georgia O'Keeffe, the painter.      BEAUMONT NEWHALL

See also PHOTOGRAPHY (History [Photography for Everyone; picture]); O'KEEFFE, GEORGIA.

**STIGMA,** in botany. See FLOWER (The Pistils; color diagram: Parts of a Flower); POLLEN AND POLLINATION.

**STIKINE RIVER,** *stih KEEN,* is an important waterway in northern British Columbia. It rises in the Cassiar Mountains and flows westward and southward for about 335 miles. It empties into the Pacific Ocean near Wrangell, Alaska. It drains an area of about 20,000 square miles. In summer, steamers once traveled up river about 170 miles to Telegraph Creek.   J. BRIAN BIRD

**STILETTO.** See DAGGER.

**STILL.** See DISTILLATION.

**STILL, ANDREW TAYLOR.** See OSTEOPATHY (History).

**STILLMAN COLLEGE.** See UNIVERSITIES AND COLLEGES (table).

**STILLWATER,** Minn. (pop. 8,310; alt. 690 ft.), is 18 miles northeast of St. Paul. It was one of the earliest settlements in the state. It was established in 1839. For many years Stillwater served as an important logging center for lumbering in the nearby pine forests. The city lies on the boundary between Minnesota and Wisconsin near the mouth of the St. Croix River, at a point where the river widens into a lake (see MINNESOTA [map]). Stillwater is called the *Birthplace of Minnesota.* The convention that formed the territory of Minnesota met there in 1848. The city has a mayor-council form of government.      HAROLD T. HAGG

**STILLWATER,** Okla. (pop. 23,965; alt. 870 ft.), depends on the rich surrounding farm lands for most of its

S. A. Grimes
**The Stilt Is a Wading Bird With Long, Slender Legs.**

trade and industries. Stillwater lies about 65 miles northeast of Oklahoma City and about 50 miles southeast of Enid. Oklahoma State University is in Stillwater. Lake Carl Blackwell nine miles west of the city is a vacation spot. Stillwater has a council-manager government. The seat of Payne County, the city was chartered in 1889.     JOHN W. MORRIS

**STILT** is a wading bird with long, slender legs. These slender legs make it look as if it walks on stilts. The stilts are related to the avocets, and live in both the Eastern and Western hemispheres. The *black-necked stilt,* the only American stilt, is about 15 inches long. The upper part of its body is black, and the under part is white. Its long legs are bright red. The stilt builds its nest by lining a low place in the ground with grasses. The female stilt lays 3 or 4 eggs of an olive or buff color, thickly spotted with chocolate tones. The bird lives along shallow ponds in fresh and salt marshes.

**Scientific Classification.** The stilt belongs to the stilt and avocet family, *Recurvirostridae.* The black-necked stilt is genus *Himantopus,* species *H. mexicanus.*   ALFRED M. BAILEY

See also AVOCET.

**STILTS** are two long poles that allow a person to walk with his feet some distance above the ground. Each stilt has a footrest fastened to it. A stilt walker stands on the footrests, keeps the top of the stilts in his armpits, and grips the stilts with his hands. With each step he moves a stilt forward with his hands. Some stilt walkers strap their legs to the stilts so they can use the motion of their legs to operate the stilts.

Stilts are used chiefly for amusement. Children like to walk on them. Some circus performers entertain by walking on stilts.

No one knows when stilt walking began. Hundreds of years ago, people in some areas used stilts to walk above water during floods. A legend dating from the 1600's tells of soldiers using stilts in Namur, Belgium. Some farmers in parts of Gascony, France, once used stilts to wade in marshland and cross streams. These farmers could run on stilts with remarkable speed and ease.

**STILWELL, JOSEPH WARREN** (1883-1946), commanded all the United States forces in the China-Burma-India theater of war during World War II. He also served as chief of staff to Generalissimo Chiang Kai-shek, supreme commander of the Chinese theater, and was the first American general to command a Chinese army. Stilwell won the nickname of *Vinegar Joe* because of his forthright manner.

Stilwell was sent to Burma in 1942 to assist the Chinese and British troops defending Burma against Japan. When the Allied forces were defeated in Burma, Stilwell retreated to India, a distance of about 140 miles through the jungle. In India, he trained several Chinese divisions to recapture Burma and open a line of communication to China. With these forces and a small American force called "Merrill's Marauders," Stilwell opened a route to China late in 1944. Stilwell and Chiang Kai-shek disagreed on military policy, and Stilwell was shifted to Washington, D.C., in October, 1944. In June, 1945, Stilwell took command of the U.S. Tenth Army on Okinawa. After the war ended, he held an Army command in the United States.

Stilwell was born in Palatka, Fla. He was graduated from the United States Military Academy in 1904. He served with the American Expeditionary Forces in France during World War I. He studied Chinese, and served as a military attaché in China from 1935 to 1939.   MAURICE MATLOFF

**STILWELL ROAD.** See WORLD WAR II (The China-Burma-India Theater).

**STIMSON, HENRY LEWIS** (1867-1950), was an American statesman. As secretary of state under President Herbert Hoover, he opposed Japan's seizure of Manchuria in 1931 by a warning known as "The Stimson Doctrine." This stated that the United States would not recognize any changes made there in violation of treaties. Hoover refused to permit him to use an economic boycott against Japan. But, in 1940, as secretary of war under President Franklin D. Roosevelt, Stimson successfully urged such a boycott. Japan refused to yield to any pressure and struck Pearl Harbor, opening war against the United States. Stimson served as secretary of war from 1940 to 1945 under Presidents Franklin D. Roosevelt and Harry S. Truman.

He was President William Taft's secretary of war from 1911 to 1913 and promoted "dollar diplomacy" to aid defense. Stimson acted as President Calvin Coolidge's mediator in Nicaragua in 1927. He was born in New York City.   HARVEY WISH

**STIMULANT** is a substance which excites the nerves and some of the organs of the body. Excited nerves send messages to and from the brain swiftly. This makes a person think and act more rapidly than normal. Common stimulants include the drugs *caffeine* (sometimes called *theine*), found in coffee and tea, and *nicotine*, found in tobacco. Stimulants are often habit-forming and may be unhealthful. However, doctors may use some stimulants to save lives. For example, the drugs digitalis and adrenalin will make the heart pump faster. See also ADRENALIN; CAFFEINE; DIGITALIS; NICOTINE; TONIC; AMPHETAMINE.   G. W. BEADLE

**STIMULUS.** See REFLEX ACTION; PSYCHOLOGY (Behaviorism); LEARNING (How We Learn).

**STING.** See ANT (Abdomen); BEE (Sting); MOSQUITO; SCORPION; WASP.

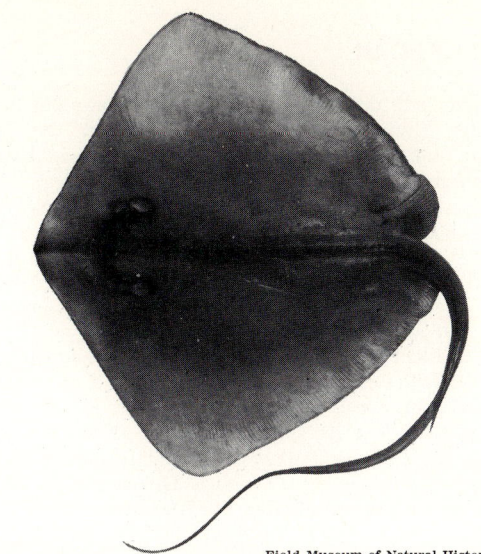

Field Museum of Natural History

**The Flat-Bodied Sting Ray,** *above,* can inflict a serious wound with the strong, sharp spine on its whiplike tail.

**STING RAY,** also called STINGAREE, is a ray, or flatish sea fish. Its long, flexible tail has one or two sharp spines on the back of the tail near the middle. These spines have teeth along their edges. At the base of these teeth are poisonous glands. When bathers disturb or step on the sting ray, it swings its tail upward. In this way, it causes a most painful wound that is nearly as dangerous as a poisonous snake bite. The fish live on sandy to muddy bottoms in all warm shallow parts of the ocean and in bays. In South America, small, freshwater sting rays infest the rivers flowing into the Atlantic Ocean. They live as far as 2,000 miles above the mouth of the Amazon River. A sting ray that lives in the waters off Australia reaches a length of 14 feet.

**Scientific Classification.** Sting rays belong to the sting ray family, *Dasyatidae*. There are about 50 species of sting ray. The common sting ray is classified as genus *Dasyatis*, species *D. centrourus*.   LEONARD P. SCHULTZ

**STINKBUG** is one of a family of insects that can spray bad-smelling odors. They have scent glands near their hind legs or on their abdomens. When stinkbugs are

**The Southern Green Stinkbug Sucks Sap from Plants.**
USDA

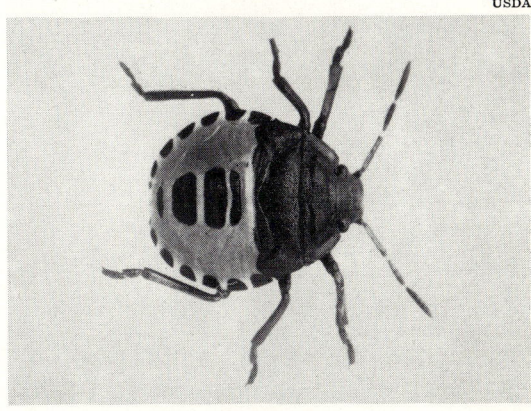

703

# STINKHORN

frightened, they open the glands and spray out a bad odor. Many stinkbugs are brown or green, but some are brilliantly colored. One kind, the red and black *harlequin bug*, damages cabbage.

**Scientific Classification.** Stinkbugs belong to the order *Hemiptera*. They are members of the stinkbug family, *Pentatomidae*. The harlequin bug is classified as genus *Murgantia*, species *M. histrionica*. LEWIS J. STANNARD, JR.

**STINKHORN.** See MUSHROOM (Poisonous Mushrooms).
**STIPULE.** See LEAF (The Stipules).
**STIRRUP.** See EAR (The Middle Ear; pictures).
**STITCH.** See SEWING (Basic Stitches).
**STOAT.** See ERMINE.
**STOCK** is a name given to three different garden flowers. The *Grecian stock* bears fragrant lilac or purple flowers which open at evening. This small, branching annual plant comes from southern Europe. Its pods have two noticeable horns on the end. The *Virginian stock* is another annual with small white, red, or lilac-colored flowers. It has a short stalk and pods with no horns. The *Brampton*, or *common*, *stock* is a straight, sturdy plant about 2 feet high. It bears fragrant white, pink, red, purple, or yellow blossoms.

**Scientific Classification.** The stocks belong to the mustard family, *Cruciferae*. Grecian stock is genus *Matthiola*, species *M. bicornis*. Brampton stock is *M. incana*. Virginian stock is *Malcolmia maritima*. DONALD WYMAN

**STOCK, CAPITAL,** is a right of ownership in a corporation. The stock is divided into a certain number of *shares*, and the corporation issues each stockholder one or more *stock certificates* to show how many shares he holds. The stockholders own the company and elect a board of directors to manage it for them.

**The Stockholder** may sell his stock whenever he wants to unless the corporation has some special rule to prevent it. Prices of stock change according to general business conditions and the earnings and future prospects of the company. If the business is doing well, the stockholder may be able to sell his stock for a profit. If it is not, he may have to take a loss.

Large corporations may have many thousands of stockholders. Their stock is bought and sold in market places called *stock exchanges*. When a sale is made, the seller signs the certificate. The buyer turns this over to the corporation and gets a new certificate.

When the corporation has made a profit, the directors may divide the profit among the stockholders as *dividends*, or they may decide to use it to expand the business. Dividends may be paid only out of the corporation's profits. When profits are used to expand the business, the directors and stockholders may decide to issue more stock to show that there is more money invested in the business. This new stock will be divided among the stockholders as a *stock dividend*.

**Kinds of Stock.** The Articles of Incorporation—papers signed when the corporation is formed—may specify the different kinds of stock. *Par stock* must be issued for not less than a set price, called the *par value*, for each share. If the articles provide for *no-par* stock, the directors determine the issuing price of the stock and may change it whenever they wish.

All shares of stock have equal dividend and voting rights unless the articles provide differently. There may be different classes of stock, such as *voting* and *non-voting*. Many articles provide for *common* and *preferred* stock. Preferred stock is entitled to a preference on dividends. That is, the directors must pay a certain amount—usually a percentage of par value—to the holders of preferred stock before they pay anything to the holders of common stock. If the preferred-stock holders share with the common-stock holders in dividends beyond the specified percentage, the stock is called *participating preferred*.

Preferred stock may also be *cumulative*. That is, if there are no dividends given in a year, the preferred-stock holders must be given double their dividend the next year. This double dividend is paid before anything is paid to the common-stock holders. It will continue to multiply for as many years as dividends are not paid.

When a corporation goes out of business, it divides its property among the stockholders. This process is called *liquidation*. When a company liquidates, the preferred-stock holders may be given the par value of their stock before the common-stock holders are given anything. This preferred stock is said to be *preferred up to par on liquidation*. ROBERT E. RODES, JR.

See also the articles INVESTMENT and STOCK EXCHANGE, with their lists of Related Articles.

**STOCK, FREDERICK AUGUST** (1872-1942), conducted the Chicago Symphony Orchestra from 1905 to 1942. Stock joined the orchestra in 1895. In 1899, he became assistant to Theodore Thomas, the director. He became director after Thomas died. Stock was born at Jülich, near Aachen, Germany. He graduated from the Cologne Conservatory. DAVID EWEN

**STOCK CAR RACING.** See AUTOMOBILE RACING.

**A Stock Plant Bears a Mass of Fragrant Blooms.**
J. Horace McFarland

The New York Stock Exchange in Wall Street Is Often Called the *Nation's Market Place*.

**STOCK EXCHANGE** is a market place where member *brokers* (agents) buy and sell stocks and bonds of American and foreign businesses on behalf of the public. A stock exchange provides a market place for stocks and bonds in the same way a board of trade does for commodities. The stockbrokers receive a small commission on each transaction they make.

### How a Stock Exchange Operates

Federal laws regulate the issuance, listing, and trading of most securities. The Securities and Exchange Commission administers these laws.

**Listing Stocks.** Stocks handled by one or more stock exchanges are called *listed stocks*. A company that wants to have its stock listed for trading on an exchange must first satisfy the exchange that it has enough paid-up capital, is a lawful enterprise, and is in good financial condition. Specific listing requirements vary among exchanges. On the New York Stock Exchange a corporation must have 1,500 stockholders who together hold at least 600,000 shares, as well as a yearly earning power under competitive conditions of over $1,200,000. Major exchanges suspend trading in certain stocks which no longer meet minimum requirements.

Unlisted securities are bought and sold in *over-the-counter* trading. All bank and insurance company stocks and many bonds are sold in this way. Many unlisted industrial securities are more speculative than listed ones. They are usually not traded on any exchange.

All stocks *fluctuate* (change) in value. Unforeseen circumstances may have lessened the earning power of a company and thus lowered the price that people are willing to pay for shares. Prosperous times or better management may increase values.

**Trading.** A person who wishes to buy stock places an order with his brokerage house. The broker gets a *quotation* (price) by telephone or telegraph, and relays the order to the firm's partner on the floor of the exchange. He negotiates the sale, and then notifies the brokerage house. Such a transaction may take only a few minutes. It is recorded on tape, and sent by *stock ticker* to brokerage firms over a nationwide network.

Each year, investors trade several billion shares worth hundreds of billions of dollars. In the early 1960's, about 1,500 stocks were listed on the New York Stock Exchange. Stock prices often reflect what is happening in the economy. If business conditions are good, stock prices tend to rise, creating a *bull market*. If conditions are poor, stock prices drop, causing a *bear market*.

**Memberships** in exchanges are worth substantial sums of money because only a limited number are avail-

# STOCK-MARKET CRASH

able. Each new member must meet a number of requirements and be formally recommended and approved by the exchange's Board of Governors before he can buy a *seat* (membership) and operate on the stock exchange. Seat owners hold their places personally. The majority of them are partners or voting stockholders in brokerage firms or corporations which are known as *member organizations*. Many firms have more than one member on the Exchange. Neither industrial corporations nor their representatives can own seats.

Some exchange members, called *specialists*, concentrate on a limited group of securities assigned by the exchange. They also act as agents for other brokers. Others are *odd-lot dealers*, who transact amounts less than the regular trading unit, such as 1 to 99 shares for 100-share units. *Floor brokers*, or "$2 brokers," are unaffiliated with exchange firms, and assist *commission house* (member firm) brokers with their firm orders.

The value of memberships depends largely on current business conditions, the volume of transactions, and the market level of securities. The New York Stock Exchange has 1,366 members and 672 member organizations with about 3,400 offices throughout the nation. The price on this exchange has varied from $17,000 in 1942, during a business recession, to a high of $625,000 in 1929. Memberships on other exchanges may be worth from $1,500 to more than $275,000.

### History

The first European stock exchange was established in Antwerp, Belgium, in 1531. There were no stock exchanges in England until the 1700's. A man wishing to buy or sell shares of stock had to find a broker to transact his business for him. In London, he usually went to a coffeehouse, because brokers often gathered there. In 1773, the brokers of London formed a stock exchange where buyers and sellers could conduct their business.

In New York City, brokers met under an old buttonwood tree in Wall Street. They organized the New York Stock Exchange in 1792. The American Stock Exchange, second largest in the United States, was formerly called the Curb Exchange because of its origin on the streets of New York City. Today, seventeen exchanges are located in various cities in the United States. These cities include Boston, Pittsburgh, Detroit, Salt Lake City, Cincinnati, and Honolulu. Stock exchanges are also located in such cities as Montreal, Toronto, Paris, and Tokyo.  G. KEITH FUNSTON

**Related Articles** in WORLD BOOK include:

| | | |
|---|---|---|
| Bears and Bulls | Bucket Shop | Securities and |
| Blue-Sky Laws | Dow Jones Index | Exchange |
| Board of Trade | Investment | Commission |
| Bond | Banking | Stock, Capital |
| Bourse | Margin | Stock Ticker |

**STOCK-MARKET CRASH.** See UNITED STATES, HISTORY OF (The Great Depression).

**STOCK RAISING.** See LIVESTOCK.

**STOCK TICKER** is a teletype machine that prints a record of the purchase and sale of stock. The machine prints up to 900 characters or figures per minute on a one-inch wide tape, often called *ticker tape*. About 3,800 tickers are in use in the United States. The New York Stock Exchange owns and maintains about 1,000 in the New York financial district. The Western Union Telegraph Company owns and maintains the others.

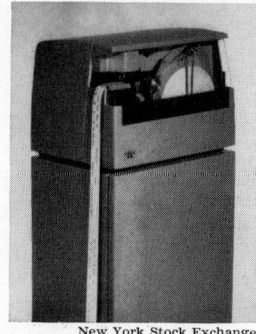

New York Stock Exchange
**A Stock Ticker**

The ticker works through a computer. A stock broker telephones or teletypes an order to the trading floor of the Exchange. A broker representing the firm buys or sells the stock. An Exchange employee records the transaction on a special IBM card. This card contains the stock symbol listing the corporate title of the security, the number of shares involved, and the price. The card is placed in a *card reader* device located at each trading post on the Exchange floor. The device transmits the trading data into a computer complex. The computer converts the data into telegraphic signals that go over the Exchange's nationwide stock network. The report of a transaction appears on the ticker network a few seconds after the data has been fed into the computer.

The Stock Exchange first used tickers in 1867. Before that time, information was carried by mail or by messenger.  G. KEITH FUNSTON

See also STOCK EXCHANGE; TELEGRAPH; EDISON, THOMAS ALVA (Early Inventions).

**STOCKADE.** See PIONEER LIFE IN AMERICA (Indian Attacks).

**STOCKHOLDER.** See STOCK, CAPITAL.

**STOCKHOLM,** *STAHK home* (pop. 793,714; met. area pop. 1,179,340; alt. 46 ft.), is the capital and largest city of Sweden. It is called the *Venice of the North* because of its many waterways.

**Location and Description.** Stockholm lies on Sweden's east coast, at the point where Lake Malar meets the Baltic Sea. The city is built on a dozen islands and along the shores of Lake Malar. See SWEDEN (political map). Nearby are more than a thousand small islands that lie in Saltsjön Bay. Wide beaches on many of the islands are popular with sunbathers and swimmers during the summer. Ice hockey and skiing are popular winter sports. The sparkling cleanliness of its streets and buildings, the magnificence of its old palaces and churches, and the sharp clean lines of its office buildings make the city an expression of Swedish character.

Stockholm has a stadium which was the site of the 1912 summer Olympic Games. The city has athletic fields, children's playgrounds, clubs for most kinds of sports, and parks for walking and horseback riding.

The vast Djurgården park has been a pleasure resort of the people of Stockholm since the 1600's. The park contains a zoo and a large open-air museum. The buildings of the museum represent different provinces and historical periods of Sweden. They include an old pharmacy from the royal palace at Drottningholm, a combmaker's workshop, and a glassmaker's house.

The Town Hall, completed in 1923, with its three golden crowns, is one of the finest buildings in Sweden. But many other historical buildings are also distinguished. The Riddarholm Church was founded in the 1200's and has been the burial place of Sweden's rulers

**Vällingby Shopping Center** in Stockholm is typical of new developments in the city's suburban areas.

Lennart Olson, Pix

since the 1500's. Storkyrkan, Stockholm's oldest church, was also founded in the 1200's. The greatest treasure of Storkyrkan is its statue of Saint George and the Dragon. Sten Sture commissioned it to commemorate a Swedish victory over the Danes in 1471. On a nearby island stand the *Riksdag* (parliament building), and the *Riksbank,* the world's oldest government-owned bank.

**Industry and Commerce.** Stockholm is Sweden's most important industrial center. The three chief manufactured products, in order of their importance, are metal goods, paper, and foods. Many kinds of consumers' goods also are manufactured in the city. Stockholm is Sweden's second largest port, and large ocean-going ships tie up at its docks. The Göta Canal connects Stockholm with Göteborg on the west coast, and provides pleasure-boat trips through southern Sweden.

**History.** Birger Jarl, one of Sweden's greatest statesmen, is believed to have founded Stockholm in the early 1250's. From the 1200's to the 1500's, the Swedes fought many battles with the Danes in Stockholm in winning independence from the Danish rulers. King Christian II of Denmark and Sweden had the chiefs of the rebelling Swedish nobility beheaded in the so-called "Stockholm Blood Bath of 1520." The city became Sweden's capital in the 1600's. Stockholm celebrated its 700th anniversary in 1953.        JAMES J. ROBBINS

See also SWEDEN (color pictures).

**STOCKINGS** are coverings worn over the feet and legs. Some of the first stockings worn by men were trouser legs strapped tight around the ankles and knees with leather thongs. Tight-fitting breeches replaced the trousers, and, when breeches were shortened, long cloth stockings were worn to cover the feet and legs. Knitted stockings were introduced in England and other parts of Europe during the 1500's. Kings and queens may have been the first to wear silk stockings, but the invention of knitting machines in 1589 made them available to other persons as well.

*Full-fashioned stockings* are knitted flat, then seamed up the back. The foot part is knitted separately, and customers should be sure that no stitches were dropped during the joining process. *Seamless* stockings and socks for men, women, and children are usually knitted on a circular machine as a tubelike *hose.*

Manufacturers use various terms to designate weight and fineness of stitch. *Denier* refers to the fineness of rayon and nylon thread. Yarn of 15 denier is finer than that of 20 or 30 (see DENIER). Denier is measured by the weight of 9,842 yards of yarn. *Gauge* refers to the number of stitches across $1\frac{1}{2}$ inches of knitting. The higher the gauge, the more stitches, and the closer and finer the knitted fabric. A 51-gauge stocking has more stitches than a 45-gauge stocking.

*Thread* refers to the number of *filaments* (threads) which are twisted together to make a single strand of knitting yarn. The more durable nylon stockings are knitted from yarn of two threads. Silk stockings may be knitted of yarn of from one to seven filaments. Yarn made of more than one filament must be twisted together. Some threads are given five turns to the inch. High-twist yarns receive an additional 20 to 25 turns to each inch. See THREAD.

*Size.* Hosiery should be $\frac{1}{2}$ to $\frac{3}{4}$ of an inch longer than the foot. Otherwise the threads may break from the movement of the foot. Stockings that are too short or too long receive extra strain when the person wearing them walks.        ELIZABETH CHESLEY BAITY

See also KNITTING MACHINE.

**STOCKS** are an old device used for punishment. Stocks are a wooden framework with holes for the legs of the victim, and sometimes for the arms and neck. Persons were placed in the stocks for minor offenses, such as drunkenness, for periods of a few hours to several days.

Stocks were commonly used for punishment in American colonial days. In the North, women charged with being "common scolds" were sometimes punished in the stocks. In the South, disobedient slaves often were placed in the stocks. The use of stocks did not disappear until the early 1800's.        MARVIN E. WOLFGANG

See also PILLORY, with picture.

**STOCKTON,** Calif. (pop. 97,680; met. area 249,989; alt. 20 ft.), is the state's only inland seaport. It is 78 miles east of the Golden Gate of San Francisco Bay (see CALIFORNIA [political map]). It was named by its

## STOCKTON, FRANK RICHARD

founder, Captain Charles M. Weber, in honor of Commodore Robert Stockton of the U.S. Navy. The channel connecting San Francisco and Stockton is deep enough to accommodate the largest vessels of the American Merchant Marine. Shipments from the port include farm products of the surrounding valley, paper, cedar lumber, and farm machinery. Stockton was chartered as a city in 1850. It is the home of the University of the Pacific, founded in 1851. The city has a council-manager form of government. GEORGE SHAFTEL

**STOCKTON, FRANK RICHARD** (1834-1902), an American author, wrote humorous, fanciful tales. He first became known for his short fairy stories for children. Stockton's first collection of fairy tales, *Ting-a-Ling*, appeared in 1870. Some of his stories were published in the *St. Nicholas* magazine, which he helped edit from 1873 to 1881. His other collections of stories include *The Floating Prince and Other Fairy Tales* (1881) and *The Bee Man of Orn and Other Fanciful Tales* (1887).

He published his first book for adults, *Rudder Grange*, in 1879. It is a novel of the absurd, fantastic adventures of a young couple living in a houseboat. He established his reputation when his best-known short story, "The Lady or the Tiger?" appeared in 1884. This story, which is famous for its unusual ending, has been translated into many languages. The story was followed in 1886 by *The Casting Away of Mrs. Lecks and Mrs. Aleshine*. Stockton was born in Philadelphia, Pa. JEAN THOMSON

**STOCKTON, RICHARD** (1730-1781), was a New Jersey signer of the Declaration of Independence. He served in the Continental Congress in 1776 and, in the same year, became chief justice of the New Jersey Supreme Court. He was responsible for securing John Witherspoon to serve as president of the College of New Jersey (see WITHERSPOON, JOHN). Stockton was born in Princeton. New Jersey has placed a statue of him in Statuary Hall in Washington, D.C. CLARENCE L. VER STEEG

**STOCKYARDS.** See MEAT PACKING (The Marketing of Livestock); KANSAS CITY (picture).

**STODDARD, WILLIAM OSBORN** (1835-1925), was an American author, journalist, and inventor. He was among the first to write that Abraham Lincoln should be elected President of the United States. He served as one of Lincoln's private secretaries from 1861 to 1864. He was United States marshal in Arkansas from 1864 to 1866. Stoddard patented nine inventions and wrote 76 books, including five on Lincoln, 10 on other United States Presidents, and many novels for boys. He was born in Homer, N.Y. WILLIAM H. GILMAN

**STODDERT, BENJAMIN** (1751-1813), America's first secretary of the navy, built the Navy up to some 50 vessels and 6,000 seamen. He pushed the purchase of navy yard sites and began basic construction of shore facilities at Portsmouth, N.H.; Charlestown, Mass.; Brooklyn, N.Y.; Philadelphia, Pa.; and Gosport, Va. He served from 1798 to 1801. Stoddert, born in Charles County, Maryland, was a merchant shipper. He served in the Revolutionary War. RICHARD S. WEST, JR.

**STOIC PHILOSOPHY** flourished from about 300 B.C. to A.D. 300. It began in Greece and then spread to Rome. The Stoic philosophers believed that each man has within himself reason, which relates him to all other men and to the Reason (God) that governs the universe. This belief provided a theoretical basis for *cosmopolitanism*—the idea that men are citizens of the world rather than of a single nation or area. This view also stimulated the belief in a natural law that stands above civil law and provides a standard by which men's laws may be judged. The Stoics felt that man achieves his greatest good—which is happiness—by following reason, freeing himself from passions, and concentrating only on things he can control.

The Stoic philosophers had their greatest influence on law, ethics, and political theory, but they also formulated important views on logic, the theory of knowledge, and natural philosophy. Zeno is considered the founder of Stoic philosophy. The early Stoics, particularly Chrysippus, were interested in logic and natural philosophy as well as ethics. The later Stoics, especially Seneca, Marcus Aurelius, and Epictetus, emphasized ethics. JOSIAH B. GOULD

See also ZENO; EPICTETUS; MARCUS AURELIUS; SENECA, LUCIUS ANNAEUS.

**STOKE-ON-TRENT** (pop. 275,730; alt. 485 ft.), the pottery center of England, lies on the Trent River about 35 miles south of Manchester (see GREAT BRITAIN [political map]). Josiah Wedgwood introduced fine chinaware at Stoke in the 1700's, and the potteries still form the main industry of Stoke-on-Trent. Wedgwood, Spode, and Staffordshire ware all come from this city. This district is the setting for Arnold Bennett's novels of the "Five Towns." FRANCIS H. HERRICK

**STOKER.** See HEATING (Coal and Coke).

**STOKER, BRAM** (1847-1912), a British author, wrote *Dracula* (1897), one of the most famous horror stories of all time. Count Dracula, the book's main character, is a nobleman who is really a *vampire* (blood-sucking killer). He lives in Transylvania (now part of Romania), and is several hundred years old. At night, he changes into a huge bat, and flies about the countryside drawing blood from the necks of sleeping victims. Dracula moves to England and terrorizes the people there. He is finally killed by a stake driven through his heart. *Dracula's Guest*, a continuation of *Dracula*, was not published until 1937. Stoker's other books include *The Mystery of the Sea* (1902), *The Jewel of Seven Stars* (1904), and *Famous Imposters* (1910).

Stoker was born in Dublin, Ireland. He was manager for actor Sir Henry Irving, and wrote *Personal Reminiscences of Henry Irving* (1906). JAMES D. MERRITT

**STOKES, CARL BURTON** (1927-    ), became mayor of Cleveland in November, 1967. A Democrat, he was the first Negro elected to head a major American city.

Stokes was born in Cleveland. His family was poor, and Stokes left high school at age 17 to go to work. He served in the Army from 1944 to 1946. After leaving the Army, he finished high school and worked his way through college. He graduated from the University of Minnesota and from Cleveland-Marshall Law School. He became a lawyer in 1957.

Stokes was elected to the Ohio House of Representatives in 1962. He was re-elected twice. In 1965, he ran for mayor of Cleveland as an independent, but lost. In the 1967 election for mayor, he defeated Republican Seth C. Taft, a grandson of President William Howard Taft. EDGAR ALLAN TOPPIN

**STOKOWSKI,** *stoh KAWF skee,* **LEOPOLD ANTONI STANISLAW** (1882-    ), a famous conductor, gained renown for his dramatic conducting style. He served as an organist in New York City until he became conductor of the Cincinnati Symphony Orchestra in 1909. He directed The Philadelphia Orchestra from 1912 to 1936, presenting new program arrangements and playing the music of unknown composers.

Houston Symphony Society
**Leopold Stokowski**

Stokowski conducted the National Broadcasting Company Symphony Orchestra from 1941 to 1944. He founded the New York City Symphony Orchestra in 1944, and later became a conductor of the New York Philharmonic Orchestra. In 1955, he became permanent conductor of the Houston Symphony Orchestra. Stokowski also appeared in motion pictures, and wrote the book, *Music for All of Us* (1943).

He was born in London, England, and studied at the Royal College of Music. Stokowski came to the United States in 1905.                IRVING KOLODIN

**STOL.** See CONVERTIPLANE.

**STOLA.** See TOGA.

**STOMACH** is an enlarged part of the alimentary canal. It lies between the *esophagus* and the small *intestine* (see ESOPHAGUS; INTESTINE). In man and most animals, it is a simple baglike organ. In cows, sheep, and other *ruminants* (animals that chew their cud), the stomach has four compartments and is more complicated than man's stomach (see RUMINANT).

Man's stomach is shaped much like a *J*. In most persons, it is located in the upper left side of the abdomen. But the position can vary. The upper end of the stomach connects with the esophagus. The lower end opens into the *duodenum*, the upper end of the small intestine. The stomach is a muscular organ. This allows it to churn and mix its contents and fit its shape to the amount of food it holds. The average adult stomach can hold a little more than a quart, but the stomachs of individuals differ. Tall, thin persons usually have long, narrow stomachs. Short, stocky persons usually have short, wide stomachs.

**The Stomach's Work.** The stomach serves as a storage place for food, so that a large meal may be eaten at one time. It also helps digest food.

Glands in the stomach wall secrete mucus to lubricate the food. Other glands give off hydrochloric acid and the enzyme pepsin to partially digest the food. The hydrochloric acid is very strong and kills any *microorganisms* (tiny living organisms such as bacteria) in the food.

The stomach muscles churn the food and digestive juices into a pulpy liquid. Then the muscles squeeze the liquid toward the *pyloric* (intestinal) end of the stomach by ringlike contractions of the muscles. These contractions, called *peristaltic waves*, occur about 20 seconds apart. They start at the top of the stomach and move downward. The *pylorus*, a ringlike muscle around the duodenal opening, keeps food in the stomach until

# STOMACH

it is a liquid. Then the pylorus relaxes and lets some of the *chyme* (liquid digested food) pass into the small intestine.

The churning action of the stomach tends to begin at our usual mealtimes. When a person says his stomach is "growling," he is referring to these peristaltic waves. Sometimes, these movements grow so strong that they squeeze acid gastric juice up into the lower part of the esophagus. This irritates the tissues there and causes discomfort.

The pylorus allows water to pass through almost as soon as it enters the stomach. But the length of time that the stomach retains food varies. On the mixed diet that most persons eat, the stomach empties in three to five hours.

When food enters the stomach, it contains *ptyalin*, an enzyme in saliva that partially digests starch. This action is stopped immediately by the hydrochloric acid in the stomach. No further digestion of starch occurs until the chyme enters the small intestine. For this reason, salivary ptyalin is not very important to digestion.

The enzymes secreted in the stomach are *pepsin*, which partially digests proteins and clots milk; and *rennin*, which also clots milk. Rennin is probably important only in infants. Infants also have *gastric lipase*, an enzyme that digests fat in the stomach. In adults, fat digestion occurs in the small intestine.

Although the stomach performs several useful functions, it is not absolutely essential for life. Many persons lead long lives after their stomachs are either partially or wholly removed because of cancer or ulcers.

**Stomach Diseases.** Many foods irritate the mucous membrane that lines the stomach. Such foods include highly spiced foods, extremely hot foods, and some alcoholic drinks. Rough and dry food that is not well chewed can irritate the stomach. Fear, anger, or constant tension can cause an excessive secretion of stomach juices even when no food is present. This greatly irritates the stomach and the duodenum. If made worse by

## THE STOMACH

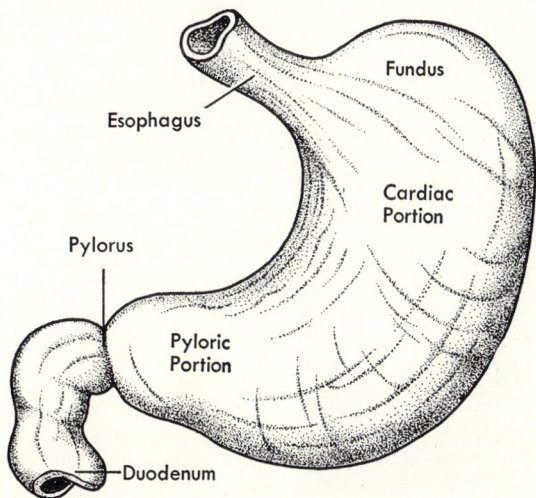

709

## STOMACH-ACHE

hastily eaten coarse food, a person can develop ulcers in the stomach or duodenum. Duodenal ulcers almost always result from too much secretion in the stomach. Excessive smoking and drinking of beverages that contain alcohol or caffeine make a person more susceptible to ulcers. Ulcers often heal themselves if the patient eats a simple diet, usually containing milk, and avoids tension. In severe cases, doctors treat ulcers by surgery. TERENCE A. ROGERS

**Related Articles.** See the Trans-Vision three-dimensional color picture with HUMAN BODY. See also:

| | | |
|---|---|---|
| Alimentary Canal | Food | Nausea |
| Animal (How Animals Eat) | Gastritis | Ruminant |
| | Gastroscope | Ulcer |
| | Ileum | Vomiting |
| Digestion | | |

**STOMACH-ACHE.** See INDIGESTION.

**STOMATA.** See LEAF (The Leaf as a Food "Factory").

**STONE.** See BUILDING STONE; ROCK.

**STONE** is a unit of weight. See WEIGHTS AND MEASURES (Avoirdupois Weight).

**STONE, EDWARD DURELL** (1902-    ), is an American architect who gained fame for harmonizing buildings with their cultural surroundings. For example, Stone adapted elements of Indian architecture for his United States embassy building in New Delhi, India (see NEW DELHI [picture: The U.S. Embassy Building]). In this and other buildings, Stone made extensive use of grillwork. He also designed the U.S. pavilion at the 1958 Brussels Worlds Fair, the Museum of Modern Art in New York City, the North Carolina State Legislative Building in Raleigh, and the John F. Kennedy Center for the Performing Arts in Washington, D.C. His book *The Evolution of an Architect* was published in 1962. Stone was born in Fayetteville, Ark. He studied at the University of Arkansas and at Harvard and M.I.T. HUGH MORRISON

**STONE, HARLAN FISKE** (1872-1946), served as chief justice of the United States from 1941 until his death. The years he served as chief justice on the Supreme Court were marked by changing constitutional views and by division within the court. Stone became an associate justice in 1925. Although a conservative, Stone often joined Louis D. Brandeis and Oliver Wendell Holmes in upholding liberal, progressive measures.

Stone was born at Chesterfield, N.H., the son of a farmer. He was graduated from Amherst College in 1894, and then studied at the Columbia University Law School. From 1899 to 1905, he taught law at Columbia. For a time he practiced law in New York City, and became a noted corporation lawyer. Stone served as dean of the Columbia University Law School from 1910 to 1923. He became attorney general of the United States in 1924 and cleaned up scandals in the Department of Justice. MERLO J. PUSEY

**Harlan F. Stone**
Wide World

**STONE, IRVING** (1903-    ), is an American biographer and novelist. His first important work was *Lust for Life* (1934), a novel about Vincent van Gogh, the painter. He also wrote *Sailor on Horseback* (1938), the story of Jack London's life; *The President's Lady* (1951), the life of President Andrew Jackson's wife; *Love Is Eternal* (1954), about Mary Todd Lincoln; and *The Agony and the Ecstasy* (1961), a story of Michelangelo's life. Stone was born in San Francisco. GEORGE J. BECKER

**STONE, LUCY** (1818-1893), was the first American woman to lecture on woman's rights, and probably the first married woman to keep her maiden name. She became a famous antislavery and woman-suffrage speaker, and converted Susan B. Anthony and Julia Ward Howe to her cause. She helped organize associations for woman's rights. Miss Stone was born in West Brookfield, Mass., and was graduated from Oberlin College. LOUIS FILLER

**STONE, MELVILLE ELIJAH** (1848-1929), one of the great newspapermen of his day, founded the *Chicago Daily News* in 1876. He made the *Daily News* a leader in journalism. As general manager of the Associated Press (AP) from 1893 to 1921, he established the principles which govern it today. As the AP general manager, he helped save the treaty negotiations that ended the Russo-Japanese War in 1905. Stone was born in Hudson, Ill. JOHN TEBBEL

**STONE, PRECIOUS.** See GEM.

**STONE, THOMAS** (1743-1787), was a Maryland signer of the Declaration of Independence. Although he favored independence for the colonists, he urged negotiation with Great Britain instead of war. Stone served in the Second Continental Congress and helped frame the Articles of Confederation. He was elected to the Maryland Senate three times. He died during his third term. Stone was born in Charles County, Maryland, and studied law at Annapolis. RICHARD B. MORRIS

**STONE AGE** is a term used to designate the period in all human cultures when men used stone, rather than metal tools. The Stone Age began more than $1\frac{1}{2}$ million years ago when human beings first began to make crude chopping tools from pebbles. It first ended in Mesopotamia and Egypt about 3000 B.C., when people began to use bronze (see BRONZE AGE).

Scientists divide the Stone Age on the basis of toolmaking techniques into three periods, the Paleolithic, Mesolithic, and Neolithic. The *Paleolithic* period (Old Stone Age) lasted from more than $1\frac{1}{2}$ million years ago to 8000 B.C. The *Mesolithic* period (Middle Stone Age) lasted from 8000 B.C. to 7000 B.C. The *Neolithic* period (New Stone Age) began about 7000 B.C., and lasted until the invention of metals. For additional information on the Stone Age, see PREHISTORIC MAN.

Many peoples were still in the Stone Age when Europeans began their voyages of exploration and discovery in the A.D. 1400's. The aborigines of Tasmania and Australia were using techniques of the Old Stone Age when white men discovered them in the 1700's. White men found the African Bushmen living in the Middle Stone Age. Islanders of the South Pacific Ocean and most American Indians had progressed to the New Stone Age. A few tribes in New Guinea and Australia are still in the Stone Age. CARLETON S. COON

See also FAMILY (picture: A New Stone Age Family).

**STONE CHINA.** See POTTERY (European Pottery).

# STONEHENGE

**The Stone Fly Is Usually Found Near Brooks or Streams.** USDA

**STONE FLY** is a weak-flying insect. Stone flies are usually found in great numbers along the shores of moving water, where they breed. The name stone fly refers to the fact that the *nymphs* (young) live under stones until they mature. Trout and other game fish eat the nymphs. Adult stone flies vary in color to match their surroundings. They may be from $\frac{1}{2}$ to $2\frac{1}{2}$ inches long. They feed on water insects and plants.

**Scientific Classification.** Stone flies make up the order *Plecoptera*. E. G. LINSLEY

**STONE FRUIT.** See FRUIT (picture: Nature Designs the Fruits).

**STONE MARTEN.** See FUR (Names of Furs).

**STONE MOUNTAIN** is a huge, rounded mass of light-gray granite, about 16 miles east of Atlanta, Ga. It is the largest stone mountain in North America. At its highest point, 1,683 feet above sea level, it rises over 700 feet above the surrounding terrain. It measures about two miles long and one mile wide. On clear days, it can be seen from 30 miles away. Together with many other granite outcrops in northern Georgia, it supports an exotic vegetation. A kind of cactus plant grows on thin pockets of soil which lie on top of the solid granite. For the location of Stone Mountain, see GEORGIA (physical map).

In 1923, an ambitious sculpturing project was undertaken on Stone Mountain. It was designed as a memorial to the heroic struggle of the South during the Civil War. That same year, Congress authorized the minting of a Stone Mountain half dollar in connection with the project. Gutzon Borglum was the first sculptor to work on the monument, but he left Stone Mountain to undertake work on the famous Mount Rushmore carvings (see BORGLUM, GUTZON). Henry A. Lukeman also worked on the project. The work was discontinued in 1928 because of lack of funds.

In September, 1958, Georgia purchased 1,613 acres, including Stone Mountain, in order to establish a state park there. DeKalb County donated another 400 acres. A lake built at the base of the mountain, and a skylift that can carry 50 people to the top, are features of the park. Other features are also planned. They include a theater, a chapel, beaches, museums, an amphitheater, and golf courses.

In 1963, work on the sculpturing project was resumed under the direction of a new sculptor, Walter Kirkland Hancock. The finished sculpture will include Jefferson Davis, Stonewall Jackson, and Robert E. Lee, on horseback. The figures are so large that when the Lee carving was unveiled, 30 persons could get on the shoulder. A picture of the Lee carving appears in the GEORGIA article. The project was expected to be completed about 1970. DAVID J. DE LAUBENFELS

**STONE OF DESTINY.** See SCONE, STONE OF.

**STONECHAT** is the name of a small European bird of the thrush family. Its name comes from its peculiar note, a sound like that of two stones struck together. The male has a black head and throat and chestnut underparts. The female is duller in coloring. The stonechat is restless and active, and usually lives in open, grassy locations. It builds its nest on the ground, under a tuft of grass, and feeds on insect larvae, worms, beetles, and seeds. It lays from four to six greenish-blue, faintly spotted eggs. The bird winters in Africa.

Eric Hosking, NAS

**The Stonechat** gets its name from its peculiar call.

**Scientific Classification.** The stonechat belongs to the thrush family, *Turdidae*. It is genus *Pratincola*, species *P. rubicola*. LEONARD W. WING

**STONECROP.** See SEDUM.

**STONEHENGE,** *STOHN henj*, is an ancient monument on Salisbury Plain in Wiltshire, England. It is a group of huge, rough-cut stones. No one knows exactly who placed them there.

In 1950, archaeologists from Edinburgh University discovered two underground holes which had probably served as ritual pits. They sent charcoal from one of the pits to the University of Chicago for analysis by the radioactive-carbon method. The charcoal was found to date from 1848 B.C., plus or minus 275 years. Carvings found on the stones in 1953 also indicate that the stones may be more than 3,500 years old. Some stones are of a kind found only in western Wales, about 300 miles away. They were probably carried to the site.

For hundreds of years, the great stones gradually fell, or people carried them away to make bridges and mill dams. But from the positions of many of the stones still in place, scholars can guess what the monument probably looked like originally. An earth wall about 320 feet in diameter surrounded the monument. Thirty blocks of gray sandstone, each standing about $13\frac{1}{2}$ feet above the ground and averaging 28 tons, stood in a circle about 97 feet in diameter. A continuous circle of smaller blocks stood on top of them. Inside was a circle of about 60 blue stones. Inside this circle were two horseshoe-shaped sets of stones, one inside the other, opening toward the northeast. Near the center curve of the inner horseshoe was a flat sandstone block 16 feet long. This was probably an altar, and may have stood upright. A stone marker 80 yards east of the altar was set to cast a shadow on it at dawn of the summer solstice, about June 21. For this reason, some scholars say that Stonehenge was connected with sun worship.

In 1963, Gerald S. Hawkins of the Smithsonian Astrophysical Observatory calculated the directions of

British Ministry of Public Buildings and Works

**The Monument at Stonehenge,** *above,* may have been an ancient astronomical observatory. Scientific studies have shown that the positions of the huge stone slabs indicate the places on the horizon where the sun and moon rise and set about June 21 and December 21. The drawing, *right,* shows what scholars believe was the original arrangement of the stones.

lines joining various stones at Stonehenge. He found that the monument may have served as an accurate astronomical calendar, capable of predicting the seasons of the year and even eclipses of the sun and moon. Using an electronic computer, he found a remarkable correlation between the directions of these lines and the directions of the rising and setting of the sun and moon about 1500 B.C. The chances of such correlations being coincidental is about one in 100 million.

In 1922, the British government began to restore Stonehenge. Some of the scattered stones were put back as they had been originally. The government now takes care of this monument. Woodhenge, also in Wiltshire, is a 3,000-year-old wooden monument similar to Stonehenge. ROBERT S. HOYT

See also PREHISTORIC MAN (picture: The Massive Sandstone Blocks of Stonehenge).

**STONEHILL COLLEGE.** See UNIVERSITIES AND COLLEGES (table).

**STONES RIVER, BATTLE OF.** See CIVIL WAR (Murfreesboro, or Stones River).

**STONEWALL JACKSON.** See JACKSON, "STONEWALL," THOMAS JONATHAN.

**STONEWARE** is a type of pottery used for jugs, crocks, various types of heavy dishes, and vessels for chemicals. Stoneware is hard and strong. Potters use clays that they can bake in great heat. Heat causes stoneware to *vitrify* (become glossy). This ware does not absorb liquids, does not leak, and does not need expensive glazes, although sometimes potters apply colored glazes.

Many large, thick-walled vessels used in factories, hotels, restaurants, and on farms are made of stoneware. They are used for mixing and storing food. Stoneware is also used for art pottery.

Early American stoneware included such articles as churns, butter pots, bean pots, mugs, jugs, and pitchers. Sometimes the potters applied designs in cobalt blue. Large potteries in Ohio and West Virginia make most of the stoneware produced today. EUGENE F. BUNKER, JR.

See also POTTERY.

**STONY BROOK, STATE UNIVERSITY OF NEW YORK AT.** See UNIVERSITIES AND COLLEGES (table [New York, State University of]).

**STOPE.** See MINING (Mining Terms).

**STORAGE BATTERY.** See BATTERY.

**STORE.** See BUSINESS; CHAIN STORE; COOPERATIVE; DEPARTMENT STORE; FOOD (Marketing).

**STORIED PROVINCE.** See QUEBEC (province).

**STORK** is a large bird with long legs and strong wings. It looks for its food in marshes and swamps, but often nests on roofs and chimneys.

The best-known stork is the *white stork*. It lives in most parts of Europe and Central Asia in the summer and in Africa and northern India in the winter. This stork is white with black markings on its wings. Its beak is red and its long legs and feet are a reddish pink. A pair of storks will return year after year to the same nest. The female stork lays from three to five white eggs. Storks eat eels, frogs, reptiles, young birds, and small mammals.

Other storks of the Eastern Hemisphere are the *Japanese stork,* the *black stork,* the *white-necked stork,* and the *adjutant.* The *maguari* and the *jabiru,* a bird 5 feet high, are found in South America. The *wood ibis* of the southern United States is also a true stork.

**Stoneware** has been a popular type of pottery for many years. The English salt-glazed stoneware figure, *left,* was made about 1750. The American pitcher, *right,* was made in the 1800's.

Metropolitan Museum of Art

712

Seidenstücker, Black Star

**The White Stork,** *left,* seeks out cities and towns with chimneys and crannies in which to nest. It rears its family in such high places. The black stork, *above,* shuns such nesting places.

Black Star

The stork is a respected and protected bird in many places. The Germans and the Dutch like storks because they destroy insects and reptiles. They also believe that the stork brings good luck. The faithfulness of a pair of storks is considered a model of married happiness. The familiar legend that the stork brings the new baby into the home arises from the fact that the stork takes loving care of its own young.

**Scientific Classification.** The stork belongs to the stork family, *Ciconiidae.* The white stork is classified as genus *Ciconia,* species *C. ciconia.*  ALFRED M. BAILEY

See also ADJUTANT; BIRD (color picture, Birds of Other Lands); JABIRU; MARABOU.

**STORM** is a disturbance of the atmosphere. Storms are usually marked by strong winds, rain, snow, or hail, or by a combination of two or more of these. Storms would never occur if the temperature of the air everywhere were equal. The air in low latitudes becomes heated, however, while that in high latitudes is cooled. The air over oceans stays warmer in the winter, and cooler in summer, than that over land. These differences in temperature also result in differences in pressure. Over warm areas the pressure remains relatively low, while over colder areas it is high.

As cold air accumulates in the high latitudes, large masses of it tend to spread out toward the equator. Eventually these large masses break off into separate, wandering masses of cold air which move generally eastward and southward. In the middle latitudes, these masses of cold air usually meet warm air masses that have come up from low latitudes. Wherever warm and cold air masses meet, a struggle develops, which may result in storms. Differences in temperature, pressure, and humidity cause all the many different kinds of storms.  GEORGE F. TAYLOR

Related Articles in WORLD BOOK include:

| Air | Hurricane | Thunder |
| Barometer | Lightning | Tornado |
| Blizzard | Rain | Typhoon |
| Cloudburst | Sandstorm | Waterspout |
| Cyclone | Sleet | Weather |
| Dust Storm | Snow | Whirlwind |
| Hail | Sunspot | Wind |

**STORM TROOPS.** See HITLER, ADOLF (Birth of the Nazi Party); GESTAPO.

**STORMALONG, ALFRED BULLTOP,** an American folklore character, was the gigantic hero of sailors' tall tales about a huge ship named the *Courser.* The *Courser* was so big that the officers and men on watch rode horseback on deck. Its masts were hinged to bend so they could let the sun and moon pass. Sailors who climbed its rigging as young men came down with gray beards. Stormalong performed amazing feats of seamanship aboard the ship. He suggested soaping the sides of the *Courser* to ease it through the English Channel. It was such a tight squeeze that the soap scraped off on the cliffs of Dover, leaving them white.  B. A. BOTKIN

**STORMY PETREL.** See PETREL.

**STORTING.** See NORWAY (Parliament).

**STORY, JOSEPH** (1779-1845), served as an associate justice of the Supreme Court of the United States from 1812 to 1845. As an outstanding member of the Supreme Court, he followed closely in the footsteps of John Marshall (see MARSHALL, JOHN). His *Commentaries,* a series of important legal essays, helped shape American concepts of the common law.

Story was born at Marblehead, Mass., and was graduated from Harvard University in 1798. He began to practice law in 1801 and later served in Congress. He was also a professor of law at Harvard University from 1829 until his death.  JERRE S. WILLIAMS

# STORYTELLING

Treasure Island

**Storytelling from Memory** is the oldest and most interesting way to hear adventure stories and travel tales. An old sailor's stories are exciting to a small boy.

H. Armstrong Roberts

**STORYTELLING** is an art that entertains people of all ages. It is as old as language. All stories are subject to change by the teller and by the writer, who may publish a new collection or may edit an old one. Stories are constantly changing, and the anecdote of today may become folklore tomorrow.

## How to Tell a Story

**Selection.** Take care in selecting materials for storytelling. Folk tales were meant to be heard. Their style, characters, and incidents reflect the places and people from which they came. There are good editions of folk tales from many lands. Some of these are listed at the end of this article. But any story rich in imagination, with a clearly defined plot, plenty of action, and universal appeal, provides good material for telling. Poetry is also well suited for use in storytelling. Good poetry is often unappreciated because it is not read aloud. See POETRY (Enjoying Poetry).

A storyteller should select stories that are worth the time of preparation. They should have qualities that inspire or delight him as well as his listeners, and give everyone something to remember and to carry away. A storyteller increases interest through his enthusiastic interpretation. Enjoyment grows out of the delight shared by listeners and teller. Young children enjoy animal stories with much repetition, while myths and hero tales appeal to the older child. Search for stories among the folklore of your own background—your region, your ancestry, and nationality. You are likely to tell this type of story most easily at first. Then work to widen your appreciation of different types of stories, and offer variety in your repertoire of stories.

**Preparation.** Begin by reading over the chosen story. The number of readings depends upon the length and involvement of the story. Then think the story through as a series of episodes or pictures from beginning to end. Read it again to see if you recall all important episodes or pictures, and repeat this thinking and reading as often as necessary. Now reread for style, recalling

714

# STORYTELLING

those particularly effective phrases and repeated verses or expressions which especially appeal to you.

Do not memorize the story word for word. Tell much of it in your own words. Your success will depend on you. If you have read well and widely, have a good vocabulary, and are sensitive to style, it is likely that your selection of words will fit in with the story and with the phrases you have kept as written. A wide vocabulary makes it possible to paint richly varied word pictures.

Tell the story over and over again until you can tell it with enthusiasm, confidence, and without thought of yourself. As you repeat it to yourself, say it aloud sometimes, to gain the proper timing and voice quality. When you tell the story to listeners, look at each person in your group, and time your telling to the individuals' reactions. This will be easy as you relive the story with them.

It is important that your story have variety in tempo, and that your voice be low and pleasant, with variety in volume and pace. Some gestures and mimicry, if natural, contribute to the telling. Make the story a part of you, and then relive the story you are telling, not only for the listeners, but with them.

## Storytelling Around the World

**The Mediterranean and Middle East** have inspired many fine stories that are still being told. Homer, who lived in Greece probably about 900 B.C., is generally accepted by scholars as the author of the *Iliad* and the *Odyssey*. He is believed to have traveled in and around Greece, reciting his poems publicly for a fee. Homer's stories later inspired the *Aeneid*, written by the Roman poet Virgil around the 30's B.C. Scholars believe that a Greek slave named Aesop wrote the famous *Fables* in the 500's B.C.

An ancient Egyptian record, *The Tales of the Magicians*, written about 4000 B.C., collected several tales around a central theme. This device has been followed ever since. One such collection is *The Arabian Nights*, first written in Arabic but originating from various Middle Eastern sources.

The great Persian contribution to the literature of storytelling was the epic *Shāh Nāmah*, or *Book of Kings*, written by Firdausi in about A.D. 1000. One episode from this epic was the source of Matthew Arnold's *Sohrab and Rustum*.

**India.** The *Mahabharata*, written in Sanskrit about 200 B.C., has for its theme the career of the Pandavas, five brothers. The *Bhagavad-Gita*, one of its great poetic passages, describes vividly the growth of the human soul. Another great Indian epic is Valmiki's *Ramayana*, a romantic tale of an incarnation of Vishnu.

The Buddhist *Jataka Tales*, written in Pali, a language similar to Sanskrit, came first from Ceylon. In these tales, Buddha recalls earlier incarnations in the forms of animals. Each tale has a moral, making the collection somewhat like Aesop's *Fables*. The *Jatakas* were followed about A.D. 500 by the *Panchatantra*, a collection of animal stories which inspired many later tales, including the fables of La Fontaine.

**China.** The story of *Gessar Khan* is a favorite Chinese hero tale. It is said to have come into being because

Al Daigle

Little Red Riding Hood

Aladdin and the Genie

**Storytelling from Books** draws the interest of most small children. All games end quickly when it's storytelling time. A teacher often shows the children pictures in the book as she tells a story.

# STORYTELLING

Buddha showed the need for a hero to inspire the followers of his religion.

**Europe.** The German *Nibelungenlied* became the counterpart of the stories of the gods and goddesses conceived by Homer. The legend, written between 1100 and 1300, tells of the *Nibelungs* (dwarfs), some historical characters, and a huge treasure.

The Icelandic sagas were sung and told from about the 1100's to the 1300's. They were obviously drawn from Greek and German mythology, but were also influenced by Christianity. Two collections are the *Poetic Edda* and the *Prose Edda*. See EDDA.

It is thought that the Viking storytellers may have borrowed their literary form from the Irish. There are two Irish sagas. One is the Red Branch, or Ulster Cycle, with Cuchulainn and Deirdre as the best known characters. The other is the Fenian Cycle, in which appear the *High Deeds of Finn*. Both were written before 1500. The Fenian Cycle is believed to be the later one, since its paganism is modified by Christian influences.

The Finnish epic, the *Kalevala*, was spread by storytellers for hundreds of years. Zacharias Topelius published part of it in 1826. After gathering information around the country, Elias Lönnrot printed his final edition of the epic in 1849, having added 12,000 lines. The *Kalevala* contains mythology and folklore. Henry Wadsworth Longfellow used the same meter for *Hiawatha*.

The *Mabinogion*, which, translated literally, means *tale of youth* or *tale of a hero*, is a collection of Welsh stories of the 1200's and 1300's. It is divided into four branches that tell of tasks and achievements. King Arthur is presented in an unusual light in some of these stories.

The outstanding French epic of the Middle Ages is the *Song of Roland*, written about 1050. It is one of the many epics of the time about the Frankish King Charlemagne. The *Poem of the Cid*, written by an anonymous author in the 1100's, glorifies the life and accomplishments of Rodrigo Díaz, a great national hero of Spain.

**The United States** has several famous tales which might be classified as either hero or tall tales. One is the story of Paul Bunyan, the fabulous lumberjack. Another is the saga of Pecos Bill, the cowboy of great prowess. The United States has many folk tales based on the life of the Negroes, the Creoles, and the Indians, and has many variations on tales from other lands.

## History

**The Earliest Storytellers.** Storytelling is thousands of years old. Tales of personal exploit are the earliest form of storytelling. They began when man recognized the forces of nature as power and action outside himself. He expressed his fear and awe in the myth and hero tale. These tales tell of sacred beings, of semidivine heroes, and of the origins of all things.

As time went on, people learned to farm, and settled in communities. This made possible specialization in arts and industries. Each person had a particular responsibility, such as sowing, reaping, cooking, or even storytelling. A particular person might be chosen as storyteller because of his reliable memory and his ability to hold the interest of listeners. The development of literary form began with the selection of specialists to tell stories.

Early folk tales, because of their underlying meanings, helped explain to the members of the community their relationships to each other and to nature. Tales told them what was right and wrong, how they happened to live where they did, and what would happen after death. Sharing these stories helped unite and entertain people.

**The Great Era of Storytelling** lasted from the 1000's to the 1500's. Most storytellers enjoyed the patronage of a king or a noble who engaged the storyteller to live at his castle. These men wrote ballads and songs describing important events, and recited them for the entertainment of the family and guests. They usually told the stories to a musical accompaniment. In southern France, such storytellers were called *troubadours*. In northern France, they were called *trouvères*. Scandinavia had its *skalds*, Wales its *bards*, and England its *minstrels*. The storytellers of Ireland, called *ollamhs*, were organized into nine groups, each of which told a different kind of tale. Germany first had the *minnesingers*, who were singers of romantic love ballads. The *mastersingers*, who belonged to musical and poetic guilds, followed in the 1300's.

All these storytellers, as well as gypsies, pilgrims, crusaders, and ordinary travelers, moved about and took their stories with them, exchanging them with other peoples. Because of this continuous exchange and adaptation of stories, it is difficult to know where particular stories, elements of stories, and variants of stories originated.

**Collecting Stories.** During the 1700's and 1800's, collectors set many of the old stories down in books. Readers were astonished to discover the similarities between stories of several countries. The collections of Jakob and Wilhelm Grimm in Germany and Peter Asbjørnsen and Jørgen Moe in Norway left a lasting influence. Later collectors followed the stories as the people told them, instead of rewriting them. During this period, people also began to write specifically for children. The Mother Goose tales, published in 1697 by Frenchman Charles Perrault, appeared in an English translation by John Newbery in the 1700's. Hans Christian Andersen wrote his famous fairy tales in the early 1800's.

**Storytelling Today** has been kept alive by a few storytellers. Marie Shedlock, an Englishwoman, was noted for her ability to interpret the fairy tales of Hans Christian Andersen. Gudrun Thorne-Thomsen has made phonograph records of the Icelandic eddas and Norwegian folk tales. Other famous storytellers include Ruth Durand Sawyer, Sara Cone Bryant, Mary Gould Davis, and Frances Clarke Sayers. Storytelling is also kept alive in homes, libraries, schools, and recreation centers. Radio and television often make use of folk tales and other good story material. Children's librarians make important contributions to the art of storytelling. Story hours are a recognized part of the services of a good library.   SARA H. WHEELER

**Related Articles** in WORLD BOOK include:

FAMOUS CHARACTERS AND STORIES

| | | |
|---|---|---|
| Aeneid | Amadís of Gaul | Canterbury |
| Aesop's | Arabian Nights | Tales |
| Fables | Arthur, King | Cid, The |
| Aladdin | Candide | Cinderella |

# STORYTELLING

| | | |
|---|---|---|
| Courtship of Miles Standish | Hiawatha | Odyssey |
| Cuchulainn | Huckleberry Finn, Adventures of | Peter Pan |
| Don Quixote | Iliad | Ramayana |
| Evangeline | Lancelot, Sir | Rip Van Winkle |
| Galahad, Sir | Lochinvar | Robin Hood |
| Grimm's Fairy Tales | Mahabharata | Robinson Crusoe |
| | Mother Goose | Round Table |
| Gulliver's Travels | Nibelungenlied | Santa Claus |
| | | Scheherazade |

### STORYTELLERS

| | | |
|---|---|---|
| Andersen, Hans C. | Mastersinger | Perrault, Charles |
| Bard | Minnesinger | Skald |
| Grimm (family) | Minstrel | Troubadour |

### OTHER RELATED ARTICLES

| | |
|---|---|
| Bible (The Bible for Children's Use) | Literature for Children |
| | Mythology |
| Caldecott Medal | Newbery Medal |
| Christmas (Literature) | Nursery Rhyme |
| Folklore | Regina Medal |

### Outline

I. **How to Tell a Story**
   A. Selection     B. Preparation
II. **Storytelling Around the World**
   A. The Mediterranean and Middle East
   B. India
   C. China
   D. Europe
   E. The United States
III. **History**
   A. The Earliest Storytellers
   B. The Great Era of Storytelling
   C. Collecting Stories
   D. Storytelling Today

### Questions

How have stories traveled throughout the world?
What community service offers storytelling today?
What qualities should the storyteller look for in selecting a story?
When did people begin collecting and comparing tales from different countries?
Where can storytellers obtain materials?
When was the great era of storytelling?
What two famous stories come from the folklore of the United States?
What are important points to remember in telling a story?
How do the *Jataka* tales resemble *Aesop's Fables*?
Why were folk tales important to early communities?

### Books to Read

#### How to Tell Stories

EASTMAN, MARY H., comp. *Index to Fairy Tales, Myths, and Legends.* Faxon, 1926. Supplement, 1937. Second supplement, 1952.
SAWYER, RUTH. *The Way of the Storyteller.* New enl. ed. Viking, 1962.
SHEDLOCK, MARIE L. *The Art of the Story-Teller.* 3rd ed. rev. Dover, 1952.
TOOZE, RUTH. *Storytelling.* Prentice-Hall, 1959.

#### Folk Stories from Many Lands

**Around the World**

ASSOCIATION FOR CHILDHOOD EDUCATION INTERNATIONAL. *Told Under the Green Umbrella: Old Stories for New Children.* Macmillan, 1962.
BAKER, AUGUSTA, comp. *The Golden Lynx and Other Tales.* Lippincott, 1960. Favorite tales of Europe and Asia.
BELTING, NATALIA M. *Elves and Ellefolk.* Holt, 1961. Brief stories of wee people with magical power.
BLEECKER, MARY N., comp. *Big Music: or, Twenty Merry Tales to Tell.* Viking, 1946.
COURLANDER, HAROLD. *The Tiger's Whisker and Other Tales and Legends from Asia and the Pacific.* Harcourt, 1959. These 31 stories reflect the uniqueness of the cultures represented.
DALGLIESH, ALICE, ed. *The Enchanted Book.* Scribner, 1958. Tales of enchantment.
DE LA MARE, WALTER. *Tales Told Again.* Knopf, 1959. A famous poet retells beloved tales.
FILLMORE, PARKER H. *The Shepherd's Nosegay: Stories from Finland and Czechoslovakia.* Harcourt, 1958. Favorites from collections now out of print.
HAZELTINE, ALICE I., ed. *Hero Tales From Many Lands.* Abingdon, 1961.
HUTCHINSON, VERONICA S., comp. *Chimney Corner Stories: Tales for Little Children.* Putnam, 1925. An attractive collection for the newcomer to folk tales.
LANG, ANDREW, ed. *The Blue Fairy Book.* New ed. McKay, 1948.
ROSS, EULALIE S., comp. *The Buried Treasure and Other Picture Tales.* Lippincott, 1958. Selected from out-of-print sources by an experienced storyteller.
WILLIAMS-ELLIS, AMABEL. *Round the World Fairy Tales.* Warne, 1966.

**Africa**

ARNOTT, KATHLEEN. *African Myths and Legends.* Walck, 1963. Well-told stories from 13 countries of Africa.
COURLANDER, HAROLD, comp. *The King's Drum and Other African Stories.* Harcourt, 1962.
COURLANDER, HAROLD, and HERZOG, GEORGE. *Cow-Tail Switch, and Other West African Stories.* Holt, 1947. More Anansi stories and others from African storytellers.
COURLANDER, HAROLD, and LESLAU, WOLF. *Fire on the Mountain, and Other Ethiopian Stories.* Holt, 1950. Tales with the unique flavor of Ethiopian life and customs.
COURLANDER, HAROLD, and PREMPEH, A. K. *Hat-Shaking Dance, and Other Tales from the Gold Coast.* Harcourt, 1957. Gay stories about the wily spider Anansi.
SHERLOCK, PHILIP M. *Anansi, the Spider Man.* Illus. by Marcia Brown. Crowell, 1954.
STURTON, HUGH. *Zomo the Rabbit.* Atheneum, 1966. Gay trickster tales.

**Arabia**

*Arabian Nights.* Ed. by Andrew Lang. New ed. Longmans, 1946. *The Arabian Nights: Their Best-Known Tales.* Ed. by Kate Douglas Wiggin and Nora A. Smith. Illus. by Maxfield Parrish. Scribner, 1929. *Arabian Nights: Tales of Wonder and Magnificence.* Ed. by Padraic Colum. Illus. by Lynd K. Ward. Macmillan, 1953.
*Sindbad, the Sailor. The 7 Voyages of Sindbad the Sailor.* Atheneum, 1962. All the Sindbad adventures.

**Australia**

PARKER, K. LANGLOH. *Australian Legendary Tales.* Viking, 1966.

**British Isles**

*England*

CHAUCER, GEOFFREY. *Tales from Chaucer: The Canterbury Tales Done into Prose.* Retold by Eleanor Farjeon. Illus. by Marjorie Walters. Branford, 1959.
HOSFORD, DOROTHY G. *By His Own Might: The Battles of Beowulf.* Illus. by Laszlo Matulay. Holt, 1947.
JACOBS, JOSEPH, ed. *English Folk and Fairy Tales.* Putnam, 1904. *More English Folk and Fairy Tales.* Many of the stories in this sensitively chosen collection are suitable for younger children. Comp.: *Favorite Fairy Tales Told in England.* Retold by Virginia Haviland. Illus. by Bettina. Little, Brown, 1959.
MALORY, SIR THOMAS. *The Boy's King Arthur.* Ed. for boys by Sidney Lanier. Illus. by N. C. Wyeth. Scribner, 1933. *The Book of King Arthur and His Noble Knights: Stories from Sir Thomas Malory's Morte d'Arthur.* By Mary Mcleod. Lippincott, 1949.
MANNING-SANDERS, RUTH. *Peter and the Piskies: Cornish Folk and Fairy Tales.* Roy, 1966.
PYLE, HOWARD. *The Story of Sir Launcelot and His Companions.* Scribner, 1907. *The Story of King Arthur and His Knights.* 1933. *The Story of the Champions of the Round Table.* 1933. *The Story of the Grail and the Passing of Arthur.* 1933. *The Merry Adventures of Robin Hood of*

717

NBC

**Storytelling on Television** often makes use of actions as well as words. Skillful puppeteers tell fanciful stories, using comically dressed hand puppets to entertain thousands of youngsters.

*Great Renown in Nottinghamshire.* New ed. 1946.
STEEL, FLORA A. *English Fairy Tales.* Macmillan, 1962.
SUTCLIFF, ROSEMARY. *Beowulf; Retold.* Dutton, 1962.
Ireland
COLUM, PADRAIC. *The King of Ireland's Son.* Macmillan, 1962.
HAVILAND, VIRGINIA. *Favorite Fairy Tales Told in Ireland; Retold From Irish Storytellers.* Little, Brown, 1961.
JACOBS, JOSEPH, ed. *Celtic Folk and Fairy Tales.* Putnam, 1923. A rich source of ancient Celtic tales.
MACMANUS, SEUMAS. *The Well o' the World's End.* Devin-Adair, 1949. *Bold Heroes of Hungry Hill, and Other Irish Folk Tales.* Farrar, Straus, 1951. The charm of the Irish people is skillfully woven into these tales which were told around Irish turf fires. *Hibernian Nights.* Macmillan, 1963.
YOUNG, ELLA. *The Wonder Smith and His Son: A Tale from the Golden Childhood of the World.* Illus. by Boris Artzybasheff. McKay, 1957. The glorious adventures of Ireland's master builder, Gubbaun Saor.
Scotland
HAVILAND, VIRGINIA. *Favorite Fairy Tales Told in Scotland.* Little, Brown, 1963.
LEODHAS, SORCHE N., ed. (pseud. of L. G. ALGER). *Heather and Broom: Tales of the Scottish Highlands.* Holt, 1960. *Thistle and Thyme.* 1962. A variety of previously unpublished stories of romance, humor, and magic.
Canada
BARBEAU, MARIUS. *The Golden Phoenix, and Other French-Canadian Fairy Tales.* Walck, 1958.
CARLSON, NATALIE S. *The Talking Cat, and Other Stories of French Canada.* Harper, 1952.
HOOKE, HILDA M. *Thunder in the Mountains: Legends of Canada.* Oxford, 1948. Action and magic.

MACMILLAN, CYRUS. *Glooskap's Country, and Other Indian Tales.* Walck, 1956. Fairy tales and legends of the Canadian Indian before the white man came.
China
BIRCH, CYRIL. *Chinese Myths and Fantasies; Retold.* Walck, 1961.
CARPENTER, FRANCES. *Tales of a Chinese Grandmother.* Doubleday, 1937.
CHRISMAN, ARTHUR B. *Shen of the Sea: A Book for Children.* Dutton, 1925. Newbery medal winner.
LIN, ADET. *The Milky Way and other Chinese Folk Tales.* Harcourt, 1961.
Czechoslovakia
HAVILAND, VIRGINIA. *Favorite Fairy Tales Told in Czechoslovakia.* Little, Brown, 1966. Handsome smattering of humorous tales.
Finland
BOWMAN, JAMES C., and BIANCO, MARGERY, comps. *Tales from a Finnish Tupa: From a Translation by Aili Kolehmainen.* Whitman, 1936. Folk tales and fables.
DEUTSCH, BABETTE. *Heroes of the Kalevala: Finland's Saga.* Illus. by Fritz Eichenberg. Messner, 1940.
France
CHANSON DE ROLAND. *Song of Roland.* Trans. by Merriam Sherwood. Illus. by Edith Emerson. McKay, 1938. *The Story of Roland.* Retold by James Baldwin. Scribner, 1930. *The Song of Roland; A new abridged translation in verse by Hilda C. Price.* Warne, 1961.
DELARUE, PAUL. *The Borzoi Book of French Folk-Tales.* Knopf, 1956. A representative selection.
PERRAULT, CHARLES. *All the French Fairy Tales.* Retold by Louis Untermeyer. Illus. by Gustave Doré. Didier, 1946. Here are Cinderella, the Sleeping Beauty, and many other beloved tales. *Favorite Fairy Tales Told in*

718

*France*. Ed. by Virginia Haviland. Illus. by Roger Duvoisin. Little, Brown, 1959. An attractive collection that maintains the spirit of the original versions.

**Germany**
BALDWIN, JAMES. *The Story of Siegfried*. Illus. by Peter Hurd. Scribner, 1956. This is a good choice for a telling of the Siegfried legends.
GRIMM, JAKOB LUDWIG and WILHELM KARL. *Household Stories*. Macmillan, 1954. Three popular collections all edited and illustrated by Wanda Gág are: *Tales from Grimm*. Coward-McCann, 1936. *More Tales from Grimm*. 1947. *Three Gay Tales from Grimm*. 1960. Selections retold by Virginia Haviland and illustrated by Susanne Suba are presented in: *Favorite Fairy Tales Told in Germany*. Little, Brown, 1959.

**Greece**
CHURCH, ALFRED J. *The Iliad and the Odyssey of Homer: Retold*. Macmillan, 1964. The story of the Trojan War and the adventures of Odysseus.
COLUM, PADRAIC. *The Golden Fleece and the Heroes Who Lived Before Achilles*. Macmillan, 1962. *The Adventures of Odysseus and the Tales of Troy*. Illus. by Willy Pogany. 1962.
D'AULAIRE, INGRI M. and EDGAR P. *Book of Greek Myths*. Doubleday, 1962.
GRAVES, ROBERT. *Greek Gods and Heroes*. Doubleday, 1960. A crisp, colorful style brings new life to these tales of struggle among the gods.
MANNING-SANDERS, RUTH. *Damian and the Dragon: Modern Greek Folk Tales*. Roy, 1966.

**Haiti**
COURLANDER, HAROLD. *Uncle Bouqui of Haiti*. Illus. by L. H. Crockett. Morrow, 1942. *The Piece of Fire, and Other Haitian Tales*. Harcourt, 1964.

**India and Pakistan**
BELING, MABEL A. *The Wicked Goldsmith and Other Tales of Ancient India*. Harper, 1941. Ancient stories in this collection are some of today's story-hour favorites.
GAER, JOSEPH. *The Adventures of Rama*. Little, Brown, 1954. This version of a Hindu epic story tells of a prince banished from his kingdom. *The Fables of India*. 1955. These tales are retold from three great ancient collections, the Panchatantra, the Hitopadesa, and the Jatakas.
JACOBS, JOSEPH, ed. *Indian Folk and Fairy Tales*. Putnam. These selections from ancient and modern sources are especially suitable for children.
JATAKAS. *Jataka Tales retold by Ellen C. Babbitt*. Appleton, 1912. *More Jataka Tales*. 1950. These animal fables are engagingly simple.
RYDER, ARTHUR W., tr. *The Panchatantra*. Univ. of Chicago Press, 1956. Wit and wisdom distinguish this collection, translated from the Sanskrit.
SEDDIQUI, ASHROF and LERCH, MARILYN. *Toontoony Pie and Other Tales from Pakistan*. World, 1961.
SEEGER, ELIZABETH. *Five Brothers: The Story of the Mahabharata*. Day, 1948. An adaptation of the great epic of India particularly suited for storytelling.
TURNBULL, E. LUCIA. *Fairy Tales of India*. Criterion, 1960. Hindu legends and animal fables.

**Indonesia**
COURLANDER, HAROLD. *Kantchil's Lime Pit, and Other Stories from Indonesia*. Harcourt, 1950. A tiny mouse deer outwits larger animals in these humorous tales.

**Iran.** See *Persia*, below.

**Italy**
CAPUANA, LUIGI. *Italian Fairy Tales*. Dutton, 1929. Humor pervades most of these stories translated by Dorothy Emmrich.
JAGENDORF, MORITZ A., comp. *The Priceless Cats, and Other Italian Folk Stories*. Vanguard, 1956. Sly humor and unusual twists to events make many of the stories in this collection story-hour favorites.

**Japan**
HEARN, LAFCADIO. *Japanese Fairy Tales*. New ed. Liveright, 1948.

# STORYTELLING

UCHIDA, YOSHIKO. *The Dancing Kettle, and Other Japanese Folk Tales*. Harcourt, 1949. The simplicity of language and varieties of plot of these tales make them good reading. *The Magic Listening Cap: More Folk Tales from Japan*. 1955. *The Sea of Gold*. Scribner, 1965.

**Korea**
CARPENTER, FRANCES. *Tales of a Korean Grandmother*. Doubleday, 1947. Fact, fancy, and folklore are blended in these 32 tales.
JEWETT, ELEANOR M. *Which Was Witch?* Viking, 1953.

**Latin America**
BRENNER, ANITA. *The Boy Who Could Do Anything, and Other Mexican Folk Tales*. Illus. by Jean Charlot. W. R. Scott, 1942. A collection of 24 Mexican folk tales.
FINGER, CHARLES J. *Tales from Silver Lands*. Doubleday, 1924. South American Indian legends and tales.
HENIUS, FRANK, comp. & tr. *Stories from the Americas*. Illus. by Leo Politi. Scribner, 1944. Favorites from 20 Latin-American countries.
JAGENDORF, MORITZ A., and BOGGS, R. S. *The King of the Mountains: A Treasury of Latin-American Folk Stories*. Vanguard, 1960. More than 50 stories from the vast Latin-American region.
JORDAN, PHILIP D. *Burro Benedicto, and Other Folktales and Legends of Mexico*. Coward-McCann, 1960. The history, religion, humor, and kindness of the people of Mexico are shown in these varied tales.
SHERLOCK, PHILIP M. *West Indian Folk-Tales*. Walck, 1966. Tales of African and South American Indian origins.

**Persia** (now Iran)
KELSEY, ALICE G. *Once the Mullah*. McKay, 1954. The priest-teacher-judge sometimes outwits others, and sometimes finds himself outwitted.
MEHDEVI, ANNE S. *Persian Folk and Fairy Tales*. Knopf, 1965. Varied tales told by an old nurse.

**Poland**
BERNHARD, JOSEPHINE B., tr. *The Master Wizard, and Other Polish Tales*. Knopf, 1934. This is a fine collection for older boys and girls.
BORSKI, LUCIA M., and MILLER, K. B. *The Jolly Tailor, and Other Fairy Tales*. Illus. by Kazimir Klepacki. McKay, 1957.
HAVILAND, VIRGINIA. *Favorite Fairy Tales Told in Poland*. Little, 1963.

**Russia**
CARRICK, VALERY. *Picture Tales from the Russian*. Stokes, 1920. The humor and simplicity of these tales make them popular with listeners.
FORD, NANCY K. *Baba Yaga and the Enchanted Ring*. Lippincott, 1960. Russian folk tales both humorous and full of suspense.
GOTTSCHALK, FRUMA K. *The Runaway Soldier, and Other Tales of Old Russia*. Knopf, 1946.
HAVILAND, VIRGINIA. *Favorite Fairy Tales Told in Russia*. Little, Brown, 1961.
RANSOME, ARTHUR. *Old Peter's Russian Tales*. Nelson, 1938. Humor is combined with unusual plots in these stories.
WHEELER, POST. *Russian Wonder Tales*. Rev. ed. Yoseloff, 1957. These stories are well liked for their rhythmic beauty.

**Scandinavia**
ASBJØRNSEN, PETER C. and MOE, JØRGEN, comps. *Norwegian Folk Tales*. Illus. by Erik Werenskiold and Theodor Kittelsen. Viking, 1961.
FRENCH, ALLEN. *The Story of Grettir the Strong*. 8th ed. Dutton, 1950. This is a vigorous retelling of the ancient Norse legend.
HATCH, MARY C. *13 Danish Tales: Retold*. Harcourt, 1947. *More Danish Tales: Retold*. 1949.
HAVILAND, VIRGINIA. *Favorite Fairy Tales Told in Norway*. Little, Brown, 1961.
HOSFORD, DOROTHY G. *Thunder of the Gods*. Holt, 1952.

# STORYTELLING

Thorne-Thomsen, Gudrun. *East o' the Sun and West o' the Moon, with Other Norwegian Folk Tales: Retold.* Row, Peterson, 1946. A great storyteller has here retold the folk tales of her country with spirit, rare understanding, and humor.

Undset, Sigrid, ed. *True and Untrue, and Other Norse Tales.* Knopf, 1945. "The husband who was to mind the house" is a representative favorite in this collection.

**Spain**

Boggs, Ralph S., and Davis, Mary G. *Three Golden Oranges.* McKay, 1936. These tales reflect the romantic atmosphere of Spain.

Cid, The. *The Tale of the Warrior Lord.* Trans. by Merriam Sherwood. Illus. by H. C. Pitz. McKay, 1957. This fine prose version describes the deeds of the great Spanish hero, the Cid.

Davis, Robert. *Padre Porko, the Gentlemanly Pig.* Holiday, 1948. These gay tales have a fairy pig as hero.

Haviland, Virginia. *Favorite Fairy Tales Told in Spain.* Little, Brown, 1963.

Irving, Washington. *The Alhambra: Palace of Mystery and Splendor.* Illus. by Louis Slobodkin. Macmillan, 1953. This version, edited by Mabel Williams, preserves the beauty and romance of medieval Spain.

Sawyer, Ruth. *Picture Tales from Spain.* Lippincott, 1936. Wise riddles and sayings alternate with simple and humorous tales.

**Switzerland**

Duvoisin, Roger A. *Three Sneezes, and Other Swiss Tales.* Knopf, 1941. Action and humor enliven these simple tales.

**Turkey**

Kelsey, Alice G. *Once the Hodja.* Illus. by Frank Dobias. McKay, 1943. Rollicking stories of a foolish character appear in this collection.

**United States**

Bowman, James C. *Pecos Bill, the Greatest Cowboy of All Time.* Whitman, 1937. *John Henry: The Rambling Black Ulysses.* 1942. Tall tales of extraordinary heroes.

Carmer, Carl. *America Sings: Stories and Songs of Our Country's Growing.* Knopf, 1942. Lumberjacks, miners, and other American work heroes from all parts of the country.

Chase, Richard, ed. *Jack Tales.* Houghton, 1943. These North Carolina folk tales describe the great deeds of Simple Jack. *Grandfather Tales.* 1948. These are more Jack stories to bring a chuckle to the most serious listener.

Colum, Padraic. *Legends of Hawaii.* Yale Univ. Press, 1937. Princesses and sharks, sufferings and great deeds, are plentiful in this rich and varied collection.

Cothran, Jean, ed. *With a Wig, With a Wag, and Other American Folk Tales.* McKay, 1954. *The Magic Calabash: Folk Tales from America's Islands and Alaska.* 1958. Jaunty, little-known tales appear in these lively collections.

Courlander, Harold. *Terrapin's Pot of Sense.* Holt, 1957. Folk tales of the American Negro.

Credle, Ellis. *Tall Tales from the High Hills.* Illus. by Richard Bennett. Nelson, 1957. These 20 tales come from the Carolina mountains.

Felton, Harold W. *Pecos Bill, Texas Cowpuncher.* Knopf, 1949. Slue Foot Sue and other characters are described with humor. *New Tall Tales of Pecos Bill.* Prentice-Hall, 1958. *Bowleg Bill, Seagoing Cowpuncher.* 1957. Tall tales of a cowpuncher who became a sailor. Ed.: *Legends of Paul Bunyan.* Illus. by Richard Bennett. Knopf, 1947.

Gillham, Charles E. *Beyond the Clapping Mountains: Eskimo Stories from Alaska.* Macmillan, 1943. *Medicine Men of Hooper Bay.* 1966. Stories of magic, talking animals, and heroic deeds.

Grinnell, George B. *Blackfoot Lodge Tales.* University of Nebraska Press, 1962. Indian hero tales.

Harris, Joel Chandler. *Uncle Remus: His Songs and His Sayings.* New rev. ed. Appleton, 1947. These humorous stories from the Negro of the southern plantation are rich in charm, wit, and wisdom. *Nights with Uncle Remus.* Routledge, 1951. A selected group of favorites with the weaker animals outwitting the stronger.

Jagendorf, Moritz A. *New England Bean-Pot: American Folk Stories to Read and to Tell.* Vanguard, 1948. *Sand in the Bag, and Other Folk Stories of Ohio, Indiana, and Illinois.* 1952.

McCormick, Dell J. *Paul Bunyan Swings His Axe.* Caxton, 1936. The giant woodsman and his blue ox enchant children with their deeds of superhuman strength.

Malcolmson, Anne. *Yankee Doodle's Cousins.* Houghton, 1941. Stories of real and legendary American heroes.

Manning-Sanders, Ruth. *Red Indian Folk and Fairy Tales.* Roy, 1960.

Rounds, Glen. *Ol' Paul, the Mighty Logger.* Holiday House, 1949. The legendary lumberjack appears again in these well-told tales.

Seeger, Ruth P. *American Folk Songs for Children in Home, School and Nursery School.* Illus. by Barbara Cooney. Doubleday, 1948. *Animal Folk Songs for Children: Traditional American Songs.* 1950.

Shapiro, Irwin. *Yankee Thunder: The Legendary Life of Davy Crockett.* Messner, 1944. This is a vigorous retelling of some of the tall tales about Davy Crockett.

Shephard, Esther. *Paul Bunyan.* Illus. by Rockwell Kent. New ed. Harcourt, 1941. Lumberjack vernacular in this version delights older children and adults.

Thompson, Vivian L. *Hawaiian Myths of Earth, Sea and Sky.* Holiday, 1966.

**West Indies**

Sherlock, Philip M. *Anansi, the Spider Man.* Crowell, 1954. These sly, humorous tales tell how the weaker animals outwitted the mighty.

## Other Stories to Tell

Andersen, Hans Christian. *It's Perfectly True, and Other Stories.* Trans. from the Danish by Paul Leyssac. Harcourt, 1938. This translation is well-suited for telling aloud. These are not folk tales, but they have folklore qualities. *Fairy Tales.* Trans. by L. W. Kingsland. Illus. by Ernest Shepard. Walck, 1962. This includes many stories not in the above selection.

Arbuthnot, May H. *Time for Fairy Tales, Old and New.* Rev. ed. Scott, Foresman, 1961. An extensive collection of fables, folk tales, myths, legends, epics, and modern fantasy selected for the storyteller.

Association for Childhood Education International. *Told Under the Blue Umbrella: New Stories for New Children.* Macmillan, 1962. *Told Under the Magic Umbrella: Modern Fanciful Stories for Young Children.* 1962. These stories have been selected with a sensitivity for children's responses.

Cathon, Laura E., and Schmidt, Thusnelda, comps. *Treasured Tales: Great Stories of Courage and Faith.* Abingdon, 1960.

Child Study Association of America, Inc. *Castles and Dragons.* Illus. by William Pène du Bois. Crowell, 1958. These favorites from many sources and lands are charmingly illustrated.

Davis, Mary G., comp. *A Baker's Dozen: Thirteen Stories to Tell and to Read Aloud.* Illus. by Emma Brock. Harcourt, 1930. Many types of stories, some of them folklore, which the collector found popular among her own story listeners.

Dobbs, Rose, ed. *Once Upon a Time.* Random House, 1950. Here are some of the most frequently requested "repeats" by story-hour listeners. *More Once-Upon-a-Time Stories.* 1961. Twenty short easily-told tales.

Eaton, Anne T., ed. *The Animals' Christmas.* Viking, 1944. Poems and stories in which animals have roles.

Farjeon, Eleanor. *The Little Bookroom.* Oxford, 1956. Stories of fantasy, humor, and wisdom offer delight in this volume, which won the first International Children's Book Award.

FENNER, PHYLLIS R., ed. *Time to Laugh: Funny Tales from Here and There.* Illus. by H. C. Pitz. Knopf, 1942. Twenty tales, old and new. Comp.: *Feasts and Frolics: Special Stories for Special Days.* 1948. *Ghosts, Ghosts, Ghosts: Stories of Spooks and Spirits, Haunts and Hobgoblins, Werewolves and Will-O'-The-Wisps.* Watts, 1952.

GRUENBERG, SIDONIE M., ed. *Favorite Stories Old and New.* Illus. by Kurt Wiese. Rev. & enl. ed. Doubleday, 1955. *More Favorite Stories Old and New.* Rev. ed. 1960.

HARPER, WILHELMINA, comp. *Merry Christmas to You! Stories for Christmas.* Dutton, 1935. *Ghosts and Goblins: Stories for Hallowe'en and Other Times.* 1936. *The Harvest Feast: Stories of Thanksgiving, Yesterday and Today.* 1938. *Easter Chimes: Stories for Easter and the Spring Season.* Illus. by Wilfred Jones. 1942.

HAZELTINE, ALICE I., and SMITH, E. S., eds. *The Easter Book of Legends and Stories.* Lothrop, 1947.

JOHNSON, SALLY P. *The Princesses.* Harper, 1962.

KIPLING, RUDYARD. *Just So Stories.* Illus. by J. M. Gleeson. Doubleday, 1946. The author tells how the camel got his hump, how the elephant got his trunk, and other nonsense tales.

PYLE, HOWARD. *Pepper and Salt: or, Seasoning for Young Folks.* Illus. by the author. Harper, 1923. Charm and wit characterize this collection. *The Wonder Clock: or, Four and Twenty Marvelous Tales, Being One for Each Hour of the Day.* Illus. by the author. These familiar tales are retold with lightness and humor.

RACKHAM, ARTHUR, comp. *The Arthur Rackham Fairy Book.* Lippincott, 1950. Fairy tales old and new skillfully illustrated by the compiler.

ROLLINS, CHARLEMAE, comp. *Christmas Gif': An Anthology of Christmas Poems, Songs, and Stories Written by and About Negroes.* Follett, 1963.

ROSS, EULALIE S., ed. *The Lost Half Hour.* Harcourt, 1963. Selections based on the collector's experience in telling stories in libraries.

SANDBURG, CARL. *Rootabaga Stories.* Illus. by Maud and Miska Petersham. Harcourt, 1922. These are short, gay stories by a master of American prose.

SAWYER, RUTH. *This Way to Christmas.* Harper, 1937. The flavor of Ireland enlivens these stories. *The Long Christmas.* Illus. by Valenti Angelo. Viking, 1941. Little known legends are beautifully told. *Joy to the World: Christmas Legends.* Little, Brown, 1966.

SECHRIST, ELIZABETH H. *It's Time for Thanksgiving.* Macrae Smith, 1957. *It's Time for Christmas.* 1959. Comp.: *13 Ghostly Yarns*, rev. ed. 1963.

SMITH, ELVA S., and HAZELTINE, A. I., comps. *The Christmas Book of Legends and Stories.* Lothrop, 1944.

WILDE, OSCAR. *The Happy Prince and Other Fairy Tales.* Duckworth, 1952. These stories by a great writer of fantasy have pathos, power, and beauty.

### Poems to Read

ADSHEAD, GLADYS L., and DUFF, ANNIS, eds. *Inheritance of Poetry.* Houghton, 1948.

ASSOCIATION FOR CHILDHOOD EDUCATION INTERNATIONAL. *Sung Under the Silver Umbrella: Poems for Young Children.* Macmillan, 1962. A collection of about 200 poems.

AUSLANDER, JOSEPH, and HILL, F. E., eds. *The Winged Horse Anthology.* Doubleday, 1929. A well-known storyteller chose these poems.

BENÉT, ROSEMARY C. and STEPHEN VINCENT. *Book of Americans.* Illus. by Charles Child. Rinehart, 1933. Famous Americans are portrayed in verse.

BREWTON, JOHN E., comp. *Under the Tent of the Sky: A Collection of Poems About Animals Large and Small.* Macmillan, 1937.

DE LA MARE, WALTER, ed. *Come Hither: A Collection of Rhymes and Poems for the Young of All Ages.* Illus. by Warren Chappell. 3rd ed. Knopf, 1957.

FERRIS, HELEN, ed. *Favorite Poems Old and New.* Doubleday, 1957. A full collection of children's favorites.

FIELD, EUGENE. *Poems of Childhood.* New ed. Scribner, 1925. This collection contains "The Duel"; "Wynken, Blynken, and Nod"; and "Little Boy Blue."

LINDSAY, VACHEL. *Johnny Appleseed, and Other Poems.* Illus. by George Richards. Macmillan, 1928.

LONGFELLOW, HENRY WADSWORTH. *Children's Own Longfellow.* New ed. Houghton, 1920. Six complete poems and parts of two others: *Evangeline* and *Hiawatha. Song of Hiawatha.* Illus. by Frederic Remington and N. C. Wyeth. 1929.

LOVE, KATHERINE I., ed. *A Pocketful of Rhymes.* Crowell, 1946. Poems selected for beauty and enjoyment.

MASEFIELD, JOHN. *Salt-Water Poems and Ballads.* New ed. Macmillan, 1953.

MILLAY, EDNA ST. VINCENT. *Poems: Selected for Young People.* Illus. by J. Paget-Fredericks. Harper, 1929.

MILNE, ALAN ALEXANDER. *The World of Christopher Robin.* Illus. by E. H. Shepard. Dutton, 1958. The delightful poems of *When We Were Very Young* and *Now We Are Six* are complete in this volume.

READ, HERBERT, ed. *This way, Delight.* Pantheon, 1956. A remarkable collection that lives up to its title.

SANDBURG, CARL. *Early Moon.* Illus. by James Daugherty. Harcourt, 1930. This volume contains 70 poems.

STEVENSON, BURTON E., comp. *Home Book of Verse for Young Folks.* Illus. by Willy Pogany. Rev. & enl. ed. Holt, 1929. A standard book for older children.

STEVENSON, ROBERT LOUIS. *A Child's Garden of Verses.* Numerous editions.

THOMPSON, BLANCHE J., comp. *Silver Pennies.* Macmillan, 1925. A choice collection for little folk.

UNTERMEYER, LOUIS, ed. *This Singing World.* Harcourt, 1923. *Rainbow in the Sky.* Illus. by Reginald Birch. 1935. *Stars to Steer By.* Illus. by Dorothy Bayley. 1941. All are treasure houses of fine poetry.

**STOSS,** shtohs, **VEIT** (1440?-1533), was a German sculptor. His works have a rich, complex appearance and a clear pattern. Stoss and his fellow German sculptor Tilman Riemenschneider used a late Gothic style. Both used Christian themes almost entirely, but Stoss's work is more dramatic and expressive than Riemenschneider's.

Stoss was born in Germany, and received his early training in southern Germany. He went to Kraków, Poland, in 1477 and worked there for almost 12 years on what is probably his masterpiece. It is a huge altar more than 42 feet high and 36 feet wide in the Church of St. Mary representing the life of the Virgin. Stoss later settled in Nuremberg, Germany. ROBERT R. WARK

**STOUT.** See BEER.

**STOUT, REX TODHUNTER** (1886-    ), is an American detective-story writer. He created the fat, beer-drinking, orchid-loving detective Nero Wolfe. Wolfe stays home and sends his able assistant Archie Goodwin out for clues. Later, while sitting with a glass of beer and a potted orchid, Wolfe solves the mystery. Wolfe first appeared in *Fer-de-Lance* (1934). Stout's many other Nero Wolfe mysteries include *The League of Frightened Men* (1935), *Before Midnight* (1955), and *A Right to Die* (1964).

Stout was born in Noblesville, Ind. He devised a school banking system which he set up in about 400 cities and towns between 1917 and 1927. Profits from the system made him wealthy and enabled him to devote his time to writing. Stout published his first novel in 1929. PHILIP DURHAM

**STOUT STATE UNIVERSITY.** See UNIVERSITIES AND COLLEGES (table [Wisconsin State University]).

# STOVE

Gladys Müller, Museum of The Franklin Institute

**The Franklin Stove,** invented by Benjamin Franklin, made use of the fireplace, but warmed a room better because of its greater radiating surface.

**STOVE.** The first stoves probably were made in Europe in the 1400's. These stoves were built of brick and tile, like many of the stoves in Europe today. They had no handy means of getting rid of the ashes resulting from a fire. The wood used as fuel was placed in an opening at the top, which was covered by a lid.

The early stoves proved so unsatisfactory that for nearly 200 years most persons continued to use the fireplace for cooking and heating. The first stoves produced in the United States were made at Lynn, Mass., in 1642. They were little more than cast-iron boxes fitted with lids. Benjamin Franklin invented the Franklin stove in 1744. This cast-iron stove was built into the wall like a fireplace, but extended out into the room so that three sides gave off heat.

**Heating Stoves.** At first, stoves were separated into special types for heating and others for cooking. About 1800, Isaac Orr of Philadelphia made the first round heating stoves. These stoves had grates through which the ashes could be shaken, and openings that controlled the supply of air reaching the fire.

Wood served as the most common stove fuel until the development of the baseburner, patented by Jordan L. Mott of New York in 1833. The baseburner was filled with coal from the top, and was arranged so that only a small amount of coal would be fed to the fire as required. The baseburner also made full use of the

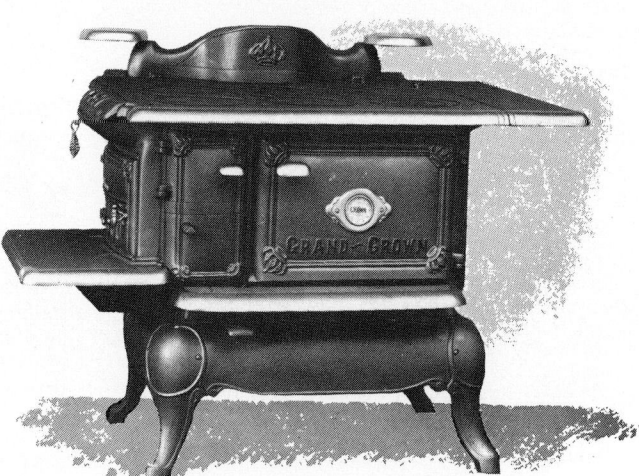

Crown Stove Works

**The Cast-Iron Cooking Range** was widely used in the 1800's. It burned coal, coke, or wood, and had surface cooking plates and a baking oven.

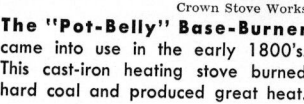

Crown Stove Works

**The "Pot-Belly" Base-Burner** came into use in the early 1800's. This cast-iron heating stove burned hard coal and produced great heat.

**A Popular Gas Range in 1925** had a side oven, instead of one under the burners. The gas line that fed the burners ran along the stove front.

Chambers Built-ins, Inc.

722

# STOVE

principles of radiation and convection to spread heat over a wide area (see HEAT [How Heat Travels]). Many principles of the early baseburner are still used in the modern "parlor heater" which heat small homes quite well, especially if the house is well insulated.

Few changes in basic design have been made since the early appearance of coal stoves. However, manufacturers have produced stoves that can burn even the poorest grades of bituminous (soft) coal without any objectionable smoke.

Kerosene and oil heating stoves also were developed during the 1800's, but they never proved as popular as coal-heating stoves, except in rural areas. Electric stoves have been developed for small homes, and electric heaters are widely used to heat single rooms in homes where the central heating system does not operate efficiently in cold weather.

Central heating, provided by warm-air furnaces or steam boilers, has replaced the heating stove in most houses and buildings. See BOILER; FURNACE.

**Cooking Stoves.** The coal range developed when the round stove of the 1800's made it necessary to have another stove for cooking purposes. From the beginning, these cast-iron ranges had cooking plates and an oven for baking. Many of them also had a reservoir for keeping rain water warm.

The first oil stoves resembled large lamps, with one wick and a metal plate over the flame for holding a single pot or pan. Later these stoves had three or more burners and a larger fuel tank. Naphtha stoves turned the naphtha into vapor and mixed it with air to produce a hot flame.

Gas stoves came into common use in the United States about 1860. Natural gas, coal gas, or a mixture of the two was fed into a burner ring that had tiny holes. Gas-flame heat proved to be quick, clean, and fairly cheap. Modern improvements in the gas range include pilot lights that start the stove without a match; automatic shutoffs that turn off the stove when food has cooked long enough; controls to provide the right cooking temperature for particular foods; insulated ovens that hold in the heat; a broiler; and a storage drawer below the ovens.

Electric ranges were generally introduced into homes and restaurants in the United States during the 1930's. The cooking unit consists of a coil of some metal that does not conduct electricity. At first, electric stoves had only one heat stage, and cooked food slowly in comparison to gas ranges. But the modern electric range has three or more heat stages, and cooks food in about the same time as the gas flame. A. P. KRATZ

See also HEATING.

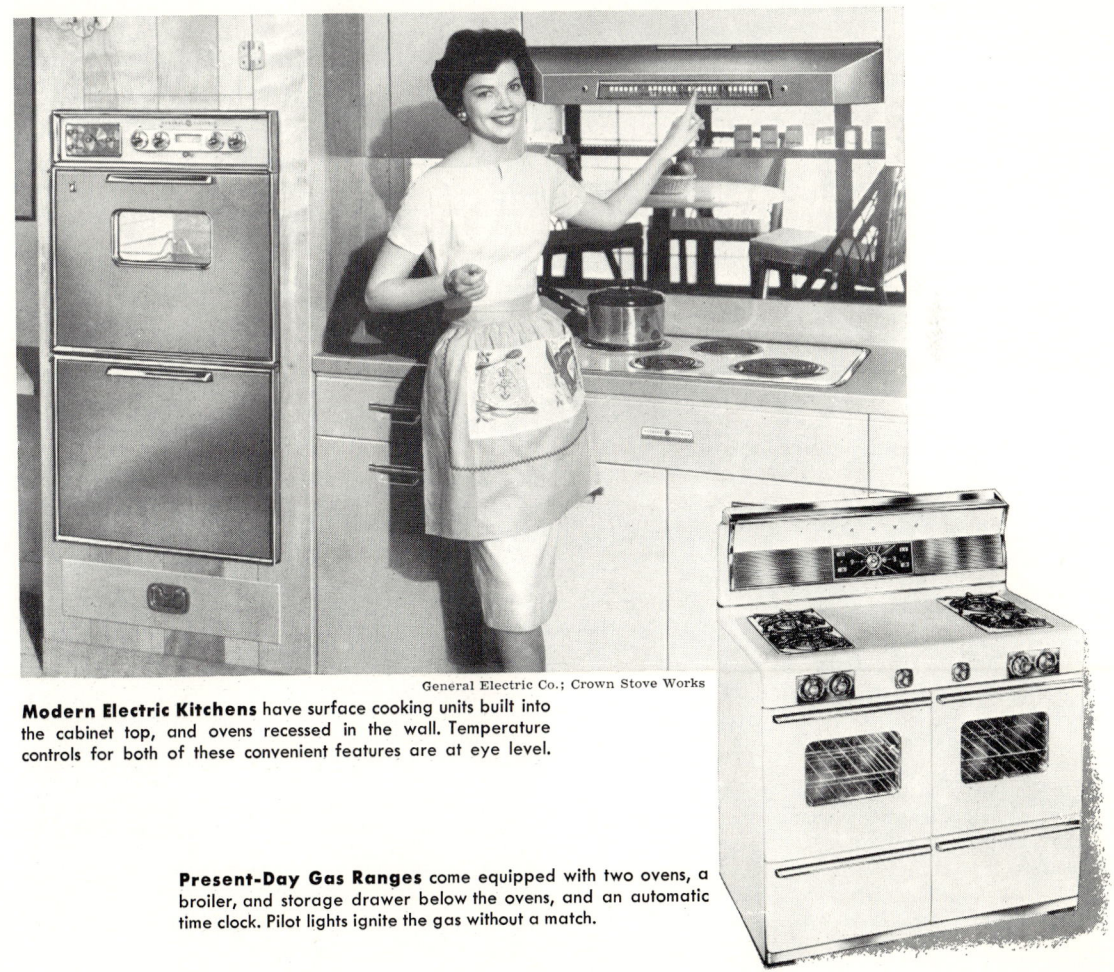

General Electric Co.; Crown Stove Works

**Modern Electric Kitchens** have surface cooking units built into the cabinet top, and ovens recessed in the wall. Temperature controls for both of these convenient features are at eye level.

**Present-Day Gas Ranges** come equipped with two ovens, a broiler, and storage drawer below the ovens, and an automatic time clock. Pilot lights ignite the gas without a match.

# STOWE, HARRIET BEECHER

Brown Bros.
**Harriet Beecher Stowe**

**STOWE, HARRIET ELIZABETH BEECHER** (1811-1896), is remembered chiefly for her antislavery novel, *Uncle Tom's Cabin*, first published in 1851. When most people think of the book's famous characters, Uncle Tom, Little Eva, Topsy, and Simon Legree, however, they are not remembering the book. They are thinking instead of George L. Aiken's play of 1852, or those crude and violent spectacles, the "Tom Shows," which once played every small town in the North. Aiken's play and the Tom Shows only faintly suggest Mrs. Stowe's book. *Uncle Tom's Cabin* is often melodramatic and sentimental, but it is more than a melodrama. It re-creates characters, scenes, and incidents with humor and realism. It analyzes the issue of slavery in the Middle West, New England, and the South during the days of the Fugitive Slave Law. The book intensified the disagreement between the North and the South which led to the Civil War. Mrs. Stowe's name became hated in the South.

**Other Works.** Mrs. Stowe's works, dealing with New England in the late 1700's and early 1800's, are important for anyone who wants to understand the American past. These include *The Minister's Wooing* (1859) and *Oldtown Folks* (1869), both novels; and *Sam Lawson's Oldtown Fireside Stories* (1872), a collection of stories. They present everyday life of the New England village, and make clear the positive and negative aspects of Puritanism. As in *Uncle Tom's Cabin*, the characters come alive to the reader as soon as they begin to talk.

Of her later books, the most shocking to her contemporaries was *Lady Byron Vindicated* (1870). It told of Lady Byron's separation from her husband, the famous poet, Lord Byron. Mrs. Stowe's account was based on Lady Byron's talk with her in 1856, and is supported by later investigation.

**Her Life.** Mrs. Stowe was born on June 14, 1811, in Litchfield, Conn., where her father, Lyman Beecher, was minister of the Congregational Church. She was educated at the academy there and at Hartford Female Seminary. From 1832 to 1850 she lived in Cincinnati, Ohio, where her father served as president of Lane Theological Seminary. In 1836, she married Calvin Stowe, a member of the Lane faculty. Her years in Cincinnati furnished her with many of the characters and incidents for *Uncle Tom's Cabin*, which she wrote at Brunswick, Me. After the publication of *Uncle Tom's Cabin*, Mrs. Stowe became famous overnight. On a visit to England, she was welcomed by the English abolitionists.

Mrs. Stowe was the mother of seven children, and the sister of the clergyman Henry Ward Beecher and the reformer and educator Catharine Beecher (see BEECHER). CHARLES H. FOSTER

See also ABOLITIONIST; UNCLE TOM'S CABIN.

**STRABISMUS.** See CROSS-EYE.

**STRABO,** *STRAY boh* (63 B.C.?-A.D. 24?), was a Greek geographer and historian. He became famous for his 17-volume *Geography*, which described all parts of the known world. These volumes are the best source of geographical information about the Mediterranean countries at the beginning of the Christian Era. Strabo also wrote a lengthy history that is now lost. He was born in Amasia, Pontus. He studied in Rome and Alexandria, and traveled in Arabia, southern Europe, and northern Africa. J. RUSSELL WHITAKER

**STRACHEY,** *STRAY chih*, **LYTTON** (1880-1932), won renown as the originator of a new type of biography. In his *Eminent Victorians* (1918), he omitted dull facts, and wrote biographies in the style of a novel. This set a fashion during the 1920's for fictionalized biography.

In his biographical essays Strachey recorded the thoughts and feelings his characters presumably had, as well as their actions and expressions. Strachey was born in London. His other books include *Queen Victoria* (1921) and *Elizabeth and Essex* (1928). R. W. STALLMAN

**STRADIVARI,** *STRAH dee VAH ree*, **ANTONIO** (1644?-1737), was one of the greatest violinmakers of all time. He made his finest instruments between 1700 and 1725. They were not only brilliant in tone and power, but also had excellent form and were exact in every detail. At the time of his death, many unfinished instruments were found in his workshop. These were completed either by his sons or by his pupils, but his name appeared on the labels.

Prices of genuine Stradivari violins now range from about $15,000 to $65,000. Unsuspecting purchasers have been deceived into buying instruments which have the outward appearance of his violins. But scholars

**Stradivari at Work on a Violin** in the early 1700's. This Italian made such perfect violins that today they are worth many thousands of dollars. It is the ambition of almost every concert violinist to own a Stradivari instrument.

Culver

estimate that Stradivari made 1,116 instruments, and of these instruments only a very few genuine specimens remain.

Stradivari's birthplace is not known, but he was an Italian. As a boy, he was apprenticed to Nicolo Amati, the famous master of violinmaking. By 1666, Stradivari was making violins under his own label. DOROTHY DELAY

See also AMATI; VIOLIN.

**STRAFFORD, EARL OF** (1593-1641), THOMAS WENTWORTH, was an English statesman. From 1614 to 1628 he was a leader of Parliament in its struggle with the Stuart kings. He was not a Puritan, however, and gradually drew away from his parliamentary friends as they became more vigorous in their criticism of King Charles I. In 1628, he went over to the king's side and in 1633, became Lord Deputy of Ireland. His administration was extremely harsh.

Wentworth returned to England in 1639. He became one of King Charles' chief advisers in his struggle against Parliament. Parliamentary leaders saw him as the greatest threat to their safety, and in 1640 decided to impeach him. He returned to London on Charles I's guarantee of safety. But, instead of an impeachment, Parliament passed a bill of attainder (see ATTAINDER). Charles, fearing mob violence, signed it, and two days later Strafford was executed. W. M. SOUTHGATE

**STRAIGHT TICKET.** See VOTING MACHINE; BALLOT.

**STRAIN.** See STRENGTH OF MATERIALS; ELASTICITY.

**STRAIT** is a narrow channel of water between two large bodies of water. Many wars have been fought and many treaties negotiated for the control and use of the world's important straits. Well-known straits include the Strait of Gibraltar between the Atlantic Ocean and the Mediterranean Sea, and the straits of Bosporus and Dardanelles between the Mediterranean and Black seas. The Strait of Magellan at the tip of South America is the only strait between the Atlantic and Pacific oceans. SIGISMOND DE R. DIETTRICH

See also the separate articles in WORLD BOOK on the various straits, such as GIBRALTAR, STRAIT OF.

**STRAITS SETTLEMENTS,** in southeastern Asia, were part of colonial British Malaya. The British East India Company formed the settlements in 1824. They included Singapore, Malacca, and Penang-Wellesley. The islands of the Dindings district were added in 1826 and the mainland in 1874. Christmas Island joined the settlements in 1900; Cocos Islands, in 1903; and Labuan Island, in 1907. During World War II, the settlements and Malaya were occupied by the Japanese.

The Straits Settlements colony was dissolved in 1946. Singapore, with Cocos and Christmas islands, became a separate colony, and Labuan Island was added to North Borneo. In 1957, the British ceded Penang and Malacca to the Federation of Malaya. In 1963, the former Straits Settlements, Malaya, Singapore, Sarawak, and Sabah (North Borneo) merged to form the Federation of Malaysia. Singapore became an independent country in 1965. GEORGE F. DEASY

**STRAMONIUM.** See JIMSON WEED.

**STRAND.** See LONDON (The City).

**STRANGLES.** See DISTEMPER.

**STRANGULATION.** See FIRST AID (Stoppage of Breathing); HERNIA.

**STRASBOURG,** *strahz BOOR,* or *STRAS burg* (pop. 228,971; met. area 302,303; alt. 450 ft.), is a trading

Strasbourg's Cathedral, one of Europe's most famous Gothic buildings, towers over the city. The spire is about 465 feet high. Work on the cathedral started in the 1000's.

center in France. Its location on the Ill River and its canal link with the Rhine make it an important "ocean port." It stands 250 miles east of Paris (see FRANCE [political map]). Its plants produce beer, tobacco, leather, petroleum, and automobiles.

Strasbourg is an old city

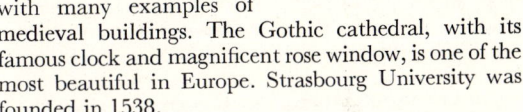
French Government Tourist Office

with many examples of medieval buildings. The Gothic cathedral, with its famous clock and magnificent rose window, is one of the most beautiful in Europe. Strasbourg University was founded in 1538.

The location of Strasbourg near the German-French border has made the city important commercially, but it has also made it a prize of war for many years. It was a German free town until 1681, when it was united with France. During the French Revolution in 1792, "The Marseillaise," the French national anthem, was written in Strasbourg. After the Franco-Prussian War in 1870, France ceded Strasbourg to Germany. The city became French again after the Treaty of Versailles in 1919. German troops occupied it in 1940, and Allied troops freed it in 1944. It has been headquarters of the Council of Europe since 1949. EDWARD W. FOX

**STRASS.** See GEM (Imitation and Artificial).

**STRASSMANN, FRITZ** (1902- ), is a German radiochemist. With Otto Hahn, another German radiochemist, he split the uranium atom in 1938. Strassmann and Hahn bombarded uranium atoms with neutrons and produced an element that they identified as barium. The importance of their work was revealed in 1939 by the Austrian physicists Lise Meitner and Otto R. Frisch. Meitner and Frisch explained that the neutrons had split the uranium atoms into fragments, producing barium and other elements.

Strassmann was born in Boppard, Germany. He taught at a technical high school in Hannover. In 1929, he joined Otto Hahn's laboratory staff in the Kaiser Wilhelm Institute for Chemistry (now Max Planck Institute) in Berlin-Dahlem. AARON J. IHDE

See also ATOM (Splitting the Atom); HAHN, OTTO; MEITNER, LISE.

**STRATEGIC AIR COMMAND (SAC)** is the long-range bomber and missile force of the United States Air Force. Its combat-ready air forces can strike anywhere in the world. SAC includes the Second, Eighth, Fifteenth, and Sixteenth air forces. It has about 1,300 jet bombers and tanker airplanes. SAC uses several types of missiles, including intercontinental ballistic missiles.

## STRATEGIC SERVICES, OFFICE OF

SAC's communications network can mobilize the entire command within seconds after a warning. A bomber force can be on the way to its targets within 15 minutes after a warning. If an enemy attack were to destroy SAC's ground control centers, retaliatory attacks would be directed from an airborne command plane. One of these planes is in the air at all times. SAC was organized in 1946, and has headquarters at Offutt Air Force Base, Nebr.  THOMAS S. POWER

See also OFFUTT AIR FORCE BASE; WESTOVER AIR FORCE BASE.

**STRATEGIC SERVICES, OFFICE OF (OSS),** was a secret intelligence agency of the United States government during World War II. William J. Donovan headed the office under the direction of the Joint Chiefs of Staff. It was organized in 1942 to gather and analyze information, and conduct psychological and guerrilla warfare. Experts in many fields performed heroic acts, often behind enemy lines.

The OSS was dissolved after the war ended in 1945. Its functions were divided between the Department of State and the War Department. In 1947, the Central Intelligence Agency (CIA) was formed to unify all government intelligence agencies (see CENTRAL INTELLIGENCE AGENCY).  MAURICE MATLOFF

**STRATFORD FESTIVAL.** See CANADA (picture: Theater); CONNECTICUT (Annual Events; color picture: Shakespeare Festival Theater); SHAKESPEARE, WILLIAM (Recent Performances); STRATFORD-UPON-AVON.

**STRATFORD-UPON-AVON** (pop. 18,600; alt. 170 ft.) is a quiet English market town. It has become famous as the birthplace of William Shakespeare.

Stratford-upon-Avon is one of the oldest towns in England. It lies in the green valley of the River Avon, 8 miles southwest of Warwick. For location, see GREAT BRITAIN (political map). High-peaked Old English style houses line the narrow streets.

The house where Shakespeare was born has been kept as a memorial. It is always open to visitors. At Shottery, a mile west of Stratford, is the thatched-roof cottage which was the home of Anne Hathaway, Shakespeare's wife. The Guild Hall and Grammar School are kept as they were in Shakespeare's day. Visitors to the Shakespearean memorials also go to nearby Wilmcote to see the cottage of Mary Arden, Shakespeare's mother. Another popular tourist spot is the chancel of Holy Trinity Church, where Shakespeare and his wife are buried.

In 1879, a Shakespeare Memorial was completed on the riverbank above the church. It includes a theater, a museum, and a library which contains valuable books and manuscripts having to do with Shakespeare and his life. The theater burned in 1926, but people immediately donated funds to rebuild it. The new theater was designed by Elisabeth Scott and opened in 1932. It seats about 1,000 persons.

Each summer, a Shakespeare festival is held in Stratford. England's leading actors perform many of Shakespeare's plays. At first, the festival lasted only a week. But it now lasts from April to November. American citizens gave funds to build a fountain and a clock tower in Stratford.  FREDERICK G. MARCHAM

See also SHAKESPEARE, WILLIAM (pictures).

Consulate General of Canada
**Baron of Strathcona**

**STRATHCONA AND MOUNT ROYAL, BARON OF** (1820-1914), DONALD ALEXANDER SMITH, was a Canadian fur trader, railroad builder, financier, statesman, and philanthropist. He was closely associated with the Hudson's Bay Company from 1838 until his death, and became a governor of the company in 1889. He went to Labrador when he was 18 and became a fur trader. Afterwards, he moved to Canada and became interested in the development of the Northwest Territories.

When Manitoba was organized as a province, Smith was elected to the Manitoba Assembly. The next year he was appointed commissioner for the Northwest Territories and was also elected to the Dominion House of Commons, serving from 1871 to 1880 and from 1887 to 1896.

Smith was the chief promoter of the Canadian Pacific Railway. He served as president of the Bank of Montreal and as chancellor of McGill University. From 1896 to 1906, he acted as Canadian High Commissioner in London.

Smith was a man of strong personality, vision, and great charm. Many educational and charitable institutions took advantage of his generosity. He was born in Forres, Morayshire, in Scotland.  JEAN BRUCHESI

**STRATIFIED ROCK** consists of layers, or *strata*. Each individual layer is called a *stratum*. Most sedimentary rocks, such as shale, sandstone, conglomerate, and limestone, are stratified.

Originally all strata were more or less horizontal. However, folding of the earth's crust in many places has thrown the rocks out of their former position. The angle at which these layers incline to the horizontal plane is called the *dip*. The dip may range from 0 to 90 degrees (vertical). Sedimentary rocks are stratified on land because rivers and wind spread them in layers. They are stratified on lake and ocean bottoms by currents of the water.  A. J. EARDLEY

See also ROCK.

**STRATIGRAPHY.** See ARCHAEOLOGY (Relative Chronology).

**STRATOSPHERE** is a layer of the *atmosphere* (air around the earth). It lies between the *troposphere* (lowest layer) and the *mesosphere* (middle layer). The stratosphere begins about 5 miles above the earth in regions near the poles, and about 10 miles above the earth near the equator. It ends about 30 miles above the earth.

On the average, the temperature throughout the lower part of the stratosphere is constant at about $-70°$ F. This part of the stratosphere is called the *constant temperature region* or the *isothermal layer*. In the upper part of the stratosphere, the temperature increases with height. Clouds rarely form in the stratosphere, because there is practically no *convection* (rising of warmer air).

Scientists constantly seek new information about the

stratosphere and higher regions of the atmosphere. In 1961, a manned balloon reached a height of $21\frac{1}{2}$ miles. Unmanned balloons and rockets, and manned spacecraft have reached even greater heights. WALTER J. SAUCIER

See also AIR (color picture: The Stratosphere); BALLOON (Balloon Explorations of the Stratosphere); IONOSPHERE; TROPOSPHERE.

**STRATTON, CHARLES SHERWOOD** (1838-1883), was an American midget who became best known by his circus name, General Tom Thumb. Stratton was a dwarf (see DWARF). His small, doll-like body was perfectly formed. As a youth, Stratton was only 25 inches tall and weighed 15 pounds. He was so bright mentally that at the age of six he was exhibited by Phineas T. Barnum as though he were a full-grown man.

Charles S. Stratton became internationally famous by the name, General Tom Thumb. *Brown Bros.*

In later years, Stratton grew to be 40 inches tall and weighed 70 pounds.

Stratton was born in Bridgeport, Conn., to parents of normal height. Barnum persuaded Stratton's parents to let the boy join the museum in New York City in 1842.

Barnum took him to Europe in 1844, where he entertained royalty and caused a sensation. In 1863, Stratton married Lavinia Warren (1841-1919), another one of Barnum's midgets. F. B. KELLEY

**STRATUM.** See STRATIFIED ROCK.

**STRATUS** is a kind of cloud. See CLOUD (Kinds of Clouds; picture).

**STRAUS, OSCAR** (1870-1954), was a Viennese composer of operettas, of which *The Chocolate Soldier* and *The Waltz Dream* are the best known. Straus was not related to the Viennese "waltz kings," Johann Strauss and his sons. It was mainly through the many operettas that he wrote that Straus gained his fame and great fortune.

Straus studied composition with Max Bruch in Berlin. He played the piano and composed songs and sketches for Baron Ernst von Wolzogen's Überbrettl theater, which brought him his first success. In 1929 and 1931 he wrote motion-picture scores in Hollywood. When Adolf Hitler came to power in 1933, Straus left Berlin for Austria. He fled to Paris and then to the United States. Straus was born in Vienna. HALSEY STEVENS

**STRAUSS,** *shtrous,* was the name of an Austrian family of composers, a father and three sons. They became famous for their waltzes and operettas. All of them were born and lived in Vienna, then considered one of Europe's gayest and most romantic capitals. The Strausses wrote music that captured this "spirit of Vienna."

The Strausses began composing after a musical form called the *Walzer* had developed into a ballroom dance in $\frac{3}{4}$ time. The four men—particularly Johann Strauss,

## STRAUSS, FRANZ JOSEF

Jr.—were noted for the waltzes they composed for dancing. In addition, no other composers have rivaled them in the quality of orchestral waltzes intended for concert performance. See WALTZ.

**Johann Strauss, Sr.** (1804-1849), was the son of a dance- and beer-hall operator. After studying music and becoming a performing violinist and conductor, he began composing waltzes in 1825. He organized his first orchestra in 1826, and toured successfully. In 1845, Strauss was appointed conductor for the Vienna court balls. His many compositions greatly improved the status of dance music. He wrote about 250 pieces, including waltzes, polkas, galops, and marches. He is best known for the "Radetzsky March."

**Johann Strauss, Jr.** (1825-1899), became known as the "Waltz King." His most famous work was "On the Beautiful Blue Danube." He was the most talented and best-known member of the family.

Strauss became a musician against his father's wishes. In 1844, he formed an orchestra that he combined with his father's orchestra in 1849. After gaining international fame as both a conductor and composer, he turned the orchestra over to his brothers in 1862. Following visits to England, France, and Italy, he conducted concerts in Boston and New York City in 1872.

Strauss was a great success as a composer of operettas, especially *Die Fledermaus* (*The Bat*, 1874), *A Night in Venice* (1883), and *The Gypsy Baron* (1885). Of his nearly 500 compositions, almost all the most popular ones are concert waltzes that show his gift as a writer of melodies and his brilliance as an orchestrator. Strauss's waltzes include the "Emperor Waltz," "Artist's Life," "Tales from the Vienna Woods," "Vienna Blood," and "Wine, Women, and Song."

**Joseph Strauss** (1827-1870) was trained as an architect but studied music secretly. He was also a poet, painter, and inventor. He became famous as a conductor of the Strauss family orchestra, and composed nearly 300 pieces, including the familiar "Pizzicato-Polka," which he wrote with his brother Johann.

**Eduard Strauss** (1835-1916) conducted his own orchestra when he was 27. In 1870, he succeeded his brother Johann as director of the Vienna court balls. Strauss wrote many compositions, but he had neither the genius of his father and brother Johann, nor the talent of his brother Joseph. Eduard's son, Johann Strauss III (1866-1939), became a successful conductor of light entertainment music. HERBERT WEINSTOCK

**STRAUSS, FRANZ JOSEF** (1915-    ), is a West German politician. He became finance minister of West Germany in 1966. As minister of defense from 1956 to 1962, he had an important role in building a modern defense force for West Germany. Strauss served as minister for special tasks from 1953 to 1955, and as minister for atomic affairs from 1955 to 1956.

Strauss was born in Munich, and attended the university there. During World War II he rose to the rank of lieutenant in the artillery. He was taken prisoner near the end of the war. After the war, Strauss helped organize the Christian Social Union political party, the Bavarian branch of the Christian Democratic Union. He has served in the Bundestag, a house of Parliament, since 1949.

# STRAUSS, RICHARD

**STRAUSS,** *shtrous,* **RICHARD** (1864-1949), was one of the greatest composers of recent times. He devoted himself mainly to composition, but his brilliant ability as a conductor would alone have assured him of world fame. His early work showed the influence of Johannes Brahms, but soon he was "struck by the lightning" of Richard Wagner's music dramas.

Strauss characterized himself as "a composer of expression," and his colorful orchestration and intense emotionalism bear this out. His symphonic poems were once controversial, but now they are fixed in the orchestral repertory. These tone poems include *Don Juan* (1888), *Death and Transfiguration* (1889), *Till Eulenspiegel's Merry Pranks* (1895), *Thus Spake Zarathustra* (1896), and *Don Quixote* (1897). He also wrote two autobiographical works for orchestra. *A Hero's Life* (1898) is a flattering self-portrait cast in the heroic mold, and the *Domestic Symphony* (1903) is a realistic account of an ordinary day in the Strauss household.

Ewing Galloway
**Richard Strauss**

His operas employ the Wagnerian principles of music drama, but in a more compact form (see WAGNER, RICHARD). *Salome* (1905) was based on Oscar Wilde's version of the Biblical story. It includes the "Dance of the Seven Veils," and Salome's love scene with the severed head of John the Baptist. This opera was so sensational that it was banned in New York City and Chicago after the first performances. Since then, however, it has entered the standard repertory of opera companies and has been produced on television (see OPERA [Some of the Famous Operas]). Strauss' next opera, *Elektra* (1909), also dealt with a sordid subject. But he surrounded both dramas with the glowing beauty of his magnificent orchestration. This process of alternate repulsion and attraction violently stirs the listener's emotions.

*Elektra* was the first Strauss opera to use a libretto by Hugo von Hofmannsthal. This libretto was so skillful that Strauss worked with Von Hofmannsthal until the author's death in 1929 (see HOFMANNSTHAL, HUGO VON). Their next opera, *Der Rosenkavalier* (1911), with its famous waltzes, evoked the spirit of old Vienna. *Ariadne auf Naxos* (1912) is an operatic comedy.

In his last years, Strauss turned once more to instrumental music and songs. His final works include *Metamorphoses* (1945) and *Concerto for Oboe* (1946). Strauss was born in Munich, Germany. WILLIAM FLEMING

**STRAVINSKY,** *struh VIN skih,* **IGOR FYODOROVICH** (1882- ), a Russian composer, greatly influenced the course of contemporary music. He decided on music as a career in 1903, when he became a pupil of the composer Nicholas Rimsky-Korsakov. In 1910, Stravinsky became famous overnight when his ballet *The Firebird* was performed by Sergei Diaghilev's Russian Ballet in Paris. Two more ballets, *Petrouchka* (1911) and *The Rite of Spring* (1913), followed. *The Rite of Spring* created a scandal because of its complex rhythms, fragmentary and repetitive melodies, and *polytonal harmonies* (harmonies in two or more keys at once). Despite this, it has influenced most later composers. Stravinsky later approached the clarity of music of the classical period in his *The Story of the Soldier* (1918) and *Octet for Wind Instruments* (1923).

Schaal, Pix
**Igor Stravinsky**

Stravinsky was born near St. Petersburg (now Leningrad). He lived in Switzerland from 1914 to 1920, and later in France, where he became a citizen in 1928. He went to Harvard University in 1939 to give a series of lectures, but he could not return to Europe because of World War II. He settled in the United States and became a citizen.

Stravinsky remains one of the most significant figures in contemporary music. Some of his later works, such as the *Symphony of Psalms* (1930) and the *Mass for Mixed Chorus and Wind Instruments* (1948), have a deeply religious quality. He continued writing music for the stage, including such ballets as *Agon* (1957). He also wrote the opera *The Rake's Progress* (1951). In his later works, he used some of Arnold Schönberg's 12-tone principles (see SCHÖNBERG, ARNOLD). HALSEY STEVENS

**STRAW** consists of the dried stems of such grains as wheat, rye, oats, and barley. Straw has many different uses. Farmers use it as bedding for animals, and for soil improvement. Manufacturers use straw to make hats, baskets, saddles, bottle covers, paper, suitcases, and strawboard for mounting and binding. In the chemical laboratory, straw is used to produce carbon, phenol oil, pitch, and acetic acid.

Wheat straw makes the best hats. The stalks are pulled out of the ground, cut into short lengths, and laid in the sun. The sun bleaches the straw almost white. The leaves are then pulled off, leaving only the stem, which is bleached again with sulfur. The straw is sorted according to color and is ready for weaving into hats. In some countries, mechanical looms do the weaving. But in many parts of Europe, Japan, and China, the work is done by hand. Some of the best hand-braided straw comes from Tuscany, Italy, where Leghorn straw braids are made from a special kind of straw. Panama hats are not made from a straw, but from the leaf fiber of a tropical tree. Straw is different from hay, which is dried young grasses or other plants that are used as feed for domestic animals. RICHARD W. POHL

**STRAWBERRY,** a small plant belonging to the rose family, is grown for its tasty fruit. The strawberry plant grows close to the ground, and has a short woody stem. The leaves grow on the stem in groups of three. The strawberry has short roots and small white flowers that have a pleasant odor. The greenish white fruits turn to a rich red color when they ripen. These berries give off a pleasant fragrance and have a delicious taste. They are among the earliest fruits in the garden. The berries seem to be *strewn* (scattered) among the leaves of the plant. For this reason, the plant first had the name *strewberry,*

728 | Year Book Close-Up
**STRAVINSKY, IGOR**
1972 Year on File (Deaths)

STREAM

**The Heart-Shaped Juicy Strawberry** has a delicious flavor and aroma. Strawberries are often eaten as dessert.

which, in time, gradually came to be called *strawberry*.

The fruit of the strawberry differs from the true berry, such as the huckleberry. The strawberry does not have an outer skin around the seed. It has a fleshy, swollen fruit with dry yellow seeds on the outside. When the strawberry ripens, the petals of the flower fall off and all that remains is the *calyx*, a leafy substance shaped like a star. Not every strawberry flower produces fruit, however. Some flowers do not have stamens. These must be planted near plants that have stamens, so that their pollen can fertilize the seeds. This type of pollination is known as *cross-pollination*.

The strawberry plant does not reproduce by seeds. During the season when the fruit is developing, the plant sends out slender growths called *runners*. These look like strings. They grow on the ground and send out roots in the soil. The roots produce new plants which grow and bear fruit. Sometimes these plants are taken from the soil and replanted to start a new plantation of strawberry plants.

The strawberry fruit is considered one of the most important small fruits grown in the Western Hemisphere. It grows both as a wild plant and as a cultivated plant. The strawberry was originally grown in northern Europe, but wild species also are found in Russia, Chile, and the United States. The first American species of strawberry was cultivated about 1835. Today, every state in the United States and every province in Canada grows the strawberry plant.

Strawberry plants can be planted in any garden soil. But the richer the soil, the larger the crop. The plant grows best in a cool, moist climate and does not do well in warm temperatures. The strawberry is planted in rows. Young plants are used for setting the rows. The rows are usually 3 feet apart and the plants are set 18 inches apart in the rows. The plants may be planted in the spring or fall, but if the temperature is too cold, fall planting requires a great deal of care. Some strawberries, called *everbearing*, produce berries throughout the summer and fall.

The strawberry fruit can be prepared in many tasty dishes. The fruit is a good source of vitamin C. Strawberries are exceptionally well adapted to quick freezing. The frozen berries, like the fresh ones, are used in ice cream, pastries, and jellies.

**Scientific Classification.** The strawberry belongs to the rose family, *Rosaceae*. Strawberries make up the genus *Fragaria*. Common American plants include genus *Fragaria*, species *F. virginiana* and *F. chiloensis*.  LEE A. SOMERS

See also PLANT (color picture: Some Members of the Rose Family).

### LEADING STRAWBERRY GROWING STATES AND PROVINCES

Crates (36 pounds) of strawberries grown in 1967

|  |  |
|---|---|
| California | 5,800,000 crates |
| Oregon | 2,528,000 crates |
| Washington | 996,000 crates |
| Michigan | 812,000 crates |
| Florida | 489,000 crates |
| British Columbia | 456,000 crates |
| Louisiana | 327,000 crates |
| Quebec | 307,000 crates |
| Ontario | 283,000 crates |
| New Jersey | 253,000 crates |

Sources: U.S. Department of Agriculture; Dominion Bureau of Statistics

**STRAWFLOWER** is a tall annual herb with yellow, orange, red, or white flowers. People dry them and use them as winter bouquets. The strawflower originated in Australia, and is now raised in gardens in Europe and America. The plant reaches a height of 3 feet and produces flowers from 1½ to 2½ inches wide. It grows from seeds.

**Scientific Classification.** The strawflower belongs to the composite family, *Compositae*. It is genus *Helichrysum*, species *H. bracteatum*.  ALFRED C. HOTTES

**STREAM.** See RIVER.

**The Strawflower** has yellow, orange, red, or white flowers.

# STREAMLINING

**STREAMLINING** is the shaping of a body so that it meets the smallest amount of resistance as it moves through a *fluid* (liquid or gas). The best streamlined shape for a body depends on whether it is to travel slower or faster than sound through the fluid. For *subsonic* (slower than sound) travel, a body should be somewhat blunt and rounded in front, and then taper to a point at the tail. Submarines and subsonic airplanes have this shape. In nature, fish have this type of streamlining. For *supersonic* (faster than sound) travel, a body should have a sharply pointed front. Supersonic airplanes and rockets have this shape.

**The Streamlined Body of a Fish** has a shape like a raindrop. This shape offers the least resistance to movement in the water.

The resisting force acting on a body as it travels through a fluid is called *drag*. The amount of drag depends on how smoothly the fluid flows around the body. The path that any bit of fluid follows around the body is called a *streamline*. If a body is streamlined, the streamlines separate smoothly at the front, pass smoothly around the body, and meet again at the tail. But if the body is not streamlined, the fluid may swirl and twist violently as it passes around the body. These motions are called *eddy currents*. The fluid may separate from the surface of the body and cause a partial vacuum behind it. The amount of drag increases because of the lack of pressure behind the body to balance pressure in front.

The effects of streamlining can be measured in a *wind tunnel*. In the tunnel, air is blown past a body so the drag can be measured. Streamlines can be made visible by adding smoke to the air at several points. When a flat plate is tested in the tunnel, streamlines can be seen curving around the edges of the plate. The air behind it is disturbed, forming eddy currents and a partial vacuum. The drag on the plate is relatively large. The streamlines can be seen following the surface more smoothly on a properly streamlined body. No eddy currents are produced, and there is less drag.

In addition to a body's shape, three other factors affect the drag: (1) the density of the fluid, (2) the amount of the body's area that meets the fluid, and (3) the speed of the body through the fluid. The drag doubles if either the fluid's density or the area of the body meeting the fluid is doubled. Doubling the speed of the body multiplies the drag by four. WILLIAM L. HULL

See also AERODYNAMICS; WIND TUNNEL.

**STREET** is a road within a town or city. Streets lead out of the cities and towns, through the surrounding suburban areas, and connect with roads and highways (see ROADS AND HIGHWAYS). Streets serve both the people who live in cities and towns and the people who only work there. They also serve the people who come from farms and other nearby places for shopping, business, and fun. In some places, the streets are used almost entirely by pedestrians. This is particularly true in some foreign countries where there are few automobiles.

*Arterial* streets are those which carry the most traffic and provide routes to the most important sections. Many of them are wider than other streets. Sometimes they are divided in the center to separate the lines of traffic going in opposite directions. *Avenue* and *boulevard* are names sometimes given to important arterial streets, including those with center dividers. *Parkways* run through parks, or parklike areas, and usually are limited to passenger cars only. *Expressways* and *freeways* are divided in the center, and crossings of other heavily traveled streets are always on different levels. To arrange for these crossings, dry-land bridges, called *grade separations*, are built. At the most important grade separations, ramps are built so that vehicles can get to and from the expressways and the other streets without crossing in front of each other.

There are about 521,000 miles of streets in the United States. This is more than 14 per cent of the total United States street, road, and highway mileage. New York City has 6,000 miles of streets—more than any other city in the United States.

## How Streets Are Built

**Planning.** Street planning is difficult. This is because great numbers of cars and trucks use the streets. Many streets were laid out before there were automobiles. They are narrow and twisting. Large and valuable buildings are close to the edges of many streets. If the streets are widened, many such buildings must be torn down. This is very expensive.

Good street planning begins with a general plan for a beautiful and useful city. This plan shows the areas for businesses, factories, stores, parks, public buildings, and homes. It also includes a layout of streets serving the city and the surrounding suburban communities. Counts of traffic and other studies show where traffic comes from, where it goes, and in what volume. With this information, engineers plan important streets that will take people where they want to go with the least interference. The large number of cross streets, and the need for streetcars and buses, parking space, and sidewalks make the planning job very complicated, especially in the older parts of cities.

Traffic engineers try to make existing streets as useful as possible. As traffic increases, some streets carry more vehicles than they were first designed to handle. Engineers must then find ways to provide more street space for vehicles to use at faster speeds. Sometimes streets can be widened by moving the edges of the streets closer to buildings. Dead-end streets can be connected with other streets. Or pairs of one-way streets can be created. In larger cities, expressways or freeways may be built.

Cables and pipelines carrying electricity, telephone wires, gas, water, and sewage run under city streets.

# STREETS NEED CONSTANT CARE

**Asphalt Joints Between Concrete Slabs** must be repaired regularly. The joints keep water, snow, and ice from seeping between the slabs and cracking them.

**Replacing a Concrete Slab.** When a single concrete slab wears out it is necessary to cut out the old piece and pour in new concrete.

**Resurfacing an Old Street** with an asphalt mixture. Many miles of old concrete, brick, and block streets are saved for further use in this way every year.

Fruehauf Trailer Co.; The Texas Co.; Bureau of Public Roads

Martin J. Schmidt

## MEN AND NATURE CAUSE DAMAGE TO STREETS

**Salt and Other Chemicals,** spread on streets to prevent skidding in icy weather, cause wear to pavement.

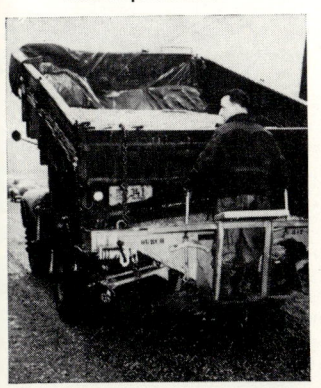

**Extremes of Heat and Cold** may cause pavement to crack so that the street must be resurfaced.

**Heavy Automobile, Bus, and Truck Traffic** is a major cause of wear on streets. Only automobiles and light trucks are allowed on some busy streets, reducing wear on pavement.

# STREET

Covered manholes in the streets make it possible to service these utilities. In large cities subways sometimes run underneath the streets (see SUBWAY).

**Draining.** Much of the rainfall in cities and towns cannot sink into the ground. So it runs onto the streets. Most streets have gutters along the sides which are lower than the street level. The water runs into the gutters and along them into openings called *catch basins*, connecting with underground sewers. Smaller towns and suburbs sometimes have shallow ditches instead of paved gutters. In such places, the ditches may be carried under driveways and cross streets by pipes, called *culverts*.

**Surfacing.** Most city streets are paved with brick, *bituminous* materials, or concrete. Brick pavements usually are laid on sand spread over the ground or over a concrete foundation. Bituminous materials are made of asphalt or tar mixed with stone and sand. They are usually black in color. Concrete is made of cement, sand, gravel, or stone, and water. Both bituminous and concrete pavements usually are laid with machines. The pavement, as well as the foundation underneath, is of different thickness depending on the firmness of the ground and the type and volume of traffic expected. Some streets, usually in outlying sections, are surfaced with gravel or stone. Sometimes the gravel or stone is topped with a coating of oil, tar, or asphalt.

**Intersections.** Places where streets meet one another are called *intersections*. When the streets are on the same level, the intersections may be the scene of accidents and traffic jams. At many intersections, traffic signals let traffic from each street take turns crossing the intersection. Sometimes, circles or islands are built to help channel traffic into the correct lanes. These are used especially at wide intersections and where more than two streets meet. Expressways and freeways, with intersecting streets at different levels, have the safest kind of crossings.

**Lighting.** Much of the light on streets at night comes from the vehicles being driven along them. But most streets also are lighted with lights on poles along the curbs. The most modern street lights have mercury vapor in the lamps, which are much brighter than the incandescent type used in our homes. Good lighting systems help reduce crime as well as traffic accidents at night.

## How Streets Are Maintained

**Repairing and Resurfacing.** Weather and traffic gradually cause the street surface to wear out or become uneven as it grows older. Holes and breaks in the surface are usually filled with the same kind of material from which the streets were built. Cracks and joints in concrete are filled with bituminous materials. Black-top pavements are occasionally sealed with a thin coating of bituminous material. This waterproofs the existing pavement and helps preserve it.

When most of a street surface gets in bad shape, an inch or more of new material may be added over the entire surface. This is called *resurfacing*. It smooths rough pavements and saves the base for further use. Existing curbs, gutters, and sidewalks seldom can be raised, and it often is necessary to strip off and replace the old surface. Sometimes the foundation must be repaired also.

On streets which are covered with gravel or stone, the surface must be reshaped from time to time, especially after wet weather. This usually is done with a scraping machine called a *motor grader*. This work, along with the addition of new material at intervals, helps keep the surface smooth.

**Clearing Ice and Snow.** Rain or sleet may freeze on

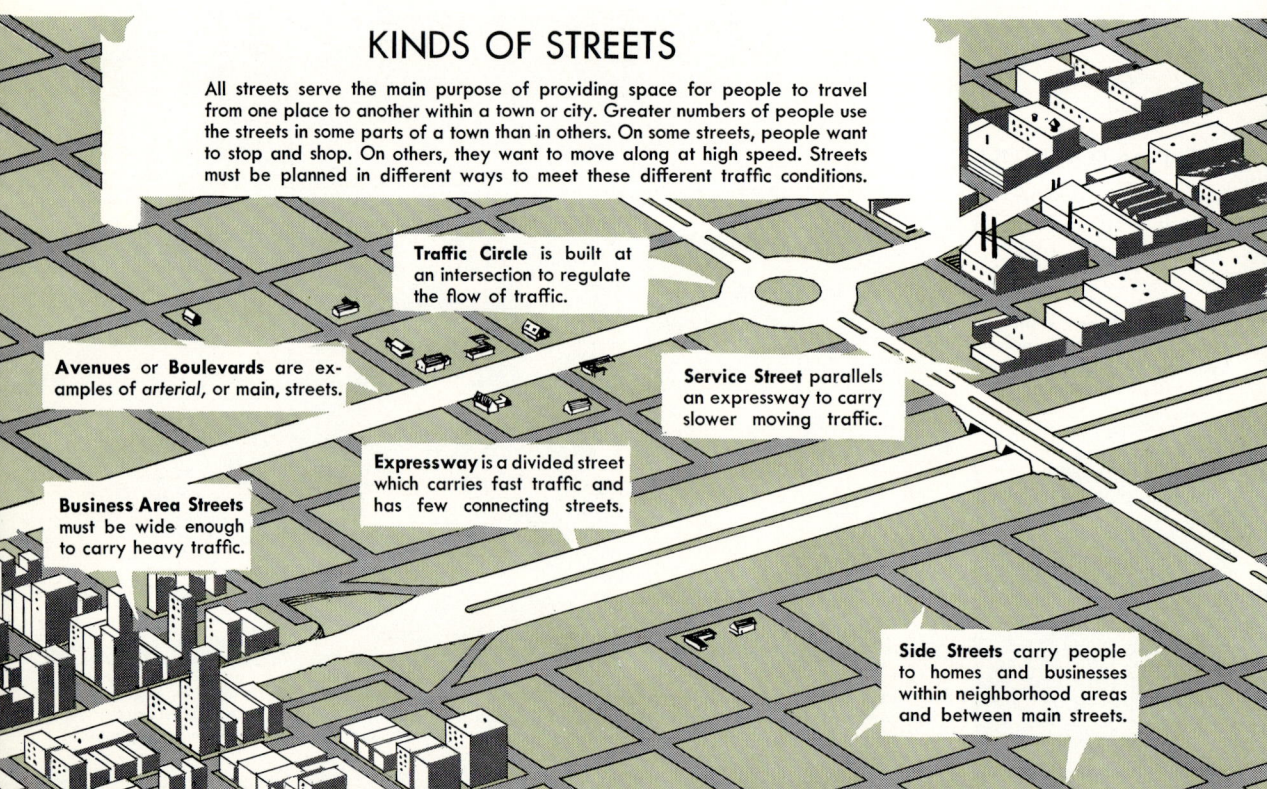

### KINDS OF STREETS

All streets serve the main purpose of providing space for people to travel from one place to another within a town or city. Greater numbers of people use the streets in some parts of a town than in others. On some streets, people want to stop and shop. On others, they want to move along at high speed. Streets must be planned in different ways to meet these different traffic conditions.

**Traffic Circle** is built at an intersection to regulate the flow of traffic.

**Avenues or Boulevards** are examples of *arterial*, or main, streets.

**Service Street** parallels an expressway to carry slower moving traffic.

**Expressway** is a divided street which carries fast traffic and has few connecting streets.

**Business Area Streets** must be wide enough to carry heavy traffic.

**Side Streets** carry people to homes and businesses within neighborhood areas and between main streets.

## STREET

streets. Then, salt or other chemicals may be spread to melt the ice. Often, these chemicals are mixed with sand or cinders which provide better traction for tires.

In northern climates, snow frequently blocks streets and must be removed or pushed off to one side. This is done with motor graders or with plows fastened to the fronts of trucks. Often, special crews of men are hired to load the snow into trucks so it can be hauled away. The loading is done by hand shovels or by elevating loaders. Elevating loaders are a system of buckets rigged on an endless chain. These "eat" into a snowbank and dump the snow into the trucks. Rotary plows sometimes are used to clear snow. The rotary plows have a big screw on the front. This screw feeds the snow through a spout and into a truck or off to the side of the street. A city such as New York may hire thousands of temporary workers to help clear millions of tons of snow from the streets after a heavy snowfall.

**Cleaning.** Streets get dirty from trash, leaves, and cinders. Maintenance crews often use machines equipped with large brushes to sweep the streets. Some of these machines are like big vacuum cleaners which suck up the dirt and dust. Every once in a while, streets may be flushed with water from trucks. This washes the dirt into the gutters and on into the sewers. Some machines have water, brushes, and vacuum all combined in one. In some places, men sweep the gutters with a brush and load the dirt into trucks or small pushcarts.

### How Streets Are Paid For

Most streets are paid for largely from taxes paid by people who live in the cities and towns. A part of every property owner's taxes goes for construction and maintenance of streets. In addition, many of the local, or residential, streets are paid for by special taxes, called *assessments*, on the property served by the streets.

In recent years, cities and towns have received a greater share of the gasoline taxes and license fees collected by the state. The state legislature usually decides how much cities and towns are to be given from such funds. The money usually is divided according to population. Some cities also have their own special license fees and other taxes for street maintenance.

Some state highway departments build and maintain certain arterial streets that are extensions of the roads and highways leading into a city. The federal government also helps pay for some arterial streets. The state and city, or town, provide additional amounts.

Many cities borrow money so that street work can be done sooner than it could if they had to wait until the money were saved up from taxes. The borrowed money is repaid as taxes are collected.

| MONEY SPENT FOR CITY STREETS IN THE UNITED STATES | |
|---|---|
| Year | Total |
| 1921 | $ 346,000,000 |
| 1930 | 860,000,000 |
| 1940 | 611,000,000 |
| 1950 | 1,144,000,000 |
| 1960 | 3,160,000,000 |
| 1967 | 5,111,000,000 |
| Source: U.S. Bureau of Public Roads | |

### History of Streets

Streets are as old as cities and towns. Greek, Roman, and other ancient cities had some paved streets and many unpaved streets. These streets often were very narrow and winding. Sometimes they were as steep as a flight of stairs. In the 1200's, the rapid growth of towns created a need for paving the main streets. A leader in the movement to pave streets in western Europe in the 1200's was King Philip Augustus of

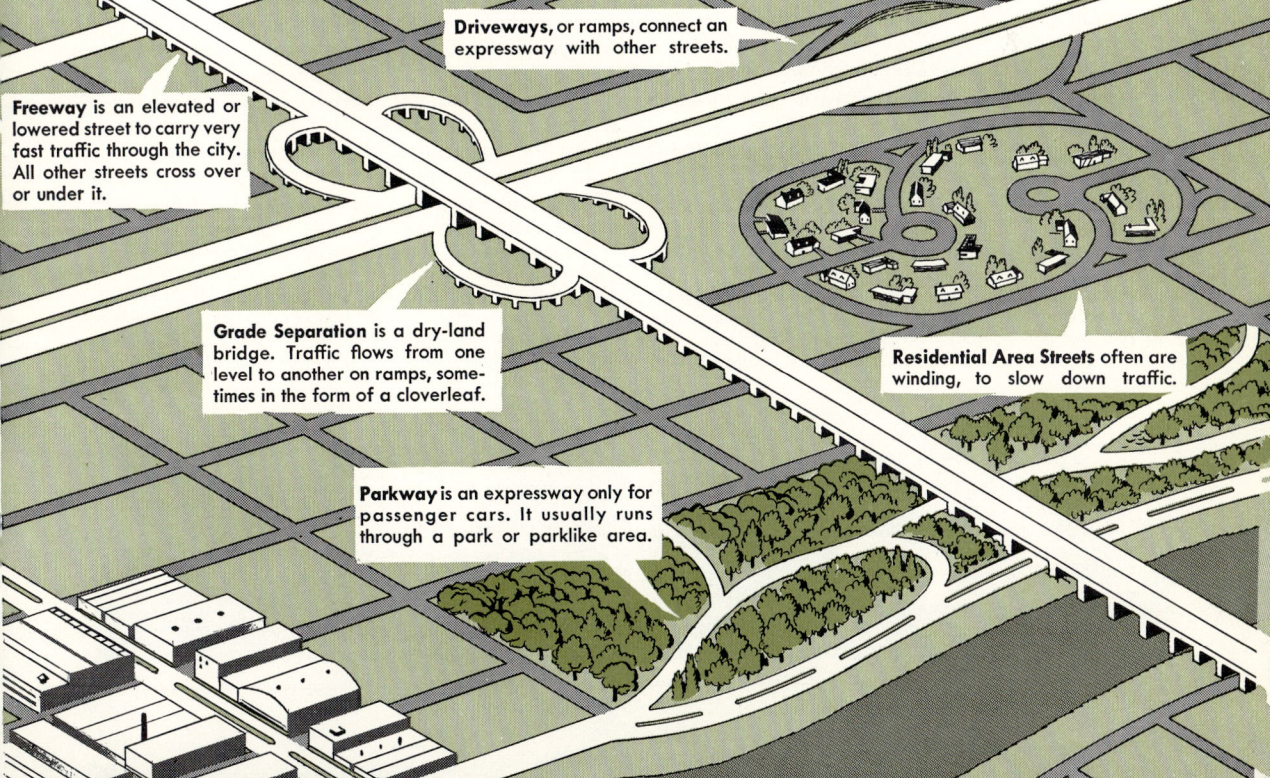

**Freeway** is an elevated or lowered street to carry very fast traffic through the city. All other streets cross over or under it.

**Driveways,** or ramps, connect an expressway with other streets.

**Grade Separation** is a dry-land bridge. Traffic flows from one level to another on ramps, sometimes in the form of a cloverleaf.

**Parkway** is an expressway only for passenger cars. It usually runs through a park or parklike area.

**Residential Area Streets** often are winding, to slow down traffic.

# STREET

France. He had the street in Paris in front of his castle and palace, the Louvre, paved with stones. Before this, the street was little more than an open sewer, and his immediate reason for having it paved probably was to overcome the bad odor. Undoubtedly, another reason for paving was to obtain a smooth surface for travel. In England, the first paved street was laid in London in 1417. The laying-out of city streets at right angles to each other, in a gridiron pattern, developed from the feudal town arrangement of the Middle Ages.

In some early American cities, many of the streets may have followed cowpaths of the original farming villages. The streets in some cities were laid out in advance. One of these cities is Washington, D.C., the nation's capital. There the Capitol is in the center of the city, with avenues leading out like spokes in a wheel. Other streets form a checkerboard or grid pattern. Circles were built at many points where avenues intersect streets. Supposedly, these circles were planned as places of defense in the event of an enemy attack.

Street widths vary from narrow ones like those in downtown Boston, Philadelphia, and New York City, to broad ones like those in Washington, D.C., and Salt Lake City. Brigham Young, the Mormon leader who laid out Salt Lake City, is credited with deciding the width of the streets. We are told that he ordered a team of horses pulling a big wagon to turn around. Then he settled on the space it took to complete the turn as the width of the streets.

Sometimes it is possible to learn a city's history by reading the names of the streets, which often are named after local pioneers or early leaders.

Many early streets in America were surfaced with round, uneven cobblestones and wood blocks. The first successful brick pavement was laid in Charleston, W. Va., in 1873. Stone blocks somewhat thicker and wider than bricks were another early paving material for streets. These still may be seen in use, especially between streetcar tracks. A bituminous pavement was patented in 1834 but was not used generally until many years later. The first concrete pavement was laid in Bellefontaine, Ohio, in 1893.

In recent years, more and more cities have found it necessary to widen old streets and build new expressways to handle the increasing traffic. HENRY A. BARNES

See also ROADS AND HIGHWAYS with its list of Related Articles.

**STREETCAR.** The first streetcars were pulled by horses. They were called *horsecars*. Later, a *cable car* was invented. It was pulled by a cable, which was drawn by steam power. The cable ran through a small trench in the surface of the ground. The streetcar attached itself to the cable by means of a gripping device. Therefore it was also called a "grip" car.

In the early 1800's, inventors began trying to use electric power. But for many years the cost of generating electricity was too great to be practical. The invention of the electric generator solved this problem, and by the 1880's a number of electric cars were exhibited. The first commercial electric railway was operated in Lichterfelde, Germany, in 1881. In 1888, Frank J. Sprague opened the first successful electric "street railway" in the United States, in Richmond, Va. Electric cars immediately began to replace cable cars and horsecars.

The modern streetcar gets its power from an overhead line by means of a long trolley pole. The current is generated in a central powerhouse and passes along heavy copper wires which make up the overhead line. The usual type of car has a small trolley wheel, or *shoe*, which rides along the line, conducting the current to the trolley pole, down which it passes to the motors under the car. The current leaves the motors by means of the tracks, and passes back to the central generator to complete the circuit.

The electric motors are attached to the driving axles of the car by gears. The motorman controls the speed by regulating the current with a control lever.

Each car has seats for 50 or more people. Straps hang from the ceiling in the front and rear aisles for people who are unable to find a seat.

The streetcar was important in the growth of cities. For years, it was one of the chief means of transportation in such places as Chicago and also in the smaller cities and in towns. Almost every large city was veined with a great network of streetcar lines. The streetcar also was used for transportation between cities and towns in some areas before the automobile came into wide use. Only San Francisco, where there are many steep hills, continues to use the cable car.

The trolley bus, introduced in 1913, replaced the streetcar in some cities. It has a bus body and gets its power from an overhead trolley, but does not use a track.

By the late 1930's, the streetcar became less important. But some cities continued to use them. Faster, quieter models replaced old cars. FRANKLIN M. RECK

See also CABLE CAR; ELECTRIC RAILROAD.

**The Horsecar Was a Forerunner of Today's Streetcar.** The horsecar of 1878 was a swaying, noisy car which ran on two rails and was pulled by horses. A small stove, and straw scattered on the floor, kept the passengers warm in cold weather.

**The Modern, Fast-Moving Streetcar** has little trouble in icy or rainy weather. Electric heating, defrosters, air brakes, and silent operation insure riding comfort and safety. Overhead trolleys pick up the electric power that turns the wheels.

Chicago Transit Authority

# HOW STRENGTH OF MATERIALS IS TESTED

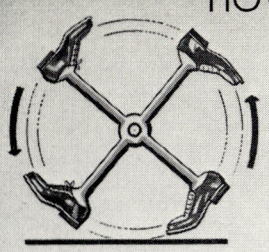

Both strength and wearing qualities of such items as shoes and tires are tested on machines. Such machines duplicate within the laboratory the actual conditions of ordinary use.

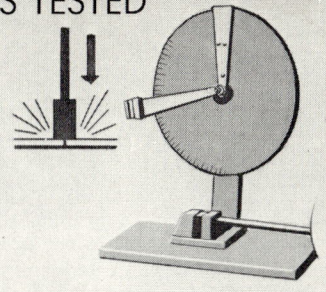

Resistance of plastic materials to crushing is determined by the heavy blows of this machine.

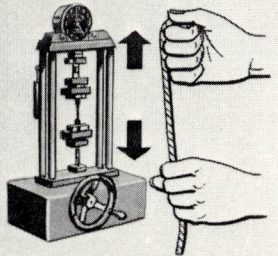

Tensile strength of thin metal strips is tested much as one tests the strength of cord.

Compression resistance is tested by machines that crush materials under tremendous pressures.

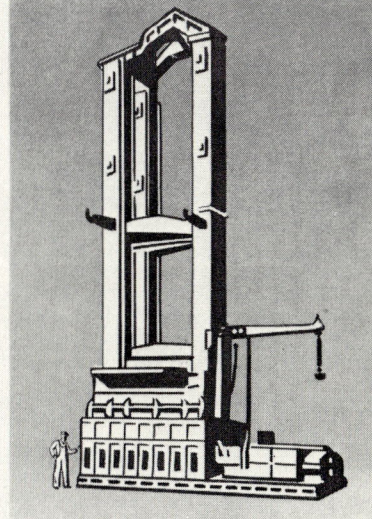

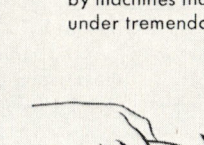

The ability of materials to resist twisting, or torsion, is recorded in machines that measure the force necessary to twist apart anything from fine wires to great bars of steel.

Some testing machines can exert a pull of more than 2,000,000 pounds.

**STRENGTH OF MATERIALS** is the term engineers use in determining how much force a material will take without breaking, and how much it will change in shape and size when an outside force is applied to it. When a force is applied to a material, as when a weight is put at the end of a rope, certain forces inside the rope cause it to stretch. The heavier the weight, the more the rope will stretch. In mechanics, the weight that is applied is called the *load*. The force within the rope that causes it to stretch is called the *stress*. The actual change, in this case the stretching, is called the *strain*. A material can undergo three changes due to stress. It can stretch, it can get shorter, or it may divide into layers. The stress that causes a material to stretch is called *tensile* stress. The stress that causes a material to get shorter is called *compressive* stress, while the stress that causes a material to divide into layers is called *shearing* stress. *Flexural* or bending loads, and *torsional* or twisting loads, produce combinations of the other types of stress that can affect various materials.

Every material offers a certain amount of resistance, or opposition, to changing its size and shape. How much resistance a material offers depends upon its strength, hardness, stiffness, elasticity, and flexibility. These *mechanical properties* are different for each material. For example, steel, wood, concrete, and cast iron differ greatly in their mechanical properties. The strength of a material will also depend on the kind of stress and type of load that is put on it.

The strength of materials can be tested in the laboratory by special machines that test the resistance of a material to strain. For example, ropes, wires, belts, and cables are tested for their tensile strength. In this test, the material is tested to see how much it can be stretched before breaking. The *elastic limit* of a wire, for example, has been exceeded when the wire does not return to its original shape when the stretching force is removed. The compression strength of such bodies as pillars, posts, and foundations is tested to see whether or not they can hold up the load they will be required to hold up in actual operation. Propeller shafts on ships are tested to see that they do not twist as they revolve. All these tests help in the selection of a proper material for a certain structure or function.

## STREPSIPTERA

In constructing a structure or a machine, the engineer must first compute the amount of stress that is applied by the load. He then selects the material that will best withstand the conditions that will have to be met. Sometimes conditions require that a material have a great deal of either tensile or compressive strength and yet weigh little. For lightness, metal may be cast in a hollow form. Engineers always use a material that is strong enough to carry several times the load expected.

### STRENGTH OF MATERIALS
(In Pounds Per Square Inch)

| MATERIAL | TENSILE | COMPRESSIVE | SHEARING |
|---|---|---|---|
| Aluminum | 58,000 | 35,000 | 35,000 |
| Brass, cold-drawn | 96,700 | 49,000 | |
| Brick | | 1,500-3,000 | |
| Bronze, cold-drawn | 85,000 | | |
| Cast iron | 60,000 | 145,000 | 70,000 |
| Concrete | | 2,000 | |
| Copper, cold-rolled | 50,000-70,000 | | |
| Steel, cast | 80,000 | 45,000 | |
| Steel, forged-rolled | 125,000 | 65,000 | 75,000 |
| Steel, nickel | 115,000 | | 92,000 |
| Stone | | 8,000 | |
| White oak | | | |
|   Parallel to grain | | 7,440 | 2,000 |
|   Across grain | 800 | | |
| White pine | | | |
|   Parallel to grain | | 4,840 | 860 |
|   Across grain | 300 | | |
| Wrought iron | 48,000 | 25,000 | 38,000 |

The measurements that are obtained from the testing machines are not exact. The values may change under different conditions. For example, small pieces of dry wood have a compressive strength of 3,000 to 10,000 pounds per square inch. But when there is moisture in the wood, the strength of the wood is lessened. Concrete made from portland cement has a compressive strength of 2,000 to 5,000 pounds per square inch. This strength increases with age and varies according to the amount of water and cement used in the concrete. Engineers have also found that a hollow shaft is stronger per pound of material than a solid shaft. ROBERT F. PATON

See also TENACITY.

**STREPSIPTERA** is an order of insects that are parasites of other insects. They are sometimes called *stylops* or *twisted-winged insects*. The males live only one or two days. They have large, fan-shaped hind wings. The front wings look like small clubs. The females have no eyes, wings, or legs. They live in the bodies of bees, wasps, crickets, and other insects. See also INSECT.

**STREPTOCOCCUS,** STREP *toh KAHK us* (plural, streptococci, STREP *toh KAHK sy*), is a type of bacteria which causes several serious diseases. Bacteria are sometimes considered the lowest form of plants. The streptococci are shaped like spheres and live together, forming chains. They infect the body by growing in it and producing poisons, called *toxins*. Sometimes a colony grows in one place, but some types of streptococci may spread through the body. The type *Streptococcus pyogenes* include the bacteria of septicemia (blood poisoning), impetigo, erysipelas, puerperal fever, septic sore throat, and scarlet fever. *Streptococcus pneumoniae*, called *pneumococcus*, is the cause of one kind of pneumonia. GEORGE L. BUSH

See also BACTERIA; DISEASE (table); TOXIN.

**STREPTOMYCIN,** STREP *toh MY sin*, is a drug that fights the bacteria that cause many diseases. It is said to be successful against infections that resist sulfa drugs and penicillin. It is the first drug that has found extensive application in the treatment of tuberculosis. See PENICILLIN; SULFA DRUGS.

Streptomycin is produced by a tiny plant that grows in the soil, a microorganism named *Streptomyces griseus*. In 1939, Selman A. Waksman of Rutgers University began to test microscopic growths to find a substance that could be used against disease germs. The best substance he found was formed by a microbe belonging to the group of actinomycetes, of the genus *Streptomyces*. It was named *streptomycin*.

Streptomycin is given off into a broth in which the microorganisms are grown. The impure drug is separated from the broth first as a solution, then as a solid. Then the drug is purified to small crystals of its salts, which form a white powder.

Chemically, streptomycin is an organic base, and forms several salts. The solid drug can be stored in a refrigerator for six months. Solutions keep their power for a considerable time, even when heated.

Streptomycin can be injected into the muscles, under the skin, or it can be taken by mouth or sprayed into the lungs. It is reported to have checked types of streptococcus and staphylococcus, Gram-negative and Gram-positive bacteria, and mycobacteria.

Streptomycin acts by interfering with the growth of the microbes. This effect is *bacteriostatic*. It kills bacteria, a *bactericidal* action. Streptomycin is effective in the treatment of tuberculosis, infections of the urinary passages, typhoid fever, pneumonia, dysentery, undulant fever, and such wound infections as gas gangrene. It may supplement the action of other drugs. SELMAN A. WAKSMAN

See also ANTIBIOTIC; WAKSMAN, SELMAN ABRAHAM.

**STRESEMANN,** SHTRAY *zuh mahn*, **GUSTAV** (1878-1929), a German statesman, was one of the authors of the Locarno Pact (see LOCARNO CONFERENCE). Elected to the Reichstag (the lower house of the German parliament) in 1906, he became the leader of the National Liberal party and, later, of the German People's party. In 1923, he became Chancellor and Foreign Minister, and he secured Germany's admission to the League of Nations in 1926. Stresemann received the 1926 Nobel peace prize. He was born in Berlin. GABRIEL A. ALMOND

**STRIAE.** See GLACIER (Erosion).

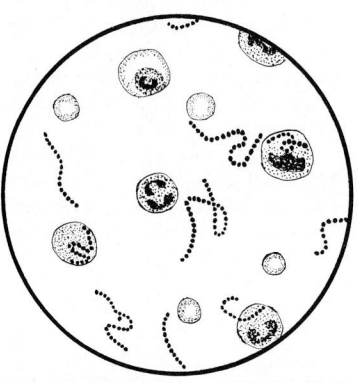

American Medical Association
**The Black, Beadlike Chains Are Streptococcus Germs.**

**STRIKE** is a means of attempting to force an employer to grant certain changes demanded by his workers. Strikes are usually called because the employer refuses to give his workers higher wages or increased benefits, or because he refuses to make changes in working conditions. Strikes have also been called to protest the decision of a labor arbitrator.

The right to strike has been upheld by the courts. The Taft-Hartley Act of 1947 forbids certain kinds of strikes, including (1) strikes by federal government employees, (2) strikes over union jurisdiction, and (3) strikes called within the 80-day "cooling off" period during which a new contract is being discussed. See TAFT-HARTLEY ACT.

**Kinds of Strikes.** Union officers may order a *called strike* if employers violate a union contract or cannot agree on a new contract. In some unions, a majority of the union members must agree to call a strike, or to allow their officers to call it. When local unions or smaller groups of union members strike without authorization, the strike is called a *wildcat strike*. A strike in which workers stop their labor, but do not leave their place of employment, is called a *sit-down strike*. A *sympathy strike* is one in which a group of workers strike against their employer because they sympathize with the demands of another group of workers striking against another employer. The purpose of the sympathy strike is to bring pressure from one employer on another to end the work stoppage. A *jurisdictional strike* is called when one union believes that the employer has given some of its work to another union. A *general strike* is one which involves all the workers within a particular industry, community, or country.

**Strike Strategy.** Most workers do not have enough savings to provide for themselves and their families through a long strike. Many unions have special *strike funds* which they use to help support the strikers. Other unions and the general public often donate money.

Lines of workers, called *picket lines*, usually walk up and down around the employers' place of business. The purpose of the picket line is to discourage workers from seeking jobs, to discourage customers, and to keep goods from being taken into or out of a factory.

**Strike Settlements.** A strike may be *broken* if the employer succeeds in hiring other workers, called strikebreakers or *scabs*, to carry on his business. Or the strikers may become unable to carry on without regular income. They may lose their jobs or be forced to go back to work under their former working conditions. The strike may end in compromise, or the strikers may win.

The methods of reaching a settlement include negotiation, conciliation or mediation, and arbitration. In *negotiation*, the employer discusses the workers' demands with representatives of the strikers. In *conciliation* or *mediation*, a third party meets with the employer and the workers. In *arbitration*, a third party settles the strike.    ROBERT D. PATTON

See also ARBITRATION; HOMESTEAD STRIKE; LABOR; LOCKOUT; PULLMAN STRIKE.

**STRINDBERG, AUGUST** (1849-1912), a Swedish writer, is one of the key figures in the history of modern drama. His experiments in dramatic form, his dynamic expression, and his brilliant language influenced the development of both naturalism and expressionism in drama. Strindberg also wrote novels, short stories, essays, poetry, and autobiographical works.

JOHAN AUGUST STRINDBERG was born in Stockholm. After some university training, he became a freelance journalist in Stockholm. He began writing plays in 1870, and completed a fine historical drama, *Master Olof*, in 1872. He gained fame with the publication of *The Red Room* (1879), a novel about the rackets of Stockholm.

Strindberg returned to playwriting with his famous naturalistic drama *The Father* (1887). This play tells how a wife destroys her husband by forcing him to doubt that he is the father of their daughter. *Miss Julie* (1888), a naturalistic play of social criticism, describes the tragedy of a woman of the Victorian age who loves a man beneath her social class. *The Creditors* (1888) describes the hate and pain which three persons can inflict upon one another.

Strindberg suffered much emotional and physical distress following two divorces in the 1890's. But by 1898 he had begun a new style of playwriting with *To Damascus* (parts I and II, 1898; part III, 1904). In this expressionistic trilogy, Strindberg portrayed himself as the "Unknown One," and expressed his lifelong spiritual uncertainty in dreamlike scenes and moods. In the delicate symbolic play *Easter* (1901), however, he faithfully presented Christian principles.

After the cold, brutal domestic drama *Dance of Death* (1901) and the romantic tragedy *The Bridal Crown* (1902),

Stratford Festival Theater, Stratford, Ontario

**Dance of Death** by August Strindberg, *right*, is a drama about a marriage that wavers between love and hate. Bitter conflict between husband and wife is a common theme in Strindberg's plays.

# STRING

Strindberg again turned to an expressionistic form in *A Dream Play* (1902). This play consists of short scenes and speeches that trace the search for happiness by the daughter of the Indian god Indra. Only one other Strindberg play, *The Spook Sonata* (1907), has less plot and a more pessimistic view of life. *The Spook Sonata* is the strangest and one of the most influential of Strindberg's plays. Its disconnected dialogue, mystical images, and distorted characters had a strong influence on expressionist drama. FREDERICK J. HUNTER

See also NATURALISM; EXPRESSIONISM.

**STRING.** See TWINE.

**STRING QUARTET.** See CHAMBER MUSIC.

**STRINGED INSTRUMENT.** See MUSIC; ORCHESTRA; SOUND (Musical Sounds).

**STRINGER, ARTHUR JOHN ARBUTHNOTT** (1874-1950), was a Canadian poet, novelist, and playwright. He wrote biography, criticism, adult and juvenile fiction, and plays for the stage and motion pictures. His books include *The Moon of Destiny* (1898), *The Prairie Wife* (1915), *The Mud Lark* (1931), and *The Cleverest Woman in the World and Other One Act Plays* (1939).

Stringer was born in Chatham, Ontario. He became a journalist, and was associated with the Montreal *Herald*, the American Press Association, and *Success* magazine. During his later life, he was a free-lance writer in New Jersey. DESMOND PACEY

**STRIP MINE.** See COAL (Mining Methods).

**STRITCH, SAMUEL A. CARDINAL** (1887-1958), was named a cardinal of the Roman Catholic Church by Pope Pius XII in February, 1946. In 1958 he was named pro-prefect of the Vatican's Sacred Congregation for the Propagation of the Faith.

Cardinal Stritch was born in Nashville, Tenn. He was an excellent student, and was graduated from high school when he was 14. At 17, he received his B.A. degree, and after two years of study at the North American College in Rome, received his Ph.D. degree. A special dispensation was secured to permit him to be ordained a priest when he was 23.

United Press Int.
**Samuel Cardinal Stritch**

The future cardinal first served in Tennessee. He became bishop of Toledo, Ohio, in 1921, the youngest American ever to become a bishop. In 1930, he was named archbishop of Milwaukee, and in 1939, archbishop of Chicago. FULTON J. SHEEN

**STROBILE.** See CONE-BEARING TREES.

**STROBOSCOPE,** *STRAHB oh skohp*, is an optical device for making swiftly rotating machinery seem to stand still. It depends on the principle that the eye must take a fraction of a second to see an object.

If a machine in rapid motion is viewed by ordinary light, the moving parts are seen only as blurred masses. No details of their shapes can be seen. The eye can see only about 16 impulses per second. Faster than this it does not see anything clearly. But now, instead of using ordinary light, let us illuminate the moving machine with a single flash of lightning. The flash is bright and comes fast. As it shines on the moving machinery, everything seems to stand still.

Illumination by lightning is not practical, but artificial lightning can be made that will give bright flashes as often as we need. If the flashes are timed to synchronize with the rotation of the machine, the eye sees the machine as standing still, even though the wheels are in rapid motion. If the flashes are timed a little slower than the rotation of the machine the wheels appear to be running slowly in one direction, while if we time the flashes a little faster than the rotation, the machine appears to be running in the opposite direction. Any unwanted motion in a machine can be discovered quickly by using a stroboscope. The stroboscope also is often used to provide the lighting for high-speed photography (see PHOTOGRAPHY [Artificial Lighting]). PALMER H. CRAIG

See also DUCHAMP, MARCEL (picture).

Gjon Mili
**Split-second Flashes of Light from a Stroboscope** make it possible for a photographer to record a basketball player's action as he dribbles down the floor and takes a shot.

**STROKE.** See APOPLEXY.

**STROMBOLI,** *STRAHM boh lih*, is an island in the Tyrrhenian Sea off the northeastern coast of Sicily. The island covers 4.7 square miles and has 559 people. It is famous for its volcano, which rises 3,038 feet high. The volcano is one of the few in Europe that are constantly active. Ancient writers reported this activity centuries ago. Disastrous eruptions rarely occur because the lava flows freely instead of building up internal pressure for violent eruptions. For location, see ITALY (color map). SHEPARD B. CLOUGH

**STROMEYER, FRIEDRICH.** See CADMIUM.

**STRONG, SIR SAMUEL HENRY** (1825-1909), served as the chief justice of the Supreme Court of Canada from 1892 to 1902. He became one of its first members when the court was established in 1875. Strong was a judge of the Court of Chancery from 1869 to 1874. He was knighted in 1893, and sworn into the Imperial Privy Council in 1897. He was born in Poole, Dorsetshire, England. J. E. HODGETTS

**STRONTIUM,** *STRAHN shee um*, a chemical element, is a soft, silvery, or yellowish metal. Strontium exists as many *isotopes* (atoms with the same atomic number but different atomic weights). Strontium-90 is a dangerous radioactive isotope found in the fallout from some nuclear explosions. In men and animals, the radioactivity of strontium-90 destroys the tissues that make blood.

Strontium is found in the minerals celestite and strontianite. Strontium combines readily with oxygen, nitrogen, and hydrogen. Strontium nitrate (Sr[NO$_3$]$_2$) burns with a crimson flame, and is used in flares and fireworks.

Strontium has the chemical symbol Sr. Its atomic number is 38 and its atomic weight is 87.62. It melts at 769° C. and boils at 1384° C. It was discovered in 1790 by Adair Crawford of Ireland. WARREN S. PETERSON

**STRUCTURAL ENGINEERING.** See ENGINEERING (Civil Engineering).

**STRUCTURAL FORMULA.** See CHEMISTRY (Structural Formulas).

**STRUCTURALISM.** See PSYCHOLOGY (History).

**STRUGGLE FOR EXISTENCE.** See EVOLUTION (Darwin's Theory); NATURAL SELECTION.

**STRUTT, JEDEDIAH.** See KNITTING MACHINE.

**STRUVE,** *SHTROO vuh,* **OTTO** (1897-1963), was an American astronomer. He contributed greatly to knowledge of stellar evolution. Struve was director of the Yerkes Observatory from 1932 to 1947, and of the McDonald Observatory from 1939 to 1947. Struve became professor of astronomy and director of the Leuschner Observatory at the University of California in 1950. He was born in Russia. HELEN WRIGHT

**STRYCHNINE,** *STRICK neen* (chemical formula, $C_{21}H_{22}N_2O_2$), is a bitter and poisonous drug obtained from the seeds of plants such as the *nux vomica* tree, found in India and Indonesia. Strychnine comes in colorless crystals. A large dose of strychnine causes a serious case of poisoning, resulting in convulsions. The usual symptoms are twitching, difficulty in swallowing, and a sudden backward bending of the body. If a person has taken strychnine, call a doctor immediately. If the victim is not having convulsions, try to make him vomit by touching the back of his throat with the blunt end of a spoon or your finger. The victim should be kept warm and as quiet as possible. A. K. REYNOLDS

See also NUX VOMICA.

**STUART, CHARLES EDWARD LOUIS** (1720-1788), was a pretender to the English throne. He also was known as "Bonnie Prince Charlie," "The Young Pretender," and "The Young Chevalier." Stuart was born in Rome, the oldest son of James Edward Stuart and the grandson of the deposed James II of England. In 1745 he tried to win back the English throne with the aid of the Highland clans of Scotland, but his army was decisively defeated on Culloden Moor. Stuart escaped to France after his defeat, and lived in Europe the rest of his life. See STUART, HOUSE OF. W. M. SOUTHGATE

## STUART, GILBERT CHARLES

**STUART, GILBERT CHARLES** (1755-1828), was an American artist. He became famous for his unfinished portrait of George Washington, probably the best-known portrait in America.

Stuart was born near Newport, R.I., and began painting at the age of 13. His early works were simple, thinly painted portraits. In 1775 he went to London for five years to serve as assistant to artist Benjamin West. A Stuart portrait, *The Skater*, was exhibited at the Royal Academy in 1782. This graceful, luminous picture received so much praise that Stuart opened his

Redwood Library and Athenaeum
**Gilbert Stuart's Self-Portrait** shows how he concentrated on facial expression and neglected the background in his works.

own portrait studio in London. For the next 10 years, the wealthy of England and Scotland sat for him. However, Stuart lived in high style and spent some time in British debtors prisons because of his extravagant living.

In 1792, Stuart returned to the United States. He planned to get money to pay his debts by painting Washington's portrait. Washington sat for three different portraits in 1795 and 1796. The "Vaughan" type is a completed painting of bust length. "Lansdowne" is a full length. "Athenaeum" is the familiar unfinished oval of Washington's head. Stuart sold many copies of the portraits that he, his daughter, and others made.

Stuart spent the last half of his life as a portrait painter. He became noted for his charm, his ability to complete portraits quickly, and his advice to young artists. "Paint what you see," he told a beginner, "and look with your own eyes." EDWARD H. DWIGHT

For color reproductions of Stuart's works, see WASHINGTON, GEORGE; JEFFERSON, THOMAS. See also pictures with ADAMS, JOHN; ASTOR.

739

# STUART, HOUSE OF

**STUART, HOUSE OF.** Stuart is the name of a royal family of England and Scotland. The Stuarts were kings of Scotland from 1371 to 1603, and kings of England and Scotland from 1603 to 1714. Their rule of the two countries in the 1600's was characterized by their insistence on the Divine Right of Kings (see DIVINE RIGHT OF KINGS).

James VI of Scotland, the son of Mary, Queen of Scots, became king of England at the death of his cousin, Queen Elizabeth I, in 1603. He took the title of James I. His son Charles I succeeded him. Charles's attempt to rule as a dictator brought on the English Revolution. He was beheaded in 1649.

England again became a monarchy in 1660 under Charles II, the son of Charles I. When Charles II died in 1685, his brother, James II, became king. James was determined to rule as a dictator and to restore the Roman Catholic religion in England, even though England was committed to parliamentary government and was strongly anti-Catholic. As a result of this conflict, James was forced to leave the throne in the bloodless revolution of 1688. Parliament gave the crown to his daughter Mary and her husband, William of Orange.

Anne Stuart, Mary's sister, became queen in 1702. She was the last Stuart ruler. During her reign, England and Scotland were united as a single nation known as Great Britain. W. M. SOUTHGATE

**Related Articles** in WORLD BOOK include:
Anne
Charles (I; II) of England
James (I; II)
Mary (II)
Mary, Queen of Scots
Scotland (The House of Stuart)

**STUART, JAMES EWELL BROWN** (1833-1864), was a Confederate cavalry general. "Jeb" Stuart distinguished himself in the first Battle of Bull Run (Manassas). He served with "Stonewall" Jackson at Chancellorsville and commanded Jackson's corps for a short time after Jackson was wounded. In command of all General Robert E. Lee's cavalry, Stuart fought several successful actions in the Wilderness Campaign in 1864. But he had gained his widest fame for his two daring rides "around McClellan" in which he took his division of cavalry all the way around the Union Army.

Brown Bros.
**"Jeb" Stuart**

Stuart became the center of a great controversy following the Battle of Gettysburg. He had taken his command off on an independent operation while General Lee invaded the North, and Stuart's absence deprived Lee of the "eyes" of his army. Stuart was killed at Yellow Tavern, Va., in 1864 in the battle for Richmond.

Stuart was born in Patrick County, Virginia, and was graduated from the United States Military Academy. He served in Kansas and on the frontier from 1855 to 1861. He resigned from the United States Army in 1861, and joined the Confederacy. FRANK E. VANDIVER

**STUART, JESSE HILTON** (1907-    ), an American writer, became famous for his stories and poems about Kentucky. He wrote *Taps for Private Tussie* (1943) and *Hold April* (1962). He published more than 200 short stories within 20 years. In 1961, he won an award for distinguished achievement in poetry from the Academy of American Poets. Stuart was born near Riverton, Ky., and became a writer and teacher. GEORGE J. BECKER

**STUART, JOHN M.** See NORTHERN TERRITORY.

**STUART, JOHN TODD.** See LINCOLN, ABRAHAM (Study).

**STUART, MARY.** See MARY, QUEEN OF SCOTS.

**STUCCO,** *STUCK o*, is a plasterlike material applied to outside walls. It forms a hard protective covering. Stucco usually consists of sand, water, and a cementing mixture. Workers usually apply three coats, using trowels. The first two coats are each about $\frac{3}{8}$ of an inch thick. The finish coat is from $\frac{1}{8}$ to $\frac{1}{4}$ of an inch thick. Stucco can be applied in a variety of finishes and colors. See also PLASTERING. GEORGE W. WASHA

**STUCK, HUDSON.** See MOUNT MCKINLEY.

**STUD.** See HOUSE (House Building Terms); CHAIN.

**STUDBOOK.** See DOG (Dog Terms).

**STUDEBAKER** is the name of a family that became famous as makers of wagons and other vehicles. Their company, Studebaker Corporation, merged with Packard Motors, Inc., in 1954. In 1966, the firm stopped making automobiles. It continued to make automobile parts and other products, and in 1967 merged with Worthington Corp. to form Studebaker-Worthington, Inc.

**Clement Studebaker** (1831-1901), with his brother Henry, opened a blacksmith and wagon shop in South Bend, Ind., in 1852. The Studebaker Brothers Manufacturing Company was organized in 1868, with Clement as its first president. The company became the largest wagon manufacturer in the country, and had a world market. Studebaker was born in Pinetown, Pa.

**John Mohler Studebaker** (1833-1917), a brother of Clement Studebaker, moved to California in 1853 during the Gold Rush. There he made wheelbarrows for the miners. When he had saved enough money, he returned to South Bend and bought his brother Henry's interest in the Studebaker firm. John Studebaker became president of the company after Clement died. In 1902, the firm made its first electric-powered vehicles, and in 1904 it began making gasoline-powered cars. By 1920, the Studebaker company was producing automobiles and trucks exclusively. Studebaker was born in Gettysburg, Pa. V. E. CANGELOSI and R. E. WESTMEYER

**Clement Studebaker**
Studebaker-Worthington, Inc.

**John M. Studebaker**
Studebaker-Worthington, Inc.

740

**STUDENT GOVERNMENT** is an activity in which students take part in the government of their school, college, or university. This activity usually takes place through a student organization. The organization may be called a *student cabinet, student congress, student legislature,* or *G.O.* (general organization). But most are called *student councils.* Most high schools, colleges, and universities have some form of student government.

Students elect representatives to the council, and the council works to promote student welfare. The council meets with the faculty and school administration to discuss curriculum, student life, alumni relations, and other matters which are of interest to the students. A faculty member serves as the council sponsor or adviser. Council activities in school include directing assembly programs, planning and directing honor study halls, coordinating student activity programs, helping to manage the school cafeteria, arranging celebrations for special days, and directing awards programs. The student council may also join in community improvement projects and conduct leadership and citizenship education programs.

About 10,000 high schools in the United States belong to the National Association of Student Councils (NASC), which distributes information about student government. Headquarters of the National Association of Student Councils are at 1201 Sixteenth Street NW, Washington, D.C. 20036.

About 340 collegiate student organizations belong to the United States National Student Association (USNSA). USNSA sponsors student exchange programs and meetings on current student and world problems. USNSA delegates may also represent United States students at international meetings. GORDON J. KLOPF

**STUDENT NATIONAL EDUCATION ASSOCIATION.** See FUTURE TEACHERS OF AMERICA.

**STUDENT NATIONAL COORDINATING COMMITTEE (SNCC),** also called "Snick," is a civil rights organization in the United States. White and Negro students founded SNCC in 1960 as the Student Nonviolent Coordinating Committee. The group adopted its present name in 1969. In the early 1960's, SNCC organized peaceful protests and demonstrations to speed desegregation in the South. In 1964, SNCC sponsored the Mississippi Project, in which about 800 volunteers helped thousands of Negroes register to vote.

Under the leadership of Stokely Carmichael, SNCC abandoned its policy of nonviolence in 1966. It adopted a strong antiwhite attitude, and discouraged white membership. Carmichael criticized the civil rights movement, and called for "Black Power." Carmichael resigned as leader of SNCC in 1967. He denounced the United States during a tour of the world. His successor, H. Rap Brown, continued the strongly militant program started by Carmichael. RICHARD BARDOLPH

**STUDENT PROTEST.** See EDUCATION, HISTORY OF (Recent Developments); RIOT (The 1960's).

**STUDENTS FOR A DEMOCRATIC SOCIETY.** See EDUCATION, HISTORY OF (Recent Developments).

**STUDIO.** See MOTION PICTURE (A Trip to a Motion-Picture Studio); RADIO (A Visit to a Radio Station); TELEVISION (A Trip to a Television Station).

**STUDY** means to apply the mind to any subject in order to learn about it. Study is accomplished mostly by means of reading, observation, questioning, and reflec-

Lars Hedman

**A Good Encyclopedia** is a collection of man's knowledge. It is an invaluable study aid for almost every subject.

tion. It is a part of the process of learning. The purpose of study is the discovery of information. A good student obtains facts and skills by which he can organize and express his thoughts and talents.

**Effective Study**

Effective or successful study consists of much more than merely memorizing facts. It calls for knowing where and how to obtain facts, and the ability to make intelligent use of them. It means that the student must be able to organize, classify, and arrange facts in their proper relationship to the subject being studied. To study successfully, a student must decide what is important information, and then form opinions concerning it. All these things must be done to the best of his ability in the shortest possible amount of time. Because knowledge is very important to every person, it is wise to learn how to study in the most effective way. See LEARNING (Efficient Learning).

**Aids to Effective Study**

**Good Physical Condition.** The mind works best when the body is in good physical condition. Good health demands that we eat properly and get enough rest, sleep, exercise, and recreation. Certain physical defects make study especially difficult. Poor eyesight, for example, can be a great hindrance to study, and should be corrected. But many physical handicaps need not prevent one from learning to study efficiently. A crippled child, for example, may learn to study as well as anyone.

**Favorable Surroundings.** Every child needs a place where he can study regularly without interruptions. He must have a desk or table to write on and a chair. Both must be of the proper height to fit his body. Both children and grownups grow tired less quickly when sitting straight in a comfortable chair. Good light, either daylight or artificial light, is necessary to prevent eyestrain. The desk or table should be located so that the light will fall over the left shoulder on the reading matter. The amount of light should be enough to read by easily, but

# STUDY

not so much as to cause glare, which results in eye fatigue. Noise and other distractions should be eliminated. Some people feel that they can study better with soft music in the background. But most people find the radio and television a distraction. Room temperature should be neither too hot nor too cold.

**Study Materials.** Certain study materials are usually required by the student. These usually include pencils, pens, ink, erasers, paper, notebooks, scratch-pads, scissors, rubber bands, a paper punch, and paper clips. Additional equipment will be needed for certain subjects. Geometry may call for a compass, a ruler, and a protractor. Besides the required textbooks, a good dictionary, a readable encyclopedia, maps, and other reference works will give valuable aid. Some provision should be made for keeping notes and work papers in orderly arrangement so that they are ready for quick reference. File folders, properly labeled and indexed, are useful for this purpose. A bookshelf and drawers for storing materials encourage neatness and systematic work. A typewriter may help some students to do more work in less time, but it is not necessary.

**Regular Habits.** Every human being is subject to habits, and the sum of his habits determines his character. The body and mind perform various functions more easily when they are taught to do so at regular intervals. For example, if we are accustomed to eating dinner at a certain hour, we normally become hungry at that time. Likewise, if a definite period of the day is set aside for study, the mind is more likely to be ready for study. The art of studying effectively can be acquired only with regular practice. If we neglect to study one day, it is easier to neglect to study on the following day.

**Reading Ability.** Effective study depends more than anything else on the ability to make the best use of the printed word. Rapid reading is essential in order to cover as much ground as possible without wasting time. The art of reading rapidly, and with understanding, can be developed with practice. Every student should try to improve his reading by improving his vocabulary, his speed, and his comprehension. See READING.

The student cannot always determine immediately how helpful a book may be to the subject being studied. In that case, it is better to skim through the book quickly at first, instead of reading it word by word. In this way, the main points and general meaning are quickly grasped. If the material proves to be helpful, a second and more careful reading can follow.

Too many students fail to understand all that they have read because they do not know the meanings of some words. If a word is unfamiliar, it is a good habit to take time to look it up in the dictionary and learn its meaning. By analyzing the organization of material, a picture of what has been read can be formed in the mind. Try to grasp essential facts and sort these out in some kind of order. The important thing is to remember the idea, rather than the author's exact words.

Read critically in order to compare the statements of one author with those of another. A subject can often be presented from different points of view. The student should not form an opinion until the subject has been considered from more than one angle. Nor should he believe everything he sees in print.

If there are questions at the end of a lesson or chapter, it is a good idea to try answering the questions *first*, on the basis of what you know. The actual reading of the lesson then becomes a process of checking and making certain the answers are correct.

**Studying Together.** Two or three students can often get good results and save a great deal of time by studying together. One interesting and effective method is for each student to prepare each day's lesson not by "studying" it, but by going through it rapidly in order to prepare a test or examination for the others. Each one then takes the test prepared by the others. The whole group scores its papers together.

**Efficient Use of Text and Reference Books.** Text and reference books contain many aids to study. An index at the back of a textbook gives an alphabetical list of names and subjects referred to in the book, with the pages where the topics may be found. The table of contents in the front of the book lists the chapters, and often provides a brief description of what each contains.

An encyclopedia may be *self-indexing*. This means that the reader can find an article, or a reference to an article, in its proper alphabetical place. In using THE WORLD BOOK, for example, he does not have to use a separate index. Both encyclopedias and dictionaries contain many *cross references* and related subjects. These aids lead the reader from the article he is reading to other articles that will provide him with additional information.

Encyclopedias and textbooks often contain *bibliographies*. A bibliography is a list of books on the subject for further reading. Reference books also have charts, diagrams, and outlines. These should be studied because they are the author's means of summarizing information. Other aids to study include vocabulary lists, pronunciation guides, photographs, and maps.

Cultivate the habit of using these aids to locate material quickly. Learn how to use such basic reference materials as an atlas, an almanac, and the card catalog in the library (see LIBRARY).

**Understanding the Assignment.** No subject can be studied effectively unless the student has a clear understanding of the work he is supposed to do. Write out each day's assignment, and make a note of what is to be read, the problems to be worked out, and what must be prepared in writing. Ask the teacher to explain any points which are not clear. Take advantage of any directions or suggestions which are offered.

**Planning the Work.** Plan carefully how to use your time to best advantage. Some students take a few minutes each morning to plan a schedule of their day's activities. Many students find it helpful to make a weekly schedule allowing adequate time for study. A study program should be kept flexible so that adjustments can be made as they are needed.

Schedule your study for a time when you are least tired. Study your most difficult subject first when you are freshest mentally and physically. The easiest subjects should ordinarily be left to do last, unless you become inclined to pass over them too lightly just because they are so easy. Plan to keep your study periods short and take a few minutes of rest between subjects.

**Taking Notes.** Cultivate the habit of taking notes in outline form both while reading and during classroom work. Notes provide a ready source of reference and they also help you to fix a subject in mind. Do not attempt to write down every word you read or hear. Instead, learn to select essential facts and sum them up in the fewest possible words, using key phrases and abbreviations. To do this efficiently requires considerable practice. But a few well chosen words can serve as pegs on which to hang ideas. After class, look over your notes and fill in any material you may have missed. The process of reducing a subject to outline form will help considerably in learning how to take effective notes. The outline should be well organized and clear. A good outline is brief enough to allow the student to learn the concepts easily. See OUTLINES AND OUTLINING.

Develop some system of filing notes so that they can be easily located when they are needed. No elaborate filing system is needed, but the exact method to use depends on the type of work being done. Perhaps all that is needed is a single folder to hold the notes for each of your subjects.

**Keeping Work Up to Date.** Nothing can be gained by putting off work from one day to another. You cannot study twice as hard in one day to make up for time lost during another. Each day's lesson must be prepared regularly for rapid progress. But sometimes you may miss work because of illness or for some other unavoidable reason. In that case, extra study time must often be allowed in order to bring the work up to date. Special assistance from your teachers or parents may be needed if you have missed a number of lessons.

**Concentration.** It is essential to keep in mind the subject to be studied. This can be accomplished only by mental discipline. The mind is often tempted to wander, sometimes even from an interesting subject. Mental discipline is a habit which can be cultivated only through constant effort. Concentration means that you must think only about the work at hand. If part of the mind is waiting for a telephone call or listening to the radio or television, the rest of the mind cannot concentrate on study.

Some subjects stimulate us naturally, and we enjoy studying them. Others may require a real effort of the will. But no subject need be dull if it is approached with a determination to master it. A subject sometimes only seems dull because we do not understand the reasons for studying it. After its purpose is explained, it may become very interesting.

Reference books often contain material other than that about the subject being studied. Sometimes such material may seem so interesting that we are distracted from the work at hand. This temptation must be vigorously resisted until the necessary tasks are accomplished. After the assignment is finished, it may be profitable to turn our attention to any subject we care to pursue. Investigation of this kind can be very stimulating to the mind. But to indulge in such relaxing reading before our work is done is as unwise a practice as eating candy before dinner.

**Frequent Review.** Each day's study should begin with a quick review of the previous lesson. This helps to fix in mind the points already learned and to form a bridge to the next assignment. All the work covered during a semester should be reviewed at regular and frequent intervals. Well-kept notes are very helpful for this purpose. Never wait until the day before an examination to review the work for an entire period. "Cramming" is the most inefficient method of study, and what is learned in this way is usually soon forgotten. Remember that passing examinations is not the most important purpose of study.

**Observation.** Not all study should be made from books. Everything about us is material for study. We can learn much about nature by reading books. But we can learn even more by observation. It is not enough merely to look. We may look without actually seeing. Instead, we must look carefully and think about what we see. Then we begin to wonder and to ask ourselves questions. The answers may be found in books or we may discover them for ourselves. Knowledge found in this way becomes a permanent part of us.

Museums offer rich sources of material for study. Some of them are mines of information about the past. History comes to life when we see actual examples of furniture, clothing, or painting and sculpture that were used or made by people in other times.

We can learn more about animals by studying live ones in zoos than by looking at pictures in books. And natural history museums present realistic exhibitions of stuffed animals in their natural settings, which zoos can seldom do.

**Application.** Study has much more meaning if what has been learned is applied to a practical purpose. For example, you might put arithmetic to use by offering to add and check the family grocery bill. A student of domestic science may be able to suggest improvements in the family's diet. All recreational activities offer opportunities to put into use something which has been learned in the classroom.

**Discussion and Self Tests.** We gain better understanding of a subject when we learn to express our ideas about it in our own words. This should be done both in writing and orally. Oral discussion stimulates quick thinking and a written analysis aids careful thinking. You should test your knowledge of a subject by asking yourself questions and then checking the answers with what you have already studied.

Discussions may take place in class. But they also may be continued outside of class with fellow students, members of the family, or older friends.

**Mental Attitude.** A happy outlook of mind helps you to study better. Worries or fear prevent concentration. The cause of a worry may exist only in your mind and can often be overcome by discussing it with parents or teachers. Fear of failing in your lessons can sometimes actually prevent effective study. But common sense and reason can help to dispel such fears. Seek the advice of parents and teachers or of someone in whom you have confidence. Your counselor or school adviser will often be able to help you understand your problems more clearly. Having faith in yourself is important to successful study.   WILLIAM H. NAULT

**Related Articles** in WORLD BOOK include:

| | |
|---|---|
| Bibliography | Encyclopedia |
| Dictionary | Outlines and Outlining |
| Education | Reading |

**STUKA.** See AIR FORCE (color picture: Fighting Planes).

**The Rock Sturgeon** has armor of bony plate to protect its head and body. Sturgeon eggs are used to make caviar.

New York Zoological Society

**STURGEON,** *STUR jun,* is the common name of a family of large fishes living in the fresh waters and seas of the North Temperate Zone. They are caught for their flesh, which is usually smoked, and for their eggs, which are used in the preparation of caviar. A superior quality of isinglass is obtained from the air bladder of the Russian sturgeon. These fish have slender bodies covered with rows of bony plates. Beneath the long snout there is a small, toothless mouth with thick, sucking lips. There are four *barbels* (fleshy projections) in front of the mouth. The head, like the body, is well protected with plates. A single dorsal fin rises from the back, and the body extends into the long upper part of the tail fin. Most of these fish migrate from salt water into streams in the spawning season, but some species live permanently in fresh waters. Sturgeon suck food into their mouths.

Sturgeon belong to a very ancient group of fish. Early ancestors of the sturgeon appeared during the Devonian Period (see EARTH [table]). The sturgeon's sucking mouth and plated body are features that developed later.

One of the best-known sturgeon is the *common sturgeon.* It lives in European waters and along the North American coast from Labrador to the Gulf of Mexico. The largest specimens may be over 10 feet long and weigh more than 1,000 pounds. The *white sturgeon* of the American Pacific Coast is the largest American fish of this group. The *lake* or *rock sturgeon* lives in the Great Lakes and the Mississippi Valley waters. Scientists consider the *beluga*, a giant sturgeon of Russia, the largest fresh-water fish. It may grow as long as 14 feet and weigh more than 3,000 pounds. The beluga produces most of the European caviar. Another Russian sturgeon, the small *sterlet,* is also a source for this delicacy. The North American sturgeons were abundant once, but overfishing, dams, and pollution have greatly reduced their number.

**Scientific Classification.** The sturgeon belongs to the sturgeon family, *Acipenseridae.* The common sturgeon is genus *Acipenser,* species *A. sturio;* the white sturgeon, *A. transmontanus;* the lake or rock sturgeon, *A. fulvescens;* the sterlet, *A. ruthenus.* The beluga is genus *Huso,* species *H. huso.*     CARL L. HUBBS

See also CAVIAR; IRAN (picture: Sturgeon Fishermen).
**STURGEON, WILLIAM.** See ELECTROMAGNET.
**STURGES, PRESTON** (1898-1959), was an American motion-picture writer and director. He became famous for films that brilliantly satirize aspects of American life. *The Great McGinty* (1940) satirizes crooked politicians. *Sullivan's Travels* (1941) attacks the false values Sturges saw mirrored in Hollywood. *The Miracle of Morgan's Creek* (1944) and *Hail the Conquering Hero* (1944) deal with small-town politics and the worship of military heroes. Sturges also wrote and directed *Christmas in July* (1940), *The Lady Eve* (1941), and *Unfaithfully Yours* (1948). All show Sturges' skill at writing witty dialogue and creating slapstick comedy.

Sturges was born in Chicago. He wrote several Broadway plays before going to Hollywood in 1932. They include the Broadway comedy hit *Strictly Dishonorable* (1929).     RICHARD GRIFFITH

**STURLUSON.** See SNORRI STURLUSON.
**STURT, CHARLES.** See AUSTRALIA (Exploration).
**STURTEVANT, ALFRED H.** See HEREDITY (Genetics).
**STUTTERING AND STAMMERING** are two terms used to describe a certain form of defective or disordered speech. Formerly the words were taken to mean two different defects. *Stuttering* was the repetition of sounds or syllables. *Stammering* was regarded as a continuous *block* that resulted in inability to utter any sound. Present-day specialists in speech correction do not recognize a difference between stuttering and stammering. The experts use the words interchangeably, but the term *stuttering* is preferred.

An example of one form of stuttering is the inability to say clearly such words as *don't* or *animal.* The stutterer says d-d-d-don't and a-a-a-animal. A sentence spoken by a stutterer might then sound something like this: "M-m-m-mother, m-m-m-may Bob-bob-Bobby have a d-d-d-doughnut?"

In stuttering there may also be a spasm of the speech muscles that prevents talking, sometimes almost entirely. Often the difficulty in speaking then results in grimacing and other facial contortions which are caused by contractions of the speech muscles.

No one knows the specific causes of stuttering. Speech experts have various theories as to what causes it and many methods have been used to correct it. Shyness and lack of self-confidence often accompany it, but they are not believed to cause it. About 4 to 6 times more males than females are afflicted by stuttering. It is most common in young children. If stuttering is not overcome, it may seriously handicap a person in his own development and in his relations with other persons. Stuttering can become so serious that it makes a vocational failure of even a talented person. It is not associated with any lack of mental ability.

Children often lose *fluency* (smoothness of speech) when they try to speak too rapidly, or if they are upset and excited. The condition is made worse if the speaker is aware of his defective speech. He strains to avoid the stuttering, and the effort tightens the muscles in his face and throat. This makes his speech worse. He may become panicky because of his difficulty, and thus increase the stuttering. He will gain fluency only when he stops struggling and learns to control his fear of what may happen.

There are different ways in which many stutterers can use the voice easily, without stuttering. These include reading in unison, singing, speaking to groups before whom they have self-confidence, and speaking to themselves when they are alone. In general, persons who stutter find it very difficult to speak in public or in any situation in which they feel insecure.

Treatment of speech disorders is often a matter of training the mental processes and emotions, as well as retraining the speech of the individual. Each case must be treated individually, according to the person's needs. Children who stutter sometimes outgrow the defect. It is advisable not to call attention to children's stuttering and to exercise calmness and patience when they speak, in order to help them establish fluency and self-confidence. VIRGIL A. ANDERSON

See also LISPING; SPEECH THERAPY.

**STUTTGART,** *SHTOOT gahrt* (pop. 632,727; alt. 853 ft.), is the capital of the West German state of Baden-Württemberg (see GERMANY [political map]). Stuttgart was formerly capital of the state and kingdom of Württemberg. The city is the center of the printing and publishing industry of southern Germany. Stuttgart lies near the Neckar River. Hills covered with vineyards and woods surround the city. It has several attractive suburbs, including Bad Cannstatt on the Neckar. Many buildings in Stuttgart are fine examples of Renaissance architecture. There are many statues, parks, gardens, churches, and schools. Stuttgart was the birthplace of the philosopher G. W. F. Hegel.

Bombers hit Stuttgart heavily during World War II because it contained machine-tool, ball-bearing, and internal-combustion engine factories. Many of its famous buildings were damaged. French troops entered Stuttgart on April 21, 1945. The city was in the American zone of occupation after the war. The *Läuderrat* or Council of States for the American zone was established in Stuttgart on Oct. 17, 1945. It was the first German organization above the state level to be established after the war. JAMES K. POLLOCK

**STUYVESANT,** *STI vuh s'nt*, **PETER** (1610?-1672), was the last Dutch governor of New Netherland, an area that included land in present-day New York and several nearby states (see NEW NETHERLAND). Stuyvesant was born in West Friesland, the son of a minister. He became a soldier as a young man, and in 1635 entered the service of the Dutch West India Company. In 1643, he became governor of Curaçao and nearby Dutch possessions. The next year, he led an attack against the island of Saint Martin and lost a leg in the battle.

In 1646, Stuyvesant became governor of New Netherland. He arrived in New Amsterdam (now New York

New York Historical Society
**Peter Stuyvesant**

# STYRIA

City) in May, 1647, and immediately began to make enemies by his harsh methods. But he restored order and business, and made friends with the Indians. His settlement in 1650 with the New England colonists of the eastern boundaries of the Dutch colony angered the Dutch because they thought he gave the Puritans too much territory. Five years later, he captured all New Sweden, which included lands in what are now New Jersey, Delaware, and Pennsylvania. He made New Sweden a part of New Netherland.

Stuyvesant refused to share his power with anybody. When a convention of Long Island citizens demanded a share in the government, he replied, "We derive our authority from God and the West India Company, not from the pleasure of a few ignorant subjects." In 1664, an English fleet ordered the surrender of the city. The citizens refused to support Stuyvesant, and he was forced to give in. Stuyvesant was sent to Holland in disgrace, but he returned to New York after a few years and settled on his *bouwerij* (farm), part of which later became the Bowery of New York City. Stuyvesant died there and lies buried on the site of Saint Mark's Church. He is one of the characters in Washington Irving's *Knickerbocker's History of New York.* IAN C. C. GRAHAM

See also NEW YORK CITY (History); NEW SWEDEN.

**STY** is an infection of one of the glands in an eyelid, usually around an eyelash. The infection, which resembles a small boil, is usually caused by a *staphylococcus* bacteria. The germs enter the root of the eyelash, grow there, and form pus. Some experts believe eyestrain is an indirect cause of sties. When people with eyestrain rub their eyes too much, germs from their hands may cause infection. White blood cells in the body usually kill the germs that cause a sty. Then the sty softens, breaks, lets out the pus, and heals. Hot moist applications held against the sty can make it break more quickly. Sties often come one after another. Doctors can inoculate the patient with a vaccine made from the staphylococcus germs. When sties continue for a long time, doctors may treat them with germ-killing drugs. WILLIAM F. HUGHES

See also BOIL.

**STYLE,** in literature and the arts, is the way thoughts or ideas are expressed by the writer or artist. See also CLOTHING; FASHION; LITERATURE (Style).

**STYLE,** in botany. See FLOWER (The Pistils; picture: Parts of a Flower).

**STYLUS** was a sharp-pointed writing instrument used by peoples of ancient times. It was made of metal, bone, or reed, and was used to engrave characters on wax or moist clay tablets. The cutting instrument that makes the grooves in a phonograph record, and the phonograph needle are called *styluses.*

**STYRENE.** See RUBBER (Synthetic).

**STYRIA,** *STIR ee uh,* now a province in the southeastern part of the Austrian Republic, was ruled by Austrian

745

**STYRON, WILLIAM**

princes for many centuries. Its area is 6,326 square miles, and it has a population of 1,137,865. It has iron ore deposits. Graz is the capital. See also GRAZ.

**STYRON, WILLIAM** (1925-        ), an American novelist, became one of the most promising writers to appear since 1950. His works are noted for their distinctive style and often for their Southern setting.

Styron's first novel *Lie Down in Darkness* (1951) describes the decline of a Southern middle-class family. The short novel *The Long March* (1953), set in a Marine Corps training camp, raises serious questions about the value of military discipline and routine. *Set This House on Fire* (1960) is an original and powerful novel of conflict in a small Italian town. *The Confessions of Nat Turner* (1967) re-creates the 1831 revolt of Virginia slaves led by an educated Negro minister who was dedicated to the destruction of the white man. The novel won the 1968 Pulitzer prize. Styron was born in Newport News, Va.                                ROBERT A. CORRIGAN

**STYX,** *stiks*, was a dark and dreary river in Greek and Roman mythology. The boatman Charon carried the souls of the dead across either the River Styx or the Acheron River to the Lower World. The gods took their most sacred oaths by the name of the River Styx.

The kingdom of Pluto was on the other side of the Styx. After Pluto judged the dead souls, they were sent either to the happy Elysian Fields or to the dismal valley of Tartarus. A high waterfall in Arcadia, an ancient Greek state, also was called the Styx. People believed its waters were poisonous and that the entrance to the Lower World lay behind it.                                PADRAIC COLUM

See also CHARON; ELYSIAN FIELDS; TARTARUS; MYTHOLOGY (picture: Arriving in the Underworld).

**SUÁREZ,** *SWAH rayth*, **FRANCISCO** (1548-1617), was a great Spanish theologian, and a founder of the philosophy of international law. In his famous treatise *On Laws*, he attacked the theory of the divine right of kings, and insisted on the necessity of the consent of the people in a just political order. Suárez saw that the medieval idea of a Christian empire was no longer possible with the emergence of self-governing national monarchies. Suárez was born in Granada. He became a Jesuit in 1564.                   JAMES A. CORBETT and FULTON J. SHEEN

**SUBCLAVIAN ARTERY.** See ARTERY (Principal Arteries); BLOOD (color picture).

**SUBCONSCIOUS** is a term used to describe mental processes such as thoughts, ideas, and feelings that go on in a person's mind without his being aware of them. Psychiatrists, psychoanalysts, and psychologists generally use the term *unconscious* to mean the same thing that most nonmedical persons mean by *subconscious*. Other words that once had the same meaning include *coconscious* and *paraconscious*.

The existence of mental processes that are active in the mind without being conscious was first studied scientifically by the French neurologist Jean Charcot and his pupils in the 1800's. They studied the unconscious by means of hypnosis (see HYPNOTISM). Soon after, doctors realized many mentally ill persons, such as those with hysteria, were influenced by unconscious thoughts and feelings (see HYSTERIA; MENTAL ILLNESS).

The doctor who first realized clearly the importance of unconscious thoughts and feelings in human psychology was Sigmund Freud of Austria. He developed the method of *psychoanalysis* for treating mentally ill patients (see PSYCHOANALYSIS). This method also serves as a way of learning what goes on unconsciously in a patient's mind. By using psychoanalysis, Freud was able to prove that unconscious thoughts and feelings not only produce the symptoms of many types of mental illness, but that they are also of basic importance in the way the minds of normal people work. This knowledge has enabled doctors to make great advances in the treatment of the mentally ill. Freud compared the mind to an iceberg. An iceberg floats with seven-eighths of it below the water and one-eighth of it above the surface. In the same way, the mind is seven-eighths unconscious, and only one-eighth conscious.                                CHARLES BRENNER

**Related Articles** in WORLD BOOK include:

| | | |
|---|---|---|
| Dream | Nightmare | Sleepwalking |
| Freud, Sigmund | Phobia | Subliminal |
| Neurosis | Psychotherapy | |

**SUBINFEUDATION.** See FEUDALISM (Knighthood Under Feudalism).

**SUBJECT.** See CITIZENSHIP (Modern Times).

**SUBJECT,** in grammar. See SENTENCE (Parts).

**SUBJUNCTIVE MOOD.** See MOOD.

**SUBLETTE,** *SUB let*, **WILLIAM LEWIS** (1799?-1845), was an American fur trader and merchant. He was born in Lincoln County, Kentucky, but grew up in St. Charles, Mo. He left Missouri in 1822 to become a trapper. He and his two partners were successful, and in 1831 their fantastic catch brought $170,000. Sublette next operated trading posts on the Platte and Upper Missouri rivers. He helped open the Oregon Trail by using wagons in the Rocky Mountains, and by finding a shortcut, *Sublette's Cutoff*.                                HOWARD R. LAMAR

**SUBLIMATION,** *SUB luh MAY shun*, is the process by which a solid substance changes into a gas, or vapor, without first becoming a liquid. There are a few substances, such as iodine, arsenic, camphor, and dry ice, which change into a gas without first melting. These substances are said to *sublime*. The most familiar example of sublimation can occur when wet clothes are hung out on the line on a winter day when the temperature is below freezing. The water on the clothes freezes and then evaporates into vapor without melting. Solid iodine will change into a vapor when it is warmed without becoming a liquid. Then, when the vapor is cooled, the iodine will change back into crystals. This change of a vapor back into a solid also is part of sublimation.

Sublimation is used in industry to purify substances. When a solid changes directly into a vapor, only the pure substance evaporates and the impurities remain. Pure sulfur (called *flowers of sulfur*), benzoin, and sal ammoniac are made by this process.                                RALPH G. OWENS

See also EVAPORATION; VAPOR.

**SUBLIME PORTE.** See TURKEY (The Ottoman Empire).

**SUBLIMINAL,** *sub LIHM ih nul*, refers to stimuli that are so weak or last so short a time that a person is not aware of them. Such stimuli are said to be *subliminal* (below the threshold of consciousness). The consciousness threshold varies from person to person and from time to time, even in the same person. Psychologists have been trying to determine whether subliminal stimuli can influence people, perhaps through the unconscious. Some use has been made of such subliminal stimuli in advertising.                                RUSSELL M. CHURCH

**Ballistic-Missile Subs** such as the U.S.S. George Washington can fire long-range ballistic missiles at distant shore targets from under the surface of the sea.

Electric Boat Div., General Dynamics

**SUBMARINE,** *SUB* muh REEN, first achieved widespread use as a weapon of war during World War I. Almost immediately, it proved its worth as a vessel that could hide beneath the surface of the sea and attack enemy warships and merchant ships. Submarines played an even greater role during World War II. The United States Navy estimates that submarines are responsible for three-fourths of all damage inflicted on ships at sea during wartime. During World War II, U.S. Navy submarines accounted for two of every three large Japanese merchant ships sunk and about one of every three Japanese warships.

Submarines are becoming even more important. With nuclear power, they can cruise underwater for almost indefinite periods. Some naval authorities believe that ballistic missile submarines will be the most important strategic force in an all-out nuclear war.

### What a Submarine Is

A submarine is a ship designed and built to operate under water. Its shape is quite different from that of a surface ship. Most submarines are shaped much like a cigar, with tapered ends and an almost round body. They have propellers and steering gear at one end, and diving planes near the other. Many submarines have a tall *conning tower* from which the ship is navigated when it is on the surface. The conning tower also contains the periscope for observing the surface when the submarine is submerged. Many recent submarines have a tall streamlined *sail* instead of a conning tower. The sail contains the submarine's bridge and navigation room, and is used both on and under the surface.

The U.S. Navy has developed a "new look" in submarines, with a rounded, fish-shaped body and a blunt, round nose. These submarines create less water-resistance than surface ships, and can go faster under water.

Every submarine has a double *hull* (shell) with a space in between for air or water. The inner hull must be extremely strong in order to withstand the great pressure of water when it is below the surface. This pressure reaches 88.9 pounds per square inch of hull surface at a depth of 200 feet. The space between the hulls fills with water, so the outer hull does not have to withstand such pressure, because it is surrounded by water.

**Power.** Prior to nuclear power, all submarines had diesel or gasoline engines for surface operations, and electric motors for underwater operations. They had to use the electric motors under water, because electric motors do not require air in order to operate. They used electric batteries to run their motors, and had to spend much of their time on the surface, recharging the batteries. They could travel about 20 knots on the surface, but only about 10 knots submerged.

German submarines used the *snorkel*, a long breathing tube, to provide air for the engines under water. The intake and exhaust valves are contained in a device that takes in a constant supply of air. R. J. J. Wichers of The Netherlands developed the snorkel. Snorkel-equipped submarines could stay under longer, and move faster, than regular submarines.

Atomic power gives submarines far greater possibilities for operations under water. Nuclear power plants do not need oxygen to work, so submarines can stay under water for an almost unlimited time. And nuclear power can produce far greater speeds than conventional power. Nuclear-powered submarines have broken all earlier records for speed, endurance, and time submerged. See ATOMIC ENERGY (Uses).

**Purposes.** Submarines serve several basic purposes. The most common use in World Wars I and II was to submerge and attack warships and merchant ships on the surface. With the development of ballistic missiles, the navy worked on submarines that could fire weapons with atomic warheads at targets as much as 1,500 miles

## SUBMARINE

away. And, with the growing threat of enemy submarines, navy planners worked on submarines designed to attack and destroy enemy submarines under water.

Submarines have also been used for many other kinds of work. They can lay mines, land small groups of men for work ashore, pick them up, pick up survivors, and act as sentries to guard shipping lanes.

### How a Submarine Operates

**On the Surface,** a submarine behaves much like any other ship. It has a rudder at the stern, and can be handled like other surface ships. But, to submerge, the submarine uses *ballast tanks* which can be filled with water or emptied, causing the submarine to submerge or surface. When a submarine is in proper readiness for diving from the surface, the total volume of the main ballast tanks that can be flooded exactly equals the unsubmerged volume of the submarine above the waterline. This condition is called *diving trim*. Submarine officers must constantly check the everyday changes in weight that result from using fuel, ammunition, and food, in order to vary the water ballast necessary to keep the ship in diving trim.

**Diving,** the submarine takes water into its ballast tanks by releasing the air pressure that kept the water out. If it fills only the main ballast tanks, it will soon reach a condition of *neutral buoyancy* and hover just below the surface. To submerge more quickly and to go deeper, the diving control officer also floods the *negative tank*. The water in this tank gives the submarine enough added weight to sink to the desired depth. Officers also control the diving planes to set the angle at which the submarine will sink. When the submarine reaches the desired depth, the diving control officer blows the water out of the negative tank with air pressure and resets the diving planes, and the ship levels off. Most navy submarines can dive to a depth of 60 feet in this way in about 30 seconds.

**Submerged,** a conventional submarine switches to its battery-driven electric motors. Nuclear-powered submarines continue to use their normal engines. From *periscope depth*, the ships officers can watch activity on the surface with the reflecting mirrors of the periscope. By adjusting its diving planes, the submarine can move up or down in the water. To dive much deeper, it must again flood the negative tank until it reaches the new depth, and again blow the tank. *Trim tanks* at each end of the ship, and others on each side, help keep the submarine on an even keel.

**Surfacing,** the submarine sets its diving planes to rise to the surface and blows all the water from its ballast tanks. The diving control officer can regulate the speed and angle of the ship's rise by varying the

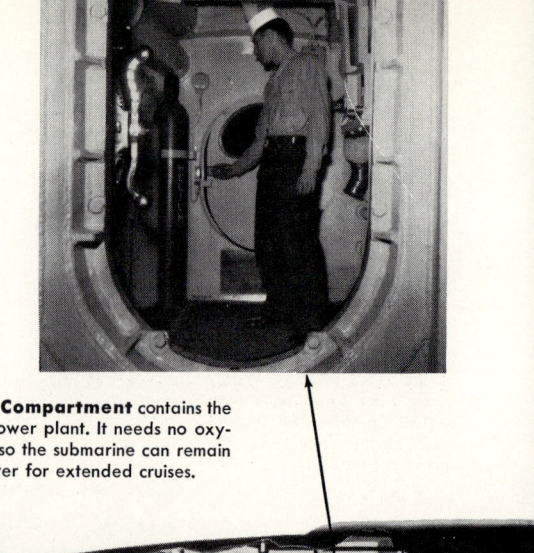

**Reactor Compartment** contains the nuclear power plant. It needs no oxygen, and so the submarine can remain under water for extended cruises.

**Life on a Nuclear Submarine,** such as the *George Washington,* a fleet ballistic-missile submarine, is shown in pictures taken aboard the *Nautilus, Skate,* and *Seawolf.*

## HOW SUBMARINES DEVELOPED

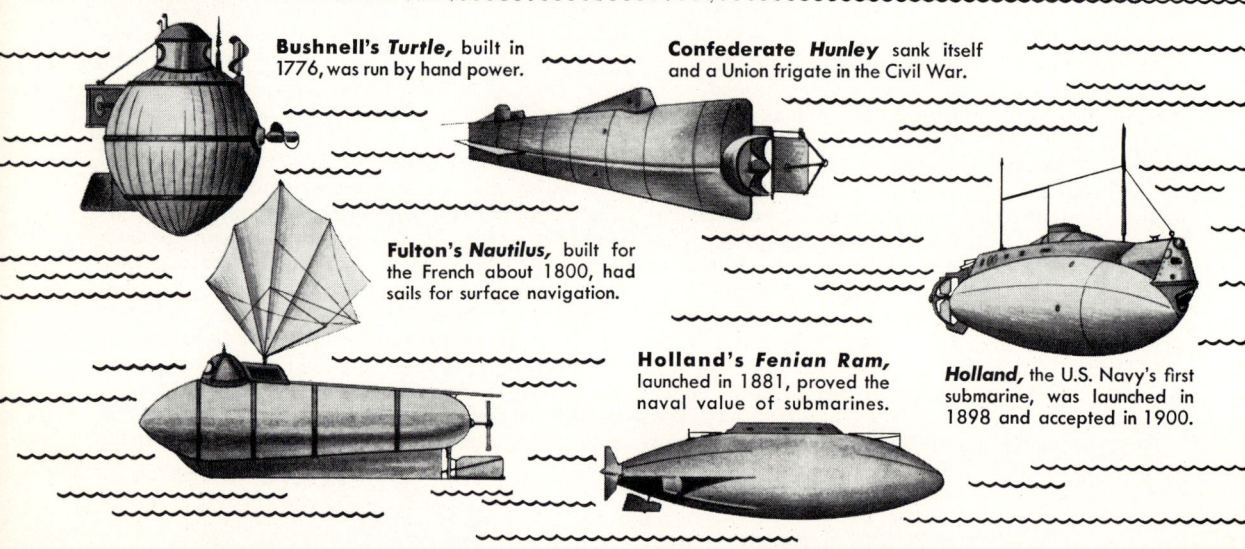

**Bushnell's *Turtle,*** built in 1776, was run by hand power.

**Confederate *Hunley*** sank itself and a Union frigate in the Civil War.

**Fulton's *Nautilus,*** built for the French about 1800, had sails for surface navigation.

**Holland's *Fenian Ram,*** launched in 1881, proved the naval value of submarines.

**Holland,** the U.S. Navy's first submarine, was launched in 1898 and accepted in 1900.

**In the Conning Tower,** the gunnery officer searches for potential targets on the surface with the periscope.

**Diving Control Center** gauges air and water pressure in the submersion tanks that give the submarine buoyancy.

**Crew's Quarters** may seem cramped, but they are more comfortable than similar quarters on other submarines.

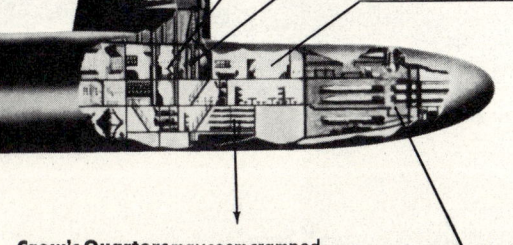

**Officers' Wardroom** shows some of the comforts of sailing aboard a nuclear submarine. More than 100 officers and men live in fairly close quarters.

**Torpedo Tubes** are the guns of most submarines. *George Washington* and other new submarines fire ballistic missiles.

Wide World; Electric Boat Div., General Dynamics

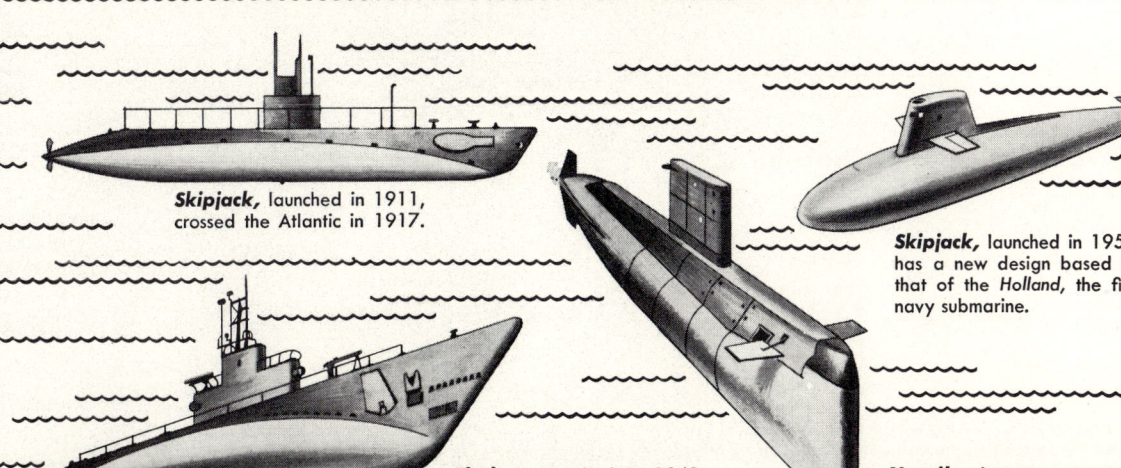

*Skipjack,* launched in 1911, crossed the Atlantic in 1917.

*Flasher,* launched in 1943, was a typical fleet submarine.

*Skipjack,* launched in 1958, has a new design based on that of the *Holland,* the first navy submarine.

*Nautilus* began operating with nuclear power in 1955.

**The Nuclear-Powered *Triton* Was the First Submarine to Go Around the World Without Surfacing.**

angle of the diving planes and the pressure used to blow the main ballast tanks. Back on the surface, the submarine will continue to float as long as air pressure keeps water out of the tanks.

### Life Aboard a Submarine

Life on a submarine is not a pleasure cruise. Even on nuclear-powered ships, there is little room for living quarters. When they must conserve oxygen, the men lie on their bunks, sleeping, reading, or playing cards, and moving as little as possible.

To offset these unpleasant factors, submarine sailors are given the finest possible food, much time off, and extra pay. Each submarine equipped with Polaris missiles has a *blue* crew and a *gold* crew of over 100 men each. They take turns on the ship so it can stay at sea almost all the time. All men on submarines are volunteers. They develop a feeling for their ship and crew that enables them to take many difficulties in stride.

In wartime, submarine duty is extremely dangerous, as well as hard. The crew keeps constant watch on the movements of other ships, and listens with sonar for the approach of potential enemies.

### Development of the Submarine

**Early Efforts.** The first submarine was a leather-covered rowboat which Cornelius van Drebbel, a Dutch scientist, demonstrated in England about 1620. But little was done with submarines until the Revolutionary War in America. David Bushnell (1742?-1824) built the *Turtle*, a one-man ship that submerged when he filled ballast tanks with water. The *Turtle* made an unsuccessful attack on a British man-of-war in New York harbor —the first recorded submarine attack on a warship.

Robert Fulton built the *Nautilus*, a copper-covered submarine 21 feet long, in 1800. Fulton tried to interest the French in his craft. They were not impressed, even though Fulton blew up a sloop in a demonstration.

During the Civil War, the Confederate *Hunley* made the world's first successful attack on a warship. In 1864,

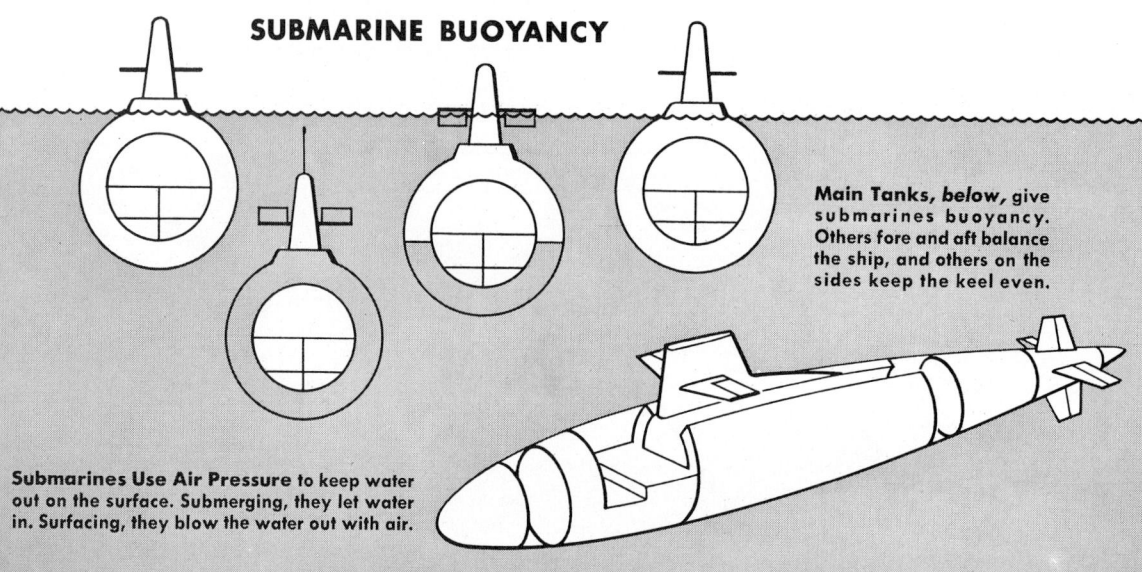

**SUBMARINE BUOYANCY**

**Main Tanks, *below*,** give submarines buoyancy. Others fore and aft balance the ship, and others on the sides keep the keel even.

**Submarines Use Air Pressure** to keep water out on the surface. Submerging, they let water in. Surfacing, they blow the water out with air.

the *Hunley* rammed the Federal corvette *Housatonic* in Charleston harbor. A torpedo on the *Hunley's* spar exploded, sinking both ships. Experiments continued after the war, spurred by the development of a self-propelled torpedo in the late 1860's. Two designers concentrated on submarines. Simon Lake (1866-1945) worked out the idea of submerging by negative buoyancy, which is used today. Lake also built wheels on one submarine for travel on the ocean floor. John P. Holland experimented in other directions, and won a U.S. Navy contract in the late 1890's.

Holland's submarine, launched in 1898, was commissioned the U.S.S. *Holland* in 1900—the navy's first submarine. It was 53 feet long and displaced 75 tons. It used a gasoline engine on the surface and an electric motor when submerged, and could speed at 7 knots on the surface. It had a torpedo tube, but no periscope.

**During World War I,** German submarines, called *Unterseebooten* or U-boats, quickly demonstrated the importance of undersea warfare. One U-boat sank three British cruisers in one engagement. The Germans soon began enforcing their blockade of Great Britain with U-boat attacks on merchant ships and passenger liners. Public feeling ran high against the Germans when they torpedoed the British *Lusitania* in the Atlantic in May, 1915. The United States entered the war partly because of Germany's unrestricted submarine warfare.

**In World War II,** all the warring nations used submarine fleets. The Germans again used submarines to try to enforce their naval blockade of Great Britain. They developed *wolf packs*, teams of from 2 to 40 submarines operating together, to attack convoys in the North Atlantic Ocean. Snorkel-equipped German submarines became a menace. The Allied nations developed new convoy techniques to meet the submarine challenge. They also speeded the construction of *subchasers*, or fast escort vessels. The development of radar and sonar provided new ways of locating submarines.

The Japanese used midget submarines and extra-large submarines. The United States Navy worked on fleet submarines, larger and more powerful than earlier American undersea craft. Some American submarines made history with their exploits. The U.S.S. *Barb* is generally credited with firing the most valuable six-torpedo salvo in submarine history. The torpedoes sank a Japanese escort carrier and a tanker. The *Barb* later became the first submarine to fire rockets at targets ashore.

**New Developments.** After World War II, designers worked on craft that could move faster and stay under water longer. The British launched a submarine powered with hydrogen peroxide, the *Explorer*, in 1954.

In the United States, a joint project of the navy and the Atomic Energy Commission produced the *Nautilus*, the world's first nuclear-powered warship, in 1955. The *Nautilus* made history by sailing under the North Pole in 1958. The navy tested a new fish-shaped hull in the *Albacore*, and later adopted it for the nuclear submarine *Skipjack*.

In 1960, the *Triton*, powered by twin nuclear plants, traveled around the world under water. It covered 41,500 miles in 84 days. The nuclear submarine *Seadragon* made the first underwater trip through the Northwest Passage the same year. It traveled from the Atlantic to the Pacific Ocean through the Canadian Archipelago.

During the 1960's, the U.S. Navy developed and put on duty several classes of nuclear-powered submarines. These classes include the *Lafayette, Ethan Allen, George Washington,* and *Thresher*. The United States planned for a fleet of more than 100 nuclear submarines by the early 1970's. Over 40 of these would carry *Polaris* ballistic missiles, which can be fired from under water.

The United States has more nuclear-powered submarines than any other nation, but Russia has the largest submarine fleet. By the late 1960's, Russia had about 380 submarines of all types, compared to about 210 for the United States.   RAYMOND V. B. BLACKMAN

**Related Articles** in WORLD BOOK include:
| | |
|---|---|
| Convoy | Rickover, Hyman G. |
| Depth Charge | Sonar |
| Holland, John P. | Torpedo |
| Inertial Guidance | World War I (The Submarine |
| Mine Layer | Menace; picture) |
| New London Naval Submarine Base | World War II (The Battle of the Atlantic) |
| Periscope | |

**SUBMARINE MINE.** See MINE, MILITARY.

**SUBMARINO.** See DIVING, UNDERWATER (Diving in Oceanographic Submarines).

**SUBPOENA,** *sub PE nuh*, is a legal notice to appear and give testimony in court. The name comes from two Latin words, *sub*, which means *under*, and *poena*, which means *penalty*. A person who receives a subpoena must obey the command *under penalty* of being held in contempt of court (see CONTEMPT). The *subpoena duces tecum* (Latin for *bring with you under penalty*) requires a person to bring into court with him certain specified things, such as papers, books, financial records, or other documents. See also WITNESS.   THOMAS A. COWAN

**SUBSET.** See SET THEORY.

**SUBSIDY,** *SUB suh dih*, is a money payment or other form of aid which the government gives to a person or organization. Its purpose is to encourage some needed activity by furnishing funds, free land, or legal rights that might otherwise be lacking.

In the 1800's, the United States government gave large tracts of land to the railroads on the condition that they would build lines across the continent. Altogether, the railroads received nearly 160,000,000 acres of land in this way. The government also granted subsidies to telegraph and cable companies. In the 1920's, the government granted subsidies to ship companies. It gave them generous mail-carrying contracts and allowed them to buy government-owned ships at a fraction of their actual cost. Government air-mail contracts have also aided the airlines since the 1920's.

The government has granted farm subsidies to farmers and food processors for the production of certain foods. It adopted this measure to stimulate production and to lower the market price of these foods. Subsidies may be of great benefit if the government grants them wisely. Food prices would have risen much more rapidly than they did during World War II if farmers had not been receiving subsidies. But subsidies can be abused, if politicians make them too generous in order to gain votes from the farmers.   ROBERT D. PATTON

See also AGRICULTURE (Surpluses); PARITY.

**SUBSOIL.** See SOIL (Depth).

# SUBTRACTION

H. Armstrong Roberts

**SUBTRACTION** is a way of taking away a number of things from a larger number. You take them away to find how many things are left. Only *like things* can be subtracted. That is, you cannot subtract apples from pencils.

Suppose you have a set of 8 oranges.

Suppose you want to take away a set of 5 oranges.

You find that you have 3 oranges left.

### Learning To Subtract

A question such as "3 from 6 is how many?" is a subtraction problem. To find out how many things are left in a subtraction problem, you can *count* or find the answer by *thinking*.

**Subtraction by Counting.** Here are two groups of chocolate cupcakes.

---- **SUBTRACTION TERMS** ----

**Borrow** in subtraction means to change a 10 in the minuend into 1's, to change a 100 into 10's, or to change a 1,000 into 100's, and so on.

**Difference.** In 12−7=5, the number 5 is the difference. It means that 12 and 7 are being compared.

**Minuend.** In 12−7=5, the number 12 is the minuend.

**Minus** in subtraction means *less* or *take away*. For example, 12 *minus* 7 is 5.

**Remainder.** In 12−7=5, the number 5 is the remainder. It is the answer to the subtraction problem.

**Subtraction Fact** is a basic statement in subtraction. For example, 16−9=7 and 4−3=1 are two subtraction facts.

**Subtrahend.** In 12−7=5, the number taken away (7) is the subtrahend.

How many cupcakes are there in the first group? Count them. There are 6 cupcakes in the first group. Mary took 3 cupcakes from the second group. How many cupcakes are left in the second group? Count them. There are 3 cupcakes left. You counted to find how many cupcakes are left if you take 3 from 6. You discovered that 3 taken from 6 leaves 3.

**Subtraction by Thinking.** Tommy has 5 pennies.

He wants to spend 2 pennies for a pencil. How many pennies will Tommy have left? Cover 2 pennies in the picture. You should be able to tell how many pennies are left by just looking at the picture, without counting. You should learn to *think* "2 from 5 leaves 3." This article will show you the facts you need to know to subtract by thinking. Thinking the answer is a quicker way of subtracting than counting.

You can learn to think the answer to a subtraction problem from what you know about addition. For example, you know that 3 and 2 are 5. This means that if you take 2 from 5, you have 3. You can practice by writing the addition and subtraction facts in groups of four.

3 and 4 are 7    4 from 7 leaves 3
4 and 3 are 7    3 from 7 leaves 4

**Subtraction Questions.** Subtraction tells you how many things are left when you take away one set of things from another. It also lets you *compare* two sets of things. Suppose Mary has 5 balloons and Sue has 3 balloons.

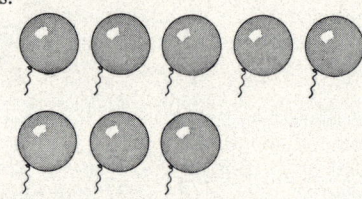

To compare the two sets of balloons, you must find the *difference* between the two sets. You can find the difference by subtracting. When you subtract 3 from 5, you

752

discover that the difference between the two sets is 2 balloons, or 2.

You can also use subtraction to find out how many more things are needed. Suppose John needs 12 pennies. He has 5 pennies. How many more pennies does he need?

When you subtract 5 from 12, you discover that John needs 7 more pennies to make 12.

Subtraction can tell you (1) how many things are left, (2) what the difference is, and (3) how many more things are needed.

**Writing Subtraction.** It is best to write your subtraction problems and their answers. This gives you a record of your thinking.

You can make a record with pictures.

The picture shows that 3 taken from 5 leaves 2.
You can write this in numbers and words.

### 3 from 5 leaves 2

But you must learn to write with numbers and signs.

$$5-3=2$$

The $-$ sign means to subtract or take away. So $5-3$ means "3 taken from 5." We call the $-$ sign the *minus sign*, and read $5-3$ as "5 minus 3." The $=$ sign means that the sets on one side of the $=$ sign are *equal* to the sets on the other side. Here is how it works:

There is another way to use numerals and signs.

$$\begin{array}{r} 5 \\ -3 \\ \hline 2 \end{array}$$

Most people use this form when working out problems in subtraction.

Each part of a subtraction problem has a name. When we are subtracting to find out how many things are left, we call the answer the *remainder*. When we are subtracting to compare two groups or to find how many more things are needed, we call the answer the *difference*. We call the number being taken away or subtracted the *subtrahend*. The number from which the subtrahend is taken is called the *minuend*.

$$\begin{array}{r} 5 \\ -3 \\ \hline 2 \end{array}$$ ← Minuend
← Subtrahend
← Remainder or Difference

# SUBTRACTION

**Subtraction Facts.** By subtracting one group from another, you discover that $8-5=3$, $6-3=3$, and $12-5=7$. We call these *subtraction facts*.

Each subtraction fact consists of a minuend, a subtrahend, and a remainder, or difference. There are 81 subtraction facts. You can discover each one of them for yourself by counting and taking away one set of things from another. For example, you can practice by crossing off squares as you have seen crossing off done in an earlier example.

### The 81 Subtraction Facts

| 2 | 3 | 4 | 5 | 6 | 7 | 8 | 9 | 10 |
|---|---|---|---|---|---|---|---|---|
| −1 | −1 | −1 | −1 | −1 | −1 | −1 | −1 | −1 |
| 1 | 2 | 3 | 4 | 5 | 6 | 7 | 8 | 9 |

| 3 | 4 | 5 | 6 | 7 | 8 | 9 | 10 | 11 |
|---|---|---|---|---|---|---|---|---|
| −2 | −2 | −2 | −2 | −2 | −2 | −2 | −2 | −2 |
| 1 | 2 | 3 | 4 | 5 | 6 | 7 | 8 | 9 |

| 4 | 5 | 6 | 7 | 8 | 9 | 10 | 11 | 12 |
|---|---|---|---|---|---|---|---|---|
| −3 | −3 | −3 | −3 | −3 | −3 | −3 | −3 | −3 |
| 1 | 2 | 3 | 4 | 5 | 6 | 7 | 8 | 9 |

| 5 | 6 | 7 | 8 | 9 | 10 | 11 | 12 | 13 |
|---|---|---|---|---|---|---|---|---|
| −4 | −4 | −4 | −4 | −4 | −4 | −4 | −4 | −4 |
| 1 | 2 | 3 | 4 | 5 | 6 | 7 | 8 | 9 |

| 6 | 7 | 8 | 9 | 10 | 11 | 12 | 13 | 14 |
|---|---|---|---|---|---|---|---|---|
| −5 | −5 | −5 | −5 | −5 | −5 | −5 | −5 | −5 |
| 1 | 2 | 3 | 4 | 5 | 6 | 7 | 8 | 9 |

| 7 | 8 | 9 | 10 | 11 | 12 | 13 | 14 | 15 |
|---|---|---|---|---|---|---|---|---|
| −6 | −6 | −6 | −6 | −6 | −6 | −6 | −6 | −6 |
| 1 | 2 | 3 | 4 | 5 | 6 | 7 | 8 | 9 |

| 8 | 9 | 10 | 11 | 12 | 13 | 14 | 15 | 16 |
|---|---|---|---|---|---|---|---|---|
| −7 | −7 | −7 | −7 | −7 | −7 | −7 | −7 | −7 |
| 1 | 2 | 3 | 4 | 5 | 6 | 7 | 8 | 9 |

| 9 | 10 | 11 | 12 | 13 | 14 | 15 | 16 | 17 |
|---|---|---|---|---|---|---|---|---|
| −8 | −8 | −8 | −8 | −8 | −8 | −8 | −8 | −8 |
| 1 | 2 | 3 | 4 | 5 | 6 | 7 | 8 | 9 |

| 10 | 11 | 12 | 13 | 14 | 15 | 16 | 17 | 18 |
|---|---|---|---|---|---|---|---|---|
| −9 | −9 | −9 | −9 | −9 | −9 | −9 | −9 | −9 |
| 1 | 2 | 3 | 4 | 5 | 6 | 7 | 8 | 9 |

It is best to learn the subtraction facts so that you can recall them without stopping to work them out. You can use them to solve problems right away.

To learn the harder facts, it is sometimes useful to *regroup*. For example, many persons find it easier to subtract numbers from 10. Suppose you wanted to solve the problem $14-7$. You know that 14 is the same as one 10 and four 1's. So you could regroup it like this.

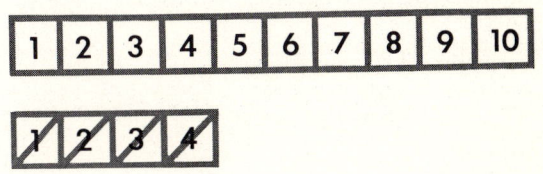

## SUBTRACTION

First, you can take away 4. You know that 7−4=3, so you must still take away 3. Subtracting 10−3 is easy.

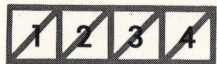

You can see that 10−3=7. So 14−7=7.

You can probably invent other ways to help you learn the subtraction facts.

### Subtracting Larger Numbers

Subtracting larger numbers is not difficult, if you know the subtraction facts and understand the number system.

**Subtracting 10's and 100's.** Suppose you have 5 dimes. This is the same as 50¢. Suppose you want to spend 3 dimes on a book. This is the same as 30¢. How much money will you have left? The problem is 5 dimes−3 dimes or 50¢−30¢. You can find the answer by counting.

You can also find the answer by using the subtraction facts and thinking.

```
  5 dimes        50¢
 −3 dimes       −30¢
  2 dimes        20¢
```

If you know that 5−3=2, you can see that 3 dimes taken from 5 dimes leaves 2 dimes. A dime is 10¢, so you can see that 50−30=20. The subtraction fact 5−3=2 helps you find the answer. *You subtract 10's the same way that you subtract 1's. But you must write the remainder in the 10's place.* And you must remember to write in a zero to show that the remainder is 10's, not 1's.

Subtracting 100's is done in the same way. Suppose you had to subtract 3 dollars from 5 dollars.

```
  5 dollars      500¢        500
 −3 dollars     −300¢       −300
  2 dollars      200¢        200
```

You subtract 100's (and 1,000's and so on) the same way that you subtract 1's and 10's. Once again, you can see how the subtraction fact helps you find the answer to the subtraction example.

**Subtracting 10's and 1's.** Tom had 45 tickets to sell. He sold 23 of them. How many tickets should he have left? That is, what is 45−23? We call numbers such as 45 and 23 *two-place* numbers, because 45 has two places, four 10's and five 1's; and 23 has two places, two 10's and three 1's.

```
 4 tens and 5 ones       45
−2 tens and 3 ones      −23
 2 tens and 2 ones       22
```

To subtract one two-place number from another, you begin by subtracting the 1's: 5−3=2. Write the 2 in the 1's place in the remainder.

```
 45
−23
  2
```

Next, subtract the 10's: 4−2=2. Remember that the 4−2 stands for 10's, not 1's. Write the 2 in the 10's place in the remainder.

```
 45
−23
 22
```

So Tom should have 22 tickets left.

Here is an example of subtracting *three-place numbers*.

```
 647
−123
 524
```

First, subtract the 1's: 7−3=4. Write the 4 in the 1's place of the remainder. Next, subtract the 10's: 4−2=2. Write the 2 in the 10's place in the remainder. Next, subtract the 100's: 6−1=5. Write the 5 in the 100's place in the answer. Subtracting two- and three-place numbers is easy, but you must remember two things. You must subtract the 1's, 10's, 100's, 1,000's, and so on, *in that order.* Always begin at the right—in the 1's place—and work to the left. Second, you must write your work carefully, so that the numbers of the remainders are in the proper places.

**How to Borrow.** When you subtract larger numbers, you often cannot solve a problem unless you know how to *borrow*. For instance, look at the example 62−27. How can you subtract seven 1's from two 1's? Borrowing helps solve this kind of example.

To understand borrowing, you must follow an example step by step. In the example 62−27, the first step is to write the numbers as 10's and 1's.

```
  62      →    6 tens 2 ones
 −27           −2 tens 7 ones
```

You cannot subtract seven 1's from two 1's. *But you can take one of the 10's in the minuend and change it into 1's.* Now you can solve the problem.

```
 6 tens 2 ones    5 tens 10+2 ones    5 tens 12 ones
−2 tens 7 ones   −2 tens    7 ones   −2 tens  7 ones
                                      3 tens  5 ones
```

So 62−27=35. There were too many 1's in the subtrahend to subtract. You "borrowed," or changed a 10 from the 10's part of the minuend into the 1's. This is what borrowing means. You can also borrow 100's, 1,000's, and so on, in solving problems.

You do not have to write out a problem every time you borrow. You can *think* the steps and write in little numbers as a guide. Here is the same example:

```
 62
−27
```

First, you study the example. "I cannot take 7 from 2," you think, "so I must change a 10 to 1's." You draw a

754

line through the 6 in the minuend and write a 5 above it. This means that there are now five 10's in the 10's place instead of six. Next, you write a little 1 just above and to the left of the 2. This means that there are now twelve 1's, instead of two.

$$\begin{array}{r}\overset{5}{\cancel{6}}\overset{1}{2}\\-27\\\hline\end{array}$$

Now you can do the subtraction. "Seven 1's from twelve 1's leave 5," you think, and write a 5 in the 1's place of the remainder. "Two 10's from five 10's leave 3," you think, and write a 3 in the 10's place of the remainder. This completes the example.

$$\begin{array}{r}\overset{5}{\cancel{6}}\overset{1}{2}\\-27\\\hline 35\end{array}$$

The same method of "borrowing" a 10 can be used for 100's and 1,000's.

$$\begin{array}{r}628\\-361\\\hline 7\end{array}$$

First, you subtract one 1 from eight 1's, and write a 7 in the 1's place of the remainder. But you see that you cannot subtract six 10's from two 10's. You must borrow a 100, or ten 10's, from the six 100's in the minuend.

$$\begin{array}{r}\overset{5}{\cancel{6}}\overset{1}{2}8\\-361\\\hline 7\end{array}$$

You draw a line through the 6 in the minuend and write a 5 above it. This means that there are now five 100's in the 100's place, instead of six. Next, you write in a little 1 just above and to the left of the 2. This means that there are now twelve 10's, instead of two. Now you can finish the subtraction. Six 10's from twelve 10's leaves six. You write a 6 in the 10's place of the remainder. Three 100's from five 100's leaves two. You write a 2 in the 100's place of the remainder.

$$\begin{array}{r}\overset{5}{\cancel{6}}\overset{1}{2}8\\-361\\\hline 267\end{array}$$

You use the same method for 1,000's. You borrow a 1,000 just as you borrowed a 10 or a 100.

### Checking Subtraction

You should always check your work in subtraction to make sure that you have done it correctly.

**Checking by Subtraction.** One way to check a subtraction problem is to subtract the remainder from the minuend.

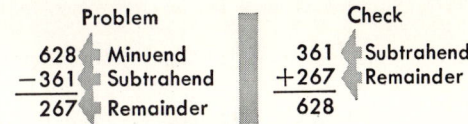

The new remainder should be the same as the old subtrahend. This checks your work.

**Checking by Addition.** A good way to check subtraction problems is by addition, because addition is the

## SUBTRACTION

opposite of subtraction. You add the subtrahend and the remainder.

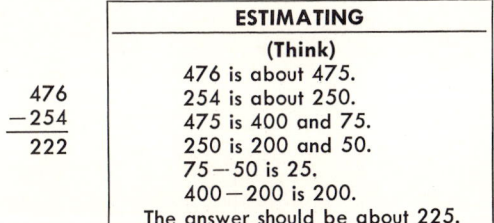

The sum of the addition should be the same as the old minuend in the subtraction problem.

**Estimating** helps you know if your answer is reasonable. Try to estimate the answer *before* you work the problem. Here is an example:

|  | ESTIMATING |
|---|---|
|  | (Think) |
| 476 | 476 is about 475. |
| −254 | 254 is about 250. |
| 222 | 475 is 400 and 75. |
|  | 250 is 200 and 50. |
|  | 75 − 50 is 25. |
|  | 400 − 200 is 200. |
|  | The answer should be about 225. |

This is almost the exact answer. You can estimate in larger numbers. For example, 476 is about 500, and 254 is about 250. Subtracting 500 − 250 gives you 250. This gives you a good idea of what the answer should be. Estimating the answer before you work a problem will save you time if you make a mistake, because you know about what the answer should be.

### Subtraction Rules To Remember

Here are six rules that will help you solve subtraction problems.

1. Remember what subtraction means. You can find the answers to subtraction problems by counting. But it is quicker and easier to *think* the answers.

2. Learning the 81 subtraction facts will help you think the answers to subtraction problems quickly.

3. Subtraction is the opposite of addition. Because of this, addition will help you learn the subtraction facts and check problems.

4. The subtraction facts help you subtract larger numbers to solve problems.

5. You can only subtract quantities of the same kind. That is, you must subtract 1's from 1's and 10's from 10's.

6. Subtraction answers three kinds of questions: how many are left, what is the difference, and how many more are needed.

### Other Ways To Subtract

There are several ways of thinking out a subtraction problem. The method we have used is called the "*take-away-borrow*" method. Here is another example:

$$\begin{array}{r}72\\-28\\\hline\end{array} \Rightarrow \begin{array}{r}\overset{6}{\cancel{7}}\overset{1}{2}\\-28\\\hline 4\end{array} \Rightarrow \begin{array}{r}\overset{6}{\cancel{7}}\overset{1}{2}\\-28\\\hline 44\end{array}$$

First, you see that you cannot take eight 1's from two 1's. You borrow a 10, making the minuend six 10's and twelve 1's. Then you subtract eight 1's from twelve

755

# SUBTRACTION

1's: 12−8=4. You write the 4 in the 1's place in the answer. Next you subtract two 10's from six 10's: 6−2=4. You write the 4 in the 10's place in the answer.

Another method is called the *"addition-borrow" method*.

$$\begin{array}{r}72\\-28\\\hline\end{array} \Rightarrow \begin{array}{r}72\\-28\\\hline 4\end{array} \Rightarrow \begin{array}{r}72\\-28\\\hline 44\end{array}$$

The numbers are the same as in the "take-away-borrow" method, but the *thinking* is different. You see that you cannot take eight 1's from two 1's, and borrow a 10. Instead of subtracting eight 1's from twelve 1's, you think "what *added* to 8 makes 12?" You know that 8+4=12, so you write the 4 in the 1's place in the answer. Instead of subtracting two 10's from six 10's, you think "what *added* to 2 makes 6?" You know that 2+4=6, so you write the 4 in the 10's place in the answer.

A third method is called the *"addition-carry" method*.

$$\begin{array}{r}72\\-28\\\hline\end{array} \Rightarrow \begin{array}{r}\overset{\cdot}{7}2\\-28\\\hline 4\end{array} \Rightarrow \begin{array}{r}\overset{\cdot}{7}2\\-38\\\hline 44\end{array}$$

First, you see that you cannot take eight 1's from two 1's. Instead of borrowing, you add ten 1's to the two 1's: 2+10=12. Next, you think "what *added* to 8 makes 12?" You know that 8+4=12, so you write the 4 in the 1's place in the answer. Now you think "I added a 10 to the 1's, so I must subtract a 10 from the 10's." To do this, you change the two 10's in the subtrahend to three 10's. You think "what *added* to 3 makes 7?" You know that 3+4=7, so you write the 4 in the 10's place in the answer.

## Fun with Subtraction

Many games that can be played with the addition, multiplication, and division facts can be changed a little for the subtraction facts.

To play a game called *More or Less*, make a pack of 36 cards. Write the numbers from 1 to 18 separately on two sets of cards. This means that there are two cards for each number. Shuffle the cards and place the pile face down. The leader of the game takes the first card and holds it up for the players to see. Suppose it is 14. The first player takes a card from the pile and shows it. Suppose it is 6. He compares it with the 14 card and says "It is less." Then he must tell how much less. In this case, he would say "It is 8 less than 14." He must find the answer by thinking the subtraction. Suppose the next player turns up 17. He compares it with the first card. He must say "It is more. It is 3 more than 14." If a player gives the wrong answer, he is out of the game. When you have gone through the cards once, you can mix them up and go through the game again with new numbers.

CHARLOTTE JUNGE

**Related Articles** in WORLD BOOK include:

| Addition | Decimal | Fraction |
| Algebra (Subtraction) | Numeral System | Mathematics |
| Arithmetic | Division | Multiplication |

### Outline

**I. Learning To Subtract**
   A. Subtraction by Counting    D. Writing
   B. Subtraction by Thinking       Subtraction
   C. Subtraction Questions    E. Subtraction Facts

**II. Subtracting Larger Numbers**
   A. Subtracting 10's and 100's    C. How to Borrow
   B. Subtracting 10's and 1's

**III. Checking Subtraction**
   A. Checking by Subtraction    C. Estimating
   B. Checking by Addition

**IV. Subtraction Rules To Remember**
**V. Other Ways To Subtract**
**VI. Fun with Subtraction**

---

### PRACTICE SUBTRACTION EXAMPLES

1. 8 − 5 =
2. 7 − 4 =
3. 8 − 6 =
4. 18 − 5 =
5. 17 − 4 =
6. 18 − 6 =
7. 15 − 9 =
8. 15 − 7 =
9. 15 − 6 =
10. 7 − 5 =
11. 7 − 2 =
12. 9 − 6 =
13. 9 − 3 =
14. 14 − 8 =
15. 14 − 6 =

16. 5 −2
17. 50 −20
18. 8 −3
19. 80 −30
20. 12 −3
21. 120 −30
22. 8 −4
23. 80 −40
24. 6 −4
25. 9 −3
26. 90 −30
27. 7 −4
28. 70 −40
29. 84 −22
30. 95 −34
31. 67 −23
32. 628 −115
33. 843 −531
34. 6725 −3513
35. 52 −26
36. 83 −48
37. 65 −39
38. 625 −241
39. 729 −381
40. 90 −36
41. 923 −465
42. 307 −186
43. 503 −280
44. 700 −265
45. 900 −189

### ANSWERS TO THE PRACTICE EXAMPLES

1. 3
2. 3
3. 2
4. 13
5. 13
6. 12
7. 6
8. 8
9. 9
10. 2
11. 5
12. 3
13. 6
14. 6
15. 8
16. 3
17. 30
18. 5
19. 50
20. 9
21. 90
22. 4
23. 40
24. 2
25. 6
26. 60
27. 3
28. 30
29. 62
30. 61
31. 44
32. 513
33. 312
34. 3,212
35. 26
36. 35
37. 26
38. 384
39. 348
40. 54
41. 458
42. 121
43. 223
44. 435
45. 711

**SUBURB,** *SUB uhrb,* refers to a community located on the outskirts of a major city. *Suburbanites* (people who live in the suburbs) travel to the city to work, and for many recreational, business, and cultural activities. Suburban areas usually have a greater percentage of high income families, children, owner-occupied homes, and automobiles than the central cities do. Many suburbs, such as Palo Alto, Calif., are uncrowded residential areas. But other suburbs, such as Yonkers, N.Y., are crowded, and have large industrial areas.

Many suburbs have independent municipal governments. But some suburban areas are governed by suburban county governments. As the central cities have grown, they often surround the suburban areas. Some suburbs have been annexed by the central city in order to reduce the conflict of overlapping authority.

Since the 1900's, the most important population shift in the United States has been the steady flow of people from cities to surrounding suburbs. WILLIAM L. C. WHEATON

See also CITY; COMMUNITY; METROPOLITAN AREA.

**SUBVERSIVE ACTIVITY.** See UN-AMERICAN ACTIVITIES COMMITTEE.

**SUBWAY** is an underground railway. In New York City, London, Paris, and Moscow, the subway system is a great, complicated network of tunnels. London was the first city to have a subway, and now has seven systems that provide quick and cheap transportation to all parts of the city and suburbs. London subways are called *tubes*. Some are so far underground that passengers go down on elevators. The first subway built in London was operated by steam locomotives, and opened in 1863. The first deep-level tube was opened in 1890, and had electric locomotives. All subways since that time have been operated by electricity.

In Spain, Madrid opened a short subway in 1919, and Barcelona in 1924. The subway in Sydney, Australia, was completed in 1926. In South America, Buenos Aires has a subway dating from 1928. Moscow's subway was opened in 1935. Tokyo's system was opened in 1927, Toronto's in 1954, and Montreal's in 1966.

In the United States, New York City, Philadelphia, Boston, and Chicago have subway systems. Boston was the first American city to have a subway, opening its line of $1\frac{1}{2}$ miles in 1897. The subway in New York City is the largest in the world, and is probably the best example of passenger-subway construction. This system is so large that a person can travel from the New Jersey shore, under the city, beneath two rivers into Long Island, without once seeing daylight. The first sections of the subway were opened in 1904. Chicago's subway runs through 9 miles of tunnel. The first part was opened in 1943. A section was added in 1951, and another was scheduled for completion in 1969.

There are two types of subways. One is called the *open cut*. The construction crew tears out the streets, and builds the subways in deep ditches. If two lines are going to cross, the crew digs one roadbed deeper than the other so one line can pass under. They then lay pavement over the subway. The other form of subway, called a *tube*, is constructed by boring through the earth at the desired depth without disturbing the surface. This type of construction is for one or two tracks.

The tunnels of an open-cut subway are rectangular in form. The tunnels of the other subway are usually circular or semicircular in shape. New York City's subway is rectangular and London's is semicircular.

Subways must be built so that ventilation is good. Stale air is carried off through vents. Fresh air may be brought into the system by means of fans.

The cost of construction of a subway is very high. The New York City system cost between $2 million and $3 million a mile. FRANKLIN M. RECK

See also ELECTRIC RAILROAD; NEW YORK CITY (picture); TUNNEL.

**SUCCESSION, PRESIDENTIAL.** See PRESIDENTIAL SUCCESSION.

**SUCCESSION WARS.** Wars growing out of disputes over who should *succeed to* (inherit) a throne are called *succession wars*. Four important conflicts in European history are known by this name. They are the War of the Spanish Succession, the War of the Polish Succession, the War of the Austrian Succession, and the War of the Bavarian Succession.

**The War of the Spanish Succession** began in 1701 and lasted until 1714. Its American phase was known as Queen Anne's War (1702-1713).

Chicago Transit Authority

**The Chicago Subway** runs through a semicircular tunnel over most of its route. The Monroe station is one of 18 along the 9 miles of subway tunnel. Thousands ride the subway every day.

757

## SUCCESSION WARS

Charles II, king of Spain, had no children, and all Europe was interested in the question of who would be his successor. The laws governing succession were so involved, and the claims of the different heirs were so conflicting, that it is almost impossible to say who rightfully should have worn the Spanish crown.

When King Charles II died in Spain on November 1, 1700, he left a will which gave the crown to the French prince, Philip of Anjou. Philip's grandfather, Louis XIV of France, then proclaimed him king of Spain, and declared that the Pyrenees no longer separated the two kingdoms. Since French power was already feared in Europe, other countries were alarmed at the prospect that France might annex the Spanish Empire.

Almost immediately the Grand Alliance was formed by England, The Netherlands, Prussia, Austria, and most of the other states of the Holy Roman Empire. This alliance sought to prevent Philip of Anjou from becoming king of Spain, and to put the Archduke Charles of Austria on the throne instead. War broke out between France and the Grand Alliance. The French were defeated decisively in the battles of Blenheim, Ramillies, Oudenarde, and Malplaquet. The English general, the Duke of Marlborough, and the imperial general, Prince Eugene of Savoy, commanded the forces of the Grand Alliance.

In 1711, Joseph I, the Holy Roman Emperor and ruler of Austria, died. He was succeeded by his brother, the Archduke Charles, who was the allies' candidate for the Spanish throne. It then became clear that the balance of power would be even more seriously threatened if Charles got Spain as well as Austria than it would be if Philip became king of Spain. Charles as ruler of Austria would be placed in a position where he would control Spain as well as the Holy Roman Empire. In 1713, Louis XIV used skillful diplomacy to bring about the Peace of Utrecht, under which he obtained fairly favorable terms. His grandson, Philip, was recognized as king of Spain on the condition that Spain and France would never be united. Charles refused to sign the Treaty of Utrecht and did not make peace until a year later. Then he found it necessary to give way and sign the Treaty of Rastatt, which was almost exactly the same as the Peace of Utrecht.

**The War of the Polish Succession** (1733-1735) was caused when Polish nobles elected Stanislaus Leszczynski, father-in-law of Louis XV of France, as king of Poland. Russia and Austria forced the Poles to accept the Elector Augustus of Saxony as king. War followed between France, aided by Spain, and Russia, aided by Austria. The outcome was a damaging blow to French prestige. Augustus of Saxony remained king of Poland.

**The War of the Austrian Succession** (1740-1748) was known in America as King George's War. It was caused by the death of the Austrian ruler Charles VI, who had no sons and left his dominions to his daughter Maria Theresa. The great powers of Europe had guaranteed that a daughter of Charles could succeed him by the terms of the Pragmatic Sanction. But they broke their words and tried to take Maria Theresa's lands. See PRAGMATIC SANCTION.

The first to attack Maria Theresa was Frederick the Great, king of Prussia, who conquered the province of Silesia. In 1741 he strengthened his hold upon the territory by an overwhelming victory at Mollwitz. France, Spain, Bavaria, Saxony, Sardinia, and Poland joined Prussia, and for a time Maria Theresa was threatened with the loss of her dominions. But she contrived to save her crown and most of her lands by her own great courage and vigorous leadership. Her appeal to the Hungarians won her the powerful support of this chivalrous people. Maria Theresa was further aided by an alliance with the great maritime powers, England and Holland, which crushed the power of France at sea. She separated Frederick the Great from his allies by giving him Silesia. The Treaty of Aix-la-Chapelle, signed in 1748, finally ended the war.

**The War of the Bavarian Succession** (1778-1779) was a short quarrel between Prussia and Austria over the succession to the throne of Bavaria and the disposition of some Bavarian territory. In 1777, the Elector of Bavaria, Maximilian Joseph, died and left no direct heirs. Austria then attempted to control the affairs of Bavaria and to dictate the succession. This aroused the jealousy of Frederick the Great. Armed forces from Prussia and Austria invaded Bavaria, and war seemed inevitable.

But neither Austria nor Prussia was anxious for war. No battles were fought, and the war is often called "the potato war." Hungry soldiers spent their time searching for food in the fields. Catherine II of Russia mediated peace. In the Treaty of Teschen, signed in 1779, both Austria and Prussia were satisfied with certain territorial gains.  ROBERT G. L. WAITE

**Related Articles** in WORLD BOOK include:
Aix-la-Chapelle, Treaties of
Blenheim, Battle of
Charles (VI) of the
 Holy Roman Empire
French and Indian Wars
 (Queen Anne's War;
 King George's War)
Louis (XIV)
Maria Theresa
Marlborough, Duke of
Seven Years' War
Utrecht, Peace of

**SUCCORY.** See CHICORY.

**SUCCOT.** See SUKKOT.

**SUCCULENT,** *SUK yoo lunt*, is the name for a fleshy plant, such as the cactus, which has large stems or leaves in which to store water. Succulent plants grow in deserts and other dry places in the world where there is little water. Desert plants have large stems or leaves in which to store water.

Succulent plants often have odd shapes. The *cactus* is perhaps the best-known succulent that stores its water in the stems. It has a thick stem and tiny leaves that look and feel like thorns. Plants that store water in their leaves include *hen-and-chickens*, *stonecrops*, and *iceplants*. Succulent plants sometimes look like stones on the ground. The *Living Rock* of South Africa is an example of this type. Other succulents, especially the *sedums*, have leaves that look like tiny beads on a long slim stem.

Succulent plants grow wild in the western part of North America, in certain parts of Africa, and in Central Asia. Many of these succulents are grown as house plants. They require little care and water. Many of them have bright, colorful flowers.  MARCUS MAXON

See also CACTUS; SEDUM; SPURGE FAMILY.

**SUCHOU.** See SOOCHOW.

**SUCKER** is the name given to several kinds of fish closely related to the minnow family. Most of them have mouths with thick, fleshy lips that help them suck up animal and plant life on the bottom of lakes and

# SUCTION PUMP

The Sucker has thick lips on the underside of the snout. Its mouth has no teeth, but its throat is lined with thin, comblike spines. Suckers live in lakes and streams.

*National Film Board*

streams. Except for a few kinds in eastern Asia, all the suckers are native to North America. These fish are dull-colored except in the spring, when the males of some species have a rose or orange stripe. The larger kinds of suckers are food fishes. They have a sweet-tasting, but bony, flesh. In the Mississippi Valley, fishermen catch large, carplike suckers known as buffalo fishes.

**Scientific Classification.** The sucker belongs to the sucker family, *Catostomidae*. The common sucker is genus *Catostomus*, species *C. commersonii*. The bigmouth buffalo fish is *Megastomatobus cyprinella*; the smallmouth buffalo fish, *Ictiobus bubalus*; and the black buffalo fish is classified as *I. urus*. CARL L. HUBBS

**SUCKLING, SIR JOHN** (1609-1642), was the most famous member of the *Cavalier poets*, a group associated with the court of King Charles I of England. Suckling's poetry is seldom serious, but its amateur quality has its own charm. Suckling's best verse has a witty and knowing quality, as in:

'Tis not the meat, but 'tis the appetite
Makes eating a delight.

Suckling's plays include *Aglaura* (1637). His short poems were published four years after his death in a collection of his writings titled *Fragmenta Aurea*. Suckling's ability as a literary critic can be seen in "A Session of Poets" (1637), a verse review of poetry in his day.

Suckling was born in Middlesex, and served in the army. In 1641, he was accused of plotting to gain control of the army for the king. He fled to Paris and died there, perhaps as a suicide. RICHARD S. SYLVESTER

**Sempervivum Is an Example of a Succulent Plant.**

*J. Horace McFarland*

**SUCRE,** *SOO kray* (pop. 59,701), is the capital of Bolivia. But all of the government offices except the Supreme Court are located in La Paz. The government moved its offices from Sucre in 1898 because La Paz had better transportation connections with the rest of the country.

Sucre lies in central Bolivia in the *Cordillera Real* (Royal Range) of the Andes Mountains, at an altitude of 8,950 feet above sea level. For location, see BOLIVIA (color map). Sucre is the chief cultural center of the country.

Sucre is sometimes called the *city of four names*. When Spanish settlers founded Sucre in 1538, they called it La Plata. Later, its name was changed to Charcas and then to Chuquisaca. In 1826, it was named Sucre for General Antonio José de Sucre, the first president of Bolivia (see SUCRE, ANTONIO JOSÉ DE). The University of San Francisco Xavier, founded in 1624, is located in Sucre. The university is among the oldest western schools. ARTHUR P. WHITAKER

**SUCRE,** *SOO kray*, is a standard coin in Ecuador. The sucre is named after the South American patriot, Antonio José de Sucre. One hundred centavos equal one sucre.

For the value of a sucre in dollars, see MONEY (table: Values of Monetary Units).

**SUCRE,** *SOO kray*, **ANTONIO JOSÉ DE** (1795-1830), liberated Ecuador and Bolivia from Spain and served as the first president of Bolivia. He was one of the ablest generals of his time. His victory over the Spaniards at Ayacucho in 1824 put an end to Spanish rule in South America.

When Bolivia became a separate state, Sucre became its first president in 1826. He was an able administrator. He resigned the presidency in 1828 to prevent war with the Peruvians who objected to his friendship with Simón Bolívar (see BOLÍVAR, SIMÓN). Sucre was killed by an assassin in 1830. Bolivia named one of its most important cities in honor of him.

*Culver*

**Antonio José de Sucre**

Sucre was born in Cumaná, Venezuela. He joined the revolutionary army when he was 15. He soon became Bolívar's trusted friend and chief lieutenant, and when Bolívar sought to free Ecuador, Sucre scored a victory at Pichincha in 1822. His strategy at Ayacucho freed Upper Peru, now Bolivia (see BOLIVIA [Independence]). HARVEY L. JOHNSON

**SUCROSE** is the chemical name for common table sugar. It has the chemical formula $C_{12}H_{22}O_{11}$. It is extracted from sugar beets and sugar cane and is the cheapest pure chemical produced on a large scale. Chemically, sucrose has certain properties of an alcohol, and it will form esters with organic acids (see ESTER). See also SUGAR.

**SUCTION PUMP.** See PUMP (Reciprocating Pumps [The Lift Pump]).

759

# SUDAN

- ★ Capital
- • Other City or Town
- —— Road
- ―+― Rail Line
- ▲ MOUNTAIN
- ～ River
- = Cataract

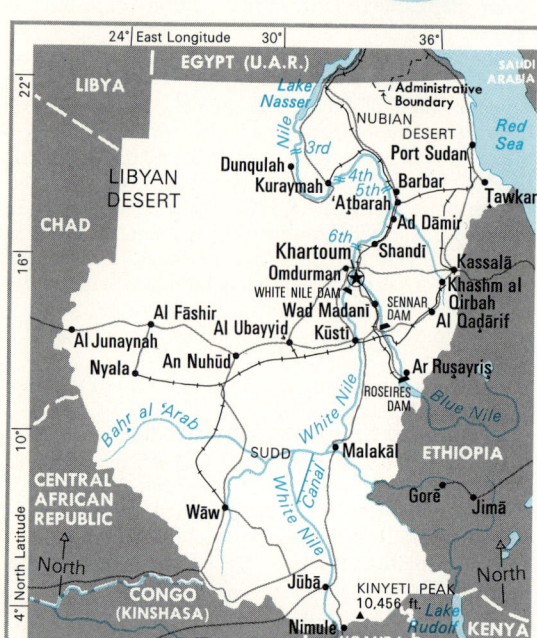

WORLD BOOK map-FHa

**SUDAN,** *soo DAN,* is the largest country in Africa. It lies in the northeastern part of the continent, and has a 400-mile coastline on the Red Sea. The Sudan is a land with widely differing people and geography. It sprawls across three distinct natural regions, ranging from bleak desert in the north to grassy plains in central Sudan and a great swamp and steaming tropical rainforest in the south.

Most of the people live near the Nile River or one of its branches, or near wells that can supply water for them and their crops. Only *nomads,* who wander about in search of water and grazing land for their camels, sheep, goats, and cattle, live in many parts of the sandy north.

In the south, the swamp and the equatorial forest produce little food or cash crops. But big game, including the rare rhinoceros, lions, leopards, elephants,

*The contributor of this article, K. D. D. Henderson, a former member of the Sudan Political Service, is the author of* Survey of the Anglo-Egyptian Sudan, The Making of Modern Sudan, *and* Sudan Republic.

buffalo, giraffe, and other animals, roams there.

The people of the Sudan are sharply divided, and this split caused civil war in the 1960's. Arabs, *Nubians* (brown-skinned people related to the early Egyptians), and some African Negro tribes live in the northern and central parts of the country. In the southern part, several different tribes of African Negroes have lived isolated from the rest of the world for generations. They were opposed to independence, and continue to oppose union with their northern countrymen. Most of the southerners speak tribal languages and cling to tribal customs.

The history of this ancient land dates back to Biblical times. The *pharaohs* (rulers) of ancient Egypt carried off valuable supplies of gold, the land's only mineral wealth. The Sudan was invaded and conquered by Egyptians, Romans, and Turks. Later, it was ruled jointly by Great Britain and Egypt for more than 50 years. During this period, it was called *Anglo-Egyptian Sudan.* It finally gained independence on Jan. 1, 1956. Its official name in Arabic, the official language, is JAMHURYAT ES-SUDAN (REPUBLIC OF THE SUDAN). Khartoum, a city on the Nile River in central Sudan, is the country's capital and leading city.

**Government.** The Sudan's government has been overthrown several times since the nation became independent in 1956. Power has passed back and forth between civilian and military rulers. A temporary constitution was suspended in 1958, restored in 1964, and suspended again in 1969. The drafting of a permanent constitution has been delayed by disagreement over the form the government should take. Some Sudanese want a parliamentary government similar to Great Britain's. Others want a presidential government like that of the United States. Opinion is also divided on the role of the Moslem religion in the government.

**People.** Most of the people in the Sudan are farmers or herders. The herders keep camels in the northern parts of the country, and those in the southern parts keep cattle.

Arabic-speaking Moslem people make up about two-

---
**FACTS IN BRIEF**

**Form of Government:** Republic. *Head of State*—Supreme Council of State (5 members).

**Capital:** Khartoum.

**Official Language:** Arabic.

**Area:** 967,500 sq. miles. *Greatest Length*—1,600 miles. *Greatest Width*—1,200 miles. *Coastline*—400 miles.

**Population:** *1956 Census*—10,262,536; distribution, 92 per cent rural, 8 per cent urban. *Estimated 1970 Population*—15,595,000; density, 16 persons to the square mile. *Estimated 1975 Population*—17,904,000.

**Chief Products:** *Agriculture*—cassava, corn, cotton, dates, hides and skins, melons, millet, peanuts, sesame, wheat. *Forest Industry*—gum arabic, hardwood. *Manufacturing and Processing*—beer, cement, salt, shoes, soap, textiles.

**Flag:** Three stripes, blue (for the Nile), gold (for the desert), and green (for vegetation). See FLAG (color picture: Flags of Africa).

**Money:** *Basic Unit*—Sudanese pound. See MONEY (table: Values).

thirds of the population, and most of them live in the northern two-thirds of the country. Descendants of Nubians and African Negroes, they have inter-married with Arab peoples and adopted their language and religion. Most of these people live in the Nile River valley and make their living as farmers. Some Beja tribes wander about the Red Sea hills with their herds.

Most of the people in northern and central Sudan live in square, flat-roofed houses that are made out of sun-baked bricks. The houses have narrow windows to keep out the heat. The nomads who live on the desert have no permanent homes because they continuously move their herds in search of water and grass. These nomads wear flowing robes to protect themselves from the sun and sand.

About one-third of Sudan's people are African Negroes. Most of the Negroes live in the southern part of the country south of the great swamp area. Some of these are among the tallest people in the world.

Negro tribes lived isolated from the rest of the world for hundreds of years, cut off by the great swamp of central Sudan and the thick rainforests. In the early 1800's, Egyptians and others invaded the swamps and jungles searching for slaves. This made the Negroes bitter and suspicious of other people. They have resisted efforts by northerners to convert them to the Islamic faith and to teach them to speak Arabic. Most of these tribesmen speak their own tribal languages, and practice tribal religions. They wear very little clothing, and live in small houses that have mud walls and thatched roofs.

Water is scarce in most parts of the Sudan. Because of this, the people dig ditches to store rainwater and bank dirt around their fields to hold rainwater on the fields. In some parts of western Sudan, the people sometimes scoop out the *pith* (soft center) of tree trunks and use the trees as water tanks. The rain runs down the branches into the hollow trunks. The people build big mud saucers at the roots of the trees, so they can haul the water up in leather buckets.

In areas that receive little rainfall, watermelons are important to the people. The watermelons, which go on growing after the rains stop, can be stored and eaten later.

In most parts of the country, the people can make pancakes from sorghum or millet flour and eat this with highly spiced vegetable soups. They add eggs and meat to their soup if they have them. The nomads live on milk most of the time.

Only about half the people of the Sudan can read and write. Most of the towns and rural areas have schools, but only about half the school-age children attend classes. The Sudan has two universities, the University of Khartoum and the Islamic University of Omdurman. Khartoum also has a branch of Egypt's Cairo University.

**Land.** The Sudan has four main natural regions ranging from north to south: (1) the desert region, (2) the steppe region, (3) the savanna region, and (4) the equatorial region.

The *desert region*, in the north, covers about a third of the country. The Libyan and Nubian deserts, which are part of the Sahara, cover most of this region. Vegetation grows only in the Nile River valley and in a few scattered *oases* (watering places).

The *steppe region* lies in central Sudan. The vast *steppes* (plains) are covered with short, coarse grass and small bushes. The *savanna region* lies south of the steppes. It is an area of tall bushes and thick, green grass (see SAVANNA).

The *equatorial region*, much of it thick tropical forest, covers nearly a third of the country in the south. The Sudd area, one of the largest marshes in the world, lies in the center of the Upper White Nile basin. The country's chief highland areas lie in the far west, on the Red Sea coast, and around the southern

Marc & Evelyne Bernheim, Rapho Guillumette

**Ruins in Northern Sudan** date from about the A.D. 200's. They stand about 35 miles from Shandi, north of Khartoum.

## SUDAN

rim of the marsh. Mount Kinyeti rises 10,456 feet on the border between the Sudan and Uganda.

The Nile River system flows through the country from south to north. The White Nile and the Blue Nile rivers meet at Khartoum to form the Nile River.

Summers are hot throughout the country, with temperatures of about 100° F. Winter temperatures vary from about 60° F. in the north to about 80° F. in the south. Almost no rain falls in the far north. Rainfall in southern Sudan averages about 40 inches a year.

**Economy.** In most of the Sudan, life centers around the water supply. People are forced to live near the rivers, water holes, and *well fields* (areas containing large amounts of water). Many of the people may spend half of each day at the well. Farmers harvest crops quickly,

United Nations
**Women Shoppers in Southern Sudan** board a Nile River ferry, carrying purchases home in the earthenware pots.

before the pools of water dry up. Planters and families use water very carefully. All building developments start with planning for dams, cisterns, and other water storage facilities.

Irrigation of such areas as the Gezira Plain, which lies between the Blue Nile and the White Nile, has made the Sudan the world's second largest producer of Egyptian cotton (see COTTON [Egyptian Cotton]). Canals have been built in this area south of Khartoum and Omdurman to distribute water to the fields. The water to irrigate the million-acre cotton region is provided by the Sennar Dam, a 3,300-foot span that blocks the Blue Nile. The dam creates a reservoir that extends over 93 miles up the river.

However, the competition of *synthetic* (artificial) fabrics and uncertain cotton prices hurt the country. When cotton crops are poor, or cotton prices are low, the country suffers economically.

Sudan's forests provide some hardwood. Nearly 90 per cent of the world's production of gum arabic, which is used in making perfumes and candy, come from forests in the Sudan (see GUM ARABIC). Farmers also produce some cassava, sesame, corn, rice, peanuts, coffee, and sweet potatoes. Of these, only peanuts are grown in sufficient amount to be an important export.

The Sudan has a good network of roads in the northern part of the country. But in the marshy southern region, roads are expensive to build and maintain. The country has about 2,800 miles of narrow-gauge railroads, and about 3,000 miles of navigable rivers. An airline provides service to the main towns.

**History.** The area that is now northern Sudan was invaded many times by Egypt after about 3000 B.C. About 750 B.C., two Sudanese kingdoms emerged in the area. Two Christian kingdoms, one in the north and one in the center, grew up in the A.D. 500's. But Arabs captured the northern kingdom in the 1200's, and the other kingdom was captured in the 1500's by a joint force consisting of Arabs and an African tribe called the Fung.

Egypt conquered the Sudan in 1821. In 1881, a Moslem leader named Muhammed Ahmed proclaimed himself the *Mahdi* (guide), and led a successful revolt against the Egyptians. His successor, Khalifa Abdullahi, ruled the Sudan until 1898, when British and Egyptian troops reconquered the country.

In 1899, Great Britain and Egypt made the Sudan a protectorate. The British appointed a governor-general and provided most of the important officials. Some Egyptian nationalists opposed British domination of Sudan. In 1924, Egyptian troops in the Sudan mutinied against the British. The mutiny failed, and most Egyptian officials were expelled from the Sudan. Egypt took no further part in governing Sudan until 1936, when it signed a new agreement with Great Britain.

After World War II, educated Sudanese began to demand independence. In 1953, Great Britain and Egypt agreed on steps leading to self-government for the Sudan. The Sudan officially became an independent country on Jan. 1, 1956, despite the objections of the people living in southern Sudan.

The Sudan has been plagued by political unrest and civil war since independence. In 1958, Ibrahim Abboud, an army general, seized control of the government. He dissolved parliament and banned all political parties. Meanwhile, a revolt of Negroes in the south against domination by the Arabs had developed into a civil war. Abboud failed to settle the conflict, and he was forced to resign in 1964. The Sudan returned to civilian government. But the new government was unable to settle the unrest in the south and also failed to solve economic problems.

In 1967, Prime Minister Sadiq Al-Mahdi, great grandson of the Mahdi, lost his support in parliament and resigned. He was succeeded by Muhammed Ahmed Mahjoub. In 1969, Mahjoub's government was overthrown by junior military officers and left wing intellectuals. The former chief justice of the Sudan, Abu Bakr Awadullah, formed a new government with army support. Awadullah suspended all representative institutions of government. K. D. D. HENDERSON

**Related Articles** in WORLD BOOK include:

| | | |
|---|---|---|
| Arab League | Nile River | Omdurman |
| Gordon, Charles G. | Nubia | Port Sudan |
| Khartoum | | |

Sudan Grass makes excellent forage for livestock. It grows in almost any kind of soil, and also in semiarid land regions.

J. Horace McFarland

**SUDAN GRASS** is a hay plant that the Department of Agriculture introduced into the United States in 1909 from Khartoum, Sudan. It was first tested in Texas, and gave excellent results. Farmers planted thousands of acres in the South and Southwest in irrigated sections and where rainfall is adequate. Eventually it spread to nearly all parts of the country. It is one of the best drought-resisting plants known to American farmers. Sudan grass has a fibrous root system. It is an annual, which means that seed must be planted every year. It looks like other tall grasses. Farmers cultivate the grass for stock feed and for its seed. Sudan hay has a higher feeding value than timothy. Livestock, especially hogs, like it.

**Scientific Classification.** Sudan grass belongs to the grass family, *Gramineae*. It is genus *Sorghum*, species *S. vulgare*, variety *sudanense*. ROY G. WIGGANS

**SUDBURY,** Ontario (pop. 84,888; met. area 117,075; alt. 856 ft.), is the center of the world's nickel industry. Sudbury lies about 250 miles northwest of Toronto. For location, see ONTARIO (physical map).

Gold and copper mines are found near the city. By-products of the copper-nickel industry, such as sulfuric acid, are made in the district. Iron ore is recovered from the slag of the nickel operations. Other industries include agriculture, and the manufacture of forest products and chemicals.

Laurentian University and a technical and mining institute are located in Sudbury. Founded in 1883 as a railway divisional point, Sudbury received a city charter in 1930. The city has a mayor-council form of government. D. M. L. FARR

See also NICKEL (Mining Nickel).

**SUDERMANN, HERMANN** (1857-1928), was a German dramatist and novelist associated with the naturalism movement. *Dame Care* (1887), his best-known novel, concerns a young man burdened with his father's failure in life. Through sacrifice, the son must master fate's repeated challenges. *Regina* (1890) is a historical novel showing an individual's struggle against the prejudices of his community.

Sudermann gained fame in Europe with his plays *Honor* (1889) and *Magda* (1893). In these dramas he stripped away the pretenses of the middle-class society of the late 1800's. Sudermann's *Lithuanian Tales* (1917) skillfully portray working-class characters and carry a genuine sense of tragedy. Sudermann was born in Matzicken in East Prussia. WALTHER L. HAHN

**SUDETENLAND,** *soo DAY t'n land*, is a region located on the slopes of the Sudetes Mountains. It lies in Czechoslovakia, on the borders of Bohemia, Moravia, and Germany. Many Germans once lived in Sudetenland. The treaties of Versailles and St. Germain in 1919 gave the area to Czechoslovakia. The Munich Agreement of 1938 gave the area and other Czech areas to Germany. In 1945, the Allies restored Sudetenland to Czechoslovakia and the Germans were expelled and replaced with the Czechs and Slovaks. M. KAMIL DZIEWANOWSKI

**SUDETES MOUNTAINS,** *soo DE teez*, a European mountain range, separate northeastern Czechoslovakia and southwestern Poland. The highest part of the Sudetes is the Riesengebirge, which means *giant mountains*. The highest point, Schneekoppe (Snow Peak), is 5,259 feet above sea level. Pine forests cover most of these rugged peaks. The lower slopes of the Sudetes in Poland have coal. FRANKLIN C. ERICKSON

**SUEDE,** *swayd*, is a soft leather that has a nap on one side. Suede is made by holding the flesh side of tanned animal hide against a buffing wheel. The rough surface of the wheel raises the nap. Items made from suede include shoes, gloves, hats, and coats.

**SUESS,** *zyoos*, **EDUARD** (1831-1914), an Austrian geologist, became famous for his work on changes of the earth's surface. His most important book was the four-volume *Face of the Earth* (1885-1901). He served as an assistant at the Hofmuseum in Vienna from 1852 to 1862, and taught at the University of Vienna from 1857 to 1901. He was an inspiring teacher of advanced students. From 1869 to 1896, he served as leader of the Liberal party in the Austrian Parliament. Suess was born in London. CARROLL LANE FENTON

**SUET,** *SYU et*, is the hard, white fat around the loins and kidneys of some animals, especially cattle and full-grown sheep. Melted suet forms tallow, which is used in making candles and soap. Beef suet is used for frying and other cooking methods. Many people use suet as bird feed in the winter. JOHN C. AYRES

**SUETONIUS,** *swee TOH nih us* (A.D. 69?-140), a Roman author, wrote a series of biographies of Roman emperors from Julius Caesar to Domitian in his *Lives of the Caesars*. This work is important not only for the information it gives us about these men, but also because it had a great influence on the writing of biography in ancient times and in the Middle Ages. All his other works are lost except his lives of grammarians, orators, and some other literary men. THOMAS A. BRADY

763

# SUEZ

**SUEZ**, soo EZ (pop. 219,000; alt. 30 ft.), is an Egyptian seaport at the southern entrance to the Suez Canal. In Arabic, its name is As SUWAYS. It lies about 80 miles east of Cairo (see EGYPT [political map]). Suez is a refueling station for ships passing through the canal. Railroads link the city with Cairo. Leading industries include oil refining and fertilizer production.

**SUEZ CANAL**, soo EZ, is a narrow, man-made waterway that extends about 100 miles to join the Mediterranean and Red seas. In normal times, it is the busiest interocean canal in the world. The canal runs north and south across the Isthmus of Suez, between the cities of Port Said and Suez. It shortened the route between England and India by 6,000 miles.

The Suez Canal has no locks, because there is no great difference between the levels of the Red Sea and the Mediterranean Sea. At first, the canal was built to a depth of 26 feet, a bottom width of 72 feet, and a surface width of nearly 230 feet. Later, the canal was widened and deepened several times to handle larger ships and more traffic. Today the canal has a depth of 46 feet, a bottom width of 118 feet, and a surface width of more than 390 feet. Most of the canal can handle only single-lane traffic. Dredges operate at all times to remove the sand that blows in from the desert. In the early days, a ship took 40 hours to pass through the canal. Today, this can be done in less than 15 hours. The estimated cost of the canal is more than $100 million. The Suez Canal is twice as long as the Panama Canal, but cost only a third as much because it required less digging and no locks.

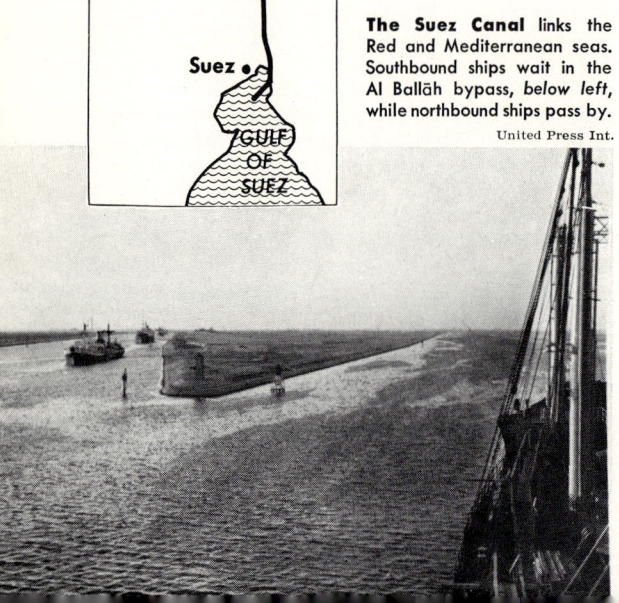

**The Suez Canal** links the Red and Mediterranean seas. Southbound ships wait in the Al Ballāh bypass, *below left*, while northbound ships pass by.
United Press Int.

**History.** Canals were built to connect the Nile River and the Red Sea hundreds of years before the time of Christ. For a time in the A.D. 600's, the Red and Mediterranean seas were joined by a canal. Napoleon I saw advantages of a waterway across the Isthmus of Suez when he visited Egypt in 1799. But Ferdinand de Lesseps, a French diplomat and engineer, carried out the plan. He got permission for the project from Mohammed Said (Pasha), the Viceroy of Egypt, in 1854. An International Technical Commission met in 1855 to plan the route of the canal. By 1858, a company had been organized with a capital stock of about $40 million. Frenchmen and the Ottoman Empire owned most of the stock. The construction of the canal was started on April 25, 1859. The canal was opened to traffic on Nov. 17, 1869. The Suez Canal Company was given a 99-year concession ending in 1968.

Although Britain gained more from the construction of the canal than any other country, it had no part in building the canal, and bought none of the original shares of stock. However, in 1875, Great Britain bought the shares of the Khedive of Egypt, Ismail Pasha, who had succeeded Mohammed Said (Pasha) as viceroy in 1863. After that, a commission composed mostly of British and French directed management of the canal.

In 1888, an international convention agreed that the canal should be open to all nations in peace and in war. However, Great Britain stationed troops near the canal for its defense in World War I, and kept ships of nations at war with Britain from using the waterway. Axis ships were denied use of the canal in World War II. In 1950, as a result of the Arab-Israeli war (1948-1949), Egypt banned Israeli ships from the canal.

Under the terms of a 1954 agreement with Egypt, British troops left the canal zone in June, 1956. In July, the United States and Great Britain withdrew offers to help finance the Aswan High Dam across the Nile River. This and other factors, including a strong Egyptian nationalist movement, led to the seizure of the canal by Egyptian President Gamal A. Nasser on July 26. Nasser announced that Egypt would use the canal tolls to build the dam. Great Britain, France, and other Western nations protested the seizure.

After years of border clashes, Israel invaded Egypt on Oct. 29, 1956. Great Britain and France attacked Egypt on October 31 in an effort to restore international control of the waterway. United Nations action ended the fighting on November 6. A United Nations police force restored peace in the canal area. The waterway was reopened in March, 1957, under Egyptian management. The canal was blocked by sunken ships during the Arab-Israeli war in June, 1967.   GEORGE H. T. KIMBLE

See also DE LESSEPS, FERDINAND MARIE; EGYPT; UNITED NATIONS (Suez Canal Crisis).

**SUFFIX.** See SPELLING (Spelling Rules).
**SUFFOLK.** See ENGLAND (color map: The 38 Counties of England).
**SUFFOLK.** See SHEEP (Medium-Wooled Sheep).
**SUFFOLK UNIVERSITY.** See UNIVERSITIES AND COLLEGES (table).
**SUFFRAGE.** See VOTING.
**SUFFRAGE, WOMAN.** See WOMAN SUFFRAGE.

764

# SUGAR

Grant Heilman

Utah-Idaho Sugar Co.

**Most Sugar Comes from Sugar Cane and Sugar Beets.** Workmen cut the sugar cane stalks with sharp steel knives, *top.* Farmers use machines, *bottom,* to pull sugar beets out of the ground and load them on wagons.

Tate & Lyle, Ltd.

**Raw Sugar Is Stored in Huge Warehouses.** Later, trains and trucks carry the raw sugar to refineries, where it is made suitable for eating.

**SUGAR** is one of man's most important foods. It is so important that it sometimes has been called the *foundation of life.* Sugar supplies energy and heat for the body much as gasoline provides power and heat for an automobile.

In addition to being important as a food, sugar is tasty. People like the sweet taste of sugar and use it to improve the flavor of many other kinds of food. All green plants make sugar. Most of the sugar we use for sweetening comes from sugar cane and sugar beets. Other sources of sugar include the maple tree, corn, grapes, and milk.

Sugar is distributed to industrial and home users in several forms. These include liquid, powdered, and various sizes of crystallized sugars. Pure white sugar and several brown sugars are produced. The sugars are delivered in packages varying in size from one-sixth of an ounce to 100-pound bags. Bulk shipments of sugar are transported by truck or railroad freight car.

## Properties of Sugar

Sugar is a sweet solid or liquid substance that is white or colorless when it is pure. Sugar is a *carbohydrate* (see CARBOHYDRATE). It furnishes energy faster than any other food. One teaspoonful of sugar contains

*Neil L. Pennington, the contributor of this article, is General Manager of California and Hawaiian Sugar Refining Corporation, Ltd., in Crockett, Calif.*

16 Calories of energy. One pound of sugar contains about 1,750 Calories.

Chemists call the sugar that people keep in a sugar bowl *sucrose* (chemical formula, $C_{12}H_{22}O_{11}$). By means of chemical methods, they can break it down into two other sugars that are simpler in chemical makeup (chemical formula, $C_6H_{12}O_6$). One of these is *glucose* (sometimes called *dextrose*). The other is *fructose* (also called *levulose*).

## Uses of Sugar

**As a Food.** On the average, a person in the United States uses about 95 pounds of sugar a year. The most familiar form of sugar is the white granular kind used to flavor such foods as cereal, coffee, and tea. But most of the sugar used in the U.S. never appears in the sugar bowl. More than half of it is used in five types of food products. They are (1) soft drinks; (2) baked goods; (3) confectionery, including chocolates; (4) canned fruit, including jams, jellies, and marmalades; and (5) frozen desserts, mostly ice cream. Sugar is used to bring out the taste and smell of fruits, and to cover up the bitter taste of drugs.

**In Industry.** Many products are manufactured from sugar and its by-products. Manufacturers make nylon from *furfural* obtained by treating sugar-cane fibers with acid. *Monosodium glutamate,* a widely used substance for bringing out the flavor of food, may be made from beet molasses. Chemists make a *plasticizer,* a material that makes plastics tougher and less brittle, from sugar. One of the ingredients used to make carbon paper is cane wax, a whitish, powdery material that coats sugar-cane stalks. Some phonograph records con-

## SUGAR

tain a resin made from sugar-cane fiber. Paper and wallboard are made from this fiber. Many cosmetics, drugs, and dyes contain sugar. Sugar is also an important ingredient in the manufacture of synthetic rubber. Raw cane sugar is used to keep tobacco from drying out while it is in storage.

### Sources of Sugar

Sugar cane and sugar beets produce most of the sugar for commercial use. All other plants also produce sugar. Other sources of sugar are the maple tree, milk, and cornstarch.

**Sugar Cane and Sugar Beets.** Sugar cane grows in tropical or subtropical climates. The sugar beet thrives in temperate zones. When the sugar is *refined* (purified), there is no difference in the chemical composition of sugar obtained from either of these plants. For more detailed information on these sources of sugar, see SUGAR CANE; SUGAR BEET.

**Plants.** Almost all plants manufacture sugar. The plants' green leaves use energy from sunlight, water from the soil, and carbon dioxide from the air to form sugar and oxygen. This process is called photosynthesis. See PHOTOSYNTHESIS.

It has been estimated that all of the plants on earth make about 400 billion tons of sugar in a year. About 80 per cent of the food energy of fruits comes from their sugar content. Sugar is found in such familiar foods as carrots, nuts, onions, and spinach.

The type of sugar found most often in plants is sucrose. It is found throughout the stems and leaves of plants. Glucose and fructose also occur widely in nature. For example, honey and sweet fruits such as grapes are made up mostly of glucose and fructose. A mixture of equal parts of glucose and fructose is called *invert sugar*. Invert sugar is formed during the canning, preserving, and bottling of foods.

**Maple Sugar and Syrup** are obtained by collecting the sap of the sugar maple tree and refining it. The sap is boiled in an *evaporator*. See MAPLE; MAPLE SUGAR.

**Milk Sugar** is found in the milk of all mammals (milk-giving animals). Chemists call it *lactose*. Milk sugar for commercial use is usually obtained as a by-product of cheese manufacture. Cheese makers need only the milk solids. They separate the *casein* (protein) which forms the *curd* (solids), from the liquid called *whey* (see CHEESE). The whey contains the milk sugar, which can be obtained by drying and refining. Milk sugar is much less sweet than cane, beet, or maple sugar. It is valuable when only a little sweetness is wanted. For example, when a drug maker wants to dilute a powerful drug, he often uses milk sugar. By mixing the powdered drug with large amounts of milk sugar, he can make a small pill that is not too sweet.

**Corn Sugar and Syrup.** Manufacturers make corn syrup from cornstarch. To obtain the sugar, weak solutions of an acid are added to cornstarch. The acid used is hydrochloric acid, which is also found in the stomachs of human beings. It helps to digest food (see HYDROCHLORIC ACID). The cornstarch, acid, and water are heated until they boil. Workers pour the hot liquid through filters to remove impurities. Huge tanks keep the liquid hot and evaporate the water until the syrup becomes thick enough for use.

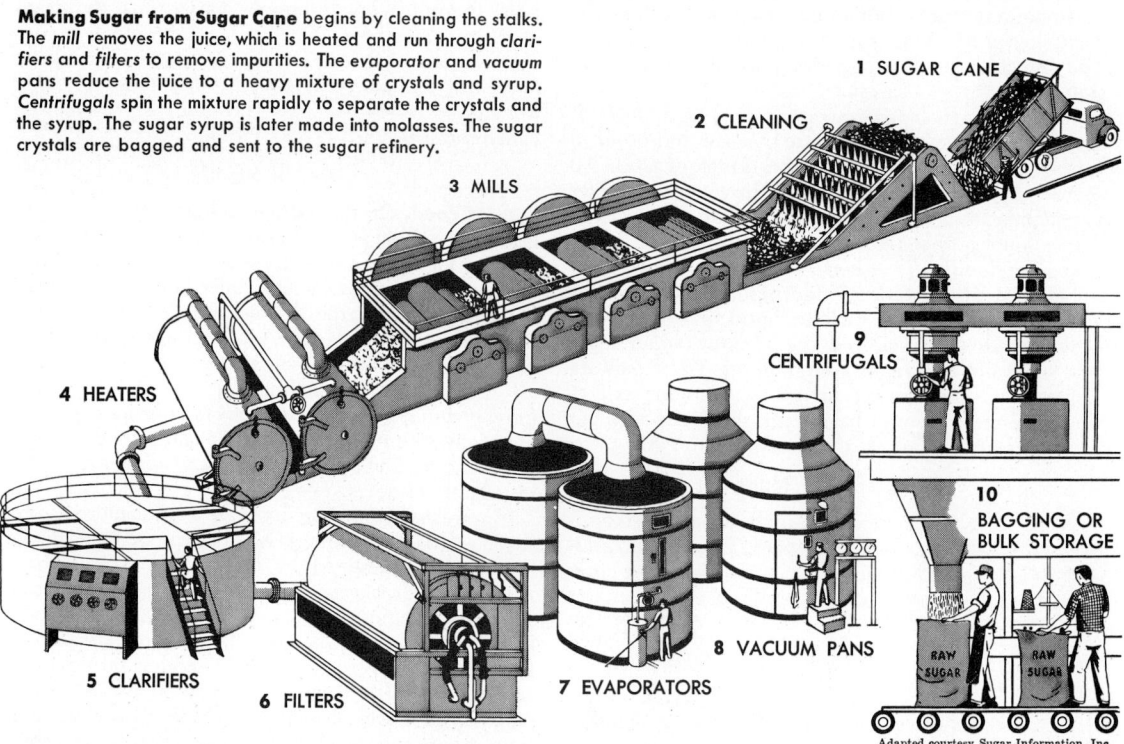

**Making Sugar from Sugar Cane** begins by cleaning the stalks. The *mill* removes the juice, which is heated and run through *clarifiers* and *filters* to remove impurities. The *evaporator* and *vacuum pans* reduce the juice to a heavy mixture of crystals and syrup. *Centrifugals* spin the mixture rapidly to separate the crystals and the syrup. The sugar syrup is later made into molasses. The sugar crystals are bagged and sent to the sugar refinery.

Adapted courtesy Sugar Information, Inc.

## LEADING SUGAR PRODUCING COUNTRIES
Tons of raw beet and cane sugar produced in 1967

|  |  |
|---|---|
| Russia | 11,500,000 tons |
| Cuba | 5,700,000 tons |
| United States | 5,313,000 tons |
| Brazil | 5,075,000 tons |
| India | 3,095,000 tons |
| Australia | 2,708,000 tons |
| Mexico | 2,530,000 tons |
| Germany (West) | 2,270,000 tons |
| Poland | 2,100,000 tons |
| South Africa | 2,009,000 tons |

Source: U.S. Department of Agriculture

## LEADING SUGAR PRODUCING STATES
Tons of raw beet and cane sugar produced in 1967

|  |  |
|---|---|
| Hawaii | 1,191,000 tons |
| Louisiana | 710,000 tons |
| Florida | 660,000 tons |
| California | 544,000 tons |
| Colorado | 414,000 tons |
| Idaho | 319,000 tons |
| Minnesota | 204,000 tons |
| Montana | 172,000 tons |
| Michigan | 153,000 tons |
| Washington | 149,000 tons |

Sources: U.S. Department of Agriculture; U.S. Beet Sugar Association

Corn sugar is commercially produced *glucose*. Corn syrup and sugar are widely used in candy, canned fruit, and bread. They are not as sweet as cane sugar, but are sweeter than milk sugar. Manufacturers who make syrups for pancakes or waffles often add cane sugar to the corn syrups to make them sweeter.

**Molasses** is a by-product of cane sugar and beet sugar. It contains from 36 to 50 per cent sugar. Chemists and drug manufacturers use it to make many chemical products, including industrial alcohol. Molasses yields large amounts of citric acid, the ingredient that gives a tart flavor to lemons and oranges. Makers of soft drinks use the citric acid from molasses in beverages. Low-grade molasses, called blackstrap, is fed to livestock.

Molasses that is to be eaten contains much sugar, so it tastes sweet. It lends flavor to cookies and candy. Special kinds of bacteria act upon molasses so that *riboflavin* (vitamin B$_2$) can be made from it. See MOLASSES; VITAMIN (Vitamin B Complex).

**Honey** serves as another source of sugar. It does not need refining. Honey is sold in its liquid form, just as it is taken from the comb where the bees have stored it. See HONEY.

### Making Cane Sugar

**Planting the Cane.** Planters put short pieces of cane stalks in the ground and cover them lightly with earth. In a short time, new stalks grow from the joints of the old cane. They grow 7 to 15 feet high. After the growing season, which may be from 7 to 22 months, workers usually cut the cane by hand. Machines are also used. Trucks, tractors, or trains take the cut cane to a sugar mill.

**Processing the Cane.** When the cane arrives at the sugar mill, it goes through a washing machine. After a thorough washing, the cane moves to a shredding machine, where knives shred the stalks. The shredded stalks are then put into a crushing machine. This machine has a series of revolving, heavy steel rollers that squeeze the cane under heavy pressure. The pressure bursts the cells inside the cane, squeezing out sweet juice. Sprays of water dissolve more sugar from the shredded stalks. The mixture of water and juice is then taken away for purifying. The fibers that remain are *bagasse*, which is either used as fuel for boilers in the mill or made into paper, wallboard, or furfural.

**Obtaining Raw Sugar.** The cane juice, still diluted with water, is heated. Lime added to the juice settles out some of the impurities. Workers put the juice in huge evaporator tanks. There, most of the water evaporates and the juice becomes thick and syrupy. However, more water must be taken out of the syrup so that crystals will form. Because sugar and sugar syrup scorch easily, the syrup is heated in great dome-shaped vacuum pans to remove excess water. The vacuum lowers the boiling point of the syrup so that even though heating is continued, the syrup will not scorch.

Large sugar crystals soon begin to form in the thick syrup. To separate the crystals from the molasses, workmen put the mixture in a *centrifuge*. This machine turns around and around at exceedingly high speeds and spins most of the molasses from the sugar (see CENTRIFUGE). What remains is called *raw sugar*, which contains from 97 to 99 per cent sucrose. Exporters ship sugar in this form from one country to another. But to make it suitable for food, raw sugar must be further refined.

**Refining Cane Sugar.** To obtain pure white sugar for table use, the yellowish-brown raw sugar must go through several more steps. First, the molasses film, which gives the raw sugar its color, must be rinsed off. Then the sugar crystals are dissolved in water and this solution is poured through filters. The filters usually contain boneblack or some form of carbon. When a clear, colorless liquid is obtained, the evaporating proc-

# SUGAR

ess is repeated until crystals form again. Once more, the centrifuge spins the syrup from the crystals, and sparkling white, pure crystalline sugar flows from the machine to drying drums. In these drums, heated air absorbs any moisture that remains. Conveyors move the sugar to packaging machines, which automatically weigh and package it for market.

But all of the syrup is not formed crystals during this procedure. So the remaining syrup goes back through the evaporation and spinning processes again. Another batch of white sugar crystals is formed. The remaining syrup is processed for the third and last time. From this, brown sugar is made.

### Making Beet Sugar

The sugar beet is related to the red garden beet, but it is white and has a high sugar content. Farmers grow sugar beets from seeds. They plant the seeds, and when the plants begin to grow, some of them are removed so that the remaining beets will have plenty of room. At the end of the growing season, the beet tops are removed and used as cattle feed. Machines pull up the roots and haul them to the sugar-making factory.

**Removing Beet Sugar.** In the factory, washing and cutting machines clean the beets and slice them to about the size and shape of shoestring potatoes. The *cossetts* (beet slices) are put in *diffusers* (vats of hot water) to soak. This soaking removes the sugar from the slices. The *pulp* (beet slices) that remains is removed and dried. The dried pulp is sometimes made into pellets for other uses, such as cattle feed. Usually, the final molasses obtained after beet sugar is refined is added to the beet pulp to make it a more valuable feed for cattle.

**Refining Beet Sugar.** The solution obtained by soaking the beets is treated with lime and carbon dioxide. Filters remove the impurities. The sugar is crystallized by evaporating the water, much as in the making of cane sugar. However, in the United States, beet-sugar processing is carried out in a single operation. Beet-sugar factories produce no raw sugar. The centrifuge spins off the molasses and leaves behind a white, sparkling sugar that contains about 99.96 per cent sucrose.

### History

Sugar cane was known at the time of Alexander the Great. Records of one of his expeditions down the Indus River in 325 B.C. show that "honey-bearing reeds" were found. The Bible mentions sugar as an article of great value. Dioscorides, a Greek physician who lived during the time of the Roman emperor Nero, wrote: "There is a sort of hard honey which is called saccharum (sugar) found upon canes in India. It is grainy like salt and brittle between the teeth, but of sweet taste withal."

The Moors brought sugar cane with them when they overran Spain in the A.D. 1000's. For the next 200 years, the only sugar raised in Europe was that in Spain. From the 900's through the 1100's, the city of Venice became the center of a flourishing sugar trade. The Venetians brought sugar from the Tigris-Euphrates Valley, and from Egypt and Syria. It was sold to tradesmen throughout Europe. But because of the difficulty of obtaining the sugar, prices were very high and the quantities were limited. For these reasons, sugar plant-

## LEADING SUGAR BEET GROWING STATES
### Tons of sugar beets grown in 1967

|  |  |
|---|---|
| California | 3,983,000 tons |
| Idaho | 2,912,000 tons |
| Colorado | 2,105,000 tons |
| Minnesota | 1,422,000 tons |
| Michigan | 1,256,000 tons |
| Washington | 1,052,000 tons |
| Montana | 1,007,000 tons |
| Nebraska | 853,000 tons |
| Wyoming | 849,000 tons |
| North Dakota | 848,000 tons |

Source: *Crop Production, 1968 Annual Summary*, U.S. Department of Agriculture

ing started in southern France and Italy, throughout North Africa, and on islands in the Atlantic Ocean near Spain in the early 1300's.

In Venice during the 1400's, an inventor molded sugar into loaves and cones. For more than 400 years afterwards, all refined sugar was molded before it was sold. Although sugar had been known and used in Europe since the Middle Ages, crude refining methods and distribution made it an expensive luxury. In London in 1742, sugar sold for the equivalent of $2.75 a pound.

Columbus brought cuttings of sugar cane to the Western Hemisphere on his second voyage. He planted it in Santo Domingo in what is now the Dominican Republic. The first sugar mill in the Western Hemisphere was built in 1508 in Isabela, a village near Santo Domingo.

After his conquest of Mexico, Cortes established two plantations. From these beginnings, the cultivation of sugar cane spread to Brazil, Peru, and Argentina. By the middle of the 1600's, tropical America became the greatest sugar-producing area in the world.

Jesuit missionaries introduced sugar cane into Louisiana in 1751. The first sugar mill in North America was set up at New Orleans by Antonio Mendez, in 1791. Étienne de Boré produced the first granulated sugar in 1795 (see BORÉ, ÉTIENNE DE).

In 1794, Andreas Marggraf, a German scientist, first took sugar from beets. In 1838, sugar beets were planted in Massachusetts. The first successful factory was established in Alvarado, Calif. Twenty-two states in the United States now grow sugar beets. One-third of the sugar consumed in the United States is beet sugar.

NEIL L. PENNINGTON

**Related Articles** in WORLD BOOK include:

| | | |
|---|---|---|
| Candy | Honey | Saccharin |
| Carbohydrate | Maltose | Sucrose |
| Cellulose | Maple Sugar | Sugar Beet |
| Dextrose | Molasses | Sugar Cane |
| Glucose | | |

Grant Heilman

**Sugar Beets** rank second only to sugar cane as a source of sugar. The silvery-white beet is the enlarged upper part of the root. Farmers feed the green leaves and beet tops to livestock.

### LEADING SUGAR BEET GROWING COUNTRIES
Tons of sugar beets grown in 1967

|  |  |
|---|---|
| Russia | 95,460,000 tons |
| United States | 19,365,000 tons |
| Germany (West) | 15,102,000 tons |
| Poland | *15,013,000 tons |
| France | 14,040,000 tons |
| Italy | 12,897,000 tons |
| Czechoslovakia | *8,556,000 tons |
| Great Britain | 7,584,000 tons |
| Germany (East) | *7,287,000 tons |
| Netherlands | 5,593,000 tons |

*1966, latest available figures

Source: *Bulletin of Agricultural Economics and Statistics*, Feb., 1968, FAO

**SUGAR BEET** is grown for the sugar that is obtained from its root. It is a *biennial* plant, because it takes two years for the plant to mature. During the first year, it grows a large fleshy root, a fleshy stem, and a cluster of leaves. The silvery-white beet is the enlarged upper part of the root, weighing 2 pounds or more. The rest of the root tapers down from the beet. It is long and slender, with many threadlike branches. This taproot grows 2 to 7 feet straight into the ground. The top of the beet is called the *crown*, and is very short. It sends out bunches of brilliant, rich green leaves, about 14 inches long. At the end of the first year of growth, the sugar beet is usually dug up and sent to the sugar refinery. If left in the ground for the second year, the plant sends out long branches that produce tiny flowers containing seeds. These flowers may be either reddish or greenish. Sugar beets are most profitably grown where there are six frost-free months each year. An average summer temperature of 67° F. to 72° F., with cool nights and warm days, is considered most favorable.

The fleshy root of the sugar beet ranks second only to sugar cane among important sources of sugar. The beet contains from 13 to 22 per cent sugar. It is made up of small cells and large cells. The small cells contain the sugar and the large cells store water. These cells are arranged in rings called *cambium* rings. The rings can be seen when the beet is cut crosswise. Beets are planted, thinned, topped, and loaded mechanically.

Sugar is taken from the beets by washing the beets and cutting them into thin slices. These slices are put into hot water, which soaks the sugar from the beets. The syrup is purified mechanically, filtered, and boiled to sugar. The sugar is dried for market and packaged.

The entire sugar-beet plant is put to good use. The leaves of the plant are cooked as greens, or used like hay for their protein. The crown, or stem, can serve as food for cattle, sheep, hogs, and other animals. The pulp of the beet that remains after the sugar is extracted also is used as feed to fatten animals. The residue from the sugar-refining process is called *molasses*. Farmers use molasses to feed cattle and other livestock.

Several diseases attack sugar beets. These include leaf spot, black root, root rot, and curly top. Crop rotation and the planting of disease-resistant varieties of beets help control disease.

The sugar beet grew wild in Asia and was cultivated in ancient times in southern Europe and North Africa. Its first modern use for sugar came about 1800 in France and Germany. During the middle 1800's, the plant was brought to the United States. But sugar beets did not become an important source of sugar in the United States and Canada until after World War I. Their use greatly increased during World War II.

**Scientific Classification.** The sugar beet belongs to the goosefoot family *Chenopodiaceae*. It is classified as genus *Beta*, species *B. vulgaris*. NEIL L. PENNINGTON

See also BEET.

**SUGAR BOWL.** See NEW ORLEANS (Visiting New Orleans); FOOTBALL (table).

**SUGAR CANE** is a tall grass plant that grows in tropical and semitropical countries. It produces sturdy stalks 7 to 15 feet high, and about 2 inches in diameter. These stalks contain a large amount of sugary juice from which sugar and syrup are made.

Sugar cane grows from a thick, solid rootstock. The numerous stalks have no branches, but have long, narrow leaves which are arranged in two rows. The stalk is divided into several sections, like a bamboo cane. These sections are called *internodes*. Each node bears a small bud which looks much like a potato eye. The color of the stem varies from yellow to reddish.

Sugar cane first grew in India. It has been cultivated in India and China since early times. After the Crusades, travelers brought it to Europe. Colonizers brought sugar cane to America and the West Indies during the 1500's. Today, the leading sugar-cane growing nations

769

## LEADING SUGAR CANE GROWING COUNTRIES
### Tons of sugar cane grown in 1967

|  |  |
|---|---|
| India | 102,213,000 tons |
| Brazil | 83,542,000 tons |
| Cuba | 58,422,000 tons |
| Pakistan | 33,270,000 tons |
| Mexico | 29,762,000 tons |
| China (Mainland) | 27,558,000 tons |
| United States | 23,650,000 tons |
| Australia | 18,727,000 tons |
| Colombia | 17,637,000 tons |
| South Africa | 15,546,000 tons |

Source: *Production Yearbook, 1967*, FAO

Werner Stoy, Camera Hawaii

**A Cane Worker in Hawaii** holds the sugar-rich section of a sugar cane stalk. Sugar is made from the sweet juice of the stalk.

include India, Brazil, Cuba, Pakistan, Mexico, Mainland China, and the United States. Hawaii, Louisiana, and Florida rank as the leading sugar cane producers in the United States. The American people use so much sugar that nearly all the United States supply must be imported from Puerto Rico, the Philippines, and other countries.

**Growth and Cultivation.** The best soil for sugar cane is a fertile soil that can hold a large amount of moisture. The plant needs much water; growers must irrigate the plants if the region has little rainfall. The soils of Louisiana and of the Florida peninsula yield excellent crops. The soils of the Hawaiian Islands are rich in lime, potash, phosphoric acid, and nitrogen. The Hawaiian plantations yield the richest crops of sugar cane in the world.

Sugar cane is grown chiefly from stem cuttings. Great furrows from 5 to 7 feet apart are dug in the field. The cuttings are laid horizontally in the furrows. Some planters use only the upper part or the matured part of the cane. Others use the entire cane.

After the cuttings have been planted, soil is thrown over the furrows until the cane is covered. In a short time the buds borne on the nodes swell and burst, and young stalks of cane emerge from the soil. Soon the leaves appear, and in a few weeks the stalks have developed nodes and internodes.

**Harvesting.** In Hawaii and Louisiana, machines are used to cut off the cane stalks. But in most other sugar-cane growing areas, workers cut the cane by hand. Each cutter uses a large steel knife which has a blade 5 inches wide and 18 inches long, with a hook on the back. As the cutters move down the rows, they cut the cane close to the ground, strip off the leaves with the hook, and cut off the top of the stalk at the last matured joint.

The cut stalks are thrown into heaps called *windrows*, and then gathered up into carts or narrow-gauge railway cars that take them to the sugar factory. The stubble left in the field produces two or three crops in Louisiana. It produces from five to ten crops in tropical regions.

**Scientific Classification.** Sugar cane belongs to the grass family, *Gramineae*. It is classified as genus *Saccharum*, species *S. officinarum*. NEIL L. PENNINGTON

See also CUBA (pictures: Farmers Harvest Sugar Cane); HAWAII (Agriculture); PUERTO RICO (color picture: Cutters Harvest Sugar Cane); SUGAR.

**SUGAR LOAF MOUNTAIN.** See RIO DE JANEIRO (picture).

**SUGAR OF LEAD.** See LEAD (Uses).

**SUGAR STATE.** See LOUISIANA.

**SUGARBERRY.** See HACKBERRY.

**SUGGESTION,** in psychology, is the acceptance of an idea by the mind without critical thought. For example, if someone merely makes a throwing motion, many observers will be sure that something actually left his hand. They get this impression because the mind tends to complete a partial picture. Similarly, if a child says he feels ill, his mother may touch his forehead and assure herself that he has a fever, even though a thermometer would show that his temperature is normal.

A professional magician relies on suggestion for most of his effects. If he goes through the motion of tossing a coin into a cup, and if people in the audience hear the expected jingling sound, they assume the coin is in the cup. Advertisers use suggestion in many ways. No advertiser would dare guarantee that a girl will become popular by using his brand of soap or toothpaste. But his slogans may strongly suggest this result.

Children accept suggestions more easily than adults do, because they are less critical and less experienced. Most uneducated or prejudiced people also accept suggestion easily. People are more suggestible when they are worried, tired, or ill. FRANK J. KOBLER

See also HYPNOTISM; MAGIC.

**SUHARTO,** soo *HAR* toe (1921-    ), became president of Indonesia in 1968. He and other top military officers seized power from President Sukarno after they put down a Communist uprising in 1965. Sukarno was allowed to keep the title of president until 1967.

Under Suharto's leadership, Indonesia ended border fighting with Malaysia and rejoined the United Nations. Sukarno had withdrawn Indonesia from the UN in 1965.

Suharto was born on the island of Java. As a young man he served in the colonial army The Netherlands kept in Indonesia, then a colony called The Netherlands (Dutch) East Indies. But later, he fought the Dutch for Indonesian independence. After independence, he rose to the rank of lieutenant-general in the Indonesian armed forces. See INDONESIA (Recent Events); SUKARNO.

**SUICIDE.** A person who deliberately kills himself commits suicide. Many authorities think that suicide becomes more common as life grows more complex. Primitive peoples rarely commit suicide. City dwellers are far more likely to commit suicide than rural people. Laborers are much less likely to kill themselves than business and professional men.

Throughout the world, three or four times as many men as women kill themselves. Male suicides generally hang themselves, or use a knife or a gun. Women often choose drowning or poison as the means of death. Women who commit suicide usually do so much younger than men. Both men and women are less likely to kill themselves if they are married. Year after year, the number of suicides has always increased during the late spring and early summer months. The rate of suicide is highest among people in the age group between 55 and 65.

Various groups have held widely different attitudes toward suicide. Many ancient peoples held that a person's life was his own, to keep or give up as he pleased. Some persons in Japan consider suicide, called *hara-kiri*, a method of avoiding disgrace (see HARA-KIRI). Christianity has always considered suicide a sin, and many Christians have believed that the person who committed suicide gave up his hope of getting to heaven. Many churches still hold this view. Roman Catholics are less likely to commit suicide than Protestants. Jews have a still lower suicide rate. Suicide is against the law, but the would-be suicide knows he will be beyond the reach of the law if he succeeds in killing himself. The law sometimes punishes attempted suicide.    JOHN W. WADE

**SUIT,** *soot*. When a person seeks the help of a court of law to enforce his rights, he is said to "bring suit." Someone who has suffered injury at the hands of another may bring suit for damages. A person also may bring suit to recover property, to collect money, to enforce the terms of a contract, or to accomplish one of many other purposes. A city, state, or other governmental unit may bring suit in the same way as a private person or a corporation. In general, a suit is any civil action brought before a court of law. Criminal prosecutions are not spoken of as suits.    THOMAS A. COWAN

See also COURT (How a Court Works); STATUTE OF LIMITATIONS.

**SUITE,** *sweet*. There are two kinds of *suites* in music: classic and modern. The classic suite is a collection of dances grouped together for their contrasting style and rhythms. One dance may be slow and the next fast, one stately, and another gay, but they are all played in the same key. The classic suite was most popular in the 1600's and 1700's, and influenced the development of the *sonata*. The modern suite is a sequence of contrasting sections, usually connected by some idea or story, such as the *Nutcracker Suite* of Peter Ilich Tchaikovsky.

Suite also has other meanings, such as a suite of rooms or a set of matched furniture.    RAYMOND KENDALL

See also GIGUE; SONATA.

**SUKARNO** (1901-    ) was president of Indonesia from 1945 to 1967. Anti-Communist military leaders took power from him in 1966, after Communists tried to overthrow the government. Sukarno retained the title of president until 1967. Indonesia was officially a "neutral" nation under Sukarno. But his statements and policies showed a leaning toward Communist China and Russia.

Sukarno was born in Surabaja, Java. He formed the Partai Nasional Indonesia (P.N.I.) in 1927, seeking independence from The Netherlands. After independence, Sukarno called for a "guided democracy" for Indonesia. By 1960, he held unrestricted power.

Sukarno brought *West Irian* (West New Guinea) under his control. He refused to recognize the Federation of Malaysia, claiming that Sabah should be part of Indonesia. He threatened to crush Malaysia, and began raids on the federation in 1964. He withdrew Indonesia from the United Nations in 1965 after Malaysia was seated on the Security Council.    GEORGE E. TAYLOR

See also INDONESIA (Government; History).

**SUKKOT,** *sook OHT*, or FEAST OF TABERNACLES, is a Jewish festival that originally celebrated the end of the harvest season. It begins on the 15th day of the Hebrew month of Tishri, and lasts nine days. Jews in Israel and Reform Jews celebrate it for only eight days. The eighth day of Sukkot is called *Shemini Atzeret*. The ninth is *Simhat Torah* (see SIMHAT TORAH). During the festival, traditional Jews live in huts called *sukkot* as a reminder of the huts in which their ancestors lived during their wanderings in the wilderness.

The ancient Hebrews celebrated Sukkot as a festival of thanksgiving, and brought sacrifices to the Temple in Jerusalem. They formed joyous parades carrying *lulabs* (palm branches), *etrogs* (citrons), and myrtle and willow branches. These plants are still used in the celebrations today.    LEONARD C. MISHKIN

**SUL ROSS STATE COLLEGE.** See UNIVERSITIES AND COLLEGES (table).

**SULAWESI** is the Indonesian name for the island of Celebes. See INDONESIA (The Islands; table).

**SULEIMAN I,** *soo lay MAHN* (1494-1566), became known in the Western world as THE MAGNIFICENT, but among his own people as THE LAWGIVER. He was the 10th ruler of the Ottoman Empire. He led armies into Hungary, and stormed the walls of Vienna. In Asia, his armies invaded Persia (Iran) and captured Tabriz and Baghdad. Suleiman's fleets dominated the Mediterranean Sea, the Red Sea, and the Persian Gulf. His sailors held North Africa, and raided the coasts of Spain, France, and Italy. Suleiman took Rhodes from the Knights of Saint John (see KNIGHTS OF SAINT JOHN). He revised the legal system. He quarreled with several of his sons, and executed two of them. See also TURKEY (The Ottoman Empire).    SYDNEY N. FISHER

## SULFA DRUGS

**SULFA DRUGS**, or SULFONAMIDES, are a group of chemicals that are used to fight bacteria and some other organisms that cause disease in the body. Thousands of lives have been saved with this valuable group of chemicals. Before scientists discovered the sulfonamides, about 12 of every 100 pneumococcal pneumonia victims died in spite of the use of a serum for pneumonia. After doctors began to use sulfa drugs, the death rate dropped to about 5 out of 100. Penicillin, which is not a sulfonamide, further reduced the death rate to from 3 to 5 in 100 cases. The use of sulfa drugs reduced the death rate in one form of meningitis from 35 to 50 out of every 100 cases to about 5 out of 100. These drugs contributed remarkably to the saving of lives in World War II.

**Uses in Treating Diseases.** The sulfa drugs are most commonly taken by mouth or by injection into the blood. They may also be applied directly to the skin as ointment or powder. However, some patients have *allergic* (sensitive) reactions when they are applied in this way. Sometimes sulfa drugs *crystallize* (solidify) in a patient's urine. For this reason, doctors may instruct patients taking sulfa drugs to drink large amounts of liquids to keep the kidneys clear.

In general, sulfa drugs are used to treat diseases, such as pneumonia, dysentery, meningitis, blood poisoning, urinary tract infections, and some venereal diseases. Other diseases treated with sulfa drugs are erysipelas, cellulitis, bubonic plague, and cholera.

Sulfonamides are not effective against all bacteria. For example, they are not effective against organisms causing tuberculosis. Therefore, the physician often must identify the type of bacteria that is causing an infection before he knows whether to use a sulfa drug. To be effective, a certain concentration of sulfa must be kept in the body. Because of this, most physicians examine the blood and body fluids regularly to determine how much of the drug is in the body.

Normally, sulfa drugs do not actually kill bacteria. Instead, they prevent the bacteria from multiplying. Then the body's regular defenses usually kill the bacteria. Many bacteria need a chemical called *para-aminobenzoic acid* (PABA) to multiply. PABA acts like a necessary vitamin for these bacteria. The sulfonamide drugs have a chemical structure similar to PABA, but they have sulfur atoms where PABA has carbon atoms. Bacteria cannot tell the difference between the two and absorb the sulfa drug rather than the PABA. The sulfur atoms then stop one or more of the growth processes of the bacteria, and the bacteria cannot multiply.

All sulfa drugs contain sulfur, nitrogen, hydrogen, and oxygen. They are called sulfur drugs or sulfonamides because of their similar chemical makeup. But each one is a little different in structure from the other.

**Development of the Sulfa Drugs.** Knowledge of the possible benefits of the sulfonamides dates back to 1908. In that year Paul Gelmo, a German chemist who was looking for better dyes for woolen goods, discovered chemicals that eventually led to the sulfa drugs. But it was not until the early 1930's that sulfonamides could be used in medicine. In 1935, a German bacteriologist named Gerhard Domagk reported that the sulfonamide drug *Prontosil* killed streptococcal bacteria in mice. He was offered the Nobel prize in medicine for 1939 for his discovery, but the Nazi regime in Germany would not allow him to accept it.

Research in this new chemical spread quickly after Domagk's discovery. Researchers, particularly in France, England, and the United States, investigated thousands of related chemicals before they found the few which were the most useful.

Prontosil and Neoprontosil are trade names for two of the earliest sulfonamides. In the body, they release *sulfanilamide*, the active substance fighting against bacteria. Sulfanilamide, sulfapyrazine, and sulfathiazole were among the earliest sulfa drugs put into general use. But in time they were largely replaced by other sulfonamides that were more effective and less harmful.

The sulfa drugs now used for general body infections include sulfadimethoxine, sulfamethazine, sulfisoxazole, and sulfadiazine. Sulfa drugs that are used for infections in the intestinal tract include succinylsulfathiazole and phthalylsulfathiazole.      SOLOMON GARB

**SULFATE** is a salt of sulfuric acid. As a rule, sulfates are stable compounds, formed in crystals. Most of them are fairly soluble in water. But such sulfates as barium, strontium, and lead sulfates, do not dissolve in water. Heavy spar is a sulfate of barium; gypsum is a sulfate of calcium; celestite is a sulfate of strontium; and Epsom salt is a sulfate of magnesium. Sulfates have important industrial uses. Copper sulfate, or blue vitriol, is used in many industries, including dyeing and calico printing. Iron sulfate is used in making ink and as a medicine. Manganese sulfate is used in calico printing. Zinc sulfate is used in surgery as an antiseptic, in calico printing, and in drying oils for varnishes. Some baking powders contain *alum*, a double sulfate of potassium and aluminum. Every sulfate contains a group of associated atoms of sulfur and oxygen known in chemistry as the *sulfate radical* ($-SO_4$). See also ALUM; GYPSUM.

**SULFIDE** is a group of compounds of sulfur with some other elements, usually metals. All sulfides contain the sulfide ion, in which sulfur has the valence of minus 2. The chemical symbol for this ion is $S^{--}$.

Sulfides are important in chemistry and industry. Hydrogen sulfide, a poisonous gas, is used in the laboratory to test for various metals. Hydrogen sulfide in the air tarnishes silver. Carbon disulfide is a solvent of rubber and sulfur, and a local anesthetic. It has been used to kill animal and insect pests. Deposits of metallic sulfides are important ores of the metals. Examples are the sulfides of zinc (zinc blende), lead (galena), mercury (cinnabar), and copper (chalcocite). Several colored sulfides are pigments in paints.

See also CARBON DISULFIDE; HYDROGEN SULFIDE.

**SULFONAMIDES.** See SULFA DRUGS.

**SULFUR** (chemical symbol, S) is a solid, nonmetallic element. It has an atomic number of 16 and an atomic weight of 32.064. It is found in many vegetables, such as onions, cabbage, and horseradish. It is necessary for the growth of plants and animals. Eggs also contain sulfur. In the mineral world, sulfur is found in large quantities both in a pure state and in combination with other substances. Sulfur occurs in a pure state in places where there are volcanoes. It combines with metals to form certain valuable metal ores such as *sphalerite, galena,*

## A FEW COMMON COMMERCIAL USES OF SULFUR

**Commercial Use of Sulfur** is among the widest of any of the elements. Sulfur is an important part of thousands of products and manufacturing operations.

Matches and Gunpowder

Rubber

Medicines

Insecticides and Plant Medicines

---

cinnabar, and *stibnite*. Gypsum, or *calcium sulfate*, is an important mineral that contains sulfur.

**Forms of Sulfur.** Sulfur comes in three forms, known as *allotropic* forms (see ALLOTROPY). Allotropic forms of an element have different physical forms. But they have the same chemical properties and are in the same state of matter. Sulfur comes in rhombic crystals, monoclinic crystals, and amorphous, or plastic, form. The *rhombic* crystals have three unequal axes, each of which is at right angles to the other. *Monoclinic* crystals are very transparent and are shaped like prisms. That is, two of the axes are at right angles with the third axis. *Amorphous*, or *plastic*, sulfur that may be formed by dropping molten sulfur into cold water, readily changes to the crystalline, rhombic form. Ordinary lump sulfur occurs in either rhombic or monoclinic crystals. It is pale yellow in color, though sulfur may sometimes be greenish, brownish, or reddish.

**Properties of Sulfur.** Sulfur is brittle and has almost no taste. When it is rubbed or melted, it gives off a "rotten egg" odor. It does not dissolve in water but dissolves readily in carbon disulfide.

Rhombic sulfur melts at 112.8° C. (235° F.) and monoclinic melts at 119.0° C. (246.2° F.). When heated above its melting point, sulfur becomes syrupy or a solid. When the temperature reaches about 250° C. (482° F.), the sulfur becomes so thick that it cannot be poured from the vessel. Above 250° C., the sulfur changes back into a liquid. The boiling point of sulfur is 444.6° C. (832° F.). When it boils it gives off a yellowish-brown vapor. This vapor *sublimes* (condenses) into fine yellow grains of powder known as *flowers of sulfur*. The roll sulfur that is used commercially is made by pouring liquid sulfur into cylinder-shaped molds to harden.

Sulfur ignites at a low temperature and burns very quickly. It burns in air with a pale-blue flame and gives off *sulfur dioxide*, a colorless gas. When sulfur dioxide is exposed to moist air, it mixes with the moisture in the air and forms *sulfurous acid*. Both sulfur dioxide and sulfurous acid are constantly being formed in the air in cities that burn a large amount of coal and gas.

**Sources.** Before 1900 almost all sulfur came from Sicily. Today the United States produces much sulfur, chiefly in Texas and Louisiana. Sulfur also is found in Spain, Mexico, Japan, and Italy.

The most common method of mining sulfur is called the *superheated water method*. This method was invented about 1900 by the American scientist Herman Frasch (see MINING [diagram]). By this method, sulfur deposits are heated beyond the melting point, known as *superheating*. Water is superheated under increased pressure so that its boiling point rises above sulfur's melting point. Four pipes, one inside the other, bore into the sulfur deposit. The two outside pipes force the hot water into the sulfur, causing the sulfur to melt. The fourth (innermost) pipe sends down compressed air into the deposit. This causes the melted sulfur to form a froth. The increased air pressure forces the froth up the third pipe. All other substances that have a higher melting point remain. Sulfur of about 99 per cent purity is obtained in this way. The frothy sulfur is sprayed into bins and allowed to dry thoroughly in the open air. By another and newer method, the sulfur cools and solidifies on a conveyer belt moving over shallow tanks of cold, running water.

Sulfur may be recovered in acid form from gases at metallic sulfide smelters. Sulfur as an element may be obtained from some natural gases and from refinery gas.

**Uses.** Sulfur has many commercial uses. Pure sulfur is used to make up a group of valuable substances known as *sulfur compounds*. These sulfur compounds include sulfuric acid, the sulfite salts, and sulfur dioxide. Sulfur mixes with saltpeter and charcoal to form gunpowder, and is used to some extent in the manufacture of matches. For the farm, sulfur is used in the manufacture of fertilizers, and in preparations that destroy in-

773

## SULFUR DIOXIDE

sects and plant pests. The lime-sulfur spray is especially used as an insecticide. Sulfur also has an important use in the making of paper pulp, which is produced by the action of calcium bisulfite on wood cellulose. Sulfur is used in various medicines and is considered helpful in certain skin diseases. Photographers use a sulfur compound, *sodium thiosulfate*, to fix photographic images after development.

GEORGE L. BUSH

**Related Articles** in WORLD BOOK include:
| | | |
|---|---|---|
| Brimstone | Sulfate | Sulfur Dioxide |
| Sulfa Drugs | Sulfide | Sulfuric Acid |

**SULFUR DIOXIDE,** *dy AHK side*, is a colorless, poisonous gas with a sharp odor of burning sulfur. Polluted air in cities often contains sulfur dioxide, which can damage the lungs. The gas forms from burning coal or other fuel containing large amounts of sulfur.

Industries combine sulfur dioxide with water to make sulfurous acid ($H_2SO_3$). This acid is used as a bleach and as a food preservative. Industries also combine sulfur dioxide with oxygen to make sulfur trioxide ($SO_3$). Sulfur trioxide combines with water to form sulfuric acid ($H_2SO_4$). Sulfur dioxide changes to a liquid under pressure, or when cooled to $-10°$ C. ($+14°$ F.). In liquid form, sulfur dioxide serves as a refrigerant.

Sulfur dioxide is found in volcanic gases and mineral waters. Manufacturers make it by burning sulfur or by heating metallic sulfur compounds. It is made in the laboratory by mixing acids with sulfite compounds. Sulfur dioxide has the chemical formula $SO_2$. It is about twice as heavy as air.

OTTO THEODOR BENFEY

See also AIR POLLUTION; SULFURIC ACID.

**SULFURIC ACID** (chemical formula, $H_2SO_4$), is a heavy, oily liquid that is strongly corrosive. Alchemists used to call it *oil of vitriol* (see ALCHEMY). Chemists classify sulfuric acid with the mineral acids because it comes from sulfur, a mineral. Some sulfuric acid contains excess amounts of *sulfur trioxide*. It is then called *oleum* or *fuming sulfuric acid*, because this kind of sulfuric acid fumes when exposed to the air.

### Uses

Almost every manufactured article in common use depends in some way on sulfuric acid for its production.

**In Industry,** the largest use of sulfuric acid is in the manufacture of fertilizers. Its second largest use is in the refining of petroleum, especially in the purification of gasoline. Sulfuric acid plays an important part in the manufacture of all other mineral or inorganic acids. Large quantities of sulfuric acid are used in the steel industry, in the production of other metals, and in electroplating. Along with nitric acid, it must be used in producing TNT, nitroglycerin, picric acid, and other explosives (see TNT; NITROGLYCERIN). Sulfuric acid is also used in automobile batteries (see BATTERY).

**In Chemistry.** Sulfuric acid plays an important part in the production of many organic chemicals. Ethyl alcohol and other alcohols are made from petroleum with the help of sulfuric acid. When ethylene, a chemical obtained from petroleum, is treated with sulfuric acid, it reacts with water to form ethyl alcohol (see ALCOHOL [Ethyl Alcohol]; ETHYLENE). Substances derived from benzene react with sulfuric acid to form sulfonates, which are widely used in detergents (see DETERGENT AND SOAP). Aromatic compounds such as toluene react with nitric and sulfuric acids to form nitro compounds. Some nitro compounds are useful as explosives. For example, TNT is a tri*nitro*toluene. Nitro compounds are also needed to prepare dyes and other chemicals.

### Chemical Action

Sulfuric acid is a strong acid and has a high boiling point. Because of this, it is useful in making other acids.

Sulfuric acid dissolves many metals and metal oxides to form sulfate salts. Metal sulfates thus formed have

SOME USES OF SULFURIC ACID

Textiles — Paints and Pigments — Explosives — Coal Products — Chemicals

Fertilizer — Petroleum Refining — Metallurgy — Rayon and Cellulose — Synthetic Rubber

many uses in industry. For example, barium sulfate, which does not dissolve in water, is used in the manufacture of paper.

Water can be mixed with sulfuric acid. But the mixing must be done carefully because of the great amount of heat released when the liquids mix. When concentrated sulfuric acid is to be diluted with water, the acid is always added to the water. If the water is added to the acid, dangerous spattering results.

Sulfuric acid combines quickly with water. Because of this, chemists often use it as a drying and dehydrating agent. An experiment can be performed with sulfuric acid and cane sugar. If the acid is poured on the sugar, the sugar becomes hot, swells, and finally turns into a black, spongy mass. Sulfuric acid has removed all the water from the sugar and left a mass of black carbon.

### Making Sulfuric Acid

Millions of tons of sulfuric acid are produced every year in the United States. Manufacturers usually use the lead-chamber process or the contact process. In each process, sulfur dioxide must first be obtained either by burning sulfur or by roasting metallic sulfides.

**The Lead-Chamber Method.** A mixture of sulfur dioxide, air, steam or water, and an oxide of nitrogen are put in lead-lined chambers. Chemical action of the ingredients with steam produces sulfuric acid.

**The Contact Method** is a newer process in which a mixture of sulfur dioxide and air is converted to sulfur trioxide. This is done by passing the gas mixture through a heated tube that contains a catalyst (see CATALYSIS). The sulfur trioxide produced combines with water to form sulfuric acid. However, this reaction takes place with explosive violence. So manufacturers first dissolve the sulfur trioxide in concentrated sulfuric acid to avoid explosions. Sulfuric acid produced by this method is more highly concentrated and more pure than that produced by the lead-chamber process.   JAMES S. FRITZ

See also ACID; BLEACHING; SULFATE.

**SULGRAVE MANOR** is an estate in Northamptonshire, England, which is regarded as the home of George Washington's ancestors. The Washington family owned it from 1539 to 1610, when Robert Washington and his son Lawrence sold it. Lawrence Washington built the manor house in the 1500's. In 1914, the British government bought the house to celebrate 100 years of peace between Britain and the United States. The house is still fairly well preserved. American patriotic societies helped furnish and restore the interior.   ALAN K. LAING

**SULLA, LUCIUS CORNELIUS** (138-78 B.C.), reformed the Roman government. He was the first Roman general to use his army against his political opponents. Later politicians, including Julius Caesar, followed this example.

Sulla was a member of a *patrician* (aristocratic) family. In 88 B.C., he was a *consul* (chief government official) and commander of a Roman army. When Mithridates VI, king of Pontus (in Asia Minor) attacked Roman lands in Asia, the Roman Senate put Sulla in command of an army to fight him. But the Assembly overruled the decision, and voted the command to Gaius Marius. Sulla was driven out of Rome. He returned with his army and drove out Marius, then went to fight Mithridates.

In 87 and 86 B.C., Sulla attacked Athens, an ally of Pontus, and then defeated two of Mithridates' armies. When Sulla entered Asia, Mithridates asked for and got peace.

Sulla hurried back to Rome, because Marius and other "popular" leaders had returned and killed many of his supporters. Marius was dead when Sulla returned in 83 B.C., but Sulla fought and won a civil war against Marius' followers. As dictator from 82 to 79 B.C., Sulla reorganized the state. He destroyed the power of the *tribunes* (representatives of the people), and gave the Senate control of Rome. After Sulla retired in 79 B.C., most of his reforms were discarded.   HENRY C. BOREN

**SULLIVAN, ANNE.** See KELLER, HELEN ADAMS.

**SULLIVAN, SIR ARTHUR SEYMOUR** (1842-1900), was a British composer. His fame rests largely on the operettas that he wrote with William S. Gilbert. Sullivan composed the music, and Gilbert wrote the words (see GILBERT, SIR WILLIAM S.). The operettas include such permanent favorites as *Trial by Jury* (1875), *H.M.S. Pinafore* (1878), *The Pirates of Penzance* (1879), *Patience* (1881), *Iolanthe* (1882), *Princess Ida* (1884), *The Mikado* (1885), *Ruddigore* (1887), *The Yeomen of the Guard* (1888), and *The Gondoliers* (1889).

Chicago Historical Society
**Sir Arthur Sullivan**

Sullivan's song "The Lost Chord" and the hymn tune "Onward, Christian Soldiers" are also remembered (see HYMN [Some World-Famous Hymns]). The rest of his large output faded quickly. Sullivan was born in London, and became a learned musician. He taught and conducted as well as composed music. Queen Victoria knighted him in 1883.   HERBERT WEINSTOCK

**Sulgrave Manor,** in Northamptonshire, England, was the comfortable home of George Washington's ancestors.
Gendreau

# SULLIVAN, JOHN

**SULLIVAN, JOHN.** See NEW HAMPSHIRE (The Revolutionary War).

**SULLIVAN, JOHN L.** (1858-1918), was a famous bareknuckle fighter and world heavyweight boxing champion. He won the heavyweight title from Paddy Ryan in 1882 in Mississippi City, Miss., on an eighth-round knockout. Sullivan fought his most famous fight with Jake Kilrain in 1889. They fought 75 rounds (2 hours, 16 minutes) before Sullivan won on a knockout. He lost the championship to Jim Corbett in 1892. He retired in 1905, and appeared on the stage. Sullivan was born in Roxbury, Mass.
LYALL SMITH

See also BOXING (picture).

**SULLIVAN, LOUIS HENRI** (1856-1924), an architect, during his lifetime was America's greatest advocate of a modern architectural style. He was an outspoken critic of the imitation of historic styles that dominated architecture in the 1800's and early 1900's.

Louis Sullivan
Elmslie

He was born in Boston, and studied at Massachusetts Institute of Technology, École des Beaux Arts in Paris, and in the office of William Le Baron Jenney (see JENNEY, WILLIAM LE BARON). Most of his buildings were designed in partnership with Dankmar Adler between 1891 and 1895 (see ADLER, DANKMAR). These include the Auditorium building located in Chicago, and skyscrapers in Chicago, St. Louis, and Buffalo. In these, Sullivan created a new style expressive of modern functional needs. His masterpiece was the Carson Pirie Scott store in Chicago.

Sullivan wrote books and articles, calling for a new architectural style to express the times. He insisted that a modern bank should not look like a Greek temple, and a present-day warehouse should not be disguised as a medieval castle. He tried to suit the needs of his time and fought borrowing designs from past periods. He published *The Autobiography of an Idea* (1924), an account of his life.

Sullivan's theory of functionalism was not widely accepted during his lifetime. He had few commissions during his last years, and he died in poverty. Since then, however, the world has recognized him as a great architectural pioneer. He was named winner of the Gold Medal of the American Institute of Architects in 1943, and, in 1956, the 100th anniversary of his birth, a large exhibition of his work was shown internationally. The architect, Frank Lloyd Wright, was his pupil (see WRIGHT, FRANK LLOYD).
HUGH MORRISON

**SULLIVAN, MARK** (1875-1952), was an American author, newspaper columnist, magazine editor, and writer for more than 60 years. He became best known for his syndicated political column, begun in the middle 1920's. He also wrote *Our Times* (1926-1936), a six-volume chronicle of American history. Sullivan, an Irish farmer's son, was born in Avondale, Pa. He began his magazine career on the *Ladies' Home Journal* in 1904. Sullivan joined the staff of *Collier's* magazine in 1906, and became the editor of the magazine in 1914.
JOHN TEBBEL

The Art Institute of Chicago

**The Carson Pirie Scott** store in Chicago, designed by the architectural firm of Adler and Sullivan, was named one of *The Seven Wonders of American Architecture* in 1958. It is one of the best designed early skyscrapers.

SUMAC

Museum of Fine Arts, Boston

Metropolitan Museum of Art

*The Torn Hat* by Thomas Sully, *above*, is a study of this American artist's son. The winsome face, torn hat, and simple charm of the boy have made this a favorite among paintings of children. Sully painted the self-portrait, *left*, in the early 1800's.

**SULLY, DUKE OF.** See FRANCE (The Age of Absolutism).

**SULLY, THOMAS** (1783-1872), an American painter, was noted for his elegant and refined portraits. Sully painted delicate, fragile portraits of women that glowed with life. His portraits of men were elegant but sturdier. Portraits by him appear in the ADAMS, JOHN QUINCY, and HENRY, PATRICK articles.

Sully was born in Horncastle, England, and came to America when he was 9. He began studying painting when he was about 12. Sully moved to New York City in 1806, then settled permanently in Philadelphia in 1808. He visited London in 1809 and 1810, and met the painters Benjamin West and Sir Thomas Lawrence, who greatly influenced his style. Sully enjoyed great success after that and was sent to London in 1838 to paint a portrait of Queen Victoria. FREDERICK A. SWEET

**SULLY-PRUDHOMME,** *syoo LEE pryoo DAWM*, **RENÉ FRANÇOIS ARMAND** (1839-1907), a French poet, won the 1901 Nobel prize for literature. His early collections of verse, including *Les Épreuves* (1866) and *Les Solitudes* (1869), deal with the sufferings of love. His later poems express the conflicts of science and religion. He also wrote several books on philosophy and psychology. He was born in Paris. As a young man, he studied engineering. HASKELL M. BLOCK

**SULPHUR.** See SULFUR.

**SULPICIAN SEMINARY OF THE NORTHWEST.** See UNIVERSITIES AND COLLEGES (table).

**SULTAN** is a title of honor given to Moslem princes and rulers. The word means *sovereign*, but in ancient days it meant merely someone who was stern and mighty. The title has been used since about A.D. 900. The ruler of old Turkey was the greatest of the sultans. Today, many sultans have wealth, but few have the power of the ancient princes. See also SERAGLIO. SYDNEY N. FISHER

**SULU ARCHIPELAGO.** See PHILIPPINES (The Islands).

**SULU SEA** is also called the SEA OF MINDORO. It lies between the Philippine Islands and Borneo. The Sulu Sea is surrounded by the Visaya Islands on the northeast, Borneo on the southwest, and the Sulu Islands on the southeast. Straits connect the Sulu Sea with the South China Sea and the Pacific Ocean. The sea has an average depth of 14,600 feet. Near the western coast of Mindanao, it is more than 16,000 feet deep. For location, see PHILIPPINES (color map). F. G. WALTON SMITH

**SULZBERGER, ARTHUR HAYS** (1891-1968), an American newspaperman, was publisher of *The New York Times* from 1935 to 1961. He succeeded his father-in-law, Adolph S. Ochs. Sulzberger carried on the great tradition of that influential newspaper. Under his direction, the *Times*' staff became the largest in the world. Sulzberger championed the cause of free and responsible journalism. Born in New York City, he joined *The Times* in 1918. He continued as chairman of the board after he retired as publisher in 1961. ALVIN E. AUSTIN

**SUMAC,** *SHOO mack*, or *SOO mack*, or SUMACH, is a group of about 120 kinds of small trees or shrubs that grow in temperate regions. Many have commercial uses.

**Common Sumacs.** One of the best known of the North American sumacs is the *staghorn sumac*. It grows from southern Canada to Georgia and Mississippi. It is an attractive flat-topped tree, growing 30 to 35 feet high. The tree bears small, greenish flowers and tiny red

**Sumac Has Narrow Leaves and Clusters of Berries.**
J. Horace McFarland

# SUMATRA

berries. Its fernlike leaves are velvety dark green above, and pale beneath. In autumn, the leaves turn scarlet, orange, and purple. The forked branches of immature trees have a velvety down. The berry clusters and leafstalks are hairy. The brittle wood has no practical use.

The *dwarf*, *black*, or *mountain sumac* is as pretty as the staghorn. It grows throughout the eastern United States and from the Mississippi River west to the Rockies. The dwarf sumac is usually a shrub, although in the Tennessee and North Carolina mountains it grows as tall as the staghorn. Its leaves contain much tannin and are used in tanning leather. They also provide a yellow dyestuff. The *smooth-leaved sumac*, which usually grows only about 3 feet high, is found east of the Rocky Mountains, from Arizona to British Columbia. The unripe summer berries make a refreshing drink that tastes something like lemonade. Some American Indians used the bark, leaves, and berries of the smooth-leaved sumac as a medicine.

**Poisonous Sumacs** have berries that hang in drooping clusters. The red berries of the harmless sumacs are in dense, erect clusters. The *poison sumac*, also called *poison elder*, has white berries. It grows in swampy land from New England to Minnesota and from Georgia to Texas. *Poison ivy* and *poison oak* have white berries. They are beautiful in autumn, with scarlet and orange foliage. The *varnish tree*, also called the *lacquer tree*, and the *wax tree* grow in Japan, China, and the Himalaya. The lacquer tree provides fine lacquer, and the wax tree is used in making candles.

**Scientific Classification.** The sumacs belong to the cashew family, *Anacardiaceae*. They make up the genus *Rhus*. The staghorn sumac is species *R. typhina*. The shining sumac is *R. copallina;* the smooth is *R. glabra;* and the poison is *R. vernix*.   J. J. LEVISON

See also POISON IVY.

**SUMATRA,** in Indonesian, SUMATERA. See INDONESIA (The Islands).

**SUMBA.** See INDONESIA (table: Chief Islands).

**SUMBAWA.** See INDONESIA (table: Chief Islands).

**SUMER,** *SOO mur*, was a region settled before 3500 B.C. in the lower part of Mesopotamia (now Iraq). The people who settled it probably came from the highlands of present-day Turkey or Iran. They are often pictured with long skirts, shaven heads, and sometimes with beards. Scholars do not know the exact origin of their racial or language group.

The Sumerians developed a brilliant civilization in Mesopotamia. Their small settlements grew into cities and city-states. The more powerful city-states conquered their neighbors and created small kingdoms, including Kish, Lagash, Nippur, Umma, Ur, and Uruk (Warka).

The Sumerians developed an economy based on farming. They built a great network of irrigation canals to water their fields, and grew barley, date palms, wheat, and many kinds of vegetables. They used domestic animals such as donkeys, goats, and sheep. Their society included priests, soldiers, traders, freemen, and slaves.

The Sumerians invented a system of writing, probably before 3000 B.C. Their *cuneiform*, or *wedge-form*, writing became one of the most important systems of writing in the ancient world (see CUNEIFORM). Thousands of clay tablets and inscriptions that have been preserved tell about the Sumerian government, law, business practices, and religion. The tablets also show that the Sumerians had some knowledge of mathematics, astronomy, and medicine.

The Sumerians built great temples and palaces in their cities. Skilled craftsmen made beautiful art objects and household equipment out of copper, gold, silver, and stone. They wove fine cloth, and made armor, chariots, spears, and swords for their armies. Many Sumerian industries were identified with specific towns. Ur was known for its metalworks and Umma for its textiles.

Much of the Sumerian culture was absorbed by Se-

**An Ancient Sumerian Grave** yielded the headdress and jewelry, *left*, of Queen Shub-ad, who lived about 5,500 years ago. The well preserved, pictorial shell plaque, *right*, came from the grave of a Sumerian king who reigned about 3500 B.C.

University Museum, Philadelphia

mitic invaders who moved into Mesopotamia and slowly took over the region. By 2000 B.C., the Sumerians had lost political power, but they furnished the base on which the impressive Babylonian and Assyrian civilizations developed. JOHN W. SNYDER

See also ASSYRIA; BABYLONIA; UR; HARP (picture).

**SUMMA CUM LAUDE.** See DEGREE, COLLEGE.

**SUMMARY** is a brief restatement of important points for emphasis. See also OUTLINES AND OUTLINING.

**SUMMER** is the warm time of the year when the sun shines most directly on one-half of the world. Summer in the Northern Hemisphere begins about June 21, the date of the summer solstice (see SOLSTICE). It ends about September 23, the date of the autumnal equinox (see EQUINOX). Usually, July and August are the hottest months of the summer season. Field crops, trees, and other plants reach their fullest maturity in summer.

When the sun is highest over the Northern Hemisphere, it is lowest in the Southern Hemisphere. The warmest months in the United States are the coldest months in Australia, and in the southern part of South America and Africa. December, January, and February are the growing season in such lands. PAUL SOLLENBERGER

See also AUGUST; DOG DAYS; JULY; JUNE; SEASON.

**SUMMERSIDE,** Prince Edward Island (pop. 10,042; alt. 21 ft.), is a port and a center for breeding silver foxes. It stands on Bedeque Bay, about five miles south of Malpeque Bay, which is famous for fine oysters (see PRINCE EDWARD ISLAND [map]). Summerside is in the richest farmlands of the island. It was once called Green's Shore, but was renamed because it lies on the warmer, or "summer," side of the island. Large amounts of farm and fish products are shipped from Summerside. The Canadian National Silver Fox Breeders' Association and the Dominion Fox Experimental Station headquarters are there. Summerside has a council-manager form of government. FRANK MACKINNON

**SUMMIT CONFERENCE,** or SUMMIT MEETING, is a meeting of two or more heads of state. It usually refers to a conference attended by Communist and Western democratic leaders. A 1955 conference in Geneva, Switzerland, is widely regarded as the first summit conference. See also COLD WAR (The Spirit of Camp David).

**SUMMONS** is an order *served* (delivered) by a sheriff or some other officer of a court. The summons notifies the person named in it that a complaint has been made against him, and that he must come to court to answer it. In some jurisdictions, the plaintiff's attorney or the court clerk may issue the summons. A summons also may be issued by other governmental agencies, such as congressional committees. See also SUBPOENA; WRIT.

**SUMNER, CHARLES** (1811-1874), was an American statesman and antislavery leader. After the Civil War, he advocated treating the South harshly. He led the Senate's opposition to President Abraham Lincoln's moderate plans for reconstruction. Later, he also opposed President Andrew Johnson's plans.

Sumner was born in Boston and was educated at Harvard University. He first won attention as a lecturer on peace and abolition. He was elected United States senator from Massachusetts in 1851. In the Senate, he vigorously attacked the South. In 1856, Sumner made a Senate speech which included several sneering references to Senator Andrew P. Butler of South Carolina. Three days later, Representative Preston S. Brooks (1819-1857), Butler's nephew, attacked Sumner in the Senate, beating him senseless.

Sumner helped found the Republican party, and during the Civil War was one of the most powerful men in the Senate. He favored freeing the slaves and giving them the right to vote. He opposed President Ulysses S. Grant's plan for annexing Santo Domingo (see GRANT, ULYSSES S. [Foreign Relations]). W. B. HESSELTINE

**SUMNER, JAMES BATCHELLER** (1887-1955), an American biochemist, crystallized the first enzyme (see ENZYME). He extracted the enzyme urease from the jack bean, and converted the crude material into pure crystals. His success stimulated John Howard Northrop to crystallize other important enzymes, and Wendell Meredith Stanley to crystallize the first virus. The three men shared the 1946 Nobel prize in chemistry. Sumner's work proved that enzymes were chemicals. He was born in Canton, Mass. HERBERT S. RHINESMITH

**SUMNER, WILLIAM GRAHAM** (1840-1910), was a noted American sociologist and economist in the late 1800's. His ideas about society reflected biologist Charles Darwin's findings about evolution.

Sumner believed the phrase "survival of the fittest" applied to man in society as well as to animals in nature. He believed that hard work results in wealth, and that poverty is the result of bad habits and laziness. He argued that reformers who tried to change society or to aid the poor were dangerous. This philosophy became known as Social Darwinism.

Sumner was born in Paterson, N.J. He taught at Yale University. His most important book, *Folkways* (1907), was a study of society. CHARLES FORCEY and LINDA FORCEY

**SUMP.** See GASOLINE ENGINE (Lubrication System).

**SUMPTUARY LAW,** *SUMP tyoo ER ih.* The word *sumptuary* comes from a Latin word which means *expenditure.* In ancient Greece and Rome, laws limited the amount of money that anyone could spend on private luxuries. Laws of this kind were called *sumptuary laws.*

Similar laws have been common at various times in England, France, Scotland, Spain, and Italy. From the days of Edward III (1327-1377) until the Reformation in the early 1500's, the English Parliament restricted the number of courses of a meal to two, except on holidays. It also regulated the amount that members of each class of society could spend on clothes. ERWIN N. GRISWOLD

See also BLUE LAWS; PROHIBITION.

**SUMTER,** S.C. (pop. 23,062; alt. 170 ft.), is the county seat and marketing center of Sumter County, which is one of the leading farming and lumbering regions of South Carolina. The city lies about 40 miles east and south of Columbia (see SOUTH CAROLINA [political map]). The chief industries include woodworking; the manufacture of furniture, barrels, concrete blocks, and bricks; steel fabrication; and machinery making. Sumter is a large livestock and turkey market. Founded in 1785, Sumter was named for Brigadier General Thomas Sumter, the *Gamecock* of Revolutionary War fame. His home is nearby. Shaw Air Force Base stands near the city. Sumter has a council-manager government.

**SUMTER, FORT.** See FORT SUMTER.

**SUMTER, THOMAS.** See SOUTH CAROLINA (History); SUMTER.

779

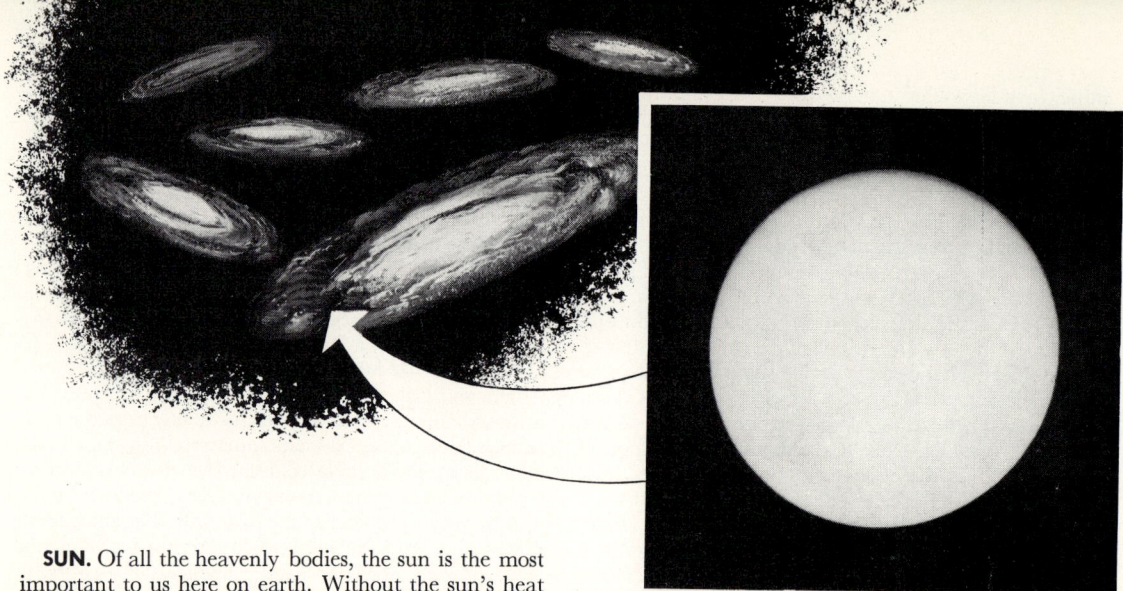

The sun is only a dwarf star in a great whirling "star island" containing billions of stars. There are countless other star islands in space. But, to man, the sun is the most important object in the sky, because...

... it gives us light and warmth

... it makes our weather

... its rays store energy in our food

**SUN.** Of all the heavenly bodies, the sun is the most important to us here on earth. Without the sun's heat and light, man, animals, and plants could not live and grow.

The sun is the center of the solar system, for the earth and all the other planets move in great circles around it. Yet the sun is only one among countless billions of stars in the heavens.

Of all the stars, the sun is nearest to the earth. That is why it looks so much bigger and brighter than any other star. If it were as far away from the earth as the stars in the Big Dipper are, the sun would be so small we could not see it without using a telescope. At that distance, too, the brightest star in the Dipper would be nearly 14,000 times brighter than the sun.

――――― FACTS IN BRIEF ABOUT THE SUN ―――――

**What Is the Sun Made Of?** The sun is a glowing ball of hot gases. These gases are made up of about the same chemical elements we find in the crust of the earth. The most common elements in the sun are hydrogen, helium, calcium, sodium, magnesium, and iron.

**How Large Is the Sun?** The diameter of, or distance through, the main ball of the sun is about 865,000 miles. This is 109 times the diameter of the earth and 400 times the diameter of the moon.

Many stars are larger than the sun. The diameter of Betelgeuse, a bright red star in the constellation Orion, is about 400 times as large as the sun's diameter. If the sun were placed at the center of Betelgeuse, the planets Mercury, Venus, Earth, and Mars could all revolve about the sun at their present distances and remain within the surface of that huge star.

**How Heavy Is the Sun?** The gases at the center of the sun are dense and heavy, but the gases at the surface are much lighter. For its size, the sun is much lighter than the earth. A bucket of average earth material would weigh about $5\frac{1}{2}$ times as much as a bucket of water. A bucket of average sun material would weigh only about $1\frac{1}{2}$ times as much as a bucket of water. But the sun is so big that its total mass, or weight, is 331,950 times that of the earth. The force of gravity at the surface of the sun is about 28 times as great as the force of gravity which holds things to the earth. A man who weighs 150 pounds on the earth would weigh about two tons on the sun.

**How Hot Is the Sun?** The temperature at the surface of the sun is about 11,000° Fahrenheit. At the center of the sun, it is probably about 36,000,000°F.

**How Far Away Is the Sun?** Its average distance from the earth is 92,956,000 miles. At times, it comes as near as 91,402,000 miles. Its farthest distance from the earth is 94,512,000 miles.

**How Long Does Light from the Sun Take to Reach the Earth?** About $8\frac{1}{3}$ minutes.

**How Much Energy Does the Sun Give to the Earth?** About 126,000,000,000,000 horsepower, or 54,000 horsepower for every man, woman, and child on earth. Yet this vast amount of energy is only one two-billionth of the total energy sent out by the sun. All the planets together receive less than one two-hundred-millionth of the sun's energy. The rest is lost in space.

780

# THE SUN IN STORY AND LEGEND

Man recognized the importance of the sun long before he learned to understand it through science. He made up stories about the sun's travels through the sky, and he sometimes worshiped the sun.

**THE HORSE-DRAWN SUN**
The ancient Greeks believed the sun god Helios drove the sun chariot through the sky.

**THE SUN'S GIFTS TO MAN**
Ancient Egyptians worshiped a sun god. They believed he brought the gift of life to the earth. This carving was made about 3,300 years ago.

**WHERE DOES THE SUN GO AT NIGHT?**
The Eskimo thought it took a boat trip under the northern horizon, and that the northern lights came from the hidden sun.

**SUN WORSHIP BY THE INCAS**
The Incas of Peru, like many other primitive peoples, worshiped the sun as a god and made sacrifices to him.

**WHY DOES THE SUN TRAVEL SLOWLY ACROSS THE SKY?**
The Maoris of New Zealand said one of their heroes fought the sun and made it lame, so that it took all day to limp across the sky.

# WHY THE SUN APPEARS RED AT SUNSET

The earth's atmosphere scatters the sun's blue and violet light rays. When the sun is directly overhead, its rays follow a relatively short path through the earth's atmosphere. Few blue and violet rays are scattered during this short trip, and the sun looks white. At sunset, however, when the sun is near the horizon, its rays must follow a longer path through the atmosphere to reach the earth. As a result, more of the blue and violet rays are scattered and the sun looks red.

### Does the Sun Move?

Long ago, people believed that the sun rose in the east, traveled across the sky, and then sank down behind the land to the west. We now know that it only seems to do this because the earth on which we stand is spinning toward the east.

But the sun does move. It moves in two ways. First, it is speeding along at about 43,000 miles an hour among the billions of other stars in the Milky Way. It carries with it the earth and all the rest of the solar system. Second, the sun spins on its axis.

The sun goes at tremendous speed on its path through space—about 12 miles a second. But we need not worry that the sun might hit another star. The nearest star to our sun, Proxima Centauri, is over twenty-five trillion, sixty-three billion miles away. This is so far that light, which travels 186,282 miles in a single second, takes more than four years to get from this star to the earth. It would take the earth about 65,000 years to reach Proxima Centauri if it were headed in that direction, which it is not.

The sun also rotates (spins around) like a giant, flaming top. But, instead of turning around once in twenty-four hours as the earth does, it takes about twenty-five days for one rotation. And because the sun is made of gas, parts of it spin around in less time than other parts. The equator turns around in the least amount of time.

### How the Sun Affects Our Earth

**What the Earth Would Be Like Without the Sun.** If it were not for the sun, there probably would be no earth. Most scientists believe that the earth and all the other planets of the solar system were once part of the sun.

But can you imagine what it would be like on the earth if the sun were suddenly to disappear? The sun's powerful gravitational pull is what causes the earth to move in a great oval path, or *ellipse*, around the sun. With the sun gone, the earth would stop circling and shoot off into space. This would be much as if you were whirling a ball fastened to a string, and the string suddenly snapped. The tides would be different, too, with the sun gone. Both the sun and the moon pull the oceans up a little, to make the bulges of water we call tides.

Our moon would seem to disappear, if the sun were gone. The moon shines only because it reflects light from the sun. The earth would be almost completely dark. Only the feeble light of the stars would reach it. The skies would be jet black, both day and night. Not even the northern lights and the southern lights would light the skies above, for they are caused by radiant energy from the sun (see AURORA BOREALIS).

However, there would be no living things on earth to miss the beautiful sunsets or the moonlit skies. Without the sun, the earth would quickly cool to a coldness greater than man has ever been able to produce with his best cold-making machines.

For just a little while, there would still be air to breathe, but there would be no winds, and soon there would be no weather changes. Winds are made as the sun heats the air. And weather is made as warm air rises, cools, and drops its moisture onto the earth. With no sun to heat the air, the cold, dark world would be blanketed in a completely still mass of air. But only for a little while. The water vapor in the air would freeze almost immediately and fall to the earth in a blanket of snow. Soon even the oxygen, nitrogen, and other gases that make up our air would settle as a solid frost upon the surface of the dark, cold, dead world below.

**Sunlight—the Miracle Worker.** The earth is so small and so far away from the sun that it receives only about one two-billionth part of the heat and light that the sun gives out. Yet this extremely narrow beam of light and heat rays makes all the difference between a dark, dead world and the warm, beautiful earth of color, light, and life that we all know.

Light and heat from the sun are called *solar energy*, from the Latin name *Sol* which the Romans gave to the sun. They reach the earth by what is called *radiation*.

Much of the radiation that streams from the sun to the earth is bounced back into space by the atmosphere, which acts like a giant mirror. But the comparatively

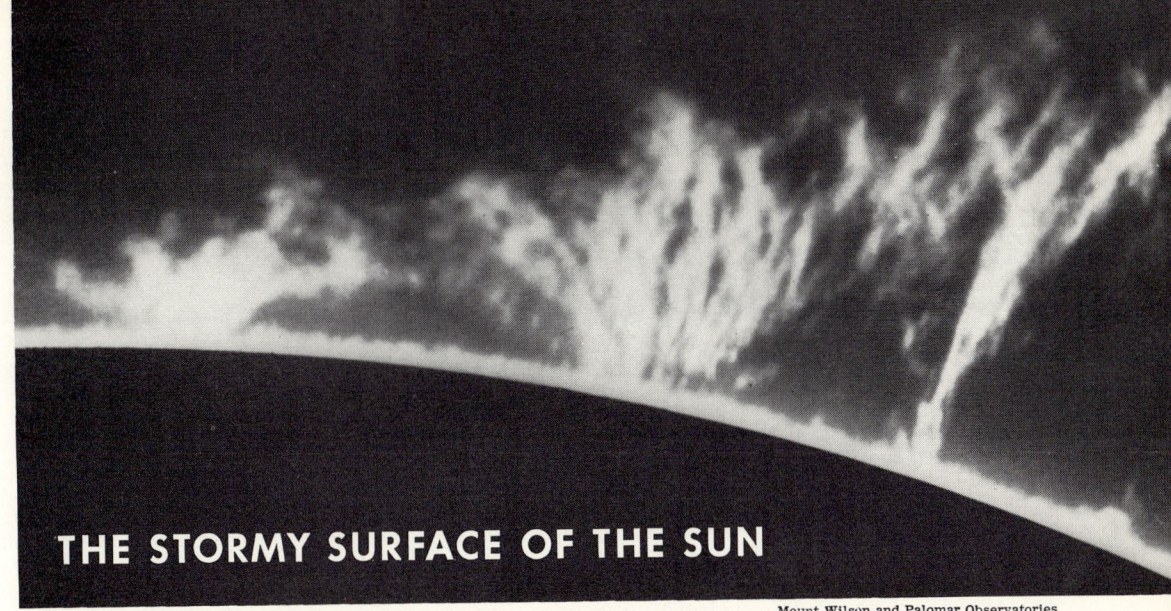

# THE STORMY SURFACE OF THE SUN

Mount Wilson and Palomar Observatories

**Prominences** are flamelike bursts of gas that shoot out as far as 250,000 miles from the sun's surface.

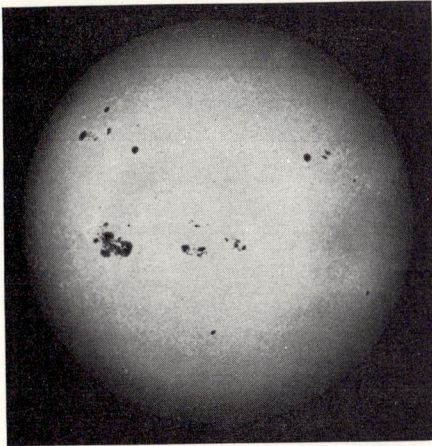

**Sunspots** are storm centers in the sun's atmosphere. We see them as dark spots. When there are many sunspots, magnetic storms "jam" radio channels.

**The Corona** is a fiery ocean of gases that surrounds the sun as the atmosphere surrounds the earth. Men can see it well only during a total eclipse of the sun. The corona may be a million miles "deep."

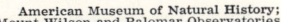
American Museum of Natural History;
Mount Wilson and Palomar Observatories

small amount that does reach the earth provides us with practically all the energy we have. This energy works many miracles on the earth. See RADIATION (How Radiation Affects Life on the Earth); SOLAR ENERGY.

**Why Food Is Called "Stored Sunlight."** There would be no food to eat without the sun. Plants manufacture food, and they must use the sun's radiant energy to do so. The raw materials of food-making are water and a gas called *carbon dioxide*. When the sun shines, the plant goes to work. It changes the water and carbon dioxide, which have no energy, into sugar, which is full of energy. We might say that the green plant traps the sunlight and stores it in the sugar. Then it makes some of the sugar into other products. Animals eat the plants, and change the sugar and plant tissues into body tissues, or use the sugar to make the energy they need to move about. Man eats plants, and also eats meat from animals. His body receives energy from both. The energy in both plant and animal foods came first from the sun. When you eat food, you are eating "stored sunlight." See LEAF (The Leaf as a Food Factory); PHOTOSYNTHESIS.

**Coal and Petroleum Are Trapped Sunlight.** Millions of years ago, giant ferns and similar plants lived and died on earth. When they were alive, they trapped the sun's energy, and then manufactured food which they stored in their tissues. When they died, they sank down into swampy soil. After millions of years, they were changed into coal. When coal is burned, it releases the light and radiant heat of the sun which the plants trapped many millions of years ago.

Something similar probably happened to make petroleum. Scientists believe that tiny plants died and their tissues were changed into oil deep in the ground. Now, when we pump oil out of the ground and use it to make fuel, we are releasing the trapped energy of sunlight. When you see a car roar down the highway, or an airplane rush through the skies above, keep in mind that it is really "sun power" that makes them go.

**Other Ways We Use the Sun's Energy.** There are many other ways in which we use the sun's energy. Windmills are sun engines, because the sun makes the

783

# SUN

winds. The sun lifts millions of tons of water into the air and makes rain. The rains spill the water back to the earth, and it forms rivers. Where there are waterfalls in the rivers, or dams across them, the falling water turns turbines that make electricity. When we burn wood in a campfire or fireplace, the light and heat we get is sunlight stored by the tree when it was alive.

Every square yard of the earth on which the sun shines could give us an average of one and a half horsepower of energy if we knew how to use it. See RADIATION (Radiant Energy as a Direct Source of Power).

**Invisible Sunlight and Health.** We can see the visible light that comes to us from the sun. But the sun also sends out radiations that we cannot see. Some of these, called *ultraviolet light*, cause sunburning and suntanning. But we could not live without ultraviolet light. Plants absorb it and make vitamin D, the "sunshine vitamin." Our bodies, and the bodies of animals, do the same thing. If we did not get out into the sunlight and make vitamin D in our bodies, or eat fresh vegetables and other foods which contain it, we would become sick and die. See VITAMIN (Vitamin D).

Ultraviolet rays streaming down on the top layers of the atmosphere highly electrify, or *ionize*, the atmosphere. In doing this, they provide an electrical "ceiling" from which the long-distance radio waves are reflected back to earth. This makes our world-wide radio communication possible.

We receive invisible *infrared* rays from the sun. Infrared rays, also called *heat rays*, change to heat when they hit something. The infrared rays keep the earth warm.

## How to Look at the Sun

It is not safe to look directly at the sun because the sun's rays can cause serious damage to the eyes. Sunglasses, smoked glass, and other types of filters do not provide adequate protection. Looking at the sun with binoculars, telescopes, or mirrors can cause even more serious damage because these objects concentrate the sun's rays, thereby making them more intense.

Much of the bright light of the sun has been absorbed by the earth's atmosphere just after sunrise or before sunset. At these times you can usually look at the red disk of the sun without danger of injuring your eyes.

## Parts of the Sun

The bright disk of the sun which gives off light and heat is called the *photosphere*, which means *light ball*. This is the part of the sun you can see through smoked glass. Around the photosphere is a layer of gas, made up chiefly of hydrogen and calcium. It is brilliant red in color, but ordinarily it can be seen only during total eclipses of the sun. This layer is called the *chromosphere*, which means *color ball*. It corresponds to the atmosphere on earth. Fiery streamers of hydrogen gas shoot out from the chromosphere. Sometimes they rise a hundred thousand miles or more into space, then fall back into the sun. Outside the chromosphere of the sun there is still another layer of gas that is called the *corona*. This can be seen during total eclipses of the sun. It is yellowish to pearly green in color, and it stretches away from the sun in all directions for distances as great as a million miles and more.

## The Stormy Surface of the Sun

**Sunspots.** If you could look through a certain kind of telescope, you might see the sun's surface covered with dark specks or blotches. These are called *sunspots*. Sometimes these spots are big enough to be seen with the naked eye through smoked glass.

Sunspots move slowly across the sun's disk. This movement shows that the sun is rotating. Sunspots should be called *sun storms*. They are really storms of twisting, whirling masses of electrified gases.

As the sunspots move across the sun, they produce tremendous magnetic effects. These magnetic forces are so great that they affect magnets and electrical instruments here on the earth. Sunspots sometimes make compass needles swing around crazily, instead of pointing steadily toward the north.

Even radios are affected during the great sun storms. Scientists think that the storm centers on the sun shoot electric particles toward the earth. These fill the upper atmosphere with electricity and cause the magnificent displays we call the northern lights, or *aurora borealis*, and southern lights, or *aurora australis*. When sunspots are very active, long-distance radios may become useless. The radio sound becomes distorted or stops. Sometimes a great explosion seems to occur in a sunspot. All radio communication on the earth suddenly blacks out for a little while. A sunspot may last for a few days or for several months. See SUNSPOT.

Seen through a telescope, a typical sunspot has a dark-appearing center called the *umbra*, surrounded by an irregular, brighter ring called the *penumbra*. Bright patches called *faculae* may be found near sunspots. A large umbra may measure 50,000 miles across, and a penumbra, 100,000 miles.

On Jan. 1, 1964, scientists from more than 50 nations began the International Years of the Quiet Sun. This 2-year project studied how the sun affects conditions in the earth's atmosphere. See INTERNATIONAL YEARS OF THE QUIET SUN.

**More than a Million Earths Would Fit in the Sun,** just as it takes a million balls to fill this glass bowl.
UFA from Penguin

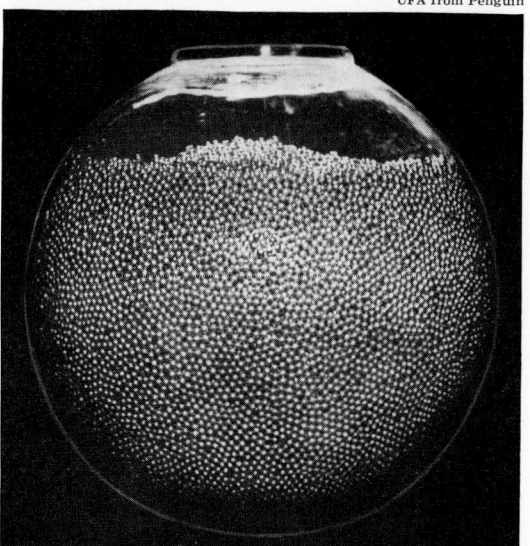

## HOW MAN CAN HARNESS THE POWER OF THE SUN

**The Sun Helps Heat the Solar House.** This kind of house is built with large windows facing south, under overhanging "sun-visor" eaves. In the Northern Hemisphere in winter, the sun is far to the south. Its rays flood the windows with warm sunshine. In summer, when the sun is high overhead, the eaves keep the hot sun rays from entering.

George Fred and William Keck, Architects, Hedrich-Blessing

**The "Noisy Sun."** Scientists have discovered an amazing thing, since the development of radar and modern types of short-wave radio receivers. The sun is a powerful "broadcasting station" that sends out noisy, high-frequency radio signals. This jumble of "solar noise" that affects radio receivers often accompanies outbursts of sunspots and great solar flares.

### Where the Sun Gets Its Heat

Scientists say the earth is about $4\frac{1}{2}$ billion years old. For most of this time, the earth has received about the same amount of light and heat from the sun that we receive today. Where does this heat come from? If the sun were a solid lump of burning coal, it would have burned up in about 1,500 years.

We now know that the sun is a kind of atomic furnace. Solar energy comes from the energy of atoms which are being changed into different forms. What happens on the sun is quite complicated, but it results in the change of hydrogen atoms into helium atoms. The hydrogen atom is the simplest of all atoms. The next simplest is helium. We think that hydrogen is constantly being changed into helium, inside the sun. When four atoms of hydrogen unite to make one atom of helium, almost 1 per cent of the original weight or mass of the hydrogen material is changed into light and heat.

For every four hundred pounds of hydrogen changed into helium, about three pounds of matter are changed into light and heat energy. The sun is changing its matter into energy so fast that it is losing weight at the rate of about four million tons a second. But the sun is so huge that scientists believe it will keep sending out heat and light at its present rate for another thirty-five billion years.

### The Sun in Art

The sun has affected man's arts since ancient times. Several designs used in ancient art, such as the hooked cross, came from man's attempts to make pictures or carvings of the sun. A circular sun-ray design from ancient times is much used today by artists, especially in decorative metalwork and in some kinds of sculpture.

Many of our most famous painters have attempted to capture the beauty, color, and warmth of the sun on their canvases. In Vincent van Gogh's brilliant landscapes, you can almost feel the warmth of the sunshine. Landscapes by Joseph M. Turner, the great English landscape painter, capture the beauty of sun-bathed earth and sea.

Music has been enriched as a result of man's admiration of the sun. One of the most beautiful songs in opera is "Hymn to the Sun" from the opera *The Golden Cockerel*, by the composer Nicholas Rimsky-Korsakov.

HARLAN T. STETSON and R. WILL BURNETT

**Related Articles** in WORLD BOOK include:

| | | |
|---|---|---|
| Astronomy | International | Rainbow |
| Aurora Borealis | Geophysical | Solar Energy |
| Corona | Year | Solar System |
| Earth | Magnetic Storm | Solstice |
| Eclipse | Midnight Sun | Sun Worship |
| Equinox | Planet | Sunspot |
| Gravitation | Radiation | |

### Outline

I. **Does the Sun Move?**
II. **How the Sun Affects Our Earth**
   A. What the Earth Would Be Like Without the Sun
   B. Sunlight—the Miracle Worker
   C. Why Food Is Called "Stored Sunlight"
   D. Coal and Petroleum Are Trapped Sunlight
   E. Other Ways We Use the Sun's Energy
   F. Invisible Sunlight and Health
III. **How to Look at the Sun**
IV. **Parts of the Sun**
V. **The Stormy Surface of the Sun**
   A. Sunspots
   B. The "Noisy Sun"
VI. **Where the Sun Gets Its Heat**
VII. **The Sun in Art**

### Questions

How far is the earth from the sun?
Is the sun a star or a planet?
How does the sun move?
How would our earth be different if there were no sun?
What is meant by *solar energy*?
How does man use the sun's energy?
What is a sunspot? How may sunspots affect the earth?

# SUN BATH

**SUN BATH** is the exposure of the body to sunlight or to sun lamps. Sunlight is made up of many different kinds of light rays. *Infrared rays* (heat rays) penetrate deeply into the body. They benefit the circulatory system and the muscles. *Ultraviolet rays* are chiefly absorbed by the skin, and may cause sunburn and tanning. They also cause chemicals in the skin to produce vitamin D, the sunshine vitamin. Sun lamps produce ultraviolet rays.

See also INFRARED RAYS; SUN (Invisible Sunlight and Health); SUN LAMP; SUNBURN; ULTRAVIOLET RAYS.

**SUN DANCE** was the most important religious ceremony of many Plains Indian tribes. The Sioux called it the *sun gazing dance*, and performed it annually. They believed it would keep away enemies and famine.

All the scattered hunting bands of the tribe gathered in summer and pitched their tepees in a great camp circle. In the center of this circle they built a large, open enclosure of upright posts and rafters connected to a tall, forked center pole. Within the enclosure, Indian men taking part painted their bodies, fasted, and danced, always facing the sun. The ceremonies lasted several days. The dance itself was simple. The dancers merely rose on their toes to the tune of music played on eagle bone whistles. At the end of the dancing, some of the young men underwent severe tortures in fulfillment of vows. The United States government prohibited the sun dance for several years because of these cruelties. A few tribes, such as the Blackfoot, still perform the sun dance, but without the tortures. JOHN C. EWERS

See also BUFFALO CEREMONIALS.

**SUN GOD.** See SUN WORSHIP.

**SUN HIGHWAY.** See ITALY (picture: The Sun Highway).

**SUN LAMP** is a common name for a device that gives off artificial ultraviolet radiation. Ultraviolet rays are found in natural sunlight, and they produce a tan on human skin. These rays cannot be seen by the human eye. They have a shorter wave length than the visible violet light. There are two general types of ultraviolet generators, sun lamps and therapeutic lamps. A person can use a sun lamp in the home without the supervision of a physician. Therapeutic lamps require professional supervision, to avoid hazards of overexposure.

The professional therapeutic lamp gives off powerful ultraviolet radiation and can produce a sunburn in a period as short as one-half to one minute. The sun lamp is not as powerful. It requires 10 or 15 minutes to produce a light sunburn.

There are several sources of artificial ultraviolet radiation. The carbon arc is a readily available source. Its ultraviolet radiation is made more intense by impregnating the cores of the carbons with certain salts of metals. The mercury arc inside a quartz tube is a common source. Another source looks like an ordinary large incandescent lamp. Inside the special glass bulb is a small mercury arc in a tiny quartz tube. Also inside the bulb is a tungsten filament. The lamp screws into any ordinary socket of 115-volt alternating current power supply. The light from this source resembles the light from an ordinary incandescent lamp, but it is enriched with ultraviolet radiation.

Direct exposure of the skin to ultraviolet rays from the sun or from artificial sources results in the formation of vitamin D. There is no evidence that ultraviolet radiation increases or improves the tone of the tissues of the body as a whole, stimulates metabolism, acts as a tonic, increases mental activity, or tends to prevent colds as many persons believe. HOWARD A. CARTER

See also GERMICIDAL LAMP; ULTRAVIOLET RAYS.

**SUN MOTOR.** See SOLAR ENERGY (Solar Engines).

**SUN VALLEY,** Idaho (pop. 317; alt. 6,000 ft.), a famous resort, lies in the Sawtooth Mountains of south-central Idaho (see IDAHO [political map]). In 1936, Averell Harriman, chairman of the board of directors of the Union Pacific Railroad, picked the site for development as a winter-sports center because of its brilliant sunshine and frequent winter snowfalls. The hotels at Sun Valley are the Sun Valley Lodge and Challenger Inn. Eight electric chair lifts serve over 40 ski runs. Other sports include skating, sleighing, and bowling. WILLIAM S. GREEVER and JANET GROFF GREEVER

See IDAHO (A Visitor's Guide; color picture).

Sun Valley News Bureau

**The Ski Slopes of Sun Valley,** in Idaho's Sawtooth Mountains, rank as one of the world's most popular winter sports centers.

**SUN WORSHIP** developed in some lands as people came to associate the sun with the growing season and with warmth. It developed among agricultural peoples, who needed sunshine for their crops, but not among hunters or seed-gatherers, who did not depend on sunlight for their food supply. Sun worship was important in the cultures of ancient Egypt, Babylonia, Persia, and northern India. The peoples of Scandinavia also worshiped the sun. Teutonic peoples named the first day of the week for the sun.

Sun worship was important to American Indians in the agricultural lands that are now the southeastern and southwestern United States. It also grew up among the Aztec, Inca, and Maya peoples who lived in Central and South America.

Kings and princes in some lands believed themselves to be brothers or children of the sun, and they came to be worshiped as gods. For hundreds of years, the Japanese worshiped their emperor as a descendant of the sun goddess, Amaterasu-O-Mi-Kami.

See also APOLLO; HELIOS; RE; SUN (picture: The Sun in Story and Legend).

**SUN YAT-SEN,** *soon yaht-sen* (1866-1925), a Chinese statesman and revolutionary leader, fought to establish a republic of China. He is generally called the *Father of the Revolution.* Sun was too idealistic to be an effective political leader. But his *Three People's Principles* (nationalism, democracy, and socialism) became the guiding principles of the Chinese republic, established in 1912.

Brown Bros.
**Sun Yat-sen**

Sun was born of humble parents in the Chungshan district of Kwangtung Province. He was educated at mission schools in Hong Kong and Honolulu, and became a doctor. From 1895 to 1911, he toured the United States, Japan, and Europe to organize sympathy for republican principles and to seek financial aid for his revolutionary movement against the Manchu dynasty. He was aided by Chinese overseas communities and English, American, and Japanese sympathizers.

**The Kuomintang Party,** headed by Sun, became a political entity in 1911 after the Wuhan uprising to overthrow the Manchu regime. From 1911 to 1922, Sun tried to unite China and establish a stable government. His party adopted a constitution, and Sun became the temporary president of the Chinese republic in 1912. The political situation at the time was turbulent. To further insure the unity of China, Sun resigned as president in favor of Yüan Shih-k'ai after only six and one-half weeks in office.

**His Later Efforts.** In 1913, Sun disagreed with Yüan's policies and organized a revolt. He fled to Japan, and the Kuomintang members of parliament were thrown out of office. Once again, the revolutionists assembled to set up a separate government under the 1912 constitution. In 1921, Sun became president of this government in Canton. He was driven out of his capital in 1922, but returned in 1923.

Sun continued to work for the unification of China.

After failing to get assistance from Western powers, he turned to Russia. With funds and help from Russia, he reorganized the Kuomintang party and army in 1923. He set up the Whampoa Military Academy, with Chiang Kai-shek as superintendent. Sun died of cancer while attending a conference in Peking in 1925.

In 1929 Sun's body was transferred to a mausoleum erected in his honor in Nanking. Politically, he was more effective after his death. His principles became the slogans of his followers. Chiang Kai-shek, during the 1930's and 1940's, achieved the unification under a central government that Sun had sought in vain to accomplish.

IMMANUEL C. Y. HSU

See also CHIANG KAI-SHEK; CHINA (History); SOONG CHING-LING.

**SUNBIRD** is the common name of a group of tiny tropical birds of Asia and Africa. They resemble the hummingbirds of the Western Hemisphere in size and in the gay color of the male's feathers. They are larger than most hummingbirds. Their bills are curved instead of straight, like those of the hummingbird. They feed mostly on flower nectar, but they also eat tiny insects that fly about flowers.

**Scientific Classification.** Sunbirds belong to the order *Passeriformes.* They are members of the sunbird family, *Nectariniidae.*

ARTHUR A. ALLEN

See also BIRD (Building the Nest).

**SUNBURN** is an inflammation of the skin caused by exposure to the sun's rays. A sun tan may be healthful, but a sunburn can be serious. The victim may suffer severe pain and discomfort. He may feel ill and have a fever. Even on cloudy days, it is possible to get a severe sunburn. The sun rays filter through the clouds. Sun rays reflecting from a body of water, or from ice, snow, or sand, increase the amount of burning. Such a burn is usually first or second degree.

Sunburn can be prevented by gradual exposure to the sun. If extensive exposure to the sun is unavoidable, a robe or covering of some kind should be worn part of the time. Olive oil or a good sun-tan ointment on the skin also helps as a preventive. A new pill developed in the late 1950's makes it possible for a person to build up a

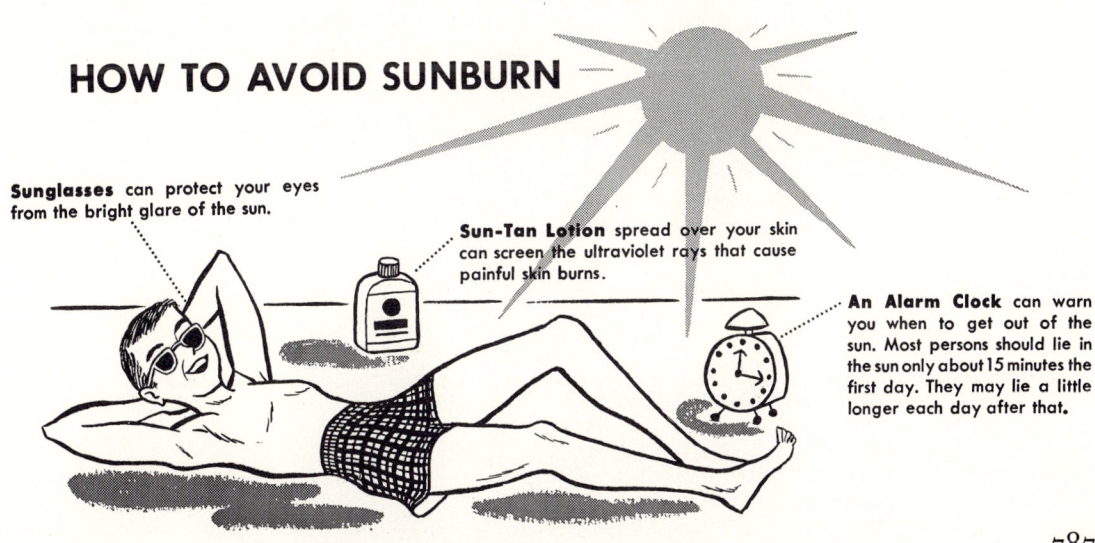

## HOW TO AVOID SUNBURN

**Sunglasses** can protect your eyes from the bright glare of the sun.

**Sun-Tan Lotion** spread over your skin can screen the ultraviolet rays that cause painful skin burns.

**An Alarm Clock** can warn you when to get out of the sun. Most persons should lie in the sun only about 15 minutes the first day. They may lie a little longer each day after that.

# SUNDA ISLANDS

resistance to sunburn. The pills are taken about two hours before exposure to the sun. They help promote a tan, and make the skin less sensitive to the sun.

Sunburn should be treated as you would treat any other kind of burn. If the skin blisters, apply a clean, dry gauze dressing over the burn. Make it tight enough so that it will not rub over the area. The dressing helps to protect the burn and keep it clean. Do not use lotions and oils on burns. Butter is particularly bad because the salt particles may irritate the burned area and cause more pain than the burn. BENJAMIN F. MILLER

See also SUN LAMP.

**SUNDA,** or **SOENDA, ISLANDS.** See INDONESIA (Islands).

**SUNDAY** is the first day of the week among Christian peoples. It is the day set aside for rest and for worship of God. Sunday was the day sacred to the sun among the old Teutonic peoples, and its name means the "day of the sun." The French call Sunday *dimanche*, the Spanish call it *domingo*, and the Italians call it *domenica*. These three names all come from the Latin words *dies dominica*, which means Lord's Day.

The early Christians lived hard lives, and had to work on Sunday as well as the other days in the week. But they made Sunday a day for special worship, because the resurrection of Jesus occurred on that day. By the A.D. 300's, both the church and the state officially recognized the day as a day of rest in Europe.

In the United States, some states have laws that forbid labor on Sunday. All government agencies and banks are closed on Sundays. A few states and communities have laws that prohibit such amusements as ball games and motion pictures on Sunday. Such laws are called *Blue Laws*. GRACE HUMPHREY

See also BLUE LAWS.

Brown Bros.
**Billy Sunday**

**SUNDAY, BILLY** (1862-1935), was a baseball player who became a famous evangelist. He used his baseball background, slangy language, flamboyant manners, and highly developed promotional methods to become the most popular evangelist of the time. He was supposed to have preached to over 100 million persons, and to have converted over a million in his campaigns.

WILLIAM ASHLEY SUNDAY was born in Ames, Iowa. His early years were spent with his grandparents and at an orphans home. He played professional baseball for the Chicago White Stockings, Pittsburgh Pittsburgs, and the Philadelphia Phillies, from 1883 to 1891. During these years he was converted, and began working with the YMCA. He became a Presbyterian minister in 1903. L. J. TRINTERUD

**SUNDAY ISLAND.** See KERMADEC ISLANDS.

**SUNDAY SCHOOL,** an observance usually connected with Protestant churches, teaches Bible study and religion. Such schools may have existed as early as the 1500's. But the present-day Sunday-school movement was started in Gloucester, England, by the publisher Robert Raikes. In 1780, he launched his "Ragged School." He tried to aid the children of the poor in his community by teaching them reading, writing, and the principles of religion. The schools received publicity through Raikes' newspaper. With the great "foreign" missionary work of the 1800's and 1900's, the schools spread to all parts of the world. When Raikes died in 1811, 400,000 children were enrolled in Sunday schools.

H. Armstrong Roberts

**Sunday-School Children** learn to understand and appreciate God through prayers, songs, and stories. Often a project helps make a lesson clearer. If the children are learning about the way God works through nature, for instance, they may cut out pictures of flowers and bring them to Sunday School.

Today, about 42,740,000 children and adults attend more than 437,000 Protestant Sunday schools. The Roman Catholic Church has a similar type of school. Sunday or Sabbath schools also are maintained by Jewish and other religious groups.

In America, the Sunday-school movement became widespread after the Revolutionary War. The American Sunday School Union was formed in 1824. Its missionary workers founded Sunday schools throughout the country. The International Sunday School Association served the United States and Canada. In 1922, this organization became the International Council of Religious Education. This organization became part of the National Council of the Churches of Christ in the United States of America in 1950 as a result of the merger of various religious groups.

The present-day Sunday school is divided into departments for students of various ages. In a large school, a superintendent directs each department and a teacher is in charge of each class. A uniform course of lessons is widely used in the United States and Canada. It is outlined by the International Council of Religious Education, which also prepares outlines for graded lessons used by many schools. Other features of current Sunday school work are circulation libraries, classes for teachers, conventions, and Sunday school workers' institutes that help train the teachers and enable them to exchange ideas.

See also RAIKES, ROBERT; RELIGIOUS EDUCATION.

**SUNDEW** is an unusual plant that traps and digests insects. It gets its name because drops of sticky fluid produced by glands appear on its leaves. In the sunlight, these drops glitter like drops of dew. Sundews live in bogs and marshes throughout the world. The *round-leaved sundew*, the most common kind, thrives in moist, acid soil in all but the southwestern part of the United States. This plant also grows in parts of Canada, Europe, and Asia.

The slender stem of the sundew is topped by small white flowers. A cluster of flat, rounded leaves grows at the base of the stem, close to the ground. These leaves are the size of a small coin. They are covered with small red gland-bearing hairs. An insect may easily become stuck to the drops of sticky fluid on the leaves. Then the hairs fold in around the insect and hold it. Fluid covers the insect and eventually suffocates it. The glands produce juices that then digest the victim.

**Scientific Classification.** The sundews are in the sundew family, *Droseraceae*. They form the genus *Drosera*. The round-leaved sundew is genus *Drosera*, species *D. rotundifolia*.
ROBERT W. HOSHAW

See also CARNIVOROUS PLANT.

**SUNDIAL** is the oldest known device for the measurement of time. It is based on the fact that the shadow of an object will move from one side of the object to the other as the sun moves from east to west during the day. The sundial is believed to have been used in Babylon at least as early as 2000 B.C.

The earliest description of a sundial comes from Berossus, a Chaldean astronomer who lived about 300 B.C. His sundial was a hollow half-sphere, or dome, set

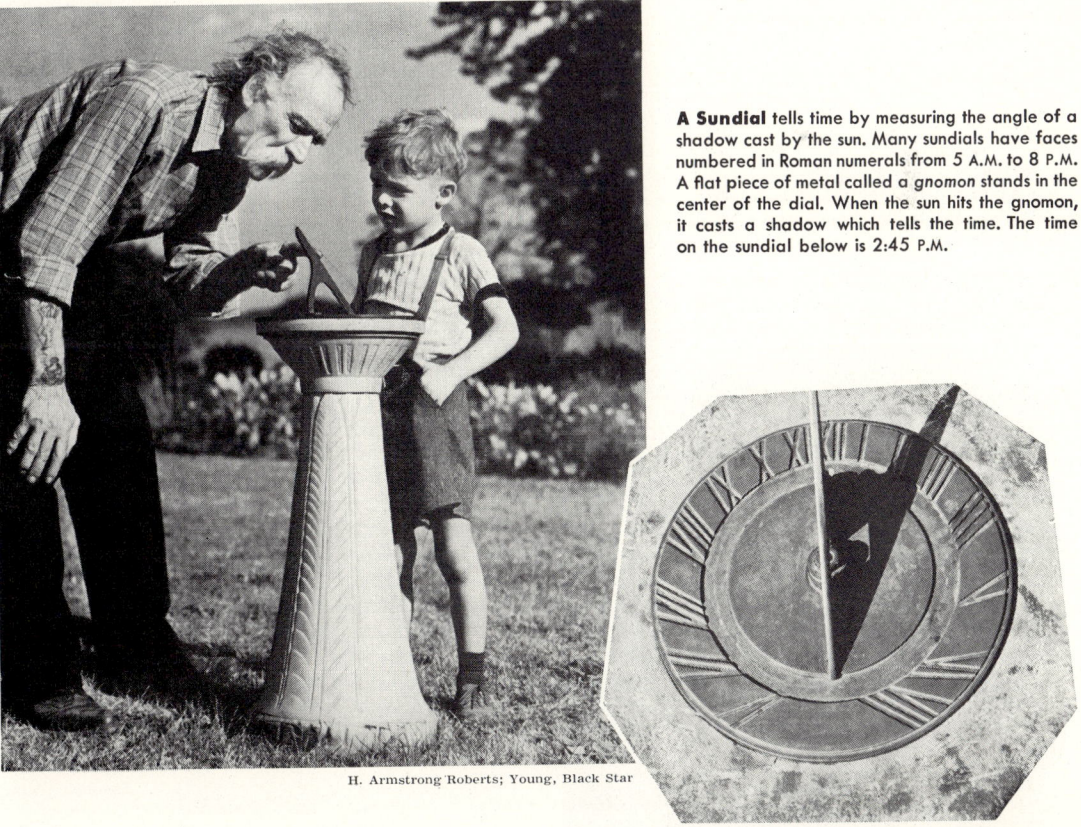

**A Sundial** tells time by measuring the angle of a shadow cast by the sun. Many sundials have faces numbered in Roman numerals from 5 A.M. to 8 P.M. A flat piece of metal called a *gnomon* stands in the center of the dial. When the sun hits the gnomon, it casts a shadow which tells the time. The time on the sundial below is 2:45 P.M.

H. Armstrong Roberts; Young, Black Star

# SUNDOG

with its edge flat and with a small bead fixed at the center. During the day the shadow of the bead moved in a circular arc, divided into 12 equal parts. These were called *temporary hours* because they changed with the seasons. *Equal hours* were decided upon about A.D. 1400, when clocks were invented.

A sundial consists of the *plane* (dial face) and the *gnomon* (style). The dial face is divided into hours and sometimes half and quarter hours. The gnomon is a flat piece of metal set in the center of the dial. It points toward the North Pole in the Northern Hemisphere and toward the South Pole in the Southern Hemisphere. The upper edge of the gnomon must slant upward from the dial face at an angle equal to the latitude of the location of the sundial.                ARTHUR B. SINKLER

**SUNDOG.** See HALO.

**SUNFISH** is a name for several kinds of fish. In the fresh waters of North America, the sunfishes are a group of small, bright-colored food fish, rarely over 10 inches long. Their color changes according to conditions of health, food, and temperature. The males become brightly colored in the breeding seasons. They clear out a nest on the bottom of a lake or stream and guard the eggs against intruders. The most widely favored game fish among the sunfishes proper (except for the black basses, which belong to the same family) is the *bluegill*. The pumpkin seed, a kind of sunfish, is found abundantly in brooks and ponds from Maine to Florida, and in the northern part of the Mississippi Valley. It has a roundish body and considerable orange in its color. There is a bright red spot on the ear flap. This fish is about 8 inches long and weighs from 6 to 8 ounces. Boys enjoy fishing for it, because it bites with so much vigor. These sunfish are usually caught with worms as a bait. Other species also are common. Some of the smaller, more brilliant kinds are kept in home aquariums.

The name sunfish also is given to a group of grotesque-appearing ocean fish. Their bodies are scaleless, silvery, and clumsy, and seem to consist of one great head with small fins. They often rest on the surface in sunny weather, with one fin above the water. Ocean sunfish may weigh 1,000 pounds. They are never eaten. They are not closely related to fresh-water sunfish.

**Scientific Classification.** Ocean sunfish belong to the mola family, *Molidae*. The common kind is genus *Mola*, species *M. mola*. Fresh-water sunfish make up the family *Centrarchidae*. The bluegill is genus *Lepomis*, species *L. macrochirus*. The pumpkin seed is *L. gibbosus*.   CARL L. HUBBS

See also CRAPPIE; FISH (Reproduction); FISHING (table, Game-Fishing World Records [Bluegill]).

**SUNFLOWER** is a large flower. It has a great sunlike flower head with surrounding "rays" of yellow petals.

The annual garden sunflower is one of the best known of several kinds. When cultivated, its flower heads may grow to be a foot in diameter. These heads are flattened disks. The outer circle in each head is a row of large, yellow petals. The other petals are small, tubular flowers which form row after row of circles in the center of the head. The plant has a rough, hairy stem from 6 to 10 feet high, and coarse, heart-shaped leaves. Many leaflike bracts surround the disk, and help to protect the more delicate parts of the flower.

Some sunflowers come up every year, but growers must raise the garden variety from seed each year. The perennial species are excellent to plant against walls and fences. Farmers grow sunflowers for the seeds, and feed them to cattle and poultry. In some parts of Europe, people use the stalks as fuel and eat the seeds.

**Scientific Classification.** Sunflowers belong to the composite family, *Compositae*. The common annual is genus *Helianthus*, species *H. annuus*. Among the perennials are *H. orgyalis* and *H. decapetalus*.   MARCUS MAXON

**SUNFLOWER STATE.** See KANSAS.

**SUNG DYNASTY,** *soong,* ruled China from 960 to 1279. The Chinese made great urban and commercial expansion during this period. Their painting, ceramics, book printing, and philosophy reached a new high point in development. A general, Chao K'uang-yin, founded the dynasty and served as its first emperor. He succeeded in creating a strong, centralized dynasty. The Sungs controlled most of China, except the northeast, until 1127. Then the Jurchens from Manchuria seized North China. In 1279, the Mongols conquered southern China and ended the dynasty.   H. F. SCHURMANN

**SUNNITE.** See ISLAM (Sects).

**SUNNYVALE,** Calif. (pop. 52,898; alt. 75 ft.), is a residential and industrial city 37 miles southeast of San Francisco. Its industries manufacture electrical equipment, processed foods, machinery, and chemicals. It is a center for both guided missile research and satellite tracking operations. The city was incorporated in 1912. It has a council-manager government. For location, see CALIFORNIA (political map).   GEORGE SHAFTEL

**SUNSET CRATER NATIONAL MONUMENT** is near Flagstaff, Arizona, and was established in 1930. The volcanic cinder cone for which the monument was named ranks as its chief feature. The monument has a large crater with a brilliantly colored summit and extensive lava flows. It also contains an ice cave that is cold the year around. Ponderosa pine trees grow in the 3,040-acre area.   C. LANGDON WHITE

**The Black-Banded Sunfish** ranges from New Jersey to Maryland. It grows about 4 inches long and has a pearly luster in reflected light. Sunfishes eat such things as insects and small shellfish. Most sunfishes lay their eggs in shallow water.
Gene Wolfsheimer

**The Bold, Brilliant Sunflower,** with its huge green leaves and towering height, brightens roadsides and gardens in summer. The gigantic plant, *left*, grew to a height of 14½ feet. The enormous sunflower head, *above*, measured 17½ inches in diameter. It had a 4-inch stem at its base. Dewdrops cover the petals of a sunflower not yet in full bloom, *below*.

United Press Int.; Crog, Black Star

791

# SUNSHINE SKYWAY

**SUNSHINE SKYWAY** is one of the longest overwater crossings in the United States. It stretches 15 miles across Tampa Bay in Florida. It consists of filled-in causeways and six steel and concrete bridges. Opened in 1954, it links St. Petersburg and Bradenton.

**SUNSHINE STATE.** See FLORIDA; SOUTH DAKOTA.

**SUNSPOT** is a dark, relatively cool area on the sun. The temperature in a sunspot is nearly 2000° C. lower than the surrounding surface of the sun. But sunspots are intensely hot and look dark only by contrast. In a well-developed spot, the *umbra* (dark central region) is surrounded by a *penumbra* (grayish border). Most sunspots last for only a few days, but some occasionally last more than a month. Sunspots appear in two bands across the sun, between 5 and 35 degrees north and south of the sun's equator. The size and number of sunspots vary greatly. The largest spots are many times the size of the earth. The number of sunspots reaches a maximum about every 11 years. For example, periods of maximum sunspot activity occurred in 1947 and in 1957-1958. The sunspot activity of 1957-1958 far exceeded that of any previously recorded period.

No one knows exactly what causes sunspots, but they seem to be related to the strong magnetic fields that have been detected where they occur. The sunspot cycle indicates that these magnetic disturbances are related to the sun's rotation. The disturbances probably arise deep within the sun's interior. According to one theory, the strong magnetic field prevents the normal violent motion of the hot solar gases, so that sunspots may be relatively calm areas.

Sunspots seem to be related to various physical changes both on the sun and in the earth's atmosphere. The magnetic fields influence the shape of the sun's *corona*, a bright area around the sun that is visible during an eclipse. During a period of maximum sunspot activity, the corona is fairly uniform. During minimum sunspot activity, the corona sometimes extends outward several solar diameters at the equator, and appears as short tufts at the poles of the sun (see CORONA [picture]). The magnetic fields of sunspots also are important in controlling the ejection of electrons and protons from the sun. During a period of maximum sunspot activity, great numbers of these particles strike the upper atmosphere of the earth, causing beautiful displays of the *auroras* (northern and southern lights). Sunspot activity also seems to influence the strength and direction of the earth's magnetic field. Violent changes in the earth's field are called *magnetic storms*. They can disrupt the transmission of radio signals. The kind of radiation produced by the sun also seems to be affected by sunspot activity. Changes in the sun's radiation affect the average temperature and rainfall on the earth, which in turn control the growth-rate of some trees.

Observation of sunspots indicates that the sun rotates. The motion of sunspots near the sun's equator indicates a rotation time of about 25 days. Sunspots farther from the equator indicate a longer rotation time, so that the sun does not appear to rotate as a solid body. Galileo was the first person to study sunspots systematically and to show that the sun rotates. R. WILLIAM SHAW

See also AURORA BOREALIS; MAGNETIC STORM; SUN.

**SUNSTROKE** is the common name for conditions that result from overheating the body. Doctors usually use the more specific terms *heatstroke* and *heat exhaustion*. Sunstroke is a form of heatstroke caused by being exposed to the sun too much or too long.

**Heatstroke** usually results when the heat-regulating mechanisms of the body break down. The body maintains its normal temperature in several ways. Among them is the cooling effect that results when sweat evaporates. Researchers found that people who work in excessive heat for a long time sweat less and less. They may stop sweating altogether and their body temperature rises to dangerous levels. Doctors consider true heatstroke a medical emergency because the high body temperatures cause brain damage.

Persons with heatstroke rarely are aware that they have stopped sweating. But they suddenly become conscious of a rapid rise in temperature. The body temperature of a patient may be 112°F. His skin feels hot and dry. His breathing is regular, and his pulse full and pounding. Soon the breathing becomes irregular, the pulse weakens, and coma develops (see COMA).

Victims of heatstroke need immediate treatment. Those who are not treated may die. A doctor should be called at once. The most important thing is to reduce the temperature as quickly as possible. Doctors often place the patient in a bathtub filled with cold water. They apply cold compresses or ice packs to the head and neck. When the patient's temperature drops to about 102°F., the drastic cooling measures usually are stopped. Most persons who have had heatstroke become ill quickly when they are exposed to heat again.

**Heat Exhaustion,** or *heat prostration*, is less severe than heatstroke. It generally occurs in persons who work near boilers, or in places with high temperatures and humidity. Victims become weak and dizzy and fall into a stupor. They usually perspire freely, and their temperature drops below normal. Their condition is like that of a person in shock (see SHOCK). These persons should be removed to a cooler location. But because of their subnormal temperature, they should be kept warm. Persons who work under conditions that might produce heat exhaustion drink large amounts of water and often take salt tablets to replace salt lost from their body when they sweat. LOUIS D. BOSHES

**SUOMI.** See FINLAND.

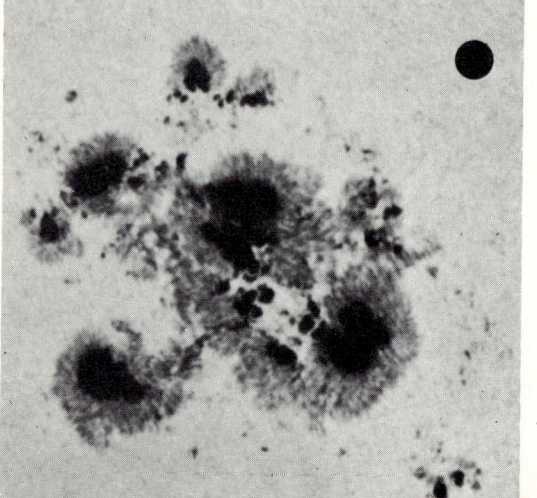

**Sunspots** may cover an area of the sun many times greater than the size of the earth. The black circle, *upper right*, shows the approximate size of the earth compared with that of sunspots.
Mt. Wilson Observatory

**SUPERCHARGER** is a device that adds power to a gasoline or diesel engine. It does this by compressing, or squeezing, the air fed into the cylinders. The extra air helps the fuel burn more completely, and makes the engine produce more power.

An understanding of how the supercharger works can be gained through an experiment with a drinking glass and a few sheets of paper. Crumple the paper into several large wads. One of the wads will almost completely fill the glass. Next, squeeze the paper wads until they are smaller. Now several wads will fit in the glass.

A cylinder in a gasoline engine is like the drinking glass. It can be filled with a "loose" amount of air like the one larger paper wad. But if the air is squeezed by a supercharger, just as the paper wads were squeezed, then the cylinder can hold several times as much air.

Superchargers are particularly useful on airplane engines. This is because the air pressure decreases as an airplane goes higher. In other words, the air becomes more loosely packed, like the big paper wad. At high altitude the supercharger packs the air tightly to keep the gasoline burning well. Superchargers are sometimes used in boat and automobile engines.

Sometimes gears connected to the engine drive the supercharger. *Turbosuperchargers* are driven by a gas turbine turned by the engine exhaust.

An airplane pilot may shift gears on some superchargers so that the speed of the supercharger may be increased at higher altitudes. Other superchargers have automatic controls to make them go faster when the outside air pressure decreases. H. S. STILLWELL

See also DIESEL ENGINE; GASOLINE ENGINE.

**SUPERCONDUCTIVITY.** See CRYOGENICS; CRYOTRON.

**SUPEREGO.** See FREUD, SIGMUND.

**SUPERHETERODYNE.** See ARMSTRONG, EDWIN H.; RADIO (Vacuum Tubes).

**SUPERHIGHWAY** is any highway with four or more traffic lanes, that has eliminated crossings with other highways and railroad tracks. Some superhighways stretch well over 100 miles in length. Automobile traffic can often travel safely on such roads at speeds from 60 to 80 miles an hour. Direct intersections with other traffic are avoided by underpasses, overpasses, or curving intersections laid out in the shape of a clover leaf. Among famous superhighways in the United States are the Pennsylvania, New Jersey and Ohio turnpikes, and the Governor Thomas E. Dewey Thruway.

See also ROADS AND HIGHWAYS; NEW JERSEY (Transportation); PENNSYLVANIA TURNPIKE; TURNPIKE.

**SUPERINTENDENT OF DOCUMENTS** is the sales agent for United States government publications. His office prepares official catalogues and indexes, including a monthly catalogue of all government publications, and a biweekly list of selected publications. His office also sends publications to libraries, mails them for other federal departments, and receives surplus copies of government literature from these agencies for sale or other distribution. Critically reviewed by SUPERINTENDENT OF DOCUMENTS

See also GOVERNMENT PRINTING OFFICE.

**SUPERIOR,** Wis. (pop. 33,563; alt. 630 ft.), is a port on Lake Superior, opposite Duluth, Minn. Superior and Duluth form a metropolitan area with 276,596 persons. Superior has one of the largest ore docks in the world. The docks store 550,000 tons of iron ore. Superior's grain elevator holds 13 million bushels of grain. It is one of the largest in the United States. One of the largest farmers' grain cooperatives in the United States does more than $3 million worth of business a year in Superior. Shipbuilding is an important industry of the city. Superior also has large flour mills, railroad and machinery shops, woodworking factories, canneries, and breweries. The city is the home of Wisconsin State University at Superior. Fur traders camped on the site of the city in 1662. In 1883, iron ore was discovered in the area. The city of Superior has a council-manager form of government. JAMES I. CLARK

**SUPERIOR, LAKE.** See LAKE SUPERIOR.
**SUPERLATIVE.** See COMPARISON.
**SUPERMAN.** See NIETZSCHE, FRIEDRICH.
**SUPERMARKET** is a large retail store that provides a one-stop food-shopping service. It offers foods of all kinds in one location. Five principal characteristics of a modern supermarket are its large size, the wide variety of foods it offers, its self-service system for shoppers, sales on a cash-and-carry basis, and its many nonfood items. Nonfood items include housewares and kitchen aids, cosmetics and beauty aids, magazines, and, sometimes, hardware, cutlery, and lawn-care materials. Some supermarkets provide snack bars, playgrounds and entertainment facilities for children, and parking areas for cars.

Supermarkets, originally found chiefly in the United States, now are found in many parts of Europe and Latin America. E. E. HARGRAVE

See also FOOD (picture: Supermarkets); TRADING STAMPS.

**SUPERNATURALISM** is the belief in a being or beings higher than or superior to what man calls nature. Supernaturalism is one of the oldest philosophic theories. The ancient Greeks and Romans believed that the gods, who lived in regions above the earth, controlled the destinies of men. Things that pertained to that realm were above (Latin *super*) the natural (Latin *naturalis*) things of earth. Supernaturalism is also identified with the term *theism* (belief in a god or gods).

Supernaturalism refers to events, qualities, or things that do not conform with natural laws. For example, miracles are events which cannot be explained entirely by natural means. Many persons believe that miracles have a supernatural origin and that they are caused by God (see MIRACLE).

Primitive societies believe in magical agencies, or "souls," which manifest themselves within natural objects. This belief is called *animism*. For example, many persons believe that stones of a particular shape or color have supernatural power. They use these stones as amulets or charms (see ANIMISM). The belief in *fetishes* (objects supposed to have magical powers) is an outgrowth of animism (see FETISH).

*Naturalism* is the opposite of supernaturalism. It contends that the natural world is the whole of reality, and that there is no supernatural or spiritual value, creation, control, or significance. WILSON D. WALLIS

**SUPERREGENERATION.** See ARMSTRONG, EDWIN HOWARD.

**SUPERSONIC FLIGHT.** See AERODYNAMICS (Supersonic Flight); AIRPLANE (Supersonic Flight; Research for the Future); WIND TUNNEL.

# SUPERSTITION

**SUPERSTITION,** soo pur STISH un. Man has learned very slowly to understand the world about him. For many thousands of years, strange or mysterious events or circumstances troubled or frightened him. He believed they were caused by good or evil forces, which could be controlled if he had the power to do so. These beliefs, now generally no longer held, are called *superstitions*. The word means *that which stands above*, or *survives*.

Present-day science believes that everything in nature has a natural cause, and a knowledge of nature's laws helps to explain every cause and effect. Scientific men arrive at this conviction through observation and reason. Scientific thinking helps to destroy superstition.

All peoples use the scientific method to some extent. But many superstitious notions and customs persist. Some of these are odd or amusing, and many of them are harmless. Even at best such superstitions show an uncritical attitude of mind, and some of them are harmful.

## Forms of Superstition

Many superstitious customs come from ancient times. A common source of superstition arises from a real or fancied resemblance between objects, persons, or events. The resemblance suggests a relationship between things which are similar. One is believed to influence the other. The apparent increase in the size of the moon, from new moon to full moon, is believed to influence favorably the growth of plants. Such superstitions are called *sympathetic* magic.

Many superstitions utilize charms and spells, call on good or evil spirits, foretell the future, or give magic powers to certain forces or objects.

**Sympathetic Magic.** There is a widespread conviction that nature affects human conduct in mystic ways, in addition to the obvious physical effects of heat, cold, storm, and other conditions and forces. The belief that occupational or ceremonial movements must correspond to movements in nature is widespread. For example, circular religious processions follow the direction of the sun, from east to south, west, and north, in a clockwise direction. In rural districts of North Europe, batter is stirred in this direction. If the direction is reversed, bad luck will follow, or the batter will be spoiled, according to superstition. The reversal of the usual procedure is supposed to bring bad luck.

**The Left Side.** The use of the right hand is normal for most persons. For this reason, the substitution of the left hand is forbidden, because it offsets the good. A reference to the left shoulder is supposed to reverse the meaning or the results of a falsehood. The literal meaning of the word *sinister* is *left*. The later and present meaning of threatening or evil is due to awkward associations with the left hand.

The unusualness of the left gives it a magic quality. The left hind foot of a rabbit becomes a charm. One must see the new moon for the first time over the left shoulder, and turn the silver in one's pocket, to have good luck. Often a superstition spreads out in many directions.

**Astrology.** Men observe the changes and the courses of sun, moon, stars, and planets. Their positions are believed to influence human life. The knowledge gained by studying the heavens developed into an elaborate system of foretelling the future, a *pseudo*, or false, science, known as *astrology*. Babylonians gave the planets the names of gods or goddesses. A person born under the planet Mars would have a violent disposition like that of Mars, the god of war.

Astrology became a very complex form of superstition. But the careful study of the heavens which it fostered led to the true science of *astronomy*.

**Evil Magic.** Magic is commonly used for working evil, casting a spell, or bewitching. An evildoer makes an image of the victim in wax or clay. Then he burns, buries, or pierces it with thorns or pins. Thus he and others believe that he injures the victim and causes his death. This is a common belief of the followers of the voodoo magic of Africa.

**Protection by Charms.** Misfortunes were commonly believed to be the result of evil influences. Objects credited with power to protect one against these harmful forces or beings are called *charms*. A charm may be a formula, a piece of metal, a stone, or some other object which is believed to bring luck. Charms are common today. They include *fetishes*, or good-luck objects such as a rabbit's foot, and *amulets*, or charms supposed to have magic power.

*The Evil Eye.* Belief that evil can be transmitted by the eyes of certain people is an ancient and now widespread superstition. It exists in Europe, especially in Italy, and throughout the Moslem world. Many kinds of charms are used to counteract the effect of the evil eye. Moslems believe that the five fingers of the hand, or any design or phrase associated with the number five, will protect against it. Another powerful charm is an image or design of an eye, which is supposed to throw back the evil to its source.

*Evil Spirits.* Some charms keep away evil spirits. A horseshoe over a door is supposed to do this. The horseshoe is now a symbol of good luck. Many superstitions have gathered about it. In some places, one who finds a horseshoe must return at once to his house, without speaking to anyone, and hang it over the door, prongs up. If hung prongs down, the luck will fall out. It must be fastened with three nails, each driven in by three blows of the hammer. Belief in the mystic power of three probably comes from the Trinity of God the Father, God the Son, and God the Holy Ghost. The origin of the superstitions regarding the horseshoe is not known. It appears to have started in comparatively recent times.

**Names and Words.** Primitive peoples regard the name as an intimate part of the person. One's actual name is sometimes kept secret, since by means of it another person might bewitch the owner. Some peoples do not give a child the name of a living relative, for fear the relative will die. There are holy names, particularly the name of a deity, which may not be spoken. Magic words when uttered summon spirits, protect against danger, or give power to medicine or to ceremonies. *Abracadabra* was at first uttered to ward off disease. But now it is a synonym for silly, empty, or meaningless words. *Open Sesame* were the magic words which opened the door to the den of the thieves in the *Arabian Nights'* tale of "Ali Baba and the Forty Thieves."

The belief that the mention of misfortune or evil will bring misfortune on one is another form of belief in the power in words. This idea is found in the common superstition of touching wood after making a statement. Some

# SOME COMMON SUPERSTITIONS

People once believed that spirits lived in an image. Today, many persons think that breaking a mirror is bad luck.

Old legends claimed that spirits lived in trees. Many still think that knocking on wood will keep away bad luck.

**BELIEF IN SPIRITS**

## BELIEF IN GOOD-LUCK CHARMS

Horseshoe

Rabbit's foot

Other good luck tokens

## SUPERSTITIONS ABOUT FOOD

Spilling salt is bad luck

Telling fortunes by tea leaves

Always stir batter in the same direction

Bubbles in coffee mean money

Some believe that the position of the stars and the time of birth influence a person's destiny

## SUPERSTITIONS ABOUT THE SKY

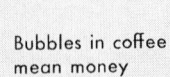 

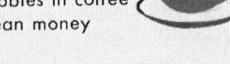

Some think the moon influences growth of crops

Many look at the new moon over their left shoulders

Many believe a wish made on a falling star comes true

## BELIEF IN BAD-LUCK SIGNS

Opening an umbrella indoors is bad luck

Black cat crossing a traveler's path

Bad luck to walk under a ladder

Friday the 13th is believed to be unlucky

Stepping on sidewalk cracks brings bad luck

# SUPERSTITION

scholars believe this is a substitution for an earlier custom of making the sign of the cross. For example, a traveler states that he has never been in a railway accident. To prevent this misfortune in the future, he touches wood. Under similar circumstances Germans say "Unberufen" (*uncalled for*), and Moslems, "Bismillah" (*in the name of God*).

**Belief in Spirits.** In all parts of the world men believe in spirits. Some, especially fairies, elves, and sprites, are helpful to human beings. Gnomes and goblins are full of mischief. For example, they cause milk to sour.

Spirits dwell in trees, rocks, springs, caves, rivers, or underground. Belief in spirits or spiritual existence is called *animism*. Evil spirits are thought to spread disease.

*Driving evil spirits out of a body* in the belief that they have caused illness, is a practice common among primitive tribes where the basic causes of disease are unknown. The medicine man of a tribe attempts to expel or destroy the evil spirits or "devils" by reciting chants and magic words. He also uses charms, fetishes, and wild dances. Sometimes he strikes or rubs the afflicted person while trying to persuade the devils to leave the body. Mental illness in particular is believed to be caused by evil spirits which have entered the head of the victim. Often a small opening is cut in the skull so that the devils can escape. See TREPHINING.

*Sneezing* is almost everywhere an omen. Some believe that in a sneeze a spirit leaves the body. Italians, to turn it into a good omen, say "Felicità" (*blessing*, or *good luck*). Germans say "Gesundheit" (*your health*). Sometimes English-speaking people say "God bless you" when someone sneezes.

*Pictures.* A picture or a reflection of a person is believed to possess part of his spirit, or to be his spirit or soul. This belief led to the practice of covering mirrors at time of death, or on certain other occasions. It is responsible for the superstition that breaking a mirror brings bad luck. Primitive people often object to having their picture taken. They are afraid they may part with a portion of themselves, or that they will be bewitched by means of the picture.

*Dreams.* A dream is regarded as an experience in which the soul of the sleeper leaves the body. For this reason, one should not waken a sleeper suddenly. His soul might not find its way back to the body. There is also belief in the return of the spirit, or ghost, of the dead to its former haunts. This idea has played a large part in superstition. It has led to trying to please dead ancestors, to the belief that the spirit of an ancestor returns in a newborn child, and to some modern cults, for example, spiritualism. Sometimes a child is named after the ancestor whose returned soul is supposed to have been recognized in the child.

*Jinn.* Moslems believe in spirits called *jinn*, or *genii*, who existed before man. The jinn live underground or in the sea, but often come to the upper world. They sometimes take the forms of cats, dogs, or other creatures. Sometimes they have human form. Most jinn are evil. They cause storms, whirlwinds, shipwrecks, disease, and a variety of misfortunes. There are also good jinn, who sometimes help men. Aladdin, in the tales of the *Arabian Nights*, summoned a jinni by rubbing a magic lamp. Each house has its jinn owners in addition to the human owners. The threshold is a favorite spot of the jinn. A bride is carried over the threshold, for fear a jinni might be sitting there. Protection against these beings is secured by various means. Recitation of passages from the Moslem holy book, the *Koran*, is considered particularly effective.

**Salt.** Salt is widely regarded as possessing magic qualities. Its power to check decay may be partly responsible for the superstitions connected with it. It is believed to ward off many kinds of spirits, including jinn. The European custom of throwing a pinch of salt over the left shoulder is a means of keeping the devil at a distance. If salt is spilled, this signifies that there will be a quarrel. Offering salt to a guest indicates a spirit of friendly hospitality.

**Medical Superstitions.** Many folk treatments are based on a likeness between the thing prescribed as medicine and the afflicted part of the body. For example, walnuts are supposed to be good for diseases of the brain. The kernel has the form of the brain, and the shell resembles a skull. The Chinese physician administers the tops, middle portions, and roots of plants for diseases of head, chest, and legs, respectively.

Sometimes the weapon which inflicts a wound is treated. The wound is healed by applying salve to the weapon. The phrase "to take a hair of the dog that bit you" reflects the same notion that one can cure the bite by means of a hair from the biter.

The fact that a magnet attracts particles of iron has led to the belief that it will also draw rheumatism out of the body. Magnets were once very rare, and were believed to possess magic powers. European peasants carried them to avoid or to cure disease. They also wore about the neck, or carried, a bag of bad-smelling plant substance called *asafetida*, to ward off disease.

Belief that unusual objects have powerful medical effects led to the practice of brewing repulsive mixtures as medicines. An example is the witches' brew described in Shakespeare's *Macbeth*.

Astrology was early associated with medicine and the theory of disease. An example is the belief that the moon causes insanity. The term *lunatic*, which comes from *luna*, the Latin word for moon, comes from this notion. Each part of the body was associated with certain heavenly bodies. Medical treatment was given only when the heavenly bodies were in favorable position.

Patients who believed strongly enough in such superstitious medical practices sometimes improved. Perhaps an induced optimistic mental state assisted in recovery.

## Present-Day Superstitions

**Common Ideas and Practices.** The tendency to cling to superstitious beliefs is strong among people who have little or no education. However, many educated people are also superstitious. They may not believe fully in their superstitions, but they conform with them because of a feeling that possibly it is safer to do so.

Many superstitions which in themselves are fairly innocent interfere little with otherwise reasonable thought or behavior. But they sometimes influence conduct.

Hotel rooms, steamship cabins, and city houses sometimes skip the number thirteen, because many persons believe it is unlucky. Friday is also thought to be rather unlucky, and a Friday which falls on the thirteenth day of the month is considered especially unlucky.

A blister on the tongue means that one has told a lie. If four people cross one another's hands when they shake hands, there will be a wedding. If your ears burn, someone is talking about you. Cold shivers indicate that someone is walking over the spot that will be your grave. If you step on a crack, you will fail in your lessons. The gift of a knife cuts friendship. Bad luck follows if one breaks a mirror, walks under a ladder, postpones a wedding, or opens an umbrella indoors. It is unlucky to turn back from a journey, to stub the toe, to wear clothes inside out, to wear a peacock feather, to meet a black cat or a funeral procession, to leave a house through a window, or to sit on a table. It is supposed to be good luck if a person finds a four-leaf clover or a horseshoe, picks up a pin, or returns money in payment of a debt.

**Foretelling the Future.** Some superstitious practices are less innocent. Especially so are those by which fortunetellers and palmists claim to predict future events, read character, or communicate with the dead. Belief in fortunetelling is very old. The ancient Romans and Greeks had their oracles and augurs. The French believed in the prophecies of Nostradamus, and the English followed Mother Shipton. Nowadays, persons in all walks of life are relieved of hundreds of thousands of dollars each year by fortunetellers. Fortunetelling is often harmful to the one whose fortune is told. But to many persons it is merely a form of entertainment and is not taken seriously. However, many people consult fortunetellers for advice on many things.

Some fortunetellers claim to possess special powers which enable them to foretell the future. Some rely on various systems of divination which are supposed to reveal a person's characteristics or proclaim his fate. Fortunetelling by cards is an example of this method. The lines in the palm of the hand are supposed to indicate personal characteristics, abilities, or fate. This method of divining is called *palmistry*. Tea-leaf reading, crystal gazing, astrology, taking omens from dreams, and *necromancy* (spirit communication) are other forms of these pseudosciences.

Many otherwise logical persons cling to superstitious beliefs because they hope that influences which lie outside their normal experience affect human life and destiny. But the development of modern education and the discoveries of scientists and scholars have helped to check the growth of superstition. WILSON D. WALLIS

**Related Articles** in WORLD BOOK include:

| | | | |
|---|---|---|---|
| Amulet | Evil Eye | Magic | Pioneer Life |
| Astrology | Exorcism | Mental Illness | in America |
| Augur | Fetish | (History) | (Caring for |
| Birthstone | Fortune- | Necromancy | the Sick) |
| Blarney | telling | Occult | Voodoo |
| Stone | Genii | Omen | Witchcraft |
| Divination | Ghost | Palmistry | |

**SUPERSTRUCTURE.** See BUILDING CONSTRUCTION (Parts of a Building).

**SUPPÉ,** *ZOO pay*, **FRANZ VON** (1819-1895), was an operetta composer. He produced large quantities of music in many forms during his lifetime. But of his great output, only a group of overtures has remained in active use. Such familiar overtures as *Poet and Peasant* (1846); *The Beautiful Galatea* (1865); *Light Cavalry* (1866); *The Jolly Robbers* (1867); *Fatinitza* (1876); *Boccaccio* (1879); and *Morning, Noon, and Night in Vienna*

## SUPREME COURT OF CANADA

are performed regularly. Suppé was born in or near Spalato (now Split), Yugoslavia. HERBERT WEINSTOCK

**SUPPLY AND DEMAND** are economic forces that determine the amount of a product that is produced and its price. The *supply* of a product is the amount of it that businessmen are willing to produce and sell. Generally, the higher the price is, the greater the supply will be. Similarly, the *demand* for a product is the amount of it that users would like to buy. Demand also depends on the price, but in the opposite way. Usually, demand is lower at high prices than at low ones. Because the amount that producers actually sell must be the same as the amount that users actually buy, the only price at which everyone can be satisfied is the one for which supply equals demand. This is called the *equilibrium price*.

The supply and demand diagram with this article shows how these economic forces operate. Using the market for onions as an example, the *supply curve SS'* shows the number of pounds that farmers will produce each month at every possible market price. Higher prices encourage farmers to produce more onions, and low prices discourage production. Consumers' reactions are shown by the *demand curve DD'*, which shows how many pounds of onions customers want to buy each month at every possible price. At low prices, they want a great many onions. At high prices, they use other vegetables instead.

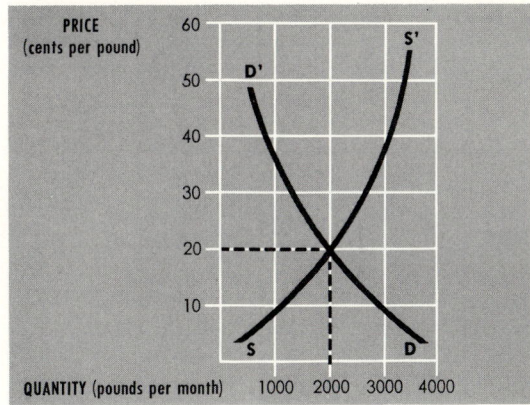

The supply and demand curves cross at a certain price (20¢ a pound in the example). When this is the market price, suppliers will offer just the quantity that users wish to buy. At any higher price, farmers will produce more onions than consumers are willing to buy, and competition among farmers will force the price down. At prices lower than equilibrium, purchasers will demand more onions than are available, and the scarcity of onions will drive the price up. ROBERT DORFMAN

See also ECONOMICS; FREE ENTERPRISE SYSTEM; INTERNATIONAL TRADE; PRICE.

**SUPRARENAL GLAND.** See GLAND (Adrenal Glands).

**SUPREME COUNCIL OF THE ROYAL ARCANUM.** See ROYAL ARCANUM, SUPREME COUNCIL OF THE.

**SUPREME COURT OF CANADA.** See CANADA, GOVERNMENT OF (The Supreme Court of Canada).

# SUPREME COURT OF THE UNITED STATES

**SUPREME COURT OF THE UNITED STATES** is the highest court in the nation. One of its basic duties is to determine whether federal, state, and local governments are acting according to the United States Constitution. The Supreme Court does its job by deciding specific legal cases on the basis of established legal rules. Much of the court's work involves rules that are laid down in the Constitution. Although many of these rules are stated in words that are not entirely clear, the Supreme Court must determine their meaning and apply them to the cases presented for decision. For a discussion of the relationship between the Supreme Court and the Constitution, see the article GOVERNMENT (Constitutional Government).

A Supreme Court decision has great importance. Once a decision has been reached by the court, all other courts throughout the United States are required to follow the decision in similar cases. In this way, the Supreme Court helps guarantee equal legal justice to all Americans. The court is not required to consider every case presented to it. It accepts only a few, most of which involve problems of national importance.

The Supreme Court heads the judicial branch of the federal government. It is the only court specifically created by the Constitution. The judicial system of each state is also headed by a supreme court. In some states, the court is known by another name, such as

*William Ray Forrester, the contributor of this article, is Dean of the Cornell University Law School, and the author of* Cases and Materials on Constitutional Law. *The article was critically reviewed by Byron R. White, Associate Justice of the Supreme Court of the United States.*

*court of appeals.* For the most part, state courts hear cases concerning state laws. However, the U.S. Supreme Court may review the decisions of the highest state courts that involve the U.S. Constitution or acts of Congress. This article deals only with the U.S. Supreme Court. For information on the entire federal court system and on the state courts, see the article COURT.

The role of the Supreme Court and its interpretation of the law change occasionally. These changes depend partly on the political, social, and economic beliefs of its members, and partly on the national conditions of the time. In our early days as a nation, for example, the court concerned itself chiefly with the proper division of authority between the federal government and state governments. A major concern today is the protection of the rights and liberties of individuals.

## How the Supreme Court Is Organized

Article III of the Constitution provides for the creation of the Supreme Court and states the limits of its jurisdiction. But details of the court's exact organization and the work it can do are left largely to Congress. Congress established the federal court system in the Judiciary Act of 1789. This act included provisions governing the Supreme Court.

**Membership.** The Supreme Court has nine members —a chief justice and eight associate justices. The exact number is set by Congress and has changed through the years. The first Supreme Court had six members. Since 1869, the court has consisted of nine members.

The Constitution sets no qualifications for justices, but states that they shall be appointed by the President, with the advice and consent of the Senate. However, all members have had some legal training and experience, and most justices have been prominent

From "Equal Justice Under Law"

**Courtroom** of the Supreme Court Building in Washington, D.C., is shown here as the justices see it from the bench. Spectators sit in the rear of the courtroom. The space between the spectators and the bench is reserved for lawyers pleading cases, for other members of the bar, and for the press. The building, completed in 1935, was designed by Cass Gilbert.

# THE SUPREME COURT

The Supreme Court has nine members. After Associate Justice Abe Fortas resigned from the court in 1969, and before President Richard M. Nixon's appointment of a new associate justice, the court had only eight members.

**Chief Justice Warren E. Burger**

**Hugo L. Black**

**W. J. Brennan, Jr.**

**William O. Douglas**

**John M. Harlan**

**Thurgood Marshall**

**Potter Stewart**

**Byron R. White**

Harris & Ewing; United Press Int.; Wide World

judges, lawyers, law teachers, or government officials.

Once appointed, justices may remain in office for life, or "during good behavior," and Congress cannot reduce their salary. These provisions protect the justices from political control, and help ensure the independence of the court.

**Salary and Terms.** The Court meets regularly in the Supreme Court Building in Washington, D.C. The annual term of the court begins the first Monday in October and usually ends in June.

The chief justice receives $62,500 a year, and each associate justice receives $60,000. A justice 70 years of age, who has served 10 or more years, may retire and continue to receive his salary. A justice may also retire at 65 if he has served at least 15 years.

## Authority of the Supreme Court

The Supreme Court declares what the law is only when an actual case comes before it under established rules of legal procedure. A matter before the court must involve a real dispute between opposing parties. The court does not give legal advice or advisory opinions, even if requested by the President or Congress.

The Constitution permits the court to decide cases "arising under" the Constitution, federal laws, and treaties. The court also decides disputes involving the United States or two or more states. The most important of these cases are those that require the court to interpret the Constitution or the laws enacted by Congress.

The Supreme Court has the power to decide whether a federal or state law or executive action is constitutional. This power, known as *judicial review*, is not expressly granted in the Constitution. However, the Constitution by its own terms is the "supreme law of the land." The court has ruled that it must review conflicts between the Constitution and an act of Congress or of a state legislature.

Most of the work of the Supreme Court comes under its *appellate jurisdiction*. This is the authority to confirm or reverse the decisions of lower courts. Appellate courts can call a lower court decision up for review when requested to do so by the losing party. The appeal is usually made on grounds that the judge has made an error in declaring the law that applies to the facts of the case. Most cases reviewed by the Supreme Court come from the federal courts of appeals and the highest state courts. The decisions of federal district courts are normally reviewed first by the courts of appeals. But in a few cases, the Supreme Court reviews the decisions of federal district courts directly. It also reviews the decisions of the federal Court of Claims and the Court of Customs and Patent Appeals.

The Supreme Court may try a few types of cases from their beginning. This authority is called *original jurisdiction*. The court has original jurisdiction in cases ". . . affecting ambassadors, other public ministers and consuls, and those in which a state shall be party. . . ." These cases, however, make up only a small fraction of the court's workload.

## The Court in Action

**Accepting Cases.** The Supreme Court cannot possibly review all the cases decided by lower courts. It can select only a few that it considers to be of sufficient importance. Questions of individual justice are most often left to the judgment of lower courts.

However, Congress has provided that the Supreme Court must grant review in a few types of cases. Such cases are brought to the court by *appeal*.

Most cases are brought before the court by a *writ of*

799

## U.S. SUPREME COURT JUSTICES

| Name | Term | Appointed By |
|---|---|---|
| **CHIEF JUSTICES** | | |
| *John Jay | 1790-1795 | Washington |
| *John Rutledge | 1795 | †Washington |
| *Oliver Ellsworth | 1796-1800 | Washington |
| *John Marshall | 1801-1835 | J. Adams |
| *Roger B. Taney | 1836-1864 | Jackson |
| *Salmon P. Chase | 1864-1873 | Lincoln |
| *Morrison R. Waite | 1874-1888 | Grant |
| *Melville W. Fuller | 1888-1910 | Cleveland |
| *Edward D. White | 1910-1921 | Taft |
| *William H. Taft | 1921-1930 | Harding |
| *Charles E. Hughes | 1930-1941 | Hoover |
| *Harlan F. Stone | 1941-1946 | F. D. Roosevelt |
| *Frederick M. Vinson | 1946-1953 | Truman |
| *Earl Warren | 1953-1969 | Eisenhower |
| *Warren E. Burger | 1969- | Nixon |
| **ASSOCIATE JUSTICES** | | |
| *James Wilson | 1789-1798 | Washington |
| *John Rutledge | 1790-1791 | Washington |
| William Cushing | 1790-1810 | Washington |
| *John Blair | 1790-1796 | Washington |
| *James Iredell | 1790-1799 | Washington |
| *Thomas Johnson | 1792-1793 | Washington |
| *William Paterson | 1793-1806 | Washington |
| *Samuel Chase | 1796-1811 | Washington |
| Bushrod Washington | 1799-1829 | J. Adams |
| Alfred Moore | 1800-1804 | J. Adams |
| William Johnson | 1804-1834 | Jefferson |
| H. Brockholst Livingston | 1807-1823 | Jefferson |
| Thomas Todd | 1807-1826 | Jefferson |
| Gabriel Duval | 1811-1835 | Madison |
| *Joseph Story | 1812-1845 | Madison |
| Smith Thompson | 1823-1843 | Monroe |
| Robert Trimble | 1826-1828 | J. Q. Adams |
| John McLean | 1830-1861 | Jackson |
| Henry Baldwin | 1830-1844 | Jackson |
| James M. Wayne | 1835-1867 | Jackson |
| Philip P. Barbour | 1836-1841 | Jackson |
| John Catron | 1837-1865 | Van Buren |
| John McKinley | 1838-1852 | Van Buren |
| Peter V. Daniel | 1842-1860 | Van Buren |
| Samuel Nelson | 1845-1872 | Tyler |
| Levi Woodbury | 1845-1851 | Polk |
| Robert C. Grier | 1846-1870 | Polk |
| Benjamin R. Curtis | 1851-1857 | Fillmore |
| John A. Campbell | 1853-1861 | Pierce |
| Nathan Clifford | 1858-1881 | Buchanan |
| Noah H. Swayne | 1862-1881 | Lincoln |
| Samuel F. Miller | 1862-1890 | Lincoln |
| *David Davis | 1862-1877 | Lincoln |
| *Stephen J. Field | 1863-1897 | Lincoln |
| William Strong | 1870-1880 | Grant |
| Joseph P. Bradley | 1870-1892 | Grant |
| Ward Hunt | 1873-1882 | Grant |
| *John M. Harlan | 1877-1911 | Hayes |
| William B. Woods | 1881-1887 | Hayes |
| Stanley Matthews | 1881-1889 | Garfield |
| Horace Gray | 1882-1902 | Arthur |
| Samuel Blatchford | 1882-1893 | Arthur |
| *Lucius Q. C. Lamar | 1888-1893 | Cleveland |
| David J. Brewer | 1890-1910 | Harrison |
| Henry B. Brown | 1891-1906 | Harrison |
| George Shiras, Jr. | 1892-1903 | Harrison |
| Howell E. Jackson | 1893-1895 | Harrison |
| *Edward D. White | 1894-1910 | Cleveland |
| *Rufus W. Peckham | 1896-1909 | Cleveland |
| Joseph McKenna | 1898-1925 | McKinley |
| *Oliver W. Holmes, Jr. | 1902-1932 | T. Roosevelt |
| William R. Day | 1903-1922 | T. Roosevelt |
| William H. Moody | 1906-1910 | T. Roosevelt |
| Horace H. Lurton | 1910-1914 | Taft |
| *Charles E. Hughes | 1910-1916 | Taft |
| *Willis Van Devanter | 1911-1937 | Taft |
| Joseph R. Lamar | 1911-1916 | Taft |
| Mahlon Pitney | 1912-1922 | Taft |
| *James C. McReynolds | 1914-1941 | Wilson |
| *Louis D. Brandeis | 1916-1939 | Wilson |
| John H. Clarke | 1916-1922 | Wilson |
| *George Sutherland | 1922-1938 | Harding |
| Pierce Butler | 1923-1939 | Harding |
| Edward T. Sanford | 1923-1930 | Harding |
| *Harlan F. Stone | 1925-1941 | Coolidge |
| *Owen J. Roberts | 1930-1945 | Hoover |
| *Benjamin N. Cardozo | 1932-1938 | Hoover |
| *Hugo L. Black | 1937- | F. D. Roosevelt |
| Stanley F. Reed | 1938-1957 | F. D. Roosevelt |
| *Felix Frankfurter | 1939-1962 | F. D. Roosevelt |
| *William O. Douglas | 1939- | F. D. Roosevelt |
| *Frank Murphy | 1940-1949 | F. D. Roosevelt |
| *James F. Byrnes | 1941-1942 | F. D. Roosevelt |
| *Robert H. Jackson | 1941-1954 | F. D. Roosevelt |
| Wiley B. Rutledge | 1943-1949 | F. D. Roosevelt |
| Harold H. Burton | 1945-1958 | Truman |
| *Tom C. Clark | 1949-1967 | Truman |
| Sherman Minton | 1949-1956 | Truman |
| *John M. Harlan | 1955- | Eisenhower |
| *William J. Brennan, Jr. | 1956- | Eisenhower |
| *Charles E. Whittaker | 1957-1962 | Eisenhower |
| *Potter Stewart | 1958- | Eisenhower |
| *Byron R. White | 1962- | Kennedy |
| *Arthur J. Goldberg | 1962-1965 | Kennedy |
| *Abe Fortas | 1965-1969 | Johnson |
| *Thurgood Marshall | 1967- | Johnson |

*Has a separate biography in WORLD BOOK.   †Appointment not confirmed by the United States Senate.

*certiorari* (pronounced *ser shee uh RARE ee*). This is a written order to call a case up from a lower court for review. The opposing attorney is given copies of the petition for certiorari and the supporting *brief* (written reasons for appeal). He has a short time to file a brief in opposition. If four justices vote to grant the petition, the court agrees to hear the case. The court controls its work load by granting only a small percentage of the requests for a writ of certiorari.

**Pleading Cases** before the Supreme Court is normally done by attorneys who have been admitted to the bar of the court. However, a *litigant* (person engaged in a lawsuit) may argue his own case. Each litigant usually hires and pays his own attorney. If a litigant has no money, free legal service may be provided.

When the United States government has an interest in a case before the Supreme Court, it is represented by the solicitor general or members of his staff. The attorney general of the United States may also argue important cases.

**Deciding Cases.** The justices decide a case after they have considered written and oral arguments from each side. During oral arguments, the justices are free to interrupt and to ask questions.

After the attorneys' oral arguments, the justices discuss the case *in conference* (in private). The chief justice begins the discussion. Then, in order of seniority, each associate justice gives his opinion. After discussion ends, the justices vote in reverse order of seniority. The latest member to be appointed to the court votes first.

800

The chief justice votes last, immediately after the associate justice who has served longest on the court. Cases are decided by majority vote.

If the chief justice has voted with the majority, he selects a justice to write the *opinion of the court*. This opinion is also called the *majority opinion*. If the chief justice has not voted with the majority, the senior justice of the majority assigns the opinion. A justice who disagrees with this opinion may write a *dissenting opinion*. A justice may write a *concurring opinion* if he agrees with the conclusion but not with the reasons for reaching it, or if he wishes to express similar reasons in his own words. Authors of the opinions announce them in a public session. All opinions are published in the *United States Reports*. The practice of putting opinions in writing requires the justices to explain and justify their decisions. Any citizen is free to read and criticize the opinions. This is an important tradition in a free society, and a strong safeguard against unreasonable use of power. The publishing of opinions also enables the public to know and understand the decisions of the court.

**Effects of Decisions.** Supreme Court decisions have importance far beyond the particular facts and parties involved. Once the court decides a case, lower courts are required to follow the decision in similar cases. The Supreme Court itself usually follows its earlier decisions. The policy of following rules laid down in previous decisions is known as *stare decisis*. This practice lends stability and predictability to the law. It allows persons to plan their future knowing that the rules will not be changed without a good reason.

The Supreme Court, however, is not bound by an earlier decision if it is convinced that an error has been made or that changed circumstances require a different approach. This provides for the court's recognition of social, political, and economic change.

### Landmark Decisions

**The Marshall Court.** Many of the most important and historic Supreme Court opinions were written by John Marshall, one of the most famous of all American judges. Marshall served as chief justice from 1801 to 1835. The Supreme Court during those years is sometimes referred to as the "Marshall court."

Marshall's most historic opinion was written in 1803, in the case of *Marbury v. Madison*. His majority opinion stated that the court may rule an act of Congress unenforceable if the act violates the U.S. Constitution. This power of *judicial review* is *implied* (expressed indirectly) but not clearly granted in the Constitution. See MARBURY V. MADISON.

Some persons have protested vigorously against the court's exercise of judicial review. However, this power has become firmly established as a basic part of the American constitutional system.

Several other Marshall court decisions also have had far-reaching application. In 1819, in *Dartmouth College v. Woodward*, the court ruled that private charters are contracts. It held that the Constitution protects such charters against violation by the states. This decision strengthened the rights of private property. See DARTMOUTH COLLEGE CASE.

Also in 1819, in *McCulloch v. Maryland*, the court supported the doctrine of implied powers. It ruled that the federal government possesses powers in addition to those specifically granted in the Constitution. It said that the U.S. government has any powers that are necessary and proper in carrying out its specified powers. This decision broadened the scope of the federal government. See MCCULLOCH V. MARYLAND; MARSHALL, JOHN.

**Regulating Commerce.** An important concern of the court has been the proper relationship between government and business. The Constitution gives Congress the power to regulate interstate commerce. In 1824, in *Gibbons v. Ogden*, the Marshall court gave a broad interpretation to the word *commerce*. Since the mid-1930's, the court has interpreted the commerce clause in a way that gives Congress wide regulatory powers in matters affecting business. See GIBBONS V. OGDEN; SCHECHTER V. UNITED STATES; INTERSTATE COMMERCE.

**Civil Rights and Liberties.** Through the years, the role and interpretations of the Supreme Court have shifted with changes in national conditions and public opinion. This has been true of the court's position on civil rights, especially in the area of race relations.

In 1857, in *Dred Scott v. Sandford*, the court held that Negroes were not and could not become U.S. citizens (see DRED SCOTT DECISION). But the 14th Amendment to the Constitution (1868) made all former slaves citizens and gave them full civil rights. In 1896, in the case of *Plessy v. Ferguson*, the court upheld a law providing for "separate but equal" public facilities for the white and Negro races. But in 1954, in *Brown v. Board of Education of Topeka*, the court ruled that racial segregation in public schools is unconstitutional. In 1964, in *Atlanta Motel v. United States*, the court upheld the Civil Rights Act of 1964. This act prohibits racial discrimination in many public accommodations.

Several cases in the 1960's dealt with voting rights. In 1962, the court ruled in *Baker v. Carr* that unfair districting of state legislatures could be challenged in federal courts. It ruled in other cases that congressional districts must be about equal in population, and that state legislatures and local governing bodies must be apportioned on the basis of equal population.

Several recent decisions have dealt with the rights of persons accused of crimes. In 1963, in *Gideon v. Wainwright*, the court held that states must provide free legal counsel to any person accused of a felony who is without funds. In 1964, in *Escobedo v. Illinois*, the court ruled that a confession cannot be used as evidence if it is obtained after the defendant has been denied permission to see his lawyer. The court went even further in the 1966 case of *Miranda v. Arizona*. It held that prior to any questioning, the defendant must be informed of his constitutional rights, including the right to remain silent. But in 1968, Congress passed a law removing this requirement for federal trials.

Other important civil rights decisions have dealt with Bible reading and prayers in public schools, freedom of speech and of the press, and pretrial publicity that is *prejudicial* (unfair) to the accused.

See also FLETCHER V. PECK; GRANGER CASES; LOCHNER V. NEW YORK; MILLIGAN, EX PARTE.

### Controversy on the Court

The Supreme Court has been sharply divided on some cases brought before it. This has been especially true of

## SUPREME SOVIET

cases involving questions that have divided the American public, such as minority rights. The court's lack of complete agreement in such cases is not unexpected nor undesirable. It reflects the seriousness of the cases and the presence of different points of view.

Since the Supreme Court was established, a strong debate has continued concerning the extent of its power. One side has insisted that the court should interpret and apply the Constitution to agree with the meaning and intent of those who wrote it. Another group has insisted on a more creative role for the court. They would interpret the Constitution so that it would apply to the new and changing problems of the nation. The second group also draws support from the original intent of the founding fathers, but disagrees as to the scope and meaning of that intent. Outstanding judges and legal scholars have been found on both sides of this debate.

The Supreme Court possesses great power over the Constitution and the nation. But this power is based on the respect of the American people. Throughout most of its history, the court has held the streams of government within their proper channels. It has largely succeeded in the delicate task of protecting the rights of unpopular minorities while relying for its support on the approval of the majority.   WILLIAM RAY FORRESTER

*Critically reviewed by* BYRON R. WHITE

See the separate biographies in WORLD BOOK for the justices listed in the *table* in this article. See also CHIEF JUSTICE; COURT; ROOSEVELT, F. D. (The Supreme Court); UNITED STATES CONSTITUTION; WASHINGTON, D.C. (color picture: the Supreme Court Building).

**SUPREME SOVIET.** See RUSSIA (Government).

**SUR.** See TYRE.

**SURABAJA,** SOOR *uh BAH yuh* (pop. 1,007,945; alt. 20 ft.), is the second largest city in Indonesia. It lies along the Kali Mas River in eastern Java, about 420 miles east of Djakarta (see INDONESIA [color map]). It is an important port and naval base, and has shipbuilding, textile, chemical, and petroleum industries.

**SURAKARTA,** SOOR *uh KAHR tuh* (pop. 367,626; alt. 430 ft.), lies in a rich agricultural area in Indonesia. For location, see INDONESIA (color map). The city is famous for its gold, textile, and copper handicraft industries. It includes the *Kraton*, a former palace of the susuhunan, or sultan. Since 1949, it has been part of the province of Central Java.   JUSTUS M. VAN DER KROEF

**SURCOAT.** See CLOTHING (The Middle Ages).

**SURETY BOND.** See BONDING.

**SURFACE MEASURE.** See SQUARE MEASURE.

**SURFACE TENSION** is a force that makes the surface of a liquid act like an elastic film. Because of surface tension, a steel needle carefully laid on water will not sink. Also, some insects can walk on water, supported by the apparent film.

Surface tension is caused by cohesive forces that attract the molecules of the liquid to each other (see COHESION). Surface molecules are attracted mainly downward, because there are no molecules of liquid above them. Cohesion makes the surface molecules resist forces that change their position. The needle and insects are supported at the surface because they push some of the molecules out of position.   CLARENCE E. BENNETT

**SURFING** is a thrilling water sport for persons of all ages. In *surfboard riding*, the surfer stands on a board that skims along the *crest* (top) of a wave. However, body surfers are swept along by the wave without using a board. Both kinds of surfing demand split-second timing. The surfer must have sharp reflexes to maintain the delicate balance he needs for a thrilling ride.

Surfers usually train for surfboard riding by body surfing. To body surf, a surfer swims out from the shore a few hundred yards and waits for a high wave. When a high wave starts in toward the shore, he does a *scissors kick* (spreads his legs apart and kicks them together) in the direction of the shore and swims a few strokes at the crest. He then puts his head down, arches his

*Sam J. Greller, the contributor of this article and a coach in water sports, is a member of the Water Polo Committee of the Amateur Athletic Union of the United States.*

**Catching A Wave,** the surfer paddles with his hands to gain speed. When the wave lifts the board, he stands up and puts his weight on his front foot, aiming the board toward the shore.

802

Don James

**Surfing** requires good balance and quick reflexes. The two men on the right are riding a wave into shore. The man on the left is paddling out to catch another wave. Surfers should be good swimmers.

back, and puts his hands at his sides. The wave sweeps him toward shore in this position. As it dies out, the surfer pushes his hands out and spreads his legs to slow down. The feel of the surf and the sense of balance gained is good training for surfboard riding.

For a surfboard ride, the surfer lies on his stomach on the board and paddles out to the area where the waves build up. When a big wave starts in toward shore, the surfer paddles his board ahead of it. As the wave begins to carry the board toward shore, the surfer stands up. He tries to guide the board across the face of the wave by shifting the weight of his body. Expert surfers

---
### SURFING TERMS
---

**Backwash, Rip,** or **Riptide** is a current that reverses itself and moves out from the shore.

**Big Gun** is a heavy surfboard used on big waves.

**Break** is the point in shallow water where a wave slows and builds up, then scatters.

**Cornering** occurs when a surfer shoots across a wave at an angle to the shoreline.

**Crack a Wave** means to ride a big wave successfully.

**Dumper,** or **Fall** is a wave that builds up sharply and drops straight down into shallow water.

**Going Down the Mine** occurs when a surfer misses the proper take-off point in a wave and is thrown in front of the wave.

**Green Wave** is a long, uninterrupted wave.

**Hanging Five,** or **Ten** occurs when the surfer hooks his toes over the end of the board.

**Hot Dogger** is an expert surfer who can do gymnastic and balancing tricks on the board.

**Howler,** or **Zipper** is a big wave that only an expert can ride.

**Pig Board,** or **Tear Drop** is a board that is shaped like a pie wedge.

**Roller** is a long, smooth wave that rolls to the shore line.

**Wipe Out** occurs when a rider is bumped from a board by a wave.

---

may move to the front of the board, but most surfers stand at the middle or rear of the board to keep it from turning over. A long rolling wave will bring a surfer onto the sands of the shore. The bigger the wave, the better the ride will be.

Surfing began in Hawaii hundreds of years ago. The sport is now popular in most parts of the world. Surfing in the United States centers on the beaches of Hawaii and southern California. Many styles of surfboards are used, but most U.S. surfers use a fiberglass board that is tapered at both ends. It is about 10 feet long, 30 inches wide, 3 inches thick, and weighs from 8 to 15 pounds. SAM J. GRELLER

See also HAWAII (color picture: Riding the Surf).

**SURGEON.** See SURGERY; MEDICINE (Specialists).

**SURGEON BIRD.** See JAÇANA.

**SURGEON GENERAL.** See PUBLIC HEALTH SERVICE.

**SURGEONFISH.** See DOCTORFISH.

**SURGEONS, AMERICAN COLLEGE OF,** is an organization of surgeons of the United States and Canada. Its purposes are to advance the science and art of surgery and to improve the surgical care of patients. The organization holds regional meetings each year. Its annual Clinical Congress is the world's largest gathering of surgeons at which scientific papers and exhibits are presented. The official surgical journal of the College is *Surgery, Gynecology & Obstetrics*. The college was founded in 1913 and has about 30,000 members. Headquarters are at 55 E. Erie Street, Chicago, Ill. 60611. LOYAL DAVIS

**SURGEONS, INTERNATIONAL COLLEGE OF,** is an organization of qualified surgeons that was founded in 1935 in Geneva, Switzerland. Its purpose is to improve and spread surgical knowledge throughout the world. About 12,000 surgeons from 47 countries belong to the organization. There are regional federations in North America, Latin America, Europe, and Asia. The organization publishes a monthly journal and bulletin. Headquarters are at 1516 N. Lake Shore Drive, Chicago, Ill. 60610, where an International Surgeons Hall of Fame has been established. HENRY W. MEYERDING

# SURGERY

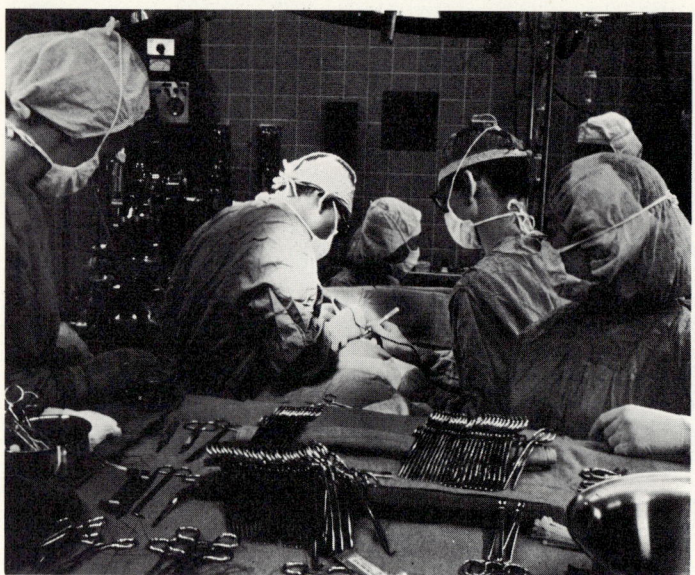
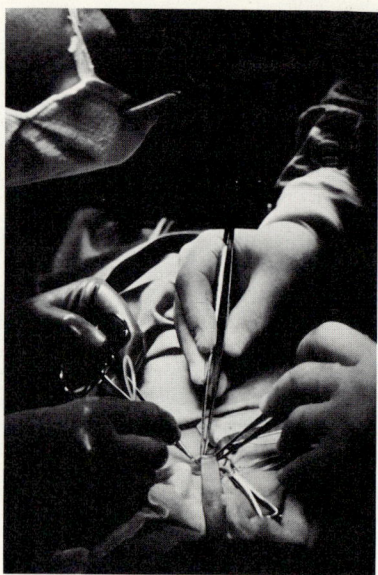

WORLD BOOK photos by E. F. Hoppe

**Modern Surgery** is a team effort, *left*. A surgeon and his assistant perform the operation, *right*, while nurses keep them supplied with the instruments they need. An anesthetist completes the team.

**SURGERY** is the branch of medicine that deals with the treatment of disease, deformities, or injuries by operations. The doctor who performs the operation is called a *surgeon*. Every physician has some training in surgery and is qualified to perform simple operations. But the surgeon is specially trained so that he has the judgment and skill to perform complicated operations on any part of the body. Four or five years of additional training after internship are necessary to qualify a doctor for general surgery. The doctor may train even longer if he wishes to enter one of the special fields of surgery.

### The Surgeon's Tools

A surgical operation is complicated. Many persons, medicines, and techniques are used to assure the greatest safety and comfort for the patient and to help the surgeon in his work. Anesthesia, the prevention of infection, and many laboratory tests are important aids to the surgeon. A qualified *surgical team* is essential to the successful performance of an operation. This team usually consists of at least a surgeon, a first assistant, an anesthesiologist, and a nurse.

**Anesthesia.** Before the discovery of anesthesia in 1842, operations were very painful. Because of this, surgeons could perform only very short operations. They tried to deaden the pain by giving large quantities of wine or other alcoholic beverages. Sometimes compounds containing opium were used. But the relief from pain was not complete and lasted only a short time.

Since the discovery of anesthesia, researchers have studied drugs and gases and developed more satisfactory anesthetics. Modern surgeons use *general anesthetics*, such as nitrous oxide, ether, and halothane, to put the patient to sleep. These may be used alone or in combination with one another. General anesthesia is also produced by injecting drugs such as pentothal sodium (see PENTOTHAL SODIUM). Sometimes a *local anesthetic*, such as novocain, which affects only the area near the place of injection, is used (see NOVOCAIN). Local anesthetics injected into the spinal canal produce anesthesia in specific parts of the body. One drug, curare, was used centuries ago by South American Indians (see CURARE). They put the drug on the tips of their arrows to paralyze or kill small animals and birds. Modern surgeons use it to relax the abdominal muscles in many serious operations. See ANESTHESIA.

**Antiseptics and Asepsis.** Infection once was a great danger in surgery. Even though the surgery was successful, patients often died because of infection. But in 1865, Joseph Lister of Great Britain introduced methods for preventing infection. He used various antiseptics to kill germs in the operating room during the course of an operation. He often sprayed carbolic acid about the room to kill the germs. Later, the method of *aseptic* (completely sterile) surgery was developed. In this method all germs that cause infection are kept out by cleaning and sterilizing all equipment used in the operating room. Instruments and linens are completely sterilized before the operation. Thus, while antiseptics kill germs that are present, asepsis keeps them out altogether. See ANTISEPTIC; LISTER, SIR JOSEPH.

**Instruments.** A surgeon uses many instruments in the course of a single operation. Sharp instruments include scissors and *scalpels* (knives). There are also holders for needles and sponges, *clamps* to grasp blood vessels, *retractors* to hold back folds of skin, and many others.

Modern instruments have advanced the growth of surgery. Perhaps one of the most useful of these, the X-ray machine, is seldom thought of as an "instrument." But this device, which permits the doctor to see inside the human body, is probably one of the most valuable tools for diagnosis. By this means, the surgeon can detect broken bones, and diagnose many of the important diseases of the internal body organs. Other instruments have been useful in looking into body cavities. The *bronchoscope* is used to examine the lungs, and to perform a *biopsy* (remove small pieces of lung tissue for study and diagnosis). Doctors use the *cystoscope* to examine the bladder. A modern surgical knife uses very short radio waves to cut body tissues.

**Sutures** are threads used to tie an open wound or incision together so that the tissues heal better. Modern surgery would be impossible without them. Some kinds of sutures, such as catgut, are absorbed by the body. Others, such as nylon or silk, must be removed after several days. See SUTURE.

**Technique.** In the early days of surgery, the operator's technique was considered most important. Only the most skilled surgeon could perform an operation in the least possible time. For example, these doctors could perform an amputation in two or three minutes. Modern surgery stresses adequate diagnosis of the disease and proper care of the patient before and after the operation. Thus, the surgeon needs not only knowledge of surgery itself, but also a wide knowledge of physiology, chemistry, and pathology. However, technique remains an important tool in surgery.

In 1874, a leading British surgeon spoke of "those portions of the human frame that will ever remain sacred." He said that "the abdomen, the chest, and the brain would be forever shut from the intrusion of the wise and humane surgeon." Since that time, the surgeon has been able to operate successfully upon all parts of the human body, including these. For example, a present-day surgeon can remove several feet of diseased intestines and sew the remaining intestinal sections together. The body will function normally after the operation. A kidney, or even a major part of the stomach, can be removed by an operation. Surgeons have been able to operate successfully on the heart. In such surgery, a doctor may lift the heart out of the body, operate on it, and then replace it. Extensive surgery on the lungs and ribs is often part of the treatment of tuberculosis. A surgeon can successfully remove an entire lung that has been diseased by cancer. A brain surgeon can remove brain tumors, repair head injuries, and cut nerves to correct certain conditions.

Transplanting organs is one of the newest types of operations. In this operation, the surgeon takes a healthy organ from one person and uses it to replace the diseased organ in another person. But the tissues must be able to exist together, or the patient's body will reject the new organ. See TISSUE TRANSPLANT.

Cryosurgery makes use of extreme cold in surgery. It usually involves freezing tissues. Cryosurgery has been suggested to cure duodenal ulcers. Surgeons sometimes use cold probes on the brain to treat Parkinson's disease. Cold probes are also used to treat detached retinas and remove cataracts. See CRYOBIOLOGY.

### A Typical Operation

Perhaps the best way to understand what is involved in a surgical operation is to consider a typical one. After a thorough examination, including laboratory tests, the doctor diagnoses the disease as an infected appendix. The patient is brought to the hospital and prepared for the operation. Sedative drugs are given to relax the patient before the operation.

The operating room has been prepared for the patient's arrival by a thorough cleaning and scrubbing. All equipment not to be used for the operation has been removed. A large table is set up near the operating table. This will hold all the sterilized instruments and sponges that the surgeon might need during the operation. A second table, a small one on an L-shaped stand, is also set up. This fits over both the operating table and the patient. It holds all the instruments and sponges immediately needed by the surgeon. A nurse has charge of these tables.

The patient is usually put to sleep in a room that is designed for this purpose. The anesthetist needs a lot of equipment such as anesthetics, anesthetic machines, masks, sterile syringes, a stethoscope, and an apparatus that measures blood pressure. A tank of oxygen and a mask for giving the gases are always present. Also at hand are small flasks of stimulant drugs.

Meantime the doctors and nurses on the surgical team prepare for the operation. They spend 8 to 10 minutes scrubbing their hands and forearms to remove germs. In addition to this, they wear sterilized rubber gloves because the skin cannot be made completely sterile even with strong antiseptics. The members of the surgical team put on sterilized gowns to cover their clothing and caps to cover their hair. They also wear masks of gauze or other material to cover their mouths and noses so that they will not breathe germs into the area.

Nurses and orderlies bring the patient into the operating room and make him comfortable on the operating table. The anesthetist takes and records the rate of the patient's pulse, respiration, and blood pressure. The anesthetist keeps a constant check on these throughout the operation. Nurses place sheets over the patient in such a manner that the area in which the *incision* (opening) is to be made is left open. This area is thoroughly cleansed, antiseptics are applied, and the area is again draped with sterile sheets. Nurses place the sterile instruments on the tables, and put the small table over the operating table, within easy reach of the surgeon. If gas is the anesthetic, the anesthetist places a mask over the patient's face and opens the valves of a complicated machine, thus allowing the patient to breathe the anesthetic. He soon feels no pain.

The surgeon starts the operation by making an incision in the skin of the abdomen. He extends this through the layer of fat that lies directly beneath the skin. He pulls back the muscle tissue, and places retractors in position to hold the tissue out of the way. This exposes the appendix and that part of the intestine to which it is attached.

As he works, the surgeon clamps the ends of small blood vessels with forceps, or with devices called *hemostats*. Thus very little bleeding takes place during the operation. *Sponges*, which are actually pieces of gauze folded into small pads, are used to remove any surplus blood. The surgeon quickly removes the appendix, ties the stump that remains with a suture and *inverts* (turns) the stump into the large intestine. Then the "closing-up" procedure begins.

805

# SURGERY

The sponges are removed. The surgeon takes the clamps off the blood vessels and ties the vessels so there will be no bleeding. He then removes the retractors, and the muscles move back into their normal position. The surgeon brings the tissues together with sutures. Finally, he sews the edges of the cut skin together.

During the course of the operation, the anesthetist has been careful to give exactly the right amount of anesthetic to the patient. The various nurses assist the surgeon like members of any well-drilled team.

At the end of the operation, the doctor applies a gauze bandage to the incision area and nurses remove the sheets used for draping. Doctors and nurses return the patient to his hospital bed and he usually recovers uneventfully. Yet such a routine operation would have been impossible a hundred years ago.

## Surgical Specialties

As in other branches of medicine, special branches of surgery have developed. These specialties came about because of the need for specialized types of surgery for specific areas of the body. Surgeons in these fields often take additional training. Frequently, new equipment is developed for use in the specialty fields.

**Ophthalmology,** a specialty in treating diseases of the eyes, has developed a distinct field of surgery. Surgeons cure blindness that results from *cataracts* (a clouding of the eye lens) by removing the lens. They also operate on the muscles of the eye to correct a condition known as cross-eyes. See OPHTHALMOLOGY.

**Plastic Surgery** can produce exceptional results by removing scars and blemishes. Plastic surgeons often graft skin. World War II gave great impetus to the development of plastic surgery. Men who were seriously disfigured in battle had their deformities corrected by means of surgery. Surgeons made new noses or new ears even though the original ones were completely destroyed. They built new jaws from living bone and cartilage and flesh. See PLASTIC SURGERY.

**Gynecology,** which deals with diseases of women, has also developed a special surgical field. The Caesarean section in childbirth once resulted in the death of about 86 of every 100 women on whom it was performed. In some modern hospitals not even two die of every 100 women on whom such operations are performed. See also HYSTERECTOMY.

**Other Specialty Fields.** There are many other fields in which special types of surgery have developed. The *thoracic* surgeon operates on the chest. In *urologic* surgery, the surgeon operates on the kidneys and bladder. The *otolaryngologist* takes care of diseases of the ears, nose, and throat. The *orthopedist* operates on bones. The *proctologist* treats diseases of the lower bowel and anus. *Brain surgeons* and *heart surgeons* need particular skills and training. In each field, new knowledge and techniques have brought great progress (see HEART [Heart Surgery]).

## History

Surgery has been known since ancient times. The first surgeon's tool was probably a piece of flint stone. Some skeletons of Stone Age men show evidence of *trephining*. In this operation, a hole was cut in the head of the patient to relieve pressure from a fracture. Primitive tribes fixed broken legs with splints. Even in the earliest times, *cautery* (searing the flesh) was used to stop bleeding. Circumcision, performed during certain religious rites, was one of the earliest operations.

Some operations were known to the ancient Babylonians, Greeks, and Romans. Military surgery has been important for two or three thousand years. The early Hindus were expert surgeons. They knew at least 125 different surgical instruments. They also developed plastic surgery to replace noses and ears that had been cut off. In the Middle Ages, surgeons were often confused with barbers. Both had the right to perform operations. But only the barber did bloodletting, for the surgeon thought it beneath him. It is from this bloodletting that the red and white striped pole of the barber developed—the red standing for blood and the white for the bandage.

Among the many famous surgeons of the past was the Frenchman, Ambroise Paré, who lived in the 1500's. He has been called the father of military medicine. He abolished the harmful practice of pouring boiling oil on wounds to sterilize them. John Hunter (1728-1793), an English pathologist, was the founder of experimental surgery. In the United States, Ephraim McDowell (1771-1830) of Kentucky performed the first successful operation to remove a tumor of the ovary in 1809, the beginning of successful abdominal surgery. Crawford Long (1815-1878) of Georgia is credited with having first used ether as an anesthetic in 1842.

Many of the great modern surgeons have been Americans. William Halsted (1852-1922) devised many new surgical procedures and techniques. He introduced the use of sterile gloves in aseptic surgery. Fred H. Albee (1876-1945), an orthopedist, brought bone grafting into practical use. Chevalier Jackson (1865-1958) developed the first practical lighted *esophagoscope*, an instrument used to examine the throat. Other modern surgeons are the famous Mayo brothers, William and Charles, both of whom made many contributions; Harvey Cushing, the great brain surgeon; and Evarts Graham. This pioneer thoracic surgeon in 1933 became the first man to remove an entire cancerous lung.

Modern surgery has advanced in five main ways. These are (1) the development of aseptic surgery; (2) the technical improvements in surgical instruments; (3) the increased knowledge of body processes; (4) anesthesia; and (5) the use of chemicals to prevent and treat infections.  WARREN H. COLE

**Related Articles** in WORLD BOOK include:

BIOGRAPHIES

| | |
|---|---|
| Billroth, Albert | Lister, Sir Joseph |
| Carrel, Alexis | Long, Crawford W. |
| Colles, Abraham | Mayo (family) |
| Crile, George W. | McDowell, Ephraim |
| Cushing, Harvey | Murphy, John B. |
| Drew, Charles R. | Paré, Ambroise |
| Forssmann, Werner | Warren, John C. |
| Kocher, Emil T. | |

OTHER RELATED ARTICLES

| | | |
|---|---|---|
| Amputation | Bronchoscope | Surgeons, International College of |
| Anatomy | Gastroscope | |
| Anesthesia | Ligature | Trephining |
| Bandage | Medicine | Vivisection |
| Barber | Surgeons, American College of | X Rays |
| Bloodletting | | |

# SURINAM

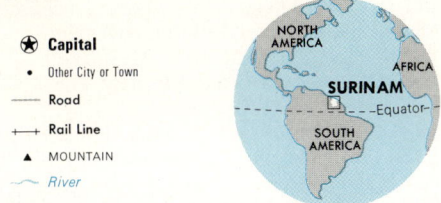

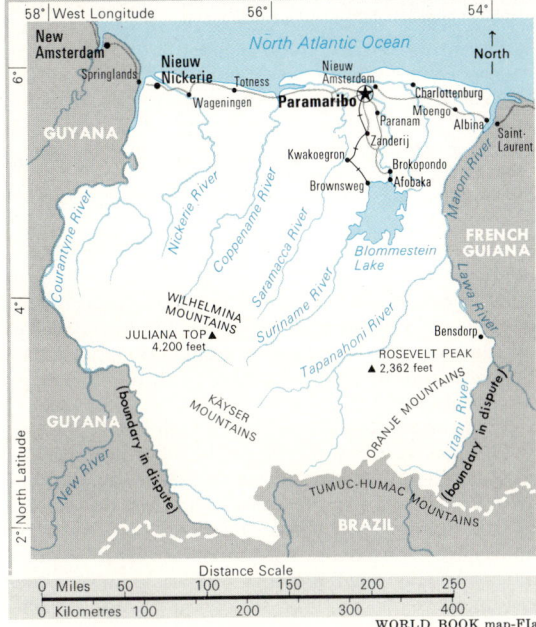

WORLD BOOK map-FIa

**SURINAM,** *SOOR uh nam,* is an overseas territory of The Netherlands. It is also called DUTCH GUIANA. Surinam lies on the northeastern coast of South America, between Guyana and French Guiana. Dense mountain forests separate Surinam from Brazil on the south. Surinam covers 63,039 square miles. Paramaribo is the capital and largest city of the territory (see PARAMARIBO).

The coast of Surinam is flat swampland. The inhabited sections along the lower parts of the rivers are protected by dams and drained by canals. Swamps and forests limit agriculture almost entirely to these regions. Mountains and thick forests cover the interior of the country. Interior forests yield dyewoods, and hardwoods such as mahogany and teak.

**The People and Their Work.** Surinam has a population of about 402,000, including about 38,000 Negroes and American Indians who live in the interior. The *Bush Negroes* are descendants of African slaves who escaped into the jungles before slavery was abolished in the mid-1800's. Indians who descended from the earliest Indian settlers live along the rivers in the interior. People from India, Indonesia, and descendants of Negro slaves form the largest population groups. Dutch is the official language of Surinam.

Agriculture and mining are the chief industries. Farm products include bananas, cacao, citrus fruits, coffee, maize, rice, and sugar. Surinam has vast deposits of bauxite, a mineral used in making aluminum, and is a leading bauxite producer (see ALUMINUM [table]). During World War II, Surinam provided over half the bauxite used by the United States. In the mid-1960's, Afobaka Dam was built on the upper Suriname River to supply power for the Suralco Company's aluminum smelter and alumina plant.

**Cities.** The chief cities of Surinam are Paramaribo (the largest city), Moengo, Nieuw Nickerie, and Totness. Other towns include Albina, Kwakoegron, Nieuw Amsterdam, and Paranam.

**Government and History.** Surinam is governed under the constitution of 1950. In 1955, The Netherlands gave Surinam complete control over its domestic affairs but retained control of foreign affairs and defense. The Dutch monarch appoints a governor for Surinam. He serves an indefinite term. A 21-member legislative council, elected by the people, serves a four-year term.

The English settled the area in 1651. By the Treaty of Breda, ending an Anglo-Dutch war in 1667, Great Britain gave the area to the Dutch in exchange for what is now New York state. The English occupied the area during the Napoleonic Wars, but Surinam reverted to the control of the Dutch government after the wars ended in 1815.

ARTHUR P. WHITAKER

**Small Villages in Surinam** with thatched-roof houses nestle along the main rivers and streams. Dense tropical growth laced with palms, banana trees, and brightly hued flowers almost hides the towns from view in some places.

Virginia Moore

807

## SURINAM TOAD

**SURINAM TOAD** is an odd-shaped toad that is known for the unusual way it raises its young. It is named for Surinam (Dutch Guiana), in South America, where man first discovered it. The Surinam toad is flat, and has a head shaped like a triangle. It has small eyes, and no tongue or teeth. The long, thin fingers of its front legs are not webbed, but its hind feet have large webs between the toes.

The Surinam toad lives in the water and has rough, brown skin. At breeding time, the female's skin grows thick and spongy. The female lays each egg while she and her mate turn over in the water. The egg sinks into the skin of the female's back. The young pass the tadpole stage in the mother's back. They come out of the skin when they are about 2½ months old or older.

**Scientific Classification.** The Surinam toad is in the Surinam toad family, *Pipidae*. It is classified as genus *Pipa*, species *P. pipa*. W. FRANK BLAIR

**The Back of the Female Surinam Toad** provides a living place for the young toads until they are large enough to take care of themselves.

American Museum of Natural History

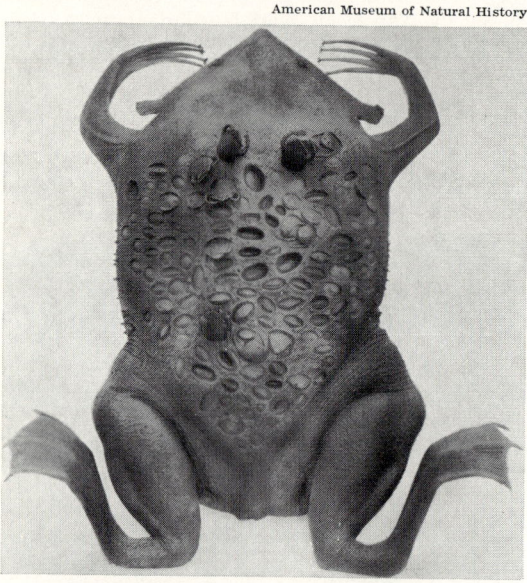

**SURNAME.** See NAME, PERSONAL (Beginnings).

**SURREALISM,** *suh REE ul iz'm*, is a movement in art and literature that attempts to express the subconscious mind. Surrealist painters intend to show their freedom from inhibitions and conventions by what they term *automatic painting*. That is, they paint as if without any conscious plan or preconceived notion of procedure, and use images and ideas taken from dream experiences. Surrealists often present these dream images with superrealistic, or surrealist, precision. In order to shock the observer into a keener awareness, surrealist painters place familiar images in immense spaces and puzzling and incongruous relationships.

Surrealism began in Paris in 1924. André Breton was its leader, and other members in the movement included Max Ernst, Yves Tanguy, and André Masson. Salvador Dali popularized surrealism in the U.S. (see DALI, SALVADOR [picture]). Giorgio de Chirico, Pablo Picasso, Paul Klee, Marc Chagall, and Marcel Duchamp are regarded as the forerunners of the movement. PETER SELZ

See also DADAISM; PAINTING (After 1900).

**SURREY.** See ENGLAND (color map: The 38 Counties of England).

**SURREY, EARL OF** (1517?-1547), HENRY HOWARD, is usually linked in literary history with Sir Thomas Wyatt. They are considered the two greatest English poets at the dawn of the English Renaissance. Surrey, a courtier and military commander during the reign of Henry VIII, was the originator of blank verse. He and Wyatt introduced the Italian sonnet form into English poetry. Their poems were first published in *The Book of Songs and Sonnets* (1557). This book is usually called *Tottel's Miscellany*. Surrey was beheaded in 1547 on a charge of high treason. PAUL M. KENDALL

**SURTAX.** See INCOME TAX.

**SURTSEY.** See VOLCANO (Famous Volcanic Eruptions).

**SURVEYING** is the technique of measuring to determine the position of points, or of marking out points and boundaries. The points may be on, beneath, or even above the earth's surface. Surveying is as old as civilization. It began in Egypt. Every year, after the Nile River overflowed its banks and washed out boundaries on the rich farmlands, the Egyptians fixed new boundaries by surveying.

**Types of Surveys** depend upon their uses.

The *land survey* is the type with which people are most familiar. It is used to fix boundaries and to find the areas of plots of ground. In Canada and the western United States, the boundaries and divisions of public lands have been fixed by government surveyors. A *plane survey* is used on small plots of ground only, since it does not take into consideration the curvature of the earth's surface. A *geodetic survey* allows for curvature and is used to find large areas or long boundaries.

The *topographical survey* includes the measuring of altitudes of elevations and depressions within the region for the purpose of making maps. The U.S. Geological Survey makes and publishes topographic maps of the United States.

*Engineering surveys* are made where buildings, bridges, roads, canals, and other man-made objects are to be built. *Underground surveys* determine where pipes are to be laid or tunnels dug. *Nautical*, or *hydrographic*, *surveys* map out the bed of a river or lake or ocean. By studying riverbeds, man can learn to control the flow of water and erosion. Both have greatly helped navigation.

*Aerial survey*, or *photogrammetry*, determines distances on the ground by means of photographs taken from airplanes. These photographs include a great amount of detail that a ground observer either cannot or does not get. Aerial surveying is almost always used for topographic mapping of large areas.

**Surveying Tools.** The most important of all tools used by the surveyor is the *transit*. This is a small telescope set up on a *tripod* (three-legged stand). To it are attached both horizontal and vertical arcs, used to measure horizontal and vertical angles. It has vernier scales by which the surveyor can read very small fractions of degrees (see VERNIER). Both the tripod and the telescope may be made level with the aid of attached *spirit levels*. These levels are similar to those used by carpenters. A *plumb bob* (weight) hangs from the tripod's

**A Surveyor's Transit** is the most important instrument used for surveying land. It serves a number of purposes. It is used to measure horizontal and vertical angles, judge distances, and determine where ground must be leveled.

H. Armstrong Roberts

center and points to the exact spot where the surveying instrument is set up.

Besides measuring and setting out angles, the transit judges distances. With the use of the telescope and levels, the surveyor can also determine where ground must be leveled. Some transits have compasses attached. A surveyor can plot a north-south line simply by pointing his telescope directly north and having a helper place a stake in line with the vertical hair which crosses the center of the telescope.

Surveyors use a long *steel tape* to measure or set out distances. Most steel tapes are 50, 100, or 200 feet long. Surveyors use an *invar tape* when making extremely precise measurements. Invar tapes are made of nickel and steel. They are less affected by changes in temperature than are steel tapes.

**The Basis of Surveying** is geometry. Angles and triangles play a very important part in the work. A surveyor must have a thorough knowledge of geometry and trigonometry. He must be able to use delicate instruments with precision and accuracy. For a diagram of how surveying works, see PARALLAX.

**Careers in Surveying.** Modern surveying is closely connected with the various branches of engineering, especially civil engineering. Surveyors find work to do whenever there are roads, dams, and bridges to be built. They determine the boundaries of the property held by individuals, as well as the boundaries of various political divisions. B. AUSTIN BARRY

**Related Articles** in WORLD BOOK include:

| | | |
|---|---|---|
| Alidade | Coast and Geodetic | Plane Table |
| Base Line | Survey | Public Lands |
| Bench Mark | Geodesy | Surveyor's Compass |
| Chain | Level | Theodolite |
| Chart | Photogrammetry | Transit |

**SURVEYOR'S COMPASS** is an instrument used for determining magnetic directions. Although engineer's transits often have a compass, the true surveyor's compass has no telescopic sighting device. Pointings are made by open sights similar to rifle sights.

The magnetic needle is the essential part of a surveyor's compass. This piece of hard steel, that is magnetized and balanced, swings in a plane parallel to the horizon. The needle generally pivots on a jeweled bearing to reduce swinging friction to a minimum. The ends of the needle, sharpened to knifelike edges, pass near ruled degree markings. At present, engineers use the surveyor's compass only in surveying land of little value, since this instrument is inferior in precision to the engineer's transit. See TRANSIT.

A surveyor must allow for the errors of a compass. For example, the balance of the needle on its pivot can be for only one zone of magnetic dip. Lines of magnetic force come up out of the earth as well as from the magnetic poles. Therefore, a free-moving needle always will dip as well as swing. Also, the lines of magnetic force from the earth are not constant in direction. They vary from day to day and even from hour to hour. Sunspots may cause this variation. The magnetic quality of nearby rocks also will affect the compass needle. The man at the compass can carry no iron. All metal likely to disturb the magnetic needle, such as knives and steel-rimmed glasses, must be left behind. B. AUSTIN BARRY

See also COMPASS.

**SURVEYOR'S MEASURE.** See WEIGHTS AND MEASURES (Linear Measure-Surveyor's, or Gunther's Chain; Square Measure-Surveyor's).

**A Surveyor's Compass** has a mirror on the inside lid which makes it possible to read the compass face while sighting objects.

Charles Bruning Co.

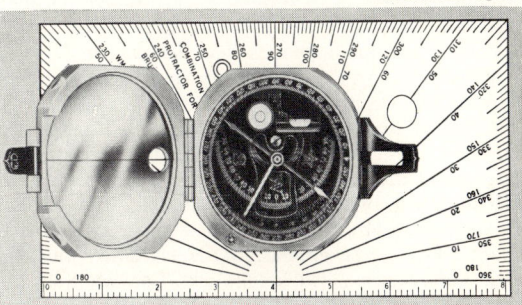

# SURVIVAL OF THE FITTEST

**SURVIVAL OF THE FITTEST.** See NATURAL SELECTION.

**SUSA,** *SOO zuh,* or SHUSH, was once the capital of the ancient Kingdom of Elam and the Persian Empire. The partly uncovered ruins of this city lie in the province of Khuzistan, in southwestern Iran. Susa appears several times in the Bible, where it is called *Shushan*. The Old Testament story of Esther took place in Susa. The tomb of Daniel is said to be in Susa. Archaeologists found the famous *Code of Hammurabi*, a collection of Babylonian laws, in the ruins of Susa in 1901. See ESTHER; DANIEL; HAMMURABI.

Susa flourished until about 640 B.C., when the Assyrians plundered it. Darius I built palaces in the city in the early 500's B.C., and made it one of the capitals of the Persian Empire. Susa declined after the Greeks, under Alexander the Great, conquered it in the late 300's B.C. RICHARD N. FRYE

**SUSPENDED ANIMATION** describes a condition in which the vital functions of the body are stopped for brief periods of time. Suspended animation occurs in drowning. Rescuers find that the drowned person's breathing has stopped. They cannot feel his pulse nor can they hear his heart beat. The person will die unless the rescuers start artificial respiration (see ARTIFICIAL RESPIRATION).

Sometimes during a surgical operation the patient's heart stops beating. In such an emergency, the surgeon makes an opening in the chest wall and massages the heart muscle itself until it begins to beat.

Suspended animation also describes conditions in which a person cannot move and seems to be in a deathlike trance. This occurs in some types of mental illness and is called catalepsy (see CATALEPSY). Fakirs can produce this condition in themselves (see FAKIR).

**SUSPENSION** is a mixture of solid particles in a gas or a liquid. Smoke particles form a suspension in air, and muddy water is a suspension of tiny dirt particles in water. A suspension differs from a *solution*, another kind of mixture. The substances in a suspension can usually be separated by mechanical methods, such as filtration. But the substances in a solution must be separated chemically or by distillation. A mixture of two liquids that do not dissolve in each other, such as oil and water, is an *emulsion*.

The molecules of liquids and gases are in constant motion. The effects of this motion on the particles in a suspension can be seen through a microscope. The moving molecules bump into the larger suspended particles, making the larger particles move in a fast, jiggling manner. This motion of suspended particles was first described in 1827 by Scottish physicist Robert Brown. It became known as *Brownian motion*.

Eventually, gravity makes the particles in a suspension *settle* (separate from the surrounding substance). The rate of settling depends partly on the size of the particles. Large particles settle faster than small particles. Road dust settles rapidly after being suspended briefly in air by a passing automobile. But smaller smoke particles may remain in the air until rain washes them down to the ground. Extremely small particles may remain suspended indefinitely. For example, the tiny fat particles in homogenized milk remain suspended, instead of rising and forming a layer of cream. The only motion of these suspended fat particles is their Brownian motion. JOHN P. FACKLER, JR.

**SUSPENSION BRIDGE.** See BRIDGE (The Suspension Bridge).

**SUSQUEHANNA RIVER,** *SUS kwuh HAN uh*, is a swift but shallow waterway flowing through one of the most important industrial regions in the eastern United States. The river rises at Otsego Lake in central New York state. It flows southward across Pennsylvania into Maryland, where it empties into Chesapeake Bay at Havre de Grace. For location, see MIDDLE ATLANTIC STATES (color map).

The river is 444 miles long. Its chief tributaries are the Chemung, the West Branch, and the Juniata rivers. Important cities on the river include Binghamton, N.Y., and Wilkes-Barre, Berwick, Sunbury, and Harrisburg, Pa. The river's swift current, rock obstructions, and shallow bed discourage shipping. However, the Susquehanna presents the greatest water-power potential of the rivers in the northeastern United States. Hydroelectric projects have been developed at Safe Harbor and Holtwood, Pa., and at Conowingo, Md. The Susquehanna Basin contains important *anthracite* (hard coal) deposits. E. WILLARD MILLER

**SUSQUEHANNA UNIVERSITY.** See UNIVERSITIES AND COLLEGES (table).

**SUSSEX.** See ENGLAND (color map: The 38 Counties of England).

**SUSSEX,** New Brunswick (pop. 3,607; alt. 72 ft.), is the center of a rich farming district about halfway between Saint John and Moncton in Canada (see NEW BRUNSWICK [political map]). Gently sloping hills, fertile valleys, and many small streams make the Sussex region excellent for cattle grazing. Sussex is known for its production of milk, butter, and soft drinks. It has a variety of small industries, the most important of which are lumbering and the manufacture of ice cream. The town lies on the main highway of the province. Once known as Sussex Vale, it was founded by United Empire Loyalists in 1783. Sussex has a mayor-council form of government. W. S. MACNUTT

**SUSSEX SPANIEL** originated in England, and gets its name from the county of Sussex, in southern England.

**The Sussex Spaniel**
WORLD BOOK photo by C. F. Williams

It is a strong stocky dog with short legs. The Sussex weighs from 35 to 45 pounds. Its coat is usually a golden liver color. The Sussex is intelligent and willing to learn. But the breed has never been popular in the United States. MAXWELL RIDDLE

**SUTHERLAND, GEORGE** (1862-1942), served as an associate justice of the Supreme Court of the United States from 1922 to 1938. During the dispute over the validity of New Deal legislation, he voted regularly to hold the measures unconstitutional. In the famous "Scottsboro" case of 1932, his opinion advanced the constitutional rights of persons accused of crime. Sutherland served as a Republican congressman from Utah, and as a United States senator. He was born in Buckinghamshire, England. JERRE S. WILLIAMS

**SUTHERLAND, JOAN** (1926- ), an Australian operatic soprano, won acclaim for her brilliant vocal technique. Her voice has a depth and richness not usually associated with the ornate style of her operatic roles. She ranks among the greatest singers of her time for her range, flexibility, and ease of singing in rapid passages of pinpoint precision. She enjoyed great success in London and New York City. Italian opera audiences nicknamed her "La Stupenda," *the stupendous one*.

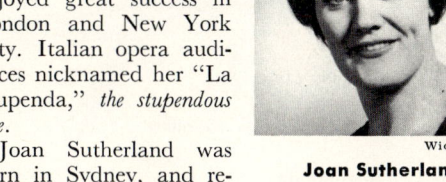
Wide World
**Joan Sutherland**

Joan Sutherland was born in Sydney, and received her early training there. She moved to London in 1951 and made her operatic debut at the Covent Garden Opera in the title role in *Lucia di Lammermoor* in 1959. She first appeared in the United States in 1961. MAX DE SCHAUENSEE

**SUTHERLAND FALLS** is the fifth highest mountain waterfall in the world. It lies 16 miles from the head of Milford Sound, in the Southern Alps of South Island, New Zealand. Its waters plunge down a mountainside in three leaps from a height of 1,904 feet. The first leap is 815 feet; the second, 751 feet; and the third, 338 feet. Water from melting glaciers forms Sutherland Falls. The waters of Sutherland Falls eventually flow into Milford Sound. See also WATERFALL (picture chart: Waterfalls of the World). J. B. CONDLIFFE

**SUTLEJ RIVER**, *SUT lej*, is the most easterly of the five waterways of the Punjab region of Pakistan. It ranks as the largest branch of the Indus, the chief river of the province of West Pakistan. The Sutlej rises in the plateau of Tibet, nearly 3 miles above sea level. The river winds its way through the passes of the Himalaya mountains and crosses northwestern India. Then it flows in a southwesterly direction through the Punjab region of West Pakistan. It joins the Indus in the east-central part of the province. The Sutlej is about 950 miles long. It is an important source of water for the dry Punjab plains. One of the world's highest dams, the Bhākra Dam, rises 740 feet above the river near Bhākra, India. J. E. SPENCER

**SUTTEE**, *suh TEE*, is a Hindu custom that people once practiced in India. Its name comes from the Sanskrit word *sati*, which means *faithful wife*. By the custom of suttee, a widow allows herself to be burned to death beside her husband's body on the funeral pyre. The pyre is a pile of material that burns easily. No one knows how the custom began. An ancient book states that a widow should lie by her husband's body on the funeral pyre. A few widows, especially the wives of kings, refused to leave the pyre and burned to death. In 1829, the British, then the rulers of India, made suttee illegal. WILFRID D. HAMBLY

**SUTTER, JOHN AUGUSTUS.** See CALIFORNIA (The Gold Rush); SACRAMENTO.

**SUTURE**, *SOO tyoor*, is the line formed where bones are joined in an immovable joint, as in the skull. It is also the sewing-up of an *incision*, or opening, in surgery. Doctors call the material used for sewing an incision a suture, too. This material is made of catgut, fine silk, linen, wire, or nylon. See also LIGATURE.

**SUVA** (pop. 54,900; alt. 31 ft.) is the capital and largest city of the Fiji Islands in the South Pacific. Suva is the chief seaport and commercial center of the islands. It lies on the southeastern coast of Viti Levu, the largest of the islands. Ships stop at Suva to load shipments of *copra* (dried coconut meat), tropical fruit, gold, and sugar. Factories there make coconut oil and soap. Suva's Fiji Museum stands inside the Botanical Gardens. See also FIJI ISLANDS.

**SUWANNEE RIVER** winds for about 190 miles through southern Georgia and northern Florida and empties into the Gulf of Mexico. Stephen Foster, who called the river *Swanee*, made it famous. His song, "Old Folks at Home," opens with the words:

Way down upon de Swanee Ribber
Far, far away,
Dere's whar my heart is turnin' ebber
Dere's whar de old folks stay.

The river rises south of Waycross, Ga. It helps drain the Okefenokee Swamp, and flows in a winding course past many small communities. Only very small boats can navigate the Suwannee. In northern Florida, the river forms parts of the boundaries of eight counties. It reaches the Gulf of Mexico at Suwannee Sound, where Hog Island divides the river into two distributaries (see FLORIDA [physical map]). JOHN H. GARLAND

**SUZERAIN**, *SOO zuh rayn*, was a name sometimes given to a feudal lord in medieval times. Today, the term refers to a state which has political control, or *suzerainty*, over another state.

**SVALBARD**, *SVAHL bahr*, is a group of islands in the Arctic Ocean, about midway between Norway and the North Pole. The islands belong to Norway, and Svalbard is their Norwegian name. They are sometimes called by their German name, Spitzbergen. Svalbard has five large islands and many smaller ones. The main islands are West Spitzbergen, North East Land, Edge Island, Barents Island, and Prince Charles Foreland. Svalbard covers 23,957 square miles. It is about 700 miles from the North Pole (see ARCTIC OCEAN [color map]). Svalbard has no permanent residents, but boats stop there each year when the harbors are free of ice. Svalbard has been the base for many Arctic explorations.

Norse Vikings probably visited the islands. Early Norwegian stories mention Svalbard. In the Middle Ages, the Norwegian kings claimed Svalbard. A Dutch

**These Are Leading Members of the Swallow Family.**

expedition under Willem Barents rediscovered the islands in 1596 (see BARENTS, WILLEM). Henry Hudson saw them in 1607. No one settled on the islands until after the Norwegians began mining coal there in the 1890's. In 1920, other countries formally recognized Norway's claim to the islands. OSCAR SVARLIEN

**SVEDBERG,** *SVAY BAR'y,* **THEODOR** (1884-    ), a Swedish chemist, became famous for developing the ultracentrifuge. This apparatus can spin materials so fast that they have 500,000 times the force of gravity acting upon them. It made it possible to determine the molecular weights of proteins and aided the study of the colloidal state. Svedberg is also known for preparing colloidal solutions of metals using an electric arc. He received the 1926 Nobel prize in chemistry. Svedberg was born in Valbo, near Gävle, Sweden. K. L. KAUFMAN

**SVENGALI.** See DU MAURIER.

**SVERDLOVSK,** *svehrd LAWFSK* (pop. 897,000; alt. 860 ft.), is a trading and manufacturing center in the Ural Mountains of Russia. The city is located on the eastern slope of the Ural Mountains, about 1,200 miles northeast of Moscow (see RUSSIA [political map]). Sverdlovsk is a major railroad center and the largest city in the Urals. It has a machine-building industry.

After the Russian Revolution, the Bolsheviks murdered Czar Nicholas II and his family on July 16, 1918, at Sverdlovsk, where they were imprisoned. The city was then called *Ekaterinburg*. THEODORE SHABAD

**SWAHILI,** *swah HEE lee,* people belong to an eastern division of the Eastern Bantu of Africa. The word *Swahili* means *coast people.* The Swahili language is spoken throughout eastern Africa, east of the Congo to the coast, and as far south as the northeastern coast of Madagascar. The Swahili are of greatly mixed stock, but basically they are Arab plus Bantu. As a rule, they tend to be Negroid in appearance, but many persons called "Swahili" are Arab in appearance. See also BANTU. WILTON MARION KROGMAN

**SWAINS ISLAND** lies in the South Pacific Ocean, 200 miles north of Samoa. For location, see PACIFIC ISLANDS (color map). The 800-acre island is composed of a ring of sand and coral surrounding a brackish lagoon. Coconut palms cover the island. The islanders make and export copra. The island has a population of over 100, and was placed under the jurisdiction of American Samoa in 1925. It was formerly part of the Tokelau Islands. See also SAMOA. EDWIN H. BRYAN, JR.

**SWALLOW** is a small, graceful bird. It has long, powerful wings, and small, weak feet suited only for perching. It has a large mouth adapted to catching flying insects, which make up nearly all its food. It eats many mosquitoes.

Swallows are found in all parts of the world. Most of them fly long distances to avoid cold or to find a food supply. So far as is known, they *migrate* (travel) by day. They fly together in large numbers, and spend the nights in woods or marshes. Some swallows nest in pairs, and some in colonies. Some make their homes in holes in banks or trees. Others build rough nests of clay or mud on beams of bridges, on rafters in barns, or under the eaves. Several kinds of swallows have changed their nesting habits through their contact with man.

812

Female swallows lay 3 to 9 eggs which are pure white, or white spotted with brown. Swallows twitter rather than sing. Some species of swallow have distinctive forked tails, which are called "swallowtails."

The swallows of North America include the *barn swallow*. The barn swallow has a steel-blue back, chestnut-colored breast, and deeply forked tail. Some of these swallows travel as much as 10,000 miles in yearly migrations. The *cliff swallow* has a square tail and a light-brown patch on its rump. The *tree swallow* often nests in birdhouses. The *bank swallow*, or *sand martin*, is the smallest of the family. The *purple martin* also is a member of the swallow family.

**Scientific Classification.** The swallows belong to the swallow family, *Hirundinidae*. The barn swallow is genus *Hirundo*, species *H. erythrogaster;* the cliff swallow, *Petrochelidon pyrrohonta;* the tree swallow, *Iridoprocne bicolor;* the bank swallow, *Riparia riparia*. ARTHUR A. ALLEN

See also BIRD (Bird Migration; color pictures: Bird Nests, Wings in Flight); MARTIN.

**SWALLOWING** is the process of taking food and saliva from the mouth to the stomach through a tube called the *esophagus* (see ESOPHAGUS). A mucous membrane lines the esophagus so that food can slide down without sticking to the sides. After a person chews food, he swallows it. The muscles of the walls of the esophagus perform the swallowing process. These muscles *contract* (shorten). The muscles wave or ripple, normally in a downward direction toward the stomach. This movement is called *peristalsis*. When the muscles in the esophagus cause abnormal wavelike movements upward toward the mouth, vomiting may take place. When the food reaches the lower end of the esophagus, a ringlike muscle opens and allows the food to pass into the stomach.

The presence of certain diseases, or of nervousness, such as stage fright, may cause difficulty in swallowing. Growths, such as tumors or cancers on the esophagus, may also cause the difficulty. In these cases, the esophagus may close. Then food is prevented from entering the stomach. WILLIAM C. BEAVER

See also ALIMENTARY CANAL.

**SWAMMERDAM,** *SWAHM ur dahm,* **JAN** (1637-1680), was a Dutch anatomist and zoologist. He pioneered in the study of minute anatomy, especially the anatomy of insects. He used specially designed scissors, and knives so tiny that they had to be sharpened under a microscope. His observations on the life histories of bees and mayflies are classics, and his work in classifying formed the basis of entomology, the study of insects. A prodigious worker, Swammerdam also made important early observations on the physiology of nerves and muscles. Swammerdam was born in Amsterdam. He studied medicine, and soon began anatomical studies, which he pursued with such intensity that he ruined his health. Much of his most important work was not published until more than 50 years after his death. But his *Historia Insectorum*, a study of the metamorphoses of insects, the effects on animals of the deprivation of blood, and similar subjects was published in 1669. Swammerdam's *Bijbel der Nature*, a report on his observations on red blood corpuscles in animals, was published in 1737. ROGERS McVAUGH

**Jan Swammerdam**
Brown Bros.

**SWAMP** is land which is more or less completely soaked with water. It is always damp and muddy. A swamp is usually on low ground, near the shore of some large body of water, but there are some swamps on hills. Sometimes the soil on a hill drains poorly, while water from springs keeps it swampy. Swamps are also formed in lake basins which have become filled with plant life. This kind of swamp is given an Indian name, *muskeg*. A swamp is much like a peat bog, but the swamp's lower layers of soil are not acid like those of a peat bog. Wet or inundated swamps are termed *marshes*. Mosquitoes often breed in these. In England, particularly near Cambridge and Ely, some marshes are called *fens*. One of the largest swamps in the United States is Okefenokee in Georgia. ELDRED D. WILSON

See also DISMAL SWAMP; EVERGLADES; MARSH; OKEFENOKEE SWAMP; PONTINE MARSHES.

**SWAMP FOX.** See MARION, FRANCIS.
**SWAMP HICKORY.** See BITTERNUT.
**SWAMP ROSE MALLOW.** See HIBISCUS.

**SWAN** is a stately water bird closely related to geese and ducks. The swan has snowy white feathers and a long graceful neck. Many poets and composers have written about the swan, and it often appears in legends, as in Richard Wagner's opera, *Lohengrin*. Fairy tales sometimes feature the swan, as in Hans Christian Andersen's "The Wild Swans."

The swan group consists of seven *species* (kinds) that live in various parts of the world. They fly in V-shaped flocks, and utter loud, trumpetlike notes while flying. They eat worms and shellfish and the seeds and roots of water plants. They dip their long, curving necks far into the water in search of food.

**The American, or Whistling, Swan** nests around the Arctic Ocean and the Hudson Bay region. It has decreased sharply in number. In winter, it flies as far

**The Trumpeter Swan** was once almost extinct. But national parks now protect its breeding grounds from hunters.
Fish & Wildlife Service

813

# SWAN

**Stately Mute Swans** are the kind commonly seen on ponds in parks and zoos. The *cygnet* (baby swan) takes its first swim soon after hatching. But it rides on its mother's back when it becomes tired.

© J. Newman

south as the Carolinas. Between October and April, flocks of whistling swans fly southward. Observers report they can fly at speeds of 40 to 50 mph. As they fly, the swans fill the air with a wide range of whistling sounds. Whistling swans make their nests out of water plants and line them with down from their bodies. Their nests sometimes stand 2 feet high and measure 6 feet across. The female lays five to seven white eggs in June. The young, called *cygnets*, are covered with grayish-brown down at first. They become snow white by the end of a year. The male swan is called a *cob*, and the female a *pen*.

**The Black Swan** is found only on the Australian continent. This water bird has a scarlet bill that is banded with white.

Arthur H. Fisher

The whistling swan grows a little less than 5 feet long. It is white except for a yellow spot between the nostrils and eyes. The legs, feet, and bill are black. The *trumpeter swan*, once almost extinct, resembles the whistling swan. It weighs up to 40 pounds, making it the heaviest flying bird in North America. Its call sounds clear and shrill. The *black-necked swan* is a waterfowl that lives in South America.

**Swans of the Eastern Hemisphere** include the *European whistling swan*, the *mute swan* and *Bewick's swan*, which is a smaller bird. The mute swan, considered a royal bird in England since 1462, can be seen in zoological gardens, parks, and estates there. It is said that this swan never uses its voice in captivity. The *black swan*, marked by a scarlet bill banded with white, lives in Australia.

**Scientific Classification.** Swans belong to the swan, goose, and duck family, *Anatidae*. The mute swan is genus *Cygnus*, species *C. olor*. The black swan of Australia is *C. atratus*. The whistling swan is *Olor columbianus;* the trumpeter swan is *O. buccinator*.   RODOLPHE MEYER DE SCHAUENSEE

See also BIRD (color picture: Birds of Other Lands).

**SWANSEA,** *SWAHN see* (pop. 170,940; alt. 30 ft.), is the second largest city in Wales. It lies about 45 miles west of Cardiff on Swansea Bay. For location, see GREAT BRITAIN (political map).

The city was founded in the 1000's. It became important in the 1800's, after the development of the hard-coal trade and the smelting industry. The use of tin cans for preserving fruits and vegetables brought prosperity to the city. Swansea became the chief British center for the shipping of tin plate. It was once called the "tin plate center of the world." Other industries in Swansea include the refining of nickel, zinc, and petroleum. The city has modern docks which cover 281 acres. DAVID WILLIAMS

**SWARM.** See BEE (Swarming).

**SWARTHMORE COLLEGE** is a coeducational school at Swarthmore, Pa., 11 miles southwest of Philadelphia. The college offers courses in liberal arts and has a division of engineering. Courses lead to B.A., B.S., M.A., and M.S. degrees.

Honors work enables superior juniors and seniors to advance as quickly as their abilities permit. Instead of regular classes, they attend small seminars twice a week. Visiting examiners give written and oral examinations to candidates for the degree with honors.

The college has a generous scholarship program to help students reduce their college expenses. Most students live in dormitories on the campus. The school color is garnet. The best-known song is the "Alma Mater." Swarthmore was founded in 1864 by members of the Society of Friends, but is not controlled by that society. For enrollment, see UNIVERSITIES AND COLLEGES (table). GILMORE STOTT

**SWARTHOUT, GLADYS** (1904-1969), was an American mezzo-soprano. She first sang in public at the age of 12. She studied voice in Chicago and, in 1924, joined the Chicago Opera Company. In 1929 she first sang with the Metropolitan Opera Company.

In addition to opera, Miss Swarthout made many concert tours of America and was seen in several successful motion pictures. She was born in Deepwater, Mo., on Dec. 25, 1904, and attended the Bush Conservatory of Music in Chicago. MARTIAL SINGHER

**SWASTIKA,** *SWAHS tih kuh,* is an ancient symbol often used as an ornament or a religious sign. The swastika is in the form of a cross with the ends of the arms bent at right angles in a given direction, usually clockwise. The swastika has been found on Byzantine buildings, Buddhist inscriptions, Celtic monuments, and Greek coins.

SWASTIKA

Oriental and American Indian — Nazi

Swastikas were widely used symbols among the Indians of North America and South America. The clockwise swastika was adopted in 1920 as the symbol of the National Socialist party of Germany. As such it came to be one of the most hated symbols in the history of man. It came to stand for all the evil associated with the Nazis as they gained control of Europe before and during World War II. After the Allies defeated Germany in 1945, they banned the display of the swastika emblem. JOSEPH WARD SWAIN

**SWATANEY.** See SHIKELLAMY.

# SWAZILAND

⊛ Capital
• Other City or Town
— Road
⊢⊣ Rail Line
▲ MOUNTAIN
～ River

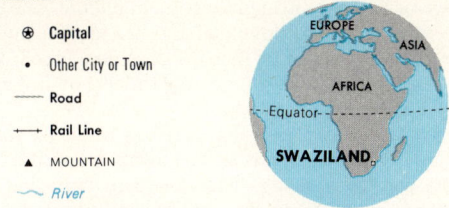

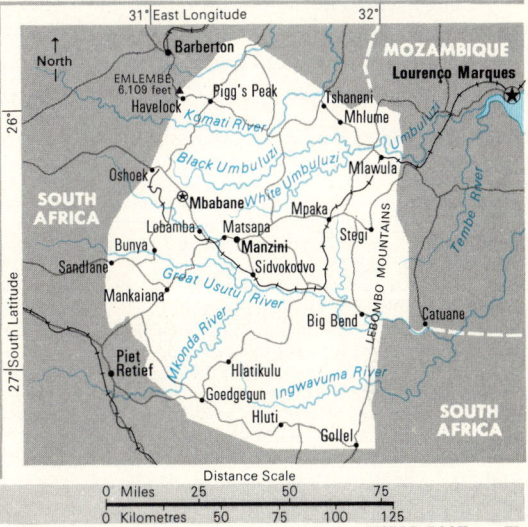

WORLD BOOK map-FIa

**SWAZILAND,** *SWAH zee land,* is a beautiful little country in southern Africa. It is surrounded by the Republic of South Africa on three sides and by Mozambique on the east. Swaziland is about as big as Hawaii, but it has only about half as many people as that state.

Swaziland has rich mineral deposits, large forests, and good farm and ranch land. But most of the mines, processing plants, and profitable farms are owned by Europeans. Most of the *Swazi* (Negro Africans) who live there are peasant farmers.

Swaziland was formerly a British protectorate. It became independent in 1968 as the KINGDOM OF SWAZILAND. Mbabane, with a population of about 14,000, is the administrative capital and largest town (see MBABANE).

**Government.** The *Ngwenyama* (hereditary leader of the Swazi) rules as king. He appoints a prime minister and Cabinet to help him govern. Parliament passes laws for the nation, but the king must approve them. The Parliament consists of a House of Assembly and a Senate. The people elect 24 members of the House, and the king appoints 6 members. The king appoints six members of the Senate, and the House elects six.

The constitution allows the Ngwenyama and the *Ndlovukazi* (queen mother) to decide all matters involving Swazi laws and customs. The Swazi National

*Hilda Kuper, the contributor of this article, is Professor of Anthropology at the University of California at Los Angeles and the author of* An African Aristocracy: Rank Among the Swazi *and* The Swazi: A South African Kingdom.

814a

# SWAZILAND

Council helps them make their decisions. When the Ngwenyama dies, his family council chooses one of his wives as the next Ndlovukazi and her son becomes the Ngwenyama. All Swazi men are considered members of the national council. The council meets at Lobamba, the Swazi traditional capital.

**People.** About 9 out of 10 persons in Swaziland are Negro Africans called Swazi. The Swazi are proud, handsome, courteous people. Most of them farm and raise livestock. They prize their cattle, and respect a man with a large herd. They rarely kill their cattle for food, but some are sacrificed at tribal ceremonies. When a Swazi man marries, he gives his wife's family a gift of cattle.

Swazi men may have more than one wife. The ideal family includes a man, his wives, his unmarried children, and his married sons and their families. Each family lives in a separate homestead that consists of huts built around a cattle pen. For generations, the Swazi built circular, beehive-shaped huts. But now many live in Western-style houses.

Each wife has her own sleeping, cooking, and storage huts. She also has garden plots within walking distance of the homestead. There she cultivates grains such as corn and millet, and other crops including beans, gourds, and peas. The men and boys tend the cattle.

Some Swazi farmers now plant crops that they can sell for cash. A few hundred Swazi have moved to towns where they work in shops and offices.

Many Swazi wear clothes made from animal skins. They also wear brightly colored cloths and beautiful bead ornaments. They speak *siSwati*, a Bantu language much like Zulu.

Each Swazi man belongs to an *age group* organized by the Ngwenyama. All the men in a particular group are about the same age. Formerly, the age groups served as military regiments. Today, they sometimes work for the royal family. Different age groups have special parts in Swazi ceremonies.

Most Swazi practice a religion based on ancestor worship. Some belong to various Christian groups.

Four out of five adults in Swaziland cannot read or write. But about 48,000 children were attending school there in the late 1960's. Classes are taught in Zulu.

About 8,000 Europeans and *Eurafricans* (people of mixed descent) also live in Swaziland. The Europeans own farms, mines, and forests. Many Eurafricans work for the Europeans. Others are farmers and craftsmen.

**Land.** Mountains about 3,500 to 4,500 feet above sea level rise along Swaziland's western border. Vast pine forests cover much of the land there. Temperatures average 60° F., and from 45 to 75 inches of rain falls

---

### FACTS IN BRIEF

**Capitals:** Mbabane (administrative) and Lobamba (traditional).
**Official Languages:** English and siSwati.
**Form of Government:** Constitutional monarchy.
**Head of State:** King.
**Parliament:** *Senate*—12 members (5-year terms); *House of Assembly*—30 voting members (5-year terms).
**Political Divisions:** Eight districts each headed by a commissioner or assistant commissioner.
**Area:** 6,704 square miles. *Greatest Distances*—(north-south) 120 miles; (east-west) 90 miles.
**Elevation:** *Highest*—Mount Emlembe, 6,109 feet above sea level. *Lowest*—70 feet above sea level.
**Population:** *1966 Census*—374,697; distribution, 97 per cent rural, 3 per cent urban. *Estimated 1969 Population*—390,000; density, 58 persons to the square mile. *Estimated 1974 Population*—474,000.
**Chief Products:** *Agriculture*—corn, sugar cane, cotton, rice, tobacco, citrus fruits, hides and skins. *Manufacturing*—wood products. *Mining*—asbestos, iron ore.
**Flag:** Five horizontal stripes. The top and bottom stripes are blue (for peace). The wide center stripe is red (for past battles) with a black and white shield, spears, and staff. Between the blue and red stripes are yellow stripes (for natural resources). See FLAG (color picture: Flags of Africa).
**Money:** *Basic Unit*—South African rand. For its value in dollars, see MONEY (table: Values [South Africa]).

---

David Goldblatt, Pix from Publix

**The People of Swaziland** wear both traditional tribal costumes and European clothing. These Swazis are lined up to vote in Manzini, a leading commercial center.

814b

during the year. Rolling, grassy midlands lie east of the mountains. More people live in this region than in any other part of the country. Temperatures average 66° F. and from 30 to 45 inches of rain falls there each year. Further east, the land levels off into a low plain covered with bushes and grass. Temperatures average 72° F. and only about 20 inches of rain falls there during a year. The land rises along the eastern border to the high, narrow Lebombo Mountains.

Swaziland is one of the best watered areas in southern Africa. Four main rivers flow eastward across the country. They are the Ingwavuma, Komati, Umbuluzi, and Great Usutu. The rivers supply water to irrigate crops and to run hydroelectric power plants.

**Economy.** Europeans own nearly half of the land in Swaziland. Most cash crops, including sugar cane, rice, and citrus fruits, are raised on European-owned farms and plantations. European ranchers raise cattle for meat, skins, and hides.

Since the 1940's, Europeans have planted large areas of barren mountainous land with pine and eucalyptus trees. Today, the area has the largest man-made forest in Africa. European-owned saw mills and a pulp mill process wood pulp and other forest products there.

Rich mineral deposits lie in the mountains, and about half the nation's income comes from the European-owned mining industry. Asbestos and iron ore are leading exports. Swaziland also has deposits of coal, gold, *barite* (ore used in making barium), and *kaolin* (clay used in making pottery).

A few Swazi farmers raise cash crops such as tobacco and cotton in the midlands. But most graze cattle and struggle to raise enough food for their families. Throughout the year, many Swazi men work on European-owned farms, forests, plantations, and mines. About 9,000 Swazi work in the gold mines of South Africa.

Swaziland has about 800 miles of tar or gravel roads. Winding footpaths run between most homesteads. A railroad connects Mbabane with the port at Lourenço Marques, capital of Mozambique. Air service links Mbabane with South Africa and Lourenço Marques.

**History.** According to the legends of the Swazi, the tribe once lived near what is now Lourenço Marques. In the late 1700's the Swazi chief Ngwane II led a small band of people over the mountains to what is now southeastern Swaziland. There they found other African tribes. Ngwane II and the chiefs who ruled after him united several of these tribes with the Swazi.

British traders and *Boers* (Dutch farmers from South Africa) first came to Swaziland in the 1830's. In the 1880's, the settlers discovered gold. Hundreds of prospectors rushed into the region. They asked the Swazi chief and his advisers to sign documents granting them rights to mine minerals and to use land for farming and grazing. The Swazi could not read and did not realize that they were giving up control of the land.

In 1894, the British and Boers agreed that the South African Boer Republic would govern Swaziland. But in 1902, the Boers lost a war with the British, and Great Britain took control of Swaziland in 1903. Great Britain ruled Swaziland until the 1960's. In 1967, Swaziland gained control over its internal matters. It received full independence on Sept. 6, 1968, with King Sobhuza II as its head of state. On Sept. 24, 1968, Swaziland was admitted to the United Nations. HILDA KUPER

# SWEATSHOP

**SWEAT.** See PERSPIRATION.
**SWEAT GLAND.** See GLAND; PERSPIRATION.
**SWEATSHOP.** The word *sweatshop* suggests a place of grinding toil. It is a term for makeshift factories where poverty-stricken people—mostly women and children—work at top speed for 12 or more hours a day in an effort to earn a living wage.

The sweatshop, often called the *sweating system*, began when the factory system developed in the early 1800's. Often, factory buildings were not large enough to house all the workers. So factory owners sublet contracts for part of the work. The other manufacturers then set up makeshift factories in dimly lighted and poorly ventilated buildings. They hired workers for low wages and long hours on a piecework basis.

As early as 1830, Americans began to object to sweatshops. But the problem did not become serious until after 1880, when large numbers of immigrants began to come to America. The owners of sweatshops took advantage of the immigrants' ignorance and poverty to get them to work for low wages. The cigar making and clothing and needlework industries, and some of the mechanical industries, used the sweating system.

In the 1900's, states began to pass laws prohibiting workers from carrying on work outside the factory in industries where sweatshops were most common. They also passed minimum wage laws which made it impractical for factories to sublet work. Laws limiting the number of hours women could work and abolishing child labor were heavy blows to the sweatshop system. Another factor which hastened its decline was the increased interest which women showed in metalworking and other trades where they could not take work outside the factory. Today, there are few sweatshops left in the world. In most countries, such practices have been made illegal. ROBERT D. PATTON

See also CHILD LABOR; WAGES AND HOURS.

**Sweatshops** employed people for very low pay. Workers put in long hours in makeshift factories under miserable conditions.
Brown Bros.

815

WORLD BOOK photo by Tore Johnson

**The Rugged Wilderness** of northern Sweden has long, cold winters and is thinly populated. Most of the people are lumberjacks or miners.

# SWEDEN

**SWEDEN** is a prosperous industrial nation in northern Europe. The Swedes have developed great industries based on their country's three chief natural resources—timber, iron ore, and water power.

The Swedish standard of living is one of the highest in the world. Sweden has more automobiles, telephones, and radios in relation to its population than any other European nation. Among all the countries of Europe, only tiny Monaco has more television sets in relation to population. Another measure of Swedish prosperity is the fact that Swedes spend more money per person on vacations than any other Europeans. About 350,000 Swedish families, or a fifth of the nation's families, have country homes where they can spend weekends and vacations.

Sweden's way of life has often been called the "middle way," because it combines private enterprise with a government that greatly influences the development of the economy. The Swedish government operates one of the most far-reaching social security systems in the world. The government provides free education and largely free medical service. It pays pensions to old people, widows, and orphans. After most Swedes retire, they receive annual pensions of about 60 per cent of their average earnings during their 15 highest paid years. The government also provides health insurance and financial aid for housing.

Sweden is the fourth largest country in Europe, after Russia, France, and Spain. Sweden is a little larger than California, but it is thinly populated and has only about half as many people as that state. Forests cover more than half of Sweden, and only about a tenth of the country is farmland. Sweden is also a land of beautiful lakes, snow-capped mountains, swift rivers, and rocky offshore islands. Stockholm, Sweden's capital and largest city, stands on the coast of the Baltic Sea and includes a number of small offshore islands. Almost a sixth of the Swedish people live in Stockholm or its suburbs.

The northern seventh of Sweden lies inside the Arctic Circle in a region called the *Land of the Midnight Sun.*

*The contributors of this article are Torsten Henriksson, First Secretary of the Swedish Institute in Stockholm; Johan Norrbin, a Stockholm geography teacher; István Vukovich of the Swedish International Development Authority; and Carl-Christian Wallén, Deputy Director of the Swedish Meteorological and Hydrological Institute.*

Pictorial Parade

**Sandy Seaside Beaches** help make Falsterbo, on the southwestern tip of Sweden, a popular vacation area.

John LaDue

**Downtown Stockholm** has a modern business area. Automobiles, not permitted on the street level, are parked underground.

There, for long periods in summer, the sun shines 24 hours a day. Above the Arctic Circle is part of an unspoiled wilderness called Lapland. This region extends into Finland, Norway, and Russia. For hundreds of years, people called Lapps have led a wandering life with their herds of reindeer.

Sweden, together with Denmark and Norway, is one of the Scandinavian countries. Swedes, Danes, and Norwegians speak similar languages and can usually understand each other. The three Scandinavian nations have close economic and cultural ties, and their histories are closely linked.

---
FACTS IN BRIEF
---

**Capital:** Stockholm.

**Official Language:** Swedish.

**Official Name:** *Konungariket Sverige* (Kingdom of Sweden).

**Form of Government:** Constitutional monarchy. *Head of State*—King or Queen. *Head of Government*—Prime Minister (appointed by the monarch). *Parliament* (Riksdag)—Upper House (151 members, 8-year terms); Lower House (233 members, 4-year terms). *Political Divisions*—24 counties and Stockholm.

**Area:** 173,666 square miles. *Greatest Length*—977 miles. *Greatest Width*—310 miles. *Coastline*—4,700 miles.

**Elevation:** *Highest*—Mount Kebnekaise, 6,946 feet above sea level. *Lowest*—sea level along the coast.

**Population:** *1965 Census*—7,765,981; distribution, 77 per cent urban, 23 per cent rural. *Estimated 1970 Population*—8,083,000; density, 47 persons to the square mile. *Estimated 1975 Population*—8,454,000.

**Chief Products:** *Agriculture*—barley, livestock (cattle, hogs), milk and other dairy products, oats, potatoes, rye, sugar beets, wheat. *Fishing*—cod, herring, mackerel, salmon. *Forestry*—fir, pine, spruce. *Manufacturing*—agricultural machinery, aircraft, automobiles, ball bearings, diesel motors, electrical equipment, explosives, fertilizers, furniture, glass, matches, paper and cardboard, plastics, plywood, precision tools, prefabricated houses, ships, steel, steelware, telephones, textiles, wood pulp. *Mining*—copper, gold, iron ore, lead, uranium, zinc.

**National Anthem:** "*Dugamla, du fria, du fjällhöga Nord*" ("Song of the North").

**National Holiday:** Flag Day, June 6.

**Money:** *Basic Unit*—krona. One hundred öre equal one krona. For the value of the krona in dollars, see MONEY (table: Values). See also KRONA.

817

# SWEDEN / Government

Sweden is a constitutional monarchy with a king, a prime minister and cabinet, and a parliament. The Swedish constitution was adopted in 1809. Only the United States has an older written constitution.

The 1809 constitution gave the king most of the executive power of the government, but the parliament was responsible for taxation. The power of the parliament gradually increased, and parliamentary rule was adopted in 1917. Today, a 16-member cabinet headed by the prime minister has the actual executive power.

**King** of Sweden is the head of state. Any bill passed by the parliament must receive his approval before it becomes law. According to the constitution, the king still has executive power. But the king always accepts the wishes of the cabinet, which he presides over at weekly meetings.

**Prime Minister and Cabinet.** The king appoints as prime minister the leader of the majority party or group of parties in the parliament. The prime minister selects the other 15 members of the cabinet.

**Parliament** of Sweden is called the *Riksdag*. It consists of two houses with equal power. All laws must be approved by both houses. The election of members of both houses is based on proportional representation (see PROPORTIONAL REPRESENTATION). The Upper House has 151 members elected to eight-year terms by the members of county and city councils. About an eighth of the members of the Upper House are elected every year. The people elect the 233 members of the Lower House to four-year terms. All men and women at least 20 years old may vote.

**Ombudsmen.** The Riksdag appoints an official called an *ombudsman* to investigate complaints by citizens against government actions or decisions. Sweden created this office in 1810, and was the first country to have an ombudsman. The Riksdag appoints a second ombudsman to investigate complaints against military authorities. This office was created in 1914. See OMBUDSMAN.

**Politics.** The Social Democratic party has controlled the Swedish government since 1932, except for a short period in 1936. The Social Democrats established Sweden's welfare system. Other parties include the Center, Conservative, and Liberal parties. In 1965, to encourage political activity, the Riksdag approved an annual government payment totaling about $5 million to political parties. Each party receives a share based on its number of seats in the Riksdag.

**Local Government.** Sweden's 24 counties and the city of Stockholm have separate governments. Each county is administered by a governor appointed by the government and a council elected by the people. Stockholm is administered by a governor appointed by the government.

**Courts.** District courts serve the towns and counties of Sweden. Regional courts of appeal hear appeals from the district courts. The Supreme Court hears final appeals in important civil and criminal cases.

**Armed Forces.** Swedish men between 18 and 47 are required to serve at least 10 months in the armed forces. The nation's army, navy, and air force have a total of about 750,000 men.

WORLD BOOK photo by Hans Malmberg

**Parliament Building** in Stockholm is the meeting place of Sweden's two houses of parliament, called the *Riksdag*.

**The Swedish Flag,** first used in the mid-1400's, was made official in 1663. The colors come from the coat of arms.

**Sweden's Coat of Arms** features the three small crowns added by King Albert in 1364. It was made official in 1908.

WORLD BOOK photo by Hans Malmberg

**Gustaf VI,** seated center, became king of Sweden in 1950. The king presides at ceremonies that open sessions of the parliament.

**Sweden** is nearly 6 per cent as large as the United States, not counting Alaska and Hawaii. The country lies just east of Norway.

WORLD BOOK map

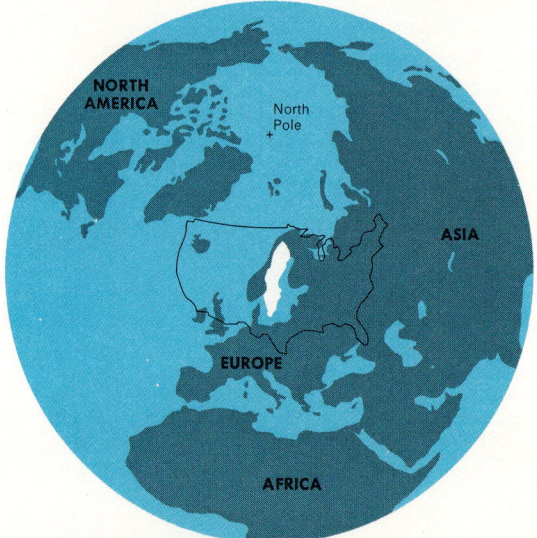

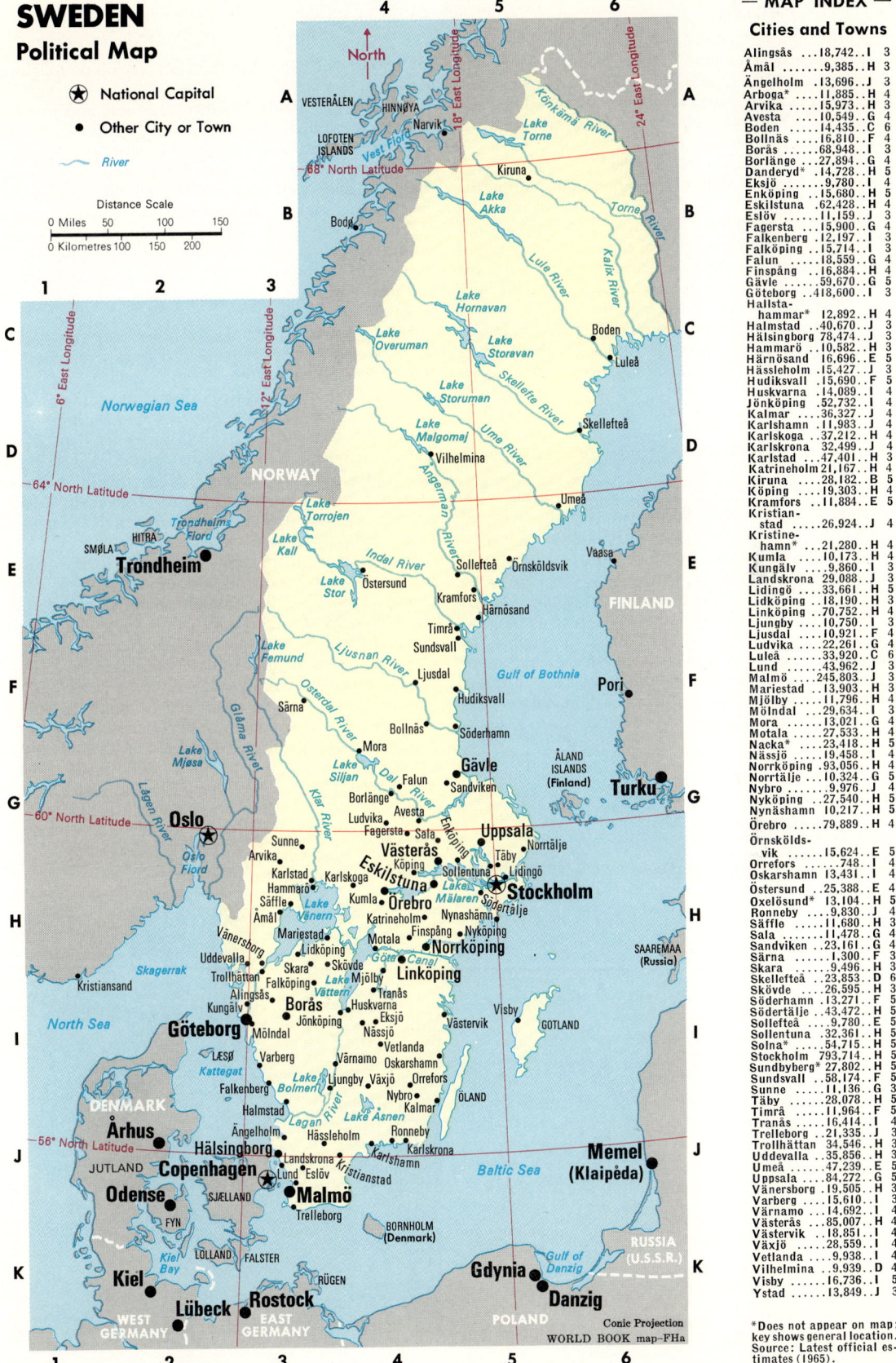

# SWEDEN / People

The Swedes are closely related to the Danes and Norwegians. Most Swedes are tall, with fair or brown hair and blue eyes. Since World War II ended in 1945, about 500,000 persons from other European countries have settled in Sweden.

About three-fourths of Sweden's people live in cities and towns, mainly in the center and south of the country. About a fourth of the people live in the three largest cities—Stockholm, Göteborg, and Malmö—and their suburbs. Sweden is one of the most thinly populated countries in Europe, with an average of 47 persons to the square mile. Only Iceland, Finland, and Norway have fewer persons to the square mile.

The Lapps, who live in the far north, differ in appearance, language, and way of life from most other Swedes (see LAPLAND). About 10,000 of these short, stocky people live in Sweden. Most Lapps are miners or lumberjacks. About 2,000 of them live as their ancestors did, wandering over the land with their herds of reindeer. About 30,000 Swedes of Finnish origin also live in the north.

**Language.** Swedish is a Germanic language that resembles Danish and Norwegian. People from all three countries can usually understand each other. Some people of Finnish origin who live in Sweden still speak their own language. The Lapps speak a language related to Finnish. Most Swedes speak some English.

**Religion.** The Lutheran Church is the state church of Sweden, and about 98 per cent of the people are members. The king must be a member. All Swedes whose parents belong to the Lutheran Church become members automatically at birth. They remain so unless they apply to withdraw. Most Swedes do not attend church regularly, but the churches are full on religious holidays.

Sweden has about 10 other large religious groups, and some of their members belong to the Lutheran Church as well. These groups, in order of size, include the Missionary Union, the Pentecostal Movement, Baptists, and Methodists. Other religious groups in Sweden include Roman Catholics and Jews.

The churches pioneered much welfare work in the country, but the government has taken over most of this work. Swedish churches have a long tradition of missionary activities, particularly the Lutheran Church in India and South Africa.

**Food.** Sweden is famous for *smörgåsbord*, an assortment of cold and hot foods placed on a large table for self-service. Swedes often eat the foods in a certain order. First they eat cold fish dishes, including anchovies, eels, herring, salmon, sardines, and shrimp. They follow the fish with such cold meats as liver pâté, smoked reindeer, and ham with vegetable salad. Next come small hot dishes, such as meatballs, omelets, sausages, and anchovies or herring cooked in breadcrumbs. Desserts include cheese and fresh fruit, fruit salad, and pastry.

**Education.** The Swedish government, with the goal of expanding and improving educational services, completely reorganized the nation's school system during the 1960's. Most children receive a free education at schools operated by the government. The government also operates all the universities and most of the technical and other specialized colleges.

Many children under the age of 7 attend kindergartens run by private persons or organizations. The government assists the kindergartens, but attendance is not required.

Children from 7 to 16 must attend a school called

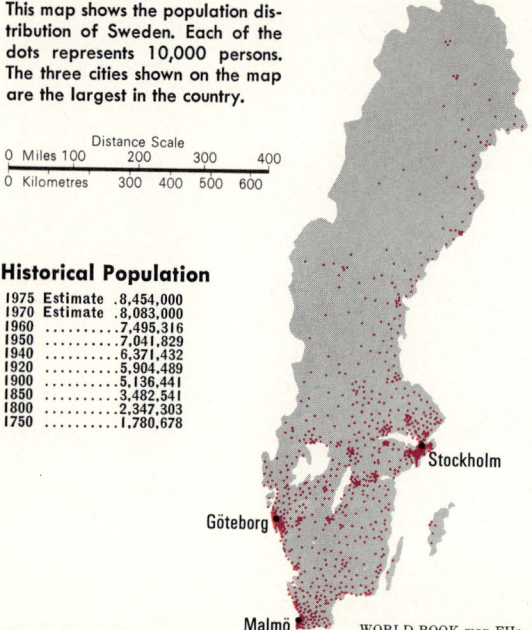

**POPULATION**

This map shows the population distribution of Sweden. Each of the dots represents 10,000 persons. The three cities shown on the map are the largest in the country.

Distance Scale
0 Miles 100  200  300  400
0 Kilometres  300  400  500  600

**Historical Population**

| | |
|---|---|
| 1975 Estimate | 8,454,000 |
| 1970 Estimate | 8,083,000 |
| 1960 | 7,495,316 |
| 1950 | 7,041,829 |
| 1940 | 6,371,432 |
| 1920 | 5,904,489 |
| 1900 | 5,136,441 |
| 1850 | 3,482,541 |
| 1800 | 2,347,303 |
| 1750 | 1,780,678 |

Stockholm
Göteborg
Malmö
WORLD BOOK map-FHa

**Farm Families** own about 80 per cent of Sweden's farms, and rent the rest. Most of them live in the southern third of the country. Less than 10 per cent of the labor force are farmers.

WORLD BOOK photo by Nils-Johan Norenlind

818b

a *grundskola*. The grundskola system, which was introduced in 1962, has three three-year divisions. The *junior stage* consists of first grade through third grade, and the *intermediate stage* covers fourth grade through sixth grade. The *senior stage* consists of seventh through ninth grade. In the seventh and eighth grades, students begin to choose their own subjects. In the ninth grade, they select one of nine courses of study. Most pupils continue their general education. Others also learn such practical skills as home economics or workshop methods. Some select special courses in languages, technology, or commerce. Every child in the fourth through seventh grade is required to study English, and about 90 per cent continue English after that.

Following the grundskola, some children go to a secondary school. Since 1966, there have been three kinds of secondary schools. The three-year *upper secondary schools* prepare students to attend a university. The two-year *continuation schools* give courses in social, economic, and technical subjects. The *vocational schools* offer day and evening courses for one to three years in such subjects as industry, handicrafts, and home economics.

Sweden has five universities—in Göteborg, Lund, Stockholm, Umeå, and Uppsala. The oldest, the University of Uppsala, was founded in 1477.

**Libraries and Museums.** Sweden has four general research libraries—the Royal Library in Stockholm and the university libraries in Göteborg, Lund, and Uppsala. The Royal Library, established in the 1600's, has

**Swedish Lumberjacks** often float logs down rivers to coastal sawmills. About half of Sweden's forests are privately owned, mostly by farmers. Many farmers work part time as lumberjacks.

Franklin Photo Agency

Franklin Photo Agency

**Vacation Lodges** dot much of the Swedish countryside. About 350,000 families own vacation homes. The Swedes spend more money per person on vacations than any other Europeans.

Fritz Henle, Photo Researchers

**Swedish Schoolchildren** visit the public square of the old section of Stockholm. There, in 1520, King Christian II of Denmark executed many Swedes who had rebelled against Danish rule.

**Gymnastics** are required in Swedish schools. Many adults do these graceful exercises during lunch-hour drills. Music for gymnastics is broadcast daily for housewives.

C. A. Peterson, Rapho Guillumette

a large collection of early Swedish manuscripts. Sweden also has about 3,800 public libraries.

Leading museums include the Skansen open-air museum, which exhibits old Swedish houses, and the National Museum, which has a fine collection of Swedish sculpture and paintings. Both these museums are in Stockholm.

**Sports.** The Swedes are an athletic people and like outdoor activities. Many spend their vacations by the sea or on the country's offshore islands. Others relax near one of Sweden's many lakes or in the vast wilderness that covers the northern part of the country. Tourists enjoy three-day trips along the Göta Canal, which flows 240 miles across southern Sweden. This canal links lakes and rivers, and connects Göteborg with the Baltic Sea.

Cross-country skiing and hockey are the chief winter sports. Every March, thousands of Swedes take part in a 55-mile-long ski run called the Vasa Race, held in the province of Dalarna. Sportsmen hunt deer, fox, moose, and various wildfowl, and fish for pike, salmon, and trout. When the rivers are frozen, fishermen cut holes in the ice and drop their lines through them. The people also like hiking and camping, soccer, swimming, and yachting. Graceful gymnastics called *calisthenics* are popular in Sweden, and are a feature of school training.

**Holidays.** The main winter festivals in Sweden take place in December. On December 13, the Swedes celebrate St. Lucia Day, the Festival of Light. Before dawn, young girls dress in white with a crown of evergreen leaves. They awaken their families with a traditional song and serve them hot coffee and buns. The main Christmas celebration is on Christmas Eve. Families gather for dinner, which usually includes ham and a fish course. After dinner, everyone receives his presents. See CHRISTMAS (color picture: A Swedish Boy).

Midsummer's Eve festivities are held on the Friday between June 19 and 26. The people celebrate the return of summer to Sweden. They stay up most of the night and dance around gaily decorated maypoles. Flag Day, the national holiday, is June 6. The king presents the national flag to Swedish organizations and societies at a special ceremony.

**Social Welfare.** The Swedes pay high taxes, but the government provides many welfare benefits. Every family receives an allowance for (1) each child under 16 and (2) each child in a secondary school or university. The government helps newly married couples by providing loans for home furnishings. In some cases of hardship, it pays up to a fourth of a family's rent. The government guarantees every employed person a four-week annual vacation with pay. Some housewives with low incomes receive allowances for vacations with their children.

Swedes who lose their jobs receive unemployment benefits representing a high proportion of their former earnings. The people have largely free medical service. After retirement, most Swedes receive annual pensions of about 60 per cent of their average earnings during their 15 highest paid years. The government also provides pensions for widows, orphans, and children who have lost one parent.

## SWEDEN/Arts

Most Swedish art forms have long been influenced by artistic developments in other parts of Europe. During the 1900's, distinctive Swedish styles have appeared in the fields of architecture and design. Swedish architects and town planners have worked together to create towns and suburbs. These communities have won international fame as models of architectural planning and design.

In 1964, the government set up a system of grants to increase the income of artists who need help. The government also supports three theater schools and a motion-picture school.

The playwright August Strindberg, who wrote *The Father* and *Miss Julie*, was the first Swedish writer to win international fame. The novelist Selma Lagerlöf wrote charming, romantic novels and a classic children's book, *The Wonderful Adventures of Nils*. She was the first Swedish writer to win a Nobel prize.

During the 1600's and 1700's, French painters working in Sweden greatly influenced the development of Swedish painting. Alexander Roslin, who produced brilliant portraits, is the best-known Swedish painter of

**The Plays of August Strindberg** are performed in most parts of the world. He wrote *Miss Julie*, one of his most famous dramas, in 1888. Strindberg was also a novelist and story writer.
The Royal Dramatic Theater, Stockholm (Swedish Tourist Bureau)

**Swedish Motion Pictures** are known for their high quality. *The Seventh Seal* and other films directed by Ingmar Bergman are especially outstanding. Bergman writes most of his own scripts.
A. B. Svensk Filmindustri

that period. French impressionism inspired Karl Fredrik Hill and Ernst Josephson in the late 1800's. Some critics consider them Sweden's greatest painters. Today, most Swedish painters follow international trends in abstract art.

The Swedish sculptor Carl Milles worked for many years in the United States, where he achieved a worldwide reputation for outdoor sculptures, particularly fountains. Most other leading Swedish sculptors use abstract forms in their work.

Swedish designers have produced home furnishings of artistic merit. Many homes in the United States are furnished in a style known as *Swedish modern*. Swedish furniture is simple in style, and most of it is made of light-colored wood. Designers use pleasant, bright colors for upholstery and drapery materials. Other Swedish furnishings with international fame for beauty include glassware, pottery, and silverware. Swedish glass vases, bowls, and other products are especially famous for their graceful design and high quality. The towns of Kosta and Orrefors, in southeastern Sweden, are the country's main glassmaking centers.

Fritz Henle, Photo Researchers

**Statues by Carl Milles** attract many visitors to Millesgården, a park near Stockholm that includes his old home and studio.

**Lapp Handicrafts,** produced in Lapland in northern Sweden, feature beautifully carved bone and wood.

Pal-Nils Nilsson, J. D. Studios Ltd.

**A Great Cultural Movement** took place in Sweden during the rule of King Gustavus III (1771-1792). Literature especially flourished. This painting shows the crowning of Gustavus, who wrote poems and plays.

*Coronation of Gustavus III* by Carl Gustav Pilo. Nationalmuseum, Stockholm

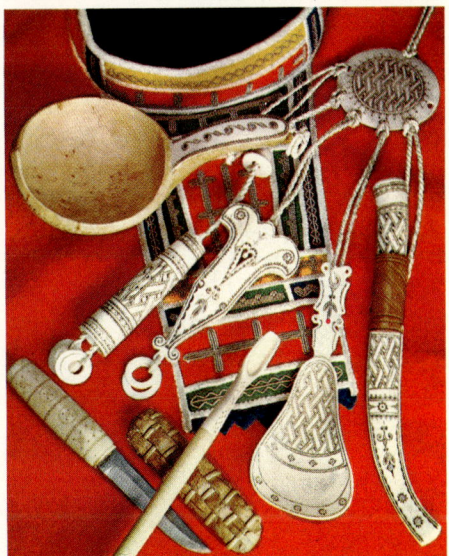

**Swedish Industrial Arts,** including home furnishings, are known for their simple, graceful design.

J. D. Studios Ltd.

# SWEDEN / The Land

Sweden occupies the eastern part of the Scandinavian peninsula. From Sweden's hilly and, in parts, mountainous border with Norway, the land slopes gently eastward to the Gulf of Bothnia and the Baltic Sea. The country's scenery varies from the unpopulated, treeless Kölen Mountains in the northwest to the fertile plains in the south. Thousands of lakes cover about a twelfth of the country's area.

The long Swedish coastline has sandy beaches in the south, and rocky cliffs in parts of the west and north. Many groups of small islands lie off the coast. Sweden's largest islands are Gotland, a fertile island covering about 1,160 square miles, and Oland, which has an area of about 520 square miles. Both these islands are in the Baltic Sea.

Sweden has four main land regions: (1) the Mountain Range, (2) the Inner Northland, (3) the Swedish Lowland, and (4) the South Swedish Highland.

**The Mountain Range** is part of the Kölen Mountains. Sweden's northern boundary with Norway runs through these mountains, which Norwegians call the Kjølen Mountains. Hundreds of small glaciers cover the higher slopes of the snow-capped range. Sweden's highest mountain, 6,946-foot Mount Kebnekaise, is in this rugged region.

The land is completely treeless above about 1,600 feet in the northernmost part of the mountains. There, the climate is too cold for trees. Some birch trees grow on the warmer lower slopes.

**The Inner Northland** is a vast, thinly populated, hilly region. Great forests of pine and spruce trees cover most of the land, and lumbering is an important industry. Many swift rivers flow southeast across the Inner Northland, and provide much hydroelectric power. The rivers have formed deep, narrow valleys, some of which have long lakes. The valleys broaden toward the coast of the Gulf of Bothnia. Most of the region's people live in these valleys or on the coast.

The Torne River forms part of the boundary between the Inner Northland and Finland. Other rivers in the region include the Lule, the Ume, the Ångerman, and the Dal rivers. Bergslagen, a hilly area rich in minerals, lies south of the Dal River in the southernmost part of the Inner Northland.

**The Swedish Lowland** has more people than any other part of the country. This region includes the central and southern plains of Sweden. The broad central plains are broken by lakes, tree-covered ridges, and small hills. Farmland covers more than 40 per cent of these plains. Sweden's largest lakes, Vänern and Vättern, are there. Lake Vänern covers 2,156 square miles, and is one of the largest lakes in Europe. Lake Vättern has an area of 738 square miles.

The southern plains include some of Sweden's most fertile land, especially in Skåne in the extreme south. Farmland and beech woods cover most of Skåne, the most thickly populated and richest farming area of Sweden.

**The South Swedish Highland,** also called the *Götaland Plateau,* is a rocky upland that rises to about 1,200 feet above sea level. This thinly populated area has poor, stony soils, and is covered mostly by forests. The southern part of the region is flat, with small lakes and swamps.

**The Swedish Lowland** includes most of Sweden's croplands, such as these fertile plains near Lake Vättern. Many lakes and small hills break up the region's central plains.

Herbert Fristedt from Carl Ostman

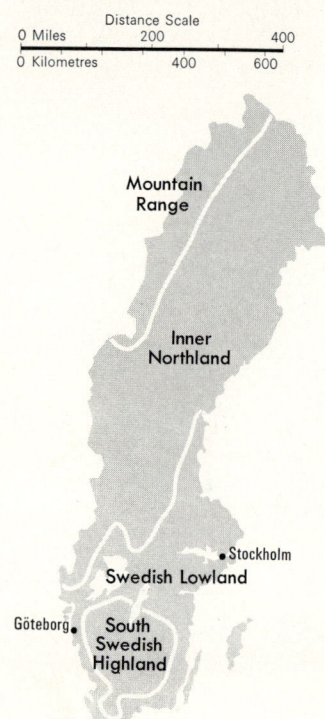

**LAND REGIONS OF SWEDEN**

WORLD BOOK map-FHa

# SWEDEN / Climate

The climate of Sweden varies greatly between the southern and northern parts of the country. Southwesterly winds from the Atlantic Ocean give southern Sweden pleasant summers and mostly mild winters. Northern Sweden has pleasant summers but cold winters. The Atlantic winds are blocked by the Kölen Mountains, and have less effect on northern Sweden.

In the extreme south, average temperatures in January and February, the coldest months, are around 32° F. In Kiruna, in the far north, temperatures average about 10° F. during these months. In July, Sweden's warmest month, temperatures average from 59° to 63° F. in the south, and 54° to 57° F. in the north. In winter, eastern air masses may cause the temperature in Stockholm to drop to −10° F., and as low as −45° F. in the northern part of the country.

Rainfall is generally greater in the Kölen Mountains and the southern highlands than on the plains that border the Gulf of Bothnia. In the south, snow covers the ground in January and February. The north has snow from mid-October through mid-April.

Pictorial Parade

**Cross-Country Skiing** is a favorite sport in Sweden, where snow covers the ground from two to six months a year.

### AVERAGE JANUARY TEMPERATURES

| Degrees Fahrenheit | Degrees Centigrade |
|---|---|
| above 25 | above -4 |
| 18 to 25 | -8 to -4 |
| 10 to 18 | -12 to -8 |
| below 10 | below -12 |

### AVERAGE JULY TEMPERATURES

| Degrees Fahrenheit | Degrees Centigrade |
|---|---|
| above 61 | above 16 |
| 57 to 61 | 14 to 16 |
| 54 to 57 | 12 to 14 |
| below 54 | below 12 |

### AVERAGE YEARLY PRECIPITATION
(Rain, Melted Snow, and Other Moisture)

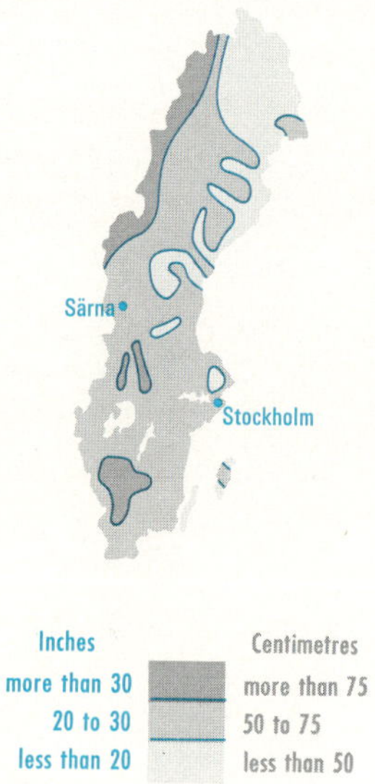

| Inches | Centimetres |
|---|---|
| more than 30 | more than 75 |
| 20 to 30 | 50 to 75 |
| less than 20 | less than 50 |

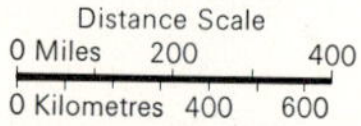

Distance Scale
0 Miles 200 400
0 Kilometres 400 600

### MONTHLY WEATHER IN STOCKHOLM AND SÄRNA

| | JAN | FEB | MAR | APR | MAY | JUNE | JULY | AUG | SEPT | OCT | NOV | DEC | Average of: |
|---|---|---|---|---|---|---|---|---|---|---|---|---|---|
| Stockholm | 31 | 31 | 37 | 45 | 57 | 65 | 70 | 66 | 58 | 48 | 38 | 33 | High Temperatures |
| | 23 | 22 | 26 | 32 | 41 | 49 | 55 | 53 | 46 | 39 | 31 | 26 | Low Temperatures |
| | 8 | 7 | 7 | 6 | 8 | 7 | 9 | 10 | 8 | 9 | 9 | 9 | Days of Rain or Snow |
| Särna | 8 | 5 | 5 | 7 | 6 | 11 | 13 | 12 | 10 | 9 | 9 | 9 | Days of Rain or Snow |
| | 19 | 24 | 33 | 42 | 56 | 63 | 69 | 65 | 54 | 42 | 30 | 24 | High Temperatures |
| | 4 | 5 | 11 | 23 | 32 | 41 | 46 | 44 | 36 | 28 | 19 | 11 | Low Temperatures |

Temperatures are given in degrees Fahrenheit

Sources: Meteorological Office, London; U. S. Navy.

WORLD BOOK maps-FHa

# SWEDEN / Economy

Sweden's economy is based mainly on its three most important natural resources—timber, iron ore, and water power. The large Swedish merchant shipping fleet transports cargoes to and from all parts of the world, and provides an important source of income for the nation. About 90 per cent of Swedish industry is privately owned. For Sweden's rank in the output of various products, see the articles listed under Products and Industry in the *Related Articles* at the end of this article.

**Natural Resources.** The raw materials for Sweden's industries come chiefly from the country's vast forests and rich deposits of iron ore. Waterfalls, rapids, and dams provide most of the nation's electricity. Although

## FARM, MINERAL, AND FOREST PRODUCTS

This map shows where the leading farm, mineral, and forest products of Sweden are produced. Most Swedish agriculture is in the southern parts of the country and on the central plains. The map also shows five important manufacturing centers.

## SWEDEN'S GROSS NATIONAL PRODUCT IN 1965
Total gross national product—$19,498,000,000

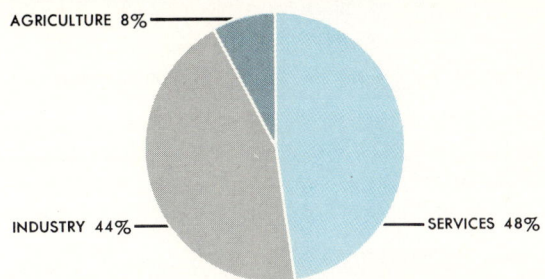

AGRICULTURE 8%
INDUSTRY 44%
SERVICES 48%

The Gross National Product (GNP) is the total value of goods and services produced by a country in a year. The GNP measures a nation's total annual economic performance. It can also be used to compare the economic output and growth of countries.

### Production and Workers by Economic Activities

| Economic Activities | Per Cent of GNP Produced | Labor Force Number of Persons | Per Cent of Total |
|---|---|---|---|
| Manufacturing | 33 | 1,496,000 | 44 |
| Trade | 14 | 442,000 | 13 |
| Government | 12 | 340,000 | 10 |
| Transportation & Communication | 9 | 272,000 | 8 |
| Agriculture, Forestry, & Fishing | 8 | 340,000 | 10 |
| Construction | 8 | — | — |
| Other Services | 7 | 510,000 | 15 |
| Housing | 6 | — | — |
| Utilities | 3 | — | — |
| Total | 100 | 3,400,000 | 100 |

Source: *Facts About Sweden*, The Swedish Institute, 1966.

**Paper Production** is the fastest-growing branch of Sweden's forest products industry. Much of the paper is exported. Sweden is one of the leading paper producers in the world.

Herbert Fristedt from Carl Östman

WORLD BOOK map-FHa

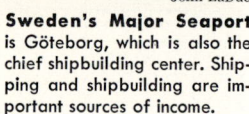

**Sweden's Major Seaport** is Göteborg, which is also the chief shipbuilding center. Shipping and shipbuilding are important sources of income.

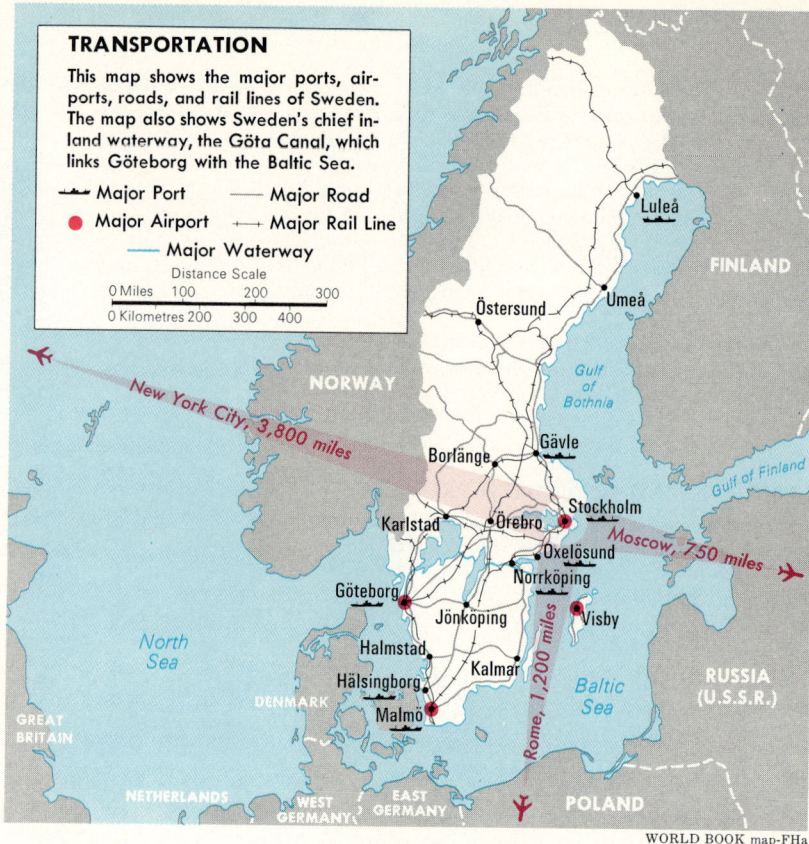

WORLD BOOK map-FHa

most of Sweden is too cold and infertile for farming, farmers produce most of the people's food.

*Forests* cover more than half of Sweden, and more than a fourth of the nation's exports are lumber or products made of wood. The main lumber regions are in the north and north-central sections, where the most important trees include fir, pine, and spruce. Much lumber is carried to manufacturing plants by truck and railroad. Logs are also floated down the rivers to sawmills on the coast, where some lumber is exported and the rest is sent to industrial centers. Forestry is less important in southern Sweden, even though oak, beech, and other trees cover large areas.

*Minerals.* Sweden has some of the richest iron ore deposits in the world. The country's total iron ore resources have been estimated at almost $3\frac{3}{4}$ billion tons, of which about 60 per cent is near Kiruna in Lapland. The Lapland mines have some of the world's best high-grade ores. Most of the Lapland ore is exported. The Swedish iron and steel industry gets most of its ore from the Bergslagen district, south of the Dal River. The Skellefteå region in northern Sweden has deposits of copper, lead, gold, and silver. Some low-grade uranium ore is mined in central Sweden. The country also has a few deposits of low-grade coal.

*Water Power* provides about 95 per cent of Sweden's electricity. The largest hydroelectric power stations are in northern Sweden. Most of them are underground, and can be operated throughout the year. Other important power stations are in central and southern Sweden, including a large station at Trollhättan.

*Farmland* covers only about 10 per cent of Sweden. A region called Skåne, in the extreme south, has a good climate and is the most fertile area. Other agricultural areas are in the south and around the lakes in central Sweden. Less than 1 per cent of the Inner Northland region is cultivated.

**Manufacturing** industries are scattered throughout central Sweden and western Skåne, and along the coast. The iron and steel industry produces high-quality steel, which is used for such products as ball bearings, stainless steel goods for the home, precision tools, and watch springs. Steel is widely used in the engineering industry, which accounts for more than a third of Sweden's total industrial production and for two-fifths of its exports.

Important Swedish engineering products include agricultural machinery, aircraft, automobiles, and ships. Linköping is the chief center of the aircraft industry, and Trollhättan has aircraft engine and diesel motor plants. Stockholm, Göteborg, and Linköping have major automobile plants. Nearly half the automobiles made in Sweden are exported to the United States. Sweden ranks second only to Japan in the number of ships it builds for export. The main shipbuilding centers are Göteborg and Malmö. The electrical engineering industry makes equipment for power supplies and communications, and telephones are an important export.

Sweden produces about 10 per cent of the world's

wood pulp. Other important products based on timber include paper and cardboard, prefabricated houses, plywood, and furniture.

The Swedish chemical industry imports most of its raw materials. The chief products include explosives, fertilizers, plastics, and safety matches. Safety matches were invented in Sweden in 1844, and the country is still one of the world's leading producers.

**Agriculture.** Dairy farming and livestock raising are the main sources of income for Swedish farmers. Milk and meat are the leading farm products. The chief crops include barley, oats, potatoes, sugar beets, and wheat. Almost all the farmers belong to Sweden's agricultural cooperative movement, which collects, processes, and markets farm products (see COOPERATIVE).

**Mining.** Sweden's most important mineral is iron ore. The country is a leading producer of this mineral, which accounts for 6 per cent of Sweden's exports. Most of the exported ore comes from mines in Lapland. In summer, the Lapland ore is shipped from the port of Luleå, on the Gulf of Bothnia. In winter, Luleå's harbor is icebound, and the ore must be carried across the mountains to the ice-free port of Narvik in Norway.

**Foreign Trade.** The value of Sweden's imports is greater than that of its exports. But in most years, income from the country's merchant shipping fleet makes up most of the difference. The chief Swedish exports include engineering products, wood pulp, paper and other wood products, iron ore, and steel. Imports include coal, petroleum, and foodstuffs.

West European nations, including Denmark, West Germany, Great Britain, The Netherlands, and Norway, account for more than 80 per cent of Sweden's exports and more than 75 per cent of its imports. Sweden also has important trade with the United States. Sweden is a member of the European Free Trade Association (see EUROPEAN FREE TRADE ASSOCIATION).

**Transportation.** The government owns about 95 per cent of Sweden's 8,450 miles of railways. Only a little more than half are electrified, but electric trains carry about 90 per cent of the total railroad traffic. Ferries connect Swedish railroads with those in Denmark and Germany. Sweden has a network of good roads and highways, and trucks carry almost as much freight as the railroads do.

Stockholm has an international airport at Arlanda. Other important airports serve Göteborg and Malmö. Swedish ships carry raw materials between coastal towns.

**Communication.** Sweden has about 160 daily newspapers, with a total daily circulation of more than 4 million. *Expressen* of Stockholm, with a circulation of about 455,000, is the largest newspaper in Sweden. Most of Sweden's newspapers are privately owned. Freedom of the press is guaranteed by law, and government censorship is forbidden even in wartime.

The Swedish Broadcasting Corporation, which operates three radio stations and one television channel, is the only broadcasting system. It is run partly by the government, but is nonpolitical. The government does not permit advertising on radio or television.

Sweden's telephone and telegraph services are operated by the government. In the mid-1960's, Sweden had about 460 telephones for every 1,000 persons, the highest proportion in the world after the United States.

## SWEDEN / History

**Early Times.** Sweden was one of the last regions to lose the ice that covered most of Europe thousands of years ago. The ice had melted by about 6000 B.C., and hunters and fishermen from south of the Baltic Sea settled in the southern tip of Sweden. People moved farther north as the climate improved.

Beginning about 50 B.C., the people traded with the Roman Empire. They exchanged furs and amber for glass and bronze objects and silver coins. The Romans were the first people to make written records about the Swedes. About A.D. 100, the Roman historian Tacitus wrote about the Svear, a Scandinavian people. *Sverige* (Sweden) means *land of the Svear*.

**The Swedish Vikings.** Beginning about A.D. 800, Scandinavian adventurers called *Vikings* sailed to many parts of the world. They acquired wealth by trade and conquest. Most of the Norwegian and Danish Vikings sailed westward. The Swedish Vikings went eastward across Russia, as far as the Black and Caspian seas. The Swedes traded slaves and furs for gold, silver, and luxury goods. The Viking expeditions lasted until the 1000's. Much of Sweden's trade with the east then came into the hands of German merchants, who settled in the town of Visby on the island of Gotland. See VIKING (The Swedish Vikings); RUSSIA (Early Days).

**The Early Kingdom.** Christianity was first preached in Sweden in A.D. 829 by Ansgar, a Frankish monk. Ansgar's missionary work began a struggle between Christianity and paganism that lasted about 200 years. The first Christian king of Sweden was Olof Skotkonung, who ruled from the late 900's until the early 1000's. Christianity brought about great changes in Sweden. The clergy founded schools, encouraged the arts, and set down Sweden's laws in writing.

By the 1000's, Sweden, Denmark, and Norway had become separate kingdoms. Sweden began to develop along partly feudal lines (see FEUDALISM). There were three social classes—the clergy, the nobles, and the

**Picture Stones** were carved by Swedish Vikings, usually as memorial monuments for heroes. This picture dates from the A.D. 700's.

Picture stone from Gotland. Historiska Museet, Stockholm

**Battle of Hangö,** during the Great Northern War, ended in victory for Russia's navy over the Swedish fleet in 1714.

peasants. Above them was the king, who was elected by the provincial lawmaking assemblies. In 1249, Sweden conquered much of Finland.

**Union with Norway and Denmark.** During the 1200's and 1300's, constant struggles took place between the rulers of Sweden and the nobles. In 1388, to oppose the growing German influence in Sweden's affairs, the nobles turned for help to Queen Margaret of Denmark and Norway. The Germans were defeated in 1389, and the three Scandinavian countries were united under Margaret in 1397.

A treaty called the *Union of Kalmar* laid down the conditions of the union between the three countries. This treaty provided for a common foreign policy, but separate national councils and the continuation of existing laws in each country. Except for a few short periods of separation, the union lasted over 100 years.

Under the influence of German merchants, Sweden's economy developed considerably during the 1200's and

---
**IMPORTANT DATES IN SWEDEN**
---

**c. 6000 B.C.** The first settlers came to Sweden.

**c. A.D. 800's to 1000's** Swedish Vikings attacked other countries, and traded and colonized.

**c. 1000** Christianity was introduced into Sweden.

**1397** Sweden, Denmark, and Norway were united in the Union of Kalmar.

**1523** Gustavus Vasa was elected king and Sweden became independent.

**c. 1540** Lutheranism became Sweden's official religion.

**1630-1632** Gustavus Adolphus won victories for Sweden in the Thirty Years' War (1618-1648).

**1709** Swedish power declined after the Battle of Poltava.

**1809** Sweden lost Finland to Russia. A new constitution was adopted.

**1814** Sweden gained Norway from Denmark.

**1905** Norway dissolved its union with Sweden.

**1914-1918** Sweden was neutral in World War I.

**1920** All persons at least 21 years old received the vote.

**1939-1945** Sweden remained neutral in World War II.

**1959** Sweden and six other nations formed the European Free Trade Association.

**1963** Atomic power was used to heat some Swedish homes.

**1965** The voting age was lowered to 20 years.

**1967** Sweden changed its traffic system from driving on the left side of the street to the right.

822

1300's. These merchants developed Sweden's mineral resources and controlled Swedish trade. Plague wiped out a large part of Sweden's population in 1350, and caused an economic decline. The German merchants, with their powerful association called the Hanseatic League, increased their control of Swedish trade (see HANSEATIC LEAGUE).

During the late 1400's, the *Riksdag* (parliament) developed into a lawmaking and tax-raising body. Members of a new social class, the merchants, joined the other three classes as members of the Riksdag.

**The Beginnings of Modern Sweden.** The union with Norway and Denmark continued throughout most of the 1400's. But many struggles took place between supporters and opponents of the union. Gustavus Vasa, a Swedish noble, finally broke away from the union in 1523 after defeating the Danes. He became King Gustavus I of independent Sweden that year. Norway remained under Danish rule.

Gustavus encouraged the followers of Martin Luther, the German religious reformer, to spread their ideas. About 1540, the Lutheran religion became the state religion of Sweden. Gustavus also increased the power of the throne and laid the foundations of the modern Swedish state. He centralized the administration, dealt harshly with revolts, built an efficient army, and encouraged trade and industry. See GUSTAVUS (I).

**The Age of Expansion.** Beginning in the late 1500's, the Swedes fought a series of wars to gain control of the lands surrounding the Baltic Sea. King Gustavus Adolphus won many victories for Sweden and the Protestant cause in the Thirty Years' War (see THIRTY YEARS' WAR). Sweden gained new possessions in Europe, and these led to continual wars against Denmark, Poland, and Russia. In 1658, under the Treaty of Roskilde, the Swedes forced the Danes to give up their provinces on the Swedish mainland.

Charles XII, who ruled from 1697 to 1718, won many victories, and for a time made Sweden one of the greatest powers in Europe. But in 1709, Czar Peter the Great of Russia defeated the Swedes in the Battle of Poltava. During the next few years, Sweden lost most of its European possessions. See CHARLES (XII).

**The Age of Liberty.** Charles XII died in 1718. Before agreeing to elect a new king, the Riksdag insisted that any monarch chosen should accept a new constitution.

This constitution, which was passed in 1720, transferred many of the crown's powers to the Riksdag. The period of parliamentary government that followed was called the Age of Liberty, and lasted until 1772. That year, an unsuccessful war in Germany and serious economic and political troubles at home resulted in a peaceful revolution that re-established the power of the king.

**The Napoleonic Wars.** Because of its growing trade with Great Britain, Sweden became involved in wars against the French Emperor Napoleon in the early 1800's. As a result of these wars, Sweden lost Finland to Russia, but gained Norway from Denmark. In 1809, Sweden adopted a new constitution which, in a modified form, is still in effect. In 1818, Jean Baptiste Bernadotte, a former French general who had become *regent* (acting ruler) of Sweden during the Napoleonic Wars, was elected king of Sweden as Charles XIV. Sweden's present royal family is descended from him.

**Industrial Growth.** Great economic and social changes occurred in Sweden during the 1800's. More land was brought into use for farming. But food was often in short supply because of a great increase in the population. There were not enough jobs for all Sweden's people, and nearly 450,000 persons left the country between 1867 and 1886. Most of them went to the United States and settled mainly in the Midwest.

Emigration gradually decreased after Sweden developed manufacturing, mining, and forest industries. During the 1860's and 1870's, engineers built many railroads, and Sweden's vast lumber resources were put into use. In 1867, Alfred Nobel, a Swedish chemist, invented dynamite, which speeded the growth of mining. Engineering industries based on iron and steel were developed, and by 1900, Sweden had become an important industrial nation.

In 1905, Norway broke away from Sweden. The Norwegians elected a Dane as their king, and Sweden recognized Norway's independence. See NORWAY (Independence).

Sweden was neutral during World War I (1914-1918) and World War II (1939-1945). After Germany conquered Norway in 1940, Sweden allowed German occupation troops to pass through on their way to Norway. Many Swedes opposed this policy, and Sweden stopped it in 1943. Sweden joined the United Nations in 1946.

**Sweden Today** is one of the most prosperous countries in the world. The Swedish economy grew rapidly during the 1960's—about 5 per cent a year. In the late 1960's, however, the nation faced sharply rising prices and a severe housing shortage. Sweden's high standard of living is spread throughout the lower income groups by means of a huge government welfare system. This program, rapidly developed since the mid-1940's, accounts for about a third of the national budget.

Some critics of the government welfare program say it gives the people too much security and makes their lives empty and boring. But most Swedes support the system, and deny it has that effect.

In September, 1967, Sweden changed its traffic system to driving on the right side of the street. Until then, Sweden was the only country on the European continent that had driving on the left side. The change was made to reduce accidents by motorists entering or leaving Sweden.

TORSTEN HENRIKSSON, JOHAN NORRBIN, ISTVÁN VUKOVICH, and CARL-CHRISTIAN WALLÉN

# SWEDEN / Study Aids

**Related Articles** in WORLD BOOK include:

### BIOGRAPHIES

| | |
|---|---|
| Andrée, Salomon A. | Lagerlöf, Selma |
| Arrhenius, Svante A. | Lind, Jenny |
| Bergman, Ingmar | Linnaeus, Carolus |
| Bernadotte, Folke | Milles, Carl W.E. |
| Bernadotte, Jean B.J. | Nilsson, Birgit |
| Berzelius, Jöns J. | Nobel, Alfred B. |
| Bjoerling, Jussi | Nordenskjöld, Nils A. |
| Buxtehude, Dietrich | Oscar (Swedish Kings) |
| Charles (Swedish Kings) | Scheele, Carl W. |
| Christina | Seashore, Carl E. |
| Ericsson, John | Siegbahn, Karl M.G. |
| Garbo, Greta | Söderblom, Nathan |
| Gullstrand, Allvar | Strindberg, August |
| Gustavus | Svedberg, Theodor |
| Hammarskjöld, Dag | Swedenborg, Emanuel |
| Hedin, Sven A. | Tenggren, Gustaf |
| Karlfeldt, Erik A. | Theorell, Hugo |
| Kreuger, Ivar | Tiselius, Arne |
| Lagerkvist, Pär F. | Zorn, Anders L. |

### CITIES AND TOWNS

Göteborg    Malmö    Orrefors    Stockholm

### HISTORY

Denmark (History)    Norway (History)
Goth    Viking

### PHYSICAL FEATURES

Baltic Sea    Lake Vänern    Torne River
Kattegat    Skagerrak

### PRODUCTS AND INDUSTRY

For Sweden's rank among other countries in production, see the following articles:
Automobile    Lumber    Ship and Shipping
Iron and Steel    Match

### OTHER RELATED ARTICLES

Air Force (Sweden)    Furniture (Modern)
Christmas (In Sweden; color    Glassware
  picture: A Swedish Boy)    Scandinavia

### Outline

I. **Government**
II. **People**
   A. Language    E. Libraries and Museums
   B. Religion    F. Sports
   C. Food    G. Holidays
   D. Education    H. Social Welfare
III. **Arts**
IV. **The Land**
V. **Climate**
VI. **Economy**
   A. Natural Resources    E. Foreign Trade
   B. Manufacturing    F. Transportation
   C. Agriculture    G. Communication
   D. Mining
VII. **History**

### Questions

Who founded Sweden's present royal family?
What is the principal religion of Sweden?
How did Sweden get its name?
Why did many Swedes emigrate in the late 1800's?
What are Sweden's three chief natural resources?
What are Sweden's two largest lakes and islands?
Who was the first Swedish writer to win world fame?
Why are Sweden's forests important to its economy?
When was Sweden's constitution adopted?
What is smörgåsbord?

## SWEDENBORG, EMANUEL

Brown Bros.
**Emanuel Swedenborg**

**SWEDENBORG,** *SWE dun bawrg*, or, in Swedish, *SVAY dun BAWR y*, **EMANUEL** (1688-1772), was a Swedish scientist, inventor, and mystical religious leader. He became an authority on mathematics, astronomy, metallurgy, anatomy, and geology, and was named a member of the Swedish State Council of Mines. He is credited with a number of inventions, and drew plans for a submarine, an airship, and a magazine-type gun, all forerunners of those of today.

Swedenborg, son of a bishop and nobleman, was born in Stockholm. He turned to religion in middle age, although he retained his scientific interests. He wrote a number of books setting forth what he called his "heavenly doctrines." He claimed that they were based on Bible teachings which had been interpreted to him through direct communication with the spiritual world. His views brought him much criticism.

Swedenborg did not intend to found a separate religious body, but, soon after his death in London, some of his followers began to form churches founded on his views. They became known as the Church of the New Jerusalem. F. A. NORWOOD

See also SWEDENBORGIANS.

**SWEDENBORGIANS,** *SWEE dun BAWR jih uns*, look to the formulation of Christian doctrine as set forth by Emanuel Swedenborg, a Swedish theologian. A church based on this doctrine was organized in London in 1787, and in the United States in 1792. Churches in the United States and Canada set up the General Convention of the New Jerusalem in 1817. A separate body, formed in 1890, took the name General Church of the New Jerusalem. For membership of the Churches of the New Jerusalem in the United States, see RELIGION (table). Swedenborgians have societies and missions in many parts of the world, usually affiliated with the American bodies or with the Conference of the New Church in Great Britain.

Swedenborg's teachings emphasize one God, the Lord and Savior Jesus Christ, in whom is the Trinity: Father, Son, and Holy Spirit. Swedenborgians believe that the Holy City, New Jerusalem, is symbolic of an ideal human society. They regard Jesus as truly *Immanuel*, or *God with us*. They believe that Swedenborg was called by God to reveal deeper spiritual meanings in scripture, and that, when mankind accepts and practices these truths, Jesus Christ makes his second coming in spirit, not in person. DAVID P. JOHNSON

**SWEDISH NIGHTINGALE.** See LIND, JENNY.
**SWEEPER.** See CARPET SWEEPER.
**SWEET ADELINES, INC.** See BARBERSHOP QUARTET SINGING.

**SWEET ALYSSUM,** *uh LIS um*, is a low, spreading plant with clusters of tiny lavender or white flowers. It is a hardy plant that gardeners can sow in early spring. Sweet alyssum usually blooms within six weeks after planting. Some varieties are dwarfed, and others grow 8 or 10 inches high.

**Scientific Classification.** Sweet alyssum belongs to the mustard family, *Cruciferae*. It is classified as genus *Lobularia*, species *L. maritima*. ROBERT W. SCHERY

**SWEET BRIAR COLLEGE** is a liberal arts college for women at Sweet Briar, Va. It offers courses leading to the A.B. degree. Sweet Briar administers the Junior Year in France, a foreign study program for men and women.

The college was chartered in 1901, and opened in 1906. For enrollment, see UNIVERSITIES AND COLLEGES (table).

**SWEET CHERVIL.** See CICELY.
**SWEET CORN.** See CORN.

**SWEET FLAG** is a tall reedlike plant of the arum family. It grows along brooks and in marshy places in almost all parts of the Northern Hemisphere. Its leaves are flat and 2 to 6 feet long. They are shaped like a two-edged sword. The stems of the sweet flag are almost like the leaves, but are stiffer and bear spikes of small green blossoms near the top. The leaves and stems rise directly from the thick, fleshy underground rootstock. The rootstock is the calamus root. It is used as a tonic and in the manufacture of perfume and other toilet preparations. In Europe, the rootstock is valued as a food.

**Scientific Classification.** The sweet flag is in the arum family, *Araceae*. It is genus *Acorus*, species *A. calamus*. HAROLD NORMAN MOLDENKE

**Sweet Flag** is a useful marsh herb. Its flower spikes, *inset*, are about 2 inches long.
L. W. Brownell; Carl L. Howard

John H. Gerard; W. Atlee Burpee Co.
**Sweet Alyssum** produces clusters of tiny white flowers, *inset*. A low plant, it has long been popular for garden borders.

# SWEET POTATO

Leaves of the Sweet Gum, or Red Gum, are among the most brilliant in autumn. The tree is tall and stately.

L. W. Brownell

**SWEET GUM,** also called RED GUM, is a tall, stately tree. It grows from Connecticut and southern New York to Florida and westward to southern Illinois, Oklahoma, and eastern Texas. Normally, it reaches a height of 80 to 100 feet. When mature, its straight trunk is 3 to 4 feet thick at the base. Sweet gum leaves are deeply lobed, and turn a deep crimson in autumn. The fruit is a brownish, spiny ball that remains on the tree through the winter. The sweet gum is so named because it produces a gummy compound, called *storax*, that is used in making perfumes, adhesives, and salves. Sweet gum wood is fairly hard and heavy. People use it to make veneer, cabinets, and other products.

**Scientific Classification.** Sweet gum trees belong to the witch hazel family, *Hamamelidaceae*. They are genus *Liquidambar*, species *L. styraciflua*.    T. EWALD MAKI

**SWEET PEA** is a favorite garden flower that belongs to the same family as the kind of pea that we eat. People grow the sweet pea for the beauty and delightful fragrance of its flowers. The sweet pea is one of the special flowers for the month of April. Sweet pea flowers are blue, red, pink, purple, and white. Some persons think they look like butterflies. There are more than 1,000 varieties of sweet pea. In some varieties, the flower petals are smooth and velvety. In others, they are crinkled and wavy. The plants may be *dwarf*, which grow only a few inches high, or *climbing*, which grow along strings or trellises.

Rich, well-drained soil, plenty of sunshine, and free circulation of air are needed to raise sweet peas successfully. Gardeners should sow the seed in April. They use one ounce of seed to 30 feet of row. The plants should be at least 2 inches apart in the row, and the rows should be 4 feet apart. As soon as the plants appear above ground, the gardener should cultivate the ground. He should stir the soil lightly every week, preferably after a rain, and keep the rows free of weeds. Once a week he should feed the plants with a liquid fertilizer.

The vines should be trained on strings. Wire trellises may absorb too much heat. The gardener should not allow the flowers to go to seed, but should pick them as they open.

**Scientific Classification.** Sweet peas belong to the pea family, *Leguminosae*. Common garden sweet peas are genus *Lathyrus*, species *L. odoratus*.    DONALD WYMAN

**SWEET POTATO** is an annual vine related to the morning-glories. It produces fleshy roots which are a valuable food. The vines rise from the main stem and lie along the ground. Some varieties have pale green vines with small pointed leaves. Others have purple vines with large leaves. Some of the roots become large and fleshy. Juicy specimens are often called *yams*, but the real yam belongs to a different family, and yams grow only in the tropics. Most sweet potatoes are dry and grainy, like the Jersey Yellow or Triumph, or damp and sweet like the Porto Rico.

The sweet potato has high energy value. Only dry beans and peas yield more energy. Sweet potatoes also contain much vitamin A and a good amount of vitamin C. They rank as one of the most important commercial vegetables. They are sometimes used to make starch and alcohol. They may be cooked fresh, or canned or dehydrated. Sweet potatoes first grew in the tropics of the Western Hemisphere. They were raised in Virginia in the early 1600's. The scientist George Washington Carver discovered 118 products that could be made from sweet potatoes.

Sweet potatoes are grown from roots placed in moist, warm, sandy soil in greenhouses or hotbeds about four weeks before planting time. Buds just below the skin of the planted root produce new plants, called *slips*, that grow up through the soil. They are removed and planted 12 inches apart in rows that are 3 feet apart. The rows are usually ridged to help the water drain. Some hoeing is necessary at first to control weeds.

Harvesting is best done before frost. The roots must

## LEADING SWEET POTATO GROWING STATES
Bags (100 pounds) of sweet potatoes grown in 1967

|  | |
|---|---|
| Louisiana 4,116,000 bags | 🥔🥔🥔🥔🥔🥔🥔🥔🥔🥔🥔 |
| North Carolina 2,185,000 bags | 🥔🥔🥔🥔🥔🥔🥔 |
| Virginia 1,656,000 bags | 🥔🥔🥔🥔🥔🥔 |
| Mississippi 1,105,000 bags | 🥔🥔🥔🥔 |
| Texas 810,000 bags | 🥔🥔🥔 |
| California 760,000 bags | 🥔🥔🥔 |
| Georgia 720,000 bags | 🥔🥔🥔 |
| New Jersey 610,000 bags | 🥔🥔 |
| Alabama 464,000 bags | 🥔🥔 |
| Maryland 420,000 bags | 🥔🥔 |

Source: *Potatoes and Sweetpotatoes*, August, 1968, U.S. Department of Agriculture

N.Y. Botanical Garden

**The Toothsome Sweet Potato** has long been associated with holiday feasts. It has great commercial importance.

be handled carefully to prevent bruising. They are *cured*, or dried, and then they are stored in a dry place where there is no danger of freezing.

Sweet potatoes have a common enemy, the fungus disease, a wilt called *stem rot*. It can be controlled with disease-free seed and by rotating the crop.

**Scientific Classification.** The sweet potato belongs to the morning-glory family, *Convolvulaceae*. It is genus *Ipomoea*, species *I. batalas*.   ARTHUR JOHN PRATT

See also CARVER, GEORGE WASHINGTON; CONVOLVULUS; YAM.

**SWEET WILLIAM** is a popular garden plant that is native to northern Europe and Asia and to the United States. The plant usually grows about 2 feet high and bears dense, round clusters of velvety flowers. The flowers range in color from white to pink, rose, or purple. Some are red with white spots. Cultivated plants may bear double flowers. Gardeners usually cultivate sweet William as a *biennial* (a plant that requires two years to mature).

**Scientific Classification.** Sweet William is in the pink family, *Caryophyllaceae*. It is genus *Dianthus*, species *barbatus*.   H. D. HARRINGTON

**Sweet William Blossoms** form large velvety clusters at the end of the stem. One cluster may have flowers in many shades.

J. Horace McFarland

**SWEETBREAD** is a tasty meat that comes from certain glands in young animals. The thymus gland in the throat of young calves produces sweetbread that is sold in fine restaurants. The pancreas of older calves is called *stomach sweetbread* or *belly sweetbread*. It is much like the sweetbread of the thymus gland.

Butchers divide the thymus gland into the throat sweetbread and the heart, or breast, sweetbread. Heart sweetbread is larger and more tender than throat sweetbread.

The best sweetbread is that taken from baby calves, because the thymus gland gradually shrinks and disappears after the animal feeds on grass. Lamb sweetbread is too small to be sold in markets.   JOHN C. AYRES

**SWEETBRIER.** See EGLANTINE.

**SWELLFISH.** See PUFFER.

**SWIFT** is the name of a family that developed one of the world's leading meat-packing companies. Two generations of that family guided the company from a small New England firm to world leadership in the industry.

**Gustavus Franklin Swift** (1839-1903) started working for his brother, a butcher, at 14, and went in business for himself at the age of 17. Before he was 35, he was a cattle exporter and a wholesale meat dealer. Association with the meat business from 1855 until his death made him an expert judge of cattle.

**Gustavus Swift**

Swift saw the need to eliminate excessive transportation costs. In 1875 he went to Chicago and became the first to slaughter meat there for shipment east. At first this activity had to be confined to the cooler months, but the use of the refrigerator car made it a year-round business.

On April 1, 1885, Swift & Company was formed. Because of the continuous growth of Swift's company in an expanding industry, he had to use unusual methods in raising additional capital. He became famous for his emphasis on cost-cutting and his insistence on the full use of by-products. He was born in Cape Cod, Mass.

**Louis Franklin Swift** (1861-1937), the oldest son of Gustavus Franklin Swift, became president of Swift & Company when his father died, and served until 1931. Later he served as chairman of the board of directors. Under his leadership, the company established a pension trust and made other advances in labor relations. Swift was active in company expansion plans, opening plants in the United States, and in South America, Australia, and New Zealand. These foreign operations were separated from Swift & Company in 1918, and became Compania Swift Internacional. Louis Swift was born at Sagamore, Mass.

**Edward Foster Swift** (1863-1932), the second son of Gustavus Franklin Swift, worked closely with his older brother in formulating company policies. He served as vice-president of the company and as president of Compania Swift Internacional and other company affiliates. He was born at Barnstable, Mass.

SWIFT

**Charles Henry Swift** (1872-1948), the fourth son of Gustavus, succeeded Louis Franklin Swift as chairman of the board of directors of Swift & Company in 1932. He encouraged the branch-house system of distribution, which increased the efficiency of the company's marketing system. He was born at Lancaster, Mass.

**Gustavus Franklin Swift, Jr.** (1881-1943), the seventh son of Gustavus Franklin Swift, became president of Swift & Company in 1931, and served until 1937. He took a leading part in the organization of the American Meat Institute. He was born in Chicago, Ill.

**Harold Higgins Swift** (1885-1962), the youngest son of Gustavus Franklin Swift, served as vice-president in charge of industrial relations. He became chairman of the board in 1948 and honorary chairman in 1955. He became a member of the University of Chicago board of trustees in 1914, and served as its chairman from 1922 to 1949. He was a director of the Rockefeller Foundation. He was born in Chicago. W. H. BAUGHN

For further information about Swift & Company, see FOOD (25 Largest Food-Processing Companies in the United States).

**SWIFT** is a small bird that can fly for many hours with its long, strong wings. Swifts capture their insect food while flying. They almost always return at dusk to the cave, chimney, cliff, or hollow tree where they live in flocks. A chimney swift may fly an estimated 135,000 miles a year. Swifts build odd nests made of sticks that they cement together with their saliva. Some of these nests are almost entirely made up of saliva. They resemble the bird's nests of east Asia that people eat.

More than 75 different kinds of swifts live in various parts of the world. They are sooty-brown or greenish-black. Some swifts have white throats or rumps. Their song, continually repeated, is little more than short, indistinct sounds.

The chimney swift of eastern North America almost always builds its nest in chimneys. Vaux's swifts of western North America and chimney swifts may roost by the thousands in large chimneys while migrating. They perform spectacular maneuvers in the air as they descend into the chimneys for the night.

**Scientific Classification.** Swifts make up the swift family, *Apodidae*. The chimney swift is genus *Chaetura*, species *C. pelagica*. Vaux's swift is *C. vauxi*. LEONARD W. WING

See also ANIMAL (color picture: Animals of the Mountains); BIRD (Building the Nest; Interesting Facts About Birds [Fastest Flier]); BIRD'S-NEST SOUP.

**SWIFT** is the name of certain small lizards that are unusually active. Swifts live on dry land in the western part of North America and in Central America. They have tiny scales with sharp points that often look like spines. There are about 50 different kinds of swifts.

**Scientific Classification.** Swifts belong to the New World lizard family, *Iguanidae*. They are classified in the genus *Uta* and in the genus *Sceloporus*. CLIFFORD H. POPE

**Swifts Are Strong, Fast Fliers.** Some of them can travel over 100 miles per hour for short distances. They feed on insects while in the air and some swifts spend the night in flight.

**Swifts Usually Roost on Vertical Surfaces,** clinging with sharp toenails and using the tail as a prop, *below*. They rarely perch on branches because their feet and legs are small and weak.

Eric Hosking, Photo Researchers

Treat Davidson, NAS

827

# SWIFT, JONATHAN

**SWIFT, JONATHAN** (1667-1745), an English author, wrote the story *Gulliver's Travels* (1726), a masterpiece of literature. Swift is called a great *satirist* because of his ability to ridicule customs, ideas, and habits he considered silly or harmful. His satire is often bitter, but it is also often humorous. Swift was deeply concerned about the welfare and about the behavior of his fellow men, and he used his talent to strike out against those men, institutions, and ideas that he considered foolish.

*Jonathan Swift* by Charles Jervas. National Portrait Gallery, London

**Jonathan Swift**

Swift's life was interesting and useful. Swift was a Protestant preacher who became a hero in Roman Catholic Ireland. He wrote many pamphlets to protest the sufferings of the Irish under their British rulers. He was also a friend of important English statesmen and a writer on English political issues.

**His Life.** Swift was born in Dublin on Nov. 30, 1667. His parents were of English birth. Swift was graduated from Trinity College in Dublin, and moved to England in 1689. He was secretary to the distinguished statesman Sir William Temple from 1689 until 1699, with some interruptions. In 1694, Swift became a minister in the Church of England.

While working for Temple, Swift met a young girl named Esther Johnson, whom he called Stella. He and Stella became lifelong friends, and some persons believe they were married. There is no proof of their marriage, however. Swift wrote long letters to Stella during his busiest days. The letters were published after Swift's death as the *Journal to Stella*.

After Temple died in 1699, Swift became pastor of a small Protestant parish in Laracor, Ireland. He began to play an important part in church life, and his skill as a writer became widely known. He visited England often between 1703 and 1710, conducting church business and winning influential friends. In 1710, he became a powerful supporter of the new Tory government in England. Through his many articles and pamphlets in defense of Tory policies, Swift became one of the most effective public relations men any English administration has ever had.

Queen Anne recognized Swift's political work in 1713 when she made him *dean* (supervisor) of St. Patrick's Cathedral in Dublin. The queen died in 1714, and George I became king. The Whig party won control of the government in the same year. These changes ended the political power of Swift and his friends.

Swift spent the rest of his life—more than 30 years—as dean of St. Patrick's. In many ways, these years were disappointing. Swift was unhappy because his political efforts had amounted to so little. He also missed his exciting friends in England. But it was as dean that Swift wrote *Gulliver's Travels* and that he became the champion of the Irish cause.

Swift's health declined in his last years and finally his mind failed. He died on Oct. 19, 1745. He left his money to start a hospital for the mentally ill.

***Gulliver's Travels*** is often described as a book children read with delight, but which adults find serious and disturbing. However, even young readers usually recognize that Swift's "make-believe" world sometimes resembles their own world. Adults recognize that, in spite of the book's seriousness, it is also amusing.

*Gulliver's Travels* describes four voyages that Lemuel Gulliver, who was trained as a ship's doctor, makes to strange lands. Gulliver first visits the *Lilliputians* (pronounced *lil eh PEW shuns*)—tiny people whose size and surroundings are only $\frac{1}{12}$ those of normal people and things. The Lilliputians treat Gulliver well at first. Gulliver helps them, but after a time the Lilliputians turn against him and he is happy to escape from them.

Gulliver's second voyage takes him to the country of *Brobdingnag* (pronounced *BROB ding nag*), where the people are 12 times larger than Gulliver and greatly amused by his puny size.

Gulliver's third voyage takes him to several strange kingdoms. The conduct of the odd people of these countries represents the kinds of foolishness Swift saw in his world. For example, in the academy of Lagado, scholars spend all their time on useless projects such as getting sunbeams from cucumbers. Here Swift was satirizing impractical scientists and philosophers.

In his last voyage, Gulliver discovers a land ruled by wise and gentle horses called *Houyhnhnms* (pronounced *HWIN ems*). Savage, stupid animals called *Yahoos* also live there. The Yahoos look like human beings. The Houyhnhnms distrust Gulliver because he resembles the Yahoos. Gulliver wishes to stay in the agreeable company of the Houyhnhnms, but they force him to leave.

Some persons believe Swift was a *misanthrope* (hater of mankind), and that the ugliness and stupidity in his book reflect his view of the world. Other persons argue that Swift was a devoted and courageous Christian who could not have held such bitter opinions about his fellow man. They claim that in *Gulliver's Travels*, Swift is really urging us to avoid the extremes between the boringly perfect Houyhnhnms and wild Yahoos and to lead moderate, sensible lives.

Scholars are still trying to discover all the ways in which real persons, institutions, and events are represented in *Gulliver's Travels*. But readers need not be scholars to find pleasure in the book and to find themselves set to thinking about its distinctive picture of human life.

**Swift's Other Works.** "A Modest Proposal" (1729) is probably Swift's second best-known work. In this short essay, Swift pretends to urge that Irish babies be killed and eaten. They would be as well off, says Swift bitterly, as those Irish who grow up in poverty under British rule. Swift hoped this outrageous suggestion would shock the Irish people into taking sensible steps to improve their condition.

*A Tale of a Tub* (1704), on the surface, is a story of three brothers arguing over their father's last will. But it is actually a clever attack on certain religious beliefs and on man's false pride in his knowledge.

In *The Battle of the Books* (1704), a lighter work, Swift imagines old and new books in a library waging war on each other. This work reflected a real quarrel

# SWIFT, JONATHAN

between scholars who were proud of being "modern," and scholars who believed the wisdom of the ancient thinkers could not be bettered.

Swift wrote many pamphlets in support of his political views. *The Drapier's Letters* (1724) are probably the most notable. Writing in the character of a simple dry-goods merchant, Swift urged the Irish to boycott the use of copper money, which England was trying to force on them.

Swift could also be very playful. He loved riddles, jokes, and hoaxes. One of his best literary pranks was the so-called *Bickerstaff Papers* (1708). In this work, he ridiculed a popular astrologer and almanac writer by publishing his own wildly improbable predictions.

Swift wrote a great deal of poetry and light verse. Much of his poetry is humorous, and it is often sharply satirical as well. But many of his poems, both comic and serious, show his love for his friends.

**Swift's Personality.** Whether Swift hated mankind or whether he mocked men to reform them is still disputed. However, there are some things Swift clearly hated and loved.

He hated those who attacked religion, particularly when they pretended to be religious themselves. He also hated the tyranny of one nation over another nation. Above all, he hated false pride—the tendency of men to exaggerate their own accomplishments and overlook their own weaknesses.

Swift loved his religious faith. He also loved liberty, simplicity, honesty, and humility. His writings—whether bitter, shocking, or humorous—ask the reader to pursue these virtues.

*Critically reviewed by* EDWARD ROSENHEIM, JR.

**The Battle of the Books,** *right*, ridicules scholars who argued the relative merits of ancient and modern writers. This picture shows a battle between ancient and modern books in a library.

Engraving by Bernard Lens the elder for the 1710 edition of *The Battle of the Books.* Newberry Library, Chicago

**Gulliver's Travels** is Swift's most famous book. In its best-known episode, Gulliver is shipwrecked in the country of Lilliput where the people are only 1/12 his size. He awakes to find that the Lilliputians have tied him down with hundreds of tiny ropes.

*Swimming Pool Age*

# SWIMMING

**SWIMMING** is one of the most popular and healthful sports. Every year, millions of persons enjoy swimming in oceans, lakes, and rivers in all parts of the world. Indoor pools in schools and recreation centers make swimming a year-round sport. Swimming uses most of the body's muscles, and develops grace and strength.

Swimming ranks as one of man's oldest sports. Cave drawings made in the Libyan Desert about 11,000 years ago show people swimming. An Egyptian nobleman who lived about 2160 B.C. recorded that his children took swimming lessons. About 880 B.C., Assyrian warriors used a crawl-type stroke to swim across streams.

Organized swimming contests began in Great Britain during the 1880's. In the United States, athletic clubs first held swimming meets in the early 1900's. Today, thousands of swimmers compete in meets held by high schools, colleges, and swimming clubs throughout the United States, Canada, and other countries. Long-distance swimmers often attempt such feats as swimming the English Channel or one of the Great Lakes.

### How to Swim

The ability to swim does not come naturally to man, as it does to fishes, frogs, and many other animals. People must learn to swim. The best and safest way to learn is under the guidance of a trained instructor. No swimmer, skilled or unskilled, should ever swim alone. An adult swimmer or lifesaver who can help in an emergency should always be present.

**Entering the Water.** Swimming lessons should start at a pool or beach protected by lifeguards. The beginner, with his instructor, enters the water gradually. He splashes himself gently, and finally goes into the water up to his neck. Bobbing in shallow water can help teach the proper way to breathe while swimming. To bob, the beginner takes a deep breath through his mouth when his head is above water, and breathes out through his mouth and nose under water. The use of swimming aids such as life jackets can also help develop a beginner's confidence in the water.

**Floating** is the next step in learning how to swim. The beginner starts with the *jellyfish float*. From a standing position in waist-deep water, he takes a deep breath and bends at the waist until his head and the upper part of his body are in the water. At the same time, he moves his hands from his waist, down along his legs, to his ankles and feet. When this is done, his feet automatically lift off the ground and he finds himself floating.

Next, the student learns the *prone float*, or *dead-man's float*. He takes a deep breath and puts his face in the water. Then he stretches his legs as far backward as possible and extends his arms forward beyond his head. To do the *prone glide*, or *moving dead-man's float*, he (1) leans forward with his arms extended over his head, and hands together; (2) lowers his shoulders below the surface of the water; (3) takes a deep breath; (4) puts his

## LEARN TO FLOAT

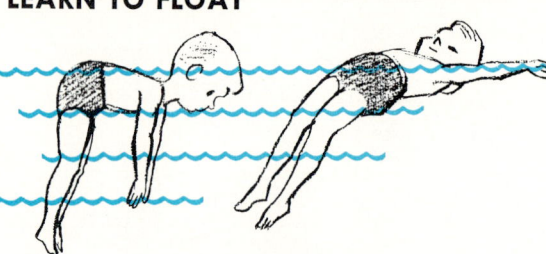

**Floating** is the first step in swimming. Begin with the *jellyfish float*, far left. Next, try the *prone*, or *dead-man's*, *float*, above. You should also learn the restful *back float*, left.

The Athletic Institute

## THEN TO GLIDE AND STROKE

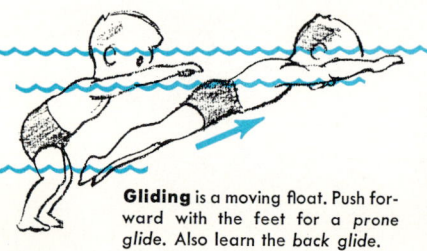

**Gliding** is a moving float. Push forward with the feet for a *prone glide*. Also learn the *back glide*.

**Arm Strokes** can be practiced easily while standing on the side of a pool, *right*, or in waist-deep water. Bend over, and reach alternately forward with each hand. Press each hand straight down and back until it points downward.

830

# SWIMMING

face in the water; and (5) pushes forward with his feet. To stand up, he pulls his knees under his body, pushes his hands down, and lifts his head.

The beginner must also learn the *back float* and *back glide*. These provide restful positions in the water and allow easy breathing, because the face is above water. To float on his back, the student squats in a sitting position in waist-deep water. His shoulders should be below the surface of the water. Next, he stretches his hands sideward with the palms up under the water, tilts his head back, and looks straight up. Then he lifts his hips as close to the surface as possible. His legs should be extended and relaxed. The beginner can do the back glide by pushing backward with his feet from the squatting position. To stand up, he pulls his knees up, moves his hands forward, and bends his head down.

**Kicking** is the next step in learning to swim. The student can practice kicking by first holding onto the side of a pool or by floating in shallow water with his hands on the bottom. He thrashes his legs up and down in whiplike movements. The legs should be moved only far enough to feel the knees pass each other. The knees should bend slightly, and the ankles should be relaxed with the feet *pigeon-toed*, or turned in. The power in the kick comes from the hips.

After the beginner masters the kick, he should combine it with the prone glide to propel himself through the water. He should also practice a similar kick on his back, and combine it with the back glide.

**The Arm Stroke.** After learning to float and kick, the beginner is ready for the *dog paddle* or *human stroke*. The student does this stroke from the prone glide and moves his arms in much the same way that a dog moves its legs in swimming. He reaches forward first with one arm and then the other, and presses each arm in turn straight down and back until it points downward from his shoulder. One arm should be going forward while the other is going down and back. The hands should be relaxed, with the fingers slightly separated. The beginner can get the feel of this arm stroke by walking bent over while stroking under water. Finally, he combines the arm stroke with the prone glide and kick.

**The American Crawl** is the fastest stroke. It combines a hand-over-hand arm stroke with a flutter kick, the feet lashing upward and backward. All breathing is done on the same side.

**The Breast Stroke** is one of the most restful strokes. Extend the arms forward, then sweep them out and back, drawing up the legs, knees out. Sweep legs together as arms go forward again.

## AMERICAN CRAWL

## BREAST STROKE

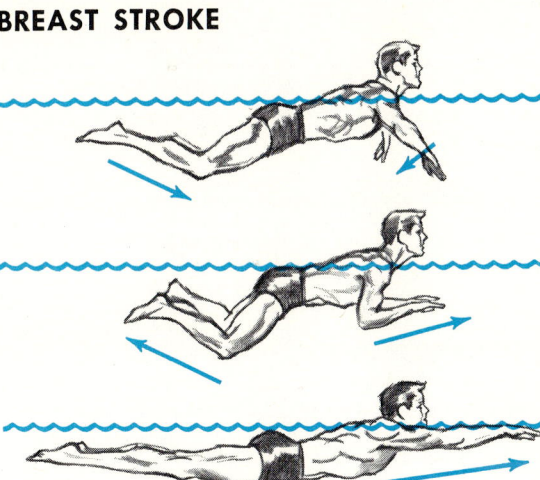

**The Butterfly** is a racing stroke. Lift both arms from the water, then lash them down and back to the waist. Use a *dolphin kick*, flutter-kicking both legs up and down at the same time.

## BUTTERFLY

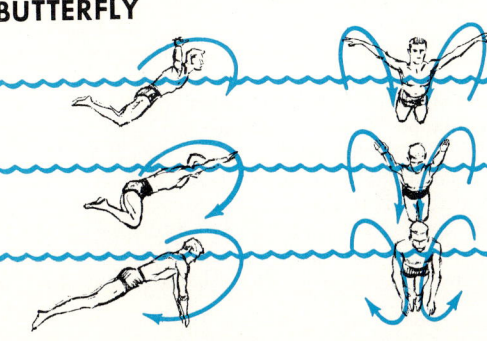

## BACKSTROKE

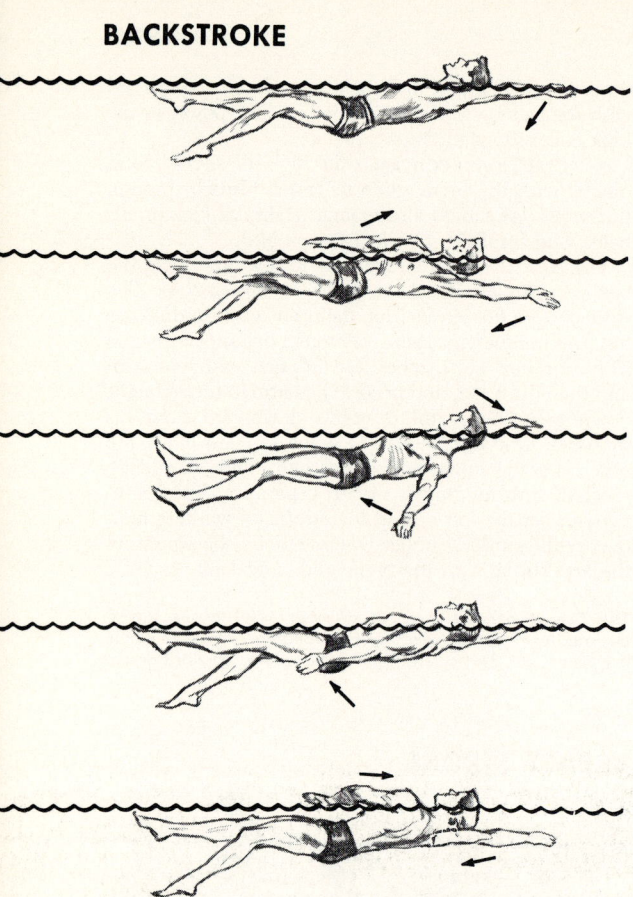

**The Backstroke** is much like the crawl turned upside down. The swimmer uses a flutter kick, and alternately stretches each arm straight back, then pulls it in a straight line to his hips.

**Rhythmic Breathing** must be learned to complete the dog paddle. This can be practiced by standing in chest-deep water or by kneeling in shallow water. The beginner starts the dog-paddle arm stroke, then takes a deep breath and puts his face in the water. He breathes out into the water through his mouth and nose as his left hand slides forward. Then he turns his face out of the water to the left side and breathes in through his mouth as his right hand slides forward. Some persons find it easier to turn the head to the right and inhale as the left hand slides forward.

After the student has learned to coordinate his arm strokes and breathing, he is ready to try the complete dog paddle. First, he does the prone glide and kick. Next, he adds the arm stroke, and then he starts rhythmic breathing. When the beginner can swim 25 yards with the dog paddle, he has a good foundation for learning the standard swimming strokes.

**Swimming Strokes.** There are five basic swimming strokes: (1) the American crawl, or free style; (2) the breast stroke; (3) the butterfly stroke; (4) the backstroke; and (5) the side stroke.

*The American Crawl*, or *Free Style*, is the fastest stroke. It combines a *flutter kick*, each foot lashing backward and upward, with a hand-over-hand arm stroke and rhythmic breathing. The American crawl developed from a racing stroke introduced about 1900 by Richard Cavill, an Australian swimmer.

*The Breast Stroke* is one of the most restful strokes. The swimmer extends his arms, then sweeps them out and back so that the palms press against the water. He draws up his legs with the knees thrust sideways. Then he pushes his legs out and sweeps them together as he extends his arms forward again. Swimmers have used the breast stroke since at least the 1500's.

*The Butterfly Stroke* is a racing stroke. The swimmer lifts both arms forward out of the water, then lashes them back toward his waist. Many swimmers use a *dolphin kick* with the butterfly. This is a double flutter kick. Both legs are whipped up and down together. The regular breast-stroke kick is also used. Jack Sieg, a University of Iowa swimmer, developed the butterfly stroke in 1935.

*The Backstroke* is much like the crawl turned upside down. It combines a flutter kick with a hand-over-hand arm stroke. This stroke originated as a stunt stroke about 1902.

*The Side Stroke* is a restful stroke and is not used for racing. The swimmer does a scissors kick. He floats on one side, draws up his upper leg, thrusts it forward and out, then snaps his legs together. As the swimmer snaps his legs together, he extends his lower hand forward from his chin and pulls his upper hand straight back from his chin. The side stroke probably developed from the breast stroke.

*Other Important Strokes* include (1) the trudgen crawl, and (2) the victory backstroke.

The *trudgen crawl* is a regular crawl with a scissors kick added at regular intervals. J. Arthur Trudgen, an amateur English swimmer, introduced this crawl in 1873. Trudgen learned the stroke from Indians in South America.

The *victory backstroke* is much like the regular breast stroke turned upside down. But the swimmer moves his

**The Side Stroke** uses the scissors kick. Draw up the upper leg and thrust it out. Move the hands to the chin. Snap the legs together, and pull back the upper arm and extend the lower arm.

## SIDE STROKE

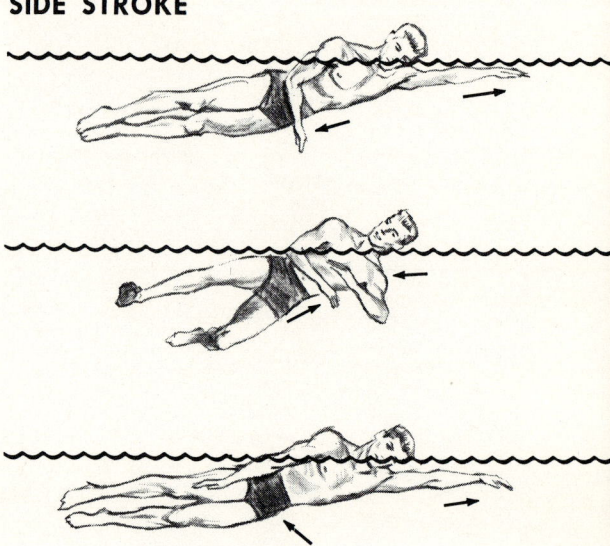

832

# SWIMMING

arms and legs at the same time, rather than alternately as in the breast stroke. This stroke always keeps the swimmer's face out of the water. It received its name because it was taught to United States servicemen during World War II.

## Swimming as a Sport

**Swimming Meets.** The Amateur Athletic Union (AAU) establishes the rules for swimming meets in the United States. It recognizes records for races ranging from 50 yards to 4 miles, and from 100 to 1,500 meters. Free-style (crawl) races are held at all these distances. (A *free-style race* can also be a contest in which the swimmers use any stroke or strokes they desire.) Backstroke, breast stroke, butterfly, relay, and medley races cover only certain distances. In an *individual medley* race, each swimmer must use three or four different strokes—butterfly, backstroke, breast stroke, and crawl. The breast stroke is used only in four-stroke relay races. In a *medley-relay* race, each member of the four-man relay team swims a different stroke. See AMATEUR ATHLETIC UNION OF THE UNITED STATES.

In Canada, the Canadian Amateur Swimming Association establishes the rules for swimming meets. The International Amateur Swimming Federation sets the rules for recognizing world swimming records. See *World Swimming Records* table with this article. For Olympic swimming records, see OLYMPIC GAMES (table: Swimming).

**Water Ballet,** or *synchronized swimming*, is especially popular with women. One or more swimmers glide through graceful formations, often accompanied by music. The swimmers "dance" in water much as ballerinas dance on a stage. They often perform the same strokes and formations at the same time. Many high schools and colleges in the United States and Canada have water-ballet groups. Judges of ballet contests award points under a scoring system similar to that used in diving (see DIVING [Competitive Diving]).

## Famous Swimmers

**Chadwick, Florence** (1918-    ), became the first woman to swim the 19-mile English Channel in both directions. She swam from France to Great Britain in 1950, and from Britain to France in 1951. In 1952, she became the first woman to swim the 21 miles from Catalina Island to the mainland of California. Miss Chadwick also conquered the Strait of Gibraltar, the Bosporus, and the Dardanelles. She was born in San Diego, Calif.

**Crabbe, "Buster," Clarence** (1908-    ), won fame as a world-champion swimmer and motion-picture and television star. Crabbe won the 400-meter free-style race in the 1932 Olympic Games. He was the first Olympic champion to swim this race in less than five minutes. Crabbe set five world records during his swimming career. He was born in Oakland, Calif.

**Ederle, Gertrude,** was the first woman to swim the English Channel. See EDERLE, GERTRUDE CAROLINE.

**Geraghty, Agnes** (1907-    ), ranked as one of the greatest woman breast-stroke swimmers in the United States during the 1920's. Miss Geraghty held the 200-yard indoor breast-stroke title in 1924 and 1925, and the 100-yard indoor breast-stroke crown in 1926 and 1927. She was born in New York City.

**Holm, Eleanor** (1913-    ), won fame as a backstroke swimmer in the 1930's. She held 12 national titles and won the 100-meter backstroke race in the 1932 Olympics. She was born in Brooklyn, N.Y.

**Kahanamoku, Duke** (1890-1968), was one of the early great crawl swimmers in the United States. Kahanamoku, who was born in Honolulu, Hawaii, held the 100-yard record from 1913 to 1921.

**Kiefer, Adolph** (1918-    ), ranked as one of the world's all-time great backstroke swimmers. He broke a world swimming record for the first time at the age of 15, and held every world backstroke record for more than 10 years. He was born in Chicago.

**Kiphuth, Robert J. H.** (1890-1967), was one of the most successful swimming coaches in the United States. During a 40-year career as swimming coach at Yale University, his teams won more than 500 meets and lost only 12 from 1918 to 1958. Kiphuth was born in Tonawanda, N.Y.

**McIver, Helene Madison** (1913-    ), reigned as the

*Swimming Pool Age*

**Swimming Races** furnish exciting tests of the skill and endurance of accomplished swimmers. As a race starts, above, the contestants plunge forward from short platforms in flat racing-dives. Ropes divide the pool into lanes, one for each of the swimmers.

833

## WORLD SWIMMING RECORDS

| Distance | Time | Holder | Nation | Year | Time | Holder | Nation | Year |
|---|---|---|---|---|---|---|---|---|
| **MEN'S FREE STYLE** ||||| **WOMEN'S FREE STYLE** ||||
| 100 Meters | *52.9s. | Alain Gottvalles | France | 1964 | 58.9s. | Dawn Fraser | Australia | 1964 |
| 110 Yards | 52.6s. | Ken Walsh | U.S. | 1967 | 59.5s. | Dawn Fraser | Australia | 1962 |
| 200 Meters | 1m. 55.7s. | Don Schollander | U.S. | 1967 | 2m. 09.7s. | Pam Kruse | U.S. | 1967 |
| 220 Meters | 1m. 57.0s. | Don Schollander | U.S. | 1966 | 2m. 11.6s. | Dawn Fraser | Australia | 1960 |
| 400 Meters | 4m. 08.2s. | Greg Charlton | U.S. | 1967 | 4m. 29.0s. | Debbie Meyer | U.S. | 1967 |
| 440 Yards | 4m. 12.2s. | Greg Charlton | U.S. | 1966 | 4m. 38.8s. | Kathy Wainwright | Australia | 1966 |
| 800 Meters | 8m. 42.0s. | Francis Luyce | France | 1967 | 9m. 22.9s. | Debbie Meyer | U.S. | 1967 |
| 880 Yards | 8m. 55.5s. | Murray Rose | Australia | 1964 | 9m. 44.1s. | Debbie Meyer | U.S. | 1967 |
| 1,500 Meters | 16m. 34.1s. | Michael Burton | U.S. | 1967 | 17m. 50.2s. | Debbie Meyer | U.S. | 1967 |
| 1,650 Yards | 17m. 11.0s. | Jon Konrads | Australia | 1960 | *18m. 51.1s. | Patricia Caretto | U.S. | 1965 |
| **MEN'S BREAST STROKE** ||||| **WOMEN'S BREAST STROKE** ||||
| 100 Meters | 1m. 06.7s. | Vladimir Kosinsky | Russia | 1967 | 1m. 14.6s. | Catie Ball | U.S. | 1967 |
| 110 Yards | 1m. 08.2s. | Ian O'Brien | Australia | 1966 | 1m. 17.0s. | Catie Ball | U.S. | 1967 |
| 200 Meters | 2m. 27.8s. | Ian O'Brien | Australia | 1964 | 2m. 39.5s. | Catie Ball | U.S. | 1967 |
| 220 Yards | 2m. 28.0s. | Ian O'Brien | Australia | 1966 | 2m. 46.9s. | Catie Ball | U.S. | 1967 |
| **MEN'S BUTTERFLY STROKE** ||||| **WOMEN'S BUTTERFLY STROKE** ||||
| 100 Meters | 55.7s. | Mark Spitz | U.S. | 1967 | 1m. 04.5s. | Ada Kok | Neth. | 1965 |
| 110 Yards | 56.3s. | Mark Spitz | U.S. | 1967 | 1m. 05.1s. | Ada Kok | Neth. | 1964 |
| 200 Meters | 2m. 05.7s. | Mark Spitz | U.S. | 1967 | 2m. 21.0s. | Ada Kok | Neth. | 1967 |
| 220 Yards | 2m. 08.4s. | Kevin Berry | Australia | 1963 | 2m. 21.0s. | Ada Kok | Neth. | 1967 |
| **MEN'S BACKSTROKE** ||||| **WOMEN'S BACKSTROKE** ||||
| 100 Meters | 58.4s. | Roland Matthes | E. Germany | 1967 | 1m. 07.1s. | Elaine Tanner | Canada | 1967 |
| 110 Yards | 1m. 00.1s. | Roland Matthes | E. Germany | 1967 | 1m. 07.5s. | Karen Muir | South Africa | 1967 |
| 200 Meters | 2m. 07.9s. | Roland Matthes | E. Germany | 1967 | 2m. 20.4s. | Elaine Tanner | Canada | 1967 |
| 220 Yards | 2m. 12.0s. | Peter Reynolds | Australia | 1966 | 2m. 27.7s. | Karen Muir | South Africa | 1967 |
| **MEN'S INDIVIDUAL MEDLEY** ||||| **WOMEN'S INDIVIDUAL MEDLEY** ||||
| 200 Meters | 2m. 11.3s. | Greg Buckingham | U.S. | 1967 | 2m. 25.0s. | Claudia Kolb | U.S. | 1967 |
| 400 Meters | 4m. 45.4s. | Dick Roth | U.S. | 1964 | 5m. 08.2s. | Claudia Kolb | U.S. | 1967 |
| 440 Yards | 4m. 50.8s. | Peter Reynolds | Australia | 1966 | 5m. 25.1s. | Mary-Ellen Oleese | U.S. | 1965 |
| **MEN'S MEDLEY RELAYS** ||||| **WOMEN'S MEDLEY RELAYS** ||||
| 400 Meters | 3m. 56.5s. | R. Matthes, E. Henninger, H. Gregor, F. Wiegand | E. Germany | 1967 | 4m. 30.0s. | K. Moore, C. Ball, E. Daniel, W. Fordyce | U.S. | 1967 |
| 440 Yards | 4m. 03.2s. | P. Reynolds, I. O'Brien, M. Dunn, M. Wenden | Australia | 1966 | 4m. 37.4s. | P. Watson, C. Ball, E. Daniel, J. Barkman | U.S. | 1967 |
| **MEN'S FREE-STYLE RELAYS** ||||| **WOMEN'S FREE-STYLE RELAYS** ||||
| 400 Meters | 3m. 32.6s. | K. Walsh, D. Havens, G. Charlton, Z. Zorn | U.S. | 1967 | 4m. 03.5s. | L. Gustavson, N. Ryan, L. Fritz, P. Watson | U.S. | 1967 |
| 440 Yards | 3m. 35.6s. | G. Ilman, M. Wall, M. Spitz, D. Schollander | U.S. | 1967 | 4m. 10.8s. | E. Tanner, J. Hughes, L. Kennedy, M. Lay | Canada | 1966 |
| 800 Meters | 7m. 52.1s. | S. Clark, R. Saari, G. Ilman, D. Schollander | U.S. | 1964 | 9m. 00.1s. | P. Caretto, D. Pfeiffer, M. Campbell, J. Hallock | U.S. | 1965 |
| 880 Yards | 7m. 59.5s. | M. Wenden, P. Reynolds, D. Dickson, R. Windle | Australia | 1966 | | (No Women's Race) | | |

Source: International Amateur Swimming Federation. The federation recognizes only records set in 50-meter or 55-yard pools.     *Record later tied.

top woman swimming star of the early 1930's. In 1932, she held 15 of a possible 16 world free-style records for women. She was born in South Bend, Wash.

**Weissmuller, "Johnny," John** (1904-    ), set more than 50 American and world swimming records during the 1920's. He broke the 100-yard free-style mark five times between 1922 and 1927. In the 1930's, Weissmuller achieved fame in the motion-picture role of *Tarzan*. He was born in Windber, Pa.

### Water Safety

Safety in the water depends on many skills. These include a knowledge of basic water-safety rules, the ability to swim, and training in lifesaving. Every year, about 6,500 persons drown in the United States and about 1,000 in Canada. Many accidents of this sort would not happen if more people knew how to swim and how to behave in or near the water.

**Water-Safety Rules.** Many water accidents could be avoided if everyone followed these simple rules:

Learn to swim.
Swim only in areas protected by lifeguards.
Swim with someone who can help in an emergency.
Never jump into strange waters. Always check for depth and look for underwater obstacles.
Never leave a small child alone in or near the water.
Always swim parallel to and close to the shore.
Do not swim in or near areas where people are diving.
Enter cold water gradually.
Do not swim for at least one hour after eating.
Do not enter water during storms.
Obey rules posted at beaches and pools.

# SWIMMING

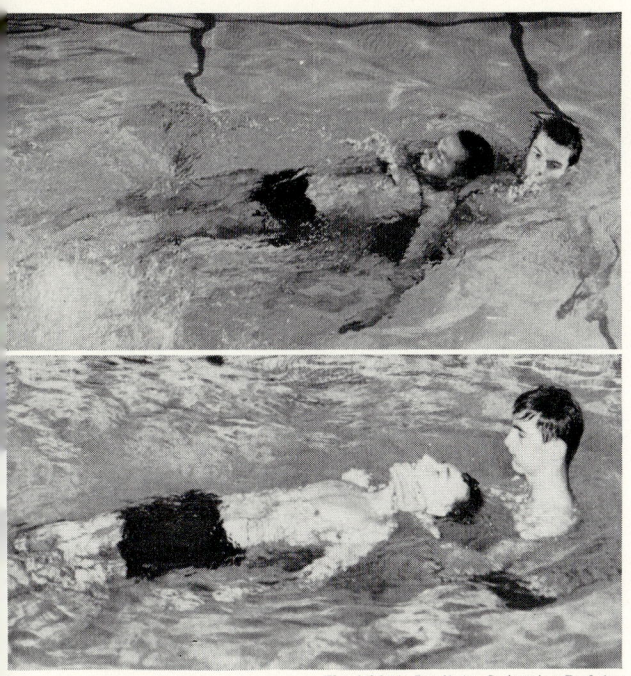

The Athletic Institute; *Swimming Pool Age*

**Lifesaving Strokes** include the *cross-chest carry, top,* and the *head carry, bottom.* In the cross-chest carry, the rescuer clamps an arm across the victim's chest and does a side stroke. In the head carry, the rescuer grips the victim's head in his hands, tilting it upward. He then swims backward in a sitting position and uses either a scissors kick or the regular breast-stroke kick.

**Lifesaving.** To earn a Red Cross Lifesaving badge, a swimmer must be able to use all the basic swimming strokes. He must also know a variety of skills, including swimming rescues, nonswimming rescues, and how to apply artificial respiration. Young persons from 12 to 15 years old can earn Red Cross Junior Lifesaving badges. Those 16 years old or older can earn Senior Lifesaving badges.

Only trained lifesavers should attempt a swimming rescue. Even a trained lifesaver should never make a swimming rescue if a safer method can be used. For example, the rescuer, without going into the water, may be able to extend an arm, leg, branch, towel, oar, or fishing rod to a drowning victim. But all lifesavers must know how to make swimming rescues. Two of the most widely used lifesaving strokes are the cross-chest carry and the head carry. The *cross-chest carry* can be used if the victim becomes violent with fear. The rescuer reaches across the victim's shoulder from behind, grasps him across the chest with one arm, and swims to shore with a modified sidestroke. The *head carry* might be used in rough water or after the victim has calmed down. The rescuer grips the victim's head in his hands and swims backward in a half-sitting position. This carry allows the rescuer to keep both his head and the victim's head above water. For descriptions of these strokes, see the pictures with this article.

The Water Safety Service of the American Red Cross offers educational programs in all phases of water safety. Other organizations with water-safety programs include high schools, colleges, the YMCA, the YWCA, the

*Swimming Pool Age*

**Water Ballet,** or *synchronized swimming,* has become a popular sport in the United States and Canada, especially for girls. The swimmers glide through graceful formations, often to music. Judges grade the swimmers in solo, duet, and team performances.

835

# SWIMMING POOL

*Swimming Pool Age; Parade;* Thomas Airviews, Bayside, N.Y.

**Outdoor Swimming Pools** afford hours of enjoyment on hot summer days. Huge public pools, *above,* are usually located in parks and can accommodate hundreds of swimmers. Smaller backyard pools designed for family groups have become increasingly popular in the United States. These range from small, portable pools erected above the ground, *lower left,* to larger, tile pools with fancy shapes, *upper left.* Many schools and recreational agencies also have indoor pools for year-round swimming.

Boy Scouts and Girl Scouts, and the Boys' Clubs of America. ADOLPH KIEFER

**Related Articles** in WORLD BOOK include:

| | |
|---|---|
| Artificial Respiration | Olympic Games |
| Baths and Bathing | Safety (Water Safety) |
| (Modern Public Baths) | Skin Diving |
| Diving | Swimming Pool |
| Drowning | Undertow |
| Life Jacket | Water Polo |

### Outline
I. **How to Swim**
  A. Entering the Water
  B. Floating
  C. Kicking
  D. The Arm Stroke
  E. Rhythmic Breathing
  F. Swimming Strokes
II. **Swimming as a Sport**
  A. Swimming Meets
  B. Water Ballet
III. **Famous Swimmers**
IV. **Water Safety**
  A. Water-Safety Rules
  B. Lifesaving

### Questions

What are the five basic swimming strokes?
What are seven water-safety rules?
What are two widely used lifesaving strokes?
What is the *jellyfish float?*
What kind of float starts from a squatting position?
When might a lifeguard use the *cross-chest carry?*
Who was the first woman to swim the English Channel in both directions?
About how many persons drown in the United States every year? How many in Canada?
What is an advantage of the *victory backstroke?*
What is a *medley swimming race?*

**SWIMMING POOL.** From ancient Greece to modern times, the swimming pool has played an important part in man's culture and society. Swimming pools were common throughout the Roman Empire. Many Roman cities had public "baths," or pools. Their indoor pools were heated by wood-burning furnaces under the floor.

Today, hundreds of cities and towns throughout the United States and Canada operate public pools for the benefit of their citizens. Many private clubs have recreational pools. The private family pool has become the center of family social life in thousands of communities. Family pools, usually lined with concrete, may be built in almost any shape to fit the terrain. But for championship swimming meets, the rules of the Amateur Athletic Union (AAU) of the United States specify that "the end walls of the pool shall be parallel and vertical, and so constructed that the competitors can push off in turning with the hands or feet."

For indoor competitive swimming pools, the AAU rules recommend a length of 75 feet and a width of 42 feet, to permit six lanes, each 7 feet in width. The pool should be at least 4 feet deep at the shallow end, and at least 10 feet deep at the diving end.

For outdoor competitive swimming pools, the AAU rules recommend a length of 50 meters (about 55 yards), and a width of 75 feet. The pool should be at least 4 feet deep at the shallow end. The diving end should be at least 10 feet deep for springboard diving and 14 feet 3 inches deep for platform diving. ESTHER WILLIAMS

**SWINBURNE, ALGERNON CHARLES** (1837-1909), was an English poet of the late Victorian period. Unconventional in his views and personal life, he said he wrote against an age that "has room only for such as are content to write for children and girls." His play, *Atalanta in Calydon*, shocked the people of his time by its implicit rejection of Christianity. In his *Poems and Ballads* (1866), Swinburne shocked them by his attitude toward morality.

Publication of his work *Atalanta in Calydon* in 1865 brought fame to the English poet. His *Poems and Ballads* appeared the next year. Then followed various works that showed Swinburne's love of liberty and hatred of oppression. He also wrote many fine lyrics which reveal his great gift for making music of words. His verse is described as a series of melodies. He imitated the rhythms of Greek poetry. He shared some of the views of the Pre-Raphaelites, a group of artists and writers who favored a return to the art forms used before the time of the Italian Renaissance artist Raphael.

Swinburne was born in London, and was educated at Eton College and Oxford University. He left Oxford without a degree and settled in London in 1861, amidst the Pre-Raphaelites. Dissipation undermined his health, and for the last 30 years of his life, he lived quietly at Putney. C. L. CLINE

**SWINE.** See HOG (Hog Terms).

**SWING**, in music. See DANCING (The 1900's); JAZZ (The Swing Era); POPULAR MUSIC.

**SWISS** is a fine, sheer cotton cloth that was first made in Switzerland. The fabric may be plain, figured, or may have woven or paste dots. Swiss may be processed to remain crisp and stiff after washing. It is used in making dresses, aprons, and curtains. It comes in widths of 28, 32, and 36 inches for dresses and aprons. Curtain swiss comes in 36-inch to 40-inch widths. Wider widths are also available for bedspreads. K. R. FOX

**SWISS CHARD** is a garden vegetable plant. Its leaves are eaten as greens. Swiss chard is related to the common beet plant. It resembles the beet, except that it does not have a large fleshy root. Swiss chard has a small woody root which cannot be eaten. The vegetable has fleshy leaf-stems, large leaves, and a dark green color. Some varieties of Swiss chard have pale yellow leaves and others have bright red leaves and leaf-stems. The plant has attractive, brilliant colors.

Swiss chard is one of the few garden greens that grow constantly throughout the summer. The seeds are sown in the spring. The large outer leaves are harvested as soon as they develop. Later the inner leaves are taken, and the harvest continues until frost kills the plant.

People grew Swiss chard as long ago as 350 B.C. It is a favorite crop in Switzerland and was introduced in the United States in 1806. Massachusetts is one of the leading states in growing Swiss chard.

Swiss chard is an excellent source of vitamin A and contains a fair amount of vitamins of the B complex and C. Like most leafy vegetables, Swiss chard is also rich in minerals.

**Scientific Classification.** Swiss chard belongs to the goosefoot family, *Chenopodiaceae*. It is genus *Beta*, species *B. vulgaris*, variety *cicla*. ERVIN L. DENISEN

See also PLANT (color picture: Vegetables Unknown to Our Forefathers).

**Large, Shiny Leaves of Swiss Chard** have an attractive appearance in the garden. The plant is hardy and nutritious. USDA

**SWISS FAMILY ROBINSON.** See WYSS (family).

**SWISS GUARDS.** This famous body of Swiss soldiers grew out of a group of 250 Swiss who were picked to guard the pope in the late 1400's. In the early 1500's, Pope Julius II secured the position of the Swiss Guards by a treaty with the Swiss cantons of Zurich and Lucerne. According to the terms of the agreement, the cantons supplied 250 men to serve as a bodyguard for the pope from that time on. Since then the pope has always had a body of Swiss Guards around him at the Vatican. But through the years, the number of guards has been reduced and their type of service changed. Today, they are called the Papal Swiss Guard.

Another body of Swiss soldiers, called Swiss Guards, or Switzers, was organized in 1616 to protect King Louis XIII of France. These soldiers served France for 175 years. On August 10, 1792, during the French Revolution, most of them were killed while defending the royal palace in Paris from attack by an angry mob.

The memory of these Swiss Guards is preserved in the famous "Lion of Lucerne," which is carved in the face of a rock at Lucerne, Switzerland. It bears the words, "To the Fidelity and Courage of the Helvetians." See THORVALDSEN, BERTEL (picture).

King Louis XVIII formed a second corps of Swiss Guards in 1815. They were defeated in the Revolution of 1830, and the corps disbanded. THOMAS E. GRIESS

**SWITCH, ELECTRIC.** See ELECTRIC SWITCH.

**SWITCHBOARD.** See TELEPHONE.

**SWITHIN,** or **SWITHUN, SAINT,** was a bishop of Winchester, England. He was a faithful adviser to Egbert and Ethelwulf, kings of the West Saxons. Swithin died in 862 and was canonized in the 900's. St. Swithin's Day is July 15. According to an old rhyme, if the weather is fair that day, it will be fair for the next 40 days. If it rains on July 15, it will rain each day for the following 40 days. FULTON J. SHEEN

See also SAINT SWITHIN'S DAY.

# SWITZERLAND / The Land

Switzerland has three main land regions: (1) the Jura Mountains, (2) the Swiss Plateau, and (3) the Swiss Alps. The two mountain regions make up about 70 per cent of Switzerland's area. But the plateau between them has about two-thirds of the country's population.

**The Jura Mountains** consist of a series of parallel ridges that are separated by narrow valleys. These ridges extend along Switzerland's western border with France. Within Switzerland, the highest mountain of the range is 5,518-foot Mont Tendre. The Jura Mountains are the home of Switzerland's important watch-making industry. Other industries in the region include dairy farming and lumbering. See JURA.

**The Swiss Plateau** is a hilly region with rolling plains. It lies from 1,200 to 2,200 feet above sea level. The movement of ancient glaciers formed many lakes, including Lake Constance and Lake Geneva. Switzerland's richest croplands and grazing lands are in this region, as well as most of the large cities and manufacturing industries. See LAKE CONSTANCE; LAKE GENEVA.

**The Swiss Alps** are part of the mighty Alps, the

## SWITZERLAND MAP INDEX

### Cantons†

| | | |
|---|---|---|
| AARGAU (ARGOVIE) | 409,000 | A 4 |
| APPENZELL Ausser Rhoden‡ | 63,900 | A 5 |
| Inner Rhoden‡ | 13,400 | |
| BASEL (BÂLE) | 422,200 | A 3 |
| Basel-Landt‡ | 188,800 | |
| Basel-Stadt‡ | 233,400 | |
| BERN (BERNE) | 980,000 | B 3 |
| FRIBOURG (FREIBURG) | 170,000 | B 3 |
| GENÈVE (GE-NEVA) | 309,600 | A 2 |
| GLARUS (GLARIS) | 41,500 | A 5 |
| GRAUBÜNDEN (GRISONS) | 145,000 | B 5 |
| LUZERN (LUCERNE) | 278,000 | A 4 |
| NEUCHÂTEL (NEUENBURG) | 164,000 | B 2 |
| ST. GALLEN (ST. GALL) | 369,000 | A 5 |
| SCHAFFHOUSEN (SCHAFFHOUSE)‡ | 72,000 | A 4 |
| SCHWYZ | 84,000 | A 4 |
| SOLOTHURN (SOLEURE) | 223,000 | A 3 |
| THURGAU (THURGOVIE) | 185,000 | A 5 |
| TICINO (TESSIN) | 230,000 | B 4 |
| UNTERWALDEN Nidwalden‡ | 24,200 | |
| Obwalden‡ | 24,700 | |
| URI | 33,000 | B 4 |
| VALAIS (WALLIS) | 185,000 | B 3 |
| VAUD (WAADT) | 493,000 | B 2 |
| ZUG (ZOUG) | 63,900 | A 4 |
| ZÜRICH | 1,066,000 | A 4 |

### Cities and Towns

| | | |
|---|---|---|
| Aarau | 17,500 | |
| Aarburg* | *49,200 | A 4 |
| Adliswil | 5,303 | A 3 |
| Altdorf | 13,700 | A 4 |
| Altstätten | 16,300 | A 5 |
| Amriswil | 7,477 | B 4 |
| Appenzell | 8,751 | A 5 |
| Arbon | 6,752 | A 5 |
| Arlesheim* | *5,082 | A 3 |
| Arosa | 13,100 | |
| Baar | 2,600 | A 4 |
| Baden | 15,000 | A 3 |
| Balsthal | *6,200 | A 3 |
| Basel | 212,100 | A 2 |
| Bellinzona | *358,700 | B 4 |
| Biberist | *27,200 | A 3 |
| Biel | *254,900 | A 3 |
| Binningen | 7,188 | A 3 |
| Birsfelden | 66,800 | |
| Bolligen | 49,800 | A 3 |
| Brugg | 13,100 | A 3 |
| Buchs | 23,200 | A 4 |
| Buchs* | 6,683 | A 5 |
| Bülach | 6,345 | A 4 |
| Bulle | 5,734 | B 3 |
| Burgdorf | 10,600 | A 4 |
| Carouge | 5,983 | B 2 |
| Cham | 16,000 | A 3 |
| Chêne-Bougeries | 14,000 | B 2 |
| | 5,232 | B 2 |
| Chiasso | 5,027 | C 4 |
| Chur | 7,377 | B 5 |
| Davos | 29,600 | B 5 |
| Delémont | 11,400 | A 3 |
| Dietikon | 21,300 | A 4 |
| Dübendorf | 17,500 | A 4 |
| Einsiedeln | 8,792 | A 4 |
| Emmen | 21,800 | A 4 |
| Flawil | 7,256 | A 5 |
| Frauenfeld | 17,100 | A 4 |
| Freienbach* | 5,520 | A 4 |
| Fribourg | 40,000 | B 3 |
| Frutigen | 5,565 | B 3 |
| Geneva (Genève) | 170,500 | |
| | *301,000 | B 2 |
| Glarus | 5,232 | A 5 |
| Goldach | 6,400 | A 5 |
| Gossau | 16,400 | A 5 |
| Grenchen | 20,300 | A 3 |
| Henau | *24,100 | A 5 |
| Herisau | 7,828 | A 5 |
| Horgen | 15,400 | A 4 |
| Horw* | 7,638 | A 4 |
| Illnau | 6,160 | A 4 |
| Ingenbohl* | 5,046 | A 4 |
| Interlaken | *4,738 | B 3 |
| Jona* | 5,686 | A 4 |
| Kilchberg | 6,784 | A 4 |
| Kirchberg | 5,554 | A 3 |
| Kloten | 15,600 | A 4 |
| Kreuzlingen | 15,000 | A 5 |
| Küsnacht | 31,500 | A 4 |
| Küsnacht am Rigi | 12,400 | A 4 |
| | 6,287 | A 4 |
| La Chaux-de-Fonds | 43,100 | A 2 |
| Lancy | 18,300 | B 2 |
| Langenthal | 12,700 | B 3 |
| Langnau im Emmental | 9,201 | B 3 |
| La Tour-de-Peilz | 6,820 | B 2 |
| Lausanne | 136,600 | |
| | *210,800 | B 2 |
| Le Chenit | 15,242 | B 2 |
| Le Locle | 14,442 | A 2 |
| Lenzburg* | 6,378 | A 3 |
| Liestal | 11,200 | A 3 |
| Littau | 12,100 | A 4 |
| Locarno | 13,200 | B 4 |
| Lucerne (Luzern) | 73,700 | |
| | *146,700 | A 4 |
| Lugano | 22,200 | |
| | *53,900 | B 4 |
| Lyss | 5,616 | A 3 |
| Männedorf | 6,192 | A 4 |
| Martigny | 8,203 | B 3 |
| Meilen | 5,254 | A 4 |
| Mels | 5,109 | A 5 |
| Mendrisio | 12,300 | C 4 |
| Meyrin | 6,834 | B 2 |
| Monthey | 19,900 | B 3 |
| Montreux | 20,800 | |
| | *11,200 | B 2 |
| Morges | 7,472 | B 2 |
| Moutier | 14,000 | A 3 |
| Münchenstein | 6,483 | A 3 |
| Münsingen | 11,600 | A 3 |
| Muri bei Bern | 6,051 | B 3 |
| Muttenz | 7,855 | A 3 |
| Neuchâtel | 14,600 | |
| | 36,600 | |
| Neuhausen am Rheinfall* | 53,600 | B 3 |
| Nyon | 12,100 | B 4 |
| Oberriet | 10,800 | B 2 |
| Oftringen | 7,731 | A 5 |
| Olten | 21,100 | A 4 |
| Onex* | *47,600 | A 3 |
| Opfikon* | 7,749 | B 2 |
| Payerne | 6,024 | A 4 |
| Pfäffikon | 7,095 | B 3 |
| Pratteln | 12,500 | A 4 |
| Prilly | 12,300 | A 3 |
| Pully | 15,700 | B 2 |
| Rapperswil | 7,585 | B 2 |
| Reinach | 15,504 | A 4 |
| Renens | 16,200 | A 3 |
| Rheinfelden | 5,197 | B 2 |
| Richterswil | 5,842 | A 3 |
| Riehen | 20,300 | A 4 |
| Romanshorn | 7,755 | A 3 |
| Rorschach | 12,500 | A 5 |
| Rothrist* | *24,400 | A 5 |
| Rüti | 8,282 | A 4 |
| Saanen | 5,048 | B 3 |
| St. Gall | 78,200 | |
| | *146,500 | A 5 |
| St. Imier | 6,704 | A 3 |
| St. Moritz | 3,751 | B 5 |
| Ste. Croix | 6,925 | B 2 |
| Sarnen | 6,554 | B 4 |
| Schaffhausen | 38,200 | |
| | *58,500 | A 4 |
| Schlieren | 10,900 | A 4 |
| Schwyz | 12,200 | A 4 |
| Sierre | 11,200 | B 3 |
| Sion | 20,000 | B 3 |
| Solothurn | 18,900 | |
| | *36,900 | A 3 |
| Spiez | 8,168 | B 3 |
| Stäfa | 6,947 | A 4 |
| Steffisburg | 12,200 | B 3 |
| Suhr | 5,525 | A 3 |
| Sumiswald | 5,324 | A 3 |
| Teufen | 13,000 | A 5 |
| Thalwil | 13,000 | A 4 |
| Thun | 34,700 | |
| | *58,100 | B 3 |
| Tramelan | 5,567 | A 3 |
| Trimbach | 5,784 | A 3 |
| Uster | 21,100 | |
| | *30,400 | A 4 |
| Vernier | 17,000 | B 2 |
| Vevey | 30,400 | A 4 |
| Wädenswil | 14,600 | A 4 |
| Wald | 7,778 | A 4 |
| Walli-sellen* | 10,200 | A 4 |
| Wattwil | 7,480 | A 5 |
| Weinfelden | 6,954 | A 4 |
| Wettingen | 20,000 | A 4 |
| Wetzikon | 13,600 | A 4 |
| Wil | 6,398 | A 5 |
| Windisch* | 5,377 | |
| Winterthur | 91,000 | |
| | *103,100 | A 4 |
| Wohlen | 11,000 | A 4 |
| Worb* | 19,985 | B 3 |
| Yverdon | 8,779 | B 2 |
| Zofingen | 6,323 | A 3 |
| Zollikofen | 12,400 | A 3 |
| Zollikon | 22,500 | A 4 |
| Zuchwil | *663,900 | A 3 |
| Zug | | |
| Zurich | | |

### Physical Features

| | | |
|---|---|---|
| Aare River | | A 3 |
| Bernese Alps (Mts.) | | B 3 |
| Bernina Pass | | B 6 |
| Birs River | | A 3 |
| Bodensee, Lake Constance | | A 5 |
| Broye River | | B 2 |
| Chasseral (Mtn.) | | A 3 |
| Dent du Midi (Mtn.) | | B 3 |
| Diablerets (Mtn.) | | B 3 |
| Dom (Mtn.) | | B 3 |
| Doubs River | | A 2 |
| Dufourspitze, see Monte Rosa | | |
| Engadine (region)* | | B 5 |
| Finsteraarhorn | | B 4 |
| Furka Pass | | B 4 |
| Glärnisch (Mtn.) | | B 4 |
| Grand Combin | | C 3 |
| Grand Dixence | | B 3 |
| Great Saint Bernard Pass | | C 3 |
| Great Saint Bernard Pass Tunnel | | C 3 |
| Hallwilersee (Hallwil Lake) | | A 4 |
| Inn River | | B 5 |
| Jungfrau (Mtn.) | | B 3 |
| Jura Mountains | | B 3 |
| Lac Léman (Lake Geneva) | | B 2 |
| Lake Ageri (Ägerisee) | | A 4 |
| Lake Biel | | A 3 |
| Lake Brienz (Bielersee) | | B 3 |
| Lake Bienz (Brienzersee) | | B 3 |
| Lake Constance, see Bodensee | | |
| Lake Geneva, see Lac Léman | | |
| Lake Joux (Lac de Joux) | | B 2 |
| Lake Lugano | | C 4 |
| Lake Maggiore | | B 4 |
| Lake Morat | | B 3 |
| Lake Murtensee (Lac de Neuchâtel) | | B 2 |
| Lake of Lucerne | | A 4 |
| Lake of Thun (Thunersee) | | B 3 |
| Lake Sarnersee | | B 4 |
| Lake Wallen (Wallensee) | | A 5 |
| Lake Zug (Zugersee) | | A 4 |
| Lepontine Alps | | B 4 |
| Lötschberg Tunnel (Mts.) | | B 3 |
| Matterhorn (Mtn.) | | C 3 |
| Monte Rosa (Mtn.) | | C 3 |
| Pennine Alps (Mts.) | | B 3 |
| Rhaetian Alps | | B 5 |
| Rhine River | | B 5 |
| Rhône River | | B 3 |
| Saint Gotthard Tunnel | | B 4 |
| Simplon Pass and Tunnel | | B 3 |
| Splügen Pass | | B 5 |
| Staubbach (Waterfall)* | | B 3 |
| Tendre, Mont (Mtn.) | | B 2 |
| Ticino River | | B 4 |
| Trümmelbach (Waterfall) | | B 3 |
| Zürich Lake (Zürichsee) | | A 4 |

†Name in German, French, or Italian, according to most spoken language; key shows general location.
*Half-Cantons.
‡Population of metropolitan area, including suburbs.
*Does not appear on map; key shows general location.
Sources: 1968 official estimates for cantons and cities over 10,000; 1960 census for other places.

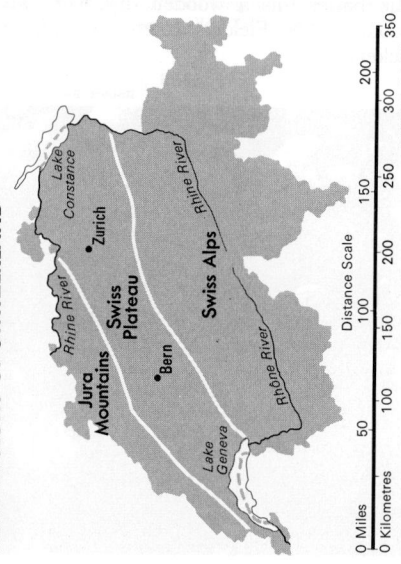

## LAND REGIONS OF SWITZERLAND

840b

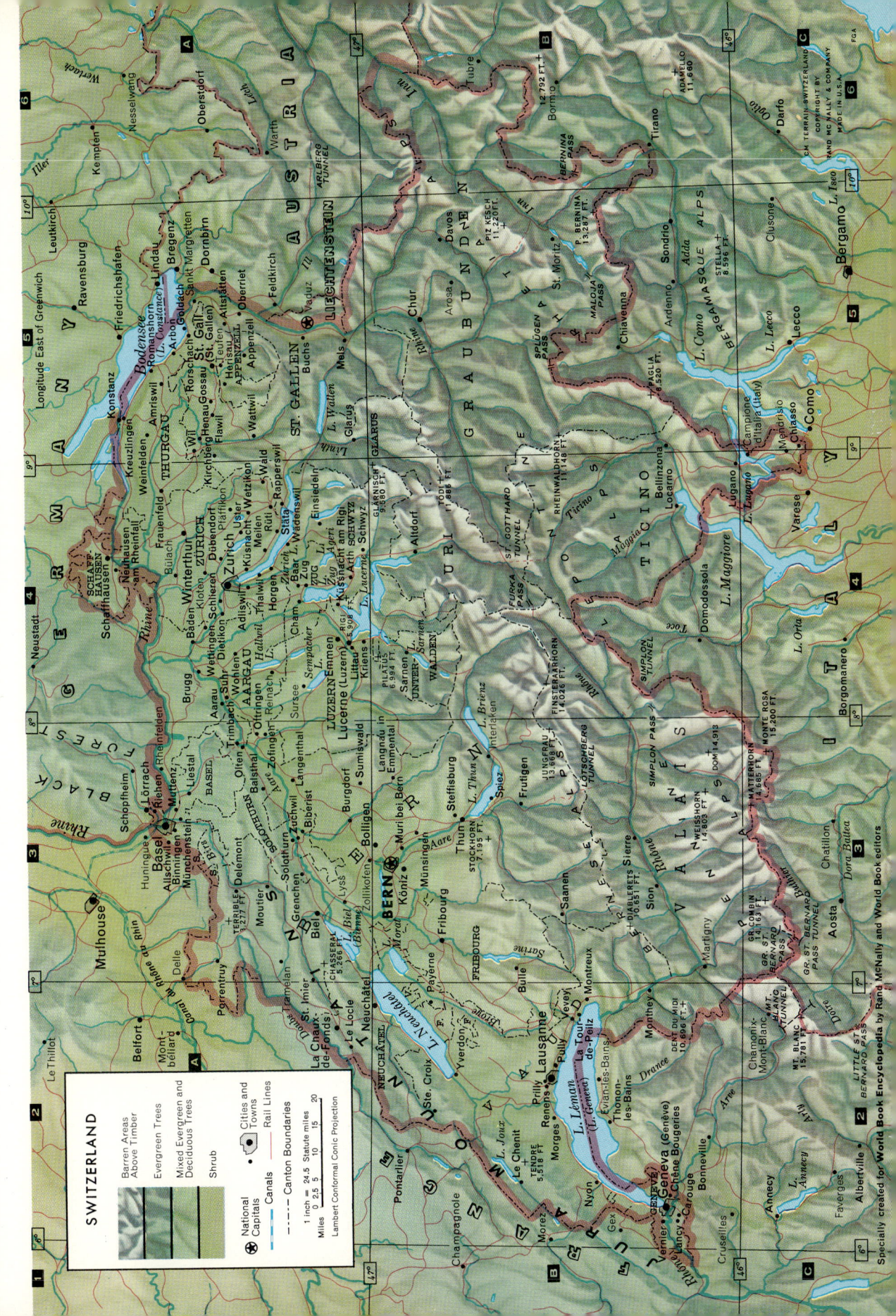

# SWITZERLAND

largest mountain system in Europe. This high, rugged region covers about 60 per cent of Switzerland, but less than a fifth of the people live there. There are glaciers as low as 3,500 feet above sea level, and snow blankets most of the region from three to five months a year. Much of the region is forested. The forests help prevent snow from sliding down to the valleys, but avalanches sometimes occur.

The upper valleys of the Rhine and Rhône rivers divide the Swiss Alps into a northern and a southern series of ranges. These ranges include the Bernese, Lepontine, Pennine, and Rhaetian Alps. Ancient glaciers carved out sharp peaks, jagged ridges, and steep gorges. Many mountain streams form plunging waterfalls. The highest waterfall is the 980-foot Staubbach in the Bernese Alps. The Pennine Alps include Switzerland's highest peak, the 15,200-foot Dufourspitze of Monte Rosa. The spectacular beauty of the Swiss Alps helps make them a major vacationland for tourists from all parts of the world. See ALPS.

**Rivers.** The Swiss Alps form part of Europe's main drainage divide. They are the source of rivers that flow in all directions. The Rhine and the Rhône rivers rise within 15 miles of each other in the Alps, but they flow in opposite directions. The Rhine flows into the North Sea, and the Rhône into the Mediterranean Sea. The Inn River winds into the Danube River, which goes into the Black Sea. The Ticino River is a tributary of the Po River, which flows into the Adriatic Sea. See INN RIVER; RHINE RIVER; RHÔNE RIVER.

**Ticino, the Southernmost Swiss Canton,** is the warmest part of the country. It has hot summers and mild winters.

## SWITZERLAND / Climate

The climate of Switzerland varies greatly from area to area because of the country's wide variety in altitude. In general, temperatures decrease about 3° F. with each 1,000-foot increase in elevation, and higher areas receive more rain and snow. Cold air from nearby mountains often settles over lower areas, producing extreme dampness and fog. Fog sometimes covers the entire Swiss Plateau like a sea of clouds. Some low areas may be covered as many as 120 days a year.

January temperatures average from 29° F. to 33° F. on the central plateau and in the mountain valleys. In winter, there is colder though drier and sunnier weather above the layer of fog than below it. In summer, the plateau is warm and sunny, but severe storms may occur. July temperatures on the plateau average from 65° F. to 70° F. Many sheltered valleys sometimes become uncomfortably hot. In summer, the higher slopes are cool or even cold, and cloudy. The canton of Ticino, which extends southward to the Italian plains, has hot summers and mild winters.

The central plateau receives from 40 to 45 inches of *precipitation* (rain, melted snow, and other forms of moisture) a year. Sheltered valleys usually have less. In some high areas, the yearly precipitation totals more than 100 inches. Above 6,000 feet, snow covers the ground at least six months a year.

A dry, warm southerly wind called the *foehn* sometimes blows into valleys in the Swiss Alps. It causes rapid changes in temperature and air pressure, which makes many people uncomfortable. This wind also may melt mountain snows earlier than usual, causing severe avalanches.

### MONTHLY WEATHER IN BERN AND LUGANO

| | JAN | FEB | MAR | APR | MAY | JUNE | JULY | AUG | SEPT | OCT | NOV | DEC | Average of: |
|---|---|---|---|---|---|---|---|---|---|---|---|---|---|
| **Bern** | 35 | 40 | 48 | 56 | 64 | 70 | 74 | 73 | 66 | 55 | 44 | 36 | High Temperatures |
| | 26 | 27 | 33 | 39 | 46 | 52 | 56 | 55 | 50 | 42 | 34 | 27 | Low Temperatures |
| | 11 | 10 | 12 | 14 | 15 | 14 | 13 | 12 | 11 | 12 | 12 | 12 | Days of Rain or Snow |
| | 7 | 6 | 9 | 11 | 14 | 12 | 11 | 10 | 9 | 11 | 10 | 8 | Days of Rain or Snow |
| **Lugano** | 43 | 48 | 56 | 63 | 70 | 78 | 83 | 82 | 75 | 63 | 52 | 45 | High Temperatures |
| | 29 | 30 | 36 | 43 | 50 | 56 | 60 | 59 | 54 | 46 | 38 | 31 | Low Temperatures |

Temperatures are given in degrees Fahrenheit

Source: Meteorological Office, London

WORLD BOOK map-GJa

# SWITZERLAND / Economy

Switzerland is a prosperous country with one of the world's highest standards of living. In spite of limited natural resources, the nation's highly specialized industries are extremely profitable. Switzerland has more jobs than its own people can fill. Workers from other countries make up about a fifth of the Swiss labor force.

Switzerland trades mainly with Western European countries and the United States. The Swiss import more goods than they export. They make up the difference with income from tourism and from banking, insurance, and transportation services to foreign persons or firms.

**Natural Resources.** Switzerland lacks important deposits of coal, iron ore, petroleum, and other minerals on which heavy industry is based. The country's limited mining activity largely involves salt and such building materials as limestone and sandstone.

Most of the land is too high or too rugged to be good farmland. In addition, the climate is generally better for growing hay and other livestock feeds rather than such crops as wheat and fruit. Crops are raised on only about a tenth of Switzerland's total area, chiefly on the Swiss Plateau. More than 40 per cent of the country consists of meadows or grazing land, much of which can be used only in summer. Forests cover about a fourth of Switzerland.

Switzerland's greatest natural resource is perhaps its rushing mountain rivers. These rivers generate more hydroelectric power per person than those of any other European country except Norway and Sweden. Almost all the power produced in Switzerland is generated at power stations on the rivers.

**Manufacturing.** Switzerland is one of the most industrialized countries in the world. Its manufacturing industries are based on the processing of imported raw materials into high-quality products for export. To keep the cost of materials and transportation as low as possible, these industries specialize in highly skilled workmanship on small, valuable items. In Switzerland's watchmaking industry, for example, the cost of materials is only about one-twentieth the cost of labor. More than 95 per cent of the watches are exported.

The Swiss make such engineering products as generators and other electrical equipment, industrial machinery, machine tools, precision instruments, and transportation equipment. Other major products are chemicals, paper, processed foods including cheese and chocolate, and silk and other textiles.

Most Swiss factories are small or medium-sized, because of the stress on quality goods rather than mass production. In addition, hydroelectric power is widely distributed. For these reasons, there are factories in small towns and even in villages throughout the country. The use of hydroelectricity, rather than coal or oil, to power the factories and railroads helps keep the busiest industrial centers almost free of smoke.

**Agriculture** in Switzerland supplies only about three-fifths of the people's needs. The rest of the nation's food must be imported. Livestock raising is the most important agricultural activity because of the limited cropland resources and the climate. It provides about 75 per cent of Switzerland's farm income, largely through dairy farming. Farmers also raise hogs, goats,

Alan Band Associates

**Switzerland's Watchmaking Industry** is world famous. Almost all Swiss watches are exported to other countries.

### SWITZERLAND'S LABOR FORCE IN 1960

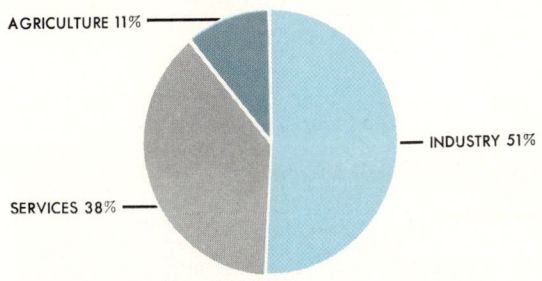

AGRICULTURE 11%
INDUSTRY 51%
SERVICES 38%

**Workers by Economic Activities**

| Economic Activities | Labor Force Number of Persons | Per Cent of Total |
|---|---|---|
| Manufacturing | 999,555 | 40 |
| Other Services | 479,550 | 19 |
| Trade & Financial Institutions | 346,215 | 14 |
| Agriculture, Forestry, & Fishing | 280,191 | 11 |
| Construction | 239,454 | 10 |
| Transportation & Communication | 135,078 | 5 |
| Utilities | 21,758 | 1 |
| Mining | 6,483 | * |
| Unemployed | 4,127 | * |
| Total | 2,512,411 | 100 |

*Less than 1 per cent
Source: *Year Book of Labour Statistics, 1968,* ILO

841

# SWITZERLAND

and sheep. Most of the dairy cattle graze on the high mountain pastures in summer, and are brought down to the valleys in winter. Much of the milk is used to make cheeses for export. These cheeses include Emmentaler, also known as *Swiss cheese*, and Gruyère, which are sold in all parts of the world.

Swiss farms are small, averaging only 8 acres. Farmers work the land carefully to make it as productive as possible. Crops include fruits, wheat and other grains, and potatoes. Grapes are grown near Lakes Geneva, Lugano, and Maggiore, and in other sunny areas. Olive trees are cultivated in the canton of Ticino.

**Tourism.** Since the early 1800's, increasing numbers of tourists have come to Switzerland. Today, more than 5½ million tourists from all parts of the world visit the country yearly. The busy tourist industry adds over $350 million to Switzerland's annual national income.

Switzerland has thousands of hotels and inns for tourists. Sports centers in the Alps, including Davos and St. Moritz, attract many vacationers. Skiing is especially popular. Most of the ski runs are free of trees because they are higher than the elevation at which trees stop growing. In summer, guides take tourists mountain climbing. Many visitors come for the healthful clear, dry, mountain air, as well as to enjoy the beauty of the Alps. Water sports on Lake Geneva and other lakes are also popular vacation attractions. Favorite lake resorts include Montreux and Vevey.

**Banking** adds more than $150 million a year to the national income. Swiss banks attract deposits from people in many other countries. The banks are probably the safest in the world, partly because of the nation's neutrality.

A depositor can choose to be identified by a number known only to himself and a few top bank officials. In this way, a man's private fortune can be kept secret.

Swiss law provides that any bank employee who violates this secrecy may be fined and imprisoned. However, the secrecy may be broken in the investigation of Swiss criminal cases.

**Transportation.** Switzerland has fine transportation systems in spite of the mountains, which make travel difficult. The government owns and operates almost the entire 3,150-mile railroad network. Many railroad tunnels cut through the Alps, including the Lötschberg, St. Gotthard, and Simplon tunnels. The 12.3-mile Simplon Tunnel is the longest railroad tunnel in the world.

Switzerland has more than 30,000 miles of hard-surfaced roads and highways. They provide travel even to distant mountain areas. But those that wind through the higher mountain passes are open only a few months of the year. Heavy snow makes them unusable except in summer. The 3½-mile Great St. Bernard Tunnel, opened in 1964, was the first automobile tunnel through the Alps. It links Switzerland and Italy.

The Rhine River connects Basel, Switzerland's only port, with the North Sea. Large barges can reach Basel, which handles about 8 million tons of cargo a year.

Geneva and Zurich have international airports. The privately owned Swissair, Switzerland's only international airline, flies to about 40 countries.

**Communication.** Switzerland has more than 450 newspapers. The largest daily newspaper, *Der Blick* of Zurich, has a daily circulation of about 190,000. Over half the more than 100 dailies are published in German, and the others are in French or Italian. A few of the nondaily newspapers are in Romansh.

The Swiss government owns the country's three radio stations and three television stations. Each broadcasts in one of the three official languages. A few programs are in Romansh. The government operates the postal, telegraph, and telephone services.

**Raising Dairy Cattle** ranks high among Swiss farming activities. Cattle auctions are held on Sundays during the summer.

Thomas Hollyman, Photo Researchers

**Skiing Tourists** flock to the snowy Swiss Alps. One popular ski resort is Zermatt, near the 14,685-foot-high Matterhorn, *rear*.

George Holton, Photo Researchers

# SWITZERLAND / History

**Early Days.** Before the time of Christ, a Celtic people called the *Helvetians* lived in what is now Switzerland. They were conquered in 58 B.C. by Roman armies led by Julius Caesar. The region, known as *Helvetia*, became a Roman province. By the A.D. 400's, two Germanic tribes, the Alemannians and the Burgundians, settled there. Another Germanic people, the Franks, defeated these tribes by the early 500's. The Frankish kingdom later expanded and became powerful under Charlemagne, but it broke apart during the 800's. See FRANK.

Most of present-day Switzerland became part of the Holy Roman Empire in 962, when the empire began, and the rest was part of the kingdom of Burgundy. That part came into the empire in 1033. Switzerland consisted of many territories, towns, and villages ruled by local lords, and some communities directly under the emperor. See HOLY ROMAN EMPIRE.

**The Struggle for Freedom.** By the 1200's, the Hapsburg, or Habsburg, family had gained control over much of Switzerland. The free men of what are now the *cantons* (states) of Schwyz and Uri feared the growth of the Hapsburgs' power. In 1273, Rudolf I became the first Hapsburg to rule the Holy Roman Empire. He began to take control of the two regions. In 1291, Schwyz and Uri decided to fight for freedom. They invited the nearby region of Unterwalden to join them.

Leaders of the three regions met in August, 1291, and signed the Perpetual Covenant, a defense agreement. They declared their freedom and promised to aid each other against any foreign ruler. The Perpetual Covenant was the start of the Swiss Confederation. The confederation came to be known as Switzerland. It took its name from the canton of Schwyz.

---

### IMPORTANT DATES IN SWITZERLAND

**58 B.C.** Roman armies under Julius Caesar conquered Helvetia (now Switzerland).

**A.D. 400's** Germanic tribes occupied Helvetia.

**962** Most of what is now Switzerland became part of the Holy Roman Empire.

**1291** Three Swiss *cantons* (states) signed the Perpetual Covenant, which established the Swiss Confederation.

**1315-1388** Switzerland defeated Austria in three wars of independence.

**1499** Switzerland won independence from the Holy Roman Empire.

**1515** The Swiss were defeated by the French in Italy, and began their policy of permanent neutrality.

**1648** The Holy Roman Empire recognized Swiss independence.

**1798** French forces occupied Switzerland and established the Helvetic Republic under their control.

**1815** The Congress of Vienna expanded Switzerland to 22 cantons, and restored the old confederation.

**1848** Switzerland adopted a constitution that established federal power over the confederation.

**1863** The Red Cross was founded in Switzerland.

**1874** Constitutional changes increased federal power.

**1920** The League of Nations met at its headquarters in Geneva, Switzerland, for its first session.

**1958** Basel became the first Swiss city to let women vote in local elections.

**1959** Swiss men voted against letting women vote in national elections.

**1960** Switzerland helped form the European Free Trade Association.

**1963** Switzerland joined the Council of Europe.

**1968** Geneva became the first Swiss city to have a woman mayor.

---

By an unknown artist from the *Stumpf Chronicle*. Zentralbibliothek, Zurich, Switzerland

**The Battle of Sempach** was fought in 1386 against the Austrians during the Swiss wars of independence. That battle, won by the Swiss, is shown in a woodcut dating from 1548.

843

# SWITZERLAND

The Hapsburgs ruled Austria, and the Swiss fought several wars of independence against Austrian forces. In 1315, at Morgarten, Swiss peasants trapped and defeated an Austrian army 10 times their strength. Between 1332 and 1353, five more cantons joined the Swiss Confederation. The Swiss again defeated the Austrians at Sempach in 1386 and at Näfels in 1388. See HAPSBURG.

The wars with Austria were full of dramatic incidents, and many famous stories have been told about Swiss heroes. For two exciting tales, see the articles on TELL, WILLIAM and WINKELRIED, ARNOLD VON.

**Independence and Expansion.** Switzerland became a strong military power during the 1400's. The Swiss entered several wars to gain land, and won many territories. In three battles in 1476 and 1477, the Swiss defeated Charles the Bold, duke of Burgundy. In 1499, they crushed the forces of Maximilian I, the Hapsburg ruler of the Holy Roman Empire. Switzerland won complete independence, though the empire did not officially recognize it until 1648. In 1512 and 1513, the Swiss drove French armies out of northern Italy. Almost all the lands won in these wars of expansion remained under Swiss control for nearly 300 years, and then were admitted into the confederation as cantons.

In 1515, the French defeated the Swiss at Marignano in Italy. The Swiss suffered great losses, and began to question their policy of expansion. Switzerland soon adopted a policy of permanent neutrality, and has stayed out of foreign wars ever since.

Five more cantons joined the Swiss Confederation between 1481 and 1513, making a total of 13. Each canton governed itself as it chose, almost like a separate country. Some cantons were peasant democracies, and others were governed by powerful families or by craftsmen's groups called *guilds*. Many cantons owned nearby territories either by themselves or with other cantons. The confederation had no central government. Delegates from each canton occasionally met in an assembly called the *Tagsatzung* to discuss various matters. But this assembly had no real power.

**Religious Civil Wars.** The Reformation spread quickly in Switzerland during the early 1500's. Huldreich Zwingli, one of the great leaders of the Protestant movement, preached in Zurich. John Calvin, another great Protestant leader, made Geneva an international center of Protestantism. See REFORMATION.

The Reformation split Switzerland into two armed camps, Protestant and Roman Catholic. The two groups fought in 1529, 1531, 1656, and 1712, but little change in Swiss life resulted.

**French Control.** In 1798, during the French Revolution, French armies swept into Switzerland and quickly occupied the country. The French set up the *Helvetic Republic*, and gave the new Swiss government strong central power. The Swiss cantons became merely administrative districts of the government.

The great political change caused much confusion and dissatisfaction among the Swiss. As a result, Napoleon of France re-established the 13 Swiss cantons in 1803 and created 6 new ones from their territories. He reduced the power of the central government, and restored much of the cantons' self-government.

After Napoleon's final defeat in 1815, the Congress of Vienna gave Switzerland three more cantons that had been under French control (see VIENNA, CONGRESS OF). The old confederation system was largely restored, with the central government having little power. The Congress of Vienna also guaranteed the neutrality of Switzerland. The European powers at the congress recognized Swiss neutrality as being for the good of all Europe. The neutrality of Switzerland has never since been broken.

**The Constitution of 1848.** By 1830, many Swiss had begun to demand political reforms—including individual rights and freedom of the press—and greater national unity. Governments were overthrown peaceably in some cantons, but rioting occurred in others. The reform movement grew in strength. Seven cantons banded together to oppose the changes, but were defeated in a three-week civil war in 1847.

Switzerland adopted a new constitution in 1848. This constitution set up a representative democracy with a two-house legislature like that of the United States. It established federal power over the confederation and guaranteed religious freedom and other individual rights. The constitution was changed in 1874 to increase the government's powers, especially in military and court matters.

In 1863, Jean Henri Dunant, a Swiss businessman and writer, founded the Red Cross in Geneva. The Red Cross flag was copied from that of Switzerland, with the two colors reversed. See RED CROSS.

**Neutrality in the World Wars.** World War I began in 1914, and Switzerland immediately declared its neutrality. The fighting nations respected this policy because Switzerland acted in a strictly neutral manner throughout the war. Food imports decreased during the four years of fighting, but Swiss farmers increased their grain production to feed the people. In 1920, Geneva became the headquarters of the newly created League

### EXPANSION OF SWITZERLAND—1291 TO 1815

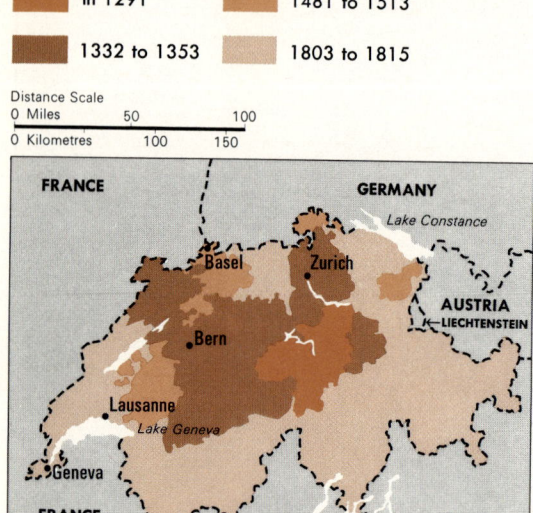

WORLD BOOK map-GJa

844

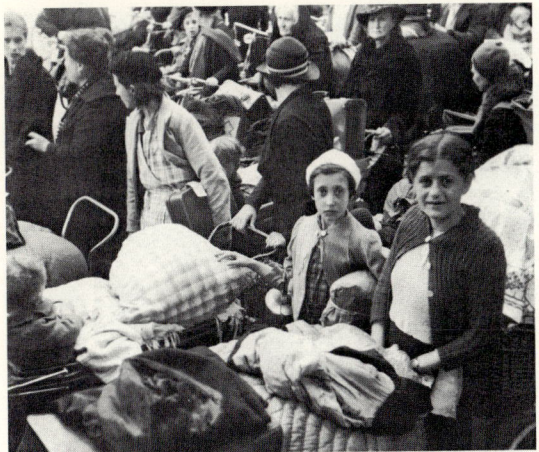

**Thousands of Refugees from War-Torn Countries** found a haven in neutral Switzerland during World War II.

Hans Steiner, Black Star

of Nations, an association of countries organized to prevent war. Switzerland was one of the original members of the League. See LEAGUE OF NATIONS.

After World War II began in 1939, Switzerland again declared its neutrality. German forces did not invade Switzerland. They feared the Swiss would blow up transportation tunnels in the Alps if they did. Switzerland became a major supply link between Germany and its ally Italy. It also represented the United States and other Allied nations in enemy countries. During the war, Switzerland cared for more than 100,000 refugees from a number of countries.

Switzerland did not join the United Nations (UN), which was founded after World War II ended in 1945. The Swiss felt that UN membership, which requires possible military action by member nations, would violate their neutrality policy. But the UN made Geneva its European headquarters, and Switzerland joined most of the UN's specialized agencies.

**Switzerland Today** still avoids membership in international organizations that might endanger its neutrality—but not so strictly as in the past. Many Swiss, especially young people, have begun to question their nation's policy of neutrality. In 1960, the Swiss helped form the European Free Trade Association, an economic organization of seven nations. Switzerland also joined the Council of Europe in 1963. This organization of 18 countries seeks to promote closer unity among its members for economic and social progress, but it has no real power.

As a neutral country, Switzerland represents about 20 nations in countries with which those nations have broken diplomatic relations. For example, it represents 10 nations, including the United States, in Cuba.

A movement to give women the right to vote is slowly making gains in Switzerland. In 1958, Basel became the first Swiss city to allow women to vote in local elections. The next year, Vaud became the first canton to grant that right. But in 1959, Swiss men voted against giving women the right to vote in national elections. In 1968, Geneva became the first Swiss city to have a woman mayor.

HEINZ K. MEIER and NORMAN J. G. POUNDS

## SWITZERLAND/Study Aids

### Related Articles in WORLD BOOK include:

#### BIOGRAPHIES

| | |
|---|---|
| Agassiz (family) | Klee, Paul |
| Ansermet, Ernest | Kocher, Emil T. |
| Barth, Karl | Le Corbusier |
| Bernoulli (family) | Mueller, Paul |
| Bovet, Daniel | Paracelsus, Philippus A. |
| Calvin, John | Pestalozzi, Johann H. |
| Dunant, Jean H. | Piccard (brothers) |
| Dürrenmatt, Friedrich | Reichstein, Tadeus |
| Euler, Leonhard | Rousseau, Jean Jacques |
| Frisch, Max | Ružička, Leopold |
| Gallatin, Albert | Spyri, Johanna |
| Graf, Urs | Tussaud, Marie G. |
| Hesse, Hermann | Werner, Alfred |
| Jung, Carl G. | Winkelried, Arnold von |
| Karrer, Paul | Wyss (family) |
| Keller, Gottfried | Zwingli, Huldreich |

#### CITIES

| | | | |
|---|---|---|---|
| Basel | Geneva | Lausanne | Saint Moritz |
| Bern | Interlaken | Lucerne | Zurich |

#### PHYSICAL FEATURES

| | |
|---|---|
| Alps | Lake of Thun |
| Engadine | Lötschberg Tunnel |
| Grand Dixence Dam | Matterhorn |
| Jungfrau | Saint Bernard, Great |
| Jura | Saint Gotthard Pass |
| Lake Constance | Saint Gotthard Tunnel |
| Lake Geneva | Simplon Pass and Tunnel |
| Lake Lugano | Staubbach |
| Lake of Lucerne | Trümmelbach |

#### OTHER RELATED ARTICLES

| | |
|---|---|
| Chillon | European Monetary |
| Clothing (color picture: Europe) | Agreement |
| Doll (color picture) | Helvetian |
| Edelweiss | Lake Dwelling |
| Europe, Council of | League of Nations |
| European Free Trade Association | Tell, William |

### Outline

I. **Government**
II. **People**
   A. Population   C. Religion   E. Arts
   B. Language   D. Education   F. Sports
III. **The Land**
   A. The Jura Mountains   C. The Swiss Alps
   B. The Swiss Plateau   D. Rivers
IV. **Climate**
V. **Economy**
   A. Natural Resources   E. Banking
   B. Manufacturing   F. Transportation
   C. Agriculture   G. Communication
   D. Tourism
VI. **History**

### Questions

What are the three official languages of Switzerland?
Where does the name *Switzerland* come from?
How much of Switzerland do the Alps cover?
What is the longest railroad tunnel in the world?
Why has Switzerland not joined the United Nations?
How did the Swiss Confederation start?
What are the only elections in which some Swiss women may vote?
In what region of Switzerland do about two-thirds of the people live?
How does Switzerland keep itself prepared for military defense?
Why are Switzerland's industrial centers almost free of smoke?

845

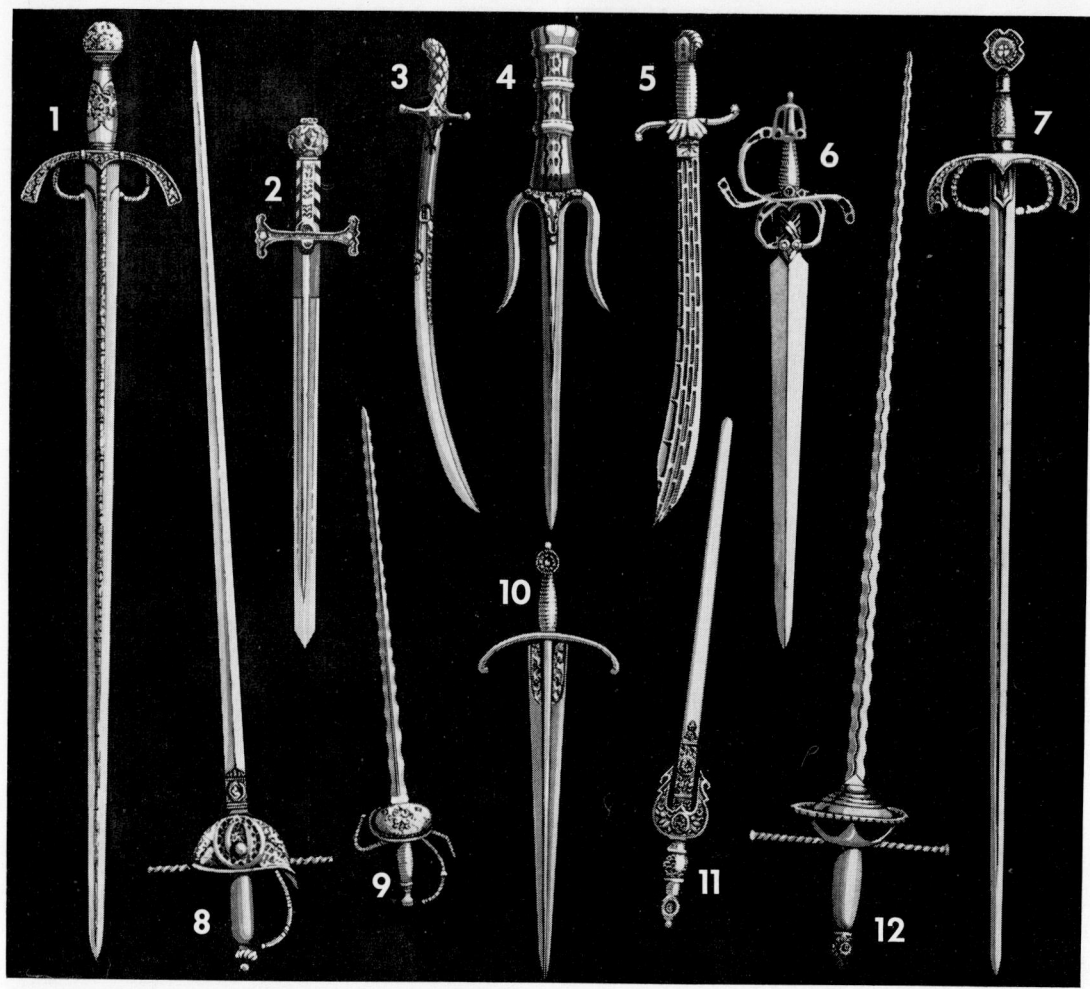

**Some Famous Swords.** (1) Sword of Isabella of Spain. (2) Sword of Francis I of France. (3) Persian sword of the 1500's. (4) Moorish boarding sword. (5) Cutlass of the 1500's. (6) Sword of the 1500's. (7) Sword of medieval naval chief. (8) Early modern sword of Scandinavia. (9) Flaming sword of Don Juan of Austria. (10) Sword of the 1400's. (11) Sword of a cardinal in the court of Philip IV of Spain. (12) Flaming sword of Philip IV of Spain, which he used in the early 1600's.

**SWORD,** *sohrd,* is one of the oldest of all fighting weapons. Man turned his skill to the art of making weapons almost as soon as he discovered the art of working metals. The earliest swords we know about were those of the Assyrians, Gauls, and Greeks. Their swords were short, two-edged weapons made of bronze. The Roman sword was a short, straight, steel weapon with a sharpened point and two cutting edges.

The *broadsword* is a broad-bladed, single-edged short sword, made for cutting but not for stabbing. The broadsword was once used by regiments of cavalry and Highland infantry in the British army. It was better for attack than defense. The *claymore,* a kind of broadsword, but double-edged and longer, was the national weapon of the Highlanders. The favorite weapon of the East was the *scimitar,* a blade with a decided curve, for which Damascus was noted. Toledo, Spain, made fine swords. The *rapier,* used in the 1500's and 1600's, was a straight two-edged sword, with a narrow, pointed blade. Swords used by cavalry during the 1800's were from $2\frac{1}{2}$ to 3 feet long and weighed about $2\frac{1}{2}$ pounds. The sword gave way to the saber in the United States Army. The saber was made for both cutting and thrusting.

There was less cavalry action in World War I and little chance to use swords. A better weapon for the charges of foot soldiers was the bayonet, a blade a foot or more long attached to the end of the rifle. The sword was also of little use in World War II, when cavalry units were mechanized. JOHN D. BILLINGSLEY

See also BAYONET; DAGGER; DUEL; FENCING.

**SWORD OF DAMOCLES.** See DAMOCLES.

**SWORDFISH** is a large ocean fish with a long, rounded body. It has a long, flattened upper jaw that looks like a sword. The swordfish is given its name because of its jaw. This fish closely resembles the marlins and sailfish, but differs from them because it has a short-based back fin. The swordfish lives in all warm seas. Its average length is 7 feet, and it usually weighs about 250 pounds. Specimens that weigh from 600 to 800 pounds and measure from 10 to 15 feet long have been caught. Swordfish are highly regarded by big-game fishermen. The swordfish is hard to catch because hooks pull out

H. Armstrong Roberts

**Swordfish Travel in Pairs** during breeding season, and a fishing boat will often hook two of the leaping, speeding sword-nosed fighters. Heavy line and a strong pole are needed for the thrilling, backbreaking fight with a "sword."

of its tender mouth easily. It is also difficult to get swordfish to take the bait.

Their "swords" are sharp-edged and strong, and half as long as the body. There have been several instances of swordfish charging boats and piercing the hulls.

Commercial fishermen catch swordfish by harpooning them from a pulpit on the bow of a sailboat. The flesh is coarse, but it has an excellent flavor when cut and cooked as a steak. Swordfish eat squid and menhaden, herring, mackerel, and other fish that travel in schools.

Two other kinds of fish have pointed, bony spikes much like those of the swordfish. The *marlins* have a long-based but low dorsal fin along the back. The *sailfish* has a long, high, sail-like fin along its back.

**Scientific Classification.** The swordfish belongs to the swordfish family, *Xiphiidae*. It is classified as genus *Xiphias*, species *X. gladius*.         LEONARD P. SCHULTZ

See also FISHING (table, Game-Fishing World Records); MARLIN; SAILFISH.

**SWORDTAIL.** See FISH (Reproduction; color picture, Tropical Fresh-Water Fishes).

**SYCAMORE** is a shade tree with reddish-brown wood. It belongs to the plane-tree family. It grows in fertile lowlands and along streams. It is found in great numbers in the United States from southern Maine to Nebraska and as far south as Texas and Florida. The sycamore may reach a height of 175 feet and be 14 feet through the trunk. The bark on the lower trunk of the tree is reddish brown, and the bark on the branches is olive green. The bark on the branches breaks off in tiny scales. When these scales break off they show an inner bark that is light cream in color. This light bark on the branches gives rise to the phrase "hoary-antlered sycamore." Some sycamores are known as *buttonwoods*, others as *plane trees*.

# SYCAMORE

The sycamore tree can be recognized by its leaves, which are broad and have large teeth. The stem of each leaf is hollow at the base where it encloses the next year's bud. The flowers of the sycamore are of two types, those that bear *stamens* and those that bear *pistils*. Each type of flower grows in separate flower heads on different parts of the same tree. The fruits of the sycamore are borne in small balls which hang from drooping stems. Each ball is made up of many tiny dry fruits known as *achenes*, which are tightly packed together.

**Scientific Classification.** Sycamores belong to the plane tree family, *Platanaceae*. They make up the genus *Platanus*. The most common sycamore tree is *P. acerifolia*.         WILLIAM M. HARLOW

See also LEAF (picture, Kinds of Leaves); TREE (picture, Tree Shapes).

George J. Baetzhold

**Sycamore Leaves,** *above left*, are broader than they are long. The fruit of the sycamore tree, *above right*, is a round ball. Its bark *below*, does not stretch as much as the bark of other trees. As the tree grows, some bark breaks off leaving exposed patches.

Rutherford Platt

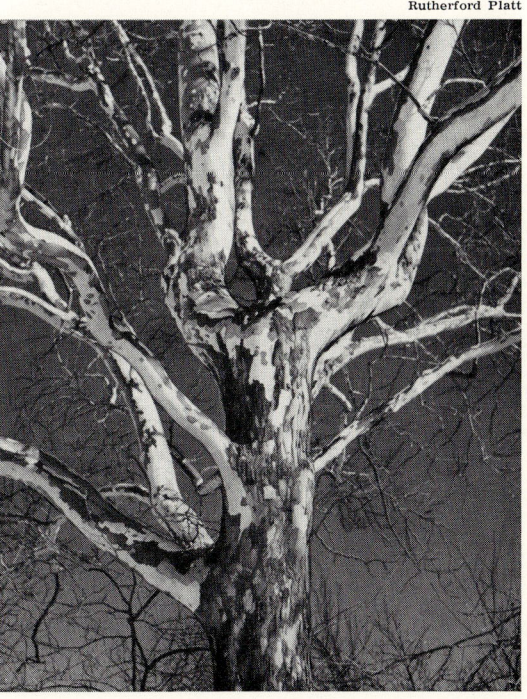

847

# SYDENHAM, BARON

**SYDENHAM,** *SIHD'n um,* **BARON** (1799-1841), CHARLES EDWARD POULETT THOMSON, was a British statesman and governor general of Canada from 1839 to 1841. He succeeded Lord Durham in Canada, and carried through the unification of Upper and Lower Canada. He was born at Wimbledon, England, and worked as a merchant. In 1826 he was elected to Parliament and in 1834 became president of the Board of Trade. JAMES L. GODFREY

**SYDENHAM, THOMAS** (1624-1689), an English physician, believed and taught that medicine could be learned only at the bedside of the patient. He was a keen observer, and gave excellent descriptions of gout, scarlet fever, measles, and influenza. He had great faith in the healing power of nature, and he felt that fever was nature's way of fighting the injurious matter that caused disease.

Brown Bros.
**Thomas Sydenham**

Sydenham was born at Wynford Eagle, Dorset, and received his degree from Oxford University. He was married about 1656, settled in London, and began to practice medicine. Success came slowly to him, but eventually he gained recognition as one of the great doctors of his time.

Sydenham prided himself on being a practical physician, and he avoided all theory. He was not interested in the developing sciences of anatomy, physiology, and chemistry, and felt that they were of little use to the practicing doctor. His practical bent is shown by his adoption of quinine for the treatment of fevers, at a time when many doctors opposed this new drug.

Even though he avoided theory, Sydenham developed a theoretical explanation of the origin and spread of epidemics. He believed that changes in the atmosphere acted on ordinary diseases at various times and made them more virulent so that they attacked many people rapidly. This theory was accepted by many physicians for several hundred years. GEORGE ROSEN

**SYDNEY** (pop. 158,801; met. area 2,444,735; alt. 35ft.) is the oldest city and the center of the largest metropolitan area in Australia. It is the capital of the state of New South Wales. Sydney lies on the southeastern coast of Australia, and has one of the finest harbors in the world. For location, see AUSTRALIA (political map). The city was founded as a penal colony on Jan. 26, 1788.

Sydney's harbor, Port Jackson, has an area of about 21 square miles and a shoreline about 150 miles long. The largest ships in the world can anchor there.

Many residential sections of Sydney lie close to the ocean beaches along the waterfront. The people enjoy swimming, fishing, and boating in the harbor. The great Harbour Bridge connects Sydney with the suburbs of the northern shore (see BRIDGE [picture]).

Sydney is an important trading center and has its own manufacturing industry. The products include textiles, chemicals, metal products, processed foods, pottery and glass, and leather. The business district centers in the heart of the city, near Martin Place. The University of Sydney was founded in 1850. The University of New South Wales, founded in 1949, and Macquarie University, founded in 1964, are located in suburbs of Sydney. The city also has several technical schools, a public library, and art galleries. Australia's first television station began operating in Sydney in 1956. C. M. H. CLARK

See also AUSTRALIA (pictures).

APF

**Downtown Sydney** centers around Martin Place and the General Post Office. Sydney is Australia's oldest city and an important trade center.

**SYDNEY,** Nova Scotia (pop. 32,767; alt. 23 ft.), is a steel center and the third largest city in Nova Scotia. It lies in a coal-mining region on the north coast of Cape Breton Island, about 210 miles northeast of Halifax. Sydney is the island's main railway terminal. Steamship lines connect the city with many important world ports. Sydney was founded in 1785. It was named for Lord Sydney, a former secretary of state for the colonies. For the location of Sydney, see NOVA SCOTIA (political map). THOMAS H. RADDALL

**SYENITE,** *SI uh nite,* is an igneous rock with a grainy texture, which is sometimes mistaken for granite. It is formed by the cooling and solidifying of molten material.

**SYLLOGISM.** See LOGIC (Deductive Logic).

**SYLVESTER** is the name of two popes of the Roman Catholic Church.

**Sylvester I** (?-335), SAINT SYLVESTER, reigned as pope from 314 until his death. According to legend, he healed the Roman emperor, Constantine the Great, of leprosy, and also baptized him. It is certain that Constantine built the basilicas of Saint John Lateran and of Saint Peter in the Vatican while Sylvester was pope. Sylvester was born in Rome.

**Sylvester II** (950?-1003) was the first Frenchman to become a pope. He reigned from 999 until his death. His ambition was to unite all western Europe into one church and one state. Sylvester was born probably in Aurillac, and was educated in the monastery of Aurillac in Auvergne. He studied mathematics, astronomy, and dialectic. GUSTAVE WEIGEL and FULTON J. SHEEN

**SYLVITE.** See POTASH.

**SYMBIOSIS,** *SIM by O sis,* means *living together.* Any two, different organisms that live together are symbiotic, whether they benefit one another, harm one another, or have no effect at all. The term is often restricted to the idea of mutual benefit. There are three forms of symbiosis: parasitism, commensalism, and mutualism.

In *parasitism,* one organism obtains food and shelter at the expense of another, sometimes destroying the host. An excellent example of parasitism is the hookworm that may live in the intestines of human beings and other animals. See PARASITE.

In *commensalism,* one organism obtains "crumbs" left over from the host's food, and is sheltered by the host. Little, if any, harm is done. For example, the remora attaches itself to the bodies of sharks and sea turtles. It gets free transportation and protection. When the hosts kill prey, the remoras detach themselves to gobble tidbits too small for the hosts (see REMORA).

In *mutualism,* both parties benefit. Man has a mutualistic relationship with his food crops and livestock. Mutualism occurs naturally when an alga and a fungus grow together to form a lichen which differs from either plant. Each organism benefits from this close association. The fungus, which cannot produce its own food, gets its food from the alga. The alga gets protection from the fungus. See LICHEN. C. BROOKE WORTH

**SYMBOL** is a sign which stands for some object or an idea. All words are symbols. Spoken words are symbols for objects and ideas. The letters of the alphabet are symbols for certain sounds. These letters are combined to form the written words which are the symbols for spoken words.

One of the most familiar symbols of all nations is the national flag. To every person the flag of his nation

# SYMBOLS

**Symbols** are signs representing objects or ideas. Some, like good-luck charms, arise from folklore and mythology. Others, such as scientific symbols, are arbitrarily assigned.

A NATION

PEACE

WAR

BUSINESS

PLENTY

GOOD LUCK

NATIONS

MUSIC

MONEY

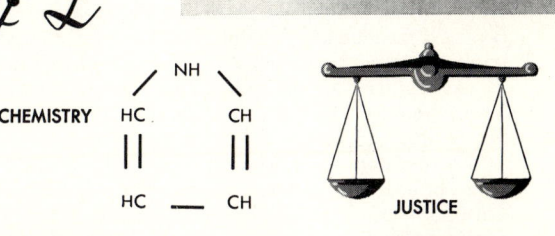
CHEMISTRY

JUSTICE

COURAGE

MEDICINE

DANGER

# SYMBOL

means "my country." The military insignia worn on the uniform of a man in the armed services are symbols. They show to which service he belongs, what rank he holds, and what his duties are.

Animals and colors have almost a world-wide symbolism. Black represents grief among Americans and Europeans, and white is the symbol of purity and innocence. In some countries, however, white stands for mourning. Blue usually stands for sincerity, and purple represents royalty. A lion is the symbol for courage, a lamb suggests gentleness, and the dove and olive branch symbolize peace. The skull and crossbones is a pictured symbol which, according to law, must be placed on all containers of poison. It stands for death.

**Religious Symbols.** Every religion has symbols, especially in pictures. The cross is the symbol of Christianity. The ship was an early Christian symbol which represented the church, in which "the faithful are carried over the sea of life." The Gospel writers are represented by symbols. The winged man is Saint Matthew, the winged lion is Saint Mark, the winged ox is Saint Luke, and the eagle is Saint John. Other saints carry symbols which distinguish them. Saint Mary Magdalene carries a box or vase (for ointment), Saint Paul carries a sword, and Saint Andrew holds a cross.

**Symbols in Mythology.** There are numerous symbols in mythology. The peacock is the symbol of Juno, and the mirror and the apple are symbols of Venus. The trident, a three-pronged spear, is the symbol of Neptune.

**Scientific Symbols.** Such sciences as mathematics, chemistry, astronomy, botany, and biology have special sets of symbols to represent the many objects, elements, and operations involved in their study. These scientific symbols are used instead of words. Some of the symbols in astronomy are so ancient that it is not known how they began. Symbols for the chief heavenly bodies are:

| Sun ☉ | Jupiter ♃ | Pallas ⚶ |
| Venus ♀ | Uranus ♅ | Vesta ⚶ |
| Moon ☽ | Mercury ☿ | Saturn ♄ |
| Ceres ⚳ | Earth ♁ and ⊕ | Neptune ♆ |
| Juno ⚵ | Mars ♂ | |

A star is represented thus: ✳.

The phases of the moon are indicated in this manner: ⏾ new moon; ☽ moon in first quarter; ☺ full moon; ☾ moon in last quarter.

There are many mathematical symbols. First, there are the symbols of value, the Arabic and Roman numbers, and the letters of the alphabet. Then there are the symbols of operation, such as $+$, the sign of addition; $-$, subtraction; $\times$, multiplication; and $\div$, division. The symbol $\pi$, called pi, stands for the number 3.1416. See ALGEBRA (Symbols in Algebra).

In chemistry, an element is designated by its first letter, or its first letter and another letter of its English, Latin, or German name. Two symbols taken from the Latin are $Hg$, the symbol for mercury, and $Fe$, the symbol for iron. $H$ stands for hydrogen, and $O$ for oxygen. $H_2O$ is the symbol for water. EDITH LILLIAN SMITH WEBSTER

**Related Articles** in WORLD BOOK include:
Advertising (Earliest Uses)
Alphabet
Cartouche
Christmas (Christmas Symbols)
Color (table: Color in Religious Symbolism)
Crescent
Easter (Easter Symbols)
Element, Chemical (tables)
Flag
Heraldry
Insignia
Liberty Cap
Map (Symbols)
Pennant
Ranching (picture: Brands of the Old West)
Seal
Shorthand
Swastika

**SYMBOLIC LOGIC.** See LOGIC; SET THEORY (History).

**SYMBOLISM** is a literary movement started by a group of French poets between 1885 and 1895. Stéphane Mallarmé was the leader of the symbolist movement, but the poetry of Paul Verlaine was more widely imitated. Leading theorists of symbolism included René Ghil, Gustave Kahn, Jean Moreás, and Charles Morice. Many European poets of the early 1900's followed the symbolist style.

Symbolism gave a spiritual atmosphere to the world by attributing to it a sacred, mystical quality. This central idea comes from the philosophy of Emanuel Swedenborg, a Swedish religious leader. According to him, visible realities are symbols for the invisible world of the spirit. In his sonnet "Correspondences," French poet Charles Baudelaire pictured man as walking in "a forest of symbols" which speak to him in words he cannot quite understand.

Symbolist verse usually presents a poetic image that can be interpreted many ways. The symbolists searched for the musical quality in words. They expressed themselves in metaphors and created technical modifications in existing verse forms. Some critics have called the movement decadent because of its obsession with death and its general pessimism over the frailty of the human condition. ANNA BALAKIAN

See also MALLARMÉ, STÉPHANE; VERLAINE, PAUL.

**SYMINGTON, STUART** (1901- ), a Missouri Democrat, has served in the United States Senate since 1953. Symington previously held several other government posts. He took charge of the Surplus Property Board, which disposed of surplus war material, in 1945. Then he served as assistant secretary of war for air from 1946 to 1947, and as the first secretary of the Air Force from 1947 to 1950. Symington also headed the National Security Resources Board from 1950 to 1951 and the Reconstruction Finance Corporation in 1951 and 1952. He was a candidate for the 1960 Democratic presidential nomination. WILLIAM STUART SYMINGTON was born in Amherst, Mass. He moved to Missouri in 1938, and was president and chairman of the board of the Emerson Electric Manufacturing Company in St. Louis from 1938 to 1945. WILLIAM E. PARRISH

**SYMMETRY,** *SIHM uh tree*, means equal or balanced proportions. Man and many animals have symmetrical proportions. For example, a line from a man's nose to the ground would divide him into two equal parts. This is called *bilateral symmetry*. Some animals, such as the starfish, have the symmetry of a wheel. This is called *radial symmetry*.

**SYMPHONIC POEM,** *sim FAHN ik*, is a fairly long orchestral work in one movement, usually built upon a story. Many symphonic poems follow the form of *sonata-allegro* movements as developed in symphonies, but they are predominantly emotional and dramatic in content. A number of composers who used the free form of symphonic poems developed the *leitmotiv* (repeated short melodic phrase or passage) as a means of unifying the work. The symphonic poem form became popular in the middle 1800's. Franz Liszt and Richard Strauss are noted for their symphonic poems.   GRANT FLETCHER

See also STRAUSS, RICHARD.

**SYMPHONY,** *SIM fuh nee*, is a form of music written for orchestra in which composers present their most highly organized and expressive musical ideas. The standard pattern of four movements usually includes a fast movement, a slow one, a dance form, and a final movement, usually fast. In classical symphonies, these four movements are often a *sonata-allegro* form; a *three-part song* form; a *minuet* and a *trio;* and a *rondo.*

Joseph Haydn began the formal experimentation that developed the symphony. His ideas were expanded by later composers, principally Wolfgang Amadeus Mozart, Ludwig van Beethoven, and Johannes Brahms. Haydn and Mozart wrote *classic* symphonies developed from the earlier *sinfonia,* a short orchestral interlude. These works followed a set pattern. Beethoven made several changes in developing the *romantic* symphony, following a sonata-allegro with a large song form, a *scherzo,* and a rondo or another sonata-allegro.

As the power and size of the symphony orchestra developed, symphonic compositions became more complex. Peter Ilich Tchaikovsky and Brahms constructed larger and longer forms, and sometimes mixed the basic forms or switched the order of movements. Anton Bruckner and Gustav Mahler wrote huge *post-Wagnerian* symphonies. Composers today often write short symphonies, or write only for chamber orchestras.

Significant developments include *cyclic* forms, in which a single theme binds each movement together; *single movement* forms, in which the symphonic plan is condensed into one movement; and *symphonic suites,* or loosely-constructed works of symphonic proportions. Few new ideas have gone beyond the basic forms developed by the German masters.   GRANT FLETCHER

See also MUSIC (Orchestral Music; History); ORCHESTRA; SONATA.

**SYMPOSIUM** is a discussion of a subject by a group of persons. Each of the speakers talks about the general subject or a part of it. When the parts are put together, the whole subject is covered. Then the audience asks the speakers to answer questions.

For example, a symposium might be held on Scouting. Four speakers might talk on the following parts of the subject: (1) The Origin and Development of Scouting; (2) Ideals of Scouting; (3) Results of Scout Training; and (4) Problems Facing Scouting.

A symposium usually gives better coverage of a subject and arouses more audience discussion than a single speech. Symposiums are often used in clubs, schools, and in public meetings. The chairman introduces the subject and the speakers. He also directs the question-and-answer period at the end.   J. V. GARLAND

See also PANEL DISCUSSION.

**SYNAGOGUE,** *SIN uh gahg,* is a Jewish house of worship. Synagogues are believed to have been started during the Babylonian captivity in the 500's B.C. At the time of Jesus there were synagogues wherever the Jews had settled. Synagogues also served in early days as law courts and places of religious instruction.

The ancient synagogue was built so that the worshiper, on entering or at prayer, faced in the direction of Jerusalem. The most important articles included the chest, known as the Holy Ark, in which the rolls of Scripture were kept, a lamp that burned all the time to symbolize the presence of God, and candlesticks for use on the Sabbath and festival days. The head of the synagogue was responsible for the conduct of the service. He chose members to lead the prayers, read from the *Torah* (Scriptures), and preached. The congregation was divided by a screen, with the men sitting on one side of it and the women on the other.

The modern synagogue has kept such self-governing features as a board of directors, known in early days as the board of elders. Most synagogues require a quorum of 10 men to begin services.   LOUIS L. MANN

See also JEWS (pictures); RHODE ISLAND (picture).

**SYNAGOGUE COUNCIL OF AMERICA** is the united voice of American Jewry in all matters in which religion plays an important role. It is made up of the six leading national Jewish organizations in the United States, including three rabbinic bodies and three laymen's groups. The Rabbinical Council of America and the Union of Orthodox Jewish Congregations in America represent Orthodox Jews in the Synagogue Council. The Rabbinical Assembly of America and the United Synagogue of America represent the Conservative Jews. The Central Conference of American Rabbis and the Union of American Hebrew Congregations represent the Reform group. The council was founded in 1926 and has headquarters at 235 Fifth Ave., New York, N.Y. 10016. It cooperates with the U.S. government, the United Nations, and Protestant, Catholic, and other groups on social and moral matters.   WILLIAM F. ROSENBLUM

**SYNAPSE.** See NERVOUS SYSTEM (Nerve Cells).

**SYNCHRO-CYCLOTRON,** *SING kroh SYE kloh trahn,* is a *nuclear accelerator,* or atom smasher, used to produce high-speed nuclear particles. The particles, including protons and alpha particles, are used in nuclear research to bombard the nuclei of atoms.

The synchro-cyclotron is an improved form of the cyclotron (see CYCLOTRON). Both devices are cylindrical machines that use electrical fields to *accelerate* (speed up) the particles. Magnetic fields guide the particles around circular paths. However, the synchro-cyclotron produces much higher energies than the cyclotron. A cyclotron cannot accelerate protons to energies greater than about 25 million electron volts (written 25 Mev). A synchro-cyclotron at the University of California produces 740 Mev. Others include a 680-Mev machine in Russia.

The final energy produced by a cyclotron is limited because above about 20 Mev, protons tend to get out of *phase* (step) with the voltage applied as they spiral within the machine. This is due chiefly to an increase in mass resulting from the increased velocity, as explained by the theory of relativity (see RELATIVITY [Special Theory of Relativity]). In 1945, Edwin M. McMillan of the United States and V. Veksler of Russia, working independently, showed that particles could be accelerated to still higher energies by adjusting the frequency of the machine's voltage so that it remained in step with the spiraling particles. The frequency is *synchronized* with the particles, hence the name *synchro-cyclotron.*   ROBERT L. THORNTON

See also ATOM SMASHER; LAWRENCE, ERNEST ORLANDO.

**SYNCHROTRON**

**SYNCHROTRON,** *SIN kroh trahn*, is a machine for accelerating atomic particles to high energies. In a synchrotron, the particles are bent by a magnetic field to move at almost a constant radius inside a vacuum chamber. As the energy increases, the magnetic field must also increase to keep this radius constant.

Synchrotrons can accelerate electrons to many hundred millions of electron volts (Mev). When the electrons strike a target, an intense beam of X rays is produced. These rays have sufficient energy to cause nuclear reactions and to produce mesons. See MESON.

Einstein's theory of relativity states that a particle increases in mass as its velocity rises (see RELATIVITY [Special Theory of Relativity]). The percentage increase in mass of the electrons is much larger than for heavier particles, such as protons. Thus an electron accelerated to 300 Mev has a mass 600 times greater than when it is at rest.

Edwin M. McMillan built the first 335 million-electron-volt synchrotron at the University of California (see McMILLAN, EDWIN MATTISON). ROBERT L. THORNTON.

See also ATOM SMASHER with its list of Related Articles.

**SYNCLINE,** *SING kline*, is the name for the *concave* (down-arched) part of a fold in rock structures. The folds are wrinkles that occurred during the time when the rocks were forming.

**SYNCOPE.** See ELISION.

**SYNDICALISM,** *SIN dih kul iz'm*. Various groups are unwilling to trust private persons. The syndicalists agree with the socialists that it is not safe to trust private owners with the great power that comes from ownership of important industries and public utilities. They differ from the socialists in that they are equally unwilling to trust government.

There are many kinds of syndicalists, but all agree that force is the basis of society. They believe power should never be centralized, and that general strikes should be used to achieve the ends of their movement.

Syndicalism began in France in 1892. It has made little advance in the world. PAYSON S. WILD, JR.

**SYNDICATE.** See CARTEL; NEWSPAPER SYNDICATE; TRUST.

**SYNECDOCHE.** See METONYMY.

**SYNGE,** *sing*, **JOHN MILLINGTON** (1871-1909), was an Irish dramatist. Most of his plays are set among Irish peasant characters, and are written in a vigorous poetic language based on folk speech.

Synge had a particular genius for tragicomedy. Like other Irish writers of his time in Ireland, he dealt imaginatively with heroism and the apparent gap between the real and the ideal. This gap forms the theme of *In the Shadow of the Glen* (1903), *The Well of the Saints* (1905), and *The Playboy of the Western World* (1907). Synge wrote two tragedies, *Riders to the Sea* (1904) and *Deirdre of the Sorrows* (performed after his death). In both plays, heroism is tied to the central character's confrontation with mortality.

Synge also wrote verse, and sketches of peasant life in the Aran Islands and other parts of Ireland. He was born in Rathfarnam, a suburb of Dublin. MARTIN MEISEL

**SYNGE, RICHARD LAURENCE MILLINGTON** (1914- ), a British biochemist, shared the 1952 Nobel prize for chemistry for the invention of partition chromatography. This is a method for analyzing substances in small samples of complicated mixtures. Each substance in a drop of solution is allowed to move at its own rate when placed on specially prepared filter paper. Then the structure of important large molecules can be inferred. Synge was born in Liverpool.

See also MARTIN, ARCHER J. P.

**SYNOD,** *SIN ud*, is an assembly, or council, of representatives of a church. It is sometimes composed of both clergymen and laymen. Synods meet for the purpose of discussing and deciding on matters of discipline, faith, and morals. See also PRESBYTERIANS.

**SYNODIC MONTH.** See MOON (The Moon's Movements).

**SYNONYM,** *SIN oh nim*, is a word that has the same, or nearly the same, meaning as another word. It comes from two Greek words meaning *associated* and *name*. There are many cases when one word will serve the same purpose as another. For example, *small* boy and *little* boy; *smart* idea and *clever* idea; *kill* a man and *slay* a man. But although two words may be synonymous, or used in the same way, in one sense, they are not synonymous in another sense. For example, *dull* and *stupid* may both be used to describe a person. But one does not use the word *stupid* to describe the *dull* blade of a knife. Synonyms enrich the language by helping the speaker or writer to use words with distinct and definite meanings and associations. They also make it possible to avoid the monotony of repetition. See also ANTONYM.

**SYNOVIAL FLUID.** See JOINT.

**SYNTAX,** *SIN tax*, is a description of the way words are put together to make sentences. It describes the order of the subject and verb, the position of auxiliary words and objects, and the relation of modifiers to the words they modify.

Word order is not the same in all languages. In English, we say "I gave Jim the ball." In another language, the order might be "I the ball Jim gave." When we put words together in proper order, they express our meaning correctly. In "I was shown a book by a clerk in a red leather binding," it seems that the clerk has a red binding, not the book.

Syntax is one of the three divisions of grammar. The others are *phonology*, the study of vowels, consonants, and intonation; and *morphology*, the study of words and their parts. PAUL ROBERTS

See also GRAMMAR; PARSING; PARTS OF SPEECH; SENTENCE.

**SYNTHESIS,** *SIN thee sis*, means bringing together two or more ideas or elements to form a new unity. In the chemical industry, coal and air and other substances are combined to synthesize nylon. Many persons have spoken of America as a synthesis of different races and nationalities. Philosophers often bring together many ideas. The combination of ideas is known as a synthesis. LOUIS O. KATTSOFF

**SYNTHETICS,** *sin THET icks*, are man-made substances in which two or more elements, or parts, are combined to make a new compound. A chemist can put two or more simple chemical compounds together to make a more complex product that will have properties different from the original parts. For example, he can combine hydrogen with oxygen to make synthetic water. Or, if he combines carbolic acid with formaldehyde under special conditions, he will obtain bakelite plastic resin. The development of nylon began when research workers tried to reconstruct the protein products in the human body. By combining the basic elements of the body proteins, they obtained nylon fiber. Synthetic fabrics are replacing many natural ones because they are stronger and cost less.

Synthetic products are developed when natural sources are unsatisfactory or cannot be obtained. Synthetics are also developed to use the by-products of other processes. Synthetic mica and synthetic rubber were made when it was difficult to get the natural products during wartime. Each of these was so superior to the natural product that the synthetics have continued in use even when natural products are plentiful. Among the typical synthetic products are dyes, food, furs and fabrics, micas, sponges, bristles, diamonds, rubbers, and varnishes.

Plastics are often called synthetics because they are man-made. All plastics are produced by combining chemically the molecules of simpler substances, such as some petroleum products, into more complex compounds. They can be tailored to have the properties needed by industry. Synthetic resins are called plastics because manufacturers can shape them into products by many methods. Some resins are brittle solids, some are like rubber, and others are liquids.     J. HARRY DuBois

**Related Articles** in WORLD BOOK include:

| | | |
|---|---|---|
| Acrilan | Orlon | Resin, Synthetic |
| Dacron | Plastics | Rubber |
| Dynel | Plexiglas | Silicone |
| Fiber Glass | Rayon | Vinyl |
| Nylon | | |

**SYPHILIS.** See VENEREAL DISEASE.

**SYR DARYA,** *sir DAHR yuh,* is one of the longest rivers in the world. It runs 1,770 miles, from Fergana Valley in Russia to the Aral Sea. It is important for irrigation, but is too shallow to be navigable. See also ARAL SEA; RIVER (color chart, Longest Rivers).

**SYRACUSE,** *SIHR uh kyoos,* on the southeastern coast of Sicily, was one of the most powerful cities of the ancient Greek world. Greeks from Corinth founded Syracuse about 734 B.C. The city grew rapidly. It became a cultural center under Hiero I, who built an empire in southern Italy.

A democracy was established at Syracuse after Hiero's death. It defeated a strong Athenian force that besieged the city from 415 to 413 B.C. But internal troubles and threats from Carthage brought to power a harsh military ruler—Dionysius I. After Dionysius' death in 367 B.C., Syracuse declined.

About 345 B.C., the Corinthian general Timoleon defeated the Carthaginians and rebuilt the city. During the rule of Hiero II, in the 200's B.C., Syracuse was allied with Rome. But the city later sided with Carthage, and Romans captured it in 211 B.C., after a three-year siege. The mathematician Archimedes aided the defenders during the siege with several defensive devices he invented (see ARCHIMEDES). Syracuse then became the capital of the Roman province of Sicily. In A.D. 878, the Saracens destroyed Syracuse. The town of Siracusa now stands on its site.     DONALD W. BRADEEN

See also DAMOCLES.

**SYRACUSE,** N.Y. (pop. 216,038; met. area 563,781; alt. 400 ft.), is an important industrial center in the heart of a rich farming region. It is the fourth largest city in New York. It was once known as the *Salt City* because it produced so much salt. The city is host to many state conventions, because it lies near the center of New York.

**Location, Size, and Description.** Syracuse lies near Onondaga Lake, about 150 miles west of Albany, in the lake region of New York. For location, see NEW YORK (political map). The city covers nearly 26 square miles. Downtown Syracuse centers around Clinton Square and Saint Mary's Circle.

**Cultural Life.** Syracuse University is the most important educational institution in the city. It includes the State University College of Forestry. Other schools are Le Moyne College (Jesuit), Pebble Hill School, the Manlius School, and the New York State College of Medicine. The Court of Appeals Law Library there has a collection of about 90,000 volumes. The city is the See of the Roman Catholic diocese and state headquarters of the Baptist and Congregationalist churches. The Syracuse Museum of Fine Arts was founded in 1896. It had the first permanent collection in the United States devoted entirely to works by American artists.

**Recreation.** Syracuse has 173 parks that cover more than 2,300 acres. Thornden Park, with its amphitheater and famous Mills Rose Garden, is one of the city's most scenic parks. Among the nearby lakes are Ontario, Oneida, Cazenovia, and the Finger Lakes. State parks near Syracuse include Clark Reservation at Jamesville, Green Lakes State Park at Fayetteville, Chittenango Falls State Park near Cazenovia, and Selkirk Shores State Park on Lake Ontario. The Onondaga Indian Reservation, the capital of the Iroquois Confederacy, lies south of the city.

**Industry and Trade.** Syracuse is the market center for a large farming region. Syracuse factories make air-conditioning machinery, air-cooled engines, automobile parts, roller bearings, farm machinery, foundry and machine-shop products, electrical appliances, steam clothes-pressing machines, typewriters, tin cans, chinaware, wax candles, and shoes. Syracuse has been called the electronics capital of the world.

**History.** The first settler, Ephraim Webster, opened a trading post in 1786. The village was incorporated in 1825. In 1847, Syracuse annexed the village of Salina and was chartered as a city. Syracuse has a mayor-council form of government.     WILLIAM E. YOUNG

**SYRACUSE, BATTLE OF.** See ARMY (Famous Land Battles of History).

**SYRACUSE UNIVERSITY** is a private coeducational school at Syracuse, N.Y. It offers courses in business administration, citizenship, education, engineering, fine arts, home economics, journalism, law, liberal arts, library science, nursing, public administration, social work, and speech and dramatic art. Forestry courses are taught at the State University College of Forestry on the Syracuse campus. The university also directs a four-year liberal arts college at Utica, N.Y.; and University College, an adult education division, in downtown Syracuse. University College coordinates Syracuse educational programs at centers in New York and in Caen, France; Stratford-on-Avon, England; Florence, Italy; and in Guatemala. Syracuse University was founded in 1870. For enrollment, see UNIVERSITIES AND COLLEGES (table).     KENNETH G. BARTLETT

*A Syrian Village* in the Anti-Lebanon Mountains near the Syria-Lebanon border, lies one hour by car from Damascus.

**SYRIA,** *SIHR ee uh,* is an Arab country at the eastern end of the Mediterranean Sea. It lies at a strategic point on ancient trade routes linking the country with Europe, Asia, and Africa. For thousands of years, Syrians have been famous as merchants and traders, moving goods back and forth between Asia and Europe. Some of Syria's ancient cities are among the oldest in the world. Damascus, Aleppo, and Palmyra were probably founded as early as 2000 B.C. These cities grew up on caravan routes and became important trading centers.

Most of Syria's people depend on farming for a living. Syrian farmers raise grains and other food crops on fertile plains in northern and eastern Syria. This land lies at the western end of a stretch of rich farmland known for centuries as the *Fertile Crescent* (see FERTILE CRESCENT). Some Syrian tribes still wander across the Syrian Desert and east of the Euphrates River in search of water and grazing land for their herds of goats and sheep.

Syria has been part of many empires since it was

*Christina Phelps Harris, the contributor of this article, is Professor Emeritus of Political Science in the Division of International Relations at Stanford University and author of* The Syrian Desert.

854

first settled about 3000 B.C. The writings of the Greek historian Herodotus in the 400's B.C. indicate that all the land between what is now Turkey and Saudi Arabia was once called Syria.

Modern Syria as an independent country dates from 1945. The country's official name in Arabic, the official language, is AL-JUMHURIA AL-ARABIA AL-SURIA (THE SYRIAN ARAB REPUBLIC). Damascus is the capital and the largest city.

### The Land

**Size and Surface Features.** Syria is about as big as the state of North Dakota. Rolling plains cover northern Syria. Plains called the *Jazīrah* lie east of the Euphrates River. The Syrian Desert stretches south and west of the Euphrates, and ends to the west in the plains of the Ḥawrān and the Anti-Lebanon Mountains, which form part of the border with Lebanon. Towards the south, the Syrian Desert extends deep into northern Saudi Arabia. The plains of the Ḥawrān contain the *Jabal ad Durūz* (Mountain of the Druse).

The Euphrates River, which rises in Turkey, is the longest waterway in Syria. For over 300 of its 1,700 miles, the river flows south, east, and then southeast through Syria's plains and desert. The Orontes River rises in Lebanon and flows north through Syria. The River Jordan rises in southern Syria, where it is fed by the snows of Mount Hermon. The Yarmūk River forms part of the boundary between Syria and Jordan.

**Climate.** Temperatures often rise above 110° F. in the inland plains and desert regions of Syria in the summer. They drop to about freezing in these regions in the winter. The coast has a mild climate most of the year. The rainy season throughout Syria occurs between late October and May. But the desert may get less than 4 inches of rain a year, while as much as 40 inches often falls along the coast. From May through September, a scorching desert wind called the *khamsin* sometimes blows across the Syrian Desert into the coastlands.

**Natural Resources.** Syria's farmland forms most of the country's natural wealth. The plains produce most of Syria's livestock and crops. Syria has few minerals,

--- **FACTS IN BRIEF** ---

**Capital:** Damascus.
**Official Language:** Arabic.
**Form of Government:** Republic.
**Head of State:** President.
**Area:** 71,498 square miles. *Greatest Distances*—(east-west) 400 miles; (north-south) 310 miles. *Coastline*—100 miles.
**Elevation:** *Highest*—Mount Hermon, 9,232 feet above sea level. *Lowest*—sea level, along the coast.
**Population:** *1960 Census*—4,565,121; distribution, 61 per cent rural, 39 per cent urban. *Estimated 1970 Population*—6,101,000; density, 83 persons to the square mile. *Estimated 1975 Population*—7,039,000.
**Chief Products:** *Agriculture*—barley, cotton, fruits, livestock, olives, pulses, sugar beets, wheat, wool. *Manufacturing and Processing*—cement, dried fruits, leather, processed food oils, soap, sugar, tobacco. *Mining*—asphalt, building stone, gypsum, oil.
**National Anthem:** "Homat El Diyar" ("Guardians of the Homeland").
**Flag:** The flag has three horizontal stripes of red, white, and black with three green stars on the white stripe. See FLAG (color picture: Flags of Asia).
**National Holiday:** Evacuation Day, April 17.
**Money:** *Basic Unit*—Pound. See MONEY (table: Values).

but it has a large supply of asphalt and building stone. It also has gypsum, natural gas, salt, some lignite, and a little chromium and iron ore. Oil deposits were discovered in the northeast part of the country in 1956 and 1960, and a refinery built at Homs with the help of Czechoslovakia now provides many petroleum products.

**Conservation.** Farmers till only about half the land suitable for farming. But more land is gradually being put into use. In the 1950's, about 100,000 acres of new farmland became available when engineers finished draining a swamp area on the Orontes River called the *Ghab*. In 1966, the Soviet Union agreed to help Syria build a dam on the Euphrates River west of Ar Raqqah. The project includes construction of several pumping stations and an electric power station. The irrigation this project provides will turn about 260,000 acres of unused plains into productive farmland.

### The People and Their Work

**Most Syrians are Arabs.** There are some non-Arab groups, including Kurds, Armenians, and a few Turks. About 6 out of 10 persons in Syria are farmers or shepherds. Their main crops are wheat, barley, and cotton, but they also raise fine quality figs, grapes, melons, olives, onions, lettuce, potatoes, sugar beets, and tobacco. Some large landowners use irrigation pumps, tractors, and other modern farm machinery. But farming methods in many parts of the country are still old-fashioned. Many Syrian farmers still plod along behind crude wooden plows drawn by oxen. Most of Syria's shepherds are wandering Bedouins. They raise sheep, goats, and cattle.

**Manufacturing.** The textile industry is Syria's largest single industry. Other large Syrian industries are those for making cement, sugar, and soap and for processing food oils and preserved fruits. Chief industrial centers are Damascus, Aleppo, Homs, and Latakia.

Syrian craftsmen are famous for their fine leather goods, brocades and embroideries, inlaid metalwork, and inlaid woodwork. Some silversmiths, leather craftsmen, and metal workers still work in open shops in the bazaars in many Syrian towns.

**Trade.** Most of Syria's foreign trade passes through Latakia, the country's main port. A second Syrian port is being planned at Tartūs. Syria's chief exports are raw cotton, wool and other textiles, livestock, grains, and foodstuffs. The leading imported products are machinery and small cars, metals and minerals, and textiles other than cotton and silk. Most of Syria's foreign trade is with France, Great Britain, Italy, Russia, the United States, West Germany, Lebanon and other nearby countries, and the Communist countries in eastern Europe.

**Transportation.** For thousands of years, traders and conquerors traveled across Syria because it was a "land bridge" between Asia, Africa, and Europe. Caravans crossed the Syrian Desert plains and grasslands to avoid the mountains in the north and the rocky, waterless desert in the south. The routes linked the Nile River Valley and countries on the Mediterranean Sea in the west with the valley of the Euphrates and Tigris rivers and the Persian Gulf in the east. Syria's importance as a trade center decreased after the Portuguese explorer Vasco da Gama discovered a sea route around Africa in 1498. In the years that followed, the country lost much of its population and wealth. In the 1700's and 1800's, Syria only partially regained its importance as a trade center.

Mattson, Black Star

**Covered Streets** shelter the bazaars of Damascus. Shopkeepers and pushcart peddlers sell products from all parts of the world.

Modern Syria has more than 4,000 miles of surfaced roads and highways. During the dry season, cars can cross the desert over many of the wide routes that were packed and flattened by the plodding camels in ancient caravans. Railroads link Syria with Lebanon, Turkey, Iraq, and Jordan. An airport near Damascus provides international air service. Two oil pipeline systems cross Syria's deserts, one from Iraq and the other from Saudi Arabia. Transit fees for the pipelines, which carry oil to Mediterranean ports, are a major source of income for Syria. Together with Lebanon, Syria has become an important trade center for the Middle East since the

**Syria** is about 50 times smaller than the United States.

**Syria** lies in the southwestern part of the continent of Asia.

**The Modern Campus** of Damascus University is much like those of many universities in the United States. Graduates of the university have taken an important part in developing many Middle Eastern countries.

Consulate General of Syria

closing of the Suez Canal during the 1967 Arab-Israeli war.

### Social and Cultural Achievements

**Education.** Syria has over 4,000 primary schools and about 400 secondary schools. About 12 per cent of the schools in Syria are either private or foreign-operated schools. Elementary and secondary education is free in all the state schools. Children between the ages of 6 and 11 must attend school. But there are many people living in the desert or in the remote mountain villages of the country who cannot read or write.

Syria has two universities, Damascus University and the University of Aleppo. The Damascus University Faculty of Medicine, opened in 1901 is the only medical school in the world that gives its courses in Arabic. The Academy of Damascus, a learned society, was founded in 1919.

**The Arts.** Syrian authors and poets have written many famous works. The most noted Syrians include the philosopher al-Farabi (872-950) and the poet al-Mutanabbi (915-965). Well-known poets today include Shafiq Jabri, Omar Abu-Rishe, Khalil Mardam, and Nizar Kabbani. Syria's many accomplished novelists and short-story writers include Shakib Jabri and Tawfik Awad. Said Taqieddine is a noted playwright. Mohammed Kurd Ali, a former president of the Academy of Damascus, was a distinguished historian.

The Arab's love of his language and the graceful nature of Arabic lettering have led to highly developed *calligraphy*, the art of beautiful writing or penmanship. Designs of Arabic lettering decorate buildings and jewelry and many other things in Syria.

Two well-known Syrian artists are Rafat Buhairi and Michel Kurshe. Wadi Sabra has been the chief leader of a recent movement to develop Syrian musical talent. He has composed operas in Arabic and French. The violinist Alexis Butros founded the first Syrian national conservatory of music in 1924.

**Religion.** About seven out of every eight Syrians are Moslems. There are more than 2,300,000 Sunni, or Orthodox Moslems, who form the largest group. There are also more than 400,000 Alawis and about 115,000 Druses, members of two strong unorthodox Islamic sects. About one out of every 12 persons in Syria is a Christian. There are nine important Eastern Christian denominations in Syria, including the Greek, Armenian, and Syrian Orthodox churches.

### History and Government

**Early Days.** Early Syria lay between the Egyptian civilization in the valley of the Nile River and the Sumerian and Babylonian civilizations in the valleys of the Euphrates and Tigris rivers. Syria's great stretches of grassland and rich soil made it a valuable prize. As a result, Syria was a constant battleground, and became part of many empires.

The first people to settle in Syria were Arab nomads, who probably came from Arabia about the year 3000 B.C. These nomads gradually settled in the Fertile Crescent, which formed three-fourths of a circle around the Syrian Desert.

The Amorites were the first nomads to settle west of the desert. The Phoenicians who came from the Persian Gulf area, drifted across the Syrian Desert into the coastal regions of what is now northern Syria, Lebanon,

---

**IMPORTANT DATES IN SYRIA**

**c. 2300 B.C.** An Arab ruler of Babylon, Sargon of Akkad, controlled northern Syria.
**c. 1000 B.C.** The Aramaeans established kingdoms in Syria.
**720 B.C.** The Assyrians conquered Syria.
**538 B.C.** Cyrus the Great added Syria to the Persian Empire.
**333 B.C.** Alexander the Great defeated the Persians at the Battle of Issus and conquered Syria.
**64-63 B.C.** Pompey made Syria a Roman province.
**A.D. 636** Moslem Arabs defeated the Christians of the Byzantine Empire at the Battle of the Yarmuk.
**1516** The Ottoman Turks conquered Syria.
**1916** The Arabs revolted against Turkish rule.
**1920** France took Syria as a League of Nations mandate.
**1945** Syria became an independent republic.
**1958** Syria and Egypt formed the United Arab Republic.
**1961** Syria withdrew from the United Arab Republic.
**1967** Syria, Egypt, and Jordan were defeated by Israel in a six-day war.

## Cities and Towns

| Name | Pop. | Grid |
|---|---|---|
| 'Abtīn | 4,340 | A 2 |
| Abū Kamāl | 7,031 | B 4 |
| Ad Dānā* | 3,297 | A 2 |
| 'Adhrā* | 3,196 | C 2 |
| Afrīn | 5,662 | A 2 |
| Al Bāb | 27,866 | A 2 |
| Aleppo | 528,618 | A 2 |
| Al Ḥaffah | 4,778 | B 2 |
| Al Ḥarrah | 3,266 | C 2 |
| Al Ḥasakah | 23,495 | A 4 |
| Al Jayyid | 7,359 | B 2 |
| Al Kanīsah* | 4,081 | B 1 |
| Al Kiswah | 4,894 | C 2 |
| Al Mu'azz- amīyah* | 5,372 | C 2 |
| Al Qāmishlī | 31,266 | A 4 |
| Al Qaryatayn | 5,246 | B 2 |
| Al Qunay- ṭirah | 19,752 | C 1 |
| Al Quṣayr | 6,666 | B 2 |
| Al Quṭayfah | 5,095 | C 2 |
| 'Āmūdā | 12,557 | A 4 |
| An Nabk | 16,884 | B 2 |
| An Nakhl | 3,946 | C 2 |
| Anṣārī | 3,976 | A 2 |
| Arīḥā* | 9,226 | B 2 |
| Armanāz* | 3,445 | A 2 |
| Ar Raqqah | 12,570 | B 3 |
| Ar Rastan | 8,690 | B 2 |
| Ar Ruḥaybah | 5,228 | C 2 |
| Arwād | 3,558 | B 1 |
| Ash Shaykh Miskīn | 3,769 | C 2 |
| As Safīrah | 5,944 | A 2 |
| Aṣ Ṣanamayn | 3,574 | C 2 |
| Aṣ Ṣaqla- bīyah | 4,663 | B 2 |
| As Suwaydā' | 17,357 | C 2 |
| At Tall* | 9,706 | C 2 |
| 'Ayn al 'Arab | 4,596 | A 3 |
| A'zāz | 14,504 | A 2 |
| Az Zabdānī | 9,968 | C 2 |
| Bāb Bīlā* | 3,670 | C 2 |
| Bāb 'Umar* | 5,734 | B 2 |
| Bāniyās | 9,087 | B 1 |
| Binnish | 4,355 | B 2 |
| Blūdān* | 3,387 | C 1 |
| Buṣrā ash Shām | 4,523 | C 2 |
| Dā'il* | 4,480 | C 2 |
| Damas- cus | 544,712 | C 2 |
| Damsarkhū | 4,298 | B 1 |
| Dar'ā | 21,009 | C 2 |
| Dārayyā | 15,135 | C 2 |
| Darbāsīyah | 6,412 | A 4 |
| Dār Ta'izzah | 3,642 | A 2 |
| Dayr 'Aṭīyah | 5,177 | B 2 |
| Dayr az Zawr | 61,728 | B 4 |
| Dayr Ba'albah | 5,434 | B 2 |
| Dayrīk | 6,656 | A 5 |
| Dūmā | 31,379 | C 2 |
| Dumayr | 4,738 | C 2 |
| Fīq | 2,545 | C 1 |
| Fū'a* | 3,353 | B 2 |
| Hama | 126,364 | B 2 |
| Ḥammūrīyah* | 2,828 | C 2 |
| Ḥarastā al Basal | 9,740 | C 2 |
| Harim | 6,927 | A 2 |
| Homs | 175,303 | B 2 |
| Idlib | 38,500 | B 2 |
| 'Irbīn* | 9,202 | C 2 |
| Izra' | 3,306 | C 2 |
| Jablah | 16,439 | B 1 |
| Jarābulus | 8,613 | A 3 |
| Jaramānah* | 6,480 | C 2 |
| Jawbar | 27,289 | C 2 |
| Jayrūd | 5,799 | C 2 |
| Jisr ash Shughūr | 13,562 | B 2 |
| Judaydat 'Arṭūz* | 3,420 | C 2 |
| Kafr Baṭnā* | 3,005 | C 2 |
| Kafr Buhum | 3,550 | B 2 |
| Kafr Lāḥah | 3,395 | B 2 |
| Kafr Nabal* | 3,417 | B 2 |
| Kafr Takhārīm | 4,539 | A 2 |
| Khān ash Shaykh | 3,611 | C 2 |
| Khān Shay- khūn | 5,710 | B 2 |
| Latakia | 75,363 | B 1 |
| Ma'arrat an Nu'mān | 17,005 | B 2 |
| Ma'arrat Miṣrīn | 5,284 | A 2 |
| Maḍāyā* | 4,209 | C 2 |
| Manbij | 14,096 | A 2 |
| Ma'rātah | 4,607 | A 2 |
| Maṣyāf | 7,448 | B 2 |
| Mayādīn | 12,808 | B 4 |
| Minīn | 3,594 | C 2 |
| Muḥassan | 4,114 | A 3 |
| Muḥradah | 8,514 | B 2 |
| Mulayḥah* | 3,170 | C 2 |
| Nawā | 8,115 | C 2 |
| Nayrab | 13,076 | A 2 |
| Nūbul | 4,021 | A 2 |
| Palmyra | 10,744 | B 3 |
| Qal'at al Madīq* | 3,992 | C 2 |
| Qārā | 4,283 | B 2 |
| Qardāḥah* | 3,107 | B 1 |
| Qāsim | 4,542 | C 2 |
| Qaṭ'ah | 2,915 | B 4 |
| Qaṭanā | 8,793 | C 2 |
| Qulayḍīn | 4,722 | B 2 |
| Rānkūs* | 2,883 | C 2 |
| Ra's al 'Ayn | 5,450 | A 4 |
| Ṣadad | 3,471 | B 2 |
| Ṣāfīṭā | 10,350 | B 2 |
| Salamīyah | 26,771 | B 2 |
| Ṣalkhad | 5,387 | C 2 |
| Salqīn | 7,575 | A 2 |
| Saqbā* | 4,181 | C 2 |
| Sarāqib | 5,153 | B 2 |
| Sarmīn | 3,800 | B 2 |
| Shahbā* | 3,432 | C 2 |
| Shaḥīl | 2,924 | B 4 |
| Shīn | 3,619 | B 2 |
| Sirghāyā* | 2,846 | C 2 |
| Subaykhān | 3,913 | B 4 |
| Ṣūrān | 5,029 | B 2 |
| Tādif | 5,611 | A 2 |
| Ṭafas | 5,070 | C 2 |
| Tall Bīsah | 6,508 | B 2 |
| Tall Kalakh | 6,428 | B 2 |
| Tall Rif'at | 3,969 | A 2 |
| Ṭarṭūs | 19,996 | B 1 |
| Tasīl | 2,842 | C 1 |
| Ṭayyibat al Imām* | 3,363 | B 2 |
| Yabrūd | 9,528 | C 2 |
| Yaldā* | 2,818 | C 2 |
| Zakīyah | 2,912 | C 2 |

Source: Census figures and official estimates.
*Does not appear on the map; key shows general location.

## Physical Features

| Feature | Grid |
|---|---|
| Anti-Lebanon Mts. | C 2 |
| Euphrates River | B 3 |
| Galilee, Sea of | C 1 |
| Jabal ad Durūz (Mtn.) | C 2 |
| Khābūr River | B 4 |
| Mediterranean Sea | B 1 |
| Mt. Hermon | C 2 |
| Orontes River | B 2 |
| Syrian Desert | C 3 |

857

# SYRIAC

**SYRIAC,** *SIR ih ak*, is one of the dialects of the Aramaic language. Many early Syriac manuscripts are versions of parts of the Bible. The use of this dialect declined after the 1300's. Today, a few tribes in Turkey and Iran speak a language called Syriac. It is quite different from the old Syriac. See also ARAMAIC.

**SYRIAN DESERT** is a triangular desert plateau that extends northward from the Nafud desert of northern Arabia. For location, see ARABIA (map). It lies roughly between 30 and 36 degrees north latitude. The Syrian Desert plateau is between 2,000 and 3,000 feet above sea level on the west. It slopes downward to the Euphrates River, which forms its eastern boundary. The southern two thirds of the plateau is rocky. A volcanic zone on the west is dotted with huge boulders of black basalt. The *Jabal Anaiza*, a mountainous area about 3,000 feet high, stands high above the central part of the plateau. Deeply cut *wadis* (dry watercourses) wind down from it to the Euphrates.

The northern third of this triangular plateau is a flat sandy plain that forms the natural bridge between Syria and Iraq. A chain of limestone hills rises along the western edge of the plain. The desert contains historic ruins and several towns that have grown up around *oases* (watering places). The famous caravan city of Palmyra is the best known of these towns.

Two motor highways have been built across the desert. Pipelines connect the oil fields of northern Iraq and of eastern Saudi Arabia with the Mediterranean. Many international and local airlines also fly across the desert. CHRISTINA PHELPS HARRIS

**Ruins of an Old Palmyrene Castle in the Syrian Desert** overlook the burial towers in the Valley of Tombs.
Inge Morath, Magnum

**SYRINGA.** See MOCK ORANGE.

**SYRINGE** is a pumplike device. It is a tube, tapered at one end, with a plunger or soft, hollow bulb at the other. The plunger or bulb either creates suction or forces fluid from the syringe. Syringes are used to spray or inject liquids, or to remove them by suction.

See also HYPODERMIC INJECTION; INTRAVENOUS INJECTION.

**SYRINX,** or PIPES OF PAN. See ORGAN (History); PAN.

**SYRUP,** or SIRUP. See CORN (Uses of Corn); MAPLE SUGAR; SORGHUM; SUGAR.

**SYSTEM,** in biology. See BIOLOGY; HUMAN BODY (Systems).

**SYSTEMIC CIRCULATION.** See CIRCULATION.

**SYSTOLIC PRESSURE.** See BLOOD PRESSURE.

**SZEGED,** *SAY gad* (pop. 110,600; alt. 300 ft.), is one of the largest cities in Hungary. It lies on the west bank of the Tisza River, 188 miles southeast of Budapest (see HUNGARY [color map]). The city is the commercial center of a fertile farming area and it has a prosperous trade in grain, wool, and tobacco. The city is also a manufacturing center, producing textiles, food, tobacco, and brooms. A church tower built in the 1200's is Szeged's oldest monument. After a disastrous flood in 1879, the city was rebuilt with broad streets and beautiful public squares. Szeged has a university and an art museum. R. JOHN RATH

**SZELL,** *zell*, **GEORGE** (1897-    ), is a prominent symphonic and operatic conductor. He did outstanding work in many central European theaters between 1920 and 1937, and then came to the Metropolitan Opera Company of New York City in 1942. In 1946 he became musical director of the Cleveland Orchestra. He was born in Budapest. IRVING KOLODIN

**SZENT-GYÖRGYI,** *SENT DYER dee*, **ALBERT** (1893-    ), an American biochemist, discovered actin, a muscle protein. He received the 1937 Nobel prize in physiology and medicine. Through his research, Szent-Györgyi explained the catalytic action in cellular oxidation, the role of vitamins in metabolism, and the chemistry and structure of muscle tissue. He wrote *Chemistry of Muscular Contraction* (1947). Szent-Györgyi was born ALBERT SZENT-GYÖRGYI VON NAGYRAPOLT in Budapest, Hungary. He came to the United States in 1947, and became a citizen in 1955. PAUL R. FREY

**SZIGETI,** *sih GET ih*, **JOSEPH** (1892-    ), is a distinguished Hungarian concert violinist, noted as a scholarly musician and a gifted, imaginative performer. He made his debut at the age of 11 in Budapest. His success led to concerts in Berlin, Dresden, London, and other European cities. In 1917, he became professor of violin at the Geneva Conservatory. Szigeti made his United States debut in Philadelphia in 1925. He was born in Budapest. DOROTHY DELAY

**SZILARD,** *ZIL ahrd*, **LEO** (1898-1964), an American physicist, pioneered in the development of atomic energy. With Enrico Fermi, he originated the method of arranging graphite and uranium which made possible the first self-sustaining nuclear reactor in 1942. In July, 1939, Szilard and Eugene Wigner visited Albert Einstein. Einstein then wrote to President Franklin D. Roosevelt and initiated federal support of atomic energy. Szilard was born in Budapest, Hungary. He became a United States citizen in 1943. He and Wigner shared the 1959 Atoms for Peace Award. CHALMERS W. SHERWIN

860